INTERNATIONAL
WHO'S WHO
IN MEDICINE

INTERNATIONAL
WHO'S WHO
IN MEDICINE

SECOND EDITION

International Biographical Centre
Cambridge England

First Edition
1987

Second Edition
1995

ISBN 0 948875 91 7

Printed and bound in the United Kingdom by: Bath Press, Lower Bristol Road, Bath, Avon BA2 3BL

INTERNATIONAL WHO'S WHO IN MEDICINE

Director General
Nicholas S Law

Assistant Publisher:
Christopher Bosman

Editorial/Production Manager:
Jocelyn Timothy

Assistant Editors:
Sheryl Rigby
Rebecca Thompson

All communications to: International Who's Who in Medicine
International Biographical Centre
Cambridge CB2 3QP, England

INTERNATIONAL BIOGRAPHICAL CENTRE
RANGE OF REFERENCE TITLES

From one of the widest ranges of contemporary biographical reference works published under any one imprint, some IBC titles date back to the 1930's. Each edition is compiled from information supplied by those listed, who include leading personalitites of particular countries or profession. Information offered usually includes date and place of birth; family details; qualifications; career histories; awards and honours received; books published or other creative work; other relevant information including postal address. Naturally there is no charge of fee for inclusion.

New editions are freshly compiled and contain on average 80-90% new information. New titles are regularly added to the IBC reference library.

Titles include:

Dictionary of International Biography
Who's Who in Australasia and the Pacific Nations
Who's Who in Western Europe
Dictionary of Scandinavian Biography
International Who's Who in Art and Antiques
International Authors and Writers Who's Who
International Leaders in Achievement
International Who's Who in Community Service
International Who's Who in Education
International Who's Who in Engineering
International Who's Who in Medicine
International Who's Who in Music and Musicians' Directory -
    Volume One - Classical and Light Classical
International Who's Who in Music - Volume Two - Popular Music
Men of Achievement
The World Who's Who of Women
The World Who's Who of Women in Education
International Youth of Achievement
Foremost Women of the Twentieth Century
International Who's Who in Poetry and Poets' Encyclopaedia

Enquiries to:
International Biographical Centre
Cambridge CB2 3QP
England

FOREWORD

It was eight years ago the International Biographical Centre published the First Edition of *International Who's Who in Medicine*. Such has been the demand the general acceptance of the title over those eight years that we were encouraged to produce and publish a Second Edition. This new edition is an expansion and enhancement of the First Edition in that we have incorporated entries from those who embrace 'Contemporary' Medicine such as Laboratory Science, Chiropody, Orthoptics, Physiotherapy, Dietics, Acupuncture, Medical Hypnosis, as well as numerous other areas which are highlighted in the book.

Obviously doctors in general practice, surgeons, consultants, administrators, and senior teaching staff, are included as well as nurses, dentists, and those concerned with public health and rehabilitation, mental health and research.

No work, however large, can include all the world's senior medical professional and staff. Our editors have attempted to include biographies in this Second Edition from as many different countries and fields of medicine as possible in order to reflect the work being done by as wide a variety of individuals as possible; future editions will offer relatively few updated entries, space being given instead to additional individuals. Selection has, for this edition, been made on the grounds of interest to the general read as well as to those within the profession, the amount of information offered, and the status of each person within a section or level of the medical and allied professions, and within the country in which they work.

The co-operation of thousands of individuals and hundreds of health authorities and professional societies, institutes and association is gratefully acknowledged by the International Biographical Centre, its researchers and editors.

Readers are encouraged to propose the names and addresses of those they feel have been omitted from this edition; these will be invited to submit material for future publication.

It must be emphasized that no charge or fee is made for inclusion in *Internaitonal Who's Who in Medicine*.

Whilst every effort has been made to ensure a high standard of accuracy in editing and publishing this edition, it is possible that occasional errors may occur in a work of this nature. In this event we apologize in advance.

DEPUTY DIRECTORS GENERAL OF THE IBC

Dr Sonia Udechuku Ewo, LFIBA, DDG, *Nigeria*
Mr Samir Qasim Fakhro, *Bahrain*
Prof Gong-Xiu Fan, FIBA, DDG, *China*
Mr Jacob Feldman, FIBA, DDG, *Australia*
Mr Shun-Hua Feng, LFIBA, DDG, *China*
Prof Franja Ferenci, LFIBA, DDG, IOM, *Yugoslavia*
Ms Anne-Marie Ferrand-Vidal, FIBA, DDG, IOM, *France*
Mrs Betty Jean Fessler, DDG, IOM, OIF, *USA*
Dr David E Flinchbaugh, LFIBA, DDG, *USA*
Dr Jean D Floresco, FIBA, DDG, *France*
Mr Wilhelm Flöttman, LPIBA, IOM, DDG, *Germany*
Mrs Vivian E S Fox, LPIBA, DDG, *USA*
Dr Charlotte A Frick, FIBA, DDG, *USA*
Mr Hunter John H Fry, DDG, *Australia*
Prof Tanefusa Fukatsu, LPIBA, DDG, IOM, OIF, *Japan*
Mr T Funahashi, LPIBA, DDG, *Japan*
Mr Stanley Gavac, LFIBA, DDG, *USA*
Mr Sylvestre Gbewonyo, LFIBA, DDG, *Kenya*
Dr Curtis A Gibson, LFIBA, DDG, *USA*
Prof Makram Girgis, LFIBA, DDG, *Australia*
Mrs M Goldston-Morris, LFIBA, DDG, *Australia*
Mr Isaac Thomas Goodine, DDG, IOM, *West Indies*
Ms Joanne Greene, DDG, *USA*
Prof Dr Ovidiu N Grivu, LFIBA, DDG, *Romania*
Prof S S Grozdanic, FIBA, DDG, *Yugoslavia*
Mrs Padmin Gunaratnam, DDG, *Republic of Singapore*
Mrs Mildred Gunn, FIBA, IOM, DDG, *Canada*
Prof Guillermo T Gutierrez, DDG, IOM, *Philippines*
Ms M D C Gwinn, LFIBA, DDG, IOM, *USA*
Prince A A Haastrup, LPIBA, DDG, *Nigeria*
Prof G Haddad, LPIBA, DDG, *Iraq*
Dr Gerardo W Hahn, LFIBA, DDG, *Argemtina*
Dr Thomas J Hammons, LPIBA, DDG, *Scotland*
Miss L Harris, LPIBA, LFWLA, DDG, IOM, *USA*
Mr Kiyoshi J Hasegawa, DDG, IOM, OIF *Japan*
Dr Kazuyuki Hatada, LFIBA, DDG, IOM, *Japan*
Ms Susanne Sally Hathaway, LPIBA, *USA*
Prof Simon John Haynes, DDG, *Canada*
Mr Peter J Heine, DDG, *Germany*
Dr Leonard W Henderson, LFIBA, DDG, *England*
Mr Robert A Hendrickson, DDG, *USA*
Dr Axel Ernst Hesse, DDG, IOM, *Spain*

Prof Hamed Shillmi Abbas, DDG, *Kingdom of Saudi Arabia*
Mr Shung Pun Ho, DDG, *Hong Kong*
Ms E D Hoffleit, LPIBA, IOM, DDG, OIF, *USA*
Dr R G L Holland, HLFIBA, DDG, *Canada*
Mr Franz Holler, DDG, IOM, *Luxembourg*
Dr Branton K Holmberg, FIBA, DDG, *USA*
Mrs M Horswell-Chambers, DDG, IOM, *USA*
Prof Zuey-Shin Hsu, LFIBA, DDG, IOM, OIF, *Taiwan, China*
Ms Catherine Harding Hudgins, DDG, *USA*
Dr Norman N Huff, LPIBA, DDG, *USA*
Mr Charles Orvis Hunter, DDG, *USA*
Rev Dr Prof Tzu-Yang Hwang, LPIBA, DDG, OIF, *USA*
Alhaji Idris Ibrahim, LFIBA, DDG, *Nigeria*
Prof Dr Kazuyosi Ikeda, LPIBA, LFWLA, DDG, IOM, OIF, *Japan*
Mr Masamichi Ishihara, LFIBA, DDG, *Japan*
Prof S Issaragrisil, LFIBA, DDG, IOM, *Thailand*
Rev Anath E Jackson, LFIBA, DDG, *USA*
Prof Dr Drs H-J Jacobs, LPIBA, DDG, OIF, *Germany*
Dr Jørgen Jensen, LFIBA, DDG, *Denmark*
Ms Margaret H Johnson, LFIBA, DDG, *USA*
Chief Charles Joshua, FIBA, DDG, IOM, *USA*
Dr Mirja A Kalliopuska, DDG, IOM, OIF, *Finland*
Prof Jawahar Kaira, DDG, *Canada*
Dr George Akaki Kanzaki, LPIBA, DDG, IOM, OIF, *USA*
Dr Richard Willy Kanzler, DDG, IOM, OIF, *Republic of South Africa*
Ms Marlene M Katchur, LPIBA, DDG, OIF, *USA*
Dr Shriniwas K Katti, DDG, *USA*
HSH Prince Dr George King de Santorini, Count de Florina, DDG, *USA*
Dr Algee Golden Kirby, FIBA, DDG, *USA*
Dr Samson B M Kisekka, LPIBA, DDG, IOM, *Uganda*
Prof Hisatoki Komaki, LFIBA, DDG, *Japan*
Dr Alfred V Kottek, LFIBA, DDG, IOM, *Austria*
Marvin Z Kurlan, MD, FACS, LFIBA, DDG, IOM, *USA*
Mr Kisho Kurokawa, LFIBA, DDG, IOM, *Japan*
Ms Tuulikki Kyllönen-Heikel, LFIBA, DDG, IOM, *Finland*
Mr Billy Lam, LFIBA, DDG, *Hong Kong*
Dr Luc Johan Lambrecht, LPIBA, DDG, OIF, *Belgium*
Dr V Landers, LPIBA, LFWLA, DDG, OIF, *USA*
Dr Harry C Layton, FIBA, DDG, IOM, *USA*
Dr William A Leavell, DDG, *USA*
Dr Charles L Leavitt, LPIBA, DDG, *USA*

Mr Don Yoon Lee, LFIBA, DDG, *USA*
Dr Irene Lee, DDG, *USA*
Dr Lee Kam-To, LFIBA, DDG, IOM,
Hong Kong
Prof Liang Dan-Fong, LPIBA, DDG, *Taiwan, China*
Eusebio G Lim, MD, LFIBA, DDG, *USA*
Ms Joan Pek Bee Lim, LFIBA, DDG, IOM,
Malaysia
Dr Phillip K Lim, LPIBA, DDG, *USA*
Prof Chung-sheng Lin, DDG, *China*
Prof Jong-Teh Lin, LFWLA, DDG, *Taiwan, China*
Prof Ping-Wha Lin, DDG, *USA*
Ms J C McKee Lindsay, LPIBA, DDG, IOM,
USA
Prof Liu Chung Chu, DDG, *China*
Dr Letha M Wayne, LFWLA, FIBA, DDG,
USA
Mrs Julia M LoTempio, FIBA, DDG, *USA*
Dr Frederick Lundell, LFIBA, DDG, IOM,
Canada
Ms Joan Mahaffey, LPIBA, DDG, IOM, *USA*
Dr Virendra B Mahesh, LPIBA, DDG, IOM,
MOIF, *USA*
Mr Umaru-Sanda Maigida, LFIBA, DDG,
IOM,
Nigeria
Dr C O Majekodunmi, DDG, *Nigeria*
Dr Clarkson Majomi, LFIBA, DDG, *England*
Dr Howard Malin, LPIBA, LFWLA, DDG, IOM,
USA
Mrs Louise Martin, DDG, *USA*
The Hon John Ross Matheson, LFIBA, DDG,
Canada
Mr Yoshihiko Matsui, LPIBA, DDG, *Japan*
Dr Patricia J Maybin, DDG, IOM, *USA*
Mr Francis C Meddleton, LFIBA, *USA*
Mr Paul J Meyer, LFIBA, DDG, IOM, *USA*
Mrs Pearl D Michaels, LPIBA, DDG, *USA*
Mr T E Miller, LFIBA, LFWLA, DDG, *USA*
Ms Carol Ann Mills, FIBA, DDG, *USA*
Dr Tsutomu Mimura, LPIBA, DDG, IOM,
Japan
Ms Hildegard M Minchenko, LFIBA, DDG,
IOM, *USA*
Dr Elpis Mitropoulou, DDG, *Greece*
Dr Victoria I Mojekwu, LFIBA, DDG, *Nigeria*
Mr Ralph E Montijo, LPIBA, DDG, IOM, *USA*
Prof Mineo Moritani, DDG, *Japan*
Prof E R Moses, LFWLA, LFIBA, DDG,
IOM, *USA*
Dr Edwin Muniz Jr, DDG, *USA*
Mr Edahiko Murakami, FIBA, IOM, DDG,
Japan
Mr James F O Mustaffah, *Ghana*
Mr George K Mwai, LPIBA, DDG, IOM,
Kenya

Mr Jack Charles Myers, FIBA, DDG, *USA*
Mrs Yong-Gyun Nah, LFIBA, DDG, *Korea*
Dr Shrinivas H Naidu, LFIBA, DDG, *USA*
Sir Saburo Nakagawa, LPIBA, DDG, *Japan*
Dr Shigehisa Nakamura, LFIBA, DDG, IOM,
Japan
Mr Kadaba V Narain, DDG, IOM, *Japan*
Mr Shiv Sahai Naraine, FIBA, DDG,
S America
Mr Frederick L Neff, FIBA, DDG, *USA*
Miss Elizabeth Nelson, LFIBA, DDG, *USA*
Prof Thu The Nguyen, DDG, *USA*
Dr Hiroshi Niimura, LFIBA, DDG, *Japan*
Dr Rev R N Nnamdi, DDG, *Germany*
Mrs Bessie Wherry Noe, DDG, *USA*
Dr Khalida I Noor, LPIBA, DDG,
Kingdom of Saudi Arabia
Senator Cyrus N Nunieh, DDG, *Nigeria*
Ms Mary Devon O'Brien, LFIBA, DDG, *USA*
Ms Rosa Margot Ochoa, FWLA, DDG,
Mexico
Dr Wilson R Ogg, LPIBA, LFWLA, DDG,
USA
Prof U Okeke, DDG, *Nigeria*
Dr Pritam S Panesar, LFIBA, DDG, *Kenya*
Prof Sutokusumo Parangtopo, *Indonesia*
Dr Lucy T Parker, LPIBA, DDG, *USA*
Dr Eugenia Pasternak, CM, PhD, LPIBA,
DDG, IOM, *Canada*
Dr Howard John Peak, DDG, *Australia*
Ms Lou Peel, DDG, *USA*
Lt Col Ralph M Persell, LFIBA, DDG, *USA*
Mr Gavin Alexander Pitt, DDG, *USA*
Ms Dorothea Porter, LFIBA, DDG, *USA*
Dr M L Porter, LPIBA, DDG, *USA*
Mr Malcolm Frederick Potter, DDG, *Australia*
Ms Carol R Proctor, FIBA, *USA*
Dr Svein D Prydz, LPIBA, DDG, IOM, *Norway*
Dr Jerzy Z Przybojewski, DDG, FIBA,
Republic of South Africa
Mrs Lois Kathryn Pullig, DDG, *USA*
Mr Robert Pwee Kong Joo, FIBA, DDG, IOM,
Republic of Singapore
Ms Sherry S Raatz, LPIBA, DDG, *USA*
Dr Srinivas S Rajan, LFIBA, DDG, *India*
Orlando M Recinos Arguello, DDG,
El Salvador
Dr Lonnie Royce Rex, FIBA, DDG, *USA*
Jerome Reyda, QC, *Canada*
Mr Eugene E Rhemann, LPIBA, DDG, *USA*
Ms C L Richards, FWLA, DDG, *USA*
Ms Janet G Riebold, LFIBA, DDG, *USA*
Dr A Robertson-Pearce, FIBA, DDG, IOM,
England
Dr Ralph R Robinson, DDG, IOM, OIF, *USA*
Ms Trudy Langsjoen Rodine, DDG, *USA*
Dr M H Rosen, LFIBA, LFWLA, DDG, *USA*
Prof Julius L Rothman, FIBA, DDG, *USA*

Ms Cecile I Rouchdy, LFIBA, OIF, *Kingdom of Saudi Arabia*
Dr P A Rubio, MD, PhD, LPIBA, DDG, *USA*
Mr R P Sabaratnam, FIBA, DDG, *Hong Kong*
Mr E F Sanguinetti, FWLA, DDG, *Argentina*
Ms Geraldine Ogden Savari, DDG, *USA*
Ragnhild Schioldborg, LFIBA, DDG, *Norway*
Prof Judith T Scholl, LFIBA, DDG, *USA*
Mrs Marjorie M Schuck, DDG, *USA*
Mr Ainsworth D Scott, LPIBA, DDG, IOM, *West Indies*
Mr Dennis Screpetis, LPIBA, DDG, *USA*
Mr Roderick Eli Seeley, LFIBA, DDG, *USA*
Jukka Tapani Seppinen, FIBA, DDG, *Finland*
Dr Shirish Shah, LFIBA, DDG, *USA*
Dr Isadore Shapiro, DDG, IOM, *USA*
Mr Ralph Albert Sheetz, DDG, *USA*
Dr Muhammad M Mukram Sheikh, HLFIBA, DDG, IOM, *Southern Africa*
Ms Bat-Sheva Sheriff, LFWLA, DDG, IOM, *Israel*
Prof Koki Shimoji, DDG, *Japan*
Mr Louis Smith, LFIBA, *USA*
Mrs Edwina Christine F Snow, DDG,· *USA*
Miss Callie J Spady, FIBA, DDG, *USA*
Mr Francis M J Spencer, LFIBA, DDG, *USA*
Ms Linda Spencer, DDG, *USA*
Mr Peter Stadler, DDG, *Denmark*
Mrs Joan E Starr, FWLA, DDG, *Australia*
Mr R St J Stephens, FIBA, DDG, *England*
Mrs E V Stewart, LFIBA, DDG, *USA*
Ms M Strandell Thamm P E, DDG, *USA*
Dr H Chien-Fan Su, FIBA, DDG, IOM, OIF, *USA*
Mrs B Sutton, LPIBA, FWLA, DDG, *England*
Dr Srikanta M N Swamy, LFIBA, DDG, IOM, *Canada*
Prof Emeric Szegho, LPIBA, DDG, *USA*
Dr Emmanuel H Tadross, LPIBA, DDG, *Canada*
Neva B Talley-Morris, FIBA, DDG, *USA*
Prof Giulio F Tarro, DDG, IOM, *Italy*
Mrs Nellie J Taze, LFIBA, DDG, *USA*
Dr Goh Han Teng, DDG, *Singapore*
Mr Patrick C Thauberger, DDG, IOM, *Canada*
Mr Francis M C Thomas, LFIBA, DDG, *Sri Lanka*
Dr Walter Dill Thomas, LFIBA, DDG, *USA*
Ms Mary J Thornton, LPIBA, DDG, IOM, *USA*
Mr Gary L Tipton, LFIBA, DDG, *USA*
Prof J H Tisch, LPIBA, LFWLA, DDG, *Australia*
Dr Ljerka Tiska-Rudman, FIBA, DDG, *Yugoslavia*
Dr Wolfgang Töglhofer, LFIBA, DDG, *Switzerland*
Mr Criton P Tomazos, DDG, England

Dr Tran Quang Hai, LFIBA, DDG, *France*
Dr Orville W Trosper, FIBA, DDG, *USA*
Prof Pars Tuglaci, FIBA, LFWLA, DDG, IOM, OIF, *Turkey*
Prof Arbo Valdma, LFIBA, DDG, *Germany*
Constantin K Vereketis, LPIBA, DDG, *Greece*
Ms Morwenna A Vincent, FIBA, DDG, *Australia*
Dr Steven A Vladem, LFIBA, DDG, IOM, *USA*
Prof R F Vliegen, LFIBA, DDG, IOM, *Japan*
Mt Rev Dr Robert A Voice, DDG, *Canada*
Dr Mary L S Wainwright, LFIBA, DDG, IOM, *USA*
Ms Annita C Walker, FIBA, DDG, *USA*
W W Walley, MD, DDG, *USA*
Mr Chang Wan-Hsi (Mo jen), DDG, *Taiwan, China*
Mr Rollin M Warner Jr, LFIBA, DDG, *USA*
Mr Norman Sidney Weiser, FIBA, DDG, *USA*
Ms Lois Campbell Wells, LPIBA, IOM, OIF, *New Zealand*
Ms Nancy Weniger-Phelps, DDG, *USA*
Dr Don B Wethasinghe, LPIBA, DDG, *Sri Lanka*
Dr M R Wiemann Jr, LPIBA, LFWLA, DDG, IOM, *USA*
Miss Annie J Williams, LPIBA, DDG, IOM, *USA*
Dr Joseph R Williams, FIBA, DDG, *USA*
Mrs Jeanne P Wilson, LFIBA, DDG, *Jamaica*
Mr Emmanuel A Winful, LPIBA, DDG, *Ghana*
Dr Abund Ottokar Wist, LPIBA, DDG, *USA*
Dr Sophie M Wolanin, LPIBA, LFWLA, DDG, IOM, *USA*
Dr Azi Wolfenson, LPIBA, DDG, *USA*
Mr Wong Chin Wah, FIBA, DDG, *Republic of Singapore*
Mr Vincent W S Wong, LPIBA, DDG, IOM, *West Malaysia*
Prof Ichiro Yamashita, LFIBA, DDG, IOM, *Japan*
Mr Yan Yi, LFIBA, LFWLA, DDG, IOM, *China*
Prof Chen-Chung Yang, LFIBA, DDG, *China*
Dr Chi-Tung Yeh, LPIBA, DDG, IOM, *China*
Mr Yew Mui Leong, LPIBA, DDG, *Hong Kong*
Prof Yulong Yin, DDG, *China*
Prof Dr K Yoshihara, LPIBA, DDG, IOM, MOIF, *Japan*
Mrs Florence S Young, LFIBA, DDG, *USA*
Mr Zhongguang Zhang, LFIBA, DDG, *China*
Prof Zhang Zhixiang, DDG, IOM, *China*
Dr Jamil Gad Zilkha, DDG, *Israel*

HONORARY AND ANNUAL RESEARCH ASSOCIATES

RESEARCH FELLOWS OF THE IBC

Professor Antoine Abondo, *Cameroon*
Dr Anna J Allen, *USA*
Dr Rowland Iwu Amadi, *West Africa*
Mr Mario V Arroyo-Gomez, *Gibraltar*
Professor Ba En-Xu, *China*
Mrs Katarina E Bader-Molnar, *Switzerland*
Margaret Baender, *USA*
Dr Isabel R Baumann, *Switzerland*
Ms Sheila Bellamy, *Australia*
Dr Guy Boillat, *France*
Dr Georges Antoine Borel, *Switzerland*
Ms Judith Anne Brooks, *USA*
Captain F W Brown, *USA*
Mrs Gertrude Esther Carper, *USA*
Professor Chung-Yi Chen, *Taiwan, China*
Mr James Dzu-Biao Chen, *Hong Kong*
Mr Michael Kuo-Hsing Ch'in, *Taiwan, China*
Dr C Juliana Ching, *Hong Kong*
Dr Frederick Foo Chien, *China*
Professor Kyu-bok Chung, *South Korea*
Mr Leonc Jusz Ciuciura, *Poland*
Ms Nancy Patricia Coe, *USA*
Ms Iris Colvin, *USA*
Dr Francesco De Napoli, *Italy*
Ms Panayote Elias Dimitras, *Greece*
Mr Eric Dixon-Cave Hiscock, *Canada*
Mr Robert Charles Dorion, *Central America*
Prof Hermann W Eichstaedt, *Germany*
Mr Ole Kristian Ersgaard, *Denmark*
Professor Litian Feng, *China*
Dr Marianne B Fleck, *USA*
Mr Wilhelm Flöttmann, *Germany*
Mrs Vivian E S Fox, *USA*
Professor Gao Hongxun, *China*
Dr Erwin E Girod, *USA*
Goh Han Teng, PhD, *Republic of Singapore*
Dr M Goldston-Morris, *Australia*
Mr Isaac Thoman Goodine, *Philippines*
Dr Francis Walter Graham, *Australia*
Dr Rhoda Grant, *USA*
Mrs Padmin Gunaratnam, *Singapore*
Ms Nancy L Thompson Gunnoe, *USA*
Ms Darlene Midori Hayashi, *USA*
Joy Alice Holm, PhD, *USA*
Mr Virapong Hongyok, *South Thailand*
Professor Dr Sadao Hoshino, *Japan*
Professor Zuey-Shin Hsu, *Taiwan, China*
Mr Louis Lim Kim Huat, *Dar es Salaam*
Ms Mildred F Hutchins, *USA*
Professor Dr Kazuyosi Ikeda, *Japan*
Mr Ramnath Jeetah, *Mauritius*
Dr Mirja A Kalliopuska, *Finland*
Mrs Puriko Kase, *Japan*
Ms Marlene H Katchur, *USA*
Dr Jerry Alvin Kirk, *USA*

Dr Samson B H Kisekka, *Uganda*
Professor Gerrit K L'Abbé, *Belgium*
Dr Philip Lai, *Hong Kong*
Professor Li Ji-Ren, *China*
Professor Li Yiyi, *China*
Professor Li Yonming, *China*
Dr Joanne L Linn, *USA*
Mr Grigori Loutchansky, *Austria*
Mr Edward James MacGilfrey, *USA*
Ms Joan Mahaffey, *USA*
Mr Umaru-Sanda Maigida, *Nigeria*
Dr Francisca Martin-Molero, *Spain*
Professor Masaie Matsumura, *Japan*
Mr Joseph M Mayo, *USA*
Professor Ebden Lizo Mazwai, *South Africa*
Mr Paul J Meyer, *USA*
Dr Isutomu Mimura, *Japan*
Ms Hildegard-Kauth Minchenko, *USA*
Professor Iwao Miyachi, *Japan*
Ms Martha A Moore, *USA*
Ms Karen Wigley-Morrison, *USA*
Professor Dr Emil Mosonyi, *Germany*
Dr John Edward Mulvihill, *USA*
Professor Henry Ian A Nowik, *USA*
Ms Helen Mary Odamtten, *Ghana*
Professor Hidemichi Ota, *Japan*
Dr Danny Shiu-Lam Paau, *Hong Kong*
Dr Eugenia Pasternak, *Canada*
Dame Gwendolyn Brown Shepley Peacher, *USA*
Professor Tadeusz Popiela, *Poland*
Mr Nader E Rastegar, *USA*
Mr Robert John Richardson, *Canada*
Dr Ralph R Robinson, *USA*
Ms Donna Jo Rolland, *USA*
Dr Jim R Ropchan, *USA*
Professor Julius L Rothman, *USA*
Dr Violet D Schaefer, *USA*
Mr Werner N W Schramm, *Germany*
Mr Clayton Winfield Scott, *USA*
Dr Isadore Shapiro, *USA*
Professor Shen Xiuzhi, *China*
Ms Anna Pearl Sherrick, *USA*
Dr V Maxine Shipley Stock, *USA*
Mr Ah-Tee Sim, *Singapore*
Mr Henri Martokoesoemo Soekrisno, *Indonesia*
Mr Haji Soemario, *Indonesia*
Mr Peter Stadler, *Denmark*
Ms Carlene Stinnette, *USA*
Dr Helen Chien-fan Su, *USA*
Dr Masuichi Takino, *Japan*
Professor Giulio Filippo Tarro, *Italy*
Mr Walter D Thomas, *USA*
Professor R F Vliegen, *Japan*

CONTENTS

A

AABY Peter Schepelern, b. 6 Nov 1944, Lund, Sweden. Epidemiologist. m. Ida Maria Lisse, 1 s. Education: MSc, Anthropology, University of Copenhagen, 1974; DMSc, Medicine, University of Copenhagen, 1988. Career: Social Scientist, Guinea-Bissau, 1978-81; Senior Lecturer, Anthropology, University of Copenhagen, 1981-91; Senior Researcher, Statens Serum Institut, 1991-. Publications: Over 95 articles in professional journals including: Co-author, Reduced childhood mortality following standard measles vaccination at 4-8 months compared to 9-11 months of age, in British Medical Journal, 1993; Author, Assumptions and contradictions in measles and measles immunization research: Is measles good for something?, in Social Science Medicine, in press. Memberships: International Union for Scientific Study of Populations; Committee on Anthropological Demography. Address: Statens Serum Institut, Artilleri Vej 5, 2300 Copenhagen S, Denmark.

ABBOTT William M, b. 14 Apr 1936, San Francisco, CA, USA. Surgeon. m. Cynthia, 14 Jan 1978, 1 s, 1 d. Education: AB, Stanford University, 1958; MD, Stanford University School of Medicine, 1961; MA, Harvard University, 1961. Appointments include: Research fellow in Surgery, 1965-66, Instrucor in Surgery, 1971-73, Assistant Professor of Surgery, 1973-76, Associate Professor of Surgery, Massachusetts general Hospital, 1976-82, Associate Professor of Surgery, 1982-89. Professor of Surgery, 1989-, Harvard Medical School; Research Affiliate, Massachusetts Institute of Technology, 1978-; Chief of Vascular Surgery, Massachusetts General Hospital. Publications: Contributor of over 200 professional articles, reviews, monographs and book chapters. Honours include: Bausch and Lomb Award in Science, 1954; Merck Award for Outstanding Scholarship in Medicine, Stanford University, School of Medicine, 1961. Memberships include: American Association for the Advancement of Science; International Society for Parenteral Nutrition; American College of Surgeons; American Trauma Society; Charter Member, New England Society for Vascular Surgery; International Cardiovascular Society; American Heart Association; Society for Vascular Surgery; European Society for Vascular Surgery; Society of Vascular Technology; Association of Program Directors in General Vascular Surgery. Address: Massachusetts General Hospital, 15 Parkman St WAC 458, Boston, MA 02114, USA.

ABBRECHT Peter H, b. 27 Nov 1930, Toledo, Ohio, USA. Professor. Education: BS, Purdue University; MS, PhD, MD, University of Michigan. Appointments: Professor of Medicine and Physiology, Chairman, Bioengineering Programme, University of Michigan, 1963-80; Director, Physiology and Biomedical Engineering Programme, National Institute general Medicine and science, 1977-78; Professor of Medicine and Physiology, Chairman, Department of Physiology, Uniformed Services University. Publications: Contributor of 90 articles and book chapters. Honours: Michigan Heart Association Outstanding Research Award, 1960; NIH Research Career Development Award, 1968-75. Memberships: AAAS; American Physiological Society; American College of Physicians, Fellow; Fellow, American College Chest Physicians; American Thoracic Society; Biomedical Engineering Society. Address: Uniformed Services University of Health Sciences, 4301 Jones Bridge Road, Bethesda, MD 20814-4799, USA.

ABDEL GADIR Ahmed, b. 25 July 1947, Sudan. Gynaecologist. m. Hayat Salih El Obeid, 11 Aug 1975, 1 son, 2 daughters. Education: MBBS; PhD, Glasgow University, Scotland, 1978; MRCOG, 1981, FRCOG, 1994. Appointments: Medical Director, Hallam Medical Centre, Harley Street, London, England; Honorary Senior Lecturer, Royal Free Hospital, London; Currently Consultant Gynaecologist and Medical Director, Female and Male Fertility Centre, Highgate Private Hospital, London. Publications: Book chapters: Hormonal changes following laparoscopic ovarian electrocautery in patients with polycystic ovarian syndrome (co-author), 1991; Surgery and the polycystic ovarian syndrome (with R W Shaw), 1992; Ovarian surgery in control and stimulation of follicular growth, 1993; Numerous articles, mainly on Reproductive Endocrinology; Conference papers mainly on Reproductive Endocrinology and Infertility. Honours: Senior British Council Scholarship for postgraduate studies, 1974-77. Memberships: British Fertility Society; American Society for Reproduction Medicine; European Society of Human Reproduction and Embryology; New York Academy of Sciences. Hobby: Music. Address: 40 Brook Avenue, Edgware, Middlesex HA8 9XF, England.

ABDULLAH Syed, b. 22 May 1928, India. Psychiatrist. m. Bilquis Abdullah, 4 Feb 1953, 1 son, 2 daughters. Education: MD. Appointments: Assistant Clinical Professor, Columbia University School of Medicine, New York City, New York, USA, 1969-88; Currently: Private Practitioner; Co-Editor, Synapse Newsletter. Memberships: American Psychiatric Associaiton; Ex-President, West Hudson Psychiatric Society. Hobbies: Reading; Writing; Gardening; Jogging. Address: 2 Hawk Street, Pearl River, NY 10965, USA.

ABE Kazuhiko, b. 16 Mar 1933, Kurume, Japan. Psychiatrist. m. Hiroko Kumamaru, 26 Jan 1969, 1 son. Education: MD, Kyushu University School of Medicine, 1958; DMS, Osaka City Medical School, 1965. Appointments: Visiting Researcher, Institute of Psychiatry, London, 1966-68; Associate Professor, Psychiatry, Osaka City University Medical School, 1969-77; Professor of Psychiatry, University of Occupational & Environmental Health, 1978-. Publications: Numerous papers on child psychiatry and psychiatric genetics. Memberships: Trustee, Japanese Society of Biological Psychiatry, 1991-; Councilor, Japanese Psychiatric Association. Honours: Recipient of Research Grant, Ministry of Health & Welfare, Tokyo, 1976-78, 1990-92. Hobbies: Music; Travel; Cycling; Languages. Address: Department of Psychiatry, University of Occupational & Environmental Health, Yahata-Nishiku, Kitakyushu 807, Japan.

ABE Muneaki, b. 11 Feb 1941, Ehime, Japan. Orthopaedic Surgeon. m. 25 Sept 1971, 1 son, 1 daughter. Education: Graduated, Osaka Medical College, 1966; MD; PhD; Approved Orthopaedic Surgeon, Approved Rheumatologist, Approved Sports Doctor, Japanese Orthopaedic Association. Appointments: Instructor, 1970, Assistant Professor, 1979, currently Associate Professor, Osaka Medical College. Publications: Arthrography of the normal and post-traumatic wrist, 1989; Replacement of the lumate by the posiform in Kienbock disease, 1992; Forearm lengthening by callus distraction, 1993. Memberships: Société Internationale de Chirurgie Orthopédique et de Traumatologie; SIROT; International Federation of Societies for Surgery of the Hand; International Wrist Investigators Workshop. Hobbies: Tennis; Golf. Address: Department of Orthopaedic Surgery, Osaka Medical College, 2-7 Daigakucho, Takatsuki, Osaka 569, Japan.

ABEL Francis Lee, b. 12 Apr 1931, Iowa City, Iowa, USA. Physician. m. Anne Elizabeth Sutherland, 16 June 1974, 1 son, 3 daughters. Education: AA, Creston Junior College, 1950; BA, University of Kansas, 1952; MD, Harvard University, 1957; PhD, University of Wisconsin, 1960. APpointments: Professor, Department Physiology, Indiana University School of Medicine, 1962-75; Interim Dean, University of South Carolina School of Medicine, 1976; Visiting Professor, Department Physiology, University of Limburg, Maastricht, Netherlands; Professor, Chairman, Department of Physiology, University of South Carolina School of Medicine, Columbia. Publications: Cardiovascular Function: Principles and Applications, Co-author, 1979; Functional Aspects of the Normal Hypertrophied and Failing Heart, Co-editor, 1984. Honours: USPHS Career Development Award, 1968-73; Dean's Distinguished Service Award, USC School of Medicine, 1987; National Research Service Award, National Institutes of Health, USPHS, 1989-90. Memberships: Institute of Electrical and Electronics Engineers; American Physiology Society; Committee Chair, 1985, Shock Society; Basic Science Council; American Heart Association; Biomedical Engineering Society. Hobbies Skiing; Fishing. Address: Department of Physiology, School of Medicine, University of South Carolina, Columbia, SC 29208, USA.

ABELLI Luigi, b. 12 Feb 1957, Rome, Italy. Biologist. m. Angela Vittoria Goletti. Education: Degree cum laude, Biological Sciences, La Sapienza University, Rome, 1981. Appointments: Research Fellow, 1982-87, Supervisor, Respiratory Disease Unit, 1988-90, Department of Pharmacology, Menarini Ricerche Sud, Pomezia, Roma; Research Fellow, Faculty of Sciences, Tuscia University, Viterbo, 1991-; Visiting Scientist, Department of Histochemistry, Royal Postgraduate Medical School, Hammersmith Hospital, London, England, 1993-94. Publications: More than 50 articles in international scientific journals; Co-author, articles in scientific books. Memberships: New York Academy of Sciences; European Neuropeptide Club; European Society of Comparative Endocrinology; National Geographic Society. Hobbies: Diving; Painting. Address: via Monfalcone 2/B, 01100 Viterbo, Italy.

ABRAHAM Abe Samuel, b. 2 Oct 1917, Bentleyville, Pennsylvania, USA. Psychiatrist. Education: BS, Westminster College, New Wilmington, Pennsylvania, 1938; MD, George Washington University

School of Medicine, 1950. Appointments include: Medical technologist, Prospect Heights Hospital, Brooklyn, New York, 1941-42; Control Chemist, American Cyanomid Corporation, Boundbrook, New Jersey, 1942-46; Internship: St Elizabeths Hospital, Federal Service Agency, 1950-52; Psychiatric Residency, 1952-55, Staff Psychiatrist, 1955-69, Veterens Administration, Brenwood Hospital, Los Angeles; Served to Captin, US Air Force; Clinical Instructor, UCLA School of Medicine, Department of Psychiatry, Los Angeles, 1958-69; Associated Clinical Professor of Psychiatry, George Washington University, School of Medicine, Department of Psychiatry, Washington DC, 1970-79; Staff Psychiatrist, USPHS-NIMH, 1969-88; Retired, 1988. Publications: Development of Criteria for Evaluating Psychiatric Educational Programs, Co-author, 1976; Characteristics of Psychiatric Residency Programs, Co-author, 1977. Honour: Diplomate in Psychiatry. Memberships: American Psychiatric Association, Life Fellow; World Federation for Mental Health; American Medical Association. Address: 12534 Montellano Terrace, San Diego, CA 92130, USA.

ABRAM Maie, b. 7 Dec 1939, Valgs District, Estonia. Anaesthesiologist. m. Arnold Abram, 3 Mar 1963, 1 son. Education: Graduated, Tartu University Faculty of Medicine, 1965; MD, 1986. Appointments: Anaesthesiologist, Pärnu Town Hospital, 1965-77; Head, Department of Anaesthesiology, 1977-91, currently Anaesthesiologist, Tartu University Hospital, Tartu. Publications: Abstracts in publications of of 8th European Congress of Anaesthesiology, 1990, and World Congress of Anaesthesiology, 1992. Memberships: Estonian Society of Anaesthesiology (now section of World Society of Anaesthesiologists); World Society of Pain. Hobby: Orienteering. Address: Tartu University Hospital, 8 Puusepp Street, EE 2400 Tartu, Estonia.

ABRAMOWICZ Helen, b. 24 May 1943, New Haven, Connecticut, USA. Psychiatrist. m. Mark Abramowicz, 1 June 1969, 2 sons, 1 daughter. Education: AB, Smith College, 1964; MD, Albert Einstein College of Medicine, 1986; Diplomate: American Board of Psychiatry and Neurology; American Board of Child Psychiatry; American Board of Pediatrics. Appointments: Intern and Resident in Paediatrics, Bronx Municipal Hospital; Fellow, Paediatric Developmental Disabilities, Albert Einstein College of Medicine; Resident in Psychiatry, Montefiore Hospital; Fellow, Child Psychiatry, New York Hospital; Currently: Psychiatrist in private practice; Assistant Professor of Psychiatry, Cornell University Medical Center. Publications: Increased cerebrospinal fluid protein following isopropyl alcohol intoxication (with P Visudhiphan), 1971; The Epidemiology of Severe Mental Retardation in Children (with S Richardson); Reproductive Ability of Adults (with Nitowsky). Honours: Fellow, American Psychiatric Association, 1988-. Memberships: Phi Beta Kappa; American Psychiatric Association, Westchester District Branch, President 1989-90; Fellow, American Academy of Child Psychiatry. Hobbies: Travel; Gardening; Opera; Reading. Address: 19 Locust Avenue, Larchmont, NY 10538, USA.

AÇIKALIN Hatice Aliye, b. 19 March 1911, Istanbul, Turkey. Retired. Education: Doctor of Medicine, University of Istanbul, 1932; Specialisation in Cardiology, University of Paris, France, 1939. Appointments: Head, Internal Medicine Service, Cerrahpasa Hospital, Istanbul, 1939-72. Publications: Anklostomiase et Asystolie, 1952; Elektrokardiografi, 1964; Apeksokardiogram - Fono kardiografi - Karotidogram, 1974. Memberships: Société de Cardiologie, France; Founder, Member, Turkish Cardiological Society. Hobbies: Reading; Gardening. Address: Yaliboyu Cevatbey Apt 162/2, Bebek, Istanbul 80810, Turkey.

ACKERMAN Marvin, b. 18 Apr 1926, Bronx, New York, USA. Physician. m. Susan Patricia Lester, 8 Aug 1957, 4 children. Education: Student, CUNY, 1945-47; BA, Western State College, 1949; Postgraduate, University Colorado, 1949-50; Bachelor in Medical Sciences, University Geneva, 1952, MD, 1955. Appointments incl: Intern, Harper Hospital, Detriot, 1956; Resident, Dermatology, Manhattan VA Hospital, New York, Skin & Cancer Hospital, Bellevue Hospital, 1957-60; Private Practice, Dermatology, New York City, 1958-59, Bronx, 1959-61, Mamaroneck, New York, 1960-, Scarsdale, New York, 1961-. Publications: Contributor of articles to professional journals. Memberships incl: Fellow, American Academy of Allergy & Immunology; American Association of Immunology Allergy; AMA; Westchester Allergy Society; American Venereal Disease Association. Address: 829 Wilmot Road, Scarsdale, NY 10583-6526, USA.

ACKERMAN William E, b. 28 Aug 1945. Medical Doctor; Director. m. M Gretchen Ackerman, 29 Jan 1972, 2 sons, 1 daughter. Education: School of Medicine, University of Louisville. Appointments: Director, University School of Medicine, Cincinnati, 1987-90; Director, Obstetrics, Anesthesia, Norton Hospital, Louisville, 1990-93. Publications: Numerous publications and articles in various journals. Memberships: American Society of Regional Anesthesia; American Society of Anesthesia; International Anesthesia Research Society. Honours: Nominated, Research Award, Southern Medical Journal, 1992. Hobbies: Swimming; Golf; Oil Painting; Playwriting. Address: 6605 Harrods View Circle, Prospect, KY 40059, USA.

ACKLIN Thomas Patrick, b. 6 Jan 1950, Sewickley, Pennsylvania, USA. Certified Psychoanalyst. Education: BA, Philosophy, 1971, MA, Philosophy, 1975, Duquesne University, Pittsburgh, 1971; MDiv, Saint Vincent Seminary, Latrobe, Pennsylvania, 1978; Psychoanalytic training, Belgian School of Psychoanalysis, 1980-82; PhD, Theology, Psychology of Religion, 1982, STD, 1983, University of Louvain, Belgium; Diploma, Pittsburgh Psychoanalytic Centre, 1985; Certification in Psychoanalysis, American Boards for Accreditation and Certification, National Association for the Advancement of Psychoanalysis, 1985; Graduate, Pittsburgh Psychoanalytic Institute, 1994. Appointments: Private practice as Psychotherapist, 1982-; Psychotherapist, Counselling Centre, Saint Vincent College, Latrobe, Pennsylvania, 1982-91; Psychotherapist, 1983-85; Psychotherapist, Pittsburgh Psychoanalytic Center, Pittsburgh, Pennsylvania; Licensed Psychotherapist, Latrobe Psychotherapy Associates, Latrobe, 1990-. Memberships: Member, American Psychoanalytic Association; Corresponding Member, Belgian School of Psychoanalysis; National Association for the Advancement of Psychoanalysis; Pittsburgh Psychoanalytic Society; International Psychoanalytic Association. Hobbies: Travel; Hiking; Reading; Writing. Address: Saint Vincent, 300 Fraser Purchase Road, Latrobe, PA 15650-2690, USA.

ADAM John Edward, b. 25 Oct 1936, Welland, Ontario, Canada. Dermatologist. m. Susan Swiggum, 16 Dec 1988, 2 sons, 2 daughters. Education: MD, Queens University, Kingston, Ontario; MHA, University of Ottawa; FRCP(C); Fellow, Royal College of Physicians and Surgeons of Canada. Appointments: Currently Professor, Chairman, Division of Dermatology, University of Ottawa. Invention: Developed Unbiased Double Blind Procedure used in Clinical Drug Trials. Publications: Over 50 articles on dermatology; Most significant: Erathroderma, Sporotrichosis and the Technique of Curettage Surgery; Contributed chapters to 2 dermatology textbooks. Honours: Honorary Member, Irish Dermatology Association; Honorary Surgeon, 78th Fraser Highlanders, 2nd Battalion, Ottawa. Memberships: Vice-President, Canadian Association of Medical Students of Canada; Vice-President, Canadian Dermatology Foundation; Vice-President, Canadian Dermatology Association; Board of Trustees, Ottawa Civic Hospital; President, Atlantic Dermatology Association; American Academy of Dermatology; Canadian Medical Association; American Medical Association. Hobbies: Gardening; Golf. Address: Suite 507, 1081 Carling Ave, Ottawa, Ontario, Canada K1Y 4G2.

ADAM John Lewis, b. 7 May 1950, Cleveland, Ohio, USA. Registered Nurse. m. Joan Pomiecko, 6 Nov 1982, 2 daughters. Education: BSN, Ursuline St John's College; BA, History, Borromeo Seminary; Certification in Mental Nursing, American Nursing Association. Appointments: Staff Nurse, Advanced Clinical Nurse, University Hospitals, Cleveland; Nurse Manager, Administrative Director of Psychiatry, St Vincent Charity Hospital; Director of Operations, Psychiatry and Chemical Dependency, Advantage Behavioral Health Network; Currently, Director of Nursing for Mental Health Services, Santa Barbara Cottage Hospital, Santa Barbara, California. Publication: Nursing Management of Neuroleptic Malignant Symdrome, in Clinical Modulities in Psychiatric Mental Health Nursing. Honours: Clinical Excellence Award, University Hospitals, Cleveland, 1978; Olive Schlink Nursing Excellence Award, St Vincent Charity Hospital, 1992. Memberships: Charter Member, American Association of Psychiatric Nurses; Fellow, American Orthopsychiatric Association; Associate Member, National League Nurses. Hobbies: Swimming; Film; Raising canines. Address: 800 Guildford Boulevard, Medina, OH 44256, USA.

ADAMS Lily Jean, b. 22 Jan 1948, New York City, USA. Registered Nurse. m. Jim Adams, 1 May 1972, 1 son, 1 daughter. Education: Diploma, Nursing; Associate in Arts & Liberal Arts; BA, Psychology; MA, Developmental Psychology. Appointments: Private Consultant on PTSD; Private Counselor; Float Nurse; Recovery/ICU Nurse Specialist for Open Heart Surgery; ICU/Triage Combat Nurse. Publications: So Proudly We

Hai!; Visions of War, Dreams of Peace. Honours: Outstanding Young Woman of America, 1983; Army Commendation Medal; Affelder Memorial Award. Memberships: International Society of Traumatic Stress Studies; American Holistic Nurses Association. Hobbies: Writing; Reading Novels; Music; Gardening; Her Children.

ADAMS Liza Maria, b. 13 Sept 1968, Brighton, England. Associate in Private Practice; Volunteer Therapist, Medical Foundation for the Care of Victims of Torture. Education: Diploma of Osteopathy, British School of Osteopathy, 1986-90; MSc, Experimental Methods in Psychology, University College, London; 1993-94 Appointments: Medical Director, London Gators American Football Club, 1990-92. Memberships: Osteopathic Association of Great Britain; General Council & Register of Osteopaths; Student Subscription, British Psychological Society. Hobbies: Hand Gliding; Martial Art. Address: 73 Darwin Road, South Ealing, London, W5 4BB, England.

ADAMS Raymond Edward, b. 22 Sept 1933, Trenton, New Jersey, USA. Ophthalmologist. m. Barbara May Stone, 2 Aug 1958, 2 sons, 1 daughter. Education: BA, Gettysburg College, Gettysburg, Pennsylvania; Postgraduate studies, Franklin Marshall College, Lancaster, Pennsylvania; MD, New York Medical College; PA, University of Pennsylvania School of Medicine, Philadelphia; Certificate of Completion, Wills Eye Hospital, Philadelphia. Appointments: Chief Resident, Wills Eye Hospital, 1963-64; Chief Ophthalmologist, USAF Hospital, Chanute, Rantoul, Illinois, 1964-66; Surgical Staff, Cooper Hospital, Camden, New Jersey, 1966-77, 1985-90; Chief of Ophthalmology, West Jersey Health System, Marlton, New Jersey, 1973-89; Acting Ophthalmologist in Chief, Wills Eye Hospital, 1985-; Medical Staff, West Jersey Health System, Voorhees, New Jersey, 1986-; Clinical Assistant Professor, Department of Surgery, University of Medicine and Dentistry of New Jersey, 1988-. Publications: Ocular Hypotensive Effect of Introvenously Administered Mannitrol (with Robert Kirschner and I Leopold); Treatment of Trichinosis (with G Spaeth and A Soffe). Memberships include: American Academy of Ophthalmology; American Medical Association; American Intraocular Implant Society; New Jersey, Camden and Christian Medical Societies; Delaware Valley Ophthalmology Society; Fellow, American College of Surgeons; New Jersey Academy of Ophthalmology and Otolaryngology; Ophthalmic Club of Philadelphia; Philadelphia College of Physicians, President 1992-; Wills Eye Society of Ex-Residents; College of Physicians of Philadelphia, President, Ophthalmology Section, 1991-93. Hobbies: Member: Air Force Association; Aircraft Owners and Pilots Association (1978-); Flying Physicians Association (1983-88). Address: 741 W Marlton Pike, Rt 70, Cherry Hill, NJ 08002-3590, USA.

ADCOCK David, b. 19 Sept 1938, Columbia, South Carolina, USA. Physician; Educator. Education: BS, 1958; MD, 1962; MPH, 1986; Certified, American Board of Radiology, American Board of Nuclear Medicine, American Board of Preventive Medicine. Appointments: Associate Professor, Radiology, University of South Carolina; Director of Nuclear Medicine, Richland Memorial Hospital; Currently Professor, Chairman, Radiology Department, University of South Carolina. Publications include: Commentary: Preventive Services In a Hybrid Capitation Fee-for-Service Setting, 1989; Marketing: Good Medicine or Good Business, 1989; Are Clinical Trials Cost-Effective, 1990; Co-author: The Cost of Excess Radiation Exposure from the Continued Use of Chest Fluoroscopy in China, 1984; A Method to Label Cigarette Smoke with 99m Technetium, 1985; Ultrasound lumbar canal measurement in hospital employees with back pain, 1988; Ultrasonic Measurement of Lumbar Canal Diameter: A Screening Tool for Low Back Disorders?, 1989; Ownership of the Medical Radiograph, 1991. Honours: Alpha Omega Alpha, 1961; Delta Omega, 1988; Luther Terry Preventive Medicine Fellowship, 1988. Memberships: American College of Preventive Medicine; American Public Health Association; Society of Chairmen of Academic Radiology Departments. Hobbies: Horticulture; Apiculture. Address: 2308 Longtowsn Road East, Blythewood, SC 29016, USA.

ADDO Samira Elias, b. 23 June 1949, Ghana. Gynaecologist. m. Isaac, 18 Aug 1976, 3 sons, 1 daughter. Education: MB; ChB; MRCOG. Appointments: Research Fellow; Senior Registrar; Consultant. Memberships: British Fertility Society; British Medical Association. Address: Bourn Hall Clinic, Bourn, Cambs CB3 7TR, England.

ADEBONOJO Festus Olumuyiwa, b. 6 May 1931, Lagos, Nigeria. Medicine. m. Leslie Goodale, 26 Nov 1989, 4 s. Education: BS, 1956, MD, 1960, Yale University; Diploma, American Board of Pediatrics,

1965. Career: Associate Professor Pediatrics, University of PA, 1976-77; Professor and Chairman, Department of Pediatrics, University of Ife, Nigeria, 1977-78; Dean, Faculty of Health Sciences, 1978-80, Professor of Pediatrics, 1982-84, Cornell Medical College; Professor and Chairman, Meharry Medical College, 1984-89; Professor and Chairman, Pediatrics, East TN State University, 1989-. Publications: Author, How Baby Grows, 1985; 36 Scientific Journal Articles. Memberships: American Pediatric Society; Sigma Xi. Address: East Tennessee State University, James H Quillen College of Medicine, PO Box 70578, Johnson City, TN 37614-0578, USA.

ADELIZZI Raymond A, b. 20 Aug 1947, Philadelphia, Pennsylvania, USA. Physician. m. Catherine Adelizzi, 15 Apr 1978, 2 sons. Education: BS, St Joseph's College, Philadelphia, 1969; DO, Philadelphia College of Osteopathic Medicine, 1973; Internship, 1973-74; Residency, 1974-76; Fellowship, Rheumatology, Hahnemann Medical College and Hospital, Philadelphia, 1976-78; Fellow, American College of Rheumatology; Fellow, American College of Osteopathic Internists, 1988. Appointments include: Chief, Section of Rheumatology, Kennedy Memorial Hospitals, University Medical Center, Stratford, New Jersey, 1978-; Clinical Assistant Professor, 1981-82, Acting Chief, Division of Rheumatology, 1981-83, University of Medicine and Dentistry, Stratford, New Jersey; Assistant Professor, 1982-87, Head, Division of Rheumatology, 1983-93, Associate Professor of Medicine, 1987-, Clinical Associate Professor of Medicine, 1994-, School of Osteopathic Medicine, University of Medicine and Dentistry of New Jersey; Director, Arthritis Center of South Jersey, Stratford, 1993-. Publications include: Over 30, mainly in field of rheumatology including diagnosis and treatment; Clinical Recognition of the Rheumatic Diseases (guest editor), 1987; Radio presentations on arthritis recognition, osteoporosis, systemic lupus. Honours: Inducted as Fellow, Philadelphia College of Physicians, 1993; Many awards. Memberships include: American College of Rheumatology; Philadelphia Rheumatism Society; New Jersey Association of Osteopathic Physicians; Arthritis Foundation, New Jersey Chapter; Founder, New Jersey Osteoporosis Society; Lyme Disease Foundation. Hobbies: Jogging; Basketball; Tennis; Golf. Address: 215 E Laurel Rd, Stratford, NJ 08084, USA.

ADER Robert, b. 20 Feb 1932, New York City, New York, USA. Psychologist. m. Gayle Simon, 2 June 1957, 4 daughters. Education: BS, Tulane University, 1953; PhD, Cornell University, 1957. Appointments: Instructor, 1957-61, Assistant Professor, 1961-64, Associate Professor, 1964-68, Professor, Psychiatry, Psychology, Medicine, Department of Biochemistry, 1968-, now George L Engel Professor, Psychosocial Medicine, Director of Division of Behavioural and Psychosocial Medicine, Director, Center for Psychoneuroimmunology Research, University of Rochester School of Medicine and Dentistry; Visiting Professor, Rudolf Magnus Institute for Pharmacology, University of Utrecht, Netherlands, 1970-71; Fellow, Center for Advanced Study in the Behavioral Sciences, Stanford, California, 1992-93. Publications: Psychoneuroimmunology (editor), 1981, 2nd edition (co-editor), 1991; Experimental Foundations of Behavioral Medicine (co-editor), 1988; About 200 papers in scientific journals. Honours include: Salmon Lecturer, New York Academy of Medicine, 1989; Fellow, The Fetzer Institute, Kalamazoo, Michigan, 1990-; MD honoris causa, University of Trondheim, Norway, 1992; Member, several editorial boards, 1964-; Editor-in-Chief, Brain, Behavior, and Immunity, 1986-; Associate Editor, Advances in Neuroimmunology, 1990-. Memberships: Psychoneuroimmunology Research Society, Founding President 1993-94; Founding Member, Fellow, Academy of Behavioral Medicine, President 1984-85; Fellow, Society of Behavioral Medicine; American Association of University Professors; American Psychosomatic Society, President 1979-80; International Society for Developmental Psychobiology, President 1981-82; Psychonomic Society; American and Eastern Psychological Associations. Hobbies: Photography; Tennis; Fishing; Gardening, Address: Department of Psychiatry, University of Rochester Medical Center, 300 Crittenden Boulevard, Rochester, NY 14642, USA.

ADESOLA Akinpelu Oludele, b. 6 Nov 1930, Nigeria. Physician. m. Bola Sodeinde, 22 Dec 1959, 2 daughters. Education: MB, BCh; BAO (Belfast), 1956; MCh (Belfast); FRCS; FACS; FWACS. Appointments: Senior Surgical Tutor, Queen's University of Belfast, Northern Ireland, 1961; Senior Buswell Fellow, University of Rochester, New York, USA, 1963; Professor of Surgery, University of Lagos College of Medicine, 1967; Visiting Professor of Surgery, McGill University, Canada, 1987; Currently Consultant Surgeon/Gastroenterologist, Bay Clinic, Lagos, Nigeria. Publications: Coronary Thrombosis: The Influence of

Meteorological Changes, 1960; Co-author: Adult Intussusception in Western Nigeria, 1964; Parathyroids, Calcium and Gastric Secretion in Man and Dog, 1964; Influence of Vaso-active Agents on Ascites, 1965; Tropical Surgery, book, 1970; Chronic Gastritis and Duodenal Ulcer in Nigerians, 1974; Acute Abdomen in Lagos, Nigeria: Changing Pattern in an African Community, 1980. Honours: President, West African Society of Gastroenterology, 1967-72; President, Nigerian Surgical Research Society, 1975-79; President, West African College of Surgeons, 1975-77; Fellow, Nigerian Academy of Science, 1986; Honorary LLD, Queen's University of Belfast, 1989; Adesuyi Prize for Outstanding Contribution to Health Care in West Africa, awarded by West African Health Community, 1993. Memberships include: Surgical Research Society of Great Britain; British Society of Gastroenterology; West African Society of Gastroenterology. Hobbies: Golf; Swimming; Classical music. Address: PO Box 51218, Ikoyi, Lagos, Nigeria.

ADIBI Siamak, b. 17 Mar 1932, Tehran, Iran. Physician. m. Joan Foedisch, 15 June 1963, 1 son, 2 daughters. Education: BA, Johns Hopkins University, USA, 1955; MD, Jefferson Medical College, 1959; PhD, Massachusetts Institute of Technology, 1967. Appointments: Assistant Professor of Medicine, 1966-71, Head, Gastroenterology Unit, 1966-81, Associate Professor of Medicine, 1971-74, Professor of Medicine, 1974-, University of Pittsburgh, Pennsylvania, USA; Director, Clinical Nutrition Research Unit, University of Pittsburgh School of Medicine. Publications: Over 135 scientific papers; Editor, books: Branched-Chain Amino and Keto Acids in Health and Disease, 1984; Dipeptides as New Substrates in Nutrition Therapy, 1987. Memberships: Association of American Physicians; American Society for Clinical Investigation; American Physiological Society; American Institute of Nutrition; American Gastroenterological Association. Hobbies: Tennis; Sailing; Biking; Kayaking. Address: Clinical Nutrition Research Unit, Montefiore University Hospital, University of Pittsburgh Medical Center, 200 Lothrop Street, Pittsburgh, PA 15213-2582, USA.

ADIMOOLAM Seetharaman, b. 15 June 1947, India. Allergologist and Immunologist. m. Kalaivani Adimoolam, 21 Feb 1977, 1 son, 1 daughter. Education: MD. Appointments: Formerly President, American Lung Association of Brooklyn, New York, USA; Currently Chief of Allergy and Immunology. Publications: Study of Intercity Asthma, in Journal of Allergy; Review of Theophylline Usage, in Journal of Foreign Medical Graduates. Honours: Several honours and awards during medical school years. Memberships: American College of Allergy and Immunology; American Academy of Allergy and Immunology; Asthma and Allergy Foundation of America; New York Allergy Society; Joint Counsel of Allergy and Immunology; Richmond County Medical Society, State of New York; Board of Directors, ALA, Brooklyn. Hobbies: Travel; Watch collecting. Address: 30 Charter Oak Road, Staten Island, NY 10304, USA.

AFRA Dénes, b. 3 Apr 1927, Pécs, Hungary. Neurosurgeon. m. Magda Csörögi, 11 Aug 1963, 1 daughter. Education includes: MD, Semmelweiss Medical School, 1951; PhD. Appointments: Assistant Professor, Anatomical Institute, Semmelweiss Medical School; Assistant, currently Vice-Director, National Institute of Neurosurgery, Budapest. Publications: Supratentorial Recurrences of Gliomas (with W Müller and R Schröder), 1977; Combined radiotherapy with dibromodulcitol (co-author), 1983; Recurrent low grade gliomas, 1991. Memberships: Hungarian Neurosurgical Society; EORTC Brain Tumour Study Group. Hobby: Swimming. Address: Maros u 34, H-1122 Budapest, Hungary.

AGAPITOS Peter J, b. 25 July 1957, Westmount, Quebec, Canada. Assistant Professor of Ophthalmology. m. Ginette Dion, 22 May 1982, 3 daughters. Education: MD, University of Ottawa, 1982; FRCSC, 1988; DIPL ABO, 1988. Appointments: Assistant Professor, Department of Ophthalmology, University of Minnesota, 1989-91; Assistant Professor of Ophthalmology, University of Ottawa, 1991-. Publications: Traumatic Hyphema in Children, 1987; Analysis of Astigmatic Keratotomy, 1989; Anatomical Study of Transclerally Sutured Intraocular Lens Implantation, 1989; Secondary Intraocular Lens Implantation, 1990; Cataract Surgical Techniques, 1991; Looped Posterior Chamber Intraocular Lenses, 1991; Cataract Surgical Techniques and Adjuncts, 1992; Effects of Insulin and EGF on DNA Synthesis in Bovine Endothelial Cultures: Flow Cytometric Analysis, 1994. Memberships: Canadian Ophthalmologic Society; American Society of Cataract & Refractive Surgery; Association for Research in Vision & Ophthalmology. Honours: Fellow, American Academy of Ophthalmology, 1988. Hobbies: Music; Racquet Sports. Address: 406-267 O'Connor Street, Ottawa, Ont K2P 1V3, Canada.

AGBOTON Hippolyte, b. 13 Aug 1948, Dakar, Senegal. Professor of Cardiology. m. Esther Aihtson, 1974, 2 daughters, 1 son. Education: MD, 1974; French National Diploma of Cardiology, 1978; Diplomas: Exotic and Tropical Medicine, 1974; Biology and Sport Medicine, 1975; Haematology, 1977; Aeronautical Medicine, 1979; Legal Reparation of Body Injury, 1980; Sailing Medicine, 1980. Appointments: Specialist in Cardiology, 1978; Editor, Le Benin Medical, 1982; Head, Scientific Affairs Unit, Ministry of Education and Scientific Research, 1983; Head, Department of Cardiology, Faculty of Health Sciences and Head, Cardiology Unit, National Teaching Hospital, Cotonou, 1984-; Professor, Cardiology, 1986-; Technical Adviser to Minister of Health, 1990-; International Board Examiner, IPSEN Foundation for African Cardiology Award, 1990. Publications: Valvular heart diseases in Benin, 1983; Blood cholesterol levels in Beninese children, 1984; Blood cholesterol in Beninese adults, 1984; High blood pressure in Benin, 1984; Acute pericarditis in West Africa, 1984; Blood pressure in Beninese children, 1985; Congenital heart diseases in Benin, 1985; Cardiovascular morbidity and mortality in Beninese adult patients, 1985; Myocardiopathies in Benin, 1986; Bundle branch blocks in Benin, 1990; Blood pressure normal values in newborns and infants in Benin, 1993. Honours: French Order of Merit, 1992. Memberships: Founder Member, West African Society of Cardiology, President 1982-92; Panafrican Society of Cardiology, Assistant General Secretary 1985-93; Rotary Club, Cotonou Lagune, Past President; Expert Member of Cardiology, World Health Organization Panel; New York Academy of Sciences; Founder Member: Medical Society of Benin; Confederation of African Medical Associations and Societies; Francophone Society of Anesthetists for Subsaharian Africa. Hobbies: Football; Music; Photography; Address: BO 1880, Cotonou, Republic of Benin, West Africa.

AGER Alastair Kenneth St Clair, b. 24 June 1956, Birmingham, England. Professor of Applied Psychology. m. Wendy Sadler, 15 July 1978, 1 son, 1 daughter. Education: BA, Keele University, 1978; PhD, University of Wales, 1983; MSc, University of Birmingham, 1985. Appointments: Clinical Psychologist, North Warwickshire Health Authority, 1985-86; Lecturer in Clinical Psychology, University of Leicester, 1986-88; Senior Lecturer in Psychology, University of Malawi, 1988-92; Currently Professor of Applied Biology, Queen Margaret College, Edinburgh, Scotland. Publications: The Life Experiences Checklist, 1990; Microcomputers and Clinical Psychology, 1991; Perception of Risk for Malaria and Schistosomasis in Rural Malawi, 1992; Mental Health Issues in Refugee Populations: A Review, 1994. Memberships: Associate Fellow, British Psychological Society; Chartered Psychologist. Hobbies: Golf; Skiing; Various church activities. Address: Queen Margaret College, Edinburgh EH12 8TS, Scotland.

AGHAHOWA Ekinadoese Juliana, b. 7 July 1958, Lagos, Nigeria. Consultant Radiologist, Head of Radiology Department, University of Benin Teaching Hospital. 3 daughters. Education: MBBS, University of Benin, 1980; Fellowship, West African College of Surgeons, 1986. Appointments: House Officer, UBTH, 1980-81; National Youth Service Corps, 1981-82; Senior House Officer, UBTH, 1982-83; Registrar, UBTH, 1983-85; Senior Registrar, UBTH, 1985-86; Senior Registrar, UBTH, 1986-87; Consultant Radiologist, Lecturer, 1988-. Publications: Bronchography, 1987; Hilar Enlargement in Respiration by Syncytial Virus Pneumonia Europ, Journal of Radiology, 1989. Memberships: West African College of Surgeons; Secretary, Radiology Faculty Board of West African College of Surgeons; Examiner, West African College of Surgeons; Nigerian Society of Radiologists; Association of Radiologists of West Africa; Nigerian Medical Association; Nigerian Institute of Management; Academic Board, University of Benin. Honours: Federal Government of Nigeria Scholar, 1969-73; Benin Area Joint Board Award, 1974-75; Federal Government of Nigeria Scholar, 1976-80; University of Benin Academic Award, 1980; Travel Fellowship Award (Trust Fund for Medical Research in the West African States within the Commonwealth), 1991. Hobbies: Piano; Reading. Address: Department of Radiology, UBTH, PMB 1111, Benin City, Nigeria.

AGRAS William Stewart, b. 17 May 1929, London, England. Physician. m. Mary Jocelyn Jenkins, 15 Jan 1955, 2 s, 2 d. Education: MD, London, 1955; Diploma, Psychiatry, McGill University, 1960; FRCP(C), 1972. Appointments: Instructor to Professor of Psychiatry, University of Vermont, 1961-69; Professor and Chairman, Department of Psychiatry, University of Mississippi Medical Center, 1969-73; Professor of Psychiatry, Stanford University School of Medicine, 1973-. Publications: Panic, 1985; Eating Disorders: Management of Obesity, Bulimia and Anorexia Nervosa, 1987; Numerous Scientific Publications;

Editor, Journal of Applied Behavior Analysis, 1974-77. Honours: Fellow, Center for Advanced Study in The Behavioral Sciences, 1976-77, 1990-91. Memberships: Society for Behavioral Medicine; Association for the Advances of Behavior Therapy. Address: Department of Psychiatry, Stanford University, School of Medicine, Stanford, CA 94305, USA.

AGRE James Courtland, b. 2 May 1950, Northfield, Minnesota, USA. Physician. m. Patti Dee Soderberg, 6 Aug 1982. Education: BA, Augsburg College, Minneapolis, 1972; MD, 1976, PhD, 1985, University of Minnesota, Minneapolis. Appointments: Instructor, Department of Physical Medicine and Rehabilitation, University of Minnesota, 1979-84; Assistant Professor, 1984-90, Associate Professor, 1990-93, Professor, Chairman, 1993-, Department of Rehabilitation Medicine, University of Wisconsin Medical School, Madison. Publications: Neuromuscular function comparison of symptomatic and asymptomatic polio subjects to control subjects, 1990; Late effects of polio: critical review of the literature, 1991. Honours: Licht Award for Excellence in Scientific Writing, 1988; Award for Best Paper Published in the Peer-Reviewed Literature, American Academy of Physical Medicine and Rehabilitation and ERF, 1990; New Investigator Award, American Congress of Rehabilitation Medicine, 1991. Memberships: American Academy of Physical Medicine and Rehabilitation; American Congress of Rehabilitation Medicine; American College of Sports Medicine; American Association for the Advancement of Science; New York Academy of Sciences. Hobbies: Cross country skiing; Cycling. Address: 600 Highland Avenue, Madison, WI 53792, USA.

AGUILO Francisco, b. 6 Oct 1934, Ponce, PR, USA. Medicine. m. Carmen Santana, 27 Jul 1961, 1 d. Education includes: Diplomate, Internal Medicine and Endocrine/Metabolism. Career: Assistant Professor, 1967-74, Associate Professor, 1974-79, Currently, Professor and Head, Division of Endocrinology, Diabetes, Metabolism, University of Puerto Rico School of Medicine. Publications: 50 papers and abstracts; Poetry books: Poemario en el Tiempo, 1989, Vox Nova, 1991, Lustro Secular y Otros Fonemas, 1993. Honours: Alpha Omega Alpha, 1958; Thompson Travelling Scholar, American College of Physicians, 1976; Mobil Award, 1989; Fellow, American College of Physicians. Memberships: American Diabetic Association; ASBMR; Endocrine Society. Hobbies: Poetry Writing; Liturgy. Address: University of Puerto Rico School of Medicine, PO Box 5067, San Juan, PR 00936, USA.

AH-MOYE Michael, b. 13 Feb 1951, Victoria, Seychelles. Gynaecologist. m. Shirley Liao, 30 August 1986, 2 daughters. Education: MB, BS, London University, 1976; MRCOG, 1982. Appointments: Lecturer in Obstetrics and Gynaecology, Oxford University and John Radcliffe Hospital, Oxford, England; Consultant Gynaecologist, Fertility and IVF Unit, Humana Hospital, Wellington, London; Currently Medical Director, Holly House Hospital Fertility Centre, Essex. Publications: Co-author: The GIFT Technique - A New Fertility Option, 1988; The Use of GMRH Analogue for Ovulation Induction for Tubal Gamete Transfer, 1988; Analysis of 1071 GIFT Procedures - The Case for a Flexible Approach to Treatment, 1989. Honours: Serono Fertility Award for Excellence in the Provision of Assisted Conception Services. Memberships: American Fertility Society; British Fertility Society; European Society of Human Reproduction and Embryology. Hobbies: Gardening; Travel; Photography. Address: 14 Ossulton Way, Hampstead Garden Suburb, London N2 0DS, England.

AHLGREN Johan G A, b. 26 Sept 1924, Linköping, Sweden. Professor Emeritus of Orthodontics. m. Margareta Westeson, 5 May 1958, 3 daughters. Education: DDS, University of Lund, 1952; Diploma, University of Michigan, Ann Arbor, USA, 1958; Diplomate (Specialist), Swedish Board of Orthodontics, 1962; Odont dr, University of Lund, 1966. Appointments include: Head of Orthodontic Clinic, Stockholm; Assistant Professor, School of Dentistry, University of Lund; Associate Professor, School of Dentistry, University of Gothenburg; Professor, Chairman, 1973-93, currently Professor Emeritus, School of Dentistry, University of Lund. Publications: Mechanism of Mastication. Electromyographic and cinematographic studies, 1966; Masticatory movements in Man, 1976; Activator treatment. Theory and practice, 1980; A ten-year evaluation of the quality of orthodontic treatment, 1993. Honours: Awards, University of Michigan, 1958-59. Memberships: British Society of Orthodontics; European Orthodontic Society; Swedish Orthodontic Society; Swedish Dental Society. Hobby: Golf. Address: School of Dentistry, S-21421 Malmö, Sweden.

AHMAD Zahida, b. 13 Feb 1931, Delhi, India. Medical Doctor. Education: MBBS (Karachi); DRCOG (London); MRCOG (London);

FRCOG (London). Appointments: Associate Professor, Obstetrics and Gynaecology, Liaquat Medical College, Jamshore, Pakistan; Associate Professor, Professor, Obstetrics and Gynaecology, Dow Medical College, Karachi; Prof, Lyari General Hospital, Karachi; Obstetrician, Gynaecologist, Mehran Hospital, Karachi; Currently Retired Professor, Dow Medical College. Publications: Maternal mortality in an obstetric unit, 1985; Abdominal Pregnancy, 1985; Primary Carcinoma of Vagina Complicating Procedentia, 1985; Uterovaginal Prolapse at Civil Hospital, Karachi, 1985. Memberships: Pakistan Society of Obstetricians and Gynaecologists; Canadian Medical Association; British Medical Association; Pakistan Reference Committee for MRCOG. Hobbies: Reading; Gardening. Address: 62 B, Block 2, PECH Society, Karachi 29, Pakistan.

AHN Chul, b. 28 Sept 1956, Seoul, Korea. Biostatistician; Researcher. m. Sunhee Choi, 25 Nov 1980, 2 sons. Education: BS, Seoul National University, 1979; MS, Georgia Institute of Technology, USA, 1982; MS, 1985, PhD, 1986, Carnegie Mellon University. Appointments: Biostatistician, Western Psychiatric Institute and Clinic, USA; Assistant Professor, Albert Einstein College of Medicine; Currently Research Scientist, City of Hope Medical Center, Duarte, California. Publications: Nonparametric mixture logistic regression models for clinical disposition, 1994; Effect of propranolol versus no antiarrhythmic drug, 1994; High dose chemotherapy, 1994; Estimation of a common odds ratio under binary cluster sampling, 1995. Memberships: American Statistical Association; Society for Clinical Trials, Steering Committee of Postprandial Hypotension Study. Hobbies: Travel; Running. Address: City of Hope Medical Center, 1500 E Duarte Rd, Duarte, CA 91010, USA.

AI Zhong-Li, b. 27 Dec 1935, Wuhan, Hubei, China. Surgeon. m. 18 June 1959, 1 son, 2 daughters. Education: Graduated, Hubei Medical University, 1959. Appointments: Assistant in Surgery, Lecturer, Professor, Second Affiliated Hospital, Hubei Medical University; Hospital Director, Second Affiliated Hospital, Hubei Medical University, 1984-93; Currently Professor of General Surgery. Publications: Combined Portacaval Shunt and Livcer Arterilization in the Treatment of Portal Hypertension (1st author), 1982; Co-author: Geriatric Emergency, 1989; Abdominal Emergency Medicine, 1990; Surgery, textbook compiled by 20 medical universities, 1993. Honours: Chinese Government Scholarship, 1992. Memberships: Chinese Medical Association; The International Association of Surgeons. Hobbies: Playing basketball, football and volleyball; Reading. Address: 20 Donghu Road, Wuchang, Wuhan 430071, China.

AIDID Sharifah Barlian, b. 26 Dec 1944, Malaysia. University Professor. m. T S Chee, 26 Feb 1972, 2 sons. Education: BSc Hons (Australia); Dip Ed (Australia); PhD (England). Appointments: Currently: Director, National Science Centre of Malaysia, Kuala Lumpur; Professor of Biophysics and Medical Physics, Universiti Kebangsaan Malaysia, Bangi. Publications: Determination of Trace Elements in Leaves of Tropical Trees in Malaysia by Neutron Activation Analysis, 1988; Multielement Distribution in Different Plant Organs, 1988; Trace Element Concentrations in the Scalp Hair and Fingernails of a Biliary Atresia Infant and His Family, 1990; Effects of Lead, Cadmium and Zinc on the Electric Membrane Potential at the Xylem/Symplast Interface and Cell Elongation of Impatiens balsamina (with H Okamoto), 1992; Response of Elongation Growth Rate, Turgor Pressure and Cell Wall Extensibility of Stem Cells of Impaties balsamina (with H Okamoto), 1993; Rare Earth Elements Abundances and Distribution Patterns in Plant Materials, 1994. Membership: Fellow, Institute of Physics, Malaysia. Hobbies: Jogging; Swimming. Address: Physics Department, Universiti Kabangsaan Malaysia, Bangi 43600, Malaysia.

AIKEN Robert Dennis, b. 4 Sept 1950, Detroit, Michigan, USA. Neurologist. m. Ellen Warren, 27 Nov 1980, 1 son, 1 daughter. Education: BS, University of Michigan, Ann Arbor; MD, Wayne State University School of Medicine, Detroit. Appointments: Instructor, Neurology, Cornel University Medical College, 1981-82; Assistant Professor, Neurology, 1982-89, Associate Professor, Neurology, 1990-, Jefferson Medical College; Associate Professor, Neurology, Thomas Jefferson University Hospital. Publications: Several. Memberships: Fellowship, College of Physicians of Philadelphia; ARNMD; ASCO; American Academy of Neurology; IASP. Address: 1015 Chestnut Street, Suite 617, Philadelphia, PA 19107-4306, USA.

AINSCOUGH Carolyn Elizabeth, b. 16 Sept 1957, Bolton, Lancashire, England. Clinical Psychologist. Education: MA (Hons),

University of St Andrews, 1980; MSc, University of Leeds, 1985. Appointments: Community Worker, Salford Social Services; Education Tutor, YMCA, Manchester; Currently Consultant Clinical Psychologist. Publications: Premenstrual Emotional Changes. A Prospective Study of Symptomatology, article, 1990; Breaking Free. Help for Survivors of Child Sexual Abuse (with Kay Toon), book, 1993. Honours: James Mencher Prize for Research, Leeds University, 1985. Membership: Associate Fellow, British Psychological Society. Hobbies: Talking; Walking; Gardening. Address: Clinical Psychology Department, H Gwynne Jones Centre, Stanley Royd Hospital, Wakefield, West Yorkshire WF1 4DG, England.

AIRAS-EHRNROOTH Christel Maria, b. 28 Dec 1944, Sweden. Psychoanalyst. m. 17 Sept 1966, divorced 1993, 1 son, 2 daughters. Education: FM, Psychologist, Psychoanalyst; Child Analyst. Appointments: Private Practice Psychoanalyst. Memberships: Finnish Psychanalytical Society; International Psychoanalytical Association. Hobbies: Art; Literature. Address: Kapteeninkatu 3 B 15, 00140 Helsinki, Finland.

AISENSTEIN-AVEROFF Marilia, b. 11 Mar 1946, Alexandria, Egypt. Psychoanalyst. m. Leo Aisenstein, 18 June 1971, 1 son. Education: Master's degree, Psychology; PhilD. Appointments: Officer, 1990-, then Treasurer, currently Training Analyst and General Secretary, Paris Society of Psychoanalysis. Publications: The work of Hypochondria, 1991; Psychosomatic solution or somatic outcome: The Man of Burma, 1993; L'Interprétation au carré, 1993; D'un certain regard sur la question Psyché-soma, 1993. Honours: Prix Maurice-Bouvet for Psychoanalysis, for study on Regression, 1993. Memberships: Full Member: International Psychoanalytic Association; Psychosomatic Institute. Hobbies: Riding; Classical music; Opera; Literature. Address: 72 rue d'Assas, 75006 Paris, France.

AKAHOSHI Masazumi, b. 13 Feb 1952, Nagasaki, Japan. Physician (Cardiology, Hypertension). m. Shoko Saito, 26 Mar 1983, 1 sons, 1 daughter. Education: MD, 1977, PhD, 1993, Nagasaki University School of Medicine. Appointments: Resident, Nagasaki University School of Medicine; Resident, Tokyo Metropolitan Geriatric Hospital; Internist, 3rd Department of Internal Medicine, Nagasaki University School of Medicine; Research Fellow, Henry Ford Hospital, Detroit, Michigan, USA; Currently Assistant Chief, Department of Clinical Studies, Radiation Effects Research Foundation. Publications: Body fluid volume and angiotensin II in maintenance of on-kidney, one clip hypertension, 1989; Contribution of the central interaction between calcium and sodium to hemodynamic regulation in SHR, 1992; Chronic hyperinsulinemia augments deoxycorticosterone acetate-salt hypertension, 1994. Memberships: Japanese Society of Internal Medicine; Japanese Circulation Society; Japanese Society of Hypertension; Japan Geriatrics Society. Hobby: Fishing. Address: Ote-machi 2-25-5, Nagasaki 850, Japan.

AKAY Metin, b. 1 Jan 1958, Turkey. Biomedical Engineer. m. Yasemin M Akay, 20 July 1981, 1 son. Education: BS, 1981, MS, 1984, Bogazici; PhD, Biomedical Engineering, Rutgers University, USA, 1990. Appointments: Graduate Assistant, 1986-90; Research Associate, Rutgers University, 1990-91; Visiting Professor. Publications: Biomedical Signal Processing, 1994; Detection and Estimation of Biomedical Signals, 1995; Noninvasive detecting of Coronary Artery Disease Using Neural Networks, 1992. Memberships: Senior member, IEEE; Sigma Xi; American Heart Association; New York Academy of Sciences. Hobbies: Reading; Tennis; Running. Address: 267 Crosspoint Drive, East Brunswick, NJ 08816, USA.

AKCHURIN Renat Suleimanovich, b. 2 Apr 1946, Andizhan, Russia. Surgeon. m. Natalia P Zhivilova, 24 Feb 1972, 2 sons. Education: MD. Appointments: Physician, 1971-73; Junior, Senior Scientific Worker, Moscow Research Center of Surgery, 1973-75; Surgeon, Moscow Research Center of Surgery, 1975. Publications: Multifocal Atherosclerosis Disease and Vascular Surgery, 1990; Modern tendencies in the development of coronary surgery, 1991; Reversibility of Myocardial Dysfunction. Honours: State Prize Winner, 1982. Memberships: International Union of Angiology; International Society of Artificial Organs; National Society of Cardiovascular Surgeons. Address: 3-d Cherepkovskaya Str 15A, 121552 Moscow, Russia.

AKERS Tina Welcher, b. 25 July 1963, Christiansburg, Virginia, USA. Registered Nurse. m. Gary Eugene Akers, 26 Mar 1988. Education: BSN; Emergency Medical Technician, Shock Trauma.

Appointments: Obstetrics and Gynaecology Nurse; Quality Assurance/Discharge Planner; Adult Home Administrator; Director of Nursing, longterm care facility; Currently Pheresis Nurse, American Red Cross. Membership: Sigma Theta Tau, International Honour Society of Nursing. Hobbies: Hiking; Nature; Photography; Reading; Volunteer Rescue Squad. Address: 3891 Flatwoods Road, Elliston, VA 24087, USA.

AKESON Wayne Henry, b. 5 May 1928, Sioux City, Iowa, USA. Orthopedic Surgeon; Orthopedic Educator. m. June Austin, Mar 1969, 3 sons, 1 daughter. Education: BS, University of Iowa, 1948; MD, University of Chicago, 1953; Intern, Billings Hospital. Appointments includ: eAssistant Professor, Orthopedics, 1959-61; Assistant Professor, Orthopedics, Creighton University, 1961; Professor, Orthopedics, University of Washington, 1961-70; Professor, Head Orthopedics, UCSP, 1970-96, Acting Chairman, Department of Surgery, 1981-83, Chairman, Faculty, 1984-85, Acting Dean, School of Medicine, 1986-88, Practice medicine Specializing in Orthopedic Surgery, San Diego. Publications: Numerous professional articles to scientific journals. Honours include: Kappa Delta Award, 3X for Research Excellence, 1967; Award, Distinction in Sports Medicine Research, American Orthopedic Society Sports Medicine, 1983; Bristol Meyers/Zimmer Award for Distinguishing Research Career, 1989; Honorary MO Degree, University of Göthenberg, 1995. Address: University of California, San Diego Medical Center, Department of Orthopaedics, 200 Arbor St #8894, San Diego, CA 92103, USA.

AKHTAR Salman, b. 31 July 1946, Lucknow, India. Psychoanalyst. m. Raj Akhtar, 4 Sept 1973, 1 son, 1 daughter. Education: MD, Aligarh Muslim University, 1968; MD, Psychiatry, Institute of Postgraduate Medical Education and Research, Chandigarh, 1986; Diplomate, American Board of Psychiatry and Neurology; Certified, Adult Psychoanalysis. Appointments: Assistant Professor, Department of Psychiatry, University of Virginia School of Medicine, Charlottesville, USA, 1976-79; Associate Professor, Psychiatry, Department of Psychiatry and Human Behaviour, 1979-84; Professor, Psychiatry, 1984-, Jefferson Medical College, Thomas Jefferson University, Philadelphia, Pennsylvania; Training and Supervising Analyst, Faculty, Philadelphia Analytic Institute, 1988-. Publications: Over 80 scientific publications including: Broken Structures: Severe Personality Disorders and Their Treatment, 1992; Editor or co-editor: New Psychiatric Syndromes: DSN-III and Beyond, 1983; The Trauma of Transgression: Psychotherapy of Incest Victims, 1991; Beyond the Symbiotic Orbit: Advances in Separation-Individuation Theory -- Essays in Honor of Selma Kramer MD, 1992; When the Body Speaks: Psychological Meanings in Kinetic Clues, 1992; Mahler and Kohut: Perspectives on Development, Psychopathology and Technique, 1994. Memberships: American College of Psychiatrists; International Psychoanalytic Association; Group for Advancement of Psychiatry; Pennsylvania and Philadelphia Psychiatric Societies; Philadelphia Analytic Society, committees; Philadelphia Foundation for Psychoanalysis; World Federation of Mental Health; Forum for Psychoanalytic Study of Film; Board of Directors, Margaret S Mahler Psychiatric Research Foundation. Hobby: Writing poetry (4 volumes published). Address: Jefferson Psychiatric Associates, 1201 Chestnut Street, Room 1503, Philadelphia, PA 19107, USA.

AKINLA Oladele, b. 28 Apr 1924, Ondo, Nigeria. Physician. m. Oluyemi Adedeji, 18 July 1953, 2 sons, 2 daughters. Education MB BS, London; FRCS(Edinburgh); FRCOG; FMCOG(Nigeria); FWACS; FICS. Appointments: Senior Lecturer, Associate Professor, Professor, Obstetrics and Gynaecology, Head of Department, College of Medicine, University of Lagos; Retired. Publications: Postabortal and Postpartum Tetanus, 1970; Pregnancy and the Skeletal Complications of Sickle Cell Disease, 1973; Important Factors in the Use-Effectiveness of the Ca-T-200 IUCD, 1975; Intravaginal Contrception with the Synthetic Progestogen R-2323, 1976; Reproductive Performance after Repair of Obstetric Vesico-Vaginal Fistulae, 1978; Co-author: Plasma Cortisol (11-Hydroxyxorticosteroid) During and After Pregnancy, 1971; Carcinoma of the Vulva in Childhood, 1972; A Comparative Study of the Clinical Performance of Two Copper-Releasing IUD's Nova-T and Copper T-200 in Lagos, Nigeria, 1980. Honour: American Medical of Honour, American Biographical Institute, 198. Memberships: Nigerian Medical Association; Past President, Society of Gynaecology and Obstetrics of Nigeria. Hobbies: Cine Photography; Swimming; Sauna Baths; Reading. Address: 72 Femi Ayantuga Crescent, PO Box 4807, Surulere, Lagos, Nigeria.

AKIYAMA Hideki, b. 4 Mar 1952, Tokyo, Japan. Staff Doctor. m. 23 Apr 1983, 3 sons. Education: MD, Tokyo Medical & Dental University, 1977. Appointments: Tokyo Metropolitan Institute of Medical Science, 1979-81; Wayne State University, 1981-84; Temple University, 1984-86; Fellow, Johns Hopkins University, 1986-89; Fellow, Tokyo Metropolitan Komagome Hospital, 1989-. Publications: Analysis of cellular events involved in T cell stimulation, 1983; Mechanism of activation of coagulation factor XT, 1986; Systemic infection due to atypical mycobacteria, 1991; Fluconazole vs oral amphotericin B, 1993. Address: 3-18-22 Honkomagome, Bunkyo, Tokyo 113, Japan.

AKSAKOGLU Gazanfer, b. 4 Feb 1950, Turkey. Professor of Community Medicine; Director, Health Education & Research District. m. Iltekin Cagatay, 19 July 1974, 2 daughters. Education: MD, Hacettepe University, Ankara, Turkey; Specialist in Community Medicine, Hacettepe University. Appointments: Lecturer, Liverpool University, 1979; Vice Medical Director, Dok Eyl Un Hospital, 1985; Vice Director, Institute of Postgraduate Health Sciences, Doh Eyl University, 1985. Publications: Principles of Controlling Communicable Diseases, 1983; Narlidere District: Five Years' Experience, 1989; Pneumonia on Primary Health Care, 1991; Domiciliary Health Care, 1993; Co-author: AIDS Prevention: Guidelines for MCH, 1990. Memberships: Turkish Medical Association; International Epidemiological Association; Association for the Study of Medical Education; World Federation for Medical Education. Hobbies: Photography; Archeology. Address: 1747 Sokak No 44/4, Karsiyaka, Izmir 35530, Turkey.

AKVAMA Jeff, b. 24 Aug 1936, Ghana. Health Officer. m. Jennifer Akvama, 8 Dec 1990, 1 son, 3 daughters. Education: Cand Med MD: Zurich, Switzerland 1964, Kiel, Germany, 1969; Jus: Denmark, 1970, Norway, 1990; Training in Alternative and Comparative Medicine, London, England, 1987-88; Specialist in General Medicine: Denmark, 1994, Norway, 1994. Appointments: Surgical Department, various hospitals, Denmark, 1965-71; District Medical Officer, Sweden, 1971-72; Electro Acupuncture, 1971-; General practice: Solrod Strand, Denmark, 1972-85, Värnamo and Gnösjö, Sweden, Meloy, Norway, 1988-; Lectures in Medicine and Medicina Alternativa, California, 1981, Western Medicine versus Medicina Alternativa, Singapore, 1982, Tropical Medicine, Accra, Ghana, 1985-87. Publications: Achalasia Oesophagi and Associated Diseases, 1969; Achalasia Oesophagi. Results of the Heller Operation, 1971; Cases of Reversible Radialis Paralyssis, 1976; Vaginitis Chemicalis, 1977; Subcutaneous impressions in babies, 1977; Safety belts and traffic, 1978; Pains syndrome, 1991; Trends in death of patients with various carcinomas 1993-. Honours: DSc, Open University for Complementary Medicines, Certificate issued by Government Parliamentary University, Colombo, 1991; Visiting Professor degree, Medicina Alternativa Institute, Sri Lanka, 1991. Memberships: Danish Medical Association; Medical Council, Ghana; Norwegian Medical Association; British Acupuncture Association. Hobbies: Scientific research; Football; Athletics. Address: Birklis 7, 8160 Glomfjord, Norway.

AL-KARMI Mutaz Zuhair, b. 8 Apr 1949, Jordan. Plastic Surgeon. m. Rula Al-Karmi, 20 July 1984, 2 sons, 1 daughter. Education: MB, ChB, A!exandria University, Egypt, 1972; FRCS, Jordanian Board of Plastic Surgery. Appointments: Consultant General Surgeon; Consultant Plastic Surgeon; Chief of Professional Training Division, Directorate of the Royal Medical Services; Consultant, Head of Plastic Surgery Department, King Hussein Medical Centre. Publications: Metopic Suture Synostosis, 1988; A Status Report on Artificial Hearts, 1989; Computed Tomography Imaging of Maxillofacial Injuries, 1989; Hydatid Cyst of Infratemporal Fossa, 1994; Facial Duplication, Case Reports and Literature Review, 1994; Tissue Expansion, Review of Five Years Experience, 1994. Memberships: Jordan Medical Association; Jordanian Surgical Society; Jordanian Society of Plastic Surgeons; American Society of Plastic & Reconstructive Surgeons. Honours: Five Army Medallions, 1984, 1986, 1988, 1990, 1993. Hobbies: Sports; Travel. Address: PO Box 9468, Amman 11191, Jordan.

AL-NASSER Abdallah Abdalrahman, b. 19 May 1958, Al-Dawadmmi, Saudi Arabia. Physician. m. Layla A Al-Gwaiz, 1983, 3 sons. Education: MBBS (Hons), 1982; Internship, Residency, King Khalid Hospital, King Saud University, Riyadh, 1982-84; Residency, University of Alabama, Children's Hospital of Alabama, USA, 1984-87; Fellowship, National Institutes of Health, National Cancer Institute, USA, 1987-90; American Board in Pediatrics, 1988; American Board in Pediatric Hematology-Oncology, 1990. Appointments: Currently Consultant Paediatric Haematologist-Oncologist, Saudi Arabia.

Publications: Lancet, 335:808-11, 1990; Pathobiology, 61:3-4, 1993; Annals of Saudi Medicine 13 (11):321-327, 1993; Leukemia Research, 18 (12):881-883, 1994. Honours: Excellent with 1st Class Honours, MBBS; Distinction Award, Okaz newspaper, 1982. Memberships: American Academy of Pediatrics; American Society of Pediatric Hematology-Oncology. Hobbies: Travel; Reading; Sport. Address: PO Box 75250, Riyadh 11578, Saudi Arabia.

AL-ROOMI Khaldoon, b. 4 June 1960, Bahrain. Doctor. Education: MD (Honours), 1982; MPH, 1985; PhD, 1989; FRSH, 1990. Appointments: Medical Researcher, University of Newcastle, New South Wales, Australia; Assistant Professor in Community Medicine, Arabian Gulf University, Bahrain; Currently Assistant Professor in Clinical Epidemiology. Publications: Hypertension control and the risk of myocardial infarction and stroke, 1990; The importance of hypertension in the aetiology of infarctive and haemorrhagic stroke, 1992; Lifestyle patterns and the risk of myocardial infarction in a Gulf Arab population, 1994. Memberships: International Epidemiological Association; Society for Epidemiologic Research; American Public Health Association; royal Society of Tropical medicine anf hygiene; Royal Society of Health. Public Health Association of Australia. Hobbies: Swimming; Jogging; Stamp collection. Address: PO Box 1099, Manama, Bahrain.

ALAGARATNAM Thevakaruna Thavaratnarajah, b. 30 Apr 1935, Sri Lanka. Surgeon. m. Malini Perinpanayagam, 15 Aug 1962, 1 son, 1 daughter. Education: MBBS (Sri Lanka), 1960; FRCS (England), FRCS (Edinburgh), 1969. Appointments: Registrar, West Kent Hospital, Maidstone, England, 1971; Lecturer, 1973, Senior Lecturer, 1980, currently Reader in Surgery, University of Hong Kong. Publications: Wound Implantation - A Surgical Hazard, 1977; Tuberculosis of Breast, 1980; Paraffinoma of the Breast, 1983; Co-author: Psychosocial Effects of Mastectomy, 1986; Risk Stratification in Perforated Duodenal Ulcers, 1987; Benign Breast Disorders in Chinese Women, 1989. Hobbies: Swimming; Bridge. Address: University Department of Surgery, Queen Mary Hospital, Hong Kong.

ALAYZA MUJICA Fernando, b. 4 Nov 1947, Lima, Peru. Psychoanalyst. m. Sonia Prager, 25 Apr 1977, 1 son, 1 daughter. Education: Psychologist, Catholic University; Psychoanalyst, Peruvian Institute of Psychoanalysis; Master in Psychology. Appointments: Professor of Psychology and Psychoanalysis, Catholic University, San Marcos University; Professor of Psychoanalysis, Peruvian Institute of Psychoanalysis. Honours: Member, Executive Council, Federacion Psicoanalitica de America Latina, 1992-94. Memberships: International Psychoanalytical Association; Peruvian College of Psychologists. Hobbies: Scuba diving; Cycling; Camping; Archaeology; Arts. Address: Los Manzanos 178, Lima 27 (San Isidro), Peru, 407727.

ALBALA A Ari, b. 2 Mar 1947, Coronel, Chile. Physician; Psychiatrist. m. Barbara Pirnstein, 20 Oct 1970, 1 s, 2 d. Education: MD, University of Tel-Aviv, Israel; Resident and Research Fellow, Department of Psychiatry, University of MI, 1975-80; Diplomate, American Board of Psychiatry and Neurology in Adult and Geriatric Psychiatry. Career: Assistant Professor, University of MI, 1981-84; Currently, Associate Clinical Professor, University of CA, San Diego. Publications: Editorial Board, Convulsive Therapy, 1985-89. Honour: Fellow, American Psychiatric Association. Memberships: Israel Medical Association; San Diego Society of Psychiatric Physicians; Society of Biological Psychiatry; Chilean Society of Neurology, Psychiatry and Neurosurgery; World Psychiatric Association; San Diego County Medical Society; National Alliance for the Mentally Ill. Hobbies: Skiing; Reading; Computers. Address: 765 Third Avenue No 301, Chula Vista, CA 91910, USA.

ALBERTI Peter William, b. 23 Aug 1934, Coblence, Germany. Surgeon. m. Elizabeth Smith, 5 Aug 1991, 2 daughters. Education: MB BS, Durham, 1957; PhD, Washington University, St Louis, 1963; FRCS(London), 1965; FRCS(Canada), 1968. Appointments: First Assistant, ORL, University of Newcastle; Clinical Teacher, 1967, Assistant Professor, 1968, Associate Professor, 1970, Professor, 1977, Department Chairman, Otolaryngology, University of Toronto; General Secretary, International Federation ORL Societies. Publications: Hearing Protection in Industry, Editor, 1981; Clinical Otoscopy, 1984, 1992; Otologic Medicine and Surgery, Co-editor, 1989; Contributor of over 150 scientific articles. Honours: President, Canadian Society of ORL, 1989-90; Vice President, Eastern Section, Otological Soceity, 1989-90. Memberships: BMA; CMA; Canadian Society ORL; Triological Society;

Otological Society. Hobbies: Sailing; Travel. Address: 7-229 EN, 200 Elizabeth Street, Toronto M5G 2C4, Canada.

ALDERMAN Amelia Anne, b. 4 Sept 1953, Rome, GA, USA. Psychiatrist. m. Albert B Gill, 28 Aug 1982, 1 son, 1 daughter. Education: AB, Wesleyan College, 1975; MD, Medical College of Georgia, 1981; University of Florida Psychiatric Residency Training Program, 1985. Publications: Combined Trazodone-Lithium Therapy for Refractory Depression, 1983; Functional Level Equation in Comprehensive Treatment Planning, 1984; Holiday Depression, 1990. Honours: Wesleyan Scholar Award, 1971-75; Pi Delta Epsilon Honorary Journalism Fraternity, 1973-75; Diplomate, American Board of Psychiatry and Neurology, 1987; ASAM, 1992; Certificate, Addiction Psychiatry, 1993. Memberships: American Psychiatric Association; American Medical Association; American Society of Addiction Medicine; American Academy of Psychiatrists in Alcoholism and Addictions. Address: 330 Hospital Drive, Suite 315, Macon, GA 31201, USA.

ALDERMAN JoAnn Ortgiesen, b. 12 July 1936, Hildreth, Nebraska, USA. Nursing Consultant. m. 5 Oct 1969, 1 son. Education: BSN, University of Nebraska School of Nursing, 1958; MSN, School of Nursing, Medical College of Georgia, 1983; Certified Risk Manager, State of Florida; Certified Case Manager, Insurance Rehabilitation Specialist Commission, 1993. Appointments include: Director of Nursing Service: John Knox Village, Pompano Beach, Florida, 1985-86; Palm Court Nursing Home, Fort Lauderdale, Florida, 1986; Harbor Beach Convalescent Home, Fort Lauderdale, 1986-89; Manor Care Nursing Center, Plantation, Florida, 1989; Quality Assurance and Risk Management Coordinator, Equicor Health Plan of South Florida, Fort Lauderdale, 1990-91; Consultant, Private Care and Case Geriatric Care Management and Geriatric Medical-Legal Consulting, Alderman's Inc (own business), Fort Lauderdale, 1991-. Honours: Optimist Scholarship, Omaha, Nebraska, 1955; US Traineeship for graduate education, 1981. Memberships: Sigma Theta Tau; National Association of Professional Care Managers; Florida Geriatric Care Managers Association; American Association of Legal Nurse Consultants. Hobbies: Physical fitness; Yoga; Music; Reading. Address: 4031 NE 15th Avenue, Fort Lauderdale, FL 33334-4642, USA.

ALDERSON Philip O, b. 8 Aug 1944, San Francsico, CA, USA. Physician. m. Marjorie J Hawkins, 13 Jun 1970, 2 d. Education: AB, 1966, MD, 1970, Washington University, St Louis. Career: Instructor of Radiology, Washington University, 1975; Assistant Professor, Associate Professor, Johns Hopkins Medical Institutions, 1976-80; James Picker Professor and Chairman, Department of Radiology, Columbia University, 1980-. Publications: Over 140 journal articles, 40 book chapters and 4 books. Honours: Over 200 invited lectures including 4 named lectureships and over 10 international lectureships. Memberships: President, NY Roentgen Society, 1990-91; President, NY State Radiology Society; President, Society Chairmen Academic Radiology Departments; Vice President, Society of Nuclear Medicine, 1984; Board of Chancellors, American College of Radiology. Address: Columbia Presbyterian Medical Center, 622 West 168th Street, New York NY 10032, USA.

ALDRETE Joaquin S, b. 2 Mar 1936, Mexico City, Mexico. Surgeon. m. Melinda L Santoyo, 5 June 1960, 1 s. Education: BS, Biology, Centro Universitario Mexico, 1952; MD, National University of Mexico, 1959; MS, Surgery, University of Minnesota, USA, 1968. Appointments: Professor and Vice Chairman, Department of Surgery, School of Medicine, University of Alabama at Birmingham. Publications: Contributor of 110 articles in professional journals and 12 chapters in surgical books. Honour: Best Doctors in the USA, 1994. Memberships: American College of Surgeons; American Surgical Association; Society of University Surgeons; Southern Surgical Association. Hobbies: Tennis; Travel. Address: Department of Surgery, University of Alabama at Birmingham, Birmingham, AL 35294, USA.

ALEXANDER Steven Roy, b. 1 Sept 1945, Portsmouth, VA, USA. Paediatric Nephrologist. m. Jeanette E Kennedy, 1 s, 2 d. Education: Stanford University, 1963-64; BS, cum laude, Rice University, Houston, 1967; MD, Baylor College of Medicine, Houston, 1967-71. Appointments include: Professor of Paediatrics, University of Texas Southwestern Medical Centre; Director, Dialysis and Renal Transplantation, Childrens Medical Centre of Dallas. Publications: Contributor of numerous articles, chapters in books, reports, lectures and scientific presentations. Honours: Jesse H Jones Scholar, 1963-67; National Association of Corrosion Engineers Scholar, 1963-67; Special Award for Excellence in

Teaching and Housestaff Education, Paediatric Housestaff, Baylor College of Medicine, 1978; Joseph B Bilderback Faculty Teaching Award, Department of Paediatrics, Oregon Health Sciences University, 1984; The Best Doctors in America, Paediatric Nephrology, 1992, 1994. Memberships include: International Paediatric Nephrology Society; Texas Transplantation Society; American Academy of Paediatrics; Greater Dallas Paediatric Society. Hobbies: Fly Fishing; Travel; Running. Address: Department of Paediatrics, UT Southwestern Medical Centre, 5323 Harry Hines Blvd, Dallas, TX 75235-9063, USA.

ALEXEJEVICH Korolev Boris, b. Dec 1909, Kazan, Russia. Education: Graduated, Gorky Medical Training Institute, 1934. Appointment: Professor of Hospital Surgery Chair, Chief of Cardiovascular Surgical Clinic, Medical Training Institute, Nizhny, Novgorod, Russia. Publications: 424 professional publications, including: Diagnosis of Congenital Heart Diseases and the Results of Surgical Treatment, 1968; Surgery of Liver; Abdominal Surgery. Honours: Honoured Citizen of Nizhny Novgorod, 1976; Order of Lenin, 1960, 1984; Order of the Red Banner of Labour, 1969; Order of the October Socialist Revolution; 7 Medals. Memberships incl: International Society of Surgeons; International Society for Cardiovascular Diseases; All-Russian Society of Anesthesiologists-Resuscitators. Address: Medical Training Institute, Cardiovascular Surgical Cilinc, Nizhny, Novgorod, Russia.

ALEXIS John Bernard, b. 17 Aug 1960, Trinidad. Pathologist. Education: MB Ch B, 1984. Career: Assistant Clinical Professor of Pathology and Clinical Instructor in Dermatology and Cutaneous Surgery, University of Miami School of Medicine; Associate Attending in Pathology, and Director of Dermatopathology, Mount Sinai Medical Centre of Greater Miami. Publications include: Acupuncture and Non A, Non B Hepatitis, 1988; An Unusual Case of Phormia Regina Myiasis of the Scalp, 1988; Enteritis Cystica Profunda in a Patient With Crohn's Disease, 1989; Cutaneous Periarteritis Nodosa, 1990; Congenital Self Healing Reticulohistiocytosis, 1991. Memberships: American and Canadian Academy of Pathology; ASCP; CAP; FSP; SMA; ISD; Miami Dermatological Society; FMA; DCMA; NMA. Address: 4300 Alton Road, Miami Beach, FL33140, USA.

ALEXOPOULOS George S, b. 30 Dec 1946, Salonica, Greece. Psychiatry. m. Christina Alexopoulos, 1 s, 1 d. Education: MD; Further qualification in Geriatric Psychiatry, 1992. Appointment: Director, Cornell Institute of Geriatric Psychiatry, Cornell Medical Center, White Plains, NY; Director, Clinical Research Center for Geriatric Affective Disorders. Publications: Numerous. Honours: Editor, US, International Journal of Geriatric Psychiatry; NIMH Merit Award. Memberships: American College of Neuropsychopharmacology; Sigma Xi; American Psychiatric Association; American Psychopathological Association; American Association of Geriatric Psychiatry; Gerontological Society of America; American Geriatrics Society; Executive Committee, Geriatric Psychiatry Section, World Psychiatric Association. Hobby: Running. Address: Cornell Medical Center NY Hospital, 21 Bloomingdale Road, White Plains, NY 10605, USA.

ALI Jehan, b. 19 Feb 1948, Carapichaima, Trinidad. Obstetrician and Gynaecologst. m. Savitri Jagdipsingh, 27 Nov 1977, 3 daughters. Education: MBBS University of the West Indies; DGO, University of the West Indies; MRCOG. Appointments: Internship to Specialist Medical Officer, General Hospital, San Fernando, 1973-; Specialist Medical Officer, Ministry of, Health, Trinidad; Senior House Officer, UK, 1980-81. Memberships: Postgraduate Institute of Obstetrics and Gynaecology of Trinidad and Tobago; Gynaecology and Obstetrics Society of Trinidad and Tobago; Society of Surgeons of Trinidad and Tobago. Hobbies: Cricket; Soccer. Address: General Hospital, San Fernando, Trinidad, West Indies.

ALI Maqbool B, b. 15 May 1943. Obstetrician and Gynaecologist. m. Syed Masood Ali, 23 Nov 1971, 1 son, 1 daughter. Education: MBBS, Dow Medical College, Karachi, Pakistan, 1966; Diploma, Anaesthesiology, Royal College of Surgeons, London, 1970; DRCOG, London, 1970; Fellow, American College of Obstetricians and Gynecologists, 1980; Board Certified, American Board of Obstetricians and Gynecologists, 1981; MRCOG, London, 1975; FRCOG, London, 1988. Appointments: Assistant Professor, Department of Obstetrics and Gynaecology, University of Illinois School of Medicine, Peoria, USA, 1977-; Staff, St Francis Medical Center, Peoria, 1979-; Staff, Methodist Medical Center, Peoria, 1979-; Obstetrician and Gynaecologist in private practice, Peoria, 1979; Secretary, Central Illinois OB/GYN, 1982-90;

Staff, Proctor Community Hospital, 1984-; President, Greater Peoria OB/GYN Corporation, 1990-. Memberships: Peoria Medical Society, Past President; Illinois State Medical Society; American Medical Association; Peoria Gynecological Society; American Women's Medical Association; Fertility Society; American Association of Gynecological Laparoscopy; World Medical Association; International Correspondence Society of OB/GYN; Fellow, Vice-Regent for Illinois, International College of Surgeons; Women Surgeons Association; Fellow, Royal Society of Medicine, London; Urogynecological Society. Hobbies: Community work. Address: 4930 N Executive Drive, Peoria, IL 61614, USA.

ALI Qurashi M, b. 9 Dec 1950, Gezira, Sudan. Professor. m. Ameera Abdalla Makki, 12 Aug 1977, 4 sons, 2 daughters. Education: BSc (Khartoum), Basic Medical Sciences; PhD (London), Human Anatomy; MBBS (Khartoum); MMRD (Alexandria), Radiology. Appointments: Lecturer, Anatomy, 1981-86, Associate Professor, Anatomy, 1986-91, Professor, Human Anatomy, 1991-; Seconded to Sultan Qaboos University, Oman, 1989-94; Consultant in Radiodiagnosis. Publications include: Evaluation of anatomy content in an integrated curriculum, 1986; Sonographic anatomy of the rectus sheath: indications for terminology and implications of rectus flaps, 1993; Co-author: Ultrasound volumetry in Hemato-metrocolpos, 1988; The paratemporal segment of the maxillary sinus: A new sign for assessment of size, 1990; Ultrasonographic evaluation of gallbladder function in patients with Schistosoma mansoni infection, 1990; Ultrasonographic investigation of periportal fibrosis in children with Schistosoma mansoni infection: reversibility of morbidity months after treatment with Praziquantel, 1990; The use of diagnostic ultrasound in schistosomiasis; standardization of methodology, 1992; Post-splenectomy abdominal ultrasound in Schisto-somiasis in Sudan, 1992; Three dimensional CT of the middle ear and adjacent structures, 1993; The pattern of skull fracture: A three-dimensional CT study; Echogenicity of the telencephalic choroid plexus as a developmental landmark; Books: Human Clinical Anatomy, 1991; Neurological Anatomy, 1992; Routine Ultrasonography, 1993. Memberships: Afro-Asia-Oceania Association of Anatomists; American Association of Clinical Anatomists; American Institute of Ultrasound in Medicine. Addres: Faculty of Medicine, University of Gezira, Wad Medani, Sudan.

ALI Tahir Osman, b. 12 Apr 1950, Simit, Sudan. Anatomist; Sports Injury Specialist. m. Ashma Abdalla Ali, 10 Apr 1981, 4 sons, 1 daughter. Education: MBBS University of Khartoum, 1976; PhD, University of London, England, 1984; Diploma of Sports Medicine, University of London, 1988. Appointments: Medical officer, Ministry of Health, Sudan; Teaching Assistant, Lecturer, Assistant professor of Anatomy, University of Khartoum; Assistant Professor, Department of Anatomy, Sultan gaboos University, Oman. Publications: Human Anatomy, Systemic and Applied; Heat Effects on Somite Mesoderm of Xenodus Laevii Embryos, 1993. Memberships: Sudan Association of Doctors; Anatomical Society of United Kingdom. Hobbies: Reading; Swimming. Address: University of Khartoum, College of Medicine, PO Box 102, Khartoum, Sudan.

ALKON Ellen S, b. 10 Apr 1936, Los Angeles, California, USA. Physician. m. Paul Kent Alkon, 30 Aug 1957, 3 daughters. Education: BA, Stanford University, 1955; MD, University of Chicago, 1961; MPH, University of California, Berkeley, 1968. Appointments: Director, Maternal and Child Health, 1973-75, Commissioner Of Health, 1975-80, Minneapolis Health Department; Chief Preventive Public Health, Coastal Region, Public Health Chief, Medical Director Public Health, Coastal Cluster Health Centres, LA County DHS. Memberships: American College of Preventive Medicine, Region, Region 8, 1992-; California Conference of Local Health Officers, President, 1990-91; California Academy of Preventive Medicine, President, 1989-92; Southern California Public Health Association, President, 1986. Address: 1333 Chestnut Avenue, Long Beach, CA 90813, USA.

ALLAN Garry Lindsay, b. 21 Oct 1958, Melbourne, Victoria, Australia. Lecturer in Nuclear Medicine. Education: BSc (Hons), PhD, University of Melbourne; Australian National Postdoctoral Research Fellow, Department of Nuclear Physics, Australian National University. Appointments: Currently Lecturer, Nuclear Medicine, Royal Melbourne Institute of Technology. Honours: Commonwealth Postgraduate Research Award; National Postdoctoral Fellowship, Australian Research Council. Memberships: Australian Institute of Physics; Australian and New Zealand Society of Nuclear Medicine. Hobbies: Computers; Behavioural psychology. Address: 12 Donald Street, Highett, Victoria 3190, Australia.

ALLAN Norman James Wilson, b. 23 Apr 1922, Dufftown, Scotland. Obstetrician and Gynaecologist. Education: MA (Aberdeen); LRCP; FRCS (C); FRCOG; FSA (Scotland). Appointments include: Associate Professor of Obstetrics and Gynaecology, University of Ottawa, Canada; Consultant Ostetrician and Gynaecologist, Ottawa General Hospital. Now retired. Publications: Genetal Tuberculosis and Pregnancy, 1961; Uterus Didelphys with Unilateral Imperforate Vagina, 1963; Membranous Occlusion of the Cervix in Pregnancy, 1972; Pseudomyxoma Peritonei et Ovarii with Occult Neoplasms of Appendix, 1973. Honours: Councillor, Grampian Regional Council, 1986. Memberships: Royal College of Obstetricians and Gynaecologists; Royal College of Surgeons of Canada. Address: 2 Campbell Street, Banff AB45 1JR, Scotland.

ALLEN Linda Graves, b. 8 Oct 1959, Indianapolis, Indiana, USA. Registered Nurse. m. William Allen, 16 Nov 1985, 2 sons. Education: BSN, University of Missouri, Columbia, USA; Certified Emergency Nurse; Trauma Nurse Specialist. Appointments: Staff Nurse, St John's Mercy Medical Center, 1981-92; Trauma Service Manager, Barnes Hospital, MO, USA, 1992-. Memberships: Emergency Nurses Association; Society of Trauma Nurses; American Trauma Society; American Association of Critical Care Nurses. Hobbies: Reading; Needlepoint; Racquetball; Swimming. Address: Barnes Hospital, 1 Barnes Hospital Plaza, St Louis, MO 63110, USA.

ALLEN Marshall Bonner Jr, b. 19 Oct 1927, Long Beach, Mississippi, USA. Neurosurgeon. m. Dorothy Herron, 12 Oct 1957, 2 sons, 1 daughter. Education: BA, Biology, University of Mississippi, 1949; MD, Harvard Medical School, 1953; Certification, American Board of Neurological Surgery, 1964. Appointments include: Fellow in Neurophysiology (US Public Health sponsored), Hôpital Henri Rousselle, Paris, France, 1961-62; Professor of Surgery, Chief, Section of Neurosurgery, Medical College of Georgia Hospital and Clinic, Augusta, 1965-94; Consultant: Georgia State Prison, Reidsville, 1965-80; VA Medical Center, Augusta, 1965-94; Central State Hospital, Millegeville, Georgia, 1967-94; Dwight David Eisenhower Army Medical Center, Fort Gordon, Georgia, 1970-. Publications: Book chapters and contributions to refereed journals in field of neurosurgery; Coauthor, books: A Manual of Neurosurgery, 1974, 1977; Atlas of Polytome Pneumography: with particular reference to the midline ventricles of the brain, 1977; Co-editor: The Pituitary, A Current Review, 1977; Essentials of Neurosurgery, 1994. Memberships include: American Academy of Neurology; American Association for the Advancement of Science; American Association of Neurological Surgeons; American College of Surgeons; American Association of Neuropathologists; Congress of Neurological Surgeons; Medical Association of Georgia; Royal Society of Medicine; Sigma Xi; National Rehabilitation Society; Eastern Association of Electroencephalographers; American Epilepsy Society. Address: Section of Neurosurgery, Medical College of Georgia, Augusta, GA 30912-4010, USA.

ALLEN Stephen Charles, b. 2 July 1952, Bristol, England. Physician. m. Julia Caroline Parr, 18 Aug 1973, 2 sons, 1 daughter. Education: BSc (Hons), Medical Biochemistry, 1973; MBChB (Hons), 1976, MRCP, 1978, MD, 1981, Manchester University; FRCP (Edinburgh), 1991; FRCP (London), 1993. Appointments: Currently Consultant Physician and Clinical Director. Publications: Various research papers on pneumonia, asthma, the physiological changes of old age; 2 textbooks, 3 chapters. Hobbies: Fine art; Mountaineering; Cycling; Wine. Address: Royal Bournemouth Hospital, Bournemouth, Dorset, England.

ALLISON David B, b. 2 Feb 1963, New York, NY, USA. Scientist. Education: BA, Psychology, Vassar College, New York, 1985; MA, Clinical and School Psychology, 1987, PhD, Clinical and School Psychology, 1990, Hofstra University, Hempstead, NY. Career includes: Applied Behavior Specialist, PLUS Group Homes, Westbury, NY, 1988-90; Adjunct Faculty, 1990, Adjunct Assistant Professor, 1992-, St John's University, Queens, NY, 1990; Associate Research Scientist, New York Obesity Research Center, St Luke's/Roosevelt Hospital Center, 1994-. Publications: Over 40 peer reviewed publications; Numerous abstracts, presentations, book chapters and books including: Co-author, Nutritional support of obese patients, in Parenteral Nutrition, 1993, Co-author, Obesity: Socio-Cultural Perspectives, in Eating Disorders Anthology, in press, Editor, Methods for the Assessment of Eating Behaviors and Weight Related Problems, in press. Honours include: Many grants; Merit Citation, Society for Behavioral Medicine, 1992; Clinical Nutrition Fellows Award, American Society for Clinical Nutrition, 1992; Finalist, Young Investigator Award, North American

Association for the Study of Obesity, 1993; Theodorec Tjossom Postdoctoral Award, 1994. Memberships include: AAAS; New York Academy of Science; APA; American Psychological Society; American Association of Applied and Preventive Psychology; American Diabetes Association; European Association for Study of Obesity; The Behavior Genetics Association; The Classification Society of North America. Address: Obesity Research Center, St Luke's/Roosevelt Hospital, Columbia University, College of Physicians and Surgeons, 411 West 114th Street, Suite 3D, New York, NY 10025, USA.

ALLISON David John, b. 21 Mar 1941, Leeds, England. Director, Diagnostic Radiology. m. Deirdre Mary Allison, 16 Apr 1966, 1 son, 2 daughters. Education: BSc, Kings College, London; MBBS, Kings College Hospital; MRCS, LRCP, St Bartholomew's Hospital; DMRD, FFR, Hammersmith Hospital. Appointments: Consultant Radiologist, Hammersmith Hospital, London. Publications: Diagnostic Radiology, 1985, 2nd edition, 1992; Over 300 original articles and 50 book chapters on radiology and physiology. Memberships: President, CIRSE; Executive Board, EAR; RCR; BIR; Chairman, Editorial Board, Journal, International Radiology. Honours: President, Cardiovascular & Interventional Radiological Society of Europe, 1991-94. Hobbies: Gardening; Food & Wine. Address: Department of Diagnostic Radiology, Royal Postgraduate Medical School, London W12 0NN, England.

ALLISON Henry Wayne, b. 28 July 1962, Gallipolis, Ohio, USA. Registered Nurse. Education: Diploma, Buckeye Hills School of Practical Nursing; Applied Associates of Science in Nursing, Regents College University, NY. Appointments: Supervisor, Clearview Convalescent Center; Staff, Medical Plaza Hospital; RN, Unit Supervision, Wilson N Jones Hospital; RN, Hemodialysis, Wilson N Jones Hospital; RN, Director of Oncology, Wilson N Jones Hospital. Hobbies: Sculpting; Growing Bonsais; Painting; Designing & Creating Dolls. Address: Rt 2, Box 266 T, Pottsboro, TX 75076-9802, USA.

ALMAZOU Vladimir, b. 27 May 1931, Tver, USSR. Physician. Education: DSc, Medical University, St Petersburg, 1954. Appointments: Intern, Postgraduate, Assistant Professor, Associate Head, Head, Department of Internal Medicine, St Petersburg Medical University; Director, Institute of Cardiology, St Petersburg. Publications: Leucopenias, Co-author, 1981; Hemopoietic Stem Cells, 1985; Complexities in Diagnostics in Cardiology, 1985; Regulation of Blood Pressure, 1983; Baroreceptor Reflexes, 1988; Borderline Arterial Hypertension, 1992. Memberships: St Petersburg Society of Cardiologists; Russian Society of Cardiologists; Russian Society of Internal Medicine; Russian Medical Academy; New York Academy of Science. Hobbies: Boating; Skiing. Address: ul Monetnaya 32-28, St Petersburg 197061, Russia.

ALMOND Richard Julian, b. 19 Jan 1938, Chicago, Illinois, USA. Psychiatrist. m. Barbara Rosenthal, 16 Dec 1962, 3 sons. Education: AB; MD; American Board of Psychiatry and Neurology; San Francisco Psychoanalytic Institute. Appointments: Assistant Professor of Psychiatry, 1969-73, Clinical Associate Professor, 1973-85, Clinical Professor, 1985-, Stanford University Medical School, California; Faculty, San Francisco Psychoanalytic Institute, 1990-; Private practice. Publications: The Healing Community, book, 1974; Psychological Change in Jane Austen's Pride and Prejudice, 1989. Memberships: American Psychiatric Association; American Psychoanalytic Association. Hobby: Singing. Address: 550 Hamilton Ave 339, Palo Alto, CA 94301, USA.

ALNAES Randolf, b. 21 Dec 1926, Norway. Professor Emeritus; Psychiatrist. Education: Dr med; Professor. Appointments include: Head of Outpatient Department, Psychiatric Clinic, University of Oslo, 1973-91; Professor Emeritus; Psychoanalyst, IPA. Publications: Langden D, Alnæs R. Avespenning ved konsentrasjon. Autohypnoide metoden. Oso: Fabritius, 1964. Alnæs, Johnsen G. editors. Psykoterapi. Synspunkter og metoder. Bd1, II og III. Oslo: Fabritius, 1966, 1968, 1971. Alnæs R, et al, editors. Poliklinikken psykiatrisk klinikk, Vinderen 25 ar. Festkrift. Oslo: Lobo grafisk, 1990. Alnæs R. Norsk psykoanalyse i mellomkrigsarene. Internasjonale strφmninger. Otto Fenichel og Wilhelm Reich. Stavanger: Psykiatrisk opplysningsfond, 1995. Co-morbidity of psychiatric disorders in an outpatient department, doctoral thesis, 1989; Psychoanalysis in Norway, 1994. Memberships: Norwegian Psychiatric Association; Swedish Psychoanalytic Association. Address: Biskop Heuchsv 4, 0871 Oslo, Norway.

ALPERS David Hershel, b. 9 May 1935, Philadelphia, Pennsylvania, USA. Physician; Professor of Medicine. m. Melanie Ann Goldman, 12 Aug 1977, 3 daughters. Education: BA magna cum laude, Harvard University, 1956; MD, Harvard Medical School. Appointments: Asst Prof of Med, Harvard Univ, 1967; Asst Prof of Med, 1969, Assoc Prof of Med, 1971, Prof of Med, 1973, Chief, Div of Gastorenterology, 1969-, Washington Univ Sch of Med, St Louis, Missouri. Publications: Manual of Nutritional Therapeutics (with W F Stenson and D M Bier), 3rd Edition, 1995; Associate editor: Physiology of Gastroenterological Tract, 3rd edition, 1994; Textbook of Gastroenterology, 2nd edition, 1995. Honours: Henry Asbury Christian Award for Excellence in his Studies, Harvard Medical School. Memberships: Am Gastroenterological Assn, President 1990-91; Assn of Am Physicians; Am Soc for Clinical Investigation; ASBCMB; ASCB; AIN. Hobbies: String quartet playing (cello); Tennis; Swimming. Address: Department of Medicine, Box 8124, Washington University School of Medicine, 660 S Euclid Avenue, St Louis, MO 63110, USA.

ALSUP Thomas D, b. 25 Aug 1950-, Helena, USA. Registered Nurse. m. Martha L Alsup, 6 Apr 1974, 2 sons. Education: AAS, Nursing; EMT-A; EMT-Advanced; CPR 1st Aid Instructor; Interior Firefighter; Certified in Audiometry & Pulmonary Function Testing. Appointments: EMT-A, Helena Hospital; Operating Room Staff Nurse, Helena Hospital; Operating Room Staff Nurse, FT Jackson, SC; Occupational Health Nurse, Westinghouse; Occupational Health Nurse Manager, Spring Industries, Columbia. Memberships: AAORN; AAOHN; ARC; NFPA; NREMTA; CAOMC; SC Firemans Association. Hobbies: Music; Coaching Little League Baseball. Address: 316 Thornside Road, Columbia, SC 29223, USA.

ALTEMBURGER Karl M, b. 13 Nov 1949, Coral Gables, Florida, USA. Physician. m. Carol Bauer, 25 May 1974, 4 daughters. Education: BA, Zoology, 1971, MA, College of Medicine, 1974, University of South Florida; Internship, Residency, Paediatrics, University of Colorado Medical Center, 1975-76; Fellowship, Allergy and Immunology, National Jewish Hospital and Research Center, The National Asthma Center and University of Colorado Medical Center, Denver, 1978-81; Board Certified in Paediatrics, 1980, Allergy and Immunology, 1981. Publications: Book chapters: The Complement System and Its Disorders in Man (with R B Johnston), 1983; Chronic Nonallergic Rhinitis, 1984; Asthma: General Evaluation and Assessment, 1984; Adverse Reactions to Local Anesthetics, 1984; Adverse Reactions to Immunizing Agents, 1984; Asthma in Childhood, 1988, 1989; Contributions to journals. Honours: Alpha Omega Alpha. Memberships: Florida Allergy and Immunology Society, President 1993-94, Executive Committee Member 1990-96; Board of Trustees, American Lung Association of Central Florida, 1985-93; Marion County Medical Society, Board of Directors 1983-88, President 1985-86, Bulletin Editor 1986-89; Fellow, American Academy of Allergy and Immunology; Fellow, American College of Allergy and Immunology; Fellow, American Academy of Pediatrics; American Medical Association; Florida Medical Association; University of South Florida College of Medicine Alumni Association, President 1983-87; Southeastern Allergy Association; American Association for the History of Medicine. Address: 1800 SE 17th Street, Office 300, Ocala, FL 34471-4100, USA.

ALTER Milton, b. 11 Nov 1929. Clinical Professor of Neurology. m. 31 Aug 1952, 4 sons, 1 daughter. Education: MD; PhD. Appointments include: Chief of Neurology, Minneapolis Veterans Administration Hospital, Minnesota, 1967-76; Chairman of Neurology, Temple University Hospital, 1976-87; Currently Clinical Professor of Neurology, Medical College of Pennsylvania, Philadelphia. Publications: More than 200 articles, chapters and books; Handbook of Neuroepidemiology, 1994. Honours: Phi Beta Kappa, 1947; Alpha Omega Alpha, 1955. Memberships: American Academy of Neurology; American Neurological Association; American Society of Epidemiology. Hobby: Travel. Address: Medical College of Pennsylvania, 3300 Henry Avenue, Philadelphia, PA 19129, USA.

ALTMAN Lawrence Kimball, b. 19 June 1937, Boston, USA. Physician; Journalist. Education: AB, cum laude, Harvard University, 1958; MD, Tufts University, 1962. Appointments: Diplomate, American Vetinary Epidemiology Society; Intern, Mt Zion Hospital, San Francisco, 1962-63; USPHS Epidemic Intelligence Service Officer, Centers for Disease Control, Atlanta, 1963-66; Medical Resident, Fellow, University Washington Hospital, Seattle, 1966-69; Medical Correspondent, Columnist, The Doctors World, New York Times, 1969-; Associate Professor, Medicine, New York University, 1970-; Visiting Physician,

Serafimer Hospital, Karolinska Institute, Stockholm, Sweden, 1973; Visiting Scientist, University Washington, 1971; Chancellor's Distinguishing Lecture for Public Universtanding of Science, University California, San Francisco, 1989. Publications: Science of The Times, 1981; Who Goes First? The Story of Self-Experimentation in Medicine, 1987; Contributor of chapters to books, articles to professional journals. Honours include: Recipient, Howard W Blakeslee Award, American Heart Association, 1982, 1983, 1994; Claude Bernard Award, National Society of Medical Research, 1971, 1974; Walter C Alvarez Award, American Medical Writers Association, 1980; Journalism Award, American Academy of Pediatrics, 1982; Journalism Award, College of American Pathologists, 1985; Public Service Award, National Kidney Foundation, George Polk Award, 1986; Vincent Downing Award, American Medical Writers Association, 1988; Media Excellence Award, Friends of National Library of Medicine, 1993; Fellow, American College of Physicians; Fellow, American College of Epidemiology; Fellow, New York Academy of Medicine. Memberships include: American Society of Tropical Medicine & Hygiene; Institute of Medicine of the National Academy of Sciences; Society for Epidemiologic Research. Address: New York Times Science News Department, 229 W 43rd Street, NY 10036, USA.

ALTMAN R Peter, b. 13 Apr 1934, New York City, USA. Physician; Surgeon. m. Hanna Diamond, 23 Aug 1964,2 s. Education: AB, Colgate University; MS, University of Rochester School of Medicine; MD, New York Medical College. Appointments: Professor of Surgery, George Washington University; Rudolph N Schullinger Professor of Surgery and Paediatrics, College of Physicians and Surgeons, Columbia University; Director, Paediatric Surgery, Surgeon in Chief, Babies and Childrens Hospital of New York, Columbia Presbyterian Medical Centre. Publications: Contributor of over 150 professional works. Honours: Alpha Omega Alpha. Memberships: American Surgical Association; Society University Surgeons; International College of Surgeons; Fellow, American College of Surgeons; Fellow, American Academy Paediatrics; American Paediatric Surgical Association; British Association Paediatric Surgeons. Hobbies: Skiing; Music; Golf. Address: Babies Hospital (N204), 3959 Broadway, New York, NY 10032, USA.

ALTSHULER Kenneth Z, b. 11 Apr 1929, Paterson, NJ, USA. Psychiatrist. m. Ruth Collins Sharp, 5 Dec 1987, 1 s, 2 d. Education: BA, Cornell University, 1948; MD, University of Buffalo, 1952; Columbia University Psychoanalytic Clinic, 1962. Career: Chief Psychiatrist, Isabella Geriatric Center, 1958-77; Professor of Clinical Psychiatry, Columbia University, College of Physicians and Surgeons, 1974-77; Professor and Chairman, Department of Psychiatry, University of TX Southwestern Medical School, 1977-. Publications: Managing Complaints of Sleep and Wakefulness, 1982; Depression: Basic Mechanisms, Diagnosis and Treatment, 1985; On The Question of Bisexuality, in American Journal of Psychotherapy, 1984; Whatever Happened to Intensive Psychotherapy, in American Journal of Psychiatry, 1990. Honours: Wilson Award in Genetics and Preventive Medicine, 1961; DSc, Honoris Causa, Gallaudet College, 1972; Stanton Sharp Chair in Psychiatry, University of TX Southwestern, 1983; Distinguished Alumnus Award, University of Buffalo, 1993. Memberships: AAAS; American College of Psychoanalysts; American College of Psychiatrists; Association of Academic Psychiatrists. Hobbies: Tennis; Symphony; Arts. Address: University of Texas Southwestern, 5323 Harry Hines Boulevard, Dallas, TX 75235-9070, USA.

ALVARES Olav, b. 1 Nov 1939, Bombay, India. Dentist; Associate Professor. m. Dorothea Ann, 20 June 1974, 1 son, 1 daughter. Education: BDS, University of Bombay, 1961; MS, University of Detroit, USA, 1963; PhD, University of Illinois Medical Centre, 1971; Fellow, American Academy of Oral Pathology. Appointments: Assistant Professor, University of Illinois Medical Centre, 1972-74; Research Associate Professor, University of Washington, 1974-81; Associate Professor, University of Texas Health Science centre, San Antonio, 1981-. Publications: Growth Factor Effects on the Expression of Collagenase and Timp-1 in Periodontal Ligament Cells, CO-author, 1995; An Overview of Chronic Adult Periodontitis: Implications for the Elderly, 1988; Regional Differences in Response to Mild Zinc Deficiency, Co-author, 1968. Honours: Consultant, National Institutes of Health, 1993-94; Chairman, Oral Biology Section, 1984-85, Biochemistry and Nutrition section, 1989-90, American Association Dental Schools; Executive Board, American Association Oral Biology, 1990-; Editor, Critical Review in Oral Biology and Medicine, 1987-; NIH-NIDR Research Career Development Award, 1976-81; NIH-NIDR Senior

Fellowship, 1993-95. Memberships: International Association Dental Research; American Association Dental Schools; American Academy Oral Pathology; American Association Oral Biology; Federation American Society Experimental Biologists. Hobbies: Bridge; Reading. Address: 2015 Morning Dove, San Antonio, TX 78232, USA.

ALVERSON Dale Clark, b. Detroit, MI, USA. m. Jennifer Bean-Alverson, 1 s, 4 d. Education includes: MD, cum laude, University of MI, Ann Arbor, 1974; Diplomate, National Board of Medical Examiners, 1975; Diplomate, Certified, American Board of Pediatrics, 1980. Career includes: Private Practice, Marquette, MI, 1977-80; Staff Physician, Pediatrics and Perinatology, Marquette General Hospital, MI, 1977-81; Associate Professor of Pediatrics, 1986-, Director, Division of Neonatology, 1988-, University of NM School of Medicine, Albuquerque, NM; Many invited eduational lectures and presentations. Publications: Reviewer for various professional journals; Many books, chapters, reviews, abstracts and other publications including: Co-author, Hemolytic disease of the newborn: Management and prevention, chapter in Principles of Transfusion Medicine, 1991; Co-author, Multi-center controlled trial comparing high-frequency jet ventilation and conventional ventilation in newborn infants with pulmonary interstitial emphysema, in Journal of Pediatrics, 1991. Honours include: Alpha Omega Alpha, 1973; Galens Honorary Medical Society, 1972; Lange Award, 1974; Glenn T Peake GCRC Clinical Investigator Award, 1988; Distinguished Achievement Award, AHA, NM Affiliate,, 1992; Outstanding Media Person, NM Hospital Association, 1993. Memberships include: AMA; Fellow, American Academy of Pediatrics; Western Society for Pediatric Research; Society of Critical Care Medicine; American Institute of Ultrasound in Medicine; European Society for Pediatric Research; Academy of Radio and Television Health Commentators. Address: University of New Mexico School of Medicine, Department of Pediatrics, Albuquerque, NM 87131, USA.

ALVIR Jose M J, b. 19 Nov 1951, Manila, Philippines. Biostatistician; Epidemiologist. m. Gloria Sotelo, 12 Jan 1980, 1 d. Education: BA, magna cum laude, Sociology, University of The Philippines, 1974; MPH, 1981, Dr PH, 1985, Columbia University. Career: Research Scientist, NY State Research Foundation for Mental Hygiene, 1981-85; Currently, Research Scientist, Assistant Professor of Psychiatry. Publications include: Co-author, Clozapine-induced agranulocytosis: incidence and risk factors in the United States, in New England Journal of Medicine, 1993; Co-author, Editorial: A reevaluation of the clinical characteristics of clozapine-induced agranulocytosis in light of the US experience, in Journal of Clinical Psychopharmacology, 1994; Co-author, Agranulocytosis: incidence and risk factors, in Journal of Clinical Psychiatry, 1994 in press. Memberships: American Statistical Association; International Society for Pharmaepidemiology; Society for Clinical Trials. Hobbies: Singing; Running. Address: Hillside Hospital - Research, PO Box 38, Glen Oaks, NY 11004, USA.

ALWASIAK Janusz, b. 3 Dec 1932, Pabianice, Poland. Physician. m. Barbara Pacha, 15 Oct 1957, 1 son, 3 daughters. Education: Diploma of Physician, Medical Faculty Medical Academy, Lodz, 1957. Appointments: Assistant, Department of Pathological Anatomy, Medical Academy, Lodz, 1964-75; Assistant, Department of Pathology, Leiden University, Holland, 1971-72; Assistant Professor, Professor, Department of Oncology Medical Academy, Lodz, 1976-; Consultant, Department of Pathology, University Hospital, Tromsф, Norway, 1985-86. Publications: Microscopic appearance of recidivant and incompletely removed supratentorial gliomas, 1970; Co-author: Rosenthal fibers, gliofibrillary changes and intracellular homogenous conglomerates in tissue culture of gliomas, 1971; Co-author: Creutzfeldt-Jakob disease with plaques and paired helical filaments, 1987. Memberships: Polish Society of Pathology; Polish Society of Oncology; Society of Polish Neuropathologists; European Academy of Pathology. Honours: Polish Society of Neuropathology Award, 1970. Hobbies: Skiing; Football; Gardening. Address: 173 Moniuszki Street, 93-250 Pabianice, Poland.

AMANNEPESOV Kakabai Amannepesovich, b. 8 Oct 1937, Turtkul, Uzbekistan. Phisiologist. m. Klychdurdyeva Sapargul, 8 June 1957, 1 son, 3 daughters. Education: MD, Turkmen Medical Institute, 1960. Appointments: Physician, Chief Physician, Central Regional Hospital; Senior Scientific Worker, Assistant Director, Institute of Physiology.. Publications: Radiocardiography & Study of Distant Results of Surgical Treatment of Artrial Septal Defect, 1970; Atresia of Tricuspid Valve. Honours: Medal For Labour Valour, 1965. Memberships: Academy of Medical Sciences of Turkmenistan; Scientific Society of Physiologists of

Turkmenistan; International Society of Pathophysiology. Hobbies: Music. Address: 744027 Turkmenistan, Ashgabat, Gaudan A-8-20.

AMAR Michel Félix Louis, b. 26 July 1946, Lyon, France. Psychiatrist. m. Dominique Leclercq, 20 Sept 1975, 2 sons, 2 daughters. Education: MD; Ancien interne, Hôpitaux de Bordeaux; Ancien Chef de Clinique, Université de Bordeaux; DEA, Clinical Psychology and Psychopathology;HDR; Psychoanalyst Member, Paris Psychoanalytical Society; Psychoanalyst Associate Member, International Psychoanalytic Association. Appointments: CCA, University of Bordeaux II; Chief, Infant and Child Psychiatry Department, Bourges; Chief, Infant, Child and Adolescent Psychiatry Department, Rouen; Currently Chef de Service, Child and Adolescent Psychiatry. Publications: L'évolution des troubles psychiatriques de l'enfance, 1990; Le Bébé Sage: Neuropsychiatrie de l'Enfance et de l'Adolescence, 1992; Les interactions en Accueil Familial, 1993; Editor, Rivages journal. Honours: 1st Prize for Confrontations - Psychiatriques, 1975; Groupe Haut Normand de Pédopsychiatrie Fondation, 1987. Memberships include: French Society for Child and Adolescent Psychiatry; International Society for Adolescent Psychiatry; World Association for Infant Mental Health. Hobby: Ornithology. Address: 276 Allée du Clair Vallon, 76230 Boisguillaume, France.

AMARALDIAS Carlos Augusto, b. 26 Aug 1946, Coimbea, Portugal. Psychoanalyst. Divorced, 1 son, 2 daughters. Appointments: Assistant Professor, Faculty of Medicine, University of Coimbea, 1972; Professor of Medical Psychology, Oporto University, 1982; Full Professor, Dynamic Psychiatry, Coimbra University. Publications: The Prevention of Drug Dependance, 1979; Precis Iestoxicomanies, 1984; Portuguese and Barzilian Aventurns de Ali Barba, 1992. Memberships: Sociedade Portuguesa Psiquiatria; Associatao Portuguesa Psiquiatria; International Portuguesa de Psicoframa Psicanalitico de Grub. Honours: Honorary President, Portuguese Group Psychoanalytical Psychodrama Society. Hobbies: Music; Literature. Address: Rua Machado de Castro 62, 3000 Coimbra, Portugal.

AMARIN Zouhair, b. 25 Nov 1948, Jordan. Gynaecologist. 2 sons, 1 daughter. Education: Medical Diploma; MSc, Medical Science; FMGEMS; MRCOG. Appointments: Lecturer, University of Glasgow, Scotland; Senior Lecturer, University of Nottingham, England; Currently Consultant Gynaecologist, Manor House Hospital, London. Publications: Use of prophylactic antibiotics in surgery; Hypogammaglobulinaemia in pregnancy; Embryological disorders of the ovary; In Vitro Fertilisation and CA 125. Honours: Merit Award in undergraduate studies. Memberships: British Fertility Society; American Fertility Society; ESHRE; British Society of Colposcopy; NAC. Hobby: President, West End Chess Club. Address: Flat 22, Milford House, 7 Queen Anne Street, London W1M 9FD, England.

AMBACHE Stella, b. 12 July 1917, Lastingham, Yorkshire, England. Psychoanalyst. m. Nachman Ambache, 14 Sept 1942, 2 sons, 1 daughter. Education: MB BCh. Appointments: Psychoanalyst in private practice. Membership: British Psychoanalytical Society. Hobbies: Reading; Painting. Address: Clifton Royal Parade, Chislehurst, Kent BR7 6NJ, England.

AMEDOFU Kwabla Geoffrey, b. 21 Sept 1947, Inoe-Keta (VR), Ghana. Audiologist. m. Doris Kafui Ziwu, 2 sons. Education: BA; MA; PhD. Appointments: Teaching, Ghana; Teaching Assistant, Research Assistant, Clinical Assistant, Michigan University, USA; Currently Clinical Audiologist and Research Fellow. Publications: Audiological Provisions for Hearing Impaired in Ghana, 1986; Extending Augmentative Communication Devices to New Language Communities, 1988. Honours: Ghana Government Scholarship, 1982-85; Cash Award, Grange Society, Michigan, USA, 1985; Phi Beta Delta, 1989. Memberships: American Auditory Society; International Hearing Society. Hobbies: Walking; Lawn tennis; Table-tennis. Address: Department of Eye, Ear, Nose and Throat, School of Medical Sciences, University of Science and Technology, Kumasi, Ghana, West Africa.

AMER Diane Hiemenz, b. 8 Apr 1951, Renton, Washington, USA. Nursing Consultant. m. Gregory Amer, 20 Dec 1975, 2 daughters. Education: RN; AD, Nursing, St Mary's Campus, College of Catherine, Minneapolis, 1972; BA, Psychology, Hamline University, St Paul, Minnesota, 1979; MA, Organisational Leadership, College of St Catherine, St Paul, 1992. Appointments: Staff Nurse, 1972-84; Public Relations Specialist, Minnesota Nurses' Association, 1984-89; Independent Nursing Consultant, Diane Amer Consulting Services

(Self-Empowerment Resources for Health, Life and Work), Roseville, Minnesota, 1990-. Honours: Editor of Minnesota State Nursing Journal, The Accent, won 4 American Journal of Nursing Awards, 1987 (2), 1990 (2). Memberships: American Nurses' Association; Minnesota Nurses' Association; American Holistic Nurses' Association. Hobbies: Photography; Travel; Jogging; Biking. Address: 2154 So Rosewood Lane, Roseville, MN 55113, USA.

AMINO Nobuyuki, b. 4 Dec 1940, Kobe, Japan. Medical Doctor. m. Masae Tanaka, 1 son, 1 daughter. Education: MD; PhD; Graduate, Osaka University Medical School. Appointments: Assistant Professor, Osaka University Medical School, 1978-89; Associate Professor, Osaka University Medical School, 1989-92; Professor, Osaka University Medical School, 1992. Publications: Autoimmune Endocrine Disease, 1983; The Thyroid, 1986. Honours: The First Annual Award of Japan Endocrine Society, 1981; Prize, Asia Oceania Thyroid Association, 1989. Memberships: American Endocrine Society; American Association for Clinical Chemistry; American Thyroid Association. Hobbies: Swimming; Bird Watching. Address: Department of Laboratory Medicine, Osaka University Medical School, 2-2 Yamadaoka, Suita, Osaka 565, Japan.

AMLER Robert William, b. 21 Apr 1952, New York City, New York, USA. Physician. m. Susan Rosinski, 1975, 2 sons, 2 daughters. Education: AB, Dartmouth College, 1972; MMS, Rutgers Medical School, 1974; MD, Robert Wood Johnson Medical School, 1976. Appointments include: Associate Director, Paediatrics, Adolescent Medicine, US Public Health Service, National Health Service Corps Field Station, 1979-81; Epidemic Intelligence Service Officer, 1981-83, Medical Epidemiologist, 1983-87, Centers for Disease Control; Senior Medical Officer, 1987-90, Chief, Health Investigation Branch, 1990-93, Chief Medical Officer, DHS, 1993-, Agency for Toxic Substance and Disease Registry; Adjunct Professor, Uniformed Services University of the Health Sciences, Bethesda, Maryland, USA; Clinical Professor, Emory University School of Medicine. Publications include: Imported measles in the United States, 1982; Measles in Pregnancy, 1983; Aerosol measles vaccine, 1983; Measles in young adults, 1985; Special communication: Carter Center health policy consultation report, 1985; Closing the Gap: The Burden of Unnecessary Illness. 1987; Healthier People: The Carter Center Health Risk Appraisal Program, Guidelines and Documentation, 1988; ATSDR-ASTHO National Health Risk Communications Training Program for State Health Agency Personnel, 1992; Adoption of an adult environmental neurobehavioral test battery, 1994. Honours include: Honorary Life Member, Georgia PTA, 1989; National School Volunteer, 1990; Distinguished Service, 1990, International Service, 1991, Rotary; Public Health Service Medals, 1991, 1992; Surgeon General's Certificate of Appreciation, 1992; Outstanding Physician, Egleston Children's Hospital, 1993. Memberships: Past President, Commissioned Officer Association, Atlanta Branch; Rotary International; Association of Military Surgeons of US; American Management Association; American Medical Association; Fellow: American Academy of Pediatrics; American College of Preventive Medicine. Hobbies: Theatre; Skiing; Tennis. Address: 1600 Clifton Road (E31), Atlanta, GA 30333, USA.

AN Xinhai, b. 18 June 1964, Xinxiang, Henan Province, China. Research Fellow. m. Tian Qing, 30 Dec 1991, 1 son. Education includes: MB, Hubei Medical University, 1987; Master's degree, Anatomy, 1992, PhD in progress, Anatomy, 1992-, Beijing Medical University. Publications: The distribution of Leu-Enkephalin immunoreactive fibers and neurons in the central amygdaloid nucleus of the rat, 1993; The direct projections from the rat's central amygdaloid nucleus to the dorsal vagal complex, 1994. Honours: Guanghua Prize, 1991. Hobbies: Swimming; Skating; Dancing. Address: Department of Anatomy, Beijing Medical University, Beijing 100083, China.

ANAND Kanwaljeet, b. 29 Nov 1957, Ludhiana, India. Physician. m. Itinder Kaur, 6 Apr 1986, 1 daughter. Education: MBBS, Mahatma Gandhi Memorial Medical College, Indore; DPhil, Jesus College, University of Oxford; FAAP, Children's Hospital and Harvard Medical School, Harvard University, Boston. Appointments: Rhodes Scholar, University of Oxford, England; Research Fellow, Department of Paediatrics, John Radcliffe Hospital, Oxford; Research Fellow, Department of Anaesthesia, Children's Hospital, Boston, Massachusetts, USA; Clinical Fellow, Neonatal and Paediatric Intensive Care Units, Massachusetts General Hospital, Boston; Attending Intensivist, Egleston Childrens Hospital, Atlanta, Georgia; Currently Asssistant Professor of Paediatrics, Anaesthesia, and Psychiatry Emory University School of

Medicine, Egleston Childrens Hospital, Atlanta. Publications: Senior Editor, Pain in Neonates, 1993; Handbook of Paediatric Critical Care, forthcoming. Honours Include: University Medal for Anatomy, University of Indore, 1977; University Medal for First in Anatomy, University of Indore, India, 1977; Blacow Award, British Paediatric Association, 1986; Keynote Address, 1st International Congress in Paediatric Pain, Maastricht, 1988; Keynote Address at the First European Conference on Paediatric Pain, Maarstricht, Netherlands, June 1989; Scientific Committee, 3rd International Meeting of Paediatric Intensive Care, Padova, Italy, 1993; The First Young Investigator Award in Paediatric Pain, International Association for the Study of Pain, Special Interest Group on Pain in Children; Moderator for Maternal and Newborn Health Symposium in Child Health 2000, 2nd World Congress and Exposition, Vancouver (BC), Canada, May 30-June 3, 1995. Memberships: British Paediatric Association; The Neonatal Society, UK; National Neonatal Forum, India; International Association for the Study of Pain; American Academy of Paediatrics; Society of Critical Care Medicine, American Association for the Advancement of Science, Hobbies: Hymn singing; Yoga and meditation. Address: Division of Critical Care Medicine, Egleston Childrens Hospital, 1405 Clifton Road NE, Atlanta, GA 30322, USA.

ANANIEV Vladimir Anatolievitch, b. 21 Aug 1945, Tomsk, Russia. Teacher of Palaeobotany, Ecology and Nature Protection. m. Lidija Petrovna Ananieva, 17 May 1946, 1 son, 1 daughter. Education: Diploma, University of Tomsk, 1967; Doctor's Diploma, 1975; Docent's Diploma, 1981. Appointments: Engineer, 1967-75; Teacher, Doctor, 1976-; Leader of Chair, 1988-89. Publications: Lower carboniferous floras of the North Minusinsk trough, 1979; Earth crust interior protection, 1986; Problems of ecology education, 1991. Honours: Medal, Nature Protection Society, 1984; Honorary Sign, For Nature Protection of Russia, 1987; Many diplomas. Memberships: Societies of Palaeontology, Botany, Ecology and Nature Protections. Hobbies: Sport; Travel; Music. Address: Lebedeva street II, 52, 634061 Tomsk, Russia.

ANANTH Jambur, b. 27 Apr 1932, Hassan, India. Psychiatrist. m. Kamala Ananth, 1 son. Education: MBBS, Kasturba Medical College; Karnatic University, Manipal; DPM; FRCP. Appointments: Associate Professor of Psychiatry, McGill University, Canada, 1974-81; Senior Psychiatrist and Chief, Biological Psychiatry Unit, Allan Memorial Institute, Montreal, 1974-81; Professor of Psychiatry, University of California Los Angeles; Director, Psychopharmacology Unit, Harbor-UCLA Medical Centre. Honours: President, Quebec Branch, APA, 1979-80; Best Teacher Award, Harbor-UCLA Medical Centre Department of Psychiatry, 1983-86; Examiner, American Board of Psychiatry and Neurology, 1991. Memberships: Chairman, Asian American Committee, APA, 1992-94; Scientific Advisory Committee, American Association of Physicians from India, 1988-; President, Kasturba Medical College Alumni Association, 1988-. Address: Harbor-UCLA Medical Centre, 1000 W Carson Street, Building 1-South, Torrance, CA 90509-2910, USA.

ANCHELL Melvin, b. 23 Aug 1919, Baltimore, Maryland, USA. Physician; Author. m. Janice Ruth Levick, 6 July 1948, 3 sons, 2 daughters. Education: BS; MD. Appointments: Self-employed Physician, now retired. Publications: 6 books; Articles published internationally in professional and trade journals. Memberships: Fellow, AAPM; Fellow, American Society of Psychoanalytic Physicians; Fellow, American Board of Family Practitioners; Counsel Member, PAMA; Los Angeles (California) Medical Association; OCMA; Californian Medical Association. Hobbies: Golf; Riding.

ANCHIN Jack Charles, b. 1 Dec 1951, Oceanside, LI, NY, USA. Clinical Psychologist. m. Christine Cornwell, 19 Dec 1976, 2 sons. Education: BA summa cum laude, Adelphi University, USA, 1973; MS, Virginia Commonwealth University, USA, 1975; Intern in Clinical Psychology, Brown University Medical School, 1977-78; PhD, Virginia Commonwealth University, USA, 1978. Career: Staff Psychologist & Research Coordinator, South Shore Mental Health Center, Quincy, MA, USA; Adjunct Faculty, Massachusetts School of Professional Psychology, Newton, MA, USA; Assistant Professor of Psychology, SUNY College at Buffalo, NY, USA; Clinical Psychologist, Manager of Clinical Services & Coordinator of Clinical Supervision, Western New York Institute for the Psychotherapies; Clinical Psychologist in Private Practice. Publications: Co-editor, Handbook of Interpersonal Psychotherapy, 1982; Co-author, Interpersonal Communication, Relationship and the Behavior Therapies, 1976; Author, Functional Analysis and the Social-Interactional Perspective: Toward an Integration in the Behavior Change Enterprise, 1987; Author, Sequence, Pattern and Style: Integration and Treatment Implications of Some Interpersonal Concepts, 1982; Author, Interpersonal Approaches to Psychotherapy: Summary and Conclusions, 1982. Honours: Departmental Honors, Delta Tau Alpha for Outstanding Academic Achievement; Psi Chi, National Honorary Fraternity in Psychology; Phi Kappa Phi, National Honor Society. Memberships: Invited Charter Member, Society for the Exploration of Psychotherapy Integration; Fellow, International Academy of Eclectic Psychotherapists; Psychological Association of Western New York; American Psychological Association. Hobbies: Music; Athletics. Address: 376 Maynard Drive, Amherst, NY 14226, USA.

ANDARY Michael Thomas, b. 10 Oct 1957, USA. Associate Professor. Education: BS, Michigan State University; MS, University of Washington; MD, Wayne State University. Appointments: Instructor, University of Washington; Currently Associate Professor, Michigan State University College of Osteopathic Medicine, East Lansing. Publications: Co-editor: Electrodiagnosis of Carpal Tunnel Syndrome, 1992; Physical Medicine and Rehabilitation Clinics of North America: Outpatients Management of Pain, 1993. Memberships: American Association of Physical Medicine and Rehabilitation; American Association of Electrodiagnostic Medicine; International Association for the Study of Pain. Address: B-401 West Fee Hall, Michigan State University, College of Osteopathic Medicine, East Lansing, MI 48824, USA.

ANDERSON Christopher, b. 17 Oct 1958. Physician. Education: BS, Chemical Engineering, Utah, 1981; MD, University of Utah, 1988. Appointments: Field Engineer, Schlumberger, 1981-84; Pulmonologist, McGill University, Montreal, Canada, 1993-. Membership: Fellow, Royal College of Physicians and Surgeons of Canada. Hobbies: Skiing; Mountaineering. Address: c/o James Upper Pastor Road, Norwich, VT 05055, USA.

ANDERSON David Coussmaker, b. 1 Dec 1940, Farnham, England. Doctor. m. Jennifer Calderwood, 18 July 1965, 3 sons. Education: MB ChB, St Andrews University; MD; MSc; FRCP; FRCPE; FRCPath. Appointments: Medical registrar, Hammersmith Hospital, 1967-71; Lecturer, St Batholomew's Hospital, 1971-75; Goldsmith's Research Fellow, UCSD, 1973-74; Senior Lecturer, University of Manchester, 1975-84; Reader, University of Manchester, 1984-86; Professor of Endocrinology, University of Manchester, 1981-81; Professor of Medicine, Chinese University of Hong Kong, 1991-94; Private Specialist, Internal Medicine and Endocriinology, Hong Kong. Publications: Darenal Cortex, 1985; Contributor of 174 original articles and chapters on endocrinology and metabolic bone disease, especially Paget's Disease of bone; Medical Education: Medi-Vision, videotapes, Medical Director of 15, 1993 and 11, 1994. Memberships: Society for Endocrinology; American Endocrine Society; American Society for Bone amd Mineral Research; Association of Physicians. Hobbies: Art; Music. Address: 403 Pacific House, 20 Queen's Road, Central, Hong Kong.

ANDERSON Iain George, b. 31 July 1953. Orthodontist. m. Nicola Vogt, 12 May 1989, 1 son, 1 daughter. Education: Bachelor of Dental Surgery, University of Edinburgh; Fachzahnarzt für Kieferorthopädie (Orthodontist), Hamburg University. Appointments: Assistant, Orthodontic Department, Hamburg University, Germany; Currently Private Practitioner. Publications: Eine Methode zur Analyse der Gesichtsharmonie mittels verberserte Harmonie Box und euer Koverianz Matrix. Memberships: BDK; EOS. Hobbies: Sailing; Squash. Address: Rosengarten 5, 22880 Wedel, Germany.

ANDERSON Ian George, b, 13 Aug 1910, London, England. Medical Practitioner. m. Jill Jones, 11 Aug 1950, 1 son. Education: MRCS (Eng), LRCP (London), 1933; MB, BS (London), 1934. Appointments: General practice, Shanghai, China, 1936-41; Honorary Surgeon, Russian Orthodox Confraternity Hospital, Shanghai, 1937-41; Royal Army Medical Corps, 1941-45; Singapore, 1947-49; Southern Rhodesia (now Zimbabwe), 1949-85; Currently: Medical Officer to group of 5 factories; Medical Referee to Local Authorities Pension Fund, Government of Zimbabwe. Publications: Surgical Treatment of Hypertension, review article, 1940; History of Esher, 1948; Mas'Aniello: verse-play, unpublished, 1978; Scotsmen in the Service of the Czars, book, 1990; Recollected in Tranquillity, memoirs for private circulation, 1994. Hobbies: Gardening; Music; Literary pursuits. Address: 33 Bath Road, Avondale, Harare, Zimbabwe.

ANDERSON James Wingo, b. 6 Aug 1936, Hinton, WV, USA. Physician; Educator. m. Gay V Anderson, 7 Jun 1957, 1 s, 1 d. Education: MS, Mayo Graduate School. Appointment: Professor of Medicine and Clinical Nutrition, University of Kentucky. Publications: Hypercholesterolemic Effects of Different Bulk Forming Fibers, in Archives Internal Medicine, 1991; Metabolic Effects of High Carbohydrates High Fiber Diets, in Journal of American Clinical Nutrition, 1991; Safety and Effectiveness of Very Low Calorie Diets, in Journal of American Diabetes Association, 1991; Prospective Randomized Controlled Comparison of the Effects of Low-Fat plus High Fiber Diets on Serum Lipid Concentrations, in American Journal of Clinical Nutrition, 1992. Memberships: American Diabetes Association; Fellow, American College of Nutrition; American Society of Nutrition; Fellow, American College of Physicians. Hobbies: Walking; Collecting Recipes. Address: VA Medical Center, Leestown Road 111C, Lexington, KY 40511-1093, USA.

ANDERSON Malcolm Francis, b. 7 Mar 1935, Leeds, Yorkshire, England. Radiologist. m. Valerie Anderson, 3 June 1961, 1 son, 1 daughter. Education: BSc; MB, BS; FRCR. Appointments: House Officer positions: St George's Hospital, London, England, 1960-64; Addenbrooke's Hospital, Cambridge, 1965-72; Assistant Professor, Stanford University, Stanford, California, USA, 1972-84; Currently Professor of Clinical Radiology and Assistant Dean, University of California, San Francisco. Publications: Several articles on radiology and hepatic blood flow. Memberships: AUR; APDR; SGIR. Hobbies: Reading; Travel. Address: VA Medical Center (11), 2615 E Clinton Avenue, Fresno, CA 93703, USA.

ANDERSON Mary Margaret, b. 21 Dec 1932, Forres, Morayshire, Scotland. Obstetrician and Gynaecologist. Education: MBChB; FRCOG. Appointments: House Appointments: Scotland; Registrar, Senior Registrar, St Marys Hospital, London; Consultant, Lewisham Hospital, London, 1968; Consultant. Publications: Author of several books on gynaecology; Contributor of chapters in books. Memberships: RSM; Hunterian Society; South East Gynaecological Society. Address: Reading; Music; Gardening. Address: Green Roof Cottage, 1 Heather Avenue, Blackheath, London SE3 7AN, England.

ANDERSON O(rvil) Roger, b. 4 Aug 1937, Illinois, USA. Professor of Natural Sciences; Researcher. Education: Baccalaureate, 1959, Master's degree, 1961, Doctorate, 1964, Washington University, St Louis, Missouri. Appointments: Assistant Professor of Natural Sciences, 1964-67, Associate Professor of Natural Sciences, 1968-70, Professor of Natural Sciences, 1971-, Columbia University Teachers' College; Research Associate, 1965-70, currently Senior Research Scientist, Biological Laboratories, Columbia University Lamont-Doherty Observatory; Visiting Professor, Tübingen University, Tübingen, Federal Republic of Germany, 1979, 1984, 1986. Publications: Cytomechanics (editor), 1987; Comparative Protozoology, 1988; Neurocognitive Models of Information Processing and Knowledge Acquisition, paper, 1991; Numerous research articles in field of eukaryotic microbiology and neurocognitive science. Honours: New diatom species Cocconeis Andersonii named in recognition of his research on symbiosis, 1989; President-Elect, 1992, President, 1994, Sigma Xi, Columbia University Chapter. Memberships: Sigma Xi; American Institute of Biological Sciences; Institute of Biology, London, UK; Fellow, American Association for the Advancement of Science; Society of Protozoologists; Freshwater Biological Association, UK; New York Academy of Sciences. Hobby: Horticulture. Address: 501 W 120th Street (3W), New York, NY 10027, USA.

ANDERSON Richard L, b. 24 Feb 1945, Iowa, USA. Oculoplastic Surgeon. m. Susan Anderson, 31 Jul 1992, 1 s, 1 d. Education: BA, Chemistry, Grinnell College, IA, 1967; MD, Medicine, College of Medicine, University of IA, 1971; Board Certified, Ophthalmology and Ophthalmic Plastic and Reconstructive Surgery, 1976. Appointments include: Chief, Department of Ophthalmology, VA Hospital, Iowa City, 1976-; Director of Oculoplastics Service, 1976-; Director of Orbital Service, 1978-; Director of Oncology Service, 1982-; Professor of Ophthalmology, 1984-; Chief, Division of Ophthalmic Plastic, Orbital and Reconstructive Surgery, 1989-; Department of Ophthalmology, University of Utah. Publications include: Over 195 articles in professional journals, 26 book reviews, over 550 papers delivered at meetings, 2 books in field, many book chapters and a teaching video. Honours include: Heed Fellowship, 1975; Fight for Sight Clinical Research Award, 1980; Professorship Awards, 1982, 1985, 1986, 1987, 1989; Keynote Speaker, New Orleans Academy of Ophthalmology, 1989; Royal College

Speaker, Canadian Ophthalmological Society, 1992; Senior Honors Award, American Academy of Ophthalmology, 1994. Memberships include: Fellow, American College of Surgeons; Fellow, American Academy of Facial Plastic and Reconstructive Surgery; Fellow, International College of Surgeons; Orbital Society; International Society for Orbital Disorders; Honorary Member, Canadian Society of Oculoplastic Surgeons. Hobbies: Skiing; Mountain Biking; Boating. Address: 1002 East South Temple 308, Salt Lake City, UT 84102, USA.

ANDERSON Timothy Donald, b. 16 Oct 1925, Croydon, Surrey, England. Medical. m. Frances Elizabeth Garrad, 24 Nov 1956, 1 s, 3 d. Education: MA; MB; BCh; FRCS (England); FRCOG. Appointments: Surgical House Officer, St Thomas's Hospital, London; Surgical Registrar, King Edward VII Hospital, Windsor; House Officer, Obstetrics & Gynaecology, Queen Charlottes & Samaritan Hospitals, London; Obstetrics & Gynaecological Registrar, St Barts Hospital, London; Senior Registrar, Obstetrics & Gynaecology, Charing Cross Hospital, London; Consultant Obstetrician & Gynaecologist, East Berkshire District; Consultant Obstetrician & Gynaecologist with VSO in Cambodia, 1991-93; Now Retired. Publications: Contributed to Cyclophosphamide on Ovarian Cancer, 1964; Papers on Cervical Immunology & Infertility, 1974, 1977; Papers on Sport in Pregnancy. Memberships: Royal Society of Medicine. Hobbies: Skiing; Mountain Walking; Tennis; Painting. Address: Eastbank River Road, Taplow, Maidenhead, Berkshire SL6 0BG, England.

ANDRADE Victor Manoel, b. 23 Aug 1937, Cachoeiro de Itapemirim, Brazil. Training Analyst, Rio de Janeiro Psychoanalytic Society. m. Magaly das Merces Andrade, 16 July 1960, 2 sons, 1 daughter. Education: MD, Psychiatrist & Psychoanalist. Publications: Book: Psicanálise de Amplo Espectro, 1993; Articles: Nascimento Violencia e Poder, 1980; Repressao Sublimaçao e Cultura, 1989; O Mundo Interno como Afeto e Representaçao, 1991; Que es la Neurosis para el Psicoanalisis de la Actualidad, 1992. Memberships: Rio de Janeiro Psychoanalytic Society; Brazilian Association of Psychoanalysis; International Psyco-Analytical Association; Rio de Janeiro Psychiatric Association. Honours: Brazilian Association of Psychoanalysis Award. Hobbies: Music; Opera; Cinema; Literature. Address: Estrada do Guanumbi 435, Jacarepagua, 22745-200 Rio de Janeiro RJ, Brazil.

ANDREASEN Nancy Coover, Psychiatrist; Educator. 1 s, 1 d. Education: BA, summa cum laude, 1958, PhD, 1963, University of NE; MA, Radcliffe College, 1959; MD, University of IA, 1970. Career includes: Assistant Professor, 1973-77, Associate Professor, 1977-81, Professor of Psychiatry, 1981-, Director, Mental Health Clinic Research Center, 1987-, University of IA; Senior Consultant, Northwick Park Hospital, London, 1983; Academy Visitor, Maudsley Hospital, London, 1986. Publications: Author, The Broken Brain, 1984; Editor, Can Schizophrenia be Localized to The Brain?, 1986; Editor, Brain Imaging: Applications in Psychiatry, 1988; Author, Introductory Psychiatry Textbook, 1991; Book Forum Editor, 1988-93, Deputy Editor, 1989-93, Editor, 1993-, American Journal of Psychiatry. Honours: Woodrow Wilson Fellow, 1958-59; Fulbright Fellow, Oxford University, England, 1959-60; Honorary Fellow, Royal College of Physicians and Surgeons, Canada; Fellow, American Psychiatric Association; Fellow, American College of Neuropharmacologists. Memberships include: President, 1989-90, American Psychopathological Association; Institute of Medicine of NAS. Address: University of Iowa Hospitals and Clinics, 200 Hawkins Drive, Iowa City, IA 52242-1057, USA.

ANDREWS Billy F, b. 22 Sept 1932, Alamance County, North Carolina, USA. Professor of Paediatrics. m. Faye Rich, 25 Dec 1953, 2 sons, 1 daughter. Education: BS cum laude, Wake Forest College, Wake Forest, North Carolina, 1953; MD, Duke University, Durham, North Carolina, 1957. Appointments: Assistant Professor, Paediatrics, 1964-66, Associate Professor, Paediatrics, 1966-68, Professor, Paediatrics, 1968-, Chairman of Paediatrics, 1969-93, Emeritus Chairman, Paediatrics, 1993-, University of Louisville School of Medicine, Kentucky; Chief-of-Staff, Kosair Children's Hospital, 1969-93; Director, Children and Youth Project. Publications: The Children's Bill of Rights, 1968; Editor: Small-for-Date Infants, 1970; The Newborn, 1977; Aphorisms, Tributes and Tenets of Billy F Andrews, 1986; Ideals and Inspiration, 1993; Words to Live By, 1993. Honours: Alpha Omega Alpha Service Award, University of Louisville, 1989; Staley Distinguished Christian Scholar at Mary Baldwin College, Washington DC and School of Medicine, University of Virginia, 1990; Wisdom Award of Honour, Eminent Fellow, 1991, Winston Churchill Medal, 1993, The Wisdom Society; The Compassionate Paediatrician Award, 1993 Senior Resident

Class, University of Louisville; Visiting Scholar, Green College, Oxford, England, 1993; Billy F Andrews MD Endowed Chair in Paediatrics, University of Louisville, 1993. Memberships: Fellow, American College of Physicians; Fellow, American Academy of Pediatrics; Fellow, Royal Society of Medicine, London; Founding Member, Southern Society for Pediatric Research; American Pediatric Society; American Osler Society; Founding Member, National Association of Children's Hospitals and Related Institutions Inc. Hobbies: Growing dwarf fruit trees and flowers; Reading; Writing; Riding. Address: Department of Paediatrics, School of Medicine, University of Louisville, 404 Alliant Service Building, 610 S Floyd Street, Louisville, KY 40292, USA.

ANDREWS Janet L, b. 30 Jan 1949, Kansas City, MO, USA. Assistant Professor of Nursing. m. Larry L Andrews, 13 Oct 1990, 2 d. Education: BSN, Graceland College; MSN, University of MO; Obstetrics and Gynaecology Nurse Practitioner; Currently pursuing PhD in Nursing at Medical College of Georgia. Career: Instructor, St Luke's School of Nursing, 1981-86; Instructor, Webster University, 1981-91; Assistant Professor, Research College of Nursing, 1986-91; Assistant Professor, Emory University, 1991-92; Currently, Assistant Professor, Perinatal, Women's Health Program. Honours: Teacher of Year, 1988; Nominee, Collegiate Nurse Educator of Year, 1989. Memberships: Sigma Theta Tau; AWHONN; Society of Rogerian Scholars; Southern Nursing Research Society. Hobby: Raising American Quarter Horses. Address: 2071 Highway 142 East, Covington, GA 30209, USA.

ANDREWS John Scott Jr, b. 23 Dec 1946, Tifton, Georgia, USA. Physician. m. Linda Anne Laurel, 23 June 1979, 1 son, 2 daughters. Education: BA, Wesleyan University; MD, Case Western Reserve University; MPH, Johns Hopkins University. Appointments: Epidemic Intelligence Service, Medical Epidemiologist, Assistant Division Director, Division Director at the Centers for Disease Control, 1975-77, 1980-89. Publications: Tetra chlordibenzo-p-dioxm levels in adpose tissue of exposed persons and in persons with no known exposure, 1989; Does Good Peer Review Assure Good Epidemiology?, 1991. Honours: US Public Health Service Outstanding Service Medal, 1992; Surgeon General's Exemplary Service Medal, 1992; member, Collegium Ramazzini Council of Fellows, 1992. Memberships: Royal Society of Tropical Medicine & Hygiene; International of Epidemioligical Association; International Society for Environmental Epidemiology; American College of Occupational & Environmental Medicine. Hobbies: Music; Tennis; Outdoors. Address: Agency for Toxic Substances & Disease Registry, Mailstop E-28, 1600 Clifton Road NE, Atlanta, GA 30333, USA.

ANDRIANO Kirk Patrick, b. 10 Nov 1956, Boise, Idaho, USA. Bioengineer. m. Elizabeth W Young, 1 Aug 1992, 1 daughter. Education: BS, Utah State University, 1980; MS, 1985, PhD, 1990, University of Utah. Appointments: Postdoctoral Fellow, University of Utah School of Medicine, Division of Orthopaedic Surgery, 1990-91; Fogarty Fellow, Tampere University of Technology, Finland, 1991-92; Postdoctoral Fellow, APS Research Institute, California. Publications: Development of Phosphate Microfiber reinforced Poly(Ortho Ester) For Absorbable Orthopedic Fixation Devices, 1995. Honours: Fogarty International Fellowship, 1991-92; Nominated American Men and Women of Science, 1994. Memberships: Biomedical Engineering Society; Society for Biomaterials. Hobbies: Climbing; Kayaking; Skiing; Running. Address: APS Research Institute, 3696 Haven Avenue, Redwood City, CA 94063, USA.

ANG Lee Cyn, b. 3 Dec 1949, Malaysia. Pathologist. m. Liang Low, 4 June 1976, 2 sons, 1 daughter. Education: MBBS, University of Singapore, 1974; LMCC; MRCPath, 1982; FRCPC, 1987; FRCPath, 1994. Appointments: Medical Officer, Ministry of Health, Singapore, 1977-84; Assistant Professor of Pathology, 1988-92, Associate Professor of Pathology, 1992-93, University of Saskatchewan, Canada; Consultant Neuropathologist, Sunnybrook Health Sciences Centre; Associate Professor of Pathology, University of Toronto, 1993-. Publications: Neurite Promoting Activity of Insulin, IGF and NGF on Spinal Motoneuron, 1993; Effects of Astrocytes, Insulin and IGF on Motoneuron, 1992; Delayed Changes of Chromogronin A in Human Striate Cortex; Papillary Tumor of CNS. Honours: Mary Tom Award, Canadian Association of Neuropathologists, 1986; Weil Award, American Association of Neuropathologists, 1991; Cum Laude Citation, American Society of Neuropathologists, 1994. Memberships: Canadian Association of Neuropathologists; American Association of Neuropathologists; American Academy of Neurology; Canadian Neurological Society. Hobbies: History; Table-tennis. Address:

Department of Pathology, Sunnybrook Health Sciences Centre, University of Toronto, 2075 Bayview Avenue, North York, Ontario M4N 3M5, Canada.

ANGELINI Corrado, b. 3 Aug 1941, Padova, Italy. Physician. m. Eicke Angelini, 18 June 1974, 1 son, 2 daughters. Education: MD maxima cum laude, 1965. Appointments: Director, Neuromuscular Center; Currently Professor of Neurology. Publication: Muscular Dystrophy Research, from molecular diagnosis towards therapy, 1991. Honours: Lions Club Host, 1980. Membership: American Neurological Association. Hobbies: Skiing; Hiking.

ANGERSTEIN Rebecca Lea, b. 18 Nov 1959, Akron, Ohio, USA. Registered Nurse. m. 29 June 1979, 1 son. Education: BSN, University of Akron; MA, Education, Kent State University; Critical Care Registered Nurse; RN, C (Certified in Nursing Continuing Education and Staff Development). Appointments: Staff Registered Nurse, Critical Care; Staff Development Educator, Critical Care; Currently Supervisor, Staff Development. Publication: Staff Development Core Curricula (chapter writer), 1994. Honours: Member, Sigma Theta Tau. Membership: National Nursing Staff Development Organization. Hobbies: Exercise; Aerobics; Weightlifting. Address: 3279 Higgin's Drive. Norton, OH 44203, USA.

ANGLE Carol R, b. 20 Dec 1927, NY, USA. Professor of Pediatrics. 1 s, 2 d. Education: BA, Wellesley College, 1948; MD, Cornell Medical School, 1951. Career: Instructor, 1954-57, Assistant Professor, 1957-68, Professor of Pediatrics, 1971-, Chairman, Department of Pediatrics, 1981-85, University of Nebraska College of Medicine. Honours: President of AAPCC, 1975-76; Alpha Omega Alpha, 1979; President, Metals Section, Society of Toxicology, 1982. Memberships: Alpha Omega Alpha; American Academy of Clinical Toxicology; American Academy of Pediatrics; American Association of Poison Control Centers; Society of Toxicology. Address: Department of Pediatrics, University of Nebraska, College of Medicine, 600 South 42nd Street, Omaha, NE 68198-6055, USA.

ANISMAN Arlene, b. 12 July 1949, Toronto, Canada. Psychotherapist. m. David Reiner, 20 Mar 1983, 2 daughters. Education: BA; MEd. Appointments: Private Practice, Psychotherapist, past 17 years. Memberships: American Orthopsychiatric Association; International Transactional Analysis Association and The Ontario Society of Psychotherapists. Hobbies: Horseback Riding; Reading; Films. Address: 489 Windermere Avenue, Toronto, Ontario M6S 3L5, Canada.

ANKNEY Claude Davison, b. 20 Sept 1946, Cleveland, Ohio, USA. University Professor. m. Sandra Johnson, 15 July 1976. Education: BS, Michigan University; PhD, University Western Ontario. Appointments: Assistant Professor, Zoology, University Western Ontario, 1977-80; Associate Professor, Zoology, University Western Ontario, 1980-86; Professor of Zoology, University Western Ontario, Canada. Publications: Nutrient reserves and reproductive performance of female Lesser Snow Geese, co-author, 1974; Sex differences in brain size: The mismeasure of woman, too?, 1992. Honours: Citation Classic Award, 1992; Fellow, American Ornithologists Union, 1992. Memberships: AAAS; Human Behavior & Evolution Society; American Ornithologists Union; Canadian Society of Xoologists; The Wildlife Society. Hobbies: Hunting; Fishing; Golf. Address: 1249 Hillcrest Avenue, London, Ontario N5Y 4N2, Canada.

ANNAN Henry George, b. 23 Oct 1945, Accra, Ghana. Consultant Obstetrician and Gynaecologist. m. Zetha Cofie, 11 Aug 1973, 4 sons, 1 daughter. Education: Cambridge University; St Bartholomew's Hospital, London; BA (Cantab), 1969; MA (Cantab), 1973; MB BChir, 1973; MRCOG, 1978; FRCOG, 1992; MFFP, 1993. Appointments: Rotating Registrar, Obstetrics, Gynaecology, St George's/St Helier Hospitals, 1978-80; Registrar, Obstetrics, Gynaecology, St Mary's Hospital, London, 1980-81; Rotating Senior Registrar, Obstetrics, Gynaecology, Addenbrookes Hospital, Cambridge and St Mary's Hospital, London, 1982-86; Currently: Consultant Obstetrician and Gynaecologist, Forest Healthcare Trust, Whipps Cross Hospital, London; Honorary Senior Lecturer, Obstetrics, Gynaecology, University of London. Publications: Trends in Births by Caesarian Section, 1982; Chapters in Forest Healthcare Trust. Handbook and Formulary, 1994; Co-author: Internal urethrotomy in management of impaired voiding in the female, 1980; The Cook Report: Assisted conception, 1991; Is the use of Ritodrine at the time of cervical cerclage necessary, 1994; ITP in

Pregnancy, 1994. Honours: Council Member: Royal Society of Medicine, 1987-92; Selwyn College Association, 1989-91; Examiner, Royal College of Obstetricians & Gynaecologists, 1989-. Memberships: British Medical Association; Faculty of Family Planning and Reproductive Health, Royal College ofObstetricians & Gynaecologists; Fellow, Royal Society of Medicine; Charter Member, Society for Minimaly Invasive Therapy; British Society for Gynaecological Endoscopy; British Society for Colposcopy and Cervical Pathology. Hobbies: Tennis; Cricket; Golf; Squash; Clay pigeon shooting; Photography; Theatre; Cinema; Gardening; Culture and history of other countries. Address: Bachelors Hall, York Hill, Loughton, Essex IG10 1HZ, England.

ANTIA Noshir Hormasji, b. 8 Feb 1922, Bombay, India. Plastic Surgeon. m. Arnie, 6 Oct 1956, 1 s, 1 d. Education: MBBS; FRCS(Eng); FACS(Hon). Appointments: Honorary Professor of Plastic Surgery, Grant Medical College, Bombay, 1960-80; Honorary Plastic Surgeon, Tata department of Plastic Surgery, JJ Group of Hospitals, Bombay, 1958-80; Director, The Foundation for Medical Research and Foundation for Research in Community Health, Bombay. Publications: 268 Scientific Publications including: The Surgical Management of Deformities in Leprosy and Other Peripheral Neuropathies, 1993; People's Health in People's Hands, 1994. Honours: Padma Shri for Significant Contribution in the Field of Plastic Surgery, 1990; G D Birla International Award for Humanism, 1994. Memberships: British Association of Plastic Surgeons; Association of Plastic Surgeons of India. Hobbies: Photography; Natural history. Address: The Cliff, 27 Pochkhanawala Road, Worli, Bombay 400025, India.

ANTONUCCI Toni, b. 9 Sept 1948, Brooklyn, New York, USA. Research Scientist. m. James S Jackson, 12 Jan 1979, 2 daughters. Education: BA; MA; PhD; National Institutes of Health Training Fellow. Appointments: Teaching Assistant, Wayne University, 1969-73; Assistant Professor, Syracuse University, 1973-79; Lecturer, University Michigan, 1979; Associate Professor, Family Practice, School of Medicine, University Michigan, 1979-88; Assistant Research Scientist, ISR, University Michigan, 1979-82; Chair, Behavioral & Social Science, Gerontological Society of America, 1993-94; Fogarty Senior International Fellow, 1992-94; Visiting Scholar, INSERM, Paris, France, 1992-94. Publications: Social Supports and Social Relationships; The Handbook of Aging and the Social Sciences; A Life-span View of Women's Social Relations. Honours: Research Career Development Award. Memberships: Gerontological Society of America; American Psychological Society; International Society for the Study of Behavioral Development; Society for Research in Child Development. Hobbies: Skiing; Jogging; Tennis; Sailing. Address: Institute for Social Research, PO Box 1248, Ann Arbor, MI 48106-1248, USA.

ANWAR Mir N, b. 13 Dec 1951, Noakhali, Bangladesh. Paediatrician. m. Nilufar, 15 June 1980, 2 sons. Education: MBBS (Bangladesh), DCH(Ireland); MRSH (London); FICA (USA); FRSTM & H (UK). Career: Registrar Paediatrics, Holy Family Red Cross Hospital, Bangladesh; Consultant Paediatrician, Maternity & Children Hospital, Makkah KSA; Consultant Paediatrician & Child Neurologist, Well Baby Clinic, Dhaka, Bangladesh. Publications include: Immunization in Bangladesh-Recent Trend, 1990; Febrile Convulsion-Management & It's Outcome-A Study Report', Dhaka, 1990; Seizure Post Immunization-Rare in Bangladesh, 1991; Management of Convulsion by Rectal Diazepam - A Comprehensive Study in BD. Honours: AOCCN, Bangkok, 1992; American Medical Association Physician Award, 1994. Memberships: ICNA; BPA; BMA; BPMPA. Hobbies: Travel; Photography. Address: Well Baby Clinic, 13 Green Super Market, Green Road, Dhaka 1205, Bangladesh.

ANZIL Archinto Peter, b. 29 Jan 1930, Treppo Grande, Italy. Physician. m. Doris Ennis, 11 Feb 1961. Education: MD, Padua University School of Medicine, Italy, 1954. Appointments: Chef des Travaux, Div Autonome de Neuropathol, CHUV, Lausanne, Switzerland; Wissenschaftlicher Ass, Max-Planck Inst fuer Psychiatrie, Munich, Germany; Associate Professor of Pathology, Medical College of Pennsylvania, Philadelphia; Professor of Clinical Pathology, State University of New York Health Science Center, New York; Director of Neuropathology, Kings County Hospital Center, New York, USA. Publications: Spinal Cord Pathology, 1994; Prominent white matter cavitation in an infant with Alexander's disease, 1994; Over 100 original papers. Memberships: American Association of Neuropathologists; Société Française de Neurologie. Hobbies: Reading. Address: Department of Pathology, Box 25, SUNY-HSCB, Brooklyn, NY 11203-2098, USA.

AOKI Thomas T, b. 12 June 1940, Oakland, California, USA. Endocrinologist. m. Susan K Aoki, 3 Aug 1963, 3 daughters. Education includes: MD. Appointments: Associate Physician, Brigham and Women's Hospital, 1982-84; Associate Physician, 1984-, currently Professor of Medicine, Chief, Divison of Endocrinology, University of California, Davis; Consultant, Medicine (Endocrinology), Veterans Administration Hospital, Martinez, California, 1984-. Publication: Long term intermittent intravenous insulin therapy and type I diabetes mellitus, 1993. Honours: Moseby Award for Scholastic Excellence, Yale University School of Mecicine, 1965. Memberships: American Diabetes Association; American Federation of Clinical Research; Endocrine Society; Western Associates of Physicians. Hobbies: Wine collecting and running. Address: University of California, Davis, Medical Center, Division of Endocrinology, 4301 X Street, Building FOLB II-C, Sacramento, CA 95817, USA.

APPELBAUM Paul S, b. 30 Nov 1951, Brooklyn, New York, USA. Psychiatrist. m. Diana Appelbaum, 2 sons, 1 daughter. Education: AB, Columbia College, 1972; MD, Harvard Medical School, 1976; Special student, Harvard Law School, 1979-80; Special student, Graduate School of Public Health, University of Pittsburgh, 1983-84. Appointments: Assistant to Associate Professor of Psychiatry and Law, University of Pittsburgh; Pennsylvania; Associate Professor of Psychiatry, Harvard Medical School; Cambridge, Massachusetts; Currently Professor, Chairman, University of Massachusetts. Publications: Clinical Handbook of Psychiatry and Law (with T G Gutheil), 1982, 2nd edition, 1991; Informed consent: Legal Theory and Clinical Practice (with C W Lidz and A Meisel), 1987, Japanese Edition, in press; Almost a Revolution: Mental Health Law and the Limits of Change, 1994. Honours: Manfred S Guttmacher Award, American Psychiatric Association, 1983. Memberships: American Psychiatric Association; American Academy of Psychiatry and Law; International Academy of Law and Mental Health. Hobby: Writing. Address: Department of Psychiatry, University of Massachusetts Medical Center, 55 Lake Avenue North, Worcester, MA 01655, USA.

APPREY Maurice, b. 2 Dec 1947, Ghana. Child Psychoanalyst. m. Zane S Apprey, 22 Oct 1973, 1 son. Education: PhD, Saybrook Institute & Research Centre, San Fransisco. Appointments: Consultant, Clinical Infant Development Program, National Institutes of Health, 1980-82; Visiting Faculty, Medical College of Virginia, 1985-90; Professor of Psychiatry, University of Virginia. Publications: Co-author, From Metaphor to Meaning; Clinical Stories and Their Translations; English Language Translator of, G Politzer's, Critique Des Fondements De La Psychologie; Author, Intersubjectivity, Projective Identification and Otherness. Memberships: Executive Council, Association of Child Psychoanalysts; Board of Editors, Psychoanalytic Study of Society; American Academy of Psychoanalysis; Association of American University Professors; American Psychological Association. Address: Office of the Dean, McKim Hall, University of Virginia School of Medicine, Box 458, Health Sciences Centre, Charlottesville, VA 22908, USA.

APTER Jeffrey T, b. 14 Dec 1950, Johannesburg, South Africa. Physician. Appointment: President, Princeton Biomedical Research PA, Princeton. Honour: Distinguished Service Award, American Academy of Clinical Psychiatry, 1993. Memberships: APA; New Jersey Medical Society; AACP; ACP. Address: Princeton Biomedical Research PA, 330 North Harrison Street, Suite 6, Princeton, NJ 08540, USA.

APUZZIO Joseph, b. 6 Oct 1947, Elizabeth, New Jersey, USA. Physician. m. Marili Bernardo, 12 Oct 1980, 1 son, 1 daughter. Education: BA; Certified: American Board of Obstetrics and Gynaecology; American Board of Maternal and Fetal Medicine. Appointments: Currently Professor of Obstetrics, Gynaecology and Radiology, UMD New Jersey Medical School, Newark. Publications: Operative Obstetrics, 2nd Edition. Honours: Phi Beta Kappa; Alpha Omega Alpha. Memberships: American College of Obstetrics and Gynaecology; American College of Surgeons. Hobby: Jogging. Address: UMD - New Jersey Medical School, Department OB/GYN, 185 South Orange Ave, Newark, NJ 07103, USA.

AQUAVELLA James V, b. 5 Feb 1932, New York City, USA. Physician. Education: MD. Appointments: Director of Ophthalmology, Park Avenue Hospital; Director of Ophthalmology, Park Ridge Hospital; Director of Ophthalmology, ROA Ambulatory Center; Professor of Ophthalmology, University Rochester. Publications: 335 publications to date. Honours: American Academy of Ophthalmology Honour Award,

1982; American Academy of Ophthalmology Senior Honour Award, 1988. Memberships: American Academy of Ophthalmology; International Association of Ophthalmology; Pan American Association of Ophthalmology; New York State Ophthalmological Society. Address: 919 Westfall Road, Rochester, NY 14618, USA.

ARBULU VILLASIS Oscar, b. 24 Mar 1938, Chiclayo, Peru. Physician. m. Carlota Bravo, 15 Feb 1969. Education: MD, Universidad Nacional de Cordoba, Argentina, 1963; Geriatric Psychiatry, University of Miami, USA. Appointments: Psychiatrist, Universidad Peruana Cayetano Heredia; Medical Assistant, Psychiatric Hospital Victor Larc Herrera; Associate Professor of Psychiatry, Universidad Nacional Mayor de San Marcos; Psychiatrist, Hospital Rebagliati. Publications: History of Geriatrics in Peru, 1993; Geriatric Depression, 1993; Sexual Aspects in Old Age, 1988. Memberships: Peruvian Psychiatric Association; Peruvian Geriatric Association; French Psychogeriatric Association; International Psychogeriatric Association. Hobby: Running. Address: Los Alamos 603, Residencial San Felipe, Jesus Maria, Lima, Peru.

ARCHAKOV Alexander Ivanovich, b. 10 Jan 1940, Kashin, Russia. Biochemist. m. Leskova Svetlana, 4 Dec 1963, 1 d. Education: Professor of Biochemistry; Postgraduate, Department of Biochemistry, 2nd Moscow Medical Institute. Career: Research and Teaching Assistant of Biochemistry, Lecturer, Biochemistry, Head of Laboratory of Enzymology and Bioenergetics, Professor of Biochemistry, Currently, Head of Department of Biochemistry, 2nd Moscow Medical Institute; Currently, Director, Institute of Biomedical Chemistry. Publications: Microsomal Oxidation, book, 1975; Oxygenases of Biological Membranes, book, 1983; Cholesterolosis, book, 1984; Cytochrome P-450 and Active Oxygen, book, 1990; Editor, Phosphatidylcholine: Effects on Cell Membranes and Transport of Cholesterol, 1989. Honours: Bach Prize of Russian Academy of Sciences, 1982; Russian State Prize, 1985, 1989; Academician, Russian Academy of Medical Sciences. Memberships: Biochemical Society of Russia; Biochemical Society of Great Britain; New York Academy of Science; International Advisory Committee of Cytochrome P-450; Scientific Committee on Oxygenases of IUB; International Centre of Advanced Studies on Molecular Biophysics and Biology. Hobby: Football. Address: Institute of Biomedical Chemistry, Russian Academy of Medical Sciences, Pogodinskaya Str 10, Moscow 119832, Russia.

ARCHIE Carol Louise, b. 18 May 1957, Detroit, Michigan, USA. Physician; Educator. m. Professor Edward L Keenan III, 6 Mar 1993. Education: BA, History, University of Michigan; MD, Wayne State University; Diplomate, American Board of Obstetrics and Gynaecology; ABOG Division of Maternal Foetal Medicine. Appointments: Assistant Professor, Department of Obstetrics/Gynaecology, University of California, Los Angeles. Publications: The Effects of Methadone Treatment on Reactivity of the Nonstress Test, 1989; Drug Dependency in Pregnancy: Managing Withdrawal, 1993; Methadone in Management of Narcotic Addiction in Pregnancy, 1994; Substance Abuse in Pregnancy, 1993. Honours: Berlex Faculty Development Award, 1992; Invited Speaker, INternational Conference Women's Health, 1993. memberships American College of Obstetrics and Gynaecology; Society of Perinatal Obstetricians; Royal Society of Medicine; National Medical Association; AMA. Hobbies: Time with family and friends; Travel; Theatre; Museums; Books. Address: Dept OB?GYN, UCLA School of Medicine, Room 22-132CHS, 10833 Le Conte Avenue, Los Angeles, CA 90024, USA.

ARDILA Carlos Luis, b. 1 Sept 1952, Bucaramanga, Colombia. Psychoanalist. m. Renate Biela, 18 July 1981, 1 son, 2 daughters. Education: MD, Universidad Javerina; Psychoanalist, International Psychoanalitical Association. Appointments: Teacher, School of Medicine, University Javeriana; Chairman, Drug Addiction & Alcoholism Department, Hospital Psiquiatrico San Camilo; Chairman, Psychotherapy Department, Hospital Psiquiatrico Universitario San Camilo; Visiting Scientist Program, USA, 1989; Publications: Translation and adaption to Spanish of, I'm Special, 1991. Memberships: International Psycho Analytical Association; Sociedad Colombiana de Psicoanalisis; Sociedad Psiquiatrica Javeriana. Honours: NIDA First International Drug Abuse Prevention Research Symposium, 1991. Hobbies: Music; Literature; Exercise. Address: Carrera 29 No 50-39 Piso 2, Bucaramanga, Colombia.

ARELLANO-OCAMPO Francisco, b. 14 Oct 1934, Guerrfro, Mexico. Professor. m. Amicla Arellano, 20 May 1959, 4 sons, 3 daughters. Education: Doctorate. Appointments: Medicine School, University of

Puebla; Residency, General Hospital of Mexico; Professor, University of Puebla. Publications: Toxic Epidermic Necrolisys, 1977; Cromo Micosis, 1977; Dermatology Complication in the Diabetic Patient, 1977; Dermatology for the Students (Ansilary Methods), 1977. Memberships: Fellow, British Society for Allergy & Clinical Inmunology; Fellow, American Society for Dermatology Surgery; European Academy of Allergology & Clinical Inmunology. Honours: Medical Award, IMSS, 1972; Nestle Pediatric Foundation Award, 1972; Ibero-Latinamerican College Distinction, 1979. Hobbies: Photography. Address: 20 Sur No 2539, Puebla, Pue CP 725500, Mexico.

ARGENTA Louis Charles, b. 28 Dec 1942, Michigan, USA. Professor of Plastic and Reconstructive Surgery. m. Mary Jo Finan, 24 Feb 1968, 5 sons, 1 daughter. Education: BS, 1965, MD, 1969, University of Michigan. Appointments: Associate Professor, Interim Head, Section on Plastic Surgery, University of Michigan; Currently Professor, Chairman, Department of Plastic Surgery, Bowman Gray Medical School, Winston-Salem, North Carolina. Publications: Craniosynostosis and its Surgical Correction in Infancy; Clinical Tissue Expansion; 130 refereed publications in journals. Honours: Frederick Collar Travelling Scholar, 1968; Merit Award, American Cancer Society, 1990; Medical Device of the Year, American Society of Medical Inventions, 1993. Memberships: American College of Surgeons; American Association of Plastic Surgery; American Society of Plastic Surgeons; Cleft Palate Society; International Craniofacial Surgery Society; American Burn Association. Hobbies: Oil painting; Travel; Mountain climbing. Address: 525 Knobview, Winston-Salem, NC 27103, USA.

ARGENTIERI BONDI Simona, b. 19 Jan 1940, Florence, Italy. Psychoanalyst. m. Raffaele Argentieri, 15 Mar 1965, 1 son. Education: MD; Training Analyst, Associazione Italiana di Psicoanalisi; Training Analyst, International Psychoanalytical Association. Publications: Freud a Hollywood, 1988; Freud e l'Arte, 1990; The Babel of the Unconscious (co-author), 1993; L'uomo nero, 1994. Membership: Psychotherapist, Albo dell' Ordine dei Medici. Hobby: Applied psychoanalysis, especially cinema and psychoanalysis. Address: via Giovan Battista Martini 6, 00198 Rome, Italy.

ARLING Mi, b. 9 July 1942, Arjeplog, Sweden. Psychotherapist. m. Sten Arling, 11 July 1970, 1 son, 1 daughter. Education: PhD; Licensed Clinical Psychologist; Licensed Psychotherapist; Authorised Teacher and Supervisor of Psychotherapy. Appointments: Currently Training Director, Centrum för Integrativ Psykoterapi. Publications: Ethics in Supervision, Reflections on Respect, 1992; Supervision in groups - a learning experiment, 1994. Memberships: Sveriges Psykologförbund; Sveriges Förening för Klinisk och Experimentell Hypnos; Riksföreningen Psykoterapicentrum; Psykoterapihandledarnas Intresseföreningen; European Association for Integrative Psychotherapy; World Council for Psychotherapy. Hobbies: Painting; Gardening; Country-house activities; Zonta Club. Address: Norra Klaragatan 8, S-653 40 Karlstad, Sweden.

ARM Robert N, b. 21 Feb 1947, Bronx, New York, USA. Dentist; Professor. m. Rhonda Bestreich, 24 June 1972, 1 son, 2 daughter. Education: BA, Queens College, New York; Diplomate, American Board of Oral Medicine; Diplomate, American Academy of Pain Management; Fellow, American Association of Hospital Dentists; Certificate of Training, Oral Pathology; Certificate of Training, Oral Medicine; Dental Internship, 1972-73, Residency, Oral Medicine, 1973-74, Philadelphia General Hospital; Residency, Pathology, Hospital of University of Pennsylvania, 1974-75; Doctor of Dental Medicine, University of Pennsylvania School of Dental Medicine. Appointments: Assistant Professor, University of Louisville School of Dentistry, 1976-79; Chairman, Department of Dentistry, 1979-, Educational Director, General Practice Residency, 1980-, Medical Center of Delaware, Wilmington; Clinical Professor of Oral Medicine, Temple University School of Dentistry. Publications: Skin Diseases and Their Oral Manifestations, section in Internal Medicine for Dentistry, 1983, 2nd edition update, 1987. Memberships: Vice-President, American Academy of Oral Medicine; American Academy of Oral Pathology; Treasurer, Northeast Craniomandibular Society; American Association of Dental Schools; American Association of Hospital Dentists; American Academy of Pain Management; International Association for Dental Research; IASP. Hobbies: Camping; Boy Scouts; Palaeopathology and archaeology; Computers. Address: Medical Center of Delaware, Department of Dentistry, 501 W 14th Street, Wilmington, Delaware, USA.

ARMATA Jerzy Józef, b. 20 Dec 1928, Jaslo, Poland. Physician. m. Teresa Armata, Oct 1952, 1 daughter. Education: Diploma of Physician, Collegium Medicum, Jagiellonian University, Cracow, 1952; MD, 1963; Associate Professor, 1968; Professor, 1982; Full Professor, 1992. Appointments: Associate, Department of Medicine, 1968, Head, Department of Haematology, 1976-, Collegium Medicum, Jagiellonian University, Cracow. Publications: Co-author: MVPP chemotherapy combined with radiotherapy in the treatment of Hodgkin's disease in children, 1978; The physician's hands and early detection of neuroblastoma, 1994. Honours: Polcul Foundation, 1992. Memberships: American Society of Pediatric Hematology and Oncology; Polish Paediatric Association. Hobby: Creative writing. Address: Polish-American Children's Hospital, Collegium Medicum, Jagiellonian University, 265 Wielicka Street, 30-663 Cracow, Poland.

ARMSTRONG David Holmes, b. 2 Feb 1933, Torrance, California, USA. Gynaecologist. m. Joan Diana Cosgrove, 18 Dec 1954, 3 sons, 1 daughter. Education: MD, 1957; FACOG; FACS. Appointments include: Intern, Paediatrics, 1957-58, Resident, Ob-Gyn, 1958-59, University of California at Los Angeles; Rotation General Ob-Gyn, Harbor General Hospital, 1960; California Institute of Technology Linus Pauling Chemistry Laboratory, 1961; General Surgery-Oncology, Gynaecologic Oncology, City of Hope, 1961; Chief Resident, Ob-Gyn, 1962, Clinical Instructor, 1964-70, Assistant Clinical Professor, 1970-80, Department Ob-Gyn, University of California, Los Angeles; Assistant Clinical Professor, 1979-94, Associate Clinical Professor, 1994-, Department of Ob-Gyn, University of California, Irvine; Private Practice, 1962-. Publications: A Quantitative Study the Fate of Recently Absorbed Food Iron, 1958; Bacteriuria During Pregnancy, 1963; A Comparison of the Percentage of Fetal Hemoglobin in Human Umbilical Cord Blood as Determined by Chromatography and by Alkali Denatureatin, 1963; Inflammation of the Umbilical Cord and Neonatal Illness, 1964; Prolonged Rupture of Fetal Membranes-Effect on the Newborn Infant, 1964; Antepartum Detection of Congenital Complete Fetal Heartblock: A Case Report, 1976; Regionalized Care: Obstetrical/Gynecological Society Role, 1977. Memberships include: American Medical Association; California Medical Association; American Association of Gynaecological Laparoscopists; Orange County OB-GYN Society, Past President; Dan Morton Society; Los Angeles OB-GYN Society. Hobbies: Walking; Jogging; Swimming; Reading; Theatre; Cinema. Address: 2720 North Harbor Boulevard, Suite 130, Fullerton, CA 92635, USA.

ARMSTRONG David William, b. 29 Jan 1954, Ottawa, Ontario, Canada. Biomedical Researcher. m. Elaine Robertson, 10 June,1978, 1 daughter. Education: BSc (Hons), 1978; MSc, University of Ottawa, 1980; Registered Specialist, Microbiology (Canadian College Microbiologist), 1982; PhD, Carleton University, 1984. Appointments: Advisor, Biomedicine and Biotechnology, Canadian Space Agency, 1985-88; Currently Head, Tissue Regeneration Laboratory, Institute for Biological Sciences, National Research Council, Ottawa. Publications: US Patent, Cell Cultivation Device for Human and Animal Cells; Novel Living Skin Replacement and Biotherapy, International PCT, 1992. Honours: Ontario Scholar, 1973; Recipient, Ontario Graduate Scholarship, 1979-80. Membership: Canadian College of Microbiologists. Hobby: Ballroom dancing. Address: Institute for Biological Sciences, National Research Council of Canada, 1200 Montreal Road, Ottawa, Ontario, Canada K1A 0R6.

ARNASON Barry Gilbert Wyatt, b. 30 Aug 1933, Winnipeg, Manitoba, Canada. Neurologist. m. Joan Morton, 27 Dec 1960, 2 sons, 1 daughter. Education includes: MD, University of Manitoba, 1957. Appointments: Assistant Professor of Neurology, 1964-71, Associate Professor of Neurology, 1971-76, Harvard Medical School, USA; Professor, Chairman, Department of Neurology, University of Chicago, Illinois, 1976-; Director, Brain Research Institute, 1985-93. Publications: Over 300 articles in the areas of neurology and immunology. Memberships: American Neurological Association; American Society of Clinical Investigation; American Academy of Neurology. Hobby: Sailing. Address: Department of Neurology, University of Chicago, 5841 S Maryland Avenue, Chicago, IL 60637, USA.

ARNOLD Anthony Christopher, b. 17 June 1949, Santa Monica, California, USA. Physician. Education: MD, University of California Los Angeles School of Medicine, 1975. Appointments: Chief, Neuro-Ophthalmology, Wilford Hall USAF Medical Centre, San Antonio, Texas, 1983-86; Chief, Neuro-Ophthalmology Division, Director, UCLA Optic Neuropathy Centre. Publications: retinal Periphlebins and Retinitis in Multiple Sclerosis, 1984; Neuro-Ophth Manifestiation of Pituitary

Tumors, 1994; Fluorescein Angiography in Acute Nonarteritic Anterior, 1994. Honours: Associate Examiner, American Board Ophthalmology, 1988-; American Academy Ophththalmology Honour Award, 1992/ Memberships: American Academy Ophthalmology; American Board Ophthalmology; North American Neuro-Ophthalmology Society; International Neuro-Ophthalmology Society; AMA; CMA; LACMA. Address: Jules Stein Eye Institute, 100 Stein Plaza, UCLA, Los Angeles, CA 90024-7005, USA.

ARNOLD Phillip Gordon, b. 24 Sept 1941, Lincolnton, North Carolina, USA. Surgeon. m. Susan E BonDurant, 18 June 1966, 2 sons. Appointments: Fellow, Plastic & Reconstructive Surgery, Emory University, 1974-76; Consultant, 1976-, Professor & Chief, 1989-, Plastic Surgery, Mayo Clinic. Publications: 4 books. Memberships: Fellow, American College of Surgeons; Southern Surgical; ASPRS; AAPS. Hobby: Fishing. Address: Mayo Clinic, 200 1st St SW, Rochester, MN 55905, USA.

ARNOLD Watson Caulfield Jr, b. 1 Dec 1945, Waco, Texas, USA. Paediatric Nephrologist. m. Tricia, 2 s. Education: BA, Tulane University, 1963-66; MD, University of Texas at dallas, Texas Southwestern Medical School, 1966-67; Intern, 1970-71, Residency, 1973-75, Medical College of Virginia, Richmond, Virginia. Appointments: Assistant Professor of Paediatrics, 1977-83, Associate Professor of Paediatrics, 1983-90, Director, renal Section, 1986-80, Director, Metabolic Division, 1987-90, University of Arkansas for Medical Sciences; Director, Paediatric Nephrology, 1978-90, Medical Director, Paediatric Dialysis Unit, 1979-88, Director of Transplantation, 1986-90, Arkansas Children's Hospital, Little Rock, Arkansas; Director of Paediatric Nephrology, Cook-Fort Worth Children's Medical Centre, Fort Worth, Texas, 1990-. Publications include: Characteristics of Renal Insufficiency in Children, Co-author, 1978; Insulin-Mediated Amino Acid Uptake in Tissue and Serum in Uremic Rats, 1979; Effect of Growth Hormone and Organ Size in Growing Uremic Rats, Co-author, 1989; Peritoneal Equilibration Test in Paediatric Dialysis Patients, Co-author, 1990. Memberships include: American Institute of Nutrition; American Society of Nephrology; Chairman, Executive Committee, 1989-92, American Academy of Paediatrics, Section on Nephrology; International Society of Paediatric Nephrology; Fort Worth Paediatric Society. Address: Cook-Fort Worth Children's Medical Centre, 801 Seventh Avenue, Fort Worth, TX 76104-273, USA.

ARNOTT Ellen Marie, b. 28 Apr 1945, Berwyn, USA. Occupational Health. m. John M Arnott, 16 Dec 1967, 1 son, 1 daughter. Education: BSN, Seton Hall University, New Jersey; MA, Corporate Health Education, Texas Woman's University. Appointments: Community Health Nursing, 1982-83; AT & T Disability Assistance Nurse, 1983-84; Manager of Health Service, Lone Star Gas Co, 1985-86; Manager of Health Service, Abbott Laboratories, 1986-88; Nursing Supervisor, J C Penney Corporate, 1988-89. Publications: Monthly Health Services Newsletter; Nurse Case Management of Workers' Compensation injuries: A strategy toward corporate cost containment, 1991; Coordinated Action Eases the Pain for all Victims, 1992. Honours: Texas State Achievement Award for Excellence in Occupational Health, 1990; Recognized as a Great One-Hundred Nurse for 1991, Dallas. Memberships: American Association of Occupational Health Nurses; Texas State Association of Occupational Health Nurses; Dallas Texas Association of Occupational Health Nurses; American Nurses Association; Texas Nurses Association; Case Management Society of America; Amicron Delta Epsilon; American Cancer Society Education Committee; American Cancer Society Skin Cancer Committee. Hobbies: Golf; Travel. Address: Arnott & Assoc Inc, 111 Pebble Beach Drive, Trophy Club, TX 76262, USA.

AROOR Suresh, b. 17 Jan 1952, Mangalore. Doctor; Pediatric Neurologist. m. Sujatha, 2 Dec 1982, 1 son, 1 daughter. Education: MBBS, DCH, MD (Paed); DM (Neuro). Career: Professor and Head, Department of Neurology, Manipal Hospital, Bangalore. Publications: Contributor of Chapter, Diseases of the Central Nervous System, in Diseases of Children in the Subtropics & Tropics; Co-author of Text-book, Seizure Disorders in Childhood & Pediatric Neuro Infection. Honours: Started the First Department of Pediatric Neurologyin the Country; Founder, Treasurer and Secretary, Child Neurology Chapter, Indian Academy of Pediatrics (IAP). Memberships: Indian Academy of Pediatrics; Child Neurology Chapter of IAP; Neurologic Society of India. Hobby: Golf. Address: Parijma Medical Centre, BTS Depot Road, Wilson Garden, Bangalore, 560-027.

ARPELS John Claude, b. 13 June 1940, New York City, USA. Menopausal Gynecology. Education: MD. Appointments: Associate Clinical Professor, University California, San Francisco Medical Center. Publications: Experimental Irradiated Nerve Heterografts, 1966; Gonadal Hormones & Breast Cancer Risk: The Estrogen Window Hypothesis Revisited, 1994; Ovarian Hormones and the Female Brain: From PMS to Menopause, 1994. Honours: Special Recognition Award, Excellence in Teaching & Practice of Medicine, Association of the Clinical Faculty, University California, 1994. Memberships: Fellow, American College of Obstetricians & Gynecologists; Association of the Clinical Faculty, University California, San Francisco School of Medicine; San Francisco Gynecology Society; North American Menopause Society; American Society of Breast Disease. Address: 3838 California Street, San Francisco, CA 94118, USA.

ARREAZA Eduardo Enrique, b. 18 Sep 1953, Caracas, Venezuela. Physician. m. Maria Fontes, 16 Oct 1982, 1 son, 2 daughters. Education: MD, Universidad de Carabobo, Valencio, 1977; FACP; Fellow, American Academy of Allergy and Immunology. Appointments: Assistant Professor of Medicine, University of Texas Medical Branch, Galveston, Texas, USA, 1985-88; Assistant Professor of Medicine, Cornel Medical College, 1988-90; Clinical Assistant Professorof Medicine, University of Rochester School of Medicine. Publications: Hereditary Angioderma: Clinical and Biochemical Heterogeneity, Co-author, 1988; Penicillin Allergy: A Review, 1989; Refractory Cholinergic Urticaria Successfully Treated with Ketotifen, Co-author, 1989; Network Regulation of the Immune Resonse, CO-author, 1989; Lower Antibody Response to Tetanus Toxoid Associated with Higher Auto-Anti-Idiotypic Antibody in Old Compared with Young Humans, Co-author, 1993. Memberships: Monroe County Medical Society. Hobbies: Jogging; Computers. Address: 220 Alexander Street, Suite 604, Rochester, NY 14607, USA.

ARSLAN Gülnaz, b. 15 Jan 1941, Istanbul, Turkey. Medical Doctor. m. Yilmaz Arslan, 26 Aug 1965, 1 s, 1 d. Education: PhD. Career: Associate Professor of Anesthesia, Hacettepe University School of Medicine; Director of Pediatric Anesthesia, Ankara; Currently, President, Anesthesiology and Reanimation Association, Ankara; Chairman of Anesthesiology, Baskent University Hospital, Ankara. Publications include: Pulmonary embolism during surgery for wilms tumour, in British Journal of Anesthesia, 1981; Co-author, Living related donor kidney transplantation at a Turkish Center, in Transplantation Proceedings, 1992; Segmental living liver transplantation in children and adults, in Transplantation Proceedings, 1993. Memberships: International Anesthesiology Research Society; European Dialysis and Transplant Association; Turkish Society of Anesthesiology and Reanimation; Middle East Society of Organ Transplantation; Turkish Transplantation Society; Anesthesiology and Reanimation Association. Hobby: Reading. Address: Baskent University Hospital, Department of Anesthesiology, Bahgeliever, Ankara, Turkey.

ARU Gabriele, b. 27 Oct 1951, Milan, Italy. Surgeon. m. Laura Zamperetti, 22 July 1989. Education: Degree in Medicine and Surgery, Milan University, 1976; Specialist in Otorhinolaryngology, 1979, Odontostomatology, 1983, Orthodontics, 1986, Sports Medicine, 1990. Appointments: Lecturer in Surgery, Niguarda Hospital, Milan, 1977; Lecturer in Otorhinolaryngology, Fatebenefratelli Hospital, Milan, 1978; Assistant Professor of Paediatic Dentistry, Cagliari University, 1992. Publications: Nuovo Glossario della Terminologia odontostomatologica, 1987; Co-author: Le Agenesie Dentali, 1988; Compendio di Odontoiatria Infantile Pratica, 1992; Odontoiatria Infantile Pratica, 1992. Honours: Knight of Italian Republic, 1991; Bronze Star of Sporting Merit, 1992; Cross of Health Merit, 1992. Memberships: European Orthodontist Society; Italian Poedodontic Society; Italian Dental Surgeons Association; Italian College of Otorhinolaryngology. Hobbies: Fencing; Parachutist; Bridge; Journalism. Address: Via A Saffi 6, 20123 Milan, Italy.

ASCHER John Albert, b. 23 Mar 1949, New York City, USA. Pharmaceutical Physician. m. Marilyn Loftis, 1 Oct 1988. Education: AB, psychology; MD. Appointments: Senior Clinical Research Scientist, Assistant Director, Associate Director, Department of Neurology/Psychiatry, Burroughs Wellcome Company. Memberships: AMA; American Psychiatric Association; North Carolina Psychiatric Association; North Carolina Medical Society. Hobby: Gardening. Address: Glaxo Wellcome Company, 3030 Cornwallis Road, Research Triangle Park, NC 27709, USA.

ASH Alok Kumar, b. 27 Jan 1952, India. Gynaecologist. m. Dalia Ash, 6 Mar 1987, 1 son, 1 daughter. Education: MD; MRCOG. Appointments: SHO, Obstetrics & Gynaecology; Registrar, Obstetrics & Gynaecology. Honours: Jr Prosector's Prize, 1970; Best Dissector's Medal, 1970; Goodeve Scholarship in Obstetrics & Gynaecology, 1974; Gold Medal in Obstetrics & Gynaecology, 1975. Membership: Royal College of Obstetricians & Gynaecologists. Hobbies: Calligraphy; Photography; Travel. Address: Department of Obstetrics & Gynaecology, Lister Hospital, Coreys Mill Lane, Stevenage, Herts SG1 4AB, England.

ASHBURN Shirley Faye Smith, b. 11 May 1945, Anderson, Indiana, USA. Health Educator. m. 22 Apr 1972, 1 daughter. Education: BSN, 1967, MS, 1970, Ohio State University. Appointments: Instructor, Ohio State University, 1970-76; Assistant Professor, Capital University, Bexley, Ohio, 1976-80; Inservice Education Instructor, Children's Hospsital, Orange COunty, California, 1980-82; Professor of Nursing, Cypress College, New York Regents College at State University of New York and California State University at Domingues Hills. Publications: The Process of Human Development, 3 Editions. Honours: Mortar Board, 1966; Sigma Theta Tau, 1967; Outstanding Teacher of the Year, Ohio State University, 1972-76. Memberships: American Nurses' Association; National Education Association. Hobbies: Music; Dancing; Humour; Aerobic Exercise. Address: 9200 Valley View Street, Cypress, CA 90630, USA.

ASHMAN Robert Frederick, b. 7 Oct 1938, Buffalo, New York, USA. Professor of Medicine and Microbiology. m. Claire Bergsma, 2 sons, 1 daughter. Education: BA, Wabash College, 1960; BA, 1962, MA, 1966, Balliol College, Oxford University, England; MD, Columbia University, USA, 1966. Appointments: Assistant Professor, University of California, 1972-79; Associate Professor, University of California at Los Angeles, 1979-80; Professor, Director, Department of Medicine and Microbiology, University of Iowa. Publications include: Textbook of Internal Medicine, contributor of 2 chapters, 2nd edition, 1992; Regulation of Apoptosis in Vitro in Mature Murine Spleen T Cells. Co-author, 1993; Apoptosis in Splenic B Lymphocytes: Regulation by Protein Kinase C and IL-4, Co-author, 1993; Deceased membrane Phospholipid Packing and Decreased Cell Size Precede DNA Cleavage in Mature Mouse B Cell Apoptosis, Co-author, 1994. Honours: Rhodes Scholarship. 1960; Danforth Fellowship, 1960; Helen Hay Whitney fellowship, 1970; American Society for Clinical Investigation, 1981; Editorial Board, Journal of Laboratory and Clinical Medicine, 1991. Memberships: American College of Rheumatology; American Association of Immunologists; American Federation Clinical Research; American Society Clinical Investigation; Central Society for Clinical Research; Clinical Immunology Society. Hobbies: History of Art and Architecture; Astronomy; Orinthology. Address: Department of Internal Medicine, Division of Rheumatology, College of Medicine, University of Iowa, Iowa City, IA 52242, USA.

ASKENASE Philip, b. 7 June 1939, Brooklyn, New York, USA. Scientist; Professor; Physician. m. Marjorie Dobkin, 2 daughters. Education: BA, Brown University, 1961; MD, Yale University School of Medicine, 1965. Appointments: Chief, Section of Allergy and Clinical Immunology. Publications: Contributor of numerous professional works. Honours: Laurens Hammond Grant for Cancer Research, 1975; NIH Merit Award, MIAID, Immunology, Allergic and Immunologic Diseases Programme, 1977; Foreign Corresposndent, Member, Polish Academy of Arts, 1987-. Memberships: American Society for Clinical Investigation; Medical Research Council; NIH MIAID Allergy Immunology and Transplantation Comm, 1992-96; US-Israel Binational Science Foundation; Phi Beta Kappa. Address: Yale University School of Medicine, Department of Immunology/LCI 904, 333 Cedar Street, New Haven, CT 06520-8013, USA.

ASOTRA Satish, b. 8 Feb 1954, Ganguwal, Pubjab, India. Scientist. m. Neeru Asotra, 14 Oct 1985, 2 daughters. Education: BSc, 1974, MSc, 1976, Himachal University, Simla; PhD, Reproduction Physiology, H P Agricultural University, Palampur. Appointments: Scientist, Council of Scientific and Industrial Research, New Delhi; Visiting Scientist, Georgetown University Medical School, Washington, District of Columbia, USA; Assistant Professor, Faculty of Dentistry, University of Toronto, Toronto, Onntario, Canada; Currently Writer, Genpharm Inc, Etobicoke, Ontario. Memberships: American Medical Writers Association; American Society of Bone and Mineral Research. Hobbies: Hiking; Fishing; Cricket. Address: 105 Aloma Crescent, Bramalea, Ontario, Canada L6T 2N8.

ASPÖCK Horst, b. 21 July 1939, Budweis. University Professor. m. Dr Ulrike Pirklbauer, 16 Nov 1963, 1 son. Education: PhD, University of Innsbruck, 1962; Habilitation, University of Vienna, 1970. Appointments: Head, Department of Medical Parasitology, Institute of Hygiene, University of Vienna, 1963-; Publications: Author or Editor of 10 books; Contributor of over 400 scientific articles. Honours: Wander Prize, 1972; Kulturpreis des Landes Oberösterreich für Wissenschaft, 1987; Excellenti in Scientia Entomfaunistica, 1991. Memberships: Board, Austrian Society of Tropical Medicine and Parasitology, President, 1981-83; Board, Austria Society of Entomology, President, 1990-93. Hobby: Music. Address: Department of Medical Parasitology, Institute of Hygiene, University of Vienna, Kinderspitalgasse 15, A-1095 Vienna, Austria.

ASSER Toomas, b. 14 July 1954, Johvi, Estonia. Associate Professor. m. Karin Ernstson, 21 Mar 1981, 2 sons, 1 daughter. Education: MD, 1979, PhD, 1986, Medical Faculty, University of Tartu. Appointments: Medical Intern, 1979-80; Military Medical Officer, 1980-82; Assistant, Department of Neurology and Neurosurgery, 1982-88, Associate Professor, Department of Neurology and Neurosurgery, 1989-, University of Tartu. Publications: The Influence of the Localized Acute Brain Damage on the CBF in Dogs, Co-author, 1987. Memberships: Secretary, Ludvig Puusepp Society of Estonian Neurologists and Neurosurgeons; Board Member, Baltic Neurosurgical Association; European Federation of Neurological Societies. Hobbies: Cross-country Skiing; Singing. Address: Department of Neurology and Neurosurgery, University of Tartu, 2 Ludvig Puusepp Street, EE2400 Tartu, Estonia.

ASSORGI Salvatore C, b. 22 July 1941, Brooklyn, New York, USA. Osteopath. m. Ruth A Fattinosky, 28 Nov 1963, 4 daughters, 1 dec. Education: BS, Mahlereberg College, 1963; DO, Kirksville College of Psteopathic Surgery, 1967. Appointments: General Practitioner Osteopath, 1968-; Medical Director, Lehigh Valley Addictions Treatment Services, 1968-93; Medical Director, Council on Alcohol and Drug Abuse, 1985-93; Medical Director, Lehigh Valley Methadone Programme, 1975-85. Honours: Board Certification, 1986; Membership, Allentown Osteopathic Medical Hospital for 25 years. Memberships: American Osteopathic Association; American Academy of General Practice in Osteopathic Medicine; Pennsylvania Osteopathic Medical Association; Lehigh valley Osteopathic Society; Pennsylvania Academy of General Practice and Osteopathic Medicine. Hobbies: Sailing; Furniture making; Scuba Diving; Camping; Skiing; Reading. Address: 1129 Walnut Street, Allentown, PA 18102, USA.

ATHANASIADOY Emily, b. 4 Dec 1951, Famagusta, Cyprus. Psychologist. m. Eleftherios Mairopoulos, 5 Sept 1987, 1 son. Education: Teaching Diploma in English, Eastbourne, England, 1974; BA, Psychology, Sociology, Dree College, 1974; BSc, MSc, Clinical Psychology, Leeds University, 1981. Appointments: Currently Clinical Psychologist in private practice. Memberships: British Psychological Society; Chartered Psychologist; Greek and Cypriot Psychological Societies; Training, International Psychoanalytic Society, 1987-. Hobbies: Singing; Swimming; Gardening; Travel. Address: Petropouloy 7, Melissia, Athens 151-27, Greece.

ATHANASIOU Athanasios, b. 26 Sept 1955, Patras, Greece. Associate Professor; Specialist in Orthodontics. Education: DDS, 1979, Dr of Dentistry, 1991, University of Athens; MSD, Temple University, USA, 1985. Appointments: Associate Professor, Programme Director, Department of Orthodontics, Aarhus University, Aarhus, Denmark, to 1993; Currently Associate Professor of Orthodontics, School of Dentistry, Aristotle University of Thessaloniki, Greece. Publications: More than 70 including: Orthodontic Cephalometry, 1995. Honours: Edward Cherkas Award, 1985; Zendium Prize, 1990. Memberships: American Association of Orthodontists; European Orthodontic Society; American Cleft Palate-Craniofacial Association; International Association for Dental Research; Other national and international groups. Hobbies: Reading; Music; Travel. Address: Department of Orthodontics, School of Dentistry, Aristotle University of Thessaloniki, GR-54006 Thessaloniki, Greece.

ATIT Madhusudan B, b. 18 June 1931, Bombay, India. Obstetrics & Gynaecology. m. Dr Sudha, 28 Apr 1958, 1 son, 1 daughter. Education: BSc, University Bombay, 1952; MBBS, University Bombay, 1957; DRCOG, London, 1960; MRCOG, London, 1965. Appointments: Senior Registrar, St james University Hospital, Leeds, 1962-65; Senior Honorary Gynaecologist, Jascok Hospital Research Center, Bombay,

1973-90; Senior Consultant Obstetrician & Gynaecologist. Publications: Several professional scientific articles in journals. Honours: Fellowship, Royal College of Obsetrics & Gynaecologists, 1981; Chairman, West Zone R.C.O.K India Chapter, 1981-86. Memberships: Founder Fellow, RCOG Association of India; International Federation of Obstetricians & Gynaecologists; Bombay Obstetricians & Gynaecologists Society. Hobbies: Reading; Swimming; Travel. Address: 2A Balmoral Hall, 7 Mt Mary Road, Bandra, Bombay 400050, India.

ATKINS Robert Charles, b. 6 June 1939, Australia. Physician. 1 s, 3 d. Education: MB BS, Melbourne; MSc, Colorado; DSc, Monash; FRACP. Appointments: Medical Officer, Alfred Hospital, 1963, 1964, 1966, 1967; Research fellow, University of Colorado, USA, 1968; University of Washington, 1969; University of Montpellier, 1970; University of Oxford, 1971; Director of Nephrology; Professor of Medicine, 1972-. Publications: Progress in Glomerulonephritis, 1979; Peritoneal Dialysis, 1981; T-Cells and Macrophages and Their Role in Renal Injury, 1992; Macrophages in Renal Injury, 1994. Honours: President, Australian and New Zealand Society of Nephrology, 1980-81; President Elect, Asian Pacific Society of Nephrology, 1993; Australian Kidney Foundation Kincaid-Smith Medal, 1994. Memberships: International Society of Nephrology; Asian Pacific Society of Nephrology; Australia and New Zealand Society of Nephrology; International Transplantation Society; International Society for Peritoneal Dialysis. Hobbies: Royal Tennis; Farming; Jazz. Address: Department of Nephrology, Monash Medical Centre, 246 Clayton Road, Clayton 3168, Australia.

ATKINSON Richard L, b. 15 May 1942, Petersburg, Virginia, UWSA. Professor of Medicine and Nutritional Sciences. m. Susan Stayner Hume, 13 Aug 1966, 3 daughters. Education: BA, Virginia Military Institute, Lexington, 1960-64; MD, Medical College of Virginia, Richmond, 1964-68. Appointments: Chief, Department Medicine, US Army Hospital, Ft Campbell, Kentucky, 1973-74; Adjunct Assistant Professor of Medicine, School of Medicine, University of California, Los Angeles, 1976-77; Assistant Professor of Internal Medicine, Director, Clinical Nutrition Centre, University of Virginia, Charlottesville, 1977-83; Associate Professor of Internal Medicine, Director, Clinical Nutrition Centre, University of California, Davis, 1983-87; Associate Chief of Staff for Research and Development, Virginia, Hampton, 1987-93; Professor of Internal Medicine, Chief, Division of Nutrition, VA MED, Norfolk, Virginia, 1987-93; Professor of Medicine and Nutritional sciences, Director, Clinical Nutrition Centre, University of Wisconsin-Madison. Publications: Contributor of over 100 articles in scientific journals. Honours: President, ASCN, 1994-95; President, North American Association for Study of Obesity, 1990-91; Chairman, NIH Nutrition Study Section, 1993-95. Memberships: AAAS; Fellow, American College of Physicians; American Diabetes Association; American Federation for Clinical Research; American Institute of Nutrition; American Society for Clinical Nutrition; American Society for Parenteral and Enteral Nutrition; Endocrine Society; North American Association for the Study of Obesity; Western Society for Clincal Investigation. Address: University Widsonsin-Madison, Department of Nuritional Sciences, 1415 Linden Drive, Madison, WI 53706, USA.

ATKINSON Roland Moore, b. 19 Feb 1936, San Jose, California, USA. Psychiatrist. 3 sons, 1 daughter. Education: AB, Stanford, 1957; MD, Stanford Medical School, 1961; Internship, Medicine, Residency, Psychiatry, UCLA, 1961-65; Board Certified in Psychiatry, American Board of Psychiatry and Neurology, 1970; Added Qualification, Geriatric Psychiatry, 1991. Appointments: US Public Health System, 1965-67; UCLA Faculty in Medicine, 1967-70; University of California, Irvine, Faculty in Medicine, 1971-76; Professor, Head, Division of Geriatric Psychiatry, Oregon Health Sciences University and Veterans Medical Centre, Portland, Oregon, 1976-. Publications Contributor of over 60 professional papers, chapters in books and monographs. Memberships: American Psychiatric Association, Fellow; American Association for Geriatric Psychiatry; International Psychogeriatrics Association. Hobbies: Mask Collecting and Crafting; Hiking; Cycling; Volleyball. Address: Veterans Affairs Medical Centre (116A), 3710 SW Veterans Hospital Road, Portland, OR 97201, USA.

ATKINSON Stephanie Ann, b. 7 Feb 1949, Guelph, Ontario, Canada. University Professor. m. Peter Y Atkinson, 2 Oct 1971. Education: BA, Nutrition, University of Western Ontario, 1968; PhD, Nutritional Sciences, Faculty of Medicine, University of Toronto, 1980; Postdoctoral Fellow, Endocrinology, Hospital for Sick Children, Toronto, 1980-82. Appointments include: Clinical Nutritionist, The Hospital for

Sick Children, Toronto, Ontario; Associate Professor, Paediatrics, currently Director, Paediatric Nutrition and Metabolism Group, Faculty of Health Sciences, Associate Member, Biochemistry, Professor, Paediatrics, Faculty of Health Sciences, McMaster University, Hamilton; Adjunct Professor, University of Guelph, Ontario, 1986. Publications: Numerous journal articles, book chapters, abstracts, mainly on infant nutrition and human lactation. Honours: Heinz Research Award, 1975-77; Graduate Student Award, Nutrition Society of Canada, 1980; Postdoctoral Research Fellowships: Restracom, 1980-81, Kidney Foundation of Canada, 1981-82; Career Scientist Award, Ministry of Health, Ontario, 1982-92; Schering Travel Fellowship, Canadian Society for Clinical Investigation, 1992; Alberta Heritage Foundation Visiting Lectureship, 1993. Memberships: Canadian Society for Nutritional Sciences; Canadian Society for Clinical Investigation; Canadian Federation for Biological Sciences; American Institute of Nutrition; American Society for Clinical Nutrition; Fellow, American College of Nutrition; American Society for Bone and Mineral Research; Canadian Dietetic Association; International Society for Research in Human Milk and Lactation. Hobbies: Music; Tennis. Address: Department of Paediatrics, HSC 3V42, McMaster University, 1200 Main Street W, Hamilton, Ontario, Canada L8N 3Z5.

ATTAPATTU John Ashmore Florian, b. 17 Nov 1934, Sri Lanka. Obstetrician; Gynaecologist. m. Maya Chandrani Attapattu 31 Dec 1963, 2 daughters. Education: MBBS (Ceylon), 1960; MOG (Ceylon), 1969; FRCOG (UK), 1984; FCOG (Sri Lanka), 1985; Certifications: Laparoscopy, St Louis, USA, 1979; Family Planning, Ministry of Health, Sri Lanka, 1984; Microsurgery, Cairo, Egypt, 1986. Appointments: Consultant, hospitals, Sri Lanka, 1974-84; Senior Consultant Obstetrician and Gynaecologist, General Hospital North, Colombo, 1984-85; Director, 1985-90, Consultant Obstetrician and Gynaecologist, 1985-90, Senior Consultant, 1990, Castle Street Hospital for Women, Colombo; Lecturer, Obstetrics, Gynaecology, 1991-94, Senior Lecturer, 1994-, University of the West Indies, Barbados; Consultant Obstetrician and Gynaecologist, 1991-, Department Head, 1994-, Queen Elizabeth Hospital, Barbados. Publications: Over 2 dozen including: Assessment of Fetal Maturity, 1976; Choriocarcinoma with pulmonary and vaginal metastases, 1980; Pregnancy Induced Hypertension, 1986; Heart Disease complicating Pregnancy, 1987; Abdominal Pregnancy, 1993; Garrulitas Vulvae: The involuntary Passage of Vaginal Flatus, 1994. Honours include: Gold Medal, Murugesar Sinnetamby Oration, 1975; Gold Medal, Richard Caldera Oration, 1985; Gold Medal, 3 WHO Fellowships. Memberships include: Foundation Fellow, Past Secretary, Past Vice President, Past President, Life Member, Sri Lanka College of Obstetricians and Gynaecologists; Ceylon Medical Association; Asia Oceania Federation of Obstetricians and Gynaecologists; Technical Advisory Panel, Sri Lanka Association for Voluntary Surgical Contraception. Hobbies: Gardening; Collecting old books; Scrabble; Bridge. Address: 12 South Bend Road, Pine Gardens, Barbados, West Indies.

ATTAR Mariam, b. 25 Feb 1964, Slovenia. Medical Physicist. m. 7 Oct 1993. Education: BA, Physics; Diploma in Philosophy. Appointments: Currently Physicist in Radiotherapy. Membership: International Organization of Medical Physics. Hobby: Reading. Address: Al-Rashir Hospital, Amman, Jordan.

ATTERBURY Colin Elliott, b. 2 Mar 1943. Physician. Education: BA, Yale University, 1965; MD, University of MO, Columbia, 1969. Appointments: Professor of Medicine, Hepatology and Associate Dean, Veterans Affairs, Yale University School of Medicine; Chief of Staff, West Haven VA Medical Center, CT. Publications: Over 50 publications on liver disease. Honour: Honorary MA, Yale University, 1990. Memberships: Fellow, American College of Physicians; American Association for Study of Liver Disease; International Association for Study of Liver Disease; Society for Law, Medicine and Ethics. Address: 440 Wallingford Road, Cheshire, CT 06410, USA.

ATTOH AHUMAH-ACQUAH Samuel Richard Brew, b. 19 February 1946, Cape Coast, Ghana. Executive Director; Psychologist; Counselor. m. Emeline S Acquah, 24 December 1969, deceased, 1 son, 1 daughter. Education: PhD; DO; SLitt; DLitt; Board Certified Acupuncturist; OMB; AA; Member of The American Academy of Medical Hypnoanalysts. Appointments: Missionary of Free Protest Episcopal Church of England; Principal and Administrator of St John Episcopal High School. Publications: Research work in Chronic Pains, Mind-Body Connection. Memberships: British Acupuncture Association; World Acupuncture Orginazation; International Acupuncture Society. Hobbies: Reading;

Running; Research in Physical Medicine and Acupuncture. Address: Holistic Health Center & Acupuncture Clinic, 511 West Main Street, Ashland, OH 44805, USA.

ATULUGAMA Nandana Gamini, b. 25 Sep 1950. Surgeon Captain. m. 15 Mar 1980, 1 son, 1 daughter. Education: MBBS, Ceylon; MD, Colombo; MCMA, Sri Lanka. Appointments: Command Medical Officer, Eastern Naval Area, 1979-86; Deputy Director, Medical Services, 1986-91; Senior Registrar in Radiology, University Hospital of Wales, Cardiff, 1991-92; Director, Naval Health Services, Consultant Radiologist, Sri Lanka Navy. Honours: Long Service Medal, 1992; Poorna Boomi Medal, 1983. Memberships: College of Radiologists; Sri Lanka Medical Association. Hobbies: Travel; Rowing. Address: 106/1A Ragama Road, Kadawatha, Sri Lanka.

ATWOOD M Luretta Barnes, b. 18 June 1945, Lincoln, USA. Nurse (RN). m. Mark Atwood, 30 Mar 1986, 1 son, 1 daughter, 2 step-daughters. Education: BS; BA; RN. Appointments: Secretary, Medical Technology, 1979-86; Staff Nurse, RN, Neuroscience. ASDAN-NAD. Honours: Alice B Olsen Scholarship Award, 1989. Hobbies: Music; Camping; Bicycling; Reading. Address: 14 Lakeside Apartments, Enfield, NH 03748, USA.

AUER Roland Nikolaus, b. 22 Aug 1954, Edmonton, Alberta, Canada. Neuropathologist. m. Iwona Anna, 6 July 1985, 3 sons. Education: BSc, 1975, MD, 1977, University of Alberta; PhD, Medical Science, University of Lund, Sweden, 1985. Appointments: Resident Neuropathology, University and Victoria Hospitals, London, Ontario, 1978-81; Resident, Paediatric Neuropathology, Hospital for Sick Children, Toronto, 1981; MRC Fellow, Laboratory of Experimental Brain Research, University of Lund, Sweden, 1982-85; Associate Professor. Publications: Contributor of over 60 scientific articles including: Cerebellar Astrocytoma with Benign Histology and Malignant Clinical Course, Co-author, 1981; Frontal Lobe Perivascular Schwannoma, Co-author, 1982; The Distribution of Hypoglycaemic Brain Damage, Co-author, 1984; The Temporal Evolution of Hypoglycemic Brain Damage II Light and Electron Microscopic Findings in the Rat Hippocampus, 1985; The Spread of Brain Edema in Hypertensive Brain Injury, Co-author, 1986; Neuropathologic Findings in Three Cases of Profound Hypoglycemia, Co-author, 1989; Delayed Symptoms and Death Following Minor Head Trauma with Occult Vertebral Artery Injury, Co-author. Honours: Alberta Heritage Foundation for Medical Research Scholarship, 1985; Medical Research Council of Canada Fellowship, 1981; R W Tegler Undergraduate Scholarship, 1973. Memberships: American Association of Neuropathologists; Society for Cerebral Blood Flow and Metabolism; Canadian Association of Neuropathologists; Canadian Diabetes Association; College of Physicians and Surgeons of Alberta; International Brain Research organisation. Hobbies: Old Canadian Stamps; Racquet sports; Cycling. Address: Calgary, Alberta, Canada.

AUERBACH Robert, b. 24 Apr 1932, New York City, New York, USA. Dermatologist. m. Arleen Daniels, 6 Aug 1958, 1 son, 1 daughter. Education: BA magna cum laude, honours in Chemistry and Mathematics; MD. Appointments include: Currently: Dermatologist; Clinical Professor of Dermatology, New York University. Memberships: Dermatology Society of New York; American Academy of Dermatologists; American Medical Association; New York State Dermatology Society; New York State Medical Society. Hobbies: Reading; History. Address: 440 East 57th Street, New York, NY 10022, USA.

AUGSBURGER James J, b. 21 June 1948, Bluffton, Ohio, USA. Ophthalmologist. m. Emma Jane Bentzel, 18 June 1972, 2 sons, 1 daughter. Education: BS, Heidelberg College, Tiffin, Ohio, 1970; MD, 1974, Resident, Ophthalmology, 1975-78, University of Cincinnati, 1974; Fellow, Vitreo-Retinal Diseases, Wills Eye Hospital, 1978-80. Appointments: Attending Surgeon, Associate Clinical Professor, Ophthalmology, Wills Eye Hospital, Philadelphia, Pennsylvania, 1980-. Publications: Over 200 including: Fine needle aspiration biopsy of solid intraocular tumors: indications, instrumentation and techniques, 1984; Fine needle aspiration biopsy in the diagnosis of intraocular cancer. Cytologic-histologic correlations, 1985; Enucleation vs cobalt plaque radiotherapy for malignant melanomas of the choroid and ciliary body, 1986; Clinical parameters predictive of enlargement of melanocystic choroidal lesions, 1989; Cobalt-60 plaque radiotherapy vs enucleation for posterior uveal melanoma, 1990; Clinical prognostic factors in patients with posterior uveal melanoma, 1990; Impact of delayed treatment in growing posterior uveal melanoma, 1993; Combined iodine-125 plaque irradiation and indirect ophthalmoscope laser therapy of choroidal malignant melanomas: comparison with iodine-125 and cobalt-60 plaque radiotherapy alone, 1993; Is observation really appropriate for small choroidal melanomas?, 1993; Visual function following enucleation of episcleral plaque radiotherapy for posterior uveal melanoma, 1994. Honours: Alpha Omega Alpha, 1974; Honour Award, American Academy of Ophthalmology, 1985; Brady Cancer Research Institute Award, 1986; Golden Apple Award, Wills Eye Hospital, 1988. Memberships: American Academy of Ophthalmology; American Ophthalmological Society; Association for Research in Vision and Ophthalmology; Retina Society. Hobby: Baseball. Address: Oncology Unit, Retina Service, Wills Eye Hospital, 900 Walnut Street, Philadelphia, PA 19107-5598, USA.

AUSTEN K Frank, b. 14 May 1928, Akron, Ohio, USA. Physician. m. Jocelyn Chapman, 11 Apr 1959, 2 sons, 2 daughters. Education: BA, Amherst College, 1950; MD, Harvard Medical School, 1954. Appointments include: Intern, 1954-55, Assistant Resident, 1955-56, Senior resident, 1958-59, Chief Resident, 1961-62, Medicine, Massachusetts General Hospital; Assistant, 1961, Instructor, 1961-62, Associate, 1962-64, Medicine, Assistant Professor of Medicine, 1965-66, Associate Professor of Medicine, 1966-68, Professor of Medicine, 1969-72, Theodore Bevier Balyes Professor of Medicine, 1972-, Harvard Medical School; Chairman, Rheumatology and Immunology, Brigham and Wome's Hospital, Boston, 1980-. Publications include: Biochemistry of the Acute Allergic Reaction, Co-editor, 1968; Symposium of the Immunobiology of Complement, Editor, 1974; The Chemistry and Biology of the Kallikrein-Kinin System in Health and Disease, Co-editor, 1976; The Eosinophil in Health and Disease, Co-editor, 1980; Biochemistry of the Acute Allergic Reactions, Co-editor, 1981; Dermatology in General Medicine Textbook and Atlas, Co-editor, 1979, 1987, 4th edition, 1993; Immunological Diseases, Co-editor, 3rd edition, 1978, 4th edition, 1988; Advances in Immunology, Co-editor, 1989; Contributor of numerous professional articles and reports. Honours include: 2nd International Geigy Rheumatism Prize, International League Against Rheumatism, 1973; Distinguished Service Award, International Association of Allergology and Clinical Immunology, 1988; Distinguished Investigator Award, American College of Rheumatology, 1993; International Association of Allergology and Clinical Immunology Scientific Achievement Award, 1994; Honorary Master of the American College of Rheumatology, 1994; Arthritis Foundations Lee C Howley, Sr., Prize for Arthritis Research, 1994; Lilly Lecturer, Royal College of Physicians, London, England, 1995; Memberships: Numerous professional societies. Address: Seeley G Mudd Building, Room 604, 250 Longwood Avenue, Boston, MA 02115, USA.

AVERY Daniel Mason Jr, b. 8 December 1950, Tuscaloosa, Alabama, USA. Obstetrician and Gynaecologist. m. Rhonda Prewitt, 26 May 1971, 1 son, 2 daughters. Education: BS; PA; MD; FACOG; FACS; FSOGC; FICS; FRSM; OBG; PSFOG; FACFE; BCFE. Appointments: Board Certified Forensic Examiner; Assistant Chief of Obstetrics and Gynaecology; Founder, Medical Director, Forensic Obstetrics and Gynaecology of North America; Deputy Coroner, Senior Partner, Princeton Obstetrics and Gynaecology. Publications: Neonatal Intensive Care Medicine, 1981; Handbook of Obstetrics and Gynaecology, 1987, 2nd edition, 1989; Editor: Medicolegal OB/Gyn Newsletter. Memberships: American Medical Association; American College of Obstetricians & Gynaecologists; American College of Surgeons; American College of Legal Medicine. Hobbies: Gardening; Classical Music; Sporting Events for Children. Address: 817 Princeton Avenue, Suite 120, Birmingham, AL 35211, USA.

AVETISOV Eduard Sergeyevich, b. 23 Dec 1921, Samarkand, Uzbekistan. Ophthalmologist. m. Amalia Mosesova, 7 July 1946, 2 sons. Education: Candidate, Samarkand Medical Institute, 1950; DMedSci, 1964. Appointments: Assistant, Ophthalmological Clinic, Samarkand Medical Institute, 1950-57; Senior Researcher, 1957-62, Professor, Head, Department of Child Vision Care, 1962-, Deputy Director, 1966-, Helmholtz Institute of Ophthalmology, Moscow. Publications: Disbinocular amblyopia and its treatment, doctoral thesis, 1964; Children's Vision Care, 1975; Concomitant Squint, 1977; Myopia, 1986. Honours: Prize, USSR Academy of Medical Science. Membership: International Ophthalmological Academy. Address: Ramenky Street 11-3, ap 629, 117607 Moscow, Russia.

AVNER-GUTTMANN Neta, b. 3 Mar 1947, Cairo. Psychologist. m. Joseph, 23 Sept 1980, 2 sons. Education: PhD, University of Geneva.

Appointments: Chief Psychologist, Sourasky Medical Center, Tel-Aviv; Head, Clinical Unit for Infant Psychiatry. Honours: J L Claparede Award, Geneva University, 1978. Memberships: International Psychonalisis Association; World Association of Infant Psychiatry & Allied Disciplines; Israel Psychological Association. Address: 13 Gruner Street, Tel-Aviv 69498, Israel.

AWADZI Gabriel Kwablahvi, b. 31 Jan 1961, Lagos, Nigeria. Gynaecologist. m. Hyacinth Mohammed, 7 Oct 1986, 2 sons. Education: MBBS, Jbadan; MRCOG. Appointments: SHO Obstetrics, 1987-88; SHO Gynaecology, 1989-90; SHO Anaesthetics, 1990-91; Registrar, Obstetrics & Gynaecology, 1991-93; Staff Gynaecologist, Frenchay Hospital, Bristol. Memberships: Royal College of Obstetricians & Gynaecologists; Medical Defense Union. Hobbies: Photography; Travel; Motorsport. Address: 19 Ellicks Close, Bradley, Stoke North, Bristol BS12 OE9, England.

AWON Maxwell Philip, b. 10 Mar 1920, Port of Spain, Trinidad, West Indies. m. Sylvia Hawthorne, 28 July 1956, 4 children. Education: BSc; MSc; LAH; MBBCh; LM; MRCOG; MRCP; FRCS; FRCP; FRCOG; FACOG. Appointments incl: General Hospital, Port of Spain, 1966; Specialist Medical Officer, Government of Trinidad & Tobago, 1961-66; Registrar, Surgery, Whiston Hospital, Prescott, 1960-61; Registrar, Royal Salop Infirmary, Shrewsbury, 1958-60; Trinidad & Tobago Medical Association, 1965-; Treasurer, Manager, Medical Co-operative Society Limited, 1993. Publications incl: Association Between Climacteric Haemorrhage, Carcinoma of The Body of The Uterus and Diabetes, 1957; Retention of Urine in Obstetrics and Gynaecology, 1964; The Vacuum Extractor - Experimental Demonstration of Distortion of the Foetal Skull, 1964; The Management System, 1980. Honours incl: Ambrose Birmingham Gold Medal in Anatomy, 1949; Medical Society Silver Medal for Student Paper, 1950. Memberships incl: Trinidad & Tobago Scientific Association; The American Association of Gynaecologic Laparoscopists; Trinidad Rifle Association; National Stick-Fighting Association; Trinidad & Tobago Chamber of Commerce. Address: 1 Alexandra Street, St Clair, Port of Spain, Trinidad, West Indies.

AXELL Tony Emil, b. 21 Oct 1939, Liungby, Sweden. Oral Surgeon. m. Elisabeth Ahlqvist, 21 June 1961, 1 son, 2 daughters. Education: DDS, 1967; Specialist Oral Surgery, 1977; Odont Dr. Appointments: Acting Chairman, Department of Oral Surgery and Oral Medicine, Chairman, Head, department of Oral Diagnosis, Faculty of Dentistry, University of Malmö; Head, Gerodontol Section, Faculty of Dentistry, University of Oslo, Norway; professor of Odontology, Specialist in Gerodontology. Publications: Clinical Diagnosis and Treatment of Oral Mucosal Lesions, 1980-83; Textbook of Oral Surgery, Co-author, 1986; Clinical Skills, Co-author, 1993; Allergy, 1993; Oral Medicine, 1994; COntributor of over 100 scientific articles in professional journals. Honour: Forssberg's National Prize, 1992. Memberships: Swedish Oral Medicine Society, President; International Association for Dental Research; International Dental Association. Hobbies: Golf; Bridge; Mountain walking; Music. Address: Munkhätteg 10, S-21456 Malmö, Sweden.

AYARS Garrison H, b. 18 Apr 1950, Sunnyside, WA, USA. Physician. m. Wendy Ann Westland, 28 Dec 1974, 1 s, 1 d. Education: BS, Molecular Biology; MD, Phi Beta Kappa, Magna Cum Laude, University of Washington; Board Certified in Internal Medicine, 1980; Board Certified in Infectious Diseases, 1982; Board Certified in Allergy & Clinical Immunology, 1985. Appointments: Fellowship in Infectious Diseases, 1980-82; Fellowship in Allergy, 1982-84; Clinical Associate Professor, University of Washington; Allergist, Private Practice. Publications: include, Incidence of Thrombocytopenia in Medical Patients on Mini-Dose Heparin Prophylaxis, 1980; The Injurious Effect of Neutrophils on Pneumocytes in Vitro, 1984; A Comparative Tolerance Study of Terfenadine/Pseudoephedrine Combination Tablets and Pseudoephedrine Tables in Patients with Allergic or Vasomotor Rhinitis, 1988; An Outbreak of Illness among Aerospace Workers, 1990; Once-a-Day Dosing with Theophylline: A Comparison of Four Sustained-Release Products, 1992; Hypersensitivity Pneumonitis, Allergic Bronchopulmonary Aspergillosis and Sarcoidosis, 1993. Honours: Fellow, American College of Physicians: Fellow, American Academy of Allergy & Immunology, Memberships: American Academy of Allergy & Immunology; American College of Physicians; American Medical Association. Hobbies: Running; Snow Skiing. Address: 901 Boren Avenue, Seattle, WA 98004, USA.

AZIZ Fachroel, b. 31 Mar 1946, Siak, Indonesia. Paleontologist; Geologist. m. Zainab Sulung, 31 Mar 1974, 2 sons, 1 daughter. Education: BSc, Academy of Geology and Mining, Bandung, 1970; Micropaleontology Course Certificate, Japex, Tokyo, Japan, 1979; Certificate, Advanced Course, Vertebrate Paleontology, Utrech University, The Netherlands, 1985; DSc. Appointments: Geologist, Paleontologist, Geological Research and Development Centre, Bandung, 1970-. Memberships: Indonesian Association of Geologists; Permanent Advisory Committee, International Association for Study Human Fossils. Hobbies: Music; Gardening. Address: Idi adimaja ii, No 6, Bandung 40275, Indonesia.

AZZIZ Ricardo, b. 5 Mar 1958, Montevideo, Uruguay. Physician. 1 daughter. Education: MD; MPH. Appointments: Instructor, Johns Hopkins University School of Medicine, Baltimore, Maryland, USA, 1985-87; Assistant Professor, 1987-91, Associate Professor, 1991-95, Director, Reproduction Endocrinology Fellowship Programm, 1992-, University of Alabama at Birmingham. Publications: Practical Manual of Operative Laparoscopy and Hysteroscopy, Co-Editor, 1992; Non-Class Adrenal Hyperplasia: Current Concepts, 1994; 21-Hydroxylase Deficiency in Female Hyperandrogenemia: Screening and Diagnosis, 1989. Honours: Cheston M Berlin Award, Penn State College of Medicine Alumni Society for Outstanding Service, 1992; Honorary Member, Argentinian Society of Sterility and Fertility, 1994. Memberships: Society for Gynaecologic Investigation; The Endocrine Society; American College of Surgeons; American Society for Reproductive Medicine; American Medical Association. Hobby: Art Collector. Address: The University of Alabama at Birmingham, 618 South 20th Street, OHB 549, Birmingham, AL 35233-7333, USA.

B

BABA Shozo, b. 3 Jan 1933, Tokyo, Japan. Professor; Doctor of Medicine. m. Kiyoko Baba, 8 Apr 1963, 4 daughters. Education: Degree in Medical Science; MD. Appointments: Assistant Professor, Keio University; Associate Professor, Hamamatsu University School of Medicine; Currently Professor, Chairman, Second Department of Surgery, Hamamatsu University School of Medicine. Publications include: Hereditary Colon Cancer, 1990. Honours: Award, Japanese Society of Coloproctology, 1988; Saito Chion Award, 1990; Chunichi Press Award, 1993. Memberships: Fellow, American College of Surgeons; Fellow, Royal Society of Medicine; Fellow, SAGES; Fellow, Japan Surgical Society; Fellow and Regent, Japan Society of Coloproctology; Fellow, Japan Society of Gastroenterology; ISUCRS: SIC; CICD; American Society of Colorectal Surgeons; Society for Surgical Oncology; Regent, International College of Surgeons. Hobbies: Travel; Gardening. Address: Second Department of Surgery, Hamamatsu University School of Medicine, 3600 Handa-cho, Hamamatsu 431-31, Japan.

BABAYEVA Aksoltan, b. 9 Aug 1929, Kazanjik City, Turkmenistan. Physician. m. Kafurov Oraz Mukhamed, 25 Jul 1959, 1 s, 1 d. Education: Master of Medical Science, Turkmen State Medical Institute, 1957; Doctor of Biological Science, 1971. Career: Senior Researcher, Chief of Physiological Section, 1957-62; Head of Institute of Regional Medicine, Academy of Science of Turkmenistan, 1962-; Corresponding Member, Academy of Science, 1975-; Senior Researcher, Scientific Research Institute of AMS. Publications: Cycle of works, Physiological mechanisms of adaptation to the hot climate of Turkmenistan. Honours: Badge of Honour, 1968; State Medal, 1970; Turkmenistan State Prize Laureate, 1970. Memberships: Chairman, Turkmen Biochemical Society; Corresponding Member, Academy of Science of Turkmenistan; Academy of Medical Sciences. Hobby: Reading Books. Address: 50 Years of Turkmenistan Street 42, Ashgabat 744000, Turkmenistan.

BABCOCK Dorothy Ellen Kreinbihl, b. 10 July 1931, Philadelphia, Pennsylvania, USA. Professor of Nursing. m. Clarence O Babcock, 28 June 1958, 3 daughters. Education: Diploma in Nursing, Misericordia Hospital School, 1952; MSc, Catholic University of America, 1958; BSNEd, University of Pennsylvania, 1956. Appointments: Clinical Instructor, Clinical Specialist in Psychiatric Nursing; Professor of Nursing. Publications: Client Education Theory and Practice, 1994; Raising Kids OK, Co-author, 1986; Developing Skills as Public Speaker, 1981; Parenting the Adolescent, 1978. Honours: Sigma Theta Tau; Pi gamma Mu; Clinical Practice Award, University of Colorado Health Science Centre, 1978. Memberships: American Association Marriage and Family Therapy; American Nurses Association; National League for Nursing; Nurse Healers Professional Association. Address: 5 South Flower Street, Lakewood, CO 80226, USA.

BACH Jovanka, b. 23 Jun 1936, MI, USA. MD; Dermatology; Dermatopathology. m. John Bach, 2 d. Education: BA, UCLA; MD, UCLA Medical School; Board Certified in Dermatology, 1962, Dermatopathology, 1975. Career: Assistant Professor, Medicine, Dermatology, USL, Los Angeles City Medical Center, 1969; Assistant Professor, UCLA Medical Center, 1979; Currently, Private Practice in Santa Monica and Assistant Clinical Professor, UCLA. Publications: Eczema and Common Skin Disorders, 1987; Pregnancy and Childbirth, 1988. Honours: Phi Beta Kappa; Israel Levin Scholarship. Membership: Los Angeles Metropolitan Dermatology Association. Hobbies: Playwright; Writer. Address: 1301 20th Street 520, Santa Monica, CA 90405, USA.

BACHYRYCZ Frank J, b. 22 Oct 1948, Danbury, Connecticut, USA. Pharmacist. m. Maryanne Cristaldi, 29 Aug 1970, 2 sons, 2 daughters. Education: BSc, University of Connecticut, School of Pharmacy, Storrs; MS, Western Connecticut State University, Danbury; RPh; Fellow, American Academy of Pain Management. Appointments: Pharmacist, Norwalk Hospital Pharmacy department; Pharmacy Supervisor, Homecare Co-ordinator, Danbury Hospital Pharmacy department. Honours: Rho Chi, 1970; Star Award, American Pharmaceutical Association, 1985; Innovative Achievement Award, Connecticut Society Hospital Pharmacy, 1986. Memberships: Connecticut Society of Hospital Pharmacists; Greater Danbury Pharmaceutical Association; American Academy of Pain Management. Hobbies: Photography; Reading; Travel.

Address: Danbury Hospital Pharmacy Department, 24 Hospital Avenue, Danbury, CT 06810, USA.

BACKUS Varda Peller, b. 5 Aug 1931, Tel Aviv, Israel. Psychiatrist. m. (1) Leo Ganz, 18 June 1953, 1 son, 1 daughter, (2) George Backus, 8 Jan 1977. Education: BS, Cum Laude, 1953; MD, 1957. Appointments: Teaching Fellow in Psychiatry, Harvard University, 1958-60; Instructor in Psychiatry, State University of New York, Downstate Medical Centre, 1966-67; Clinical Assistant Professor of Psychiatry, Stanford University, 1968-75; Clinical Associate Professor of Psychiatry, Stanford University, 1975-77; Clinical Associate Professor of Psychiatry, University of California at San Diego, 1986-. Publications: Couple Therapy in Psychiatric Treatment, 1975; Friends and Lovers in the College Years, 1983; Psychotherapy with College Students, 1990. Honours: Sigma Alpha, 1952; Appreciation For Excellent Teaching, UCSD, 1985-86; Fellow, APA, 1982; LF, APA, 1994. Memberships: Group For The Advancement of Psychiatry; American College of Psychiatry; APA; San Diego Psychiatric Society. Hobbies: Reading; Music; Skiing; Swimming; Cooking. Address: 10666 N Torrey Pines Road, La Jolla, CA 92037, USA.

BADELLINO Fausto, b. 26 June 1928, Torino, Italy. Surgical Oncologist. m. Marielisa Moro, 14 Sep 1960, 2 d. Education: Medicine, University of Torino, 1951. Appointments: Deputy Director, Division of Surgery, Institute of Oncology, Torino; Chief, Division of Surgical Oncology, Tumor Institute, Genoa. Memberships: President, Italian Society Surgical Oncology; Membr Council, Italian Society of senology; Chairman, Detection and Diagnosis Program, UICC; SSO. Hobby: tennis. Address: Division of Surgical Oncoloy - 1ST, V.le Benedetto XV, n 10-16132 genoa. Italy.

BAENA-CAGNANI Carlos E, b. 11 May 1951, Córdoba, Argentina. Medical Doctor. m. Cecilia M Patiño, 28 Sept 1990, 2 sons, 2 daughters. Education: MD, National University of Córdoba, 1976; Fellow, Department of Allergology, University of Navarra, Spain, 1976-80; Research Scholar, University of South Florida, USA, 1991. Appointments: Assistant Professor of Medicine, Allergology, University of Navarra, Spain, 1979-80; Assistant Professor of Paediatrics, University of Córdoba, Argentina, 1980-; Head, Division of Clinical Immunology, Hospital Infantil Municipal, Córdoba, 1985-. Publications: More than 70 abstracts, original papers, book chapters, others. Honours: 2nd Prize, Argentinian Allergy and Immunology Association, 1991; Special Award, Argentinian Congress of Allergy and Immunology, 1993. Memberships: President, Latin American Society of Allergy and Immunology; Argentinian Association of Allergy and Immunology; American Academy of Allergy and Immunology. Hobbies: Rugby; Music; Running. Address: Santa Rosa 381, Córdoba 5000, Argentina.

BAGG Jeremy, b. 21 Mar 1957, Brighton, Sussex, England. Consultant Oral Microbiologist. m. Mary Patscharis, 23 Aug 1980. Education: BDS (Hons), 1979, PhD, 1982, Edinburgh University; FDS RCS (Ed); MRCPath, 1987. Appointments: Leckie Mactier Research Fellow, Faculty of Medicine, University of Edinburgh, Scotland; Lecturer in Oral Medicine and Oral Pathology, Cardiff Dental Hospital and School, Wales; Currently Consultant Oral Microbiologist, Glasgow Dental Hospital and School, Scotland. Publications: The isolation and purification of a mannose-binding agglutinin from E coli strains and Corynebacterium parvum NCTC 10390 (with I R Poxton, J Doyle, P W Ross, D M Weir), 1980; The binding of group B streptococci to epithelial cells, 1984; Can the colonisation resistance of the oral microflora be reduced?, 1990; Human herpesvirus-6: the latest human herpes virus, 1991; An update on viral hepatitis, 1992; A problem that won't go away, 1993; Virology and the mouth, 1994; Co-author, nearly 50 contributions to journals including Journal of Medical Microbiology, Journal of Oral Pathology, Update, British Dental Journal. Memberships: International Association for Dental Research; British Society for Oral Pathology; British Society for Oral Medicine; British Society for Medical Mycology. Hobbies: Music; Reading; Hill-walking. Address: Oral Microbiology Unit, Glasgow Dental Hospital and School, 378 Sauchiehall Street, Glasgow G2 3JZ, Scotland.

BAGLEY William Alexander, b. 16 Aug 1919, Dunedin, New Zealand. Dental Surgeon. m. Marjory Helen Steven, 17 Mar 1945, 2 sons. Education: BDS, University of New Zealand (Otago University Dental School). Appointments: Man-powered private practice, 8 months (wartime); Army Officer, New Zealand Dental Corps; Self-employed general private practice, Dunedin; Now retired. Honours: Paul Harris Fellow, Rotary, Dunedin, 1988; Certificate of Appreciation, New Zealand

Police, Nelson, 1994. Membership: New Zealand Dental Association. Hobbies: Swimming; Yachting; Recreational walking; Garden upkeep. Address: 140 Moana Avenue, Nelson 7001, New Zealand.

BAHETI Dwarkadas Kanhayalal, b. 1 July 1945, Nandred, India. Doctor. m. Sudha, 13 Dec 1969, 2 sons. Education: MBBS; MD. Appointments: Consultant Anaesthetist, Ministry of Health, Tehran, Iran, 1977-82; Honorary Secretary, Indian Society for Study of Pain; Consultant of Pain Management, Assistant Professor of Anaesthesiology, University of Bombay. Publications: Scientific papers in international and national journals. Honours: Certificate of Merit, P.G.I.M.E.R, 1974; International Sholar, Cleveland Clinic Foundation, 1991. Memberships: Life Member, Indian Society of Anaesthetists; Life Member, Indian Society for Study of Pain. Hobbies: Watching Sports; Social Work. Address: B/2, Mahesh Apartment, B.M. Bhargava Road, Santacryz(w), Bombay 400 054, India.

BAI Huawen, b. 1930, Beijing, China. University Professor. Education: Graduate, Department of Chinese, Peking University, 1955. Appointments: Professor, Library and Information Science Department, Peking University. Publications: Author and Co-Author of 20 books including: The Refraction of Buddhist Halo, 1988; Supplement to Dun-huang Pien-wen Ji, Co-author, 1989; An Introduction to the Catalogue of Dun-huang Relics, 1992; Explanatory Notes to Ennin's Diary, 1992; Contributor of over 30 papers including: What is Pien-wen?, 1982; The Revise of 'Shou Lo Pi Ch'iu Chien Wu Pai Hsien Jen Ping Chien Yueh Kuang Tung Tzu Ching, 1990; From the Immortal Yi Jiao to the Monk Jue Ming, 1992. Address: Apt 306, Building 103, Chengzeyuan, Peking University, Beijing 100080, China.

BAI Ren-xiao, b. 27 June 1949, Tianjin, China. Medical Doctor. m. Fan Wei-chan, 27 March 1977, 1 son. Education: Graduated, Tianjin Medical University, 1977. Appointments: Orthopedist, Tianjin Hospital, 1977-93; Associated Medical Professor, Tianjin Hospital, 1993-; Vice President, Tianjin Jinhua Rheumatism Hospital, 1990-. Publications: Rheumatic Diseases Treated with Traditional Chinese and Western Medicine, 1989; Prevention and Treatment of Rheumatic Diseases, 1992; Surgical Treatment of Serious Deformity of Hip in Ankylosing Spondylitis, 1993. Honours: Title, Internationally Recognized Expert in Oriental Medicine, US Chinese Medical Association, 1994. Memberships: Director, Secretary, Chinese Academic Committee of Rheumatism; Vice President, Tianjin Academic Committee of Rheumatism; US Chinese Medical Association. Hobbies: Music. Address: No 2 Daxing Street, Tianjin 300021, China.

BAI Yao, b. 7 Dec 1931, Bao Tou City, China. Physician. m. Ms Shi-min Zhao, 8 Mar 1958, 1 son, 1 daughter. Education: MD, Beijing Medical University, China. Career: Resident, Chief Resident, Department of Medicine, PUMC Hospital, 1956-61; Chief Resident, Attending Physican, Associate Professor, Chief of Thyroid Unit, Deputy Director, Department of Endocrinology, 1961; Professor, Department of Endocrinology, PUMC Hospital, PUMC, currently. Publications: 80 papers, 1961-; 10 chapters of medical books edited and published. Honours: Prize awarded from PUMC, 1987-92; Prize awarded from National Ministry of Health, 1991. Memberships: Standing Committee, Chinese Medical Association of Endocrinology; President, Beijing Medical Association of Endocrinology. Hobbies: Taking Photo; Learning Geography. Address: Department of Endocrinology, Peking Union Medical College Hospital, Beijing 100730, China.

BAINTON Dorothy Ford, b. 18 June 1933, Magnolia. Pathologist. m. Cedric R Bainton, 28 Nov 1959, 3 sons. Education: BS, Millsaps College, 1955; MD, Tulane University School of Medicine, 1958; MS, University of California, 1966. Appointments: Postdoctoral Resident Fellow, UCSF, 1963-69; Postdoctoral Resident Pathologist, 1966-69; Assistant Professor of Pathology, 1969-75; Associate Professor of Pathology, 1975-81; Professor of Pathology, 1981-; Chair, Pathology Department, 1987-94; Vice Chancellor, Academic Affairs, 1994-. Publications: Identification of Neutrophil Gelatinase-Associated Lipocalin as a Novel Matrix Protein of Specic Granules in Human Neutrophils, 1994. Memberships: American Society for Cell Biology; American Society for the Advancement of Science; American Heart Association; American Association of Pathologists; Association of American Physicians; American Society of Hematology. Honours: Alpha Omega Alpha, 1957-; NIH Career Development, 1970-75; Millsaps College Alumna of the Year, 1978; NHI Grantee, Cancer Research, 1978-87; NHI Merit Award HLB, 1986-96. Hobbies: Gardening. Address: University of California, San Francisco, Medical Sciences Building, Rm

115, San Francisco, CA 94143-0400, USA.

BAIR Byron Dee, b. 3 Aug 1956, Tremonton, UT, USA. Medicine. m. Lenis Allen, 1978, 1 s, 5 d. Education: BS, Utah State University; MD, University of Utah; Residency, Internal Medicine and Psychiatry, West Virginia University. Career: Chief Resident, Internal Medicine, Clinical Instructor, West Virginia University; Chief Resident, Psychiatry, University of West Virginia; Currently, Assistant Professor, Internal Medicine, Psychiatry, University of Utah; Director, Geriatric Medicine and Psychiatry. Honour: Alpha Omega Alpha. Memberships: American Geriatric Society; Association of Internal Medicine and Psychiatry. Address: Salt Lake City VAMC, GRECC (182), 500 Foothill Boulevard, Salt Lake City, UT 84148, USA.

BAIRD David Tennent, b. 13 Mar 1935, Glasgow, Scotland. Medical Practitioner. 2 sons. Education: BA; MBChB; FRCP(Edinburgh); FRCOG; DSc; FRSE. Appointments: Junior Hospital Appointments, Edinburgh and London, 1959-65; MRC Travelling Fellowship, Staff Scientist, Worcester Foundation for Experimental Biology, Massachusetts, USA, 1965-68; Lecturer, Senior Lecturer, Department Obstetrics and Gynaecology, 1968-72, Professor of Obstetrics and Gynaecology, 1977-85, Clinical Research Professor of Reproductive Endocrinology, University of Edinburgh. Honours: Society for Endocrinology Medal, 1975; Clinical Endocrinology Medal, 1984; Fellow, Royal Society of Edinburgh, 1990. Memberships: Society for Endocrinology; Endocrine Society, USA; Society for the Study of Fertility, Chairman, 1981-84; Royal Society of Medicine; Blair Bell Research Society; Australian Society for Reproductive Biology; Edinburgh Obstetrical Society, President, 1992-94. Hobby: Skiing. Address: Department of Obstetrics and Gynaecology, Centre for Reproductive Biology, University of Edinburgh, 37 Chalmers Street, Edinburgh EH3 9EW, Scotland.

BAJUSZ Cecilia, b. 7 Mar 1956, Yugoslavia. Dental Surgeon. m. Dr George Sandor, 2 daughters. Education: HBSC; DDS. Publications: Oral Surgery: Treatment of the Geriatric Patient, 1988. Memberships: Academy of General Dentistry; Canadian Dental Association. Honours: Kennedy Trophy, 1975; ; Ontario Scholarship, 1978; Ryan Medal, 1978; Canadian Association of Oral & Maxilofacial Surgeons Award, 1984; Hobbies: Opera; Ballet; Classical Literature; Painting. Address: 215 Wynford Drive, Don Mills, Ontario M3C 3P5, Canada.

BAJWA Kulwinderjeet Singh, b. 16 Dec 1968, Punjab, India. registered Osteopath. m. Parmeet Gill, 13 Dec 1992. Education: Diploma in Osteopathy, British School of Osteopathy, 1991. Appointment: Principal, Registered Osteopath, Slough Clinic of Osteopathy. Memberships: Osteopathic Association of Great Britain; General Council and register of Osteopaths. Address: The Slough Clinic of Osteopathy, 12 Bourne Road, Slough, Berkshire SL1 2PA, England.

BAKER Carleton Harold, b. 2 Aug 1930, Utica, New York, USA. Medical Physiologist. m. Sara Johnson, 20 July 1963, 2 daughters. Education: BA, Syracuse University, 1952; MA, 1954, PhD, 1955, Princeton University. Appointments: Assistant Professor, Associate Professor, Professor, Medical College of Georgia, 1955-67; Professor, University of Louisville Health Sciences Centre, 1967-71; Professor, Chairman, University of South Florida College of Medicine, 1971-92; Deputy Dean, Research and Graduate Affairs, 1980-82; Member of several professional journal Editorial Boards, 1966-94. Publications: Microcirculatory Technology, Editor, 1986; Contributor of numerous professional articles, 1953-94. Honours: Florida Heart Association, Bronze, 1974, Silver, 1977; University of South Florida Distinguished Scientist Award, 1981; Founder Award, 1992; Phi Kappa Phi Artist Scholar Award, 1991. Memberships: American Physiological Society; Microcirculatory Society; European Society for Microcirculation; American Heart Association; Shock Society; AAAS; Society for Experimental Biology and Medicine. Hobbies: Golf; Fishing; Model building. Address: Department of Physiology and Biophysics, College of Medicine, Box 8, University of South Florida, Tampa, FL 33612, USA.

BAKER F M, b. 15 Sept 1942, New York City, New York, USA. Geriatric Psychiatrist. Education: BA, Hunter College, 1964; MD, University of Rochester School of Medicine and Dentistry, 1975; MPH, Johns Hopkins University School of Hygiene and Public Health, 1985. Appointments: Assistant Professor, Department of Psychiatry, Yale University School of Medicine, 1975; Associate Professor, Department of Psychiatry, University of Texas Health Science Center, San Antonio, 1987; Currently Associate Professor, Department of Psychiatry,

University of Maryland School of Medicine, Baltimore; Exchange Faculty Member, Erasmus University School of Medicine, Rotterdam, Netherlands, 1994-95. Publications: Co-author: Geriatric psychopathology: an American perspective on a selected agenda for research, 1992; Acute care of the African American elder, 1993; Depression among elderly African Americans and Mexican Americans, letter, 1993; Depression in African American medical patients, 1994. Honours: Elected to Hunter College Hall of Fame, 1984; Fellow, American Psychiatric Association, 1990. Memberships: Board Member, American Association for Geriatric Psychiatry; International Psychogeriatric Association. Hobbies: Walking; Music; Art museums. Address: Department of Psychiatry, University of Maryland School of Medicine, 645 West Redwood Street, Baltimore, MD 21201-1549, USA.

BAKER Frank, b. 23 Feb 1936, Dallas, Texas, USA. Professor of Psychology. m. Adrienne Polland, 20 Mar 1960, 2 sons, 1 daughter. Education: BA cum laude, Vanderbilt University, 1958; MA, 1962, PhD, 1964, Northwestern University. Appointments: Assistant Professor, Lehigh University, 1963-65; Assistant Professo, Harvard Medical School, Massachusetts, 1965-74; Professor, State University of New York, Buffalo, 1974-85; Professor, Chairman, Behavioural Sciences Department, 1985-87, Professor, Director, Health Psychology, 1987-, Johns Hopkins School of Hygiene and Public Health, Baltimore, Maryland. Publications: Industrial Organizations and Health, 1969; Systems and Medical Care, 1970; Organizational Systems, 1973; The Mental Hospital and Human Services, 1975; Program Evaluation in the Health Fields, 1979; Helping: Human Services for the 80's, 1981; Work, Health and Productivity, 1991. Honours: Sigma Xi, 1961; Delta Omega, 1985. Memberships: American Association for Advancement of Science; Fellow, American Orthopsychiatric Association; Fellow, American Psychological Association; American Public Health Association; Society of Behavioral Medicine. Address: The Johns Hopkins School of Hygiene and Public Health, Department of Environmental Sciences, 615 N Wolfe Street, Suite 7513, Baltimore, MD 21205, USA.

BAKER Joel Wilson, b. 17 Jan 1905. Surgeon. m. Elizabeth Russell, 26 July 1934, 4 s. Education: MD, University of Virginia; Honorary LLD, University of Alaska. Appointments: Chief of Surgery, Virginia Mason Medical Centre; Chairman, The Mason Clinic; President, Virginia Mason Hospital; Retired. Publications: Contributor of 136 professional works. Honours: Honorary FRCS, England, 1970; Honorary FRCS, Edinburgh, 1974; Honorary Alaska State Medical Association, 1964. Hobbies: Golf; Hunting; Bridge. Address: 2171 38th Avenue East, Seattle, WA 98112, USA.

BAKER Joyce Carla, b. 4 Sep 1950, Denver, USA. Natural Health Care Consultant. m. Charles Gary Baker, 14 Oct 1973, 3 sons. Education: BSN; Diplomate in Homeopathy; Level I and II Certificates in Energetic Medicine & Electro Dermal Screening. Appointments: Assistant Head Nurse; Director of Nursing, Monte Vista, Colorado; Director of Nursing, American Nursing Care; Natural Health Care Consultant; Guest Lecturer. Publications: Articles pending on ADD and Homeopathy; Pesticides, Heavy Metals and Yeast. Honours: American Heart Association Honorary Volunteer, 1980. Memberships: CHADD; National Center of Homeopathy; National Health Federation; AARP. Hobbies: Music; Travel. Address: 7954 Brookpoint Place, Westerville, OH 43081-5008, USA.

BAKER Lauren, b. 10 Oct 1960, Brockton, Massachusetts, USA. Biomechanical Engineer. m. David Baker, 25 Apr 1987, Education: BS, Chemical Engineering; MS and PhD, Mechanical Engineering. Appointments: Research Assistant Professor, Department of Surgery, University of Massachusetts Medical School, Worcester; Assistant Professor, Department of Mechanical Engineering, Worcester Polytechnic Institute; Currently Pre-Clinical Programme Manager. Publications include: Non Invasive Detection of Arterial Occlusive Disease: A Theoretical Model and Study, MS thesis, 1985; The Development of an Analytical and Experimental Model to Study Arterial Pulse Wave Propagation in Health and Disease. PhD dissertation, 1988; Co-author: A Digitally Controlled Wave Form Generator for Model Studies of the Circulation, 1988; The Role of the Peripheral Vascular Bed in Arterial Pulse Wave Propagation, 1988; Maintenance of Arrest During Reperfusion Accelerates Recovery from Stunning Only in the Presence of Hyperkalemic Depolarization, 1989; Assessment of Myocardial Ischemia by Fourier Analysis of Cardiac Signals, 1990; Tumor Necrosis Factor (TNF) Causes Diastolic Creep and Reversible Left Ventricular (LV) Systolic Dysfunction in Conscious Dogs, 1990; The Correction of Intramyocardial Respiratory Acidosis with Sodium

Bicarbonate (NaHCO3), 1990; The Correction of Intramyocardial Hypercarbic Acidosis With Sodium Bicarbonate, 1994. Honours: Master's Thesis of the Year, Worcester Polytechnic Institute, 1985. Memberships: American Society of Mechanical Engineers; Institute of Electrical and Electronics Engineers; Society for Clinical Trials. Hobbies: Swimming; Rowing. Address: 7 Barrows Road, Shrewsbury, MA 01545, USA.

BAKER Roger, b. 31 July 1946, London, England. Clinical Psychologist. m. Ann Baker, 3 Aug 1968, 4 daughters. Education: BA, Bangor, Wales; PhD, Leeds; C.Psychol; FBPS. Appointments: Research Co-ordinator, Grampian Health Board; Honorary Senior Lecturer, Department of Mental Health, Aberdeen Unversity; Consultant Clinical Psychologist, Grampian Health Board; Head, Research Support Unit, Dorset Healthcare NHS Trust. Publications: Rehab: Rehabilitation Hall and Baker, 1984; Panic Disorder: Theory Research And Therapy, 1989; Understanding Panic Attacks And Overcoming Fear, 1995. Memberships: Fellow, The British Psychological Society; The British Association of Behavioural & Cognitive Psychotherapies. Hobbies: Tennis; Writing. Address: Department of Psychology, Branksome Clinic, Layton Road, Parkstone, Poole, Dorset, England.

BAKER Suzanne Schneider, b. 14 Sept 1947, Marietta, Ohio, USA. Nurse. m. David Bigelow Baker, 19 Aug 1967, 1 son, 1 daughter. Education: Diploma in Nursing; Certified Chemical Dependency Counsellor. Appointments: Physician Assistant, Marietta Ob/Gyn Incorporated, 1969-87; Staff Nurse, Case Manager. Memberships: NAACOG; NCCDC. Hobbies: Gardening; Gourmet Cooking; Furniture Refinishing. Address: 108 Bittersweet Trail, Marietta, OH 45750, USA.

BAKER William Henry, b. 24 May 1937, Chicago, Illinois, USA. Vascular Surgeon. m. Ann Velde, 6 Sept 1958, 3 daughters. Education: BA, Knox College, Galesburg, Illinois; MD, University of Chicago. Appointments: Associate Professor of Surgery, Chief, Section Peripheral Vascular Surgery. Publications: Contributor of over 100 articles in major surgical and vascular surgical journals. Memberships: American Surgical Association; Central Surgical Association Midwest Surgical Association, Past President; Midwestern Vascular Surgery Society; Society for Vascular Surgery; ISCVS, NA Chapter. Hobbies: Golf; Tennis; Biking. Address: 2160 S 1st Avenue, Maywood, IL 60153, USA.

BAKHSH Ahmed, b. 1 Mar 1958, Anga, Punjab, Pakistan. Physician. m. Adeeba Malik, 21 Sept 1989, 2 daughters. Education: MBBS. Appointments: House Surgeon, Holy Family Hospital, Rawalpindi, 1985-86; Medical Officer, General Hospital, Rawalpindi, 1986-89; Community Medical Officer, Rural Areas, 1989-90; Research Fellow in Neurosurgery, Quaid-Azam Postgraduate Medical College, Islamabad. Memberships: International League Against Epilepsy; International Bureau for Epilepsy; Epilepsy Foundation of America; British Epilepsy Association; Epilepsy Foundation of Australia; Swiss League Against Epilepsy. Address: Z-1119 Ratta Road, Rawalpindi, Pakistan.

BALCH Charles M, b. 24 Aug 1942, Milford, DE, USA. Surgeon. 3 s, 1 d. Education: BS; MD. Appointments: Intern in Surgery; Resident in General Surgery; Fellow in Immunology; Program Specialist, Military; Staff Surgeon; Chief of Oncology Research; Associate Scientist; Scientist; Senior Investigator; Associate Director for Clinical Studies; Acting Director; Assistant Professor; Associate Professor; Professor; Chief of Section of Surgical Oncology; Associate Chairman, department of general surgery; Professor of Immunology; Chairman, Department of General Surgery; Head, Division of Surgery, Vice President for Hospital and Clinics; EVP for Health Affairs. Publications: Principles and Practice of Research: Strategies for Surgical Investigators, 1991; Cutaneous Melanoma: Clinical Management and Treatment Results Worldwide, 1992; Efficacy of 2cm Surgical Margins, 1993. Honours: Chair, Senator A M Aikin Jr; Board of Directors, Space Centre Houston; Board of Visitors, Trinity University. Memberships: AACR; ACS; ASCO; SSO; WHO Melanoma Group. Address: The University of Texas A M Anderson Cancer Centre, 1515 Holcombe Blvd, Houston, TX 77030, USA.

BALCH Henry H, b. 11 June 1917, Paraguay. General Surgeon. m. Julester Lina Post, 19 Aug 1944. Education: MB; BCh; MA; MSc; MC. Appointments: Assistant Professor, Surgery, New York University Medical Center; Associate Professor, Surgery, Georgetown University Medical Center; Clinical Professor of Surgery, Georgetown University Medical Center. Publications: 40 scientific papers on Host Resistance to Infection and on Surgical Subjects. Honours: Commonwealth Fund

Fellow in Surgery, 1947; Markle Scholar in Medical Science, 1948-53. Memberships: American Surgical Association; Fellow, American College of Surgeons; Society of University Surgeons; International Society of Surgeons. Hobbies: Piano; Boating. Address: 1726 Hoban Road NW, Washington, DC 20007, USA.

BALDWIN John Charles, b. 23 Sep 1948, Ft Worth, TX, USA. Surgeon; Researcher. m. Christine Janet Stewart, 31 Mar 1973, 3 s. Education: BA, summa cum laude, Harvard University, 1971; MD, Stanford University, 1975; MA Privatim (hon), Yale University, 1989; Diplomate: American Board Internal Medicine; American Board of Surgery; American Board Thoracic Surgery. Appointments include: Professor Surgery and Chief Cardiothoracic Surgery, Yale University, New Haven, 1988-94; Cardiothoracic Surgeon-in-Chief, Director Thoracic Surgery Residency Program, Yale, New Haven Hospital; DeBakey/Bard Professor and Chairman, Baylor College of Medicine and Chief of Surgical Services, The Methodist Hospital, 1994-. Publications: Co-editor, Oxford Textbook of Surgery, 1989-; Editorial Board: Journal Thoracic and Cardiovascular Surgery, 1990-; Transplantation, 1990-; Transplantation Science, 1992-; Numerous professional articles and Book Chapters. Honours include: John Harvard Scholar, 1969, 1970; Wendell Scholar, Harvard University, 1969; Medaille de la Ville de Bordeaux, French Thoracic Society, 1987; Travelling Fellow, ACS, 1989; Master Teacher Award, Cardiovascular Revs and Reports, 1990. Memberships include: Fellow ACP, Royal College Surgeons; American College of Angiology; American College Cardiology; Board of Governors, American College Surgeons, 1993-; AMA; American Association Thoracic Surgery; American Society Transplant Surgeons; American Heart Association; American Society Extracorporeal Technology; New Haven Lawn Club; Yale Club New Haven. Address: Baylor College of Medicine, Dept Surgery, One Baylor Plaza, Houston, TX 77030, USA.

BALE Sereima D Komaivunuku, b. 11 Sep 1945, Koro Island, Fiji. Anaesthetist. m. Qoriniasi Bale, 2 sons, 2 daughters. Education: DSM, Fiji School of Medicine, 1969; DA, College of Medicine, University of Philippines, 1975; FPBA, Diplomate, Philippines. Appointments: registrar in Anaesthetics, 1971, Senior registrar, 1975, Consultant Anaesthetist, 1988, Colonial War Memorial Hospital, Suva, Fiji. Publications: Pacific Society of Anaesthetists' Journal, Co-editor; Pain Relief in Terminal Cancer in the Pacific, 1992. Memberships: President, Pacific Society of Anaesthetists, 1990-93; Fiji Medical Association; Associate Member, NZSA; Assocation of Women Graduates, Fiji; Fiji Cancer Society. Hobby: Golf. Address: Colonial War Memorial Hospital, Suva, Fiji Islands.

BALELE Yohana Daudi Majola (Colonel), b. 1 Mar 1948, Bariadi, Tanzania. Medical Doctor. m. edda Balele, 1978, 2 sons. Education: MD, University of Dar-es-Salaam, 1975; MRCOG, Royal College of Obstetricians and Gynaecologists, London, 1983. Appointments: Medical Officer, Korogwe Hospital; Chief Adviser to Chief of Medical Servics, Uganda Army; Senior House Officer, Withington and Stepping Hill Hospitals, England; Director of Medical Services, Tanzania Defence Forces; Currently: Consultant Obstetrician and Gynaecologist; Commandant, Tanzania Military Medical Academy. Memberships: Tanzania Medical Association; Tanzania Association of Obstetricians and Gynaecologists. Hobbies: Nature study. Address: Lugalo General Military Hospital, PO Box 60126 (Kawe), Dar-es-Salaam, Tanzania.

BALEN Adam H, b. 30 Apr 1960, London. Reproductive Medicine. m. Dr Frances Hunt, 17 Jul 1988, 1 s. Education: MB; BS; MD; MRCOG. Appointments: Research Fellow, Middlesex Hospital, London; Subspecialist Senior Registrar, Nuffield Department of Obstetrics & Gynaecology, Oxford, UK. Publications: The CTG In Practice, 1992; Papers on Polycystic Ovary Syndrome, Ovulation Induction, Hypersecretion of LH, Gonadotsophin Surge Attenuating Factor, IVF, 1990-95. Memberships: Royal Society of Medicine; British Fertility Society. Hobbies: Travel; Fine Wine; Jazz. Address: 3 Westbury Grove, Woodside Park, London, N12 7PE, England.

BALOGIANNIS Stavros, b. 24 Aug 1944, Thessaloniki, Greece. Professor of Neurology. m. Heleni Bozini, 1965, 1 son, 3 daughters. Education: MD, 1968; PhD, 1975; BTheol, 1979. Appointments: Postdoctoral Fellow, National Hospital, Queen's Square, London, 1973-74; Researcher, Louvain, 1976; Fellow, University of Pennsylvania. Publications: An Overview of Psychology, 1982; Clinical Neuropathology, vol 1-111, 1984; Psychology, 1985; Psychiatry and Pastoral Psychiatry, 1986; Muscular Diseases, 1989; 250 articles.

Memberships: President, Hellenic Society of Neuropathology; Founding Member, European Society of Neuropathology; American Association of Neuropathology. Honours: Greek State Scholarship, 1973-76; Gold Medal of St Demetions; Gold Medal of St Paul; Gold Medal of Holy Vision. Hobbies: Classical Music; Poetry; Linguistics; Mathematics. Address: Angelaki 5, Thessaloniki 54621, Greece.

BALSDON Michael John, b. 18 Aug 1940, Sutcombe, England. Gynaecologist. m. Maria Isabel Herane, 21 Nov 1992. Education: BA, Open University; MB BS, London University; MD, University of Chile; MRCS, LRCP (Conjoint Board); FCA, Institute of Chartered Accountants; FRCOG, Royal College of Obstetricians and Gynaecologists. Appointments: Consultant, Gynaecology and Genito-Urinary Medicine, Southampton and Portsmouth; Currently Gynaecologist, Santiago, Chile. Publications: Contributions in field of Endocrinology and Genito-Urinary Infection, to American Journal of Obstetrics and Gynecology, Lancet, Genito-Urinary Medicine, Dermatologia, other journals. Honours: Consultant, Royal Navy, England. Memberships: British Medical Association; Colegio Medico de Chile. Hobbies: Cyclamens; Butterflies; Statistics. Address: Carmen Sylva 2552, Dpto 52, Providencia, Santiago, Chile.

BANAFAA Omar Saleh Abdulla, b. 12 Feb 1944, Aden, Yemen. Obstetrician and Gynaecologist. Education: FRCOG, UK; MBChB, St Andrews; DObst RCOG, UK; DTM&H, Liverpool; MFFP, UK. Appointments: registrar, Bangour General Hospital, Scotland; Registrar, Glasgow Royal Maternity Hospital; Registrar, Bellshill Maternity Hospital and Monklands General Hospital, Lanarkshire; Consultant Obstetrician and Gynaecologist, Head of department of Obstetrics and Gynaecology. Memberships: British Medical Association; European Society for Human Reproduction and Embryology. Hobbies: Poetry; Tennis; Music. Address: Al-Mana General Hospital, PO Box 1364, Al-Khoba 31952, Saudi Arabia.

BANG Ki Moon, b. 2 Oct 1940, Korea. Medical Epidemiologist. m. Hanok Kim, 30 May 1969, 2 sons. Education: PhD; MPH; MS; BS. Appointments: Chief, Research & Statistics Division, National Institute of Tuberculosis, 1966-72; Professor, Howard University, 1985-; Adjunct Professor, West Virginia University, 1993-; Chief, Surveillance, NIOSH/CDC, US Department of Health & Human Services, 1993-. Publications: Principles of Biostatistics, 1968; Environment and Health, 1980; Handbook of Black American Health, 1993; Article: Chronic Bronchitis, 1990. Honours: Elias Hochman Memorial Award, 1980; Don Savage Memorial Award, 1992. Memberships: The Society for Epidemiologic Research; The American Public Health Association. Hobbies: Tennis; Judo; Classical Music. Address: 4110 Casey Ct, Alexandria, Virginia, USA.

BANJOKO Moses Okunuga, b. 20 September 1935, Odogbolu, Nigeria. Doctor of Medicine. m. Justina Olufunke Odubote, 22 September 1962, 3 sons, 3 daughters. Education: Bachelor of Medicine; Bachelor of Surgery; MB CHB, Manchester; Licentiate of the Royal College of Physicians; Member, Royal College of Surgeons; FRCOG; FMCOG; FICS. Appointments: House Officer, Park Hospital, Manchester, 1966-68; Senior House Officer, Royal Manchester Childrens Hospital, 1968; Senior House Officer, St Mary's Hospital, Manchester, 1969; Registrar, Stepping Hill Hospital, Stockport, 1970; Senior Registrar, Lagos University Teaching Hospital, 1974; Lecturer, University of Lagos, Senior Lecturer, University of Lagos, 1978. Publications: Management of Unstable Lie in Pregnancy, 1973; Problems of Prematurity in Obstetric, 1974; The Obstetric Performance of Nigerian Primigravide Age 16 and Under, 1975. Memberships: Nigeria Medical Association; New York Academy of Sciences; Society of Gynaecology and Obstetrics of Nigeria; Fellow, International Foundation of Obstetrics and Gynaecology. Hobbies: Reading; Table Tennis; Football. Address: Mainland Specialist Hospital, 9 Solabomi Crescent, Aguda, Surulere, Nigeria.

BANKS Archibald Walker, b. 20 Mar 1920, Glasgow, Scotland. Surgeon. 1 daughter. Education: LMSSA, 1944; MBBS, London, 1947; MRCOG 1954; FRCS(Edinburgh), 1963; FRCOG, 1980. Appointments: RAMC, 1944-47; Consultant Surgeon, Ministry of Health, Libya, 1968-70; Surgeon, Waipawa Hosdital Board, New Zealand, 1970-72; Emeritus Consultant in Obstetrics and Gynaecology, Rotherham Area. Publications: Skin Grafting in the Radical Vulva Operation, 1964; A Case of Peutz-Segher's Syndrome in Early Pregnancy Mimicking Hyperomesis Gravidarum, 1974; Libya in Retrospect, 1973. Honour: Defence Medal, 1947. Memberships: British Medical Association;

Society of Apothecaries of London, Liveryman. Hobbies: Sailing; Music; Radio; Astronomy. Address: 5 Slayleigh Avenue, Sheffield S10 3RA, England.

BANKS-TARR Sharon E, b. 5 Apr 1950, Pittsburgh, Pennsylvania, USA. Registered Nurse. m. Paul D Tarr, 10 Nov, 1 son, 1 daughter. Education: Master of Nursing, 1980; BSc Nursing, 1974. Appointments: Vice President, Pittsburgh Area Nurse Recruiters, 1993; Midatlantic Regional Representative, National Association of Health Care recruiters; Lieutenant Commander, US Navy; Clinical Nurse Manager. Honours: Navy Achievement Award for Professional Achievement. Memberships: Association of Clinical Nurse Specialists; National Association Female Executives. Hobbies: Reading; Downhill skiing; Sailing; Golf; Family outings. Address: National Naval Medical Centre, 8901 Wisconsin Avenue, Bethesda, MD 20889, USA.

BANKSON Daniel Duke, b. 27 Jun 1956, Moscow, ID, USA. Clinical Chemist. m. Dr Anne M Baribault, 29 May 1982, 1 s, 1 d. Education: BSc, Biochemistry, University of BC, 1978; SM, Nutritional Biochemistry and Metabolism, 1982, PhD, Nutritional Biochemistry and Metabolism, 1985, MA Institute of Technology. Career: Research Assistant, Teaching Assistant, MIT, 1978-82; Research Assistant, Research Associate, Tufts University, 1982-86; Fellow, University of NC, 1986-89; Associate in Cancer Prevention, Fred Hutchinson Cancer Research Center, 1989-93; Currently, Assistant Chief, Clinical Chemistry, VA Medical Center, Seattle, and Assistant Professor, Laboratory Medicine, University of WA, Seattle. Publications: Numerous papers published in the field of nutrition, endocrinology, clinical biochemistry, 1978-. Honours: Young Investigator Award, Academy of Clinical Laboratory Physicians and Scientists, 1987; Fellow, Academy of Clinical Biochemistry; Diplomate, American Board of Clinical Chemistry. Memberships: American Association for Clinical Chemistry; American Institute of Nutrition; American Society for Clinical Nutrition; National Academy of Clinical Biochemistry. Address: Veterans Affairs Medical Center, 1660 South Columbian Way 113, Pathology and Laboratory Medicine Service, Seattle, WA 98108, USA.

BAO Shi-yao, b. 18 Sept 1939, Shaoxing, Zhejiang, China. Professor of Neurology. m. Xu Duan-fang, 19 Aug 1968, 1 daughter. Education: MB. Suzhou Medical College, 1964; Research Fellow, National Cardiovascular Centre, Japan, 1983-85. Appointments include: Associate Professor, Chief, Department of Neurology, 1st Affiliated Hospital, 1986, Professor, Chief of Neurology, Chairman, Neurology Teaching and Research Section, 1988, currently President, 2nd Affiliated Hospital, Suzhou Medical College; Currently: Director, Master of Medicine course, Suzhou Medical College; President, Sino-France Friendship Hospital. Publications: Susceptibility difference of juvenile brain and adult brain to post-ischemic cerebral edema, 1988; The effect of high hematocrit and low MABP in cerebral ischemia in gerbils, 1988; Influence of hyperglycemia on the prognosis significance of acute cerebral infarction, 1990; The changes of regional cerebellum blood flow after vertebral artery occlusion and anastomosis, 1990; Effects of Ligustrazine and salvia miltiorrhizae on blood flow, energy metabolism in gerbil brains following experimental cerebral ischemia and post-ischemic reperfusion, 1991; The study of cervical spondylosis and anatomy of cervical spine, 1991; Studies of platelet surface glycoproteins in patients with acute cerebrothrombosis, 1993. Honours: Expert who has made special contributions, State Council of China; Scientific Achievement Prizes for 3 projects, 1990, 1992, 1993; Government Special Subsidy, 1992-. Memberships: Suzhou Standing Council, Jiangsu Council, Chinese Medical Association; Standing Editorial Board, Journal of Clinical Neurology; Editorial Board, Journal ot Neuroimaging, USA. Hobbies: Reading; Playing table-tennis. Address: Second Affiliated Hospital, 181 San Xiang Road, Suzhou 215004, China.

BAQAI Zahida, b. 29 October 1935, Faridpur, Bangladesh. Gynaecologist. m. Dr F.U. Baqai, 25 February 1966, 1 son. Education: MBBS, 1958; DRCOG, 1964; MRCOG, 1966; FICS, 1968; FRCOG, 1981. Appointments: Consultant Gynaecologist, Obstetrician & Head of the Department, Baqai Hospital, 1969-; Consultant Gynaecologist & Obstetrician, P.N.S. Shifa, Pakistan Naval Service, 1966-71; Honorary Consultant, Lady Daffrin Hospital, Karachi, 1966; Registrar, Obstetrics & Gynaecology, Southpost Royal Infirmary, Lancashire, England, 1963. Publications: Conquest of Diabetes, 1966; Management of Prolapsed Umbilical Cord, 1967; Incidence of Pelvic Tuberculosis, 1969; Ten Year Statistical Study of Obs & Gynae cases at a Private Hospital, 1979. Memberships: Royal College of Obstetricians & Gynaecologists, London; Society of Obstetricians & Gynaecology of Pakistan; Society of

Surgeons of Pakistan; Diabetic Association of Bangladesh; Private Hospitals Association. Hobbies: Listening to Music. Address: D-136 Block B, North Nazimabad, Karachi, Pakistan.

BARANOV Alexander E, b. 18 Mar 1938, Crimea, Russia. Physician. m. Flora Kudriavzeva, 27 Apr 1962, 2 sons. Education: Crimean Medical Institute, 1961; Postgraduate in Haematology, Central Postgraduation Institute, Moscow, 1966; DMS, 1983. Appointments: Head, Haematological Department, Central Railway Hospital No 2, Moscow, 1967; Head, Haematological Department, Clinic of Institute of Biophysics, Moscow, 1969-. Publications include: Evaluation of the Dose and Prognosis of the Dose and Prognosis of the Time Course of Neutrophil Count by Haematological Indexed with Specifically Reference to Gamma-irradiation of Man, 1981; Total-Body Gamma Therapeutic Irradiation in a Dose of 3Gy in Acute Leukaemia - Haematological and Clinical Aspects of the Bone Marrow Syndrome, 1987; Treatment of Acute Radiation Disease (ARD) - Experience from Chernobyl, CO-author, 1988; Haematological Effects in a Population Irradiated at the Accident of the Chernobyl Atomic Power Station, CO-author, 1989. Address: Clinical Department of the Institute of Biophysics, Zhivopisnaya 46, 123182 Moscow, Russia.

BARANOVSKY Max Gregory, b. 7 Aug 1944, Tashkent, Uzbekistan. Psychiatrist. m. Tatiana Godlevsky, 26 July 1968, 2 sons. Education: MD, Pavlov Medical School, St Petersburg, Russia, 1967; Fellowship, 1970-74; Psychiatric Residency, Tufts Medical School, USA, 1980-83; Diplomate, ABPN in General and Geriatric Psychiatry. Appointments: Currently Chief, Geropsychiatric and Dual Diagnosis Services, St Elizabeth's Medical Center, Boston, Massachusetts, USA. Publications: 6 articles. Memberships: American Psychiatric Association; International Geriatric Psychiatric Society. Hobbies: Jazz; Volleyball; Photography. Address: Department of Psychiatry, St Elizabeth's Medical Center of Boston, 736 Cambridge St, Boston, MA 02135, USA.

BARANOWSKA-GEORGE Teresa, b. 24 Jan 1926, Piotrkrów-Trybunalski, Poland. Ophthalmologist. m. Stefan George, 23 Dec 1961, 1 daughter. Education: MD; PhD. Appointments: Assistant, 1952, First Assistant, 1955, in Ophthalmologic Clinic, Szczecin; Head, Ophthalmologic Department, Piotrkow-Trybunalski, 1970-72; Assistant Professor, Professor, Ophthalmologic Clinic, Medical Academy, Szczecin. Publications: Prismatic hypercorrection in treatment of the squints, 1967, 1968, 1969; The symptom of deviation and of secondary false localization in squinters treated by localization method with alternate obturation of the eyes, 1968-69; The problem of the treatment of eccentric fixation by the application of a prism in front of the cross-eye and occlusion of the fixin eye, 1970; New trial of treatment of aniseiconia by means of localization exercises, 1970; Penalization in treatment of squint by the localization method, 1973, 1974; Dependence of results in operations on straight and oblique muscles of eyeball in the mode of their incision, 1989; Prophylacic examinations of visual organ in infants between 10-14 weeks of life, 1990; Prophylaxis in school age myopia 1990 and 1994, 1992; Surgery of open angle glaucome; Treatment of squint with special reference to Szczecin method, Sylwjana - Szczecin, 1993/94, translated in Polish and French. Honours: Merited Teacher, Polish People's Republic, 1983; Gold Cross of Merit, 1973; Cross of Poland's Restitution, 1980; Medal of National Education, 1987. Memberships: State Railway Consultant, Ophthalmology; Chairman, Szczecin Ophthalmologic Association; Szczecin Scientific Society; Polish Ophthalmologic Society; European Strabismological Association; Vice Chairman, Strabismological Section, Polish Ophthalmologic Society. Address: Powstancòw Wielkopolskich Str 72, 70-111 Szczecin, Poland.

BARANY (Franz) Peter, b. 26 Oct 1955, Stockholm, Sweden. Physician. m. Asa Wallje, 3 May 1986, 2 d. Education: MD, 1987, Dr Med Sc, 1993, Karolinska Institute, Stockholm; Speciality Training in Nephrology, Huddinge University Hospital, 1987-94. Appointments: Specialist in Nephrology, Department of Renal Medicine, Huddinge University Hospital. Publications: Contributor of 17 professional papers. Memberships: European Dialysis and Transplantation Association; European Renal Association; International Society of Nephrology; International Society for Peritoneal Dialysis; American Society of Nephrology. Hobby: Sports. Address: Department of Renal Medicine, Huddinge University Hospital, S-141 86 Huddinge, Sweden.

BARBACH Lonnie, b. 6 Oct 1946, Newark, New Jersey. Author; Psychologist. 1 daughter. Education: BS, Simmons College, Boston, Massachusetts, 1968; MA, Wright Institute, Berkeley, California, 1972;

PhD, Wright Institute, Berkeley, California, 1974. Appointments: Co-Director, Clinical Training, University California Medical Center, 1973-76; Associate Professor, Antioch College West, San Francisco, 1977-78; Monthly Column in Playgirl Magazine, 1982-84; Co-Founder, Focal Point Productions, Sausalito, California, 1985-90; Monthly Column in New Woman Magazine, 1993-94; Quarterly Column in Eternelle Magazine, 1994-; Assistant Clinical Professor of Medical Psychology, University California Medical School, San Francisco, 1978-; Psychologist, Private Practice, San Francisco, 1976-. Publications incl: Erotic Interludes: Tales Told by Women, 1986; Going the Distance: Finding and Keeping Lifelong Love, 1991; The Pause: Positive Approaches to menopause, 1993; The Erotic Edge: Erotica for Couples, 1994. Honours: Simons Honors Academy, 1966, 1967, 1968; American Medical Writers Association Award, Honorable Mention, 1978; American Association of Sex Educators, Counselors & Therapists, 3rd Annual Regional Award, 1978; Co-President, Association for Humanistic Psychology, 1986-87; National Council on Family Relations Media Awards Competition, 1st Place, 1992; Selected for Gifted Woman Project by Howard Schatz Pacific Photographic Press, 1992; Award for Significiant Contributions, Santa Clara County Psychological Association, 1992. Memberships incl: American Association of Sex Therapists Counselors & Therapists; American Psychological Association. Hobbies: Skiing; Travel; Roller Blading; Playing with her Daughter. Address: 60 Palm Way, Mill Valley, CA, USA.

BARBARASH Leonid S, b. 22 June 1941, Moscow, Russia. Cardiovasccular Surgeon. m. Nina Perova, 1960, 2 daughters. Education: Can Med Sci, Kemerovo, 1973; MD, 1985. Appointments: Surgeon, Kemerovo District Hospital, 1964; Assistant Professor, 1972, Professor, 1987, Department of Surgery, Medical Institute, Kemerovo; Director, Kemerovo Cardiac Centre, 1992-. Publications: Contributor of numerous articles. Memberships: Russian Society for Cardiovascular Surgery, Kemerovo Branch Chairman; European Society for Cardiovascular Surgery. Hobbies: Gardening; Dogs. Address: Krasnaya Street 2b-19, Kemerovo 650002, Russia.

BARBENEL Joseph Cyril, b. 2 Jan 1937, London, England. Bioengineer. m. Lesley Mary Hyde Jarrett, 6 Aug 1960, 2 sons, 1 daughter. Education: BDS; BSc; MSc; PhD; LDS' RCS(Eng); CPhys FInstP; CBiol; FIBiol; CEng; FBES; FRSE. Appointments: House Surgeon, London Hospital, 1960; Lieutenant, RADC, 1960-61; Captain, RADC, Malaya, 1961-62; General Dental Practice, London, 1962-63; Nuffield Fellow, St Andrews University, 1963-66; Student, Bioengineering Unit, Strathclyde University, 1966-67; Lecturer, Dundee University, 1967-69; Lecturer, 1970, Reader, 1982, Personal Professor, 1985, Professor, 1989, Head of department, 1992, University of Strathclyde, Glasgow. Publications: Editor and Co-Editor of 5 books; Contributor of numerous chapters, papers and professional articles. Memberships: Past President, Biological Engineering Society; Past President, Society for Tissue Viability; Royal Society of Medicine; Past Member of Steering Committee, Forum on Clinical Rheology; International Society for Bioengineering and the Skin, Past member of Committee, Secretary of Standardisation; International Federation for Medical and Biological Engineering; Institute of Physical Science and Medicine; Biomedical Engineering Society, USA. Hobbies: Music; Art; Theatre; Reading; Work. Address: University of Strathclyde, Bioengineering Unit, Wolfson Centre, 106 Rottenrow, Glasgow G4 0NW, Scotland.

BARKIN Gilbert, b. 6 Feb 1929, Brooklyn, NY, USA. Medical Doctor. m. Sandra Bernice Snyder, 6 Dec 1955, 1 s, 3 d. Education: AA, BS, George Washington University, 1949; MD, George Washington University School of Medicine, 1953; Diplomate, American Boards of Medical Examiners, 1954 and Pediatrics, 1959; Board Certified in Pediatric Allergy, 1961. Career includes: Allergist, Psychophysiological Laboratory, VA Hospital, Perry Point, MD, 1962; Consultant Allergist, WA Sanitarium and Hospital, Takoma Park, MD, 1964-; Regional Consultant, Asthmatic Children's Foundation, Miami Beach, FL, 1964-. Publications include: Co-author, Do I Have An Allergy?, in NEA Journal, 1970; Author, Socioeconomics of Allergy, in Ann Allergy, 1981; Presidential Address, Ann Allergy, 1983; Asthma, Hospitalizations and Deaths are Increasing, in Montgomery County Medical Society Bulletin, 1991; Editorial Board, Immunology and Allergy Practice, 1988-. Memberships include: American Academy of Pediatrics; Various offices, American College of Allergists; American Academy of Allergy; American Association for Study of Headache; Board of Directors, WA Metropolitan Chapter of Allergy Foundation of America; Board of Directors, Joint Council of Allergy and Immunology; President, Interasma, North

American Chapter. Hobby: Grandchildren. Address: 8508 Cedar Street, Silver Spring, MD 20910, USA.

BARLOW David Hearnshaw, b. 26 Dec 1949, Glasgow, Scotland. Academic Medicine. m. Norma C Woodrow, 30 Mar 1973, 1 s, 1 d. Education: MA, Oxford University, 1985; BS, Glasgow University, 1971; MBChB, Glasgow University, 1975; MD, Glasgow University, 1981; FRCOG, London, 1993; Fellow of Oriel College, Oxford. Appointments: Clinical Reader, Department of Obstetrics & Gynaecology, University of Oxford, 1984-90; Nuffield Professor of Obstetrics & Gynaecology, University of Oxford, 1990-. Publications: Research Articles of Reproductive Medicine, particularly Fertility & IVF, Endometriosis, Menopause and HRT. Honours: MRC Training Fellowship, 1977; Hall Tutorial Fellowship, 1979; Blair Bell Memorial Lectureship, RCOG, 1985. Memberships: Fellow, Royal College of Obstetricians & Gynaecologists. Hobbies: Music; Painting. Address: Nuffield Department of Obstetrics & Gynaecology, The John Radcliffe Hospital, Oxford OX3 9DU, UK.

BARNARD Donald Roy, b. 7 June 1946, Santa Ana, California, USA. Medical Entomologist. m. Priscilla Margaret Grier, 12 Aug 1967, 1 son, 1 daughter. Education: BS, Zoology, 1969, MA, Biology, 1972, California State University; PhD, Entomology, University of California, 1977; Postdoctoral Fellow, Colorado State University, 1977-79. Appointments: Research Entomologist, Agricultural Research Service, US Department of Agriculture, Oklahoma, 1979-88; Supervisory Research Entomologist, Research Leader, Agricultural Research Service, US Department of Agriculture, Florida, 1989-. Publications: Over 60 articles in peer-reviewed scientific journals, 2 book chapters, 2 technical manuals, all on aspects of medical or veterinary entomology. Memberships: American Mosquito Control Association; Ecological Society of America; Entomological Society of America; International Organization for Biological Control. Hobbies: Sailing; Freshwater fishing; Travel; Photography. Address: Medical and Veterinary Entomology Research Laboratory, Agricultural Research Service, USDA, PO Box 14565, Gainesville, FL 32604, USA.

BARNARD Peter Deane, b. 25 Apr 1932, Canberra, Australia. Dentist. div. 1 son, 1 daughter. Education: BDS, 1954, MDS, 1967, DDSc, 1991, University of Sydney; MPH, University of Michigan, USA, 1956; FRACDS, 1965; FAPHA, 1966; FICD, 1972. Appointments: Lieutenant Colonel, Australian Army, retired; Consultant, World Health Organisation, India, 1972, Indonesia, 1974-75, Malaysia, 1984; Director, Preventive dentistry, Westmead Hospital, 1984-; Senior lecturer in Preventive Dentistry, 1961-69, Associate Professor of Preventive Dentistry, 1970-, University of Sydney. Publications: Contributor of numerous monographs and articles in professional journals. Honours: Meritorious Service Award, Australian Dental Association, 1985; Alan Docking Science Award, International Association for Dental Research, ANZ Division, 1993. Memberships include: Vice Chairman, Commission of Public Health Services, Federation Dentaire Internationale, 1970-76. Address: Dental Clinical School, Westmead Hospital, Westmead, New South Wales 2145, Australia.

BARNER Hendrick Boyer, b. 23 Feb 1933, Seattle, USA. Professor of Surgery. m. Mechthild B Boehnke, 6 Mar 1961, 3 sons. Education: BS; MD. Appointments: Professor of Surgery, St Louis University, 1973-91; Professor of Surgery, Albert Einstein College of Medicine, 1991-93; Professor of Surgery, Washington University, 1993-. Publications: Contributor of 244 articles and 20 book chapters. Memberships: American Surgical Association; American Association for Thoracic Surgery; Society of Thoracic Surgeons; Society of University Surgeons. Address: 11125 Dunn Road, St Louis, MO 63136, USA.

BARNES David L, b. 3 January 1938, Illinois, USA. Senior Vice President, Medical Affairs. m. Bobbie Ransdell, 31 December 1993, 3 sons, 3 daughters. Education: MD, Tulane School of Medicine; Surgical Residency, Indiana University Medical Center; Residency, Occupational Medicine, University of California, San Francisco; MPH, Emory University. Appointments: Staff Physician, Firestone Tyre & Rubber Company; Staff Physician, PPG Industries; Medical Coordinator, Director, Howell Medical Center. Memberships: American College of Surgeons; American College of Preventative Medicine; American College of Occupational & Environmental Medicine; International Committee on Occupational Health. Hobbies: Golf; Fishing; Hiking. Address: 4360 Chablee Dunwoody Road #202, Atlanta, GA 30314, USA.

BARNES Graham, b. 24 Oct 1936, North Carolina, USA. Psychotherapist; Hypnotherapist. 2 sons. Education includes: MA,

Abilene Christian University, 1964; STB, Harvard University, 1967. Appointments: Founder, 1969, President, Faculty, 1969-78, Co-Initiator, Experimental Graduate Programme in Psychotherapy, 1973-75, Southeast Institute, Chapel Hill, North Carolina, 1969-78; Adjunct Lecturer, Department of Psychiatry, 1973-78, Lecturer, School of Public Health, 1976, Medical School, University of North Carolina; Teacher, Supervisor, Psychotherapy programmes in Europe, 1978-89; Head, School of Psychotherapy Cybernetics, Department of Psychiatry, Medical Faculty, University of Zagreb, Croatia, 1990-; Director, Inform Lab, Solna, Sweden, 1991-. Publications: Editor, contributor: Transactional Analysis After Eric Berne, 1977; Techniques of Contractual Supervision, 1977; Co-author: Health Script: Its relationship to illness in a college population, 1978; Future of Psychotherapy Today, 1993; Co-author: Event-Related Potentials (P300) During Cognitive Processing in Hypnotic and Non-Hypnotic Conditions, 1993; Author: Justice, Love and Wisdom. Linking Psychotherapy to Second-Order Cybernetics, 1994. Memberships: Clinical Member, American Group Psychotherapy Association; Certified Teaching Member, International Transactional Analysis Association;Certified Marital and Family Therapist. Hobbies: Running; Cycling; Wine collecting. Address: Råsundavägen 152, S-171 30 Solna, Sweden.

BARNES Karen L, b. 12 Jan 1948, Pittsburg, California, USA. Nurse. m. Patrick D Barnes, 17 July 1971, divorced, 2 daughters. Education: MSc; Clinical Nurse Specialist; Registered Nurse. Appointments: Head Nurse, CCO University of Oklahoma Health Sciences Center; Project Nurse, Oklahoma Medical Research Foundaiton; Clinical Nurse Specialist, Office of Dr Carl Rubenstein, Faculty of Okahoma University. Publications: Training Methods of Competitive Swimmers, 1984; Co-author: Self-directed learning in Nursing Education: An analysis of literature 1983-1993, 1995. Memberships: American Nurses Association; Oklahoma Nurses Association; American Heart Association. Honours: Sigma Theta Tau; Parry Scholarship, 1989; Outstanding Young Women of America, 1984. Hobbies: Gardening; Swimming; Pets. Address: 2004 Ridgecrest Road, Edmond, OK 73013, USA.

BARNES Kevin William, b. 3 Jan 1945, Christchurch, New Zealand. Osteopathic Physician. Education: BSc, Chemistry and Biochemistry, Massey University; DO, European School of Osteopathy, United Kingdom. Appointments: Treasurer, New Zealand Register of Osteopaths Incorporated, 1990-91. Publications: Principles of Osteopathic Treatment of the Brachial Plexus Region, 1981. Memberships: European Society of Osteopaths; General Council and Register of Osteopaths; New Zealand Register of Osteopaths; Royal Society of Health. Hobbies: Tennis; Piano; Private Pilot. Address: 72 Rongopai Street, Palmerston North, New Zealand.

BARNET Laurel Sheppeard, b. 21 June 1964. Nursing Instructor. m. Jeffrey Barnet, 11 June 1987. Education: BS, Dallas Baptist University; MS, Texas Woman's University. Appointments: Staff Nurse, Pediatric Neurology & Orthopedic; Staff Nurse, Neonatal Intensive Care; Staff Nurse, Women & Children's Center. Hobbies: Reading; Swimming; Bicycling; Walking; Sewing; Crafts. Address: 410 Agnew, Bonham, TX 75418, USA.

BARNETT Stanley Brian, b. 29 May 1946, Essex, England. Research Scientist. m. Shirley, 1968, 2 sons. Education: BSc Hons, University of London, King's College; MSc, PhD, Pathology, University of New South Wales, Australia. Appointments: Scientist, Ultrasonics Institute, Commonwealth Department of Health, Australia; Visiting Scientist, Radiation Biology, University of Rochester, New York, USA; Project Leader, Ultrasonics Laboratory, CSIRO. Publications: Author: Sister chromatid exchanges in laboratory cultured cells after repeated exposure to pulsed ultrasound, journal of Ultrasound in Medicine, 1987; Co-author : Effects of pulsed ultrasound and temperature on development of rat embryos in culture, Teratology, 1990; Issues and Recommendations regarding thermal mechanisms for biological effects of ultrasound, Ultrasound in Medicine Biology, 1992; International perspectives on saftey and standardisation of diagnostic pulsed ultrasound in Medicine, Ultrasound in Obstetrics and Gynaecology, 1993. Honours: Medical Ultrasound Pioneer Award, 1988; Fellow, American Institute of Ultrasound in Medicine, 1988. Memberships: World Federation for Ultrasound in Medicine and Biology; Teratology Society; Australasian Society for Ultrasound in Medicine. Hobby: Sailing. Address: Ultrasonics Laboratory, CSIRO, 126 Greville Street, Chatswood 2067, Australia.

BARNHOUSE, Ruth Tiffany, b. France. Psychiatrist; Episcopal Priest. div. 6 sons, 1 daughter. Education: BA, Barnard College, USA, 1947; MD, Columbia University College Physicians and Surgeons, 1950; ThM, Weston College School of Theology, 1974. Appointments: Clinical Assistant Psychiatry, Harvard Medical School, Boston, 1959-78; Adjunct Professor, Pastoral Theology, Virginia Theological Seminary, Alexandria, Virginia, 1978-80; Ordained Priest, Episcopal Church, 1980; Professor of Psychiatry and Pastoral Care, School of Theology, SMU, Dallas, Texas, 1980-89; Private Practice. Publications: A Women's Identity, 1994; Clergy and the Sexual Revolution; Male and Female: Christian Approaches to Sexuality; Contributor of 26 articles including: The Sacred Dance of the Sexes. Honours: Training Grant, US Public Health Service, 1955; Tuition Grant, 1973; Fellow, College of Preachers, 1976; Maura Award, Women's Centre of Dallas, 1987. Memberships: American Academy of Psychoanalysis, Scientific Associate; American Psychiatric Association, Life Fellow; Royal Society of Medicine, Fellow. Hobbies: Needlepoint; Piano; Travel; Reading. Address: 100-B Turtle Creek Village #350, Dallas, TX 75219, USA.

BARNS THOMAS EVERARD Christopher, b. 6 Feb 1919, Highclere, England. Obstetrician; Gynaecologist. m. Olive Teresa Fitch, 24 May 1944, 1 son. Education: Keble College, Oxford; Oxford Medical School; BA (Oxon), 1939; BM ChB (Oxon); Postgraduate training under Sir John Stallworthy; MRCOG, 1948; MA (Oxon), 1951; FRCP (Edin), 1954; DM (Oxon), 1956. Appointments: War service, Field Surgical Unit, Burma Campaign; Senior Registrar, Radcliffe, Oxford, 1946; Research Fellow, Newcastle Medical School, 1950; State Obstetrician, HRH Sultan of Johore, 1953; Senior Consultant, Obstetrics, Gynaecology, Cumberland, 1956; Chair, Professor, Obstetrics, Gynaecology, Christian Medical College Madras Medical School, India, 1966; Associate Professor, International Health, Johns Hopkins University Medical Faculty, USA, 1969; WHO Advisor, Maternal and Child Health, South East Asia region, 1972-78; UNFPA Needs Assessment Missions to Maldives, 1978, Philippines, 1979, Syria, 1980; 6 consultancies to Egyptian Health Ministry on Rural Health Development, 1981-83; WHO Consultant, Geneva, 1984; Liverpool School of Tropical Medicine and Consultant to ODA, 1985-86; WHO deputation to World Bank Mission, Bangladesh, 1990-91. Publications: Chapters: Recent Advances in Obstetrics and Gynaecology, 1979; Field Research in 3rd World Obstetrics, 1980; Community Obstetric Care, 1982; Social Obstetrics, 1986; Community Obstetric Care, 1987; Maternal Health Care, 1994; Articles: Natural History of Pelvic Tuberculosis; Field research in delivery of Maternal Care, 1980; Obstetric Mortality in Developing Countries, 1991; Safe Motherhood in India, 1991. Honours: Blair Bell Award, Royal College of Obstetricians and Gynaecologists, 1954; Aleck Bourse Memorial Lectureship, 1969; Guest Keynote address, All India Obstetrics-Gynaecology Congress, 1974, 1984; Honorary Fellowship, Royal College of Physicians, Edinburgh, 1984; Ida Scudder Oration, 1986. Hobbies: Reading; Grandpa duty. Address: The Old Vicarage, Nether Wasdale, Nr Gosforth, Cumbria CA20 1ET.

BARRATT Paul Stuart, b. 5 Apr 1964, Chichester, England. Registered Osteopath. m. 2 Nov 1991. Education: DO; MRO; British School of Osteopathy. Membership: Register of Osteopaths. Hobbies: Playing Piano; Television; Computers. Address: 187 Dalkeith Road, Edinburgh EH16 5DS, Scotland.

BARRETT Kim Elaine, b. 21 June 1958, London, England. University Professor. m. Philip Bonomo, 2 July 1988. Education: BSc, Medicinal Chemistry, 1979, PhD, Biological Chemistry, 1982, University College, London. Appointments: Visiting Fellow, NIH, 1982-85; Assistant Research Immunologist, 1985-88, Assistant Professor of Medicine, 1988-92, Associate Professor of Medicine, UCSD School of Medicine, USA. Publications: Contributor of over 90 articles in professional books and journals. Honours: SERC Scholarship, 1979-82; Fulbright Travel Scholarship, 1982. Memberships: British Society Immunologists; British Society Cell Biology; American Association Immunologists; American Federation Clinical Research; American Gastro Association; American Academy Allergy Immunology; American Physiology Society. Address: UCSD Medical Centre, 8414, 200 West Arbor Drive, San Diego, CA 92103-8414, USA.

BARRETT Warrick Lee, b. 17 Oct 1949, Ft Dix, New Jersey, USA. Physician. m. Gail D Nash, 24 June 1978, 2 sons, 1 daughter. Education: AB, St Louis University, 1971; MD, Cornell University Medical College, 1975; Internship, Montefiore University Hospital, 1976; Residency, US Air Force Medical Center, Ohio, 1979. Appointments: Director, Hospital Services, USAF Hospital, Greenland, 1975-76; Family

Practice Resident, Staff Physician, USAF Medical Center, Wright-Patterson AFB, Ohio, 1977-81; Chairman, Department of Family Medicine & Primary Care, USAF Medical Center, Wright-Patterson AFB, 1980-81; Occupational Medical Director, United Technologies Essex, Ft Wayne, 1981-88; Staff Physician, Methodist Occupational Health Centers, Indianapolis, 1988-89; Private Practice, Occupational & Family Medicine, Indianapolis, 1989-90; Mobilization Augmentee Physician, Persian Gulf Crisis & War, 1990-91; Occupational Medical Director, Navistar International Engine Assembly Plant & Foundry, Indianapolis, 1991-93; Medical Director, Subaru-Isuzu Automotive Inc, Lafayette, 1993-. Memberships: American Medical Association; National Medical Association; American College of Occupational & Environmental Medicine; American Academy of Family Physicians; Indiana State Medical Association; Indianapolis Medical Society; Aesculapian Medical Society. Hobbies: Recreational Sports; Writing. Address: 5500 State Road 38 East, Lafayette, IN 47905-9405, USA.

BARRINS Phyllis C, b. 4 Apr 1921, Dyer, Indiana, USA. Medical Hypnotherapist. m. Edward F Barrins, 19 Sept 1942, 3 sons, 4 daughters. Education: RN Diploma; BA Sociology; BA Social Sciences; BS, Parapsychology; PhD, Clinical psychology; PhD, Clinical Hypnotherapy; MA, Sociology. Appointments: Instructor, St Johns University; Instructor, University of Phoenix; Psychologist & Nurse, Saddleback Ranch School; Freelance Writer; Medical Hypnotherapist; Researcher in Reincarnation; Mentor, Prescott College. Publications: Hypnosis: New Tool in Nursing Practice, Editor, Co-author, 1982; Author: The Birthday Present, 1992; Hee Haw Is His Name, 1992; Contributor of children's stories, articles, pamphlets. Memberships: American Association of Suicidology; American Association of University Professors; Federation of American Scientists; American Society for Psychological Research. Address: 2023 East Adams Street, Tucson, AZ 85719, USA.

BARRON Kevin, b. 21 Apr 1929, St Johns, Newfoundland, Canada. Neurologist. m. Elizabeth Grossmann, 14 June 1956, 1 son, 1 daughter. Education: MD. Appointments: Chief, Neurology Service, VAH-Hines, 1964-69; Chairman, Neurology Department, Albany Medical College, 1969-93; Professor of Neurology and Psychiatry, Northwestern Medical School, 1967-69; Professor of Neurology and Pathology, Albany Medical College. Publications: Contributor of over 150 articles in refereed journals and book chapters. Honours: Honorary Fulbright fellow, 1976; Councillor, Founding Member, Society Experimental Neuropathology; Alpha Omega Alpha, 1989; Councillor, American Neurological Association. Memberships: American Association Neuropathologists; Canadian Association Neuropathology. Hobbies: Hiking; Classical Music. Address: NY, USA.

BARRON (Solomon) Leonard, b. 29 Sep 1926, London, England. Obstetrician and Gynaecologist. m. Eleanor Evans, 9 Sep 1959, 1 son, 1 daughter. Education: MB BS, St Thomas' Hospital Medical School, 1944-49; FRCS(England); FRCOG. Appointments: Senior Registrar, St Thomas and Queen Charlotte Hospital; Consultant Obstetrician, Prince of Wales Hospital, Tottenham, London, 1962-67; Consultant Obstetrician and Gynaecologist, Royal Victoria Infirmary and Princess Mary Maternity Hospital, Newcastle-upon-Tyne; retired; Chairman, Freeman Hospital NHS Trust. Publications: Obstetrical Epidemiology, Co-author, 1983; Issues in Fetal Medicine, Co-author, 1994; Contributor of numerous medical articles. Honour: Galton Lecturer, 1992. Memberships: Blair Bell Society; Society for Social Medicine; North of England Medico-Legal Society. Hobbies: Choral Singing; Golf. Address: 34 Lindisfarne Close, Jesmond, Newcastle-upon-Tyne NE2 2HT, England.

BARSKY Howard E, b. 15 June 1924, Philadelphia, Pennsylvania, USA. Physician; Allergist. m. Shirley Kofsky, 23 Nov 1950, 2 sons, 1 daughter. Education: Pre-med, University of Perinsylvania; DO, Philadelphia College of Osteopathic Medicine; Certified, American Board of Allergy and Immunology. Appointments: Clinical Associate Professor, Temple University School of Medicine. Publications: Contributor of numerous articles including: Seasonal Allergic Rhinitis, 1975; Serum Complement Levels: Their Diagnosis and Prognostic Implications, 1977; Bronchial Asthma, 1977; Complement: Its Properties, Activation and Activities, 1978; Anaphylaxis, 1978; Anaphylactiod Reactions Associated with Infusion of Radiographic Contrast Media, 1980; Contact Dermatitis, 1981; Allergic Contact Dermatitis: Patch-Testing, 1982; Albuterol (Salbutamol), 1982; Hybridomas: An Immunologic Breakthrough, 1982; Stinging Insect Allergy-Avoidance, Identification,

and Treatment, 1987; Asthma and Pregnancy, 1991. Address: 202 Parkview Road, Cheltenham, PA 19012, USA.

BARTH Robert Henry, b. 31 October 1944, Newark, New Jersey, USA. Physician (Nephrologist). m. Elettra Nerbosi, 10 May 1976. Education: BA, Chemistry, Cornell University, Ithaca, New York, 1967; Laurea in Medicine and Surgery, cum laude, Universita' degli Studi di Bologna, Bologna, Italy, 1976. Appointments: Assistant Professor of Medicine, Associate Director of Baumritter Kidney Center, Albert Einstein College of Medicine, Bronx, New York, 1983-86; Associate Professor of Clinical Medicine, SUNY Health Science Center, Brooklyn; Chief, Hemodialysis, VA Medical Center, Brooklyn, New York. Publications: Dialysis by the numbers: The false promise of Kt/V, 1989; Hematuria, 1992, 1995; Dialysis, 1992; Urea modeling and Kt/V: A critical appraisal, 1993; High-flux hemodialysis: Overcoming the tyranny of time, 1993; Short dialysis: Big trouble in a small package, 1994; Pros and cons of short, high efficiency, and high flux dialysis, 1995. Memberships: American Society for Artificial Internal Organs; American Society of Nephrology; International Society for Peritoneal Dialysis; International Society of Nephrology; National Kidney Foundation; New York Society of Nephrology; Physicians for a National Health Plan. Hobbies: Jazz; Hiking; Skiing; Computers. Address: VA Medical Center, 800 Poly Place, Brooklyn, NY 11209, USA.

BARTON Gail Melinda, b. 20 Apr 1937, Worcester, MA, USA. Physician. m. Duncan John Kretovich (div), 1 daughter. Education: MD; MPH; AB. Appointments: Assistant Professor, University Michigan; Staff Psychiatrist, Washtenaw County Community Mental Health Center; Director of Research & Development, Department of Mental Health; Associate Professor, University Michigan; Medical Director, Howard Mental Health Center, Burlington; Associate Clinical Professor, University Vermont; Professor of Psychiatry, Dartmouth Medical School, Lebanon New Hampshire and Director of Mental Hygiene Clinic, Veterans Affairs Medical Center, White River Junction, Vermont. Publications: Mental Health Administration: Principles and Practice; Ethics and the Law for Mental Health Administrators; Handbook of Emergency Psychiatry for Clinical Administrators. Memberships: American College of Psychiatrists; American College of Mental Health Administrators. Hobbies: Photography; Canoeing; Painting; Basketmaking; Hiking. Address: Department of Psychiatry, Veterans Affairs Medical Center, White River Junction, VT 05001, USA.

BARTON Walter Earl, b. 29 July 1906, Oakpark, Illinois, USA. Physician. m. Elsa Benson, 2 July 1932, dec, 2 sons, 1 daughter. Education: BS, University of Illinois; MD, College of Medicine, University of Illinois; Neurology, National Hospital, London. Appointments: Lieutenant Colonel, US Army Medical Corps, 1942-45; Superintendent, Boston State Hospital, 1945-63; Medical Director, American Psychiatric Association, 1963-74; VA Hospital White River, Vermont, 1974-77; Professor of Psychiatry, Active Emeritus, Dartmouth Medical School. Publications: Author of 10 books including: Administration in Psychiatry, 1962; Mental Health Administration Principles and Practice, 1983; Ethics and Law in Mental Health Administration, 1984; Contributor of over 180 articles in scientific journals. Honours include: Salmon Medal; Distinctive Service Award; President's Commendation, 1994. Memberships: President, Group for Advancement of Psychiatry; Fellow, American College of Physicians; Fellow, American College of Mental Health Administration; President, American Psychiatric Association; President, American Board of Neurology and Psychiatry; FAPA; AMA. Address: RR1 Box 188, Hartland, VT 05048, USA.

BARTZ Volker Walter Paul, b. 22 May 1951, Jugenheim, Germany. Company President. m. Heidemarie Bartz, 17 Oct 1984, 1 son, 3 daughters. Education: MBA. Appointments: International Marketing Director; Currently President, Nephromed Bartz GmbH, Hüttenberg. Honours: Inventor, several patents. Membership: International Society of Peritoneal Dialysis. Hobbies: Soccer; Tennis; Family. Address: Sudetenstrasse 19, D-35625 Hüttenberg, Germany.

BARUA Arabinda, b. 1 Jan 1934, Chittagong, Bangladesh. Gynaecologist. m. 12 Mar 1962, 2 s, 1 d. Education: MBBS, Dhaka; MRCOG, London; FRCOG, London. Appointments: Professor of Obstetrics & Gynaecology, Rajshahi Medical College; Professor of Obstetrics & Gynaecology, Dhaka Medical College; Professor of Obstetrics & Gynaecology, Chittagong Medical College, Bangladesh; Now Retired. Publications: Author, Obstetrics & Gynaecology - Made Easy, 1994. Memberships: Bangladesh Medical Association; Bangladesh Medical College Teachers Association; Fellow, Royal

College of Obstetricians & Gynaecologists, UK. Hobbies: Music. Address: 4 Surson Road, Chittagong, Bangladesh.

BARULLI Sharon, b. 10 June 1948, Hartford, USA. Care Plan Coordinator. Appointments: Enterostomal Therapist. Address: 7972 SE 97th Way, Okeechobee, FL 394974, USA. 2.

BASCH-KÁHRE Eva Johanna, b. 24 Mar 1934, Vienna, Austria. Psychoanalyst. m. Björn Kåhre, 30 Dec 1955, 2 s. Education: Qualified and authorized as Doctor, 1968; Qualified as Psychoanalyst, 1974; Authorized as Psychiatrist, 1976. Career: Psychoanalyst, 1974-; Head, Institute of Psychotherapy, Riksföreningen Psychoterapilentrum; Currently, Psychoanalyst, Teacher in Psychotherapy, Supervisor in Psychotherapy. Publications include: Several papers on masculinity and femininity, thinking, psychosomatics and religion in Swedish journals, 1979-; Patterns of Thinking, in International Journal of Psychoanalysis, 1985; Forms of the Oedipus Complex, in Scandinavian Psychoanalytical Review, 1987; Female and Male Patterns, in Swedish, 1990. Honour: Honorary Member, National Society Psychotherapy Centre, Sweden. Membership: Swedish Psychoanalytical Society. Hobbies: Reading; Theatre; Music; Hiking; Travel. Address: Luntmakargatan 89, S-11351 Stockholm, Sweden.

BASH Roger L, b. 27 Feb 1947, Brooklyn, New York, USA. Neuropsychologist. m. MargoT Yunik, 14 June 1987, 1 son. Education: MA, Northeastern Illinois University, 1975; MSW, Florida University, 1985; PhD, Florida University, 1987. Appointments: Coordinator of Neuropsychology, New Medico, Philadelphia; Director of Psychology/Neuropsychology, Treasure Coast Rehabilitation Hospital, Florida, 1991-. Publications: Supervision, coaching and job placement in rehabilitation, 1985; Fundraising in career development, 1986; Revitalizing a career course: The gender roles infusion, 1988. Honours: Teaching Assistantship, UniversityIllinois, Chicago, 1970-71; Fellowship, Florida University College of Education, 1982-83; Research Assistantship, Flordia University, 1983-84; University Scholarship, Florida University, 1987; Presidents Award, Florida University Student Health & Advocacy Response Team, 1987; Outstanding Contribution to Internship Program, Florida University, 1987; Certificate of Successful Completion, 1988, 1989. Memberships: American Psychological Association; National Academy of Neuropsychology; Society for the Exploration of Psychotherapy Integration; International Association of Cognitive Psychotherapy; American Pain Society; American Academy of Pain Management; American Board of Behavioral Psychology. Address: Treasure Coast Rehabilitation Hospital, 1600 37th Street, Vero Beach, FL 32960, USA.

BASKETT Peter John Firth, b. 26 July 1934, Belfast, Ireland. Consultant Anaesthetist. Education: BA; MB; BCh; BAO; MRCP; FFARCS. Appointments: Consultant Anaesthetist, Frenchay Hospital & Royal Infirmary, Bristol, England; Senior Clinical Lecturer, Anaesthesia, University of Bristol, England. Publications: Medicine for Disasters, 1988; Immediate Care, 1972; Resuscitation Handbook, 1989. Memberships: Chairman, European Resuscitation Council; Immediate Past President, World Association for Emergency & Disasters; Immediate Past President, Association of Anaesthetists of Great Britian & Ireland; Council of Royal College of Anaesthetists. Honours: Member, Australian Society of Anaesthetists; Elected Member of the Royal College of Physicians; Award, British Association for Immediate Cases, 1990. Hobbies: Sport; Rugby; Gardening. Address: Department of Anaesthesia, Frenchay Hospital, Bristol BS16 1LE, England.

BASMAJIAN John V, b. 21 Jun 1921, Constantinople. Medical Scientist. m. Dora Lucas, 4 Oct 1947, 1 s, 2 d. Education: MD with Honors; Order of Canada; Order of Ontario; FRCP(C); FRCP & S, Glasgow; FACA; FSBM; FABMR; F Austral Fac RM; Hon Dip St LC. Appointments: Lecturer to Professor, University of Toronto; Professor & Head, Anatomy Department Queens University, Canada; Professor & Director, Emory University, Rehabilitation Center, Atlanta; Professor of Medicine, McMaster University, Canada; Director, East Seal Research Insitute. Publications: Author/Editor of more than 350 Scientific Articles, 59 Books; Series Editor of the 22 Volume, Rehabilitation Medicine Library; Producer of Motion Picture Films. Honours include: Officer of The Order of Canada; The Order of Ontario, Henry Gray Laureate of the American Association of Anatomists; Honorary Fellowship, Royal College of Physicians & Surgeons of Glasgow; Golden Key Recipient, Congress of Rehabilitation Medicine, 1977; Starr Gold Medal for Medical Research, Toronto, 1967; Kabakjian Award, New York 1967; Fellow, Royal College of Physicians and Surgeons, Canada, 1979.

Memberships: include, American Association of Anatomy; Biofeedback Society of America; International Society of Electrophysics Kinesiology. Hobbies: Travel; Gardening; Music. Address: Rehabilitation Centre, Chedoke-McMasters Hospital, Box 2000, Hamilton, Ontario, Canada, L8N 2Z5.

BASS Natalia N, b. 30 Nov 1956, Borisov, Belorussia. Physicist; Radiologist. m. Yury Bass, 22 June 1979, 2 sons. Education: Polytechnical Institute, Odessa, Ukraine, 1979. Appointments: Student, 1974; Medical Engineer, 1979; Physicist, Radiologist, Moldova Oncological Institute, 1985. Memberships: Moldova Association of Medical Physicists, 1992; IOMP. Hobbies: Travel; Reading Books. Address: Alba-Iulia Str 10 Ap 5, Kishinev 277039, Moldova.

BASSINGTHWAIGHT James Bucklin, b. 10 Sep 1929, Toronto, Canada. Pysiologist; Educator; Medical Researcher. m. Joan Elizabeth Graham, 18 June 1955, 1 son, 4 daughters. Education: BA, 1951, MD, 1955, University of Toronto; Postgraduate, Medical School, London, 1957-58; PhD, Mayo Graduate School of Medicine, University of Minnesota, USA, 1964. Appointments include: Intern, Toronto General Hospital, 1955-56; Physician, International Nickel Company, Sudbury and Matheson, Ontario, 1956-57; House Physician, Hammersmith Hospital, London, England; Teaching Assistant, Physiology, University of Minnesota, Minneapolis, 1961-62; Fellow, Mayo Graduate School of Medicine, Rochester, 1958-64; Instructor, 1964-67, Assistant Professor, 1967-69, Associate Professor, 1972; Visiting Professor of Pharmacology Institute, University of Bern, Switzerland, 1970-71; Associate Professor of Bioengineering, University of Minnesota, 1972-75; Professor of Physiology, Bioengineering, Mayo Graduate School of Medicine, 1973-75; Professor of Medicine, 1975; Professor of Bioengineering, Radiology and Biomathematics, University of Washington, Seattle, 1975-; Director, Centre for Bioengineering, 1975-80; Visiting Professor of Medicine and Physiology, McGill University, 1979-81. Publications: Contributor of articles in professional journals. Honours include: NIH Research Career Development Award, 1964-74; NIH Merit Award, 1986-; Louis and Artur Lucian Award, McGill University, 1979; Faculty Achievement Award for Outstanding Research, University of Washington College of Engineering. Memberships include: AAAS; American Physcological Society, 1965-; Biomedical Engineering Society, 1969; Muscularatory Society; ISOTT; American Heart Association, Council on Circulation, 1976-. Address: University of Washington Centre for Bioengineering, Box 35-7962, Seattle, WA 98195-7962, USA.

BASTOS Paulo de Novaes Telles de Faria Correa, b. 24 Dec 1957, Mozambique. Dentist. m. Maria Laura Costa, 18 July 1992, 1 child. Education: Medico Dentista and Bachelor of Biology, University of Oporto, Portugal. Appointments: University Monitor, Genetics Department, BioMedical Teaching Institute, University of Oporto; Currently Hospital Assistant and Private Practitioner. Memberships: Portuguese Dental Association; European Orthodontic Association; Portuguese Dento-Facial Association; Spanish Orthodontic Association; The American Prosthodontic Society. Hobbies: Numismatics; Old Portuguese furniture. Address: Rua Pedro Escobar 174-3E, 4100 Porto, Portugal.

BASU Shishta, b. 12 Oct 1951, Arrah, Bihar, India. Medical Doctor. m. Sitangshu Baso, 28 Feb 1929, 1 son. Education: MBBS; MS; MRCOG. Appointments: Medical Officer, Patna University, India, 1977-78; Civil Assistant Surgeon, Bihar State Health Services, 1980-83; Senior House Officer, Department of Obstetrics, Derby City Hospital, England, 1984; Senior House Officer, Dudley Road Hospital, Birmingham, England, 1984-88; Registrar, Dudley Road Hospital, 1984-89; Senior Consultant, Head of the Department, Narinder Mohan Hospital, Ghaziabad, 1990-92; Senior Consultant, Head of the Department, Jaipur Golden Hospital, New Delhi, 1991-. Publications: Inhibitory Effect of Amniotic Fluid on the Growth of Common Micro-organisms, 1980; The Rational use of Coagulation Studies in Obstetrics & Gynaecology, 1988; Alternative Vacuum supplies for Ventouse Deliveries, 1989; Molybdenum Co-factor Deficiency - A cause of Neonatal Death, 1989. Honours: National Merit Scholarship, Government of India, 1968; Gold Medal in Physiology, 1972; Senior Research Fellowship, Council of Scientific & Industrial Research, 1978; Hamilton Bailey Prize, 1988. Memberships: Life Member, Federation of Obstetricians & Gynaecologists; BPNI; Royal College of Obstetricians & Gynaecologists. Hobbies: Astrology; Painting; Sewing & Embroidery; Music. Address: c/o Dr N L Nadda, 109 C-13 Sector 3, Rohini, Delhi 110085, India.

BATES Andrew John Paul, b. 6 Mar 1965, Essex, England. Forensic Psychologist. Education: BA, Honours, Psychology, Exeter University, 1986; MSc Applied Criminological Psychology, London University, 1990; Currently pursuing PhD in Psychology, Loughborough University, 1993-. Career: Higher Psychologist, Feltham YOI, Middlesex, England; Currently,Senior Psychologist, HMP Grendon, England. Membership: Chartered Forensic Psychologist. Hobbies: Writing; Theatre; Cinema; Music. Address: 74B Kennington Road, Oxford, OX1 5PB, England.

BATES Jason Hamilton Tunstall, b. 22 May 1956, England. Biomedical Engineering Professor. Education: BSc, Honours, Physics; PhD, Medicine; DSc. Appointments: Associate Professor of Medicine and Biomedical Engineering, Meakins-Christie Laboratories, McGill University, Montreal, Quebec, Canada. Publications: Contributor of over 90 scientific articles in professional journals. Memberships: IEEE; American Physiological Society. Hobbies: Karate; Music. Address: Meakins-Christie Laboratories, McGill University, Montreal, Quebec H2X 2P2, Canada.

BATWALA Ignatius James, b. 10 Oct 1936, Uganda. Medical Practitioner. m. Ida Nanteza, 30 Dec 1967, 2 sons, 5 daughters. Education: MB ChB; MRCPG; FRCOG, 1987. Appointments: Medical Officer, Senior Registrar Special Grade, Consultant, Senior Consultant Obstetrician and Gynaecology, Mulago Hospital, Uganda; Currently Private Practitioner, Kampala; Deputy Minister, Uganda Government, 1986. Publications: Anaemics in Pregnancy, 1976; Cephalo Pelvic Disproportion in Uganda, 1982. Memberships: Uganda Medical Association; Uganda Association of Obstetricians and Gynaecologists. Hobby: Lawn tennis. Address: Fiona Clinic, PO Box 8349, Kampala, Uganda.

BAU Li-ling, b. 21 Sept 1930, Peking, China. Ophthalmologist. m. 1952, 1 daughter. Education: Pre-medical Department, Yanjing University, Peking, 1947-50; Peking Union Medical College, 1950-55. Appointments: Resident, Chief Resident, 1955-58, Deputy Visiting Physician, 1958-64, Ophthalmology Department, Peking Union Medical College Hospital; Deputy Visiting Physician (Associate Professor), 1964-78, Vice-Chief Physician, 1978-85, 1986-87, Chief Physician, Professor, 1988-94, Ophthalmology Department, 1st Teaching Hospital of Shaanxi Medical College, Taiyuan; Vice-Chief Physician, in charge Uveitis Clinic, Zhongshan Ophthalmic Center, Canton, 1985-86. Publications: 22 in ophthalmological field including: Uveo-encephalitis treated by combination of traditional Chinese and Western medicine, 1986; Long-term follow-up of sympathetic ophthalmia treated by combination of Chinese traditional and Western medicine, 1988; A family with Fabry's disease: Ocular manifestations and transmission electron microscopic examination of a skin lesion biopsy, 1990; Combination of traditional Chinese and Western medicine in treating acute posterior multifocal placoid pigment epitheliopathy, 1993. Honours: 2 Awards for Articles, Shaanxi Province, 1990; 2 Awards for Best Papers, Chinese and American Organising Committee, Grand Prize Contest for Best Papers on World Traditional Medicine, 1994. Memberships: Chinese Ophthalmology Association; Association of Combination of Traditional Chinese and Western Medicine; Chinese Genetics Association. Hobbies: Tennis; English translation (amateur medical English interpreter and editor of several Chinese medical journals). Address: 43 Xin Si Hu Tong, Dong Si 12 Lane, Beijing 100007, China.

BAUER Philip Joseph, b. 16 Sept 1940, Chicago, Illinois, USA. Dental Surgeon. m. Elizabeth Bauer, 2 June 1962, 2 sons, 1 daughter. Education: BA, University of Connecticut; DMD, Tufts School of Dental and Oral Surgery,; Graduate Certificate in Endocontics, Columbia School of Dental and Oral Surgery; Diplomate, American Board of Endodontics. Appointments: Adjunct Professor, Clinical Dentistry, Columbia University School of Dental and Oral Surgery, New York City; Staff, Outpatient Dental Department, Stamford Hospital, Stamford, Connecticut; Currently Endodontist and Staff, Dental Department, Greenwich Hospital, Greenwich, Connecticut. Honours: Fellow, Pierne Faucamel Academy. Memberships: Connecticut State Dental Association; American Dental Association; American Association of Endodontists; Member, Past President; Alpha Omega Fraternity, Fairfield Alumni Chapter; Stamford Dental Society; Connecticut Association of Endodontists; Greenwich Dental Society; Excellence in Endodontic Study Group. Hobbies: Biking; Tennis. Address: 125 Strawberry Hill Avenue, Stamford, CT 06902, USA.

BAUER Rudolph, b. 28 Sept 1942. Psychologist. Education: PhD; Diplomate, Clinical Psychology. Appointments: University of Maryland Medical School, USA; Director of Training, Gertolt Training Centre, Washington DC. Publications: Numerous. Memberships: APA; ASCH. Address: 1834 Swann Street NW, WEashington DC 20009, USA.

BAUMANN Klaus Ingo, b. 7 May 1945, Copenhagen, Denmark. Physiologist. m. Anna Tang, 25 Dec 1981. Education: Study of Medicine, Hamburg and Tübingen, Germany, 1964-70; MD, 1970, Habilitation in Physiology, 1978, University of Hamburg. Appointments: Lecturer in Physiology, 1972-77, Senior Lecturer in Occupational Medicine, 1977-81, University of Hamburg, Germany; Currently Reader, Department of Physiology, Chinese University, Shatin, Hong Kong. Publications: About 100 papers in Journal of Physiology, Pflügers Archiv, International Journal of Occupational Health, Brain Research, others. Memberships: American Physiological Society; German Physiological Society; Physiological Society, UK. Hobby: Sailing. Address: Department of Physiology, Chinese University, Shatin, New Territories, Hong Kong.

BAUMANN Ralf, b. 28 June 1957, Aachen, Germany. Obstetrician and Gynaecologist. m. Christine Arnemann, 5 Aug 1988, 1 son, 1 daughter. Education includes: Dr Med cum laude, 1983; Specialist Examination; Foreign Medical Graduate Examination in the Medical Sciences, USA; Research Fellow, Oxford University, 1989-90; MRCOG, 1990-. Appointments: Senior House Officer, General Surgery, Jewish Hospital, Berlin, 1983; Senior House Officer, Registrar, Obstetrics, Gynaecology, Krankenhaus am Urban, Berlin, 1983-89; Senior House Officer, Research Fellow, John Radcliffe and Churchill Hospitals, Oxford, England, 1987-90; Senior Registrar, Clemens Hospital, Münster, Germany, 1992-. Publications: Co-author: Prospective comparison of videopelviscopy with laparotomy for ectopic pregnancy, 1991; Experience with the first 250 endometrial resections, 1991. Memberships: Deutsche Gesellschaft für Gynäkologie und Geburtshilfe; Arbeitsgemeinschaft für Gynäkologische Endoskopie. Hobbies: Music (piano and violoncello); Swimming. Address: Am Kämpken 33, D-48163 Münster, Germany.

BAUMANN Robert J, b. 22 Oct 1940, Chicago, Illinois, USA. Child Neurologist. m. Judith R Kravitz, 11 Oct 1964, 1 son, 2 daughters. Education: BS magna cum laude, Tufts University, 1961; MD, Case Western Reserve University, 1965; Resident in Paediatrics, Neurology, Child Neurology, 1965-69, Fellow in Child Neurology, 1971-72, University of Chicago. Appointments: Captain, USAF Medical Corps, 1969-71; Assistant Professor, 1972-78, Associate Professor, 1989-92, Professor of Neurology and Paediatrics, 1992-, University of Kentucky, Lexington. Honours: Neuroepidemiology Consultant to Commission on Control of Epilepsy, Washington DC, 1976, to Instituto de Investigaciones, Facultad de Ciencias Medicas, Universidad Central del Ecuador, 1991, to American Academy of Pediatrics, 1991-. Memberships: American College of Epidemiology; American Academy of Neurology; American Academy of Pediatrics; Professors of Child Neurology; Child Neurology Society. Hobbies: Gardening; Travel. Address: Department of Neurology, University of Kentucky, 800 Rose Street, Lexington, KY 40536-0084, USA.

BAUMBACH H Dale, b. 13 Sept 1944, Lodi, California, USA. Neuropsychologist. Education: BA. 1969, MA, 1973, PhD, Psychology, 1975, University of California, Riverside; MA, Sociology, Loma Linda University, 1970; Clinical Psychology, Department of Psychology, University of Missouri, Kansas, 1970-71; Postdoctoral fellow in neurology, Stanford University School of Medicine, 1975-79. Appointments include: President, Sierra Institute for Medical and Neuropsychology Incorporated, 1983-; Private Practice in Clinical Neuropsychology,; COnsultant in Clinical Neuropsychology, San Joaquin County Mental Health Services, San Joaquin General Hospital, Stokton, California, 1982-; Consultant in Clinical Neuropsychology, Kentfield Medical Hospital, 1985-; Consultant in Clinical Neuropsychology, St Joseph's Parkside Hospital, Stockton, California, 1989-. Honours include: National Eye Institute Postdoctoral Research Fellowship, 1976, Postdoctoral Fellowship, 1975, NIH, Stanford University School of Medicine; Chancellor's Patient Fund Award for Dissertation Research, 1974, National Science Foundation Research Fellowship, 1968, University of California, Riverside. Memberships include: American Psychological Association; International Association for the Study of Pain; Behavioral Neurology International, Charter Member; California State Psychological Association; Institute for the Advancement of Health; American Association for the Advancement of

Science. Hobbies: Classical music; Skiing. Address: 1222 Monaco Court, Suite 17, Stockton, CA 95207, USA.

BAURES Mary Margaret, b. 13 Sept 1947, St Petersburg, Florida, USA. Psychotherapist. div. Education: BA, University of Florida, 1969; MA, 1976, EdM, 1984, Boston University; Certificate, Advanced Study in Human Development, Harvard University, 1986; Neuropsychology Intern, MEEC Clinic, Northshore Children's Hospital, Salem, Massachusetts College, 1990-91; PsyD, Antioch New England, 1994; Appointments: Instructor, Emerson College, Boston, Massachusetts, 1981-86; Counselor, Beverly (Massachusetts) Hospital, 1984-86; Emergency Service Clinician, Center for Mental Health, Waltham, Massachusetts, 1987-91; Psychotherapist, Seacoast Counseling, Danvers, Massachusetts, 1989-; Faculty, Department of Psychology, Adult Degree Programme, Vermont College, 1989-; Founder, Director, Boycott Anorexic Marketing. Publications: Undaunted Spirits: Portraits of Recovery from Trauma, 1994; Numerous articles in professional journals and magazines include: Somerset Maugham - Brilliant, Wealthy, Insufferable, 1992; Letting go of bitterness and hate, 1994. Memberships: International Society of Traumatic Stress; Harvard Faculty Club. Hobby: Oil and watercolour painting. Address: Seacoast Counseling, 85 Constitution Lane, Danvers, MA 01923-3627, USA.

BAYAT Fawzia, b. 11 Feb 1955, Stanger, South Africa. Radiographer. Education: Diploma in Radiography (Diagnostics), KEH, 1975; Diploma in Radiography (Therapy), Groote Schuur Hospital, 1978; BA, University of South Africa, 1981. Appointments: Diagnostic Radiographer, 1973; Therapy Radiographer, 1977; Diagnostic Radiographer, 1983; Currently Senior Radiographer and CT Scanner. Memberships: South African Medical and Dental Council; Society of Radiographers of South Africa. Hobbies: Reading; Tapestry making; Culinary skills. Address: PO Box 37162, Overport 4067, South Africa.

BAYES-DE-LUNA Antoni, b. 11 Mar 1936, Vic, Spain. MD. m. M Clara Genis, 2 Sept 1963, 1 s, 4 d. Education: Professor of Cardiology, University Autonomous Barcelona; Doctor of Medicine; President Elect, International Society Federation Cardiology. Appointments: Chief, Cardiac Department, Hospital Sant Pau, Barcelona. Publications: Papers in Cardiological Journals and Books on Cardiology and Clinical Electro Cardiography. Honours: Medico Delaño Espana, 1991, 1994; Catauna, 1992. Memberships: American College of Cardiology; European Society of Cardiology. Address: Department of Cardiology, Hospital Sta Creu i Sant Pau, Av S Antoni M Claret 167, E-08025 Barcelona, Spain.

BAZALGETTE Richard Anthony, b. 1 Oct 1938, Hamadan, Iran. Osteopath. m. Mary Bridget Gillespie, 1 June 1993, 2 sons. Education: DO, British School of Osteopathy, 1964; MRO. Appointments: Private Practice; Past Council Member, Osteopathic Association of Great Britain; Editor, monthly newsletter; Past Council Member, General Council and Register of Osteopaths; Past Honorary Treasurer. Honour: JP. Memberships: OAGB; GCRO; Magistrates Association. Hobbies: Squash; Tennis; Golf; Walking. Address: 1 Springfield Crescent, Parkstone, Poole, Dorset BH14 0LL, England.

BAZILE Emilio, b. 1 May 1946, L'Azile, Haiti. Psychiatrist (Geriatrics). m. Josette Bazile, 21 Aug 1976, 1 son, 2 daughters. Education: MD; LMCC; CSPQ; FRCP; VPT; Board Certified Specialist, Canada; ECGMG, USA. Appointments: Head of Psychogeriatric Programme, Pierre Janet Hospital, Quebec, Canada; Director, Psychogeriatric Inpatient Consultation Service, Head of Consultation Liaison, Ottawa General Hospital, Ottawa, Ontario; Currently Assistant Professor of Psychiatry, Researcher on Dementia, Ottawa University. Memberships: Canadian Academy of Geriatric Psychiatry; Fédération des Médecins Specialistes du Quebec; Association of Haytian Physicians; Canadian Psychiatric Association; New York Academy of Sciences; Royal College of Physicians and Surgeons of Canada; American Association for Geriatric Psychiatry; American Association of Geriatric Medicine. Hobbies: Soccer; Computers. Address: 5827 Knights Dr, Manotic, Ontario, Canada K4M 1K2.

BEAKEY James Emerson, b. 24 Nov 1965, North Carolina, USA. Healthcare Researcher. Education:BA, Psychology, East Carolina University, 1988; MA, Applied Social Science, Healthcare Research, Boston University, 1992; MBA Graduate Certificate, New Hampshire College, 1993. Appointments: Research Assistant; Research Analyst; Senior Researcher. Publications: Public Relations Practices and Management Case Studies and Problems, Contributing Author, 5th

Edition. Memberships: SPSSI; Society for the Psychological Study of Social Issues. Hobbies: Sailing; Skiing. Address: 44 Dumas Avenue, Hampton, NH 03842, USA.

BEANLANDS Donald Stewart, b. 27 Dec 1932, Halifax, Nova Scotia, Canada. Cardiologist. m. Rhona Beanlands, 3 sons, 1 daughter. Education: MDCM, Dalhousie University; Postgraduate training, Internal Medicine, Cardiology, Dalhousie University and University of Toronto; FRCPC; FACC. Appointments include: Toronto Western Hospital; Head, Division of Cardiopulmonary Medicine. Ottawa Civic Hospital; Chief, Division of Cardiology, University of Ottawa, 1975-; Deputy Director-General, University of Ottawa Heart Institute. Publications: Author or co-author, more than 100 published papers. Honours: Gold Medallist, Dalhousie University; PAIRO Award as Outstanding Teacher, University of Ottawa School of Medicine; Annual Lecture, Canadian Cardiovascular Society, 1989; Dupont Lecture, 1992; Award of Excellence, Faculty of Medicine, University of Ottawa Awards Night, 1993. Memberships: More than 40 national and international medical associations. Address: Division of Cardiology, University of Ottawa Heart Institute H202, Ottawa Civic Hospital, 1053 Carling Avenue, Ottawa, Ontario, Canada K1Y 4E9.

BEATTIE Robert Bryan, b. 15 Dec 1959, Kaduna, Nigeria. Obstetrician. m. Margaret Jean McDowell, 2 d. Education: MD, 1988; MRCOG. Appointments: Fellow, Maternal Fetal Medicine, Toronto Perinatal Complex, Toronto, Canada; Lecturer, Fetal Medicine, University of Birmingham, UK; Consultant in Fetal Medicine, University Hospital of Wales, Cardiff, UK. Publications: include, Intrauterine Growth Retardation and Prediction of Perinatal Distress by Doppler Ultrasound, 1987; Placental Blood Flow Assessed as an Antenatal Screening Tool for IUFGR and Poor Fetal Outcome, 1988; A Compound Analysis of Umbilical Artery Velocimetry in Low Risk Pregnancy, 1992; Identical Twins with Trisomy 21 Discordant for Exomphalos, 1993; Umbilical Artery Doppler Ultrasonography as a Screening Tool, 1992. Memberships: American Institute of Ultrasound in Medicine; Blair Bell Research Society; British Medical Association; British Medical Ultrasound Society; Birmingham and Midlands Obstetrics & Gynaecological Society; British Obstetric Computer Society; Irish Perinatal Society; Nuffield Obstetrics and Gynaecological Society; Society of Obstetricians & Gynaecologists of Canada; Society of Perinatal Obstetricians; Ulster Obstetric & Gynaecological Society; Welsh Obstetric & Gynaecological Society. Hobbies: Computing; Water Skiing. Address: University Hospital of Wales, Heath Park, Cardiff, CF4 4XW, Wales.

BEATUS Ben L Jr, b. 21 Sept 1936, Memphis, Tennessee, USA. Physician (Psychiatry). m. Sandra Loskovitz, 21 Dec 1958, 2 sons. Education: MD, University of Tennessee, Memphis, 1960; Internship, St Joseph Hospital, Memphis, 1961; Psychiatric Residency, University of Kansas Medical Center, 1962-64; Certified, American Board of Psychiatry and Neurology, 1969. Appointments: Captain, Chief of Psychiatry, USAF, HAFB, Florida, 1965-67; Staff Psychiatrist, Memphis Mental Health Institute, 1967-69; Private practice, part-time, 1967-69, full-time, 1969-; Clinical Instructor, 1967-71, Clinical Assistant Professor, 1971-, University of Tennessee; Consulting Staff, several hospitals. Memberships: American Psychiatric Association, West Tennessee Chapter President, 1975-76; American Medical Association; Tennesse Medical Association; Southern Medical Association; Memphis and Shelby County Medical Society; American Geriatric Society; American Association for Geriatric Psychiatry; Academy of Psychosomatic Medicine; Medical Advisory Board, Alzheimer's Disease Association, Memphis Chapter. Hobbies: Skiing; Tennis; Sailing; Travel. Address: 55 Humphreys Center, Suite 300, Memphis, TN 38120, USA.

BEATY Barry Lee, b. 11 July 1950, New Orleans, USA. Medical Doctor. m. Rita Mack, 19 Mar 1985. Education: BS, Biology, Tarleton State University, 1973; MS, Animal Physiology, Texas A & M University, 1975; DO, North Texas Health Science Center, College of Osteopathic Medicine, 1979. Appointments: Owner, Medical Director, DFW Pain Treatment Center; Clinical Associate Professor, North Texas Health Science Center, College of Osteopathic Medicine. Memberships: American Osteopathic Association; President-Elect, American Osteopathic Academy of Sclerotherapy; American Academy of Pain Management. Hobbies: Martial Arts; Scuba Diving; Photography. Address: 4455 Camp Bowie Blvd, Fort Worth, TX 76107, USA.

BECK Morris, b. 12 Oct 1927, New York City, USA. Physician. m. Hollis L Schwartz, 6 Aug 1960, 2 daughters. Education: BA; MD.

Appointments: Chief, Division of Allergy, Miami CHildren's Hospital; Assistant Professor, University of Miami School of Medicine. Publications: Editor, Allergy Edition of International Journal of Paediatrics. Memberships: American College of Allergy; American Academy of Allergy; Dade County Medical Association, Florida Medical Association. Hobbies: Photography; Fishing. Address: 7800 SW 87 Avenue, Suite B240, Miami, FL 33173, USA.

BECKER Adrian, b. 3 Aug 1939, London, England. Orthodontist. m. Sheila Eskin, 19 Sept 1965, 2 sons, 3 daughters. Education: BDS (Lond); LDS (Eng); Diploma in Dental Orthopaedics, Glasgow. Appointments: Clinical Associate Professor, Department of Orthodontics, Hebrew University-Hadassah School of Dental Medicine, Jerusalem, Israel. Publications: The median diastema, book chapter, 1978; 55 articles in international journals including: The Palatally impacted canine: a new approach to its treatment (with Y Zilberman), 1978; Periodontal status following the alignment of buccally ectopic maxillary canine teeth (with D Kohavi and Y Zilberman), 1984; Familial trends in palatal canines, anomalous lateral incisors and related phenomena (with Y Zilberman and B Cohen), 1990; The effects of infraocclusion: part I-tilting of the adjacent teeth and space loss (with R M Karnei-R'em), part 2-the type of movement of the adjacent teth and their vertical development (with R M Karnei-R'em), part 3-dental arch length and the midline (with R M Karnei-R'em and S Steigman), 1992; Orthodontics for the Handicapped Child (with J Shapira), 1994. Honours: President, Israel Orthodontic Society, 1978-80; Referee to American Journal of Orthodontics and Dentofacial Orthopedics, European Journal of Orthodontics, Angle Orthodontist journal. Memberships: Corresponding Member, British Society for the Study of Orthodontics; Full Member, European Orthodontic Society; International Member, American Association of Orthodontists. Address: Department of Orthodontics, Hebrew University-Hadassah School of Dental Medicine, PO Box 12272, Jerusalem, Israel.

BECKERMAN Robert, b. 29 Oct 1946, Brooklyn, New York, USA. Physician. 3 daughters. Education: BS, Dickinson College, Carlisle, Pennsylvania, 1968; MD, Jefferson Medical College, Philadelphia, 1972. Appointments: Assistant Professor, Paediatrics, University of Miami School of Medicine, 1978-79; Professor, Chief of Paediatrics and Physiology, 1978-, Director, Paediatric Pulmonary and Sleep Laboratory, 1980-90, Tulane University School of Medicine, New Orleans. Publications: Primary pulmonary hemisiderosis, 1990; Co-author: chapters in Respiratory Control Disorders in Children (also co-edited), 1992; Obstructive sleep apnea syndrome, and Sudden infant death syndrome, chapters 61 and 63 in Pediatric Respiratory Disease: Diagnosis and Treatment, 1993; Control of ventilation and apnea; Contributions to refereed journals including: Arthrogryposis multiplex congenita as part of an inherited symptom complex, 1978; Altered polyamine metabolism in cystic fibrosis, 1979; Brainstem auditory response in Ondine's syndrome, 1986; Obstructive sleep apnea syndrome in sickle cell disease, 1989; Influence of SKF 95587 and BN 50730 on bronchoconstrictor responses in the cat, 1990. Honours: Member, State of Louisiana Commission on Infant Apnea and Home Monitoring, 1986; Member, Research Council, Southern Society for Pediatric Research, 1987; Cystic Fibrosis Center Grant, Cystic Fibrosis Foundation, 1990-91; Training Grant, Maternal and Child Health Pediatric Pulmonary Center, 1990-95. Memberships: American Thoracic Society; Fellow, American College of Chest Physicians, Paediatric Assembly; Louisiana Lung Association; Fellow, American Academy of Pediatrics; Southern Society for Pediatric Research; Clinical Sleep Society. Address: Tulane University School of Medicine, 1430 Tulane Avenue, New Orleans, LA 70112, USA.

BECKWITH John Bruce, b. 18 Sept 1933, Spokane, Washington, USA. Professor of Pathology. m. Nancy Gay Browning, 21 June 1984, 3 daughters. Education: BA, Biology, Whitman College, 1954; MD, University of Washington School of Medicine, Seattle, 1958. Appointments: Head, Pathology, 1964-74, Director of Laboratories, 1974-84, Children's Hospital and Medical Centre, Seattle; Chairman, Pathology, Children's Hospital, Denver, Colorado, 1985-91; Assistant Professor, 1964-68, Associate Professor, 1968-74, Professor of Pathology and Paediatrics, 1974-84, University of Washington School of Medicine; Professor of Pathology and Paediatrics, University of Colorado School of Medicine, 1985-91; Professor of Pathology, Loma Linda University School of Medicine, 1991-. Publications: Atlas of Tumor Pathology, Fascicle on Renal Tumors, 2nd ed 1974, 3rd ed 1994; Sudden Infant Death Syndrome, 1970; Anencephly, 1978. Honours include: Distinguished Alumnus Award, University of Washington School

of Medicine, 1980; Honorary DSc, Whitman College, 1980; President, Society for Paediatric Pathology, 1995; Pathologist-in-Chief, National Wilms Tumor Society, 1969-. Memberships: Teratology Society; International Society Paediatric Oncology; American Medical Association; California Medical Association; College of American Pathologists; International Association of Pathologists. Hobbies: Fishing; Antiquarian Books; Teratology. Address: Loma Linda University, Department of Pathology, Division of Paediatric Pathology, AH 327, Loma Linda, CA 92350, USA.

BEDROSSIAN Edward H Jr, b. 9 Sept 1951, Philadelphia, Pennsylvania, USA. Ophthalmologist. m. Laura Bedrossian, 2 sons. Education: MD, Temple University; MA, Chemistry, Lafayette College. Appointments: Associate Professor, Ophthalmology, Temple University Medical School, Pennsylvania; Founding Director, Wills Eye Hospital Fascia Lata Bank. Publications: Cryosurgery for Recurrent Trichiasis, 1984; Removal of Small Lesions Around the Eyes, 1986; Evaluation of Orbital Injuries, 1987; Establishment of a Fascia Lata Bank, 1989; Banked Fascia Lata, 1991; The Repair of Orbital Floor Fractures in Plastic and Reconstructive Surgery of the Head and Neck, 1991; HIV and Banked Fascia Lata, 1991; Banked Fascia Lata as an Orbital Floor Implant, 1993; Co-author: Incontinentia Pigmenti Associated with Nasolacrimal Duct Obstruction, 1984; Isolated Neurofibroma of the Orbit; Medical and Surgical Treatment of Chalazia, 1986; HIV and Banked Fascia Lata, 1989; Corneal Perforation in Patients with Vitamin A Deficiency in the United States, 1990. Honours: Resident's Research Award, 1982; Distinguished Teaching Award, 1994. Memberships: American Society of Ophthalmic Plastic and Reconstructive Surgery; American Academy of Ophthalmology; American College of Surgeons. Hobbies: Skiing; Tennis; Music; Travel. Address: 4501 State Road, Drexel Hill, PA 19026, USA.

BEEBEEJAUN Mahmad Seedick, b. 14 Mar 1949, Mauritius. Obstetrician and Gynaecologist. m. Rashedah Malleck Goolab Amode, 27 July 1976, 1 son, 2 daughters. Education: MB ChB, University of Aberdeen; MRCOG (London); FRCOG (London). Appointments: House Physician and Surgeon, Aberdeen Royal Infirmary, Scotland, 1975-76; Lecturer, Department of Pathology, 1977, Research Fellow, Gynaecological Oncology, 1981, University of Aberdeen; Registrar in Obstetrics, 1978-80, Senior Registrar, Research Fellow, 1980, Aberdeen Maternity Hospitals; Currently Obstetrician and Gynaecologist, Mauritius. Memberships: Society for Minimally Invasive Therapy, London; American Institute of Ultrasound Medicine. Hobbies: Running; Swimming. Address: 18 Van Der Meersch Street, Rose Hill, Mauritius.

BEECH John Roy, b. 24 July 1949, Manchester, England. Senior Lecturer. 1 daughter. Education: BSc, City University; MPhil, Reading University; DPhil, New University of Ulster, Coleraine. Appointments: Lecturer, New University of Ulster, Northern Ireland, 1973-84; Lecturer, 1984-93, Senior Lecturer, 1993-, University of Leicester, England. Publications: Learning to Read, 1985; Co-editor: Cognitive Approaches to Reading, 1987; Assessment: Speech and Language Therapy, 1993. Membership: Fellow, British Psychological Society. Address: Psychology Department, University of Leicester, University Road, Leicester LE1 7RH, England.

BEELEY Josie Ann, b. 30 Jan 1939, Crewe, Cheshire, England. University Lecturer. m. Dr John G Beeley, 15 Sep 1965, 1 son. Education: BSc, 1st Class Honours, MSc, PhD, University of Manchester. Appointments: Lecturer in Biochemistry, University of Sheffield, 1965-67; Research Associate, University of Washington, Seattle, USA, 1967-78; Lecturer in Dental Biochemistry, Senior Lecturer in Oral Biochemistry, University of Glasgow, Scotland, 1978-. Publications: Contributor of over 100 papers in biochemical, medical and dental journals. Honours: ORCA-Rolex Prize, European Organisation for Caries Research. Memberships: Biochemical Society; British Dental Association; Royal Society of Medicine; European Organisation for Caries Research; British Electrophoresis Society; Association of Basic Science Teachers in Dentistry; International Association for Dental Research. Hobby: Tennis. Address: Department of Oral Sciences, University of Glasgow Dental School, 378 Sauchiehall Street, Glasgow G2 3JZ, Scotland.

BEIKO George H H, b. 12 May 1957, Ukraine. Ophthalmologist. m Sheila J Demsey, 30 May 1992. Education: BSc, University of Toronto, Canada, 1979; BM, BCh, Oxford University, England, 1986; FRCS (Canada), 1991. Appointments: Consultant Ophthalmic Surgeon, St John's Ophthalmic Hospital, Jerusalem, 1991; Currently Consultant

Ophthalmic Surgeon, Niagara Health Center, St Catharines, Ontario, Canada. Memberships: Ontario Medical Association; American Academy of Ophthalmology; Canadian Ophthalmological Society. Address: Suite 103, 180 Vine St, St Catharines, Ontario, Canada L2R 7P3.

BELDAVS Robert Alan, b. 18 June 1963, Ontario, Canada. Ophthalmologist. Education: FRCSC; Diplomate, American Board of Ophthalmology; Fellowship, Cornea and External Disease, Emory University, Atlanta, USA, 1991-1992. Appointments: Active Staff Misericordia General Hospital and Health Sciences Centre, Winnipeg; Instructor faculty of medicine, University of Manitoba. Publications include: Intrastromal Photorefractive Keratectomy with the Nd: YLF laser, 1994; Bilateral microbial keratitis after radial kratotomy, 1993; Comparison of laser and manual removal of corneal epithelium for PRK, 1994. Honours include: Leboldus Award for Proficiency as a Clinician, 1985; Lange Award for proficiency as a Clinician, 1986; Hurmant award in opthalmology, 1989; Upjohn Research Award, 1990; D W Mills opthalmology grand rounds award, 1991; Resident Teaching Award, 1992. Memberships: American Academy of Ophthalmology; Manitoba and Canadian Medical Associations; AOA Honour Medical Society. Hobbies: Hiking; Skiing; Mountain biking. Address: 1502-277 Wellington Crecent, Winnipeg, Manitoba, R3M 3V7, Canada.

BELENKOV Youri Nikitich, b. 9 Feb 1948, St Petersburg, Russia. Cardiologist. m. Lubov Belova, 21 Mar 1971. Education: Gorky Medical Institute, 1972; MD, 1974; PhD, 1983. Appointments: Staff Physician, 1972, Junior Resident, 1974, Senior Resident, 1977, Head of Laboratory, 1983, Director, 1987-, A L Miasnikov Scientific Research Institute of Cardiology. Publications: Ultrasound Diagnostic in Cardiology, 1981; Practical Echocardiography, 1982; Ultraschalldiagnostik Kardiovaskularer, 1983; Art: Clinical Support for Neurohumoral Concept of CHF, 1994. Honours: State Prize, 1982, 1987. Memberships: Cardiology Society of Russia; Pharmacology Society of Russia; Working Group, Congestive Heart Failure; European Society of Cardiology. Hobbies: Music; Cars. Address: 3 Cherepkovskaia 15, 121552 Moscow, Russia.

BELFORD Raphael, b. 28 Feb 1933, Berwick, PA, USA. Psychologist. m. Jeanne Reichard, 2 d. Education: BS, Psychology, Pennsylvania State University, 1955; MS, Psychology, Pennsylvania State University, 1957; Internship, Baltimore Psychiatric Institute, 1968-69; PhD, Clinical Psychology, West Virginia University, 1970. Appointments: Psychologist, State Correctional Institution, Camp Hill, Pennsylvania; Director of Treatment, State Correction Institution, Camp Hill, Pennsylvania; Psychologist, Pennsylvania Board of Probation & Parole; Deputy Superintendent for Treatment, State Correction Institution, Camp Hill, Pennyslvania; Director, Psychological Services, Pennsylvania Department of Corrections; Consultant in Private Practice. Memberships: American Psychological Association; American Society of Clinical Hypnosis; American Association of Correctional Psychologists; American Correctional Association; Pennsylvania Psychological Association. Hobbies: Photography; Travel. Address: 16 Farm House Lane, Camp Hill, PA 17011, USA.

BELL Norman Howard, b. 11 Feb 1931, Gainesville, Georgia, USA. Physician; Scientist. m. Leslie Dinsmore, 16 Dec 1972, 2 sons, 1 daughter. Education: AB, Emory University, Atlanta, Georgia, 1951; MD, Duke University, Durham, North Carolina, 1955. Appointments: Assistant Professor of Medicine, Northwestern University School of Medicine, 1966-68; Associate Professor of Medicine, 1968-71, Professor of Medicine, 1971-79, Indiana University School of Medicine; Currently Professor of Medicine and Pharmacology, Medical University of South Carolina, Charleston. Honours: William S Middleton Award, Veterans Administration, 1983; Frederic C Bartlett Award, American Society for Bone and Mineral Research, 1992. Memberships: American Society of Clinical Investigation; American Society for Bone and Mineral Research, Secretary-Treasurer 1978-85, President 1986-87; Association of American Physicians; American Society for Pharmacology and Therapeutics; Endocrine Society; Alpha Omega Alpha. Address: VA Medical Center, 109 Bee Street, Charleston, SC 29401-5799, USA.

BELL Sara Delia L'Estrange, b. 5 Feb 1961, Birmingham, England. Naturopath; Osteopath. m. 13 May 1989, 2 daughters. Education: ND; DO. Appointments: Private Practice; Wholistic Educational School for Children, 5-11yrs, Central London. Memberships: MRN; MRO; OAGB. Hobbies: Education-Wholistic for Children; Windsurfing; Interior Design;

Skiing; Art; Riding. Address: 3, St Andrews Road, London, W14 95X, England.

BELLAK Leopold, b. 22 June 1916, Vienna, Austria. Psychiatrist. div, 2 daughters. Education: MA, Boston University and Harvard University; MD, New York Medical College, 1944. Appointments: Clinical Professor of Psychiatry, G Washington University, 1971-75; Consultant to US Military Academy West Point, 1966-79; Clinical Professor of Psychiatry, Albert Einstein College of Medicine, 1975-89; Emeritus Professor of Psychiatry. Publications: Author of 35 books and contributor of 150 articles. Honours: Annual Merit Award, New York Society of Clinical Psychologists, 1964; Award for Contribution to Community Psychiatry, 1976; Frieda Fromm-Reichmann Award, American Academy of Psychoanalysis, 1981; Bruno Klopfer Award, Society for Personality Assessment, 1991; Award for Distinguished Professional Contributions to Knowledge, American Psychological Association, 1992. Memberships: Fellow, American Psychiatric Association; Fellow, American Psychological Association; American Psychoanalayutic Association. Hobbies: Karate; Akaido; Judo. Address: 22 Rockwood Drive, Larchmont, NY 10538, USA.

BELLERMANN Peter Robert Wilhelm, b. 26 Nov 1939, Friemar. President, National Neurofibromatosis Foundation, Chairman of the International Neurofibromatosis Association. m. Pamela Maniet, 8 Aug 1986, 2 sons, 1 daughter. Education: BA, University of Minnesota; MPA, Princeton University. Appointments: Assistant Vice President, Citibank; Senior Advanceman, Sen E Muskie, General Manager, PAF; Depty Director, Volunteer Consulting Group. Memberships: American Society of Human Genetics. Honours: Past Chairman, Appeals Committee, New York State Council on the Arts; Honorary Citizen, Tacoma Park, Maryland, USA. Address: 141 Fifth Avenue, Suite 7-S, New York, NY 10010, USA.

BELLINO Robert John, b. 3 June 1935, Pittsburgh, Pennsylvania, USA. Medical Doctor (Psychiatry). m. Sherry June Fuller, 8 June 1962, 2 daughters. Education: BS with honours, 1962, MD, 1966, Psychiatric Residency, 1967-70, University of Florida; Rotating Internship, St Mary's Hospital, West Palm Beach, Florida, 1966-67. Appointments: Private practice in Psychiatry. Honours: Phi Beta Kappa, 1962; Fellow, American Psychiatric Association, 1982. Memberships: American Medical Association; Florida Medical Association; Manatee County Medical Society; American Psychiatric Association; Florida Psychiatric Society; American Association of Geriatric Psychiatry; Diplomate: National Board of Medical Examiners; American Board of Psychiatry and Neurology; American Academy of Pain Management. Hobbies: Studying philosophy; Growing orchids; Raising budgies and Persian cats; Falconry. Address: 1450 59th Street W, Bradenton, FL 34209, USA.

BEN-HAIM Shlomo Abraham, b. 15 Oct 1957, Haifa, Israel. Cardiac Electrophysiologist. m. Simona Speter, 12 Aug 1980, 1 son, 3 daughters. Education: MD, cum laude, 1982, DSc, 1987, Technion-Israel Institute of Technology. Appointments: Associate Professor. Publications: Prediction of Immediate Ventricular Arrhythmias After Coronary Artery Ligation, CO-author, 1992; Periodicities of Cardiac Mechanics, 1991; Impulse Propagation in the Purkinje System and Myocardium of Intact Dogs, 1993. Honours: Bernard Elkin Prize for Surgery, 1981; Rhone Fellowship Prize, 1987; Juludan Prize for Biomedical Research, 1994. Memberships: Institute of Electrical and Electronics Engineers; North American Society of Pacing and Electrophysiology; American Heart Association; American Federation of Clinical Research; Biomedical Engineering Society; Federation of Experimental Biology; Israel Medical Association. Address: Bruce Rappaport Faculty of Medicine, Technion-Israel Institute of Technology, POB 9649, 31096 Haifa, Israel.

BENDAYAN Moise, b. 21 June 1949. Department Chairman. Education: MSc; PhD. Appointments: Assistant Professor of Anatomy, Associate Professor, Full Professor, Chairman, Department of Anatomy, University of Montreal, Canada. Publications: Contributor of 160 articles in scientific journals. Honours: M L Barr Award, 1982; Vector Award, 1983; Feulgen Award, 1984; Diabetes Award, 1993. Memberships: Histochemical Society; Canadian Electron Microscopy Society; Canadian Federation Biology Society; Canadian Association Anatomists; American Panic Association. Address: Department of Anatomy, University of Montreal, CP 6128 Montreal, Quebec H3C 3J7, Canada.

BENDICH Adrianne, b. 8 Apr 1944, New York, USA. Clinical Research Scientist. m. Dr David Kafkewitz, 5 July 1984, 1 son, 1 daughter. Education: BS, City College of New York; MS, Iowa State

University; PhD, Rutgers University. Appointments: Senior Scientist, 1981-88, Senior Clinical Research Coordinator, 1988-93, Clinical Research Scientist, 1993-, Hoffmann-La Roche Incorporated. Publications: Author of 5 books including: Micronutrients in Health and Disease Prevention; Contributor of over 60 publications. Honour: Roche Research and Development Prize, 1992. Memberships: American Association Immunologists; New York Acadeny of Sciences; American Institute Nutrition; American Soceity Clinical Nutrition; Institute Food Technologists; Sigma Xi; Oxygen Society. Address: Human Nutrition Research, Building 787/5, Hoffman-La Roche Incorporated, Nutley, NJ 07110-1199, USA.

BENENSON Michael William, b. 31 Mar 1941, New York City, USA. Physician. m. Martina Srichandra, 19 Jan 1974, 1 son, 1 daughter. Education: BA, Cornell University, 1963; MD, University of Maryland, 1968; MPH, Johns Hopkins University School of Hygiene and Public Health, 1975. Appointments: Medical Research Team, Vietnam, 1971; Epidemiologist, Seato laboratory, 1972-75; Chief, Epicon, 1975-80; Commander, AFRIMS, Bangkok, Thailand, 1980-84; Chief. Preventive Medicine, 7th Medical Command, 1984-94; Surgeon, Provide Comfort, 1991; Surgeon, Support Hope, 1994; Chief, Preventitive Medicine, 30th Medical Brigade; Colonel, US Army. Honours:"A" Designator, 1987; Legion of Merit Award, 1994; Humanitarian Medal. Memberships: American Soceity Tropical Medicine and Hygiene; American Public Health Association; American College of Preventive Medicine; American College of Epidemiology. Hobbies: Skiing; Tennis; Sailing. Address: 30th Medical Brigade, Unit 29218, APO, AE 09102, USA.

BENFIELD John Richard, b. 24 June 1931, Vienna, Austria. Thoracic Surgeon. Education: BA, Columbia University, USA, 1952; MD, University of Chicago, 1955. Appointments include: Captain, Commander, 44th Mobile Army Surgical Hospital, Korea, 1957-59; Professor of Surgery, 1988-, Chief, Thoracic Surgery, 1988-, Vice Chairman, 1988-95, University of California at Davis; Attending Surgeon, VA Martinez Medical Centre, 1988-91; Courtesy Staff, Kaiser Permanente Medical Centre, Sacramento, 1988-. Publications: The Scientific Management of Surgical Patients, Co-editor, 1983; Chest Surgery Clinics of North America, Editor, 1992; Contributor of numerous articles in professional journals and book chapters. Honours include: Sigma Xi; Distinguished Teacher Award, University of California at Los Angeles School of Medicine, 1974; Honoured Guest, Japanese Association for Thoracic Surgery, 1975; President, Western Thoracic Surgical Association, 1988-89; F Henry Ellis Lecture, New England Deaconess Hospital, Harvard, 1992; Honoured Guest, South American Congress of Thoracic Surgery, 1992; Honoured Guest Speaker, Louis Mark Lecture, ACCP Meeting, Orlando, Florida, 1993; President, Society of Thoracic Surgeons, 1995-; President, Thoracic Surgery Directors Association, 1995; Vice President, Pacific Coast Surgical Association, 1995-. Memberships include: American Association for Cancer Research; American Association for Thoracic Surgery; American College of Chest Physicians; American College of Surgeons; American Medical Writers Association; American Surgical Association; California Medical Society; International Association for the Study of Lung Cancer; Pacific Coast Surgical Association; Royal Society of Medicine, Great Britain; Society of Thoracic Surgeons; Western Thoracic Surgical Association. Address: University of California Davis Medical Centre, 4301 X Street, Sacramento, CA 95817, USA.

BENNETT J Claude, b. 12 Dec 1933, Birmingham, Alabama, USA. University President. m. Nancy Miller Bennett, 17 June 1958, 1 son, 2 daughters. Education: AB, Samford University, 1954; MD, Harvard Medical School, 1958; DSc, Honoris Causa, University of Alabama at Birmingham, 1992. Appointments include: Assistant Professor, Department of Medicine, 1965-66, Assistant Director, Division of Clinical Immunology and Rheumatology, 1966-70, Associate Professor, Department of Microbiology, 1966-70, Associate Professor, Department of Medicine, 1966-70, Senior Scientist, Cancer Research and Training Centre, 1972-, Director, Multipurpose Arthritis Centre, 1977-84, Professor, Chairman, Department of Microbiology, 1970-82, Professor of Medicine, Director, Division of Clinical Immunology and Rheumatology, 1970-82, Professor, Chairman, Department of Medicine, 1982-, President, 1993-, University of Alabama at Birmingham. Publications include: Vistas in Connective Tissue Disease, Editor, 1968; Rheumatology and Immunology, 2nd Edition, Co-editor, 1986; Cecil Textbook of Medicine 19th Edition, Co-editor, 1992; Cecil Essentials of Medicine, Co-editor, 1993; Contributor of numerous articles, book reviews, editorials, abstracts and presentations. Honours include: Fellow, American Association for the Advancement of Science, 1988;

Master, American College of Physicians, 1990; Phillips Memorial Award, American College of Physicians, 1993. Memberships include: American Academy of Allergy and Immunology; American Academy of Microbiology; American Association for the Advancement of Science. Address: University of Alabama at Birmingham, 1070 Administration Building, 701 20th Street South, Birmingham, AL 35294-0110, USA.

BENNETT Peter Brian, b. 12 June 1931, Portsmouth, England. Scientist. m. Margaret Warren, 7 July 1956, 1 son, 1 daughter. Education: PhD; DSc. Appointments include: Professor of Biomedical Engineering, Duke University, 1972-79; Director of Research, Department of Anesthesiology, Duke Medical Center, 1973-84; Professor, Anesthesiology, Duke University Medical Center, 1972-; Executive Director, National Divers Alert Network, Duke Medical Center, 1980-; Associate Professor, Department of Cell Biology, 1989-; President, International Divers Alert Network Inc, 1992-. Publications include: Physiological limitations to underwater exploration and work, 1989; Platelet count in deep saturation diving, 1992; Books incl: The Aetiology of Compressed Air Intoxication and Inert Gas narcosis, 1966; The Physiology and Medicine of Diving, 1982; Basic and Applied High Pressure Biology, 1994. Honours: Several awards, honours and grants. Hobbies: Scuba Diving; Swimming. Address: Box 3823, Duke University Medical Center, Durham, NC 27710, USA.

BENNETT William Michael, b. 6 May 1938, Chicago, Illinois, USA. Physician. m. Sandra Silen, 12 June 1977, 3 sons, 1 daughter. Education: BS, MD, Northwestern University, Chicago. Appointments: Assistant Professor of Medicine, 1970-74, Associate Professor of Medicine, 1974-78, Professor of Medicine, 1978-, Professor of Pharmacology, 1981-, Oregon Health Science University. Publications: Author of over 100 books and chapters; Contributor of over 315 scientific papers in peer review journals. Honours: Medical Research Foundation Discover Award, 1991; Gift of Life Award, National Kidney Foundation, 1992; Distinguished Service, American College of Physicians, 1989. Memberships: Fellow, American College of Physicians; Council, American Society Nephrology; American Association Physicians; President, Western Association of Physicians; American Society Transplant Physicians; American Society Clinical Pharmacology and Therapeutics. Hobby: Sports. Address: Department of Medicine, Oregon Health Sciences University, Portland, OR 97201, USA.

BENSON Patricia Mae Dimmick, b. 1 July 1956, Clinton, Iowa, USA. Registered Nurse. m. John A Benson, 2 June 1984. Education: AAS with honours, Clinton Community College, 1977; BSN magna cum laude, Marycrest College, 1978; Teacher Certification, Mt Mercy College, 1986; MA, Education, University of Iowa, 1992. Appointments: Director, Inservice Education; Health Services Supervisor; Abstractor, Health Records; Research Assistant II; Research Assistant III (Clinical Studies Coordinator); Currently Programme Associate I (Study Coordinator/Supervisor), Department of Paediatrics, University of Iowa College of Medicine. Publications: Co-author: Protamine Skin Testing Does Not Predict Immediate Adverse Systemic Reactions Following Protamine Administration, 1989; A Prospective Study of the Risk of an Immediate Adverse Reaction to Protamine Sulfate During Cardiopulmonary Bypass Surgery, 1990; A Two-Center, Double-Blind, Parallel Groups, Placebo and Positively Controlled and Randomized, Dose-Ranging Study of the Efficacy, Safety and Onset and Duration of Action of Azelastine Nasal Spray in the Treatment of Seasonal Allergic Rhinitis Using an Acute Model, 1994. Honours: Topper's Honour Society, 1975; Pi Lambda Theta, 1991; Sigma Theta Tau, 1992. Memberships include: Associate Member, American Academy of Allergy and Immunology, 1991-93; American Nurses Association, 1979-82, 1984-85; International Reading Association, 1986-87. Hobbies: Music; Crafts; Travel; Walking; Baseball. Address: 2125 Leonard Circle, Iowa City, IA 52246, USA.

BENTLEY Kenneth Chessar, b. 22 Sep 1935, Montreal, Canada. Director and Professor of Oral and Maxillofacial Surgery; Dental Surgeon in Chief. m. Jean Wadsworth, 19 Aug 1961, 1 s. Education: DDS; MD; CM. Career: McGill University and Montreal General Hospital since 1966; Dean, Faculty of Dentistry, 1977-87, now Director and Professor, Division of Oral and Maxillo-Facial Surgery, Faculty of Dentistry, McGill University; Chairman, Executive Committee of the Council of Physicians, Dentists and Pharmacists, 1988-90, now Dental Surgeon in Chief, Montreal General Hospital. Publications include: 30 articles published in professional journals, 1967- including: Co-author, An in vivo study of the effect of a Helium-Neon laser on the breaking force and histological characteristics of wounds, in Laser. Honours include: Fellowship, International College of Dentists, 1971; Fellow, Pierre Fauchard Academy, 1978; Fellowship American College of Dentists; Fellowship Royal College of Dentists of Canada; Fellowship, Academy of International Dental Studies, 1983; Arnold K Maislen Award of New York University, 1984; Distinguished Service Award of the Canadian Dental Association, 1989. Memberships include: Association of Canadian Faculties of Dentistry, President, 1974-76; Canadian Dental Association; Montreal Dental Club, President, 1992-93. Hobbies: Music; Organist; Scottish Country Dancing; Gardening. Address: 1650 Cedar Avenue, Montreal, Canada, H3G 1A4.

BENZON Honorio Tabal, b. 12 Sep 1946, Ilocos sur, Philippines. Professor of Anesthesia. m. Julieta Palpallatog, 30 May 1970, 1 s, 1 d. Education: BS, Pre Medicine, Far Eastern University, Philippines, 1962-66; MD, Feu, Philippines, 1966-71; Intern, Overlook Hospital, Summit, NJ, 1972-73; Resident Anesthesiology, University of Cincinnati. Career includes: Attending Staff, Northwestern Memorial Hospital, Chicago, 1976-; Assistant Professor, 1980-85, Associate Professor, 1985-94, now Professor of Anesthesiology, Northwestern University Medical School; Research Sabbatical, Neurophysiology, Harvard Medical School, Boston, 1985-86; Chief, Pain Management Service. Publications: Written chapters for six different medical books, 30 original articles, review articles and editorials in various professional journals. Honours: Most Outstanding Intern, St Luke's Hospital, 1971; Member, Association of University Anesthetists, 1990; Associate Editor: Pain Digest, 1994-; Editorial Board; Regional Anesthesia, 1994-; Reviewer of: JAMA, Regional Anesthesia, Pain Digest, The Clinical Journal of Pain, Journal of Cardiothoracic and Vascular Anesthesia, and Mayo Clinic Proceedings. Memberships: American Association for The Advancement of Science; International Association for the Study of Pain; American Society of Anesthesiologists; International Anesthesia Research Society; American Society of Regional Anesthesia. Hobbies: Tennis; Cinema. Address: 303 East Superior, Rm 360, Chicago, IL 60611, USA.

BERBER Arturo Cecilio, b. 7 Oct 1960, Mexico. Consultant; Researcher. m. Blanca Delrio, 1 May 1993. Education: MD, Escuela Superior De Medicina, 1985; PhD, Escuela Nacional De Ciencias Biologicas, 1989; Diplomate in Pharmacology, Facultad De Medicina, Unam, 1993. Appointments: Associate Professor, Escuela Superior De Medicina, 1986-92; Universidad Nacional Autonoma De Mexico, 1987-; Scientific Director, Apoyo Farmacologico Integral, 1988-; Clinical Studies Coordinator, Janssen Farmaceutical, Mexico, 1992-93; Medical Manager, Knoll Basf Pharma Mexico, 1993-. Publications: Contribution to the study of juvenile rheumatoid arthritis in Mexico, 1986; Detection of IgA class antibodies against Salmonela typhi LPS in serum and colostrum samples, 1988; Identification of E histolytica antigens recognized by IgA class human antibodies in sera and colostra of puerperal women using immunoblotting techniques, 1990; Secretory IgA and Seric IgG against polioviruses on surburban Mexican children, 1991; Process and presentation of antigens in the mucosal immunarity system, 1992; Comparative pharmacokinetics of two commercials forms of itraconazole in healthy individuals, 1993; Comparative study of bronchoalveolar lavages in Normal subjects and in patients with chronic pulmonar obtructive disease, 1994; Nasopharyngeal and systemic humoral responses induced by trivalent attenuated poliomielitis Vaccine in newborns, 1994; Induction of Immunitary responses in nasopharyngeal secretions after the oral immunization with bacterial lysates, 1994. Memberships: Sociedad Mexicana De Inmunologia Mucosal Immunology Society; American Association for the Advancement of Science. Hobbies: History of Art; History of Science; Comparative Technology. Address: Cruz Galvez 269, 02800 Mexico City, Mexico.

BERDANIER Carolyn Dawson, b. 14 Nov 1936, New Brunswick, New Jersey, USA. Professor of Nutrition. m. C Reese Berdanier, 2 sons, 1 daughter. Education: BS, Pennsylvania State University, 1958; MS, 1963, PhD, 1966, Rutgers University. Appointments: Research Nutritionist, USDA, 1968-75; Assistant Professor, University Maryland, 1970-75; Associate Professor, Univesity Nebraska College of Medicine, 1975-77; Professor, Head, Department Foods and Nutrition, University of Georgia, 1977-88; Professor of Nutrition, University of Georgia, 1977-. Publications include: Nutrition and Gene Expression, 1993; Is DHEA an anti obesity agent, 1993; Early renal disease in BHE/cdb rats is less in rats fed beef tallow than in rats fed menhaden oil, 1993; NIDDM in the now obese BHE/cdb rats, 1994; Mutated rat DNA, 1995. Honours include: NIH Nutrition Research Fellowship, 1963-66; NIH Postdoctoral Research Fellowship, 1966-67; Sigma Xi, 1967; Elected Fellow, American Institute of Chemists, 1970; Gamma Sigma Delta, 1981; Phi

Kappa Phi, 1981; Borden Award, AHEA, 1992. Memberships include: Society of Experimental Biology and Medicine; American Institute of Nutrition; American Society for Clinical Nutrition; American Diabetes Association. Hobby: Horses. Address: Department of Foods and Nutrition, University of Georgia, Dawson Hall, Athens, GA 30602, USA.

BERGANTINO Leonard Daniel, b. 29 May 1943. Clinical Psychologist. 1 son, 1 daughter. Education: BA, University of Connecticut, 1966; MA, Fairfield University, 1967; MSEd, EdD, University of Southern California, 1971; PhD, International College, 1977; Diplomate in Family Psychology, American Board of Professional Psychology. Appointments: High School Teacher, 1966-68; School Counsellor, 1968-71; Counselling and Clinical Psychologist, Veterans Administration Hospitals, 1971-72; Clinical Psychologist, Community Mental Health Center; Currently private practice in Clinical Psychology (In-Depth Family Therapy), West Los Angeles. Publications: Psychotherapy, Insight and Style: The Existential Moment, 1981, 1986, in German, 1992, Master Classic edition as Making an Impact in Therapy: How Master Clinicians Intervene, 1993. Memberships: American Psychological Society; American Society of Community Health; Clinical Psychology Association; Los Angeles Society of Clinical Psychology. Hobbies: Boxing; Basketball; Mandolin; Trumpet. Address: 12301 Wilshire Blvd, Ste 300, Los Angeles, CA 90025, USA.

BERGER Melvin, b. 7 March 1950, Philadelphia, PA, USA. Physician; Immunologist. div. 1 s, 1 d. Education: MD, Case Western Reserve University, 1976; PhD, Biochemistry, Case Western Reserve University, 1976. Appointments: Assistant Chief, Allergy-Immunology Service, Walter Reed Army Medical Center, Washington DC, 1981-84; Professor of Pediatrics, Case Western Reserve University; Chief, Immunology Division, Rainbow Babies & Childrens Hospital, Cleveland, Ohio. Publications: Numerous Articles on Complement, Cystic Fibrosis, Intravenous Immunoglobulin and Neutrophils. Honours: Phi Beta Kappa, 1970; Alpha Omega Alpha, 1976; Meritorious Service Medal, US Army, 1985. Memberships: American Society Clinical Investment; American Association Immunologists; American Academy of Allergy & Immunology; American Academy of Pediatrics; Society Pediatric Research. Address: 18907 Lomond Boulevard, Shaker Heights, Ohio 44122, USA.

BERGER Miriam Roskin, b. 9 Dec 1934, New York City, USA. Dance Therapist. div, 1 son. Education: BA, Bard College, 1996; DA, New York University, 1956. Appointments: Director, Creative Arts Therapies, Bron Psychiatric Centre; Consultant, Creative Arts Rehabilitation Centre; Teacher, Stockholm, Rotterdam, Bonn, Italy. Honours: 1st Prize, Paper, Medart International Congress, 1991. Memberships: President, Founder Member, American Dance Therapy Association; Former Co-Editor, American Journal of Dance Therapy. Address: School of Education, New York University, 35 W4th Street, New York, NY 10012, USA.

BERGER Richard Stanton, b. 30 July 1940. Dermatologist. m. Janice, 2 Oct 1977, 1 son, 1 daughter. Education: MD, University of Michigan. Appointments: Assistant Professor of Dermatology, University of Missouri; Associate Director of Clinical Research, Johnson and Johnson; Clinical Associate professor of Dermatology, Rutgers University; Acting Chief, Dermatology, Clinical Professor of Dermatology, Robert Wood Johnson School of Medicine. Publications: Contributor of over 60 articles and 15 scientific exhibits. Memberships: American Academy of Dermatology; Society of Investigative Dermatology; The Dermatology Foundation. Hobby: Swimming. Address: 3270 Highway 27, Kendall Park, NJ 08824, USA.

BERGER Timothy George, b. 28 Feb 1949, Fort Dix, NJ, USA. Dermatologist. m. Elizabeth Jean Hovanec, 27 Apr 1982. Education: MD. Appointments: Chief, Dermatology Service, San Francisco General Hospital; Associate Clinical Professor, University of California, San Francisco. Publications: 12 Books and part books, 16 abstracts, numerous articles in regional, national and international periodicals. Honours: Army Commendation Medal, 1981; Meritorious Service Medal, 1987; Henry J Kaiser Award for Excellence in Teaching, University of CA, San Francisco, 1989; Teacher of Year, University of CA, 1989-90; Army Achievement Medal, 1990. Memberships: Association of Military Dermatologists; American Academy of Dermatology; American Society of Dermatopathology; San Francisco Dermatological Society. Address: Dermatology Service, Building 90, Ward 92, Room 224, San Francisco General Hospital, 1001 Potrero Avenue, San Francisco, CA 94110, USA.

BERGERON Michael Joseph Robert, b. Alma, Quebec, Canada. Physician; Professor. m. Cecile Gagnon, 1 son, 1 daughter. Education: MD; MSc; Specialist in Nephrology, CSPQ. Appointment: Professor of Physiology. Publications: Contributor of over 180 publications. Memberships: Canadian Physiological Society; American Society of Nephrology. Address: Department Physiology, University of Montreal, Montreal, Quebec H3C 3J7, Canada.

BERGERON Wilton L, b. 13 Feb 1914, Scott, Louisiana, USA. Physician. m. Juanita Landey, 3 Aug 1957, 3 sons, 1 daughter. Education: MD; BS; Board Certified Allergist, American Board of Allergy and Immunology. Appointments: Practitioner. Memberships: American College of Allergy and Immunology; AMA; Catholic Physicians Guild. Hobbies: Fishing; Computers. Address: PO Box 98, Scott, LA 10583, USA.

BERGFIELD Wilma Fowler, b. 6 May 1938, Philadelphia, Pennsylvania, USA. Physician; Dermatologist. m. Dr John A Bergfield, 25 Aug 1962, 2 daughters. Education: MD, Temple University School of Medicine, 1960-64; BS, College of William and Mary, 1964; Cleveland Clinic Dermatology Residency, 1968; DP, 1969-72. Appointments: Residency, Cleveland Clinic, 1972; Head, Dermatopathology Department; Staff, Department of Dermatology, 1969, Head, 1984-, Clinical Research, CCF. Honours:Ohio Wineb Achievement, 1985; YWCA Career Women Achievement, 1988; Leadership, Cleveland, 1988; Distinguished Physician Achievement Award, Womens Dermatology Association, 1986; Alumnus, Templle University School of Medicine, 1994. Memberships: President, 1992, American Academy of Dermatology; Board of Governors, Cleveland Clinic Foundation, 1992-97. Hobbies: Home; Skiing; Boating; Reading. Address: 9500 Euclid Avenue, Cleveland Clinic Foundation, Cleveland, OH 44195-5001, USA.

BERGSJO Per Bjarne, b. 17 Mar 1932, Baerum, Norway. Professor of Obstetrics and Gynaecology; Consultant. m. Jenny Benjaminsen, 2 s, 1 d. Education: MD, 1956, PhD, 1968, Oslo University; Specialist in Obstetrics and Gynaecology, Norway, 1969. Career: Resident in Surgery, Narvik Hospital, 1959-60; Resident in Obstetrics and Gynaecology, Tonsberg Hospital, 1960, Aker Hospital, Oslo, 1966-69, Haukeland Hospital, Bergen, 1970-71; Resident in Pathology, The Norwegian Radium Hospital, 1962-63, Anesthesiology, Aker Hospital, 1969; Associate Professor, University of Bergen, 1971-72; Head, Department of Obstetrics and Gynaecology, Akershus Central Hospital, 1973-80; Professor, Head of Women's Clinic, Bergen, 1980-90; Currently, Professor of Obstetrics and Gynaecology, University of Bergen and Consultant, Women's Clinic, Haukeland Hospital, Bergen. Publications: Norwegian textbooks on Obstetrics and Gynaecology, and Pregnancy Care in General Practice; Numerous scientific articles, commentaries and editorials. Honour: Schering's Prize for Accomplishments in Obstetrics and Gynaecology, Norwegian Gynaecological Society, 1992. Memberships include: Norwegian Medical Association; Scandinavian Association of Obstetricians and Gynaecologists; Norwegian Gynaecological Society; Fellow, Royal Society of Medicine, UK. Address: Fjellveien 114, N-5019 Bergen, Norway.

BERGSTEIN Jerry Michael, b. 26 June 1939, Cleveland, OH, USA. Physician. m. Renee Hillman, 10 July 1963, 2 s, 1 d. Education: BA, UCLA, 1961; MD, University of Minnesota, 1965. Appointments: Assistant Professor and Head, Paediatric Nephrology, UCLA School of Medicine, 1973-77; Professor of Paediatric Nephrology, Indiana University School of Medicine, 1977-. Publications: Nephrologic Diseases, 1992; Role of Coagulation in Glomerular and Vascular Diseases, 1994; Plasminogen-activator Inhibitor, Co-author, 1992. Memberships: American Society of Nephrology; American Society of Paediatric Nephrology; American Soceity Investigation Pathology; Society for Paediatric Research; National Kidney Foundation. Hobbies: Gardening; Travel; Sports. Address: James Whitcomb Riley Hospital for Children, 702 Barnhill Drive, Indianapolis, IN 46202, USA.

BERK Cahit, b. 19 Sept 1944, Cyprus. Obstetrician & Gynaecologist. m. Janet Clare Griffiths, 4 Nov 1978, 1 son. Education: MD, University Istanbul, Turkey, 1968; FRCOG. Appointments: Locum, Consultant Obstetrician & Gynaecologist, Chase Farm Hospital, Enfield, Middlesex; Private Obstetrician & Gynaecologist. Publications: The diagnosis of Diaphraguich Hernia in Trauterine by Ultra-sound, 1980. Memberships: MRCOG, 1979; FRCOG, 1994. Hobbies: Golf; Reading; Travel; Music. Address: 4 The Grove, Palmers Green, London N13 5LQ. England.

BERLAND David I, b. 1 Aug 1947, St Louis, Missouri, USA. Physician. m. Elaine Prostak, 21 May 1977, 2 daughters. Education: BA, University of Pennsylvania; MD, University of Missouri. Appointments: Staff Psychiatrist, Menninger Foundation; Professor of Child and Adolescent Psychiatry, Director, Division of Child and Adolescent Psychiatry, St Louis University. Publications: Knowing and Doing Ethics, 1992; Child and Adolescent inpatient units in medical schools: staffing patterns, length of stay and utilization rates, 1992; Patient allegations of sexual abuse against psychiatric hospital staff, 1994. Honours: Diplomate, Psychiatry, 1978, Diplomate, Child Psychiatry, 1980, American Board of Psychiatry and Neurology. Memberships: Society of Professors of Child and Adolescent Psychiatry; American Academy of Child and Adolescent Psychiatry. Hobbies: Photography; Running. Address: 1221 S Grand, St Louis, MO 63104, USA.

BERLIN Michelle, b. 9 May 1958, Oakland, California, USA. Physician. m. Robert A Lowe. Education: BA, Microbiology & Immunology, University of California, Berkeley, 1980; MPH, University of California, School of Public Halth, Berkeley, 1980; MD, University of Cincinnati, College of Medicine, 1986. Appointments: Resident in Obstetrics & Gynaecology, University of Cincinnati Medical Center, Cincinnati, 1986-88; Resident in Obstetrics & Gynaecology, University of California, Davis Medical Center, Davis, California, 1988-90; Resident in Preventative Medicine, University of California, Berkeley, 1990-91; Research Fellow, Center for AIDS Prevention Studies, University of California, San Francisco, 1990-92; Assistant Professor, Department of Obstetrics & Gynaecology/Reproductive Sciences/Department of Epidemiology & Biostatistics, University of California, San Francisco, 1992-93; Assistant Professor of Obstetrics & Gynaecology, University of Pennsylvania, School of Medicine, Philadelphia, 1993-. Publications: include Efficacy of Oral-Beta-Agonist Maintenance Therapy in Preterm Labor: A Meta-Analysis; HIV-Infected Health Care Worker: Public Opinion about Testing, Disclosing and Switching, 1993; A Comparison of Local and General Anesthesia for Laporoscopic Tubal Sterilization, 1991. Memberships: American College of Obstetricians & Gynaecologists; American Medical Association; American Medical Women's Association; American Public Health Association; Society for Epidemiologic Research. Address: University of Pennsylvania, 239L NEB, 420 Service Drive, Philadelphia, PA 19085-6095, USA.

BERNHARD Jeffrey D, b. 31 Oct 1951, Buffalo, NY, USA. Dermatologist. Education: AB, Harvard College, 1973; Knox Fellow, St John's College, Cambridge, 1973-74; MD, Harvard Medical School, 1978. Appointment: Professor of Medicine, Director of Division of Dermatology, University of Massachusetts Medical School. Publications: ITCH, book, 1994; Assistant Editor, Journal of the American Academy of Dermatology. Honour: Phi Beta Kappa, 1973. Memberships: Fellow, Royal Society of Medicine; American Academy of Dermatology. Address: Division of Dermatology, University of Massachusetts Medical Center, 55 Lake Avenue North, Worcester, MA 01655, USA.

BERNSTEIN Aaron, b. 22 Dec 1936. Medical Doctor. m. Lynda Joyce Bernstein, 21 Sep 1981, 1 d. Education: BA, Distinction; MD; CM; FRCPC. Appointment: Senior Medical Officer, Department of Citizenship and Immigration, Government of Canada. Membership: Fellow, Royal College of Physicians and Surgeons of Canada. Hobbies: Music; Drama. Address: PO Box 489 H Kong, Station A Ottawa, Ontario, Canada, K1N 8V5.

BERNSTEIN David I, b. 12 Sept 1951, Cincinnati, Ohio, USA. Physician. 2 sons. Education: MD, University of Cincinnati; Residency, Internal Medicine, Cleveland Clinic, 1977-80; Residency, Allergy, Immunology, Northwestern University, 1980-82. Appointments: Assistant Professor of Medicine, 1982-89, Associate Professor of Medicine, 1989-, Division of Immunology, University of Cincinnati. Publications: Asthma in the Workplace; Author or co-author, 44 journal articles on allergic diseases, 21 chapters and reviews on allergic diseases. Memberships: Fellow, American Academy of Allergy; Fellow, American College of Physicians; American Association of Immunologists. Hobbies: Fishing; Tennis. Address: Division of Immunology ML 563, 231 Bethesda Avenue, Cincinnati, OH 45267, USA.

BERNSTEIN I Leonard, b. 17 Feb 1924, Jersey City, USA. Physician; Educator. m. Miriam Goldman, 29 Aug 1948, 2 s, 2 d. Education includes: MD, University of Cincinnati, 1949; Diplomate, American Board of Internal Medicine, American Board of Allergy and Immunology, American Board of Diagnostic Laboratory Immunology. Career includes: Fellow, Allergy and Immunology, Northwestern

University Medical School, 1955-56; Faculty, 1956-, Director of Allergy Training Program, 1958-, Director, Allergy Research Laboratory, 1958-, Trustee, Faculty Council on Jewish Affairs, 1967-75, Clinical Professor of Medicine, 1971-, Director, Allergy Clinic, 1971-, University of Cincinnati Medical Center; Director, Asthma and Allergy Treatment Center, Deaconess Hospital, 1984-93; Consultant in Field. Publications: Contributor of about 230 articles to professional journals. Honours: Grantee, National Institute of Allergy and Infectious Diseases, 1958-; EPA, 1994-, Fellow, ACP, American Academy of Allergy. Memberships: President, 1982-83, American Academy of Allergy; AAAS; American Association of Immunologists; Central Society for Clinical Research; American Thoracic Society; Society for Occupational and Environmental Health; Board of Directors, 1986-91, American Board of Allergy and Immunology; Board Governors, 1988-91, American Board of Internal Medicine. Address: 8464 Winton Road, Cincinnati, OH 45231-4927, USA.

BERNSTEIN Richard K, b. 17 Jun 1934, New York City, USA. Private Practice - Diabetes Mellitus. m. Anne E Bernstein, MD, 1956, 4 children. Education: BA, Liberal Arts and Mathematics, Columbia College, NY, 1950-54; BS, Industrial and Management Engineering, Columbia University School of Engineering and Applied Science, NY, 1953-55; Non-Matriculated Graduate Study in Theoretical Physics, 1957 and in Computer Design, Solid State Circuits and Advanced Mathematics, 1959-60, Completion of Pre-Medical Curriculum in Biology and Organic Chemistry, 1978, Columbia University School of General Studies, NY; MD, Albert Einstein College of Medicine, Bronx, NY, 1979-82. Career includes: Consultant and member Board of Directors, National Silver Industries Inc, NY, 1978-82; Consultant, Diabetes; American Foundation for The Blind, 1979, The Diabetes Research and Training Center of the Albert Einstein College of Medicine and Montefiore Hospital and Medical Center, 1979-81; Private Medical Practice in Diabetes Mellitus, 1983-. Publications: Diabetes: The Glucograf Method for Normalizing Blood Sugar, book, 1981, paperback edition, 1984; Numerous articles in professional journals, published abstracts and presentations. Honour: Alpha Pi Mu. Memberships include: European Association for Study of Diabetes; AMA; American Writers' Association; International Association of Medical Specialists; International Diabetes Federation. Hobbies: Flute; Sailing; Music - Baroque to 1946; Painting; Investments; Home and Boat Repairs; Landscape Architecture; Photography; Astrophotography. Address: 516 West Boston Post Road, Mamaroneck, NY 10543, USA.

BERRADA Abdellatif, b. 25 Dec 1936, Casablanca, Morocco. Pediatrician. m. Raymonde Mouret, 15 July 1961, 2 daughters. Education: MD, Paris University Medical School, 1964; Specialist in Pediatrics, Paris University Medical School, 1967. Appointments: House Physician, 1961; Consultant Physician, 1964-67; Head Doctor, Prematur & New Born Babies, 1967-93. Publications: Numerous publications in medical journals. Memberships: Founder Member, Moroccan Society of Pediatrics, 1965; Former Member, Moroccan Superior Medical Association, 1969; French Society of Pediatrics. Honours: Doctoral Thesis Prize, 1964; Chevalier of the Ouissan El Arch, 1992. Hobbies: Golf; Swimming. Address: 47 Bd Anfa, Casablanca, Morocco, Africa.

BERROL Cynthia Florence, b. 12 May 1934, New York, USA/ Educator; Dance and Movement Therapist; Consultant. m. Sheldon Berrol, 31 Mar 1955, dec, 2 sons, 2 daughters. Education: BA, Brooklyn College; MA, Mills College, Oakland, California; PhD, University of California, Berkeley. Appointments: Lecturer, City College of San Francisco, 1964-68; Lecturer, University of California, Berkeley, 1968-72; Lecturer, San Francisco State University, 1974-76; Professor, Department of Kinesiology and Physical Education, California State University, Hayward, 1976-. Publications include: A Neurophysiologic Approach to Dance/Movement Therapy: Theory and Practice, 1981; Trainee Attitudes Toward Disabled Persons: Effect of a Special Physical Education Program, 1984; Head Trauma: Pathophysiology and Implications for Physical Education, 1987; Head Injury rehabilitation: Chronicle of a Dance/Movement Therapist's Experience in Denmark, 1987; A View From Israel: Dance/Movement and Creative Arts Therapy in Special Education, 1989; Dance/Movement Therapy in Head Injury Rehabilitation: A Case Study, 1991; The Neurophysiologic Basis of the Mind-Body COnnection in Dance/Movement Therapy, 1992; Dance/Movement Therapy: Expressive Motion for Positive Resuslts, Co-author, 1994. Honours include: Research Scholarship, Creative Activity Grant, California State University, Harward, 1994. Memberships include: American Dance Therapy Association, Treasurer, 1990-94, Educational Research Chair, 1994-; Association for Neurologically Handicapped Children; Allied Association for Health, Physical Education, Recreation and Dance. Address: Department of Kinesiology and Physical Education, California state University Hayward, Hayward, CA 94542-3062, USA.

BERTHELSDORF Siegfried, b. 16 June 1911, Shannon County, Missouri, USA. Psychoanalyst; Psychiatrist. m. Mildred Friederich, 5 May 1945, 2 sons, 1 daughter. Education: BA, University of Oregon; MA, Anatomy, University of Oregon Medical School; Certificated Psychoanalyst, New York Psychoanalytic Institute; Certified Analyst, American Psychoanalytic Association. Appointments: Student Instructor in Anatomy, 1932-39; Supervising Psychiatrist, Manhattan State Hospital, New York; Adjunct Professor, College of Physicians and Surgeons, New York; Adjunct Professor, Clinical Professor, OHSU; Private Practice. Publications: Ansoparamedian Lobule of Cerebellum, 1941; Analysis of Addiction, 1976; Ambivalence Towards Women, 1988; Perspective at 77, 1991; Infant Stress, 1994. Honours: Phi Beta Kappa, 1934; Sigma Xi, 1934; Henry Waldo Coe Prize, 1939; Bronze Medal and Citation, Am Rhod Society, 1974; Citation, MacLaren School for Boys, 1983. Memberships: AMA; APA; American Psychoanalytic Association; International Psychoanalytic Association; New York Psychoanalytic Society; Seattle Institute for Psychoanalysis. Hobbies: Music; Farming. Address: 1125 SW Saint Clair Avenue, Portland, OR 97205, USA.

BERUBE Eric, b. 26 Mar 1959, California, USA. Education: MA, 1990, PhD, 1995, The Claremont Graduate School. Appointment: Research Design and Statistical Analysis Consultant. Publication: Co-author, The Relationship of Radiographic Fit and Eccentricity of Cementless Femoral Components with Clinical Results, in Journal of Bone and Joint Disease. Address: 5478 Carlson Drive 8, Sacramento, CA 95819, USA.

BERWA Laxmi Narain, b. 23 Mar 1947, Bandikiu, India. Consultant; Private Practioner. m. Kamlesh Berwa, 2 Sep 1975, 3 s. Education: AHIR College, Rewari, India; DAV College, Jullundlir City, Punjab, India; MBBS, All India Institute of Medical Sciences, New Delhi, India; MD; Fellow, American College of Physicians. Career includes: Major, USAF, Medical Corps, 1977-80; Staff, Department of Medicine, Section of Hematology and Oncology, Southern MD Hospital Center, 1980-; Staff, Department of Medicine, AMI Doctors Hospital of Prince Georges County, Lanham, MD, 1980-; Courtesy Staff, Department of Medicine, PG General Hospital, 1980-; Oncology Consultant, Pennsylvania Blue Shield and Medicare, Camp Hill, PA, 1983-; Physician Advisor for Delmarva Foundation, 1986-89; Various lectures given. Publications include: Co-author, Thrombocytosis in Chronic Myelocytic Leukemia and Its Management with ARA C-Infusion, presented at the 22nd Annual American College of Physicians Regional Air Force Meeting and Society of Air Force Physicians, 1980; Article written on Hypertension in 2 issues of Old Mill News, Kettering, MD. Honour: Fellow, American College of Physicians. Memberships: Chairman and Member of various committees; Elected Member, American Society of Clinical Oncology; Speakers Bureau of the American Cancer Society; Speakers Bureau of the American Heart Association, Professional and Education Committee, 1985-87, Chairman of Southern Branch, 1988; Prince George's Medical Society. Hobbies: Collecting Antique Books; Gardening; Local Basketball; Family. Address: 7700 Old Branch Avenue, Suite C-101, Clinton, MD 20735, USA.

BESCH Henry R Jr, b. 12 Sept 1942, San Antonio, Texas, USA. Professor; Researcher. m. Frankie R Drejer, 1 son. Education: BSc, Ohio State University; PhD, Ohio State University College of Medicine, 1967; USPHS Fellow, Baylor College of Medicine, 1968-70; MRC Fellow, Royal Free Hospital School of Medicine, London, England, 1970-71. Appointments include: Professor, Chairman, Department of Pharmacology and Medicine, 1977-, Senior Research Associate, Krannert Institute of Cardiology, 1977-, Showalter Professor, Pharmacology, 1980-, Indiana University School of Medicine; Assistant to the Director, 1989-91, Director, 1991-, State Department of Toxicology. Publications: About full publications including: Purification of reagents and solvents, 1964; Roles of calcium in cellular function, 1972; Co-author: Regulation of subcellular calcium pools: Membrane bases for cardiac arrhythmias, 1980; The receptor concept: Basic to clinical science, 1982; Isolation of canine cardiac sarcolemmal vesicles, 1984; Study of cardiac autonomic receptors by radiolabelled ligand binding assays, 1984; Local anesthetics, 1986; Molecular determinants of high affinity binding of ryanodine to the vertebrate skeletal muscle receptor: A comparative field analysis, 1994; Abstracts. Honours include: British Medical Research Council Fellowship, 1970-71; Canadian

Medical Research Council Visiting Professor, 1979. Memberships include: Fellow, American College of Cardiology; Sigma Xi; American Heart Association, Basic Science and Cardiology Councils; International Society for Heart Research, Executive Committee, American Section 1982-88; New York Academy of Sciences; American Association for Clinical Chemistry; National Academy for Clinical Biochemistry. Address: Department of Pharmacy and Toxicology, Indiana University School of Medicine, 635 Barnhill Drive, Indianapolis, IN 46202-5120, USA.

BEST Connie Lee, b. 18 Jan 1951, Gaffney, South Carolina, USA. Clinical Psychologist. m. Vernon Paul Harrison, 16 Feb 1991, 1 daughter. Education: BA, Psychology, University of South Carolina, 1973; MS, Clinical Psychology, 1981, PhD, Clinical Psychology, 1983, University of North Texas, Denton. Appointments: Instructor, 1983-84, Assistant Professor, 1984-90, Associate Professor, 1990-, Department of Psychiatry and Behavioural Sciences, Medical University of South Carolina, Charleston. Publications: Victims of Crime: Epidemiological and Treatment Considerations, 1988; 1st author: Medical students' attitudes about female rape victims, 1992; Accidental injury: Approaches to assessment and treatment, 1994. Honours: South Carolina Woman of the Year, 1993; Appointed to Department of Defense Advisory Committee on Women in the Services, 1994-97. Memberships: American Psychological Association; South Carolina Psychological Association; Association of Military Surgeons of the United States. Hobby: Spending time with family. Address: 3298 Mountainbrook Avenue. North Charleston, SC 29420, USA.

BETSER Jonathan, b. 3 Mar 1965, London, England. Principal of 2 Practices; Osteopath and Sports; Team Therapist. Education: Diploma in Osteopathy, British School of Osteopathy, London, 1988. Career: Principal of 2 Practices of Osteopathy, Herbal Medicine and Acupuncture; Clinical Tutor at British School of Osteopathy; Osteopath to British Trampolining Team (Including World and European Championships) Leighton Buzzard Rugby Football Club; Organising National Health Service based study into Osteopathic treatment. Memberships: Back Pain Association of Great Britain; British Association of Sports Medicine; Register of Osteopaths; National Osteoporosis Society. Hobbies: Hockey; Reading; Music;Parish Church; Council Member. Address: Woodside Clinic, Great Northern Road, Dunstable, Bedfordshire, LU5 4BT, England.

BEUTLER Larry Edward, b. 14 Feb 1941, Logan, Utah, USA. Psychologist. Education: BS, 1965, MS, 1966, Utah State University; PhD, University of Nebraska, Lincoln, 1970. Appointments: Assistant Professor, Duke University, 1970-71; Assistant Professor, Stephen F Austin State University, 1971-73; Associate Professor, Baylor College of Medicine, 1973-79; Professor, University of Arizona, 1979-90; Professor of Education and Psychology, University of California, Santa Barbara, 1990-. Publications: Systematic Treatment Selection (with J Clarkin, 1990; Integrative Assessment of Adult Personality (with M Berren), 1994; Comprehensive Textbook of Psychotherapy (with B Borger), 1994. Honours: Meritorious Service, Arizona Psychological Association, 1985; International President, Society for Psychotherapy Research, 1986-88; Research Award, ASGW, 1987. Memberships: Fellow, American Psychological Association; Fellow, American Psychological Society; Society for Psychotherapy Research. Hobby: Training and showing Arabian horses. Address: Department of Education, University of California, Santa Barbara, CA 93106, USA.

BEVAN William, b. 16 May 1922, Plains, Pennsylvania, USA. Psychologist. m. Dorothy Louise Chorpening, 17 Feb 1945, 3 sons. Education: AB, Franklin and Marshall College, 1942; MA, 1943, PhD, 1948, Duke University. Appointments: Instructor, Duke University, 1947; Instructor, Assistant Professor, Heidelberg College, 1946-48; Assistant Professor, Associate Professor, Professor, Emory University, 1948-59; Fulbright Professor, University of Oslo, Norway, 1952-53; Professor, Chairman of Psychology, Kansas State University, USA, 1959-62; Dean of Arts and Sciences, 1962-63, Vice-President for Academic Affairs, 1963-66, Kansas State University; Vice-President, Provost, Johns Hopkins University, 1966-70; Executive Officer, American Association for the Advancement of Science, 1970-74; William Preston Few Professor of Psychology, 1974-92, Provost, 1979-82, Emeritus Professor, 1992-, Duke University; Vice-President, Director of Health Programme, John D and Catherine T MacArthur Foundatin, 1982-91; Currently retired and Associate Editor, American Psychologist. Publications: Author or co-author, some 190 articles; Contemporary Approaches to Psychology (edited with Harry Helson), 1967. Honours:

Member, Institute of Medicine, National Academy of Sciences; Honorary Member, Society of Experimental Psychologists; Phi Beta Kappa; Sigma Xi. Memberships: Academy of Behavioral Medicine Research; American Psychological Association; American Association for the Advancement of Science; Federation of American Scientists; Southern Society for Philosophy and Psychology; Psychonomic Society; Association for Advancement of Psychology. Hobbies: Reading; Collecting classical compact discs. Address: 21 Stoneridge Circle, Durham, NC 27705-5510, USA.

BHAT Usha Parekh, b. 13 Dec 1940, Bangalore, India. Paediatric Neurologist. m. N S Bhat, 3 Feb 1972, 1 son, 1 daughter. Education: MBBS, University of Madras, 1963; ECFMG, USA, 1964; DCH, 1967, MD, Paediatrics, 1968, University of Bombay; Paediatric Neurology: London, 1973-74, Johns Hopkins Hospital, Baltimore; DTCH, Tropical Child Health, Tropical School of Medicine, UK, 1974; Diploma, Arabic, Qatar, 1979; Fellow, International College of Pediatrics, Washington DC, 1984; PhD, Neurodevelopmental Disorders in Children, Institute of Neurology, Madras. Appointments include: Assistant Professor, Paediatrics, 1972-73; Senior Registrar: Children's Hospital, Sheffield, England, 1973-74, Hammersmith Hospital, London, 1973-74; Consultant, Liverpool, 1974-75; Specialist, Paediatrics, Paediatric Neurology, Rehabilitation, HGH, Doha, Qatar, 1976-93; Fellow, Neurogenetics, 1994; Currently Paediatric Neurologist, Sri Ramachandra Medical College and Research Institute, Paediatrician, Apollo Hospital, Director, Amar Hospital & Usha Health Centre, Chairman, The Paediatric Specialty Center, Madras, India. Publications include: Co-author: Neurological and related Syndromes in CNS Tuberculosis: Clinical Features and Pathogenesis, 1971; Some Neurological Syndromes in CNS Tuberculosis, 1972; Posthaemorrhagic hydrocephalus: Diagnosis, differential diagnosis, treatment, and long-term results, 1974; Post Haemorrhagic Hydrocephalus, 1974; Measurements of muscle strength and performance in children with normal and disease muscles, 1976. Honours include: Tate Memorial Fellow, Neurotuberculosis, 1965-68; Commonwealth Fellow, Paediatric Neurology, 1973-74. Memberships: Indian Academy of Paediatrics; Indian College of Paediatrics; Indian Academy of Neurology; ICNA; AOCCN; Neuro Club; Madras Consultants Club, Apollo Hospitals. Hobbies: Reading, especially medical and non-medical journals and magazines; Swimming; Tennis; Bridge. Address: Amar Hospital and Usha Health Center, 154 Poonamallee High Road, Madras 600 100, India.

BHATHENA Sam Jehangirji, b. 18 Sept 1936, Bombay, India. Researcher. m. Pauruchisty Kias, 13 July 1975. Education: BSc, 1961; MSc, 1964; PhD, Medical Biochemistry, 1970. Appointments: Postdoctoral Fellow and Research Associate, National Institutes of Health, USA, 1971-74; Research Biochemist, Veterans Administration Medical Center, Washington DC, 1974-83; Assistant Professor, Georgetown University, 1974-83; Research Associate Professor, University of Maryland, 1990-; Research Chemist, Lead Scientist, Metabolism and Nutrition Interaction Laboratory, Beltsville Human Nutrition Research Center, USDA. Publications: Over 180 in scientific and medical journals including papers, reviews, book chapters and abstracts. Honours: Pandit Dube Scholar, 19675-69; Outstanding Research Scientist, Beltsville Human Nutrition Research Institute, 1988. Memberships: The Endocrine Society; American Diabetes Association; American Institute of Nutrition; American Federation of Clinical Nutrition; Society for Experimental Biology and Medicine. Hobbies: Playing chess; Reading. Address: Metabolism and Nutrient Interaction Lab, Beltsville Human Nutrition Research Center, USDA, BARC-E, Beltsville, MD 20705, USA.

BHATTACHARYA Jayashree, b. 30 Aug 1947, Dehradun, India. Gynaecologist. m. S S A Husain, 15 Dec 1975, 1 son, 1 daughter. Education: BScI; MBBS; D(Obst)RCOG; MRCOG. Appointments: Senior House Officer, Obstetrics and Gynaecology, King's College and University College Hospitals, London, England, 1974-75; Senior Registrar, Riyadh Alkhari Hospital Programme, Saudi Arabia, 1979-82; Consultant, Obstetrics and Gynaecology, Security Forces Hospital (AMI), Riyadh; Currently Consultant Gynaecologist, England. Publications include: A comparison of implantation rates and multiple pregnancy rates between the transfer of fresh embryos in superovulated cycles and frozen thawed embryos in natural or artificial cycles, 1990; Isn't IVF the treatment of choice for infertility caused by endometriosis, 1992; Role of ovum donation in assisted reproductive technology, 1994; Periovulatory ultrasonography may predict a non-receptive endometrium, 1994; The role of IVF in the treatment of infertility caused by endometriosis, 1994; Endometrial ossification: A cause of secondary infertility, 1994. Memberships: General Medical Council; Medical Protection Society; British Fertility Society; American Fertility Society; European Society of Human Reproduction and Embryology. Hobbies: Gardening; Reading; Psychoanalysis. Address: Bourn Hall Clinic, Bourn, Cambridge CB3 7TR, England.

BHATTACHARYYA Jharna, b. 4 July 1946, Calcutta, India. Scientist. Education: BSc, MSc, Physiology; PhD, Physiology. Appoinments: Senior Scientific Assistant, Scientist B, Scientist C, Indian Institute of Chemical Biology. Publications: Environment and Physiology, 1994; Contributor of 25 articles in scientific journals. Memberships: Society of Biological Chemists; Indian Science Congress Association; Indian Physiological Society; Association of Physiologists and Pharmacologists of India. Hobbies: Music; Drama. Address: Indian Institute of Chemical Biology, 4 Raja SC Mullick Road, Jadarpur, Calcutta 700032, India.

BHONSLE Rajan, b. 15 June 1959, Maharashtra, India. Radiologist & Sonologist. m. Minnu, 22 May 1985, 1 son. Education: MD Radio Diagnosis with 1st rank, Bombay University, India. Career: Consulting Radiologist, Motiben Dalyi Hospital, Bombay, 1985-87; Consulting Hon Radiologist, Jane Patrao Hospital, 1987-90. Publications: Several. Honours: Several. Membership: Indian Radiological & Imaging Association. Hobbies: Singing; Meditation. Address: 122 Sainara, Cuffe Parade, Bombay 400005, India.

BHUIYA Badrul Amin, b. 6 Apr 1951, Dhaka, Bangladesh. Teacher. m. Bilkis Banu, 4 Mar 1979, 1 son, 1 daughter. Education: MSc, University of Dhaka, 1974. Appointments: Lecturer in Zoology, Assistant Professor of Zoology, Associate Professor of Zoology, University of Chittagong. Publications: Biology of Rice Pest Parasitoid, 1984; A New Genus and Species of Pteromalidae from Bangladesh. 1990. Memberships: Zoological Soceity of Bangladesh; Bangladesh Entomological Society; European Network of Bangladesh Studies; International Society of Hymenopterists. Hobbies: Music; Travel; Painting. Address: Block B, House 51, Paharika Housing Estate, Post Office, University of Chiitagong, Chittagong 4331, Bangladesh.

BIBBY Ronald Edward, b. 23 July 1950, Rainhill, England. Orthodontist. m. Norma Cameron, 17 July 1976, 1 son, 2 daughters. Education: BMSc (Hons), Biochemistry, Oral Anatomy, 1972, BDS, 1974, MMSc Orthodontics, 1977, University of Dundee; MDent (Orthodontics), University of the Witwatersrand, 1979. Appointments: Professor of Orthodontics, University of the Western Cape, South Africa; Currently Specialist Practitioner of Orthodontics, Scotland. Publications: Dissertations: The effect of selected decalcifying agents on the results obtained with certain stains; A cephalometric appraisal of normal incisor relationships; Journal articles: The epithelial attachment, 1972; A cephalometric study of sexual dimorphism, 1979; Incisor relationships in different skeletofacial patterns, 1980; The hyoid triangle, 1981; The calibrated facebow, 1983; Relation between edentulous rest position and complete denture intercuspal position, 1984; The hyoid bone position in mouthbreathers and tonguethrusters, 1984; The ala-tragus line in complete denture prosthetics, 1985. Memberships: European Orthodontic Society; British Orthodontic Society. Hobbies: Sport especially triathlon; Music; Other creative pursuits. Address: 25 Barossa Place, Perth PH1 5HH, Scotland.

BICK Claus Heinrich, b. 9 July 1935, Dahn, Germany. MD Consultant; Professor. Education: Medicine & Psychology, University of Heidelberg, 1958; MD, Innsbruck and Würzburg Medical University, 1968. Appointments: Researcher in Hypnosis, 1968; Director of Bick-Krankenhaus, 1972; Director, Bick Institute, 1984; Director, Assistant Professor, European Academy of Medical Hypnosis, 1985; MD, Consultant in Nature Cures; Professor ho in Humanistic Disciplines. Publications: Neurohypnase Ullstein-Verlag, 1983; Discovering of the cerebral shifting in EEG in hypnotic state, 1985; EEG-Mapp in Hypnosis, 1989. Honours: President, International Society on Cerebral Dominances, 1988; President, European Society of Medical Hypnosis, 1990. Memberships: International Society on Cerebral Dominances; European Society of Medical Hypnosis; American Academy of Medicine; International Society of Prenatal Psychology. Hobbies: Literature; Art; Research in Reincarnation. Address: Professor h.c. Claus Bick, MD, Baermann str 27, D81245, Munich, Germany

BICKERS David Rinsey, b. 23 Sep 1941, Richmond, VA, USA. Physician. m. Melinda Jaegar McKenzie, 30 May 1970, 1 d. Education: AB, Georgetown University, Washington, DC, 1963; MD, University of VA, Charlottesville, 1967. Career includes: Chief of Staff and Senior VP,

Medical Affairs, University Hospital of Cleveland, 1990-93; Professor and Chairman of Department of Dermatology, Case Western Reserve; Currently, Carl Truman Nelson Professor and Chairman of Department of Dermatology, Columbia-Presbyterian Medical Center, NY. Publications: Numerous books, chapters, articles and abstracts including: Photosensitivity Diseases: Principles and Diagnosis and Treatment, 1981, 2nd edition, 1989; Clinical Pharmacology of Skin Disease, 1984; Dermatopharmakologie and Dermatotherapie, 1992. Honours include: Career Scientist, 1974-77; R J Reynolds Scholar in Clinical Medicine, 1976-77; Alpha Omega Alpha, 1986; Honorary Member, German Dermatology Society, 1988. Memberships include: Secretary Treasurer, Society for Investigative Dermatology; Advisory Council, NIAMS, 1988-92; Associate Editor, Journal of Investigative Dermatology, 1987-. Address: Columbia-Presbyterian Medical Center, Department of Dermatology, 161 Ft Washington Avenue, 14th Floor, New York, NY 10032, USA.

BIDDLE Stuart James Hamilton, b. 4 July 1954. University Lecturer. m. Fiona Biddle, 1 Sept 1984, 2 sons. Education: BEd; MSc; PhD; Chartered Psychologist. Appointments: Lecturer, North Staffordshire Polytechnic, 1979; Lecturer, 1988, currently Senior Lecturer, University of Exeter. Publications: Books: Psychology of physical activity and exercise: A health-related perspective, 1991; European perspectives on exercise and sport psychology (editor), 1994. Memberships: Fellow, Physical Education Association; British Association of Sport and Exercise Sciences; British Psychological Association. Hobbies: Exercise (jogging, cycling, weight training); Beer making. Address: School of Education, University of Exeter, Heavitree Road, Exeter EX1 2LU, England.

BIEK Richard William, b. 16 Nov 1931, Chicago, Illinois, USA. Physician. m. Gail S Biek, 10 Jan 1981, 2 sons, 2 daughters. Education: BA, cum laude; BS; MD; MPH; FACPM; Certified, American Board of Preventive Medicine. Appointments: Medical Superintendent, Evangelical Presbyterian Church Hospital, Worawora, Ghana; Director, Bureau of State-Local Relations, Division of Health, State of Wisconsin, USA; Clinical professor, University of Wisconsin Medical School; Chief Medical Officer, Deputy Commissioner, City of Chicago; Lieutenant Colonel, Senior Medical Officer, 33rd Infantry, Ilarne. Publications: Foodborne Illness, 1993; Immunization Barriers, 1990; Chicago Measles Outbreak, 1990; Insomnia, 1986; High Blood Pressure, 1984; Ainhum, 1975; Periodic Screening, 1973; Acute Diarrhea, 1969; Schistosomiasis, 1965. Honours: Alumnus of Distinction, University of Dubuque, Iowa, 1968; Army Achievement Medal, 1990. Memberships: Associate, World Medical Association; American Medical Association; Illinois State Medical Society; Chicago Medical Society; American Public Health Association; Illinois Public Health Association. Address: 4217 North Sheridan Road, Unit 1R, Chicago, IL 60613-1677, USA.

BIELORY Leonard, b. 17 Nov 1954, Neptune, NJ, USA. Medical Director; Consultant Allergist and Immunologist. Education: BS, Fundamental Science, Lehigh University College of Engineering, Bethlehem, PA, 1976; MS, Molecular Biology, Lehigh University Graduate School of Molecular Biology, Bethlehem, PA, 1976; MD, UMDNJ, NJ Medical School, Newark, NJ, 1980; Diplomate, Internal Medicine, 1984, Allergy and Immunology, 1985, Diagnostic Laboratory Immunology, 1986. Appointments include: Consultant in Allergy and Immunology, St Barnabas Medical Center, Livingston, NJ, 1985-, East Orange Veterans Administration Medical Center, NJ, 1985-; Director, Division of Allergy and Immunology, Department of Medicine, 1985-; Co-Director Immuno-Ophthalmology Service, Department of Ophthalmology, 1991-; Member of various committees; Reviewer, Associate Editor and Editorial Board Member of various professional journals; Numerous invited lectures and meetings. Publications: Numerous articles, books, monographs, chapters, abstracts, reviews and reports including: Allergic Diseases of the Eye, in Current Practice of Medicine, 1993. Honours include: Phi Beta Kappa, 1975; Physician's Recognition Award, AMA, 1983, 1986, 1989; Dean's Award of Clinical Excellence, UMDNJ, NJ Medical School, 1986; Alpha Omega Alpha, 1990. Memberships include: NY Academy of Sciences; Fellow, NY Academy of Medicine; American Federation of Clinical Research; Fellow, American Association of Certified Allergists; Fellow, American Academy of Allergy and Immunology; Fellow, American College of Physicians. Address: Division of Allergy and Immunology, UMD New Jersey Medical School, 90 Bergen Street, DOC 4700, Newark, NJ 07103-2499, USA.

BIERENBAUM Marvin Leonard, b. 30 Aug 1926, Philadelphia, Pennsylvania, USA. Physician; Researcher. m. Nettie Bella Eiser, 1 July 1951, 1 son, 1 daughter. Education: BS, Biology, Rutgers University, New Jersey, 1947; MD, Hahnemann Medical College, Pennsylvania, 1953. Appointments: Consultant in Cardiology and Internal Medicine, Montclair, New Jersey, 1957-58; Director, Kenneth L Jordan Cardiac Research Group, Montclair, 1959-; Clinical Associate Professor of Medicine, University of Medicine and Dentistry, New Jersey, 1965-; Regional Medical Advisor, Social Security Administration, 1973-85; Professor, Community Medicine, Seton Hall University, 1988-. Publications: 150 articles in professional journals. Honours: Elected Fellow, American College of Physicians, 1963; Fellowship, Milbank Fund, 1965; Resident Consultant to Netherlands Heart Association, 1976-77; Elected Fellow, American College of Cardiology, 1978; Honorary Professor of Medicine, Chongqing Medical School, China, 1987. Memberships include: American Health Association Council on Epidemiology; American Health Association Council on Atherosclerosis; American Society of Clinical Nutrition; American College of Nutrition. Hobby: Sports. Address: Kenneth L Jordan Heart Fund and Research Group, 48 Plymouth Street, Montclair, NJ 07042, USA.

BIGGS Max W, b. 4 Aug 1920, Cleveland, Ohio, USA. Doctor of Medicine. m. Joanne Whitecotton, 24 Aug 1947, 2 sons, 1 daughter. Education: MD, Harvard Medical School, 1945; PhD, Medical Physics, University of California, Berkeley, 1954. Appointments: LLNL, 1955 (40 years); Medical Director, Lawrence Livermore National Laboratory, ret'd. Address: 4616 Las Lomitas Drive, Pleasanton, CA 94566, USA.

BIGOTTE DE ALMEIDA Luis, b. 21 Jan 1948, Guarda, Portugal. Medical Doctor. m. Natalia Astrid Bigotte, 27 Jan 1973, 1 son. Education: MD, University of Lisbon; PhD, University of Uppsala, Sweden, 1983. Appointments: Neurologist, Hospitais Civis de Lisboa, Hospital dos Capuchos; Researcher, Institute of Pathology, University of Uppsala, Sweden; Neurologist, Hospital de Vila Franca de Xira; Head, Laboratory of Neuropathology, Hospital dos Capuchos, Lisbon; Director, Department of Neurology, Hospital Garcia de Orta, Almada Publications: Co-Author: Toxic Affects of adraimycin on the central nervous system: Ultrastructural changesin some circumventricular organs of the mouse after IV administration of the drug, 1983; Co-author: Cytotoxic effects of adriamycin on the central nervous system of the mouse: Cytofluorescence and electron-microscopic observations after various modes of administration, 1984; Author: Morphofunctional methods for the study of peripheral neuropathy, 1986. Co-author: Degeneration of trigeminal ganglion neurons caused by retrograde axonal transport of doxorubicin, 1987; Author: Neuropatologia, 1988; Co-author: Distribution and toxic effects of IV injected epirubicin on the central nervous system of the mouse, 1989; . Honours: Sandoz Award of Neurology, 1985; Vasconcellos Marques Award of Neurosurgery, 1985. Memberships: Portuguese Medical Association; Portuguese Society of Neurology; Portuguese Society of Neuropathology; International Society of Neuropathology; European Neuroscience Association; Brain Research Organization; European Neurological Society. Hobbies: Drawing; Painting; Travel. Address: Rua Prof Mira Fernandes Lote 2-7E, P-1900 Lisbon, Portugal.

BIGRIGG Margaret Alison, b. 26 Sept 1958, Whitehaven, Cumbria, England. Clinical Director. m. James Browning, 1 daughter. Education: BM, Southampton University, 1982; FRCS, Edinburgh, 1986; MRCOG, 1989; MD, 1993. Appointments: Consultant Senior Lecturer, Southmead Hospital, Bristol; Currently Clinical Director, Greater Glasgow Community Trust, Scotland. Publications: Menstrual Disorders: A guide to hysterectomy and alternative therapies (with J Smith), book; Overview of Clinical Experience to Date, chapter, 1992; Treatment of Cervical Intra-epithelial Neoplasis (CIN) (with J Browning), chapter, 1993; Patient acceptance of diathermy loop treatment, letter, 1990; Co-author: Three cases of recovery of IUCD from sigmoid colon, 1988; Disseminated intravascular coagulation associated with group A Streptoccal infection in pregnancy, 1988; Cervical screening and Government policy, 1989; 1000 patients undergoing colposcopic diagnosis and treatment of cervical dysplasia at a single clinic visit, using the low voltage diathermy loop, 1990; Listeriosis in twin pregnancy, 1990; Use of intramyometrial 15m PGF2 alpha to control atonic PPH following vaginal delivery and failure of conventional therapy, 1991; Management of women referred to early pregnancy asessment unit: care and cost effectiveness, 1991; Pregnancy following loop diathermy excision of cervical dysplasia, 1991; Pregnancy following large loop excision of the transformation zone, 1993; Efficacy and safety of large-loop of the transformation zone, 1994. Address: 2 Claremont Terrace, Glasgow G3 7XR, Scotland.

BILLINGSLEY Peter Francis, b. 30 Sept 1958, Birmingham, England. Medical Entomologist. Education: BSc (Hons), Agricultural Zoology, University of Leeds, 1981; PhD, Biology, Queen's University, Canada, 1985; Royal Society Research Postdoctoral Fellow, 1986, Postdoctoral Fellow, 1986-88, Swiss Tropical Institute, Basel. Appointments: Currently Royal Society University Research Fellow, Imperial College of Science, Technology and Medicine, London. Memberships: Fellow, Royal Entomological Society; Fellow, Royal Society of Tropical Medicine and Hygiene. Hobbies: Folk musician; Photography. Address: Department of Biology, Imperial College of Science, Technology and Medicine, Prince Consort Road, London SW7 2BB, England.

BILSTROM David E, b. 5 Sep 1944, Chicago, IL, USA. Allergy Specialist. m. Leanne Miller, 11 Apr 1969, 3 s. Education. BA, Grinnell College; MD, University of Iowa; Intern, Duke University; Residency, UCLA; Fellowship, Georgetown. Career: US Navy, 1972-77; Currently, Allergy Specialist. Memberships: Oregon Allergy Society, President, 1991-; AMA; Oregon Medical Association; Multnomah County Medical Association; American Association of Allergy and Immunology; Oregon Allergy Society. Address: 9370 SW Greenburg Road, Portland, OR 97223, USA.

BIMLER Hans Peter, b. 10 Dec 1916, Obenigk. Orthodontist. m. Erika Boenisch, 28 Apr 1959, 1 son, 2 daughters. Education: MD; DDS. Appointments: Major, Medical Corps; Private Practice. Publications: Contributor of ver 100 professional publications, 1950-. Honours: Professor Honoris Causa, Sao Paulo, 1989; Honorary Membership in French, Spanish and Suth American Societies . Memberships: AAo; IAO; EOS. Hobby: Kayaking. Address: Wilhelmstrasse 40, 65183 Wiesbaden, Germany.

BIRD Arthur Richard, b. 27 Oct 1947, Cape Town, South Africa. Haematologist. m. Susan Bird, 6 June 1980, 1 son, 2 daughter. Education: MB ChB; MMed, Pathology; FFPath (South Africa). Appointments: Intern, Medicine, Surgery, 1973, Registrar, Pathology, Haematology, 1974-76, Senior Specialist, Department of Haematology, 1984-89; Groote Schuur Hospital; Senior Specialist, Department of Pathology, Red Cross War Memorial Children's Hospital, 1979-83; Currently Medical Director, Chief Executive, Western Province Blood Transfusion Service. Publications: Approximately 45 articles and letters in field of haematology and blood transfusion. Honours: Elected to International Society of Blood Transfusion Council as Councillor for African Region, 1992. Memberships: Western Province Blood Transfusion Service, Old Mill Road, Pinelands 7450, Cape Town, South Africa.

BIRK (Carl) Lee, b. 8 February 1935, New Albany, Indiana, USA. Professor, Doctor of Psychiatry. m. (1) Enily Perkins Gantt, 21 June 1958, (2) Ann Wegner Birk, 15 June 1973, 1 son, 3 daughters. Education: BA, Chemistry, Zoology, Valparaiso University; MD, Johns Hopkins, 1960; Psychiatry, Harvard, 1961-66; Boarded in Psychiatry, 1970. Appointments: Chief of Behaviour Therapy, Group, Family & Covile Therapy, Massachusetts General Hospital, 1971; Clinical Director, Founder, Learning Therapies Inc, 1972-87; Associate Psychiatirst, Beth Israel Hospital, 1974-; Associate Clinical Professor of Psychiatry, Harvard. Publications: Behavior Hterapy in Clinical Psychiatry, 1972; Biofeedback-Behavioral Medicine, 1973; Psychoanalysis and Behavior Therapy, 1993; Shifting Gears in Sex Therapy, 1980; Psychatherapy within Social Systems, 1994. Honours: Henry Strung Denison Fellow in Psychiatry, 1959-60; First Annual Rhoads Lecturer, Duke University, 1994. Memberships: American College of Psychiatrists; American Family Therapy Association; Society for Exploration of Psychotherapy; International American Society of Clinical Psychopharmacology. Hobbies: Skiing; Economics; Hiking. Address: 91 Main Street, Concord, MA 01742, USA.

BIRKBECK John Addison, b. 24 Jan 1933, Scotland. Nutritionist; Educator. m. Adele Cholmondeley-Smith, 23 Jan 1959, 3 sons, 1 daughter. Education: MB, ChB (Edinburgh); FRCP (C); Certified, American Board of Pediatrics; MNZIFST. Appointments: Assistant Professor, Paediatrics, 1962-67, Associate Professor, Paediatrics, Human Nutrition, 1968-72, University of British Columbia, Canada; Senior Lecturer in Paediatrics, University of Southampton, England, 1973-75; Professor, Chairman, Department of Human Nutrition, University of Otago, New Zealand, 1975-86; Currently: Medical and Scientific Director, New Zealand Nutrition Foundation; Clinical Reader, Auckland Medical School. Publications: Metrical growth and skeletal development of the human fetus, 1976; New Zealanders and their Diet, 1979; Fetal growth and endocrinology, 1981; Diet Survey, 1991; The Life Diet, 1991. Honours: Queen Elizabeth II Fellow, 1960-62; Markle Scholar in Medical Science, 1964-68. Memberships: American Society of Clinical Nutrition; Nutrition Society, UK; Australasian Clinical Nutrition Society; Paediatric Society of New Zealand. Hobbies: Computer (databases and interactive media); Music especially keyboard. Address: InforMed Systems, PO Box 17, Waikauku, New Zealand 1250.

BISHOP George D, b. 30 May 1949, South Haven, USA. University Professor. m. Jane Andrew, 9 June 1973, 1 son, 1 daughter. Education: BA, magna cum laude, Hope College; MS, Yale University; PhD, Yale University. Appointments: Research Psychologist, Department of Psychiatry, Walter Reed Army Institute of Research, Washington, 1975-79; Visiting Assistant Professor of Psychology, Department of Sociology, Anthropology & Psychology, The American University in Cairo, Egypt, 1979-81; Assistant Professor of Psychology, 1981-87, Associate Professor of Psychology, 1987-93, Division of Behavioral & Cultural Sciences, The University of Texas, San Antonio; Visiting: Senior Teaching Fellow, Department of Social Work and Psycology, National University of Singapore, 1991-93; Associate Professor, Department of Social Work and Psycology, National University of Singapore, 1993-. Publications Include: Book: Health Psychology: Integrating Mind and Body, 1994; Articles: Responses to persons with AIDS: Fear of contagion or stigma?, 1991; Understanding the understanding of illness: Lay disease representations, 1991; Lay disease representations and responses to victims of disease, 1991; Cognitive organization of disease, 1992; Sense of coherence as a resource in dealing with stress, 1993. Honours: National Science Foundation Fellow, 1971-74; Sigma Chi Research Award, 1971; S J Stringer, Junior Psychology Award, 1970. Memberships: Singapore Psychological Society; Society for Behavioral Medicine; American Psychological Association; American Psychological Society; Society for Personality and Social Psychology; Society for the Psychological Study of Social Issues. Address: Department of Social Work & Psychology, National University of Singapore, 10 Kent Ridge Crescent, Singapore 0511, Singapore.

BISWAS Arijit, b. 22 Sep 1955, Asansol, India. Obstetrican; Gynaecologist. m. Dr Tapati Biswas, 28 feb 1981, 1 daughter. Education: MBBS, Calcutta University; MD, All India Institute of Medical Sciences; Dip NB, National Board of Education, India; MRCOG London. Appointments: registrar, Obstetrics and Gynaecology, Dartford, Kent, England, 1988; Registrar, Obstetrics and Gynaecology, University of Liverpool, 1990; Lecturer, Honorary Consultant of Obstetrics and Gynaecology, Narional University of Singapore. Publications: Breech and Pelvimetry, 1993; Platelet Disorders in Pregnancy, 1994. Honours: Gold Medal in Obstetrics and Gynaecology, Calcutta University, 1980; Goodeve Scholar, 1978/ Memberships: Obstetrical and Gynaecological Society of Singapore. Hobbies: Stamp collecting; Table Tennis. Address: Department of Obstetrics and Gynaecology, National University Hospital, National University of Singapore, Lower Kent Ridge Road, 0511 Singapore.

BISWAS Tuli, b. 8 Mar 1953, Calcutta, India. Research Scientist. m. Amit K Biswas, 27 Apr 1978, 1 son. Education: MSc; PhD, 1984. Appointments: Research Associate; Currently Scientist B, Department of Physiology, Indian Institute of Chemical Biology. Publications: 11 original articles. Honours: National Scholarship for Merit, 1974. Memberships: Indian Science Congress Association; Society of Biological Chemists; Physiological Society of India. Hobbies: Reading story-books; Listening to music. Address: Department of Physiology, Indian Institute of Chemical Biology, 4 Raja S C Mullick Road, Jadavpur, Calcutta 700 032, India.

BIZER Vladimir Alexandrovich, b. 22 Apr 1929, Kherson, USSR. Professor of Oncology. m. Antonina Sakunova, 2 June 1955, 1 daughter. Education: Kiev State Medical Institute; Doctor of Medical Sciences. Appointments: General Surgeon; Chief, Department of Bone and Joint Surgery; Scientific Worker, Research Institute of Traumatology and Orthopaedics; Currently Professor of Oncology and Leading Scientific Worker, Medical Radiological Research Centre, Russian Academy of Sciences, Obninsk. Publications: Homotransplantation of bone tissue in children, 1969; Combination therapy for osteogenic sarcoma, 1989; Reconstructive treatment of bone sarcoma in childhood, 1992. Membership: Association of Orthopaedic Surgeons. Hobby: Fishing. Address: ul Koroliova 1, app 68, 249020 Obninsk, Kaluga Region, Russia.

BJORKLUND Geir, b. 20 Apr 1969, Mo i Rana, Norway. Medical Free-lance Journalist. Education: Currently: External Candidate, Moheia videregående skole, Mo i Rana. Publications: Many articles in medical journals and magazines. Memberships: American Institute of Biomedical Climatology; International Society of Biometeorology. Hobbies: Stamps; Economics; Literature; Nature. Address: Toften 24, N-8610 Grubhei, Norway.

BLACKBURN Ronald, b. 20 Oct 1938, Stockton-on-Tees, England. Clinical Psychologist. m. Celia Bannister, 28 Feb 1964, 2 sons, 1 daughter. EducationL: MA, Cambridge University, 1961; MSc, Birmingham University, 1966; PhD, Southampton University, 1973; FBPsS; FIOP; Chartered Psychologist. Appointments: Principal Psychologist, Rampton Hospital, 1971-74; Senior Lecturer in Clinical Psychology, Aberdeen University, 1974-81; Chief Psychologist, Park Lane Hospital, Liverpool, 1981-90; Professor of Clinical and Forensic Psychological Studies, University of Liverpool; Director of Research, Ashworth Hospital. Publications: The Psychology of Criminal Conduct, 1993; Contributor of numerous papers and chapters in books. Honours: Fellow, British Psychological Soceity, 1976; Fellow, International Organisation for Psychophysiology, 1982. Memberships: British Psychological Society; International Organisation for Psychophysiology. Hobbies: Music; Travel; History; Food. Address: Research Unit, Ashworth Hospital, Maghull, Liverpool L31 1HW, England.

BLACKLOW Neil Richard, b. 26 Feb 1938, Cambridge, MA, USA. Academic Physician. m. Margery Brown, 2 Jun 1963, 2 s. Education: BA, Harvard College; MD, Columbia University. Career: Virologist, National Institutes of Health, 1965-71; Associate Professor of Medicine, Boston University, 1971-76; Director, Division of Infectious Diseases, 1976-90, Chair, Department of Medicine, 1990-, University of Massachusetts Medical School. Publications include: Author or Co-author of 165 published articles; Co-editor of Textbook "Infectious Diseases", 1992. Honour: Richard M Haidack Distinguished Professor of Medicine, University of Massachusetts Medical School, 1990-. Memberships: Association of American Physicians; American Society for Clinical Investigation; Association of Professors of Medicine; American Clinical and Climatological Association. Hobbies: Tennis; Music. Address: Department of Medicine, University of Massachusetts Medical Center, 55 Lake Avenue North, Worcester, MA 01655, USA.

BLAHOS Jaroslav, b. 3 June 1930, Horazdovice, Czechoslovakia. Professor of Internal Medicine. m. Simonetta Cusan, 1966, 2 sons. Education: Corresponding Member, French National Medical Academy. Appointments: Research Worker, Research Institute of Endocrinology; Professor, Head, Department of Internal Medicine, University Hospital, Prague. Publications: Textbook on Endocrinology, 1985, 1989; 394 papers in Czechoslovakia and foreign journals. Honours: 2 Medals, Charles University, Prague; Medal of the Czechoslovakia Medical Association. Memberships: Czechoslovakia Medical Association; Czechoslovakia Literary Foundation; French & Rome Endocrinology Society. Hobbies: Music. Address: Vychodni 30, 16200 Prague 6, Czechoslovakia.

BLAKE Douglas Harold, b. 6 Nov 1921, Worcester, England. Specialist. m. Olive May Lister, 21 June 1950, 2 sons. Education: MB, ChB, MRCS, LRCP, Birmingham University Medical School; MRCPEd, Edinburgh University; Postgraduate Course, Glasgow University. Appointments: Assistant Chest Physician, Markfield Hospital Leicestershire, 1952-62; First Chest Physician, Northern Territory of Australia, 1963; First Specialist Geriatrician, Bendigo Home & Hospital for the Aged, 1967-72. Publications: The Treatment of Chronic Cavitating Pulmonary Tuberculosis by long term Chemotherapy, 1961; A Geriatric Day in Hospital, the first 12 months, 1968; Geriatrics & Rehabilitation, 1972; The Geriatric Medicine Book, 1991. Honours: Carter Downs Medical Prize, 1939; Bertram Windle Prize, Birmingham University, 1941. Memberships: British Medical Association; British Thoracic Society; British Geriatrics Society; Australian Association of Gerontology; Australian Society for Geriatric Medicine. Hobbies: Music; Photography; Philately. Address: 150 Bardwell Drive, Mickleham, Melbourne, Victoria, Australia.

BLAKLEY Brian, b. 16 Feb 1952, Minneapolis, MN, USA. Medical Doctor. m. Joan Blakley, 2 s, 1 d. Education: BSc; MD, Medicine; PhD, Otolaryngology; Fellowship - Neurotology, University of Toronto. Career: Instructor, University of Minnesota; Currently, Associate Professor, Otolaryngology, Wayne State University. Publications: Otolaryngology fr the House Officer, 1989; Feeling Dizzy, 1994; 32 articles in peer reviewed journals. Honours: Resident Teaching Award, 1984; General Research Awards. Memberships: AMA; AAO-HNS; MSMS; MOS; Triological; ANS; AAAS. Hobbies: Music; Tennis. Address: Wayne Sate University, Department of Otolaryngology, Ste 5E UHC, 540 East Canfield, Detroit, MI 48201, USA.

BLANDINO Joyce Kwok Hing, b. 26 Dec 1962, Hong Kong. Scientist. m. Joseph R Blandino, 8 June 1991. Education: BS, University of Illinois at urbana-Champaign, USA, 1986; MS, 1988, PhD, 1992, University of Virginia. Appointments: Lecturer, Piedmont Virginia Community College; Postdoctoral Fellow, University of Virginia School of Medicine; Visiting Assistant Professor, James Madison University. Publications: Short-term Effect of Hepatic Arterial Versus Portal Venous Repertusion on the Energy Levels of the Liver Tissue, 1990; Lambert-Eaton Syndrome IgG Inhibits Dihydropyridine-Sensitive Slowly inactivating Calcium Channels in Bovine Adrenal Chromaffin cells, Co-author, 1993; Inhibitory Action of Lambert-Eaton Syndrome IgG on Calcium Currents in a Thyroid C-cell Line, Co-author, 1993; Effects of Lambert-Eaton Syndrome Serum and IgG on Calcium and Sodium Currents in Small-Cell Lung Cancer Cells, Co-author, 1993; Voltage-dependent Sodium Channels in Human Small-Cell Lung Cancer cells: Role in Action Potentials and Inhibition by Lambert-Eaton Syndrome IgG, Co-author, 1995. Honours: Dean's list, 1984-85, 1985-86; Dean's Fellowship, 1986-87; Graduate Research Assistantship; 1986, 1987-92; High Blood Pressure Research training Grant, 1992-93; Phi Kappa Phi; Tau Beta Pi. Memberships: Biomedical Engineering Society; American Association for the Advancement of Science; Cardiovascular Training Grant, 1993-95 Hobbies: Cooking; Hiking. Address: 3870 Cadet Ct, Penn Laird, VA 22846, USA.

BLANK Arthur S, b. 7 Jan 1936, Oil City, Pennsylvania, USA. Psychiatrist. m. Donna H Blank, 25 Apr 1970, 2 daughters. Education: BA, Allegheny College, 1957; MD, Case Western Reserve University, 1961; Psychiatric Residency, Yale University, 1962-65. Appointments: Clinical Director, Yale Psychiatric Institute, 1967-72; Assistant Professor of Psychiatry, University of Minnesota; National Director, War Veteran Counseling Center, US Department of Veterans Affairs, 1982-94; Clinical Professor of Psychiatry, Georgetown University, Washington DC; Clinical Professor of Psychiatry, Uniformed Services University of Health Sciences, Bethesda, Maryland; Psychiatry Service, Veterans Affairs Medical Center, Minneapolis, Minnesota. Publications: The Trauma of War (edited with Stephen Sonnenberg and John Talbott), 1985; Clinical Detection, Diagnosis, and Differential Diagnosis of Post-traumatic Stress Disorder, 1994. Honours: William Porter Award for Achievement in Psychiatry, Association of Military Surgeons of the United States, 1993. Memberships: American Psychiatric Association; International Society for Traumatic Stress Studies; International Society for the Study of Dissociation. Address: Psychiatry Service (116A), VA Medical Center, Minneapolis, MN 55409-2319, USA.

BLASER Martin Jack, b. 18 Dec 1948, New York City, New York, USA. Physician. m. Ronna Wineberg, 3 Sept 1979, 1 son, 2 daughters. Education: BA, University of Pennsylvania, 1969; MD, New York University, 1973. Appointments include: Associate Professor of Medicine, University of Colorado School of Medicine, 1985-89; Chief, Infectious Disease Section, Veterans Administration Medical Center, Denver, Colorado, 1985-89; Currently Addison B Scoville Professor of Medicine, Director, Division of Infectious Diseases, Vanderbilt University, Nashville, Tennessee. Publications: Campylobacter pylori in gastritis and peptic ulcer disease (editor), 1989; Co-editor: Campylobacter jejuni: current strategy and future needs, 1992; Infections of the gastrointestinal tract, 1995. Honours: Young Investigator Award, Western Society for Clinical Investigation, 1989; Squibb Award, Infectious Diseases Society of America, 1992. Memberships: American Society for Clinical Investigation; American Society for Clinical Research, National Councillor 1986-90; Infectious Diseases Society of America, National Councillor 1993-96. Hobbies: Running; Hiking. Address: Division of Infectious Diseases, Vanderbilt University School of Medicine, Nashville, TN 37232, USA.

BLAUSTEIN Mordecai P, b. 19 Oct 1935, NY, USA. Professor and Chairman. m. Ellen R Baron, 21 Jun 1959, 1 s, 1 d. Education: BA, Honours, Zoology, Cornell University, Ithaca, NY, 1957; MD, Washington University School of Medicine, St Louis, MO, 1962. Career: Teaching Assistant in Zoology, Cornell University, NY, 1956-57; Senior Research Fellow, Cambridge University, Cambridge, England, 1966-68; Associate Professor, Physiology and Biophysics, Washington University School of Medicine, 1968-75; NATO Senior Fellow in Science, Guest Scientist,

Switzerland, 1971; Guest Scientist in England, 1973; Professor of Physiology and Biophysics, Washington University, 1975-80; Currently, Professor and Chairman, Department of Physiology, University of Maryland School of Medicine. Publications: Over 185 articles published in scientific journals and books; 3 Books edited; Holder of 2 US Patents. Honours: Current Contents Citation Classics, 1974, 1977; Robert J and Claire Pasarow Foundation Award, 1990; Alexander von Humboldt Sr, US Scientist Award, 1993; Heart to Heart and International Society on Hypertension in Blacks, Humanitarian Cardiology Award, 1993. Memberships: American Association for the Advancement of Science; American Heart Association; American Physiological Society; Biophysical Society; International Society on Hypertension in Blacks, NY Academy of Sciences; Society for Neuroscience. Hobbies: Bicycling; Book Collecting. Address: Department of Physiology, Rm 5-009, Bressler Building, University of Maryland, School of Medicine, 655 West Baltimore Street, Baltimore, MD 21201-1559, USA.

BLAZER Dan German, b. 23 Feb 1944, Nashville, Tennessee, USA. Psychiatrist; Professor. m. Sherrill Blazer, 1 son, 1 daughter. Education: BA, Biology, Vanderbilt University, 1965; Harding Graduate School of Religion, Memphis, Tennessee, 1966; MD, University of Tennessee College of Medicine, 1969; Resident, Psychiatry, Duke University Medical Center, 1973-75; MPH, Epidemiology, 1989, PhD, Epidemiology, 1980, University of North Carolina, Chapel Hill. Appointments: Assistant Professor, Psychiatry, 1976-80, Assistant Professor, Community and Family Medicine, 1980-88, Associate Professor, Psychiatry, 1980-85, Head, Division of Social and Community Psychiatry, 1981-85, Professor, Psychiatry, 1985-90, Director, Affective Disorders Programme, 1985-92, Head, Division of Geriatric Psychiatry, 1988-92, Professor, Community and Family Medicine, 1988-, J P Gibbons Distinguished Professor, Psychiatry, 1990-, Dean, Medical Education, 1992-, Duke University Medical Center; Adjunct Professor, University of North Carolina, Chapel Hill, 1986-. Publications: Books include: Healing the Emotions, 1979; Handbook of Geriatric Psychiatry, 1980; Depression in Late Life, 1982, 2nd Edition, 1993; Life is Worth Living, 1987; Born to Work, 1992; Chapters, over 250 articles, over 130 abstracts. Honours include: Diplomate, American Board Psychiatry and Neurology; Fellow, American College of Psychiatry; Alex Haley Award, Gerontology, 1986; Jack Weinberg Award, Geriatric Psychiatry, American Psychiatric Association; Alpha Omega Alpha, 1993-. Memberships include: American Association for the Advancement of Science; Fellow: American and Southern Psychiatric Associations; American Geriatric Society; Gerontological Society; American Psychopathological Association. Address: 203 Midenhall Way, Cary, NC 27513, USA.

BLESSING-MOORE Joann, b. 21 Sept 1946, Tacoma, Washington, USA. Medical Doctor. m. Robert C Moore, 1 daughter. Education: MD, Health Science Center, Syracuse, NY, USA; BA, Syracuse University. Appointments: Clinical Professor, Children's Hospital, Stanford; Staff MD, Palo Alto Medical Foundation, Clinical Associate Professor, Stanford; Private Practice. Publications: Abstracts and journal articles plus editor of 2 journal supplements. Memberships: America Academy of Allergy Immunology; America College of Allergy Immunology; America Thoracic Society; America College of Chest Physicians. Hobbies: Hiking; Photography; Music; Scuba Diving; Travel; Horses; Sailing. Address: 770 Welch Road 232, Palo Alto, CA 94304, USA.

BLOCH Silvia Margit Anna Becker, b. 10 Dec 1955, Mainz, Germany. Psychiatrist. m. Hans Bloch, Aug 1981, 1 son. Education: MD; ABPN, general and Geriatric Psychiatry. Appointments: Director, Geriatric Evaluation Unit and Staff Psychiatrist, Dora Veterans Hospital; Clinical Assistant Professor, Department Neuropsychiatry, USCSM, USA. Honour: Psychiatric Chief Resident, 1985. Memberships: AMA; APA; AMWA; AAGLP; AAGP; Columbia Medical Society. Hobbies: Watersports; Arts; Theatre. Address: 1116 Blanding Street, Suite 2B, Columbia, SC 29201, USA.

BLOCK Andrew Robert, b. 3 Mar 1952, Cincinnati, OH, USA. Director of Behavioral Medicine; Editor in Chief. Education: BA, Psychology, Haverford College; PhD, Applied Experimental Psychology, Dartmouth College. Career: Director of Rehabilitation, The Spine Institute, Carmel, IN; Assistant Professor of Psychology, Purdue University, IN; Currently, Director of Behavioral Medicine, Texas Back Institute and Editor in Chief, Spine Rehabilitation. Publications: An investigation of the response of the spouse to chronic pain behavior, in Psychosomatic Medicine, 1981; Presurgical Psychological Screening, in Rehabilitation of The Spine, 1993. Honour: NIH Postdoctoral Fellow in Neuro-Behavioral Science, 1981. Memberships: American Psychological Association; International Association for The Study of Pain. Hobbies: Camping; Baseball; Cooking. Address: Texas Back Institute, 3801 West 15th Street, Plano, TX 75093, USA.

BLOKHINA Irina Nikolaevna, b. 21 Apr 1921, Nizhni Novgorod, Russia. Microbiologist. m. Andrey G Ugodchikov, 2 July 1941, 2 sons. Education: Diploma, Institute of Medicine, Gorky; MD; Professor; Academician, Russian Academy of Medical Sciences. Appointments: Hospital Nurse, 1941; Physician, Blood Transfusion Station, 1942-45; Scientist, 1946-53; Laboratory Head, 1954; Director, Research Institute of Epidemiology and Microbiology, Nizhni Novgorod, 1955-. Publications: Genosystematics (with G Levanova), 1976; Dysbacteriosis (with V Dorofeychuck), 1979; Control for Microorganism Cultivation Process (with V Ogarkov and G Ugodchikov), 1983; Systematics of Bacteria (with G Levanova and A Antonov), 1992. Honours: Medal for Labour Valour, 1946; Order of Lenin, 1966; Order of the Red Banner of Labour, 1970; Order of the October Revolution, 1981. Memberships: Society of Epidemiology; Society of Microbiology. Hobbies: Music; Sport. Address: Research Institute of Epidemiology and Microbiology, Gruzinskaya St 44, 603025 Nizhni Novgorod, Russia.

BLOOM Sherman, b. 26 Jan 1934, Brooklyn, NY, USA. Physician; Pathologist. m. Miriam Fishman, 11 Feb 1994, 1 d. Education: AB, New York University, College of Arts and Sciences, 1955; MD, New York University School of Medicine, 1960. Career: Instructor in Pathology, New York University School of Medicine, 1965; Assistant then Associate Professor of Pathology, University of Utah College of Medicine, 1966; Associate then Professor of Pathology, University South Florida College of Medicine, 1974; Professor of Pathology, George Washington University College of Medicine, 1977; Currently Professor and Chair, Department of Pathology, University of Mississippi School of Medicine. Publications: Myocardial Injury in Magnesium Deficiency, 1989; Trans-cellular desmin-lamon intermediate filament network in cardiac myocytes, in Journal of Molecular Cellular Cardiology, 1993. Memberships: NY Academy of Science; College of American Pathologists; Society for Cardiovascular Pathology; American College of Nutrition; International Academy of Pathology. Hobbies: Hiking; Fishing; Hunting. Address: Department of Pathology, University of Mississippi Medical Centre, 2500 North State Street, Jackson, MS 39216-4505, USA.

BLOWS Johanna Maria, b. 24 Aug 1939. Psychologist. m. Mark W Blows, 6 Feb 1960, 2 d. Education: MA Honors, Anthropology, 1982; MA, Psychology, 1990. Appointments: Tutor, School of Behavioral Sciences, Macquarie University, 1970-76; Senior Tutor, 1977-78; Psychologist, Private Practice. Publications: Co-Author, Clenched Hand/Open Hand, 1989; Author, Eagle and Crow: An Exploration of an Australian Aboriginal Myth, 1995. Hobbies: Reading; Music; Theatre; Swimming. Address: 16 Campbell Road, Kenthurst, NSW 2156, Australia.

BLOWS Mark William, b. 22 Apr 1936, Sydney, New South Wales, Australia. Clinical Psychologist. m. 6 Feb 1960, 2 daughters. Education includes: MA, Honours in Psychology, University of Sydney. Appointments: Senior Clinical Psychologist, Cumberland Hospital, Parramatta, New South Wales; Currently in private clinical practice. Publications: "Clenched Hand/OPEN HAND": A MODERN VERSION of an Ancient Yogic Relaxation Technique (co-author), 1989; Lifting the Mask, 1992; Editor: Perspectives on Relaxation and Meditation, 1992; Proceedings of a Workshop: Towards The Whole Person: Integrating EASTERN & WESTERN APPROACHES TO BODY-MIND SKILLS, 1993. Memberships: Australian Psychological Society; Institute of Private Clinical Psychologists of Australia; Transnational Network for the Study of Physical, Psychological and Spiritual Wellbeing. Hobbies: Gardening; Amateur wine-making; Classical music. Address: 16 Campbell Road, Kenthurst, New South Wales 2156, Australia.

BLUESTEIN Danny, b. 4 Nov 1955, Montevideo, Uruguay. Biomedical Engineer. m. Rita Goldstein, 21 Jan 1991. Education: BSc; MSc; PhD. Appointments: Aeronautic Engineer, IAI; Adjunct Assistant Professor of Biomedical Engineering, University of Miami, USA; Assistant Professor of Mechanical Engineering, Florida International University. Publications: Contributor of articles in professional journals. Honours: Phi Beta Delta; Outstanding International Scholar, 1993. Memberships: BMES; Israeli Society of Biomedical Engineers. Hobbies: Music; Sports. Address: 1000 West Avenue #615, Miami Beach, FL 33139, USA.

BLUETT Desmond G, b. 7 Oct 1926, London, UK. Gynaecologist. m. Elizabeth Ward-Booth, 12 Sept 1953, 1 d. Education: MD; FRCOG; FACS; MB; BS; DObstRCOG; LRCP; MRCS; LMSSA; FICS. Appointments: House Appointments, Guys Hospital; General Practice; Ships Surgeon; Specialist Gynaecologist Royal Navy; City of London Maternity; Addenbrookes Hospitals Registrar in Obstetrics & Gynaecology; Attending Surgeon, Metropolitan Hospital, New York; Associate Director, Research Ortho Pharmaceutical/Diagnostics, USA; Consultant in Obstetrics & Gynaecology, Royal Navy; Private Practician, Gynaecology and Medico-Legal Litigation. Publications: Infant Resuscitation, 1962; Prolapse in Pregnancy, 1963; Iniencephaly Causing Obstructed Labour, 1964; Intrauterine Devices, 1972; Sundry Publications on Cystitis, STD, Infertility. Memberships: Fellow, Royal Society of Medicine; International Fertility Association; Society Abdominal Surgeons of America; Pacific Coast Fertility. Hobbies: Polo; Horse Riding; Shooting; Photography. Address: 21 Devonshire Place, London, W1N 1PD, England.

BLUMBERG Jeffrey Bernard, b. 31 Dec 1945, San Francisco, CA, USA. Nutritionist. m. Dorothy Eleanor Frost, 4 Sep 1971, 2 s. Education: BS, Psychology, BPharm, Washington State University; PhD, Pharmacology, Vanderbilt University. Career: Assistant Professor, Pharmacology, 1976-78, Director, Toxicology Program, 1978-80, Associate Professor, 1979-81, Head, Pharmacology Section, 1980-81, Northeastern University; Associate Professor, Nutrition, 1981-88, Assistant Director, Human Nutrition Research Center, 1981-, Acting Associate Director, 1985-87, Associate Director, 1989-, Professor, Nutrition, 1989, Tufts University. Memberships: AAAS; New York Academy of Science; Fellow, American College of Nutrition; American Institute of Nutrition; American Society for Clinical Nutrition; Union of Concerned Scientists; American Aging Association; American Society for Parenteral and Enteral Nutrition; The Oxygen Society; International Society for Free Rad Research; Gerontological Society of America. Address: Tufts University, 711 Washington Street, Boston, MA 20111, USA.

BLUMENFIELD Michael, b. 14 Jun 1938, NY, USA. Psychiatrist. m. Susan Gronen, 24 Jun 1962, 2 s, 1 d. Education: BA; MD. Career: Professor of Psychiatry, Medicine and Surgery, New York Medical College. Publications include: Numerous publications including, Psychological Care of the Burn and Trauma Patient, book. Memberships: APA(F); ACP(F); American Association of Psychosomatic Medicine (F). Address: 16 Donellan Road, Scarsdale, NY 10583-2008, USA.

BOADU Kwasi Okyere, b. 9 May 1944, Essuowin, Ghana. Obstetrician, Gynaecologist. m. Belinda, 22 Dec 1985, 3 sons, 4 daughters. Education: MRCOG, 1976; FRCOG, 1989; FWACS, 1985; FICS, 1994. Appointments: Consultant, Police Hospital, Ghana, 1980; Consultant, Mpilo Hospital, Zimbabwe, 1985; Consultant, Proprietor, Accra Clinic, 1982-85; Consultant, Specialist, Proprietor, Aboraa Hospital, Accra. Publications: Medical Correspondent and Consultant, Private Weekly Newspaper, Ghana. Memberships: Ghana Medical Association; Society of Obstetricians & Gynaecologists, Ghana; Fellow, Royal College of Obstetricians & Gynaecologists; Fellow, International College of Surgeons; Fellow, West African College of Surgeons. Hobbies: Rose Gardening; Hockey. Address: Aboraa Hospital, Ring Road Central, PO Box 3781, Accra, Ghana.

BOARDMAN Lesley Anne, b. 9 Dec 1953, London, England. Superintendent Physiotherapist. m. Christopher John Boardman, 31 Aug 1974, 1 son, 1 daughter. Education: Diploma, Physiotherapy, Acupuncture. Appointments: Basic Grade Physiotherapist; Senior Grade Phsiotherapist; Brief Locums in Industry. Memberships: Chartered Society of Physiotherapy; British Acupuncture Association. Hobbies: Water Sports: Water Skiing, Windsurfing, Swimming; Running; Horse Riding. Address: The Hampshire Clinic, Basing Road, Basingstoke, Hants RG24 0AL, England.

BOBILA Ramon, b. 28 Mar 1951, Manica, Philippines. Consultant Physician, Allergy & Clinical Immunology. m. Aurora Manalo, 1980, 1 son, 2 daughters. Education: BS, Biology, 1972; MD, 1976. Appointments: Chief Resident, Pediatrics, New York, 1984; Clinical Instructor & Research Fellow, University of Medicine & Dentistry, New Jersey, 1984-86. Publications: Thymic Biopsy in Children with AIDS, 1986; Epidermological Features of Pediatric AIDS, 1985; Chronic EBU Syndrome, 1986. Memberships: American College of Allergy & Immunology; New Jersey Medical Society. Hobbies: Sking; Tennis.

Address: 1601 White Horse Mercerville 4, Hamilton, NJ 08619, USA.

BOCHKOV Nikolay, b. 19 Oct 1931, Tambov, Russia. Geneticist; Physician. m. Diana Efanova, 12 Sep 1953, 1 son, 1 daughter. Education: MD, Moscow Medical School; PhD, Postgraduate study, Institute of Experimental Biology; DD. Appointments: Research Worker, 1958-59; senior Research Worker, 1960-68; Director, Institute of Medical Genetics, 1968-89; Head, Department of Medical Genetics, 1990-. Publications: principles of Human Cytogenetics, 1969; Human Chromosomes and R Diation, 1971; Human Genetics, 1978; Medical Genetics, 1984; Human Heredity and Environmental Mutagens, 1989. Honour: Governmental Prize, 1983. Memberships: Vavilov Society of Geneticists; Russian Medical Genetics Society; European Environmental Mutagen Society; Russian Academy of Medical Sciences. Hobbies: Photography; Nature. Address: Moskvorechie st 1, Moscow 115478, Russia.

BOCK Samuel Allan, b. 28 Apr 1946, Baltimore, Maryland, USA. Physician. m. Judith Bock, 19 Oct 1985. Education: AB, Washington University, St Louis, 1964-68; MD, University of Maryland School of Medicine, Baltimore, Maryland, 1968-72; Internship, University of Maryland Hospital, Baltimore, Maryland, 1972-73; Residency, Pediatrics, University of Colorado Medical Center, 1973-74. Appointments: Senior Staff Physician, Department of Pediatrics, National Jewish Center for Immunology and Respiratory Medicine, 1976-1984; Pediatric Allergist, Department of Pediatrics, Department of Health & Hospitals, 1976-84; Assistant Professor of Pediatrics, University of Colorado Medical Center, 1976-82; Associate Clinical Professor, Department of Pediatrics, University of Colorado Health Center, 1982-90; Clinical Professor, Department of Pediatrics, University of Colorado Health Sciences Center, 1990-. Publications: Quantitative Measurement of Thalidomide by Gas-Liquid Chromatography, 1964; Adverse Reactions to Food due to Hypersensitivity, 1978; Usefulness of Measurement of Antibodies in Serum in Diagnosis of Sensitivity to Cow Milk and Soy Proteins in Early Childhood, 1980; Natural History of Severe Reactions to Foods in Young Children, 1985; The Natural History of Peanut Allergy, 1989. Honours: Alpha Omega Alpha, 1972; Jacob E Finesinger Prize for Excellence in Psychiatry, 1972. Memberships: Fellow, American Academy of Allergy & Immunology; Fellow, American Academy of Pediatrics; Diplomate, American Board of Pediatrics; Diplomate, American Board of Allergy & Clinical Immunology. Hobbies: Skiing; Hiking; Biking; Jazz. Address: Boulder Valley Asthma & Allergy Clinic, 3950 Broadway, Boulder, CO 80304-1199, USA.

BODE Christoph Albert Maria, b. 15 Aug 1955, Cologne, Germany. Cardiologist. m. Brigit Bode, 24 May 1983, 2 sons, 1 daughter. Education: MD, University of Cologne Medical School, 1981. Appointments: Physician, Military Service, Germany, 1981-82; Research Fellowship, University of Cologne, 1982-83; Resident in Medicine, Department of Internal Medicine, Cardiology, University of Heidelberg, 1983; Research Fellow, Medicine, Massachusetts General Hospital & Harvard Medical School, 1984-86; Assistant in Medicine, Department of Medicine, Cardiology, University of Heidelberg, 1986-92; Invited Scientist, Cardiac Unit, Massachusetts General Hospital & Harvard Medical School, 1987; Board Certification for Internal Medicine, 1991; Medical Faculty, Habilitation, 1991; Oberarzt, Department of Internal Medicine, Cardiology, University of Heidelberg, 1992; Venia Legendi for Internal Medicine, Privatdozent, 1992; Board Certification for Cardiology, 1993. Publications: Patents: Heterobifunctional antibodies and method of use, 1988; Platelet specific immunoconjugates, 1989; Fibrin-targeted antithrombins and method of use, 1993. Memberships: Marburger Bund, 1979-; American Academy for the Advancement of Science, 1984-; American Federation for Clinical Research, 1985; Thrombosis Section, American Heart Association, 1985-; Deutsche Gesellschaft für Herz-und Kreislaufforschung, 1986-; Ärztekammer Nordbaden, 1986-; Deutsche Gesellschaft für Gerinnung und Haemostase, 1991-; International Society for Fibrinolysis, 1992-. Honours include: Heilmayer Award, 1988; Alexander Schmidt Award, German Society for Thrombosis & Hemostasis, 1992; Alexander Schmidt Memorial Lecturer, German Society for Thrombosis & Haemostasis, 1993; Fericus Award, 1994. Hobbies: Travel; Tennis. Address: Medical Clinic III, University of Heidelberg, Berheimerstrasse 58, Heidelberg 6900, Germany.

BODE Gerd, b. 27 Jan 1940, Germany. Toxicologist & Pathologist. m. Lis Bode-Diesney, 7 June 1973, 2 daughters. Education: MD, Universities in Germany & Austria. Appointments: Head of Toxicology & Pathology, 1982-86; Head of Medical Research, Bochringer Mannheim Gmblt; Vice President, International Toxicology of Boehringer Mannheim Gmblt. Publications: About 80 papers. Memberships: Many national and international societies of Toxicology and Pathology. Hobbies: Swimming; Art. Address: Herzberger Landstr 93, D-37085 Göttingen, Germany.

BOGOLEPOV Nikolai N, b. 30 Nov 1933, Moscow, Russia. Neuromorphologist. m. Ribina Lidia N, 5 Nov 1968, 2 daughters. Education: MD, Medical Institute, Moscow. Appointments: Head, Electron Microscopy Laboratory Brain Research Institute, Moscow, 1967-; Deputy Director, Brain Research Institute, 1970-82, 1992-94. Publications: Ultrastructure of Synapses in Health and Disease, 1975; Ultrastructure of the Brain in Hypoxia, 1983; Morphinism, 1984. Honours: Prize, V M Bechterev's name for best publication in Neuropathology, Russian Academy of Medical Sciences, 1987. Memberships: Editorial Board, Journal of Anatomy, Histology & Embriology & Journal of Neuropathology & Psychiatry. Hobbies: Theatre; Concerts. Address: Brain Research Institute, per Obucha 5, Moscow 103064, Russia.

BOISROND Jean, b. 2 Dec 1946, Cap-Haitien, USA. Professor; President. m. Claude Aline Leveille, 8 Oct 1988, 1 son. Education: Grossesse a Risques,Strasbourg, France; Infertility, John Hopkins University; Training in Vasectomy, Pro-Pater, Brasil; Health Care Administration & Hospital Management, Haifa, Israel. Appointments: Former Minister of Public Health and Population, General Director State University Hospital; Medical Director, University Hospital; Assistant Director, University Hospital; Attending Department of OB-GYN; Professor of OBST-GYN, National School of Nurses; Professor of STD & Contraceptive Techniques, National Institute of Community Health; Professor, President, Meres et Enfants D'Haiti. Publications: Formule de Johnson Modifiee, 1987; Hemoglobinopathies et Grossesse A L'Hueh. Memberships: De L'Association des Obstetriciens Francais; De La Societe Haitienne D'Obstetrique-Gynecol. Hobbies: Tennis; Travel. Address: Angle Des Rues, Saint Honore Et Honseigneur Guilloux, Port-Au-Prince, Haiti, WI.

BOLEN Jean Shinoda, b. 29 June 1936, Los Angeles, California, USA. Psychiatrist. 1 son, 1 daughter. Education: BA, University of California, Berkeley, 1958; MD, University of California, San Francisco, 1962. Appointments: Clinical Professor of Psychiatry, University of California Medical Center, San Francisco; Private Practice. Publications: The Tao of Psychology, 1979; Goodnesses in Everywoman, 1984; Gods in Everyman, 1989; Ring of Power, 1992; Crossing to Avalon, 1994. Memberships: Fellow, American Psychiatric Association; Fellow, American Academy of Psychoanalysis; International Association of Analytical Psychology. Hobbies: Travel. Address: 2021 Webster Street, San Francisco, CA 94115, USA.

BOLINSKE Robert Edward, b. 6 Oct 1924, Wisconsin, USA. Medicine. m. 20 Oct 1951, 1 s, 4 d. Education: MD, Medical College, Wisconsin, 1948. Appointments: Private Practice, Clinical Professor, St Louis University, School of Medicine, St Louis, Missouri. Memberships: Fellow, American Academy of Allergy & Immunology; Fellow, American College of Allergy. Hobbies: Swimming. Address: 56 Portland Drive, St Louis, MO, USA.

BONFILS Pierre, b. 11 May 1957, Alger. ENT Doctor. m. Brigitte Bauer, 21 Jun 1986, 2 children. Education: MD; PhD. Career: ENT Professor, Faculty Necker - Enfants Malades, Paris, 1992-. Memberships: Association for Research in Oto Laryngology. Hobbies: History; Tennis; Golf. Address: Hospital Boucicaut, 78 rue de la Convention, 75015 Paris, France.

BONIFAZIO Juan Lorenzo, b. 9 Mar 1935. Medical Doctor. Widower, 1 daughter. Education: Medical School, University of Montevideo, Uruguay; Postgraduate in Endocrinology & Internal Medicine. Appointments: Assistant Professor of Endocrinology. Publications: Numerous articles in professional journals. Memberships: Sociedad Argentina Etica y Moral Medica; Asociacion Medicos Catolicos Del Uruguay. Hobbies: Piano. Address: C.M.C.U, Secretaria, Juan B Blanco 1047, Apto 603, Montevideo, Uruguay.

BONK Arnold Eli, b. 6 Aug 1951. Dentist. m. Helen Bonk, 29 Aug 1972, 1 son, 1 daughter. Education: DMD; FAGD; Diplomate, ABOI. Appointments: Clinical Instructor; Staff, Montefore Hospital. Honours: Numerous in the field of Oral Implantology. Memberships: AAID; ABOI; ADA; CSDA; ICOI; ACOI. Address: 2226 Black Rock Tpk, Fairfield, CT 06430, USA.

BONNER Jack W III, b. 30 July 1940, corpus Christi, Texas, USA. Psychiatrist. m. Myra T Bonner, 1 son, 2 daughters. Education AA, Del Mar College, 1960; BA, University of Texas, Austin, 1961; MD, University of Texas Southwestern Medical School, 1965. Appointments include: Consultant, Physicians Advisory Committee, Sierra Medical Centre, El Paso, Texas, 1991; COnsulting Staff, St Joseph's Hospital, Asheville, North Carolina, 1980-92; Consulting Staff, Memorial Mission Hospital of Western North Carolina Incorporated, 1980-92; Active Medical Staff, The Oaks Psychiatric Health System, Austin, Texas, 1992-; Clinical Associate professor of Psychiatry, University of Texas Medical School, San Antonio, 1970-71, 1993-. Publications: The Psychology of Discipline, Co-Editor, 1983; Unmasking thr Psychopath: Antisocial Personality and Related Syndromes, Co-Editor, 1986; Contributor of numerous articles in professional magazines and chapters in books. Memberships include: Fellow, American Psychiatric Association; American Group Psychotherapy Association; American Medical Association; Buncombe County Medical Society; North Carolina Medical Society; North Carolina Psychiatric Association; Fellow, Southern Psychaitric Association; Fellow, American Association for Society Psychiatry; Fellow, American Orthopsychiatric Association; Fellow, American College of Mental Health Administration; Texas Society of Psychiatric Physicians. Address: The Oaks Psychiatric Health System, 1407 West Stassney Lane, Austin, TX 78745-2998, USA.

BONO Gregory Louis, b. 14 May 1951, Kansas City, MO, USA. Occupational Medicine Physician. m. Emily Therese Prather, 3 Nov 1979, 2 d. Education: MD, University of Kansas, 1978; MPH, University of California, 1984; BS, Regis College, 1973; Certified by American Board of Preventive Medicine in Occupational Medicine; Fellow, American College of Occupational and Environmental Medicine, 1988. Appointments: California Industrial Medical Clinics : Staff Physician, Peninsula Industrial Medical Clinic, 1980; Staff Physician Santa Clara, 80-81; Assistant Medical Director, Santa Clara, 1981-82; Medical Director, Fremont, 1982-83; Staff Physician, San Jose, 1983-84; Medical Director, Redicare Center, New United Motor Manufacturing Inc, Fremont, California, 1984-85; Staff Physician, Occupational Medicine Associates, North Kansas City, Missouri, 1986-88; Staff Physician, St Luke's Occupational Medicine, Lenexa, Kansas, 1988-. Honours: Program Director, 14th Annual Carroll P Hungate Postgraduate Seminar on Occupational Health, 1991; Alpha Sigma Nu, 1972; Award for receiving highest grade on comprehensive General Chemistry Examination, Chemical Rubber Company, 1970; Received a four year Academic Scholarship to attend Regis College, 1969; Dean's List, Rockhurst High School, 1965-69. Memberships: California Medical Association; Santa Clara County Medical Association; Alameda-Contra Costa Medical Association; American College of Occupational and Environmental Medicine; Western Occupational Medicine Association; American Medical Association; Metropolitan Medical Society of Greater Kansas City. Hobbies: Tennis. Address: 14115 West 95th Street, Lenexa, KS 66215-5207, USA.

BONORIS Athanasios I, b. 8 Nov 1953, Argos, Greece. Critical Care, Internal Medicine, Cardiology & ER Physician. Education: BS, Biological Sciences, University of Illinois, 1971-75; Graduate Studies, University of Illinois, 1975-76; MD, University of Athens School of Medicine, 1976-82. Appointments: Critical Care, Internal Medicine, Cardiology & ER Physician, St Mary's Holy Cross, Ingalls & Great Lakes Hospital. Memberships: ACP; ACC; Council on Geriatric Cardiology. Honours: Dean's List, 1972-75; Recorded in the Book of Academic Honours, 1975. Hobbies: Swimming; Travel; Theatre; Movies; Soccer; Basketball; Photography. Address: 1726 S Elm Street, Des Plaines, IL 60018, USA. 152.

BOOTH David Allenby, b. 1 Aug 1938, Newark, Nottinghamshire, England. Professor. m. Frances Ruth Booth, 10 Aug 1966, 2 sons. Education: BA, Chemistry, 1958, BSc, 1960, MA, 1963, Oxford University; BA, Psychology, Philosophy, 1962, PhD, Biochemistry, 1964, London University; DSc, Psychology, Birmingham University, 1977; Chartered Psychologist (with Practising Certificate); Accredited Nutritionist. Appointments: Research Worker, Institutes of Psychiatry and Neurology, London University, 1959-65; Research Faculty, Yale University, USA, 1964-66; Assistant Professor, Rockefeller University, 1966; Research Fellow, Sussex University, England, 1966-72; Currently Professor of Psychology (Personal Chair), School of Psychology, University of Birmingham. Publications: Psychology of Nutrition, 1994; Editor: Hunger Models, 1978; Neurophysiology of Ingestion, 1993; Co-author, over 200 research papers in scientific journals and books. Honours: Fellow, British Psychological Society. Memberships:

Experimental Psychology Society; Society for Neuroscience; Nutrition Society of Great Britain; European Chemoreception Research Organisation; Society for Chemical Industry; Society for Study of Ingestive Behavior Inc. Address: School of Psychology, University of Birmingham, Edgbaston, Birmingham B15 2TT, England.

BOR Robert, b. 13 Oct 1959, Cape Town, South Africa. Clinical Psychologist. Education: MA, Clinical Psychology; DPhil; Chartered Psychologist; AFBPsS; Chartered Clinical and Conselling Psychologist; UKCP Family Psychotherapist; Family Therapy Qualification. Appointments: University College Hospital, London, England, 1985-86; Royal Free Hospital, London, 1986-91; Currently Reader in Psychology, City University, London. Publications: AIDS: A Guide to Clinical Counselling, 1988; Internal Consultations in Health Care Settings, 1990; A testing time for doctors, 1991; Theory and Practice of HIV Counselling (co-author), 1992. Honours: Churchill Fellow, 1989. Memberships: British Psychological Society; United Kingdon Council for Psychotherapy; British Association for Counselling; Institute of Family Therapy. Hobbies: Ndebele art; Mountain biking; Travel. Address: Psychology Department, City University, London EC1V 0HB, England.

BORDEN Ernest Carelton, b. 12 July 1939, Norwalk, Connecticut, USA. Professor. m. Louise Dise, 24 June 1967, 2 daughters. Education: AB. Harvard University, 1961; MD, De University, 1966. Appointments: Professor, Departments Medicine Paediatrics and Microbiology, Director, cancer Centre, medical College of Wisconsin, 1990-94; Professor, Division of CLinical Oncology, University Hospitals and School of Medicine and University of Wisconsin Clinical Cancer centre, University of Wisconsin, Madison, 1983-90; Director, cancer Centre, University of Maryland; Professor of Medicine, Oncology, Microbiology and Pharmacology. Publications: Alpha Interferon - Further Benefits in Combination with Cytotoxic Chemotherapy in Patients with low and Intermediate Grade Non-Hodgkin's Lymphoma: an ECOG Study, Co-author, 1992; Interferons - Exanding Therapeutic Roles, 1992; Differentiation Therapy of Cancer - Laboratory and Clinical Investigations, Co-author, 1993; Williamsburg Conference on Biological and Immunological Treatments for Cancer, 1993; Challenges of Modern Medicine, Volume 2, Molecular Diagnosis and Monitoring of Leukemia and Lymphoma, Co-Editor, 1994. Honours include: American Cancer Society Professor of Clinical Oncology, 1984-94; Davison Scholar, Oxford University, 1966; SIngapore Malaysia Academy of Medicine, Silver Medal, 1990. Memberships: Fellow, American College of Physicians; American Association Immunologists; President, 1988-89, International Society of Interferon Research; President, 1987-88, Fellow, Society for Biological Therapy; American Soceity of Hematology. Address: University of Maryland Cancer Centre, 22 South Greene Street, Baltimore, MD 21201-1595, USA.

BORGLUM Keith C, b. 13 Aug 1951. Vice President, Professional Management and Marketing. Career: Managing Director, Alliance for Dental Management; President, Health Pro Technologies. Publications include: Many including: Ten Telephone Time Savers, 1987; What Does Your Receptionist Tell Patients About Your Practice?, 1988; How The "Baby Bust" Affects Staffing Your Practice, 1990; Practice Management Headache, 1991; Managing Personnel, 1991; Software Solutions: Things Your System Will Not Do, 1992; Anatomy of a Physician-Consultant Relationship, 1992; What Lies Ahead for the Dental Profession in 1993. Honours: Board of Editorial Advisors, Physician's Marketing, Eyecare Management Update; Editor, California Physician's Business Advisor. Memberships: Affiliate, Medical Group Management Association; California Medical Group Management Association; Society of Medical-Dental Management Consultants; Founding Member, Academy of Dental Management Consultants; Professional Association of Heath Care Office Managers. Hobbies: Fishing; Wild mushroom hunting; Rare fruit tree gardening. Address: 3468 Piner Road, Santa Rosa, San Francisco, Ca 95401, USA.

BORIEL Aladin M, b. 31 July 1957, Suez, Egypt. Bioengineer. m. Jani McKenna Boriek, 8 Aug 1985. Education: BSc, 1980, Graduate Diploma, 1982, Helwan Institute of Technology, Cairo; MSc, University of Michigan, USA, 1984; MSc, 1989, PhD, 1990, Postdoctoral Training in Mechanical Engineering, 1989-90, Rice University. Appointments: Teaching Assistant, University of Michigan, 1984-85; Research Associate, 1990-92, Research Instructor, 1992-94, Assistant Professor of Medicine, Pulmonary and Critical care, Baylor College of Medicine. Publications include: Setting Stress Distribution in Particle Reinforced Polymer Composites, CO-author, 1988; A Mathematical Model and Numerical Estimation of Setting Stresses in Polymer Composites

Molded Under Hydrostatic Pressure, Co-author, 1992; Displacements and Strains in the Costal Diaphragm of the Dog, CO-author, 1994; Inferences on Diaphragm Mechanics from Gross Anatomy, Co-author, 1994; Inferences on Passive Diaphragm Mechanics from Gross Anatomy, Co-author, 1994. Honour: Valedictorian, Helwan Institute of Technology, Cairo, Egypt, 1992. Memberships include: American Thoracic Society; American Physiological Society; Biomedical Engineering Society; Society of Industrial and Applied Mechanics American Soceity for Mechanical Engineers; Society of Materials in Engineering; American Society of Zoology. Hobby: Tennis. Address: Pulmonary and Critical Care, Baylor College of Medicine, 1 Baylor Plaza, Suite 520B, Houston, TX 77030, USA.

BORNSTEIN Philipp E, b. 14 Jan 1941, St Louis, MO, USA. Education: BS Sciences, TX Western College of University of Texas, 1962; Extern in Pathology, R E Thomason General Hospital, El Paso, Texas, 1965; Extern in Anesthesiology, Barnes Hospital, St Louis, 1967; MD, Washington University School of Medicine, St Louis, 1967. Career includes: Staff Psychiatrist 1981-, Medical Director for Psychiatric Services 1985-, President Elect Medical Staff 1988-, President Medical Staff 1990-92, Past President Medical Staff 1993-94, St John's Hospital, Springfield, IL, USA. Publications: A Note on Stress and Sex Determination, 1974; Debate: Electroconvulsive Therapy: Yes, 1979; Philosophy in Medicine, 1983; A Trip to Druk Yul Land of the Thunder Dragon, 1988. Honours: Men of Mines (Outstanding Senior Male Graduates), Texas Western College, 1962; Outstanding Graduate Chemisty, 1962. Memberships include: American Chemical Society, 1961-62; Illinois State Psychiatric Society, 1973-; American Academy of Clinical Psychiatrists, Founding Member 1975, President 1978-80, Board of Directors 1981-82, Chairman, Ways and Means Co 1987-; American Academy of Forensic Sciences, 1978-. Address: Vine Street Clinic, 301 N 6th Street Suite 220, Springfield, IL 62701 1098, USA.

BORODIN Yury Ivanovich, b. 22 Mar 1929, Blagoveshensk, Russia. Anatomist; Lymphologist. m. 11 Aug 1953, 1 son, 1 daughter. Education: MD. Appointments: Aspirant, 1953; Assistant, 1956; Docent, 1958; Professor, 1971; Member, Russian Academy of Medical Sciences, 1975; Academician, 1980. Publications: Methods of investigations of lymphatic system, 1976; Microlymphology, 1983; Lymphatic node at circular disturbances, 1986; General anatomy of lymphatic system, 1990; Functional anatomy of lymphnode, 1992; Functional Morphology of immune system, 1987; Particular anatomy of lymph system, 1995. Honours: Orders of USSR, 1961, 1980; Order of Russia, 1994; Order of Bulgar, 1988; Medal of Academician Vavilov SI, 1979; Reward of Academician Vorobjev VP, 1984. Memberships: Russian Society of Anatomists; Presidium, Russian Academy of Medical Sciences. Hobbies: Books; Sciences and Cultures; Rest in the Country. Address: Timakov Street 2, Novosibirsk 630117, Russia.

BORSON Soo, b. 5 Apr 1942, San Francisco, CA, USA. Psychiatry and Geriatrics. 2 s. Education: MD, Stanford, 1969; Psychiatry Residency, 1979, Geriatric Psychiatry Fellowship, 1981, University of Washington, Seattle; Certified by ABPN in Psychiatry, 1985 and Geriatric Psychiatry, 1991. Career: Instructor, 1981-84; Assistant professor, 1984-87; Associate Professor of Psychiatry and Behavioral Science, University of Washington School of Medicine, 1987-. Publications include: Over 30 publications including: 1st author: Chronic anorexia nervosa: Medical mimic, in West Journal of Medicine, 1981; Behcet Disease as Psychiatric Disorder in American Journal of Psychiatry, 1982; Depression in elderly medical outpatients, in JAGS, 1986; Antidep resistant depression in elderly, in JAGS, 1986; Psychiatry and Nursing home, in American Journal of Psychiatry, 1987; Impaired SNS in AD, Journal of Gerontology, 1989; Improvement in function with nortriptyline, in COPD-Psychosom, 1992. Honours: Alpha Omega Alpha, 1968; Borden Award for Clinical Excellence, 1969; Sandoz Academic Award, 1979; Citation for Excellence in Medical Student and Resident Teaching, 1989 and 1992; Fellow, Geront Society of America, 1991; Journal Paper Award for 1992, Academy of Psychosom Medicine. Memberships include: American Psychiatric Association; American Association of Geriatric Psychology; Society for Neuroscience; Gerontol Society of America. Hobbies: Music; Poetry; Dance. Address: RP-10, PB Sci, University of Washington School of Medicine, 1959 NE Pacific Street, Seattle, WA 98195, USA.

BORUS Jonathan Frederick, b. 4 May 1941, Washington, District of Columbia, USA. Psychiatrist. m. Dixie Lee Nelson, 13 June 1964, 3 sons. Education: MD, University of Illinois College of Medicine, 1965. Appointments: Research Psychiatrist, Walter Reed Army Institute of Research, 1969-72; Instructor, Johns Hopkins University Medical School, 1972; Co-Director, Freedom Trail Clinic, Lindemann Center, 1973-76; Director of Training, Massachusetts General Hospital, 1976-90; Currently: Professor of Psychiatry, Harvard Medical School; Psychiatrist in Chief, Brigham and Women's Hospital, Boston. Publications: Coordinated Mental Health Care in Neighborhood Health Centers, book, 1979; Deinstitutionalization of the chronically mentally ill, 1981; The transition to practice, 1982; Are we training too many psychiatrists?, 1989; Economics and psychiatric education, 1994; Editor, Academic Psychiatry, 1989-. Honours: Distinguished Psychiatric Lecturer, American Psychiatric Association, 1987; Outstanding Psychiatric Educator, Association for Academic Psychiatry, 1992; Pfizer Visiting Professor, 1993; Honorary MA, Harvard University, 1944. Memberships: Association for Academic Psychiatry, President 1986-88; Fellow, American Psychiatric Association; Fellow, American College of Psychiatrists. Hobbies: Musical comedies; Running; Sports; Gardening. Address: Brigham and Women's Hospital, 75 Francis Street, Boston, MA 02115, USA.

BOSCH Carles, b. 18 Aug 1960, Olot, Girona, Spain. Orthodontist. Education: MD; DDS; MS, Honorary Research Associate, University of Witwatersrand, Johannesburg, South Africa. Career: Emergency Service, Hospital Sant Jaume, Olot, Girona, Spain; Specialist in Stomatology, Primary Health Service, Ripoll, Spain; Visiting Assistant Professor, Department of Orthodontics and Center for Craniofacial Anomalies, University of CA, San Francisco, USA; Currently, Assistant Professor, Royal Dental College, Aarhus, Denmark. Publications: Bone Healing Following Delayed Osteosynthesis After Separation of the Bone Fragments, 1991; Data and Patterns Transverse Dentofacial Structure, 1993. Honours: Honorary Member, Medical Students Association, La Garrotxa, 1984; Recognition in Excellence of Teaching, School of Dentistry, University of CA, 1992. Memberships: American Cleft Palate and Craniofacial Anomalies; European Orthodontic Society; Medical Sciences Academy of Catalonia; Danish Orthodontic Society; Spanish Orthodontic Society. Hobby: Squash. Address: Department of Orthodontics, Royal Dental College, Faculty of Health Sciences, Aarhus University, Vennelyst Boulevard, DK-8000 Aarhus C, Denmark.

BOSCHAN Pedro Jorge, b. 11 Sep 1939, Budapest, Hungary. Psychoanalyst. m. Lidia Scalozub, 2 Nov 1971, 1 son, 1 daughter. Education: MD, University of Buenos Aires Medical School; Research Fellow, NIH, USA. Appointments: Research Fellow in psychosomatics, State University of New York Upstate Medical Centre, 1965-68; Training Analyst, Asocacion Psiconalitica de Buenos Aires; professor of Mental Health, Medical school, University of Buenos Aires and University Maimonides. Publications: Dependence and Narcissistic Persistances, 1987; Attention, Interpretation, Identify and Narcissism, 1989; Temporality and Narcissism, 1990. Honour: Tepal Award, 1984. Memberships include: Intrnational Society for the Study of Time. Hobbies: Sculpture; Woodcarving; Tennis. Address: Malabia 2330, 1425 Buenos Aires, Argentina.

BOSE Sudhir Chandra, b. 6 Mar 1910, India. Medical. m. Shirley Joy Campbell, 11 Oct 1961, 1 s. Education: MB, Calcutta University, 1934; LRCP, Edinburgh, 1953; LRCS, Edinburgh, 1953; LRFPS, Glasgow, 1953; DRCOG, 1948; MRCOG, 1949; FRFPS, Glasgow, 1952; FRCS, Edinburgh, 1954; FRCS, Glasgow, 1962; FRCOG, 1968. Appointments: Resident House Officer in Hospital Carmichael Medical College, Calcutta, India; Served in Indian Medical Service (Army) 1941-46; Served with 8th Army in North Africa and Italy; Registrar in Obstetrics & Gynaecology, Hartlepool Group Hospitals, St James' Hospitals, Leeds, UK; Obstetrician & Gynaecologist in West Africa for 11 years; Obstetrician & Gynaecologist in Hospitals in Wales; Now Retired. Memberships: British Medical Association. Address: Sherwood, 16 Bosvean Gardens, Truro, Cornwall TR1 3NQ, England.

BÖSENBERG Adrian Thomas, b. 7 Nov 1949, Cape Town, South Africa. Anaesthesiologist. m. Beverley Gray, 2 Dec 1972, 1 son, 1 daughter. Education: MB ChB (Cape Town); DA (SA); FFA (SA). Appointments: Fellow, Paediatric Anaesthesia, University of Washington, Seattle, USA, 1983-84; Clinical Instructor, Children's Hospital and Medical Centre, Seattle, 1984; Currently Associate Professor in Anaesthesia (Paediatrics), University of Natal, South Africa. Publications: Thoracic Epidural Anaesthesia via Caudal Route, 1988; Strenuous Exercise Causes Endotoxaemia, 1988; Oesophageal Atresia: Caudo-Thoracic Epidural Anaesthesia Reduces Need for Post-Op Ventilatory Support, 1992. Memberships: Association of Paediatric Anaesthetists of Great Britain and Ireland; American Society of Regional

Anesthesia; European Society of Regional Anaesthesia. Hobbies: Philately; Arctophily; Cycling. Address: 20 Argyll Road, Pinetown, 3610 South Africa.

BOSTICK Roberd (Robin) Maner, b. 21 Aug 1951, Beaufort, SC, USA. Family Practice; Cancer Epidemiology. m. Rita Gay Thetford, 17 Jun 1973, 1 s, 1 d. Education: BS, magna cum laude, Wofford College, MD, 1976; MD, Medical University of SC, 1976; MPH, University of MN, 1990. Career: Private Practice of Family Medicine, 1979-88; Assistant Professor, Family Practice and Community Health of Epidemiology, University of MN, 1990-94; Currently, Associate Professor of Public Health Sciences-Epidemiology and of Family and Community Medicine, Wake Forest University, NC. Honours: Phi Beta Kappa, 1973; Alpha Omega Alpha, 1976; Lester Breslow Scholar Award for Excellence in Health Promotion, Disease Prevention, 1990; New Faculty Award, Society of Teachers of Family Medicine, 1992; Merck Society of Epidemiologic Research Clinical Epidemiology Fellowship Award, 1994; Delta Omega Honorary Society in Public Health, 1995. Memberships: American Association for Cancer Research; American Society of Preventive Oncology; Society for Epidemiologic Research; Society of Teachers of Family Medicine; American Academy of Family Physicians. Hobbies: Backpacking; Gardening. Address: Department of Public Health Sciences, Bowman Gray School of Medicine, Wake Forest University, Medical Center Boulevard, Winston-Salem, NC 27157, USA.

BOTO Paulo Alexandre Faria, b. 27 Jan 1971, Lisbon, Portugal. Medical Student. Education: Medical Student, Faculdade de Medicina de Lisboa, Universidade de Lisboa, 1989-. Honours: Honorary Life Member, International Federation of Medical Students Associations, 1994. Memberships: Executive Board, local Students Union, 1991-93; Executive Board, Portuguese Medical Students International Committee, 1992-93; Executive Board, International Federation of Medical Students Associations, 1992-94. Hobbies: Listening to music; Reading. Address: Rua Eng Duarte Pacheco 1 A, 1 dto, 2700 Amadora, Portugal.

BOUCHIER Ian Arthur Dennis, b. 7 Sept 1932, Cape Town, South Africa. Academic Physician. m. Patricia Norma Henshilwood, 5 Sept 1959, 2 sons. Education: MBChB, 1954, MD, 1960, University of Cape Town; FRCP; FRCPE; FFPHM; Honorary FCP (South Africa); FRSA; FIBiol; FRSE. Appointments: Senior Lecturer in Medicine, 1965-70, Reader in Medicine, 1970-73, University of London, England; Professor of Medicine, University of Edinburgh, Scotland, 1973-86. Publications: 500 scientific papers and reviews in gastroenterology and general medicine; Editor: Davidson's Principles and Practice of Medicine, 17th edition, 1991; Gastroenterology, Clinical Science and Practice, 2nd edition, 1993. Honours: CBE, 1990. Memberships: British Society of Gastroenterology; American Society of Gastroenterology; Association of Physicians of Great Britain and Ireland. Hobbies: Music; History of whaling; Cooking. Address: Department of Medicine, Royal Infirmary, Edinburgh EH3 9YW, Scotland.

BOUDAGOV Robert Surenovich, b. 4 July 1949, Samarkand, Uzbekistan, USSR. Professor of Radiobiology. m. Zinaida Boudagova, 6 Sept 1969, 2 sons, 1 daughter. Education: Samarkand Medical Institute, 1972; DrMedSc, Radiobiology, Obninsk, Russia, 1987. Appointments: Scientist, Head, laboratory modelling radiation and non-radiation effects, Vice-Director for research work, Medical Radiological Research Centre, Russian Academy of Medical Sciences, Obninsk. Publications: Co-author: The pathogenesis and treatment of combined radio-thermal injuries, 1989; Rationale for the methods of prevention and treatment of toxic infectious complication of combined radiation and thermal injuries, 1992; Combined radiation injuries: pathogenesis, clinic and treatment, 1993; Pecularities of the development of bacterial enteroendotoxemia after the combined effect of radiation and burns, 1993. Membership: Russian Association of Radiobiology. Hobbies: Music; Fishing. Address: Medical Radiological Research Centre of Russian Academy of Medical Sciences, Koroliov str 4, 249020 Obninsk, Kaluga Region, Russia.

BOULTER Donald, b. 25 Aug 1926, Cambridge, England. Scientist. m. Margaret Eileen Boulter, 1 Aug 1956, 4 daughters. Education: Christ Church, Oxford University; BA, MA, DPhil, Oxford. Appointments: Lecturer, University of Liverpool, 1957-66; Head, Department of Botany, then Biology, University of Durham, 1966-91; Currently Emeritus Professor, Consultant and non-Executive Director. Publications: Over 300 papers in leading scientific journals. Honours: Seesel Fellow, Yale University, 1953-56; Commander, Order of the British Empire. Memberships: Royal Society of Arts; Institute of Biologists; Biochemical

Society; Society of Experimental Biology. Hobbies: Travel; Reading. Address: 5 Crossgate, Durham DH1 4PS, England.

BOUNOURE Guy-Marie, b. 22 Mar 1946, Strasbourg, France. Specialist in Orthodontics. m. Christine Amans, 3 Nov 1990, 2 sons, 1 daughter. Education: Diploma in Dental Surgery, Strasbourg University, 1970; Doctor of Dental Surgery, Toulouse University, 1976-. Qualified Orthodontist Specialist, National Board, 1982. Appointments: Research in Fluorides, Orthodontics, Dento-Facial Orthopaedics; Publications: Author or co-author, over 50 publications in various French or foreign scientific journals, 1976-; Over 50 conference papers, posters and various scientific contributions, 1977-. Honours: Judicial Expert, 1989; Expert for Social and Private Insurances, 1989. Memberships: Executive Committee, French Society of Dento-Facial Orthopaedics; President, Executive Committee Member, Assistant Editor, Association of the French Review for Dento-Facial Orthopaedics; Honorary Member of Executive Committee, French Bioprogressive Society; European Orthodontic Society; American Foundation for Orthodontic Research. Hobbies: Painting; Music; Walking; Skiing. Address: 2 avenue Gambetta, 81000 Albi, France.

BOURNE Lyle E(ugene), b. 12 Apr 1932, Boston, MA, USA. Professor. Education: BA, Distinction, Psychology, Brown University, Providence, RI, 1953; MS, 1955, Phd, Psychology, 1956, University of Wisconsin, Madison. Career includes: Associate then Professor of Psychology, University of Colorado, 1963-; Visiting Professor at various American universities, 1966-74; Director, Institute of Cognitive Science, University of Colorado, 1980-83; Chair, Department of Psychology, University of Colorado, 1983-91; Numerous professional talks. Publications include: Numerous publications in various journals, 1955-, including: Cognitive Psychology: A brief overview, in Psychological Science Agenda, 1992; Co-author, Training and retention of simple mental multiplication skill, in Applied Cognitive Psychology: Applications of Cognitive Theories and Concepts, 1993; Co-author, Psychology: The diverse science, in preparation. Honours: Francis Whelan Scholar, Brown University; Fellow, Rhode Island State Board of Education; Elected Member, Society of Experimental Psychologists, 1972; Social Science Writing Award, University of Colorado, 1988; Consulting Editor: Psychological Reports, 1960-, Journal of Clinical Psychology, 1975-; Editor: Science Watch Section, American Psychologist, 1992- and Advanced Psychology Texts Series, Sage Publications, 1992-. Memberships include: Board of Scientific Affairs, American Psychological Association, 1990-93, Chair, 1992-93; Member various committees; President, Federation of Behavioral, Psychological and Cognitive Sciences, 1994-. Address: Department of Psychology, University of Colorado, Boulder, CO 80309-0345, USA.

BOWDEN Gillian Elaine, b. 18 Aug 1962, South Yorkshire, England. Clinical Psychologist. m. George Core, 16 Mar 1991, 1 d. Education: BA, Honours, Psychology, Manchester Polytechnic; Diploma in Clinical Psychology, South East Thames Regional Training Scheme in Clinical Psychology. Appointments: Clinical Psychologist, Ravensbourne NHS Trust; Clinical Psychologist, West Lambeth Community Care NHS Trust. Publications: Work Stress Burnout and Coping: A Review and Emprical Study of Staff in Supported Housing, 1994. Membership: British Psychological Society. Hobbies: Cooking; Travel. Address: 24 Girton Road, London SE26 5DH, England.

BOWDLER Anthony John, b. 16 Oct 1928, England. Professor of Medicine. m. 2 children. Education: University College, London; University College Medical School; BSc, 1st class honours, 1949, MB, BS, 1952, MD, 1963, PhD, 1967, University of London. Appointments: House appointments, Registrarship, University College Hospital, Hammersmith Hospital, Brompton Hospital, London, 1952-60; Haematology Fellow, University College Hospital Medical School, London and University of Rochester, New York, 1962-64. Senior Lecturer, University College Hospital Medical School, 1964-67; Associate Professor, 1967-71, Professor, 1971-80, Michigan State University College of Medicine, East Lansing, USA; Professor of Medicine, Marshall University School of Medicine, Huntington, West Virginia, 1980-94. Publications: The Spleen: Structure, Function and Clinical Significance (editor), 1990; 73 original articles, reviews and abstracts on scientific and clinical subjects. Honours: Fellowes Silver Medallist, University College Hospital Medical School, 1950; MB Gold Medallist and Prizeman, University of London, 1952; Fulbright Scholar, 1962-64; Buswell Senior Fellowship, University of Rochester, 1962-64. Memberships: Fellow, Royal College of Physicians; Fellow, Royal College of Pathologists; Fellow, American College of Physicians;

Medical Research Society; American Society of Hematology; American Society of Clinical Oncology. Hobby: Gardening. Address: 2 Compton Court, Milton, WV 25541, USA.

BOWEN-SIMPKINS Peter, b. 28 Oct 1941, United Kingdom. Gynaecologist. m. Kathrin Ganguin, 19 Aug 1967, 2 daughters. Education: MA, MB, BChir, Cambridge University; LRCP, MRCS, Guy's Hospital Medical School, London; FRCOG; MFFP. Appointments: Lecturer in Anatomy, Guy's Hospital Medical School; RMO, Queen Charlotte's Maternity Hospital; RSO, Samaritan Hospital for Women; Registrar, Lecturer, Senior Registrar, Middlesex Hospital and Hospital for Women, London; Consultant Gynaecologist. Publications: Pocket Examiner in Obstetrics and Gynaecology, 1993; Contributor of chapters in books and numerous articles and papers. Honour: Handcock Prize for Surgery, RCS, 1966. Memberships: Council, 1993-, RCOG; Foundation Board Member, 1994-, Faculty of Family Planning and Reproductive Health, RCOG; British Fertility Society; BMA. Hobbies: Fly Fishing; Golf; Tennis; Sailing; Skiing; Opera. Address: 38 Walter Road, Swansea SA1 5NW, Wales.

BOWIE E J Walter, b. 10 Mar 1925, England. Physician. m. Gertrud Susi Ulrich, 22 Dec 1949, 3 s, 1 d. Education: MA, Wadham College, Oxford, England, 1950; BM & BCh, Wadham College, Oxford, England, 1952; MS In Medicine, University of Minnesota, Mayo Graduate School, 1961; DM, Oxford University, England, 1981; FRC, Pathology; FACP. Appointments: Consultant in Hematology, Department of Medicine, Mayo Clinic, Rochester, Minnesota, 1961-71; Head, Section of Hematology Research, Mayo Clinic, Rochester, Minnesota, 1971-89; Consultant in Hematology, Mayo Clinic, Rochester, Minnesota, 1989-. Publications: 293 Manuscripts; 208 Abstracts; 5 Books; 48 Book Chapters. Honours: Trotter Medal in Surgery, University College Hospital, 1951; Judson Daland Travel Award, Mayo Foundation, 1963; Distinguished Investigator of the Mayo Foundation, 1987; Distinguished Career Awd, International Society of Thrombosis and Hemostasis, 1991. Memberships: American Association for Advancement of Science; American Association of Pathologists; American College of Physicians; American Federation for Clinical Research; American Medical Association; American Society of Hematology; Central Society for Clinical Research; International Society & Federation of Cardiology; International Society on Thrombosis & Haemostasis. Hobbies: Reading; Skiing; Travel; Pottery. Address: Mayo Clinic, Hilton 1020, 200 First Street SW, Rochester, MN 55905, USA.

BOWMAN Elizabeth Sue, b. 9 Mar 1954, Roanoke, VA, USA. Psychiatrist. m. Philip M Coons, MD, 5 Sep 1981. Education: BS, Chemistry, Purdue University, 1976; MD, Indiana University, 1980; STM, summa cum laude, Christian Theological Seminary, IN, 1987. Career includes: Assistant then Associate Professor of Psychiatry, Indiana University School of Medicine, 1984-; Course Director, Psychiatry resident Religion and Psychiatry Course, 1985-; Over 100 continuing education lectures, 1985-; Outpatient Clinic Attending Psychiatrist, Indiana University Hospital, 1990-. Publications include: 1 Book Chapter and over 15 articles in refereed journals, 1976-, including: Co-author, Diagnostic Interview for Genetic Studies: Rationale, Development, Training and Reliability, Archives of General Psychiatry, in press. Honours: George Sheldon Rader Award for Outstanding Graduating Resident in Psychiatry, Indiana University, 1984; Theta Pi, 1987; Student Association Award, Christian Theological Seminary, 1987. Memberships include: American Psyciatric Association, Fellow; Indiana Psychiatric Society, President, International Society for the Study of Multiple Personality and Dissociation, President, Treasurer. Hobbies: Gardening; Photography. Address: Indiana University School of Medicine, 541 Clinical Drive, Room 291, Indianapolis, IN 46202, USA.

BOWSHER David (Richard), b. 23 Feb 1925, Amesbury, Wiltshire, England. Director of Research; Honorary Consultant Neurologist. m. (1) Anna Meryl Reid, 27 Sep 1952, dissolved 1959, (2) Doreen Arthur, 1 Apr 1969, 1 s. Education: BA, Honours, MA, MB, BChir, MD, Gonville and Caius College, Cambridge; University College Hospital, London; Harvard Medical School (MA General Hospital); PhD, Faculty of Medicine, University of Liverpool; FRCPEd; FRCPath. Career: House Officer, United Liverpool Hospitals; Assistant Lecturer, Lecturer, Senior Lecturer, Reader, Faculty of Medicine, University of Liverpool; Honorary Clinical Assistant, Mersey Regional Neurological and Neurosurgical Unit; Professor, Associé à la Faculté des Sciences de Paris; Professor, Associé à la Faculté des Sciences de Marseille; Honorary Consultant Neurologist, Mersey Regional Centre for Pain Relief; Currently, Director of Research, Pain Research Institute, both at Walton Hospital, Liverpool.

Publications: 6 Books; 13 Chapters in multi-author textbooks; Over 190 articles in medical and scientific journals. Memberships include: International Association for the Study of Pain, former President of British and Irish Section; North of England Neurological Association, former President; BMA, former Chairman, Liverpool Division; British Neuropathological Association; Brain Research Association. Hobbies: Uxoriousness; Music; Language and Languages; Travel; Walking. Address: Pain Research Institute, Walton Hospital, Liverpool, L9 1AE, England.

BOXX Pamela Whyte, b. 5 May 1939, Dundee, scotland. Physician. m. J A Boxx, 30 June 1973. Education: MBChB, St Andrews University, 1963; DRCOG, 1967; MRCOG, 1973; FRCOG, 1985. Appointments: Royal Air Force Medical Officer, based in Aden, El Adem, Muharraq, Singapore, Cyprus, 1965-90; Consultant in Obstetrics and Gynaecology, RAF Hospitals in Ely, Wegberg, Germany, Akrotiri, Cyprus, 1977-; Acupuncturist. Publication: Acupuncture in Obstetrics, 1983. Honour: Honorary fellow, RCOG, 1985. Memberships: Royal Society of Medicine; British Acupuncture Society; British Acupuncture Association. Hobbies: Drama; Ballet; Singing; Walking; Crosscountry Skiing. Address: Alderdale, Inverness Road, Carr-Bridge PH23 3AU, Scotland.

BOYANOWSKY Ehor Orest, b. 9 Jun 1943, Toronto, Canada. Psychology. m. Vicky Mullholland, 1 Dec 1985, 1 s, 2 d. Education: BA, University of Western Ontario; MS, PhD, University of Wisconsin, Madison. Career: Professor in Psychology: Dalhousie University, 1970-74, University of British Columbia, 1975, Simon Fraser University, 1975-, London School of Economics, 1980; Currently, Associate Professor of Criminology. Publications: 30 articles, chapters and reports including: Co-author, Toward a thermoregulatory model of violence, in Journal of Environmental Systems, 1981. Honours: Honour Society, University of Western Ontario, 1966; Providence of Ontario Government Fellowship, 1966; Canada Council Fellow, 1969-70; SSHRC Fellow, 1980. Memberships: American and Canadian Psychological Associations; International Society for Research on Aggression. Hobbies: Freelance Writing; Fly Fishing; Photography. Address: School of Criminology, Simon Fraser University, Burnaby BC, Canada, V5A 1S6.

BOYER Thomas David, b. 10 Oct, Tacoma, WA, USA. Physician. m. Carol Kaempfer, 1 s, 1 d. Education: BS, University of Redlands, CA, 1965; MD, University of Southern CA, Los Angeles, 1969. Career: Clinical Instructor, 1977-78, Assistant Professor, 1978-84, Associate Professor, 1984-89, Professor of Medicine, 1989-90, University of California, San Francisco; Professor of Medicine, currently Director of Digestive Diseases and Associate Professor of Biochemistry, Emory School of Medicine, Atlanta, GA, 1990-. Publications: Co-editor, Hepatology: A Textbook of Liver Diseases, 3rd edition in preparation. Memberships: American Gastroenterological Association; International Association for Study of Liver Diseases; American Society for Clinical Investigation; American Association for Study of Liver Diseases; American Society for Biochemistry and Molecular Biology. Hobbies: Golf; Sailing. Address: Digestive Diseases, PO Drawer AL, Emory University School of Medicine, Atlanta, GA 30322, USA.

BOZIAN Richard C, b. 12 Aug 1919, Springfield, Massachusetts, USA. Medical Educator and Researcher. m. Marguerite L Wilkinson, 31 Aug 1951, 3 sons, 2 daughters. Education: BS, Pharmacy, 1939; MD, 1950. Appointments: Professor of Medicine, Department of Medicine, University Clinic, College of Medicine, Cincinnati, Ohio, 1945-67; Professor Emeritus; Director of Research, Monarch Foundation, Ohio. Memberships: American Institute of Nutrition; American Society Clinical Nutrition. Hobbies: Reading; Travel; Sports. Address: 471 W Galbraith Road, Cincinnati, OH 45215, USA.

BOZYMSKI Eugene Michael, b. 29 Sep 1935. Physician; Professor. m. Mary Kay Simon, 21 June 1958, 4 sons. Education: MD; Board Certified in Internal Medical and Gastroenterology. Appointments: Instructor in Medicine, Medical College of Wisconsin. Assistant Professor, Associate professor, Professor of Medicine, Chief of Endoscopy, University of North Carolina Medical Centre; Captain, US Army Medical Corps; Chief of Infectious Disease, Kenner Army Hospital. Publications: Contributor of numerous professional articles in medical and scientific journals. Honours: Present Governor, American College of Gastroenterology for North Carolina, 1990-; Past Governor, American College of Physicians, 1988-93. Memberships: AGA; ASGE; FACG; FACP; American Motility Society; AFCR' North Carolina Medical Society; Chilean Society of Internal Medicine; Bolivian Society of Internal

Medicine. Hobbies: Family; Tennis; Fishing. Address: Department of Medicine, Division of Gastroenetrology. University of North Carolina, Chapel Hill, NC 27514, USA.

BRAASCH John William, b. 11 Dec 1922, Rochester, Minnesota, USA. Surgeon. m. Nancy Wheeler King, 21 Mar 1946, 1 son, 3 daughters. EducationL BS, Yale University; MD, Harvard University; MS, University of illinois; PhD, University of Minnesota. Appoontments: President, Boston Surgical Society, 1982; President, New Engand Surgical Society, 1984-85; Vice President, Society for Surgery of the Alimentary Tract, 1987-88; Director, American Board of Surgery, 1979-85; Editorial Board, Surgical Gastroenterology, 1982-; Chairman, Department General Surgery, Program Director, Wahey Clinic; Assistant Clinical Professor of Surgery, Harvard Medical School. Publications: Surgery of the Small Intestine in the Adult, 1968; Atlas of Abdominal Surgery, 1990; Surgical Disease of the Biliary Tract and Pancreas, Multidisciplinary Management, 1994. Honours: Mayo Clinic Alumni Association Prize for Original Research, 1955; Two Rundedone Citations. Memberships: New England Surgical Society; Society for Surgery of the Alimentary Tract; Southern Surgical Association; American Surgical Association; International Hepato-Pancreas-Biliary Association. Hobbies: Tennis; Bridge; Gardening. Address: 41 Mall Road, Burlington, MA 01805, USA.

BRADY Albert M, b. 3 Dec 1945, Omaha, NE, USA. Senior Vice-President; Medical Director Oncology. m. Jean Alison Hays, 1 s, 4 d. Education: MD, University of California, Los Angeles, School of Medicine, 1966-70; Intern, Medicine, Duke University Medical Center, 1970-71. Career includes: Research Associate in Medical Oncology, University of Minnesota, MN, 1976-77; Clinical Instructor in Medicine, Oregon Health Sciences University, Portland, OR, 1987-89; Medical Director of The Cancer Care Center, The Breast Center, Porter Home Hospice, Rural Outreach Program, Porter Memorial Hospital, Denver, Co, 1989-92; Editorial Board, Journal of Oncology Management, Cedar Knolls, NJ, 1992-94; Chairman of Many committees including Analgesic Regulatory Issues Committee, American Pain Society, 1992-; Currently, Medical Director of Oncology, Harris Methodist Health System, Fort Worth, TX. Publications: Several articles in professional journals including: Co-author, Fostering Collaboration by Understanding Physician Behavior: The Cancer Program Perspective in AHA's Hospital Technology Special Report, 1992. Honours include: Clinical Fellow, American Cancer Society; Alpha Omega Alpha; Fellow, Ford Foundation; Regents Scholar, UCLA Undergraduate and Medical School. Memberships include: Academy of Hospice Physicians; American Academy of Pain Management; American College Physicians; American Hospital Association; AMA; American Pain Society; American Society of Hematology; International Association for Study of Pain; National Hospice Organization. Address: 811 5th Avenue, Fort Worth, TX 76104, USA.

BRADY Luther Weldon, b. 20 Oct 1925, Rocky Mount, North Carolina, USA. Radiation Oncologist. Education: AA, George Washington University, 1944; AB, George Washington University, 1946; MD, George Washington University, 1948. Appointments include: George Washington University; Jefferson Medical College Hospital; University of Pennsylvania; College of Physicians & Surgeons, New York; Harvard Medical College, 1962-63; Professor, Radiology, Hahnemann Medical College & Hospital, 1963-70; Professor, Chairman, Department of Radiation Oncology & Nuclear Medicine, Hahnemann Medical College & Hospital, 1970-; Professor of Clinical Oncology, Hylda Cohn American Cancer Society, 1975-. Publications: Editor, Diagnostic & Therapeutic Radiology, 11 books, 1975-80; Co-editor, Appleton Century Croft Books in Nuclear Medicine, 1974; Co-editor, Cancer Management Series, 11 books, 1977-83; Co-editor, Principles & Practice of Radiation Oncology, 1987, 1990. Memberships: Royal Society of Medicine, Radiology Section, London, England; American College of Radiation Oncology; American Society for Therapeutic Radiology & Oncology; American Radium Society; Inter-Society Council for Radiation Oncology; Radiological Society of North America; Society of Chairmen of Academic Radiology Departments; Society of Chairmen of Academic Radiation Oncology Departments. Honours include: Honorary Degree of Doctor of Fine Arts, Colgate University, 1988; Designated Radiologist of the Year, Philadelphia Roentgen Ray Society, 1990; Distinguished Alumni Award, George Washington University, 1990; Distinguished Honoree Medal, National Philanthroph Day, Philadelphia, 1993. Address: Department of Radiation Oncology & Nuclear Medicine, Hahnemann University, Broad & Vine Streets, PA 19102, USA.

BRAGG David Gordon, b. 1 May 1933, Portland, Oregon, USA. Radiologist. m. Marcia Ann Robertson, 19 Aug 1955, 3 sons, 1 daughter. Education: Medical Degree, University of Oregon Medical School; Fellow, American College of Radiology. Appointments: Instructor in Radiology, Columbia University, New York, Radiologist, Columbia Presbyterian Medical Centre, New York, 1965-66; Assistant Professor of Radiology, Cornell University Medical College, Attending Radiologist, New York Hospital, 1966-70; Clinician, Sloan-Kettering Institute, New York, 1968-70; Associate Professor, Cornell, 1970; Professor, Chairman, Department of Radiology, Univeristy of Utah Medical School. Publications: Editor, Co-Editor, Senior Editor or Editor-in-Chief of 15 books including: Diseases of the Liver, 1977; Radiographic Atlas of Colon Disease, 1980; Cancer Medicine, 1982; Cancer: Principles and Practice of Oncology, 1985; Handbook for Chest Radiology, 1989; Manual for Oncologic Therapeutics, 1988. Honours: Teacher of Year Award, Department of Radiology, University of Utah, 1990. Memberships: AMA; ACR; Radiological Society of North America Association University Radiologists; Society of Chairmen of Academic Radiology Departments; American Roentgen Ray Society; American Academy for Advancement of Sciences; Society for Cancer Imaging. Address: Department of Radiology, University of Utah Medical Centre, 1A71 SOM, 50 North medical Drive, SLC, UT 84132, USA.

BRAGG Philip Dell, b. 2 July 1932, Gillingham, Kent, England. University Professor. m. (1) Elizabeth Steele, 1 Mar 1958, (2) Diana Crookall, 31 Dec 1988, 1 son, 2 daughters. Education: BSc, 1954, PhD, 1958, University of Bristol. Appointments: Assistant Professor, 1964-71, Associate Professor, 1971-74, Professor, 1974-, Head, Department of Biochemistry, 1987-, University of British Columbia, Vancouver, Canada. Publications: 150 refereed scientific journal articles in the areas of bioenergetics and membrane structure and function. Honours: Scholar, Medical Research Council of Canada; DSc, University of Bristol, 1986. Memberships: The Royal Society of Chemistry; American Society for Biochemistry and Molecular Biology; American Society of Microbiology; Canadian Society of Biochemistry and Molecular Biology. Hobbies: Music; Natural history. Address: Department of Biochemistry and Molecular Biology, University of British Columbia, 2146 Health Sciences Mall, Vancouver, British Columbia, Canada V6T 1Z3.

BRAND Ely, b. 29 Mar 1955, Bern, Switzerland. Surgeon. m. Nancy Messing. 30 Dec 1989, 1 d. Education: BS, Magna Cum Laude, Yale College; MS, Yale University. Appointments: Assistant Professor, University of California at Los Angeles, School of Medicine, 1985-88; Director, Gynaecologic Oncology/Assistant Professor, University of Colorado, 1988-93; Chairman, Denver Gynaecologic Oncology. Publications: include, New Treatment for Cervical Dysplasia, 1991; Laparoscopic Excision for the Adnexal Mass, 1992; Electrosurgical Advances in Gynaecology, 1992; Malignant Melanoma of The Vagina, 1987; The Argon Beam Coagulator Improves Ovarian Cancer Debulking Surgery, 1992; Genetic Therapy for Ovarian Cancer: Generation of a New Retroviral Vector, 1993; Malignancy Arising in Endometriosis Associated with Unopposed Estrogen Replacement, 1988; Cecal Rupture after Continent Urinary Diversion during Total Pelvic Exenteration, 1991. Honours: Clinical Fellow, Harvard Medical School, 1981-85; Lecturer, Tutorial System International, UK Tour 1991. Memberships: Society of Gynaecologic Oncologists; American College of Surgeons. Address: 260 Cook, Denver, Colorado 80206, USA.

BRANDSTATER Murray Everett, b. 21 Apr 1935, Tasmania, Australia. Medicine. m. Karen Pyers, 19 Apr 1962, 2 s, 1 d. Education: MBBS, Melbourne University, 1957; PhD, University of Minnesota, 1972; MRCP(London); FRCP(C). Appointment: Professor and Chairman, Department of Physical Medicine and Rehabilitation, Loma Linda University, CA, USA. Publications: Co-author, An analysis of Temporal Variables in Hemiplegic Gait, in Archives of PM and R, 1983; Co-editor, Stroke Rehabilitation, 1987; Co-author, Venous Thromboembolism in Stroke, in Archives of PM and R, 1992. Memberships: American Academy of Physical Medical and Rehabilitation; American Association of Electrodiagnostic Medicine. Address: Loma Linda University, Department of Physical Medical and Rehabilitation, 11234 Anderson Street, Loma Linda, CA 92354, USA.

BRANDT Douglas Mitchell, b. 7 Feb 1956, Atlanta, Georgia, USA. Physician (Psychiatrist). m. Catherine L Duym, 23 June 1990, 1 daughter. Education: AB summa cum laude, Chemistry, Duke University, 1977; MD, Emory University School of Medicine, 1982; Internship, St Francis Medical Center, Hartford, Connecticut, 1982; Residency, Psychiatry, Institute of Living, Hartford, 1982-86; Fellowship in Psychopharmacology, New England Medical Center, Boston, 1986-87. Appointments: Assistant Unit Chief, 1987-88, Unit Chief, Clinical Psychopharmacology Unit, 1989-91, Institute of Living, Hartford; Assistant Professor, Department of Psychiatry, University of Connecticut, 1987-91; Clinical Assistant Professor of Psychiatry, University of Pittsburgh, Pennsylvania, 1991-95; Medical Director, Psychiatry, Horizon Hospital System. Publications: A comparison of weight changes with fluoxetine, desipramine, and amitriptyline: a retrospective study of psychiatric inpatients, 1993. Honours: Class Honours, Duke University, 1974-77; Phi Eta Sigma, 1975; Phi Lambda Upsilon, 1977; Phi Beta Kappa, 1977. Memberships: American Medical Association; American Psychiatric Association; American Association for Geriatric Psychiatry; Academy of Psychosomatic Medicine; Association for Academic Psychiatry; American College of Physician Executives; Psychiatric Physicians of Pennsylvania; Western Pennsylvania Psychiatric Society; The Association for Convulsive Tnerapy; American Society of Clinical Psychopharmacology. Hobbies: Photography; Travel; Music; Cycling. Address: 60 South Race Street, Greenville, PA 16125 , USA.

BRANDT-RAUF Paul Wesley, b. 9 Oct 1948, New York, USA. Professor. m. Sherry Brandt-Rauf, 26 Jun 1974, 2 s, 1 d. Education: Columbia University: BS, 1970; MS, 1973; ScD, Applied Chemistry, 1974; MD, 1979; MPH, 1980; PhD, Environmental Sciences, 1987; Board Certified, American Board of Internal Medicine, 1984; Board Certified, American Board of Preventive Medicine, 1986. Appointments: Assistant Professor, Columbia University, 1985-89; Associate Professor, Columbia University, 1989-93; Professor of Public Health, Columbia University, 1993-. Publications: Co-Author of more that 125 Scientific Papers, including, Conformational Effects of Environmentally Induced Cancer-Related Mutations in the p53 Protein, 1994. Honours: Editor-in-Chief, Journal of Occupational and Environmental Medicine, 1992-; Robert R J Hilker Award, 1990. Memberships: American College of Physicians; American College of Preventive Medicine; American College of Occupational and Environmental Medicine; American Public Health Association; Royal Society of Medicine. Address: Division of Environmental Sciences, Columbia University, School of Public Health, 60 Haven Avenue B-I, New York 10032, USA.

BRANNON-PEPPAS Lisa, b. 19 Sep 1962, Houston, Texas, USA. Chemical Engineer. m. Nicholas A Peppas, 10 Aug 1988. Education: BS, Rice University, 1984; MS, 1986, PhD, Chemical Engineering, 1988, Purdue University. Appointments: Formulations Chemist, Eli Lilly and Company, 1988-91; President, Biogel Technology Incorporated. Publications: Absorbent Polymer Technology, 1990; Contributor of numerous articles in professional journals. Honours: Harold B Lamport Award, 2nd Prize for Best Bioengineering Research by a Scientist under 35 years of age, Biomedical Engineering Society, 1989. Memberships: American Institute of Chemical Engineers; American Chemical Society; Controlled Release Society; New York Academy of Sciences; Biomedical Engineering Society. Hobbies: Wildlife; The Arts; Travel. Address: Biogel Technology Incorporated, 9521 Valparaiso Court, PO Box 681513, Indianapolis, IN 46268, USA.

BRANSCOM Margaret Ellen, b. 2 Sept 1920, Iola, Kansas, USA. Psychiatrist. m. Nathan E Carl, 26 dec 1948, 1 son, 1 daughter. Education: AB, MD, University of Southern California; MA, University of Iowa; American Board of Medical Specialists, psychiatry. Appointments: Private practice, Los Angeles, 1950-67, Rancho Santa Fe, 1967-. Memberships: California Medical Association; American Psychiatric Association; San Diego County Medical Society. Hobbies: Gardening; Flower Arranging; Cooking; Horse Riding; Sewing; Mineral Collecting; Oriental Art Collecting; Real estate investment. Address: Box 1295 Rancho Santa Fe Medical Building, 6037 La Granada, Rancho Santa Fe, CA 92067, USA.

BRANT Jeannine M, b. 7 Mar 1962, Billings, MT, USA. Oncology CNS; Pain Consultant. m. Richard Brant, 20 Dec 1986, 1 d. Education: RN; MS, Oncology Nursing, AIDS minor, University of California, San Francisco; OCN, Oncology Certified Nurse. Career: ICU Nurse, Deaconess Medical Center, Billings, MT, 1984-86; Chemotherapy Nurse, Billings Clinic, 1986-87; Oncology Nurse, Redding Medical Center, CA, 1988-90; Pain Research Assistant, UCSF, 1990-; Oncology CNS and Pain Consultant, St Vincent Hospital, Billings, 1991-92; Currently: Oncology Clinical Nurse Specialist and Pain Consultant. Honours: Graduate Scholarship, American Cancer Society, 1990; Golden Eagle Award for Health Film, 1991; Health Education Grant for Native American Video , 1991. Memberships: Oncology Nursing Society

- Pain and Transcultural Special Interest Groups; IASP, Sigma Theta Tau. Hobbies: Snow Skiing; Bicycling; Cooking; Travel. Address: 1209 Avenue D, Billings, MT 59102, USA.

BRAY David Noel, b. 14 Feb 1941, Sheffield, England. Chiropractor; Consultant in Stress Management. m. Monica Shears, 10 Dec 1967, 1 son, 1 daughter. Education: Member, Institute of Science Technology; Doctor of Chiropractic, USA. Appointments: Research and Development, Laboratory Supervisor, to 1967; Consultant, Enton Hall Residential Clinic, 1971-73; Currently in private practice; Voluntary activities: Information Officer, International Stress Management, UK Branch, 1986-92; British Liaison Volunteer, P K Anokhin Institute of Normal Physiology, Moscow, Russia, to present; Trustee, International Academy of Science, Russia. Publications: Stress Management in Complementary Medicine, article, 1988; Stress Management in Russia, article, 1994; Biofeedback, chapter in Complementary Therapies for Nurses, 1994. Honours: P K Anokhin Medal, 1992. Memberships: British Chiropractic Association; Founder Member, ISMA, UK; American Association of Apllied Psycho-Physiology and Biofeedback. Hobbies: Music; Theatre; Desk-top publishing. Address: 25 Sutherland Avenue, Leeds LS8 1BY, England.

BREGMAN Harold, b. 9 May 1949, New York, USA. Physician. m. Judith Brown, 22 May 1977, 1 s, 1 d. Education: BS, Brooklyn College, USA, 1970; MD, SUNY Downstate Medical Center, USA, 1974; FACP, American College of Physicians; Clinical Associate Professor of Medicine, University of Chicago, USA. Appointments: Staff Nephrologist, Allegteny General Hospital, Pittsburgh, Pennyslvania, USA, 1980-83; Director, Nephrology Division, Lutheran General Hospital, Illinois. Publications: Author - Iron Overload: Associated Myopathy in Patients on Maintenence Hemodialysis, 1980; Co-author - Complications During Hemodialysis, 1994. Memberships: American Society of Nephrology; American College of Physicians: American Society of Hypertension. Hobbies: Fishing; Skiing. Address: Department of Medicine, Lutheran General Hospital, 1775 Dempster Street, Park Ridge, IL 60068, USA.

BREMAN Joel Gordon, b. 1 Dec 1936, Chicago, Illinois, USA. Physician. m. Vicki Ann Vaughan, 26 June 1966, 1 son, 1 daughter. Education: AB, University of California at Los Angeles, 1958; MD, University of Southern California, 1965; DTPh, London School of Hygiene and Tropical Medicine, University of London, England, 1971. Appointments: Chief of Project, Centres for Disease Control, USAID Smallpox Eradication and Measles Control, Guinea, West Africa, 1967-92' Research fellows in Medicine and Infectious Diseases, Boston City Hospital, USA, 1969-70; Chief, Division of Epidemiology, OCCGE, Upper Volta, 1972-76; Epidemic Intelligence Service Officer, Michigan department of Public Health, 1976-77; Deputy Director, Smallpox Project, World Health Organisation, geneva, Switzerland, 1977-80; Deputy Director, Malaria Branch, CDC, 1981-93. Publications include: Controllin Malaria in Africa: Progress and Priorities, Co-author, 1994; Addressing the Challenges of Malaria Control in Africa, Co-author, 1994; Malaria Prevention in Pregnancy: The Effects of Treatment and Chemoprophylaxis on Placental Malaria Infection, Low Birth Weight, and fetal, Infant, and Child Survival, Co-author, 1994; Where Do We Go from Here?, CO-author, 1994; Overview on Childhood Immunization Registries and report from the National vaccine Advisory Committee: Subcommittee on Vaccination registries, CO-author, 1994. Honours: Outstanding Service Medal, US Public Health Service; Order of the Leopard, Government of Zaire. Memberships include: Fellow, Infectious Disease Society of America; Fellow, American College of Epidemiology; Fellow, Royal Society of Tropical Medicine and Hygiene. Hobbies: Biking; Running. Address: 317 A Street SE, Washington DC 20003, USA.

BREMERS Louis M H, b. 6 Feb 1944, Maastricht. Orthodontist. m. E A A M Rottier, 14 Sep 1968, 4 d. Education: DDS, 1968; PhD, 1973; Orthodontist, 1973. Career: Staff, Department of Orthodontics, k u Nijmegen; Treasurer, DMO; Currently, Orthodontist in Private Practice. Publication: De Condylus Mandibulae, 1973. Memberships: DMO; EOS; NVOS; NMT; AAO. Hobbies: Golf; Hunting. Address: Groesbeekseweg 141, 6524 CV Nijmegen, The Netherlands.

BRENEMAN James C, b. 20 Mar 1922, Sherburn, MN, USA. Physician. m. Mary Jo Helmerson, 4 Oct 1946, 1 s, 1 d. Education: BA; BS; MB; MD; Diplomate of American Board of Allergy and Immunology. Career: Chairman, Food Allergy Committee, American College of Allergy and Immunology, 1969-83; Chairman, International Food Allergy Symposium, 1973-83; Vice Chairman, Michigan Board of Medicine,

1975-84; Currently, President of Midwest Immunology Centre. Publications: Basics and Food Allergy, edition 1, 1978, edition 2, 1986; Handbook of Food Allergy, 1987, Italian edition, 1991. Honours: Distinguished Fellow, American College of Allergy and Immunology; Fellow, American Academy of Allergy and Immunology. Memberships: American College of Allergy and Immunology; American Academy of Allergy and Immunology. Hobby: Travel. Address: 9880 East Michigan, Galesburg, MI 49053, USA.

BRENNAN James H, b. 18 May 1954, Lichfield, Staffordshire, England. Clinical Psychologist. m. Harriet Stuart-Menteth, 20 Apr 1991, 1 son. Education: BA (Hons), Psychology, York University, Toronto, Canada, 1977; MPhil, Clinical Psychology, Institute of Psychiatry, London University, England, 1981. Appointments: Clinical Psychologist, Enfield, Middlesex, 1981-85; Principal Psychologist, Islington Health Authority, 1985-91; Consultant Clinical Psychologist, Bristol Oncology Centre, 1992-. Publications: Organisation of Psychosocial Oncology Services, 1994. Memberships: Associate Fellow, British Psychological Society; Executive Member, Newsletter Editor, British Psychosocial Oncology Group. Address: Bristol Oncology Centre, Horfield Road, Bristol BS2 8ED, England.

BRENT Jeffrey, b. 15 Jan 1946, New York City, USA. Physician. m. Dr Laura Klein-Brent, 31 Aug 1991, 1 son. Education: MD; PhD. Appointments include: Clinical Instructor, 1987-89, Assistant Professor, Department Paediatrics, 1989-93, Assistant Professor, Department of Surgery, 1989-93, Assistant Clinical professor, Department of Paediatrics, 1993-, Assistant Clinical Professor, Department of Surgery, 1993-, University of Colorado Health Science Centre. Publications: Numerous presentations; Contributor of numerous professional papers and abstracts. Honours include: American Academy of Clinical Toxicology Research Fellowship Award, 1989-90; American College of Emergency Physicians Career Development Award, 1990-91; Fellow, American Academy of Clinical Toxicology, 1993; Nominated to Presidency, American College of Clinical Toxicology, 1993. Memberships include: American Academy of Clinical Toxicology; American College of Emergency Physicians; American College of Occupational and Environmental Medicine; Aviation Medical Association; Physicians for Social Responsibility; Society for Academic Emergency Medicine; Undersea and Hyperbaric Medical Society' Civil Aviation Medical Association. Address: 805 Coloron Road, Lookout Mountain, CO 80401, USA.

BRESLIN Nancy A, b. 18 Aug 1957, New Jersey, USA. Psychiatrist. m. Peter J Caws, 28 Nov 1987, 1 daughter. Education: MD, University of Pittsburgh; Chief Resident, George Washington University Department of Psychiatry; Senior Staff Fellow, NIMH; Board Certified, American Board of Psychiatry and Neurology, 1988. Appointment: Assistant Professor, George Washington University Department of Psychiatry. Honours: Laughlin Fellowship, American College of Psychiatrists, 1987; Alpha Omega Alpha, 1983. Memberships: AMA; APA; AAAS; NYAS; SNS. Hobbies: Travel; Painting. Address: George Washington University, Department of Psychiatry, 2150 Pennsylvania Avenue NW, Washington DC 20037, USA.

BREWER John Isaac, b. 9 Oct 1903, Milford, Illinois, USA. Professor Emeritus. m. Ruth Russell, 2 June 1928, 1 son. Education: Bradley College, Peoria, Illinois, 1921-24; BS, 1925; Enrolled, Medical School, University of Chicago, 1924-26; Clinical Medicine, Rush Medical College, 1926-28; PhD, Rush Medical College, University of Chicago, 1928; Department of Anatomy, 1936, University of Chicago. Appointments: Clinical Assistant, 1930-32, Instructor, 1932-36, Associate, Gynaecology, 1936-40, Assistant Professor, Gynaecology, Obstetrics, 1940-48, Professor, Gynaecology, Obstetrics, 1948-77, Professor Emeritus, Obstetrics, Gynaecology, 1972-, Acting Chairman, Department of Obstetrics and Gynaecology, 1972-74, Northwestern University Medical School; Assistant, Obstetrics, Gynaecology, 1930-32, Attending, 1933-42, 1945-47, St Luke's Hospital, Chicago, Illinois; Lieutenant-Colonel, US Air Force Medical Corps, 1942-45; Chief, Division of Obstetrics and Gynaecology, Passavant Hospital (later Passavant Pavilion, Northwestern Memorial Hospital), 1947-74; Editor-in-Chief, 1974-90, Editor Emeritus, 1990-, American Journal of Obstetrics and Gynecology. Publications: A Normal Human Ovum in a Stage Preceding the Primitive Streak, thesis, 1937; Books: Gynecology, 1950; Textbook of Gynecology, 1952, 4th edition, 1967; Gynecologic Nursing, 1966; 57 articles in field of obstetrics, gynaecology, cancer research. Honours include: Charter Member, Centurion Society, 1984; John and Ruth Brewer Chair in Gynaecology and Cancer Research

established, Northwestern University, 1983; Distinguished Surgeon, Society of Gynecologic Surgeons, 1989; Honorary degree in Science, Bradley University; Legion of Merit. Memberships include: American Medical Association; Chicago and Illinois State Medical Societies; Former Regent, American College of Surgeons; Former President, several organisations including American College of Obstetricians and Gynecologists. Hobby: Golf (best handicap 4). Address: 739 E Park Center Blvd, Apt 158, Boise, ID 83706-6530, USA.

BREWER Leslie George, b. 27 June 1945, Detroit, Michigan, USA. Physician. 1 son. Education: DO, Wayne State University, Kirksville College of Osteopathic Medicine and Surgery; Intern, Tucson General Hospital; Residency in Psychiatry, Lafayette Clinic, Wayne State University School of Medicine. Appointments: Executive Director, Centre for Problem Resolution, Sun Coast Hospital; Adjunct Clinical Professor, Department of Psychiatry, Southeastern and West Virginia Colleges of Osteopathic Medicine; Retired. Publications: Children of Alcoholics, 1977; Alcohol and the Elderly, 1981; Centre for Problem Resolution, 1988; Co-Dependency, 1988; Chemical Co-dependency, 1989; Treating Chemical Co-dependents in the Same Therapeutic Milieu, 1989. Honours: Honorary Staff, Sun Coast Hospital, Largo, Florida; Certification, American Board of Psychiatry and Neurology. Memberships: American College of Neuropsychiatry; American Osteopathic Academy of Addictionology; Founding Member, American Academy of Psychiatrists in Alcoholism and Addictions. Hobby: Videography. Address: PO Box 500, Arivaca, AZ 85601, USA.

BRIDGES III Robert Russell, b. 27 Jul 1954, Chattanooga, Tennessee, USA. Physician. Education: Masters in Science in Biology; MD,University of Alabama, 1982; Fellow, American College of Obstetricians & Gynaecologists; Diplomate, American Board of Obstetrics & Gynaecology. Appointments: Intern & Resident, Obstetrics & Gynaecology, George Washington University, 1982-86; Private Practice, Obstetrics & Gynaecology, 1986-. Memberships: District of Columbia Medical Society; Fellow, American College of Obstetricians & Gynaecologists; Diplomate, American Board of Obstetrics & Gynaecologists. Hobbies: Flying. Address: 2440 M St NW, Washington DC 20037, USA.

BRIGGS Daniel Arthur, b. 23 July 1959, Bangor, Maine. CEO of Religious Organizations. m. Suzanne Emily OpDyke, 5 Apr 1980, 2 sons, 2 daughters. Education: BTh, Ind Bible College, 1990; MS, Cornerstone Theol University, 1991; Student, New York University, 1992; PhD Candidate, Walden University, 1994; Lic Clin Counselor, Maine; Lic Life & Health Ins Agent, Maine; Mortgage Broker, Maine; Level II Nondestructive Radiographer; Lic Master Plumber. Appointments: Intern Clin, Theologist Apostolic Bible Way Church, Kouchabouguac, N.B, Canada, 1980; X-Ray Technician, Fiber Materials Inc, Biddeford, Maine, 1980-83; Carpenter's Helper, Energy Homes, Biddeford, Maine, 1983-84; Finance Counselor, First Investor's Corp, Portland, Maine, 1984-85; with Roto Rooter, Stoughton, Mass, 1986-87; Owner, The Drain Co Inc, Biddeford Maine, 1985-92; Clin Theologist, Pres, Founder, Maine Centre, Psychotherapy & Psychoanalysis, Augusta, Maine, 1987-93; Chairman, Board of Directors, Co-founder, Alfred Adler Institute of New England, Augusta, Maine, 1990-; Pres, Founder, Apostolic Church of Faith, Gardiner, Lewiston, Maine, 1993-; Founder, First Apostolic Church, Biddeford, 1980-; Chairman, Board Director, Founder, Institute for Theocentric Psychology, N Whitefield, Maine, 1993-; Board Director, Co-founder, World Christian Youth Association, Gardiner, Maine, 1994-. Publications: Theocentric Psychology, 1992; Disciples of Christ, vol 1 2nd ed, 1993; Integration of Adlerian and Theocentric Psychology, 1994. Memberships: National Association for Advancement of Psychoanalysis; Apostolic World Christian Fellowship. Hobbies: Chess; Racquetball; Fishing. Address: 99 Western Avenue, Augusta, ME 04330, USA.

BRIGGS Dimkpa Nimi, b. 22 Feb 1944, Port Harcourt, Nigeria. Professor. 1 s, 2 d. Education: MD; FRCPG. Appointments: Professor of Obstetrics and Gynaecology; Provost, College of Health Sciences, University of Port Harcourt. Honour: Distinction in Obstetrics and Gynaecology. Address: PO Box 124, University of Port Harcourt, Choba, Port Harcourt, Nigeria.

BRIGGS Josephine Elizabeth, b. 14 Dec 1944, Toronto, Canada. Physician. m. Jurgen Schnermann, 14 Sep 1980, 2 sons. Education: AB, 1966, MD, 1970, Harvard University. Appointments include: Associate, Internal Medicine, 1974-76, Assistant Dean of Students for the Clinical Years, 1975-76, Mount Sinai School of Medicine, New York; Research

Associate, Physiology Institute, University of Munich, Germany, 1979-85; Visiting Assistant Professor, Department Internal Medicine, University of Texas Health Science Centre, Dallas, 1983-84; Assistant Professor, 1985-88, Associate Professor, 1988-93, Division of Nephrology, Department of Internal Medicine, Associate Professor, Department of Physiology, 1990-93, Professor, Division of Nephrology, Department of Internal Medicine, 1993-, Professor, Department of Physiology, 1993-, Associate Chair for Research Programs, Department of Internal Medicine, 1993-, University of Michigan. Publications: Contributor of over 100 scientific and professional articles in journals; Numerous presentations and lectures at conferences and symposia. Honours include: Kidney Foundation Fellowship, 1976-77; Alexander von Humboldt Scientific Exchange Award, 1979-81; Established Investigator, 1983-88, Grant-in-Aid, 1985-88, American Heart Association; Volhard Prize, German Nephrological Society, 1988; Elected, American Society of Clinical Investigation, 1988; Elected to fellow, Council for High Blood Pressure Research, 1991. Memberships include: American Society of Nephrology; American Heart Association; National Kidney Foundation of Michigan Women in Nephrology. Address: Department of Medicine, Division of Nephrology, University of Michigan, 1660 MSRB II, Box 0676, Ann Arbor, MI 48109, USA.

BŘÍZOVA Eva, b. 25 Sep 1957, Havlíčkův Brod, Czech Republic. Palynologist. Education: Final Examination, Botany, Faculty of Science, Charles University, Prague, 1982; RNDr, Charles University, Prague, 1988; CSc, Paleontology, Palynology, Czech Academy of Science, 1988. Appointment: Palynologist in the Quaternary Department, Czech Geological Survey, Prague, 1982-. Membership: Botaniical Association by Academy of Science, Czech Republic. Hobbies: Palynology; Flowers; Nature; Knitting; Music; Botany. Address: Czech Geological Survey, Klárov 31 131, 118 21 Praha 1, Czech Republic.

BROADHURST Laurel Evans, b. 18 Nov 1960, Cleveland, Ohio, USA. Physician. m. Dr Richard Broadhurst, 9 June 1991, 1 son. EducationL BA, Kalamazoo College, 1983; MD, University of Cincinnati, 1987; MPH, Harvard University, 1991; Fellow, American College of Preventive Medicine. Appointments: Epidemiology Consultant to the US Army in Europe, 1992-94. Publcations: Decreases in Invasive Haemophilus Influenza Diseases uin US Army Children, 1984 Through 1991, 1993, Honours: Board Certification, American Board Preventive Medicine, 1993; US Army Meritorious Service Medal, 1994. Memberships: American Public Health Association; American Medical Association. Hobbies: Skiing; Scuba diving; Travel. Address: 6814 Thornapple Drive, Gales Mills, OH 44040, USA.

BROBBEY Yaw Safo Karikari, b. 20 Sept 1934, Kumasi, Ghana. Medical Practitioner. m. Elizabeth Abraham, 20 Mar 1964, 2 sons, 2 daughters. Education: MB BCh, Queens University, Belfast, 1963; MRCOG, 1969; FWACS, 1970; FRCOG, 1983. Appointments: Senior House Officer, then Registrar, Obstetrics and Gynaecology, Northern Ireland Hospital Authority, 1965-68; Registrar in Obstetrics and Gynaecology, Darlington Hospital, Darlington, England, 1968-69; Consultant Obstetrician and Gynaecologist, Korle Bu Teaching Hospital, Accra, Ghana, Ridge Hospital, Accra, Tema Group Hospital; Currently Consultant Obstetrician and Gynaecologist, Director, Karikari Brobbey Hospital, Accra. Publications: Vaginal Tubal Ligation - an effective supplement to the National Family Planning Programme, 1971; Evaluation of Vaginal Tubal Ligation, 1975. Memberships: Ghana Medical Association; Ghana Surgical Science Club; Ghana Society of Obstetrics and Gynaecology; American Fertility Society; West African College of Surgeons. Hobby: Lawn tennis. Address: PO Box 475, Mamprobi, Accra, Ghana.

BROBBY George Wireko, b. 9 Nov 1942, Dunkwa, Ghana. ENT Surgeon. m. Beatrice Boaheme, 28 Aug 1968, 2 sons, 1 daughter. Education: BD; MD; DDS, University of Marburg, Germany. Appointments: Consultant, ENT Surgeon, St Petrus Hospital, Germany; Head, Department of Eye, Ear, Nose & Throat, Dean, School of Medical Science. Publications: Co-author, Stuttering Sickling & Cerebral Malaria, 1974; Co-author, Bactenology of Otitis Media, 1991; The Discharging Ear in the Tropics, 1992. Memberships: Ghana Medical Association; Fellow, West Africa College of Surgeons; Fellow, International College of Surgeons. Honours: Secretary General, Pafos; President, Deaf Education in the Third World. Hobbies: Football; Cross Country Running. Address: Dean's Office, School of Medical Sciences, University of Science & Technology, Kumasi, Ghana.

BROCKHOUSE Charles L, b. 7 Apr 1959, Deep River, Ontario, Canada. Molecular Biologist. m. Abbey Ballantine, 19 Oct 1991. Education: BSc, 1982, MSc, 1964, PhD, 1991, University of Toronto; Postdoctoral Fellow, 1991-94. Publications: Sibling species and sex chromosomes in Eusimulium vernum (Diptera: Simuliidae), 1985; Co-author: The role of sex chronosomes in black fly evolution, 1989; Supernumerary chromosome evolution in the Simulium (Nevermannia) vernum group (Diptera: Simuliidae), 1989; Chromocentre polymorphism in polytenes chromosomes of Simulium costatum (Diptera: Simuliidae), 1989; A new British species of the Simulium vernum group, with comments on its ecology and life history, 1990; Simulium (Nevermannia) juxtacrenobium (Insecta, Diptera): a proposal that availability of the specific name be taken from the intended original description by Bass and Brockhouse, 1990; Molecular identification of onchocerciasis vector sibling species in black flies (Diptera: Simuliidae), 1993; Several contributions to symposia including: Molecular Studies in Black Flies, 1988; Intergenic Spacer Sequences for Species Identification, 1988; Molecular assays for the identification of sibling species of disease transmitting black flies (Diptera: Simuliidae) (with R M Tanguay), 1993; Cloning of high molecular weight sgp gene from S longistylatum and the use of sgps in sibling detection (with R M Tanguay), 1994. Honours: Postdoctoral Fellowship, Medical Research Council of Canada, 1991-94. Membership: Genetics Society of Canada. Photography; Cycling. Address: 64 Lover's Lane, Ancaster, Ontario, Canada L9G 1G6.

BRODRICK Angela, b. 2 July 1965, Whiston, England. Speech-Language Pathologist. Education: BA, Biology, University of Dallas, USA, 1987; MS, Speech-Language Pathology, Texas Woman's University, 1991; Certificate of Clinical Competence in Speech-Language Pathology, American Speech-Language Hearing Association, 1993. Appointments: Certifed Ophthalmic Assistant, Galucoma Associates of Texas, USA; Contract Speech-Language Pathologist, NovaCare Inc; Presently, Director of Rehabilitation, Beverly Rehabilitation. Publications: Professional Paper, A Sociological Approach to Aphasia Rehabilitation: The Rationale. Honours: Invited to study Voice and Drama under Dr Veronica Dunne, College of Music, VEC, Dublin, Ireland, 1987. Memberships: American Speech-Language Hearing Association; New Mexico Speech-Language Hearing Association; Texas Speech-Language Hearing Assocciation; Permanent Advisory Board Member, Texas Womans University Aphasia Centre; President, Alberquerque Speech and Audiology Professionals Association; Vice President for New Mexico Speech-Language Hearing Convention, 1995; Advisory Board for Grant-A-Wish. Hobbies: Singing; Reading; Hiking; Sailing. Address: 4909 Ridgeside Drive, Dallas, TX 75244 ,USA.

BROIDE David, b. 9 Dec 1952, Worcester, South Africa. Physician. m. Deborah Elcock, 10 Jan 1984, 1 son. Education: MBChB, University of Cape Town, 1976; Intern, Groote Schuur Hospital, 1977; Residency, Pete Bent Brigham, Boston, USA, 1978-81; Fellow, Allergy, Immunology, University of San Diego, California, 1984-87. Appointments: Assistant Professor of Medicine, University of California, San Diego, 1987-. Honours: Certified, American Board of Internal Medicine, 1981; Certified, American Board of Allergy and Immunology, 1987. Memberships: American Thoracic Society; American Academy of Allergy and Immunology. Hobby: Golf. Address: University of California at San Diego, 200 W Arbor Street, San Diego, CA 92103-8417, USA.

BROMM Burkhart F, b. 30 Jun 1935, Wilhelmshaven, Germany. Physiology; Researcher. m. Thussi Klemm, 1 s, 1 d. Education: Studied at Universities of Tübingen and Hamburg; MD, University of Kiel, 1965; PhD in Medicine and Physiology, 1968, Habilitation, 1969. Career: Professor of Physiology, Director of Electrophysiology Department, University of Bochum, Germany, 1970-73; Professor and Director of Neurophysiology Department, University of Hamburg, 1974-; Head, Institute of Physiology, 1977-. Publications: Editor: Pain Measurement in Man, book, 1984; Pain and the Brain: From Nociaphim to Cognition, book, 1995. Contributions to: Articles in professional publications. Memberships: International Association for Study of Pain, local organiser of world congress in Hamburg, 1987; European Association of Neuroscience, co-organiser of congress in Hamburg, 1983; German Society of Physiology and Pharmacology. Address: University of Hamburg, Institute of Physiology, Martinistrasse 52, D-2000 Hamburg 20, Germany.

BRONIEWSKI Michal, b. 7 Mar 1945, Bystrzyca, Poland. Physician. m. Hanna Pietrzak, 12 Feb 1983, 2 sons, 1 daughter. Education: MD, Pomeranian Medical University School, Szczecin, Poland; Specialisation in Paediatrics and Paediatric Haematology, Poland. Appointments: Currently Family and Children practice, Calgary, Canada. Address: 30 Pasadena Gardens NE, Calgary, Alberta, Canada T1Y 6L9.

BRONNER Felix, b. 7 Nov 1921, Vienna, Austria. Physiologist; Biophysicist; Educator; Painter. m. Leah Horowitz, 12 Oct 1947, 1 s, 1 d. Education: BS, University of CA, Berkeley and Davis, 1941; PhD, MIT, 1952. Career includes: Helen Hay Whitney Fellow, Arthritis and Rheumatisim Fellow, Rockefeller Institute Medical Research, NYC, 1954-56; Professor of Oral Biology, 1969-86, Professor of Nutrition Sciences, 1976-89, Professor of Biostructure and Function, 1986-89, Professor Emeritus, 1989-, University of CT; Guest Scientist, INSERM Paris, 1972, Lyon, France, 1988. Publications include: Co-Editor, Intracellular Calcium Regulation; Editorial Boards include: American Journal of Physiology (Modeling Forum), 1985-, Journal of Nutrition, 1986-90, 1991-; Numerous articles to professional journals; Paintings exhibited in 3 one-man shows, numerous juried shows. Honours include: Quaker Oats Fellow, 1950-52; André Lichwitz Prize, 1974; Prizes for Paintings. Memberships: Fellow, AAAS; American Physiology Society; Biophysical Society; Harvey Society; Experimental Biology and Medicine; American Institute of Nutrition; Orthopedic Research Society; American Federation of Clinical Research; NY Academy of Sciences; American Society of Clinical Nutrition; American Society for Bone and Mineral Research; American Society Gravity Space Biology. Address: University of Connecticut Health Center, Department of Biostructure and Function, Farmington, CT 06030, USA.

BROOKE Ralph Ian, b. Leeds, England. Dental Surgeon; University Administrator. m. Lorna Shields, 21 Apr 1963, 2 sons. Education: BCh Dentistry; LDS; MRCS; LRCP; FDSRCS; FRCD (C). Appointments: Currently Vice-Provost, Health Sciences, Dean, Faculty of Dentistry, University of Western Ontario, London, Canada. Publications: Numerous; Memberships: Numerous. Hobbies: Music; Cycling. Address: University of Western Ontario, London, Ontario, Canada N6A 5C1.

BROOKE Roger William Acton, b. 7 May 1953, South Africa. Clinical Psychologist. m. Rosalind Jones, 18 Nov 1979, 2 sons, 1 daughter. Education: BA, University of Cape Town, 1976; BA Hons, 1977, PhD, Psychology, 1989, Rhodes University; MA, Clinical Psychology, University of Witwatersrand, 1983; Chartered Clinical Psychologist, UK; Licensed Psychologist, Pennsylvania, USA. Appointments: Director, Internship programme, 1989-90, Director of Training in Clinical Psychology and Rhodes Psychology Clinic, Coordinator of PhD in Psychotherapy, 1990-93, Rhodes University; Professor, Director of Training in Clinical Psychology, Duquesne University, Pittsburgh, Pennsylvania, USA, 1994-. Publications: Jung and Phenomenology, 1991. Memberships: SAMDC. Hobbies: Running; Skiing; Camping. Address: 3803 Edinburg Drive, Murrysville, PA 15668, USA.

BROOKER Dawn June Ratcliffe, b. 25 Jan 1959, Northampton, England. Clinical Psychologist. m. Eric Brooker, 18 Nov 1991. Education: BSc (Hons), 1981, MSc, Clinical Psychology, 1984, University of Birmingham. Appointments: Clinical Psychologist, Sandwell Health Authority, 1984-86; Principal Clinical Psychologist, Central Birmingham Health Authority, 1986-90; Lecturer, Top Grade Clinical Psychologist, joint appointment, South Birmingham Health Authority and University of Birmingham, 1990-92; Currently Consultant Clinical Psychologist, Quality Assurance Projects Manager, South Birmingham Mental Health (NHS) Trust. Publications: The Behavioural Assessment Scale of Later Life (BASOLL), 1993; Review of Observational Methods of Assessing Quality of Care for Older Adults, 1994. Honours: Honorary Lecturer in Psychology, 1986-. Memberships: Division of Clinical Psychology, British Psychological Society; Psychologists Special Interest Group in the Elderly. Hobbies: Walking; Talking; Dogs. Address: Queen Elizabeth Psychiatric Hospital, Mindelsohn Way, off Vincent Drive, Edgnaston, Brimingham B15 2QZ, England.

BROOKS Clifton Rowland, b. 5 May 1923, Louisville, KY, USA. Professor; Founder and Executive Director. m. (1) Agnes J McVeigh, 1946-91, (2) Beverly Frances Persons, 14 Feb 1993, 6 s. Education: BS, Medical Science; MD, University of Wisconsin Medical School, Madison; MPH, Epidermiology, UCLA Graduate School of Public Health. Career includes: Professional Aviator and Senior Flight Surgeon; Teaching: Hunter safety, wilderness survival, aviation and basic and advanced genealogy; Genealogical Research: Registrar Grand Protector, Guild of St Margaret of Scotland, Family and Lineage Society; Administration: Federal, State, Local Government and Industry; Private Practice:

Pediatrics, Allergy, Epileptology, Clinical Immunology, Aerospace, Occupational and Environmental Health; Currently: Professor of Health Education, College of Allied Health, University of Oklahoma, Health Sciences Center; Founder and Executive Director of American Board and International Boards of Environmental Medicine. Memberships: Many Medical, Scientific, Educational, Genealogical, Lineage and Research organisations. Honours: Science Advisory Board, US Environmental Protection Agency; Founding Secretary, American Association of Clinical Immunology and Allergy; Founding President, Society for Clinical Ecology (American Academy of Environmental Medicine). Hobbies: Genealogical Research; Heraldry; The English Manorial System. Address: 1718 West Robinson Street No A, Norman, OK 73069-7311, USA.

BROUSSARD Elsie Rita, b. 30 Jan 1924, Baton Rouge, LA, USA. Physician. m. (1) Frances P Cassidy, 30 Jan 1945, (2) Lloyd Henry Cooper, 1 Jan 1972, dec 1988, 1 s, 1 d. Education: MD, Louisiana State University, 1944; MPH, University of Pittsburgh, 1962; DrPH, 1964. Appointments include: Rotating Intern, Hotel-Dieu Hospital, New Orleans, 1944-45; Admitting PHysician, Charity Hospital, New Orleans, 1945-46, 1948-49; Resident in Surgery, Children's Hospital, San Francisco, 1946; Practice Medicine specialising in Paediatrics, New Orleans, 1949-51; Assistant County Health Officer, Director, Mental Health and Maternal Child Health Programmes, Escambia County Health department, Florida, 1952-61; Resident in Public Health, Florida Board Health, Pensacola, 1959-61; Teaching Fellow in General Psychiatry, University of Pittsburgh, 1963-65; Teaching Fellow in Child Psychiatry, 1965-67, Associate professor, Public Health Psychiatry, Graduate School Public Health, 1966-71; Member of Staff, Western Psychiatric institute and Clinic, Pittsburgh, 1969-. Publications include: Broussard's Neonatal Perception Inventories, 1964; COntributor of numerous articles. Honours include: Special Award, Escambia County Mental Health Association, 1959; Lela Rowland Prevention Award, National Mental Health Association, 1983. Memberships include: Life Fellow, American Psychiatric Association; American Academy Child and Adolescent Psychiatry. Address: Graduate School of Public Health, University of Pittsburgh, 130 DeSoto Street, Pittsburgh, PA 15261, USA.

BROWE John Harold, b. 17 Nov 1915, Burlington, Vermont, USA. Physician. m. Clare Hornbeck, 23 Sep 1939, 2 sons, 2 daughters. Education: AB, MD, University of Vermont; MPH, Columbia University School of Public Health; American Board of Preventive Medicine, Public Health; American Board of Nutrition, Specialist in Clinical Nutrition. Appointments include: Research Associate in Medicine and Biochemistry, Clinical Director, Nutrition Study, University of Vermont; Medical Consultant in Nutrition, Vermont Department of Public Health; Director, Bureau of Nutrition, New York State Department of Health; Retired. Publications include: Nutrition and Family Health Service, Co-author, 1960; A Nutrition Survey of the Armed Forces of Iran, CO-author, 1961; Survival Rations and Water, 1962; Principles of Emergency Feeding, 1964, 1968. Honours: Honorary Membership, Hudson Valley Dietetic Association, 1957-; Sociedad Chilena de Nutricion, Bromatologia y Toxicologia, 1960-. Memberships include: American Public Health Association; American Institute of Nutrition; American Society for Clinical Nutrition, Charter Member; Fellow, American College of Preventive Medicine; Fellow, American Public Health Association. Hobbies: Bowling; Physical Fitness. Address: 4 Locust Avenue, Troy, NY 12180-5124, USA.

BROWMAN George Paul, b. 19 May 1945, Montreal, Quebec, Canada. Oncologist; Clinical Epidemiologist. m. Jo-anne Gauzer, 3 sons. Education: BSc, 1967, MD, CM, 1971, McGill University; MSc, 1985 McMaster University. Appointments: Head, Laboratory Research, 1981-86, Head, Laboratory and Clinical Research, 1982-86, Ontario Cancer Foundation, Hamilton Regional Centre, 1987-92; Head, Service of Clinical Haematology, Hamilton Civic Hospital, 1989-; Professor and Chair, Department of Clinical Epidemiology and Biostatistics, McMaster University. Publications: Controversies in patient management: Evidence based recommendations against neoadjuvant chemotherapy for routine management of patients with squamous cell head and neck cancer; Predicting remission outcome in acute nonlymphocytic leukemia: General principles and their application to residual marrow leukemia, 1992; The HNRQ (Head and Neck Radiotherapy Questionnaire): A Morbidity/Quality of Life Instrument for Clinical Trials of Radiation Therapy in Locally Advanced Head and Neck Cancer, 1993; Influence of cigarette smoking on the therapeutic efficacy of radiation therapy in head and neck cancer, 1993; Standard chemotherapy in squamous cell head and neck cancer: What we have learned from randomized trials, 1994. Memberships: Ontario Medical Association; Canadian Oncology Society; American Association for Cancer Research; American Society of Clinical Oncology; American Association for the Advancement of Science. Hobbies: Baseball; Tennis. Address: Department of Clinical Epidemiology and Biostatistics, Faculty of Health Sciences, 2C10B, McMaster University, 1200 Main St West, Hamilton, Ontario, Canada L8N 3Z5.

BROWN Calvin Reed, b. 11 Jul 1926, Koosharen, Utah, USA. Geneal Surgeon. m. Barbara Jane Jenkins, 24 Dec 1948, 1 s, 3 d. Education: BA; MA; MD; PhD; LCB; DABOM; GCPA; Board Certified in Surgery, Proctocology; Occupational Medicine; Preventative Medicine and Family Practice. Appointments: Instructor, Anatomy, University of Utah College of Medicine; Chief of Surgery/Chief of Staff, Lark Ellen Hospital; Medical Director, Utah State Department of Correction & NICC Airforce Base; Chief Occupational Physician; Now Retired. Publications: 50 Medical Articles in Various Journals; 6 Books, including, Answer To Cancer; Luke The Greek Physician; Paradox; The Gospel in Poetry. Honours: Surgeon General, Vassar; Distinguished Alumnus, Snow College. Memberships: include, American Medical Association; American Academy of Preventative Medicine; Utah Academy of Preventative Medicine; American Academy of Family Practitioners. Hobbies: Writing; Skiing; Hunting; Fishing; Golf; Travel. Address: 4275 White Way, Salt Lake City, Utah 84117, USA.

BROWN Charles McDonnell, b. 14 Jun 1921, Nanchang, Kiangsi, China. Surgeon, retired. m. Dorothy Gene Spencer, 25 Jan 1945, 3 s, 3 d. Education: AB, 1943, MD, 1946, Syracuse University; Assistant Resident in Surgery, Upstate, 1949-53; Chief Resident and Instructor in Surgery, 1953-54. Career: Internship, Wesley Memorial, Chicago, 1946-47; Military Service, 1st Lt to Captain AUS, 1947-49; Surgery Staff, Rome and Murphy Memorial Hospital, Rome, NY, 1954-89, retired. Memberships: Oneida County Medical Society; New York Medical Society; American Medical Association; American College of Surgeons. Hobbies: Skiing; Golf; Gardening. Address: 604 North George Street, Rome, NY 13440, USA.

BROWN Wendy Joan Weinstock, b. 9 Dec 1944, New York, NY, USA. Physician. m. Dr Barry D Brown, 2 May 1971, 1 s, 3 d. Education: MD, Women's Medical College of Pennsylvania, 1966-70; Intern, University of Illinois Affiliated Hospitals, 1970-71; Resident, Medical College of Wisconsin Affiliated Hospitals, 1971-74; Fellowship in Nephrology, Medical College of Wisconsin, Milwaukee, 1976-78. Appointments include: Associate Professor in Internal Medicine, St Louis University Health Sciences Centre; Staff Physician, 1978-, Acting Chief, Haemodialysis Section, 1983-85, Chief, Dialysis Renal Section, 1985-90, Director, Clinical Nephrology, 1990-, St Louis Department of Veterans Administrative Medical Centre. Publications: The History of the National Kidney Foundation: The First Forty Years, Co-editor and author, 1990; Medical Student Education: Meeting the Challenges of Life-Threatening Illness, Death and Bereavement, Co-editor, 1992; Expert Consultations and Hospice Care. Co-Editor; Contributor of numerous articles and chapters in books. Honours include: Distinguished Service Award, The National Kidney Foundation, Baltimore, 1992; Alpha Omega Alpha, Delta Chapter, Medical College of Pennsylvania, 1994. Memberships include: American Society of Nephrology; International Society of Nephrology; St Louis Society of the American Medical Women's Association. Address: 100 Frontenac Forest, St Louis, MO 63131, USA.

BRUCE Joanna Frances Mary Solan, b. 23 July 1960, Plymouth, England. Acupuncturist. m. Jeremy McLaren Bruce, 21 Sept 1985, 3 sons. Education: RGN, Royal Berkshire Hospital, Reading, 1981; Psychiatric Certificate, Fulbourn Hospital, Cambridge, 1982; BAc, International College of Oriental Medicine, East Grinstead. Appointments: Private practice, Westminster, London, and Martock, Somerset, 1986-87; Founder, Director, Westminster Natural Health Centre, London, 1987-91; Currently in private practice, Herefordshire. Honours: Practice of the Year, 1989, 1990. Membership: International Register of Oriental Medicine. Hobbies: Riding; Swimming; Reading. Address: Oaklands, Kinton, Leintwardine, Nr Craven Arms, Salop SY7 0LT, England.

BRUCE-LOCKHART Patrick, b. 25 May 1918, Warborough, England. Obstetrician & Gynaecologist. m. Eve Didychuk, 3 Aug 1963, 4 s, 2 d. Education: MBChB, Edinburgh; MRCOG, 1953; FRCOG, 1968; FRCSC, 1974. Appointments: Obstetrician & Gynaecologist, Sudbury Memorial Hospital & Sudbury General Hospital, 1954-; Chief of Staff,

Sudbury Memorial Hospital, 1960-61, 1988-90. Honours: Honory Fellow, Huntingdon College Laureuliah University, 1984. Memberships: President, OMA, 1961-63; Chairman, OMA Council, 1972-82; Deputy Speaker, CMA General Council, 1983-85; Speaker, 1986-91. Hobbies: Sailing; Golf; Music. Address: 263 St Charles Lake Road, Sudbury, Ontario, P3E 5G6, Canada.

BRUCKER Hannelor A, b. 7 Apr 1940, Stuttgart, Germany. Allergist. m. Heinrich Brucker, 1965, 1 son, 3 daughters. Education: American Board of Internal Medicine, 1974-83; University Tuebingen, Germany. Appointments: Private Physician. Publications: Numerous articles to professional journals. Memberships: ACP; AAAI. Honours: FACP, 1991. Hobbies: Music; Gardening; Reading; Art. Address: 4010 W 65th St, Southdale Allergy & Asthma Clinic, Minneopolis, MN 55435, USA.

BRUCKER Heinrich Karl, b. 15 Mar 1940, Plochingen, Germany. Physician. m. Hannelore A Brucker, 28 May 1965, 1 s, 3 d. Education: Doctor of Medicine, Technische Universitat, München, Germany. Appointments: Department Head, Radiology, Hospital for Skin Diseases, Stuttgart, Germany, 1972-75; Private Practice. Publications: Thesis: Enzyme Histochemical Investigation Pertaining to Viomycin Nephrosis; Co-Author, Correlation of Skin Test Reactions to House Dust and Cats; Co-Author, Nasal Cytology Ag Tool in the Differ Diagnosis of Non Allergic Rhinims. Honours: Received prize for thesis from Technische Universitat, München, Germany. Memberships: Fellow, American Academy of Allergy & Immunology; American College of Allergy & Immunology; American Association of Certified Allergists. Hobbies: Computers. Address: 4010 W 65th Street, #221, Minneapolis, MN 55435, USA.

BRUHN John Glyndon, b. 27 Apr 1934, Norfolk, Nebraska, USA. University Adminstration. Education: BA, University Nebraska, 1956, MA 1958; PhD, Medical Sociology, Yale University, 1961. Appointments incl: Research Sociologist, Department of Psychological Medicine, University of Edinburgh, Scotland, 1961-62; Assistant Professor 1963-64, Assistant Professor of Preventive Medicine & Public Health 1964-67, Associate Professor of Sociology in Medicine 1967-72, Professor & Chairman, Department of Ecology, 1969-72; Dean, School of Allied Health Sciences & Special Assistant to the President for Community Affairs, 1981-. Publications incl: Author or co-author of 128 articles in professional journals; 45 invited conference papers; 13 book chapters; Co-author of 5 books incl: The Roseto Story: An Anatomy of Health, 1979; Medical Sociology: An Anotated Bibliography, 1972-82, 1985. Honours incl: Career Development Award, National Heart Institute, 1968-69; Danforth Foundation Associate, 1973; Katherine & Nicholas C Leone Award for Administrative Excellence, 1983; J Warren Perry Distinguished Author Award, Journal of Allied Health, 1984. Memberships incl: American Heart Association, Fellow; American Public Heath Association, Fellow; Royal Society of Health, Fellow; American Psychosomatic Society; American Association of University Professors. Hobbies: Stamp & Coin Collecting; Travel; Theatre. Address: University of Texas, El Paso, TX 79968-0501, USA.

BRUN Arne Erik, b. 10 Jul 1930, Mariestad, Sweden. Doctor; Pathologist. m. Inger Brun, 4 Jan 1954, 2 s, 2 d. Education: MD; PhD. Career: Pathologist, Neurologist, University of Lund, Sweden; Research Associate in Neuropathology, Harvard University, Boston, MA; Instructor of Pathology, Associate Professor, University of Lund, Sweden; Currently, MD, and Professor at University of Lund. Publications: Thesis, 1965; About 300 papers, book chapters and reviews. Honour: Chairman, Swedish Association for Pathologists. Memberships: Swedish Association for Pathologists; International Association of Neuropathologists; Royal Physiographic Society of Lund; Rotary International; French Foundation for Alzheimer Research, International Board. Address: Department of Pathology, Division of Neuropathology, University Hospital, S-22185 Lund, Sweden.

BRUWER Maria P (Mari), b. 1 Feb 1951, Bloemfontein, Republic of South Africa. Radiographer. m. André Bruwer, 25 Sept 1981, 2 sons, 2 daughters. Education: Diploma, Diagnostic Radiography, 1971, Diploma, Therapeutic Radiography, 1973, BRad, Diagnostic, 1982, BRad (Hons), Diagnostic, 1984, MRad, Diagnostic, 1986, University of Orange Free State; Management courses. Appointments: Therapeutic Radiographer, National Hospital, Bloemfontein, 1974; Diagnostic Radiographer, Kimberley Hospital, 1974-77; Senior Radiographer, specialised units, National Hospital and Universitas Hospitals, Bloemfontein, 1978-79; Chief Radiographer, Lecturer, specialised units for University students, Universitas Hospital, Bloemfontein, 1979-89; Control Radiographer,

Pelonomi Hospital, Bloemfontein; Control Radiographer, Sub-Directorate for Radiographic Services, Health Services, Province of Orange Free State, 1991-. Publications: The Application of Cineangiography in Congenital Heart Lesions Using a Modern Bi-plane Cardiovascular Angiographic Unit, 1986; Aksiale Cineangiografie in Kongenitale Hart Letsels, 1988; Cine Image Quality Control (with A D Bruwer), 1989; State of the Art Processor Quality Control as done at Pelonomi Hospital (with P Charles), 1992. Honours: Medical Research Council Grant in Diagnostic Radiography, 1986-87; Maybaker Award, 1987. Memberships: International Society of Radiographers and Radiological Technologists; Society of Radiographers, Republic of South Africa, Education Committee Chairman, Orange Free State Branch; South African Medical and Dental Council. Hobbies: Golf; Needlework. Address: c/o Department of Pediatric Cardiology (G69), PO Box 339, L1OFS, Bloemfontein 9301, Republic of South Africa.

BRYAN Charles Stone, b. 15 Jan 1942, Columbia, South Carolina, USA. Physician. m. Donna Hennessee, 30 Nov 1982, 2 daughters. Education: MD, Johns Hopkins University School of Medicine, 1967. Appointments: Fellow, Infectious Diseases, Vanderbilt University; Director, Infectious Diseases, Heyward Gibbes Distinguished Professor of Medicine and Chair, Department of Medicine, University of Carolina School of Medicine. Publications: Comparably Massive Penicillin G Therapy in Renal Failure, Co-author, 1975; The Clinical Significance of Positive Blood Cultures, 1989; What IS the Oslerian Tradition?, 1994. Honours: William Osler Medal, American Association for the History of Medicine; Laureate Award, American College of Physicians; President's Award, South Carolina Medical Association; Alpha Omega Alpha. Memberships: Fellow, American College of Physicians; Fellow, Infectious Diseases Society of America; American Osler Society; Association of Professors of Medicine. Hobbies: Medical History; Golf; Jogging. Address: 2 Richland Medical Park, Suite 502, Columbia, SC 29203, USA.

BRYCHTA Pavel, b. 27 Feb 1957, Velké Mezirici, Czech Republic. Plastic Surgeon. m. Marie Brychtova, 12 Apr 1980, 1 son, 1 daughter. Education: MD, Masaryk University, Brno, 1982; PhD, Plastic Surgery. Appointments: Fellowship in Plastic Surgery, Clinic of Plastic Surgery, Brno; Resident, Plastic Surgery and Burns, Traumatologic Research Institute, Brno; Currently Chief, Burns and Reconstructive Surgery Centre, University Hospital, Brno-Bohunice. Publications: Percutaneous Detection of Free Flap Vascular Pedicles Using a Doppler Ultrasonic Velocimeter, 1987; Kultivierte Hautzellen - wichtiger Bestandteil der Verbrennungsmedizin, 1994. Memberships: Secretary, Czech Society of Burns Medicine; National Representative of Czech Republic, European Burns Association. Hobby: Sport. Address: Centrum pro popalené, FNsP Brno-Bohunice, Jihlavska 20, 639 00 Brno, Czech Republic.

BUCHANAN Mary Jo, b. 6 Dec 1952, Sinton, Texas, USA. Registered Nurse. m. Frank Buchanan, 24 Jun 1990, 3 s, 2 d. Education: BS, Nursing, University of Texas, 1975; Certified Nephrology Nurse, 1388. Appointments: Director of Nursing, Matagorda General Hospital Dialysis Facility; Director of Nursing, Angleton Dialysis Clinic, 1982-86; Director of Nursing, Fondren Dialysis Clinic, 1985-86; Chief Executive Officer, Houston Kidney Center, 1996-; Chief Executive Officer, Northwest Kidney Center, 1991-; Chief Executive Officer, Houston Kidney Center Southeast, 1993-; Chief Executive Officer, North Houston Kidney Center, 1994-; Chief Executive Officer, Houston Kidney Center Intergrated Service Network, 1994-. Honours: BS in Nursing with Honors, University of Texas, 1975. Memberships: American Nephrology Nurses Association; National Renal Administrators Association. Hobbies: Family; Flower Gardening; Painting. Address: 1200 Binz, Suite 300, Houston, Texas 77004, USA.

BUCHENHORNER Marianne, b. 15 Sept, Budapest, Hungary. Psychotherapist. m. Thomas L Jacobs, 19 Oct 1990. Education: Certificate in Psychtherapy & Psychoanalysis; MS, Social Work; PsyD, Psychoanalysis; Certificate, Supervision of Psychotherapy & Psychoanalysis; Certificae, Mental Health Consultation. Appointments: Social Worker, Community Service Society, 1966-69; Supervisor, Downstale Medical Center, 1969-71; Director, Multiple Service Center, New York, 1971-72; Private Practice, 1972-; Director, Counseling Postgraduate Center, 1976-81; Supervisor, Teacher, Postgraduate Center, 1974-89; Supervisor, Institute of Contemporary Psychotherapy, 1993-. Memberships: NPAP; NASW; AGPA; Professional Board of Postgraduate Center; Society of Clinical Social Work Psychotherapists;

Society for Psychoanalytic Training. Hobbies: Art; Tennis. Address: 196 East 75th Street, New York, NY 10021, USA.

BUCHWALD Henry, b. 21 June 1932, Vienna, Austria. Surgeon. m. Emilie D Bix, 6 June 1954, 4 daughters. Education: BA, Columbia College; MD, College of Physicians and Surgeons, Columbia University; MS, Biochemistry, PhD, Surgery, University of Minnesota. Appointments include: Currently Professor of Surgery and Biomedical Engineering, University of Minnesota, Minneapolis. Publications: First author: A Totally Implantable Drug Infusion Device, in Diabetes Care, 1980; Report of the Program on the Surgical Control of the Hyperlipidemias, in New England Journal of Medicine, 1990; Hypothesis Cholesterol Inhibition, Cancer, and Chemotherapy, in Lancet, 1992. Honours: Samuel D Gross Award, Philadelphia, American College of Surgeons, 1969; Distinguished Service Award, Association for Academic Surgeons, 1976; Inventor of the Year, 1988; Outstanding Achievement Award, Minnesota Medical Alley, 1989. Memberships: American Surgical Association; American College of Surgeons; Society of University Surgeons; Central Surgery Association; Association for Academic Surgeons; American College of Cardiology; American Heart Association; Minneapolis Surgery Society. Hobbies: Running; Riding; Music; Reading. Address: Box 290, UMHC, University of Minnesota, Minneapolis, MN 55455, USA.

BUCK Steven L, b. 7 Jul 1949, Urbana, Illinois, USA. Professor. m. Jeanette Norris, 11 Sept 1982, 1 s. Education: BA, Reed College, 1971; MA, University of California, San Diego, 1974; PhD, University of California, San Diego, 1976. Appointments: Associate Professor of Psychology, University of Washington, Seattle. Publications: Cone-Rod Interaction Over Time and Space, 1985; Cone Pathways and the PI-O and PI-O Rod Mechanisms, 1993; The Range of Scotopic Contrast Colors, 1994. Honours: Phi Beta Kappa, Reed College, 1971; NIH Research Grant, Interaction in the Visual System, 1979-. Memberships: American Psychological Association; Association for Research in Vision & Ophthalmology; Optical Society of America. Hobbies: Food; Wine; Gardening. Address: Department of Psychology, NI-25, University of Washington, Seattle, WA 98195, USA.

BUCKLEY Sean Michael, b. 30 Apr 1957, Washington DC, USA. Environmental Hygienist. m. Lynn Conlon, 27 Feb 1982, 1 son, 1 daughter. Education: BS, Richard Stockton College, 1982; MPH, Yale University, 1992; Certified Safety Professional, 1992. Appointments: Industrial Hygienist, US Department of Transportation, 1991-93; Junior Research Fellow, University of Otago Medical School, 1989-90; Research Associate, Yale Medical School, 1988-89; Chief, Port Operations, US Coast Guard, Javeau, Hong Kong, 1986-87; Industrial Hygienist, US Army Medical Department Activity, Fort Monmouth, New Jersey. Publications: Falls from Moving Motor Vehicles, 1993; Injuries Due to Falls from Horses, 1993. Honours: Fulbright Travel Grant, 1989-90; USCG Commandant's Letter of Commendation Ribbon, 1987. Memberships: American Industrial Hygiene Association; American Society of Safety Engineers. Hobby: Watersports. Address: 615 Shore Road, Linwood, NJ 08221, USA.

BÜCKMANN Detlef, b. 4 Nov 1927, Helgoland, Germany. Biologist. m. Erika, 26 Aug 1959, 1 s, 1 d. Education: Dr.rer.nat, Mainz, 1952; Abitur Hamburg, 1947; Promotion Mainz, 1952; Habilitation Mainz, 1957. Appointments: Privatdozent Mainz, 1958-59; Göttingen, 1959-63; Apl Professor, Göttingen, 1963-65; Ordinarius, Gießen, 1965-69; Ulm, 1969-; Rector of the University, Ulm, 1979-83; Full Professor of Zoology. Publications: Articles in Die Naturwissenschaften, Journal of Comparative Physiology, Z Naturforschung, Roux Archives, General and Comparative Endocrinology. Honours: Verdienstorden der Bundesrepublik Deutschland, 1987. Memberships: Deutsch Zoologische Gesellschaft; Ges dt Naturforscher und Ärzte; Verband Deutscher Biologen; European Society of Comparative Endocrinology. Address: Universität Ulm, Abt. Allgemeine Zoologie, D89069, ULM, Germany.

BUCUR Eugen Ovidiu, b. 8 Apr 1941, Bucharest, Romania. Veterinary Surgeon. m. Cornelia Bogdan, 4 Aug 1976, 1 daughter. Education: PhD; DVM. Appointments: Veterinarian, Chief Territorial Inspector, Sprancenata, 1967-71; Chief Epidemiologist, Ulmeni, Giurgiu District, 1971-75; Scientific Researcher, Pasteur National Institute for Veterinary Medicine, 1975-. Publications: Co-author: Animal normal and pathological cytology, 1980; Co-author: Embryonic mortality in pigs: The deficiency in vitamin E and selenium - one of the possible causes, 1981; Dietary liver necrosis in the pig, 1982; Co-author: Harderian gland response to the aerosol vaccination against Newcastle disease, 1982;

Co-author: Elements of compared histopathology in scanning (SEM), 1985; Morphopathological aspects concerning the correlation between salmonellosis and weaning stress in swine, 1990; Neuropathological changes in swine acute septicaemic salmonellosis, 1990. Memberships: Romanian Veterinary Medical Association; Romanian Circle of Neuropathology; Romanian National Society of Cellular Biology; The International Society of Neuropathology. Hobbies: Rugby; Jogging; Mountaineering. Address: Pasteur National Institute for Veterinary Medicine, Calea Giulesti 333, Sector 6, Cod 77826, Bucharest, Romania.

BUDELMANN Bernd Ulrich, b. 1 Apr 1942, Hamburg, Germany. Neuroscientist. Education: Dr rer nat, University of Munich, 1970; Habilitation, University of Regensburg, 1975. Appointments: Assistant Professor, 1972-79, Associate Professor, 1979-87, University of Regensburg; Associate Professor, 1987-93, Professor, Department of Otolaryngology, 1993-, University of Texas Medical Branch, Galveston, USA; Member, Marine Biomedical Institute, University of Texas Medical Branch; Member, Scientific Advisory Board, Stazione Zoologica Anton Dohrn, Naples, Italy, 1991-; Executive Secretary, Cephalopad International Advisory Council, 1994-. Publications: Over 50 in professional journals and books. Honours: Heisenberg Fellow, 1979-84; National Institutes of Health Grantee, 1989-; Wellcome Trust Grantee, 1991. Memberships: American Society for Gravitational and Space Biology; American Society of Zoologists; Bárány Society; Deutsche Zoologische Gesellschaft; Förderverein Ernst Haeckel Haus, Jena; Gesellschaft Deutscher Naturforscher und Ärzte; International Brain Research Organisation; J B Johnson Club; Neuroootological and Equilibriometric Society; Sigma Xi, University of Texas Medical Branch Secretary; Society for Experimental Biology; Society for Neuroscience; Verband Deutscher Biologen. Hobbies: Art; Music; Travelling; Hunting. Address: Marine Biological Institute, University of Texas Medical Branch, 301 University Blvd, Galveston, TX 77555-1163, USA.

BUEHLMANN Thomas Walter, b. 26 Jan 1947, Berne, Switzerland. Dentist. m. Suzanne Elsaesser, 31 Aug 1973, 2 d. Education: Orthodontics and Child Dentistry. Career: Dentist in Private Practice. Memberships: European Orthodontic Society; Schweizerische Gesellschaft für Kieferorthopäedie. Hobbies: Music; Horse Riding; Skiing. Address: Wildhainweg 19, 3012 Berne, Switzerland.

BUGENTAL James F T, b. 25 Dec 1915, Fort Wayne, IN, USA. Psychologist. m.(1) Mary Edith (Smith) 1939, divorced 1967, (2) Elizabeth Keber Bugental, PhD, 23 May 1968, 1 s, 2 d. Education: BS, Education, West Texas State Teachers College, 1940; MA, Sociology, George Peabody College, 1941; PhD, Psychology, Ohio State University, 1948. Career includes: Consultant in Futures Studies, Stanford Research Institute; Faculty: University of California, Los Angeles, US International University, Ohio State University, Georgia School of Technology, and JFK University, Evolution of Psychotherapy, 1985, 1990, 1995; Director of Inter/Logue, Santa Rosa; Lecturing and teaching in over 200 various educational and medical institutions in 5 countries; Associate Clinical Professor now Emeritus Clinical Faculty in Psychiatry, Stanford Medical School; Emeritus Professor, Saybrook Institute, San Francisco; Distinguished Adjunct Professor, California School of Professional Psychology, Berkeley/Alameda. Publications include: 9 Books and 1 book length monograph published and one in preparation "Theory into Practice"; About 70 articles in professional and technical journals and periodicals; Over 40 reprintings of articles for inclusion in other books; About 30 chapters and forewards; Editorial boards of 11 journals in psychology and related fields; His work has been reprinted into several languages. Honours include: US Public Health Fellow, Ohio State University, 1946-48; Recognition Certificate, Division of Clinical Psychology, APA, 1986; Rollo May Award, Mentor Society, 1987; Pathfinder Award, Association for Humanistic Psychology, 1991; DHL, Saybrook Institute, 1993. Memberships include: Fellow, American Psychological Association, 1943-. Address: 24 Elegant Tern, Novato, CA 94949, USA.

BUIE Robert, b. 7 Jun 1926, Quebec City, Canada. Psychiatrist. m. Edith Edwards, 11 Aug 1962, 1 s, 2 d. Education: Psychoanalyst. Career: Professor, University of Montreal, 1962-72; Professor, University of New Mexico, 1972-85; Professor, University of McMaster Hamilton, Ontario, 1986-93; Currently in Private Practice. Memberships: Fellow, American Psychiatric Association; Canadian Psychoanalytic Society, 1985-92. Hobbies: Reading; Music; Bicycling. Address: 440 Elizabeth Street Suite 303, Burlington, Ontario, Canada, L7R 2M1.

BULAT Marin, b. 28 Jan 1936, Bisko, Croatia. Professor of Pharmacology. m. Mirjana Bodakos, 23 July 1966, 1 daughter. Education: MD, 1962, MSc, 1964, PhD, 1966, University of Zagreb. Appointments: Resarch Associate, Rudjer Boskovic Institute, Zagreb, 1964-72, 1976-80; Visiting Professor, Chicago Medical School, Chicago, Illinois, USA, 1973-76; Professor of Pharmacology, Chairman of Pharmacology Department, University of Zagreb, 1980-. Publications: Co-author: Fate of intracisternally injected 5-HT in brain, 1966; Origin of 5-HIAA in spinal fluid, 1971; Author: Monoamine metabilites in CSF, 1974; On the cerebral origin of 5-HIAA in lumbar CSF, 1977; Dynamics and statics of CSF: The classical and a new hypothesis, 1993. Memberships: Croatian Pharmacological Society, President 1980-85, 1992-; Collegium Internationale Neuro-Pharmacologicum; European College of Neuropsychopharmacology. Address: Bartolici 7, 41000 Zagreb, Croatia.

BULKLEY Gregory B, b. 28 Apr 1943, Spokane, Washington, USA. Surgeon. m. Jacqueline Graham, PhD, 19 Sept 1993, 1 d. Education: AB, Princeton University, 1965; MD, Harvard, 1970; Fellow, American College of Surgeons. Appointments: Ravitch Professor of Surgery, Johns Hopkins University, School of Medicine. Address: Blalock 685, Johns Hopkins Hospital, 600 North Wolfe Street, Baltimore, MD 21287 4685, USA.

BULL Peter Edward, b. 24 Apr 1949, Exeter, Devon, England. Psychologist. m. Ann Rose Gore, 15 Dec 1980. 1 son. Education: BA, MA, Modern History (Oxon); BA, PhD, Psychology (Exeter). Appointments: Currently Senior Lecturer in Psychology, University of York. Publications: Books: Graded objectives and tests for modern languages: an evaluation, 1981; Body Movement and Interpersonal Communication, 1983, paperback, 1984, Japanese translation, 1986; Posture and Gesture, 1987; Conversation: an interdisciplinary approach (edited with D B Roger), 1989; Contributions to books and journals include: An appraisal of the current status of communication skills training in British medical schools (with L G Frederikson), 1992. Honours: Fellow, British Psychological Society, 1989. Memberships: European Association of Experimental Social Psychology; British Psychological Society. Hobby: Early music. Address: Department of Psychology, University of York, Heslington, York YO1 5DD, England.

BULLARD Dennis Eugene, b. 6 Oct 1950, Wynne, Arkansas, USA. Neurosurgeon. m. 20 May 1975, 2 daughters. Education: MD, St Louis University; BA, University of Southern California. Appointments: Associate Professor, Neurological Surgery, Director, Brain Tumor Clinic, Duke Medical Center; Clinical Professor, University of North Carolina; Chief of Surgery, Rex Hospital. Publications: Approximately 100 publications. Memberships: AANS; CNS; RSM; SUN; SNS. Honours: Swiss Medical Research Award. Address: Department of Neurosurgery, Raleigh Neurosurgery Clinic, 3009 New Bern Avenue, Raleigh, NC 27620, USA.

BUNATIAN Armen, b. 30 Sept 1930, Erevan, Armenia. Anaesthetist. m. Anna Bunatian, 5 June 1953, 1 daughter. Appointments: Professor, Chairman, Chair of Anesthesiology & Internal Care, Postgraduate Faclty Moscow Medical Academy, 1992-. Publications: Numerous professional publications in scientific journals. Honours: State Prize Winner, 1983, 1988. Memberships: Royal College of Anesthetists. Address: Abrikosovski per 2, 119874 Moscow, Russia.

BUNDY Kirk Jon, b. 21 May 1947, Highland Park, Michigan, USA. Biomedical Engineer. m. Pia Ilmalahti, 12 Dec 1974, 1 son, 1 daughter. Education: BS, Michigan State University, 1968; MS, 1970, PhD, 1975, Materials Science and Engineering, Stanford University. Appointments: Scientific Associate, swiss Federal Institute of Technology, Zurich, Switzerland, 1971-75; Postdoctoral fellow, Georgia Tech, USA, 1975-78; Assistant Professor, Johns Hopkins University, 1978-83; Associate and Full Professor, Tulane University, 1983-. Publications: Contributor of 115 articles, book chapters. abstracts, presentations and reports. Honours: T J Watson Memorial National Merit Scholarship, 1965-68; International Nickel fellowship, 1969-70; Honours College, Michigan State University, 1965-68; NIH Fogarty Senior International Fellowship, 1990. Memberships: Society for Biomaterials; Biomedical Engineering Society; Society for Environmental Geochemistry and Health; Society of Environmental Toxicology and Chemistry. Hobbies: Reading; Movies. Address: Biomedical Engineering Department, Tulane University, New Orleans, LA 70118, USA.

BUNNELL William P, b. 9 Feb 1942, Montrose, PA, USA. Orthopaedic Surgeon. m. Marcia Bunnell, 2 d. Education: BS, Houghton College, NY, 1964; MD, Temple University School of Medicine, PA, 1968. Career includes: Professor of Orthopaedic Surgery, Jefferson Medical College, 1987-; Surgeon, Loma Linda Community Hospital, 1987-, Loma Linda University Medical Center, 1987-; Veterans Administration, Loma Linda, CA, 1987-; Professor of Pediatrics and Orthopaedic Surgery, Chairman, Department of Orthopaedic Surgery, Loma Linda University Medical Center, CA, 1987-. Publications: Numerous articles in professional journals and several book chapters including: Adolescent Idiopathic Scoliosis: Patient Evaluation, Seminars in Spine Surgery, 1991; Co-author, Orthopaedics in The Pediatric Office, in Current Problems in Pediatrics, 1992; Outcome of Spinal Screening, in Spine, 1993. Honours: Giannestras-Schmerge Traveling Fellowship, 1975; Award for Spinal Research, Eastern Orthopaedic Association, 1979. Memberships include: American Academy of Cerebral Palsy and Developmental Medicine; American Academy of Orthopaedic Surgeons; AMA; American Orthopaedic Association; CA Medical Association; Christian Medical Society; International Society of Orthopaedic Surgery and Traumatology; Pediatric Orthopaedic Society; Scoliosis Research Society. Address: Orthopaedic Surgery, Loma Linda University School of Medicine, Loma Linda, CA 92350, USA.

BURCHELL Howard Bertram, b. 28 Nov 1907, Athens, Ontario, Canada. Physician. m. Margaret Helmholz, 14 Aug 1942, 4 d. Education: MD; PhD. Appointments: Instructor of Medicine, University of Pittsburgh; Consultant in Medicine, Mayo Clinic; Professor of Medicine, University of Minnesota; Editor, Circulation. Professor of Medicine Emeritus, University of Minnesota. Honours: Guest Lecturer, London, Edinburgh, St Andrews, Boston, Stanford, University of Arizona. Memberships: American Phsylogical Society; Association of American Physicians; Canadian Cardiovascular Society; Osler Society. Hobbies: History of Medicine - A C Doyle, Ben Franklin. Address: 260 Woodlawn Avenue, St Paul, MN 55105, USA.

BURDICK William MacDonald, b. 24 Apr 1952, Providence, Rhode Island, USA. Biomedical Engineer. Education: BS, Physics, 1975; MEng, 1981; Biomedical Engineering and Mechanical Engineering, 1982-86. Appointments: USAF, Tyndall AFB, Florida, 1976-78; Biomedical Engineer, Scott and White Memorial Hospital and Clinics, 1981; Engineering Analyst, WEAC(FDA), 1988-90; Medical device Reviewer, FDA neurological devices, 1990-94; Medical Device Reviewer, FDA, General Hospital and Personal use Devices, 1994-. Publications: Contributor of articles and poetry. Honours: FDA Group recognition Award, 1990; WEAC Top Performers Award, 1990; CFC Certification of Appreciation, 1990; Commendation for Presentation, Editor's Choice Award, The National Library of Poetry, 1994. Memberships: Biomedical Engineering Society; International Platform Association; Research Board of Advisors, ABI. Hobbies: Reading; Writing; Sports; Outdoor recreations; Gardening. Address: HHS/PHS/FDA/ODE, HFZ-410, 9200 Corporate Boulevard, Rockville, MD 20850, USA.

BURGERS Myrle, b. 1 Nov 1931, Volksrust, South Africa. Radiographer. m. Ben Burgers, 5 Nov 1960, 1 s, 1 d. Education: DR, 1952, DTE, 1983, Pretoria University. Appointments: Radiographer, 1952-60, 1980-82; Tutor Radiographer, 1983-86; Head Radiographer, Training, 1986-, Military Hospital. Memberships: South African Society of Radiographers; International Society of Radiographers and Radiologic Technologists. Hobbies: Ballet; Crochet; Learning French Conversation. Address: Kruinsig, Faerie Glen, Pretoria 0043, South Africa.

BURGESS Ellen Diane, b. 9 November 1953, Winnipeg, Manitoba, Canada. Physician. m. Graham Larking, 17 May 1986, 1 son, 1 daughter. Education: MD, University of Manitoba, 1976. Appointments: Associate Professor, Division of Renal Medicine, Faculty of Medicine, University of Calgary. Publications: Canadian Erythropoietin Study Group: Effect of recombinant human erythropoietin therapy on blood pressure in hemodilaysis patients, 1991; Co-author: Aluminum absorption and excretion following sucralfate therapy in chronic renal failure, 1992; 70 abstracts, 54 papers, 3 book chapters. Honours: Fellow, Royal College of Physicians & Surgeons of Canada, 1982; Fellow, American College of Physicians, 1986. Memberships: Canadian Hypertension Society; Canadian Bioethics Society; International Society of Hypertension; American Society of Hypertension; International Society of Nephrology; American Society of Nephrology. Hobbies: Exercising. Address: 1403 29th Street, NW, Calgary, Alberta, T2N 2T9, Canada.

BURK John Robert, b. 19 Feb 1944, Fort Worth, TX, USA. Physician. m. Stephanie Steves Burk, 25 Sept 1982, 3 s, 2 d. Education: BS, Washington and Lee University, Lexington, VA, 1966; MD, University of Virginia School of Medicine, 1970. Career includes: Clinical Instructor, Medicine, University of Texas Health Science Center, Dallas, 1977-; Medical Director, Critical Care, 1978-, Medical Director, Cardiopulmonary Department, 1978-, Co-Medical Director, All Saints Sleep Disorders Diagnostic and Treatment Center, 1982-, All Saints Episcopal Hospital; Co-Director, Advanced Cardiac Life Support Provider and Instructor Courses, 1986-, Affiliate Facility, 1987-, ACLS Advisory Committee, 1992-, American Heart Association; Emergency Physicians Advisory Board,, 1989-, Executive Committee, 1993-, City of Fort Worth, Tarrant County. Publications: Many presentations, clinical trial reports and articles in professional journals. Honours include: Intern of Year, Ochsner Foundation Hospital, New Orleans, 1973; Trustees Award for Excellence in Medical Writing, Ochsner Foundation Hospital, 1973; Life and Breath Advocate Award, American Lung Association of Texas, 1988. Memberships include: American Thoracic Society; American College of Chest Physicians; American College of Physicians; Society of Epidemiologic Research; American Medical Association; National Association of Medical Directors of Respiratory Care. Address: Pulmonary Consultants of Texas, PA, 1521 Cooper Street, Fort Worth, TX, USA.

BURNETT Leslie, b. 9 Sep 1954, Sydney, Australia. Clinical Associate Professor. m. Ruth Pojer, 1 s, 1 d. Education: BSc, Medicine, 1st Class Honours, 1978, MBBS, 1st Class Honours, 1980, PhD, 1986, University of Sydney; Business Management Certificate, Australian Institute of Management, 1994. Appointments: Professorial Resident, 1980; Resident Registrar, 1981-85, Research Fellow, 1986, Royal Prince Alfred Hospital; Pathologist, 1987-88, Managing Pathologist, 1989, Sugerman's Pathology Pty Ltd, Hurstville; Director of Clinical Chemistry, 1990-95 Western Sydney Area Pathology Service, Institute of Clinical Pathology and Medical Research, Westmead Hospital; assistant Director, Institute of Clinical Pathology and Medical Research. Publications: About 45 scientific papers. Honours: AMSA Lilly Research Fellow, 1978; Wellcome Prize, 1984. Memberships: Australasian Association of Clinical Biochemists; Fellow, Royal College of Pathologists of Australasia; Fellow, Quality Society of Australasia; Fellow, Australian Institute of Management. Hobbies: Contract Bridge; Classical Music; Bushwalking. Address: Inst of Clinical Pathology and Medical Research, Westmead Hospital, Westmead, NSW 2145, Australia.

BURNS Rosalie A, b. 29 July 1932, Philadelphia, PA, USA. Physician. m. Dr Herbert I Goldberg, 8 Sep 1957, 1 s, 1 d. Education: BA, Smith College; MD, Yale University School of Medicine. Appointments: Instructor in Neurology, Cornell University School of Medicine, 1962-64; Instructor in Neurology, Medical College of VA, 1964-65; Assistant Professor, 1966-70, Associate Professor, 1970-74, Professor, 1974-, Chair, Department of Neurology, Medical College of PA. Publications include: Cerebral Ischemia in Surgery, Co-author, 1961; Cranio-Metaphyseal Dysplasia, Co-author, 1966; Basilar-Vertebral Artery Insufficiency as a Cause of Vertigo, Co-author, 1973; Characteristics of Tenion Headache-A Profile of 1420 Cases, Co-author, 1979; Vascular Diseases of the Central Nervous System, 1983; Section on Neurologic Diseases, Editor, 1983; Introduction to Neurology, 1983; Stroke in Young Adults, 1984; Section on Neurologic Diseases, Editor, 1990; Introduction to Neurology, 1990. Honours: Lindback Award for Distinguished Teaching, 1969. Memberships: Association of University Professors of Neurology, Past President; American Academy of Neurology, Former 2nd Vice President; American Neurological Association; Director, American Board of Psychiatry and Neurology. Hobbies: Swimming; Skiing; Reading. Address: 3300 Henry Avenue, Philadelphia, PA 19129, USA.

BURR David Bentley, b. 28 Jun 1951, Findlay, OH, USA. Professor. 1 s, 1 d. Education: BA, Beloit College, 1973; MA, University of Colorado, 1974; PhD, University of Colorado, 1977. Career: Instructor in Anatomy, 1977-78, Assistant Professor of Anatomy, 1978-80, University of Kansas Medical Center; Assistant Professor, 1980-83, Associate Professor, 1983-86, Professor, 1986-90, of Anatomy and Orthopedic Surgery, West Virginia University, Medical Center; Currently, Professor and Chairman of Anatomy and Professor of Orthopedic Surgery, Department of Anatomy, Indiana University School of Medicine. Publications: Structure, Function and Adaptation of Compact Bone, book, 1989; Over 80 peer reviewed full length manuscripts. Memberships: Orthopedic Research Society; American Society Bone

Min Research; Sigma Xi; American Society of Space Biology; American Anatomy Association. Hobbies: Piano; Racquetball; Reading; Stamps. Address: Department of Anatomy, MS259, Indiana University School of Medicine, 635 Barnhill Drive, Indianapolis, IN 46202, USA.

BURRI Betty Jane, b. 23 Jan 1955, San Francisco, CA, USA. Chemist. m. Kurt R Annweiler, 1 Dec 1984. Education: BA, Physiology, San Francisco State University, 1976; MS, Biochemistry, CA State University, Long Beach, 1978; PhD, Chemistry, University of CA, San Diego, 1982. Career: Research Associate, Scripps Clinic and Research Institute, La Jolla, CA, 1982-85; Currently, Research Chemist, Western Human Nutrition Research Center, San Francisco, CA. Publications: Contributor to various professional journals including: Lancet, 1982; American Journal Clinical Nutrition, 1988; Nutritional Biochemistry, 1992; Ann New York Academy of Science, 1993. Honours: Special Service Award, ARS, 1992; Adjunct Professor, University of Nevada, Reno, 1993. Memberships: Association for Women in Science; American Institute of Nutrition; American Society of Clinical Nutrition. Address: Western Human Nutrition Research Center, USDA, ARS, PWA, PO Box 29997, Presidio of San Francisco, CA 94129, USA.

BURRIDGE Michael John, b. 27 Apr 1942, St Albans, England. Veterinarian. m. Karen Maureen Pleskovich, 1 Jan 1983, 1 daughter. Education: BVMS, Edinburgh University, Scotland, 1966; MPVM; PhD, University of California (Davis), USA, 1976. Publications: Co-inventor of attractant decoy for controlling bont ticks; Co-inventor of self-medicating applicator for controlling pests on animals. Memberships: Royal College of Veterinary Surgeons, England; American Veterinary Medical Association; American Association for Advancement of Science; Council for Agricultural Science & Technology; American Society of Tropical Medicine & Hygiene; Phi Kappa Phi. Hobbies: Horse Breeding; Horse Driving; Gardening. Address: Department of Pathobiology, College of Veterinary Medicine, University of Florida, PO Box 110880, Gainesville, FL 32611-0880, USA.

BURROWS Barbara Ann, b. 15 Dec 1947, Columbia, SC, USA. Veterinarian. m. Richard M Dhemmler, 31 Aug 1969, divorced Aug 1975, 1 s. Education: BA, cum laude, Biology, Hartwick College, Oneonta, NY; VMD, University of Pennsylvania School of Veterinary Medicine. Career: Bacteriologist, Johnson and Johnson, NJ, 1970-71; Microbiologist, Ciba-Geigy, NJ, 1973-79; Veterinarian, Amboy Avenue Veterinary Hospital, Metuchen, NJ, 1983-84; Veterinarian, Small Animal Practitioner, Black Horse Pike Animal Hospital, Turnersville, NJ, 1984-. Memberships: American Veterinary Medical Association; American Animal Hospital Association; American Association of Feline Practitioners; Association of Women Veterinarians; New Jersey Veterinary Medical Association; Southern New Jersey Veterinary Medical Association. Hobbies: Dancing; Racquetball; Music; Reading. Address: 406 Cedar Avenue, Collingswood, NJ 08108, USA.

BURSZTAJN Harold J, b. 18 Nov 1950, Lodz, Poland. Associate Clinical Professor. Education: Diploma, Eastside High School, Paterson, New Jersey, 1968; AB, Princeton University, Princeton, New Jersey, 1972; MD, Harvard Medical School, Boston, Massachusetts, 1977; Resident in Pediatrics, Children's Hospital Medical Center, 1977-78; Resident in Psychiatry, Massachusetts Mental Health Center, 1979-82; Chief Resident, Program in Psychiatry and the Law, Massachusetts Mental Health Center, 1981-82. Appointments: Clinical Instructor, Department of Psychiatry, Harvard Medical School, 1982-84; Assistant Clinical Professor, Department of Psychiatry, Harvard Medical School, 1984-90; Associate Clinical Professor, Department of Psychiatry, Harvard Medical School, 1990-. Publications: include, Books: Divided Staffs, Divided Selves: A Case Approach to Mental Health Ethics, 1987; Medical Choices, Medical Chances: How Patients, Families, and Physicians can Cope with Uncertainty, 1990; Decision Making in Psychiatry and the Law, 1991; Numerous Reports & Book Chapters. Honours: University Scholar, Princeton University, 1968-72; Phi Beta Kappa, 1972; Magna Cum Laude, Department of Philosophy, Princeton University, 1972; Cum Laude Honors Thesis, Harvard Medical School, 1977; Co-Winner, Soloman Award, Massachusetts Mental Health Center, 1981; Second Place, Soloman Award, Massachusetts Mental Health Center, 1983. Memberships: include, Society for Health & Human Values, 1976-; Society for Medical Decision Making, 1979-; American Academy of Psychiatry and the Law, 1980-; American Society of Law and Medicine, 1981; American Psychoanalytic Association. Address: 96 Larchwood Drive, Cambridge, MA 92138-4639, USA.

BURTON Richard Michael, b. 28 july 1926, Newcastle-under-Lyme, Staffordshire, England. Obstetrician and Gynaecologist. m. Antoinette Brenda Grant, 26 July 1985, 1 son, 3 daughters. Education: MA; FRCS; FRCOG; MMSA. Appointments: Consultant Obstetrician and Gynaecologist, Hillingdon and Ealing, London; Commanding Officer, 257 (Southern) General Hospital, RAMC(V), Territorial Army; Commanding Officer, 357 Field Surgical Team RAMC(V); Retired. Honours: C St J; TD; KLJ. Memberships: British Medical Association; Hospital Consultants and Specialists Association; Worshipful COmpany of Barbers; Society of Apothecaries. Hobbies: Bowls; Orienteering; Swimming. Address: Briar Close, 16 Latchmoor Avenue, Gerrards Cross, Buckinghamshire SL9 8LJ, England.

BUSKIRK Elsworth Robert, b. 11 Aug 1925, Beloit, Wisconsin, USA. Physiologist. m. Mable Heen, 28 Aug 1948, 2 daughters. Education: BA magna cum laude, Biology, Physical Education, St Olaf College, Northfield, Minnesota, 1950; MA, Physical Education, Physiological Hygiene, 1951, PhD, Physiological Hygiene, 1954, University of Minnesota, Minneapolis. Appointments: Professor, Applied Physiology, Director, Noll Laboratory of Human Performance Research, Pennsylvania State University, 1963-88; Marie Underhill Noll Professor, Human Performance (now Emeritus), Director, Laboratory for Human Performance Research, College of Health and Human Development, Pennsylvania State University, 1988-. Publications: Over 230 including: Obesity, 1993; Energetics and Climate with Emphasis on Heat: An Historied Perspective, 1993; Obesity and Weight Control, 1994; Co-author: Fat-free mass in relation to stature: ratios of fat-free mass to height in children, adults, and elderly subjects, 1991; Ventilatory response of moderately obese women to submaximal exercise, 1991; Body composition and the expiratory reserve volume of pre-pubertal lean and obese boys and girls, 1992. Honours include: Honorary Associate Fellow, American Academy of Physical Education, 1970; Honours: Research Citation, American College of Sports Medicine, 1973; Honor Award, American College of Sports Medicine, 1984; NATO, Senior Fellowship in Science, 1977; National Fitness Leaders Association, 1992, Environmental and Exercise Section, American Physiological Society, 1993; Editorial Service Award, American College of Sports Medicine, 1993. Memberships include: American Academy of Physical Education; American College of Sports Medicine; American Heart Association, Epidemiology and Respiratory Disease Councils; American Physiological Society; Sigma Xi; New York Academy of Sciences; American Institute of Nutrition; Gerontology Society of America; International Society of Biometeorology; American Federation of Aging Research, National Scientific Advisory Council. Hobbies: Golf; Tennis; Hunting; Fishing; Reading. Address: 119 Noll Laboratory, The Pennsylvania State University, University Park, PA 16802, USA.

BUSSE Ewald William, b. 18 Aug 1917, St Louis, Missouri, USA. President, Institute of Medicine. m. Ortrude Schnaedelbach, 18 July 1941, 1 son, 3 daughters. Education: AB, Westminster College, 1938; MD, Washington University, 1942. Appointments include: Chairman, Department of Psychiatry, 1953-74, Dean of Medical and Allied Health Education, 1974-82, Associate Provost, 1974-87, Dean Emeritus, 1982-87, Duke University, Durham, North Carolina; President, Chief Executive Officer, North Carolina Institute of Medicine, 1987-. Publications: Cerebral Manifestations of Episodic Cardiac Dysrhythmias (editor), 1979; Co-editor: Handbook of Geriatric Psychiatry, 1980; The Duke Longitudinal Studies of Normal Aging 1955-1980, 1987; Geriatric Psychiatry, 1989. Honours: ScD (Honorary) Westminster College, 1960; Salmon Award, New York Academy of Medicine, 1980; Brookdale Foundation Award, Gerontological Society of America, 1982; Sandoz Prize for Interdisciplinary Research on Aging, 1983; Pioneer Award, Government Commission on Reduction of Infant Mortality, 1993. Memberships: Institute of Medicine; Gerontological Society of America; International Association of Gerontology; American Geriatric Society; American Psychiatric Association. Hobbies: Tennis; Sailing; Skiing. Address: Duke University Medical Center, Box 2948, Durham, NC 27710, USA.

BUTLER Gillian, b. 13 Apr 1942, Longparish, England. Clinical Psychologist. m. Christopher Butler, 25 June 1966, 2 daughters. Education: BA (Hons), 1st Class, Experimental Psychology, St Anne's College, Oxford, 1974; MSc, Abnormal Psychology, Oxford, 1976; PhD, Open University, 1990. Appointments: Research Associate, Department of Psychiatry, Oxford University, 1979-88; Currently Consultant Clinical Psychologist. Publications: Co-author: Exposure and anxiety management in the treatment of social phobia, 1984; Anxiety management for persistent generalised anxiety, 1987; A comparison of behaviour therapy and cognitive behaviour therapy in the treatment of generalised anxiety disorder, 1991. Memberships: British Psychological Society; British Association for Behavioural and Cognitive Psychotherapy; Society for the Exploration of Psychotherapy Integration. Hobbies: Walking; Gardening; Reading; Cooking; Travel; Cinema; Music. Address: Department of Psychology, Warneford Hospital, Headington, Oxford OX3 7JX, England.

BUTLER Neville Roy, b. 6 July 1920. Paediatrician. m. Jean Ogilvie, 14 May 1954, 2 daughters. Education: MB BS, Charing Cross Hospital Mwedical School. Appointments: Captain, RAMC; 1st Assistant, Paediatric Unit, University College Hospital, 1950; Medical Registrar and Pathologist, Hospital for Sick Children, Gt Ormond Street, 1953; Consultant Paediatrician, Oxford and Wessex RHB, 1957-63; Director, Perinatal Mortality Survey, National Birthday trust Fund, 1958; Consultant Physician, Hospital for Sick Children, Gr Ormond Street, Senior Lecturer, Institute of Child Health, University of London, 1963-65; Co-Director, National Child Development Study, 1965-75; Professor of Child Health, University of Bristol, 1965-85; Emeritus Professor, 1985-; Director, Child Health and Education Study, 1970-85; International Centre for Child Studies, 1982-; Youthscan UK, 1985-. Publications: Perinatal Mortality, Co-author, 1963; 11,000 Seven Year Olds, 1966; Perinatal Problems, 1969; From Birth to Seven, 1972; ABO Haemolytic Disease of the Newborn, 1972; The Social Life of Britain's Five Year Olds, 1984; From Birth to Five, 1986. Memberships: Vice President, RCM, 1972-; Vice Prtesident, HVA, 1975-; BPA; Neonatal Society; Cuban Paediatric Society; Hungarian Paediatric Society. Hobby: Running a Charity. Address: Vice Cottage, Seagry Road, Sutton Benger, Chippenham, Wiltshire, England.

BÜTOW Kurt Wilhelm, b. 1 Apr 1948, Windhoek, Namibia, South Africa. Maxillo-Facial & Oral Surgeon. m. Lucille du Toit, 13 Nov 1976, 2 daughters. Education: BSc, Faculty of Natural Science, Rand Afrikaans University, South Africa, 1970; BChD, Faculty of Dentistry, University of Stellenbosch, 1976; MChD, MFOSurg, Faculty of Dentistry, University of Stellenbosch, 1980; Dr Med Dent, Faculty of Medicine, Friedrich-Alexander University of Erlangen-Nuremburg, Germany, 1983; PhD, Faculty of Dentistry, University of Pretoria, 1988. Appointments Include: Lecturer, University of Stellenbosch, 1976; Lecturer, University of Western Cape, 1978; Head, Professor, Chief Specialist, University of Pretoria, 1984, 1993-; Professor, Chief Specialist, University of Pretoria, 1983-84, 1992-93. Publications: 140 publications including 2 books and 1 chapter in a 2 books, 2 doctorate dissertations, scientific abstracts and scientific reports. Honours: 2nd Prize, University of Stellenbosch, 1974; Johnson & Johnson Dental School Award, 1975; Elida-Ponds Research Award, 1984; Elida-Ponds Fellowship Research Grant, 1986; Deans Award, 1988; Silver Medal Award, Outstanding Research, University of Pretoria, 1989; Awd, Top Achiever, University of Pretoria, 1989, 1992, 1993. Memberships: South African Dental Association; International Association of Dental Research; International Association of Oral & Maxillo-Facial Radiology; International Association of Oral & Maxillo-Facial Surgery, Life Fellow; British Association of Oral & Maxillo-Facial Surgery; South African Society of Maxillo-Facial & Oral Surgery. Address: PO Box 1266, Pretoria 0001, South Africa.

BUTTERWORTH Robert Roman, b. 24 June 1946, Pittsfield, USA. Psychologist; Researcher; Media Therapiest. Education: BA, SUNY, 1972; MA, Marist College, 1975; PhD, Clinical Psychology, California Graduate Institute, 1983. Appointments: Assistant Clinical Psychologist, New York Department of Mental Hygiene, Wassaic, 1972-75; President, Contemporary Psychology Associates, Inc, Los Angeles & Downey, California, 1976-; Consultant, Los Angeles County Department of Health Services; Staff Clinician, San Barnardino County Department of Mental Health, 1983-85; Staff Psychologist, California Department of Mental Health, 1985-. Publications: Numerous publications in scientific journals. Memberships: America Psychology Association for Media Psychology; California Psychology Association; National Accreditation Association. Address: 431 South Kingsley Drive, Apartment 308, Los Angeles, CA-90020-3289, USA.

BUXTON Edward John, b. 20 Oct 1956, Birmingham, UK. Consultant Gynaecological Oncologist; Gynaecologist. Education:MBChB, University of Birmingham, UK, 1980; MRCOG. Appointments: Lecturer in Gynaecological Oncology, University of Birmingham, UK; Consultant Gynaecological Oncologist/Gynaecological Surgeon, The General Infirmary, Leeds, UK. Publications: Author of Articles on Chemotherapy in Cervical, Ovarian and Edometrial Cancer; Author of Articles on Treatment of Cervical Pre-Cancer; Author of Chemotherapy in Gynaecological Malionancy in Gynaecological Oncology, 1987; Author of Presentation and Staging of Endometrial Cancer in Textbook of Gynaecological Oncology, 1991. Memberships: International Gynaecological Cancer Society; British Gynaecological Cancer Society; British Society for Colposcopy & Cervical Pathology; British Medical Association. Hobbies: Game Fishing; Equestrian Activities. Address: Department of Gynaecological Oncology, Clarendon Wing, The General Infirmary at Leeds, Belmont Grove, Leeds LS2 9NS, England.

BUYUKUNAL S N Cenk, b. 3 Dec 1952, Gallipoli, Turkey. Professor in Paediatric Surgery. m. 22 Oct 1976, 1 d. Education: 1st Degree Graduation, Cerrahpasa Medical Faculty, with High Honour, 1976. Career: Assistant Professor in Paediatric Surgical Department, 1980-83; Military Duty in Kasimpasa Navy Hospital, 1983-84; Associate Professor, 1985-90, Professor in Paediatric Surgery, 1990-, Department of Paediatric Surgery, Cerrahpasa Medical School, Istanbul University; Publications: Antenatal Diagnosis and Treatment, book, 1992; 140 Articles on paediatric trauma, paediatric urology and oncology. Honours: Eczacibasi Medical Research Prize, 1987 and 1989; Medal of History of Pediatric Surgery, BAPS Meeting in Athens, Greece, 1988. Memberships: Turkish Association of Paediatric Surgeons; British Association of Paediatric Surgeons; International Society Paediatric Oncology (SIOP); International Paediatric Surgical Oncologists; Turkish Association of General Surgeons; Asian Association of Paediatric Surgeons. Hobbies: Music; Travel; Medical puppets and babies collection. Address: Haciemin sok Ersek Apt 30, D-3 Nisantasi, 80200 Istanbul, Turkey.

BYK Christian, b. 5 May 1955, Paris, France. Judge; Professor of Law. m. Dominique Dolcet, 4 Oct 1982, 1 d. Education: LLB, 1978, LLD, cum laude, 1991, Hab Jur, 1992, Universite de droit, d'economie et de Sciences Sociales de Paris, Pantheon Assas. Appointments: Member, Steering Committee on Bioethics, Council of Europe, 1983-91; Special Adviser on Bioethics to the Secretary General of the Council of Europe, 1991-93; Judge, Paris; Professor of law, University of Poitiers. Publications: Reproductive Medicine: What About Ethics and Law, 1989; Law Reform and Human Reproduction, Co-author, 1992; Bioethics and the European Convention on Human Rights, 1994; Dictionnaire Permanent Bioethique, Co-author, 1994; International Journal of Bioethics, General Editor, 1990-. Honours: Member, Czech Central Ethical Commission, 1992; Honorary Member, Romanian Academy of Medical Sciences. Memberships: COuncil of International Organisations of Medical Sciences, Executive Committee; International Association of Law Ethics and Science, Secretary General; French Centre of Comparative Law, Executive Board. Hobbies: Garden Art; Photography. Address: 62 Blvd de Port-Royal, 75005 Paris, France.

BYRNE Edward, b. 15 Feb 1952, England. Neurologist. m. Melissa Byrne, 1974, 3 sons, 1 daughter. Education: BSc; B Med Sc; MBBS; Diploma, Clinical Science; MD; FRACP. Appointments: Resident Registrar, Royal Adelaide Hospital; Registrar, Research Fellow, National Hospital for Nervous Diseases, London; Currently, Professor Clinical Neurosciences, University of Melbourne & Director Melbourne Neuromuscular Reserach Centre. Publications: Over 100 publications in major journals, special interest in Muscle Diseases. Memberships: Royal Society of Medicine; Royal Australian College of Physicians; Australia Association of Neurologists. Honours: Queen's Square Prize for Neurological Research, 1982. Hobbies: Reading; Chess. Address: St Vincents Hospital, Melbourne, Vic 3065, Australia.

BYRNE Neville John, b. 26 Aug 1951, Melbourne, Australia. Physician. m. Janet Liddle, 9 Apr 1983, 1 s, 2 d. Education: MB BS, Monash University, 1974; FACOM, 1986. Appointments: Medical Officer, Qantas, Sydney, 1982-88; Senior Occupational Physician, British Airways, London, England. Publications: Comparison of Airline Passenger Oxygen Systems. Memberships: SOM; IAPOS. Hobbies: Biographies; Tennis; Travel. Address: British Airways Health Services, PO Box 10, Heathrow Airport, TW6 2JA, England.

BYYNY Richard Lee, b. 6 Jan 1939, CA, USA. MD. m. Jo Ellen Garverick, 25 Aug 1962, 1 s, 2 d. Education: BA, History, 1960, MD, 1964, University of Southern California. Career: Assistant Professor, 1971-75, Associate Professor of Medicine, 1975-77, University of Chicago; Professor of Medicine, Executive Vice Chancellor, 1994-, University of Colorado, Health Sciences Center. Publications include: Co-author, A Clinical Guide for the Care of Older Women, 1990. Honours: Merck Award, 1964; American Council on Education

Fellowship, 1992. Memberships: Alpha Omega Alpha; Society of General Internal Medicine, Past President; American Society of Hypertension; Endocrine Society. Hobbies: Skiing; Sailing; Running. Address: 4200 East 9th Avenue, Box A-095, Denver, CO 80262, USA.

C

CABERNITE Leao, b. 8 May 1923, Cairo, Egypt. Psychiatrist; Psychoanalist. m. Sara Ita, 16 June 1951, 1 son, 1 daughter. Education: Medicine, 1948; Philosophy, 1954; Psychoanalysis, 1959; Group Therapy, 1962; Nuclear Medicine, 1968. Appointments: Director, Pedro II Hospital, Mental Health Division, 1957; Professor, Psychiatry, Ministry of Health, 1957; Director, Health Education Division, Ministry of Health, 1959; Assistant Professor, 1st Clinical Department of the Surgical & Medical School, 1960; President, Officer, Several Medical & Psychoanalytical Societies, 1972-81; Editor, Several Publications, 1972-80; Clinical Coordinator, Pinel Hospital, 1991; Training Analyst, Teacher, Psychoanalytic Teaching Institute. Publications: Medicine Teaching in Brazil, 1967; Absence Defence in Psychoanalysis, 1970; Oedipus Complex in Psychoanalysis & Group Therapy, 1972; The Therapeutic Group and Psychoanalysis, 1974; 88 articles published or lectured on Medicine, Psychiatry, Psychology, Psychoanalysis. Honours: Honour Diploma, Almofariz Order, 1951; Medal, Medical Sciences Integration, 1958; Commendatary of the St Paul Order, 1960; Honour Merit, Joana D'Arc Order, 1968. Memberships: International Psychoanalitical Association; New York Academy of Science; American Group Psychotherapy Association; Rio de Janeiro Psychoanalytic Society; Brazilian Psychoanalytic Association; Brazilian Medical Association. Integration, 1958; Commendatary of the St Paul Order, 1960; Honour Merit, John D'Arc Order, 1968. Hobbies: Swimming. Address: Rua Aires Saldanha 66, Apto 701, 22060-030 Rio de Janeiro RJ, Brazil.

CADDELL Joan Louise, b. USA. Medical Researcher. Education: BA; MD; Board Certification in Paediatrics; Board Certification in Paediatric Cardiology. Appointments: Instructor, Paediatrics, Yale University, 1960-62; Rockefeller Foundation Fellow to Uganda, 1962-63, to Nigeria, 1963-65; Assistant Professor, St Louis University, Missouri; National Institutes of Health Fellow to Thailand, 1970-72; Research Professor, Paediatrics, St Louis University, 1980; National Institutes of Health Adjunct Scientist, 1980-89; Currently Research Professor, Paediatrics, Thomas Jefferson University, Philadelphia, Pennsylvania. Publications: Metabolic and nutritional diseases, chapter in Heart Diseases in Infants, Children and Adolescents, 1968, 1977, 1983, 1989, 1994; Diseases of the cardiovascular system, chapter in Diseases of Childhood in the Subtropics and Tropics, 1970, 1978, 1980. Memberships: American Institute of Nutrition; Society for Experimental Biology and Medicine; American Pediatric Society; American Society of Clinical Nutrition. Hobbies: Piano; Swimming. Address: Department of Paediatrics, Thomas Jefferson University, Philadelphia, PA 19107-5541, USA.

CADIEUX Roger Joseph, b. 7 Feb 1945, Physician; Mental Health Care Executive. 1 s, 1 d. Education includes: BS, Northwestern State University, 1973; MD, LA State University, 1977; Diplomate, American Board Psychiatry and Neurology. Appointments include: Physician Consultant, PA Department of Aging, 1987-; PACE Therapeutic Advisory Committee, 1992-; National HCFA Advisory Committee for Applying Drug Use Review (DUR) in a Medicare/Medicaid Population, University of MD Ct Public Policy, 1992-; Director, Geriatric Assessment Clinic, PA State University College of Medicine, Hershey, PA, 1992-; President, Commonwealth Affiliates, PC, 1992-; Psychiatric Consultant, The Homeland Nursing Home of Harrisburg, PA State University, Department of Psychiatry's Teaching Nursing Home Program, 1993-; Associate Professor, Department of Psychiatry, PA State University, College of Medicine, Milton South, Hershey Medical Center, 1993-. Publications: 56 articles in professional journals including: Co-author, Sleep Disorders in the Elderly: Conservative Treatment is Usually Enough, in Postgraduate Medicine, 1992; Author, Geriatric Psychopharmacology: A Primary Care Challenge, in Postgraduate Medicine, 1993; Author, Psychiatric Disorders in the Elderly, in Patient Care, 1993. Honours include: Alpha Omega Alpha and Honor's Council, LA State University of Shreveport School of Medicine, 1976; Rock Sleyster Scholar in Psychiatry, AMA Education and Research Foundation, 1976. Memberships include: APA; American Geriatric Society; American Association for Geriatric Psychiatry; Academy of Sleep Disorders Medicine. Address: Suite 38 Northwood Office Center, 2215 Forest Hills Drive, Harrisburg, PA 17112, USA.

CADY Blake, b. 27 Dec 1930, Washington DC, USA. Surgical Oncologist. m. Elizabeth Wilder, 1 Oct 1960, 1 s, 2 d. Education: BA, Amherst College; MD, Cornell University Medical College. Career: Professor of Surgery, Harvard Medical School, 1967-81; Chief, Surgical Oncology, New England Deaconess Hospital. Publications: Books, Surgery of the Thyroid and Parathyroid Glands, 1991; Atlas of Surgical Oncology, 1992; Surgical Oncology Clinics of North America, 1992; General Surgical Oncology, 1992; Articles, Technical and Biological Factors in Disease-Free Survival After Hepatic Resection for Colorectal Cancer Metastases, 1991; New Therapeutic Possibility in Primary Invasive Breast Cancer, 1993; An Expanded View of Risk Group Definition in Differentiated Thyroid Carcinoma, 1988. Honours: Lemuel Shattuck Medal, Massachusetts Public Health Association, 1983; Annual National Division Award, Massachusetts Division American Cancer Society, 1984; Henry D Chadwick Medal, Massachusetts Thoracic Society, 1994. Memberships: American Cancer Society; Society of Surgical Oncology; Boston Surgical Society; Society of Head and Neck Surgeons; New England Cancer Society; American College of Surgeons; New England Surgical Society. Hobbies: Sailing; Reading. Address: 110 Francis Street, Suite 2H, Boston, MA 02215, USA.

CAHAN William George, b. 8 Feb 1914. Surgeon. m. Grace Mirabella, 24 Nov 1974, 2 s. Education: BS, Harvard College, 1935; MD, Columbia University, New York, 1939. Appointments include: Professor of Surgery, 1974-80, Emeritus Professor, Surgery, 1980-, Cornell University Medical College; Consultant, Thoracic Service, 1985-86; Attending Surgeon, 1986-90, Memorial Hospital, New York City; Emeritus Attending Surgeon, Memorial Hospital, New York, 1991-. Publications: Contributor of numerous professional articles including: Cancer in the Armed Forces, 1944; Description and use of the Breast Clamp, 1951; Cancer of the Lung, 1963; Multiple Primary Cancers, One of Which is Lung, 1969; Multiple Primary Cancers of the Lung, Esophagus and Other Sites, 1977; Post-Radiation Osteogenic Sarcoma of Bone and Soft Tissues: A Clinicopathologic Study of 66 Oatients, Co-author, 1985; Post-Radiation Sarcomas Involving the Spine, Co-author, 1986. Honours include: Honorary Academician, Faculty of Physical Mathematical and Natural Sciences, Noble Academy of Empress St Theodora, Rome, 1968; Distinguished Service Award, American Cancer Society, 1982. Memberships include: New York Surgical Society; New York Society for Thoracic Surgeons; New York Surgical Society; Society of Surgical Oncology; Association for the Advancement of Medical Instrumentation. Address: 1275 York Avenue, New York, NY 10021, USA.

CAI Chongyang, b. 16 Oct 1934, Guangdong, China. Associate Research Professor. m. Shangqi Chen, 18 Aug 1962, 2 s. Career: Geology Department, Changchun University of Earth Science, 1956-60; Assistant Professor and Head of Geology Section of Mining Department, Iron and Steel Institute of Baotou, 1960-63; Postgraduate student of Palaeobotany, Nanjing Institute of Geology and Palaeontology Academia Sinica, 1963-67; Postdoctoral study at Palaeontology Institute of Bonn University, 1980-82; Currently, Associate Research Professor and Head of Palaeozoic Section of Palaeobotany Department, Nanjing Institute. Publications include: Co-author, Recent advances in the study of the Wutung Formation of the Lower Yangtze Valley, 1984. Honours: 2nd Prize, Natural Science Jiangsu Committee of Science and Technology, 1979; 2nd Prize, Natural Science of Academia Sinica, 1987. Memberships: Corresponding Member, SDS of IUGS; Member of Professional Group on Devonian System of All-China Stratigraphy Committee; Geological Society of China; Palaeontoloy Society of China; Botany Society of China. Hobbies: Stamp Collecting; Sport. Address: Nanjing Institute of Geology and Palaeontology, Academia Sinica, Chimingsu, Nanjing 210008, China.

CAI Dung Van, b. 10 Oct 1942, Binh-Dinh, Vietnam. Physician. m. Ngoc Hong Truong, 1 Dec 1965, 2 s, 3 d. Education: Vietnamese Medical Doctor; Board Certified Obstetrics & Gynaecology; Fellow, American College of Obstetricians and Gynaecologists. Appointments: Vietnamese Medical Doctor, 1968-75; Intern at Lower Bucks County Hospital, Bristol, Pennsylvania; Resident in Obstetrics & Gynaecology, Presbyterian Hospital, Philadelphia, Pennsylvania; Resident and Chief Resident, Obstetrics & Gynaecology, Albany Medical College, Albany, New York; Solo Practice of Obstetrics & Gynaecology, San Jose, California, 1984-. Memberships: CMA; Santa Clara County Medical Association; Shufelt Society of Gynaecologists; Vietnamese Physician Association; Fellow of American College of Obstetrics & Gynaecology. Hobbies: Fishing; Dancing; Reading. Address: 259 Meridian Avenue, Suite 5, San Jose, CA 95126, USA.

CAI (TSAI) Ru-Sheng, b. 25 Dec 1915, Fukien, China. Physician. m. Wu Shou-Rou, 1 son, 1 daughter. Education: MD. Appointments: Currently: Professor of Medicine, Peking Union Medical College; Deputy Director, Cardiovascular Institute and Fu Wai Hospital, Chinese Academy of Medical Sciences. Publications: Recent Advance in Research of Cor Pulmonale in China, 1994; Co-author: Chest Disease, 1959; Respiratory Disease. Membership: Chinese Medical Association. Hobby: Soccer. Address: Fu Wai Hospital, Cardiovascular Institute, Beijing, China.

CAI Shi Wen, b. 13 June 1933, Fujian, China. Professor of Hygiene. m. Zheng Jia Ji, 22 Aug 1962, 2 sons. Education: Graduate, Beijing Medical University, 1956; PhD, Leningrad Medical College, Russia, 1962. Appointments: Research Assistant, Institute of Health, Chinese Academy of Medical Sciences, 1962; Visiting Physician, Tianshui Prefecture Hospital, 1970; Associate Professor, Institute of Health, Chinese Academy of Preventive Medicine, 1981; Professor, Director, IEHE, Chinese Academy of Preventive Medicine, 1987-. Publications: A Bacteriological and Helminthological Investigation on Sewage Irrigated Area in Beijing Suburb, 1988; Cadmium Exposure and Health Effects among Residents in Irrigation Area with Ore Dressing Wastewater, 1989; A Judgement for Attribution of Increase in urine ß2-Microglobulin After Environmental Cadmium Exposure, 1992. Honours: Consultant, Advisory Committee on Public Health, Ministry of Public Health, China, 1988; Scientific Advisor, Environmental Protection Committee, The State Council, China, 1991. Memberships: Chinese Medical Association; Chinese Association of Preventive Medicine. Address: Institute of Environmental Health and Engineering, CAPM, 29 Nan Wei Road, Beijing 100050, China.

CAI Wen-Qin, b. 11 Jan 1935, Nanjing, China. Professor. m. Ke-Cheng Zhang, 30 Dec 1962, 1 son, 2 daughters. Education: MB, 3rd Military Medical University, 1957; PhD, University College, London, England, 1983. Appointments: Lecturer, Department of Histology and Embryology, 1973-83, Professor, Department of Histology and Embryology, 1983-, 3rd Military Medical University. Publications: Practical Immunocytochemistry, 1987; Applications of Electron Microscopy on Clinical Medicine, 1987; Practical Immunocytochemistry and Nucleic Acid Hybridisation, 1994; Enteric Nervous System, 1990. Memberships: President, Neuroscience Society Chongqing; Councillor, China Anatomy Society; Chinese Electron Microscopy Society; Chinese Histochemistry Society. Hobbies: Literature; Sightseeing; Travel; Swimming; Sports. Address: Department Histology and Embryology, The 3rd Military Medical University, Chongqing 630038, China.

CAI Xiao-Sun, b. 19 December 1923, Shanghai, China. Chinese Herb Doctor. m. Wang Huei Feng, 20 August 1943, 2 sons, 1 daughter. Education: Graduate, College of Medicine, China. Appointments: Deputy Chief Chinese Herb Gynaecologist, 1986; Chief Chinese Herb Gynaecologist; Expert Committee, Shanghai Chinese Medicine University. Publications: Chief Editor: The Gynaecology Volume of the Complete Book of Chinese Herb Prescriptions, 1989; Chief Editor: Female Sterility Treatment with Chinese Medicine, 1989; Chief Editor: Chinese Medicine Treatment to Gynaecology. Honours: Special Bonus, State Council of China for Outstanding Contribution to Medical and Health Development of the Country, 1992. Memberships: Medical Science Committee of China; Advisor, Chinese Medicine Society of Shanghai; Deputy Chief Committeeman, Gynaecology Committee of Chima; Photography Society of Shanghai. Hobbies: Photography; Tourism; Hunting. Address: Room 402, No 33, The 19th Lane, Zhao Yuan Road, Shanghai, China.

CAI Xue Lin, b. 15 Feb 1935, Renshow County, Sichuan, China. Committee Member; Professor of Geology. m. 25 Dec 1961, 3 s, 1 d. Education: Graduate, Beijing College of Techology, 1958; Masters Degree, Tectonic Geology, Beijing College of Geology, 1964. Career: Vice-Director, Physical Geology Teaching Section, Chengdu College of Geology, 1976-83; Science Committee, Chengdu College of Geology, 1978-83; Member, Pre-Cambrian Course of State Council in China, 1978-82; Member and Vice-Director, Structural Geology Course and Teaching Guide Committee, Ministry of Geology and Mineral Resources of China, 1981-91; Currently, Tectonic Professional Committee of Geological Society of China; Tectonophysics Professional Committee of Seismological Society of China; Director of Structural Geology Course and Teaching Guide Committee of Ministry of Geology and Mineral Resources of China; Professor of Chengdu College of Geology, 1966-93. Publications include: Structural Geology, 1988; Three Methods for Determining Structural Shapes of Folds in the Metamorphic rock region and Their Theoretical Foundation, in Science in China, Series B, volume 33, No 4, 1990. Honours: Science Prize of China, 1978; Best Book Prize for Structural Geology, Geology and Mineral Resources of China, 1988; Winner 4 times of Science and Technology Achievement, 1988-91; Outstanding Achievement by a Chinese Scientific Expert, 1992. Hobbies: Chess; Reading. Address: Department of Geology, Chengdu College of Geology, Shilidian, Chengdu, Sichuan 610059, China.

CAI Youling, b. 15 July 1927, Tiantien, China. Professor of Dermatology. m. Loa Chen, 18 Dec 1954, 1 son, 1 daughter. Education: MD, Beijing University Medical College, 1955. Appointments: Currently Professor of Dermatology, Beijing Red Cross, Chanyong Hospital. Publications: A study on the allergenicity of the volatile elements of Chinese lacquer, 1985. Honours: 2nd Place, Science and Technology Award, Ministry of Public Health, 1984. Membership: Chinese Medical Association. Hobby: Enjoying music. Address: Beijing REd Cross, Chanyong Hospital, Beijing, China.

CALACHE Michel, b. 13 Oct 1953, Alexandria, Egypt. Psychiatrist. m. Lisa Calache, 18 July 1987, 1 s, 1 d. Education: MD; FRCP(C); Board Certified, American Board of Psychiatry and Neurology. Appointments: Staff Psychiatrist, Marion VA Medical centre, IN, USA. Publications: Contributor of several professional articles and book chapters. Memberships: American Psychiatric Association; American Association for Geriatrics Psychiatry; Fellow, Royal College of Physicians of Canada. Hobbies: Music; Travel; Walking; Fine Art. Address: 1700 East 38th Street, Marion, IN 46953, USA.

CALDERON Eduardo G, b. 19 Mar 1953, Tacna, Peru. Medical Doctor. m. Martha I Arrieta, 31 Aug 1984, 1 son, 1 daughter. Education: MD, San Agustin National University, 1987. Appointments: Visiting Fellow, 1988-90, Research Associate, 1991-92, Assistant Professor of Medicine, 1994-, Division of Allergy and Immunology, University of South Florida, Tampa, USA; Associate Professor, Department of Physiological Sciences, San Agustin National University, Arequipa, Peru, 1993-94. Publications: Co-author: New approaches to the treatment of HIV infection, 1991; Methotrexate in bronchial asthma, 1991, 1992; Is there a role for cyclosporine in asthma?, 1992; A possible role for adhesion molecules in asthma, 1992; Cyclosporine G in the treatment of psoriasis or psoriatic arthritis in HIV infected patients; Modulation of endothelin-1 production by a pulmonary epithelial cell line. Memberships: American College of Physicians; American Academy of Allergy and Clinical Immunology; Peruvian College of Physicians. Hobbies: Music; Literature; Astronomy. Address: 13000 Bruce B Downs Blvd, VAR 111 D, Tampa, FL 33612, USA.

CALDERONE Salvatore, b. 24 May 1928, Cefalu', Palermo, Italy. Orthodontist. m. Antonella Polito, 29 July 1965, 2 daughters. Education: MD, University of Palermo, 1951; Specialist, Dentistry, University of Bologna, 1953; Licensed to practise in Orthodontics. Appointments: Private practice in Orthodontics; Instructor, European Postgraduate in Edgewise Therapy Course, 1974-; Instructor, Tweed International Foundation for Orthodontic Research, Tucson, Arizona, USA, 1988-. Publications: Cuspid retraction; Stability of orthodontics treatment by Tweed-Merrifield mechanics; Mandibular response during and follcwing class II treatment by Tweed-Merrifield philosophy; Class III orthodontic-surgical treatment by Tweed-Merrifield philosophy. Honours: Award of Special Merit, C Tweed International Foundation, 1990. Memberships: Società Italiana Ortodonzia; Collège Européen d'Orthodontie; European Orthodontics Society; Tweed International Foundation for Orthodontics Research; Fouchard Academy. Hobbies: Swimming; Sailing; Cross-country. Address: Via La Marmora 82, 90143 Palermo, Italy.

CALL Justin David, b. 7 Aug 1923, Salt Lake City, Utah, USA. Psychoanalyst. m. Barbara Weaver, 25 Aug 1952, 3 daughters. Education: MD, University of Utah; Boards in Paediatrics, Adult and Child Psychiatry; Certified in Adult and Child Psychoanalysis, American Psychoanalytic Association. Appointments include: Associate Professor, Director of Child Psychiatry training, University of California, Los Angeles, 15 years; Professor, Chief of Child and Adolescent Psychiatry, 25 years, now Professor Emeritus of Psychiatry, University of California, Irvine, 25 years; Founding President, World Association for Infant Psychiatry (now World Association for Infant Mental Health), 1980. Publications: Frontiers in Infant Psychiatry; Approach Behavior in the New Born, 1964; Psychiatric Syndromes in Infancy, 1987; 100 others. Honours: Listed as Psychiatrist, Child Psychiatrist and Psychoanalyst in

Best Doctors in America. Memberships: American Psychoanalytic Association; Fellow, American Academy of Pediatrics; Fellow, American Academy of Child and Adult Psychiatry; American Medical Association; Fellow, American Psychiatric Association. Hobbies: Skiing instruction; Piano. Address: 1958 Galaxy Drive, Newport Beach, CA 92660, USA.

CALLOW Allan Dana, b. 9 Apr 1916, Somerville, MA, USA. Surgeon. m. Una Scully Ryan, 26 May 1989, 1 s 4 d. Education: MD; PhD; DSc, Honours; MS. Appointments: Professor and Chair of Surgery, Tufts University School of Medicine; Research Professor, Washington University Medical School; Research Professor, boston University. Publications: Author of 2 textbooks; Contributor of over 200 articles and 50 chapters in books. Honours: Cleveson's Award, Japan, 1989; President's Medal, Tufts, 1993. Memberships: American Surgical Association; Society Vascular Surgeons; Massachusetts Medical Society. Hobbies: Writing; Gardening. Address: 209 Sargent Drive, Brookline, MA 02166, USA.

CAMERON Alan D, b. 26 Jun 1957, Dundee, Scotland. Obstetrician. m. Philomena Cameron, 8 Aug 1985, 1 s, 1 d. Education: MBChB, Glasgow University, 1975-80; MD, 1991; MRCOG. Career: Lecturer, Department of Obstetrics, University of Glasgow; Fellow in Maternal-Fetal Medicine, University of Calgary, Alberta, Canada; Currently, Obstetrician and Gynaecologist, Director of Fetal Medicine, Queen Mother's Hospital, Glasgow, Scotland. Publications: Chapters in books, Prenatal Diagnosis; Peer reviewed articles in American Journal of Obstetrics and Gynaecology, British Journal of Obstetrics and Gynaecology. Memberships: GMC; MDDUS; British Medical Association; RCOG; Blair Bell Society; Munro Kerr Society; Society of Perinatal Obstetricians; British Medical Ultrasound Society. Hobbies: Sport; Art; Classic Cars. Address: Strathallan, 15 Greenock Avenue, Glasgow G44 5TS, Scotland.

CAMPBELL Doris Margaret, b. 24 Jan 1942, Aberdeen, Scotland. Doctor. m. Alasdair J Campbell, 3 Aug 1968, 1 son, 1 daughter. Education: MB ChB, 1967, MD|, 1973, Aberdeen University; DRCOG, 1969; MRCOG, 1975; FRCOG, 1990. Appointments: include: Lecturer, Obstetric and Gynaecology/Physiology, 1974-84; Registrar, Obstetrics and Gynaecology, Grampian Health Board, 1969-74; Research Fellow, Department Obstetrics and Gynaecology, University of Aberdeen, 1969-73; Senior Lecturer, Obstetrics and Gynaecology and Reproductive Physiology, University of Aberdeen, 1984-. Publications: Twinning and Twins, Co-Editor, 1988; Contributor of over 150 scientific papers in journals and books. Memberships: International Society for the Study of Hypertension in Pregnancy; International Society for Twin Studies, Multiple Pregnancy Group; Nutrition Society; Blair Bell Research Society; Society for Higher Education. Hobbies: Bridge; Hillwalking; Badminton; Reading. Address: 77 Blenheim Place, Aberdeen AB2 4DZ, Scotland.

CAMPBELL Kathleen C M, b. 20 Mar 1952, Sioux Falls, South Dakota, USA. Director of Audiology. m. Craig Campbell, 1975. Education: BA, Communication, Education; MA, Audiology, University of South Dakota, 1977; Doctoral Fellow, Health Services Research and Development, Veterans Administration, Iowa, 1987-88; PhD, Audiology, Hearing Science, University of Iowa, 1989. Appointments: Regional Audiologist II, British Columbia Ministry of Health, Canada, 1977-82; Audiologist II, Department of Otolaryngology, Head and Neck, University of Iowa, USA, 1983-88; Associate Professor, Division of Otolaryngology, Southern Illinois University School of Medicine, Springfield, 1989-; Adjunct Associate Professor, Gerontology Programme, Sangamon State University. Publications: Co-author, contributions to: Journal of American Academy of Audiology, 1993; Otolaryngology Clinics of North America, 1993; Annals of ORF, 1994. Honours: CIDA and SBIR Grants, National Institutes of Health, 1990: Alzheimer Disease Center Core Grant, National Institute of Audiology, 1992; Children's Miracle Network Telethon, Southern Illinois University, 1993-94. Memberships: American Speech and Hearing Association; AAS; American Association of Audiology; Association for Research in Otolaryngology; CDRF; Women in Neuroscience; AAO-HNS; SHHH. Address: Southern Illinois University School of Medicine, PO Box 19230. St John's Pavilion 5B, Springfield, IL 62794-9230, USA.

CAMPBELL Sandra Joan, b. 1 December 1957, Sydney, Australia. Nursing. Education: Post Basic Nephlology Certificate, 1984; General Nursing Certificate, High Distinction, 1978; Graduate Diploma of Applied Science (Advanced Clinical Nursing) Sydney University, 1992; Master of Clinical Nursing, Sydney University, 1994. Appointments: Clinical Nurse Consultant, CAPD, 1986; Renal Service, 1993; Registered Nurse, CAPD, 1994. Memberships: Secretary, New South Wales Branch of Renal Society of Australasia; International Society for Peritoneal Dialysis. Hobbies: Reading; Walking; Swimming; Golf. Address: 489 Rocky Point Road, Sans Soug, Sydney NSW 2219, Australia.

CANTEZ Talat, b. 15 December 1933, Konya, Turkey. Medical Doctor. m. Sema Goney, 12 June 1966, 2 daughters. Education: MD; FAAP; FACC. Appointments: Chairman, Department of Pediatrics, Director of Pediatrics, Cardiology, Turkey, 1983; Christ Medical Center, Rush University, Chicago, USA, 1975-80; Dean, Faculty of Pharmacy, Chairman of Medical Sciences, ITA (Marmara University, 1980-81); Vice Rector, Dicle University, Diyarbakir, Turkey, 1983. Publications: Pediatrics (textbook), 1971; 130 original articles in professional medical journals with 80 paper presentations. Honours: Valedictorian of Military Medical School, 1957; Istanbul Teacher of the Year, 1976, 1977, 1979; Christ Medical Center, Rush University, Chicago, Best Doctors in America, 1978; Physician Recognition Awards. Memberships: American Academy of Pediatrics; American College of Cardiology, Turkish Cardiology Society; European Pediatric Cardiology Association; Turkish Pediatric Association; Turkish Radiologic Society. Hobbies: Photography; Travel; Fishing. Address: Vanikoy Cad 17/1, Kandilli-Anadolu Hisari, Istanbul, Turkey 81620, Turkey.

CAO Daidi, b. 9 Apr 1950, Chen County, China. Doctor. m. He Guoxin, 28 Dec 1980, 1 daughter. Education: Bachelor Degree, Hunan Traditional Chinese Medical College, 1975. Appointments: Associate Chief Physician of Traditional Chinese Medicine. Publications: Chinese Traditional Medical Classification of Chronic Bronchitis and Blood Flow Changes, 1992; Macroscopic Analysis and Microscopic Combination of Gastric Disease, 1994. Memberships: Chinese Traditional Medical Academic Society of Hunan Province. Address: 2nd Hospital attached to Hengyang Medical College, Hengyang City, 421001 Hunan, China.

CAO Guang-Cheng, b. 28 Feb 1962, Shanxi, Xin Jiang City, China. Doctor. m. Wo Jun Ying, 28 Nov 1985, 1 son, 1 daughter. Education: Chang Zhi Medical College, China, 1988. Appointment: Director of Hospital. Publications: Handbook of Treatment on Cerbrovascular, 1988; Gere Indicational of Emery Treatment Internal Medicine, 1991. Honour: Advanced Science & Technology Worker, 1991. Membership: Red Cross. Address: No 64, Cheng Bei Da Jie, Xinjiang County, Shanxi Province, China.

CAO Hongxin, b. 10 Feb 1958, Harbin, China. Medical Doctor. m. Tian Huiping, 4 Mar 1984, 1 daughter. Education: BA, 1983, MA, 1986, PhD, MD, 1991, Heilongjiang College of Traditional Chinese Medicine. Appointments: Associate Professor, 1991; Assistant Leader, Basic and Diagnostic Office of Traditional Chinese Medicine, 1992; currently Professor, Tutor of Master Candidates, Assistant President of Heilongjiang College of Traditional Chinese Medicine, Harbin. Publications: Assistant Chief editor: Encyclopaedia of Traditional Chinese Medicine Treatment, Diagnosis and Prevention, 1989, 1990, 1991; Chief Editor: Children's Therapy, 5 copies, 1993; Diagnostic and Treating Handbook for Diseases of Liver and Gallbladder, 1994. Honours: Voted 1 of 10 Greatest Outstanding Youth of Harbin, 1992; Voted 1 of 10 Greatest Outstanding Youth of Heilongjiang Province, 1994. Membership: Vice-Chairman, Traditional Chinese Medicine Research Committee. Hobby: Swimming. Address: Heilongjiang College of Traditional Chinese Medicine, 14 Heping Road, Harbin 150040, China.

CAO Qi Long, b. 29 May 1928, Soochow, China. m. 8 Mar 1955, 2 d. Education: MD, Peking Union Medical College. Appointments: Doctor and Chief Doctor, Department of Neurology, PUMC Hospital, 1954-58; Professor and Chief Doctor, Department of Neurology, General Hospital of PLA. Honours: include, Distinguished Honourship for Military Geriatric Health Service, 1992; MSTA 2nd Degree, Research for Traditional Medical Pulse Diagnosis in 100 CVD Patients, 1989; Beijing Scientific Technological Award, Health EEG Normal Value in Beijing Province, 1988; Chinese Medical Academy Award, Beijing Branch for Excellent Academic Thesis, 1990; Distinguished Educational Prize for High Qualified Postgraduates among Military Colleges and Universities, 1993. Memberships: Chinese Medical Academy; Chinese Brain Ultrasound Diagnostic Association; Chinese Electric Bio-Impedance Association; Chinese Neuro-Rehabilitation Association; National Medicine Drug Bureau; Chinese EEG and Epilepsy Association; Beijing EEG Association; Chinese Medical Academy, Beijing Branch; Beijing Anti-Epilepsy Association; Chinese Ultrasound Technological

Association; Chinese PLA Neurological Association. Hobbies: Classical Music; Tropical Fish; Stamp Collecting. Address: 28 Fuxing Avenue, PLA General Hospital, 4th Building, Room 504, Beijing 100853, China.

CAO Zhi-Chen, b. 2 Jul 1948, Tianjin, China. Doctor and Professor. m. Xiujun Song, 21 Jul 1977, 1 d. Education: MD, Tangshan Medical College, China, 1976. Appointments: Resident and Assistant, Surgical Department, Affiliate of Tangshan Medical College, 1976-79; Resident and Assistant, Department of Internal Medicine, 3rd Affiliate Hospital of Hebei Medical College, 1979-84; Chief Resident and Lecturer, Department of Internal Medicine, 3rd Hospital of Hebei Medical College, 1984-85; Assistant Professor, Hebei Medical College, 1986-93; Associate Professor, Hebei Medical College, 1993-. Publications: Observation for Sero Magnesium in the Patients with Viral Hepatitis, 1990; Toxic Shock Syndrome, 1990; The Clinical Significance of Examining NAG in Urine of the Patients with EHF, 1990; The Influence of Sero Lipid Peroxides on Liver Function in Patients with Viral Hepatitis, 1993; Observation of Insular Function in the Patients with Hepatitis B and Diabetes, 1994. Honours: Recipient of Award of Provincial Achievement in Scientific Research, 1993, 1994. Memberships: Chinese Medical Association. Hobbies: Basketball; Beijing Opera. Address: 16 Weiming Street, Shijiazhuang, Hebei 050051, China.

CAPLAN Arthur L, b. 31 Mar 1950, Boston, MA, USA. Bioethicist. m. Janet Caplan, 1 s. Education: BA; MA; MPhil; PhD, Columbia University. Appointments: Associate Director, The Hastings Center, 1985-87; Director, Center for Biomedical Ethics, University of Minnesota, 1987-94; Currently, Director, Center for Bioethics, University of Pennsylvania. Publications: If I Were a Rich Man, 1992; When Medicine Went Mad, 1992; Prescribing Our Future, 1993. Membership: President, American Association of Bioethics, 1993-94. Address: Centre for Bioethics, University of Pennsylvania, 3401 Market Street, Suite 320, Philadelphia, PA 19104, USA.

CAPLAN Louis R, b. 31 Dec 1936, Baltimore, MD, USA. Physician. Neurologist. m. Brenda Fields Caplan, 28 Nov 1963, 5 s, 1 d. Education: BA, cum laude; MD, summa cum laude. Career: Chief of Neurology, Beth Israel Hospital; Assistant Professor of Neurology, Harvard University; Neurologist in Chief, Michael Reese Hospital; Professor of Neurology, University of Chicago; Currently, Professor and Chairman of Neurology, Tufts University; Neurologist in Chief, New England Medical Center, Boston. Publications: 300 Articles and 105 abstracts published; 14 Books including: Editor, Brain Ischemia: From Basic Science to Treatment, 1994; Co-author, The American Heart Association Family Guide to Stroke: Treatment, Recovery and Prevention, 1993; Author, Posterior Circulation Vascular Disease, in press. Honours: Phi Beta Kappa, 1957; Alpha Omega Alpha, 1961; Gold Key Award, 1990; Distinguished Achievement Award, American Heart Association, 1993. Memberships: American Academy of Neurology; American Neurological Association; American Heart Association; American College of Physicians; Honorary Member, Australian and German Neurological Associations. Hobbies: Sport; Reading. Address: New England Medical Center, 750 Washington Street, Boston, MA 02111, USA.

CAPLIS Michael E, b. 25 Jul 1938, Ypsilanti, MI, USA. Biochemist; Toxicologist. m. Lucille M Truitt, 3 s, 4 d. Education: BSc, Chemistry, Eastern Michigan University, 1962; MSc, Biochemistry, 1964, DPhil, Biochemistry, 1970, Purdue University, West Lafayette, IN; Post Doctorate, St Mary Medical Center, Gary, IN, 1969-72; Continuing education in various fields, 1969-90. Career includes: Director, Clinical Biochemistry Laboratories, St Mary Medical Center, Hobart and Gary, IN, 1969-83; Director and Founder, Great Lakes Laboratories, Michigan City, IN, 1970-; Adjunct Professor, Indiana University Northwest School of Medicine, 1979-; Founder and Director, Northwest Criminal and Toxicology Laboratory, IN. Publications: Over 30 publications in scientific journals and books. Honours include: Diplomat, American Board of Forensic Toxicology; Indiana Criminal Justice Planning Agency Federal Grant, 3 years; Fellow, Academy of Clinical Toxicology; Fellow, American Academy of Forensic Science; Fellow, National Academy of Clinical Biochemists; Fellow, American Institute of Chemists. Memberships include: American Association for the Advancement of Science; American Chemical Society; Association of Official Analytical Chemists; American Association of Crime Laboratory Directors; New York Academy of Sciences; Tissue Culture Association. Hobbies: Woodworking; Boating; Hunting. Address: 118 East 8th Street, Michigan City, IN 46360, USA.

CARDILLO Kenneth R, b. 12 Sept 1951, White Plains, New York, USA. Psychoanalyst. m. Paulette Grondin, 27 Dec 1975, 3 sons. Education: BA, Philosophy, Fordham University, 1973; MS, Psychology, Southern Connecticut University, 1978; Certificate, The West Chester Institute for Training in Psychoanalysis & Psychotherapy, 1978. Appointments include: Staff Psychotherapist, Hudson River Counseling Service; Faculty, West Chester Institute; Staff Psychologist, Monroe School System & Norwalk School System, Connecticut; Founder, Casco Bay Counseling Service, 1981; Founder, Consulting Associates, 1991. Memberships: National Association for the Advancement of Psychoanalysis; American Orthopsychiatric Association; The Institute for Global Ethics. Hobbies: Skiing; Mountain Climbing; Sailing; Family Adventures. Address: 16 Madokawando Landing, Falmouth, Maine 04105, USA.

CARDOZO J J Bosco, b. 26 Sep 1936, Zanzibar. Physician. m. Hazel Cardozo, 2 Jan 1965, 5 s, 1 d. Education: MD; FRCOG; Board Certified, Obstetrics and Gynaecology. Career: Obstetrician and Gynaecologist. Honour: Charles Gold Medal in Anatomy, 1956. Membership: Fellow, Royal College of Obstetricians and Gynaecologists. Hobbies: Gardening; Cycling; Cuisine. Address: Dunning Street, Claremont, NH 03743, USA.

CAREY Larry C, b. 5 Nov 1933, Coral Grove, OH, USA. Surgeon. m. Christina Green, 17th Sep, 2 s, 3 d. Education: BS, 1955, MD, 1959, Ohio State University. Career includes: US Navy, Lt Commander, 1965-70; Professor and Chairman, 1975-85, Robert M Zollinger Professor of Surgery, 1977-87, Clinical Professor, Department of Surgery, 1987-90, Ohio State University; Director of Medical Affairs, Grant Medical Center, 1987-90; Professor and Chairman, Department of Surgery, University of South FL, College of Medicine, 1990-; Chief of Surgery, Tampa General Hospital, 1991-. Publications include: Over 190 articles in professional journals, 1959-93, including: Co-author, Impact of staging on treatment of pancreatic and ampullary cancer, in Endoscopy, 1993, Health Care Costs and Us, in the HCMA Bulletin, 1993; Over 50 books, chapters and monographs incuding: Co-author, Surgical Treatment of Digestive Disease, 1989; Editorial Boards: American Journal of Surgery, 1976-; Surgery, 1984-; Hillsborough County Medical Association - The Bulletin, 1991-. Honours include: Navy Commendation Medal, 1968; Honorary Professor, Mirizzi Postgrauate School of Surgery, Argentina, 1985; Various Honorary Memberships. Memberships include: Alpha Omega Alpha; Various positions American Board of Surgery; Fellow, American College of Surgeons; AMA; ASA; American Trauma Society; International Hepato-Biliary Pancreatic Association; International Society of Surgery; Society of Military Surgeons; Founding member, Surgical Biology Club III. Address: Harbourside Medical Tower, 4 Columbia Drive, Suite 430, Tampa, FL 33606, USA.

CAREY Robert Munson, b. 13 Aug 1940, Lexington, Kentucky, USA. Professor of Medicine. m. Theodora Hereford, 24 Aug 1963, 1 son, 2 daughters. Education: MD, Vanderbilt University, 1965; Internship in Medicine, University of Virginia; Residency in Medicine, New York Hospital-Cornell Medical Center; Fellow, American College of Physicians. Appointments: Assistant Professor, Associate Professor, Full Professor of Medicine, currently James Carroll Flippin Professor of Medical Science, Dean, University of Virginia School of Medicine, Charlottesville. Publications: Over 200 scientific publications; 2 books. Honours: Distinguished Alumnus Award and Founder's Medal, Vanderbilt University, 1994; Institute of Medicine, National Academy of Sciences, USA; Association of American Physicians. Memberships: American Society for Clinical Investigation; American Clinical and Climatological Association. Hobbies: Running; Hiking; Camping; Fishing; Tennis. Address: Pavilion VI, East Lawn, Charlottesville, VA 22903, USA.

CARLETON Richard Allyn, b. 15 Mar 1931, Providence, Rhode Island, USA. Cardiologist. m. April Michele Carleton, 29 Jan 1975, 1 son, 4 daughters. Education: BA summa cum laude, Dartmouth College, 1952; MD cum laude, Harvard Medical School, 1955. Appointments: Professor of Medicine, University of Illinois, Rush Medical College, University of California at San Diego, Dartmouth Medical School; Currently Physician-in-Chief, Memorial Hospital of Rhode Island. Publications: Over 250 scientific papers and chapters, 1960-. Honours: Teacher of the Year, 1966, 1968, 1970, 1972, 1988; Gold Heart Award, American Heart Association, 1993. Memberships: American Society of Clinical Investigation; American College of Cardiology; Association of University Cardiologists; American Heart Association. Hobbies: Sailing;

Gardening; Running. Address: 32 S Meadow Lane, Barrington, RI 02806, USA.

CARLISLE William, b. 12 Aug 1927, Montgomery, Alabama, USA. MD. m. Mary Elizabeth Jackson, 6 Nov 1951, 1 s, 1 d. Education: BS; MD; FACOG Diploma, American Board of Obstetrics & Gynaecology. Appointments: MD, United States Air Force, 1954-56; Fellow; Obstetrics & Gynaecology Ochswer Foundation: Private Practice, Tuscaloosa, Alabama. Memberships: ACOG Diploma, American Board of Obstetrics & Gynaecology. Hobbies: Golf. Address: 920 Overlook Road N, Tuscaloosa, Alabama 35406, USA.

CARLSTON John A, b. 9 Nov 1932, New York City, New York, USA. Allergist. m. Jean L Carlston, 21 June 1958, 3 daughters. Education: MD, Yale University, 1958; Board Certified, Allergy and Immunology, 1974, 1977, 1980, 1983, 1987, 1994. Appointments: Instructor in Medicine, University of Illinois, 1962-65; Associate in Medicine, Northwestern University School of Medicine, 1965-69; Associate Professor of Medicine (Allergy), Eastern Virginia Medical School, 1972-. Publications: Hay fever, 1980; Many articles in Annals of Allergy. Memberships: Fellow, American Academy of Allergy and Immunology; Fellow, American College of Allergy and Immunology; Fellow, American Association of Certified Allergists; Fellow, Southeastern Allergy Association; Fellow, International Correspondence Society of Allergists. Hobbies: Go; Bridge; Golf; Tennis; Skiing; Sailing; Travel. Address: 1704 Sir Wm Osler Drive, Virginia Beach, VA 23454, USA.

CARMICHAEL Stephen Webb, b. 17 July 1945, Detroit, Michigan, USA. Professor of Anatomy. m. Susan L Stoddard, 16 May 1992, 1 son. Education: AB with honours, Kenyon College; PhD, Anatomy, Tulane University; DSc. Appointments include: Currently Professor, Chair, Department of Anatomy, Mayo Clinic, Rochester, Minnesota. Publications: 100 articles; 6 books. Address: Department of Anatomy, Mayo Clinic, Rochester, MN 55905, USA.

CARONE Anna Rita, b. 30 July 1948, Italy. University Teacher. m. William Craig, 8 Dec 1984, 2 sons. Education: University Degrees in Psychology; Postgraduate in Psychotherapy. Appointments: Researcher, Teacher, Medicine Faculty & School of Post-degrees in Clinical Psychology, Criminology & Alcolism. Publications: Element Di Biologia Del Comportamento e Di Psicologia, 1994. Memberships: Italian Association of Alcolism; EATA; ITAA; USA Transactional Analysis Association. Hobbies: Reading; Travel; Plants. Address: Clinica Psichiatrica, Facolta Di Medicina, F Chirungia, Univerita, Bari, Italy.

CARONE Patrick Francis, b. 1 Oct 1944, NY, USA. Physician. m. Lucia Machado, 17 Apr 1971, 1 s, 1 d. Education: BSc, cum laude, Georgetown University, Mineola, NY, 1966; MD, Johns Hopkins University School of Medicine, Baltimore, MD, 1970; Rotating Internship, Saint Vincent's Hospital and Medical Center of NY, 1970-71; Master of Public Health, Epidemiology and Public Health, Yale University School of Medicine, New Haven, CT, 1977; Diplomate in Psychiatry, 1977; Certified Mental Health Administrator, 1981. Career includes: Board for Medicine, NY State Education Department, 1984-; Director of Psychiatry, Mercy Hospital, Rockville Center, NY, 1985-; Visiting Associate Clinical Professor, NY College of Osteopathic Medicine, 1987-; Consultant in Psychiatry, Associated Staff, NYSA, ILA Medical Center of NY, 1988-; Neuropsychiatric Consultant, Nassau County Police Department, NY, 1991-; President Elect, Nassau County Medical Society, 1993-; Member and Advisory Board, Board of Professional Medical Conduct, 1993-; Currently, Head of Psychiatry, Mercy Medical Center. Publications include: Over 10, 1968-1990 including: Professionalism - The Forgotten Factor, in The News Bulletin of the Professions, 1990. Honours include: Army Commendation Medal, 1974; Fellow, Federation of State Medical Boards, 1984; Fellow, American Psychiatric Association, 1986; Knight, 1988-92, Knight Commander 1992-, Equestrian Order of Holy Sepulcher of Jerusalem; Knight, American Association of the Sovereign Military Order of Malta, 1993-. Memberships include: American College of Physician Executives; APA; AMA; Alliance for the Mentally Ill. Address: 2000 North Village Avenue, Suite 305, Rockville Centre, NY 11570, USA.

CARPENTER Charles C J, b. 1 May 1931, Savannah, GA, USA. Professor of Medicine. m. Sally Fisher, 3 s. Education: BA, Princeton University, 1952; MD, Johns Hopkins University School of Medicine, 1956. Career: Physician in Chief, Baltimore City Hospitals, 1969-73; Professor of Medicine, Johns Hopkins University, 1969-73; Professor and Chairman, Case Western Reserve University, 1973-86; Currently,

Professor of Medicine, Brown University. Publications: Co-editor, Cecil Essentials of Medicine, 1986, 2nd edition, 1990, 3rd edition, 1993. Honours: Member, Institute of Medicine, National Academy of Sciences, 1988-; Medical Alumni Service Award for Distinguished Contributions to Johns Hopkins University SOM, 1991; Joseph E Smadel Award for Outstanding Contributions to Public Health, 1991. Memberships: Secretary, 1975-81, Councillor, 1981-87, President, 1987-88, Association of American Physicians; Board of Directors, 1976-84, Executive Committee, 1978-83, Chairman, 1983-84, American Board of Internal Medicine; Master, American College of Physicians. Hobbies: Cycling; Skiing; Fishing. Address: Brown University, The Miriam Hospital, 164 Summit Avenue, Providence, RI 02906, USA.

CARPENTER Genevieve Castrodale, b. 7 Nov 1931, Dallas, TX, USA. Psychologist. Education: BS, Psychology, PA State University, 1953; Diploma in Abnormal Psychology, 1954, PhD, Psychology, 1959, University of London, England. Appointment: Lecturer, Institute of Psychiatry, University of London; Assistant Programme Director for Psychobiology, National Science Foundation, Washington DC; Senior Psychologist, Royal Free and Memorial Hospitals, London; Scientist Administrator, Research Fellowships in Psychology and Psychiatry, National Institutes of Health, Bethesda, MD; Assistant Professor, Child Development Research Unit, Boston University Medical Centre; Senior Lecturer, Behaviour Development Research Unit, St Marys Medical School, University of London; Consultant Psychologist, Sutton Hospital, Sutton, Surrey; Private Consultancy. Publications: Differential Visual Behaviour to Human and Humanoid Faces in Early Infancy, Co-author, 1970; Differential Response to Mother and Stranger Within the First Month of Life, 1973; Visual Regard of Moving and Stationary Faces in Early Infancy, 1974; Contributor of book chapters. Honours: Phi Beta Kappa; Phi Kappa Phi; Psi Chi; Rotary Business and Professional Women's Scholarship, 1953-54; British Medical Research Council Scholarship, 1958-59; Co-investigator, National Institute of Mental Health Research Grant, Bethesda, MD, 1967-70. Memberships: Associate Fellow, British Psychological Society; American Psychological Association. Hobbies: Piano; Travel; Countryside. Address: 8 Roland Gardens, London SW7 3PH, England.

CARRICK-SMITH Leslie, b. 10 July 1945, Oldham, Lancashire, England. Chartered Forensic Psychologist; Chartered Educational Psychologist. Education: BA, Open University, 1973; Fellow, College of Preceptors, 1977; MEd, Manchester University, 1980; MSc, Sheffield University, 1983; Chartered Psychologist. Appointments: Teacher, later Chief Examiner, 1963-80; Currently Principal, L Carrick-Smith and Associates, Chartered Psychologists (specialising in trauma). Membership: Associate Fellow, British Psychological Society. Hobbies: Church music; Electronics; Canoeing. Address: Highfields House, Sheffield Road, Clowne, Chesterfield S43 4AP, England.

CARROLL Kenneth Kitchener, b. 9 Mar 1923, Carrolls, New Brunswick, Canada. University Professor. m. Margaret Ronson, 26 Aug 1950, 3 sons. Education: BSc, 1943, MSc, 1946, DSc, Honorary, 1993, University of New Brunswick; MA, University of Toronto, 1946; PhD, University of Western Ontario, 1949. Appointments: Assistant Professor of professor, Head, Department of Medical Research, 1954-68; Professor, Department of Biochemistry, 1968-88, Professor Emeritus, 1988-, Director, Centre for Human Nutrition, University of Western Ontario. Publications: Editor of several books including: Lipids and Cancer, 1975; Diet, Nutrition and Health, 1989; Nutrition and Disease Update - Cancer, Heart Diseases, 1994; Author or Co-author of over 250 papers and review articles. Honours: Fellow, American Institute of Nutrition, 1993; Fellow, Chemical Institute of Canada; Fellow, Royal Society of Canada, 1982; Earle Willard Henry Award, Canadian Society for Nutritional Sciences, 1987. Memberships include: American Institute of Nutrition; Canadian Society Nutritional Science; American Oil Chemists' Society. Hobbies: Curling; Sailing. Address: 561 St George Street, London, Ontario N6A 3B9, Canada.

CARRUTHERS S George, b. 18 Sep 1945, Londonderry, Northern Ireland. Professor of Medicine. m. Gillian Devon, 4 Oct 1969, 3 sons, 1 daughter. Education: MB BCh BAo, Queen's University of Belfast, 1969; MD; FRCPC; FRCP; FACP; FCP. Appointments: Assistant to Full Professor of Medicine and Pharmacology, University of Western Ontario, Canada, 1977-88; Professor, Head, Department of Medicine, Dalhousie University. Publications: Handbook of Clinical Pharmacology, Co-author, 1978. Honours: Piafsky Young Investigator, 1982, Distinguished Service Award, 1992, Canadian Society Clinical Pharmacology. Memberships: Vice President, Canadian Association of

Professors of Medicine; American Society of Clinical Pharmacology and Therapeutics; British Pharmacological Society. Hobbies: Reading; Travel. Address: Department of Medicine, 442 Bethune, Victoria General Hospital, 1278 Tower Road, Halifax, Nova Scotia B3H 2Y9, Canada.

CARSON Jeffrey L, b. 11 Oct 1951, Pennsylvania, USA. Professor of Medicine. m. Susan Batoff, 18 May 1977, 1 son, 2 daughters. Education: BA, University of Rhode Island, 1978; MD, Hahnemann Medical College, 1977; Internship, Residencies, Hahnemann Medical College and Hospital, 1977-80; Henry J Kaiser Family Foundation Fellowship in Internal Medicine, Hospital of University of Pennsylvania, 1980-82. Appointments: Assistant Professor, University of Medicine and Dentistry New Jersey-Rutgers Medical School, 1982-87; Adjunct Assistant Professor, 1983-88, Adjunct Associate Professor, 1988-, University of Pennsylvania; Associate Professor, 1987-94, Chief, Division of General Internal Medicine, 1987-, Professor, 1994-, University of Medicine and Dentistry New Jersey-Robert Wood Johnson Medical School; Hospital positions: Cooper Hospital/University Medical Center, 1982-87; Robert Wood Johnson University Hospital, 1987-. Publications include: Over 50 articles; Early Experience with the COMPASS data base, in Pharmocoepidemiology, 1989; Co-author, contributions to: Medical Care of the Surgical Patients; Pharmacoepidemiology: The Science of Post-Marketing Drug Surveillance; Pharmocoepidemiology; Side-Effects of Anti-Inflammatory Durgs 3; Drug Epidemiology and Post-Marketing Drug Surveillance; Perioperative Care, Principles of Geriatric Medicine and Gerontology. Honours: Golden Apple Award, 1985-, 1986; Special Student Teaching Award, 1987. Memberships: Phi Kappa Phi (Rhode Island), 1973; Fellow, American College of Physicians, 1991-. Hobbies: Racquetball; Sailing; Coaching soccer, Little League and softball. Address: 97 Paterson Street, New Brunswick, NJ 08903-0019, USA.

CARTER Daniel John, b. 13 June 1956, Wisconsin, USA. Pathologist. Education: BA, Brown University, 1978; MD, 1984, Pathology Resident, 1984-88, Medical College of Wisconsin; Surgical Pathology Fellow, Memorial Sloan-Kettering Cancer Center, 1988-90; Dermatopathology Fellow, New York University, 1990-91. Appointments: Currently: Chief of Anatomic Pathology, Berkshire Medical Center, Pittsfield, Massachusetts; Associate Clinical Professor of Pathology, University of Massachusetts. Publications include: Lymphadenopathy and enterovesical fistula in Fabry's disease, 1988; Primary adenocarcinoma of ileostomy sites, 1988; Atypical apocrine metaplasia in sclerosing lesions of breast, 1991. Honours: Holteman Fellow in Dermatopathology, New York University, 1990-91. Membership: College of American Pathologists. Address: Pathology Department, Berkshire Medical Center, 725 North Street, Pittsfield, MA 01201, USA.

CARTER-POKRAS Olivia Denise, b. 1 June 1957, Ridgewood, New Jersey, USA. Epidemiologist. m. Robert Pokras, 22 May 1988. Education: BS, Biology; MHS, Biostatistics, PhD, Epidemiology, Johns Hopkins University. Appointments: Peace Corps Volunteer, 1979-81; Mathematical Statistician, National Institutes of Health, 1982; Health Statistician, National Centre for Health Statistics, 1982-91; Public Health Analyst, Office of Minority Health, 1991-. Publications include: gallstone Size and the Risk of Gallbladder cancer, Co-author, 1984; Alanine Aminotransferase (ALT) Levels in Hispanics, 1993; Health Profile of Latinos; Appendix: Using Vital Statistics to Assess Health Status; Numerous presentations. Honours include: OASH Special recognition Award, 1993; Surgeon General's Certificate of Appreciation, 1993; NCHS Directors Award, 1993. Memberships: American Public Health Association; Society for Epidemiologic Research. Hobbies: Violin; Horse riding. Address: 9509 Saginaw Street, Silver Spring, MD 20901, USA.

CARTERETTE Edward Calvin Hayes, b. 10 Jul 1921, NC, USA. Professor of Cognitive Pscychology. m. Noel Louise McSherry, 3 Apr 1981, 1 s. Education: BA, Mathematics, University of Chicago, 1949; BA, cum laude, Psychology, Harvard University, 1952; MA, 1954, PhD, 1957, Experimental and Mathematical Psychology, Indiana University. Appointment: Professor of Cognitive Psychology and Member, Brain Research Institute, University of California, Los Angeles; Research Professor, University of Virginia, Charlottesville. Publications: Editor, Brain Function, volume III: Speech Language and Communication, 1966; Co-author, Informal Speech, 1974; Co-editor, Handbook of Perception, 11 volumes, 1973-78; Co-author, The role of auditory feedback in the vocalization of cats, in Experimental Brain Research, 1987; Co-author, The effects of articulation on the acoustical structure of feline vocalizations, in Journal of the Acoustical Society of America, 1991. Honours include: NSF Postdoctoral Fellow in Physics, Royal Institute of

Technology, Stockholm, Sweden, and Cambridge University, England, 1960-61; Senior Fellow, Institute for Mathematical Studies in the Social Sciences, Stanford University, 1964-65. Memberships: Fellow, Acoustical Society of America; Fellow, American Association for the Advancement of Science; Fellow, American Psychological Society; Fellow, Vice-President, 1989-, Society for Music Perception and Cognition. Hobbies: Flying; Art; Music. Address: 118 Maid Marion Place, Williamsburg, VA 23185, USA.

CASEMENT Patrick John, b. 27 Aug 1935, Woldingham, England. Psychoanalyst. m. Margaret Rose lloyd, 12 Nov 1966, 2 d. Education: MA, Cantab; Diploma in Public and Social Administration, Oxford. Appointments: Probation Officer, 1963-66; Family Social Worker, Family Welfare Association London, 1966-70; Principal Family Social Worker, Family Welfare Association, London, 1970-73; Training and Supervising Analyst, British Psycho-Analytical Society. Publications: On Learning from the Patient, 1985; Further Learning from the Patient, 1990. Memberships: British Psychoanalytical Society. Hobbies: Music; Photography. Address: 122 Mansfield Road, London NW3 2JB, England.

CASSEM Edwin, b. 24 Jan 1935, Omaha, Nebraska, USA. Psychiatrist. Education: AB, 1959; PhL, 1960; MA, 1961; MD, 1966; BD, 1970. Appointments: Director of Residency Training, Psychiatry, Massachusetts General Hospital, 1974-76; Chief, Psychiatric Consultation Service, Massachusetts General Hospital, 1977-90; Acting Chief, Department of Psychiatry, Massachusetts General Hospital, 1988-90; Chief, Department of Psychiatry, Massachusetts General Hospital, 1990-. Publications: Original Report, The Coronary Care Unit: An Appraisal of its Psychological Hazards, 1968; Use of High-Dose Intravenous Haloperidol in the Treatment of Agitated Cardiac Patients, 1985; Depression and Anxiety Secondary to Medical Illness, 1990; Book, Massachusetts General Hospital Handbook of General Hospital Psychiatry, 1991. Honours: Moses Maimonides Award, Greater Boston Medical Society, 1966; Honorary Member of Medical Staff, Youville Hospital Cambridge, Massachusetts, 1988-; Thomas P Hackett Memorial Award, Academy of Psychosomatic Medicine, 1989; Alumnus of the Year, Creighton Preparatory School, Omaha, Nebraska, 1991. Memberships: include, Massachusetts Medical Society; American Medical Society; American Heart Association; Fellow, Royal Society of Health, Massachusetts Psychiatric Society; American Psychosomatic Society; Fellow, American Psychiatric Association; American Society of Law Enforcement Trainers; Society of Biological Psychiatry; New York Academy of Medicine; Fellowship Committee, Massachusetts Psychiatric Society; Academy of Psychosomatic Medicine. Address: Department of Psychiatry, Massachusetts General Hospital, 55 Fruit Street, Bulfinch 351, Boston, MA 02114, USA.

CASSIMATIS N Emmanuel G, b. 17 Oct 1944, Athens, Greece. Physician. m. Patricia Cutler, 26 Dec 1968, 1 son, 1 daughter. Education: BA, University of Chicago, 1967; MD, Harvard Medical School, 1971; Internship in Paediatrics, Yale New Haven Hospital, 1971-72; Residency in Psychiatry, Massachusetts Mental Health Center, 1972-75. Appointments: Director of Psychiatric Education, Chief of Outpatient Psychiatry, Walter Reed Army Medical Center; Chief, Department of Psychiatry, US Army Hospital, Berlin, Germany; Deputy Commander for Clinical Services, Frankfurt Army Regional Medical Center; Psychiatry Consultant to Army Surgeon-General; Chief, Medical Education Division, Office of the Surgeon General, Department of the Army, Washington DC; Associate Dean and Professor of Clinical Psychiatry, School of Medicine, Uniformed Services University of the Health Sciences. Publications: Mental Health Viewed as an Ideal, 1979; The False Self: Existential and Therapeutic Issues, 1984. Honours: Phi Beta Kappa and President, Maroon Key Society, University of Chicago, 1966, 1967; National Scholarship, Harvard Medical School, 1967-71; Order of Military Medical Merit, US Army, 1989; The Legion of Merit, 1991; The Surgeon General's "A" Proficiency Designator. Memberships: Section Council on Federal and Military Medicine, and House of Delegates, American Medical Association; American Psychiatric Association; American Psychoanalytic Association; International Psychoanalytic Association. Hobbies: Travel; Gardening; Swimming; Reading. Address: 9619 Kingston Road, Kensington, MD 20895, USA.

CASSORLA Fernando, b. 28 Aug 1948, Chile. Clinical Director. Education: MD, University of Chile, 1973. Career: Senior Investigator, Developmental Endocrinology Branch, 1986-90, Clinical Director, 1990-, National Institute of Child Health and Human Development. Publications: Over 110 publications and over 70 abstracts including: Telarquia precoz, in Revista Chilena de Pediatria, 1992; Adrenal maturation during childhood and adolescence, in Reproductive Disorders during Adolescence, in press; Co-author, Abolition of the sex specific response of bone to gonadal steroids in androgenized female rats and in testicular feminized male rats, in press. Honours: Director's Award, NIH, 1991; Annual Distinguished Clinical Teacher, NIH, 1991. Memberships include: American Academy of Pediatrics; Endocrine Society; Society for Pediatric Research. Hobbies: Skiing; Travel; Photography. Address: Building 10, Room ION262, National Institutes of Health, Bethesda, MD 20892, USA.

CASTEÑEDA DIAZ Cesar Abel, b. 25 Jan 1954, Cajamarca, Peru. Medico Neurologo. m. Gilda, 17 Nov 1976, 1 s, 1 d. Education: Courses inNeurophysiology; University Professor. Appointments: Medicine Internist; Specialist in Neurology; Investigator in Neurophysiology. Publications: Medical Urgencies, 1991; Several Articles of interest in Neurology. Memberships: Peruvian Neurology Society; Prevention and Treatment of Epilepsy Committee. Hobbies: Sports: Fisicoculturism. Address: Moquegua 3660, San Martin de Porres, Lima, Peru.

CASTLEDINE Christopher John, b. 23 Oct 1954, Skegness, Lincolnshire, England. Dentist. m. Patricia Gerry, 6 Apr 1963, 2 s. Education: BDS; Dental, Holistic and Philosophical Courses. Appointments: Practising Dentist. Membership: British Dental Association. Hobbies: Tennis; Chess; Walking. Address: 20 Grounds Road, Four Oaks, Sutton Coldfield B74 4SE, England.

CASTLEMAN Lawrence Dennis, b. 11 Feb 1942, Michigan, USA. Hair Transplant Surgeon. m. Diana Locks, 24 July 1965, 1 son, 2 daughters. Education: BS, University of Michigan, 1962; MD, 1966, Residency, 1972, Wayne State University; American Board of Ophthalmology, 1974; American Board of Eye Surgeons, 1990; Fellow, Marzola Institute for Hair Restoration. Appointments: Currently: Director, Castleman Ambulatory Surgical Center; Director, LaserGraft Hair Center. Publications: Text for Choyce Lens Implantation, 1978; Posterior Intra-Ocular Lens Implantation, manual 1982; Complications of Pupillary IOL's, 1986; Inventor, 5 US Patents for Lens Implants, 1984, 1986. Honours: Alpha Omega Alpha, 1966; Pioneer Award for introduction of advanced surgical techniques, Cavityon Corporation, 1991. Memberships: International Society of Cosmetic Laser Surgeons; International Society of Hair Restoration Surgery; American Academy of Otolaryngology and Ophthalmology. Hobby: Oil painting. Address: 100 E Big Beaver Road, Troy, MI 48084, USA.

CASTRONOVO Frank Paul, b. 2 Jan 1940, Newark, NJ, USA. Professor. m. Judith Anne Belli, 3 Apr 1977, 1 s, 2 d. Education: BS, Pharmacy, MS, Health Physics, Rutgers University; PhD, Radiological Science and Radiopharmacology, Johns Hopkins University. Appointments: Instructor in Radiology, Harvard Medical School, 1970-76; Radiopharmacologist, Mass General Hospital, 1980-87; Assistant Professor, 1976-86, Associate Perofessor, 1986-, Director, Health Physics and Radiopharmacology, 1989-, Brigham and Womens Hospital. Publications: Contributor of 98 articles, 1961-; US Patent, Labelled Phosphonic Acid Composition for Investigation of In-vivo Deposits of Calcium. Honours: A De Rose Memorial Award, 1959; Parenteral Drug Association National Award, 1969; Fellow, American Society of Hospital Pharmacists, 1994. Memberships: APhA; Health Physics Society; Society of Nuclear Medicine; AAPM; ASHP. Hobbies: Volunteer, Museum of Science; Ethnopharmacy. Address: Department of Health Physics and Radiopharmacology, Brigham and Womens Hospital, Harvard Medical School, 75 Frances Street, Boston, MA 02115, USA.

CATANZARITE Valerian, b. 7 June 1954. Perinatologist. m. Karen Watson, 15 Aug 1982, 1 s, 1 d. Education: BS with Honors, Mathematics & Biology, California Institute of Technology, Pasadena, 1971-74; MD, University of California, San Diego Medical School, 1974-80; PhD, Biophysics, University of California, Berkeley, 1977-80; Board Certified in Obstetrics & Gynaecology & Maternal Fetal Medicine. Appointments: Assistant Professor of Obstetrics & Gynaecology/Director, Obstetrics Special Care Unit, University of New Mexico Medical Center, 1986-87; Assistant Professor of Obstetrics and Gynaecology/Perinatal Consultant, Arkansas Perinatal Outreach Education Program, University of Arkansas for Medical Sciences, 1988-89; Director, The Perinatal Center, San Diego, California, 1989-90; Director of Perinatal Imaging, Sharp Perinatal Center, 1990-. Publications: include, The Biosynthesis and Turnover of NAD in Enucleated Culture Cells, 1974; Computer Consultation in Neurology: Subjective and Objective Evaluations of the Neurologist System, 1982; Management of Pregnancy Subsequent to

Rupture of an Intracranial Arterial Aneurysm, 1984; Determinants of Visualization of Fetal Anatomy at Second Trimester Sonography, 1990. Honours: include, California Institute of Technology Schlor, 1971-74; University of California Regents' Scholar, 1974-80; California State Scholar, 1971-74. Memberships: American Association for Medical Systems and Informatics; American College of OB/GYN, Fellow; California Medical Association; San Diego County Medical Society; Society of Perinatal Obstetricians. Hobbies: Distance Running; Foreign Languages; Weightlifting; Cycling. Address: 8010 Frost #M, San Diego, California 92123, USA.

CAUCHOIX Jean M, b. 19 Jan 1912, Paris France. Orthopaedic Surgeon. m. Huguette Alavoine, 30 Aug 1940, 1 s (dec), 3 d. Education: Honory Professor of Orthopaedic Surgery, Paris VII University; X BICHAT, School of Medicine. Appointments: Retired. Publications: include, Surgical Managment of Thoracic Potts Disease, 1957; Management of Open Leg Fractures, 1957; Leg Length Discrepancy following Hip TB in Children, 1958; Surgical Management of Vertabral Bodies Tumours, 1959; Scoliosis: An Original Method of Connection and Fusion, 1959; Experimental Scoliosis, 1960; Lumbar Spinal Stenosis, 1974; Results of Electro-Magnetic Bone Stimulation on Long Union after Ununited Fractures, 1980-81. Honours: Offices de la Legion d'honneur. Memberships: include, National Association of Medicine, Paris; American Association of Orthopaedic Surgeons; International Study of Lumbar Spine, Sofot. Hobbies: Alfinism; Skiing; Sailing; Gardening. Address: 114 Rue de Bac, 75007 Paris, France.

CAVALLETTO Bartolomeo P, b. 6 Jul 1965, Lipari, Italy. Clinical Nurse Consultant. m. Catherine A R Cavalletto, 19 Aug 1989, 1 s, 1 d. Education: Graduate Diploma, Nursing Management, UTS; RN, Paediatric and General Nursing. Career: Nurse, 1987-90, Clinical Nurse Specialist, Pain Management, 1990-92, Clinical Nurse Conclutant, Pain Management, 1992-, Royal Alexandria Hospital for Children. Memberships: Pain in Children Group, International Association for Study of Pain; Australian Pain Society; Australian Confederation of Paediatric Nurses; Paediatric Nurses Association, NSW. Address: Royal Alexandria Hospital for Children, PO Box 34, Camperdown, NSW 2050, Australia.

CAVENAR Jesse O Jr, b. 6 June 1939, Batesville, Arkansas, USA. Physician. m. Mary Gibson, 30 June 1964, 1 son, 1 daughter. Education: BS, 1959, MD, 1963, University of Arkansas; Psychiatry Residency, University of North Carolina, 1968-71; Psychoanalytic training, University of North Carolina-Duke Psychoanalytic Institute, 1968-75. Appointments: Associate Chief of Staff for Education, Veterans Administration Medical Center, Durham, North Carolina; Captain, Medical Corps, US Naval Reserve; Currently Professor of Psychiatry, Duke University, Durham. Publications: 118 professional publications; Editor, 11 textbooks. Honours: Certified, American Board of Psychiatry; Certified, Board of Professional Standards, American Psychoanalytic Association. Hobbies: Tennis; Birdwatching; Travel. Address: 1509 Cumberland Road, Chapel Hill, NC 27514, USA.

CAVENDER Finis Lynn, b. 13 May 1938, Amarillo, USA. Consultant; Educator. m. Jeanie Woodson, 20 Feb 1959, 3 sons. Education: BS, MS, PhD, Texas Technical University, University of Georgia, Cornell University. Appointments: Manager of Toxicology, Becton Dickinson & Co; Director of Inhalation Studies, Toxigenics; Principal Scientist, Dynamac Corp; Associate Professor of Environmental Sciences. Publications: Environmental Toxicology, 1981. Honours: Speakers Bureau, American Chemical Society, 1980; Fellow, American Academy of Clinical Toxicology, 1987. Memberships: American Acadmy of Clinical Toxicology; Society of Toxicology; American Industrial Hygiene Association; American Thoracic Society; Tox Masters International. Hobbies: Wood Carving; Golf; Running; Skiing; Camping. Address: 103 Quarterpath, Cary, NC 27511-9791, USA.

CAWKWELL Barry William, b. 20 Sept 1935, Grimsby, Lincolnshire, England. Child/Educational Psychologist. m. Sheila Margaret Bayne, 21 Dec 1968, 1 daughter. Education: DipSc, Bristol University, 1960; BSc (Hons), London University, 1972; MSc, University of East London; Chartered Psychologist. Appointments: Experimental work, Atomic Energy Research Establishment, Harwell; Science Master, Rye Grammar School, Rye, Sussex; Tutor, Open University; Currently Senior Educational Psychologist, Norfolk; Currently Consultant Child and Educational Psychologist in East Anglia. Memberships: Associate Fellow, British Psychological Society; Fellow, Royal Society of Health. Hobbies: Music; Travel; Stock Market trading; Collecting pre-18th century silver spoons. Address: 6 Oak Wood, Blofield, Norwich, Norfolk NR13 4JQ, England.

CERRONI Lorenzo, b. 24 Jan 1959, Rome, Italy. Medical Doctor. Education: MD; Specialist in Dermatology. Appointments: Currently Assistant Professor, University of Graz, Austria. Publications: Clinicopathologic and immunologic features of transformation of mycosis fungoides in large cell lymphoma, 1992; Pitfalls in Histopathologic Diagnosis of Malignant Melanoma, 1994; Bcl-2 expression and 14:18 interchromosomal translocation in cutaneous lymphomas and pseudolymphomas, 1994. Memberships: American Academy of Dermatology; International Society for Dermatopathology; American Society for Dermatopathology; European Association for Haematopathology. Hobbies: Tennis; Jogging; Music; Reading. Address: Department of Dermatology, University of Graz, Auenbruggenplatz 8, A-8036 Graz, Austria.

CHADWICK Peter Kenneth, b. 10 July 1946, Manchester, England. Lecturer in Psychology; Writer. m. Rosemary Jill McMahon, 27 Aug 1983. Education: BSc, University College of Wales, 1967; MSc, Imperial College, University of London, 1968; Diploma, Imperial College, 1968; PhD, University of Liverpool, 1971; BSc, University of Bristol, 1975; PhD, University of London, 1989. Appointments: Senior Demonstrator, Experimental Psychology, University of Liverpool, 1975; Lecturer, Psychology, University of Strathclyde, 1976; Lecturer, Psychology, Birkbeck College, University of London, 1982; Lecturer, Psychology, Goldsmith College, University of London, 1984; Tutor, Psychology, The Openm University, London Region, 1989; Lecturer, Psychology, The City Literary Institute, London, 1990; Professor, Community Psychology, Boston University (British Programmes), 1991. Publications: Scientists can have Illusions Too, 1977; Borderline: A Psychological Study of Paranoia and Delusional Thinking, 1992; A First-hand Phenomenological Account of a Schizoaffective Psychotic Crisis, 1993. Honours: Royal Society European Programme Research Fellowship, University of Uppsala, Sweden, 1972-73; Bristol University Postgraduate Scholarship, 1975; British Medical Association Exhibition, 1985. Memberships: Associate Fellow, British Psychological Society; Scientific & Medical Network, Middlesex. Hobbies: Cycling; Walking; Reading; Writing Short Stories; Modern Art. Address: 45 Post Office Close, Lingwood, Norwich, Norfolk NR13 4EW, England.

CHAEFSKY Robert Louis, b. 21 Feb 1940, Philadelphia, PA, USA. Psychiatrist. m. Sandra M Chaefsky, 2 Aug 1964. 2 s. Education: AB, Temple University, 1962; MD, Temple University School of Medicine, 1966; Residency, Temple University Hospital, 1972. Appointments: Indian CHealth Service, US Public Health Service, 1967-69; Clinical Assistant Professor, Department of Psychiatry, Temple University School of Medicine. Honours: Charter Member, American Academy of Psychiatrists in Alcoholism and the Addictions. Membership: American Psychiatric Association. Hobbies: Music; Sport; Travel. Address: 2432 Bristol Road, Bensalem, PA 19020, USA.

CHAI Xiangshu (Siangshu), b. 12 Dec 1932, Jinan, China. Researcher in Physiology. m. Qiang Yi Jun, 30 Nov 1965, 1 son. Education: MD, Shandong Medical University, 1953. Appointments: Lecturer, Assistant Professor, Shandong Medical University, 1953-65; Associate Research Scientist, Senior Research Scientist, Head, Department of Physiology, Shandong Academy of Medical Sciences, Jinan, 1965-94; Senior Visiting Scholar, University of Michigan, USA, 1986-89. Publications: Extracellular calcium, contractile activity and membrane potential in tail arteries from genetically hypertensive rats, 1992; Potassium Channel Antagonists and Vascular Reactivity in SHRSP, 1993; Proteinkinase C activator and contractile responses to lead in rabbit arteries, 1994. Honours: Several Scientific Awards, Cninese Government, 1986, 1990; National Special Allowance of China, 1992. Memberships: Vice-Chairman, East China Physiological Society; American Physiological Society. Hobbies: Table-tennis; Soccer. Address: Department of Physiology, Shandong Academy of Medical Sciences, 89 Jing 10 Road, Jinan, Shandong 250001, China.

CHAKRABARTI Biman Kumar, b. 1 Sept 1931, India. Consultant Obstetrician and Gynaecologist. m. Chandan Chakrabarti, 11 July 1962, 1 son. Education: MBBS, DGO, Calcutta University; MRCOG (London); FRCOG; FACS (USA); Postdoctoral Fellow, Johns Hopkins Institute, Baltimore, USA; FIMA, Academy of Medical Specialities, New Delhi. Appointments: Lecturer, Assistant Professor, Associate Professor, Professor, Medical College, Calcutta; Practising Consultant Gynaecologist and Obstetrician; Senior Visiting, Thakurpukur Cancer

Hospital, Calcutta. Publications: Editor, Manual of MTP, 2nd Edition, 1993; Over 30 articles in all-India journals; Contributor in Maternal physiology and pathology, Volume IV, Proceedings of XIIIth World Congress of Gynaecology and Obstetrics, Singapore. Honours: Delivered 1st Dr Jajneswar Chakrabarty Memorial Oration, Calcutta, 1994; C S Dawn Presidential Award, 1994. Memberships: Ex-President, Bengal Obstetrics and Gynaecology Society; Federation of Obstetrics and Gynaecology Society of India; FIGO; American Fertility Society; Asia Oceania Society. Hobbies: Sports; Literature; Travel; Social service (Rotarian). Address: 6 Sunny Park, Apartment 17/4, Calcutta, India.

CHALMERS Thomas Clark, b. 8 dec 1917, New York City, USA. Physician. m. Frances Talcott, 31 Aug 1942, 2 sons, 2 daughters. Education: MD. Appointments: Chief of Medical services, Shattuck Hospital, Boston, 1955-68; Associate Chief Medical Director for Research and Education, United States Veterans Administration; Director of Clinical Centre, Associate Director, Clinical Care, National Institutes of Health; President, Mt Sinai Medical Centre; Dean, Mt Sinai School of Medicine, New York; Chairman, Meta Works Incorporated; Adjunct Professor of Medicine, Tufts and Dartmouth Medical Schools; Adjunct Lecturer, Harvard School of Public Health; Lecturer, Department of Epidemiology and Biostatistics, Boston University School of Medicine. Publications: Over 300 articles in professional journals. Memberships: American Society for Clinical Investigation; Association of American Physicians; American Federation for Clinical Research; American Gastroenterological Association, Past President; Association for the Study of Liver Diseases, Past President; Society for Clinical trials, Past President. Address: 32 Pinewood Village, West Lebanon, NH 03784, USA.

CHAMBERLAIN David B, b. 27 Feb 1928, West Haven, Connecticut, USA. Psychologist. m. Jane Mayo, Sept 1950, 2 sons. Education: AB, Randolph-Macon College, 1949; MDiv, Boston University School of Theology, 1953; PhD, Boston University Graduate School, 1958; Licensed Psychologist, California, 1970-. Appointments: Director of Counselling, United Methodist Church, Ohio Area, 1963-69; Clinical Director, Anxiety Treatment Center, San Diego, California, 1970-80; Psychologist in private practice, 1970-. Publications: Babies Remember Birth, book, 1988; 30 published papers including: Consciousness at birth: A review of the empirical evidence, 1983; The mind of the newborn: Increasing evidence of competence, 1986; The cognitive newborn: A scientific update, 1987; The expanding boundaries of memory, 1989, 1990; Is there intelligence before birth?, 1991, 1992; The sentient prenate: What every parent should know, 1994. Honours: Omicron Delta Kappa, for Collegiate Leadership, 1949; Pi Delta Mu, 1949. Memberships: President, Association for Pre- and Perinatal Psychology and Health; American Psychological Association; California Psychological Association; San Diego Psychological Association. Hobbies: Carpentry; Gardening. Address: 909 Hayes Avenue, San Diego, CA 92103, USA.

CHAMBERLAIN Geoffrey Victor Price, b. 23 Apr 1930, Hove, Sussex, England. Physician. m. Jocelyn Kerley, 23 June 1956, 3 sons, 2 daughters. Education: MB, MD, London; FRCS(England); FRCOG; FACOG; FSLCOG. Appointments: Residencies, Royal Postgraduate Medical School, Great Ormond Street, King's College Hospital, 1955-70; Consultant, Queen Charlotte's and Chelsea Hospitals, 1970-83; Chairman, Head of Department of Obstetrics and Gynaecology, St George's Hospital Medical School, London University; President, Royal College of Obstetricians and Gynaecologists. Publications include: Pregnancy Care, 1986; Birthplace, 1987I; Lecture Notes in Gynaecology, Co-author, 1988; Obstetrics, Co-author, 1989; Obstetrics by Ten Teachers, 15th Edition, Co-author, 1989; Gynaecology by Ten Teachers, 15th edition, Co-author, 1989; Modern Fetal Antenatal Care, 1990; How to Avoid Medico-Legal Problems in Obstetrics and Gynaecology, 1991; Preparing for Pregnancy, 1991; Clinical Physiology in Obstetrics, Co-author, 2nd Edition, 1991; Lecture Notes in Obstetrics, Co-author, 6th Edition, 1992; ABC of Antenatal Care, 1992; Pregnancy in the 1990s, Co-author, 1992; Pain and its Relief in Childbirth, Co-author, 1993. Honours: RD, 1975; Thomas Eden Fellowships, RCOG, 1964; Fellow, UCL, 1989; Fellow, Medical Academy of Poland, 1989; Fellow, American College of Obstetricians, 1990. Memberships: RCOG; BMA; RSM; Blair Bell Society; Neonatal Society. Hobbies: Opera; Gardening; Editing British Journal of Obstetrics and Gynaecology. Address: St George's Hospital Medical School, Cranmer Terrace, London SW17 0RE, England.

CHAMBERS Ann F, b. 4 Apr 1948, Evanston, IL, USA. Professor of Oncology. m. Philip Shirley, 1977, 1 son. Education: BA Botany 1973, PnD Zoology 1978, Duke University. Career: Professor & Head, Div of Experimental Oncology, Department of Oncology, University of Western Ontario and Career Scientist, London Regional Centre. Publications: Ras-Responsive Genes and Tumor Metastasis, 1993; Recombinant GST-human Osteopontin Fusion Protein is Functional in RGD-Dependent Cell Adhesion, 1994; Reduced Malignancy of Ras-Transformed NIH 3T3 Cells Expressing Antisense Osteopontin RNA, 1994. Memberships: American Association for Cancer Research; American Association for the Advancement of Science; American Society for Cell Biology; American Society for Microbiology; Canadian Society for Cell Biology; Metastasis Research Society. Address: London Regional Cancer Centre, 790 Commissioners Road East, London, Ontario N6A 4L6, Canada.

CHAMPION Geoffrey David, b. 16 May 1937, Parramatta, NSW, Australia. Physician. m. Caroline Mayhew Thompson, 3 May 1962, 1 s, 2 d. Education: MBBS; FRACP. Career includes: Visiting Physician, Repatriation General Hospital, Concord, NSW, 1972-77; Honorary, Visiting Physician in Rheumatology, St Vincent's Hospital, Sydeney, Chairman, Department of Rheumatology, 1973-85, President, St Vincent's Society, 1992, 1973-; Honorary, Visiting Consultant Physician in Paediatric Rheumatology, Prince Henry and Prince of Wales Hospitals, 1974-. Publications: Over 90 including: Co-author, The faces pain scale for the self-assessment of the severity of pain experienced by children: development, initial validation, and preliminary investigation for ratio scale properties, in Pain, 1990; Co-author, Variable disease and variable response to second line agents, in Second-Line Agents in The Rheumatic Diseases, 1991; Author, Unproven remedies, alternative and complementary medicine, in Rheumatology, 1993, in press. Honours include: Research Award, Southern Californian Rheumatism Society, 1971; Abbott Fellowship, Royal Australasian College of Physicians, 1971; Tweedle Fellowship, Part-Time Research Grant, Royal College of Physicians, 1975. Memberships include: Australian Medical Association; Various offices, Royal Australasian College of Physicians; Associate Member, 1967, Chairman, NSW Branch, 1978-79, NSW representative on Council, 1976-79, Therapeutics Sub-Committee, 1977-87, Australian Rheumatism Association; Various offices, Arthritis Foundation of Australia; International Association for Study of Pain; Scientific Program Commit6tee, World Pain Congress, 1993-. Hobbies: Music; Books; Tennis; Golf. Address: St Vincent's Clinic, 438 Victoria Street, Darlinghurst, NSW 2010, Australia.

CHAMUEL Fred, b. 30 Apr 1930, Cairo, Egypt. Physician. m. Marlene, 1 Oct 1980, 2 d. Education: MD. Appointments: Private Obstetrician & Gynaecologist. Honours: Former Associate Professor in University of Miami Medical School. Memberships: American College of Obstetricians & Gynaecologists; American College of Surgeons. Hobbies: Tennis; Photography; Classical Music. Address: 8960 SW 87 Court, Miami, Florida 33176, USA.

CHAN Anthony Kam Chuen, b. 4 Aug 1961, Hong Kong. Paediatrician. m. Cindy Y Y Ng, 25 May 1991, 1 s, 1 d. Education: MB BS; FRCP(C). Appointments: Paediatric Haematology/Oncology Fellow. Memberships: Canadian Paediatric Society; American Academy of Paediatrics. Address: 77 Elm Street Apt 509, Toronton, Ontario M5G 1H4, Canada.

CHAN Chok Leung, b. 24 Feb 1954, Hong Kong. Medical Physicist. Education: BSc; MPhil; Chartered Engineer; MIEE. Appointments: Physicist; Senior Physicist; Department Manager, Department Radiotherapy and Oncology, Queen Elizabeth Hospital, Kowloon. Publications: Contributor of scientific papers in professional journals. Memberships: Chairman, Hong Kong Association of Medical Physics; Ex-Officio Member, Radiological Protection Advisory group, Hong Kong Government; Irradiating Apparatus Working Party; Government Steering Group on Radioactive Waste Management; Hong Kong Anti-Cancer Society; Hong Kong Society of Nuclear Medicine; Hong Kong Society of Radiation Therapy and Oncology. Hobbies: Go Chess; Table Tennis; Bridge; Basketball. Address: Department of Radiotherapy and Oncology, Queen Elizabeth Hospital, Kowloon, Hong Kong.

CHAN James, b. 27 Dec 1937, Hong Kong. Physician. m. Winnie M Y Chan, 15 June 1968, 1 daughter. Education: MD. Appointments: Assistant Professor, University of South Carolina, USA; Associate Professor, George Washington University; Chief of Nephrology, Children's Hospital, National Medical Center; Vice-Chairman,

Paediatrics, currently Professor, Chairman, Division of Paediatric Nephrologyu, Medical College of Virginia; Visiting Scientist, National Institutes of Health. Publications: Kidney Electrolyte Disorders, 1990; Phosphate in Pediatric Health and Disease, 1993; 281 articles in various journals. Honours: Best Teacher's Award, Medical College of Virginia, 1978-79; Chairman, Advisory Committee, International Symposium, Hong Kong, 1986; Alpha Omega Alpha Faculty Award, 1987. Memberships: National Institutes of Health Consultant and Reviewer; Extramural Reviewer, Veterans Administration; Executive Committee, American Academy of Pediatrics; Medical Direction, NKF of Virginia; Growth Advisory Board, Genentech Inc; Editorial Board: Kidney International: Acta Paediatrica Sinica; Journal of Optimum Nutrition; Nephron (Section Editor). Address: Medical College of Virginia, Box 980498, MCV Station, Richmond, VA 23298, USA.

CHAN Kin-Wei Arnold, b. 23 Nov 1960, Hong Kong. Physician; Epidemiologist. m. Hui-Ru Rachel Chang, 7 Feb 1988, 1 son, 1 daughter. Education: MD, National Taiwan University; ScD, Harvard University, USA. Appointments: Assistant Director, Epidemiology and Statistics, Pharmaceutical Division, Ciba-Geigy Corporation; Associate Professor, Institute of Epidemiology, National Taiwan University College of Public Health. Publications: Patterns of Interchange in the Dispensing of Non-Steroidal Anti-Inflammatory Drugs, Co-author, 1992; An Equilibrium Model of Drug Utilization, Co-author, 1993; Incidence of Rheumatoid Arthritis in Central Massachusetts, Co-author, 1993; The Lag Time Between Onset of Symptoms and Diagnosis of Rheumatoid Arthritis Patients and its Determinants, Co-author, 1994. Memberships: Jogging; Swimming. Address: 1 Jen-Ai Road, Section 1, Room 1551, Taipei, Taiwan, China.

CHAN Kiong Kong, b. 22 June 1945, Singapore. Gynaecological Surgeon and Oncologist. m. Patricia Anne Phillips, 17 July 1971, 2 sons, 1 daughter. Education: MB BS, London; FRCS; FRCOG. Appointments include: Former Senior Lecturer, University of Birmingham, England; Currently Consultant Gynaecological Surgeon and Gynaecological Oncologist. Publications: Management of Ovarian Cancer; Numerous articles and chapters on gynaecological oncology. Memberships: International Gynaecological Cancer Society; British Gynaecological Cancer Society; British Society for Colposcopy and Cervical Pathology. Hobbies: Skiing; Golf; Chess; Bridge; Music. Address: 81 Harborne Road, Birmingham B15 3HG, England.

CHAN Yee-Shing Alvin, b. 26 Jan 1954, Hong Kong. Medical Doctor. m. Karen Lo, 21 Mar 1981, 1 son, 1 daughter. Education: MBBS (HK); MRCP (UK); DCH (Glasgow); FHKAM (Paediatrics). Career: Private Practitioner in Pediatric Neurology; Honorary Consultant in Paediatrics, Hong Kong Baptist Hospital. Publications: Report of a Chinese Boy with Mitochondrial Cytopathy, Journal of Paediatrics, 1985; Co-author: Drugs in Paediatric Neurology, Analgesics And Sedatives, in Paediatric Manual, 1986; Sparganosis of the Brain, Journal of Neurosurgery, 1987; The Hong Kong Myasthenia Gravis Data Bank, Journal of the Hong Kong Medical Association, 1989. Honour: Honorary Secretary, Hong Kong Neurological Society, 1992-94. Memberships: Hong Kong Neurological Society; Hong Kong Paediatric Society; The Hong Kong Society of Child Neurology and Developmental Paediatrics. Hobbies: Swimming; Singing; Writing Songs; Ball Games. Address: Suite 1816, Argyle Centre, Phase I, 688 Nathan Road, Kowloon, Hong Kong.

CHAN Yim Hung, b. 24 Jan 1959, Hong Kong. Physician. Education: BA, Cornell University, 1981; MD, Albany Medical College, 1986; Diplomate, American Board of Psychiatry & Neurology, 1993. Appointments: Clinical Instructor, University of California, San Francisco, 1990-92; Clinical Assistant Professor of Psychiatry, University of California, San Francisco, 1992-. Publications: Chapters published in American Psychiatric Press, 1996. Honours: Family Service Agency Board Director Certificate of Recognition as Vice President, 1995. Memberships: American Psychiatric Association; Northern California Psychiatric Society; Association of Clinical Faculty; California Psychiatric Society. Hobbies: Cycling; Running; Painting; Travel. Address: 3527 Sacramento Street, Suite 104, San Francisco, CA 94118, USA.

CHANDORA Deen B, b. 23 Mar 1943, Jodhpur, Raj, India. Medicine. m. Savitri Swami, 8 Feb 1966, 2 s, 1 d. Education: MBBS, 1964; MD, 1967; Diplomate, American Board of Psychiatry, 1978; Certificate, Addiction Medicine. Career: Tutor in Medicine, S P Medical College, Bikaner, Raj, India, 1968-74; Assistant Clinical Professor, Psychiatry, Medical College of GA, 1978-84; Assistant Professor of Psychiatry,

Emory School of Medicine, Atlanta, GA, 1984-87; Medical Director, Clayton Center, 1987-; Currently, Internist, Psychiatrist, Addiction Medicine Specialist. Publications include: Mobile Opium Deaddiction Camps of Manaklao, India, 15th International Institute on Prevention and Treatment of Drug Dependence, Amsterdam, The Netherlands, 1986; Socially Sanctioned Euthanasia, in Clinical Psychiatry News, 1993; Co-author, Assessment of Splanchic Blood Flow in Alcohol and Drug Abuse Using Radionuclide Angiography, in Journal of Substance Abuse, 1993. Honours: Performance Awards, 1980, 1981, Suggestion Award, 1981, VA Medical Center, Augusta, GA. Memberships: American Society of Clinical Psychopharmacologists; Fellow, American College of International Physicians. Hobbies: Photography; Gardening. Address: 112 Broad Street, Jonesboro, GA 30236, USA.

CHANDRAN Krishnan Bala, b. 16 May 1944, Madurai, India. Professor. m. Vanaja, 22 June 1972, 2 daughters. Education: DSc; MS; BTech; BSc. Appointments: Hindustan Motors Limited, Calcutta, 1966-67; Research Associate, 1972-74, Assistant Professor, 1974-78, Associate Professor, 1978, Tulane University School of Medicine, New Orleans, USA; Research Engineer, Bendix Corporation, Instruments and Life Support Division, Davenport, Iowa, 1980; Associate professor, Division of Materials Engineering, 1978-84, Professor, Department of Biomedical Engineering, 1984-, University of Iowa. Honours include: Merit Scholarship, Indian Institute of Technology; NATO fellowship, Houston, Texas, 1975; Old Gold Fellowship, University of Iowa, 1979; Borelli Award, American Soceity of Biomechanics, 1988; Fellow, American Society of Mechanical Engineers, 1989; Senior member, Biomedical Engineering Society, 1992; Fellow, American Institute of Medical and Biological Engineers, 1995. Memberships include: American Academy of Mechanics; Charter Member, American Society of Biomechanics; American Society of Engineering Education; American Heart Association; American Society of Civil Engineers; Cardiovascular Systems Dynamics Society. Hobbies: Reading; Tennis; Racquetball. Address: Department of Biomedical Engineering, 1202 Engineering Building, University of Iowa, Iowa City, IA 52242, USA.

CHANDRAN Ravi, b. 25 May 1958, Kuala Lumpur, Malaysia. Obstetrician and Gynaecologist. m. Shashi Kalia, 2 July 1984, 2 sons. Education: MB, BS (Malaya), 1982; MRCOG (UK), 1988; MOG (Malaya), 1989; AM (Malaya), 1993; FICS (USA), 1994. Appointments: Registrar, Obstetrics and Gynaecology, North Staffordshire Maternity, England; Lecturer, Obstetrics and Gynaecology, National University of Malaysia; Clinical Research Fellow, Nuffield Department of Obstetrics and Gynaecology, University of Oxford, England; Currently: Associate Professor, National University of Malaysia; Consultant Obstetrician and Gynaecologist. Publications include: Co-author: Perforating invasive mole masquerading as an ovarian tumour, 1991; Effect of a fetal surveillance unit on admission of antenatal patients to hospital, 1991; Fetal and umbilical artery blood flow velocity waveforms in intrauterine growth retardation, 1992; Diagnosis of the placental antecedents of preeclampsia, 1992; Study of the utero-placental and fetal blood circulation using Doppler: techniques and applications, 1992; Fetal cerebral Doppler in the recognition of fetal compromise, 1993; CLASP: a randomised trial of low-dose aspirin for the prevention and treatment of pre-eclampsia among 9364 pregnant women, 1994; Middle cerebral artery flow velocity waveforms: Part 1-The Fetus, 1995. Honours: Young Investigator Award, Obstetrics and Gynaecology Society of Malaysia, 1993. Memberships include: Malaysian Medical Association; Obstetrics and Gynaecology Society of Malaysia; Academy of Medicine, Malaysia; American Institute of Ultrasound in Medicine. Hobbies: Reading; Squash. Address: 6 Jalan Sri Hartamas 13, 50480 Kuala Lumpur, Malaysia.

CHANEN William, b. 6 May 1927, Australia. Gynaecological Surgeon. m. Ann Mordech, 8 June 1960, 2 sons, 1 daughter. Education: MBBS, 1951; Diploma, Obstetrics and Gynaecology, University of Melbourne, 1956; MRCOG, 1956; FRCS(Edinburgh), 1957; FRACS, 1964; FRCOG, 1971; FRACOG, 1979. Appointments include: Honorary Consulting Surgeon, Royal Women's Hospital, 1988-; Member of Editorial Board, The Cervix and Lower Female Genital Tract, 1991-; Immediate Past President, Australian Society for Colposcopy and Cervical Pathology, 1993-; Assistant Secretary, Executive Board, International Federation for Cervical Pathology and Colposcopy, 1993-; President, 9th World Congress, International Federation for Cervical Pathology and Colposcopy, 1993-. Publications include: A Clinical and Pathological Study of Adenocarcinoma of the Uterine Body, 1960; An Endocervical Speculum, 1979; The Positive Papanicolaou Smear: Indications for Treatment, 1984; Symposium on Cervical Neoplasia:

Electrocoagulation Diathermy, 1984-85; The Efficacy of Electrocoagulation Diathermy Performed under Local Anaesthetic for the Eradication of Precancerous Lesions of the Cervix, 1989; The CIN Saga. The Biologic and Clinical Significance of Cervical Intraepithelial Neoplasia, 1990; Contributor of papers and chapters in books; Lecturer in field. Memberships include: Australian Society for Colposcopy and Cervical Pathology; International Society of Cervical Pathology and Colposcopy; Australian Society of Gynaecologic Oncologists; Clinical Oncology Society of Australia; Australian Medical Association; Honorary Member, canadian Society of Colposcopists. Address: cardigan House Medical Suites, Suite 2, 96 Grattan Street. Carlton, Melbourne 3142, Australia.

CHANG Luke Sien-Shih, b. 26 June 1942, Hunan, China. University Teacher; Surgeon. m. Pai-Ho Chen, 10 June 1973, 2 sons, 1 daughter. Education: MD, National Defense Medical Centre, Taipei, Taiwan, 1967; Fellow, Columbia University, New York City, 1978-79, Appointments include: Lecturer, Associate Professor of Surgery and Urology, National Yang-Ming Medical College, Taipei, Taiwan; Attending Surgeon, Chief, Division of Urology, Department of Surgery, Chief, Emergency Unit, Veterans General Hospital, Taipei; Currently: Dean, School of Medicine, Professor, Chairman, Department of Surgery, National Yang-Ming University and Veterans General Hospital, Taipei. Publications: About 128 in field of urology in journals including Journal of Urology, Journal of Urology ROC, Chinese Medical Journal, Clinical Medicine, Journal of the Surgical Association ROC, European Urology, Journal of Formosan Medical Association, British Journal of Urology. Honours: Outstanding Talents Prize in Science and Technology, Republic of China, 1987. Memberships: Surgical Association, ROC; Chinese Medical Association; President, Urological Association, ROC; Endocrine Society, ROC; Biomedical Engineering Society, ROC; Chinese Society of Clinical Oncology; American Urological Association Inc; International College of Surgeons; International Society for Laser Surgery and Medicine; Asian Surgical Association. Hobbies: Music; Golf. Address: Dean's Office, School of Medicine, National Yang-Ming University. 155 Li-Nong Street, Section 2, Taipei, Taiwan 11221, China.

CHANG Nianjia, b. 4 Dec 1924, Yanzhou, Jiangsu Province, China. Teacher. m. 31 Oct 1949, 1 daughter. Education: Graduated, Jiangxi Medical College, 1949; Completed: Anatomical Teaching Class, Union Medical College, Beijing, 1950; Neuroanatomical Teaching Class, Huanan Medical College, 1955. Appointments: Surgeon, Nanchang People's Hospital, Jiangxi, 1949; Instructor of Anatomy, Jiangxi Medical College, 1956; Associate Professor, Vice-Principal, Yichun Branch College, 1982; Professor of Anatomy, Head, Anatomical Department, Yichun Medical College, 1987-. Publications: Observation and Measurement of Chinese Sacrals, 1956; Variations of Cystic Artery, 1958; Observation on the Branches of Coeliac Artery, 1958; Observation of Branches of Superior and Inferior Mesenteric Arteries, 1963; Co-author: Vascular Anatomy of Abdominal and Pelvic Region, 1987; Analysis of Correlative Factors of Mandibular Bone, 1987. Honours: Teaching Model, Jiangxi Province, 1985; Teaching Results Prize, 2nd degree, High Schools of Jiangxi Province, 1988; Labour Model, Chinese Educative System, 1989; Scientific Progress Prize, 3rd degree, Chinese Education Commission, 1990; Special Prize, Chinese Government. Memberships: Chinese Association of Anatomy; Vice-President, Jiangxi Anatomical Association. Hobby: Beijing theatre. Address: Yichun Medical College of Jiangxi Province, Yichun, Jiangxi 336000, China.

CHANG Shu Shi, b. 22 Feb 1952, Taiwan, China. Dean, Chang's Neuropsychiatric Clinic; Associate Professor, Chinese Medical Technologic College; Lecturer, Chinese Medical College. m. Chien Hui Yu, 29 Mar 1991. Education: MD, Chinese Medical College. Appointments: Resident, Neurologic Department, Changhua Christian Hospital; Director, Neurologic Department, Suin-Ten Hospital. Publications: The Molluscan Neuropeptide FMR Famide Stimulates the Release of R14CJ Acetylocholine from isolated ideal Synapotosomal Preparations of Guinea Pig, 1989. Memberships: Clinical Associate Member, American Academy of Neurology. Hobbies: Golf. Address: 199 Chung-Sen Road, Taichung, Taiwan, China.

CHANG Thomas Ming Swi, b. 8 Apr 1933, Swatow, China. Medical Scientist. m. Lancy Yan, 21 June 1958, 2 sons, 2 daughters. Education: BSc (honours Physiology), MD, CM (Medicine), PhD (Research on Artificial Cells), McGill University, Canada; FRCP (C) (Medicine), Royal College of Physicians of Canada. Appointments: Fellow, 1962-65, Scholar, 1965-68, Career Investigator, 1968-, Medical Research Council of Canada; Assistant Professor, 1966-69, Associate Professor, 1969-72;

Full Professor of Physiology, 1972-, Full Professor of Medicine, 1975-, and Full Professor of Biomedical Engineering, 1990-, McGill University, Montreal; Director, Artificial Cells and Organs Research Centre, McGill University. Publications: 21 books or symposium volumes, including: Artificial Cells, 1972; Biomedical Applications of Immobilized Enzymes and Proteins, 1977; Microencapsulation, 1984; Blood Substitutes, 1992; 391 full papers. Honours: First Incentive Lectures, 1969; Clemson Award, 1980; 125th Anniversary of Canada Confederation Medal Award, 1993; Officer, Order of Canada, 1993; Honorary Professor, Nankai; Inventor of Artificial Cells. Memberships: Honorary President, International Society for Artificial Cells, Blood Substitutes and Immobilization Biotechnology; President, International Society for Artificial Organs; Editor-in-chief, Journal of Artificial Cells, Blood Substitutes and Immobilization Biotechnology. Hobbies: Classical music; Tennis; Microcomputer; Weight training. Address: Artificial Cells and Organs Research Centre, Faculty of Medicine, McGill University, Montreal, PQ, Canada H3G 1Y6.

CHANG Tou Choong, b. 17 Nov 1962, Malaysia. Obstetrician and Gynawecologist. m. Jacqueline Loh, 8 Oct 1988, 1 son. Education: MBBS, 1985, MD, 1994, University of London, England; FRCGS(Glasgow), 1990; MRCOG(London), 1990. Appointments: Specialist Obstetrician and Gynaecologist, Kandang Kerbau Hospital, Singapore. Publications: Serial Ultyrasound Assessment of Fetal Weight in the Diagnosis of Fetal Growth Retardation, Co-author, 1993; Doppler Ultrasound and Fetal Growth, 1944. Memberships: Affiliate Member, Society of Perinatal Obstetricians, USA. Hobby: Golf. Address: Department of Obstetrics and Gynaecology, Kandang Kerbau Hospital, 1 Hampshire Road, 0821 Singapore.

CHANG Ying-Shan, b. 29 Aug 1925, Huang Sian, Shantong, China. Physician. m. Zhou Wen Yan, 22 Mar 1952, 2 s. Education: BS, Yenching University; MD, Peking Union Medical College. Appointments: Professor of Biochemistry; Head, Division of Biochemistry. Publications: Proteoglycans Synthesized by Smooth Muscle Cells Derived From Monkey (Macaca Nemestrina) Aorta, Co-author, 1983; Human Aortic Proteoglycans, Part 2, Proteoglycans From Normal Tissue and Atherosclerotic Lesions, Co-author, 1988; Proteoglycans of Human Aorta, III; Self-reaggregation and Reaggregation With Exogenous Hyaluronic Acid, Co-author, 1990; Human Aortic Proteoglycans of Subjects From Districts of High and Low Prevalence of Atherosclerosis in China, Co-author, 1991; Contributor of 30 other professional works. Honours: Recipient of 2 Prizes of 3rd Awards for Research Work. Memberships: Chinese Biochemical Society; Atherosclerotic Professional Committee, Chinese Pathophysiological Society, 1987-. Hobbies: Gardening. Address: Biochemical Division, Cardiovascular Institute and Fu Wai Hospital, CAMS and PUMC, 167 Beilishi Road, West District, Beijing 100037, China.

CHAO Zhen Nan, b. 24 Oct 1924, Jing De Zhen, China. Professor of Hepatobiliary Surgery. m. Yu Li Qing, 27 Jan 1944, 2 s, 1 d. Education: MD, Zhong Shan University College of Medicine, China, 1949. Appointment: Professor of General Surgery, Xijing Hospital, Fourth Military Medical University, China. Publications: First author of articles in Chinese Medical Journal: Biliary Ascariasis: Endoscopic Worms Removal under Radiological Versus Ultrasonic Control, 1986, Diagnosis and Management of Intrahepatic Retained Stones Through a Subcutaneoulsy Placed Afferent Loop of Roux-En-Y Choledochojejunestomy, 1987, Choledochoscopy in Management of Retained Biliary Stones and Recurrent Lesions, 1990; Chief Editor, Abdominal Endoscopic Surgery, 1990; Chief Editor, Emergency Medicine, 1995; Journal Editor: Hepatobiliary Surgery, Journal of Hepatobiliary, Pancreatic and Splenic Surgery, Journal of Endoscopic Surgery, China. Membership: Chinese Medical Association. Address: Xijing Hospital, 4th Military Medical University, Xian 710032, China.

CHAPIN Steven Lynn, b. 11 Apr 1957, Evanston, IL, USA. Clinical Psychologist. m. Mary Kaler, 13 July 1991, 1 d. Education: MA, Psychology; ScB, University of Texas at Dallas; MS, Human Development, 1988; PhD Clinical Psychology; Brown University, Providence, Rhode Island. Appointments: Staff Psychologist, Adolescent Chemical Dependency Unit, Brookside Hospital, Nashua, New Hampshire, 1988-89; Psychologist, North Middlesex Regional High School, Townsend, Massachusetts, 1989-90; Staff Psychologist, Herbert Lipton Community Medical Health Centre, Ayer and Clinton, Massachusetts, 1989-. Memberships: American Psychological Association; Massachusetts Psychological Association; Soceity for the

exploration of Psychotherapy Integration. Hobbies: Hiking; Canoeing. Address: Lipton centre, 180 Groton Road, Ayer, MA 01432, USA.

CHAPMAN Antony John, b. 21 Apr 1947, Canterbury, England. Psychologist. m. Siriol David, 1 June 1994, 2 sons, 2 daughters. Education: BSc, 1968, PhD, 1972, University of Leicester; Fellow, British Psychological Society; Chartered Psychologist. Appointments: Lecturer, 1971-78, Senior Lecturer, 1978-83, Institute of Science and Technology, University of Wales, Cardiff; Currently Dean of Science, Leeds University. Publications: 13 books; 3 book series. Address: Psychology Department, Leeds University, Leeds LS2 9JT, England.

CHAREONTHAITAWEE Pradit, b. 5 Oct 1932, Pathumthani, Thailand. Medical Doctor. 4 daughters. Education: Pre-Medicine, Chulalongkorn University, 1950; MD, Faculty of Medicine, Siriraj Hospital, University of Medical Science, 1954; DA, Royal College of Surgeons, England, and Royal College of Physicians, London, 1960; FFARCS, Anaesthesiology, Royal College of Surgeons, England, 1962; Diploma, Thai Board of Anaesthesiology, Medical Council, 1969. Appointments: Instructor, Department of Surgery, 1957, Instructor, Department of Anaesthesiology, 1960, Chairman, Department of Anaesthesiology, 1980, Assistant Dean for Administration, Chief of Secretariat Office, 1982, Professor, Department of Anaesthesiology, 1986-, Dean, Faculty of Medicine, 1989-, Faculty of Medicine, Siriraj Hospital, Mahidol University; President, Mahidol University. Publications include: Textbook of Anaesthesia. Honours: Order of the Crown of Thailand, 1979; Ratanaporn Medal, 1984; Liberation of Kuwait, 1992; Officier, Ordre National de Merit; Order of the Royal White Elephants; Order of Chulachomkloa; Nepal Order. Memberships include: Board Committee, Heart Foundation of Thailand; Conference of Thai University Faculty Senate; Board Committee, Mahidol University Council; Honorary Fellow, Royal College of Surgeons of Thailand, 1983-. Address: 198/2 Somdej-prapinklao Road, Bangplad District, Bangkok 10700, Thailand.

CHARIEV Mukhametashir, b. 15 Mar 1938, Turkmenistan. Cardiologist. m. Saparova Ene, 4 Aug 1958, 2 sons, 1 daughter. Education: MD, Turkmen Medical Institute. Appointments: Assistant of Therapy, Sub-Faculty, Head, Therapy Sub-Faculty, Tukmen Medical Institute; Vice-Minister of Health; Director of Research Institute Preventive and Clinical Medicine. Publications: Gas Exchange at Arterial Hypertension and Ischemic Heart Disease in Moderate and Hot Climate, 1985; Contributor of over 160 scientific articles in professional journals. Honours: Academician of Turkmen Medical Academy, 1992; Honoured Man of Science of Turkmenistan, 1994. Memberships: Association of Cardiologists of CIS; International Society of Angiologists; Chairman, Society of Physicians in Turkmenistan. Hobbies: Running; Chess. Address: 2 Warsharskij pr 14, Ashgabat 744000, Turkmenistan.

CHARKVIANA Levan Ioseph, b. 24 Jan 1923, Kutaisi, Georgia. Gynaeologist-Oncologist. m. Memnune Ustiachvili, 2 Jan 1949, 1 son, 1 daughter. Education: Graduate, Therapy Department, Tbilisi Medical Institute, 1944; Candidate's Degree, 1952; Doctorate, 1963. Appointments: Director, District Health Department, 1945-47; Head Physician, Batumi Republic Hospital, 1948-54; Head Physician, Maternity Hospital, Batumi, 1954-64; Head, Gynaecology Clinic, Ybilisi Oncological Research Centre, 1964-. Publications: Author of 12 monographs. Honours: State Prize, 1982; Honorary Scientist of Georgia, 1988; Honorary Doctor of Adjaria, 1963; Academician, Academy of Medical Science of Republic of Georgia, 1994. Memberships:Board, European Society of Gynaecologists and Oncologists; Honorary Member, Italian, Belorussian, Kazakh Oncological Societies. Hobbies: Cinematographic Art; Photography; Tourism. Address: Chikovani Street 20 Fl 56, Tbilisi 380015, Georgia.

CHARLESWORTH Maxwell John, b. 30 Dec 1925, Victoria, Australia. Professor of Philosophy. m. Stephanie Armstrong, 18 Feb 1950, 2 s, 5 d. Education: MA, University of Melbourne; PhD, University of Louvain. Career includes: Chairman, Department of Philosophy, University of Melbourne, Australia; Dean, School of Humanities, Deakin University, Australia; Now retired. Publications include: Life Among the Scientists: An Anthropological Study of an Australian Scientific Community, 1989; Life, Death, Genes and Ethics, 1989; Distributing Health Care Resources: Ethical Assumptions, 1992. Honour: Officer of the Order of Australia, 1989. Membership: Australian Bioethics Association. Hobbies: Walking; Sailing. Address: 86 Lang Street, North Carlton, Victoria 3054, Australia.

CHASE Robert Arthur, b. 6 Jan 1923. Professor of Surgery, Stanford. m. Ann Parker, 3 Feb 1946, 1 s, 2 d. Education: BS; MD; MSc, Honours. Appointments: Emile Holman Professor of Surgery, Stanford; President and Director, National Board of Medical Examiners; Professor of Surgery and Anatomy, Stanford. Publications: Atlas of Hand Surgery, 1984; Bassett Atlas of Human Anatomy, 1989; A Stereoscopic Atlas of Human Anatomy: The Bassett and Gruber Legacy, 1994; Contributor of numerous professional articles, book chapters and papers. Honours: Recipient of numerous awards and honours including: First Emile Holman Professor of Surgery, Stanford, 1972; Honorary DSc, University of New Hampshire, 1993. Memberships include: President American Society for Surgery of The Hand; President American Association of Clinical Anatomists; President, 1970, California Academy of Medicine; Fellow, America College of Surgeons; National Centre for Health Services Research Consultant; National Research Council; New England Society of Plastic and Reconstructive Surgery; Phi Beta Kappa, University Newhampshire; Sigma Xi, Yale Chapter; Society of Clinical Surgery; Western Surgical Association; Serves on several Editorial Boards. Hobbies: Woodworking; Photography. Address: Anatomy MSOB 327, Stanford, CA 94305, USA.

CHATEAU Peter de, b. 4 Mar 1937, Den Haag, Netherlands. Child Psychiatrist. m. Viveca Lindskog, 1 Sept 1962, 2 sons, 1 daughter. Education: MD, University of Leyden; ECFMG, USA, 1972; PhD, University of Umeå, Sweden, 1976. Appointments: Assistant Professor, Paediatrics, University of Umeå; Assistant Professor, Child Psychiatry, Karolinska Institute, Stockholm; Currently Professor, Chairman, Department of Child Psychiatry, University of Nijmegen, Netherlands. Publications: 85 in professional journals on paediatrics and child psychiatry, especially early development, parent-infant attachment, infant psychopathology. Honours: Ronald MacKeith Memorial Lecture, Oxford, 1982; Queen Elizabeth II Lecture, Royal College of Physicians, Canada, 1991. Memberships include: Vice-President, World Association for Infant Mental Health; Swedish Medical Association; Dutch Medical Association; Dutch Royal College of Psychiatry. Hobbies: Classical music; Reading; Fungi; Outdoor life. Address: Verloren Land 67, 6596 CL Milsbeek, Netherlands.

CHATTERJEE Tapan Kumar, b. 14 Jan 1937, Calcutta, India. Obstetrician and Gynaecologist. m. Jayashi Chatterjee, 3 Mar 1972, 3 daughters. Education: MBBS; DGO, 1961; MRCOG (UK), 1965; MD, Sheffield University, 1970; FRCS (Edinburgh), 1970; FRCOG (UK), 1979. Appointments: Associate Professor, Head of Gynaecology, Zambia University; Director of WHO Clinical Research Center, Zambia; Associate Professor, Obstetrics and Gynaecology, King Faisal University, Saudi Arabia; Consultant, Rubi General Hospital, Calcutta, India. Publications include: A randomized double blind study of six combined oral contraceptives, 1982; IUD Insertion following termination of pregnancy: A clinical trial of the Cu T, 220C, Lippes Loop D and Copper 7, 1983; Multinational comparative clinical trial of long acting injectable contraceptives: norethisterone enanthate and depot-medroxyprogesterone acetate. Final report, 1983; Socioeconomic and demographic characteristics of induced abortion cases, 1985; Group B streptococci colonization among Saudi women in labour and neonatal acquisitation, 1985; Phaechromocytoma in pregnancy, 1985; Co-author: Vaginal administration of 15(S)15 methyl F2 alpha methyl ester for induction of abortion, 1970; Gonococcal infection in women with PID in Zambia, 1980; IUD insertion following abortion, 1983. Memberships include: Life Member, Indian Medical Association; Bengal Obstetrics and Gynaecology Society. Hobby: Photography. Address: 24 Deshbandhu Road (East), Calcutta 700035, India.

CHAU Sun-Sung, b. 13 Mar 1934, Auckland, New Zealand. Obstetrician and Gynaecologist. m. Soong Chin, 9 Dec 1961. Education: MB ChB, University of New Zealand; Diploma of Obstetrics, Auckland; MRCOG; FRCOG; FRNZCOG. Appointments: Formerly Obstetrician and Gynaecologist, St Helen's and Waitakere Hospitals, Auckland; Co-Founder, Director, currently Chairman, Obstetrician and Gynaecologist, Artemis Medical and Surgical Centre, women's health centre, Takapuna, Auckland; Director, Artemis North Shore Fertility Associates in high birth technology; Director, Urodynamic Services; Director, Artemis Day Hospital; Currently: Senior Gynaecologist and Colposcopist, National Women's Greenland Hospital, Auckland; Senior Obstetrician, North Shore Obstetrics Hospital. Memberships: Founder, Secretary, Past President, North Shore Obstetrics and Gynaecology Society; Past President, New Zealand Obstetrics and Gynaecology Society; Past President, New Zealand Medical Association, North Shore Division; Past Councillor, Glenfield County Town. Hobbies include:

Fencing (Auckland University and Otago Blues, Auckland Province Junior Champion); Swimming; Tramping; Fishing; Skiing; Classical music (violin); International travel. Address: Artemis Medical and Surgical Centre, 2 Pupuke Road, Takapuna, Auckland, New Zealand.

CHAUDHURI Paresnath, b. 28 Sept 1947, West Bengal, India. Obstetrician and Gynaecologist. m. Mridula Chaudhuri, 16 Jan 1971, 1 son, 1 daughter. Education: MBBS, University of Calcutta; DObst, 1974, MRCOG, 1975, FRCOG, 1990, Royal College of Obstetricians and Gynaecologists, London. Appointments: Associate Professor, Obstetrics and Gynaecology, Erasmus University, Rotterdam, Netherlands, 1978-80; Obstetrician and Gynaecologist, Ministry of Health, Singapore, 1981-86; Professor in Obstetrics and Gynaecology, M S Ramaiah Medical College, Bangalore, India, 1989-93; Consultant Obstetrician and Gynaecologist, Bangalore. Publications: Brain Tumour and Pregnancy, 1980; Acute Third Degree Inversion of Uterus, 1985; Chlamydia Trachomatis Infection in Unmarried Women Seeking Abortions, 1986; 25 other articles. Honours: Gold Medal in Obstetrics and Gynaecology, N R S Medical College, Calcutta, 1969; Benjamin Henry Shears Memorial Lecture Award, Obstetrical and Gynaecological Society of Singapore, 1984. Memberships: Bombay Society of Obstetrics and Gynaecology; Bangalore Society of Obstetrics and Gynaecology. Hobbies: Countryside driving; Bird watching; Reading; Writing; Singing. Address: The Women's Clinic, 606 Barton Centre, 84 M G Road, Bangalore 560 078, India.

CHAVKIN Wendy, b. 17 Feb 1952, New York City, USA. Physician. m. Nicholas Frevdenberg, 1 s. Education: Master of Public Health; MD. Appointments: Director, Bureau of Maternity Services & Family Planning, New York City Department of Health, New York, 1984-88; Editor in Chief, Journal of the American Medical Women's Association; Senior Research Associate, Chemical Dependency Institute, Beth Israel Medical Center; Associate Professor, School of Public Health, Columbia University. Publications: include, Double Exposure: Women's Health Hazards on the Job and at Home, 1985; Motherhood in Question: The Complicated Issue of Pregnancy and AIDS Prevention, 1987; Women, Alcohol and Other Drugs, 1995; Abortion and Public Health, 1995; Reproductive Hazards: Not For Women Only, 1993; Neural Tube Defects: A Comparison of Data Sources, 1983. Honours: Research Fellow, Rockefeller Foundation, 1988-89; Public Service Science Fellow, National Science Foundation, 1980. Memberships: American Medical Women's Association; American Public Health Association. Address: Columbia University, School of Public Health, 60 Haven Avenue, B-3, New York 10032, USA.

CHEEK David Bradley, b. 22 May 1912, Singapore. Physician. m. June Prince, 6 May 1942, 1 s, 1 d. Education: BA, Cum Laude, Harvard, 1934; MD, University of California, San Francisco, 1942; Fellow, American College of Surgeons; Fellow, American College of Obstetricians & Gynaecologists. Appointments: Instructor, Department Gynaecology, Johns Hopkins Hospital, 1942-44; University of California, Medical School, San Francisco, 1956-57; Contract Instructor, California School of Professional Psychology: San Francisco Campus, 1971-73; Berkeley Campus, 1975-76; Fresno Campus, 1985-86; Now Retired. Publications include: Pathologic Findings in Genital Bleeding Two or More Years after Spontaneous Cessation of Menstruation, 1946; Hypnosis: An Additional Tool in Human Reorientation to Stress, 1958; Possible Uses of Hypnosis in Dermatology, 1961; The Anesthetized Patient Can Hear and Remember, 1962; Surgical Memory and Reaction to Careless Conversation, 1964; Significance of Dreams in Initiating Premature Labor, 1969; Short Term Hypnotherapy for Frigidity Using Exploration of Early Life Attitudes, 1976. Honours: President, American Society of Clinical Hypnosis, 1965-66; Citation of Excellence, American Society of Clinical Hypnosis, 1970; Lifetime Contributions Citation by California School of Professional Psychology, 1985. Memberships: include, American Medical Association; San Francisco County Medical Association; International Society for Investigative and Forensic Hypnosis; American Society for Clinical Hypnosis. Address: 1140 Bel Air Drive, Santa Barbara, CA 93105, USA.

CHEN Bao-wen, b. 15 Jan 1937, Guandong, China. Physician. m. Shi Ting-Sen, 51 Feb 1965, 1 son, 1 daughter. Education: Bachelor Degree, Beijing Medical School. Appointments: Resident Physician, Physician 1960-68, Assistant, Lecturer 1969-84, Associate Professor 1985-90, Professor 1991-, Division of Gastroenterology, First Teaching Hospital, Beijing Medical University. Publications: Sucralfate increase gastric mucosal blood flow in rats, 1989; The modulation action of Molatonin on serotonin induced aggravation of ethanol ulceration and changes of gastric mucoasl blood flow in rat stomach, 1989; The Role of Gastric Mucosal Blood Flow in Cytoprotection Digestion, 1991; Nicotine induced gastric injury. A quantitive macroscopic and microscopic analysis of protective effects of sucralfate and feeding, 1991. Memberships: Chinese Gut Hormone Association; Traditional Medicine-Western Medicine Association of Beijing Medical University. Hobbies: Beijing and Guangdong Opera; Music. Address: Beijing Medical University, First Teaching Hospital, No 8 Xi Shen Ku Street, Beijing 100034, China.

CHEN Chang, b. 21 Jan 1933, Jiangsu Province, China. Pharmacuetical Researcher. m. Zheng Xian-Yu, 1 Jan 1959, 2 sons. Educationl Graduate, Department Pharmacuetical Chemistry, East China College of Pharmacy. Appointments: Vice Chief, Malaria Research Department, 1972-75, Institute Parasitic Diseases, Vice Chief, Department Pharmaceutical Chemistry, 1976-83, IPD; CAMS; Chief, DPC IPD, Chinese Academy Preventive Medicine, 1984-. Publications: Insecticides for Sanitary Uses, Co-author, 1959; Control and Research of Malaria in China, Co-author, 1991; Contributor of entries in encyclopaedias. Honours: Important Achievement Prize of Science and Technology, Shanghai, 1977; National Scientific Conference Prize, 1978; 3rd Award, Chinese Invention, 1985. Memberships: Advisory Committee, Experts in Malaria, Ministry of Public Health of China. Hobbies: Reading; Watching Television. Address: 207 Rui Jin Er Lu, Shanghai 200025, China.

CHEN Changzhao, b. 8 Aug 1948, Shandong Province, China. Teacher. m. Meixian Liu, 1 Dec 1977, 1 d. Education: BA, Shandong Medical University, 1973. Appointments: Professor of Pathology; Dean of Department of Pathology. Publications: A Textbook of Pathology, Chief Editor, 1992; Ovarian Tumors in Children and Adolescents, 1986; Ovarian Neoplasm in Children and Adolescents in Yimeng District. 1987; Intestinal Malignant Lymphoma, 1987. Honours: Leading Qualified Scientist of the Medical Department of Shandong Province, 1992. Memberships: Chinese Medical Association; China Anti-Cancer Association. Hobbies: Fishing; Running. Address: Department of Pathology, Linyi Medical School, 24 Qingnian Road, Linyi, Shandong 276002, China.

CHEN Chao, b. 5 July 1963, Wunzhou City, Zhejiang, China. Doctor. Education: BS, Medicine, 1985, MD, Acupuncture, Clinical Medicine, 1988, OMD Certification, 1989, Zhejiang College of Traditional Chinese Medicine (TCM); Certified Acupuncture Physician, China, USA; Qi Gong Master. Appointments: Practitioner, Lecturer, Oriental Medicine; Acupuncturist, Teachers Committee Chair, Academic Dean, Acupuncture Department, Professor, Oriental Medicine, Zhejiang College of TCM; Professor, International Centre for Study of Oriental Culture, Qianjiang Medical College; Director, Institute of Acupuncture and Oriental Medicine, Florida, USA. Publications: Research on Natural Therapy, 1989; Practical Chinese-English Acupuncture Manual, 1990; Videos: Chinese Acupuncture Science, 1990; Guide to International Exam of Acupuncture (chief lecturer), 1991; Articles include: Research on Model-HY Laser Acupuncture Instrument, 1987; Research on Human Laser, 1989; Clinical Observation and Experimental Research on Laser Acupuncture for Treatment of Chronic Prostatitis, 1990; Chinese Qigong: a skill to recharge your energy, 1993. Honours: Famous Contemporary Doctor of TCM; Excellent Teacher of Provincial Universities; Excellent Teacher of the College; Nominee, National Excellent Teacher. Memberships: Vice President, Zhejiang Clinical Acupuncture Research Association; All China Association of Acupuncture; All China Association of Qi Gong Science; All China Association of TCM; All China Association of Integrated Traditional and Western Medicine; All China Association of Future Research; American Asssociation of Acupuncture and Oriental Medicine; International Medical and Beauty Association; American Society for Psychical Research. Hobbies: Qigong exercise; Meditation; Reading; Singing. Address: Zhejiang Traditional Chinese Medical College, Qinchung Road, Hangzhou 310009, China.

CHEN Char-Nie, b. 19 July 1938, Hai-Chen, Fujian, China. Professor of Psychiatry. m. Chou-May Chien, 1 son, 2 daughters. Education: MB, National Taiwan University, Taipei, 1964; CPM, 1972; MRCPsych, 1973; MSc, 1974; MRANZCP, 1981; FRANZCP, 1983; FRCPsych, 1985; Specialist Psychiatrist, 1992. Appointments: Intern, 1964-65, Resident, 1965-68, National Taiwan University Hospital; Senior House Officer, Morgannwg Hospital, Bridgend, South Wales, Registrar, Lecturer, Senior Lecturer, St George's Hospital Medical School, London, 1969-80; Professor, Founding Chairman, Department of Psychiatry, Chinese University of Hong Kong, 1981-94; Founding Head, Shaw College,

Chinese University of Hong Kong. Publications: Over 70 in learned journals including: Plasma tryptophan and sleep, 1974; Carbohydrate-rich diet and nocturanl growth hormone secretion, 1977; Sleep, depression and antidepressants, 1979; The use of clomipramine as a REM sleep suppressant in narcolepsy, 1980; The effect of maprotiline on rapid eye-movement (REM) sleep, 1981; The gradual metamorphosis of psychiatry, 1982; Behavioural sciences: Plural or singular?, 1984; Psychiatry in transition, 1985; Two stage screening in community survey: Report of a pilot study, 1989; Evidence for and against the notion that a shortened REM latency is a biological marker for depressive illness, 1991; Sleeping and dreaming, 1992; Shatin Community Mental Health Survey in Hong Kong: II. Major findings, 1993; The epidemiology of poor sleep, 1994. Memberships: British and Hong Kong Medical Associations; European and Asian Sleep Research Societies; Hong Kong Society of Sleep Medicine; Royal and Hong Kong Colleges of Psychiatrists; Society of Psychiatry, Taiwan; Collegium Internationale Neuro-Psycho-Pharmacologicum; International Brain Research Organization. Address: c/o Department of Psychiatry, Faculty of Medicine, Chinese University of Hong Kong, Shatin, NT, Hong Kong.

CHEN Chien-Jen, b. 6 June 1951, Kaohsiung, Taiwan. Epidemiologist. m. Fong-Ping Lo, 14 Aug 1977, 2 daughters. Education: MPH, National Taiwan University, 1977; ScD, Johns Hopkins University, USA, 1982; Fellow, American College of Epidemiology. Appointments: Professor, Director, Institute of Epidemiology, National Taiwan University, Taipei; Research Fellow, Academia Sinica, 1988-; Adjunct Professor, Tulane University School of Public Health, USA, 1994-; Senior Associate, Johns Hopkins University School of Hygiene and Public Health, 1994-. Publications: 160 refereed journal articles, 23 full conference papers, 8 books or book chapters. Honours: Outstanding Research Awards, National Science Council, Republic of China, 1986-96; Fogarty International Research Fellowship Award, US National Institutes of Health, 1989-90. Memberships include: American Association for Cancer Research; International Society for Environmental Epidemiology; National Public Health Association, Republic of China. Hobbies: Jogging; Mountain hiking. Address: Institute of Epidemiology, College of Public Health, National Taiwan University, 1 Jen-Ai Road Section 1, Taipei 10018, Taiwan, China.

CHEN Chui-Ju, b. 21 Nov 1941, Ningpo, China. Professor of Vascular Surgery. m. Li Hong Chang, 24 Apr 1969, 2 sons, 1 daughter. Education: MB, Zhejiang Medical Universioty, 1965. Appointments: Resident Doctor, 1965-80; Doctor-in-Charge, 1980-89, Professor of Vascular Surgery, 1989-, Kunming General Hospital, Chengdu Military Command. Publications: Ringing of Femoral Veins for Primary Valvular Incompetency of Deep Veins of Lower Extremity, 1988; Full-Valve Annuloplasty in treatment of Primary Deep Venous Valvular Incompetence of the Lower Extremities, 1992; The New Way of Digestive Tract Reconstructed with Full Gastrectomy, 1992; Management of Variceal Ulcer in Lower Extremities, 1993; Prevention and Treatment of Iatrogenic Vascular Injuries, 1994. Honours: 3rd Class Prize of Military Science and Technology Progress for Full-Valve Annuloplasty in treatment of Primary Deep Venous Valvular Incompetence of the Lower Extremities, 1989; 2nd Class Prize of Military Science and Technology Progress for Study on Primary Deep Venous Valvular Incompetence of the Lower Extremities, 1992; Merit Citation, Class 3, 1992. Membership: Committee Member, Chinese Vascular Surgery Institute. Hobbies: Climbing; Cooking. Address: Kunming General Hospital, Chengdu Military Command, Kunming 650032, China.

CHEN Ci-Ling, b. 21 July 1924, Fujian, China. Physician. m. M D Jian, 20 June 1951, 3 daughters. Education: MD, Urology; Postgraduate Course, PUMC, Beijing. Appointments: Head, Urological Department, 1979; Vice Chairman, Chinese Medical Association, Jiangsu Branch, 1983; Professor of Surgery, Chief Surgeon of Urology, Suzhou Medical College. Publications: Bio-Medico-Physical Research, Chief Editor; Practical Surgery. Honour: National Scientific and Technological Award, 1993. Hobby: Photography. Address: 96# Shi Zi Street, First Affiliated Hospital, Suzhou Medical College. Suzhou 215006, China.

CHEN Dagong, b. 4 Oct 1933, Tian-Tai, Zhejiang, China. Professor of Colo-proctology. m. Bixuan Mei, 14 Feb 1961, 1 son, 1 daughter. Education: Undergraduate, Zhejiang Medical University of China, 1960. Appointments: Chief Doctor of Colo-proctology Department of People's Hospital of Zhejiang Province China. Publications: Atlas of Surgical Operation, 1974; Illustration of Minor Operations, Co-author 1986; Atlas of Operation for Colo-proctological Diseases, Co-author, 1988; Measurement of Pressure in Anal Canal and Rectum in Colo-proctology,

1988; A New Surgical Procedure in Familial Polyposis of Colon in Colo-proctology, 1991. Honours: 2nd Scientific and Technological prize of Zhejiang, 1989, 1993; National Special Allowance Award, 1993. Memberships: Council of Chinese Colo-proctology Association; Head, Chinese Monographic Group on Anal Fissure. Hobby: Fishing. Address: 1-2-(Room) 101 Dormitory of Zhejiang People's Hospital, Hangzhou, Zhejiang 310014, China.

CHEN Dazhong, b. 6 June 1909, Wuxi, China. Professor of Acupuncture (retired). m. Zhou Wen-Zui, 29 Sept 1932, 1 daughter. Education: Certificate of Traditional Chinese Medicine, Public Health Ministry; Director Doctor. Appointments: Physician, Traditional Chinese Medicine and Acupuncture, Wuxi, 1936-43; Deputy Head, Traditional Chinese Medicine Department, Guangxi Hospital. Publication: A Handbook of Clinical Treatment by Acupuncture and Moxibustion, 1961. Honours: Invited to be Honorary Chairman, Italian Acupuncture Association, 1961. Membership: All-China Acupuncture Association. Address: Room 201, No 9 Building, No 1 Jian De Road, Shanghai 200025, China.

CHEN Dechang, b. 16 Jan 1932, Shanghai, China. Surgeon. m. Prof Jia-Qi Pan, 1 Feb 1964, 2 daughters. Education: Aurdra University (French Catholic University), 1947-52; MD, Second Shanghai Medical College, 1953. Career: Senior Surgeon, Burn Unit, Second Shanghai Medical College, 1959-64; Department of Surgery, Peking Union Medical College Hospital, 1964-84; Chairman, Department of Critical Care Medicine, Peking Union Medical College Hospital, 1984-. Publications: Sepsis, Cytokines & Multiple Organ Failure, 1991; Multiple Organ Failure: Challenge & Strategy, 1993; Nosocomial Infection, 1993; Chief-Editor, Textbook of Critical Care Medicine, in press. Honours: Ministry of Health Prize, China, 1959. Memberships: American Society for Microbiology; World Federation of Societies of Critical Care Medicine (Delegate of China); American Association for the Advancement of Science. Hobbies: Photo; Tourism. Address: Department of Critical Care Medicine, Peking Union Medical College Hospital, Beijing 100730, China.

CHEN Doreen Guo-Fong, b. 4 Oct 1932, Hongkong, China. Acupuncturist. m. Dr Shi-Yuan Yang, 5 Aug 1962, 2 sons, 1 daughter. Education: MD, Peking Union Medical College; Licensed Acupuncturist, New York State, USA. Appointments: Attending Physician, Institute of Paediatrics, CAMS, China; Research Associate, Acupuncture Centre of New York, USA; Research Assistant, UAB, Cardiovascular Research Centre; Visiting Scholar, New York Hospital Department of Paediatrics; President, Doreen Chen Acupuncture Centre. Publications: Contributor of articles in professional journals; Research papers presented at international conferences. Honours: National Research Award, Ministry of Health, China; Acupuncturist of Year, American Association of AScupuncture and Oriental Medicine, 1994. Memberships: Secretary, New York State Licensed Acupuncturist Association;; Research Committee, AAAOM; Chinese Medical Society; Chinese Paediatric Society. Hobbies: Music; Sport. Address: 392 Central Park West, Apt 18N, New York, NY 10025, USA.

CHEN Feng, b. 29 Mar 1942, Liuzhou, Guangxi, China. Chief Physician; Professor of Traditional Chinese Medicine. m. Deng Xiuzhen, 1 son, 1 daughter. Education: BA, Guangxi College of Traditional Chinese Medicine, 1965. Appointments: Chief Physician, Hospital of Traditional Chinese Medicine. Publications: Diagnosis and Treatment of Miscellaneous Traditional Chinese Medical Diseases, Co-author, 1994; Treatment of Heart Disease by Removing Blood Stasis, 1993; Treatment of Heart Disease with Promoting Blood Circulation by Removing Blood Stasis-investigation and Analysis of Pharmacy, 1994; Treatment of Coronary Heart Disease with Di Ao Xin Xue Kang and Treatment Experience of 53 Cases, 1994; Treatment of Yeng Edema with Decoction of Ephedra, Forsythia Fruit and Red Bean - 44 Cases, 1982. Memberships: Academic Board of Traditional Chinese Medicine of China. Hobbies: Medicine; Chinese Handwriting. Address: The Municipal Hospital of Traditional Chinese Medicine, 32 Jiefangbeilu, Liuzhou, Guangxi, China.

CHEN Fusheng, b. 26 July 1935, Fuzhou, China. Professor. m. Suwen Liu, 1 July 1962, 2 d. Education: Graduate, Nanjiang University, 1958. Appointments: Lecturer, 1979; Associate Professor, 1982; Professor, 1985; Teacher of Postgraduate, 1985; National Exemplary Teacher, 1990; Teacher of DSc, 1993. Publications: Fluctuation in Helium Nuclear Reaction-Diffusion Systems in Astrophysics and Space Science, Co-author, 1992; Chaotic Pulsation in Variable, 1993; On

Fluctuation in Reaction-Diffusion Systems Affected by Pressure, 1994. Honours: National Exemplary Teacher, Medal and Bonus, 1990; Special Allowance from Government, 1992. Memberships: Chinese Physical Society; Jiangxi Science and Technology Society. Hobbies: Table Tennis; Bicycling; Music. Address: Department of Physics, Jiangxi University, Nanchang, Jiangxi 330047, China.

CHEN Guanghua, b. 2 Aug 1936, Xian, Shaanxi, China. Physicist. m. 1 July 1962, 1 s, 1 d. Education: BS, Lanzhou University, 1958; MS, Jilin University, 1967. Appointments: Lecturer, 1978; Associate Professor, 1981; Full Professor, 1986-; Professor, Shantou University, 1991-; Shanghai Scientific Technological University, 1992-; Sichuan University, 1990-; Huazhong Normal University, 1994-; Chairman, Physics Department, Head of PhD, 1990-, Head, Institute of Electronics Materials, Lanzhou University. Publications: Amorphous Semiconductor Physics, 1989; Contributor of over 250 scientific articles in professional journals. Honours: Nominator, Japan Prize, Science and Technology Foundation of Japan, 1985-94; Prominent Education Expert, State of China. Memberships: American Physics Society; Chinese Physics Society; Chinese Solar Energy Society; Chinese Electronic Society; Member of Council, Chinese Ceramics Society; Amorphous Material and Physics in China. Hobby: Badminton. Address: Department of Physics, Lanzhou University, Lanzhou 730000, China.

CHEN Guo Rui, b. 18 Oct 1931, Fujian, China. Doctor. m. Zhou Minghui, 31 Mar 1957, 1 s, 1 d. Education: BA, Shandong Medical University, 1955. Appointment: Professor of Orthopaedics. Publications: Experimental and Clinical Study of Homologous Alcohol, in Chinese Medical Literature, 1981; Transplantation of preserved Homologous Half-Joint, report of 56 cases, 1981. Honour: Country Scientific Prizes, 1978, 1984. Membership: Chinese Medical Association. Hobby: Sport. Address: Affiliated Hospital, Shandong Medical University, Jinan, Shandong 250012, China.

CHEN Hao-Hui, b. 9 May 1936, Jawa, Indonesia. Surgeon. m. Zhang Ji Ying. Education: MD, Beijing Medical College, China, 1958. Appointments include: Professor, Chief, Department of Critical Care Medicine; Professor, Director, Department of Surgery, District 3, 3rd University Hospital, Beijing Medical University, China; Associate Research Professor of Surgery, State University of New York, Buffalo, USA, 1983; Vice-President, 1985-88, Chief, Department of General Surgery, Director, Surgical Intensive Care Unit, 1989-92, currently Professor, Chief, Department of Critical Care Medicine, Professor, Director, Director of Surgery (District 3), 3rd University Hospital, Beijing Medical University, China; Visiting Professor of Surgery, University of Southampton School of Medicine, England, 1992-93; Member, Editorial Board: Clinics in General Surgery; Resuscitation. Publications: The relation of cholic acid and bilirubin to bile pigment precipitation, 1980; Large dose atropine alkaloids in shock therapy, 1982; 22-year experience with the diagnosis and treatment of intrahepatic calculi, 1984; Integrating ancient and modern medicine in Chinese Hospitals, 1987; Splenic conservation surgery using microwave regulator, 1993. Honours: Awards for research on Gallstones, City of Beijing, 1985, 1989. Memberships: Fellow, China Association of Surgery; Fellow, China Association of Emergency Medicine. Hobbies: Music; Sports; Travel. Address: 3rd University Hospital of Beijing Medical University, 49 North Garden Road, Beijing 100083, China.

CHEN Ji-Zhong, b. 24 Mar 1941, Anhui, China. Ophthalmologist. m. Ru-yong Song, 1 May 1967, 1 son, 1 daughter. Education: Graduated, Department of Medicine, Anhui Medical University, 1963. Appointments: Physician-in-charge and Lecturer, Vice-Director and Associate Professor, Director and Professor, Anhui Medical University, Hefei. Publications: Co-author, books: Atlas of Ocular Diseases, 1985; The pediatric diagnostics of physical examination, 1994; Encyclopedia of science and technology summary, 1994; Articles: Cataract operation after the retinal detachment re-attachment surgery; More than 20 other academic theses. Membership: Chinese Ophthalmology Institute, Anhui Branch. Hobbies: Art, especially drawing for atlas of ocular diseases; Chinese literature. Address: The Department of Ophthalmology, The Affiliated Hospital of Anhui Medical University, Hefei, Anhui, China.

CHEN Jia-Wei, b. 25 Dec 1930, Shanghai, China. Physician. m. Yu-Chen Bi, 16 Feb 1958, 1 daughter. Education: Graduate Diploma, Shanghai Second Medical College, 1957; Postgraduate Diploma. Appointments: Resident Doctor, 1957-62; Visiting Doctor, Assistant, 1962-78; Consultant Physician, 1978-; Associate Professor, 1978-86; Professor, 1986-. Publications: Lipoatrophic Diabetes, 1964; Pancreatic

Cholera, 1977; 17α-hydroxylase Deficiency, 1980; Cyclic Cushing's Disease, 1987. Memberships: Standing Committee, Endocrine Society, Chinese Medical Association; Standing Committee, Diabetes Society, Chinese Medical Association; IDF. Address: 300 Guangzhou Road, Nanjing 210029, China.

CHEN Jia-Yi, b. 27 Jun 1922, Pingding County, Shangsi Provinces, China. Doctor. m. 4 May 1951, 1 s, 2 d. Education: Graduated, Beijing Medical University, Beijing, 1944-50. Appointments: First Teaching Hospital, Beijing Medical University, 1950-53; People's Hospital of Lahsa, Tibet, 1953-62; Professor, Department of Ophthalmology, First Teaching Hospital, Beijing Medical University, Beijing, 1962-. Publications: Editor, Modern Handbook of Ophthalmology, 1993; Hemangioma of Optic Disc, 1993; Retinopathy of Acute Panereatitis, 1993. Honours: Advanced Worker, People's Hospital of Lahsa, Tibet, 1956. Memberships: Chinese Medical Association, 1950-; Editor of Journal of Traditional Chinese Ophthalmology. Hobbies: Reading; Collecting Stamps. Address: No 37, Xi-Shi-Ku Street, West City, Beijing, China.

CHEN Jiande, b. 4 Dec 1956, Zhejiang, China. Biomedical Researcher. m. Xiuxia Du, 6 Feb 1983, 2 sons, 1 daughter. Education: BS; PhD, Applied Science. Appointments: Assistant Professor of Medicine, Director, Electrophysiology Laboratory, Assistant Professor of Electrical Engineering, University of Virginia, USA. Publications: Electrogastrography: Principles and Applications, Editor, 1994; Contributor of 31 peer-reviewed papers in journals and 26 book chapters and conference papaers. Honour: Scholarship, Catholic University of Leuven, 1984-89. Memberships: Senior member, IEEE; American Gastroenterological Association; American Federation of Clinical Research. Hobby: Musical Instruments. Address: Institute for Healthcare Research, Baptist Medical Centre, 3300 NW Expressway, Oklahoma City, OK 73112, USA.

CHEN Jiatang, b. 27 Aug 1936, Shanghai, China. Doctor. m. 24 Sept 1963, 1 son, 1 daughter. Education: University Graduation. Appointments: Docotr; Associate Professor; Professor of Paediatrics. Publications: Books, Paediatrics Lecturer, co-author, 1982; Paediatrical Manual, co-author; Child Cerebral Palsy Treatment Manual, co-author; Articles, The Genetics Discussion on Four Cases of Girl Progressive Muscular Dystrophy, 1992; The Clinic Summary of Epilepsy in the Cerebral Palsy Child, 1994; Result Analysis of Child Cerebral Palsy and Parents, 1994; Discussion on Etiology of Twins Child Cerebral Palsy, 1993. Honours: Award, China Association of Acupuncture, 1992; Excellent Paper Award, China Association of Rehabilitation; Award, Advance of Science & Technology, Provincial Government, 1993. Memberships: Asian & Oceanian Child Neurology Association; China Association of Rehabilitation; Zhejiang Association of Rehabilitation. Hobbies: Reading; Walking. Address: Childrens Hospital of Zhejiang Medical University, Hangzhou, China.

CHEN Jihuei, b. 10 February 1935, Fuzhou, Fijian, China. Professor. Appointments: Lecturer, 1982; Associate Professor, 1985. Publications: The medicinal study on ant, 1983; The wholesome function and trace element of leaves in artifical sexual propagation of camellia chrysantha (HU) Tuyama (golden camellia), 1994; Determination of trace germanium in herbal medicine by graphits furnace atomic absorption spectrometry, 1991. Honours: 3rd Prize, Guangxi Provincial Scientific and Technical Advancement, 1992. Memberships: The Medical Society of China. Hobbies: Singing. Address: The Traditional Medical College of Guangxi, 135 Box, Nanning, Guangxi 530001, China.

CHEN Jinchang, b. 19 Dec 1936, Shanghai, China. Professor of Physics. m. Yijun Yan, 12 June 1977, 1 daughter. Education: MS, 1961; Chinese Academy of Sciences. Appointments: Assistant Professor, Institute of Modern Physics, Chinese Academy of Sciences; Associate Professor, Central Iron and Steel Research Institute; Professor, Beijing Teachers College, Capital Normal University. Publications: Co-author: Amorphous Physics, 1988; Amorphous Alloys, 1989; Mean-field analysis of a ferrimagnetic mixed spin system, 1991; Electronic Structure of Atom Cluster Fe4B', 1992. Honours: Beijing Science and Technology Progress, 3rd Award, 1987, 1989, 2nd Award, 1993; 2nd Award of Natural Sciences, Chinese Academy of Sciences, 1994. Memberships: Physics Association of China; Metal Association of China. Hobbies: Basketball; Swimming. Address: Department of Physics, Capital Normal University, Beijing 100037, China.

CHEN Jiuru, b. 11 Dec 1932, Shanghai, China. Doctor. m. Tongmin Zhu, 1 Oct 1959, 1 s, 1 d. Education: BA, Shanghai Medical University, China, 1959. Appointments: Chief Doctor, Department of Radiology, Zha-Bei Central Hospital, 1987-; Professor and Tutor of Master Degree, Department of Radiology, Medical College of Shanghai Railway University, 1990-; Professor, Department of Radiology, SuZhou Medical College, China, 1995-; Assistant Chief Editor, Chinese Journal of Computed Medical Imaging, 1995-. Publications: Co-Chief Editor, The Principle and Diagnosis of Gastrointestinal Radiography, 1995; Author, Tuberous Sclerosis, in Chinese J Radiol, 1984; Clinical Investigation of Scapulohumeral Periarithritis with Aethrography, in Chinese J Radiol, 1986; The X-Ray Diagnosis of Gastric Varices, in J Clin Radiol, 1987; Double Contrast Barium Meal of Esophagogastric Junction, in J Clin Radiol, 1988; The Mass Screen for Gastric Carcinoma with Double Contrast Radiography, in Chinese J Radiol, 1989; Gastroesophageal Reflux, in Chinese J Radiol, 1989; Differential Diagnosis between Benign and Malignant Gastric Ulcer, in Chinese J Radiol, 1989; Multiple Primary Carcinoma (MPC) in Gastric-Intestinal Tract, in Chinese J Radiol, 1990; Clinical Investigation on the Application of 654-2 and Its Adverse Reactions during Double-Contrast Gastrointestinal Studies, in Chinese J Radiol, 1992; Clinical and Radiological Diagnosis of Gastric Early Carcinoma (Type I), in J Clin Radiol, 1994. Honours: National Advanced Science Award, Experimental and Application of Gastrointestinal, Double Contrast Roentgenography, 3rd Prize, 1993. Memberships: Chinese Medical Association. Hobbies: Reading; Music; Bridge. Address: Xi-Zang Bei Road, Lane 225-1, No 1603, China.

CHEN Jun-qing, b. 29 Nov 1928, Huhehote, China. Medical Doctor; Professor. m. Huang Hua-Lu, 1 Oct 1956, 4 daughters. Education: MD. Appointments: Doctor, 1st Affiliated Hospital, 1956, Lecturer, 1970, Professor, 1981-, China Medical University, Shenyang; Chairman, Institute of Cancer. Publications: Co-author: Surgical treatment of gastric cancer, 1964; Surgical classification of advanced gastric cancer, 1980; Principle of resection of gastric cancer based on the biologic behavior, 1982; Pathologic characteristics and the rational surgical treatment of the rectal carcinoma, 1985; Serosa typing in gastric cancer and its significance, 1986; Gastric Cancer, book, 1987; Some problems in the surgical treatment of gastric cancer, 1991; The killing effect of hypo-osmolar solutions and hyperthermia on gastric cancer, 1991; Biologic behavior of gastric cancer and its application, 1993; Identification and classification of serosal invasion, as it relates to cancer cell shedding and surgical treatment in gastric cancer, 1994; Current Surgery of Cancer, book, 1994. Honours: 2nd Prize in Science and Technology Achievement, Ministry of Health, China, 1988; 1st Prize in Science and Technology Achievement, Shenyang Municipal Government, 1989. Memberships: Councillor, Chinese Cancer Research Foundation; Editorial Board, NATL Medical Journal, China. Hobbies: Calligraphy; Running. Address: Cancer Institute, China Medical University, 155 Nanjing North Street, Shenyang, Liaoning 110001, China.

CHEN Ke-Yun, b. 21 Apr 1934, Hui An, Fujian, China. Associate Professor; Physician. m. He Chun Chi, 22 June 1974, 1 son. Education: MD, Zhejiang Medical University; Research Fellow, Physician, University of Southern California School of Medicine Medical Center, Los Angeles, USA. Appointments: House Physician, Senior House Physician, 1955-60, Assistant, Probational Research Fellow, Physician, Nuclear Medicine, 1960-77, Lecturer, Doctor in charge of Nuclear Medicine, Associate Director, 1977-82, Experimental and Clinical Associate Professor of Nuclear Medicine, 1982-94, Zhejiang Medical University, Hangzhou. Publications: Experimental research of I-131-CUN-1 labelled lung cancer monclonial Antibody, 1994; Co-author: Preliminary observation of Cs-131 distribution in experimental acute myocardial infarction and coronary insufficiency treated with root of salvia miltiorrhiza, flower of chrysanthemum morifolium and chrysanthemum indicum, 1983; Experimental research of LYM-1 monoclonal antibody, 1988; I-131-LYM-1 MOAb radioimmunotherapy and LYM-1 MOAb immunotherapy in implanted nude mice model, 1988; Experimental study of I-131-LYM-2 monoclonal antibody, 1989; Preliminary observation on the diagnostic significance of quantitation of serum CA50 and carcinoembryonic antigen in 732 patients with colorectal cancer, 1993. Honours: Scientific and Technical Advanced Prize, Zhejiang, 1977, 1979; Excellent Achievement of Science and Technology, Zhejiang, 3rd Class Prize, 1981. Memberships: Nuclear Academy of China, Zhejiang Branch; Nuclear Medical Academy in China, Zhejiang Branch; Chinese Medical Academy, Zhejiang Branch. Hobby: Chinese curios. Address: Apartment

601, Building 49, District 6, Chao-Fei New Village; Tain-Shui Bridge, Hangzhou, Zhejiang 310014, China.

CHEN Linda Li-yueh, b. 22 Mar 1937, Tokyo, Japan. Professor. m. Biris Yuen-jien Chen, 23 Dec 1961, 2 daughters. Education: BS, Pharmacy; PhD, Biochemistry; Board Certified Nutritionist. Appointments: Research Associate, Department of Biochemistry, University of Louisville, Louisville, Kentucky, USA, 1964-66; Assistant Professor, 1967-72, Associate Professor, 1972-79, Professor, 1979-, Chair, 1983-87; Director, Nutritional Sciences Program, 1989-, Univesity of Kentucky, Lexington. Publications: Nutritional Aspects of Aging, Volumes I and II, Editor, 1986; Nutritional Biochemistry - Laboratory Methods Experiments and Exercises, 1972; Contributor of over 100 research articles in professional journals. Honour: Borden Award for Nutrition Research in North America, 1990; Editorial Board, Arch Gerontal Geriatr Memberships: American Institute of Nutrition; American Aging Association; American Society for Clinical Nutrition; Gerontological Society of America. Hobbies: Music; Reading. Address: 204 Funkhouser Building, Department of Nutrition and Food Science, University of Kentucky, Lexington, KY 40506-0054, USA.

CHEN Meng-Chin, b. 1 May 1925, Hunan, China. Professor of Physiology. m. Hui-Zhen Lu, 15 Mar 1953, 2 s, 1 d. Education: MD, National Central University, School of Medicine, 1951. Appointments: Teaching Assistant, 1953-56, Lecturer, 1956-78, Associate professor, 1978-85, Professor, 1985-, Peking Union Medical College and Chinese Academy of Sciences. Publications: The Developmental Strategy of Physiology in China, Chief Editor, 1994; A History of Chinese Physiology, Vice Chief Editor, 1994; Contributor of 140 professional papers in Chinese journals. Honours: Honorary President, Beijing Association for Physiological Sciences, 1992-. Memberships: President, Chinese Association for Physiological Sciences, 1989-. Address: Department of Physiology, Institute of Basic Medical Sciences, Chinese Academy of Medical Sciences, 5 Dong Dan San Tiao, Beijing, China.

CHEN Menglin, b. 5 February 1954, Changde, Hunan, China. Associate Professor of Medicine. m. 1 May 1982, 1 son. Education: Graduated, Hengyang Medical College, 1977; MS, Traditional Chinese Medicine, 1993. Publications: The Comparative Analysis of Traditional Chinese Medicine and X-rasy's characteristic, 1994; The curative effects on treating 54 cases of leukopenia with Yulu-Soup, 1994; Relation between the chest Z-ray chotography of bronchial asthma and difference of syndromes infection, 1994. Memberships: Chinese Association of the Integration of Traditional and Western Medicine. Hobbies: Running. Address: 1st Municipal Hospital of Traditional Chinese Medicine, Changde City, Hunan 415000, China.

CHEN Miao-Lan, b. 14 July 1931, Guang Dong, China. Professor of Pathology. m. Dr Yong-su Zhen, 19 Nov 1955, 2 sons. Education: MD, Sun Yat-sen Medical College, Guangzhou, 1954. Appointments: Vice President, Chinese Academy of Medical Sciences, 1985-93; Associate Dean, Peking Union Medical College, 1985-93; Deputy Head, National Leading Group for Cancer Control, 1985-94; Chairperson, Expert Advisory Committee for the Ministry of Health, 1987-94; Editor-in-Chief, United Press of Peking Union Medical College and Beijing Medical University; Vice Chairperson, National Expert Committee for AIDS Control. Publications: Local Factors on Induction of Cervical Carcinoma, Co-author, 1962; Experimental Esophageal Cancer and Precancerous Changes, CO-author, 1980; Cancer Pain Control in China, 1989; Cancer Control in China, 1994. Memberships: Western Pacific Advisory Committee on Health Research of World Health Organisation; World Health Organisation Expert Advisory Panel on Cancer; Board Member, Chinese Medical Association. Hobby: Music. Address: Chinese Academy of Medical Sciences, 9 Dong Dan San Tiao, Beijing 100730, China.

CHEN Ming Sen, b. 10 May 1937, Wu Han, China. Surgeon. m. Dr Wenrong Liu, 20 May 1967, 1 son, 1 daughter. Education: Postdoctoral Research Work Fellowship, Spleen and Liver Centre of PLA, 1972-75. Career: Surgeon, 30 yrs; Director of General Surgery. Publications: Dictionary of Practical Medicine (co-author), 1989; The Treatment of Air Force Pilots' Spleen Disease, 1988; Disection of Whole Stomache, 1988; Collection of Bill, 1988. Honours: Fellowship of Peking Union Medical College, 1962; The Famous Surgeon Award, 1972; Excellent Director Award in PLA, 1982. Memberships: Membership of Commitee of Chinese Medicine; Membership of Committee of Spleen and Liver Therapy. Hobbies: Golf; Swimming; Fishing. Address: General Surgery,

The General Surgery of General Hospital of PLA Air Force, 30 Xi Diao Yu Tai, Beijing 100036, China.

CHEN Nailing, b. 17 Nov 1937, Tianjin, China. Physician. m. Wang Hua Lin, 1 Jan 1972, 1 son, 2 daughters. Education: Graduate, National Tianjin Medical College, 1957-63; Expert in Gastroendocopic Examination, Endoscopic Papillotectomy, Liver Disease. Appointments: Vice Director, Gastroenterology Department, Beijing General Hospital, 1978-84; Vice-Director, 1984-94, Director, 1994-, Institute of Liver Diseases, PLA. Publications: A Long Term Follow-up Study of the International Metaplasia and Hyperplasia of Mucosa of Chronic Gastritis, 1984; Experience of Practicing SUZUKI's Method of Sclerotherapy, 1986. Memberships: Beijing China Medical Association. Hobbies: Cooking; Travelling; Gardening. Address: Institute of Liver Diseases, No.5 Nan Men Cang Dongsi Beijing, 100700 Beijing, China.

CHEN Ning-Sheng, b. 3 Sep 1933, Nanjing, China. Physician. m. Yang Bing-Xiu, 6 Aug 1961, 2 sons. Education: BA, Guangzhou College of Traditional Chinese Medicine, 1955-61. Appointments: Professor, Director, Internal Medicine department, Director, Department of Infectious Diseases, professor, Director, Liver Disease Laboratory, First Affiliated Hospital of Hunan College of Traditional Chinese Medicine. Publications: The Viewpoint on the Development of TCM, 1981; Study on the Regularity of Differentiation and Treatment in Ascites due to Cirrhosis, 1986; The Treatment of Chronic Hepatitis with TCM, 1989. Honours: 1st award of Traditional Chinese Medicine Science and Technology of Hunan Province, 1993; 3rd Award of World Traditional Medicine, Las Vegas, USA, 1994. Memberships: Committee, Liver Diseases of All-China TCM Association; Committee, Internal Medicine of Hunan TCM Association. Hobbies: Swimming; Table Tennis. Address: The First Affiliated Hospital of Hunan College of Traditional Chinese Medicine, 105 Shaoshan Road, Changsha, China.

CHEN Peng, b. 25 Oct 1935, Xinyu, Jiangxi, China. Cardiothoracic Surgeon. m. Rizhen Huang, 2 Feb 1962, 3 sons. Education: BA, Jiangxi Medical Science College; Visiting Scholar, School of Medicine, University of Pittsburgh, USA, 1991-92. Appointments include: Assistant Professor, Department of Human Anatomy, Jiangxi Medical Science College, 1956-58; Currently Professor, Chairman, Department of Cardiothoracic Surgery, Tutor of Master students, 2nd Affiliated Hospital, Jiangxi Medical College, Nanchang. Publications: Introduction of Congenital Heart Disease, 1962; Surgical Treatment of Carotid Aneurysm, 1978; Prosthetic Heart Valvulitis, 1991. Honours: Science Meeting Award, Jiangxi Medical College, 1978; National Special Allowance, State Council, China, 1992. Memberships: Chairman, Association of Thoracic Cardiovascular Surgery, Jiangxi Province; Standing Committee, Association of Surgery, Jiangxi Province. Hobbies: Chinese calligraphy; Music. Address: Department of Cardiothoracic Surgery, 2nd Affiliated Hospital, Jiangxi Medical College, Nanchang, Jiangxi 330006, China.

CHEN Qi-rong, b. 7 Oct 1930, Pinyang, Zhejiang, China. Senior Engineer. m. Miss Jin, 20 Mar 1960, 1 son, 1 daughter. Education: Graduated, Department of Pharmacy, Beijing Medical University; Master's degree, Academy of Pharmaceutical Industrial Research, Beijing. Appointments: Academy of Pharmaceutical Industrial Research, Beijing; Xinhua Pharmaceutical Works, Sandong; 2nd Traditional Chinese Medicinal Factory, Hangzhou; Currently Professor, Institute of Foodstuffs, Hangzhou. Publications: The chemical constituents of traditional Chinese medicine, the alkaloids on Sinomenium actum, 1962; Studies on the chemical structure of Astralgus membranaceus polysaccharides, 1985; Chemistry of food additives, 1990. Memberships: Chinese Pharmaceutical Society; Food Society, Zhejiang. Hobby: European classical music. Address: East No 104, No 6 Building, Songmu Chang Hedong, Hangzhou, Zhejiang 310007, China.

CHEN Quan Xin, b. 10 Sep 1933, Guangzhou, China. Doctor. m. Hao Ying, 3 May 1962, 1 son, 1 daughter. Education: BM, Guangdong Special School of Traditional Chinese Medicine, 1955. Appointments: Resident Physician, 1955, Attending Physician, 1968, Associate Professor, 1982, Professor, 1991-, Guangdong Hospital of Traditional Chinese Medicine; Visiting Professor, Acupuncture College of Britain, America and Singapore. Publications: New Clinical Acupuncture and Moxibustion, 1983; Principle of Research on Differentiation and Treatment of Bi-syndrome, 1980; Study of Special Acupoint, 1993; The Needle Insertion by Twirling and Rotating-Flying Puncture, 1994. Honour: Famous Doctor of Traditional Chinese Medicine of Guangdong, 1993. Memberships: President, Acupuncture and Moxibusion

Association of Guangdong; Director, Acupuncture and Moxibustion Association of China. Hobbies: Swimming; Music. Address: Acupuncture Department of Guangdong Provincial Hospital of Traditional Chinese Medicine, 111 Dade Road, Guangzhou 510120, China.

CHEN Rei Qi, b. 26 Dec 1937, Tianjin, China. Doctor of Traditional Chinese Medicine. m. Yang Jin-lin, 1 Oct 1978, 2 sons, 1 daughter. Education: MD, Traditional Chinese Medicine. Appointments: Head, Department of Emergency; Professor of Traditional Chinese Medicine, 2nd Hospital att to Tianjin College of Traditional Chinese Medicine, China; Senior Physician, Chinese Medical Centre. Publications: Clinic Application of Five Elements, 1985. Honours: Award of Advanced Research in acute somach pain, National Institute of Traditional Chinese Medicine, Beijing, 1990. Memberships: Secretary General, Chinese National Medical Society for Stomach & Splean Conditions, 1986-90; Chinese National Scientific Research Co-operative Group for Pain, 1994-; Director, Association of Traditional Chinese Medicine, England. Hobbies: Athletics; Dance. Address: 5 Catherine Place, Bath, BA1 2PR, England.

CHEN Rendun, b. 1 Oct 1926, Hangzhou, China. Professor of Medicine; Research Professor of Nutrition. m. Wang Zheng Xian, 1953, 2 daughters. Education: MD, Shanghai Medical College; United Nations Senior Fellow, University of Harvard School of Public Health and Nutrition and Food Sciences Department, Massachusetts Institute of Technology. Appointments include: Associate Research Professor of Nutrition, Academy of Military Medical Sciences; Visiting Scientist, Massachusetts Institute of Technology, USA; Visiting Professor, Medical College of Georgia; Currently Chief, Section of Nutrition, Member of Expert Group, 302 Hospital, Beijing. Publications: The recent advance in nutrition, 1964; Suggestions for Chinese Dietary Guidelines, 1988; Advances in Free Radical Biology and Medicine, 1991. Honours: 2 Awards, State Scientific and Technological Commission, 1966; 3 Awards for Advancement of Science and Technology, People's Liberation Army, 1989, 1991, 1992. Memberships: Society for International Nutrition Research; Federation of American Societies for Experimental Biology; American Institute of Nutrition; American Society of Clinical Nutrition. Hobby: Computer programmes. Address: 302 Hospital, 26 Feng Tai Road, Beijing 100039, China.

CHEN Rouze, b. 19 Aug 1937, Guandong Province, China. University Teacher. m. Shen Youmon, July 1963, 1 son, 1 daughter. Education: Graduate Diploma, Guangxi Medical University. Appointments: Assistant, Pathology Department, 1961-79, Lecturer, Pathology Department, 1979-85, Associate Professor, Pathology Department, 1985-92, Professor of Pathology, Head, Department of Electron Microscopy, 1992-, Guangxi Medical University, Nanning. Publications: Electron Microscopic Observation on the Morphological Change of Fibroblast, 1988; Study on Biopsy Specimens from Endomyocardium - Analyses of 106 Cases, 1990; Ultrastructure Studies of Human Hepatocellular Carcinoma and Surrounding Nontumourous Liver, 1993. Memberships: Pathology Association of China; Electron Microscopy Association of China; Vice-Chairman, Guangxi Electron Microscopy Association. Hobby: Listening to Music. Address: Department of Electron Microscopy, Guangxi Medical University, Nanning, Guangxi 530027, China.

CHEN Rusong, b. 5 Mar 1932, Zhejiang, China. Scientist; Professor of Radiation Medicine and Radiotoxicology. m. Huang Qi, 30 Jan 1960, 2 sons, 1 daughter. Education: Graduated, Shanghai First Medical College, 1956. Appointments: Assistant Research Fellow, Atomic Energy Institute, China Academy of Sciences, 1956-64; Associate Research Fellow, then Research Fellow, Professor of Radiation Medicine and Radiotoxicology, China Institute for Radiation Protection, Taiyuan, Shanxi, 1964-. Publications: Co-author: Revisory suggestion for hygienic standards of natural uranium, 1975; Osteosarcoma-inducing effect of plutonium nitrate in rats, 1985; Clinical medicine for over-exposed workers of China, 1989; Toxicological study of plutonium, 1992; Study on setting of Reference Chinese Man, 1993. Honours: Awards of national or ministerial level for about 10 achievements in scientific research, 1980-93. Memberships: Chinese Association of Radiological Medicine and Protection; Vice-Chairman, Shanxi Branch, Chinese Association of Radiological Medicine and Protection; Shanxi Anticancer Association. Hobby: Travel. Address: Xuefu Street 270, Taiyuan PO Box 120, Shanxi, China.

CHEN ShengXi, b. 21 Oct 1944, Tao Yuan, Hunan, China. Cardiothoracic Surgeon. m. Y H Wang, 30 Dec 1970, 2 sons. Education includes: Japan Centre of Circulatory System Study for Coronary Surgery and PTCA, Osaka. Appointments: Instructor, then Visiting Doctor, 1981-91; Associate Professor, Director of Cardiothoracic Surgery, Vice-Directorof Surgery, Hsiang Ya Hospital, Changsha, 1991-. Contributor to Operative Surgery, 5th chapter of Cardiothoracic Surgery, 1990. Honours: 3rd Degree Honour, 2 4th Degree Honours, Provincial Scientific and Technological Advances, 1989, 1990 (2); Award for Department's Successful Heart Transplantation, Hunan Province Health Department, 1994. Membership: Vice-Director, Chinese Cardiothoracic Association, Hunan Branch. Address: Surgery Building, Ward 22, Hsiang Ya Hospital, Changsha 410078, China.

CHEN Shi Shu, b. 11 Nov 1929, Fujiang, China. Professor of Molecular Biology. m. Xue Yi Ding, 11 Aug 1986, 4 daughters. Education: MD, Shanghai Second Medical College, 1955; PhD, Beijing Medical College, 1959. Appointments: Visiting Professor, Mt Sinai Medical Centre, New York, USA, 1986-87; Visiting Professor, Rockefeller University, New York, 1981-82; Visiting Researcher, Memorial Sloan-Kettering Cancer Centre, New York, 1980-81; Director, Research Centre for Human Gene Therapy, Chairman, Professor, Department Biochemistry and Laboratory of Molecular Biology, Shanghai Second Medical University, China. Publications: Tumor and Immunity, Co-editor, 1982; Medical Cell and Molecular Biology, Chief Editor, 1994; Contributor of over 60 papers in professional journals. Honours: Model Worker of Shanghai City; National Progressive Educator; Awards for Distinguished Achievements of Science and Technology; Permanent awards, State Council of China, 1992. Memberships: President, Shanghai Biochemical and MOlecular Biology Society, 1989-92; Standing Committee, Chinese Biochemistry and Molecular Biology, 1989-; Committee, Chinese Association for Biotherapy, 1994. Hobbies: Reading; Watching Television. Address: Shanghai Second Medical University, 280 Chongqing Road, Shanghai 200025, China.

CHEN Shou Po, b. 7 July 1928, Shanghai, China. Physician. m. Ming Jiang, 29 Sept 1959, 2 daughters. Education: MD, Peking Union Medical College, 1957. Career: Attending Physician; Co-Director, Department of Medicine; Co-Chief, Division of Gastroenterology; Professor of Medicine. Publications: 76 scientific papers in medical journals, 1980-93; Associate Editor-in-Chief, Advances in Clinical Medicine. Honours: Second Grade Reward, Ministry of Public Health, 1985, 1993. Memberships: Member, Editorial Board, Chinese Journal of Internal Medicine & Journal of Clinical Gastroenterology. Address: Department of Gastroenterology, Peking Union Medical College Hospital, 1 Shuai Fu Yuan, Beijing 100730, China.

CHEN Shui-Cheng, b. 29 Mar 1939, Xiamen, China. Doctor of Chinese Medicine. m. Huang Mei Zhen, Feb 1969, 2 sons. Education: Bachelor's degree, Department of Bone Trauma, Fujian College of Traditional Chinese Medicine, 1967. Appointments include: Physician in charge, Traditional Chinese Medicine; Chief Physican, Traditional Chinese Medicine; Deputy Chief Doctor of Traditional Chinese Medicine. Publications: Scientific Nature of Yin-Yang Theory Observation on the Treatment of Injury with Gupi Decoction, 1994. Honours: Gold Medal, International Traditional Medicine Research Institute and Organisation of Exhibition of Excellent Results of International Medicine, 1994. Hobbies: Stamp collecting; Miniature trees and rockery. Address: Room 201, Zhong Hua Lu No 2, Gulangyu, Xiamen 361002, China.

CHEN Shuzhou, b. 17 Apr 1941, Anhui, China. Chief and Professor of Surgery. m. 15 Jun 1969, 1 s. Education: Nanjing Medical University, 1965. Career: Resident and Assistant of Surgery, 1965; Attending Doctor and Lecturer, 1980; Associate Professor of Surgery, Vice Chief Surgeon, 1987; Head of Office of Medical Affairs of Affiliated Hospital, 1985; Head, Department of Medical Education and Scientific Research, 1989; Chief Doctor, Professor of Surgery, Affiliated Hospital, 1994-. Publications include: Aneurysm of the Abdominal Aorta Complicated by Marfan's Syndrome, in Chinese Journal of Surgery, 1981; Surgical Treatment of Bile Duct Cancer - A Report of 43 Cases, in Jiangsu Medical Journal, 1992; Given emergency treatment to severe patients with trauma in abdominal organs, in Chinese Journal of Traumatology, 1992. Honour: Copper Medal for Intubating Forceps, Beijing International Exhibition of Inventions, 1988. Memberships: Red Cross Society of China; Chinese Medical Association; All-China Society on Integration of Traditional Chinese Medicine and Western Medicine; Chinese Anticancer Association. Hobbies: Music; Art; Sport. Address: Department of Surgery, Affiliated Hospital, Nantong Medical College, Jiangsu 226001, China.

CHEN Su Zhen, b. 21 Feb 1921, Shenyang, China. Director of Doctor Research Fellows. m. Chang Jun Yang, 13 Sep 1952, 1 s. Education: PhD. Career: Registrar in Surgery, 1944-49, Lecturer in Surgery, 1949-54, Vice Professor, 1953, Chief of Surgical Department, 1955-83, Professor, 1980, Currently, Director of Doctor Research Fellows, China Medical College; Chief Editor, Journal of Practical Surgery, 1980-83. Publications: The etiology, diagnosis and treatment of massive haemorrhage of the liver, in special publication of National Journal of China, 1964; The study of morphology and distribution of inorganic elements on the fractured surface of gallstones, in Chinese Journal of Surgery, 1984; The Acute Abdomen, 1990. Honours: First Female Surgical Professor in China; 1st Class Prize for teaching film on gallstones, China Hygienic Ministry, 1983; 2nd Class Prize for prevention and treatment of gallstones in China, China Hygienic Ministry, 1984. Memberships: Founder Member, IHPB Association, 1987-; Chinese Medical Association. Hobby: Social Work. Address: Surgery Department, Second Third Attached Hospital to China Medical University, 36 Shanhao Street, Heping Distict, Shenyang, China.

CHEN Wei J, b. 1 July 1959, Taiwan. Epidemiologist. m. Suh-Fong Jeng, 6 July 1986, 1 son. Education: MD, National Taiwan University College of Medicine, 1984; ScD, Harvard School of Public Health, USA, 1992. Appointments: Postdoctoral Research Fellow, Department of Epidemiology, Harvard School of Public Health; Lecturer, Institute of Public Health, College of Medicine, Associate Professor, Institute of Epidemiology, College of Public Health, National Taiwan University. Publications: Linkage Studies of Schizophrenia: A Simulation Study of Statistical Power, Co-author, 1992; Estimating Age at Onset Distributions: The Bias From Prevalent Cases and Its Impact on Risk Estimation, Co-author, 1993. Membership: International Genetic Epidemiology Society. Hobbies: Swimming; Running; Movies. Address: 1 Jen-Ai Road, Section 1, Taipei 100, Taiwan, China.

CHEN Wei-Cheng Jacok, b. 13 Aug 1931, Shanghai, China. Chief Physician. m. Lin Zhi Fen, 1 Oct 1957, 1 son, 2 daughters. Education: Graduated, Peking Union Medical College, 1957. Appointments include: Currently Chief Physician, Professor, Yancheng Third People's Hospital, Yancheng. Address: Department of Internal Medicine, Yancheng Third People's Hospital, Yancheng, Jiangsu, China.

CHEN Wenbin, b. 15 June 1932, Fuzhou, Fujian, China. Professor. m. Dezhen Chen, 30 July 1959, 1 s, 1 d. Education: MD, School of Medicine, Fujian Medical College, 1950-55. Appointments: Resident, 1955-58; Chief Resident, 1958-59, Department of Intern Medicine College Hospital, Sichuan Medical College; Senior Fellow, 1959-61, Instructor, 1962-80, Division of Pulmonology, College Hospital, SMC; Associate Professor, Department of Internal Medicine, University Hospital, WCUMS, 1980-86; Visiting Associate Professor, Division of Pulmonology, Tulane University, USA, 1982-83; Professor, Department of Internal Medicine, University Hospital, WCUMS, 1986-; Director of Pulmonology. Publications: Contributor of 118 professional articles in national journals and chapters in numerous books. Honours: Scientific Progress Awards for several book chapters from Sichuan Province. Memberships: Committee Member, Chinese Medical Association, Internal Medicine and Respiratory Medicine, 1986-, Chengdu and Sichuan Branch, 1956-. Address: Division of Pulmonology, First University Hospital, West China University of Medical Sciences, 37 Gou Xue Xiang, Chengdu, Sichuan 610041, China.

CHEN Wenxian, b. 26 Apr 1932, Fujian, China. Doctor; Professor. m. 1 Jan 1959, 2 sons, 1 daughter. Education: MD, Medical College of Nanjing University, 1954. Appointments: House Surgeon, Department of ENT, Xijing Hospital of 4th Military Medical University; Lecturer, Xijing Hospital; Associate Professor, Vice Chairman, Chairman, Department of ENT, Tangdu Hospital. Publications: Co-author: The Standard of Clinical Diagnosis and Therapy, 1982; A Modern Clinical Medical Dictionary, 1993; Operative Surgery, Surgery of the Ear, Nose and Throat, 1994. Honours: Advanced Health Workers award, 1959, 1993; 2nd, 3rd Awards of Achievement of Scientific Research, 1983-93. Memberships: Vice Chairman, Society of ENT, Shanxi Branch, CMA; Director, Xian Branch, CMA; HOnorary Chairman, Society of ENT. Xian Branch, CMA. Hobbies: Sport; Music. Address: Department of Otolaryngology, Tangdu Hospital, 4th Military Medical University, Xian 710038, China.

CHEN Wufan, b. 15 Oct 1949, Hunan Province, China. Professor. m. Kang Xingmei, 23 Sept 1978, 1 son. Education: BA, 1975, MD, 1981, Beijing University of Aeronautics and Astronautics. Appointments:

Lecturer, Department of Aeronautics and Astronautics, Changsha Institute of Technology, Hunan Province; Associate Professor, Department of Computer Application, currently Professor of Medical Image and Signal Processing, Department of Biomechanical Engineering, The First Military Medical University, Guangzhou, Guangdong Province. Publications: A generalized variational principle of N-S equations of steady and incompressible flow and its finite element analysis, 1988; The implicit difference scheme and the analysis of stability of an improved Pajneshu system, 1989; An approximate solution of blood flow problem in the aorta, 1989; Optimal division of soft-classification problem for fuzzy cluster, 1993; A new algorithm of detecting edges for medical color image: generalized fuzzy operator, 1994. Memberships: Guangdong Province Biomechanics Society; National Society of Image and Graphics of China; National Computer Society of China; Technologists for Estimation and Approval, National Natural Science Foundation of China; Technologists for Estimation and Approval, National Scientific Research Outcomes of China. Hobbies: Writing Chinese poetry; Drawing Chinese pictures. Address: Department of BME, The First Mlitary Medical University, Guangzhou, Guangdong 510515, China.

CHEN Xin, b. 28 June 1924, Beijing, China. Professor of Space Medicine. m. 30 Apr 1949, 2 sons, 1 daughter. Education: Medical College, University of Japan. Appointments: Vice Director, Institute of Space Medico-Engineering, 1966; Director, Institute of Space Medico-Engineering, 1983; Chairman, Chinese Society of Somatic Science. Publications: Theory of Man-Machine-Environment System Engineering, 1987. Honours: State Award for Scientific & Technological Progress, 1985; State Prize, Outstanding Contributions in Research Work, 1991. Memberships: Honourable Member, Chinese Society of Aeronautics & Astronautics; Academician Member of International Academy of Astronautics. Hobbies: Scientific Thinking. Address: PO Box 5104, Beijing 100094, China.

CHEN Xing-Rong, b. 4 July 1931, Sichuan, China. Professor of Radiology. m. An-Zhong Zhang, 14 July 1956, 1 son, 1 daughter. Education: BA, 1956, PhD, MD, 1966, Shanghai 1st Medical College. Appointments: Resident, Shanghai 1st Medical College, 1956-62, Physician-in-charge, Shanghai 1st Medical College, 1962-80, Chairman, Department of Radiology, 1962-92, currently President, Hua Shan Hospital; Associate Professor, 1980-86, Professor of Radiology, 1986-, Shanghai Medical University; Chairman, Shanghai Radiology Society, 1989-93. Publications: 12 monographs and 150 papers including: Interventional Radiology, 1989; Selective angiography, 1990; CT and MRI of central nervous system, 1992; CT and MRI of whole body, 1994. Honours: Outstanding Professor of Graduate Education, Shanghai Medical University, 1985; Outstanding Doctor of National Department of Health, Ministry of Public Health, China, 1988. Memberships: Vice-Chairman, Chinese Radiological Society; Corresponding Member, RSNA; Editorial Boards: Journal of Clinical Radiology; Foreign Medical Clinical Radiology Fascicule; Shanghai Medicine; Chinese Journal of Radiology (vice-chief editor); Journal of Interventional Radiology (chief editor). Hobby: Swimming. Address: Lane 170, 10 Ping Jiang Road, Shanghai 200032, China.

CHEN Xuemin, b. 16 Jan 1936, Hunan Province, China. Teacher. m. Wu Minjie, 8 Dec 1960, 1 son, 1 daughter. Education: MD, Tongji Medical University, 1957. Appointments: Assistant Teacher, 1957-79, Lecturer, 1979-85, Associate Professor, 1985-89, Professor, 1989-, Tongji Medical University. Publications: Environmental Hygiene (co-author), in Chinese Encyclopedia of Medicine, 1985; Modern Environmental Hygiene (chief author), 1995. Memberships: Vice-Chair, Chinese Association of Environmental Health; Chair, Chinese Association of Preventive Medicine, Wuhan Branch. Hobbies: Reading; Table-tennis. Address: Department of Environmental Health, Tongji Medical University, 13 Hang Kong Road, Wuhan 430030, China.

CHEN Yifeng, b. 8 Oct 1938, Anhui, China. Professor of Genetics. m. 23 Mar 1968, 1 s, 1 d. Education: Fudan University, Shanghai, 1963. Appointments: Assistant Professor, Kunming Institute of Zoology, Academia Sinica, 1978; Professor of Genetics and Cell Biology, Nanjing Normal University, 1986-. Publications: 6 Books and 65 Articles including; Chromosomes of the Primates in China, Co-author, 1981; Studies of the Homology of Chromosomes Between Human Being and Rhesus Monkey with Chromosomal in Situ Suppression Hybridization, Co-author, 1993. Honour: Title of Outstanding Scientist of China, 1986. Memberships: Chinese Society for Genetics; Chinese Society for Cell

Biology. Hobbies: Running; Swimming. Address: Department of Biology, Nanjing Normal University, Nanjing 210024, China.

CHEN Yiren, b. 5 July 1924, Shuyang County, Jiangsu, China. Archiater; Professor. m. Weizheng Du, July 1945, 3 sons, 2 daughters. Education: BD, Traditional Chinese Medicine, Jiangsu Advanced School of Traditional Chinese Medicine. Appointments: Doctor of Traditional Chinese Medicine, 1945-55; Teacher, Traditional Chinese Medicine, 1956-80; Associate Professor, Traditional Chinese Medicine, 1981-85; Archiater, Professor, Nanjing College of Traditional Chinese Medicine, 1986; Specialised in treating angiocardiopathy, cerebrovascular disease and disorders of the nervous system. Publications: Discussion of Treatise on Febrile Diseases, 1990; Translation and Explanation of Treatise on Febrile Diseases, 1992. Honours: 1st Prize for Outstanding Teaching, Nanjing College of Traditional Chinese Medicine, 1987; Prize for Excellent Edition of Teaching Material, 1990; Prize for Excellent Academic Thesis, 1991; Prize for Outstanding Teaching, Jiangsu Educational Committee, 1992. Memberships: National Academic Committee of Zhongjing's Theory; Council Member, Jiangsu Research Institute of Zhongjing's Theory. Hobbies: Chinese chess; Calligraphy. Address: PO Box 70, Nanjing College of Traditional Chinese Medicine, Nanjing 210029, China.

CHEN Yuan, b. 1 Feb 1930, China. Professor of Biochemistry. m. Zhou Mei, 5 Feb 1956, 1 son, 1 daughter. Education: MD, Medical College of Nian-Jien University, 1954. Appointments: Assistant, Department of Biochemistry, 1954-64, Lecturer, 1964-86, Associate Professor, 1987, Professor of Biochemistry, 1988-95, Head, Laboratory of Free Radical Medicine, First Military Medical University of PLA. Publications: Free Radical Medicine, Chief Editor, 1991; Lipoperoxidation and Coronary Heart Disease, 1988; Lipoperoxidation and Experimental AS, 1993; LDL Modified by UV and Cu2+, 1993; Prevention of Lipoperoxidation by PSK, 1995. Honours: 2nd Award, General Logistics Department of PLA in Medical Science Research, 1989, 1992; Outstanding Product Award, National Nature Science Foundation of China, 1995. Memberships: Chinese Medical Society; Chinese Free Radical Biology and Medicine Society; Chinese Atherosclerosis Society; International Atherosclerosis Society. Address: Research Laboratory of Free Radical Medicine, The First Military Medical University, Guangzhou 510515, China.

CHEN Yunzhen, b. 25 Feb 1925, Fuzhou, China. Physician. m. Chen Shizhi, 1 July 1955, 2 sons, 1 daughter. Education: BM in MD, Fujian Medical College, Fuzhou, China, 1950; Attending Advanted Hematologic Course, Shanghai First Medical College, Zhong Shan Medical Hospital, Shanghai, 1956-57. Career: Assistant Physician 1951, Resident Physician 1952, Attending Dr 1957, Vice Chief Physician 1979, Chief Physician 1987, Fujian Provincial Hospital. Publications: Co-author, Clinicohematology, 1980; Co-author, Health Care and Longevity of Senior, 1987; Co-author, Handbook of Diagnosis and Treatment with Combining Traditional Chinese and Western Medicine, 1989. Honours: Honourable Certified for Progressive Prize, Fujian Science and Technology, 1991, 1992; Honourable Certified and Bonus, Chinese State Council, 1993. Memberships: Association of Geriatric Medicine, Chinese Medical Association; Head, Geriatric Society, Fujian Branch of CMA; Vice Director, Geriatric Society, Fujian Branch of Chinese Association of Rehabilitation Medicine. Hobbies: Recreation; Sports; Electronic Games. Address: Fujian Provincial Hospital, Fuzhou 350001, China.

CHEN Yuquan, b. 14 Oct 1928, Qidong, Jiangsu, China. Chief Surgeon; Professor of General Surgery. m. Hu Wenxiu, 8 Feb 1953, 3 daughters. Education: BM, Nantong Medical College; Residency in General Surgery; MD. Appointments: Resident Surgeon, 1953, Associate Professor, 1979, Professor, Chief Surgeon, 1986-, Nantong Medical College, Nantong. Publications: Exclusion of Stomach in the Treatment of Postoperatve Recurrent Hemorrhage due to Portal Hypertension, 1987; Study of the Experimental and Clinical Value of Serum PGGT Level and PGGT/TGGT Ratio in Diagnosis of the Pancreatic Head Cancer, 1992. Honours: Medal and Certificate, Ministry of Public Health, 1958; Certificate of Honour, 8th Asian Conference of Surgery in Fukuoka, Japan, 1991. Memberships: International Society of Surgery; Medical Society of China, Jiangsu Branch. Hobby: Light music. Address: 20 West Temple Road, Nantong, Jiangsu, China.

CHEN Zaijid, b. 16 May 1928, Hubei, China. Cardiologist. m. Professor |ZXijing Zhang, 1 Oct 1955, 2 daughters. Education: MD. Appointments: Assistant resident, Resident, Visiting Physician, Vice

Head, Department of Internal Medicine, Head, Department of Coronary Heart Disease, Professor of Medical Sciences, Cardiovascular Institute and Fu Wai Hospital, Chinese Academy of Medical Sciences, Peking Union Medical College. Publications: Coronary Heart Disease, Chief Editor, 1994; Angina Pectoris; Disease of Aorta, 1994. Honours: 2nd Award, Scientific and Technological Progress, Ministry of Health and Hygiene, 1986; National Excellent Teacher, 1991. Hobbies: Reading; Television. Address: Fu Wai Hospital, Beilishi Road No 167, Beijing 100037, China.

CHEN Zhan, b. 10 Feb 1931, China. Professor of Medicine. m. Yao Xian-En, 30 Jan 1957, 1 s, 1 d. Education: MD, Shanghai Second Medical University, 1955. Appointments: Professor of Medicine, Director of Cardiology, Capital Medical University, An-Zhen Hospital. Publications: Current Management of Heart Disease, 1993; Auscultation of the Heart, 1958; Arrthymia and Clinical Electrophysiology, Co-author. Memberships: Society of Cardiology; Beijing Medical Association; Chinese Medical Association; Society of Pacing and Electrophysiology. Address: An Din Men Wai, An-Zhen Li, District 4, Building 5# Room 9-1, Beijing 100029, China.

CHEN Zhizhou, b. 19 Jan 1940, Zhejiang Province, China. Medical researcher. m. Fan Zhenfu, 1 Jan 1966, 1 son, 1 daughter. Education: BA, Shanghai First Medical University, 1962; MSc, Peking Union Medical College, Beijing, 1966. Appointments: Assistant Researcher of Endocrinology, Peking Union Hospital, CAMS, 1966; Lecturer, 1978, Associate Professor, 1985, Professor of Experimental Nuclear Medicine, 1990-, Cancer Institute, CAMS. Publications: Radioisotopes in Biology and Medicine, Co-author, 1976; Radioinoassay in Medicine, 1991; Immunoradiometric Assay of Tumor Marker CA50, 1988; IRMAs of CA242, CA125, CA19-9, PSA, 1992, 1993, 1994. Honours: State and Technology Prizes, Health Ministry, 1983, 1993; Special Honour of State Council, 1992. Memberships: China Medical Association; China Immunology Society; China Anti-Cancer Association; Editorial Board, Labelled Immunoassays and Clinical Medicine. Hobbies: Running; Table Tennis; Badminton. Address: Cancer Institute (Hospital), Chinese Academy of Medical Sciences, PO Box 2258, Panjiayao, Beijing 10021, China.

CHEN Zhong Wei, b. 1 Oct 1929, Zhejiang, China. Professor. m. Dr Yin Hui Zhu, 1 July 1954, 1 s, 1 d. Education: Shanghai Second Medical University. Appointments: Resident Surgeon to Head of Orthopaedic Department, Shanghai Sixth People's Hospital, 1954-84; Professor of Orthopaedics, Zhong Shan Hospital, 1984-94; Visiting Professor of 12 International Medical Centres including New York University, Harvard, London University and Osaka City University. Publications: replantation of Severed Limb, 1964; Microsurgery, 1985. Honour: Replantation of Extremity, National Science Congress Award, 1981. Memberships: Executive Member, International Society of Reconstructive Microsurgery; Chinese Academy of Science. Hobbies: Tennis; Fishing; Motocycles. Address: 136 Medical College Road, Shanghai 200032, China.

CHEN Zi-Long, b. 29 Oct 1962, Xiangtan City, Hunan Province, China. Professor; Doctor. m. Chen Bo, 30 Dec 1987, 1 s. Education: BEng, 1982, MEng, 1985, PhD, 1993, Central-South University of Technology. Appointments: Teacher, 1985-90, Professor, 1993-, Department of Geology, Central-South University of Technology. Publications: Studies on the Geological and Geochemistrical Features of Denfuxian Tungsten Ore Deposits and Their Origin, 1991; Experimental Study on the Partitioning of W and Sn Granitic Silicate Melts and Aqueous Fluids, Co-author, 1993; Experimental study of the partitioning of W and Sn between two seperated melts in the sytems of aqueous gramitic silicate melt, 1994; Experimental results for the beginning melting of tin-bearing gramites in Guangxi and their geological significance, 1994; etc totalling in 40 papers. Honours; CNNC Prize for Science and Technology, 1990; CSUT Prize for Science and Technology, 1989. Memberships: International Association on the Genesis of Ore Deposits; Mineralogical-Petrological-Geochemistrical Society of China; Gem jade Association of Hunan Province. Hobbies: Table Tennis; Swimming; Basketball; Running. Address: Department of Geology, Central-South University of Technology, Changsha, Hunnan 410083, China.

CHENEY Mack Lowell, b. 27 Dec 1955, Sherman, TX, USA. Facial Plastic Surgeon. m. Wendy Burns, 7 May 1982, 2 s, 1 d. Education: BS, Honours Cum Laude, Biology, Millsaps College, Jackson, 1978; MD, University of MS Medical School, Jackson, 1982. Career includes:

Director, Facial Plastic and Reconstructive Surgery Services, Department of Otolaryngology, 1988-; Director, Otolaryngology Emergency Services, 1990-, Associate Surgeon, 1994-, MA Eye and Ear Infirmary, Boston, MA; Instructor, 1988-90, Assistant Professor, 1990-, in Otology and Laryngology, Harvard Medical School, Boston, MA; Many presentations and invited lectures. Publications: Many articles in professional journals, books and chapters including: Co-author, Illustrated Atlas of Cutaneous Surgery, 1991; Co-author, Surgical Atlas of Pedicled and Free Flap Transfers for Head and Neck Reconstruction, in press. Honours: Athletic Scholarship, Millsaps College, 1974; Oak Ridge National Research Center Scholarship, 1977; Millsaps College Biology Research Award, 1978; Millsaps College Honors Degree, 1978. Memberships include: Fellow, American Academy of Otolaryngology; Fellow, American College of Surgeons; Fellow, Amerian Academy of Facial Plastic and Reconstructive Surgery; AMA; American Society of Peripheral Nerve; European Academy of Facial Surgery; Sir Charles Bell Society. Address: Massachusetts Eye and Ear Infirmary, Facial Plastic and Reconstructive Surgery, 243 Charles Street, Boston, MA 02114, USA.

CHENG Gregory, b. 26 Oct 1954, Hong Kong. Physician. Education: MD, PhD, University of Toronto, Canada; FRCP(Canada), 1983; ABIM, Haematology, 1984, Medical Oncology, 1983, Internal Medicine, 1982. Appointments: Deputy Director, Ottawa Red Cross; Assistant Professor, Department of Medicine, University of Ottawa; Senior Clinical Pathologist, Queen Mary Hospital, Hong Kong. Publications: Audit Use of Synthetic Colloids and Blood Alternatives, 1993; Guidelines for the Use of Fresh-Frozen Plasma, Cryoprecipitate and Platelets, 1994; Transient Myeloproliferative Disorder in a Down's Neonate with Rearranged T Cell Receptor ß Gene and Evidence of In Vivo Maturation Demonstrated by Dual Colour Flow Cytometric DNA Ploidy Analysis, 1994; Evaluation of the Gel Test for Antibody Screening in a Tertiary Hospital in Hong Kong: Insensitivity for Some Cold Antibodies That Are Reactive at 37 degress C by Conventional Indirect Antiglobulin Tests, 1994; Type and Screen of Blood Units at a Teaching Hospital, 1994. Honours: Terry Fox Fellowship, 1984-86; Medical Research Council Canada Research fellowship, 1986-89. Membership: Chairman, Hong Kong Blood Transfusion Society. Hobbies: Tennis; Travel. Address: 140 Pokfulam Road, Unit 31, Hong Kong.

CHENG Li-qun, b. 9 Mar 1964, Fushun, Liaoning, China. Doctoral Student. m. Education: BM, 1987, Master's degree, Digestive Pathopathology, 1990, Dalian Medical College; Digestive Endoscopy, Dalian Municipal Central Hospital, 1990-; PhD and MD in progress, Department of Surgery, Queen Mary Hospital, University of Hong Kong, 1994-. Publications: Effect of Jin Shi San on Gallstone Dissolution in Guinea Pigs, 1990; Omeprazole in the treatment of peptic ulcer, 1991; Cholelitholysis with complex MTBE emulsion. An experimental study, 1992; One case of ileocaeca enterocyst excised by endoscopic high frequency electrocoagulation, 1992. Molecular Mechanisms of Cholesterol Gallstone Formation, forthcoming. Honours: Olympus Scholarship Programme Study, Showa University Fujigaoka Hospital, Japan, 1993. Memberships: Society of Medicine, Chinese Medical Association; Chinese Biophysical Society; Pan-Pacific Surgical Association. Hobbies: Sport (member of baseball and swimming teams, Medical School); Photography. Address: Department of Endoscopy, Dalian Municipal Central Hospital, Dalian 116033, China.

CHENG Shi, b. 20 June 1937, Beijing, China. Professor of Biophysics. m. Zhu Yuan Xiang, June 1965, 2 sons. Education: MD, Beijing Medical University, 1960. Appointments: Assistant, Lecturer, Associate Professor, currently Professor of Biophysics, Department of Biophysics, Beijing Medical University. Publications: EM observation on platelet aggregation groups, 1981; Study on erythrocytes of patients with cirrhosis of liver, 1983; Study on erythrocyte membrane fluidity by laser Raman spectroscopy, 1988; Metallothionein and free radical scavenger, 1991; Quench effect of metallothionein on free radical signal in postischemic reperfusion of isolated rat hearts, 1992; Protective effects of metallothionein on cardiac myocytes against hydroxyl radicals by ESR spin label method, 1993; Biological Membrane and Disease, 1994. Honours: Prize for Achievements in Academic Research, Beijing, 1981; Prize for Achievements in Scientific Research, Beijing Medical University, 1993. Memberships: National Biophysical Association; National Cell Biology Association; National Medical Association; Society of Beijing Physiology. Hobbies: Enjoying music; Reading novels. Address: Department of Biophysics, Beijing Medical University, Beijing 100083, China.

CHENG Stephen Wing Keung, b. 9 May 1960, Hong Kong. Surgeon. Education: MBBS, 1984, MS, 1993, University of Hong Kong; FRCS, Edinburgh, 1988. Appointments: Lecturer, 1990-94, Senior Lecturer, 1994-, Department of Surgery, University of Hong Kong. Publications: Co-author: Peptic ulcers and abdominal aortic aneurysms, 1992; Infected femoral pseudoaneurysms in intravenous drug abusers, 1992; Thoracic outlet syndrome: supraclavicular approach, 1994; Neurogenic thoracic outlet syndrome, 1994; Supraclavicular reoperation for neurogenic thoracic outlet syndrome, 1994; Abdominal aortic aneurysms in Hong Kong, 1994; Optimal exposure of the proximal abdominal aorta: A critical appraisal of transabdominal medical visceral rotation, 1994. Address: Department of Surgery, The University of Hong Kong, Professorial Block, Queen Mary Hospital, Pokfulam Road, Hong Kong.

CHENG Wei, b. 10 Oct 1957, Bijie City, Guizhou, China. Charge Nurse. m. Zhing QinShu, 12 Dec 1982, 1 son. Education: Graduated, Bijie Prefecture Medical Middle School, 1988. Appointments: Currently Charge Nurse, Bijie Prefecture Hospital, Guizhou. Publications: Pursuit and Discussion of the Management of Graded Quality Nursing, 1992; Nurse Ethics (co-author), 1992. Membership: Bijie Prefecture Nurses Association. Hobby: Riding. Address: Bijie Prefecture Hospital, Guizhou, China.

CHERNIACK Neil Stanley, b. 28 May 1931, Brooklyn, New York, USA. Physician. m. Sandra Cherniack, 1955, 2 sons, 1 daughter. Education: BA; MD; Doctor of Medicine, Karolinska Institutet, Stockholm. Appointments: Assistant Professor of Medicine, Chicago, Illinois, 1964-68; Clinical Associate Professor of Medicine, University of Illinois, 1968-69; Associate Professor of Medicine, 1969-73, Professor of Medicine, 1973-77, University of Pennsylvania; Professor of Medicine, 1977-, Dean, School of Medicine, 1990-95, Case Western Reserve University, Cleveland, Ohio; Professor and Director of Clinical Services and Research, University of Medicine and Dentistry School of Medicine of New Jersey, 1995-. Publications: The Lung, 1990; Control of Breathing, 1991; Chronic Obstructive Pulmonary Disease, 1991, Italian edition, 1992; Future directions in sleep research; a respiratory physician's perspective, 1993; The role of ventral medulla in hypoxic respiratory depression and sympathetic excitation (co-author), 1993. Memberships: Central Society for Clinical Research; Society for Neuroscience; American Thoracic Society; American College of Chest Physicians. Hobby: Painting (watercolour and oils). Address: University of Medicine and Dentistry of New Jersey, 185 So Orange Avenue, Newark, NJ 07103, USA.

CHERNOGORENCO Vasily B, b. 14 Jan 1926m Ismail, Ukraine. Chemist Inorganic. m. Maria Bidulina, 5 July 1956, 1 son. Education: PhD, Kiev, 1955. Appointments: Senior Researcher, Institute for Problems of Materials Science, National Academy of Sciences of Ukraine; Deputy Head, Ukrainian Phosphorus Expert-Consultation Section, Ministry of Industry, Ukraine. Publications: About 200 scientific works and 40 patents, incl: Bismuthides, 1977; Development of chemical technology in Ukraine, 1976; The properties of elements, 1976; Definition of the chemical compound, 1978; Preparation of phosphides in the combustion regime, 1981; Scientometric estimation of present-day study on phosphides, 1981. Honours: Medal, Academy of Sciences, 1983; 10 decorations for participation in World War II. Memberships: D Mendeleev Chemical Society; Scientific Council, Institute for Problems of Materials Science. Address: Semashko Str 16, Apt 16, Kiev 142 252142, Ukraine.

CHERTKOV Joseph L, b. 28 Mar 1927, Odessa, Russia. Hematologist. m. Veits Inessa, 24 July 1950, 1 son, 1 daughter. Education: MD, Moscow Medical University, 1947; PhD, Moscow Medical University, 1950; DSc, Russia Academia of Medicine, 1961. Appointments: Assistant Professor, Minsk Medical University; Senior Researcher, Moscow Institute of Meat Production; Professor, National Hematological Scientific Center. Publications: Blood Expanders, 1958; Properdin System, 1961; Pathogenetic Basis of Radiation Disease, 1965; Cellular Basis of Immunity, 1969; Cellular Basis of Hematopoiesis, 1977; Hematopoietic Stem Cell and Its Microenvironment, 1984. Honours: 3 Medals, 1970, 1977, 1980; Honour Medal of Pulmonology Society, Russia; Honour Medal, Charles University, Prague. Memberships: Society of Experimental Hematology; Society Hematology & Transfusiology, Russia. Address: Leningradsky Prospect 28, Apt 16, Moscow 125040, Russia.

CHEUNG Lim Kwong, b. 18 Sept 1958, China. Oral & Maxillofacial Surgery. m. Dr Maria Wong, 6 Jan 1985, 1 son, 1 daughter. Education:

BDS; FFDRCS; FDSRCPS; FRACDS; FRACDS (OMS); FHKAM (DS). Career: Senior Lecturer. Publications: The Use of Mouldable Acrylic for Restoration of the Temporalis Flap Donor Site, 1994; Reconstructive Options for Maxillary Defects, 1994; Mandibular Reconstruction with Dacron Tray - Radiological Assessment of Bone Remodelling, 1994; 3 Dimensional Stability of Maxillary in Cleft Palate Patients with Residual Alveolar Cleft, 1994. Honours: Memberships: Life Fellow, International Association of Oral & Maxillofacial Surgeons; Asian Association of Oral & Maxillofacial Surgeons; Hong Kong Association of Oral & Maxillofacial Surgeons; Hong Kong Dental Association. Address: Department of Oral & Maxillofacial Surgery, University of Hong Kong, Prince Philip Dental Hospital, 34 Hospital Road, Hong Kong.

CHEUNG Man Ban William, b. 9 Nov 1962, Hong Kong. Clinical Psychologist. Education: B Soc Sc, 1984, M Soc Sc, Clinical Psychology, 1987, University of Hong Kong; Registered Psychologist, Hong Kong Psychological Society; Chartered Psychologist, British Psychological Society. Appointments: Co-ordinator, Clinical Psychological Service, Hong Kong Family Welfare Society. Memberships: Associate Fellow, Hong Kong Psychological Society; British Psychological Society. Hobby: Performing Arts. Address: Hong Kong Family Welfare Society, Clinical Psychological Service, G/F 106 Kwai Yan House, Kwai Fong Estate, Kwai Chung, New Territories, Hong Kong.

CHEVALIER Robert L, b. 25 Oct 1946, Chicago, USA. Paediatric Nephrologist. m. Janis S Slezak, 23 Dec 1970, 1 d. Education: BS, Zoology, 1968, MD, 1972, University of Chicago; Genentech Professor of Paediatrics. Appointments: Assistant Professor of Paediatrics, 1978, Associate Professor of Paediatrics, 1983, Chief of Paediatric Nephrology, 1978-92, Professor and Vice Chair, Department of Paediatrics, University of Virginia, 1988-. Publications: Pathophysiology of Obstructive Uropathy, 1994; Renal Physiology and Function, 1992. Honours: Louis Welt Fellowship, 1975-77; Established Investigator, American Heart Association, 1983-88. Memberships: American Society of Paediatric Nephology, President, 1991-92; Southern Society Paediatric Research, President, 1990-91; Society for Paediatric Research; American Paediatric Society. Hobbies: Classical Music; Antiquarian Books and Maps. Address: Department of Paediatrics, Box 386, University of Virginia School of Medicine, Charlottesville, VA 22908, USA.

CHEZ Ronald August, b.17 Aug 1932, Chicago, Illinois, USA. Professor of Obstetrics and Gynaecologist. 1 son, 1 daughter. Education: MD, 1957. Appointments: Professor and Chair, Obs/Gyn, Pennsylvania State University; Professor, Obs/Gyn, University of Pittsburgh' Clinical Dir4ector, NICHD-NIH; Branch Chief, Pregnancy Research Branch, NICHD, NIH; Professor and Vice Chair, Obs/Gyn, New Jersey Medical school; Professor of Obstetrics and Gynaecology, University of South Florida. Publications: Contributor of 271 professional works. Memberships: American College of Obstetrics and Gynaecology; Society Gynaecological Investigation; American Gynaecology and Obstetrics Society; Society Perinatal Obstetrics. Address: Suite 500, 4 Columbia Drive, Tampa, FL 33606, USA.

CHI David Shyh-Wei, b. 7 July 1943, Taiwan, China. Educator. m. Sue-Yue Lin, 19 Dec 1982, 1 son, 1 daughter. Education: BS;' MA; PhD; CLD. Appointments: Research Assistant Professor, department Pathology, New York University, USA, 1977-80; Associate Professor, Department Internal Medicine, 1980-86, Professor, 1986-, Director, Clinical Immunology Laboratory, 1980-, Chief, Division Biomedical Research, 1981-, East Tennessee State University. Publications: Contributor of 44 articles in journals, 126 abstracts and presentations and 5 book chapters. Honours: New Investigation Research Award, NCI, 1980; Ruth R Harris Endowment, 1989; Dean's Excellence in Teaching Award, 1992; Fellow, American Academy Microbiology, 1988; Fellow, Association Medical Laboratory Immunologists, 1987. Memberships: Sigma Xi; American Society Microbiology; The Harvey Society; American Association Immunologists; Society Experimental Biological Medicine; North American Taiwanese Professor's Association; Clinical Immunology Society; American Society Histocompatibility and Immunogenetics; International Neuropeptides Society. Hobbies: Painting; Cooking; Music. Address: Department of Internal Medicine, Box 70622, James H Quillen College of Medicine, East Tennessee State University, Johnson City, TN 37614-0622, USA.

CHIANG Cheng Wen, b. 24 Oct 1943, I-Lan, Taiwan. Physician. m. Mei Yu Yang Chiang, 8 Nov 1972, 2 s. Education: MD. Career:

Currently, Director of 1st Cardiovascular Division, Chang Gung Memorial Hospital; Associate Professor, 1982-88, Professor, Internal Medicine, 1989-, Chang Gung Medical College. Honours: Best Medical Physician Award, Chang Gung Memorial Hospital, 1977; Cheng Hsing Medical Award, Medical Association, Taiwan, 1979. Memberships: American College of Chest Physicians; Vice President, ROC Society of Cardiology; President, Society for Ultrasound in Medicine of the ROC; Western Pacific Association Critical Care Medicine, Taiwan. Hobbies: Music; Boating. Address: 1st Floor, 23, Lane 165, Kwang Fu North Road, Taipei, Taiwan.

CHIDAMBARAM Balasubramaniam, b. 11 June 1957. Physician. m. Sandhya. Education: MBBS, Madras Medical College, 1974-81; MCh. University of Madras, 1986. Appointments include: Clinical Postdoctoral Fellow, Paediatric Neurosurgery, Department of Neurosurgery, Baylor College of Medicine, Houston, Texas, USA, 1988-89; Registrar in Neurosurgery, Regional Neurosciences Centre, Newcastle General Hospital, Newcastle-upon-Tyne, England, 1990. Publications include: Neurolysis in the Management of Certain Nerve Injuries, CO-author, 1980; Unusual Presentation of Subdural Haematoma. Co-author, 1983; technical Notes - Repair After Removal of Facia Lata, CO-author, 1983; Management of Myelomeningocele - Selection Policy and Indication for Surgery, Co-author, 1985; Operative Sonography in Neurosurgery - A Preliminary report, Co-author, 1986; Metatstatic Compression of Spinal Cord, Co-author, 1988; COngenital Arachnoid Cysts in Children, Co-author, 1989; Enterogenous Cyst of Spinal Cord - A Case Report, Co-author, 1993; Diastematomyelia (Split Cord Malformation), 1994; Contributor of numerous conference papers. Memberships include: International Society for Pediatric Neurosurgery; International Member Congress of Neurological Surgeons; Life member, Neurological Society of India; Life Member, Child Neurology Chapter, Indian Academy of Paediatrics; Life Member, Association of Surgeons of India; Life Member, Indian Medical Association; Life Member, Indian Academy of Neurosciences; Life member, Association of Trauma Care of India; Indian Society of Paediatric Neurosurgery. Address: Ranga Nursing Home, 36 TTK Road, Alwarpet, Madras 600018, India.

CHIGBUH Alexander Ekenwa, b. 2 Oct 1940, Ahiazu Mbaise, Nigeria. Medicine. m. Eucharia Chigbuh, 10 Sep 1985, 2 s, 5 d. Education: MD; DSc; Diploma SOG; FICS. Career: Head, Department of Obstetrics and Gynaecology, Queen Elizabeth Specialist Hospital, Umuahia; Head, Department of Obstetrics and Gynaecology, General Hospital, Aba; Currently, Medical Director, Gabriel N'Elizabeth Chigbu Hospital, Nigeria. Publications: The African Woman Towards Motherhood; Motherhood, Pregnancy and Childcare. Honour: FICS, 1977. Memberships: International College of Surgeons; International Society of Hypnosis and Handwriting Psychology. Hobbies: Photography; Lawn Tennis. Address: Gabriel N'Elizabeth Chigbu Hospital, Obohia, Ahiazu Mbaise, IMO State, Nigeria.

CHIKEZIE Alfred Ikem, b. 14 May 1935, Nigeria. Medical Director. m. Monica Chikezie, 27 Feb 1966, 4 daughters. Education: MD, Colombia; FRMS; LLB, London, England; BL, London, England; BL, Nigeria. Appointments: Solicitor & Advocate, Nigeria Supreme Court; Barrister-at-Law, Grays, London, England. Memberships: British Acupuncture Association. Hobbies: Swimming; Reading; Tennis. Address: Alphonso Chikezie Memorial Hospital, PO Box 460, Nnewi, Nigeria.

CHILD Elizabeth Anne, b. 17 Mar 1941, Croydon, Surrey, England. Psychologist; Therapist. m. John Child, 31 July 1965, 1 son, 1 daughter. Education: Certificate in Social Studies, University of Durham, 1963; Certificate in Youth Work, Cambridge Education Committee, 1964; BA, Social Studies, University of Newcastle, 1965; PhD, University of Aston, 1983. Appointments: Personal Secretary, 1960-61; Research Officer, Department of Zoology, 1963-64, Research Officer, Department of Applied Economics, 1965, University of Cambridge; Assistant Youth Leader, Coleridge Evening Centre, Cambridge, 1963; Children's Play Officer, Telford Development Corporation, 1965-69; Part-time Research Officer, Nuffield College, Oxford, 1976-77; Tutor, Aston University, 1978-83; Private practice in Hypnotherapy and Psychotherapy, 1983-, Alternative Medicine, 1989-; Development of Crystal Healing Practice, 1990-; Joint Manager, New Age Days, lectures and counselling group, 1991-. Publications: Provision for pre-school children's play with special reference to toddlers' play spaces, 1969; Children and leisure, 1973; Play as a social product, 1981; Play and culture: a study of English and Asian children, 1983; Theories of Play, 1984; Books in progress: The Crystal Dream: A Comprehensive Study of Crystals and their Uses; The

Golden Dream. Membership: Associate Fellow, British Psychological Society. Hobby: Riding. Address: Tudor Croft, Tanners Green Lane, Earlswood, Solihull, West Midlands B94 5JT, England.

CHIN William Waiman, b. 20 Nov 1947, New York, USA. Molecule Geneticist; Physician. m. Denise Jean-Claude, 1 son, 1 daughter. Education: AB, Columbia College, New York, 1968; MD, Harvard Medical School, Boston, 1972. Appointments: Assistant Professor of Medicine, Harvard Medical School, 1981-84; Associate Professor of Medicine, Harvard Medical School, 1984-93; Chief, Director of Genetics, Senior Physician, Brigham & Women's Hospital; Investigator, Howard Hughes Medical Institute; Professor of Medicine, Harvard Medical School. Publications: Over 200 professional publications. Honours: Bowditch Lecturer, American Physiology Society, 1984; Van Meter 1986, & Ingbar 1992, Awards, American Thyroid Association; AFCR Award for Clinical Research, 1988; Boots Pharmaceuticals Mentor Award, Endocrine Society, 1993. Hobbies: Tennis; Skiing; Walking. Address: Division of Genetics, Thorn 919, Brigham & Women's Hospital, 75 Francis Street, Boston, MA 02115, USA.

CHIORAZZI Nicholas, b. 2 Oct 1945, Weehawken, NJ, USA. Physician. m. M Lorraine Dziadowicz, 19 June 1971, 1 s, 1 d. Education: AB, College of the Holy Cross; MD, Georgetown University. Appointments include: Visiting Investigator, 1974, Postdoctoral Fellow, 1976-77, Assistant Professor, 1977-82, Associate Professor, 1982-87, Deputy Head, Laboratory of Immunology, 1984-87, Adjunct Professor, 1987-93, Rockefeller University; Professor of Medicine, 1987-, Member of Immunology Program, Graduate School of Medical Sciences, 1987-, Cornell University Medical College; Chief, Division of Rheumatology and Allergy, Clinical Immunology, North Shore University Hospital, Manhasset, NJ. Publications: Contributor of numerous professional articles including: In Vivo and Post Mortem Dissolution Rates of Pulmonary Emboli and Venous Thrombi in the Dog, Co-author, 1973; Human Monoclonal Antibodies as Probes to Study Autoimmune and Allergic Disorders, 1986; Variant Transcripts of CD79a and CD 79b in Human B Cells, Co-author, 1994. Honours include: National Research Service Award, NIH, 1975-77; Fellow, Arthritis Foundation, 1977-80; Marcia Whitney Schott Scholar in Clinical Science, The Rockefeller University, 1980-82. Memberships include: Fellow, American Academy of Allergy and Immunology; Charter Member, Clinical Immunology Society; New York Rheumatism Society; New York Academy of Sciences; American Federation for Clinical Research; American Association of Immunologists; American College of Physicians. Address: North Shore University Hospital, Cornell University School of Medicine, 300 Community Drive, Manhasset, NY 11030, USA.

CHISWELL Douglas Albert, b. 29 Dec 1921, Sheerness, Isle of Sheppey, Kent. Obstetrician; Gynaecologist. m. Joan, 25 Aug 1947, 2 s. Education: MB, London University; BS, London University; LRCP; MRCS; DTM&H, Liverpool; FRNZCOG; FRCOG. Appointments: Medical Officer, Colonial Medical Service, Kenya; Registrar, Harari Hospital, Salisbury, South Rhodesia; Surgeon/Superintendant, Bay of Islands Hospital, Kawakawa, New Zealand; Now Retired. Hobbies: Sailing; Amateur Radio. Address: The Bullock Track, RD3, Warkworth, New Zealand.

CHO Chi Hin, b. 25 Apr 1949, Canton, China. Reader in Pharmacology. m. Agnes Yuen Wah Chan, 14 July 1978, 1 daughter. Education: BPharm, National Defence Medical Center, Taiwan, 1972; PhD, University of Hong Kong, 1978. Appointments: Research Associate, University of Toronto, Ontario, Canada, 1979-81; Associate Professor, National Yang Ming Medical College, Taiwan, 1981-84; Research Professor, Veterans General Hospital, 1982-84; Lecturer, 1984-89, Senior Lecturer, 1989-92, Reader in Pharmacology, 1992-, University of Hong Kong. Publications: Effects of zinc chloride on gastric secretion and ulcer formation in pylorus-occluded rats, 1976; Current views of zinc as a gastro-hepatic protective agent, 1989; Differential mechanisms of mild irritants on adaptive cytoprotection, 1994. Memberships: Executive Member, Gastrointestinal Section, International Union of Pharmacology; Executive Member, International Conference for Ulcer Research. Hobbies: Running; Soccer. Address: Department of Pharmacology, Faculty of Medicine, The University of Hong Kong, 5 Sassoon Road, Hong Kong.

CHO Nam Han, b. 10 Nov 1958, Seoul, Korea. Professor of Medicine. m. Heomin Kim, 8 Aug 1984, 1 s, 1 d. Education: BS, 1982, MS, 1982, East TN State University, USA; PhD, University of Pittsburgh, 1989. Appointments: Board Director, Senior Citizen Centre of Chicago, 1990;

Chicago Public School Council, 1991; Professor of Medicine, Obstetrics and Gynaecology, Northwestern University Neonatal School. Publications: Spontaneous Whole Blood Platelet Aggregational Triopathy of IDDM, 1992; Spontaneous Whole Blood Platelet ASggregation in IDDM, 1989; Weight of Insulin Secretion at Diagnosis of GDM, Co-author, 1993; The Prevalence of GDM, Co-author, 1991. Honours: Epsilon Eta, 1983; Key to the City of Miami, 1992; Community Service Award, City of Johnson City, 1981; National Dean's List, 1982. Memberships: American Diabetes Association; Society for Epidemiologic Research. Hobbies: Golf; Skiing. Address: #1211 Maetan-Dong, Paldal-Gu, Hankuk Apt 106-404, Suwon 442-370, Korea.

CHOBLI Kpadonou Martin, b. 28 May 1948, Niaouli, Benin. Professor of Anaesthesiology. m. Linda Kpenou, 1982, 1 son, 2 daughters. Education: MD, 1976; French National Diploma of Anaesthesiology, 1978; Diploma of Disaster Medicine, Bordeaux, 1986; Diploma of Anaesthesiology in Coelioscopic Surgery, 1991. Appointments: Specialist in Anaesthesiology, 1978-; Professor of Anaesthesiology, 1986-; Head, Faculty and Hospital. Publications: Management of multiple injuried patients, 1983; Anaesthesia in new born, 1984; Morbidity and mortality in anesthesia, 1986; Training system in anesthesia in Africa, 1990; Anaesthesia practice in Subsaharian Africa today. Honours: Order of Merit, Ivory Coast, 1993. Memberships: President, National Society of Sport Medicine; Secretary, African Society of Anaesthesiology; West African Society of Anaesthesiology; French Society of Anaesthesiology; Society of Anaesthesiology of Subsaharian Africa; West African College of Surgery. Hobbies: Football; Music. Address: BP No 03 0631, Cotonou, Republic of Benin.

CHODERA Joseph Dezider, b. 10 nov 1923, Tepla. Physician. m. Dr M M Chodera, 26 Feb 1964, 1 s, 1 d. Education: MD, PhD, Prague; Med Spec, Prague. Appointments: Assistant, Charles University, Prague; Scientist, CS Academy of Science, Prague' Director of Prosth Research centre, Prague; Principal Research Fellow, DHSS, London; Consultant Physician, Queen Mary's Unviersity Hospital, Roehampton; Senior Research Fellow, UCL, London; Medical Practitioner. Publications: Rehabilitation in Nervous Diseases; Contributor of 113 articles, papers and 5 patents. Honours: Laufberger's Medal, Academy Science, Czechoslovakia, 1984; Honorary Member, Purkynie Society, 1993. Memberships: BMA; Rheumatology Society; ISPO, Switzerland. Address: 19 Buxton Drive, New Malden, Surrey KT3 3UX, England.

CHODOROW Joan, b. 29 May 1937. Psychoanalyst; Dance Therapist. m. Dr Louis H Stewart, 23 June 1985, 1 stepson, 1 stepdaughter. Education: MA, Goddard College, 1972; PhD, The Union Institute, 1988; Postgraduate Diploma in Analytical Psychology, C G Jung Institute of Los Angeles, 1983. Appointments: Founder, Teacher, Community Dance Studio, Los Angeles, 1957-64; Dance Therapist, Child psychiatric Unit, County Hospital, Los Angeles, 1964-66; Dance Therapist, Psychiatric Medical Group, Santa Barbara, 1968-73; Dance Therapist, Cottage Hospital, Santa Barbara, 1968-83; Jungian Analyst in Private Practice, Fairfax, California, 1983-. Publications: Dance Therapy and Depth Psychology - The Moving Imagination, 1991; What is Dance Therapy, Really?, Editor, 1973. Honours: International Dance Therapy Conference in Berlin, Germany, Keynote Speaker, 1994. Memberships: President, 1974-76, American Dance Therapy Association; Analyst Member, International Association for Analytical Psychology and the C G Jung Institute of San Francisco; American Psychological Association. Address: 272 Cascade Drive, Fairfax, CA 94930, USA.

CHOI Bernard C K, b. 17 Feb 1953, Hong Kong. Associate Professor of Epidemiology. m. Anita Pak, 1 June 1986, 1 son, 1 daughter. Education: BSc, Chinese University of Hong Kong, 1977; MSc, University of Aston, Birmingham, England, 1978; PhD, University of Toronto, Canada, 1983. Appointments: Assistant Professor, currently Associate Professor, University of Toronto, Canada. Publications include: Index for rating predictive accuracy of screening tests, 1982; N-nitroso compounds and human cancer: A molecular epidemiologic approach, 1985; Erythema Multiforme (Stevens-Johnson Syndrome): A chart review of 123 hospitalized patients (with J R Nethercott), 1985; The economic impact of smoking in Canada (with J R Nethercott), 1988; Microscopic hematuria as a predictor of urologic diseases among steel workers (with J A Farmilo), 1990; Mass screening for rectal neoplasm in Jiashan County, China (with G Zheng, X Yu, R Zou, Y Shao, X Ma), 1991; Sensitivity and specificity of a single diagnostic test in the presence of work-up bias, 1992; Definition, sources, magnitude, effect modifiers, and strategies of reduction of the healthy worker effect, 1992.

Memberships: Society for Epidemiologic Research; Biometric Society; International Society for Preventive Oncology; International Society of Doctors for the Environment. Hobbies: Badminton; Flute. Address: 247 Rushton Road, Toronto, Ontario, Canada M6G 3J4.

CHOLE Richard A, b. 12 Oct 1944, Madison, WI, USA. Otolaryngologist. m. Cynthia Beiseker, 27 Dec 1969, 2 s, 2 d. Education: MD; PhD. Career: Assistant Professor, Associate Professor, Currently, Professor and Chair, Department of Otolaryngology, Head and Neck Surgery, University of California, Davis School of Medicine. Publications: 112 publications, 1975- including: Gerbil model of aural cholesteatoma, chapter in Cholesteatoma and Mastoid Surgery, 1992; Bone resorption in aural cholesteatoma, chapter in Cholesteatoma and Mastoid Surgery, 1992; Cholesteatoma, chapter in Current Therapy in Otolaryngology, 5th edition, 1994. Honours: 1st Place Award for Basic Research in Otolaryngology, American Academy of Ophthalmology and Otolaryngology, 1977; Elected to Membership of Collegium Otorhinolaryngologicum Amicitiae Sacrum, 1991; Research Award, UC Davis School of Medicine, 1992-93. Memberships: American Academy of Otolaryngology, Head and Neck Surgery; American Triological Society; American Otological Society; American Society for Bone and Mineral Research. Address: Otolaryngology Research Laboratories, University of California, Davis, 1515 Newton Court, Room 209, Research Park, Davis, CA 95616-8647, USA.

CHOMICKI Oskar Adolf, b. 20 May 1931, Warsaw, Poland. Medical Physicist. m. Janina Dabrowski, 7 Aug 1954, 1 son. Education: BA, MSc, Warsaw University. Appointments: Assistant, Warsaw University, 1952-56; Researcher, Institute of Tuberculosis, Warsaw, 1956-59; Lecturer, 1959-69. Senior Lecturer, 1969-92, Postgraduate Medical School, Warsaw; Secretary-General, Marie Sklodowska-Curie Memorial Foundation, , 1992-; Consultant, Institute of Banking and Insurance, 1992-. Publications: Contributions to books: Medical Scientigraphy, 1970; Dictionary of Radiology, 1975; Encyclopaedia of Physics, 1983; Over 50 papers in national and international medical and physics journals. Honours: 3rd Degree Award, Atomic Agency, 1972; Numerous awards for research, Ministry of Health, 1960-90. Memberships: American Association of Physics in Medicine; International Organisation for Medical Physics; International Union for Physical and Engineering Sciences; Polish Society of Medical Physics. Hobbies: Foreign languages; Watching TV; Reading crime stories. Address: Lowicka 21a, m 2, 02-502 Warsaw, Poland.

CHORBA Terence Louis, b. 10 Feb 1950, Yonkers, New York, USA. Physician. m. Linda Grabbe PhD, 2 s, 1 d. Education: BA, Columbia University, USA, 1971; MD, State University of New York at Buffalo, USA, 1979; BA, Oxford University, England, 1975; MPH, University of North Carolina, 1988; MPA, Harvard University, USA, 1993. Appointments: Medical Epidemiologist, Centers for Disease Control, Atlanta, USA. Publications: Co-Author: Recent Changes in Longevity and Causes of Death Among Persons with Hemophilia A, 1994; The Role of Parvovirus B19 in Aplastic Crisis and Erythema Infectiosum, 1986. Memberships: American College of Physicians; American Public Health Association; Association for the Advancement of Automotive Medicine; Infectious Diseases Society of America. Address: Almaty (I D), Department of State, Washington DC 20521-7030, USA.

CHOU James Ching Yung, b. 4 Jun 1959, Philadelphia, PA, USA. Psychiatrist. m. Emily Yi Min Chen, 18 Jul 1981, 2 d. Education: MD. Appointments: Assistant Professor of Psychiatry, NY University; Research Psychiatrist, Nathan Kline Institute. Publications: Pass The Boards! Videotaped Psychiatry Oral Board Exams, videotape, 1992; Contributing Editor, Pocket Handbook of Emergency Psychiatric Medicine, 1993; Articles and book chapters published including: Co-author, Treatment Approaches for Acute Mania, in Psychiatric Quarterly, 1993. Memberships: American Psychiatric Association; American Medical Association. Address: Nathan Kline Institute, Orangeburg, NY 10962, USA.

CHOU Pesus, b. 9 Nov 1948, Taiwan, China. Professor. Education: DrPH, National Yang-Ming University, Taipei. Appointments: Director, Preparatory Office of the School of Public Health, Dean of Student Affairs, National Yang-Ming University. Publications include: Screening for Cervical Cancer in Taiwan from 1974-1984, Co-author, 1989; A Community-Based Screening for Liver, Cervical and Colorectal Cancer in Taiwan, 1990; Review on Risk Factors of Cervical Cancer, 1991; Community-Based Epidemiological Study on Diabetes in Pu-Li, Taiwan, Co-author, 1992; Review on Cervical Cancer Screening Programs in

Various Countries, Co-author, 1993; Parkinson's Disease in Kin-Hu, Kinmen: A Community Survey by Neurologists, Co-author, 1994. Honours: Outstanding Young Women in the Republic of China, 1984; Tulane Medical Alumni Association Student Recognition Award, 1985; Delta Omega, 1985; Honorary Citizen in Kinmen, 1992. Memberships: President, Chinese Society of Preventive Medicine. Address: National Yang-Ming University, Shih-Pai, Taipei, Taiwan.

CHOU Shelley Nien Chun, b. 6 Feb 1924, Chekiang, China. Neurosurgeon; Academic Administrator; Medical Educator. m. Jolene Johnson, 24 Nov 1956, 2 s, 1 d. Education: BS, St John's University, Shanghai, China, 1946; MD, University of Utah, 1949; MS, 1954, PhD, 1964, University of Utah. Career includes: Clinical Assistant, College Medical Univerity of Utah, 1956-58; Visiting Scientist, National Institutes of Neurological Diseases and Blindness, NIH, 1959; Faculty, 1960, Associate Professor, 1965-68, Professor, 1968-92, Head of Department of Neurosurgery, 1974-89, Professor Emeritus, 1992, Interim Dean of Medical School and Deputy Head for Medical Affairs, 1993-, University of Minnesota; American Board of Neurological Surgery, 1974-79; Research RVWCMT ACGME, 1984-90; Chairman, 1987-89. Publications: Numerous articles to professional journals; Publications on studies of intracranial lesions using radioactive angiography techniques, malformations of cerebral vasculature, neurological dysfunctions of urinary bladder. Memberships include: AMA; Graduate Medical Ed CMT, 1984-, Advisory Council Neurosurgery, 1981-87, ACS; Congress Neurological Surgery; President, 1978-79, Society Neurological Surgeons; President Elect, 1985-86, President, 1986-87, American Academy of Neurological Surgery; Society of Nuclear Medicine; Various offices, American Association of Neurological Surgeons; AAAS; PHI; RHO; Sigma. Address: D429 Mayo, 420 Delaware Street SE, Minneapolis, MN 55455-0374, USA.

CHOU Yi Je, b. 20 Dec 1939, Shang Dong, China. Professor of Ophthalmology. m. Gao Yin, 10 Mar 1970, 1 s. Education: BA, Qing Dao Medical College, 1965. Appointment: Director of Ophthalmology Department, Affiliated Hospital of Qing Dao Medical College. Publications: The effect of laser to liver carcinoma cell extrasomatic cultured, 1982; Study of the skill of treatment of eye diseases with laser, 1993; Study of the technique of two ways of retrobulbar anesthesia, 1993. Memberships: Shang Dong Medical Association; Shang Dong Ophthalmology Association. Hobby: Swimming. Address: Ophthalmology Department, Affiliated Hospital of Qing Dao Medical College, 16 Jiangsu Road, Qing Dao 266003, China.

CHOW Anthony W, b. 9 May 1941, Hong Kong. Physician. m. 20 May 1967, 2 sons. Education: MD; Fellowship in Infectious Diseases; FRCP (C); FACP. Appointments: Assistant Professor of Medicine, 1972-77, Associate Professor of Medicine, 1977-78, University of California, Los Angeles, USA; Professor of Medicine, University of British Columbia, Vancouver, Canada, 1979-. Publications: 298 scientific papers; 2 books; 157 abstracts. Honours: Canadian Infectious Diseases Society Award, 1984; Schering Fellowship Award, 1987, 1994; Academic Award for Scientific Achievement, Vancouver General Hospital, 1992; Canadian Institute of Academic Medicine, 1993; International Courvoisier Leadership Award, 1993. Memberships: Canadian Infectious Disease Society; Infectious Disease Society of America; American Society of Microbiology; Western Society for Clinical Research; Western Association of Physicians. Hobbies: Cycling; Tennis. Address: Division of Infectious Diseases, Department of Medicine, G F Strong Research Laboratory, Vancouver Hospital and Health Sciences Centre, Rm 452, D Floor, 2733 Heather Street, Vancouver, BC, Canada V5Z 3J5.

CHRETIEN Jacques, b. 23 Jan 1922, Ciré d'Aunis, France. Professor. m. Paule Lequitte, 31 July 1945, 3 sons, 2 daughters. Education: Faculty of Medicine, Paris; FRCP London. Appointments: Non-Resident, 1946; Resident, 1949, Assistant, 1959, Physician, 1963, Hospitals of Paris; Professor of Medicine, 1961; Physician, Centre hospitalier de Créteil, 1970; Professor, Pneumophtisiology Clinic, 1976; Physician, Laennec Hospital, 1976; Member, National Academy of Medicine, France; Ex-Executive Chairman, IUATLD. Honour: Croix de Guerre. Hobbies: Painting; Music. Address: 286 Boulevard Raspail, F-75014 Paris, France.

CHRISTENSON Randall Mark, b. 29 Dec 1951, Wichita, KS, USA. Psychiatrist. m. Anne Louise Meyer. 20 Oct 1979, 2 s, 2 d. Education: BA, Bethany College, 1973; MD, Creighton University, 1978. Career: Senior Staff Psychiatrist, 1983-93, Chief of Medical Staff, 1987-91,

Currently, Program Director, Older Adult Program, Pine Rest Christian Hospital; Clinical Assistant Professor, 1983-90, Clinical Associate Professor, 1990-, Michigan State University College of Human Medicine. Publications: Co-author, Reactivation of Traumatic Conflicts, in American Journal of Psychiatry, 1981; Epidemiology of Persecutory Ideation in an Elderly Community Population, in American Journal of Psychiatry, 1984; Assessing Pathology in Separation - Individuation Process by Inventory, in The Journal of Nervous Mental Disease, 1985. Honour: Fellow, American Psychiatric Association, 1994. Memberships: American Psychiatric Association; American Association for Geriatric Psychiatry; Kent County Medical Society; Michigan State Medical Society; Michigan Psychiatric Society. Hobbies: Flower Gardening; Walking. Address: 300 68th Street SE, Grand Rapids, MI 49501-0165, USA.

CHRISTIAN Joe Clark, b. 12 Sep 1934, Marshall, OK, USA. Physician. m. Shirley Yancey, 6 May 1960, 2 s. Education: BS, OK State University, 1956; MS, 1959, PhD, 1960, MD, 1964, University of KY. Career: Assistant Professor, Associate Professor, Professor, 1966-94, Currently Professor and Chairman, Department of Medical and Molecular Genetics, IN University School of Medicine. Memberships: American Society of Human Genetics; Research Society on Alcoholism. Hobby: Farming. Address: 975 West Walnut Street, Room 130, Indianapolis, IN, 46202-5251, USA.

CHRISTOPHER John Chambers, b. 29 Mar 1962, Baltimore, Maryland, USA. Counselling Psychologist. Education: AB, University of Michigan; MEd, Harvard University, 1987; PhD, University of Texas, 1992; APA Internship, University of Missouri Counselling Centre. Appointments: Assistant Professor of Counselling, University of Guam. Publications: The Influence and Early Experience on Personality development, Co-author, 1994; The Persistence of Basic Mistakes, Co-author, 1994; Splitting Kernberg, Co-author, 1992; Social Theory as Practice, Co-author, 1994. Honour: University Fellowship, University of Texas, 1988. Memberships: American psychological Association; American Anthropological Association. Hobbies: Hiking; Scuba Diving; Cycling; Yoga. Address: College of Education, University of Huam, Mangilao, Guam 96923, USA.

CHRYSANTHOPOULOS Chris, b. 17 Sep 1939, Greece. Physician. m. Tina Sarafuanou, 28 Aug 1971, 2 daughters. Education: MD; PhD. Appointments: Assistant Professor, Medical College of Wisconsin, USA; Director, Allergy Department, PED, DPT, MCV, USA; Professor of Technological Institute, Greece; Assistant Professor, Medical School, Salonica. Publications: Pediatrics: Primary Care; Contributor of professional articles. Memberships: FAAP; FAAA; Greek Paediatric Association; Greek Allergy Association. Address: Agia Sofias 213, Salonica-Macedonia, 54623 Greece.

CHU Chia-Ming, b. 9 Sept 1951, Taichung, China. Physician. m. Meei-Yue Tung, 1 June 1983, 1 son, 1 daughter. Education: MD, National Taiwan University. Appointments: Attending Physician, Chang Gung Memorial Hospital; Lecturer, China Medical College; Associate Professor, Chang Gung Medical College; Chief, Division of Hepatogogy, Chang Gung Memorial Hospital; Professor and Chairman, Department of Internal Medicine, Ghang Gung Memorial Hospital, Chang Gung Medical College. Publications: Over 100 papers, mostly related to acute and chronic hepatitis published in journals including Gastroenterology, Hepatology, Gut, Dig Dis Sci, Cell Immunol, J Clin Pathol. Honours: Research Award, National Science Council of China, 1987-94. Memberships: International Association for the Study of Liver; Asia-Pacific Association for the Study of Liver; The Gastroenterological Society of Taiwan. Hobbies: Travel; Chinese Chess. Address: Liver Unit, Chang Gung Memorial Hospital, 199 Tung Hwa North Road, Taipei, Taiwan 10591.

CHU Ren-jun, b. 8 Feb 1931, Rongchen County, China. Professor of Gastroenterology. m. Li Chang-tai, 26 June 1956, 5 sons. Education: BS, The Sixth Military Medical College, 1956; Advanced Study, Tianjing Haematology Research Institute, 1959; Advanced Study, Gastroenterology and Cardiovascular Disease, Zhongshang Hospital, Shanghai First Medical University, 1962-63; Advanced Study, Sichuan Chinese Traditional Medicine Institute, 1980. Appointments: Professor of Gastroenterology, Director, Department of Gastroenterology, Chengdu General Hospital. Publications: Result Analysis of Fibrogastroscopic Examination to 1562 Cases, 1986; Study on Clinical Significance of Slight Hyperbilirubinemia/GPT (Glutamic-Pyruvic Transaminase) Raising, 1987; Report on 2579 Cases of Gastric Ulcer and Duodenal

Ulcer by Endoscopic Examination at Different Elevations, 1990; A Study of the Liver Cancer-Associated Antigen HAg18-1 ELA Kit Applied in Patients with Hepatocellular Carcinoma, 1991; Endoscopic Radiofrequency Therapy for upper Gastroenterologic Diseases, 1993. Memberships: Vice Head, Gastroenterology Branch of Sichuan, China Medical Association; Standing Member, PLA Association of Gastroenterology; Sichuan Association of the Combination of Chinese Traditional and Western Medicine. Hobbies: Growing fragrant Thoroughwort; Football. Address: Department of Gastroenterology, Chengdu General Hospital, Tian Hui Town, Chengdu, Sichuan 610083, China.

CHU Taiming, b. 20 June 1960, China. Teacher; Researcher. Education: BS; MS; PhD, College of Engineering, University of Akron, Ohio, USA. Appointments: Teaching Assistant, Department of Mathematics; Technical Assistant, Engineering Computer Graphics Facility; Research Assistant, Institute of Biomedical Engineering Research; Postdoctoral Research Fellow, Institute of Polymer Engineering Research; Postdoctoral Research Fellow, Institute of Rehabilitation Engineering Research, Houston, Texas. Publications: Three Dimensional Finite Element Stress Analysis of Polypropylene Ankle-Foot Orthosis: Static Analysis, 1995; A Lumped Parameter Mathematical Modeling of Splanchnic Circulation, 1992. Honours: Honorary membership, Sigma Xi; Sigma Xi GIAR Biomedical Research Award. Memberships: ASME; BMES; ASEE; ACRM; RESNA; AAUP; CAST. Hobbies: Music; Swimming. Address: 28 Queensbridge Drive, East Hanover, NJ 07936, USA.

CHU Xiu Zhen, b. 20 Nov 1964, Shanghai, China. Clinician. m. Huruixin Chu, 7 Sep 1990. Education: BA, Shanghai Medical University, China. Appointment: Clinician of Anesthesia, Cancer Hospital, Shanghai Medical University. Publication: Analysis for blood in operating. Memberships: International Association for Study of Pain; Chinese Association for Study of Pain. Address: Department of Anesthesia, Cancer Hospital, Shanghai Medical University, 399 Lin Lin Road, Shanghai 200032, China.

CHUANG De-Maw, b. 12 Oct 1942, Tainan, Taiwan. Pharmacologist. m. KLin-Whei L Chuang, 8 June 1968, 2 sons. Education: BS, Oharmacy; PhD, Biochemistry. Appointments: Postdoctoral Fellow, Roche Institute of Molecular Biology, Nutley, New Jersey, USA, 1971-73; Staff Fellow, Laboratory of Preclinical Pharmacology, NIMH, 1974-77; Chief, Section on Molecular Neurobiology, NIMH, Bethesda, Maryland. Publications: Contributor of articles in professional journals. Honours: Invited Speaker to numerous international symposia; Invited Reviewer for several scientific journals. Memberships: American Society for Pharmacology and Experimental Therapeutics; American Society of Biological Chemistry and Molecular Biology; Society for Neuroscience. Hobbies: Dancing; Playing Tennis. Address: 6909 Bright Avenue, McLean, VA 22101, USA.

CHUANG Tsu-Yi, b. 21 May 1946, Amoy, China. Physician. m. Lydia Chuang, 22 Dec 1973, 1 son, 1 daughter. Education: BMed (equivalent to MD); MPH; Diploma of Dermatology; Diploma of Preventive Medicine. Appointments: Assistant Professor of Dermatology, 1984, Associate Professor of Dermatology, 1990, University of Wisconsin, Madison, USA; Associate Professor of Dermatology, 1990, currently Professor of Dermatology, Wright State University, Dayton, Ohio. Publications: Parasitic Diseases of the Skin, 1992; Puva and Skin Cancer, 1992; Keratoacanthoma in Kauai, Hawaii, 1993. Honours: Badge of Honour for Outstanding Student, National Taiwan University, 1969; Special Lecturer Awards, Chinese Dermatological Society, 1985, 1987, 1989, 1991. Memberships: American Academy of Dermatology; American College of Preventive Medicine; Society for Epidemiologic Research; Society for Investigative Dermatology. Hobbies: Stamp collection; Basketball; Pop music. Address: 702 Grants Trail, Centerville, OH 45459, USA.

CHUDWIN David Scott, b. 11 July 1950, Chicago, USA. Assistant Professor of Allergy. m. Claudia Chudwin, 1 Oct 1983, 1 son, 1 daughter. Education: BS, 1972, MD, 1976, University of Michigan; Fellowship, Immunology, University of California, San Francisco, 1979-82. Appointments: Private Practice, Allergy Consultant; Assistant Professor of Immunology, Rush Medical College, Chicago. Publications include: Activiation of the Alternative Complement Pathway by Red Blood Cells from Patients with Sickle Cell Disease, 1994. Honour: Fellow, American Academy of Allergy and Immunology, 1990. Memberships: American Association of Immunologists; American

Academy of Allergy and Immunology; American College of Allergy. Address: 500 Skokie BOulevard, Suite 140, Northbrook, IL 60062, USA.

CHUNG Sheung-Chee Sydney, b. 29 Oct 1954, Hong Kong. Surgeon. m. 14 Aug 1982, 2 d. Education: MD (CUHK); FRSC(Ed); FRCS(Glas); MRCP(UK); MB BCh; BAO; LRCPI; LRCSI. Appointments include: Team Head, Department of Surgery, 1987-, Surgeon-in-Charge, Combined Ulcer Clinic, 1985-, Consultant in Gastroenteric Surgery, 1988-, Director, Endoscopy Centre, The Chinese University of Hong Kong, 1991-, Professor of Surgery, The Chinese University of Hong Kong, 1994-, Prince of Wales Hospital, Shatin. Publications include: Practical Management of Acute Gastrointestinal Bleeding, Co-author; Contributor of numerous professional book chapters, papers, abstracts and letters; Several professional video tapes. Honours include: Francisco Roman Memorial Lecturer, Philippines Society of Gastroenterology and Philippines Society of Gastrointestinal Endoscopy, 1993; J Mitra Orator, Society of Gastrointestinal Endoscopy of India, 1993; Abraham Colles Medal, Royal College of Surgeons in Ireland, Dublin, 1993; Visiting Professor to several Institutions. Memberships include: Secretary, 1992-, Hong Kong Society of Digestive Endoscopy; American Society of Gastrointestinal Endoscopy, 1992-; Society of American Gastrointestinal Endoscopic Surgeons; Hong Kong Society of Gastroenterology. Address: Department of Surgery, The Chinese University of Hong Kong, Prince of Wales Hospital, Shatin, Hong Kong.

CHURCH William Kimball, b. 13 Dec 1926, Spokan, Washington, USA. Osteopathic Physician. m. Rosemary Heath, 7 Aug 1947, 3 s, 1 d. Education: BSc, Northeast Missouri State University; DO, Kirksville College of Osteopathic Medicine; Doctor of Osteopathy. Appointments: President, Ontario Osteopathic Association; Secretary/Treasurer, Ontario Osteopathic Association; Private Practice of Osteopathy. Publications: Articles in Health Magazine; DQ Magazine; Journal of American Osteopathic Association. Memberships: American Osteopathic Association; Canadian Osteopathic Association; Ontario Osteopathic Association. Hobbies: Sailing; Drawing; Painting; Skiing; Golf. Address: 93 Neywash Street, Orillia, Ontario L3V 1X4, Canada.

CIACCIO Thomas J, b. 28 May 1939, Brooklyn, New York, USA. Physician. Education: MD. Appointment: Staff, Ob-Gyn, Kaiser Hospital. Memberships: Los Angeles County Ob-Gyn Society; Fellow, American College Ob-Gyn. Address: CA, USA.

CICCONE J Richard, b. 21 Mar 1943, New York, USA. Psychiatrist. m. Natalie A Caputo, 2 sons, 1 daughter. Education: AB, Columbia University, 1963; MD, University of Pittsburgh, 1968. Appointments: Instructor, 1972; Assistant Professor, 1974-80; Associate Professor, 1980-89; Professor of Psychiatry, 1989-. Publications: Forensic Psychiatry and applied Clinical Ethics: Theory and Pracitce, 1983; About 46 papers and book chapters. Memberships: American Psychiatric Association; American Academy of Psychiatry & Medical Law. Honours: AAPL Silver Apple, 1987; Pollacik Award, 1993. Address: University of Rochester Medical Center, 300 Crittenden Blvd, Rochester, NY 14642-0001, USA.

CLARE Geoffrey R, b. 5 Jul 1917, Kingsdown, Kent, UK. Medical Practitioner. m. Dr Lenorah Attkins, 12 Jun 1945, 1 s. Education: MRCS; LRCP; D OBST; K COG; FRCOG; FRACOG. Appointments: HS, St Mary;s Hospital, London; Surgeon Lieutenant, RNUR; Queen Charlottes Hospital, London; University College Hospital, London; Alfred Hospital Melbourne; Queen Victoria Hospital, South Australia; Now Retired. Memberships: Royal Australian College of Obstetricians & Gynaecologists, Australia. Address: Unit 2, 8 Clarke Street, Bowral, NSW 2576, Australia.

CLARK Beverly Wyone Babst, b. 10 Sept 1948, Seattle, Washington, USA. Nutritionist; Administrator. m. Barry Allan Clark, 30 Dec 1978, 1 son, 2 daughters. Education: BS, Foods and Nutrition; MPH, Nutrition; Registered Dietitian. Appointments: Dietary Consultant, 7 convalescent hospitals; Instructor, Home Economics, San Jose College, California; Nutritionist, Contra Costa County; CARE Nutritionist; WIC Director and Nutritionist for Alameda and Contra Costa Counties; Public Health Programme Specialist II. Memberships: Bay Region Dietetic Association; California Dietetic Association; American Dietetic Association; California WIC Association. Hobbies: Travel; Doll collecting; Swimming; Walking. Address: 400 Read Drive, Lafayette, CA 94549, USA.

CLARK Michael Robert, b. 13 Jun 1960, IA, USA. Assistant Professor. m. Kyle Jacqueline Zimmer, 18 Apr 1987. Education: BS, High Distinction, Biochemistry, University of IA, 1982; MD, WA University School of Medicine, St Louis, MO, 1986; MPH, Epidemiology, University of WA School of Public Health, Seattle, 1992. Career includes: Acting Instructor, Psychiatry and Senior Research Fellow, University of WA Medical Center, Seattle, 1990-92; Currently, Assistant Professor, Psychiatry, Department of Psychiatry and Behavioural Sciences, Johns Hopkins Medical Institutions. Publications include: Psychiatric and Medical Factors Associated with Disability in Patients with Dizziness, 1992, in press; Chronic Fatigue: Predictors of Persistent Symptoms in a Three-Year Follow-Up Study, 1993, in press; The Relevance of Psychiatric Research on Somatization to the Concept of Chronic Fatigue Syndrome, 1993, in press. Memberships: International Association for Study of Pain; American Pain Society; Academy of Psychosomatic Medicine; American Psychosomatic Society; American Psychiatric Association; MD Psychiatric Society. Address: Meyer 4-181, Department of Psychiatry and Behavioural Sciences, The Johns Hopkins Hospital, 600 North Wolfe Street, Baltimore, MD 21287-7481, USA.

CLARK Orlo Herrick, b. 7 Aug 1941, Brooklyn, New York, USA. Surgeon. m. Carol Zeller, 22 Aug 1964, 1 son, 2 daughters. Education: BA, Cornell University, Ithaca, New York, 1963; MD, Cornell Medical College, New York City, 1967; Surgical Residency, University of California, San Francisco, 1967-70, 1971-73; Registrar, Endocrine Surgery, Royal Postgraduate Medical Centre, London, England, 1970-71. Appointments: Assistant Professor, Associate Professor, currently Professor, Vice-Chair, Department of Surgery, University of California, San Francisco; Staff Surgeon, Veterans Administration Medical Center, San Francisco; Currently Chief of Surgery, Mt Zion Medical Center, University of California, San Francisco. Honours: President, San Francisco Surgical Association; President, Northern California Chapter, American College of Surgeons; President, American Association of Endocrine Surgeons, 1993-94; President Elect, International Association of Endocrine Surgeons, 1994-95. Memberships include: Society of University Surgeons; American Surgical Society; Pacific Coast Surgical Society; Western Surgical Society; International Society of Surgeons; SSO; SHNS; Western Society of Clinical Investigators; Endocrine Society; ASBMR; ASCR. Hobbies: Tennis; Gardening; Music. Address: UCSF/Mount Zion Medical Center, 1600 Divisadero Street, San Francisco, CA 94115, USA.

CLARK Robert Roy, b. 23 Mar 1945, Winchester, Massachusetts, USA. Clinical Psychology. m. Lynn Monahan, 7 June 1975, 1 son, 1 daughter. Education: AB cum laude, Social Relations, Harvard University, 1967; PhD, Clinical Psychology, Columbia University, 1974. Appointments: Group Therapist, Butabika Mental Hospital, Kampala, Uganda, 1967-68; Director of Smoking Cessation, American Health Foundation, 1972-79; Consultant, Fortune Society for Exoffenders, 1979-89; Private Practice; Adjunct Clinical Supervisor, Yeshira University. Publications: Smoking: A Social Interaction Theory of Cigarette Smoking and Quitting, 1977; African Healing and Western Psychotherapy, 1982; The Socialzation of Clinical Psychologists, 1973. Honours: Rotary Fellowship for Study Abroad, 1967-68; National Institute for Mental Health Fellowships, 1969-72. Memberships: American Psychological Association; Society for the Psychological Study of Social Issues. Hobbies: Forestry; Running; Sports. Address: 295 Central Park West, New York, NY 10024, USA.

CLARKE Cyril Astley, b. 22 Aug 1907, Leicester, England. Consultant Physician. m. Frieda Margaret Mary Hart, 27 Dec 1935, 3 sons. Education: MD, ScD, Cambridge University; FRCP London; FRCP Edinburgh; FRS London, 1970; FRSE; 10 Honorary ScD, Edinburgh, Leicester, East Anglia, Birmingham, Liverpool, Sussex, Hull, Wales, London, College of William and Mary, Williamsburg, USA. Appointments: House Physician, Guy's Hospital, 1932; Medical Specialist, RNVR, 1939-46; Medical Registrar, Queen Elizabeth Hospital, Birmingham, 1946; Consultant Physician, United Liverpool Hospitals, 1946-72; Professor of Medicine, Liverpool, 1965-72; Retired. Publications: Genetics for the Clinician, 1962; Selected Topics in Medical Genetics, Editor, 1969; Human Genetics and Medicine, Co-author, 1970, 3rd edition, 1987; Prevention of Rhesus Haemolytic Diseases, 1972; Rhesus Haemolytioc Disease, Selected Papers and Extracts, 1975; Contributor of articles in medical and scientific journals. Honours: Gairdner Prize, 1977; Lasker Prize, 1980; Artois Baillet Latour Prize, 1981; Buchanan Medal, Royal Society, 1990. Hobbies: Entomology; Sailing small boats. Address: 43 Caldy Road, West Kirby, Wirral L48 2HF,Enfgland.

CLARKE Paul Stephen, b. 27 Jul 1914, Enniskillen, Northern Ireland. Physician. m. Madeline Widdas, 14 Feb 1948. Education: MBBS; FRACGP; FRCGP; FAAAI; FACAI. Career: Chief Medical Officer, Tingri Medical Association; Visiting Specialist Allergy, Royal Hobart Hospital, Specialist Allergist, Veteran's Affairs; Private Practice now retired. Publications: 28 publications including: Serological (Schultz-Dale) Test for Carcinoma, in Medical Journal of Australia, 1964; Dangers of Immunotherapy for the treatment of asthma in children, in Medical Journal of Australia, 1990; Peak Flow Charts Replace the Stethoscope in the Diagnosis and Management of Asthma, in Journal of Allergy and Clinical Immunology, 1992. Honour: Winner, Faulding Memorial Prize, 1970. Memberships: British Medical Association; Australian Medical Association; Australasian Thoracic Society; Australian Society Clinical Immunology and Allergy. Hobbies: Wining and Dining; Sailing; Trout Fishing. Address: 15 Amaroo Drive, Buderim, Queensland, Australia, 4556.

CLAUSEN Robert William, b. 18 Jun 1947, Englewood, NJ, USA. Physician. m. Barbara Ann Kraemer, 3 Aug 1975, 1 d. Education: BSc, Valparaiso University; MBBS, Kasturba Medical College, University of Mysore, India, 1974. Appointments include: Attending Physician, Memorial Hospital and St Joseph's Medical Center, South Bend, IN, 1982-; Guest Assistant Professor, Biological Sciences, University of Notre Dame, IN, 1984-; Clinical Assistant Professor of Medicine, IN University School of Medicine, South Bend Center for Medical Education, Notre Dame, IN, 1986-; Course Director, Immunology and Allergy, IN University Senior Student Elective, St Joseph's Medical Center, South Bend, IN, 1986-. Publications: Many articles, abstracts, and scientific presentations including: Venom in the Treatment of Insect Sting Allergy, in Hospital Formulary, 1981; Allergic Reactions to Insect Stings - A Clinical Review, in Journal of Family Practice, 1982; Co-author, Immune Complex-mediated Disease not a factor in patients on maintainance immunotherapy, in Journal of Allergy Clinical Immunology, 1983. Honours include: Pi Delta Epsilon, 1967; Anatomy Honorary Club, Kasturba Medical College, India, 1969; Fellowship, American College of Allergy and Immunology, 1983, American College of Physicians, 1984, American Academy of Allergy and Immunology, 1985; Lutheran Academy for Scholarship, 1985; Distinguished Alumni Award, Kasturba Medical College, 1989. Memberships include: AMA; Clinical Immunology Society; Association of Indian Physicians of America; National Hospice Organization. Hobbies: Music; Hiking; Fishing; Racquetball; Train Spotting. Address: Allergy and Clinical Immunology, The South Bend Clinic, 211 North Eddy Street at LaSalle, South Bend, IN 46634-1755, USA.

CLEARY Paul D, b. 14 May 1948, Toronto, Canada. Professor. m. Cynthia F Barnett, 20 May 1982, 1 s, 1 d. Education: BS; MS; PhD. Appointments: Assistant, Associate Professor and Graduate, School of Social Work, Rutgers University, 1979-82; Assistant, Professor, Department Health care Policy, Harvard Medical School, 1982-. Publications: The Three Mile Island Nuclear Accident: Population Impact, Co-author, 1988; Contributor of numerous professional articles, abstracts, book reviews, papers and reports. Memberships: American Sociologic Association; American Association Advancement of Science; American Public Health Association; American Association Health Service Research. Hobbies: Flying; Scuba Diving. Address: Department of Health Care Policy, Harvard Medical School, 25 Shattuck Street, Boston, MA 02115, USA.

CLEMENT Peter, b. 11 Nov 1941, Belgium. Physician. div, 2 sons. Education: MD, University of Brussels; ENT Training, University of Amsterdam, 1967-70. Appointments include: ENT Specialist, Municipal Hospitals, Brussels; Professor of Otorhinolaryngology, Free University of Brussels; Head, ENT Department, Free University of Brussels, 1979-. Publications include: Objectivation of the Therapeutic Effect of Aerosol Therapy in Allergic Rhinopathy. Summary, Co-author, 1973; Rhinomanometry and Nasal Provocation, Co-author, 1975; ENT Diseases of Allergic Origin, 1978; Allergic origin, 1979; The Use of a Mathematical Model in Rhinomanometry, 1980; Conservative Treatment of Sinusitis in Children, 1981; The Diagnostic Value of a Cytogram in Rhinopathology, Co-author, 1981; Nasal Provocation Testing Held Safe and Reliable; The Management of Seanosal Rhinitis, 1986; The Influence of Formaldehyde on the Nasal Mucosa, Co-author, 1987; CT-Scan of the Incidence of Sinus Involvement and Nasal Anatomic Variations in 196 Children, Co-author, 1990; Symposium 4 Rhinomanometry, 1992. Memberships include: Royal Society of Medicine; Secretary general, Treasurer, International Rhinologic Society; Council for International Organisations of Medical Sciences; Board

Member, Medical Trends; Board Member, Journal of Head and Neck Pathology. Hobbies: Scuba Diving; Astronomy. Address: Prof P. Clement, ENT Departement, AZ-VUB, Laarbeeklaan 101, 1080 Brussels, Belgium.

CLOSE Benjamin, b. 2 Jan 1961, California, USA. Physician. m. Karen Mimi, 13 Aug 1983, 1 son, 1 daughter. Education: BS, 1983, MD, 1987, Louisiana State University. Appointments: Private Practice, 1992-. Honours: Board Certified, Internal Medicine, 1990; Board Certified, Allergy and Immunology, 1993. Memberships: AMA; American Academy of Allergy and Immunology' American College of Allergy and Immunology; American College of Physicians. Hobbies: Sport; Reading. Address: 3311 Prescott Road, Suite 210, Alexandria, LA 71303, USA.

CLOUGH Anne Virginia, b. 13 Jan 1959, Cambridge, Massachusetts, USA. University Professor. m. Peter J Tonellato, 28 Dec 1985, 2 sons. Education: BSc, Mathematics, McGill University, Montreal, Canada, 1981; PhD, Applied Mathematics, University of Arizona, 1986. Appointments: Visiting Associate Professor, Center for Bioengineering, University of Washington, Seattle; Currently Associate Professor of Mathematics and Biomedical Engineering, Marquette University, Milwaukee, Wisconsin. Publications: An Algorithm for Angiographic Estimation of Blood Vessel Diameter, 1991; Regional Transit Time Estimation from Image Residue Curves, 1994. Memberships: Society for Industrial and Applied Mathematics; Biomedical Engineering Society; Review Board, Annals of Biomedical Engineering Society. Hobbies: Skiing; Hiking. Address: Department of Mathematics, Marquette University, PO Box 1881, Milwaukee, WI 53201, USA.

COETZER Bernardus Rudolf, b. 27 Nov 1962, Cape Town, South Africa. Clinical Psychologist. m. Susan Meyer, 6 Oct 1990. Education: BA with distinction, 1984; BA (Hons) with distinction, Clinical Psychology, 1985; MA with distinction, Clinical Psychology, 1987. Appointments: Clinical Psychologist, South African Medical Services, 1988-89; Psychologist, Old Mutual Group Schemes and part-time private practice, 1990-92; Currently Clinical Psychologist, Lecturer, Stikland Hospital and University of Stellenbosch. Memberships: Registered Clinical Psychologist, South African Medical and Dental Council; International Council of Psychologists; British Psychological Society. Hobbies: Photography; Running. Address: Department of Psychiatry, University of Stellenbosch, Faculty of Medicine, PO Box 19063, Tygerberg, 7505 South Africa.

COFFMAN Sandra Jeanne, b. 31 May 1945, San Antonio, Texas, USA. Psychologist. m. David W Hutchinson, 2 sons. Education: BA, English & French, Purdue University, 1967; MA, International Studies, The American University, 1969; PhD, University of Washington, 1978. Appointments: Clinical Supervisor, Psychologist, University of Washington and NIMH, Seattle, 1984-87; Clinical Associate Professor, University of Washington, Seattle, 1988-; Clinical Consultant, Eastside Domestic Violence Project, Bellevue, Washington, 1987-; Co-Director, Women's Counseling Group, Seattle, 1981-90. Publications: Co-author: Talking It Out, 1984; a chapter in:- Social Learning-Based Earital Therapy and Cognitive Therapy as a Combined Treatment for Depression; Co-author: You Don't Have To Take It!, 1993. Memberships: American Psychological Association; Feminist Therapy Institute; Association for the Advancement of Behavior Therapy. Address: 2003 Western Avenue #340, Seattle, WA 98121-2114, USA.

COGGAN Ruth Evelyn, b. 8 Jul 1940, Toronto, Canada. Gynaecologist. Education: MB; CLB; FRCOG. Appointments: Gynaecologist, Pennell Memorial Hospital, Bawnu, NWFP, Pakistan; Gynaecologist, Bach Christian Hospital, P O Qalanderabad, Pakistan. Honours: OBE, 1981; SQA, 1983. Memberships: Royal College of Obstetricians & Gynaecologists. Hobbies: Music; Reading; Walking. Address: Bach Christian Hospital, P O Qalandarabad, District Hazara, Pakistan 22000.

COGILL Stephen Richard, b. 4 June 1946, Scarborough England. Group Analyst; Psychologist. m. Julie, 1 son, 2 daughters. Education: BA, Honours, Psychology; MPhil, Group Analysis Clinical Psychology; ABPsS; Member IGA. Appointments: Consultant Psychologist, University College Hospital; Chair, Institute of Group Analysis. Publications: Impact of Maternal Postnatal Depression on Cognitive Development of Young Children, 1986. Memberships: British Psychological Society; Group Analytic Society; Institute of Group Analysis. Hobbies: Cinema; Theatre; Sailing; Walking. Address: 60 Ranelagh Road, London W5 5RP, England.

COHEN Alfred Martin, b. 3 Nov 1941, New York, USA. Surgeon. m. Constance Hurley, 11 Sep 1983, 1 s, 1 d. Education: BA, Cornell University, 1963; MD, Johns Hopkins University Medical School, 1967. Appoinments include: Massachusetts General Hospital, 1976-86; Associate Member, 1986-89, Member, 1989-, Associate Attending Surgeon, Colorectal Service, 1986-89, Attending Surgeon, Colorectal Service, 1989-, Chief, Colorectal Service, 1986-, Department of Surgery, Memorial-Sloan Kettering Cancer Centre, New York City. Publications: Contributor of numerous professional articles, reports and abstracts. Honours include: Recipient of numerous Grants; Henry Strong Denison Scholar in Medical Research, Johns Hopkins University School of Medicine, 1966; James McLaughlin Research Award, Resident Fellow, Student American Medical Association, 1972; Ira Nathanson Scholar in Cancer Research, Massachusetts Division, American Cancer Society, 1976-86; Outstanding Teacher Award, MSKCC Surgical Fellows, 1990. Memberships include: Membership Committee, 1981-83, American Society of Clinical Oncology; Cancer Liaison, Commission on Cancer, American College of Surgeons, 1987-. Address: Memorial Sloan-Kettering Cancer Centre, 1275 York Avenue, New York, NY 10021, USA.

COHEN Chaim, b. 26 Oct 1955, Israel. Physician. m. Iris, 12 Aug 1979, 2 sons. Education: MD; MSc, Occupational Health; Board Certification in Occupational Medicine, American Board of Preventive Medicine. Appointments: Occupational Physician, Kupat Holim, Tel-Aviv District; Occupational Physician, Mor, Institute for Medical Data, Bnei-Brak; Clinical Scholar, University of Kentucky, Department of Preventive Medicine, USA. Publications: Liver Disease Following Occupational exposure to 1,1,1-trichloroethane, 1993; Arsenic Poisoning in Central kentucky, Co-author, 1993; Serum Copper Level in Gynecologic Malignancies, Co-author, 1987. Memberships: American College of Occupational Medicine; AMA; Israeli Medical Association; Israeli Society of Occupational Health Physicians. Hobby: Swimming. Address: 13 Vitkin Street, Tel-Aviv 63474, Israel.

COHEN Gerald N, b. 25 June 1929, Chicago, Illinois, USA. Physician. Education: MD; MS, Physiology; MA; Board Certified, Allergy, Clinical Immunology and Asthma. Honour: Alhpa Omega Alpha. Memberships: American Academy of Allergy, Fellow; American College of Allergy and Clinical Immunology, Fellow; American College of Chest Physicians, Fellow. Address: 1029 W Howard Street, Evanston, IL, USA.

COHEN Harvey Jay, b. 21 Oct 1940, Brooklyn, New York, USA. Professor of Medicine, Director. m. Sandra Helen Levine, June 1964, 1 son, 1 daughter. Education: BS, Brooklyn College, 1961; MD, Downstate Medical Center, State University of New York, 1965. Appointments incl: Chief Medical Service, 1976-82; Associate Chief Staff of Education, 1982-84; Director of Geriatric Research, Education & Clinical Center, 1984-, VA Medical Center, Durham, North Carolina; Professor of Medicine 1980-, Director of Center for Aging 1982-, Duke University, Durham. Publications incl: Medical Immunology, 1977; An Approach to Monoclonal Gammopathies in the Elderly, 1982; Effect of Age on Response to Treatment and Survival in Multiple Myeloma, 1983; Comparison with Two Long-Term Chemotherapy Regimens, With or Without Agents to Modify Skeletal Repair, 1984; Aging and Neoplasia, 1984; Carbohydrate Metabolism in Transforming Lymphocytes from the Aged, 1985; The Essential Role of L-Glutamine in Lymphocyte Differentation in Vitro, 1985. Honours incl: Physicians Recognition Award, American Medical Association, 1984-87. Memberships: Fellow, American Geriatrics Society; American Society of Clinical Oncology; American Association of Hematology; American Association of Cancer Research; Alpha Omega Alpha; Fellow, American College of Physicians. Address: Center for the Study of Aging, Box 3003, Duke University Medical Center, Durham, NC 27710, USA.

COHEN Helen, b. 2 Feb 1954, New York City, New York, USA. Occupational Therapist; Neurobiologist. Education: BS, Occupational Therapy, Tufts University, Medford, Massachusetts, 1976; MA, Motor Learning, 1981, EdD, Motor Learning, 1986, Columbia University, New York City. Appointments: Occupational Therapist, Visiting Nurse Service, New York City, 1982-89; Research Association, Mt Sinai School of Medicine, New York City, 1985-89; Assistant Professor, Programme in Rehabilitation Science and Department of Otolaryngology, Medical College of Ohio, Toledo, 1989-91; Assistant Professor, Department of Otorhinolaryngology, Baylor College of Medicine, Houston, TX, 1991-. Publications: Vestibular rehabilitation reduces functional disability, 1992; Habituation and adaptation of the vestibulo-ocular reflex: a model of differential control by the

vestibulo-cerebellum (co-author), 1992; Neuroscience for Rehabilitation, 1993. Memberships: Barany Society; American Occupational Therapy Association; Society for Neuroscience; Association for Research in Otolaryngology. Hobbies: Sailing; Music; Knitting. Address: Department of Otorhinolaryngology, Baylor College of Medicine, One Baylor Plaza, Houston, TX 77030, USA.

COHEN I Kelman, b. 30 Mar 1935, New York, USA. Plastic Surgeon. m. Merna Sallop, 1 Jan 1993, 1 s, 1 d. Education: BS; MD; PhD with Honors. Appointments: Professor and Chairman, Plastic Surgery Medical College of Virginia, Virginia Commonwealth University, Richmond, Virginia. Honours: PhD Honors, Kenyon College, 1987; Distinguished Medical Alumni Award, University of North Carolina, School of Medicine, 1993. Address: Medical College of Virginia, MCV Station, Box 980154, Richmond, VA 23298, USA.

COHEN Kenneth David, b. 16 Mar 1928, Philadelphia, PA, USA. Physician. m. Ann Fedorka, 13 Mar 1955, 3 s. Education: BA; MD, University of Health Sciences, The Chicago Medical School, 1953; PHILA, University of Pennsylvania, 1949. Appointments: Clinical Director, Belmont Treatment Center, Philadelphia, 1973-80; Associate Director of Psychiatry, Presbyterian University of Pennsylvania Medical Center, 1980-83; Clinical Professor, Psychiatry, Department of Psychiatry, University of Pennsylvania, School of Medicine, 1991-; Private Practice, Psychiatry & Psychoanalysis. Publications: include, Significance of Illness to the Patient,1960; Post-Partum Psychosis following Pregnancy by Artificial Insemination, 1966; Doctor-Patient Relationship and Its Role in Compliance, 1980; A Verification of Freud's Grandest Clinical Hypothesis: The Transference, 1985; Orality and the Oedipus, 1987. Honours: include, Fellow, American Psychiatric Association, 1972; Fellow, College of Physicians of Philadelphia, 1978; Earl D Bond Award - Excellence in Education, 1988. Memberships: American Psychoanalytic Association; Philadelphia Association for Psychologists; American Psychiatric Association; Psychiatric Physicians of Pennyslvania; Philadelphia Psychiatrical Society; American Medical Association; Pennsylvanian Medical Society; Philadelphia County Medical Society. Address: Suite 116, 191 Presidential Boulevard, Bala Cynuyd, PA 19004, USA.

COHEN Sheldon G(ilbert), b. 21 Sep 1918, Pittston, Pennsylvania, USA. Physician; Medical Scientist. Education: BA, Syracuse University, 1936-37, Ohio State University, 1937-40; MD, New York University College of Medicine, 1943. Appointments include: Research Associate in Immunology, 1951-56, Associate Professor of Biological Research, 1957-62, Professor of Biological Research, 1962-68, Professor of Experimental Biology, 1968-72, Wilkes College, Pennsylvania; Adjunct Professor of Medicine, 1988-, Adjunct Professor of Paediatrics, 1989-91, Northwestern University, Chicago; Adjunct Professor of Immunology, Wilkes University School of Science and Engineering, 1992-; Medical Services, Chief of Allergy, 1951-72, Chairman, Committee on Medical School-Hospital Complex, 1972, Mercy Hospital, Wilkes-Barre, Pennsylvania; Scientific Advisor, National Institutes of Health. Publications include: The Chicken in History and in the Soup, 1991; Discovery and Rediscovery, 1992; Spain, Portugal, Christopher Columbus and the Jewish Physician, 1993; Fish In and Out of Water, Food, Toxins, Allergens, 1993; Immunologists Honored by Commemorative and Special Issues of Postage Stamps, Co-author, 1993; Discovery and Rediscovery (Part 2), 1993. Honours include: Distinguished Service Award, American Academy of Allergy, 1971; Distinguished Service Award, Asthma and Allergy Foundation of America, 1981; Achievement Award, International Association of Allergology and Clinical Immunology, 1988; Alumni Leadership Award, New York University School of Medicine, 1992. Memberships include: Association of American Physicians; American Association of Immunologists. Address: Solar Building, Room 2C37, National Institutes of Health, Bethesda, MD 20892, USA.

COHEN Theodore Benjamin, b. 4 Feb 1923, New York City, USA. Psychoanalyst. 1 son. Education: MA, Psychology, MD, University of Pennsylvania; Board Certified, Child and Adolescent Psycotherapy and Child and Adult Psychoanalysis. Appointments: Assistant, University of pennsylvania department of Psychiatry, 1952-60; Associate Professor, Temple University, 1956-90; Clinical Professor, Jefferson Medical School Department of Psychiatry, 1979-. Publications: The Vulnerable Child, Co-editor, 1993, volume 2, 1994; Vulnerable and High Risk Children, 1980. Honours: President, Regional Council of Child Psychiatry, 1974; Bnai brith Vocational Guidance Award, 1986. Memberships: International psychoanalysis Association; Israeli

Psychoanalytic Society; American Psychoanalytic Society; Philadelphia Psychoanalytic Society. Hobbies: Tennis; Snorkelling; Table Tennis. Address: 421 Hidden River Road, Narberth, PA 19072, USA.

COLBERT Charles, b. 19 Feb 1919, Minneapolis, Minnesota, USA. Medical Physicist. m. Rita Rubin, 4 Feb 1945, 3 s, 2 d. Education: BS, Electrical Engineering, 1940; PhD, Medical Physics, 1973. Appointments: Radio Engineer, US Army/US Air Force, 1941-54; Consulting Engineer, 1954-73; Founder & Chief Executive Officer, Wastgate Laboratories, 1956-62; Consulting Engineer, 1963-66; Director, Radiology Research Laboratory, 1966-85; Founder/Director, Foundation of Skeletal Health Research, Pres Engineering Corporation, 1985-; Associate Clinical Professor, Radiological Sciences, Wright State University, School of Medicine. Publications: Chapter Author, Radiographic Absorptiometry; Renal Osteodystrophy: Bone Mineral Loss and Recovery with Treatment, 1990. Honours: Eta Kappa Nu, National Honor Society for Achievement in Electrical Engineering, 1940; Dr Fritz Russ Award, Institute of Electrical & Electronic Engineers for Achievement in Bio-Engineering. Memberships: Institute of Electrical & Electronic Engineers; American Society of Artificial Internal Organs; American Association of Physicists in Medicine. Hobbies: Archaeology; Ancient History; Ancient Numismatics. Address: Foundation for Skeletal Health Research, Yellow Springs, Ohio 45387-0561, USA.

COLICE Gene, b. 1 May 1950, New York, NY, USA. Physician. m. Elizabeth O'Hare, 3 June 1973, 2 s, 1 d. Education: MD; FCCP. Appointments: Assistant Professor of Medicine, University of South Florida Medical School, 1982-85; Assistant Professor, Dartmouth Medical School, 1985-91; Associate Professor of Medicine, Dartmouth Medical School, 1991-93; Associate Consulting Professor of Medicine, Duke Medical School, 1994-; Associate Director, Pulmonary/Critical Care, Burroughs Welcome Company. Publications: Contributor of numerous professional articles and reviews including: Airway Effects of Low Concentrations of Sulfur Dioxide: Dose Response Characteristics, Co-author, 1984; An Unusual Cause of Unilateral Hyperlucent Lung, Co-author, 1988; Resolution of Laryngeal Injury Following Translaryngeal Intubation, 1992; Susceptibility to Monocrotaline and High Altitude Induced Pulmonary Hypertension in Two rat Strains, Co-author, 1994. Memberships: American Thoracic Society; American College of Chest Physicians, Fellow, 1983; American College of Physicians. Address: Burroughs Welcome Company, 3030 Cornwallis Road main Building, RTP, NC 27709, USA.

COLLAZOS GONZALEZ Julio, b. 11 Mar 1955, Tordehumos, Valladolid, Spain. Internist; Researcher. Education: MD, Complutense University, Madrid, 1978; Fellowship, Specialty in Internal Medicine, 1980-84, PhD with honours, 1990, Autonomous University, Madrid; Resident, Jimenez Diaz Foundation, Madrid, 1980-84. Appointments: Attending Physician, Provincial Hospital, Alicante, 1984-87; Attending Physician, Galdacano Hospital, Vizcaya, 1987-9; Chief, Infectious Diseases Section, Hospital de Galdacano. Publications: Tumour Markers in Benign Liver Diseases, Doctoral Thesis, 1990; Numerous scientific articles. Membership: New York Academy of Sciences. Hobbies: Sports; Computers; Photography. Address: Servicio de Medicina Interna, Hospital de Galdacano, 48960 Vizcaya, Spain.

COLLIER Gary James, b. 15 Jul 1947, USA. Professor. m. Bernadette Gillis, 9 Jun 1983, 2 s, 1 d. Education: BA, University of Massachusetts; MSC, University of Alberta; PhD, University of Alberta. Appointments: Research Associate, Department of Psychiatry, University of Alberta; Assistant Professor, St Mary's University, Hallifax; Assistant, Associate & Full Professor of Psychology, University College of Cape Breton. Publications: Emotional Expression; Currents of Thought in American Social Psychology; Social Origins of Mental Ability. Memberships: American Psychological Association. Hobbies: Running; Climbing; Canoeing; Skiing. Address: Department of Behavioural and Life Science, University College of Cape Breton, Sydney, Nova Scotia, Canada B1P 6LZ.

COLLINS Carol Fundak, b. Lorain, Ohio, USA. Physician. m. Daniel E Collins, 17 June 1978, 3 daughters. Education: MD; BS; MS; MPH. Appointments: Flight Surgeon, United Airlines; Chief Staff Physician, California Pacific medical Centre; Physician, Lawrence Berkeley Laboratory, Unviersity of California, Berkeley; Associate Physician, Ford Motor Company, Cleveland, Ohio. Honours: Board Certified, American Board of Preventive Medicine in Occupational Medicine, FACPM; Board Elected, American Board of Internal Medicine. Memberships: American College of Preventive Medicine, Fellow; American College of

Occupational and Environmental Medicine; American College of Physicians. Hobbies: Reading; Snow skiing; Miniature horses. ADdress: 29323 Regency Circle, Westlake, OH 44145, USA.

COLLINS Graham John, b. 31 Mar 1955, Chatham, England. Clinical psychologist. m. Jacqueline Wynne Davie3s, 28 Apr 1984, 1 son, 2 daughters. Education: MA, Cambridge University, 1977-81; MA, Sheffield University, 1978; MPsychol, Liverpool University, 1980. Appointments: Senior Clinical psychologist, Barnardo's NW, 1980-82; Clinical Psychologist, Head of Speciality, St Helens and Knowsley Health Authority, 1982-86; Consultant Clinical Psychologist, Central Nottinghamshire Healthcare (NHS) Trust, 1986-. Publications: foster Parents Teaching Programs, 1983; Evaluating Community Care, 1984; Moving From a Problem Ward to Staffed Flat, 1987; Staff Support, 1990. Memberships: Associate Fellow, British Psychological Society, Division of Clinical Psychology. Hobbies: Running; Wine making. Address: Clinical Psychology Services, Department of Clinical Psychology, Central Notts Healthcare Trust Headquarters, Southwell Road West, Mansfield, Nottinghamshire NG18 4HH, England.

COLLINS Ingrid Josephine, b. 30 Dec 1943, Leeds, Yorkshire, England. Consultant Chartered Educational Psychologist; Spiritual Healer. m. Malcolm M Collins, 30 Dec 1973. Education: BSc (Hons), Psychology, Manchester University; Diploma in Educational Psychology, London Child Guidance Training Centre; Advanced Consultation and Training in Community and Mental Health, Tavistock Institute, London. Appointments: Teacher, Leeds County Council, 1965-71; District Educational Psychologist, Surrey County Council, 1972; Consultant Educational Psychologist to Westminster County Council, 1983-88; Senior Career Educational Psychologist, Inner London Education Authority, 1986-90; Currently: Consultant Chartered Educational Psychologist in private practice; Visiting Lecturer, School of Teaching Studies, University of North London; Co-Director, Education Management Unit, Kensington Consultation Centre, London; Spiritual Healer. Publications: NESISEN Special Needs Training Programme (co-author), 1982; The Gift of Spiritual Healing, 1991; Soul Therapy, 1994. Honours: Honorary Consultant, Fitness on 5, London Hilton on Park Lane, Aug 1993. Memberships: Associate Fellow, British Psychological Society; Affiliate Member, Association of Educational Psychologists; Jewish Association of Spiritual Healers. Hobbies: Spending time with family, friends and pets; Theatre; Canal boat sailing; Fitness training; Arts. Address: 28 Fortismere Avenue, Muswell Hill, London N10 3BL, England.

COLLINS John Alfred, b. 2 Oct 1936, Kitchener, Ontario, Canada. Obstetrician and Gynaecologist. m. Carole Joanne Sedwick, 1 son, 2 daughters. Education: MD. Appointments: Clinical Research Fellow, Ontario Cancer Foundation London Clinic, 1967-76; Department of Obstetrics and Gynaecology, 1967-77, Assistant Dean of Undergraduate Education, Faculty of Medicine, 1975-77, University of West Ontario; Professor, Head of Obstetrics and Gynaecology, Dalhousie University, 1977-83; Professor, Chairman, Department of Obstetrics and Gynaecology, McMaster University, Hamilton, 1983-93. Publications: Author or co-author, various medical papers and publications. Memberships: Canadian Medical Association; Society of Obstetricians and Gynecologists, Canada; Canadian Fertility Society; American College of Obstetricians and Gynecologists; American Fertility Society; Royal College of Physicians and Surgeons, Canada. Address: 261 MacNab Street, Hamilton, Ontario, Canada L8P 3E2.

COLLINS Sara, b. 24 Nov 1946, Jerusalem. Psychoanalytic Psychotherapist. m. Lawrence A Collins, 6 July 1982, 1 son, 1 daughter. Education: BA, MSSc with distinction, Hebrew University, Jerusalem; Postgraduate Training in Community Mental Health, Fulbourn Hospital, Cambridge, England; Psychoanalytic Psychotherapy Training, British Association of Psychotherapists. Appointments: Head, Psychology Department, Chase Farm Hospital, Enfield, Middlesex; Psychoanalytic Psychotherapist, The Portman Clinic, Hampstead, London; Currently Clinical Tutor, Training Adviser, Freudian Training Committee, British Association of Psychotherapists. Publication: Repetitiveness and Boredom as a Challenge to Growth, 1985. Honours: British Council Scholarship for Postgraduate Training in Community Mental Health, 1975-76. Memberships: Full Member, British Association of Psychotherapists; British Confederation of Psychotherapists; Associate Fellow, British Psychological Society. Hobbies: Gardening; Cake design. Address: 102 South Hill Park, Hampstead, London NW3 2SN, England.

COLLINS William John Neilson, b. 25 Mar 1940, Scotland. Dental Surgeon. m. Vanda, 16 Oct 1963, 1 s, 2 d. Education: BDS, University of St Andrews; MSc, London; FDSRCPS, Glasgow; FETC; TD. Appointments: Dental Officer, Royal Army Dental Corps, 1963-79; Director, School of Dental Hygiene, Glasgow Dental Hospital, 1979-90; Chief Dental Officer, Northern Ireland, 1990-. Publications: Handbook for Dental Hygienists, 1992; Dental Hygienists Self-Assessment Manual, 1984; Guide to Periodontics, 1991. Honours: TD, 1993. Memberships: British Dentists Association; Irish Dentists Association; British Dentist & Hygienists Association; British Periodontal Society; British Association for Study of Community Dentistry. Hobbies: Golf. Address: Brucefield, Marjoribanks Street, Bathgate, West Lothian, EH48 1AH, Scotland.

COLMAN Michael D, b. 5 Dec 1942, Detroit, Michigan, USA. Psychoanalyst. m. Claire S Patt, 15 June 1980, 3 sons, 1 daughter. Education: MD; Graduate, Adult and Child/Adolescent Psychoanalytic Training Programmes, Michigan Psychoanalytic Institute. Appointments: Inpatient Programme Director, Children's Psychiatric Hospital, Ann Arbor, Michigan; Clinical Instructor, University of Michigan, Ann Arbor; Clinical Assistant Professor, Wayne State University, Department of Psychiatry, Detroit; Private Practice in Psychoanalysis and Psychotherapy with Adults and Children. Publications: Group Therapy for Physically Handicapped Toddlers with Delayed Speech and Language Development, 1976; The Residential Treatment of a Consciously Rejected Child, 1980. Honour: Alpha Omega Alpha. Memberships: American Psychoanalytic Association; Michigan Psychoanalytic Society; American Psychiatric Association; Michigan Psychiatric Society; Michigan State Medical Society. Hobbies: Travel; Swimming; Woodworking. Address: 2725 Endsleigh Drive, Bloomfield Township, MI 48301-2676, USA.

COLMORGEN Garrett Hubbard Chasey, b. 9 July 1951, New Jersey, USA. Physician. m. Martha Ann Zazzarino, 28 July 1979, 1 daughter. Education: BS, Centre College of Kentucky, 1969-73; MD, College of Medicine and Dentistry of New Jersey New Jersey Medical School, 1973-78. Appointments include: Assistant Professor, Obstetrics and Gynaecology, Jefferson Medical College, Philadelphia, 1985-; Director, Maternal-Foetal Medicine, department of Obstetrics and Gynaecology, 1986-, Chairman, Ambulatory Services Committee, Medical-Dental Staff, 1989-, Chairman, Obstetrics-Gynaecology Newborn Care Committee, 1990-, Medical Director, Outpatient Services Department, 1991-, Associate Attending Physician, Department of Obstetrics and Gynaecology, 1991-, Medical Centre of Delaware; ACOG Advisory Council, Delaware section, District 3, Wilmington, 1994-. Publications: Contributor of numerous professional articles and abstracts in professional and scientific journals. Honours include: Nelson Allen Chemistry Award, Centre College of Kentucky, 1973; hi Beta Kappa, 1973; Robert A MacKenzie Award in Obstetrics and Gynaecology, Monmouth Medical centre, 1982; Service Excellence award, Medical Centre of Delaware, 1993; Distinguished Service Award, Perinatal Association of Delaware, 1994. Memberships include: National Perinatal Association; Fellow, American College of Obstetricians and Gynaecologists; American Medical Association; Society of Perinatal Obstetricians. Address: Department dof Obstetrics-Gynaecology, Medical centre of Delaware, 4755 Stanton-Ogletown Road, PO Box 6001, Newark, DE 19718, USA.

COLOMBO John Louis, b. 9 Sep 1949, Omaha, Nebraska, USA. Physician. m. Marcia Lee Meredith, 10 Sep 1976, 1 daughter. Education: BA, Psychology, 1971; MD, 1975, Paediatric Residency, 1975-78, University of Nebraska Medical Centre; Fellowship, Pulmonology, Tulane University, 1978-81. Appointments: Associate Professor of Paediatrics. Publications: Injuries to Children with Chronic Lung Disease, 1985; Aspiration Lung Injury, 1993; Aspiration Syndromes: Pediatric Respiratory Medicine; Contributor of numerous articles in professional journals. Hobbies: Skiing; Writing; Golf. Address: 600 South 42nd Street, Box 985190, Omaha, NE 68198-5190, USA.

COLOVER Jack, b. 5 Sept 1913, London, England. Neurologist. m. Sarina Politi, 9 Mar 1952, 1 son, 1 daughter. Education: MD; FRCP; University College Hospital, London. Appointments: Squadron Leader, Royal Air Force; Consultant Neurologist, SE Thames Regional Neurological and Neurosurgical Units, The Brook Hospital, Woolwich, London; Professor of Neurology, Memorial University, Newfoundland, Canada; Currently Research Assistant, Department of Immunology, Rayne Institute, St Thomas Hospital, London. Publications: Various on sarcoidosis of the nervous system, chemistry of tubercle bacillus, experimental demyelination, multiple sclerosis, P2 myelin protein in spinal fluid, Cri-du-Chat syndrome, proteins of spinal fluid; Functional Dualism of the The Nervous System. Honours: Mentioned in despatches, Royal Air Force, 1943. Memberships: Association of British Neurologists; British Neuropathological Society; British Society of Immunology. Hobby: Fishing. Address: 56 Eyre Court, Finchley Road, London NW8 9TU, England.

COLTEN Harvey Radin, b. 11 Jan 1939, Houston, Texas, USA. Pediatrician; Educator. m. Susan J Kaplowitz, 29 Jul 1959, 1 s, 2 d. Education: BA, Cornell University, 1959; MD, Western Reserve University, 1963; MA (Honorary), Harvard University, 1978; Diplomate, American Board of Allergy & Clinical Immunology, American Board of Pediatrics, Intern-in-Pediatrics University Hospital, Cleveland, 1963-64; Resident in Pediatrics, 1964-65; Resident in Pediatrics, Children's Hospital of Washington DC, 1968-69. Appointments: Research Associate, National Insitute of Child and Human Development, NIH, Bethesda, Maryland, 1965-67; Assistant Professor, Pediatrics, George Washington University, 1969-70; Assistant Professor, Pediatrics, Harvard University, 1970-73; Associate Professor, 1973-79; Professor, 1979-86; Chief, Division of Cell Biology/Director, Cystic Fibrosis Program, Children's Hospital Medical Center, Boston, 1976-86; Harriet B Spoehrer Professor/Chairman, Department of Pediatrics, Washington University Medical School, St Louis, 1986-1995; Pediatrician-in-Chief, Children's and Barnes Hospitals, 1986-1995; Jewish Hospital, 1986-90; Harriet B Spoehrer Professor of Pediatrics, WA University School of Med, 1995-. Publications: Contributor of Articles to Professional Journals; Associate Editor of numerous journals including, Journal of Allergy & Clinical Immunology, 1977-80; Journal of Clinical Investigation, 1982-85; Journal of Immunology, 1971-74; New England Journal of Medicine, 1978-81. Honours: E Mead Johnson Award, 1979; Recipient, Spl Faculty Research Award, Western Reserve University, 1963. Memberships: include, American Academy of Allergy & Immunology; American Academy of Pediatrics; American Association for the Advancement of Science; American Association of Immunologists; American Pediatric Society; Institute of Medicine. Address: Department of Pediatrics; Washington University, School of Medicine, 1 Children's Place, St Louis, MO 63110, USA.

COLWELL John Amory, b. 4 Nov 1928, Boston, Massachusetts, USA. Physician. m. Jane Kuebler, 19 June 1954, 2 sons, 2 daughters. Education: AB, Princeton University, 1950; MD, 1954, PhD, 1968, Northwestern University Medical School. Appointments: residency, Internal Medicine, 1955-57, Fellowship, Endocrinology and Diabetes, 1960-63, Assistant to Associate Professor of Medicine, 1963-71, Northwestern University Medical School; Professor of Medicine, 1971-, Director, Endocrinology Diabetes Metabolism Division, Medical University of South Carolina. Publications: Contributor of over 100 scientific articles, 2 books and 40 book chapters in medical scientific literature, mainly on diabetes and its vascular complications. Honours: President, 1987-88, Banting Award, 1988, Outstanding Physician Educator, 1992, American Diabetes Association. Memberships: American College of Physicians; American Diabetes Association; Endocrine Society. Hobby: Golf. Address: Medical University of South Carolina, 171 Ashley Avenue, Charleston, SC 29425, USA.

COMER James Pierpont, b. 25 Sep 1934, East Chicago, Indiana, USA. Child Psychiatrist. m. Shirley Ann Arnold, 20 June 1959, dec, 1 son, 1 daughter. Education: AB, Indiana University, 1956; MD, Howard University College of Medicine, 1960; MPH, University of Michigan School of Public Health, 1964. Appointments: Staff Member, National Institute of Mental Health, Washington DC, 1967-68; Assistant Professor of Psychiatry, 1968-70, Associate Professor of Psychiatry, 1970-72, Associate Professor of Psychiatry with tenure, 1972-75; Professor of Psychiatry, 1975-, Maurice Falk Professor of Child Psychiatry, 1976-, Associate Dean for Student Affairs, 1969-, Director, School Development Programme, 1973-, Yale University Child Study Centre and School of Medicine. Publications: Beyond Black and White, 1972; Black Child Care, 1975, 1976; Raising Black Children, 1992; School Power: Implications of an Intervention Project, 1980, 1993; Maggie's American Dream: The Life and Times of a Black Family, 1988; Contributor of numerous articles in professional journals. Honours include: Recipient of numerous honorary degrees from national institutions; John and Mary Markle Foundation Scholar in Academic Medicine, 1969-74; Phi Delta Kappa Distinguished Fellow Award, Connecticut Chapter, 1984; Agnes Purcell McGavin Award, American Psychiatric Association, 1985; Neal-Marshall Alumnus of Year Award, Indiana University, 1989; President's Award, Connecticut Association for Human Services, 1992; Fellow, American Academy of Arts and

Sciences, 1994. Memberships include: National Medical Association; American Orthopsychiatric Association. Address: Yale Child Study Centre, 230 South Frontage Road, PO Box 207900, New Haven, CT 06520-7900, USA.

CON Vu Quang, b. 1 July 1944. Entomologist. m. Ing Le Thanh Hang, 12 Feb 1990, 2 daughters. Education: Bach of Biol Science; PhD; DSc. Career: Head, Department of Insect Ecology, Institute of Ecology & Biological Resources, NCNST. Publications: 72 publications: Interrelation of Host and Parasite of Insects, 1979; Host-Parasite Relationship of Rice Lepidoptenous Pest and Their Parasites in Vietnam, Senkt-Peterburg, RAS, 1992; 70 other manned articles. Memberships: Council Member, Biology of Vietnam; General Secretary, Entomological Society of Vietnam. Hobbies: Ornament Tress; Flower Trees. Address: Institute of Ecology & Biological Resources, National Centre for Natural Science and Technology of Vietnam, Nghia do, Tu liem, Hanoi, Vietnam.

CONDON Mark Casey, b. 2 Feb 1969, Washington DC, USA. Researcher. Education: MA; PhD Candidate. Appointment: Assistant. Hobby: Juggling. Address: PO Box 313, Urbana, IL 61801-0313, USA.

CONDON Robert E, b. 13 Aug 1929, Albany, New York, USA. Surgeon. m. Marcia Jane Pagano, 16 Jun 1951, 2 s. Education: AB, University of Rochester, 1951; MD, 1957; MS, University of Washington, 1965; Diplomate, American Board of Surgery, National Board Medical Examiners. Appointments: Resident, Department of Surgery, University of Washington, School of Medicine, 1958-65; Postdoctoral Research Fellow, National Heart Institute, 1961-63; Assistant Professor of Surgery, Baylor College of Medicine, Houston, 1965-67; Associate Professor of Surgery, University of Illinois, College of Medicine, Chicago, 1967-69; Professor, 1969-70; Professor/Head of Department of Surgery, University of Iowa, College of Medicine, 1971-72; Professor of Surgery, Medical College, Wisconsin, 1972-; Chairman, Department of Surgery, 1979-; Chief, Surgical Services, Wood VA Hospital, Milwaukee, 1972-81; Attending Surgeon, Milwaukee County General Hospital, Columbia Hospital, 1972-; Froedtert Memorial Lutheran Hospital, 1982-; Consultant, Mount Sinai, Samaritan, St Luke's, St Mary, St Joseph Hospitals, Milwaukee. Publications: Author, Abdominal Pain: A Guide to Rapid Diagnosis, 2nd Edition, 1995; Manual of Surgical Therapeutics, 8th Edition, 1993; Hernia, 4th Edition, 1995; Surgical Care, 1980. Honours: include, Recipient Senior Class Award as Outstanding Faculty Member, Baylor University, 1966; Excellence in Teaching Award, Phi Chi, 1967; Teacher of the Year Award, 1972. Memberships include: Society Clinical Surgery; Western Surgical Association; Milwaukee Academy of Medicine; Royal Society of Medicine; American Association Surgery of Trauma. Address: Department of Surgery, The Medical College of Wisconsin, 9200 West Wisconsin Avenue, Milwaukee, WI 53226, USA.

CONGDON Peter John, b. 12 Jan 1935, Plymouth, England. Educational Psychologist. m. Audrey Mary Abraham, 8 Aug 1964, 2 sons, 2 daughters. Education: BA (Hons), MA, Educational Psychology, PhD, Educational Psychology, London University; Diploma in Educational Psychology, University of Wales; Certificate of Education, University of Exeter; AFBPsS. Appointments: Director, Lozells Child Guidance Clinic, 1969-71; Senior Educational Psychologist, Warwickshire, 1971-89; Director, Gifted Children's Information Centre, Solihull, 1989-. Publications: Helping children of high intelligence, 1978; Dyslexia: towards a better understanding, 1981; Lefty, a story of left-handedness, 1989; Dyslexia: a pattern of strength and weaknesses, 1989. Honours: Barnes Memorial Scholarship, Exeter, 1954. Membership: British Psychological Society. Hobbies: Victorian art; Genealogy. Address: Hampton Grange, 21 Hampton Lane, Solihull B91 2QJ, England.

CONLEY Susan B, b. 3 Feb 1948. Paediatrician. Education: Md, University of Michigan, 1973. Appointments: Instructor in Paediatrics, Washington University School of Medicine, St Louis; Assistant and Associate Professor, Vice Chairman, Department of Paediatrics, University of Texas Medical School at Houston; Director, Paediatric Renal Centre, Pacific Medical Centre, San Francisco; Professor of Paediatrics, Stanford University Medical School. Publications: Contributor of over 60 professional articles and book chapters. Honours: Distinguished Service Award, National Kidney Foundation, 1993. Memberships: American Academy of Paediatrics; American Society of Paediatric Nephrology; American Society of Nephrology; International Society of Nephrology; American Association Transplant Physicians.

Address: Stanford University Medical Centre, Department of Paediatrics, Stanford, CA 94305-5119, USA.

CONNER Christine Evelyn, b. 13 Dec 1963, Omagh, Co Tyrone, Northern Ireland. Physician. m. Dr M J Metcalfe, 2 May 1992. Education: MbChB, Edinburgh University, Scotland, 1987; MRCOG, 1993. Appointments: Career rergistrar, Aberdeen Royal Infirmary, 1992-94; Wellbeing Research Fellow, 1994. Honours: MRCOG Prize Medal, 1993; Lawson Gifford Prize in Obstetrics and Gynaecology, Edinburgh University, 1987. Memberships: BA; Edinburgh Obstetric Society. Hobbies: Hillwalking; Cookery; Skiing. Address: 9 Rosslyn Terrace, Dowanhill, Glasgow G12 9NA, Scotland.

CONTRADA Richard Jude, b. 11 Sept 1954, Brooklyn, New York, USA. Associate Professor of Psychology. Education: BA; PhD. Appointments: Research Associate; Medical Psychology, Uniformed Services University of Health Sciences, Bethesda, Maryland; Associate Professor, Psychology, Rutgers State University. Publications: Over 40 articles and chapters published. Honours: Member of Academy of Behavioral Medicine Research. Memberships: American Psychology Association; American Psychology Society; SESP; SMB. Hobbies: Running; Painting; Guitar Playing. Address: Department of Psychology, Tillet Hall, Rutgers University, New Brunswick, NJ 08903, USA.

CONWAY David Ian, b. 21 Apr 1948, Prestbury, Cheshire, England. Gynaecologist. m. Pauline Newman, 23 Oct 1975, 3 sons, 4 daughters. Education: MD, Manchester University; FRCOG. Appointments: Consultant Gynaecologist, Monklands Hospital, Airdrie and Glasgow Nuffield Hospital, Glasgow, Scotland. Hobbies: Family; Investment. Address: 53 Kirkintilloch Road, Lenzie, Glasgow G66 4LB, Scotland.

CONWAY Patrick John Kenneth, b. 29 Nov 1941, Dublin, Ireland. Obstetrician and Gynaecologist. m. Frances Brigid Keane, 26 June 1974, 1 son, 3 daughters. Education: MB BCh; BAO; DPH; FRCOG. Appointments: Registrar, Obstetrics and Gynaecology, St James Hospital, Dublin, 1971-73; Registrar, Rotunde, Dublin, 1973-75; Registrar in Gynaecology, Mater, Dublin, 1976; Consultant, Obstetrics and Gynaecology, St Lukes Hospital, Anua Uyo, Akwa Ibom State, Nigeria, 1977-79; Consultant, Obstetrics and Gynaecology, Midland Health Board, Port Laoise, Ireland, 1980-. Publications: Annual Clinical Report, Portlaoise General Hospital Maternity, 1980-93. Memberships: Royal College Obstetricians and Gynaecologists' Institute Obstetricians and Gynaecologists Ireland; Laois Clinical Society. Hobbies: jogging; Horse Management. Address: Kilminchy, Portlaoise, Co Laois, Ireland.

CONWELL Yeates, b. 21 Feb 1953, Delaware, USA. Physician. m. E Gay Mills. Education: AB, Princeton University, 1976; MD, University of Cincinnati, 1980. Appointments: Resident in Psychiatry, 1980-84, Fellow, Senior Instructor, Department of Psychiatry, 1984-85, Yale University; Assistant Professor of Psychiatry, School of Medicine, 1985, Associate Professor of Psychiatry, 1991-, University of Rochester. Publications: Completed Suicide at Age 50 and Over, 1990; Suicide and Cancer in Late Life, 1990; Rational Suicide and the Right to Die, 1991. Honours: ABPN Certification, 1985; Added Qualifications in Geriatric Psychiatry, 1991. Memberships: American Psychiatric Association; American Association of Geriatric Psychiatry; International Psychogeriatric Association; American Association of Suicidology. Address: University of Rochester Medical Centre, 300 Crittenden Boulevard, Rochester, NY 14642, USA.

CONYNGHAM Bruce, b. 3 Jan 1928, Wellington, New Zealand. Obstetrician and Gynaecologist. m. Janet Hodson, 9 July 1960, 1 son, 3 daughters. Education: MB ChB, Otago; FRCOG; FRNZCOG; GRCS Edinburgh; FRACS; MPH, JOhns Hopkins University, USA. Appointments: Assistant Professor in Obstetrics and Gynaecology, CMC Ludhiana, Punjab, India; Consultant, England and New Zealand; Private Practice Visiting Specialist, Health Wattemata. Publications: Norehisterone in Menorrhagia, 1963; Contributor of professional articles in journals, 1965-68. Memberships: New Zealand Medical Association; New Zealand Family Planning Association; New zealand Ob-Gyn Society. Hobbies: Smallholding Life; Philately; Card Collecting; Books; Geneaology. Address: Springhill, 59 Mahoenui Valley Road, Coatesville, RD3, Albany, New Zealand.

COOK Ralph Richard, b. 21 Feb 1939, Detroit, Michigan, USA. Education: BA, Hope College, Michigan, 1961; MD, Wayne State University, School of Medicine, Michigan, 1968; MPH, University of Michigan, School of Public Health, 1971. Appointments: Orderly, Harper

Hospital, 1957; Deckhand, M Y Marco Polo, England, 1961; Bus Repairman, City Transportation Authority, Michigan, 1964; Staff Physician, Michigan Division, Dow Chemical USA, 1972-77; Research Physician, Health & Environmental Research, Dow Chemical USA, 1975-77; Director of Epidemiology, Health & Environmental Sciences, The Dow Chemical Company, 1978-86; Corporate Director of Epidemiology, Health & Environmental Sciences, The Dow Chemical Company, 1986-87; Corporate Director of Epidemiology, Director H&ES Research Computer Systems, 1988-92; Director of Epidemiology, The Dow Corning Corporation, 1992-94; Corporate Director of Occupational Health & Epidemiology, The Dow Corning Corporation, 1994-. Publications include: An Update of Mortality Among Chemical Workers Potentially Exposed to the Herbicide 2,4-Dichlorophenoxyacetic Acid and Its Derivatives, 1993; Biological Effects of Low Level Exposures. Memberships include: American College of Epidemiology, Fellow; American Medical Association; American Public Health Association; Society for Epidemiologic Research. Address: Corporate Occupational Health, Dow Corning Corporation, Mail #C01120, Midland, MI 48686-0994, USA.

COOLEY Arthur Leland, b. 25 Nov 1931, Stanford, CA, USA. Physician. Education: BA, Stanford University; MD, Stanford University. Appointments: Assistant Clinical Professor, Obstetrics & Gynaecology, Stanford University School of Medicine; Practicing Gynaecologist. Honours: Dermatology & Radiology Prizes, Stanford University, 1958. Hobbies: Surfing; Skiing; Gardening; Carpentry; Piano Music. Address: 14215 Squirrel Hollow, Saratoga, CA 95070, USA.

COOPER Cary Lynn, b. 28 Apr 1940, Los Angeles, California, USA. University Professor. m. Rachel Davies, Aug 1984, 1 son, 3 daughters. Education: BS, MBA, University of California, Los Angeles; MSc, Manchester University, England; PhD, Leeds University; FBPsS; FRSA; FRSM. Appointments: Lecturer in Social Psychology, University of Southampton, England; Professor of Organisational Psychology and Pro Chancellor, University of Manchester Institute of Science and Technology. Publications: 80 books including: Aging, Stress and Health, 1989; Cancer and Stress, 1991; The Workplace Revolution, 1994; Research Methods in Stress and Health Psychology, 1995. Honours: Fellow, British Psychological Society; Fellow, Royal Society of Arts; Fellow, Royal Society of Medicine; Editor-in-Chief, Journal of Organizational Behavior; Co-Editor, Stress Medicine. Memberships: British Academy of Management; Academy of Management, USA; International Association of Applied Psychology; American Psychosomatic Society. Hobbies: Raising children; Playing the piano; Soccer. Address: Manchester School of Management, UMIST, PO Box 88, Manchester M60 1QD, England.

COOPER Colin, b. 1 Feb 1954, Enfield, England. Psychologist. Education: BSc, 1st Class, 1976, PhD, 1983, University of Exeter. Appointments: Psychologist, Ministry of Defence, 1976-79; Research Fellow, University of Exeter, 1983-86; Lecturer, University of Ulster, Northern Ireland, 1986-91; Lecturer, School of Psychology, Queen's University, Belfast. Publications: Contributor of over 40 articles in professional journals including: Affect Intensity: Factor or Artifact? Co-author, 1993; Mood Variability and Personality, Co-author, 1992. Memberships: Associate Fellow, British Psychological Society. Address: School of Psychology, Queen's University, Belfast BT7 1NN, Northern Ireland.

COOPER Donald Stewart, b. 21 Dec 1940, Newport News, Virginia, USA. m. Margaret W Thompson, 29 June 1963, 3 sons. Education: BA, magna cum laude, Harvard College, 19962; PhD, Harvard University, 1971; MA, UNiversity of Iowa, 1981. Appoiontments: Assistant Research Scientist, University of Iowa, 1981-83; Director, Laboratory for Laryngeal Physiology, University of Southern California. Publications: Comparison of EMG Signals from Different Electrode Placements in the Palatoglossus Muscle, 1985; Antoine Ferrein and the Formation of the Human Voice, 1989; Fatigue-Resistance of Canine Vocal Fold Muscle, 1990; Thyroarytenoid Intramuscular Pressures, 1993; Muscle Energetics, Vocal Efficiency, Laryngeal Biomechanics, 1993. Honours: National Institutes of Health Research Support, 1992-; Voice Foundation Research Support, 1989-90. Memberships: Acoustical Society of America; American Speech-language-Hearing Association; Association for Research in Otolaryngology. Hobbies: History of laryngeal and phonatory physiology. Address: 903 Hoffman Building, 2025 Zonal Avenue, University of Southern California School of Medicine, Los Angeles, CA 90033, USA.

COOPER James Nelson, b. 8 June 1938, Staten Island, New York, USA. Doctor of Medicine. m. Carolyn Olverson, 1965, 3 sons, 1 daughter. Education: BA, Columbia University; MD, New York University. Appointments: Currently Chairman, Department of Medicine, Fairfax Hospital, Falls Church, Virginia. Hobbies: Golf; Tennis; Reading. Address: Fairfax Hospital, 3300 Gallows Road, Falls Church, VA 22046, USA.

COOPER Louis Zucker, b. 25 Dec 1931, Albany, GA, USA. Phusician; Paediatrician. m. Madeline W Appell, 2 s, 2 d. Education: BS, MD, Yale University. Appointments: Professor of Paediatrics, Columbia University; Director of Paediatrics, St Luke's-Roosevelt Hospital Centre, New York. Publications: Contributor of numerous works. Memberships: American Academy of Paediatrics; America Pediatric Society; Infectious Disease Society of America; Society for Paediatric Research. Address: St Luke's-Roosevelt Hospital Centre, 1111 Amsterdam Avenue, New York, NY 10025, USA.

COOPER Max Dale, b. 31 Aug 1933, Hazlehurst, Mississippi, USA. Professor of Medicine. m. Rosalie Lazzara, 2 June 1960, 3 sons, 1 daughter. Education: MD, Tulane University, 1957; Diplomate, American Board of Paediatrics. Appointments include: Paediatric Allergy Fellow, University of California, San Francisco Medical Centre, 1962-63; Instructor, Department of Paediatrics, Tulane Medical School, New Orleans, 1962-63; Medical Fellow Specialist, Assistant Professor, Department of Paediatrics, University of Minnesota, 1963-67; Professor of Paediatrics and Microbiology, 1967-, Senior Scientist, Comprehensive Cancer Centre, 1971-; Director, Cellular Immunobiology Unit, Tumour Institute, 1976-; Director, Division Developmental and Clinical Immunology, 1987-, Howard Hughes Investigator, 1988-, University of Alabama at Birmingham; Visiting Scientist, Tumour Immunology Unit, Department of Zoology, University College of London, England, 1973-74; Visiting Professor, Institute of Embryology and Pasteur Institute, Paris, France, 1984-85. Honours: Samuel J Meltzer Founder's Award, Society for Experimental Biology and Medicine, 1966; 3M Life Sciences Award, 1990; Sandoz Prize for Immunology, 1990; American College of Physicians Award, 1994. Memberships: President, 1988-89, American Association of Immunologists; American Society for Clinical Investigation; Vice President, 1978, Society for Paediatric Research; President, 1993-94, Clinical Immunology Society; National Academy of Sciences; Institute of Medicine. Address: 378 Wallace Tumour Institute, Division Developmental Clinical Immunology, University of Alabama at Birmingham, Birmingham, AL 35294-3300, USA.

COOPER Reginald Rudyard, b. 1 June 1932, Elkins, West Virginia, USA. Physician; Orthopaedist. m. Jacqueline Smith, 22 Aug 1954, 3 sons, 1 daughter. Education: BA; BS; MD; MS. Appointments: Orthopaedic Surgeon, US Naval Hospital, Pensacola, Florida, 1960-62; Associate in Orthopaedics, 1962-65, Assistant Professor of Orthopaedics, 1965-68, Associate Professor of Orthopaedics, 1968-71, State University of Iowa College of Medicine; Professor of Orthopaedics, 1971-; Acting Chairman, Department of Orthopaedics, 1973; Chairman, 1973-, University of Iowa College of Medicine. Publications: The Validity of Orthopedic In-Training Examination Scores, Co-author, 1981; Long Term Follow Up of Fascia Transfer for the Paralytic Hip in Myelodysplasia, Co-author, 1982; Hip Disarticulation: A Prosthetic Follow Up, Co-author, 1984. Honours: Kappa Delta Award for Outstanding Basic Research in Orthopaedics, 1970-71; Alpha Omega Alpha; President, American Academy of Orthopaedic Surgeons, 1987-88; President, Orthopaedic Research Society, 1974. Memberships: Chairman, Journal of Bone and Joint Surgery Board of trustees; Chairman, National Orthopaedic Residency Review Committee; Past President, American Academy of Orthopaedic Surgeons; Past President, Orthopaedic Research Society. Hobbies: Travel; Photography. Address: Department of Orthopaedics, University of Iowa Hospitals and Clinics, 200 Hawkins Drive, Iowa City, IA 52242, USA.

COOPER Sharon P, b. 7 Nov 1952, Baton Rouge, Louisiana, USA. Epidemiologist. m. Charles Cooper, 3 sons. Education: BA, University of Texas, 1973; MS, University of Oklahoma, 1975; MS, Harvard School of Public Health, 1976; PhD, University of Texas, 1982. Appointments: Faculty Associate, 1976-85, Research Assistant Professor, 1985-90, University of Texas; Visiting Scholar, University of Houston, 1992-93; Assistant Professor of Epidemiology. Publications: The Relation Between Degree of Blood Pressure Reduction and Mortality Among Hypertensives, Co-author, 1988. Honours: Phi Beta Kappa, 1973; Harriet Cunningham Citation for Meritorious Scientific Writing, 1988, 1989; Outstanding Faculty Award, 1992. Memberships: Society for

Epidemiologic Research; American Public Health Association; Texas Public Health Association. Hobby: Walking. Address: PO Box 20186, Houston, TX 77225, USA.

COOPER Wayne Douglas, b. 2 Apr 1947, Jersey City, New Jersey, USA. Physician. m. Barbara Joan Weiss, 20 Oct 1979, 1 s, 2 d. Education: BA, Alfred University, Alfred, New York, 1969; MD, George Washington University, Washington DC, 1973. Appointments: Resident at George Washington University in Obstetrics & Gynaecology, 1973-76; Private Practice of Obstetrics & Gynaecology, 1976-. Honours: Kane-King-Dodek, Obstetrical Honor Society. Memberships: Washington Gynaecology Society; DC Medical Society; Jacobi Medical Society. Hobbies: Softball; Scuba; Basketball; Travel. Address: 2400 Pennsylvania Avenue, NW #108, Washington DC 20037-1714, USA.

COOPERMAN Jack M, b. 13 Jan 1921, New York City, New York, USA. Nutritionist. m. Ruth E Drucker, 11 July 1949, 1 son. Education: BS, City College of New York; MS, PhD, Postdoctoral Fellow, University of Wisconsin, Madison. Appointments: Director, Nutrition Research Hoffman-La Roche, Nutley, New Jersey, 1946-57; Assistant Professor, Paediatrics, 1957-64, Associate Professor, 1964-74, Professor, Community and Preventive Medicine, Paediatrics, 1976-, New York Medical College; Visiting Professor, University of West Indies, 1960; Visiting Professor, All-India Institute of Medical Sciences, 1978; Lederle Lecturer in Nutrition, Israeli Dietetic Association, 1988; Lecturer in Nutrition, Catholic Medical College of Korea, Seoul, 1989. Publications: 150 scientific papers; 14 books. Memberships: American Institute of Nutrition; American Society of Clinical Nutrition; American Chemical Society; Fellow, New York Academy of Sciences; Fellow, American Association for the Advancement of Science; Biochemical Society of Great Britain. Hobbies: Walking; Literature; Theatre; Music. Address: 43-10 Kissena Boulevard, Flushing, NY 11355, USA.

COPLAND-GRIFFITHS Michael Charles, b. 7 November 1946, Newbury, Berkshire, England. Chiropractor. m. Noelle Mary (Penny) Spencer, 6 December 1980. Education: DC, Bradfield College, Anglo-Euro College of Chiropractic. Appointments: Faculty Member, Anglo-Euro College of Chiropractic, 1977-81; Member of Council, AECC, 1978-80; Member of Council, British Chiropractic Association, 1979-91, 1993-; Member of Advisory Committee and Education Committee, Institute for Complementary Medicine, 1982-85; Vice President, AECC Alumni Association, 1982-91; Committee Member, Council for Complementary & Alternative Medicine, 1982-89; Vice Chairman, CCAM, 1986-89; Member, Finance & General Purposes Committee, BCA, 1986-88, 1993-94, Chairman, 1986-87; Member, Parliamentary Committee, BCA, 1987-; Board Member, Chiropractic Registration Steering Group, 1994-; Chairman CRSG, 1994-; Member, Working Party on Current Parameters for Safe and Competent Practice in Chiropractic, 1994-95. Publications: Dynamic Chiropractic Today - The Complete and Authoritave Guide, 1991. Honours: President's Award for Outstanding Service to the Profession, 1991. Memberships: British Chiropractic Association; European Chiropractors Union. Hobbies: Archaeology; Post Medieval Country Pottery; History; Natural History; British Heritage; Organic Gardening; Contemporary Ceramics. Address: Trowle House, Wingfield, Trowbridge, Wiltshire BA14 9LE, England.

COPPERI Maria Teresa, b. 26 May 1940, Torino, Italy. Psychologist and Psychotherapeutist; m. Alessandro Tolio, 4 July 1963, 2 sons. Education: Doctor of Philosophy, University of Turin, 1963. Appointments: Professor at the International University of New Medicine, Milan, Italy. Publications: Let's Revalue Our Stress; Transgression Obesity; Mental Computer Programming, 1988. Memberships: Italian Society of Psychology; Italian Society of Clinical Sexuology; Order of Psychologists; The International Society for Medical & Psychological Hypnosis. Hobbies: Swimming; Reading. Address: Via Harar 29, 20153 Milano, Italy.

CORAN Arnold Gerald, b. 16 Apr 1938. Paediatric Surgeon. m. Susan Williams, 2 sons, 1 daughter. Education: AB cum laude, Harvard College, 1959; MD cum laude, Harvard Medical School, 1963; Residencies, Surgery: Peter Bent Brigham Hospital, Boston, 1964-68, 1969, Children's Hospital Medical Center, Boston, 1965-68; Paediatric Surgical Registrar, Rikshospitalet, Oslo, 1969. Appointments: Lieutenant-Commander, Medical Corps, US Navy, 1970-72; Consultant, Paediatric Surgery, National Naval Medical Center, Bethesda, Maryland, 1970-72; Assistant Clinical Professor, George Washington University School of Medicine, 1970-72; Head Physician, Paediatric Surgery, Los Angeles County-University of Southern California Medical Center,

1972-74; Assistant Professor, 1972-73, Associate Professor, 1973-74, University of Southern California School of Medicine; Professor, Surgery, Head, Section of Paediatric Surgery, 1974-, Professor, Paediatrics, 1983-, University of Michigan Medical School, Ann Arbor; Surgeon-in-Chief, C S Mott Children's Hospital, Ann Arbor, 1981-. Publications: 15 books including: Profiles in Nutritional Management: The Infant Patient, 1980; Peri-operative Problems in Pediatrics, 1987; Hirschsprung's Disease (with E Elhalaby), 1994; Over 300 chapters and journal contributions. Honours include: Bronze Medal, Scandinavian Society of Paediatric Surgery; Dozer Visiting Professor, Ben Gurion University, Israel, 1990. Memberships: Alpha Omega Alpha; American Academy of Pediatrics; American College of Surgeons; American College of Chest Physicians; Vice Regent, New York Academy of Sciences; Collegium Internationale Chirurgiae Digestivae; Many more. Hobbies: Golf; Running. Address: University of Michigan, Mott Children's Hospital, 1500 Medical Center Drive, Room F3970, Ann Arbor, MI 48109-0245, USA.

CORBETT James John, b. 2 July 1940, Chicago, Illinois, USA. Physician. m. Joyce Zymali, 29 Dec 1962, 1 son, 2 daughters. Education: BA, Brown University; MD, Chicago Medical School. Appointments: Clinical Assistant Professor of Neurology, Jefferson Medical School, 1974-77; Assistant Professor of Neurology, University of Iowa Medical School, 1977-80; Associate Professor, Neurology and Ophthalmology, 1980-85, Professor, Neurology, Ophthalmology, 1985-90, University of Iowa; Professor, Chairman of Neurology, Professor of Ophthalmology, University of Mississippi. Honours: Silversides Lecture, Toronto, 1981; Geoff Whiston Memorial Lecture, Halifax, 1993. Memberships: American Academy Neurology; Americal Neurological Association; North American Neuro-ophthalmology Society; AMA; Association of University Professors of Neurology. Hobbies: Fly Fishing; Reading; Travel. Address: 2500 North State Street, University of Mississippi Medical Centre, Department of Neurology, Jackson, MS 39216-4505, USA.

CORDERO Manuel Raul, b. 29 Oct 1931, Lima, Peru. Medical Doctor. m. Aida Garcia-Zapatero, 21 June 1957, 2 sons. Education: BS, 1955, MD, 1957, San Marcos University, Lima; Diplomate, American Board of Ophthalmology. Appointments: Ophthalmologist, Anglo-American Hospital, Lima; Chief of Service, Ophthalmology, Social Security Hospital, Lima; Currently Professor of Ophthalmology, University of San Marcos, Lima. Publications: Several papers in Peruvian Ophthalmological Journal. Memberships: Former President, Peruvian Ophthalmological Society; Fellow, American Academy of Ophthalmology; Fellow, American College of Surgeons. Hobby: Playing the piano. Address: Tudela y Varela 138-303, San Isidro, Lima, Peru.

COREY Jacquelynne Perou, b. 10 Jun 1953, Chicago, IL, USA. Otorhinolaryngologist. m. (2) Timothy C Hain, MD, 29 Sep 1990, 2 s, 1 d. Education: BA, Carleton College; MD, University of Illinois; FAAOA; FACS. Career includes: Assistant Professor, West Virginia University; Assistant Professor, 1987-95, Associate Professor, University of Chicago. Publications include: Numerous articles in professional journals, presentations at meetings, invited lectures and abstracts; Editor, Home Study in Otolaryngic Allergy, 1990, 1995. Honours: Diplomate, 1985, Guest Examiner for Oral Examination, 1991, 1992, American Board of Otolaryngology; Fellow, Academy of Otolaryngic Allergy; Fellow, American Academy of Otolaryngology, Head and Neck Surgery; Fellow, American College of Surgeons; Fellow, American In Vitro Allergy Immunology Society; Fellow, American Rhinologic Society. Memberships include: American Association of Medical Colleges; American College of Allergists; AMA; American Medical Women's Association; Founding Member, Foundation for Allergy Care and Treatment; Performing Arts Medical Association; Voice Foundation; Treasurer, 1994, American Academy of Otolaryngic Allergy; Vice President, 1994, President, 1995, American In Vitro Allergy Immunology Society. Hobbies: Opera; Skiing. Address: University of Chicago - OHNS, 5841 South Maryland Avenue, MC 1035, Chicago, IL 60637, USA.

CORLEY Barbara Margaret Gianetta, b. 4 July 1939, Cheshire, England. Psychologist. Education: MA, Oxford University, 1961; Diploma in Education, 1962; MSc, 1975, PhD, Education, 1992, London University. Appointments: Assistant Education Officer, The Spastics Society, 1970-75; Divisional and Specialist Psychologist, Inner London Education Authority, 1975-90; Currently Independent Consultant. Publications: The spelling competence of partially sighted children, 1993; Co-author: Partially Sighted Children, 1989; Oral reading errors of partially sighted children, 1993; Reading strategies in partially sighted children, 1993. Membership: Associate Fellow, British Psychological Society. Hobbies: Genealogy; Travel. Address: 208 Gilbert House, Barbican, London EC2Y 8BA, England.

CORNEIL Donald Wayne, b. 13 May 1943, Ottawa, Canada. Director. m. Carole-Ann Lanose, 18 July 1983, 1 son. Education: MSW, Carleton University, Ottawa, 1983; ScD, School of Hygiene and Public Health, Johns Hopkins University, Baltimore, USA, 1993. Appointments: Director, Employee Assistance Service, Government of Canada; Project Director, WHO-ILO Project on Alcohol in Employment Settings; Director, Occupational Health, Health Canada. Publications: Alcohol in Employment Settings, 1994; Health Promotion and Protection Ethics. Honours: EAP Hall of Fame, 1994; Dr John Hume Award for Doctoral Research, Johns Hopkins University, 1993; Campus Safety Award, National Safety Council, 1990. Hobby: Collecting antique fire engines. Address: 1071 Grenoble Crescent, Orleans, Ontario K1C 2CS, Canada.

CORREA Adolfo, b. 2 Mar 1946, Mazatlan, Mexico. Paediatrician; Epidemiologist. m. Ana I Alfaro, 2 July 1978. Education: BS, San Diego State University, 1969; MS, 1970, MD, 1974 University of California, San Diego; MPH, 1981, PhD, 1987, The Johns Hopkins University. Appointments: Assistant Professor, Department of Epidemiology, Johns Hopkins University. Publications: Epidemiology of Congenital Heart Disease: The Baltimore-Washington Infant Study, 1981-89, 1993; Science and Practice of Cancer Prevention and Control, Co-author, 1994; Total Anomalous Pulmonary Venous Return: Familiar and Environmental Factors, Teratology, 1991; Ebstein's Anomaly of the Tricuspid Valve: Genetic and Environmental Factors, Teratology, 1994; Exposure Measurement in Case Control Studies and Reported Methods and Recommendations, 1994. Honours: National Science Foundation Traineeship, 1967-68; First Independent Research Support and Transition Award, NIEHS, NIH; Delta Omega, Alpha Chapter, 1994. Hobby: Classical Guitar. Address The Johns Hopkins School of Hygiene and Public Health. Department of Epidemiology, 615 N Wolfe Street, Baltimore, MD 212905, USA.

CORTNER Jean Alexander, b. 10 Nov 1930, Nashville, TN, USA. Educator; Physician. m. Jeanne Gibson Morgan, 24 Mar 1956, 2 s, 1 d. Education: BA, Chemistry, Vanderbilt University, 1952; MD, 1955; Diplomate, American Board of Pediatrics. Career includes: NIH Visiting Fellow, Departments of Pediatrics and Biochemistry, Babies Hospital and Columbia, 1961-63; Chief, Department of Pediatrics, Roswell Park Memorial Institute, Buffalo, 1963-67; Professor, Chairman, Department of Pediatrics, SUNY, NY, 1967-74; Physician in Chief, Children's Hospital, Buffalo, 1967-74; Physician in Chief, 1974-86, President of Medical Staff, 1990-92, Children's Hospital of PA; Professor of Pediatrics in Human Genetics, University of PA School of Medicine, 1975-89. Publications: Contributor of articles to scientific journals. Honours: Phi Beta Kappa, 1952; Sigma Xi, 1963; Fellow, College of Physicians of Philadelphia, 1975; Distinguished Medical Alumni Award, Vanderbilt University, 1986. Memberships include: Society for Pediatric Research; Pediatric Travel Club; American Pediatric Society; Peripatetic Club; Fellow, American Academy of Pediatrics; AAAS; AAUP; AHA; Committee on Social Issues, 1970-76, on Genetic Services, 1982-86, American Society of Human Genetics; Society for Study of Inborn Errors of Metabolism. Address: Lipid-Heart Research Center, Children's Hospital of Philadelphia, 34th Street and Civic Center Boulevard, Philadelphia, PA 19104, USA.

COTTON Robin T, b. 13 May 1941, Manchester, England. Physician. 5 children. Education: MA, University of Cambridge; MA, University of Birmingham; Ped-Oto Fellowship, University of Toronto, Canada; H&N Fellowship, University of Cincinnati, USA. Appointments: Director, Paediatric Otolaryngology, Children's Hospital; Professor, Department of Otolaryngology, University of Cincinnati. Publication: A Practical Approach to Pediatric Otolaryngology. Honours: 7th World Congress of Bronchoesophgology Seymour Cohen Lecture, 1992. Memberships: ACS; ABO; AMA; AAFPRS; ABEA; ARO; SUO; TRIO; ASHNS; ASPO; COS. Hobbies: Running; Boating; Music. Address: Childrens Hospital Medical Centre, 3333 Burnet Avenue, Cincinnati, OH 45229-3039, USA.

COUBLE Pierre Marie, b. 2 July 1949, Violay, France. Research Director. m. Marie-Lise Foussal, 8 Sept 1977, 2 daughters. Education: Docteur de spécialité, 1974, Docteur-ès-Sciences, 1982, Lyon University. Appointments: Currently CNRS Research Director, Centre for Molecular and Cellular Genetics, Claude Bernard University, Villeurbanne. Publications: Co-author: Specific expression of a silk

encoding gene of Bombyx in the salivary gland of Drosophila, 1990; P25 gene regulation in Bombyx, 1992. Honours: Japanese STA Award, 1993. Hobbies: Painting; Running; Skiing. Address: 203 Avenue Fleming, 69300 Caluire, France.

COULSTING Frank Noel, b. 24 Dec 1920, Macclesfield, Cheshire, England. Osteopath. m. Jean Marian Manger, 20 July 1950, 1 son, 2 daughters. Education: Diploma in Osteopathy, 1951; MRO. Appointments: Tutor Operator, British School of Osteopathy; Pioneer of Co-Communication Therapy, CCT. Publications: The Cranial Approach to Osteopathy, 1985; Yoga/Meditation/Healing. Memberships: Register of Osteopaths. Hobbies: Yoga; Gardening. Address: 12 Tekels Park, Camberley, Surrey GU15 2LF, England.

COURTNEY Richard James, b. 2 July 1941, Greenville, Pennsylvania, USA. Scientist. m. Diana Powers, 11 June 1966, 2 daughters. Education: BS, Grove City College, 1963; MS, 1966, PhD, 1968, Syracuse University; Postdoctoral Fellow, Department of Virology and Epidemiology, Baylor College of Medicine, 1968-70. Appointments: Assistant Professor, 1970-76, Associate Professor, 1976-77, Department of Virology and Epidemiology, Baylor College of Medicine, Houston, Texas; Associate Professor, 1978-81, Professor, 1981-85, Department of Microbiology, Cell and Molecular Biology Programme, University of Tennessee, Knoxville; Professor, Chairman, Biochemistry and Molecular Biology, Louisiana State University School of Medicine, Shreveport, 1985-91; Professor, Chairman, Microbiology and Immunology, Pennsylvania State University College of Medicine, Hershey, 1991-. Publications: About 80 including: Herpes simplex virus protein synthesis in the presence of 2-deoxy-D-glucose, 1976; Co-author: The gA and gB glycoproteins of herpes simplex virus type 1: two forms of a single polypeptide, 1980; Inducible expression of the herpes simplex virus type 2 glycoprotein gene, gG-2, in a mammalian cell line, 1988; Identification and characterization of the herpes simplex virus type 1 virion protein encoded by the UL35 open reading frame, 1992. Honours: NCI Fellowship, 1968-70; Chair-Elect, Division S (DNA Viruses), American Society of Microbiology, 1993-94; Fellow, American Academy of Microbiology, 1994-. Memberships: American Society for Biochemistry and Molecular Biology; American Society for Microbiology; American Society for Virology. Hobbies: Reading; Golf; Skiing. Address: Department of Microbiology and Immunology, The Pennsylvania State University College of Medicine, 500 University Drive, Hershey, PA 17033, USA.

COUSENS Emma Schwichtenberg, b. 15 Mar 1949, Winston, Salem, USA. Home Care Specialist; Consultant. m. Nicholas A Cousens, 2 Nov 1976, deceased, 1 son. Education: Associate Degree, Nursing Science; Matriculating Student, Framingham State College. Appointments: Medical Case Management, Catastrophic Medical Cases; Coordination & Management, Direct Hospice Services, Metro West Hospice; Home Care & Public Health Administration of Services; Elected Member, Chair Woman, Bellingham Board of Health, 1980-92. Publications: Contributor to monthly Massachusetts Association of Health Boards News Letter, 1986-. Memberships: Bellingham Democratic Committee; Associated Boards of Health; Executive Board, Massachusetts Association of Heath Boards, Norfolk County; Executive Member, Massachusetts-Ukrain Citizens Bridge. Honours: Appointed Member, Massachusetts Right to Know Task Force, 1984; Governors Award, Excellence in Volunteerism, Govenor Michael Dukakis, 1985; Massachusetts Salute to Excellence Award, Dedicated Leadership, 1985; Appointed Member, Massachusetts Cancer Care Coordinating Committee, 1988; Lobbist, Massachusetts Association of Health Boards, Environmental & Public Health Issues; Bernardine McQueeny Dedication Award, Outstanding Service to the Central Massachusetts Association of Health Boards, 1991-92. Hobbies: Camping; Gardening; Travel. Address: 148 Caroline Drive, Bellingham, MA 02019-0138, USA.

COUSTAN Donald Ross, b. 18 Oct 1943, Chicago, Illinois, USA. Physician. m. Terri Distenfield Coustan, 20 May 1965, 1 son, 2 daughters. Education: BA, Psychology, Magna cum laude, Yale College, 1964; MD, Yale Medical School, 1968. Appointments: Assistant Professor of Obstetrics and Gynaecology, Yale Medical School, 1975-80; Associate Professor, 1980-82, Associate Professor of Obstetrics and Gynaecology, Brown University Programme in Medicine, 1982-86; Professor, 1986-, Department Chair, 1991-; Chief of Obstetrics and Gynaecology, Woman and Infant's Hospital of Rhode Island. Publications include: Symposium on Gestational Diabetes, 1976; The Baby Team: A Positive Approach to Pregnancy with Diabetes, Co-author, 1979; The Pregnant Patient with Overt Diabetes: Practical

Guide to Management, Part II, 1981, 1982; Home Glucose Monitoring Becomes More Sophisticated, 1983; Pregnancy in a Young Diabetic, 1989; Diagnosis of Gestational Diabetes: What Are Our Objectives?, 1991 Gestational Diabetes, 1993; Contributor of numerous presentations, abstracts, book reviews and letters. Honours include: Phi Beta Kappa, 1964; Sigma Xi, 1964. Memberships include: Fellow, American College of Obstetricians and Gynaecologists; American Diabetes Association; American fertility Society; Society of Perinatal Obstetricians; Association of Professors of Gynaecology and Obstetrics; Perinatal Research Society' Society for Gynaecologic Investigation; American Gynaecological and Obstetrical Society. Address: Department of Obstetrics and Gynaecology, Woman and Infant's Hospital of Rhode Island, 101 Dudley Street, Providence, RI 02905-2401, USA.

COUTINHO Roeland Arnold, b. 4 Apr 1946, Laren, The Netherlands. Microbiologist; Epidemiologist. m. Johanna Wiggelendam, 21 Mar 1970, 1 son, 1 daughter. Education: MB,1967, MD, 1972, PhD, 1984, University of Amsterdam. Appointments include: Doctor-in-Charge, Hospital, Ziguinchor, South Senegal, 1973-74; General Practitioner, Netherlands, 1974; Head, Department of Infectious Diseases and Environmental Health, Municipal Health Service of Amsterdam, 1977-; Advisor, Infectious Diseases, Dutch National Institute of Public Health, Bilthoven, 1988-90; Professor, Epidemiology and Control of Infectious Diseases, University of Amsterdam, 1989. Publications: Contributor of 228 articles in professional and scientific journals including: High Mortality Among HIV-Infected Injecting Drug Users without AIDS Diagnosis: Implications for HIV Infection Epidemic Modellers:, Co-author, 1994; Do Bisexual Men Play a Significant Role in the Heterosexual Spread of HIV?, Co-author, 1994; The Amsterdam Cohort Study on HIV Infection Among Drug Users. Evaluation of Prevention Programs, Co-author, 1994. Memberships include: Medical Society for the Study of Venerreal Diseases, Great Britain; Dutch Society for Microbiology; Dutch Society for the Study of Venereal Diseases; Dutch Society for Infectious Diseases; American Public Health Association; International Epidemiological Association; International AIDS Society; American Society for Epidemiologic Research. Hobbies: Soccer; Reading; Music. Address: Municipal Health Service, Nieuwe Achtergracht 100, 1018 WT Amsterdam, The Netherlands.

COWAN David Neal, b. 29 May 1947, Richmond, Virginia, USA. Epidemiologist. m. Jane Ward Ellis, 10 June 1977, 1 son, 1 daughter. Education: BS, Old Dominion University; MPH, Tulane University; PhD, University of Massachusetts, Amherst. Appointments: Major, Medical Service Corps, US Army Reserve; Senior Scientist, SRA Technologies Incorporated. Publications: Contributor of numerous articles in professional journals. Memberships: American College of Epidemiology; Society for Epidemiologic Research; Association of Military Surgeons of the US; Homicide Research Working Group. Hobbies: Gardening; Boating; Fishing; Hunting. Address: 10711 Margate Road, Silver Spring, MD 20901, USA.

COWAN Tony Michael, b. 26 Feb 1969, New Zealand. Dental Surgeon. m. Allison Black, 29 Jan 1994. Education: BDS, Otago, 1991. Membership: New Zealand Dental Association. Hobbies: Skiing; Golf; Theatre; Cricket. Address: Okere Falls, PO Box 2008, Rotorua, New Zealand.

COWIN Stephen Corteen, b. 26 Oct 1934, Elmira, New York, USA. Engineer; Educator. m. Martha Agnes Eisel, 10 Aug 1956, 1 son, 1 daughter. Education: BSE, Civil Engineering, 1956, MS, Civil Engineering, 1958, Johns Hopkins University; PhD, Engineering Mechanics, Pennsylvania State University, 1962; Postdoctoral study, University of Nottingham, 1967-68; Basic Medical courses in Anatomy and Physiology, School of Medicine, Tulane University, 1979-80. Appointments include: Professor, Mechanics, Department of Biomedical Engineering, 1977-85, Adjunct Professor, Department of Orthopaedics, School of Medicine, 1978-88, Professor, Applied Statistics, 1979-88, Alden J Laborde Professor of Engineering, 1985-88, Tulane University; Distinguished Professor, Department of Mechanical Engineering, City College, City University of New York, 1988-; Adjunct Professor, Orthopaedics, Mt Sinai School of Medicine, New York City, 1989-. Publications include: The Mechanical Properties of Bone (editor), 1981; Functional Adaptation Bone Tissue (co-editor), 1984; Strain Assessment by Bone Cells, 1988; Bone Mechanics (editor), 1989; The Structural Adaptation of Bones, 1990; Properties of Cortical Bone and The Theory of Bone Remodeling, 1990; Nature's Structural Engineering of Bone on a Daily Basis, 1992. Honours: Numerous including Best Paper Award, American Society of Mechanical Engineers, Bioengineering Division,

1992; European Society of Biomechanics Research Award, 1994. Memberships: Alpha Mu Beta; American Association for Dental Research; Fellow, American Association for the Advancement of Science; Senior Member, Biomedical Engineering Society; American Society of Biomechanics; New York Academy of Sciences; Orthopaedic Research Society; Sigma Xi. Address: Department of Mechanical Engineering, City College, City University of New York, 138th and Convent, New York, NY 10031, USA.

COX Barbara, b. 13 Feb 1932, Milwaukee, Wisconsin, USA. Medical Editor and Writer. 2 daughters. Education: BS, Honours, Iowa State University; MS, Ohio State University; EdS, University of Florida. Appointments: Editor, M D Anderson Hospital, Houston, Texas, 1961-62; Freelance Medical Editor and Writer, 1962-72; Editor, Writer, Mayo Clinic, Rochester, Minnesota, 1973-77; Manager, Biomedical Publications, Ross Laboratories, Columbus, Ohio, 1978-81; Director, MedEdit Associates, 1985-. Publications: Understanding Allergy, 1979; Living with Lung Cancer, 1987; Contributor of numerous articles in medical journals and newspapers. Honour: Award of Distinction, Society for Technical Communications, 1980. Memberships: Fellow, American Medical Writers Association; Council of Biology Editors. Hobbies: Pkayaing Guitar; Camping. Address: 5429 SW 80 Street, Gainesville, FL 32608, USA.

COX Robert Sayre Jr, b. 30 Jan 1925, San Francisco, California, USA. Pathologist. m. Brenda Kay Cox, dec 25 Nov 1989, 2 sons, 2 stepsons, 3 daughters. Education: Massachusetts Institute of Technology, 1943; University of Idaho, Moscow, 1943-44; Stanford University, 1944; St Louis University School of Medicine, 1945-46; BA, Distinction, 1946, BA, 1948, MS, 1948, PhD, Biochemistry, 1952, Stanford University; MD, University of Chicago School of Medicine, 1952. Appointments include: Chief, Clinical Pathology and Research and Development, Letterman Army Hospital, 1957-59; Chief, Pathology Service, Rodriguez Army Hospital, 1959-62; Director of Laboratories, Santa Clara Valley Medical Center, 1962-80; Chair of Pathology, Creighton University, 1980-91; Professor of Pathology, 1980-95; Emertus 1995-. Publications include: Pathology, Co-Editor, 1974; Manual for Laboratory Workload Recording Method, Co-author and Co-editor, 1972-90; Decisive Laboratory Management Today - The CAP Workload Recording Method Applied, Co-author, Co-Editor, 1985; Advanced Management Strategies Using CAP Workload Recording, Co-author, Co-editor, 1988; Patient Preparation and Specimen Handling, Fascicle VI: Chemistry, Co-author, Co-Editor, 1992; Patient Preparation Preparation and Specimen Handling Fascicle I: Immunology, Co-author, Co-editor, 1993; Patient Preparation and Specimen Handling Fascicle VII: Molecular Pathology and Flow Cytometry, Co-author, Co-editor, 1995. Honours include: Phi Beta Kappa; Phi Lambda Upsilon; Sigma Xi; Alpha Omega Alpha; Owen F Thomas Award, California Blood Bank Society, 1993. Memberships include: Fellow, New York Academy of Sciences; American Medical Association. Society. Address: Creighton University Department Pathology, Saint Joseph Hospital 6343B, 601 North 30 Street, Omaha, NE 68131, USA.

CRAIG Joseph Kevin, b. 20 Apr 1924, Newcastle-upon-Tyne, England. Surgeon. m. Dr Pat O'Sullivan, 1 Oct 1961, 2 sons, 2 daughters. Education: MB ChB, 1946; DRCOG; MRCOG; FRCS Edinburgh; FRCS England; FRCOG. Appointments: Senior Registrar, Lecturer in Obstetrics and Gynaecology, Bristol; Retired. Publications: Anxieties in Pregnancy, Co-author, 1984; Medical Mediation, 1993. Memberships: Northern England Obstetrics and Gynaecology Society; South west Obstetrics and Gynaecology Society; MEDACT; IPPNW, UK Councillor. Address: Orchard Hill, Corston, Bath BA2 9AR, England.

CRAIG Timothy John, b. 13 Jan 1959, Oceanside, New York, USA. Immunologist. m. Jill Craig, 24 Dec 1975, 2 sons, 1 daughter. Education: AAS; BA; DO. Appointments: Staff Internist; Allergist; Assistant Professor. Publications: Drug Toxicity, 1980-89; Hypersensitivity Pneumonitic, 1992; Vocal Cord Dysfunctions, 1992; Psitticosis, 1989; Asthma Care, 1993; Immunodeficiency, 1992. Honours: UpJohn Achievement Award, 1984; Sandoc Award, 1984; Nasal Commendation, 1987; Bailey Ashford Award, 1992; Dara Award, 1993; Army Commendation, 1993. Memberships: AOA; ACAI; AAAI; ACP; ACOI. Hobbies: Canoeing; Hiking; Skiing. Address: 2 Bristol Circle, Charleston, SC 29407, USA.

CRAIGHEAD Claude Claiborne, b. 30 Aug 1914, Shreveport, Louisiana, USA. Physician. m. Edith Dorrell, 16 Nov 1943, 1 son, 2 daughters. Education: MD, 1939; BA, 1934. Appointments: Clinical

Instructor of Surgery, 1949-55; Clinical Assistant Professor of Surgery, 1955-60; Clinical Associate Professor of Surgery, 1960-68; Clinical Professor of Surgery, 1968-84; Acting Chief, Thoracic Surgery, 1981-; Chief, Thoracic Surgery, 1969-73; Chief, Section of Peripheral Vascular Surgery, 1968-; Professor, 1984-. Publications: Contributor of over 70 articles. Honours: Claude C Craighead Endowed Chair, 1992; Listed Wall of Healing, New Orleans Hadassah; Dr Ernest Lederle Award for Excellence in Research Education and Patient Care, 1993; Outstanding Alumnus, 1993. Memberships: American College of Chest Physicians; American College of Surgeons; Surgical Association of Louisiana Southern Surgical Association; American Medical Association; New Orleans Surgical Society; James D Rives Surgical Society; AOA Medical Honour Society. Address: Department of Surgery, Louisiana State University School of Medicine, 1542 Tulane Avenue, New Orleans, LA 70112, USA.

CRAINZ Franco, b. 18 May 1913, Rome, Italy. Retired University Professor. Education: MD, Rome, 1936; FRCOG. Appointments: Professor of Obstetrics and Gynaecology, Novara, 1956-64, Gagliari, 1964-66, Medduk, 1966-67, Bari, 1967-72, Rome, 1972-88; Emeritus Professor, 1988-. Publications: An Obstetric Tragedy, 1977; Birth of an Heir, 1988; La Societa Italiana, 1992; Contributor of papers. Honours: Honorary member, Past President, Italian Society of OAG; Honorary member, Austrian, Portugese, Romanian, Spanish and Swiss Societies; Corresponding Member, German Society. Hobbies: History; Music. Address: Via P Mascagni 124, 00199 Rome, Italy.

CRAWFORD E David, b. 6 June 1947, Cincinnati, Ohio, USA. Physician; Surgeon. m. Barbara L Crawford, 28 June 1969, 3 sons. Education: MD. Appointments: Professor of Urology, University of Mississippi; Chairman, Division of Urology. Publications: Editor, Genitourinary Cancer Surgery, 1st, 2nd Editions. Honours: Chairman, National Prostate Cancer Education Council; Chairman, Genito-Urinary Cancer Committee, Southwest Oncology Group. Memberships: American Urological Association; ACS. Hobby: Skiing. AddressL UCNSC, 4200 East 9th, Denver, CO 80262, USA.

CRAWFORD Fred A Jr, b. 17 Oct 1942, Columbia, South Carolina, USA. Cardiothoracic Surgeon. m. Mary Jane Dantzler, 11 June 1966, 1 son, 1 daughter. Education: MD, Duke University, 1967. Appointments include: Assistant Professor, 1976-78, Chief, Division of Cardiac Surgery, 1976-79, Associate Professor, 1978-79, University of Mississippi; Professor, Head, Division of Cardiothoracic Surgery, 1979-; Chairman, Department of Surgery, 1988-, Medical University of South Carolina, Charleston. Honours: Governor, American College of Cardiology, 1987-92; Member, Board of Directors, American Board of Thoracic Surgery, 1991-. Memberships include: American Surgical Association; American Association for Thoracic Surgery; American College of Surgeons; Society of Thoracic Surgery; Southern Surgical Association; Thoracic Surgical Directors Association. Hobbies: Hunting; Fishing. Address: Medical University of South Carolina, 171 Ashley Avenue, Charleston, SC 29425, USA.

CRAWFORD Michael Howard, b. 10 July 1943, Madison, WI, USA. Physician. m. Janis Kirschner, 23 June 1968, 1 s, 2 d. Education: AB, University of California, Berkeley, 1965; MD, University of California, San Francisco, 1969. Appointments: Assistant Professor of Medicine, University of California, San Diego, 1974-76; Assistant to Professor of Medicine, University of Texas Health Science Centre, San Antonio, 1976-89; Robert S Flinn Professor and Chief of Cardiology, University of New Mexico, 1989-. Publications: Current Diagnosis and Treatment in Cardiology, Editor, 1995; Contributor of over 200 original articles, reviews and book chapters. Honours: Paul Dudley White Award, Association Military Surgeons of the US, 1981. Memberships: FACC; FACP; SSCI; WAP; AFCR; Fellow, AHA Clinical Council; ASE; ASNC. Hobbies: Classic British Automobiles; Skiing. Address: University of New Mexico Hospital, 2211 Lomas NE, Albuquerque, NM 87131, USA.

CREEVY Donald Charles, b. 22 Apr 1936, Minneapolis, MN, USA. Physician; Obstetrician; Gynaecologist. m. 17 Jan 1987, 1 s (dec), 2 d. Education: BA, University of Minnesota; BS, University of Minnesota; MD, University of Minnesota; Diplomate, American Board of Obstetrics & Gynaecology, Stanford University, School of Medicine. Appointments: Fellow, National Foundation; Clinical Teaching Assistant & Clinical Instructor, Department of Gynaecology & Obstetrics, Stanford University School of Medicine; Deputy Chief, Department of Gynaecology & Obstetrics, Stanford University School of Medicine; Member, Medical Board, Stanford University Hospital; Chairman & Member, Perinatal

Care Committee, Stanford University Hospital; Clinical Assistant Professor in Obstetrics & Gynaecology, Stanford University School of Medicine. Publications: include, Proceedings of the Fifth International Congress of Psychosomatic Obstetrics and Gynaecology, 1978; Report of the Committee to Study Alternative Birthing: A Report to the 1978 Legislature on Alternatives in Maternity Care, 1978; The Relationship of Obstetrical Trauma to Learning Disabilities: An Obstetrician's View, 1986; Birth Without Surgery, 1987. Memberships: Santa Clara County Medical Association; California Medical Association; American Medicial Association; American College of Obstetricians and Gynaecologists; Audio Engineering Society. Hobbies: Music; Sound Reproduction; Travel. Address: 4370 Alpine Road, Portola Valley, CA 94028, USA.

CREWS Douglas E, b. 16 Oct 1950, Toledo, OH, USA. Professor of Anthropology and Preventive Medicine. 2 s, 1 d. Education: BA, 1976, MA, 1980, PhD, 1985, Penn State University. Appointments: Research Assistant Professor, Northwestern University Medical School, Department of Community Health and Preventive Medicine, 1987-80; Assistant Professor, Loyola University Medical School, Department of Preventive Medicine, 1990-91; Associate Professor of Athropology and Preventive Medicine, Ohio State University. Publications include: Multiple Caises of Death, Chronic Diseases and Aging, 1990; Ethnicity as a Taxonomic Tool in Biomedical and Biosocial Research, 1991; Population Genetics of Apolipoprotein E, A-IV, and H Polymorphisms and Effect on Lipids, 1993; Biological Anthropology and Human Aging: Some Current Directions in Aging Research, 1993; Correlates of Blood Pressure in Yanomami Indians of Northwestern Brazil, 1993; Human Evolution and the Genetic Epidemiology of Chronic Degenerative Diseases, 1991; Obesity and Diabetes, 1994; Why Are Chronic Degenerative Diseases and Aging Related?, 1994; Biological Anthropology and Aging: An Emerging Synthesis, Co-Editor, 1994. Memberships include: American Heart Association Council on Epidemiology, 1987-; American Anthropological Association-Biological Anthropology, 1990-; American Association of Physical Anthropologists, 1980-. Hobbies: Water Skiing; Downhill Skiing; Travel; Racquetball. Address: Department of Preventive Medicine, Ohio State University, B-107 Starling-Coving Hall, 320 West 10th Avenue, Columbus, OH 43210, USA.

CRIPPS Derek James, b. 17 Sept 1928, London, England. Physician. m. Eileen Cripps, 21 Dec 1963, 2 sons, 2 daughters. Education: MB, BS, University of London, 1953; MSc, University of Michigan, 1961; MD (London), 1965; FACP. Appointments: Senior Registrar, St John's Hospital for Diseases of the Skin, London, 1962-65; Assistant Professor, 1965-68, Associate Professor, 1968-72, Professor, Head of Dermatology, 1972-, University of Wisconsin, Madison, USA. Publications: Erythropoietic Protoporphyria, MD thesis, 1965; Author or co-author, articles including: Biochemical and fluorescence microscopy screening tests for erythropoietic protoporphyria, 1965; Hepatobiliary changes in erythropoietic protoporphyria, 1965; Porphyria and photosensitivity, 1967; Syphilis maligna praecox. Syphilis of the great epidemic?; Absorption and action spectra studies on bithionol and halogenated salicylanilide photosensitivity, 1970; Sunscreens: Skin types and protection factor, 1979; Instrumentation and action spectra in light-associated diseases, 1981; Porphyria turcica due to hexachlorobenzene: a 20 to 30 year follow-up study on 204 patients, 1984. Memberships: American Academy of Dermatology; British Association of Dermatology; Society for Investigative Dermatology; European Society for Dermatologic Research; Central Society for Clinical Research. Hobbies: Travel; Classical music; Swimming (Great Britain 1950-52). Address: University Station Clinics, 2880 University Ave, Madison, WI 53705, USA.

CRIST William Miles, b. 21 July 1943, Florence, South Carolina, USA. Professor of Paediatrics. m. Helen Lucille Valle Crist, 5 June 1971, 1 son. Education: BA, cum laude, Central Methodist, Fayette, 1965; MD, University of Missouri, Columbia, 1969; Board Certified Paediatric Haematology and Oncology. Appointments: Chief, Paediatric Service, Carswell AFB, Ft Worth, Texas, 1972-74; NCI Trainee, Oncology Research, Washington School of Medicine, Missouri, 1974-75; Associate Scientist, Comprehensive Cancer Centre, 1975-78, Acting Director, Paediatric Haematology/Oncology, Children's Hospital, 1976-78, Director, Paediatric Haematology/Oncology, Children's Hospital, 1978-85, University of Alabama at Birmingham; Chairman, Member, Department of Haematology/Oncology, St Jude Children's Research Hospital, Memphis, Tennessee, 1985-1995; Director, Extramural Programs and Chief, Leukemia/Lymphona Division, St Jude Children's Res Hospital, Memphis, TN, 1995-; Professor of Paediatrics,

University of Tennessee, Memphis, College of Medicine. Publications: Contributor of articles to professional journals. Honours: Omicron Delta Kappa; Sigma Epsilon Pi. Memberships: Vice Chairman, 1985-90, Paediatric Oncology group; Associate Chairman, 1985-, Biologic Studies of ALL, POG; Vice Chairman, 1991-92, Paediatric Oncology Group. Address: St Jude Children's Research Hospital, Department of Haematology/Oncology, PO Box 318, 332 N Lauderdale, Memphis, TN 38105-2794, USA.

CRONENWETT Jack L, b. 13 Dec 1946, Ludington, Michigan, USA. Vascular Surgeon. m. Debra A Cote, 26 Sep 1981, 2 daughters. Education: BS, University of Michigan, 1969; MD, Stanford University, 1973. Appointments: Assistant, Associate Professor of Surgery, University of Michigan Medical Centre; Professor of Surgery, Dartmouth Medical School; Chief, Section of Vascular Surgery, Dartmouth-Hitchcock Medical Centre. Publications: Contributor of over 100 scientific articles and book chapters in vascular surgery, 1976-. Honours: Phi Beta Kappa, 1968; Senior Surgical Award, Stanford, 1969; Conrad Jobst Award for Vascular Research, 1977; Resident Research Award, Association Academy Surgery, 1977. Memberships: Society for Vascular Surgery; New England Society for Vascular Surgery' Society of University Surgeons; New England Surgical Society; International Society for Cardiovascular Surgery. Hobbies: Tennis; Skiing. Address: Section of Vascular Surgery, Dartmouth Hitchcock Medical Centre, 1 Medical Centre Drive, Lebanon, NH 03756, USA.

CROSS Herbert James, b. 18 Mar 1934, Ashland, Virginia, USA. Psychologist. m. Sharon Willard, 17 Jan 1993, 1 son, 1 daughter. Education: BA, Psychology, Randolph-Macon College, 1958; MA, Psychology, University of Richmond, 1960; PhD, Psychology, Syracuse University, 1965. Appointments include: Instructor in Psychology, University of Richmond, Virginia, 1959-61; Assistant Professor, Associate Professor, University of Connecticut, 1965-72; Associate Professor, 1972-75, Professor of Psychology, 1975-, Co-Coordinator, Medical Psychology Practicum, 1989-93, Director, Human Relations Center, 1993-, Washington State University; Numerous Consulting positions. Publications include: Post traumatic stress disorder in Vietnam veterans: Social factors, 1990; Co-author: The influence of the 1960's on adolescence, 1985; Malpractice in psychotherapy and psychological evaluation, 1987; The modification of hypnotic susceptibility by social skills training, 1988; Hypnotically Created Pseudomemories: Further Investigation into the "Memory Distortion of the Response Bias" Question, 1992. Honours: US Public Health Service Fellow, 1964-65; Henry Guze Award, 1989; President, Washington State Psychological Association. Memberships: American Psychological Association; American Society of Clinical Hypnosis; Washington State Psychological Association, President-Elect 1993, Executive Board 1989-90; Eastern and Western Psychological Associations; Society for the Scientific Study of Sex; Association of Scientist-Practitioners in Psychology; American Association of Applied and Preventive Psychology. Hobby: Pistol and rifle shooting. Address: NE 703 Maple Street, Pullman, WA 99163, USA.

CROWTHER Patricia Anne, b. 21 May 1925, Derbyshire, England. Clinic Consultant. m. Dr Henry S Cecil, 19 Sep 1961, 1 daughter. Education: MD, USA. Appointments: Chief Child Psychiatrist, Board of Education, Philadelphia, Pennsylvania, 22 years; Consultant to 4 Mental Health Clinics. Publications: Child Welfare; Mental Hygiene; International Congress of Mental Health, United Kingdom; Mental Health Congress, Cannes, France. Memberships: Regional Council of Child Psychiatry; Academy of Child and Adolescent Psychiatry; American Psychiatric Association. Hobbies: Opera; Gardening; Birdwatching.

CRUE Benjamin Lane Jr, b. 22 May 1925, Rahway, New Jersey, USA. Emeritus Professor. m. Beverly Marie Malyon, 22 Sep 1943, 1 son, 3 daughters. Education: Deepsprings College, 1942-43; University DePauw, 1943-44; BS, MD, University of Chicago, Chicago, 1944-48. Appointments: Professor of Neurology, Chairman, California College of Medicine, Los Angeles, 1962-64; Emeritus Professor, (Clinical) of Neurosurgery, University of Southern California Medical School, Los ASngeles, 1986-; Medical Director, Durango Pain Rehabilitation Centre; President, Neurology, Neurosurgery Association PC Durango, Colorado. Publications: Contributor of numerous articles in professional journals. Memberships: La Platco County Medical Society; Colorado State Medical Society; AMA; American Pain Society; American Academy Pain Medicine; FACS; Medical Staff, Mercy Medical Centre, Durango; Western Pain Society. Address: 1130 Main Avenue, Durango, CO, USA.

CRUICKSHANK Derek James, b. 4 Mar 1957, Aberdeen, Scotland. Doctor. m. Rose Elliott, 4 Mar 1985, 1 s, 1 d. Education: MB; ChB; MRCOG. Appointments: Consultant of Obstetrics & Gynaecology. Publications: CA125 in Ovarian Cancer, 1987; Familial Epithelial Ovarian Cancer, 1992; Ovulation and Ovarian Cancer, 1992. Memberships: Royal College of Obstetricians & Gynaecologists; British Gynaecological Cancer Society; BSCCP. Hobbies: Blues Music; Golf; Real Ale. Address: South Cleveland Hospital, Marton Road, Middlesborough, England.

CRUMLEY Roger L, b. 10 Aug 1941, Perry, Iowa, USA. Head and Neck Surgeon. m. Janet L Conant, 13 Oct 1987, 2 daughters. Education: BA, Simpson College, 1972; MD, 1967, MS, 1975, University of Iowa. Appointments: Chief, Otolaryngology, San Francisco General Hospital, 1975-80; Professor, Chair, Department of Otolaryngology, Head and Neck Surgery, University of California, Irvine. Honours: Harris P Mosher Award for Excellence in Research (Otolaryngology); President, American Academy of Facial Plastic and Reconstructive Surgery, 1994-95. Hobbies: Skiing; Running; Golf; Jazz Trumpet and Piano. Address: University of California Medical Centre, 101 City Drive, Orange, CA 92668, USA.

CRUNDWELL Jane Kim, b. 16 Nov 1968, England. Psychologist. Education: BSc (Hons), Psychology, Marketing, 1991, PhD, Psychology, 1994, Lancaster University. Appointments: Currently Research Psychologist. Publications: Fluoxetine and Suidical Idepition: A Review of the Literature, 1992; Suicide in Western History, 1992; Lithium and Its Potential Benefit in Reducing Increased Mortality Rates Due to Suicide, 1994. Membership: British Psychological Society. Hobbies: Travel; Crafts; Reading; Writing. Address: Department of Psychology, Fylde College, University of Lancaster, Lancaster LA1 4Yf, England.

CRUZ Norma Irene, b. 23 Dec 1952, Cuba. Plastic Surgeon. m. Leo Korchin, 22 Dec 1990. Education: BS, 1972, MD, 1976, Residency, General Surgery, 1976-81, University of Puerto Rico; Residency, Plastic Surgery, Yale University, 1981-83. Appointments: Chief of Plastic Surgery, Associate Professor of Plastic Surgery, University of Puerto Rico, 1984-; Director, Surgical Research Laboratories, 1984-. Publications: Management of Contaminated Bone Grafts, 1981; An Experimental Model to Determine the Level of Antibiotics in Irradiated Tissues, 1984; Evaluation of Fibrin Glue in Rat Sciatic Nerve Repairs, 1986; Muscle Flaps in the Management of Vascular Grafts in Contaminated Wounds: An Experimental Study in Dogs, 1988; Accelerated Healing of Full Thickness Burns by the Use of High Voltage Pulsed Galvanic Stimulation in the Pig, 1989; The Effect of Isotretinoin and Triamcinolone Acetonide on Human Skin Fibroplasts In-Vitro, 1993. Honours: President, Puerto Rico Plastic Surgery Society, 1994. Memberships: American Society of Plastic and Reconstructive Surgeons; American College of Surgeons; The Society of Head and Neck Surgeons. Hobbies: Painting (acrylic over canvas); Tennis. Address: Division of Plastic Surgery, University of Puerto Rico, PO Box 365067, San Juan, PR 00936-5067, USA.

CRYER Philip Eugene, b. 5 Jan 1940, El Paso, Illinois, USA. Academic Physician. 1 son, 1 daughter. Education: BA, 1962, MD, 1965, Northwestern University Medical School. Appointments: Resident, Medicine, Barns Hospital, Fellow in Endocrinology and Metabolism, Washington University, St Louis, 1965-69, 1971-72; US Navy, 1969-71; Instructor, 1971, Assistant Professor, 1972, Associate Professor, 1977, Professor, 1981; Irene E & Michael M Karl Professor of Endocrinology & Metabolism, 1995, Faculty, Washington University School of Medicine. Publications: Diagnostic Endocrinology, 1976, 1979; Contributor of over 250 articles and 55 book chapters. Honours: Phi Beta Kappa, 1961; Alpha Omega Alpha, 1964; Rorer Award of the Endocrine Society, 1987; Rumbaugh Award, Juvenile Diabetes Foundation, 1989; Banting Medal, American Diabetes Association, 1994. Memberships: American Federation Clinical Research; American Society Clinical Investigation; Association American Physicians; Endocrine Society; Juvenile Diabetes Foundation; American Diabetes Association, Editor, Diabetes, 1992-, President Elect, 1995. Hobby: Music. Address: Campus Box 8127, Washington University School of Medicine, 660 South Euclid Avenue, St Louis, MO 63110, USA.

CSILLAG Veronica Maria, b. 13 May 1928, Budapest, Hungary. Consultant; Medical Doctor. m. György Vikar, 5 May 1953, 2 sons. Education: Medical Diploma, Special Training with exams in Neurology, EEG, Psychiatry, Psychoanalysis. Appointments: Medical Doctor, Several Hospitals, Szombathely, Balassagyarmat, OTKI, ORFI;

Specialist, Polyclinics; Chief Medical Officer, Department for Neurotic People, Kerepestarcsa. Publications: Annotations for students at the University of ELTE, Psychology, from the lectures in the topic on EEG, 1969-70; Das Persönlichkeitsprofil schwerer Epileptiker, Was misst der Bear Fedio Fragebogen?, 1984. Memberships: Society of Hungarian Medicine, H Elektrophysiological Society; Hungarian Psychoanalytic Society; International Psychoanalytic Association. Hobbies: Music; Reading Literature; Travel. Address: Rhedey u 5, H1026 Budapest, Hungary.

CSILLIK Bertalan, b. 10 Nov 1927, Szeged, Hungary. Professor of Anatomy, Project Director. m. Elizabeth Knyihar-Csillik, 30 Apr 1972, 2 daughters. Education: |MD, Szeged, 1954; PhD, Budapest, 1962; DSc, Budapest, 1968. Appointments: Instructor of Anatomy, 1950-59; Assistant Professor of Anatomy, 1960; Assistant Professor, Pharmacology, University of Pennsylvania, USA, 1962-63; Associate Professor of Anatomy, Szeged, 1964-68; Professor of Neuropathology, Harvard University, Boston, USA, 1977-78; Professor of Anatomy, Chairman, 1968-93; Professor of Anatomy, Harvard University Medical School, Boston, 1993-94; Project Director, Bay Zoltan Institute of Biotechnology. Publications: The Post Synaptic Membrane, 1965, German, 1987; The Protean Gate, 1986. Honours: Silver Medal of Labour, 1986; International Peace Award, Albert Einstein Academy, USA, 1991. Laureate of the Hungarian Academy of Sciences, 1993. Memberships: Consultant Member, Hungary Academy of Science; Corresponding Member, Belgium Royal Academy; Leopoldine Academy, Germany. Hobbies: Classical Music. Address: Bay Zoltan Institute of Biotechnology, 2 Derkovits Fasor, H-6726 Szeged, Hungary.

CUBA RODRIGUEZ Juan Manuel, b. 2 June 1928, Cajabamba, Cajamarca, Peru. Medical Doctor; Professor of Neurology. Education: MD. Appointments include: Assistant Etranger, Hôpital de la Salpêtrière, 1959; Currently: Chief, Department of Neurology; Principal Professor of Neurology. Publications: Les Formations Non-Segmentaires du Tronc Cérébral de l'Homme, 1962; L'Anatomie et Physiologie Normal et Pathologique du Système Nerveux, 1966, by Fundamenyos de Semiología Neurológica, 1989; Revue Neurologique, 1985, 1986; Aproximación Anatomofuncional del Tronco Cerebral, 1995. Honours: Scientific Investigation National Award, 1962; Teaching and Investigation Award, Peruvian Medical College, 1994. Memberships: Société Française de Neurologie; Peruvian Society of Neurology; National Academy of Medicine. Hobby: Literature. Address: Jr José Maria Eguren 110, Magdalena, Lima, Peru.

CUELLO Augusto Claudio Guillermo, b. 7 Apr 1939, Buenos Aires, Argentina. Medical Research Scientist. m. Martha Maria J Kaes, 10 Mar 1967, 2 daughters. Education: MD, University of Buenos Aires, 1965; MA (hon), 1968, DSc, 1986, Oxford University; Dr hc, Federal University of Ceara, Brazil, 1991. Appointments: Assistant Professor, School of Biochemistry, University of Buenos Aires, 1974-75; Staff Scientist, Neurochemical Pharmacology, Medical Research Council, Cambridge, England, 1975-78; Lecturer, Department of Pharmacology and Human Anatomy, Oxford University; Medical Tutor, E P Abraham Senior Research Fellow, Lincoln College, Oxford, 1978-85; Professor, Chairman, Pharmacology and Therapeutics, McGill University, Montreal, Canada, 1985-; Consultancies. Publications include: Editor: Co-Transmission 1, 1982; Immunohistochemistry, 1983; Brain Microdissection Techniques, 1987; Pain and Mobility, 1987; Substance P and Neurokinins, 1987; Neuronal Cell Death and Repair: Restorative Neurology, 1993; Immunohistochemistry II, 1993; Cholinergic Function and Dysfunction: Progress in Brain Research, 1993. Honours: Estela A de Goytia Prize, Argentinian Association for Advancement of Science, 1968; Postdoctoral Fellow, National Institutes of Health, 1970-72; Professor A Rosenblueth Award, Grass Foundation, 1979; Robert Feulgen Prize, Gesellschaft für Histochemie, 1981; Honorary Professor: Buenos Aires University, 1992; Norman Bethune University of Medical Science, China, 1992; Honorary Citizen, New Orleans, 1992. Memberships include: American Society for Neuroscience; Brain Research Association; Canadian College of Neuropsychiatry; International Society of Neuroendocrinology; British Pharmacological Society; Canadian Pain Society. Address: 73 Rosemont Crescent, Montreal, Quebec, Canada H3Y 2C8.

CUI Dejian, b. 14 Jun 1934, Beijing, China. Physician. m. Li Zhanliang, 17 Sept 1960, 1 son, 1 daughter. Education: Physician, Kharkov Medical School, Ukraine, 1960; MD, Military Postgraduate Medical School, China, 1980; Postdoctoral Fellowship, Duke University Medical Center, USA, 1985-86. Appointments: Chief, Division of

Respiratory Medicine, General Hospital of PLA, Beijing, China, 1983-87. Publications: co-author: Geriatric Cardiology, 1987; Effect of sub-human lung fibroblasts, in J Appl Physiol, 1987; Effect of 70% oxygen on postresectional lung growth in rats, in J Toxicol Env Health, 1988; Changes of glucocorticold reseptor of lung tissue in Guinea pig asthma models, in Am Rev Resp Dis, 1993; A plasma amino acid study of patients with COPD and cor pulmonale, in Europ Resp J, 1993. Honours: Armed Forces Science and Technology Advances Prizes, grade 2, 1992, grade 3, 6 times, 1988-94. Memberships: Summit Respiratory Medicine Society, PLA; Chinese Medical Association; Western Returned Student Association. Hobbies: Swimming; Travelling. Address: Div of Respiratory Medicine, 304th Hospital, 51 Fucheng Road, Beijing 100037, China.

CUI Keming, b. 14 Mar 1941, Shangdong Province, China. Professor. Education: Studied Botany, Department of Biology, Peking University, China, 1960-66. Career: Professor, Department of Plant Molecular and Developmental Biology, College of Life Sciences, Peking University, China. Publications: More than 40 papers published in Scientia Sinica, Acta Botsanica Sinica, Plant Physiology, Plant, Cell and Environment, Trees and IAWA Bull. Membership: Chinese Society of Botany; China Eucommia Comprehensive Development Association. Address: Department of Plant Molecular and Development Biology, College of Life Sciences, Peking University, Beijing 100871, China.

CULBERTSON Frances Mitchell, b. 31 Jan 1921. Psychologist. m. John M Culbertson, Aug 1947, 1 son, 3 daughters. Education: BS, Psychology, 1947; MS, Psychology, 1949; PhD, Psychology, 1955; Postdoctoral training, 1959-61. Appointments: Clinical Psychologist, Chair, Psychology, 1965-66, University of Wisconsin, Madison; Researcher, Child Psychiatry, NMIH, 1966-67; School Psychologist, 1967-68; Professor, University of Wisconsin, Whitewater, 1968-88; Clinical Psychologist, Hypnotherapist, 1988-. Publications: Voices in International School Psychology, 1985; Relaxation Strategies for Children, 1990; Relaxation Strategies with an Anxious Child, 1990; Stresses, Strains and Adaptive Responses of Women - International Report, 1993. Honours: Pi Lambda Theta, 1949; Sigma Xi, 1950; Diplomate, American Board of Professional Psychology, 1972; Fellow, American Psychological Association, 1979; Honorary President, Brazilian Clinical Psychology, 1979; Psi Chi, 1986. Memberships: American Psychological Association; International Council of Psychologists; International Association of Applied Psychology; Wisconsin Psychological Association; American Society of Clinical Hypnosis. Hobbies: Cross-country skiing; Hiking; Reading; Chorus. Address: 5305 Burnett Drive, Madison, WI 53705, USA.

CUMMING David Crosbie, b. 15 May 1944. Professor of Obstetrics & Gynaecology. m. Ceinwen Ovens, 1 Apr 1967, 1 s, 1 d. Education: MB; ChB; FRCOG; FRCSC. Appointments: Assistant Professor, 1981-83; Associate Professor, 1983-90; Professor of Obstetrics & Gynaecology and Medicine, Division of Endocrinology. Publications include: Hysteroscopy in 100 Patients, 1979; Combined Laparoscopy and Hysteroscopy in the Investigation of the Ovulatory Infertile Female, 1980; Acute Suppression of Circulating Testosterone Levels by Cortisol in Man, 1983; The Effect of Acute Exercise on LH Pulsatile Release in Women Runners, 1985; Assessment of Premenstrual Complaint with the Prementrual Assessment form: Comparison of Two Populations, 1991; Evidence of Autonomic Dysreflexia during Functional Electrical Stimulation in Individuals with Spinal cord Injuries, 1993; Urinary Free Cortisol as an Indicator of Exercise Training Stress, 1994. Memberships: Canadian Fertility and Andrology Society; American Fertility Society; Society of Obstetricians and Gynaecologists of Canada. Hobbies: Travel; Reading. Address: IDI Walter Mackenzie Health Sciences Centre, University of Alberta, Edmonton, Alberta, Canada T6G 2R7.

CUMMING Robert Graham, b. 10 Feb 1956, Sydney, Australia. Epidemiologist. m. Anne Nunan, 6 Apr 1985, 2 d. Education: MPH, PhD, University of Sydney; MB BS. Appointments: Senior Lecturer in Epidemiology. Publications: Calcium Intake and Bone Mass: A Quantitative Review of the Evidence, 1990; Case-Control Study of Risk factors for Hip Fractures in the Elderly, 1994. Memberships: Society for Epidemiologic Research; Public Health Association of Australia. Hobbies: Travel; Reading; Skiing. Address: Department of Public Health, A27 University of Sydney, Sydney, Australia.

CUNNINGHAM Erik, b. 5 Nov 1962, Helsinki, Finland. Physician in General Practice. m. Susan P McKay, 2 Aug 1990, 1 daughter. Education: MD, University of British Columbia, Canada, 1987.

Appointments: Currently: Private Family Practice and Active Staff, Prince Rupert Regional Hospital, British Columbia, Canada. Memberships: Prince Rupert Medical Society; British Columbia Medical Association; British Columbia College of Physicians and Surgeons. Hobbies: Swimming; Running; Piano; Guitar.

CUNNINGHAM Valorie, b. 26 Mar 1964, Kingston, Ontario, Canada. Physician. m. William Joseph Cunningham, 27 Mar 1993. Education: BSc, Pharmacology, University of British Columbia, 1986; MD, University of British Columbia, 1990. Appointments: Private Family Practice Physician; Emergency Department Physician, Whitehorse General Hospital; Physician, Medevac Services, Yukon; Health Promotions Committee, Yukon Medical Association; Medical Advisor, Thomson Centre Extended Care & Rehabilitation Facility; Advisor, Pharmacare & Chronic Disease Program. Publications: Toxins from Marine Invertebrates, 1990. Memberships: Yukon Medical Association; Canadian Medical Association; BC College of Physicians & Surgeons; BC Medical Association. Hobbies: Cross Country Skiing; Camping; Hiking; Whitewater Canoeing & Kayaking; Volleyball. Address: 406 Lambert Street, Whitehorse, Yukon Y1A 1Z7, Canada.

CURATI-ALASONATTI Walter, b. 8 Nov 1943, Geneva, Switzerland. Physician. m. Judith A Payne, 28 Aug 1993. Education: MD, University of Geneva Medical School, 1973; PhD, University of Geneva Medical School, 1980. Appointments: Associate Professor, University of Geneva, 1980; Professor, University of Mainz, 1987. Publications: More than 100 professional articles. Memberships: RSM; FRCR; RSNA; SSRMN; AIUM; BMA. Honours: FRCR, 1992. Hobbies: Languages and Dialects; Architecture. Address: Royal Postgraduate Medical School, Du Cane Road 150, London W12 0HS, England.

CURRIMBHOY Zinet E, b. 28 June 1925, Bombay, India. Physician. Education: BSc DCH, MD, Paediatrics, Bombay; MD, Toronto, Canada; American Board of Paediatrics USA; American Board of Paediatric Haeatology/Oncology USA. Appoinments: Provisional Assistant Paediatrician and Fellow in Paediatric Haematology, New York University; Research Associate in Paediatric Haematology Oncology and Instructor in Paediatrics, Chicago; Associate Attending, Attending, Chicago; Assistant Professor in Paediatrics, Philadelphia; Associate Professor, Cornell University; Associate Professor, Tulane University School of Medicine, New Orleans; Head of Paediatric Haematology/Oncology, Wadia Children's Hospital, Bombay, India. Publications: Fletcher factor Deficiency and Myocardial Infarction, Co-author, 1976; An Outbreak of an Infection Association with Circulating Activiated Monocytes and Hemophycyoctes in Children, 1991. Memberships: American Society of Haematology. Hobby: Music. Address: Sekhsaria Sadan, 20 Nepean Sea Road, Bombay 6, India.

CURTIS John Joseph, b. 16 Jan 1944, Rochester, New York, USA. Physician. Education: BS, University of Scranton, 1966; MD, Georgetown University, Washington DC, 1970. Appointments: Assistant Professor of Medicine, University of Kentucky Medical Centre, 1974-79; Associate Professor of Medicine, 1979-85, Professor of Medicine, Professor of Surgery, Programme Director, GCRC, University of Alabama at Birmingham. Publications: Contributor of over 122 works including professional articles and book chapters. Memberships: American Society of Nephrology; International Society of Nephrology; American Society of Transplant Physicians; European Dialysis and Transplant Association; Transplantation Society; AFCR; Southern Society for Clinical Research; American Society of Hypertension. Address: University of Alabama at Birmingham, Division of Nephrology, Birmingham, AL 35294-0007, USA.

CURTIS Kenneth William, b. 11 Sept 1952, Calgary, Alberta, Canada. Senior Consultant; Forensic Consultant, Ernst & Young, Canada; Clinical Psychologist. m. Patricia Anne McGeady, 7 July 1973, 1 daughter. Education: MA, Psychology, University of Regina; BA, Honours in Psychology, University Regina; BA, Athabasca University, Alberta; Diploma, Neuropsychology, Neuropsychopathology, Drexel University, Philadelphia, USA; Board Certified in Rehabilitation Counselling; Board Certified Pain Practitioner. Appointments: Corporate President, Red Deer, Alberta, Canada, 1976-81; Research Assistant, Red Deer College, Alberta, Canada, 1983; Teaching Assistant, University Regina, 1985-88; Clinical Psychologist & Psychological Associate, Regina Mental Health Clinic, Family Violence Unit, Regina Mental Health Clinic, Sask, Canada, 1986-89; Clinical Psychologist & Researcher, IWP, Wascana Rehabilitation Centre, Wascana Hospital, Regina, 1989-93. Publications: Chronic Disability Syndrome: Canadian

Family Physician, 1991; Treatment Readiness Index, 1993; Editor, Saskatchewan Psychologist, 1990-92. Memberships: Fellow, American Academy of Pain Management; International Association for the Study of Pain; Canadian Psychological Association; Psychological Society of Saskatchewan; Canadian Association of Rehabilitation Personnel; Commission on Rehabilitation Counsellor Certification. Honours: Civic Commendation for an Act of Courage, Alberta, 1977; President's Award, Academic Excellence, 1985; Member, Guest Lecturer, International Delegation of Medical Specialists to Russian I M Sechenov 1st Moscow Medical Academy, Eastern Europe & Hungary, 1992. Hobbies: Flying; Scuba Diving; Family; Travel; Boating; Golf. Address: 32 Dowie Bay, Regina, Saskatchewan S4R 5W3, Canada.

CUTLER David Lloyd, b. 17 Feb 1940, Cleveland, Ohio, USA. Psychiatrist. m. Nancy Lee Mantz, 15 June 1967, 2 sons, 1 daughter. Education: MD, Ohio State University, 1967; Psychiatry training, University of Washington, Seattle, 1968-70, University of California, Irvine, 1970-71. Appointments: Professor of Psychiatry; Editor, Community Mental Health Journal; Director, Public Psychiatry Training Programme, Oregon Health Sciences University, Portland, Oregon. Publications: Contributor of numerous articles in professional journals. Membership: American Association of Community Psychiatrists. Address: Oregon Health Sciences University, 3181 Sam Jackson Road, Portland, OR 97201-3011, USA.

CUTLER Jay B, b. 7 Sept 1930, Brooklyn, New York, USA. Attorney. m. Randy Cutler, 5 Apr 1952, 2 daughters. Education: BS, Business Administration, New York University, 1951; JD, Brooklyn Law School, 1956. Appointments: Attorney in Private Practice, 1958; Attorney and Public Affairs TV Producer, 1958-68; Senate Minority Counsel, Health Subcommittee, 1968-77; US Senate Minority Counsel, Alcoholism and Narcotics Subcommittee, 1972-77; US Senate Minority Counsel and Staff Director, Labour and Human Resource Committee, 1975-77; Currently Special Counsel and Director, Government Relations. Publications: Analysis for Comprehensive Manpower Training Act, 1970; College of American Pathologists Legislative Update Presentation, 1975; Conference on Licensure, New York Medical Training Registry, 1975; CHF Testimony to Senate Health and Scientific Research Committee, 1979. Honours: Honorary Doctor of Humane Letters, 1978; APA Special Presidential Commendation, 1985; Certificate of Excellence, American Society of Association Executives, 1985; Visiting Professor, Cleveland Clinic, 1990. Memberships: American Bar Association; Women in Government Relations; American Academy of Health Administration; American Academy of Law and Psychiatry. Hobbies: Biking; Reading; Swimming; Travel. Address: 1400 K Street NW, Washington, DC 20005, USA.

CUTTING Robert Thomas, b. 28 Oct 1929, Winchendon, MA, USA. Physician. m. Frances Clark Smith, 16 May 1992, 3 s, 4 d. Education: BS, Holy Cross College, 1951; MD, Boston University, 1955; MPH, Harvard University, 1959; Diploma, US Army Command & General Staff College, 1945; Diploma, Industrial College of the Armed Forces, National Defense University, 1976; Diploma, American Board of Preventative Medicine; Fellow, American College of Preventative Medicine. Appointments: Chief Surgeon, US Army Security Agency; Battalion Commander, US Army, Alaska; Chief, Preventative Medicine Research Division, Office of the Surgeon General; Chair, Walter Reed Army Medical Research Team, Vietnam; Chair, Division of Surgery, Walter Reed Army Institute of Research; Director, Health and Environment/Director, Health Care, Office the Surgeon General; Chief Surgeon, US Army Medical Command; Commanding General, DD Eisenhower Army Medical Center; Senior Physician, Westinghouse. Memberships: include, American Medical Association; American Public Health Association; American Society of Tropical Medicine and Hygiene; International Health Society. Hobbies: Gardening; Archery; Birding; Fishing. Address: Medical Department, Savannah River Site, Aiken, SC 29808, USA.

CYNADER Max Sigmund, b. 24 Feb 1947, Berlin, Germany. Educator; Research Scientist. 3 daughters. Education: BSc, McGill University, Canada, 1967; PhD, Massachusetts Institute of Technology, USA, 1972. Appointments: Assistant Professor of Psychology, 1973, Associate Professor, 1977, Professor, 1981, Associate Professor of Physiology, 1979, Professor, 1984, Killam Research Professor, 1984-88, Dalhousie University, Halifax, Nova Scotia; Professor, Director of Research, Department Ophthalmology, Professor of psychology, Professor of Physiology, University of British Columbia. Publications: Author and Co-author of over 160 scientific papers and book chapters.

Honours: EWR Steacie Fellowship, Natural Sciences and Engienering Research Council of Canada, 1979-81; Appointed Fellow, Canadian Institute for Advanced Research, 1986-; Elected Fellow, Royal Society of Canada, 1987; Killam Research Prize, 1989-91, Distinguished Medical Research Lecturer, 1992, University of British Columbia. Memberships: Society for Neuroscience; Association for Research in Vision and Ophthalmology; Association for Research in Otolaryngology; International Brain Research Organization; International Strabismological Association. Hobbies: Skiing; Racquetball; Bridge. Address: Department of Ophthalmology, University of British Columbia, 2550 Willow Street, Vancouver, British Columbia V5Z 3N9, Canada.

CYWES Sidney, b. 1 Jan 1931, Paarl, South Africa. Professor of Paediatric Surgery. m. Marlene Voges, 16 Oct 1960, 1 son, 1 daughter. Education: MBChB, University of Cape Town, 1953; MMed, University of Cape Town, 1958; FACS, 1974; Certified Paediatric Surgeon, South Africa Medical & Dental Council, 1983; FRCS, 1992. Appointments: Lecturer, Surgery, University of Cape Town, 1961; Senior Lecturer, Associate Professor, 1969; Charles FM Saint Professor of Paediatric Surgery, Head, Department of Paediatric Surgery, Chief Paediatric Surgeon, 1975-. Publications Include: Haemoperitoneum in the newborn, 1967; The surgical management of massive bowel resection, 1968; The surgeon and the child, 1976; Blunt liver trauma in children: nonoperative management, 1985; The birth of a child with a congenital anomaly, 1985; Degenerative leiomyopathy with massive megacolon-myopathic form of chronic idiopathic intestinal pseudo-obstruction occuring in indigenous Africans, 1987. Memberships Include: The South African Oncology Association, 1987-; Executive Council, World Federation of Associations of Paediatric Surgeons, 1989-; Founder, Child Safety Center, University Cape Town & Red Cross Children's Hospital. Honours Include: President's Citation Award, Paarl Gymnasium Old Boys' Union, 1992; Fellowship, Royal College of Surgeons, Edinburgh ad hominem, 1992; Elected Vice President, World Federation of Associations of Paediatric Surgeons, 1992. Hobbies: Horticulture; Mountain Walking; Hiking. Address: 24 Monterey Drive, 7800 Constantia, South Africa.

CZYŻEWSKA Krystyna, b. 6 Feb 1948, Sopot, Poland. Assistant Professor. m. Andrzej Czyżewski, 14 Jun 1969, 1 s, 1 d. Education: Gdansk University, Poland, 1974; PhD, Adam Mickiewicz University, Poznan, Poland, 1979; Dr hab biol med, Karol Marcinkowski University Medical School, Poznań, Poland, 1993. Assistant Professor, Pathophysiology, Dr hab biol med, Karol Marcinkowski University Medical School, Poznań, Poland. Publications: Structure and Function of Mammals Mesothelium, in Post Biol Kom, 1990; Co-author, Change in the transport of uric acid under the influence of pyrazinoic acid: In vitro studies with human and rabbit peritoneum, in Perit Dial Intern, 1989; Co-author Methotrexate influences peritoneal permeability, in Ambulatory Peritoneal Dialysis, 1990; Function of Peritoneal Mesothelium: The study of problems in experimental medicine, PWN 1992; Functions of Peritoneum in Hyperglicemic condition in Post Hig Med Dos'w, 1994. Memberships: International Society for Peritoneal Dialysis; Polish Physiological Society; Polish Society of Nephrology; Polish Biochemical Society. Hobbies: Forest; Bicycle; Garden. Address: 61-885 Poznań, Pòtwiejska 23/3, Poland.

D

D'ABREU Aloysio Augusto, b. 8 Jan 1940, Rio de Janeiro, Brazil. psychoanalyst. m. 10 Oct 1968, 2 daughters. Education: Physiotherapy, 1966; MD, 1967; Specialized in Psychiatry, Universidade Federal de Rio de Janeiro, 1968; Specialized in Psychoanalyses, Brazilian Psychoanalytic Society of Rio de Janeiro, 1975. Appointments: Full member and Training Psychoanalyst, Brazilian Psychoanalytic Society of Rio de Janeiro. Publications: Theoretics and Philosophical Bases of Self-Psychology, Co-author, 1987; Interpretation: A Shared Emotional Experience, 1991; Winnicett and Kobut A Comparative Study, 1993. Honour: Sacerdoti Prize, 37th IPA Congress, Buenos Aires, 1991. Memberships: Associate Member, International Psycho-Analytical Association. Hobby: Scuba Diving. Address: Praia de Botafogo, 422/605 Rio de Janeiro, Botafogo 22250-040, Brazil.

D'ANGIO Guilio John, b. 2 May 1922, New York USA. Physician. Education: AB, Columbia University, 1943; MD, Harvard Medical School, 1945. Appointments include: Assistant in Radiology, 1953-56, Instructor in Radiology, 1956-62, Clinical Associate in Radiology, 1962-64, Harvard Medical School; Professor of Radiology, Director, Division of Radiation Therapy, University of Minnesota Hospitals, 1964-68; Professor of Radiology, Cornell University Medical College, 1968-76; Chief, Division of Radiotherapy Research, Memorial Sloan-Kettering Cancer Centre, 1968-76; Professor of Radiology, Professor of Radiation Oncology, Professor of Paediatric Oncology, University of Pennsylvania School of Medicine, 1976-; Department of Radiation Oncology, Hospital of University of Pennsylvania, Philadelphia, 1992-; Division of Oncology, The Childrens Hospital of Philadelphia, 1992-. Honours include: Phi Beta Kappa; Annual Award, The Emmanuel Cancer Foundation, 1985; Unicef Health prize, 1987; Distinguished Career Award, American Society of Paediatric Haematology/Oncology, 1990; W W Sutow Professorship Award, University of Texas M D Anderson Cancer Centre, Houston, 1991. Memberships include: American Association for Advancement of Science; American Association for Cancer Research; American College of Radiology; American Society of Clinical Oncology; American Radium Society; Sigma Xi. Address: 518 Cedar Lane, Swarthmore, PA 19081, USA.

D'SILVA Henry Ignatius, b. 15 Jul 1947, Bombay, India. Renal Medicine. m. Ann M Spirito Santo, 2 May 1981, 2 s. Education: Intermediate Science; MD. Appointments: Clinical Assistant Professor of Medicine, Albany Medical College, 1982-84; Currently, Private Practice in Nephrology. Publications include: Pharmacokinetics of Cefagolin in Peritoneal Dialysis, Abstract in American Society of Nephrology, 1978, Kidney International, 1979; Pharmacokinetics in Continuous Anibulatory Peritoneal Dialysis, in American Journal of Kidney Disease, 1983. Memberships: International Society of Nephrology; International Society of Peritoneal Dialysis. Hobbies: Photography; Museums; Horticulture. Address: 1205 Langhorne Newtown Road, Suite 404, Langhorne, PA 19047, USA.

DA COSTA Domingos Jr, b. 17 Aug 1931, Belém, Pará, Brazil. Medical Doctor; University Professor. m. Wolitza Sidrim da Costa, 30 Jan 1962, 2 daughters. Education: MD, State University of Pará, 1958; Appointments include: Currently: Professor, Medicine Clinic, State University of the Pará; Haematologist, Ministry of Health; Oncohaematologist, Ofir Loyola Institute. Publications: Hemoglobinopathies, 1974; Virus and Oncogen, 1983; Haemorrhagic Syndrome of Altamira, encyclopaedia entry, 1993; Co-author: Haemorrhagic Syndrome of Altamira, in Lancet, 1974; Acute Lymphoblast Leukemia in Native, 1983; Haemorrhagic Syndrome of Altamira, in Infectious and Parasitic Desease, 1982; Haemorrhagic Syndrome of Altamire in 50 years, 1986; Haemorrhagic accident to larva of Lonomia, 1986; Haemorrhagic accident to larva of Lonomia, in Poisonous Plants and Animals, 1992. Memberships: American Society of Clinical Pathologists; International Society of Hematology; Brazilian Society of Cancerology; Brazilian School of Hematology; International Society of Thrombosis and Haemosthasis; World Federation of Hemophilia; International Society for Preventive Oncology; Brazilian Society of Clinical Oncology; Latinoamerican Society of Pediatric Oncology; American Heart Association; New York Academy of Sciences; European Society for Medical Oncology; Latinoamerican Federation of Cancerology. Address: Avenida Governador José Malcher, Apto 301, Belém, Pará 66055-260, Brazil.

DADA Timothy Ekundayo, b. 18 Feb 1924, Nigeria. Consultant Obstetrician and Gynaecologist. 1 son. Education MB ChB, Bristol, England; MRCS(Eng); LRCP(London); MMSA(London); FWACS; FMCOG; FRCOG; FICS. Appointments: Secretary, Exaiming Board in Obstetrics and Gynaecology; Examiner, National Postgraduate Medical College in Obstetrics and Gynaecology; Chief Consultant, Lagos Island Maternity Hospital, Nigeria. Memberships: Royal Society of Medicine, London; New York Academy of Sciences, USA. Hobbies: Lawn Tennis; Golf. Address: Maria Lodge, 10 Amodu Tijani Street, Victoria Island, Lagos, Nigeria.

DADELSZEN Peter von, b. 20 Oct 1959, Hamilton, New Zealand. Obstetrician and Gynaecologist. m. Kim Marie Hughes, 20 Jan 1983, sep. 1 son, 1 daughter. Education: Canterbury University, 1978; BMedSc, 1981, MB ChB, 1984, Diploma, Obstetrics, 1987, Otago University; MRCOG, 1991; MRNZCOG, 1992; MCR, Oriel College, Oxford University, 1993-. Appointments: House Surgeon, 1984-86, Senior House Officer, Obstetrics, Gynaecology, 1987, Otago Hospital Board; Registrar, Obstetrics, Gynaecology, 1988, Research Fellow, 1989, Christchurch Women's Hospital; Registrar, Obstetrics, Gynaecology, Oxford Regional Health Authority, England, 1990-92; Currently: Clinical Research Fellow; Honorary Senior Registrar. Publications include: Co-author: Increased retention of intrauterine contraceptive devices medicated with indomethacin and medroxyprogesterone acetate, 1981; Influence of ethylene oxide exposure on the extraction of indomethacin from silastic polymer rods, 1982; Pulmonary thromboembolism complicating recurrent placental abruption at 29 weeks gestation, 1990; Endometrial hyperplasia and adenocarcinoma during Tibolone (Livial) therapy, 1994. Honours: Scholar, Summer Scholar, Medical Research Council, New Zealand, 1981; Summer Research Fellow, Faculty of Medicine, Otago, 1982; Doris Gordon Fellow, 1989, Auckland Travelling Scholar, 1990-91, New Zealand Obstetrics and Gynaecology Society; Research Training Fellow, Action Research, 1993-95; Girdlers Research Fellow, Green College, Oxford, 1994-95; Richard Doll Travel Award, Green College, Oxford. Memberships: British Medical Association; New Zealand Medical Association; British Society of Immunology. Hobbies: Travel; Skiing; Cycling; Squash; Music; Drama. Address: Nuffield Department of Obstetrics and Gynaecology, John Radcliffe Hospital, Oxford OX3 9DU, England.

DAGSLAND Helga, b. 28 May 1910, Norway. Nurse. Education: Nursing Education, Bergen, 1937; Administration and Organisation, Oslo, 1946-47; Columbia University, New York, USA, 1952-53, 1958-59; BSc, 1953; MA, 1959; Pedagogics, University of Oslo, 1972. Publications: To Be Sick; School Administration; The Area of Light; Gold and Gravel; Nursing as Therapy; Leaders and Humanity; Poems; Novels From Everyday Life; CARITAS. Honours: Florence Nightingale Medal; Kings Medal, Knight of St Olav's Order, First Class; Scholarship, Columbia University; Scholarship, Norwegian Nurses Association; Honorary Member; Association of Nurses in Geriatrics; Attended congresses and meetings worldwide. Address: Sorhaugget 222, N-5500 Haugesund, Norway.

DAHLIN-WIDSTRÖM Barbro Elisabeth, b. 28 Mar 1940, Stockholm, Sweden. Writer; Psychoanalyst. m. Anders Widström, 15 Aug 1961, 1 son, 1 daughter. Education: MD. Appointments: Assistant Professor, University Clinic, Sankt Görans Hospital; Currently Writer and Psychoanalyst. Publications: 12 books (mainly poetry), 1959-88. Memberships: International PEN; Swedish Psychoanalytical Society. Hobbies: Poetry; Music; Bird-watching. Address: Skirnervägen 9, 18263 Djursholm, Sweden.

DAI Fugui, b. 18 July 1935, Sichuan, China. Leprologist. m. Rao Wen Qi, 16 Dec 1955, 3 sons, 2 daughters. Education: Guiyang College of Medicine. Appointments: Head, Leprosy Hospital of Salaxi, Guizhou; Teacher, Second Medical and Health School of Bie-Jie Prefecture, Guizhou; Assistant Chief Physician. Publications: Leprologia, textbook. Memberships: Society of Leprosy, Guizhou Province; Society of Dermatology, Guizhou Province. Hobby: Basketball. Address: Second Medical and Health School of Bie-Jie, Guizhou, China.

DAI Long Ji, b. 8 Feb 1947, Chengdu City, Sichuan Province, China. Librarian. m. Qing Ming Li, 22 Feb 1974, 1 d. Education: BA, Peking University, China, 1982. Appointments: Lecturer, Department of Library and Information Science, Peking University, 1986; Associate Professor, Peking University Library, 1991; Deputy Director, Peking University Library. Publications: Co-Author, Introduction to Reference Sources in

Western Languages, 1987; Almanac, Annual and Yearbook Studies, 1991; Automation and Library Development, 1993. Memberships: Vice President, Library and Information Committee for University and College in Beijing Area. Hobbies: Stamp Collecting. Address: Peking University Library, Beijing 100871, China.

DAI Rong-Xi, b. 23 Nov 1931, An-Hui, China. Professor. m. Liang Su-Xiang, 1 June 1957, 2 sons, 1 daughter. Education: BA, Shandong University, 1956; Postdoctoral Fellowship, Georgetown University Medical School, 1985-87. Appointments: Research Assistant, Shanghai Institute of Cell Biology, 1956-77; Associate Professor, Shanghai Institute of Cell Biology, 1989. Publications: A Study of Artifertility of Gossypol, 1978; Endocytic Activity of Sertolic Cells Grown in Bicameral Cuntural Chambers, 1987; Studies on the Mechanism of Specific Influence of Trichosanthin on Trophoblast Cells, 1993. Honours: Award of National Congress of Sciences, 1978; 1st Grade Award of the Important Achievement of Scientific Research, Academia Sinica, 1983. Memberships: Chinese Society of Cell Biology; Chinese Society of Reproductive Biology. Hobbies: Painting; Music. Address: 320 Yo-Yang Road, Shanghai, China.

DAI Ruping, b. 1 May 1939, Beijing, China. Professor of Radiology. m. 8 May 1969, 1 son. Education: MD, Beijing Medical University, 1962. Appointments: Currently Professor of Radiology, Cardiovascualr Institute and Fu Wai Hospital, Chinese Academy of Medical Sciences, Beijing. Publications: Interventional Treatment, 1993; Co-author: A Current Treatment of Medicine, 1992; Percutaneous transseptal Balloon valvuloplasty for treatment of mitral stenosis, 1993. Honours: 1st and 2nd Award, Ministry of National Health, 1986, 1987, 1993; National Medical Specialist Award, Chinese Government, 1994. Memberships: Cardiovascular and Interventional Radiological Society of Europe; Radiological Society of North America; Radiological Society of China. Hobbies: Music; Sport; Trips. Address: Department of Radiology, Cardiovascular Institute and Fu Wai Hospital, Chinese Academy of Medical Sciences, 167 Bei Li Shi Street, Fu Wai Avenue, Beijing 100037, China.

DAI Shouzhi, b. 6 July 1935, Shanghai, China. Immunologist. m. Zou Yichun, 2 May 1969, 2 sons. Education: Graduate, Shanghai Medical University, 1959; Advanced Immunology Course, Karolinska Institute, Sweden, 1979-81. Appointments: Assistant, Lecturer of Biochemistry, 1959-79, Associate Professor, Professor of Immunology, 1981-, Ningxia Medical College. Publications: The Degree of Clonal Elimination in Various Types of Specific Immunologic Unresponsiveness, 1982; Antigen-Antibody Complex-Induced Immunosuppression, 1988. Honours: National Advanced Element in Sciences, Special Allowance for Scientists, State Council of China. Memberships: Scandinavian Society for Immunology; Asian-Pacific Association for the Study of the Liver. Hobbies: Table Tennis; Beijing Opera. Address: Department of Immunology, Ningxia Medical College, Yinchuan 750004, Ningxia, China.

DAI Yong, b. 15 Sept 1962, Hubei, China. Nephrologist. m. Hong-mei Zuo, 23 Feb 1992. Education: BA, Tongji Medical University, 1983; MD, 1989, PhD, 1992, Sun Yat-Sen University of Medical Sciences. Appointments: Resident, 1983-89, General Resident, 1989-90, First Affiliated Hospital of Sun Yat-Sen University of Medical Science; Head and Professor, Nephrology Department, Shenzhen People's Hospital. Publications: Observation on Cell Immunity Function of Uremic Patient, 1990; Relationship Factors of Left ventricular Hypertrophy in End-Stage Renal Disease, 1993; Chief Editor, Shenzhen Medical Journal, 1994. Memberships: Chinese Medical Association; Shenzhen Nephrology Society Branch, Deputy Chairman. Hobbies: Music; Swimming. Address: No 3 Dongmen North Road, Shenzhen, Guangdong, China.

DAI Yu-Cheng, b. 15 Oct 1936, Gansu, China. Hematologist. m. Heng-Zhen Mao, 1 May 1966, 1 son, 1 daughter. Education: MD, Jiangxi Medical College, 1963. Career: Resident Doctor, China, 1964; Visiting Scholar, Canada, 1979; Assistant Professor, China, 1982; Visiting Professor, Canada, 1986; Professor of Medicine and Director, China, 1987. Publications: Co-author, Lymphoid Progenitors in Culture Technology for Hemopoietic Cells, 1984; Co-author, The Assay for Lymphoid Progenitors in Transplantation Base for Hemopoietic Cells, 1988. Honours: Received Title, National-Level Outstanding Young and Middle-Aged Scientist, 1984; Editorial Board, China Journal Int Medicine, 1985. Memberships: Chinese Medical Association; Chinese Society of Physiology; International Society of Experimental Hematology. Hobby: Swimming. Address: Jiangxi Institute of Medical

Sciences, 155 Bayi Road 330006, Nanchang, Jiangxi Province, China.

DAI Yue-Su, b. 22 Apr 1953, Kunming City, Yunnan, China. Computer Engineer. m. 1981, 1 daughter. Education: University Diploma; Master in Computers. Appointments: Assistant Engineer, 1880-87; Engineer, 1987-93; Currently Senior Engineer, First Affiliated Hospital Computer Office, Henan Medical University. Publications: Medical Computer Basis (chief editor); WY-200 Hospital Bookkeeper Training Teaching Material (vice chief editor). Honours: Award for Teaching Results, Henan Medical University, 1989; 4 Awards for Computer Application in Diagnosis System, Henan Province, 1990-92; 2 major projects, Henan Province, 1992-93. Memberships: Chinese Computer Institute, Henan Branch; China Health Economics, Henan Special Reporter. Hobbies: Music; Reading novels. Address: First Affiliated Hospital Computer Office, Henan Medical University, Henan 450052, China.

DAI Zhi, b. 6 Dec 1935, Chongqing, China. Prevention & Treatment of Short Stature. m. Zhang Zhengfang, 1 Jan 1958, 2 s, 2 d. Education: BA, Chongqing Medical College, 1962; Associate Professor, Pioneers of Short Stature Treatment in China. Appointments: Radiologist, Director of Radiological Department, Changhang Hospital; Head, Chongqing Dwarf Research Institute. Publications: Chief Author, Subject of Preventional & Treatment on Dwarf, 1990; Co-Author, Prevention and Treatment of Short Stature, 1991; Co-Author, Recent Scientific Technology on Human Growth, 1993; Co-Author, X-Ray Anatomy Atlas, 1985. Honours: Gold Medal of Achievements in Medical Articles for Health and Hygiene of Science & Peace; Silver Medal of Zhong-Jing Cup on the China International Fair. Memberships: China Medical Association; American-Seni Medical Association. Hobbies: Swimming; Photography. Address: Chongqing Dwarf Research Institute, No 162 Daping Main Street, Chongqing 630041, China.

DAMANI Lyaqatali A, b. 15 June 1949, Kalisizo, Uganda. University Senior Lecturer. Education: BPharm; MSc; PhD; MRPharmS. Career: University of London, England, 1977-78; University of Manchester, 1978-85; University of London, 1986-92; Senior Lecturer. Publications include: Urinary Metabolic Profiles in Man and Rat of 1,2-dimethyl and 1,2-diethyl Substituted 3-hydroxypyridin-4-ones, 1992; High-performance Liquid Chromatographic Determination of 1,2-diethyl-3-hydroxypyridin-4-one and Its 2-(1-hydroxyethyl) Metabolite in Rat Blood, 1992; Species Variability in the Stereoselective N-oxidation of Pargyline, 1994. Hobbies: Music; Bridge. Address: Chinese University of Hong Kong, Department of Pharmacy, Faculty of Medicine, Shatin, NT, Hong Kong.

DAMSEY Joan, b. 9 Dec 1931, Jamestown, NY, USA. Medical Management Consultant. m. Lloyd Damsey MD (dec), 6 Nov 1955, 2 s, 2 d. Education: BA; MA; FACMPE. Appointments: American Red Cross, Buffalo, NY, 1953-55; Gimbels, NY, 1955-57; Administrator, The Medical Clinic, FL, 1957-80; Damsey Consultant Services, FL, 1970-81; Currently: Director of Practice Management, Eastern VA Graduate School of Medicine; President and CEO, Damsey and Associates Ltd, Medical Management Consultants. Publications: 22 Articles in Medical Literature; Newsletter, Practice Management Tips, Bi-monthly since 1981; Increasing Referrals (book), 1993; Marketing The Product (chapter), 1993. Honours: Outstanding Contribution Award, Eastern VA Medical School, 1993; President Elect, St Mary's Infant Home. Memberships: Board of Directors, American College of Medical Practice Executives; St Mary's Hospital; Chesapeake Bay Foundation; MG MA; SMD. Hobbies: Fishing; Travel; Opera. Address: 444 Crawford Street, Portsmouth, VA 23704, USA.

DANEV Stoyan, b. 10 Jan 1932, Sofia, Bulgaria. Physician. m. Maria Daneva, 11 Aug 1963, 1 daughter. Education: DMS; PhD; DSc; Sofia University; Sofia Medical University; WHO Fellowship, Copenhagen, Denmark, 1968. Appointments: Assistant and Associate Professor, Postgraduate Medical Institute, Sofia, 1966-74; WHO Teacher, Sofia, 1982, 1985, Lisbon, Portugal, 1985; Chairman, Clinical Laboratory and Clinical Immunology Chair, Medical Faculty, Sofia; Coordinator of TEMPUS Project on teaching in Molecular Biology and Medicine (jointly with Bulgaria, Belgium and Germany), 1994. Publications include: Clinical Enzymology, 1974; Immune Deficiency Diseases, 1975; Inborn Metabolic Errors, 1976. Honours: 100 Years Bulgarian Public Health Medal, 1979; Medal for Professional and Teaching Achievement, 1987. Memberships: IFCC National Representative; International Society of Clinical Enzymology, Founding Member; Balkan Clinical Laboratory Federation, President, NYAS; Association of Clinical Biochemists, UK;

Culture Centre de Rougemont, Vice President. Hobbies: Music; Art; Pets; Skiing; Swimming; Travel; Linguistics. Address: Chair of Clinical Laboratory and Clinical Immunology, Medical Faculty, 1431 Sofia, Bulgaria.

DANIEL Christopher John, b. 12 May 1955, Birkenhead, England. Psychologist. Education: MA, Psychology; MA, Criminology; Chartered Psychologist. Appointments: Head of Psychological Services, Glen Parva, Young Offender and Remand Centre, Leicester; Head of Psychological Services, HM Prison, Wakefield; Currently Head of Research and Development, Psychological Services, Dorset Prisons Psychological Services, Portland YO1, Easton Dorset. Publications: A Review of the Current Literature on Arson and Incendiarism - Part 1, 1980; Unit 3: An Evaluation of a token Economy Approach within Glen Parva Young Offender Centre, 1982; Shame Aversion Therapy and Social Skills Training with an Indecent Exposure, 1986, 1987; A Stimulus Satiation Treatment Programmme with a Young Male Firesetter, 1986, 1987; An Evaluation of a Contingency Contracting Training/Hospital Unit at Glen Parva Young Offender Centre (October 1986-October 1987), 1988; Covert Sensitisation Treatment of an Incarcerated Heroin Addict with a Criminal History of Aggravated Burglaries on Chemists' Shops, 1988, 1990; Anger Control Bibliotherapy with a Convicted Murderer under Life Sentence: A Clinical Report, 1992; Author or co-author, several more. Memberships: British Psychological Society; Editorial Board, Journal of Offender Rehabilitation. Hobby: Pedigree dogs (showing and judging). Address: HM Young Offender Institution, Easton, Portland, Dorset DT5 1DL, England.

DANIELL Harry, b. 3 Aug 1928, East Millinocket, ME, USA. Doctor. m. Barbara, 22 June 1952, 2 d. Education: MD. Appointments: Clinical Professor, Department of Family Practice, University of CA Medical School at Davis; Private Practice. Publications include: Smoking Associations with Skin Troubles; Osteoporosis; Obesity Relations to Osteoporosis; Breast cancer; Prostate Cancer; Etiology of Periodontitis. Address: 2626 Edith Avenue, Redding, CA 96001, USA.

DANNENBERG Andrew L, Education: BA, Swarthmore College, 1974; MD, Stanford University, 1979; MPH, Johns Hopkins University, 1983. Appointments: Family Practice Resident, Medical University of South Carolina, 1979-82; Clinical Instructor 1984-86, Clinical Assistant Professor 1986-89, Department of Community & Family Medicine, Georgetown Medical School; Medical Staff Fellow 1982-85, Medical Epidemiologist, USPHS Commissioned Corps 1985-89, Epidemiology & Biometry Program, National Heart, Lung & Blood Institute, Maryland; Assistant Professor, Department of Health Policy & Management, & Department of Epidemiology, Johns Hopkins School of Public Health, 1989-; Director, Johns Hopkins General Preventive Medicine Residency, 1989-; Member, Core Faculty, Johns Hopkins Injury Prevention Center, 1989-. Publications: Bicycle Helmet Laws and Educational Campaigns: An Evaluation of Strategies to Increase Children's Helmet Use, 1993; Intentional and Unintentional Injuries in Women: An Overview, 1994; Homicide and Other Injuries as Causes of Maternal Mortality in New York City 1987-1991, 1995. Honours: Phi Beta Kappa, 1974; Delta Omega, 1983; US Public Health Service Citation, 1989; Teaching Quality Award, Johns Hopkins School of Hygiene & Public Health Student Assembly, 1993. Address: Department of Health Policy & Management, Johns Hopkins University School of Public Health, 624 North Broadway, Room 545, Baltimore, MD 21205, USA.

DARNEY Philip Dempsey, b.27 Feb 1943, Oklahoma, USA. Gynaecologist. m. Uta Landy, 13 Oct 1995, 3 daughters. Education: MSc, London School of Hygiene and Tropical Medicine 1972; MD, University of California, San Francisco; AB, University of California, Berkeley; Resident in Preventive Medicine, Centres for Diseqase Control, Atlanta, 1972-73; Resident in Obstetrics and Gynaecology, Brigham and Women's Hospital, Boston, 1974-77. Appointments: Deputy Director, Division of Reproductive Health, Centres for Disease Control, 1972-74; Assistant Professor of Obstetrics and Gynaecology, Harvard Medical School, 1977-78; Associate Professor of Obstetrics and Gynaecology, Oregon Health Science University, 1979-80; Professor of Obstetrics, Gynaecology and Reproductive Science, University of California at San Francisco, 1981-. Publications: Clinical Guide to Contraception, 1993; Gynaecologic Surgery, 1995; Contributor of over 100 professional articles. Honours: Outstanding Young Professional, American Public Health Association, 1983. Memberships: American College of Obstetricians and Gynaecologists; American College of Preventive Medicine; American Public Health Association; American Society for Reproductive Medicine. Hobbies: Sculling; Sailing; Surfing.

Address: Department Obstetrics and Gynaecology, San Francisco General Hospital 6D, San Francisco, CA 94110, USA.

DARWOOD John, b. 6 Feb 1956, Van Wert, Ohio, USA. Physician. Education: BS, Biology, University of Toledo, 1978; MD, Wright State University, 1983; MS, Aerospace Medicine, Wright State University, 1989; Family Practice Residency, Dayton, Ohio, 1986. Appointments: Occupational Medicine Physician, Industrial Medical Center, Dayton, Ohio, 1986-90; Occupational & Aerospace Medicine, Kennedy Space Center, 1990-. Publications: Mass Discrimination Under GZ Acceleration, 1991. Honours: Board Certifications - Family Practice, 1986, 1992; Occupational Medicine, 1992; Aerospace Medicine, 1994. Memberships: American College of Occupational and Environmental Medicine; American Academy of Family Physicians; Aerospace Medical Association; American College of Preventative Medicine. Hobbies: Flying; Scuba; Raquetball; Running. Address: EG & G Florida, P O Box 21296, BOC-005/500, Kennedy Space Center, Florida 32815, USA.

DASANANJALI Thamrong, b. 4 Sep 1946, Bangkok, Thailand. Doctor. m. Dr Krongkarn, 3 June 1978, 1 d. Education: MD; LLB; MPA; Certificate of Proficiency in Psychiatry. Appointments: Clinical Assistant, Institute of Psychiatry, University of London, 1975; Director, Suanaranrom Mental Hospital, 1981; Director, Forensic Psychiatric Hospital, 1984; Director, Division for the Coordination of Drug Abuse Treatment, 1989; Chief Medical Officer, Department of Medical Services. Publications: Contributor of numerous articles on law, mental health and substance addiction. Honours: Secretary General, ASEAN Federation for Psychiatry and Mental Health, 1985. Memberships: British Academy of Forensic Sciences; American Academy of Psychiatrists on Alcoholism and Addiction. Hobbies: Travel; Reading. Address: 100/23 "Kamonkarn", Tha-it Road, off Rattanathibeth Road, Nonthaburi 11000, Thailand.

DASMAHAPATRA Tapasranjan, b. 14 Jan 1939, Midnapur, West Bengal, India. Specialist in Obstetrics and Gynaecology. m. 22 July 1969, 1 son, 1 daughter. Education: MBBS, Honours, Calcutta University; DGO; MD; DCH; DRCOG; MAMS; FICS' FRCOG. Appointments: Registrar, Clinical Tutor, Resident Surgeon, for MCh Calcutta and NRS MCH Calcutta; Registrar, Clinical Tutor, Hull and Wakefield Hospitals, England; Obstetrician and Gynaecologist, Digha, India. Publications: Thesis in Anaemia in Pregnancy; Contributor of professional articles. Honours: Gold Medal in Forensic Medicine; Certificate of Honours in Midwifery and Dental Surgery. Memberships: Indian Medical Association. Hobbies: Writing; Gardening; Social welfare. Address: The Nest, New Digha, PO NTS Digha, Via Contai, District Midnapur, West Bengal 721428, India.

DATTA Asoke Gopal, b. 20 Jan 1928, Calcutta, India. Professor, Research and Teaching. m. Anima Datta, 22 May 1955, 1 son. Education: MSc, Calcutta University; PhD, Calcutta University. Appointments: Assistant Director, Indian Institute of Chemical Biology, 1968; Deputy Director, Indian Institute of Chemical Biology, 1978; Scientist Directors Grade, Indian Institute of Chemical Biology, 1985; Emeritus Scientist, Indian Institute of Chemical Biology, 1988; Visiting Professor, Jadarpus University, 1993. Publications: More than 100 original papers in International journals and few Review Articles. Honours: Fellow, Indian Academy of Science, 1980; BD Chopra Oration, INSA, 1981; Fellow, Indian National Science Academy, 1982; Visiting Scientist, Roche Institute of Molecular Biology, 1973-74, 1979-80. Memberships: Life Member, Indian Science Congress; Indian Academy of Sciences; Indian National Science Academy; Society of Biological Chemist & Physiological Society of India. Hobbies: Music; Sports. Address: 9A Ballygunge Place, Calcutta 700019, India.

DATTENBERG-DOYLE Susann Rosina, b. 28 Nov 1958, Ludwigshafen, Germany. Psychologist. m. 29 Aug 1992, 2 sons, 1 daughter. Education: BSc (Hons), Psychology, Aston University, England; Dr Phil, Social Psychology, Ruprecht Karls Universität, Heidelberg, 1989. Appointments: Chief of Training, Alexander Proudfoot, 1986; Corporate Director of Organisational Development, IMPAC, 1992; Currently Behavioural Sciences Director, Cannizaro Consulting Co, Dublin, Republic of Ireland. Publication: The Impact of Stereotypes on Personal Judgement, 1989. Memberships: Bund Deutscher Psychocogen; British Psychological Society. Address: Ladenburgerstrasse 1, D-69120 Heidelburg, Germany.

DATTWYLER Raymond J, b. 9 Aug 1945, New York, USA. Physician. m. Patricia Hoehman, 10 June 1973, 1 son, 1 daughter. Education: BA, Hofstra University, 1967; MS, State University of New

York at Buffalo, 1970; State University of New York, 1973. Appointments: Instructor of Medicine, Harvard University School of Medicine, Boston; Assistant Professor of Medicine, Associate Professor of Medicine, State University of New York at Stony Brook. Publications: Borreliosis, Co-author, 1991; Lyme Diseases, Co-author, 1993. Honours: NIH Predoctoral fellowship, 1969; Clara A March Scholarship, 1973; NIH Postdoctoral Fellowship, 1974-76. Memberships: World Health Organisation COmmittee on Lyme Borreliosis; CDC and FDA on Lyme Disease Tests; NIH Diagnosis and Treatment of Lyme Disease, Panel Member. Hobbies: Soccer; Scuba Diving; Wine. Address: State University of New York, Division of Allergy and Clinical Immunology, Stony Brook, NY 11794-8161, USA.

DAUTERMAN Walter C, b. 10 June 1932. Toxicologist. m. Barbara Roper, 7 Apr 1963, 2 sons. Education: BS, 1954, MS, 1957, Rutgers University; PhD, University of Wisconsin, 1959. Appointments: Currently Professor of Toxicology and Entomology, North Carolina State University, Raleigh. Memberships: American Chemical Society; Sigma Xi; Society of Toxicology; Entomological Society of America. Address: Department of Toxicology, North Carolina State University, Box 7633, Raleigh, NC 27695, USA.

DAVEY Kenneth George, b. 20 Apr 1932, Chatham, Ontario, Canada. Professor. m. Jeannette Evans, 28 Jan 1954, div, 1 son, 2 daughters. Education: BSc, 1954, MSc, 1955, University of Western Ontario; PhD, Cambridge University, England, 1958. Appointments: NRC Postdoctoral fellow, University of Toronto, 1958-59; Drosier Fellow, Gonville and Caius College, Cambridge University, England, 1959-63; Associate Professor of Parasitology, 1963-66, Director, Institute of Parasitology, 1964-74, Professor of Parasitology and Biology, 1966-74, McGill University, Canada; Professor of Biology, 1974-, Chair, Department of Biology, 1974-81, Dean, Faculty of Science, 1982-85, Distinguished Research Professor of Biology, 1984-, Vice President, Academic Affairs, 1986-91, York University. Publications: Reproduction in the Desert, 1964; Contributor of over 200 learned articles; Editor or Editorial Board member on several professional journals. Honours include: Fellow, Royal Society of Canada, 1975; Fellow, Entomological Society of Canada, 1976; Queen's Silver Jubilee Medal, 1977; Gold Medal, Entomological Society of Canada, 1984; Fry Medal, Canadian Society of Zoologists; Gold Medal, Biological Council of Canada, 1987; Distinguished Biologist, Canadian Council of University Biology Chairs, 1992. Memberships include: Vice President, 1979-81, President, 1981-82, Canadian Society of Zoologists; Entomological Society of Canada; Society for Experimental Biology; International Society for Invertebrate Reproduction; Entomological Society of Ontario; European Society of Nematology. Hobbies: Food and Wine; Hand Weaving. Address: Department of Biology, York University, North york, Ontario M3J 1P3, Canada.

DAVIDSON Glen William, b. 26 July 1936, Wendell, Idaho, USA. Professor; Dean. m. Shirlee Proctor, 26 Nov 1971, 2 daughters. Education: BA, University of the Pacific; MDiv, Drew University; PhD, Claremont Graduate School. Appointments: Assistant Professor, Associate Director of Professional Degrees, University of Chicago; Professor, Chair, department of Medical Humanities, Professor of Psychiatry, Chief of Thanatology, Southern Illinois University School of Medicine; Doane Professor, Vice President for Academic Affairs, Dean of College, Doane College; Adjunct Professor of Preventive and Societal Medicine, University of Nebraska Medical Centre. Publications: The Hospice, revised edition, 1985; Living with Dying, revised edition, 1990; Understanding Mourning, revised edition, 1995; Human Beings: Contemporary Issues, 1990; Disinfected Mail, 1992. Honours: Distinguished Alumnus, Claremont Graduate School, 1982; Award of Merit, American Association for State and Local History, 1988; Award of Merit, American Association of Museums, 1992, 1994; Silver Medal, American Philatelic Congress, 1992; Canadian Philatelic Exhibition, 1993. Memberships: American Academy of Religion; American Association of Historians of Medicine; American Council of Academic Deans; American Association of Marriage and Family Therapists; Medical Museums Association; Society for Health and Human Values. Address: 125 Lakeview Circle, Crete, NE 68333, USA.

DAVIDSON Hilary Lorna, b. 26 Apr 1947, Birmingham, England. Acupuncturist. m. 13 July 1968, 2 daughters. Education: BA, Open University; SRN, Ipswich Hospital; LicAc, British College of Acupuncture. Appointments: Staff Nurse, 1968-72; Acupuncturist. Publications: Contributor of professional articles. Honours: Prize in Clinical Ecology, Action Against Allergy, 1982. Memberships: British Acupuncture

Association and Register; Registered, UKCCN. Hobbies: Swimming; Travel. Address: 521 Foxhall Road, Ipswich, Suffolk IP3 8LW, England.

DAVIDSON Leah, b. 1 June 1926, Chelm, Poland. Psychiatrist. m. Esmond Davidson, 25 June 1947, 2 sons, 1 daughter. Education: BSc, University of Witwatersrand, Johannesburg, South Africa, 1944; MBBCh, Johannesburg, 1951; Psychiatric Residency, Bronx Veterans Administration and Psychiatric Institute, New York, USA, 1965-68; Certificate in Psychoanalysis, White Institute, New York, 1971; Board Certified in Psychiatry and Neurology, 1978. Appointments: Currently in private practice. Publications: Numerous including many papers on cross culture, religion, women. Honours: President, William Alanson White Society, 1985-88; Fellow, American Psychiatric Association, 1986. Memberships include: Life Fellow, American Academy of Psychoanalysis. Hobbies: Championship ballroom dancer; Poet. Address: 602 West 231st Street, New York, NY 10463, USA.

DAVIDSON Robin, b. 4 July 1950, Belfast, Northern Ireland. Clinical Psychologist. m. Patricia, 25 Aug 1975, 3 s. Education: BSc; MSc; MSc (Clinical Psychology); DPhil; ABPS. Appointments: Principal Psychologist, Leeds; Member, Mental Health Commission, Northern Ireland, 1986-94; Head of Psychology Service, Northern Health and Social Services Board. Publications: Alcoholism-Drug Abuse Addiction, 1986; Counselling Problem Drinkers, 1992; Contributor of numerous articles on addiction in journals. Honour: Former Vice Chairman, Mental Health Commission, Northern Ireland. Membership: British Psychological Society. Hobbies: Squash; Golf; Music. Address: Department of Clinical Psychology, Holywell Hospital, Antrim, Northern Ireland.

DAVIES Robert James, b. 24 Feb 1943, Taffs Well, Wales. Professor of Respiratory Medicine. m. Karen Henley, 2 sons. Education: BA, 1964, MB, MA, 1968, MD, 1977, Cambridge University; MRCP, 1970, FRCP, 1982, Royal College of Physicians, London; Fellowship, American Academy of Allergy and Immunology, USA. Appointments: Research Fellow, Brompton Hospital, London, 1971-73; Lecturer, Senior Registrar, St Thomas' Hospital, London, 1973-76; Medical Research Council Travelling Fellow, Tulane University, USA, 1976-77; Reader in Respiratory Medicine, 1977-78, Consultant Physician, 1978-, Senior Lecturer, 1983-90, Professor of Respiratory Medicine, 1990-, St Bartholomew's Hospital, London, England. Publications: Allergy: The Facts, 1989; Editor, Respiratory Medicine journal, 1987-94. Honours: Dorothy Temple Cross Travelling Fellowship, 1976; Medal, Faculty of Medicine, University of Montpellier, France. Memberships: International Association for Allergology and Clinical Immunology, 3rd Vice-President; British Society for Allergy and Clinical Immunology, President 1987-90. Address: Department of Respiratory Medicine and Allergy, St Bartholomew's Hospital, West Smithfield, London EC1A 7BE, England.

DAVIS Barry Robert, b. 2 Jun 1952, Brooklyn, New York, USA. Professor of Biometry and Public Health. m. Wallis Lowenthal, 30 Jun 1974, 1 s, 1 d. Education: BS, Massachusetts Institute of Technology; MS, University of California, San Diego School of Medicine; ScM, Brown University; PhD, Brown University. Appointments: Assistant Professor, University of Texas, School of Public Health, 1983-88; Associate Professor, University of Texas, School of Public Health, 1988-92; Professor of Biometry and Public Health, University of Texas, School of Public Health, 1992-. Publications include: Co-Author: The Association of Systolic Blood Pressure Change and Mortality in Persons with Diastolic Hypertension: The HDFP Experience, 1987; The Multicenter Trial of Cryotherapy for Retinopathy of Prematurity: Three-Month Outcome, 1990; Prevention of Stroke by Antihypertensive Drug Treatment in Older Persons with Isolate Systolic Hypertension, 1991; The Effect of Captopril on Morbidity and Mortality in Patients with Left Ventricular Dysfunction Following Myocardial Infarction, 1992; Reduction in Long-Term Antihypertensive Drug Requirements: Effects of Weight Reduction by Dietry Intervention in Overweight Persons with Mild Hypertension, 1993. Honours: Outstanding Faculty Award, University of Texas, Health Science Centre, 1993, 1994. Memberships: American College of Preventive Medicine; American Public Health Association; American Heart Association, Council on Epidemiology; Society for Clinical Trials. Hobbies: Reading; Computers; Tennis; Travel. Address: 1200 Herman Pressler Street, #801, Houston, TX 77030, USA.

DAVIS David, b. 12 Mar 1948, New York City, USA. Psychiatrist. m. Dr Robin Mintzer, 29 Jan 1994. Education: MD; Board Certified Psychiatry; FAPA. Appointments: Director, Orange County Institute of Short-Term Dynamic Psychotherapy; Assistant Professor, Clinical

Psychiatry, UCIMC; Private practice, general Psychiatry and Psychoanalysis. Publications: Contributor of articles in professional journals. Memberships: AMA; APA; CSIMS; American Psychoanalytic Association. Hobbies: Golf; Tennis; Theatre. Address: 20101 SW Birch Street, Suite 100, Newport Beach, CA 92660, USA.

DAVIS Devra Lee, b. 7 June 1946. Epidemiologist. m. 19 Oct 1975, 1 son, 1 daughter. Education: BS, MA, University of Pittsburgh, USA; MPH, Johns Hopkins University; PhD, University of Chicago. Appointments: Assistant Professor, Queens College, 1970-75; Scientific Director, Environmental Law Institute, 1977-82; Director, Board of Environmental Studies and Toxicology, Scholar-in-Residence, National Academy of Sciences, 1983-93; Advisor to Assistant secretary of Health. 1993-94; Presidential Appointee, National Chemical safety Board, 1994-95. Publications: Trends in Cancer, 1990; Patterns in Cancer, 1988, 1990; Trends in Cancer, 1994. Membership: Collegium Ramazzini. Hobbies: Hiking; Skiing; Cello; Torah. Address: 324 Maryland NE, Washington DC 20002, USA.

DAVIS Hilton Mark, b. 19 Sept 1947, Moorends, Yorkshire, England. Psychologist. m. Liz Tait, 7 Sept 1974, 1 son, 2 daughters. Education: BA, University College of Swansea; Diploma in Clinical Psychology, Oxford; Chartered Psychologist; FBPsS; PhD, London University. Appointments: Clinical Psychologist, Rampton Hospital; Lecturer in Abnormal Psychology, The City of London Polytechnic; Lecturer in Health Psychology, currently Reader in Health Psychology, London Hospital Medical College; Clinical Director of Child Mental Health. Publications: Working with Parents (with C Cunningham), 1985; Counselling and Communication in Health Care (with L Fallowfield), 1991; Counselling Parents of Children with Chronic Illness or Disability, 1993. Membership: British Psychological Society. Hobbies: Cooking; Spanish. Address: 10 Elderslie Road, London SE9 1UE, England.

DAVIS Jessica Grosof, b. 3 Apr 1934, Brooklyn, New York, USA. Physician. m. 17 June 1956, 1 son, 1 daughter. Education: BA, Wellesley College, 1955; MD, College of Physicians and Surgeons, Columbia University, 1959. Appointments include: Instructor, Assistant Professor, Albert Einstein College of Medicine; Associate Professor of Clinical Paediatrics, Cornell University Medical College; Co-Director, Division of Human Genetics, Cornell Medical Centre. Publications include: factors Influencing Mammalian X Chromosome, Condensation and Sex Chromatin Formation I. The Effect of in Vitro Cell Density of Sex Chromatin Frequency, Co-author, 1968; Infantile Spasms in Down Syndrome: A Report of 5 Cases and Review of the Literature, Co-author, 1978; De Novo Duplication of the 7Q11q22 Region, Co-author, 1983; Genetic Counselling: A Clinician's Perspective, 1992; reproductive Technologies for Prenatal Diagnosis, 1993; Genetic Services: A National Survey, 1995. Honours: President, COuncil of Regional Networks of Sactic Services; Board of Directors, American College of Medical Genetics. Hobbies: Gardening; Native American Pottery. Address: 525 East 68th Street, New York, NY 10021, USA.

DAVIS Jonathan Robert, b. 25 June 1954, Boston, Massachusetts, USA. Research Scientist. Education: BA, History, Biology, Presbyterian College, Clinton, South Carolina, 1976; MS, Medical Entomology, Clemson University, South Carolina, 1980; PhD, Immunology, Infectious Diseases, Johns Hopkins Univ School of Hygiene and Public Health, Baltimore, Maryland, 1987. Appointments include: Research Assistant, Department of Immunology and Infectious Diseases, 1982-86, Associate, Department of Molecular Microbiology and Immunology, 1994-, Johns Hopkins University School of Hygiene and Public Health; Research Analyst, Department of Epidemiology, 1986-87, Instructor, 1987-88, currently Assistant Professor, University of Maryland School of Medicine, Baltimore. Publications: Over 55 papers and abstracts on malaria vaccine development including: Safety and immunogenecity in man of a synthetic peptide malaria vaccine against Plasmodium falciparum sporozoites, 1987; Conserved repetitive epitope recognized by CD4+ clones from a malaria-immunized volunteer, 1989; Successful immunization of humans with irradiated sporozoites: Humoral and cellular responses of the protected vaccinees, 1991; Plasmodiun falciparum: In vitro characterization and human infectivity of a cloned line, 1992; Evaluation of ingested human anti-sporozoite sera on Plasmodium falciparum sporogony in Anopheles stephensi, 1993; Laboratory methods for the conduct of experimental malaria challenge of volunteers, 1994. Honours: Outstanding Young Alumnus Award, Presbyterian College, 1992. Membership: Selection Committee, Young Investigator Award, American Society of Tropical Medicine and Hygiene. Hobby: Competitive javelin throw. Address: Center for Vaccine

Development, Department of Medicine, Division of Geographic Medicine, University of Maryland School of Medicine, 10 South Pine Street, Baltimore, MD 21201-1192, USA.

DAVIS Larry E, b. 16 Aug 1940, New York City, USA. Neurologist. Education: MD, Stanford University; Residency, Johns Hopkins Hospital, 1980-83; Diplomate, American Board of Psychiatry and Neurology, 1985. Appointments: Professor of Neurology and Microbiology, University of New Mexico School of Medicine. Publications include: Neurocysticerosis, 1990; Acute Bacterial Meningitis, 1992; Viral Meningitis and Encephalitis, 1992; Tuberculous Meningitis in the United States, 1992; Central Nervous System Infections; Botulinum Toxin: From Poison to Medicine, 1993; Neurologic Aspects of AIDS: An Overview; Cysticercosis of the Nervous System; Treachery of the Hysterical Diagnosis. Honours: Moore Award, 1979, Weil Award, 1984, American Neuropathology Association; Apple Teacher Award, University of New Mexico, 1992. Memberships: Fellow, American College of Physicians; Fellow, American Neurological Association. Hobbies: Tennis; Hiking. Address: Chief Neurology Service, VA Hospital, 2100 Ridgecrest Drive, Albuquerque, NM 87108, USA.

DAWN Chitta Sankar, b. 1 Aug 1926, Calcutta, India. Gynaecologist. m. 4 Jun 1950, 2 s, 1 d. Education: MD; PhD; FRCOG, London; FICMCH; DR BC Roy. Appointments: Teacher/Assistant Professor/Professor, 1954-84; Retired Professor & Head, Department of Obstetrics & Gynaecology, Medical College, Calcutta; Professor, Indian College of Maternal & Child Health, Calcutta. Publications: Author of Textbook of Obstetrics & Gynaecology, 1st Edition, 1958, 12th Edition, 1994; Textbook of Gynaecology & Contraception, 1st Edition, 1958, 11th Edition, 1994. Honours: National Awardee for Best Teacher in India, 1981. Memberships: Founder President, National Association for Voluntary Sterlisation & Family Welfare of India. Hobbies: Reading. Address: 25B, CIT Road, Calcutta 700014, India.

DAWSON Richard William Kyle, b. 21 Dec 1926, Lower Hutt, New Zealand. Psychologist. m. Mary Mhyfanwy McNamara, 21 Jan 1953, 2 daughters. Education: Teachers Certificate, 1949, Diploma, Teaching, 1954, Advanced Diploma, Teaching, 1963, New Zealand Department of Education; BSc (High Distinction), Educational Psychology, MA, Educational Psychology, Minnesota University, USA; DipEd, Counselling Psychology, Massey University, New Zealand; DipPsych, Applied Psychology, Adelaide University, Australia; PhD, Psychology, Flinders University, Australia, Chartered Psychologist. Appointments: Primary School Teacher, 1949-52; Principal Infant School Teacher, 1952-54; Junior High School Teacher, 1954-56; Senior Assistant Teacher, 1956-58; Research Fellow, University of Minnesota, USA, 1958-62; Senior Psychologist in charge, New Zealand Department of Education, 1963-69; Director of Counselling and Psychological Services, Flinders University of South Australia, 1970-81; Retired, 1981; Editor, Journal of Australian and New Zealand Student Services Association; International Correspondent, Forward Trends, London; Honorary Adviser. Publications include: Culturally Disadvantaged Children, 1969; The Rise and Fall of the Guidance Counsellor in the New Zealand Secondary School, 1972; On Guidance Counsellors and Careers Advisers, 1973; Craik's Premise: Men and Machines Can Be Specified in the Same Terms, 1974; Integrating Welfare Resources on a University Campus, 1979. Memberships: Associate Fellow, British Psychological Society; Senior Member, Flinders University Convocation; South Australian Psychological Association; South Australian Musicians Association. Hobbies: Classical clarinet; Jazz tenor saxophone. Address: 34 Ridgefield Avenue, Seaview Downs, South Australia 5049, Australia.

DE ALMEIDA Altair, b. 20 Jan 1956, Nairobi, Kenya. Acupuncturist; Shiatsu. m. Iona Courtenay, 30 June 1986, 1 d. Education: Licentiate in Acupuncture, 1988; Diploma in Shiatsu, 1991; First degree Reiki. Appointments: Principal and Founder, Inner Dance School of Tai Chi and Qigong, 1988; Co-Founder and Chairman, Malvern Natural Health Centre, 1990-93; European School of Shiatsu, Malvern Hills Branch Director, 1992; Acupuncturist, Shiatsu Practitioner, Private Health Centre and NHS Pain Clinic. Creative Works: Taichi, video, 1992; Qigong, video, 1994. Memberships: Traditional Acupuncture Society; Teacher Member, Register of Shaitsu Society. Hobbies: Agate Stone Collecting and Cutting; Holistic Medicine. Address: Sunflower, 218 Elgar Avenue, Malvern, Worcestershire WR14 2HB, England.

DE BARSY Thierry, b. 22 Jan 1941, Berchem, Antwerp. Professor; Doctor. m. A M de Cannart d'Hamale, 17 July 1965, 2 daughters. Education: MD; Neurologist; Rehabilitation; Professor. Appointments:

Research Fellow, Fonds National de la Recherche Scientifique; Associate Professor; General Coordinator, Centre of Neurology, W. Lennox. Publications: More than 120. Memberships: American Academy of Neurology; Belgium Academy of Medicine. Honours: Officer, Order of Leopold II, 1986; Commandeur de l'ordre du St Sepulcre, 1977, Knight, 1990. Hobbies: Reading; Gardening. Address: Zurenborgstraat 46, B-2018 Antwerp, Belgium.

DE BOER Robert, b. 19 June 1947, Haarlem, The Netherlands. Research Scientist. m. W Secherling, 4 Nov 1976, 1 son, 1 daughter. Education: MSc, 1976, PhD, 1981, University of Amsterdam. Appointments: Research Scientist in Medical Entomology. Publications: The Control of House Dust Mite Allergens in Rugs, 1st author, 1990; The Woodmouse as a Reservoir of Tick-Transmitted Species, 1993; The Decay of House Dust Mite Allergens, 1994; Genotypic and Phenotypic Analysis of Borrelia Burgdorferi, 1994. Memberships: Netherlands Entomological Society. Hobbies: Outdoor sports; Cycling; Birdwatching. Address: Section Populationbiology (FTO), University of Masterdam, Kruislaan 320, 1098 SM Amsterdam, The Netherlands.

DE COURCY-WHEELER Richard Horatis Beresford, b. 31 Jan 1960, Borehamwood, England. Obstetrician & Gynaecologist. m. Rose McMillen, 20 May 1989, 1 s, 1 d. Education: MA, Royal College of Surgeons, Ireland, 1984; BAO; BCh; LRCP + SI; MRCOG, 1990. Appointments: Rotunda Hospital, Dublin, 1989; Hammersmith Hospital, London, 1989; Registrar, St Thomas' Hospital, London, 1990-91; Research Fellow, St Thomas' Hospital, London, 1992-93; Senior Registrar Obstetrics and Gynaecology, Northern Ireland. Publications: Contraceptive Use in Young Women, 1991; Small Fetal Transcerebellar Diameter: A Screening Test for Spina Bifida, 1994; Association Between Small Size for Gestational Age and Death, 1994. Memberships: Royal Society of Medicine; Ulster Obstetrics & Gynaecology Society; Irish Perinatal Society; Blair-Bell Research Society; Simpson Club. Hobbies: Riding; Fishing; Shooting. Address: 2 Windsor Hill, Carnreagh, Hillsburough. BT26 2RL, Ireland.

DE CRESPIGNY Lachlan James, b. 25 Mar 1948, Melbourne, Australia. medical Practitioner. m. Margaret Robertson, 31 July 1991. 3 sons, 1 daughter. Education: MD; BS; FRCOG; FRACOG; DDu; COGUS. Appointments: Lecturer, Department Obstetrics and Gynaecology, University of Melbourne, 1981-82; Assistant Obstetrician, Ultrasound Department, Royal Women's Hospital, 1983-85; Specialist in Ultrasound, Royal Women's Hospital, Melbourne. Publications: Which Test for My Unborn Baby? A Guide to Prenatal Diagnosis, 1991; Contributor of numerous articles in professional journals. Memberships: Australian Society for Ultrasound in Medicine; Human Genetic Society of Australia; Fertility Society of Australia; Australian Perinatal Society. Hobbies: Tennis; Reading; Theatre. Address: 3 Lawnhill Road, Malvern, 3144 Victoria. Australia.

DE LORIMIER Alfred A, b. 30 May 1931, Washington, District of Columbia, USA. Surgeon. m. Sandra Marie de Lorimier, 21 Nov 1954, 1 son, 2 daughters. Education: AB, Zoology, University of California, Berkeley, 1952; MD, University of California, San Francisco, 1956; Certifications: American Board of Surgery, 1963, 1987; Special Competence in Paediatric Surgery, 1975, 1985; Surgical Critical Care, 1986. Appointments: Assistant Professor, Surgery, 1964-771, Chief, Division of Paediatric Surgery, 1965-88, Associate Professor, Surgery, 1971-80, Professor, Surgery, Division of Paediatric Surgery, 1980-, Professor, Paediatrics, 1988, University of California, San Francisco; Attending Surgeon, several hospitals, San Francisco, 1964-; Chief, Division of Paediatric Surgery, San Francisco General Hospital, 1965-88; Consultant Paediatric Surgeon, Letterman Army Medical Center, San Francisco, 1972-90. Publications: Author or co-author, about 150 articles, papers, chapters, including: The Modified Puestow Procedure for Chronic Relapsing Pancreatitis in Children, 1990; Tracheobronchial obstruction in infants and children, 1990; Carotid Artery Reconstruction Following Extracorporeal Membrane Oxygenation, 1990; A Comparison of Four Staging Systems of Localized and Regional Neuroblastoma: A report from The Children's Cancer Study Group, 1990; Amnion Inversion in the Treatment of Giant Omphalocele, 1991. Honours: Helmut Fesca Award for Outstanding Surgical Resident, 1962. Memberships: American Surgical Association; American Academy of Pediatrics; American College of Surgeons; Society of University Surgeons; American and California Medical Associations; San Francisco Surgical and Medical Societies; Many others. Hobby: Grape grower (de Lorimier Winery). Address: 533 Parnassus Avenue, San Francisco, CA 94143, USA.

DE MANIELLE Margaretha Elizabeth, b. 13 Jan 1971, Paarl, South Africa. Radiographer. m. Francois de Manielle, 2 Oct 1993. Education: Diploma in Diagnostic Radiography, Cape Technicon, 1991. Appointments: Radiographer, Tygerberg Hospital. Hobbies: Horse Riding; Running; Swimming. Address: Knolvlei, Posbus 9043, Klein-Drakenstein 7628, South Africa.

DE SILVA Pinnaduwage Ariyaratne, b. 26 Nov 1944, Narigama, Sri Lanka. Consultant in Genito-Urinary Medicine. m. Thavamanidevi Krishnan, 22 Dec 1971, 2 sons. Education: MBBS (Ceylon); 1969; D(OBS), RCOG, 1976; MROCG, 1977; FRCSE, 1978; FRCS, RCPS (Glasgow), 1978; MCOG (Sri-Lanka), 1984; Diploma in Genito-Urinary Medicine, University of London, 1989; FRCOG, 1993; MFFP (RCOG), 1993. Appointments: Former District Chairman, Family Planning Association; Consultant Obstetrician and Gynaecologist attached to Ministry of Health, 1983-89, as Visiting Obstetrician and Gynaecologist, Base Hospitals, Matale and Nuwara-Eliya, Sri Lanka; Currently Consultant Physician in Genito-Urinary Medicine, Dewsbury Health Care, Dewsbury and Clayton Hospital, Wakefield, West Yorkshire, England. Publications: Co-author: STD in Rape Victims, 1991; Chemical Burns in Colposcopy, 1994; History of Venereal Diseases Yaws (Parangi) in Sri-Lanka, 1994. Memberships: British Medical Association; Medical Society for the Study of Venereal Diseases; Association of Genito-Urinary Medicine; NGUPCG; BSCCP. Hobbies: Calligraphy; Table-tennis. Address: 46 Mountbatten Avenue, Sandal, Wakefield, West Yorkshire, England.

DE SPEVILLE Carol, b. 24 Apr 1943, London, England. Educational Psychologist. m. Bertrand de Speville, 22 July 1967, 1 s, 1 d. Education: BSc, London University, 1964; Postgraduate Training in Educational Psychology, The Tavistock Centre, London, 1967-68. Appointments: Educational Psychologist, London Borough of Hounslow, 1968-81; Educational Psychologist in Private Practice. Memberships: Associate Fellow, British Psychological Society, Chartered Psychologist; Affiliate C Psychologica Aff; Association of Educational Psychologists; Associate Fellow, Hong Kong Psychological Society. Hobbies: Sailing; Cooking; Theatre. Address: 76 J Peak Road, Hong Kong.

DE VECCHI Amedeo Franco, b. 26 Jan 1948, Milan, Italy. Nephrologist. m. Franca Carandente, 6 Mar 1976, 2 s. Appointments: Professor in Experimental Endocrinology; Professor in Endocrinology, University of Milano. Publications: Co-author: Comparison between immunofixation and crossed IEP for the detection of C3 activation products, in Clin Chim Acta, 1979; Long term comparison between single morning daily or alternate day steroid in cadaver kidney transplantation, in Transplant Proc, 1980; Renal Disease in essential mixed cryoglobulinemia, in Q Journal Medicine, 1981; A survey of current steroid regimens for transplant patients, in Heart Transplant, 1982; Oral phosphatidilcholine administration in CAPD patients with reduced ultrafiltration, in Peritoneal Dialysis Intern, 1989; Plasma and dialysate IgG in CAPD, in American Journal Nephrology, 1980; The Oreopoulos and the Y set techniques for long term prevention of peritonitis in CAPD patients, in Nephrology, 1990; Nutritional assessment of CAPD patients, in American Journal of Kidney Disease, 1991. Honour: Fellowship in Nephrology. Memberships:Societa Italiana di Nefrologia; International Society for Peritoneal Dialysis; International Society for Chronobiology. Hobbies: Scuba Diving; Skiing; Walking in Mountains; Sailing. Address: Divisione di Nefrologia e Dialsi, IRCCS Ospedale Maggiore, Via Commenda 15, 20122 Milano, Italy.

DEAN Joseph Oral Jr, b. 21 Jun 1940, Birmingham, Alabama, USA. Pharmacist; Educator. m. Judith Yarborough, 20 Aug 1960, div 8 Jul 1977. m. Carol Deigrosso Davis, 17 Dec 1977, 1 Step s, 2 d. Education: BS, Pharmay, Samford University, 1962; MEd, University of Montevallo, 1980; PhD, University of Alabama, 1985; Licensed Pharmacist in Alabama and Tennessee, USA. Appointments: Owner, Helena Drug Company, 1967-72; Director of Professional Affairs - Pharmacy, Samford University, 1975-84; Coordinator of Grants and Special Academic Projects, Samford University, 1981-84; Vice President for University Relations, Samford University, 1984-86; Vice President for Development, Charleston Southern University, 1986-89; President, Samford University Foundation, 1989-93; Dean, School of Pharmacy, Samford University, Birmingham, Alabama, 1993-. Publications: Journal of American Pharmaceutical Education, 1994, 1995; Southern Baptist Educator, 1987; Journal of Council for Advancement and Support of Education, 1985. Honours: Bowl of Hygeia, Alabama, 1972. Memberships: American Pharmaceutical Association; International Pharmacy Federation; American Association of Colleges of Pharmacy.

Hobbies: Travel; Reading. Addrress: 3545 Brookfield Road, Birmingham, AL 35226-2038, USA.

DEAN Paul Rudyard, b. 14 Feb 1947, Cardiff, Wales. Psychotherapist. m. Sally, 1 son, 1 daughter. Education: Diploma, Analytical Group Psychotherapy, 1981; Diploma, Systemic Integrative Psychotherapy, 1993; Postgraduate Diploma in Art Therapy, 1983. Appointments: Senior I Art Therapist, Basingstoke District Hospital, 1987-89; Referring Psychotherapist, Metanoia Psychotherapy Institute, 1989-92; Core Tutor, Professional Counselling Course, Kingston College, 1987-95. Publications: Theme - Centred Groupwork, 1990; An Archetypal Self Model in a TA Frame of Reference, 1992. Memberships: United Kingdom Council for Psychotherapy; Society for Existential Analysis; British Association of Art Therapists. Hobbies: Reading; Films; Music; Art. Address: 74 Lincoln Avenue, Twickenham, Middlesex TW2 6NP, England.

DEBAKEY Michael E, b. 7 Sept 1908, Lake Charles, Louisiana, USA. Surgeon; Educator; Baylor College of Medicine Chancellor. m. Katrin Fehlhaber, 4 sons, 1 daughter. Education: BS, 1930, MD, 1932, MS, 1935, Tulane University, New Orleans. Appointments include: Professor, Chairman, Cora and Webb Mading Department of Surgery, 1948-93, Distinguished Service Professor, 1968-, Vice-President for Medical Affairs, Chief Executive Officer, 1968-69, President, 1969-79, Chancellor, 1978-, Olga Keith Wiess Professor of Surgery, 1981-, Baylor College of Medicine, Houston, Texas; Clinical Professor of Surgery, University of Texas Dental Branch, Houston, 1952-; President, The DeBakey Medical Foundation, Houston, 1961-; Distinguished Professor of Surgery, Texas A&M University, College Station, 1972-; Director, The Debakey Heart Centre, Houston, 1985-. Creative works: Many professional books and book chapters; Over 1500 journal articles; Developed roller pump for heart-lung machine, Dacron artificial arteries and Dacron-velour arteries for artery replacement, first successful patch-graft angioplasty, fundamental concept of therapy in arterial disease, left ventricular bypass pump for cardiac assistance and its first successful clinical application; Performed first successful resections and graft replacements in aortic, thoracoabdominal and renal aneurysms; Many other achievements. Honours: 44 honorary degrees, US and foreign universities; Nearly 200 honours and awards, US and global institutions and organisations including: Gold Heart Award, American Heart Association, 1968; President's Distinguished Service Award, Baylor College of Medicine, 1992; American Heart Association Lifetime Achievement Award, 1994. Memberships: Numerous including: American Heart Association; American Medical Association; New York Academy of Science; International Platform Association; American Surgical Association; Michael E Debakey International Surgical Society; International Cardiovascular Society; Southern Surgical Association. Address: Baylor College of Medicine, One Baylor Plaza, Houston, TX 77030, USA.

DEBAS Haile Tesfaye, b. 25 Feb 1937, Asmara, Eritrea. Doctor of Medicine. m. Ignacia Kim, 23 May 1969. Education: BSc; MD; CM; FACS; FRCS(C). Appointments: Assistant Professor of Surgery, University of British Columbia, 1971; Associate Professor of Surgery, UCLA, 1980; Professor of Surgery, UCLA, 1981; Professor, Chief of Gastrointestinal Surgery, University of Washington, 1985; Professor, Chiar, Department of Surgery, UCSF, 1987; Dean, School of Medicine, UCSF, 1993. Memberships: Royal College of Surgeons; American College of Surgeons; American Surgical Association; American Gastroenterological Association; International Hepato-Biliary Association. Hobbies: Reading; Writing; Travel; Modern History. Address: Deans Office, University of California School of Medicine, 513 Parnassus Avenue, S-224, San Francisco, CA 94143 0410, USA.

DEBELIC Mladen Juraj, b. 13 July 1933, Zagreb, Croatia. Physician. m. Jutta Fox, 11 Dec 1965, 2 sons. Education: MD. Appointments: Chief, Clinic for Lung, Senior Consultant, Allergic Diseases. Publications: Editor, Bronchitis im Kindes, 1986; Co-editor, Asthma, 1988; 255 publications. Memberships: European Society of Resp Diseases; American Academy of Allergy & Immunology; German Society of Allergy & Clinical Immunology. Honours: Honorary Member, Czechoslovakia Society of Allergy & Clincial Immunology, 1989; Honorary Member, Hungarian Society of Allergy & Clinical Immunology, 1989; Honorary Member, Croatian Society of Allergy & Clinical Immunology, 1990. Address: Cecilienallee 6-8, D-33175 Bad Lippspringe, Germany.

DEBUSK Franklin Lafayette, b. 13 Dec 1922, Gainesville, Florida, USA. Physician. m. Elizabeth Anne Tisdale, 2 June 1945, 2 sons, 1 daughter. Education: BS, University of Florida; MD, Johns Hopkins University School of Medicine, 1946; Intern, Children's Medical Service, Massachusetts General Hospital, 1946-47; Resident, 1948-49; Fellow in Paediatrics, Ochsner Foundation of Tulane, New Orleans, 1951. Appointments: Chief of Paediatrics, Oliver General Hospital, Army of US, Augusta, Georgia, 1948-49; Private Practice, Paediatrics, Pensacola, Florida, 1952-66; Assistant Professor of Paediatrics, 1966-69, Associate Professor of Paediatrics, 1969-73, Professor of Paediatrics, 1975-, University of Florida. Publications: Section on Hutchinson-Gilford Progenia Syndrome; The Hutchinson-Gilford Progenia Syndrome, 1972. Honours: Phi Beta Kappa; Phi Kappa Phi; Alpha Omega Alpha; Hippocratic Award, University of Florida, 1982. Memberships: Florida Medical Association; Fellow, American Academy of Paediatrics; Florida Paediatric Society; Society for Paediatric Dermatology. Hobbies: Reading; Sailing; Log-splitting. Address: Department of Paediatrics, University of Florida College of Medicine, PO Box 100296, Gainesville, FL 32610, USA.

DECI Edward L, b. 14 Oct 1942, Clifton Springs, New York, USA. Psychologist. Education: AB, Hamilton College; MBA, University of Pennsylvania, Philadelphia; MS, PhD, Carnegie-Mellon University; Postdoctoral Fellow, Stanford University. Appointments: Professor of Psychology, University of Rochester, New York. Publications: Intrinsic Motivation, 1975; Psychology of Self-Determination, 1980; Intrinsic Mot and Self-Determination in Human Bevahior, 1985. Honours: Grantee, NIMH, 1977-78, 1989-94, 1991-93; National Science Fund, 1981-83; National Institutes Child Health and Human Development, 1986-90, 1990-95. Memberships: American Psychological Association; American psychological Society. Hobby: President, Monhegan Museum Association. Address: Department of Psychology, University of Rochester, Rochester, NY 14627, USA.

DEES William Hunter, b. 28 Nov 1955, Raleigh, North Carolina, USA. Medical Entomologist. m. Wendy Gulick, 18 Dec 1982, 1 son. Education: BS, The Citadel, 1978; MS, Clemson University, 1980; PhD, Old Dominion University, 1986. Appointments: Entomologist, Navy Environmental and Preventive Medicine Unit, Norfolk, Virginia; Research Entomologist, Naval Medical Research Unit, Cairo, Egypt; Operations Officer, Navy Disease Vector Ecology and Control Centre, Alameda, California; Entomology Department Head, Navy Environmental Health Centre, Norfolk, Virginia. Publications: Biochemical Changes in Hyalomma Dromedarii Embryos and Effect of 20-Hydroxyecdysone Applied to the Mother, Co-author, 1990; Cutaneous Leishmaniasis in the Peace Keeping Force in East Sinai, Co-author, 1989; Contributor of 14 other articles. Honours: Navy Commendation Medal, 1991, 1993; Navy Achievement Medal, 1993; Humanitarian Service Medal, 1990; Sigma Xi Research Award, 1978. Memberships: Acarological Society of America; Society for Vector Ecology; Sigma Xi; Association of Military Surgeons of the United States; American Society of Tropical Medicine and Hygiene. Hobbies: Astronomy; Paleontology; Reading; Jogging; Hiking; Boating. Address: Navy Disease Vector Ecology and Control Centre, Naval Air Station, Box 43, Jacksonville, FL 32212-0043, USA.

DEHOVITZ Jack Alan, b. 8 Dec, Oceanside, California, USA. Physician. m. Jana Novotna, 31 May 1992, 1 daughter. Education: MD; MPH. Appointments: Clinical Assistant Professor of Community & Preventive Medicine, New York Medical College; Associate Professor, Preventive Medicine & Community Health. Publications: Clinical Performance and Quality Health Care, 1994. Honours: Alpha Omega Alpha, 1979; Edward Randall Medal for Academic Excellence, 1979. Memberships: Association of Teachers of Preventive Medicine; American College of Physicians; New York Academy of Medicine; Infectious Diseases Society of America. Address: Downstate Medical Center for Preventive Medicine & Community Health, 450 Clarkson Avenue, Box 43, Brooklyn, NY 11203, USA.

DELAVEAU Pierre Georges, b. 4 June 1921, Charenton, France. Lecturer; Searcher. m. Christiane Gautier, 18 June 1949, 3 sons, 1 daughter. Education: Pharm D, 1953; MD, 1954; DSc, 1967. Career: Professor Dr of Pharmacognos, University René Descartes, Paris. Publications: Films: Medicinal Plants, 1985; More than 10 books: History and Revival of Medicinal Plants, 1982; Guide for Dangerous Plants, 1983; Spices, 1987; Etymology of 3000 Scientific Names, 1992, reedited 1995. Honours: Laureate of Faculties of Medicine and Pharmacy, Academy of Medicine & Pharmacy; Chairman, Society Bot France, 1987-89; Correspondent of Koninklijke Academie voor Genesskunde van België, 1987; Dr Honoris Causa, Un Liege (Belgium), 1995. Memberships: Academie Nationale de Pharmacie, 1970; Academie

Nationale de Medecine, 1992. Hobbies: Gardening; Plant Photography. Address: Rue Soufflot 13, Paris 75005, France.

DELFOSSE Patricia, b. 21 Aug 1956, Ashford, Kent, England. Traditional Acupuncturist. Hobbies: BA (Hons), Psychology; LicAc; MTAcS; Certificate, Traditional Chinese Medicine; JTEC. Appointments: Rsearcher, Lecturer in Social Psychology, Sheffield Hallam University; Community Broadcaster; Acupuncturist, The Acupuncture Practice, Sheffield. Membership: Traditional Acupuncture Society. Hobbies: Tai Chi; Astrology; Batik; Travel; Reading; Writing. Address: The Acupuncture Practice, 133 Pomona Street, Sheffield S11 8JN, England.

DELGADO Pedro L, b. 17 Dec 1956, Iguara, Cuba. Physician. m. Sandra M Walsh, 22 Dec 1979, 2 sons, 1 daughter. Education: BS summa cum laude, University of Houston, USA, 1979; MD, 1983, MA, Pharmacology, 1984. University of Texas Medical Branch. Appointments: Assistant Professor of Psychiatry, Yale University School of Medicine, USA, 1987-92; Currently Associate Head, Director of Research, Department of Psychiatry, AHSC, Tucson, Arizona. Publications: Co-author: Journal of Psychiatry and Disease, 15:55-60, 1988; Life Science, 45:2323-2332, 1989; Archives of General Psychiatry, 47:411-418, 1990; Archives of General Psychiatry, 51:865-874, 1994. Honours: Alpha Epsilon Delta, 1976; Rock Sleyster Scholarship, 1983; Joseph Kasi Award, 1983; Alpha Omega Alpha, 1983; Lustman Award, 1988. Memberships: American Psychiatric Association; American College of Neuropsychopharmacology; Society for Neuroscience. Hobby: Hiking. Address: Department of Psychiatry, AHSC, 1501 N Campbell Avenue, Tucson, AZ 85724, USA.

DELMAR Kim, b. 23 Aug 1955, Viborg, Denmark. Chiropractor. m. Thora Pedersen, 21 May 1988, 1 son. Education: DC; Diploma of Roentgenology; Diplomate, AECC; Accredited, DKF, DANUH. Address: Odense, Norway.

DELMONTE Michael M G S, b. 20 Sep 1947, The Hague, Netherlands. Clinical Psychologist. m. Patricia G Bes, 4 July 1973, 3 d. Education: BSc; HDE; MA; MSc; MPsych Sc; PhD. Appointments: Research Fellow, Trinity College, Dublin, Ireland; Senior Psychologist, Psychosomatic Unit, Senior Clinical Psychologist, St Patrick's Hospital, Dublin. Publications: Author of 4 chapters in books and contributor of over 50 articles in professional journals. Memberships: Associate Fellow, Psychological Society of Ireland; Associate Fellow, British Psychological Society. Hobbies: Folk History; Languages; Horse Riding; Foreign Travel. Address: 10 Trafalgar Terrace, Monkstown, County Dublin, Ireland.

DELROY Sandra Estelle, b. 26 Mar 1945, Leeds, England. Chartered Clinical and Counselling Psychologist. Education: BS, Psychology, 1976, MA, Educational Psychology, 1980, John Carroll University; PsyD, Clinical Psychology, Illinois School of Professional Psychology, 1984; Diploma, Counselling Psychology, British Psychological Society, 1992. Appointments: Senior Clinical Psychologist, Mental Health Unit, Barnet Health Psychology; Currently Head, Clinical Psychology Services for People with Physical Disabilities and AIDSLINE, Enfield Community Care, National Health Service Trust; Consultant Clinical Psychologist, The King Oak Private Hospital, Enfield. Memberships: British Psychological Society; British Association for Counselling; International Round Table for the Advancement of Counselling. Address: 3 Northumberland House, 237 Ballards Lane, Finchley, London N3 1LB, England.

DEMARIA Peter A Jr, b. 15 Nov 1958, PA, USA. Psychiatrist. Education: MD. Appointments: Assistant Professor of Psychiatry and Human Behaviour, Jefferson Medical College. Honours: Board Certified in Psychiatry, added Qualification in Addiction psychiatry; Certified in Addiction Medicine, American Society of Addiction Medicine. Memberships: American Academy of Psychiatrists in Alcoholism and Addictions; American Society of Addiction Medicine; Association for Medical Education and Research in Substance Abuse; American Psychiatric Association; American Medical Association. Address: 1201 Chestnut Street, 15th Floor, Philadelphia, PA 19107, USA.

DEMICK Jack, b. 18 May 1952, Hartford, Connecticut, USA. Clinical Psychology. m. Joan Kellerman, 1 s, 1 d. Education: BA, Psychology, Yale University, 1974; MA, Psychology, Clark University, 1977; PhD, Psychology, Clark University, 1981; Postdoctoral Fellow, Child Psychology and Psycoeducation, McLean Hospital, 1981-82. Appointments: Chief of Psychology, Fuller Memorial Hospital, South

Attleboro, Massachusetts, 1982-84; Assistant Professor, Department of Psychology, Emmanuel College, Boston, Massachusetts, 1984-86; Visiting Associate Professor, Departments of Psychology and Education, Clark University, Worcester, Massachusetts, 1986-89; Associate Professor and Chair, Department of Psychology, Suffolk University, Boston, Massachusetts, 1989-94; Professor and Chair, Department of Psychology, Suffolk University, Boston, Massachusetts, 1994-. Publications: include, The Clinician's World of Action as an Approach to Teaching Abnormal Psychology, 1978; Relations between Experience and Action: Automobile Seat Belt Usage in Japan and the United States, 1986; Cherished Possessions and Adaptation of Older People to Nursing Homes, 1990. Honours: Fellow, Clark University, 1976-78, 1979-80; Scholar, Clark University, 1975-76; Graduated Magna Cum Laude with Honors in Psychology, Yale University, 1974. Memberships: include, American Psychological Association; Eastern Psychological Association; Society for Research in Child Development; Psychonomic Society; Society for the Psychological Study of Social Issues. Hobbies: Movies; Television. Address: Suffolk University, Department of Psychology, 41 Temple Street, Boston, MA 02114, USA.

DEMUTH Donald Lynn, b. 23 May 1951, Philadelphia, Pennsylvania, USA. Businessman. m. Nancy Marwick DeMuth, 18 Dec 1977, 2 sons. Education: BA, Franklin and Marshall College, 1972; Wharton School, University of Pennsylvania, 1976; MBA; Certified Public Account/Personal Financial Specialist; Certified Professional Business Cnsultant. Appointments: Senior Accountant, Touche Ross and Company CPAs, 1972-75; Teaching Fellow of Accounting, Wharton School of University of Pennsylvania, 1975-76; Assistant Professor of Accounting and Finance, Pennsylvania State University, 1976-80; Adjunct Assistant Professor of Finance and Accounting, Franklin and Marshall College, 1976-78; Owner, Donald L DeMuth Professional Management COnsultants, 1976-. Publications: Physician's Guide to the Tax Reform Act of 1986, 1987; 1988 Tax Planning Strategies for Dentists (Featuring the Revenue Act of 1987 and the Tax Reform Act of 1986), 1988; Contributor of over 35 professional articles, 1977-. Honours: Wall Street Journal Award, Franklin and Marshall College, 1972; Pi Gamma Mu, 1972. Memberships: Institute of Certified Professional Business Cnsultants; Society of Medical-Dental Management Consultants; American and Pennsylvania Institutes of Certified Public Accountants; Central Pennsylvania Estate Planning Council. Hobbies: Baseball; Weightlifting; Jogging. Address: 129 Montsera Road, Carlisle, PA 17013, USA.

DEMYER William, b. 8 July 1924, South Charleston, West Virginia, USA. Paediatric Neurologist. m. Marian Kendall, Sept 1952, 2 sons. Education: BS, Anatomy, Physiology, 1949, MD, 1952; Residency, Neurology, Indiana University Medical Center, 1953-56; Diplomate, American Board of Psychology and Neurology, 1958; Certified, Child Neurology, 1968. Appointments include: Director, Neuroanatomy Laboratory, Department of Neurology, 1954-, Professor of Neurology, 1965-, Indiana University School of Medicine, Indianapolis; Consultant in Neurology: Wishard Memorial Hospital, Veterans Administration Medical Center and Larue Carter Memorial Hospital. Publications: Neurohistology for Clinical Medicine, 4th edition, 1979; Psychiatry/Neurology: PreTest Self-Assessment and Review (with M DeMyer), 1982; Neuroanatomy, 1988; Technique of the Neurologica Examination: A Programmed Text, 4tn edition, 1993; Author or co-author, more than 75 scientific articles, textbook contributions and others. Honours: Special Fellow, National Institutes of Health, 1962-68; Voted Outstanding Teacher in Clinical Sciences, 1972, 1974, 1976, 1978, 1980, 1981, 1983, 1984, 1985; Award for Most Outstanding Teacher in Medical School, Classes of 1972, 1975, 1982, 1983; Frederick Bachman Leiber Award for Outstanding Teaching, 1981. Memberships: Fellow, American Academy of Neurology; Professors of Child Neurology; Child Neurology Society; American Association of Neuropathologists; Alpha Omega Alpha; International Association for the Advancement of Science. Hobbies: Competition ballroom dancing; Tennis. Address: Department of Neurology, Indiana University Medical School, 702 Barnhill Drive, Indianapolis, IN 46202, USA.

DENG Gui-Fen, b. 22 Dec 1928, Shun-te County, China. Professor. m. Zhu Jia-Kai, 27 Mar 1952, 2 s. Education: Graduated from Medical School of Zhong-Shan University, 1952; Refreshed at UCLA, Division of Behavioral Sciences and Health Education. Appointments: Professor and Head Department of Hygiene of Children & Adolescents, School of Public Health, Sun Yat-sen University of Medical Sciences; Standing Member of Executive Committee of Children and Adolescents Society of China Medical Association. Publications: Over 52 Articles Published,

1964-94. Honours: 5 Awards from Chinese Government, 1981-94. Memberships: Chinese Medical Association. Hobbies: Stamp Collecting. Address: Department of Children & Adolescents Health, School of Public Health, Sun Yat-sen University of Medical Sciences, Guangzhou 510089, China.

DENG Qi-Hui, b. 27 Oct 1942, Li Ling, Hunan, China. Teacher. m. Xin-Wu Zhong, 27 Oct 1967, 1 s, 1 d. Education: BS, Hunan Medical University, 1966. Appointments: Resident Doctor of Medicine, University Hospital, 1966-74, Assistant, department of Physiology, 1974-81, Instructor, Department of Physiology, 1981-88, Associate Professor, Department of Physiology, 1989-, Hunan Medical University. Publications include: Effect of Allium Scorodoprasum on Lysozyme Activity of Pulmonary Alveolar Macrophages, Co-author, 1988; 5000 Questions and Answers of Physiology, 1982; Laboratory Manual of Physiology, 1983; Preview Lecture is a Good Step to Improve Teaching Quality, 1994. Honours: Awards of Literature, 1986, 1988. Memberships: Chinese Association of Physiological Sciences; Chinese Somatic Sciences; Head, Hunan Medical University Qigong Research Society; Director, Hunan Women Association of Culture Communication. Hobbies: Qigong; Swordplay; Raising Pets; Writing. Address: Department of Physiology, Hunan Medical University, Zhangsha 410000, China.

DENG Shao Qing, b. 14 July 1944, Chongqing, China. Surgeon. m. Mei-Rei Lu, 1 Oct 1968, 2 sons. Education: Masters degree in surgery; Postgraduate of Surgery. Appointments: Lecturer in Surgery, 1981; Associate professor of Surgery, 1988; Vice Chairman of General Surgery, Director, Endoscopic Surgery, Beijing Medical University. Publications: Plasma Shock Lithotripsy of Gallstone - Animal Experiment and Clinical Application, 1991; Gallbladder Mycin and Cholesterol and Pigment Stone Formation in Hamsters, 1984. Honours: Honoured Master Degree recipient with Prominent Contributions, National Education Committee of China, 1991; Excellent Teacher of Medicine, Ministry of Public Health of China. Membership: Chinese Medical Association. Hobbies: Classical Music; Jogging; Tabletennis. Address: Third Teaching Hospital of Beijing Medical University, 49 North Garden Road, Haidian District, Beijing 100083, China.

DENG Yi Ping, b. 8 Feb 1928, Shanghai, China. Researcher. m. Bing Kun Xu, 25 Dec 1951, 1 s. Education: MD, Medical College of Lingnan University, Ganton, China. Career: Assistant, 1952, Lecturer, 1956, Associate Professor, 1978, Professor, 1985-, Sun Yat-sen University of Medical Sciences, Guangzhou. Publications include: Co-author, The effect of hyperlipidemic and normal serum on vascular and plague segment smooth muscle cell, in Morphology and Protein Synthesis, 1987; Co-author, The scanning electron microscopy of aortic endothelium in different age under hyperlipidemic action, 1989; Co-author, The effect of Panax notoginseng saponins on tissue-type plasminogen activator activity of endothelial cells in vitro, 1994; Neuron, in reference book of histology, 1993. Memberships: Chinese Anatomical Association; Chinese Cell Biology Society; Chinese Medical Association; Chinese Pathophysiology Society. Hobbies: Classical Music; Photography; Travel. Address: Department of Histology and Embryology, Sun Yat-Sen University of Medical Sciences, Guangzhou, China.

DENG Zhong-duan, b. 6 Oct 1927, Nan Ning, China. Teacher. m. Dong-Yuan Che, 22 Jan 1955, 1 s. Education: Graduate, Guang Xi Medical College, 1952. Appointments: Assistant, 1953, Docent, 1966, Associate Professor, 1980, Professor, 1983, Professor of Pathology, Department of Pathology and Chairman, Institute of Cardiovascular Pathology, Tongji Medical University; Guest Professor, Institute of Pathology, Heidelberg University, Germany, 1980. Publications: Diseases of Cardiovascular System, Co-author, 1990; Diseases of Digestive System, Retroperitoneum and Pharynx, Co-author, 1978. Honours: Scientific Prize, Hubei Province, 1993. Memberships: Committee Member, Society of Pathology; Chinese Medical Association; Chairman, Society of Pathology; CMA Hubei Division. Hobby: swimming. Address: Department of Pathology, Tongji Medical University, Hang Kong Road 13, Wuhan 430030, China.

DENNO Gordon James, b. 21 Feb 1938, MI, Battle Creek, USA. Podiatric Medicine & Surgery. m. Marilyn Richter, 14 July 1962, 2 sons. Education: DPM, Illinois College of Podiatric Medicine, 1962; FACFAS; FACPP; FASPM; FAAHP, Geriatric Scholar, Great Lakes Geriatric Education Center, Chicago, 1988. Appointments: Clinical Preceptor, USA Academy of Health Sciences, Texas, 1973-87; Orthopaedic

Surgery Staff, Tripler Army Medical Centre, Hawaii, 1980-83; Auxiliary Clinical Assistant Professor, Scholl College of Podiatric Medicine, Chicago, 1985, 1986, 1987;Chairman and Associate Professor, Department of Medicine, Scholl College of Podiatric Medicine, Chicago, 1987-93; Professor, Department of Medicine, Scholl College of Podiatric Medicine, chicago, 1993-; Chairman, Department of Surgery, SCPM, Chicago, 1994. Publications Include: Safeguarding Your Children's Feet, 1972; Improved Combat Physical Fitness Reserve: The Running Shoe, 1976; Which Running Shoe is Best For You, 1980; Infectious Diseases of the Lower Extremity, 1990; Intravenous Fluid Management for the Podiatric Physician, 1991; Common Sense in Taking Cultures, 1991; Could It Be Malignant Melanoma?, 1992; Amniology Coside Toxicity and Control, 1992; A Look at Podiatric Medicine, 1993; The Clinical Significance of Fungus Infections of the Toenails in the Elderly: A Response to the Health Care Financing Administration Midcare Policy, 1994. Memberships Include: American College of Podiatric Physicians; American College of Foot and Ankle Surgeons; American Board of Podiatric Surgery; American Podiatric Medical Specialities Board; American Society of Podiatric Medicine; American Association of University Professors. Honours Include: Durlacher National Scholastic Honour Society, 1959-62; Army Commendation Medal, 1975; Meritorious Service Medal, 1983; Distinguished Service Award, HPA, 1983; Legion of Merit, USA, 1988; Illinois Podiatric Medical Students Association Appreciation Plaque, 1992.Who's Who in American Education, 1994; Address: 953 Moccasin Ct, Carol Stream, IL 60188, USA. 15.

DEPAOLA Dominick P, b. 29 Dec 1942, Brooklym, New York, USA. Dental Educator. m. Rosemary Elizabeth Femiano, 2 Aug 1969, 1 daughter. Education: BS, St Francis College; DDS, New York University; PhD, Massachusetts Institute of Technology. Appointments: Dean, Dental School, University of Texas Health Science Center at San Antonio, 1983-87; Dean, New Jersey Dental School, University of Medicine and Dentistry of New Jersey, 1988-90; President, Dean, Baylor College of Dentistry, Dallas, Texas, 1990-. Publications: The Influence of Food Carbohydrate on Dental Caries, in Food Carbohydrates, 1982; Forward, in Nutrition in Oral Health and Disease, 1985; Nutrition in Relation to Dental Medicine, in Modern Nutrition in Oral Health and Disease, 1993. Honours: Member, Council on Dental Education, American Dental Association, 1992-; Alumni Achievement Award, New York University College of Dentistry, 1993. Memberships: National Council for Research on Women Presidents Roundtable; Association of Governing Boards and Universities; Texas Dental Association; American Association of Dental Schools; American Dental Association. Hobbies: Golf; Hiking. Address: Baylor College of Dentistry, Office of President and Dean, PO Box 660677, Dallas, TX 75266-0677, USA.

DEPPE Gunter, b. 30 Sept 1943, Heiligenstadt, Germany. Gynaecologic Oncologist. div., 2 sons, 1 daughter. Education: MD; Board Certified, Obstetrics and Gynaecology, 1976, Gynaecologic Oncology, 1979. Appointments: Associate Professor, Mount Sinai Medical Center, New York City, USA; Chief, Gynaecology, Gynaecologic Oncology, Mount Sinai, Chicago, Illinois; Currently Director of Gynaecologic Oncology, Professor, Wayne State University, Detroit, Michigan. Publications: Chemotherapy of Gynecologic Cancer (editor), 1984, 2nd edition, 1990; Female Cancer (edited with S B Gusberg and W M Shingleton). Honours: Solomon Silver Award in Clinical Medicine, 1977; Certificate of Appreciation for Moving Detroit Forward, 1993. Memberships: American College of Obstetrics and Gynecology; American College of Surgeons; Society of Gynecologic Oncologists; International Gynecologic Cancer Society; European Society of Gynaecologic Oncologists. Hobbies: Stamp collecting; Swimming. Address: 4707 St Antoine, Detroit, MI 48201, USA.

DERGACHEV Anatoly Ivanovich, b. 21 May 1947, Port-Artur, Russia. Physician. m. Inna Berdnikova, 31 Apr 1983, 1 son. Candidate of Medical Sciences, Crimea State Medical Institute, 1971; Postgraduate course, Research Institute of Medical Radiology, USSR Academy of Medical Sciences, 1979. Appointments: Roentgenologist, 1976; Scientific Worker, currently Senior Scientist, Medical Radiology Research Centre, Russian Academy of Medical Sciences, Obninsk. Publications: Ultrasound Biometry of Abdominal and Retroperitoneal Organs and Vessels, 1989; Handbook on the Ultrasound Diagnosis of Abdominal and Retroperitoneal Diseases, 1993. Hobbies: Gardening; Motor-cars. Address: ul Koroliova 4, 249020 Obninsk, Kaluga Region, Russia.

DESAI Veena Balvantrai, b. 10 May 1931, Kasvan, Gujarat, India. Physician. m. Vinay Gandevia, 19 Sep 1964, 1 son. Education: MB BS; DGO; MD; FRCOG(London); DABOG; FACOG; FACS; FICS. Appointments: Chief of Ob-Gyn, West Anaheim Medical Centre, USA; Associate Clinical professor, Boston University and University of California, Irvine; Vice Chief Medical Staff, West Anaheim Medical Centre. Publications: Dystocia due to Sacro-Coccygeal Teratoma, 1968; Endometriosis in Fruit, Flora and Fauna Forms, 1994; Pseudomigration of Cu7 Due to Contractile Round Ligaments. 1994. Honours: Medal of Merit, 1982; President Regan Medal of Freedom, 1994; Order of Liberty, 1993. Memberships: President, Buena Park Rotary Club; Inner Circle Republican Party. Hobbies: International Politics; Travel. Address: Desai Medical Corporation, Suite 110, 3010 W Orange Avenue, Anaheim, CA 92804, USA.

DESCOEUDRES Claude Eric, b. 10 Aug 1939, Amsterdam, Netherlands. Physician. m. Katharina Lehmann, 28 Apr 1967, 2 s. Education: MD, University of Basel, 1967. Appointments: Lecturer in Nephrology, University of Berne; Director of Haemodialysis, Inselspital, Bern, Switzerland. Publications: Co-author, Heroin associated nephropathy, in Clinical Nephrology, 1979; Langzeitdialysemethoden, in Reubi F, Nierenkrankheiten, 1982; Co-author, Human recombinant erythropoetin, in Nephrology Dialysis Transplant, 1988; Hyperkaliemie, in Medicine et Hygiene, 1993. Memberships: Swiss Society of Nephrology; International Society of Nephrology; French Society of Nephrology; International Society of Peritoneal Dialysis. Hobbies: Stamp Collecting; Books, Classic Literature. Address: Choisystrasse 14, CH-3008 Bern, Switzerland.

DESCOTES Jacques Georges, b. 1 April 1951, Lyon, France. Professor of Pharmacology. m. Christiane Souillet-Desert, 30 June 1973, 1 son, 1 daughter. Education: MD, 1976; PharmD, 1980; PhD, 1988. Appointments: Professor of Pharmacology, Faculty of Medicine, A Carrel Lyon University; Head, Lyons Poison Information Center, France. Publications: Author: Immunotoxicology of Drugs and Chemicals, 1986, 1988; Drug Induced Immune Diseases, 1990; Editor: Human Toxicology, 1995. Memberships: French Society of Toxicology; Eurotox; The Society of Toxicology; Indoor Air International; European Association of Poisons Centers and Clinical Toxicologists. Address: Le Bletinet, 38480 St Jean d'Avelanne, France.

DESHPANDE Jayant Krishnanath, b. 8 May 1952, Bombay, India. Medical Doctor. 2 sons. Education: AB, Boston University, USA; MD, University of Tennessee, Memphis. Appointments: Assistant Professor, Department of Anaesthesiology and Critical Care Medicine, Associate Director, Paediatric Intensive Care Unit, The Johns Hopkins Hospital, Baltimore, Maryland, USA; Currently Director, Paediatric Critical Care and Paediatric Anaesthesia, Associate Professor, Paediatrics, Anaesthesiology, Vanderbilt University Medical Center, Nashville, Tennessee. Honours: Teacher of the Year Award, Department of Anaesthesiology and Critical Care Medicine, The Johns Hopkins School of Medicine, 1987; Fellow, American Academy of Pediatrics, 1988; W M Keck Clinician Scientist Award, The Johns Hopkins University, 1988-89, 1989-90. Memberships: Association of University Anesthesiologists; American Society of Anesthesiologists; American Academy of Pain Management; Society of Neuroscience; Society for Pediatric Anesthesia; Society of Critical Care Medicine. Address: Vanderbilt University Medical Center, Division of Pediatric Critical Care and Anesthesia, Medical Center North, T-0118, Nashville, TN 37232-2591, USA.

DESNICK Robert J, b. 7 Dec 1943, Minneapolis, Minnesota, USA. Geneticist. m. Julie Herzig, Oct 1988, 1 son. Education: BA, University of Minnesota, Minneapolis, 1965; PhD, Genetics, University of Minnesota Graduate School, 1970; MD, University of Minnesota Medical School, 1971; Diplomate, National Board of Medical Examiners; Fellow, American Academy of Pediatrics; Diplomate, Certified in Clinical Genetics and Biomedical Genetics, American Board of Medical Genetics. Appointments include: Professor, Paediatrics, University of Minnesota, 1977; Arthur J and Nellie Z Cohen Professor, Paediatrics, Genetics, Chief, Division of Medical and Molecular Genetics, 1977-, Professor, Human Genetics, Chairman, Department of Human Genetics, 1993-, Mount Sinai School of Medicine, New York City; Attending Physician, Paediatrics, Mount Sinai Hospital, 1977-; Consultant Physician, Paediatric Genetics, Beth Israel Hospital, City Hospital Center at Elmhurst. Publications: Over 350, including many regarding metabolic diseases and human genetics. Honours include: US Public Health Service Fellowship in Genetics, 1968-70; Ross Award in Pediatric Research, 1972; C J Watson Award, 1973; National Institutes

of Health Career Development Award, 1975-80, National Institutes of Health Merit Award, 1992-. Memberships include: Founding Fellow, American College of Medical Genetics; American Society for Clinical Investigation; Society for Glycobiology; Genetics Society of America; American Society of Human Genetics; Genetics Society of America; Society for Inherited Metabolic Diseases, President, Vth International Congress of Inborn Errors of Metabolism, 1990; American Society of Biochemistry and Molecular Biology; Founding Member and President Elect, Association of Professor of Human/Medical Genetics; Society for Pediatric Research; American Association of Physicians; American Association for the Advancement of Science; Many editorial boards. Address: Mount Sinai School of Medicine, Department of Human Genetics, Box 1203, Fifth Avenue and 100th Street, New York, NY 10029, USA.

DETELS Roger, b. 14 Oct 1936, Brooklyn, New York, USA. Professor. m. Mary M doud, 14 Sept 1963, 2 s. Education: BA, Harvard University, Cambridge, Massachusetts, 1958; MD, New York University, New York, 1962; MS, Preventative Medicine, University of Washington, Seattle, Washington, 1966; FAAS; FFPHM (Hon). Appointments: Medical Officer, US Naval Medical Research Unit, Taipei, Taiwan, 1966-69; Medical Officer, Research, Epidemiologist, National Institute of Neurological Disease and Stroke, Bethesda, Maryland, 1969-70; Associate Professor of Epidemiology, UCLA School of Public Health, 1970-73; Acting Head, Department of Epidemiology, UCLA School of Public Health, 1970-72; Head, Division of Epidemiology, UCLA School of Public Health, 1972-80; Dean, UCLA School of Public Health, 1980-85; Professor of Epidemiology, UCLA School of Public Health, 1973-. Publications: include, Books: Oxford Textbook of Public Health: History Determinants, Scope and Strategies, Vol 1, 1984; Oxford Textbook of Public Health: Processes for Public Health Promotion, Vol 2, 1985; Numerous Research Papers and Chapters. Honours: include, Fellow, Society for Epidemiologic Research, 1969; Sigma Xi, 1971; Delta Omega, 1971; Fellow, American College of Epidemiology, 1984; Distinguished Alumnus Award, School of Public Health, University of Washington, 1983; Faculty Award, UCLA School of Public Health, Alumni Association, 1992. Memberships: include, American Association for the Advancement of Sciences, 1969-; American College of Epidemiology; American Heart Association; American Public Health Association. Address: University of California, Los Angeles School of Public Health, Department of Epidemiology, 10833 Le Conte Avenue, Los Angeles, CA 90024-1772, USA.

DETMER Don Eugene, b. 3 Feb 1939, Winfield, Kansas, USA. Medicine. m. Mary Helen McFerson, 26 Aug 1961, 2 d. Education: MD, Durham University, 1965; University of Kansas; Surgical Training, Johns Hopkins, Duke, National Institutes of Health. Appointments: Professor of Surgery and Preventative Medicine, University of Wisconsin, Madisson, USA; Professor & Vice President, Health Sciences, University of Utah, Utah, USA. Publications: In Vivo Stability of Segmented Polyurethane, 1970; The Ambulatory Surgical Unit, 1972; Heuristics and Biases in Medical Decision Making, 1978; Improved Results in Acute Appendicitis Care following Areawide Review, 1984; An Administration Medicine Program for Clinician-Executives, 1981; Ambulatory Surgery: A More Cost-Effective Treatment Strategy?, 1994. Honours: AOA, Kansas, 1965; Distinguished Teacher, University of Madisson; Distinguished Alumnae, Duke University, Alumni Association. Memberships: include, Chair, Board on Health Care Services; Special Medical Advisory Board; Veterans Administration; Trustee, China Medical Board; Association for Health Services Research; American Colleges of Surgeons, Medical Informatics, Physician Executives and Sports Medicine; American Surgical Association. Hobbies: Fly Fishing; Needlework; Painting; Biography; Reading. Address: University of Virginia, Box 179, Health Sciences Center, Charlottesville, Virginia 22908, USA.

DETRE Katherine, b. 28 Apr 1926, Budapest, Hungary. Physician. m. Thomas P Detre, 16 Sep 1956, 2 s. Education: BA; MD; DrPH. Appointments: Internship, Residency, Queen's University Medical School, 1952-56; Research Associate, Yale Medical School, 1956-60; Biostatistician, West Haven, VA, 1967-; Associate Professor, 1974-79, Professor, 1979-, University of Pittsburgh. Publications: Contributor of over 200 articles, reports, letters, book chapters and abstracts including: What Can Comparative Databases Contribute to the Evaluation of New Technology?, 1993; Report from the Pitt-UNOS Liver Transplant Registry, Co-author, 1993. Honours: ACC Fellowship, 1992; Fellow, AAAS, 1992; Phi Beta Kappa, 1989; Women in Science Award, 1987. Memberships: ASA; Biometric Society; NIH Advisory Committees; SCT;

AHA; ACE; AES. Hobbies: Symphony and Music Theatre. Address: University of Pittsburgh, Department of Epidemiology, Graduate School of Public Health, 130 DeSoto Street, A531 Crabtree Hall, Pittsburgh, PA 15261, USA.

DEURZEN-SMITH Emma van, b. 13 DEc 1951, The Hague, Netherlands. Professor of Psychotherapy and Counselling. m. David Livingston Smith, 19 Sept 1980, 1 son, 1 daughter. Education: LicPhil; LicPsy; MPhil; MPsy; Chartered Psychologist. Appointments: Psychotherapist, Hospitals of Saint-Alban and Ageu, France; Director in Psychology of Therapy and Counselling, Antioch University, Massachusetts, USA; Currently Academic Dean, School of Psychotherapy and Counselling, Regent's College, London, England. Publications: Existential Counselling in Practice, 1988; Existential Therapy, in Individual Therapy: A Handbook, 1990; Hard-Earned Lessons from Counselling in Action, 1992. Honours: Chair, Society for Existential Analysis, 1988-93; Chair, UK Council for Psychotherapy, 1993-. Memberships: Associate Fellow, British Psychological Society; Registered Existential Psychotherapist, UK Council for Psychotherapy. Hobbies: Ice-dancing; Singing. Address: School of Psychotherapy and Counselling, Regent's College - Inner Circle, Regent's Park, London NW5 1NS, England.

DEVER G E Alan, Edpidemiology. m. Georgia Armstrong, 17 Aug 1963, 1 son, 1 daughter. Education: MT, Belleville General Hospital School of Medical Technology, Canada; BA, 1967, MA, 1968, State University of New York at Buffalo, USA; PhD, University of Michigan, 1970; Honorary MPH, Emory University, 1977; PhD, Donsbach University, 1982. Appointments: State Epidemiologist, Division of Physical Health, Georgia Department of Human Resources, Georgia, 1972-77; Director, Office of Health Services Research and Statistics, Georgia; Director, Nutrition Consultant, Centre for Preventive Medicine Incorporated, Decatur, Georgia, 1982-86; Director, Clinical Epidemiology and Biostatistics, Mercer Univeristy School of Medicine. Publications Epidemiology in Health Services Management 1984, 1987; Community Health Analysis: Global Awareness att the Local Level, 2nd edition, 1991; Quality of Life and the Distribution of Physicians in Georgia: A Disturbing Paradox, 1989; Community Health Analysis: A Holistic Approach, 1980; Passages: Predictable Mortality Through the Life Stages, 1980; Linking Vital Statistics to Marketing Data, Co-author, 1994. Honours: Grassmann Chair of Rural Medicine, Mercer University School of Medicine, 1991; Rural Health Research of the Year. Memberships: American Public Health Association;National Rural Health Association. Address: Mercer University, School of Medicine, 1550 College Street, Macon, GA 31207, USA.

DEVEREUX Richard Blyton, b. 23 Oct 1945, Philadelphia, Pennsylvania, USA. Physician. m. Corinne Keating Devereux, 3 Oct 1970, 1 son, 1 daughter. Education: BA, Yale University, 1967; MD, University of Pennsylvania, 1971; Certified, American Board of Internal Medicine, 1974 and Cardiovascular Diseases, 1977. Appointments: Assistant Professor of Medicine, 1978-83, Associate Professor of Medicine, 1983-92, Professor of Medicine, Cornell Medical College. Publications: Contributor of 320 research papers and chapters and 360 research abstracts. Honours: Spencer Morris Prize, University of Pennsylvania, 1971; Antione Morfan Award, National Warfan Foundation, 1987. Memberships: American Federation Clinical Research; American Heart Association, Circulation and High Blood Pressure Research; American College of Physicians, Fellow; American College of Cardiologists, Fellow; International Society of Hypertension; Association of University Cardiologists. Hobbies: Sking; Theatre. Address: New York Hospital-Cornell Medical Centre, 525 East 68th Street, New York, NY 10021, USA.

DEVOE Lawrence Daniel, b. 11 May 1944, Chicago, Illinois, USA. Medical Doctor. m. Anne Hester Devoe, 1 daughter. Education: BA, Anthropology, Pre-Med, Harvard University, 1966; MD; Internship, 1970-71, Residency, 1973-76, Maternal-Fetal Medicine Fellowship, 1978-79, University of Chicago. Appointments: Assistant Professor, Department of Obstetrics and Gynaecology, University of Chicago In-Lying Hospital and Clinic, Chicago, Illinois, 1976-83; Associate Professor, 1983-89, Director, Maternal-Foetal Medicine, 1984-, Department of Obstetrics and Gynaecology, Medical College of Georgia, Augusta. Publications: Computer Applications for Perinatology, 1993; Medical-Legal Considerations in Antepartum Fetal Surveillance: Computerized, 1994. Honours: Purdue Frederick Award, 1981; 2nd place paper, 1986, 3rd place paper, 1987, Southern Perinatal Association; 3rd place paper, 1990, 1st place paper, Purdue Frederick

Award, 1991, American College of Obstetrics and Gynecology. Memberships: Fellow, American College of Obstetrics and Gynecology; Chicago Gynecologic Society; The Society of Perinatal Obstetricians; Southern Atlantic Association of Obstetrics and Gynecology. Hobby: Running. Address: Medical College of Georgia, 1120 15th Street, Augusta, GA 30912, USA.

DEWAN Mantosh Jaimani, b. 22 July 1951, Bombay, India. Psychiatrist. m. Anita Lall, 10 June 1975, 1 son, 1 daughter. Education: MBBS, Bombay University, 1974; Diplomate, American Board of Psychiatry & Neurology, 1982. Appointments: Assistant Professor 1979, Associate Professor 1985-, Professor 1992, Vice Chairman, 1994, SUNY Health Sciences Center, Syracuse; Staff Psychiatrist, 1979-85, Acting Chief of Psychiatry, Syracuse Veterans Medical Center, 1985-89. Publications include: Toward a definitive diagnosis of Alzheimer's Disease, 1992; A Direct Comparison of the Defense Mechanisms of Non-depressed People and Depressed Psychiatric Inpatients; A comparison of three depression rating scales, 1992; Factitious disorders with psychological symptoms; Antidepressant side effects and physician prescribing patterns, 1993; Factors associated with antidepressant choice. Honours: Fellow, American Psychiatric Association, 1992; Exemplary Psychiatrist Award, 1994, by the National Alliance for the Mentally Ill. Memberships: American Psychiatric Association; Society for Biological Psychiatry; American Association of Directors of Psychiatry Residency Training; American Association of Psychiatrists from India. Hobbies: Alpine Skiing; Tennis; Travel. Address: Department of Psychiatry, SUNY Health Sciences Center, 750 East Adams Street, Syracuse, NY 13210, USA.

DEWEESE James Arville, b. 5 Apr 1925, Kent, Ohio, USA. Surgeon. m. Patricia Bidwell, 5 Apr 1962, 2 s, 4 d. Education: MD. Appointments: Surgeon, Strong Memorial Hospital, 1968-95; Cardiothoracic, Surgeon-in-Chief, Professor of Surgery, 1969-; Chair, Division Cardiothoracic Surgery, 1975-91; Associate Chair, Department of Surgery, 1986-91; Chief, Section of Vascular Surgery, 1987-91; Professor of Surgery, Chief Emeritus of Cardiothoracic Surgery and Vascular Surgery, University of Rochester, New York, 1991-. Publications: Editor of Operative Surgery; 254 Articles in Medical Journals, 1951-; 82 Chapters in Books; 3 Movies; 1 Instructional Tape. Hobbies: Golf. Address: University of Rochester, 601 Elmwood Avenue, Rochester, New York 14642, USA.

DEWEY Clarence Forbes, b. 27 Mar 1935, Pueblo, Colorado, USA. Professor. m. Carolyn Miller, 3 Aug 1963, 1 s. Education: BE, Yale University, 1956; MS, Stanford University, 1957; PhD, California Institute of Teaching, 1963. Appointments: Associate Professor, University of Colorado, 1963-68; Associate Professor, Massachusetts Institute of Technology, 1968-75; Visiting Professor, Imperial College, 1992; Associate in Pathology, Brigham Women's Hospital, 1982-; Professor of Mechanical Engineering, Massachusetts Institute of Technology. Publications: Over 100 Articles in Reviewed Journals and Proceedings in the Field of Arterial Flow and Medical Imaging. Honours: Founding Fellow, American Institute of Medical Biological Engineering, 1992; Faculty Fellow, University of Colorado, 1966-67; Senior Member, Medical Engineering Society, 1993. Memberships: American Institute of Medical Biolgical Engineering; APS; BME Soc. Hobbies: Skiing; Tennis; Travel. Address: Room 3-254, Massachusetts Institute of Technology, 77 Massachusetts Avenue, Cambridge, MA 02139, USA.

DÉZSI Zoltán, b. 13 Dec 1928, Magyarbikal, Rumania. Physicist. m. Mária Szihalmy, 31 July 1954, 1 son, 1 daughter. Education: Diploma as High School Teacher of Mathematics and Physics, Faculty of Natural Science, Kossuth Lajos University, Debrecen, 1951; Diploma, Candidate of Science, 1979; PhD; Fellow, Institute of Physics. Appointments: Lecturer, Institute of Experimental Physics, Kossuth Lajos University, 1950-; Radiology Clinic, Debrecen Medical University, 1963-. Publications: Optimal clinical-radiation physical and radiation biological conditions of telecobalt treatment, 1979. Honours: Honoured for Excellent Work, Kiváló Munkáért, 1981. Memberships: International Organization for Medical Physics; Secretary, Medical Physics Section, Hungarian Association for Biophysics; Hungarian Radiological Society. Hobbies: Stamp-collecting; Gardening. Address: Egyetem sugárut 4.I/3. H-4027 Debrecen, Hungary.

DHALIWAL Amrit, b. 25 Nov 1942, Punjab, India. Physician. m. Kulwant S Dhaliwal, 25 Sept 1972, 1 s, 1 d. Education: MBBS; MD. Appointments: Practicing Allergist. Hobbies: Gardening. Address: 4906 39th Avenue, Kenosha, WI 53142, USA.

DHALIWAL Kulwant S, b. 29 Mar 1937, Punjab, India. Physician. m. Amrit K Dhaliwal, 25 Sept 1972, 1 s, 1 d. Education: MBBS; MRCP; Board Certified in Allergy & Immunology. Appointments: Practicing Allergist & Immunologist. Hobbies: Reading; Photography. Address: 4906 39th Avenue, Kenosha, WI 53144, USA.

DI Rongqing, b. 2 Feb 1930, Heilongjiang, China. Surgeon. m. Li Wenxiu, 2 Feb 1957, 1 son, 1 daughter. Education: Graduated, Surgery Department, Chinese Medical University, 1948. Appointments: Surgeon, Hospital affiliated to 6th Military Medical University, 1950-60; Visiting Surgeon, Nanjing Gulou Hospital, 1960-74; Chief Surgeon, Nanjing 1st People's Hospital, 1975-; Professor, Nanjing Railway Medical College, 1988-. Publications: Surgical Treatment of Interhepatic Biliary Duct Stone Complicated by Stricture, 1980; Treatment of Portal Hypertension by Side-to-Side Meso-Caval Anastomosis, 1981; Anastomosis of Thoracic Duct and Internal Jugular Vein for Ascites Due to Late Hepatic Cirrhosis, 1982; Surgery Management of Pancreatic Trauma, 1987; An Experimental Study on the Role of Beta-Endorphin in the Pathogenesis of Acute Pancreatitis and the Effect and Mechanism, 1990; Emergency of Abdomen, 1990; Current Surgery of Liver Billiary Pancreas and Spleen, 1992; Practical Collections of Chinese Surgical Specialist, 1993. Honours: Distinguished Medical Specialist, certifed by State Council of China, 1992; 12 Science Progress Awards, Nanjing Municipality and Jiangsu Province, 1978-92. Memberships: China Medical Association; Biliary Study Committee, China Medical Association; Director, Jiangsu Branch, China Medical Association; Standing Director, Nanjing Sub-Committee, China Medical Association; Editorial Boards: Chinese Journal of Practical Surgery; Journal of Clinical General Surgery. Hobbies: Literature; Music. Address: 68 Changle Road, Nanjing 210006, Jiangsu, China.

DI BENEDETTO Margarete, b. 27 oct 1925, Germany. Physician. m. Philip J Di Benedetto, 24 Aug 1952, 1 son, 1 daughter. Education: Albertus University, Königsberg, East Prussia, 1942-44; Friedrich Alexander University, Erlangen, 1948-51. Appointments: Assistant professor, Cleveland Metro Hospital, Case Western Reserve University, USA, 1967-70; Sinai Hospital, Baltimore, 1970-71; Assistant Professor, Boston University, Boston-West Roxbury VA, Harvard Medical School, 1971-77; Associate Professor, Professor, Medical College, Wisconsin Milwaukee Medical Centre, 1977-80; Professor, USHSUS, US Army, Walter Reed Army Medical Centre, 1980-86; Professor, Georgetown University; Clinical Investigator, Eisenhower Army Medical Centre, 1986-87; Colonel, US Army Training Command, Fort Monroe, 1987-89; Professor, Chair, UVA Health Science Centre, 1989-. Publications: Contributor of numerous articles in medical journals. Honour: President, American Society for Clinical Evoked Potentials, 1986-87. Memberships: AAEM; ACSM; AAPHR; ACRM; AAP; IMSP. Address: Box 30 BRH UVA Health Science Centre, Charlottesville, VA 22901, USA.

DI GEORGE Angelo Mario, b. 15 Apr 1921, Philadelphia, USA. Pediatric Endocrinologist. m. Natalie J Picarello, 5 May 1951, 2 sons, 1 daughter. Education: BA, Temple University, 1943; MD, Temple University, 1946. Appointments: Assistant Professor, 1958-61; Associate Professor, 1961-67; Professor, 1967-91; Emeritus Professor, 1991-. Publications: Over 100 publications in Pediatric Endocrine, Metabolic and Genetic Disorders. Honours: Cystic Fibrosis Foundation, 1959; Corresponding Member, Societe Francaise de Pediatrie, 1967; Distinguishing Service Award, Philadelphia Endocrine Society. Memberships: American Pediatric Society; The Endocrine Society; American Diabetes Association; Sigma Xi; American Society for the Advancement of Science. Hobbies: Gardening; Medical History. Address: St Christophers Hospital for Children, Erie Ave at Front Street, Philadelphia, PA 19134-1095, USA.

DIAMOMD Leonard, b. 7 Aug 1929, Brooklyn, New York, USA. Physician; Psychiatrist. m. Ruth Carrel Finger, 9 Apr 1954, 1 son, 3 daughters. Education: BA; MD; Certificate in Psychoanalytic Medicine, Columbia University Center for Psychoanalytic Training and Research; Board Certified in Psychiatry and Psychoanalysis. Appointments: Supervising and Training Analyst, Columbia University Center for Psychoanalytic Research and Training; Currently: Assistant Clinical Professor of Psychiatry, Columbia University College of Psychology; Solo private practice. Memberships: American Psychiatric Association; American Psychoanalytic Association. Hobby: Music. Address: 29 South Main STreet, New Medford, CT 06776, USA.

DIAO Yuechi, b. 23 Aug 1931, Rangcheng Country, Hebei Province, China. Professor. m. Yang Jinxian, 10 Oct 1950, 3 sons, 2 daughters.

Appointments: Currently Section Chief, Pharmacy Department, 1st Hospital of Tianjin College of Traditional Medicine. Memberships: Communist Party of China. Hobby: Running. Address: Anshan West Road, Nankai District No 314, Tianjin, China.

DIASPRO Alberto Giovanni Mario, b. 7 Apr 1959, Genoa, Italy. Electronic Bioengineer. m. Teresa Cassano, 10 Mar 1984, 1 daughter. Education: Laurea, Electronic Engineering, University of Genoa, 1983; Abilitation for Professional Activity, 1983. Appointments: Technical, scientific and research activities, University of Genoa, including Research Associate, Institute of Biophysics, School of Medicine, 1985-, Research Associate, Department of Physics, University of Genoa, 1985-1994, and Faculty Member (Professore a Contratto), Biomedical Computer Science, Faculty of Medicine and Surgery, 1986-89, University of Genoa; Consultant in Electronic Engineering: Orsi Automazione, Genoa, 1983-86; Esacontrol Biomedicale, Genoa, 1985-86; Ge-Ancifap, Rome; Aeritalia SaiPa, Turin, 1987-88. Publications: Author or co-author, over 100 including: Medical and Biological Engineering and Computing, 23-I:263-64, 1985; Cell Biophysics, 10(2):45-60, 1987; Computer Methods and Programs in Biomedicine, 27:75-78, 1988, 31:225-236, 1990; Cell Biophysics, 15(3): 1989-200, 1989; Image Vision and Computing, 8(2):130-134, 1990; Pattern Recognition Letters, 11:553-556, 1990, 14:861-868, 1993; IEEE Transactions on Biomedical Engineering, BME-38(7):670-678, 1991; Biochemical and Biophysical Research Commission, 177(3):1313-1318, 1991; Journal of Microscopy (OXF), 165(2):311-324, 1992; Ultramicroscopy, 42/44:1668-1670, 1992; Signal Processing, 32(3):357-366, 1993; Sensors and Actuators A, 37/38:557-581, 1993; Bioimaging, 2(1), 1994. Honours: Admission to several schools on Pure and Applied Biostructures, E Majorana ERICE-NATO Advanced School; Guest Editor of IEEE-EMBS Magazine; Editorial Board of the International Journal Microscopy Research and Techniques. Memberships: Italian Group of Cytometry; Senior Member, Institute of Electrical and Electronics Engineers-EMBS; SPIE; New York Academy of Sciences; Biomedical Engineering Society; Italian Society of Pure & Applied Biophysics. Hobbies: Chess; Music; Reading; Judo; Stamp collection. Address: Via Lomellini 4-6, 16124 Genova, Italy.

DIAZ-BUXO Jose Antonio, b. 6 Feb 1946, Caguas, Puerto Rico. Nephrologist. m. Sandra Diaz, 2 d. Education: BS, Biology, University of Puerto Rico, San Juan, 1967; MD, Medicine, University of Puerto Rico, San Juan, 1970; MS, Physiology, University of Minnesota, 1975; Residency, Internal Medicine, Mayo Graduate School of Medicine, Rochester, 1970-73; Fellowship, Nephrology, Mayo Graduate School of Medicine, Rochester, 1973-75. Appointments: Clinical Instructor, Department of Medicine, University of North Carolina, 1975-76; Associate Attending, Internal Medicine and Nephrology, Charlotte Memorial Hospital, North Carolina, 1975-79; Nephrology Consultant, Nalle Clinic Kidney Center, Charlotte, North Carolina, 1975-82; Clinical Assistant Professor of Medicine, University of North Carolina, 1977-78; Clinical Associate Professor of Medicine, Department of Medicine, University of North Carolina, 1979-1994; Attending, Internal Medicine and Nephrology, Carolinas Medical Center, North Carolina, 1980-90; Director, Home Dialysis, Metrolina Kidney Center, North Carolina, 1986-; Chief, Nephrology Division, Carolinas Medical Center, North Carolina, 1991-; Senior Attending, Internal Medicine and Nephrology, Carolinas Medical Center, North Carolina, 1991-; Clinical Professor of Medicine, University of North Carolina, 1995-. Publications: Over 150 including, Acute Renal Failure Following Excretory Urography in Azotemic Diabetes, 1975; Continuous Cyclic Peritoneal Dialysis, 1990. Honours include: Alpha Omega Alpha, 1969; Sigma Xi, 1975; Fellow, American College of Physicians, 1977. Memberships include: American Society of Nephrology; International Society of Nephrology; International Society of Artificial Organs; American Medical Association; North Carolina Kidney Foundation. Hobbies: Music; Hunting. Address: Medical Director, Home Dialysis, Metrolina Kidney Center, 928 Baxter Street, Charlotte, NC 28204, USA.

DIBNER Harold, b. 15 Sept 1945, Waterbury, USA. Psychologist. Education: BA, Psychology, Boston University; MA, PhD, Counseling Psychology, Columbia Pacific University. Appointments: Chief of Therapeutic Services, YWCA, Ft Worth, Texas; Consulting Psychologist. Publications: Evaluation YWCA Intervention Center Program, Attorney General State of Texas, 1975. Memberships: Clinical Member, International Transactional Analysis Association. Honours: Trustee Scholarship, Boston University, 1964. Hobbies: Skiing; Golf; Audio. Address: 4212 Stonedale Road, Fort Worth, TX 76116, USA.

DICKERSIN Kay, b. 10 Nov 1951, Philadelphia, Pennsylvania, USA. Epidemiologist. m. Robert A Van Wesep, 30 June 1973, 2 sons. Education: BA, Zoology, 1974, MA, Cell Biology, 1975, University of California, Berkeley; PhD, Epidemiology, Johns Hopkins University School of Hygiene and Public Health, 1989. Appointments: Assistant Professor, Director of Clinical Trials Unit, Department of Ophthalmology, 1989-92, Graduate Faculty, 1991-, Assistant Professor, Department of Epidemiology and Preventive Medicine, 1992- University of Maryland School of Medicine, Baltimore; Lecturer, Department of Epidemiology, 1991-, Faculty, Center for Clinical Trials, 1991-, Johns Hopkins University School of Hygiene and Public Health, Baltimore; Director, Baltimore Cochrane Center, 1993-. Publications include: Author, co-author, chapters: Pharmacological Control of Pain in Labor, 1989; The existence of publication bias and risk factors for its occurrence, 1991; Research Registers, 1993; Death, 1994; Measles and Mumps Vaccines, 1994; Publication Bias: The problem that won't go away, 1994; The accessible biomedical literature represents a fraction of all studies in a field. Philosophical, ethical and practical aspects of editing refereed science journals, 1994; Meta-analysis: Nuisance or new science?, 1994; Reinventing medical research, 1994. Honours: Howard Hughes Medical Fellowship, Harvard Medical School, 1971; Traineeship in Public Health, Johns Hopkins University, 1980-81; Frohlich Fellowship, New York Academy of Sciences, 1993-97; Woman of Excellence, National Association of Women Business Owners, Baltimore Chapter, 1994. Memberships: Society for Epidemiologic Research; Society for Clinical Trials; American Association for the Advancement of Science; Association for Vision and Research in Ophthalmology. Address: Department of Epidemiology and Preventive Medicine, University of Maryland School of Medicine, 660 W Redwood Street, Baltimore, MD 21201, USA.

DICKERSON Omar Bruce, b. 27 Feb 1936, Hayti, Missouri, USA. Occupational Medicine. m. Mimi Haggerty, 11 July 1964, 1 s. Education: MD; Master of Public Health; BA, Chemistry; Boards in Occupational Medicine. Appointments: Corporate Director of Health & Safety, IBM Corporation, 1980-87; President, Dickerson Occupational Health Services Inc, 1987-. Publications: Co-Editor, Occupational Medicine, 1994. Honours: Past President, College of Preventive Medicine; Past President, American College of Occupational and Environmental Medicine. Memberships: American College of Occupational and Environmental Medicine; Human Factors & Ergonomics Society; American Industrial Hygiene Agency. Hobbies: Golf; Gardening. Address: 41 Thrush Lane, New Canaan, Conneticut 06840, USA.

DICKINSON Kathy Lee, b. 6 Jul 1954, Hopkinsville, Kentucky, USA. Certified Ophthalmic Technician. m. Paul R Dickinson, 7 Aug 1992, 1 d. Education: Ophthalmic Certification Assistant and Technician. Appointments: Business Administrator, Bailey Plumbing & Electric Service; Certified Ophthalmic Technician. Publications: Tennessee Ophthalmic Personnel Society Newsletter - Activated Leadership, 1990; Tennessee Ophthalmic Personnel Society Newsletter - Keratometer Steps, 1994. Honours: Kentucky Jaycee Top Ten President, 1989; Kentucky Jaycee Program Manager of the Year, 1990; Kentucky Jaycee District Manager of the Year, 1991. Memberships: Tennessee Ophthalmic Society; Associated Technical Personnel in Ophthalmology; Joint Commission of Allied Health Personnel in Ophthalmology; Tennessee Opthalmic Society President, 1991; Todd Co American Red Cross Director, 1995; Todd Co High School PTO President, President, 1995. Hobbies: Reading; Hiking; Cooking. Address: P O Box 144, Elkton, KY 42220-0144, USA.

DIEBSCHLAG Francesca, b. 18 Feb 1950, Illinois, USA. Practitioner of Traditional Chinese Medicine; Lecturer in Chinese Medicine and Research Methodology; Research Consultant; Researcher. m. Hans Diebschlag, 14 Apr 1979, 1 son. Education: BAc, International College of Oriental Medicine, 1987; BPhil, University of Exeter, 1993. Appointments: Director of Research, International College of Oriental Medicine; Lecturer in Research Methodlogy, London School of Acupuncture and Traditional Chinese Medicine, England; Research Consultant, College of Traditional Chinese Acupuncture; Research Consultant, The Letchworth Centre for Complementary Medicine; Currently: Director, The West View Clinic of Oriental Medicine; Independent Lecturer in Alternative Systems of Health Care. Publications: Placebo Acupuncture, 1993; Types of Research Designs, 1994. Memberships: International Register of Oriental Medicine, UK; Register of Chinese Herbal Medicine. Address: 2 West View Gardens, East Grinstead, West Sussex RH19 4EH, England.

DIGGS Carter Lee, b. 31 Dec 1934. Physician. m. virginia Mabry, 6 June 1956, 2 sons, 1 daughter. Education: MD; PhD. Appointments: Director, Division of Communicable Diseases & Immunology, Walter Reed Army Institute of Research; Associate Director, Walter Reed Army Institute of Research. Publications: More than 50 scientific articles. Honours: Phi Beta Kappa, 1975. Memberships: American Association of Immunologists; American Society of Tropical Medicine & Hygiene; American Society of Microbiologists. Hobbies: Flying; Music. Address: 11202 Landy Court, Kensington, MD 20895, USA.

DIMSDALE Joel A, b. 16 Apr 1947, Sioux City, Iowa, USA. Physician. m. Nancy Kleinman, 17 Sep 1979, 1 son. Education: BA, 1965, MA, 1970, MD, 1973, Stanford University. Appointments: Instructor, Assistant Professor, Associate Professor of Psychiatry, Harvard Medical School, 1976-85; Associate Professor, Professor of Psychiatry, University of California San Diego, 1985-. Publications: Survivors, Victims and Perpetrators, Editor; Quality of Life in Behavioral Medicine Research, Editor; Contributor of over 100 research articles; Editor-in-Chief, Psychosomatic Medicine, 1992-. Honours: Sigma Xi; Clinician Scientist Awardee, American Heart Association, 1979-84 Fellow, American Psychiatric Association, 1987; President, Academy of Behavioural Medicine Research, 1991. Memberships: American Psychosomatic Society; Academy of Behavioural Medicine Research; American Psychiatric Association; Society of Behavioural Medicine. Hobbies: Reading; Skiing. Address: Department of Psychiatry, UCSD, La Jolla, CA 92093-0804, USA.

DING Hongcai, b. 9 May 1914, Jiangsu, China. Oral and Maxillofacial Surgeon. m. 1937. 1 son, 3 daughters. Education: MD, College of Medicine, National Central University, 1941. Appointments: Assistant Professor, 1941-44, Lecturer, 1944-50, Associate professor, 1951-60, Professor of Oral and Maxillofacial Surgery, 1960-, Fourth Military Medical University. Publications: Oral Embryology and Histology, 1957; The Submicroscopic Structures of the Cancer Cells of Oral and Maxillofacial Region Before and After Cryosurgery, 1981; Biologic Effect of Freezing on Tissues of the Maxillofacial Region, 1985; The Biologic Effect of Alkaline Phosphatase After Freezing, 1993. Honours: Recipient, Scientific Progress Award and Scientific Accomplishments, 9 times, 1982-93. Memberships: Director, Cryobiological Association, 1981-87; Honourable President, Head and Neck Oncological Surgeons, 1989-; CI Committee, International Institute of Refrigeration, 1984-87; Vice President, Shanxi Institute of refrigeration of China, 1979-92. Address: College of Stomatology, Fourth Military Medical University, Xian, Shanxi 710032, China.

DING Jin-bang, b. 21 Dec 1938, Sanyuan County, Shaanxi, China. Acupuncturist. m. Xu Cai-yun, 1 May 1967, 1 son, 1 daughter. Education: BA, Xian Medical University, 1963; Shaanxi College of Traditional Chinese Medicine. Appointments: Micro-Organism Section, Basic Department, Xian Medical University, 1963-70; Vice Head, Professor, Acupuncture and Moxibustion Department, Shaanxi College of Traditional Chinese Medicine, 1971-. Publications: Treating Stroke by Acupuncture, 1985; Treating Color Blindness by Acupuncture, 1974; The Text Book of Acupuncture Treatment, The Surgical and The Five Sense Organs Parts, 1982. Honours: Honorary Professor, Xijing Suen Simiao Self-Teaching College of Traditional Chinese Medicine; Scalp Acupuncture video won Best Video Teaching Film, 1993. Memberships: Developing and Researching Society of Xijing Traditional Chinese Medical Science and Technology. Hobbies: Reading; Running. Address: Department of Acupuncture and Moxibustion, Shaanxi College of Traditional Chinese Medicine, No 1 Weiyang Road, 712083 Xianyaang, Shaanxi, China.

DING Shihai, b. 17 Jan 1931, Tsingtao, China. Professor of Human Anatomy. m. Ke Yan, 19 Mar 1955, 1 son, 1 daughter. Education: BA, Shandong University, 1953; MD, Peking Medical College, 1954. Appointments: Associate Professor, Chairman, Department of Anatomy, Yishui School of Medicine, 1978; Dean of Studies, Yishui School of Medicine, 1978; Chief Editor, Journal of Yishui School of Medicine, 1979. Publications: Textbook of Human Anatomy, 1974; Survey of Anatomical Data Variations of Chinese, 1986; The measuring and calculating method of some cranial angles, 1983; Sexual diagnosis of Chinese crania from discriminant function analysis, 1989; Human Anatomy, 1990; Over 60 articles. Honours: Advanced Teacher of Shandong, 1988; National Advanced Worker, 1988; Model of Labour of Qingdao, 1993. Memberships: Chinese Society for Anatomical Sciences; Vice Chairman, Anthropological Committee; Vice Chairman, Shandong Society of Anatomy. Hobbies: Singing; Table Tennis;

Philately. Address: Department of Anatomy, Qingdao Medical College, 16 Songshan Road, Qingdao 266021, Shandong, China.

DION Kenneth Lucien, b. 7 Oct 1944, New Hampshire, USA. Professor of Psychology. m. Karen Kisiel, 16 Mar 1968. Education: BA, University of New Hampshire, 1967; PhD, University of Minnesota, 1970. Appointments: Associate Editor, Journal of Experimental Social Psychology, 1977-79; Consulting Editor, Canadian Psychology, 1986-90; Psychology for Women Quarterly, 1986-93; Journal of Personality and Social Psychology, 1990-95; Professor of Psychology, University of Toronto, Canada. Publications: The Phenomenology of Being a Target of Prejudice, CO-author, 1975; Intergroup Conflict and Intragroup Cohesiveness, 1979; Belief in a Just World and Physical Attractiveness Stereotyping, Co-author, 1987; Romantic Love: Individual and Cultural Perspectives, CO-author, 1988; Personality-based Hardiness as a Buffer for Discrimination-Related Stress in Members of Toronto's Chinese Community, Co-author, 1992. Honours: Fellow, American Psychological Association; American Psychological Society; Canadian Psychological Assocaition; Arts and Science Excellence Awards, 1992, 1994. Memberships: Society of Experimental Social Psychology; European Association of Experimental Social Psychology. Hobbies: Travel; Reading; French culture and cuisine. Address: Department of Psychology, University of Toronto, Toronto, Ontario M5S 1A1, Canada.

DIRIK Eray, b. 25 June 1947, Cyprus. Medical Doctor. m. Gurvan Dirik, 28 Feb 1975, 1 son, 1 daughter. Education: Pediatrician; PED Neurologist. Appointments: Associate Professor, Department of Child Health & Pediatrics, Dokuz Eylul Medical University Faculty. Publications: Incontinensia Pigmenti Acromians, 1989; Menkes Kinky Hair Syndorme, 1989. Memberships: Turkish Pediatric Societies. Hobbies: Painting; Travel. Address: Mustafa Kemal Sahil Bulvari Sahil/Apt No 255, Guzelyali, Izmir, Turkey.

DODD Karen Deborah Sklayne, b. 10 Oct 1957, London, England. Clinical Psychologist. m. Howard Dodd, 20 Mar 1983, 2 d. Education: BSc Psychology, University College, London, 1979; PhD, University of Manchester, 1982; MSc Clinical Psychology, University of Surrey, 1984. Appointments: Clinical Psychologist, Richmond, Twickenham and Roehampton Health Authority, 1984-90; Principal Clinical Psychologist, Surrey Heartlands. Publications: The Relationship Between Social Class and Educational Psychological and Physical Aspects of Spina Bifida and Hydrocephalus, Co-author, 1980; The Effects of Selective Surgery on the Self Concept and Attainments of Children with Spina Bifida and Hydrocephalus, 1981; Where Should Spina Bifida Children Go To School?, 1984. Memberships: Associate Fellow, British Psychological Society; British Association for Behavioural and Cognitive Psychotherapy. Hobbies: Cross-stitch Embroidery; Picture Framing. Address: Department of Psychology, St Ebba's, Hook Road, Epsom, Surrey, England.

DODERO Danilo, b. 10 Oct 1949, Genova, Italy. Gynaecologist. m. 7 Apr 1979, 1 son, 1 daughter. Education: MD, 1974; Specialist in Obstetrics and Gynaecology, 1978, Appointments: Assistant Obstetrics and Gynaecology, E O Galliera Hospital, Genova, 1975; Consusltant, 1985; Chief, Head, Department bstetrics and Gynaecology, Chiavari/Lavagna Hospital, Genova, 1994-. Publications: Author of over 200 works including books and videotapes of surgical operations. Honours: Professor of Foetal medicine, Universita La Sapienea, Rome, 1994. memberships: National Board, Italian Society of Perinatal Medicina. Hobby: Sailing. Address: Via Antica Romana di Quinto 101, 16166 Genova, Italy.

DOEGE Theodore C, b. 11 Dec 1928, Lincoln, Nebraska, USA. Physician; Scientist. m. Ann Elizabeth Edmondsou, 23 June 1957, 1 son, 1 daughter. Education: MS, Preventive Medicine, University Washington, Seattle; AB, Oberlin College; MD, University Rochester. Appointments: Associate Professor, Epidemiology Biometry Program, School of Public Health, University Illinois, Chicago, 1972-; Senior Scientist, American Medical Association, Chicago, 1984-. Publications: Author, editor or contributor to more than 80 medical scientific publications. Memberships: American Medical Association; Sigma Xi; American Association for Advancement of Science; Fellow, American College of Preventive Medicine; Fellow, American Public Health Association. Address: 515 No State St, Chicago, IL 60610, USA.

DOLAN John Patrick, b. 23 Jan 1935. Psychiatrist. m. Margaret Abel, 6 Sep 1974, 1 s, 1 d. Education: MD, New Jersey College of Medicine, 1962. Appointments: Assistant Professor of Psychiatry, St Louis University School of Medicine; Associate Professor, Department of Psychiatry, New York Medical College; Chairman, Department of Psychiatry, St Vincent's Medical Centre, Bridgeport, CT. Honours: President, Bridgeport Psychiatric Society, 1987-. Memberships: American Psychiatric Society; Bridgeport Psychiatric Society; New York Academy of Science. Address: 2800 Main Street, Bridgeport, CT 06606, USA.

DOLEN William Kennedy, b. 16 Oct 1952, Memphis, USA. Physician. m. Carolyn Canon, 21 Dec 1974, 1 son, 1 daughter. Education: BS, Rhodes College, 1974; MD, University of Tennessee Center for the Health Sciences, 1977. Appointments: Associate Professor, Pediatrics & Medicine, Medical College of Georgia. Publications: Immunoassay of specific IgE: low level assays require measurement of allergen specific background, 1992; Use of standard and conventional extracts in prick skin testing, 1992; Common allergenic pollen and fungi, 1994. Memberships: American Academy of Allergy & Immunology; American Medical Association; European Academy of Allergy & Clinical Immunology. Honours: Board of Regents, ACAI, 1993; Editorial Board, Annals of Allergy. Hobbies: Music. Address: Allergy Immunology BG-247, Medical College of Georgia, Augusta, GA 30912, USA.

DOLGIKH Robert, b. 20 Mar 1942, Chimkent, Kazakhstan. Physician, Stomatology. m. 6 Jul 1973, 2 d. Education: Diploma, Almatinskiy State Medical Institute. Appointments: Senior Laboratory Assistant, Faculty of Therapeutic Stomatology, 1973; Assistant of Faculty, 1977; Head of Laboratory of Laser Medicine Equipment, 1978-. Publications: Experimental Grounds for YAG: Laser Application to Dentistry, 1989; The Mechanism of Action of YAG from Laser, 1989; The Action of Eradiation of YAG from Laser on Tooth Tissue, 1992. Memberships: International Society of Laser Optics. Hobbies: Horticulture; Growing Citrus Plants. Address: Pos Aktas d.5, Kv 19, Talgar, Almatinskaya Oblast, Kazakhstan.

DOLOVICH Jerry, b. 2 Apr 1936, Winnipeg, Canada. Physician. m. Myrna Gersovitz, 2 July 1963, 3 daughters. Education: MD; FRCPC. Appointment: Professor of Paediatrics, McMaster University. Memberships: American Academy of Allergy and Immunology. Address: Room 3V41 McMaster Medical Centre, 1200 Main Street West, Hamilton, Ontario L8N 3Z5, Canada.

DOLUISIO James T, b. 28 Sep 1935, Bethlehem, PA, USA. Educator. m. Phyllis Doluisio, 2 s, 1 d. Education: BS, Pharmacy; MS, Pharmacy; PhD, Physical Pharmacy. Appointments: Assistant and Associate Professor, Philadelphia College of Pharmacy and Science, 1961-67; Professor and Assistant Dean, University of KY, 1967-73; Dean, University of TX College of Pharmacy, 1973-. Publications: Over 90 papers on bioequivalency and drug absorption, biopharmaceutics, pharmacokinetics, physical pharmacy, pharmacy education, and various pharmacy issues for national and international journals, textbooks and conferences. Honours: Honorary Doctorate, DSc, Philadelphia College of Pharmacy and Science; American Pharmaceutical Association, Remington Honor Medal. Memberships: US Pharmacopeial Convention Board of Trustees Chairman; American Pharmaceutical Association; American Colleges of Pharmacy; American Society of Hospital Pharmacists; American College of Apothecaries; NARD; Federation Internationale Pharmaceutique; TX Pharmacy Association; TX Society of Hospital Pharmacists. Address: University of Texas College of Pharmacy, Austin, TX 78712, USA.

DOMOTO Douglass T, b. 17 Sep 1943, Elgin, IL, USA. Physician. m. Betsy Ann Hall, 19 Jun 1970, 1 d. Education: MD, Yale University; Juris Doctorate, St Louis University, 1995. Appointments: Assistant Professor, University of Chicago, 1978-82; Associate Professor Medicine, St Louis University, 1982-. Memberships: American Society of Nephrology; International Society of Nephrology; International Society of Peritoneal Dialysis. Address: 3635 Vista, St Louis, MO 63110, USA.

DONAHOO James Saunders, b. 30 Sept 1937, Jackson, TN, USA. Cardiothoracic Surgeon. m. Carol Manasco, 24 June 1961, 1 son, 1 daughter. Education: AB, Birimingham Southern College, 1959; MD, Medical College of Alabama, 1963. Appointments: Associate Professor of Surgery, Johns Hopkins University School of Medicine, 1971-82; Associate Professor of Surgery, Jefferson Medical College, 1982-89; Professor, Chief, Cardiothoracic Surgery, New Jersey Medical School. Publications: Systemic Pulmonary Shunts in Neonates and Infants using PTFE, 1980; Combined Aortic and Mitral Valve Repalcement, 1985;

Co-author, Ultrasound Decalcification of Aortic Valve Stenosis, 1992. Memberships: Fellow, American College of Surgery; Southern Surgical Association; American Association for Thoracic Surgery; Society of Thoracic Surgeons. Honours: Alpha Omega Alpha, 1962; Osler Abbot Award, 1982; Army Achievement Medal, 1991; Congressional Certificate of Merit, 1992; President, New Jersey Society of Thoracic Surgeons, 1994. Hobbies: Polo; Foxhunting; Opera; 19th Century Oil Paintings. Address: UMD New Jersey Medical School, 185 South Orange Avenue, Newark, NJ 07103, USA.

DONEGAN William Laurence, b. 3 Nov 1932, Jacksonville, Florida, USA. General Surgeon. m. Judith Higgins, 21 Dec 1963, 1 son, 1 daughter. Education: MD; FACS; BA. Appointment: Professor of Surgery, medical College of Wisconsin. Publications: Cancer of The Breast. Honours: Fulbright Lecturer to Yugoslavia, 1988; Professor of Clinical Oncology, American Cancer Society, 1975-82. Memberships: American Surgical Association; Central Surgical Association; Society of Surgical Oncology; American College of Surgeons. Hobby: Travel. Address: 950 N 12th Street, Milwaukee, WI 53201, USA.

DONG Cheng, b. 19 July 1959, Shanghai, China. Researcher; Educator. m. Rita Marie Chenoweth, 8 Oct 1988, 1 son, 1 daughter. Education: BS, Engineering Science, Jiao-Tong University, 1982; MS, Bioengineering, 1984, PhD, Bioengineering, 1988, Columbia University, USA. Appointments: Assistant Research Bioengineer, University of California, San Diego, USA, 1988-90; Staff Fellow, National Institutes of Health, 1990-92; Lecturer, Catholic University of America, 1991; Currently Assistant Professor of Bioengineering and Engineering Science, Pennsylvania State University, University Park. Publications: Computers in Biomedicine; Recent Advances in Coronary Circulation; Cell Mechanics and Cellular Engineering; Papers in Biophysical Journal, Biorheology, Journal of Theoretical Biology, Annals of Biomedical Engineering, Journal of Biomechanical Engineering, Microvascular Research, Journal of Cell Physiology, other journals. Honours: Best Journal Paper Award in Bioengineering, 1989; Melville Medal, American Society of Mechanical Engineers, 1990; Lamport Young Investigator Award, Biomedical Engineering Society, 1992; Junior Faculty Research Award, American Cancer Society, 1994. Memberships: American Society of Mechanical Engineers; Biomedical Engineering Society; North American Society of Biorheology; Microcirculation Society. Hobbies: Reading; Music; Hiking; Biking; Photography; Travel. Address: 7 Sandra Circle, State College, PA 16801, USA.

DONG Chuanren, b. 28 September 1935, Hubei, China. Professor. m. Zhang Youyun, 8 September 1959, 2 sons, 1 daughter. Education: BA, Hubei Medical University, China, 1959. Appointments: Assistant of Pathophysiology, Hubei Medical University, 1959; Lecturer of Pathophysiology, Hubei Medical University, 1967; Associate Professor, Director, Department of Pathophysiology, Hubei Medical University, 1978; Director, Department of Scientific Research, Hubei Medical University, 1983-. Publications: Co-author, Pathophysiology, 1990, 1993; The Alterations of Coagulation, An-coagulation in EHF, 1989; Role of Soyabean Phospholipid Liposome in Reperfusion Membrane Injury, 1992; The Myocardial Membrane Injury in Infraction, 1990. Honours: Government Special Subsidy for Outstanding Contribution, 1994. Memberships: Standing Director, Chinese Medical Association, Wuhan, Hubei Branch; National Society of Microcirculation; International Society of Hearth Research. Hobbies: Running; Basketball. Address: Department of Pathophysiology, Hubei Medical University, Wuhan, Hubei 430071, China.

DONG Hanji, b. 17 Nov 1921, Panyu, Guangdong, China. Professor of Pathology. m. Qin Dai, 27 Mar 1951, 2 sons. Education: MD, West China Union University Medical College, 1950. Appointments: Assistant Lecturer, Pathologist, Department Head, Pathology, Guangdong Medical College; Associate Professor, Professor, Consultant Pathologist, Pathology Department, Affiliated Hospital, Guangdong Medical College; Retired. Publications include: Soft Tissue Tumor Pathology, Co-author, 1981; Numerous articles in professional journals. Honours: Recipient of honours and awards for professional services. Memberships: Chinese Medical Association. Hobbies: Baseball; Tennis. Address: Building 17, Guangdong Medical College, Zhengjiang 524023, Guangdong, China.

DONG Jun, b. 20 Sept 1927, Hebei, China. Professor of Pathology. m. Ho Pun-mui, 2 Jan 1957, 2 sons. Education: Tung Chi University Medical College, Shanghai, 1946-52. Appointments: Assistant, 1953-56, Lecturer, 1956-78, Associate Professor, 1978-1983, Professor of Pathology, 1983-, Sun Yat-Sen University of Medical Sciences,

Guangzhou. Publications: Editor-in-chief: Pathology, 1978; Pathology volume, Chinese Encyclopaedia of Medicine; Co-author: The relationship between HBV-infection, liver cirrhosis and hepatoma in China, 1980; Cytotoxic action of natural killer cells on CNE-2 nasopharyngeal carcinoma cells, 1989; Immunohistochemical study on the proliferative activity of rat liver in hepatocarcinogenesis, 1991; Evolution and biological behaviors of natural killer-resistant subline of B16-melanoma cells, 1993. Memberships: Chinese Society of Pathology; International Academy of Pathology. Hobbies: Classical music; Beijing Opera. Address: 31 Zhu Si Village, Zhi Xin Road, Guangzhou 510080, China.

DONG Yao Jun, b. 8 Mar 1936, Hebei, China. Oral Surgery. m. Jiang hui Zhong, 5 Aug 1965, 1 son, 1 daughter. Education: DDS, Faculty of Dentistry, West China Medical University. Appointments: Department of Oral Maxillofacial Surgery College of Stomatology, Hubei Medical University; Associate Dean, College of Stomatology, Hubei Medical University. Publications: Practical Orthognathic Surgery, 1987; Fundmentary of Oral Biology, 1993. Honours: Governmental Allowance, 1991-. Memberships: Vice Chairman, Association of Chinese Reconstructive Surgery, Hubei Branch; Chairman, Wuhan Stomatological Branch. Hobbies: Table Tennis; Jogging. Address: College of Stomatology, Hubei Medical University, No 65 Luoyu Road, Wuhan, Hubei 430070, China.

DOOUSS Karen Elizabeth, b. 11 Nov 1964, London, England. m. John Merlop, 2 Dec, 1 son, 1 daughter. Education: BDS. Appointments: General Practice, 1988-. Memberships: New Zealand Dental Association. Hobbies: Going to the Gym; Playing Guitar; Singing. Address: 20 Wilkes Street, Richmond, Nelson, New Zealand.

DORIA-MEDINA EGUIA Roberto, b. 6 Mar 1925, Bolivia. Professor; Doctor. m. Carmen Ponce, 21 Feb 1951, 2 sons, 3 daughters. Education: MD, Especisigst en Psiquiatria; PhD, Universidad de Buenos Aires. Appointments: Jefe de Servicio Hospital Bordz; Coordinator, Docencia e Investigacion Hospital Borda. Publications: Angustia; Boderlines, 1992; Arte Prehispano Vision Psyicoanalitica, 1993. Memberships: Association Psicoanalitica Argentina; Association Medica. Honours: Premio Blecjer Association Psicoanalitica, 1977. Address: Arenales 1330 P6, 1061 Buenos Aires, Argentina.

DORIAN William, b. 4 Mar 1921, Timisoara, Romania. Physician. m. Helen Dorian, 28 June 1944, 2 sons. Education: MD, CM, 1948; FRCP(C), 1972. Appointments: Assistant Professor of Medicine, University Cluj; Executive Director of Medical Research, Merck-Frosst Labs, Montreal, Canada; Lecturer, McGill University, Montreal, Canada; Staff, Montreal General Hospital; Wellesley Hospital, Toronto. Publications: Infectious Hepatitis, 1953; Chronic Hepatitis, 1958; Posthepatitic Cirrhosis, 1957. Memberships: Royal College of Physicians & Surgeons; Canadian Society for Clinical Pharmacology; American Society for Clinical Pharmacology; American Academy of Allergy. Honours: Service Award, Canadian Society for Clinical Pharmacology, 1989. Hobbies: Cycling; Hiking; Swimming; Computers; Photography. Address: 3303 Don Mills Road, Apt 1003, Willowdale, Ont M2J 4T6, Canada.

DOROHOV Vitaly Vladimirovich, b. 23 June 1947, Waldenburg, Russia. Physician. m. Anna Dorohova, 12 May 1950, 1 son, 1 daughter. Education: MD, Moscow State Medical Institute, 1975; Superior Category in Psychiatry; PhD. Appointments: Head, department of Psychiatric Hospital, Bryansk, 1991; Deputy Head Doctor, Bryansk Diagnostic Centre. Publications: Thyroid pathology in Children and Adolescents in the Most Radio-Contaminated Areas of the Bryansk Region (Russia) After the Chernobyl Accident, Co-author, 1994. Memberships: International Consortium for Research on the Health Effects of Radiation. Hobbies: Sailing. Address: 2 Bejiyzkaya Str, bryansk 241007, Russia.

DOUGLAS Thomas Scott, b. 3 Jan 1948, Scott County, USA. Physician. m. Sandra Berge, 7 July 1979, 1 son, 2 daughters. Education: BA, Augustana College; MD, University Iowa. Appointments: Associate Consultant, Mayo Clinic; Assistant Medical Director, Consultant, Occupational Medicine. Publications incl: Brucellosis: An Unusual Cause of Post Operative Fever, 1973; Hyperpyrexia in Catatonic States, 1976; Hematology Review Quiz, Resident and Staff Physician, 1976; An Evaluation of Excess Colorectal Cancer Incidence Among Workers Involved in the manufacture of Polypropylene, 1988; Factors Associated with Participation in an Occupational Program for Colorectal Cancer

Screening, 1989; Assessment of Colorectal Cancer Screening Outcomes among Baytown Chemical Plant Polyolefin Unit Workers, 1989. Honours: Beta Beta Beta; Bortz Award for Outstanding Medical Student Research, University Iowa College of Medicine, 1974; AMA Physician Recognition Awards (Annually). Memberships: American College of Physicians, Fellow; American College of Occupational Medicine, Fellow; American College of Preventative Medicine, Fellow; Mayo Alumni Association; Central States Occupational Medicine Association; American Medical Association. Hobbies: Fishing; Medical Stamp Collecting. Address: East Range Clinic, Department of Occupational Medicine, 910 6th Avenue North, Virginia, MN 55792, USA.

DOVE Colin Ivor, b. 6 Apr 1932, Plaistow, London, England. Osteopath. m. Mary Grace Dove, 30 May 1959, 1 son, 2 daughters. Education: Diploma in Osteopathy, British School of Osteopathy, 1956. Appointments: Principal, 1968-77, Head, Department of Postgraduate Studies, 1980-87, Director, Postgraduate Studies, 1987-90, British School of Osteopathy; Private Practice. Honours: Littlejohn Award, osteopathic Association of Great Britain, 1977; Honorary Life Membership, Cranial Academy, USA, 1987; Honorary Fellow, British School of Osteopathy, 1991. Memberships: General Council and register of Osteopaths. Hobbies: Fellwalking; Cycling; Photography; Model Making. Address: 70 Eastern Road, Romford, Essex RM1 3QA, England.

DOVE James T, b. 2 Aug 1939, Norwalk, Ohio, USA. Cardiologist. m. Carol Ann Proctor, 27 Aug 1960, 1 son, 1 daughter. Education: BA, Wittenberg University, 1961; MD, Case Western Reserve University, 1965. Appointments: Clinical Assistant Professor of Medicine; Clinical Professor of Medicine; Chief, Division of Cardiology; President, Prairie Cardiovascular Consultants Ltd. Publications: Introduction in Cardiac Pacing, 1983; A Practical Guide to Cardiac Pacing, 1987; Thrombolytic Therapy for Acute Myocardial Infarction, 1992. Honours: Cum Laude, Wittenberg University, 1961; Mead Johnson Schoalrship Award, 1968-69; American College of Physicians Laureate Award, 1992. Memberships: American College of Physicians; Governor, Downstate Illinois, 1988-92; American Heart Association; American College of Cardiology; American College of Chest Physicians. Address: Prairie Cardiovascular Consultants Limited, PO Box 19420, Springfield, IL 62794-9420, USA.

DOVE Lorraine, b. 20 Feb 1960, Pennsylvania, USA. Nurse Consultant. Education: Diploma, Reading Hospital School of Nursing; Certification, Gerontological Nursing, American Nurses' Association. Appointments: Staff Nurse, Reading Hospital, 1982-83; Charge Nurse, Lebanon Valley General, 1983; ADON Leader, Nursing Center, 1983-84; Head Nurse, Springfield Municipal, 1984; Senior Medical Coordinator, Medical Personnel Pool, 1986; Director of Nursing, Sunrise Manor, 1986-88; ADON, Palm Garden, 1988; Director of Nursing, Vero Beach Care, 1988-92; Director of Nursing, Okeechobee Health Care, 1992-94; Regional Nurse Consultant, Patient Care Pharmacy, 1994-95; CQI/RA Coordinator, Colonial Palms East, 1995-. Memberships: Florida and National Associations of Directors of Nursing Administration; Intravenous Nurses Society; FHCA District XIII AIDS Task Force; District XV Health and Human Services Board Aging and Adult Committee; AIDS Consortium of the Treasure Coast. Hobbies: Cooking; Artwork; Crafts. Address: 6103 Boca Colony Drive, Apartment 1411, Boca Raton, FL 33433, USA.

DOW Julian Alexander Thomas, b. 9 May 1957, Cheltenham, England. Biologist. m. Fiona Lyall, 25 Apr 1987. Education: BA, 1977, MA, 1981, PhD, 1981, Cambridge University. Appointments: Research Fellow, St Catherine's College, Cambridge, 1981-84; Harkness Fellow, 1981-83; Senior Lecturer. Publications: Contributor of 45 papers. Honour: President's Medallist, Society for Experimental Biology, 1992. Memberships: Society for Experimental Biology; British Society for Cell Biology; Fellow, Royal Entomological Society. Hobbies: Skiing; Wines; Golf; Travel. Address: Department of Cell Biology, University of Glasgow, Glasgow G12 8QQ, Scotland.

DOWNER Roger George Hamill, b. 21 Dec 1942, Belfast, N. Ireland. Professor of Biology. m. Jean Taylor, 2 Apr 1966, 1 s, 2 d. Education: BSc, Belfast; MSc, Belfast; PhD, Western Ontario; DSc, Belfast; Fellow of Royal Society of Canada. Appointments: Assistant Professor, 1970-76; Associate Professor, 1976-81; Professor, 1981-; Chair of Biology, 1986-89; Acting Dean of Science, 1989; Vice-President, University Relations, University of Waterloo. Publications: 4 Edited

Books; 150 Refereed Papers and Book Chapters. Honours: Fry Medal, Canadian Society of Zoologists, 1991; Gold Medal, Entomolgical Society of Canada, 1992, Memberships: Past-President, Canadian Society of Zoologists; Past-President, Canadian Council of University Biology Chairs. Hobbies: Squash; Golf; Theatre; Reading; Walking. Address: University of Waterloo, Waterloo, Ontario, Canada N2L 3G1.

DOYLE David, b. Edinburgh, Scotland. Neuropathologist. m. Dr Janet Caryl Doyle, 24 Oct 1964, dec 1984, 5 sons. Education: RD; DFM; MD; CBiol; FIBiol; F(FPath)RCPI. Appointments: House Officer, Royal Infirmary, Edinburgh, 1961-62; Demonstrator, Anatomy and neuroanatomy, Edinburgh, 1962; Senior House Officer, Surgical Neurology, Edinburgh, 1963; Lecturer, pathology, Edinburgh, 1964-65; Senior Registrar, Pathology and Neuropathology, Kings College Hospital, 1966-71; Head, Department of Neuropathology, Glasgow. Honours: Reserve Decoration, 1972, Bar, 1982. Hobbies: Bagpiping; Dinghy Sailing; Aviation. Address: Neuropathology, Institute of Neurological Sciences, Southern General Hospital, Glasgow G51 4TF, Scotland.

DRACUP Angela Pauline, b. 31 Jan 1943, Bradford, West Yorkshire, England. Educational Psychologist. m. Frank Dracup, 2 Jan 1965, 1 daughter. Education: BA Honours, Psychology, University of Sheffield; Diploma, Educational Psychology, University of Manchester. Appointments: Educational Psychologist, Bradford Local Education Authority, 1967-75; Senior Lecturer, Educational Psychology, 1975-78; Educational Psychologist, North Yorkshire County Council, 1978-93; Currently Consultant Psychologist in private practice. Publications: 4 mainstream fiction novels for adults and young adults. Honours: Honorary Tutor, University of Manchester, 1992. Memberships: Associate Fellow, British Psychological Society; Association of Educational Psychologists; Authors' Society. Hobbies: Writing; Walking her dogs; Music; Research. Address: 6 Lancaster Road, Harrogate, North Yorkshire HG2 0EZ.

DRAYTON Keith Douglas, b. 2 May 1923, Christchurch, New Zealand. Obstetrician and Gynaecologist. m. Norma Chalmers Pugh, 3 daughters. Education: MB ChB, Otago, 1949; MRCOG, 1955; FRCOG, 1967; FRNZCOG(F). Appointments: Visiting Obstetrician and Gynaecologist, Christchurch Hospital, 1958-88; Chairman of Staff, Christchurch Womens Hospital, 1979-88; Head, Department of Obstetrics and Gynaecology, Canterbury Area Health Board, 1980-88; Retired. Publication: Cruising Banks peninsula, 2nd edition, 1992. Honour: OBE, 1993. Memberships: Royal College of Obstetricians and Gynaecologists; Royal New Zealand College of Obstetricians and Gynaecologists. Hobbies: Marine Communications; Search and Rescue; Sailing. Address: 5 Webb Street, Christchurch, New Zealand 8001.

DREBORG Sten, b. 4 Apr 1933, Sodertälje, Sweden. Physician. m. Britta Dreborg, 24 Aug 1958, 1 son, 2 daughters. Education: MD; PhD. Appointments: Paediatrics, Falun, Sweden, 1961-65; Paediatrics, University of Uppsala, 1965-69; Head, Department Paediatrics, Boden, 1969-79; Medical Director, Pharmacia Diagnostics, 1979-89; Associate Professor, University Hospital, Paediatric Allergology, Linkoping. Publications: Contributor of over 140 professional articles. Honours: Fellow, AAAI; Distinguished Fellow, ACAI; Honorary Secretary and Treasurer, ESPACI. Memberships: ESPACI; EAACI; ESR; AAAI; ACAI. Hobby; Horse Breeding. Address: Department Paediatrics, Level 14, University Hospital of Linkoping, S-58185 Linkoping, Sweden.

DRESKIN Stephen C, b. 11 Aug 1949, Chicago, Illinois, USA. Physician Scientist. m. June K Innzuka, 5 Aug 1982, 1 s, 2 d. Education: BA, University of Pennsylvania, 1971; PhD, Physiology, Emory University, 1975; MD, Emory University, 1977. Appointments: Medical Staff Fellow, National Institute of Allergy and Infectious Diseases, Bethesda, Maryland, 1981-85; Guest Researcher, National Institute of Arthritis, Musculoskeletal and Skin Diseases, National Institute of Health, Bethesda, Maryland, 1985-88; Assistant Professor of Medicine and Microbiology/Immunology, University of Colorado School of Medicine, Denver, Colorado, 1989-. Publications: include, Research in Macromolecular Chemistry: A New Approach to an Undergraduate Biochemistry Laboratory, 1971; Effects of Acute Growth Hormone Treatment on Rat Skeletal Muscle Ribosomes, 1980; The Metabolism of IgE in Patients with Markedly Elevated Serum IgE Levels, 1987; Only The Smile is Left, 1988; The Receptor with High Affinity for IgE: The Next Steps, 1989. Honours: Arthritis Investigator Award, 1985-88; Burroughs Wellcome Developing Investigator Award, 1990-95. Memberships: American Academy of Allergy & Immunology; Western

Society of Clinical Investigation; American Association for the Advancement of Science. Hobbies: Tennis. Address: Campus Box B164, University of Colorado, Health Sciences Center, 4200 East Ninth Avenue, Denver, CO 80262, USA.

DRESSER Iain, Psychoanalyst. Education: MA; BM; BCh; MPhil. Appointment: Psychoanalyst. Membership: British Psychoanalytical Society. Address: 23 Highbury Villas, Bristol BS2 8BY, England.

DREWES Lester Richard, b. 11 Apr 1943, Deshler, Ohio, USA. Professor. m. Rose, 3 children. Education: BS, Capital University; PhD, University of Minnesota. Appointments: Postdoctoral Fellow, Assistant Scientist, University of Wisconsin, Madison; Professor, Head, Department of Biochemistry and Molecular Biology, University of Minnesota. Publications include: Frontiers in Cerebral Vascular Biology: Transport and Its Regulation, Co-Editor, 1993; Contributor of numerous chapters in books and over 100 articles in journals and papers read at professional meetings. Honours: National Cancer Institute Postdoctoral Fellow, 1971-72; Alexander von Humboldt Fellowship Award, 1982-83; Bacaner Award, Minnesota Medical Foundation, 1990; Frederick C Goetz Award, American Diabetes Association-Minnesota Affiliate, 1993. Memberships: American Society of Biochemistry and Molecular Biology; American Society for Neurochemistry; American Association for the Advancement of Science; Sigma Xi; International Society for Cerebral Blood Flow and Metabolism; International Society for Neurochemistry. Address: University of Minnesota, Department of Biochemistry and Molecular Biology, 10 University Drive, Duluth, MN 55812, USA.

DREYER Nancy A, b. 30 Apr 1950, New York City, USA. m. Kenneth J Rothman, 30 Aug 1980, 3 d. Education: BA, Brandeis University, 1972; MPH, University of North Carolina, 1976; PhD, Epidemiology, University of North Carolina at Chapel Hill, 1978. Appointments: Epidemiologist, Duke University Medical Centre, 1977-79; Director of Epidemiology, Equifax, 1979-80; CEO and President, Epidemiology Resources Inc, 1980-. Publications include: Low-level Ionizing Radiation: Just How Great IS The Cancer Risk?, 1982; Analgesic-associated Nephropathy: Aetiology or Tautology?, 1985; Ethical Forum: Publication Rights-A Case Study, 1992; An Epidemiologic View of Causation: How It Differs From the Legal, 1994; Maintaining Radiation Protection Records, 1992. Honours: Kammer Merit in Authority Award, American Occupational Medical Association, 1984. Memberships: Society for Epidemiologic Research; International Society of Environmental Epidemiology; Health Physics Society; International Epidemiology Association. Hobbies: Skiing; Gardening. Address: ERI, 1 Newton Executive Park, Newton, MA 02162-1450, USA.

DREYFUS Claude E, b. 7 Sept 1929, Geneva, Switzerland. Chiropractor. m. Aviva Hauptman, 1 son, 1 daughter. Education: Doctor of Chiropractic. Appointments: Assistant, Chicago General Health Clinic, Illinois, USA; Assistant, Los Angeles Chiropractic Clinic, California; Assistant to Professor W H Illi, Centre pour l'Etude de la Statique et de la Dynamique du Corps Humain, Geneva, Switzerland; Counsel to Genevan Sick-Insurance Federation; Currently: Own practice; Director of Radiology Service. Publications: About 60, mainly popular educative and informative articles in general and specialised newspapers and magazines; Some professional papers. Honours: Henry Dunant Medal. Memberships: Founding Member, Dean, Association des Chiropraticiens du Canton de Genève; Swiss Chiropractors Association; European Chiropractors Union; Some State Commissions on Public Health and Welfare. Address: Rue du Mont-Blanc 7, CH-1201 Geneva, Switzerland.

DROSSMAN Douglas, b. 20 Mar 1946. Physician; Academics. m. Deborah Ducoff, 3 Jun 1970, 2 s. Education: BA, Cum Laude, Hofstra University, 1966; MD, Albert Einstein College of Medicine, 1970; FACP; FACG. Appointments: Intern & Residency, Internal Medicine, University of North Carolina, 1970-72; Residency in Medicine, New York University, Bellevue Medical Center, 1972-73; Chief, Internal Medicine, USAF Hospital, Bergstrom Airforce Base, Texas, 1973-75; Fellow in Psychosomatic Medicine, University of Rochester, 1975-76; Fellow in Gastroenterology, 1976-78; Faculty, University of North Carolina: Instructor, 1977-78; Assistant Professor, 1978-83; Associate Professor, 1983-90; Professor, 1990-. Publications: Functional Gastrointestinal Disorders: Diagnosis, Pathophysiology, Treatment, 1994; Over 200 Publications including Scientific Articles, Video Tapes and Other Media. Memberships: American College of Physicians; American College of Gastroenterology; American Gastroenterological Association; American Psychosomatic Society; Functional Brain Gut Research Group. Hobbies: Jogging; Tennis; Magic. Address: Division of Digestive Diseases, 420

Burnett Womack CB#7080, University of North Carolina, Chapel Hill, NC 27599-7080, USA.

DRUCKER William R, b. 5 Apr 1922, Chicago, Illinois, USA. Professor of Surgery. m. Barbara, 3 sons, 1 daughter. Education: MD; FACS; BS. Appointments: Professor, Chairman, Department of Surgery, University of Toronto, 1966-72; Dean, School of Medicine, University of Virginia, 1972-77; Professor, Chairman, Department of Surgery, University of Rochester, 1977-87. Publications: Over 120 professional publications. Honours: Phi Beta Kappa; Alpha Omega Alpha; Finley Scholar, 1954-57; Markil Scholar, 1958-63; 2nd Vice President, ACS, 1988-89; Honorary Fellow, Royal College of Surgeons, 1988. Memberships: AAST; ACS; AFCR; AJS; APS; AFIP; AAMC; CJS; CSCR; NAS; NBME; NIH; SEBM; NLM. Hobbies: Diving; Photography; Woodworking. Address: USUHS School of Medicine, Department of Surgery, 4301 Jones Bridge Road, Bethesda, MD 20814, USA.

DRURY Michael, b. 5 Aug 1926, Birmingham, England. Professor. m. Joan Williamson, 7 Oct 1950, 3 s, 1 d. Education: MB ChB, Honours, Birmingham; FRCP; FRCGP; FRACGP. Appointments: Professor of General Practice, University of Birmingham; President, Royal College of General Practitioners; Member, General Medical Council; Emeritus Professor of General Practice, University of Birmingham. Publications: Treatment, A Textbook on Drug Therapy, 1973-94; The Practice Manager, 3rd Edition, 1994; Contributor of various chapters in books. Honours: OBE, 1978; Knight Bachelor, 1988. Memberships: BMA; RSM. Hobbies: Gardening; Talking. Address: Rossall Cottage, Church Hill, Belbroughton, West Midlands DY9 0DT, England.

DRUT Ricardo, b. 19 Oct 1944, La Plata, Argentina. MD, Pathologist. m. Marta Jones Bernal, 20 Dec 1973, 3 sons. Education: MD, University of La Plata School of Medicine, Argentina, 1968. Appointments: Resident, Chief Resident, Staff Member, Department of Pathology, Hospital General San Martin, La Plata, Argentina; Chief, Department of Pathology, Hospital de Ninos, La Plata, Argentina. Publications: Co-author: Mucoepidermoid Carcinoma of the Liver, 1975; Solitary Keratoacanthoma of the nipple in a male, 1976; Oat-cell carcinoma and mixed oat-cell eoidermoid carcinoma of the esophagus, 1978; Co-author: Pleomorphic xanthoastrocytoma, 1983; Ectopic immature renal tissue, 1984; Co-author: Herpes-virus infection diagnosed by cytology of tracheal aspirates, 1985; Anaplastic Wilms' tumor first suggested by fine-needle aspiration cytology and biopsy, 1987; Co-author: Incidence of childhood cancer in La Plata, Argentina, 1977-1987, 1990; Co-author: Congenital pancreatoblastoma in Beckwith-Wiedemann syndrome: an emerging association, 1988. Memberships: Sociedad Argentina de Patologia; Sociedad Latinoamericana de Patologia; Society for Pediatric Pathology; International Pediatric Pathology Association; College of American Pathologists. Honours: Co-awarded, National Academy of Medicine, 1988. Hobbies: Fishing. Address: Department of Pathology, Hospital de Ninos, Calle 13 entre 65 y 66, 1900 La Plata, Argentina.

DU Fuchang, b. 18 Aug 1931, Zhejiang Province, China. Physician. m. Wang Quanzhong, 1 Jan 1959, 2 daughters. Education: Undergraduate, Nanjing Medical University, 1950-55; Graduate, Postgraduate Research Institute, Shanghai Medical University, 1965. Apointments: Resident Doctor, 1955; Physician in Charge, 1960; Chief Doctor of Cardiology, 1978; Lecturer, 1982, Associate Professor, 1987, Professor, 1989-, Nanjing Medical University. Publications: The Longterm Prognosis Following Myocardial Infarction, 1965; A Five-Year Prospective Study on Risk Factors in the Development of CHD, 1987; A Population-Based Study on Incidence of ICM, 1992. Honours: Advanced Medical Worker of Jiangsu Province, 1978; Advanced Scientific and Technological Worker of Higher Education System, 1992; Certificate of Outstanding Contribution to Public Health and Undertaking, Chinese State Council, 1992. Membership: Chinese Hypertension League. Hobby: Cultivating flowers. Address: The Cardiovascular Institute, Nanjing Medical University, No 300 Guanzhong Road, Nanjing, China.

DU Ruofu, b. 3 Aug 1930,Shangyu County, Zhejiang, China. Professor of Human Genetics. m. Chen Zhenghua, 3 July 1954, 2 d. Education: Graduate, Beijing Agriculture University, 1950; PhD, Leningrad Agriculture College, 1958. Appointments: Research Assistant, Associate Professor, Professor, Institute of Genetics, Chinese Academy of Sciences, Beijing, 1958-. Publications: Radiation Genetics and Breeding, 1981; Karyotype and Chromosome Evolution of Deer, 1988; Ethnic Groups in China, 1993; Contributor of 120 articles. Honours:

Certification of Merit of Great Scientific Achievements, CHinese Academy of Sciences, 1979. Memberships: Permanent Committee, Chairman of Committee of Human Genetics, Genetics Society of China; Permanent Committee, Chinese Society of Medical Genetics. Hobbies: Stamp and Coin Collecting. Address: Institute of Genetics, Bldg 917 Datun Road, Beijing 100101, China.

DU Xinping, b. 5 Apr 1951, Hungwu County, Hupeh, China. Physician in Charge. m. Ban Ya Fang, 28 Apr 1981, 1 d. Education: Diploma, Mdicine. Career: Apprentice, 1969, Intern, 1974, Physician, 1982, Physician in Charge, 1992-, Chinese Traditional Medicine Department, The 6th Hospital of Wuhan, China. Publications: Books include: Collections for Clinical Experience on Spleen-Gastric; Try to Talk About Falling into a Coma; Articles: Essay on typhoid, Chou Y practice divination's relation, 1991; Liver pain and cure. Honours: Advanced Worker, 1977, 1985, 1991, 1992, 1993. Membership: Chinese Traditional Medicine Association of China. Hobby: Chess. Address: The 6th Hospital, Wuhan 430015, China.

DU Yuan, b. 25 February 1932, Chengdu, Sichuan, China. Docotr; Professor of Medicine. m. Sun Bi-ru, 1 August 1956, 1 son, 1 daughter. Education: Graduate, Sichuan Medical College, 1952-54; Advanced Studies, First Shanghai Medical College, 1957-58. Appointments: Resident Physician, Kunming 298 Hospital, Yunnan, 1954-56; House Resident Surgeon, Shanghai Hospital of Public Security, 1956-58; House Resident Surgeon, Hong Kou District Central Hospital of Shanghai, 1958-73; House Resident Surgeon, No 3 People's Hospital of Chengdu, 1973-75; Visiting Surgeon, No 3 People's Hospital of chengdu, 1975-78; Vice Chief Surgeon, Deputy Director of Surgical Department, No 3 People's Hospital of Chengdu, 1978-81; Chief Surgeon, Director, Surgical Department and Cardiothoracic Department, No 3 People's Hospital of Chengdu, 1981-88; Chief Surgeon, President, No 2 People's Hospital of Chengdu, 1988-. Publications Include: Diagnosis and treatment of Atrial septal defect, 1983; Resuscitation of Heart, Lung and Brain, 1991; Surgical treatment of mitral valve of rheumatic valvular heart disease, 1991; Laparoscopic cholecystectomy - 270 cases, 1993; Smoking hazard and the tobacco economic problem, 1994. Honours Include: Honourable title of Advanced Medical Worker in the Hospitals, 26 times, every year from 1958 to 1965 and from 1975 to 1993. Memberships Include: Standing Committee, Chinese Association of Emergency Medicine; Standing Committee, Sichuan Association of Cardiothoracic Surgery; Committee, Appraising Medical Thesis Submitted for Master and Doctors Degrees of West China University of Medical Sciences. Hobbies: Reading; Table Tennis; Tennis. Address: No 2 Peoples Hospital of Chengdu, 10 South Qing Yun Street, Chengdu, Sichuan, China.

DU PLESSIS Daniel Paul, b. 19 Oct 1937, De Aar, Republic of South Africa. Medical Technologist. m. Ena Du Plessis, 1 Sept 1976, 1 son, 1 daughter. Education: National Diploma in Histopathological Techniques. Appointments: Control Technologist, 1980, Assistant Director, 1988, Anatomical Pathology Department, Medunsa; Currently Deputy Director, Pathology Laboratories, Ga-Rankuwa Hospital. Publications: Lichen Planus Dermopathy: Demonstration of Lichen Planus Specific Epidermal Antigen in Affected Patients, 1983; Indirect Immunofluorescence Microscopy of Lichen Planus, 1984; Serum from Lichen Planus Patients Reacts with Fetal Skin Tissues, 1984; Serological and Virological evidence of human T-lymphotrophic virus in systematic Lupus Erythematosis, 1987. Honours: Ames National Award for Histopathology, 1986, 1988; South African Scientific Award, 1993. Memberships: International Association of Tumour Marker Oncologists; Society of Medical Laboratory Technology of South Africa. Hobbies: Photography; Travel; Rotary. Address: Department of Anatomical Pathology, PO Box 213, Medunsa 0204, Republic of South Africa.

DU PLESSIS Peter Francois, b. 3 Sept 1957, Welkom, South Africa. Chartered Clinical Psychologist. Education: BA; BA (Hons), Psychology; MSc, Medical Psychology; Statement of Equivalence, British Psychological Society. Appointments: Clinical Psychologist, Lecturer, Addington Hospital and University of Natal, Durban; Senior Clinical Psychologist, Principal Clinical Psychologist, Guy's Hospital, London, England; Currently Principal Clinical Psychologist, Head of Speciality. Publications: HIV Education and Young People, 1993. Honours: Associate Fellow, British Psychological Society, 1992. Memberships: British Psychological Society, Chair, Division of Clinical Psychology Special Group (HIV/AIDS), Member, Division of Counselling Psychology. Address: 5 Belsize Court, Wedderburn Road, Hampstead, London NW3 5QL, England.

DUA Jagdish, b. 5 Feb 1942, India. Psychologist. m. Sushma Dua, 1970, 2 sons, 1 daughter. Education: BSc, Physics, Honours; MA, Psychology; MSc. Psychology; PhD, psychology. Appointments: Lecturer in Psychology, University of Delhi, 1963; Casual Tutor in Psychology, University of Sydney, Australia, 1964-67; Lecturer in psychology. 1968, Senior Lecturer in Psychology, University of New England, Armidale, New South Wales. Publications: Contributor of 7 chapters in books, monographs and over 40 articles in professional journals. Honours: Research Studentship, Sydney University, 1964-67; Fellow, International College of Psychosomatic Medicine; Invited Presenter of Symposia and Workshops at International Conferences and Workshops. Memberships: Australian Psychological Society; Australian Behaviour Modification Association. Hobbies: Classical Music; Travel. Address: Department of Psychology, University of New England, Armidale, New South Wales 2351, Australia.

DUAN Guo-sheng, b. 4 Mar 1919, Liaonng, China. Neurosurgeon. m. Zhan Feng-chin, 15 Sept 1944, 3 sons, 1 daughter. Education: MB. Appointments: Resident, Chief Resident, Liaoning Medical College Affiliated Hospital, 1943; Attending Surgeon, Neurosurgeon, Chief Neurosurgeon, General Hospital of PLA, Shenyang Unit, 1949; Chief, Professor of Neurosurgery, General Hospital of PLA, Beijing. Publications: Chief Editor, Practical Neurosurgery, 1976; Chief Editor, Operative Surgery: Neurosurgical Volume, 1994; Co-author, War Surgery, 1954, 1979; Chinese Medical Encyclopaedia Neurosurgery, 1984; Neurosurgery, 1990. Honours: Awards of National Scientific Meeting, 1978; Awards of Scientific Progress; Awards of Military Scientific Progress. Memberships: Chinese Neurosurgical Association; Academia Eurasiana Neurochirgica; World Federation of Neurosurgical Societies. Hobbies: Basketball; Reading. Address: 28 Fuxing Road, Department of Neurosurgery, General Hospital of PLA, Beijing 100853, China.

DUAN Lianrong, b. 22 July 1923, Qu County, Sichuan Province, China. Stomatologist. m. Feng Chongyin, 2 July 1949, 3 sons, 3 daughters. Education: DDS, West China Union University, 1950. Appointments include: Currently Chief Doctor of Stomatology, Bijie Prefecture Hospital, Guizhou. Publications: The Clinical Efficiency of Terraced Occlusion in Complete Denture Prosthesis, 1986; A few suggestions consulting with the authors of Full Denture Prosthodontology, 1987; The New Practical Complete Denture Prosthodontics, 1988. Memberships: Academic Committee, Chongqing City Stomatology Association; Standing Committee, Guizhou Province Stomatology Association. Address: Bijie Prefecture Hospital, Guizhou, China.

DUAN Yi-shan, b. 16 July 1940, Shanghai, China. Teacher. m. Li-ying Chen, 20 Oct 1967, 1 son, 1 daughter. Education: BA, Fudan University. Appointments: Deputy Director, Humanitic and Social Science Department; Chief Editor, Journal of Knowledge of Ancient Medical Literature; Professor of Ancient Medical Literature, Shanghai University of Traditional Chinese Medicine. Publications: Ancient Medical Literature, Co-author, 1984; Rhetiroc in Ancient Medical Chinese, 1987; Ancient Medical Literature, series, 1988; Ways of Distinguishing the Meaning of Words in Ancient Medicine Literature, 1990, 1993; A Dictionary of Famous Remarks in Traditional Chinese Medicine, 1992; Practical Ancient Medical Literature, 1993; Contributor of numerous articles. Honours: Professional Experts of Shanghai University of Traditional Chinese Medicine. Memberships: China Association of Traditional Chinese Medicine; Pharmacy Research Society of Chinese Ancient Medical Literature; Copy Editor, Committee of Planned Traditional Chinese Medicine and Pharmacy Textbooks of General Higher Education; Editor, Committee of China Association of Traditional Chinese Medicine and Pharmacy. Hobbies: Chinese Chess; Billiards; Watching sport. Address: Teaching and Research Division of Ancient Medical Literature, Shanghai University of Traditional Chinese Medicine and Pharmacy, Shanghai, China.

DUBOIS Arthur Brooks, b. 21 Nov 1923, New York City, USA. Physiologist. m. Roberdeau Callery, 21 June 1950, 2 sons, 1 daughter. Education: MD, Cornell Medical School, 1946. Appointments: Assistant Professor of Physiology, 1952, Professor of Physiology and Medicine, University of Pennsylvania; Professor of Epidemiology and Physiology, Yale Medical School, 1974-; Director, John B Pierce Laboratory, 1974-88. Publications: The Lung, Co-author, 1955; Contributor of research articles in scientific journals. Memberships: Association of American Physicians; American Physiological Society. Address: 290 Congress Avenue, New Haven, CT 06519, USA.

DUBOWSKI Kurt M, b. 21 Nov 1921, Berlin, Germany. Toxicologist. Education: AB; MSc; PhD; LLD. Appointments include: George Lynn Cross Distinguished Professor of Medicine, The University of Oklahoma College of Medicine, Oklahoma City, USA; member of Clinical Staff, The University Hospitals, 1961-; Consultant in Clinical Chemistry and Toxicology, Department of Veterans Affairs Medical Centre, Oklahoma City, 1962-; Consultant in Laboratory Medicine, Oklahoma Medical Research Foundation, Oklahoma City, 1967-; State Director of Tests for Alcohol and Drug Influence, State of Oklahoma, 1970-; Criminalist, Oklahoma Department of Public Safety and Oklahoma Highway Patrol; Visiting Professor, Indiana University, 1958-. Honours include: Certificate of Appreciation, Executive Office of the President of the United States, 1975; Outstanding Clinical Chemist Award, Texas Section, American Association for Clinical Chemistry, 1981; Distinguished Service Award, American Board of Forensic Toxicology, 1986; Elected Distinguished Fellow, American Academy of Forensic Sciences, 1991; Presidential Citation, American Association for Clinical Chemistry, 1992; Robert F Borkenstein Award, National Safety Council, 1992. Memberships include: Academy of Clinical Laboratory Physicians and Scientists; Fellow, American Academy of Clinical Toxicology; American Association of University Professors; Life Fellow, American Institute of Chemists; American Medical Association; Charter Member, American Society of Crime Laboratory Directors. Address: Department of Medicine, The University of Oklahoma, Health Sciences Centre, Research Building, 38-R, PO Box 26901, Oklahoma City, OK 73190-3000, USA.

DUCOIN Francis John, b. 23 Jan 1950, Camden, New Jersey, USA. Dental Implantology. m. Mary Jane, 3 Apr 1993, 3 sons, 3 daughters. Education: BS, Drexel University, 1972; MS, Drexel University, 1973; DMD, University of Pennsylvania, 1982. Appointments: Private Practice, Stuart, Florida; Co-Director, Implant Section, ACRC. Publications: Associate Editor, Journal of Implant Dentistry. Honours: OKU National Dental Honor Society, 1982; Diplomate, ICOI, 1989; Fellow, AGD, 1990. Memberships: ADA; AGD; ICOI; ACOI; AO; AAID; ABOI; AI&T; AAIP. Hobbies: Golf. Address: 800 East Ocean Blvd, Stuart, FL 34994, USA.

DUDANI Niranjan, b. 31 Dec 1926, Larkana, Sindh. Medicine. m. Krishna, 4 May 1955, 2 sons. Education: Flight Surgeon Diploma, US Navy Institute of Aviation Medicine, 1962; Diploma, Public Health, Bombay University, 1968; MD, Massachusetts, 1974; Diplomate, American Board of Allergy & Immunology, 1984. Appointments: Specialist in Allergy/Immunology, Allergy Medical Associates Inc, 1975-; Private Practice, General Medicine, Marblehead, 1984-; Medical Docotr, Middlesex Regional Alcohol Treatment Center, Waltham, 1985-; Senior Aviation Medical Examiner, FAA, 1968-; Town Physician, Marblehead, 1984-; Reviewing Physician, PSRO of Massachusetts Medical Society, 1987-90; Member, Geriatric Committee, American College of Allergists, 1983-; Hospital Appointment with Atlantic Care Hospitals, Lynn Memorial & Union Hospitals, 1985-. Publications incl: Experiences in Medical Coverage of Airport Disasters at Logan International Airport in Boston, 1983; Ancestral Agony - Book of Poems in English, 1976; Phengoon, Collection of Poems, Short Stories and Essays; Sindh Jee Zeenat, novel, 1992. Memberships: Fellow, American College of Allergists; Fellow, Massachusetts Medical Society; Fellow, American Association of Certified Allergists; Fellow, American Association of Allergists & Immunologists; American Academy of Allergy & Immunology; Society of US Navy Flight Surgeons; Patron Member, American Association of Physicians of India. Address: 214 Ocean Street, Lynn, MA 01902, USA.

DUDAR Thomas E, b. 12 Nov 1956, Brooklyn, NY, USA. Product Development. m. Mary Susan Kelly, 23 Jul 1983, 1 d. Education: BS, Bioengineering, Columbia University, 1978; MS, Chemical Engineering/Biomedical Engineering, Carnegie-Mellon University, 1980; PhD, Chemical Engineering-Biomedical Engineering, Carnegie-Mellon University, 1982. Appointments: Engineering Assistant, Brooklyn Union Gas Company, 1977; Research Assistant, Columbia University, 1978; Teaching Assistant and Calculus Teacher, Carnegie-Mellon University, 1978-80; Baxter Healthcare Corporations, 1983-, Positions include: Principal Engineer, Artificial Organs Division, 1983-84; Senior Principal Engineer, Parenterals Division, 1985-87; Section Manager, Parenterals Division, 1988-90; Manager, Technical Development, I V Therapy Division, 1991-92; Director, Product Development, I V Systems Division, 1992-93; Director, Research & Development, IV Systems Division, 1994-. Publications: Differential Response of Normal and Tumor Microcirculation to Hyperthermia, 1984; Mathematical Models for Microcirculatory Flow Modifications in Normal and Neoplastic Tissues During Hyperthermia, 1983; Microcirculatory Flow Changes During

Tissue Growth, 1983. Honours: include, Baxter Dave Winchell Patent Award; Baxter Corporate Distinguished Technical Awards; Baxter Corporate Outstanding Technical Award; Parenterals Division Technical Award; NASA Certificates of Recognition; National Institutes of Health Traineeship. Memberships: include, Biomedical Engineering Society; American Institute of Chemical Engineers; Sigma Xi; Phi Lambda Upsilon. Address: Baxter Healthcare Corporation, Route 120 & Wilson Road, Round Lake, IL 60073, USA.

DUDLEY Hugh Arnold Freeman, b. 1 July 1925, Dublin, Ireland. Retired Professor of Surgery. m. Jean B L Johnston, 17 July 1947, 2 sons, 1 daughter. Education: MBChB, Edinburgh, 1947; FRCSE, 1951; ChM, Edinburgh, 1958; FRACS, 1965; FRCS, 1973; Hon F SA College Surgeons; Hon F American Surgical Association. Appointments: Lecturer in Surgery, Edinburgh, 1954-58; Senior Lecturer in Surgery, Aberdeen, 1958-63; Foundation Professor of Surgery, Monash University, Melbourne, Australia, 1963-73; Professor of Surgery, St Marys Hospital Medical School, London University, England, 1973-88; Retired. Publications: Operative Surgery, Editor, 3rd and 4th editions; Emergency Surgery, Editor, 10th and 11th editions; An Aid to Clinical Surgery, Editor, 2nd and 3rd editions; Contributor of numerous articles in professional journals. Honour: CBE, 1988. Memberships: Surgical Research Society of Great Britain and Ireland, President, 1981; Surgical Research Society of Australasia, President, 1968; Biological Engineering Society of Great Britain, President, 1981-82. Hobbies: Writing; Shooting. Address: Broombrae, Glenbuchat, Strathdon, Aberdeenshire AB36 8UA, Scotland.

DUDRICK Stanley John, b. 9 Apr 1935, Nanticoke, Pennsylvania, USA. General Surgeon. m. Theresa Monica Keen, 14 June 1958, 2 sons, 4 daughters. Education: BS, Franklin and Marshall College, 1957; MD, 1961, Residency in Surgery, Fellowship in Surgical Research, 1967, University of Pennsylvania; Diplomate, American Board of Surgery, 1968; FACS; FACN; FAAP (Hon); FPCS (Hon, Philippines). Appointments: Professor of Surgery, University of Pennsylvania, Chief of Surgery, Philadelphia Veterans Administration Hospital, 1967-72; Professor, Chairman, Department of Surgery, 1972-80, currently Professor of Surgery, University of Texas Medical School, Houston; Chief of Surgery, 1972-80, Surgeon-in-Chief, 1990-, Hermann Hospital, Houston; Director of Nutritional Support, St Luke's Hospital, Hermann, 1981-88; Professor, Chairman, Department of Surgery, Pennsylvania Hospital, Philadelphia, 1988-90. Publications: Editor or co-editor: Manual of Surgical Nutrition, 1965; The Management of Difficult Surgical Problems, 1981; Manual of Pre-Operative and Post-Operative Care, 1983; Practical Handbook of Nutrition in Clinical Practice, 1994. Honours: Phi Beta Kappa, 1957; Sigma Xi, 1970; Alpha Omega Alpha, 1975; Brookdale Award in Medicine, American Medical Association, 1975; Grace Goldsmith Award, American College of Nutrition, 1982; Ladd Medal, American Academy of Pediatrics, 1988; Many others. Memberships: American College of Surgeons; American Surgical Association; Society of University Surgeons; American Board of Surgery; American Medical Association; 60 others. Hobbies: Sailing; Skiing; Tennis; Writing; Reading. Address: 3050 Locke Lane, Houston, TX 77019, USA.

DUGAN Charles Clark, b. 24 Jan 1921, USA. Medicine & Surgery. m. Eugenie Pounds, & Ruth L Fugh, both deceased, 5 sons. Education: AA, Wentworth Junior College, 1940; AB, Cornell University, 1942; MD, Jefferson Medical College, 1946. Appointments include: Good Samaritan Hospital, West Palm Beach; Palm Beach Gardens Community Hospital; Consultant, Bethesda Memorial Hospital, Banyan Psychiatric Institute. Publications incl: Some Modifications in the Preparation of the Leucite Calvarium for Large Monkeys; Effect of the Anti-Stress Formula on B-47 Aircrews Under Non-operational Flying; Genes and Their Disease Association; Dermbrasion and Facial Toning; Hair Transplant Surgery. Honours include: Key of Success Award, American Biographical Institute; Professional Award Citation 35 years, Federal Aviation Agency, 1991; Surgeon of the Year, FSDS, 1991-92; Practitioner of the Year, 1993-94, Florida Society of Dermatology. Memberships include: American Medical Association; Florida Medical Association; Florida Society of Dermatology; Iberiam Congress of Dermatology; American Academy of Facial Plastic & Reconstructive Surgery; International Society of Dermatopathology. Hobbies: Computers; Philately; Swimming; Scuba Diving; Tennis; Flying; Boating; Golf; Building. Address: 8696 Thousand Pines Circle, West Palm Beach, FL 33411, USA.

DUHL Leonard J, b. 24 May 1926, New York City, New York, USA. Physician; Psychiatrist. m. Lisa Shippee, 8 June 1980, 1 son, 4 daughters. Education: AB, Columbia University, 1945; MD, Albany Medical College, 1948; Fellow, Menninger School of Psychiatry, 1954; Graduate, Washington Psychoanalytic Institute, 1964. Appointments include: Chief of Planning, National Institute of Mental Health, Bethesda, Maryland, 1964-66; Assistant Secretary, Department of Housing and Urban Development, Washington DC, 1966-68; Professor, Public Health, City Planning, 1968-91, Professor, Public Health, 1991-, University of California, Berkeley; Clinical Professor, Psychiatry, University of California, San Francisco, 1968-. Publications: Approaches to Research in Mental Retardation, 1959; The Urban Condition: People and Policy in the Metropolis, 1963; Health Planning and Social Change, 1986; The Social Entrepreneurship of Change, 1990; Environmental Health in Urban Development, Co-author, 1991; Health and the City: The Governance of Diversity, 1991; Co-author: Mental Health and Urban Social Policy, 1964; The City and the University, 1969; Technology and Learning Disabilities, 1983; The 1982 California Health Care Reform, A Case Study in Policy Analysis, 1983; The Mental Health Complex: It's a New Ball Game, 1986; New Boundaries to Health, videotape series, 1978; Book chapters, articles, papers. Memberships: American College of Psychiatry; former Fellow, American Orthopsychiatric Association; Life Fellow, American Psychiatric Association; American Public Health Association, former Fellow; Group for the Advancement of Psychiatry, Past Chairman, Committee on Preventive Psychiatry; International Association for Child Psychiatry and Allied Professions, Assistant Secretary General 1962-63; National Conference for International Health; Northern California Psychiatric Society; Society for Health and Human Values. Address: 410 Warren, School of Public Health, University of California, Berkeley, CA 94720, USA.

DUMLER John D, b. 16 Apr 1926, Baltimore, USA. Gynaecologist. m. Patricia Jones, 25 Jun 1949, 4 s, 2 d. Education: BS; MD. Appointments: Private Practice, 1957-70; Associate Chief, Obstetrics & Gynaecology Department, St Agnes Hospital, Baltimore, 1971-72; Gynaecology Clinician, Maryland State Health Department, 1973-81; Program Director, Obstetrics & Gynaecology, 1982-88; Gynaecology Clinician, 1989-95. Publications: Carcinoma in Situ of the Uterine Cervix, 1957. Memberships: American College of Obstetrics & Gynaecology; American College of Surgeons. Hobbies: Books. Address: 117 East of the Sun, Fenwick Island, DE 19944, USA.

DUNAYEVSKY Oleg Arssenievich, b. 18 Feb 1928, Belgi, Russia. Physician; Professor. m. Ludmila Ossadohaya, 22 Oct 1954, 2 daughters. Education: Graduate, Leningrad Medical Institute, 1955; Clinical Studies, Department of Infectious Diseasesof the Institute, 1955-57; Candidate of Medicine, 1964; MD, 1973. Appointments: Physician, Leningrad Hospital of Infectious Diseases, 1957-62; Assistant, Department of Infectious Diseases, Leningrad Institute of Advanced Studies for Doctors, 1962-68; Head, Department of Infectious Diseases and Epidemiology, 1968-, Rector, 1974-87, Professor of Medicine, Tver Medical Academy. Publications: Diagnosis Based on the Formula in Patients with Acute Epidemic Hepatitis and Obstructive Jaundice Originating from Newgrowths, Co-author, 1966; Differential Diagnostics of Jaundice, 1977; Pecularities in the Course of Infectious Diseases in Elderly and Old Persons, Co-author, 1982; Differential Diagnostics of Liver Diseases, 1985; Alcohol as a Pathological Factor in Patients with Acute and Chronic Hepatitis and Cirrhosis of the Liver, Co-author, 1987; Mathematics Simulation of Treatment of Jaundice in Patient in Infectious Department, Co-author, 1989; Viral Hepatitis and Differential Diagnostics of Liver Diseases, 1993. Honour: Honoured Scientist of Russian Federation, 1992. Memberships include: Chairman, Oblast region Association of Physicians Infectious Diseases; Scientific Body, Tver Medical Academy; Editorial Body, Russian Medical Journal; Chairman, Tver Department of Russian Children Fund; International Academy of Informatization; Corresponding Member, Russian Academy of Medicine. Address: Ploschad Slavy, dom 1, KV 178, 170000 Tver, Russia.

DUNCAN Bruce Bartholow, b. 22 Apr 1949, Nashville, TN, USA. Physician. m. Maria Ines Schmidt, 9 Jun 1979, 1 s, 1 d. Education: BA, Williams College, 1971; MD, MPH, Johns Hopkins University, 1979; PhD, University Fed Rio Grande Do Sul, 1991. Appointments: Resident, North Carolina Memorial Hospital, 1979-82; Research Assistant Professor, department Epidemiology, UNC, 1982-83; Associate Professor, Department Social Med, University Federal do Rio Grande do Sul, Brazil 1984-; Visiting Associate Professor, Department Epidemiology, UNC, 1992-93. Publications: Medicina

Ambulatorial-Condutas Clinicas Em Atencao Primaria, Editor, 1990. Memberships: American College of Physicians; Society for Epidemiological Research; International Epidemiology Association; Hobbies: Camping; Hiking. Address: Rua Ramiro Barvellos 2600/414, Porto Alegre, RS 90035-003, Brazil.

DUNGY Claibourne Ira, b. 29 Oct 1938, Chicago, Illinois, USA. Pediatrician. m. Madgetta Thornton, 2 daughters. Education: BS, Eastern Illinois University, 1962; MD, University Illinois, Chicago, 1967; MPN, Johns Hopkins University, 1971. Appointments incl: Chief, Division of General Pediatrics, Department of Pediatrics, University of California, Irvine, 1985-88; Associate Professor, Department of Pediatrics, University of Iowa College of Medicine, 1988-; Director, Division of General Pediatrics, University of Iowa Hospitals & Clinics, 1988-; Professor, Department of Pediatrics, University of Iowa College of Medicine, 1993-. Publications incl: The effect of discharge samples on duration of breastfeeding, 1992; Do physicians treat their own children?, 1993; Behavioral problems among twins, 1993; Nitrate in baby food: Adding to the nitrate mosaic. Honours: Beta Beta Beta, 1961; Outstanding Young Men of the Year, National Jaycees, 1973; Orange County Partners for Progress Achievement Award, Medicine, 1977; Distinguished Alumnus Award, Eastern Illinois University, 1979; Alpha Kappa Alpha, 1985; Distinguished Service Award, UCI-CCM Black Medical Students, 1987. Memberships incl: American Public Health Association; Ambulatory Pediatric Association; American Academy of Pediatrics; International Society for System Science in Health Care. Address: University of Iowa, 200 Hawkins Drive, IA 52242-1083, USA.

DUNN Peter Macnaughton, b. 23 June 1929, Birmingham, England. Physician. m. Judy Lunt, 22 July 1961, 2 sons, 1 daughter. Education: MA, MB, BChir, MD, Cambridge University; FRCP; FRCOG; DCH, London. Appointments: Senior Research Fellow, Cardiovascular Research Unit, University of California, San Francisco, USA, 1966-67; Emeritus Professor of Perinatal Medicine and Child Health, University of Bristol, England. Publications: Author of over 350 books and articles on perinatal matters. Honours: President, BAPM, 1981-84; FRCOG ad Iundem, 1983; Gold Medal, British Orthopaedic Association, 1983; DESNOO[van't Hoogerbuijs Stickling Prize and Medal, The Netherlands, 1983. Memberships: BPA; RCP; RCOG; BAPM; Neonatal Society. Hobbies: Golf; Fly Fishing; Walking; Chess. Address: Tramore, 173 Henbury Road, Henbury, Bristol BS10 7AD, England.

DUNN (Rudolf) Walter, b. 21 Nov 1915, Leipzig, Germany. Physician. m. Joyce Williams, 24 Sep 1949, 2 sons, 2 daughters. Education: MB BChir, Cambridge University, England; FRCOG(England); FRCS(Canada); LRCP; MRCS(London). Appointment: Retired. Memberships: Canadian Medical Association; British Columbia Medical Association. Hobbies: Music; Stamps; Travel. Address: 125 Pacific Carlton, 15366 17th Avenue, South Surrey, British Columbia V4A 1T9, Canada.

DUNPHY Bruce Cox, b. 13 May 1957, Paisley, Scotland. Physician. m. Linda McCallum, 1 Feb 1985, 2 sons, 1 daughter. Education: MB, ChB, 1980; MD (Aberdeen), 1989; MRCOG; FRACOG. Appointments: Lecturer, University of Sheffield, England; Currently Associate Professor, Chief of Gynaecology, Foothills Hospital, Calgary, Alberta, Canada. Publications: Book chapters: Clinical aspects of ovulation (co-author), 1990; The management of acute pelvic pain (with M D G Gillmer), 1994; Over 3 dozen contributions to journals including Human Reproduction, Andrologia, Fertility and Sterility, Journal of Obstetrics and Gynaecology, Journal of Society of Obstetricians and Gynecologists of Canada. Memberships: Society of Reproductive Surgeons; International Society of Gynaecological Endoscopy; American Fertility Society. Hobbies: Cycling; Golf; Reading; Walking. Address: Department of Obstetrics and Gynaecology, Foothills Hospital, Calgary, Alberta, Canada T2N 2T9.

DUNSTAN Gordan Reginald, b. 25 Apr 1917, Plymouth, Devon, England. Clerk in Holy Orders; University Teacher. m. Ruby Maud Fitzer, 23 Aug 1949, 2 sons, 1 daughter. Education: CBE; MA; DD; LLD; FSA. Appointments: Professor of Moral & Social Theology, Kings College, University of London, 1967-82; Hon Research Fellow, University of Exeter, 1982-. Publications: The Artifice of Ethics, 1974; Doctors' Decisions, 1989. Memberships: Hon Fellow, Royal Society of Medicine; Hon Fellow, Royal College of Physicians; Fellow ad eundem, Royal College of Obstetricians & Gynaecologists; Hon Fellow, Royal College of General Practioners. Address: 9 Maryfield Avenue, Exeter EX4 6JN, Devon, England.

DURAK Hatice Sagun, b. 6 Feb 1959, Istanbul. Professor of Nuclear Medicine. m. Ismet Durak, 7 Sept 1983, 1 son. Education: MD, Hacettepe University, Ankara, Turkey. Appointments: Resident, Specialist, Department of Nuclear Medicine, Hacettepe University, 1985-89; Research Fellow, Johns Hopkins Medical Institute, Division of Nuclear Medicine, USA, 1991; Assistant Professor of Nuclear Medicine, Dokuz Eylul University, 1992; Director, Department of Nuclear Medicine, Dokuz Eylul University. Publications: 99m Tc-aD-Glucose 1-Phosphate imaging in lung cancer, 1988; Functional asplenia and portal hypertension in patient with primary splenic angiosarcoma, 1990; Evaluation of 99m Tc labelled vitamin K4 for testicular imaging, 1991; Giant rhabdomyosarcoma with necrosis visualized with Thallium-201 chloride, 1991; Thallium-201 uptake in brown tumors of hyperparathyroidism, 1991; Quantitative maxillary sinus scintigraphy with 99m Tc DTPA following Caldwell Luc surgery, 1991; A case of parathyroid adenoma with brown tumors diagnosed by 201 Thallium 99m Technetium subtraction scintigraphy, 1991; Diuretic renography in children: A noninvasive method for the assessment of upper urinary tract pathologies, 1991. Memberships: Turkish Society of Nuclear Medicine; European Association of Nuclear Medicine; American Society of Nuclear Medicine. Hobbies: Astronomy; Travel; Cooking. Address: Mithatpasa Caddesi No 259/8, Balcova 35340, Izmir, Turkey.

DURDEN Lance Anthony, b. 26 Sep 1955, Sale, Cheshire, England. Medical Entomologist. m. Susan Sutter, 29 Aug 1981. Education: BSc, Zoology, 1977, PhD, Zoology, 1981, University of London. Career: ResearchAssociate, Vanderbilt University Medical School, Nashville, TN, 1982-87; Research Associate, Smithsonian Institution, Washington DC, 1987-; Senior Fellow, US Army Medical Res Institute of Infectious Diseases, Fort Detrick, Frederick, MD, 1990-92. Publications include: Co-author, Ectoparasites of commensal rodents in Sulawesi: Utara with notes on species of medical importance, in Medical and Veterinary Entomology, 1991; Co-author, Experimental transmission of Langat virus by the soft tick Ornithodoros sonrai, in Journal of Medical Entomology, 1994; Co-editor, A Textbook of Medical and Veterinary Entomology, Entomological Society of America, 1995. Honour: Editorial Board, Medical and Veterinary Entomology, 1991-. Memberships: American Society of Tropical Medicine and Hygiene; American Society of Parasitologists; American Committee on Medical Entomology; American Committee on Arthropod-borne Viruses; Royal Entomological Society of London; Society for Vector Ecology. Hobbies: Running; Soccer; Writing. Address: Institute of Arthropodology and Parasitology, Georgia Southern University, LB 8056, Statesboro, GA 30460, USA.

DURFEE Michael John, b. 4 May 1942, Worcester, Massachusetts, USA. Director, Child Abuse Prevention Program, LA County Department of Health Services. m. Deanne Tilton, 2 sons, 1 daughter. Education: MD. Appointments: Child Psychiatrist, Medical Director, MacLaren Hall, Placement for Foster Children, 1975-79; Director of Child Abuse Prevention Programm, Los Angeles County Department of Mental Health, 1980-81; Director, Child Abuse Prevention Program, Los Angeles County Department of Health Services, 1981-; Co-Principal Investigator, National Training Grant for Child Death Review Teams, 1995-. Publications: Clinical Intervention With Young Molested Children; Origins and Clinical Relevance of Child Death Review Teams. Honours: President's Commission on Child & Youth Deaths, 1989; Spectrum Institute Award for the Prevention of Abuse of the Developmentally Disabled, 1991; National Maternal & Child Health Advisory Task Force on Fatal Child Abuse, 1992; California Department of Corrections Award for Prevention of Prenatal Substance Abuse, 1992; California Consortium for the Prevention of Child Abuse Lifetime Achievement Award, 1993; Assistant Clinical Professor of Psychiatry & Pediatrics at the University of Southern California School of Medicine, 1980. Memberships: Child Abuse Section, American Academy of Pediatrics; Local, State & National Commissions on Child Abuse & Neglect. Hobbies: Swimming; Jogging. Address: 241 North Figueroa Street, Room 306, Los Angeles, CA 90012, USA.

DURNOV Lev, b. 21 Dec 1931, Moscow, Russia. Paediatric Oncologist. m. Valentina Darnova, 2 daughters. Education: MD, Second Medical Moscow School, 1956; PhD. Appointments: Paediatric Surgeon, 1959-62; Head, department of Paediatric Oncology, 1962-; Director Institute of Paediatric Oncology of Cancer Research Centre, Russian Academy of Medical Sciences. Publications: Author of 22 books on paediatric oncology and contributor of over 300 professional articles. Honour: SIOP Member, 1990-. Membership: SIOP. HobbiesL Hunting; Art; Dogs. Address: Kashirskoye Str 24, 115478 Moscow, Russia.

DURVE Mohan, b. 9 July 1948, Bombay, India. Physician. m. Jayshree, 3 daughters. Education: MBBS, Gordhandas Sundardas Medical School, Univeersity of Bombay, 1966-71. Appointments include: Family Practice, Pune, India, 1973-74; Paediatric Residency, CHildrens Hospital Medical Centre, Boston, Massachusetts, USA, 1974-75; Paediatric Fellowship, Cleveland Clinic Foundation, Cleveland, Ohio, 1975-77; Assistant Clinical Professor. Department of Paediatrics, Case Western Reserve University School of Medicine, Cleveland, Ohio. Publications: Skin test for Gluten-sensitive Enteropathy Using Subfractions of Gluten, 1980; Contributor of articles in newspapers and magazines. Honours include: Fellowship, American College of Allergists, 1980; Fellowship, American Association of Certified Allergists, 1981; Fellowship, American Academy of Allergy-Immunology, 1985; Delegate, People to People Allergy Delegation to India People to People International, 1987; Affiliate Fellow, Cleveland Clinic, Cleveland, Ohio, 1987; Elected President, Association of Indian Physicians of North East Ohio, 1992; Elected President, Association of Marathi Physicians of America, 1994. Memberships include: Fellow, American Academy of Allergy-Immunology; Fellow, American College of Allergy-Immunology; Fellow, American Association of Certified Allergists; Cleveland Allergy Society; American Society of Internal Medicine; Northern Ohio Paediatric Society; Academy of Medicine of Cleveland. Hobbies: Swimming; Travel; Photography. Address: 8789 Ridge Road, Cleveland, OH 44129-5635, USA.

DUTTA Bishnupada, b. 15 Mar 1938, India. Medical Practitioner. m. Jayati Ghosh, 28 July 1963, 1 son, 1 daughter. Education: MBBS (Calcutta), 1962; DCP course, Indian Armed Forces Medical College, Poona, 1963-65; DCP, Poona, 1965; FRCPA, Australia, 1974. Appointments: Resident Medical Officer, 1962-65, Pathologist, 1965-70, Indian Army hospitals, 1962-65; Tutor in Pathology, University of New South Wales, Australia, 1970-72; Pathology Registrar, Royal Prince Alfred Hospital, Sydney, New South Wales, 1972-74; Private practice in Pathology (Consultant Histopathologist), 1975-. Memberships: International Academy of Pathology; Australian Society of Dermatopathology; American Society of Dermatopathology; British Society of Dermatopathology; International Society of Dermapathology. Hobbies: Theatre; Opera; Drama; Fiction; History; Philosophy; Travel. Address: Epping, New South Wales 2121, Australia.

DÜVEL Hercules Morkel, b. 6 July 1963, Pretoria, South Africa. Physician. m. Esmé Düvel, 11 Nov 1989, 1 daughter. Education: MBChB, Pretoria. Appointments: Family Physician. Memberships: MASA; MMA. Hobbies: Golf; Skiing; Baseball. Address: Rossburn Medical Clinic, PO Box 40, Rossburn, Manitoba, R0J 1V0, Canada.

DUYZIKOV Alexander, b. 21 Oct 1941, Volgograd, Russia. Cardiosurgeon. m. Rita Lipovetskaya, 3 Aug 1963, 2 sons. Education: Higher Education, 1965, Graduate School, 1967-69, MD, 1980 Rostov State Medical Institute. Appointments: Chief Doctor, Rostov Hospital region, 1965-67; Graduate School, 1967-69; Surgeon, Submarines, SU Army, 1969-72; Cardiosurgeon, 1972-; Chief, Regional Cardiovascular Centre, 1973-. Publications: Author of 4 books; Contributor of 94 scientific articles; 4 Inventions: Homotranspantation of the Arteries, 1982, Diagnostic and Treatment of the Stenosis of the Lower Limbs, 1984, Treatment of Abdominal and Carotid Ischemia, 1986, 1987. Honours: The Order of Honour, 1984; Honorary Doctor of Russia, 1985. Memberships: Management, Cardiovascular Society of Russia; International Academy of Information. Hobby: Swimming. Address: Regional Clinical Hospital, Blagodatnaya 170, Rostov on Den 344085, Russia.

DWOSKIN Joseph Y, b. 14 July 1935, Chicago, Illinois, USA. Clinical Assistant Professor. 4 daughters. Education: BS, Springfield College, 1961; MD, Jefferson Medical College, 1965. Appointments: Assistant Professor, Department of Urology, SUNY, 1970-74; Assistant Attending, Children's Hospital, Buffalo, 1970-78; Acting Chief, Urology, Children's Hospital, 1978-83; Chief, Department of Urology, Children's Hospital, 1983-84; Clinical Assistant Professor, SUNY; Chief, Department of Urology, Mercy Hospital, Buffalo; Attending Staff, Children's Hospital & Mercy Hospital; Consulting Staff, Millard Fillmore Hospital, Buffalo. Publications incl: Vesicoureteral reflux in Children, 1985; Sibling uropathology, 1986; Vesicoureteral Reflux, 1990. Memberships: American Academy of Pediatrics; American College of Surgeons; American Medical Association; American Urological Association; Society of Pediatric Urology; Society Internationale d'Urologie; European Society of Paediatric Urology; Society of GURS. Address: 313 Elmwood Avenue, Buffalo, NY 14222-2399, USA.

DWYER Johanna T, b. 20 Oct 1938, Syracuse, NY, USA. Professor. Education: DSc; MSc; MS; BS. Appointments: Assistant Professor, Harvard School of Public Health, 1970-74; Associate Professor, Tufts Medical School, 1974-83; Professor of Medicine and Community Health, Tufts Medical School and Tufts School of Nutrition and adjunct Profesor Maternal & Child Health Harvard School of Public Health. Publications include: Food and Nutrition Policy in a Changing World, Co-author, 1979; Screening Older Americans' Nutritional Health, 1991; Contributor of 86 research articles, 185 reviews and reports, 15 book reviews, 11 abstracts and 14 videotapes. Honours: President, American Institute of Nutrition, 1994; President, Society for Nutrition Education, 1976; Secretary American Society of Clinical Nutrition, 1990-93. Memberships: American Institute of Nutrition; American Dietetics Association; Food and Nutrition Board, National Academy of Sciences. Hobby: Archaeology. Address: 750 Washington Street, Boston, MA 02111, USA.

DWYER Karinski Debra Ann, b. 10 Dec, Long Beach, California, USA. Registered Nurse. m. John T Dwyer, 21 Dec 1991, 1 daughter. Education: BSN; MS Program for Maternal Child Health. Appointments: RN in Pediatric ICU. Memberships: ANA. Hobbies: Antiques; Hiking. Address: PO Box 5024, Coreene, RI 02827, USA.

DYKEN Mark L, b. 26 Aug 1928, Laramie, Wyoming, USA. Professor of Neurology. m. Beverly Joan All, 6 Aug 1951, 3 sons, 3 daughters. Education: BS, Indiana University, 1951; MD, Indiana University Medical School, 1954. Appointments: Clinical Director, Director of Research, New Castle State Hospital, 1958-61; Active Staff, Henry County Hospital, New Castle, 1958-61; Chairman, Section of Neuropsychiatry, 1959-61; Professor, Chairman, Department of Neurology, Indiana University. Publications: Over 200 articles, books, abstracts and editorials publised in cerebral vascular disease. Honours: The Henry Barnett Stroke Lecturer, Toronto, Canada, 1992; The Willis Lecturer, 18th International Joint Conference on Stroke & Cerebral Circulation, Miami, Florida, 1993; Provenzano Lecturer, Neurology Center of Fairfax Limited, Virginia, 1993. Memberships: AMA; AHA; ANA; ABPN; ABMS; Association of University Professors of Neurology. Address: Department of Neurology, Indiana University Medical Center, 545 Barnhill Direve, EM-125, Indianapolis, IN 46202-5124, USA.

DYSINGER Paul William, b. 24 May 1927, Burns, Tennessee, USA. Physician. m. Yvonne M Minchin, 11 May 1958, 3 sons, 1 daughter. Education: BA summa cum laude, Southern College of SDA, 1951; MD, Loma Linda University School of Medicine, 1955; MPH, Harvard University School of Public Health, 1962. Appointments: Medical Officer, US Public Health Service, 1956-58; Medical Officer, US State Department, Phnom Penh, Cambodia, 1958-60; Associate Dean and Professor, Loma Linda University, California, 1961-88; Senior Health Advisor, Adventist Development and Relief Agency, 1988-93; Chief Executive Officer, Senior Health Advisor, Development Service International, 1993-. Publications include: How We Can Keep Well, and Why Diseases Come, in Way to Health and Happiness, 1965; The Mission's Medical Contributions to East Africa, in Seventh-Day Adventist Contributions to East Africa 1902-1983, 1985; Management of First Level Care and Referral (with Wayne S Dysinger), in Guidelines on Obstetric Emergencies, 1993; Pulmonary Emphysema in a Non-smoking Population (co-author), 1963; Health Problems of the Waha (co-author), Part IV, 1964, Part V, 1972; Modern Medical Missions, 1971; Ecology Can Be a Way of Medical Practice, 1972; AIDS and Child Survival, 1989. Memberships: Fellow, American Public Health Association; Fellow, American College of Preventive Medicine; Fellow, Royal Society of Tropical Medicine and Hygiene; National Council for International Health, Board Member 1988-89; International Health Society, President 1991-93, Vice-President; Adventist International Medical Society. Hobbies: Travel; Philately; Photography. Address: PO Box 210, Williamsport, TN 38487, USA.

DYSKEN Maurice William, b. 16 June 1942, Dayton, Ohio, USA. Physician. m. Signe Midelfort, 8 June 1968, 1 son, 1 daughter. Education: AB, Oberlin College; MD, Case Western Reserve University. Appointments: President, Minnesota Psychiatric Society, 1992-93; Director, GRECC Program, Minneapolis VA Medical Center; Professor of Psychiatry, University of Minnesota. Publications: 1 book, 81 papers, 15 book chapters, 103 abstracts. Honours: Member, NIA Study Section, 1993-97. Memberships: American Psychiatric Association; Psychiatry Research Association. Hobbies: Piano; Running; Tennis. Address: GRECC Program (11G) MN VA Medical Center, One Veterans Drive, Minneapolis, MN 55417, USA.

E

EASTCOTT Harry Hubert Grayson, b. 17 Oct 1917, Montreal, Canada. Education: Latymer School, North London; St Mary's Hospital and Postgraduate Medical Schools, London; Qualified MB, BS, London, 1941. Appointments: Royal Naval Volunteer Reserve, 1943-46; FRCS England, 1946; Surgical Research Fellow, Harvard Medical School, 1949-50; Assistant Director, Surgical Unit, St Mary's Hospital, London, 1950-55; Full Staff Appointment, St Mary's Hospital, London, 1955-82; Consultant in Surgery and Vascular Surgery, Royal Navy, 1957-82; Consultant Surgeon, Royal Masonic Hospital, London, 1964-80; Consultant Surgeon, King Edward VII Hospital for Officers, London, 1965-87. Publications: Author, Arterial Surgery, 3rd Edition, 1969; Various Articles on General and Vascular Surgery, including The First Carotid Artery Reconstruction for Threatened Stroke, 1954. Honours: Fothergillian Gold Medal, Medical Society of London, 1974; King's Fund Australasian Travelling Fellowship, 1973; Cecil Joll Prize, RCS England, 1984; Galen Medal, Worshipful Society of Apothecaries of London, 1993. Memberships: include, Society for Vascular Surgery; Royal Society of Medicine; American Surgical Association. Address: 47 Chiltern Court, Baker Street, London NW1 5SP, UK.

EBERTS Brian W, b. 22 June 1960, Carnegie, Pennsylvania, USA. Psychiatrist. m. Gina Micarelli, 21 May 1987. Education: MD, University of Pittsburgh, 1986; Board Certified, 1992. Appointments: Chief, Division of Mental Health Service, 1990-94; Currently Locum Tenens. Membership: American Medical Association. Address: PO Box 6024, Englewood, CO 80155-6024, USA.

ECALE Carol Lynn, b. 20 May 1956, Elmhurst, Illinois, USA. Research Scientist. m. Shijun Zhou, 16 Aug 1993. Education: BS, Chemistry, 1979; MA, Russian, 1983; PhD, Entomology, 1993. Appointments: Molecular Biologist, Sandoz, 1985-88; Currently Postdoctoral Research Associate, University of Missouri, Columbia. Publications: The Happiest Day, translation from Russian of Viktoria Tokareva's Samyj Scastlivyj Den, 1990; A Characteristic Body Posture of the Potato Leafhopper is Correlated with Probing, 1994; Time Course of Anatomical Changes to Stem Vascular Tissues of Alfalfa, Medicago Sativa L, from Probing Injury by the Potato Leafhopper, Empoasca Fabae, 1995; Honours: Phi Kappa Phi, Purdue University, 1983; Haseman Outstanding Graduate Student Award, University of Missouri, 1993. Memberships: American Association for the Advancement of Science; Entomological Society of America; American Phytopathological Society; American Association for the Advancement of Slavic Studies. Hobbies: Chinese herbal medicine; Massage therapy. Address: 1-87 Agriculture Building, University of Missouri, Columbia, MO 65211, USA.

ECHENBERG Dean Fredric, b. 10 Oct 1941, Sherbrooke, Quebec, Canada. Physician. 1 s. Education: BS, Wayne State University, Michigan, 1962; MD, Wayne State University, Michigan, 1966; MPH, University of California at Berkeley, 1980; PhD in Epidemiology, University of California at Berkeley, 1982. Appointments: Military Service, US Air Force, 1967-69; Staff Physician, Detroit General Hospital, Emergency Department, Michigan, 1971; Private Practice, Family Medicine, San Francisco, 1971-77; Consultant, International Longshoremen's and Warehousemen's Union, San Francisco, 1971-79; Principal Investigator, Research Grant, National Institute of Aging, 1979; Consultant, US Agency for International Development, 1982; Director, Medical and Scientific Affairs, Western Consortium for the Health Professions Inc, San Francisco, 1982-84; Director, Population Studies, Bay Area Human Nutrition Center, University of California, San Francisco, 1982-84; Direcotr, Bureau of Disease Control, Department of Public Health, City and County of San Francisco, 1984-89; International Medical Volunteer, 1989-91; Director, Central and Eastern Europe, Project Hope, Prague, Czech Republic, 1992-. Publications: include, Nutritional Status and Severity of Diarrhea, 1981; Malnutrition in American Children using the Paradigm Seen in Less Developed Countries: A Study of Infection and Growth, 1982; Aids: The Making of a Chronic Disease, 1992; Nutritional Assessment of Immigrant Children: Physical Assessment, 1985. Memberships: include, International Institute of San Francisco; Fellow, American Academy of Family Practice; American Public Health Association. Address: 406 Arkansas, San Francisco, CA 94107 2814, USA.

ECKETY William Gamm, b. 23 July 1926, New Jersey, USA. Forensic Pathologist. m. Haroldine Laugel, 21 June 1952, 1 son, 1 daughter. Education: BA, Medical School; MD. Appointments: Chief Medical Examiner, Norfolk, 1958; Hospital Pathologist, Forensic Pathologist, Tampa, 1959-64; Hospital Pathologist, Forensic Pathologist, Orlando, 1964-67; Hospital Pathologist, Forensic Pathologist, Wichita, 1967-83; Medicolegal, Forensic Sciences International Director, Forensic Pathologist, Kansas, 1983-; Director, International Reference Organization in Forensic Medicine. Publications: Three Volume Text, Forensic Medicine & Trauma; Editor Emeritus, Founder, American Journal of Forensic Pathology and Medicine; Introduction to Forensic Sciences; Interpretation of Blood Stain Evidence; Numerous Articles. Memberships: American College of Pathologists; American Academy of Forensic Sciences; National Association of Medical Examiners; American College of Legal Medicine. Honours: Silver Medal, Oscar Freire Institute, Sao Paulo, Brazil; Center Named After Him, Mogi Das Cruzes, Brazil; First Criminal Justice Award, Kansas; The Amazing People of Kansas Award. Hobbies: History; Plants; Animals; Aviation. Address: 146 Derby Woods Drive, Panama City, FL 32444, USA.

ECONOMIDES Demetrios Leonidas, b. 14 Oct 1956, London, England. Gynaecologist. m. Daphne, 2 d. Education: MBBS; MD; MRCOG. Appointments: Research Fellow, Harms Birthright Centre for Fetal Medicine; Lecturer, Nuffield Department of Obstetrics & Gynaecology, Oxford, England; Consultant & Senior Lecturer, Department of Obstetrics & Gynaecology, Royal Free Hospital, London, England. Publications: On Fetal Metabolism and Endocrinology. Memberships: Royal College of Gynaecologists; British Medicine Association; Royal Society of Health. Hobbies: Walking; Photography. Address: Royal Free Hospital, Pond Street, London, NW3 2QG, England.

EDELMANN Robert Joel, b. 21 Jul 1951, Basingstoke, Hampshire, England. Clinical Psychologist. m. Mary Bernadette Edelmann, 27 May 1989, 2 d. Education: BSc, Geography, Geology, 1972, BSc, Psychology, 1977, MPhil, Clinical Psychology, 1984, PhD, Psychology, 1981, University of London. Career: Lecturer in Psychology, Bulmershe College of Higher Education, Reading, England, 1981-82; Lecturer in Psychology, University of Sheffield, 1984-86; Lecturer, 1986-93, Senior Lecturer in Clinical Psychology, 1993-, University of Surrey, Guildford; Currently, Course Director, MSc Health Psychology. Publications: The Psychology of Embarrassment, 1987; Coping With Blushing, 1990; Anxiety: Theory Research and Intervention in Clinical and Health Psychology, 1992; Interpersonal Conflicts at Work, 1993; Numerous articles in academic journals mainly on anxiety, infertility and endometriosis. Memberships: Fellow, British Psychological Society; British Association of Behavioural Psychotherapy; Society of Reproductive and Infant Psychology. Address: Department of Psychology, University of Surrey, Guildford, Surrey, GU2 5XH, England.

EDEN Osborn Bryan, b. 2 Apr 1947, Birmingham, England. Professor of Paediatric Oncology. m. Randi Forsgren, 15 May 1970, 1 son, 1 daughter. Education: MB BS, London, 1970; DRCOG, 1972; MRCP (UK), 1974; FRCPE, 1983; FRCP, 1992; Postdoctoral Fellow, Stanford University, California, USA. Appointments: Senior House Officer and Registrar, Royal Hospital for Sick Children, Edinburgh, Scotland; Consultant Paediatric Haematologist, Edinburgh; Currently Professor of Paediatric Oncology. Publications: Over 100 papers and chapters on paediatric haematology and cancer. Memberships: Chairman, Medical Research Council Working Party on Childhood Leukaemia; COMARE; British Paediatric Association; SIOP; BSH; Paediatric Research Society. Hobbies: Hill walking; Literature; Politics; Photography. Address: 5 South Gillsland Road, Edinburgh EH10 5DE, Scotland.

EDERER Fred, b. 5 Mar 1926, Vienna, Austria. Epidemiologist. m. Hilda Tomar, 30 Mar 1958. Education: BS; MA, American University, Washington DC, USA; FACE. Appointments: Statistician, Associate Director for Biometry and Epidermiology, National Eye Institute; Senior Epidemiologist, The Emmes Corporation; Board of Editors, American Journal of Ophthalmology, American Journal of Epidemiology; Visiting Professor of Epidemiology, Johns Hopkins University. Publications: Contributor of over 100 articles in scientific journals and chapters in books. Honours: David Rumbaugh Scientific Award, Juvenile Diabetes Association; Superior Service Award, Department of Health Education and Welfare. Memberships: Society for Epidemiologic Research; American College of Epidemiology; Society for Clinical Trails. Hobbies: Playing Viola in String Quartets; Tennis. Address: 5504 Lambeth Road, Bethesda, MD 20814, USA.

EDGINGTON Kenneth, b. 15 Sep 1940, London, England. Physician. m. Heathr Oswald, June 1981, 2 sons, 2 daughters. Education: MRCS; LRCP; FFOM; DAvMed; FRAeS. Appointments: Colonel, Royal Army Medical Corps; Consultant Adviser in Aviation Medicine, Army, 1979-86; Head, UK Health Services, British Airways, 1988-92; Currently Chief Medical Officer, UK Civil Aviation Authority; Honorary Civilian Consultant to the Royal Navy and Army in Aviation Medicine; Reader in Civil Aviation Medicine, Royal Air Force. Publications: Contributor of numerous papers on aviation medicine topics. Memberships: Royal Society of Medicine; Royal Aeronautical Society; International Academy of Avition and Space Medicine; Aerospace Medical Association. Hobbies: Sailing; Skiing; Squash. Address: CAA Aviation House, Gatwick Airport South, West Sussex RH6 0YR, England.

EDMONDS Douglas Keith, b. 23 July 1949, London, England. Obstetrician and Gynaecologist. m. Gillian Linda Rose, 13 Oct 1990, 2 sons. Education: MBChB, University of Sheffield; FRCOG; FRACOG. Appointments: Senior Registrar, Princess Anne Hospital, Southampton; Senior Registrar, Queen Elizabeth Hospital, Adelaide, South Australia; Currently Consultant, Queen Charlotte's and Chelsea Hospital, London. Publications: Spontaneous and Recurrent Abortion, 1986; Practical Paediatric and Adolescent Gynaecology, 1988; Dewhurst's Postgraduate Obstetrics and Gynaecology (editor); Numerous papers on reproductive medicine and paediatric and adolescent gynaecology. Memberships: Royal Society of Medicine; American Fertility Society; British Fertility Society; Blair-Bell Society; Ovarian Club; Gynaecological Club. Hobbies: Sport; Wine; Gastronomy. Address: 78 Harley Street, London W1N 1AE, England.

EDRISSIAN Gholam Hossein, b. 23 Aug 1931, Sanandadj, Iran. Professor of Medical Parasitology. m. Mehrnoush Mohtadi 8 Oct 1966, 1 s. Education: DPharm, Teheran University, 1956; MSc, Medical Parasitology, London School of Hygiene and Tropical Medicine, 1969; Board of Clinical Laboratory Science, Teheran University Medical Science, 1965. Career includes: Training and research mainly on malaria and leishmaniases, 1957-, Resident and Technologist, 1957-63, Assistant Professor, 1964-69, Associate Professor, 1970-75, Professor, 1976-, Currently Professor and Director of Protozoology Unit, School of Public Health and Institute of Public Health Research. Publications: 50 Articles in scientific journals or presented at international scientific meetings including: Principal-author, An endemic focus of visceral leishmaniasis in Meshkin-shahr, E Azerbaijan province, in Bulletin Society Path Exot, 1988; Principal-author, Bacterial infection in the suspected cutaneous leishmaniasis, Bulletin World Health Organization, 1990. Honour: Distinguished Professor, Teheran University Medical Science, 1992. Memberships: Iranian Public Health Association; Royal Society of Tropical Medicine Hygiene; Iranian Academy of Medicine Basic Sciences; Secretary, Board of Medical Parasitology; Expert Advisory Panel on Malaria, World Health Organization. Address: School of Public Health and Institute of Public Health Research, Teheran University of Medical Sciences, PO Box 6446, Teheran 14155, Iran.

EDWARDS David John Arthur, b. 13 Oct 1943, Newbury, England. University Professor; Clinical Psychologist. 2 sons, 1 daughter. Education: BA, 1966; MA, 1973; PhD, 1978. Appointments: Lecturer in Psychology, Rhodes University, 1972-80; Senior Lecturer in Psychology, Rhodes University, 1981-84; Professor of Psychology, Rhodes University, 1985-; Head, Department of Psychology, Rhodes University, 1986-93. Publications incl: The challenge of hypertension to South African health psychology, 1992; Psychology: An introduction for students in Southern Africa, 1993; Psychometric properties of the Right Wing Authoritarianism scale in black and white South African Students, in press. Memberships: South Africa Medical & Dental Council; Psychological Society of South Africa; South African Society for Clinical Psychology; Association for Transpersonal Psychology; British Psychological Society; Society for the Exploration of Psychotherapy Integration; Association for Past Life Research & Therapy; International Association of Cognitive Psychotherapy. Address: Department of Psychology, Rhodes University, Grahamstown 6140, South Africa.

EDWARDS Susan J, b. 7 Nov 1947, York, PA, USA. Psychologist. Education: MC, MEd, Arizona State University; PhD, AR State University; Postdoctoral Fellow, Rutgers University; Licensed Psychologist. Appointments: Over 20 years service in the mental health field including: Community Psychology; Education; Academia; Private Practice Psychology. Publications: Former columnist, Portland Business Journal; Numerous Track Journal Articles; Management Psychology Columnist, Custom Builder Magazine; When Men Believe in Love, 1995.

Honours include: Best Program, Arizona Personnel and Guidance Association, 1976. Memberships: American Counselling Association; American Psychological Association; American Association of Press Women. Hobbies: Horseback Riding; Writing. Address: 515 Executive Drive, Montgomery Commons, Princeton, NJ 08540, USA.

EFIONG Ekpo Ita, b. 21 July 1932, Calabar, Nigeria. Obstetrician and Gynaecologist. m. 22 Oct 1960, 1 son, 1 daughter. Education: MBBS (London); LRCP (England); MRCS (London); Fellow, Royal College of Gynaecologists, London; Fellow, College of Surgeons, Edinburgh. Appointments: Senior Lecturer in Obstetrics and Gynaecology, University of Lagos; Examiner for Nigerian Medical Council; Currently Consultant Obstetrician and Gynaecologist. Publications: Pregnancy in the Overweight Nigerian, 1975; A prospective study of postpartum menstrual function in S Nigerians, 1977; Co-author: The Obstetric Performance of Nigerian Primigravidae Aged 16 and Under, 1975; A prospective study of the effect of intravenous encormethiazole in eclamptic patients, 1975. Honours: Prize in Obstetrics and Gynaecology, West London Hospital, 1959. Memberships: Fellow, International Federation of Obstetricians and Gynaecologists; Fellow, West African College of Surgeons. Hobbies: Walking; Swimming. Address: PO Box 3813, Festac, Lagos, Nigeria.

EGELER Rudolph Maarten, b. 6 Sept 1955, Amsterdam, Netherlands. Paediatric Oncologist. m. Amy Sanders, 7 Sept 1985, 2 sons. Education: MD; PhD; Residency in Paediatrics, University of Amsterdam, 1985-90; Research Fellowship, Erasmus University of Minnesota, USA, 1991-93. Appointments: Staff Paediatric Oncologist, University of Rotterdam, Sophia Children's Hospital, 1993-. Publications: Current concepts and treatment in Langerhans cell histiocytosis (with M E Nesbit Jr), 1992; The association of LCH with malignant neoplasms (co-author), 1993; LCH: a continuing challenge (with G J D'Angio), 1995. Honours: Fellow Research Award, 1st Prize, University of Minnesota, 1992; Young Author Award, 1st Prize, NTVG (Dutch Journal of Medicine), 1993. Memberships: Histiocyte Society; International Society of Pediatric Oncology; American Society of Pediatric Hematology and Oncology. Hobbies: Rugby; Mountaineering; Skiing. Address: Erasmus University Rotterdam, Sophia Children's Hospital, Paediatric Hematology-Oncology, Dr Molewaterplein 60, 3015 GJ Rotterdam, Netherlands.

EHLERS Anke, b. 11 Jan 1957, Kiel, Germany. Clinical Psychologist. Education: Dipl Psych, 1983; DSoc Sc, 1985; Dr Habil Rer Nat, 1989. Appointments: Assistant Professor, University of Marberg, 1985-90; Professor, University of Göttingen, 1991-93; Welcome Principal Research Fellow, 1993-. Publications: Increased Cardiac Awareness in Panic Disorder, Co-author, 1992; Anxiety Induced by False Heartrate Feedback in Panic Disorder, Co-author, 1988. Honours: Young Psychologist, German Psychological Society, 1986; Faculty Award, Social Sciences, TÜbingen, 1987. Memberships: German Psychological Society; British Psychological Society; American Psychological Association; Society for Psychophysiological Research. Hobbies: Art; Theatre; Films. Address: Department of Psychiatry, University of Oxford, Warneford Hospital, Oxford OX3 7JX, England.

EHRENKRANZ Richard Allan, b. 28 Jul 1946, Newark, NJ, USA. Physician; Neonatologist. m. Ellen Barbara Swerdel, 25 Aug 1960, 2 s. Education: BS, Life Sciences; MD. Appointments: Attending Physician, Pediatrics, 1978-, Clinical Director, Newborn Special Care Unit, 1982-, Yale, New Haven Hospital; Professor of Pediatrics and Obstetrics and Gynaecology, Yale University School of Medicine, 1988-. Publications include: Many articles, chapters, proceedings, and abstracts including: Co-author, Low dose indomethacin and extension of intraventricular hemorrhage: A multicenter randomized trial, in Journal of Pediatrics, 1994 in press; Iron requirements of preterm infants, in Nutrition, 1994 in press. Honours: Diplomate, National Board of Medical Examiners, 1973; Public Policy Fellow, Office of Government Affairs, March of Dimes Birth Defects Foundation, 1992-93. Memberships: Alpha Omega Alpha; American Academy of Pediatrics; New England Perinatal Society; Fellow, American College of Nutrition; Sigma Xi; AAAS; Society for Pediatric Research; American Society for Clinical Nutrition. Hobbies: Snow Skiing; Biking; Gardening. Address: Department of Pediatrics, Yale University School of Medicine, PO Box 208064, 333 Cedar Street, New Haven, CT 06520-8064, USA.

EICHELMAN Burr S, b. 20 Mar 1943, Hinsdale, Illinois, USA. Physician; Psychiatrist. m. Anne C Gonzalez-Hartwig, 30 Dec 1982, 2 sons, 1 daughter. Education: SB, hons, University of Chicago, 1964; MD,

University of Chicago, 1968; PhD, Biopsychology, University of Chicago, 1970. Appointments: Intern, Pediatrics, University of California, San Francisco, 1969-70; Staff Associate, Lab of Clinical Psychobiology, NIMH, Maryland, 1970-72; Resident, Fellow, Psychiatry, Stanford School of Medicine, 1972-75; Kennedy Fellow in Medicine Law & Ethics, Stanford, 1975-76; Assistant Professor, University of Wisconsin, 1976-79; Associate Professor, 1979-84; Professor, 1984-88; Professor of Psychiatry, University of North Carolina, Chapel Hill, 1988-90; Professor, Chairman, Dept of Psychiatry, Temple, Philadelphia, PA, USA. Publications: Terrorism: Interdisciplinary Perspectives, 1983; Aggresive Behavior - From Laboratory to Clinic. Honours: Valedictorian, 1961; Sigma Xi, 1969; Alpha Omega Alpha, 1968; A E Bennett Award, Society of Biol Psychiatry, 1972; Falk Fellow, American Psychiatric Association, 1973. Memberships: American Psychiatric Association; American Psychology Association; American College of Neuropsychopharmacology; AAAS; International Society for Research of Aggression. Hobbies: Piano; Voice; Tennis; Skiing. Address: Department of Psychiatry, Temple University School of Medicine, 3401 North Broad Street, Philadelphia, PA 19140, USA.

EIGEN Michael Edward, b. 11 Jan 1936, New Jersey, USA. Psychologist. m. Betty Gitelman, 27 Dec 1981, 2 sons. Education: AB, University of Pennsylvania, 1957; PhD, New School for Social Research, 1974. Appointments: Faculty, New York University Postdoctoral Program & National Psychological Association for Psychoanlysis. Publications: Over 100 papers in professional journals, 4 books: The Psychotic Cure, 1986; Coming Through the Whirlwind, 1992; Electrified Tightrope, 1993; Reshaping The Self, 1995. Honours: Phi Beta Kappa, 1956. Memberships: American Psychological Association; National Psychological Association for Psychologists. Hobbies: Music; Family. Address: 225 Central Park West, Apt 101A, NY 10024, USA.

EILBER Frederick R, b. 17 Aug 1940, Detroit, MI, USA. Physician. m. Harriet Eilber, 4 s. Education: MD, University of MI Medical School, 1961. Appointments: Assistant Professor of Surgery, 1973-75, Associate Professor of Surgery, 1975-79, UCLA School of Medicine; Professor of Surgery, UCLA, 1979-91; Currently, Professor of Surgery, Chief Division of Surgical Oncology, UCLA. Publications: 3 Books; 63 Book Chapters; 128 Published Articles. Honours: Golden Scapel Award in Teaching, UCLA, 1978, 1979, 1980; Distinguished Alumni Award, MD Anderson Hospital and Tumor Institute, 1985. Memberships: American Surgical association; Society of University Surgeons; Society of Surgical Oncology; Society of Head and Neck Surgeons. Address: UCLA School of Medicine, Department of Surgery/Oncology, Room 54-140 CHS, 10833 Le Conte Ave, Los Angeles, CA 90024-1782, USA.

EINAV Shmuel, b. 30 Oct 1942, Tel Aviv, Israel. Scientist. m. Chasia Einav, 26 May 1964, 3 daughters. Education: BSc; MSc; PhD. Appointments: Professor: Massachusetts Institute of Technology, University of California at Berkeley and University of California at Los Angeles, USA; Technical High School, Aachen and University of Karlsruhe, Germany; Currently Chairman, Department of Biomedical Engineering, Tel Aviv University. Publications: About 100 papers in scientific journals. Honours: Miller Professorship for Distinction in Science. Memberships: International Federation of Medical and Biological Engineering; New York Academy of Sciences; American Society of Mechanical Engineers; American Institute of Aeronautics and Astronautics. Hobby: Playing the violin. Address: Department of Biomedical Engineering, Tel Aviv University, Tel Aviv 69978, Israel.

EINHORN Carl Murray, b. 21 Oct 1922, NY, USA. Psychologist. m. Dr Ruth A Hollender, 16 Mar 1947, 1 s, 2 d. Education: BA, Yeshiva University, 1945; MA, 1950, PhD, 1955, University of MI; Postdoctoral study, NY University, 1957-59; Diplomate, Counselling Psychology. Career includes: Unit Psychologist, Veterans Administration Medical Center, Lyons, NJ, 1970-83; Director, Center for Human Relations, Medical Arts Center at Colonial Oaks, NJ, 1977-88; Director, Central Jersey Biofeedback and Stress Control Center Inc, NJ, 1984-89; Currently, Adjunct Professor, Union for Experimenting Colleges and Universities, Cincinnati, OH; Consulting Psychologist, Social Security, Newark, NJ; Director, Center for Psychological Services, NJ; Executive Director, Center for Health Psychology Inc, NJ. Honours: Recognition Award, NJ Academy of Psychology, 1982; Distinguished Senior Contributor to Counselling Psychology, American Psychology Association, 1990. Memberships: American Psychological Association; American Association for Counselling and Development; NJ Psychological Association; International Society for Clinical and Experimental Hypnosis; Board of Trustees, NJ Academy of Psychology;

Elected, Congress of Rehabilitation Medicine; American Academy of Medical Hypnoanalysts; Certified Hypnotherapist, American Association of Professional Hypnotherapists. Hobbies: Travel; Golf. Address: 44 Yorktown Road, East Brunswick, NJ 8816, USA.

EINZIG Stanley, b. 25 Jul 1942, Brooklyn, NY, USA. Pediatric Cardiology. Education: MD; PhD; FACC. Career: Associate Professor, University of MN; Professor, WV University; Currently, Vice Chairman for Research, Department of Pediatrics; Professor of Pediatrics and Physiology, Chief, Pediatric Cardiology, WV University, Morgantown. Publications: 88 Publications in referred journals. Memberships: American Physiological Society; Society for Pediatric Research; Fellow, American College of Cardiology. Hobby: Golf. Address: West Virginia School of Medicine, Department of Pediatrics, Morgantown, WV 26506, USA.

EISDORFER Carl, b. 20 Jul 1930, Bronx, NY, USA. Medicine. m. Susan Elizabeth Gadsby, 4 s, 1 d. Education: BA, 1951, MA, 1953, PhD, 1959, NY University; MD, Duke University School of Medicine, Durham, NC, 1964. Appointments: Director, Alzheimer's Disease and Memory Disorders Centers, University of Miami and Mount Sinai Medical Center, FL, 1986-; Director, University of Miami Research Center for Biopsychosocial Studies of AIDS, 1986-; Director, University of Miami Center on Adult Development and Aging, 1986-; Professor and Chairman, Department of Psychiatry, University of Miami School of Medicine, 1986-; Professor of Psychology, University of Miami, Coral Gables, FL, 1986-; Professor, Family Medicine and Community Health, 1993-; Executive Vice President and Chief Clinical Officer, Mental Health and Primary Health Care Services, 1993-; Associate Director, University of Miami Center for Applied Gerontology. Publications include: Over 260 publications including: Co-author, Psychopathology Associated with Alzheimer's Disease and Related Disorders, in Journal of Gerontology, 1993. Honours include: Fellow, AAAS, 1977; Alpha Omega Alpha, 1978; Potamkin Prize for Outstanding Contributions to Research in Dementia, 1982; Jack Weinberg Memorial Award for Excellence in Geriatric Psychiatry, 1984; Outstanding Contributions to Aging Award, American Society on Aging Award, 1987; William C Menninger Memorial Award, American College of Physicians, 1990. Memberships include: Various offices, Alzheimer's Disease and Related Disorders Society; American Geriatric Society; APA; National Academy of Sciences. Hobbies: Fishing; Reading; Travel. Address: 1425 NW 10th Avenue, Suite 206, Miami, FL 33136, USA.

EISENBRUCH Maurice, b. 8 Oct 1948, Melbourne, Australia. Psychiatrist. m. Renata Volich, 26 jan 1994. Education incl: Master of Educational Studies, Monash University, 1984; MD, University of Melbourne, 1982; PhD, University Cambridge, 1982; MA, University of Melbourne, 1977. Appointments: Senior Research Fellow in Anthropology, Department of History & Philosophy of Science, University Melbourne, 1993-. Publications: The role of cultural bereavement for the health transition in a multicultural society, 1990; Is western mental health care appropriate for refugees, 1991; L'espace rituel et les guérisseurs traditionnels au Cambodge, 1994. Honours: John Adey Prize in Psychiatry, University Melbourne, 1972; Exhibitioner, Queen's College, University Melbourne, 1968. Memberships incl: Royal Anthropological Institute, England; American Psychiatric Association; Australian College of Paediatrics; Royal Society of Victoria. Address: 2 Carrefour De L'Odeon, Paris 75006, France.

EKWEMPU Christopher Chigbo, b. 7 Mar 1936, Nigeria. Professor of Obstetrics and Gynaecology. m. Faith Okoli, 19 Mar 1966, 2 sons, 1 daughter. Education: MB, BS, London University; FRCOG; FMCOG (Nigeria); FWACS (West Africa); FICS. Appointments: Consultant, Pumwani Maternity Hospital, Nairobi, Kenya, 1971-74; Senior Lecturer, Consultant, 1974-79, Reader, Obstetrics, Gynaecology, 1980-81, Professor, Obstetrics, Gynaecology, 1981-92, Ahmadu Bello University, Zaria, Nigeria; Professor, Consultant, Goroka Base Hospital, Goroka, Papua New Guinea, 1992-. Publications: Determinants of Maternal Mortality in Zaria Area of Nigeria (co-author), book contribution, 1992; Sections in Textbook of Obstetrics and Gynaecology for Medical Students, Vol I, 1988, Vol II, 1989; Contributions to learned journals include: Embryotomy in the management of obstructed labour, 1977; Co-author: Endometriosis among the Hausa/Fulani Population of Nigeria, 1979; Puerperal asymptomatic Bacteraemia. A problem in tropical environments, 1984; Antenatal care, formal education and childbearing, 1985; Three years experience with Norplant contraceptive implants in Nigeria, 1992; A multicentre clinical trial in Nigeria with a low-dose oral contraceptive, Marvelon, 1993. Honours: Best Student of

Year Award, Grammar School, 1950-54; Athletics Blue, University of Ibadan, 1960, 1961, 1962. Memberships include: Nigerian Medical Association; British Medical Association; New York Academy of Sciences; Fertility Association of Nigeria; Society of Gynaecology and Obstetrics of Nigeria; International AIDS Society; New York Academy of Sciences. Hobbies: Gardening; Classical music; Anthropology; Travel. Address: Goroka Base Hospital, PO Box 392, Goroka, Papua New Guinea.

EL-AZGHAL Hussein Ibrahim, b. 28 Sept 1933, Alexandria, Egypt. Obstetrician and Gynaecologist. m. Aziza Hussein, 21 Feb 1961, 2 sons, 3 daughters. Education: MBChB, 1957, Diploma, Obstetrics and Gynaecology, 1959, Diploma, Surgery, 1961, Ain Sham University, Cairo; FRCS (Edinburgh), 1963; MRCOG, 1970; MRCP (UK), 1973; ECFMG (USA), 1973; FRCOG, 1985. Appointments: House Officer; Resident, Obstetrics, Gynaecology; Specialist, Obstetrics, Gynaecology; Clinical Demonstrator, Obstetrics, Gynaecology; Registrar and Lecturer, Obstetrics, Gynaecology; Assistant Professor, Obstetrics, Gynaecology; Consultant in Gynaecology and Obstetrics. Publications include: Studies on Serum Magnesium Level in Normal Pregnancy and in Patients with EPH Gestosis, 1971; Stress Incontinence during Pregnancy. Its Pathogenesis and Management, 1972; Clonazepan in the Control and Prevention of Eclampsia, 1978; Co-author: Treatment of uterine hypoplasia, 1961; Norethisterone. A cervical blocking agent, 1965; The Stein-Leventhal Syndrome. The Rationale of Treatment by Surgery, 1965; Congenital Alresia Vaginae. A sinplified technique for vaginal reconstruction, 1967; Serum Iron in Newborn Infants and Their Mothers in Egypt, 1971; Studies of Maternal Serum Magnesium during pregnancy and labour and its correlation with foetal serum level. Honours: Gold Medal, Ain Sham University Faculty of Medicine, 1957; Prizes for Anatomy, Bacteriology, Pathology and Hygiene, 1957. Memberships: Egyptian Medical Association; British Microsurgical Society; Fallopius International Society; Middle East Fertility Society. Hobbies: Agriculture; Horticulture. Address: 12 Sheikh Bashir Neema Street, Nozha, Heliopolis, Cairo, Egypt.

EL-IBRASHY Mohamed Talaat, b. 15 Aug 1935, El-Mansoura, Egypt. Entomologist. m. Sohair El-Ibrashy, 10 Apr 1959, 1 son, 1 daughter. Education: BSc, 1957, MSc, 1961, University of Cairo; PhD, Wageningen Agricultural University, Netherlands, 1965. Appointments: Research Assistant, 1958-66, Researcher, 1966-72, Associate Research Professor, 1972-77, Head, 1972-, Professor of Insect Physiology, 1977-, Cairo. Publications: Over 60 including: Hormonal manipulation of insect reproduction in IPM systems: Recent developments and future trends, 1990; Hazardous effects of GMO on the ecosystem, 1992. Honours include: State Prize of Biological Sciences, 1983; 1st Rank Order of Sciences and Arts, Egypt, 1985; Einstein Diploma, 1985. Memberships include: Society of Physiological Sciences; Entomological Society of Egypt; Fellow, Royal Entomological Society, London; Malaysian Plant Protection Society; European Society for Comparative Endocrinology; International Society of Invertebrate Reproduction. Hobbies: Running; Volleyball; Flippers; Travel; Dancing (discotheque). Address: Insect Physiology Unit, Plant Protection Department, National Research Centre, Tahrir Street, Dokki, 12622 Cairo, Egypt.

EL-SHEIKH Mohamed Ahmed Ali, b. 1 January 1947, Kagmar, North Kordofan, The Sudan. Obstetrics and Gynaecology. m. Ehsan Gasmalla Mohamed, 20 June 1974, 3 sons, 2 daughters. Education: MBBS, Khartoum, Sudan; FRCOG, London, England. Appointments Include: House Officer, Khartoum Teaching Hospital, 1970-71; Medical Officer, El Obied General Hospital, 1971-72; Senior Medical Officer, Talodi General Hospital, 1972-73; Visiting Consultant Obstetrician & Gynaecologist, Magadishu, Somalia, 1980; Vice Chancellor, University of Juba, 1991-. Publications Include: Twin Pregnancy: A Four Year Report, 1982; LH Pulse frequency in relation to positive Oestrogen, Gonadotrophin feedback in amenorrhoea, 1983; Modulation of the pulsatile release of gonadotrophine by Exogenous Steroids in amenorrhoeic women with characterised functional defects, 1983; Reproductive hormonal profile in regularly menstrating Sudanese Women, 1984; Pathological mechanisms in Polycystic ovary syndrome: Modulation of LH pulsatility by progesterone, 1984; Emergency Hysterectomy in Obstetrics practise in Almadina Al Munawarah, Saudi Arabia, 1992. Memberships: Sudan Medical Association; Sudanese Society of Obstetricians & Gynaecologists; American Fertility Society. Hobbies: Reading; Tennis. Address: University of Juba, Khartoum Centre, PO Box 321/1, Khartoum, The Sudan.

EL-ZIBDEH Mazen Yousef, b. 5 Nov 1947, Jaffa, Jorden. Gynaecologist. m. May Sallam, 28 July 1982, 2 sons, 2 daughters. Education: MB; BCH; FICS; MRCOG; FRCOG. Appointments: Registrar, Obstetrics & Gynaecology, Glasgow Royal Infirmary & St Bartholomews Hospital, London; Assistant Professor, King Faisal University, Saudi Arabia; Assistant Professor, University Science & Technology, Irbid, Jordan; Senior Consultant, Head of Department, Islamic Hospital, Amman, Jordan. Publications: Diagnostic Laparoscopy, 1986; Perinatal Mortality, at King Fahd Hospital, 1988; Co-author, Obstetric Implications of Pregnancy in Adolescence, 1986; Co-author, Fetus Acardins Amorphus, 1987. Memberships: American Fertility Society; Falolopins International Society; Jordanian Society of Obstetricians & Gynaecologists. Address: PO Box 910201, Amman, Jordan.

ELAD David, b. 30 Apr 1951, Haifa, Israel. Professor of Biomedical Engineering. m. Pnina Kuperhmit, 6 Aug 1972, 2 daughters. Education: BSc, 1973, MSc, 1978, DSc, Biomedical Engineering, 1982, Technion, Israel. Appointments: Visiting Research Fellow, Imperial College, London, England, 1982-83; Postdoctoral Fellow, Massachusetts Institute of Technology, USA, 1983-85; Visiting Associate Professor, Northwestern University, 1989-91; Professor of Biomedical Engineering, Department of Biomechanical Engineering, Tel Aviv University, Israel. Publications: Mathematical Simulation of Forced Expiration, 1988; Three-Dimensional Measurement of Biological Surfaces, 1990; Modeling Forced Expiration, 1991; Air Flow in the Human Nose, 1993; Intravenous Infusion, 1994. Memberships: Biomedical Engineering Society; American Society of Mechanical Engineers; Israel Society of Biomedical Engineering. Hobbies: Swimming; Music. Address: Department of Biomedical Engineering, Faculty of Engineering, Tel Aviv University, Tel Aviv 69978, Israel.

ELGART Mervyn L, b. 12 Aug 1933, New York City, USA. Medicine - Dermatology. m. Sheila Ruth Cliff, 13 Jun 1954, 5 s. Education: AB, summa cum laude, Honours in Biology and Chemistry, Brooklyn College; MD, Cornell University Medical College, 1957; Special Competance in Dermatopathology, American Board of Dermatology, 1982. Career: Chief of Dermatology, Andrews AFB Hospital, 1964-66; Chief of Dermatology, VA Hospital, Washington DC, 1966-67; Assistant Professor, 1967-70, Associate Professor, 1970-74, Professor of Dermatology, Medicine and Pediatrics, 1974-, Chairman, Dermatology, 1975-, George Washington University Medical School, Washington DC. Publications: Co-author, Erythroplasia of Querat, in JAMA, 1975; Co-author, Manual of Fungi for Dermatologists, 1982; Insect Bites and Stings, Dermatologic Clinics, 1990. Honours: Phi Beta Kappa, 1952; Alpha Omega Alpha, 1974; Golden Apple Award, George Washington University School of Medicine, Sciences. Memberships: American Academy of Dermatology; Washington DC Dermatological Society; Society of Investigative Dermatology; International Society of Dermatology; American Society Dermatopathology; American Society of Dermatological Surgery; Association of Professors of Dermatology. Hobbies: Golf; Classical Music; Opera. Address: George Washington University Medical Center, Department of Dermatology, 2150 Pennsylvania Avenue NW, Washington DC 20037, USA.

ELIAS Jack A, b. 10 Apr 1951. Physician; Researcher; Educator. m. Sandra Elias, 1 Dec 1980, 1 daughter. Education: MD, University of Pennsylvania. Appointments: Assistant Professor, University of Pennsylvania School of Medicine; Associate Professor, University of Pennsylvania School of Medicine; Professor of Medicine and Chief of Pulmonary and Critical Care Medicine, Yale Univeristy School of Medicine. Honours: E L Trudesu Scholar, American Lung Association; Career Investigator, American Lung Association; Member, American Society of Clinical Investigation. Memberships: American Lung Association; American Thoracic Society. Hobbies: Hiking. Address: 333 Cedar Street, New Haven, CT 02520-8057, USA.

ELIAS Merrill Francis, b. 17 Apr 1938, Pittsburgh, USA. Behavioral Enidomiology & Experimental Neuropsychology. m. Penelope K Elias, 2 sons, 1 daughter. Education: BA, Allegheny College, 1960; MS, Purdue University, 1961; PhD, Purdue University, 1963. Appointments: Second Lt, USAF, 1960-63; First Lt to Captain, USAF, Air Force Systems Command, Griffis AFB, Rome, New York, 1963-66; Assistant Professor of Psychology, Allegheny College, 1966-69; NIH Postdoctoral Fellow, Duke University Medical School, 1969-71; Assistant Professor of Medical Psychology, Duke University Medical Center, Co-ordinator, Research Training Program in Aging, 1971-72; Associate Professor of Psychology, West Virginia University, 1972-73; Associate Professor of Psychology, Syracuse University, Associate Director for Research

All-University Gerontology Center, 1973-77; Professor of Psychology, University of Maine, 1977-. Publications Include: Determining neuropsychological cut scores for older, healthy adults, 1990; Special features of hypertension in the elderly, 1992; Hypertension effects neurobehavioral functioning: So What's New, 1993; Cognitive function and cardiovascular responsivity in subjects with a parental history of hypertension, 1993; Unmedicated blood pressure levels and quality of life in elderly hypertensive women. Honours: Distinguished Military Graduate, Allegheny College, 1960; Honours in Psychology, Allegheny College, 1960; BA Cum Laude, Allegheny College, 1960; Presidential Research & Achievement Award, University of Maine, 1991. Memberships Include: Society of Hypertension; Fellow, American Psychological Association. Hobbies: Canoe; Hiking; Cycling. Address: Department of Psychology, University of Maine, Clarence Cook Little Hall, Orono, ME 04469-0140, USA.

ELIASHOF Byron Amdur, b. 28 Feb 1935, Pittsburgh, Pennsylvania, USA. Psychiatrist. m. Pamela Audrey Deakin, 1960, 2 sons. Education: AB, Yale University, 1956; MD, Albert Einstein College of Medicine, 1961. Appointments include: Teaching Fellow in Psychiatry, Harvard Medical School, 1962-65; Chief Resident, Clinical Research Center, Massachusetts Mental Health Center, 1963-64; Psychiatry Staff, Queen's Medical Center, Honolulu, 1967-; Associate Clinical Professor, Department of Psychiatry, University of Hawaii, 1970-; Lecturer, School of Social Work, University of Hawaii, 1971-76; Board Director, Hawaii Mental Health Center. Publications: The Role of Stress in Workers; Short Term Psychotherapy of an Outpatient, 1967; Chronic Schizophrenia and the Demands of an Intensive Treatment Center, 1968. Memberships: American Academy Disability Evaluating Physicians; Honolulu County Medical Society; Hawaii State Medical Society; American Society for Clinical Hypnosis; American Academy Psychiatry & the Law; Association for Applied Psychophysiology & Biofeedback; Hawaii Psychiatric Society; American Medical Association; American Psychiatric Association. Hobbies: Music; Travel; Cooking; Photography. Address: Suite 1306, 1441 Kapiolani Blvd, Honolulu, HI 96814, USA.

ELITHORN Alick Cyril, b. 16 Dec 1920, Southsea, Hampshire, England. Researcher. m. Sheila Pusinelli, 2 sons, 2 daughters. Education: MA; MD; DPM; FRCP; FBPsS; CPsychol. Appointments: Life Tenured Member, Medical Research Counxcil Neurological Research unit; Member of Scientific Staff, MRC; Consultant Physician, National Hospital for Nervous Diseases, Royal Free Hospital; Honorary Research Fellow, Department of Statistics, University of California; Adviser, Department of Mathematics, St Josephs University, Philadelphia; Department of Psychology, University College London. Address: Galton Laboratory, Department of Genetics and Biochemistry, University College, London, England.

ELKIND Arthur H, b. 28 Oct 1932, New York City, NY, USA. Director. m. Arlene R, 3 Jul 1955, 1 s, 2 d. Education: BA, Columbia University, 1949-53; MD, State University of New York, College of Medicine, 1957-58. Appointments: Junior Assistant, Medical Resident, Maimonides Hospital, Brooklyn, New York, 1958-59; Assistant & Senior Medical Resident, Montefiore Hospital, Bronx, New York, 1958-61; Public Health Service Fellow, Medical Division, Montefiore Hospital, Bronx, New York, 1961-62; Physician, Montefiore Hospital, Bronx, New York, 1962-; Assistant Attending Physician/Associate Attending Physician/Attending Physician, Mount Vernon Hospital, New York, 1962-63, 1963-64; 1965-; Physician, Headache Unit, Montefiore Hospital, Bronx, New York, 1962-73; Acting Director, Heahache Unit, Montefiore Hospital, Bronx, New York, 1973-75; Director of Headache Univ, Department of Neurology, Montefiore Hospital, Bronx, 1975-78; Practice: Internal Medicine, Mount Vernon, New York, 1962-; Research Group for Study of Headache, World Federation of Neurology, 1976-; Clinical Assistant Professor of Medicine, New York Medical College, 1984-. Publications include: Muscle Contraction Headache: Overview and Update of a Common Affliction, 1987; Headache and Facial Pain Associated with Head Injury, 1989; Drug Abuse in Headache Patients, 1989; Drug Abuse and Headache, 1991; Posttraumatic Headache, 1992. Memberships: include, Chairperson of Headache Section of American Society of Clinical Pharmacology & Therapeutics, 1988-91; Board Member Secretary of Executive Board of National Headache Foundation, 1990-; American Medical Association. Hobbies: Old Master Prints; Photography; Music. Address: 20 Archer Avenue, Mount Vernon, New York, 10550, USA.

ELLIOTT Claire Baker, b. 13 Dec 1923, Clayton, Alabama, USA. Physician. m. Howard C Elliott, 24 Apr 1958, 5 daughters. Education: AB, University of Alabama; MD, George Washington University of Medicine. Appointments include: Chairman, Department of Pathology, Honorary Professor, University of Alabama School of Medicine; President of Medical Staff, Baptist Medical Center, Montclair; Now retired. Publications: American Journal of Surgery, 1989; Clinical Biotechnology, 1992; American College of Surgeons Exhibit, 1992; American Journal of Clinical Pathology, 1994. Honours: Board Certifications in Anatomic Pathology, Clinical Pathology and Dermatopathology. Memberships: Diplomate, American Society of Clinical Pathologists; Diplomate, American Society of Dermatopathology; Diplomate, College of American Pathology. Hobbies: Study; Beachcombing. Address: 4260 Sharpsburg Drive, Birmingham, AL 35213, USA.

ELLIS F Henry Jr, b. 20 Sept 1920, Washington DC, USA. Thoracic Surgery. m. Mary Jane Walsh, 4 Dec 1978, 3 sons, 5 daughters. Education: AB; MD; PhD. Appointments: Chief of Thoracic Surgery, Mayo Clinic; Chief of Thoracic & Cardiovascular Surgery, Lahey Clinic; Chief of Cardio Thoracic Surgery, Deaconess Hospital, 1971-90; Chief Emeritus, 1990-. Publications include: Esophageal hiatal hernia, 1972; Caritas Chirurgie, 1978; Surgery for short esophagus with stricture: An experimental and clinical manometric study, 1978; Reoperative Achalasia Surgery, 1986; Limited Esophagogastrectomy for Carcinoma of the Cardia: Indications, Technique and Results, 1988; The Nissen Fundoplication, 1992; Oesophagomyotomy for Achalasia: A 22 year experience. Honours: Billings Gold Medal, AMA, 1955. Memberships: Society of Clinical Surgery; American Surgical Association; Society of Thoracic Surgeons; American Association of Thoracic Surgery; European Association for Cardiac Thoracic Surgery. Hobbies: Tennis; Skiing. Address: 21 Fairmount Street, Brookline, MA 02146, USA.

ELLIS Marcia, b. 24 Apr 1948, San Francisco, USA. Clinical Forensic Psychologist. m. 23 May 1987. Education: BA, cum laude, Stanford University; PhD, Psychology, University of California. Appointments: Psychologist, Stanford Medical Center; Psychologist, Affiliated Psychologist, Mental Research Institute. Publications: International Journal of Clinical & Experimental Hypnosis, 1975. Honours: Honours Program in Psychology, Stanford University, 1968-70; President, Ventura County Psychological Association, 1993. Memberships: American Psychological Association; California Psychological Association. Address: 4482 Market St #408, Ventura, CA 93003, USA.

ELSAYED Said, b. 29 Nov 1935, Cairo, Egypt. Professor. m. 19 Apr 1961, 1 son, 1 daughter. Education: BSc, MSc, PhD; Member of the European Academy of Allergy; Member of the American Academy of Allergy; Member of the Federation of the European Biochemical Societies; Member of the Scandinavian Society of Immunology. Appointments: Research Associate, University of Oslo Faculty of Medicine, Pediatric Research Institute, Rikshospitalet, Oslo, Norway, 1966-72; Research Biochemist, University Hospital of Bergen, 1972; Professor of Clinical Biochemistry, 1989. Publications: Published over 100 publications in International Allergy Journals, 1966-94; Published many chapters in Allergy Books. Memberships: Norwegian Professor Union; Norwegian Researcher Association. Hobbies: Rowing; Reading; Classical Music; Mountain Climbing. Address: Gronnegrend No 11, N-5040 Pradis, Bergen, Norway.

ELTOFT Anita, b. 27 May 1961, Oslo, Norway. Chiropractor. Education: Doctor of Chiropractic. Memberships: Norwegian Chiroractic Association; European Chiropractic Association. Hobbies: Bicycling; Art; Reading. Address: Sandakerveien 76, Oslo 4, 0483 Norway.

ELWOOD James Mark, b. 27 Aug 1946, Belfast, Northern Ireland. Professor of Medicine. m. Candace Trip, 1974, 1 s, 1 d. Education: MD; DSc; FFPHM, UK; FFPHA, Australia/New Zealand; FRCP, Canada; FACE. Appointments: Head, Epidemiology Cancer Control Agency of British Colombia, Canada; Professor & Chair, Department of Epidemiology & Community Medicine, Nottingham, England; Professor, Cancer Epidemiology, University of Otago, Dunedin, New Zealand. Publications: Casual Relationships in Medicine, 1988; Epidemiology and Control of Neural Tuba Defects, 1980, 1993; Epidemiology of Melanoma, 1993. Memberships: Vice President, Australasian Epidemiological Association; Member, New York Academy of Sciences; Fellow, American College of Epidemiology; Fellow, Royal Statistical Society. Hobbies: Home & Family. Address: Hugh Adam Cancer Epidemiology Unit, P O Box 913, Dunedin, New Zealand.

ELY Jorge Fonseca, b. 11 May 1930, Porto Alegre, Brazil. Plastic Surgeon. Education: Medical Doctorate, Faculdade de Medicina da Universidade Federal do Rio Grande doSul, 1954. Appointments: Director of Plastic Surgery & Burns Unit, Pronto Socorro Hospital; Head of Plastic Surgery Unit, Santo Antonio Childrens Hospital; Professor, Head of Plastic Surgery, Fundacao Faculdade Federal de Ciencias Médicas; Chief of Plastic Surgery Unit, Santa Casa Hospital; Post-graduate Professor for the area of Plastic Surgery, Universidade Federal do Rio Grande do Sul; Director, Clinica Sul-Brasileira de Cirurgia Plastica, Porto Alegre, Brazil. Publications: Cirurgia Plastica, 1965; Editor, Transactions of the XIII Brazilian Congress of Plastic Surgery and First Brazilian Congress of Aesthetic Plastic Surgery, 1976; Editor of the 'Transactions of the Seventh Congress of The International Confederation for Plastic, Reconstructive and Aesthetic Surgery', 1980; 33 medical articles published in Brazil and 22 outside. Memberships include: Fellow, Royal Society of Medicine; Fellow, International College of Surgeons; International Confederation for Plastic, Reconstructive & Aesthetic Plastic Surgery; American Society of Aesthetic Plastic Surgery; Brazilian Society of Mastology; Brazilian Society of Cancerology; Brazilian Society of Reconstructive Microsurgery. Honours: Award, Brazilian Section of the International College of Surgeons, 1980; Plaque, Pioneer of Microsurgery in Brazil, 1987; Special Honour Certificate, Brazilian Plastic Society Congress, 1989; Gold Medal, Argentinean Society of Plastic Surgery, 1991; Award & Medal, Humboldt University, Berlin, 1992. Hobbies: Art; Tennis; Water Skiing. Address: Rua André Puente 396, Porto Alegre, RS 90035-150, Brazil.

EMEAGWALI Dale Brown. Education: BA, Biology, Coppin State College, Baltimore, USA, 1976; PhD, Microbiology, Georgetown University School of Medicine, Washington DC, 1981. Appointments: Postdoctoral Fellow, NIH, bethesda, 1981-84; Postdoctoral Fellow, Department of Pathology, Uniformed Services University of Health Sciences, bethesda, 1985-86; University of Wyoming, Laramie, 1986-87; Assistant Research Scientist, University of Michigan, Ann Arbor, 1987-92; Teacher, Researcher, University of Minnesota, Twin Cities Campus, 1994-. Publications include: Evidence of a Constitutive and Inducible Form of Kynurenine Formamidase in an Actinomycin-producing Strain of Strepomyces Parvulus, Co-author, 1980; A Possible Role of d-Valine and Related d-Aminoo Acides in Repression of Enzyme and Actinomycin Synthesis, Co-author, 1989; Differential Expression of c-myc, c-myb, and Erythopoeitin Receptor in Two Murine Erythroleukemia Cell Lines, Co-author, 1993; Regulation of Tryptophan Metabolism and Its relationship to Actinomycin d Synthesis, Co-author, 1983. Honours include: Sigma Xi; Biomedical Research Awardm Coppin State College, 1976; Postdoctoral Fellow, American Cancer Society, 1981. Memberships: American Association for the Advancement of Science; American Society of Microbiology; National Technical Association. Address: 1180 Cushing Circle, Suite 113, St Paul, MN 55108-5015, USA.

EMERSON Bryan Thomas, b. 5 Sept 1929, Townsville, Queensland, Australia. Professor of Medicine. m. Elva Brett, 28 Apr 1955, 2 s. Education: Fellow of the Royal Australasian College of Physicians, 1967; Member of the Royal Australiasian College of Physicians, 1957; Bachelor of Medicine and Bachelor of Surgery, University of Queensland, 1952; MD, University of Queensland, 1962; PhD, University of Queensland, 1973. Appointments: Junior Resident Medical Officer, Brisbane General Hospital, 1953-54; Medical Registrar, Brisbane General Hospital, 1955-56; Teaching Medical Registrar, Medical Professorial Unit, Brisbane General Hospital, 1957-59; Senior Lecturer in Materia Medica and Therapeutics, University of Queensland, 1960-62; Research Associate, Medical Professorial Unit, Westminster Hospital Medical School, University of London, 1963; Reader in Medicine, University of Queensland, Princess Alexandra Hospital, 1964-73; Professor, 1974-94 & Head, 1985-94, Professor Emeritus, 1995-, Department of Medicine, University of Queensland. Publications: Hyperuricaemia and Gout in Clinical Practice, 1983; Numerous Contributions to Post Graduate Textbooks in Medicine, Nephrology and Rheumatology and to Scientific Medical Literature. Honours include: Weinholt Prize, University of Queensland, 1950; Parr Prize for Research in Rheumatic Diseases, Australian Rheumatology Association, 1966; US Public Health Services Postdoctoral International Fellowship, 1967; Honorary Fellow, Queensland Institute of Medical Research. Memberships include: Australian Medical Association; Australian Society for Clinical and Experimental Pharmacology. Hobbies: Music; Swimming; Antique Collecting. Address: Department of Medicine, 5th

Floor, Princess Alexandra Hospital, Ipswich Road, Woolloongabba, Queensland 4102, Australia.

EMERSON Catherine Mary McGirr, b. 18 Dec 1961, Belfast, Northern Ireland. Physician. m. Duncan Emerson, 16 July 1993, 1 son. Education: BSc, Honours, Pharmacology, 1983; MBBS, London, 1986; MRCOG, 1992; MFFP, 1993. Appointments: Senior Registrar in Obstetrics and Gynaecology, Newcastle-upon-Tyne. Memberships: RCOG; BMA. Hobbies: Skiing; Hockey; Tennis; Squash; Aerobics. Address: 92 East Boldon Road, Cleadon, Sunderland, Tyne and Wear SR6 7TD, England.

EMERY Paul Emile, b. 2 May 1922, Montreal, Canada. Physician. m. Virginia Olga Kenwick, 27 Jul 1979, 3 s, 2 d. Education: BA, Cum Laude, University of Montreal, 1942; Premedical Certificate, University of Montreal, 1943; MD, Cum Laude, University of Montreal, 1948. Appointments: US Army, Division of Psychiatry, Washington, 1953-55; Consultant, Veterans Administration, New Hampshire, 1962-64; Consultant, New Hampshire Division of Public Health, 1962-71; Private Practice, Concord, New Hampshire, 1962-85; Consultant, St Paul's School, Concord, New Hampshire, 1971-78; Medical Director, Forensic Univ, New Hampshire Hospital, 1980-82; Medical Director, New Hampshire Forensic Center, 1980-85; Consultant, New Hampshire Hospital, Concord, 1982-86; Consultant, Veterans Administration Hospital, New Hampshire, 1982-85; Consultant, Concord Hospital, New Hampshire, 1980-85; Clinical Director/Director for Stress Recovery, BA Medical Center, Ohio, 1985-87, 1987-88; Chief, Psychiatry Service, VA Medical Center, New Hampshire, 1989-. Publications: Journal Articles including, Secondary Mania in Late Life, 1994; Predisposing Variables in PTSD Patients, 1991; Clinical Indications for Inpatient Treatment of PTSD, 1988; The Task of Defining Stress, 1987. Honours: include, Winter Soldier Award for Intellectual and Clinical Leadership, Center for Stress Recovery, 1986; Certificate of Commendation, New Hampshire Medical Society, 1972; Salutation Plaque, New Hampshire Program on alcoholism and Drug Abuse, 1971. Memberships: include, American Psychiatric Association; National Association of VA Physicians; New Hampshire Medical Society. Address: VA Medical Center, 718 Smyth Road, Manchester, NH 03104, USA.

EMMETT Edward Anthony, b. 29 Feb 1940, Sydney, Australia. Medicine. m. Mary Emmett, 27 Dec 1975, 2 sons. Education: MB, BS, University of Sydney, 1964; MS, University of Cincinnati, 1975. Appointments: Resident Medical Officer, Royal Prince Alfred Hospital, Sydney, 1964-66; Repatriation General Hospital Concord, Australia, 1967-69; Fellow, University of Cincinnati, 1970; Assistant to Associate Professor, University of Cincinnati, 1971-78; Professor, Johns Hopkins University, 1978-88; Chief Executive, National Occupational Health & Safety Commission, Australia, Professor, University of Sydney, Sydney, Australia, 1989-. Publications: Editor-in-Chief, Year Book of Occupational Environmental Medicine, 1990-95; Over 100 articles and book chapters. Honours: Fight for Sight Citation for Clinical Research, 1987. Memberships: Royal Australian College of Physicians; American College of Occupational Environmental Medicine; Society of Toxicology; Society for Investigative Dermatology. Hobbies: Travel; Tennis; Golf. Address: 86 Glassop Street, Balmain, NSW 2041, Australia.

ENARI Tor-Magnus, b. 8 Oct 1928, Turku, Finland. Research Director (retired). m. Nita Enari, 17 June 1950, 1 son, 1 daughter. Education: Dr phil, Biochemistry, University of Helsinki, 1958. Appointments: Director, 1967-79, Research Director for Process Technology, 1983-93, VTT - Technical Research Centre of Finland; Research Professor, Academy of Finland, 1979-83; Currently Consultant. Publications: About 200 scientific articles in various journals of biotechnology, biochemistry and brewing. Honours: A I Virtanen Prize, 1983; Horace Brown Medal, 1987. Memberships: Societas Scientarum Fenniae; Finnish Academies of Technology, Chairman 1992-95; Fellow, Institute of Brewing. Address: Pohjoiskaari 13 A 1, FIN-00200 Helsinki, Finland.

ENDLER Norman Solomon, b. 2 May 1931, Montreal, Canada. Psychologist. m. Beatrice Kerdman, 26 Jun 1955, 1 s, 1 d. Education: BSc; MSc; PhD; Registered Psychologist, Ontario, Canada. Career: Psychologist, PA State University, 1958-60; Lecturer, Psychology, York University, Downsview, Ontario, 1960-62; Assistant Professor, 1962-65, Associate Professor, 1965-68, Professor, 1968-, York University; Consultant, Toronto East General Hospital, 1964-84. Publications: Co-author, Personality and Behavioural Disorders, 1977; Holiday of Darkness, 1982, revised, 1990; Co-author, Electroconvulsive therapy:

Myths and Realities, 1988; Co-author, Depression: New Directions, 1990. Honours: Canadian Council, 1969-78; Canadian Silver Jubilee Medal, 1978; Social Sciences and Humanities Research Council, 1979-80; SSHRC, 1991-94, 1994-97. Memberships: Fellow, Canada Council; Fellow, American Psychological Association; Canadian Psychological Association; Ontario Psychological Association; Royal Society of Canada. Hobbies: Reading Mystery Novels; Tennis; Travel. Address: Psychology Department, York University, North York, Ontario, Canada, M3J 1P3.

ENDO Banri, b. 16 Sept 1934, Tokyo, Japan. Professor. m. Sechie Endo, 12 Apr 1957, 1 son, 1 daughter. Education: Graduate School, Tokyo University. Appointments: Associate Professor, currently Professor, Tokyo University. Membership: Anthropological Society of Nippon. Address: Nakaochiai 2-20-2, Shinjuku-ku, Tokyo 161, Japan.

ENESCU Elena Simina, b. 9 Apr 1937, Gherla, Club, Rumania. Stomatologist. m. Dan Enescu, 28 May 1970, 1 daughter. Education: Specialisation in Prophylaxis and Implantology, Faculty of Stomatology, Bucharest, 1965. Appointments: Stomatologist; Chief, Vitan Dental Hospital; Methodologist, Prophylactic Oral Diseases, Bucharest; Currently Chief, Prophylactic Section, Founder, Vice-President, AMSLPR. Publications: Our Teeth, 1985; Who Knows Gains: The Golden Toothbrush, 1988; Articles include: Fluorization in the Prevention of Tooth Decay, 1982; Immediate Prothesis, 1983. Honours: National Champion and Record Holder in Skating; Patents: Reveplac, Rezisim, Simident, Andasim. Memberships: Founder Member, Health Messenger; Honorary Member, American Society of Implantology; Honorary Member, American Dental Society. Hobbies: Faith in God; Seaside. Address: Victoriei Street 224, Bl D5, Et 7, Ap 27, Bucharest Sector 1, Rumania.

ENGEL Marvin Leroy, b. 12 May 1936, Kansas City, MO, USA. Physician; Dermatologist. m. Sara Mizrachi, 24 Jul 1967, 1 s, 3 d. Education: BA, 1956, MD, 1959, Stanford University. Appointments: Clinical Associate Professor, University of CA, San Francisco; Private Practice. Memberships: AMA; CA Medical Association; American Academy of Dermatology; San Francisco Dermatology Society. Hobbies: Photography; Computers; Reading. Address: Building 2, Suite 110, 130 La Casa Via, Walnut Creek, CA 94598, USA.

ENGEL Tibor, b. 8 Mar 1938, Czechoslovakia. Physician. m. Renee Engel, 17 Feb 1972, 1 stepson, 2 daughters, 1 stepdaughter. Education: BA, Texas Western College, USA; MD, University of Texas Medical Branch. Appointments: Assistant Director, Obstetrics and Gynaecology, Denver General Hospital, Denver, Colorado; Clinical Professor, Obstetrics and Gynaecology, University of Colorado Health Sciences Center, Denver. Publications: 30 in various medical journals. Memberships: American College of Obstetricians and Gynecologists; American Fertility Society; American Association of Gynecologic Laparoscopists; Endocrine Society. Hobby: Collecting art. Address: 4500 E 9thAvenue, Denver, CO 80220, USA.

ENGEL W King, b. 19 Nov 1930, St Louis, USA. Neurologist; Medical Doctor. Education: BA, The Johns Hopking University, 1951; MD, CM, McGill University Faculty of Medicine, 1955. Appointments: Clinical Professor of Neurology, George Washington University School of Medicine, 1970-81; Professor of Neurology & Pathology, University of Southern California School of Medicine, 1981-. Publications: Basic concepts in the understanding of epilepsy, 1954; An inherited disease similar to amyotrophic lateral sclerosis: An intermediate form?, 1959; Some properties of cultured chick skeletal muscle with particular reference to fibrillation potential, 1959; Vascular deposits of immunoglobin and complement in idiopathic inflammatory myopathy, 1972; Ultrastructural development of explanted human skeletal muscle in tissue culture, 1972; Increased plasma enzyme concentrations in rats with functional ischemia of muscle provide a possible model of Duchenne musclar dystrophy, 1972; Twisted tubulofilaments in inclusion-body myositis muscle resemble paired helical filaments of Alzheimer brain and contain hyperphosphorylated tau, 1994; Apolipoprotein E immunoreactive deposits in inclusion-body muscle diseases, 1994. Memberships: Include: American Medical Association; American Academy of Neurology; American Neurological Association; Histochemical Society; American Society for Cell Biology. Address: 637 South Lucas Avenue, Los Angeles, CA 90017, USA.

ENGEL-HILLS Penelope Claire, b. 21 Oct 1955, Zambia. Radiographer. m. Colin Arthur Engel, 7 Apr 1990, 1 daughter. Education:

Diploma in Teaching Radiography, 1985, BScMed (Hons), Radiotherapy, 1989, University of Cape Town; Higher Diploma in Radiography (Therapy), SAMDC, 1986. Appointments: Radiographer, Rotterdam Radiotherapeutisch Instituut, 1970-80; Senior Radiographer, Zeeuws Radiotherapeutisch Instituut, 1980-81; Chief Radiographer, Groote Schuur Hospital, Observatory, 1982-91; Senior Lecturer, Peninsula Technikon, 1992-. Publications include: Neutron Therapy: Handbook, 1989; Chapter in "Radiation Therapy in Oncology for Health Care Professionals", 1995. Honours: Hospital Merit, 1987; Maybaker Award, 1989; Joyce Runnals Award, 1989. Memberships: Professional Board for Radiography, 1989-; Society of Radiographers of South Africa. Hobbies: Sailing; Hiking. Address: Radiography Education E45 OMB, Groote Schuur Hospital, Observatory 7925, South Africa.

ENGSTROM Hans Holger Helmer, b. 19 Oct 1912, Älgarås, Sweden. Researcher, University of Uppsala. m. Marianne Älberg, 3 Oct 1941, 1 son, 4 daughters. Education: MD, 1941; Jub Dr Member, Royal Society of Science. Appointments: Assistant Professor, Histology, Karoliosta Institute, Stockholm; Associate Professor, Gothenburg; Professor, University of Uppsala, Sweden, 1968. Publications: Otosclerosis, 1941; Structural Pattern of the Organ of Carti, 1966; Over 150 articles on the structure and ultrastructure of the ear. Memberships: Royal Society of Sciences, Uppsala; Royal Society of Medicine, London, England. Honours: Shambaugh Prize; Guyot Prize; Toynbee Prize; Amplifon Prize. Hobbies: Golf; Philately. Address: Börjegatan 1 B, 75373 Uppsala, Sweden.

EPSTEIN Leon J, b. 7 June 1917, Jersey City, New Jersey, USA. Psychiatrist. m. Ellen Buchanarı, 2 June 1984, 1 son, 1 daughter. Education: MD; PhD. Appointments: Staff Psychiatrist, St Elizabeth's Hospital, 1954-56; Deputy Director, California Department Mental Hygiene, 1956-61; Professor, Associate Director, Department of Psychiatry, 1961-83, Interim Chair, Psychiatry, 1985-86, Professor Emeritus, Department of Psychiatry, 1987-, University of California at San Francisco. Publications: Author of numerous books and articles in psychogerontology and psychopharmacology. Honours: J Elliott Royer Award, 1976; Outstanding Achievement Award, NCPS, 1985; Establishment of Leon J Epstein Chair in Geriatric Psychiatry, University of California San Francisco, 1986. Memberships: American Board of Psychiatry and Neurology; American College Neuropsychopharmacology; American College of Psychiatrists; American Geriatrics Society; American Psychiatric Association; Gerontological Society of America; North California Psychiatric Society. Address: 350 Parnassus Avenue, Suite 309, San Francisco, CA 94117, USA.

EPSTEIN Marsha, b. 4 Feb 1945, Chicago, IL, USA. Physician. m. Syyed Tariq Mahmood, 14 Jun 1975, 1 s. Education: BA, Reed College, 1966; MD, University of California, San Francisco, 1969; MPH, University of California, Berkeley School of Public Health, 1971. Fellowship in Family Planning, University of California at Los Angeles, Department of Obstetrics & Gynaecology, 1973-74. Appointments: Physician Specialist, Los Angeles County, 1974-75; Physician Coordinator, University of California at Los Angeles, Family Planning Nurse Practitioner Program, 1975-77; Private Practice as General Practitioner, 1978-82; District Health Officer, Inglewood District, Los Angeles County, 1982-. Publications: Co-Author: Reduction of High Risk Sexual Behavior among Heterosexuals Undergoing HIV Antibody Testing: A Radomized Clinical Trial, 1991. Memberships: American Medical Women's Association; American Public Health Association; American College of Physician Executives. Address: 123 W Manchester Blvd, Inglewood, CA 90301, USA.

EPSTEIN Richard S, b. 28 Nov 1939, New York, USA. Psychiatrist. Education: MD, Washington University, School of Medicine, St Louis, MD, USA; BS, Yale University, 1960; Psychiatric Resident, Johns Hopkins; Clinical Associate in Psychiatry, National Institute of Mental Health. Appointments: Private Practice, Psychiatry, 1969-; Clinical Professor, Georgetown University, School of Medicine; Clinical Professor, Uniformed Services University of the Health Sciences. Publications: Keeping Boundaries: Maintaining Safety and Integrity in the Psychotherapeutic Process, 1994; Co-Author, Anxiety Disorders. Memberships: Fellow, American Psychiatric Association; Washington Psychiatric Society; American Medical Association; American Academy of Psychiatry and the Law. Address: 10401 Old Georgetown Road, Bethesda, MA 20814-1911, USA.

ERÄNEN Liisa Maria, b. 27 Sep 1955, Hämeenlinna, Finland. Researcher. m. Simo Eränen, 18 July 1980, 1 son, 1 daighter. Education: MA, Social Psychology and Social Work, University of Helsinki. Appointments: Researcher, University of Helsinki; Researcher, Ministry of Interiors, Rescue Department; Therapist, Helsinki Youth Clinic. Publications: Disaster Psychology, 1991; Coping with Disaster, Helping Behaviour of Individuals and Societies, Co-author, 1993; Psychological Consequences of Accidents and Disasters, 1993; Reactions of a Society in Exceptional Situations. Memberships: European Society for Traumatic Stress Studies, Board Member; International Society for Traumatic Stress Studies; International Association of Trauma Counsellors. Hobbies: literature; Music. Address: Department of Social Psychology, POB 4, FIN-00014 University of Helsinki, Finland.

ERIJMAN Mauricio Oscar, b. 9 Sept 1944, Buenos Aires, Argentina. Medical Doctor. m. Helida Teakinski, 24 June 1972, 1 son, 1 daughter. Education: MD; Certified Cardiologist. Appointments: Resident, Internal Medicine, Buenos Aires, 1969; Fellow, Cardiology, Potah Tirva, Israel, 1974; Private Practice, Buenos Aires. Publications: Several professional publications in journals. Memberships: New York Academy of Sciences. Hobbies: Golf; Travel. Address: Juncal 1695 6/K, Buenos Aires 1062, Argentina.

ERLICH Sara Riwka, b. 23 Aug 1938, Recife, Pernambuco, Brazil. Psychiatrist; Psychoanalyst; Writer. Widow. Education: MD, Federal University of Pernambuco; Specialisation in Child and Adolescent Psychiatry; Training in Rehabilitation Medicine; Complete Psychoanalytic Training. Appointments: Co-Founder, Assistant Director, Northeast Rehabilitation; Department Chief, State Mental Hospital, Pernambuco; Currently Training Analyst, Teacher, Supervisor, Recife. Publications: Stories That Had To Be Told, 1982; The Time of the Acacias: On the Way to Shechinah, 1982; Uma Introducâo ad Estudo da Psicanalise e do Pensar, 1985; Relatos Psicanaliticos, 1991; Psychiatric and psychoanalytic articles in journals. Honours: Graduated in 1st place, Faculty of Medicine, 1958; Guest, Psychoanalytical Society of Israel, 1987; Member: Asociacion Internacional de Escritores Judios en Lengua Hispana y Portuguesa, 1987; Academia Cabofriense de Letras, Rio, 1991; International Association of Medical Writers in the Portuguese Language, 1993. Memberships: Brazilian Medical Association; Brazilian Psychiatric Association; Full Member, Brazilian Psychoanalytic Society, Rio; Full Member, Psychoanalytic Study Group, Recife; Society for Adolescent Medicine, USA; International Rehabilitation Medicine Association. Hobbies: Reading; Cinema; Music; Walking; Travel. Address: Av Rosa e Silva 1350, 6o, Apt 604, Edificio Pedro Mello-Aflitos, CEP 52050-020, Recife, Pernambuco, Brazil.

ERVERDI Nejat, b. 5 Sept 1957, Ankara, Turkey. Orthodontist. m. Feryal Erverdi, 5 Sept 1984. 1 son, 1 daughter. Education: Dentist, 1981, Orthodontist, 1988, Hacattepe University. Appointments: Research Assistant, Hacettepe University, 1981-85; Military service, 1985-87; Assistant Professor, 1987-89, Associate Professor, 1989-94, Professor, 1994-, Marmara University. Publications: Comparison of two different expansion techniques from the point of root resorption, 1994; Cephalometric Investigation of the Clinical Effects of the Elastic Bite Block Appliance, 1994. Honours: Best Academician of the Year Award, Marmara University, 1993. Memberships: European Orthodontics Society; Turkish Orthodontic Society. Hobbies: Skiing; Tennis; Swimming. Address: Büyükçiftlik sok 24/10, 80200 Nisantasi, Istanbul, Turkey.

ERYUKHIN Igor Aleksandrovitch, b. 28 Dec 1936, St Petersburg, Russia. General Surgeon. m. Svetlana Ivanova, 13 Aug 1968, 2 daughters. Education: Military Medical Academy, 1960. Appointments: Medical Officer, Paratroop Battalion, 1960; Chief of Postgraduate Surgery Department, Military Medical Academy, 1977; Chief of Field Surgery Department, 1985. Publications: Bleedings in gastro-intestinal diseases, co-author, 1987; Inflammation as a general biological reaction. On the model of acute peritonites, 1989; Acute ileus, 1989; Textbook on Field Surgery, 1995; Endotoxicosis in Surgical Clinic, 1995. Honours: Order, The Red Star, Military Medals. Memberships: President, Pirogov Surgical Society; Member of Government, Russian Surgical Society; Deputy Editor, Vestnik chirurgii im I. I. Grecova. Hobbies: Classical Music. Address: Military Medical Academy, Botkinskaya St 20, St Petersburg 194175, Russia.

ESHER Frederick Justus Swinton, b. 11 Jun 1903, London, England. Psychiatrist. m. (1) Phyllis Binfield Shammon, 1 Jun 1935, 1

d, (2) Edith Nicholls Whitehead, 10 Jun 1983. Education: Universities of Birmingham, Leeds and Nottingham; MBChB; MRCS; LRCP; DPM; FRCPsych; Chartered Psychologist. Career: GP, Staffordshire, 1926-29; AMO, Nottinghamshire County Mental Hospital, 1929-32, Calderstones Institute for Mental Defectives, 1932-36, Manchester Child Guidance Clinic, 1933-39; Director, Sheffield Child Guidance Clinic, 1937-39; Medical Director, Sheffield Mental Health Services, 1937-66; Senior Lecturer in Psychiatry, Sheffield University, 1938-66, Osmania University, India, 1944-46; Consultant to EMS, Sheffield, 1940-42; Major, RAMC, 1942-46; Psychiatrist to Scientific Committee, Home Office and Civil Defence; Psychiatrist, Sheffield Hospital Board, 1947-57; Senior Lecturer in Psychiatry, University of Saskatchewan, 1966-68; Consultant, University Hospital on loan to WHO for Caribbean survey on mental hospital facilities, 1972; Psychiatrist Emeritus, Sheffield Hospitals for the Mentally Subnormal, 1967. Memberships: Royal College of Psychiatrists; Geographical Society; British Psychological Society. Hobbies include: Travel; Photography; Electronic Organs. Address: 3 Montrose Court, Hill Turrets Close, Bents Green, Sheffield, S11 9RF, England.

ESPINOZA Luis R, b. 3 Jul 1943, Peru. Medical Doctor. m. Carmen G Espinoza, 20 Dec 1969, 1 s, 1 d. Education: MD. Career: Resident in Medicine, Barnes Hospital, St Louis, MO; Fellow in Rheumatology, Washington University, St Louis, MO; Fellow in Immunology, Rockefeller University; Assistant Professor, Medicine, McGill University; Associate Professor, Medicine, University of South FL College of Medicine; Currently, Professor and Chief, Section of Rheumatology, LSU Medical Center. Publication: Infections in the Rheumatic Diseases, Psoriatic Arthritis. Memberships: American College of Rheumatology; American College of Physicians. Hobbies: Music; Reading. Address: LSU Medical Center, 1542 Tulane Avenue, New Orleans, LA 70112-2822, USA.

ESTRIDGE Trudy D, b. 12 Dec 1961, Olney, Texas, USA. Biomedical Engineer. Education: BSc, Bioengineering, Texas A&M University, Texas, 1983; MSc, Bioengineering, Texas A&M University, Texas, 1988; PhD, Biomedical Engineering, University of Alabama, Birmingham, Alabama, 1991. Appointments: Research Scientist. Publications: A Quantification of Vascular Ingrowth into Dacron Velour, 1991; A Comparison of Three Techniques to Study Vascular Ingrowth into Dacron Velour, 1988; Techniques to Quantify Vascular Ingrowth into Porous Biomaterials, 1988; The Use of Oxygen to Activate Fibroblasts in Non-Healing Wounds, 1988; Quantifying Vascular Ingrowth into Dacron Velour, 1988; The Effects of Chelated Silver on the Success of Percutaneous Devices, 1988; Microcasting: A Technique to Study Vascular Ingrowth of Biological Implants, 1985. Honours include: University of Alabama Dean's Award for Engineering Graduate Student, 1990; Department of Biomedical Engineering Outstanding Graduate Student Award, University of Alabama, 1989-90, 1990-91; National Collegiate Engineering Award, 1990; Tau Beta Pi, 1989; Sigma Xi, 1988; Distinguished Student Award, Texas A&M University, 1983; Texas A&M University Opportunity Award, 1980; Southland Corporation Scholarship, 1979-81; Scott Whitaker Memorial Scholarship, 1979. Memberships: Society for Biomaterials; American Society of Testing and Materials; The Biomedical Engineering Society; Controlled Release Society; Tissue Culture Association. Hobbies: Computers. Address: Collagen Corporation, 2500 Faber Place, Palo Alto, CA 94303, USA.

ETTINGER Lawrence Jay, b. 17 Dec 1947, Brooklyn, NY, USA. Physician. m. Alice Renick, 16 Nov 1986. Education: BA, cum laude, Biology, 1969, MD, 1973, Case Western Reserve University, Cleveland, OH. Appointments include: Member of various committees; Associate Professor of Pediatrics, University of Medicine and Dentistry of NJ, Robert Wood Johnson Medical School, 1984-; Attending physician at various hospitals including: St Peter's Medical Center, 1985-; Consultant for various medical centers including: CentraState Medical Center, 1991-, Muhlenberg Regional Medical Center, 1993-. Publications include: 116 presentations, 59 abstracts, chapters in books, over 50 articles in professional journals including: Hematology-Oncology, in A Core Textbook of Pediatrics for Medical Students, 1994 in press. Honours include: Phi Beta Kappa, 1970; UMDNJ University Excellence Award for Patient Care, 1991; Governor's Awards, The Pride of NJ, The Clara Barton Medical Service Award for Outstanding Contributions to Welfare of Human Life, 1992; NJ Pride Award for Health, 1993. Memberships include: Childrens Cancer Group; Fellow, American Academy of Pediatrics; American Society of Clinical Oncology; American Society of Hematology; AMA; American Association for Cancer Research; Pediatric Hematology Oncology Network of NJ; Academy of Medicine of NJ. Hobbies: Travel; Photography. Address:

Department of Pediatrics, University of Medicine and Dentistry of New Jersey, Robert Wood Johnson Medical School; 1 Robert Wood Johnson Place, CN19, New Brunswick, NJ 08903-0019, USA.

ETZEL Ruth Ann, b. 6 Apr 1954, Milwaukee, WI, USA. Pediatrician; Epidemiologist. Education: BA Summa Cum Laude, Biology, University of Minnesota, Minneapolis, 1973-76; MD, University of Wisconsin, School of Medicine, Madison, 1976-80; Pediatrics Resident, North Carolina Memorial Hospital, North Carolina, 1980-83; PhD, Department of Epidemiology, School of Public Health, University of North Carolina, North Carolina, 1983-85; Robert Wood Johnson Clinical Scholar, University of North Carolina, North Carolina, 1983-85. Appointments: Epidemic Intelligence Service Officer, Center for Environmental Health, Centers for Disease Control, Atlanta, Georgia, 1985-87; Medical Epidemiologist, Center for Environmental Health and Injury Control, Centers for Disease Control, Atlanta, Georgia, 1987-90; Chief, Air Pollution and Respiratory Health Branch, National Center for Environmental Health, Centers for Disease Control and Prevention, Atlanta, Georgia, 1991-. Publications: Author: Passive Smoking and Middle Ear Effusion Among Children in Day Care, 1992. Honours: Phi Beta Kappa, University of Minnesota, 1976; Arthur S Flemming Award, Scientific Category, 1991; J D Lane Clinical Society Open Award for most significant contribution in original health research, 1992. Memberships: Ambulatory Pediatric Association; American Academy of Pediatrics; American Public Health Association; American College of Epidemiology; Physicians for Social Responsibility; Society for Epidemiologic Research; Society for Pediatric Epidemiologic Research. Hobbies: Skiing. Address: Centers for Disease Control and Prevention, Mailstop F-39, 4770 Buford Highway, NE, Chamblee, Georgia 30341-3724, USA.

EUZÉBY Jacques Achille, b. 11 Aug 1920, Bagnols, Céze, France. Emeritus Professor. m. Renee Gayte, 20 May 1944, 2 sons, 4 daughters. Education: DVM; MSc, Biology. Appointments: Assistant Lecturer in Parasitology; Lecturer in Parasitology; Docent in Parasitology; Professor of Parasitology and Parasitic Diseases; Emeritus Professor of Parasitology and Parasitic Diseases, Ecole Veterinaire de Lyon. Publications: Author of 11 books on parasitology, 1956-89; Author of 2 books of medical mycology, 1993, 1994; Contributor of over 400 articles on parasitology. Honours: Doctor, Honoris Causa, Universities Torino and Timisoara, Romania 1969; Membre de l'Academie Nationale de Medecine; Membre de l'Academie Veterinare de France, 1985; Membre de l'Academie Royale des Sciences Veterinaires d'Espagne, 1993; Prix de Parasitologie Emile Brumpt and Pfizer, 1993; Former President, World Association for the Advancement of Veterinary Parasitology, 1965-69. Hobbies: Literature; Poetry; History. Address: 149 Rue Vauban, 69006 Lyon, France.

EVANS Frederic M, b. 18 July 1926, Iowa, USA. Doctor of Psychiatry & Psychoanalysis. m. Mary Hawkins, 2 sons. Education: MD; FAPA. Appointments: Private Practice, Psychiatry & Psychoanalysis. Memberships: Winchester Psychoanalytic Association. Hobbies: Sailing. Address: 74 Cross Pond Road, Pound Ridge, NY 10576, USA.

EVANS Mark Ira, b. 14 May 1952, Brooklyn, NY, USA. Physician. m. Wendy J Evans, 5 Sep 1981, 2 d. Education: BS, magna cum laude, Tufts University, MA, 1973; MD, Distinction in Research, SUNY, Brooklyn, NY, 1978. Career: Resident, University of Chicago, 1978-82; Fellow, National Institutes of Health, Bethesda, 1982-84; Currently: Professor and Vice Chief, Obstetrics and Gynaecology, Professor of Molecular Medicine and Genetics, Professor of Pathology, Wayne State University. Publications: Co-author, Fetal Diagnosis and Therapy, 1989; Author, Reproductive Risks and Prenatal Diagnosis, 1992. Honours: President, International Fetal Medical Surgery Society, 1987 and 1997; Central Award, Obstetrics and Gynaecology, 1988. Memberships: American College of Obstetrics and Gynaecology; Society of Gynaecologic Investigation; Society Perinatal Obstetricians; American Society Human Genetics; American College of Medical Genetics; American Gynaecological & Obstetrical Society. Hobby: Golf. Address: Department of Obstetrics and Gynaecology, Hutzel Hospital, Wayne State University, 4707 St Antoine, Detroit, MI 48201, USA.

EVERETT Warren Douglas, b. 8 Apr 1945, Wichita, Kansas, USA. Physician. divorced. 3 sons. Education: BS; BMS; MPH; MD. Appointments: US Air Force, 1964-88; Residency Director, John Peter Smith Hospital, Ft Worth, Texas; Chief, Family Practice Program, University of Alabama, Huntsville. Publications: Numerous publications in professional scientific journals. Memberships: American Academy of Family Practice; Aerospace Medical Association; Society of Teachers of Family Medicine. Address: 201 Governor's Drive, Huntsville, AL 35801, USA.

EVERSON Richard B, b. 20 Dec 1946, New York, USA. Physician. m. May 1979, 3 s. Education: BS; MD; MPH. Appointments: Medical Officer, US Public Health Service, National Institute of Environmental Health Sciences and National Cancer Institute; Medical. Epidemiologic Research. Publications include: Enzymatic Determinants of Responsiveness of the LPC-1 Plasma Cell Neoplasm to Fluorouracil and Fluorodeoxyuridine, Co-author, 1970; Late Mortality in Wilm's Tumor, 1975; Individuals Transplacentally Exposed to Maternal Smoking May Be At Increased Cancer Risk in Adult Life, 1980; Passive Smoking in Adulthood and Cancer Risk, Co-aithor, 1985; The Effect of Chemotherapy on the In Vivo Frequency of Glycophorin, Co-author. Memberships: American Association Cancer Research; Society for Epidemiologic Research. Address: 115 Burnwood Ct, Chapel Hill, NC 27711, USA.

EVERY Ronald Gresham, b. 30 September 1912, Dunedin, New Zealand. Thegotist. m. Ferne Sollenberger, 12 May 1938, 2 sons, 2 daughters. Education: BDS, Otago University, 1936; DDS, Northwestern University, USA, 1938. Appointments: Private Dental Practice, Christchurch, 1939-64; Honorary Research Fellow, University of Canterbury, 1964-80; Lecturer, Departments of Anatomy and Dental Anthropology, University of Chicago, USA, 1966, 1968; Research Affiliate, Vertebrate Paleontology, Yale University, USA, 1966; Guest Professor, Geologisch-Palaontologisches Institut, Freie Universitat, Berlin, 1967-68; Lecturer in Zoology, University of Canterbury, 1970-71. Publications: The Significance of Extreme Mandibular Movements, 1960; The Teeth as Weapons: Their Influence on Behaviour, 1965; Sharpness of Teeth in Man and Other Primates, 1970; A New Terminology for Mammalian Teeth: Founded on the Phenomenon of Thegosis, 1972; Thegosis in Prosimians, 1974; Significance of Tooth Sharpness for Mammalian, Especially Primate Evolution, 1975. Honours: Sydney Fellow, University of Otago School of Dentistry, 1976; Honorary Life Member, Canterbury Branch of New Zealand Dental Association. Hobbies: Photography; Sailing; Skiing. Address: 9 Clifton Spur, Sumner, Christchurch, New Zealand.

EWBANK Josephine Alice, b. 28 Aug 1917, Hong Kong. Obstetrician and Gynaecologist. m. 9 Oct 1976, 1 daughter. Education: MB ChB; MD; FRCOG. Appointments: Resident Obstetric Officer, Resident House Surgeon, Simpson Maternity Pavillion, Edinburgh, Scotland; Resident House Surgeon, Senior Obstetric and Gynaecology, Cumberland Infirmary, Carlisle; Retired. Publications: Vitamin B and Toxaemia of Pregnancy, 1943; Report of 2 Cases of Precocious Puberty, 1955; An Assessment of the Value of Hypnosis in Pregnancy and Labour, 1962; Problem of Abortion, 1972. Honours: Aunandale Gold Medal for Surgery; Buachanan Prize for Midwifery and Gynaecology, 1941; Vaughan Scholarship for Midwifery and Forensic Medicine, 1941. Memberships: Chairman, Medical Staff Committee, 1974; Chairman, DMC, 1975; President, Medical Staff, 1972. Hobbies: Cine Photography; Sailing; Lapidary. Address: Flat 7 Castle Court, Castle Street, Carlisle, Cumbria CA3 8TP, England.

EXELBERT Lois Love, b. 11 Dec 1948, Brooklyn, NY, USA. Registered Nurse. Div, 3 s, 1 d. Education: BS, Nursing, Hunter College, NY, 1970; Certified, Childbirth Educator, 1980; ADA Post Graduate Course, Orlando, FL, 1982; MS, Adult Education, FL International University, 1982. Appointments include: Staff, Jefferson Medical College Hospital, PA, 1968-70; Various positions including: Diabetes Teaching Coordinator, 1972-85; ASPO Childbirth Educator, 1978-; Co-Developer and Instructor, Prenatal-Postnatal Fitness Program, 1982-; Visiting Nurse; Administrator, Joslin Diabetes Clinic, 1991-, Baptist Hospital of Miami Inc. Publications include: Co-author of many publications including: An Interagency Effort for Media Development (article), in Diabetes Educator, 1982; Parenting During Pregnancy, newsletter series, 1982; Over 30 lectures given, 1972-. Memberships include: Florida Organization of Nurse Executives; Aerobics and Fitness Association of America; American Diabetes Association; American Society for Psychoprophylaxis in Obstetrics; Advisory Board, FL International University School of Nutrition and Diabetes; President, Baptist Hospital's Toastmasters Club, 1991. Hobbies: Painting; Poetry; Writing; Film Review. Address: 9405 SW 89th Street, Miami, FL 33176, USA.

EXTEIN Irl Lawrence, b. 3 Mar 1948, St Louis, MO, USA. Psychiatrist. m. Barbara Sundheimer, 6 Feb 1974, 3 s, 1 d. Education: BA, University of Chicago; MD, Yale University, 1974. Appointments: Residency in Psychiatry, Yale, 1975-77; Clinical Associate, NIMH, 1977-79; Director, Neuropsychiatric Evaluation Unit, Fair Oaks Hospital, NJ, 1979-82; Medical Director, Falkirk Hospital, NY, 1982-84; Medical Director, Fair Oaks Hospital, FL, 1984-92; Private Practice. Publications: Hypothyroidism and Depression, 1981; The TRH Test in Mani and Schizophrenia, 1982; Medical Mimics of Psychiatric Disorders, Co-Editor, 1986. Honours: Best Doctors in America, 1993; Editorial Board, Psychosomatics. Memberships: AMA; APA; Society of Biological Psychiatry. Hobbies: Sports; Kids. Address: 16244 S Military Trail #280, Delray Beach, FL 33484, USA.

EYSENCK Hans Jürgen, b. 4 Mar 1916, Berlin, Germany. Psychologist. m. 4 sons, 1 daughter. Education: BA; DSc; PhD. Appointments: Researcher, 1942-48; Reader, 1949-55; Professor, 1955-83. Publications: Many publications in professional journals. Memberships: American Psychological Association; British Psychological Society; German Psychological Society. Hobbies: Tennis; Squash; Reading; Thinking. Address: 10 Dorchester Drive, London SE24 0DQ, England.

EYSENCK Sybil Bianca Giuletta, b. Vienna, Austria. Psychologist. m. Prof H J Eysenck, 30 Oct 1950, 3 s, 1 d. Education: BSc; PhD. Appointments: Justice of The Peace; Psychologist now retired. Publications: Co-author, Personality Structure and Measurement, 1969; Co-author, Psychoticism as A Dimension of Personality, 1976; Co-author, Individual Differences in Children and Adolescents, 1988; 178 Articles in psychological journals. Membership: Fellow, British Psychological Society. Address: 10 Dorchester Drive, Herne Hill, London, SE24 0SQ, England.

EZEILO Bernice Nwakaego, b. 7 Apr 1943, Nanka, Nigeria. Clinical Psychologist. m. Gabriel C Ezeilo, 17 Oct 1963, 3 sons, 1 daughter. Education: SRN, School of Nursing, University College Hospital, Ibadan, 1965; BSc, Psychology, Zoology, 1971, MA, Abnormal and Clinical Psychology, 1975, University of Zambia, Lusaka; PhD, Clinical Psychology, University of Nigeria, Nsukka, 1984. Appointments: Clinical Instructor, 1967-69, Tutor, School of Nursing, 1971-75, University Teaching Hospital, Lusaka; Assistant Lecturer, 1975-76, Lecturer II, 1976-79, Lecturer I, 1979-81, Senior Lecturer, 1981-86, Reader, Clinical Psychologist, Coordinator of Clinical Training Programme, 1986-, Department Head, 1991-94, Department of Psychology, University of Nigeria, Nsukka. Publications include: The Identification and Assessment of the Mentally Retarded in Africa, 1979; Assessing Weight Conservation Nonverbally: The Problem of Conceptualization among African Children, 1981; Age, Sex and Self Concepts in a Nigerian Population, 1983; School Psychology in Nigeria, 1989; Self Concept and Psychopathology, 1990; Psychology and Health in Africa, 1990; Western Psychological Therapies and the African Client, 1994. Honours: Chartered Psychologist, British Psychological Society, 1989. Memberships: Associate Fellow, British Psychological Society; Secretary, Nigerian Association of Clinical Psychologists; Secretary, Nigerian Psychological Association; American Psychological Association. Hobbies: Singing, choral and solo (soprano); Reading; Writing. Address: Department of Psychology, University of Nigeria, Nsukka, Nigeria.

EZERIETIS Evalds, b. 26 December 1913, Gulbene, Latvia. Professor of Surgery. m. Velta Svarcbach, 1 son, 1 daughter. Education: Graduate, Faculty of Medicine, Latvian University. Appointments: Secretary General, Latvian Association of Surgeons, 1960-74. Publications: Numerous professional publications. Honours: Honorary Member, Latvian Academy of Sciences, 1992. Hobbies: Long Distance Walking. Address: Latvian Academy of Medicine, The Chair of Surgery No 2, 16 Dzirciema Str, LV 1007 Riga, Latvia.

F

FABB Wesley Earl, b. 19 Mar 1930, Ultima, Australia. Medicine. m. Marian Clara Fabb, 21 Feb 1987, 4 s, 2 d. Education: MB, BS, University of Melbourne, 1955; MRACGP, 1967; FRACGP, 1971; FCGPS, 1974; FFGP, South Africa, 1975; MCFPC; 1979; FRCGP, 1986; FHKCGP, 1990; FCGPSL, 1992; FRNZCGP, 1992. Appointments include: Visiting Assistant Physician, Alfred Hospital, Melbourne, 1972-93; Numerous Educational and Administrative Posts, Consultancies and Assignments, 1966-; Currently: Professor of Family Medicine, Chinese University of Hong Kong; Honorary Clinical Associate Professor, Department of Community Medicine, Monash University, Melbourne. Publications include: Over 80 publications, 1967-, including: Co-author, Principles of Practice Management, 1984; Co-author, The Nature of General Family Practice, 1983; Numerous national and international addresses given, 1972-93. Honours include: ANZAME Award of Achievement in Medical Education, 1983; Member of the Order of Australia for Services to Medicine and Health Education, 1987; Royal Australian College of General Practitioners Rose Hunt Award and Medal, 1991. Memberships include: Honorary Secretary and Treasurer, 1980-93, Chief Executive Officer, 1993-, World Organization of Family Doctors, WONCA; Affiliate Royal Society of Medicine, 1976-; Editorial Board, Family Practice, 1982-; Editorial Board, The Medical Annual, 1990-; Chairman Academic Board, Executive Council, Hong Kong Institute of Family Medicine. Hobbies: Travel; Computers. Address: Dept of Community and Family Medicine, Chinese University of Hong Kong, 4th Floor, Lek Yuen Health Centre, Shatin NT, Hong Kong.

FADEL Hossam Eldin, b. 15 Oct 1940, Cairo, Egypt. Obstetrician; Gynaecologist. m. Skina Ibrahim Fuoad Fadel, 25 Aug 1965, 2 sons. Education: MB BCh; D Ob Gyn; DS; PhD, Cairo; Board Certified in Obstetrics and Gynaecology; Board Certified in Maturnal Fetal Medicine, USA. Appointments: Instructor, Tutor, Ob-Gyn Department, Ain Shames University, Cairo; Assistant Professor, Ob-Gyn Department, Rush Medical College, Chicago, USA; Assistant Professor, Associate Professor, Professor, Ob-Gyn Department, Medical College of Georgia, Augusta, Georgia; Director of Perinatology, University Hospital; Clinical Professor of Ob-Gyn, University Hospital and Medical College of Georgia. Publications include: Diagnosis and Management of Obstetric Emergencies, 1982. Memberships: American Medical Association; Society of Perinatal Obstetricians; Society of Gynaecological Investigation; Fellow, American College of Obstetricians and Gynaecologists; Islamic Medical Association of America; National Perinatal Association. Address: University Professional Centre II, Suite 200, 818 Sebastian Way, Augusta, GA 30901, USA.

FADEM Stephen Zale, b. 18 May 1948, Tulsa, Oklahoma, USA. Medical Doctor. m. Joyce Abramson Fadem, 2 sons, 1 daughter. Education: MD, Univeristy of Oklahoma College of Medicine, 1973. Appointment: Nephrologist, Medical Director, Houston Kidney Center Integrated Systems. Publications: Numerous professional publications in scientific journals. Honours: Sir Alexander Fleming Scholarship Finalist, 1965; American Heart Association, Council on the Kidney Traveler's Scholarship, 1977; Physician's Recognition Award; National Service Research Award, 1976-77; Distinguished Service Award, National Kidney Foundation, 1989; Myron D Jenkins Award, National Kidney Foundation of Southeast Texas, 1991. Memberships: American Society of Internal Medicine; American Colelge of Physicians, Fellow; Harris County Medical Society; Houston Kidney Internal Medicine; American Medical Association; Texas Medical Association; Texas Medical Foundation; American Federation Clinical Research; American Society of Nephrology; International Society of Nephrology; American Heart Association. Hobbies: Computer Graphics; World History; Fishing. Address: 1200 Binz, Suite 300, Houston, TX 77004, USA.

FAERSTEIN Saul J, b. 17 Nov 1943, New York, USA. Forensic Psychiatry. m. Victoria Rothberg, 30 Mar 1969, 1 s, 1 d. Education: AB, Brandeis University, 1964; MD, New York University, 1968; Fellowship, USC, School of Medicine, Institute of Psychiatry and Law, 1974-75. Appointments: Assistant Director, USC Institute of Psychiatry and Law, 1975-80; Assistant Clinical Professor of Psychiatry, University of California at Los Angeles, School of Medicine. Honours: Fellow, American Psychiatric Association, 1994. Memberships: APA; AAPL. Hobbies: Tennis. Address: 360 North Bedford Drive, Beverly Hills, VA 90210, USA.

FAIRWEATHER-TAIT Susan Jane, b. 17 July 1949, King's Lynn, Norfolk, England. Research Scientist. m. Christopher McEvoy, 17 May 1986, 1 son. Education: BSc, Food Science; MSc, Distinction; PhD. Appointments: Research Nutritionist, Beecham Products, 1978-79; Senior Scientific Officer, Institute of Food Research, 1979-86; Principal Research Scientist, Institute of Food Research, 1986-. Publications: Dietary Reference Values for Food Energy and Nutrients for the United Kingdom, 1991; The Metabolism of Iron and Its Bioavailability in Foods, 1992. Honours: Honorary Lecturer, University of East Anglia, 1990-. Memberships: American Institute of Nutrition; American Society for Clinical Nutrition; European Academy of Nutritional Scientists. Hobbies: Gardening; Reading; Swimming; Entertaining 7 year old Son. Address: Institute of Food Research, Norwich Laboratory, Norwich Research Park, Colney, Norwich NR4 7UA, England.

FALKNER Frank Tardrew, b. 27 Oct 1918, Hale, England. Physician. m. June Dixon, 21 Jan 1948, 1 s, 1 d. Education: MRCS; LRCP (Lond); MD, KY, USA; MRCP(Lond); FRCP(Lond). Career: First Assistant, Institute of Child Health, Hospital for Sick Children, University of London; Chair, Department of Pediatrics, University of Louisville School of Medicine; Associate Director, National Institute of Child Health, Public Health Service, USA; Director, Fels Research, Institute Ohio; Chair, MCH Program, University of CA, Berkeley; Currently, Professor Emeritus. Publications: Co-editor, Human Growth, 2nd edition, 1986; Editor, Infant and Child Nutrition Worldwide, 1991; Co-author, Prenatal Influences on Postnatal Growth. Honours: Markle Scholar in Medical Science, 1957-62; Fellow, American Academy of Pediatrics, 1966; Diplomate, American Board of Clinical Nutrition, 1967; Senior Member, Institute of Medicine National Academy of Science, 1985. Memberships: Vice President, American Memorial Hospital Board; Editor in Chief, International Child Health, International Pediatric Association; College Overseas Advisor, Royal College of Physicians, UK. Hobbies: Music; Motor Racing. Address: International Child Health, University of California, 308 Warren Hall, Berkeley, CA 94720, USA.

FALKOWSKI Wojciech, b. 17 June 1930, Poland. Medical Doctor. m. M B McManus, 8 Sept 1959, 2 sons. Education: MB; BCh; BAO; LM; MRCGP; MPhil; FRC Psychiat. Appointments: Examiner, Royal College of Psychiatrists; Co-founder, Editorial Board, British Journal of Psychotherapy; Vice President, Center for Psychoanalytic Psychotherapy; Chairperson, Polish Medical Association; Pro-Rector, Polish Universities Abroad. Publications: Group psychotherapy for alcoholics and drug addicts, 1991; Other chapters and articles in journals on psychotherapy, addiction and other topics. Memberships: Royal College of Psychiatrists; Polish Medical Association; Royal Society of Medicine. Honours: Polonia Restituta, Polish Second Highest Civil Award, 1991; First Prize, British Arts Council, Kensington & Chelsea, England, 1991. Hobbies: Music; Painting. Address: 1 Eardley Road, London SW16 6DA, England.

FALVO Cathey, b. 6 Dec 1941, New York City, USA. Physician. 1 d. Education: MD, SUNY at Syracuse, 1968; MPH, Columbia University School of PUblic Health, 1977. Appointments: Assistant Director, Child and Youth Project, Roosevelt Hospital, NY, 1973-78; Director Paediatrics, Ossming Open Door Health Centre, 1978-92; Director, Epidemiology, New York Medical College, 1981-93; Medical Consultant, Westchester County Department of Health, 1979-81; Program Director, International and Public Health. Publications: Immunizations: An Ongoing Need, 1975; CHAP: A Study in Duplication and Fragmentation of Services, 1979; Rubella Screening and Immunization in Adolescent Clinic, 1979; Reversible Quadraplegia in acHild with H.Inf, 1987; Adverse Reactions Associated with Simultaneous Multiple Vaccines in Travelers, 1994. Memberships: Fellow, American Academy Pediatrics; Fellow, American College Preventive Medicine; American Public Health Association; National Council for International Health; International Edipemologic Association; Society Epidemological Research. Hobbies: Cooking; Skiing; Chamber Music. Address: Graduate School Health Centre, New York Medical College, Valhalla, NY 10595, USA.

FAN Jia-Jun, b. 21 Mar 1934, Nanjing, China. Professor. m. Liu Cai-yun, 1 Aug 1963, 2 s. Education: BS, Beijing University, 1959. Appointments: Assistant, 1961, Lecturer, 1979; Associate Professor, 1987, Professor, 1992, 4th Military Medical University. Publications: Casson Viscosity and Casson Yield Stress, 1992; Changes of Hemorheological Indices Induced by Intracardiac Surgery Under Extracorporeal Circulation, 1992; Hemorheological Changes Induced by Atriopeptin III in Anesthetized Rates, Co-author, 1991; Investigations of Electromagnetic Radiation and Luminous Phenomena in the State of

Qigong Function, 1990; Basis and Clinical Practice of Hemorheology, Chief Editor, 1995. Honours: Excellent Teacher, Headquarters of Logistics Department of PLA China, 1993. Memberships: Chinese Medical Society; Society of Chinese Biomedical Engineering; Chinese Society of Biophysics. Hobby: Qi-gong. Address: Department of Physics, 4th Military Medical University, Xi'an 710032, China.

FAN Jing Yu, b. 7 Jul 1937, Haerbin, China. Professor of Biophysics. m. Zhang Xiu Hui, 28 Jul 1963, 2 d. Education: Diploma, Beijing Medical College, China, 1961. Appointments: Assistant, Beijing Medical University, 1961-78; Lecturer, Beijing Medical University, 1978-85; Associate Professor, Beijing Medical University, 1985-89; Professor, Department of Biophysics, Beijing Medical University, 1989-. Publications: More than 60 Papers including, Receptor-Mediated Endocytosis of Insulin: Role of Microvilli Coated Pits and Coated Vesicles, 1982; Immunoelectron Microscopic Localization of Human Skeletal Muscle Myosis, 1988; The Role of Gap Junctions in Determining the Skin Conductance and their Possible Relationship to the Acupuncture Points and Meridians, 1990. Honours: First Class Awards for Science and Technology Progress, National Sports Committee, China, 1993. Memberships: Biophysical Society of China; Cell Biology Society of China; Electron Microscopy Society of China; Stereology Society of China. Address: Department of Biophysics, Beijing Medical University, Beijing 100083, China.

FAN Ping-Chin, b. 20 Mar 1922, Hopei, China. Professor of Parasitology. m. Mrs Hung-Chun Lang, 17 Apr 1955, 1 son. Education: MB, National Defense Medical Center, China, 1948; MD, Yonsei University, Korea, 1975. Career: Assistant, Lecturer, Associate Professor, Professor & Chairman, Parasitology, NDMC, China, 1948, 1962, 1976; Professor & Chairman, Department of Parasitology, National Yangming Medical College, NYMC, China, 1976-90; Professor, Department of Parsitology, NYMC, China, 1990-92; Professor Emeritus, National Yangming University, 1992-. Publications include: Helminthic Infections of Appendix, 1963; Prevalence of Pediculus Humanus Capitis Among School Girls of Chuang-Wei and Nan-Ao Districts in Ilan County and Man-Chow District in Ping-Tung County, Taiwan, 1981; Medically Important Snails of Kinmen (Quemoy) Islands, 1985; Clinical Manifestations of Taeniasis in Taiwan Aborigines, 1992; Parasite Infection of Foreign Laborers in Taiwan, 1993. Honours: Award for distinguished sciences and technology, Executive Yuan, China, 1978; Award for basic medical sciences & teaching in NYMC, Ministry of Education, 1987; Award for distinguished research, NSC, China, 1994. Memberships: American Society of Parasitology; American Society of Tropical Med Hygiene; Royal Society of Tropical Med Hygiene; Chinese Medical Society; Chinese Society of Microbiology; Korean Society of Parasitology; Chinese Society of Parasitology. Hobby: Chinese Chess. Address: Department of Parasitology, National Yangming University School of Medicine, 155, Section 2, Li-Nung Street, Shih-Pai Taipei, 11221, Taiwan, China.

FAN Zhenfu, b. 10 May 1935, Hebei, China. Medical Research. m. Chen Zhizhou, 1 Jan 1966, 1 son, 1 daughter. Education: BA, Beijing Medical University, 1962; Visiting Scientist, Deutsches Krebsforschungs Zentrum, Heidelberg, 1979-81. Appointments: Assistant Researcher, Radiation Medicine Institute, CAMS, 1962; Lecturer, Cancer Institute, CAMS, 1978; Associate Professor, Cancer Institute, CAMS, 1985; Professor, Cancer Institute, CAMS, 1990. Publications: China Medical Encyclopedia, co-author, 1983; Radioimmunoassay in Medicine, 1991; Radioimmunoassay of Spermine, 1982; Immunoradiometricassays of CA242, CA125, Cal9-9, PSA, 1992, 1993, 1994. Honours: Science & Technology Prizes, Health Ministry of China, 1983, 1985, 1993; Special Honour, State Council, 1992. Memberships: China Medical Association; China Immunology Society; Deputy Chief Editor, Labelled Immunoassays and Clinical Medicine. Hobbies: Running; Violin. Address: Cancer Institute (Hospital), Chinese Academy of Medical Sciences, PO Box 2258, Panjiayao, Beijing 100021, China.

FANCHER Edwin, b. 29 Aug 1923, Middletown, NY, USA. Psychologist. m. Vivian Kramer, 8 Nov 1969, 1 s, 1 d. Education: MA, Psychology. Career: Staff Psychologist, Central NJ Mental Hygiene Clinics, 1954-58; Founding Co-Director, Washington Square Institute for Psychotherapy and Mental Health, 1960-70; Founding President, NY School for Psychoanalytic Psychotherapy and Psychoanalysis, 1977-. Publications: A Training Analysis for Psychoanalytic Psycotherapists, in Psychoanalytic Review, 1990; Discussant on Symposium on Psychoanalytic Education, in Psa Review, 1993. Memberships: NY Freudian Society; International Psychoanalytic Association; American Psychological Association; American Board of Medical Psychotherapists; American Orthopsychiatric Association. Hobbies: Travel; Photography. Address: 33 Greenwish Avenue, New York, NY 10014, USA.

FANG Chun-Wang, b. 5 Mar 1915, Changshan, Zhejiang, China. Professor. m. Xu Bi-wu, 1934, 4 sons, 1 daughter. Education: MB, National Shanghai Medical College, 1943. Appointments: Doctor, Affiliated Hospital of National Shanghai Medical College, 1943; Dean, Bethune Medical College of East China, 1946; Professor of Communicable Disease & Epidemiology; Dean, 1953, Vice President, 1957, President, 1984-, Shandong Medical College; Internal Dean of Shandong Provincial Hospital; Vice Dean of Shandong Academy of Medical Science; President of Shandong Medical University. Publications: Practical Communicable Disease, 1948; Communicable Disease and Epidemiology, 1981; Chief Editor, Practical Clinical Epidemiology, 1986. Honours: Honorary President, Shandong Medical University, 1986. Memberships: Committee of Medical Science, Ministry of Public Health of China; Standing Committee, Medical Education Institute of Chinese Medical Academy; Vice Chairman, Chinese Medical Association, Shandong Branch; Shandong Sciences & Technology Association; Chinese International Education Intercourse Association. Hobbies: Reading; Walking; History. Address: Department of Epidemiology, Shandong Medical University, Jinan 250012, China.

FANG Da Chao, b. 16 Oct 1924, China. Professor of Pharmacology. m. Liu De Show, 27 Aug 1947, 2 s, 1 d. Education: MD; PhD. Appointments: Assistant of Pharmacology, 1952-60; Lecturer of Pharmacology, 1960-80; Associate Professor. 1980-83, Professor of Pharmacology, Tongji Medical College, 1983-. Publications: Action of Tetrandrine, 1986; A New Calcium Antagonist of Chinese Medicinal Origin-Tetradrine; Blocking Action of Berberine on Alpha-Adrenoceptors. Honours: Vice President, Chinese Society of Cardio-Vascular Pharmacology, 1987-91; China National Prize for Calcium Antagonist Action of Tetrandrine, 1986. Memberships: Chinese Pharmacological Society; Chinese Society of Cardiovascular Pharmacology. Hobbies: Radio Amateur; Dancing. Address: Department of Pharmacology, Tongji Medical College, 13 Hankong Road, Wuhan 430030, China.

FANG Jiming, b. 24 Jan 1964, Tianjing, China. Teacher. m. Cunjie Zhang, 4 jan 1988, 1 s. Education: BA, 1985, MS, 1988, PhD, 1992, Beijing Normal University. Appointments: Assistant Lecturer, Department of Biology, 1988, Associate Professor in Animal Behaviour, Department of Biology, 1992-, Beijing Normal University. Publications include: Seasonal Changes of Brandt's Voles and Their Relation to Burrows, 1989; The Role of Substrate Odours in Maintaining Social Tolerance Between male House Mice, 1993; Animal Parentage Test and DNA Fingerprinting, 1994; The Mating System and Reproduction of Brandt's Voles, 1994;Analysis of relative Fatness Indexes of Animal, 1995; Analysis of Relative Fatness of Brandt's Voles and Comparison Between Relative Fatness K and Kwl (weight/length index) of Small Mammals, 1995. Honours: 2nd Class Award of Science and Tecnology, Ministry of Agriculture in China, 1991. Memberships: Ecology Society of China; Mammalogy Society of China. Address: Running; Swimming; Classical Music. Address: Department of Biology, Beijing Normal University, Beijing 100875, China.

FANG Kun-Hao, b. 19 Sept 1928, Guangdong, China. Radiologist. m. Li-Yin Niu, 1 Nov 1955, 2 s, 1 d. Education: Sun Yat-Sen University of Medical Sciences, 1954; Professor and Chief Doctor of Radiology. Appointments: Associate Professor, Department of Radiology, Xinjiang Medical College, 1980; Professor of Radiology, Sun Yat-sen University of Medical Sciences, Guangzhou. Publications: Diagnostic Radiology of Human Echinococcosis, 1978; Diagnostic Radiology in Uro-Surgery, 1979; Co-Author, Principles and Practice in Biliary Surgery, 1991; Radiological Diagnosis of Reflux Nephropathy, 1992. Honours: Chairman of Guangdong Provincial Radiological Society; Committee Member of Chinese Radiological Society. Memberships: Chinese Medical Association; Chinese Association of Imaging Technology & Research. Hobbies: Tennis; Swimming. Address: Department of Radiology, First Affiliated Hospital, Sun Yet-sen, University of Medical Sciences, Guangzhou 510080, China.

FANG Li-Di, b. 8 Jan 1938, Quang Zhou, China. Doctor. m. 6 May 1967, 2 sons. Education: Graduated, Shanghai Second Medical University. Resident, Surgical Department, Rui-Jin Hospital, 1962-65; Attending Surgeon, Cardiothoracic Surgery, Ru-Jin Hospital, 1966-85; Chief, Cardiothoracic Surgery, Shanghai Yang-Pu Central Hospital,

1986-90; Professor, Chief, Cardiothoracic Surgery, Shanghai Ninth Peoples Hospital, Shanghai Second Medical University. Memberships: Chinese Association of Cardiothoracic Surgery. Address: Room 501, 10 Lane, 89 Huai-Hai Dong Road, Shanghai 200021, China.

FANG Qi-Sheng, b. 13 Nov 1929, Ningpo, China. University Teacher; Researcher. m. Wang Qi Lin, 17 May 1957, 2 sons. Education: Diploma, Dalian Medical College; Master's degree, Shanghai First Medical College. Appointments: Chief of Teaching, Research Group, Nanjing Medical College; Professor of Environmental Hygiene, Researcher of Environmental Medicine, Nanjing Medical University. Publications: Guidelines on Studies in Environmental Epidemiology, 1985; Health Effects of Electro-Magnetic Wave and Its Environmental Health Standards, 1989; Health Effects of Ozone and Its Environmental Health Standard, 1992. Honours: Award for Outstanding Hygienic Standard, Ministry of Public Health, 1990; Special State Council Subsidy, 1993. Memberships: Managing Councillor, Chinese Medical Trace Element Association; Councillor, Chinese Environmental Health Association; Editorial Committee, Chinese Journal of Preventive Medicine. Hobbies: Playing chess; Swimming. Address: Department of Environmental Health, Nanjing Medical University, Nanjing 210029, China.

FANG Shan De, b. 15 Feb 1932, Shanghai, China. Professor of Surgery. m. Bessie Wan, 10 Oct 1959, 1 s. Education: School of Medicine, St John's University; Graduate, Shanghai Second Medical College. Appointment: Professor of Surgery, Tongi Medical University. Publications: Contributor to 15 surgical books; Editor of 5 books including: Reoperative Abdominal Surgery, 1989; Principle and Practice of Biliary Surgery, 1991, Reoperative Surgery and Gynaecology, 1994; Co-editor, Surgical Journal of the Liver, Biliary Tract and Pancreas. Membership: Deputy Chief, Society of Biliary Surgery, Chinese Medical Association. Address: Department of Surgery, Tongi Medical University, Wuhan, Hubei 430030, China.

FANG Xian Ping, b. 2 Feb 1925, Hanco, Hubei, China. Physician. m. Kung Zheng Xu, 24 Feb 1950, 2 sons. Education: MD, Siang Ya Medical University, 1950. Appointments: Doctor, First Affiliated Hospital of Hunan Medical University, 1952; Doctor, 1983, Professor, 2nd Affiliated Hospital of Hunan Medical University. Publications: The Diagram of Liver, Pancreas and Spleen Operation, Examine Approver, 1993; Elder Health Protection, Co-author, 1993; Experimental and Clinical Observations of Effects of Propranolol on Portal Vein Pressure, 1987; Current Viewpoint of Breast Cancer Operation, 1992; The Differential Diagnosis of Breast Mass, 1994. Honours: National Excellent Teacher and Doctor, 1991; Achievement in Scientific Research, 1990. Memberships: Chairman, Hunan General Surgery, Chinese Medical Association; Vice Chairman, Hunan Anticancer Association; ESPEN, Germany. Hobbies: Sport; Basketball; Music. Address: Second Affiliated Hospital of Hunan Medical Univerwsity, Changsha 410011, China.

FANG Zeng, b. 19 Jan 1930, Shang-Dyn, China. Professor of Medical Information. m. Chang Jin, 20 Aug 1955, 3 daughters. Education: Graduated, Beijing Foreign Languages College, 1953. Appointments include: Vice-Director, East-Asia Institute of Special Chinese Medicine, 1993; Currently Director, Shaanxi Medical Informational Centre. Publications: Method of Studies and Research on Chinese Medicine, 1987. Honours: National Award for Advancement of China Science Information, 1986. Memberships: Chinese Medical Association; Shaanxi Science Information Association. Hobby: Stamp collector. Address: Shaanxi Institute of Chinese Medicine, Bing-Zhou West STreet 10, Taiyuan, Shaanxi, China.

FANG Zhen, b. 20 June 1941, Beijing, China. Professor. m. Shu-ying Chen, 1 Oct 1966, 2 daughters. Education: BM, Tianjin Medical University, 1964; MD, Gastroenterology (Digestive Endoscopy) and Critical Care Medicine. Appointments include: Chief Physician, Internal Medicine, Tianjin Gong-An Hospital, 1987; Professor, Internal Medicine, Tianjin 2nd Medical College, 1992; Vice-President, 3th Hospital, Tianjin Medical University, 1993-. Publications include: Gastric Carcinoid, 1983; Acute Pump Failure, 1989; Removal of Foreign Bodies in the Upper Gastrointestinal Tract with Endoscope, 1991; Diagnosis and Management of acute gastrointestinal bleeding with emergency endoscopy in 428 cases, 1991; Nifedipine or indomethacin and ureteral colic, 1991; Influence of Oral Feeding of Basic Ferric Sulphate Solution on the Mucosa of Upper Gastrointestinal Tract of Mice, 1992; Diagnosis and Treatment of UGMB; Gastroscopy for Emergency; Thrombin and Reptilase; Developing a specially designed gastric tube accompanied with gastroscopy in treating upper gastric massive bleeding, 1993;

Influence of emergency endoscopy on cardiovase of UGIB patients, 1994; Endoscopic variceal ligation for active esophageal variceal bleeding, 1994. Honours: Scientific Progress Award, 3rd Class, Tianjin Municipal Government, 1993; Scientific Progress Award, 2nd Class, Tianjin Municipal Health Bureau, 1993. Memberships: Society of Critical Care Medicine, USA; Standing Committee, Tianjin Society of Gastroenterology and Digestive Endoscopy; Standing Committee, Emergency Medicine, Chinese Medical Association; Editor, Chinese Critical Care Medicine Journal. Hobbies: Chinese music; Sports. Address: 91 Ma Chang Road, Tianjin 300203, China.

FANIBUNDA Kersi, b. 4 Nov 1936, Bombay, India. Oral Surgeon. m. Mingi Chinoy, 1 son. Education: BDS, University of Bombay, 1958; LDSRCS, England, University of Leeds, 1961; FDSRCS(Eng), 1964; MDS, Newcastle, 1976. Appointments: House Officer, Registrar, Leeds Area Health Authority; Lecturer, Senior Lecturer, Honorary Consultant Oral Surgeon, Newcastle-upon-Tyne; Consultant in Administrative Charge, Department of Oral Surgery, RVI; Consultant in Administrative Charge, Department of Admissions, Dental Hospital, Newcastle; Acting Head, Department of Oral Surgery, Dental School. Memberships: British Dental Association; British Association of Oral and Maxillofacial Surgeons; Council Member, President Elect, North of England Odontological Society; British Association of Dental and Maxillofacial Radiologists. Address: Department of Oral Surgery, The Dental School, University of Newcastle upon Tyne, Framlington Place, Newcastle upon Tyne NE2 4BW, England.

FARBER Eugene Mark, b. 24 July 1917, Buffalo, New York, USA. President. 3 sons, 2 daughters. Education: AB, Oberlin Coll, 1939; MD, University of Buffalo, 1943; Fellow, Mayo Clinic, 1944-48; MS, University of Minnesota, 1946. Appointments: Clinical Instructor of Dermatology, Stanford University, 1948-49; Clinical Assistant, Professor of Dermatology, Stanford University, 1949-50; Assistant Professor, Pathology, Stanford University, 1949-50; Clinical Professor, Director, Division of Dermatology, Stanford, 1950-59; Professor of Dermatology, Chairman, Department of Dermatology, Stanford University, 1959-86; President, Psoriasis Research Institute, 1986-. Publications include: The application of sulfonamides to gastrointestinal disease, 1945; Benadryl in the treatment of urticaria, 1945; Evaluation of Beta-dimethylaminoethyl benzhydryl ether hydrochloride, 1946; Effect of low molecular weight dextran on acrocyanosis and scleroderma, 1969; Program for veneral diseases education in secondary schools, 1970; Hospital treatment of psoriasis: A modified anthralin program, 1970; The Rare Coexistence of Leprosy and Psoriasis, 1992; Nail Psoriasis, 1992; European Journal of Dermatology, 1992. Memberships: American Academy of Dermatology; American Dermatological Association; Pacific Dermatology Association; Society for Investigative Dermatology; Space Dermatology Foundation. Honours Include: Order of Andres Bello, Banda de Honor, President of Venezuela, 1984; Advisory Vice President, Pan American Medial Association, 1984; The City of Paris Medal, 1991; American Medical Association Physician's Recognition Award, 1991-94. Address: 600 Town and Country, Palo Alto, CA 94301, USA.

FARKAS Hazel Daphne, b. 17 Apr 1937, St Albans, England. Psychiatrist. m. hanson Farkas, 27 Apr 1963, 3 daughters. Education: MB; ChB. Appointments: Rotating Intern, Norwalk Hospital, 1962-63; Resident in Psychiatry, University Louisville, 1964-67; District Psychiatrist, Western Kentucky, 1967-69; Medical Director, Duphi Co MHC, North Carolina; Spring Grove State Hospital, Maryland; Private Practice, Catonsville; Staff Psychiatrist, MVPC then Central NYPC; Team, Outreach Program of MVPC. Publications: Various journal articles. Memberships: American Psychiatric Association; CNY Academy of Medicine. Hobbies: Gardening; Walking; Snorkelling. Address: 1400 Noyes Avenue, Utica, NY 13502, USA.

FARR Robert MacLaughlin, b. 10 Dec 1935, Belfast, Northern Ireland. Psychologist. m. Ann-Marie Wood, 3 Sep 1966, 1 s, 1 d. Education: BA, 1957, MA, 1959, DSc, 1992, Queen's University, Belfast; Divinity Testimonium, Trinity College, Dublin, 1962; PhD, University of London, 1977. Career: Assistant Lecturer, Queen's Belfast, 1962-64; Research Officer, Science 4 (RAF), Ministry of Defence, 1964-66; Lecturer, University College, London, 1966-79; Professor of Psychology, University of Glasgow, 1979-83; Currently, Professor of Social Psychology, London School of Economics. Publications: Guest Editor, special issue, British Journal of Social Psychology, 1983; Co-Editor, Social Representations, 1984; Guest Editor, special issue, Journal for the Theory of Social Behaviour, 1987. Honours: Fellow, British

Psychological Society, 1977; President, British Psychological Society, 1985-86. Memberships: Honorary Life Member, British Psychological Society; European Association of Experimental Social Psychology; Academia Europaea. Hobbies: Reading; Walking; Gardening. Address: Apt 8, 1 Avenue Elmers, Surbiton, Surrey, KT6 4SP, England.

FARRELL Richard Alfred, b. 22 Apr 1939, Providence, Rhode Island, USA. Physicist. m. Marie Joan Hetu, 17 June 1961, 1 son, 1 daughter. Education: BS, Providence College, 1960; MS, University of Massachusetts, 1962; PhD, Catholic University of America, 1965. Appointments: Teaching Assistant, University of Massachusetts, 1960-62; Research Associate, Catholic University, 1962-64; Physicist, Newport (RI) Underwater Ordnance Station, 1960-61; Physicist, JHU/APL, 1965-; Principal Physicist, 1970-; Group Supervisor, 1977-; Chairman, Part-Time Masters degree Programme, Engineering and Applied Physics Biomedicine, Johns Hopkins University. Publications: Light Scattering in the Cornea, Co-author, 1969; Wavelength Dependencies of Light Scattering in Normal and Cold Swollen Rabbit Corneas and Their Structural Implications, Co-author, 1973; A Variational Principle for Scattering from Rough Surfaces, Co-author, 1977; Coexistence Curves for Fourth-Neighbor Ising Models on the Face-Centred-Cubic Lattice, CO-author, 1979; Stromal Damage in Rabbit Corneas Exposed to CO_2 Laser Radiation, Co-author, 1983; A Variational Principle for the Scattered Wave, Co-author, 1990; Corneal Transparency, 1994. Honours: NSF Grantee, 1962-64; NASA Postdoctoral Grantee, 1964-65; Alcon Research Institute Award for Outstanding Research in Vision and Ophthalmology, 1990. Memberships: Associaion Research in Vision and Ophthalmology; American Physical Society; Optical Society of America; Biomedical Engineering Society; International Society for Eye Research. Hobby: Golf. Address: 10757 West Crestview Lane, Laurel, MD 20723, USA.

FARRINGTON David Philip, b. 7 Mar 1944, Ormskirk, Lancashire, England. Psychologist. m. Sally Chamberlain, 30 July 1966, 3 daughters. Education: BA, Psychology, Cambridge University, 1966; MA, PhD, Psychology, Cambridge University, 1970. Appointments: Staff, Cambridge University Institute of Criminology, 1969-. Publications: 13 books, over 150 articles, latest book: Psychological Theories of Crime, 1994. Honours: Sellin-Glueck Award, American Society of Criminology, 1984. Memberships: British Society of Criminology; European Association of Psychology & Law. Address: Institute of Criminology, 7 West Road, Cambridge CB3 9DT, England.

FARRY Malcolm Saba, b. 28 Nov 1940, New Zealand. Dental. m. Lyn, 11 Jan 1969, 3 sons, 5 daughters. Education: BDS, Otago. Appointments: Clinical Lecturer, Faculty of Dentistry, 1978-; Member, Postgraduate Committee, Faculty of Dentistry, 1981-88; External Examiner, Faculty of Dentistry, 1987-89; Lecturer, Practice Management, Faculty of Dentistry, 1991-. Memberships: New Zealand Dental Association; New Zealand Perio Society; New Zealand Endodontic Society. Hobbies: Family; Sport; Skiing; Physical Fitness; Music; Church Affairs. Address: 516 George Street, PO Box 686, Dunedin, New Zealand.

FASHING Norman James, b. 14 Aug 1943, Walker, MN, USA. College Professor. m. Gisela Anna Krueger, 26 Aug 1969, 2 s, 1 d. Education: BA, 1965, MA, 1967, California State University at Chico; PhD, Kansas University, 1973. Appointments: Instructor, Chico State University, 1966-67; Visiting Associate Professor, Oregon State University, 1980; Visiting research Professor, Griffith University, Brisbane, Australia, 1994; Professor of Biology, College of William and Mary, USA. Publications: Contributor of 28 professional articles, 17 abstracts and 50 presentations at scientific meetings and congresses including: Dispersal Behavior and Vector Potential of Aedes cantator (Diptera:Culicidae) in Southern Maryland, Co-author, 1981; House Dust Mites in Williamsburg, Virginia, Co-author, 1990; The Dental Needs of High School Students in Newport News, Virginia: A Pilot Study, Co-author, 1993. Honours: Recipient of Grants from NSF and the Smithsonian Institute. Memberships: Acarological Society of America; Entomological Society of America; European Acarological Society; Central States Entomological Society; Virginia Academy of Sciences. Hobbies: Camping; Hiking; Gardening; Photography. Address: Department of Biology, College of William and Mary, Williamsburg, VA 23187, USA.

FATHALLA Mahmoud Fahmy, b. 1 May 1935, Egypt. Obstetrics & Gynecology. m. Wafaa Hammad, 4 Oct 1964, 2 sons. Education: Doctor Degree, Obstetrics & Gynecology, Cairo University, 1962; PhD,

Edinburgh University, 1967. Appointments: Director, WHO Special Programme of Research, Development & Research Training in Human Reproduction, 1989-92; Professor of Obstetrics & Gynecology. Publications: Editor, FIGO Manual on Human Reproduction, 3 volumes with teaching slides. Honours: Doctor Honous Causa, Uppsala University, Sweden. Memberships: President, International Federation of Gynecology & Obstetrics. Address: PO Box 30, Assiut, Egypt.

FAULK Elizabeth H, b. 18 May 1925, Jacksonville, Florida, USA. Clinical Psychologist. Education: BA, Connecticut College, 1947; MA, University of Florida, 1950; PhD, University of Florida, 1955. Appointments: Staff, Menninger Clinic, Kansas, 1961; Psychology Service, Virginia Hospital, Kansas, 1961-65; Chief Clinical Psychologist, Juvenile Court Psychiatric Clinic, Florida, 1965; Senior Clinical Psychologist, Director of Psychological Training, Guidance Center, Daytona Beach, 1965-68; Private Practice, Boca Katon, Florida, 1968-90; Private Practice, Deerfield Beach, Florida, 1990-. Publications: Group Counseling in Diverse Population. Honours: Outstanding Women of the Year-Soroptimist, 1974; Psychologist of the Year, Florida Psychological Association, 1981; J C Penny Golden Rule Award, 1986; harriet Buescher Lawrence 34 Prize, 1993. Memberships: APA; FPA; Fellow, KPA; Diplomate in Clinical Psychology, ABPP & American Academy of Psychotherapists; American Psychotherapy Association. Hobbies: Tennis; Golf; Boating. Address: 550 North Ocean Blvd #11, Deerfield Beach, FL 33441, USA.

FAWCETT Angela Jocelyn, b. 6 Sep 1944, London, England. Research Psychologist. m. David Fawcett, 30 Sep 1967, 1 s, 1 d. Education: BA, Psychology, 1986, PhD, Psychology, 1990, University of Sheffield. Career: Research Associate, Leverhulme Trust, 1990-92, Research Fellow, Leverhulme Trust, 1992-93, Lecturer in Orthoptics, 1993, Research Fellow, Medical Research Council, 1993-, University of Sheffield. Publications include: Co-author, Automaticity: a new framework for dyslexia research, in Cognition, 1990; Co-author, Reaction times and dyslexia, in Quarterly Journal of Experimental Psychology, 1994; Co-author, Event-related potentials and dyslexia, in Annals of New York Academy of Sciences, 1994; Co-editor, Dyslexia and Skill: Multidisciplinary Perspectives, 1994; About 30 articles and book chapters co-authored. Honours: Harry Kay Prize, 1986; Parker Habershon-Rhodes Scholarship, 1986. Memberships: Chartered Psychologist, British Psychological Society; Experimental Psychology Society; Rodin Remediation, Switzerland; Cognitive Science Society, USA. Address: 37 Tapton Crescent Road, Sheffield, S10 5DB, England.

FAY Roger Andrew, b. 25 Mar 1949, Sydney, New South Wales, Australia. Obstetrician and Gynaecologist. 2 daughters. Education: MB, BS, Sydney University, 1974; MRCOG, 1980; FRACOG, 1982. Appointments: Clinical Lecturer, Department of Obstetrics and Gynaecology, University of Sydney; Currently Obstetrician and Gynaecologist. Publications: Sole or senior author: Failure with the new triphasic oral contraceptive Logynon, 1982; Feto-maternal haemorrhage as a cause of fetal morbidity and mortality, 1983; Platelets in pregnancy: hyperdestruction in pregnancy, 1983; Platelets and uric acid in the prediction of pre-eclampsia, 1985; Uric acid in pregnancy and pre-eclampsia: an alternative hypothesis, 1990; Ponderal Index: a better definition of the 'at risk' group with intrauterine growth problems than birthweight for gestational age in term infants, 1991; Categories of intrauterine growth retardation, 1993; Colour Doppler imaging of the uteroplacental circulation in the middle trimester: observations on the development of a low resistance circulation, 1994; Colour Doppler imaging of the uteroplacental circulation in the middle trimester: features of the uterine flow velocity waveform that predict abnormal pregnancy outcome, 1994. Honours: T B Walley Research Fellowship in Obstetrics and Gynaecology, University of Sydney, 1982. Memberships: Australian Perinatal Society; Australian Gynaecological Endoscopic Society. Hobbies: Meditation and Eastern philosophy; Wine appreciation. Address: "Westbank", 2 Nepean Street, Emu Plains, NSW 2750, Australia.

FAZIO Antonio L S, b. 6 Feb 1945, Catania, Italy. Psychoanalyst. m. Maria Oliveri, 27 Dec 1971, 3 sons. Education: MA, Sociology, Trento University; Therapist training, London Centre for Psychotherapy. Appointments: Psychiatric Social Worker; Child and Family Psychotherapist; Consultant Psychotherapist, Therapeutic Communities; Clinical Assessor, London Centre for Psychotherapy; Currently Clinical Associate in Psychotherapy, University College Hospital, London. Publications: Family Therapy with School Phobic Adolescents, 1977; The Role of the Psychotherapist in the Psychiatric Team with Special

Reference to Staff Training, 1980; One for All, book, 1990; The Psychodynamic Family Treatment of Adolescence's Problems. Memberships: Italian Register of Psychologists, Psychotherapy Section; Associate Member, British Psychoanalytical Society; Associate Member, Italian Psychoanalytical Society; Associate Member, Group Analytic Society, London; British Confederation of Psychotherapists. Hobbies: Sailing; Skiing; Classic cars. Address: 35 The Park, Golders Green, London NW11 7ST, England.

FEDER Robert, b. 8 July 1951, Detroit, Michigan, USA. Psychiatrist. m. Marsha Cooper, 13 Aug 1974, 1 son, 1 daughter. Education: BS with high honours, University of Michigan; MD, University of Washington; Postdoctoral Fellow, Yale University. Appointments: Medical Director, Psychiatric Unit, Beverly Hospital, 1981-83; Chief Psychiatrist, Matthew Thornton Health Plan, 1983-86; Chairman, Department of Psychiatry, Nashua Memorial Hospital, Nashua, New Hampshire, 1988-93; Director, Partial Hospitalisation Programme, Nashua Brookside Hospital, 1989-1995; Associate Medical Director, Nashua Brookside Hospital, 1992-95; Director, Partial Hospitalization Program, Optima Health, 1995-. Publications: 24 articles in psychiatric journals. Honours: Exemplary Psychiatrist Award, Alliance for the Mentally Ill, 1992; Fellow, American Psychiatric Association, 1993. Memberships: American Psychiatric Association; American Medical Association; New Hampshire Psychiatric Society, President, Chairman for Public Affairs. Hobbies: Skiing; Computer art; Music; Boogie boarding. Address: 100 McGregor Street, Manchester, NH 03102, USA.

FEDOROV Vladimir Dmitrievich,b. 21 March 1933, Moscow, Russia. Surgeon. m. Fedozova (Alybina) Maina V. 10 January 1953, 1 son, 1 daughter. Education: MD, II Medical Institute, Moscow, Russia, 1960. Appointments: Professor, Moscow Medical Academy, 1960-71; Director, Scientific Research Institute of Proctology, 1972-88; Director, A.V. Vishnevsky Institute of Surgery. Publications: Surgical treatment of diffuse colon polyposis: Analysis of 500 cases, 1987; Moderate and hard simultaneous combined operations, 1993. Memberships: International Society of Surgery, 1983; International HBP Association, 1990. Address: 27 B Serpukhovskaya Str, 113811 Moscow, Russia.

FEDSON David S, b. 19 Nov 1937, Austin, Minnesota, USA. Physician. div. 1 son, 2 daughters. Education: BA, Yale, 1959; MD, Yale University School of Medicine, 1965. Appointments: Associate professor of Medicine, University of Virginia School of Medicine, 1982-88; Assistant and Associate Professor of Medicine, University of Chicago, 1972-82; Chief Medical Resident, University of Chicago, 1971-72; Clinical Associate and Senior Staff Fellow, NIAID, NIH, 1968-71; INtern, Resident, Osler Medical Service, The Johns Hopkins Hospital, Baltimore, 1966-68; Harry T Peters Jr Professor of Internal Medicine, University of Virginia Medical School, Charlottesville. Publications include: Pneumococcal Vaccine, Co-author, 1993; Immunization for Healthcare Workers and Petients in Hospitals, 1992; Guide for Adult Immunization, Editor, 1990; Pneumococcal Vaccination in the Prevention of Community-Acquired Pneumonia: An Optimistic View of Cost-Effectiveness, 1993; Clinical Effectiveness of Influenza Vaccination in Manitoba, CO-author, 1993; Influenza Vaccination Rates and Risks for Influenza-Associated Hospital Discharge and Death in Manitoba, CO-author, 1992; Clinical Practice and Public Policy for Influenza and Pneumococcal Vaccinations of Elderly Persons, 1992; Hospital-based Pneumococcal Immunization: Epidemiologic Rationale from the Shenandoah Study, Co-author, 1990. Memberships include: Fellow, American College of Physicians; Fellow, Infectious Diseases Society of America. Hobbies: Music; Reading; Gardening. Address: Box 494, University of Virginia School of Medicine, Charlottesville, VA 22908, USA.

FEE Willard E Jr, b. 10 Jun 1943, Porchester, NY, USA. Physician; Surgeon. m. 1 s, 1 d. Education: MD, cum laude; BS, cum laude. Appointments: Assistant Professor of Surgery, 1974-80, Associate Professor of Surgery, 1980-86, Currently, Professor and Chairman, Otolaryngology, Head and Neck Surgery, Stanford University. Publications: Over 90 articles in professional journals, 1970-93, including: Co-author: The Electrophysiologic and Histologic Effects of the Argon Beam Coagulator on Peripheral Nerves, in Larynscope, 1992; Proceedings of the Third International Conference on Head and Neck Cancer: Nasopharyngeal Carcinoma, in Head and Neck Cancer, 1993; Current Issues in Nerve Repair, in Arch Otolaryngology head Neck Surgery, 1993; 11 Chapters in Books, 1982-94. Honours: Alpha Omega Alpha, 1969; Outstanding Intern Award, 1969-70; Lederle Research Award, 1968; Collegium ORL Amicitiae Sanctum-Member USA, 1984-.

Memberships: Director, American Board of Otolaryngology, 1985-; American Academy of Otolaryngology, Head and Neck Surgery; American College of Surgery; Society of Otolaryngologists; Paul H Ward Society; American Laryngological Association. Hobbies: Fly Fishing; Skiing; Scuba Diving; Restoring Classic Automobiles. Address: Stanford University Medical Center, Division of Otolaryngology, Head and Neck Surgery, 300 Pasteur Drive, Edwards R135, Stanford, CA 94305-5328, USA.

FEENEY John Anthony, b. 10 May 1954, Stafford, England. Education: BSc Hons, Psychology, City University, London, England, 1978; MSc Occupational Psychology, University of Hull, England, 1984. Career: Occupational Psychologist, Training Services, Broadgreen, Liverpool, England, 1981-84; Psychologist, National Health Service, 1984-90; Independent Chartered Psychologist. Publications: Co-author, Task Analysis in Rehabilitation, 1993; Occasional articles. Membership: British Psychological Society. Hobbies: Walking; Touring; Selected Reading. Address: 41 Kirkstall Avenue, Highfields, Stafford ST17 9FW, England.

FEI Ding-Yu, b. 13 Apr 1942, Zhejiang, China. Medical Imaging. m. Guang-Ming Wu, Jan 1971, 1 son. Education: BS and PE, Electronic Engineering, Tsinghua University, Beijing, China, 1965; PhD, Bioengineering, Pennsylvania State University, 1986. Career: Director, Division of Electronic Measurements and Instrumentation, Shanghai University of Science and Technology, 1971-81; Assistant Professor in Biomedical Engineering, Virginia Commonwealth University, 1989-. Publications: Co-author: Angle Independent Doppler Color Imaging: Determination of Accuracy and a Method of Display, Ultrasound in Med & Bio, 1994; CA: The Effect of Angle and Flow Rate Upon Hemodynamics in Distal Vascular Graft Anastomoses: A Numerical Model Study, 1994; Author: A Theory to Correct the Systematic Error Caused by the Imperfectly Matched Beam Width to Vessel Diamter Ratio on Volumetric Flow Measurements Using Ultrasound Techniques, 1995. Honour: Principal Investigator, Whitaker Foundation, USA, 1991-94. Memberships: IEEE Engineering in Medicine and Biology Society; Biomedical Engineering Society; American Institute of Ultrasound in Medicine. Address: Box 980694, MCV Station, Richmond, VA 23298-0694, USA.

FEINSTEIN Alvan Richard, b. 12 Apr 1925, Philadelphia, Pebnsylvania, USA. Professor; Physician. 1 son, 1 daughter. Education: BS; MS, Mathematics; MD. Appointments include: Sterling Professor of Medicine and Epidemiology, Yale University School of Medicine. Publications include: Clinical Judgement, 1967, reprinted, 1974; Clinical Biostatistics, 1977; Clinical Epidemiology. The Architecture of Clinical Research, 1985; Clinimetrics, 1987; Contributor of over 300 articles in professional journals. Honours: Recipient of numerous honours and awards for professional services. Memberships include: Association of American Physicians; Fellow, American College of Physicians; American Society for Clinical Investigation; American Epidemiological Society; Institute of Medicine; Interurban Clinical Club; Connecticut Academy of Science and Engineering; Fellow, Institute of Statisticians; Fellow, American College of Epidemiology; Fellow, American Association for the Advancement of Science; American Medical Association; American Heart Association; Alpha Omega Alpha; Sigma Xi; Fellow, Jonathan Edwards College, Yale University. Address: Yale University School of Medicine, 333 Cedar Street, New Haven, CT 06520-8025, USA.

FEIRSTEIN, Frederick, b. 2 Jan 1940, New York City, New York, USA. Psychoanalyst. m. Linda Bergton, 9 June 1963, 1 son. Education: BA, University of Buffalo, 1960; MA, New York University, 1961; NCPsyA, National Psychological Association for Psychoanalysis, 1984. Appointments: Currently: Psychoanalyst in private practice, New York City; Faculty, Training Analyst, Supervisor, National Psychological Association for Psychoanalysis and Institute for Expressive Analysis. Publications: The Family Circle, play, 1974; Survivors, poems, 1975; Manhattan Carnival, poems, 1981; Fathering, poem, 1982; Family History, poems, 1986; Expansive Poetry, essays, 1989; City Life, poems, Ending the Twentieth Century, poems; Numerous play productions. Honours: OADR Award in Playwriting, 1976; Guggenheim Fellowship in Poetry, 1979-80; Collady Prize, 1986, 1994. Memberships: National Psychological Association for Psychoanalysis; National Accreditation Association for Psychoanalysis; Institute fo Expressive Analysis. Hobby: Playing basketball with his son David. Address: c/o Egon Dumler, Dumler & Giroux, New York, USA.

FEIXAS-VIAPLANA Guillem, b. 19 Sept 1961, Barcelona, Spain. Psychologist. m. Nuria Gallinat-Serrano, 19 Oct 1985, 1 son, 1 daughter. Education: Doctor in Psychology, 1988. Appointments: Pre-doctoral Fellow, University Barcelona; Post-doctoral Fellow, Memphis University, USA, 1988-89; University Professor, Universitat de Barcelona. Publications: Aproximaciones a la priesterapia, 1993; Constructiuismo y Psicoterapia, 1990; A Manual for the Pepertory Grid, 1994; Personal Construct Theory & Systemic Therapis, 1990. Memberships: Society for the Exploration of Psychotherapy Investigation; Society for Psyche Therapy Research. Hobbies: Music; Cinema; Outdoor Walks & Sports. Address: Torre Dels Pardals 65 At-2, Barcelona 08032, Spain.

FELDMAN Elaine, b. 9 Dec 1926, New York, NY, USA. Medical Professor Emeritus. m. 19 Jul 1957, 2 s, 1 d. Education: Medical Degree, NY University School of Medicine, New York City. Career includes: International Lecturer on Nutrition; Currently, Professor Emeritus of Medicine and Physiology and Endocrinology, Medical College of GA, Augusta; Director Emeritus, College's GA Institute of Human Nutrition. Publications: Over 80 articles in biomedical journals including The New England Journal of Medicine, Journal of Nutrition, Journal of Lipid Research; Editorial Board, American Journal of Clinical Nutrition; Consulting Editor, Journal of the American College of Nutrition. Honours: Goldberger Award, American Medical Women's Association; Calcium Nutrition Education Award, American Medical Women's Association; National Dairy Council's Award for Excellence in Medical Nutrition Education, American Society for Clinical Nutrition. Memberships: Fellow, American Heart Association's Council on Arteriosclerosis; Fellow, American College of Physicians; American Society for Clinical Nutrition; American Medical Women's Association; American Medical Association. Address: Medical College of Georgia, CJ106, Augusta, GA 30912-3102, USA.

FENCHEL Gerd H, b. 29 Mar 1926, Berlin, Germany. Psychologist; Psychoanalyst. m. Leslie Spitz, 30 Jun 1991, 1 s, 1 d. Education: BS, 1949, MS, 1951, City of New York College; PhD, New York University, 1959. Fellow, Psychology Department, City College, 1946-50; Assistant Dean, Alfred Adler Institute, 1955-73; Supervisor, Director of Group Psychotherapy, Long Island Consultant Centre, 1953-60; Faculty, Institute for Analytical Psychotherapy, 1960-71; Contributing Editor, GROUP journal, 1984-94; Currently, Dean, Director, Washington Square Institute for Psychotherapy. Publications: Co-author, The Developing Ego and The Emerging Self, 1987; Editor and Contributor, Psychoanalysis at 100, 1994; Many articles in GROUP, and Psychoanalytical Psychology. Honour: Fellow, American Group Psychotherapy Association. Memberships: American Psychological Association; Eastern Group Psychotherapy Society; NY State Psychological Association; PA Psychological Association; International Council of Psychologists; American Group Psychotherapy Association; National Association for Advancement of Psychoanalysis. Hobbies: Stamp Collecting; Photography; Travel. Address: 41-51 East 11th Street, New York, NY 10003, USA.

FENG Chongyin, b. 18 June 1930, Anyao County, Sichuan, China. Chief Nutritionist. m. Duan Lianrong, 2 July 1949, 3 sons, 3 daughters. Education: BA, West China Union University, 1950. Appointments include: Currently Chief Nutritionist, Bijie Prefecture Hospital, Guizhou. Publications: Observation of the Pupils' Cerebral Cortex Functional Efficiencies Adjusted with Break Refreshments, 1985; The Survey Report of the Children's Nutrition in Several Specific Nurseries of Bijie Prefecture, 1985; Textbook of Hygiene (chief editor), 1986. Membership: Guizhou Province Hygiene Association. Hobby: Shadow boxing. Address: Bijie Prefecture Hospital, Guizhou, China.

FENG Ji-Liang, b. 7 Aug 1931, Shandong, China. Physician. m. Liu Xi Ying, 1 May 1958, 1 son, 1 daughter. Education: Bachelor's degree, Shandong Medical College, 1954; Bachelor's degree, Shandong Chinese Traditional Medical College, 1977. Appointments: Resident Doctor, 1944, Doctor in charge, 1960, Associate Professor and Deputy Chief Physician, 1982, Professor, Chief Physician, Anorectum Department, 1987-, Affiliated Hospital, Shandong Traditional Chinese Medical College. Publications: Chief editor: Selected Works of Chinese Traditional Medical Prescription, 1977; Chinese Traditional Medical Manual for Treating Common Rural Disease, 1977; Practical Anorectum Surgical Science, 1991; Learned articles include: Dialectically Change Dressings; Dialectical Fumigation; Dialectical Surgical Operation; Articles at international academic conferences: Treating Anal Fistula with Acupuncture and CO2 Laser, 1983; Dialectical Surgical Operation on Removal of Rectum Carcinoma and Remaking Anus, 1990. Honours:

Numerous Merits, China; Participant: 2nd International Scientific Conference on Lasers, 1983; 2nd China-Japan Discussion Meeting on Cancer of the Large Intestine, 1990. Memberships: Director, Anorectum Branch, Chinese Traditional Medical Association; Editorial Board, Journal of Anorectum Disease in China; Committee Member, Shandong Anorectum Branch, Chinese Traditional Medical Association; Director, Shandong Branch, Combined Chinese and Western Medical Association; Director, Shandong Laser Institute; Editorial Board, Journal of Shangdong Laser. Hobbies: Making friends; Travel; Appreciating antiques. Address: 154 Lishan Road, Jinan, Shandong, China.

FENG Lida, b. 23 Nov 1925, Beijing, China. Immunologist; Medical and Qigong Expert. m. Luo Yuanzheng, 1947, 1 s. Education: Studied at Medical College of Qi Lu University, 1944-46, Biology Department of University of CA, Berkeley, 1946-49; PhD, Immunology, Medical College of Lenningrad University, 1958. Appointments: Profesor, Deputy Director, General Navy Hospital, Beijing; Director of China Immunology Centre. Publications: General Introduction of Contemporary World Immunology, 1980; Relationship between Chinese Medicine and Immunity of Organisms, 1980; Chinese Clinical Qigong Science, 1988; Chinese Medical Qigong Science, 1989; Modern Qigongology, 1994. Honour: Outstanding Scientist, State Council of China, 1993. Memberships: Honorary Professor of Traditional Chinese Medical College; Professor of Carders Management College of Chinese Academy of Sciences; Vice Chairman, International Federation of Qigong Science. Hobbies: Sport; Music. Address: General Hospital of Navy, Beijing 100037, China.

FENG Yuzeng, b. 10 July 1933, Wuxi, China. Professor. m. Shen Ru Quan, 28 Apr 1957, 1 daughter. Appointments: Professor of Obstetrics & Gynecology, Jian Nan University; Professor of Obstetrics & Gynecology, Shanghai Medical University. Publications: Chemotherapy and Conservative Surgery in a Case of Late Chorivcarcinoma with Pelvic Arteris-venous Fistula and Fertility Preservation, 1983; Primary Ovarian Pregnancy and IMD, 1984. Memberships: Chinese Medical Association; Jiansu Provincial Medical Association; Shanghai Association of Obstetrics & Gynecology. Address: 190 North Suzhow Road, Shanghai, China.

FENNESSY John James, b. 8 Mar 1933, Republic of Ireland. Professor of Radiology. m. Ann M O'Sullivan, 20 Aug 1960, 4 sons, 3 daughters. Education: MB, BCh; BAO. Appointments: Acting Chief, Diagnostic Radiology, 1973-74; Chairman, Department of Radiology, 1974-84; Currently Professor of Radiology, University of Chicago, IL, USA. Publications: The Radiology of Lung Cancer, 1975; Irradiation Damage to the Lungs, 1987; Various on transbronchial lung biopsy techniques, 1966-; Others on inflammatory bowel disease, lung cancer and radiation injury. Honours: Fellow, Royal College of Surgeons in Ireland, 1978. Memberships: Chicago Radiology Society; American College of Radiology; Thoracic Radiology Society; Radiology Society of North America; Fleischner Society. Hobbies: Swimming; History. Address: University of Chicago, Department of Radiology, 5841 S Maryland Avenue, Chicago, IL 60637, USA.

FERGUSON Alexander Cunningham, b. 4 July 1943, Scotland. Paediatrician. Education: MB ChB; FRCPC; DCH; DABAI; University of Glasgow; University of Western Ontario, Canada; University of Toronto; University of California at Los Angeles, USA. Appointments: Intern, Resident in Paediatrics, University of Glasgow; Hospital for Sick CHildren, Toronto; Research Fellow, Paediatric Allergy and Immunology, University of California; Lecturer, Queen's University, Ontario; Assistant, Associate, Professor, University of British Columbia. Publications: Contributor of numerous peer reviewed works in field. Honours: Mead Johnson Fellowship, Canadian Paediatric Society, 1972; Ross Award, Canadian Paediatric Society, 1974. Memberships: Canadian Medical Association; Royal College of Physicians of Canadian; American Academy of Allergy and Immunology; Canadian Society for Allergy and Clinical Immunology; Western Society for Paediatric Research. Hobbies: Sailing; Hiking; Skiing; Golf; Reading. Address: Department of Paediatrics, British Columbia Children's Hospital, 4480 Oak Street, Vancouver, British Columbia V6H 3V4, Canada.

FERGUSON-SMITH Malcolm Andrew, b. 5 Sep 1931, Glasgow, Scotland. Medical Geneticist. m. 11 July 1960, 1 son, 3 daughters. Education: MB, ChB; MA; DSc; FRCPath; FRCP; FRCOG; FRSE; FRS. Appointments: Professor of Medical Genetics, University of Glasgow, 1973-87; Honorary Consultant in Medical genetics, Director, West of Scotland Regional Genetics Service, Rioyal Hospital for Sick Children,

Glasgow; Professor of Pathology, University of Cambridge, England; Director, East Anglian Genetics Service; Honorary Consultant in Medical Genetics, Addenbrookes NHS Trust, Cambridge. Publications: Essential Medical Genetics, 4th Edition, 1993; Prenatal Diagnosis and Screening, 1993. Honours: Macdougall-Brisbane Prize, 1984-86; San Remo International Prize for Genetic Research, 1990. Memberships: British, European and American Societies of Human Genetics; Genetical Society; Pathological Society; Zoological Society. Hobbies: Swimming; Sailing; Fishing. Address: Department of Pathology, University of Cambridge, Tennis Court Road, Cambridge CB2 1QP, England.

FERNANDEZ Louis A V, b. 30 May 1944, Karachi, Pakistan. Physician. m. Virginia Fernandez, 17 Nov 1973, 1 s, 1 d. Education: MBBS; FRCPC; FACP. Career: Assistant Professor, 1976-81, Associate Professor, 1981-89, Professor of Medicine, 1989-, Dalhousie University. Publications: Aggressive Natural Killer Cell Leukemia Blood, 1986; Infiltration of human B cell chema lymphocytic leukemia by a antibody, International Journal of Cancer, 1994. Memberships: Fellow, American College of Physicians; Fellow, Royal College of Physicians and Surgeons of Canada; American and Canadian Hematology Societies; Canadian Society for Clinical Investigation. Hobby: Tennis. Address: Camp Hill Medical Centre, 1763 Robie Street, Halifax, NS, Canada, B3H 3G2.

FERNANDEZ-MADRID Felix, b. 28 Nov 1927, Buenos Aires, Argentina. Physician. m. Ana M Berger, 14 Oct 1954, 2 sons, 2 daughter. Education: MD, University of Buenos Aires, 1953; PhD, Physiology, Cellular and Molecular Biology, University of Miami, Coral Gables, Florida, 1966. Appointments: Instructor of Medicine, University of Buenos Aires, 1953-57; Assistant Professor of Medicine and Physiology, University of Miami, Florida, USA, 1966-68; Currently Professor of Internal Medicine, Chief of Rheumatology Division, Wayne State University, Detroit, Michigan. Publications: Treating Arthritis, Medicine, Myth and Magic, 1989. Honours: Fellow, American College of Physicians; Fellow, American College of Rheumatology. Memberships: Michigan Rheumatism Society; Arthritis Foundation; Detroit Medical Club. Hobbies: Chess; Tennis. Address: 18531 Wiltshire, Lathrup Vill, Michigan, USA.

FERNANDO Athula J, b. 2 Apr 1933, Sri Lanka. Professor of Physical Therapy. 2 sons. Education: BPT (Man); DipTP (England); MEd, University of Manitoba. Appointments: Currently Professor, Head, Physical Therapy, University of Manitoba, Canada. Publications: From Professionalism to Professionalization, 1987; Planned Professionalization of the Student Physiotherapist, beyond casual enculturation, 1991. Honours: Queen's Silver Jubilee Medal. Memberships: Former President, Canadian Physiotherapy Association; President, World Confederation for Physical Therapy. Hobbies: Reading; Travel. Address: Apt 907, 277 Wellington Crescent, Winnipeg, Manitoba, Canada R3M 3V7.

FERNANDO Emerick Martin, b. 14 June 1931, Sri Lanka. Obstetrician and Gynaecologist. m. Monica Ranasuriya, 23 Oct 1958, 2 sons. Education: MBBS, Ceylon, 1957; MOG(Sri Lanka), 1970; Dep Acupuncture, China, 1977; FRCOG, 1987. Appointments: Consultant Obstetrician and Gynaecologist: Anuradhapura, Badulla, Kurunebara, Colomboo; Professor of Obstetrics and Gynaecology, Tripoli, Libya. Memberships: Royal College of Obstetricians and Gynaecologists; Sri Lanka College of Obstetricians and Gynaecologists. Hobbies: Photography; Scrabble. Address: 8 Rajapihilla Road, Kurunegala, Sri Lanka.

FERNANDO Wellege Hemachandra, b. 1 July 1927, Sri Lanka. Obstetrician and Gynaecologist. m. S N De Silva, 1951, 1 son, 1 daughter. Education: MBBS; FRCS(England); FRCOG; FCOG; FCS(Sri Lanka). Appointments: Consultant, De Soysa Hospital for Women, Colombo; Consultant. Memberships: Life Member, Sri Lanka Medical Association; Sri Lanka College of Obstetricians and Gynaecologists; Life member, Ceylon College of Surgeons. Hobbies: Books; Travel. Address: 73 Isipathana Mawatha, Colombo 5, Sri Lanka.

FERRE Richard C, b. 4 Jul 1942, Salt Lake City, Utah, USA. Psychiatrist. m. Janis Madsen Baker, 12 Jun 1970, 3 s. Education: Biology, Stanford University, 1964; Medicine, University of Utah, 1970; Internship & Residency, Emory Univesity, 1971-74; Child Psychiatry Fellowship, University of Utah, 1974-75; Adult Psychiatry & Neurology, Board Certified, 1978; Child Psychiatry & Neurology, Board Certified, 1979. Appointments: Institute for the Study of Health & Society,

Washington DC, 1970-71; Medical Director of Inpatient Services, Primary Children's Medical Center, 1975-91; Medical Director of Residential Treatment Center, Primary Children's Medical Center, 1975-; Chairman, Department of Child Psychiatry, Primary Children's Medical Center, 1987-; Associate Clinical Professor, Department of Child & Adolescent Psychiatry, University of Utah School of Medicine, 1986-. Publications: include, Tourette's Disorder and the Use of Clonidine, 1982; Case of Giles De La Tourette's Syndrome or Oedipus Revisited, 1980; Updating the Norms for the Achenbach: Child Inpatients, 1990; Child Abuse among Child Inpatients, 1984. Memberships: American Psychiatry Association; American Academy of Child & Adolescent Psychiatry. Address: 100 North Medical Drive, Salt Lake City, Utah 84113 1103, USA.

FIELDING Jonathan E, b. 4 Oct 1942, Nyack, New York, USA. Professor. m. Karin Barter, 19 Sep 1976, 2 sons. Education: MD; MPH; MBA. Appointments: Principal Medical Services Officer, National Job Corps Programme, 1971-73; Director, Division of Quality Assurance, Bureau of Quality Assurance, DHEW, 1974-75; Commissioner of Public Health, Commonwealth of Massachusetts, 1975-79; Co-Director, UCLA Centre for Health Enhancement Education and Research, 1979-82; Founder and CEO, US Corporate Health Management Incorporated, 1983-87; Vice President, Health Director, Johnson and Johnson Health Management Incorporated, 1986-93; Vice President for Health Policy, Johnson and Johnson Corporate, 1979-; Professor of Health Services and Paediatrics, UCLA Schools of Public Health and Medicine. Publications: Author of numerous books and learned articles. Honour: Porter Prize, 1994. Memberships: American Academy of Paediatrics; American Association of Public Health Physicians; American College of Preventive Medicine; American Peer Review Association; American Public Health Association; Association for Health Services Research; California Academy of Preventive Medicine; International Union for Health Promotion and Education; Worksite Health promotion Alliance. Hobbies: Bicycling; Photography. Address: UCLA School of Public Health, 10833 Le Conte Avenue, Los Angeles, CA 90095, USA.

FIELDING Richard, b. 15 June 1952, Ripon, England. Psychologist. m. Sarla Kukadia, 4 Aug 1986, 2 daughters. Education: BA, honours, London; Dip. Clin Psychology; PhD, Sheffield, England. Appointments: Clinical Psychologist, Bolton Health Authority, England; Senior Clinical Psychologist, Bolton Health Authority; Lecturer in Health Psychology, The University of Hong Kong; Head, Behavioral Sciences Unit, The University of Hong Kong. Publications: Depression & Myocardial Infarction: A Review & Reinterpretation, 1991; Symptoms, Blood Pressure Information & Mood Effects on Subsequent Symptom Recall, 1992; Clinical Communication Skills, 1995. Memberships: Associate Fellow, British Psychological Society; Fellow, Hong Kong Psychological Society. Hobbies: Painting; Textiles; Scuba Diving; Running; Yoga. Address: Department of Community Medicine, The University of Hong Kong, Patrick Manson Southwing, 7 Sassoon Road, Hong Kong.

FILLER Robert Martin, b. 5 Mar 1931, Brooklyn, NY, USA. MD; FRCS (C). 3 s. Education includes: AB, Cornell University, 1952; MD cum laude, WA University School of Medicine, 1956; Diplomate, National Board of Medical Examiners, 1957; FACS, 1968; FRCS (C), 1977. Appointments include: Chief Resident in Surgery, Children's Hospital Medical Center, MA, 1963-64; Professor, Department of Surgery, University of Toronto, 1977-; Chair, Pediatric Surgery, University of Toronto, 1981-; Surgeon-in-Chief, Hospital for Sick Children, Toronto, 1977-94; Head, Division of General Surgery, 1977-94, 1995-; Consultant, Pediatrics, Women's College Hospital, Toronto, 1984-; Associate Staff, Mount Sinai Hospital, Toronto, 1989-. Publications include: 170 Peer reviewed publications, 1960-, including: A forum for progress in pediatric surgery, in Journal of Pediatric Surgery, 1992; Co-author, Severe tracheomalacia associated with esophageal atresia: Results of surgical treatment, in Journal of Pediatric Surgery, 1992; 17 Non Peer Reviewed Publications, 1972-91; Numerous books, chapters in books and proceedings, 1966-; Numerous invited visits and lectures to hospitals, universities, conferences and symposia, 1977-; Numerous scientific papers read; Scientific films and videotapes. Honours include: Numerous research awards; Cross of Merit for Outstanding Achievement, 1979; 1st Recipient, Sir James Carreras Award, Variety Clubs International, 1986; President, American Pediatric Surgical Association, 1990. Memberships include: Numerous Surgery Committees; Board of Directors, Alpha Omega Alpha, 1986-; American College of Surgeons; Many Editorial Advisory Boards; International Society of Surgery, 1988-. Address: The Hospital for Sick Children, 555 University Ave, Toronto, Ontario, Canada, M5G 1X8.

FINDLAY C Edward, b. 1 Nov 1958, Peterboro, Canada. Osteopathic Physician. Education: BSc; DO; CCFP. Appointments: Private Practice, Family Medicine, Osteopathic Therapy. Publications: The Canadian Healthcare System, 1992. Honours: Certificate of Special Competence, Osteopathic Manual Medicine, 1994. Memberships: President, Prairie Osteopathic Association; College of Family Physicians, Canada; American Osteopathic Association; Canadian Osteopathic Association. Hobbies: Skiing; Hiking; Rock Climbing; Cycling; Kayaking. Address: 1603-20 Avenue North West, Calgary, Alberta, T2M 1G9, Canada.

FINE Richard N, b. 3 Oct 1937, Philadelphia, Pennsylvania, USA. Medical Doctor. m. Shawney Wagner, 28 Aug, 2 sons, 2 daughters. Education: BS, Muhlenburg College, 1958; MD, Temple University Medical School. Appointments: Instructor in Pediatrics, USC; Assistant Professor of Pediatrics, USC; Associate Professor of Pediatrics, USC; Professor of Pediatrics, USC; Professor of Pediatrics, UCLA; Vice Chairman for Clinical Affairs, Department of Pediatrics, UCLA. Publications: Co-author, Dialysis Therapy, 1993; Co-author, Growth after recombinant human growth hormone in children with chronic renal failure: Report of a multicenter randomized double-blind placebo-controlled study, 1994; Co-author, Five years experience with recombinant human growth hormone treatment of children with chronic renal failure, 1994. Honours: National Medical Award in Nephrology, National Kidney Foundation of New York & New Jersey, 1992; SUNY Stony Brook School of Medicine Award for Excellence in Teaching, 1993. Memberships: AMA; American Society of Nephrology; American Society for Pediatric Nephrology; American Pediatric Society; National Kidney Foundation; American Academy of Pediatrics; American Federation for Clinical Research. Address: Department of Pediatrics, University of New York at Stony Brook, Stony Brook, NY 11794-8111, USA.

FINK George, b. 13 Nov 1936, Austria. Director; Honorary Professor. m. Ann Elizabeth Langsam, 1959, 1 son, 1 daughter. Education: MB, BS, 1960, MD, 1978, University of Melbourne; DPhil, Hertford College, University of Oxford, 1967. Appointments: Junior, Senior House Officer, Royal Melbourne & Alfred Hospitals, Victoria, Australia, 1961-62; Demonstrator in Anatomy, Monash University, Victoria, Australia, 1963-64; Nuffield Dominions Demonstrator, Oxford University, 1965-67; Senior Lecturer in Anatomy, Monash University, 1968-71; University Lecturer, 1971-80; Director, MRC Brain Metabolism Unit; Honorary Professor, University of Edinburgh. Publications: Neuropeptides: Basic and Clinical Aspects, 1982; Neuroendocrine Molecular Biology, 1986; Neuropeptides: A Methodology, 1989; Over 300 scientific publications mainly on neuroendocrinology and neuroendocrine molecular biology. Honours: Royal Society-Israel Academy Exchange Fellow, Weizmann Institute, 1979; Walter Cottman Fellow & Visiting Professor, Monash University, 1985, 1989; Arthur Fishberg Professor, Mt Sinai Med School, New York, 1988; Prosector in Anatomy, Melbourne University, 1986; Wolfson Lecturer, University of Oxford, 1982; First GW Harris Leture, Phys Soc, Cambridge, 1987. Memberships incl: European Neuroendocrine Associaton; Trustee of JI of Neuroendocrinology. Hobbies: Skiing; Swimming. Address: MRC Brain Metabolism Unit, University Department of Pharmacology, 1 George Square, Edinburgh EH8 9JZ, Scotland.

FINK Jordan Norman, b. 13 Oct 1934, Milwaukee, Wisconsin, USA. Physician. m. Phyllis Mechanic, 26 Aug 1956, 1 son, 2 daughters. Education: BS, 1956, MD, 1959, University of Wisconsin. Appointments: Fellow, Allergy and Immunology, Northwestern University; Associate Professor of Medicine, currently Professor of Medicine, Medical College of Wisconsin, Milwaukee. Publications: Hypersensitivity Pneumonitis in Allergy, Principles and Practice, 1993. Honours: Phi Beta Kappa, 1955; Alpha Omege Alpha, 1959. Memberships: American Academy of Allergy and Immunology; Association of American Physicians; American Association of Immunology. Hobbies: Swimming; Travel. Address: Medical College of Wisconsin, 870-0 W Wisconsin Avenue, Milwaukee, WI 53226, USA.

FINKELSTEIN Stanley M, b. 16 Jun 1941, Brooklyn, NY, USA. Biomedical Engineering. Education: BS; MS; PhD. Appointments: Assistant/Associate Professor of Operations Research and Systems Analysis and Bioengineering, Polytechnic Institute of Brooklyn; Associate Professor/Professor of Laboratory Medicine and Pathology, University of Minnesota. Publications: Over 120 Articles, Chapters and Abstracts. Honours: NDEA Fellow, 1962-65; NSF Faculty Fellow in Science, 1975-77; NIH and NSF Research Grants. Memberships: IEEE Engineering in Medicine and Biology Society; Biomedical Engineering Society; AAAS; Association for Advancement of Medical Instrumentation; New York Academy of Sciences. Hobbies: Jogging; Biking; Cross Country Skiing. Address: University of Minnesota, Department of Laboratory Medicine and Pathology, Division of Health Computer Sciences, Box 511 Mayo, Minneapolis, MN 55455, USA.

FINKLESTEIN Jerry, b. 28 Apr 1938, Montreal, Quebec, Canada. Physician. m. Marilyn Solowey, 20 Nov 1966, 2 daughters. Education: BSc, MD, CM, McGill University, Montreal; FAAP. Appointments: Currently: Professor of Paediatrics, University of California at Los Angeles School of Medicine, USA; Medical Director, Jonathan Jaques Children's Cancer Center, Long Beach. Publications: Over 100 articles and abstracts in peer review journals, 1969-94. Honours: American Board of Pediatrics, 1968; American Board of Pediatrics, Haematology and Oncology, 1974. Memberships: American Academy of Pediatrics; American Society of Pediatric Hematology and Oncology; American Society of Clinical Oncology; American Society of Hematology. Hobbies: Skiing; Tennis; Archaeology. Address: 2653 Elm Avenue 200, Long Beach, CA 90806, USA.

FINLAY Jonathan Lester, b. 16 Oct 1948, Manchester, England. Associate Professor; Vice Chairman. m. Diane Papalia Finlay, 19 July 1976, 1 daughter. Education: MB, ChB, University of Birmingham Medical School, England, 1973; BSc, hons, Biochemistry, 1990. Appointments: Assistant Professor of Pediatrics, Stanford University Medical Center, 1980-82; Assistant Professor of Pediatrics, University Wisconsin Medical School, Madison, 1982-85; Associate Professor of Pediatrics, University of Wisconsin, Madison, 1985-87; Associate of Pediatrics, University of Pennsylvania School of Medicine & The Children's Hospital of Philadelphia, 1987-89; Chairman, Brain Tumor Strategy Group of the Childrens Cancer Group, 1985-92; Vice Chairman, Brain Tumor Strategy Group, 1992-. Publications: Over 50 peer-reviewed original articles, mainly concerning therapy of brain tumors and childhood non-Hodgkin's lymphoma; Additionally, review articles, book chpters, symposia reports and abstracts of oral presentations numbering over 80, 1980-. Memberships: American Society of Clinical Oncology; American Society of Hematology; American Society of Pediatric hematology & Oncology; International Society for Experimental Hematology; International Society of Paediatric Oncology; Childrens Cancer Group of North America. Hobbies: Philately; Movies; Opera; Classical Music; Fine Wines & Food. Address: Department of Pediatrics, Room H1408, Memorial Sloan-Kettering Cancer Center, 1275 York Avenue, NY 10021, USA.

FINLEY Dorothy Ann, b. 17 July 1943, Berkeley, California, USA. Editor, Nutrition. 2 sons. Education: BS, high honours, University of California, Davis; MS, University of California, Daivs; PhD, University of California, Davis. Appointments: Associate Editor, The Journal of Nutrition, 1969-90; Manuscripts Editor, American Journal of Clinical Nutrition. Publications: Co-author, Effects of magetarian duts upon composition of human milk, 1986. Memberships: American Institute of Nutrition; American Society for Clinical Nutrition; Council of Biology Editors. Address: Department of Nutritional Sciences, 109 Morgan Hall, University of California, Berkeley, CA 94720-3104, USA.

FISCH Richard, b. 15 Dec 1926, New York City, New York, USA. Psychiatrist. 2 sons, 2 daughters. Education: BA, Colby College, Waterville, Maine, 1949; MD, New York Medical College, New York, 1954; Psychiatric Residency, Sheppard and Enoch Pratt Hospital, Towson, Maryland, 1955-58; American Board of Psychiatry and Neurology, 1962. Appointments: Currently Psychiatrist in private practice, Palo Alto, California and Senior Research Fellow, Mental Research Institute. Publications: Change - Principles of Problem Formation and Problem Resolution (with P Watzlawick and John Weakland), 1974; The Tactics of Change - Doing Therapy Briefly (with John Weakland and Lynn Segal), 1982. Honours: Award for Distinguished Achievement in New Directions in Family Therapy, American Family Therapy Association, 1981. Hobbies: Private pilot; Photography. Address: 555 Middlefield Road, Palo Alto, CA 94301, USA.

FISHER Benjamin, b. 24 May 1928, Jerusalem, Israel. Physician. 2 sons, 1 daughter. Education: MD; FRCP(C). Appointments: Assistant Professor of Medicine, University of Calgary Medical School, 1970-73; Chief of Dermatology Department, Chaim Sheba Medical Centre, University of Tel-Aviv Medical School, 1973-75; Professor, University of Toronto Medical School. Publications: Co-author: Gross and Microscopic Pathology of the Skin, 1988; Co-author: Cutaneous

Manifestations of the Acquired Immunodeficiency Syndrome Update, 1987; Co-author: Neurotic Excoriations, 1974. Honours: Canadian Dermatological Association Research Award, 1972; Nominated, Practitioner of the Year, Division of Dermatology, University of Toronto, 1993. Memberships: Canadian Medical Association; Canadian Dermatological Association; American Academy of Dermatology; American Society of Dermatopathology; International Society of Tropical Dermatology. Address: Suite 326, Jones Bldg, The Wellesley Hospital, 160 Wellesley Street East, Toronto, Ontario M4Y 1J3, Canada.

FISHER Bernard, b. 23 Aug 1918, Pittsburgh, USA. Surgeon. m. Shirley Kruman, 5 June 1947, 1 son, 2 daughters. Education: BS, Chemistry, MD, University of Pittsburgh; Diplomat, American Board Surgeons. Appointments: Assistant Professor of Surgery, 1953, Associate Professor of Surgery, 1956, Professor of Surgery, 1959; Chairman, National Surgical Adj Breast Project, NSABP, 1967-94; Distinguished Service Professor, 1986. Publications: Contributor of over 480 works including: Comparison of Radical Mastectomy with Alternative Treatments for Primary Breast Cancer: A First Report of Results from a Prospective Randomized Clinical Trial, 1977; Five Year Results of a Randomized Clinical Trial Comparing Total Mastectomy and Segmental Mastectomy with or without Radiation in the Treament of Breast Cancer, 1985; A Randomized Trial Evaluating Tamoxifen in the Treatment of Patients with node-negative Breast Cancer who have Estrogen-receptor-positive Tumors, 1989; The Evolution of Paradigms for the Management of Breast Cancer: A Personal Perspective, 1992. Honours: Albert Lasker Research Award; American Cancer Society Medal of Honour; Bristol Myers Squibb Award; General Motors Cancer Research Foundation Kettering Prize. Memberships: ASCO; AACR; American College of Surgeons; American Surgical Association; Society of Surgical Oncology; NABCO; Y-ME. Address: University of Pittsburgh, School of Medicine, Department of Surgery, 914 Scaife Hall, 3550 Terrace Street, Pittsburgh, PA 15261, USA.

FISHER Robert, b. 5 Jan 1955, Auburn, New York, USA. Physician. m. Bonnie Helfgott, 8 Aug 1982, 2 d. Education: BA, Haverford College; MD, University of Rochester; Certified Internal Medicine, Washington University; Clinical Immunology, Johns Hopkins University. Appointments: Assistant Professor, East Carolina University School of Medicine; Associate Professor of Medicine. Publications: Association of Penicillin Allergy with Urticalis, 1993; Mediator Fundions of Platelets, 1994. Honours: Phi Beta Kappa, 1977; American Academy of Allergy Young Investigator, 1987; Davis Fellowship, 1989. Memberships: American Academy of Allergy & Immunology; American College of Allergy & Immunology; Clinical Immunology Society; American Thoracic Society. Hobbies: Tennis; Computers. Address: Allergy & Asthma Center, Medical College of Wisconsin, P O Box 1997, Milwaukee, WI 53201, USA.

FITZ-GERALD Mary Jo Juneau, b. 20 Oct 1954, Lake Charles, Louisiana, USA. Psychiatrist. m. Michael S Fitz-Gerald, 1 son, 2 daughter. Education: BS, McNeese State University, Lake Charles, 1976; MD; Louisiana State University Medical Center, Shreveport, 1980. Appointments: Assistant Professor, Clinical Psychiatry, 1983-93; Director of Inpatient Service, 1989-90; Director of Psychiatry Consultation Liaison, 1990-94; Currently Associate Professor, Clinical Psychiatry, Residency Training Director, Louisiana State University Medical Center, Shreveport. Publications: Premenstrual Symdrome, 1990; Co-author: Longitudinal Quantitative EEG Findings After Acute Carbon Monoxide Exposure: Two Case Studies, 1991; Differences in Complex Reaction Time Between THC Users and Non-User Controls, 1992; Multi-System Screening in Selecting Normal Ss for Drug Abuse Research: How Normal is Normal?, 1993; Time Distortion as a Persistent Sequelae of Chronic THC Use, 1993; Performance of Chronic Daily Marijuana Users on Neuropsychological Tests, 1993; Altered Quantitative EEG Topography as a Seuence of Chronic THC Exposure: A Replication Using Screen Normal Subjects, 1993. Memberships: American Psychiatric Association; Louisiana Psychiatric Medical Association; Association; ASAM; AADPRT; Shreveport Medical Society; Fellow, APA, 1993; LSMS; President, LPMA, 1995-96; Aera V Rep to the JCPA, 1994-. Hobbies: Children; Travel. Address: Department of Psychiatry, Louisiana State University Medical Center, 1501 Kings Highway, POB 33932, Shreveport, LA 71130-3932, USA.

FITZGERALD Jeanne Tashian, b. 18 Apr 1946, Chicago, Illinois, USA. Medical Writer; Consultant. 1 s, 1 d. Education: BA, 1967, AM, 1969, University of Chicago; Postgraduate Studies, University of Michigan, 1971-73. Appointments: Assistant Editor, Michigan Academy

of Science, 1970-73; Associate Editor, Department of Surgery, University of Michigan Medical Centre, 1973-84; Administrative Editor, Annals of Thoracic Surgery, 1973-84; President, Communication Consultants for Health Care and Business. Publications: Editor of numerous books; Contributor of numerous articles; Every Woman's Pharmacy: A Guide to Safe Drug Use, Co-author, 1984; The Women's Health and Drug Reference, Co-author, 1993. Honours: Fellow, AMWA, 1982; Apollo Award for Excellence in Writing, SE Michigan Hospital Public Relations Association, 1986; Award of Merit, Society for Technical Communications, 1989. Memberships: American Medical Writers Association; American Association of Medical Society Executives. Hobbies: Foreign Languages; Breeding Himalayan Cats; Golf; Ballroom Dancing. Address: 821 Hewett Drive, Ann Arbor, MI 48103, USA.

FITZGERALD Raymond James, b. 27 Aug 1941, Dublin, Republic of Ireland. Consultant Paediatric Surgeon. m. Joy Carson, 17 Aug 1968, 2 sons, 1 daughter. Education: BA, 1965, MB BCh, BAO, 1967, MA, 1968, Trinity College, Dublin University; Fellow, Royal College of Surgeons in Ireland, 1972; Fellow, Royal College of Surgeons in England, 1972; Fellow (Paediatric Surgery), Royal Australasian College of Surgeons, 1977. Appointments: Intern, Adelaide Hospital, Dublin; Surgeon Lieutenant (Surgical Specialist), Royal Navy; Surgical Registrar, Broad Green Hospital, Liverpool, England; Senior House Officer, Hospital for Sick Children, Great Ormond Street, London; Senior Research Fellow, Senior Registrar, Our Lady's Hospital for Sick Children, Dublin; Registrar, Royal Children's Hospital, Melbourne, Victoria, Australia; Senior Registrar, The Children's Hospital, Temple Street, Dublin; Currently Consultant Paediatric Surgeon, The Children's Hospital, Temple Street and Our Lady's Hospital for Sick Children, Dublin. Publications: Over 65 on different aspects of paediatric surgery. Memberships: British Association of Paediatric Surgeons; Society for Research into the Hydrocephalus of Spina Bifida, Ex Treasurer; Fellow, Royal Academy of Medicine in Ireland; International Society of Paediatric Oncology; President, Association for the Welfare of Children in Hospital. Hobbies: Private pilot; Game shooting; Walking; Skiing. Address: 9 Orwell Park, Rathgar, Dublin 6, Ireland.

FITZPATRICK Thomas Bernard, b. 19 Dec 1919, Madison, Wisconsin, USA. Physician; Educator. m. Beatrice Devaney, 27 Dec 1944, 3 sons, 1 daughter. Education: BA, Honours, University of Wisconsin, 1941; MD, Harbard University, 1945; Fellow, Mayo Foundation, 1948-51; PhD, University of Minnesota, 1952; Fellow, Commonwealth Fund, Oxford, England, 1958-59; DSc, Honorary, University of Massachusetts, 1987. Appointments: Intern, 4th Medical Service, Boston City Hospital, 1945-46; Biochemist, Army Medical Centre, Maryland, 1946-48; Assistant Professor of Dermatology, University of Michigan Medical School, 1951-52; Professor, Head, Division Dermatology, University of Oregon Medical School, 1952-58; Edward Wigglesworth Professor of Dermatology, Harvard Medical School, 1959-60; Professor Emeritus, 1990-; Department Head, 1959-87; Chief, Dermatology Service, Massachusetts General Hospital, Boston, 1959-87; Prosser White Orator, St John's Dermatology Society, London, 1964; Dohi International Exchange Lecturer, Dermatology, Japan, 1969; Special Consultant, USPHS, NIH; Consultant, Peter Bent Brigham Hospital, Children's Hospital Medical Centre, Boston, 1962. Publications include: Year book Dermatology, Editor, 1984-; Dermatology in General Medicine, Chief Editor, 1971, 3rd Edition, 1987. Honours include: Officer, Order of Rising Gold Rays, Japan; Mayo Foundation Alumni Research Award; Distinguished Service Award, Dermatology Foundation, 1989; Distinguished Service Award, University of Wisconsin, 1989. Memberships include: Associate of Professors of Dermatology; International Pigment Cell Society; President, 1971, Dermatology Foundation. Address: 209 Newton Street, Weston, MA 02193-2338, USA.

FJELD Anne, b. 30 may 1953, Oslo, Norway, Orthodontist. m. Sigmund Hov Moen, 1 s. Education: Cand Odont, Oslo, 1977; postgraduate Student, 1985; Orthodontic Specialist, 1993. Appointments: Private Practice. Memberships: European Orthodontic Society. Hobbies: Running; Skiing. Address: Dr Dedichensv 82, 0675 Oslo, Norway.

FLANDERS Douglas Roy, b. 22 Apr 1967, San Antonio, Texas, USA. Physician. m. Jennifer Lyn Cowan, 15 Aug 1978, 3 sons 1 daughter. Education: BS, Biology, Dallas Baptist University, 1988; MD, University of Texas Southwestern Medical Center, 1992; Internship, Internal Medicine, St Paul Medical Center, Dallas, 1992-93; Resident in

Anaesthesiology, Parkland Memorial Hospital, 1993-. Appointments: Teaching Assistant, Department of Cell Biology, University of Texas Southwestern Medical Center, autumn 1991; Associate Physician, The University Medical Group, 1993-. Honours: Marshal O Bell Scholarship, 1985-89; Louis Barckman Scholarship, 1991-92. Memberships: American Medical Association; Texas Medical Association; American Society of Anesthesiologists. Hobbies: Running; Tennis; Writing. Address: 2004 Eastbrook Circle, Mesquite, TX 75150, USA.

FLANIGAN Michael John, b. 27 Apr 1948, Milwaukee, WI, USA. Physician. m. Jane Ann Miller, 11 Aug 1971, 3 s, 1 d. Education: BS, MD, University of WI; MD. Appointment: Assistant Professor of Medicine, University of IA. Memberships: Alpha Omega Alpha; American College of Physicians; International Society of Nephrology; International Society of Peritoneal Dialysis; American Society of Artificial Internal Organs; National Kidney Foundation; American Society of Transplant Physicians. Address: W 346 GH, Department of Medicine, University of Iowa Hospitals, Iowa City, IA 52240, USA.

FLANIGAN Robert Charles, b. 2 May 1946, Lima, Ohio, USA. Urologist. 2 children. Education: BA, College of Wooster, 1968; MD, Case Western Reserve University, 1972. Appointments: Assistant, Associate Professor, Surgery, University of Kentucky, 1980-86; Professor, Chairman, Department of Urology, Loyola University Medical Center 1986-. Publications: Prostrate Trans Cell Cancer, 1982; Therapy in Surgery, 1991; Numerous publications and articles in journals. Memberships: Editorial Board, Kidney Cancer Journal. Honours: WMA Award, College of Wooster, 1968; Airforce Commendation Medal, 1980; Golden Apple Award, 1981. Hobbies: Sports; Tennis; Golf. Address: 2160 South 1st Avenue, Maywood, IL 60153, USA.

FLATT Jean Pierre, b. 3 Mar 1933, Basel, Switzerland. Biochemist. m. Ann Elizabeth Holmes, 21 Dec 1963, 1 s, 2 d. Education: Chemical Engineering Diploma, Ecole Polytechnique, University of Lausanne, Switzerland, 1956; Dr Es Sciences, Chemistry, University of Lausanne, Switzerland, 1959; Post Doctoral Research Fellow, Department of Biology Chemistry, Harvard Medical School, Boston, MA, USA, 1960-63. Career: Chef de Travaux, Lecturer in Biochemistry, Faculty of Sciences, University of Lausanne, Switzerland, 1963-67; Research Associate, Instructor, Assistant Professor, Associate Professor of Physiological Chemistry, Department of Nutrition and Food Services, MA Institute of Technology, Cambridge, MA, 1967-73; Currently, Professor of Biochemistry and Molecular Biology, University of MA Medical School, Worcester, MA. Publications: Contributor to: Journal of Biological Chemistry, 1966, 1969, Journal of Lipid Research, 1970, Diabetes, 1972, Journal of Clinical Investigation, 1985; American Journal of Clinical Nutrition, 1974, 1987, Diabetes, Mat Rev, 1988, Journal of Nutritional Biochemistry, 1991, Ann NY Academy of Science, 1993. Hobbies: Hiking; Skiing; Biking; Music; Chess. Address: Department of Biochemistry and Molecular Biology, University of Massachusetts Medical School, Worcester, MA 01655, USA.

FLEMING Lora Elderkin, b. 1 Jan 1957, Los Angeles, USA. Epidemiology. m. M Outiz, 1 daughter. Education: AB, Radcliffe College, Harvard University, 1978; MSc, Imperial College, London University, England, 1979; MD, MPH, Harvard Medical School & Harvard School of Public Health, 1984. Appointments: Intern, Oil, Chemical & Atomic Workers Union, Watertown, 1980; Residency Training, Montefiore Hospital, New York, 1984-87; Fellowship Training, Yale University School of Medicine, 1987-1989; Assistant Professor, Department of Epidemiology & Public Health, University of Miami School of Medicine, 1989-. Publications include: Disease Clusters: A Central and Ongoing Role in Occupational Medicine, 1991; Disease Clusters in Occupational Medicine: A Protocol for their Investigation, 1992; Organochlorine Pesticides and Parkinsons Disease, 1994. Honours incl: NIOSH Career Development Award, SERCA, 1993-94; Enviro-Hero Award, Arise Foundation, Miami, 1993. Address: c/o Department of Epidemiology, University of Miami School of Medicine, PO Box 016069, Miami, FL 33101, USA.

FLEMING William Hare, b. 1 May 1935, Columbus, Ohio, USA. Surgeon. 2 sons, 1 daughter. Education: BA, Yale University, 1957; MD, Columbia University, 1961. Appointments: Assistant Professor of Surgery, Emroy University; Chief, Thoracic Surgery Section, Atlanta, VA; Adjunct Senior Research Scientist, Georgia Institute of Technology; Associate Professor of Surgery, UNMC; Chief, Thoracic-Cardiac Surgery Section, UNMC; Professor of Surgery, UNMC; Professor of Pediatrics, UNMC; Director of Pediatric Cardiovascular Surgery,

Childrens Memorial Hospital, 1985-93; Medical Director, Division of Clinical Perfusion Education, School of Allied Health Professions, UNMC, 1989-92. Honours: President's Award, Southern Thoracic Surgical Association to Co-authors & Dr Fleming for their paper on Carcinoma of the Pulmonary Sulcus, 1979. Memberships: Metropolitan Omaha Medical Society; Nebraska Medical Association; American Academy of Pediatrics; American Association for Thoracic Surgery; American College of Cardiology; American College of Chest Physicians; American College of Surgeons. Hobbies: Tennis; Jet-skiing; Sailing. Address: 8300 Dodge Street, Suite 302, Omaha, NE 68114-4112, USA.

FLETCHER David J, b. 30 Sept 1954, Cleveland, Ohio, USA. Physician. m. Wanda E Fletcher, 22 Mar 1978, 1 son, 1 daughter. Education: MD; MPH. Appointments: Medical Director, DMH Corporate Health Services, 1986-89; US Army Preventive Medicine Officer; Director, Midwest Occupational Health Associates. Publications: Management of Multi-Site Occupational Health Services, in Journal of Occupational Medicine, 1994. Memberships: American College of Occupational & Environmental Medicine; American College of Preventive Medicine; ATPM. Hobbies: Prairie Restoration; Hiking. Address: 1770 E Lake Shore Drive, Suite 200, Decatur, IL 62521-3809, USA.

FLETCHER William Sigourney, b. 17 May 1927, Arlington, Massachusetts, USA. Surgeon. 1 son, 2 daughters. Education: AB, Dartmouth College, cum laude; MD, Harvard Medical School. Appointments: Instructor, Surgery, Oregon Health Sciences University, 1960-62; Assistant Professor, Surgery, Oregon Health Sciences University, 1962-65; Associate Professor, Surgery, Oregon Health Sciences University, 1965-70; Professor, Surgery, Oregon Health Sciences University, 1970-; Head, Surgical Oncology, Oregon Health Sciences University, 1975-. Publications incl: Cyclophosphamide, Methotrexate and 5-Fluorouracil in the Treatment of Metastatic Prostate Cancer, 1993; Pharmacokinetics and Results of Dose Escalation in Cis-platin Hyperthermic Isolation Limb Perfusion, 1994; Didemini B in Metastatic Malignant Melanoma: A Phase II Trial of the Southwest Oncology Group, 1994; Results of Cisplatin Hyperthermic Isolation Perfusion for Stage IIIA and IIIAB Extremity Melanoma, 1994; Colorectal Cancer in Young Patients: Characteristics and Outcome, 1994. Memberships incl: American Association for Cancer Education; American Association for Cancer Research; American Surgical Association; Multnomah County Medical Society. Hobbies: Raising and Training Labrador Retrievers; Bird Hunting; Beach; Reading; Writing. Address: 1600 South West 88th Portland, OR 97225, USA.

FLICK Ferdinand Herman, b. 19 Feb 1917, New York City, USA. Physician; Surgeon. m. Marie T Pinto, 20 Apr 1945, 2 sons, 2 daughters. Education: BS, MS, Fordham University; MD, Yale University. Appointments: Assistant Professor, University California, Berkeley; Teaching Fellow, Fordham University; Division Surgeon, US Army; Attending Physician, Presbyterian Hospital, New York; Chief Plant Physician, Edison Assembly Plant, Ford Motor Company. Publications: Pelvic Congestion Syndrome, 1955; Prolongation of Anesthesia by Tetraethyl Thivram Disalfide, 1951. Honours: Sigma Xi; Meritorious Service Medal, US Army Medical Corps. Memberships: Fellow, American Society of Abdominal Surgeons; Fellow, American College of Preventive Medicine; Fellow, American College of Occupational & Environmental Medicine. Hobbies: Golf; Skiing; Stamp Collecting. Address: 21 Miara Street, Parlin, NJ 08859-1815, USA.

FLORENZANO Ramon V, b. 28 Dec 1944, Santiago de Chile, Chile. Medical Doctor. m. Macarena Valdes, 20 Mar 1970, 3 sons, 3 daughters. Education: MD, University of Chile, 1968; MPH, University of North Carolina, USA, 1968; Diplomate, American Board of Psychiatry, 1977. Appointments: Resident in Psychiatry, North Carolina Memorial Hospital, 1973-75; Assistant Professor, 1975-77, Clinical Professor, 1988-89, University of North Carolina Medical School, 1975-77; Head of Psychiatry, Hospital del Salvador, Santiago, Chile, 1978-83; Full Professor, Chairman, Department of Psychiatry, University of Chile Medical School, Santiago, 1983-. Publications: Tecnicas de Psicoterapias Dinamicas, 1984; Salud Familiar, 1986; Atencion Primaria y Salud Mental, 1989. Memberships: International Psychoanalytical Association; American Psychiatric Association; Chilean Neuropsychiatric Association. Hobbies: Tennis; Reading. Address: Ricardo Matte 584, Santiago, Chile.

FLYNN Janet, b. 24 Jan 1958, Wigan, England. Family Physician. m. W Patrick Lewis, 13 Jul 1991. Education: BA, University of Western

Ontaria, 1976; MD, McMaster University, 1988; Clinical Fellowship in Palliative Care, London, Ontario, 1990-91; Qigong for Healths Healing, University of Hawaii, Manoa, 1992. Appointments: Family Physician, London Intercommunity Health Centre, London, Canada. Publications: A Putative Role for Human Retro Viruses in the Cause of Multiple Sclerosis, 1987; Management of Intractable Nausea & Vomiting in Terminally Staged Aids; The Management of Advanced Cancer. Honours: Ontario Scholar, 1972; Faculty Scholarship, University of Western Ontaria, 1975; Embassy Scholarship, University of Western Ontario, 1976; Dean's Honors Roll, University of Western Ontario, 1972-77. Memberships: Ontario/Canadian Medical Associations; Native Physicians Association of Canada; Canadian Physicians for Aid & Relief; Ontario Herbalists Association; International Society for Traumatic Stress Studies; Physicians for the Environment. Hobbies: Music; Tennis; Running. Address: JK International Trauma Counselling Services, Suite 417, 981 Wellington Road South, London, Ontario, Canada N6E 3A9.

FOGEL-DE KORC Eva, b. 16 June 1928, Roumania, (Uruguayan Citizen). Professor of Clinical Toxicology. m. Israel Korc, 31 Jan 1953, 1 son, 1 daughter. Education: MD, Faculty of Medicine, University of Uruguay, 1955. Appointments: Assistant Professor, Internal Medicine, Pneumology; Associate Professor, Emergency Medicine; Full Professor, Toxicology; Director, Poison Control Center, Faculty of Medicine, University of Uruguay. Publications: Manejo del enfermo grave en emergencia, 1981; Chemical Emergency Preparedness, 1984; Patologia de las intoxicaciones, 1993. Memberships: American Academy of Toxicology; Latin American Association of Toxicology; Uruguayan Society of Toxicology; Uruguayan Society of Emergency Medicine & Surgery; World Federation of Poison Control Centers. Honours: Prize, National Academy of Medicine, Uruguay, 1982; Prize, 50 Years of the Ministry of Public Health, Uruguay, 1984. Address: Gabriel A Pereira 3247, Apt 201, 11300 Montevideo, Uruguay.

FOLLIN Marie, b. 13 May 1947, Sweden. Orthodontist. Education: DDS; LDS; OD. Appointments: Associate Professor, Orthodontic Department, University of Goteborg. Memberships: EOS; SOF. Hobby: Sailing. Address: Orthodontic Department, Faculty of Odontology, Medicinaregatan 12, S-41390 GÖteborg, Sweden.

FOMON Samuel Joseph, b. 9 Mar 1923, Chicago, IL, USA. Physician. 2 s, 3 d. Education: AB, cum laude, Harvard University; MD, University of Pennsylvania, Philadelphia. Appointments: Assistant Professor, 1954-57, Associate professor, 1957-61, Professor, 1961-93, Department of Paediatrics, College of Medicine, University of Iowa; Director, Program in Human Nutrition, University of Iowa, 1980-88; Professor Emeritus, University of Iowa. Publications Infant Nutrition, 1967, 2nd edition, 1974; Nutrition of Normal Infants, 1993. Honours: USPH Career Development Award, 1962-67; Borden Award, American Academy of Paediatrics, 1966; Rosen von Rosenstein Medal, Swedish Paediatric Society, 1974; McCallum Award, American Society for Clinical Nutrition, 1979; Honorary member, American Dietetic Association, 1985; Fellow, American Institute of Nutrition, 1989; Conrad A Elvejhem Award, American Institute of Nutrition, 1990; Nutricia Research Foundation Award, Netherlands, 1991; Bristol-Myers Squibb/Mead Johnson Award for distinguished Achievement in Nutrition Research, 1992; Doctor Honoris Causa, Argentina. Memberships: American Academy Paediatrics; American Paediatric Society; American Society for Clinical Nutrition, President, 1981-82; American Institute of Nutrition, President, 1989-90; Midwest Society for Paediatric Research, President, 1963-64; Society for Paediatric Research. Hobby: Gardening. Address: 415 Windsor Drive, New Braunfels, TX 78132, USA.

FONSEKA Merrennage Neil Thomas, b. 19 July 1940, Colombo, Sri Lanka. Professor of Surgery. m. Pushpa Fonseka, 6 Aug 1970. Education: FRCS, 1972; FRCS, 1972; FRCOG, 1993. Appointments: Registrar in Surgery, St Bartholomews Hospital, London, 1971-72; Senior Registrar in Surgery, Charing Cross Hospital, London, 1973-76; Surgeon, Limb Center & Hon Consultant Surgeon, Brighton Health District, 1977-79. Publications: A Students Guide to History Taking and Examination in Surgery, handbook for Medical Undergraduates, 1992; Basic Principles in Surgery, 1995. Honours: Commonwealth Open Scholarship for Surgery, 1970. Memberships: Board Member, Study in Surgery, Postgraduate Institute of Medicine, Colombo, Sri Lanka; Life Member, College of Surgeons of Sri Lanka; Life Member, College of Obstetricians & Gynaecologists of Sri Lanka. Address: Department of Surgery, Faculty of Medicine, University of Ruhuna, PO Box 70, Galle, Sri Lanka.

FONTÁNYI Sándor, b. 30 Jan 1926, Szolnok, Hungary. Surgeon. m. Ilona Kolozsi, 30 Dec 1961, 1 son, 2 daughters. Education: Semmelweis University of Medicine, Budapest, Hungary, 1951; Department of Cardiovascular Surgery, 1953. Appointments: Department of Surgery, Péterfy Hospital, Budapest. Publications: Co-author: Acute arteriovenous anastomoses, 1980; Author: Modification and diagnostic value of vein percussion, 1982; Co-author: TPM/Toe-Plethysmometry in diagnosis of peripheral occlusive arterial disease, 1986. Honours: Award, Péterfy S Hospital, 1970. Memberships: Hungarian Association of Surgeons of Angiology. Hobbies: Skiing; Sailing; Surfing; Riding; Biking; Music; Guitar. Address: 14/a Károlyi M, u Budapest 1053, Hungary.

FORD Linda Lou Hooton, b. 14 Aug 1948, Tipton, Oklahoma, USA. Dietitian. m. Gary Leroy Ford, 21 Dec 1973, 2 daughters. Education: AA, Altus Junior College, 1968; BSc, Summa Cum Laude, Harding College, 1970; Dietetic Internship, UO Health Sciences Centre, 1971; Registration, American Dietetic Association, 1971; Licensure, Oklahoma, 1980. APpointments: Therapeutic, Travelling, Managing Dietitian, ARA Services, 1971-73; Dietary Department Head, Jackson County Memorial Hospital, 1974-77; Consulting Dietitian, 1975-84; OSDH Nutritionist, 1986-. Memberships: American Dietetic Association; Okloahoma Dietetic Association. Hobbies: Bible Study; Walking. Address: 1905 North Oregon Avenue, Mangum, OK 73554, USA.

FOREMAN John William, b. 23 June 1947, Washington DC, USA. Pediatric Nephrology. m. Linda Poffenberger, 29 May 1973, 1 son, 1 daughter. Education: BS, 1969; MD, 1973. Appointments: Intern, Resident in Pediatrics, Montreal Children's Hospital, 1973-75; Assistant Chief Resident, The Children's Hospital of Philadelphia, 1975-76; Fellow, Nephrology & Metabolism, The Children's Hospital of Philadelphia, 1976-79; Assistant Professor of Pediatrics, University of Pennsylvania School of Medicine, 1979-85; Associate Professor of Pediatrics, University of Pennsylvania School of Medicine, 1985-86; Associate Professor of Pediatrics, Medical College of Virginia, 1986-90; Professor of Pediatrics, Medical College of Virginia, 1990-93; Professor of Pediatrics, Duke University School of Medicine, 1993-; Chief, Pediatric Nephrology, Duke University Medical Center, 1993-. Publications incl: Hypoxanthine uptake in isolated rat renal cortical tubule fragments, 1979; Effects of cysteamine therapy in nephropathic cyctinosis, 1981; Effect of cystine dimethylester on renal solute handling and isolated renal tubule transport in the rat: A new model of the Fanconi syndrome, 1987; Fanconi syndrome and cystinosis, 1994. Honours: Daland Fellow, American Philosophical Society, 1990; WHO Consultant in Pediatric Nephrology to Tianjin, China, 1984. Memberships incl: American Academy of Pediatrics; American Society of Nephrology. Hobbies: Reading; Bicycling. Address: Box 3959, Duke University Medical Center, Durham, NC 27710, USA.

FORER Bertram Robin, b. 24 Oct 1914, Springfield, Massachusetts, USA. Psychologist. Education: BS, Premedical, University of Massachusetts, Amherst, 1936; MA, Psychology, Experimental Esthetics, UCLA, Los Angeles, 1938; Teaching Assistant, UCLA, Los Angeles, 1938-41; PhD, Experimental and Social Psychology, UCLA, Los Angeles, 1941. Appointments: Personnel Technician, US Civil Service Commission, Washington DC, 1941-42; US Army, 1942-46; Test & Measurement Specialist, Office of the Secretary of War, Washington DC, 1946-47; Associate Clinical Professor, UCLA, 1947-59; Private Practice, Clinical Psychology, Los Angeles and Malibu, California, 1949-84. Publications: include, A Study of Consonant Preferences, 1940; A Diagnostic Interest Blank, 1948; A Structured Sentence Completion Test, 1950; Personality Dynamics & Occupational Choice, 1951; The Stability of Kuder Scores in a Disabled Population, 1955; Framework for the Use of Clinical Techniques in Vocational Counseling, 1965; Personal Validation and the Person, 1968; One Degree of Freedom, 1982. Honours: Commendation for Training Contributions, California State Psychological Association, 1986; Commendation for Outstanding Service, American Psychological Association, 1986; Award for Distinguished Contribution to the Profession, 1994. Memberships: include, American Psychological Association; American Academy of Psychotherapists; Los Angeles Society of Clinical Psychologists; American Group Psychotherapy Association; Society for the Psychological Society and Training Faculty; Phi Delta Kappa. Hobbies: Metal Sculpting; Travel; Photography. Address: 19854 Pacific Coast Highway, Malibu, CA 90265, USA.

FORLIFER Linda Elizabeth, b. 20 Mar 1948, Baltimore, Maryland, USA. Editor; Writer. m. Robert W Cooke, 31 Aug 1968, 2 sons.

Education: BA, Washington College, Chestertown, Maryland, 1970. Appointments: Assistant Editor, Neurosurgery, Congress of Neurological Surgeons; Currently Owner, ForWords Editorial Service, Baltimore. Publications: Copyediting on Line, 1991; Improving the Clarity and Readability of Clinical Reports and NDA Documents, 1991. Memberships: American Medical Writers Association; Council of Biology Editors; Executive Women's Network. Address: 315 East 33rd Street, Suite 203, Baltimore, MD 21218-3431, USA.

FORMAN Samuel A, b. 27 Oct 1952, Philadelphia, Pennsylvania, USA. Occupational Medicine Physician. m. Linda Roth, 10 Jan 1981, 2 daughters. Education: BA, University of Pennsylvania, 1973; MPH, Harvard School of Public Health, 1977; MD, Cornell Medical College, 1977; MS, Harvard School of Public Health, 1980; MPPM, Yale School of Management, 1995. Appointments: Associate Medical Director, Proctor & comisio Company, 1986-93; US Navy Medical Corps, 1977-86; Associate Professor of Environmental Medicine, University of Cincinnati Medical College. Publications: Occupational Medicine Staffing in Large US Corporations, 1994; An Early Study of Pulmonary Asbestosis Among Manufacturing Workers; Review of Papylong Glycol Dinitrate Toxicology and Epidomology. Honours: Magna Cum Laude Academic Honours, 1973; Navy Commendation Medal, 1985. Memberships: Fellow, American College of Occupational & Environmental Medicine; American Medical Association. Hobbies: Writing Fiction; History; Antiques; Travel. Address: Yale School of Management, New haven, CT 06520, USA.

FORREST Katherine Alden, b. 19 Feb 1942, Ohio, USA. Medical Consultant. m. Leonard M Salle, 30 July 1989, 2 sons. Education: BA, Harvard University; MD, Harvard Medical School; MPH, Harvard School of Public Health; Board-Certified in Preventive Medicine. Appointments: Research Associate, Harvard School of Public Health; Assistant Professor, Yale University School of Medicine; Medical Director, Planned Parenthood, San Jose, California; Associate Director, Clinical Investigation, Syntex; Associate Medical Director, International Marketing and New Product Planning, Syntex; Currently: Principal Research Scientist, American Institutes for Research, Palo Alto, California; Independent Medical Research and Marketing Consultant. Publications: Men's Reproductive Health, book, 1984; Condom failure: Laboratory testing and clinical considerations, 1989; Vaginal douching and pelvic inflammatory disease, 1989; College students' knowledge and attitudes about HIV and changes in HIV-preventive behaviors Co-author, 1990; Norms and beliefs related to AIDS prevention among California Hispanic men Co-author, 1993. Honours: General Motors National Scholarship, 1959-63; Raddcliffe Institute Macy Scholar, 1966-69. Memberships: American Public Health Association; American Fertility Society; Medical Marketing Association; Northern California Pharmaceutical Discussion Group. Hobbies: Singing; Hiking. Address: 150 Erica Way, Portola Valley, CA 94028-7440, USA.

FORRESTER Michael Anthony, b. 21 Mar 1953, Glasgow, Scotland. Psychologist. Education: BA, Honors, Psychology; PhD, Developmental Psychology. Appointments: Senior Lecturer in Psychology. Publications: The Development of Young Children's Social-Cognitive Skills; Hove-Lawrence Earlsbaum. Address: Department of Psychology, University of Kent, Canterbury, Kent CT2 7LZ, UK.

FORTNER Victoria Gene, b. 15 Jan 1954, St Louis, Missouri, USA. Herbist. Education: University of Missouri, St Louis, 1972-74, 1976-77, 1978-82; University of Texas, Arlington, 1977; Michigan State University, 1975; Lansing Community College, Michigan, 1974. Appointments include: Laboratory Manager, Contact Lens Specialist, Dr R I Myers OD, 1982-83; Certified Ophthalmic Medical Technician, Senior Technician, West County Ophthalmology Incorporated, 1984-91; Self Employed; Lecturer; Facillator; Counsellor; Artist; Craftperson; Restorer; Herbist. Publications include: Shamanism, 1986; The Old Ways, 1988; Sharing the Old Medicine Ways, 1988; Instant Enlightenment, 1993; Indian Givers Part 1-4, 1993; Gone But Not Forgotten, 1994; GE Brings Good Things to the Native Community, 1994. Hobbies: Native American dancing; Traditional Native Crafts. Address: 8219 Jefferson Avenue, St Louis, MO 63114, USA.

FORTNEY Judith A, b. 28 Jan 1938, Cheshire, England. Edipemiologist. m. Dr L R Fortney, 15 Apr 1962. 1 s, 1 d. Education: BSc, London School of Economics; PhD, Duke University, Durham, NC, USA. Appointments: Adjunct Professor of Epidemiology, University of North Carolina; Corporate Director of Scientific Affairs. Publications: Contributor of numerous professional articles in journals including:

Childbirth in Developing Countries, Co-Editor, 1983; Contraception for American Women Forty and Over, 1987; The Importance of Family Planning in Reducing Maternal Mortality, 1987; Contraception-A Lifelong Perspective, 1989. Honours: Fellow, American College of Epidemiology. Memberships: American Public Health Association; American College of Epidemiology; International Epidemiologic Society; Society for Epidemiology Research. Address: Family Health International, PO Box 13950, Research Triangle Park, NC 27709, USA.

FOUREL Genevieve Gilberte Marie, b. 19 Jan 1965, Neuilly, France. Researcher. Education: License Matrise, Paris VI University. Appointments: Predor, GR Crabtree Laboratory, Stanford, 1986; Student, I Meo laboratory, 1987, PhD Student, P Trollaic Laboratory, 1992, Group Leader, Institut Pasteur, Paris. Publications: Contributor of articles in journals. Honours: Prix Jeune Cherchen de la fondation pour la Recherche Medicale, 1992. Hobbies: Triathlon; Piano. Address: Institut Pasteur, 28 rue du Dr Roux, 75724 Paris cedex 15, France.

FOURNIER Etienne, b. 24 Nov 1923. Professor of Clinical Toxicology. m. Marielle Boy, 27 Apr 1947, 3 sons, 1 daughter. Education: MD; PhD. Appointments: Dean, Medical School Lariboisiue Saint Louis, Paris; Foundation Member, International Union of Toxicologists; Professor of Medicine; Physician, Hospital Fernand Widol. Publications: Contributor of papers and books on toxicology. Honours: Orpla Prize, 1987; Memberm National Academy of Medicine, France. Memberships: President, Societe Medecin Legal et Criminologie; Permanent Expert, European Community; Head, National Professional Disease Commission. Hobbies: Skiing; Travel. Address: 160 Boulevard Malesherbes, 75017 Paris, France.

FOWINKLE Eugene W, b. 2 Sept 1934, Memphis, Tennessee, USA. Medical Administration. m. Ruby Youngblood, 3 daughters. Education: MD, University of Tennessee, 1958; MPH, University of Michigan, 1962. Appointments: Director of Communicable Disease Control, Memphis & Shelby County Health Department, 1962-65; Assistant Director, 1965-66; Director, 1966-69; Clinical Instructor, University of Tennessee, 1964-65; Assistant Professor, 1965-74; Clinical Professor of Cummunity Medicine, 1974-83; Commissioner of Public Health, State of Tennessee, 1969-83. Publications: Numerous articles to professional journals. Honours: President's Award, Tennessee Hospital Association, 1983; Distinguished Service Award, Memphis Medical Society, 1982; Distinguished Service Award, University of Tennessee College of Medicine Alumni Association, 1982; Physician of the Year, Tennessee Association for Home Health, 1983. Memberships: Fellow, American College of Physicians; AMA; American Public Health Association; American College of Preventive Medicine; Southern Medical Association; Wilderness Society; Nashville Academy of Medicine; Tennessee Public Health Association. Hobbies: Hunting; Running; Music; Residential Construction. Address: Vanderbilt University Medical Center, D-3300 Medical Center North, Nashville, TN 37232-2104, USA.

FOX Roger W, b. 13 Jan 1949, Belleville, Illinois, USA. Physician. 2 sons, 1 daughter. Education: BA, Drake University, 1971; MD, St Louis University, 1975; Internship, Residency, 1975-78, Fellowship, Allergy, Clinical Immunology, 1978-80, University of South Florida Affiliated Hospital; Fellow, American Academy of Allergy and Immunology, 1985; Fellow, American College of Physicians, 1985. Appointments: Assistant Professor, Medicine, 1980-88, Associate Professor, Medicine, 1988-, Associate Professor, Public Health, 1993-, University of South Florida College of Medicine, Tampa; Physician, 1980-, Director, Allergy and Immunology Clinic, 1991, James A Haley Veterans Administration Hospital, Tampa. Publications: Textbook chapters including: Immediate Hypersentivity and Immune Complex Disease, 1982; The Effects of Age and Circadian Rhythm on Theophylline Pharmacokinetics in Normal Subjects, 1986; Environmental Control of Indoor Air Pollution, 1992; The Role of Immunotherapy in Asthma, 1994; Urticaria and Angioedema, 1994; Numerous articles and abstracts in the field of allergy and immunology; Tape recordings: Journal Club Allergy: Discussion based on selections from current literature, 1981; Treatment of Mild to Severe Chronic Urticaria with Astemizole, 1986. Honours: Beta Beta Beta, 1972. Memberships: President, Florida Allergy Society; American Medical Association; American Association for Clinical Immunology and Allergy; Florida Medical Association; Fellow, American Association of Certified Allergists. Hobbies: Running; Tennis; Golf; Boating; Water-skiing; Skiing. Address: 13801 Bruce B Downs Boulevard 502, Tampa, FL 33613-3923, USA.

FOX Steven H. Education: BS, Swarthmore College, Stanford University; MD, SM, University of Chicago; MPH, University of Washington. Appointments: Medical Epidermiologist; Agency for Health Care Policy and Research, USPHS. Address: AHCPR, 2101 East Jefferson St, Suite 605, Rockville, MD 20852, USA.

FOY Hjordis Mannbeck, b. 28 June 1926, Stockholm, Sweden. Professor of Epidemiology. m. Robert Eugene Foy, 23 Nov 1956, 3 daughters. Education: MD, Karolinska Institute, Stockholm; MS, PhD, University of Washington, USA. Appointments: Staff (Resident), Infectious Diseases and Internal Medicine, Stockholm, 1953-56; Intern, Fellow, Internal Medicine, Johns Hopkins Hospital, Baltimore, Maryland, USA, 1956-59; Staff Physician, Outpatient Clinic, Station Hospital, Ft George G Meade, 1960-61; Senior Fellow, Instructor, Department of Preventive Medicine, 1966-67, Professor, Department of Epidemiology, 1976-, University of Washington, Seattle. Publications: Adenoviruses, in Viral Infections of Humans: Epidemiology and Control, 3rd edition, 1989; Mycoplasma pneumoniae, in Bacterial Infections of Humans, 2nd edition, 1991. Honours: Fellow, Infectious Disease Society of America; Fellow, American College of Preventive Medicine. Memberships include: American Epidemiological Society; Society for Epidemiological Research; International Organisation of Mycoplasmologists. Hobby: Hiking. Address: Department of Epidemiology, SC-36, University of Washington, Seattle, WA 98195, USA.

FRANCESCHINI José A, b. 20 Mar 1949, Puerto Rico, USA. Medical Doctor; Psychiatrist. m. Angelisa Bonilla, 18 Apr 1981, 1 son, 2 daughters. Education: MD, Universidad Central del Caribe, 1980; Board Certified in Psychiatry and Geriatric Psychiatry. Appointments: Instructor in Psychiatry, 1984, Assistant Professor in Psychiatry, 1985, University of Alabama, Birmingham, USA; Chief, Geriatric Psychiatry, State Hospital, Alabama, 1985; Chief, Geriatric Psychiatry, Veterans Administration San Juan Medical Center, Puerto Rico, 1986; Director, Geriatric Programme, First Hospital Panamericano, Puerto Rico, 1988; Mbr, Executive Committee, 1991, Chairman, Department of Psychiatry, 1991-, University Hospital, Universidad Central del Caribe; Member, Puerto Rico Alzheimer's Disease Advisory Board, 1993. Publications: Co-author: The Elderly Coronary Bypass Patient: A Focus on Psychiatric Morbidity, 1984; Hyperparathyroidism and Paranoid Psychosis: Case Report and Review of Literature, 1984; Psychogeriatrics: Relationship between Consultant-Liaison and Inpatient Psychiatry. Honours: Alpha Omega Alpha, 1993. Memberships: American Psychiatric Association; American Psychiatry Association of Chairmen; American Academy of Psychiatry and Law; American Association of Partial Hospitals; American Association for Geriatric Psychiatry. Hobbies: Racketball; Tennis; Riding; Skiing. Address: Edificio Medico Sta Cruz, Suite 201, Sta Cruz St No 73, Bayamon, PR 00959, USA.

FRANCIS Leslie John, b. 10 Sept 1947, Colchester, Essex, England. Academic. Education: BA, 1970, MA, 1974, BD, 1990, Oxford University; MTh, Nottingham, 1976; PhD, Cambridge University, 1976; MSc, London, 1977; FBPsS, British Psychological Society, 1988. Appointments: Leverhulme Research Fellow, London; Senior Research Officer, Culham College Institute; Mansel Jones Research Fellow, Trinity College, Carmarthen, Wales; D J James Professor of Pastoral Theology, University of Wales, Lampeter and Trinity College, Carmarthen. Publications: Tennage Religion and Values, 1995; Psychological Perspectives on Christian Ministry, 1995; Churches in Fellowship, 1991; Religion in the Primary School, 1987; Teenagers and the Church, 1984; Young and Unemployed, 1984. Memberships: British Psychological Society; British Educational Research Association; Religious Research Association; Society for the Scientific Study of Religion. Address: Trinity College, Carmarthen, Dyfed SA31 3EP, Wales.

FRANCO Eduardo Luis Fabiano, b. 26 Mar 1953, Campinas, Brazil. Epidemiologist. m. Eliane Duarte, 27 July 1979, 3 s, 1 d. Education: BSc, Campinas State University, 1975; MPH, 1982; DrPH, 1984, University of North Carolina, USA. Appointments: Visiting Scientist, Centres for Disease Control, Atlanta, USA, 1980-84; Senior Researcher, Ludwig Institute for Cancer Research, Sao Paulo, Brazil, 1984-89; Professor of Epidemiology, University of Quebec, Canada, 1989-95; Adjunct Professor, Department of Epidemiology; Director, Division of Epidemiology, Department of Oncology, McGill University, Montreal, 1995-. Publications include: Epidemiological Correlates of Cervical Cancer, 1989; Sexually Transmitted Disease Model for Cervical Cancer: Incoherent Epidemiologic Findings and the Role of Misclassification of Human Papillomavirus Infection, 1991; Multiple Cancers of the Upper Aero-Digestive Tract: The Challenge of Risk factor Identification, 1991;

The Role of Epidemiology in the Study of Cancer Causes and Prognostic Factors. Honours: Research Scholar Award, FRSQ, Canada, 1993; Superior Performance Award. CDC, Atlanta, USA, 1981; Associate Editor, American Journal of Epidemiology, 1993; Editorial Board Member, Epidemiology, 1993. Memberships: Society for Epidemiologic Research; American Association Cancer Research; International Epidemiological Association. Hobbies: Computers; Reading; Soccer. Address: 129 Highgate Avenue, Pointe-Claire, Quebec H9R 2X5, Canada.

FRANKEL Herman Morris, b. 30 Mar 1938, Brooklyn, New York, USA. Physician; Educator. m. Ruth Ellen Wallach, 2 daughters. Education: BA, Columbia College, Columbia University, 1958; MD, Columbia University College of Physicians and Surgeons, 1962; Intern, Montefiore Hospital and Medical Center, New York, 1962-63; Paediatric Resident, New York Hospital, Cornell Medical Center, 1963-65; Fellow, Language and Communication Disorders in Children, University of Oregon Medical School, 1965-68. Appointments: Instructor, University of Oregon Medical School, Portland, 1968-69; Director, Prescriptive Education Programme, Portland Public Schools, 1969-73; Paediatrician, Kaiser-Permanente Medical Care Programme of Oregon, Portland, 1974-77; Senior Investigator, Kaiser-Permanente Health Services Research Center (now Center for Health Research), 1977-84; Programme Director, Portland Health Institute Inc, 1984-. Publications: Why teach them to read? A commentary on education as empowerment, 1971; Kaiser Permanente Freedom From Fat Program. Health Counts: Fat and Calorie Counting Made Easy, 1987; Workshop manuals with J C Staeheli: Moving Toward Health: A Two-Part Workshop, Practical Physiology for Clinical Personnel, and Helping People Develop and Maintain New Habits and Expectations, 1991; Preventing Burnout: Helping Patients and Clinicians Succeed Without Exhaustion, 1991; Journal contributions; Presentations. Honours: Phi Beta Kappa, 1958; US Secretary of Health and Human Services Award for Excellence in Community Health Promotion and Disease Prevention, 1983; Highly Rated Faculty, Young Presidents Organization, 1994. Memberships: Multnomah County Medical Society; Portland Academy of Hypnosis; Physicians for Social Responsibility; International Physicians for the Prevention of Nuclear War. Hobbies: Walking; Travel; Bread-baking; Reading. Address: 3310 NW Savier Street, Portland, OR 97210, USA.

FRANKEL Steven, b. 21 Aug 1942, New York City, USA. Psychiatrist. m. Ellen Barbara Silver, 4 June 1968, 1 son, 1 daughter. Education: MD; Board Certified in General Psychiatry; Board Psychiatry in Child and Adolescent Psychiatry; Certified, American Psychoanalytic Association. Appointments: Assistant Professor, University of Michigan Medical School; Co-Ordinator, Services for Children, Mount Zion Hospital, San Francisco; Private Practice; Associate Clinical Professor, University of California Medical School. Publications: Intricate Engagements: The Collaborative Basis of Therapeutic Change, 1995; Contributor of 15 professional articles. Honours: Outstanding Child Psychiatrists in USA, Town and Country Magazine, 1990. Memberships: American Psychoanalytic Association; American Psychiatric Association; Sigma Xi. Address: 1044 Sir Francis Drake Boulevard, Kentfield, CA 94904, USA

FRANKENHAUSER Marianne, b. 30 Sept 1925, Helsinki, Finland. Professor Emeritus. m. Bernhard Frankenhauser, 7 June 1946, 1 daughter. Appointments: Currently Professor Emeritus. Publications: Estimation of Time. An experimental study, 1959; Behavior and circulating catecholamines, 1971; Psychoneuroendocrine approaches to the study of emotion as related to stress and coping. 1978; The psychophysiology of workload, stress and health: comparison between the sexes, 1991; Women, Work and Health. Stress and Opportunities (edited with U Lundberg and M A Chesney), 1991. Hobbies: Writing popular science; Sailing. Address: Vårgårdsvägen 75, S-113 36 Saltsjöbaden, Sweden.

FRANKLAND Alfred William, b. 19 Mar 1912, Bexhill, England. Consulting Physician and Allergist. m. Pauline Jackson, 7 May 1941, 1 son, 3 daughters. Education: BCh; DM; MA (Oxon); FRLP. Appointments include: Director, Allergy Department, St Mary's Hospital, London, 1951-77; Honorary Consultant Allergist, Middlesex Hospital, London, 1977-81; Honorary Consulting Allergist, Guy's Hospital, London, 1977-; Honorary Secretary, Asthma Research Council, UK, 35 years. Publications: Over 100 scientific articles; Chapters of various books. Honours: Allergy Clinic, St Mary's Hospital, London, named The Frankland Clinic, 1988. Memberships: British Allergy Society, Secretary 18 years, President 1963-66; International Association of Allergology and Clinical Immunology, Secretary General 1967-70; Royal Society of Medicine, President, Section of Allergy and Clinical Immunology, 1978-80, Council Member, Section of History, 1991; European Academy of Allergology and Clinical Immunology, President 1978-80; Honorary Member, Past President, International Association of Aerobiology; British Medical Association, St Marylebone Division, Executive Council 1980-; Harveian Society of London, Council Member 1992; National Asthma Campaign, Vice-Chairman 1991-92, Vice-President 1992; Honorary Member, Japanese Allergy Society; Honorary Fellow: American College of Allergy and Immunology; American Academy of Allergy and Immunology; British Society of Allergy and Clinical Immunology. Address: 139 Harley Street, London W1N 1DJ, England.

FRASER David Ben, b. 20 Oct 1926, Houston, Texas, USA. Psychiatrist. m. Nell Brumley, 30 June 1979, 2 sons, 2 daughters. Education: BA, University of Texas, 1948; MD, University of Texas, 1952. Appointments: Client Day Treatment & Outpatient Department, Virginia Hospital, Arkansas, USA; Medical Director, South Arkansas Regional Health Center, El Dorado. Publications: Use of Lithium Corbonate in Affective Disorders, 1969. Honours: Arkansas Council Community Mental Health Center Distinguished Service Award, 1984; Life Fellow, American Psychiatric Association, 1995. Memberships: American Psychiatric Association; Arkansas Psychiatric Society; Arkansas Medical Association; Union County Medical Society. Hobbies: Camping; Fishing; Hunting. Address: 715 North College, El Dorado, AR 71730, USA.

FRASER Thomas Morris, b. 31 Jan 1922. Physician; Engineer. m. Joan Doone, 17 May 1947, 2 sons, 1 daughter. Education: MB, ChB, University of Edinburgh, 1944; MSc, Ohio State University, 1960; FACPM; PEng, University of Waterloo, 1970. Appointments: Medical practice, London, 1948-52; Royal Canadian Air Force, 1952-62, including Officer Command School of Aviation Medicine, 1960-62; Member, Lovelace Foundation for Medical Education and Research, Albuquerque, New Mexico, USA, 1962-67; Professor, Chairman, University of Waterloo, Ontario, Canada, 1967-87; Now retired. Publications: Books: Sustained Acceleration, 1963; The Worker at Work, 1989; Fitness for Work, 1992; Work, Productivity and Human Performance, 1994; 2 others. Honours: Numerous fellowships. Memberships include: Ontario Medical Association; Canadian Medical Association; Professional Engineers of Ontario; Human Factors Association, USA; Human Factors Association of Canada. Hobbies: Writing; Golf. Address: Box 1606, Niagara-on-the-Lake, Ontario, Canada L0S 1J0.

FRAYN Douglas Harmon, b. 3 Jan 1936, Kingston, Ontario, Canada. Psychoanalyst. m. Eileen Frayn, Jul 1982, 1 s, 1 d. Education: MD, Queen's University; Institute of Living, University of Toronto; FRCP(C); FAPA. Career: Head, Outpatient Department, Clarke Institute; Director, Toronto Institute of Psychoanalysis; Associate Professor of Psychiatry, University of Toronto; Consultant in Psychotherapy, Clarke Institute, Toronto Hospital; Currently, Associate Director, Canadian Psychoanalytic Institute. Publications: 2 Book articles and 15 published articles including: Enactments and other forms of regressive acting out, Contemporary considerations influencing psychoanalytic interventions, An analyst's Regressive Reverie, Premature termination in PSA control cases. Honour: Miguel Prados Award in Psychoanalysis, 1989-90. Memberships: Canadian and International Psychoanalytic Societies; Canadian and American Psychiatric Associations; Ontario Psychiatric Association. Hobbies: Squash; Blackjack. Address: 315 Avenue Road 2, Toronto, Ontario, Canada, M4V 2H2.

FRAZER Malcolm Ian, b. 24 Mar 1957, Felling, England. Urogynaecologist. m. Linda Ann Hardy, 30 Mar 1982, 3 sons. Education: MB ChB, 1980, MD, 1988, Birmingham University, 1980. Appointments: Lecturer, Obstetrics and Gynaecology, University of Liverpool, 1986-88; 1st Assistant, University of Newcastle, 1988-90; Staff Specialist, Obstetrics and Gynaecology, 1990-94; Currently: Private practice, Southport, Queensland, Australia; Associate Clinical Professor, University of Queensland. Publications: An Introduction to Clinical Gynaecological Urology (co-author); Numerous papers on female bladder function and urinary incontinence. Honours: Fellow, Certified Urogynaecologist, Royal Australian College of Obstetricians and Gynaecologists. Memberships: Royal College of Obstetricians and Gynaecologists; International Incontinence Society; International Urogynaecological Association. Hobbies: Piano; Writing. Address: Suite 4, Allamanda Medical Centre, Spendelove Avenue, Southport, Queensland 4215, Australia.

FREEDMAN Alfred M, b. 7 Jan 1917, Albany, NY, USA. Psychiatrist. m. Marcia Kohl, 24 Mar 1943, 2 sons. Education: AB, Cornell University; MD, University of Minnesota. Career: Assistant Professor, New York University College of Medicine, 1950-55; Associate Professor, State University of New York, 1955-60; Chair of Psychiatry, New York Medical College, 1960-89; Visiting Professor, Harvard Medical School, 1988-93; Roche Visiting Professor, Australia & New Zealand, 1988; Professor Emeritus, New York Medical College, currently. Publications: Comprehensive Text Book of Psychiatry, Edition I, 1967, II 1975, III 1980; Psychopathology of Adolescence; Opiate Addiction: Origins and Treatment; 12 other books; 237 scientific articles. Honours: Lapinlahtimdedal, Helsinki, 1990; Wyeth Ayerst Award, 1989; Jeanne Knudson Award, 1988; Terence Cardinal Cooke Medal, 1985; Samuel Hamilton Award. Memberships: American Psychiatric Association, President 1973-4; American College of Neuropsychopharmacology, President 1971-72; President, Academia Psychiatrae et Medicinae. Hobbies: Photography; Sailing; Opera; Music; Travel. Address: 1148 5th Avenue, New York, NY 10128, USA.

FREEDMAN Michael Leonard, b. 12 Dec 1937, Newark, NJ, USA. Physician. m. Cora Singer, 24 Jun 1962, 1 s, 1 d. Education: AB, Honours, Colgate University, 1959; MD, cum laude, Tufts University School of Medicine, 1963. Career: Intern and Resident, NY University Medical Center, 1963-65, 1968-69; Research Associate, 1965-67, Staff Investigator, 1967-68, National Institute of Health, NCI; Assistant Professor, 1969-74, Associate Professor, 1974-77, Professor of Medicine, 1977-, Currently, Diane and Arthur Belfer Professor of Geriatric Medicine, NY University Medical Center. Publications include: Various Editorial Boards; 156 publications including: Anemias, in Merck Manual of Geriatrics, 1993 in press; Hematologic Malignancies and Myeloproliferative Disease, in Merck Manual of Geriatrics, 1993 in press; Numerous abstracts and presentations, over 500 invited lectureships. Honours include: Alpha Omega Alpha, 1963; Best Teacher Award, NYU School of Medicine, 1982; Heroes of Bellevue Award, 1987; Wholeness of Life Award, The Hospital Chaplincy, 1988. Memberships include: Fellow, American College of Physicians; American Society of Biochemistry and Molecular Biology; Fellow, International Society of Hematology; AAAS; Fellow, NY Academy of Sciences; Fellow, American Geriatrics Society; Fellow, American Gerontological Society of America; AMA. Hobby: Travel. Address: New York University Medical Center, 550 First Avenue, New York, NY 10016, USA.

FREEMAN Carolyn R, b. 2 Jan 1950, England. Radiation Oncologist. m. Juan Carlos Negrete, 1981, 1 son, 1 daughter. Education: MB, BS; FRCP (C). Appointments: Currently Professor, Rosenbloom Chairman, Department of Oncology, Division of Radiation Oncology, Montreal General, Montreal, Canada. Publications: Book chapters: The Management of Recurrent Melanoma (with J K MacFarlane and M P Thirlwell), 1979; Tumors of the Central Nervous System, in Principles and Practice of Pediatric Oncology, 1989, 1992; Radiotherapy dose-fractionation schedules. Hyperfractionation and accelerated regimens (with R S Lehnert), 1991; Over 40 articles in peer-reviewed journals. Memberships: American Society for Clinical Education; Canadian Association of Radiation Oncologists; American Society for Therapeutic Radiology and Oncology; American Society for Clinical Oncology-American Radium Society; European Society for Therapeutic Radiology and Oncology. Address: Montreal General, Radiation Oncology, 1650 Cedar Avenue, Montreal, Quebec, Canada H3G 1A4.

FREEMAN David Franklin, b. 13 Apr 1925, Raleigh, NC, USA. Psychoanalyst; Child Psychiatrist. m. Constance Covell, 28 Mar 1953, 1 s, 2 d. Education: BS, Wake Forest University, 1948; MD, Bowman Gray School of Medicine, 1951; Diplomate, Adult and Child Psychiatry; Certified in Adult and Child Psychoanalysis; Training Analyst. Career: Assistant Professor to Clinical Professor, University of NC School of Medicine, 1961-80; President of NC Council of Child Psychiatry, 1971; President of NC Psychoanalytic Society, 1980-82; Currently, Director, University of NC, Duke Psychoanalytic Education Program; Private Practice. Honour: Alpha Omega Alpha, 1950. Memberships: American Psychoanalytic Association; International Psychoanalytical Association; Association for Child Psychoanalysis; American Academy of Child and Adolescent Psychiatry; American Psychiatric Association. Hobbies: Carpentry; Sailing; Gardening; Music. Address: 101 Ashe Place, Chapel Hill, NC 27514, USA.

FRENCH Pauline Mary, b. 27 Dec 1952, Salisbury, Wiltshire, UK. Acupuncturist. m. John French, 19 Sept 1987, 3 s, 1 d. Education: SRN; RSCN; Lic Ac. Appointments: Traditional Acupuncturist. Memberships:

Traditional Acupuncture Society; Royal College of Nursing. Hobbies: Walking; Observing Wildlife. Address: The Mill House, Shaftesbury Road, Compton Chamberlayne, Salisbury, Wiltshire, SP3 5DW, England.

FRICK Oscar Lionel, b. 12 Mar 1923, NY, USA. Medicine. m. Mary Hubbard Frick, 2 Sep 1954. Education: AB, Art and Science, Cornell University, 1944; MD, Cornell Medical School, 1946; MMS, University of Pennsylvania, PA, 1960; PhD, Stanford University, CA, 1964. Appointments: Intern, Pediatrics, 1946-47; Residency, Pediatrics, 1950-51; Private Practice, Pediatrics, NY, 1951-58; Postdoctoral Fellow, McGill University, Canada, 1958-59; Postdoctoral Allergy Fellow, UCSF, 1959-60; Institut d'Immunobiologie, Paris, France, 1960-62; Assistant, Associate, Professor of Pediatrics, UCSF, from 1965; Sabbatical, Inselspital Bern, Switzerland, 1991-92; Now Professor of Pediatrics Emeritus. Publications: Over 120 research articles in Journal of Allergy and Clinical Immunology, Annals of Allergy, and Journal of Immunology; Over 30 book reviews. Memberships: President, American Academy of Allergy and Immunology, 1977-78; Secretary General, International Association of Allergology and Clinical Immunology, 1985-91; American Association of Immunologists; American Academy of Pediatrics; American Pediatrics Society; American College of Allergy and Immunology; Collegium Internationale Allergologicum; American Thoracic Society. Hobbies: Hiking; Sailing. Address: Box 0546, HSW 1404A, Dept Pediatrics, University California, San Francisco, CA 94143, USA.

FRIED Floyd Alan, b. 23 Mar 1936, Brooklyn, New York, USA. Physician. m. Ellen Shapiro, 1 July 1962, 1 son, 1 daughter. Education: BS, Brooklyn College, 1957; MD, University of Chicago, 1961; Teaching Scholar, University of North Carolina, 1991. Appointments: Assistant Professor, Surgery, University of Chicago, 1967-70; Associate Professor, Surgery, Chief of Urology, University of North Carolina, 1970-74; Professor of Surgery, Chief of Urology, University of North Carolina, 1974-93; Professor of Surgery, 1993-. Publications: 70 articles in professional journals. Honours: Teaching Scholar, University of North Carolina, Chapel Hill, 1991. Memberships: American Medical Association; American Urological Association; american College of Surgeons; American Association of Medical Colleges. Hobbies: Fly Fishing. Address: University of North Carolina, Division of Urology, CB#7235, Cahpel Hill, NC 27599-7235, USA.

FRIEDEL David Hugh, b. 5 July 1943, Malverne, New York, USA. Optometrist. 1 son. Education: OD; FAAP; FCOVD' BS; FBNT. Appointments: Clinical Instructor, State University of New York School of Optometry, Staff Optometric Centre of New York; Chief Paediatric Optometry, Wilson A Hospital, Fort Dix, New Jersey; Staff, Department of Health, New York City; Private Practice. Publications: A New Vision Therapy Technique, 1967; With Your Eyes Wide Open, pamphlet, 1970; Improving Visual Performance, pamphlet, 1993. Honours: Citation, US Army, 1970. Memberships: FCOUD; FAAO; Diplomate, DFNT; AOA. Hobbies: Scuba diving; Motocross; Motorcycles; Tai Chi; Yoga; Tennis. Address: 2407 East 4th Street, Tucson, AZ 85719, USA.

FRIEDEL Robert Oliver, b. 4 Aug 1936, Corona, New York, USA. Physician. m. Susanne Weber, 1 son, 3 daughters. Education: BS, Duke University, 1958; MD, Duke University School of Medicine, 1964. Appointments include: Professor, Chairman, Department of Psychiatry, Medical College of Virginia, 1977-84; Professor, Chairman, Department of Psychiatry, University of Michigan, Ann Arbor, 1984-85; Vice-President, Psychiatry, Medicine and Research Charter Corporation, Macon, Georgia, 1985-90; Currently Heman E Drummond Professor, Chairman, Department of Psychiatry, University of Alabama, Birmingham. Publications: Acetylcholine action: Biochemical aspects (with J Durell and J T Garland), 1969; Prediction of tricyclic antidepressant response: A critical review (with R J Bielski), 1976. Honours: L A Smith Scholastic Award, 1961; Alpha Omega Alpha, 1963; Virginia Ware Gibbons Scholar in Biologic Psychiatry, 1969-70; Falk Fellow, American Psychiatric Association, 1969-70; National Institute for Mental Health Research and Scientific Development, 1970-75; National Mental Health Association for Volunteer Services, 1990. Memberships: Fellow, American Psychiatric Association; American Medical Association; American College of Neuropsychopharmacology, Group for Advancement of Psychiatry; American Society of Pharmacology and Experimental Therapeutics; American Society of Neurochemistry; American Association for the Advancement of Science; American Federation for Clinical Research. Hobby: Golf. Address: Smolian

Psychiatric Clinic, Room 113, 1700 7th Avenue South, Birmingham, AL 35294-0018, USA.

FRIEDMAN Matthew Joel, b. 10 Mar 1940, Newark, New Jersey, USA. Psychiatrist; Pharmacologist. m. Gayle Marie Smith, 2 Oct 1976, 1 s, 3 d. Education: AB, Dartmouth College, 1961; PhD, Pharmacology, Albert Einstein College of Medicine, 1967; MD, University of Kentucky, Lexington, 1969. Appointments: Intern, University of Kentucky Medical Center, 1969-70; Resident in Psychiatry, Massachusetts General Hospital, Boston, 1970-72; Dartmouth Hitchcock Medical Center, 1972-73; Assistant Professor, Psychiatry & Pharmacology, Dartmouth Medical School, 1973-78; Associate Professor, Dartmouth Medical School, 1978-88; Professor, Psychiatry & Pharmacology, Dartmouth Medical School, 1988-; Staff Psychiatrist, VA Hospital, 1973-78; Chief Psychiatry, 1978-89; Executive Director, National Center for PTSD, 1989-. Publications: Numerous Peer Reviewd Journal Articles, Book Chapters, Technical Reports on Post Traumatic Stress Disorders, Biological Psychiatry; Psychopharmacology and Treatment outcome research; Two Books in Press, Neurobiological & Clinical Consequences of Stress: From Normal Adaptation to PTSD; Ethnocultural Aspects of Post Traumatic Stress Disorders. Honours: Recipient National Commanders Award DAV, 1975, 1983; Significant Achievement Certificate, Hospital & Community Psychiatry Institute, 1988; William C Porter Lecture Award, 1988; Outstanding Federal Employee of VT, 1989; Special Recognition Award, Vietnam Veterans of America, 1993. Memberships: American Psychiatric Association; International Society for Traumatic Stress Studies; Society of Biological Psychiatry. Hobbies: Skiing; Horses; Gardening; Jogging; Reading. Address: National Center for Post-Traumatic Stress Disorders, VAM & ROC (116D), Hartland Road, White River Junction, VT 05009, USA.

FRIEDMAN Paul Jay, b. 20 Jan 1937, NY, USA. Medicine. m. Elisabeth Clare Richardson, 18 Jun 1960, 1 s, 3 d. Education: BS, University of WI, 1955; Oxford University, Balliol, 1957-58; MD, Yale University Medical School, 1960; AOA; PBK. Appointments: Chief of Radiology, USN Station Hospital, New London, CT, 1964-66; Picker Fellow in Radiology, Yale University, 1966-68; Assistant, Associate, and Professor of Radiology, Dean for Academic Affairs, University of California San Diego, School of Medicine 1968-. Publications: 85 Refereed articles, 25 Editorials, 18 Book Chapters mainly concerning Pulmonary Radiology and Research Ethics, 1 journal supplement edited. Honours: Markle Scholar, 1969-74; Chair, Council of Academic Societies, Association of American Medical Colleges. Memberships: President, Fleischner Society, 1994-95; Association of University Radiologists; Radiological Society of North America; Roentgen Ray Society. Hobbies: Choral Singing; Gardening; Hiking. Address: 5644 Soledad Road, La Jolla, CA 92037-7048, USA.

FRIEDRICH Joan, b. 3 March 1952, New York City, USA. Health Consultant. Education: MA, Counselling Psychology; PhD, Clinical Nutrition; CCN; BCIAC; NBCCH. Appointments: Director, Atkins Centre Complementary Medicine Nutrition Counselling Programme, 1990-92; President, New York State Biofeedback Society, 1990-91. Publications: Be Well..Stay Well!; Lifetime Wellness; Relax and Release: Discover Inner Calm; Contributor of numerous articles in professional and consumer journals. Memberships: International and American Associations Clinical Nutritionists; American College Nutrition; Association Applied Psychophysiology and Biofeedback. Hobbies: Sport; Outdoors; Photography; Music. Address: Life-Line, PO Box 482, Bronxville, NY 10708, USA.

FRINDEL François, b. 3 Mar 1950, Strasbourg, France. Orthodontist Specialist. 1 son, 1 daughter. Education: DDS, University of Nancy, 1974; Qualified Orthodontist Specialist, National Board, 1982; Expert for Social and Private Insurances, 1984. Appointments: Private Practice. Publications: Author or co-author, more than 30 in French scientific journals, 1976-; More than 30 conferences, posters in Europe, 1976-. Honours: Vice-President, French National Bioprogressive Society, 1989-93. Memberships: Titular Member, French Society of Dento-Facial Orthopaedics; Titular Member, French Bioprogressive Society; Foundation for Orthodontic Research; European Orthodontic Society. Hobby: Collecting. Address: 17 rue des Drs Charcot, 42100 St-Etienne, France.

FRISANCHO Andres Roberto, b. 4 Feb 1939, Cuzco, Peru. Professor of Anthropology; Research Scientist. m. Hedy G Frisancho, 13 Sep 1964, 2 s. Education: BH, National University of Cuzco, Peru, 1962; MA, 1966, PhD, 1969, Biological Anthropology, PA State

University. Career: Instructor, Anthropology, PA State University, 1967-68; Lecturer, 1968-69, Assistant Professor, 1969-73, Associate Professor of Anthropology, 1973-78, Currently, Professor of Anthropology and Research Scientist, Center for Human Growth and Development, University of MI. Publications: Anthropometric Standards for the Evaluation of Growth and Nutritional Status, 1990; Human Adaptation and Accomodation to Environmental Stress, 1993; Increased serum cholesterol associated with truncal fat distribution among Mexican-American males, in American Journal Human Biology, 1994. Fulbright Fellow, 1963-64; President, American Human Biology Council, 1988-90. Memberships: American Association of Anthropology; American Association of Physical Anthropologists; Fellow, American Association for Advancement of Science; Fellow, Human Biology Council. Hobbies: Tennis; Chess. Address: Center for Human Growth and Development, University of Michigan, 300 North Ingalls, Ann Arbor, MI 48109-0406, USA.

FRISCH Jonathan David, b. 4 Oct 1963, Oakland, CA, USA. Epidemiologist. Education: AB, Biophysics, Medical Physics, 1985, MPH, Public Health, 1987, PhD, Epidemiology, 1990, University of California, Berkeley. Career includes: Part-time Graduate Student Instructor, 1985-90, Adjunct Lecturer, 1991-93, Adjunct Assistant Professor, 1994, University of California, Los Angeles, CA; Part-time Research Assistant, CA Birth Defects Monitoring Program, Emeryville, CA, 1986-90; Senior Epidemiologist, 1990-92, Senior Staff Epidemiologist, 1992-93, Manager, Epidemiology Programs, 1993-, UNOCAL Corporation. Publications: Various papers presented including: The Spatial Evaluation of Neighbourhood Clusters of Birth Defects, MI State University Epidemiology Group, East Lansing, MI, 1990; Spatial Clustering in Industrial Epidemiology: A Methodology, Industrial Epidemiology Forum, Seattle, WA, 1993. Honours: Sealbearer, CA Scholarship Federation, 1981; Outstanding Graduate Student Instructor, University of California, 1988; Sigma Xi, 1989-; Elected Member, American College of Epidemiology, 1993. Memberships: Society for Epidemiologic Research; American Public Health Association; Society for Risk Analysis. Address: UNOCAL Corporation, Mailstop 5M-44, PO Box 7600, Los Angeles, CA 90051, USA.

FROJMOVIC Maurice Mony, b. 2 Feb 1943, Belgium. Professor. m. Vivian Saginur, 1 son, 2 daughters. Education: BSc, Chemistry, McGill University; PhD, Chemistry, McGill University. Appointments: Postdoctoral Fellow, NATO; Biodynamics, MC, Berkeley. Publications: Dynamics of Platelet and Blood Cell Receptor Expression and Aggtregation in Flour, 1995. Hobbies: Squash; Skiing; Biking; Reading. Address: Physiology Department, McIntyre Medical Science Building, 3655 Drummond #1137, Montreal H3G 1Y6, Quebec, Canada.

FRY Donald E, b. 16 August 1946, Marion, Ohio, USA. Surgeon. m. Rosemary Jollis Fry, 7 September 1968, 1 son, 1 daughter. Education: MD, Ohio State University; BSc, Ohio State University. Appointments: Staff Surgeon, VA Medical Center, Louisville, Kentucky, 1977-82; Director, Price Institute of Surgical Research, Louisville, Kentucky, 1980-82; Chief, Surgical Service, VA Medical Center, Cleveland, Ohio, 1982-87; Professor, Chairman, Department of Surgery, University of New Mexico Health Sciences Center, Albuquerque, 1987-. Publications Include: Dissemination and causes of infection, 1976; The role of colonic bacteria in the pathophysiology of fecal peritonitis, 1977; The major deterrent to improve results, 1978; Missile tract infections following transcolonic gunshot wounds, 1978; Occult diverticulities: A cause of retroperitoneal fibrosis, 1980; Antibiotic pharmacokinetics in surgery, 1990; Reoperation for intra-abdominal abscess, 1991; Obligatory negative nitrogen balance following spinal cord injury, 1991. Memberships: American College of Surgeons; American Trauma Society; American Surgical Association; Association for Academic Surgery; Surgical Infection Society; Shock Society; Society of University Surgeons; Western Surgical Society. Address: Department of Surgery, University of New Mexico Health Sciences Center, 2211 Lomas Boulevard NE, Albuquerque, New Mexico, USA.

FU Congyuan, b. 11 June 1923, Wuhan City, China. Professor. m. Li Qun, 3 Sep 1949, 4 daughters. Education: BSc, National Central University, Nanjing, 1947. Appointments: Assistant, Biology and Histology, National Central University, 1947-51; Instructor of Physiology, China Central Academy of Health, 1951-56; Institute of Experimental Medicine, CAMS, 1956-59; PUMC, 1959-72; Assistant Professor, 1978, Professor, 1982-, Beijing College of Traditional Chinese Medicine. Publications: Experiment Research on TCM Pulse-Patterns, 1993. Honour: China Ministerial Scientific and Technological Award, 1988.

Memberships: Chinese Physiological Society; Chinese Association of the Integration of Traditional and Western Medicine. Hobbies: Table-Tennis; Reading; History. Address: Department of Basic Medical Sciences, Brijing Traditional Chinese Medicine University, Beijing 100029, China.

FU Jingfen, b. 2 Dec 1951, Tianjin, China. Associate Professor of Infectious Diseases. m. Zhang Chongzhi, 13 July 1979, 2 daughters. Education: MD, Ningxia Medical College, 1977. Appointments: Doctor, Lecturer, currently Associate Professor, Ningxia Medical College. Publications: 22 learned articles on infectious diseases, 1978-94; Practical Integrated Medicine (co-author), 1992. Honours: 6 Scientific Achievement Awards; International Gold Research Award, ICIM, USA, 1994. Memberships: Committee Member, CAID and CAIM, Ningxia Branch. Address: Ningxia Medical College, Yinchuan 750004, China.

FU Karen K, b. 15 Oct 1940, Shanghai, China. Radiation Oncologist. Education: AB cum laude, Physics, Barnard College, Columbia University, NY, 1963; MD, College of Physicians and Surgeons, Columbia University, NY, 1967; Certified, Therapeutic Radiology, American Board Radiology. Appointments include: Residency, Stanford University Medical Center, CA, 1969-71; Research Associate, Cancer Research Institute, 1972-; Consultant: Veteran's Administration Hospital Tumour Board, 1972-; Mt Zion Hospital, Zellerbach-Saroni Tumour Institute, 1973-; San Francisco Regional Tumour Foundation, 1974-; Research Associate, Laboratory of Radiobiology, 1974-; Professor, 1982-, Vice Chair, 1994-, Department of Radiation Oncology; University of California, San Francisco; Consultant, Marin General Hospital, San Rafael, CA, 1993-. Publications include: 84 Professional publications, 1965-, including: Integration of chemotherapy and radiotherapy for organ preservation in head and neck cancer, in Head and Neck Cancer, 1993; Neck node metastases from unknown primary: Controversies in management, in Frontiers in Radiology Ther Oncology, 1994; Over 30 Book Chapters. Honours include: Mabel Mead Scholarship, 1963-67; American Cancer Society Junior Faculty Fellowship, 1976-79; Distinguished Physician Award, Chinese American Physicians' Society, 1993; MacLaren Lecturer. Memberships include: American Medical Women's Association; Radiation Research Society; American College of Radiation; Cell Kinetics Society; American Association Cancer Research; Society of Chinese Bioscientists in America. Hobbies: Hiking; Writing; Reading; Travel; Walking; Opera; Ballet; Theatre; Swimming; Address: UCSF Radiation Oncology Dept, 505 Parnassus Ave, L-08, San Francisco, CA 94143-0226, USA.

FU Shigui, b. 4 July 1919, Nanchang, Jiangxi, China. Professor; Chief Doctor. m. Defen Li, 4 Aug 1948, 1 son, 4 daughters. Education: MB, Zhong Zheng Medical College, 1943. Appointments: Lecturer, Assistant Professor, National Zhong Zheng Medical College, and Resident, Visiting Doctor, Affiliated Hospital 1943-49; Assistant Professor, Visiting Doctor, 6th Military Medical University and Affiliated Hospital, 1949-53; Assistant Professor, Professor, Jiangxi Medical College, 1953-; Chief Doctor, Vice-President, Jiangxi Maternal and Child Health Hospital, 1953-. Publications include: The Physiology and Pathology of Menstrual Cycle at the standpoint of combination of Western and Chinese Medicine, 1973; The Surgical Operation of Female Urinary Fistulas, 1979; The Operative Treatment of Female Urinary Fistulas, book, 1981; Report of 36 cases of Turner's Syndrome, 1987; Co-author: The Pathological Physiology, book, 1958; Encyclopedia of China, obstetrics and gynaecological sections, 1980; The Practice and Theory of Obstetrics and Gynecology, book, 1982; The Gynecology of Combination of Western and Chinese Medicine, 1993; The Gynecological Neoplasm, 1993. Honours: National Model Worker, State Council of China, 1979; Certificate of Merit, Bonus, for invention of Receptor of urine for patients with urinary incontinence, 1989; Monthly Monetary Award for Scientist with Important Contributions, State Council of China, 1991-. Memberships: Obstetrics and Gynaecology Committee, National Health Bureau; National Committee of Combination of Western and Chinese Medicine; Jiangxi Hereditary Association, Vice-President 1981-91; Women Scientists and Technologists Friendship Association, Jiangxi, President 1980-90. Hobbies: Travel; Table-tennis. Address: Jiangxi Medical College, Box 28, 161 Bayi Avenue, Nanchang, Jiangxi 330006, China.

FU Wenbin, b. 16 Nov 1963, Hainan, China. Physician. m. Xie Xiaoqi, 8 July 1991. Education: MB; Specialist of Acupuncture. Appointments: Resident Physician, Guangdong Provincial Hospitala of TCM, 1987; Attending Physician, Senior Lecturer in Acupuncture; Director, Acupuncture and Moxibustion Association of Guangdong

Province. Publications: Clinical Application of Siguan (Four-gate) Points with Case Studies, 1991; Clinical Practice of Eye-Acupuncture, 1991; Treatment 136 Sciatica Patients Main with Eye-Acupuncture, 1992; Eye-Acupuncture in Treatment of Acute Asthma Attack, 1993; Clinical Immediately Observation on Acute Asthma Attack 76 Visits Controlled by Eye-Acupuncture, 1993; Clinical Application of Regulative Liver Methos in Acupuncture and Moxibustion, 1994; Chinese-English handbook of Acupuncture and Moxibustion, 1995; Clinical Research Anti-asthmatic with Eye-Acupuncture, 1995. Honours: Famous Doctor of Acupuncture and Moxibustion, 1995. Memberships: Acupuncture and Moxibustion Association of China. Hobby: Bowling. Address: Acupuncture Department, Guangdong Provincial Hospital of Traditional Chinese Medicine, 111 Dade Road, Guangzhou 510120, China.

FUJIKI Norio, b. 17 Nov 1928, Kobe, Japan. Professor Emeritus. m. 30 Oct 1955, 3 sons. Education: MD 1952, PhD Medicine 1956, Kyoto Prefectural University of Medicine. Career: Emeritus Professor, Fukui Medical School; Medical Advisor, Gene Analysis Laboratory, Toyobo Tsuruga. Publications: Editor & Contributor, Human Dignity & Medicine, 1987; Isolation, Migration & Health, 1991; Human Genome Research & Society, 1992; Medical Genetics & Society, 1992; Intractable Neurological Disorders, Human Genome Research & Society, 1993; Illustrated Medical Genetics, 1995; Introduction of Medical Genetics, Kimpodo, 1988; Clinical Genetics, Igaku Shoin, 1969. Memberships: Expert Advisory Panel on Human Genetics, WHO; HUGO Pacific; Vice President, International Bioethics Committee, UNESCO. Hobbies: Handmade Paper; Haiku. Address: 1009 Nakano 2 chome, Fukui City, 910-37, Japan.

FUJISAWA Kohshiro, b. 7 July 1933. Neuropathologist. 1 daughter. Education: MD, University of Tokyo School of Medicine. Appointments: Research Staff, Institute of Brain Research, School of Medicine, University of Tokyo; Senior Research Staff, Department of Neuropathology, Tokyo Metropolitan Institute for Neuroscience; Chief, Department of Neuropathology, Tokyo Metropolitan Institute for Neuroscience; Associate Director, Tokyo Metropolitan Institute for Neuroscience. Publications: On the advantage of using semiultrathin plastic sections for electronmicroscopic neuropathology, 1993. Memberships: Japanese Society of Neuropathology; International Society of Neuropathology; Japanese Society of Neurology; Japanese Society of Geriatric Medicine. Hobbies: Classical Music; Reading. Address: B-502 Miyamaé-daira Palm House, 6-15-1 Tsuchi-hashi, Miyamaé-ku, Kawasaki-shi, Kanagawa-ken 216, Japan.

FUKUYAMA Yukio, b. 28 May 1928, Miyazaki, Japan. Medical Doctor. m. Ayako Arai. Education: MD; PhD; Postgraduate Course, Faculty of Medicine, University of Tokyo. Appointments: Clinical Associate, Department of Paediatrics, University of Tokyo, 1957-60; Assistant Professor, 1960-64; Associate Professor, 1964-65; Chief Paediatrician, National Children's Hospital, 1965-67; Professor and Chairman, Department of Paediatrics, Tokyo Womens Medical College, 1967-94; Chairman, Board of Trustees, Japanese Society of Child Neurology, 1968-93; President, International Child Neurology Association, 1982-86; President, Asian & Oceanian Association of Child Neurology, 1983-90. Publications: Child Neurology, 1982; An Atlas of Clincial Child Neurology, 1986; Epilepsy Bibliography, 1989; Modern Perspectives in Child Neurology, 1991; Fetal and Neonatal Neurology, 1992. Memberships: Japanese Society of Child Neurology; Japanese Society of Neurology; Japan Paediatric Society; International Child Neurology Association; Asian & Oceanian Association of Child Neurology. Hobbies: Philately; Cinema; Music; Baseball. Address: 6-12-16 Minami-Shinagawa, Shinagawa-ku, Tokyo 162, Japan.

FULLERTON Gary D, b. 10 Nov 1939, Santa Paula, CA, USA. Medical Physicist. m. Nancy Fullerton, 2 d. Education: BA, MS, PhD, University of WI and University of CA. Career includes: Assistant Professor, Therapeutic Radiology, University of MN, 1975; Assistant Professor, Radiology, 1978, Associate Professor, Radiology, 1982, UTHSC; Associate Professor and Chief, 1985, Professor and Chief, 1987, Radiological Sciences Division, Department of Radiology, UTHSCSA. Publications include: Co-editor, Biological Risks of Medical Irradiation, 1980; Co-author, Method to Improve the Accuracy of Membrane Osmometry Measures of Protein Molecular Weight, in Journal of Biochemistry Biophysics Meth, 1993. Honours: President, Society of Magnetic Resonance Imaging, 1986; Founding Editor, Journal of Magnetic Resonance Imaging, 1990; President, American Association of Physicists in Medicine, 1991; Robert J Shalek Award for Achievement in Medical Physics, 1992; Malcolm Jones Professor of Radiology,

University of TX HSCSA, 1992. Memberships: Delegate of American Association of Physicists to International Organization of Medical Physics, 1986-92; Secretary, 1982-84, American Association of Physicists in Medicine; Board, 1982-84, Society of Magnetic Resonance Imaging. Hobbies: Skiing; Travel; Reading. Address: Radiology Department, University of Texas HSCSA, 7703 Floyd Curl Drive, San Antonio, TX 78284, USA.

FULOP George, b. 17 Aug 1954, Budapest, Hungary. Psychiatrist. m. Andrea Leigh Zuckerman, 1 son. Education: Ba, Columbia University, USA, 1976; MD, Albert Einstein College of Medicine, Bronx, 1980; MPH, Mt Sinai Medical Centre, 1986. Appointments: Intern in Medicine, Montefiore Hospital, Bronx, 1980-81; Resident in Psychiatry, Mt Sinai School of Medicine, New York City, 1981-84; Faculty Fellow, General Preventive Medicine, 1984-86; Instructor of psychiatry, 1984-86, Assistant Professor of Psychiatry, 1986-93, Associate professor, 1984-. Publications: Contributor of 35 articles to professional journals and 7 chapters in books; Journala reviewer. Honours: NIMH Grantee, 1989-. Memberships: AMA; Society Liaison Psychiatry; Association Geriatric Psychiatry; American Geriatric Society; American Psychiatric Association. Hobbies: Art History; Swimming. Address: Mt Sinai School of Medicine, Box 1228, 1 Gustav Levy Place, New York, NY 10029, USA.

FUNDER John Watson, b. 26 dec 1940-, Adelaide, South Australia, Australia. Physician. m. Kathleen Rose Brennan, 11 Dec 1964, 2 sons, 1 daughter. Education: MD, PhD, Melbourne; FRACP. Appointments: Deputy Director, Prince Henry's Institute of Medical Research, 1980-90; Director, Baker Medical Research Institute. Publications: Contributor of 400 scientific papers in endocrinology, hypertension and bioethics. Honours: SusmanMedal, Royal Australasian College of Physicians, 1983; Wellcome Australia Medal, 1987. Memberships: Honorary Life Member, Australian Society for Medical Research; Executive Committee, International Society of Endocrinology. Hobbies: Reading; Cooking; Travel; Wine. Address: 1022 Drummond Street, North Carlton, 3054 Victoria, Australia.

FUTAGI Yasuyuki, b. 15 Apr 1947, Hyogo, Japan. Child Neurologist. m. Chieko Yamada, 27 Oct 1973, 2 sons, 1 daughter. Education: MD, Osaka University, 1973. Appointments: Resident in Paediatrics, Osaka University, 1973-74; Medical Staff in Paediatrics, Osaka Keisatsu Hospital, 1974-75; Medical Staff in Paediatrics, Mimihara Hospital, 1974-75; Director, Division of Paediatric Neurology, Osaka Medical Centre and Research Institute for Maternal and Child Health, Osaka. Publications: Cerebral Blood Flow and Brain Shrinkage Seen on CT During ACTH Therapy, 1986; Primitive Reflex Profiles in Infant, 1992. Honours: Nagashima Prize, Japanese Society of Child Neurology, 1987. Memberships: International Child Neurology Association; Society for Developmental Paediatrics; Japanese Society of Child Neurology; Japanese Society of Paediatrics. Hobbies: Writing; Swimming. Address: 3-3-12 Horiagemidorimachi, Sakai, Osaka 593, Japan.

FUXA James R, b. 26 Jan 1949, Lincoln, Nebraska, USA. Professor of Insect Pathology. m. Diann M Treptow, 20 May 1972, 2 sons. Education: BS, University of Nebraska, 1971; MS, Oregon State University, 1975; PhD, North Carolina State University, 1978. Appointments: Head, Department of Entomology, Louisiana University, 1990-91; Professor of Insect Pathology, Louisiana State University. Publications: Senior Editor, Epizootiology of Insect Diseases, 1987, Chinese Edition, 1992; Insect Control with Baculoviruses, 1991; Environmental Risks of Genetically Engineered Entomopathogens, 1990; Release and Transport of Entomopathogenic Micro-organisms, 1991. Honours: Environmental Science & Engineering Fellow, American Association for the Advancement of Science, 1987. Memberships: Society for Invertebrate Pathology; Entomological Society of America; International Organization for Biological Control. Address: Department of Entomology, Louisiana State University, Baton Rouge, LA 70803, USA.

FÜZÜN Mehmet, b. 2 Jan 1952, Akhisar, Turkey. General Surgeon. m. Sema Füzün, 11 July 1974, 2 daughters. Appointments: Medical Doctor, 1975; Surgeon, 1980; Associate Professor, 1986; Professor, 1993. Publications: Over 70 articles in general surgery. Memberships: International Society for Regional Cancer Therapy; Turkish Surgical Society; Turkish Society of Endoscopic Laparascopic Surgery; European Association of Video-Surgery. Hobbies: Running; Basketball. Address: Dokuz Eylul University Hospital Inciralti, Izmir, Turkey.

G

GABBARD Glen Owens, b. 8 Aug 1949, Charleston, Illinois, USA. Psychiatrist. m. Joyce Davidson, 14 June 1985, 1 son, 3 daughters. Education: BS, Eastern Illinois University, 1972; MD, Rush Medical College, 1975; Karl Menninger School of Psychiatry, Residency, 1978; Psychoanalytic Training, Topeka Institute for Psychoanalysis, 1984. Appointments: Medical Direcor, C F Menninger Memorial Hospital, 1989-94; Vice President for Adult Services, The Menninger Clinic, 1991-94; Callaway Distinguished Professor, Karl Menninger School of Psychiatry. Publications: Psychodynamic Psychiatry in Clinical Practice: The DSM-IV Edition, 1994; Treatments of Psychiatric Disorders: The DSM-IV Edition, 1995. Honours: Psychiatric Times Teacher of the Year Award, 1992; Sigmund Freud Award of the American Society of Psychoanalytic Physicians, 1992; Edward Strecker Award, 1994. Memberships: American College of Psychiatrists; Group for the Advancement of Psychiatry; Benjamin Rush Society. Hobbies: Golf. Address: Menninger Clinic, Box 829, Topeka, KS 66601, USA.

GABOW Patricia A, b. 8 Jan 1944, Starke, Florida, USA. Physician. m. Harold N Gabow, 21 June 1971, 1 son, 1 daughter. Education: BA; MD. Appointments include: Instructor in Medicine, 1973-74, Assistant Professor of Medicine, 1974-79, Associate Professor of Medicine, 1979-87, Professor of Medicine, 1987-, Division of Renal Diseases, University of Colorado Health Sciences Centre; Chief, Renal Disease, 1973-81, Clinical Director, Department of Medicine, 1976-81, Director of Medical Services, 1981-91, Denver General Hospital; Deputy Manager of Medical Affairs, 1989-92, Manager, Medical Director, 1992-, Denver Health and Hospitals; Appointment to Mayor's Cabinet, City and County of Denver, 1992-; Faculty Associate, University of North Carolina at Chapel Hill, 1992-93. Publications include: Fluid and Electrolytes: Clinical Problems and Their Solution, 1983; Disorders of Potassium Metabolism, Co-author, 1980; Polycystic Kidney Disease, Co-author, 1993l; Case Study on Autosomal Dominant Poycystic Kidney Disease, 1993; Cystic Diseases of the Kidneys, Co-author; Cystic Disease of the Kidney. Honours include: Alpha Omega Alpha, 1969; Kaiser Permanente award for Excellence in Teaching, 1976; Seton Hill College Distinguished Alumna Leadership Award, 1990. Memberships include: Diplomate, American Board of Internal Medicine; Denver Medical Society; American Society of Nephrology; International Society of Nephrology; American College of Physicians; American Federation of Clinical Research; American Physiological Society; Association of American Physicians. Hobbies: Reading; Biking; Gardening; Cooking. Address: Denver General Hospital, 777 Bannock Street, Denver, CO 80204-4507, USA.

GAHBAUER Reinhard A, b. 14 Feb 1944, Augsburg. Radiation Oncology. 1 s, 1 d. Career: Cleveland Clinic, 1978-84; Currently, Director, Radiation Oncology, A James Cancer Hospital, OH State University, Columbus. Publications: International Journal Radiation Oncology, 1993, 1994; Strahlentherapy, 1993. Memberships: ACR; ACRO; ESTRO; Radiation Society; Radiation Research Society; International Society Boroz Neutron Capt. Address: Ohio State University College of Medicine, 200 Meiling Hall, 370 West 9th Avenue, Columbus, OH 43210, USA.

GAIER Harald Camillo, b. 6 Dec 1938, Vienna. Consultant Allergist. m. Sabine Anna Elisabeth Gaier, 12 Sept 1979, 4 sons. Education: MD, SA Faculty of Homoeopathic Medicine; ND, Naturopathic Coll; DO, International College of Osteopathy. Appointments: Member of Professional Committee's Working Party; Invited to Address the Royal Society of Medicine, London. Publications: Talking Health, 1988; Thorsons Encyclopaedic Dictionary of Homoeopathy, 1991; Articles published in Complementry Medical Research. Memberships: Secretary, International Federation of Practitioners of Natural Therapeutics; Fellow, SA Homoeopathic Association; Associate Member, The World Medical Association; Registered Member, Homoeopathic Medical Association, England; Register of Osteopaths, England; Register of Naturopaths, England. Honours: SAHA Fellowship, 1985. Hobbies: Languages; International Medical Politics. Address: 46 Pulens Crescent, Sheet, Petersfield, Hampshire GU31 4DH, England.

GAJADHARSINGH Gerry John Michael, b. 9 Mar 1963, Trinidad, West Indies. Osteopath. Education: BSc, Natural Science, University of West Indies, Trinidad, 1982-83; Diploma in Osteopathy, British School of Osteopathy, London, 1983-87. Appointments: Guest Lecturer in

Osteopathic Technique, European School of Osteopathy and various Colleges and Universities in Belgium, France, Spain, Sweden, Guadeloupe, 1988-; Private Practice in West End of London, 1987-; Lecturer, British School of Osteopathy, 1987-; Council Member of the General Council and Register of Osteopaths, 1991; Osteopath to London & South East Division Rugby Colts, 1989-. Honours: Finals Prize for Osteopathic Technique, British School of Osteopathy, 1987. Memberships: General Council & Register of Osteopaths. Hobbies: Snow-Skiing; Horse-Riding; Travel; Fencing. Address: 27 Bickenhall Mansions, Bickenhall Street, London, W1H 3LE, UK.

GALATZER-LEVY Robert M, b. 26 July 1944, New York, USA. Psychiatrist. m. Susan Jeanne Galatzer-Levy, 22 June 1974, 4 sons, 1 daughter. Education: BA; MS; MD. Appointment: Private Practice Psychoanalysis, Child Adolescent Psychoanalysis. Publications: The Essential Other: A Developmental Psychology of the Self, 1993; Contributor of articles to professional journals. Memberships: American Psychoanalytic Assoication; American Society of Adolescent Psychiatry; Chicago Society of Adolescent Psychiatry; Chicago Psychoanalytic Society; American Society of Child Adolescent Psychiatry. Address: 180 N Michigan Avenue, Chicago, IA 60601-7401, USA.

GALIONI Elmer Francis, b. 17 Jan 1924, San Francisco, CA, USA. Physician. m. Avis J Hardin, 8 Dec 1962, 1 s, 2 d. Education: MD, Medical School; Diplomate, American Board Psychiatry and Neurology; Certified in Mental Health Administration. Appointments: Medical Officer, LT, US Navy, MC, 1946-49; Associate Medical Director, Stockton State Hospital, CA, 1950-61; Deputy Director, CA Department Mental Health, 1961-72; Director, Mental Health Service, American River Hospital, Carmichael, 1972-83; Private Practice, 1983-; Now, Semi-Retired. Publications: Intensive Treatment of Back-Ward Patients, in American Journal Psychiatry, 1953; Evaluation of a Treatment Program for Chronically Ill Schizophrenic Patients, Chronic Schizophrenia, 1960; La Personalita Multipla, in Trattato di Criminologia, Medicina Criminilogica e Psychia Forense, Italy, 1990. Honours: Fellow, American Psychiatric Association, 1958; Life Fellow, APA, 1990; Fellow, American Association River Hospital of Science, 1961. Memberships: AMA; American Association for Geriatric Psychiatry; American Academy Psychiatry and Law; Fellow, AAAS; Life Fellow, APA. Hobbies: Photography; Cooking. Address: 708 Elmhurst Circle, Sacramento, CA 95825, USA.

GALLAGHER Richard Paul, b. 3 Dec 1944, Barking, England. Epidemiologist. m. Deborah Dueckman, 31 Aug 1968, 1 s, 1 d. Education: BSc, University of BC, 1967; MA, University of West WA, 1973. Appointments: Clinical Associate Professor, Department of Health Care and Epidemiology, University of BC, 1985-; Associate Professor, Division of Dermatology, University of BC Faculty of Medicine, 1988-; Associate Professor, Department of Ophthalmology, Faculty of Medicine, University of BC; Currently, Head, Section of Epidemiology, BC Cancer Agency. Publications: Epidemiology of Malignant Melanoma, 1986; Epidemiological Aspects of Cutaneous Melanoma, 1994; Over 100 scientific articles. Memberships: Board of Directors, Canadian Society for Epidemiology and Biostatistics; Fellow, American College of Epidemiology; International Epidemiologic Association. Hobbies: Skiing; Mountaineering. Address: British Columbia Cancer Agency, 600 West 10th Ave, Vancouver, BC V5Z 4E6, Canada.

GALLUP Donand G, b. 20 June 1939, Youngstown, Ohio, USA. Gynaecologist, Oncologist. 1 son, 1 daughter. Education: BS; MD. Appointments: Flight Surgeon, 1964-67; Flight Surgeon, Naval Station Mayport, Florida, 1967-68; Staff, Ob/Gyn Naval Hospital, Taipei, Taiwan, 1971-73; Staff, Director, Gynecologic Oncology, naval Regional Medical Center, Portsmouth, Virginia, 1975-84; Assistant Professor, Eastern Virginia Medical School, 1977-79; Associate Professor, Eastern Virginia Medical School, 1979-84; Associate Professor, Medical College of Georgia, 1984-89; Director, Section of Gynecologic Oncology, Medical College of Georgia, 1988-; Professor, Medical College of Georgia, 1989-. Publications: Discussion DNA ploidy and S phase fraction are not significant prognostic factors for patients with cervical cancer, 1994; Abdominal Incisions and Complications, 1994; GU Injuries, Prevention and Therapy, 1994. Honours incl: National Defense Medal; Vietnam Service Medal; Vietnam Campaign Medal; Torpin Award, Faculty of the Year in Department of Obstetrics & Gynecology, Medical College of Georgia, 1985, 1987, 1990. Memberships incl: International Gynecologic Cancer Society; American College of Surgeons, Fellow; American Society of Clinical Oncology. Hobbies: Golf; Tennis. Address: Medical

College of Georgia, School of Medicine, Department of Obstetrics & Gynecology, Augusta, GA 30912, USA.

GALTON Elizabeth, b. 16 June 1941, Evesham, England. Psychiatrist; Analyst. m. John Dunkelberger, 25 June 1977, 1 daughter. Education: MD, University of Kansas School of Medicine, 1967; Graduate, Los Angeles Psychoanalytic Institute; Fellow, American Psychiatric Association. Appointments: President, Southern California Psychiatric Society; Private Practice of Psychiatry & Psychoanalysis, University California, Los Angeles. Honours: Fellow, APA, 1989. Memberships: APA; South California Psychiatric Society; LA Psychoanalytic Institute; Clinical Faculty, University of California, Los Angeles; Graduate Center, Child Development & Psychotherapy Faculty. Hobbies: Viola. Address: 2901 Wilshire Blvd, Ste 449, Santa Monica, CA 90403, USA.

GAMBERT Steven R, b. 22 Aug 1949, New York City, New York, USA. Professor of Medicine. m. Gry Biong, 15 Oct 1972, 1 son, 1 daughter. Education: AB with honours, University College, New York University; MD, Columbia University. Appointments: Associate Professor, Director of Geriatrics, Medical College of Wisconsin; Director, Center for the Study of Aging, New York Medical College; Acting Chairman, Professor, Department of Medicine, New York Medical College, Valhalla. Publications: Contemporary Geriatric Medicine, 1989; Diabetes Mellitus in the Elderly, 1991; Author of over 300 articles. Honours: NIA Academic Award, 1984; President, American Aging Association, 1989; Chair, Clinical Medicine, Gerontological Society of America. Memberships: American College of Physicians; American Gerontology Society; Gerontological Society of America. Hobbies: Karate; Saxophone; Running. Address: New York Medical College, Valhalla, NY 10595, USA.

GAMBUTI Gary, b. 27 Sept 1937, Paterson, New Jersey, USA. Hospital President. m. Linda Lewis, 6 Oct 1979. Education: BA, 1959; MPA, 1961. Appointments: Senior Vice President, 1967-75; Executive Vice President, 1975-77; President, St Lukes-Roosevelt, 1977. Memberships: Chairman, Society of New Jersey Hospital Association; Chairman, Hospital Associates of New York; Chairman, American Hospital Association Committee of Communications. Address: 1111 Amsterdam Avenue, New York, NY 10025, USA.

GAMELLI Richard Louis, b. 18 Jan 1949, Springfield, MA, USA. Physician; Surgeon. m. Mary, 7 Jul 1973, 3 d. Education: AB, Chemistry, Magna Cum Laude, St Michael's College, Colchester, Vermont, 1966-70; MD, University of Vermont, College of Medicine, 1970-74; Straight Surgical Internship, Medical Center Hospital of Vermont, 1974-75; Surgical Resident, Medical Center Hospital of Vermont, 1975-79. Appointments: University of Vermont College of Medicine: Assistant Professor of Surgery; Associate Professor of Surgery; Professor of Surgery; Director, Surgical Research Laboratories; Director, House Staff Training Programme, 1985-90; Medical Center Hospital of Vermont: Associate Surgeon-in-Chief; Attending in Surgery; Director and Founder, Burn Program; Director, Nutritional Support Services; Director, Resident Teaching Conference; director, Burn-Shock-Trauma Service, 1988-90; Professor, Department of Surgery & Pediatrics, Stritch School of Medicine, Loyola University Medical Center, 1990 and 1994; Director/Founder, Shock-Trauma Institute, Loyola University Medical Center, 1990; Chief, Burn Center, Foster G McGaw Hospital, Loyola University Medical Center, 1990; Director of Surgical Research, Department of Surgery, 1994. Publications: Numerous Articles, Book Chapters, Abstracts, Books, Book Reviews. Honours: include, Dr John C Hartnett Lectureship, St Michael's College, 1983; 1st Recognition Award for Teaching, Department of Surgery, University of Vermont, 1990. Memberships: include, American Association for the Surgery of Trauma; American Burn Association; Association for Academic Surgery; Central Surgical Association. Hobbies: Skiing. Address: Loyola University Medical Center, 2160 South First Avenue, Shock Trauma Institute, Maywood, IL 60153, USA.

GAMM Stanford R, b. 14 Aug 1917, Chicago, IL, USA. Psychiatrist. m. Ethel Anita Thompson, 24 Apr 1943, 3 d. Education: Attending Psychiatric VA Research Hospital, Chicago, Illinois; Psychiatric Residency, Michael Reese Hospital, Chicago, 1946-69; Graduate, Chicago Institute for Psychoanalyses. Appointments: Chief, Outpatient Psychiatric Clinic, Michael Reese Hospital, Chicago, Illinois; Attending Psychiatrist, Michael Reese Hospital; Assistant Clinical Professor, Northwestern University School of Medicine, Chicago; Attending Psychiatrist, VA Research Hospital, Chicago, 1956-73; Solo Proprietor,

Private Practice, Psychiatry & Psychoanalysis, California. Publications: 7 Papers in Various Psychiatric Publications. Honours: Presidential Unit Citation, US Navy, USS Harry F Bauer, 1945. Memberships: American Psychiatric Association; Chicago Psychoanalytic Society; American Academy of Psychoanalysis; California Psychiatric Association; Northern California Psychiatric Society. Hobbies: Walking; Bicycling; Gardening; Reading. Address: 20 Hoods Point Way, San Mateo, CA 94402-4011, USA.

GAN Hui-Fang, b. 11 Mar 1930, Chang-Chun, Jilin, China. Teacher; Professor. m. Bao-qi Gang, 3 Mar 1951, 1 son, 1 daughter. Education: Harbin Medical University, 1950. Appointments: Paediatrician, Department of Pediatry, China Medical University, Shenyang, 1950-55; Assistant, 1955-60, Lecturer, 1960-80, Associate Professor, 1980-85, Professor, 1985-, Department of Preventive Toxicology, Harbin Medical University. Publications: Practical Handbook of Preventive Toxicology, Vice Chief Editor, 1991; Preventive Toxicology, Vice Chief Editor, 1992. Honours: Award of Scientific Progress, Provincial Government of Heilongjiang, 1985, 1987, 1991, 1993. Memberships: Standing Committee, Association of Preventive Toxicology; China Preventive Medicine Association; Chairman, Association of Preventive Toxicology of Heilongjiang Province; Director, Department of Preventive Toxicology, Harbin Medical University. Hobby: Music. Address: Heilongjiang 150001, China.

GANAPATI R, b. 6 July 1930, Tamil Nadu, India. Director, Bombay Leprosy Project. Education: BSc, Madras University; MBBS, Madras Medical College, 1955; Postgraduate Diploma, Dermatology, Bombay, 1972. Appointments: Research Officer, Acworth Leprosy Hospital, 1963-75; Project Director, Gremaltes, GLRA, 1975-76; Director, Bombay Leprosy Project, 1976-. Publications: Contributed over 200 articles published in various national and international journals as well as chapters in 12 books. Honours: Padma Shri, 1983; Yodh Memorial Gold Medal, 1983; Garware Medical Sciences Oration Award, 1986; Jalma Trust Fund Oration Award (ICMR), 1987; Ambady Oration Award, (IADVL) 1988; ND Diwan Memorial Award, (NASEOH) 1989-90; Fr Maschio Humanitarien Award, 1991; Manav Mitra Award, 1994; Association of Leprologists (MP) Appreciation Award, 1994; Indian Leprosy Foundation Award for Excellence, 1994. Memberships: WHO Expert Advisory Panel on Leprosy; National Leprosy Fradication Commission; Maharashtra State Leprosy Council; Governing Bodies of NASEOH, VRC, 3R Society; Independent Evaluation Team of NLEP, Govt of India, 1990, 1991, 1995; WHO Consultant for Assessment of Training Centres in 1986 and MDT Districts in India since 1987. Address: Vidnyan Bhavan, 11, VN Purav Marg, Sion-Chunabhatti, Bombay 400 022, India.

GANDEVIA Bryan Harle, b. 5 Apr 1925, Melbourne, Australia. Consultant Physician. m. Dorothy V Murphy, 25 Aug 1953, 2 s. Education: MBBS, 1948; MD, Melbourne University, 1953; FRACP, 1953; FFOM; RCP. Appointments: Captain, RAAMC, Japan and Korea, 1949-50; Various postgraduate appointments Melbourne and London, England, 1950-57; Melbourne University and Consultant Appointments, 1957-63; Chairman and Associate Professor, Department Respiratory Medicine, University of NSW Teaching Hospitals, 1963-85; Consultant Physician, 1985-. Publications include: Numerous publications in medical and specialist journals concerning respiratory medicine and history of medicine; Senior author, Annotated Bibliography of the History of Medicine in Australia, 1984. Honour: AM, Order of Australia. Memberships: International Commission on Occupational Health; British and Australian Thoracic Societies; International Society of History of Medicine. Hobbies: Books; Wine; Watching Cricket. Address: 69 Arthur Street, Randwick, New South Wales, Australia, 2031.

GANGAL Sudha, b. 25 Aug 1934, Pune, Maharashtra State, India. Scientist. m. Gajanan A Gangal, 10 May 1952, 2 d. Education: MSc; PhD; Fellow of Indian Academy of Sciences; Fellow of Indian National Science Academy; Fellow, Maharashira Academy of Sciences. Appointments: Cancer Research Institute, Bombay, India: Scientific Officer SF, Head Immunology Division, 1984-88; Scientific Officer SG, Head Immunology Division, 1988-91; Scientific Officer G, Head Immunology Division, 1991-93. Publications: Research Articles in Journals; Chapters in Books. Honours: Shakuntala Amirchand Award, 1964; Raja Ravi Sher Singh Khalsia Memorial Cancer Research Award, 1974; Ranabaxy Award for Applied Medical Research, 1992. Memberships: Fellowships of Academies; Indian Immunology Society; Indian Association for Cancer Research; Indian Women Scientist's Association; International Cell Research Organization. Hobbies: Social

Work in Tribal Areas of India; Indian Classical Music. Address: 3 Shakuntal, Sahitya Sahawas, Bandrac (East), Bombay 400081, India.

GANGAROSA Raymond Eugene, b. 1 Jul 1951, Rochester, NY, USA. Medical Epidemiologist. Education: BA, Emory University, 1970; MSc, Electrical Engineering, GA Institute of Technology, 1976; MD, Medical College of GA, 1980; Master of Public Health, Emory University, 1990. Appointments: Research Technician, Electromagnetic Sciences Inc, Atlanta, 1973-74; Resident, University of MD, 1980-81; Senior Clinical Scientist, Picker International, Cleveland, 1981-88; Consultant for Novel Magnetic Resonance Imaging Design Team, 1987-88; Visiting Scientist, Centers for Disease Control and Prevention, Atlanta, 1990-93; Currently, Medical Epidemiologist Office of Perinatal Epidemiology, Georgia Division of Public Health; Reserach Fellow, Emory University Ethics Center; PhD Candidate in Epidemiology, Emory University, Atlanta, GA. Publications: 6 Patents in Magnetic Resonance Imaging Techniques and Expert Systems; Editor and/or Author of regulatory volumes, training manuals, user manuals, newsletter, and product design specifications; Publications on Magnetic Resonance Imaging, epidemiology of gastroenteritis, impact of harmful products on health care infrastructures public health law. Honours include: Regional campaign director, NC State Senate candidate, Chapel Hill, 1972; Secretary and Charter Member of Citizen's Agenda. Memberships: Director, Alcohol, Tobacco and Drug Control, 1989-; American Association for Advancement of Science; NY Academy of Sciences; Society for Epidemiologic Research; American Public Health Association. Hobbies: Sculpture; Drawing; Cartooning; Music; Writing; Snorkeling; Sailing; Computers; Electronics; Chess; Bridge. Address: 2833 Royal Path Court, Decatur, GA 30030-4168, USA.

GANGULI Mary, b. 17 Feb 1952. Psychiatrist; Epidemiologist. Education: MBBS, University of Madras, India; FRCP(C) in Psychiatry; Diplomate, ABPN, Psychiatry; MPH in Epidemiology, University of Pittsburgh. Appointments: Medical Demonstrator, Department of Psychiatry, Christian Medical College, Vellore, India, 1975; Assistant Professor of Psychiatry, University of Pittsburgh, School of Medicine, Department of Psychiatry, 1979-; Medical Staff, Department of Psychiatry, Western Psychiatric Institute and Clinic, 1979-92; Medical Staff, Department of Psychiatry, Western Psychiatric Institute and Clinic of Presbyterian University Hospital, 1992-; Chief Psychiatrist, Benedum Geriatrics Center, University of Pittsburgh Medical Center, 1986-93; Assistant Professor of Psychiatry & Epidemiology, University of Pittsburgh, School of Medicine, Department of Psychiatry and Graduate School of Public Health, Department of Epidemiology, 1986-; Director of Psychiatry, Benedum Geriatrics Center, University of Pittsburgh Medical Center, 1993-. Publications: include, Psychoanalytic Case Studies of Political Phenomena: The Perils of this Approach, 1983; Prevalance and Prognostic Value of Neurological Abnormalities in Alzheimers Disease, 1990. Memberships: Canadian Psychiatric Association; Indian Psychiatric Society; American Psychiatric Association; American Public Health Association; Society for Epidemiological Research; American Geriatrics Society; Canadian Academy of Geriatric Psychiatry; American Association for Geriatric Psychiatry; Gerontological Society of America. Address: WPIC, 3811 O'Hara Street, Pittsburgh, PA 15213, USA.

GANIN Gennady Nikolaevich, b. 1 Jan 1959, Ukraine, USSR. Zoologist-Ecologist. m. Natalia Kosigina, 25 July 1989, 2 sons. Education: BA, Dnepropetrovsky State University, Ukraine, 1981; Doctor's degree, Russian Academy of Sciences, 1989. Appointments: Senior Research Scientist, Institute of Water and Ecological Problems, Khabarovsk. Publications: Co-author: Soil invertebrates of Far East, 1989; Pedogenesis in Priamurje, 1989; Biogeochemical consultant's investigation of environment, 1993; Biogeochemical indication for protected and developed territories, 1993. Honours: G Soros International Science Foundation, 1993. Memberships: Society of Entomology; Society of Pedology; Secotox International Society. Hobbies: Kong-fu; Travel. Address: Institute of Water and Ecological Problems, 65 Kim Yu Chen St, Khabarovsk 680063, Russia.

GANLEY James Powell, b. 25 Apr 1937, Altadena, California, USA. Physician; Teacher. m. Anne Hay Hunter, 7 Aug 1965, 4 daughters. Education: BS, Mount St Mary's College, 1959; MD, Georgetown University, 1963; MPH, 1969, DrPH, 1972, Johns Hopkins University. Appointments: Senior Staff Fellow, National Eye Institute; Assistant Professor, University of Arizona Medical Center; Currently Professor, Chairman, Department of Ophthalmology, Louisiana State University Medical Center, Shreveport. Publications: Epidemiologic Characteristics of Presumed Ocular Histoplasmosis, 1973; Co-author: Presumed Ocular

Histoplasmosis, 1972; The Framingham Eye Study, 1977; Uveitis, perivenous sheathing and multiple sclerosis, 1978; Toxoplasmosis and Cats, 1980; Aspirin and recurrent hyphema from blunt trauma, 1983; Isolation of a herpes simplex virus that is retinovirulent in mice, 1989; Ophthalmic Epidemiology journal (editor-in-chief), 1993-. Memberships: American Academy of Ophthalmology; American College of Preventive Medicine; American College of Epidemiology; American Public Health Association; International Eye Foundation; Treasurer, International Society of Geographic and Epidemiologic Ophthalmology; International Uveitis Study Group; American Uveitis Society; Program Planning Committe-Association for Research in Vision and Ophthalmology;President, Shreveport Medical Society; Louisiana State Medical Society;Past President, Louisiana Association for the Blind. Hobbies: Sailing; Tennis; Photography. Address: Department of Ophthalmology, Louisiana State University Medical Center-Shreveport, PO Box 33932, Shreveport, LA 71130-3932, USA.

GAO Cong Guang, b. 25 December 1935, Huaiyin, Jiangsu, China. Professor of Cardiology. m. Xiao Jie Fang, 1 October 1961, 1 son, 1 daughter. Education: MD, Zhejiang Medical University. Appointments: Intern, Staff, Visiting Doctor, Associate Professor, Ningbo No 2 Hospital; Head of Medicine, Li Huili Hospital, Ningbo. Publications: Co-author, Cardiology, 1979; Author, Anisodamine in the treatment of acute pancrestitis, 1982; Left ventricular false tendone and ventricular premature beats, 1993. Honours: 6 times Research Award, Ningbo Hospital. Memberships: Chinese Medical Association. Hobbies: Sports. Address: Li HuiLi Hospital, Ningbo, Zhejiang 315040, China.

GAO Cong-Yuan, b. 10 Apr 1939, Jiangsu, China. Professor of Pharmacy and Analytical Chemistry. m Wang Jiayu, 10 Mar 1962, 1 son, 1 daughter. Education: BA, Beijing Medical University, 1960; Senior Visiting Scholar, University of Pittsburgh, USA, 1985. Appointments include: Currently Professor of Pharmacy and Analytical Chemistry, Director of Analytical Computational Centre and Spectral Analysis Laboratory, Beijing Medical University; National Grade Adjuster of, Chinese Measurement Accreditation. Publications include: 1st author: Fluorometric Determination of Free Salicylic Acid in Preparations of Acetylsalicylic Acid, 1983; The Study of Analytical Method for Preparation of Chinese Herbal Medicines, 1985; Quaternary Alkaloids of Thalictrum Cultratum, 1986; NMR Indentification of 2-0 Acetyl and 3-0-Acetyl-4, 6-Benzylidene-&-D Methyl Glucopyranoside, 1988 Study and Identification of the Chemical Structure of a New Component in Glycyrrhiza Uralensis Fisch by NMR Methods, Alkaloids of Thalictrum Delavayi, NMR Study on Fluorosonucleosides (I), 1990; NMR Study on the Structure of a New Phytocodysteroid: NMR Study on Configuration and Conformation of Fluoroisonucleosides (II), 1991; NMR Study on the Chemical Structure of a New Flavonoloside, 1994; Co-author: The Study of Chromatography and Spectrometry for Chinese Medicines, 1984; New Bisbenzylisoquinoline Alkaloids from Pycnarrhena Manillensis, 1987; New Bisbenzylisoquinoline Alkaloids from Daphnadra Dielsii, 1989; Structure Investigation of a New Alkaloid from Zanthoxylum Schinifolium Sieb et Zucc, 1992; 13 C-NMR Study on 2,4-Diamino-5-Methyl-6-Substituted-Benzyl-Pyrido-(2,3d)-Pyrimidines, Structure Determination by NMR, 1993. Memberships: Chinese Pharmaceutical Association; Beijing Chemical Association; Chinese Analytical Measurement Association; Beijing New Drugs Committee for Examination and Approval. Hobbies: Swimming; Chinese chess; Table-tennis. Address: PO Box 219, Beijing Medical University, 38 Xueyuan Road, Beijing 100083, China.

GAO Feng-Ming, b. 9 Mar 1931, Fengren County, China. Pathology. m. Shu-Lan Wang, 21 Feb 1957, 3 s. Education: Hebei Medical College, 1951-56; Postgraduate, 1962-64; Beijing College of Linguistics, 1973-74; Master's Degree in Cancer Pathology; Visiting Scholar, King's and Guy's Hospital, London 1974-75. Appointments: Teacher and Research Worker in Pathology, 1956; Associate Professor, 1982; Professor of Radiopathology, 1986-. Publications: More than 80 Papers published including, Late Effect of Female Sex Hormones Combined with Gamma Rays and Cellular Kinetics, 1987; Experimental Canine, 1981. Honours: Advanced Research Worker offered by Laboratory of Industrial Hygiene, 1988-90; National Advanced Worker, 1988-1990; 3rd Prize for Scientific and Technical Progress, 1987, 1993. Memberships: The Society of Radiation Research & Radiation Processing; Chinese Society of Environmental Mutagens; Beijing Society of Environmental Mutagens. Hobbies: Photography; Touring; Cooking. Address: Laboratory of Industrial Hygiene, Ministry of Public Health, 2 Xinkang Street, Deshengmenwai, 100088 Beijing, China.

GAO Ji, b. 1 December 1926, Tianjin, China. Professor; Researcher on Human Reproduction. m. Ru Fu Zhang, 19 April 1952, 1 son, 1 daughter. Education: MD, Cheeloo University, China; Postgraduate Programm, Peking Union Medical College, China. Appointments: Teaching Assistant, 1953; Lecturer, 1960; Associate Professor and Researcher, 1976; Professor, Director and Senior Researcher, 1979-91; Retired. Publications: Menstrual blood loss in healthy Chinese women, 1981; Effect of intrauterine devices on menstrual blood loss, 1982; A randomized comparative clinical evaluation of the Steel Ring, VCu200 and TCu220c IUDs, 1986; Menstrual blood loss and haematological indices in healthy Chinese women in Beijing, 1987; Prevention and treatment of IUDs induced menorrhagia, 1988; Pregnancy interruption with Ru486 in combination with d1-15-methyl-prostaglandin-F2a-methyl ester: The Chinese experience, 1988; Three years experience with Levonorgestrel-releasing IUD and Norplant-2 implants: A randomized comparative study, 1992. Honours: Awarded, National Advanced Team for Family Planning, National Family Planning Commission, 1986; Awarded Four and Third Prizes of Achievement on Science and Technology, National Family Planning Commission, 1985, 1986, 1987, 1993. Memberships Include: Chinese Medical Association; Academic Committee, National Research Institute for Family Planning, Beijing; Board Member, Society of Family Planning, Beijing Branch; World Health Organization Consultant Group on Human Reproduction. Hobbies: Music; Literature; Travel. Address: 96 Westpointe Crescent, Nepean, Ontario K2G 5Y8, Canada.

GAO Meihua, b. 24 Aug 1954, Dongying, Shandong, China. Teacher. m. Li Wuxiu, 18 Nov 1979, 1 d. Education: Qingdao Medical College. Appointments: Institute of Microbiology in China; Institute of Immunology in China. Publications: Chief Editor of 4 works, 1987-94; 95 Professional Publications including: Effect of IL-2 Gene with Tumour Mice by Laser, in Journal of Microbiology and Immunology, 1994; The Influence of IL-2 Activity on Stomach Cancer Transplant Mice, in Journal of Physical Therapy, 1994; Chief Editor and Editor of 4 Journals. Honours: Model Teacher; Advanced Worker; The Mainstay of Learning and Guide of Subject in University, Shandong Province. Memberships: Institute of Microbiology; Institute of Immunology. Hobby: Badminton. Address: 522 no 3 Huanghe Road, Binzhou, Shandong 256603, China.

GAO Runlin, b. 4 May 1941, Hebei, China. Cardiologist. m. Yuhuan Du, 12 Sept 1968, 1 daughter. Education: BA, Beijing Medical University, 1965; MSc, MD, Peking Union Medical College, 1981; Special Fellow, Loma Linda University School of Medicine, California, USA, 1985. Appointments: Attending Physician, 1981, Associate Professor of Medicine, 1987, currently Professor of Medicine, Director, Department of Cardiology, Deputy Director, Fu Wai Hospital, Chinese Academy of Medical Sciences, Beijing. Publications: Evaluation of clinical criteria of coronary recanalization in acute myocardal infarction, 1991; Intravenous recombinant tissue-type plasminogen activator in acute myocardial infarction, 1991; Reperfusion arrhythmias in acute myocardial infarction, 1993; Co-author, contributions to Coronary Heart Disease, 1994: Coronary angiography; Percutaneous transluminal coronary angioplasty; Syndrome X; Cardiogenic shock. Honours: 3rd Award of Advances in Science and Technology, Ministry of Public Health, China, 1991; 3rd Award of Advances in Science and Technology, Chinese Academy of Medical Sciences, 1991. Memberships: Council Member, Chinese Medical Association, Beijing Branch; Standing Committee, Chinese Society of Cardiology. Hobby: Music. Address: Fu Wai Hospital, 167 Bei Lishi Road, Beijing 100037, China.

GAPONOV Serge Petrovich, b. 3 Dec 1964, Voronezh. Biologist; Parasitologist. Education: Voronezh University, 1986; Postgraduate Course of Voronezh University, 1989. Career: Doctor Ph., Lecturer, Voronezh University, 1989-. Publications: Tachinid Egg Morphology, 1989; Eggs of Phasiinae, 1992; Exochorion Morphology in Some Species of the Sub Family Tachininae (Diptera, Tachinidae), 1993. Honour: Holder of Honour Stipend of Russian Academy of Sciences, 1994-96. Memberships: Russian Entomological Society; Active member, the New York Academy of Sciences, 1994; Russian Parasitological Society. Hobbies: Figure Skating; Classic Music; Travel. Address: Revolution Avenue, House 26/28, Apt 98, 394000 Voronezh, Russia.

GARCIA Mary Katherine, b. 9 Jan 1947, Chicago, IL, USA. Nursing. m. John E Garcia, 7 May 1969, 1 s, 1 d. Education: BSN, Villanovall; MN, UCLA; RN; CS. Career includes: Consultant, Program Coordinator, LA Chapter of AAFA, 1984-87; Consultant, National Programs and Services, AAFA, Washington DC, 1987-88; Coordinator of support group for parents of children with asthma and allergies, Presenter of workshops, 1988-; Psychotherapist, Houston Child Guidance Clinic, 1992-93; Program Administrator, TB at American Lung Association of TX, Houston and SE Region, 1993-. Publications include: Co-author, Asthma in the School: Improving Control with Peak Flow, 1989; Forging an Alliance with School Nurses, in American Journal of Asthma and Allergies for Paediatricians, 1989; Editor in Chief, School Asthma News, 1991; Commentary on guidelines for dx and management of asthma, in Abstracts of Clinical Care Guidelines, 1991. Memberships include: American Nurses Association; TX State Nurses Association; Food and Drug Adminstration, 1990-93; Pulmonary-Allergy Drugs Advisory Committee; Children's Lung Health Committee, 1989-93; Quality of Care of Asthma Committee, Chairman of Non Physician Ed Subcommittee, American Academy of Allergy and Immunology; Expert Consultant to National Asthma Education Program of NHLBI. Address: 14 Muirfield, Sugar Land, TX 77479, USA.

GARDNER Brian Patrick, b. 17 July 1948, Fort Jameson, Zambia. Doctor. m. Stephanie Faller, 18 October 1980, 3 sons, 4 daughters. Education: BA, MA, Oxon; BM; BCh; MRCP; FRCS. Appointments: Registrar, Neurosurgery, Royal Victoria Hospital, Belfast, Ireland; Senior Registrar, Southport Spinal Injuries Centre; Consultant Surgeon in Spinal Injuries. Publications: Various professional publications in medical journals; Several chapters in books on Spinal Cord Injuries. Memberships: British Medical Association; International Medical Society of Paraplegia. Hobbies: Family; Local Schools; Local Church. Address: National Spinal Injuries Centre, Stoke Mandeville Hospital, Aylesbury, Bucks HP21 8AL, England.

GARDNER Elizabeth Mary, b. 17 Aug 1965, PA, USA. Postdoctoral Research Associate. BS, Chestnut Hill College; PhD, Medical College of PA, 1994. Career: Senior Research Assistant, Department of Biochemistry, Currently, Postdoctoral Research Associate, Department of Immunology, Medical College of PA. Publications: Co-author, Dietary vitamin A restriction produces marginal vitamin A status in young rats, in Journal of Nutrition, 1993; Co-author, The function of vitamin A in development and growth during pregnancy and lactation, in Proceedings of Conference on Nutrient Regulation during Pregnancy, Growth and Lactation, 1994. Honour: Howard Heinz Predoctoral Training Fellowship in Biomedical Nutrition. Memberships: American Institute of Nutrition; American Society for Clinical Nutrition; PA Interurban Nutrition Club. Hobby: Travel. Address: Department of Microbiology and Immunology, Medical College of Pennsylvania, 2900 Queen Lane, Philadelphia, PA 19129, USA.

GARDNER Russell, b. 19 Mar 1938, Granton, WI, USA. Professor of Psychiatry. m. Suzanne Gardner, 1 s, 2 d. Education includes: MD, University of Chicago, 1962; Graduate, Psychoanalytic Institute. Career includes: Professor of Psychiatry, Departments of Neuroscience, 1974-84, of Family Medicine, 1980-84, University of ND School of Medicine, Fargo, ND; Senior Examiner, American Board of Psychiatry and Neurology, 1983-; Professor of Psychiatry and Behavioral Sciences, 1984-, Director, Consultation-Liaison Service, 1988-93, UTMB, Galveston, TX. Publications include: Many articles in peer reviewed journals, books, chapters, forewards and abstracts including: Co-editor, Psychotropic Drugs and Dysfunctions of the Basal Ganglia. A Multidisciplinary Workshop, 1969; Co-author, Behavioral Principles in Medical Rehabilitation: A Practical Guide, 1983. Honours include: Golden Apple Award for Outstanding Preclinical Professor, University of ND School of Medicine, 1977; Fellow, APA, 1980; Invited Speaker, APA Presidential Conference on The Future of Psychiatric Education, 1986; Fellow, American College of Psychiatrists, 1988. Memberships include: President, 1984-86, Association for Academic Psychiatry; Program Chairman, 1989, 1990, 1991, 1992, Titus Harris Society; Sigma Xi; American Psychosomatic Society; Human Behavior and Evolution Society; International Society for Human Ethology; AAAS; Co-Founder, Secretary, Newsletter Editor, International Association of Comparative Psychopathology. Hobbies: Swimming; Painting; Sculpture. Address: Department of Psychiatry and Behavioral Science D28, University of Texas Medical Branch, Graves Building Rm 4 450, Galveston, TX 77555, USA.

GAREFIS Paris, b. 3 June 1942, Greece. Dentist. 2 sons, 1 daughter. Education: Dental School, Aristotelion University, Thessaloniki, Greece, 1960-66; Residency, Oral Surgery Department, 424 Military Hospital, Thessaloniki, Greece, 1969-94. Appointments: Private Clinic. Publications: Numerous scientific articles and publications in the field of Oral Implants. Memberships: Greek Dental Association; American

Prosthodontic Society; American Endodontic Society; American Academy of Implant Dentistry; International Congress of Oral Implantologists; Dental Foundation of California, USA; Fellow, Italiano Study Implantari; Honorary, Argentina Instituto de Implantologia; American College of Imlantology; Fellow, American Endodontic Society; Master, American Endodontic Society. Hobbies: Tae Quan Do; Basketball; Piano. Address: 7 Ippokratous St Marousi, Athens 151-23, Greece.

GARFEIN Arthur Douglas, b. 29 Oct 1942, Brooklyn, NY, USA. Psychiatrist; Psychoanalyst. m. Anita Burnett, 17 Nov 1967, 1 s, 1 d. Education: MD; Certificate, Psychoanalytic Training. Career: Chief of Psychiatry, Porter Memorial Hospital, 1977-79; Psychiatric Consultant, CO State Board of Medical Examiners, 1980-; Peer reviewer, National CHAMPUS Project, American Psychiatric Association, 1983-88; Chairman, Peer review Committee, CO Psychiatric Society, 1984-86; President, CO Psychiatric Care, 1994; Currently, Medical Director, Behavioral Health Services, Porter Memorial Hospital, Denver, CO; Clinical Assistant Professor of Psychiatry, University of CO Health Sciences Center, Denver, CO. Honours: Diplomate, American Board of Psychiatry and Neurology, 1974; Fellow, American Psychiatric Association, 1983. Memberships: CO Medical Society; American Psychiatric Association; American Psychoanalytic; International Psychoanalytic Association. Hobbies: Biking; Hiking; Reading; Opera; Bluegrass Music; Theatre; Symphony. Address: 191 East Orchard Road, Suite 202, Littleton, CO 80121, USA.

GARFINKLE Ely, b. 13 Apr 1949, Montreal, Canada. Psychiatrist; Psychoanalyst. m. Linda Dansky, 7 Dec 1980, 3 sons, 1 daughter. Education: BSc, 1971; MD, 1973; Diploma Medicine (Psychiatry), McGill University, 1980; FRCP, 1981. Appointments: Staff Psychiatrist, McGill University Health Services, 1981-85; Secretary, International Psychoanalytic Studies Organization, 1985-87; Private Psychoanalytic Practice. Publications: Remembering and Repeating in Multiple Personality in Psychoanalytic Psychotherapy, 1989. Memberships: College of Physicians & Surgeons of Ontario; Canadian Medical Association; Ontario Medical Association; Professional Corporation of Physicians & Surgeons of Quebec; Federation of Medical Specialists of Quebec; Royal College of Physicians & Surgeons of Canada. Address: 72A Fourth Avenue, Ottawa, Ontario K1S 2L2, Canada.

GARRETTSON Lorne Keith, b. 2 Mar 1934, California, USA. Medicine; Pediatrics. m. Elizabeth Miller, 20 Apr 1963, 3 d. Education: BA, Pomona College; MD, Johns Hopkins University; Postdoctoral Training, Clinical Pharmacology. Appointments: Assistant Professor, SUNY, Buffalo; Associate Professor, Pharmacy and Pharmaceutics, Pediatrics, VA Commonwealth University; Associate Professor of Pediatrics and Medical Director, Georgia Poison Center. Memberships: American Academy of Clinical Toxicology; American Association of Poison Control Centers; American Academy of Pediatrics; American College of Medical Toxicology; ASPET; AAAS. Hobbies: Cycling; Woodworking. Address: Dept of Pediatrics, Emory University School of Medicine, 69 Butler Street, Atlanta, GA 30303, USA.

GARRIDO Patricio Jose, b. 17 Mar 1940, Granada, Spain. Physician. m. Carmen Martin, 9 Sep 1968, 1 son, 2 daughters. Education: University of Barcelona School of Medicine; EPidemiology Summer Programme, University of Massachusetts, USA; Epidemiology Programme, Johns Hopkins University School of Medicine. Appointments: General Practitioner; Physician, Family and Community Practice; Chief, Epidemiology, Department of Public Health f Cataluna, Spain; Director, International Travel and Health for Cataluna; Professor of Public Health, University of Barcelona. Publications: Preventive Medicine and Public Health, Co-author, 1991; The Control of Tuberculosis, 1992; Food Poisoning Control and Prevention, Co-author, 1992; The Epidemiological Method in Mental Health, Co-author, 1993; Utility of the Sanitary Information Diseases System, 1989; Diet and Colon Cancer in Spain, Ecological Study, 1991; Epidemiology of Mushroom in Spain, 1992. Honours: Fulbright Grant, 1985; Award, Life to the Years and Years for to Live, Barcelona College of Physician Work, 1990. Memberships: American Public Health Association; American Society for EPidemiological Research. Hobbies: Photography; Music; Philosophy; Painting. Address: Travessera de las Corts 350, Barcelona 08029, Spain.

GARZULY Ferenc, b. 21 Dec 1937, Bratislava, Hungary. Neurology. m. Maria Geszler, 11 May 1967, 1 d. Education: MD, Specialist in Neurology and Neuropathology, Pécs Medical University, 1962;

Candidate, Medical Science, 1989. Appointment: Chief of Department of Neurology, County Hospital, Szombathely, Hungary. Publications: Co-author, Subacute spongius encephalopathy, in Arch Psychatr Nervenkr, 1971; Morbid changes in Lowe's oculo-cerebro-renal syndrome, in Neuropädiatrie, 1973; Neuronale migration disturbance in Zellweger syndrome, in Neuropädiatrie, 1974; Pathological features of neuro-leukemia: Changes and lessons, in Orv Hetil, 1994. Honours: Special Neurological Collegium; Leadership Member, Hungarian Stroke Association and Hungarian Neurologic and Psychiatric Society. Hobby: Bicycling. Address: Markusovszky Hospital, Department of Neurology, H-9701 Szombathely, PO Box 143, Markusovszky u 3, Hungary.

GASSILIN Vladimir S, b. 9 Jan 1929, Samara, Russia. Professor. m. Vera Komarova, 4 Mar 1956, 2 daughters. Education: BA, 1952; MD, 1965. Appointments: Assistant Professor of Medicine, University Samara, 1952; Professor of Medicine, University Kursk, 1966; Professor of Government Medical Center. Publications: 11 books in Russian, 240 articles and studies in Russian, 10 in English; Geriatric Aspects of Internal Diseases, co-author, 1995. Honours: Award, Russian Academy of Medical Sciences After Languages, After Myasnicov. Memberships: Russian Academy of Medicine; Russian Medical Association; Society of Russian Cardiologists. Hobbies: Gardening. Address: ul Vozdvijenka 6, Moscow 103875, Russia.

GATTONE Vincent Henry, b. 6 June 1951, Philadelphia, PA, USA. Medical School Professor. m. Diane M Wehrle, 26 Dec 1977, 2 s, 3 d. Education: BS, Chemistry, Ursinus College, Collegeville, Pennsylvania, 1973; MS, Anatomic Pathology, George Washington University, Washington DC, 1975; PhD, Medical Science Anatomy, Medical College of Ohio, Toledo, Ohio, 1980; Postdoctoral Fellow, Indiana University, School of Medicine, Indianapolis, 1980-83. Appointments: Assistant Professor, Milton S Hershey Medical Center, Pennsylvania State University, Department of Anatomy, 1983-86; Assistant Professor, University of Kansas Medical Center, Department of Anatomy & Cell Biology, 1986-89; Associate Professor, University of Kansas Medical Center, Department of Anatomy & Cell Biology, 1989-1995; Professor, University & Kansas Medical Center, Department of Anatomy & Cell Biology, 1995. Publications: Numerous Research Publications in Renal Cell Biology & Pathophysiology. Honours: Student Voice Teaching Awards, 1991, 1992, 1994. Memberships: American Association of Anatomists; American Society of Nephrology; International Society of Nephrology; International Society of Pediatric Nephrology; American Association for the Advancement of Sciences; Society for Neurosciences; American Heart Association; Sigma Xi. Hobbies: Photography. Address: Department of Anatomy & Cell Biology, University of Kansas Medical Center, 3901 Rainbow Boulevard, Kansas City, KS 66160-7400, USA.

GAUCAN Constantin, b. 14 June 1940, Ploiesti, Romania. Professor. m. Maia, 10 July 1964, 1 son, 1 daughter. Education: PhD, DDS, University of Medicine, University of History & Philosophy, Bucharest. Appointments: Dental Technician, 1960; University of Medicine, 1967; Assistant Professor, 1973; Postgraduate Clinics, University of History & Philosophy, 1979. Publications: 189 Scientific articles and lectures in Romania and abroad; 2 books: Odontollogy, 1979; Restorative Procedures in Large Crown Distructions, 1989. Memberships: RDA; FDI; ORE. Hobbies: History; Skiing; Fishing; Mountain Climbing. Address: No 8 Hristo Boteu Street, Sector 3, Apt 1, Bucharest, Romania.

GAVIN John Bevan, b. 14 May 1935, Matamata, New Zealand. Experimental Pathologist. m. Irene Jones, 21 May 1960, 1 son, 3 daughters. Education: BDS, New Zealand, 1959; DDS, Otago, 1964; PhD, Otago, 1968; DSc, Otago, 1988; Postdoctoral Research Fellowship, Northwestern University, USA; Fellow, Royal College of Pathologists. Appointments: Lecturer, then Senior Lecturer in Basic Dental Science, University of Otago; Associate Professor of Anatomy, University of Saskatchewan, Canada; Currently Professor of Experimental Anatomy, Assistant Vice-Chancellor, University of Auckland, New Zealand. Publications: 3 doctoral theses and over 200 published papers on dental and oral pathology, cardiovascular research and medical education. Honours: Honorary Life Membership, Cancer Society of New Zealand; Honorary Member for Life, New Zealand Dental Association. Memberships: President, Australia and New Zealand Microcirculation Society; President, Australasian Section, International Society for Heart Research; Deafness Research Foundation of New Zealand. Hobby: Woodworking. Address: Department of Pathology,

University of Auckland School of Medicine, Private Bag 92019, Auckland, New Zealand.

GAYDOS Joel Carl (Colonel), b. 7 Apr 1942, Edenborn, Pennsylvania, USA. Physician. m. Charlote Ann Klaus, 5 June 1965, 2 sons, 2 daughters. Education: AB, 1964, MD, 1968, West Virginia University; MPH, Epidemiology, University of Pittsburgh Graduate School of Public Health, 1972. Appointments include: Chief, Department of Epidemiology, 1976-77, Chief, Department of Advanced Preventive Medicine Studies, 1977-79, Walter Reed Army Institute of Research, Washington DC; Epidemiologist, US Army, Europe, 1979-82; Chief, Occupational and Environmental Medicine Division, 1982-83, Director, Occupational and Environmental Health, 1983-85, Medical Director, 1993-, US Army Environmental Hygiene Agency, Aberdeen Proving Ground, Maryland, USA; Consultant, 1985-89, Chief of Preventive Medicine, 1988-89, Department of the Army, Office of The Surgeon General; Associate Dean (Acting), Uniformed Services University of the Health Sciences, F Edward Hébert School of Medicine, Bethesda, Maryland, 1992-93. Publications: Textbook of Military Medicine, Vol 2 - Occupational Health: The Soldier and the Industrial Base (associate specialty editor), 1993; Military Participation in Emergency Humanitarian Assistance (co-author), 1994; About 20 articles. Honours include: Order of Military Medical Merit, 1989; Superior Service Medal, US Department of Defense, 1993. Memberships include: Fellow, American College of Preventive Medicine; Fellow, American College of Occupational and Environmental Medicine; Association of Military Surgeons of the United States; American Medical Association; American Society of Tropical Medicine and Hygiene. Hobbies: History; Wildlife conservation; Soccer. Address: US Army Environmental HygieneAgency, Center for Health Promotion and Preventive Medicine, Aberdeen Proving Ground, MD 21010-5422, USA.

GAYLIN Willard, b. 23 Feb 1925, Cleveland, OH, USA. Psychiatrist. m. Betty Schofer, 2 d. Education: BA, Harvard College; MD, Western Reserve Medical School; Certificate, Psychoanalytic Education, Columbia Psychoanalytic School. Career: Co-founder, President, 1969-93, Currently, Chairman, The Hastings Center, NY; PPFA's AIDS Advisory Panel; Board of Directors, Planned Parenthood Federation of America, Helsinki Watch, Medical/Scientific Board of National Aphasia Association; Currently, Private Practitioner, Psychiatry and Psychoanalysis; Clinical Professor of Psychiatry, Columbia College of Physicians and Surgeons. Publications: 15 books including: The Male Ego, Adam and Eve and Pinocchio: On Being and Becoming Human, Rediscovering Love, The Rage Within, Caring, Feelings: Our Vital Signs, The Killing of Bonnie Garland: A Question of Justice; Author or editor of over 100 articles. Honours include: Elected Member, Institute of Medicine; Fellow, APA; Fellow, NY Psychiatric Society; George E Daniels Medical for Contributions to Psychoanalytic Medicine; Van Gieson Award for Outstanding Contributions to Mental Health Sciences; Chubb Fellow, Yale; Henry Beecher Award for Life-Achievement in Bioethics. Memberships: Past Chairman, Human Rights Task Force, APA; Human Rights Committee, Institute of Medicine. Address: 111 East 65th Street, Apt 2A, New York, NY 10021, USA.

GBOLADE Babatunde Abiodun, b. 1953, Jos, Nigeria. m. Linda Ibidunni, 5 Dec 1981, 1 s, 2 d. Education: MBBS, University of Ibadan, Nigeria, 1978; LM, 1983; DGO, Trinity College, University of Dublin, 1983; MRCOG, 1992; MFFP, 1993; MRCPI, 1994. Appointments: House Officer, 1978-79; Medical Officer, 1979-85; Registrar, Obstetrics and Gynaecology, 1985-92; Registrar, Genito-Urinary Medicine, 1992-93; Currently, Lecturer in Family Planning and Reproductive Healthcare, Department of Obstetrics and Gynaecology, University of Manchester. Publications: Traumatic Injuries of the Female Genital Tract, in Journal Tropical Obstetrics and Gynaecology, 1990; Urethrocliesis: Treatment for Genuine Stress Incontinence?, in Journal of Obstetrics and Gynaecology, 1993; Recurrent Lower Motor Neurone Facial Paralysis in Successful Pregnancies, in Journal of Laryngology and Otology, 1994. Honours: Federal Government Undergraduate Award, 1974; Ogun State Postgraduate Scholarship for Obstetrics and Gynaecology, 1979. Memberships: Fellow, Royal Society of Health; Royal College of Obstetricians and Gynaecologists; Royal College of Physicians, Ireland; Faculty of Family Planning and Reproductive Health Care (RCOG). Hobbies: Classical Music; Medical Computing; Video Photography; Swimming. Address: 108 Lily Hill Street, Whitefield, Manchester, M45 7SG, England.

GE Hong, b. 1 May 1932, Beijing, China. Director Doctor. m. Shao Meng-ru, 19 Sep 1959, 1 daughter. Education: MD, Peking Union Medical College, 1957. Appointments: Doctor of Cardiology, Lanzhou General Hospital, 1957-85; Doctor od Cardiology, 514 Hospital, Beijing, 1985-94; Doctor of Cardiology, Cardiovascular Disease Hospital, 1994-. Publications: The Management of the Organs' Failure, Co-author, 1992; The Refractory Heart Failure Treated with the Hemodialysis, 1994. Honours: One of the Honour Papers, 4th Cardiovascular Congress Meeting of China, 1993. Memberships: Beijing Cardiologic Association; Chinese Medical Association; World Hypertension League; Chinese Hypertension League. Hobbies: Classical Music; Ceramic Art. Address: 9 De-Wai An-xiang North Road, Beijing 100101, China.

GE Jiou-yu, b. 16 Sept 1953, Nanjing, Jiangsu, China. Dental Surgeon. m. Tie-mei Wang, 1 May 1983, 1 son. Education: BA, Nanjing Medical University. Appointments: Resident Physician, 1983, Visiting Physician, 1988, Department Head, 1988, currently Vice-Chief Physician, Nanjing Stomatological Hospital; Associate Professor. Publications: Root canal therapy, book, 1994; Articles: A possible prognostic indicator for periodontal breakdown, 1994; A study on SOD in normal and inflamed human dental pulp tissue (co-author), 1994. Honours: Excellent Award for Research, 1985, for Work, 1993, Nanjing Stomatological Hospital. Membership: Chinese Medical Association. Hobbies: Tavle-tennis; White and black; Watching TV; Fishing. Address: 30 Zhong Yang Road, Nanjing, Jiangsu 210008, China.

GEENEN Vincent Gaston Marcel, b. 6 Feb 1958, Verviers, Belgium, Associate Professor. m. Isabelle Jasselette, 27 Oct 1979, 2 sons. Education: MD, PhD, University of Liege Medical School. Appointments: Research Assistant, 1982-86, Senior Research Assistant, 1986-88, Research Associate, 1988-94, Research Associate Professor, 1994-, Belgian National Fund for Scientific Research; Assistant Professor, Internal Medicine, Endocrinology, University Hospital of Liege-Sart Tilman. Publications: More than 50 articles in professional journals; Co-editor: Horizons in Endocrinology, 1991; Regulatory Peptides special issue, 1993; Thymus - Journal of T-Cell Biology. Honours: Semper Prize, Belgian NFSR, 1988; Smith Kline-Beecham Prize, Royal Academy of Medicine, Brussels, 1992; Alumni Prize, Belgian University Foundation, 1993. Memberships: Endocrine Society, USA; International Society of Neuroimmunomodulation; International Society of Molecular Evolution; New York Academy of Sciences; European Foundation of Immunogenetics; Société Française d' Immunologie. Hobbies: Country biking; Cultural sightseeing. Address: Department of Endocrinology, Institute of Pathology CHV-B23, University of Liege, B-4000 Liege-Sart Tilman, Belgium.

GEERLINGS Peter Johannes, b. 13 Nov 1939, Jakarta, Indonesia. Psychiatrist. m. Eugenie, 24 Feb 1965, 3 daughters. Education: MD. Appointments: Head, Department of Psychiatry, University of Amsterdam, 1984-91; Associate Professor, Department of Psychiatry; Medical Director, Jellinek Clinic, Amsterdam. Publications incl: Alcoholism: social consequences and clinical definitions, 1991; Psychiatrische stoornissen en druggebruik: diagnostiek en behandeling, 1993; Low-threshold and high-threshold methadone programmes, 1993; Hersenen en Verslaving, 1993; Eens verslaafd altijd verslaafd? Determinanten van het therapeutisch beloop, 1993. Memberships: Dutch Psychoanalysis Association; National Council of Health. Hobbies: Cycling; Classical Music; Reading. Address: Jellinck Clinic, Jacob Obrechtstraat 92, 1071 KR Amsterdam, The Netherlands.

GEHA Alexander Salim, b. 18 Jun 1936, Beirut, Lebanon. Surgeon. m. Diane L Redalen, 25 Nov 1967, 3 d. Education: BS, summa cum laude, 1955, MD, summa cum laude, 1959, American University of Beirut, Lebanon; MS, Surgery and Physiology, University of MN, Mayo Graduate School of Medicine, MN, 1967; MA, Privatum, Yale University, 1978. Appointments include: Professor and Director, Cardiothoracic Surgery, Case Western Reserve University, Cleveland, OH, 1986-; Attending Surgeon and Director, Cardiothoracic Surgery, University Hospitals of Cleveland, 1986-; Consultant in Surgery, Wade Park Veterans Administration Hospital, OH, 1986-; Attending Surgeon, Cleveland Metropolitan General Hospital, OH, 1986-; Consultant, Cardiothoracic Surgery, Mt Sinai Hospital, OH, 1989-. Publications include: Over 140 publications in professional journals, 1962-, including: Co-author, Blood Lost and Blood Transfused in Coronary Artery Bypass Graft Surgery: Implications for Blood Conservation Strategies; Over 80 abstracts, 1965-; Many text books; 2 Medical films, 1970, 1978; 3 Medical book reviews; Many invited lectureships. Honours include: Society of Sigma Xi, 1968. Memberships include: Various committees, 1986-; American Association for Thoracic Surgery; American College of Cardiology; AMA; AHA; American Surgical Assoc; International

Association for Cardiac Biological Implants; International Society for Heart Transplantation; Lebanese Order of Physicians; Halsted Society; Pasteur Club; Societe Internationale de Chirurgie; Society for Vascular Surgery. Address: 11100 Euclid Avenue, Cleveland, OH 44106, USA.

GEIRSSON Reynir Tomas, b. 13 May 1946, Reykjavik, Iceland. Doctor. m. Steinunn Sveinsdottir, 21 Mar 1971, 2 d. Education: Doctor of Medicine, University of Iceland, 1986; FRCOG, 1993. Appointments: Clinical Lecturer, University of Dundee, Scotland, 1982-84; Consultant Obstetrician/Gynaecologist, National University Hospital, Reykjavik, Iceland, 1984-93; Senior Lecturer, (Sabbatical) University of Edinburgh, Scotland, 1989-90; Professor and Chairman, Department of Obstetrics & Gynaecology, Iceland. Publications include: Growth of Total Intrauterine, Intra-Amniotic and Placental Volume in Normal Singleton Pregnancy Measured by Ultrasound, 1985; The Relation of Birthweight to Histological Appearances in Vessels of the Placental Bed, 1986; Intrauterine Volume in Pregnancy, 1986; Total Intrauterine Volume and Symphysis-Fundus Height, Is there a Relation?, 1987; Can We Produce Perinatal Mortality Still Further?, 1989; Familial and Genetic Predisposition to Eclampsia and Preeclampsia in a Defined Population, 1990. Honours: Regional Councils Gold Medal, Membership Exam, RCOG, 1981. Memberships: Royal College of Obstetricians & Gynaecologists; Nordic Association of Obstetricians & Gynaecologists; Icelandic Medical Association. Hobbies: Skiing; Music; History. Address: Department of Obstetrics & Gynaecology, National University Hospital, 101 Reykjavik, Iceland.

GELB Adrian Walter, b. 28 Oct 1948, South Africa. Anaesthetist. m. Lola Katz, 17 Dec 1972, 3 daughters. Education: MBChB, University of Cape Town, 1972; DA (England), 1974; FRCPC (Canada), 1979. Appointments: Currently Professor, Chairman, Department of Anaesthesia, University of Western Ontario, London, Canada. Publications: Local anesthetics in cerebral ischemia, 1989; Co-author: Ventilatory responses to hypoxia and hypercapnia during halothane sedation and anesthesia in man, 1978; Cardiovascular effects of isoflurane-induced hypotension for cerebral aneurysm surgery, 1983; Primate brain tolerance to temporary focal cerebral ischemia during isoflurane- or sodium nitroprusside-induced hypotension, 1989; The multiple organ donor: identification and management, 1989. Honours: Parker B Francis Fellowship, 1979-80. Memberships: Canadian Anaesthetists Society; American Society of Anesthesiologists; International Anesthesia Research Society; Society of Neurosurgical Anesthesia and Critical Care. Hobbies: Reading; Music. Address: Department of Anaesthesia, University Hospital, 339 Windermere Road, London, Ontario, Canada N6A 5A5.

GELBIER Stanley, b. 26 Nov 1935, London, England. Public Dental Health Educator. m. Marilyn Jeanette Joseph, 8 Jul 1962, 1 s, 1 d. Education: LDS,1961, DDPH,1969, FDS, 1993, Royal College of Surgeons; PhD, Council for Academic Awards, London, 1980; DHSMA, Society Apothecaries, London, 1980. Career includes: Lecturer, Child Dental Health, London Hospital, 1963-67; Chief Dental Officer, Borough of Hackney, London, 1967-74; Area Dental Officer, Lambeth Health Authority, London, 1974-82; Consultant, Dental Public Health, 1982-90, Director, Primary Care, 1987-91, Camberwell Health Authority; Professor of Dental Public Health, University of London, 1990-. Publication: Handbook for Dental Surgery Assistants, 2nd edition, 1977. Honour: Fellow, British Institute of Management. Memberships: Deputy Curator Museum, 1983-87, Curator, 1988-, British Dental Association; Secretary, 1972-75, President, 1976, British Paediatric Dentistry Society; Treasurer, 1973-78, President, 1987, British Association of Community Dentistry; American Academy History of Dentistry. Hobbies: Photography; Swimming; Travel. Address: King's College London, Caldecot Road, London, SE5 9RW, England.

GENEFKE Inge, b. 6 July 1938, Copenhagen, Denmark. Medical Doctor. m. Bent Sorensen, 30 May 1991. Education: Graduated in Medicine, 1965, Fellowship, Institute of Pharmacology, 1968-72, University of Copenhagen, 1965; Postgraduate course, Medical and Technical Biochemistry, Strasbourg University, France, 1966; Research, Strasbourg, Munich, Fellowships, Switzerland, Italy, 1965-69; Specialisation in Neurology, Rigshospitalet and other Copenhagen University hospitals, 1972-82. Appointments: Initiator, Medical Director: Rehabilitation and Research Centre for Torture Victims, Copenhagen, 1981-, and International Rehabilitation Council For Torture Victims, 1988-. Publications: Torturen i verden-den angår os alle; Contributor to: Torture and its consequences: current treatment approaches; American Journal of Public Health; American Journal of Social Psychiatry; British

Journal of Psychiatry; Jahrbuch für Psychopatologie und Psychoterapie; Scandinavian and Danish journals. Honours include: Dane of the Year, International Press Center, 1982; Låt Leva-priset, Human Rights Award, Sweden, 1983; Vikingepris, Hobro Town Council, 1985; Aristoteles Prize, Onassis Foundation, Greece, 1986; Human Rights Achievement Award, Walter Briehl Human Rights Foundation, USA, 1988; The Right Livelihood Honorary Award, 1989; Honorary degree, Medicine, Surgery, University of Bologna, 1989; Ebbe Munck-Prisen, 1990; Grants and scholarships. Memberships: Co-founder of Danish Medical Group, Amnesty International, President, Medical Advisory Board, Amnesty International, Co-founder, Board Member, Anti-Torture Research; International Society for Traumatic Stress Studies; European Society for Traumatic Stress Studies; Executive Council, OMCT/SOS-Torture, Geneva; Co-founder, Physicians for Human Rights, Denmark. Hobbies: Reading; Swimming; Walking in the nature; Art exhibitions. Address: Borgergade 13, PO Box 2107, DK-1014 Copenhagen, Denmark.

GENING Tatiana Petrovna, b. 3 Sept 1950, Semipalatinsk, Kasachstan. Biologist. m. Ivan I Gening, Mar 1991, 1 daughter. Education: Ural State University. Appointments: Engineer, Semipalatinsk Medical Institute Experimental Laboratory; Senior Teacher, Semipalatinsk Medical Institute; Professor, Head of Normal Physiology & Microbiology Department. Publications incl: Dinamika nekotorykh fermentov v processe Khronizatsil gepatita, 1977; Fiziologia vydelenia, 1993; Napravlennyi transport somatotropnogo gormona s ispolzovaniem yeritrotsitarnykh nositelei, 1994; Yeritrotsitarnye nositeli v napravlennom transporte gormonov, 1994. Honours: Soros Grant, 1993; Grant, Ulyanovsk Branch Moscow State University, 1994. Memberships: Russian Physiological Society. Hobbies: Gardening. Address: Gargarin Str 9/10-24, Ulyanobsk 431002, Russia.

GENTRY John T, b. 31 Dec 1921, St Louis, MO, USA. Physician. Education: MD; MPH. Appointments incl: Adjunct Professor of Hospital Administration, 1970-75, Adjunct Professor of Physicial Therapy, 1972-75, Duke University, North Carolina; Commissioner of Health, Erie County Department of Health, Buffalo, 1976-81; Consultant, Health Data Institute, Lexington, 1985. Publications incl: Studies on the Epidemiology of Sarcoidosis in the United States: The Relationship to Soil Areas and to Urban-Rural Residence; An Epidemiological Study of Congenital Malformations in New York State; Low Level Radiation Effects; The Study of Innovation and Diffusion in Health Care Organizations: A Summary and Evaluation of Research; Attitudes and Perceptions of Health Service Providers; Evaluation and Measurement of the Quality of Health Care; Health Service Indicators as Components of a Health Status Index. Memberships: American Public Health Association; American Association for the Advancement of Science. Hobbies: One Design Sailing Competitions. Address: 258 Atlantic Road, Gloucester, MA 01930-4256, USA.

GEORGE Mary, b. 12 Dec 1953, India. Gynaecologist. m. R Jacob George, 28 Feb 1982, 1 son. Education: BSc; MBBS; MRCOG. Appointments: House Officer, 1979; Resident Medical Officer, 1982; Residency in Obstetrics & Gynaecology, 1986; Consultant in Obstetrics & Gynaecology, Liberia, 1986; Sho/Acting Registrar in Obstetrics & Gynaecology, 1988; Registrar in Obstetrics & Gynaecology, 1989-91; Supernumerary Registrar in Urogynaecology, 1991-92; Registrar in Gyn Oncology, 1992. Honours: BSc, 1st rank. Memberships: MRCOG. Hobbies: Cooking; Needlework; Sports; Reading. Address: 40 Jubilee Road, Gosforth, Newcastle-upon-Tyne, NE3 3UR, England.

GERRARD John Watson, b. 14 Apr 1916, N Rhodesia, Zambia. Medicine. m. Lilian Elisabeth Whitehead, 28 Aug 1941, 3 s. Education: BA; BM; BCh; DM, Oxon; FRCP, Canada and UK. Appointments: First Assistant, Faculty of Medicine, University of Birmingham, UK; Professor of Pediatrics, Faculty of Medicine, University of Saskatchewan; Professor Emeritus, Canadian Pediatric Society; Currently, semi-retired. Publications: Numerous publications; 2 Books. Honours: John Scott Award, 1962; Ross Award, Canadian Pediatric Society, 1985. Memberships: Royal College of Physicians, London, UK; Royal College of Physicians and Surgeons, Canada. Hobby: Ornithology. Address: 809 Colony Street, Saskatoon, Sask, Canada, S7N 0S2.

GERSH Richard, b. 26 Nov 1957, MA, USA. Physician. m. Jane Russin, 9 Mar 1991, 2 sons. Education: AB, Harvard, 1979; MD, NY Medical College, 1983. Appointments: Unit Chief, Department of Psychiatry, St Vincent's Hospital, NY; Currently, Chief, Ambulatory Care Service, Department of Psychiatry, St Vincent's Hospital. Publication: Suicide in Children and Adolescents, chapter in, Forensic Psychiatry: A

Comprehensive Textbook, 1993. Memberships: American Psychiatric Association; American Society for Adolescent Psychiatry; American Association for Geriatric Psychiatry. Hobbies: Art; Theatre; Music. Address: 203 West 12th Street, New York, NY 10011, USA.

GERSHENGORN Marvin Carl, b. 26 May 1946, NY, USA. Physician. m. Janet Smolofsky, 21 Jun 1969, 1 d. Education: MD. Appointment: Professor of Medicine, Director of Division of Molecular Medicine, Cornell University Medical College, NY. Address: Cornell University Medical College, 1300 York Avenue, New York, NY 10021, USA.

GERSIE Alida, b. 10 Mar 1947, Heusden, The Netherlands. Dramatherapist. Education: MO, Cultural Pedagogy, Rjksuniversiteit Amsterdam; Pg Dip Arts Administration, ACDS. Appointments: Social Worker, Family Welfare Association, 1979-82; Director, Community Centre, London Borough of Islington, England, 1976-79; Director of Srtudies, Postgraduate Arts Therapies Programme. Publications: Storymaking in Education and Therapy, Co-author, 1990; Storymaking in Bereavement, 1991; Earthtales, Storytelling in Times of Change, 1992. Memberships: BADth; NADth; International Society for Traumatic Stress Studies. Hobbies: Weaving; Mountain walking. Address: 31 Gordon Road, Enfield, Middlesex EN2 0PU, England.

GERSON Lowell Walter, b. 26 Sep 1942, NY, USA. Epidemiologist. m. Francine Goldstein, 16 Aug 1964, 1 s, 1 d. Education: AB, Western Reserve University, 1964; MA, Western Reserve University, 1966; PhD, Case Western Reserve University, 1970. Appointments: Assistant Professor, John Carroll University, 1968-70; Assistant and Associate Professor, Medical Sociology, Memorial University of Newfoundland, 1970-75; Associate Professor, Epidemiology, McMaster University, 1975-78; Professor of Epidemiology, Associate Director, Division of Community Health Sciences, Northeastern OH Universities College of Medicine, 1978-. Publications: Several Books, Book Chapters and Monographs including: Alcohol and Other Drug Related Problems, 1977; Epidemiology, in Alcoholism: New Perspectives, 1984; Numerous Professional Articles, 1967-94. Honours: AKD, Sociology Honorary, 1965; PLDE Journalism Honorary, 1965. Memberships: American Association for Advancement of Science; American Public Health Association; Association for Medical Education and Research in Substance Abuse; Association of Teachers of Preventive Medicine; Gerontological Society of America; International Epidemiological Association; National Council on Alcoholism, OH; Governing Council, OH Public Health Association; Director, Northeast Branch, OH Public Health Association; Society for Epidemiologic Research; Society for Academic Emergency Medicine. Hobbies: Sailing; Bicycling; Reading. Address: PO Box 95, Rootstown, OH 44272, USA.

GERSTNER Natalie Kathryn, b. 20 Aug 1963, Winnipeg, Canada. Paediatrician. m. Dr Thomas Victor Gerstner, 4 May 1991. Education: BSc, 1984; MD, 1989; FAAP, 1992; FRCPC, 1993. Career: Ukranian Dance Instructor; Ukranian School Teacher; PALS Instructor; House Officer, NICU; Currently, Paediatrician; Associate Professor, Child Health, Health Science Centre and St Boniface Hospital. Memberships: MMA; CMA; MPS; CPS; CMPA; MOCOMP; AAP. Hobbies: Swimming; Skiing; Piano and Flute Music; Reading; Camping. Address: Winnipeg Clinic, 425 St Mary Avenue, Winnipeg, MB, Canada, R3C 0N2.

GERVACIO Abner, b. 13 Apr 1967, Manila, Philippines. Medical Doctor. Education: BS, Medical Technology; Registered Medical Technologist; MD, 1995. Appointments: Part-time Staff Medical Technologist, Perpetual Help Medical Center. Memberships: American Medical Technologists; Philippine Association of Medical Technologists. Hobbies: Cycling; Swimming; Golf. Address: 66 Aniban, Bacoor, Cavite, Philippines 4102, USA.

GEVA Pinhas, b. 22 Jul 1949, Ramat, Gan, Israel. Pediatrician. m. Dalia Geva, 18 Jan 1977, 1 s, 2 d. Education: MD, Sackler School of Medicine, Tel-Aviv, Israel; Board Certified in Pediatrics and Pediatric Nephrology. Appointments: Fellow, Division of Pediatric Nephrology, UCLA, 1985-87; Fellow, Albert Einstein College of Medicine, 1987-88; Currently, Attending Physician in Pediatric Nephrology. Memberships: International Pediatric Nephrology Association; ASAIO; ISAIO; International Society for Peritoneal Dialysis. Hobbies: Sport; Reading. Address: 324 3rd Avenue, Pelham, NY 10803, USA.

GHOSH Asish, b. 15 Feb 1938, Rourkella, India. Scientist. Education: BSc, Honours; MSc; PhD. Career: Lecturer in Zoology, Ripen College, University of Calcutta; Research Associate, Department of Entomology, University of WI, Madison, USA; Chief Research Officer, Department of Zoology, University of Calcutta; Deputy Director; Joint Director, ZSI; Currently, Director, Zoological Survey of India, Ministry of Environment, Government of India. Publications: 220 publications in 15 countries including 6 volumes on Fauna of India, Insecta, Homoptera, Aphidoidea, 1980-93. Honours: Fellow, Entomology Society of India; Fellow, Zoological Society; Fellow, School of Fundamental Research, Calcutta; Rockefeller Foundation; Fulbright Scholar; Field Travel Grantee. Memberships: Bombay National History Society; Zoological Society; Entomological Society of India; Aphidological Society; Institute of Landscape Ecology. Hobbies: Music; Reading. Address: 329 Jodhpur Park, Calcutta 700068, India.

GIANNIKOPOULOS Ioannis, b. 1 Nov 1943, Olympia, Greece. Medical Doctor. m. Hope Gotsis, 16 June 1974, 2 sons, 1 daughter. Education: MD, National and Kapodistriakon University of Athens, 1967; Residency, 1976-79; G I Fellowship, 1979-92, Certification in Internal Medicine, American Board of Internal Medicine, 1984; Board Certification in Gastroenterology, 1985; Research, 1988; Fellow, American College of Gastroenterology, 1993. Appointments: Fellow, 1979-82; Assistant Medical Director, 1983; Research Associate, Clinical Investigator, 1984; Assistant Professor of Medicine, 1984, Acting Chairman of Gastroenterology, 1990, currently Chairman of Gastroenterology, King/Drew Medical Center, Los Angeles, California. Publications: Ranitidine in Duodenal Ulcer, 1983; Co-author: Prostaglandins and chemotherapy induced ulcers in dogs, 1985; Prostaglandins in Duodenal Ulcer, 1986. Honours: Rotary Club of Athens, 1967; Honorary discharge, Greek Army, 1968; 3rd Fellow Essay Award, 1982; King/Drew Medical Center, 1992. Memberships: American Medical Association; American Gastroenterology Association; ASGE; Endoscopy, APA; American College of Gastroenterology. Hobbies: Reading; History; Outdoors. Address: 12021 South wilmington Ave, MP 11, AHB 2199, Los Angeles, CA 90059, USA.

GIBBS Frederic Andrews, b. 28 Mar 1941, Boston, MA, USA. Radiation Oncology. m. Priscilla Fabing, 3 Jul, 1 s, 1 d. Education: BS, CA Institute of Technology, 1963; MD, 1969 and Residency, Stanford University. Appointment: Professor, Radiation Oncology, University of Utah Medical Center. Honour: Fellow, American College of Radiology, 1993. Memberships: American College of Radiology; American Society of Therapeutic Radiology and Oncology; Radiation Research Society; North American Hyperthermia Society. Address: Radiation Oncology, University Hospital, Salt Lake City, UT 84132, USA.

GIBERT Barton, b. 28 Oct 1908, London, England. Retired Obstetric & Gynaecological Surgeon. m. Rosamund, 3 June 1940, Twin Sons. Education: BSc; MD, London; FRCS, England; FRCOG; MSc. Appointments: Residences; House Surgeon; Casualty Officer; Res Anaesthetist, St Thomas Hospital, London, 1932-33; Clinical Assistant, Children's & X-Ray Departments; General Practice; Junior and Senior R.M.O, Chelsea Hospital for Women. Publications: Study of Ac Mastitis of Pueperium, 1935; Origin of Cysts of Broad Ligament, 1948; Numerous other professional publications. Memberships: Fellow, Royal Society of Medicine. Hobbies: Numisatics; Heraldry; Fishing, Gardening. Address: Tower 1, 24055 Paseo Del Lago West, Laguna Hills, CA 92653, USA.

GILBERT Gregory Eastham, b. 30 Mar 1965, Boston, MA, USA. Biostatistician. m. Sharon Lynn McFadden, 3 Jun 1989. Education: BA, Psychology; MSPH, Biostatistics and Epidemiology. Career: Biostatistician: SC Department of Health and Environmental Control, 1991, Medical University of SC, Charleston, 1991-93, SC Department of Natural Resources, Charleston, 1993-95, NCGS and Associates Inc, 1995-; Adjunct Faculty, University of Charleston, SC, 1992-94. Publications: Comparison of Intraocular Lens Fixation Techniques Performed During Penetrating Keratoplasty, in American Journal of Ophthalmology, 1991; Electrocardiographic Abnormalities and 30 Year Mortality Among White and Black Men of the Charleston Heart Study, in Circulation, 1993. Memberships: American Public Health Association; Biometrics Society; Society of Epidemiological Research; American Association for Advancement of Science. Hobbies: Skeet Shooting; Fishing; Backpacking; Cooking; Reading. Address: 2344 South England Street, Charleston, SC 29414-5522, USA.

GILBERT Harriet S, b. 22 Jun 1930, Philadelphia, PA, USA. Physician. m. 3 Jan 1957, 2 s, 1 d. Education: AB, Bryn Mawr College, 1951; MD, Columbia University College of Physicians and Surgeons, 1955. Career includes: Associate Program Director, Clinical Research Center, MSMC, 1979-86; Professor of Medicine, 1981-86, Associate

Dean for Research, 1981-86, Currently Lecturer, MSSM; Attending Physician for Hematology, MSH, 1981-; Albert Einstein College of Medicine, Montefiore Medical Center and Bronx Municipal Hospital Center, 1986-; Founding President and Director, Myeloproliferative Disease Research Center Inc, 1989-; Clinical Professor of Medicine, Albert Einstein College of Medicine, Yeshiva University, 1991-. Publication: Diagnosis and Treatment of Polycythaemia Vera, Agnogenic Myeloid Metaplasia, and Essential Thrombocythemia, in Neoplastic Diseases of the Blood, 2nd edition, 1991. Honours include: Diplomate, Internal Medicine, 1965, Hematology, 1972; Fellow, American College of Physicians, 1966; Grantee, National Cancer Institute, NIH, 1982-86. Memberships include: Biomedical Advisory Committee, 1977-82, Chair, 1982-84, NY Academy of Sciences; American Society Hematology; American Institute of Nutrition; American Federation Clinical Research. Address: 950 Park Avenue, New York, NY 10028-0320, USA.

GILL Becky Lorette, b. 16 Mar 1947, Phoenix, AZ, USA. Addictionist. m. Jim S Gill, 5 Aug 1978. Education: BA, Biology, Stanford University, CA, 1968; Doctor of Medicine, University of AZ College of Medicine, 1973; Numerous Licensures and Board Certifications. Appointments include: Head, Alcohol Rehabilitation Service, Substance Abuse Department, Chief of Psychiatry, Naval Hospital, Millington, TN, 1985-88; Director, Medical Services, 1986-88, Director, Surgical Services, 1986; Head, Alcohol Rehabilitation Department, 1988-94, Naval Hospital, Long Beach, CA; Medical Director, 1992-94; Head, Navy Addictions Rehabilitation and Education Department, Camp Pendleton, CA, 1994-. Memberships include: American Society of Addiction Medicine, 1977-; Association of Military Surgeons of The US, 1977-; Various Offices, Addiction Professionals of NC, 1978-; National Association of Alcoholism and Drug Abuse Counselors, 1979-; Founding Member, American Academy of Psychiatrists in Alcoholism and Addictions, 1985-; CA Association of Alcohol and Drug Counselors, 1988-; Alcohol and Drug Council of NC, 1994-. Hobbies: Tennis; Jogging. Address: 32155 Corte Florecita, Temecula, CA 92592-6319, USA.

GILLENWATER Jay Young, b. 27 Jul 1933, Kingsport, TN, USA. Urologist. m. Shirley Brockman, 22 Jun 1955, 1 s, 2 d. Appointments: Chairman, Department of Urology, University of VA Medical School, 1967-; Editor, Journal of Urology. Publications: Editor of: Adult and Pediatric Urology, Journal of Urology, Urology Year Book. Honours: President, American Foundation Urological Disease; Past President, American Urological Association. Hobby: Gardening. Address: Department of Urology, University of Virginia Medical School, Box 422, Charlottesville, VA 22908, USA.

GILLESPIE Arnold, b. 29 Sep 1936, Sydney, Australia. Associate Professor. Education: MBBS; RSc; FRCOG; FRACOG. Appointments: Lecturer, University of London, Queen Charlotee's and Chelsea Hospital for Women; Associate Professor, Department Obstetrics and Gynaecology, Adelaide University. Hobbies: Travel; Computing. Address: Women's Health Centre, Royal Adelaide Hospital, Adelaide, South Australia, Australia.

GILLHAM M Beth, b. 29 Jul 1940, Clarendon, TX, USA. Education: Dietetics. Education: BS, Nutrition and Home Economics Education, TX Technological College, 1962; PhD, Nutrition, IA State University, Ames, 1975. Career: Dietician, St Luke's Hospital, Denver, CO; Teacher, Jefferson County Public Schools, Golden, CO; Assistant Professor, IA State University, Ames, IA; Associate Professor, Director of Coordinated Program in Dietetics, Department of Human Ecology, University of TX, Austin, 1981-. Publications include: Co-author, Nutritional Treatment for The Alcoholic Patient, in Critical Care Quarterly, 1986; Sources of nutrition information for rural and urban elderly adults, in Journal of American Dietetic Association, 1990; Peer involvement in the nutrition education of college students, in Journal of American Dietetic Association, 1992. Honours: Many grants, 1979-92; Distinguished Dietician, TX Dietetic Association, 1989; Medallion Award, American Dietetic Association, 1991. Memberships: American Institute of Nutrition; American Dietetic Association; American Society for Parenteral and Enteral Nutrition; Society for Nutrition Education. Hobbies: Travel; Music. Address: Department of Human Ecology, University of Texas, Austin, TX 78757, USA.

GILLMER Michael David George, b. 17 Jan 1945, Pretoria, South Africa. Obstetrician and Gynaecologist. m. Janet Yvonne Davis, 17 Aug 1968, 1 son, 1 daughter. Education: MB, BS, London; LRCP, MRCS, 1968; MRCOG, 1972; MA, Oxford, 1979; MD, London, 1979; FRCOG,

1984. Appointments: Lecturer in Obstetrics and Gynaecology: University of Natal, 1975-76; St Mary's Hospital, University of London, England, 1976-79; Clinical Reader in Obstetrics and Gynaecology, University of Oxford, 1979-84; Currently Consultant, Women's Centre, John Radcliffe Hospital, Oxford; Honorary Lecturer, University of Oxford. Publications: 100 Cases for Students of Medicine, 1979; 100 Case Histories in Obstetrics and Gynaecology, 1991; Articles on diabetes in pregnancy, contraception, abortion and hysteroscopic surgery. Honours: Gold Medal, MRCOG, 1972. Memberships: Gynaecological Visiting Society of Great Britain and Ireland; Blair Bell Society; London Obstetric and Gynaecological Society; Spencer Wells Society. Address: Felstead House, 23 Banbury Road, Oxford OX2 6NX, England.

GILLOCK Margaret Ring, b. 19 Apr 1957, Bethesda, Maryland, USA. Science Writer; Editor. m. Oliver P Gillock, 10 Apr 1988. Education: Bachelors Degree, Biology & English, Northwestern University; Candidate for MS, Technical & Science Communications. Appointments: Marketing Editor, Journal of Analytical Toxicology, American Association for Medical Assistants, Director of Editorial Services, Editorial Manager, National Committee for Clinical Laboratory Standards, Science Writer. Memberships: American Medical Writers Association; American Society for Information Science. Address: 540 Conshocken State Road, Bala Cynwyd, PA 19004, USA.

GILMAN Sid, b. 19 Oct 1932, Los Angeles, CA, USA. Physician. m. Carol G Barbour, PhD, 1 s. Education: BA, University of CA, Los Angeles, 1954; MD, University of CA, Los Angeles, 1957. Appointments: Instructor to Associate in Neurology, Harvard Medical School, 1965-68; Assistant Professor to Professor, Neurology, Columbia University, 1968-76; H Houston Merritt Professor of Neurology and Professor of Anatomy, Columbia University, 1976-77; Professor and Chair, Department of Neurology, University of MI, 1977-. Publications: Disorders of the Cerebellum, 1981; Manter and Gatz's Essentials of Clinical Neuroanatomy and Neurophysiology, 8th edition, 1992; Clinical Brain Imaging, 1992; Over 300 publications in scientific books and journals. Honours: Phi Beta Kappa, 1954; Alpha Omega Alpha, 1957; Research Career Development Award, National Institutes of Health, 1966-68; Lucy G Moses Prize, Columbia University, 1973; Weinstein-Goldenson Prize, United Cerebral Palsy, 1981. Memberships: Past President, MI Neurological Association; Past President, American Neurological Association; American Academy of Neurology; American Society for Clinical Investigation; American Physiological Society; American Association for Advancement of Science. Address: University of Michigan Medical Center, 1500 E Medical Center Drive, 1914 Taubman Center, Ann Arbor, MI 48109-0316, USA.

GILMAN Susan Chernow, b. 22 Dec 1948, New York, USA. Psychiatrist. m. Peter M Gilman, 3 Feb 1979, 3 sons. Education: BA, Psychology, Beloit College; MD, Albert Einstein College of Medicine. Appointments: Director, Senior Adult Services, Fairmount Institute; Director, Older Adult Partial Program, Belmont Comprehensive; Geriatric Clinical Board Certified, 1994. Memberships: American Psychiatric Association; American Geriatric Psychiatric Association. Hobbies: Reading; Tennis; Aerobics. Address: 27 Wiltshire Road, Wynnewood, PA 19096, USA.

GINEVAN Michael Edward, b. 22 Oct 1946, Amsterdam, New York. Biostatistician. m. Jean Anderson, 27 Dec 1970, 1 s. Education: BS, Biology, State University of NY, Albany, 1968; MS, Zoology, University of MA, Amherst, 1971; PhD, Mathematical Biology, University of KS, 1976; New England Epidemiology Institute, 1981. Appointments include: Biostatistician, United States Nuclear Regulatory Commission, 1982-86; Senior Science Advisor, Biostatistics, Environ Corporation, 1987-88; Senior Scientist, Biostatistics, Risk Focus Division, Versar Inc, 1988-90; Principal Scientist, Biostatistics, Risk Focus Division, Versar Inc, 1990-91; Deputy Director, US Department of Energy, 1991-93; Managing Principal, Step 5 Corporation, 1993-94; Principal, ME Ginevan and Associates, 1991-. Publications include: 51 Professional publications, 1976-93, including: Co-author, Human exposure assessment 1: Understanding the uncertainties, Toxicology and Industrial Health, 1992; Assessment of the Possible Health Effects of Ground Wave Emergency Network, 1993; Author, Bounding the mean concentration for environmental contaminants when all observations are below the limit of detection, 1993. Honours: NY State Regents Scholar, 1964-68; Tri Beta, 1967; Hungerford Memorial Fellowship, 1973-74; University of KS Dissertation Fellowship, 1975-76; Sigma Xi, 1978; Distinguished Achievement Medal, American Statistical Association, 1993. Memberships: AAAS; American Statistical Association;

International Environmetrics Society; Sigma Xi; Society for Epidemiologic Research; Charter Member, Society for Risk Analysis. Hobbies: Golf; Hiking; Computer Science; Oenology; Cooking. Address: 307 Hamilton Ave, Silver Spring, MD 20901, USA.

GIRARD Janice Hagen, b. 5 Jan 1966, Missoula, Montana, USA. Ophthalmic Technician. m. Timothy S D Girard, 16 June 1984, 1 daughter. Education: Certified Ophthalmic Medical Technician. Appointments: Optician; Refractive Surgery Co-ordinator; Ophthalmic Medical Assistant; Director, Ophthalmic Technical Review. Memberships: Joint Commission Allied Health Personnel Ophthalmology; Montana Association Ophthalmic Personnel, Co-Founder. Hobbies: Crosscountry Skiing; Watersports; Hiking. Address: 2140 Oriole, Missoula, MT 59802, USA.

GIRVIN John Patterson, b. 5 Feb 1934, Detroit, MI, USA. Neurosurgery. m. Bettye Ruth Parker, 13 Sep 1959, 2 s, 1 d. Education: MD, University of Western Ontario, 1958; PhD, McGill University, 1965; FRCS(C), 1968. Career: Lecturer, Department of Physiology, McGill University, 1962-63; Assistant Professor, Associate Professor, Professor, Departments of Physiology and Clinical Neurological Sciences, 1968-, Currently, Professor and Chairman, Division of Neurosurgery, Department of Neurological Science, University of Western Ontario. Memberships: Congress Neurological Surgeons; Canadian Neurological Society; American Association of Neurological Surgeons; American Epilepsy Association. Hobbies: Woodworking; Canoeing. Address: University Hospital, 339 Windermere Road, London, Ontario, N6A 5A5, Canada.

GISE Leslie Hartley, b. 13 Jul 1942, Ayer, MA, USA. Physician. m. Thomas Worthington, 24 Jun 1981, 1 d. Education: AB, cum laude, Psychology, Bryn Mawr College, PA, 1963; MD, Columbia University, College of Physicians and Surgeons, NY, 1967. Career includes: Private Practice, NY, 1973-95; Associate Director, Behavioural Medicine and Consultation Psychiatry Division, 1979-90; Associate Attending, Department of Psychiatry, Department of Obstetrics, Gynaecology and Reproductive Science, Mount Sinai Hospital, Associate Clinical Professor, Department of Psychiatry, Department of Obstetrics, Gynaecology and Reproductive Science, Mount Sinai School of Medicine, 1979-95; Psychiatrist, Department of Obstetrics, Gynaecology and Reproductive Science, 1984-95; Director, Premenstrual Syndromes Program, 1985-95; Medical Staff, Gracie Square Hospital, 1987-95. Publications: Reviewer for several professional journals; Editorial Board, Health Care for Women International, 1984-; Editor, Premenstrual Syndromes: New Findings and Controversies, 1988; Many refereed publications, abstracts, chapters, reviews and numerous presentations. Honours: Fellow, American Psychiatric Association, 1986; Fellow, Academy of Psychosomatic Medicine, 1991; 25 Year Service Award, Associated Alumni of Mount Sinai Medical Center, 1992; Physicians Recognition Award, AMA. Memberships include: American College of Psychiatrists; Various offices, American Society of Psychosomatic Obstetrics and Gynaecology; Program Committee, 1983-84, American Psychosomatic Society; Founding Member, 1989-, North American Menopause Society. Address: 233 Naalae Road, Kula, Maul, HI 96790, USA.

GISOLF Aart Cornelis, b. 10 Sep 1937, Haarlem, Netherlands. Medical Journalist. 1 d. Education: MD, University of Amsterdam, 1965. Appointments: General Practitioner, Amsterdam, 1965-69; Director, Audiovisual Centre, Erasmus University, Rotterdam, 1969-82; Broadcaster, NOS-TV, Hilversum, 1972-86; Technical Correspondent, Algemeen Dagblad, Rotterdam, 1975-; Producer of Medical Program, SDR-TV, Stuttgart, 1986-. Memberships: Dutch Medical Association; Dutch Association Cinematographers; Past President, International Science Film Association. Hobby: Musician. Address: Werder Str 17, D-68165, Mannheim, Germany.

GISSURARSON Loftur Reimar, b. 11 July 1961, Reykjavik, Iceland. Psychologist. m. Johanna M Thorlacius, 21 June 1983, 2 sons. Education: BA, University of Iceland, 1984, Teacher Credentials, 1986, University of Iceland; PhD, University of Edinburgh, Scotland, 1989; Chartered Psychologist, Iceland and UK. Appointments: Research Fellow, University of Edinburgh; General Psychologist, currently Chief Psychologist, Reykjavik's Regional Office for the Affairs of the Disabled, Iceland. Publications: Some PK Attitudes as Determinants of PK Performance, 1990-91; The Psychokinesis Effect: Geomagnetic Influence, Age and Sex Differences, 1992; Studies into Methods of Enhancing and Potentially Training Psychokinesis: A Review, 1992;

Reported Auditory Imagery and Its Relationship with Visual Imagery, 1992; Co-author: Does Geomagnetic Activity Affect Extrasensory Perception?, 1987; Volition and Psychokinesis: Attempts to Enhance PK Performance through the Practice of Imagery Strategies, 1990; A Proposed Research Paradigm for the Study of Volitional Mentation, 1994. Honours: Completed BA degree with highest marks to be given in Psychology, University of Iceland, 1984. Memberships: British Psychological Society; Icelandic Psychological Society; Parapsychological Association. Hobbies: Swimming; Reading; Writing. Address: SKAL, Krokabyggd 1A, 270 Mosfellsbaer, Iceland.

GITTELMAN Martin, b. 24 Sept 1930, New York, USA. Professor of Clinical Psychiatry. m. Lourdes, 1987, 2 daughters. Education: MS, CUNY, 1960; PhD, Columbia University, 1966. Appointments: Assistant Professor, Einstein Medical College, 1961-66; Associate Professor, New York School of Psychiatry, 1970-74; Associate Professor, New Jersey Medical School, 1974-84; Professor of Clinical Psychiatry, New York Medical College; Editor in Chief, International Journal of Mental Health; Foreign Editor, Hospital & Community Psychiatry. Publications: Strategic Intervent for Hyperactive Children, 1980; Lo Stato Dell'Arte Della Riabilitazione, 1992. Honours: President, Psy Sans Frontieres, 1991-; President, World Association for Psychiatric Social Rehabilitation, 1991-93; Reconnaisance Meritee, Rep Mali. Memberships: World Psychiatric Association; American Public Health Association; Fellow, Academia, Medicinae & Psychiatriae. Hobbies: Reading; Hiking; Skiing. Department of Psychiatry, Rm 932, New York Medical College, 234 East 149th Street, Bronx, NY 10451, USA. 6.

GLANTZ Kalman, b. 13 Oct 1937. Psychotherapist. m. Lorraine Fine, 15 Apr 1986, 1 son. Education includes: BA, Hebrew University, Jerusalem, 1958; PhD, Clinical Psychology, Union Graduate School, USA, 1987. Appointments include: Lecturer, Instructor, Assistant Professor, Lesley College, Cambridge, Massachusetts, 1977-85; Psychotherapist, private practice, 1977-; Psychotherapist, Tri-City Mental Health Center, Everett, Massachusetts, 1987-91; Psychotherapist, Himber Practice, Concord, Massachusetts, 1991-. Publications: Exiles From Eden: Psychotherapy from an Evolutionary Perspective (with John K Pearce), 1989; Staying Human In The Organization (with Gary Bernhard), 1991; Articles and contributions to books. Memberships: Human Behavior and Evolution Society; Massachusetts Mental Health Counselors Association; Society for the Exploration of Psychotherapy Integration; New England Society for the Study of Multiple Personality and Dissociation. Hobbies: Tennis; Running. Address: 12 Kinnaird St, Cambridge, MA 02139, USA.

GLASER Anthony Nicholas, b. 29 Aug 1954, London, England. Psychologist. m. Marlene Wellington, 9 Aug 1986. Education: BA, 1976, PhD, 1980, Sussex University; MS, 1993, MD, 1995, American University of the Caribbean. Career: Social Therapist, Henderson Hospital, 1979; Lecturer in Social Psychology, University of Sussex, 1980; Assistant Professor, 1981-83, Associate Professor, 1983-87, Currently, Professor of Medical Psychology, American University of the Caribbean. Publications: Therapeutic Communities and Therapeutic Communities, in International Journal Therapeutic Communities, 1982; Drive Theory of Social Facilitation, in British Journal of Society of Psychology, 1982; Biostatistics for the Medical Boards, 1994. Honours: University of Sussex Adam Weiler Prize, 1976; President of Faculty, American University of The Caribbean, 1987, 1988, 1989. Memberships: British Psychological Association; Association of Therapeutic Communities. Hobbies: Amateur Radio; Windsurfing. Address: Providence Estate House, St Peter's Village, Montserrat, West Indies.

GLENN James Francis, b. 10 May 1928, Lexington, Kentucky, USA. Surgeon. m. Gale Morrison, 29 December 1948, 2 sons, 2 daughters. Education: BA, Rochester; MD, Duke; FACS; FRCS. Appointments: Chairman, Urology, Duke, 1963-80; Dean, Emory University School of Medicine, 1980-83; President, Sinal Medical Center, New York, 1983-87; Chief of Staff, Dean, Clinical Affairs, University of Kentucky Medical Center, 1987. Publications: Numerous professional articles. Honours: Honorary Fellow, Royal College of Surgeons, England, 1987. Memberships: Various associations and Societies. Hobbies: Tennis; Farming; Thoroughbred Racing. Address: 2600 Basin Springs Road, Winchester, KY 40391, USA.

GLENN Jules, b. 27 Oct 1921, Brooklyn, NY, USA. Physician. m. Sylvia Graver, 16 Jun 1943, 2 s, 2 d. Education: BA, Columbia College, 1942; MD, NY University School of Medicine, 1946; Graduate of NY Psychoanalytic Institute, 1957 and in Child Analysis, 1962. Career:

Rotating Intern, Jewish Hospital of Brooklyn; Intern, Neurology, Belleview Hospital, NYC; Resident, Psychiatry, US Public Health Service Hospital, Fort Worth, TX; Training and Supervising Analyst, Psychoanalytic Institute, NYU Medical Center; Associate Editor, Journal of American Psychoanalytic Association; Currently, Clinical Professor of Psychiatry, NY University Medical Center, Private Practice of Psychiatry and Psychoanalysis. Publications: Editor, Child Analysis and Therapy, 1978; Co-editor, Freud and His Self Analysis, 1979; Co-editor, Freud and His Cases, 1980; Assistant Editor, Psychoanalytic Case Studies. Honours: Diplomate, Psychiatry, National Board of Psychiatry and Neurology, 1957; Freud Lecturer, Psychoanalytic Association of NY, 1990; Marianne Eris Lecturer, Association for Child Psychoanalysis, 1991. Memberships: American Psychoanalytic Association; Fellow, American Psychiatric Society; Former President, Association for Child Psychoanalysis; American Academy of Child and Adolescent Psychiatry. Hobbies: Travel; Photography; Tennis. Address: 8 Preston Road, Great Neck, NY 11023, USA.

GLORIG Aram, b. 8 June 1906, Manchester, England. Otologist. div., 2 daughters. Education: BS, Atlantic Union College, South Lancaster, Massachusetts, USA, 1931; MD, Loma Linda University, Los Angeles, 1938; Intern, Lawrence Memorial Hospital, New London, Connecticut, 1939-40; Resident: Willard Parker Hospital, New York City, 1939-40, Henrietta Egleston Hospital, Atlanta, 1940-41; Preceptorships: Emory University School of Medicine, 1941-42, Cancer Memorial Hopsital, 1946, Los Angeles Foundation of Otology, 1948. Appointments include: Director, 1964-77, Director Emeritus, 1977-, Callier Center for Communication Disorders; Professor, Otolaryngology, University of Texas Southwestern Medical School, 1964-77; Professor, Department of Communication Disorders, 1973-77, Dean, School of Human Development, 1975-77, Dean Emeritus, 1977-, University of Texas, Dallas; Consultant, Industrial and Forensic Otology, House Ear Clinic and Senior Research Advisor, House Ear Institute, Los Angeles, California, 1977-; Continuing Education for Registered Nurses, California State Board of Registered Nursing, 1981-83. Honours: Carhart Memorial Award, 1979, Lifetime Achievement Award, 1992, American Auditory Society; Honorary Awards, House Ear Institute, 1985, 1991; Health Achievement in Occupational Medicine Award, American College of Occupational and Environmental Medicine, 1994; Many others. Memberships: Founder, American Auditory Society; American Medical Association; Founding Member, International Society of Audiology; Fellow: Acoustical Society of America; American Academy of Ophthalmology and Otolaryngology; American Otological Society; American Speech and Hearing Association; Many more. Address: House Ear Clinic Inc, 2100 West Third Street, Los Angeles, CA 90057, USA.

GLOVSKY M Michael, b. 15 Aug 1936, Boston, USA. Clinical Professor of Medicine; Physician. m. Carole I Parks, Oct 1988, 3 sons, 2 daughters. Education: MD, BS, magna cum laude, Tufts University & Tufts Medical School. Appointments: Chief, Allergy & Immunology, Kaiser Medical Group, Los Angeles, 1974-84; Professor of Medicine & Pathology, USC School of Medicine, 1984-89; Clinical Professor of Medicine, USC Medical School; Medical Director, Asthma & Allergy Center. Publications: Author, Co-author of 63 articles in Medical Journals; Topics: Complement in Disease; Complement Inhibitors; Anaphylotoxins; Asthma & Allergy Mechanisms. Memberships: American Academy of Allergy & Immunology; American Association of Immunology; American College of Allergy & Immunology; American Thoracic Society; American Association for the Advancement of Science. Hobbies: Photography; Travel; Reading. Address: Huntington Memorial Hospital, Asthma & Allergy Center, 39 Congress Street, Pasadena, CA 91105, USA.

GLUHOVSCHI Gheorghe, b. 2 July 1940, Andrieseni, Iasi, Rumania. Medical Doctor. m. Lucia Gluhovschi, 25 Aug 1965, 1 daughter. Education: MD, Faculty of General Medicine, University of Medicine; Specialist, Internal Medicine; Qualified as Professor. Appointments: General Practitioner, 1963-67; Assistant Professor, 1967-90; Associate Professor, 1990-93; Professor of Nephrology, 1993-. Publications: Co-author: Nefrologie Clinica, 1979; Imunopatologia bolilor renale, 1988; Nefrologie Vol I, 1992; Infectia tractului urinar în practica medicala, 1992; Ghid de ecografie abdominala, 1993; Ghid de nefrologie. Diagnostic si tratament, 1993; Actualitati în medicina interna, 1993; Nefropatia endemica balcanica (Endemic Balkanic nephropathy), in English and Rumanian, 1994; Actualitati în imunologia clinica, 1994. Honours: Gh Marinescu Prize for book Nefrologie Clinica, Academy of Rumania, 1979. Memberships: European Dialysis and Transplant Association;

Europeabn Renal Association. Hobbies: History; Geography; Football; Volleyball. Address: Calea Aradului No 8, Etaj I Ap 16, Timisoara, COD 1900, Rumania.

GODDARD Jerome, b. 12 Apr 1957, Booneville, MS, USA. Medical Entomologist. m. Rosella Blackman, 19 May 1979, 2 s. Education: BAE, 1979, MS, 1981, University of Mississippi; PhD, Medical Entomology, Mississippi State University, 1984. Career: Medical Entomologist, USAF, 1986-89; Clinical Assistant Professor of Preventive Medicine, University of Mississippi Medical School, 1991-; Currently, Medical Entomologist, Mississippi Department of Health. Publications: Ticks and Tickborne Diseases, book, 1988; Physicians' Guide to Arthropods of Medical Importance, book, 1993; Arthropods in Human Health - Series, in Laboratory Medicine. Honours: Company Grade Officer of Year, School of Aerospace Medicine, 1988; Best Academic Instructor, School of Aerospace Medicine, 1988. Memberships: American Society of Rickettsial Diseases; Sigma Xi; American Mosquito Control Association. Hobbies: Fishing; Camping. Address: Bureau of Environmental Health, Mississippi State Department of Health, PO Box 1700, Jackson, MS 39215, USA.

GODDARD Sally Anne Dalzel, b. 13 Apr 1957, Cheltenham, England. Developmentalist. m. (1) 4 Aug 1979, (2) Peter Blythe, 20 Oct 1994, 2 sons, 1 daughter. Education: Development Therapist Training, Institute for Neuro-Psychological Psychology, Chester, 1987. Appointments: development Therapist and Co-Director, International School for Research and Training in Developmental Delay. Publications: The Fear Paralysis Reflex and Its Interaction with The Primitive Reflexes, 1989; A Developmental Basis for Learning Difficulties and Language Disorders, 1990; Developmental Milestones: A Blueprint for Survival, 1990; Elective Mutism: The Unchosen Silence, 1991; The Foundations for Life and for Living, 1991; The Effect of Reflex Activity Upon Oculo-Motor and Visual-Perceptual Performance, 1992; Reflexes-The Basis of Education. Memberships: Associate, Institute for Neuro-Psychological Psychology, Chester. Hobbies: Music, Piano, Clarinet and Choral; Fine Arts; Walking. Address: 4 Stanley Place, Chester CH1 2LU, England.

GOERDT Ann Renee, b. 3 May 1943, Dubuque, IA, USA. Physical Therapist. Education: MA, Education and Anthropology, 1972, PhD, International Community Health Education, 1984, NY University; BS, Physical Therapy, St Louis University, 1986. Career: Physical Therapist, Rusk Institute, NY, 1966-69; Supervisor, Clinical Education, Goldwater Memorial Hospital, NY University Medical Center, 1969-72; Faculty, NY University Physical Therapy Department, 1973-80; Rehabilitation Consultant, International and American nongovernmental organizations for rehabilitation, 1981-85; Consultant, 1986-88, Scientist, 1988-, Rehabilitation Unit, World Health Organization. Publications include: Social Integration of the Physically Disabled in Barbados, in Social Science and Medicine, 1986; Co-author, Training in the Community for People with Disabilities, WHO, 1989; Other publications include articles in World Health Magazine and congress proceedings. Honours: Organization of American States Fellowship, 1980; Fulbright Grant for Graduate Study, 1980; National Research Award, NIMH, USA, 1981. Membership: American Physical Therapy Association. Hobbies: Dance; Golf; Travel. Address: Rehabilitation Unit, World Health Organization, CH-1211 Geneva 27, Switzerland.

GOETZ Karl Georg, b. 24 Dec 1930, Berlin, Germany. Physicist. m. Ulrike Goetz, 19 May 1962, 1 s, 3 d. Education: Diploma in Physics, University of Goettingen, 1961; PhD, Physico-Chemistry, University of Goettingen, 1961. Career: Research Associate, 1961-68, Currently, Director, Max-Planck Institute for Biological Cybernetics, Tuebingen, Germany. Honours: Honorary Professor, University of Tuebingen, 1974; Corresponding Member, Academie der Wissenschaften, Mainz, 1983-; Boris Rajewsky Award for Biophysics, 1989. Membership: European Molecular Biology Organization. Address: Max-Planck Institute for Biological Cybernetics, Spemann Str 38, D-72076 Tuebingen, Germany.

GOGGIN Michael James, b. 9 Apr 1934, Doncaster, England. Consultant Nephrologist. m. Cynthia Mary Ward, 8 Oct 1994, 2 sons, 1 daughter. Education: MB, BS; MRCS; LPCP; MRCP; FRCP. Appointments: Lecturer in Nephrology, Institute of Urology and Nephrology, London University, 1968-71; Currently Consultant Nephrologist. Publications: Isotopic and Radiological Investigation of Renal Function for Hypertension, 1970; A Cooperative Study on Clinical Value of Dynamic Renal Scanning with Deconvolution Analysis, 1982.

Hobbies: Travel; Music. Address: 32 Dover Street, Canterbury, Kent CT1 3HQ, England.

GÖKCE Özcan, b. 19 June 1956, Izmir, Turkey. General Surgeon. m. Cigdem Erdogmus, 8 July 1983, 1 son, 1 daughter. Education: MD, 1980, Specialist in General Surgery, 1985, Hacettepe University; Passed Professorship Examination, 1988. Appointments: Associate Professor in General Surgery, Department Head, Firat University, 1988-91; Senior Registrar in Transplantation Surgery, Addenbrooke's Hospital, Cambridge, England, 1992-93; Professor of General Surgery, Dokuz Eylul University, Izmir, Turkey, 1993-. Publications: Use of Random Urine Samples to Estimate Total Urinary Calcium and Phosphate Excretion (co-author), 1991; Comparison of the Noxious Effects of Various Scolocidal Agents on Liver Parenchyma, 1991; Povidone-Iodine in Experimental Peritoneal Hydatidosis, 1991; Preventive Effect of Nicardipine on Hyperplastic Changes in Venous Bypass Grafts, 1993. Honours: Awarded titles: Second Most Successful Medical Graduate of Hacettepe University, 1980; Best Medical Doctor in Temporary Military Service in 1985. Memberships: International Society of Surgery; Transplantation Society. Hobbies: Computer programming; Designing tools. Address: Dokuz Eylul University, Faculty of Medicine, Balcova, 35340 Izmir, Turkey.

GOLD Bernard L, b. 6 Jan 1950, Dallas, TX, USA. Allergist. 1 s, 1 d. Education: BA, Honours, University of Montana, 1973; MD, Baylor College of Medicine, Houston, 1977; Board Certified, Internal Medicine, 1981, Allergy and Immunology, 1985. Appointments include: Clinical Instructor, Internal Medicine, University of MI Medical School, 1986-93; Director, Allergy Clinic, University of MI Health Services, 1986-; Private Practice, Ypsilanti, MI, 1990-; Teaching Faculty, St Joseph Mercy Hospital, 1992-; Clinical Assistant Professor, Internal Medicine, University of MI, 1993-. Honour: Charles Waters Award for Distinction in Botany, University of Montana, 1973. Memberships: Fellow, American Academy of Allergy and Immunology; Fellow, American College of Allergists; American College of Physicians; MI State Medical Society; Washtenaw County Medical Society; John M Sheldon Society. Hobbies: Horses; Golf; Tennis; Skiing; Cooking; Wine; Photography; Art. Address: 4870 Clark Road, Ypsilanti, MI 48197, USA.

GOLDBERG Jane G, b. 31 May 1946, New Orleans, Louisiana, USA. Psychoanalyst. 1 daughter. Education includes: PhD. Appointments: Research Associate: New School for Social Research, New York City, 1971; City University of New York, 1972-76; Faculty: 5th Avenue Center, New York City, 1982-85; Center for Modern Psychoanalytic Studies, 1984-; Boston Center for Modern Psychoanalytic Studies, 1984-; Treatment and Referral Service, 1984-. Publications: Psychotherapeutic Treatment of Cancer Patients, 1981; Deceits of the Mind (and their effects on the body), 1991; The Dark Side of Love, 1993; The Contagion of Death; Building a Psychological Immune System. Memberships: Society of Modern Psychoanalysts; National Association for Accreditation of Psychoanalysts. Address: 222 Park Avenue S, 6D, New York, NY 10003, USA.

GOLDBERG Mark Steven, b. 4 Jan 1952. Epidemiologist. 1 son, 1 daughter. Education: BSc honours, Physics, MSc, Epidemiology, Biostatistics, PhD, Epidemiology, Biostatistics, McGill University. Appointments: Epidemiologist: Mt Sinai Hospital, Montreal, Canada; Hôpital du Sacré-Coeur, Montreal; Public Health Department, Maisonneuve-Rosemont Hospital, Montreal. Publications: Retrospective cohort study of a synthetic textiles plant in Quebec, 1994; The Ste-Justine adolescent idiopathic cohort study, 1994. Honours: Russel Hibbs Award, Clinical Category, Scoliosis Research Society, 1993. Memberships: Society for Epidemiologic Research; Biometric Society; International Epidemiological Association. Hobbies: Golf; Tennis; Children. Address: Public Health Department, Maisonneuve-Rosemont Hospital, 75 de Port-Royal E, Montreal, Quebec, Canada H3L 3T1.

GOLDBERG Richard J, b. 14 Mar 1949. Psychiatrist. m. Sandra K Livingston, 23 Jan 1971, 2 daughters. Education: AB, Cornell University; MD, University of New York. Appointments: Psychiatrist-in-Chief, Rhode Island Hospital & Women & Infants Hospital, Providence, Rhode Island. Publications: Books, The Psychosocial Dimensions of Cancer: A Practical Guide for Health-Care Providers, 1984; Psychiatric Aspects of Cancer, Volume in Advances in Psychosomatic Medicine Series, 1988; Practical Guide to the Care of the Psychiatric Patient; Papers: Managing Medicare Reimbursement on Medical-Psychiatry Units, 1991; The Psychosocial Review of Systems, 1992; Integrating the Mental Status Examination into the Medical Interview, 1992; Depression in Medical Patients, 1993; Major Depressive Disorder in Patients with the Implantable Cardioverter Defibrillator: A Report of Two Cases Treated with Electroconvulsive Therapy, 1993. Honours: Falk Fellowship, AAA, 1979. Memberships: APA. Hobbies: Piano. Address: Rhode Island Hospital, 593 Eddy Street, Providence, RI 02903, USA.

GOLDEN Barbara Elaine, b. 24 Apr 1945, Cookstown, Northern Ireland. Paediatrician. m. Michael H N Golden, 29 June 1968, 1 son, 1 daughter. Education: BSc, hons; MBBCh; BAO; MD; DCH Appointments: House Officer, Royal Victoria Hospital & Royal Belfast Hospital for Sick Children, 1969-72; Casualty Officer & Part-time GP, Belfast & London, 1972-74, Clinical Research Fellow and Lecturer, Jamaica, 1974-92; Clinical Lecturer, University of Aberdeen, 1992-93; Senior Lecturer, University of Aberdeen, 1993-99. Publications: Numerous professional publications. Honours: Queen's University of Belfast Foundation Scholarship, 1965; Ulster Hospital Gold Medal in Paediatrics, 1969; Victoria Colman Gold Medal in Psychiatry, 1969. Memberships: American Institution of Nutrition; American Society for Clinical Nutrition; The Nutrition Society; British Paediatric Assocaition; Scottish Paediatric Society. Hobbies: Bridge; Reading; Walking. Address: Department of Child Health, University of Aberdeen Medical School, Foresterhill, Aberdeen AB9 2ZD, Scotland.

GOLDENBERG Gerald Joseph, b. 27 Nov 1933, Brandon, Manitoba, Canada. Physician. m. Sheila Claire Melmed, 4 Jan 1959, 1 s, 3 d. Education: MD, University of Manitoba, 1957; PhD, University of MN, 1965; FRCP(C), 1973; FACP, 1985. Career includes: Lecturer, Department of Medicine, 1964-66, Assistant Professor, 1966-70, Associate Professor, 1970-75, Professor, 1975-90, University of Manitoba, Winnipeg; Professor, Departments of Medicine and Pharmacology, Director of Interdepartmental Division of Oncology, Assistant Dean, Oncology, University of Toronto, 1990-. Publications include: Co-author, Evidence for a mutant allele of the gene for DNA topoisomerase II in adriamycin-resistant P388 murine leukemia cells, in Cancer Research, 1989; Co-author, Increased expression of cytosolic glutathione S-transferases in drug-resistant L5178Y murine lymphoblasts: chemical selectivity and molecular mechanisms, in Cancer Research, 1993; Co-author, Characterization of a DNA topoisomerase IIa gene rearrangement in adriamycin-resistant P388 leukemia: expression of a fusion mRNA transcript encoding topoisomerase IIa and the retinoic acid receptor-a locus, in Cancer Research, 1993. Honour: Gold Medal, University of Manitoba, 1957. Memberships: Canadian Oncology Society; Canadian Society Clinical Investigation; Clinical Research Society of Toronto; American College of Physicians; American Society for Experimental Pathology; American Association for Cancer Research. Hobbies: Bridge; Golf; Tennis. Address: University of Toronto, 92 College Street, Toronto, Ontario, M5G 1L4, Canada.

GOLDMAN Armond Samuel, b. 26 May 1930, San Angelo, TX, USA. Physician. m. Barbara Goldman, 31 Jul 1950, 4 s, 1 d. Education: MD, University of TX School of Medicine, Galveston, 1953. Appointments: Instructor, Pediatrics, 1958-59; Assistant Professor, Department of Pediatrics, 1959-66; Director, Division of Immunology and Allergy, Department of Pediatrics, 1959-; Associate Professor, Department of Pediatrics, 1966-72; Professor, Department of Pediatrics, 1972-; Professor, Department of Human Biological Chemistry and Genetics, 1973-; Professor, Department of Pathology, 1980-; Professor, Department of Microbiology and Immunology, 1990-; University of TX Medical Branch, Galveston. Publications: Co-author: Human milk feeding enhances the urinary excretion of immunologic factors in low birth weight infants, in Pediatric Research, 1989; A novel X-linked combined immunodeficiency disease, in Journal of Clinical Investigation, 1990; Tumor necrosis factor-α in human milk, in Pediatric Research, 1992; Activated-memory T lymphocytes in human milk, in Cytometry, 1992; Interleukin-6 in human milk, in Journal Reproductive Immunology, 1993; The immune system of human milk: Antimicrobial, antiinflammatory and immunomodulating properties, in Pediatric Infectious Disease Journal, 1993. Memberships: President Elect, International Society for Research in Human Milk and Lactation; Society for Pediatric Research; American Association Immunology; American Pediatric Society. Hobbies: Bird Watching; Violin. Address: Pediatric Immunology and Allergy Division, Room 2,360 Childrens Hospital, University of TX Medical Branch, 301 University Blvd, Galveston, TX 77555-0369, USA.

GOLDMAN Craig, b. 2 Sep 1962, Binghamton, NY, USA. Physical Education Director. m. Andra Vlosky, 18 Jun 1989, 1 s. Education: BSE,

Physical Education; MS, Health Service Administration. Career: Physical Education and Health Director; Teen Services Director; Children's Director; Physical Education Director and Director of Summer Programming. Memberships: AAHPERD; AJCP. Hobbies: Running; Basketball. Address: 1478 West Terrace Circle, Apt 3, Teaneck, NJ 07666, USA.

GOLDSCHMIDT Ernst Walter Matthias, b. 24 Aug 1933, Frankfurt, Germany. Professor of Ophthalmology. Education: MD, University of Copenhagen, Denmark, 1958; Specialist in Ophthalmology, 1966. Appointments: Head, Department of Ophthalmology, Odense University Hospital, Denmark, 1971-83; Head, Department of Ophthalmology, Hilleroed, Denmark, 1983-92; Professor of Ophthalmology, Odense University, 1979-84; Currently, Professor of Ophthalmology, University of Hong Kong. Publications: Thesis, On The Etiology of Myopia, 1968; Myopia in Humans: Can progression be arrested?, Ciba Foundation Symposium, 1990. Memberships: Danish Ophthalmological Society; German Ophthalmological Society; Hong Kong Ophthalmological Society. Hobbies: Classical Music; Skiing. Address: Skovvej 9, DK-2950 Vedbaek, Denmark.

GOLDSMITH Gary N, b. 30 Oct 1948, Brooklyn, NY, USA. Psychoanalyst; Psychiatrist. Education: BA; MD. Appointments: Faculty, Psychoanalytic Institute of New England East; Clinical Instructor in Psychiatry, Harvard Medical School. Memberships: American Psychoanalytic Association; American Psychiatric Association. Address: 1419 Beacon Street, Brookline, MA 02146, USA.

GOLDSMITH John R, b. 5 Feb 1922, Portland, OR, USA. Epidemiologist. m. Dr Naomi Fried Goldsmith, 21 Dec 1947, 2 s, 2 d. Education: BA, Physics, Reed College, Portland, 1942; MD, 1945, MPH, 1957, Harvard University; Board Specialist in Internal Medicine, US, and Public Health, Israel. Appointments: Ward Physician, US Veterans Hospital; Medical Residency, Fellowship in Physiology, University of WA, Seattle; Head, Research on Air Pollution Health Effects, California Department of Public Health; Currently, Professor of Epidemiology, Faculty of Health Science, Ben Gurion Universzity of the Negev. Publications: Environmental Epidemiology, Community Studies of Environmental Health Problems; Editorial Boards: Public Health Reviews; Science of the Total Environment; Archives of Environmental Health. Honours: Fellowship in Preventive Medicine, Harvard Medical School. Honours: AOA; PBK; Clean Air Award, CA Lung Association; US Environmental Protection Agency, Distinguished Visiting Scientist Award. Memberships: International Society for Environmental Epidemiology; International Epidemiological Society; AMA; American Public Health Association. Hobby: Singing with Light Opera Group. Address: POB 473, Omer 84965, Israel.

GOLDWASER Alberto Mario, b. 23 Mar 1951, Buenos Aires, Argentina. Physician. m. Indig L Goldwaser, 17 Nov 1984, 3 s. Education: Psychiatry; Psychoanalysis; BS. Appointments: Faculty Department of Psychiatry, New York University Medical Center; Secretary, New Jersey Psychoanalytic Society. Memberships: American Psychiatric Association; American Psychoanalytic Association; International Psychoanalytic Association; American College of Physicians. Hobbies: Tennis; Soccer. Address: 60 West Ridgewood Avenue, Ridgewood, NJ 07450, USA.

GOLIGHER John Cedric, b. 13 Mar 1912, Londonderry, Northern Ireland. Surgeon. m. Gwendoline Nancy Williams, 17 Mar 1952, 1 son, 2 daughters. Education: ChM Edinburgh; FRCS Edinburgh and England. Appointments: Consultant Surgeon, St Mary's Hospital, and St Mark's Hospital, London, 1947-54; Professor of Surgery, University of Leeds, 1954-77; Retired; Emeritus Professor of Surgery, Leeds University; Consulting Surgeon, St Mark's Hospital, London. Publications: Surgery of Anus Rectum and Colon, 5th edition, 1983. Publications: Contributor of numerous professional articles in books and journals. Honours: Hon MD Göteborg, 1973; Hon DSc, Leeds, 1979; Hon MD, Belfast, 1980-; Hon MD, Uruguay, 1982; Lister Award, RSC England, 1981; Linton Award, RCS Edinburgh, 1979; Honorary Fellow, American College of Surgeons, Australian College of Surgeons, 1973. Memberships: Association of Surgeons of Great Britain and Ireland, Past President; British Society of Gastroenterology. Past President; Section of Coloproctology, Royal Society of Medicine, Past President. Hobbies: Music; Reading; Tennis; Travel; Gastronomogy and Oenology. Address: Ladywood, Orchard Drive, Lonton, Yorkshire LS22 4HP, England.

GOLTZMAN David, b. 22 Sept 1944, Montreal, Quebec, Canada. Physician; Medical Researcher; Educator. m. Naomi Lyon, 29 Dec 1968, 2 sons, 1 daughter. Education: BSc, McGill University, 1966; MD, McGill University, 1968; Fellow, Royal College of Physicians & Surgeons of Canada, 1974. Appointments: Instructor in Medicine, Harvard Medical School, 1974-75; Assistant Professor of Medicine, McGill University, 1975-78; Associate Professor of Medicine, McGill University, 1978-83; Professor of Medicine, McGill University, 1983-; Professor, Chairman, Department of Physiology, McGill University, 1988-93; Chairman, Department of Medicine, McGill University, 1994-. Publications: The Parathyroids: Basic and Clinical Concepts, 1994; Principles and Practice of Endocrinology and Metabolism, 1994; Author of numerous articles on clinical and basic endocrinology research. Honours: Holmes Gold Medal, McGill University, 1968; Scientist Award, Medical Research Council of Canada, 1983; Prix André Lichtwitz of Inserm, France, 1987; Fellowship, Royal Society of Canada, 1995. Memberships: American Society for Bone & Mineral Research; Endocrine Society; Canadian Society of Endocrine & Metab; American Association of Phys; Canadian Association of Academic Medicine. Hobbies: Classical Music; Gardening; Tennis. Address: Royal Victoria Hospital, Room A309, 687 Pine Avenue West, Montreal, Quebec H3A 1A1, Canada.

GOMBEROFF JODORKOVSKY Mario, b. 16 Dec 1936, Santiago, Chile. Physician. m. Liliana Pualuan H, 19 Oct 1972, 3 sons. Education: University of Chile Medical School; Chilean Psychoanalytic Institute. Appointments: Professor of Psychiatry, Psychology School, Catholic University; Director, Department of Psychiatry, Faculty of Medicine (Oriente), University of Chile; Currently: Psychiatrist in Chief, Clinical Division B, J Horwitz B Psychiatric Institute; Professor of Psychiatry, Head of Psychiatry Committee, Postgraduate School, Faculty of Medicine, University of Chile; Training and Supervising Psychoanalyst, Chilean Psychoanalytic Institute and Association; Member, Psychiatric Committee, National Corporation of Medical Specialists. Publications: Psychiatry (editor, co-author), 1982; Co-author: Affects in Clinical Practice, 1988; Correio da Fepal, 1988; Superior Education in Mental Health, 1993; Children and Adolescents in Latin-America, 1994; Many papers in national and international journals. Memberships: Neurologic, Psychiatric and Neurosurgical Society; Mental Health Society; Chilean Psychoanalytic Institute and Association; Latinoamerican Psychoanalytic Federation; International Psychoanalytic Association. Address: Ingeniero Pedro Blanquier 5572, Las Condes, Santiago, Chile.

GOMEZ-CABAL Fernando, b. 24 Jan 1951, Bogotá, Colombia. Doctor; Psychoanalyst. m. Maria Chiappe, 20 Nov 1991, 4 s. Education: Doctor en Medicina y Cirugia; Psychoanalyst. Career: Instructor, Fisiologia, Col My del Rosario; Faculty of Medicine, Instructor, National University of Colombia; Faculty of Medicine, Assistant Professor con funciones de Director, Department of Psiquiatria, Colegio Mayor de Nuestra Señora del Rosario; Currently, Full Time Psychoanalyst. Publications: El Mito de Yurupary y el tabu de la Virginidad; Encuadre y Proceso I; Las fobias en Freud hasta 1900; Comentarios a algunos consejos technicos de Freud en el caso Juanito, in Rev Soc Col Psicoan. Memberships: Titular Member, Sociedad Colombiana de Psicoanalisis; International Psychoanalytical Association. Hobbies: Tennis; Golf; Lectures; Classical and Operatic Music. Address: Av 13 No 86-86, Bogotá, Colombia, SA.

GONEYALI Serupepeli Daunikucu, b. 21 Dec 1939, Fiji. Anesthetist. m. Noame Cavuinaxesi, 4 Apr 1970, 3 sons, 1 daughter. Education: Diploma of Surgery & Medicine, Fiji School of Medicine; Diploma of Anaesthesia, University of Philippines; Diploma, Philippine Board of Anesthisiology; Diploma, Hospital Care & Health Management. Appointments: General Medical Officer, Natocosa Health Center, Buala District Hospital, Maliu District Hospital, 1963-69; Anaesthitic Registrar, Lautoka District Hospital, 1970-86; Consultant Anesthetist, 1987-94; Medical Superintendent, Lautoka Hospital, 1989-. Honours: Australian Society of Anaesthetist (Baxter) Travel Award, 1986. Memberships: Fiji Medical Association; Pacific Society of Anaesthetists. Hobbies: Reading; Music; Gardening. Address: Department of Anesthesia, Lautoka Hospital, Fiji.

GONG Bin, b. 8 Jan 1942, San Dong, China. Teacher; Medical Researcher. m. Qizhong Mo, 28 Dec 1967, 1 son, 1 daughter. Education: BS, Molecular Genetics, Beijing University, 1966; Advanced study: Immunological Institute, 1977-79, Endocrinological Institute, 1979-80, Shanghai Second Medical College. Appointments: Associate Professor, Molecular Pharmacology, Endocrine-Immunology, 1988; Professor, Molecular Pharmacology, Endocrine-Immunology, Shanghai

University of Traditional Chinese Medicine, 1993-. Publications: 86 papers in domestic and foreign journals, 1980-; Co-author: Effect of Heart and Kidney Benefiting Chinese Herbal Medicine in the Functions of Adrenergic Receptor in Brain Tissues of Analogous Dementia in Rats, 1992; Effect of Er-Xian Decoction and its Separation Prescription on Plasma and Nuclear Sex Hormone Receptor of Uterus and Prostate in Old Rats, 1992; Effect of 861 on Gonadal Hormone in Plasma and its Receptor of Uterus Muscle Tumor of Patients, 1993; Effect of Kidney-Benefiting Chinese Herbal Medicine on the Functions of Neurotransmitters Receptor in Brain and Immunization Organ after Immunizing Rats by SRBC, 1993; Effect of Kidney-Benefiting Chinese Herbal Medicine on Neurotransmitters in Brain Spleen after Immunizing Rats by SRBC, 1994; Effect of Needling Point Zusanli on Immunologic Function in Rats, 1994; Immunoassay - A Practical Guide (translator, editor), 1992; 2 books, 1990. Honours: 10 2nd and 3rd Science and Technology Progress Awards, Ministry of Public Health and Shanghai Science and Technology Commission, 1980-; Honour for Special Contribution in Biomedical Science, Chinese State Council, 1992. Memberships: Director, Chinese Senile Drugs Association; Chinese Immunological Association; Chinese Association of the Integration of Traditional and Western Medicine. Hobbies: Running; Swimming; Classical music. Address: Shanghai University of Traditional Chinese Medicine, 530 Ling-Ling Road, 200032 Shanghai, China.

GONG Chuan Bin, b. 13 May 1934, Jilin, China. Professor. m. Sun Jing, 3 August 1959, 1 son, 1 daughter. Education: Department of Medicine, Jilin Medical University, 1958-62. Appointments: Professor of Biochemistry, Jilin Medical University, 1962-87; Centre of Clinical Labs, Jilin, 1987-. Publications: Lab Technology of Clinical Biochemistry, 1984; Numerous professional articles. Honours: Scientific Research Prizes, China, 1978. Hobbies: Music. Address: No 33 Gongnong Street, Centre of Clinical Lab, Changchun, Jilin, China.

GONG Jin-han, b. 7 June 1927, Shanghai, China. Professor of Medicine. m. Gao Bin-chun, 12 July 1953, 2 sons. Education: MD, College of Medicine, Tong-Ji University, Shanghai, 1951. Appointments include: Director, Department of Underwater Medicine, 1964-82, Senior Research Professor, Department of Underwater Medicine, 1979-, Vice-Director, 1982-85, Naval Medical Research Institute, Shanghai; Visiting Professor, 2nd Military Medical University, 1991-; Editor-in-Chief, Chinese Journal of Nautical Medicine. Publications: Experimental Study on the 350 m Simulated Heliox Saturation-370 m Excursion Diving, 1992; Editor-in-chief, monographs: Diving Medicine, 1985; Nautical Medicine, 1994. Honours: Winner, Special Lifelong Government Subsidy for Men of Achievement, 1992; National Awards for Scientific Technology Progress, A Grade, 3 C Grades, and People Liberation Army's Awards for Scientific Technology Progress, 2 A Grades, 3 B Grades, 1985-93. Memberships: Executive Member, Chinese Nautical Medical Association; Trustee, Chinese Medical Association, Shanghai Branch; Vice-President, Chinese Ocean Engineering Society. Hobby: Classical music. Address: Naval Medical Research Institute, 880 Xiang Yin Road, Shanghai 200433, China.

GONG Qirong, b. 28 Oct 1938, Qidong, Jiangsu, China. Ophthalmologist. m. Shi Binglu, 29 Oct 1941, 2 sons. Education: BA, Medicine, Nanjing Medical College, 1964. Appointments: Resident, Assistant; Attending Doctor, Lecturer, Vice-Archiater; Currently Professor of Ophthalmology, Archiater, Vice-Superintendent, Nantong Affiliated Hospital of Medical College, Jiangsu. Publications: Books: Operative Surgery of the Retinal Detachment, 1986; Operative Surgery of the Cataract, 1990; Learned articles: Ophthalmic manifestation of histiocytomatosis, 1982; Treatment to secondary glaucoma of refractory traumatic hyphema, 1985; Surgical treatment of congenital nystagmus associated with abnormal head position, 1985; Prophylaxis and treatment for continuous hyperpressure after acute bout of angle-closure glaucoma, 1992; Invention of electric coagulation iris scissors, 1990, 1992. Memberships: Chinese Medical Association; Jiangsu Ophthalmologic Institute; Jiangsu Prevention of Blindness Organization; East China Infection Control Organization; Editorial Committees: Chinese Journal of Ocular Fundus Diseases; Journal of Clinical Ophthalmology; Acta Academiae Nantong. Hobby: Running. Address: Jiangsu Nantong Affiliated Hospital of Medical College, Jiangsu 226001, China.

GONG Wei-bing, b. 10 Mar 1949, Hunan Province, China. Associate Professor of Ultrasound. m. Wei-kang Li, 12 June 1976, 1 son, 1 daughter. Education: Medical Master, First Military Medical University, 1980. Appointments: Physician, Department of Cardiology, 1974,

Lecturer, Department of Ultrasound, 1987, Associate Professor, 1992-, Nanfang Hospital, First Military Medical University. Publications: Analysis of 98 Cases of Congenital Heart Diseases by Imaging Diagnosis, 1989; Patterns of Dilated Cardiomyopathy in Endocardiography, 1990; Renal Allograft Rejection Detected by Two-Dimensional, 1991, 1992, 1993; Groups of Color Doppler Flow Image in the Transplanted Kidney, 1994. Memberships: Medical Ultrasound Society of PLA; Permanent Member, Guang Dong Ultrasound Society of Chinese Medical Association; General Member, AIUM. Hobbies: Chinese Literature; Jogging. Address: Department of Ultrasound, Nanfang Hospital, Tonghe, Guangzhou 510515, China.

GOODHEART Barbara, b. 13 Jul 1934, Chicago, IL, USA. Author. m. Clyde Goodheart MD, 26 Dec 1953, 1 s, 2 d. Education: BA, Biology, Northwestern University. Career: Author. Publications: A Year on the Desert, 1969; Diabetes, 1990; Contributor to 6 books. Honours: GCAC Sound, Sight Award, American Medical Writers Association, 1986; Beth Fonda Award, Honourable Mention, 1991. Memberships: Chairperson, 1974-75, 1982-83, Co-President, 1994-95, Mid West, American Society of Journalists and Authors; Board, GCAC American Medical Writers Association, 1988-89; Board, Independent Writers of Chicago, 1991-93. Hobbies: Sailing; Travel. Address: 15 Sheffield Court, Lincolnshire, IL 60069, USA.

GOODILL Sharon Wood, b. 27 Mar 1956, Florida, USA. Dance/Movement Therapist and Educator. m. John J Goodill MD, 27 Dec 1981, 2 d. Education: BA, Psychological Services and Theatre Arts, Dance, Hollins College, VA, 1978; Master's Creative Arts in Therapy, Hahnemann Medical College, 1980. Appointments: Dance/Movement Therapist: JFK MH/MR Center, Philadelphia; Terry Children's Psychiatric Center, Delaware; New Bedford Area Center for Human Services; Meadowood Hospital, Delaware; Currently, Director, Dance/Movement Therapy Education, Hahnemann University. Publications: Co-author, Dance/Movement Therapy with Abused Children, in Journal of Arts in Psychotherapy, 1987; Co-author, The Role of Dance/Movement Therapy with Medical Involved Children, in International Fraternity of Arts Medicine, 1994. Honours: Phi Beta Kappa, 1978. Memberships: Academy of Dance Therapists; Chair, Committee on Approval of Graduate Programs, American Dance Therapy Association. Address: MS 905, Creative Arts in Therapy Program, 1427 Vine St, Hahnemann University, Philadelphia, PA 19102-1192, USA.

GOODMAN Warren Harvey, b. 10 Nov 1935, New York City, NY, USA. Physician; Psychiatrist. m. Dr Beverly Hullquist Goodman, 27 Nov, 3 d. Education: AB, Columbia College, Columbia University; MD, SUNY Downstate Medical Center; Certified in Psychoanalysis, SUNY Downstate Medical Center. Career: President, Nassau Psychiatric Society, 1983; Currently, Faculty, Departments of Psychiatry, Cornell University Medical College, NY University Medical College, Albert Einstein College of Medicine. Publications: Contributor, Psychoanalytic Terms and Concepts, 1990; Psychotherapy with Borderline Patients, chapter in Dynamic Psychotherapy: The Analytic Approach, 1992; Many book reviews in Psychoanalytic Quarterly, 1984, 1985, 1987, 1990, 1993. Honours: Fellowship, American Psychiatric Association, 1977; Fellowship, Nassau Academy of Medicine, 1984. Memberships: 3 Weigt Court, Great Neck, NY 11021, USA.

GOONEWARDENE Indra Malik Rodrigo, b. 20 Jun 1953, Colombo, Sri Lanka. Consultant Obstetrician and Gynaecologist. m. Anula Ratnayaka, 4 Jun 1982, 3 s. Education: MBBS, Honours, University of Ceylon, Colombo, 1976; MS, Obstetrics and Gynaecology, Postgraduate Institute of Medicine, University of Colombo; MRCOG, UK. Appointments: Internship, Teaching Hospital, Colombo; Senior Medical Officer, District Hospitals of Moratuwa and Panadura; Registrar, Lecturer, Senior Lecturer, Head of Obstetrics and Gynaecology, Teaching Hospital, Galle; Currently, Senior Lecturer, Consultant Obstetrician and Gynaecologist, University of Ruhuna, Galle. Publications: Gestational Trophoblastic Tumours, 1991; Severe Preeclampsia, 1993; Contraception, 1993; Publications in Ceylon Medical Journal: Haemoglobin levels and iron stores in pregnant women, 1994; Pure Choriocarcinoma of Ovary, 1994; Efficacy of routine antenatal care, submitted; Maternal and cord blood haemoglobin and ferritin levels, submitted; Eclampsia, in Sri Lanka Journal of Obstetrics, 1985. Honours: Commonwealth Medical Scholarship, 1985-86; World Health Organization Fellowship, 1988; Young Gynaecologists Educational Grant, FIGO Congress, 1991; Commonwealth Medical Fellowship, 1994-95. Memberships: Sri Lanka Medical Association; Sri

Lanka College of Obstetrics and Gynaecology; Royal College of Obstetrics and Gynaecology, UK. Hobbies: Swimming; Chess; Snooker; Billiards. Address: 26A Hotel Road, Mt Lavinia, Sri Lanka.

GORBUSHIN Nikolai Grigorievich, b. 21 May 1935, Cheliabinsk, Ural. Scientist. m. Svetlana Stepanov, 9 Dec 1961, 3 sons. Education: Candidate of Technical Science. Appointments: N V Timofeev-Resovskii, 1961-81; Leader, Information group, Medical Radiological research centre of RAMS. Publications: The Information and Communication Property of the International economic Data Base, 1994. Memberships: Association of Information Workers; Philosophical Society; Society of Medicine and Radiology. Hobby: Bicycling. Address: Sovhoznaia Str 23/9 Fl 33, 252142 Kiev-142, Ukraine.

GORDON Alan George, b. 26 Oct 1929, Belfast, Northern Ireland. Gynaecologist. m. Mary Lilian Naylor, 20 Aug 1963, 1 son, 2 daughters. Education: MB BCh, BAO, Queen's University, Belfast; FRCS(Ed); FRCOG. Appointments: Senior Tutor, Royal Maternity Hospital, Belfast, 1961-64; Lecturer, Queen's University, Belfast, 1964-65; Consultant Obstetrician and Gynawecologist, Princess Royal Hospital, Hull, England, 1965-92. Publications: Gynaecological Endoscopy, 1988, 2nd Edition, 1995; Tubal Infetility, 1989; Practical Laparoscopy, 1993; Practical Hysteroscopy, 1993; Endometrial Ablation, 1995. Memberships: British Society Gynaecological Endoscopy, President, 1990-92; European Society Gynaecological Endoscopy, President, 1992-94; International Society Gynaecological Endoscopy, President, 1993-95. Hobbies: Fell Walking; Association Croquet. Address: BUPA Hospital, Anlaby, Hull Hu10 7AZ, England.

GORDON George, b. 4 Sept 1936, Fife, Scotland. Consultant Obstetrician and Gynaecologist. m. Rosemary Hutchison, 11 June 1966, 1 son, 1 daughter. Education: MB, ChB; FRCS (Edinburgh); FRCOG; Fellow, British Medical Association. Appointments: Senior Registrar, Western General Hospital, Edinburgh; Currently Consultant Obstetrician and Gynaecology, Dumfries and Galloway. Honours: British Medical Association Fellowship, 1987; Chairman, Confidential Enquiry into Maternal Deaths, Scotland. Memberships: Gynaecological Travellers Club; British Fertility Society; British Endoscopy Society. Hobbies: Golf; Music; Gardening; Scots literature. Address: Netherwood Bank, Dumfries DG1 4TY, Scotland.

GORDON John Robert, b. 23 May 1952, New Brunswick, Canada. Research Immunologist. m. Audrey E Gordon, 7 May 1983, 1 son, 1 daughter. Education: BSc, University of Saskatchewan, 1977; PhD, University of Saskatchewan, 1984. Appointments: Staff Scientist, National Institute for Medical Research, Mill Hill, England, 1984-87; Instructor in Pathology, Harvard Medical School, Boston, USA, 1987-91; Associate Professor, Veterinary Microbiology, University of Saskatchewan, Canada. Publications: Mast cells as a source of both pre-formed and immunologically inducible tumor necrosis factor alpha, 1989; Mast cells as a source of multifunctional cytokines, 1990; Mast cell and eosinophil cytokines in allergy and inflammation, in press; Human eosinophils express transforming growth factor B, 1991; Human eosinophils can express the cytokines TNF and MIPI, 1993. Memberships: American Association of Immunologists; Canadian Society of Immunologists; American Academy of Allergy & Immunology. Hobbies: Cross Country & Telemark Sking; Hiking; Painting. Address: Department of Veterinary Microbiology, University of Saskatchewan, Saskatoon, Canada.

GORELICK David Alan, b. 30 May 1947, Brooklyn, New York, USA. Physician. m. Naomi Feldman, 7 Apr 1973, 5 s, 2 d. Education: BA, Cornell University, 1968; MD, Einstein College of Medicine, 1976; PhD, Pharmacology, Einstein College of Medicine, 1976. Appointments: Associate Clinical Professor of Psychiatry, University of California at Los Angeles, School of Medicine; Assistant Chief, Alcohol & Drug Treatment Program, West Los Angeles Veterans Affairs Medical Center; Chief, Treatment Branch, Intramural Research Program, National Institute on Drug Abuse; Adjunct Professor of Psychiatry, University of Maryland, School of Medicine. Publications: Overview of Pharmacological Treatment Approaches for Alcohol & Other Drug Addiction, 1993; Recent Developments in Pharmacological Treatment in Alcoholism, 1993. Honours: Research Career Development Award, 1980-83. Memberships: American Psychiatric Association; American Society of Addiction Medicine; Research Society on Alcoholism; Society for Neuroscience. Address: P O Box 5180, Baltimore, MD 21224, USA.

GOREVALOVA Larisa Vasil'evna, b. 9 Aug 1935, Goltsovo village, Ryazan region, Russia. Otolaryngologist. m. Nicolay N Gorevalov, 20 June 1960, 1 son. Education: Graduated, 2nd Moscow Medical Institute N I Pyrogov; Postgraduate intern courses in Children's Otolaryngology, Children's Filatov Hospital, Moscow; Advanced courses in Children's Otolaryngology, Moscow and Alma-Ata. Appointments: District Paediatrist; Operating Otolaryngologist; Currently working alternately at Children's Polyclinic and at Otolaryngologic Branch, Obninsk Town Hospital. Honours: Numerous letters of thanks; Veteran of Labour; Her professional activity mentioned in local newspapers. Memberships: Moscow Scientific Society of Otolaryngologists; Kaluga Scientific Society of Otolaryngologists. Hobbies: Reading belles-lettres; Scientific and philosophical literature; Theatre; Music; Poetry. Address: Lenin prospect 28-34, Obninsk 249020, Kaluga Region, Russia.

GORNEY Roderic, b. 13 Aug 1924, Grand Rapids, Michigan, USA. Professor of Psychiatry. m. Carol Ann Sobel, 13 Apr 1986. Education: BS, 1948, MD, 1949, Stanford University; PhD, Psychoanalysis, Southern California Psychoanalytic Institute, 1977; Diplomate, American Board Psychiatry and Neurology, 1955. Appointments: Assistant, Associate, Professor of Psychiatry, University of Calaifornia Los Angeles, 1962-80; Professor of Psychiatry, 1980-, Director, Psychosocial Adaptation and the Future Program, 1971-. Publications: The Human Agenda, 1972; Cultural Determinants of Achievement, Aggression, and Psychological Distress, 1980; Impact of Dramatized Television Entertainment on Adult Males, 1977. Honour: Essay Prize, American Psychiatric Association, 1971. Memberships: Fellow, AAAS; Academy of Psychoanalysis; American Psychiatric Association; Group for Advancement of Psychiatry. Hobbies: Trail Riding; Guitar; Singing. Address: UCLA Neuropsychiatric Institute, 760 Westwood Plaza, Los Angeles, CA 90024-1759, USA.

GORSKI Peter Andrew, b. 12 Apr 1949, New York, NY, USA. Developmental Pediatrician. m. Sandra Lee Reed, 8 Jul 1978, 2 s, 1 d. Education: AB, Haverford College; MD, Tufts University School of Medicine; MPA, Harvard University, JFK School of Government. Career: Fellow in Medicine, Harvard Medical School; Assistant Professor of Pediatrics, University of CA, San Francisco; Assistant Professor of Pediatrics and Psychiatry, Northwestern University; Currently, Director, Blake Newborn Family Unit, Massachusetts General Hospital and Harvard Medical School. Publications: 20 publications, 1979-94. Memberships: President Elect, Society for Developmental and Behavioural Pediatrics; Board of Directors, National Perinatal Association. Hobbies: Sailing; Music; Fine Art. Address: General Pediatrics Research, WACL-715, Massachusetts General Hospital, Boston, MA 02114, USA.

GOSAVI Shrikant Madhusudan, b. 10 April 1954, Bombay, India. Consultant. m. Dr Anjali, 16 Dec 1985, 2 sons. Education: MBBS, MD, Obstetrics, Gynaecology, Grant Medical College and J J Group of Hospital, University of Bombay; DGO, Obstetrics, Gynaecology, DFP, Obstetrics, Gynaecology, FCPS, Obstetrics, Gynaecology, College of Physicians and Surgeons, Bombay; DObstRCP (Eire); MRCOG (UK); Senior House Officer, St George's Hospital, 1977-78, Registrar, 1978-80, J J Group of Hospitals; Senior House Officer, George Eliot Hospital, Nuneaton, England, 1981-83; Registrar, Rutherglen Maternity Hospital, Victoria Infirmary, Royal Samaritan Hospital for Women, Glasgow, Scotland, 1983-84. Appointments: Teaching medical students, Universities of Bombay and Glasgow; Private practice as Consultant in Obstetrics and Gynaecology, Nasik, 1985-. Publications: Shake test for foetal pulmonary maturity, 1979; Miconazole in Vaginal moniliasis, 1979; Heart disease in pregnancy, 1980; Malignant mixed mesodermal tumour in a 13 year old girl (Youngest patient reported), 1984. Honours: Gold Medal and Dina Patel Prize for highest aggregate and marks in FCPS Examination, 1980. Memberships: Indian Medical Association, Nasik Branch; Nasik Obstetrics and Gynaecological Society. Hobbies: Music; Badminton. Address: 1370 G Shivaji Road, Nasik City 422001, Maharashtra, India.

GOSEN Karen, b. 26 Nov 1954, Minneapolis, Minnesota, USA. Psychiatrist. m. Greg Gosen, 4 Feb 1978, 1 son. Education: BS, Pharmacy, Drake University, 1978; MD, University of Minnesota, 1982; Resident, Mayo Graduate School of Medicine, 1982-86. Appointments: Psychiatrist, Gundersen Clinic Ltd, 1986-91; Medical Director, Lutheran Recovery Centers, 1987-91; Currently: Psychiatrist, Clinical Director, Fountain Lake Treatment Center, Minnesota; Psychiatrist, Naeve Behavioral Health, Minnesota. Honours: Admitted, Rho Chi, 1976; Admitted, Alpha Omega Alpha, 1982; Diplomate, Psychiatry, 1988,

Diplomate, Psychiatry with added qualification in Addiction Psychiatry, 1993, American Board of Psychiatry and Neurology; Certification, American Society of Addiction Medicine, 1991. Memberships: American Psychiatric Association; Minnesota Psychiatric Society; American Academy of Psychiatrists in Alcoholism and Addiction; American Society of Addiction Medicine. Hobbies: Reading; Needlework; Ranching. Address: 414 Park Avenue, Albert Lea, MN 56007, USA.

GOTTHEIL Edward, b. 8 Jun 1924, Montreal, Quebec, Canada. Professor of Psychiatry. m. Ruth Irene Ranville, 1 Jul 1951, 1 s, 1 d. Education: BA, Queen's University, 1946; MA, McGill University, 1948; PhD, University of Texas, 1951; MD, Southwestern Medical School, University of Texas, 1955; Internship, Roanoke Memorial Hospital, 1955-56; Psychiatry Residency, Letterman General Hospital, San Francisco, 1956-59. Appointments: Teaching Fellow, University of Texas, 1948-50; Chief Psychologist, Austin State Hospital, 1949-51; Psychologist, Beverly Hills Sanitarium, 1952-55; US Army Post Psychiatrist, Irwin Army Hospital, Kansas, 1960-62; Associate Professor, Department of Continuing Education, Kansas State University, 1961; Chief, United States Military Academy, New York, 1962-64; Jefferson Medical College, Philadelphia: Associate Professor, Psychiatry, 1964-69; Professor of Psychiatry, 1969-; Coordinator, Department of Psychiatry, 1964-67; Director, Department of Psychiatry and Human Behavior, 1967-83; Director of Alcohol & Drug Abuse Services, 1973-; Attending Psychiatrist, Thomas Jefferson University Hospital, Philadelphia, 1965-. Publications: Numerous Publications, 1951-94, including, Sociometric Technique and Experimental Method in Social Psychology, 1952; The Military Effectiveness of Men with Criminal Histories, 1961; The Medical Student and His College Environments, 1967. Honours: C Nelson Davis Award, Philadelphia County Medical Society, 1993. Memberships: include, American College of Psychiatrists; National Council on Alcoholism; Pennsylvania Medical Society; Alpha Omega Alpha; Sigma Xi; Medical Society of Pennsylvania. Hobbies: Reading; Theater. Address: 1201 Chestnut Street, 15th Floor, Philadelphia, PA 19107, USA.

GOTTLIEB A Arthur, b. 14 Dec 1937, USA. Professor of Medicine. m. Dr Marise S Gottlieb, 1958, 2 d. Education: AB, summa cum laude, Distinction in Chemistry, Columbia College, 1957; MD, NY University School of Medicine, 1961. Career includes: Associate Professor, 1969-72, Professor of Microbiology, 1972-75, Institute of Microbiology, Rutgers University, New Brunswick, NJ; Currently, Professor and Chairman, Department of Microbiology and Immunology, Professor of Medicine, Tulane University School of Medicine, New Orleans, LA. Publications: Numerous publications including: Co-author, Clinical and biological effects if IMREG-1 and IMREG-2, two immunologically active components of leukocyte dialysates in Recent Advances, in Transfer Factor and Dialyzable Leukocyte Extracts, 1991; Author, Clinical and immunologic observations in patients with AIDS-related Complex treated with IMREG-1, in International Journal of Immunopharmacology, 1991. Honours include: Phi Beta Kappa, 1956; Sigma Xi, 1972; Frances Stone Burns Award, American Cancer Society, 1968; Travelling Fellow, Royal Society of Medicine; Fellow, American College of Physicians; Fellow, American Academy of Microbiology; Mayor's Certificate of Merit, City of New Orleans, 1985. Memberships include: AAAS; American Association for Cancer Research; American Chemical Society; American Society for Cell Biology; International Association for Comparative Research on Leukemia and Related Diseases; Chairman, Councillor, Association of Medical School Microbiology. Address: Department of Microbiology and Immunology, Tulane University School of Medicine, 1430 Tulane Aveune, New Orleans, LA 70112, USA.

GOTTLIEB Gary Lloyd, b. 6 May 1955, New York, NY, USA. Physician; CEO. m. Dr Derri Shtasel, 13 Jun 1981, 1 s, 1 d. Education: BS, cum laude, Rensselaer Polytechnic Institute, Troy, NY, 1975; MD, Albany Medical College of Union University, NY, 1979; MBA, Distinction, Health Care Administration, Wharton Graduate School of Business Administration, University of PA, 1985. Career includes: Attending Physician, 1984-94, Director, Geriatric Psychiatry, 1986-94, Executive Director of Clinical Practices, Psychiatry, 1988-94, Associate Professor of Psychiatry in Medicine, 1989-94, Associate Professor of Psychiatry, 1989-94, Hospital of University of PA, Philadelphia; Clinical Professor of Psychiatry, Univ of Pennsylvania, 1994-; Director and Chief Executive Officer, Firends Hospital, Phila, PA, 1994-; Advisory Panel on Alzheimer's Disease, Department of Health and Human Services, 1993-; Associate Dean for Managed Cure, Univ of PA Health System, 1992-94. Publications include: Editorial Board, International Journal of Geriatric Psychiatry, 1988-; Assistant Editor, American Journal of Geriatric Psychiatry, 1992-; Numerous publications in professional journals, presentations and abstracts. Honours include: Beta Gamma Sigma, 1985; Earl Bond Award for Teaching Excellence, Department of Psychiatry, University of PA, 1989; Christian R and Mary F Lindback Foundation Award for Distinguished Teaching, University of PA, 1991. Memberships include: Scientific Advisory Committee, Alzheimer's Association Inc; Various offices, American Association for Geriatric Psychiatry; APA; Association for Academic Psychiatry; Gerontologic Society of America; Society for Health and Human Values. Hobbies: Tennis; Skiing; Literature; Music. Address: Friends Hospital, 4641 Roosevelt Boulevard, Philadelphia, PA 19124-2399, USA.

GOTTLIEB George Robert, b. 29 July 1946, New York City, USA. Physician. m. 2 sons, 1 daughter. Education: BEng, City University of New York, 1968; MD, Honours, New York University School of Medicine, 1975; Intern, Residency, New York Hospital, Cornell Medical School, 1977. Appointments: Emory University School of Medicine; Dekalb Medical Centre; Egleston Medical Centre; Gwinnett Medical Centre; Private Practice for Allergy and Immunology. Memberships: Fellow, Ame4rican Academy of Allergy and Immunology; Fellow, American College of Allergists; Fellow, American Academy of Paediatrics. Address: 2675 North Decatur Road, Suite 404, Decatur, GA 30030, USA.

GOTTSCHALK Alexander, b. 23 Mar 1932, Chicago, IL, USA. Radiologist. m. Jane Rosenbloom, 13 Aug 1960, 1 s, 2 d. Education: MD; BS; DABR; DABR NM; FACR; FCCP; Honorary MA, Yale. Appointments: Professor and Chairman of Radiology, University of Chicago; Professor of Radiology, Yale University; Professor of Radiology, Michigan State University. Publications: 168 Published scientific articles; 92 Published abstracts; Senior Editor, Diagnostic Nuclear Medicine, 1988. Honours: Fleischner Lecture and Medal, 1983; Gold Medal, Association of University Radiologists, 1987. Memberships: Fellow, ACR; Past President, AUR; Past President, Fleischner Society; Past President, SNM; RSNA; ARRS; Fellow, ACCP. Hobbies: Skiing; Golf. Address: 4246 Van Atta Road, Otemos, MI 48664, USA.

GOTTSCHALK Louis A, b. 26 Aug 1916, St Louis, Missouri, USA. Psychiatrist; Neurologist. m. 24 July 1944, 1 son, 3 daughters. Education: MD; PhD, psychoanalysis. Appointments: Research Associate, Michael Reese Hospital, Chicago, 1948-51; Research Psychiatrist, National Institute of Mental Health, Bethesda, Maryland, 1951-53; Research Professor of Psychiatry, University of Cincinnati, 1953-67; Founding Chairman, Professor, department Psychiatry and Human Behaviour, College of Medicine; Professor Emeritus of Psychiatry and Social Science, University of California, Irvine. Publications: Author or editor of 22 books and contributor of over 200 articles in refereed journals. Honours: Hofheimer Award for Research in Psychiatry, 1955; Research Career Award, USPHS, University of Cincinnati COllege of Medicine, 1961-67; Foundation Fund for Research in Psychiatry Award, American Psychiatric Association, 1978; Dan Aldrich Award for Distinguished University Service, 1993. Memberships: American Psychiatric Association; American Psychoanalytic Association; American College of Neuropsychopharmacology; Association for Research in Nervous and Mental Disease; American Medical Association; Southern California Psychoanalytic Society. Address: Department of Psychiatry and Human Behaviour, College of Medicine, University of California, Irvine, CA 92717, USA.

GOU Sheng-Liang, b. 23 Dec 1947, Nei County, Shaanxi Province, China. Professor. m. 1977, 1 son, 3 daughters. Education: Graduate, Shaanxi Traditional Medical School, 1972. Appointments: Chinese Medical Doctor, Huai-Ya Towns Clinic, 1972-82; Advanced Studies, Shaanxi Academy of Traditional Chinese Medicine, 1983-85; President, Visiting Physician, Mei COunty Hospital of Combined Traditional Chinese and Western Medicine, 1985-90; Director, Professor, Physician-in-Chief, Xi'An Institute of Hepatic Diseases, 1990-. Publications: Contributor of 5 research articles. Honours: Golden Cup Prize, Malaysia International Fair of New Science and Technology, 1993; Golden Prize, Third Chinese Fine-Products Fair of Medicine and Health Protection, 1994; 1st Class Academic Paper Prize, 1st China Academic Symposium for Difficult and Complicated Illness. Memberships: All China Association of Traditional Chinese Medicine; President, Hu County Hospital for Digestive Diseases; Specialist, China Clinical Centre for Difficult and Complicated Cases. Hobbies: Music; Calligraphy; Painting. Address: Xi'an Institute of Hepatic Diseases, 201 ZhuQue Street, Xi'an, Shaanxi province 710061, China.

GOURLEY Dick R, b. 26 Dec 1944, Franklin, KY, USA. Pharmacy. m. Greta Ann Kimbrough, 07 Dec 1968, 1 d. Education: BS, Pharmacy, 1969, Pharm D, 1970, University of TN; Certificate in Health Systems Management, Harvard University, 1980. Appointments: Assistant Professor, Mercer University, 1970-72; Assistant Professor, Associate Professor, Professor and Chairman, University of NE College of Pharmacy, 1972-84; Professor and Dean, Mercer University School of Pharmacy, 1984-89; Provost, Mercer University, 1987-89; Professor and Dean, University of TN College of Pharmacy, 1990-. Honours: Rho Chi National Honour Society; Phi Lambda Sigma; Honorary Membership, Hospital Society of Australia, 1981; Outstanding Service Award, NE Society of Hospital Pharmacists, 1984; Special Recognition Award, Atlanta Academy of Institutional Practitioners, 1989. Memberships: American Pharmaceutical Association; American Association of Colleges of Pharmacy; American Society of Hospital Pharmacists; Federation of International Pharmaceutique; American College of Clinical Pharmacy; International Foundation for Pharmacy Education; TN Pharmacists Association. Hobbies: Miniatures; Antique Collecting; Reading; Travel; Golf; Numismatist. Address: University of Tennessee, College of Pharmacy, 847 Monroe, Memphis, TN 38163, USA.

GRAFTON-WASSERMAN Deborah Angela, b. 19 May 1952, New York, USA. Epidemiologist. m. Glenn M Wasserman, 7 Jul 1985, 1 d. Education: BS, Trinity College, Washington DC, 1979; MPH, University of Hawaii, 1982; PhD, University of Hawaii, 1988; Fellow, Thomas J Watson Foundation, 1979. Appointments: Biologist, Laboratory of CNS Studies, NINCDS, National Institute of Health, 1980; Consulting Epidemiologist, South Pacific Commission, Noumen, New Caledonia, 1985; Infectious Disease Epidemiologist, Monterey County, California Health Department, 1988; Consulting Infectious Disease Epidemiologist, Washington DC Commission of Public Health, 1990; Consulting Epidemiologist specialising in Disease Surveillance Activities. Publications: Co-Author, Fertility and Contraception in the Marshall Islands, 1988; Co-Author, Marshall Islands Women's Health Survey, 1985; Co-Author, Elemental Content of Scalp Hair in Guamanian Chamarros with Amyotrophic Lateral Sclerosis and Parkinsonism Dementia, 1984. Memberships: Society for Edpiemiologic Research; American Public Health Association. Hobbies: Yoga; Fabric Marbling. Address: 303 La Jolla Avenue, Sun City Center, FL 33573, USA.

GRAHAM Ian Davidson, b. 20 Mar 1934, Ontario, Canada. Psychoanalyst. m. Suzanne Blomer, 17 Sept 1960, 2 sons, 1 daughter. Education: MD, University of Western Ontario, 1958; Psychiatric Residency, University of Rochester, New York, USA, 1962; Diploma, Post Residency Fellow, Adult Psychiatry, Mennineer Foundation, 1964; Diploma, Psychoanalysis, Toronto Institute of Psychoanalysis, 1972. Appointments: Assistant Professor, Psychiatry, University of Toronto; Director, Canadian Institute of Psychoanalysis; Director, Toronto Institute of Psychoanalysis. Publications: The Personal Myth in Psychoanalysis. Memberships: Ontario & Canadian Psychiatric Associations; Ontario & Canadian Medical Associations; Toronto & Canadian Psychoanalytic Institutes & Societies. Hobbies: Writing; Tennis. Address: 206 St Clair Avenue West, Toronto, Ontario M4V 1R2, Canada.

GRAHAM Sam Dixon, b. 13 Feb 1949, Philadelphia, PA, USA. Urology. m. Sally L Kauffman, 25 May 1974, 3 d. Education: BS, Honours, Economics; MD. Career: Intern and Resident of Surgery, Strong Memorial Hospital, Rochester, NY; Resident, Urology, Duke University, Durham, NC; Currently, Professor and Chairman, Urology, Emory University, Atlanta, GA. Honours: Dupont Scholar, 1967; AFUD Scholar, 1980-82. Membership: American Urology Association. Hobbies: Sailing; Golf; Tennis. Address: Emory University School of Medicine, 1365 Clifton Road North East, Atlanta, GA 30322, USA.

GRAHAM-POLE John Richard, b. 23 Feb 1942, Devon, England. Professor of Pediatrics. m. Sheila Eyberg, 10 Nov 1985, 1 s, 1 d. Education: MBBS, University of London, 1966; MRCS; LRCP, England, 1966. Career: Consultant Pediatrician and Senior Lecturer, St Bartholomew's Hospital, London, England, 1977-78; Associate Professor, Department of Pediatrics, Case Western Reserve University, Cleveland, OH, 1978-81; Currently, Professor of Pediatrics, Hematology and Oncology, University of Florida. Publications include: Myeloablative Treatment Supported by Marrow Infusions for Children with Neuroblastoma, in High Dose Cancer Therapy: Pharmacology, Hematopoietins, Stem Cells, 1992; A Healthy Society, in Healing, 1993; Co-author, Development of an Art Program on a Bone Marrow Transplant Unit, in Cancer Nursing, 1994. Honours: Donald Patterson Prize, British Paediatric Association, 1977; Doctorate of Medicine Thesis, University of London, 1978; University of FL Superior Accomplishment Award, 1994. Memberships include: American Society of Pediatric Hematology and Oncology; American Society of Clinical Oncology; International Society of Experimental Hematology; Institute of Noetic Sciences; International Bone Marrow Transplant Registry; Society for Health and Human Values; International Arts-Medicine Association. Hobbies: Poet; Clown; Gardening; Meditating; Acting. Address: Pediatric Hematology and Oncology, University of Florida, PO Box 100296, Gainesville, FL 32610-0296, USA.

GRAN Petter, b. 19 Oct 1951, Oslo, Norway. Chiropractor. m. Karin Gran, 11 Oct 1973, 1 son, 1 daughter. Education: Doctor of Chiropractic, Palmer College of Chiropractic, Davenport, Iowa, USA, 1974. Appointments: Chiropractor in private practice. Memberships: Norwegian Chiropractic Association; European Chiropractors Union. Hobbies: Skiing; Tennis; Watersports; Wine-tasting; Lions Club. Address: Hönengt 46, 3500 Hönefoss. Norway.

GRANDWILEWSKI DE POCIECHA Waldemar Joseph, b. 5 Mar 1949, Inowroclaw, Poland. Doctor of Medicine. m. Janine-Anne Wilk, 16 Dec 1972, 2 sons. Education: University of Wroclaw, 1969-71; MD, Academy of Medicine, Warsaw, 1978; General Surgery, Academy of Medicine, Gdansk and Bydgoszcz, 1981; University of Western Ontario, London, 1985-87; Family Medicine, Queen's University, Kingston, Ontario, 1987-89; Orthopaedic Surgery, McMaster University, Hamilton, Ontario, 1989-93. Appointments: Clinical Surgical Assistant, Researcher, Scarborough General Hospital, University of Toronto, Ontario, Canada, 1984-85; Medical Consultant, Examiner, Meditest Medical Services Company, Toronto, 1984-85; Currently: President, SA-CA-POL Pharmacy Corporation, Canada; Clinical Fellow, Department of Orthopaedics, McMaster University, Hamilton. Publications: Diagnosis of Peripheral Vascular Disease, Determination of the level of amputation, in lower extremities using a Doppler Ultrasound (Doppler XV), 1981; Complication of Forearm-Plate Removal (with Drew Bednar), 1992; Anterior and Posterior Spinal Fusion, Comparison of One-Stage and Two-Stage Procedures (with G Richard Viviani), 1993; Research papers: Pulmonary Embolus in Emergency Care, 1989; Review of Intra-articular Fractures of the Distal Radius (Study in Adults over 40), 1990; Single versus Double Plate Fixation in Supracondylar Fracture of the Femur, 1993. Memberships: College of Physicians and Surgeons of Ontario; Canadian College of Family Medicine; Canadian Orthopaedic Association; Ontario Medical Association; American Academy of Orthopedic Surgeons; Ontario Genealogical Society of Canada. Hobbies: History; Biography; Skiing; Hunting. Address: 51-255 Mount Albion Rd, Hamilton, Ontario, Canada L8K 6K1.

GRANT Clive Stannard, b. 23 May 1949, Denver, CO, USA. Professor of Surgery. Education: BA, University of Northern CO, 1971; MD, University of CO, 1975. Appointments: Professor of Surgery, Mayo Medical School; Vice Chairman, Department of Surgery, Mayo Clinic. Honour: Alpha Omega Alpha, 1975. Memberships: Honorary Member, Denver Academy of Surgeons; Honorary Member, St Paul Surgical Society; Honorary Member, Scott and White Surgical Society; AAES; ACS; SSAT; IAES; Central Surgical Society; Western Surgical Society; AACE. Address: Mayo Clinic, 200 1st Street SW, Rochester, MN 55905, USA.

GRANT Donald Charles, b. 19 Dec 1936, South Australia. Psychiatrist; Psychoanalyst. m. Katherine White, 25 Sep 1973, 2 s. Education: MBBS, Adelaide University; DPM, Melbourne University; FRANZCP; MRCPsych. Career: Consultant Psychiatrist, St Vincent's Hospital, Melbourne, 1967-88; Consultant Psychiatrist, Health Department, Victoria, 1988-93; Currently in Private Practice. Publications: Misreading Freud - Some Thoughts on Adolf Grünbaum's "Tally Argument", in Psychoanal and Contemporary Thought, 1990; Psychiatry in Search of Self, in ANZJP, 1994. Memberships: Australian Medical Association; Australian Psychoanalytical Society; International Psychoanalytic Association. Hobbies: Ancient Mediterranean and Middle Eastern Pottery. Address: 291 Flemington Road, North Melbourne, Victoria 3051, Australia.

GRASBY Ernest Dudley Yarnold, b. 23 Nov 1903, Teignmouth, Devon, England. Surgeon. m. Margare Coldicott, 9 Sep 1930, 1 son, 1 daughter. Education: MB BS, London; MRCS, England; LRCP, London; FRCOG. Appointments: Consultant Gynaecologist and Obstetrician, Tunbridge Wells Group of Hospitals; Surgeon Superintendent, 1939-48;

Pembury Hospital, Kent; Examiner, University of London; Retired. Hobbies: Music; Painting. Address: Fothersby West, Rye Road, Hawkhurst, Kent TN18 5DB, England.

GRAVETT Peter James, b. 17 Nov 1946, London, England. Haematologist. m. Maureen Gravett, 6 June 1975, 1 son. Education: MB BS (London); MRCS (England); LRCP; FRCPath; MBACA, British Acupuncture Association. Appointments: Regimental Medical Officer, 1/2nd Gurkha Rifles, 1970-73; Specialist Pathologist, Royal Army Medical Corps, 1973-80; Consultant Haematologist, Lieutenant-Colonel, Royal Army Medical Corps, Officer-in-charge, John Boyd Laboratory, Queen Elizabeth Military Hospital, 1980-84; Consultant Haematologist, The London Clinic, 1985-. Publications: Use of English in Alternative Medicine, 1993; Contributor to Cambridge Encyclopaedia, 1993; Author or joint author, articles relating to bone marrow transplantation. Honours: Honorary Consultant Haematologist to Westminster Hospital, 1981. Memberships: Fellow, Royal Society of Medicine; Founder Member, British Blood Transfusion Society; British Society of Haematology. Hobby: Instructor, WV Style, Tai Chi Chuan. Address: 15 Harmont House, 20 Harley Street, London W1N 1AN, England.

GRAY Genevieve Isabel, b. 23 Jan 1943, Rocdale, New South Wales, Australia. Professor. Education: FCN (New South Wales); FRCNA; Diploma, Nursing Education, Diploma, Advanced Nursing Studies, MSc, Nursing, Manchester University. Appointments: Head, Faculty of Health Studies, Assistant Professor, Dean of Nursing, Flinders University, South Australia; Currently Professor of Nursing, Dean, Faculty of Nursing and Health Studies, University of Western Sydney-Nepean, New South Wales. Publications: Co-editor: Towards a Discipline of Nursing, 1991; Co-editor: Scholarship in the Discipline of Nursing, 1995; Co-author: A Successful Guide to Grant Applications; Across the Spinifex - Registered Nurses Working in Rural and Remote Australia; Co-Editor: Issues in Australian Nursing Series, Volume 2, 1989, Volume 3, 1992, Volumes 4 and 5, 1995. Honours: Yvonne International Nursing Fellow, League of Red Cross Societies, Geneva, 1976. Memberships: Royal College of Nursing, Australia, President 1991-1992, 1993-94; Research Society, Royal College of Nursing, Australia; Editorial Advisory Boards: Asian Journal of Nursing; Collegian, Royal College of Nursing. Hobbies: Photography; Travel. Address: Faculty of Nursing and Health, University of Western Sydney-Nepean, Westmead Campus, Westmead, NSW 2145, Australia.

GRAY Jean Dorothy, b. 2 July 1942, Redhill, England. Physician. m. Michael W Gray, 31 Aug 1968, 2 daughters. Education: BSc; MD; FRCPC. Appointment: Visiting Assoiciate Professor, Stanford, 1984; Professor, Medicine & Pharmacology, Dalhousie, 1990; Active Medical Staff, Victoria General Hospital & Camp Hill Medical Center; Associate Dean, Postgraduate Medical Education, Dalhousie University. Publications: Drugs and Therupeutics for Maritime Practitioners; Therapeutic Choices, editor-in-chief, 1995; Criteria for Selection and Evaluation of Good Teaching Cases, 1992. Honours: Searle Distinguished Achievement Award, Canadian Society of Clinical Pharmacology, 1990; Canadian Progress Club Woman od Distinction Award, 1991; Royal College of Continuing Education Fellowship, 1994; University of Alberta Medical Alumni Association Outstanding Achievement Award, 1994. Memberships: AOA; Royal College of Physicians of Canada; CSCP; CSCI; ASCPT; CSIM; Canada Hypertension Society; CAME; CFMW. Hobbies: Reading; Needlework; Hiking. Address: Camp Hill Medical Center, 1763 Robie Street, Halifax, NS B3H 3G2, Canada.

GRAY Maria Danuta, b. 1 April 1937. Gynaecologist. Education: LRCP&LM; LRCSI&LM (1962); DRCOG (1966); MRCOG (1968); FRCOG. Appointments: Dr Steven's Hospital, Dublin; Steppinghill, Stockport; Newcastle-upon-Tyne; Registrar, East Birmingham; Senior Registrar, East Birmingham and Marston General; Consultant Gynaecologist, Birmingham Nuffield Hospital. Publications: Endometrial Hyperplasia & Adend Carcinoma During Tibolone (Livial) Therapy, 1994. Memberships: British Menopause Society; North American Menopause Society; International Menopause Society; International Society of Gynaecological Endocrinology. Hobbies: Reading; Painting; Philately; Ornithology; Astronomy; Gardening. Address: 14 St Mary's Road, Harborne, Birmingham B17 0HA, England.

GRAY Nicola Susan, b. 21 Oct 1964. Psychologist. Education: BSc, Honours, Psychology; MSc, Clinical Psychology; PhD, Psychology; Chartered Psychologist. Appointments: Postdoctoral Research Psychologist, Schizophrenia; Currently, Psychologist. Publications:

Co-author, Behavioural Brain Sciences, 1991; Co-author, Psychopharmacology; Co-author, Schizophrenia Research, in press. Memberships: British Psychological Society; British Association of Psychopharmacology; British Neuropsychiatry Association. Hobby: Scuba Diving. Address: Institute of Psychiatry, De Crespigny Park, Camberwell, London, SE5 8RQ, England.

GRAYSON Leonard D, b. 20 Aug 1921, Brooklyn, NY, USA. Physician. m. Rosalin Berman, 25 Dec 1946, 1s, 3 d. Education: BS; MB, MD, Chicago Medical School; Board Certified, Dermatology, 1957, Allergy and Immunology, 1974. Career: NY State University College of Medicine, 1954-55; WA University Medical School, 1963-70; Allergist, Clinical Immunologist, Dermatologist, Southern IL University Medical School, 1979-. Publications: 35 published articles. Honour: Enid Ireland Award, 1993. Memberships: American Academy of Dermatology; American Academy of Allergy; American Medical Writers Association; American College of Allergies; American Association of Certified Allergists; American Geriatric Society. Hobbies: Tennis; Music; Golf; Computers. Address: Quincy Medical Group, 1101 Maine Street, Quincy, IL 62301, USA.

GREEN André, b. 12 Mar 1927, Cairo, Egypt. Psychoanalyst. m. Litza Guttieres, 13 May 1989, 3 s. Education: MD, Faculty of Paris, France. Career: Director, Paris Psychoanalytical Institute; Vice President, International Psychoanalytic Association; Professor, Freud Memorial Chair, University College, London; President, Paris Psychoanalytical Society; Currently, Training Analyst, Paris Institute of Psychoanalysis. Publications: Un oeil en trop, 1969; Le Discours Vivant, 1973; Narcissisme de Vie - Narcissisme du Mort, 1983; La folie privée, 1990; Le travail du nigatif, 1993. Memberships: Paris Psychoanalytical Society; International Psychoanalytical Association. Hobby: Music. Address: 9 Avenue de l'Observatoire, Paris 75006, France.

GREEN David Marvin, b. 7 June 1932, Jackson, MI, USA. Graduate Research Professor. m. Marian Heinzmann, 7 June 1980, 3 s, 1 d. Education: BA, University of Chicago, 1952; BA, 1954, MA, 1955, PhD, 1958, University of MI; MA, University of Cambridge, England, 1973; MA, Harvard University, 1973. Appointments include: Consultant, Bolt Beranek and Newman Inc, MA, 1958-; Associate Professor Psychology, Vice Chairman, University of PA, 1963-66; Professor of Psychology, University of CA, 1966-73; Professor Psychophysics, 1973-85, Chairman, Department of Psychology and Social Relations, 1978-81, Harvard University; Graduate Research Professor, University of FL, 1985-. Publications include: Numerous professional publications, 1957-94, including: A theory of community annoyance created by noise exposure, in Psychological Acoustics, 1993; Sound's Effects on Marine Mammals Need Investigation, EOS, 1994. Honours include: Sigma Xi; Guggenheim Fellowship, 1973-74; Overseas Fellow, St John's College, Cambridge, England, 1973-74; Distinguished Scientific Contribution Award, American Psychological Association, 1981; Fellow, All Souls College, Oxford, England, 1981-82; Javit's Award, National Institute of Health, 1987-94; Gold Medal, Acoustical Society of America, 1994. Memberships include: Society of Experimental Psychologists; Psychonomic Society; Psychometric Society; American Association of University Professors; President, Acoustical Society, 1981. Hobby: Gardening. Address: University of Florida, Dept of Psychology, Psychoacoustic Lab, Gainesville, FL 32611-2250, USA.

GREEN Frank, b. 3 Sep 1946, Gainesville, FL, USA. MD. m. Catherine West, 27 Dec 1969, 1 s, 1 d. Education: MD, University of PA; BS, Washington University; Subspeciality Training in Pediatrics and Neonatology. Appointment: Professor of Pediatrics and Nutritional Sciences, Meriter Hospital, Madison, WI. Publications: Over 75 publications. Memberships: Society for Pediatric Research; American Institute of Nutrition; American Society for Bone and Mineral Research. Hobbies: Horticulture; Skiing; Biking. Address: Wisconsin Perinatal Center, Meriter Hospital, Madison, WI 53715-1596, USA.

GREEN George R, b. 14 Oct 1934, Philadelphia, PA, USA. Physician. m. Trudy King, 19 May 1962, 3 s, 1 d. Education: BS; MD; FACP; FAAAI. Career includes: Physician in Chief, Division of Allergy and Immunology, Department of Medicine, Abington Memorial Hospital; Assistant Professor, 1969-76, Associate Clinical Professor, 1976-88, Clinical Professor of Medicine, 1988-, University of PA School of Medicine. Publications include: Antibiotic Therapy in Patients with a History of Penicillin Allergy, chapter in Penicillin Allergy, Clinical and Immunology Aspects, 1970; Adverse Reactions to Drugs, in Conn's Current Therapy, 1989; Original papers include: Penicillin Allergy in a

Patient with Chronic Osteomyelitis, in Current Issues in Allergy and Immunology, 1992. Honours: Alpha Omega Alpha, 1962; Award of Merit, Boy Scouts of America, 1987; Community Service Award, Boy Scouts of America, 1989. Memberships include: American College of Physicians; American Academy of Allergy and Immunology; Philadelphia College of Physicians; Hospital Medical Staff Delegate, 1987-, AMA; President, NE Region, 1972-75, Flying Physicians Association; Clinical Immunology Society. Hobbies: Flying; Boy Scouts; Hunting. Address: 1235 Old York Road Ste 222, Abington, PA 19001, USA.

GREEN Hubert Gordon, b. 31 Oct 1938, Dallas, TX, USA. Physician. m. Jean Ann Hunter, 7 Jun 1969, 1 s, 3 d. Education: BA, William M Rice University; MD, University of TX Southwestern; MPH, University of CA, Berkeley. Career: Assistant Professor of Pediatrics and Biometry, University of Arkansas; Medical Director, Arkansas Children's Hospital; Deputy Director, Region 6, US Public Health Service; Director, Dallas County Health Department; Currently, Dean, University of TX Southwestern Allied Health Sciences School. Publications: Cretinism, 1971; Handicapped Barriers, 1973; Infants of Alcoholic Mothers, 1974; Education Via Television, 1976; 2,4,5-T, 1979; Facial Clefts, 1979; Chylothorax, 1980, 1990; Babies DOE, 1985, 1990; AIDS, 1987, 1989. Honours: Alpha Omega Alpha, 1968. Memberships: American Academy of Pediatrics; AMA; American Public Health Association; Association of Schools of Allied Health Professions. Hobbies: Teleology; Cosmology. Address: University of TX, SW Medical Center, 5323 Harry Hines Boulevard, Dallas, TX 75235-9082, USA.

GREEN Larry Alton, b. 27 Mar 1948, Oklahoma, USA. Physician. m. Margaret Joyce Ball, 27 Mar 1971, 1 s, 1 d. Education: BA, Psychology, University of OK; MD, Baylor College of Medicine; Residency in Family Medicine, University of Rochester and Highland Hospital; Diplomate, American Board of Family Practice. Appointments: Practice, Van Buren, AR; Assistant Professor and Residency Director, University of CO; Director, Mercy Family Medicine Residency, Denver; Woodward-Chisholm Chairman and Professor, Department of Family Medicine, University of CO. Publications: Numerous articles published concerning family medicine and practice based research. Memberships: Institute of Medicine, 1991-; American Academy of Family Physicians; Society of Teachers of Family Medicine; North American Primary Care Research Group; Association of Departments of Family Medicine. Hobbies: Fly Fishing; Tennis. Address: Center for Studies in Family Medicine, 1180 Clermont, Denver, CO 80220, USA.

GREEN Lawrence Winter, b. 16 Sep 1940, Bell, CA, USA. Public Health. m. Judith Ottoson, 1 May 1982, 2 d. Education: BS, 1962, MPH, 1966, DPH, 1968, University of CA School of Public Health, Berkeley. Career: Assistant Professor, Associate Professor, Professor, Johns Hopkins University; Director, US Office of Health Promotion; Visiting Lecturer, Harvard University; Professor, University of Texas; Vice President, Kaiser Family Foundation; Currently, Professor and Director, Institute of Health Promotion Research, University of British Columbia, Canada. Publications: Over 380 articles and chapters published; Books: Measurement and Evaluation in Health Education and Health Promotion, 1986, Health Promotion Planning, 2nd edition, 1991, Preventing Drug Abuse, 1993, Community Health, 7th edition, 1994. Honours: Distinguished Fellow, Society for Public Health Education, 1986; Alumnus of Year, University of CA, Berkeley, 1994; Award of Excellence, American Public Health Association, 1994. Memberships: Fellow, American Public Health Association; Society of Public Health Education; Society of Behavioral Medicine; Academy of Behavioral Medicine Research; International Union for Health Promotion and Education. Hobbies: Computers; Gardening. Address: Institute of Health Promotion Research, University of British Columbia, 6248 Biological Sciences Road, Vancouver, BC, Canada, V6K 1J7.

GREEN Wesley Frederick, b. 11 Sept 1930, Sydney, New South Wales, Australia. Medical Scientist. m. Maureen Woodward, 1 Apr 1970, 1 son. Education: Diploma in Medical Technology, Sydney University; Master of Medical Science, Sydney University, 1995. Appointments: Currently: Professional Officer, Department of Medicine, Sydney University; Research Scientist, Institute of Respiratory Medicine, Royal Prince Alfred Hospital, Sydney. Publications include: Precipitins against a fungus, Phoma violacea, isolated from a mouldy shower curtain in sera from patients with suspected allergic alveolitis, 1972; The house dust mite, Dermatophagoides farinae, in Australia, 1983; Abolition of allergens by tannic acid, 1984; Co-author: Tyrophagus putrescentiae: an allergenically important mite, 1978; Asthma in a rural highland area of

Papua New Guinea, 1981; House dust mites in blankets and houses in the highlands of Papua New Guinea, 1982; Reduction of housedust mites and mite allergens: effects of spraying carpets and blankets with Allersearch DMS, an acaricide combined with an allergen reducing agent, 1989; House dust mites and mite allergens in public places, 1991; House dust mite increase in Wagga Wagga houses, 1993. Membership: Institute of Respiratory Medicine, Sydney. Hobbies: Cave exploring; Anthropology; Music (cellist). Address: 57 Sun Valley Road, Valley Heights, New South Wales 2777, Australia.

GREENBAUM Joseph, b. 28 Mar 1946, Poland. Physician. Education: BSc, Honours; MD; FRCPC Internal Medicine; FRCPC Clinical Immunology. Appointment: Assistant Clinical Professor of Medicine. Memberships: American Academy of Allergy; American College of Allergy; Canadian Society of Allergy; British Society of Allergy. Address: 25 Charlton Avenue East, Suite 805, Hamilton, Ontario, Canada, L8N 1Y2.

GREENBERG Mark Lawrence, b. 12 June 1944, Johannesburg, South Africa. Pediatric Oncologist. m. Corin Jowell, 15 June 1969, 1 son, 1 daughter. Education: MBchB; FRCP(C); FAAP. Appointments: Director, Postgraduate Training Programme Pediatrics; Associate Chair, Department of Pediatrics; Professor of Pediatrics & Surgery, University of Toronto; Director, Division of Oncology, Hospital for Sick Children, Toronto. Publications: Continuous Infusion Pre-operative Chemotherapy for Hepatoblaspoma; Pre-operative Chemotherapy for Wilms Tumor; Optic Gliomas-Survaillance or Treatment; Care of the Dying Child. Honours: President, Canadian Society of Pediatric Hemato/Oncology; Chair, Pediatric Oncology Group of Ontario. Memberships: American Society of Pediatric Hemato/Oncology; American Society of Clinical Oncology; American Society of Hemalology; International Society of Pediatric Oncology; Canadian Society of Pediatric Hemato/Oncology. Hobbies: Music; Running; Squash. Address: Hospital for Sick Children, 555 University Avenue, Toronto M5G 1X8, Canada.

GREENBERG Michael R, b. 22 Aug 1943, Bronx, New York, USA. Professor of Public Health. m. Gwen Greenberg, 19 Jan 1978, 1 son, 3 daughters. Education: BA, Hunter College, CUNY; MA, PhD, Columbia University. Appointments: Assistant Professor, Columbia University, New York City, 1969-71; Associate Professor, Full Professor, Rutgers University, 1971-. Publications: Urbanization and Cancer Mortality, 1983; Public Health and the Environment, 1987; Environmental Risk and the Press, 1987. Honours: Special Award of Merit for Research and Education, US EPA, 1977; Award for Research, 1984, Award for Public Service, 1991, Rutgers University Board of Trustees; Special Award for Journalism, Sigma Delta Chi, 1988, 1989. Memberships: American Association for the Advancement of Science; AAG; Society for Epidemiologic Research; Society for Risk Analysis. Hobbies: Walking; Exercising; Reading. Address: 228 Lawrence Ave, Highland Park, NJ 08904, USA.

GREENBERG Raymond Seth, b. 10 Aug 1955, Chapel Hill, North Carolina, USA. Professor; Provost. m. Leah Daniella Greenberg, 23 Oct 1988. Education: BA with highest honours, 1976, PhD, 1983, University of North Carolina; MD, Duke University, 1979; MPH, Harvard University, 1980. Appointments: Assistant Professor, Community Health, 1983-86, Deputy Director, Winship Cancer Center, 1985-90, Associate Professor, Community Health, 1986-87, Associate Professor, Chair, Epidemiology and Biostatistics, 1987-90, Dean, School of Public Health, 1990-95, Emory University, Atlanta, Georgia; Vice President for Academic Affairs and Provost, Medical University of South Carolina, Charleston, South Carolina, 1995-. Publications: Co-author: Racial Differences in Survival of Women with Breast Cancer, 1986, 1995; Breast Self-Examination and Survival from Breast Cancer, 1988; Race Nutritional Status and Survival from Breast Cancer, 1990; Medical Epidemiology, 1992; Environmental Tobacco Smoke and Lung Cancer in Non-Smoking Women, 1994; Epidemiología Médica, 1995. Honours: Phi Beta Kappa, 1975; Sigma Xi, 1976; Delta Omega, 1983; American Epidemiological Society, 1989; Chair, Preventive Medicine/Public Health Test Committee, National Board of Medical Examiners, 1990-93; Chair, Epidemiology and Disease Control Study Section, National Institutes of Health, 1992-94; Chair, Advisory Council, Prudential Center for Health Care Research, 1994-; Advisory Committee on Research and Medical Grants, American Cancer Society, 1994-; Board of Scientific Counselors, National Institute for Dental Research, 1995-. Memberships: American College of Epidemiology, President 1990-91; Society for Epidemiological Research; American Public Health Association; American Statistical Association.

Address: Medical University of South Carolina, 171 Ashley Avenue, Charleston, SC 29425, USA.

GREENBERGER Norton Jerald, b. 13 Sep 1933, Cleveland, OH, USA. Physician. m. Joan Narcus, 10 Aug 1964, 3 d. Education: MD, Case Western Reserve University. Appointments: Professor and Chairman, Department Internal Medicine, KS University School of Medicine. Publications: Author and co-author of about 200 original articles and 5 textbooks. Honours: Honorary Fellowships: Royal Australasian College of Medicine; Royal College of Physicians and Surgeons of Ireland; College of Physicians of South Africa. Memberships: President, 1990-91, American College of Physicians; President, 1984-85, American Gastroenterological Association; President, 1980-81, Central Society for Clinical Research; President, 1986-87, Association of Professors of Medicine; American Society of Clinical Investigation; Association of American Physicians. Hobbies: Jogging; Swimming; Bridge; Classical Music. Address: University of KS, School of Medicine, 39th and Rainbow Blvd, Kansas City, KS 66103, USA.

GREENE Frederick L, b. 18 Dec 1944, Norfolk, Virginia, USA. Physician. m. Donna Greene, 21 June 1970, 1 son, 1 daughter. Education: BA, University of Virginia; MD, University of Virginia. Appointment: Professor of Surgery, University of South Carolina. Publications: Endoscopic Surgery, 1994. Memberships: American College of Surgeons; Society of Surgical Oncology. Hobbies: Travel; Golf. Address: 2 Medical Park, Suite 402, Columbia, SC 29203, USA.

GREENFIELD Joseph C Jr, b. 20 Jul 1931, Atlanta, GA, USA. Physician. m. Mary Ruth Fordham, 13 Aug 1955, 3 d. Education: AB, History, Emory University, Atlanta, GA, 1952; MD, Emory University School of Medicine, Atlanta, GA, 1956. Appointments: Graduate Faculty, 1968-, Associate Professor of Cell Biology (Physiology), 1978-, Duke University; Professor of Medicine, 1970-, Director, Heart Station, 1971-, James B Duke Distinguished Professor, 1981-, Chairman, Department of Medicine, 1983-, Duke University Medical Center; Currently, Dean, University of TX Southwestern Allied Health Sciences School. Publications include: Various Medical Journal Editorial Boards; Over 150 research publications including: Co-author, Inter- and Intra- observer variability performing continuously updated ST-segment recovery analysis following thrombolytic therapy for myocardial infarction, in Journal of Electrocardiology, 1994, in press; Co-author, Regional changes in myocyte structure in a model of canine right atrial hypertrophy, in American Journal Physiology, 1994, in press; Many case reports, editorials, clinical reviews and book chapters. Honours: Phi Beta Kappa; Alpha Omega Alpha; Career Development Award, National Heart Institute, 1966-75; Eugene A Stead Award for Excellence in Teaching, Duke Medical Housestaff, 1984; Distinguished Scientist Award, American College of Cardiology, 1985; Merit Award, National Heart, Lung and Blood Institute, 1986-96; Institute of Medicine of the National Academy of Sciences, 1990. Memberships include: Fellow, American College of Cardiology; Fellow, American College of Physicians; AHA. Hobby: Quail Hunting. Address: Duke Medical Center, PO Box 3246, Durham, NC 27710, USA.

GREENSPAN Barney, b. 28 Mar 1943, Miami Beach, FL, USA. Clinical Psychologist. 3 s. Education: PhD, MI State University, 1970; Child Psychoanalyst; Diplomate in Clinical Psychology. Appointments: Postdoctoral Fellowship in Psychotherapy, Advance Behavioural Science Center, Grosse Pointe, MI, 1970-72; Director, Psychological Services, Belle Faire Residential Treatment Center, Cleveland, OH, 1972-79; Private Clinical Practice, 1979-89; Chief of Psychological Services, North Central Human Service Center, Minot, ND, 1989-. Publications: Articles in Journal of Contemporary Psychotherapy, 1971, and Adolescence, 1977, 1979; Book Reviews in the Family Coordinator, Journal of Personality Assessment, Child Welfare, Readings, 1971-93. Memberships: American Psychological Association; Association for Child Psychoanalysis; American Orthopsychiatric Association. Hobbies: Exercising; Sport; Reading. Address: 1805 2nd Avenue SW no 208, Minot, ND 58701-3474, USA.

GREENWALD Gilbert, b. 24 Jun 1927, USA. Physiologist. m. Pola Gorsky, 8 Sep 1950, 1 s, 2 d. Education: PhD, Zoology, University of CA, Berkeley, 1954. Appointments: Instructor, Assistant Professor, Anatomy, University of WA, Seattle, 1956-61; Professor of Anatomy, KUMC, 1965-77; Research Professor, Human Reproduction, University of KS Medical Center, 1966-71; Chairman, Physiology, 1977-93; Currently, Distinguished Professor of Physiology, 1973-. Publications:

Editor, Biology of Reproduction, 1974-77; Editor, Factors Regulating Ovarian Function, 1983; Associate Editor, Physiology of Reproduction, 1988, 2nd edition, 1993. Honours: Higuchi Award, University of KS, 1984; Carl Hartman Award, Society Study Reproduction, 1993. Memberships: Society Study of Reproduction, President, 1971; British Society for Study of Fertility; American Physiological Society; Society for Experimental Biological Medicine, Council, 1991-95. Hobbies: Reading; Classical Music. Address: Department Physiology, University of KS Medical Center, Kansas City, KS 66103, USA.

GREENWAY Frank L, b. 15 Jan 1945, Petaluma, CA, USA. Physician. m. Teresa Greenway, 3 Jan 1977, 2 s, 1 d. Education: BA, Biology, Stanford University, 1966; MD, University of CA School of Medicine, Los Angeles, 1970; Fellowship in Endocrinology and Metabolism. Career: Instructor, 1975-77, Assistant Clinical Professor, 1977-85, Associate Clinical Professor, 1985-93, Clinical Professor of Medicine, 1993-, University of CA School of Medicine, Los Angeles; In Private Practice of Internal Medicine, Endocrinology and Metobitism. Publications: Manuscript Reviewer; Over 30 publications including: Clinical Studies with Phenylpropanolamine: A Meta Analysis, in American Journal of Clinical Nutrition, 1992; Co-author, Higher Calorie Content Preserves Myocardial Electrical Activity During Very-Low-Calorie Dieting, In Obesity Research, 1994. Honours include: Student Research Award, 2nd Place, UCLA School of Medicine, 1968; Alumni Award, UCLA School of Medicine, 1970; Merit Award, Los Angeles Surgical Society, 1975; Distinguished Teaching Award, Harbor-UCLA Medical Center, 1986. Memberships: CA Medical Association; Los Angeles County Medical Association; American Diabetes Association; American Federation of Clinical Research; Fellow, American College of Physicians; North American Society for Study of Obesity; American Institute of Nutrition; American Society for Clinical Nutrition. Hobby: Car Restoration. Address: 4560 Admirality Way 301, Marina Del Ray, CA 90292, USA.

GREER David Steven, b. 12 Oct 1925, NY, USA. Dean of Medicine Emeritus. 1 s, 1 d. Education: BS, University of Notre Dame; MD, University of Chicago School of Medicine, IL. Appointments include: Associate Dean Medicine, 1974-81, Chairman, Section of Community Health, 1978-81, Professor of Community Health, 1975-, Dean of Medicine, 1981-92, Currently, Dean Emeritus, Brown University. Publications: Over 40 articles published in professional journals, 1959-90, including: Co-author, Charting the Winds of Change, in Academic Medicine, 1990; Hospice Care for the Elderly, in Improving the Health of Older People: A World View, 1990; Altering the Mission of the Academic Health Center: Can Medical Schools Really Change?, in Education of Physicians to Improve Access Care for the Underserved?, Proceedings of the Second HRSA Primary Care Conference, 1990. Honours: Alpha Omega Alpha, 1953; Outstanding Service Award, MA Easter Seal Society, 1970; Meritorious Service, National Rehabilitation Association, 1972; Outstanding Citizen Award, Jewish War Veterans Auxiliary, 1973; Distinguished Service Award, University of Chicago Medical Alumni, 1973; MA, ad eundem, Brown University, 1975; Cutting Foundation Medal, Andover Newton Theological Seminary, 1976; Honorary DHL, Southeastern MA University, 1981. Memberships include: Institute of Medicine; AMA; Gerontological Society; Diplomat, American Board of Internal Medicine; American College of Physicians; International Society of Rehabilitation Medicine. Hobbies: Squash; Racquets; Reading. Address: Brown University, Box G-B221, Providence, RI 02912, USA.

GREGER Janet L, b. 18 Feb 1948, Joliet, IL, USA. Professor. Education: BS, University of IL, 1970; MS, 1971, PhD, 1973, Cornell University. Career: Assistant Professor, Purdue University, 1973-78; Assistant Professor, 1978-79, Associate Professor, 1979-83, Professor, 1983-, Currently, Associate Dean, Graduate School, University of WI, Madison. Publications: Nutrition for Living, textbook, 1985, 2nd edition, 1988, 3rd edition, 1991, 4th edition, 1994; Over 130 research articles in peer reviewed journals, 1975-94. Honour: AAAS Congressional Science and Engineering Fellow, 1984-85. Memberships: Council on Government Relations, Board of Management, 1993-96; Board of Directors, 1992-94; American Association for Accreditation of Laboratory Animal Care; American Institute of Nutrition; American Society for Clinical Nutrition; AAAS. Hobbies: Reading; Travel. Address: Department of Nutritional Sciences, University of Wisconsin, 1415 Linden Drive, Madison, WI 53706, USA.

GREGOR Anna, b. 13 Aug 1948, Prague. Senior Lecturer. m. Neil Pollock Magee, 9 May 1983, 2 s. Education: MRCP; FRCR.

Appointments include: Registrar, 1977-80, Acting Senior Registrar, 1980, Department of Radiotherapy and Oncology, Royal Marsden, London; Research Fellow, Imperial Cancer Research Fund, and Honorary Senior Registrar, Department Clinical Oncology, University of Edinburgh, Western General Hospital, 1980-83; Consultant Radiotherapist and Oncologist, Western Infirmary, Glasgow, 1983-87; Currently, Senior Lecturer, University Department Clinical Oncology, Honorary Consultant, Lothian Health Board. Publications: 7 Articles published in professional journals, 1979-92, including: Cranial Irradiation in small cell lung cancer, Guest Editorial British Journal of Cancer, 1991; Co-author, The treatment of primary malignant brain tumours, in Journal of Neurology, Neurosurgery and Psychiatry, 1991; Co-author, Phase II study of Tauromustine in malignant glioma, in European Journal of Cancer, 1992. Honours: Richardson-Kuhlman Prize, 1973; AID Travelling Scholarship, 1977; Jan Evangelista Purkyne Medal, 1991. Memberships include: British Association for Cancer Research; BMA; Royal Society of Medicine; European Association of Therapeutic Radiology and Oncology; International Society for Paediatric Oncology; European Neuroblastoma Society; Founder Member, British Oncological Association, Scientific Chairman, 1989, Board, 1985-90; Scottish Radiological Society. Hobbies: Family; Music; Travel. Address: 45 Spylaw Bank Road, Edinburgh, EH13 0JF, Scotland.

GREGORY Gertrude B, b. 21 May 1933, Freeport, New York, USA. Physician. m. Ralph L Gregory, 20 Jan 1957, 1 son, 1 daughter. Education: BA, Hofstra University; MD, Wayne State University College of Medicine. Appointments: Occupational Physician, Marygrove Clinic; Chief Physician, Ford Motor Co Tractor Division; Part-time Staff, Henry Ford Hospital; Semi Retired. Memberships: ACOEM; AMA; Michigan Medical Society; Macomb Co Medical Society. Hobbies: Landscaping; Gardening; Refinishing Furniture. Address: 68135 Frampton Drive, Romeo, MI 48095, USA.

GRIBBLE T John, b. 6 Apr 1937, Cardiff, Wales. Pediatric & Hematology Doctor. m. Geraldine Godek, 26 Nov 1966, 2 sons, 1 daughter. Education: MD, Stanford University, California, 1964. Appointments: Instructor, Pediatrics, Stanford University, 1968-69; Assistant Professor, Pediatrics, Stanford University, 1969-74; Senior Attending & Clinical Associate Professor, Pediatrics, Stanford University, 1974-76; Associate Professor, Pediatrics, University of New Mexico, 1976-. Publications incl: Hematogones: A Multiparameter Analysis of Bone Marrow Precursor Cells, 1989; Geographic Variability of Hemophilia-Associated AIDS in the United States: Effect of Population Characteristics, 1989; Use of Porcine Factor VIII for Surgical Procedures in Hemophilia A Patients with Inhibitors, 1993; HIV Associated Malignancy in Hemophiliacs - Preliminary Report of the Hemophilia Malignancy Study, 1991; Acquired Immunodeficiency Syndrome-Associated Non-Hodgkin's Lymphomas and Other Malignancies in Patients with Hemophilia, 1993. Honours incl: Phi Beta Kappa, 1959; Alpha Omega Alpha, 1964; Faber Pediatric Award, Stanford, 1964; Special Teaching Award, Sickle Cell Council of New Mexico, 1990. Memberships: Western Society for Pediatric Research; The American Society of Hematology; American Academy of Pediatrics; New Mexico Pediatric Society; Hemophilia Research Society; World Federation of Hemophilia; American Academy of Pediatrics. Hobbies: Photography; Woodworking. Address: Department of Pediatrics, University of New Mexico, Albuquerque. NM 87131-5311, USA.

GRIECO Michael Henry, b. 10 Aug 1932, NY, USA. Medicine. m. Dorothy Grieco, 26 Nov 1960, 1 s, 2 d. Education: MD, State University of NY, 1957; JD, Fordham University; Professor of Clinical Medicine, Columbia University College of Physicians and Surgeons. Appointments: Director, Department of Medicine, St Lukes-Roosevelt Hospital Center, NY. Publications: 18 Books and Book Chapters, 1975-92, including: Approach to the immunocompromised patient, in Infectious Diseases, 1992; 120 Articles published in professional journals, 1963-92, including: Co-author, Effect of foscarnet therapy on HIV P24 antigen levels in AIDS patients with CMV retinitis, in Journal of Infectious Diseases, 1992. Memberships: American Association of Immunologists; American Society of Microbiology; American Academy of Allergy and Immunology; Infectious Diseases Society of America. Hobbies: Aviation; Anthropology. Address: St Lukes-Roosevelt Hospital Center, 1000 10th Avenue, New York, NY 10019. USA.

GRIEVE Andrew Robert, b. 23 May 1939, Stirling, Scotland. Dentistry. m. Frances Ritchie, 26 Sept 1963, 2 d. Education: BDS, University of St Andrew, 1961; FDSRSC, Education, 1965; DDS, University of Birmingham 1974. Appointments: Junior Hospital Appointments and General Dental Practice, 1961-63; Lecturer, University of St Andrew, 1963-65; Lecturer, University of Birmingham, 1965-75; Senior Lecturer, University of Birmingham, 1975-80; Professor and Head of Department of Conservative Dentistry and Dean of Dentistry, University of Dundee. Publications: Numerous publications in Scientific Journals related to the field of Conservative Dentistry. Memberships: British Dental Association; Royal Odonto-Chirurgical Society of Scotland; British Society for Dental Research; British Society for Restorative Dentistry. Hobbies: Hill Walking; Woodwork; Gardening; DIY. Address: 20 Albany Road, West Ferry, Dundee DD5 1NT, Scotland.

GRIFFIN Bob Taylor, b. 6 Dec 1945, Oklahoma, USA. Healthcare Executive. m. Gwen Hanners, 23 Aug 1969, 1 son. Education: BS, West Texas University, 1968; MS, Abilene Christian University, 1975; MSHA, Texas Woman's University, 1981. Appointments: Chief Executive Officer, Rio Vista Rehabilitation Hospital; CEO, South Texas Rehabilitation Center; CEO, Josephine Memorial Hospital; COO, Tidelands General Hospital. Publications: Unit Dose Medications, 1974. Memberships: American College of Healthcare Executives; Medical Group Management Association; Southwest Healthcare Executives. Hobbies: Golf; Vertibrate Paleontology. Address: 7205 San Marino, El Paso, TX 79912, USA.

GRIFFIN Gregory Crawford, b. 1 Aug 1952, Richmond, VA, USA. Pediatrician; Hematology and Oncology. Education: BA, Dartmouth College, Hanover, NH, 1973; MD, Jefferson Medical College, PA. Appointments: Director, Pediatric Hematology and Oncology, David Grant USAF Medical Center Travis AFB, CA; Assistant Professor of Clinical Pediatrics, University of CA, Sacramento, CA; Currently, Clinical Associate Professor of Pediatrics, Jefferson Medical College. Publications: Ganglioneuroblastoma and Persistent Ataxia, in Clinical Pediatrics, 1982; Yolk Sac Carcinoma of The Testis in Children, in Journal of Urology, 1987. Honours: Phi Beta Kappa, 1973; Meritorious Service Medal, USAF, 1989; UC Davis Teaching Award, 1990. Memberships: American Academy of Pediatrics; American Society of Pediatric Hematology and Oncology; American Society of Clinical Oncology. Hobbies: Running; Tennis. Address: A I du Pont Institute, 1600 Rockland Rd, Wilmington, DE 17803, USA.

GRINER Paul F, b. 1 Jan 1933, Philadelphia, PA, USA. Physician. m. Miriam Millard, 1 s, 1 d. Education: BA, Harvard University, MA, Honours, 1954; MD, University of Rochester, NY, 1959. Career includes: Assistant Professor, 1967-69, Associate Professor, 1969-73, Samuel E Durand Professor of Medicine, 1973-, University of Rochester School of Medicine and Dentistry; Currently, General Director and Chief Executive Officer, Strong Memorial Hospital, University of Rochester. Publications: 97 Publications including: Technology assessment in a teaching hospital, in Decisions in Imaging Economics, 1992; Co-author, Cost-effective health care: The Rochester experience, in Health Affairs, 1993; Additional perspectives on global budgeting: The Rochester, New York, experience, in Changing the Health Care System: Models from Here and Abroad, 1994. Honours: Doran Stephens Prize, 1959; Alpha Omega Alpha, 1959; Air Force Commendation Medal, 1964; University Mentor Award, University of Rochester, 1982; Honorary Fellow, Venezuelan Society of Internal Medicine, 1988, Academy of Medicine of Malaysia, 1993; Lifetime Achievement Award, Arthritis Foundation, 1993; President, 1993-94, Master, 1994, American College of Physicians. Memberships include: AAAS; American Society of Hematology; Fellow, American College of Physicians; International Society for Technology Assessment in Health Care; Sigma Xi; Institute of Medicine of the National Academy of Sciences. Hobbies: Reading; Fishing; Tennis. Address: University of Rochester School of Medicine and Dentistry, 601 Elmwood Avenue, Rochester, NY 14642, USA.

GRINKER Joel, b. 11 Jul 1939, Chicago, IL, USA. Professor and Director, Human Nutrition. Education: BA, Psychology, Wellesley College, MA, 1961; PhD, Experimental Social Psychology, NY University, 1967; Russell Sage Postdoctoral Fellow, Rockefeller University, 1967-69. Career includes: Assistant Professor, 1971-75, Associate Professor, 1975-82, Rockefeller University, NY; Visiting Associate Professor, College du France, Paris, 1980; Professor of Nutrition, Department of Pediatrics and Communicable Diseases, 1983-, Member, Center for Human Growth and Development, 1983-, Professor and Director, Program in Human Nutrition, School of Public Health, 1982-, University of MI; Visiting Scientist, USDA Human Nutrition Research Center on Aging, Tufts University, 1993-. Publications: Reviewer for many professional journals; Numerous publications and abstracts including: Body Composition Measurement: Accuracy, validity and comparability, in Body Composition and Physical Performance, 1992; Co-author, Learned control of meal-size in spontaneously obese and non-obese bonnet macaque monkeys, in Physiology and Behaviour, 1993. Honours: Creative Talent Award Program, Dissertation, American Institutes for Research, 1967; Future Leaders Award, Nutrition Society, 1973-76; Institute of Behavioral Medicine, 1981. Memberships include: Fellow, AAAS; Fellow, APA; American Psychosomatic Society; American Institute of Nutrition; American Public Health Association; European Society for Study of Obesity; Fellow, NY Academy of Sciences; Sigma Xi; Society for Neuroscience. Address: Program in Human Nutrition, School of Public Health, The University of Michigan, Ann Arbor, MI 48109-2029, USA.

GRINSTEIN Alexander, b. 21 Aug 1918, Russia. Psychoanalyst. m. Adele Brotslaw, 27 Sep 1941, 2 s. Education: BA; MD. Appointments include: Training and Supervising Analyst, MI Psychoanalytic Institute, 1960-; Clinical Associate Professor, Wayne State University Medicine, 1969-73; Clinical Professor of Psychiatry: Wayne State University School Medicine, 1973-; Detroit Psychiatric Institute, 1973-; President and Chair Educational Committee, MI Psychoanalytic Institute, 1985-87. Publications: 17 Professional articles, 1951-90; 8 Book Reviews, 1967-84; 12 Books and Book Chapters, 1974-, including: The Index of Psychoanalytic Writings, 14 Volumes, 1956-75; Understanding Your Family, 1957; On Sigmund Freud's Dreams, 1968; Freud at the Crossroads, 1990; Conrad Ferdinand Meyer and Freud: The Beginnings of Applied Psychoanalysis, 1992; The Remarkable Beatrix Potter, in press. Honours: Sigma Xi, Wayne State University, Detroit, 1960; Grant, Mental Health, National Institute WA, 1968-73; Grant, McGregor Foundation, Detroit, 1964; Grant, Foundation for Research in Psychoanalysis, NY, 1959-73. Memberships: International Psychoanalytical Association; Life Member, American Psychoanalytic Association; Life Fellow, American Psychiatric Association; Life Member, MI Psychiatric Society; Life Member, MI Psychoanalytic Society and Institute; Life Member, Oakland County Medical Society; Life Member, MI State Medical Society; President, 1972-74, MI Association for Psychoanalysis. Hobbies: Photography; Playing Violin; Horseback Riding. Address: 31510 East Bellvine Trail, Beverly Hills, MI 48025-3705, USA.

GRISANTI Giorgio, b. 4 Aug 1929, Palermo, Italy. Professor of Audiology. m. Marina Scaduto, 24 Jun 1963, 2 s, 1 d. Education: Medical Diploma, 1952; ENT Specialization, 1957. Appointments: Assistant, ENT Department, 1957, Associate Professor, Audiology, 1967, Professor of Audiology, 1967-, Chairman, Department of Audiology, 1981-, University of Palermo. Publications: The embryological development of the limbus and the lateral and anterior wall of ductus cochlearis in the rabbit, in Acta Otolar, 1967; Handbook of Audiology, 1980; An automatic test for frequency discrimination, in British Journal of Audiology, 1987; Artificial intelligence techniques for audiological diagnosis, in Otorhinolaryngology, Head and Neck Surgery, 1990; An Expert System for the diagnosis of genetic deafness, In Audiology in Europe, 1992. Memberships: President, 1987-1989, Italian Society of Audiology; President, 1990-, International Association of Physicians in Audiology; International Society of Audiology; Bureau Internationale d'Audiophonologie. Hobby: Classical Music. Address: Via Giusti no 33, I-90144 Palermo, Italy.

GRIVU Ovidiu Nicolae, b. 29 Aug 1931, Sasciori, Alba, Rumania. Dentist. m. Maria Grivu, 24 July 1955, 1 daughter. Education: MD, University of Medicine, Timisoara, 1955; DSS, University of Medicine, Bucharest, 1959; DSc, Dental Faculty of Targu Mures, 1971. Appointments: Assistant, 1963, Lecturer, 1969, Assistant Professor, 1971, Professor of Orthodontics, 1990-, University of Medicine, Timisoara. Publications: Books: Stomatologie pediatrica, 1975; Tehnica ortodontica, 1994; Articles: Über störende Einflüsse auf die Entwicklung der Kiefer und Zähne im Wechselgebiss, 1979; Aspectos ergonomicos del consultario dental, 1979; Carie des dents temporaires, 1979; Ultrastructure des dents incluses, 1980; The Psychological Conditioning of Children to Dental Treatment, 1991. Honours: Scientific Delegate for Balkan countries, Revista Europea de Estomatologia, Barcelona, 1993. Memberships: International Association of Paediatric Dentistry; European Orthodontic Society; Association Stomatologique Internationale. Hobbies: Painting; Writing; Listening to classical music. Address: Str Snagov 5, 1900 Timisoara, Rumania.

GROBOIS Brian Saul, b. 12 July 1957, New York City, USA. Physician. m. Susan B Schnitzer, 16 Dec 1989, 1 son, 1 daughter. Education: BA, University of Pennsylvania, Philadelphia, 1978; MD,

Sackler School of Medicine, Tel Aviv University, New York State Program, Ramat Aviv, Israel, 1983; Certified, American Board of Psychiatry and Neurology, 1989, Geriatric Psychiatry, 1992, Addiction Psychiatry, 1993. Appointments include: Assistant Attending Psychiatrist, Montefiore Medical Centre, Bronx, New York, 1987-; Instructor in Psychiatry, Cornell University Medical College, New York, 1990-92; Clinical Assistant Professor in Psychiatry, Mount Sinai School of Medicine, New York, 1992-; Associate Chief of Psychiatry for Psychopharmacology and Addiction Services, Jewish Board of Family and Children's Services, New York, 1993-; Private Practice, New York City, 1993-. Publications: The Identification of PTSD in Cancer Survivors, Co-author. Honours: Valedictory Address, Sackler School of Medicine, 1983; Cum Laude, University of Pennsylvania, 1978; Sphinx Senior Society, 1977; Mortar Board, 1977; Alpha Epsilon Delta, 1976. Memberships: American Psychiatric Association; Academy of Psychosomatic Medicine; American Academy of Psychiatrists in Alcoholism and Addictions; American Association for Geriatric Psychiatry; American Academy of Child and Adolescent Psychiatry. Hobbies: Music; Films. Address: 26 Lovell Road, New Rochelle, NY 10804-2115, USA.

GROEN Elaine Sharon, b. 28 Feb 1944, Artesia, CA, USA. Registered Dietician. m. Glenn Groen, 4 Sep 1965, 1 d. Education: BA, cum laude, Home Economics, CA State University, Long Beach, CA, 1970; Dietetic Internship, Loma Linda University Medical Center, 1971. Career: Consulting Dietician, Capistrano by the Sea Psychiatric Hospital, 1971-72; Clinical Dietician and Assistant Food Service Manager, South Coast Community Hospital, 1972-74; Medical Sales Representative, 1974-75, Nutritional Sales Specialist, 1975-77, Sales Training Associate, Home Office, 1977-79, Regional Consultant Dietician, 1979-80, Mead Johnson Nutritional Division, Bristol-Myers; Consulting Nutritionist in Private Practice, 1980-. Publications include: Co-author, Healthy Cooking on the Run, 1983, 1992; Co-author, Fabulous Fiber Cookery, 1988; Columnist, Nutri-Chat, Rossmoor News, 1983-; Writer for various publications. Honours: Phi Kappa Phi, 1968; Omicron Nu, 1968; Crisco Award for Outstanding Student in Home Economics, 1970. Memberships include: American Dietetic Association; American Society for Female Executives; American Association University Women; National Society Against Health Fraud. Hobbies: Snowskiing; Reading; Gardening; Travel. Address: 33 Quail Court, Ste 201, Walnut Creek, CA 94596-5594, USA.

GRÖNLUND Erna Caresia, b. 19 Jul 1938, Stockholm, Sweden. Dance Therapist. m. Rune Grönlund, 20 Sep 1961, 1 d. Education: MA, Stockholm University, 1974; Professor of Dance Education; Psychotherapist, 1991; DTR, 1990; PhD, Education, Stockholm, 1994. Appointments: Professor and Leader of Department for Dance Education and Dance Therapy, University College of Dance, Stockholm. Publications: Dance Playing for Handicapped Children, 1988; Co-author, Psychosomatic Healing Art, 1991; Dance Therapy - Introduction to an Expressive Therapy, 1991; Co-author, Dance in the World, 1992; Children's Emotions Processed in Dance (Dissertation), 1994. Memberships: American Dance Therapy Association; Dance and The Child International; Founder and Chairman, Swedish Association for Dance Therapy, 1985-90. Hobbies: Walking; Poetry; Music. Address: Byvagen 40, 13334 Saltsjobaden, Sweden.

GROSS Earl G, b. 19 Jul 1943, NY, USA. Physician. m. Elaine Hersey, 1973, 1 s, 1 d. Education: BA, Denison University, 1965; MS, Syracuse University, 1968; MD, Temple University, 1971; Board Certified in Dermatology and Dermatopathology. Career: Medical Director, Kahaluu Medical Clinic, Hawaii; Fellow Dermatopathology, Cleveland Clinic; Medical Specialist, Derm Branch NCI, NIH and Cancer Prevention Branch NCI, NIH, Bethesda, MD; Currently, Associate Professor at UCHC; Chief, Dermatology, VAMC, Newington. Publications: Co-author, Chemoprevention of Basal Cell Carcinoma with Isotretinoin; Changes in plasma cholesterol and triglycerides following treatment with Isotretinoin; Retinoids and The Eye, in Dermatologic Clinics. Memberships: American Academy of Dermatology; Society for Investigating Dermatology; American Society of Dermatopathology; American Society for Clinical Investigation; Dermatology Foundation; New England Dermatologic Society. Address: University of Connecticut Health Center, Division of Dermatology, PO Box 4040, Farmington, CT 06034-4040, USA.

GROSS Myron, b. 9 Apr 1952, Jamestown, USA. University Professor. m. Michelle Gross, 20 Dec 1977. Education: BS, MS, North Dakota University, 1974, 1977; PhD, University of Minnesota, 1985.

Appointments: Research Fellowship, Mayo Clinic, Endocrine Research Unit, 1984-87; Research Associate, Epidemiology, University of Minnesota, 1987-90; Assistant Professor, Epidemiology, University of Minnesota, 1990-. Publications incl: The Formation of Stable Acetaldehyde-Hemoglobin Adducts in Red Blood Cell Model, 1992; Evidence for the formation of multiple types of acetaldehyde-haemoglobin adducts; Immunomodulating actions of carotenoids: Enhancement of in vivo and in vitro antibody production to T-dependent antigens; The highly efficient production of full-length and mutant rat brain calcium-binding proteins in a bacterial expression system. Honours: Sigma Xi; Graduate Student Research Award, American Institute of Nutrition; Alpha Zeta Alimni; National Research Service Award. Memberships: The Protein Society; American Society of Biochemistry & Molecular Biology; New York Academy of Sciences; American Association for Clinical Research; American Association for the Advancement of Science; American Institute of Nutrition; American Society for Clinical Nutrition; Council on Undergraduate Research. Address: Division of Epidemiology, University of Minnesota, 1300 South Second Street, Suite 300, MN 55454-1015, USA.

GROSSBERG George Thomas, b. 20 Aug 1948, Hungary. Geriatric Psychiatrist. m. Darla Jean Brown, 13 June 1976, 3 sons, 2 daughters. Education: BA, Yeshiva University, 1971; MD, St Louis Medical School, 1975. Appointments: Instructor, St Louis University Medical Center, 1978-81; Assistant Professor, St Louis University Medical Center, 1982-86; Associate Professor, 1987-89; Professor, 1990-. Publications: 70 chapters and papers on geriatric psychiatry; Editor, 4 books. Honours: Falk Fellowship, 1977-79; Alzheimer's Association Public Service Award, 1988. Memberships: American Association of Geriatric Psychiatry; American Geriatric Society; American Psychiatry Association, Fellow. Hobbies: Skiing; Antique Collecting. Address: St Louis University Health Sciences Center, Department of Psychiatry & Human Behavior, 1221 South Grand, St Louis, MO 63104, USA.

GROVER Frederick L, b. 27 Oct 1938. Cardiothoracic Surgeon. m. Carol Grover, 2 s. Education: AB, Chemistry, 1960, MD, 1964, Duke University. Career includes: Instructor of Surgery, Professor and Head of Division of Cardiothoracic Surgery, University of CO Health Sciences Center; Assistant Professor, Associate Professor, Professor of Surgery, University of TX Health Sciences Center, San Antonio; Chief, Cardiothoracic Surgery, Audie L Murphy VA Hospital; Chief, Cardiothoracic Surgery, Denver VA Hospital; Currently, Professor of Surgery, Head of Division of Cardiothoracic Surgery, Chief, Surgical Services, University of CO School of Medicine. Publications include: 128 publications in professional journals, 29 book chapters, 22 invited lectures and 21 films in field. Honours include: QIA Advancement for Superior Performance, 1986; VA Chief Medical Director's Commendation Award for Outstanding Achievement as a Member of Cardiac Surgery Special Review Site Visit Team in Conducting Quality Assurance, 1987. Memberships include: American Board of Surgery; American Board of Thoracic Surgery; American Heart Association; International Society for Cardiovascular Surgery; Fellow, American College of Surgeons; American Trauma Society; Fellow, American College of Chest Physicians; Fellow, American College of Cardiology; American Surgical Association; AMA. Hobbies: Fly Fishing; Skiing. Address: University of Colorado School of Medicine, 4200 East 8th Avenue C310, Denver, CO 80262, USA.

GRUNDFAST Kenneth M, b. 12 Mar 1944, Brooklyn, NY, USA. Physician. m. Ruthanne Blatt, 26 May 1974, 2 d. Education: BA, Liberal Arts, Johns Hopkins University, Baltimore, MD, 1965; MD, State University of NY, 1969; Professor of Otolaryngology and Pediatrics, George Washinton University School of Medicine. Appointments include: Clinical Assistant Professor, 1980-88, Clinical Associate Professor, 1988-93, Georgetown University Medical Center; Visiting Investigator, National Institute of Health, 1989-90; Clinical Professor, Georgetown University Medical Center, 1993-; Currently, Co-Chairman, Department of Otolaryngology. Publications include: Ear Infections in Your Child, 1987; Otolaryngology - Head and Neck Surgery in Children - Staying Out of Trouble, 1994; 19 Book Chapters; 64 Peer Reviewed Articles in Professional Journals, 1978-; 84 Invited and Funded Lectures, 1978-93; Numerous Seminars, Scientific Presentations and Non-Funded Invited Lectures, 1977-93. Honours include: Humanitarian Award, AMA, 1973; Honor Award, 1986; Fellow of Intitut Georges Portmann, Bordeaux, France, 1993-. Memberships include: AMA; Alexander Graham Bell Association for The Deaf; Fellow, American Academy of Pediatrics; American Society of Pediatric Otolaryngology; American Bronchoesophagologic Association; Fellow, American College of

Surgeons. Hobbies: Bicycling; History of Medicine. Address: Children's Hospital National Medical Center, Otolaryngology, 111 Michigan NW, Washington DC 20010, USA.

GRUZOVA Mira, b. 3 Aug 1932, Chelijabinsk, Russia. Cytologist. m. Apr 1964, 1 s, 1 d. Education: Diploma, Leningrad State University; PhD; Doctor of Biology. Career: Research Associate, 1955-57; Graduate Student, 1958-61; Junior Scientist, 1961-72; Senior Scientist, 1972-80; Professor, Head of Group, Institute of Cytology, Academy of Science, St Petersburg, Russia, 1980-. Publications: Functional organization of the oocyte nucleus of Chrysopa, in Chromosoma, 1972; The nucleus during oogenesis with special reference to extrachromosomal structures, in Oocyte growth and maturation, 1988; Karyosphere in oocenesis and intranuclear morphozenesis, in International Rev Cytology, 1993. Membership: Anatomy, Gistology and Embryology Society. Address: Institute of Cytology, Academy of Science of Russia, Jikhoretsky Ave 4, 194064 St Petersburg, Russia.

GRYGIERS Tadeusz, b. 10 Feb 1915, Warsaw, Poland. Professor. m. P A Sandiford, 29 Sep 1953, 1 s, 1 d. Education: Diploma, Political Science and Economics, Cracow, 1935; LLM, Warsaw, 1936; PhD, London, 1950. Appointments: Junior Barrister, Warsaw, 1936-39; Clinical Psychologist, Choroszcz, 1939-40; Acting Psychiatrist, Siktivkar, 1940-41; Clinical Psychologist, Banstead, 1953-60; Professor, 1960-; Currently, Professor Emeritus, University of Ottawa; Professor of Jurisprudence, Polish University Abroad, London, England. Publications: Oppression: A study in social and criminal psychology, 1954; The Dynamic Personality Inventory, 1962; Criminology in Transition, 1965; Questionnaire de Préférence, 1971; Zbior Zasad Obrony Soleczhej, 1976; The Dynamic Approach to Personality Assessment, 1976; Social Protection Code; a new model of criminal justice, 1977. Honours: Pinsent-Darwin Studentship, 1947, 1948; Rockefeller Fellowship, 1947, 1948, 1952-3. Hobby: Yachting. Address: Dept of Criminology, Faculty of Social Sciences, Univ of Ottawa, Ottawa, Ontario, Canada, K1N 6N5.

GRZEGORZEWSKA Alicja Ewa, b. 18 Nov 1949, Poznan, Poland. Nephrologist. m. Wlodzimierz Grzegorzewski, 2 Apr 1972, 1 son, 1 daughter. Education: MD, 1973; Specialist in Internal Medicine II and Nephrology; PhD, 1981; Habilitation, 1989. Appointments: Department of Nephrology, University of Medical Sciences, Poznan, 1973-, currently Assistant Professor. Publications: Contributions to Advances in Peritoneal Dialysis, 1981, 1988, 1990, 1992-94; Artifical Organs, 1982; Peritoneal Dialysis Bulletin, 1983, 1986, International Urology and Nephrology, 1989; Peritoneal Dialysis International, 1989, 1990, 1994; Kidney International, 1991; ASAIO Journal, 1992, 1993; Polish scientific journals. Honours: Scientific Award, Ministry of Health and Social Care, 1992. Memberships: International Society for Peritoneal Dialysis; European Dialysis and Transplant Association; President, Regional Association, Polish Society of Nephrology. Hobbies: Literature; Gardening. Address: Department of Nephrology, Al Przybyszewskiego 49, 60-355 Poznan, Poland.

GU Baisheng, b. 8 Dec 1940, Shanghai, China. Professor of Urology. m. Shen Jinghua, 8 Mar 1968, 2 sons. Appointments: Paediatrics Surgery, Urology Department, Shanghai Rai-Jin Hospital, 1965-84; Vice Professor, Guangzhou Medical College, Ji Nan University; MD Consultant, The Hong Kong (China) Traumatology and Osteopathic Association Limited; Chief Doctor, Urology Department, Shenzhen People's Hospital, 1984-. Publications: Surgical Treatment for Primary Aldosteronism, 1982; ERFH Treatment for Disease of Prostate, 1992. Membership: Chinese Medical Learned Society. Hobbies: Stamp Collecting; Music. Address: 602 East 11 Building No 3, North Dongmen Road, Shenzhen 518020, China.

GU Kai-Shih, b. 13 Jan 1913, Shanghai, China. Cardio-thoracic Surgeon. m. Y C Cheng MD, 5 Nov 1941, 1 s, 1 d. Education: Docotr of Medicine, National Medical College of Shanghai, 1938. Appointments: Resident Surgeon, Teaching Hospital, National Medical College, Shanghai, 1938-40; Visiting Surgeon, Teaching Hospital, National Medical College, Shanghai, 1940-42; Chief Surgeon, Shanghai Nan-Yang Hospital, 1942-47; Fellow, Mayo Clinic Medical Center, USA, 1947-48; Fellow, of MGH, School of Medicine, Harvard University, USA, 1948-49; Superintendent, Shanghai Nan-Yang Hospital, 1949-56; Chairman of Professor for Postgraduate Class of Thoraco-Cardiac Surgeons, 1957-66; Founder of Shanghai Chest Hospital, 1956-57; Director/Chief Surgeon, Shanghai Chest Hospital, 1957-; Vice President/Professor of Thoracic Surgery, Shanghai Railway College, 1980-83; Honorable President, Shanghai Railway College, 1983-;

Honorable Professor, Chun-Cheng Medical University, 1984-. Publications: Therapy of Pulmonary Tuberculosis of Lung, 1955; Clinical Cardiovascular Surgery, 1965; Operative Surgery of Thoraco-Cardio-Vascular Diseases, 1982, 1991. Honours: Received Award for Prominent Achievement, Shanghai Municipal Committee, 1955, 1956, 1957; Received Medal Award during World Conference on Open Heart Surgery in India, 1985. Memberships: Chinese Medical Association of Shanghai; Society of Surgery; Society of Thoracic Surgery, Shanghai; Society of Thoracic Surgery, USA. Address: 45/10 Tai Yuan Road, Shanghai 200031, China.

GUAN Cuong Wen, b. 20 Sep 1930, Heilongjiang Province, China. Doctor. m. Huang Miao Juan, 1 Sept 1956, 2 d. Education: Graduate from China University of Medicine. Appointments: Physician and Physician-in-Charge in ShenYan, Guangzhou and Changcheun, 1952;Vice Chief Physician, Shanghai, 1986-; Currently, Director, Laser-Safety Research Group, Shanghai Institute of Optics and Fine Mechanics Academia Sinica. Publications: Laser Safety in China, in Chinese Journal, 1980; Study on the protection of eyes against, in Chinese Journal, 1985; Laser Safety in China, in Laser Therapy, 1991; Book in progress. Honour: Wise Elder, Shanghai 1993. Memberships: National Institute of Electromedical Information Inc, USA, 1987-; Society of Labour Protection Science and Technology of China; Optical Society of China, Shanghai Branch; China Medical Society; Shanghai Laser Society. Hobby: Swimming. Address: Shanghai Institute of Optics of Fine Mechanics Academia Sinica, PO Box 800-211, Shanghai, 201800, China.

GUAN Weiyi, b. 15 Apr 1937, Ashan, Liaoning, China. Chief Physician. m. Jingzhen Guan, 10 Aug 1962, 2 sons, 1 daughter. Education: BM, Dalian Medical College, 1963; Further Study, No 3 Army Medical University, 1963-73. Appointments: Physician in Medical Department, 1978; Vice Head of the Medical Department, 1991; Head of the Medical Department, 1991; Professor, Medical Department for Digestive System. Publications: The Clinical Type of Orginal Liver Cancer, 1988; Irritable Bowel Syndrome of Old Men, 1991; Sclerotherapy for Haemorrhage Digestive Tract Ulcer, 1993; Emergency Treatment for High Concentration Glacial Acetic Acid Poisioning, 1993. Honours: Advanced Medical Worker, 1992, 1993. Memberships: China Medical Association, Liaoyang Branch; Specialized Group of Digestive Medical Department of Shenyang Military Command. Hobbies: Running; Football. Address: No 146 Weiguo Road, Liaoyang City, Liaoning Providence, China.

GUAN Xiao Hong, b. 23 Sept 1946, Jiangsu, China. Teacher. 1 daughter. Education: MD, Peijing Union Medical Schoo, 1970; PhD, Nanjing Medical University, 1985. Career: Ophthalmologist, 1970-78; Graduate for PHD, 1978-85; Lecturer, 1985-87; Associate Professor, 1987-94; Professor of Parasitology Department, Nanjing Medical University, currently. Publications: An Immunoregulatory Human Monoclonal Antibody in Schistosomiasis Japonica Hum Antiobod Hybridomas, 1991; The Establishment and Characterization of the Anti-Idiotypic Monoclonal Antibody, 1991. Hobbies: Pets; Reading; Shopping. Address: 45 Mei Yuan Xin Cun, Nanjing, Jiangsu 210018, China.

GUAN Yi Jun, b. 1 Apr 1936, Qingdao, Shandong, China. Doctor. m. Liu Shulian, 1 Dec 1962, 3 d. Education: BA, Shandong Medical University, 1961. Appointment: Professor. Publications: Study on the relationship between the glomerulonephritis diseases and the learning ability, in National Medical Journal of China, 1991; Effect of cordyceps sinesis on T-lymphocyte subsets in chronic renal failure, in Chinese Journal of Integrated Traditional and Western Medicine, 1992. Honours: 2nd Award, Science and Technology Achievement, Shandong, 1992; Honoured, The Super Person in Science and Technology Achievement of Shandong Province. Memberships: Chronic Renal Failure and Chronic Glomerulonephritis Association. Hobby: Inventor of kind of Traditional Chinese Medicine to deal with chronic renal failure and chronic glomerulonephritis. Address: 115 Culture Western Road, Jinan, China.

GUAN Zhi-ping, b. 14 Sept 1937, Hong Kong. Professor of Paediatrics. m. 22 July 1965, 1 son. Education: Zhongshan Medical College, China, 1960; Visiting Scholar, University of Cincinnati Medical Centre, USA, 1981-83; Research Scholar, Children's Hospital, Medical Centre, USA, 1983. Appointments: Paediatrician; Assistant Professor, Associate Professor; Professor of Paediatrics. Publications: Clinical Neonatalogy, Co-author, 1988; Growth Failure and Decreased Bone

Mineral of Newborn Rats with Chronic Furosemide Therapy, Co-author, 1986; Rickets with Large Dose of Vitamin D Therapy: Effects On 25-OHD, Ca Mg and P Concentrations, 1990; Prevention of Rickets, 1994. Honours: Medical Achievement, 3rd Class, 1992, 1994; Research Achievement, 2nd Class, 1986, 1st Class, 1991. 3rd Class, 1994. Memberships: Chinese Medical Association; Guangdong State Paediatric Association. Hobby: Music. Address: Department of Paediatrics, First Affiliated Hospital, Sun Yat-Sen University of Medical Sciences, Guangzhou, China.

GUDEMAN Steven Kent, b. 5 Mar 1950, Watseka, IL, USA. Neurosurgeon. m. Cynthia White, 1 s, 2 d. Education: AB, 1972; MD, 1976. Appointments: Professor and Chief, Division of Neurosurgery, 1991-, Van L Weatherspoon Jr Distinguished Professor of Neurosurgery, 1991-, Acting Director, Neurosurgical Residency Program, Division of Neurosurgery, 1991-, Medical Director, Department of Physical Medicine and Rehabilitation, 1993-, University of NC, Chapel Hill; Attending Physician, University of NC Hospitals, Chapel Hill, 1991-. Publications: Numerous publications, abstracts, books and chapters including: Co-author, Proton MR spectroscopic characteristics of a presumed giant subcortical heterotopia, in AJNR, 1993. Honours: Alpha Omega Alpha; Vice President, Alpha Epsilon Delta; Continuing Medical Education Award, American Association of Neurological Surgeons and Congress of Neurological Surgeons; Blue Key Treasurer, AMA; Distinguished Alumni Scholarship; Herman B Wells Award; Hoosier Scholarship; Indiana Memorial Union Service Award. Memberships include: Fellow, American College of Surgeons; American Association of Neurological Surgeons; AMA; Nathan A Womack Surgical Society; North American Skull Base Society; Pediatric Oncology Group; Society of Critical Care Medicine. Address: University of North Carolina, 148 Burnett-Womack, CB 7060, Chapel Hill, NC 27599-7060, USA.

GUDJONSSON Birgir, b. 8 Nov 1938, Akureyri, Iceland. Consultant. m. Heidur A Vigfusdottir, 7 Oct 1961, 1 s, 2 d. Education: Graduate, Linguistic Department, Reykjavik Gymnasium, 1958; MD, University of Iceland, 1965; FACP; FRCP. Appointments include: Assistant Professor of Medicine, Yale University School of Medicine, New Haven, CT, 1972-73, 1977-78, 1982; Consultant, Attending City Hospital Reykjavik, 1974-77; Currently, Consultant Attending Medical Clinic Reykjavik; Private Practice, Internal Medicine and Gastroenterology, 1974-. Publications: 16 Articles published in professional journals, 1975-90, including: Cancer of the pancreas: 50 years of surgery, in Cancer, 1987; Cancer of the Pancreas: Need for standardisation of therapeutic results (abstract), Proceedings of the World Congress of Gastroenterology, Australia, 1990. Memberships: Fellow, American College of Physicians; American Gastroenterological Association; American Society for Gastrointestinal Endoscopy; Fellow, Royal College of Physicians; British Society of Gastroenterology; Royal Society of Medicine; NY Academy of Sciences; British Association of Sport and Medicine; World Association of Hepato-Pancreato-Biliary Surgery; American College of Sports Medicine; International Association of Pancreatology. Hobbies: Judge in athletics and gymnastics. Address: The Medical Clinic, Alfheimum 74, 104 Reykjavik, Iceland.

GUENTHER Donna Marie, b. 20 Oct 1938, Meadville, Pennsylvania, USA. Physician. 1 son. Education: BS, Allegheny College, 1960; MD, temple University School of Medicine, 1967; Certified, American Board of Paediatrics; Certified, American Board of Allergy and Immunology. Appointments include:Chief, Allergy and Immunology, Children's Hospital Medical Centre, Oakland, California, 1973-85; Assistant Clinical Professor of Paediatrics, University of California, San Diego, 1976-86; Assistant Clinical Professor of Paediatrics, 1977-86, Associate Clinical Professor of Paediatrics, 1986-92, University of California, San Francisco; Medical Consultant, Institute for Shipboard Education, University of Pittsburgh, 1987; Career Physician, Participant Physician, South San Francisco, 1985-88, Participant Physician, Senior Physician, 1988-90, Martinez and Antioch, Senior Physician, Antioch, 1990-, Chief of Allergy, Antioch, 1993-, Kaiser Permanente Medical Group. Publications include: Prevention of Delayed Foreign Marrow Reaction in Lethally Irradiated Mice by Early Administration of Methotrexate, CO-author, 1962; Objective Evaluation of the Status of Patients with Chronic Asthma, Co-author, 1972; Peripheral Blood Eosinophils in Graft Versus Host Disease in Rodents, Co-author; An Epistemology of Healing, 1989. Honours include: Kappa Kappa Gamma; Phi Beta Phi; Kappa Kappa Gamma. Memberships include: Fellow, American Academy of Paediatrics, Section on Allergy; Fellow, American Academy of Allergy and Immunology; Fellow, American College of Allergy and Immunology; Allergy Association of Northern California. Address: Kaiser

Permanente Medical Group, 3400 Delta Fair Boulevard, Antioch, CA 94509, USA.

GUERNINA Zoubida, b. Algeria. Chartered Psychologist. Education: BSc, hons; Master Degree; PhD. Appointments: Psychologist, Ethnic Micoutres; Lecturer in Psychology; Consultant in Transcultural Issues; Therapist in Multi Cultural Meetings. Publications: Human Development Avebury Counseling Immigrants; Transcultural Approaches; Counseling Psychology Quarterly; Percepters of Other Cultures. Memberships: Brithis Psychological Society; British Association of Counselling; Psychotherapy Section (BPS) Health Psychology (BPS). Hobbies: Community Work; Languages. Address: University of Humberside, Pyschology Department, Fuglenive Avenue. Hull HU5 7LV, England.

GUGGENHEIM Frederick Gibson, b. 7 July 1935, Chicago, Illinois, USA. Psychiatrist. m. Olivia Rogers, 24 Apr 1984, 2 children. Education: BA, cum laude, Yale College; MD, Columbia University College of Physicians & Surgeons. Appointments: Instructor, Assistant Professor, Harvard Medical School, 1969-79; Associate Professor, University of Texas, Southwestern Medical School, Dallas, 1979-85; Marie Wilson Howells Professor and Chairman, Department of Psychiatry, University of Arkansas for Medical Sciences, 1985-. Publications: Major Psychiatric Disorders, 1982; Manual of Psychiatric Consultants in Emergency Care, 1984; Psychological Aspects of Surgery, 1985; Chapter on Somatoform Disorders in Kaplean and Saddock, Comprehensive Textbook of Psychiatry, Edition VI, 1995. Honours: Exemplary Psychiatrist, National Alliance for the Mentally Ill, 1993. Memberships: American Psychiatric Association; American College of Psychiatrists; Association for Academic Psychiatry. Hobbies: Fine Art; Photography. Address: University of Arkansas for Medical Sciences, 4301 West Markham Street, Slot 554, Little Rock, AR 72205, USA.

GUIDOTTI Tee Lamont, b. 14 May 1949, Glendale, California, USA. Physician. Education: BS, Biological Sciences, University of Southern California, 1971; MD, University of California, San Diego, 1975; MPH, Johns Hopkins University, 1981; Fellow, Royal College of Physicians and Surgeons of Canada; Certificant, Canadian Board of Occupational Medicine. Appointments: Professor, Head, Division of Occupational and Environmental Health, San Diego State University, San Diego, California, 1980-84; Adjunct Associate Professor, University of California at San Diego School of Medicine, 1982-84; Professor of Occupational Medicine, Department of Health Sciences, University of Alberta, Edmonton, Canada, 1984-; Acting Chairman, Department of Public Health Sciences, University of Alberta Faculty of Medicine, Edmonton, 1993-94. Publications: Numerous in occupational and environmental medicine, recently including: Mortality of urban firefighters in Alberta, 1927-1987, 1993; Lung cancer among tin miners in southeast China: Silica exposure, silicosis, and cigarette smoking (co-author), 1994; Field performance of dermal patches in pesticide exposure determination (co-author), 1994; Trends in mortality from COPD in Alberta: back to the future?, 1995. Honours: Fellow: American College of Physicians, 1982; Royal Society of Medicine, 1982; American College of Occupational and Environmental Medicine, 1982; American College of Chest Physicians, 1986; H Siemens Memorial Award, Alberta Occupational Health Society, 1989. Memberships include: American Association for the Advancement of Science; Board of Directors, Canadian Occupational Health Association; Sigma Xi; Past President, Alberta Occupational Health Society; Alberta Medical Association. Address: 1 Tweedsmuir Crescent, Edmonton, Alberta, Canada T6G 2G3.

GUIERRE Alain, b. 4 Feb 1965, France. Osteopath. m. Claudia Sauer, 14 Aug 1993. Education: Diploma of Osteopathy. Memberships: The General Council & register of Osteopaths. Hobbies: Rowing; Skiing. Address: L'Eldorado, 9 Boulevard Moneghetti, Beausoleil, Monte Carlo 06240, France.

GUILL Margaret Frank, b. 18 Jan 1948, Atlanta, Georgia, USA. Physician. m. Marshall A Guill, 6 Jul 1974, 1 s, 1 d. Education: BA, Agnes Scott College, 1969; MD, Medical College of Georgia, 1972. Appointments: Assistant Professor of Pediatrics, Medical College of Georgia, School of Medicine, 1981-86; Tenure & Associate Professor of Pediatrics, 1986-93; Professor of Pediatrics, 1993-; Assistant Professor of Internal Medicine, 1981-88; Associate Professor of Internal Medicine, 1988-; Cystic Fibrosis Center, Medical College of Georgia: Assistant Director, 1982-87; Interim Director, 1988-90; Director, 1990-; Associate Director, Allergy-Immunology Training Program, 1990-92; Chief, Pediatric Pulmonology, 1992-; Director, MCG Asthma Center, 1990-; Consultant, Department of Medicine, Eisenhower Army Medical Center;

Consultant, Department of Medicine, VA Medical Center, Augusta, GA; Consultant, Walton Rehabilitation Hospital, Augusta, GA. Publications: include, Emergency Treatment of Insect Sting Reactions - Should Adrenaline be Available in Schools & Camps? 1981; Evaluation of Primary Immune Deficiency Disorders, 1984; Investigating an Immunodeficieny Disease, 1991; Junctional Epidermolysis Bullosa - Treatment with Phenytoin, 1983. Honours: Alpha Omega Alpha, 1972; Mosby Book Award, 1973; Hal Davison Award, Southeast Allergy Association, 1985; Distinguished Faculty - Patient Care, Medical College of Georgia, 1990. Memberships include: American Academy of Pediatrics; American College of Chest Physicians; American Academy of Allergy & Immunology; American College of Allergy & Immunology. Hobbies: Homemaking; Outdoor Sports. Address: BG 240 Medical College of Georgia, Augusta, GA 30912, USA.

GUINAN John Joseph, b. 12 Mar 1941, Philadelphia, PA, USA. Scientist. m. Ellen Harrison, DDS, 6 Jan 1979, 5 d. Education: BS, Electronic Engineering, MIT, 1963; MS, Electronic Engineering, MIT, 1964; PhD, Communications Biophysics, MIT, 1968. Appointments include: Principal Research Scientist, Department of Electrical Engineering and Computer Science, and Research Laboratory of Electronics, MA Institute of Technology, 1985-; Lecturer, Harvard University, MA Institute of Technology, 1992-; Associate Director, Eaton-Peabody Laboratory, MA Eye and Ear Infirmary, 1992-; Associate Professor, Department of Otology and Laryngology, Harvard Medical School, 1993-. Publications: 22 Original reports, 1967-, including: Co-author, Acoustic-reflex frequency selectivity in single stapedius motoneurons of the cat, in Journal Neurophysiology, 1992; Motoneuron axon distribution in the stapedius muscle of the cat: An intracellular labeling study, submitted; Several procedures of meetings, reviews and abstracts. Honour: Eta Kappa Nu. Memberships: Institute of Electronic and Electrical Engineers; American Association for The Advancement of Science; Acoustical Society of America; Society for Neuroscience; Association for Research in Otolaryngology; American Speech-Language-Hearing Association. Hobbies: Tennis; Classical Guitar. Address: 68 Chester Street, Newton, MA 02161, USA.

GULASEKARAM Bala, b. 10 Mar 1946, Sri Lanka. Psychiatrist. m. 7 Dec 1972, 1 son, 1 daughter. Education includes: Board Certified in Psychiatry, American Board of Psychiatry and Neurology. Appointments: Currently Senior Psychiatrist, Metropolitan State Hospital, Norwalk, California, USA. Memberships: American Medical Association; American Psychiatric Association. Hobby: Tennis. Address: 16510 Bloomfield Avenue, Cerritos, CA 90703, USA.

GULAY Huseyin, b. 18 Feb 1954, Rize, Turkey. General Surgeon. m. Zeynep Gulay, 5 Apr 1983, 2 daughters. Education: MD, Hacettepe University, Ankara, 1978; General Surgeon, Hacettepe University Hospital, 1983; Associate Professor of Surgery, 1988; Professor of Surgery, 1994. Appointments: General Surgeon, Gölcük Navy Hospital, 1983-84; General Surgeon, Giresun State Hospital, 1984-86; Transplant Co-ordinator & Surgeon, Turkish Transplantation & Burn Foundation Hospital, Ankara, 1986-91; Faculty Member, Dokuz Eylül University, School of Medicine, Izmir, 1992. Publications: Co-author: Cadaver Kidney Transplantation with Prolonged Cold Ischemia Time, 1988; Urological Complications in 350 Consecutive Renal Transplants, 1990; Bilateral Brest Carcinoma: 28 years Experience, 1990; Living Related Kidney Transplantation in 349 Concecutive Recipients, 1991; Management of Nipple Discharge, 1994. Memberships: Turkish Transplantation Society; Middle East Society for Organ Transplantation; International Society of Surgery. Hobbies: Hunting; Travel; Pingpong. Address: 101 Sokak 15/10, 35290 Göztepe, Izmir, Turkey.

GUMERMAN Mary L Van Horn, b. 24 Mar 1943, Milwaukee, WI, USA. Health Information Manager. m. Douglas Gumerman, 24 Aug 1968, 3 d. Education: McGill University, Harvard University; BS, RRA, St Louis University, 1976; MPH, Tulane University, 1993. Appointment: Health Information Manager, Epidemiology and Biostatistics of International Health. Memberships: American Health Information Management Association; Society for Epidemiological Research; International Society of Travel Medicine. Hobbies: Gardening; Investing; Travel; Volunteering. Address: 435 South Old Orchard, Webster Groves, MO 63119, USA.

GUMP Dieter Walter, b. 28 Mar 1933, New York, USA. Physician. m. Valerie P Waite, 22 Jan 1983, 2 sons 1 daughter. Education: BA, Smithmore College, 1955; MD, Johns Hopkins University School of Medicine, 1960. Appointments: Assistant Professor, 1966; Associate

Professor, 1977; Professor of Medicine & Microbiology & Molecular Genetics, 1980. Publications: Co-author: Legionnaires Disease in Patients with Associated Serious Disease, 1979; Co-author: Evidence of Prior Pelvic Inflammatory Disease and its relationship to C Trachomatis antibody and intrauterine contraceptive device used in infertile women. Memberships: Fellow, American College of Physicians. Hobbies: Cross Country Skiing; Hiking; Bicycling; Bird Watching. Address: University of Vermont, Infectious Disease Unit, Given C-247, Burlington, VT 05405-0068, USA.

GUNARATNE Austin Ananda Herat, b. 24 July 1927, Sri Lanka. Obstetrician and Gynaecologist. m. Sita Chrystle Sandaratne, 17 Dec 1958, 1 daughter. Education: MBBS, Ceylon; D Obst RCOG, Great Briatin; FRCOG(England) FCOG(Sri Lanka). Appointments: Registrar in Obstetrics and Gynaecology. Women's Hospital, Liverpool, England, North London Hospital, Forest Gate Hospital, London, Lewisham Hospital, London, St Stephens Hospital, London, Ealing Hospital, London; Consultant Obstetrician and Gynaecologist, Ministry of Health, Sri Lanka, 1970-87. Publications: Lippes Loop in Peritoneal Cavity, 1974; Case of gangrene Following Partus, 1974; Choriocarcinoma with Metastasis in the Spine, 1975. Honours: Fellowship, Royal College of Obstetricians and Gynaecologists, Great Britain, 1983; Fellowship, Sri Lanka College, 1989. Memberships: Life Member, Council Member, Sri Lanka College Obstetricians and Gynaecologists; Council Member, Ceylon Medical Association, 1973-77. Hobbies: Tennis; Television; Reading journals. Address: 72 Kuruppu Road, Colombo 8, Sri Lanka.

GUNARATNE Mahasara, b. 7 Sept 1934, Galle, Sri Lanka. Doctor; Professor. m. Chulanie Silva, 18 Jan 1968, 2 d. Education: MBBS, Ceylon; MS, Ceylon; FRCOG, England; Senior Professor, University of Peradeniya, Sri Lanka. Appointments: Senior Professor. Publications: Childlessness - The Laymans Guide; Five Dons; Mechanics of Translocation of the IUCD, 1973. Honours: Vice President, Sri Lanka College of Obstetrics & Gynaecology, 1994-. Memberships: Sri Lanka College of Obstetrics & Gynaecology; Sri Lanka Medical Association; Royal College of Obstetrics & Gynaecology, England. Hobbies: Music; Art. Address: Rambert, 33/2A Riverdale Road, Aniewatte, Kandy, Sri Lanka.

GUNASEKARA Mahendrapala Dias Abeywickrama, b. 3 Nov 1940, Sri Lanka. Medical Officer. m. Mangalika Gunasekara, 29 Nov 1973, 1 s, 1 d. Education: MS, Sri Lanka; MBBS, Sri Lanka; MRCOG, United Kingdom. Appointments: Resident Obstetrician and Gynaecologist; Currently, Consultant Obstetrician and Gynaecologist. Address: 1B Edward Place, Sunandarama Road, Kalubowila, Dehiwala, Sri Lanka.

GUNDERSON Carl Harmon, b. 6 Nov 1933, South Bend, IN, USA. Neurologist. m. Anne Bruner, 6 Sep 1957, 1 s, 2 d. Education: BS, University of Notre Dame, South Bend, IN, 1954; MD, MS, University of Chicago, IL, 1958. Appointments: Resident and Fellow in Neurology, Yale, New Haven Medical Center, 1959-62; Chair, Neurology Service, Womack Army Hospital, Fort Bragg, NC, 1962-64; Chair, Psychiatry and Neurology Branch, Medical Field Service School, Fort Sam Houston, TX, 1964-67; Assistant Chair, Neurology Service, LAMC, 1967-70; Chair, Neurology Service, BAMC, 1970-80; Chair, Neurology Service, WRAMC, 1980-; Chair, Department of Neurology, USUHS, 1983-. Publication: Quick Reference to Clinical Neurology, 1982; Essentials of Clinical Neurology, 1989. Memberships: Fellow, American Academy of Neurology; American Medical Association; American Neurological Association; Association of Military Surgeons. Address: Neurology Uniformed Service, Univ of Health Science, FEH School of Medicine, 4301 Jones Bridge Road, Bethesda, MD 20814-4799, USA.

GUNDERSON John G, b. 20 Jun 1942, Two Rivers, WI, USA. Psychiatrist. m. Susan Gunderson, 25 Jul 1965, 1 s, 1 d. Education: MD; Dartmouth Medical School; Harvard Medical School; American Psychoanalytic Association, Boston. Appointments: Assistant Director, Center for Studies of Schizophrenia, NIMH; Director, Psychotherapy; Director of Psychosocial Research, McLean Hospital; Currently, Associate Professor in Psychiatry, Harvard Medical School. Publications: Borderline Personality Disorder; Psychotherapy of Schizophrenia; Principles and Practice of Milieu Therapy. Memberships: International Society Study of Personality Disorders; American Psychiatric Association; American Psychoanalytic Association; Psychotherapy Research Society. Hobbies: Fly Fishing; Painting; Basketball; Tennis. Address: McLean Hospital, Belmont, MA 02178, USA.

GÜNERLI Ali, b. 13 Jan 1946, Izmir, Turkey. Associate Professor, Anesthesiology. m. Rukiye Günerli, 10 Feb 1972, 1 son, 1 daughter. Appointments: National Service, Health Directorate Ministry of Defense, 1970-72; Physician, Health Service, Turkey, 1972-76; Resident of Anesthesiology, Dean, St Elisabeth Hospital, Julich & Medical Faculty Chair of Anesthesiology, 1977-83; Senior Resident, 1985-87; Assistant Professor, 1987-89; Associate Professor, Anesthesiology, Dokuz Eylul Medical University Faculty, 1989-. Publications: Co-author, Oxygen Theropy and Inhalation Therapy, 1992; Co-author, Nutrution in Patients with Hepatic Insufficiency, 1993. Memberships: Turkish Anesthesiology Society; European Society of Intensive Care Medicine; ESPEN. Hobbies: Music; Football; Reading. Address: 1783 Sok No 25/7 Lavent Apt, 35540 Karsiyaka, Izmir, Turkey.

GUNN Albert Edward Jr, b. 31 Oct 1933, Port Washington, NY, USA. Physician. 3 s, 3 d. Education: BSc, Fordham College; LLB, Fordham Law School; MBBCh, BAO, National University of Ieland; LRCP(Lon); MRSC(Eng). Career: Assistant Director, Governmental Relations, American Medical Association; Medical Director, Geriatric Services, Suffolk County, NY Health Services; Departmental Chairman, Board of Regents, National Library of Medicine, NIH, 1986-87; Currently, Associate Dean for Admissions, University of TX, Medical School, Houston. Publications: Editor and Contributor, Cancer Rehabilitation, 1984; AIDS in Africa, 1988. Memberships: President, 1990, Houston Academy of Medicine; Society or Surgical Oncology; Fellow, American College of Physicians. Hobbies: Reading; Travel. Address: University of Texas Medical School, 6431 Fannin Street G024, Houston, TX 77030, USA.

GUO Cheng Jie, b. 3 Dec 1920, Fuping County, Shaanxi Province, China. Doctor. m. Wang Ju, 6 Oct 1937, 1 son, 1 daughter. Education: Bachelor of Medicine. Career: Head of Clinic and Teaching Section, Shaanxi College of Traditional Chinese Medicine; Head of Meridian Research Section of Shaanxi College of Traditional Chinese Medicine; Dean of Acupuncture Department, Shaanxi College of Traditional Chinese Medicine. Publications: Chief Editor, Selection of Acupuncture Literature; Selection of Acupuncture Classics; Author, Mammary Hyperplasia Treated by Acupuncture; Co-author, Summary of Contemporary Meridian Research in China. Honours: Summary of Contemporary Meridian Research of China, won Second Reward of Shaanxi Government, 1979; Clinic Efficacy and Mechanism of Hyperplasia Treated by Acupuncture, won Second Reward of Traditional Chinese Medical Bureau, 1987. Memberships: Standing Member, Acupuncture Association of China; Vice Chairman, Acupuncture Association of Shaanxi; Vice Director, Shaanxi Traditional Chinese Medical Journal. Hobby: Writing. Address: Shaanxi College of Traditional Chinese Medicine, Xianyang, Shaanxi, China.

GUO De-Wen, b. 18 Sept 1926, Shanghai, China. Physician; Professor of Radiology. m. Chen Ying-Zhen, 30 Nov 1949, 2 sons, 1 daughter. Education: BS, St John's University, 1947; MD, St John's University Medical School, 1950. Appointments: Resident, Visiting Doctor, Department of Radiology, St Elizabeth Hospital, Shanghai, 1950-59; Chief, 1959-88, Chairman, 1988-, Department of Radiology, Shanghai Chest Hospital; Professor of Radiology, Shanghai 2nd Medical University, 1988-. Publications: Splenoportography, 1954; Double-outlet Right Ventricle, 1984; Clinical Investigation on Coronary Arteriography, 1985; Aneurysm of Sinus of Valsalva, 1987; Aortico-left Ventricular Tunnel, 1989. Honours: Fellow, American College of Chest Physicians, 1982-; Fellow, International College of Angiology, 1987-. Memberships: Committee Member, Shanghai Branch, Radiologic Society, Chinese Medical Association; Member, American College of Chest Physicians; Member, International College of Angiology. Hobbies: Amateur radio; Music. Address: 9-101, Lane 3671, Zhong Shan Road (North), Shanghai 200062, China.

GUO Feng, b. 8 Sept 1939, Yellow Mountain, Anhwei, China. Professor of Immunology. m. Wei-xiou Wu, 26 Feb 1968, 1 son, 1 daughter. Education: BA, Shanghai Medical University, 1965; MSc, Institute of Microbiology and Epidemiology, Academy of Military Medical Sciences, Beijing, 1968. Appointments: Researcher in Virology, Institute of Microbiology and Epidemiology, Academy of Military Medical Sciences, Beijing, 1968-74; Physician, Associate Professor, Professor, Changhai Hospital, Shanghai, 1975-94. Publications: Co-author: Preliminary study on the immune function of human red cells, 1982; Enhancement of Therapeutic Effect and Red Cell Immune Function by Radix Trichosanthis in Mice Bearing Ehrlich Ascites Carcinoma, 1989; Detection of erythrocyte immune function and CIC in myasthenia gravis,

1990; Advance of Red Cell Immunology Research, book, 1993. Honours: Second Award of Military Science and Technology Progress, for clinical red cell immune function research, 1991. Memberships: Shanghai Society for Immunology; Chinese Society for Immunology. Hobby: Travel. Address: Laboratory of Immunology, Changhai Hospital, 2nd Military Medical University, Shanghai 200433, China.

GUO Jie, b. 18 Mar 1932, Shandong, China. Surgeon. m. Ai Mei Duan, 21 May 1955, 2 s, 2 d. Education: BSc; BM; MD. Appointments: Vice Chairman, now Chairman, Standing Committee of Thoraco-Cardio-Vascular Surgery, Tsingtao. Publication: Bronchoplasty and pulmonary arterioplasty with lobectomy in the treatment of central type lung carcinoma, in Chinese Journal of Surgery, 1991 and Medline, USA, 1992. Honour: Well Known-Famous Surgeon of 1st Session, Tsingtao, 1988. Memberships: Chinese Medical Association; Chinese Surgical Association; Chinese Cancer Control Association. Hobbies: Basketball; Tennis. Address: 1 Jiao Zhon Rd, Tsingtao 266011, China.

GUO Jisheng, b. 6 Nov 1939, Shijiazhuang, Hebei, China. Doctor of Traditional Chinese Medicine. m. Lang Xiuwen, 1 Jan 1962, 1 daughter. Education: Graduate, Academy of Traditional Chinese Medicine. Appointments: Doctor, Shijiazhuang Infectious Disease Hospital; Head, Shijiazhuang Medical Institute; Vice Dean, Hua Fu Hospital. Publications: The Academic Thoughts Research of Hebei's Famous Doctors Through The Ages, 1991; A Report on Treatment of 1412 Cases of Juvenile Myopic Eyes Using Acupuncture and Electromagnet Wave Irrodiation on Local Points, 1990. Honours: Excellent Intellectual of Hebei Province, 1989; 2nd Prize of Gold Cup, First World's Traditional Medical Science Conference, 1994. Memberships: Hebei Cerebrorascular Disease Research and Connection Center; Hebei Cardiovascular Cerebrorascular and Pheumvascular Diseases Preventive and Treated Office. Hobbies: Music. Address: Shijiazhuang Medical Science Research Institute, 77 Gongnong Road, Hebei 050051, China.

GUO Shao-Lun, b. 18 Oct 1917, Liaoning, China. Medical Doctor. m. Xiu Qin Ji, 1 May 1944, 2 sons, 1 daughter. Education: BA, 1941, MD, 1945, Manchuria Medical University; Studied Digital Imaging, Wisconsin Medical College, USA, 1985. Appointments: Assistant, Manchuria Medical University; Lecturer, Shenyang Medical College; Associate Professor, China Medical University; Professor, Beijing, Beijing Railway Medical College; Chief Physician, Beijing Railway General Hospital; Now retired. Publications include: Award-winning articles: CT study of mediastinal mass, 1990; CT diagnosis of sellar and parasellar diseases, 1992; Co-author: Radiological study on 35 cases of benign gastric tumors, 1979; Evaluation of diagnostic capability of counter table for solitary round shadow in the lung fields, 1984; Evaluation of hepatocholecystopathy by MRI, 1990; Investigation on the diagnosis of some rare splenic diseases, 1992; MRI manifestations of abnormal lumbar intervertebral disk, 1993; CT and MR diagnosis of intracranial vascular malformations, 1994; Comparative study between clinical and imaging manifestations in brain stem disease, 1994. Honours: Advanced Worker Award, Beijing Railway General Hospital, 1986; Awards for 30 Years of Great Contributions to Radiology of China, Chinese Journal of Radiology, 1993; Excellent Article Awards, Beijing Railway General Hospital, also National Radiological Meetings, 1979, 1984, 1990 (2), 1992 (2), 1993, 1994 (2). Memberships: Chinese Radiological Association; Beijing Tumor Association; Editorial Boards: Chinese Journal of Radiology; Journal of Clinical Radiology. Hobbies: Swimming; Travel. Address: Beijing Railway General Hospital, Beijing 100038, China.

GUO Shou-yan, b. 10 Oct 1923, Tienjin, China. Pathologist. m. Bao Mei Wang, 15 Jan 1956, 1 d. Education: BS, Catholic University, Peking, 1946; MD, Peking Union Medical College, 1952. Appointments: Vice Chairman, 1976-82, Chairman, 1983-93, Currently Professor, Department of Pathology, Shanghai Second Medical University. Publications: over 40 Professional publications including: Scanning electron microscopic study of intermingled skin grafts of severe burn patients, in Treatment and Research in Burns, 1983; Effect of ageing on aortic morphology in populations with high and low prevalence of hypertension and atherosclerosis, in American Journal Pathology, 1991. Honours: Award of Chinese Ministry of Public Health, 1978; Award of Shanghai Bureau of High Education, 1979; Award of Shanghai Science and Technology, 1979. Memberships: Chinese Society of Pathology, Chairman, 1988-94, Standing Committee, Council, 1986-90, Currently Advisor, Shanghai Society of Pathology; Chinese Medical Association; International Academy of Pathology; Asia Pacific Association of

Societies of Pathologists; Chinese Society of Immunology. Hobbies: Music; Sport. Address: 280 South Chongqing Road, Dept of Pathology, Shanghai Second Medical University, Shanghai 200025, China.

GUO Suiji, b. 4 Feb 1928, Beijing, China. Otolaryngology. m. Baolu Yao, 8 Aug 1956, 2 d. Education: Graduate, Peking Union Medical College, 1955; Postdoctoral training, research scholar, School of Medicine, University of Southern CA, USA, 1979-81. Career: Associate Professor, 1982, Vice Head of ENT Department, 1983-84, Professor of Otolaryngology, 1987-, Peking Union Medical College Hospital. Publications include: Co-author, Sound localization ability in cochlear implant patients, a preliminary study, in Chinese Journal of Otorhinolaryngology, 1983; Co-author, Wegener's granulomatosis and midline necrotizing granuloma, in Chinese Journal of Internal Medicine, 1984; Co-author, ENT Diseases, in Emergency Treatment and Self-Saving, 1990. Honours: Member of Cochlear Implant Research Project winning 2nd and 3rd class prizes, Ministry of Public Health, 1982, 1987. Membership: Chinese Medical Association. Hobbies: Reading; Traditional Chinese Shadow Boxing. Address: Apt 405, Entrance 1, Building 5, No 2 Nanwei Road, Xuan Wu District, Beijing, 100050, China.

GUO Wan Hua, b. 8 Sept 1928, Guangzhou, China. Professor of Medicine. m. Zhi-Chien He, 1 Jul 1951, 2 d. Education: MB, Zhongshan Medical College. Appointments: Assistant; Lecturer; Associate Professor; Professor & Director. Publications: Nerve Tissue, Development of Nervous System, 1988; The Effect of Macrophage Conditioned Medium on the Survival of Cerebellar Cortical Neuron, 1992; Glia Cells and Nerve Regeneration, 1993. Honours: The Award of Medical Science and Technology, 1992. Memberships: The Chinese Society of Anatomy; The Chinese Society for Cell Biology. Hobbies: Classical Music; Swimming. Address: Division of Neurosciences, Department of Histology and Embryology, Sun Yat-Sen University of Medical Sciences, Guangzhou 510089, China.

GUO Yuan Ji, b. Fujian, China. Medical Director. m. Yu Fen Li, 1 s, 1 d. Education: Graduate, Shanghai Second Medical University, 1962; Appointments: Studied Measles Virus and Interferon, Department of Immunology, Institute of Virology, 1962-71; Studied Molecular Biology of Influenza Viruses, National Institute for Medical Research Council, London, England, 1974-75; Research, Department of Influenza, Institute of Virology, Beijing, 1976-; Studied Influenza C Viruses, University of Glasgow, 1983-84; Editor: Journal of Experimental and Clinical Virology; Disease Surveillance and Medical Virology of Overseas. Honours: 6 Certificates of Merit, Chinese Government and Institute. Memberships: Beijing Branch, Chinese Medical Association; Medical Virology Society. Address: Institute of Virology, Chinese Academy of Preventive Medicine, Beijing 100052, China.

GUO Zhen-Qiu, b. 30 Dec 1926, Wang Cheng Chang Sha, Hunan, China. Professor; Doctor's Advisor. m. Luo Xin-Yuan, 1 Dec 1947, 1 s, 2 d. Education: Master's Degree in Chinese Medicine; Professor & Doctor's Advisor of Microcosmic Differential Diagnostics; Founder of Diagnostics of TCM; Medical Scientist. Appointments: Lecturer, Hunan HengYang Medical College, 1948-61; Associate Professor, Hunan Chinese Medical College, 1962-77; Professor & Doctor's Advisor, Hunan College of TCM, 1978-. Publications: Co-Author, Diagnostics of TCM, 1987; Author, Review and Prospects for the Study of Microcosmic Differential Diagnostics, 1991; Author, Scientific tradition and Scientific Development, 1991; Author, A Series of Subjects of Microcosmic Differential Diagnostics Are Emerging, 1993; Co-Author, Clinic and Experimental Studies on Chronic Schisto Somiasis Japonica Hepatic Fibrosis, 1994; Author, The Latest Annotation On Differentiation and Therapeutics of Paediatrics of TCM, 1994. Honours: Award for Great Contribution to Development of Higher Education, 1991; Top Prize for Research of Microcosmic Differential Diagnostics, Scientific and Technological Development, State Educational Committee of China, 1992. Memberships: Editorial Board of Chinese Medical Encyclopaedia; Committee of Compiling Traditional Medical Teaching Materials Under The Health Ministry of China; Theoritical Research Committee; All-China Association of TCM. Hobbies: Music; Painting; Poetry. Address: Hunan College of TCM, No 107 Shao Shan Road, ChangSha, Hunan 410007, China.

GUO Zu Chao, b. 20 Jan 1912, China. Teacher. m. Huang Wan Ying, 29 Dec 1936. Appointments: Lecturer, Associate Professor, Department of Public Health, Medical College, National Central University, 1943-49; Professor of Statistics, Department Public Health, Medical College,

National Central University, 1951; Professor of Health Statistics, 5th Military Medical University, 1951-54; Professor of Health Statistics, 4th Military Medical University, 1954-; Tutor, Medical Statistics and Health Statistics, 1981-. Publication: Statistical Methods for Medical and Biological Science. Membership: ASA, 1948-50. Address: 4th Military Medical University, Xian, China.

GUPTA Anil, b. 13 Feb 1955. Physician. m. Dr Sindhu Gupta, 25 Feb 1985, 2 sons. Education: MD; Fellow, American College of Allergy and Immunology. Appointments: Director, Allergy, Jamaica Hospital, New York, USA; Clinical Instructor, North Shore University Hospital, Cornell University Medical College. Publications: A Biochemical Marker of Fetal Wellbeing, 1982; Dermatological Manipulations of Pediatric HIV Infection, 1989. Memberships: AAAJ; ACAJ. Address: 1807 Randall Avenue, Bronx, NY 10473, USA.

GUPTA Janesh Kumar, b. 22 Nov 1963, Mombasa, Kenya. Obstetrics and Gynaecology. m. Namrta R Dhir, 26 Aug 1990, 2 s. Education: MSc; MRCOG; MB CHB. Appointments: Research Fellow, O & G, 1990; Senior House Officer, O & G, 1990-91; Regional Registrar, O & G Yorkshire Region, 1991-93; Senior Registrar, O & G, Ninewells Hospital, Dundee, Scotland, 1993-. Publications: Effect of Mifepristone on Dilation of Pregnant and Non-Pregnant Cervix, in Lancet, 1990; Assessment of Congenital Abnormalities of Fetal Brain, in Fetal and Neonatal Neurology and Neurosurgery, 2nd edition, 1995; Are Fetal Choroid Plexus Cysts a Marker for Amniocentesis, 1995. Memberships: Royal College of Obstetrics and Gynaecologists; General Medical Council. Hobbies: Squash; Photography; Do-it-Yourself. Address: 25 Rosehall Gardens, Dundee, DD2 4UE, Scotland.

GUPTA Laxmi Chand, b. 10 Jul 1939, Gwalior, India. Medicine. m. Kusum Gupta, 19 Feb 1967, 2 s. Education: MD, Radiology; DMRE; MD, PSM. Career: GDO GDII, 1966; GDO GDI, 1969; Chief Medical Officer, 1981; DY Director, 1990; Director of Medicine, 1995. Publications: 135 scientific papers in Indian and foreign journals, and 65 Medical Books including: Differential Diagnosis, 1984, 5th edition, 1994; X-Ray Diagnosis, 1988-93; Diagnostic Ultrasound, 1994; CT Scan, 1995. Honours: BC Roy National Award, 1988; President's Police Medal for Distinguished Services, 1993; World Record for writing 65 medical books, 1994. Memberships: Fellow: College of Chest Physicians, 1974, Association of Public Health, 1990, International Academy of Medical Sciences, 1991, Indian Association of Social and Preventive Medicine, 1991; Indian Radiological and Imaging Association; Indian Society of Health Administration; Nutrition Society of India; National Association of Critical Care Medicine; Indian Association of Sports Medicine; Indian Association of Rehabilitation; Indian Association of Sports Statistics; Indian Society of Communicable Diseases; Indian Association of Hospital Administration. Hobbies: Painting; Sculpturing. Address: DII 322 Vinay Marg, Chankyapuri New Delhi 21, India.

GUPTA Prakash C, b. 4 July 1944, India. Research Scientist. m. Alka, 19 June 1977, 2 sons. Education: DSc, Johns Hopkins University; MSc, Bombay University; Fellow, Overseas American College of Epidemiology. Appointment: Senior Research Scientist. Publications: About 90 Research Papers. Honours: TAKEMI Fellowship, Harvard School of Public Health, 1984-85; Visiting Scientist Award, International Agency for Research on Cancer, Lyon, France. Memberships: International Epidemiological Association; American Public Health Association; Indian Society of Oncology. Hobby: Reading. Address: Tata Institute of Fundamental Research, Homi Bhabha Road, Colaba, Bombay 400005, India.

GUPTA Rajinder Mohan, b. 16 May 1939, Farid Kot, India. Educational Psychologist. m. Jessie Beatrice Gupta, 30 Dec 1967, 1 son, 3 daughters. Education: MA; MEd(Exon); MEd (Manchester); Diploma, Experimental Psychology; PhD. Appointments: Lecturer; Teacher; Psychologist; Honorary Research Fellow; Member, Special Educational Needs Tribunal, Department for Education. Publications: CORE, 1987; Cultural Diversity and Learning Efficiency: Recent Developments in Assessment (edited with P Coxhead), 1988; Intervention Strategies With Children: Some Practical Approaches (edited with P Coxhead), 1990; Home Based Reinforcement Programmes: An Acceptable and Practical Approach to Learning and Behaviour Difficulties (editor); Articles include: Visual discrimination in good and poor readers (with S J Ceci and Slater), 1978; The assessment of the learning efficiency of Asian children (with P Coxhead), 1983; Learning Efficiency Versus Low IQ and/or Teachers ratings as predictors of reading ability of "Mentally Defective" children:

a longitudinal study, 1985; A Survey of Educational Psychologists' Views on the Delivery of Behaviour Modification (with P Coxhead), 1989; Fear of failure (with J B Gupta), 1992. Hobbies: Listening to Indian classical music; Walking; Cooking. Address: 204 Little Sutton Lane, Four Oaks, Sutton Coldfield, West Midlands B75 6PH, England.

GUPTE Suraj, b. 2 Oct 1946, Jammu, India. Paediatrician. m. Shamma Bakshi, 1 Nov 1981, 1 son, 1 daughter. Education: MD, Postgraduate Institute of Medical Education and Research; Visiting Training Fellowships: Paediatric Gastroenterology, Stockholm, Sweden, 1974; Infant Nutrition, Hyderabad, India, 1974; Diarrhoeal Diseases, Hong Kong, 1981; Medical Journalism, Malmo, Sweden, 1983. Appointments: Lecturer, 1973-74, Assistant Professor, 1974-87, Associate Professor, 1987-89, Professor, 1989-, Paediatrics, Head, Unit of Paediatrics, Government Medical College, Jammu; Visiting Fellowships: Diarrhoeal Disease and Infant Nutrition, Kuala Lumpur, Malaysia, 1979-80; Paediatrics Education, Taiwan, China, 1988; Child Neurology, Tokyo, Japan, 1990. Publications: The Short Textbook of Paediatrics, 7th edition; Differential Diagnosis in Paediatrics, 2nd edition; Instructive Case Studies in Paediatrics, 2nd edition; Paediatric Drug Directory, 7th edition; Infant Feeding; Baby Book; Childcare: Everything You Wanted to Know; MCQs in Paediatrics; MCQs in Medicine; Recent Advances in Paediatrics, Editor; Paediatric Yearbook, Editor; Newer Horizons in Tropical Paediatrics, Editor; Paediatrics Today, Editor; Contributor of over 150 professional articles in national and international journals; Presented over 100 scientific papers, chaired sessions, given guest lectures/orations and acted as resource authority at several national and international conferences, workshops and symposia worldwide. Honours: Fellowship, Indian Academy of Paediatrics, 1991; Fellowship, Royal Society of Tropical Medicine and Hygiene, 1976; Fellowship, Child Health Study Group, 1982. Memberships: Indian Academy of Pediatrics; APSSEAR; International Child Neurology Association, ICNA; Royal Society of Tropical Medicine and Hygiene; International College of Paediatrics and Child Care. Hobbies: Writing; Cricket; Painting; Travel. Address: Gupte House, 60 Lower Gumat, Jammu, Jammu and Kashmir 180001, India.

GUR Dan, b. 16 Jun 1957, Israel. m. Merav Gur, 19 Oct 1982, 1 s, 1 d. Education: DO, London; Diploma of Naturopathy, London; Merchant Officer, Deck Department Course, Israel. Appointments: Diving Safari Guide; Deck Officer in Merchant Navy. Memberships: General Council and Register of Osteopaths, UK; General Council and Register of Naturopaths, UK; British Naturopathic Association; International Association of Natural Hygienists. Hobbies: Sport; Sailing. Address: 16A Yocheved St, Haifa 34-674, Israel.

GURUBACHARYA Vijaya Lall, b. 2 May 1938, Kathmandu, Nepal. Doctor. m. Baba Maiya Gurubacharya, 1969, 2 s, 1 d. Education: MBBS, India; DTM & H, Liverpool; DCP, London University; DPath, London. Appointments: Medical Officer; Pathologist; Medical Superintendent; Consultant. Publications: Incidence of Cancer, 1983; Prevalence of Intestinal Parasites & Problems Associated with it, 1989. Honours: Two Decorations by HM The King, Nepal. Memberships: Nepal Medical Association. Hobbies: Reading; History; Listening to Music. Address: Bakhun Dole, Pulchowk, Kathmandu, Nepal.

GUSBERG Saul Bernard, b. 3 Aug 1913, New Jersey, USA. Professor of Obstetrics & Gynaecology. m. Dorothy C Gusberg, 17 June 1938, 1 son. Education: MD, Harvard University; DSc, Columbia University. Appointments: Research Fellow, Harvard University; Clinical Professor of Obstetrics & Gynaecology, Columbia University; Distinguished Professor, Chairman, New York School of Medicine; Consultant, American Cancer Society. Publications: Numerous professional publications. Honours: Phi Beta Kappa, 1933; Sigma Xi Silver Medal, Columbia University. Memberships: Past President, New York Academy of Medicine; Society of Pelvic Surgeons; American Association of Obstetrics & Gynaecology. Hobbies: Music; Art. Address: 257 Palisade Avenue, Dobbs Ferry, NY 10522, USA.

GUSEVA Zynaida Alexandrovna, b. 24 Jan 1934, Brjansk Region, Russia. Physician. m. K P Gusev, 28 Apr 1977. Education: Smolensk Medical Institute, 1958; Advanced Professional Qualification, Biophysics Institute, Moscow, 1966-68; Postgraduate Course, 1968-71. Appointments: Practical Doctor, 1958-61; Clinical Doctor, 1966-71; Head, Functional Diagnosis Department, Medical Radiological research centre RAMS, 1971-. Publications: Contributor of professional articles in journals. Honour: Doctor of the Highest Category, 1985-. Hobbies:

Cooking; Working in the Country. Address: Marx Str 34-133, Kaluga Region, 249020 Obninsk, Russia.

GUSKOVA Angelina, b. 29 Mar 1924, Krasnoyarsk, Russia. Physician. Education: DMS; Medical High School Diploma Physician; Postgraduate Training, Inneural Disease Clinics and Neurosurgery. Appointments: Head, Neurological Department, Occupational Disease Hospital, Majak Nuclear Facility, Chelyabinsk, 1949-57; Collaborator, Institute of Biophysics, Ministry of Health of USSR, 1957-61; Head, Radiological Department, Institute of Hygiene and Occupational Disease, Academy of Medical Sciences of USSR, 1961-74; Head, Clinical Department, Institute of Biophysics of Minsitry of Health, Russia, 1974-. Publications: Two Cases of Radiation Disease, 1954; Radiation Disease of Man, 1974; Manual of Radiation Accidents, 1988. Honours: Lenine's Prize, 1963; Honourable Scientist of the USSR, 1976. Memberships: Haematology Society of Russia; UNSCEAR Adviser for Russian Delegation, ICRP, 1987-92. Hobbies: History of Science; Music; Travel. Address: Givopisnaya 48-17, 123098, Moscow, Russia.

GUTH Paul S, b. 29 May 1931, New York, NY, USA. Pharmacology. m. Marilena Terrell, 31 Dec 1979, 4 s. Education: BSc, Fordham University; MSc, Pharmacology, Philadelphia College Pharmacology and Science; PhD, Hahnemann Medical College. Appointments: Associate in Pharmacology, Hahnemann Medical College; Currently, Professor of Pharmacology, Tulane University Medical School. Publications: 92 Professional publications; 5 Review articles and 2 patents issued. Honours: Outstanding Alumnus, Hahnemann, 1970; Wellcome Senior Research Fellow, 1973; Fogarty Senior International Fellow, 1983; Citation Classic Article, 1986. Memberships: American Society Pharmacology and Experimental Therapeutics; Society for Neuroscience; AAAS. Hobbies: Music; Sailing. Address: Dept of Pharmacology, Tulane University School of Medicine, 1430 Tulane Ave, New Orleans, CA 70112, USA.

GUTIERREZ Guillermo, b. 10 Mar 1946, Palma Soriano, Cuba. Professor of Medicine. m. Marian E Wulf, 18 Jun 1983, 1 s, 3 d. Education: MD; PhD, Engineering. Appointments: Assistant Professor, 1983-89, Associate Professor, 1989-91, Currently Professor of Medicine, Director, Pulmonary Division. Publications: 14 Professional publications 1993-, including: Sepsis and Cellular Metabolism, in Sepsis, 1994; Derangements in oxygen transport in shock states and sepsis, in Intensive Care Medicine, in press. Honours: General Motors Scholar, 1971-76; Outstanding Young Engineer of Year, Engineering Society of Detroit, 1979; American Lung Association Career Investigator Award, 1990-95; Dean's Teaching Excellence Award, UTHSC, 1990, 1991, 1992, 1993. Memberships: American College of Physicians; American College of Chest Physicians; American Physiological Society; American Society for Clinical Investigation; American Thoracic Society; Society of Critical Care Medicine. Hobbies: Sailing; Skiing; Music; Reading. Address: University of TX Health Science Center, 6431 Fannin, Ste 1274, Houston, TX 77030, USA.

GUTTMAN Helene A Nathan, b. 21 Jul 1930, New York City, USA. Science Administrator; Regression Therapist. Education includes: BA, Biology, Brooklyn College, 1951; AM, Medical Sciences, Harvard University, 1956; MA, Botany, Columbia University, 1958; PhD, Microbiology, Rutgers University, 1960; Intensive Bioethics Course, Human, 1988, Animal, 1989, Georgetown University; Certification Program, Past Life Regression Therapy and Hypnotherapy, Inner Guidance Center, 1993. Career includes: Coordinator, Human Nutrition, Biotechnology, Food Production and Protection, SEA/USDA, 1980-82; Nutrition Scientist, CSRS/USDA, 1982-83; President, HNG Associates, 1983-; Associate Director, Beltsville Human Nutrition Research Center, 1983-89, National Animal Care Coordinator, 1989-, ARS/USDA. Publications include: Co-author, Microbiology in Your Future, 5th edition, 1985; Co-editor, Science and Animals: Addressing Contemporary Issues, 1989; Editor, Guidelines for the Well-Being of Rodents, 1990; Co-editor, Rodents and Rabbits: Current Research Issues, 1994 in press. Honours include: Fellow, Sigma Delta Epsilon, 1953; Andelot Fellow in Medical Sciences, Harvard Medical School, 1954-55; Fellow, AAAS, 1958; Sigma Xi, 1965; Fellow, American Institute of Chemists, 1969; Fellow, American Academy of Microbiology, 1973; Fellow, NY Academy of Sciences, 1976; Chartered Chemist, Royal Society of Chemistry, UK, 1982. Memberships include: Neurosciences Society; American Society of Biology Chemistry and Molecular Biology; American Society of Cell Biology; Society In Vitro Biology; Association of Past Life Research and Therapy; National Guild of Hypnotherapy.

Hobbies: Gardening; Constructive Arts. Address: 5607 McLean Drive, Bethesda, MD 20814, USA.

GUTU William, b. 14 May 1962, Zimbabwe. Radiographer. m. Josephine Gutu, 12 Dec 1984, 1 s, 2 d. Education: Diploma in Medical Radiography, Diagnostic; DCR, London, England; Gold Diploma in Refridgeration and Air Conditioning, ICS London, England. Appointments: High School Teacher, 1983-84; Trainee Radiographer, 1985-87; Currently, Senior Radiographer at MPILO Central Hospital, Bulawayo, Zimbabwe. Memberships: Health Professions Council, Zimbabwe; Zimbabwe Society of Radiographers; President, Hospital Radiographers Association, Zimbabwe. Hobbies: Chess; Kung Fu; Listening to Soukos and Country Music. Address: 574 New Luveve, Bulawayo, Zimbabwe.

GUZMAN-MORENO Luis David, b. 16 Dec 1952, San Luis Potosi, Mexico. Neurosurgeon. m. Rosa Ortega Ruiz, 25 June 1986, 2 sons, 2 daughters. Education: Physician, Surgeon, Autonomous University, San Luis Potosi, 1978; Training, Clinical Hypnosis, Autonomous University, 1979; Family Physician, The Mexican Institute of Social Security, 1980; Certificate, Educational Council for Foreign Medical Graduates, 1985; Neurosurgeon, Western Medical Center, Guadalajara, 1991. Appointments include: Professor, Hystology, Dental School of Autonomous University; Professor, Neuroanatomy & Psychofarmacology, Psychology School of Autonomous University; Professor, Clinical Neurology & Neurosurgery, Mexican Institute of Social Security; Chief, Neurosurgical Department, Mexican Institute of Social Security; Professor, Neurology, Mexican Institute of Social Security; Medical Director, Special Projects, Megabrain Unlimited Company; Advisor, Plastic Arts Supporting Group, 1994. Publications include: Producer Several Audio/Video tapes related to Hypnosis and Neurology (Clinical Exploration of the Nervous System), 1985; Introductory Manual of Ericksonian Hypnosis and Neurolinguistic Programation, Author, 1990; Introduction to Family Medicine, 1992; Hypnosis in Mexico: A personal view, 1992; Author/Producer of Book/Tape, Hypnodontics, 1993; Hypnosis and Genital Herpes, 1994; Brain Rehabilitation: The Hypnosis Link, 1994; Honey, I Hypnotized the Boy: A Brief Manual for Concerned Parents, 1994; How to Survive your Internship: A Brief Manual for the Intern, 1994. Honours: Graduated with Honours, Medicine School of Autonomous University, 1978; The A H Robins Award, Best Graduate in Medicine, 1978; The Best Students of Mexico Award, 1978; Honourary Citizenship from USA (Oaklahoma), 1985-; Diploma, Best Graduate in Neurosurgery, 1991; President, Founder, Mexican Institute of Clinical Hypnosis, 1994. Memberships include: National Atheneum of Arts, Literature, Science and Technology, 1978-; The Institute for Research in Hypnosis & Psychotherapy, New York, USA; International Society of Theoretical & Experimental Hypnosis, Prague; World Federation of Mental Health. Hobbies: Violin Player; Painting; Paleontology; Archeology. Address: Apartado Postal 1931-A, San Luis Potosi, SLP 78000, Mexico.

GYURKO George, b. 22 May 1938, Hungary. Surgeon. m. 3 Jan 1961, 1 son. Education: Specialist of Surgery, Vascular Surgery. Appointments: Medical University of Debrecen, 1961-81; County Hospital, Miskolc, 1981-86; County Hospital Salgotarjan, 1986-. Publications: 137 publications on Surgery, Vascular Surgery & Haemodynamic. Memberships: International College of Angiology; Hungarian Surgical Society; Hungarian Angiological Society. Hobbies: Travel. Address: 3121 Solgotarjan, Kodaly Z u 5/A, Hungary.

H

HA Xiao Xian, b. 18 Oct 1939, Baoding City, Hebei Pr, China. Professor of Gynaecology. m. Li Shu Ying, 10 Sept 1973, 1 son. Education: Undergraduate, Tianjin College of TCM, 1963. Career: Vice President, Tianjin Medical Research Institute of TCM; Director of Gynaecological Research Section. Publications: Selected Reports and Talk of Ha Litian on Gynaecological Case, 1982; Ha Xiao Xian's Collected Medical Treatises, 1991; Abstract on Gynaecology of the Canon of Internal Medicine, 1992; Selected Effective Prescriptions of Gynaecology of TCM, 1989. Honours: Tianjin Science and Technology Advance Award, Cert of Achievement in Scientific Research, National Level, Promulgated by State Commission of Science and Technology, 1992. Memberships: Committee Member, Gynaecological Commission, Chinese Medical and Pharmaceutical Association; Editorial Member of Magazine, Traditional Chinese Medicine of Tianjin. Hobbies: Music; Writing. Address: Tianjin Medical Research Institute of TCM, Tianjin College of Traditional Chinese Medicine, Tianjin 300193, China.

HAAS Ingrid Elizabeth, b. 5 Jun 1953, Portland, OR, USA. Physician. m. Thomas Edward Hendricks, 16 Oct 1976, 2 d. Education: BS, OR State University, 1975; MD, University of OR Medical School, 1978. Career: Physician, Cigna Healthplan, 1982-85; Chief of Staff, Healthplan, 1984-85; Board Certification, American Board of Obstetrics and Gynaecology, 1984; Private Practice, 1985-. Honours include: Phi Kappa Phi; Pi Beta Phi; Panhellenic Council Member; OSU Scholarship and Leadership Award, 1973, 1974; Mortar Board; President, Scottsdale Ranch Women's Association, 1985-86; Fellow, American College of Obstetrics and Gynaecology. Memberships: Women Emerging; Maricopa County Medical Society; Phoenix Obstetric and Gynaecologic Society; AZ Medical Association. Hobbies: Family; Skiing. Address: 10615 North Hayden Road 102, Scottsdale, AZ 85260, USA.

HABAYEH Anwar Odeh Akeel, b. 13 Apr 1941, Zerka, Jordan. Obstetrician and Gynaecologist. m. May El-Naber, 2 June 1978, 1 son, 4 daughters. Education: BSc, 1963; MD, 1968; Research Fellow in Chest Diseases, American University of Beirut, Lebanon, 1968; MRCOG, 1974; FRCOG, 1994. Appointments: Owner, Habaybeh Hospital; Consultant Obstetrician and Gynaecologist. Publications: Normal Pulmonary Function Standard - Mid-East, 1968; Practice of Obstetrics in Underdeveloped Countries (co-author), 1980. Memberships: Jordan Medical Association; Jordan Society of Obstetrics and Gynaecology. Hobbies: Swimming; Running; Tennis. Address: PO Box 928, Code No 13110, Zerka, Jordan.

HABBAL Omar, b. 12 Mar 1947, Damascus, Syria. Medical Practitioner; Lecturer. m. Eileen Dufton, 23 July 1979, 3 daughters. Education: MB ChBm Cairo, Egypt, 1972; PhD, Manchester University, England, 1986. Appointments: House Officer, Senior House Officer, registrar, Clinical Assistant, National Health Service, England; Anatomy Lecturer, Leeds and Manchester; Assistant Profesor; Associate Professor. Publications include: Lymphoid Tissue Changes During Syngeneic Pregnancy in the RTu Rat, Co-author, 1992; The Immune Response to Coitus and Conception, CO-author, 1993; A Scanning Electron Microscopy Study of Rat Serous Membranes, Co-author, 1994; Teaching of Human Anatomy: A Role for Computer Animation, CO-author, 1995; The Role of the Diaphragm in Lymphatic Absorption from the Peritoneal Cavity, Co-author, 1995. Memberships: General Medical Council, London; Anatomical Society of Great Britain and Ireland. Hobbies: Computer Programming; Reading; Swimming. Address: College of Medicine, PO Box 35 Al-Khod, Sultan Qaboos University, Muscat 123, Sultanate of Oman.

HABIBA Marwan, b. 2 Jan 1959, Cairo, Egypt. Physician. Education: MB BCh, 1982; MSc Obstetrics and Gynaecology, 1986; MRCOG, 1991. Appointments: Assistant Lecturer, Department Obstetrics and Gynaecology, Cairo University, 1989; Registrar, Obstetrics and Gynaecology, Princess Margaret Hospital, Swindon, England, 1992; Clinical Research Fellow, Obstetrics and Gynaecology. Publications: Radionuclide Through the Genital Tract, 1994; Analysis of Menstrual Calendars, co-author, 1994. Membership: British Menopause Society. Address: 19 The Fairway, Oadby, Leicestershire LE2 2HN, England.

HABIBULLA Mohammad, b. 6 Sept 1936, Proddatur, India. Professor of Neurobiology. m. Salima Begum, 9 Jan 1961, 1 son, 3 daughters. Education: BA; BSc (Honours); MA; PhD. Appointments:

Professor, University of Constantine; Professor, Jawaharlal Nehru University; Professor of Neurobiology, Dean, School of Life Sciences, JNU; Visiting Professor, Universities of Oxford, Cambridge and Edinburgh; Visiting Professor, University of Graz, Austria and OSU, USA. Publications: Realm of Differentiation, Cell Biology, Editor; Contributor of over 76 research articles in international journals. Honours: IBRO-UNESCO Fellowship Award; Royal Society United Kingdom Visiting Fellowship; DFG-INSA Visiting Fellowship/Memberships: IBRO; FAOPS; Sigma Xi; AES; AIBS; IANS; NSI; ISCAP; ESN; APSN; FIPS. Hobbies: Writing; Photography. Address: School of Life Sciences, Jawaharlal Nehru University, New Delhi 110067, India.

HABRAND Jean-Louis, b. 26 Dec 1951, Algiers, Algeria. Professor; Radiation Oncologist. Education: MD, Ancien Interne des Hôpitaux de Paris; Master, Clinical Oncology, Head and Neck Oncology and Radiobiology; Clinical and Research Fellow, MA General Hospital, Harvard Medical School, USA. Appointments: Chef de Clinique, Assistant, Faculté de Médecine de Paris, 1980; Assistant Professor, Institut Gustave Roussy, 1986; Medical Director, Centre de Protonthérapie d'Orsay, 1991; Professor Radiation Oncology, University of Paris, 1993. Publications: Contributions to: Journal Clinical Oncology, 1992; International Journal Radiation Oncology Biology Phys, 1994. Honour: Prix Lucien Mallet, Société Française de Radiothérapie Oncologique, 1990. Memberships: International Society of Pediatric Oncology; American Society of Therapeutic Radiology; European Society of Therapeutic Radiology. Hobbies: Music; Playing Clarinet; Astronomy; Golf. Address: Départment de Radiothérapie, Institut Gustave Roussy, Rue C Desmoulins, 94805 Villejuif Cedex, France.

HACHINSKI Vladimir, b. 13 Aug 1941, Ukraine. Neurologist. m. Mary Ann, 10 June 1967, 2 sons, 1 daughter. Education: BA; MD; FRCP; MSc; DSc. Appointments: Richard and Beryl Ivey Professor and Chairman, Department of Clinical Neurological Sciences; Chairman, International Stroke Conference, 1987-92. Publications: Over 200 scientific articles. Honours: Trillium Clinical Award, 1990. Memberships: Board Director, American Academy of Neurology; World Federation of Neurology. Address: 339 Windermere Road, London, Ont N6A 5A5, Canada.

HACKETT John T, b. 10 July 1951. Forensic Psychiatrist. m. Dina J Aaron, 14 Aug 1987, 3 sons. Education: BA, Chemistry; MD; American Board of Psychiatry and Neurology, with added qualification in Forensic Psychiatry. Appointments: Currently Psychiatric Director, Merced Manor, Merced, California. Membership: American Academy of Disability Evaluating Physicians. Hobbies: Skiing; Swimming; General aviation. Address: 1101 Sylvan C208, Modesto, CA 95355, USA.

HADDAD Zack H, b. 27 Jan 1938, Cairo, Egypt. Scientific Medical Professor. m. Eveline Sylvia Lifton, 21 Mar 1964, 1 son, 1 daughter. Education: PNS, Cairo, 1954; MSc, University of Cairo, 1956; MD, Sorbonne, Paris, 1964. Appointments: Chief Resident, New York University, Belleuve, 1964; USPHS-NIH Fellow, University of California, San Francisco, 1965; Assistant Professor, 1967; Associate Professor, 1970; Professor, 1976-92; Director of Allergy/Immunology, 1967-93; Co-Director, 1992-. Honours: Von Pinquet Award, 1978; Bela Shick Award, 1981. Memberships: American Academy of Pediatrics; Society for Pediatrics; American Academy of Allergy and Immunology; American College of Allergy. Hobbies: Collecting Masterpieces; Tribal African Art. Address: 6772 Shearwater Lane, Malibu, CA 90265, USA.

HADDOX Kathryn, b. 23 Aug 1962, Charleston, West Virginia, USA. Medical Assistant. m. 9 Sept 1989, 1 son. Education: Diploma, Medical Assistant; Certified Ophthalmic Assistant; Phlebotomist. Appointments: Certified Ophthalmic Assistant, Surgical Coordinator, Visual Fields, Tonographies, Phlebotomy, Chemistry, Urine and Haemoccult Testing, Eye Laser Technology; Currently Medical Assistant, Laboratory Testing Personnel. Hobbies: Cross-stitch; Dancing; Team mom for baseball. Address: 116 Hedrick Road, Scott Depot, WV 25560, USA.

HADDY Theresa Eileen Brey, b. 27 Feb 1924, Wabasso, MN, USA. Pediatrics, Hematology and Oncology. m. Francis John Haddy, 21 Sep 1946, 1 s, 2 d. Education: BS, 1944, MB, 1946, MD, 1948, University of MN; Board Certified in Pediatrics, 1957; Board Certified in Pediatric Hematology and Oncology, 1978. Appointments: Assistant Professor, University of OK; Associate Professor, MI State University; Professor, Howard University, DC; Currently, Researcher, Pediatric Branch, National Cancer Institute, NIH. Publications: Scientific papers concerning childhood cancer, iron metabolism, standard values for cellular elements in blood; Central Nervous System Lymphoma, in Journal of Clinical Oncology, 1991; Neutrophil Kinetics, 1994. Honours: Principal Investigator for Pediatric Oncology Group, 1961-66; Responsible Investigator for Children's Cancer Groups, 1985-88. Memberships: American Academy of Pediatrics; American Society of Hematology; American Society of Pediatric Hematology and Oncology; Washington Blood Club. Hobbies: Piano; Acrylic Painting; C & O Canal Association. Address: 10804 Whiterim Drive, Potomac, MD 20854, USA.

HADI Hamid A, b. 10 Jan 1938, Kabul, Afghanistan. Doctor of Medicine. m. Afifa Edisi, 22 Nov 1989. Education: MD. Appointments: Teaching Fellow, Perinatal Pathology; Assistant Professor, Obstetrics & Gynecology; Associate Professor, Obstetrics & Gynecology; Professor, Obstetrics & Gynecology; Director, Division of Maternal Fetal Medicine. Publications: Cardiac 150 Enzyme and EKG Changes, 1989; Premiture Ruptures of the Membranes, 1994. Honours: Best Teacher of the Year, Medical College of Georgia, 1982. Memberships: ACOG; SMA. Hobbies: Music; Tennis; Outdoor Camping. Address: Department of Obstetrics & Gynecology, East Carolina University School of Medicine, Greenville, NC 27858, USA.

HADJIMINAS Minas George, b. 15 Jan 1920, Ayios Amvrosios, Cyprus. Consultant Paediatrician. m. Mary Helen Kilcoyne, 12 June 1955, 2 sons. Education: MBChB, University of Brimingham, England, 1951; DCH (London), 1959; Specialisation in Medicine, 1959, Specialisation in Paediatrics, 1960, Greece. Appointments: Director, Paediatric Department, Nicosia General Hospital, 1959-80; Director, Cyprus Thalessaemia Project, 1971-89; Director, AIDS and Hepatitis B Programmes, 1982-89; Consultant to the Ministry of Health. Publications: Molecular basis of H-disease in the Mediterranean, 1979; Alpha Thalassaemia in two Mediterranean populations, 1982; Co-author: A-Thalassaemia in Cyprus, 1979; Prevention of Thalassaemia in Cyprus, 1980; Genetic abd molecular diversity on non-deletion HbH-disease, 1981. Honours: Scholarships, 1945, 1955, 1958, 1974. Memberships: British Medical Association; Cyprus Medical Association; Cyprus Paediatric Society; Cyprus Society of Allergology. Hobbies: Walking; Philately (Vice-President, Cyprus Philatelic Society); Coin collector (Member, Cyprus Numismatic Society). Address: Metochiou 38, Flat 3, PO Box 4095, Nicosia, Cyprus.

HAGERSTRÖM Lennart, b. 14 Jan 1933, Malmo, Sweden. Orthodontist. m. Britt Wallberg, 16 Jul 1960, 2 s, 1 d. Address: Hedakersvagen 29D, S-217 64 Malmo, Sweden.

HAGGARD Mark P, b. 26 Dec 1942, London, England. Founder Director. m. Liz Haggard, 22 Sep 1962, 2 s. Education: MA, Psychology; PhD, Psychology; Special Professor in Audiological Sciences, University of Nottingham. Appointments: University Demonstrator in Experimental Psychology, 1967-71; Professor of Psychology and Head of Department, 1971-76; Founder Director, MRC Institute of Hearing Research, 1977-. Publications: Screening Children's Hearing, 1991; Research in the Development of Effective Services for Hearing Impaired People, 1993. Honour: Honorary Member of Faculty of Public Health Medicine, Royal College of Physicians, 1994. Memberships: Fellow of the Royal Society of Medicine. Hobbies: Skiing; Choral Music. Address: MRC Institute of Hearing Research, University Park, Nottingham, NG7 2RD, England.

HAHN Chun Suk, b. 25 Apr 1918, Pusan, Korea. Eye Clinician. m. Eun Hee Park, 12 June 1952, 3 sons, 4 daughters. Education: MD; PhD. Appointments: Associate Professor of Ophthalmology, Seoul National University, resigned 1965; Currently: Director, Dr Hahn's Eye Clinic, Seoul; President, Hahn's (Hanil) Medical Instruments Manufacturing Co. Publications: Hahn Test Chart for 5 m, 1972; Hahn Test Chart for 3 m, 1974; Hahn Colour Vision Test, 21 plates, 1981; Hahn Double 15 Hue Test, 1981; Hahn Concise Colour Vision Test for primary school, 11 plates, 1981. Honours: Green Stripe Star Medal, Government of Republic of Korea, 1960. Membership: International Research Group on Colour Vision Deficiencies. Hobby: Photography. Address: 172-15 Dongsun Dong 5 Ga, Sungbuk Ku, Seoul 136-055, Korea.

HAIDA Michiko, b. 3 Sept 1948, Tokyo, Japan. Doctor (Internal Medicine). m. Kimishige Haida, 18 Oct 1979, 2 sons. Education: MD, Faculty of Medicine, Tohoku University; PhD, Department of Medicine and Physical Therapy, Faculty of Medicine, Tokyo University; Residency, Toranomon Hospital, 5 years. Appointments: Research Fellow, Department of Medicine and Physical Therapy, Tokyo University, 15 years; Currently Chief, Department of Internal Medicine,

Hanzomon Hospital, Tokyo. Publications: Today's Therapy (co-author), yearly revised editions, 1984-. Memberships: Japanese Society of Allergology; Japanese Society of Internal Medicine; International Congress of Allergy and Clinical Immunology. Hobby: English-Japanese-English interpretation, training to acquire techniques of simultaneous interpreting. Address: c/o Hanzonom Hospital, 1-10-5 Kojimachi, Chiyoda-ku, Tokyo 102, Japan.

HAILE MESKEL Helena, b. 27 Dec 1949, Ethiopia. Physician. 1 s. Education: MD; FRCPS(C); FCAP. Appointments: Pathologist. Publications: Bacterial Meningitis in Infancy and Childhood, 1978; ANF in the Conduction System of the Heart, Co-author, 1988; Atrial Natriuretic Factor in the Impulse-Cnduction System of Rat Cardiac Ventricles, Co-author, 1989; Processing of the Atrial Natriuretic Factor Propeptide by Atrial Cardiocytes as Revealed by Immunocryoultramicrotomy, Co-author, 1989; Atrial Natriuretic Factor in Purkinje Fibers of Rabbit Heart, Co-author, 1989; Atrial Natriuretic Factor in the Vena Cava and Sinus Node, Co-author, 1990; Immuno-Electron Microscopy of Atrial Natriuretic Factor Secretory Pathways in Atria and Ventricles of Control and Cardiomyopathic Hamsters with Heart Failure, Co-author, 1990; Metallothionein as an Epithelial Proliferative Compartment Marker for DNA Flow Cytometry, Author, 1993. Memberships: Canadian Association of Pathologists; Ontario Association of Pathologists. Address: St Catherines General Hospital, 142 Queenston Street, St Catherines, Ontario L2R 7C6, Canada.

HAINES Kathleen Ann, b. 28 Jul 1949, New York, USA. Physician. m. Emil C Gotschlich, MD, 24 May 1975, 1 d. Education: BA, Hunter College, City University of New York; MD, Albert Einstein College of Medicine; Board Certified in Pediatrics, Allergy & Immunology, Pediatric Rheumatology. Appointments: Fellow in Allergy & Immunology, Cornell University Medical Center, 1977-80; Assistant Professor of Pediatrics & Medicine, New York University Medical Center, 1983-90; Director of Pediatric Rheumatology, New York University Medical Center. Publications: Multiple publications in Professional Journals. Honours: USPHS Grant, 1993; New York Arch Foundation Grants, 1991-92. Memberships: American Association of Pediatrics; American Association of Allergy & Immunology; ASCB; ACR; AFRC; SPR. Hobbies: Golf; Needlepoint; Cooking. Address: 301 East 17th Street, Hospital for Joint Diseases, New York 10003, USA.

HAINES Stephen John, b. 4 Sep 1949, Burlington, VT, USA. Neurological Surgeon. 2 s. Education: AB, Dartmouth College, 1971; MD, University of Vermont, 1975. Appointment: Professor of Neurosurgery, Otolaryngology and Pediatrics, University of MN. Publications: Numerous professional publications. Honours: Phi Beta Kappa, 1971; Alpha Omega Alpha, 1975; Van Wagener Fellow, AANS, 1981. Memberships: CNS; AANS; ACS; Society of Neurological Surgeons; Neurosurgical Society of America; Society for Clinical Trials. Hobby: Electronic Music. Address: Box 96 UMHC, 420 Delaware St SE, Minneapolis, MN 55455, USA.

HAKAMA Matti, b. 9 Nov 1939, Oulu, Finland. Professor. m. Pirjo Sirpoma, 30 Dec 1961, 1 s, 2 d. Education: MSc, University of Minnesota; DSc, University of Helsinki. Career: Actuary, 1961-63, Head Statistician, 1963-71, Finnish Cancer Registry; Associate Professor of Biometry, University of Helsinki, 1971-75; Currently, Professor of Epidemiology, University of Tampere, School of Public Health, Finland. Publications: Publications on epidemiology of cancer and other chronic diseases. Honours: Cancer Society of Finland Award, 1982; Edgar Gentilli Prize, Royal College of Gynaecology and Obstetrics, 1982. Membership: Council, International Union Against Cancer. Address: Department of Public Health, University of Tampere, PO Box 607, FIN-33101 Tampere, Finland.

HALBERSTADT-FREUD Hendrika Clara, b. 9 Feb 1937, Amsterdam, The Netherlands. Psychoanalyst. div, 1 son, 1 daughter. Education: PhD, Psychology. Appointments: Private Practice; Training Analyst, Supervisor, Dutch Psychoanalytic Association. Publications: Freud, Proust, Perversion and Love, 1991; Postpartum Depression and Symbolic Illusion, Clare Schumann A Woman's Loves and Life. Memberships: International Psychoanalytic Association; Association for Child Psychoanalysis. Hobbies: Reading; Literature; Swimming. Address: Van Breestraat 131, 1071ZL Amsterdam, The Netherlands.

HALE Andrew Richard, b. Tonbridge, England. Professor. m. Mary Prothero 15 May 1970. Education: MA, Natural Sciences, Cantab, 1966;

PhD, Health and Safety, Aston; CPsychol; M ERG; FIOSH. Appointments: Scientific Staff, National Institute of Industrial Psychology, 1966-72; Lecturer, Senior Lecturer, Occupational Safety and Health, Aston University, 1972-84; Coordinator, Human Resources, Sonatrach Arzew, Algeria, 1980-81; Currently, Professor of Safety Science, Delft University of Technology, Netherlands. Publications: Co-author: Review of Industrial Accident Literature, 1972; Individual Behaviour in the Control of Danger, 1987; Over 200 Scientific and Professional Articles and Papers. Memberships: British Psychological Society; Ergonomics Society; Institution of Occupational Safety and Health; Dutch Safety Practitioners Society; Dutch Occupational Hygiene Society. Hobbies: Cinema; Wine; Racket Sports. Address: Safety Science Group, TV Delft, Postbus 5050, 2600 GB Delft, Netherlands.

HALE Paul Nolen Jr, b. 12 May 1941, Galveston, Texas, USA. University Educator. m. Frances Anne Andrews, 26 Jan 1968, 1 son, 1 daughter. Education: BS, Industrial Engineering, Lamar Tech; MS, Industrial Engineering, University of Arkansas; PhD, Industrial Engineering, Texas A&M University. Appointments: Assistant Professor, Industrial Engineering, Texas A&M University; Assistant Professor, Associate Professor, currently Department Head and Centre Director, Biomedical Engineering, Louisiana Tech University, Ruston. Publications: Biomedical Engineering Academic Program Annual Report (editor); Rehabilitation Technology Services (editor), 1989; Technology for the Next Decade (editor), 1989. Honours: Meritorious Service Award, Louisiana Governor's Conference, 1984; Centennial Certificate, American Society for Engineering Education, 1993; Outstanding Biomedical Educator, Biomedical Engineering Division, American Society for Engineering Education, 1993. Memberships: Board of Directors, Biomedical Engineering Society; Board of Directors, RESNA; Institute of Electrical and Electronic Engineers/EMBS, Education Committee Chair; American Society for Engineering Education, Biomedical Engineering Division; Phi Kappa Phi. Address: Biomedical Engineering Department, Louisiana Tech University, PO Box 10348, Ruston, LA 71272, USA.

HALL Alan H, b. 8 Jan 1949, South Bend, IN, USA. Medical Toxicologist. m. Priscilla K Sanders, 8 Jul 1967, 1 d. Education: BA, Honours, Sociology, IN University, South Bend, IN, 1973; MD, IN University School of Medicine, IN, 1977; Diplomate, Emergency Medicine, 1985, Medical Toxicology, 1986. Career: Part of Full Time Emergency Medicine, 1977-85; Air Force Reserve Flight Surgeon, Flight Surgeon, Chief of Aeromedical Services, 1984-89; Senior Consultant, Rocky Mountain Poison and Drug Center, University of CO Health Sciences Center, 1986-; Editor in Chief, TOMES and TOMES Plus Information Systems, Denver, CO, 1986-; Assistant Professor of Pediatrics, 1987-92, Clinical Assistant Professor of Preventive Medicine and Biometrics, 1992-, University of CO Health Sciences Center. Publications: Peer Reviewer for various medical journals including: American Journal of Medicine, Journal of Toxicology - Clinical Toxicology, Intensive Care Medicine, Annals of Emergency Medicine; Many publications and abstracts including: Ethylene glycol and methanol: Poisons with toxic metabolic activation, in Emergency Medicine Reports, 1992; Sodium Nitrate, in Antidotes for Poisoning by Cynaide, 1993. Honours: Fellow, American College of Emergency Physicians, 1985; Liberal Arts and Sciences Distingushed Alumnus Award, 1991, Distinguished Alumnus Award, 1992, IN University, South Bend, IN. Memberships include: American Academy of Clinical Toxicology; Space Medicine Branch, Aerospace Medicine Association; Society of USAF Flight Surgeons; AMA. Hobbies: Hiking; Snowskiing; Swimming; Gardening; Composing and Performing Music; Fiction Writing. Address: Toxicology Consulting and Medical Translating Services, 85 Santa Fe Mountain Road, Evergreen, CO 80439, USA.

HALL Elizabeth Helen (Liz), b. 5 Sep 1948, Lancaster, England. Clinical Psychologist. m. Dr Graham Hall, 17 Apr 1971, separated, 1 s, 1 d. Education: BA, Honours, 1969, PhD, 1973, University of Newcastle upon Tyne; Diploma in Psychotherapy, University of Aberdeen; Diploma in Clinical Psychology, British Psychological Society. Appointments include: Junior Research Associate, 1969-71, Research Associate, 1971-72, University of Newcastle upon Tyne; Clinical Psychologist, Kingseat Hospital, New,achar, 1980-83, 1983-84, Senior Clinical Psychologist, Kingseat Hospital and Community Clinical Psychology Department, 1984-86, Senior Clinical Psychologist, Community Clinical Psychology department, Community Unit, 1986-89, Principal Clinical Psychologist, Coordinator of Services to Community Agencies, 1989-91, Grampian Health Board; Consultant Clinical Psychologist, Sexual Abuse Consultant, Clinical Psychology Department, Grampian Health Board

and Grampian Healthcare NHS Trust, 1991-. Publications include: Intellect, Mental Illness and Survival in the Aged: A Longitudinal Investigation, Co-author, 1972; Surviving Child Sexual Abuse: A Handbook for Helping Women Challenge Their Past, 1989, 1990, 2nd edition, 1993, 1994; Helping Adult Survivors of Child Sexual Abuse, 1994. Memberships: Clinical Division, British Psychological Society. Hobbies: Swimming; Cycling; Reading; Foreign Travel. Address: Clinical Psychology, Royal Cornhill Hospital, Cornhill Road, Aberdeen, Scotland.

HALL Emery Alan Christopher, b. 24 Apr 1960, San Diego, California, USA. Optometrist. m. Ronda Hamilton, 19 July 1980, 1 son, 2 daughters. Education: BS, Biology, 1983; BS cum laude, Visual Sciences, 1985; Doctor of Optometry, 1987. Appointments: Currently Director of Optometric Service; Eye Physicians Medical Center. Publications: A Comparative Study of the Seiko P3 and Varilux 2 Progressive Addition Lenses, 1988. Honours: Admitted to Beta Sigma Kappa, 1987; Fellow, American Academy of Optometry, 1988; California Young Optometrist of the Year, 1993. Memberships: American Optometric Association; California Optometric Association; American Academy of Optometry; San Diego County Optometric Society. Hobbies: Tennis; Building construction. Address: 681 Third Avenue, Chula Vista, CA 91910-5703, USA.

HALL John E, b. 8 Aug 1946, Milo, VA, USA. Scientist; Educator. m. Becky Frederick, 24 Jun 1972, 2 s, 1 d. Education: BS, Kent State University, 1968; PhD, MI State University, 1974; Postdoctoral Fellow, University of MS Medical Center. Appointments: Assistant Professor, Associate Professor, Currently, Professor and Chairman, Department of Physiology and Biophysics, University of MS Medical Center. Publications: About 290 professional publications including, Renal and Cardiovascular Mechanisms of Hypertension in Obesity, Hypertension, 1994. Honours include: NIH National Research Service Award, 1975; NIH Research Career Development Award, 1979; Marion Young Scholar Award, American Society Hypertension; Harry Goldblatl Award in Cardiovascular Research, American Heart Association, 1984; Lewis K Dahl Award, American Heart Association, 1992; FAP Barnard Distinguished Professor, University of MS, 1993. Memberships: American Society Hypertension; International Society Hypertension; Council for High Blood Pressure Research; American Heart Association; Inter-American Society Hypertension; American Physiological Society; American Society Nephrology; International Society Nephrology. Hobbies: Sport; Basketball; Softball; Fishing. Address: Dept Physiology and Biophysics, University of MS Medical Center, Jackson, MS, 39216, USA.

HALL Judith, b. 3 July 1939, Boston, MA, USA. Physician; Department Head. 1 s, 2 d. Education: BA, Wellesley College, 1961; MD, MS, University of Washington; FAAP; FCCMG; FABMG; FRCP(C) Paediatrics and Medical Genetics. Appointments: Assistant, Associate, Full, Professor of Medicine and Paediatrics, University of Washington; Professor of Medical Genetics, University of British Columbia, Canada; Professor and Head of department of Paediatrics, BCCH. Publications: Human Malformations and Associated Anomalies, 1993; Handbook of Normal Physical Measurements, 1989; Contributor of numerous review articles and chapters in books. Honours: Sr Killiam Prize, 1991; Distinguished Medical Alumni, University of Washington, 1992; BC Science World Hall of Fame, 1993; March of Dimes Colonel Saunders Award, 1994; Induction in Hall of Scholars, Johns Hopkins, 1994; Women of Distinction Award, 1994. Memberships: American Society of Human Genetics, President, 1994-96; Western Society for Paediatric Research, President, 1994. Address: 4024 West 31st Avenue, Vancouver, BC V6S 1Y6, Canada.

HALL Robert Dickinson, b. 6 Mar 1947, Washington DC, USA. Entomologist. m. Melba R Hall, 24 Dec 1990, 2 daughters. Education: BA, 1973; MS, 1975; PhD, 1977. Appointment: Professor of Entomology. Publications: Over 60 professional publications mainly in Medical and Veternary Entomology. Memberships: Sigma Xi; Phi Kappa Phi; Phi Sigma; Gamma Sigma Delta; American Academy of Forensic Sciences; Entomological Society. Address: Department of Entomology, 1-87 Agriculture, University of Missouri, Columbia, MO 65211, USA.

HALPE Neil Lakshman, b. 7 Jul 1940, Kuliyapitiya, Sri Lanka. Obstetrician and Gynaecologist. m. Menaka Pilapitiya, 28 Apr 1977, 2 s. Education: MB, BS, University of Ceylon; FRCOG, Royal College of Obstetrics and Gynaecologists, London. Appointments: Senior Lecturer, University of Peradeniya, Sri Lanka; Consultant Obstetrician and Gynaecologist: Benoni Hospital, Benin City, Nigeria; General Hospital

Kandy; Base Hospital Nuwara Eliya; Base Hospital Matale; Currently, Base Hospital, Kuliyapitiya, Sri Lanka. Publication: Sensitivity to Primaquine in Ceylonese Children Due to Sensitivity to Deficiency of Glucose 6 Phosphate Dehyrogenase, in Ceylon Medical Journal, 1968. Memberships: Sri Lanka College of Obstetrics and Gynaecologists; Kandy Society of Medicine; Kuliyapitiya Clinical Society. Hobbies: Drama; Environmental Protection; Jazz. Address: 36-2 Pitakanda Road, Nittawela, Kandy, Sri Lanka.

HALPERN Georges Maurice, b. 7 Sept 1935, Warsaw, Poland. Professor of Medicine and Nutrition. m. Emiko Oguiss, 14 May 1971, 2 daughters. Education: MD, 1964; PhD, DSc, 1992. Appointments: Chief Resident, Centre Rene Huguenin, St Cloud, France, 1962-63; Clinical Assistant Professor, Gammaencephalography, La Pitie, Paris, France, 1964-66; Assistant Professor, Internal Medicine, Foundation Rothschild, Paris, France, 1966-69; Professor, Immunology, Anthropology, Paris, 1975-77; Visiting Professor, Stanford Children's Hospital, 1981-83; Professor of Medicine and Nutrition, University of California, Davis, USA. Publications: L'allergie & la peau, 1976; L'allergia e la pelle, 1977; Allergies, 1984; Bronchial Asthma, 1994. Memberships: FAAAI; FACAI; FEAACI; FSFI; FAILL; ACIC; FAIVAIS. Honours: Gold Medal, Intern Academy Lutece, 1977; Medal Vermeil, City of Paris, 1985; Czechoslovakia Medal of Honor, Purkynje, 1977; Corresponding Member, Academy of Medicine, Colombia, 1984; Guest Award, Korea Society of Immunology, 1978. Hobbies: Gourmet Cooking; Wine Tasting. Address: 9 Hillbrook Drive, Portola Valley, CA 94028-7933, USA.

HALSTEAD Scott B, b. 23 Jan 1930, Lucknow, India. Physician. m. Edna Fishburn, 28 May 1955, 2 sons, 1 daughter. Education: MD, Columbia University, 1955. Appointments: Chief, Department of Viral & Rickettsial Diseases, 406 Medical General Laboratory, Japan, 1957-59; Chief, Virology Department, SEATO Medical Laboratory, Bangkok, 1961-65; Chairman, Harvard School of Medicine, 1968-83; Acting Director, Deputy Director, Health Sciences Division, Rockefeller Foundation, 1983-95. Publications: Over 240 scientific articles Memberships: AAAS; American Society of Virology; Infectious Disease Society of America. Hobbies: Tennis; Skiing; Travel. Address: Naval Medical Research & Development Command, National Naval Medical Center, Bethesda, MD 20889-5606, USA.

HAMADEH Randah Ribhi, b. 3 June 1953, Jerusalem. Epidemiolgist. m. Dr Ahmed Al-Ansari, 8 March 1984, 1 son, 2 daughters. Education: BSc, honours, American University of Beirut, Lebanon, 1975; MSc, American University of Beirut, Lebanon, 1977; DPhil, Oxford University, England, 1988. Appointments: Assistant Manager, Office of Professional Standards & Systems Analysis, Ministry of Health, Bahrain; Assistant Professor, College of Medicine, Arabian Gulf University. Publications include: author, Space Clustering of Leukemia, Hodgkin's Disease and other Lymphomas in Bahrain, 1977; author, The Impact of Smoking in Bahrain, 1987; Co-author, Epidemiology of Non-Hodgkin's Lymphomas, in Reviews in Cancer Epidmeiology, vol 2, 1983; Author, Prevalence of Smoking in Bahrain, 1992; Smoking and Acute Myocardial Infarction in Bahrain - a case control study, 1993; Prevalence of Known Risk Factors in Hospital Cases of Acute Myocardial Infarction in Bahrain, 1993; co-author, Injury and Poisoning in Bahrain - a hospital based study, 1993; co-author, Tobacco Consumption and Chemical Analysis of Cigarettes in Bahrain in The International Journal of the Addictions, 1994; Smoking Habits of Medical Students in Bahrain, 1994; Change in Smoking Habits in Bahrain, 1981-91, 1994; Knowledge and Attitudes of Medical Students in Bahrain Towards Smoking, forthcoming. Memberships: Society for Epidemiologic Research; Society for Social Medicine; International Epidemiologic Association. Hobbies: Reading; Walking; Cooking. Address: College of Medicine, Arabian Gulf University, PO Box 22979, Manama, Bahrain.

HAMILTON Charles Richard, b. 5 Mar 1954, England. Clinical Oncologist. m. Penelope Vivien Wilkins, 29 Sep 1979, 3 s, 1 d. Education: MBBS; MRCP; FRCR. Career: Assistant Lecturer, Medical Oncology and Registrar, Radiotherapy, St Bartholomew's Hospital; Lecturer, Radiotherapy, The Royal Marsden; Leon Goldberg Fellow, The Princess Margaret, Toronto; Currently, Consultant in Radiotherapy and Oncology, Royal South Hamptonshire Hospital. Publications: Gastrointestinal Morbidity of adjunct radiotherapy in Stage I Malignant Testes, BBC Radio 1, 1987; Assistant Editor, UICC Manual of Clinical Oncology, 6th edition, 1994. Memberships: College of Physicians; College of Radiologists. Address: Healthdene, Hadrian Way, Chilworth, Southampton, England.

HAMILTON John Richard, b. 8 Mar 1934, Ontario, Canada. Professor. m. Patricia Levis, 31 Oct 1959, 3 sons. Education: MD; FRCP(C). Appointments: Director, Division of Gastroenterology, Department of Pediatrics, University of Toronto & Hospital for Sick Children, Toronto, 1969-86. Publications: Practical Pediactric Gastroenterology, 1983; Pediatric Gastroentestinas Disease, 1991. Honours: Nutrition Award, American Academy of Pediatrics; Schwachman Award, American Society of Pediatric Gastroenterology. Memberships: American Pediatric Society; Canadian Pediatric Society; Canadian Society for Clinical Investigation; Canadian Association of Gastroenterology. Address: Montreal Childrens Hospital, 2300 Tupper Street, Montreal, Quebec H3H 1P3, Canada.

HAMILTON-FARRELL Martin Robert, b. 2 Apr 1954, Newcastle Upon Tyne, England. Anaesthetist. Education: BSc, London; MB BS, London; MRCP, UK; FRCA. Appointments: Senior House Officer, Addenbrooks Hospital; Registrar, Southampton General Hospital; Senior Registrar, London Hospital Medical College; Currently, Consultant Anaesthetist, Director of Intensive Therapy Unit, Whipps Cross Hospital, London. Publications: Respiratory and Cardiac Monitoring, BJHM, 1990; Applications of Hyperbaric Oxygen, BJHM, 1992; Co-author, General Care of the Ventilated Patient, BMA, 1994; Co-author, Side Effects of General Anaesthetics and Gases, in Meyler: Elsevier, 12th edition. Memberships: British Medical Association; RCP, London; RSM; British Hyperbaric Association. Hobbies: Walking; Music. Address: 52 Ufton Road, London, N1 4HH, England.

HAMOSH Margit, b. 13 Aug 1933, Dresden, Germany. Professor of Pediatrics. m. Paul Hamosh, 21 Oct 1954, 3 d. Education: MS, Microbiology; PhD, Biochemistry. Career: Instructor, 1959, Assistant Professor, 1961-64, Biochemistry, Hebrew University, Hadassah Medical School; Visiting Scientist, NIMH, 1965-67, NIH, NIAMD, 1967-74; Professor of Pediatrics and Chief, Division of Developmental Biology and Nutrition, 1974-. Publications: Editor, Human Lactation, volume 2, 1986; Lingual and Gastric Lipases: Their Role in Fat Digestion, 1990; Co-author, Nutrition during Lactation, 1991; 180 original articles, reviews and chapters. Honour: President, International Society Research Human Milk and Lactation, 1986-88. Memberships: American Physiology Society; American Institute of Nutrition; Editorial Board, Pediatric Council, 1982-84, American College of Nutrition; American Society of Clinical Nutrition; American Pediatric Society; Council, 1983-85, Perinatal Research Society; President, 1986-88, Executive Committee, 1994-96, International Society Research Human Milk Lactation; Endocrine Society. Hobbies: Visual and Performing Arts; Ethymology. Address: Department of Pediatrics, Georgetown Univerity Medical Center, Washington, DC 20007-2197, USA.

HAMPSON Peter John, b. 29 May 1954, Leigh, lancashire, England. University Lecturer. m. Shelagh Fagan, 31 July 1981, 1 s, 1 d. Education: BSc, University of Birmingham; PhD, University of Lancaster; AFBAS; C Psychol. Appointments: Lecturer, Manchester Polytechnic, 1978-84; Statutory Lecturer in Applied Psychology, University College, Cork, Ireland. Publications: Imagery and Consciousness, Co-author; Imagery: Current Developments, Co-author; Contributor of articles. Memberships: British Psychological Society; Psychological Society of Ireland; European Society for Cognitive Psychology. Hobbies: Flying; Walking; Gardening. Address: Department of Applied Psychology, University College, Cork, Ireland.

HAMPTON Marta Toruno, b. 27 Jan 1958, Managua, Nicaragua. Dermatologist. m. Archibald A Hampton, 20 Dec 1980, 2 sons, 1 daughter. Education: BS; MD. Appointments: Clinical Researcch Assistant, University of Miami, 1985-86; Clinical Assistant Professor, Medical University of South Carolina, 1992-93; Assistant Professor, Medical University of South Carolina, 1994-. Publications: Ciguatera Fish Poisoning, 1989; Preschool Sarcoidosis Masquerading as Juvenile Rheumatoid Arthritis: Two Case Reports and a Review of the Literature, 1990; Clear Cell Hidradenoma (nodular hidradenoma), 1992; A Murine Model of the Eosinophilia-myalgia Syndrome Induced by 1,1-Ethylidenebis (L-tryptophan); Intracorneal Nuclear Dust Aggregates in Dermatitis Herpetiformis: A Clue to Diagnosis. Honours: National Honor Society, 1975; Phi Beta Kappa, 1982; Faculty Excellence Award, MUSC, 1989; Alpha Omega Alpha, 1990; Faculty Excellence Award, MUSC, 1992. Memberships: Fellow, American Academy of Dermatology; Associate, American Society of Dermatopathology; Fellow, Women's Dermatologic Society. Hobbies: Ballet; Tennis; Ceramics. Address: 4 Sayle Road, Charleston, SC 29407, USA.

HAN De Tan, b. 25 Dec 1927, Suqian, Jiangsu, China. Surgeon; Neurosurgeon. m. Zhai Yue Xian, 12 Jul 1954, 1 s, 2 d. Education: Graduate, Medical College of Cheeloo University, 1953; Postgraduate, Urology and Neurosurgery, Shanghai First Medical College, China, 1956, 1964. Career: Professor and Director, Surgical Teaching, Scientific Research Deaprtment, 1985; Editor, Academiae Medicinae, Shadong Medical University, 1986; Contributing Editor, Beijing Science and Technology, 1986; Provincial Evaluation Committee on achievement in scientific medical research, 1990; Currently, Professor, Director of Surgeru and Neurosurgery, Jinan Clinical College, Shandong Medical University. Publications: Co-author, Common Diseases of Surgery, 1966; Author, Surgical Reconstruction in Complete Traumatic Severance of Pancreas, in National Medical Journal of China, 1978; Transoral Focal Debridment Decompression and Bone Graft for Axis TB with Higher Paraplegia, in Chinese Journal of Surgery, 1987; The use of Silver-Core Silicone bulb for therapeutic embolization in cerebral arteriovenous malformation, in Chinese Journal of Neurosurgery, 1989. Honours: Government's Special Allowance, State Council of China, 1992; 2nd Award for Achievement in Teaching Research, Chinese National Education Committee, 1993. Memberships: Jinan Municipal Medical Society; Shandong Provincial Medical Association; Chinese Medical Association; Chinese Scientific Workers Society. Hobbies: Tennis; Chinese Chess. Address: Surgical Department of Jinan Municipal Zhong Xie Hospital, Jinan 250013, China.

HAN Guo-Zhen, b. 1 Aug 1929, Shandong, China. Physician. m. Lu Zhen Ping, 1 May 1955, 2 sons. Education: Graduated, Shandong Medical College, 1952; Professor, Diplomas, 1993. Appointments: Resident Physician, 1952-, Chief Resident, 1959-60, Visiting Physician, 1960-79, Head of Digestion Department, 1979-89, currently Visiting Physician, Chang Hai Hospital, Shanghai; Assistant, 1952-69, Lecturer, 1977, Professor, 1991-95, Second Military Medical College, Shanghai. Publications: Analysis of the cause of a mistake - liver Amoebiasis, 12 cases, 1963; CPC, total 9 cases, 1982, 1983, 1986; Year Book of Medicine, China, 1983, 1984, 1985; Medical Lecture, muscles and joints, 1983. Honours: 2nd Award for case report of Menetrier's disease, 1978; 30 Years of Medical Education Award. Membership: Chinese Medical Society. Hobbies: Playing ball; Tennis. Address: The Chang Hai Hospital, Second Military Medical College, Shanghai, China.

HAN Lebing, b. 28 Feb 1949, Wuhan, China. Traditional Chinese Medicine. m. Yin Zhengpu, 10 Feb 1975, 1 d. Education: Graduate Physician, Wuhan Retraining College, 1975. Career: Visiting Physician, Traditional Chinese Medicine; Currently, Associate Professor, Traditional Chinese Medicine. Publications: About 20 papers published including: Keeping intelligentsia up health. Honour: 2nd Prize for paper on Apprentice System for Traditional Chinese Medicine. Membership: Wuhan Branch, Chinese Association of Traditional Chinese Medicine. Hobbies: Table Tennis; Badminton; Swimming; Reading. Address: 49 Li Huang Pi Road, Wuhan 430014, China.

HAN Xiangyang, b. 7 Dec 1932, Liaoning, China. Obstetrician & Gynecologist. m. Lin Xioue, 8 Aug 1957, 3 daughters. Education: Graduate, Harbin Medical University, 1956. Appointments: Resident Doctor, Teaching Assistant, Visiting Physician, Lecturer, Deputy Professor, Professor, Chief Physician, Researcher, Obstetrics & Gynecology Department, First Affiliated Hospital, Harbin Medical University. Publications: 15 books incl: Family Planning Clinical Brochur & Clinical Family Planning, 1988; Over 80 papers. Honours: Provincial Young & Middle Aged Scientist, 1988; National Young and Middle Aged Scientist, 1990; National Excellent Scientific & Technological Researcher, 1992; National Examplery Dcotor in Marginal Areas, 1994. Hobbies: Swimming; Photography. Address: The First Affiliated Hopspital, Harbin Medical University, 23 Youzheng Street. Harbin 150001, China.

HAN Ying, b. 17 Feb 1933, Liaoning, China. Physician. m. Kun Lin, 1 Oct 1958, 2 daughters. Education: MD, Chinese Medical University, 1950-56. Appointments: Physician, Affiliated Hospital, Institute of Hematology, Chinese Academy of Medical Sciences, Tianjin, 1957-69; Attending Doctor, Department of Internal Medicine, 1st Hospital of Panzhihua City, Sichuan, 1970-85; Deputy Head, Department of Medical Administration, Xiqing Hospital. Tianjin, 1986-89; Assoicate Chief Physician of Testing Quality Department, Xiqing Hospital, Tianjin. Publications: The gouty arthritis complicated from chronic nephritis, 1980; Clinical characteristics of 55 elderly cases with rheumatic heart disease in the rural areas, 1991. Membership: Chinese Medical

Association. Hobby: Watching TV. Address: 343 Xiqing Road, Tianjin 300380, China.

HANCOCKS Stephen Andrew, b. 19 Aug 1953, Hemel Hempstead, Hertfordshire, England. Dentist. Education: BDS, University College Hospital Dental School, 1976; LDS, 1977; DDPH, 1981; MCCD, 1990; Royal College of Surgeons of England. Appointments: Dental Officer, Camden and Islington, London, 1977-81; Registrar in Children's Dentistry, Eastman Dental Hospital, 1981-83; Senior Dental Officer, Riverside Health Authority, 1984-88; Senior Dental Officer, West Essex Health Authority, 1989-90; Currently Publishing Manager, FDI World Dental Press; Communications Manager, General Dental Council. Publications: Editor, FDI World; Associate Editor, International Dental Journal. Honours: Runner-up, Columnist of the Year Award, UK Press Gazette, 1993. Memberships: Fédération Dentaire Internationale; British Dental Association; British Society of Paediatric Dentistry; International College of Dentists; British Association for the Study of Community Dentistry; British Dental Editors Forum. Hobbies: Writing; Theatre; Swimming; Gardening; Walking. Address: Leys View Cottage, Lower Swell, Stow-on-the-Wold, Glos GL54 1LF, England.

HAND Roger, b. 25 Sep 1938, Brooklyn, NY, USA. Physician. Divorced, 1 s, 1 d. Education: BS 1959; MD 1962. Appointments include: Assistant Professor Medicine, Rockefeller University, NY; Assistant to Full Professor of Medicine, McGill University, Montreal, Canada; Director of McGill Cancer Center, Montreal, Canada; Currently, Professor of Medicine and Chief of General Internal Medicine, University of IL College of Medicine. Publications: Over 70 professional articles published, 1971-, including: Co-author, Staging Procedures, Clinical Management and Survival Outcome for Ovarian Carcinoma, in JAMA, 1993; Overlord and operational art: AAF plan C, the proposed airborne drop at Evreux, in Military Review, in press; For female cancers, is less more?, in Irish Medical Journal, in press. Honours include: Phi Beta Kappa; Alpha Omega Alpha; Fellow, American College of Physicians; Fellow, Royal College of Physicians of Canada; Leadership Citation, American Cancer Society, IL. Memberships include: American Society of Clinical Investigation; American Society for Clinical Oncology; American College of Physician Executives; Society for General Internal Medicine. Hobby: Sailing. Address: Dept of Medicine, M/C 787, 840 South Wood Street, Chicago, IL 60612, USA.

HANDBERG OVERVAD Annjette, b. 22 Jun 1964, Denmark. Chiropractor. m. Jesper Overvad, 30 Jul 1988, 1 s, 1 d. Memberships: Danish Chiropractor Association; European Chiropractor Association. Hobbies: Training Dogs for Hunting; Hunting. Address: Vorregaards Alle 99, 8200, Aarhus N, Denmark.

HANDZEL Zeev T, b. 15 Apr 1937, Poland. Physician; Researcher. m. Ruth Handzel, 26 Aug 1958, 2 sons. Education: MD, Hebrew University Medical School, Israel, 1964; Fellow, National Institutes of Health, Bethesda, Maryland, USA, 1971-73. Appointments: Associate Professor of Paediatrics and Clinical Immunology, Hebrew University and Hadassah Faculty of Medicine; Vice-Director, Paediatric Department, Kaplan Hospital, Rehovot; Director, Paediatric Research Institute and Clinical Immunology and Allergy Unit, Kaplan Hospital. Publications: Responses of Leprosy Patients to a Protein of M Leprae (author), 1992; Pediatric Immunology (author), 1993; AIDS in Israel (co-editor), 1993; Allergy in Israel (editor), 1994. Honours: Rogodzinsky Prize, 1978; AIDS Research International Award, World Academy of Population and Health Sciences, 1987. Memberships: American Academy of Allergy and Clinical Immunology; European Group of Immunodeficiency; New York Academy of Sciences; International AIDS Society. Hobbies: Swimming; Reading. Address: Pediatric Research Institute. Kaplan Hospital. Rehovot 76100, Israel.

HANIHARA Kazuro, b. 17 Aug 1927, Fukuoka, Japan. Professor of Anthropology. m. 16 Nov 1953, 1 son, 1 daughter. Education: BSc, DSc, Faculty of Science, University of Tokyo. Appointments: Associate Professor, Sapporo Medical College; Professor, Professor Emeritus, University of Tokyo; Professor, Professor Emeritus, International Research Centre for Japanese Studies. Publications include: Introduction to Human Evolutiojn, 1972; Introduction to Dental Anthropology, 1992; Origin of the Japanese, 1994. Honours: Kyoto Press Prize for Advancement in Culture, 1991. Memberships: American Association of Physical Anthropologists; Anthropological Society of Nippon; Japanese Association of Human genetics. Hobbies: Music; Computer Programming; Horse riding. Address: 2-1-2-503 Higashi-Sakaidani-cho, Oharano, Nishikyo-ku, Kyoto, Japan.

HANIHARA Tsunehiko, b. 21 Aug 1958, Sapporo, Japan. Physical Anthropologist. m. 30 Apr 1990, 2 sons. Education: BSc, 1985, Licensed Medical Doctor, 1985, Yamagata University School of Medicine; DMS, University of Tokyo. Appointments: Research Associate, Department Anatomy, Jichi Medical School, 1985-92; Assistant Professor, Department Anatomy, Sapporo Medical University, 1992-94; Associate Professor, Department Anatomy, Tohoku University, 1994-. Publications: Contributor of articles in professional journals. Honour: Promotion Prize for a Significant Paper of Anthropological Science, 1993. Memberships: Anthropological Society of Nippon; Japanese Association of Anatomists; American Association of Physical Anthropologists; Dental Anthropology Association. Hobby: Audio. Address: Department of Anatomy, Tohoku University School of Medicine, 2-1 Seiryo-cho, Aoba-ku, Sendai 980-77, Japan.

HANIN Israel, b. 29 Mar 1937, Shanghai, China. Pharmacologist; Educator. m. Leda Toni, 12 Jun 1960, 1 s, 1 d. Education: BS, UCLA, 1962; MS, 1965; PhD, Pharmacology, 1968. Appointments: Visiting Scientist, Toxicology, Karolinska Institute, Stockholm, 1968; Staff Pharmacologist, NIMH, WA, 1969-73; Assistant Professor, Associate Professor, Psychiatry and Pharmacology, University of Pittsburgh School of Medicine, 1973-81; Professor, 1981-86; Professor and Chairman, Department Pharmacology and Experimental Therapeutics, Director, Institute Neuroscience and Aging, Director, MD PhD Program, Loyola University Chicago, Stritch School of Medicine, Maywood, IL, 1986-; NIH Study Sections Member and Chair, 1979-1982; 1987-1990. Resident, 1991-. Publications: Editor of 12 books; Contributor of articles to professional journals. Honour: Grantee, NIMH, NIH, National Institute Aging, 1965-92. Memberships: Neuroscience Society, President Pittsburgh Chapter, 1982-83, President, Chicago Chapter, 1990-91; American Chemical Society; American Society Pharmacology and Experimental Therapeutics, Co-founder Great Lakes Chapter, 1987, President, 1990-92; American Society Neurochemistry; American College Neuropsychopharmacology; Society for Neuroscience. Hobbies: Collector of Ancient Glass and Pottery; Antique Walking Sticks; First Edition Journals. Address: Pharmacology Loyola University of Chicago, 2160 South 1st Ave, Maywood, IL 61053, USA.

HANSEN Heine H, b. 1 May 1938. Director, Professor, MD, The Finsen Center. Education: MD, University of Copenhagen, 1963. Appointments include: Assistant Professor, George Washington University, USA, 1971-73; Senior Lecturer, University of Copenhagen, 1973-75, 1988-91; Professor and Chair, Clinical Oncology, University of Copenhagen, 1991; Physician-in-Chief, Department of Oncology, Rigshospitalet, Finsen Institute, Copenhagen, Denmark, 1989-1994. Publications: Co-author, Lung Cancer, in Holland JF and Cancer Medicine, Philadelphia, USA, 1982; Co-author, Lung Tumours, 1988; Management of small cell cancer of the lung, in The Lancet, 1992. Honours: Annual Honorary Award, Danish Society for Cancer Research, 1982; George Edilstyn's Memorial Award, Royal College of Radiologists, London, 1983; Honorary Award, European Society of Medical Oncology, Madrid, Spain, 1987; Vera Peter's Annual Award, Princess Margaret Hospital, Toronto, Canada, 1989. Address: The Finsen Center, Rigshospitalet, 9 Blegdamsvej, Copenhagen, Denmark.

HANSON Kaido P, b. 20 Sep 1936, Vyry, Estonia. Doctor. m. Olga Hanson, 20 Feb 1965, 1 s. Education: MD; PhD, 1964; DSc, Medicine, Leningrad, 1973; Professor, Biochemistry. Appointments: Research Fellow, CRIRR, Leningrad, 1961-64; Lecturer, Chair, Biochemistry, University of Tartu, Estonia, 1964-66; Head, Laboratory of Biochemistry, CRIRR, Leningrad, 1966-75; Head of Department and Deputy Director, 1988-91; Acting Director, N N Petrov Research Institute of Oncology, 1991-. Publications: Over 300 publications concerning molecular biology, biochemistry, molecular and cellular radiobiology and oncology; Author of 6 monographs. Honours: Russia State Prize Winner, 1987; Corresponding Member of Russian Academy of Medical Sciences, 1988. Memberships include: Scientific Council of International Agency for Research on Cancer, Lyon, France, 1990-93; Editorial Board, Radiobiologia, Moscow. Hobby: Sport. Address: N N Petrov Research Institute of Oncology. 68 Leningradskaya St, Pesochny 2, St Petersburg, 189646, Russia.

HANUS Michel Emile, b. 6 Aug 1936, France. Psychiatrist. m. Isabelle Frenay, 5 Apr 1986, 5 sons. Education: MD. Publications: Psychiatrie de l'étudiant, 1970; Drogues et drogués, 1971; La pathologie du deuil, 1976; Les deuils dans la vie, 1994. Memberships: Société de Thérapeutique et Pharmacodynamie, 1973; Société Médico-Psychologique, 1973; Association du Congres de Psychiatrie de langue francaise, 1975; Société de Psychiatrie Biologique, 1988; Association Européenne de Psychiatrie, 1988; Société Psychanalytique de Paris, 1980; Société de Thanatologie, 1974. Hobbies: Music; Gardening. Address: 6 rue Boutarel, 75004 Paris, France.

HAO Wen Xue, b. 28 july 1926, Hiacheng, Liaoning, China. Physician. m. Professor Qu Ji Hui, 13 Feb 1953, 2 daughters. Education: BM; MD, China Medical University. Appointments: Lecturer, Associate Professor, Chief Doctor, Chairman, State Pharmaceutical COmpany Limited; Director, Research Centre of Prevention and Treatment of Senile Diseases, China Medical University. Publications: The Clinical Application of Agkistrodon Halys Venom in China, 1986; Thrombosis and Antithrombotic Enzymes, 1992; Honours: Excellent Product Prize for Science and Technology in Healthcare, 40th Anniversary of the Founding oh the Country, 1989; Golden Cup and Honourable Prize, International Symposium on Gerontology, 1990; Gold Medal prize for Chinese Scientific and Technical Achievement in Indonesia, 1992. Memberships: International Society for Fibrinolysis and Thrombolysis; International Society on Toxinology; Honorary President, US Chinese Medical Association; Permament Member of COuncil, Chinese Association of Prevention and Treatment of AIDS. Hobby: Swimming. Address: Research centre of Prevention and Treatment of senile Disease, China Medical University, N 16 Xinghai Village, Fujiazhuang, Dalian, China.

HAQUE Mohammed Nur Al, b. 9 Jan 1944, Rangpur, Bangladesh. Obstetrician & Gynacologist. m. Elsie Gan, 23 July 1980, 1 son, 1 daughter. Education: BSC; MB BS; MRCOG; LRCS, LRCP&S; LMCC; FACOG; FSOGC; FRCS(C); FRCOG. Appointments: Lecturer, Obstertrics & Gynacology, University of Sheffield, England; Former Examiner of MB, CHB, University of Sheffield, England; Senior Consultant, Obstetrics & Gynacology, Medina, Saudi Arabia; Private Practice. Publications: Significance of Maternal Mid-Term AFP-Int, 1983; Post-Date Pregnancy: Is Induction Still Necessary?, 1989; Pregnancy after Infertility, 1988; Co-Relation between Fetal Breathing Studies & Maternal Mid-Trimester AFP; Ultrasound Radio Telemetry: A New Dimention of Fetal Monitoring. Memberships: Fellow, Royal College of Obstetricians & Gynacologists; American Associates of Gynacologists; Royal College of Canada; Canadian Medical Association; Sask Medical Association. Honours: Gold Medal, BS Final Examinations, 1969. Hobbies: Photography; Fishing. Address: 64 Marquis Crescent South, Yorkton, Saskatchewan S3N 3L7, Canada.

HARADA Kenichi, b. 14 Nov 1929, Maebashi City, Japan. Psychiatrist. m. Takako Kodama, 12 Apr 1957, 1 son, 2 daughters. Education: MD, School of Medicine University of Tokyo. Appointments: Chief Doctor, National Musashi Hospital for Mental Diseases; Professor, Department of Psychiatry, Shinshu University; Professor, Department of Psychiatry, Tokyo University; Honorary Professor, Shanghai Second Medical College, China; Director, Kanagawa Prefectural Center of Psychiatry. Publications: Pathohistology in CNS of systemic lupus erythematodes, 1950; On the symptomatology of symptomatic psychoses, 1967; Organic Psychoses, 1975; Emotional condition in alcohol withdrawal psychoses, 1993. Memberships: Japan Society of Psychiatry and Neurology; International Society of Neuropathology; Japan Epilepsy Society; Japan Society of Psychopathology; Neuropsychiatry Assocaition of Japan. Address: Fujimidai 2-2-10, Nerima-ku, Tokyo, Japan.

HARAHAP Marwali, b. 4 Mar 1932, Pematang Siantar, Indonesia. Medical Doctor. m. Dalina Harahap, Feb 1961, 4 sons, 1 daughter. Education: Medical degree, University of Indonesia School of Medicine, Jakarta, 1960; Certified Specialist in Dermato-Venereology, 1964; Fellow, Division of Dermatology, University of California School of Medicine, San Francisco, 1964-66; DrMedSci, University of North Sumatra, Medan, 1968; Fellow, Department of Plastic Surgery, Tokyo Women's Medical College, 1977. Appointments: Dean, 1969-73, Professor, Department of Dermatology, 1973-, University of North Sumatra School of Medicine, Medan; First Director, Founder, Academic Hospital, Rumah Sakit Umum Pusat, H ADAM MALIK, Medan, 1990-93. Publications: Author or co-author, numerous contributions to books, journals and conference proceedings in the field of dermatology and plastic surgery; Editor or co-editor, several books. Honours: Honorary Award for Scientific Contribution, Indonesian Society of Dermatology and Venereology, 1991; Honorary Award for 25 Years of Government Service, President of Indonesia. Memberships: Chairman, Founder, Indonesian Society for Dermatologic Surgery; Former Chairman, Indonesian Dermato-Venereological Association, North Sumatra Region;

Charter Member, American Dermatologic Society for Allergy and Immunology; Charter Member, International Society for Dermatologic Surgery; Fellow, International Academy of Cosmetic Surgery; American College of Cryosurgery; Association for the Study of Medical Education; American Medical Writers Association; Various others. Hobbies: Picnicking; Travel. Address: 55 Jl Ir Juanda, Medan, Indonesia.

HARALABAKIS Nikos B, b. 26 Oct 1956, Tripolis, Greece. Orthodontist. m. Maria Nina Figa, 27 Sep 1985, 2 s, 1 d. Education: DDS, University of Thessaloniki, Greece; MS, Certificate in Orthodontics, Georgetown University, Washington, DC; Dr Dent, University of Thessaloniki, Greece. Career: Dentist; Orthodontist; Lecturer in Orthodontics; Currently, Assistant Professor in Orthodontics, University of Athens, Greece. Publications: Co-author, A postero anterior cephalometric evaluation of adult open bite subjects as related to normals, in European Journal of Orthodontics, 1991; The hyoid bone position in adult individuals with open bite and normal occlusion, in EJO, 1993; Premature of delayed exfoliation of deciduous teeth and root resorption and formation, in AO, 1994; Cephalometric characteristics of open bite in adults, in IJAOOS, 1994. Memberships: Greek Dental Association; Greek Orthodontic Society; European Orthodontic Society. Hobbies: Mountain Skiing; Sailing. Address: 6 Ploutarchou Street, 10676 Athens, Greece.

HARAN Mano Vasudevan, b. 4 Mar 1949, Colombo, Sri Lanka. Specialist in Obstetrics and Gynaecology. m. Renuka Kunaratnam, 30 Jan 1988, 1 son, 1 daughter. Education: MBBS (Ceylon); LRCP, MRCS (UK); MRCOG (UK); FACVEN (Australia); St John's College; Jaffna University; University of Ceylon, Colombo. Appointments: Consultant in Genitourinary Medicine, Mid and North Staffordshire District Health Authority, England; Director, Sexual Health Services, Darling Downs Region, Queensland, Australia; Currently Director of Obstetrics and Gynaecology, Toowoomba Base Hospital, Toowoomba, Queensland. Publications: Various including: Chlamydial Infections; Chorioamnionitis; HPV Infection of the Vulva. Honours: Distinction in Obstetrics and Gynaecology; 2nd Class Honours in MBBS. Memberships include: Queensland Sexual Health Society. Hobbies: Gardening; Photography; Cricket. Address: Department of Obstetrics and Gynaecology, Toowoomba Base Hospital, Wilmot Street, Toowoomba, Queensland 4350, Australia.

HARDING Graham Frederick Anthony, b. 19 Mar 1937, Birmingham, England. Clinical Neurophysiologist. m. Pamela Francis, 20 Sept 1991, 1 son, 2 daughters. Education: BSc, hons, University College London; PhD, University of Birmingham; DSc, University of Aston. Appointments: Honorary Consultant in Neuropsychology, Birmingham Central, 1974-; Honorary Consultant in Neuropsychology, Royal Wolverhampton, 1974-; Reader in Neuropsychology, 1973-78; Head, Vision Sciences, 1981-87. Publications: Photosensitive Epilepsy; More than 150 publications in Epilepsy, Neurology and Vision. Memberships: British Society for Clinical Neurophysiology; Fellow, British Psychology Society; International Society of Clinical Electrophysiology. Hobbies: Live Steam Model Railways. Address: Vision Sciences, Aston University, Aston Triangle, Brimingham B4 7ET, England.

HARGREAVES Isabel R, b. 28 Dec 1954, Manchester, England. Clinical Psychologist. m. Trevor W Jones, 30 May 1987, 1 s, 1 d. Education: BA, 1st Class Honours, PhD, University of North Wales, Bangor; MSc, Distinction, Kings College, Aberdeen. Appointments: Top Grade Clinical Psychologist, Gwynedd Health Authority; Deputy Director, North Wales Doctoral Clinical Pathology Course. Publications: Attributions and Depression, 1985; Community Health Staff's Prejudice and Knowledge About AIDS, Co-author, 1990; The Cognitive Assessment of Vulnerability to Depression, Co-author; Adult Clinical problems: A Cognitive Behavioural Approach, Review, 1992; Neuroses: Depressive and Anxiety Disorders, Co-author, 1994. Membership: AFBPS. Address: Department of Psychology, University College of North Wales, Bangor, Gwynedd LL57 2DG, Wales.

HARICHANDRAN C Hema, b. 23 Aug 1946, Colombo, Sri Lanka. Psychiatrist. m. Dharmini Harichandran, 17 Dec 1977, 2 daughters. Education: MB BS, University of Ceylon, 1971; MD; Dual Board Certified, Psychiatry, 1988, Geriatrics, 1992. Appointments: Acting Chief, Psychiatry Service, Department of Veterans Affairs; Chief, Inpatient Psychiatry; Chief, Substance Abuse Services; Academic Psychiatrist. Memberships: American Medical Association; American College of

International Physicians. Hobbies: Tennis; Travel. Address: 3203 Ronino Way, Lafayette, CA 94549-2639, USA.

HARICHANDRAN Dharmini, b. 10 Sep 1948, Colombo, Sri Lanka. Psychiatrist. m. Hema Harichandran, 17 Dec 1977, 2 daughters. Education: MB BS, University of Ceylon; Board Certified in Psychiatry, 1987. Appointments: Chief Psychiatry, Mt Diablo Medical Centre; Private Practice, Walnut Creek, California, USA. Membership: American Psychiatric Association. Hobby: Tennis. Address: 3203 Ronino Way, Lafayette, CA 94549-2639, USA.

HARLAND Barbara F, b. 16 Apr 1925, Chicago, IL, USA. Graduate Associate Professor of Nutrition. m. James W Harland, 6 Sep 1947, 1 s, 2 d. Education: BS, Dietetics, IA State University, Ames, 1946; MS, Nutrition, University of WA, Seattle, 1949; PhD, Nutrition, University of MD, College Park, 1971; Registered Dietician; Licensed Dietician; Licensed Nutritionist. Career: Chief Dietician, Stillwater, MN, 1946-47; Chief Dietician, Swedish Hospital Medical Center, Seattle, WA, 1948-49; Instructor, Nutrition, IN University SE, New Albany, 1964-65, University of MD, College Park, 1967-69; Research Biologist, Food and Drug, A & M Washington DC, 1969-84; Currently, Graduate Associate Professor of Nutrition, Department of Nutrition Science, Howard University. Publications: Co-author, AOAC approved method for analysis of total dietary fiber, 1985; Senior Author, AOAC approved method for analysis of phytate, 1986; Senior Author, Comprehensive List of Phytates in Foods, 1986; Senior Author, Fiber and Mineral Bioavail, 1989; Vanadium, 1994. Honours: Kappa Omicron Nu, 1946; Phi Sigma, 1971; Sigma Xi, 1971. Memberships: American Dietetic Association; American Chemical Society; American Society Clinical Nutrition; Society for Experimental Biology and Medicine; American Institute of Nutrition; Society for Nutriton Education; Association of Off Analytic Chemists. Hobbies: Tennis; Skiing; Swimming; Music. Address: Department of Nutritional Science, College of Allied Health Science, Howard University, Washington DC 20059, USA.

HARMON David Eugene, b. 27 July 1951, Greenville, Tennessee, USA. Eye Specialist. Education: BS, University of Tennessee, 1973; MS, University of Tennessee, 1975; PhD, University of Georgia, 1978; OD, New England College of Optometry, 1989. Appointments: Professor, Southern Illinois University; Professor, Clemson University; Internist, Veterans Hospital; Internist, Children's Hospital; Internist, Dimock Health Center; Eye Specialist & Geneticist in Solo Practice. Publications: Co-author of 15 genetic publications and author of 26 genetic publications. Honours: Outstanding Teacher, Southern Illinois University, 1981-82; Outstanding Teacher, Clemson University, 1983-85; Highest Proficiency Examination among Accelerated Optometry Students, 1988; Highest Internist Evaluation at Eye Clinic, 1989. Memberships: American Optometric Association; American Dairy Science Association; American Society of Animal Science; Sigma Xi; Alpha Zeta; Holstein Association. Hobbies: Travel; Camping; Coin Collecting; Table Tennis; Fishing. Address: Route 5, Box 6, Greeneville, TN 37743, USA. 7.

HARMON John W, b. 22 Apr 1943, USA. Surgeon. m. Gail McGreevy Harmon, 1 s, 1 d. Education: BA, Harvard College, 1965; MD, Columbia University, College of Physicians and Surgeons, 1969; Certified in General Surgery, 1976, Certified in Surgical Critical Care, 1992, American Board of Surgery. Appointments: Surgical Investigator, Walter Reed Army Institute of Research, 1975-85; Staff Surgeon, Walter Reed Medical Center, 1977-85; Director, Division of Surgery, Walter Reed Army Institute of Research, Washington DC, 1983-85; Chief of Surgery, Veterans Administration Medical Center, Washington DC, 1985-; Professor of Surgery: Georgetown University, Washington DC, 1985-; George Washington University, 1985-; Uniformed Services University of the Health Sciences, Bethesda, 1985-; Clinical Professor of Surgery, Howard University, Washington DC, 1985-; 3rd Year Clerkship Grading Committee, Georgetown Medical School, 1985-. Honours: Davis Mason Little Award, 1965; Merck Prize, Columbia University, 1969; William Beaumont Society Annual Award for Excellence in Clinical Research in Gastroenterology, 1982; 1st Prize, Washington Academy of Surgery, 1984; Invited Scientific Presentation, Columbia College of Physicians and Surgeons, 1994. Memberships include: American College of Surgeons; Chesapeake Vascular Society; The Shock Society; American Physiological Society; Pancreas Club; Associate, Association of Program Directors in Surgery; VA Study Section, Surgical Merit Review Board, 1994-97; Public Policy Committee, Society for the Surgery of the Alimentary Tract, 1990-; Cosmos Club, Admissions Committee, 1994-97; Colonel, US Army

Reserve Medical Corps, 1987-. Address: Chief, Surgical Sve 112, VA Medical Ctr, Washington DC 20422, USA.

HAROUN Ansar M, b. 29 Nov 1947, Pakistan. Psychiatrist. m. Nasra Sawal, 1977. Education: Christ's Hospital, Sussex, England; University of London at St Thomas' Hospital and King Edward Medical College; MMed Sci, Medical School, Nottingham, 1979; ABPN Board Certified Psychiatry, 1985; Board Certified Child and Adolescent Psychiatry, 1989. Appointments: Community Physician, Medical School, Nottingham, 1976-79; Psychiatrist, Yale Medical School, USA, 1980-85; Paediatric Psychiatrist, Columbia University College of Physicians and Surgeons, New York, 1985-87; Forensic Psychiatrist, Superior Court California, San Diego, 1987-; Assistant Clinical Professor of Psychiatry, UCSD School of Medicine, Director, VA Forensic Psychiatry Clinic, San Diego; Adjunct Professor, University of San Diego School of Law. Publications: Insomnia and Depression in General Practice, 1979; Clnical Guidelines for Involuntary Outpatient Treatment, 1990. Honours include: Roosevlet Scholar; Ciba Award, Royal Society of Medicine, London; Elected Yale University Medical School Council; Elected University of Nottingham senate; Board, Faculty of Medicine and Board, Postgraduate Studies, Tutor, Lenton Hall; Fellow, Royal Society of Health, London. Memberships: American Academy Psychiatry and Law, Child Psychiatry and Law Committee; American Psychiatric Association; American Society Law and Medicine; American College of Utilization Rev Physician; American College Forensic Psychiatry. Address: 5475 Bragg Street, San Diego, CA 92122-4103, USA.

HARPER Diane Frances, b. 26 Oct 1939, London, England. Osteopath. m. R E Harper, 2 Mar 1963, 1 s, 1 d. Education: Teachers Certificate, Royal Academy of Dancing; Cert Ed, Sidney Webb College; DO MRO, European School of Osteopathy. Appointments: Teacher: Richmond Secondary School; Biddenden Primary School; Colliers Green Primary School; Supply Teaching, Kent County Council; Currently, Osteopath. Membership: GCRO. Hobbies: Reading; Tennis; Travel; Music. Address: Andred Oast, Gribblebridge Lane, Biddenden, Kent, England.

HARRIS David Joseph, b. 7 Jun 1938. Clinical Geneticist. m. Chery Hall, 28 Jun 1970, 1 s, 3 d. Education: AB, cum laude, Oberlin College; MD, University of Rochester, NY. Appointments: Investigators Program, US Public Health Service, Center for Disease; Currently, Chief, Section of Genetics, Children's Mercy Hospital, KS City, MO; Professor of Pediatrics and Biological Sciences, University of MO, Kansas City. Memberships: American Society of Human Genetics; Genetics Society of America; American Academy of Pediatrics; American College of Medical Genetics. Hobbies: Music; Violin in Orchestra; Piano; Harpsichord. Address: Children's Mercy Hospital, 2401 Gillham, Kansas City, MO 64108, USA.

HARRIS Jeffrey P, b. 10 Jul 1949, Quincy, MA, USA. Professor. m. Susan H Harris, 2 s, 1 d. Education: BA magna cum laude, Case Western Reserve University, Cleveland, OH, 1971; MD, University of PA, Philadelphia, PA, 1974; PhD, Immunopathology, University of PA, 1976; Certified, American Board of Otolaryngology, 1979. Appointments include: Clinical Fellow, Otolaryngology, Harvard Medical School, Boston, MA, 1978-79; Assistant Professor, 1979-85, Associate Professor, 1985-89, Professor of Surgery and Otolaryngology, 1989-; Chief, Division of Otolaryngology - Head and Neck Surgery, 1986-, University of CA School of Medicine, San Diego, CA. Publications: Author of 2 books, 31 book chapters and over 100 articles published in scientific journals; Manuscript Reviews and editorial board of 7 scientific journals. Honours: Phi Beta Kappa; Alpha Omega Alpha; NINCDS Teacher Investigator Development Award, 1981-86; Sam Sanders MD Award for Clinical Research in Allergy, 1985; Fellowship, Triological society; Honor Award, American Academy Otolaryngology; Collegium Oto-Rhino-Laryngologicum Amicitiae Sacrum. Memberships include: Co-Chairman, Expert Panel, Hearing and Hearing Impairment, 1992; NIH Communicative Disorders Study Section, 1992-96; Numerous committees; Fellow, American College of Surgeons; Diplomate: National Board of Medical Examiners and American Board of Otolaryngology; Pres Association for Research in Otolaryngology; AMA; American Neurotology Society; Otosclerosis Group; Assoc Examiner American Board of Otolaryngology Medical and Scientific Advisory Board, Vestibular Disorders Association, 1992. Address: UCSD Medical Center, Division of HNS, 225 Dickinson Street, San Diego, CA 92103-8895, USA.

HARRIS Thelissa Annette, b. 6 June 1949, Houston, TX, USA. Physician. Education: MD, 1976; Diplomate, American Board of Psychiatry and Neurology, 1980. Appointments: Staff Psychiatrist, The Institute of Living, Hartford, 1979-87; Private Practice of Psychiatry, 1987-. Publications: Treatments of Psychiatric Disorders, Consultant, 1990. Honours: Fellow, American Psychiatric Association, 1989. Memberships: American Psychiatric Association; Black Psychiatrists of America. Hobbies: Reading; Walking; Gardening; Cooking. Address: 682 Prospect Avenue, Hartford, CT 06105, USA.

HARRISON Robert Cameron, b. 2 Aug 1920, Lamont, Alberta, Canada. Surgeon. m. Lorraine Gershaw, 21 Apr 1947, 5 s. Education: MD, Alberta, 1943; MSc, Toronto, 1951. Appointments: Professor of Surgery and Director of Surgical Research, University of Alberta, 1952-66; Professor and Head, Surgery, 1966-76, Professor of Surgery, 1976-, UBC. Publications: Reoperative Gastrointestinal Surgery, 1973, 2nd edition, 1979, Japanese edition, 1986; Over 150 Professional Papers. Honours: Gold Medals in Surgery, RCP & S (C), 1954, 1956; Nuffield Traveling Professor in Surgery, UK, 1959; Reeve Prize. Memberships include: Past Council Member, MRC Canada; President, Janes Surgical Society, 1972; President, Canadian Association Gastroenterology, 1982-83; Royal College of Physicians and Surgeons of Canada; American Surgical Association; Society of University Surgeons; 2 Editorial Boards. Hobby: Boating. Address: UBC Dept of Surgery, 2211 Westbrook Mall, Vancouver, BC, Canada, V6T 1W5.

HARROW Martin, b. 22 Aug 1933, New York City, NY, USA. Psychologist. m. Helen Kramer, 19 Aug 1956, 4 d. Education: BA, Psychology, City University of New York, 1955; PhD, Psychology, Indiana University, 1961; Diplomate, ABPP, Psychology. Career: Instructor, Associate Professor, Department of Psychiatry, Yale University School of Medicine, 1962-73; Associate Professor, Professor, Departments of Psychiatry and Psychology, University of Chicago, 1973-90; Chief Psychologist, Michael Reese Hospital, 1973-; Principal Investigator, NIMH Research Grants on Schizophrenia, 1975-; Professor and Director of Psychology, Department of Psychiatry, University of IL College of Medicine, 1990-. Publications: Disordered Thinking and Schizophrenic Psychopathology, book, 1985; Articles: Outcome in Manic Disorders, in Archives of General Psychiatry, 1990; Psychotic Unipolar Depression at Follow-up, in American Journal of Psychiatry, 1994. Honours: Outstanding Contribution to Psychology, IL Psychological Association, 1990; Research Grant, National Institute of Mental Health Merit Award, 1992. Memberships: Fellow, American Psychological Association; Editorial Board, Clinical Psychology Review; Midwestern Psychological Association. Hobbies: Chess; Basketball; Cards; Reading; Writing. Address: Department of Psychiatry, University of Illinois College of Medicine, Chicago, IL 60612, USA.

HARSHA Brian Christopher, b. 16 Jul 1956, Portsmouth, OH, USA. Oral and Maxillofacial Surgeon. m. Judith Seville, 13 Nov 1982, 1 s, 1 d. Education: BA, University of VA, 1978; DDS, Medical College of VA, 1982; MSc, University of NC, 1986. Appointment: Private Practice. Publications: Cranial bone grafts and oral and maxillofacial surgery, 1986; Co-author, Stabilization of LeFort 1 osteotomies utilizing small bone plates, in International Journal Adult Orthodontics Orthognathic Surgery, 1986. Honours: A D Williams Award, 1979, 1981. Memberships: AAOMS; ADA; AACS. Hobbies: Skiing; Golf; Volleyball. Address: 708 21st Ave North, Myrtle Beach, SC 29577, USA.

HARTFIELD Vincent Jonathan, b. 25 Sept 1932, London, England. Obstetrician, Gynaecologist; Priest. m. Margaret Greaves, 5 July 1958, 1 son, 3 daughters. Education: MB BS, London, 1957; MRCS, LRCP, 1957; DA; FRCOG; FRNZCOG; FMC; OG (NIG) FWACS. Appointments: Obstetics & Gynaecology Surgeon, Deputy Medical Superintendent, Wesley Guild Hospital, Ilesha, Nigeria; Medical Superintendent, Ituk Mbang Hospital, Uyo, Nigeria; O & G Consultant, Wanganui Hospital, New Zealand. Publications Include: Efficacy of Measels Vaccine, 1963; Obstetrics in a Developing Country, 1964; Symphysiotomy, 1973; Antenatal Record Card for Use in Developing Countries, 1973; Dying in Hospital, 1978; Female Sterilization by the Vaginal Route, 1993. Honours: Research Prize, West African College of Surgeons, 1965. Memberships: New Zealand Medical Association; Royal New Zealand College of Obstetrics & Gynaecology; Medical Action for Global Security; Anglican Pacifist Society. Hobbies: Classical Music; Gardening; Novels; Art. Address: 6 Caversham Road, St Johns Wood, Wanganui, New Zealand 5001.

HARTMAN Lawrence Stephen, b. 27 Jan 1944, Ruislip, England. Osteopath. m. Susan Hartman, 13 Jul 1991, 1 s, 2 d. Education: DO, British School of Osteopathy; PhD, Medicina Alternativa; Member of Register of Osteopaths. Appointments: Lecturer in Osteopathic Technique, 1964-78; Head, Department of Technique BSO, Associate Professor of Osteopathic Technique, British Shool of Osteopathy, London, 1978-88; Technique Consultant, 1988-94; Currently, Private Practice, International Teaching. Publications include: Handbook of Osteopathic Technique, 1983, 2nd edition, 1986, and accompanying video, 1983, revised, 1991. Memberships: Osteopathic Association of Great Britain; General Council and Register of Osteopaths; French and Japanese Register of Osteopaths. Hobbies: Golf; Model Aircraft; Amateur Radio; Karate; Computers; DIY; Car Restoration; Writing. Address: 178 East Barnet Road, New Barnet, Hertfordshire, EN4 8RD, England.

HARTMAN William Morris, b. 28 Jul 1939, Elgin, IL, USA. Physicist. m. Christine Rein, 24 Jun 1967, 1 s, 1 d. Education: DPhil, Oxon; Theoretical Physics, 1965. Appointment: Professor of Physics, Michigan State University. Publications: 50 Publications on Psychoacoustics and Human Hearing, 1977-93. Memberships: Acoustical Society of America; Association for Research in Otolaryngology. Address: Physics Department, Michigan State University, East Lansing, MI 48824, USA.

HARTWELL Rudi, b. 8 Aug 1938, Berlin, Germany. Obstetrician and Gynaecologist. m. Anne Elizabeth, 2 Feb 1972, 1 son. Education: MBBS; LRCP; MMCS; FRCOG; FRCS (Edinburgh). Appointments: Senior House Officer, Queen Charlotte's Hospital, England, 1964; registrar, Royal London Hospital, 1967-69; Consultant Obstetrician and Gynaecologist, Princess Alexandra Health Services. Publications: Pregnancy Induced Hypertension, 1989. Membership: Royal Society of Medicine. Hobbies: Skiing; Mountain Walking; Tennis; Opera. Address: Park House, Pishiobury Drive, Sawbridgeworth, Hertfordshire CM21 0PD, England.

HARVEY Harry Martin, b. 26 Sep 1935, Enfield, Middlesex, England. Acupuncturist. m. Joan Harvey, 1964, 1 s, 2 d. Education: BA, Social Administration, Nottingham University; Diploma in Applied Social Studies; Home Office Certificate of Training in Childcare; Diploma in Adult Education; Diploma in Acupuncture, Northern College of Acupuncture, York, England. Appointments: Social Worker, 1960-71; Senior Lecturer in Social Work, Trent Polytechnic, Nottingham, 1971-86; Various Part-Time Lectureships and Training Posts, 1986-92; Private Practice, Acupuncture, 1992-. Membership: Register of Traditional Chinese Medicine. Hobbies: Folk Dancing; Furniture Restoration; Writing and Composing; Acappella Singing. Address: Leominster Community Centre, School Road, Leominster, Herefordshire, HR6 8NJ, England.

HARVEY Steve, b. 1 Nov 1949, Duluth, Minnesota, USA. Psychologist. m. 24 May 1990, 1 son. Education: BA, Stanford University, 1971; MA, Creative Arts Therapies, Lone Mountain College, 1978; PhD, University of Denver, 1981; Licensed Psychologist; Academy of Dance Therapists Registered; Registered Drama Therapist; Registered Play Therapist; Supervisor. Appointments: Staff Psychologist, NEEDs School; Adjunct Assistant Professor, University of Colorado, Colorado Springs; Adjunct Faculty, Naropa Institute, Boulder, Colorado; Currently Child Psychologist and Creative Arts Therapist in private practice, Consultant, Educator. Publications: Book chapters: Dynamic Play therapy: Expressive interventions with families; Ann: A dynamic play therapy response to ritual abuse; Sandra: A case of an adopted sexually abused child; Dynamic play therapy: Creating attachments; Creative arts therapy interventions with children and adolescents: Accent on interdisciplinary, poetic, and dramatic approaches, in press; Journal articles: Creating a family: An integrated expressive arts approach to adoption; Dynamic play therapy: An integrated expressive arts approach to the family therapy of young children. Memberships: American Psychological Association; American Dance Therapy Association; National Association of Drama Therapy; American Play Therapy Association. Hobbies: Creative drama and dance; Hiking; Camping. Address: 1605 S Tejon, Colorado Springs, CO 80906, USA.

HASHASH M Zulfikar, b. Beirut, Lebanon. Obstetrician and Gynaecologist. m. Margaret Cowen, 31 May 1980, 1 son, 2 daughters. Education: MB, BCh; Residency, Obstetrics and Gynaecology Department, American University, Beirut; MD; MRCOG. Appointments: Registrar, West Middlesex Hospital, London, England; Currently Consultant, Obstetrics and Gynaecology Department, Makassed

General Hospital, Beirut. Honours: 1 of Founders of Teaching Residency Programme, Obstetrics and Gynaecology Department, Makassed General Hospital. Hobbies: Reading; Golf; Snooker. Address: Makassed General Hospital, Beirut, Lebanon.

HASHIM BIN YAACOB, b. 12 May 1949, Kelantan, Malaysia. Professor of Oral Pathology and Oral Medicine. m. Sri Nurestri, 1979, 2 sons, 1 daughter. Education: BDS (Otago); MSc (London); FDSRCPS (Glasgow); FDSRCS (Eng); DIS (IIU). Appointments: Department Head, 1980-82, Deputy Dean, Dental School, 1983-86, Dean, Dental School, 1987-, Professor of Oral Pathology and Oral Medicine, 1987-, Dental Faculty, University of Malaya, Kuala Lumpur. Publications: 60 articles in professional and academic dental journals. Memberships: Royal College of Physicians and Surgeons of Glasgow; Royal College of Pathologists, UK; Institute of Health Education, UK. Hobbies: Writing poetry; Malay culture. Address: Dental Faculty, University of Malaya, Kuala Lumpur 58100, Malaysia.

HASKELL Neal H, b. 14 Oct 1946, Indiana, USA. Forensic Entomologist. 1 s, 1 d. Education: BS, Entomology, Purdue University; MS, 1989, PhD, 1993, Purdue University; Board Certified Entomologist. Career: Private Forensic Consultant. Publications: Co-author, Use of aquatic insects in determining submersion intervals, 1989; Co-editor, Entomology and Death: A Procedural Guide, 1990; Co-author, The black soldier fly Mermetia Illucens as a potential measure of human postmortem interval, 1993. Honours: President's Academic Award, Purdue University, 1969, 1970. Memberships: American Academy of Forensic Science; Midwestern Association of Forensic Scientists; Entomological Society of America. Hobbies: Tennis; Shooting Sport; Travel. Address: 425 Kannal Avenue, Rensselaer, IN 47978, USA.

HASLE Henrik, b. 27 Sept 1958, Denmark. Medical Doctor. 1 son, 3 daughters. Education: MD, Odense University, 1987. Appointments: Currently Clinical Research Fellow, Odense University Hospital. Publications: Thesis on Myelodysplastic Syndromes in Children and some 30 papers mainly dealing with haematology and oncology. Memberships: Danish Society of Pediatrics; Danish Society of Hematology; Nordic Organisation of Pediatric Hematology and Oncology; American Society of Pediatric Hematology and Oncology. Address: Department of Pediatrics, Odense University Hospital, 5000 Odense C, Denmark.

HASPELS Ary A, b. 27 Dec 1925. Professor of Gynaecology. m. Mrs A v Hall, 2 s, 3 d. Education: MD, 1954; PhD, 1961; FICS; FRCOG, 1989. Appointments: Registrar, Surgery, Nymeglu, 1954-56; Tropical Doctor, Indonesia, 1956-64; Registrar, Obstetrics & Gynaecology, University of Amsterdam, 1964-67; Consultant, University of Amsterdam, 1967-69; Full Professor, Obstetrics & Gynaecology, Utrecht, 1969-91; Professor of Gynaecological Research. Publications: More than 400 publications; More than 20 Books. Honours: Honorary FRCOG, London, 1989; Honorary FNCOG, 1991; Underground Resistance Cross, 1969; Commander Order of Orange, 1969; Knight Dutch Lyon, 1990. Memberships: Royal College of Obstetrics & Gynaecology, London; International Fertility Association; Netherlands College of Obstetrics & Gynaecology. Hobbies: Golf; Tennis. Address: University Hospital Utrecht, Heidelberglaan 100, P O 85500, 3508 GA Utrecht, The Netherlands.

HASSLER Ove, b. 25 June 1932, Motala, Sweden. Professor of Pathology. m. Margit Hedström, 24 June 1960, 1 son, deceased. 3 daughters. Education: MD, 1956; PhD, 1961. Appointments: Professor of Pathology, mainly Neuropathology. Publications: About 140 publications on cerebral anenrysms, cerebral arteries, microangiography on the CNS. Address: Department of Pathology, University Hospital, S90187 Umea, Sweden.

HATA Yoshinobu, b. 7 Aug 1941, Japan. Associate Professor. m. Makiko Hata, 23 Sept 1971, 1 son, 1 daughter. Education: MD, Hirosaki University School of Medicine, 1966; PhD, Hokkaido University School of Medicine, 1972. Appointments: Currently Associate Professor, First Department of Surgery, Hokkaido University School of Medicne, Sapporo. Publications: Flow cytometric analysis of the nuclear DNA content of hepatoblastoma, 1991; Surgical treatment of congenital biliary dilatation associated with pancreatico-biliary maljunction, 1992. Memberships: French Society of Pediatric Surgery; International Society of Pediatric Oncology; Pacific Association of Pediatric Surgery. Hobbies: Judo; Skiing; Tennis; Windsurfing. Address: First Department of

Surgery, Hokkaido University School of Medicine, N-15 W-7, Sapporo, 060 Japan.

HATCHER Charles Ross Jr, b. 28 June 1930, Bainbridge, Georgia, USA. Cardiothoracic Surgeon. m. (1) 1 son, 1 daughter, (2) Phyllis Gregory Slappey, 9 July 1988. Education: BS magna cum laude, University of Georgia, Atlanta, 1950; MD cum laude, Medical College of Georgia, 1954, Internship, Assistant Resident, Surgery, Halsted Resident, Surgery, Johns Hopkins Hospital; Assistant Resident, Surgery, Peter Bent Brigham Hospital. Appointments: Captain, Medical Corps, Walter Reed Army Medical Center, 1956-58; Instructor, Surgery, 1962-63, Assistant Professor, Surgery, 1963-67, Associate Professor, Surgery, 1967-71, Chief, Division of Cardiothoracic Surgery, 1971-90, Professor of Surgery, 1971-, Emory University School of Medicine, Atlanta, Georgia; Director, Chief Executive Officer, 1976-84, Chief Financial Officer, 1984-90, The Emory Clinic; Vice-President for Health Affairs, Director, The Robert W Woodruff Health Center, 1984-. Publications: Over 200 in the field, including 16 in books. Honours: Regents Scholar, University of Georgia, Atlanta; Phi Beta Kappa; Alpha Omega Alpha; Sigma Xi; President's Medal, Southeastern Surgical Congress; Silver Medallion, American Heart Association; Distinguished Service Award, Emory University School of Dentistry; Distinguished Professional Achievement Award, Emory University School of Medicine Alumni Association; Outstanding Leadership Award, Morehouse School of Medicine, 1990. Memberships: American College of Surgeons; American College of Cardiology, Board of Governors 1977-80; American College of Chest Physicians, Board of Governors and Board of Regents 1974-81; American Surgical Association; President, 1986 & 1987, Society of Thoracic Surgeons; Society for Vascular Surgery; President, 1984, Southern Thoracic Surgical Association; American Association for Thoracic Surgery; American Heart Association. Hobbies: Hunting; Reading; Travel. Address: 1440 Clifton Road NE, Atlanta, GA 30322, USA.

HATFIELD Robert Arthur, b. 2 Apr 1954, Birmingham, England. Chiropractor. m. Denise Elmer, 28 Aug 1978, 1 son, 3 daughters. Education: BSc, Honours, Aston University, 1978; DC, Anglo-European College of Chiropractic, 1985; Advanced Sacro-Occipital Technique Practitioner, 1992. Appointments: Private Practice; Principal Chiropractor, Walsgrave and Nuneaton Chiropractic Clinics. Honour:Clinical Progeny Prize, Anglo-European College of Chiropractic, 1985. Membership: British Chiropractic Association. Hobbies: French Language; Travel; Health and Fitness Training; Skiing. Address: 380 Walsgrave Road, Coventry CV2 4AF, England.

HAUGE Ståle, b. 19 June 1959, Langesund, Norway. Chiropractor. 2 sons, 1 daughter. Education: Doctor of Chiroprasctic, Anglo-European College of Chiropractic, Bournemouth, England, 1986; Certified Chiropractic Sports Physician. Memberships: Norwegian Chiropractic Association; European Chiropractors Union; FICS; ICAK-E. Hobbies: Scuba-diving; Cross country skiing. Address: PO Box 60, 3201 Sandefjord, Norway.

HAUSER Peter, b. 16 Apr 1955, Petersburg, VA, USA. Physician; Scientist. Education: BA, Distinction, German Literature, University of VA, 1976; MD, University of VA Medical School, 1981. Appointments include: Medical Staff Fellow, Biological Psychiatry Branch, National Institute of Mental Health, Bethesda, MD, 1986-88; From 1988, National Research Scholarship Award, Guest Researcher, Molecular Regulation and Neuroendocrinology Section, National Institute of Diabetes and Digestive and Kidney Diseases, Bethesda. Publications: Editor, Brain Imaging in the Affective Disorders, 1991; Numerous articles, presentations and abstracts, including: Co-author, Attention Deficit Hyperactivity Disorder in Subjects with Generalized Resistance to Thyroid Hormone, in New England Journal of Medicine, 1993. Honours: Wyethe Award for Excellence, Ontario Psychiatric Association Annual Meeting, Toronto, 1986. Memberships: Cosmos Club, Washington DC; Board Certified, Psychiatry and Neurology. Hobbies: Skiing; Woodworking; Biking; Camping; Painting. Address: 4951 Eskridge Terrace, Washington DC 20016, USA.

HAVALDAR Parvat, b. 5 June 1955, Naganur, Belgaum, India. Medical Doctor. m. Shanta Havaldar, 27 May 1980, 2 daughters. Education: MBBS, DCH, MD (Paediatrics), Karnatak University, Dharwad. Appointments: Tutor in Paediatrics, Lecturer in Paediatrics, currently Associate Professor of Paediatrics, J N Medical College, Belgaum. Publications: Brucellosis in Children, 1987; Fulminant Diphtheretic Myocarditis, 1989; Haemorrhagic Diphtheria, 1989; Chronic

Calcific Pancreatitis in Children, 1992. Honours: British Council Trainee in Maternal and Child Health. Memberships: Life Member, Indian Academy of Paediatrics; International Society of Tropical Paediatrics; Indian Medical Association. Hobbies: Cricket; Indian classical music. Address: A-9/1 Staff Quarters, J N Medical College, Nehru Nagar, Belgaum 590010, India.

HAWKINS Denis Frank, b. 4 Apr 1929, London, England. Obstetrics and Gynaecology. m. Joan Taynton, 10 Jul 1957, 1 s, 2 d. Education: BSc; PhD; DSc; MB, BS, London; MD, Mass; D Obst RCOG; MRCOG; FRCOG; FACOG. Appointments: Professor of Obstetrics and Gynaecology, Boston University School of Medicine, 1965-68; Senior Lecturer, Reader, Professor of Obstetric Therapeutics, University of London, 1965-; Editor, Journal of Obstetrics and Gynaecology; Honorary Consultant Obstetrician and Gynaecologist, Hammersmith Hospital. Publications: Obstetric Therapeutics, 1974; Gynaecological Therapeutics, 1981; Drugs and Pregnancy, 1983, 1987; Drug Treatment in Obstetrics, 1983, 1991; Recent Advances in Perinatal Medicine, 1993. Hobbies include: Greek Archaeology; Primitive Rock Carvings. Address: Blundel Lodge, Blundel Lane, Cobham, Surrey, KT11 2SP, England.

HAWKINS June, b. 6 Sept 1938, Jersey, Channel Islands. Physician. m. J Richard Hawkins-Kimmel, 1 s, 1 d. Education: LRCP, 1962; MRCS, 1962; MB, 1962; BA, 1962; Diplomate American Board of Internal Medicine, 1972; Diplomate, American Board of Allergy & Immunology, 1974. Appointments: House Surgeon, West London Hospital, Hammersmith, 1962; House Physician, St Mary Abott's Hospital, London, 1963; Obstetric Officer, Queen Elizabeth II Hospital, Welwyn, Herts, 1963; Resident in Internal Medicine, Baylor University Medical Center, Texas, 1964-65; Chief Resident in Internal Medicine, Baylor University Medical Center, Texas, 1966; Fellow, Baylor University Medical Center, Department of Pathology, 1966-68; Assistant Professor, Department of Microbiology, Baylor University College of Dentistry, 1968-69; Assistant Medical Director, Southwestern Life Insurance Company, Texas, 1969-70; Colorado Permanente Medical Group, Department of Internal Medicine, Colorado, 1971-74; Clinical Assistant/Professor of Medicine, Oregon Health Sciences University; Private Practice, Allergy & Immunology. Publications: Isolation of Dexyribonucleic Acid, 1966; Nature, 1967; Revista Medica, 1967; Immune Response in Humans to Autologous Tumor Immunizations, 1969; Computer Usage in Evaluating Medical Examiners, 1970; Humidifier Lung, 1976. Hobbies: Dancing; Golf; Tennis; Travel. Address: 9735 South West Shady Lane, Suite 303, Tigard, Oregon 97223, USA.

HAY Elizabeth Dexter, b. 2 Apr 1927, St Augustine, FL, USA. Biomedical Research. Education: AB, Smith College, 1948; MD, Johns Hopkins University, 1952; MA, Honorary, Harvard University, 1964; DSc, Honorary, Smith College, 1973, Trinity College, 1989; LHD' Honorary, 1990. Appointments include: Assistant Professor, Johns Hopkins University, Baltimore 1956-57; Assistant Professor, Cornell University Medical School, NY, 1957-60; Assistant Professor, Harvard Medical School, Boston, 1960-64; Louise Foote Pfeiffer Associate Professor of Embryology, 1964-69; Chairman, Department of Anatomy and Cellular Biology, 1975-93; Advisory Council, Johns Hopkins School of Medicine, 1982-; Board, Scientific Counselors National Institute Enviromental Health Science, NIH, 1990-. Publications: Regeneration, 1966; Co-author, Fine Structure of the Developing Avian Cornea, 1969; Editor, Cell Biology of Extracellular Matrix, 1981, 2nd edition, 1991; Articles published in professional journals. Honours: Distinguished Achievement Award, NY Hospital, Cornell Medical Center Alumni Council, 1985; Alcon Award for Vision Research, 1988. Memberships include: President 1973-74, Society for Development Biology; President 1976-77, Legislature Alert Committee, 1982-, E B Wilson Award, 1989, American Society of Cell Biology; President 1981-82, Henry Gray Award, 1992; American Association of Anatomists; National Academy of Sciences; International Society Development of Biologists. Hobby: Raising Cats. Address: Dept of Cell Biology, Harvard Medical School, 220 Longwood Ave B-1-342, Boston, MA 02115, USA.

HAYASHI Kuniaki, b. 19 Jan 1939, Nagasaki, Japan. Professor of Radiology. m. Michie Hayashi, 1 son, 1 daughter. Education: MD; Postgraduate course, Department of Radiology, Nagasaki University School of Medicine, 1965-79; Resident, Department of Radiology, Cleveland Clinic, USA, 1971-74; Certified: American Board of Radiology; Japanese Board of Radiology. Appointments: Assistant, 1969-74, Instructor, 1974-75, Associate Professor, 1975-88, Professor, Chairman, 1988-, Department of Radiology, Nagasaki University School of Medicine. Publications: Co-author: Aortographic analysis of aortic dissection, 1974; Takayasu's arteritis: Decrease in aortic wal thickening following steroid therapy, 1986; Initial pulmonary artery involvement in Takayasu's arteritis, 1986; Rounded atelectasis with emphasis on its wide spectrum, 1993. Hobby: Tennis. Address: 330-318 Koebaru, Nagasaki 851-11, Japan.

HAYES Marie J, b. 15 Aug 1951, Brookline, MA, USA. Professor of Psychology. 1 son, 1 daughter. Education: BA, magna cum laude, Boston College, 1969-73; MA, PhD, Northeastern University, 1974-79. Appointments: Instructor, Psychology, Northeastern University, 1976-79; Principal Psychologist, Glavin Regional Center, 1978-79; Postdoctoral Fellow, Boston University School of Medicine, 1979-80; Instructor in Psychology, Pennsylvania University, 1983-85; Instructor in Psychology, University of Pennsylvania, 1983-86; Research Scientist, Hospital of the University of Pennsylvania, 1986-87; Instructor in Psychology, Husson College, 1987-89; Instructor in Psychology, University of Maine, 1987-91; Assistant Professor in Psychology, University of Maine, 1991-; Allied Health Scientist, Family Practice Clinic, Eastern Maine Medical Center, 1993-. Publications: Spontaneous motor activity is affected by sleep surface quality in children, 1994; Neonatal desipramine treatment alters free-running circadian drinking rhythms in rats, 1994; Functional analysis of spontaneous movements in preterm infants. Memberships: International Society for Developmental Psychobiology; Society for Research in Child Development; Sleep Research society; International Association for Infant Mental health; Maine Association for Infant Mental Health; American Association of University Women. Address: RFD 2, Box 1748, Hampden, ME 04444, USA.

HAYES Nicola Jane (Nicky), b. 19 June 1953, Taplow, Buckinghamshire, England. Psychologist. Education: BSc (Hons), 1975, MEd, 1983, Leeds University; PGCE, Leeds University/Huddersfield Polytechnic, 1980; PhD, Council for National Academic Awards/Huddersfield Polytechnic, 1991; Chartered Psychologist. Appointments: Lecturer, Huddersfield Technical College, 1982-85; Lecturer, Researcher, Huddersfield Polytechnic, 1986-91; Consultant Chartered Psychologist, 1991-; Honorary Research Fellow, University of Huddersfield. Publications include: Teach Yourself Psychology, 1994; A First Course in Psychology, 1984, 1988, 1993; Principles of Social Psychology, 1993; Principles of Comparative Psychology, 1994; Foundations of Psychology, 1994. Honours: Honorary Life Member, Association for the Teaching of Psychology, 1985; Fellow, British Psychological Society, 1995. Memberships: British Psychological Society; Association for the Teaching of Psychology; British Association for the Advancement of Science; European Association of Work and Organisational Psychology. Hobbies: Science fiction; Ice-skating; Home preserving of fruit and vegetables; Wildlife conservation. Address: 9 Lime Street, Lockwood, Huddersfield HD1 3SN, England.

HAYNES Suzanne Groweg, b. 13 Nov 1947, Huntington Park, CA, USA. Epidemiologist. 1 d. Education: BA, University of Tennessee, 1969; MA, 1970, MPH, 1972, University of Texas; PhD, University of North Carolina, 1975. Appointments include: Research Economist, Mayor's Manpower Planning Council, Houston, TX, 1970-71; Epidemiologist, National Heart Lung and Blood Institute, Bethesda, 1975-80; Research Associate Professor, Department of Epidemiology, University of North Carolina, School of Public Health, Chapel Hill, 1983-84; Chief, Medical Statistics Branch, National Centre for Health Statistics, Hyattsville, Maryland, 1984-87;Office of Director, National Institutes of Health, Women's Health Initiative, Community Prevention Study, 1993; Office on Women's Health, Public Health Service, Office of Assistant Secretary for Health, USDHHS, National Action Plan on Breast Cancer, 1994; Chief, Health Promotion Sciences Branch, 1987-94, Chief, Health Education Section, Health Education Section, National Cancer Institute, Bethesda; Assistant Director for Science, Office on Women's Health, Public Health Service, Office of Assistant Secretary for Health, USDHSS, 1994. Publications: Contributor of numerous articles in professional journals. Honours include: Sigma Delta Epsilon; Established Investigator, American Heart Association, 1982-84; NCHS Womens Council Award for Excellence, 1987; Special Recognition Award, American Association of Physicians for Human Rights, 1994. Memberships include: Fellow, Academy of Behavioural Medicine, 1979-; Fellow, American College of Epidemiology, 1981-; Governing Council, American Public Health Association, 1986-92. Address: 12330 Shadetree Lane, Laurel, MD 20708, USA.

HAYWOOD Theodore Joseph, b. 13 Feb 1929, Monroe, North Carolina, USA. Physician. m. Nancy Hume Ferguson, 21 Dec 1959, 2 sons, 1 daughter. Education: BS, The Citadel, Charleston, 1948; MD,

Vanderbilt University School of Medicine, Nashville, 1952. Appointments: Resident Physician, Charity Hospital of Louisiana, 1954-55; Resident Physician, Massachusetts General Hospital, Boston, 1955; Director, Allergy Clinics, Osaka Army Hospital, Japan, 1955-57; Fellowship, Baylor College of Medicine, Houston, 1958-63. Publications Include: Headache in Childhood, 1961; Pediatric Allergy and Immunology, 1961; Oral Allergies, 1961; Allergy in School Age Children, 1975; Allergy: Immunologic and Psychophysiologic Aspects, 1976; Female Allergy to Seminal Fluid, 1978; Determinant Constitutional and Other Variables in the Etiology of Atopic Diseases, 1980; Allergy of the Central Nervous System, 1982. Memberships Include: Vanderbilt Medical Alumni Association, 1952-; Great Ormond Street Dining Club, 1953-; Glynn County Medical Society, 1957-58; American Academy of Allergy & Immunology; Greater Houston Allergy Society, 1973-; Texas Allergy Society, 1986-. Hobbies: Photography; Travel; Reading. Address: McGovern Allergy Clinic, 6969 Brompton Road, Houston, TX 77025, USA. 2.

HAZE Neula, b. 27 Sept 1947, Kirksville, Missouri, USA. Dance and Movement Therapist. Education: MA, Dance; MA, Counselling Psychology; Academy of American Dance Therapists. Appointments: Coordinator of Graduate Dance Therapy Programme, California State University, Hayward, 1983-93; Currently Director, Authentic Movement Institute, Oakland, California. Publications: An Interview with Janet Adler, 1994; Authentic Movement Institute Opens, 1994. Membership: American Dance Therapy Association. Address: Authentic Movement Institute, PO Box 11410, Oakland, CA 94611, USA.

HE Sheng, b. 10 Nov 1941, Chongqing, China. Surgeon. m. Liu Yongsong, 6 Jan 1969, 1 daughter. Education: MD; Fellowship, Division of Hepato-Pancreatic and Biliary Surgery, West China University of Medical Sciences. Appointments: Surgical Resident, 1965-80, Attending Surgeon, 1980-, Lecturer, 1980-87, Associate Professor, 1987-94, Professor, 1994-, School of Medicine, West China University of Medical Sciences, Chengdu. Publications: Resection of the Caudate Lobe of the Liver for Primary Hepatocellular Cancer, 1988; Hepatic Segmentectomy Using a Microwave Tissue Coagulator and Guided by Intraoperative Ultrasoundography, 1992. Honours: Technical Advancement Award, Bureau of Provincial Public Health, 1994. Memberships: Chinese Medical Assocaition; Chinese Anti-Cancer Association. Hobbies: Photography; Poetry. Address: Department of Surgery, The First University Hospital, West China University of Medical Sciences, Chengdu, Sichuan 610041, China.

HE Shiqin, b. 28 Sept 1938, Jishou, Hunan, China. Teacher; Researcher. m. Yang Linsheng, Oct 1964, 1 son, 1 daughter. Education: MB, Jiangxi Medical College, 1963. Appointments: Assistant, 1963, Lecturer, 1980, Associate Professor, 1987, currently Professor, Jiangxi Medical College, Nanchang. Publications: 3 books including: Experimental direction of microbiology; Experimental direction of virology; 40 papers; Detection of IgA antibody to EBV-VCA, 1979; Study on the etiological cervical carcinoma, 1987; HTLV-1 and human leukemia, 1992; HTLV-1 and autoimmune disease, 1992. Honours: 2nd Award, Institute of Virology, 1994. Memberships: Committee Member, Jiangxi Society of Microbiology and Immunology; Chinese Medical Association; Committee Member, Society of Chinese Medical Association. Address: Department of Microbiology, Jiangxi Medical College, 161 Bayi Main Road, Nanchang 330006, China.

HE Shou-Zhi, b. 25 Nov 1945, China. Ophthalmologist. m. 3 Oct 1971, 1 son. Education: 4th Military Medical College, Xian, 1964-69; MM, Postgraduate Medical school, Beijing, 1980-83; Institute of Clinical Ophthalmology, Gynma, Japan, 1987-88. Appointments: Doctor, Harbin, 1970; Postgraduate Student, Beijing, 1980; fellow, Institute Clinical Ophthalmology, Gunma, Japan, 1987; Director of Ophthalmic Department and Ophthalmic Centre, 1987; Director, Ophthalmic Centre. Publications: Cataract and Its Modern Surgical Treatment, 1993; Ophthalmic Microsurgery, 1994; Experiment Study of Development and reversal of the Galactose-induced Cataract; Contributor of over 30 other articles. Honours: Distinguished Service Award. Memberships: Executive Member, Chinese Ophthalmic Association; Executive Member, Cataract and IOL Association. Hobbies: Music; Playing Accordian; Swimming; Dancing. Address: No 28 Fu-xing Road, Beijing 100853, China.

HE Zeyong, b. 28 Jan 1919, Suzhou, China. Professor. m. 30 June 1954, 2 sons, 1 daughter. Education: Medical School, Keio University, Japan, 1939-43. Appointments: Instructor, Shanxi Woman's Medical

School, 1944-45; Assistant Professor, Shanxi Chuanzhi Medical College, 1946-49; Associate Professor, Professor, Shanxi Medical College, 1949-89; Professor of Histology & Embryology, Shanxi Medical College. Publications: Histology and Embryology, 1983. Memberships: Chinese Society of Anatomy. Hobbies: Music. Address: Shanxi Medical College, 86 Xinjian South Road, Taiyuan 030001, China.

HE Zhen-ping, b. 1942, China. Professor; Surgeon. Education: Graduated, Fourth Miliary Medical College, 1965. Appointments: Liver and Biliary Tract Surgical Research Centre, Southwest Hospital, Third Military Medical College, Chongqing, 1965-, currently Professor, Director Physician, Tutor of Doctoral Students. Publications include: More than 40 research papers in field of liver, gall and pancreatic surgery; Resection of carcinoma of the hepatic caudate lobe, 1989; Other reports include prevention and treatment of intrahepatic bile duct stones and related complications, treatment of hemobilia due to post protal artery, use of gall bladder to repair traumatic bile duct injury, plastic method of striatures of bile duct in high site, and treatment of non-functional pancreatic islet cell carcinoma and pancreatic stones. Honours: 7 2nd and 3rd Prizes for Military Progress in Science and Technology. Address: Liver and Biliary Tract Surgical Research Centre, Southwest Hospital, Chongqing 630038, China.

HE Zheng-xian, b. 4 Apr 1938, Guangzhou, China. Doctor. m. Jin Zhen-yun, 16 Jan 1967, 2 sons. Education: MD, Sun Yat-sen University of Medical Sciences. Appointments: Resident Doctor, 2nd & 3rd Hospital of SUMS, 1964; Attending Doctor, Lecturer, 3rd Hospital of SUMS, 1980; Associate Professor, 3rd Hospital of SUMS, 1985; Professor, 3rd Hospital of SUMS, 1993. Publications: Immune Status of Leukemia, 1982; Immune Status of Aplastic Anemia, 1983; Progress in study of sister chromatid exchange of blood disease, 1985; Observation of SCE of 54 Cases of CML with Ph Positive, 1988; A Handbook of Human Gytogenetics, 1993; Experimental Study of Effects of Dengue Virus 2 on SCE Frequency of the Lymphocytes and Bone Marrow Cell in Vitro, 1994; Hereditary Non-spherocytic Hemolytic Anemia and Clinic, 1994. Honours: Award for Immune Status of Leukemia, 1994. Memberships: Council, Society of Pediatrics, CMA, Guangdong Branch; Council, Society of Medical Genetics, CMA, Guangdong Branch; Council, Guangdong Eugetics Association. Hobbies: Writing; Music. Address: Department of Pediatrics, 3rd Affiliated Hospital, Sun Yat-sen University of Medical Sciences, Guangzhou, China.

HE Zhizhi, b. 9 Apr 1939, Pingxiang, Jiangxi, China. Physician. m. Pi Chihong, Jan 1968, 2 sons. Education MB. Appointments: Resident, Attending Doctor, lecturer, Associate Professor, Senior Doctor of Chinese Medicine, Professor of Chinese Internal Medicine, Jianxi College of Traditional Chinese Medicine. Publications: Emergency Medicine, Co-author, 1993; Handbook of TCM Emergency, Co-author, 1994; Treating Hematochezia Resulted from Spleen Deficiency by Strengthening Spleen to Remove Blood Stasis, Co-author. Honours: Several Time Recipitnet of title Advanced Medical Worker; 3rd Prize, Scientific Research Achievement, Jianxi TCM Institute. Memberships: Jiangxi Women Scientists Federqation; Jiangxi Qigong Research Society; Jiangxi Chinese Medical Society; Jiangxi Eugenics Association. Hobby: Music. Address: Yangming Road 20, Nanchang 330006, China.

HEALEY Norman John, b. 2 Sep 1940, England. Medicine. m. Maureen Anne Brock, 24 Jun 1978, 3 d. Education: Guy's Hospital; DA; DRCOG; FLCOM; ND; MRCS; LRCP. Appointments: Surgeon Lieutenant, Royal Navy; Senior House Officer, Royal Bucks Hospital, Aylesbury; Private Practice, Osteopath, 1975-; Honorary Consultant, St Luke's Hospital, London; Consultant Osteopathic Physician. Honour: Kitchener Scholarship, 1959. Memberships: Fellow, London College of Osteopathic Medicine; British Osteopathic Association, Past Honorary Secretary; Fellow, Royal Society of Medicine; British Institute of Musculo-Skeletal Medicine. Hobbies: Cricket; Rugby; Gardening; Country Walking; Swimming. Address: 16 Upper Wimpole Street, London, W1M 7TB.

HEANEY Robert Proulx, b. 10 Nov 1927, Omaha, Nebraska, USA. Physician. m. Barbara Reardon, 12 July 1952, 2 sons, 5 daughters. Education: BS 1947, MD 1951, Creighton University. Appointments: Assistant Professor, Department of Medicine, Associate Professor, Department of Medicine, Chairman, Department of Medicine, Head, Section Endocrinology/Metab, Vice President for health Sciences, John A Creighton University Professor, all at Creighton University. Publications: 3 books and over 200 original papers, chapters, monographs and reviews in scientific and educational fields. Honours:

Kappa Delta Award, 1970; Creighton Distinguished Faculty Award, 1974; Creighton University Alumni Achievement Citation, 1988; Creighton University Distinguished Research Career Award, 1991; Frederic C Bartter Award, American Society Bone and Mineral Research, 1994. Memberships: American College of Physicians; American Institute of Nutrition; American Society for Bone & Mineral Research; American Society for Clinical Investigation; American Society for Clinical Nutrition. Hobbies: Wood Working; Reading; Crossword Puzzles; Computers. Address: Creighton University, 2500 California Plaza, Omaha, NE 68178, USA.

HEAP Michael, b. 30 Apr 1949, Rossendale, England. Clinical Psychologist. m. Valerie Elliott, 2 June 1979. Education: BSc, Psychology, University of London, 1967; MSc, Clinical Psychology, London, 1978; PhD, Psychology, University of London, 1981. Appointments: Research Assistant, National Hospital, Maida Vale, London, 1970-74; Clinical Psychologist, Royal Free Hosptial, London, 1974-79; Clinical Psychologist, St Augustines Hospital, Canterbury, 1979-86; Clinical Psychologist, Sheffield Health Authority, 1986-92; Lecturer & Clinical Psychologist, 1992-. Publications: Hypnosis: Current Clinical, Experimental And Forensic Practices, 1988; Hypnosis in Therapy, 1991; Hypnotherapy: A Handbook. Memberships: Associate Fellow, British Psychological Society; British Society of Experimental & Clinical Hypnosis; International Society of Hypnosis. Hobbies: Swimming; Running; Cello; Wine-Making. Address: Centre for Psychotherapeutic Studies, University of Sheffield, 16 Claremont Crescent, Sheffield, S10 2TA, England.

HEATLEY Mallory Nina, b. 5 Jan 1954, Redhill, Surrey, England. Educational Psychologist. m. Gareth Heatley, 25 Sept 1971, 1 son, 2 daughters. Education: BA, hons, Open University; MSc, Psychology of Education, London University Institute of Education; MSc, Educational Psychology, London University College; Certificate of Education, Exeter University. Appointments: Primary Teacher, Cornwall, Somerset, Buckinghamshire, 1975-84; Educational Psychologist, Buckinghamshire, 1985-91; Chartered Psychologist. Memberships: Associate Fellow, British Psychological Society. Hobbies: Skiing; Watercolour Painting. Address: 1 Livesey Hill, Shenley Lodge, Milton Keynes, MK5 7DS, England.

HEERDEGEN Carmen, b. 20 Apr 1962, Neubrandenburg, Germany. Neurologist; Psychotherapist. m. Dietmar G Luchmann, 28 May 1986. Education: DM, Medical Academy of Magdeburg/University of Magdeburg, 1987; Certifications: Acupuncture, Medical Hypnosis, Neurology, Psychotherapy, Unconventional Medicine. Appointments: Lecturer, Institute of Anatomy, Humboldt University Medical School, Berlin; Neurological and Psychiatric Departments in Langenfeldt, Bad Neustadt, Esslingen, Nürtingen and others; Currently Medical Director, Institute of Modern Psychological Therapy and Unconventional Medicine, Stuttgart. Memberships: American Academy of Neurology; German Society of Hypnosis; German Society of Neurology. Hobbies: Literature; Yachting; Skiing. Address: Institut für Moderne Psychologische Therapie und Naturheilkunde, Waldburgstrasse 122, D-70563 Stuttgart, Germany.

HEIMBECKER Raymond Oliver, b. 29 Nov 1922, Calgary, Canada. Surgeon. m. Kathleen Jensen, 18 Nov 1950, 2 s, 3 d. Education: BA, Sask, 1944; MD, Toronto, 1947; MA, Toronto, 1949; M Surg, Toronto, 1953; FRCS (C), 1957; FACS, 1960; FACC; FCCP. Appointments: Conducted extensive pioneer research in heart transplant with first valve transplant, 1955, 1962; Autottransfusion, 1973-; Modern heart transplant and cyclosporin, clinical success, 1981; Clinical Teacher, University of Toronto and Toronto General Hospital; Senior Resident Associate, Ontario Heart Foundation; Consultant Surgeon, Wellesly Hospital; Examiner, Royal College of Surgeons, Canada; 1st Chief C U and Thoracic Surgery, University Hospital, London; Currently, Professor Emeritus, University of Western Ontario. Publications: Over 150 chapters and articles. Honours: George Peters Award, Toronto, 1950; Lister Award, Toronto, 1957; Rose Foundation, 1976; Jeddah M, 1984; Bombay, 1985; Beijing M, 1986; Special AOA, 1986. Memberships: Society of University Surgeons; Society VASC Surgeons; American Association of Thoracic Surgeons; Canadian Society of CV and Thoracic Surgeons; Society of Thoracic Surgeons, Great Britain and Ireland; American Surgical Association. Hobbies: Sailing; Water Colour Painting; Fishing; Farming; Wind Surfing. Address: RR 1 Collingwood, Ontario, Canada, L9Y 3Y9.

HEIMBÜRGER Olof Peter Erik, b. 16 May 1957, Stockholm, Sweden. MD; Nephrologist. m. Catharina Lycleeborg, 12 Sep 1987, 2 s. Education: MD 1982, PhD 1994, Karolinska Institute; Specialist in Nephrology, Huddinge Hospital, 1990. Appointment: Specialist in Nephrology, Department of Renal Medicine, Karolinska Institute. Publications: Peritoneal Transport in Patients Treated with Continuous Peritoneal Dialysis (PhD Thesis), 1994; About 30 scientific papers in field of nephrology. Memberships: International Society of Peritoneal Dialysis; Swedish Medical Society. Hobby: Opera. Address: Dept of Renal Medicine K56, Karolinska Institute, Huddinge Hospital, S-141 86 Huddinge, Sweden.

HEITLER Susan McCrensky, b. 17 Jul 1945, Alton, IL, USA. Clinical Psychologist. m. Bruce Heitler, Jun 1971, 2 s, 2 d. Education: BA, Harvard University, 1967; MEd, Boston University, 1968; PhD, NY University, 1975. Appointment: Private Practice of Clinical Psychology at Rose Medical Center. Publications: David Decides No More Thumbsucking, 1985, 93; From Conflict to Resolution, 1990; Working With Couples in Conflict (audiotape), 1992; Depression, A Disorder of Power, 1994 (audiotape); Anxiety, Friend or Foe?, 1994, (audiotape); Conflict Resolution For Couples, 1994, (audiotape). Membership: American Psychological Association. Hobbies: Tennis; Violin. Address: 4500 East 9th Ave 660 S, Denver, CO 80220, USA.

HEJTMANEK Milan, b. 3 May 1928, Olomouc, Czech Republic. Professor of General Biology. m. Nora Uhrova, 15 Dec 1951, 2 daughters. Education: RNDr, Masaryk University, Brno, 1951; Assistant Professor, 1963, Professor, 1990, Palacky University, DrSc, Czechoslovak Academy of Sciences, Prague, 1969. Appointments: Assistant, 1952-64, Assistant Professor, 1964-90, Professor, 1990-, Biology Institute, Medical Faculty, Palacky University, Olomouc. Publications: Co-author: Sexuality and Pathogenicity of Fungi, 1981; Fungal Dimorphism, 1985; Identification of Dermatophytes, 1990; Genetics of Dermatophytes, 1992; Effect of the New Fluorescent Brightener Rylux BSU on Morphology and Biosynthesis of Cell Walls in Saccharomyces Cerevisiae, 1994. Honours: Honorary Member, Society of Mycopathology, Czechoslovakia, 1987; Honorary Member, Czechoslovak Biological Society, 1993; J E Purkyne Medal. Memberships: International Society for Human and Animal Mycology; Czechoslovak Microbiological Society ; Czechslovak Science Society for Mycology. Hobbies: Photography; Tourism. Address: Hnevotinska 3, 775 00 Olomouc, Czech Republic.

HELLERSTEIN David Joel, b. 30 Dec 1953, Ohio, USA. Physician; Psychiatrist. m. Lisa Perry, 16 Oct 1983, 2 s, 1 d. Education: AB, Harvard College, 1976; MD, Stanford University Medical School, 1980; Residency, Psychiatry, NY Hospital, Cornell Medical Center, 1980-84. Career: Fellow, Psychiatry, NY State Psychiatric Institute, 1984-85; Psychiatrist, 1985-, Currently Director of Psychiatric Outpatient Services, Beth Israel Medical Center; Assistant Professor of Psychiatry, Mount Sinai School of Medicine, 1988-93, Albert Einstein College of Medicine, 1993-. Publications: Books: Battle of Life and Death, essays, 1986; Loving Touches, novel, 1987; A Family of Doctors, non-fiction, 1994; Articles include: Double blind trial of fluoxetine use placebo in dysthymia, in American Journal of Psychiatry, 1993; Contributing Editor, North American Review, 1986-. MD Magazine, 1988-; Pushcart Prize Best Essay Award, 1981. Memberships: American Psychiatric Association; Authors Guild; NY Academy of Medicine. Address: Beth Israel Medical Center, Psychiatric Outpatient Services, 1st Avenue and 16th Street, New York, NY 10003-2992, USA.

HELM Cyril William, b. 4 Sep 1951, Plymouth, England. Gynaecological Oncology. 1 s, 2 d. Education: MA; MB; BCH; FRCS ED; FRCS Eng; MRCOG. Appointments: Senior Registrar, Obstetrics and Gynaecology, Edinburgh Royal Infirmary, Scotland, 1987-89; Instructor, Gynaecologic Oncology, University of AL, Birmingham, USA, 1989-92; Director, Gynaecologic Oncology, Temple University School of Health Sciences, PA, USA, 1992-93; Consultant Gynaecologic Oncologist, Christie Hospital, Manchester, England, 1993-94; Director, Gynaecologic Oncology, Temple University School of Health Sciences, PA, USA, 1994-. Publications: 5 Contributions to Professional Journals including: Co-author, Prospective Randomized Trial of LLETZ Versus Laser Ablation in Patients with Cervical Intraepithelial Neoplasia, 1994; 2 Book chapters. Memberships: British Medical Association; British Society for Colposcopy and Cervical Pathology; Royal Society of Medicine; International Gynaecological Cancer Society; British Gynaecological Cancer Society. Hobbies: Squash; Tennis; Running. Address: Division of Gynaecologic Oncology, 719 OPB, Temple

University Hospital, Broad and Ontario Streets, Philadelphia, PA 19140, USA.

HELMICK Charles G, b. 14 Oct 1950, Ann Arbor, Michigan, USA. Medical Epidemiologist. m. April Kristy Harrison, 19 June 1982, 1 son, 2 daughters. Education: MD. Appointments: Medical Doctor, Johns Hopkins School of Medicine, 1972-76; Internal Medicine Residency, Baltimore City Hospitals, 1976-79; Centers For Disease Control & Prevention, 1979-. Publications: Perinatal risk factors for inflammatory bowel disease: A case control study, 1990; Ulcerative colitis and colorectal cancer, 1990; Stomach cancer after partial gastric resection, 1988. Honours: US Public Health Service Awards, Outstanding Service Medal, 1991, Commendations, 1989, 1990, 1992; Outstanding Unit Citation, 1995. Memberships: American Public Health Association; Society for Epidemiologic Research; Physicians for Social Responsibility. Hobbies: Soccer; History; Astronomy. Address: Center for Disease Control & Prevention, 4770 Buford Highway K51, Atlanta, GA 30341-3724, USA.

HENDEE William R, b. 1 Jan 1938, Owosso, Michigan, USA. Professor. m. Jeannie Wesley, 16 Apr 1960, 5 sons, 2 daughters. Education: Electrical Engineering, Tulane University, New Orleans, 1955-57; BS, Physics, Millsaps College, Jackson, Mississippi, 1959; Physics, Vanderbilt University, Nashville, Tennessee, 1959-60; PhD, Physics, University of Texas, Austin and Dallas, 1962. Appointments include: Chairman, Department of Radiology, University of Colorado, 1978-85; Vice-President, Science and Technology, American Medical Association, 1985-91; Adjunct Professor, Radiology, Northwestern University, 1985-91; Clinical Professor, Radiology, 1985-91, Senior Associate Dean, Vice-President, Professor, Radiology, Biophysics, 1991-, Medical College of Wisconsin, Milwaukee; Adjunct Professor, Bioengineering, Marquette University, 1994. Publications: 20 books; Over 350 scientific articles; Monographs; Editor, several books. Honours include: Omicron Delta Kappa, 1963-; Honorary DSc, Millsaps College, 1988; William D Coolidge Gold Medal, American Association of Physicists in Medicine, 1989; Institute of Medicine, Chicago, 1991-; Wright Langham Memorial Lecturer, University of Kentucky, 1991; Distinguished Service Award, American Academy of Home Care Physicians, 1991; Fellow, American Institute of Medical and Biological Engineering, 1991-; Member, World Health Organization Expert Advisory Panel on Radiation, 1992-; Co-President, World Congress on Medical Physics and Biomedical Engineering for Year 2000, 1994. Memberships include: Senior Member, Biomedical Engineering Society; Health Physics Society; American Association for the Advancement of Science; American Association of Physicists in Medicine; Society of Nuclear Medicine; American College of Radiology; Radiological Society of North America. Many committees and offices. Hobbies: Skiing; Fishing; Opera. Address: Medical College of Wisconsin, 8701 Watertown Plank Road, Milwaukee, WI 53226, USA.

HENDERSON Catherine Anna, b. 6 Dec 1942. Psychoanalyst. m. Stephen Henderson, 8 Aug 1964, 2 sons. Education: BSN; MA; PhD, Clinical Psychology, 1990. Appointments: Visiting Nurse Associate, New Haven, 1945-65; Staff Nurse, Seattle King County Public Health Department, 1965-72; School Nurse, Bellevue Public Schools, 1972-82; Psychoanalyst, 1976-. Publications include: Experience Trauma on Mother-Infant Interaction in the Homeostatic Phase of development, 1990; The Analysis of a Very Angry Boy, 1991. Honours: Diagnostic Profile Course, Anna Freud Centre, London, England, 1978-79. Memberships: Seattle Institute Psychoanalysis; Infant Research; Sigma Theta Tau' Seattle Psychoanalytic Society. Hobbies: Reading; Sailing; Cookery. Address: 1300-114 Avenue SE, Suite 210, Bellevue, WA 18004, USA.

HENDERSON (Donald) James, b. 7 Aug 1940, Sudbury, Canada. Psychoanalyst; Legislator. m. Karen Santolini, 4 Sept 1977, 3 sons. Education: MD, 1964; MPH, 1968; FRCP(C), 1969; DABPN, 1973. Appointments incl: Associate Professor, Department of Psychiatry, University of Toronto, 1981-; Consultant, Psychotherapy Clinic, Clarke Institute of Psychiatry, 1985-; Member of Legislative Assembly, Ontario Legislature, 1985-. Publications include: The Plasma Proteins, 1961; The Medical Management of Uncomplicated Peptic Ulcer, 1963; Soviet Medicine, 1968; Exorcism and Possession in Psychotherapy Practice, 1982; The Role of the Father in Separation-Individuation, 1982; Is Incest Harmful?, 1983; Humanity Is Cost Effective; The 1990 Ontario Election: Lessons for Canadians, 1991; The Role of the Father, 1991. Honours: University of Western Ontario Board of Governors Scholarship, 1958, 1960; Ontario Medical Association Prize in Public Health & Preventive

Medicine, 1963; Alpha Omega Alpha, 1963; Gold Medal, University of Toronto Diploma Course in Psychiatry, 1970. Memberships: OPA; CPA; APA; AOA; OMA; CMA. Hobbies: Travel. Address: 14 Fieldstone Road, Etobioke M9C 2J6, Canada.

HENKIN Robert Irwin, b. 5 Oct 1930, Los Angeles, CA, USA. Physician; Neuroscientist. m. Marsha Jacobs, 15 Mat. 3 s, 3 d. Education: MA, PhD, MD, UCLA; AB Cum Laude, University of Southern California, Los Angeles; Intern in Medicine, UCLA Hospital; Resident in Medicine, University of Miami Hospital. Appointments: Research Associate, NIMH, NHI, Bethesda, Maryland; Senior Investigator, NHLI, NIH, Bethesda; Chief, Section on Neuroendocrinology, NHLI, NIH, Bethesda; Associate Professor of Paediatrics and Neurology, Professor of Paediatrics and Neurology, Georgetown University Medical Centre, Washington DC; Director, The Taste and Smell Clinic, Washington DC. Publications: Zinc, 1978; Contributor of articles in professional journals. Memberships: American Society of Clinical Investigation; American Physiological Society; American Institute of Nutrition; Biophysical Society, Charter Member. Hobbies: Tennis; Running. Address: 5125 MacArthur Blvd, Suite 20, Washington DC, USA.

HENNEKENS Charles Henry, b. 6 Dec 1942, Brooklyn, New York, USA. Epidemiologist. m. Deborah Cole, 1 son, 2 daughters. Education: MD; DrPH, Epidemiology. Appointments: Professor of Epidemiology, Harvard School of Public Health, 1994-; John Snow Professor of Medicine and Ambulatory Care and Prevention, Harvard Medical School, 1994-; Chief, Division of Preventive Medicine. Publications: Author of 357 works including 300 original reports, 57 reviews and 2 textbooks. Honours: James D Bruce Memorial Award, American College of Physicians, 1992. Memberships: American Association for the Advancement of Science; American Epidemiologic Society; Association American Physicians; International Society for Nutrition and Care. Hobbies: Squash; Tennis. Address: 900 Commonwealth Avenue East, Boston, MA 02215, USA.

HENOCK Mark Lawrence, b. 31 May 1947, Bronx, New York, USA. Teacher. Medical Technologist. m. Janet Eve Gottlieb, 20 May 1973, 1 daughter. Education: BA, Biology, University of Bridgeport, 1970; Master of Professional Studies, Health Care Administration, Long Island University, 1978; Medical Technologist Certification, American Medical Technologists; Associate Member, American Society of Clinical Pathologists, 1983; Graduate work, Pathology, St John's University; Licenses: New York State Permanent Teaching Certificate, Biology, General Science, Laboratory Specialist. Appointments: Medical Technologist, Clinical Chemistry, Albert Einstein College of Medicine, 1970; Medical Technologist, Haematology, North Shore University Hospital, 1974-80; Supervisor, Group Health Inc, 1980-83; Director of Admissions, Menorah Home and Hospital, 1983-86; Teacher, Biology, Science, Medical Technology, New York City Board of Education, 1986-. Publications: The Nature of the Bacteriophage, 1970; The Aging Process, 1978. Honours: Biology Award, City University of New York. Memberships: American Medical Technologists; New York Biology Teachers Association. Hobbies: Photography; Amateur astronomy. Address: 380 Hewlett Parkway, Hewlett, NY 11557, USA.

HENRICHS Theodore Fred, b. 1 Apr 1932, Evanston, IL, USA. Psychologist. m. Margaret Ann Lusk, 19 Dec 1953, 3 s, 1 d. Education: BS, Northwestern University, 1953; MA, OH University, 1957; PhD, University of NC, Chapel Hill, 1961. Appointments: Assistant Professor, 1962-67, Associate Professor, 1968-73, Professor, 1973-, Psychiatry and Psychology, University of MO, Columbia. Publications: First Author, MMPI indices in the identification of patients inducing pseudoseizures, in Epilepsia, 1988; Author, The effect of methods of accurate feedback on clinical judgements based upon the MMPI, in Journal of Clinical Psychology, 1990. Honours: Diplomate in Clinical Psychology, 1966; Fellow of Society for Personality Assessment, 1979; Fellow, American Psychological Association, 1990. Memberships: American Psychological Association; Sigma Xi; Society for Personality Assessment. Hobbies: Reading; Hiking; Golf. Address: N120 Health Sciences Center, University of Missouri, Columbia, MO 65212, USA.

HENSCHKE Sadie Priscilla, b. 3 Mar 1935, Tumby Bay, South Australia. Counsellor; Mediator. m. Robert William, 7 Jan 1956, 2 sons, 4 daughters. Education: Accreditations in Marriage & Family Counselling, Mediation & Group Leadership. Appointments: GPO Telephonist; Nursing Training. Publications: Family Therapy Journal of Australia & New Zealand. Memberships: Australian Association of Marriage & Family Counsellors; South Australian Dispute Resolution Association; Family Therapy Association. Honours: Life Member, Marriage Guidance, South Australia. Address: 12 Payton Avenue, Dernancourt 5075, South Australia.

HENSRUD Donald Douglas, b. 6 Mar 1957, Camp Zama, Japan. Physician. m. Natasha Matt, 11 Aug 1989, 1 daughter. Education: BS, University North Dakota, 1980; MD, University of Hawaii, 1984; MPH, University of Minnesota, 1989; MS, University of Alabama at Birmingham, 1992. Appointment: Assistant Professor of Preventive Medicine & Nutrition, Mayo Medical School. Publications: A prospective study of weight maintenance in obese subjects reduced to normal body weight without weight loss training, 1994; Antioxidant status, fatty acids and cardiovascular disease, 1994; Antioxidant status, fatty acids and mortality from cardiovascular disease and keshan disease, 1994. Honours: Clinical Nutrition Fellows Award, American Society for Clinical Nutrition, 1992. Memberships: American Medical Association; Minnesota Medical Association; American College of Physicians; American Society for Clinical Nutrition; American Society for Parenteral and Enternal Nutrition. Hobbies: Exercise; Cooking; Gardening. Address: Division of Preventive Medicine, Mayo Clinic, Rochester, MN 55905, USA.

HEPBURN Mary, b. 14 Apr 1949, London, England. Obstetrician; Gynaecologist. Education: BSc, 1970; MBChB, 1973, MD, 1987, University of Edinburgh; MRCGP, 1977; MRCOG, 1981; Pre-Reg Medicine, Surgery, Edinburgh, 1973-74; General Practice Training Scheme, Aberdeen, 1974-77; Obstetrics and Gynaecology Training, Dublin and Glasgow, 1978-89. Appointments: Senior Lecturer, Women's Reproductive Health, University of Glasgow, Scotland, 1990-; Honorary Consultant Obstetrician and Gynaecologist, Greater Glasgow Health Board, 1990-. Publications: Papers including: Drug Misuse in Pregnancy, 1993; Prostitution - Would Legalisation Help, 1993; Book chapters including: Social Problems, in Antenatal Care: Clinical Obstetrics and Gynaecology, 1990; Socially Related Disorders, in High Risk Pregnancy, 1992; Pregnancy and HIV, in Working with Women and AIDS, 1993. Memberships include: British Medical Association; Glasgow Obstetrical and Gynaecological Society; Glasgow Medico-Chirurgical Society; British Federation Against Sexually Transmitted Diseases. Hobbies: Hill walking; Sailing; Swimming; Listening to music. Address: Royal Maternity Hospital, Rottenrow, Glasgow G4 0NA, Scotland.

HERDSON Peter Barrie, b. 29 Dec 1932, Auckland, New Zealand. Professor. m., 3 children, 2 stepchildren. Education: MPS (NZ); BMedSc, Auckland University, 1956; MB, ChB, University of Otago, 1959; PhD, Pathology, Northwestern University, USA, 1965; FRCPA. Appointments include: Assistant Pathologist, Henrotin Hospital Hospital, Chicago, Illinois, USA, 1964-69; Assistant Professor, 1965-67, Associate Professor, 1967-69, Northwestern University Medical School, Chicago; Foundation Professor, Chairman, Department of Pathology, University of Auckland School of Medicine, 1969-85; Visiting Professor, Duke University Medical School, Durham, North Carolina, USA, 1977; Professor, Chairman, Department of Pathology and Laboratory Medicine, King Faisal Specialist Hospital and Research Centre, Riyadh, Saudi Arabia, 1985-91; Professor, Director, Department of Pathology, Woden Valley Hospital, Woden, Australian Capital Territory, 1991-; Coroner's Pathologist, Canberra, 1991-; Professor of Pathology, University of Sydney, 1995-. Publications: Theses: The cervical region of Ophidia with reference to the parathyroids and the carotid arteries, 1956; Studies on fine structural changes induced in rat liver by partial starvation and by drug administration, 1965; Author or co-author, 89 papers with special reference to kidney and heart disease, cell injury, organisation of pathology. Honours include: John Malcolm Memorial Prize, Physiology, Biochemistry, University of Otago, and Scott Memorial Prize, Anatomy, University of Otago Medical School, 1955; Professor Emeritus, University of Auckland School of Medicine, 1985; Honorary Fellow, Royal Australasian College of Radiologists, 1986. Memberships include: New Zealand Society of Pathologists; Foundation President, Canberra Medico Legal Society; President, Royal College of Pathologists of Australasia, 1983-85; President, World Association of Societies of Pathology. Address: ACT Pathology, Woden Valley Hospital, PO Box 11, Woden, ACT 2606, Australia.

HERMANEK Paul Johann, b. 8 Mar 1924, Vienna, Austria. Professor Emeritus. m. Christine Zimmermann, 5 Mar 1955, 1 son, 1 daughter. Education: Dr med, University of Vienna. Appointments include: Head, Division of Surgical Pathology, Department of Surgery, 1969, Full Professor of Surgical Pathology, 1978, Currently Professor Emeritus, University of Erlangen, Erlangen, Germany. Publications: Illustrated synopsis of colorectal tumors, 1983; TNM Atlas, 1985, 1989, 1992;

Chirurgische Onkologie (co-author), 1986; TNM Classification of Malignant Tumors, 1987, 1992. Honours: President, German Society of Endoscopy, 1983; Vice-President, German TNM Committee, 1987; German Cancer Prize, 1988; Jubilee Prize, German Society of Surgery, 1988; Honorary Membership, Austrian Society of Pathology, 1991; European Award, European Society of Surgical Oncology, 1994; Dr med (hc), University of Munster. Memberships: German Society of Pathology; European Society of Pathology; International Academy of Pathology; European Society of Surgical Oncology. Hobbies: Music; History of art. Address: Masurenweg 15, D 91058 Erlangen, Germany.

HERMANN Robert E, b. 28 Jan 1929, Highland, Illinois, USA. Surgeon. m. Polly Fisher, 8 Mar 1986, 4 sons, 1 daughter. Education: BA, Harvard University, 1950; MD, Washington University School of Medicine, 1954; FACS. Appointments: Emeritus Consultant, Former Chairman, Department of General Surgery, Cleveland Clinic Foundation; Clinical Professor of Surgery, Case Western Reserve University School of Medicine. Publications: Author of 2 books; Contributor of 182 articles and 53 chapters in books. Honours: Honorary Member, Surgical Societies of Minnesota, Equador, British Columbia, Colombia, research Society of South Africa, Germany, Buffalo, New York, Illinois. Memberships: American College of Surgeons; Society for Surgery of the Alimentary Tract; Collegium Internationale Chirurgiae Digestivae; Surgical Biology Club III; Society of Surgical Oncology; Central Surgical Association; Southern Surgical Association; Eastern Surgical Society; James IV Association of Surgeons; International Societ of Surgery; American Surgical Association. Hobbies: Music; Tennis; Golf. Address: Department of General Surgery, Cleveland Clinic Foundation, 9500 Euclid Avenue, Cleveland, OH 44195, USA.

HERNANDEZ-PEREZ Enrique, b. 31 Jul 1939, San Salvador, Central America. Professor of Dermatology. m. Raquel de Hernandez-Perez, 17 Nov 1965, 2 s, 2 d. Education: MD, National University of De El Salvador; Professor of Dermatology. Appointments: Professor of Dermatology, National University of El Salvador; Director, Center for Dermatology and Cosmetic Surgery; President, Iberian Latin American College of Dermatology. Publications: 119 Scientific papers published; 4 Books; Several chapters in scientific books. Memberships: Iberian Latin American College of Dermatology; American Academy of Dermatology; American Academy of Cosmetic Surgery. Hobby: Reading. Address: Pasaje 1 no 137, Urbanizacion La Esperanza, San Salvador, El Salvador, Central America.

HERSCHFUS Jechiel Aaron, b. 19 Apr 1918, Rotterdam, Holland. Physician. m. Reva Weinstein, dec 9 Sept 1951, 1 s, 3 d. Education: Board Certified Allergy & Immunology; BS; BA; MD. Appointments: Vice President, 1975-76, President, 1976-77, American Association of Clinical Immunology & Allergy, North East Region; Treasurer, Medical Staff, Norwood Hospital, Norwood, MA, 1984-90; Practising MD. Publications: Author & Co-Author of more than 30 scientific papers published in national and international medical journals and texts dealing with Bronchial Asthma, Emphysemia & Pulmonary Physiology. Honours: Horizons for Youth Award, 1978. Memberships: Fellow, American College of Chest Physicians; American College of Allergists; Society of Clinical Ecology; Society of Clinical Immunology & Allergy; American Federation of Clinical Research. Hobbies: Gardening; Stamp Collecting; Classical Music. Address: 62 South Main Street, Sharon, MA 02067, USA.

HERXHEIMER Johanna Christine Gabriele, b. 23 Aug 1942, Potsdam, Germany. Psychiatric Referee, Consultant, German Embassy, London, England; Private Practice. m. Andrew Herxheimer, 24 Mar 1983. Education: Studied Medicine, University of Tübingen, 1961-64; Free University of Berlin, 1964-67; MD, magna cum laude, 1969; Psychiatrist, Neurologist, Stuttgart, Germany, 1977; Psychoanalyst, Stuttgart, 1981. Appointments: Research Assistant, Allergology, Clinical Immunology, Free University, Berlin, 1967-70; Resident, Allergology, University of Illinois, USA, 1970-71; Staff Psychiatrist, Neurologist, Academic Hospital, Stuttgart, 1972-78; Psychoanalytical Practice, 1978-. Publications including: Mites and House Dust Allergy, 1968; Potassium Iodide in Bronchial Asthma, 1969; Co-author, An Approach to Automation of Medical Interview, 1972. Memberships: Associate Member, British Psycho-Analytical Society. Hobbies: Playing the Piano; Oriental Studies. Address: 9 Park Crescent, London N3 2NL, England.

HESHIKI Zenshi, b. 10 June 1936, Brazil. Doctor. m. Shiuko Yonezawa, 29 Sept 1939, 1 son, 2 daughters. Education: MD; PhD. Appointments: Graduation, Rib. Preto Faculty of Medicine, IAMSPE

Hospital; Botucatu Faculty of Medicine; Marilia Unesp Campus; Londrina State University; Professor of Otolaryngology. Publications: Chronic tonsilitis of children, 1966; Eustachian tube and sonomanometry, 1971; Otosclerosis, 1975; Temporal bone histopathology, 1984. Memberships: Brazilian Medical Society; Institut Georges Portmann; Société Française d'ORL; Association for Research in Otolaryngology. Honours: Prix Honorio Libero, 1965; M Otoni de Rezende, 1966; Candido Rondom, 1978. Hobbies: Football; Basketball; TV; Vacations. Address: Rua Domingos Soares de Barros, 210, 18.603-590 Botucatu, Estado de Sao Paulo, Brazil.

HETHERINGTON Angela Patricia, b. 24 Mar 1952, Manchester, UK. Occupational Psychologist. 2 d. Education: PhD, Applied Psychology; MSc, Occupational Psychology; BA, Honors in Psychology. Certificate of Education. Appointments: Senior Lecturer, Occupational Psychology. Address: De Montfort University, Leicester, LE1 9BH, England.

HEWITT Stanley Ray, b. 21 Sept 1917, Birmingham, England. Obstetrician and Gynaecologist. m Myrna Russell, 16 Feb 1952, 1 son. Education: MBBS (Lond); MRCS (Eng); LRCP (Lond); FRCOG; MMSA (Lond); FRCPI. Appointments: Surgeon-Lieutenant, RNVR, 1943-46; SurgicalRegistrar, National Temperance Hospital, London; Resident Obstetrics Officer, Epsom District Hospital, Epsom, Surrey; Gynaecology House Surgeon, Southlands Hospital, Shoreham-by-Sea, Sussex; Registrar, Obstetrics, Gynaecology, St Luke's Hospital, Guildford, Surrey, Senior Registrar, Obstetrics, Gynaecology, Plymouth Clinical Area; Senior Registrar, Tutor, Obstetrics-Gynaecology Professorial Unit, University of Bristol, Southmead Hospital; Locum Consultant, Obstetrics, Gynaecology: North Gloucester Clinical Area, then Lincoln; Consultant Obstetrician and Gynaecologist, Portiuncula Hospital, Ballinasloe, Republic of Ireland, 1962-82. Publications: Skin Homograft in Prevention of Habitual Abortion. 1971; Bleeding in Mid-Pregnancy, 1974; Ectopic Pregnancy, 1976; Co-author: Prevention of Rhesus Haemolytic Disease, 1966; Report of a Failed Case (Rh), 1967; Early Primary Peritoneal Pregnancy: Report of Two Cases and Review, 1968; Extramammary Paget's Disease of the Anus, 1968; IgG Anti-D in Prevention of Rhesus Iso-Immunization-A Second Report and Review of 100 Pregnancies, 1968; Prevention of Rhesus Haemolytic Disease-A Review of Six Years Experience, 1972; A Place for Presacral Neurectomy, 1981. Memberships: British and Irish Medical Associations; Fellow, Royal Academy of Medicine, Ireland, President, Obstetrics Section 1975-77; President, Institute of Obstetrics and Gynaecology, Royal College of Physicians of Ireland, 1982-85. Hobbies: Walking; Reading; Television. Address: Mannamead, Station Road, Ballinasloe, Co Galway, Republic of Ireland.

HIBBERD Adrian Donald, b. 19 Aug 1946, Sydney, Australia. Medicine. m. Suzanne Forgan-Smith, 28 Aug 1976, 2 s, 2 d. Education: MBBS; MD, Distinction; B Med Sci; FRACS; FACS. Appointments: Senior Lecturer in Surgery, University Otago, New Zealand, 1980-84; Associate Professor of Surgery, Newcastle, Australia, 1987-93; Area Director, Transplantation/HAHS, New South Wales, Australia, 1987-; Clinical Professor of Surgery, University of Newcastle, 1993-. Publications: 65 Professional articles published, 1983-93, including: Co-author, The long-term prognosis of women with breast cancer in New Zealand: A study of survival to 30 years, in British Medical Journal, 1983; Co-author, Castanospermine modifies expression of adhesion molecules in allograft recipients, in Transplant Proc, 1993. Honour: Sir Thaddeus McNaughton Fellow. Memberships: Vice President, 1989-91, Secretary, 1991-93,Transplantation Society of Australia and New Zealand; Transplantation Society; Vascular Section, Royal Australasian College of Surgeons. Hobbies: Tennis; Surfing; Yoga. Address: Newcastle Transplant Unit, John Hunter Hospital, Locked Bag 1, Hunter Region Mail Centre, Newcastle, NSW 2310, Australia.

HIBBERD Patricia Lavonne, b. 11 Jun 1954, Sheffield, England. Physician. m. Mark G Hibberd, 19 Jul 1975, 1 s. Education: BSc, Honours, Biochemistry, Kings College, London, UK, 1975; PhD, Leicester, UK, 1978; MD, Harvard Medical School, Boston, MA, USA, 1986. Career includes: Postdoctoral Fellow, Primary Communications Research Centre, Leicester University, UK, 1978-80; Fellow, Infectious Diseases, MA General Hospital, Boston, 1988-90; Currently: Assistant Professor of Medicine, Harvard Medical School, Boston, MA; Assistant Physician, MA General Hospital, Boston; Clinical Director, Program in Transplant Infectious Diseases, MA General Hospital, Boston; Co-Director, Infectious Disease Unit, Epidemiology Program, MA General Hospital, Boston. Publications: Many articles in professional journals including: Approach to immunization in the immunosuppressed host, in Infectious Disease Clinics of North America, 1990; Clinical aspects of fungal infection in organ transplant recipients, in Clinical Infectious Diseases, 1994; Use and misuse of statistics in epidemiologic studies of multiple sclerosis, in Annals Neurology, 1994. Honours: Board Certified, American Board of Internal Medicine; Fulfilled Board Eligibility Requirements, American Board of Internal Medicine, subspeciality in Infectious Diseases. Memberships: Society for Epidemiologic Research; American College of Physicians; Infectious Disease Society of America; American Society of Transplant Physicians. Hobbies: Skiing; Ballet. Address: Infectious Disease Unit, Massachusetts General Hospital, Fruit Street, Boston, MA 02114, USA.

HICKEY Robert Cornelius, b. 9 Dec 1917, Penna, USA. Physician; Surgeon. m. Rose Van Vranken, 21 Jun 1942, 3 s, 2 d. Education: BS, Cornell University, 1938; MD, Cornell University Medical School, 1942. Appointments: Associate in Surgery to Professor, 1951-62, Associate Dean, 1955-62, University of IA; Professor and Chairman of Surgery, University of WI, Madison, 1963-68; Professor of Surgery, Director and EVP, University of TX, MD Anderson, Houston, 1968-. Publications: 150 Cancer related publications; Editor-in-Chief, (1985-88, Section Editor, 1959-), Yearbook Cancer; Current Problems Cancer, 1975-86; Various editorial boards. Honours: National Cancer Advisory Board, NCI, 1980-86; Professor Emeritus, UTMDACC, 1984-90; Distinguished Alumni, CUMC, 1985. Memberships: Harris Co Medical Society; Texas Medical Society; Houston Surgical Society; American Surgical Association; American College of Surgeons; American Association Endocrine Surgeons. Hobby: Reading. Address: 435 Tallowood, Houston, TX 77024, USA.

HICKISH Gordon Walter, b. 7 Oct 1925, London, England. Doctor. m. Aileen Hickish, 8 Jul 1949, 3 s, 3 d. Education: VRD; MB Ch B, Edinburgh; FRCGP; DCH. Appointments: (retired) Hospital Practitioner, ENT Department, St Bartholomew's Hospital, London; Currently, General Practitioner. Publications: Ear, Nose and Throat Disorders, 1985; Leading Article, Hearing Problems of Elderly People, British Medical Journal, 1989; New Tools for GP's, Medical Annual, 1993-94. Memberships: Association of Aviation; Medical Examiners Aerospace Medical Association; European Underwater and Baromedical Society; Fellow, Royal Society of Medicine. Hobbies: Beekeeping; Sailing; Crosscountry Skiing. Address: Heather Cottage, Burnt House Lane, Bransgore, Nr Christchurch, Dorset, BH23 8AL, England.

HIGGINS Millicent Williams, b. 5 Mar 1928, Halifax, England. Physician. m. Ian T T Higgins, 2 May 1964, 2 s. Education: MB; BS; MD; DPH; Honorary Fellow, American College of Chest Physicians; Professor Emeritus, University of Michigan. Appointments: Professor of Epidemiology and Internal Medicine, University of Michigan; Deputy Director, Deca, NHLBI, NIH. Publications: Smoking and Lung Function, 1993; Long Term Benefits and Adverse Effects of Weight Loss, 1993; 89 Publications. Honours: Honorary Fellow, American College of Chest Physicians. Memberships: American Heart Association; Fellow, Council on Epidemiology and Prevention; Fellow, American College of Epidemiology. Hobbies: Walking; Music; Sailing. Address: 252 Indian River Place, Ann Arbor, MI 48104, USA.

HIGGINS William Hubert, b. 21 May 1946, McKeesport, USA. Allergist. Education: BA, Youngstown University, 1968; DO, Des Moines College of Osteopathy, 1972; Diplomate, American Board, 1983. Appointments: Osteopathic Family Practice; Intern, Phoenix General Hospital, 1972-73; Private Practice, Scottsdale, 1973-; Board Director, Scottsdale Green Homeowners Association, 1987-94. Memberships: American College of Allergists; American Osteopathic Association; American College of Allergy & Immunology, 1987-94; American Osteopathic Specialists, 1989; Scottsdale Sea & Ski Club; Masons; Arizonia Osteopathic Medical Association, 1992-94. Hobbies: Scuba Diving; Snow Skiing; Softball; Racquetball; Camping. Address: 8417 E McDowell Road 103, Scottsdale, AZ 85257-3903, USA.

HILDING-HAMANN Iben, b. 2 Aug 1963, Copenhagen, Denmark. Chiropractor. m. Knud Erik Hamann, 13 Aug 1988, 1 daughter. Education: BSc, Chiropractic, 1991; DC, 1992. Appointments: Fulltime Chiropractor. Memberships: British Chiropractic Association. Hobbies: Aerobics; Country Walks; Family Life. Address: 58 Birmingham Road, Sutton Coldfield, West Midlands, B72 1QJ, England.

HILEY-YOUNG Bruce, b. 27 Dec 1949, California, USA. Social Worker. 1 daughter. Education: BS, University of Oregon, 1974; MSW, University of Hawaii, 1983. Appointments: Crisis Team Worker,

Honolulu, Hawaii, 1983-84; Clinical Social Worker, Inpatient Treatment Programme for Post-Traumatic Stress Disorders, 1984-87, Programme Coordinator, Community Services Section, Department of Psychiatry, 1987-89, Veterans Administration Medical Center, Palo Alto, California; Disaster and Community Outreach Coordinator, Education Specialist, Editor, National Center for Post-Traumatic Stress Disorder, Clinical Laboratory and Education Division, Department of Veterans Affairs, Menlo Park, California, 1989-. Publications include: Facilitating cognitive-emotional congruence in anxiety disorders during self-determination cognitive change: An integrated model, 1990; Trauma reactivation and treatment: Integrated case examples, 1992; The use of volunteers and mutual aid personnel in mental health disorders (with D Myers and P J Spofford), 1994; Warzone violence in Vietnam: a review and examination of premilitary, military, and postmilitary factors (co-author), 1994; 5 videos. Honours: Silver Apple, as co-producer of Children and Trauma: The School's Response, National Educational Film and Video Festival, 1993. Memberships: American Red Cross, Santa Cruz Chapter, Board of Directors, Advisory Council for Disaster Mental Health, Social Services Committee; American Red Cross, Disaster Services and Human Resources: Mental Health; International Society for Traumatic Stress Studies. Hobbies: Painting; Songwriting. Address: National Center for PTSD, 3801 Miranda Ave 323E, Palo Alto, CA 94304, USA.

HILL Clara E, b. 13 Sep 1948, Shivers, Mississippi, USA. Professor of Psychology. m. James Gormally, 25 May 1974, 1 son, 1 daughter. Education: BA, MA, PhD, Southern Illinois University. Appointment: Professor. Publications: Therapist Techniques and Client Outcomes: Eight Cases of Brief Psychotherapy, 1989; Editor, Journal of Counseling Psychology, 1994-99. Memberships: Society for Psychotherapy Research, President, 1994-95; American Psychological Association; Association for the Study of Dreams. Hobby: Reading. Address: Department of Psychology, University of Maryland, College Park, MD 29742, USA.

HILLER F Charles, b. 30 Jan 1942, Kansas City, KS, USA. Physician. m. Michelle Hiller, 20 Mar 1965, 3 s, 1 d. Education: AB, University of KS, Lawrence; MD, University of KS School of Medicine, KS. Appointments include: Assistant Professor, 1975-80, Associate Professor, 1980-83, Currently, Professor of Medicine, University of AR, Little Rock; Associate Professor, Department of Toxicology, 1982-83; Medical Director, Medical Intensive Care Unit and Sleep Disorders Center, 1984-; Director, Pulmonary and Critical Care Medicine Division, 1985-; Medical Director, Respiratory Therapy, LRVAMC, 1993-; Vice Chairman, Department of Internal Medicine, 1993-. Publications: 85 Professional articles published, 1977-, including: Health implications of hygroscopic particle growth in the human respiratory tract, in Journal Aerosol Medicine, 1991; Co-author, Nicotine blood levels measured after smoking cigarettes designed to release nicotine by heat vaporization instead of burning, submitted; Numerous presentations and abstracts; Co-editor book, Pulmonary Disease: Focus on Clinical Diagnosis, 1983; Editorial reviewer for several professional journals. Honours: Eagle Scout; Outstanding Young Man in America, 1977; Alpha Omega Alpha, 1979; Sigma Xi, 1984. Memberships include: American Thoracic Society; Fellow, American College of Chest Physicians; American Federation for Clinical Research; Association of Pulmonary Program Directors; Chairman, Chest Section, Southern Medical Association. Hobbies: Backpacking; Bicycling; Camping; Boy Scouts. Address: 4301 West Markham, Slot 555, Little Rock, AR 72205, USA.

HINDE Frederick Charles, b. 18 Oct 1933, Sydney, Australia. Obstetrician and Gynaecologist. m. Mary Taylor, 6 Feb 1961, 2 sons, 2 daughters. Education: MBBS, 1956, DGO, 1960, Sydney; FRCS(Ed); FRACS; FRCOG; FRACOG; FCPSP. Appointments: Visiting Gynaecologist, Royal Prince Alfred Hospital, Sydney; Visiting Gynaecologist, Masonic Hospital, Sydney; President, Royal Australian College of Obstetricians and Gynaecologists. Honours: ED, 1970; Honorary AM, Malaysia, 1994. Hobby: Music. Address: 15 Kareelah Road, Hunters Hill, 2110 Australia.

HINGORANI Vera, b. 23 Dec 1924, Bubak, India. Gynaecologist. m. 22 Apr 1954, 1 daughter. Education: FRCOG; FACS; Hon FACOG; FICS; FIMSA; FICOG. Appointments: Principal Investigator, Officer-in-Charge, Human Reproduction Research Centre of ICMR, All india Institute of Medical Sciences, New Delgi, 1982-86; Senior Vice President, Federation of Obstetrics and Gynaecological Societies of India, 1982-83; Chairman Representative, Committee of Royal College of Obstetricians and Gynaecologists, London Northern Zone, India,

1982-85; Ex-Honorary Surgeon to the President of India, 1982-85; Program Director, Post Partum Programme, All India Institute of Medical Sciences, New Delhi, 1972-86, 1986-; Clinical Director, WHO, Research Training Centre, All India Institute of Medical Sciences, New Delhi, 1972-87; Professor, Head, Department of Obstetrics and Gynaecology, All India Institute of Medical Sciences, New Delhi; Head, Department Obstetrics and Gynaecology, Batra Hospital, New Delhi. Publications: Contributor of over 300 papers in national and international journals; Contributor of chapters in books; Handbook Scientific Abstract, Chief Editor, 1992; Chief Editor of conference proceedings. Honours include: Conferred National Award of Padmashree for outstanding contribution in the service to women and the newborn by the President of India, 1984; Honorary fellowship, American College of Obstetricians and Gynaecologists, 1977; Early Fellowship, Royal College of Obstetricians and Gynaecologists, 1966; Fellowship, National Academy of Medical Sciences, 1975. Memberships include: Indian Medical Association; Indian Academy of Cytologists. Address: A-1 Batra Hospital, New Delhi 110062, India.

HINMAN Frank, b. 10 Feb 1915, San Francisco, California, USA. Urologist. m. Marion Modesta Eaves, 3 Dec 1948. Education: MD; FACS; FAAP. Appointments: Clinical Instructor, Urology, 1948-50, Assistant Clinical Professor, Urology, 1950-54, Associate Clinical Professor, Urology, 1954-62, Clinical Professor, Urology, 1962-, University of California, San Francisco; Chief, Urology Service, San Francisco General Hospital, 1958-77; Urologist-in-Chief, Children's Hospital, San Francisco, 1959-85. Publications: Hydrodynamics of Micturition (editor), 1971; Benign Prostatic Hypertrophy (editor), 1983; Atlas of Urologic Surgery, 1989, Spanish edition, 1993, German edition, 1994; American Pediatric Urology, 1991; Atlas of UroSurgical Anatomy, 1993; Atlas of Pediatric Urologic Surgery, 1994; 280 journal articles. Honours include: Hugh Hampton Award, 1977, Ramon Guiteras Award, 1985, American Urological Association; Benjamin Stockwell Barringer Medal, American Association of Genitourinary Surgeons, 1984; Honorary Fellow, Royal College of Surgeons of England; St Paul's Medal, British Association of Urologic Surgeons; Valentine Medal, New York, 1995. Memberships: Alpha Omega Alpha; Phi Beta Kappa; Fellow, American Academy of Pediatrics, Urology Section President 1987; Honorary Member, American Association of Genitourinary Surgeons, President 1980; Fellow, American Society for Study of Sterility; American College of Surgeons, Regent 1972-80, Vice-Chairman 1978-80, 1st Vice-President 1982-83; American Surgical Association; Founding Member, Society for Pediatric Urology, President, 1973; Founder, Endocrine Urology Group; Founding Member, Genito-Urinary Reconstructive Surgeons; Founding Member, Urodynamics Society, President 1980-82; Many others. Hobby: Sailing. Address: University of California, San Francisco, CA 94143-0738, USA.

HINOVA-PALOVA Dimka Valchanova, b. 30 Dec 1948, Bulgaria. Medical Doctor. m. Dr Adrian Paloff, 9 June 1976, 1 daughter. Education: MD; PhD. Career: Assistant; Assistant Professor. Publications: Reciprocal Conn Between the Claustrum and Auditory Cortical Fields in the Cat; An Experimental Study Using Light and Electron Microscopic Anterograde Degeneration Methods, 1988. Memberships: Bulgarian Society of Anatomists; Anatomische Gesellschaft; European Society of Exp Morphology; International Brain Research Organization. Hobby: Ski sport. Address: Faculty of Medicine, Department of Anatomy, Sofia 1431, Bulgaria.

HIRAIDE Fumihisa, b. 7 May 1938, Tokyo, Japan. Professor of Otolaryngology. m. Seiko Takahashi, 29 Apr 1968, 1 daughter. Education: ND, Fukushima Medical College, 1965; PhD, University of Tokyo, 1974. Appointments: Assistant Professor, University of Tokyo, 1974; Associate Professor, National Defense Medical College, 1977; Associate Professor, Jichi Medical College, 1985; Associate Professor, 1989, Professor of Otolaryngology, 1990-, Tokyo Medical College. Publications: Atlas of Otology, 1974; Dizziness, 1982; Atlas of Otolaryngologic Surgery, 1989; Atlas of ENT Diagnosis, 1991; New Atlas of Otology, 1992; Manual of ENT Diagnosis, 1994. Memberships: Japan Society of Otolaryngology; Japan Society of Otology; Japan Society of Audiology; Japan Society of Rhinology; Japan Society of Broncho-Esophagology; Japan Society of Stomato-Pharyngology; Japan Society of Head and Neck Surgery; Association for Research in Otolaryngology, USA. Hobby: Photography. Address: 3-20-10 Wakamiya, Nakano-ku, Tokyo, Japan.

HIRASHIMA Akinori, b. 11 Apr 1955, Yame City, Fukuoka, Japan. Associate Researcher. m. Mika Hirashima, 15 Sept 1987, 1 son, 1

daughter. Education: BSc; MSc; PhD. Appointments: Postdoctorate Researcher, Berkeley, California University, 1983-85; Visiting Researcher, Bayer AG Monheim, Germany, 1985-86. Publications: Advances in Second Messenger and Phosphoprotein Research: The Biology and Medicine of Signal Transduction, 1990; Frontiers and New Horizons in Amine Acid Research, 1992; Pesticides/Environment: Molecular Biological Approaches, 1993. Memberships: Pesticide Science Society of Japan; Japan Society for Bioscience; Biotechnology & Agrochemistry. Hobbies: Bicycling; Walking. Address: Department of Agricultural Chemistry, Kyushu University, Fukuoka 812-81, Japan.

HIRD David W, b. 30 June 1942, Virginia, USA. Professor. m. Shelley Carter, 15 July 1973, 1 son, 1 daughter. Education: AB, Syanford University; DVM, MPVM, University of California, Davis; PhD, University of Minnesota. Appointments: International work in Chile, Venezuela, Australia; County Veterinarian, Imperial Company, California; Professor of Epidemiology, University of California, Davis. Publications: Contributor of over 100 professional publications> Honours: Honorary Professor, University of Chile, 1993; Fulbright Scholar, 1987, 1988. Address: VM, Medicine and Epidemiology, University of California, Davis, CA, USA.

HIRSCH Samuel Roger, b. 19 Dec 1930, Chicago, Illinois, USA. Physician. m. (1) 3 sons, 2 daughters, (2) Sharon Ann Hirsch, 30 Nov 1990. Education: BA, University of Wisconsin, Madison, 1953; MD, University of Wisconsin Medical School, 1956; Intern, Resident, Illinois Research and Education Hospital, Chicago, 1956-58; Resident, Internal Medicine, Veterans Administration Center, Wood, Milwaukee, 1960-62; Allergy Fellowship, Milwaukee County Medical Complex, 1962-68. Appointments: Captain, USAF, Chief of Medicine, 2791st USAF Hospital, Hill AFB, Ogden, Utah, 1958-60; Clinic Physician, Mt Sinai Hospital, Milwaukee, Wisconsin, 1963-67; Attending Physician, 1963-78; Clinical Instructor, Marquette University School of Medicine, Milwaukee, 1963-68; Research Associate, 1964-84, Chief, Allergy and Pulmonary Research Laboratory, 1975-81, Veterans Administration Medical Center, Wood; Assistant Clinical Professor, 1968-73, Associate Clinical Professor, 1973-87, Clinical Professor of Medicine, 1987-, Medical College of Wisconsin, Milwaukee; Associate Clinical Professor of Medicine, University of Wisconsin, Milwaukee, 1976-; Private Practice. Publications: About 45 articles and book chapters in field of respiratory allergies; Over 50 abstracts. Honours: Board Certified: Internal Medicine, 1965; Allergy, American Board of Allergy and Immunology, 1972, 1977. Memberships: Fellow, American College of Physicians; Fellow, American College of Chest Physicians; Fellow, American Academy of Allergy and Immunology; FACAI. Hobbies: Music; Finance. Address: 5020 W Oklahoma Ave, Milwaukee, WI 53219, USA.

HIRSCHEL L Anne, b. 17 Apr 1926, Breslau, Germany. Dentist; Medical Writer. m. John U Hirschel, 16 Dec 1948, 1 son, 1 daughter. Education: BDS, University of London; LDS, Royal College of Surgeons; DDS, University of Michigan. Appointments: Dentist, Stonebridge Health Center, England; Dentist, City of Detroit, Michigan; Dentist in private practice; Currently Medical Writer. Publications: American Jurisprudence Proof of Facts, 1991; Contributor: Encyclopaedia Britannica Yearbook of Science-The Future, 1989; Encyclopaedia Britannica Medical Health Annuals, 1989, 1990, 1992. Honours: Florence Huson Scholar, 1950. Memberships: American Medical Writers Association; American Dental Association; Michigan Dental Association; Oakland County Dental Society; Fellow, Royal Society of Health. Hobbies: Travel; Book collecting; Video photography. Address: 20120 Ledgestone Drive, Southfield, MI 48076, USA.

HIRSCHFELD Robert M A, b. 2 Sept 1943, Alexandria, LA, USA. Psychiatrist. m. Ellen Kingsley, 2 s, 2 d. Education: MD, 1968; MS, 1972; BS, 1964. Appointments: National Institute of Mental Health, Rockville, Maryland : Research Psychiatrist, Clinical Research Branch, 1972-77; Head, Depression Section, Clinical Research Branch, 1977-78; Chief, Center for Students of Affective Disorders, Clinical Research Branch, 1978-85; Chief, Mood, Anxiety & Personality Disorders Research Branch, 1985-90; Profesor & Chairman, Department of Psychiatry & Behavioral Studies, University of Texas, Medical Branch, Galveston. Publications: Mood Disorders: Psychosocial Treatments, 1989; When the Blues Won't Go Away, 1991. Honours: ADAMHA Administrator's Award for Meritorious Achievement, 1979; Pieter Baan Lecture, Netherlands Psychiatric Association, 1988; WPA Gerald L Klerman Award for Panic Disorder, 1993. Memberships: American Psychiatric Association; American College of Psychiatry; American

College of Neuropsychopharmacology. Address: 301 University Boulevard, Galveston, TX 77555-0429, USA.

HITZIG Walter H, b. 9 May 1922, Mexico. Physician. m. Verena E Weber, 2 June 1955, 1 son, 1 daughter. Education: MD, Zürich, Switzerland. Appointments: Research Fellow, Children's Hospital, Boston, 1955-56; Lecturer, Zurich, 1961; Assistant Professor, 1963; Associate Professor, 1965; Professor, 1977; Emeritus, 1989. Publications: Agammaglobulinämie und Alymphozytose, Co-author, 1958; Hämoglobin, Co-author, 1960; Septische Granulomatose, Co-author, 1968; Primary Immunodeficiencies, Co-author, 1971; Plasmaproteine, 1977. Honours: Honorary Member of numerous paediatric and immunological societies. Address: Zurich, Switzerland.

HO Chung Yin Andrew, b. Hong Kong. Obstetrician, Gynaecologist. m. Lo Lin June Liau, 3 Sept 1967, 1 son, 4 daughters. Education: MBBS, Hong Kong; MRCOG (UK); Fellow, Hong Academy of Medicine (Obstetrics and Gynaecology). Appointments: Senior Medical Officer, Queen Elizabeth Hospital, Hong Kong; Honorary Clinical Lecturer, University of Hong Kong; Currently Honorary Consultant Gynaecologist, Hong Kong Buddhist Hospital. Memberships: Hong Kong Medical Association; Singapore Medical Association. Hobbies: Tennis; Boating; Swimming. Address: Room 705, Argyle Centre Phase 1, 688 Nathan Road, Kowloon, Hong Kong.

HO Kang-Jey, b. 2 Aug 1937, Taiwan, China. Pathologist. m. Yen-Dong Ho, 26 Dec 1969, 1 son, 1 daughter. Education: MD, National Taiwan University, 1963; PhD, Northwestern University, 1968. Appointments: Assistant Professor of Pathology, Northwestern University, 1968-70; Assistant Professor of Pathology, University of Alabama, 1970-71; Associate Professor of Pathology, University of Alabama, 1972-76; Staff Pathologist, Virginia Medical Center, 1970-. Publications: Over 200 scientific papers in the field of lipid metabolism. Honours: Best Research Paper, 1968; Schweppe Foundation Fellowship, 1973; Flonorary Professorship, Guiyang Medical College, China. Memberships: American Heart Association; American Institute of Nutrition; American Society for Clinical Nutrition; American Society for Investigative Pathology; American Association of Pathologists. Hobbies: Classical Music; Travel; Gardening; Fishing; Crafting. Address: 1583 Mountain Gap Drive, Birmingham, AL 55226, USA.

HO Nai-Kiong, b. 28 Dec 1937, Singapore. Paediatrician. m. Woon-Ho Foong, 3 June 1967, 3 sons. Education: MBBS, Singapore; MMed, Paediatrics; FRACP; FAMS. Appointments: Head, Department of Neonatology, Tao Payoh Hospital; Visiting Professor Paediatrics, Jinan University, China; Head, department of Neonatology, Kandang Kerbau Hospital, Singapore. Publications: Contributor of numerous articles in professional journals. Honours: Commander Brother of the Order of St John, 1990; Public Service Medal, Republic of Singapore, 1992. Memberships: Singapore Medical Association; Singapore Padiatric Society; Perinatal Society of Singapore. Hobby: Calligraphy. Address: 81 Hillcrest Road, Singapore 1128, Republic of Singapore.

HO Pak Chung, b. 18 May 1950, Hong Kong. Reader in Obstetrics & Gynaecology. m. Ada Yim-Ping Tse, 27 Dec 1980, 1 s, 1 d. Education: MB, University of Hong Kong, 1974; BS, University of Hong Kong, 1974; MD, University of Hong Kong, 1990; MRCOG, 1979; FRCOG, 1991. Appointments: Medical & Health Officer, 1975-76; Lecturer, 1976-82; Senior Lecturer, 1982-87; Reader of Obstetrics & Gynaecology, University of Hong Kong, 1987-. Publications: 85 Articles in Journals; 10 Chapters in Books; 36 Abstracts; including, Intrauterine Insemination is not Useful in Oligoasthenospermia, 1989; A Controlled Trial of Bestatin in Hydatidiform Mole, 1990; Intrauterine Insemination After Ovarian Stimulation as a Treatment for Subfertility because of Subnormal Semen: A Prospective Randomized Controlled Trial, 1992; A Prospective Randomized Comparison of Levonorgestrel with the Yuzpe Regimen in Post-Coital Contraception, 1993; Lymphocyte Subsets and Serum Immunoglobulins in Patients with Premature Ovarian Failure before and after Oestrogen Replacement, 1993. Memberships: Royal College of Obstetricians & Gynaecologists; American Fertility Society; Hong Kong College of Obstetricians & Gynaecologists; International Society of Reproductive Immunology. Hobbies: Table Tennis; Swimming; Music. Address: Department of Obstetrics & Gynaecology, University of Hong Kong, Pokfulam Road, Hong Kong.

HO Patrick C P, b. 24 July 1949, Hong Kong. Ophthalmologist. 1 son, 1 daughter. Education: MD, Vanderbilt University, USA; FACS; Diplomate, American Board of Ophthalmology; fellow, American Academy of Ophthalmology. Appointments: Clinical Assistant Professor, UCSF; Professor of Ophthalmology, CHinese University of Hong Kong; Honorary Consultant, Hospital Authority of Hong Kong; Honorary Professor of Ophthalmology to seven Universities in China. Publications include: Kinetics of Cornel Epithelial Regeneration and Epidermal Growth Factor, Co-author, 1974; Acute Syphilitic Optic Neuritis, Co-author, 1981; Macular Photocoagulation - Which Laser?, Co-author, 1983; Contact Lenses for Vitrectomy, Co-author, 1984; Contributor of numerous chapters in books, abstracts, reports and conference proceedings. Honours: Distinguished Service Award, Asia-Pacific Academy of Ophthalmology, 1989; Senior fellowship Scheme Award, 1992; Association of Southeast Asia Institutions of Higher Learning. Memberships: Fellow, Hong Kong College of Surgeons; Vice President, Asia-Pacific Academy of Ophthalmology. Hobby: Music. Address: 11B Entertainment Building, 30 Queen's Road Central, Hong Kong.

HOBBES Robin Russell, b. 5 Dec 1952, St Albans, England. Psychotherapist. m. Judi Ledward, 22 Jan 1986, 1 s, 1 d. Education: BA, Joint Honours, Philosophy and Politics; Diploma, Social Work, Clinical Transactional Analyst; CQSW; CTA; PTSTA. Appointments: Chairperson, British Institute of Transactional Analysis, 1985-87; Chair of Ethics, British Institute of Transactional Analysis, 1994-; Currently, Director of Training, Elan Psychotherapy Training Institute. Memberships: British Institute of Transactional Analysis; British Association of Counselling. Hobbies: Composer; Saxophonist; Go Player; Cycling. Address: 6 Clarence Rd, Hale, Altincham, Cheshire, WA15 8SG, England.

HOBFOLL Stevan Earl, b. 25 Sept 1951, Chicago, Illinois, USA. Clinical Psychologist. m. Ivonne Heras Hobfoll, 2 sons, 1 daughter. Education: BS, Magna Cum Laude, University of Illinois, Urbana, 1973; University of London, King's College, England, 1971-72; MA, 1975, PhD, 1977, University of South Florida, Tampa, USA. Appointments: Lecturer, 1980-82, Senior Lecturer, 1982-83, department of Sociology of Health, faculty of Health Sciences, Ben Gurion University of the Negev, Beersheva, Israel; Senior Lecturer, 1983-87, Professor Fellow, 1987-88, Department of Psychology, Tel-Aviv University; Professor of Psychology, Director, Applied Psychology Centre, Kent State University, Ohio, USA, 1987-. Publications include: Stress, Social Support, and Women, Editor, 1986; The Ecology of Stress, 1988; Work Won't Love You Back: A Survival Guide for Dual Career Couples, Co-author, 1994; Conservation of Resources: A New Attempt at Conceptualizing Stress, 1989; Pulse of a Nation: Depressive Mood Reactions of Israelis to the Israel-Lebanon War, Co-author, 1989; War-related Stress: Addressing the Stress of War and Other Traumatic Events, Co-author, 1991; Reducing Inner-City Women's AIDS Risk Activities: A Study of Single, Pregnant Inner-City Women, Co-author, 1994. Honours include: Ecology of Stress, selected by Encyclopeaedia Britannica 1989 Yearbook as one of 175 recent books that have been judged significant contributions to learning and understanding. Memberships include: American Psychological Association; Society for Test Anxiety Research; International Society for the Study of Personal Relationships. Address: Applied Psychology Centre, Kent State University, Kent, OH 44242, USA.

HOCHBERG Marc Craig, b. 29 June 1949, New York, NY, USA. Medicine. m. Susan Newhouse, 10 June 1973, 2 daughters. Education: MD, The John Hopkins University, 1973; MPH, 1979; FACP; FACR. Career: Associate Professor of Medicine, The Johns Hopkins University School of Medicine, 1984-91; Joint Appointment of Epidemiology, School of Hygiene and Public Health, 1979-91; Professor of Medicine and Epidemiology, University of Maryland School of Medicine. Publications: Co-authored textbook, Epidemiology of the Rheumatic Diseases, 1993; Edited Volume of Rheumatic Disease Clinics of North America, 1990; Author, over 100 articles. Honours: Arthritis Investigator Award, Arthritis Foundation, 1983-86; President, Southeast Region, American College of Rheumatology, 1991-92. Memberships: American College of Rheumatology; American College of Physicians; Society for the Epidemiology Research. Address: c/o University of Maryland School of Medicine, 419 W Redwood St, Ste 620, Baltimore, MD 21201, USA.

HODESS Arthur Bart, b. 15 Jan 1950, New York, USA. Chief, Cardiology; Chief, Critical Care; Chairman, Department of Medicine, Brandywine Hospital; President, Brandywine Valley Cardiovascular Association. m. S Christina Ellsworth, 23 Dec 1987, 4 sons. Education: BA, Boston University, 1970; MD, Columbia University College of Physicians & Surgeons, 1974. Appointments: Intern in Medicine, Hospital University of Pennsylvania, 1974-75; Resident, Hospital

University of Pennsylvania, 1975-77; Fellow, Cardiology Hospital, University of Pennsylvania, 1977-79; Assistant Instructor in Medicine, Hospital University of Pennsylvania, 1974-79; Instructor in Medicine Department, Hospital University of Pennsylvania, 1977-78; Clinical Associate in Medicine, Hospital University of Pennsylvania, 1979-81; Attending Cardiologist, Brandywine Hospital, 1979-. Publications include: Leber's optic atrophy associated with spondyloepiphyseal dysplasia, 1974; Quabain induced changes in electrophysiologic properties of neonatal, young and adult canine cardiac purkinje fibers, 1975; Cellular electrophysiology of human myocardial infarction I Abnormalities of cellular activation, 1979; Electrophysiological effects of a new antiarrhythmic agent, flecainide, on the intact cainine heart, 1979. Memberships include: Fellow, American College of Cardiology, 1984; Fellow, Clinical Council of Cardiology, 1985; Fellow, American College of Physicians; Cardiac Electrophysiology Society; American Society of Echocardiography. Honours: New York Regents Scholar, 1966-68; AOA, 1973; Physician's Recognition Award, 1978, 1981, 1985, 1988. Hobbies: Tennis; Theatre; Cinema; Opera. Address: 3025 Zinn Road, Thorndale, PA 19372, USA.

HODOBA Daniel Danilo, b. 15 Feb 1951, Sr Mitrovica, Vojvodina. Psychiatrist. m. Nevenka Hodoba, 26 Feb 1976, 1 son. Education: MD, 1975, postgraduate study in Neurology, 1979-80, MSc, 1983, DSc, 1985, University of Zagreb; Specialisation in Psychiatry, Vrapce Psychiatric Hospital, 1978-81; Primarius. Appointments: General Practitioner, 1976-78; Psychiatrist-Neurophysiologist, EEG Department, 1981-91, Head, EEG and Psychophysiology Department, Head, Department of Psychiatric Research, 1991-, Vrapce Psychiatric Hospital, Zagreb. Publications: Paradoxic sleep facilitation by interictal epileptic activity of right temporal origin, 1986; Evidence from epileptic patients on the role of the right hemisphere in REM sleep, 1992; Mental disorders in the elderly, 1994. Honours: President, Croatian Association of Sleep Research, 1994-. Memberships: Croatian Medical Association; International Psychogeriatric Association; International Society for Neuroimaging in Psychiatry. Hobbies: History of ancient civilizations; Cycling. Address: Bartolici 47, 41000 Zagreb, Croatia.

HODOBA Nevenka, b. 23 Aug 1951, Pula, Croatia. Doctor; Anaesthesiologist. m. Danilo Hodoba, 26 Feb 1976, 1 son. Education: MD; Specialist in Anaesthesiology. Appointments: General Practitioner, Zagreb; Currently Anaesthesiologist, Clinic for Thoracic Surgery, Zagreb. Membership: Croatian Association of Anaesthesiology. Hobby: Painting. Address: Bartolici 47, 41000 Zagreb, Croatia.

HOFF Charles, b. 28 Oct 1937, Newark, NY, USA. Professor. m. Marcia Jane Lasswell, 10 July. Education: BS, 1961, MA. 1968, PhD, 1972, Pennsylvania State University; Dipl Hum Biol, University of Oxford, 1968. Appointments: Professor of Paediatrics and Biostatistics and Epidemiology; University of South Alabama College of Medicine. Publications include: Altitudinal Variation in the Physical Growth and Development of Peruvian Quechua, 1974; Earlier maturation of Pregnant Black and White Adolescents, CO-author, 1985; Maternal-Fetal ABO/Rh Antigenic Dissimilarity and Human Fetal Development, Co-author, 1986; Trend Associations of Smoking with Maternal, Fetal and Neonatal Morbidity, Co-author, 1986; Does Exposure to HLA Alloantigens Trigger Immunoregulatory Mechanisms Operative in Both Pregnancy and AIDS? Co-author, 1989; Maternal-Fetal HLA-DR Relationships and Fetal Growth, Co-author, 1993; An HLA-haplotype Associated with Preeclampsia and Intrauterine Growth Retardation, Co-author, 1994. Honours: Wenner-Gren Fellowship, University of Oxford, 1967-68; NIH Traineeship, 1969; University of Oregon Academic Year Award, 1971-72, 19175-76; University of Oregon Summer Research Award, 1972; University of Oregon Group Year Award, 1972-73; NIH Grant, 1979-81; Distinguished Visiting Professor, University of Tennessee, 1983; March of Dimes Grant, 1984-85; NIH Grant, 1986-88; MBRS Visiting Professor, University of Hawaii, 1992. Memberships include: American Society of Reproductive Immunology; American Heart Society; American College of Epidemiology; Human Biology Council. Address: PO Box 40130, Mobile, AL 36640-0130, USA.

HOFFER M Mark, b. 15 Jul 1935, New York, NY, USA. Orthopedic Surgeon. m. Margo Rotman, 8 Jun 1960. Education: MD, University of Chicago, 1960; Orthopedic Residency, Oschner Clinic, 1968; Hand Fellowship, Orthopaedic Hospital, 1969; Pediatric Orthopedic Fellowship, Rancho Los Amigos Hospital, 1969. Appointments: Chairman, Orthopedics, University of CA, Irvine; Professor Emeritus, University of CA, Irvine Medical Center; Currently, Lowman Chair, University of Southern CA, Orthopedic Hospital. Honours: Kappa Delta,

1977; Richmond Award, 1991. Memberships: Board Surfing; Road Running; Masters Competitive Swimming. Address: 2300 S Flower Ste 200, Los Angeles, CA 90007, USA.

HOFFMAN Nancy Yanes, b. 2 July 1929, Boston, Massachusetts, USA. Medical Author and Editor. m. Marvin J Hoffman, 15 Aug 1949, 1 son, 2 daughters. Education: BS with high distinction; MSc. Appointments: Weekly Book Reviewer, Los Angeles Times, California; Advisory Board, Community Savings Bank, Rochester, New York; Public Relations Consultant, Ochsner Medical Institutions, New Orleans, Louisiana; Director, Philadelphia Pension Planning Group, Pennsylvania; Associate Professor of English, Rochester, New York; Currently: President, NYH Health Care Communications; Medical Author and Writer-in-Residence. Publications: Change of Heart, The Bypass Experience, 1985; Breast Cancer: A Practical Guide to Diagnosis, 1995; Doctor, I've Found a Lump!, 1996; The Season of Sexuality: Love, Sex and Intimacy for Seniors, in progress. Honours: Class Marshall, MSc class; Inducted into Phi Beta Kappa. Memberships: Authors Guild; American Medical Writers Association; American Society of Journalists and Authors; National Association of Science Writers; American Heart Association. Address: 16 San Rafael Drive, Rochester, NY 14618, USA.

HOFFMANN Klaus Hubert, b. 15 Sept 1946, Evlangen, Germany. University Professor. m. Jana Hoffmann, 19 Feb 1971, 2 daughters. Education: Diploma, University of Evlangen, 1970; PhD, University of Evlangen, 1973; Habilitation, 1977. Appointments: Professor, University of Ulm, 1978-94; Head, Department of Animal Ecology, University of Bayventh. Publications: Editor, Environmental Physiology and Biochemistry of Insects, 1985; Co-author, Physiologie oler Insechten, 1995; 100 original research papers. Honours: Merckle Research Prize in Ecophysiology, 1990. Memberships: Several national and international organizations. Hobbies: Sports.

HOGSTON Patrick, b. 16 Jul 1954, London, UK. Consultant Gynaecologist. m. Carrie, 13 Sept 1980, 1 s, 1 d. Education: BSc, University of London, 1976; MBBS, University of London, 1979; LRCP; FRCS' MRCOG. Appointments: Consultant Gynaecologist. Publications: MCQS for DRCOG; Active Management of Labor, 1993; Early Discharge After Major Gynae Surgery, 1994. Honours: Handcock Prize, 1979. Memberships: British Gynaecological Cancer Society; British Society Colposcopy/Cervical Pathology. Hobbies: Ornithology; Walking; Cycling; Music. Address: 38 St Edwards Road, Southsea, Hampshire, PO53 3DJ, UK.

HOKIN Lowell Edward, b. 20 Sept 1924, Chicago, USA. Biochemist. m. Mabel Neaverson, 1 Dec 1952, div 1973, 1 son, 1 daughters, 1 deceased. Education: MD, University of Louisville, 1948; PhD, University of Sheffield, England, 1952. Appointments: Intern, Michael Reese Hospital, 1948-49; Fellow, American Cancer Society, University of Sheffield, 1949-51; British-American Exchange Fellow, Cancer Research, University Sheffield, 1951-52; Merck Postdoctoral Fellow, Montreal General Hospital Research Institute, McGill University, 1952-53; US Public Health Service Special Fellow, Montreal General Hospital Research Institute, McGill University, 1953-54; Lecturer in Pharmacology, McGill University, 1954-55; Assistant Professor, McGill University, 1955-57; Assistant Professor, University of Wisconsin Medical School, 1957-59; Associate Professor, University of Wisconsin Medical School, 1959-61; Professor, University of Wisconsin Medical School, 1961-68; Chairman of Pharmacology, University of Wisconsin Medical School, 1968-93; Professor of Pharmacology, University of Wisconsin Medical School, 1968-; Pharmacology Study Section, NIH, 1973-77; Molecular Pharmacology Editorial Board, 1973; Archives of Biochemistry & Biophysics Editorial Board, 1967-74. Honours: US Public Health Service Lifetime Research Center Award, 1962-68; Distinguished Sciencits Seminar, University of Buffalo, 1992; Special Symposium Lecturer, 33rd Symposium of Regulation of Enzyme Activity & Synthesis in Normal & Neoplastic Tissues, 1992; Hilldale Award, 1993. Hobbies: Reading; Classical Music; Skiing. Address: University of Wisconsin Medical School, 1300 University Avenue, 3780 Medical Science Bldg, Madison, WI 53706, USA.

HOLEN Are, b. 18 Jul 1964, Oslo, Norway. Medical Doctor. m. T S Berg-Nielsen, 1 s, 1 d. Education: MD; PhD; Medical Candidate, University of Oslo, 1978; Psychology Candidate, University of Oslo, 1972. Appointments: Associate Professor of Psychiatry, Department of Psychiatry, University of Oslo; Post-Doctoral Fellow, University of California, San Francisco, Laughley Porter Psychiatric Institute; Associate Professor of Behavioral Medicine. Publications: A Long-Term

Outcome Study of Survivors from a Disaster, 1990. Memberships: Norwegian Medical Association; Norwegian Psychiatric Association; Internal Society for Traumatic Stress Studies.

HOLFORD Theodore Richard, b. 19 May 1947, Columbus, OH, USA. Biostatistics. m. Maryellen Hutchinson, 21 Dec 1969, 1 s, 1 d. Education: BA, Andrews University; PhD, Biostatistics, Yale University. Appointments: Assistant Professor, 1974-79, Associate Professor, 1979-89, Professorin Biostatistics, 1989-, Yale University. Publications: About 100 articles in refereed journals. Honours: Eleanor Roosevelt International CA Fellowship, 1981-82; Wakeman Award for Research in Neurosciences, 1990. Memberships: American Statistical Association; Biometric Society; Society for Epidemiologic Research. Hobby: Music. Address: Department of Epidemiology and Public Health, Yale Medical Science School, P O Box 208034, New Gaven, CT 06520-8034, USA.

HOLLAND Edwin Lionel, b. 20 Oct 1932, Dublin, Ireland. Obstetrician & Gynaecologist. m. Irene Francis, 4 Oct 1958, 3 s. Education: MA; MB; BCh; BAO; FRCOG. Appointments: Senior Lecturer, Queen's University, Belfast, Northern Ireland; Consultant Obstetrician/Gynaecologist. Memberships: British Medical Association; Royal College of Obstetricians & Gynaecologists; Gynae Trevellers; Ospreys; Gynae Society. Hobbies: Gold. Address: Department of Obstetrics & Gynaecology, Daisy Hill Hospital, 5 Hospital Roads, Newry, County Down, Ireland.

HOLLAND Keith, b. 3 Sep 1956. Optometrist. m. Clare Hobbs, 5 Apr 1980, 3 sons, 1 daughter. Education: BSc, Honours, City University; FBCO; DCLP, British College of Optometry. Appointments: Staff refractionist, London Refraction Hospital; Clinical Teacher, City University; Private Practice, 1984-; Consultant in Paediatrics. Publications include: Reading with Vision, 1986; Vision and Reflexes, 1994; Vision and Learning, 1993. Honours: Turville Memorial Lecture, 1990; Honorary Member, Professional Association of Teachers of Special Needs. Membership: Fellow, British College of Optometry. Hobby: Family Life. Address: 27 St George's Road, Cheltenham, Gloucestershire GL50 3DT, England.

HOLLINGWORTH Antony Arthur, b. 8 June 1954, Mansfield, Nottinghamshire, England. Doctor. m. Ann Duthie, 2 June 1984. Education: MBChB, Manchester; PhD, London; FRCS, Edinburgh; MRCOG; DHMSA. Appointments: Research Fellow, Imperial Cancer Research Fund, 1987-90; Senior Registrar, Nottingham Hospitals, 1990-94; Consultant, Whipps Cross Hospital, London, 1995-. Memberships: BSCCP; BGCS. Hobbies: Music; Reading; Weight Training. Address: Whipps Cross Hospital, Whipps Cross Road, Leytonstone, London, E11 1NR, England.

HOLLOMBY David J, b. 4 Nov 1943, Montreal, Canada. Nephrologist. m. Ellen Rowland, 8 July 1967, 1 son, 1 daughter. Education: BSc; FRCP(C); FACP. Appointments: Chair, Nephrology Division, University of Western Ontario; Chief, Nephrology Service, University Hospital. Honours: McGill University Scholar, 1971; Francis Howard Prize in Medicine, McGill University, 1971; Edward G Pleva Award for Excellence in Teaching, University of Western Ontario, 1992; Douglas Bocking Award for Excellence in Teaching, 1993. Memberships: Canadian Society of Nephrology; American Society of Nephrology; Ontario Medical Association; Canadian Medical Association; American Society of Transplant Physicians; Canadian Association for Medical Education. Address: University Hospital, Nephrology Service, 339 Windemere Road, PO Box 5339, London, Ontario N6A 5A5, Canada.

HOLLOWAY G Allen Jr, b. 14 Oct 1938, New York City, USA. Physician. m. Eileen Swanberg, 28 Mar 1987. Education: BA, Yale University, 1960; MD, Harvard University Medical School, 1964; Clinical and Research Associate, Acting Intern, Massachusetts General Hospital, Boston, 1964-65. Appointments include: Instructor, 1972-75, Assistant Professor, 1975-80, Research Assistant Professor, 1980-82, Research Associate Professor, 1982-88, Centre for Bioengineering, University of Washington, Seattle; Adjunct Professor, Department of Chemical, Bio and Materials Engineering, Arizona State University, Phoenix, 1992-; Attending Physician, 1988-, Director, Vascular Laboratory, 1988-, Director, Medical Research, 1991-, Maricopa Medical Centre, Phoenix. Publications: Contributor of numerous articles in professional and scientific journals. Honours: USPHS Fellowship, Nephrology, University of Washington, 1968-69; Research Career Development Award, NIH, 1980-85. Memberships: Biomedical

Engineering Society; Association for the Advancement of Medical Instrumentation; European Microcirculatory Society; Western Vascular Society; Wound Healing Society; Society for Vascular Medicine and Biology; Rocky Mountain Vascular Surgical Society. Address: Department of Surgery, Maricopa Medical Centre, 2601 East Roosevelt, Phoenix, AZ 85008, USA.

HOLMAN B Leonard, b. 20 Jun 1941, Sheboygan, WI, USA. Physician. m. Dale E Barkin, 2 d. Education: BS, University of WI; MD, WA University; AM, Honorary, Harvard University. Appointments: Director, Clinical Nuclear Medicine, Brigham and Women's Hospital, 1970-86; Currently, Philip H Cook Professor, Radiology, Harvard Medical School; Chairman, Department of Radiology, Brigham and Women's Hospital. Publications: 6 Books; 300 Articles in professional journals including: Co-author: Quantitative brain SPECT in Alzheimer's disease and normal aging, in Journal Nuclear Medicine, 1993; Total quality management in cardiovascular and interventional radiology, in Investigative Radiology, 1993; HMPAO brain perfusion SPECT in acute aphasia: Correlation with clinical and structural findings, in Clinical Nuclear Medicine, 1993. Honours: Herrman L Blumgart Pioneer Award, Society of Nuclear Medicine, 1986; Distinguished Educator Award, Society of Nuclear Medicine, 1992; Golden Eagle Award, CINE, Freddie Award International Health and Medical Film Festival, 1994. Memberships: President, 1987-88, Society of Nuclear Medicine; President, 1995-96, MA Radiological Society; Radiological Society of North America; American Heart Association; Fellow, American College of Radiology; Fellow, American College of Chest and Physicians. Hobbies: Digital Photography; Photography. Address: Chairman, Dept of Radiology, Brigham and Women's Hospital, 75 Francis St, Boston, MA 02115, USA.

HOLMES Judith Anne, b. 5 Sep 1948, Yorkshire, England. Therapy Radiographer. m. Mike Holmes, 9 Sep 1972, 1 s. Education: MSR (D), England; Nat Ed Dip(T), South Africa. Appointments: Chief Radiographer, Department of Radiation Therapy, Hillbrow Hospital, Wits University, South Africa; Chief Radiographer, Sandton Oncology Centre, South Africa. Publications: Contributor of various professional papers and posters presented to congresses. Honours: Transvaal Provincial Administration 1st Class Merit, 1986, 1988. Memberships: Society of Radiographers; Society of Radiation Oncologists; South African Medical and Dental Council. Hobbies: Pottery; Gardening; Reading. Address: PO Box 1447, Fourways 2055, South Africa.

HOLMES William John, b. 28 June. Dentist. m. Hazel Tyner, 9 Sep 1961, 1 s, 3 d. Education: MB; BDent Sc. Appointments: Clinical Teacher, Dublin University Dental School, Ireland; General Dental Practice. Memberships: Irish Dental Association; Royal Academy of Medicine in Ireland; Irish Endodontic Society; British Endodontic Society. Hobbies: Gardening; Dog Walking. Address: 31 Clonkeen Road, Blackrock, Co Dublin, Ireland.

HOLMSTRUP Palle, b. 4 Nov 1945, Copenhagen, Denmark. Professor of Dentistry. m. Grete Holmstrup, 14 Nov 1975, 2 sons. Education: DDS; PhD; Dr Odont; Board Certificate in Oral Surgery. Appointments: Research Associate; Associate Professor in Oral Medicine; Currently Professor, Chairman, Department of Periodontology, School of Dentistry, University of Copenhagen. Publications: Articles in international scientific journals about subjects in oral medicine and periodontology; Number of chapters in textbooks on similar subjects. Address: School of Dentistry, Faculty of Health Sciences, University of Copenhagen, 20 Noerre Allé, DK 2200 Copenhagen N, Denmark.

HOLSINGER James Wilson Jr, b. 11 May 1939, Kansas City, Kansas, USA. Physician. n. Barbara Jenn Craig, 28 Dec 1963, 4 daughters. Education: MD, 1964, PhD, 1968, Duke University; MS, University of South Carolina, 1981; Fellow, American College of Physicians; Fellow, American College of Cardiology; Fellow, American College of Healthcare Executives. Appointments include: Under-Secretary for Health, US Department of Veterans Affairs, 1990-93; Director, Veterans Administration Medical Centre, Lexington, Kentucky, 1993-94; Currently Chancellor, University of Kentucky Medical Centre, Lexington. Honours: Gold Medal, American College of Healthcare Executives, 1993; Exceptional Service Award, 1993, Distinguished Career Award, 1994, Department of Veterans Affairs. Memberships: Society of Medical Administrators; American Association of Clinical Anatomists; American Association of Anatomists. Address: University of Kentucky Medical Centre, A-301 Kentucky Clinic, Lexington, KY 40536-0284, USA.

HOLTZ Aliza, b. 10 Jan 1952, New York, USA. Biomedical Consulting & Communications. Education: PhD, Biology, Boston University, 1980. Appointments: Auxiliary Police Officer, New York, 1980-82; Board Director 1984-86, First Vice President, Board Diretor 1986-91, Arts Interaction, Washington Heights & Inwood Council for the Arts Inc. Publications incl: Test Items Book to Accompany "Elements of Biology", 1979; Study Guide and Workbook to accompany "Elements of Biology", 1979;Androgen control of an inhibitory modulator of phosphodiesterase in rat epididymis and prostate, 1981; Gastroesophageal Reflux Disease in the Elderly, 1990; Diagnosis and Treatment of Gastroesophageal Reflux Disease, 1990. Memberships: American Association for the Advancement of Science; American Medical Writers Association; New York Academy of Sciences; Sigma Xi. Hobbies: Hiking; Camping. Address: 275 Ft Washington Avenue, New York, NY 10032-1203, USA.

HONG Rong Zhao, b. 25 Jun 1945, Fu Jian Province, China. Ophthalmologist. m. Su-Wen Nie, Jul 1972, 1 s, 1 d. Education: BM, Beijing Medical University, China. Appointments: Chairman of Ophthalmic Department, Kai Yuan District Hospital, 1984-92; Currently, Head of Kai Yuan Ophthalmic Hospital. Publications: Introcular Lens Implantation, in Chinese Ophthalmic Magazine, 1992; Corneal Implantation, in New Development of Ophthalmology, 1992; RK Operation, 1992. Honours: Outstanding Technical Talent, Government Special Allowance by State Council, Fu Jian Province, 1992; Work Model of Fu Jian Province, 1992. Membership: Chinese Ophthalmic Association. Hobbies: Running; Playing Basketball; Playing Table Tennis; Singing. Address: Kai Yuan Ophthalmic Hospital, 336 Xia He Road, Xiamen, Fu Jian, China.

HONG-JIANG Yuan, b. 30 Aug 1931, Chengdu, Sichuan, China. Physician. m. Professor Chen Hui-Mai, 1 Jan 1961, 2 daughters. Education: MS, West CHina University of Medical Sciences; MD, Traditional Chinese Medicine of Chengdu; Various courses in national and international institutions. Appointments: Assistant, Resident, Department of Medicine, 1954-60, Instructor, Traditional Chinese Medicine, 1960-62, Sichuan Medical College; Attending Physician, Department of Medicine, Central Hospital of Tibet, Lhasa, Xizang, 1962-74; Vice Director, Department of Medicine, School of Public Health, 1976-83, Associate Professor of Geriatrics and Director, Geriatrics Department, 1983-85, Professor of Geriatric Gerontology, 1985-93, Vice President, Sichuan Senior Citizens' University, Director, CMB Program on Gerontology, 1993-, West China University of Medical Sciences. Publications: Geriatric Medicine, Editor, 1995; Essential KNowledge on Keeping Fit for the Elderly, Editor, 1993; An Investigation on 823 Centenarians in 1990 in Sichuan, Co-author, 1993; An Observation of Rehabilitative Effects on Chinese Traditional Exercises in Improvement of Senile Cardiovascular Function and in Treatment of Hypertension and Hyper Lipemia, Co-author, 1987. Honours: Medal and Certificate of Merit, Ministry of Public Health, 1957; 1st Award, Chinese Academy of Sciences, 1988. Memberships: Chairman of Council, Sichuan Branch, Geriatrics, Chinese Medical Association; Council, Chinese Rehabilitative Medical Association; Counci;. Chinese Geriatrics Association; Vice Secretary, general of Council, Sichuan Branch, Chinese Gerontology Association. Address: CMB Program on Gerontology, West China University of Medical Sciences, Chengdu, Sichuan 610041, China.

HONIGSZTEJN Henrique, b. 22 Mar 1935, Rio de Janeiro, Brazil. Psychoanalist. m. Daisy Aroesti Honigsztejn, 10 Feb 1972, 2 daughters. Education: Training Analist. Appointments: Internist, Clinical Assistant, Chief of Medical (Internal) Section, Iaser J Rio Instituto Assistencia Servidor Estado Rio de Janeiro, 1965-. Publications: A Psicologia Da Criacao (The Psychology of Creativity); Co-author, Freud: A Interpretacao; Co-author, A Presenca De Freud. Memberships: Brazilian Psychiatric Association; Brazilian Psycoanalitic Society. Hobbies: Reading; Writing. Address: Tonelero 265-304, Copacabana, Rio de Janeiro 22030-000, Brazil.

HONJO Tasuku, b. 27 Jan 1942, Kyoto, Japan. Professorof Biochemistry. m. Shigeko Kodani, 4 Feb 1969, 1 son, 1 daughter. Education: MD, Kyoto University Faculty of Medicine; PhD, Kyoto University Graduate School. Appointments: Professor, Osaka University Faculty of School, Department of Genetics; Professor, Kyoto University Faculty of Medicine, Department of Medical Chemistry; Director, Institute for Molecular Biology and Genetics. Publications: Immunoglobulin Genes, Editor, 1993. Honours: Asahi Award, 1981; Kihara Award, 1984; Behring-Kitasato Prize, 1992. Memberships: Honorary Member,

American Association of Immunologists; Human Genome Organisation; New York Academy of Sciences; Fogarty Scholar, National Institute of Health. Hobbies: Golf; Art; Tennis. Address: Kyoto University Faculty of Medicine, Department of Medical Chemistry, Yoshida Sakyo-ku Konoe, Kyoto 606, Japan.

HOOSHMAND Hossein, b. 21 Mar 1949, Gonabad, Iran. Researcher of Agricultural Pests. m. Talat Nozari, 21 Sep 1973, 1 s, 2 d. Education: BSc, Ferdowsi University of Mashad, Iran, 1980; MSc, Medical Entomology and Vectors Control. Career: Extension Officer in Ferdows County; Head of Office of Agriculture of Fariman; Currently, Researcher of Agricultural Pests, Research Laboratory of Mashad. Publications: Using bait traps to collect soil termites, 1990; Observation on swarming and colony foundation of Anacanthotermes, in Proceedings 19th ICE, 1992. Memberships: Entomological Society of Iran; International Isoptera Society. Hobbies: Reading; Walking; Studying Urban Entomology. Address: Plant Pests and Diseases Research Laboratory of Mashad, PO Box 149, Mashad 94735, Iran.

HOPE Katya Michèle, b. 2 April 1947, Washington, District of Columbia, USA. Psychotherapist. m. Jay Marx, 7 July 1977, 1 son, 1 daughter. Education: BA, Mills College; MSW, San Francisco State University; LCSW; MFCC; Board Certified Diplomate in Social Work; Supervisor, Play Therapy Association. Appointments: Director, Summer Art Workshop for Children, 1969-75; Co-Founder, Director, Safari School alternative junior high school, 1969-73; Director of Family Therapy, New Bridge Foundation Drug Treatment Programme, 1975-77; Co-Founder, Child and Adolescent Counseling Center, J K Kennedy University Graduate Psychology Programme; Currently: Private practice; Adjunct Professor of Clinical Psychology, J F Kennedy University. Publications: Family Therapy in Drug Treatment Program, National Drug Abuse Conference, 1977. Honours: J F Kennedy Graduate School Faculty Commendation, 1983. Memberships: Play Therapy Association; Northern California Sand Play Therapists; Diplomate, National Association of Social Workers; Northern California Therapy Association. Hobbies: Surfing; Skiing; Kids; Art. Address: 1821 Delaware Street, Berkeley, CA 94703, USA.

HOPKINSON Peter, b. 19 Jul 1949, Harrogate, Yorkshire, England. Clinical Psychologist. m. Celia Ann Hopkinson, 5 Jun 1980, 2 s. Education: BSc, Honours, Psychology, 1976, PhD, Psychology, 1988, Southampton University; MSc, Clinical Psychology, Manchester University, 1984; Advanced Certificate in Management, Leicester University, 1991. Career: Clinical Psychologist, Stockport Health Authority, 1984-88; Principal Clinical Psychologist, Northampton Health Authority, 1988-90; Consultant Clinical Psychologist, Rockingham Forest NHS Trust, Kettering, 1990-. Membership: British Psychological Society. Hobbies: Gardening; DIY. Address: Clinical Psychology Services, St Mary's Hospital, London Road, Kettering, Northamptonshire, NN15 7PW, England.

HOPPER David L, b. 28 Aug 1953, Memphis, USA. Private Practice. m. Clara Hopper, 28 Dec 1989, 3 sons. Education: Community College, Southern Nevada, 1972-75; University of Nevada, 1975-85; BS, Louisiana University, 1975-82; PhD, Columbia Pacific University, 1982-87. Appointments Include: Department Head, Blair College of Medical & Dental Assisting, Las Vegas, 1974-75; Medical Psychologist, University Medical Center, Southern Nevada, 1989-91; Consulting Somnologist, Western Region Sleep Disorders Center, Las Vegas, 1990-91; Private Practice, Behavioral Medicine Consultants, Las Vegas, 1990-; Private Practice, Life Skills Counseling Service, Las Vegas, 1991-. Publications Include: Understanding alcohol and drug abuse, 1985; Pain control, 1986; Use of biofeedback in the treatment of childhood agression; Transpersonal sexual therapy; Relationship between sleep events, mood, and urinary monoamine levels; Psychogenic sleep apnea: A case report, 1988; Sleep and pain, 1992; Sleep Hygiene, 1992. Memberships Include: Association of Applied Psychophysiology & Biofeedback; New York Academy of Sciences; American Pain Society; American Academy of Pain Management; American Association for the Advancement of Science. Honours: Fellow, American Academy of Behavioral Medicine, 1986; Fellow, American Association of Professional Hypnotherapists, 1986; Fellow, International Academy of Behavioral Medicine, Counseling & Psychotherapy, 1987; Fellow, American Academy of Somnology, 1990; Fellow, American Board of Medical Psychotherapists, 1990. Hobbies: Hiking; Music; Racquetball. Address: PO Box 29124, Las Vegas, NV 89126-3124, USA. 2.

HORAK Marita, b. 5 Aug 1937, Rep of South Africa. Radiographer. m. Dr John Horak, 23 Nov 1967, 1 son, 1 daughter. Education: BA; BA Hons; MA. Career: Radiographer; Senior Radiographer; Tutor Radiographer; Head, Department of Radiography, Port Elizabeth Technikan, currently. Publications: The Selection of Students for Radiography, 1978; The Systems Theory and Training Programmes, 1981; The Place of the Radiographer in a Changing Technology, 1984. Honours: Maybaker Award for Education, 1986; Merit Award, Society of Radiographers of SA, 1988; Chairman, Professional Board for Radiography, 1984-94. Memberships: Society of Radiographers of SA; American Registry of Radiologic Technologists. Hobbies: English Poetry; Classical Music; Gardening. Address: 3 Pari Way, Walmer, Port Elizabeth 6070, Republic of South Africa.

HORI Akira, b. 23 Oct 1941, Nagoya, Japan. Neuropathology. m. Yoshiko Hori, 25 Oct 1975, 1 d. Education: MD, Postgraduate School of Medicine, Nagoya City University. Appointments: Assistant, Department of Neuropathology, University of Göttingen; Research Fellow, Division of Neuropathology, Psychiatric Research Institute of Tokyo; Currently, Co-Chairman, Institute of Neuropathology, Hannover. Publication: Neuropathologie, 1981. Honour: Scholar of Alexander von Humboldt-Stiftung, Germany. Memberships: International Society of Neuropathology; American Society of Neuropathology; Japanese Society of Neuropathology; German Society of Neuropathology and Neuroanatomy; International Society of Child Neurology. Hobbies: Music; Archaeology; Architecture. Address: Institute of Neuropathology, Med Hochschule Hannover, D 30623, Hannover, Germany.

HORNER W Elliott, b. 8 Nov 1954, North Carolina, USA. Scientist. Education: BA, University of North Carolina, 1976; MS, University of New York College of Forestry, 1981; PhD, Virginia Polytechnic Institute & University, 1985. Appointments: Postdoctoral Fellow; Research Assistant Professor of Medicine. Publications: 27 refereed journal articles, 1 chapter, 5 reviews, 30 abstracts published on fungal and cockroach aeroallergens, fungal plant diseases and biodeterioration of natural products by fungi. Honours: Webber Award, 1985; Young Faculty Award, 1994. Memberships: American Academy of Allergy & Immunology; Mycological Society of America; International Aerobiology Association. Address: Tulane Medical Center, 1700 Perdido Street, New Orleans, LA 70112, USA.

HORNSBY Beve, b. 13 Sept 1915, Camberley, England. Psychologist; Speech Therapist. m. Jack Myddleton Hornsby, 14 July 1939, 3 sons, 1 daughter. Education: MSc; MEd; PhD; FCSLT; AMBDA; Fellow, Royal Society of Arts; Chartered Psychologist and Speech Therapist; Trainer in Instrumental Enrichment. Appointments: Head, Speech Therapy Clinic, Kingston, 1969-70; Head, Dyslexia Department, St Bartholomew's Hospital, London, 1970-80; Principal, Hornsby International Centre, London, 1984-; Principal, Hornsby House School, London, 1988-. Publications: Alpha to Omega, 1984; Overcoming Dyslexia, 1990; Before Alpha, 1993; A-Z Activity Packs, 1993. Honours: Honorary Fellow, British Dyslexia Association, 1980; Honorary Fellow, College of Speech and Language Therapists. Memberships: British Psychological Society; College of Speech and Language Therapists. Hobbies: Reading; Theatre; Walking. Address: Hornsby International Centre, Glenshee Lodge, 261 Trinity Road, London SW18 3SN, England.

HORNSTEIN Otto Paul, b. 22 Jan 1926, Munich. Dermatologist. m. Ingeborg Iris, 27 Aug 1955, 1 son, 1 daughter. Appointments: Medical Diplomate, 1951; Lecturership, Habilitation, 1958; Associate Professor, Düsseldorf, 1964-67; Professor, Chairman, University of Erlangen-Nuernberg, 1967-. Publications: Diseases of oral mucosa and lips, 1965; Inflammatory and systemic reactions of the oral mucosa, 1974; Cutaneous and Oral Manifestations of Rheumatic Diseases, 1980; Dermatological Aspects of Rheumatoid Diseases, 1989; Topical Treatment of Skin Diseases, 1985; Progress in Mycology, 1991; Viral and Bacterial Infections of the Skin, 1993; Diseases of Lip and Oral Cavity, 1994. Memberships: German Dermatological Society; German Society of Pathology; German Society of Rheumatology; Collegium Dermato-Histologicum; Hungarian Society of Dermatology; Argentina Society of Dermatology; Societé Francaise de Dermatologie. Honours: Bundesverdienstkreuz 1 Klasse, 1993. Address: Department of Dermatology, University Erlangen-Nuernberg, Hartmannstr 14, 91052 Erlangen, Germany.

HOROWITZ Benson, b. 17 May 1934, Philadelphia, Pennsylvania, USA. Physician. m. 25 Aug 1957, 1 son, 1 daughter. Education: BA; MD.

Appointments include: Associate Clinical Professor, University of Connecticut; Vulvologist. Publications: Vaginitis/Vaginosis (co-editor), 1991; Vulvar and Vaginal Disease, book chapter, 1994; AMA Drug Evaluations, Drugs used topically for infections of the skin and mucous membranes, Chapter 2 (editor); Author or co-author, articles and papers including: Some Complications of Intrauterine Contraceptive Devices, 1969; Sugar Chromatography Studies in Chronic Candidiasis, 1983; Sexual Transmission of Candida, 1987; Interferon Therapy for Condylomatous Vulvitis, 1989; The Role of non-albicans species, 1990; Candidiasis: Speciation and Therapy, 1990; Mycotic vulvovaginitis: a broad overview, 1991; Vulvar Vestibulitis and Vestibular Papillomatosis, 1991; Lactobacillus Vaginosis, 1994. Honours: Phi Beta Kappa, 1954; Alpha Omega, 1959; Chairman, Vaginitis Committee, ISSVD, 1991. Memberships: American Medical Association; American College of Obstetricians and Gynecologists; ISSVD. Hobbies: Woodworking; Antique radio restoration. Address: 449 Farmington Avenue, Hartford, CT 06105, USA.

HOROWITZ Ira, b. 17 Dec 1957, Brooklyn, New York, USA. Physician. m. Julie Ann Wood, 22 Feb 1986, 2 children. Education: BA, Biology, University of Rochester, New York; MD, Baylor College of Medicine, Houston, Texas. Appointments: Clinical Instructor, Baylor College of Medicine, 1984; Instructor, Johns Hopkins Medical Institute, 1985-87; Assistant Professor, Johns Hopkins Medical Institute, 1987-91; Associate Professor, Director, Gynecologic Oncology, Emory University School of Medicine. Publications: Plantao em ginecologia e obstetricia; Advances in Obstetrics & Gynecology; Basel Cell Carcinoma Secondary to Radiotherapy for Carcinoma of the Cervix. Memberships: American Medical Association; Society of Gynecologic Oncologists; American Society of Clinical Oncology; Georgia Obstetrical & Gynecological Society; Atlanta Obstetrical & Gynecological Society; American College of Obstetricians & Gynecologists; American College of Surgeons. Hobbies: Camping; Travel. Address: Emroy University School of Medicine, 69 Butler Street SE, Atlanta, GA 30303, USA.

HORTA E SILVA Francisco, b. 24 May 1931, Cons Lafaiete, Brazil. Psychoanalyst. div., 2 sons, 2 daughters. Education: MD; Postgraduate course in Health Sciences (Psychology). Appointments: Clinical Psychoanalyst; Professor of Psychosomatic Medicine, Brazilian Council of Professional Support for Higher Education, 1980-91; Currently Professor of Psychosomatic Medicine, Brazilian Institute of Gastroenterology. Publications: Case Record of the Brazilian Institute for Studies and Research in Gastroenterology - IBPEGE - Weekly Clinicopathology Exercises; Some Considerations Regarding the Psychosomatic Model; Psychosomatic Medicine and Psychoanalytic Interpretation. Memberships: International Psychoanalytic Association; Latin American Psychoanalytic Federation; Brazilian Association of Psychosomatic Medicine; Brazilian Association of Psychoanalysis. Hobbies: Reading; Literature; Philosophy; Travel; Music; Theatre; Cinema. Address: Alameda Lorena 205, 01424-000 Sao Paulo SP, Brazil.

HORTON Robert John Munro, b. 19 Oct 1910, Cleveland, Ohio, USA. Retired Physician and Professor. m. Beryl Cook, 1 son, 2 daughters. Education: BS; MD; MPH. Appointments include: University Professor; Now retired. Address: 142 Carol Woods, Chapel Hill, NC 27514, USA.

HORVATH Agnes, b. 14 Jan 1948, Budapest, Hungary. Pediatrician. div. 1 s. Education: MD. Appointments: Assistant Professor, Pediatrics, University of Chicago, 1987-90; Staff Physician, Orthopaedic Hospital of Los Angeles, 1990-94; Staff Physician, Eastern Manic Medical Center, 1994-. Memberships: American Society of Pediatric Hematology & Oncology. Hobbies: Music; Travel. Address: Department of Pediatrics, Eastern Manic Medical Center, 417 State Street, Suite 10, Bangor, ME 04401, USA.

HORVATH Edward Philip, b. 9 Aug 1946, Painesville, Ohio, USA. Physician. m. Wendy Joy Swanson, 28 Jun 1975, 2 sons, 1 daughter. Education: BA, Western Reserve University, 1968; MD, Ohio State University College of Medicine, 1971; MPH, University of Minnesota, 1975. Appointments: Medical Director, BP American Incorporated, Cleveland, Ohio; Section Chief, Occupational Medicine, Marshfield Clinic, Marhsfield, Wisconsin; Medical Corps, United States Navy; Director, Occupational Medicine, Cleveland Clinic Foundation. Honours: Alpha Omega Alpha, 1971; BP Chairman's Award for Achievement in Health Safety and Environmental Care, 1991. Memberships: American College of Occupational and Environmental Medicine; American College of Preventive Medicine; American Medical Association; International Commission on Occupational Health. Address: Cleveland Clinic Foundation, 9500 Euclid Avenue, Desk A-11, Cleveland, OH 44195-5008, USA.

HORWITZ Kathryn B, b. 20 Feb 1941, Sosua, Dominican Republic. Scientist. m. Lawrence D Horwitz, MD, 14 Jun 1964, 1 s, 1 d. Education: BS, Barnard College, Columbia University, 1964; MS, NY University, 1966; PhD, University of TX, Southwestern Medical School, Dallas 1975; Postdoctoral Fellow, University of TX School of Medicine, San Antonio. Appointments: Assistant and Associate Professor, University of CO School of Medicine; Currently, Professor of Medicine and Pathology, and the Molecular Biology Programs, University of CO School of Medicine, Denver. Publications: Author of over 100 publications concerning hormones and breast cancer; Editor, Endocrine Aspects of Cancer, 1993. Honours include: National Board Award, University of PA School of Medicine, 1986; Researcher of Year Award, NFCR, 1990; University of Helsinki Medal, 1993; Merit Award, NIH, 1993. Memberships: The Endocrine Society of US, Council Member, 1993; American Association for Cancer Research; American Association for Clinical Research; American Society for Biochemistry and Molecular Biology. Hobbies: Gardening; Travel; Reading. Address: Univ of CO School of Medicine, Department of Medicine Box B-151, 4200 East 9th Ave, Denver, CO 80262, USA.

HORWITZ Ralph I, b. 25 June 1947, Philadelphia, PA, USA. Professor; Physician. m. Sarah McCue Horwitz, 5 Aug 1970, 1 daughter. Education: BS, Albright College, 1969; MD, Pennsylvania State University College of Medicine, 1973; Robert Wood Johnson Clinical Scholar at Yale, 1975-77. Career: Assistant Professor of Medicine 1978-82, Associate Professor of Medicine 1982-85, Associate Professor of Epidemiology 1983-88, Associate Professor of Medicine 1985-88, Professor of Medicine & Epidemiology 1988-, Harold H Hines, Jr Professor of Medicine & Epidemiology 1991-, Yale University School of Medicine, New Haven, Connecticut; Chairman, Department of Internal Medicine, Yale University School of Medicine, currently. Publications include: Analysis of Clinical Susceptibility Bias in Case-Control Studies, 1979; An Ecogenetic Hypothesis for Lung Cancer in Women, 1988; Problems of Comorbidity in Mortality after Prostatectomy, 1992. Honours: C V Mosby Award for General Academic Excellence, Pennsylvania State University School of Medicine, 1973; Henry J Kaiser Family Foundation Faculty Scholar Award, 1981-86. Memberships: American Society for Clinical Investigation; Fellow, American College of Physicians; American Epidemiological Society, 1988; Association of American Physicians, 1993; Connecticut Academy of Science and Engineering, 1993. Address: Yale University School of Medicine, 333 Cedar Street, New Haven, CT 06510, USA.

HOSANG Robert Anthony, b. 6 Apr 1950, Kingston, Jamaica. Physician. m. Joyce Yap, 20 Oct 1984, 2 sons. Education: BSc; MBBS; DM; MPH; MBA. Appointments: Lecturer, Faculty of Medicine, University of West Indies, Jamaica, 1980-84; Senior Physician, Kaiser Permanente Medical Centre, Hayward, California, 1986-; Lecturer, School of Public Health, University California, Berkeley, 1989-. Memberships: Royal College of Obstetricians and Gynaecologists; Fellow, American College of Obstetrics & Gynecology; International Society for Gynecological Endoscopy. Hobbies: Fishing; Music. Address: 224 Encounter Bay, Alameda, CA 94502, USA.

HOTZ Werner, b. 25 Apr 1952, Stetten, Germany. Dentist. m. Ingrid Neuberger, 16 Mar 1979, 2 sons, 1 daughter. Education: Diplomate, International Congress of Oral Implantology. Appointments: Department of Oral & Maxillofacial Surgery, University of Freiburg, 1976; Thomas S Golec, Private Clinic, San Diego, California, 1986; Leonard J Linkow, Private Clinic, New York, 1988. Publications: Das Tiolox Implantat System, 1991; The Tiolox Implant System, 1991; Tiolox Implantat System, 1992; Operationsanleitung für zweiphasige Tiolox-Schrauben, 1992; Beschreibung des Tiolox-Implantat Systems am Beispiel einer Klasse II Versorgung des Unterkiefers, 1992; Tiolox Implantat System Die besonderen prothetischen Möglichkeiten, 1992; Die subantrale Augmentation mit homologem Knochen zur Schaffung eines stabilen enossalen Implantatlagers, 1992; Das Tiolox Implantat System Aktueller Stand der zahnärztlichen Implantologie, 1993; Biocompatibility of the Tiolox Implant System by using Three Different Materials, 1993; Prothetische Lösungen bei Implantaten: Fallstudie, 1993; Bioakzeptanz des Tiolox Implantates unter Verwendung verschiedener Werkstoffe, 1993. Memberships: AGI; DGZI; DZOI; ICOI; ASO; AAID. Honours: DGZI Implant Surgery Course Leader, 1988; ICOI Diplomate, 1994.

Hobbies: Skiing; Hunting. Address: Schillerstr 5, 72510 Stetten 1, Germany.

HOU Fan-fan, b. 16 Oct 1950, Shanghai, China. Doctor. m. Chang Li Wei, 20 Jan 1978, 1 son. Education: MD, The First Medical University, Guangzhou, 1973; PhD, Sun Yat-sen University of Medical Sciences, 1993. Appointments: Resident in Medicine, The 86th Hospital of Anhuei, 1976-80; Visiting in Medicine, Jinglin Hospital, Nanking, 1980-88; Professor, Medical Director, Department of Nephrology, Nanfang Hospital. Publications: Fibronectin in patients with Chronic Renal Failure undergoing Dialysis, 1990; The Diagnostic Value of Serum IgG Antibody to Purified Protein Derivatves in CRF Patients Complicated with Active Tuberculosis, 1994. Honours: Science & Technology Award of PLA, 1991; Zeng Xian Zi Prize, National Council on Higher Education, 1993. Memberships: Chinese Medical Association; Chinese Society of Nephrology; Chinese Microbiology & Immunology Association. Hobbies: Sports; Music. Address: Department of Nephrology, Nanfang Hospital, Guangzhou 510515, China.

HOU Qin-Ping, b. China. Vice-Dean. m. Bao Yong, 1 daughter. Education: BA, Chinese Medicine, Nan-Jing College of Chinese Medicine, 1982. Appointments: Currently Vice-Dean, Chinese Medical Department, Saltern General Hospital, Lian Yun-Gang, Jiangsu. Hobbies: Reading, especially poetry and novels; Riding; Tennis; Travel. Address: Saltern General Hospital, Lian Yun-Gang, 222002 Jiangsu, China.

HOUDART Raymond, b. 22 Oct 1913, France. Neurosugeon. m. 19 Sept 1940, 5 sons, 3 daughters. Publications: Numerous professional publications. Memberships: Several associations, societies and organizations. Address: 26 Quai de Bethune, 75004 Paris, France.

HOUK William Michael, b. 23 October 1940, Cleveland, Ohio, USA. Physician. Legally Separated, 14 February 1994, 3 sons, 2 daughters. Education: BSc, Loyola University of the South, 1972; MSc, University of Rochester, New York, 1967; MD, 1975. Appointments: Commanding Officer, Naval Aerospace Medical Research Laboratory, 1980-85; Commanding Officer, Naval Medical Research and Development Command, Bethesda, 1985-88; Deputy Assistant Chief, Bureau of Medicine and Surgery, Director of Medical Readiness, Washington DC, 1988-92; Staff Director, Defense Medical Standards Board. Publications: Numerous professional publications. Honours: Merit Service Medal (Three Awards). Memberships: Fellow, Aerospace Medical Association; American Medical Association; American College of Preventive Medicine; New York Academy of Sciences. Hobbies: Photography; Fishing; Music; Ice Hockey. Address: 1745 Hillmeade Square, Frederick, MD 21702, USA.

HOUNSFIELD Brian James, b. 4 Nov 1942, Epsom, Surrey, England. Registered Osteopath. m. Wendy Kimber, 6 Jun 1970, 1 s, 2 d. Education: DO; MRO. Appointment: Private Osteopathic Practice since 1966. Memberships: General Council and Register of Osteopaths; Osteopathic Association of Great Britain. Hobbies: Church activities; Sailing; Golf; Trojan Motorcars. Address: Longdown Lodge, 97 College Road, Epsom, Surrey, KT17 4HY, England.

HOUSE James Stephen, b. 27 Jan 1944, Philadelphia, PA, USA. Research Scientist; Professor of Sociology. m. Wendy Fisher, 13 May 1967, 1 s, 1 d. Education: BA, Haverford College, 1965; PhD, University of Michigan, 1972. Career: Instructor to Associate Professor of Sociology, Duke University, 1970-78; Associate Professor, Associate Research Scientist, Survey Research Center and Department of Epidemiology, University of MI, 1978-82; Associate Chair, 1981-84, Chair, 1986-90, Department of Sociology, University of Michigan; Professor and Research Scientist, 1983-, Director, 1991-, Survey Research Center, University of Michigan. Publications: Work Stress and Social Support, 1981; Social Relationships and Health, in Science, 1988; Age, Socioeconomic Status and Health, in Milbank Quarterly, 1990; Aging, Health Behavior and Health Outcomes, 1992; Sociological Perspectives on Social Psychology, 1995. Honours: Guggenheim Fellow, 1986-87; Fellow, American Association for the Advancement of Science, 1986-. Hobbies: Tennis; Travel; Gardening. Address: Institute for Social Research, University of Michigan, Box 1248, Ann Arbor, MI 48106, USA.

HOVIS Jeffery, b. 3 Apr 1956, Toledo, Ohio, USA. Optometrist. Education: OD, 1980; MS, 1986; PhD, 1986. Appointments: Associate Professor, University of Waterloo, Canada. Publications: The Ability of

Colour Vision Tests to Predict Performance on Identifying Wire Colour, 1994. Memberships: Canadian Optometric Association; Aerospace Medical Association. Address: School of Optometry, University of Waterloo, Waterloo, Ontario N2L 3G1, Canada.

HOWARD John Malone, b. 25 Aug 1919, Autuaville, Alabama, USA. Surgeon. m. Nina Abernathy, 22 Dec 1943, 3 sons, 3 daughters. Education: BS, Cum Laude, Birmingham Southern College; University of Pennsylvania School of Medicine. Appointments: Associate Professor, Baylor University, Department of Surgery, 1950-54; Professor, Chairman, Department of Surgery, Emory University, 1955-57; Chairman of Surgery, 1958-62, Professor of Surgery, 1963-74, Haneman Medical College; Director, Emergency Medical Services, Professor of Surgery, Medical College of Ohio, 1974-78; Private Practice, 1980-. Publications: Editor: Studies of Battle Casualties in Korea: Volume III, The Battle Wound, 1953, Volume I, The Systemic Response to Injury, 1955, Volume II, Resuscitative Tools, 1955, Volume IV, Post Traumatic Renal Insufficiency, 1955; Surgical Diseases of the Pancreas, Co-author, 1960; The Chemistry of Trauma, Co-author, 1963; Cardiovascular Surgery, Editor, 1963; Septic Shock, Clinical and Experimental Experiences, Co-author, 1964; Studies of Ultraviolet Irradiation: Its Efficiency in Preventing Infections in Operative Wounds, Editor, 1964; Surgical Disease of the Pancreas, Co-author, 1986; Contributor of numerous chapters in books. Honours include: Teacher of Year Award, Medical Undergraduates of Baylor University, 1954; Legion of Merit, US Army, 1954; Golden Square Slipper award to 22 Scientists in Their Salute to Medicine, 1961; Honorary Lifetime Director, American Trauma Society. Memberships include: Diplomate, American Board of Surgery; Diplomate, American Board of Thoracic Surgery. Address: 3454 Oak Alley Court, Suite 202, Toledo, OH 43606, USA.

HOWELL R(alph) Rodney, b. 10 Jun 1931, Concord, NC, USA. Paediatrician; Genetics. m. Sarah Esselstyn, MD, 19 Nov 1960 (dec), 1 s, 2 d. Education: BS, Davidson College; MD, Duke University. Appointments: Clinical Associate, National Institute of Health, Bethesda, MD; Associate Professor of Pediatrics, Johns Hopkins University, 1964-72; Professor and Chairman of Pediatrics, University of TX, Houston, 1972-89; Metabolism Study Section, NIH; Chairman, Scientific Advisory Board, Muscular Dystrophy Association, 1989-; Currently, Professor and Chairman of Pediatrics, Department of Pediatrics, Miami School of Medicine. Publications: Over 100 scientific articles and 4 books concerning pediatrics and genetics. Memberships: American Pediatric Society; Society for Pediatric Research; American College Genetics; American Board Pediatrics. Hobbies: Aviation; Raising Tropical Finches. Address: PO Box 016820 D820, University of Miami, Miami, FL 33101, USA.

HOWELL Timothy, b. 9 Mar 1947, New York, NY, USA. Geriatric Psychiatrist. m. Meg L Little MD, 21 Mar 1972, 2 s, 2 d. Education: BA, 1972, MA, 1976, MD, 1978, Stanford University, CA. Appointment: Associate Professor of Psychiatry and Medicine, University of Stanford, CA. Memberships: American Association for Geriatric Psychiatry; American Geriatrics Society; American Psychiatric Association; Gerontological Society of America. Address: Mental Health Clinic, Wm S Middleton Memorial Veterans Hospital, 2500 Overlook Terrace, Madison, WI 53705, USA.

HOWIE Peter William, b. 21 Nov 1939, Aberdeen, Scotland. Doctor. m. Anne Jardine Quigg, 25 Mar 1965, 1 son, 1 daughter. Education: MB ChB, MD, Glasgow; FRSE; FRCP(Glasgow). Appointments: Senior Lecturer in Obstetrics and Gynaecology, University of Glasgow; Clinical Consultant, MRC Reproductive Biology Unit, Edinburgh; Professor of Obstetrics and Gynaecology, University of Dundee. Publications: Contributor of numerous articles in scientific journals. Memberships: Edinburgh Obstetrical Society; British Medical Association; General Medical Council. Hobbies: Golf; Music. Address: 8 Travebank Gardens, Monifieth DD5 4ET, Scotland.

HOWSE David Charles Napier, b. 29 Nov 1936, Winnipeg, Canada. Neurologist. 1 s, 1 d. Education: BA; MD, University of Toronto; FRCP(C). Appointment: Head of Division of Neurology, Department of Medicine, Queen's University, Kingston, Ontario. Honour: Fellowship, Canadian Life Insurance, 1973-76. Memberships: Canadian Neurological Society; American Academy of Neurology. Address: 102 Stuart Street, Queen's University, Kingston, Ontario, Canada, K7L 2V6.

HOWSON Christopher Paul, b. 15 Oct 1948, Rio de Janeiro, Brazil. Epidemiologist. m. Marie I Holevoet, 1 Jan 1983, 1 daughter. Education:

BA, Swarthmore College, USA, 1971; MS, University of Oklahoma, 1976; PhD, University of California, Los Angeles, 1983. Appointments: Senior Epidemiologist, American Health Foundation, USA, 1983; Project Director, Food and Nutrition Board, National Academy of Sciences, USA, 1986; Associate Director, Division of International Health, 1991, currently Director, Board on International Health, Institute of Medicine, National Academy of Sciences. Publications: Co-author: The decline of gastric cancer: epidemiology of an unplanned triumph, 1986; Chronic arthritis after rubella vaccine, 1992; Acute encephalepathy and chronic neurologic damage after pertussis vaccine, 1993; Co-editor: Adverse Effects of Pertussis and Rubella Vaccines, 1991; In Her Lifetime: Female Morbidity and Mortality in Sub-Saharan Africa, 1995. Memberships: International Epidemiological Association; American Public Health Association. Address: Institute of Medicine, National Academy of Sciences, 2101 Constitution Avenue NW, Washington, DC 20418, USA.

HOYUMPA Anastacio M, b. 4 July 1937, Baybay, Leyte, Philippines. Physician. m. Joan Howland, 22 June 1963, 2 sons, 2 daughters. Education: MD, University of Santo Tomas, Manila, 1961; Intern, Resident, USAF Hospital, Clark Air Force Base, Philippines, 1960-62, Sinai Hospital, Baltimore, 1962-65; Gastroenterology Fellow, University of Cincinnati Medical Center, 1965-67. Appointments: Assistant Professor, University of Cincinnati, Ohio, 1968-72; Assistant Professor, 1972-76, Associate Professor, 1976-82, Vanderbilt University, Nashville, Tennessee; Chief, Gastroenterology, Veterans Administration Hospital, San Antonio, Texas, 1982-86; Professor of Medicine, University of Texas Health Science Center, San Antonio, 1982-. Publications: Mechanisms of vitamin deficiencies in alcoholism, 1986; Co-author: Thiamine transport across the rat intestine. I. Normal characteristics, 1975; Thiamine transport across the rat intestine. II. Effect of ethanol, 1975; Effect of ethanol on intestinal (Na, K) ATPase and intestinal thiamine transport in rats, 1977; Effect of ethanol on benzodiazepine disposition in dogs, 1980; Effect of short-term ethanal administration on lorazepam clearance, 1981; Effects of Liver disease on the disposition of ciramadol in humans, 1989; Is glucoronidation truly preserved in patients with liver disease?, 1991; Many others. Honours: Research and Education Associate, 1973-75, Clinical Investigator, 1976-78, Alcohol Research Investigator, 1979-81, Veterans Administration. Memberships: American Society of Gastrointestinal Endoscopy; International and American Associations for Study of Liver Disease; Research Society of Alcoholism; American Gastroenterological Association; American Society of Clinical Nutrition; American College of Physicians. Address: Department of Medicine, G1 Nutrition, University of Texas Health Science Center, San Antonio, TX 78284-0001, USA.

HSIEH Chung-cheng, b. 27 Sept 1954, Taiwan, China. Associate Professor. m. Fei-Fang Hsu, 3 July 1991, 1 daughter. Education: BS, 1976, MPH, 1978, National Taiwan University; MS, 1980, ScD, 1985, Harvard University, USA. Appointments: Assistant Professor of Epidemiology, 1985-91, Associate Professor of Epidemiology, 1991-, Harvard School of Public Health, Boston, Massachusetts, USA. Publications: Co-author: Dual effect of parity on breast cancer risk, 1994; Transient increase in risk of breast cancer following a brith, 1994. Honours: Scholarship, Ministry of Education, Taiwan, 1978; Stomatology Fellow, Project HOPE, 1987; Visiting Scientist Award, International Agency for Research on Cancer, 1988; Cancer Fellow, Project HOPE, 1991; Suzanne Sheats Fellow, Breast Cancer Research Grant, Massachusetts Department of Public Health, 1993; Citation for Excellence in Teaching, Harvard School of Public Health, 1994. Memberships: Society for Epidemiologic Research; Biometric Society. Hobbies: The art of tea-drinking; Tennis. Address: Department of Epidemiology, Harvard Univesity School of Public Health, 677 Huntington Avenue, Boston, MA 02115, USA.

HSIEH Shelton, b. 29 May 1933, Shanghai, China. Academic Professor. m. Ling Chun Liu, 3 Oct 1973, 1 son, 1 daughter. Education: BS, Natl Taiwan University, China; Title VII Fellow, US Department of Education, Washington DC, USA; MSc, McGill University, Canada; EdD, Columbia University; Diploma, Clinical Acupuncture Institute of New York. Appointments: Intern, Queen Mary veteran Hospital, Montreal; Fellow, McGill University, Royal Victoria Hospital, Montreal; Associate, Clinical Allergy Centre, Iowa; Fellow Scientist, Columbia Presbyterian Medical Centre; Adjunct Professor, St Peter's and Monclair State Colleges. Publications: Stress Issues Among Chinese People in New York, 1991; Prediction of Immunoglobulins, Co-author, 1969; Cutaneous Reaction on rat, Co-author, 1970; El Puente/Columbia University Project, Co-author, 1988. Honours: Fellow, Kappa Delta Pi Honour

Society in Education, 1991-94; Title VII fellow Award, US Department of Education, Washington DC, 1985, 1986, 1987. Memberships: Fellow, American Association for Clinical Immunology and Allergy; Scientific Fellow, American College of Allergists. Hobbies: Music; Walking. Address: 2474 Fifth Street, Fort Lee, NJ 07024, USA.

HU Fu Lian, b. 24 Aug 1940, Hunan, China. Physician. m. Shi Lin Zhou, Feb 1967, 1 daughter. Education: College of Medicine, Hunan Medical University, 1959-65. Appointments: Instructor 1983-88, Associate Professor 1988-93, Professor 1993-, Departmenmt of Gastroentorology, First Teaching Hospital, Beijing Medical University. Publications include: Should thymol turbidity test be abandoned?, 1987; Ranitidine and cimetidine in the short term treatment of duidenal ulcer and their acid inhibitory effect in duodenal ulcer patients, 1987; Antibiotics in the treatment of intractable duodenal ulcer disease complicated by Campylobacter pylori infection, 1988; A double-blind, double-dummy multicentre controlled clinical study of famotidine in the short-term treatment of gastric and duodenal ulcer, 1993. Honours: Scientific & Technological Award, Beijing, 1989; Scientific & Technological Award, Ministry of Public Health of China, 1990. Memberships: Secretary to President, Chinese Society of Gastroenterology; Editorial Board, Chinese Journal of Digestion; Editorial, Chinese Journal of Gastroenterology and Hepatology. Hobbies: Classical Music. Address: 8 Xishiku St, West City District, Beijing 100034, China.

HU Min, b. 2 July 1950, Jiangxi Province, China. Physician. m. Zhu Xuan, 16 July 1981, 1 son. Education: Bach of Medicine, Jianxi Medical College, 1983; Master of Medicine, Endocrinology & Metabolism, Hunan Medical College, 1986. Career: Farmer, Jianxi, 1966; Rural Teacher, Jiangxi, 1969; Rural Doctor, Jiangxi, 1972; Miner, Jiangxi, 1976; Medical Student of Undergraduates, Jiangxi, 1978; Postgraduate Student of Endocrinology & Metabolism, Hunan, 1983; Physician, Hunan, 1986; Doctor in Charge & Lecturer, Hunan, 1988; Associate Professor, Second Clinical College of Hunan Medical University, 1993. Publications: Co-author: The Pre and Postoperative Observation of Change of Thyroid Hormone in Acute Obstructive Suppurative Cholangitis and Cholithiasis, 1987; Effect of Propranolol on Circulating T4, T3, rT3 and TSH in Patients with Hyperthyroidism, 1987. Memberships: China Medical Association; Hunan Endocrinological Association. Hobbies: Running; Swimming. Address: Institute of Metabolism & Endocrinology, Hunan Medical University, 156 Road Renmin, 410011 Changsha, Hunan, China.

HU Ruide, b. 16 Feb 1940, Shanghai, China. Professor of Pathology. m. He An Jian, 12 Oct 1967, 1 d. Education: BA, Shanghai Second Medical College, 1963. Appointments: Professor and Vice Chairman of Pathology Department, Sun Yat Sen University of Medical Science. Co-author, Joints Diseases, in Surgical Pathology, 1977; Immunohistochemical Diagnosis of Tumours, in Immunohistochemistry, 1990; Dynamic Changes of Fibronectin and Nuclear Features during Rat Hepatocarcinogeneses, in Chinese Journal of Pathology, 1992. Memberships: Chinese Medical Association; Chinese Pathology Association; IAP Chinese Division. Hobby: Running. Address: 118-801 South Zhi Xin Road, Guangzhu, 510080, China.

HU Sheng-Shan, b. 30 Sept 1946, Jiangxi, China. Researcher. m. Wang Jing-Wu, 1 Jan 1975, 1 daughter. Education: BA, Nanjing Pharmaceutical University. Career: Pharmaceutist, Hospital, 1968-70, 1968-71; Pharmaceutical Engineer, 1972-82; Professor of Pharmacology, 1983-94; Director, Department of Pharmacology, Jiangxi, currently. Publications include: Co-author, Effects of Delsoline on Beating Rate of Cultured Rat Myocardial Cell in Acta Pharmacologica Sinica, 1986; Co-author, The Preparation of the Vidarabine Ophthalmic Ointment in Modern Applied Pharmacy, 1989; Co-author, The Determination of Vidarabine in Ophthalmic Ointment, 1989; co-author, Effects of Tetrandrine on Beating Response of Cultured Rat Myocardial Cells and Its Antagonism with Calcium in Abstract Beijing International Conference on Heart Research, 1992. Memberships: Jiangxi Branch, Chinese Pharmacological Society; Jiangxi Branch, Chinese Pharmaceutical Society. Hobbies: Singing; Journeying. Address: 97 Beijing East Street, Jiangxi Institute of Med Sci, Nanchang 330029, China.

HU Yongda, b. 24 Jan 1942, Hubei Province, China. Dentist. m. Chen Changxi, 1 Oct 1968, 2 daughters. Education: MB, Hubei Medical College, 1966. Appointments: Lecturer, 1985-90, Professor of Stomatology, 1991-, Vice Director, Stomatology Department, Sun

Yat-sen University of Medical Sciences. Publications: Orthodontics for Peridontal Disease with 78 Cases Report, 1991. Honours: Excellent Teacher, Sun Yat-sen University of Medical Sciences, 1986-88. Membership: Chinese Orthodontics Association. Hobbies: Singing; Cooking. Address: 1st Floor, 10 Building, Zhu Si Cun, Zhi Xin South Road, Guangzhou 510080, China.

HU Yongmei, b. 19 Jan 1927, Beijing, China. Professor of Biochemistry and Molecular Biology. m. 8 Feb 1956, 1 son, 3 daughters. Education: MD. Appointments: Assistant, Department of Biochemistry, Peking Union Medical College; Research Fellow, Department of Biochemistry, Institute of Experimental Medical Science, Beijing; Research Assistant, Lecturer, Vice-Professor, currently Professor, Department of Biochemistry and Molecular Biology, Institute of Basic Medical Science, Chinese Academy of Sciences, Peking Union Medical College, Beijing. Publications: Articles on comparison of serum lipids and lipoproteins between normal persons and patients with CHD and their significance in diagnosis, 1959-60, studies on coagulation and fibrinolysis (3 translated into English), 1981-83, effect of lipoproteins and apolipoproteins on lipoprotein receptors, 1981-86, preparation and purification of apoA-I, apoA-IV, preparation of their liposomes, observation of their effect on IDl receptor expression, 1987-93. Memberships: Chinese Biochemical Society; Chinese Medical Biochemical Society; FAOB; Editorial boards: Acta Academiae Medicinae Sinicae; Chinese Basic Medical Sciences and Clinics. Address: Institute of Basic Medical Sciences, Chinese Academy of Medical Sciences, Faculty of Basic Medicine, Peking Union Medical College, 5 Dong Dan San Tiao, Beijing 100730, China.

HU Zong-Han, b. 3 Jul 1936, Jilin, China. Microbiologist. m. Yi Li Lu, 20 Jun 1964, 1 s. Education: Graduate of Chinese Medical University, 1956. Appointments: Chief, National Center for Viral Hepatitis of China; Secretary, National Committee for Viral Hepatitis, Ministry of Health, China; Head, Virological Department of National Institute for the Control of Pharmaceutical & Biological Products, Beijing. Publications: The Tissue Culture Research of Poliomyelitis Virus, 1962; Experimental Diagnosis of Viral Hepatitis, 1986. Honours: Commissioner, National Committee for Viral Hepatitis, Ministry of Health, China, 1983. Memberships: Chinese Medical Association; Scientific Society of China; International Organization for Mycoplasmology. Hobbies: Basketball; Volley Ball. Address: The National Institute for the Control of Pharmaceutical & Biological Products, Temple of Heaven, Beijing 100050, China.

HUA Liansheng, b. 14 Sept 1946, Henan, China. Physiotherapist. m. Ge Xinmei, 1 Oct 1968, 1 son, 1 daughter. Education: BA, Chongqing University. Appointments: Physiotherapist, Technical Advisor on physiotherapeutic equipment maintenance, 1976-90; Developing and trading physiotherapeutic equipment, 1990=91; General Manager, Xijing Medical Corporation, Xi'an, 1991-. Publications: Hematoporphyrin derivatives high power interstitial irradiation of argon laser in the treatment of superficial transitional cell bladder tumour. Honours: Gold Medal for Application of Military Technique to Civilian Use, National Invention Fair, 1993. Memberships: Chinese Medical Association; Chinese Biomedical Engineering Association. Hobby: Studying and developing physiotherapeutic equipment. Address: Xijing Medical Equipment Corporation, Xijing Hospital, Xi'an, Shaanxi 710032, China.

HUA Yu, b. 15 Oct 1923, Hangzhou, Zhejiang Province, China. Obstetrician and Gynaecologist. m. Yu Chun-zhi. Education: BS, 1943, MD, School of Medicine, 1948, St John's University, Shanghai. Appointments: Resident Doctor, Department of Obstetrics and Gynaecology, St Elizabeth Hospital, Shanghai; Visiting Doctor, Associate Professor, currently Professor of Obstetrics and Gynaecology, Department of Obstetrics and Gynaecology, Xijing Hospital, Fourth Military Medical University, Xian. Publications: Analysis of 546 cases of breech delivery, 1957; How to lower the infant mortality rate in breech delivery, 1964; Study of G-banded chromosomes of cord blood in newborns, 1985; Clinical and cytogenetic study of XY females, 1986; Cytogenetic analysis of 312 couples with recurrent abortion, 1988; Eleven cases of abnormal karyotypes first discovered, 1988; Analysis of chromosomes of peripheral lymphocytes in 1321 cases for genetic counselling, 1989; Co-author: Pregnancy test with male toad in Shanghai, 1950; Choriocarcinoma of uterus, 1952; Preliminary report on the cytogenetic study of primary amenorrhea, 1982; Chromosome alterations of peripheral lymphocytes in patients with cervical carcinoma, 1989; Observation on the rate of satellite association in young couples with trisomy 21 offsprings, 1989; Gene diagnosis of Duchenne muscular dystrophy in three families, 1991; Analysis of chromosomes in ascitic fluid cells of ovarian carcinoma, 1993. Memberships: Chinese Medical Association; Eugenic Association of Shaanxi Province. Hobby: Music. Address: Department of Obstetrics and Gynaecology, Xijing Hospital, Fourth Military Medical University, 15 Changle West Road, Xian, Shaanxi, China.

HUANG Bingshan, b. 19 May 1934, Shandong, China. Professor; Doctor. m. Yan Shi Huang, 24 Sep 1959, 1 son, 2 daughters. Education: Heilongjiang College of Traditional Chinese Medicine; Western Doctor Study and Research, Chinese Medicine Programme; MD. Appointments: Medical Doctor, Chief Medical Doctor, Director Doctor, Lecturer, Professor, Director, Chinese Medical Department, Vice President of College. Publications include: Treatment of AIDS by Chinese Medicine, 1991; AIDS and Its Treatment by Traditional Chinese Medicine, CHief Editor, 1991; Syndromes of Traditional Chinese Medicine, Chief Editor, 1993; One Thousand Herbs and One Thousand Formulas, Chief Editor, 1993; Diagnostics in Traditional Chinese Medicine, Co-author, 1983; Analysis and Differentiation of Symptoms in TCM, editor, Co-author, 1984; Analysis and Differentiation of Syndromes and Diagnosis in TCM, Editor, Co-author, 1989; Multiple Choice Exam in TCM Diagnostics, Chief Editor; Clnical Observation on AIDS Treated with Acupuncture, 1989; Contributor of numerous professional papers. Honours: First Class Awards, Hailongjiang Chinese Medicine Bureau. Memberships: Director, Treatment Centre of AIDS with TCM; Vice Chairman, TCM Combining with Western Medicine Association of Heilongjiang. Hobbies: Beijing Opera; Table Tennis; Swimming. Address: 233 N 3rd Street #8, San Jose, CA 95112, USA.

HUANG Bingxian, b. 27 Mar 1932, Guangdong, China. Biomedical Engineer. m. 31 Dec 1965, 2 daughters. Education: Engineer, Southern China University of Technology, 1953; Graduate Programme, Institute of Automation, Academia Sinica, 1962. Appointments: Research Associate, Associate Professor, currently Professor of Biocybernetics, Institute of Automation, Academia Sinica. Publications: Quantitative Medicine (co-author), 1984; Biological Control in Medicine, 1987; The Fundamentals of Biocybernetics, 1991. Memberships: Chinese Society of Biomedical Engineering; Chinese Society of Biophysics; Chinese Association of Automation. Hobby: Chinese Classical Poems. Address: PO Box 2728, Beijing 100080, China.

HUANG Chen Ya, b. 4 Nov 1939, Shanghai, China. Medical Practitioner. m. Chak Yee Kam. Education: MBBS, 1966; BSc Sydney, 1961; MMed, Sungapore, 1971; FRACP. Appointments: Senior Consultant Neurologist, Lidcombe Hospital New South Wales, Australia, 1980; Senior Lecturer, 1981, Reader in Neurology, 1984, Consultant Neurologist, Hong Kong University. Publications: Contributor of several professional articles in journals. Honours: Member, Order of the British Empire, 1979. Memberships: American Academy of Neurology' Australian Association of Neurology; Royal Society of Medicine; Australian College of Physicians; Hong Kong Academy of Medicine. Address: 807 Melbourne Plaza, 33 Queen's Road Central, Hong Kong.

HUANG Cheng-Da, b. 1929, Canton, China. Orthopaedic Surgeon. m. 1954, 1 son, 1 daughter. Education: MD, 1954. Appointments include: Professor, 1976-, currently Tutor to candidates for Doctor's degree, Head, Department of Orthopaedic Surgery, 1st Affiliated Hospital, Sun Yat-Sen University of Medical Sciences, Guangzhou; Performed 1st-ever successful replantation of traumatic amputated leg. Publications: Metallic vertebral body prosthetic replacement for treatment of primary thoracic bone tumour complicated by paraplegia - long-term follow-up of 8 cases, 1987; Co-author: Successful restoration of a traumatic amputated leg, 1965; Experience in replantation of severed fingers, 1973; Experience with anastomoses of arteries approximately 0.2 mm in external diameter, 1982; Induced osteosarcoma in rabbits with 4-nitroquinoline-1-oxide, 1987; Analysis of 38,959 cases of tumours and tumour-like lesions of bone, 1990; Coupled suturing - A new technique for microvascular anastomosis, 1991; Telangiectatic osteogenic sarcoma, 1992; Editor: 40 articles, 1959-91; Textbook, technical book, encyclopaedia of medicine. Honours: 6 National or Guangdong Province Scientific Research Prizes, 1978, 1982, 1986, 1992, 1993. Memberships: Chinese Orthopaedic Association, Chairman, Bone Tumour Section; Chairman, Guangdong Orthopaedic Association; Orthopaedic Committee, Ministry of Health. Hobbies: Handicrafts; Reading; Sports. Address: First Affiliated Hospital, Sun Yat-Sen University of Medical Sciences, Guangzhou 510080, China.

HUANG Gang, b. 6 Jul 1961, Hunan, China. Medicine. m. Lu Yan, 28 Oct 1987, 1 d. Education: MD, Shanghai Medical University, 1988; MSc, Shanghai Medical University, 1988. Appointments: Visiting Research Scientist, Italy; Visiting Scholar, France; Associate Professor of Nuclear Medicine. Publications: 20 Thesis in Journal of Nuclear Medicine Communications, Chinese Journal of Nuclear Medicine, 1988-94. Honours: Second Prize from Chinese Health Department. Memberships: European Nuclear Medicine Association; Chinese Medical Association; Chinese Inventive Association. Hobbies: Music; Travel. Address: Department of Nuclear Medicine, Zhongshan Hospital, Shanghai Medical University, Shanghai 200032, China.

HUANG Guanghua, b. 29 Aug 1932, Philippines. Physician. m. Evelyn Hou, 16 June 1982, 2 sons. Education: BA, Zhong Shan Medical College, China, 1958; MD, University of Pennsylvania School of Medicine, USA, 1982. Appointments: Vice-Director, Medical Department, 1973-84, Hospital Vice-Director, 1984-85, Guangdong Provincial People's Hospital, China; Director, Public Health Bureau of Guangdong Province, 1985-92; Currently Chief Physician of Internal Medicine. Publications: Esophageal Manometry Study, 1985; Co-author: Bacillary Dysentery, 1976; Quantitative Infrared Spectroscopy of Common Bile Ductstones, 1988. Memberships: Chinese Medical Association; Guangdong Science and Technology Association; Chinese Association of Rehabilitation Medicine. Hobbies: Tennis; Reading. Address: Public Health Bureau of Guangdong Province, 17 Xianlienan Road, Guangzhou 510060, China.

HUANG Hua-Yu, b. 1 Sept 1936, Shanghai, China. Scientific Researcher. m. 25 Oct 1968, 1 son, 1 daughter. Education: Diploma, undergraduate study, Shanghai Medical University; Diploma, graduate study, Chinese Medical University; MD, Freiburg University, Germany. Appointments: Primary Researcher, Department of Nutrition, Chinese Academy of Preventive Medicine; Professor, Head, Neuropharmacology Group, Shanghai Institute of Physiology, Chinese Academy of Sciences. Publications: European Journal of Pharmacology, 153:175-184, 1988, 169:115-123, 1989, 206:221-230, 1991; Acta Pharmacologica Sinica, 11:494-497, 1990, 12:28-32, 1991, 12:160-163, 1992, 13:51-54, 1992, 14:35-38, 1993, 15:215-219, 1994; Neuropharmacology, 32:133-137, 1993. Memberships: Chinese Physiological Society; Chinese Biochemical Society. Address: Shanghai Institute of Physiology, Chinese Academy of Sciences, Yue Yang Road 320, Shanghai 200031, China.

HUANG Huizhao, b. 31 Oct 1924, Jiangxi, China. Professor of Infectious Diseases. m. Xu Xuehua, 6 Feb 1945, 1 s, 1 d. Education: MD, The Seventh Military University, China, 1955. Appointments: Doctor, Airforce General Hospital, China, 1955-58; Doctor, Shanxi Taigu Hospital, China, 1959-61; Doctor/Professor, Ningxia Medical College, China, 1962-94; Professor, Ningxia Medical College, China, 1995-. Publications: Series of Studies on Severe Hepatitis, Chronic Hepatitis and Cirrhosis Treated with Chinese Medicine, 1978-94. Honours: Scientific Achievement Awards, China, 1980-92; International Research Golden Award, ICIM, USA, 1994. Memberships: IASL; IRECLD; CAIED; CAIM. Hobbies: Penmanship. Address: Ningxia Medical College, Yinchuan 750004, China.

HUANG Jianfu, b. 2 Dec 1933, Fuzhou, Fujian, China. Professor of Surgery. m. 1961, 1 son, 1 daughter. Education: Bachelor of Medicine, 1962. Appointments: Surgeon, Xie He Hospital, Fuzhou, 1962-. Publications: Cholangiocholecysts cholechoscopic withdrawal of stones, 1985; Improvement of pancreatodundenectomy and pancreatocholedochojejunostomy, 1992; Blood free hepatectomy, 1993. Honours: Winner, 3rd Prize, 1988, 2nd Prize, 1990, in field of technology, Fujian. Membership: Committee Member, Fujian Hepatic Science. Hobbies: Playing bowls. Address: Xie He Hospital, Fuzhou, Fujian 350001, China.

HUANG Jianzhong, b. 20 July 1930, Chengmai, Hainan, China. Paediatrician. m. Zheng Jinying, Mar 1958, 2 sons, 1 daughter. Education: Army Medical College, 1950-53; Bachelor Degree, Lanzhou Medical College, 1973. Appointments: Middle-South Army Hospital, 1953-56; Lanzhou Hospital, 1961-62; Hainan Provincial People's Hospital, Resident Docotr 1953, Attending Doctor 1972, Vice Clinical Professor 1981, Clinical Professor 1988. Publications: Severe And Imminent Condition In Clinical Paediatrics, book; 42 essays, such as, Treatment of children's acute nephritis with anisodamine, 1983; Treatment of Nephropathy Syndrome with Traditional Chinese Medicine and Modern Medicine. Honours: Advanced Workers in the Medical Field,

1978; Hainan Excellent Specialist, 1992; The National Special Award for Outstanding Specialist, 1993. Memberships: Chief Member, Nephrosis Association of Hainan; Health Consultant, Hainan Women & Children Association; Editor, Hainan Medical Journal. Hobbies: Reading Novels; Writing. Address: Paediatrics Department, Hainan Provincial People's Hospital, Haikou 570311, China.

HUANG Jiefei, b. 26 Sept 1944, Nantong, Jiangsu, China. Professor of Gastroenterology. m. Zuxun Ge, 1 May 1969, 1 son. Education: BS, 1968, MD, 1982, Nantong Medical College. Appointments: Currently Professor of Gastroenterology, Affiliated Hospital, Nantong Medical College. Publications: The Change of Enzyme Activity of Gastric Mucosa in Gastric Disease, 1982; Sulphomucin Colonic Type Intestinal Metaplasia and Carcinoma in the Stomach (co-author), 1986; Transmucosal Potential Difference in Erosive Duodenitis and Its Changes after Treatment with Colloidal Bismuth Subcitrate, 1988; Ultrastructural Study of Gastric Musocal Capillaries in Liver Cirrhosis with Portal Hypertension, 1989; Gastroduodenal Mucosa Damage Caused by Transcatheter Arterial Chemo-embolization in Patients with Hepatocellular Carcinoma, 1994. Memberships: Society of Digestive Endoscopy, Chinese Medical Association; Editorial Board, Journal of Endoscopy, China; International Research and Exchange Center of Liver Disease, China. Hobbies: Running; Table-tennis. Address: Department of Gastroenterology, Affiliated Hospital, Nantong Medical College, Nantong, Jiangsu, China.

HUANG Jiqun, b. 5 December 1932, Jieyang, Guangdong, China. Professor of Biochemistry. m. Hu Meixiang, 25 August 1957, 1 son, 1 daughter. Education: MD. Appointments: President, Guangzhou Medical College, 1987-92; Director, Cancer Institute of Guangzhou Medical College. Publications: A new method for estimation of alpha-fetoprotein (AFP) Enzyme linked counterelectrophoresis assay on cellulose acetate membrane, 1985; Analysis of the molecular variants of alpha-fetoprotein by cross affinity enzymoimmunoelectrophoresis and its diagnostic value, 1990; Enzymorocket electrophoretic assay of alpha-fetoprotein, 1991; Enzymorocket electrophoretic assay and crossed affinity enzymoimmunoelectrophoresis and its application in diagnosis of primary liver cancer, 1994. Honours: The National Specialist with Outstanding Contributions of China, National Scientific and Technical Committee. Memberships: Chinese Medical Association; Council Member, Chinese Anticancer Association; President, Guangzhou Anticancer Association. Hobbies: Music Appreciation; Travel. Address: Guangzhou Medical College, Dongfengxi Road, Guangzhou 510182, China.

HUANG Ming Xi, b. 9 Feb 1937, WuXi, China. Epidemiologist. m. 25 Sept 1961, 2 daughters. Education: BA, Tongi Medical University, China, 1957. Career: Teaching Assistant 1957-78, Lecturer 1978-83, Associate Professor 1983-90, Professor of Epidemiology 1990-, Tongji Medical University. Publications: Editor-in-Chief, Handbook for the Control of Communicable Diseases in Man, 1st, 2nd & 3rd edition, 1964, 1977, 1981; Co-author, Epidemiology (official granted national university textbook), 1966, 1978, 1982; Management of Infectious Disease, 1990; Impacts of the Three Gorge Project on the Natural Plaguy Disease in Hubei Province, 1987. Honours: Award, National Science Congress, 1978; First Class Award, The Advanced Work in Science and Technology, Chinese Academy of Sciences, 1990. Memberships: Department of Epidemiology Standing Committee, Chinese Preventive Medicine Association; Disinfectant Society of Chinese Preventive Medicine Association. Hobbies: Music; Dance; Sport. Address: Department of Epidemiology, Tongji Medical University, Wuhan, China.

HUANG Nai Jian, b. 10 June 1935, Beijing, China. Professor. m. 18 July 1959, 1 son, 1 daughters. Education: Jining Medical College, China, 1957; Shandong College of TCM, China Head, 1962 Colo-proctological Department, Hospital Affiliated to Shandong College of Traditional Chinese Medicine. Appointments: Lecturer, 1978; Associate Professor, 1983; Professor, 1988-. Publications: Literature Researching About Colo-Proctology of Traditional Chinese Medicine, 1981; Chinese Colo-Proctology, 1994. Honours: Special Contributor of All-China Association of Colo-proctology, 1986-91; Outstanding Worker in Science and Technology Circles of Shandong, 1988; Excellent Specialist in Science and Technology Circles of Shandong, 1992. Memberships: Standing Member, Sub-Association of Colo-Proctology of Chinese Association of Traditional Chinese Medicine and Pharmacology; Chairman, Editorial Committee of Chinese Journal of Colo-Proctology; Chief Editor, Editorial Department of Chinese Journal of Colo-Proctology; All-China Association of Edit of Traditional Chinese

Medicine; Standing Member, Shandong Traditional Chinese Medicine Association; Chairman, Shandong Sub-Association of Colo-Proctology; Shandong High-Ranking Judge Committee of Medical Technology. Hobbies: Qigong; Music. Address: 32 POB Anwaixiaoyeng District of Beijing, China.

HUANG Nai-Xang, b. 28 April 1955, Liaoning, China. Professor of Cardiovascular Surgery. m. Yao Li, 12 May 1983, 1 daughter. Education: MD, Department of Cardiovascular Surgery, Tongji Medical University; BA, Jinzhou Medical College, 1982; MM, Chinese Medical University, 1989. Appointments: The First Affiliated Hospital, Jinzhou Medical College, 1982; Chinese Medical University, 1987; Union Hospital, Tongji Medical University, 1992. Publications: Percutaneous needle biopsy for lung cancer, 1989; Myocardial cell culture, 1993; The experiment methods of cardiovascular surgery, 1994. Memberships: Chinese Medical Association; Northeast Medical Image Association. Hobbies: Photography; Travel; Music; Swimming. Address: Department of Cardiovascular Surgery, Union Hospital, Tongji Medical University, Wuhan 430022, China.

HUANG Ru-Heng, b. 15 Nov 1923, Shanghai, China. Biochemical Pharmacologist. m. Ji Qing-E, 1 Jan 1954, 1 son, 1 daughter. Education: BS, Dai-Tung University, 1948; MA, Medical College of Shanghai, 1951. Career: Assistant Professor, 1951-78; Associate Professor, 1978-83; Professor (full), 1983-; Head, Department of Drug Metabolism, currently. Publications: Since 1949, published over 120 articles about: Enzymes Cholinesterast; Low Temperature Phosphorescence; Permeability of RBC Membrane; Revealed the metabolic pathway of 5 drugs, Pharmokinetics and Pharmodynamics of 10 drugs. Honours: National Prize of Natural Science (co-winner), 1986; National Prize of Progress in Science & Technology, 1987; National Prize of Progress in Science & Technology (co-winner), 1988. Address: 27 Taiping Road, Institute of Pharmacology and Toxicology, Academy of Military Medical Sciences, Beijing 100850, China.

HUANG Teng-Bo, b. 9 September 1937, Shanghai, China. Oncologist. m. 1 October 1961, 3 daughters. Education: MD. Appointments: Head, Department of Cancer Epidemiology; Head, Faculty of Design, Measurement and Evaluation in Medical Research. Publications: Clinical and Laboratory Researches on Nasopharyngeal Carcinoma, 1984; Cancer of the Nasopharynx in Childhood, 1990; Diet and Nasopharyngeal Carcinoma, 1989; Occupational and Other Non-Dietary Factors for Nasopharyngeal Carcinoma, 1990. Honours: Science and Technique Advance Award, 1993. Memberships: Chinese Medical Academy. Hobbies: Classical Music. Address: Cancer Hospital, Sun Yat-Sen University of Medical Sciences, Dong Fang Road East, Guangzhou 510060, China.

HUANG Wen-Ying, b. 9 Apr 1933, Fujian Province, China. Professor of Pathology. m. Shou Gu, 9 Aug 1973, 1 s. Education: Graduated from Zhongshan Medical College, China, 1955. Appointments: Research Assistant; Research Associate; Associate Professor; Professor and Scientist of Pathology. Publications: Proteoglycans in Human Artherosclerotic Lesions, 1984; Ultrastructural Study of Aortic Lesions in Youth, 1991. Honours: First Class Scientific Technological Awards from Chinese Academy of Medical Sciences and PUMC, 1989, 1990; Award from Ministry of Health, China, 1991. Memberships: International Atherosclerosis Society; Chinese Electron Microscopy Society; Society of Pathology; Chinese Medical Association. Address: Department of Pathology, Cardiovascular Institute and Fu Wai Hospital, CAMS & PUMC, Beijing 100037, China.

HUANG Xi, b. 31 Mar 1959, Xiangtan, Hunan, China. Doctor; Teacher. m. 15 May 1985, 1 son. Education: BS, Hunan Traditional Chinese Medical College, China, 1982; MS, Fourth Military Medical University, 1989; MD, Fourth Military Med University. Career: Resident, 1983; Lecturer, 1989; Physician-in-Charge, 1990. Publications: Studies of Metabolism and Pharmacokinetics of Extract from Malaytea Scurfpea (Psoralea Corylifolia) in Mice, 1991; Influence of Combined Salvia Miltiorrhiza and Ligusticum Wallichii on Pharmacokkinetics of Tetramethylpyrazine in Rats, 1994; Pharmacokinetic Characteristics of Tetramethylpyrazineand Study on Hemorheology in Rat Model of Spleen Deficiency Syndrome, 1994. Honours: First Award of Excellent Paper on Traditional Medicine, 1994; Paper of Excellence, National Natural Science Foundation of China, 1993. Memberships: Chinese Association of Integration of Traditional and Western Medicine. Hobbies: Playing the Violin and Erhu (a two-stringed bowed instrument); Running; Football.

Address: Department of Traditional Chinese Medicine, Xijing Hospital, Fourth Military Medical University, Xi'an 710032, China.

HUANG Yan-Ting, b. 18 Aug 1930, Guandong Province, China. General Surgeon. m. Shu-Fan Xu, 6 June 1954, 1 son, 1 daughter. Education: Beijing Medical College, 1948-54; Visiting Scholar, University of California, Medical Centre, San Diego, USA, 1984. Appointments: Resident, The First Teaching Hospital, 1954-58, Chief Resident, 1959, Attending Surgeon, 1960, Associate Professor, 1982, Professor, 1986, Chairman, Department of General Surgery, 1990, Beijing Medical University. Publications: Division of Surgery Volume of Modern Medicine, Chinese Grand Encyclopaedia, Chief Editor; Portal Hypertension, 1985; Acute necrotizing Pancreatitis, 1993. Honours: Portasystemic Shunt, National Prize of Progress in Science and Technology, 2nd Class, 1979; Residual Intrahepatic Stones, Prize of National Ministry, 1992. Memberships: Vice Editor-in-Chief, National Journal of Medicine; Chinese Medical Association; International HBP Association; Standing Committee, Chinese Surgical Association; Consulting Specialist of Medical technology, National Ministry of Public Heath. Hobbies: Reading; Classical music; Travel. Address: 35# Xishibei Santiao, Beijing 100034, China.

HUANG Yanming, b. 23 May 1964, Hubei, China. Chinese Medicine; Integrated Chinese and Western Medicine; Acupuncture and Massage; Chinese Herbal Pharmacology. m. Lan Wang, 7 Feb 1994. Education: Master of Medicine; Undergraduate Study (BM), Hubei Chinese Medical College; Postgraduate Study, Tongii Medical University; Special training of technique of DNA analysis. Career: Resident Physician, Assistant, 1989-92; Physician in Charge, Lecturer, 1992-. Publications include: Practice Cardiology of Chinese Medicine, book, 1993; Oncology of Chinese Medicine, book, 1994; 14 Articles published including: Certain Questions and Countermeasures in Hemiparalysis Forecase, 1991; Study on the red-cell immune adherence activity and its relationship with blood-stasis in the primitive hypertensive patients, 1994. Honour: Excellent Young Teacher, Hubei Education Committee. Memberships: Chinese Association of the Integration of Chinese Medicine and Western Medicine; Chinese Association of Chinese Medicine; Chinese Hemorheology Special Association. Hobbies: Mountain Climbing; Swimming; Tai Quan. Address: Division of Chinese Medicine, Xiehe Hospital, Tongii Medical University, Wuhan 430022, China.

HUANG Yaoquan, b. 25 Aug 1923, Liaoning, China. General Surgeon; Professor. m. Zhaomin Wang, 15 Nov 1944, 2 daughters. Education: MB, ChB, Liaoning Medical College, Mukdem, 1947; Intern, Tianjin Central Hospital, 1947. Appointments: Assistant Resident, Chief Resident, Visiting Surgeon, Lecturer, Tianjin Medical College Hospital, 1948-64; Visiting Surgeon, Head of Department of Surgery, Professor, Tianjin First Central Hospital, 1964-. Publications: Tumors of Head and Neck in Infant and Childhood, in Otorhinolaryngology in Infants and Children; Selective Porto-Systemic Shunts in Portohypertension, chapter in Recent Advances of Liver, Biliary Tract, Pancreas and Spleen; Diseases of Small Intestine, in Chinese Encyclopedia of Medicine, General Surgery vol; Selective Works of Dr Yaoquan Huang, 1993; Abdominal Surgery (edited with H C Wu); Member, Editorial Board: Physical Examination and Signs of Surgical Patients; Recent Advances of Diagnosis and Treatment Techniques in Surgery; About 90 papers. Honours: Tianjin Progress of Science Award, 1988; Chinese Government Award for Scientists with Special Contributions. Memberships: Vice-President, China Surgery Association; President, Tianjin Surgery Association; Vice-President, Chinese Medical Association, Tianjin Branch; Editorial Boards: Chinese Journal of Surgery; Tianjin Medical Journal; Clinic General Surgery; Apllied Journal of Surgery; Clinic China Oncology. Address: Tianjin First Central Hospital, 24 Fukang Road, Tianjin 300192, China.

HUANG Yingcai, b. 28 November 1936, Guangdong, China. Physician. m. Qin Lijun, 13 November 1965, 1 son, 1 daughter. Education: MD, Fourth Military Medical University, 1961. Appointments: Resident, Chief Resident, Visiting Doctor, Associate Professor, Professor, Department of Gastroenterology. Publications: Clinical analysis of 23 cases of hepatic tuberculosis, 1982; Evaluation of photoradiation therapy for 20 cases of malignant tumors, 1984; An experimental study and clinical application of breaking gastric bezoars endoscopically by a laster ignited mini-explosive head, 1990; Photodynamic therapy in upper gastrointestinal cancer, 1990; Endoscopic laser therapy for gastrointestinal sessile polyps, 1992; Co-author: Gastroendoscopy, 1978; Co-author: Practical Laser Medicine, 1990. Honours: Technological Progress Awards, Chinese

Military Committee, 1984, 1989, 1993; Awards, Five Times, Chinese Health Administration, 1984. Memberships: Committee Member, Beijing Laser Medicine Association; Chinese Medical Association; Editor, Chinese Journal of Lasers. Hobbies: Swimming; Travel; Dancing. Address: Department of Gastroenterology, Chinese Great Wall Hospital, Beijing 100853, China.

HUANG Zhengren, b. 10 June 1933, Singapore. Haematologist (Internal Medicine). m. Tang Guangkui, 23 July 1957, 2 sons, 1 daughter. Education: MB, Harbin Institute of Medical Sciences, 1956; Diploma, 2nd National Training Course on Haematopathy, Institute of Haematopathy, Chinese Academy of Sciences, 1960. Appointments: Medical practice, teaching, research on Haematological Internal Medicine, 1960-; Currently Professor, Chief, Department of Haematology, Guangdong Provincial People's Hospital, Guangzhou. Publications: Fetal Hepatocytic Suspension in Treating Aplastic Anemia, 1981; Progress in Treating Acute Leukemia, 1988; Autotransplantation of Bone Marrow, 1990; G-CSF, GM-CSF in Treating Acute Leukemia, 1992. Honours: Scientific Achievement Award for article Relationship between Hematopathy and Other Sciences, Guangdong Association of Science. Memberships: Chinese Medical Association; Chinese Association of Sciences; Guangdong Association of Women; Guangdong Association of Women Intellectuals. Hobby: Classical music. Address: Haematology Department, Guangdong Provincial People's Republic, Zhongshan (2nd) Road, Guangzhou 510080, China.

HUANG Zhi Qiang, b. Jan 1922, Kwangdon. Surgeon. m. Jean Yu, 20 May 1950, 2 sons. Education: MD. Career: Vice Director, Southwest Hospital; Director of Hepato Biliary Surgical Center; Professor of Surgery, currently. Publications: Operative Surgery, 1975; Biliary Tract Surgery, 1976; Hepatic Surgery, 1981; Mordern Basic Surgery, 1988; Operative Biliary Surgery, 1989. Honours: National Awards of Advancement of Technology and Science, 1986. Memberships: Chinese Medical Association; International Surgical Society. Address: Department of Surgery, Fuxin Road, General Hospital of PLA, Beijing 100853, China.

HUBBARD Richard, b. 24 Dec 1929, Battle Creek, Michigan, USA. Biochemical Nutritionist. m. Constance Gloor Hubbard, 18 Nov 1951, 2 sons, 1 daughter. Education: BA, Chemistry, Mathematics, Pacific Union College, 1951; MS, Biochemistry 1958, PhD, Biochemistry 1961, Purdue University. Appointments: Instructor, Biochemistry, School of Medicine, University of Michigan, 1960-63; Head Chrom Researchr, Beckman Instructor, Palo Alto, 1963-67; Project Leader, NASA/SRI Biosatellite Prim Programme, SRI, Menlo Park, 1967-70; Research Associate Professor of Pathology, Biochemistry & Nutrition, Schoos of Medicine & Public Health, Loma Linda University. Publications: Effect of dietary protein on serum insulin and glucagon levels, 1989; Atherogenic effect of oxidized products of cholesterol, 1989; Elevated glucagon levels in ALS, 1992; Potential of diet to alter disease, 1994. Honours: Phi Lambda Upsilon; Sigma Xi. Memberships: American Association of Clinical Chemistry; American Chemistry Society; American Society of Clinical Pathology; American Institute of Nutrition; American Society Clinical Nutrition; New York Academy of Sciences. Hobbies: Sailing; Cycling. Address: 1906 Verde Vista Drive, Redlands, CA 92373, USA.

HUBBELL F Allan, b. 13 Nov 1948, Waco, TX, USA. Physician. m. Nancy Cooper, 23 May 1975, 1 s. Education: BA, Baylor University; MD, Baylor College of Medicine; MSPH, UCLA. Appointments: Chief, Division of General Internal Medicine and Primary Care, University of CA, Irvine; Director, Center for Health Policy and Research; Director, Primary Care Internal Medicine; Residency, University of CA, Irvine. Publications: 50 Published papers and book chapters on issues related to technology assessment and access to medical care. Honours: Teacher of Year, University of CA, Irvine, 1987, 1989. Memberships: American College of Physicians; Society of General Internal Medicine; American Federation for Clinical Research. Hobbies: Skiing; Reading. Address: Dept of Medicine, UCI Medical Center, 101 City Drive, Orange, CA 92668, USA.

HUBER Donald Simon, b. 18 Apr 1929, Clarendon, Pennsylvania, USA. Physician. m. Mary Hanks, 6 Sep 1958, 2 sons, 1 daughter. Education: BA; MD. Appointments: Solo Practice in Allergy and Immunology. Memberships: AMA; ACAI; ACA. Hobbies: Reading; Baseball. Address: 502 Eustis Street, Huntsville, AL 35801, USA.

HUDD Nicholas Payne, b. 11 Oct 1945, Romford, England. Physician. m. Gwen Johnstone, 11 Oct 1969, 2 s, 1 d. Education: MA;

MB; BChir (Cantab); FRCP. Appointments: House Physician, Harlow; Medical Registrar, Basildon; Haematology Registrar, Orsett Hospital; Senior Medical Registrar, Manchester; Currently, Consultant Physician, Benenden Hospital. Memberships: British Diabetic Association; Royal Society of Medicine. Hobbies: Golf; Rose Growing; Music; History. Address: 54 Wimpole Street, London, W1, England.

HUGHES Alan Benjamin, b. 8 Jul 1947, Deep River, Ontario, Canada. Obstetrician. m. Christine Ann Freer, 8 Jul 1983, 2 d. Education: MD, University of BC, 1974; FRACGP, 1980; MRCOG, 1984; FRACOG, 1989. Appointment: Obstetrician and Gynaecologist, Senior Specialist. Memberships: Australian Medical Association; Australian Association Study of Hypertension in Pregnancy; ANZ Perinatal Society; National Association of Specialist Obstetricians and Gynaecologists; South Pacific Regional Obstetric and Gynaecologic Society; Australian Gynaecological Endoscopy Society. Address: PO Box 524, Alice Springs, NT 0871, Australia.

HUGHES John R, b. 7 June 1949, Columbia SC, USA. Physician. Education: MD. Career: Assistant Associate Professor, Department of Psychiatry, University of Vermont; Professor, Department of Psychiatry, Psychology & Family Practice, currently. Publications: Over 150 scientific articles. Honours: Ove Ferno Award, 1994; NIDA Career Development Award, 1985. Memberships: American Psychiatric Association; Society for Research on Nicotins & Tobacco. Address: Department of Psychiatry, University of Vermont, 38 Fletcher Place, Burlington, VT 05401-1419, USA.

HUGHES Stephen Edward, b. 1 Jun 1953, Newton, MA, USA. Scientist. m. Michelle R Lennartz, 30 Nov 1984, 1 s, 1 d. Education: BS, University of Miami, 1974; PhD, University of MA, Amherst, 1981; PhD, Zoology. Appointments: Postdoctoral Research Associate, University of MI, 1980-85; Assistant Research Scientist, Central Institute for the Deaf, 1985-92; Assistant Professor of Neurobiology, WA University, 1988-92; Faculty Research Associate, Albany Medical College, 1992-; Lecturer, State University of NY, 1992-; Research Assistant Professor, SUNY, 1993-; Assistant Professor, Department of Surgery, Albany Medical College. Publications: Co-author: Chronic impairment of axonal transport eliminates taste responses and taste buds, in Journal of Neuroscience, 1983; Neural induction of taste buds, in Journal of Comparative Neurology, 1987; Transplantation of photoceptors to light damaged retina, in Investigative Ophthalmology, 1989. Honours: Board, RP Foundation Fighting Blindness, St Louis Chapter, 1989-92; Sigma Xi. Memberships: American Association for the Advancement of Science; Association for Research in Otolaryngology; International Brain Research Organization; Sigma Xi; Society for Neuroscience. Hobbies: Photography; Camping; Bicycling; Woodworking. Address: Albany Medical College A-134, 47 New Scotland Ave, Albany, NY 12208, USA.

HULTCRANTZ Elisabeth, b. 24 Nov 1942, Västerås, Sweden. Associate Professor. m. Ed Paulétte, 15 May 1981, 1 son, 2 daughters. Education: MD, University of Uppsala; Med Dr (PhD) University of Uppsala; Med Lic, 1968. Appointments: Resident in Surgery, Sala, 1969; GP, Falun, 1970-71; Resident, ENT, Falun, 1972-73; Ward Physician, ENT, 1974-81; Associate Professor, Clinical Teacher, University Hospital of Uppsala, 1982-; Visiting Assistant Professor, University of Michigan, 1983. Publications: The Cochlear Blood Flow, 1978; Children with Tonsillary Obstruction, 1988; Sudden Deafness, 1990. Memberships: Swedish Medical Association; Swedish Medical Society; American Association of Research in Otology; Physics Against Nuclear Weapon Amnesty. Honours: Hwasser's Prize, 1979; Wallin's Stipend, 1979. Hobbies: Skiing; Gardening; Singing in the Choir. Address: ENT Clinic, University Hospital, S-75185 Uppsala, Sweden.

HUMBERT James Ronald, b. 7 Mar 1938. Professor of Pediatrics. Div, 3 s. Education: MD, University of Geneva, 1964; MS, University of Colorado, 1970; Privat Docent, University of Geneva, Switzerland. Appointments: Associate Professor Pediatrics, University of CO Medical Center, 1976-80; Associate Professor Pediatrics, State University of NY, Buffalo, 1976-80; Professor, Pediatrics and Microbiology, State University of NY, Buffalo, 1980-87; Professor of Pediatrics, Tulane University School of Medicine, 1987-92; Professor of Pediatrics, Wright State University School of Medicine, 1992-95; Currently, Director, Hematology and Oncology Department. Publications: Co-author, Physiology and Pathology, 1975; Co-author, Chemical Bone Marrow of Patients with Sickle Cell Disease, 1993. Honour: Best Doctors in America, 1979. Memberships include: AMA; Witebsky Center for Immunology; American Society Hematology; AFCR; SPR. Hobbies: Art

Collecting; Skiing; Classic Cars; Opera; Theatre; Music. Address: Children's Medical Center, 1 Children's Plaza, Dayton, OH 45404, USA.

HUMBLE Charles Glenn, b. 23 Mar 1947, Tennessee, USA. Epidemiologist. m. Victoria Freeman PhD, 29 Feb 1984, 2 daughters. Education: SM, Harvard School of Public Health, USA, 1980; PhD, University of North Carolina at Chapel Hill, USA, 1990. Career: Epidemiology Section Manager, New Mexico Tumor Registry, 1980-86; Burroughs Wellcome Fellow of Pharmacoepidemiology, University of North Carolina at Chapel Hill, 1991-92; Epidemiologist, Quality Management Institute & Education Center, Durham, North Carolina, currently. Publications include: Marriage to a Smoker and Lung Cancer Risk in New Mexico, 1987; Passive Smoking and Cardiovascular Disease Mortality Among Nonsmoking Wives in Evans County, Georgia, 1990; Oats and Cholesterol: The Prospects for Prevention of Heart Disease, 1991; Prevalence of Illness and Chemical Exposures Among Professional Photographers, 1988. Memberships: Society for Epidemiologic Research; American Public Health Association; North Carolina Association for Healthcare Quality; American Medical Record Review Center. Hobbies: Running; Reading; White Water Canoeing. Address: 910 Emory Drive, Chapel Hill, NC 27514, USA.

HUMMEL Robert Paul, b. 17 Sep 1928, Bellevue, Kentucky, USA. Surgeon. m. Helen Beam, 26 June 1954, 1 son, 2 daughters. Education: BS, 1947; MS, 1951; Board Certified, American Board of Surgery, 1960; FACS. Appointments: Advisory Council for General Surgery, Governor, Professional Liability Committee, Nominating Committee, American College of Surgeons; Professor of Surgery, Vice Chairman, Department of Surgery, Chief of Staff, University Hospital. Publications: Clinical; Burn Therapy - A Management and Prevention Guide, 1982; Contributor of 61 articles. Honours: Cum Laude, 1947; Alpha Omega Alpha, 1951; Sigma Xi, 1965. Memberships: American Surgical Association; American College of Physician Executives; American College of Surgeons; Central Surgical Association; Halsted Society; Southern Surgical Association. Hobbies: Golf; Horseracing. Address: Department of Surgery, University of Cincinnati, PO Box 670558, Cincinnati, OH 45267-0558, USA.

HUMPHREY Dennis Charles, b. 18 Jan 1931, London, England. Obstetrician and Gynaecologist. m. Delyth Davies, 4 Oct 1958, 1 s, 2 d. Education: MBBS(London), 1952; FRCS(Eng), 1961; MRCOG, 1965; FRCOG, 1978; FRACOG, 1979; ThA, 1993. Career includes: Senior Registrar, Obstetrics and Gynaecology, West Middlesex Hospital, 1965-67, Charing Cross Hospital, London, 1967-69; Honorary Obstetrician, Salvation Army Home, Hobart, 1969-74; Consultant Obstetrician and Gynaecologist, Royal Hobart Hospital, Tasmania, 1969-; Accredited Gynaecologist Calvary, St Helen's and St John's Hospitals, 1969-; Lecturer, Obstetrics and Gynaecology, Faculty of Medicine, University of Tasmania, 1972-. Pubications include: The Causes of Coronary Heart Disease, Guy's Hospital Reports, 1957; Localised Accidental Vaccinia of the Vulva, American Journal of Obstetrics and Gynaecology, 1963; Iron Dextrant Infusion, in Lancet, 1964; Co-author, Normal Infant after Combination Chemotherapy including Teniposide for Burkitts Lymphoma in Pregnancy, in Medical and Pediatric Oncology, 1982. Honours: Charles Forster Prize in Cardiology, 1956; Certificate Golding Bird Prize, Examination in Obstetrics and Gynaecology, 1956. Memberships include: Australian Medical Association; Australian Gynaecological Endoscopic Society; Australian Society for Colposcopy and Cervical Pathology; American Association of Gynaecologic Laparoscopists. Hobby: Bush Walking. Address: Umdruba, 22 Parliament Street, Sandy Bay, Hobart, Tasmania 7005, Australia.

HUMPHREY George Bennett, b. 9 May 1934, Chicago, IL, USA. Professor of Paediatrics. m. M B Minawska. Education: MD, 1960; PhD, 1963; Pediatrics, Pediatric Hematology and Oncology. Appointments: Assistant Professor of Pediatrics, 1970-71, Associate Professor of Pediatrics, 1971-75, University of OK; Assistant Provost, University of OK Health Science Center and Director, OK Cancer Center, OK City, 1973-80; Professor of Pediatrics, University of OK, 1975-86; Professor of Pediatrics, University of Gronengin, Netherlands, 1984-92; Professor of Pediatrics, Medical College of OH, 1992-. Publications: 6 Books including: Co-author, Hodgkin's Disease in Children: Controversies and Current Practice, 1989; 20 Book chapters, 1974-; 6 Abstracts; Over 100 professional articles including: Co-author, Parental coping with their child's death, in Counselling Psychology Quarterly, 1991. Honours: NCI Review Committee; Executive Committee, Pediatric Oncology Group. Memberships: American Academy of Pediatrics; American Society of

Hematology; American Society for Pediatric Research; International Society Paediatric Oncology; Pediatric Oncology Group. Hobbies: Wilderness Camping; Skiing. Address: Medical College of Ohio, PO Box 10008, Toledo, Ohio, USA.

HUMPHREY Valerie Barbara, b. 17 Feb 1940, Birmingham, England. Acupuncturist. m. David Humphrey, 31 Mar 1962, 1 son, 1 daughter. Education: Diploma in Acupuncture. Appointments include: Director, Shifnal Clinic, Shifnal, Shropshire. Membership: Register of Traditional Chinese Medicine. Hobbies: Golf; Swimming. Address: Telford and District Occupational Health Centre, Halesfield 13, Telford, Shropshire TF7 4QP, England.

HUNT Lindsay McLaurin Jr, b. 19 Sep 1939, Oklahoma City, OK, USA. Dental Education. m. Patricia Ann Bell, 11 Jun 1960, 2 s. Education: BA, University of OK; DDS, Baylor University; PhD, Baylor University. Appointments: Assistant Professor of Dental Research, Coordinator of Basic Health Sciences for Dentistry, Emory University; Associate Professor and Chairman, Department of Oral Biology; Associate Dean, Academic Affairs, Professor of Oral Biology; Currently, Dean, School of Dentistry, VA Commonwealth University. Publications: Co-author, Transmission of Bacteria by Nitrous Oxide Equipment, in Dental Abstracts, 1978; Co-author, A Comparison of Intra-Lingual Epienphrine Before and During Cardiovascular Depression, 1978. Honours: Fellow, American College of Dentists, 1978; Fellow, Pierre Fauchard Academy, 1988; Fellow, International College of Dentists, 1989; First Harry Lyons Endowed Professorship, 1992; Honorary Alumnus, Dental Division, Medical College of VA Alumni Association, 1993. Memberships: American Dental Association; American Association of Dental Schools; International College of Dentists; American College of Dentists; Pierre Fauchard Academy. Address: School of Dentistry, Virginia Commonwealth Univ, PO Box 980566, Richmond, VA 23298-0566, USA.

HUNTLEY James Michael, b. 25 Aug 1964, Melbourne, Australia. Psychologist. Education: BA, University of Guelph, Ontario, Canada, 1986; Master of Letters, University of New England, Armdale, NSW, 1993. Appointments: Honorary Psychiatrist, Victoria State Emergency Service; Consultant Psychiatry, St John Ambulance, Australia; Associate of Centre for Psychiatric Services, Swiabrune University, Melbourne. Publications: Traumatic Events Management, St John Ambulance National Training Log, 1993; Co-author, Supercoping: How Emergency Service Volunteers Cope with Critical Incident Stress, 1993; APS Conference, 1993. Memberships: International and Australian Societies for Traumatic Stress Studies; Australasian Critical Incident Stress Association; Australian Psychiatric Society. Hobbies: Hiking; Camping; Parachuting. Address: Centre for Psychological Services, 16 Park Street, Hawthorn, Victoria 3122, Australia.

HURVICH Marvin Samuel, b. 7 May 1930, Birmingham, Alabama, USA. Psychologist; Professor of Psychology. m. Elaine Hurvich, 1 Nov 1981, 2 sons, 1 daughter. Education: BS, University of Alabama, 1953; MA, 1955, PhD, 1960, University of Pennsylvania; Postdoctoral Certificate, Psychotherapy and Psychoanalysis, New York University, 1968. Appointments: Chief, Clinical Psychology Section, Fort Riley, Kansas, 1960-62; Director, Clinical Psychology Training, Roosevelt Hospital, New York City, 1964-73; Chairman, Department of Psychology, currently Professor of Psychology, Long Island University, 1977-80; Visiting Professor of Psychology, New York University. Publications: On the Concept of Reality Testing;, 1970; Ego Functions in Schizophrenics, Neurotics and Normals (co-author), 1973; Traumatic Moment, Basic Dangers and Annihilation Anxiety in Psychoanalytic Psychology, 1989. Honours: Phi Beta Kappa, 1952. Memberships: American Psychological Association; International Psychoanalytic Association; Institute for Psychoanalytic Training and Research; New York Freudian Society. Address: 228 West 22nd Street, New York, NY 10011, USA.

HUSAIN Oliver Anthony Nasseem, b. 25 Mar 1924, London, England. Retired Consultant Pathologist. m. Katharine Mary Regis Sangar, 25 Jan 1948. Education: Kings College London and Kings College Hospital, London; MBBS (Hons); MRCS, LRCP; MD; FRCPath; FRCOG. Appointments: Registrar, Pathology, Chelsea and Kensington Group of Hospitals, London; Major, Senior Specialist in Patholoy, Royal Army Medical Corps; Senior Registrar, Pathology, Westminster Hospital, London; Consultant Pathologist and Cytopathologist, Chelsea and Kensington Hospitals, and Charing Cross Hospital, London; Now retired. Publications: Gynaecological Cytology Atlas, 1989; Automated Cervical Cancer Screening, 1994; Over 40 chapters in books and over 100 papers, mainly on researches into cytochemistry and creation of diagnostic tests for pre- and early cancers and development of automated cell scanners and quality control procedures. Memberships: Co-Founder, Secretary, Chairman, President, British Society for Clinical Cytology; Co-Founder, Secretary-General, European Federation of Cytology Societies; Co-Founder, Chairman of Medical Advisory Committee, Women's Nationwide Cancer Control Campaign, 1964-. Hobbies: Travel; Walking; Art; History. Address: 42 Oakhill Court, Edge Hill, Wimbledon, London SW19 4NR, England.

HUSAR Walter, b. 24 Sept 1956, Jersey City, USA. Instructor, Department of Neurosciences; Staff Neurologist, Department of Veteran Affairs. Education: BS, summa cum laude, St Peter's College, 1978; MS, Rutgers University, New Brunswick, 1982; MD, UMDNJ, New Jersey Medical School, Newark, 1988. Appointments: Adjunct Lecturer in Biology, St Peter's College, Jersey City; Instructor of Neurosciences, UMD-NJ Medical School, Newark; Currently: Staff Neurologist, VA medical Centre, East Orange. Honours: Dean's List, 1974-78; Summa cum laude, 1978. Memberships: American Medical Association; Fellow, Academy of Medicine, New Jersey; Essex County Medical Society; Associate, American Academy of Neurology; Medical Society of New Jersey; Stroke Council, American Heart Association. Hobbies: Fishing; Computers. Address: 10 Christine Drive, East Hanover, NJ 07936, USA.

HUSSAIN Mohammad Ishfaq, b. 23 Jan 1950, Abbottabad, Pakistan. Physician m. Rukshanda Shah, 17 June 1985, 1 son, 2 daughters. Education: FSc, College of Abbottabad; MB BS, University of Peshawar; Khyber Medical College; FAAP. Appointments: Clinical Assistant Professor of Paediatrics, Indiana University School of Medicine, USA, 1984-; Clinical Preceptor Paediatrics for Residents Deaconess Hospital, Evansville, Indiana; Paediatric Haematologist Oncologist, St Marys Medical Centre, Evansville. Publications: Ocular Irritation from Low Dose Methotrexate Therapy, 1982; Purified Digoxin Specific Fab Fragments, Their Use in Preventing Serious Complications of Digoxin Toxicity, 1st author, 1985; Lymphocytic Leukemia, 1st author, 1987; Iron Responsive Iron deficiency Anemia in Children, 1985. Honours: Former Member, Haemophilia Advisory Commission to the Governor of Indiana, USA. Memberships: Fellow, American Acadwemy of Paediatrics; American Society of Paediatric Haematology-Oncology; Indiana State Medical Association; Association of Pakistani Physicians in North America. Hobbies: Photography; Sports; Travel. Address: 801 St Marys Drive Suite 203, Evansville, IN 47714, USA.

HUSSAIN Muhammad Anwar, b. 31 Dec 1951, Noakhali. Obstetrician and Gynaecologist. m. noor Akhter Begum, 14 Apr 1977, 2 daughters. EducationL: MBBS; MRCOG(London). Appointments: Assistant Professor, Department Obstetrics and Gynaecology, Myensingh Medical College; Associate Professor, Department Obstetrics and Gynaecology, Rajshahi Medical College; Associate Professor, Department Obstetrics and Gynaecology, Dhaka Medical College. Publications: A Clinical Guide to Obstetric Management; Contributor of 15 articles. Honours: Young Gynaecologist Award, Asia-Oceania Federation of Obstetrics and Gynaecology, 1991. Memberships: Organizing Secretary, Obstetrical and Gynaecological Society of Bangladesh; Representative Committee, RCOG Bangladesh. Hobbies: Reading; Watching Television; Gossiping with Friends. Address: Project and Commodities (BD) Limited, Sena Kalyan Bhaban, Room No 1106, 11th Floor, 195 Motijheel C/A, Dhaka-1000, Bangladesh.

HUSSERL Fred E, b. 7 Mar 1946, Bogota, Colombia. Physician. m. Consuelo Rubiano, Mar 1972, 1 son, 1 daughter. Education: Doctorate; FACP. Appointments: Staff Nephrologist, Ochsner Clinic; Medical Director, Home Dialysis Training Program. Publications sinclude: Hypertension after Clonidine Withdrawal, Co-author, 1978;; Renal Papillary Necrosis Associated with Fenoprofen Therapy, Co-author, 1981; Adverse Effects of Antihypertensive Drugs, Co-author, 1981; Erythromycin Warfarin Interaction, 1983; Toxic Nephropathies and Drug Usage in Patients with Renal Impairment, 1987; Effective Communication: A Powerful Risk Management Tool, 1993; Love; Fabry's Disease: Images in Clinical Medicine, Co-author; Contributor of numerous abstracts and presentations. Honour: Top Five Percent Throughout Medical School. Memberships include: American Medical Association; American Society of Nephrology; International Society of Nephrology; International Society for Peritoneal Dialysis; Southern Medical Association. Hobbies: Photography; Music. Address: Ochsner Clinic, 1514 Jefferson Highway, New Orleans, LA 70121, USA.

HUTCHINS Grover Macgregor, b. 17 Aug 1932, Baltimore, Maryland, USA. Professor of Pathology. m. Loretta H Bajkowska, 29 July 1956, 1 son, 2 daughters. EducationL: BA, 1957, MD, 1961, Johns Hopkins University and School of Medicine; Research Fellow, Scripps Clinic and Foundation. Appointments: Instructor, School of Medicine, 1966-67, Professor of Pathology, 1983-, Johns Hopins University; Pathologist, 1967, Assistant and Associate Professor of Pathology, Director of Autopsy Pathology, 1976, Johns Hopkins Hospital. Publications: Autopsy Performance and Reporting, Editor, 1990; An Introduction to Autopsy Technique, Editor; Contributor of 433 articles and 46 chapters in books Honours: Alpha Epsilon Delta; Alpha Omega Alpha; Phi Beta Kappa; Certificate of Excellence in Teaching; Ranice W Crosby Distinguished Achievement Award; Society for Paediatric Pathology Scroll of Appreciation. Memberships: CAP Autopsy Committee, 1986-; Advisor CAP Forensic Pathology Committee; CAP Commission on Anatomological Pathology; Chairman, CAP Autopsy Committee. Hobby: Antiques. Address: 1 Stratford Road, Baltimore, MD 21218-1145, USA.

HUTCHINSON Richard Michael Strode, b. 31 Jul 1934, Southsea, Hampshire, UK. Chiropractor. m. Yvonne Margaret Fleming, 4 Apr 1959, 1 s, 2 d. Education: Doctor of Chiropractic, Anglo-European College of Chiropractic. Appointments: Regular Commission in Royal Navy to rank of Lieutenant Commander, specialised in Submarine and Anti Submarine Warfare; Chiropractor in Private Practice. Memberships: British Chiropractic Association; European Chiropractors Union; American Chiropractic Association. Hobbies: House; Home; Garden; Dogs; Carpentry. Address: Old Manor Cottage, Meonstoke, Hampshire, SO32 3NH, UK.

HUTCHINSON Timothy Paul, b. 21 Aug 1951, Amersham, England. Statistician. Education: BA, University of Cambridge, England, 1972; PhD, University of London, England, 1976. Career: Lecturer in Statistics. Publications: Numerous journal articles; Books: Road Accident Statistics, 1987; Continous Bivariate Distributions, Emphasising Applications (co-author with C D Lai), 1990; Ability, Partial Information, Guessing: Statistical Modelling Applied to Multiple-Choice Tests, 1991; Essentials of Statistical Methods in 41 Pages, 1993. Address: School of Mathematics and Statistics, University of Sydney, NSW 2006, Australia.

HUTCHISON George Barkley, b. 18 Oct 1922, Lexington, KY, USA. Physician. Education: AB magna cum laude; MD; MPH. Appointments: Assistant Medical Director, Health Insurance Plan of Greater NY; Assistant Professor, Associate Professor, Epidemiology, Harvard University; Associate Professor of Radiology, University of Chicago; Professor of Epidemiology, Harvard University, now retired. Publications: Over 50 publications in professional journals of epidemiology, 1955-92. Honours: Phi Beta Kappa, 1943; Delta Omega, 1960; John Snow Award in Epidemiology, 1987. Memberships: American Public Health Association; American Statistical Association; American Association for Advancement of Science. Address: 115 Saint Francis Court, Apt 96, Louisville, KY 40205, USA.

HUTTENBACH Dirk Erik, b. 6 Feb 1938, Amsterdam, Netherlands. Psychiatrist. m. Muriel Patterson, 6 Jun 1964, 2 s, 2 d. Education: BSc, Case Institute of Technology, 1959; MD, State University of NY, Syracuse, 1965; FAPA; FAACAP; Intern, Kaiser Foundation Hospital, San Francisco; Residency, Psychiatry and Fellowship in Child Psychiatry, University of CA, San Francisco. Appointments: Major, US Army Medical Corp, Ft Benning, GA, 1970-72; Private Practice, Center for Interpersonal Studies, Smyrna, GA, 1972-74; Private Practice, Marietta, GA, 1974-. Publication: Adolescent Urine Drug Screen Program, A Cobb County Medical Society Program, in Journal Medical Association of GA, 1987. Honours: Fellowship: American Psychiatric Association, 1991; American Academy of Child and Adolescent Psychiatry, 1991. Memberships: AMA; APA; AAC; AAP; ASAM; ASAP. Hobbies: Reading; Classical Music. Address: 833 Campbell Hill Street, Ste 440, Marietta, GA 30090, USA.

HWANG Chi-Hwan, b. 7 Apr 1955, Seoul, Korea. Dental Clinician. m. Hong Jin-Ho, 8 Aug 1986, 2 daughters. Education: DDS; MSD; PhD. Appointments: Automobile Engineer; Dental Technician; Currently Director, Yok Kok Dental Clinic. Publications: Gnathology, 1992; Dental Photography, 1993; Holistic Dentistry, 1994. Memberships: American Academy of Implant Dentistry; International Congress of Oral Implantologists; American Academy of Functional Orthodontics and Taekeuk Dental Research; International Academy of Dental Research; Global Cooperation Society Club International; HANWOOL. Hobbies:

Golf; Climbing; Fishing. Address: Yok Kok Dental Clinic, 127 Yok Kok Dong, Pucheon Si, Kyungkido 422-090, Korea.

HWANG Kuei-Hsiang, b. 13 Jan 1951, Keelung, Taiwan, China. Physician. m. 3 children. Education: MD, 1993; PhD, American Pacific Coast University, 1993-94. Appointments: Researcher, mutual relationship between parapsychology and medical science; Invited Speaker; Columnist. Memberships: Society of Urban Plan; Society of Urban Policy; Society of Surpass Psychology; Society of Land Economics; American Association of Parapsychology; World Association of Women Journalists and Writers, Chinese Chapter. Address: 6F No 26 Lane 50 I-Hsien Road, Taipei, Taiwan, China.

HYNES Arleen (Sister), b. 3 May 1916, Sheldon, IA, USA. Librarian; Bibliotherapist. m. Emerson Hynes, 26 Jul 1941, 8 s, 2 d. Education: BS, College of St Catherine, USA, 1940; Registered Poetry Therapist. Appointments: National Chairperson, Family Life Committee, National Council of Catholic Women, 1956-62; Librarian-Bibliotherapist, The Circulating Library, St Elizabeth's Hospital, Washington DC, 1970-80; Currently, Free Lance Author, Teacher, Lecturer, Biblio-Poetry Therapist. Publications: Biblio/Poetry Therapy - The Interactive Process: A Handbook, 1986; Some considerations concerning assessment in poetry therapy and interactive bibliotherapy, 1988; Bibliotherapy: An interactive process in counseling older persons, 1990; Poetry: An avenue into the spirit, 1990; Biblio/Poetry Therapy: A Resource Bibliography, 1992. Honours: Dorothea Lynne Dix Award, St Elizabeth's Hospital, WA, 1977; National Association for Poetry Therapy Award for Pioneering Efforts in the Field, 1985; Exceptional Service Award, Association of Specialized and Cooperative Libraries, 1986. Memberships: Presdent Emerita, National Federation of Biblio/Poetry Therapy; President, Bibliotherapy Round Table; Board, National association for Poetry Therapy. Hobbies: Reading; Symphonic Music; Art Galleries. Address: 104 Chapel Lane, St Joseph, MN 56374, USA.

I

IANNI Francis Anthony James, b. 29 Mar 1929, Wilmington, DE, USA. Psychoanalyst. m. Elizabeth Reuss-Ianni, 18 Jul 1971, 3 s. Education: BS; MA; PhD, Penn State University; Graduate NY Psychoanalytic Institute; Certified, American Psychoanalytic Association. Appointments: Professor: Yale University; University of Florence; University College Addis Ababa; US Department HEW; Director, Institute for Social Analysis; Currently, Professor, Columbia University; Associate, Staff Department of Psychiatry, St Luke's Hospital. Publications: American Social Legislation, 1959; Culture, System and Behavior, 1965; A Family Business, 1973; The Search for Structure, 1990. Honour: Educator of Year, University of Pennsylvania, 1991. Memberships: American Psychoanalytic Association; American Psychological Association; New York Psychoanalytic Society. Hobby: Yachting. Address: Villa L'Acquilla, Cloupr Road, Newfoundland, NJ 07435, USA.

IBRAHIM Abel Hadi, b. 1 Jan 1957, Sudan. Doctor. m. Latifa, 15 Oct 1981, 1 d. Education: MBBS; MRCOG; FRCS, Education. Appointments: National Health Hospitals in England in Obstetrics & Gynaecology for 10 Years; General Practitioner. Memberships: General Medical Council; British Medical Association. Hobbies: Music; Travel. Address: 68 Regent Road, Warley, Birmingham, B68 1TS, UK.

IBRAHIM Mounir, b. 26 July 1948, Cairo, Egypt. Physician; Psychiatrist. Education: MB; Bch; MD. Appointments: Clinical Associate Professor of Psychiatry, Bowman & Gray School of Medicine; Private Practice. Memberships: American Medical Association; American Psychiatric Association; Christian Medical-Dental Society. Hobbies: Travel; Reading; Music. Address: 1400-A Millgate Drive, Winston, Salem, NC 27103, USA.

IGBOGBAHAKA Bertram Obiahanna, b. 21 Feb 1933, Enugu Akwu, Achi, Nigeria. Medical Practitioner. m. Grace Igbogbahaka, 28 Jan 1961, 2 sons, 3 daughters. Education: MB BS (Lond); LRCP; MRCS; DObstRCOG; FRCOG (Lond); FMCOG (Nig); FICS; FOFGO. Appointments: House Surgeon, House Physician, Bridgend General Hsopital, Wales; Post Reg House Officer, Obstetrics and Gynaecology, University College Hospital, Ibadan, Nigeria; Senior House Officer, University College Hospital, Ibadan; Registrar, St David's Hospital, Cardiff, Wales; Senior Registrar, University College Hospital, Ibadan; Consultant Gynaecologist, Queen Elizabeth Hospital, Nigeria; Consultant Gynaecologist, Medical Director, Ucheoma Hospital Ltd, Aba. Memberships: Royal College of Obstetricians and Gynaecologists, London; Medical College of Obstetricians and Gynaecologists, Nigeria; International College of Surgeons; International Federation of Gynaecology and Obstetrics. Hobbies: Reading; Chess. Address: Ucheoma Hospital Ltd, 53 Ehi Road, PO Box 1905, ABA, Abia State, Nigeria.

IIDA Nobutoshi, b. 14 Nov 1928, Hokkaido, Japan. Professor. m. Yuri Kumagai, 15 June 1952, 2 daughters. Education: MD, 1952, PhD, 1957, Hokkaido University. Appointments: Chief, Department of Nephrology, Osaka Prefectural Hospital, Osaka; Currently Professor, Nursing Department, Aino Gakuin College. Publications: Illustrated Water and Electrolytes, 1969; Standard Dialysis Therapy, 1981; Management of Renal Disease, 1992. Memberships: International Society of Nephrology; European Dialysis and Transplant Association; European Renal Association; International Society for Peritoneal Dialysis. Hobby: Travel. Address: 3-4-33 Bandai-higashi, Sumiyoshi, Osaka 558, Japan.

IKEDA Noriaki, b. 13 June 1952, Nagoya, Japan. Oral and Maxillofacial Surgeon. m. Yoko Hayashi, 19 Mar 1978, 1 son, 1 daughter. Education: DDS, 1977, PhD, 1984, Aichigakuin University; Assistant Etranger, Faculty of Medicine, Université Paris VI, 1985. Appointments: Research Associate, 1979-81, Attending Lecturer, 1981-86, Assistant Professor, Department of Oral and Maxillofacial Surgery, 1986-, School of Dentistry, Aichigakuin University; Chief Surgeon, Aichigakuin University Hospital, 1986-. Publications: Lesions précancereuses des muqueuses des voies aérodigestives supérieures (co-author), 1994; Prevalence study of oral mucosal lesions in a selected Cambodian population (main author), 1995. Memberships: International Association for Dental Research; Japanese Society of Oral and Maxillofacial Surgeons; Japanese Stomatological Society. Hobbies:

Playing the guitar; Cycling; Watching movies. Address: 2-11 Suemoridori, Chikusaku, Nagoya 464, Japan.

IKEHARA Morio, b. 1 Jan 1923, Tokyo, Japan. Director. m. 11 Nov, 2 sons. Education: Bachelor's Degree, Medical School, Tokyo University, 1945; PhD. Appointments: Resident Assistant, Tokyo University School of Medicine; Assistant Professor, Hokkaido University School of Medicine, 1955; Professor, Faculty of Pharmacy Science, Hokkaido University, 1966; Professor, Faculty of Pharmacy Science, Osaka University, 1968; Professor Emeritus, Osaka University, 1986; Director, 1986; Professor, Tokyo Science University, 1986. Publications: Nucleic Acids, 1979; Organic Chemistry of Nucleic Acids, 1979; Experimental Procedures in Protein Engineering, 1984; Methods in Protein Engineering, 1984; Chemistry of Nucleosides and Nucleotides, 1988; Nucleic Acids and Molecular Biology, 1993. Memberships: Pharmacy Society, Japan; Chemical Society, Japan; Biochemistry Society, Japan. Hobbies: Book Reading; Music; Sports. Address: 3-11-14 Hiyoshidai, Takatsuki, Psaka 569, Japan.

IKEUCHI Tatsuro, b. 20 Jan 1942, China (former Manchuria). Associate Professor. m. Nov 1976, 1 son, 1 daughter. Education: Bachelor of Fisheries, 1964, MSc, 1966, DSc, 1972, Hokkaido University. Appointments: Research Associate, Roswell Park Memorial Institute, Buffalo, New York, USA, 1968-71; Assistant Professor, 1975-79, Faculty of Science, Hokkaido University; Associate Professor, Tokyo Medical and Dental University, Japan, 1979-. Publications: Inhibitory effect of ethidium bromide on mitotic chromosome condensation and its application to high-resolution chromosome banding, 1984. Memberships: The Japan Society of Human Genetics; The Genetics Society of Japan; Japanese Cancer Association; The Society of Chromosome Research. Address: Division of Genetics, Medical Research Institute, Tokyo Medical and Dental University, 1-5-45 Yushima, Bunkyo-ku, Tokyo 113, Japan.

ILDERTON Margaret Weymoth, b. 26 Jun 1945, Gweru, Zimbabwe. Radiographer. m. Howard George Ilderton, 26 Jan 1972, 1 s. Education: Diploma in Diagnostic and Therapeutic Radiography. Appointments: Chief Radiographer, MPILO Hospital, Bulanayo, Zimbabwe, 1974-80; Principal then Chief Radiographer, Windhoek. Publication: Self Evaluation - Student Guide for Namibian Students, 1994. Memberships: South African Medical and Dental Council; Namibia Medical Board. Hobby: Gardening. Address: Radiographic Services, Ministry of Health and Social Services, PUT Bag 13198, Windhoek, Namibia, South Africa.

ILOABACHIE Gabriel Chukwubuzor, b. 12 February 1941, Ogidi, Anambra, Nigeria. Obstetrician and Gynaecologist. m. Irene N Iloabachie, 19 October 1974, 3 sons, 3 daughters. Education: MBBS, London, 1966; MRCOG, 1974; FWACS, 1981; FMCOG, 1982; FICS, 1984; FRCOG, 1986. Appointments: Senior Lecturer; Consultant. Publications Include: Masculinizing Tumors of the Ovary, 1976; Primary Ovarian Cancer Complicating Pregnancy, 1988; Two Stage Repair of Giant Vesico Vaginal Fistula. 1989; Urinary Incontinence: An Uncommon Complication of Female Circumcision - A Method of Ursthral Reconstruction from Vaginal Tissues, 1990; Trends in Caesarean Section, 1992; Medical and Sociocultural Problems of the Adolescent Proceedings of the Paediatric Association of Nigeria, 1993. Memberships: Nigerian Medical Association; Academic Staff Union of Nigerian Universities; Society of Obstetrics and Gynaecology of Nigeria; Enugu Sports Club; DMGS Old Boys Association. Hobbies: Gardening; Photography; Lawn Tennis; Jogging. Address: 4 Acres Street, Uwani, Enugu, Nigeria.

ILYIN Vladimir Nikolaevich, b. 12 Nov 1945, Moscow, Russia. Surgeon. m. Larissa Bitkova, 25 Jan 1969, 1 son, 1 daughter. Education: MD, 2nd Moscow Medical Institute, 1970; FRCS. Appointments: Resident, Cardiovascular Surgery, 1970-75, Chief Resident, 1975-80, Assistant Professor, Division paediatric Heart Surgery, 1980-89, Professor of Cardiovascular Surgery, 1990-95, Heart, Department for Heart Surgery in Infants Before 1 Year Old, Bakulev Institute of Cardiovascular Surgery, Moscow. Publications: Trend of Intracardiac Hemodynamics, Ventrical's Volume and Pumping Function in Natural History of Fallot's Tetralogy. Co-author, 1991. Memberships: Russian Society of Cardiovascular Surgeons; European Congenital Heart Surgeons' Club. Hobbies: Touring; Skiing; Sailing. Address: 1812 Year Street, 10-2-115, Moscow 121170, Russia.

IMAM Nilufar, b. 5 May 1940, Dhaka, Bangladesh. General Medical Practitioner. m. Mahbub Karim, 6 Aug 1962, 1 son, 1 daughter.

Education: MBBS, University of Dhaka, 1962; MRCOG, 1968; FRCS Edinburgh, 1971; FRCOG, 1989; MFFP, 1993. Appointments: Several house positions, Bangladesh and England, 1962-67; Registrar, Obstetrics, Gynaecology, Royal Hampshire County Hospital, Winchester, 1967-69; Medical Officer, Family Planning Association, 1969-72; Part-time General Practice and Family Planning Sessions for Medway Health Authority, 1972; Senior Partner in General Practice and Senior Instructing Family Planning Medical Officer, 1977-; Non-Executive Member, Kent Family Health Services Authority, 1992-94. Honours: Gold Medal for standing 1st in MBBS, University of Dhaka, 1962. Memberships: British Medical Association, Medway Postgraduate Executive Committee; Cervical Screening Committee, North Kent Health Care Trust; Founder Member, Faculty of Family Planning and Women's Reproductive Health; Executive Council Member, Medway Doctors on Call, Local General Practitioners Co-Op Subcommittee. Hobbies: Her family's welfare; Gardening, including plant propagation from cuttings and seeds; Overseas travel; Walking for physical fitness and appreciation of nature; Interest in the neighbourhood and environment; Governor, Byron Road Primary School, Gillingham, Kent, and Chatham Grammar School for Girls, Chaltham, Kent, 1988-90. Address: 144 Edwin Road, Gillingham, Kent ME8 0AG, England.

IMBASCIATI Antonio, b. 9 May 1936, Pisa, Italy. Professor; Psychoanalyst. m. Lucia Rapezzi, 7 Mar 1965, 2 sons, 1 daughter. Education: MD; Specialisations: Psicotecnica, Clinical Psychology, Child Neuropsychiatry; Libera Docenza (PhD equivalent), Psychology; Professore Ordinario, Clinical Psychology. Appointments: Psychoanalyst; Psychologist; Psychiatrist; Professor (ordinario), University of Brescia. Publications: 26 books including: La Consapevolezza, 1989; La donna e la bambina, 1990; Affetto e Rappresentazione, 1991; Psicologia Medica, 1993; L'oggetti e le sue vicissitudini, 1993; Fondamenti psicoanalitici della psicologia clinica, 1994; 130 papers. Memberships: Full Member, International Psychoanalytic Association; Italian SPI. Hobbies:. Science and Art.

IMBEAU Stephen Alan, b. 25 Nov 1947, Portland, OR, USA. Allergy Medicine. m. Shirley Ruth Imbeau, 17 Aug 1979, 2 s, 1 d. Education: BA, Mathematics, University of CA, Berkeley, 1969; MD, University of CA, San Francisco, 1973. Appointments: Resident, Internal Medicine, 1973-77, Clinical Instructor, Medicine, 1977-79, Elective, Infectious Disease, 1979-80, University of WI, Madison; Assistant Clinical Professor, Medical University of SC, Charleston, 1980-; Instructor in Medicine, Family Practice, Medical Teaching Service, McLeod Regional Medical Center, Florence, SC, 1987-; Currently, Private Practice, Allergist. Publications: Many professional articles published, 1972-91, including: Co-author, Acute and chronic pulmonary changes in allergic bronchopulmonary aspergillosis, in American Journal Medicine, 1979; Co-author, Asthma mythology: What do you still believe?, in SC Medical Journal, 1981; Co-author, Nasal Endoscopy: An advancement in diagnosis and treatment of sinusitis, in SC Medical Journal, 1991; Seven presentations of papers at scientific meetings; Numerous speeches and presentations of medical-political topics; A 2 year radio broadcast series, from 1992. Honours: Fellow, University of WI, Madison, 1977-79; Diplomat: Internal Medicine, 1976; Allergy and Immunology, 1979. Memberships include: AMA; Secretary, 1991-94, SC Medical Association; Fellow, American College of Physicians; Fellow, American Academy of Allergy and Immunology; American Society of Internal Medicine; Alternate Delegate to the AMA from SC, 1992-; Vice Chairman, SOCPAC, 1994-. Hobbies: Stamp Collecting; Hunting. Address: PO Box 2598, Florence, SC 29502, USA.

INDERBITZIN Lawrence Ben, b. 15 Sept 1939, Muskegon, Michigan, USA. Psychiatrist. m. Ann L Wagner, 4 June 1960, 1 son, 1 daughter. Education: MD with honours, University of Michigan. Appointments: Associate Professor, Georgetown University; Director of Student Health Psychiatry, Georgetown University, Chairman, Hoya Health, Georgetown; Teaching Analyst, Baltimore-DC Institute of Psychoanalysis; Director of Ambulatory Psychiatry, Grady Memorial Hospital, Atlanta, Georgia; Director of Outpatient Psychiatric Research, Grady Memorial Hospital; Site Director of Psychiatric Residency Training, Grady Memorial Hospital. Publications incl: EEG-averaged evoked response and perceptual variability in schizophrenics, 1972; Patient's sleep on the analytic couch, 1988; Life crises, neutrality, and caring, 1988; Unconscious Fantasy: A Reconsideration of the Concept, 1990; Psychoanalytic Psychology, 1990. Honours: Phi Kappa Phi, 1963; Alpha Omega Alpha, 1963; Journal Prize, Journal of the American Psychoanalytic Association, 1988; Commendation for Excellent Services to American Psychoanalytic Leadership Conference, 1993.

Memberships: Fellow, American Psychiatric Association; American Psychoanalytic Association; International Psychoanalytic Association; Atlanta Psychoanalytic Society; Georgia Psychiatric Association; American College of Psychiatrists; Association for Psychoanalytic Medicine. Hobbies: Travel; Gardening; Skiing; Writing. Address: 1701 Uppergate Drive, Atlanta, GA 30322, USA.

INDIRABAI K, b. 30 Aug 1927, Srikakulam, India. Medicine. Education: MBBS; DCH; MD; FAMS (India); FIMSA (India); FIAP (India); FICP (USA); FAAP (USA). Career: Assistant Professor, 1957-67, Professor of Paediatrics, 1967-. Publications include: A study of Oral Rehydration Therapy in childhood diarrhoea, in Indian Journal of Paediatrics, 1980; A study of Leprosy among school children (rural and urban) of A P, in Leprosy in India, 1982; Contributor to: Recent Advances, by Dr Suraj Gupta, 1991, 1993, Text Book, by Dr P M Udhani. Honours: World Health Organisation Fellowship, 1970, 1976, 1977, 1981; Consultant, ICDS Programme, Government of India, 1975-; President, Indian Academy of Paediatrics, 1982; B C Roy National Award, 1993. Memberships: Life Member, Indian Association for Advancement of Medical Education; Life Member, National Leprosy Organisation, India; Life Member, National Federation for Welfare of Mentally Retarded, India; National Selection Committee for National Award of Social Welfare Department, 1982; National Selection Committee for Child Health Award of World Health Organisation, 1982; International Xerophthalmia Club, UK; Indian Council, Medical Research Task Force on Indian Childhood Cirrhosis, 1982-83. Hobbies: Gardening; Reading Books; Letter Writing. Address: c/o Sri P Suresh Chander Pal, 7 2nd Main Road, Ram Nagar, Madras 82, Tamilnadu State, India.

INGALL Michael Alexander, b. 8 Jul 1940, Boston, MA, USA. Physician. m. Carol Krepon, 18 Jun 1961, 1 s, 1 d. Education: BA, Harvard College, 1961; MD, Chicago Medical School, 1966. Appointments: Medical Director, Providence Mental Health Center, 1972-84; Chief of Psychiatry, Harvard Community Health Plan, 1984-93; Staff Psychiatrist, Butler Hospital, 1978-; Staff Psychiatrist, Fuller Memorial Hospital, 1993-; Currently, Clinical Associate Professor of Psychiatry, Brown University Medical School. Honours: Roche Award, 1966; Alumni Association Award, 1966; Alpha Omega Alpha, 1966; Fellow, American Psychiatric Association, 1981. Memberships: American Psychiatric Association; American Group Psychotherapy Association; President, Legislative Representative, Public Affairs Representative, Rhode Island Psychiatric Society. Hobbies: Bicycling; Opera Singer; Shepherd. Address: 150 Upton Avenue, Providence, RI 02906, USA.

INGEL Irine Ed, b. 25 Mar 1953, Kirov, Russia. Biologist. m. Lev Kh Ingel, 5 Jan 1990. Education: Doctor of Biology, Teaching University Kaluga, 1978; PhD, Radiobiology, 1986. Appointments: Research Scientist, 1979-94, Senior Research Scientist, Laboratory of Experimental Pathomorphology, Medical Radiological Research Centre, Obninsk. Publications: Influence of Prostaglandin Biosynthesis Inhibition on Haemopoietic Recovery in Mice After Irradiation, 1984; Haemostimulating Efficiency of Non-Steroid Anti-inflammatory Drugs Under Modified Irradiation Conditions, 1988. Memberships: Society of Russian Pathophysiologists; Russian Society of Pharmacologists. Hobby: Tourism. Address: 4 Korolev Street, 249020 Obninsk, Russia.

INGELMAN-SUNDBERG Axel, b. 22 Dec 1910, Uppsala, Sweden. Gynaecologist. Professor Emeritus. m. Professor Mirjam Furuhjelm, 10 Mar 1946, 3 s, 1 d. Education: MD, Royal Caroline Institute, 1947. Career: Assistant Professor, 1947-49, Associate Professor, 1949-58, Royal Professor, 1958-77, Obstetrics and Gynaecology, Royal Caroline Institute; Chairman, Obstetrics and Gynaecology, Sabbatsberg Hospital, Stockholm, 1958-79; Visiting Professor to many universities; Consultant Physician, Sophiahemmet Hospital, 1979-88, Ersta Hospital, 1983-88. Publications: Associate Editor, International Journal of Gynaecology and Obstetrics, 1974-; Rectal Injuries following Radium Treatment of Cancer of the Cervix, book, 1947; The Childbearing Years, book, 1951; Co-author, A Child is Born, 1982; Over 190 scientific papers published on obstetrics, gynaecology, endocrinology and urogynaecology. Honours: Hwasser's Prize, 1934; The Finnish Cross of Liberty, Red Cross, 1941; Honorary Professor, University of Montevideo, Uruguay, 1962; The Order of the North Pole Star, 1964; FIGO Medal, 1994. Memberships include: President, 1961-69, Swedish Society of Obstetrics and Gynaecology; President, 1966-68, Scandinavian Association of Obstetricians and Gynaecologists; President, 1968-74, International Fertility Association; President, 1976-81, International

Urogynaecologic Association; Honorary Member of 13 national obstetric and gynaecological societies, International Federation of Fertility Societies, International Continence Society; Swedish Society of Obstetrics and Gynecology; Swedish Society of Urology. Hobbies: Fishing; Gardening. Address: Fjalarstigen 1A, S-182 64 Djursholm, Sweden.

INGLIS Donald Bain Carrick, b. 17 Dec 1941, Aberdeen, Scotland. Church of Scotland Minister. Education: MA; MEd; BD. Appointments: School Teacher, Aberdeen and Aberdeenshire; Senior Educational Psychologist, Lanarkshire and Fife Region; Assistant Church of Scotland Minister, West Lothian; Currently, Minister of St Andrew's Parish of Turriff. Membership: Associate Member, British Psychological Society. Hobbies: Violin Playing; Cycling; Hill Walking. Address: St Andrew's Manse, Balmellie Road, Turriff, Aberdeenshire, AB53 7DP, Scotland.

INGMUNDSON Paul Thoma, b. 29 Dec 1952, Detroit, Michigan, USA. Clinical Psychologist. m. Eva Cunneen Beytagh, 29 Nov 1985, 1 s, 2 d. Education: BA, Cum Laude, Psychology, Haverford College, 1975; PhD, Psychology, University of Texas at Austin, 1984. Appointments: Clinical Associate Professor of Psychiatry and Medicine (Neurology), University of Texas, Health Science Center, San Antonio; Staff Psychologist, Audie L Murphy Veterans Hospital. Honours: Professional Service Award, Association of VA Chief Psychologists, 1994. Memberships: Fellow, American Sleep Disorders Association; International Society for Traumatic Stress Studies; American Psychological Association. Hobbies: Hiking; Reading. Address: Psychology (116B), Audie L Murphy Veterans Hospital, 7400 Merton Minter Boulevard, San Antonio, Texas 78284, USA.

INGSTER Lillian May, b. 10 May 1955, New York, USA. Epidemiologist. m. W Turner Moore III, 7 Jan 1978, div. 12 Aug 1992, 3 s. Education: BA, Natural Sciences, The Johns Hopkins University, 1977; MHS, Epidemiology, The Johns Hopkins University School of Public Health, 1983. Appointments: Health Statistician, National Heart, Lung & Blood Institute, 1978-86; Research Consultant/Project Manager, Washington Consulting Group, 1990-91; Specialist Assistant to the Director. Publications: include, Drug Disorders and Cardiovascular Disease: The Impact on Annual Hospital Length of Stay for the Medicare Population; National Data Issues for Coronary Heart Disease Surveillance, in the Summary Proceedings of the Workshop on Methods for the Surveillance of Coronary Heart Disease, 1993; A Client-Based Analysis of Drug Disorder Diagnosis on Lengths of Stay and Total Charges for the Medicare Population, 1993; Use of Official Statistics to Examine Regional Differences in Incidence, Prevalence and Mortality from Ischemic Heart Disease, 1993; Representatives of the Framingham Risk Model for Coronary Heart Disease Mortality: A Comparison with a National Cohort Study, 1987. Memberships: Sigma Xi; American Public Health Association; American Heart Association; Society for Epidemiologic Research. Hobbies: Horseback Riding; Fishing; Reading; Cooking. Address: 918 Challedon Road, Great Falls, VA 22066, USA.

INWOOD David Gerald, b. 15 Mar 1946, Brooklyn, New York, USA. Psychiatrist. m. Linda Rae Freeman, 23 June 1969, 2 sons, 1 daughter. Education: BS, Temple University, Philadelphia, 1969; MD, Universidad Autonoma, Guadalajara, Mexico, 1975. Appointments: Director, Training, Child and Adolescent Psychiatry, State University of New York Health Sciences Center, Brooklyn, 1983-92; Currently Director, Child and Adolescent Outpatient Services, State University of New York Downstate Medical Center, attending Maimonides Hospital; Board of Directors, Postgraduate Training, Psychotherapy Institute, New York City, 1993-. Publications: Spectrum Post-Partum Psychiatric Disorders, 1984; Post-Partum Psychiatric Disorders: Textbook of Psychiatry, 1989; Runaway Youths, 1995; Handbook of Child and Adolescent Psychiatry. Honours: Board Examiner, Child and Adolescent Psychiatry, 1986-. Memberships: American Academy of Child and Adolescent Psychiatry; American Psychiatric Association; American Medical Association; New York Council for Child and Adolescent Psychiatry, President 1992-93. Address: 95 Pierrepoint Street, Brooklyn, NY 11201, USA.

IOSSELIANI David George, b. 3 June 1943, Tbilissi, Russia. Cardiologist. m. Chvedeliani Guranda, 17 Feb 1977, 2 sons, 1 daughter. Education: Diplomated Student, State Medical Institute, Tbilissi, 1960-66; PhD; MD. Appointments: Postgraduate Student, 1967-70; residency, fellowship, Cardiology, 1971-75, Senior Scientific Worker, 1975-82, Head, Department of Interventional Cardiology, 1982-, Bakulev Institute of Cardiovascular Surgery. Publications: Acute Coronary Circulatory Disorders, Co-author, 1988; Manual on Cardiovascular

Surgery, Co-author, 1989; New Onset Angina, Co-author, 1988; Unstable Angina: Medical or Surgical Treatment, Co-author, 1992; COntributor of 150 articles in national and international journals. Honours: State Prize Winner, 1988. Memberships: Fellow, American College of Cardiology; The New York Academy of Sciences; International Society of Cardiovascular Pharmacotherapy. Hobby: Collecting paintings. Address: Bakulev Institute of Cardiovascular Surgery, Leninsky Avenue 8, 117931 Moscow, Russia.

IRWIN Richard Stephen, b. 15 Nov 1942, New London, CT. USA. Professor of Medicine. m. Diane H Northrop, 21 Jun 1969, 4 d. Education: BS, Tufts University, Medford, MA, 1964; MD, Tufts University School of Medicine, Boston, MA, 1968. Appointments: Assistant Professor of Medicine, Brown University, Providence, RI; Director, Medical Intensive Care Unit, RI Hospital, Providence, RI; Associate Director, Pulmonary Diseases, RI Hospital, Providence, RI; Associate Professor, Medicine, University MA Medical School, Worcester, MA; Currently, Professor of Medicine, Director, Pulmonary, Allergy and Critical Care Medicine, University of MA Medical School; Co-Editor, Journal of Intensive Care Medicine. Publications: 108 Original articles, including: Co-author, The Treatment of Cough: A Comprehensive Review, Chest, 1991; 89 Chapters in Books; 2 Books including: Intensive Care Medicine, 1985, 1991. Honours: Fellow, American College of Physicians, 1978; Fellow, American College of Chest Physicians, 1979. Memberships: American Thoracic Society; American College of Chest Physicians; American College of Physicians; American Federation for Clinical Research; American Association of Cardiovascular and Pulmonary Rehabilitation; National Association of Medical Directors of Respiratory Care. Hobbies: Physical Fitness; Skiing; Gardening. Address: Pulmonary, Allergy and Critical Care Medicine, University of MA Medical Center, 55 Lake Ave North, Worcester, MA 01655, USA.

ISAKOV Yuri Fedorovich, b. 28 June 1923, Kovrov, USSR. Paediatric Professor. m. 1 son. Education: DMS, Pirogov 2nd Moscow Medical Institute, 1951. Appointments: Deputy Minister of Health of the USSR, 1981-87; Head, Chair of Paediatric Surgery, Pirogov 2nd Moscow Medical Institute, 1966-; Vice President, Russian Academy of Medical Sciences, 1990-. Publications include: Mediastinum Tumors and Cysts, 1975; Foreign Bodies in Respsiratory Tracts, 1979; Pediatric Surgery, 1983; Paediatric Surgical Disease, 1993; Infusion Therapy and Parenteral Feeding in Paediatric Surgery, Co-author, 1985. Honours: Honoured Man of Medicine, USSR State Prizewinner. Memberships: International Surgery Society; Czech Purkine Medical Society; NY Academy of Medical Sciences. Address: Presidium of the Russian Academy of Medical Sciences, Solianka Str 14, 109801 Moscow, Russia.

ISBISTER William Hugh, b. 7 Apr 1934, Manchester, England. Surgeon. m. Magdalena Richter, 31 Mar 1962, 2 s, 1 d. Education: MB Ch B, 1958, MD, 1964, Victoria University of Manchester; FRCS Ed; FRACS. Appointments include: Foundation Professor of Surgery, 1975-90, Chairman, University Department of Surgery, 1975-90, Deputy Dean, 1985-89; Wellington School of Medicine; Senior Specialist Colorectal Surgeon, 1975-90, Chairman, Department of General Surgery, 1981-88, 1989-90, Wellington Hospital; Currently, Specialist Colorectal Surgeon, Chairman, Department of Surgery, King Faisal Specialist Hospital and Research Centre. Publications: Numerous professional publications, 1965-89, including: Dealing with Piles, in Patient Management, 1986; Changing Nature of Anal Cancer, in Practice Briefs Patient Management, 1989; Colorectal Cancer, the truth, the whole truth and nothing but the truth, Annual Report of Wellington Medical Research Foundation, Wellington, 1989; Numerous papers published in abstract, 1963-93. Memberships include: British Medical Association; Fellow, American Society of Colon and Rectal Surgeons; Gastroenterological Society of New Zealand; Life Member, Surgical Research Society of Australasia; International Society of University Colon and Rectal Surgeons; Wellington Post Graduate Medical Society; The Wellington Club; Riyadh Surgical Club; Riyadh Gastroenterological Club; Association of Coloproctology of Great Britain and Ireland. Hobbies: Music, Jazz and Opera; Photography; Computing. Address: King Faisal Specialist Hospital and Research Centre, PO Box 3354, Riyadh 11211, Saudi Arabia.

ISHII Akira, b. 11 July 1937, Kochi, Japan. Professor of Parasitology. m. Fuyuko Ishii, 1968, 3 sons. Education: MD, DrMedSci, University of Tokyo; MSc, University of London. Appointments: Assistant Professor, Tokyo Medical and Dental University; Assistant Professor, Institute of

Infectious Diseases, Tokyo University; Professor, Miyazaki Medical College; Professor, Okayama University Medical School; Currently Director, Department of Parasitology, National Institute of Health, Tokyo. Publications: In Japanese: Standard Textbook of Medical Zoology (co-editor); Clinical Parasitology (chapter author). Honours: Koizumi Prize, Japan Society of Parasitology; Society Prize, Japan Society of Sanitary Zoology, 1992. Memberships: Japan Society of Parasitology; Japan Society of Sanitary Zoology; Japan Society of Tropical Medicine and Hygiene; Japan Society of Allergologists. Hobbies: Tennis; Golf; Trekking. Address: Department of Parasitology, National Institute of Health, 1-23-1 Toyama, Shinjukuku, Tokyo 162, Japan.

ISHMUKHAMETOV Irat Ismaguilovich, b. 4 Aug 1932, Ufa, Bashkiria, Russia. Physician. m. Yagudina Dina, 6 Sep 1956, 2 s. Education: Doctor of Medical Sciences; Professor; MD, Medical Training Institute, Ufa, 1956; Postgraduate, Institute of Medical Parasitology, Moscow, 1963; Institute of Medical Radiology, Obninsk, 1969. Appointments: Research Associate, Chief of Laboratory, Institute of Medical Radiology, Obninsk; Currently, Chief of Laboratory for Clinical Physiology, Nuclear Medicine and CT, 23 years. Publications: Strongyloidosis, 1965; Radioisotope studies of absorption, 1970; Nuclear medical diagnostics of digestive organs, 1979; Radionuclear and CT diagnostics in emergency medicine, 1993. Honours: Awards of Russian Economic Achievements Exhibition for Scientific Research, 1963, 1983, 1985. Memberships: All Russian Society of Roentgenologists and Radiologists; All Russian Society of Physiology. Hobbies: Table Tennis; Skiing; Reading; Science Fiction; Poetry. Address: Sklifosovsky Institute for Emergency Medicine, 3 B Sukharevskaya Square, 129010, Moscow, Russia.

ISLES Christopher G, b. 27 Jul 1952, Rochdale, Lancashire, England. Consultant Physician. m. Rosaleen Whittell, 4 Oct 1975, 2 d. Education: BSc; MD; FRCP. Appointment: Consultant Physician, Dumfries and Galloway Royal Infirmary, Scotland. Publications: Papers on hypertension and cardiovascular epidemiology. Memberships: Scottish Society of Physicians; Scottish Renal Association; British Hypertension Society. Hobbies: Hill Walking; Running; Gardening. Address: Glebe House, Kirkmahoe, Dumfries, DG1 1SY, Scotland.

ISRAELSTAM David Michael, b. 20 Jul 1939, Chicago, IL, USA. Psychiatrist. Divorced, 1 d. Education: BS; MD; PhD; Board Certified, American Board of Psychiatry and Neurology. Appointments: Delegate, State of WI to National Assembly, American Academy of Child and Adolescent Psychiatry, 1990-93; Currently, Medical Director, Grand Teton Mental Health Consultants. Publications include: LSD and Chromosomes Science, 1967; Califonia (USA) Law Review: Drug Abuse Bibliography, 1968; Perspectives in Biology and Medicine, 1972. Honour: Alumni, Dean's Men's Award, University of Chicago, 1959. Memberships: Currently, President of Southern Chapter, WI Psychiatric Association; American Psychiatric Association; WI Council of Child and Adolescent Psychiatry; American Academy of Child and Adolescent Psychiatry. Hobbies: Public Speaking; Dancing; Trick Cycling. Address: 556 Grand Canyon Drive, Madison, WI 53719, USA.

ISSARAGRISIL Surapol, b. 18 July 1950, Rajburi, Thailand. Physician; Hematologist. m. Ratana Buranayotkul, 25 Nov 1978, 1 son, 2 daughters. Education: BSc, Mahidol University, 1971; MD, Mahidol University, 1974. Appointments: Instructor, Department of Medicine, Siriraj Hospital, Mahidol University, 1978-80; Assistant Professor, 1980-83; Associate Professor, 1983-89; Professor of Medicine, 1989-. Publications: Blood Diseases in SEA, 1987; 3 books; 20 book chapters; 100 articles to professional journals. Honours: Faculty Best Research Award, 1992; Best Research Award, National Research Council, 1993; Mahidol-B Braun Prize for Medical Research, 1993; Fellow, International Biographical Association, 1994. memberships: AAAS; American Society of Hematology; Asian Pacific Bone Marrow Transplant Group. Hobbies: Reading. Address: 179/49 Bangkoknoi-Talingchan St, Bangkok 10700, Thailand.

ITAMI Jinroh, b. 21 Feb 1937, Japan. Physician. Education: Graduated, Okayama University Medical School. Appointments: Researcher, Department of Psychiatry, Okayama University; Director, Kobe Clinic; Currently: Director, Department for Intractable Diseases, Shibata Hospital, Kurashiki; Guest Researcher, Pasteur Institute, Kyoto. Publications: Meaningful Life Therapy, 1988; How to cope with cancer cheerfully, 1991. Honours: Citation for Excellent Paper, for study entitled Laughter and Immunity, Japanese Association of Psycho-Somatic Medicine, 1992. Memberships: Japanese Association of Psycho-Oncology; Japanese Congress of Morita Therapy; Japanese Association of Psycho-Somatic Medicine. Hobbies: Mountaineering; Jogging; Humour. Address: Shibata Hospital, 6108 Tamashima-Otoshima, Kurashiki 713, Japan.

IVERSEN Helle Klingenberg, b. 17 Apr 1956. Research Fellow. Education: Candidate, Medicine, University of Copenhagen, 1985; Training in Surgery, Ortopaedkirugisk afdeling T KAS Gentofte, 1985-86; Training in Neurology, 1986-87, Research Fellow, 1987-, Neuromedicinsk afdeling N KAS Gentofte. Appointment: Currently, Research Fellow. Publications: Over 25 professional publications, 1987-, including: Co-author, Regional cerebral blood flow patterns in migraine without aura: An Interictal SPECT study, in Migraine and other Headaches: The Vascular Mechanisms, 1991; Co-author, Small arteries can be accurately studied in-vivo, using high frequency ultrasound, submitted; Co-author, Symptomatic migraine due to intracranial arteriovenus malformations, submitted; 55 Congress presentations, 1987-92. Membership: Board Member, Danish Migraine Society. Address: Runebergs alle 43, 2860 Soborg, Tlf 31673502, Denmark.

IWATA Makoto, b. 5 Oct 1942, Tokyo, Japan. Physician. m. Kazuko Ogawa, 13 Mar 1966, 1 son, 1 daughter. Education: MD, PhD, Boaded Neurologist of the Japanese Society of Neurology. Appointments: Residency, Toranomon Hospital, Tokyo; Assistant, Tokyo Medical & Dental University; Research Fellow, Montefiore Hospital, New York, USA. Publications: Colour Atlas of the Pathology of the Nervous System, 1988; Kanji versus Kana: Neuropsychological correlates of the Japanese writing system, 1984. Memberships: The Japanese Society of Neurology; Japanese Neuropsychological Association. Honours: Nakayama Prize, 1992; Prix Annuel 1992 de la Société Franco-Japonaise de Médecine, 1992. Hobbies: Music; Essay Writing; Talking. Address: 3-44-10 Sakuradai, Nerimaku, Tokyo 176, Japan.

IWATANI Yoshinori, b. 16 May 1952, Osaka, Japan. Professor, Clinical Laboratory Science, Osaka University Medical School, Japan. m. Atsuko Kitamura, 24 Sept 1982, 1 son, 1 daughter. Education: MD, Kyushu University, 1979; DMS, Osaka University, 1983. Appointments: Research Fellow, University of Toronto, Canada, 1984-86; Research Assistant, Osaka University Medical School, 1983-84, 1986-89; Assistant Professor, 1989-93; Associate Professor, 1993-94; Professor, 1994-. Publications: Peripheral Self Tolerance and Autoimmunity: The Protective Role of Expression of Class II Major Histocompatibility Antigens on Non-lymphoid Cells, 1989. Memberships: Japanese Society of Clinical Pathology; Japanese Society of Immunology; Japan Endocrine Society; Japan Thyroid Association; American Endocrine Society; American Thyroid Association; American Association for Clinical Chemistry. Honours: Schichijo Prize, Japan Thyroid Association, 1989. Hobbies: Listening to Music. Address: 3-13-9 Nagaremachi, Hiranoku, Osaka 547, Japan.

IYER Rajee Srikrishmnan, b. 27 Sept 1938, Bombay, India. Obstetrician; Gynaecologist. m. 13 Oct 1982. Education: MD, G S Medical College, Bombay, 1961; FRCOG(London). Appointments include: Assistant Professor of Obstetrics and Gynaecology, University of Bombay; Solo Practice; Consultant Obstetrician-Gynaecologist, Wadia Maternity Hospital, Bombay, 1976-82; Attending Obstetrician-Gynaecologist, Staten Island University Hospital, Staten Island, USA, 1992-93; Attending Obstetrician-Gynaecologist, Woodhill Medical Associates, Brooklyn, New York. Publications include: Unruptured Rudimentary Horn Pregnancy, 1962; Continuous Lumbar Epidural Analgesia for Painless Labor, 1968; Acute Surgical Gastrointestinal Complications with Pregnancy, 1968; Clinical Correlation of Cytological Studies; Study of Uterine Sensitivity to Oxytoxic Drug - Evaluation of Symth's Test, 1966; Cervical Musous Study in Infertile Patients, 1977. Honours include: Mrs Ramabhai Nowrungay Foreign Fellowship, University of Bombay,1967; Mrs Jhhaveri Prize, 1967; Dr M A Shah Prize, 1972; Invited Lecturer, Blair Bell Research Society, Royal College of Obstetricians and Gynaecologists, London, England, 1969. Memberships: Junior Fellow, American College of Obstetrics and Gynaecologists. Hobbies: Classical music; Shakespearean plays and works; Walking. Address: 235 Evergreen Avenue, Bethpage, Long Island, NY 11714-1221, USA.

IZZO Ezio Maria, b. 24 Feb 1943, Angri, Salerno, Italy. Psychiatrist; Psychoanalyst. m. Maria Lucchi, 21 Oct 1972, 2 sons. Education: Degree in Medicine and Surgery; Specialisation in Psychiatry. Appointments: Expert Witness, appointed by Civil Tribunal, Rome; Professor, Hospital Medical School, Lazio Region; Currently Chief,

Guidonia Mental Hospital, Rome. Publications: Riabilitazione Psicosociale, 1990; Gli Affetti nella Psicoanalisi, 1991; Responsabilitá e Libertá in Psicopatologia, 1993; Contributions to: Rivista di Psicoanalisi Angosce Primarie e Processo Psicoanalitico, 1985; Gli Argonauti, I Lavoro e gli Psicotici nelle Istutuzioni, 1993; Prospettive Psicoanalitiche nel Lavoro Istituzionale, 1987, 1989, 1991; Psiche, 1993. Memberships: Medical Order of Rome; Full Member, International Psychoanalytical Association. Hobbies: Tennis; Soccer; Travel. Address: Via Ettore Ramagnoli 9, 00137 Rome, Italy.

J

JACKS Brian Paul, b. 23 May 1943, Regina, Saskatchewan, Canada. Physician; Psychiatrist. m. Nicole Jones, 11 Apr 1993. Education: MD, 1967; FAACP. Appointments include: Assistant Director, Child/Adolescent Psychiatry Outpatient Services, LAC-USC Medical Centre, 1972-76; Ward Chief, Long-Term Intensive Adolescent Inpatient Services, Director, Residency Training for Child/Adolescent Psychiatry, 1976-79; Private practice, 1979-; Clinical Professor of Psychiatry, USC; Expert Witness, 1980. Publications: Overactivity in Children, 1974; Psychopathology in Children, 1975; Psychopathology in Adolescence, 1975; Malingering, 1994; Numerous lectures and presentations. Memberships: American Psychiatric Association; American Academy of Child Psychiatry, Fellow; American Society of Adolescent Psychiatry; Past President, 1983-84, Southern California Society for Adolescent Psychiatry Executive Council; Past President, Executive Committee, 1982-83, Southern California Society for Child Psychiatry; Southern California Psychiatric Society; Psychiatric Alumni in Continuing Education, USC; California Society of Industrial Medicine. Address: 462 North Linden #254, Beverly Hills, CA 90212, USA.

JACKSON Debra Jean, b. 16 Oct 1958, Miami, FL, USA. Perinatal Epidemiologist. m. Mitchell J Besser, 22 Sep 1984, 2 s. Education: BSc, Nursing; NCC Certified Neonatal Intensive Care Nurse; MPH, Maternal and Child Health; Doctoral Student in Epidemiology and Biostatistics. Career: Neonatal, Perinatal Nurse, Shands Teaching Hospital and University of California, San Diego Medical Center; Maternal and Child Health Outreach Coordinator, Chuuk, FSM; Currently, Research Director, The Birthplace, San Diego. Publications: Co-author, Prenatal Care Manual: A Guide for Clinic Health Workers, 1988; Co-author, Making the Alternative the Mainstream, and, Use of the Nurse-Midwifery Clinical Data Set for Classification of Subjects in Birth Center Research, in Journal of Nurse Midwifery, 1994. Honours: Phi Kappa Phi, 1985; Churchill Award in Public Health Nursing, San Diego State University, 1986. Memberships: American Public Health Association; Association of Women's Health Obstetric and Neonatal Nurses; Society for Epidemiologic Research; Society for Pediatric Epidemiologic Research. Hobbies: International Travel; Scuba Diving; March of Dimes Volunteer. Address: 7511 High Avenue, San Diego, CA 92037, USA.

JACKSON Francis Charles, b. 2 Sept 1917, Rutherford, New Jersey, USA. Physician-Surgeon. m. Joan Gloria Mortenson, 1 Sept 1949, 4 sons, 3 daughters. Education: BA, Yale, 1939; MD, University of Virginia, 1943; Diplomate: National Board of Medical Examiners, 1945; American Board of Surgery, 1951. Appointments include: General and Vascular Surgery practice, Pittsburgh, Pennsylvania, 1952-70; Chief, Surgical Service, VA Hospital, Pittsburgh, 1952-70; Assistant Professor, Associate Professor, 1953-65, Professor, 1965-70, University of Pittsburgh School of Medicine; Consulting Staff, Presbyterian University Hospital, Pittsburgh, 1959-70; Clinical Professor: Georgetown University School of Medicine, 1970-75; George Washington University School of Medicine, 1971-75; Director, Surgical Service, 1970-73, Special Assistant to Chief Medical Director for Emergency and Disaster Medical Services, 1972-73, Director, Emergency and Disaster Medical Services Staff, 1973-75, VA Central Office, Washington DC; Professor, 1975-, Department Chair, 1975-80, Associate Dean, 1980-82, Assistant to Dean for VA Affairs, 1985-, Clinical Professor, 1985-, Texas Tech University School of Medicine. Publications: Role of Medicine in Emergency Preparedness, 1968; Articles. Honours: Pfizer Award of Merit, US CD Council, Minneapolis, 1960; Key to City of Louisville, 1964; Billings Gold Medal, American Medical Association, 1966; Stitt Award, Association of Military Surgeons of the US, 1968; Man of Year, Pittsburgh Academy of Medicine, 1969. Memberships include: Alpha Omega Alpha; Fellow, American College of Surgeons; American and Texas Medical Associations; American Association for the Surgery of Trauma; Founder Member, Association of VA Surgeons; Life Member, Association of Military Surgeons of the US; Senior Member, Société Internationale de Chirurgie; American Surgical Association. Hobbies: Reading; Railroading; Grandchildren. Address: Dean's Suite, Texas Tech University School of Medicine, Lubbock, TX 79416, USA.

JACKSON Peter, b. 29 Dec 1943, Harrogate, England,. Obstetrician and Gynaecologist. m. Carole Daniel, 19 Sep 1964, 1 son, 1 daughter. Education: MRCS(England); LRCP(London), 1967; MRCOG, 1971; FRCOG, 1984. Appointments: Specialist, North Battleford, Saskatchewan, Canada, 1975-76; Consultant, National Women's Hospital, Auckland, New Zealand, 1976-79; Consultant, Worksop and Nottingham, England, 1979-81; Consultant Obstetrician and Gynaecologist, Huddersfield NHS Trust. Publications: Single Dose Metronidazole Prophylaxis in Gynaecological Surgery, Co-author, 1979; A Successful Pregnancy Following Total Hysterectomy, Co-author, 1980; The Birth-Plan Experience, Co-author, 1985; Collection of Patient-Based Data, 1994; Management for Hospital Doctors, Co-Editor, 1994. Memberships: British Medical Association; Ospreys Gynaecological Society; British Association of Medical Managers. Hobbies: Skiing; Fell walking; Scottish Dancing; Photography. Address: Department of Obstetrics and Gynaecology, Huddersfield Royal Infirmary, Acre Street, Huddersfield HD3 3EA, England.

JACOBS M Kathryne, b. 6 Dec 1941, Wisconsin, USA. Psychologist. div. 1 s. Education: BA, St Mary College; MSLS, Syracuse University; PhD, University of Toledo; Consultant, American Society of Clinical Hypnosis. Appointments: Toledo Hospital, 1977-80; National Institute of Mental Health Study Center, 1980-82; Department of Psychiatry, University of Maryland, 1983-88; Private Practice, Associate Faculty of Johns Hopkins University. Honours: Assistantship, NIH, 1963; NIH Fellowship, 1964-65; HEW Fellowship, 1968-69. Memberships: include, American Psychological Association; District of Columbia Psychological Association; Maryland Psychological Association; Adoption Therapy Coalition; American Professional Society on the Abuse of Children; American Society of Clinical Hypnosis; Association for the Advancement of Psychology; Georgetown University Committee on Psychiatry and Law; International Society of Hypnosis; International Society for Infant Studies; World Association for Infant Mental Health; Society for Clinical and Experimental Hypnosis. Hobbies: Gardening; Yoga; Opera; Riding; Travel. Address: 3811 Newark Street NW, Washington DC 20016, USA.

JACOBSEN Sara Lisa, b. 22 Aug 1966, Cornwall, Canada. Chiropractor. Education: Doctor of Chiropractic, Los Angeles College of Chiropractic, USA. Appointments: Chiropractor. Honours: Dean's List, 1990, 1989; Magna Cum Laude, 1991. Hobbies: Skiing; Swimming; Skating; Aerobics; Sailing. Address: Dalgasgade 58, 7400 Herning, Denmark.

JACOBSON Jacob G, b. 17 Jun 1928, NY, USA. Psychoanalyst. m. Sarah Frye, 6 Jul 1951, 1 s, 2 d. Education: BS; MD, University of MI; Psychiatric Residency at Menninger School of Psychiatry; Psychoanalytic Training at Chicago Institute for Psychoanalysis. Appointments: Psychoanalyst; Clinical Professor of Psychiatry, University of CO Health Sciences Center. Publications: 6 Professional publications, 1960-94, including: The Structural Theory and the Representational World: Developmental and Biological Considerations, in Psychoanalytic Quarterly, 1983; Developmental Observation, Multiple Models of the Mind, and the Therapeutic Relationship, in Psychoanalytic Quarterly, 1993; Signal Affects and Our Psychoanalytic Confusion of Tongues, in Journal of the American Psychoanalytic Association, 1994; Editorial Board, Psychoanalytic Quarterly, 1985-. Memberships: Life Fellow, American Psychiatric Association; Denver Psychoanalytic Society; American Psychoanalytic Association. Address: 1636 16th Street, Boulder, CO 80302, USA.

JACOBSON Sandra, b. 21 Mar 1953, Vancouver, WA, USA. Physician. m. Dr Ronald P Hammer, 5 Dec 1986. Education: BA summa cum laude, Pscychology, University of Hawaii, 1976; MD, University of Hawaii School of Medicine, 1987; Psychiatry Residency, UCLA Neuropsychiatric Institute, 1991; Diplomate in Psychiatry, American Board of Psychiatry and Neurology, 1993. Appointments include: Staff Psychiatrist, UCLA, West Los Angeles VA Medical Center, 1992-93; Assistant Professor, Tufts University School of Medicine, 1993-; Assistant Psychiatrist, New England Medical Center, 1993-; Chief of Clinical Neuroscience, Lemuel Shattuck Hospital, 1993-; Director, EEG Laboratory, Lemuel Shattuck Hospital, 1994-. Publications include: 11 Contributions to professional journals including: Co-author, Psychiatric Care in the Nursing Home, 1994; Co-author, Delirium and Quantitive EEG, 1994; 8 Abstracts, 1987-93; Reviewer for Journal of the American Geriatrics Society, American Journal of Geriatric Psychiatry. Honours: Phi Kappa Phi, 1974; Mortar Board, 1975; Phi Beta Kappa, 1976; Laughlin Fellow, American College of Psychiatrists, 1991; Familian Foundation Research Award, UCLA, 1991. Memberships: American Psychiatric Association, 1986-; Society for Neuroscience, 1991-; West Coast College of Biological Psychiatry, 1991-; American Association for Geriatric Psychaitry, 1991; Massachusetts Psychiatric Society, 1993-. Address: Dept of Psychiatry, Tufts/New England Medical Center, 750 Washington St, Box 1007, Boston, MA 02111, USA.

JAFFE Robert, b. 18 Feb 1933, Detroit, Michigan, USA. Physician, m. Evelyn Grossman, 29 Aug 1954, 1 son, 1 daughter. Education includes: MD, University of Michigan Medical School, 1957; Intern, 1957-58, Postdoctoral Fellow, Endocrinology, 1958-59, Resident, Chief Resident, Obstetrics, Gynaecology, 1959-63, University of Colorado Medical Center; Postdoctoral Fellow, Reproductive Endocrinology, Karolinska Sjukhuset, Stockholm, Sweden, 1963-64; MS, University of Colorado, 1966; Diplomate, American Board of Obstetrics and Gynecology. Appointments: Assistant Professor, 1964-68, Associate Professor, 1968-71, Professor, 1971-73, Obstetrics and Gynaecology, University of Michigan; Professor, Chairman, Department of Obstetrics, Gynaecology and Reproductive Sciences, Director, Reproductive Endocrinology Center, University of California, San Francisco, 1973-; Visiting professorships. Publications include: Over 40 chapters and over 200 journal contributions, mainly in reproductive endocrinology; Reproductive Endocrinology: Physiology, Pathophysiology and Clinical Management (with S S C Yen), textbook, 1978, 3rd edition, 1992; Editor: Hormones in Reproduction, 1967; The endocrine milieu of pregnancy, puerperium and childhood, 1974; Prolactin, 1981; The Endocrine Physiology of Pregnancy and the Peripartal Period (co-editor), 1985. Honours include: Phi Eta Sigma; Alpha Omega Alpha; Sigma Xi; Faculty Fellow, 1966-69, Faculty Scholar, 1980-81, Josiah Macy Jr Foundation; Fred Gellert Chair in Reproductive Medicine and Biology, 1990; MERIT Award, National Institute of Child Health and Human Development, 1993. Memberships include: Institute of Medicine, National Academy of Science; American College of Obstetricians and Gynecologists, Chairman, Division of Endocrinology and Fertility; President, California Academy of Medicine; Perinatal Research Society, Steering Committee, Past President; President, San Francisco Gynecologic Society; Endocrine Society, Council Member, Secretary-Treasurer. Address: Department of Obstetrics and Gynaecology, University of California, San Francisco, CA 94143-0132, USA.

JAFFER Kulsum, b. 16 Aug 1954, Karachi, Pakistan. Medical Doctor. m. Shahid K Gill, 4 Sept 1981, 2 daughters. Education: BSc, MB BS, Karachi University; DObst (Ireland); MRCOG (England); MFFP (England). Appointments: Registrar, Obstetrics and Gynaecology, Lanarkshire Health Authority, Scotland, 1989-90; Currently SCMO, Instructing Doctor, Family Planning, England. Memberships: General Medical Council; Royal College of Obstetricians and Gynaecologists, Faculty of Family Planning and Reproductive Health Care; West Midlands Association of Family Planning Doctors. Hobbies: Reading; Sewing and embroidery. Address: 45 Alderminster Road, Hillfield, Solihull B91 3YT, England.

JAIN Kewal Krishan, b. 7 Dec 1937, Faridkot, India. Neurosurgeon; Consultant. m. Verena Pulver, 26 Sept 1976, 2 sons, 1 daughter. Education: MD; FRCS(C); FRACS; FICS; AFPM. Appointments: Consultant in Neurosurgery, Vancouver, Canada, 1964-74; Professor of Neurosurgery, SCT Postgraduate Medical Center, India, 1975-77, & University of Shiraz, Iran, 1977-78; Research Scientist, GSF Munich, Germany, 1979-80; Chief Neurosurgeon, Letterman Army Medical Center, San Francisco; US Army, 1979-83; Research Neurosurgeon, UCLA Los Angeles, 1981-86; Visiting Professor, Universities of Bonn & Dusseldorf, Germany; Consultant, Fachklinik Klausenbach, Germany, 1986-89; Consultant, Neurosurgery & Biotechnology, Basel, Switzerland, 1989-. Publications: 10 books including, Handbook of Laser Neurosurgery, 1995; Drug-induced Neurological Disorders, 1995; DNA Diagnostics, 1995; Gene Therapy, 1995. Memberships: International College of Surgeons; Association of Military Surgeons, USA; American College of Hyperbaric Medicine; Faculty of Pharmaceutical Medicine, England. Hobbies: Photography; Skiing; Middle-Distance Running. Address: Schwandstrasse 56, CH-6390 Engelberg, Switzerland.

JAIN Pramod Kumar, b. 12 Dec 1952, Nanauta, Saharanpur, UP, India. Physician; Nephrologist. m. Alka Jain, 31 Oct 1979, 1 s, 1 d. Education: MBBS; MD, Medicine; MNAMS, Medicine. Appointments: Senior Resident, Medicine, PGIMER, Chandigarh, India; Lecturer in Medicine, MLB Medical College, Jhansi, UP, India; Visiting Professor, Missouri University, Columbia, USA; Visiting Physician, Harvard Medical School, Boston, USA. Publications: 19 contributions in professional journals including: Co-author, Perinatal Outcome in Hypertensive Disorders of Pregnancy, 1991; Review Article, Continous Ambulatory Peritoneal Dialysis, in Medicine Update, 1993; Current Dialysis Techniques in Management of Renal Failure, in Journal of Internal Medicine, 1993. Honours include: Chancellor's Medal, Best Medical Student of Meerut University, 1974; Gold Medal, Best Performance in MD, Meerut University, 1979; MNAMS, General Medicine, National

Academy of Medical Science, 1981; Ghosh Oration Award, Indian Medical Association, 1983; Partial Air Travel Grants, Department of Science and Technology, Government of India, 1986, 1990. Memberships: Life Member, API, India; Indian Society of Nephrology; Indian Medical Association; Indian Academy of Medical Education; International Society of Nephrology; Asian Pacific Society of Nephrology. Hobbies: Reading Magazines; Indian Classical Music. Address: Dialysis Unit, MLB Medical College, Jhansi UP, India.

JAIN S K, b. 4 July 1949, Banda, India. Biomedical Scientist. m. Kamal Jain, 5 June 1974, 2 sons. Education: BSc, 1967; MSc, 1969; PhD, 1974. Appointments: Research Associate, Tufts Medical School, Boston; Research Associate, Harvard Medical School, Boston; Senior Scientist, National Institute of Immunology, New Delhi. Publications: Over 70 professional publications in scientific journals. Honours: Merit Scholarships, 1958-64; National Science Talent Search Scholarship, 1964-74; Consultant, WHO, 1987, 1989; Consultant, US-AID, 1991; Visiting Professor, Catholic University, Rome, 1992-93. Memberships include: Fellow, Academy of Zoology. Hobbies: Reading; Literature; Light Music; Chess. Address: Department of Biochemistry, Hamdard University, New Delhi 110062, India.

JALALI Behnaz, b. 26 Jan 1944, Iran. Psychiatrist. m. Mehrdad Jalali, 18 Sept 1968. Education: MD, 1968; Residency in Psychiatry, University of Maryland Hospital, USA, 1970-73; Board certifications: Psychiatry and Neurology, 1977; Addiction Psychiatry, 1993. Appointments: Assistant Professor of Psychiatry, Rutgers University Medical School, USA, 1973-76; Assistant Professor of Psychiatry, Yale University School of Medicine, 1976-81; Director, Family Therapy Unit, 1976-85, Associate Professor of Psychiatry, 1981-85, Department of Psychiatry, Yale University; Associate Clinical Professor of Psychiatry, 1985-94, Clinical Professor of Psychiatry, 1994-, University of California Los Angeles School of Medicine. Publications: Attitudes Towards Mental Illness, Its Relation to Contact and Ethnocultural Background, 1978; Book chapters: Iranian Families, 1982; Ethnicity: Cultural Adjustment and Behavior, 1988. Honours: Fellow: American Association for Social Psychiatry; American Orthopsychiatric Association, 1980; American Psychiatric Association, 1994. Memberships include: American Family Therapy Association; World Federation for Mental Health. Hobbies: Photography; Hiking; Cinema; Psychiatry; Painting. Address: 11301 Wilshire Boulevard, Los Angeles, CA 90073, USA.

JALNAWALLA Sarosh Framroze, b. 22 Feb 1925, Indore, India. Obstetrician and Gynaecologist. m. Mr Framroze Jalnawalla, 28 Dec 1965, 1 d. Education: MBBS, Lady Hardinge Medical College, Delhi, India; DRCOG, MRCOG, FRCOG, London. Career: RMO, Victoria Lanana Hospital, New Delhi; Obstetrician and Gynaecologist, Irwin Hospital and Safdarjung Hospital, New Delhi; Professor, Obstetrics and Gynaecology, University College of Medical Sciences, New Delhi; Currently, Consultant in Obstetrics and Gynaecology. Publications: Many articles to Indian Medical Journal, Journal of Obstetrics and Gynaecology, India, and Women's Medical Journal, India. Memberships: Fellow, Royal College of Obstetrics and Gynaecology; Federation of Obstetricians and Gynaecologists of India; Association of Medical Women. Address: 8 Clematis Gardens, 12-A Boat Club Road, Pune 411001, India.

JAMEEL Aliuthuma L M, b. 25 Dec 1939. Obstetrician; Gynaecologist. m. Haseena Rinzine Mustapha, 19 Apr 1968, 2 s, 2 d. Education: MBBS, Ceylon, 1965; Diploma Obstetrics; RCOG, UK, 1974; MRCOG, UK, 1978; FRCOG, 1995. Appointments: Resident Obstetrician, Ratnapura Hospital, 1978; Obstetrician and Gynaecologist, Consultant, Central Hospital, Kalmunai, 1979-88; Consultant Obstetrician and Gynaecologist, Taif Maternity and Childrens Hospital, Taif, Saudi Arabia, 1988-92; Currently, Managing Medical Director, Central Hospital, Kalmunai, Sri Lanka. Memberships: International College of Surgeons, USA; Council Member, Sri Lanka Medical Association; Sri Lanka College of Obstetricians and Gynaecologists; College of General Practitioners of Sri Lanka. Hobbies: Badminton; Politics; Gardening. Address: Villa Rinzine, Cassim Road, Kalmunai 6 E P, Sri Lanka.

JAMES David Edward, b. 31 July 1937, Oxford, England. University Teacher. m. Penelope Jane Murray, 30 Mar 1963, 2 sons, 1 daughter. Education: BSc, Reading, 1960; DipEd, Oxon, 1961; Diploma of Further Education, London, 1967; MEd Durham, 1968. Appointments: Lecturer, Zoology & Psychology, City of Bath Technical College, 1961-63; Lecturer, Science & Psychology, St Marys College, Newcastle-on-Tyne,

1963-64; Lecturer, Educational Psychology, University of Surrey, 1964-69; Director of Adult Education 1969-80, Professor, Head, Department of Educational Studies, 1981-93. Publications: A Students Guide to Efficient Study, 1966; Introduction to Psychology for Teachers, Nurses and Other Social Workers, 1968, 1969. Memberships: MIBiol, CBiol; AFBPsS, CPsychol; FRSA; FRSH; FIPD. Hobbies: Writing; Farming. Address: Department of Educational Studies, University of Surrey, Guildford, Surrey GU2 5XH, England.

JAMES J(ames) Frank(lin), b. 2 Sep 1937, NC, USA. Physician; Psychiatrist. 5 D. Education: BA, Comparative Literature, University of NC; MD, University of TN. Appointments: Senior Flight Surgeon, CVS G33, Vietnam, 1965-66; Resident in Psychiatry, University of NC, Duke, 1967-70; Superintendant, Cherry Hospital, NC, 1970-71; Mental Health Program Chief, Fresno County, CA, 1971-78; State Director, Mental Health, OK; Professor of Psychiatry, University of OK, 1989-89; Currently, Professor and Chairman, Department of Psychiatry, East Carolina University School of Medicine. Publications: Many professional articles including: Does the Community Mental Health Movement Have the Momentum Needed to Survive?, in American Journal Orthopsychiatry, 1987; Confronting Psychiatric Problems and Issues in Rural Areas, in North Carolina Medical Journal, 1993. Honours: Fellow; American Psychiatric Association; American College of Psychiatry; American College of Mental Health Administration; Royal College of Health; Founding Fellow, American Geriatric Association; Diplomat, American College of Healthcare Executives; Citizen of Year, State of OK, 1981; APA Gold Award, 1984; Regents-Kellog Fellow, 1988; Distinguished Service Award, National Alliance for the Mentally Ill, 1989; Citation for Contributions to the State, OK, 1989; Exemplary Program Award, 1993, Nany Roeske Award for Teaching Excellence, American Psychiatric Association, 1994. Address: Dept of Psychiatry, School of Medicine, East Carolina University, Greenville, NC 27858, USA.

JAMES Richard Clark, b. 25 Oct 1948, York, England. Holistic Medicine; Acupuncture; Psychotherapy. m. Marie Dewhurst, 20 Oct 1982, 1 s, 1 d. Education: BSc, Physiology, Royal Veteninary College, London, 1971; MBBS, University College Hospital Medical School, 1976; MBAAR;Licentiate, Acupuncture, British College of Acupuncture, 1976; Diploma in Humanistic Psychology, Institute for Development of Human Potential, 1983. Appointments: House Physician, UCH, St Pancras Hospital, 1977; House Surgeon, Whittington Hospital, 1978; Assistant in General Practice, Limes Grove, London, 1979-81; Director of Teaching Clinic, British College of Acupuncture, 1981-83; Founder, Director, Isis Centre for Holistic Health, 1982-; Freelance Teacher; Currently, Private Practice of Holistic Medicine, Acupuncture and Psychotherapy. Publication: Co-author, Medicine for Beginners, 1984. Honours: Honorary Fellow, College of Osteopaths, 1989. Memberships: British Acupuncture Association and Register; British Medical Acupuncture Society; British Holistic Medical Association; Scientific, Medical Network; Doctor, Healer Network. Hobby: Organic Gardening. Address: All Hallows House, Idol Lane, London, EC3R 5DD, England.

JANCO Orit, b. 23 July 1962, Montreal, Quebec, Canada. Dance and Movement Therapist. Education: BA, McGill University; MA, Dance and Movement Therapy, minor Counselling Psychology, Antioch Graduate School, Keene, New Hampshire, USA. Appointments: Movement Therapist, Clinical Coordinator, Outpatient Pain Programme, New England Rehabilitation Hospital, Woburn, Massachusetts, USA; Consultant, Pain Management Programme, Harvard Community Health Plan, Boston, Massachusetts. Publications: Healing in Water: Dance Movement Therapy in Water with the Chronic Pain Population, thesis, unpublished. Membership: American Dance Therapy Association. Hobbies: Travel; Hiking; Theatre; Swimming; Recycling; Foreign languages. Address: 79 Fountain Street, West Newton, MA 02165, USA.

JANECKA Ivo Peter, b. 25 Jan 1943, Hranice, Czechoslovakia. Surgeon. m. Cheryl Janecka, 26 Apr 1985, 2 sons, 1 daughter. Education: MD. Appointments: Associate Professor, University of Pittsburgh School of Medicine, 1986-93. Professor of Otolaryngology, University of Pittsburgh, 1993-. Publications: Include: Cytology of cerebrospinal fluid, 1965; Vibratory patterns observed in real time by interferometric holography, 1969; Fetal mediastinitis following retropharyngeal abscess, 1971; Facial Translocation Approach to the Cranial Base: The Anatomic Basis, 1991; Integrity of Facial Function: Its Preservation and Repair, 1991; Computerized Tomography and Magnetic Resonance Imaging Following Cranial Base Surgery, 1991; Brachytherapy for Malignances Involving the Base of the Skull, 1993; Transfacial Approaches to the Clivus and Upper Cervical Spine, 1993;

Efficacy of surgical treatments for squamous cell carcinoma of the temporal bone: A literature review, 1994. Memberships: Include: American Society of Clinical Oncology; Association for Research in Otolaryngology; Plastic Surgery Research Council; The Society of Head & Neck Surgeons; The Triological Society. Honours: Include: Deficit Reduction Award, 1989; Outstanding Medical Specialist in the US, 1989; Physician's Recognition Award, American Medical Association, 1991. Address: 203 Lothrop Street, Suite 500, Department of Otolaryngology, Pittsburgh, PA 15213, USA.

JANSEN Cornelis Antonius Maria, b. 29 Mar 1948, Uithoorn, Netherlands. Gynaecologist. Education: MD, University of Leiden; Phd, Cum Laude, IBID. Appointments: Gynaecologist; Head of IVF and ART Clinic. Publications: 140 Articles in National and International Literature. Memberships: include, European Society of Human Reproduction and Embryology; American Fertility Society; Dutch Society of Obstetrics and Gynaecology. Address: Huize Eik en Del, Van der Oudermeulenlaan 6, 2243 CS Wassenaar, The Nederlands.

JANSEN Erik Christian, b. 10 Nov 1943, Copenhagen, Denmark. Anaesthesiologist. m. Birgit Rügge, 9 May 1974, 1 son, 2 daughters. Education: MD, University of Copenhagen, 1972; Specialist in Anaesthesiology, 1981; Doctor of Medical Science, University of Copenhagen, 1988. Appointments: Resident in Anaesthesia, Surgery & Intensive Medicine, 1972-80, Senior Resident, 1980-89 at Copenhagen Hospitals; Acting Chief Anaesthesiologist, Herlev Hospital, 1984-85, National University Hospital, 1988-89; Chief Anaesthesiologist, National University Hospital, 1989-. Publications: Oxygen and carbon dioxide in long bones, 1979; Postural stability after diazepam, 1985; Analysis of gait and postural stability, 1988; Invesitgation on spelling aids for physically and mentally handicapped, 1992. Memberships: Vice Chairman, Medical Board for Outer Copenhagen Hospitals, 1974-76; Secretary, Danish Association for Transplantation, 1991-94; Chief, National Anaesthesiologists Specialists Training, 1988-92; Examiner, European Academy of Anaesthesiology, 1993-. Honours: Guest Lecturer, Dundee, 1976; Hafnia Award, 1972, 1974; Guildal Award, 1978, 1988; Lykfelts Award, 1987. Hobbies: Artic Exploration; Sailing. Address: Department of Anaesthesia, AN 2034, National University Hospital, DK-2100 Copenhagen, Denmark. 52. 139.

JASPARS-RAVENSWAAY Bertha Johanna, b. 15 May 1934, Balik Papan, Borneo. m. J M F Jaspars, 22 June 1962, 1 son, 1 daughter. Education: BA, 1957; MA, 1961. Appointments: Child Guidance Clinic, Netherlands, 1958-62; Child Psychiatry Clinic, Netherlands, 1965-69; Psychologist, Residential School for Disturbed Children, 1970-77; Educational Psychologist, Counselor, 1983-. Publications: A functional theory of attribution, some clinical applications, 1981; Commonsense and education, 1984; Cognitive processes and everyday explanations, 1986; Instrumental Enrichment Evaluation, 1986. Memberships: British Psychological Society; Interdisciplinary Society of Biological Psychiatry. Hobbies: Gardening; Swimming; Bridge. Address: 52 Salisbury Crescent, Oxford OX2 7TL, England.

JASZKOWSKI Donna M, b. 29 Dec 1953, Chicago, Illinois, USA. Doctor of Optometry. Education: AA; BS; OD. Appointments: Past Secretary of TAO; Self-Employed. Honours: Personally Collected RSO in a March of Dimes Walkathon. Memberships: HCOS; TOA. Hobbies: Snow & Water Skiing; Movies; Travel; Sight Seeing. Address: 7835 Vickijohn Drive, Houston, TX 77071, USA.

JAVID Manucher J, b. 11 Jan 1922, Tehran, Iran. Neurosurgeon. m. Lida Emma Fabbri, 19 Oct 1951, 1 s, 3 d. Education: MD, University of IL College of Medicine, Chicago, IL. Appointment: Professor and Chairman, Department of Neurosurgery, University of WI, Madison. Publications: Over 80 professional articles published. Honours: Alumnus of Year for Service to Research and Education, University of IL Medical Alumni Association, 1983; Distinguished Alumnus Award, MA General Hospital, 1989; Introduced the use of osmotic agents in Neurosurgery. Memberships: 20 Medical and Scientific Societies. Hobbies: Study of world religions especially Christianity, Islam, and the Baha'i Faith. Address: Dept of Neurological Surgery, University of Wisconsin Hospital, Madison, WI 53792-3232, USA.

JAYASINGHE Jayasinghe Mudiyanselage Ananda Chandra, b. 22 Jan 1953, Negombo, Sri Lanka. Medical Physicist. m. W R Nandawathie, 26 Aug 1987, 2 sons. Education: BSc, University of Colombo, 1974; Master's degree in Biomedical Engineering, University of New South Wales, Australia, 1984. Appointments: Currently Medical

Physicist, Nuclear Imaging Unit, General Hospital, Colombo. Publications: Master's Biomedical Engineering thesis, 1984; Artefact Reduction in dual-radionuclide Subtraction Studies (co-author), 1987. Memberships: Associate Member, Australasian College of Physical Scientists and Engineers in Medicine; International Organisation of Medical Physicists. Hobbies: Studying Sri Lankan history; Computer literacy. Address: Nuclear Imaging Unit, Department of Radiology, General Hospital, Colombo 10, Sri Lanka.

JAYASUNDERE Harischandra D, b. 12 Nov 1938, Sri Lanka. Obstetrician and Gynaecologist. m. Surangani P Weerakkody, 14 Sep 1972, 1 s. Education: MBBS(Cey); D Obs R COG(Eng); FRCOG(Eng); FSLCOG. Appointment: Consultant Obstetrician and Gynaecologist. Memberships: Royal College of Obstetrics and Gynaecology, UK; Sri Lanka College of Obstetricians and Gynaecologists; Independant Medical Practitioners Association. Hobbies: Golf; Photography. Address: 435A Havelock Road, Colombo 6, Sri Lanka.

JAYATILAKA George Kingsley, b. 21 Dec 1941, Kuala Lumpur, Malaysia. General Practitioner. m. Shalinee Abayasekara, 26 Jan 1971, 2 daughters. Education: MBBS, University of Ceylon, 1970; MRCOG, 1984. Appointments: Currently General Practitioner, England. Membership: Royal College of Obstetricians and Gynaecologists. Hobby: Stamp collecting. Address: 16 Wansfell Gardens, Thorpe Bay, Nr Southend-on-Sea, Essex SS1 3SW, England.

JELKS Mary L, b. 23 May 1929, Glava, Illinois, USA. Pediatric Allergy. m. Allen N Jelks MD, 16 Jun 1957, 2 s, 2 d. Education: BA, Cum Laude, University of Nebraska; MD, University of Nebraska. Appointments: Aerobiology Research. Publications: Allergy Plants that Cause Wheezing & Sneezing. Memberships: American Association of Allergy & Immunology; American Medical Association; Sigma Xi; FAIS. Hobbies: Plants; Environemtnal Work Horse. Address: 1930 Clematis Street, Sarasota, FL 34239 3813, USA.

JENISTA Jerri Ann, b. 18 May 1952, Florida, USA. Medical Doctor. 4 d. Education: BA, DePaul University, 1973; MS, University of Rochester, 1983; MD, University of Chicago, 1977; Pediatric Residency, University of Colorado, 1977-80; General Academic Pediatric Fellowship, University of Rochester, 1980-82; Pediatric Infectious Disease Fellowship, University of Rochester, 1982-83. Appointments: Assistant Professor, Pediatric Infectious Diseases, University of Michigan, 1983-92; Pediatrician, St Joseph Mercy Hospital, Ann Arbor, Michigan, 1992-. Publications: Medical Problems of Foreign-Born Adopted, 1987; Infectious Diseases & Internationally Adopted Children. Memberships: Ambulatory Pediatric Association; American Academy of Pediatrics; Pediatric Infectious Diseases Society; Society for International Traveler Health. Hobbies: Writing; Travel. Address: 551 Second Street, Ann Arbor, MI 48103, USA.

JENKINS David John Anthony, b. 20 Jul 1942, London, England. Professor. m. Alexandra Jenkins, 2 d. Education: BA, Animal Physiology, 1965, MA, 1970, BMBCh, 1971, DPhil, 1975, DM, 1976, DSc, 1988, Oxford University; PhD. Appointment: Professor, Nutritional Sciences and Medicine, University of Toronto, Canada. Publications include: Over 160 original papers including: Co-author, Glycemic index of 102 complex carbohydrate foods in patients with diabetes, in Nutr Res, 1994; Over 50 abstracts including: Co-author, Effect of fiber-rich foods on the composition of human intestinal microflora, CFBS, 1993; Over 85 chapters and reviews including: Co-author, Diet factors affecting nutrient absorption and metabolism, in Modern Nutrition in Health and Disease, 8th edition, 1993. Honours: Borden Award, Nutrition Society of Canada, 1983; Goldsmith Award for Clinical Research, American College of Nutrition, 1985. Memberships include: Canadian Medical Protective Association, 1982-; College of Physicians and Surgeons of Ontario, 1982-; American Society of Clinical Nutrition, 1984-; American College of Nutrition, 1985-; Nutrition Society, London, England, 1985-; Canadian Atherosclerosis Society, 1987-; Ontario Medical Association, 1989-; General Medical Council, 1991-; GI Journal Club, Toronto Hospital, 1992-. Hobbies: Museums; Art; Politics. Address: Department of Nutritional Sciences, Faculty of Medicine, University of Toronto, Ontario, Canada, M5S 1A8.

JENNISON Kathleen Mary, b. 1 Oct 1944, Carlisle, England, Medical Practitioner. Education: MB BS; FRCOG; FRCP(Glasgow). Appointments: Cnsultant Obstetrician and Gynaecologist. Memberships: BMA; Fellow, Royal Society of Medicine. Address: 'Brambles', 10a The Groved, Hartford, Huntingdon, Cambridgeshire PE18 7YD, England.

JENRETTE Joseph M, b. 24 Feb 1951, Raleigh, North Carolina, USA. Radiation Oncologist. m. Elizabeth G Chandler, 14 Aug 1976, 1 son, 1 daughter. Education: BA, University of North Carolina, 1973; MD, Medical University of South Carolina, 1979. Appointments: Chief Resident, Instructor, Assistant Professor, Radiation Oncology, Medical University of South Carolina. Publications: Role of Radiosurgery in Primary Prostate Cancer, 1994. Memberships: American Medical Association; South Carolina Medical Association; International Radiosurgery Society; American Society of Therapeutic Radiologists. Hobbies: Swimming; Reading. Address: 171 Ashley Avenue, Charleston, SC 29425, USA.

JENSEN Knud, b. 12 Jul 1932, Bramminge, Denmark. Psychiatrist; Neurologist. m. 1985, 2 d. Education: MD; PhD; Doctor of Medical Science. Appointments: Consultant, Institute for Neurochemistry & Psychopharmacology, State Mental Hospital, Aarhus, 1961-77; Consultant in Neurochemistry, Odense University Hospital, 1971-77; Psychiatric Consultant, State Prison, Sobysogaard, 1971-; Psychiatric Consultant, Department for Rehibilitation of Criminals in Odense, 1978-; Psychiatric Consultant, Psychiatric Rehabilitation Workshop, Odense, 1970-77; Psychiatric Consultant, Rehabilitation & Pension Board for Funen County Council, 1976-91; Junior Consultant, Odense University Hospital, 1970-75; Consultant to Geriatric Departments and Care Homes in Odense Municipality, 1970-77; Acting Consultant, Department of Neurology, Odense University Hospital, 1971-72; Senior Consultant, Department of Psychiatry, Odense University Hospital, 1975-; Administrative Head, Department of Psychiatry, Odense University Hospital, 1979-83, 1986-91. Publications: Commitment and Civil Right of the Mentally Ill, 1985; Mental Disorders and Cognitive Deficits in Multiple Sclerosis, 1989; Mental Disorders in Aged, 1995; Cerebrospinal Fluid Proteins in Neurological Diseases, 1978. Honours: Vice President, World Federation for Mental Health; Advisor for WHO on Mental Health Legislation. Memberships: World Federation for Mental Health; Danish Psychiatric Society. Address: Department of Psychiatry, Odense University Hospital, DK-5000 Odense C, Denmark.

JERABEK Jaroslav, b. 19 Dec 1951, Prague, Czechoslovakia. Neurologist. m. Alena Pathová, 18 Sep 1975, 2 d. Education: MD; PhD. Appointment: Assistant Professor, Neurology, 2nd Medical School, Charles University, Prague. Publications: Oculomotor Disorders, film, 1987; Co-author, The influence of sports load on the central nervous system, monograph, 1988; The Oculomotor and Vestibular Findings in Specific Developmental Dyslexia, 1989; Co-author, Decision making in neurology and child neurology, 1993. Honours: IREX Grant, 1987; Award of Czech Neurologic Society, 1988. Memberships: International Academy for Research in Learning Disabilities; Bárány Society; Czech Neurologic Society. Hobbies: Literature; Hiking; Cross Country Skiing. Address: Patockova 1707-101, 169 00 Prague 6, Czechoslovakia.

JEREB Berta, b. 25 May 1925, Dravograd, Slovenia. Radiation Oncologist. m. Marjan Jereb, 28 Sept 1961, 1 son, 1 daughter. Education: PhD. Appointments: Radiotherapist, The Institute of Oncology, Ljubljana, 1950-61, 1984-; Radiumhemmet Karolinska Sjukhuset, Stockholm, Sweden, 1961-73; Sloan Kettering Cancer Center, New York, USA, 1974-84. Publications: About 150 publications and chapters in 5 books. Memberships: International Society of Pediatric Oncology; Childrens Cancer Study Group; American Association of Radiation Oncology. Address: Slovenska 9 a, 61000 Ljubljana, Slovenia.

JI Shu Rong, b. 29 May 1942, Harbin, China. Rehabilitation and Paediatric Orthopaedic Surgeon. m. Zhang Yun Chen, 1 Oct 1967, 2 sons. Education: MM; Postgraduate Course, Beijing Institute of Traumatology and Orthopaedics; Individual training, Rehabilitation and Paediatric Orthopaedic Surgery, Japan. Appointments: Paediatric Orthopaedic Surgeon, 3rd Affiliated Hospital, China Medical University, 1965-79; Orthopaedic and Microsurgeon, Beijing Jishuitan Hospital, 1979-82; Paediatric Orthopaedic Surgeon, 3rd Affiliated Hospital, China Medical University, 1982-86; R&O Professor, CRRC, 1986-95. Publications: Free Transplantation of Venous Network Pattern Skin Flap. An Experimental Study in Rabbits, 1984; Acute Epiphyseal Osteomyelitis in Infants: A Report of 25 Cases, 1985; Post-Operative Redislocation in CDH, 1987; Rehabilitation Management Procedure for Paraplegia Patient in Hospital, 1991; Contributor of over 40 articles. Honours: 2nd Science Prize, Beijing Health Bureau, 1988; 2nd Science Prize, Liaoning Province, 1990; Government Prize, 1992; Memberships: Chinese Medical Association; Chinese Rehabilitation Association; Hobbies: Table Tennis; Skating; Dance; Singing. Address: Beijing, China.

JIA Fuzhong, b. 30 Jan 1934, Changzhou, Jiangsu, China. Physician. m. 1 Jan 1959, 1 son, 1 daughter. Education: MD; Master's degree, Faculty of Infectious Disease, Nanjing Medical College. Appointments: Physician-in-charge, First Teaching Hospital, Beijing Medical University, 1957-62; Lecturer, 1962-80, Associate Professor, 1980-82, currently Physician-in-charge, First Affiliated Hospital of Nanjing Medical College. Publications: Concanaval in A-induced Suppressor Activity, 1983; Disease of the Liver and Biliary System, book, 1984; Preliminary Evaluation on Variation of Serum ADA Lever in Patients with EHF, 1989. Honours: Praised for Outstanding Contribution to the Medicine and Health Cause, State Council. Memberships: Vice Director, Jiangsu Branch, Chinese Medical Association of Infectious Disease; Vice Director, Jiangsu Province Collaborating Group for Viral Hepatitis Prevention and Therapy; Committee Member, Chinese Medical Association of Infection and Parasitic Disease; Committee Member, International Research and Exchange Center for Liver Disease; Standing Committee, Chinese Society of Nosocomiology. Hobby: Music. Address: 300 Guangzhou Road, Nanjing 210029, China.

JIA Jing-Tao, b. 27 Aug 1927, Liaoyang, China. Professor of Forensic Medicine. m. Qing-Yu Wang, 9 May 1954, 1 son, 2 daughters. Education: BA, China Medical University, 1950; Tutor of Dr Med, 1986. Appointments include: Professor of Forensic Medicine, Department of Forensic Medicine, China Medical University; Director, Professor, Faculty of Forensic Medicine, China Medical University; Currently Honorary Dean, Faculty of Forensic Medicine, China Medical University, Shenyang. Publications: Ancient history of forensic medicine in China, 1984; Forensic Blood Group Serology, 1988; Chief author: Introduction to Forensic Medicine, 1988; Forensic Anthropology, 1993. Honours: Science and Technical Award, Ministry of Public Health, 1988; Science and Technical Award, Liaoning Province, 1989, 1991; Education Achievement Award, Liaoning Province, 1989, 1993. Memberships: China Association of Forensic Medicine; China Association of Medicine; China Health Law Society. Hobby: Swimming. Address: Chinese Medical University, Faculty of Forensic Medicine, 92 North 2nd Avenue, Heping Qu, Shenyang 110001, China.

JIA Kedong, b. 29 June 1963, Shandong, China. Physicia. m. Liu Hongjie, 22 Jan 1989, 1 s. Education: BA, Qingdao Medical College, Shandong, 1986; MD, Shandong Academy of Medical Science, 1993. Appointments: Assistant Professor. Publications: Detection of Giardia Lamblia Specific Antigen in Stool Samples by Dot Immunobinding Assy, 1994; Study on the Effect of Monoclonal Antibodies on Giardia Lamblia in Vitro, 1994. Hobby: Dancing. Address: Shandong Institute of Parasitic Diseases, Jining 272133, China.

JIA Siguang, b. 9 Jan 1924, Beijing, China. Professor of Aerospace Medicine. m. 9 Jan 1945, 1 son, 1 daughter. Education: PhD, Leningrad Academy of Military Medicine. Appointments: Director of Research Department, Institute of Aerospace Medicine, 1960; Chief of Science & Technology Commission, Institute of Space Medico-Engineering, 1983. Publications: The basic characteristics of functional ECG, 1985; Aerospace Hypoxia and Oxygen Supply - Physiology and Protective Equipment, 1989. Honours: State Award for Scientific & Technological Progress, 1985; State Prize, Outstanding Contributions in Research Work, 1991. Memberships: Vice Director, Specialized Commission of Ergonomics, Aviation Medicine & Rescue; Corresponding Member, International Academy of Astronautics. Address: PO Box 5104, Beijing 100094, China.

JIA Yu-chen, b. 14 Aug 1023, Henan Province, China. Professor. m. Zhang Shu-xiu, 20 Nov 1952, 1 son, 3 daughters. Education: National Defence Medical College, Shanghai, 1944-50; Second Military Medical University, Shanghai. Appointments: Assistant Resident Doctor, 1950; Visiting Doctor and Lecturer, 1957; Vice Director and Associate Professor, 1979; Professor, 1986-, Member of Expert group, 1988-, Consultant of Radiology, Changhai Hospital. Publications: Author of over 10 books including: Roentgenologic Atlas of Bone Tumor, 1979; Radiology of Syndromes, 1981; Comparative Study on Therapeutic Effects of TACE and TAI for HCC, 1992; Contributor of over 90 scientific papers, 1951-94. Honour: Outstanding Professor in Radiology, 1994. Memberships: Vice Chairman, Shanghai Interventional Radiology Society, 1990; Editorial Committee or Consultant: JCR, 1982, Journal of Interventional Radiology, 1992, Journal of Hepatobiliary Surgery, 1993; Committeeman, Chinese Oncological Society; Huaming (Sino-Japan) Cancer Pharmaceutical Research Society. Hobbies: Reading; Classical Music. Address: Changhai Hospital, 174 Changhai Road, Shanghai 200433, China.

JIANG Ci-Peng, b. 2 May 1933, Xiang-Xiang, Hunan Province, China. Researcher; Teacher of Masters Students. m. Hou Jia-Zhu, 26 Sept 1965, 2 d. Education: Hunan Medical University, China, 1951-56. Appointments: Lecturer & Associate Professor of Surgery, 1st Affiliated Hospital of Lanzhou Medical College, 1956-74; Professor of Parasitology, Lanzhou Medical College, 1975-89; Professor/Vice-Dean of Hunan Medical College, 1990-92; Professor/Director of Parasitology, Lanzhou Medical College, 1993-. Publications: Books, Echinococcus and Hydatid Disease, 1994; Co-Author, Clinical Hepatology, 1985; Co-Author, Chemotherapy of Parasitosis, 1988; Co-Author, Animal Models of Human Diseases, 1990; Co-Author, The Chinese Great Encyclopedia, 1993; Articles, Liver Alveolar Echinococcosis in the Northwest of China, 1981; Research on the Proliferation and Growth of Human Echinococcus, 1987; Experimental Studies of Echinococcus on White Mice, 1984. Honours: International Miguel-Benzo Extraordinary Prize Awarded at XIII International Hydatidology Congress in Spain, 1985; The 3rd Chinese Natural Science Prize Awarded in Beijing, 1988; Outstanding Expert of the National Degree Awarded by Chinese Government in Beijing, 1991. Memberships: International Hydatidology Association; World Association for the Advancement of Veterinary Parasitology; WHO International Working Group on Echinococcusis; Chinese Medical Association. Hobbies: Music; Football Match's; Photography. Address: Hydatid Research Laboratory, Lanzhou Medical College, Lanzhou, Gansu 73000, China.

JIANG Dan, b. 8 June 1952, Xi'an, China. Physician (Traditional Chinese Medicine); Physiotherapist. m. Hang Li, 25 May 1981, 1 daughter. Education: Graduated with Diploma, 1978, MMedSci, 1987, Beijing University of Traditional Chinese Medicine. Appointments: Nurse, 1969-75, Consultant, 1978-91, 1st Affiliated Hospital, Beijing University of Traditional Chinese Medicine, 1969-75; Lecturer, Beijing University of Traditional Chinese Medicine, 1978-91; Practitioner, Chinese Herbs and Acupuncture, Sheffield Clinic of Complementary Medicine, Sheffield, England, 1991-. Publications: The Effective and Proved Prescriptions of Contemporary Traditional Chinese Medicine (co-chief author), 1989; Essence of Medical Qi-gong (editor), 1990; The Main Points of Medical Massage for Baby and Child, 1991; ECIWO Biology Theory on ME Syndrome Diagnosed and Treated with Auricular Points, 1992; Analysis of 50 Cases of ME Treated with Chinese Herbs and Acupuncture, 1993; More than 10 articles including: The Clinical and Testing Research for 100 Cases of Cerebral Paralysis in Children Cured by Massage, 1989. Memberships: British Acupuncture Association; Fellowship: Association of Traditional Chinese Medicine, UK. Hobbies: Running; Swimming; Dance. Address: 378 Ecclesall Road, Sheffield S11 8PJ, England.

JIANG De Sheng, b. 18 June 1934, Ningbo, China. Professor of Medicine. m. Lin Pei Qin, 26 December 1960, 1 son, 1 daughter. Education: Ningbo Medical College, 1960. Appointments: Attending Doctor, 1978; Chief Physician, 1987; Head, Medical Department. Publications: A Clinical Study on the Bacillary Abscess of Liver, 1966; Endoscopic Manifestations of Peptic Ulcer, 1980; AGML Induced in 27 Young Students after an Examination Stress, 1981; NUD and Emotional Disorder, 1992; Athletic Stress Peptic Ulcer, 1992; Relationship between Episode of Peptic Ulcer and Climate, 1993. Memberships: China Medical Association; Chinese Anticancer Association. Hobbies: Photography; Fishing. Address: Ningbo The First Hospital, Ningbo 315010, China.

JIANG Deyong, b. 16 Dec 1945, Yantai, Shangdong, China. Ophthalmology. m. Hui Yan, 4 Oct 1972, 1 s. Education: BA, 1967, MD, 1982, Hunan Medical University China. Career: House Physician, 1967-69, House Surgeon, 1970-72, Resident in Ophthalmology, 1973-79, Visiting Doctor, Ophthalmology, 1980-86, Associate Professor, 1987-90, Professor, Ophthalmology, 1991-, Director of Department of Ophthalmology. Publications include: Effect of Panx Notoginsong and Tetrandine on Experimental Proliferative Vitreoretinopathy, in Chinese Journal of Ophthalmology, 1994; Retinal Disease, Vitreous Disease, in Ophthalmic Pathology, 1994; Co-Editor in Chief, Ophthalmic Surgery, 1994. Memberships: Vice Chairman, Hunan Society of Ophthalmology; Chinese Association of Ophthalmology; Chinese Association of Ophthalmic Pathology; Association of Ocular Fundus Disease. Hobbies: Table Tennis; Er-Hu (chinese violin). Address: Department of Ophthalmology, 2nd Affiliated Hospital, Hunan Medical University, Changsha Hunan 410011, China.

JIANG Dezhao, b. 24 Mar 1938, Hunan, China. Teacher. m. Juncheng Li, 1 Jan 1965, 1 son, 1 daughter. Career: Assistant, 1961; Lecturer, 1978; Associate Professor, 1985; Professor, 1992; Professor,

Director of Blood Physiology, Hunan Medical University, at present. Publications: An Age-related Reduction in the Replicative Capacity of Two Murine Hematopoietic Stromal Cell Types, 1992. Honours: 2nd Prize, Public Health Ministry for Prominent Science & Technique Accomplishment, 1985; 4th Prize, Hunan Public Health Bureau for Science & Technique Accomplishment, 1985. Memberships: Chinese Association of Physiological Sciences; Chinese Association of Pathophysiological Sciences. Hobby: Reading detective stories. Address: Department of Blood Physiology, Hunan Medical University, Changsha, Hunan 410078, China.

JIANG Hongchi, b. 10 Oct 1949, Heilongjiang, China. Surgeon. m. Xi Shuqin, 22 May 1969, 1 son. Education: BA, 1982, MM, 1985, Harbin Medical University; MD, Tongji Medical University, 1988; Postdoctoral training, University of London, England, 1993. Appointments: Currently Professor, Head of Abdominal Surgery, First Hospital, Harbin Medical University. Publications: Co-author: Spleen Surgery, book, 1991; Advances in treatment of abdominal surgery, 1993; Treatment of hemophilia A by living mother-to-son splenic transplantation. First case report in the world. Honours: Outstanding Young/Middle-Aged Scientist or Expert, Chinese Government, 1992. Memberships: Chinese Medical Association; Chinese Society of Splenic Surgery. Hobbies: Swimming; Playing table-tennis. Address: Department of Surgery, The First Hospital of Harbin Medical University, Harbin 150001, China.

JIANG Li-xia, b. 23 Mar 1954, Hangzhou, China. Chemist. m. Sun Mao-sen, 28 dec 1982, 1 d. Education: BA, Nanjing University, 1980; Postgraduate, Zhejiang Academy of Medicine, 1983; Training, City University, England, 1987. Appointments: Professor of Pharmaceutical Analysis. Publications: Long-Acting Contraceptive Agents: HPLC of Levonorgestrel Cyclopentylcarboxylate oxime and its Hydrolysis Products, 1987; HPLC of Cyproterone Acetate, 1989; HPLC Analysis of Injectable Contraceptive Preparation Containing Norethisterone Enanthate and Estradiol Valerate, 1990; Resolution and Identification of Steroid Oxime Syn and Anti Isomers by HPLC, 1990; Determination of Clenbuterol in its Permeated Solution Through the Human Skin, 1991; HPLC Determination of Main Nucleoside and Nucleic Acid Base in Mycelia of Cordyceps, 1993. Memberships: Chinese Chemical Society. Hobbies: Swimming; Singing; Bridge. Address: Zhejiang Academy of Medicine, 60 Tian Mu Shan Street, Hangzhou, Zhejiang, China.

JIANG Min-de, b. 1 Apr 1964, Chengdu, China. Gastroenterology. m. Sheng-hua Zhou, 12 July 1982, 1 son. Education: Bachelor of Medicine, Fourth Military Medical University, Xian, 1978-83; Master of Medicine, National Army Center on Gastroenterology, Xijing Hospital, Xian, 1985-88. Appointments: Pharmacist, Shengyang Army Hospital, 1970-78; Physician, Teacher, Internal Medicine Department, Tangdu Hospital, 1983-85; Attending Physician, Director, Department of Gastroenterology, General Hospital of Chendu Army, 1988-. Publications: Several professional articles published. Honours: Prize of Academic Thesis of Excellence, National Hygiene Department, 1989; 5 Prizes of the National Army Scientific & Technology Progress, 1990-. Memberships: Chinese Medical Association; Sichuan Branch Committee, Gastroenterology, Chinese Medical Association; Secretary, Association on Gastroenterology & Hepatology of Chengdu Army. Hobbies: Reading Books; Bridge; Music. Address: Gastroenterology Department, Chengdu Army General Hospital, Tianhui Town, Chengdu 610083, China.

JIANG Ming, b. 1 May 1930, Beijing, China. Physician. m. Shou Po Chen, 29 Sept 1959, 2 daughters. Education: MD, Peking Union Medical College, 1957. Career: Attending Physician; Visiting Scholar, University of California, Los Angeles (UCLA), Department of Rheumatology; Professor of Medicine. Publications: 74 scientific papers published in medical journals, 1980-93; Editor-in-Chief, Textbook of Rheumatology. Honour: Second Grade Reward, Ministry of Public Health, 1991. Membership: Member, Editorial Board, Chinese Journal of Internal Medicine. Address: Department of Clinical Immunology and Rheumatology, Peking Union Medical College Hospital, 1 Shuai Fu Yuan, Beijing 100730, China.

JIANG Ping, b. 14 Jan 1968, DaLian, China. Acupuncture Doctor. m. Shi Zhongwei, 5 Feb 1994. Education: Bachelor Degree, Acupuncture Department, Liaoning College of Chinese Traditional Medicine. Appointments: Resident Doctor, Acupuncture Department, The Municipal Central Hospital, Dalian. Publications: Observation To The Rehibilitation Effect Of Moving Function In Early Stage For The Hemiplegia Patients, 1994; Treating 18 Cases of Gurilain-Barre's Syndrome With Ophthalmacupuncture Therapy, 1994. Memberships: Acupuncture Institute, Liaoning, China; Research Institute for Chinese Special Acupuncture; CTM Institute, Dalian. Address: Acupuncture Department, The Municipal Central Hospital, Dalian 116033, China.

JIANG Si-Chang, b. 15 Sept 1913, Tian-Gien, China. Medical Doctor. m. Wu Yu-Lin 1 July 1941 (dec.), 3 sons. Education: Graduated, Beijing Medical University, 1938. Appointments: Professor, Chief of Otolaryngology, Nanking Central University Medical College, Nanking; Currently Professor, Ear, Nose and Throat Department, People's Liberation Army Postgraduate College; Director, Institute of Otolaryngology, Beijing. Publications: Recent Advances of Otosclerosis and Stapedectomy in China, 1979, 1993. Honours: Visiting Assistant Professor, University of Chicago, USA, 1947-48; Honorary Chairman, Chinese Otolaryngological Society and Chinese Journal of Otolaryngology. Memberships: Board Member, Chinese Medical Association. Hobby: Basketball. Address: ENT Department, 301 Hospital, Beijing, China.

JIANG Zhu Ming, b. 24 Jun 1935, China. Professor of Surgery. m. Rong Sheng Li, 1965, 1 s, 1 d. Education: MD, Shanghai Medical School, 1958; Board Certified, Beijing Surgical Association, 1978; Postdoctoral Research Training, Department of Surgery, Brigham and Women's Hospital, Harvard Medical School, 1982, 1983. Appointments: Senior Surgeon, Professor of General Surgery, Peking Union Medical College Hospital; Mentor, PhD Degree Candidates; Mentor, Postdoctoral Research Fellows. Publications: 126 Papers in China, USA and Japan concerning, Porta Hypertension, Gastric Cancer, Selective Vagotomy for Ulcer Disease, Body Fluid, Body Composition, Parenteral and Enteral Nutrition; 5 Monographs including: Co-author: Emergency Clinic, 1986; Emergency Medicine, 1991; Artificial Gut: Parenteral and Enteral Nutrition, 1993. Honours: Chinese Academy of Medical Sciences Award, Beijing, 1978; 1st Grade, Ministry of Health Award, Beijing, 1981; Scientific and Technology Committee of Beijing Award, 1983; Distinguished Service Award, Harvard Medical School Medal, 1986; National Prize of Sciences and Technology Progress, 1989; Natural Sciences Foundation of China award, 1991. Memberships: Chinese Surgical Association, 1978; Brigham Surgical Alumni Society, Boston, USA, 1982; American Society of Parenteral and Enteral Nutrition, WA, USA, 1983; FACS, Chicago, USA, 1989; European Society of Parenteral and Enteral Nutrition, UK, 1992; Editor-in-Chief, Chinese Journal of Clinical Medicine, 1993; Editorial Board: Acta Chinese Academy of Medical Sciences, 1988; Nutrition, USA, 1985; Clinical Nutrition, UK, 1995. Hobbies: Music; Computers. Address: Dept of Surgery, Peking Union Medical College Hospital, Beijing 100730, China.

JIAO Sude, b. 31 May 1922, Xinji, Hebei, China. Professor of Chinese Medicine. m. Wan Yuzhen, Jan 1951, 1 d. Education: Postgraduate Diploma of Chinese Medicine, 1958; Professor of Chinese Medicine. Appointments: Doctor of Chinese Medicine, 1941-49; Physician, Beijing No 2 Hospital, 1951-55; Lecturer/Associate Professor/Professor of Chinese Medicine/Doctor in Charge/Director, Beijing Institute of Chinese Medicine, 1958-84; MD/Director of Internal Medicine, Sino-Japanese Friendship Hospital, Beijing, 1984-94. Publications: Dialetical Therapeutics: A Case Study, 1982; Symptons & Diagnostics, 1984; Encyclopaedia of Chinese Medicine, 1989; Jiao Shude on Principals of Chinese Medicine, 1991; Ten Lectures on Chinese Medicine, 1994. Honours: Best Works Awards, 1977; Dialectical Therapeutics Awards, 1982; Advanced Individual Award, 1984; National Advanced Worker Award, 1986; Technical Development Award, 1991. Memberships: Academic Committee, Beijing Institute of Chinese Medicine; People's Congress, Beijing, China; Honorary Chairman, Association of Chinese Medicien, Japan. Hobbies: National Music; Peking Opera. Address: Beijing Sino-Japanese Friendship Hospital, Yinghua Donglu, Hepingli, Beijing 100029, China.

JIAO Tian Duo, b. 12 Aug 1932, Shanxi, China. Radiologist. m. Zhuang-Zhao Jiang, 30 Mar 1958, 1 son, 1 daughter. Education: 2nd Military Medical University, 1957. Appointments: Resident, Hangzhou 117th Central Hospital, 1957; Hospital Doctor in Charge, Shanghai Siping Street Hospital, 1983; Deputy Chief Doctor, Department of Radiology, Shanghai Central Hospital of Yangpu District, 1990. Publications: X-ray Diagnosis of Minuite Gastric Cancer, 1991; Investigation on Characteristic Appearance of Lesions Located in Ab-gravitational Wall (AW) of Stomach and Colon in Double Contrast Barium Examination, 1993. Honours: 3rd Prize, Public Health Ministry for Prominent Science & Technique Accomplishment, 1993. Memberships: Chinese Medical Association. Hobbies: Shadow Boxing.

Address: Tongji New Villages 544-3, Shanghai 200092, China.

JIN Chio, b. 8 Sept 1935, Jiangsu, Suzhou, China. Nurse Educator. m. Zang Mei-Fu, Mar 1959, 1 son. Education: Registered Nurse, Peking Union Medical College School of Nursing, 1957; Vice-Researcher. Appointments: Head Nurse, Surgical Ward and Operating Room; Teacher, Nursing School, Peking Union Medical College, 1953-90; Currently Chairman of Nursing Education, School of Nursing, Beijing. Publications: Co-author: Chronic Diseases of Elderly and Children's Nursing Care at Home, 1991-93; The Book of Nursing in China, 1993. Honours: Beijing Excellent Medical and Educational Personnel, 1959, 1983; Advanced Worker, Peking Union Medical College, 1963, 1990. Memberships: Beijing Nursing Association, Board Member, Chairman of Nursing Education; Committee of Health Bureau Centre, Chairman of Nursing Education; Advisor, Beijing Nursing Schools; Board Member, Beijing Elder Medical Workers Association; Co-worker, Chinese and Japanese Hospital Hygienic School for training in nurses' ceremony; In charge, Preparation Committee for Model Ward. Hobbies: Music; Literature. Address: 41 Dong Dan North Avenue, Dormitory, Peking Union Medical College, Beijing 100005, China.

JIN Hong-Yi, b. 11 Aug 1931, Shanghai, China. Cardiologist. Professor. m. 15 Aug 1958, 2 daughters. Education: BM, Zhejiang Medical University. Appointments: Resident Doctor, Attending Doctor, Vice-Chief of Physicians, Chief of Physicians; Visiting Professor, Zhejiang Medical University; Currently: President, Zhejiang Hospital, Hangzhou; President, Zhejiang Geriatrics Institute. Publications: Co-author: Hepatic Venous Catheterization, 1962; The Evaluation of Non-invasive Electrophysiologic Testing in the Diagnosis of Sinoatrial Node Function, 1984; Hypercoagulation in Fishermen with Hypertension, Hyperlipidemia, and Coronary Heart Disease, 1984; A Report of Hypertension Sampling Survey in Zhejiang Province in 1990, 1993. Memberships: Chinese Cardio-Vascular Disease Prevention Leading Group; Council Member, Chinese Geriatrics Association; Chairman, Zhejiang Geriatrics Association; Chairman, Zhejiang Sports Medicine Association. Hobby: Music. Address: Zhejiang Hospital, 12 Lingyin Road, Hangzhou 310013, China.

JIN Ji ling, b. 10 Jun 1946, Shaanxi Province, Xian, China. Doctor. m. Ding Song Jia, 26 Jan 1975, 1 s. Education: Master of Medicine; Graduate, Shaanxi Traditional Chinese Medical College, 1969; Graduate Student, Gynaecology, Nanjing Traditional Chinese Medical College, 1982. Career: Shaanxi Traditional Chinese Medical College, 1969-79, and following degree to 1986; Currently, 1st Teaching Hospital of Tianjin Traditional Chinese Medical College. Publications: Over 20 scientific reports including: A Selection of Questions and Answers in Traditional Chinese Medicine, 1988; Compendium of Traditional Chinese Medicine, 1993; Development of Case Reports for Clinical Practice, 1993. Honours: Excellent Thesis Prize, Tianjin, 1991; 2nd Prize for Fine Thesis, 1st International Conference of Ye Tian Shi Theory, 1993; 2nd Prize, Excellent Thesis, Liaoning Journal of Traditional Chinese Medicine, 1994. Membership: Traditional Chinese Medical Association of China. Hobbies include: Dancing; Singing; Swimming. Address: Gynaecological Department of First Teaching Hospital of Tianjin Traditional Chinese Medical College, 314 Anshan Xi Dao, 300193 Tianjin, China.

JIN Pihuan, b. 1 Dec 1929, Zhenjiang, Jiangsu, China. Teacher. m. Wenqin Ji, 1 May 1956, 2 s. Education: Diploma, Medical University of China, 1955. Appointments: Assistant, Lecturer, Department of Health organisation, Associate professor, Chief of Computer Centre, Professor of Medical Statistics, Department of Health Statistics and Social Medicine, Shanghai Medical University. Publications: Statistical Package for Medical Statistics, 1986; An Introduction to the Computer Applications in Medicine, 1989; Statistical Methods for Medical Applications, 1993. Memberships: Working Group 1, International Medical Information Association; Deputy Chairman, China Medical Information Association, Chairman, Shanghai Branch. Hobby: Model Aeroplanes. Address: Department of Health Statistics and Social Medicine, Shanghai Medical University, Shanghai 200032, China.

JIN Rui, b. 9 Aug 1948, Beijing, China. Physician. m. Shan Zhuqing, 20 Feb 1976, 1 daughter. Education: MD. Appointments: Resident Physician, No 541 General Hospital, Shang Xi, 1982-87; Lecturer, Physician-in-Charge, 1987-92, Head, Department of Liver Diseases and Digestion, You-an Hospital, Beijing, 1992-. Publications: Techniques of Clinical Diagnosis and Treatment, book, 1993; Survey on pathologic changes of upper digestive mucosa caused by severe viral hepatitis,

article, 1993. Membership: Chinese Medical Association. Hobbies: Weiqi; Chinese chess; Table-tennis; Basketball, including serving as umpire for municipal teams. Address: Apt 4, Entrance 2, No 4 Building, Hufang Road, Xuanwu District, Beijing, China.

JIN Weixin, b. 20 June 1937, Jinan, China. Professor of Obstetrics and Gynaecology. m. Qingdao, 20 Oct 1964, 1 son, 1 daughter. Education: MD, Shandong University, 1962. Appointments: Professor of Obstetrics and Gynaecology. Publications: Diagnosis and TCM Treatment of Sterility, 1992; Gynaecology of TCM. 1992; Male Insterility, 1994; Male Insterility and Dysfunction of Sex, Co-author, 1992; Study on Male Insterility Treated with Shengjing Tang and Yehua tang, 1989; Study of Female Insterility due to Dysfunction of Ovulation Treated by Luole 1991; 103 Cases of Female Tubal Obstruction Treated with Zhuyun Tongguan Tang, 1992; Diagnosis and TCM Treatment of Male and Female Insterility, 1993; Study of Non-Liquefaction of Sperm, 1993, Honours: 1st prize, National Scientific and Technological progress,, 1992; 3rd Prize, Shandong Committee of Science, 1989. Memberships: Sterility Research Association of China; Andriarty Branch, Research Association of TCM and Chinese Materia Medica; Chinese TCM Association. Hobby: Music. Address: 53 Jingshi Road, Shandong College of Traditional Chinese Medicine, Jinan, Shandong 250014, China.

JIN Zhomei, b. 5 Mar 1931, Zhejiang Pr, China. Professor. m. Lisheng Wang, 26 Aug 1958, 1 son, 1 daughter. Education: BA, Chengdu University of Science & Technology, 1956; PhD, Leningrad Chemical Engineering College, USSR, 1962. Career: Vice Director, Department of Chemical Engineering, 1965-79; Vice Director, Department of Metal Materials, 1983-85; Research Director; Consultant of Sichuan Consultative Committee of Science & Technology. Publications include: Metastable Equilbrium for Pentasystem of Sea Water Type,1980; Reaction Mechanism for the Hydrochloric Acid Leaching of Ilmenite Ores, 1980; Reaction Kinetics of the Ferric Chloride Leaching of Sphalerite, 1984; Kinetic Study of Silver Catalytic Leaching of Sulfide Ore, 1988; Silver Ion Catalysis in Leaching of Nickel Matte, 1990; An Investigation of the Electrochemical nature of the Leaching of Sphalerite, 1993; Synthesis of Potassium Hexatitanate by Melt Method, 1994; Extraction Silver from Ag-rich Complex Sulfide Ore, 1995. Honours: Awarded with 5 prizes for achievements in research, Ministry of Metallurgical Engineering & Sichuan Provincial Committee of Science & Technology, 1977, 1978, 1980, 1985. Memberships: Chairman, Academic Committee, Sichuan Society of Nonferrous Metals; Member, The Minerals, Metals and Materials Society (USA). Hobby: Running. Address: Department of Metal Materials, Chengdu University of Science and Technology, Chengdu 610065, China.

JING Dingguo, b. 26 Oct 1944, Wenzhow, Zhejiang, China. Associate Professor of Colo-proctology. m. Du Weiwei, 21 June 1964, 2 sons, 2 daughters. Education: Graduate, Traditional Chinese Medical College. Appointments: Resident Doctor, Colo-Proctologic Department, 1979, Physician-in-Charge, 1987, Associate Professor, 1992-, 2nd Affiliated Hospital, Wenzhow Medical College. Publications: Question and Answer About Colo-Proctologic Disease, 1994; Operation with remaining Dentate Line and Skin of Anal Canal for the Mixed Hemorrhoid, 1991; Interrupted Suturing Combined with High Injection in the Treatment of Internal Prolapse of Rectal Mucosa, 1994. Honours: 2nd Class prize of Success in Science and technology, Wenzhow, 1993; 3rd Class prize of Success in Science and Technology, Zhejiang Province, 1995. Memberships: Council of Zhejiang Provincial Colo-Proctologic Society of the Integration of Traditional and Western Medicine; Council of Wenzhow Association of the Integration of Traditional and Western Medicine. Hobby: Writing. Address: 46-3-203 Guihu Road, Wenzhow, China.

JING Weiben, b. Oct 1927, Beijing, China. Associate professor of Physical Chemistry. m. Xiao Gueiwen, 1 son, 2 daughters. Education: Graduate, Chemistry Department, Beijing University, 1952. Appointments: Shanxi Educational College, 1952-62; Teacher, Hunyuan Middle School, 1962-78; Dean, Chemistry Department, 1984-89; Chief Editor, Journal of Yanbei Teachers' College, 1988-; Deputy Director, Science Committee, Associate Professor of Physical Chemistry, Yanbei Teachers' College. Publications: Editor of books; Contributor of over 40 professional papers. Honours: Reputation of Splendid Teacher, Yanbei Teachers' College, 1980, 1984, 1985, 1986, 1987, 1988; 2nd Class prize for Exemplary Teaching with Positive Results, 1989. Memberships: Chemistry Committee of China; Committee of Dialectation of Nature.

Hobbies: Ballad Singing; Story telling. Address: Department of Chemistry, Yanbei Teachers' College, Datong, Shanxi, China.

JKACHENKO Boris Ivanovich, b. 27 Jan 1931, Dnepropatrovsk, Russia. Psychologist. m. Olga Menshikova, 1958, 1 son, 1 daughter. Education: Medical Institute USSr, 1955; Postgraduate, MD, 1964; PhD, Candidate of Medical Science, Instityute for Experimental Medicine, 1958. Appointments: Junior, 1958, Senior Research Fellow, 1963, Head of Laboratory, 1965, Department Head, 1973, Director, 1990-, Institute for Experimental Medicine; PProfessor, 1968; Corresponding Member, RAMS, 1978; Academicien, RAMS, 1984. Publications: Venous Circulation, Co-author, 1979; Luns Hemodynamics, Co-author, 1987; Central Regulation of Regional Hemodynamics, 1992. Honours: Academy Parin Prize, 1982; State Prize for Achievement in Science, 1989. Memberships: Russian Society of Physiologists; International Academy of Science. Hobbies: Skiing; Swimming. Address: 8 linie 3/9-20, 199034 St Petersburg, Russia.

JOGIAR Francisco, b. 1 Jan 1948, San Juan, PR, USA. Medical Doctor. m. Olga Billoch, 29 Dec 1972, 3 s, 1 d. Education: BS, Mount St Mary's College, MD, 1969; MD, University of PR, School of Medicine, 1973; Internal Medicine, 1976, Nephrology, 1978, University of PR, School of Medicine. Appointments: Assistant Professor Medicine, Associate Professor Medicine, Professor of Medicine, University of PR, School of Medicine. Publications: 5 Abstracts, 1981-93; 9 Contributions to Professional Journals including: The Significance of Pancreatitis on CAPD Patients and a CAPD Program, in Peritoneal Dialysis International. Honour: Fellow, American College of Physicians, 1993. Memberships: American College of Physicians; International Society of Nephrology; International Society for Peritoneal Dialysis; American Society of Nephrology; Puerto Rico Medical Association. Address: Clinica Las Americas Suite 108, 400 Roos Avenue, Hato Rey, PR 00918, USA.

JOHN Carolyn Henrietta, b. 28 Aug 1963, Monmonthshire, South Wales. Clinical Psychologist. Education: BSc, Bristol University; PhD, Reading University; MSc, Institute of Psychiatry, London University. Appointments: Lecturer in Clinical Psychology, Newcastle University, 1989-91; Consultant Clinical Psychologist, S. Tees. H.A; Honorary Lecturer in Psychology, Durham University. Publications: Language, Values & Intercultural Differentiation, co-author, 1986; Emotionality Ratins and Free Association Norms, 1988; Gestalt Perceptions in Schizophienia, co-author, 1992; Inductive Reasoning in Delusional Thought, co-author, 1994; Cognitive Behavior Therapy of Schizophrenia, co-author, 1994. Memberships: British Psychological Society; Division of Clinical Psychology. Hobbies: Hill Walking; Foreign Languages; Travel; Cookery. Address: Psychology & Counselling Agency, Woodlands Road Clinic, Woodlands Road, Middlesbrough, Cleveland TS1 3BL, England.

JOHNSON A Wayland, b. North Carolina, USA. Professor; Psychotherapist. 2 sons (dec.), 1 daughter. Education: BA, 1961; BD, 1964; ThM, 1969; PhD, 1993. Appointments include: Director, Department of Pastoral Care, Crownville State Hospital, Maryland; Director, Department of Pastoral Care, Washington Hospital Center, District of Columbia; Coordinator, Clinical Education, Northwestern Memorial Hospital, Chicago, Illinois; Pastoral Educator, The Royal North Shore Hospital of Sydney, Sydney, New South Wales, Australia; Director, Department of Pastoral Care and Counselling, Memorial Medical Center, Savannah, Georgia; Director, Department of Pastoral Care, Good Samaritan Medical Center, West Palm Beach, Florida; Now retired. Publications: A Study of the Demography of CPE Supervisors, 1980; A Study of the Demography of Pastoral Counselors, 1982. Memberships: Diplomate, College of Pastoral Supervision and Psychotherapy; Diplomate, American Association of Pastoral Counselors; Training Supervisor, Australia and New Zealand Council on Clinical Training; Fellow, College of Chaplains. Hobbies: Hunting; Fishing; Travel. Address: Route 1 - Box 780, Gladstone, Virginia, USA.

JOHNSON Anne Bradstreet, b. 5 Mar 1927, Boston, MA, USA. Research Physician. m. Jack Minkoff, 19 Jun 1948, 1 s, 1 d. Education: AB, Cornell University, 1948; MD, Cornell University Medical College, 1951; Certifications: Internal Medicine, 1958 and Pathology, 1976. Appointments: Teaching Fellow, Western Reserve University, OH; Fellow in Medicine, Columbia University College of P and S, NY; American Cancer Society Fellow in Biochemistry, Albert Einstein Institute College of Medicine, NY; Instructor, Assistant Professor, Currently, Associate Professor, Albert Einstein College of Medicine.

Publications: Over 50 articles in medical research journals, 1958-68. Honours: Moore Award, American Association of Neuropathologists, 1972; Grants: National Institute of Health, Multiple Sclerosis Society; Alzheimers Association; United Leukodystrophy Foundation. Memberships: American Association Neuropathologists; Histochemical Society; Society of Neuroscience; American Society Cell Biology; International Academy of Pathology; College of American Pathologists. Hobbies include: Lake Retreat; Boating. Address: Dept of Pathology - K604, Albert Einstein College of Medicine, 1300 Morris Park Ave, Bronx, NY 10461, USA.

JOHNSON Arthur Thomas, b. 21 Feb 1941, East Meadow, NY, USA. Biological Engineer. m. Cathleen May Throop, 7 Sept 1963, 2 sons, 2 daughters. Education: BA, Cornell University, 1964; MS, Cornell University, 1967; PhD, Cornell University, 1969. Appointments: Captain, US Army, 1969-71; General Engineer, Edgewood Arsenal, 1971-75; Professor, University of Maryland, 1975-; Biomedical Engineer, Maryland Institute for Emergency Medical Service Systems, 1982-83. Publications: Biomechanics and Exercise Physiology, book, 1991; 4 book chapters, 65 peer reviewed publications, 99 professional papers. Honours: Founding Fellow, American Institute of Medical Biological Engineers, 1992; Senior Member, Institute of Electric Electron Engineers, 1992; Excellence Teaching Materials Award, American Society of Engineers Education, 1992; Centennial Certificate, American Society of Engineers Education, 1993; President's Citation, ASAC, 1994. Memberships: AIHA; AIMBE; ASAE; ASEE; IEEE; BMES; Sigma Xi; Alpha Epsilon; Tau Beta Pi; Phi Kappa Phi. Hobbies: Table Tennis; Fruit Growing. Address: University of Maryland, College Park, MD 20742, USA.

JOHNSON Eric Welton, b. 8 May 1912, Hale, Cheshire. m. Madge Altrincham, 24 Aug 1938. Education: Dr AC; FBAcA; MCSP; Grand Diploma Phys. Appointment: Part Time Private Practice. Memberships: Chairman, British Acupuncture Association, and Register, 10 Years; Past President, Cheshire County Hockey Association. Hobbies: Rotary; Hockey; Golf; Bridge. Address: Stoneleigh, 218 Washway Road, Sale, Cheshire, M33 4RA, England.

JOHNSON Jean E (Irwin), b. 3 Nov 1925, Wilsey, Kansas, USA. Professor of Nursing. Education: BS, Home Economics, Nursing, Kansas State University, 1948; MS, Psychiatric Nursing, Yale University, 1965; PhD, Social Psychology, University of Wisconsin-Madison, 1971. Appointments: Instructor, various Schools of Nursing, 1948-58; Associate Professor, then Professor, Director, Center for Health Research, College of Nursing, Wayne State University, Detroit, Michigan, 1971-79; Professor, Clinical Chief and Associate Director for Oncology Nursing, University of Rochester Medical Center, Rochester, New York, 1979-93; Professor of Nursing, University of Rochester, 1993-. Publications: The effects of accurate expectations about sensations on the sensory and distress components of pain; Coping with elective surgery, 1984; Process of coping with radiation therapy, 1989. Honours: Member, Institute of Medicine, National Academy of Sciences, 1974; Fellow, American Academy of Nursing, 1978; Distinguished Contribution to Nursing Science, American Nurses Foundation Inc and American Nurses Association, 1983; Outstanding Contributions to Nursing and Health Psychology, American Psychological Association, 1993. Memberships: American Nurses Association; American Psychological Association; American Association for the Advancement of Science; Academy of Behavioral Research; American Psychological Society. Address: University of Rochester Medical Center, School of Nursing, Box SON, 601 Elmwood Avenue, Rochester, NY 14642, USA.

JOHNSON Jeffrey Vaughn, b. 6 Apr 1949, Raleigh, North Carolina, USA. Public Health Social Scientist; Educator. m. 21 Aug 1982. Education: BA, Summa Cum Laude, University of Minnesota, 1980; PhD, Johns Hopkins University, Baltimore, 1986.. Appointments: Health Scientist, US Occupational Safety and Health Administration, 1980-81; Cardiovascular Research Fellow, Johns Hopkins University, 1982-84; Work Environment Research Fellow, University of Stockholm, Sweden, 1984-85; Assistant Professor of Behavioural Sciences, Assistant Professor of Occupational Health, 1987-89. Johns Hopkins School of Public Health; Associate research Scientist, Swedish National Institute of psyuchosocial Factors and Health, 1984-94; Visiting Scientist, Statistics Sweden, 1984-94; Associate Professor of Behavioural Sciences and Occupational Health, School of Public Health, Associate Professor of Medicine, School of Medicine, Associate Professor of Sociology, School of Arts and Sciences, The Johns Hopkins University, Baltimore. Publications include: The Impact of Workplace Social

Support. Job Demands and Work COntrol Upon Cardiovascular Disease in Sweden, 1986; The Psychosocial Work Environment of Physicians, 1994; Chronic Outcomes: Cardiovascular Disease, 1995. Honours include: Cornelus W Kruse Award, Johns Hopkins University; Fellowship Award, National Heart Lung and Blood Institute, 1982-85; Grant, US National Institute of Aging, 1983-98; Recipient of numerous awards and grants for professional services. Memberships include: Society for Occupational and Environmental Health; American Public Health Association. Address: The Johns Hopkins School of ublic Health, 624 N Broadway, Room 706, Baltimore, MD 21205-1901, USA.

JOHNSON Michele Louise, b. 1 Apr 1963, Springburn, Glasgow, Scotland. Movement Psychotherapist. m. Simon Paul Johnson, 31 Aug 1991. Education: BA (Hons), Laban Centre for Movement and Dance, 1984; Postgraduate Certificate of Education, Bedford College of Higher Education, 1985; MA, Creative Arts in Therapy (Psychotherapy), Hahnemann University and Medical School, USA, 1990; Dance Therapy Registered, 1990; AFAA Personal Trainer/Fitness Counsellor, 19194. Appointments include: Dance and Movement Specialist, Steps Out Education Unit, Scottish Ballet, Glasgow, 1986-88; Movement Therapy Intern, St Elizabeth's Hospital, Washington DC, USA, 1989-90; Senior Group Worker, Alpha House Ltd, Droxford, England, 1991-94; Self-employed, SOMASIKE Personal and Professional Development of Body and Mind, 1994-; AOGB National Tutor; AOGB Regional Director for Hampshire, 1995. Publications: An Examination of the Therapeutic Process in Dance/Movement Therapy. A Single Analysis, not yet published. Honours: Duke of Edinburgh's Gold and Silver Awards, 1980; Provost Petrie Cup and Hamilton Prize for Community Work, 1980; Achievement Award for Past Work, Outstanding Women in Britain, COSMOPOLITAN, 1991. Memberships: American Dance Therapy Association; Association for Dance and Movement Therapy; British Association for Counselling. Hobbies: Artistic Director, Humdrum Amdram Theatre Co; Fitness instructor. Address: 5 Anthony Grove, Elson, Gosport, Hampshire PO12 4AR, England.

JOHNSON Philip James, b. 5 May 1948, Manchester, England. Physician. m. Susan Jean Allison, 4 Dec 1981, 2 daughters. Education: MB ChB, 1972, MD, 1991, Manchester; MRCP (UK), 1974; FRCP (UK), 1991. Appointments: Guy's Hospital, London, 1973; Royal Marsden Hospital; London Chest Hospital; National Hospital, Queen Square, London; Liver Unit, King's College London; Manchester Royal Infirmary; Institute of Liver Studies, London; Currently Professor of Clinical Oncology, Chinese University of Hong Kong. Publications: Laboratory Investigation of Liver Disease, 1989; Over 100 papers on liver disease and cancer. Memberships: American Society of Clinical Oncology; American Association for Study of the Liver; British Society of Gastroenterology. Hobbies: Chess; Piano; Running. Address: Department of Clinical Oncology, Chinese University of Hong Kong, Prince of Wales Hospital, Shatin, NT, Hong Kong.

JOHNSON Richard Greene, b. 3 June 1921, Louisville, Kentucky, USA. Physician; Psychiatrist. m. Agnes Campbell, 2 Nov 1945, 2 sons, 2 daughters. Education: BA; MD; PhD. Appointments: Medical Director, Westwood Hospital; President, California Psychiatric Society. Memberships: AMA; CMA; LACMFL. Hobbies: Golf; Tennis. Address: Suite 310, 10301 Wilshire Blvd, Los Angeles, CA 90025 1007, USA.

JOHNSON Waine C, b. 30 Sept 1928, Mt Vernon, Texas, USA. Physician. m. Deanna M Glutz, 3 daughters. Education: MD. Appointments: Assistant Director to Director of Laboratory, Skin and Cancer Hospital, Assistant Professor to Professor, Temple University Medical School, Philadelphia, Pennsylvania, 1962-78; Currently: Chairman, Department of Dermatology, The Graduate Hospital, Philadelphia; Clinical Professor of Dermatology, University of Pennsylvania, Philadelphia; President, Johnson and Griffin Dermatopathology Associates PC. Publications: 109 scientific articles in national and international journals dealing with the fields of dermatology and dermatopathology; Dermal Pathology (co-editor), 1974. Honours: Recipient of Gold Medal for Science Exhibit, American Society of Clinical Pathologists, College of American Pathologists, 1962. Memberships: Past President, American Society of Dermatopathology; Past President, Philadelphia Dermatology Society; Past Pres, Atlantic Dermatology Conference; American Registry of Pathology; American Dermatology Association; American American Association; American College of Physicians; American Academy of Dermatology; International Academy of Pathology; Society of Investigative Dermatology. Address: 137 S Easton Road, Box 8, Glenside, PA 19038, USA.

JOHNSON Warren Charles, b. 8 Jun 1923. Physician. m. Dorothy Morlin, 27 Dec 1956, 1 s, 1 d. Education: BS; MD; Certification, American Board of Psychiatry, American Psychoanalytic Association. Career: Chief Psychiatrist, HQ Command USAF; Director, Juvenile Court Guidance, NIMH; Chief Psychiatrist, Board of Police and Fire Surgeons, DC; Currently, Associate Clinical Profesor of Psychiatry, SW University Medical School. Publications include: Book review, Readings, the Osiris Complex, 1994; Understanding Human Behaviour, American Association; Industrial Nurses Journal, 1960. Honour: Certificate of Commendation, Government of DC, Metropolitan Police Department, 1983. Membership: American Psychoanalytic Association. Hobbies: Golf; Sailing. Address: 5030 Van Ness Street NW, Washington DC 20016, USA.

JOHNSON-LAIRD Philip Nicholas, b. 12 Oct 1936, Rothwell, Near Leeds, Yorkshire, England. Psychologist. m. Maureen M Sullivan, 1 Aug 1959, 1 s, 1 d. Education: BA, Honours; PhD. Appointments: Lecturer, Psychology, University College, London; Visiting Fellow, Institute for Advanced Study, Princeton; Reader, Professor, Experimental Psychology, Sussex University; MRC Applied Psychology Unit, Cambridge; Currently, Stuart Professor of Psychology, Princeton University. Publications: Co-author, Psychology of Reasoning, 1972; Co-author, Language and Perception, 1976; Mental Models, 1983; The Computer and the Mind, 1988; Co-author, Deduction, 1991; Human and Machine Thinking, 1993; Many Scientific Articles in Professional Journals. Honours: Spearman Medal, British Psychological Society, 1974; Honorary Doctorate, University of Gothenburg, 1983; FBA, 1986; Medal of Honor, University of Florence, 1989; FRS, 1991. Memberships: British Psychological Society; Experimental Psychology Society; Cognitive Science Society; Society of Experimental Psychologists; Psychonomics Society. Hobbies include: Playing Modern Jazz Piano. Address: Dept of Psychology, Princeton University, Princeton, NJ 08544, USA.

JOHNSTON Kenneth Wayne, b. 22 Feb 1943, Brantford, Ontario, Canada. Surgeon. m. Jean Turley, 11 Feb 1967, 1 son, 1 daughter. Education: MD cum laude, Toronto; FRCS (Canada), Surgery. Appointments: Currently Professor of Surgery, University of Toronto. Publications: 5-year results of a prospective study of percutaneous transluminal angioplasty (with M R N Rae, S A Hogg-Johnston, R F Colapinto, P M Walker, R J Baird, K W Sniderman, P G Kalman), 1987; Multicenter prospective study of non-ruptured abdominal aortic aneurysms. I. Population and operative management (with T K Scobie), 1988; Multicenter prospective study of nonruptured abdominal aortic aneurysms - II. Variables predicting morbidity and mortality, 1989; Ruptured abdominal aortic aneurysm: Six-year follow up results of a multicenter prospective study, 1994; Nonruptured abdominal aortic aneurysm: 6 year follow up results from the multicenter prospective Canadian aneurysm study, in press. Honours: James IV Travelling Fellowship, 1984; Recorder, International Society for Cardiovascular Surgery, 1992-. Memberships: American Surgical Association; Society for Vascular Surgery; International Cardiovascular Society; Society of University Surgeons. Hobby: Computing. Address: The Toronto Hospital, 9 Eaton Room 217, Toronto, Ontario, Canada M5G 2C4.

JOHNSTON Leland Mann Jr, b. 2 Jul 1947, Jackson, Tennessee, USA. Physician. m. Beatrice, 1 Oct 1993, 1 s. Education: MD; Certification as Psychoanalyst by American Psychoanalytic Association. Appointments: Physician. Memberships: American Psychiatric Association; American Medical Association; American Psychoanalytic Association. Hobbies: Skiing; Music. Address: 2271 NE 51st Street, Seattle, WA 98105, USA.

JOHNSTONE Lucy Clare, b. 21 Apr 1956, Dorset, England. Clinical Psychologist; Lecturer. Education: MA; AFBPsS. Appointments: Basic Grade, Senior & Principal Psychologist, Luton & Dunstable General Hospital, Barrow Hospital, Bristol Hospital. Publications: Users & Abusers of Psychiatry, 1989; Family Management in Schizophrenia: Its Criticisms & Limitations, 1993; Psychiatry: Are We Allowed to Disagree?, 1993. Address: University of The West of England, St Mattias Campus, Fishponds, Bristol BS16 2JP, England.

JOLY Jean R, b. 6 Jan 1950, Montreal, Canada. Medical Researcher. m. Johanne Hubert, 26 May 1973, 1 s, 1 d. Education: MD, 1974, FRCPC, 1979, MBA, 1993, Montreal; MSPH, Seattle, 1981. Career: Director, Department of Microbiology, Laval University, Quebec, 1989-92; Currently, Research Director, Hôpital du Saint-Sacrement, Quebec City, Canada. Publications: Monitoring for the Presence of

Legionella: Where, When and How?, State of the Art Lecture, ASM, 1993; Co-author, Estimation of HIV Seroprevalence in Quebec Using Sentinel Hospital Surveillance, in Canadian Medical Association Journal, in press. Membership: President, Canadian Society for Epidemiology and Biostatistics. Address: Research Centre, Hôpital du Saint-Sacrement, 1050 ch Ste-Foy, Quebec, Canada, G1S 4L8.

JONAS Steven, b. 22 Nov 1936, New York, NY, USA. Medicine. m. Adrienne Weiss, 4 Jul 1994, 1 s, 1 d. Education includes: BA cum laude, Columbia College, NY, 1958; MD, Harvard Medical School, Boston, 1962; Research Fellow, London School of Economics, London, England, 1964-65. Appointments include: Lecturer, Department of Community Medicine, Mount Sinai School of Medicine, NY, 1969-; Various positions, currently Professor, Department of Preventive Medicine, School of Medicine, State University of NY, Stony Brook, 1971-; Adjunct Associate Professor, Texas College of Osteopathic Medicine, Fort Worth, TX, 1980-; Associate Editor, Preventive Medicine, 1983-; Editorial Board, American Journal of Preventive Medicine, 1987-; Radio host, one hour live talk show on WUSB, Talking Politics With Dr Steve Jonas, 1992-. Publications include: Books include: Medical Mystery: The Training of Doctors in the United States, 1978; Triathloning for Ordinary Mortals, 1986; An Introduction to the US Health Care System, 3rd edition, 1992; Regular Exercise: A Handbook for Clinical Practice, 1995; 8 Books with other authors; Numerous Monographs, book chapters, edited journal issues, original papers, book forwards and reviews; Contributions to magazines and journals; Over 50 papers delivered at conferences; 13 Consultations, 1968-86. Honours include: Fellow, American Public Health Association, 1969; American Journal of Nursing, Book of Year Award, 1982; Founders' Medal for Contributions to Medical Education, 1982; Dean's Fellow, Touro College School of Law, NY, 1986-87. Memberships include: Department of Preventive Medicine Committee, 1988-; American Hospital Association; American Public Health Association. Hobbies: Triathlon Racing; Downhill Skiing; Classical Music. Address: Dept of Preventive Medicine, School of Medicine, SUNY, Stony Brook, NY 11794-8036, USA.

JONES Alan Robert Elliff, b. 22 Jul 1955, Carshalton. Psychotherapist. Education: BSc, Psychology, 1984; Advanced Diploma, Psychotherapy, 1984. Appointments: Private Psychotherapist; Founder of South London Network for Counselling and Psychotherapy; Assistant Director of Pellin Institute, London/Naples. Honours: Registered Psychotherapist, 1992. Memberships: Association of Humanistic Psychology Practitioners; Society for Existential Analysis; British Institute for Integrative Psychotherapy; UKCP; BAC; Society for Exploration of Psychotherapy Interation. Hobbies: Philosophy; Art; Music. Address: 3 Bushey Road, Sutton, Surrey SM1 1QR.

JONES Anne Patricia, b. 18 Jan 1952, Sydney, Australia. Lobbyist. m. Dr David Butt, 23 Mar 1979, 1 s, 1 d. Education: BA, Honours. Career: Researcher, Anthropology Department, Sydney University; Writer, Times Books, Singapore; Education Officer, NPWS; Campaigner, Total Environment Centre; Co-Director, Manly Environment Centre; Advisor to Independent MP, New South Wales State Parliament; Currently, Executive Director, ASH Australia. Publication: Guide to Antiques, Arts and Crafts in Singapore, 1988. Hobbies: Gym Work. Address: ASH Australia, 153 Dowling Street, Woolloomooloo 2011, New South Wales, Australia.

JONES David, b. 7 Sept 1934, England. Psychotherapist. m. Laura Donington, 4 July 1994, 2 daughters. Education: BA Degree; Diploma in Psychotherapy. Appointments: Lecturer in Psychology, London School of Economics; Private Practice. Publications: Innovative Therapy, a handbook, 1994. Memberships: British Psychological Society; Association for Humanistic Practitioners. Hobbies: Bee Keeping. Address: Ajanta Centre, 39 Blenkarne Road, London SW11 6H2, England.

JONES Ian Stuart Crawford, b. 3 Oct 1942, Romford, England. Obstetrician and Gynaecologist. m. 4 s, 1 d. Education: MBChB (Otago); Graduate Certificate Ed, Queensland; Diploma, Obstetrics, Otago; ChM, Otago; MHA, University of New South Wales; FRACOG; FRCOG; FACS. Career: Assistant Lecturer, Obstetrics and Gynaecology, 1972-73, Assistant Lecturer, Pathology, 1974, Otago University; Lecturer, Obstetrics and Gynaecology, University of Queensland, 1975-78; Senior Lecturer, 1979-88, Associate Professor, 1991-93, Professor, 1994-, Obstetrics and Gynaecology, Queensland University. Honours: Mary Rooney Weigel Honour Award, International Academy of Proctology, 1973; Reserve Force Decoration. Memberships:

Australian Perinatal Society; Australian Military Medical Association; Australian Gynaecological Endoscopy Society; Australasian Society for the Study of Hypertension in Pregnancy. Address: Department of Obstetrics and Gynaecology, Mater Mothers Hospital, South Brisbane, Queensland 4101, Australia.

JONES James Robert, b. 16 Dec 1934, Brooklyn, New York, USA. Physician. widower, 3 sons, 2 daughters. Education: BS, Manhattan College, 1965; MD, State University of New York, Brooklyn, 1960. Appointments include: Professor, Obstetrics and Gynaecology, State University of New York, Brooklyn, 1977; Professor, Chairman, Obstetrics and Gynaecology, Rutgers Medical School (now Robert Wood Johnson Medical School), 1988; Currently Professor, Chairman, Obstetrics and Gynaecology, New York Medical College, Valhalla. Publications: More than 100. Honours: Alpha Omega Alpha; Purdue Fredrick Award, 1980; Faulkner Professor, Rotunda, Dublin, 1985; Visiting Professor, 1990. Memberships: American College of Obstetrics and Gynecology; APGO; New York Obstetrical Society. Hobbies: Music; Farming. Address: New York Medical College, Munger Pavilion, Room 306, Valhalla, NY 10595, USA.

JONES Lorna, b. 17 Aug 1934, York, England. Lecturer; Consultant. m. John Fisher Jones, 11 Aug 1956, 2 sons, 1 daughter. Education: Cert Ed, Middlesbrough College of Education; BSc (Hons), Zoology, Psychology, London University External; IBiol, Sunderland External. Appointments: Lecturer, Hartlepool College of Further Education, 1978-90; Lecturer, Workers Education Association, 1990; Stress Management Consultant, 1990-. Publications: Handbook for GCE Psychology Teachers (with Sanders, Hayes and Brody), 1983; Psychology (Ed Jones and Davies) due 1996. Memberships: British Psychological Society; ISMA; BAPT. Hobbies: Badminton; Tennis; Voluntary hospice work. Address: 12 Retford Grove, Hartlepool, Cleveland TS25 2NP, England.

JONES Philip Richard, b. 5 Mar 1952, Swindon, Wiltshire, England. Counselling Health and Educational Psychologist; Physical Therapist. m. Patricia Ann, 28 June 1975, 1 daughter. Education: BSc, Honours, London; PGTC, Goldsmiths College; MSc, University of Sussex; Certificate of Educational Research, Open University; MA, PhD, University of Nottingham; AFBPS; CPsychol. Appointments include: Teacher, Brook House Comprehensive, Hackney, London, 1975-76; Play Leader, Mentally Handicapped Children, Paddington, London, 1977; Educational/Senior Clinical Psychologist, Spastics Society Residential School, 1979-81; Educational Psychologist, Nottinghamshire Local Education Authority, 1981-86; Senior Educational Psychologist, 1986-88, Staff Development Officer Kirklees Psychological Service, 1987-89, Senior educational Psychologist, Project and Early Intervention Team, 1988-89, Senior Educational Psychologist, Kirklees South, 1989-, Director for Kirklees Psychological Serivice In-Service Provision, 1990-, Kirklees Local Education Authority. Publications: Signs and Symbol Communication for Mentally Handicapped People, Co-author, 1986; Psychology and Physical Disability, Co-Editor, 1992; Contributor of numerous articles, chapters in books, research papers and radio and television programmes. Memberships include: Associate Fellow, British Psychological Society; Association of Educational Psychologists; British Society for Experimental and Clinical Hypnosis. Hobbies: Natural History; Local Politics. Address: The Psychological Service, Oastler Centre, 2nd Floor Co-Operative Buildings, 103 New Street, Huddersfield, West Yorkshire HD1 2UA, England.

JONES R Wayne, b. 24 Sep 1937, Dallas, TX, USA. School Psychology; Psychodiagnostics; Family Systems Psychotherapy. Education: BS, Tulane University, 1958; MA, Psychology, LA State University, 1960; PhD, Psychology, University of Miami, 1964; Diplomate, Clinical Psychology, 1969; Diplomate, Professional Neuropsychology, 1983. Appointments: Research Associate, State Colony and Training School, Pinesville, LA, 1959-60; Instructor, Psychology, University of Miami, FL, 1964-66; Research Instructor of Ophthalmology, Miami School of Medicine, FL, 1963-66; Assistant Professor of Child Clinical Psychology, Emory University, Atlanta, GA, 1966-69; Associate Professor, 1969-72, Professor and Director, School Psychology Training Programs, GA State University, Atlanta, 1972-; Currently, Private Practice, Paces Center for Psychological Services, Atlanta; Consultant, Westminster Schools; Principal Consultant, Pschological and Legal Consultants. Publications include: 7 Books and Book Chapters, 1964-93, including: Suicide and the School, 1993; 19 Articles in Professional Journals, 1962-91, including: Co-author, Behaviors analgous to frontal lobe dysfunction in children with attention deficit hyperactivity disorder, in Archives of Clinical Neuropsychology, 1989. Honours: Fellow, GA Psychological Association, 1969; Founding Board Director, American Board of Professional Neuropsychology, 1982-87. Memberships include: American Psychological Association; National Academy of Neuropsychologists; Advisory Board of Editors, Annual Editions Life Management Series, 1993-94. Address: Counseling and Psychological Services, College of Education, Georgia State Univ, Atlanta, GA 30303, USA.

JONES Robert Leroy, b. 28 May 1939, Allentown, PA, USA. Medical Scientist; Educator. m. Nancy H Jones, 30 May 1964, 2 d. Education: BS, Physical Science; MS, Preventive Medicine; MCP, Psychology; DEd, Medical Physiology. Appointments: Associate Professor, Plymouth State College; Research Scientist, Pillsbury Co; Chairman, Science Department, American College of Switzerland; Academic Dean, Community College; Currently, Associate Professor, Family and Community Medicine; Director, Predoctoral Education. Publications include: Exercise and Pregnancy, 1985; Is Science Value Free, 1986; Pain Management, 1991; Biology of Aging, 1994. Honours: Teaching Awards, 1971, 1983, 1987, 1989, 1993; Special Recognition Award, Teaching and Scholarship, 1992. Memberships: Society of Teachers of Family Medicine; AAAS; American Association of Public Health; North American Primary Care Research Network. Hobbies: Travel; Sport; Reading. Address: Dept of Family and Community Medicine, Pennsylvania State University, College of Medicine, Hershey, PA 17033, USA.

JOOSSENS Jozef Victor, b. 12 Feb 1915, Borgerhout. Professor of Medicine. m. Agnes Buys, 12 Sept 1942, 4 sons. Education: MD, 1939; Licentiate in Physical Education, 1941; Dr in Public Health, 1942. Appointments: Head of Internal Medicine, St Lucas Hospital, Ekeren, Antwerp, 1946-54; Leuven University, Professor of Medicine, 1954-84; Founder, Head of Cardiology, 1955-80; idem Epidemiology, 1965-84; Director of Heart Center, 1963-84. Publications: First Editor, Diet and Human Carcinogenesis, 1985; Co-editor, Epidemiology of Arterial Hypertension, 1980; Author, The Pattern of Food and Mortality in Belgium, 1977; Nutrition and Gastric Cancer, 1981. Memberships: Royal Academy of Medicine of Belgium; Fellow, American College of Cardiology; New York Academy of Sciences. Honours: Assubel Prize, Preventive Medicine, 1971; Boehringer-Pharma Prize, Fundamental Research in Atherosclerosis, 1987; Great Officer, Order of Leopold, 1987. Address: Ter Winden, Kerselarenweg 11, B-3020 Herent, Belgium. 52.

JORDAN William Stone Jr, b. 28 Sep 1917, Fayettville, NC, USA. Physician. m. Marion Anderson, 17 May 1947, 1 s, 1 d. Education: ABm University of North Carolina, 1938; MD, Harvard University 1942. Apppointments: Fellow to Associate Professor, Preventive Medicine and Medicine, Western Reserve University, 1947-58; Professor, Chairman, Department of Preventive Medicine, University of Virginia, 1958-67; Dean, College of Medicine, University of Kentucky, 1969-74; Director, Microbiology and Infectious Diseases Programme, National Institute of Infectious Diseases, NIH, 1976-87; Consultant, USPHS; Retired. Publications: Illness in the Home, CO-author, 1964; Community Medicine in the United Kingdom, 1978; Contributor of 105 articles in professional journals. Honours: Outstanding Civilian Service Medal, Department of Army, 1978, 1981; Phi Beta Kappa; Alpha Omega Alpha. Memberships include: American Association of Physicians; American Epidemiological Society; American Society Microbiology; Royal Society of Medicine. Hobbies: Photography; Travel; Swimming. Address: 9112 Charred Oak Drive, Bethesda, MD 208717-1926, USA.

JORDAO Antonio Jose Lorena, b. 8 Oct 1959, Lisboa, Portugal. Medical Doctor. m. Fatima Ferreira, 26 Aug 1993, 1 son. Education: MD, Universidade Classica de Lisboa, 1983. Appointments: CRA Euro-Labor, Grünenthal; Senior Registrar, Allergy & Clinical Immunology, Hospital de Santa Maria, Lisboa. Publications: Co-author: Phisiopathology of Urticaria, 1991; Co-author: Treatment Aspects of International Asthma: Europe in Bronchial Asthma: Principles of Diagnosis and Treatment, 1993. Memberships: SPAIC; GAILL EAACI; Interasma. Honours: Scholarship, The Danish Government, 1991; Prémio da Sociedade Nédica dos H D Zonal Sul, 1984. Hobbies: Jogging; Body Building; Soccer. Address: Rua Alexandre Ferreira, 30-R/C Esq, 1700 Lisboa, Portugal.

JORIZZO Joseph Lucius, b. 6 Oct 1951, Rochester, New York, USA. Dermatologist; Professor, Chairman, Department of Dermatology, Bowman Gray School of Medicine. divorced, 2 sons. Education: AB,

1971; MD, 1975. Appointments: Resident, Chief Resident, Department of Dermatology, University of North Carolina, 1975-79; Overseas Registrar, St John's Hospital for Diseases of the Skin, 1979-80; Assistant then Associate Professor, University of Texas, Medical Branch, 1980-86. Publications: 134 Articles; Dermalogical Signs of Diseases, 1988, 1994. Memberships: AAD; ADA; SID; BAD; Italian Society of Dermatology; French Society of Dermatology. Honours: Phi Beta Kappa; Alpha Omega Alpha; Lecturer, Royal Society of Medicine Trust, England, 1994. Address: Bowman Gray School of Medicine, Wake Forest University, Medical Centre Blvd, Winston-Salem, NC 27157, USA.

JOSEPH David Alan, b. 10 Oct 1947, Chicago, Illinois, USA. Psychiatry. m. Pamela Bodotin, 24 Aug 1969, 3 sons, 1 daughter. Education: BA, Yale University, 1969; MD, University of Health Sciences, The Chicago Medical School, 1973. Appointments: Associate, Northwestern University, Chicago, 1977-91; Associate, Rush Medical College, Chicago, 1986-91. Memberships: American Psychiatry Association; Washington Psychiatric Association; Association for Geriatric Psychiatry; International Society for the Study of Multiple Personality & Dissociation. Hobbies: Sailing; Skiing; Kayaking. Address: 13030 Military Road South #202, Seattle, WA 98168, USA.

JOSHUA Sandra Catherine, b. 2 Jan 1957, Manhattan, New York, USA. Clinical Researcher. Education: BS cum laude, Community Health Education, Hunter College, School of Health Sciences, New York City, 1979; MSPH, Department of Preventive Medicine and Biometrics, Health Science Center, University of Colorado, Denver, 1991; Academic course in Pharmacoepidemiology. Appointments include: Public Health Disease Control Specialist A, 1984-85, Public Health Disease Control Specialist B, 1985-87, Epidemiology Division, Colorado Department of Health, Denver; Epidemiology Research Associate, Epidemiology Information and Surveillance Division, 1987-89, Clinical Research Associate I, Cardiopulmonary Division, 1989-90, Clinical Research Associate II, Cardiopulmonary Division, 1990-92, Clinical Research Associate III, Cardiopulmonary Department, 1992-93, Clinical Research Associate III, Neurology and Psychiatry Department, 1994-, Burroughs Wellcome Co, Research Triangle Park, North Carolina. Publications: An Epidemiologic Study of CS: Risk indicators for the occurrence of CS in Colorado, 1988. Honours: Radio Broadcast Certification, Connecticut School of Broadcasting, 1987; Young Outstanding Women of America Award, 1986, 1987; Aerobic Instruction Certification, 1988. Membership: Society for Epidemiological Research. Hobby: Tai Chi Uon. Address: PO Box 16153, Chapel Hill, NC 27516, USA.

JUDSON Franklyn Nevin, b. 14 Apr 1942, Cleveland, OH, USA. Physician; Medical Doctor. m. Marti J Judson, 12 Dec 1981, 2 d. Education: BA, Wesleyan University, 1964; MD, University of PA, 1964; Board Certified, Internal Medicine, Infectious Diseases and Preventive Medicine. Career: Assistant Director, 1974-76, Director, 1976-86, Denver Disease Control Service; Director, Denver Public Health Department, 1986-; Currently, Professor, Departments of Medicine and Preventive Medicine, University of CO; Chief, Infectious Diseases Service, Denver General Hospital. Publications: Over 200 publications as author or co-author including editing 3 books, 112 peer reviewed articles and 24 chapters. Honour: Achievement Award, American Veneral Diseases Association, 1980. Memberships: Fellow, Infectious Diseases Society of America; Fellow, American College of Preventive Medicine; American Veneral Diseases Association; Royal Society of Medicine. Hobbies: Running; Skiing; Organic Farming. Address: 605 Bannock Street, Denver, CO 80204-4507, USA.

JÜRGENS Herbert, b. 3 July 1949, Bonn, Germany. Physician. m. Christine Jürgens, 2 sons, 2 daughters. Education: MD; Board Examination; Dr med habilitation; Medical Residency, 1975-76; Paediatric training, 1976-81; Special Fellow, Paediatric Oncology, Memorial Sloan Kettering Center, New York, USA, 1978-79. Appointments: Associate Professor; Full Professor, 1991; Currently Director, Department of Paediatric Haematology and Oncology, Klinik und Poliklinik für Kinderheilkunde, Munster. Publications: Ewing's Sarcoma, in Cancer in Children, 3rd edition; Cancer 61:23-32, 1988; Bone tumours, in Paediatric Oncology, 1992; Pathology Research Practice 189:1111-1136, 1993; Current Opinion in Oncology 6:391-396, 1994. Memberships: Board Member, German Society of Paediatric Oncology and Haematology; Chairman, National Ewing's Sarcoma Study; Board Member, SIOP; ASCO; EMSOS; UICC. Address: Klinik und Poliklinik für Kinderheilkunde, Päd Hämatologie und Onkologie, Albert-Schweitzer Str 33, 48129 Münster, Germany.

JUSSAWALLA Darab Jehangir, b. 13 Apr 1915, Bombay, ndia. Oncologist. m. Gertrud. Education: MS; FRCS; FACS; FAMS; FASc; FNA. Appointments: Director, Lady Ratan Tata Medical and Research Centre, Bombay; Head, Department of Oncology, Breach Candy Hospital, Bombay; senior Consultant, Jaslok Hospital, Bombay. Address: B/22 Darshan Apartments. Mount Pleasant Road, Malabar Hill, Bombay 400 006, India.

JUTHANI Nalini V, b. 26 Jan 1946, Bombay, India. Physician. m. Virendra Juthani, 29 Mar 1970, 1 s, 2 d. Education: MD; FAPA. Appointments: Clinical Instructor, 1978; Assistant Professor of Psychiatry, 1979; Currently, Associate Professor of Psychiatry, Albert Einstein College of Medicine, 1993-. Publication: Immigrant Mental Health: Conflicts and Concerns of Indian Immigrants in USA, 1992. Honours: Fellow, NY Academy of Medicine; Teacher of Year Award, 1990. Memberships: American Psychiatric Association; NY Academy of Medicine. Hobbies: Photography; Painting; Philosophy Groups. Address: 17 Pheasant Run, Scarsdale, NY 10583, USA.

JUTSHOUK Nikolai D, b. 27 Dec 1940, Brest, Russia. Physician. m. Valentine Raerskaya, 31 Aug 1973, 1 daughter. Education: MD, Irkutsk State Medical Institute, 1966. Appointments: Central Institute of Epidemiology, 1969; Moscow Medical Stomatological Institute, 1971; Infectionist. Publications: Salmoneleses, 1989; Manual on Infection Diseases, Co-author, 1986; Epidemiology, 1993; Bacterial Dysenteria, 1994; Co-author of over 350 works. Honours: Corresponding Member, Russian Academy of Medical Sciences, 1993. Memberships: All-Russian Scientific Society of Infectionists; Supreme Validation Commission of Russian Federation. Hobby: Swimming. Address: Russian Federation, Jygnaya Pervomay-skaya st 3-179, Moscow, Russia.

K

KABAT Elvin A, b. 1 Sept 1914, New York City, USA. Higging Professor of Mircobiology. m. Sally Lennick, 1942, 3 s. Education: BS; AM; PhD; DSc, honorary. Appointments include: Instructor in Pathology, Cornell Medical College, 1938-41; Assistant Professor of Bacteriology, 1946-48, Associate professor of Bacteriology, 1948-52, Professor of Microbiology, 1952-85, Professor of Human Genetics and development, 1969-, Higgins Professor of Microbiology, 1984-85, Professor Emeritus, 1985-, Columbia University; Microbiologist, Medical Service, Presbyterian Hospital, Neurological Institute, 1956-; Expert, OD National Institutes of Health, 1989-93. Publications: Experimental Immunochemistry, co-author, 1948; Blood Group Substances, Their Chemistry and Immunochemistry, 1956; Structural Concepts in Immunology and Immunochemistry, 1968; Variable Regions of Immunoglobulin Chains, Tabulations and Analyses of Amino Acid sequences, 1976; Sequences of Immunoglobulin Chains, Tabulation and Analysis of Amino Acid Sequences of Precursors, V-Regions, C-Regions, J-Chain and ß2-Microglobulins, 1979; Sequences of Proteins of Immunological Interest, 1987; Contributor of numerous scientific papers. Honours include: Recipient of several honorary degrees from Institutions; R E Dyer Lecture Award, National Institutes of Health, 1979; Dickson Prize in Medicine, University of Pittsburgh, 1986; National Medal of Science, 1991; Lifetime Award, American Association of Immunologists, 1995. Memberships include: NAS; Fellow, American Academy of Arts and Sciences. Address: Columbia University, 701 West 168th Street, New York, NY 10032, USA.

KABAT Hugh Francis, b. 3 Oct 1932, Manitowoc, WI, USA. Pharmacy. m. 15 Sep 1980, 6 s. Education: BS, Pharmacy; MS, Hospital Pharmacy; PhD, Pharmacy Administration. Career: Graduate Assistant, University of MI; Instructor, University of CO; Assistant, Associate, Professor, Associate Dean, University of MN; Currently, Professor, College of Pharmacy, University of NM. Publications: Clinical Pharmacy Handbook, 1969; Drug Induced Mod Laboratory Test Values, chapter in Laboratory Medicine, 1973; DUR, in SNF, 1975; UNMH/BCMC Policy and Procedural Manual, 1985; UNMH Formulary, 1986-90. Honours: ASHP Research Award, 1969; Distinguished Service Award, 1971, Fellow, 1974, APS; Fulbright Senior Scholar, 1977; Innovative Educator, 1984; Fellow, AAPS, 1985. Memberships: Board of Directors, AACP; AAHE; AAPS; AAUP; AphA; APHA; ASHP; FIP; NCIH; Fulbright Association; International Society of Chromobiology. Hobbies: International Travel; Southwest History. Address: 4 Hoptree Trail, Corrales, NM 87048, USA.

KAGAN Bruce Laurence, b. 8 Jan 1953, New York, NY, USA. Physician. Education: MD; PhD. Career: Chief, Post-traumatic Stress Disorder Unit, West LA VAMC; Currently, Associate Professor of Psychiatry, UCLA School of Medicine. Publications: Nature, 1978; PNAS USA 78, 1981; Nature, 1983; PNAS USA 87, 1990; Science 255, 1992. Honours: Medical Scientist Training Program, 1975; APA BW Fellow, 1984; Pfizer Fellow, 1985; VA Career Award, 1986; NIMH Research Scientist Award, 1994. Memberships: American Psychiatric Association; Biophysical Society; International Society for Traumatic Stress Studies. Address: 760 Westwood Plaza, Los Angeles, CA 90024, USA.

KAHAN Barry Donald, b. 25 Jul 1939, Cleveland, OH, USA. Physician; Surgeon. m. Rochelle Liebling Kahan, 5 Sep 1962, 1 d. Education: MD; PhD. Career: Assistant Professor, 1972-74, Associate Professor, 1975-76, Surgery and Physiology, Northwestern University School of Medicine, Chicago, IL; Currently, Professor of Surgery, Director of Division of Immunology and Organ Transplant, University of TX Medical School, Houston. Memberships: American Association of Immunologists; American College of Surgeons; American Society of Transplant Surgeons; American Society of Transplant Physicians; International Society of Transplantation. Address: University of Texas Medical School, 6431 Fannin Suite 6240, Houston, TX 77030, USA.

KAHANA Eva, b. 21 Mar 1941, Budapest, Hungary. Professor, Chair, Sociology. m. Professor Boaz Kahana, 15 Apr 1962, 2 children. Education: BA, Stern College for Women, 1962; MA, City College CUNY, 1965; PhD, University of Chicago, 1967; DHL, Yeshiva University, 1991. Appointments include: From Associate Professor to Professor, Director, Elderly Care Research Center, 1971-84; Professor, Case Western Reserve, University of Cleveland, 1984-; Armington Professor, 1989-90; Chairman, Department of Sociology, 1985-;

Director, Elderly Care Research Center, 1984-; Pierce and Elizabeth Robson Professor of Humanities, 1990-; Mary E Switzer Distinguished Fellow, National Institute Disability and Rehabilitation, 1992-93. Publications: Editorial Board, Gerontologist, 1975-79; Psychology of Aging, 1984-90; Journal of Gerontology, 1990-; Articles to professional journals; Chapters to books. Honours: Publisher's Prize, 1969; NIMH Career Development Grants, 1974-79; Distinguished Mentorship Award, Gerontology Society of America, 1987; National Institute Aging Merit Award, 1989-; Arnold Heller Award of Excellence in Geriatrics and Gerontology, 1992; Distinguished Gerontological Researcher in Ohio, 1993. Memberships include: American Sociological Association; American Psychological Association; Society for Traumatic Stress; Life Member, Wayne State University Academy of Scholars. Hobbies: Reading; Antiques; Travel. Address: Case Western Reserve University, Department of Sociology (Mather Mem) 226, Cleveland, OH 44106-1749, USA.

KAIRUKI Hubert Clemence Mwombeki, b. 24 June 1940, Bukoba, Tanzania. Obstetrician; Gynaecologist. m. Kokushubka Kairuki, 11 June 1967, 3 sons, 2 daughters. Education: MB ChB, Dip Obst, MMed, Makerere University; MRCOG(UK), 1974; FRCOG(UK), 1992. Appointments: Senior Lecturer, University of Dar Es Salaam, 1982; Managing Director, Mikocheni Hospital. Publications: The Place of Symphysiotomy in Obstetric Disproportion, 1974; Management of Eclampsia in Labour. Memberships: Association of Gynaecologists and Obstetricians, President, 1989-. Address: Mission Mikocheni Teaching Hospital, PO Box 65300, Dar Es Salaam, Tanzania.

KAKABADSE Andrew, b. 30 Mar 1948, Athens, Greece. Psychologist. Widower, 1 daughter. Education: BSc (Hons), Salford University, England; MA, Brunel University; PhD, Manchester University; AAPSW (Qualified Psychiatric Social Worker). Appointments: Mental Health Officer; Child Guidance Officer; Research Officer; Senior Lecturer, currently Professor of Management and Development, Cranfield University, Cranfield. Publications: Books: People and Organisations: The Practitioner's View, 1982; Stress, Change and Organisation, 1982; Culture of the Social Services, 1982; Politics of Management, 1983; Privatisation and the NHS: A Scope for Collaboration (with J Chandra), 1985; Working in Organisations (with S Vinnicombe and R Ludlow), 1987, Penguin Edition, 1988; Cases in Human Resources Management (with S Tyson), 1987; Management Development and the Public Sector - A European Perspective (with Rainer Holzer), 1989; Wealth Creators, 1991; Sabotage (with F Analoui), 1991; Using Ethnography in Small Firms Research (with G Stockport), 1992; Cases in European Human Resource (with S Tyson); Monographs; Articles; Co-editor, books: Leadership and Organisation Development, 1980; Power, Politics and Organisations: A Behavioural Science View, 1984; Future of Management Education, 1984. Memberships: Fellow, British Psychological Society; Fellow, International Academy of Management; Fellow, Royal Society of Arts, Manufacturing and Science. Hobbies: Cycling; Swimming; Travel. Address: Cranfield School of Management, Cranfield University, Wharley End, Cranfield, Bedfordshire MK43 0AL, England.

KAKETA Toshitaka, b. 11 Nov 1930, Sendai, Japan. Dentist. m. Yoshi Kaketa, 14 Nov 1961, 1 son, 2 daughters. Education: DDS, Tokyo Dental College; PhD, Nihon Medical University; Fellow, International College of Dentistry, Tokyo; Diploma, Fellow, International Congress of Oral Implantologist, USA; Advanced Leading Instructor, Japanese Society of Implantology, Tokyo. Appointments: Full Time Lecturer, Tokyo Dental College; Professor, Iwate Medical University School of Dentistry; Chairman of Prosthodoutics; Chairman, Institute of Implant Dentures; Dean, Sendai College of Dental Hygiene. Publications: Immediate Dentures, 1963; Crown and Bridge Work Prosthodentics, 1964; Mundamental and Clinical Dental Implants, 1988; Oral Implantology, 1990. Memberships: American Academy of Implant Dentistry; Asian Implant Academy; Japanese Society of Oral Implantology; Japan Society of Prosthodontics. Honours: Award of Qualified Implantologic Merits, International Research, Committe of Oral Implantology, 1991; International Education Award, The International Congress of Oral Implantologists, 1992. Hobbies: Golf; Classical Music. Address: 2-5-19 Nankodia, Minami, Lzumi-ku, Sendai 02981, Japan.

KALAKOUTIS Gabriel Michael, b. 7 Jul 1949, Nicosia, Cyprus. Medicine. m. Monica Kalakoutis, 7 Sept 1986, 1 s, 2 d. Education: BSc, Medical Science, 1971, MB, Ch B, 1974, University of Edinburgh Medical School, UK; MRCOG. Appointments: Consultant Obstetrician-Gynaecologist, Makarios Hospital, Nicosia, Cyprus.

Publication: Co-author, Cervical Pregnancy Ending in a Live Birth, in European Journal of Human Reproduction and Embryology. Memberships: International Gynaecological Cancer Society; Royal College of Obstetricians and Gynaecologists. Hobbies: Swimming; Photography. Address: 4 Menandrou Street, Makedonitissa, Nicosia, Cyprus.

KALANTAROV Karl, b. 28 Aug 1930, Bakou, Russia. Biophysicist. m. Naydenova Valentina, 5 Apr 1956, 2 s. Education: Candidate of Science, Moscow University, 1958; DSc, Biophysics. Appointments: Research Fellow, Institute for Medical Instrumentation, 1958-; Currently, Head of Laboratory for Medical Engineering, Research Institute. Publications: Optimal Configuration of System for Nuclear Medicine, Data Logging and Processing, and Basic Algorithms, Russian National Congress for Radiology, 1977. Honour: Honoured Scientist of Russia. Memberships: Russian Society of Medical Physics; Academician, Russian Academy for Medical Engineering. Hobby: Ashtray Collecting. Address: Seraphimovitcha Street, 1 Apt 279, Moscow 109072, Russia.

KALINER Michael Arun, b. 27 Apr 1941, Baltimore, Maryland, USA. Physician. m. Jean Andrews, 12 June 1972, 2 sons, 1 daughter. Education: MD, University of Maryland Medical School, 1967. Appointments: Head, Allergic Diseases, National Institutes of Health, 1975-93; President, American Academy Allergy and Immunology; Medical Director, Institute for Asthma and Allergy. Publications: Author of over 400 articles, reviews, chapters and books. Honours: Patterson Lectureship, 1989; Van Pirguet Lectureship, 1990; Jaris Lectureship, 1986, 1988; Loueg Lectureship, 1992; National Asthma Award, 1992. Memberships: Association American Physicians; American Society Clinical Investigation; American Academy Allergy and Immunology; American Thoracic Society; American Association Immunology. Address: Washington Hospital Centre, 106 Irving Street NW # 108, Washington DC 20010, USA.

KALKWARF Kenneth Lee, b. 12 Apr 1946, Lincoln, Nebraska, USA. Dentist. m. Sharon Ruta Moore, 6 July 1974, 2 s. Education: DDS, MS, University of Nebraska. Appointments: Assistant, Associate, Professor, University of Nebraska; Associate Professor, University of Oklahoma; Professor of Periodontology, Dean, University of Texas Health and Science Centre, San Antonio. Publications: Contributor of over 120 professional articles. Honours: American College of dentists, 1985; International College of Dentists, 1992; Outstanding Alumnus, University of Nebraska, 1990. Membership: American Dental Association. Hobbies: Informatics; Jogging; Spectator sports. Address: UTHSCSA, 7703 Floyd Curl Drive, San Antonio, TX 78284-7906, USA.

KALMYKOV Leonid, b. 21 Nov 1937, Kharkiv, Ukraine. Dosimetrist; Radiobiologist. m. Irina Brestovitskaya, 12 May 1973, 1 daughter. Education: Diploma in Physical and Radio Chemistry, Kharkiv State University, 1960; Candidate of Sciences, Chemistry, 1970; DSc, Biology, 1991. Appointments: Laboratory Technician, 1960-61, Scientific Worker, 1961-91, Head, Dosimetry and Radiation Safety Department, 1991-, Institute of Medical Radiology, Kharkiv. Publications: Radiobiology of bone tissue (co-author), 1986; Estimation of radiobiological constants for 210Po behaviour in organisms (co-author), 1968; Materials for thermoluminescent dose detectors and photon radiation energy detectors, 1994. Membership: Ukrainian Association of Radiologists. Hobby: Gardening. Address: ul 8 Sjezda Sovetov 9/56, Kharkiv 310058, Ukraine.

KALRA Jawahar (Jay), b. 2 Apr 1949, Aligarh, India. Professor of Pathology. m. Kamla Kalra, 26 Apr 1986, 1 son, 1 daughter. Education: BSc, Aligarh University, 1967; MSc, 1972, PhD, 1976, MD, 1981, Memorial University, Newfoundland, Canada; Certified: Canadian Society of Clinical Chemistry and Royal College of Physicians and Surgeons of Canada, 1986; FRCPC, 1986; FACB, 1987; FICA, 1988; FACA, 1989; FCACB, 1989. Appointments: Assistant Professor, 1985-88, Associate Professor, 1988-91, Professor, Head, Department of Pathology, 1991-, College of Medicine, University of Saskatchewan; Director, Pathology Laboratory, Royal University Hospital, 1991-; Chief, Department of Laboratory Medicine, Saskatoon District Health Board, 1993-. Publications include: Co-author, 12 key papers, 1989-, including: Influence of endothelin on cardiovascular function, oxygen free radicals and blood chemistry, 1991; Lipid profile in acute stroke, 1992; Oxygen free radicals and hypercholesterolemic atherosclerosis: Effect of Vitamin E', 1993. Honours: University Medal, 1969; Excellent Research Award, Eastern Student Research Forum, 1979; Med Chem Award, 1991, 1992, Excellence Research Award, 1994, Canadian Society for Clinical

Chemistry; Rotary Golden Wheel Award, 1994. Memberships: New York Academy of Sciences; International Society of Free Radical Research-Oxygen Society; American Society of Clinical Pathologists; International Society for Heart Research; National Academy of Clinical Biochemistry; American Association of Clinical Chemistry; Canadian and Saskatchewan Medical Associations; Canadian Association of Pathology; Canadian Association of Medical Biochemists; Royal College of Physicians and Surgeons, Canada. Hobbies: Badminton; Cooking. Address: 323 Coldspring Crescent, Saskatoon, Saskatchewan, Canada S7J 3M9.

KALRA Veena, b. 3 Mar 1946, Lahore. Additional Professor of Paediatrics. m. Avninder Kalra, 6 June 1973, 2 sons, 1 daughter. Education: MBBS, Delhi University, 1968; MD, All India Institute of Medical Sciences, New Delhi, 1972. Appointments: Currently Additional Professor of Paediatrics, All India Institute of Medical Sciences, New Delhi; Examiner in Paediatrics, Indian and foreign universities. Publications: Author or co-author, 78 original technical papers and 10 chapters for medical textbooks by Indian and foreign authors; Founder Editor, Neurotransmitter, newsletter of Child Neurology Chapter, Indian Academy of Paediatrics; Guide of 23 MD/PhD Thesis in Child Neurology; Children Liver Diseases; Neuro Genetic Disorders. Honours: 1st place, all university examinations; Numerous awards including: President of India's Medal and Pfizer's Scroll of Honour as Best Medical Graduate from Delhi University, 1968; Sorell Katherine Award as Best Paediatric Postgraduate from All India Institute of Medical Sciences, 1972; WHO Research Training Grantee, 1981; S T Achar Endowment Award for Best Clinical Research, Indian Academy of Paediatrics, 1983; Kanishka Award for Medical Education, Lions Club Delhi; Certificates of Merit and Recognition by International & Asian Congresses of Pediatrics, 1977, 1983, 1994. Memberships: Fellow, National Academy of Sciences, India; International Child Neurology Association, USA; Life Member, Indian Academy of Paediatrics; Asian Oceanian Association of Child Neurology, Japan; Founder Member and Executive Secretary, 1991-93, Indian Academy of Paediatrics Child Neurology Chapter; Life Member, Oxford and Cambridge Society of India; Active Member, Child Neurology Society, USA. Hobbies: Music; Driving; Travel; Watching nature; Sleeping. Address: D-II/1 Ansari Nagar, New Delhi 110 029, India.

KALSER Martin H, b. 7 Jan 1923. Physician. m. Barbara, 1 s, 2 d. Education: MD; PhD. Appointments: Professor of Medicine, Division Chief, Gastroenterology, University of Miami Schoo of Medicine, Miami, Florida, USA. Address: University of Miami School of Medicine, 1600 NW 10th Avenue, POB 016099 (R59), Miami, FL 33101, USA.

KALTENBACH James Albert, b. 31 Jan 1952, Baltimore, USA. Auditory Neuroscientist. m. 26 June 1986, 1 d. Education: BS, George Washington University, 1975; MS, Towson State University, 1980; PhD, University of Pennsylvania, 1984. Appointments: Currently, Associate Professor, Department of Otolaryngology, Wayne State University; Assistant Professor, Department of Audiology, Wayne State University, 1987-94; Postdoctoral Fellow, Department of Physiology, University of Pennsylvania. Publications: Numerous papers and book chapters. Honours: Award for Meritorious Service, Smithsonian Institution, 1970; Undergraduate Research Fellowship, National Science Foundation, 1971; Graduate Research Training Award, 1982-84; NIH Postdoctoral Fellowship, 1984-87; Chair of Education Committee for the Association for Research in Otolaryngology, 1995-; Memberships: Society for Neuroscience; International Brain Research Organisation; Association for Research in Otolaryngology; American Association for the Advancement of Science. Hobbies: Travel; Hiking; Paleontology; Music composition. Address: 1903 Pembroke, Birmingham, MI 48009, USA.

KAMDAR Rasiklal Mohanlal, b. 20 Nov 1919, Limbdi, Gujarat, India. Surgeon. m. Dr Priyamvada Kamdar, 3 Feb 1949, 1 s, 2 d. Education: MBBS; MS, Bombay University, India; FRCS, UK. Appointments: Honorary Surgeon, Sir T Hospital, Bhavnagar, 1951-76; Honorary Surgeon, Western Rly Hospital, Bhavnagar, 1962-83; Currently, Consulting Surgeon, Kamdar Hospital, Bhavnagar. Publications: Many scientific papers in various professional journals. Honours: Vice President, K J Mehta TB Hospital, Amargadh; President, Indian Medical Association, 1978; President, Gujarat Chapter, Association of Surgeons of India; President, Rotary Club for 3 terms; KN Bahadurji Scholarship for Surgery; Outstanding Activities Award, GIANTS Club; Fellow, Royal College of Surgeons, UK. Memberships: Indian Medical Association; Association of Surgeons of India. Hobbies: Music; Religious and Social

Activities. Address: Kamdar Hospital, Bhavnagar, Gujarat, 364001, India.

KAMDAR Vikram Rasiklal, b. 9 Aug 1950, Ahmedabad, India. Psychiatrist. m. Sandra June Cowen, 15 Feb 1991, 1 daughter. Education: MD, MB, BS, India; DPM, Dublin, Ireland; Board Certified in Psychiatry, Maudsley, London, England. Appointments: General Practitioner, Birmingham, England, 1982-89; Psychiatrist, Birmingham, 1989-92; Attending Consultant Staff Psychiatrist, South Arkansas Regional Health Centre, USA. Memberships: American Psychiatric Association; Arkansas Psychiatric Association. Hobbies: Cricket; Swimming; Travel; Bridge; Stamp and coin collecting. Address: South Arkansas Regional Health Centre, 715 North College, El Dorado, AR 71730, USA.

KAMEN George, b. 4 May 1942, Pleven, Bulgaria. Psychiatrist. m. Katia Bogdanova, 8 Apr 1980, 1 son, 1 daughter. Education: Higher Medical Institute, Sofia, 1969; MD, Washington Square Institute, New York, 1990. Appointments: Assistant Professor, Medical Academy, Sofia; Psychiatrist, Mariehede, Germany; Independent Scholar, Psychoanalyst, Washington Square Institute, New York; Honorary Research Fellow, Centre of Psychoanalytic Studies, University of Kent, England. Publications: Aspects of Group Psychotherapy, 1973; The Bulgarian Folk and Ritual Dances as Communication and their Therapeutic Impact, 1974; Registration and Assessment of the Dynamic Structures of a Small Group, 1974; Co-author, Attempted Self-Destruction and Nosology, 1976; Syndrome and Nosology as Indications for Group Therapy, 1978; Psychoanalysis in Bulgaria, 1992; Some Thoughts About Mentality and the Fate of Psychoanalysis in Bulgaria, 1993; The Rulers, The Victims and The Silence, 1994. Memberships: National Association for the Advancement of Psychoanalysis; New York Academy of Sciences; The American Group Psychotherapy Association; The Bulgarian Psychiatric Association. Hobbies: Travel; Arts; Books. Address: Washington Square Institute for Mental Health, 41-51 East 11th Street, New York, NY 11222, USA.

KAMENETSKY Mikhail, b. 28 Jun 1933, Chernigov, Ukraine. Physician. m. Maya Polonnikova, 17 Feb 1959, 1 s. Education: MD, Kiev Medical University, 1956; PhD, 1965, DSc, 1989, Donetsk Medical University. Career: Radiologist, Kovel, Ukraine, 1956-58; Radiologist in Chief, Donetsk, Ukraine, 1958-67; Instructor, Radiology, Associate Professor, 1987, Currently, Head of Department of Radiology, Donetsk Medical University, Ukraine. Publications: 424 publications including: Higher Medical Education, 1992; Roetgenological evaluation of susceptibility to nephrogenic lung edema, 9th European Congress of Radiology, 1995. Honour: Honoured Worker of Public Education, Ukraine, 1993. Memberships: Ukranian Association of Radiology; European Association of Radiology; President, Donetsk Regional Division of UAR. Hobbies: Music; Painting; Poetry; Sport. Address: 2A Shchorsa Str, Flat 35, Donetsk 340055, Ukraine.

KAMENEVA Marina Vitaly, b. 28 June 1944, Moscow, Russia. Biomed Scientist. m. Dr Boris A Kushner, 6 Feb 1966, 1 son, 1 daughter. Education: MS, 1968, PhD, 1972, Moscow University. Appointments: Junior Research Fellow, 1968-75, Senior Investigator, 1975-89, Moscow University; Visiting Professor of Surgery, University of Pittsburgh, USA, 1991-. Publications: Effect of Hematocrit on the Development and Consequences of some Haemodynamic Disorders, 1990; Heparin Effect on Red Blood Cell Aggregation, Co-author, 1994; Effect of Perfluorochemical Emulsion (FLUOSOL) on Blood Trauma and Hemorrheology, Co-author, 1994; Resistance-reducing Polymers and Some Hydrodynamic Problems in Atherosclerosis, Co-author, 1986; Effect of High Molecular Weight Compunds Dissolved in Blood on Hemodynamics, Co-author, 1976; Contributor of over 80 professional articles. Honours: Lomonosov Diploma, Moscow University, 1972; State Diploma of Senior Scientist, 1983. Memberships: International Society for Clinical Hemorheology; American Society for Artificial Internal Organs; Biomedical Engineering Society. Hobbies: Music; Stamp Collecting. Address: 5 Bayard Road #519, Pittsburgh, PA 15213, USA.

KAMIL Elaine, b. 26 Jan 1947, Cleveland, Ohio, USA. Pediatric Nephrologist. m. Ivan Jeffery Kamil, 29 Aug 1970, 2 sons, 1 daughter. Education: BS, magna cum laude, University of Pittsburgh, 1969; MD, University of Pittsburgh, 1973. Appointments: Acting Assistant Professor of Pediatrics, University California, Los Angeles School of Medicine, 1979-80;; Consultant in Pediatric Nephrology, Hawthorne Community Medical Group, California, 1981-; Adjunct Assistant Professor of Pediatrics, University California, Los Angeles School of Medicine,

1983-87; Medical Director, The Children's Clinic of Long Beach, 1984-87; Medical Director, Pediatric Nurse Practitioner Program, California Stae University, Long Beach, 1985-87; Adjunct Assistant Professor of Pediatrics, University of California, Los Angeles School of Medicine, 1987-88; Assistant Clinical Professor of Pediatrics, University California, Los Angeles School of Medicine, 1988-90; Associate Director, Pediatric Nephrology & Transplant Immunology, Cedars-Sinai Medical Center, 1990-; Associate Clinical Professor of Pediatrics, UCLA School of Medicine, 1991-. Publications incl: Long Term Cyclosporine A Treatment of Steroid Resistant and Steroid Dependent Nephrotic Syndrome, 1991; Treatment of Wegener's Granulomatosus (WG) with Pooled Intravenous Gammaglobulin (IVIG), 1992; Recombinant Human Growth Hormone in Pubertal Patients with Chronic Renal Disease, 1992. Honours incl: Teaching Award, University California, Irvine, 1986-87; Continuing Service Award, National Kidney Foundation of Southern California, 1991. Memberships incl: Alpha Omega Alpha; Phi Beta Kappa; National Kidney Foundation of Southern California. Hobbies: Hiking; Skiing; Travel. Address: Cedars-Sinai Medical Center, 8700 Beverly Blvd, Los Angeles, CA 90048, USA.

KAMINEK Milan, b. 12 May 1938, Kolin, Czech Republic. Dentist; Orthodontist. m. Eva Hruskova, 24 Feb 1962, 2 sons. Education: DDS, Palacky University, Olomouc, 1961; Study visit, Royal Dental Colleges, Copenhagen and Aarhus, Denmark, 1968-69; Specialist in Orthodontics, 1971; Candidate of Science, 1976; Habilitation (Docent), 1978; DSc, 1987. Appointments: Assistant Professor, Orthodontic Department, 1961-78, Docent, Orthodontics, 1978-89, Professor of Orthodontics, 1989-, Palacky University, Olomouc. Publications: Soucasné fixni ortodontické aparaty, 1976; Kieferorthopädische Therapie mit festsitzenden Apparaturen, 1980; Celustna ortopédia (co-author), 1981. Honours: Scientific Prize, Czech Stomatological Association, 1981; Honorary Member, Society for Orthopaedic Stomatology, Democratic Republic of Germany, 1989; Correspondent Member, German Society for Jaw Orthopaedics, 1993. Memberships: European Orthodontic Society; Czech Orthodontic Society; Czech Stomatological Association; Czech Stomatological Chamber; Scientific Board, Medical Faculty, Palacky University. Hobby: Music. Address: Delnicka 44, 779 00 Olomouc, Czech Republic.

KANAREK Marty Steven, b. 20 Mar 1947, Washington DC, USA. Professor. m. Frances Culwell, 29 Jul 1972, 2 s, 1 d. Education: BA, Grinnell College; MPH, University of Minnesota; PhD, Epidemiology, University of California, Berkeley. Career includes: Health Research Speciality, USEPA, 1972-78; Currently, Professor, Preventive Medicine and Environmental Studies, University of Wisconsin, Madison. Publication: Co-author, Asbestos in Drinking Water and Cancer Incidence in the San Francisco Bay Area, in American Journal of Epidemiology, 1980. Memberships: Fellow, American College of Epidemiology; Society for Epidemiological Research. Address: Department of Preventive Medicine, University of Wisconsin, 504 North Walnut Street, Madison, WI 53705, USA.

KANE Lennox, b. 7 June 1946, Ballymena, County Antrim, Northern Ireland. Obstetrician and Gynaecologist. m. vanessa Charrington, 27 Sep 1980, 1 son, 1 daughter. Education: BA, MD, 1982, Trinity College, Dublin; Mb BCh BAO, 1970; MRCOG, 1978; FRCOG, 1992. Appointments: Consultant, Clinical Director, St Albans and Hemel Hemstead, England. Publications: Contributor of papers on chlamydial infections and pelvic inflamatory disease. Hobbies: Golf; Country Pursuits; Destroying Bureaucracy. Address: Reepers Cottage, The Green, Little Gaddesden, Hertfordshire HP4 1PQ, England.

KANE Mark, b. 28 Dec 1961, Melbourne, Australia. Osteopath. Education: MAESO, Australian College of Acupuncture, 1985; Diploma in Medical Herbalism, Southern Cross School of Herbal Medicine, NSW, Australia, 1987; DO, College of Osteopaths, London, 1991; MA, Complementary Health Studies, University of Exeter Centre for Complementary Health Studies, 1994. Appointments: Faculty Lecturer MA Therapeutic Bodywork, MSc Complementary Therapy Studies University of Westminster Centre for Community Care and Primary Health; Research Fellow British School of Osteopathy; Private Practice as Osteopath and Acupuncturist. Publication: Measuring Success - What of The Patient's Perspective, in British Osteopathic Journal, 1995. Memberships: College of Osteopaths Practitioners Association; Register of Traditional Chinese Medicine. Hobbies: Skiing; Sculpture; Music. Address: 12a Thurloe Street, London, SW7 2ST, England.

KANEKO Michio, b. 28 July 1947, Sendai, Japan. Associate Professor. m. 1 May 1971, 2 s, 1 d. Education: Graduate, Faculty of Medicine, University of Tokyo, 1973. Appointments: Staff, Paediatric Surgery, Japan Red Cross Medical Centre; Staff, Surgery, National Children's Hospital; Associate of Paediatric Surgery, University of Tokyo; Assistant Professor, Associate Professor, Department of Paediatric Surgery, University of Tsukuba. Publications: Genetic Aspect of Neuroblastoma, 1988; Treatment of Advanced Neuroblastoma with Emphasis on Intensive Induction Chemotherapy, 1990. Hobbies: Mountaineering; Fishing; Cello playaing. Address: Department of Paediatric Surgery, University of Tsukuba, 1-1-1-, Tennodai, Tsukuba, Ibaraki 305, Japan.

KANG Chil-Yong, b. 28 Nov 1940, Hadong, Korea. Professor. m. 17 Dec 1966, 1 son, 2 daughters. Education: BSc; Dip Vet Sc; PhD; DSc; FRSC. Appointments: Professor, University of Texas Southwestern Medical School, USA, 1974-82; Professor, Chairman, Department of Microbiology and Immunology, University of Ottawa, Canada, 1982-92; Professor, Dean of Science, University of Western Ontario, 1992-. Publications: Contributor of 110 scientific articles in peer-review journals. Honours: national Commendation Medal of the President of Korea, 1986; DSc, Carleton University, 1991; Elected Fellow, Royal Society of Canada. Memberships: American Society Virology; American Society Microbiology; AAAS; New York Academy of Science; Genetic Society of Canada; Canadian Society Microbiology; Royal Society of Canada. Hobbies: Music; Golf. Address: Western Science Centre, The University of Western Ontario, London, Ontario N6A 5B7, Canada.

KANG Daein, b. 20 Jan 1951, South Korea. Dental Surgeon. m. Young Kim, 26 Nov 1975, 3 sons. Education: DDS; Diplomate, American Osseous Society; Fellow, International Congress of Oral Implantology; Fellow, American Academy of Implant Dentistry. Appointments: Founder, Pacific Institute of Oral Implantology, Los Angeles, California, USA. Honours: US Jaycees, 1987; Institute for Human Rights, 1990. Memberships include: American Dental Association; Californian Dental Association. Hobby: Sailing.

KANG Liangshi, b. 25 Dec 1919, Xiamen, China. Doctor of Chinese Medicine. m. Cheng Yue Qin, 14 July 1943, 5 sons, 3 daughters. Education: Chinese Medicine study under Kang Ming-Jiao, 7 years; Diploma of Doctor of Chinese Medicine, Central Test Institute, 1948. Appointments include: Vice-Director Doctor of Chinese Medicine, 1958, Director Doctor, Xiamen Chinese Medicine Hospital, 1978-; Professor of Chinese Medicine, Xiamen Chinese Medicine Institution, 1988-. Publications: 61 papers about Chinese medicine in national journals on Chinese medicine, 1958-94; 4 books, 1960-94, including: On the diagnosis and cure of Liver Diseases. Honours: 3 Science Promotion Awards of Fujian Province, 5 Science Promotion Awards of Xiamen City, 1978-90; Medal and Certificate of Merit for Contribution to Traditional Chinese Medicine, Fujian Province, 1985. Memberships: Chairman, All-China Traditional Medicine Society, Xiamen Branch; Vice-Director, Chinese Medicine Training and Exchange Centre. Hobbies: Chinese classical literature and writing arts. Address: 4 Jin Xin Street, Xiamen, Fujian, China.

KANG Tingguo, b. 2 April 1955, Liaoning, China. Professor. m. Zhu Liwa, 28 September 1983, 1 son. Education: BS, Liaoning College of Traditional Chinese Medicine, 1982. Appointments: Professor, Liaoning College of Traditional Chinese Medicine. Publications: Microidentification of Chinese Patent Medicine, 1990; TLC Identification of Chinese Patent Medicine, 1994. Memberships: Professional Committee, Chinese Drug's Identification of Traditional Chinese Medicine and Pharmacy Institute of China; Committee, China Market Institute. Hobbies: Go. Address: Liaoning College of Traditional Chinese Medicine, No 79 Chogshan East Road, Shenyang, China.

KAO Lily Ching-Chiung, b. 4 Aug 1951, Hong Kong. Neonatologist; Paediatrician. m. Dr Wen Hsien Hsu, 2 July 1983, 1 son, 3 daughters. Education: BA, Temple University, USA, 1974; PhD, University of Pennsylvania, 1978; Fellowship, Neonatology and Paediatric Pulmonology, Children's Hospital, Los Angeles, 1981-83. Appointment: Neonatologist, Children's Hospital, Oakland, California. Publications: Furosemide Acutely Decreases Airway Resistance in Chronic Bronchopulmonary Dysplasia, Co-author, 1983; Neonatal Therapuetics: Bronchopulmonary Dysplasia, Co-author, 1991; Bronchopulmonary Dysplasia: Strategies for Total Patient Care, Co-author, 1990; High-Density Lipoprotein Subclass Distribution in Premature Newborns Before and After the Onset of Enteral Feeding, Co-author, 1988; Effects of Inhaled Metaproterenol and Atropine on the Pulmonary Mechanics of Infants with Bronchopulmonary Dysplasia, Co-author, 1989. Honours: Summa Cum Laude, 1974; Phi Beta Kappa, 1974. Memberships American Academy of Paediatrics; Western Society of Paediatric Research; Society for Paediatric Research. Hobbies: Singing; Playing Piano. Address: 747 52nd Street, Children's Hospital, Oakland, CA 94609, USA.

KAO Ming-Chien, b. 3 Jan 1939, Taipei. Neurosurgeon. m. Amy Tsai, 3 Jan 1984, 1 son, 1 daughter. Education: MD; DM; Sc. Appointments: President, Laser Medicine Society, China; President, International Society for Laser Surgery & Medicine; Director, Laser Medicine Research Center; Secretary General, Neurological Society. Publications: Laser endoscopic sympathectomy using a fiberoptic CO_2 laser to treat palmar hyperhidrosis, 1992; Laser endoscopic sympathectomy for palmar hyperhidrosis, 1994; Autonomic activities in hyperhidrosis patients before, during and after endoscopic laser sympathectomy. Honours: Outstanding Achievement in Applied Science, China, 1992. Memberships: International Society for Laser Surgery & Medicine; laser Medicine Society of China; Neurological Society of China. Hobby: Golf. Address: No 7 Chung-Shan South Road, Taipei, Taiwan.

KAPLAN Berton H, b. 27 Jun 1930, Winchester, VA, USA. Social Epidemiology. m. Ellen Brauer, 15 Jun 1959, 2 s. Education: PhD, 1962. Career: Visiting Professor, Psychiatry and Behavioral Sciences, Stanford Medical School, 1975-76; Advisory Committees, Institute of Medicine, 1980-90; Currently, Professor of Epidemiology, University of NC, School of Public Health. Publications: Blue Ridge, 1971; The Urban Environment and Psychiatric Disorder, 1971; Co-author, Further Explorations in Social Psychiatry, 1976; Numerous articles published. Memberships: AAAS; American Anthropological Society; American Social Society. Hobby: Sculpting. Address: Department of Epidemiology, CB 7400, University of NC School of Public Health, Chapel Hill, NC 27599-7400, USA.

KAPLAN Michael, b. 31 Oct 1940, Tver, Russia. Physician. m. Valentina Tupikina, 25 May 1966, 1 d. Education: BA, Tver Medical College, 1957; MD, Medical Radiological Research Centre of RAMS, 1969. Appointments: Surgeon, Michoslavl Infirmary, 1963; Chief, Department of Internal Medicine. Publications: Non-Resonance Mechanism of Biostimulation Action of Low-Intensity Laser Radiation, Co-author; An Attempt in Using Superpower Laser Radiation to Treat Malignancies. Memberships: European Association of Physicians-Naturopathologists; Laser Association of Russia. Hobbies: Painting; Sculpture. Address: 38 Marksa Street, Apt 6, Obninsk 249020, Russia.

KAPPENBERG Richard, b. 5 Feb 1944, Jamaica, New York, USA. Neuropsychologist. m. Judith Nakashima, 27 Nov 1970, 1 son, 1 daughter. Education: BA, 1965, MA, 1966, Fairfield University; PhD, University of Hawaii, 1973; Diplomate: American Academy of Medical Psychotherapy; American Academy of Behavioral Medicine; American Board of Vocational Experts. Appointments: Director of Rehabilitation Service, Salvation Army; Supervising Psychologist, Salvation Army; Chairman, Department of Human Development, University of Hawaii; Chief Psychologist, Clinical Director, Head Injury Programme, Rehabilitation Hospital of the Pacific; Currently in private practice, Honolulu, Hawaii. Publications: Various articles in Encyclopedia of Psychology, 1985; Neuropsychological Assessment, 1987. Honours: Past President, Hawaii Psychological Association, 1978, 1988; Distinguished Service Award, Hawaii Psychological Association, 1988. Memberships: American Psychological Association; National Academy of Neuropsychology; Hawaii Psychological Association. Hobby: Golf. Address: 1188 Bishop St, Suite 2005, Honolulu, HI 96813, USA.

KAPUR Raman, b. 4 Jan 1958, Northern Ireland. Clinical Psychologist. m. Mary Kapur, 11 Aug 1980, 1 son, 1 daughter. Education: BSc (Hons), Psychology; MSc, Abnormal Psychology; MPhil, Psychology (Psychotherapy Research). Appointments: Clinical Psychologist, Blackburn, England; Senior Clinical Psychologist, London; Currently Consultant Clinical Psychologist, Northern Ireland Mental Health Charity (Threshold). Publications: Group Psychotherapy in Acute Psychiatry, 1986; Therapeutic Factors in In-patient and Out-patient Psychotherapy Groups, 1988; Effects of Interpretations in Groups, 1993. Membership: British Psychological Society. Hobbies: Tennis; Squash. Address: 432 Antrim Road, Belfast BT15 5GB, Northern Ireland.

KARABUS Cyril David, b. 1 Apr 1935, Beaufort West, South Africa. Paediatrician. m. Jenifer Jackson, 11 Apr 1975, 2 s, 3 d. Education: MBChB, 1957; MMed(Paed), 1964, UCTown Medical School; DCH, London, 1965; MRCP (Lond and Edin), 1965; FRCP; FRCPE. Appointments: Associate Professor of Paediatrics, Head, Hematology and Oncology Service, University of Capetown and Red Cross Children's Hospital. Publications include: Haemophilia services in South Africa, chapter in Status and Atlas of Haemophilia Worldwide, 1984; Treatment of coagulation defects, in South African Journal of Continuing Medical Education, 1993; The Interdisciplinary Team in Management: Value and Problems, chapter in Neoplastic Diseases of Childhood, 1994. Honours: President, South African Society for Haematology, 1986-88, 1995-; Founding Chairman, South African Children's Cancer Group, 1987-89. Memberships: South African Paediatric Association; South African Children's Cancer Group; South African Society for Haematology; American Society Clinical Oncology; American Society Paediatric Hematology and Oncology. Hobbies: Reading; Oenology. Address: Red Cross Children's Hospital, Rondebosch, 7700 Cape Town, South Africa.

KARAGÜLLE Müfit Zeki, b. 17 Oct 1953, Istanbul, Turkey. MD. m. Fatma Serap, 8 Sep 1979, 1 d. Education: MD. Career: General Practitioner; Chairman, Istanbul Chamber of Medicine; Professor, Istanbul Medical Faculty. Memberships: Turkish Medical Association; World Hydro-Thermal Organization. Hobbies: Football; Poetry. Address: N Erten Sok 27-16, Merter, 34101 Istanbul, Turkey.

KARON Bertram Paul, b. 29 Apr 1930, Tanton, Massachusetts, USA. Professor; psychologist. m. Mary Mossop, Sept 1957, 3 s. Education: AB, Harvard University; MA, PhD, Princeton University. Appointments: NIMH Postdoctoral Fellow, Philadelphia Psychiatric Hospital; Principal Investigator, Michigan State Psychotherapy Research Project, Michigan State University and Detroit Psychiatric Institute; Professor of Clinical Psychology, Michigan State University. Publications: pstychotherapy of Schizophrenia: The Treatment of Choice, Co-author; Contributor of over 100 articles in national and international professional journals. Honours: Raymond D Fowler Award, 1990; Michigan Psychiatric Association Master Lecturer, 1990; Distinguished Publication, Society for Psychoanalytic Training, 1982. Memberships: Past President, Division of Psychoanalysis, American Psychological Association; President, Michigan Psychoanalytic Council; Fellow, Division of Clinical Psychology and Psychotherapy, American psychological association; Past President, Psychologists Interested in the Study of Psychoanalysis. Address: Michigan State University, Department of Psychochology, East lansing, MI 48823, USA.

KARP Warren B, b. 2 Dec 1944, Brooklyn, NY, USA. Professor. m. Nancy Virginia Blanchard, 1 Apr 1976, 1 s, 1 d. Education: BS, Chemistry, Pace University, 1965; PhD, Biochemistry, OH State University, 1970; DMD, Medical College of GA, 1977; Certified, Nutrition Specialist, 1993. Appointments: Director, Clinical Perinatal Laboratory, Medical College of Georgia Hospitals and Clinics, 1977-; Professor, Oral Biology (Biochemistry), 1988-; Professor, Oral Diagnosis and Patient Care Services, 1988-; Professor, School of Graduate Studies, 1988-; Professor, Pediatrics, 1988-; Professor, Biochemistry and Molecular Biology, 1991-; Member of many committees; Numerous guest lectures and national and state presentations. Publications include: Numerous abstracts and publications in referred journals including: Nutrition for the dental health professional, in Journal California Dentist Association, in press; Contemporary Nutrition Principles, and, Nutrition Care Activites for Members of the Dental Health Care Team, invited book chapters in Clark's Clinical Dentistry, due 1995. Honours include: Many grants awarded, 1975-; Sigma Xi; Instructor of Year, Augusta Area Dietetic Internship, 1982, 1986, 1992; Excellence in Teaching Award, MCG School of Medicine, 1987. Memberships include: Committee Member, Speaker, 1988-, American Heart Association; AAAS; American Chemical Society; Various offices, Sigma Xi; New York Academy of Sciences; International Association of Dental Research; American Dietetic Association. Address: BG-114, Department of Pediatrics, Medical College of Georgia, Augusta, GA 30912, USA.

KARPOV Rostislav Sergeevich, b. 8 Sept, Tomsk, Russia. Physician. m. Galina Krikunenko, 4 May 1963, 2 daughters. Education: MD, Tomsk Medical Institute, 1960; PhD, Tomsk Medical Institute, 1966; DSc, Tomsk Medical Institute, 1974. Appointments: Intern, Fellow, Physician, Associate Professor, Professor, Therapy Faculty, Tomsk Medical Institute, 1960-79; Deputy Director, Siberian Branch of Cardiology Research Centre of the USSR Academy of Medical Sciences, 1980-86; Head, Department of Therapy, Tomsk Medical Institute, 1979-; Chief, Coronary Heart Disease Department, Institute of Cardiology, Tomsk Research Centre of Russian Academy of Medical Sciences, 1980-; Chairman, Tomsk Research Centre of Russian Academy of Medical Sciences, 1986-. Publications: Coronary heart disease diagnosis in women. True and false-positive study results', co-author, 1990; The role of immune system in hyperlipoproteinemia, co-author, 1990; Evaluation of cardiac performance in hypertension, co-author, 1992; Combined atherosclerotic lesions of coronary and major arteries: peculiarities of diagnosis and treatment, co-author, 1991. Honours: State Prize Winner, 1982. Memberships: Tomsk Clinical Pharmacology & Pharacotherapy Society; CIS Cardiology Society; Russian Society of Hypertension; International Society & Federation of Cardiology; International Union of Angiology. Hobby: Skiing. Address: Belinskaya Street 70-36, Tomsk 634004, Russia.

KARRH Bruce W, b. 29 Aug 1936, AL, USA. Physician; Executive. m. Betty Cock, 11 Nov 1956, 2 s, 1 d. Education: BS; MD. Career: Medical Supervisor, Richmond, VA-Dupont; Corporate Medical Director, DuPont Company; Vice President, Safety, Health and Environmental Affairs, DuPont Company; Currently, Vice President, Integrated Health Care, DuPont Company. Publications: Numerous. Honours: Health Achievement in Industry, ACOEM, 1977; Sappington Lecturer, ACEEM, 1982; Knudson Award, ACDEM, 1986. Memberships: Fellow, American College of Occupational and Environmental Medicine; Fellow, American Board of Preventive Medicine. Hobbies: Tennis; Travel; Reading. Address: DuPont Company Integrated Health Care, 1007 Market Street, Wilmington, NE 99848, USA.

KARRIEV Murad Orazkulievich, b. 29 Apr 1932, Bezmein, Turkmenistan. Pharmaceutical Chemist. m. Galina Karrieva, 30 Dec 1979, 1 son, 1 daughter. Education: MPharm, Tashkent Pharmaceutical Institute, 1957. Appointments: Head, Central Pharmacy Department, Ministry of Health of Turkmenistan; Junior Scientific Assistant, Senior Scientific Assistant, Chief Scientific Assistant, Head of Laboratory, Deputy Director of Botany Institute and Chemistry Institute, Head of Department, Pharmaceutical Chemistry of Medical Institute, Turkmenistan Academy of Science; General Director, "Turkmenderman", Turkmen State Scientific Production Association. Publications: Herbs of Scientific Medicine of USSR Not Included in Pharmacopoeia, 1970; Archa as the Herb, 1971; Main Herbs of Central Asia, 1984; Herbs in Scientific and Popular Medicine, 1988; Pharmacological Chemistry of the Herbs of Turkmenistan, 1991. Honours: Badge of Honour, Medal Gairat, 1993; Order for Humanism, 1994; Honoured Science and Technology Worker of Turkmenistan. Memberships: Corresponding Member, Academy of Sciences and Academy of Medical Sciences of Turkmenistan. Hobby: Chess. Address: 126/2 Dzerzhinsky Street, Ashgabat 744006, Turkmenistan.

KASIM Mehmet, b. 15 Apr 1946, Tavsanli, Turkey. Obstetrician and Gynaecologist. 1 s, 2 d. Education: MD. Career: Director, Prenatal Services, Los Angeles County Health Department; Instructor, Chicago Medical School; Assistant Clinical Professor; Currently, Director, Founder, Verdugo Women's Health and Family Medical Center. Publication: Micro Bacteriology of Amniotic Fluid. Honours: American Board of Obstetrics and Gynaecology; Turkish Board of Obstetrics and Gynaecology. Memberships: American College of Obstetrics and Gynaecology. Hobbies: Tennis; Classical Music. Address: 1510 West Verdugo Avenue, Burbank, CA 91506, USA.

KASONDE Joseph Mwenya, b. 30 Jan 1938, Mazabuka, Zambia. Medical Doctor. m. Mary Chazi Mukandi, 7 Nov 1970, 5 daughters. Education: MB, ChB (Aberdeen), 1966; MD with commendation, Aberdeen University, 1976; FRCOG (London), 1985. Appointments: Permanent Secretary, Director of Medical Services, Ministry of Health, Lusaka, Zambia, 1977-84; Chairman, Chief Executive, University Teaching Hospital, Lusaka, 1984-85; Area Manager for Africa, World Health Organization (HRP), 1985-91; Responsible Officer, Resources for Research, Special Programme of Research, Development and Research Training in Human Reproduction, World Health Organization. Publication: Economic Reality and Health Care in Developing Countries (with Curtis McLaughlin), book. Memberships: Blair Bell Research Society, UK; Association of Surgeons of East Africa. Hobby: Golf. Address: World Health Organization, 1211 Geneva 27, Switzerland.

KASPEREK Stefan Jakub, b. 23 Dec 1932, Bytom, Poland. Physician; Neurologist. m. Elisabeth Borowiak, 21 Aug 1965, 1 son, 2 daughters. Education: Education Certificat of Proficiency, Silesian Medical Academy, Katowice, Poland, 1955; MD, 1967. Appointments: Assistant, Neurological Department, Municipal Hospital, Bytom, Poland, 1955; Doctor, Lecturer, Department of Neurology, Silesian Medical Academy, Zabrze, Poland. Publications: Changes in the optic pathways in subacute sclerosing leucoencephalitis, 1968; Compulsory eugenic sterilisations in district Breslau and Opole Silesia 1934-1944, 1980; Co-author, Stiff-man syndrome and encephalomyelitis, 1971; Co-author: Retinal changes in subacute sclerosing panencephalitis, 1976; Co-author: Subacute sclerosing panencephalitis during pregnancy, 1992; Co-author: Thoracic radiation myelopathy, 1993. Memberships: Polish Neurological Society; Association of Polish Neuropathologists. Honours: Scientific Prize, Association of Polish Neuropathologists, 1986, 1993; Prize, Polish Minister of Health, 1989-90. Hobbies: Tourism; Canoeing. Address: 32/63 Chrobrego Street, 40 881 Katowice, Poland.

KASS Philip H, b. 19 Aug 1958, Los Angeles, CA, USA. Assistant Professor of Epidemiology. m. Jan Carmikle, 28 Dec 1986, 1 s, 1 d. Education: BS; DVM; MPVM; MS, Statistics; PhD, Epidemiology; Diplomate, American College of Veterinary Preventive Medicine, speciality in Epidemiology. Appointment: Currently, Assistant Professor of Analytic Epidemiology. Memberships: Society for Epidemiologic Research; American Veterinary Medical Association; American Statistical Association; Biometric Society. Address: Department of Population Health and Reproduction, School of Veterinary Medicine, University of California, Davis, CA 95616, USA.

KASTOR John Alfred, b. 15 Sept 1931, New York City, USA. Professor of Medicine; department Chairman. m. Mae Eisenberg Kastor, 4 July 1954, 1 s, 2 d. Education: AB, University of Pennsylvania, 1953; MD, New York University, 1962. Appointments: Chief, cardiovascular Section, Hospital of University of Pennsylvania, 1977-81; Professor of Medicine, University of Pennsylvania School of Medicine, 1976-83; Theordore E Woodward Professor of Medicine, 1984-, Chairman, Department of Medicine, 1984-, University of Maryland School of Medicine; Physician-in-Chief, University of Maryland hospital, 1984-. Publications: Arrhythmias, 1994; Contributor of numerous articles and chapters in electrocardiology and clinical electrophysiology. Honours: Alpha Omega Alpha; Sigma Xi. Memberships: American College of Cardiology; American College of Physicians; American Federation for Clinical Research; American Heart Association; Association of American Physicians; Association of Professors of Medicine; Association of University Cardiologists; Paul Dudley White Society. Hobbies: Biography; History; Classical Music; Swimming. Address: University of Maryland Hospital, 22 South Greene Street, Baltimore, MD 21201, USA.

KATHPALIA Satish Chander, b. 19 Aug 1943, India. Physician. m. Shashi Kathpalia, 16 Feb 1975, 1 s, 1 d. Education: MBBS; MD, Medicine; FACP; Diplomate, Boards of Internal Medicine and Internal Medicine - Nephrology. Career: Instructor in Medicine; Assistant Professor; Associate Professor of Clinical Medicine; Currently, Clinical Associate Professor of Medicine, University of IL; Chairman, Department of Medicine, St Joseph Hospital Center, Joliet, IL. Publications: 40 publications including: Co-author, Hereditary tubular disorders, in Harrison's Principals of Internal Medicine, 1990; Co-reviewer, Acetaminophen intoxication, Seminars in Dialysis, 1992; Co-author, Hereditary tubular disorders in Harrison's Principals of Internal Medicine, edition 13, 1994. Honours: FACP, 1983; Distinguished Service Award for Outstanding Alumni, 1994. Memberships: Fellow, American College of Physicians; American Society of Nephrology; Council on Kidney in Heart Disease, AHA; National Kidney Foundation; International Society of Nephrology; International Society for Peritoneal Dialysis; International Society for Artificial Internal Organs; AMA; IL Medical Society; Chicago Medical Society; Advisory Board, Kidney Foundation of IL. Hobbies: Philately; Biking; Tennis; Reading. Address: 815 North Larkin Avenue, Suite 205, Joliet, IL 60435, USA.

KATO Shiro, b. 4 Nov 1925, Dalian, China. Medical Adviser. m. Junko Shoji, Osaka, Japan, 27 May 1951, 2 daughters. Education: MD 1950, PhD 1956, Osaka University Medical School. Career: Associate Professor, 1956-64, Professor 1964-89, Director 1980-84, Research Institute for Microbiol Diseases, Osaka University; Professor Emeritus, Osaka University, 1989-; Adviser, Sumitomo Pharmaceuticals Co Ltd, 1989-93. Publications: Marek's Disease Virus, 1985; Edward Jenner, 1980, 1988; Pathogenic Virology, 1989, 1995. Honours: Prize of Princess Takamatsu Foundation for Cancer Research, 1980. Memberships: past President & Director General, Society of Japanese Virologists; Councilor, Japanese Cancer Association; Councilor, Japan

Society of Medical History. Hobbies: Medical History; Photography. Address: Fujishirodai 4-23-7, Suita, Osaka 565, Japan.

KATSUTARO Shimaoka, b. 4 Sep 1931, Nara, Japan. Medicine. m. Tomoko Suzuki, 14 May 1956, 2 d. Education: MD, Keio University, School of Medicine, Tokyo, 1955. Career: Research Assistant, University College Hospital Medical School, London, 1961-63; Associate Chief Cancer Research Clinician, Roswell Park Memorial Institute, Buffalo, NY, 1963-86; Research Professor of Medicine, State University of New York, Buffalo, 1971-; Associate Chief of Research, Radiation Effects Research Foundation, Nagasaki, Japan. Publications: Clinical differentiation between thyroid cancer and benign goiter, in JAMA, 1962; Suppressive Therapy of nontoxic goiter, in American Journal of Medicine, 1974; Carcinoma of the Thyroid, in International Adv in Surgical Oncology, 1979; Thyroid Cancer, in Current Therapy in Internal Medicine, 1987; Treatment of Thyroid Carcinoma and Hormonal Therapy, in Cancer and Hormone, 1990. Memberships: Endocrine Society; American Thyroid Association; New York Academy of Sciences; American Society of Clinical Oncology; American Association for Cancer Research; Society of Nuclear Medicine; American Society for Bone and Mineral Research; American Society for Hypertension; Japanese Endocrine Society. Hobby: Contract Bridge. Address: Radiation Effects Research Foundation, 1-8-6 Nakagawa, Nagasaki 850, Japan.

KATZ Alan R, b. 21 Aug 1954, Pittsburgh, PA, USA. Associate Professor. m. Donna Crandall, 19 Jan 1986. Education: BA, Biology, summa cum laude, University of CA, San Diego, 1976; MD, University of CA, Irvine, 1980; MPH, Epidemiology, University of HI School of Public Health, 1987; Diplomate, Medical Examiners, 1981, Preventive Medicine, 1989. Career includes: Staff Physician, Department of Emergency Medicine, Kaiser-Permanente Medical Center, Honolulu, HI, 1984-91; Director, AIDS/STD Program, State of HI Department of Health, 1987-88; Assistant Professor, Department of Public Health Sciences, UHSPH, 1988-94; Associate Professor, Department of Public Health Sciences, Director, Preventive Medicine Residency Program, UHSPH, 1994-. Publications: Textbook chapters, journal articles, conference proceedings and invited conference presentations, including: Chlamydia trachomatis: a frequently overlooked public health menace, in Hawaii Medical Journal, 1989. Honours: Fellow, American college of Preventive Medicine, 1989; University of HI Presidential Citation for Meritorious Teaching, 1989; University of HI School of Public Health Outstanding Mentor Award, 1990; University of HI Regent's Medal for Excellence in Teaching, 1992; Delta Omega, 1992. Memberships include: HI Public Health Association; HI AIDS Task Force; Amnesty International; American Public Health Association; Society for Epidemiologic Research. Address: University of Hawaii School of Public Health, Department of Public Health Sciences, 1960 East West Road, Honolulu, HI 96822, USA.

KATZ Jacob, b. 13 Jun 1933, South Africa. Pediatrician. MB B Ch; MD. Appointment: Professor of Pediatrics. Address: Department of Pediatrics, UCI Medical Center, 101 City Drive S, Orange, CA 92668, USA.

KATZ Lois Anne, b. 1 Dec 1941, Rockville Centre, NY, USA. Physician. m. Arthur Katz, 18 Aug 1962, 2 s. Education: BA, Wellesley College, 1962; MD, NY University School of Medicine, 1966. Appointments: Internship and Medical Residency, Bellevue Hospital, NY, 1966-68; Senior Assistant Resident in Medicine, NY Hospital, NY, 1968-69; Chief Resident in Medicine, 1969-70; Fellowship in Nephrology. 1970-71; Staff Physician, New York VA Medical Center, 1970-80; Associate Professor of Clinical Medicine, 1979-94; NY University School of Medicine; Associate Chief of Staff, New York VA Medical Center, 1980-; Professor of Clinical Medicine, 1994. Honours: Board Certified. Diplomate in: Internal Medicine, 1971; Nephrology, 1974; Alpha Omega Alpha Alumni. Memberships: Fellow, American College of Physicians; American Medical Women's Association; American Society of Hypertension; American Society of Nephrology. Hobbies: Cooking; Reading. Address: 423 E 23rd Street, New York, NY 10010, USA.

KATZ Ralph Verne, b. 20 Mar 1944, Jersey City, NJ, USA. Epidemiologist; Professor. m. Barbara Joan Frey, 14 July 1968, 1 s. Education: BS; DMD; MPH; PhD' FACE. Appointments: Associate Professor, Department of Health Ecology. University of Minnesota; Director, PM&R Unit, University of Minnesota Hospital; Director, NIH Postdoctoral Fellowship in Cariology, Director, Graduate Program in

Geriatric Dentistry, University of Minnesota; Chairman, department of Restorative Dentistry, Professor, University of Connecticut; Co-Director, New England Oral Epidemiology, NIH Postdoctoral Fellowship Program; Director, NIH Postdoctoral Fellowship in Oral Epidemiology, University of Connecticut. Publications: Contributor of articles and scientific abstracts; Contributor of chapters in books. Honours: US Public Health Service Fellow, 1970-74; Reserach Fellow, Gerontologic Society of America, 1982; NIH Special Grant Review Section, 1994-98. Memberships: SER; ACE; IADR; AADR. Hobbies: Tennis; Gardening. Address: Department of Behavioural Sciences and Community Health, MC 3910, School of Dental Medicine, University of Connecticut Health Centre, Farmington, CT 06030, USA.

KATZ Steven Edward, b. 10 Aug 1937, Philadelphia, Pennsylvania, USA. Psychiatrist. m. Marjorie A Billstein, 12 June 1960, 2 daughters. Education: BA, Cornell University; MD, Hahnemann University; Certificate, Psychoanalysis, Columbia University; Fellow, American College of Psychiatrists. Appointments: Director, Education and Training, 1971-74, Associate Director, 1974-79, Department of Psychiatry, Roosevelt Hospital, New York City; Director, Programme Planning, 1978-80, Medical Director, Department of Psychiatry, 1980-83, Director, Psychiatry, 1987-91, Bellevue Hospital, New York City; Associate Chairman, Department of Psychiatry, 1980-83, Executive Vice-Chairman, 1987-91, New York University Medical Centre; Commissioner, New York State Office of Mental Health, Albany, 1983-87; Medical Director, Tisch Hospital, New York University Medical Centre, Professor of Psychiatry, New York University, 1992-; Clinical Professorof Psychiatry, University of Vermont, 1994-; Currently Executive Vice-President, Medical Director, Jackson Brook Institute, South Portland, Maine. Publications: Speaking Out for Psychiatry, 1987; Intensive Treatment for the Homeless and Mentally Ill, 1992; Over 70 chapters and articles including: Public Mental Health Services in the US and Israel, 1993; Hospitalization and the Mental Health System. Honours include: Alpha Omega Alpha, 1963; League Centre Award, 1984; Alexander P Braile Award, 1986; Horace M Kallen Distinguished Service Award, American Jewish Congress, 1987; William E Byron Award, New York State Chapter, Association of Mental Health Administrators, 1987. Memberships: American Medical Association; American Psychiatric Association; American Psychoanalytic Association; Group for Advancement of Psychiatry; International Psychoanalytical Association; American College of Psychiatry; American Association of Psychiatric Admnistrators. Hobbies: Sports; Stereo; Cars. Address: Jackson Brook Institute, 175 Running Hill Rd, South Portland, ME 04106, USA.

KAUFMAN Leon, b. 8 Jan 1927, Edinburgh, Scotland, England. Anaesthetist. m. Tonia Gale, 7 Mar 1954, 1 son, 3 daughters. Education: MB, ChB, 1949; FRCA, 1956; MD, 1962. Appointments: Consultant Anaesthetist, Royal Free Hospital, London, 1962-69; Consultant Anaesthetist, University College Hospital, London, 1969-89; Consultant Anaesthetist, St Mark's Hospital, London, 1965-91; Consulting Anaesthetist, University College Hospital, London & St Mark's Hospital London, Hon Senior Lecturer. Publications: Editor & Contributor: Anaesthesia Review Series, vols 1 to 12, 1983-; Medicine in the Practice of Anaesthesia, 1989; 2 chapters in 'A Companion to Dental Studies', 1985. Honours: Pask Award, Services to Anaesthesia, 1990; Registrar's Prize, Anaesthetic Section of the Royal Society of Medicine, 1959. Memberships: Royal Society of Medicine; Association of Anaesthetists; Medical Society of Medicine; European Academy of Anaesthesiology. Hobbies: Computers; Gardening; Mediaeval and Modern Medicine. Address: 145 Harley Street, London, W1N 2DE, England.

KAVALEROV Gueni, b. 17 Oct 1925, Moscow, Russia. Metrologist. m. Melihova Galina, 8 Jun 1962, 1 s. Education: Electrical Engineer, 1949; Science Candidate, Magnetic Fields, Electrotechnical Academy of Leningrad, 1963; Doctor of Technical Science, Geophysics and Biology, 1970. Appointments: Head of Laboratory, 1949; Deputy Director, Institute for Measurement, Leningrad, 1956-68; Deputy Minister, Instrument Industry of Russia, 1969-87; Head of Technical Department; Prime Scientific Expert of Medical Engineering, Research Institute. Publications: Introduction of Information Theories of Measurement, 1974; Information of Measurement, 1983; Many articles in IMEKO - Proceedings, 1964-91. Honours: The Russian State Award of Science, 1950; Award of IMEKO, International Confederation, 1994. Memberships: President, International Society of Instrument and Metrology, Russia; Academy of Metrology. Hobby: Models of ships. Address: Smolenskaja Str 10, Apt 234, Moscow 121099, Russia.

KAY Brian Herbert, b. 2 May 1944, Prestwich, England. Entomologist. div. 3 d. Education: BSc, 1969, PhD, 1978, University of Queensland, Australia. Appointments: Joined, 1963, Chairman of Parasitology and Entomology, 1988-91, Head, Mosquito Control Laboratory, Queensland Institute of Medical Research, Brisbane; Director, Vector Control, Queensland Health Department, 1984-86; Adjunct Assoc Professor, Tropical Health Programme, University of Queensland; Head, WHO Collaborating Centre for Environmental Management for Vector Control. Publications: Contributor of 131 scientific works. Honours: Winston Churchill Memorial Fellow, 1978; World Health Organization Fellowship, 1974; Aust-Japan Foundation Fellow, 1980. Memberships: Entomological Society of Queensland, President, 1977; Australian Entomological Society; Society Vector Ecology; Mosquito Control Association of Australia. Hobbies: Fishing; Colonial Restoration; Rugby; Cricket. Address: Queensland Institute of Medical Research, 300 Herston Road, Herston, Brisbane, Queensland 4006, Australia.

KAY George, b. 17 Apr 1954, Warsaw, Poland. Doctor of Dental Medicine. m. Katherine Merolla, 14 Aug 1979, 2 sons. Education: ScB, Brown University, Providence, 1976; DMD, Harvard School of Dental Medicine, Boston, 1980; MMSc, Harvard Medical School, Boston, 1984. Appointments: Resident, Dental Department, Brockton Veterans Administration Medical Center, 1980-81; Private Practice, Dentistry, Boston, 1981-; Consultant, Johnson & Johnson, Dental Products Company, East Windsor, 1982-84; Consultant, Coors Biomedical Company, Lakewood, 1982-84; Consultant, Instron Corporation, Canton, 1983-90; Clinical Instructor, Harvard School of Dental Medicine, 1984-; Staff Associate, Center for Prosthetic Research, Forsyth Institute for Research & Advanced Study in Dentistry, Boston, 1985-; Research Affiliate, Massachusetts Institute of Technology, Cambridge, 1985-; Co-Director, Fixed Prosthodontics, Harvard School of Dental Medicine, Boston, 1987-92; Consultant, The Whitaker Foundation, Camp Hill, 1987-; Visiting Faculty, Misch Implant Institute, Dearborn, 1988-. Publications include: Ramus Implant, 1978; Studies of the Flow Phenomena Associated with Crown Cementation, 1984; The influence of some factors on crown cementation: A Computer Simulation Study, 1984; A Computer Model of Phenomena Associated with Crown Cementation, 1985; Dental Cements: Quantitative Treatment of Factors Influencing Viscosity and Setting, 1986. Memberships include: Sigma Xi; American Dental Association; Academy of General Dentistry; American Society of Osseointegration; American College of Prosthodontists; American Academy of Implant Dentistry. Honours include: 1st Place Winner, Stanley D Tylman Essay Competition, American Academy of Crown & Bridge Prosthetics, 1985; Omicron Kappa Upsilon, Faculty Member, 1987; Fellow, International Congress of Oral Implantology, 1989; Associate Fellow, American Academy of Implant Dentistry, 1992; Diplomate, American Society of Osseointegration, 1993. Hobbies: Snow Skiing; Snow Boarding; Boating; Hiking. Address: 780 Boylston Street, Boston, MA 02199, USA.

KAYE Neil S. Psychiatrist. m. Dr Susan M Donnelly. Education: BA, Skidmore College, 1980; MD, Albany Medical College, 1984; Resident, Department of Psychiatry, Albany Medical Centre Hospital, 1984-87; Fiorensic Fellowship, Department of psychiatry, Syracuse University-SUNY, 1987-88. Appointments: Assistant Instructor, Albany Medical College, Department of psychiatry, 1984-87; Teaching Assistant, Syracuse University School of Law, 1987-88; Assistant Professor of Psychiatry, University of Massachusetts, School of Medicine, 1988-90; Special Guest Instructor, Widener University School of Law, 1991-; Assistant Professor, Thomas Jefferson School of Medicine, Department of Psychiatry, 1991-; Hospital Expert Reviewer, United States Department of Justice Special Investigation Unit, 1991-. Publications include: Electroconvulsive Therapy, History and Progression to Modern Use, 1980; Sleeping Pills, 1989; SDexual Deviancy, 1990; Competency Tests, 1992; Evaluating Alleged Sexual Abuse, 1993;; A Comprehensive Textbook of Forensic Psychiatry, Co-author. Memberships include: American Medical Association; American Psychiatric Association; American Academy of Forensic Sciences; New York Academy of sciences; Massachusetts Medical Society. Hobbies: Cooking; Wine; Music; Antiques; Boating; Hiking. Address: 1601 Concord Pike, Suite 92-100, Wilmington, DE 19803, USA.

KAYNAK Süleyman, b. 24 Aug 1954, Ankara, Turkey. Ophthalmologist. m. 5 Feb 1988. Appointments: Assistant Professor, Medical School, Dokuz Eylul University, 1983-88; Associate Professor, 1988; Chief of Department, 1990-92. Publications: 156 articles published in medical journals, 18 of them International, 138 in Turkish Journals. Memberships: European Society of Cataract & Refractive Surgeons; Turkish Society of Ophthalmology. Hobbies: Photography; Travel; Literature. Address: Balcova Mithatpotsa CD 225/12, 35330 Izmir, Turkey.

KAZEM Rahnuma, b. 30 Sept 1960, Delhi, India. Obstetrician and Gynaecologist. Education: MBBS (Hons), University of Calcutta, 1983; Diploma in Obstetrics and Gynaecology, Aligarh Muslim University, 1986; MRCOG, London, 1990; Diplomate, National Board, Delhi, 1991. Appointments: Registrar, Obstetrics and Gynaecology, Grantham and Kesteven General Hospital, Grantham, Lincolnshire, England, 1989-91; Registrar, Obstetrics and Gynaecology, Southmead Hospital, Bristol, 1991-93; Clinical Research Fellow, Assisted Reproduction Unit, Aberdeen, Scotland, 1993-; Honorary Registrar. Publications: Effect of Mifepristone on GnRH-Induced LH and FSH Secretion, 1994, Current Attitudes Towards Egg Donations Among Men and Women, 1995. Honours: Honours in Biochemistry, 1st MBBS exam, 1980; Honours in Ophthalmology and Otolaryngology, 3rd professional MBBS exam, 1983. Memberships include: British Fertility Society. Hobbies: Badminton; Embroidery; Knitting; Sewing; Crochet. Address: Assisted Reproduction Unit, University of Aberdeen, Aberdeen Maternity Hospital, Aberdeen AB9 2ZD, Scotland.

KCHAIT Svetlana Yevgenjevna, b. 5 May 1939, Vladivostok, USSR. Haematologist. m. Naum Z Kchait, 15 Aug 1964, 2 sons. Education: Can Med Sci, Orenburg Medical Institute, 1956-62; Diploma, Physician Practitioner. Appointments: Postgraduate Student, 1962-65; Assistant Lecturer, Chair of Histology, 1962-76; Junior Scientific Worker, 1976-90; Senior Scientific Worker, 1990-93; Leading Resesracher, Medical Radiological Research Centre of RAMS, 1993-. Publications: Investigation of Peripheral Blood Parameters in Liquidators Living in Kaluga Region According the Data of Medical Examinations over 1991-1993, 1994; Particularities of Hemogramms in Children and Adolescents Living in Contaminated Areas of Kaluga Region, 1994. Hobbies: Travel; Music. Address: Engels Street 24, Apt 224, Obninsk 249020, Kaluga Region, Russia.

KE Ruoyi, b. 12 Nov 1926, Zhejian, China. Professor of Medicine. m. Lu Jinbo, 18 Oct 1950, 1 son, 1 daughter. Education: MB, China Medical University; Tokyo Women's Medical College. Appointments: Assistant Resident, Resident Doctor, Department of Medicine, University Hospital, China Medical University, 1949-54; Lecturer, Associate Professor, Professor, Department Head, Department of Medicine, No 1 University Hospital, Dalian Medical University, 1955-. Publications: Coronary Circulation and Its Clinical Medicine, 1990. Honours: Science and Technology Major Achievement Award, Liaoning, 1978; Science and Technology Advancement Award, 2nd Class, Liaoning, 1989. Memberships: Council Member, Chinese Medical Association; Editorial Board, Chinese Journal of Cardiology; President, Dalian Cardiovascular Society, Chinese Medical Association. Address: The No 1 University Hospital, Dalian Medical University, 222 Zhongshan Road, Dalian 116011, China.

KEDAR Amos, b. 26 Jan 1938, Tel-Aviv, Israel. Physician. m. Yardena Kedar, 5 Aug 1964, 3 d. Education: Hebrew University Hadassah Medical School, Jerusalem, Israel, 1958-64; MD, 1966. Appointments include: Head, Department Pediatrics A, Central Emek Hospital, Afula, 1985-87; Visiting Assistant Professor, Department Pediatrics, University of Florida, Gainesville, 1988-91; Assistant Professor, Department Pediatrics, University of Florida, Gainesville, 1991-. Publications: 23 Research Articles, 1979-; 18 Clinical Research Articles, 1978-93; 3 History of Medicine Articles to Koroth, 1968, 1969, 1971; Over 40 Abstract Articles and 3 Chapters in Books; Journal reviewer for Clinical Pediatrics. Honours: Various Grants, 1981-95; Distinguished Worker, Government Section, 1985. Memberships: Alachua County Medical Society; American Academy of Pediatrics; American Association for Cancer Research; American Society of Clinical Oncology; American Society of Pediatric Hematology-Oncology; Florida Medical Association; Israel Medical Association; Israel Society for Clinical Pediatrics; NY Academy of Sciences; Pediatric Oncology Group; Committees include: Sickle Cell Foundation, Scientific Advisory Board; Institutional Review Board; Shands' Cancer Committee. Hobbies: Chess; Bridge; Travel. Address: University of Florida, College of Medicine Pediatric Hematology/Oncology, Box 100296, JHMHC, Gainesville, FL 32610, USA.

KEENAN William, b. 8 Sep 1939, Rawlins, Wyoming, USA. Physician. m. Deborah Keenan, 21 Aug 1965, 5 s, 2 d. Education: BS, University of Santa Clara; MD, Loyola University. Appointments include: Research Fellow, 1967-69, Instructor in Paediatrics, Assistant Professor of Paediatrics and Obstetrics and Gynaecology, 1969-73, Assistant Professor, 1969-73, Associate Professor, 1973-78, Assistant Professor of Obstetrics and Gynaecology, 1973-79, Professor of Paediatrics and Professor of Obstetrics and Gynaecology, 1978-80, University of Cincinnati; Professor of Paediatrics, Professor of Obstetrics and Gynaecology, St Louis University Medical Centre, 1980-; Director, Neonatal Perinatal Medicine, 1980-, Director, Paediatric Fellowship Programme, 1990-, Cardinal Glennon Children's Hospital; Director, Department of Paediatrics, Saint Mary's Health Centre, St Louis, Missouri, 1981-. Publications include: Chylous Ascites, Co-author, 1966; Massive Pulmonary Hemorrhage, Co-author, 1975; Mortality and Morbidity of Exchange Transfusion, Co-author, 1985;Management of Hyperbilirubinemia, 1987; Contributor of book chapters, abstracts and videos. Honours include: Outstanding Faculty, Teaching Award, Department of Paediatrics, University of Cincinnati, 1979; Genesis Award for Outstanding Service to Women and Children, March of Dimes, 1989; Sigma Nu. Memberships include: Midwest Society for Paediatric Research; American Academy of Paediatrics; Irish and American Paediatric Society; American Society for Clinical Nutrition; American Federation Clinical Research; American Association for Advancement of Science; Missouri and Illinois Perinatal Society. Address: Cardinal Glennon Children's Hospital, 1465 So Grand Blvd, St Louis, MO 63104, USA.

KELLEY Benjamin Southerland, b. 29 Oct 1956, Troy, Alabama, USA. Biomedical and Environmental Engineering Professor. m. Kathy Fowler, 30 May 1981, 2 sons, 2 daughters. Education: BCE, Auburn University, 1979; MSME, 1980, PhD, 1983, University of Kentucky. Appointments: Head, Biomedical Engineering Section, Biomaterials Section, Polymer Development Section, Southern Research Institute, Birmingham, Alabama, 1983-88; Associate Professor and Chair, Department of Biomeedical and Environmental Engineering, Mercer University School of Engineering, Macon, Georgia. Publications: Environmental Practices in Kazakhstan, 1995; Computer Model for Lumbar Stresses, 1991; Biodegradable Composite Boneplate, 1988; Spermacide-Releasing Diaphragm, 1987. Memberships: Biomedical Engineering Society; American Society for Engineering Education. Hobbies: Gardening; Travel; College Athletics; Reading. Address: 1400 Coleman Avenue, Macon, GA 31207, USA.

KELLOGG George W, b. 21 Jan 1943, Louisiana, USA. Psychiatrist. m. Education: MD; JD; MBA. Appointments: Currently Psychiatrist in private practice. Memberships: Monterey County Medical Society; California Medical Association; Northern California Psychiatric Society; American Psychiatric Association. Address: 11A Maple Street, Salinas, CA 93901, USA.

KELLY David Thomas, b. 9 Aug 1935, Balclutha, New Zealand. Cardiologist. Education: MB ChB, Otago University, New Zealand, 1959; FRCP (Edinburgh), 1995. Appointments: Associate Professor of Medicine, Johns Hopkins University School of Medicine, USA, 1974-76; Currently Head, Department of Medicine, University of Sydney, New South Wales, Australia. Publications: Editor or co-editor, 11 books; 13 book chapters; 120 refereed journal articles; 14 editorials or invited articles; 30 published conference proceedings; 133 abstracts; 3 educational videos. Honours: Member, Order of Australia, 1995. Memberships: Honorary Member, 7 cardiac societies. Hobbies: Golf; Skiing. Address: Hallstrom Institute of Cardiology, Royal Prince Alfred Hospital, Sydney, New South Wales 2050, Australia.

KEMP Caroline Mary, b. 23 July 1960, London, England. Registered Osteopath; Registered Naturopath. Education: SRN; ND; Diploma of Osteopathy; Diploma of Naturopathy; MRO; MRN. Appointments: State Registered Nurse. Memberships: MRN; MRO. Hobbies: Films; Sport; Pottery. Address: 106 Warwick Way, London SW1V 1SD, England.

KENIGSBERG Martin Ira, b. 27 Apr 1952, New York, USA. Clinical Psychologist. m. Sharon Finkelstein, 26 June 1977, 2 sons, 1 daughter. Education: AB, with distinction & honours in Psychology, Stanford University, 1974; AM, Psychology, Stanford University, 1974; PhD, Clinical Psychology, Pennsylvania State University, 1978; Postdoctoral Fellow, Stanford University Medical Center, 1980. Appointments: Co-ordinator of Psychological Services, Center for Health Enhancement, University of California, Los Angeles; Staff Psychologist, Veterans

Affairs Medical Center, Long Beach, California; Clinical Assistant Professor, University of California, Irvine Medical Center. Memberships: American Board of Professional Psychology; Academy of Clinical Psychology; American Psychological Association; Society of Behavioral Medicine. Honours: Fellow, Academy of Clinical Psychology, 1994; Vice President, Academy of Clinical Psychology; Past President, National Organization of Virginia Psychologists. Address: Psychology Service 116B, VA Medical Center 5901, East Seventh Street, Long Beach, CA 90822, USA.

KENNEDY Gary J, b. 1 Nov 1948, Dallas, Texas, USA. Physician. m. Jenny McCord, 1 Sep 1969. Education: BA, University of Texas, 1970; MD, University of Texas Medical School, San Antonio, 1975. Appointments: Fellow, Liaison Psychosomatic Psychiatry, 1979-81, Research Fellow in Geriatric Psychiatry, 1982-84. Director, Division of Geriatric Psychiatry, Montefiore Medical Centre; Associate Professor of Psychiatry, ALbert Einstein College of Medicine, Bronx, New York. Publications: Phases of Change in Alzheimer's Diseases, Co-author, 1984; Persistence of Late Life Depression, Co-author, 1991; Depression and Mortality, Co-author, 1992. Honours: US World Health Organisation Travel Study Fellowship, 1983; New Investigator Award, National Institutes of Health, 1984; Fellow, Brookdale Centre on Aging, 1989. Memberships: American Psychiatric Association Council on Aging; Association for the Bar of the City of New York; Adjunct Member, Legal Problems of Aging. Hobbies: Running; Swimming; Gardening; Cooking. Address: Division of Geriatric Psychiatry, Montefiore Medical Centre, 111 East 210th Street, Bronx, NY 10467, USA.

KENNEDY Joseph F, b. 6 Oct 1935, New York, NY, USA. MD. m. 4 children. Education: BS, cum laude, Biology, St John's University, NY, 1957; MD, NY Medical College, 1961. Career includes: Assistant Professor, Department of Population Dynamics, Johns Hopkins University School of Hygiene and Public Health, 1969-74; Assistant Professor, 1974-78, Associate Clinical Professor, 1978-85, Clinical Professor, 1985-, Reproductive Medicine, University of CA, San Diego. Publications: Contributor of articles in professional journals including: Co-author, Pregnancy rates with fresh verses computer-controlled cyropreserved semen for artifical insemination by donor in a private practice setting, in American Journal of Obstetrics and Gynaecology, 1990; Co-author, Effect of controlled ovarian hyperstimulation on pregnancy rates following intrauterine insemination, in American Journal of Obstetrics and Gynaecology, 1992. Honours: 2 Fellowships, Johns Hopkins University, 1967-69; Fellow, American College of Obstetricians and Gynaecologists, 1968; Wyeth Award, Pacific Coast Fertility Society, 1976; Diplomate, American Board of Obstetrics and Gynaecology, 1967. Memberships: Endocrine Society; American Fertility Society; Pacific Coast Fertility Society; San Diego Reproductive Endocrinology Society; San Diego County Medical Society; CA Medical Association; Physicians in Private Practice, UCSD Network. Address: Intertil Gynaecology and Obstetrics, 9339 Genessee Avenue Suite 220, San Diego, CA 92121-2121, USA.

KENNEDY Mark Stuart, b. 1 Aug 1970, London, England. Chiropractor. m. Deborah Katherine Drury, 10 Sep 1994. Education: BSc, Chiropractic, Anglo-European College of Chiropractic, 1992; Diploma of Chiropractic, British Chiropratic Association, 1993. Appointments: Associate Chiropractor, Portsmouth Chiropractic Clinic, 1992-93; Currently, Associate Chiropractor, Kingston Chiropractic Clinic, London. Memberships: British Chiropractic Association; European Chiropractic Union; SOTO, Europe. Hobbies: Tennis; Golf. Address: Kingston Chiropractic Clinic, 1 Surbiton Crescent, Kingston Upon Thames, Surrey, KT1 2JP, England.

KENTON Jeremy Martin, b. 11 Dec 1955, Glasgow, Scotland, England. Council Member, General Council & Register of Osteopaths; Private Practice; Member, Ethics Committe; Member, PR Committee. m. Sharon Anna Calder, 21 July 1990, 2 daughters. Education: Naturopathic Diploma, Diploma in Osteopathy, British College of Naturopathy & Osteopathy, 1979. Appointments: Lecturer, Orthopaedics & Traumatology, 1979-90; Council Member, British Naturopathic & Osteopathic Association, 1980-92; Chairman, BNOA Public Relations Committee, 1981-91; Senior Clinician, BCNO Clinic, 1985-90; Council Member, Council for Complementary & Alternative Medicine, 1985-88; British Delegate, Committee Liason European Osteopathy, Brussels, 1986-; Vice President, BNOA, 1987-88; President, BNOA, 1989-90; President, General Council & Register of Naturopaths, 1989-90; Council Member, International Federation of Practitioners of Natural Therapeutics, 1989-; Elected to GCRO Council, 1990. Publications:

Regular broadcaster on local and national TV and Radio Networks. Memberships: General Council & Register of Osteopaths; General Council & Register of Naturopaths. Hobbies: Horse Riding; Theatre; Music; Reading. Address: The Loughton Clinic, 115 High Road, Loughton, Essex, England. 192.

KENWOOD Patricia, b. 29 May 1942, Sydney, Australia. Psychoanalyst. m. Alun Kenwood, 20 May 1978, 1 d. Education: BA; Memmber, Association of Child Psychotherapists; Member, Australian Psychoanalytical Association. Appointments: Seminar Leader and Tutor, Tavistock Clinic, London, England; Child Psychotherapist, Royal Children's Hospital, Melbourne, Australia; Psychoanalyst in private practice; senior Lecturer, Monash University. Publications: Short Term Therapeutic Work with a Ten Year Old Girl, 1973. Memberships: Australian Psychological Society; Association of Child Psychotherapists, UK; Australian Psychoanalytical Society; IPA; Victorian Association of Psychotherapists. Hobbies: Opera; Films; Travel. Address: 51 Cole Street, Brighton, Victoria 3186, Australia.

KEOGH Daniel Patrick, b. 31 July 1952, Norwalk, CT, USA. Environmental Toxicologist; Entomologist. Education: BS, 1975, MS, 1985, John Carroll University, Ohio; PhD, Bowling Green State University, 1991. Appointments include: Biological Lab Team Leader, Consultant, Cleveland Environmental Research Group and Environmental Resource Association, 1976-85; Research Assistant. Case Western Reserve Medical School, Dermatology Department, 1981-84; Graduate Teaching Assistant, Biology Department, John Carroll University, 1982-84; Entomologist, Case Western Reserve University, 1983-85; Graduate Teaching Fellow, Biology Department, Bowling Green State University, 1985-91; Post-doctoral Fellow, Graduate Centre for Toxicology, Instructor of Biology, University of Kentucky. Publications include: Regulation of Insect Steroid Hydroxylase Activity; Evidence for Involvement of a Neuroendocrine-Endocrine Axis During Larval-Pupal Development, 1989; Effects of Plant Flavonoids and Other Allelochemicals on Ecdysone 20-Monooxygenase, Co-author, 1993. Honours include: Sigma Xi; Graduate Research Grant, 1990; Certificate of Recognition for Outstanding Teaching Performance, Bowling Green State University, 1991. Memberships: Society of Environmental Toxicology and Chemistry; American Association for the Advancement of Science; American Museum of Natural History. Hobbies: Chess; Golf; Basketball; Music; Running; Reading; Cooking; Wines. Address: 445 S Ashland Avenue #A23, Lexington, KY 40502, USA.

KER Chen-Guo, b. 6 Oct 1947, Taiwan. Surgeon. m. Su-chuan Chen, 23 Nov 1974, 2 sons. Education: MD; PhD. Appointments: Assistant Professor, Associate Professor of Surgery, currently Professor of Surgery, Kaohsiung Medical College School of Medicine, Kaohsiung; Chief, Division of HBP Surgery, Kaohsiung Medical College Hospital. Publications: Gallstones and Choledochoscopy, 1988; Emergency Medicine Illustrated, 1993; Hepato-Bilio-Pancreatic Surgery, 1995; About 100 medical papers in world journals. Honours: Takeda Research Scholarship, Japan, 1980; Taiwan Medical Research Scholarship, 1981. Memberships: American College of Surgeons; Collegium Internationale Chirurgiae Digestivae; New York Academy of Sciences; International Surgical Society. Hobbies: Golf; Stamp collecting. Address: Division of HBP Surgery, Kaohsiung Medical College School of Medicine, Kaohsiung 80708, Taiwan, China.

KERBESHIAN Jacob, b. 21 Jan 1944. Physician. m. Lynn Anderson, 4 Feb 1968, 1 s, 3 d. Education: AB, Harvard College, USA, 1966; MD, University of Rochester, 1970; Certified, American Board of Psychiatry and Neurology in Psychiatry and Child Psychiatry. Appointments: US Air Force Medical Corps, 1975-77; Grand Forks Clinic, 1977-88; Private Practice, 1988-; Clinical Professor of Neuroscience, University of North Dakota. Publications: Gilles de la Tourette Syndrome, 1994. Memberships: American Medical Association; American Psychiatric Association; American Academy Child and Adolescent Psychiatry. Address: 2812 17th Avenue South, Grand Forks, ND 58201, USA.

KERN George Washington, b. 19 Apr 1943, Philadelphia, PA, USA. Physician; Allergist. m. Margaret Ann Browne, 10 May 1969, 5 s, 2 d. Education: AB, Biology, La Salle College, 1965; MS, University of PA, 1967; MD, Thomas Jefferson University, 1970; Board Certified in Pediatrics and Allergy and Immunology. Career: Instructor at Mercy Cathedral Medical Center, 1974-75; Instructor, St Christopher's Hospital, Thomas Jefferson University; Allergist and Immunologist. Honours: Fellow, Academy of Pediatrics; Fellow, College of Allergists; Fellow,

Academy of Allergy and Immunology; Fellow, College of Physicians of Philadelphia. Memberships: College of Allergists; Academy of Allergy and Immunology; Academy of Politics; Philadelphia Allergy Society; PA Association of Allergists. Hobby: Fishing. Address: 520 Maple Avenue Suite 6, West Chester, PA 19380, USA.

KERR Charles Morgan, b. 14 Feb 1935, Perry, Oklahoma, USA. Psychiatrist. m. Esther E Vargo, 21 Oct 1957, div, 5 s. Education: BA, Yale University, 1957; MD, Baylor College of Medicine, 1963; Graduate, School of Submarine Medicine, US Naval Submarine Base, Groton, Connecticut, 1964. Appointments include: Private Practice; Clinical Associate Professor, Department of psychiatry, University of Arizona College of Medicine; Board Certified (AMER Board of Psychiatry and Neurology), 1974. Publications: Treating the Difficult Patient, 1979. Honours include: Member of the Year Southern Arizona Roadrunners, 1978; Outstanding Citizen of Tucson, 1979; Selected as Torch Bearer, 1980 Winter Olympics, Lake Placid, New York; Dr Charles Kerr Day, declared by Mayor of Tucson, May 19th 1980; Senior resident's Award for Excellence in Psychiatric Education, 1984, 1992, 1994; Fellow, American Psychiatric Association, 1984; Golden Horseshoe Award, Odessa High School, Texas, Horatio Alger Day, 1985; Memberships include: American Medical Association; Arizona Medical Association; American Psychiatric Association; American Group Psychotherapy Association; Academy of Psychosomatic Medicine; American College of Sports Medicine; Association of Sex Therapists and Counsellors; Society for Scientific Study of Sex. Hobbies: Running; Reading; Hiking; Fishing. Address: 8230 East Broadway, Suite W-2, Tucson, AZ 85710-4044, USA.

KERR William John Stanton, b. 12 July 1941, Belfast, Northern Ireland. Professor of Orthodontics. m. Françoise Contoz, 3 July 1967, 1 d. Education: BDS, Belfast, 1965; D Orth, RCS, England, 1973; FDS, RCS, Edinburgh, 1974; FFD, RCS, Ireland, 1974; MDS, Belfast, 1976; FDS, RCPS, Glasgow, 1990; DDS, Glasgow, 1992. Appointments: Government Dental Officer, Bermuda, 1968-70; registrar, Senior registrar, School of Dentistry, Belfast, 1972-77; Senior Lecturer in Orthodontics, 1977-88, Reader in Orthodontics, 1988-93, Professor, Honorary Consultant in Orthodontics, University of Glasgow, Scotland. Publications: The Design Construction and Use of Removable Orthodontic Appliances, 1990; A Longitudinal Study of Dento-Facial Growth From 5-15 Years, 1979; A Comparison of Skeletal and Dental Changes Produced by Function Regulators (FR2 and FR3), Co-author, 1989. Memberships: British Dental Association; European Orthodontic Society; British Orthodontic Society; International Association for Dental Research. Hobbies: Music; Gardening. Address: Glasgow Dental Hospital and School, 378 Sauchiehall Street, Glasgow G2 3JZ, Scotland.

KERR-WILSON Richard Henry James, b. 10 Apr 1947, Heswall, Cheshire, England. Gynaecologist. m. Joanne Dundas, 10 Aug 1974, 3 daughters. Education: MA; MB BChir; FRCS(Edinburgh); FRCOG. Appointments: Senior Registrar, Royal Informary of Edinburgh, 1979-85; Visiting Assistant Professor, Birmingham, Alabama, USA, 1982-83; Consultant Obstetrician and Gynaecologist. Publications: Injury to the Bowel During Gynaecological Surgery, 1990; Terminal Care of Gynaecological Malignancy, 1994. Memberships: British Gynaecological Cancer Society; Gynaecological Travellers. Hobbies: Fishing; Hiking. Address: 26 Moorend Road, Leckhampton, Cheltenham, Gloucestershire GL53 0HD, England.

KETTL Paul, b. 15 July 1954, Philadelphia, PA, USA. Psychiatrist. m. Kathleen Fisher, 20 Sep 1980, 2 s, 1 d. Education: MD, Temple University; Board Certified in Psychiatry, Geriatric Psychiatry. Appointments: Psychiatry Resident, Johns Hopkins Hospital, Baltimore, 1980-84; Psychiatrist, Alaska Native Medical Centre, Anchorage, 1984-86; Director, Geriatric Psychiatry Unit, Pennsylvania State University College of Medicine. Honours: Award for Excellence in Teaching, Medical Student Class, 1991, 1992, 1993, 1994, 1995. Memberships: American Psychiatric Association; American Association for Geriatric Psychiatry. Address: Department of Psychiatry, M S Hershey Medical Centre, PO Box 850, Hershey, PA 17033, USA.

KETTLE Douglas Stewart, b. 28 Jan 1918, London, England. Medical Entomologist; Retired Academic. m. (1) Gladys Emily Horne, 5 July 1945 (dec. 1973), 2 sons, 1 daughter, (2) Ada Dora Harthoorn, 11 Dec 1974. Education: BSc, 1939, MSc, 1945, DSc, 1952, London University; CBiol; FIBiol. Appointments: Captain, RAMC, 1940-46; Entomologist, Cooper Technical Bureau, 1946-47; Department of Health

for Scotland, 1947-51; Research Worker, University College, Dundee, 1951-52; Lecturer, University of Edinburgh, 1952-61; Seconded to Ministry of Health, Jamaica, 1959-60; Foundation Professor of Zoology, University of Nairobi, Kenya, 1961-69; Professor of Entomology, 1969-83, Emeritus Professor, 1983-, University of Queensland, Australia. Publications: Medical and Veterinary Entomology, 1984, reprinted 1990. Honours: Carnegie Fellowship at University College, Dundee, 1951-52; Visiting Fellow, Corpus Christi College, Cambridge University, Cambridge, England, 1977-78. Address: 71 Riverhills Road, Middle Park, Queensland 4074, Australia.

KHAIT Naum Zemovich, b. 1 Dec 1939, Ananjev, Odessa, USSR. Psychiatrist. m. Svetlana E Arkhipova, 15 Aug 1964, 2 sons. Education: Cand Med Sci, Orenburg Medical Institute, 1956-62; Diploma Physician Practitioner; Physician of the Highest Degree. Appointments: Neurologist, 1962-67; Psychiatrist, Sexopathologist, 1967-, Chief, Psychiatric Department, Municipal Hospital and Polyclinic. Publications: Sexual Up-bringing of Teenagers, 1975; Sexual Disturbance in Male Patients with Hypothalamic Lesions, 1993. Honours: Honoured Diploma to participant of mitigation of consequences of Chernobyl accident. Hobbies: Travel; Cars; Fine Art; History. Address: Engels Street 24, Apt 224, 249020 Obninsk, Kaluga Region, Russia.

KHAN A S Serajul Islam, b. 3 Jan 1937, Mymensing, Bangladesh. Neonatologist. m. L B Khan, 10 Oct 1975, 1 daughter. Education: MBBS, Dacca, 1962; DCH (London), 1967; MRCP (UK), 1974; FRCP (London), 1987. Appointments: Registrar: Kettering General Hospital, Pontefract Infirmary, Luton and Dunstable Hospital, England; Currently Senior Neonatologist and Paediatrician, Doha, Qatar. Publications: Neonatology in Qatar, 1989; Co-author: Endocardial-Fibroelastosis, 1973; Congenital Mediastinal Cysts in the Newborn Infant, 1989; Molecular Characterization of Complex Translocation in Newborn, 1993. Membership: British Paediatric Association. Hobbies: Reading history; Swimming; Travel. Address: PB 4496, Doha, Qatar.

KHAN Aftab Ahad, b. 9 June 1945, Meerut, Pakistan. Surgeon. m. 3 Jan 1985, 2 s, 1 d. Education: MBBS; FRCS(C); Diplomate, American Board of Surgery. Appointments: Attending Surgeon, Bridgeton Hospital, USA< 1974-82; Private Practice, Karachi, Pakistan, 1982-90; Vascular Surgeon, Liaquat National Hospital, Karachi, 1983-85; Chief Surgical Unit III, Abbasi Shaheed Hospital, karachi, 1985-90; Attending Surgeon, South Jersey Hospital System, USA, 1991-. Memberships: Founding Member, Society of Gastro-Intestinal Endoscopists and Gastroenterology of Pakistan; Society of Surgeons of Pakistan; Fellow, American College of Surgeons. Hobbies: Tennis; Swimming. Address: 10 Magnolia Avenue, Suite E, Bridgeton, NJ 08302, USA.

KHAN Lakshmi Bhargava, b. 16 Aug 1938, Madras, India. Obstetrician and Gynaecologist. m. A S S I Khan, 10 Oct 1975, 1 daughter. Education: MBBS, Jaipur, 1962; MRCOG (London), 1973; FRCOG (London), 1988. Appointments: Registrar, Obstetrics and Gynaecology, Heatherwood Hospital, Ascot, England; Research-Registrar, King's College Hospital, London; Senior Consultant Obstetrician, Hamad Medical Corporation, Doha, Qatar. Honours: Invited Participant, WHO Seminar on Use of Prostaglandins, Geneva, 1973. Memberships: British Family Planning Society; General Medical Council. Hobbies: Reading; Sewing; Travel. Address: PB 4496, Doha, Qatar.

KHAN Nashi, b. 26 June 1959, Lahore, Pakistan. Clinical Psychologist. Education includes: MSc, Psychology; MSc, Clinical Psychology, University of London, England. Appointments: Trainee Clinical Psychologist, Maudsley and Bethlem Royal Hospitals, England; Currently Chartered Clinical Psychologist, Lahore, Pakistan. Honours: Distinction in Matriculation; 1st Prize in English. Memberships: British Psychological Society; Psychological Corporation, UK; Register of Chartered Psychologists; NFER-Nelson; University of London Union. Hobbies: Reading; Writing. Address: PO Box 3222, Gulberg, Lahore 54660, Pakistan.

KHANCHANDANI Baiju Ashish, b. 6 Sept 1963, Barnet, Hertfordshire, England. Chiropractor. Education: Doctor in Chiropractic, Anglo-European College of Chiropractic, Bournemouth, 1986; Certified Chiropractic Sports Physician, New York Chiropractic College, 1989; Applied Kinesiology, Basic and Advanced Seminars with David Leaf, 1990. Appointments: Chiropractor: World Squash Championship, 1987, World Armwrestling, 1987, World Games, 1989, World Powerlifting, 1991; International Federation of Sports Chiropractic: Representative to International Council for Sports Science and Physical Education,

1990-94, Representative to Commonwealth Games, 1994; Chairman, Board of Education, Italian Chiropractic Association; Member, Board of Education, European Chiropractors Union; Governor, Anglo-European College of Chiropractic. Publication: Albers-Schonberg's Disease with Multiple Level Spondylolisthesis, 1988. Memberships: Italian Chiropractic Association; European Chiropractors Union; International Federation of Sports Chiropractic; Italian Association of Applied Kinesiology. Hobbies: Squash; Football; Wine. Address: Piazzale Azzolino 22, Fermo 63023 (AP), Italy.

KHANTZIAN Edward John, b. 26 May 1935, Haverhill, MA, USA. Psychiatrist. m. Carol Anne De Andrus, 19 May 1959, 1 s, 3 d. Education: AB, Psychology, Boston University; MD, Albany Medical School; Certified Psychiatrist and Psychoanalyst; Further qualification in Addiction Psychiatry. Career: Director, Drug Treatment Programs, Associate Chief of Psychiatry, The Cambridge Hospital; Currently, Associate Chief of Psychiatry, Tewksbury Hospital, MA. Publications: The Self Medication Hypothesis of Addictive Disorders, in American Journal of Psychiatry, 1985; Addiction and The Vulnerable Self, 1990. Honours: Felix and Helene Deutsch Prize, Boston Psychoanalytic Institute and Society, 1973; Collegium of Distinguished Alumnae, Boston University, 1974; President, AAPAA. Memberships: MA Medical Society; MA Psychiatric Society; AMA; APA; APsA; AAPAA; GAP. Hobbies: Physical Fitness; Tennis; Reading; Writing. Address: 10-12 Phoenix Row, Haverhill, MA 01832, USA.

KHARDORI Romesh, b. 11 Apr 1949, Srinagar, Kashmir, India. Physician. m. Nancy Misri, 11 Oct 1973, 2 s. Education: MB, University of Jammu and Kashmir, 1972; BS; MD, All-India Institute of Medical Sciences, New Delhi, 1977; FACP; FACE; Diplomate, American Board of INternal Medicine; Diplomate, ABIM, Endocrinology and Metabolism. Appointments: Associate professor, Head, Department of Endocrinology, Sanjay Gandhi Postgraduate Institute of Medicine Sciences, Lucknow, 1987-89; Associate Professor, Endocrinology and Metabolism. Publications: Diabetes Control and Care, 1978; Practicel Biochemistry, 1983; Contributor of over 100 articles, reviews and abstracts. Honours: FACP, 1991; FACE, 1994. Memberships: AMA; ACP; Endocrine Society. USA' ADA' County and State Medical Society; American Association Clinical Endocrinologists. Hobbies: reading; Music. Address: Southern Illinois University School of Medicine, 801 N Rutledge, PO Box 19230, Springfield, IL 62794-19230, USA.

KHARKEVICH Dimitri A, b. 30 Oct 1927, Leningrad, Russia. Pharmacologist. m. Nizovtseva Elena, 1970, 1 son. Education: MD; PhD; DSc; Member, Russian Academy of Medical Science. Appointments: Assistant, Department of Pharmacology, 1st Leningrad Medical Institute, 1951-55; Senior Researcher, Institute of Pharmacology, Moscow, 1955-58; Department of Pharmacology, Moscow Medical Academy, 1958-. Publications: Ganglion-blocking and Ganglion-stimulating Agents, 1967; Pharmacology of Curare-line Agents, 1969; Pharmacology of Ganglionic Transmissions, 1980; New Neuromuscular Blocking Agents, 1986; Pharmacology, 1993, 3rd edition; Pharmacology of Myorelaxants, 1989. Memberships: Russian Pharmacological Society; IUPHAR; Eur. UPHAR. Hobbies: Fishing; Hunting; Windsurfing. Address: Leninsky Prospect 85-419, 117261 Moscow, Russia.

KHARTCHENKO Vladimir Petrovitch, b. 18 Sept 1934, Crimea, Ukraine. Thoracic and Abdominal Surgeon; Clinical Oncologist; Pulmonologist. m. R E Dontzova, 10 May 1964, 1 daughter. Education: Crimean National Medical School; Aspirant Courses, P A Gertzen Moscow Scientific Research Cancer Institute; MD; Professor. Appointments include: Chief, Department of Abdominal Surgery, P A Gertzen Moscow Scientific Research Cancer Institute; Deputy Director for Science, Moscow Research Institute of Roentgenology and Radiology; Currently: Director, Surgical Unit Head, Moscow Research Institute of Diagnosis and Surgery; Chief, Chair of Oncology and Radiology, Faculty of Medicine, International Friendship University. Publications: Monographs: Isolated Resection of Tracheal Bifurcation, 1992; Lung Cancer, 1994; Lung Oncopathology, 1994; More than 300 learned articles; 30 inventions in medicine, including 2 US Patents. Honours: Laureate, Russian State Prize, 1987. Memberships: Vice-President, Russian Association of Radiologists; Chief, Board on Diagnosis and Multidisciplinary Treatment of Cancer, National Ministry of Health. Hobby: International tourism. Address: Ul Acad Pilugina 8-486, Moscow 117393, Russia.

KHELGHATI Amrullah, b. 30 Jan 1937, Tabriz, Iran. Medicine. m. Thelma Khelghati, 9 Sep 1972, 2 s, 1 d. Education: Tehran University; MD, LA University; MPH, University of California. Appointments: Assistant Clinical Professor of Pediatrics, LA State University; Associate Pediatrician, Pediatrician, University of MA, Worcester. Publications: Review of Pediatric Hematology-Oncology, 1990, with Supplement, 1992. Memberships: American Society of Pediatric Hematology-Oncology; BAHAI; International Health Agency. Hobby: Scrabble. Address: 347 Page Street, Lunenburg, MA 01462, USA.

KHOLIN Alexander Vasilyevich, b. 16 Nov 1959, St Petersburg, Russia. Professor of Radiology. m. Maria Khvatova, 20 Nov 1988, 1 s, 1 d. Education: MD, I P Pavlov Medical Institute, St Petersburg, 1982; PhD; DSc. Appointments: Radiologist, 1982-85, Research Fellow, 1985-88, N N Petrov Oncology Research Institute, St Petersburg; Assistant Lecturer, 1989-91, Reader, 1991-93, Chairman, 1993-, Professor of Radiology, Medical Academy of Postgraduate Studies, St Petersburg. Publications: Contributor of 58 scientific papers in medical journals; Magnetic Resonance Imaging: Basics for Interpretation, 1994. Membership: Russian Radiology Association. Address: Sampsonievsky Ave 17, Apt 60, St Petersburg PO 194175, Russia.

KHOMENKO Alexander Grigoriyevitch, b. 20 Dec 1926, Kharkov, USSR. Phthisiologist. m. Nina B Pochkous, 8 Feb 1949, 2 sons. Education: MD, Kharkov Medical Institute, 1949. Appointments: Director, Ukrainian TB Research Institute, 1961-65; Medical Officer, WHO Secretariat, Geneva, Switzerland, 1965-69; Head, Chair of Phthisiology, Ukrainian Postgradduate Institute for Doctors, 1970-73; Director, Central TB research Institute, Moscow, 1973-. Publications: Tubercluosis, 1st edition, 1981, 2nd edition, 1988; Tubercluosis as an International Problem, 1991; Sarcoidosis, 1983; Hereditary in Pulmonary Diseases, 1990; Extrinsic Allergic Alveolitis, 1987. Honours: Order of the Red Labour Banner, 1981; USSR State Prize, 1982; Order of October Revolution, 1986; Order of International Friendship, 1993. Memberships: Russian Scientific and Medical Association of Phthisiologists; International Union Against Tubercluosis and Lung Disease. Hobby: Tourism. Address: Central TB Research Institute, 2 Yauzskaya Alley, Moscow 107564, Russia.

KHOO Michael C K, b. 15 Sept 1954, Hong Kong. Educator. m. Pam Khoo, 11 July 1986, 2 sons. Education: BSc (Eng), 1st Class Honours; ACGI; SM; PhD. Appointments: Research Biomedical Engineer, Veterans Administration Medical Center, West Roxbury, and Brigham and Women's Hospital, Boston, Massachusetts, USA, 1981-83; Currently Associate Professor of Biomedical Engineering, University of Southern California, Los Angeles. Publications: Modeling and Parameter Estimation in Respiratory Control, 1989; Periodic Breathing, in The Lung - Scientific Foundations, 2nd edition, 1995. Honours: Governor's Prize, Imperial College, 1976; Research Career Development Award, National Institutes of Health, 1990-96; Career Development Award, American Lung Association, 1991-96. Memberships: American Physiological Society; American Sleep Disorders Association; Biomedical Engineering Society; Institute of Electrical and Electronic Engineers. Hobbies: Reading; Skiing. Address: Biomedical Engineering Department, OHE-500, University of Southern California, Los Angeles, CA 90089-1451, USA.

KHOURI Zaf, b. 9 Dec 1955, Beirut, Lebanon. Dental Surgeon. m. Cathryn Khouri, 22 Dec 1979, 3 d. Education: BDS, New Zealand, 1979; Graduate Diploma, Forensic Odontology, Melbourne, 1991. Appointments: Dental Surgeon and Consultant Forensic Odontologist; Adviser to New Zealand Police on Forensic Dentistry. Memberships: New Zealand Dental Association; Australian and New Zealand Forensic Science Society; New Zealand Society of Forensic Dentistry; American Society of Forensic Odontology. Hobbies: Fitness; Motorsport. Address: PO Box 464, Hamilton, New Zealand.

KHOURY Antoine E, b. 24 Jul 1955, Cairo, Egypt. Surgeon. m. Shahira Khoury, 2 s, 1 d. Education: MB; BCH; FRCSC; FAAP. Appointment: Assistant Professor, Department of Surgery, Hospital for Sick Children, Toronto, Canada. Publications: Determination of the coeffeicient of kinetic friction of urinary catheter materials, 1991; A preliminary assessment of pseudomonas aeruginosa biofilm development using fluorescence spectroscopy, 1992; Prevention and control of bacteial infections associated with medical devices, 1992; Electrical enhancement of biocide efficacy against pseudomonas aeruginosa biofilms, 1992. Honours: First Prize, Research Competition, 1988; CVA Scholarship Foundation Award, 1990. Memberships: Royal

College of Physicians and Surgeons of Canada; American Urological Association; American Academy of Pediatrics. Hobbies: Tennis; Squash. Address: The Hospital for Sick Children, Urology Division, 555 University Avenue, Toronto, Ontario, Canada, M5G 1X8.

KHOUZAM Hani Raoul, b. 5 June 1950, Helipolis, Cairo, Egypt. Psychiatrist. m. Lynda Margaret Dickerson, 20 Nov 1982, 1 son, 1 daughter. Education: MBBCH, Cairo University, Egypt, 1977; MPH, Tulane University, New Orleans, Louisiana, 1981. Career: Staff Psychiatrist, Oklahoma County Crisis Intervention Center, 1987-90; Medical Director, The General Psychiatry Impatient Unit, VA Medical Center, Oklahoma City, Oklahoma, 1990-92; Director, Consultation Liaison Psychiatry, VA Medical Center, Manchester, New Hampshire, currently. Publications: Manual of Emergency Psychiatric Interventions, 1987-88; Secondary Mania in Late Life, The Journal of American Geriatric Society, 1994. Honours: Hubert Humphrey International Fellowship, 1980-81; Outstanding Instructor, Department of Psychiatry, Oklahoma College of Medicine, 1992. Memberships: Egyptian Medical Association; American Psychiatric Association; New Hampshire Medical Society; New Hampshire Psychiatric Society; World Federation of Mental Health. Hobbies: Bible Studies; Stamp Collection; Writing; Listening to Classical Music. Address: 5 Terrace Road, Concord, NH 03301-3138, USA.

KHUDAIBERGENOV Mwad Aitbaevich, b. 23 Nov 1944, Ashgabat. Physician. m. 27 June 1975, 1 son, 1 daughter. Education: The First Leningrad Medical Institute, Russia, 1969; MD, Turkmen State Medical Institute. Appointments: Physician, First Leningrad Medical Institute's Clinic, 1969-71; Postgraduate Student, The First Medical Institute, 1971-74; Candidate of M Sciences, 1975; Assistant of the Chair, 1975-81; Professor of the Chair. Publications: More than 70 professional publications incl: Synthesis of nuclear acides by blast elements of marrow of sting leucosis patients, 1973; Methabolism of nuclear acid in blood cells and marrow of sting leucosis patients, 1978. Hobbies: Fishing; Reading. Address: ul Kokandskaja 33, 744001 Ashgabat, Turkmenistan.

KIBBI Abdul-Ghani, b. 31 May 1955, Beirut, Lebanon. Dermatologist; Dermapathologist. m. Hanan Mikati, 10 Aug 1987, 1 son, 1 daughter. Education: BS, 1976, MD, 1981, American University of Beirut; Resident in Dermatology, American University of Beirut Medical Center, 1981-84; Research Fellow in Dermatopathology and Laser Pathology, Massachusetts General Hospital, Harvard Medical School, USA, 1984-86. Appointments: Assistant Professor of Dermatology, Associate Professor of Dermatology, Associate of Human Morphology, American University of Beirut, Lebanon; Visiting Professor of Dermatopathology, Massachusetts General Hospital, Harvard Medical School, Boston, USA; Consultant, Family Practice Residency Programme, Ministry of Health, Bahrein; Currently: Dermatologist, Dermapathologist, American University of Beirut, New York City; Member, Secretary, Scientific Council, Arab Board of Dermatology; Acting Chairman, Department of Dermatology, American University of Beirut, 1994-. Publications: Dysplastic Nevi, 1987; Diseases caused by protozoa (co-author), 1990; Malignant Melanoma: practical applications, 1991; Basic pathologic reactions of the skin (co-author), 1993. Honours: 1st Research Award, Clinical Medical Sciences, American University of Beirut, 1990; The Abdul-Hamid Shouman Young Scientist Research Award, Amman-Jordan, 1990. Memberships: American Academy of Dermatology; Associate, American Society of Dermatopathology; International Society of Dermatology. Hobbies: Computers; Travel; Reading. Address: Department of Dermatology, American University of Beirut, 850 Third Avenue, New York, NY 10022, USA.

KIBERD Bryce Alan, b. 3 Nov 1954, Lowell, MA, USA. Physician. m. Colleen Craig, 23 Jun 1984, 2 s, 1 d. Education: MD, University of Toronto, 1980; FRCP(C); Research Fellowship, Stanford, 1984. Appointment: Associate Professor of Medicine, Dalhousie University. Publications: Cyclosporine-induced Renal Dysfunction in Human Renal Allograft Recipients, in Transplantation, 1989; Interleukin 6 Receptor Blockage Ameliorates Murine Lupus Nephritis, in Journal American Society of Nephrology, 1993; Modulation of Glomerular Structure and Function in Lupus Nephritis by Methylprednisolone and Cyclophosphamide, in Journal Laboratory Clinical Medicine, 1994; Should Hepatitis C Infected Kidneys be Transplanted in the United States?, in Transplantation, 1994. Memberships: American Society of Transplantation; Canadian Society of Transplantation; American Society of Nephrology. Hobbies: Swimming; Running; Cycling; Pastel and Acrylic Painting. Address: 5077 Dickson Building, Victoria General Hospital, Halifax, Nova Scotia, Canada, B3H 2Y9.

KIDNER David William, b. 27 July 1947, Winchester, Hampshire, England. Psychologist; Psychotherapist. div, 1 daughter. Education: BSc, Honours; BSc, Honours; PhD. Appointments: Lecturer in Psychology,. Goldsmiths College, London University; Psychotherapist in private practice; Senior Lecturer in Psychology, Sheffield University, London University. Publications: Experimentation in Hypnosis: Towards an Adequate Methodology, 1993; Avoiding Environmental Catastrophe: What Can Psychology Offer?, 1993; The Environmental Crisis: Why Psychology is Mute, 1994; Empty Hearts and the Dream of Wholeness: Selfhood and the Regeneration of Culture, 1994; Human Intelligence and Environmental destruction; Book reviewer. Memberships: Associate Fellow, British Psychological Society; United Kingdom Training College for Hypnotherapy and Counselling. Hobbies: Squash; Running; Photography; Wilderness Hiking. Address: Department of Secondary and Tertiary Education, Nottingham Trent University, Clifton, Nottingham NG11 8NS, England.

KIEN Craig Lawrence, b. 5 Oct 1946, Cincinnati, OH, USA. Pediatrics. m. Patricia J Liddil, 3 Oct 1970, 2 d. Education: BS, Zoology, Duke University, Durham, NC, 1968; MD, University of Cincinnati College of Medicine, 1972; PhD, Nutritional Biochemistry and Metabolism, MA Institute of Technology, Cambridge, MA, 1977. Career includes: CE Compton Chair of Nutrition and Chief, Section of Clinical Nutrition, Department of Medicine, WV University School of Medicine, Morgantown, WV, 1984-87; Professor and Director, Division of Nutrition, 1988-, Professor, Department of Medical Biochemistry, 1991-, College of Medicine, OH State University. Publications: 73 Publications including: A Metabolic Bed for Collecting Excreta in Premature Infants, in Journal Pediatric Gastroenterology Nutrition, 1990; Co-author, Effects of Lactose Intake on Nutritional Status in Premature Infants, in Journal of Pediatrics, 1990; Co-author, Feeding-induced changes in energy expenditure in children with cystic fibrosis, in JPEN, 1994, in press; Editorial Board, Journal of Parenteral and Enteral Nutrition, 1991-, American Journal of Physiology, 1992-95. Honours: Future Leaders Award, The Nutrition Foundation Inc, 1980; Special Fellow, Leukemia Society of America Inc, 1981. Membership: Nutrition Study Section. Address: Department of Pediatrics, Division of Nutrition, Ohio State University, Room W209 Childrens Hospital, 700 Children's Drive, Columbus, OH 43205-2696, USA.

KIENER Cecile Alice, b. 16 May 1958, Chambery, France. Registered Osteopath. Education: Diploma in Osteopathy, European School of Osteopathy, Kent, England, 1991; License in Acupuncture, British College of Acupuncture, London, 1994. Memberships: General Council and Register of Osteopaths; Osteopathic Association of Great Britain; British Acupuncture Association. Hobbies: Sport; Chinese Medicine; Reading. Address: 248 Mierscourt Road, Rainham, Kent, ME8 8JW, ENGLAND.

KIETZMAN Deborah, b. 7 May 1954, Monroe County, Albia, Iowa, USA. Registered Nurse; Counsellor. m. Tim S Anderson, 21 May 1983, 3 daughters. Education: BS, Psychology; BA, Criminal Justice; BSN, Nursing; MA, Substance Abuse Counselling; Certified Addictions Cousellor, Level III. Appointments: Currently State Registered Nurse, Counsellor, Director, Hospice of Monroe County. Address: Monroe County Hospital, RR£, Albia, IA 52531, USA.

KIHARA Yasuki, b. 8 Feb 1955, Hiroshima, Japan. Cardiologist. m. Miho Yukitoshi, 7 Oct 1979, 1 son, 2 daughters. Education: Medical Diplomate, Japan, 1979; Junior Resident, 1979-81, Senior Resident, 1981-82, Tenri Hospital, Tenri, Nara; Specialty Board, Japan Society of Internal Medicine, 1985; Clinical Fellow, Kyoto University Hospital, 1986; Research Fellow, Harvard Medical School, USA, 1986-87; Research Fellow, PhD, Kyoto University, 1987; Specialty Board, Japanese Circulation Society, 1992. Appointments: Instructor in Medicine, Harvard Medical School, Boston, Massachusetts, USA, 1987-89; Assistant Professor, Toyama Medical and Pharmaceutical University, Toyama, Japan, 1989-93; Assistant Professor, Faculty of Medicine, Kyoto University, Kyoto, 1993-. Publications: Articles in Circulation Research, 1988, 1989, 1991, 1991, and Journal of Clinical Investigation, 1994. Honours: Research Award, Yamanouchi Foundation, 1986; Research Fellowship, American Heart Association, 1987-88; Finalist, R I Bing Award, 13th World Congress, International Society for Heart Research, 1989; Research Award, Japan Heart Foundation, 1991; Research Award, Yokoyama Foundation, 1992; Sagawa Young Investigator

Award, 10th International Conference, Cardiovascular System Dynamics Society, 1992. Memberships: Japan Society of Internal Medicine; Japanese Circulation Society, Kyoto; Affiliate, American Heart Association, Massachusetts; Associate Fellow, American College of Cardiology; American Association for the Advancement of Science; Full Member, Sigma Xi, Harvard-Radcliffe Chapter. Address: Third Division, Department of Internal Medicine, Kyoto University Hospital, 54 Shogoin-Kawaharacho, Sakyo, Kyoto 606, Japan.

KIHLE Nina, b. 18 May 1957, Skien, Norway. Dance Therapist. m. Dag Loberg, 21 Apr 1990, 1 s, 1 d. Education: Candidate Mag, University of Oslo, 1984; MA, New York University, 1985. Appointment: Dance Therapist, Telemark Central Hospital, Psychiatric Unit. Membership: American Dance Therapy Association. Hobbies: Hiking; Tennis; Music. Address: Havundv 100, 3715 Skien, Norway.

KIKUCHI Shinichi, b. 15 Dec 1946, Fujushima, Japan. Professor of Prthopaedic Surgery. m. Yumiko Suzuki, 20 Jan 1974, 2 d. Education: BA, 1971, MD, 1982, Fukushima Medical College. Appointments: Assistant Chief, Department of Orthopaedic Surgery, Japan Red Cross Medical Centre, Tokyo; Director, Fukushima Prefectural Tajima Hospital, Fukushima; Professor and Chairman, Department of Orthopaedic Surgery, Fukushima Medical College. Publications: Low Back Pain Clinic, 1986; Accepted Theory and Truth of Backache, 1994. Memberships: International Society for the Study of the Lumbar Spine; Japanese Orthopaedic Association. Hobbies: Reading; Golf. Address: 1-14-22 Noda-machi, Fukushima 960, Japan.

KILBOURNE Edwin Michael, b. 1 Oct 1953, New Orleans, Louisiana, USA. Physician. m. Barbara Kay Williams, 26 Nov 1982, 2 s, 1 d. Education: BA with Distinction, Cornell University, Ithaca, New York, 1974; MD, Cornell University Medical College, New York, 1978. Appointments: Resident in Internal Medicine, University of Alabama Hospital, Birmingham, Alabama, 1978-80, 1982-83; Epidemic Intelligence Service Officer, Center for Enrinomental Health, Centers for Disease Control, Atlanta, Georgia, 1980-82; Chief, Investigations Section, Centre for Environmental Health, Centers for Disease Control, Atlanta, Georgia, 1983-85; Medical Epidemiologist, Center for Environmental Health, Center for Disease Control, Madrid, Spain, 1985-87; Medical Epidemiologist/Chief, Health Studies Branch, Environmental Hazards and Health Effects, Center for Environmental Health and Injury Control, Atlanta, Georgia, 1987-89, 1989-90; Assistant Director for Science, Epidemiology Program Office, Centers for Disease Control & Preventation, Atlanta, Georgia, 1990-. Publications: include, Post-excitatory Depression in Thoracic Sympathetic Efferent Neural Traffic during a Cardiogenic Hypertensive Chemoreflex, 1982; Toxic-Oil Syndrome, Case Reports associated with the ITH Oil Refinery in Sevilla, 1987; A Parentally Reported Epidemic in an Elementary School, 1989; Toxic Oil Syndrome - A Current Clinical and Epidemiologic Summary, 1991. Honours: include, Alexander D Langmuir Prize, for excellence in Epidemiology, 1982; USPHA Unit Commendation, 1985; USPHS Foreign Duty Service Ribbon, 1985. Memberships: include, American College of Physicians; American Epidemiological Society. Address: 5658 Mill Trace Drive, Dunwoody, Georgia 30338, USA.

KILIARIDIS Stavros, b. 8 Oct 1955, Thessaloniki, Greece. Orthodontist. m. Anastassia Eudoridou, 25 Oct 1994. Education: DDS, Thessaloniki University, 1979; Speciality in Orthodontics, 1983, LDS, Orthodontic Doctor, 1986; Docent, University of Goteborg, Sweden, 1990. Appointments: Research Associate, 1982-86, Assistant Professor, 1986-90, Associate Professor, Orthodontics, 1990-. Publications: About 40 articles and reviews on craniofacial growth, orthodontic treatment, muscle physiology, temporomandibular disorders. Honour: European Orthodontic Society Research Award, 1988. Memberships: Swedish Dental Society; European Orthodontic Society; International Association of Dental Research. Hobbies: Music; Basket Ball; Hiking; Swimming. Address: Strofigou Kallari 1, GR-54622 Thessaloniki, Greece.

KILMORE Mearl A, b. 24 Jan 1937, Cumberland County, Pennsylvania, USA. Professor of Pharmacology. m. Hazel Derr, 4 sept 1957, 1 s, 2 d. Education: BS, franklin and Marshall College, Lancaster, Pennsylvania, 1957; MS, 1960, PhD, 1964, Thomas Jefferson University, Philadelphia. Appointments: Research Fellow, department of Anaesthesiology, Thomas Jefferson University, 1958-64; Assistant Professor, 1967-70, Associate Professor, 1970-72, Department of Pharmacology, College of Osteopathic Medicine and Surgery, Des Moines, Iowa; Professor of Physiology and Pharmacology, Professor of Physiology and Pharmacology, 1980-82, Discipline Head of Physiology and Pharmacology, 1982-86, Professor of Physiology and Pharmacology, 1986-93, University of Osteopathic Medicine and Health Sciences, Des Moines. Publications include: Effects of Respiratory Obstruction on the Brain, CO-author, 1959; Water Requirements for Running in Rats, CO-author, 1966; Comparison of Myocardial Irritability of Selected Anesthetics, Co-author, 1971; Relationship of Osteopathic Manipulative Treatment, Lordosis and Respiration, Co-author, 1982. Honours include: Consultant, AOA National Osteopathic Board of medical Examiners, Pharmacology, Physiolog; Consultant, American Association of Podiatric Boards, Pharmacology; fellow in Clinical Pharmacology. Memberships include: American Association for the Advancement of Science; Sigma Xi; American College for Clinical Pharmacology and Therapeutics; New York Academy of Sciences; American Society for Microbiology. Address: University of Osetopathic Medicine and Health Sciences, 3200 Grand Avenue, Des Moines, IA 50312-4198, USA.

KILPACK Virginia Marie, b. 3 Feb 1936, New York, USA. Nurse. m. Gilbert H Kilpack, 25 May 1973, 1 s, 3 d. Education: BSN, 1959, MSN, 1961, Case Western University; PhD, Columbia Pacific University, 1987. Appointments: Staff Nurse; Assistant Head Nurse Instructor in Nursing; Assistant Professor of Nursing; Clinical Nurse Specialist, Neuroscience. Publications Ethical Issues and Procedural Dilemmas in Measuring Patient Competence, 1984; Intershift Report: Verbal Communication Using Nursing Process, Co-author, 1987; Using Research Bases Interventions to Decrease Patient Falls, CO-author, 1991. Honours: Sigma Theta Tau Regional and International Award for Research Utilization in Nursing Practice. Memberships: American Association of Neuroscience Nurses; American Nurses Association; American Nurses Association Council of Clinical Nurse Specialists; Sigma Theta Tau International. Hobbies: Gardening; Hiking. Address: North Thetford Road, Lyme, NH 03768, USA.

KIM Christopher M-H, b. 11 Mar 1950, Seoul, South Korea. Physician. m. 13 Aug 1978, 3 daughters. Education: MD, Chung Nam University School of Medicine, 1975. Appointments: Medical Director, Monmouth Pain Institute Inc, Red Bank, New Jersey, USA, 1983-. Publications: Author: Bee Venom Therapy and Bee Acupuncture Therapy, Korean edition, 1992. Honours: National Literature Award, Cho-Sun Daily News, Korea, 1975; Special Awards from Korean Pain Society, 1988. Memberships: President, American Apitherapy Society; International Association for Study of Pain; American Pain Society; American Academy of Pain Medicine; Academy of Neuromuscular Thermography; American Academy of Thermology; American Colllege of Acupuncture. Hobbies: Research on Bee Venom and other Toxins; Outdoor sports including hunting and deep sea fishing; Classical music. Address: 252 Broad Street, Red Bank, NJ 07701, USA.

KIM Kathleen M, b. 23 Jan 1958, Baltimore, Maryland, USA. Psychiatrist. m. Dr Zachary Rattner, 15 Dec 1992. Education: AB, MD, Brown University; MPH, Harvard School of Public Health. Appointments: Director, Psychiatric Emergency Department and Outpatient Clinic, 1989-90, Director, Partial Hospital Programme, Director, Psychiatric Ambulatory Services, 1990-, Yale-New Haven Hospital. Publications: Pathologic Grief and Its Relationship to Other Psychiatric Disorders, 1991; Neuroodocrine Changes Following Bereavement, 1993. Honours: Mead Johnson Fellow, 1985-86, Chairman's Award for Excellence, 1990, American Psychiatric Association. Memberships: American psychiatric Association; American Association of Geriatric Psychiatry. Hobbies: Golf; Downhill Skiing; Gardening; Reading Fiction. Address: Yale-New Haven Hospital, 425 George Street, New Haven, CT 06511, USA.

KIM Myunghee, b. 8 Nov 1932, Pusan, Korea. Psychiatrist; Psychoanalyst. m. Dr Peter Reimann, 29 June 1992, 2 daughters. Education: MD, 1957; Psyuchoanalyst, 1981; Fellow in Child Psychiatry, New York University Medical Centre, USA, 1970. Appointments: Staff Psychiatrist, Roosevelt Hospital, New York City, 1964-65; Teaching Staff, Bergen Pine Hospital, New Jersey, 1977-85; Staff Child Psychiatrist, Child Guidance and Family Service, 1970-72; Consultant to Headstart, 1971-72; Assistant Clinical Professor, Private Practice. Publication: Dissociative Disorder in Father Daughter Incest, 1991. Memberships: American Psychiatric Association; American Psychoanalytic Association; International Psychoanalytic Association. Hobbies: Travel; Trekking; Gardening; Art Collecting. Address: 272 Short Hills Avenue, Springfield, NJ 07081, USA.

KIM Wun Jung, b. 8 Aug 1950, Seoul, Korea. Physician. m. Yongjin Kang, 10 July 1980, 2 s, 1 d. Education: MD, Seoul National University; MPH, University of Michigan, USA; Child Psychiatry, Johns Hopkins University; Board Certified in Child, Adolescent and Adult Psychiatry. Appointments: Instructor, Johns Hopkins University; Assistant Professor, Director of Adolescent Psychiatry. Associate Professor, Assistant Training Director of Child Psychiatry, Medical College of Ohio. Publications: Contributor of professional articles. Memberships: APA; AACAP; ASAP; AOA. Hobby: Sports. Address: Division of Child Psychiatry, Medical College of Ohio, PO Box No 10008, 3000 Arlington, Toledo, OH 43699, USA.

KIMBROUGH Edward Ernest, b. 29 Sept 1929, Gainesville, Georgia, USA. Orthopaedic Surgeon. m. Jeanette Ludgate, 20 Nov 1954, 1 son, 3 daughters. Education: BA, Vanderbilt University, 1950; MD, Vanderbilt Medical School, 1953. Appointments: Resident, University of Minnesota Hospital, 1953, 1954; Resident, Brook Army Hospital, 1957-60; Chief, Orthopaedics, DeWitt Army Hospital, 1960-63; Moore Clinic, 1963-83; Chair, Department Orthopaedics, University of South Carolina School of Medicine, 1983-1995. Publications: Contributor of articles on hip and knee trauma in journals and texts; Editor, Journal of South Carolina Medical Association, 1974-80; Editor, Columbia Recorder, 1970-74. Honours: Certificate, Republic of Vietnam, 1965; Certificate, State of South Carolina, 1989; Columbia Medical Society, 1980; South Carolina Medical Association, 1980. Memberships: Eastern Orthopaedic Association, President, 1991; South Carolina Orthopaedic Association, President, 1981; Columbia Medical Society, President, 1978; Southern Orthopaedic Association, President, 1994. Hobbies: Reading; Walking; Gardening. Address: 2 Richland Medical Park, Columbia, SC 29203, USA.

KIMMICH Robert André, b. 2 Nov 1920, Indianapolis, Indiana, USA. Physician; Psychiatrist. m. Nancy Earle Smith, 1945, 1 s, 1 d. Education: BS, Yale University; MD, Indiana Universityy. Appointments: Assistant Professor, yale University Medical School; Director, Hawaii State Hospital. Chief, Mental Health department, San Francisco; Director, Michigan department Mental Health; Associate Professor, Stanford University; Chair, Psychiatric Department, Children's Hospital, San Francisco; Board of Directors, Cal-Pac Medical Association; Private practice of Psychiatry. Publications: Contributor of various articles; Programming and planning the Mental Health Centre, 1965. Honours: Distinguished Service Award, Northern California Psychiatric Society, 1992; Life Fellow, APA. Memberships: AMA; American Psychiatric Association; California Medical Association; President, Northern California Psychiatric Society, 1993-95. Hobbies: Sailing; Guitar. Address: 341 Spruce, San Francisco, CA 94118, USA.

KIMURA Kunihiko, b. 25 May 1927, Tokyo, Japan. Professor Emeritus of Anatomy. m. 8 Apr 1952, 1 son. Education: BSc, 1951, DSc, 1962, University of Tokyo; PhD, Osaka City Medical School, 1957. Appointments: Professor of Anatomy, Kanagawa Dental College, 1964-65; Professor of Anatomy, Tokyo University of Education, 1965-76; Professor of Anatomy, National Defense Medical College, 1976-93; Currently: Professor Emeritus; Research Associate, Kimura Auxological Institute. Publications: Human Growth, 1963; Human Anatomy, 1969; Growth, 1979; Translations: Gray's Anatomy, 1981; Zihlman: The Human Evolution Coloring Book, 1987; Memberships: Anthropological Society of Nippon, 1947-; Japanese Association of Anatomists, 1956-; American Association of Physical Anthropologists, 1961-; American Association of Anatomists, 1975-; Society for the Study of Human Biology, 1975-. Address: Kimura Auxological Institute, 1315-71 Irumagawa, Sayama 350-13, Japan.

KIMURA Robert Shigetsugu, b. 5 June 1920, Long Beach, California, USA. Inner Ear Researcher. m. 29 Jan 1966, 2 daughters. Education: BA, Stanford University; PhD, Tokyo Medical & Dental University. Appointments: Research Assistant; Research Associate; Principle Associate; Lecturer; Associate Professor, Otology & Laryngology, Harvard Medical School; Director, Electron Microscopy Laboratory, Massachusetts Eye & Ear Infirmary. Publications: Co-author: Meniere's Disease, Pathogenesis, Diagnosis and Treatment, 1981; Chapters in Cochlear Vascular Lesion, 1973; Ultrastructural Atlas of the Inner Ear, 1984; Hearing Loss and Dizziness, 1985. Honours: Javits Neuroscience Award, 1984; Shambaugh Prize in Otology, 1988; Collegium Oto-Rhino-Laryngologicum Amicitiae Sacrum; Award of Merit, Association for Research in Otolaryngology, 1990. Memberships: Association for Research in Otolaryngology; Barany Society; Collegium Oto-Rhino-Laryngologicum Amicitiae Sacrum; American Otological

Society; American Academy of Otolaryngology; American Association of Anatomists. Address: 21 Woodchester Drive, Weston, MA 02193, USA.

KIMURA Tasuku, b. 1941, Tokyo, Japan. Professor of Morphology. m. Fujiko Kiyota, 1 son, 1 daughter. Education: BSc, MSc, DSc, University of Tokyo. Appointments: Research Assistant, University of Tokyo; Associate Professor, Teikyo University; Professor, Section of Morphology, Primate Research Institute, Kyoto University. Publications: Primate Morphophysiology, Locomotor Analyses and Human Bipedalism, Co-editor, 1985; Primatology Today, Co-editor, 1990; The Evolution and Dispersal of Modern Humans in Asia, Co-editor, 1992. Memberships: Anthropological Society of Nippon; Primate Society of Japan; Medicolegal Society of Japan; Japanese Association of Anatomists; American Association of Physical Anthropologists; International Primatological Society. Address: Primate Research Institute, Kyoto University, Inuyama 484, Japan.

KINCAID-SMITH Priscilla Sheath, b. 30 Oct 1926, Johannesburg, South Africa. Professor of Medicine. m. Dr Ken Fairley, 11 July 1958, 2 sons, 1 daughter. Education: DSc; MD; DCP; FRCP; FRCPA; FRACP. Honours: Eric Sussman, 1969; David Hume, 1989; Leon Chesley, 1990; William Upjohn, 1991; John Peters, 1993. Address: Department of Pathology, University of Melbourne, Parkville 3052, Australia.

KINDSCHI George William, b. 2 May 1940, Rochester, Minnesota, USA. Physician. m. Claire McCann, 8 June 1968, 2 sons, 2 daughters. Education: BA, 1962, MD, 1968, MS, 1981, University of Wisconsin, Madison; Board Certified in Anatomic Pathology, Clinical Pathology, 1973, Dermopathology, 1978, Medical Management, 1992. Appointments: Director of Laboratories, Naval Hospital, Great Lakes, Illinois, 1973-76; Retired as Captain, Naval Reserve, 1990; Director of Pathology, The Monroe Clinic, 1976-. Publications: Clinical Laboratory Improvement Acts, 1981; Frozen Sections, Their Use and Abuse, 1984; Abortion, Euthanasia and Malthusian Theory, 1988. Honour: Meritorious Service Award, Wisconsin State Medical Society, 1991. Memberships: Fellow, CAP; Fellow, American Society of Dermpathology; American College of Physician Executives; AMA; Wisconsin Medical Society; Green County (Wisconsin) Medical Society; Wisconsin Society Pathology. Hobbies: Boy Scouts; Travel; Reading; Family. Address: 515 22nd Avenue, Monroe, WI 53566, USA.

KING Janet, b. 3 Oct 1941, Red Oak, Iowa, USA. Professor. m. Charles King, 25 dec 1967, 2 s. Education: BS, Iowa State University; PhD, Nutrition, University of California at Berkeley. Appointments: Dietitian, Fitzsimmons General Hospital, 1964-67; USPHS Postdoctoral Fellow, department of Nutritional Sciences, 1972, Assistant Professor of Nutrition and Nutritionist, Agricultural Experiment section, 1972-78, Associate Professor, 1978-83, Professor of Nutrition, 1983-, University of California, Berkeley; Director, Western Human Nutrition Research Centre,US Department of Agriculture, San Francisco, 1995-. Memberships: American Institute of Nutrition; American Dietetic Association; American Society for Clinical Nutrition. Address: Western Human Nutrition Research Centre, PO Box 29997, Presidio of San Francisco, CA 94129.

KING Jeffrey Charles, b. 21 Nov 1949, Chicago, IL, USA. Obstetrician; Gynaecologist. m. Ruth Anne Towell, 5 May 1973. Education: MD, Rush Medical College, Chicago, USA, 1975; Postdoctoral Fellowship, Maternal-Fetal Medicine, Georgetown University, Washington DC, USA, 1981. Appointments: Instructor, Department of Obstetrics & Gynaecology, University of Louisville, Kentucky, 1979-80; Instructor, Department of Obstetrics & Gynaecology, Georgetown University, School of Medicine, 1980-82; Associate Director, Maternal-Fetal Medicine, Columbia Hospital for Women, Washington, 1981-83; Director, Perinatal Education Exchange Program, Washington, 1982-85; Associate Director, Department of Obstetrics & Gynaecology, Georgetown University, School of Medicine, Washington, 1982-85; Coordinator, Resident Training Program at Georgetown Department of Obstetrics & Gynaecology, Washington, 1985-90; Assistant Professor/Assistant Chairman/Associate Professor, Department of Obstetrics & Gynaecology, Georgetown University School of Medicine, 1982-92, 1992-93, 1992-; Director, Maternal Transport Service, Georgetown University Hospital, Washington, 1981-. Publications: Numerous Scientific Publications, Chapters, Abstracts. Honours: Academic Teracher of the Year, 1986; Commissioned Kentucky Colonel by Governor Brown, 1980; Best Physician in Washington, 1992, 1993. Memberships: include, American Institute of

Ultrasound in Medicine, 1979; The American Medical Association, 1979; The Continental Gynaecology Society; The American College of Obstetricians & Gynaecologists; Society of Perinatal Obstetricians. Hobbies: Travel; Tennis; Antiques; Wines. Address: 5151 Yuma Street, NW, Washington DC 20016, USA.

KING John William, b. 31 Aug 1946, New Orleans, Louisiana, USA. Physician. m. Dr Tanya Lunn King, 20 June 1970, 1 s, 1 d. Education: BS, Tulane University; MD, Louisiana State University Medical Centre. Appointments: Clinical Instructor, Bowman Gray School of Medicine, Winston-Salem, North Carolina, 1977-78; Assistant Professor of Medicine. 1978-82; Associate Professor of Medicine, 1982-91; Professor of Medicine, 1991-; Programme Director, Section of Infectious Diseases, Louisiana State University Medical Centre, Shreveport. Publications include: Cytological Aspects of Lipid Assimilation by Cestodes. Incorporated of Lineoleic Acid into the Parenchyma and Eggs by Hymenolepis diminuta, Co-author, 1969; A Clinical Approach to Hepatitis B, 1982; A Clinical Approach to Non-A, Non-B Hepatitis, 1983; Joys of Medical Literature, 1986; Ribavirin and Intravenous Immune Globulin Therapy of Measles Pneumonia in HIV Infection: A Case Report and Review of the Literature, Co-author, 1993; Numerous talks, symposia and educational tapes. Honours: Beta Beta Beta, 1967; Sigma Xi, 1985; FACP, 1981; Fellow, Infectious Diseases Society of America, 1992. Memberships: American Federation Clinical research; American Society for Microbiology. HobbiesL Aikido-Jujitsu; Scuba diving; Playing drums. Address; Louisiana State University Medical Centre, PO Box 33932, Shreveport, LA 71130, USA.

KING Paul Harvey, b. 4 Sept 1941, Fort Wayne, Indiana, USA. Associate Professor. m. Betty Sue Freeman, 31 Mar 1982, 2 sons, 2 daughters. Education: BS, Engineering Science, 1963, MS, Engineering, 1965, Case Institute of Technology, Cleveland, Ohio; PhD, Mechanical Engineering, Vanderbilt University, Nashville, Tennessee, 1968. Appointments: Assistant Professor, 1968-72, Associate Professor, Mechanical Engineering, Biomedical Engineering, 1972-. Chairman, Biomedical Engineering Department, 1975-76, Associate Professor, Anaesthesiology, 1987-, Director, Division of Biomedical Engineering, Department of Anaesthesiology, 1991-, Vanderbilt University. Publications include: Co-author: Computer Optimisation of Hemodialysis, 1970; Operating Room Monitoring And Record Keeping System, 1988; The Capnogram Analyser: A Real Time Expert System, 1992; Automated Record-Keeping Systems Used In Anesthesiology, 1992; Knowledge-based Flash Evoked Potential Recognition System, 1992; Clinical evaluation - continuous real-time intra-arterial blood gas monitoring during anaesthesia and surgery by fibre optic sensor, 1992; Automated Evoked Potential Monitoring, 1993; Co-patentee: Multi-crystal Tomography, 1971. Honours: Skylab Award and Skylab Achievement Award, 1975; Group Achievement Award, Skylab Medical Team, 1975. Memberships: Sigma Xi; American Society of Electrical Engineers; Full Member, Institute of Electrical and Electronic Engineers; AAMI; Full Member, BMES; International Anaesthesia Research Society; Anaesthesia Patient Safety Foundation; Editorial Board, International Journal of Clinical Monitoring and Computing. Hobbies: Photography; Gardening; Computers. Address: 6012 Sherwood Drive, Nashville, TN 37215-5733, USA.

KING Walter Wing-Keung, b. 21 January 1950, Hong Kong. Surgeon. m. May Poon, 1985, 2 sons. Education: BA, honours, University of Wisconsin, 1971; MD, Vanderbilt University, 1975; FRCS(Ed); FRCS(C); FACS. Appointments: Surgical Resident, State University of New York, Stony Brook, 1976-80; Fellow in Surgery, Harvard Medical School, 1980-82; Clinical Assistant, Massachusetts General Hospital, 1980-82; Fellow, Memorial Sloan Kettering Cancer Center, 1982-83; Chief, Head and Neck/Plastic Reconstructive Surgery, Prince of Wales Hospital, The Chinese University of Hong Kong, 1984-. Publications: Nasopharyngeal Cancer: A Chinese Perspective, 1994. Honours: American Society for Head & Neck Surgery Fellowship Award, 1984. Memberships: ISBI; ABA; SHNS; ASHNS; SIC; ASCO; AAFPRS. Hobbies: Tennis; Swimming. Address: Department of Surgery, Prince of Wales Hospital, Hong Kong.

KINGSLAND Kevin Geoffrey, b. 23 Aug 1947, UK. Psychologist. m. Venika Mehra, 23 Dec 1970, 1 s. Education: BSc, Honours; Diploma, Couns Psychology; FI Mgt; CPsychol; AFBPsS. Appointments: Director, Centre for Human Communication; Director, TSR International, Asia. Publications: Complete Hatha Yoga, 1976; Hathapradipika, 1977; The Whole Person, 1994. Memberships: Division of Counselling Psychology and Occupational Psychology, British Psychological Society; Scientific

and Medical Network, Royal Society of Health. Hobbies: Running; Performing Arts; Languages; Complexity. Address: GOA University, PO Bambolim, GOA-403 202, India.

KINGSTON Bernard William Jacques, b. 4 Apr 1949, England. Registered Osteopath; Lecturer. Education: BA, Honours, Oxford; Diploma in Osteopathy; Postgraduate Certificate in Education. Appointments: Registered Osteopath; Lecturer in Functional Anatomy, British School of Osteopathy. Memberships: Member of register of Osteopaths. Hobbies: Skiing; Marathon running; Windsurfing; Cooking; Gardening; Music. Address: 16 Northcote Road, St Margaret's, Twickenham TW1 1PA, England.

KIPEN Howard Matthew, b. 29 July 1953, Los Angeles, California, USA. Physician. m. Debra Laskin, 28 June 1987, 2 daughters. Education: BA, University of California, Berkeley, 1976; MD, University of California, San Francisco, 1979; MPH, Columbia University, 1983. Appointments include: Director, Clinical Center, Environmental and Occupational Health Sciences Institute, Piscataway, New Jersey, 1989-; Associate Professor, Departments of Environmental and Community Medicine, and of Medicine, 1991-, Director, Occupational Health Division, Department of Environmental and Community Medicine, 1994-, Robert Wood Johnson Medical School, University of Medicine and Dentistry of New Jersey; Director, Occupational Health Division, Environmental and Occupational Health Sciences Institute, 1994-. Publications include: Articles in Brain Research, American and British Journals of Industrial Medicine, Toxicology and Industrial Health, Environmental Health Perspectives, Journal of Occupational Medicine, Inhalation Toxicology, American Journal of Public Health, other refereed journals; Book chapters. Honours include: Phi Beta Kappa, 1974; Adolph G Kammer Merit in Authorship Award, American College of Occupational and Environmental Medicine, 1992; Environmental and Occupational Medicine Academic Award, National Institute of Environmental Health Sciences, 1992-97. Memberships: American College of Physicians; American Public Health Association; New Jersey Medical Society, Fellow, New Jersey Academy of Medicine; Occupational and Environmental Medicine Association of New Jersey, Program Chairman 1991, Secretary 1992, President 1994; Charter Member, International Society for Environmental Epidemiology; American Thoracic Society; New Jersey Thoracic Society, Research Grant Committee Member 1988-94; Fellow: American Colleges of Occupational Medicine, of Preventive Medicine, of Chest Physicians;. Hobbies: Jogging; Reading; Travel; Skiing. Address: EOHSI, 681 Frelinghuysen Road, Box 1179, Piscataway, NJ 08855-1179, USA.

KIPSHIDZE Nodar, b. 12 Oct 1923, Tbilisi, Republic of Georgia. Doctor. m. Lelt Cheishvilt, 15 Mar 1949, 1 s, 1 d. Education: MD; PhD; Post Graduate course, Medical Institute, Tbilisi, Aspirantura, A S of Republic of Georgia, Doctoratura, AMS Moscow. Career: Professor of Medical State Institute, 1957-60; Head of Department of Infarction, Institute of E and C Therapy, 1961-72; Head of Division of Pharmacology and Biology, World Health Organisation, 1963-65; Currently, Director, Institute of Experimental and Clinical Therapy, Tbilisi Medical Institute. Publications: Atlas of Echocardiogrqaphy, 1989; Prolapse of Mitral Valves, 1989; Cardiomyopathy, 1990; Treatment of Heart Coronary Diseases by Means of Lazer, 1993. Honours: State Award for Treatment of Myocardial Infarction, 1981; Russian AS Myasnikow Award, 1988; Russian State Award, 1989. Memberships: Head, Association of Atherosclerosis; Head, Georgian Society of Geriatrics and Gerontology; Head, Society of Internists; Russian A M S; New York Academy of Sciences; Georgian A M S. Hobby: Music. Address: 380059 Tbilisi, Lubliana ul 4, Republic of Georgia.

KIRBY Brian John, b. 25 Aug 1936, Southend-on-Sea, England. Senior Lecturer; Consultant Physician. m. Rachel Pawson, 1960, 1 s, 1 d. Education: MB ChB; FRCP. Appointments: Junior Posts, Leeds and London; Medical College of Virginia; Royal Postgraduate Medical School; University of Edinburgh; Senior Lecturer in Medicine; Consultant Physician. Publications: Contributor of professional articles. Honours: Sir Stanley Davidson Travelling Fellowship; Medicine Gilliland Travelling Fellowship. Memberships: British Cardiac Society; Association of Physicians. Hobbies: Walkng; Sailing; Skiing. Address: Postgraduate Medical School, Barrack Road, Exeter EX4 4SF, England.

KIRCH Wilhelm, b. 4 July 1947, Cologne. Physician. m. Gabriele Kirch, 17 Nov 1978, 2 daughters. Education: J Gutenberg University, Mainz, Germany; Internist; Nephrologist; Clinical Pharmacologist. Appointments: Physician, Medical University Hospitals, Germany &

Switzerland; Senior Registrar, University Hospital, Essen and Medical University Hospital, Kiel, Germany; Director, Clinical Pharmacology & Therapeutics, Technical University, Dresden, Germany, Vice Dean. Publications: Books: Internal Medicine and Dentistry; Editor: Misdiagnoses in Internal Medicine, practical drug therapy; Numerous articles in medical publications. Honours: Ludolf Krehl Prize, Southwest German Society of Internal Medicine; Prize, Regensburg Academy of Medical Sciences. (Memberships: American Society of Clinical Pharmacology Ther; British Pharmacology Society; German Society of Internal Medicine. Address: Med Hosp, Technical Univ, Fiedlerstr 27, D-01307 Dresden, Germany.

KIRKCALDY Bruce David, b. 17 Sept 1952, Wallasey, England. Clinical Psychologist. m. Elisabeth Pia Thome, 23 Dec 1988, 2 daughters. Education: MA, University of Dundee, Scotland, 1975; PhD, University of Giessen, Germany, 1986. Appointments: Research Associate, University of Birmingham, 1975-76; Research Psychologist, DSHS, Cologne University, Germany, 1979-82; University Clinic of Cologne, 1982-88; Marl Child and Adolescent Psychiatry, 1990-91; Currently: Honorary Lecturer, Ruhr University Bochum; Research Fellow, Düsseldorf University; Consultant, University of Manchester, Institute of Science and Technology, Manchester, England. Publications: Individual Differences in Movement, 1985; Normalities and Abnormalities in Human Movement, 1989; Sport and Leisure: Therapeutic aspects (editor), 1990; The impact of organisational stress on managers (co-author), 1994. Honours: Chartered Psychologist; Associate Fellow, British Psychological Society; Clinical Psychologist, BDP. Memberships: British Psychological Society; International Society for the Study of Individual Differences; German Society of Behavioural Therapy. Hobbies: Running; Swimming; Music; Sport psychology. Address: Department of Work and Organisational Psychology, Ruhr University Bochum, Bochum, Germany.

KIRKPATRICK Martha J, b. 30 Dec 1925, Oxnard, California, USA. Psychiatrist. m. Dr Seymour Pastron, 1957, div, 1977, 3 s. Education: AA, University of Michigan, 1946; MD, McGill Medical School, 1950; Psychoanalytic Training, Los Angeles Psychoanalytic Institute, 1971; Diplomate, American Board of Psychiatry and Neurology, 1959. Appointments: Clinical Professor, Department of Psychiatry, University of California at Los Angeles. Publications: Women's Sexual Development, Editor, 1980; Women's Sexual Experience, Editor, 1982. Memberships: American Psychiatry Association American Psychoanalytics Association; American Academy of Psychoanalysis; American College of Psychiatrists. Hobbies: Cooking; Skiing; Opera; Archaeology. Address: 988 Bluegrass Lane, Los Angeles, CA 90049-1433, USA.

KISHKOVSKY Albert, b. 7 Jan 1922, Kiev. Radiologist. m. Kuzminskaya Nina, 29 Apr 1951, 1 daughter. Education: Saratov Medical Institute, Russia, 1943; Research Institute of Medical Raidology, Moscow, 1947; Postgraduate, Military Medical Academy, Leningrad, 1956. Appointments: Roentgenologist, Kiev Military Hospital, 1946-52; Radiologist, Soviet Military Hospital, Poland, 1952-54; Head of Roentgeno-radiology, Chair, Military Medical Academy, St Petersburg, Chief Radiologist, Soviet Army, 1960-89; Professor, Radiology, Military Medical Academy, St Petersburg. Publications: Roentgenotherapy of Non-oncological Dieseases, (co-author), 1977; Radiodiagnosis in Military Medicine, (co-author), 1979; Differential Radiodiagnosis in Gastroenterology, 1984; Atlas of Radiodiagnostic Proceedures, 1987; Radiodiagnosis in Emergency Medicine, (co-author), 1989. Honours: Decorated with 4 Orders and 17 Medals of Russia, 1943-89; Council of Ministers Prize Winner, 1989. Memberships: Russian, European and International Associations of Radiology; Corresponding Member of Russian Academy of Medical Sciences. Hobbies: Autotouring; Gardening. Address: 194175 St Petersburg, Clinicheskaya St 6, Department of Radiology, Military Medical Academy, Russia.

KISSLO Joseph Andrew, b. 10 Aug 1941, Plymouth, Pennsylvania, USA. Professor of Medicine. m. Katherine B Kisslo, 17 Aug 1983, 1 son, 1 stepson, 2 daughters. Education: BS, University of Notre Dame, Notre Dame, Indiana, 1963; MD, 1967, Intern, 1967-68, Hahnemann University, Philadelphia; Assistant Resident, Internal Medicine, 1970-71, Postdoctoral Fellow, Paediatric Cardiology, 1971-72, Yale University; Postdoctoral Fellow, Adult Cardiology, Duke University Medical Center, 1972-74; Diplomate, National Board of Medical Examiners, 1968. Appointments include: Associate Professor of Medicine, 1977-87, Assistant Professor of Radiology, 1977-, Director, Cardiac Diagnostic Unit, 1977-83, Professor of Medicine, 1987-, Duke University Medical

Center, Durham, North Carolina; Many visiting professorships, USA and abroad. Publications include: Over 200 in journals, monographs and books such as Circulation, Ultrasound in Medicine, American Journal of Cardiology, Journal of the American College of Cardiology, An Introduction to Doppler Echocardiography (monograph with slides), Journal of Thoracic and Cardiovascular Surgery, Surgery of the Chest, Acute Coronary Care; Improved Cardiac Anthropomorphic Phantom, patent. Honours: Blue Circle Honor Society, 1961; Alpha Omega Alpha, 1965, Edelsohn and Langbord Prizes, 1967, Hahnemann; Silver Medal for Education, British Medical Society, 1981; Fellow, American College of Cardiology, 1980-; Inge Edler Lecture, University of Lund, Sweden, 1991; Edler Lecturer, American Society of Echocardiography, 1993. Memberships include: Senior Member, American Federation for Clinical Research; International Society of Intraoperative Cardiovascular Ultrasound, Chairman of Board of Directors; Fellow, American Institute of Ultrasound in Medicine; American Society of Echochardiography, President 1983-85, Vice-President 1981-83, Board of Directors; Society of Pediatric Echocardiography; Editorial boards. Address: 221 Longwood Drive, Chapel Hill, NC 27514, USA.

KITAMURA Katsutoshi, b. 11 Feb 1923, Hiroshima, Japan. Neurosurgeon. m. Yoshiko Higashiyama, 5 Jan 1951, 2 sons, 2 daughters. Education: MD; DMSc. Appointments: Professor of Neurosurgery, Kyushu University, Fukuka, Japan; Director, Shinkokura Hospital, Kitakyushu, Japan. Publications: Haemangiomas in Japan, 1986; Surgical Results for Cerebral Aneurysms in Japan, 1987; Spontaneous Occlusion of the Circle of Willis, 1993. Memberships: Honorary President, Japan Neurosurgical Society; Honorary Member, Society of Neurological Surgeons, USA. Hobbies: Fine Arts; Tennis. Address: 2-5-7 Shodai, Sawara-ku, Fukuoka 814, Japan.

KITO Shozo, b. 29 Jan 1927, Aichi, Japan. Physician; Neuroscientist. m. Sachiko Kito, 16 May 1955, 1 son. Education: MD, PhD, Tokyo University School of Medicine. Appointments: Instructor, Tokyo University School of Medicine, 1968-71; Assistant Professor, Tokyo Women's Medical College, 1971-73; Professor, Hiroshima University School of Medicine, 1973-90; Professor, The University of the Air, 1990-. Publications: Neurotransmitters Receptors, 1984; Neuroreceptors and Signal Transduction, 1988; Neuroreceptor Mechanisms in Brain, 1991; Many other publications. Memberships: American Society for Neurosciences; Japanese Society of Pharmacology; Japanese Society of Geriatric Medicine. Honours: Japanese Medical Association Award, 1976; Mitsukoshi Medical Award, 1977. Hobbies: Reading; Tennis. Address: 2-11 Wakaba Mihamaku, Chiba 261, Japan.

KITWOOD Thomas Marris, b. 16 Feb 1937, Boston, England. Psychologist. Divorced, 1 s, 1 d. Education: BA; MSc; PhD. Career: School Teaching Posts, 1960-74; Senior Research Fellow, 1974-79, Lecturer in Psychology, 1979-91, Senior Lecturer, 1991, University of Bradford; Currently, Director, Bradford Dementia Research Group. Publications: Concern for Others, 1990; The Dialectics of Dementia, American Ageing Society, 1990; Person and Process in Dementia, in International Journal of Geriatric Psychiatry. Memberships: British Psychological Society; British Association for Counselling; British Society of Gerontology. Hobbies: Walking; Painting; Music. Address: Bradford Dementia Research Group, University of Bradford, Bradford, West Yorkshire, BD7 1DP, England.

KIYU Andrew Dawie, b. 5 May 1952, Sarawak, Malaysia. Epidemiologist. m. Josephine John, 26 Apr 1980, 1 son, 1 daughter. Education: MBBS, 1976, MPH, 1981, University of Malaya; DPH with honours, Tulane University, New Orleans, USA, 1990. Appointments: House Officer, Internal Medicine, 1976-77; Medical Officer, 1977-79; Medical Officer of Health, 1979-90; Epidemiologist, 1990-. Publications: The dogs and their possible influence on the health of the longhouse people of the Seventh Division of Sarawak, 1981; The epidemiology of reported typhoid and paratyphoid fevers in Sarawak in 1979, 1981; The epidemiology of cancer in Sarawak, East Malaysia, 1985; A study of patients admitted to Miri Hospital, Sarawak, by airborne medical evacuation, 1986; Impact of rural water supply and sanitation on the health status of children under five years in Sarawak, Malaysia, 1990; Nutritional Status of Children in Rural Sarawak, Malaysia (co-author), 1991; With S Hardin: Child minding and nutritional status of children 6-12 months old in Sarawak, 1991; Functioning and utilization of rural water supply in Sarawak, Malaysia, 1992; Latrine use in rural Sarawak, Malaysia, 1993. Honours: Excellent Service Award, Ministry of Health, Malaysia, 1992. Memberships: American College of Epidemiology; Society for Epidemiologic Research; Associate, American College of

Preventive Medicine; International Epidemiological Association; Biometric Society; Society of Public Health, UK; American Public Health Association; International Council for the Control of Iodine Deficiency Disorders; Fellow, Borneo Research Council; American Medical Writers Association; Association for the Advancement of Science; Fellow, Royal Society of Tropical Medicine and Hygiene, UK; Malaysian Medical Association. Hobbies: Photography; Reading; Body building. Address: Lot 127 Hockien Road, 93000 Kuching, Sarawak, Malaysia.

KJELLSTRAND Per T T-son, b. 14 July 1941, Svenljunga, Sweden. Senior Scientist. m. Karin Anne Marie Carlsson, 29 June 1968, 1 son, 2 daughters. Education: BS, 1970, PhD, 1977, Assistant Professor 1979, University of Lund. Appointments: Research Assistant, 1967-77, Project Leader, 1977-87, University of Lund, Lund; Currently Senior Scientist, Gambro AB. Publications: About 100 scientific articles in histochemistry, toxicology, haemodialysis and peritoneal dialysis. Honours: Robert Feulgen Preis für Histochemie, 1977; Oscar II's Stipend for Scientific Achievement, 1977. Memberships: American Society of Artificial Organs; American Society of Nephrology; Swedish Society of Toxicology; Scandinavian Society of Cell Toxicology; Histochemical Society. Hobbies: Hunting; Sailing; Boat building. Address: Ekvägen 25, Södra Sandby, Sweden.

KLAHR Aryeh Leslie, b. 25 Jul 1952, Brooklyn, NY, USA. Psychiatrist. Education: BA, Yeshiva University, 1973; MD, University of Guadalajara, Mexico, 1977; Diplomate, American Board of Psychiatry and Neurology, 1989. Career includes: Resident in Psychiatry, Hillside Hospital, Division of Long Island Jewish Medical Center, Glen Oaks, NY, 1984-87; Director, Alcoholism Treatment Services, Fair Oaks Hospital, Summit, NJ, 1988-90; Medical Director, Industrial Medicine Associates, PC, White Plains, NY, 1990-; Clinical Assistant Professor, NY Medical College, Department of Psychiatry, 1991-. Publications: Contributor of articles to professional journals and chapters to medical books. Honours: Regent's Scholarship, State of NY Board of Regents, Albany, NY, 1969-73; Fellow, American Psychiatric Association; Fellow, Addictionology, Fair Oaks Hospital, Summit, NJ, 1987-88. Memberships: AMA; Medical Society of State of NY; American Society of Addiction Medicine; American Academy of Clinical Psychiatrists. Hobbies: Singing; Tennis; Skiing. Address: 280 Dobbs Ferry Road, Suite 306, White Plains, NY 10607, USA.

KLAHR Saulo, b. 8 Jun 1935, Santander, Colombia, SA. Physician. m. 29 Dec 1965, 2 s. Education: MD, Universidad Nacional de Colombia, 1959; Resident in Medicine, Universidad del Valle, 1959-61; Postdoctoral Fellow in Renal Diseases, WA University, 1961-63. Career: Instructor, Assistant Professor, Associate Professor, Professor, Joseph Friedman Professor of Renal Disease, Currently, Simon Professor of Medicine, Washington University, St Louis, MO. Publications: Over 400 scientific publications; Editor or Co-editor of 14 books on nephrology, electrolyte disorders and nutrition. Honours: Fellow, American College of Physicians; Established Investigator, American Heart Association; Uremia Award, 1989; David Hume Memorial Award, 1992; Fellow, American Association for the Advancement of Science, 1993. Memberships: American Society of Nephrology; International Society of Nephrology; Association of American Physicians; American Physiological Society; American Society for Clinical Investigation. Hobbies: Reading; Classical Music; Chess. Address: Washington University School of Medicine, St Louis, MO 63110, USA.

KLATSKY Arthur Louis, b. 24 Oct 1929, New York City, USA. Physician. m. Eileen Rohrberg, 21 June 1953, 1 s, 1 d. Education: BA, Yale, 1950; MD, Harvard, 1954; Certified in Internal Medicine and in Cardiovascular Diseases by ABIM. Appointments: Senior Consultant in Cardiology, Kaiser Foundation Hospital, Oakland, California. Publications: Contributor of over 60 articles, abstracts and book chapters. Honours: Thomas Turner Award for Excellence in Alcohol Research, Alcoholic Beverage Medical Research Foundation, 1992; Distinguished Practitioner National Academies of Practice, 1995. Memberships: Fellow, American College of Physicians; Fellow, American College of Cardiology; Fellow, Council on Epidemiology, American Heart Association. Hobbies: Running; Music; Gardening; Travel. Address: 280 W MacArthur Boulevard, Oakland, CA 94611, USA.

KLEBER Rolf Jan, b. 19 Mar 1950, Banjarmasin, Indonesia. Psychologist. Education: MS, University of Nijmegen, The Netherlands; PhD, University of Amsterdam, The Netherlands. Career: Visiting Lecturer, University of California, Irvine; Coordinator, Continuing Education, Dutch Association of Psychologists; Research Associate, Universities of Nijmegen and Wageningen, The Netherlands; Co-Founder Institute for Psychotrauma, The Netherlands; Currently, Head of Research Institute for Psychotrauma, Associate Professor of Clinical Psychology. Publications: Co-author, Brief Psychotherapy of Posttraumatic Stress Disorders, in Journal of Consulting Clinical Psychology; Author, Coping with Trauma: Theory, Prevention and Treatment, 1992; Editor, Beyond Trauma: Societal and Cultural Dimensions, forthcoming. Memberships: International Society for Traumatic Stress Studies; Dutch Association of Psychologists. Address: Institute for Psychotrauma, Justus van Effenstraat 52, 3511 HN Utrecht, The Netherlands.

KLEIN-SCHWARTZ Wendy, b. 16 Dec 1953, Baltimore, Maryland, USA. Clinical Pharmacist. m. Elliott Schwartz, 3 s, 1 d. Education: PharmD. Appointments: Director, Maryland Poison Centre; Associate professor of Pharmacy Practice and Science, University of Maryland School of Pharmacy. Publications include: Adsoprtion of Oral Antidotes for Acetaminophen Poisoning, Co-author, 1981; Poisoning in the Elderly, Co-author, 1983; Jimson Weed Intoxication in Adolescents and Young Adults, Co-author, 1984; Ipecac Administration in Children Younger than One Year Old, Co-author, 1985; Three Fatal Sodium Azide Poisonings, Co-author, 1989; Assessment of Management Guidelines, Acute Iron Ingestion, Co-author, 1990; Poisoning in the Elderly, Epidemioloical, Clinical and Management Considerations, Co-author, 1991; Simulated Acetaminophen Overdose: Pharmacokinetics and Effectivemness of Activited Charcoal, Co-author, 1991; The Effect of Milk on ipecac-induced Emesis, Co-author, 1991; Initial Symptons as Predictors of Esophageal Injury in Alkaline Corrosive Ingestions, CO-author, 1992; The Use of Activiated Charcoal in a Simulated Acetaminophen Overdose: A New Loading Dose for N-Acetylcysteine?, Co-author. Honours: Rho Chi. Memberships: American Association of PoisonControl Centres; American Academy of Clinical Toxicology; American Association of Colleges of Pharmacy. Address: Maryland Poison Centre, University of Maryland School of Pharmacy, 20 N Pine Street, Baltimore, MD 21201, USA.

KLEINMAN Susan L Rosenberg, b. 2 Jun 1942, Joplin, Missouri, USA. Dance/Movement Therapist. m. Paul Kleinman, 18 Feb 1972, 1 s. Education: MA, Academy of Dance Therapists Registered; BFA, University of Oklahoma, 1964; MA, Lone Mountain College, 1977. Appointments: Apprenticeship, St Elizabeths Hospital, 1964-65; Dance/Movement Therapist, Western Psychiatric Institute and Clinic, 1965-71; Dance/Movement Therapist, Highland Park General Hospital, 1971-86; Dance/Movement Therapist, Charter Hospital, 1986; Dance/Movement Therapist & Chairperson of National Coalition of Arts Therapies Associations. Publications: Dance Therapy: A Means of Communication, 1968; Dance Is Life; Aging Artfully; Health Benefits of Art & Dance. Memberships: American Dance Therapy Association; American Journal of Dance Therapy; National Coalition of Arts Therapies Associations. Hobbies: Art; Dance. Address: 7826 NW 40th Street, Hollywood, Florida 33024, USA.

KLIMA Karen Ann, b. 27 Nov 1960, Baltimore, MD, USA. Ophthalmic Photographer; Technician. Education: BA, College of Notre Dame, MD, 1982; Certified Retinal Angiographer, 1987; Certified Ophthalmic Technician, 1992. Appointment: Senior Ophthalmic Technician; Ophthalmic Photographer. Publication: 2nd Author, The Prevalance of Cisch Nodules and Other Ocular Findings, in NF 1. Honours: 1st and 2nd Place, Photography Awards, American Academy of Ophthalmology, 1989, 1990, 1991; Employee of Month, Wilmer Eye Institute, Johns Hopkins Hospital, 1994. Memberships: Ophthalmic Photographers Society; Joint Commission of Allied Health Professionals Organization. Hobbies: Biking; Softball; Golf. Address: 3405 Pinewood Avenue, Baltimore, MD 21206, USA.

KLIMOV Anatoli, b. 14 June 1920, Petrozavodsk, Russia. Biochemist. m. Maria Jakovleva, 2 Nov 1946, 1 son, 1 daughter. Education: MD, Military Medical Academy, Leningrad, 1960; Candidate of Medical Sciences, 1951. Appointments: Senior Teacher, Department of Biochemistry, Military Medical Academy, Leningrad; Director, Institute of Antibiotics, Leningrad; Director, Division of Biomedical Sciences, WHO, Geneva; Head, Department of Biochemistry & Lab of Lipid Metabolism, Institute of Experimental Medicine, St Petersburg. Publications: Penicillins and Cephalosporins, 1973; High Density Lipoproteins and Atherosclerosis, 1984; Lipoproteins, Dis-lipoproteinemias and Atherosclerosis, 1984; Immunoreactivity and Atherosclerosis, 1986. Memberships: Full member of Russian Academy of Medical Sciences, 1975; International Atherosclerosis Society; European Atherosclerosis Society; Russian Biochemical Society. Honours: Honourable Member, Hungarian Atherosclerosis Society, 1976; Honourable Member, Cuban Society of Angiology, 1987. Hobbies: Travel; Photography. Address: 22 Bol Monetnaya Str App 10, St Petersburg 197061, Russia.

KLYMAN Cassandra M, b. 1 Jan 1938, New York City, USA. Psychoanalyst. m. Calvin Klyman, 26 June 1994, dec, 2 sons. Education: BA; MD; FAPA; Certification in Psychoanalysis, American Academy of Psychoanalysis. Appointments: Assistant Clinical Professor of Psychiatry, Wayne State University College of Medicine, Department of Psychiatry Faculty, Michigan Psychoanalytic Institute; Chair, Committee on Education, Department of Psychiatry, Sinai Hospital of Detroit; Past President, Michigan Psychiatric Society. Publications: Pregnancy as a Run to Early Childhood Sibling Logs, 1986; Comm Parental Surrogate in the Development of the Adolescent, 1985; An Operatic Accompaniment to an Analysis, 1980. Honours: Award for Distinguished Service, Michigan Psychiatric Society, 1985, 1988, 1994; Award for Outstanding Teaching Performance and Dedication and Achievement, Sinai Hospital, detroit, 1975, 1992. Memberships: American Psychoanalytic Association; American Psychiatric Association; AMA; Michigan State Medical Society; Oakland City Medical Society; International Psycho-Analytic Association. Hobbies: Tennis; Swimming; Theatre. Address: 3060 Chickering Lane, Bloomfield Hills, MI 48392, USA.

KNIGHTON Shaun Heath, b. 19 Aug 1961, Ilkeston, Derbyshire, UK. Chiropractor. m. Christine Holroyd, 24 Sept 1994. Education: Bachelor of Business Administration, Simon Fraser University, Burnaby, BC, Canada, 1983; Doctor of Chiropractic, AECC, Bournemouth, Dorset, England, 1990. Appointments: Vice President, Quest Insurance Limited, 1981-86; Chiropractor, 1990-; Board of Directors, Soto Europe, 1993-. Memberships: British Chiropractic Association; Soto Europe. Hobbies: Fishing; Rock Music; Reading; Skiing. Address: 566A Burton Road, Litteover, Derby, DE23 5DG, UK.

KNOBLOCH Ferdinand Jiri, b. 15 Aug 1916, Praha, Czechoslovakia. Psychiatrist. m. Jirini Skorkovska, 5 Sept 1947, 2 d. Education: MD, Prague; Med ScC, Prague; MD, Canada; FRCP, Canada; Qualified Psychoanalyst/Fellow of the American Academy of Psychoanalysts. Appointments: Lecturer/Associate Professor, Department of Psychiatry, Charles University, Prague, 1946-70; Visiting Professor: Havana, Cuba, 1963; University of Illinois, Chicago, 1968-69; Columbia, 1969-70; A Einstein Medical College, 1969-70; Professor, University of British College, 1971-83; Professor Emeritus, Psychiatry, 1983-. Publications: Author, Forensic Psychiatry, 1967; Psychotherapy, 1968; Neurosis and You, 1962, 1963, 1968; Integrated Psychotherapy, 1979. Honours: Award of the Czachoslovak Medical Society for book, Forensic Psychiatry, 1968. Memberships: Psychotherapeutic Section, World Psychiatric Association; Fellow, American Psychiatric Association; American Group Psychotherapy Association; Canadian Society for Integrated Psychotherapy and Psychoanalysis. Hobbies: Music; Piano Playing; Wind Surfing. Address: 4137 W 12 Avenue, Vancouver, BC, B6R 2P6, Canada.

KNOWLES Caroline Hoffberg, b. 1 Mar 1926, New York City, USA. Psychologist. m. William Henry Knowles, 7 Jun 1971, 2 d. Education: BA, New York University; MA< Brown University; PhD, Yale University. Appointments: Assistant Professor, University of California at Riverside, 1959-61; Instructor, University of Michigan, 1961-67; Psychologist, Simmons College, 1968-69; Psychologist, Boston University, 1969-73; Visiting Psychologist, Vanuatu General Hospital, 1980-83; Private Practice, 1967-. Publications: Food Hoarding, 1960; Professional Identity and IMpulse Expression in Phantasy, Co-author, 1966; Changes in Olfactory Sensitivity during Menstrual Cycle, dissertation; Physiological Basis of Hoarding in the Albino Rat, dissertation; Presenter of several papers at professional meetings; Contributor of poetry to poetry journals. Memberships: American Psychological Association; American Society for Clinical Hypnosis; California Psychological Association; Redwood Psychological Association. Hobbies: Travel; Hiking; Swimming; Biking. Address: 1222 South Main Street, Lakeport, CA 95453, USA.

KNUTZEN Victor Keith, b. 13 May 1943, MD, USA. Medical Director. m. Helen Sheldon, 23 Apr 1966, 2 d. Education: MBChB; MD, Cape Town; FRCS(Edin); FRCOG(London); FACS; FACOG. Appointments: Assistant Professor, Obstetrics and Gynaecology, Mount Sinai, NY; Clinical Professor, Obstetrics and Gynaecology, University of Nevada,

Reno; Medical Director, Northern Nevada Fertility Center; Medical Director, Northern Nevada Medical Group. Honour: President of Society of Assisted Reproductive Technology. Memberships: American Fertility Society; Society of Assisted Reproductive Technology; Northern Nevada Obstetric and Gynaecologic Society. Hobbies: Sailing; Scuba Diving; Squash; Fishing. Address: Northern Nevada Fertility Center, Suite 801, 75 Pringle Way, Reno, NV 89502, USA.

KOBAYASHI Noboru, b. 23 Nov 1927, Tokyo, Japan. Physician. m. Shigeko, 9 Oct 1960, 1 s. Education: MD, 1954, DMS, 1960, Faculty of Medicine, University of Tokyo; Postgraduate Training, Cincinatti Children's Hospital, USA; Postgraduate Training, Hospital for Sick Children, Great Ormond Street, London, England. Appointments: Professor, Chairman, Department of Paediatrics, University of Tokyo; General Director, Children's Research Centre, President, National Children's Hospital, Tokyo; Professor Emeritus. Publications: Immune System and Immunological Diseases, 1974; Immunodeficiency, its Nature and Etiological Significance in Human Diseases, 1978; Textbook of Pediatrics, 1980; New Encyclopedia of Pediatric Medicine, 1988; Author of 90 books. Honours: Distinguished Service Prize, Japan Medical Association, 1984; Mainichi Publishing Culture Award, Mainichi News Paper Company Limited, 1985; Medal, International Pediatric Association, 1986. Memberships: Director or Councillor Member: Japan Pediatric Society; Japanese Association of Child Health; Japan Allergology Society; Japan Cancer Society; Honorary Member, American Pediatric Society; Honorary Member, British Paediatric Society. Hobbies: Music; Walking. Address: The National Children's Hospital, 3-35-31 Taishido, Setagaya-ku, Tokyo 154, Japan.

KOBOS Joseph C, b. 23 Nov 1942, Chicago, Illinois, USA. Psychologist. m. Carolyn, 28 Aug 1965, 3 s. Education: BA, St Benedict's College, 1964; MS, 1967, PhD, 1970, Ohio University; Diplomate in Clinical Psychology, American Board of Professional Psychology, 1978; Texas State Board of Examiners of Psychologists, 1971. Appointments: Assistant Professor, 1970, Adjunct Assistant Professor, 1976, Adjunct Associate professor, 1981, Trinity University; Assistant Professor, tenure, 1981, Associate Professor, 1981, Professor, 1990, UTHSCSA; Director, Counselling Service, UTHSC-SA. Publications: What is Psychotherapy? - An Interpersonal Psychological Approach, 1990; Brief Therapy-Short-Term Psychodynamic Intervention, Co-author, 1987; Aspects of Termination in Group Psychotherapy, 1993. Memberships: American Psychological Association, Fellow, 1968; American Group Psychotherapy Association, Fellow, 1986, faculty, 1981; SW Group Psychotherapy Society, fellow, 1985. Hobbies: Golf; Travel; Photography. Address: University of Texas Health Science Centre-San Antonio, 7703 Floyd Curl Drive Suite 358L, San Antonio, TX 78284-7702, USA.

KOCH Nana, b. 9 May 1948, New York City, New York, USA. Dance/Movement Therapist; College Professor. Education: EdD, Teachers College, Columbia University, 1990; MEd, Teachers College, Columbia University, 1989; MA, Elementary Education, Adelphi University, 1971; BA, Dance, Adelphi University, 1970; Certified Movement Analyst, Laban Institute of Movement Studies, 1979; Certificate in Psychomotor Therapy, Dance Therapy, New York Medical College, Flower and Fifth Avenue Hospital, 1971. Appointments: Dance Therapist, Association for the Help of Retarded Children, 1971-72; Director, Dance Therapy Department, Brooklyn Developmental Center, 1973-77; Dance Therapist, Pilgrim Psychiatric Center, 1977; Tutor and Evaluator in Dance Therapy, Empire State College, 1978-79; Advisor in Dance Therapy, New York University Gallatin Division, 1977-80; Dance Therapy Consultant, Private Practice, 1977-80; Senior Dance Therapist, Fair Oaks Hospital, 1977-80; Instructor of Effort/Shape Movement Analysis, Laban Institute of Movement Studies, 1981; Assistant Professor/Coordinator of Dance and Movement Therapy Program, Hunter College of the City University of New York, 1980-. Publications: include, AIMS; A Microsystems Analysis of A Dance/Movement Therapy Session, 1994; Sound and Movement Exploration on a City Block, 1974; Content Analysis of Leadership Variables in Dance Therapy, 1984. Honours: Intramural Faculty Development Award, Hunter College, 1985-86; Accepted into the Faculty Development Program at CUNY, 1985-86. Memberships: include, Dance/Movement Therapy Educators Council; Laban/Bartenieff Institute of Movement Studies. Address: Hunter College, 425 E 25th Street, New York City, NY 10010, USA.

KODAIRA Susumu, b. 25 Aug 1938, Tokyo, Japan. Professor of Surgery. m. Yoshiko Kodaira, 13 Oct 1985, 3 sons, 1 daughter. Education: MD, School of Medicine, Keio University, 1963.

Appointments: Assistant Professor of Surgery, Keio University School of Medicine, 1977; Currently Professor, Chairman, 1st Department of Surgery, Teikyo University School of Medicine. Publications: Immunohistologic analysis of the extra-cellular matrix components of the fibrous stromas of human colon cancer, 1993. Memberships: Japan Surgical Society; The Japan Society of Coloproctology; Japan Society for Cancer Therapy; International Society of Colon and Rectal Surgeons. Hobbies: Ice-hockey; Golf. Address: 8-19-16 Todoroki, Setagaya-ku, Tokyo 158, Japan.

KODOUSEK Rostislav, b. 1 July 1926, Zdar, Eastern Bohemia, Czechoslovakia. Pathologist. m. Vera Maturova, 5 May 1951, 1 son, 1 daughter. Education: MUDr, Charles University, 1951; Dr Sci, Charles University, 1979; University Professor, 1982. Appointments: Assistant, Institue of Pathology, Hradec, Kralove, 1951-53 and in Olomouc, 1953-74; Head, Research Lab for Cyto-Histochemistry, Ibidem, 1964-74; Head, Institue of Pathology, Palacky University, Olomouc, 1974-1994. Publications: Enzymhistochemistry of myocardial a.cerebral ischaemia, 1956; Whipples disease, 1964; Human Adiaspiromycosis, 1971; Hodgkin's disease, 1992. Memberships: J Ev Purkyne Medical Society; The Czech a Slovak Society for Cyto-Histochemistry; European Society of Pathology; International Academy of Pathology; The C Sternberg Society of Pathology. Honours: Golden Medal, Pro Meritis in Education, Science & Culture, University Olomouc, 1986; Prizes of CS Society of Pathology, Ministry of Health. Hobies: Photography; Classic Music. Address: Heyrovsky Str 12, 77900 Olomouc, Czech Republic.

KOHIYAR Gool Ardeshir, b. 4 Sept 1929, Bombay, India. Gynaecologist. Education: MD, Bombay; MRCOG, London; Dip Ven; Dip FP. Appointments: Assistant professor, Obstetrics & Gynaecology, Vadilal Sarabhai Hospital & Medical College, Ahmedabad, India; Honorary Obstetrics & Gynaecology, Nowroji Wadia Hospital, Bombay, India; Senior Registrar, St Thomas' Hospital, London, UK; Consultant, Genito-Urinary Medicine, Royal Infirmary, Edinburgh; Now Retired.Memberships: MRCOG; MSSVD. Hobbies: Music; Theatre; Art. Address: 24 Pedhall Crescent, Longstone, Edinburgh, EH14 2HU, Scotland.

KOIDE Hikaru, b. 16 Feb 1930, Hiroshima, Japan. Professor of Medicine. m. Sachiko Arai, 1 June 1963, 1 son, 1 daughter. Education: MD, University of Tokyo, 1954; Medical Residency, University of Tokyo Hospital, 1955; Fulbright Fellow, Harvard University, USA, 1964; Research Associate, Vanderbilt University, 1966. Appointments: Lecturer, Faculty of Medicine, University of Tokyo, 1967; Associate Professor, 1970, currently Chairman and Professor of Medicine, Department of Medicine, Juntendo University, Tokyo. Publications: Guanidines 2, 1989; Co-author: Cellular and Molecular Biology of the Kidney, 1991; Extracellular Matrix in the Kidney, 1994. Honours: Award, Japanese Kidney Research Foundation, 1987. Memberships: International Society of Nephrology; International Society of Peritoneal Dialysis; American Society of Nephrology; National Kidney Foundation. Hobbies: Swimming; Dancing. Address: 5-8-11 Nakaizumi, Komae-shi, Tokyo 201, Japan.

KOIVUKANGAS Timo Kalevi, b. 16 Dec 1941, Pielisensuu (now part of Joensuu), Finland. Psychoanalyst. m. Marja-Liisa Kiljala, 1 Nov 1968, 1 son, 2 daughters. Education: MD; Specialisations: Paediatrician, 1974; Child Psychiatrist, 1983; Apprentice to Professor Zvi Laron, Juvenile Diabetes, Israel Counselling Centre for Juvenile Diabetes, Beilinson Hospital, Petah Tikva, Israel, 1977-78; Psychoanalytic Training, Finnish Psychoanalytical Association, 1988-92. Appointments: Assistant in Paediatrics, Junior Lecturer in Paediatrics, Assistant in Child Psychiatry, Specialist in Child Psychiatry, District Hospital, Kemi; Head, Child Psychiatric Unit, Kemi Central Hospital, 1983-88; Assistant Doctor, Adolescent Unit, Psychiatric Department, University of Oulu, Oulu, 1988-89; Private practice, 1989-, as Therapist, then Psychoanalyst. Publications: Sjögren's Syndrome and Achalasia of the Cardia in Two Siblings (co-author), 1973; Growth Onset Diabetes Mellitus as a Therapeutic and Psychosocial Problem, doctoral thesis, 1979. Honours: Scholarship, Ministry of Health, Israel, 1977-78. Memberships: Finnish Medical Association; Finnish Paediatric Association; Finnish Child Psychiatric Association; Finnish Psychoanalytical Association. Hobbies: Books; Music; Wildlife, Hebrew. Address: Aatuntie 13, 94500 Lautiosaari, Finland.

KOKATNUR Mohan Gundo, b. 19 Mar 1930, India. Clinical Biochemist. m. Saroj Saraf, 4 Aug 1963, 2 daughters. Education: BS, Chemistry; BS, Chemical Technology; PhD, Foods, Biochemistry,

Nutrition, University of Illinois, USA, 1959; Postdoctoral Fellowship in Clinical Biochemistry, Louisiana State University Medical Center, 1978. Appointments: Fellow, Scientists Pool, Council of Scientific and Industrial Research, India, 1961-63; Postdoctoral Research Associate, University of Illinois, USA, 1963-66; Assistant Professor, 1966-72, Associate Professor, 1972-93, Professor of Pathology, 1993-, Louisiana State University Medicel Center, New Orleans. Publications: Nutrition in Coronary Heart Disease and Sudden Cardiac Death (co-ed), 1991. Memberships: American Institute of Nutrition; American Association for Clinical Chemistry. Hobbies: Travel; Photography. Address: Department of Pathology, Louisiana State University Medical Center, 1901 Perdido Street, New Orleans, LA 70112, USA.

KOKERNOT Robert Hutson, b. 14 Aug 1921, Alpine, Texas, USA. Medicine. m. Marlene, 6 May 1972, 1 son, 3 daughters. Education: Doctor of Veterinary Medicine, 1946; MD, 1950; MPH, 1953. Appointments: Staff Member, The Rockefellow Foundation; Assistant Director, University of Illinois; Professor, Chairman, Department of Pathobiology & Comparative Medicine, University of Texas School of Public Health; Chairman, Professor, Department of Preventive Medicine & Community Health, Texas Technical University, Health Sciences Center. Publications: Senior author of 34 articles. Honours: Alpha Omega Alpha, 1949. Hobbies: Gardening; Travel. Address: 1904 Summit Ridge Drive, Kerrville, TX 78028-9150, USA.

KOKKO Juha P, b. 26 Mar 1937, Helsinki, Finland. Physician. m. Nancy Radford, 21 June 1961, 2 s. Education: BA, 1959, MD, 1964, PhD, 1964, Emory University, USA. Appointments include: Inter, Residency, Osler Service, Johns Hopkins Hospital, Baltimore, 1964-66; Assistant Professor of Medicine, 1969-72, Associate professor of Medicine, 1972-74, Chief of Nephrology, department of Medicine, 1973-86, Professor of Medicine, 1974-86, University of Texas-Southwestern Medical Centre, Dallas, Texas; Professor, Chairman, 1986-, Asa G Candler Professor and Chairman, 1988-, Department of Medicine, Emory Univerity School of Medicine, Atlanta, Georgia. Publications include: Nephrology, Co-editor, 1984; Fluids and Electrolytes, Co-editor, 1986, 2nd edition, 1990; COntributor of numerous articles in professional journals and chapters in books. Honours include: Alpha Omega Alpha' Student Outstanding Faculty Award, 1982-83, 1983-84; Distinguished University decoration, University of Helsinki, 1984. Memberships include: American Society for Clinical INvestigation; American Association of Physicians; Association of Professor os Medicine; American Federation for Clinical Research; American Physiological Society; American Society of Nephrology; International Society of Nephrology. Hobbies: Golf; Hunting; Fishing; Skiing. Address: Department of Medicine, Emory University School of Medicine, 1364 Clifton Road, Suite H153, Atlanta, GA 30322, USA.

KOKOT Franciszek, b. 24 Nov 1929, Olesno SI, Poland. Physician. m. Malgorzata Kokot, 26 Dec 1955, 4 s. Education: Physician, 1953; Defence of the doctor thesis, 1957; Defence of the habilitation thesis, 1962. Career: Technician, Chemistry, 1949-50, Assistant and Senior Assistant, Pharmacology, 1950-57, Assistant Professor, Internal Medicine, 1957-62, Assistant Professor, Internal Medicine, 1962-69, Extraordinary Professor, Internal Medicine, 1968-74, Head of Nephrology Clinic, 1974-, Currently, Director, Nephrological and Sciences Clinic, Silesian School of Medicine, Katowice, Poland. Publications: Author or Co-author of 30 textbooks on internal medicine; Editorial Board of 5 international journals in nephrology. Honours: Purkyni Medal, 1980; Louis Pasteur Medal, 1985; Honorary Member of Society of Nephrology in Czechoslovakia, 1986, Bulgaria, 1986, Yugoslavia, 1983, Germany, 1979, Hungary, 1990, Italy, 1992, Macedonia; F Volhard Medal, 1991; International Distinguished Medal, USA, 1991; Doctor Honoris Causa, Medical School of Wroclaw, 1990, Silesian University Medical School, 1993; Fellow, Royal College of Physicians, 1994. Memberships: Polish Academy of Sciences; Polish Academy of Arts; International Society of Nephrology; European Society of Nephrology. Hobby: Beekeeping. Address: Al Korfantego 8-162, Katowice 40-027, Poland.

KOLAR Jaromir Jan, b. 30 July 1926, Ostrava, Czechoslovakia. Professor. m. Olga Srbova, 15 Dec 1962. Education: MD, Faculty of Medicine, Charles University, Prague, 1950. Appointments: Resident in Radiology, Usti nad Labem, 1950-55; Lecturer, Charles University, Prague, 1955-65; Associate Professor, Charles University, Prague, 1966-76; Professor, Head of Chair, Diagnostic Radiology, Postgraduate Medical School, Prague, 1976-. Publications: The Physical Agents and Bone, 1965; Whole Body Skeletal Response in Local Bone Disease,

1981; 464 articles; 16 books. Memberships: Postgraduate Medical School, Prague; Czech Radiological Society, Prague. Honours: Corresponding Member, German Radiological Society, 1986; Boris Rajewski Silver Medal, European Association of Radiology, 1993. Hobbies: Philatelist. Address: 106 00 Praha 10, Preslickova 5, Czech Republic.

KOLB Lawrence C, b. 16 June 1911, Baltimore, Maryland, USA. Physician. m. Madeleine Currie, 7 Mar 1937, 1 s, 2 d. Education: MD, Johns Hopkins University, 1934. Appointments: Professor and Chair, Department of Psychiatry, Columbia University; Director, New York State Psychiatric Institute; Commissioner, New York state Deparment Mental Hygiene; Distinguished Physician, US Department Veterans Affairs; Professor Emeritus, Columbia University; Professor of Psychiatry, Albany Medical College. Publications: Moden Clinical Psychiatry, Editions 5-10; The Painful Phantom, 1954; A Neuropsychological Hypothesis Explaining Post-Traumatic Stress Disorders, 1986. Honours: Distinguished Fellow, American Psychiatric Association; Lawrence C Kolb Professorship in Psychiatry, 1968; Lawrence C Kolb Research Building, New York State Psychiatric, 1980; Pioneer Award, International Society of Traumatic Stress. Memberships: American Psychiatric Association, president, 1968; Association Research Nerve and Mental Disorders, President, 1968; American Psychoanayltic; American Neurological. Hobbies: Golf; Fishing; Gardening. Address: 232 Van Wies Point, Glenmont, NY 12077, USA.

KOLBAS Eugene Dean, b. 6 February 1928, Petrovci, Croatia. Medical Doctor. m. Deanna F Neimar, 31 January 1961, 1 son, 2 daughters. Education: MD, Medical School, Zagreb, Croatia; Residency Training, Sarajevo, Bosnia and Pensylvania, USA. Appointments: Chief, M. Lousteau Hospital; Officer of Health, The Health Department of Kingdom of Morocco; Assistant to Dr Van De Kerckhof, Diest, Belgium; House Doctor, J. Talon Hospital, Montreal, Canada; Private Practice, Indiana, Merrilville, California, Los Angeles and several Locum Tenens work in different locations of Florida, Hawaii and at First Strategic Hospital at Vandenberg Air Force Base in California. Honours: Life Fellow, USA College of Obstratritions & Gynacologists, 1988-. Memberships: American Medical Association; California Medical Assocation; World Health Organization; American College of Obstratritions & Gynacologists. Hobbies: Music; Travel; Hunting; Fishing; Naturalist. Address: 66 Vic Capri, Rancho Palos Verdes, CA 90275, USA.

KOLESNIKOVA Antonina Ivanovna, b. 20 Sep 1940, Uljanovsk, Russia. Scientific Researcher. m. Anatoly Kolesnikov, 29 June 1962, 1 d. Education: Kuybyshev Medical Institute, 1963; Postgraduate, Moscow Biophysic Institute, 1974; Cand Med Sc, 1975; D Med Dc, 1989; Senior Researcher of Radiobiology, 1987. Appointments: Practical Doctor, 1963-69; Clinical Intern, Moscow Biophysic Institute, 1969-71; Postgraduate, 1971-74; Junior Researcher, 1972-84, Senior Researcher, 1984-91, Leading Researcher, 1991-, Medical Radiological Research Centre, RAMS. Publications include: Clonogenic Precursor-cells in the Culture, 1989; Age Dependence of the Number of the Fibroblasts (CFU-F) and Haemopoietic Stem Cells (CFU-S) in Bone Marrow and Spleen of Rats, Co-author, 1990; Radiosensitivty of Precursor-cells of Haemopoietic Stroma (CFU-F) in rat Bone Marrow, Co-author, 1992; Ability of Rat CFU-F to Recover from radiation Damages, 1993. Memberships: Moscow Society of Haematologists and Radiobiologists. Hobbies: Running; Cooking. Address: 249020 Obninsk, Kaluga Region, Marks Avenue 34-26, Russia.

KOLFF Willem Johann, b. 14 Feb 1911, Leyden, Holland. Medicine & Surgery. m. Janke C Huidekoper, 4 Sept 1937, 4 sons, 1 daughter. Education: MD; DSc; PhD. Appointments incl: Assistant, Pathology Anatomy, University Leiden, 1934-36; Assistant, Medical Department, University Groningen, 1938-41; Head, Medical Department, Municipal Hospital, Kampen, Holland, 1941-50; Private Docent, University Leiden Medical School, Holland, 1950-51; Staff, Research Division, Cleveland Clinic Foundation, 1950-63; Assistant Professor, Professor, Clinical Investigation, Education Foundation, Cleveland Clinic Foundation, 1950-67; Professor of Medicine & Surgery, Research Professor of Engineering & Bioengineering, Director of Kolff's Lab, Department of Surgery & Bioengineering, University of Utah, 1982-; Adjunct Professor, Department of Surgery, Temple University, 1985-. Publications incl: Regulation of Artificial Hearts, 1993; The Dawn of Counterpulsation, 1993; Muscle and Pneumatic-Powered Counterpulsating LVADs: A Pilot Study, 1994; Books: De Kunstmatige Nier, 1946; Artificial Organs, 1976; New Ways of Treating Uraemia, 1987; Artificial Organs and the Future,

1988. Honours incl: Christopher Columbus Discovery Award in Biomedical Research, National Institutes of Health, Washington DC, 1992. Memberships incl: American Association for Advancement of Science; American Medical Association; Biomedical Engineering Society. Address: Kolff's Lab, Department of Bioengineering, 2460-A Merrill Engineering Blvd, University of Utah, Salt Lake City, UT 84112, USA.

KOLLER PIZZANI Miriam, b. New York City, USA. Psychiatrist; Child Psychiatrist. m. Dr Eddy Pizzani, 1 October 1993, 1 s, 1 d. Education: AB, cum laude, Vassar College, 1967; MA, Rutgers University, 1969; MD, Medical College of Virginia, 1980; Board Certified in Psychiatry, 1985; Board Certified in Child Psychiatry, 1986. Honours: Fellow, American Psychiatric Associaton; Fellow, American Academy of Child and Adolescent Psychiatry. Appointments: Assistant Professor of Psychiatry, Medical College of Virginia, 1985-87; Assistant Clinical Professor of Psychiatry, 1987-; Private Practice. Publications: Lateral Ventricular Enlargement in Adolescents with Schizophreniform Disorder. Honours: President. Richmond Psychiatric Society. Memberships: AMA; APA; AACP; Virginia Council of Child Psychiatry; Psychiatric Society of Virginia; Richmond Academy of Medicine; Medical Society of Virginia; Richmond Psychiatric Society, President, 1994-95. Hobbies: Tennis; Piano; Cycling. Address: 5855 Bremo Road, Richmond, VA 23226, USA.

KOLMOS Hans Jorn Jepsen, b. 10 June 1948, Sonderborg, Denmark. Clinical Microbiologist. m. Lisbet, 10 June 1972, 1 s, 2 d. Education: MD, 1974, DMS, 1985, Odense University; Certified Specialist in Medical Microbiology, 1986; Appointments: Registrar, Odense University Hospital, 1974-83; registrar, State Serum Institute, Copenhagen, 1984-86; Consultant, State University Hospital, Copenhagen, 1986-87; Chief Physician, Department of Clinical Microbiology, Hvidovre Hospital. Publications: Hygienic Problems in Dialysis, Thesis, 1985; Contributor of numerous professional articles in journals and textbooks. Memberships: President, Danish Society for Clinical Microbiology, 1995-, (Board Member, 1984-90); Chairman, Danish Club for Central Sterilization and Hospital Hygiene, 1989-95. Hobbies: Medical History; Beekeeping. Address: Hvidovre Hospital, Department of Clinical Microbiology 445, Kettegaard alle 30, DK-2650 Hvidovre, Denmark.

KOMAROV Fedor Ivanovich, b. 26 Aug 1920, Smolensk, USSR. Professor. m. 1 daughter. Education: DMS, Navy Medical Academy, Leningrad, 1947. Appointments: Chief, central Military Medical Department, 1977-89; Head, Chair of Hospital Therapy, 1st Moscow Medical Institute, 1972-82; Chief Therapist, USSR Defence Ministry, 1972-77; Vice President, Russian Academy of Medical Sciences, 1990-; Chief, Laboratory of Chronomedicine and Clinic Aspects of Gastroenterology, 1990-. Publications include: Biochemic Research in Clinic, 1981; Pathology of Vision Organs in General Disease, 1982; Clinic Instrumental Research in Inner Organs Disease, 1989; Emergency Therapy in Military Doctor's Practice, 1993; Internal Therapy, 1981, 1990. Honours: Konchalovsky, 1979; Botkin, 1985; Leparsky, 1992; Emeritus Doctor, Greigswald University, 1977, Polish and Bulgarian Military Medical Academies; Member of International Academy of Science, 1994. Hobbies: Painting; Walking. Address: Presidium of the Russian Academy of Medical Sciencesm, Solianka Str 14, 109801 Moscow, Russia.

KOMINS Jeffry Ivan, b. 12 May 11945, Philadelphia, Pennsylvania, USA. Physician - Obstetrics & Gynaecology. m. susan Lee Komins, 11 Jun 1967, 2 d. Education: BSc, Biology, Villanova University, Villanova, Pennsylvania; MD, Hahnemann Medical College, Philadelphia, Pennsylvania, 1970. Appointments: Instructor in Obstetrics & Gynaecology, University of Pennsylvania Hospital, 1974-75; Assistant Professor, Department of Obstetrics & Gynaecology, Thomas Jefferson University, 1978; Clinical Associate Professor, Obstetrics & Gynaecology, Thomas Jefferson University, 1984; St Francis Hospital - Assistant, 1975; Associate, 1980; Attending, 1987; Wilmington Medical Center, Wilmington, Delaware - Assistant, 1975; Associate, 1982; Senior Attending, 1985; Obstetrics & Gynaecology Associates PA, 1975-94; Chairman, Department of Obstetrics & Gynaecology, Memorial Hospital of Burlington County, 1994. Publications: include, Utilization of Glucose by Normal, Defunctionalized and Denervated Bladder Muscle; Effect of Retropubic Revision of Bladder Neck Upon Electrical Stimulation of Neurogenic Bladder, 1967; Hyperthyroidism in Pregnancy, 1975; Ultrasound Assisted Amniocentesis in Prenatal Genetic Counseling, 1976; Mucinous Cystic Neoplasm of the Pancreas Demonstrated by Ultrasound and Endoscopic Retrograde

Pancreatography, 1980. Honours: Villanova Scholarship to Harrington High School; Alpha Omega Alpha, Hahnemann Chapter, Zeta; Mosby Book Scholarship, Hahnemann. Memberships: include, American College of Obstetricians & Gynaecologists; American Fertility Society; American Medical Association; Philadelphia Colposcopy Society. Address: Memorial Hospital of Burlington County, 3rd Floor South Building, 175 Madison Avenue, Mount Holly, New Jersey 08060, USA.

KONDO Kiyotaro, b. 24 May 1933, Shizuoka, Japan. Professor of Public Health. m. Yoshiko Kondo, 23 Apr 1967, 2 sons, 1 daughter. Education: MD, Tokyo niversity, 1959. Appointments: Associate Professor of Neurology, Brain Research Institute, Niigata University, 1965; Director, Department of Neurology, Tokyo Metropolitan Institute of Neuroscience, 1956; Professor of Public health, Hokkaido University School of Medicine. Publications: Neuroepidemiology, Co-editor, 1976; Neurology in Primary Care, 1991; Human Genetics, 1991; Genetics of Neurological Diseases, 1993; Co-author of 30 books. Memberships: Chairman, Research Group on Neuroepidemiology; World Federartion of Neurology. Hobbies: Collecting Butterflies and Transport Tickets. Address: 401-13 Miyanomori Shukusha, 3-10 Miyano mori, Chuo-ku, Sapporo 064, Japan.

KONDRATENKO Pyotr, b. 6 Apr 1953, Donetsk, Ukraine. Professor; Surgeon. m. Nina Dyomina, 6 Jul 1991, 1 s, 1 d. Education: Candidate's Degree, Donetsk State Medical University, 1970-77; National Research Centre of Clinical and Experimental Surgery, Kiyiv, 1977-78; Probationer, State Medical University, Kiyiv, 1987; Doctor's Degree, 1990. Career: Head, General Surgery Division, Surgery Department, 1979-85, Assistant Professor, 1985-91, Professor, Second Hospital Surgery Department, 1991-, State Medical University, Donetsk, Ukraine. Publications: Over 125 publications including: Surgery of bleeding gigantic gastric and duodenal ulcer, 1991; The mistakes and difficulties of diagnostics of acute appendicitis in women, 1992; Methods of treating patients with local festering infection, 1993; Diagnostics and treating closed abdomen injury, 1993. Honour: Golden Medal, Russian Ministry of Higher Education, 1973. Membership: Ukranian Surgeons Association. Hobbies: Badminton; Swimming; Reading; Travel; Theatre; Music. Address: 19 Bagration Street, Donetsk 340047, Ukraine.

KONOVALOV. Address: Burdenko Neurosurgical Institute, Moscow, Russia.

KOO Winston, b. 22 Apr 1949, Hong Kong. Physician. m. 6 children, 1 dec. Education: MB BS, Honours, University of New South Wales, Sydney, Australia, 1972; FRACP; Diplomate, American Academy of Paediatrics, American Board of Paediatrics, General Paediatrics, Sub-Board of Neonatal Perinatal Medicine. Appointments: Clinical Associate Physician NIH Award, 1984-86; Assistant Professor of Paediatrics, University of Alberta, Canada, 1986-90; Associate Professor of Paediatrics and Obstetrics and Gynaecology, University of Tennessee, Memphis, Tennessee, USA, 1990-95; Professor, Departments of Pediatrics and Obstetrics and Gynecology, Wayne State University, Detroit, Michigan, 1995-. Publications: Contributor of numerous book chapters, scholarly reviews and articles in refereed journals. Honours: Young Investigator Award, American College of Nutrition, 1986; Multiple Research Support, NIH, USA, MRC, Canada and Industry, 1982-. Memberships: Royal Australasian College of Physicians; Australian College of Paediatrics; American Academy of Paediatrics; American Society Bone Mineral Research; American Society Clinical Nutrition; American Institute of Nutrition; American College of Nutrition; Society Paediatric Research. Hobby: Travel. Address: Department of Pediatrics, Hutzel Hospital, 4707 St Antoine Blvd, Detroit, MI 48201, USA.

KOOKER Robert Allen, b. 17 Jan 1942, Marquette, MI, USA. Physician. m. Katharine Armstrong, 31 Oct 1963, 2 s, 1 d. Education: BA, Northwestern University, 1967; MD, University of IL, 1970; Diplomate in Psychiatry, 1978 and Addiction Psychiatry, 1993, American Board of Psychiatry and Neurology. Career: Chief, Psychiatry Service, Veteran's Administration West Side Hospital, Chicago, IL, 1974; Chairman, Department of Mental Health, David Grant USAF Medical Center, Travis AFB, CA, 1981; Medical Director, Chief Psychiatrist, Placer County Mental Health Services, CA; 1988. Publications: General and Addiction Psychiatry, 1978, 1993. Memberships: American Association of University Professors; American Society of Addiction Medicine; American Association for the Advancement of Science; American Psychiatric Association; American Medical Association. Hobbies: Golf; Fishing; Writing; Skiing; Tennis; Chamber Music; Old

Cars. Address: 3835 North Lakeshore Drive, Loomis, CA 95650-9787, USA.

KOONINGS Paul Philip, b. 1 Feb 1956, Toronto, Ontario, Canada. Physician. m. Marianne Sommerville, MD, 19 Dec 1986, 2 s, 2 d. Education: BSc, MD, University of Western Ontario; FRCS(C); FACOG. Career: Assistant Professor, Eastern Virginia Medical School, Norfolk, VA; Currently, Physician, Southern CA Kaiser Permanente Medical Group, San Diego. Publications: 40 Peer reviewed articles in professional journals. Honours: Alpha Omega Alpha, 1982; Cum Laude, 1982. Memberships: ACOG; WAGO; SGO; Alpha Omega Alpha. Hobbies: Old Car Restoration. Address: Kaiser Permanente Medical Center, Department of Obstetrics and Gynaecology, 4647 Zion Avenue, San Deigo, CA 92190, USA.

KOOP C Everett, b. 14 Oct 1916, Brooklyn, New York, USA. Senior Scholar, Koop Institute at Dartmouth. m. Elizabeth Flanagan Koop, 3 s, 1 d. Education: MD, Cornell Medical College, 1941; Doctor of Science (Medicine), University of Pennsylvania, 1947; Professor of Pediatric Surgery, School of Medicine, University of Pennsylvania, 1959; Professor of Pediatrics, 1971. Appointments: Surgeon-in-Chief, Children's Hospital of Philadelphia, 1948-81; Editor-in-Chief, Journal of Pediatric Surgery, 1964-76; Deputy Assistant Secretary for Health/Surgeon General, US Public Health Service, 1981-89; Elizabeth DeCamp McInery Professor at Darmouth. Publications: Author of more than 200 articles and books on the practice of medicine and surgery, biomedical ethics and health policy. Honours: 35 Honorary Doctorates; Awarded the Denis Brown Gold Medal by British Association of Paediatric Surgeons; Awarded the William E Ladd Gold Medal of American Academy of Pediatrics; Order of the Duarte, Sanchez and Mella, the Highest Award of the Dominican Republic for achievement in separating the conjoined Dominican twins; Awarded Medal of the Legion of Honor by France, 1980; Awarded Public Health Service Distinguished Service Medal in recognition of extraordinary leadership of the US Public Health Service. Memberships: include, American Surgical Association; Society of University Surgeons; American Pediatric Surgical Association; National Academy of Sciences; Institute of Medicine; American Philosophical Society; Fellow, American College of Surgeons; Fellow, American Academy of Pediatrics; American College of Preventive Medicine. Address: 6707Democracy Boulevard, Suite 107, Bethesda, MD 20817-1129, USA.

KOOPMAN William James, b. 19 Aug 1945, Lafayette, Indiana, USA. Meduckal Educator; Immunologist; Internist. m. Lilliane, 15 June 1968, 2 sons, 2 daughters. Education: BA, Washington University, 1967; MD, Harvard University, 1972. Appointments: Intern, Resident, Massachusetts General Hospital, Boston 1972-74; Research Fellow, NIH, Bethesda, Maryland, 1974-77; Assistant Professor, Associate Professor, Professor of Medicine, 1977-, Director, Division Clinical Immunology and Rheumatology, Director, Multipurpose Arthritis and Musculoskeletal Diseases Centre, University of Alabama at Birmingham. Publications: Arthritis and Allied Condicitions, Co-Editor, 12th Edition, 1993; Primer on the Rheumatic Diseases, Co-Editor, 1993; Arthritis and Allied Conditions, Editor, 13th Edition, 1996. Honours: Carol Nachman Research Prize, Germany, 1982. Memberships: American College of Rheumatology, Treasurer, 1992-; American Society Clinical Investigation, President, 1990-91; Assocation American Physicians; Association of Immunologists. Hobbies: Fishing; Gardening. Address: 187 Wildwood Lane, Indian Springs, AL 35124, USA.

KOPA Janos, b. 23 Oct 1935, Ujpest, Hungary. Neurosurgeon; Neurologist. m. Maria Konig, 22 Sept 1960, 1 son, 1 daughter. Education: MD, Medical University of Pecs, 1960; PhD, 1993. Appointments: Institute of Physiology, Clinic of Neurophsychiatry and Neurosurgery of the Medical University, Pecs. Publications: Description of the so called Kopa-phenomen in behavioural physiology, Epidemiology, Medical and operative treatment of the cerebral aneurysms; Description of the Decisevily Intraventricular Haemorrhages of the brain; New Methods in the Operations of the Anterior Scale and the Cervical Spine; Introducing of some micro-surgical methods in the neurosurgery. Memberships: Leading Member of the Hungarian Neurosurgical Society and Neurosurgical College of Hungary; Regional Academic Research. Honours: Honoured Professor, Medical University of Pecs, 1993. Hobbies: Hunting. Address: 48-as Ifjusag u 7, H-7400 Kaposvar, Hungary.

KOPEIKIN Vadim Nikolaevich, b. 17 Mar 1929, Moscow, Russia. MD; Dental Prosthetist. m. Malvina Malaya, 6 Nov 1974. Education:

Diploma, Moscow Medical Stomatology Institute; Candidate of Medical Sciences, Doctor of Medical Sciences, State Higher Certifying Commission, 1980. Career: Resident Dentist, 1951-54, Assistant Lecturer, 1954-64, Assistant Professor, 1964-77, Professor, Head, Clinical Prosthetic Dentistry, 1978-, Moscow Medical Stomatology Institute; Dean of Refreshment Faculty, 1968-78; Currently, Director, Research Institute of Dentistry. Publications: Co-author, Tooth Prosthetic Technique, 1964, 1968, 1978, 1985; Prosthetic Treatment of Parodontium Disease, 1977; Errors in Prosthetic Treatment, 1986; Co-author, Stomatology: Dentist's Manual, 1987; Prosthetic Denistry, textbook, 1988; Manual on Prosthetic Dentistry, 1993. Honours: Russian Medal, 1970; Honoured Dentist of Russia, 1974; Order of Honour, 1980; Russian title, Inventor, 1985; Honoris Causa in Science and Tchnology of Russia, Russian Academy of Medical Science, 1990. Memberships: Russian Dental Association; Associate Member, Cuban Dental Society. Hobbies: Fishing; Travel. Address: 125206 Moscow, Voutcheticha ul 9A, Russia.

KOPILOFF George, b. 20 Jan 1939, Argentina. Physician. m. Nelly Caceres, 19 Apr 1964, 1 son, 1 daughter. Education: MD. Career: Chief, Triage Psychiatric Clinic, Jerry L Pettis Memorial V A Hospital, Loma Linda, CA, 1979-83; Chief, Day Treatment Center, Jerry L Pettis Memorial VA Hospital, 1983-88; Medical Director, Behavioral Health Services, Hemet Valley Medical Center. Honours: Diplomate, American Board of Psychiatry & Neurology in Psychiatry; Examiner, American Board of Psychiatry and Neurology; 1993 Exemplary Psychiatry, National Alliance for the Mentally Ill. Memberships: American Psychiatric Association; South CA Psychiatric Society; American Medical Association; American Association for Geriatric Psychiatry; Union of American Physicians and Dentists. Hobbies: Soccer; Politics; History; Geography. Address: 1117 E Devonshire Avenue, Hemet, VA 92543-308, USA.

KOPYT Nelson Paul, b. 19 Nov 1951, New York City, New York, USA. Nephrologist. m. Andrea Kopyt, 23 June 1974, 2 daughters. Education: BA cum laude, University of Pennsylvania, 1974; DO (1st of 200), Philadelphia College of Osteopathic Medicine, 1979; Board Certified, Internal Medicine, 1984, Nephrology, 1986, Critical Care, 1987, American Board of Internal Medicine; Nephrology Fellow, Temple University, 1985; Fellow, American College of Physicians, 1988. Appointments: Nephrologist, private practice group on Active Staff, 6 hospitals, 1985-; Clinical Assistant Professor, 1985-92, Clinical Associate Professor, 1992-, Temple University Health Sciences Center, Philadelphia, Pennsylvania; Clinical Associate Professor, Philadelphia College of Osteopathic Medicine, 1986-; Faculty, National Bureau for Information on Coronary Heart Disease Risk, South Norwalk, Connecticut, 1991-; Teaching, Lehigh Valley Hospital, 1993-. Publications include: Co-author: Recurrent Rhabdomyolysis as a Manifestation of Alcoholic Myopathy: A Case Report, 1984; Renal Retention of Potassium in Fruit, 1985; Fluid, Electrolyte and Acid-Base Disorders in Diabetes Mellitus, 1987; Fluid, Electrolyte and Acid-Base Disorders Complicating Diabetes Mellitus, 1992. Honours: William D Reppert MD Teaching Award, St Luke's Hospital, Bethlehem, Pennsylvania, 1992; 1st of Top 20 Teachers, Lehigh Valley Hospital, Allentown, Pennsylvania, 1993. Memberships: American College of Physicians; American Society of Artificial Organs; American Medical Association; International Society of Nephrology; National Kidney Foundation; American Society of Nephrology; Renal Physicians Association; International Society of Peritoneal Dialysis; American Society of Hypertension. Hobbies: Reading; Golf. Address: 50 South 18th Street, Easton, PA 18042, USA.

KORBET Stephen Michael, b. 13 June 1953, Alton, Illinois, USA. Physician; Associate Professor. m. Barbara Trimarco, 4 July 1981. Education: BA summa cum laude, Millikin University, 1975; MD, Rush Medical College, 1979; Fellow, American College of Physicians, 1986; Internship, Residency, 1979-82, Fellowship, Nephrology, 1982-84, Rush Presbyterian St Luke's Medical Center (RPSLMC); Appointments include: Assistant Attending, 1984-88, Associate Attending, 1988-, Associate Director, 1992-, Nephrology Section, Department of Internal Medicine, RPSLMC; Medical Director, Dialysis Unit, RPSLMC, 1984-88; Assistant Professor, 1984-90, Associate Professor, Internal Medicine, 1990-, Rush Medical; Medical Director, Circle Medical Management Dialysis Facility, Chicago, Illinois, 1988-. Publications: Author or co-author, 9 book chapters including: Cryoimmunoglobulinemia, 1987; Crescentic glomerulonephritis, 1989; The value of the renal biopsy, 1992; Causes, diagnosis, and treatment of peritoneal membrane failure, 1994; Chronic renal failure; Renal disorders associated with systemic

diseases; Immunotactoid glomerulopathy; About 50 journal articles. Honours include: Alpha Omega Alpha, 1979; Outstanding Resident Award, 1982, Teaching and Service Award, 1991, Department of Internal Medicine, RPSLMC; Robert M Kark Prize for Research, Chicago Society of Internal Medicine. Memberships include: International and American Societies of Nephrology; American Medical Association; New York Academy of Sciences; Chicago and American Societies of Internal Medicine; National Kidney Foundation; Illinois State and Chicago Medical Societies; Renal Physicians Association. Address: 1653 W Congress Parkway, Chicago, IL 60612, USA.

KORDA Andrew Robert, b. 8 Mar 1942, Budapest, Hungary. Gynaecologist. m. Eleanor Segal, 17 Dec 1965, 1 son, 2 daughters. Education: MB, BS, 1966, Dip Arts, 1993, Sydney University, 1966; MRCOG, 1971; FRACOG, 1979; FRCOG, 1984; Certification, Urogynaecology, 1989. Appointments include: Visiting Gynaecological and Obstetric Surgeon, 1975, Head, General Gynaecology and Gynaecological Urology Department, 1991, King George V Hospital, Sydney, Australia; Visiting Gynaecological and Obstetric Surgeon, 1975, Clinical Supervisor, Obstetrics, Gynaecology, 1975-79, Gynaecologist, Urodynamic Unit, 1981, Head, General Gynaecology and Gynaecological Urology Department, 1991, Royal Prince Alfred Hospital, Sydney; Clinical Lecturer, University of Sydney, 1975; Partner: Private gynaecological practice, Royal Prince Albert Medical Centre, Camperdown; Sydney, Camperdown, North Shore, Bankstown, Liverpool and Penrith Urodynamic Centres. Publications: Over 60 including: The Prostaglandins. Clinical Application in Human Reproduction (co-author), 1973; Renal Physiology (with J Horvath), 1979; The Value of Clinical Symptoms and Physical Signs in the Diagnosis of Urinary Incontinence in the Female, 1983; Cystodistension in the Treatment of Detrusor Instability, 1989; The Effect of Obesity on the Outcome of Successful Surgery for Genuine Stress Incontinence, 1993; Intervention in Primigravid Women Developing Mild Hypertension (co-author), 1993. Honours: Mabel Elizabeth Leaver Memorial Prize, Obstetrics, 1966; Aisling Society of Sydney Prize for Essay. Memberships include: Honorary Treasurer, New South Wales and New South Wales State Committees, Royal College of Obstetricans and Gynaecologist; Associate, Urodynamics Society; International Continence Society; International Urogynaecological Society. Hobbies: Music; Opera; Swimming; Sailing; Books; Food; Wine History. Address: Royal Prince Alfred Medical Centre, 100 Carillon Ave, Newtown, New South Wales 2042, Australia.

KORENBERG Edward Isaevich, b. 30 Nov 1936, Odessa, Ukraine. Epidemiologist. m. Svetlana Shljapina, 26 Dec 1980, 2 s, 1 d. Education: Graduate, Department of Natural Science, Moscow Region Pedagogical Institute, 1960. Career: Senior Scientific Assistant, 1960-61, Junior Researcher, 1961-71, Senior Scientist, 1971-79, Currently, Chief of Laboratory of Vectors of Infections, Gamaleya Institute, Moscow. Publications: Biokhorological structure of the species using the taiga tick as an example, 1979; Co-author, Regionalization of the tick-borne encephalitis area, 1981. Honour: P G Sergiev Prize, Academy of Medical Science of Russia, 1982. Membership: All-Russian Society for Epidemiologists, Microbiologists and Parasitologists. Hobby: Collector of Middle-Asian Ceramics. Address: Gamaleya Institute for Epidemiology and Microbiology, Russian Academy of Medical Sciences, Gamaleya Str 18, 123098 Moscow, Russia.

KOROLEV Boris Alexejevich, b. 7 Dec 1909, Kazan, Russia. Surgeon. Education: Corky Medical Institute, 1934; Candidate Degree, Medicine, 1948; MD Degree, 1951. Appointments: Army Surgeon, 1934; City Hospital Surgeon, 1935-36; Surgeon, 7 City Hospital, 1936; Lecturer, General Surgery Chair, Medical Institute, 1939; Professor of Surgery, Cardiovascular, Thoracic & Adomin Surgery. Pubications: 424 published works, 8 monographs; Order of the Red Banner of Labour, 1969; Order of the October Socialist Revolution, 1967; Diagnosis and the results of surgical treatment of congenital heart diseases, 1968; Surgery of Liver Cirrhosis, 1973; Emergent Surgery of Biliary Tracts, 1990. Honours: Honourable Citizen, N Novgorod, 1976; Numerous other honours, awards and medals. Memberships: Board Member, All-Russian Societies of Surgeons & Cardiovascular Surgeons; Chairman, N Novgorod Society of Surgeons; Honourable Chairman, N Novgorod Society of Surgeons; Founder, Chairman, N Novgorod Society of Cardiologists. Hobbies: Skiing; Jogging; Swimming; River Trips; Gardening. Address: 83A-3 Verkhne-Volzhskaya Embankment, Nizhny Novgorod 603005, Russia.

KORTH Stuart Bryan Philip, b. 18 Oct 1942, Tunbridge Wells, Kent, England. Osteopath. m. B Christina Austin, 6 June 1963, 2 s, 1 d. Education: DO; MRO. Appointments: SCRO Examiner; Consultant to Children's Clinic, European School of Osteopathy; Director of Osteopathy, Osteopathic Centre for Children; Private Practice. Memberships: General Council and Register of Osteopaths; Osteopathic Association of Great Britain. Hobby: Music. Address: Harbour St Brides, Primrose Lane, Forest Row, East Sussex RH18 5LT, England.

KORYTOVA Louisa, b. 23 December 1937, Omsk, Russia. Radiation Therapy Professor. m. Vitalyi Korytov, 30 September 1959, 1 son. Education: PhD. Appointments: General Hospital N7 Omsk; Oncology Hospital Omsk; Central Research Institute of Roentgenology and Radiation Therapy, St Petersburg. Publications: Standard Methods of Radium Therapy, 1986; Hodgkin's Disease and Homeosasis, 1994. Memberships: Association of Radiologists of Russia; City Association of Oncologists, St Petersburg. Hobbies: Reading Science Fiction; Gardening. Address: Naberegnaja Fontanki 101, ap 27, 190031 St Petersburg, Russia.

KOSKENVUO Kimmo, b. 22 May 1936, Kangaslampi, Finland. Physician. m. Marja-Leena Lindblad, 10 Oct 1965, 1 d. Education: Licentiate of Medicine, 1962, Specialist in Public Health, 1972, MD, 1974, University of Helsinki; Administrative Qualification, 1980. Appointments: Army Physician, 1963-; Acting Professor of Public Health, Turku University, 1973; Head, Medical section of General Headquarters, Finnish Defence Forces, 1976-78; Senior Lecturer of Military Health Care, University of Helsinki, 1977; Surgeon-General, Finnish Defence Forces, 1978-. Lieutenant General, Med, 1995. Publications: Sudden Deaths among Finnish Conscripts, dissertation, 1974; Military Health and Medical Care, Editor, 1989, 1990, 1995; Field Surgery and Medicine, Editor, 1993, 1994; Contributor of over 150 professional articles. Honours: Honorary Member, Association of Military Surgeons of the United States, 1976; SL K1, Finnish bade of Honour, 1982; Honorary Member, International Committee of Military Medicine, 1984; Pohjola Award, 1991; Honorary Member, Finnish Society of Medical Officers, 1991. Memberships: Finnish Medical Association; Finnish Society of Medical Officers; Finnish Public Health Doctors; International Committee of Military Medicine; Board of the Finnish Red Cross. Hobby: Photography. Address: The Defence Staff, Finnish Defence Forces, POB 919, 00101 Helsinki, Finland.

KOSVINER Adele, b. 29 Apr 1944, Olney, Buckinghamshire, England. Clinical Psychology. m. Jerome Kuehl, 23 Jul 1976. Education: BA, Honours, Psychology, University College, London; MSc, Social Psychology, London School of Economics; MSc, Clinical Psychology. Appointments: Panel Psychologist, Civil Service Selection Board, 1984-94; Chair, Standing Committee on Psychotherapy, British Psychological Society, 1994-; Chair, Psychotherapy Section, British Psychological Society, 1993-94; Currently Consultant Clinical Psychologist, Riverside Mental Health Trust, London. Publications: Many reports and publications including: The Psychotherapies in the Curriculum of Clinical Psychologists, in Curriculum in Clinical Psychology, 1992; Smatterings, Standards and Snobbism in Psychotherapy and Psychology, inaugaural address, Chair, Psychotherapy Section, British Psychological Society, 1993; Psychotherapies within the NHS, in Handbook of Psychotherapy, 1994. Membership: British Psychological Society. Hobbies: Travel; Opera; Horse Riding; Windsurfing. Address: Chelsea and Westminster Hospital, 1 Nightingale Place, London, SW10 9NG, England.

KOTIN Joel Tepper, b. 30 June 1941, Chicago, IL, USA. Psychiatrist; Psychoanalyst. m. Dr Lyda L Hill, 13 Dec 1975, 2 s, 1 d. Education: MD; Certified in Psychiatry, American Board of Psychiatry and Neurology; Certified in Adult Psychoanalysis, American Psychoanalytic Association. Appointments: Clinical Professor of Psychiatry, University of California at Irving; Private Practice. Publications: Getting Stared: An Introduction to Dynamic Psychoanalytic Psychotherapy, 1995; Contributor to numerous articles. Memberships: American Psychoanalytic Association; International Psychoanalytic Association. Hobbies: Music; Running; Swimming; Hiking. Address: 21622 Ocean Vista Drive, Laguna Beach, CA 92677, USA.

KOTO Atsuo, b. 29 Sept 1941, Tokyo, Japan. Neurologist; Neuropathologist. m. Yuriko, 1971, 1 s, 1 d. Education: MD, Keio University School of Medicine, 1966. Appointments: Associate Professor of Neurology. Publications: Syndrome of Normal Pressure Hydrocephalus: Possible Relation to Hypertensive and Arteriosclerotic Vasculopathy, 1977; Morquio Syndrome: Neuropathy and Biochemistry, 1978; Cerebrovascular NADPH Diaphorase-Containing Nerve Fibers in the Rat, 1993. Memberships: American Association of Neuropathologists; International Association of Stroke. Address: Department of Neurology, Keio University School of Medicine, 35 Shinanomachi, Shinjuku-ku, Tokyo 160, Japan.

KOU Li Yun, b. 12 Jun 1929, Shenyang City, China. Laboratory Medicine. m. Feng Shu Tung, 30 Dec 1959, 1 s, 1 d. Education includes: 1 Year Visiting Scholar, UCSF, USA. Career: Pediatrician; Physician of Laboratory Medicine; Associate Professor, Professor, Associate Director; Currently Professor and Director of Laboratory Medicine, 3rd Teaching Hospital, Beijing Medical University. Publications: Observation of Determination of Urine Protein and Improvement of CBB Method, 1988; Laboratory Diagnostics, 1991; Determination of Serum Type 1V Collagen and the Use in Hepatic Diseases, 1993. Honours: Outstanding Thesis Award, 1988; Outstanding Teacher Award. Membership: Society of Laboratory Medicine, Chinese Medical Association. Hobbies: Reading; Travel. Address: Department of Laboratory Medicine, 3rd Teaching Hospital, Beijing Medical University, 49 North Huayuan Road, Beijing, China.

KOULACK David, b. 21 Dec 1938, New York, NY, USA. Professor. m. Jane Cahill, 21 Jul 1993, 3 s, 2 d. Education: BA; MS; PhD. Appointments: Professor, Brooklyn College, Washington State University, University of Manitoba. Publications: Dream Research, 1971; Readings in Social Psychology, 1973; Single Father's Handbook, 1979; To Catch A Dream, 1991. Memberships: Canadian Psychological Association; Canadian Sleep Society; Association for Study of Dreams. Hobbies: Walking; Reading. Address: Department of Psychology, University of Manitoba, Winnipeg, Manitoba R3T 2N2, Canada.

KOUTSILIERIS Michael, b. 10 July 1954, Piraeus, Greece. Professor of Physiology, Obstetrics-Gynaecology and Endocrinology. m. Antigone Sourla, 7 Aug 1992. Education: MD, Medical School of Athens; PhD, McGill University,Montreal, Quebec, Canada. Appointments: Research Fellow, McGill University, Montreal, Quebec Province, Canada, 1982; Lecturer, Department of Biochemistry, Faculty of Medicine, University of Sherbooke, Sherbrooke, Quebec Province, 1987; Assistant Professor of Obstetrics/Gynaecology, 1988; Professor of Physiology, Obstetrics/Gynaecology, Endocrinology, Laval University, Quebec, 1992; Publications: Prostate-derived growth factors for osteoblasts, 1991; Osteoblastic Metastasis in Advanced Prostate Cancer, 1994. Honours: Chercheur-Boursier, FRSQ and Medical Research Council of Canada; Young Investigator Award, American Society for Bone and Mineral Research, 1985. Memberships: Endocrine Society, USA; Hellenic Medical Society; Canadian Fertility and Andrology Society; Quebec Medical Association. Hobbies: Tennis; Raquetball. Address: 76 Dalhousie 504, Quebec, Quebec Province, Canada G1K 8W6.

KOVAL Galyna Julyanivna, b. 20 Dec 1925, Odessa, Ukraine. Radiology. m. Grabovezcy Anatol, 27 May 1947, 1 s, 1 d. Education: Odessa Medical Institute, Ukraine, 1948; MD, 1968, PhD, 1970, Kyiv Advanced Training Institute for Doctors. Career: Assistant Professor, 1955, Docent, 1965, Director of Division of Radiology, 1967-94, Kyiv Advanced Training Institute for Doctors. Publications: Editor and Co-author: Clinical Radiology, textbook, 1975, Röentgenodiagnostics of Skull Diseases and Trauma, 1984, Basis of Medical Techniques and Methods of Radiologic Research, 1991. Memberships: Kyiv Medical Association of Radiologists; Member of Honour, Ukraine Association of Radiologists. Hobbies: Travel; Sailing. Address: M Reuta 19, Kyiv 15, 252015, Ukraine.

KOZACHENKO Vladimir, b. 25 Mar 1932, Chernigov Region, Ukraine. Obstetrician; Gynaecologist. m. Margarita Shmarlovskaya, 18 Oct 1962, 2 sons. Education: Voronezh State Medical Institute; Dr Med Sci. Appointments: Resident, 1954, Lecturer, 1958, Assistant Professor, 1960, Head, Chair of Obstetrics and Gynaecology, 1969, Voronezh Medical Institute; Chief, Gynaecology Unit, Cancer Research Centre, Russian AMS. Publications: Dysplasia and Carcinoma in Situ of the Uterine Cervix, Co-author, 1970; Pregnancy and Labor after Cesarean Section, 1978; Cancer of the Uterus, 1983; Microinvasive Cancer of the Uterine Cervix, Co-author, 1988; Background and Premalignant Diseases of the Uterine Cervix, Co-author, 1994. Honours: Academician, Academy of Natural Sciences, 1994; Honour Member, Association of Oncologists of Georgia, 1990. Memberships: Active member, European Association of Oncological Gynaecology; Russian Association of Obstetrics and Gynaecology; Russian Association of Oncologists;

Russian Association of Gynaecologic Oncologists. Hobbies: Chess; Running. Address: 35-4-286, St Acad Millionshchikova, Moscow 115446, Russia.

KRAJINA Zvonimir, b. 12 Jan 1923, Sibenik, Croatia. Emeritus Professor of Otorhinolarygology. Education: MD, 1946; DSc, 1962. Appointments include: Assistant Professor, Medical Faculty, 1956; Ordinary Professor of Otorhinolaryngology, 1968; ENT Clinics, Göteborg and Stockholm, Sweden, 1956; Lyon, France, 1958; Washington University, St Louis, USA, 1969-70; Director, ENT Department, Medical Faculty, Zagreb, 1971-86; Dean, Medical Faculty, 1975-78; Rector, Zagreb University, 1982-86; Lectures worldwide. Publications: Author of 7 books; COntributor of 303 papers. Honours: Collegium ORLAS, 1961; Vice President, Croatian Medical Academy, 1983-93; Guest Professor, European Rhinologic Congresses and Courses, 1962-82; Republican Award Rudjer Boskovic, 1978; Life Award for Science, 1985; American Golden Mirror Award in Rhinology, 1969; Laureate, Croatian Medical Academy, 1991, Memberships: Honorary member, ENT Greece Society; Honorary member, Brazilian Rhinologic Society; Honorary Member, European Rhinologic Society; Corresponding member, Austrian ENT Society; Corresponding Member, German ENT Society. Address: Klinicki bolnicki centar, Salata 4, 41000 Zagreb, Hrvatska.

KRAMER Janet (Phillips), b. 25 Dec 1942, Pottsville, Pennsylvania, USA. Physician. m. Brian D Kramer, 10 June 1967. Education: BS, Pennsylvania State University, 1964; MD, The Women's Medical College of Pennsylvania, 1968; Intern, T M Fitzgerald Mercy Hospital, Darby, Pennsylvania; residency, Internal Medicine, Medical Centre of Delaware; Fellowship, Adolescent Medicine, Children's Hospital, Washington DC. Appointments: Medical Director, delaware Division of Substance Abuse, 1971-76; Private practice of Medicine, 1971-93; Director, Adolescent Medicine, Medical Centre of Delaware, 1985-; Clinical Assistant Professor of Family Practice, T M Jefferson University. Publications: The Five Year Experience In a Day Hospital for Chronically Ill Adolescents, CO-author, 1994; Effects of Smoking Cessation on respiratory Symptoms in a Juvenile Detention Center, Co-author, 1994; Correlates and Consequences or Norplant Use Among a Sample of Post-Partum Adolescents, Co-author, 1994; New Concepts of Anorexia Nervosa and Bulimia, 1989; Contributor of editorials and presentations. Honours: Fellowship, American Academy of Clinical Toxicology, 1974; Fellowship, Philadelphia College of Physicians, 1975; Fellowship, Society of Adolescent Medicine, 1986, 1989, 1992; Original Member, Graduate Medical Education. Memberships: American Society of Internal Medicine; Society of Adolescent Medicine; AMA; AMWA; delaware and New Castle City Medical Societies. Hobbies: History; Travel; Theatre; Hiking. Address: 3 Boysenberry Ct, Hoakessin, DE 19707, USA.

KRAMER Michael Stuart, b. 8 July 1948, New York City, USA. Paediatrician; Epidemiologist. m. Claire Sasportas, 14 June 1981, 1 s, 1 d. Education: BA, University of Chicago, 1969; MD, Yale University, 1973; National Health Research Scientist, Health Canada. Appointments: Assistant Professor, 1978-82, Associate Professor, 1982-87, Professor, Departments of Paediatrics and Epidemiology and Biostatistics, McGill University Faculty of Medicine. Publications: Determinants of Low Birth Weight, 1987; Clinical Epidemiology and Biostatistics, 1988; Nutrition During Pregnancy, 1992; Adverse Events Associated With Childhood Vaccines, 1994. Honours: Phi Beta Kappa, 1969; Sigma Xi Prize, 1969; Alpha Omega Alpha, 1972; Prix d'Excellence, 1987; APA Research Award, 1993. Memberships: SPR; APA; AAP; SER; ACE; ISRHML; SPER. Hobbies: Violin; Chamber Music; Tennis; Squash; Skiing. Address: 1020 Pine Avenue W, Montreal, Quebec H3A 1A2, Canada.

KRAMER Thomas Andrew Moss, b. 3 June 1957, Orange, New Jersey, USA. Psychiatrist. m. Dr Jane H Feldman, 8 Sept 1994. Education: BA, Harvard College, 1978; MD, New York University School of Medicine, 1983; Board Certified in Psychiatry, 1989, Addiction Psychiatry, 1993. Appointments: Assistant Director of Psychiatric Residency Training, Columbia University, 1987-89; Director of Psychiatric Reseach Training and Education, Mt Sinai School of Medicine, 1989-91; Diretor, Psychiatric Outpatient Services, University of Arkansas. Publications include: Uses and Advantages of Interactive Video in Medical Training, Co-author, 1988; Didactic Curriculum for Postresidency Fellowship Training in Psychiatric Research, Co-author, 1991; Acquired Brain Lesions and Psychiatric Illness, Co-author, 1991; Pregnancy During Graduate Medical training, Co-author, 1993; The Hierarchical Arrangement of Internalizing Cognitions, Co-author, 1994;

Residency Directors and Computer Use in Psychiatric Residency training Programs, Co-author; Integration of Positive/Negative Affectivity and Cognitive Conent Specificity: Improved Discrimination of Anxious and depressive Symptoms, Co-author; Numerous posters, abstracts and presentations. Honours: Teacher of the Year, Mt Sinai Department of Psychiatry, 1991, UAMS Department of Psychiatry, 1992. Memberships: President, 1994-95, Arkansas Psychiatric Society; Association for Academic Psychiatry; American Association of Directors of Psychiatric Residency training. Hobbies: Animals; Computers. Address: 4301 W Markham, Slot 568, Little Rock, AR 72205, USA.

KRAMER Willibald, b. 13 Apr 1915, Utrecht, Netherlands. Neurologist. m. E C C Plokker, 26 Aug 1947, 1 s. Education: Doctoranous, Doctor, State University, Utrecht. Appointments: Psychiatrist; Neurologist, Epileptic Institute, Meer en Bosch, Heemstede; Neuropathologist, University of Amsterdam; Professor of Medicine, Neurology, State University Leiden. Publications: Handbook of Neurology, Contributor; Contributor of numerous papers in national and international scientific journals. Honours: Willem Orange Award, 1949; Doctor Award, University of Batavia, Indonesia, 1949. Memberships: American Academy of Cerebral Palsy; Honorary Member, Neurological Society, France. Hobbies: Theology; Philosophy; Neuropsychiatry. Address: Apollolaan 574, 2324 CJ Leiden, Netherlands.

KRANE Robert J, b. 15 Jan 1943, New York City, USA. Urologist. m. Diane, 27 June 1964, 2 s, 2 d. Education: AB, Columbia University, 1963; MD, Albert Einstein, 1967. Appointments: Professor and Chairman, Department of Urology, Boston University. Publications: The Prostate, 1992; Clinical Urology, 1994; Male Sexual Dysfunction, 1984; Clinical Neurourology, 1979, 2nd edition, 1990. Honour: Gold Cystoscope Award, 1983. Memberships: AUA; AAGUS; ACS. Address: 720 Harrison Avenue, Suite 606, Boston, MA 02118, USA.

KRANK Daniel Frederick, b. 16 Sept 1932, Los Angeles, California, USA. Physician. m. Barbara, 21 May 1993, 2 sons, 1 daughters. Education: BS, cum laude, University of San Francisco, 1956; MD, University California, San Francisco, 1960; MPH, Harvard University, 1962. Appointments: Colonel, US Mary Medical Corps; Child Psychiatrist, Private Practice. Memberships: American Psychiatric Association; American Academy of Child & Adolescent Psychiatry; American Public Health Association. Hobbies: Travel; Hiking; Music; Classical Literature. Address: 11120 New Hampshire Avenue, Suite 509, Silver Spring, MD 20904, USA.

KRAUSZ Charles Edward, b. 25 July 1902, Philadelphia, Pennsylvania, USA. Physician. m. Alice Worrall, 25 Nov 1937. Education: Graduate in CHiropody, 1923, DSc, 1934, Temple University; DSc, Temple University, 1934; DPM, Pennsylvania College of Paediatric Medicine, 1970. Appointments: President, National Association of Chiropody, 1938-40; Dean, School of Chiropody, Temple University, 1941-60; Retired. Publications: Chiropody Quiz Compends. Honours: Honorary DEd, Ohio College of Chiropody, 1956; Honorary DHL, Pennsylvania College of Paediatric Medicine, 1976. Address: 810 Gilbert Road, Cheltenham, PA 19012, USA.

KRESH J Yasha, b. 13 July 1948, Russia. Cardiovascular Researcher; Educator. m. Myrna Blickman Masucci. Education: BSEE, New Jersey Institute of Technology, 1971; MS, Biomedical Engineering, 1973, PhD, 1976, Rutgers University. Appointments: Research Associate, Beth Israel Medical Center, Newark, New Jersey, USA, 1976-79; Director of Research, Jefferson Medical College, Philadelphia, Pennsylvania, 1979-86; Professor of Medicine, Director of Cardiovascular Biophysics and Computing, Professor and Director of Research in Cardiothoracic Surgery, Likoff Cardiovascular Institute, Philadelphia, 1986-; Lecturer in field. Publications: Over 100 in physiological cardiology and bioengineering journals; Patentee in field. Memberships: Fellow, American College of Cardiology; Senior Member, Institute of Electrical and Electronic Engineering, Biomedical Engineering Society; American Heart Association; American Society of Artificial Internal Organs; Sigma Xi; Tau Beta Pi; Eta Kappa Nu. Hobbies: Fractal art; Swimming; Sailing; Computing. Address: 816 Edgewood Road, Yardley, PA 19067-3162, USA.

KREVEL Zivan, b. 13 Aug 1959, Ljubljana, Slovenia. Acupuncturist. Education: BSc, University of Ljubljana, 1984; Medical School, 1990-; Acupuncture, Chengdu, China, 2 years. Appointments: Private Acupuncture Practice. Memberships: British Acupuncture Association and Register; Acupuncture and Traditional Medicine Association,

Slovenian Society of Medical Doctors; Slovenian Homeopathic Society; Slovenian Tai-Chi Society. Hobbies: Taijiquan (T'ai-Chi); Jogging; Tennis; Skiing. Address: Gotska 13, 61117 Ljubljana, Slovenia.

KRIEGER Nancy, b. 27 Oct 1958, New York City, USA. Epidemiologist. Education: BA, Radcliffe College, 1980; MS, University of Washington, Seattle, 1985; PhD, University of California, Berkeley, 1989. Appointments: Investigator, Division of Research, Kaiser Foundation Research Institute, Oakland; Lecturer, Epidemiology, School of Public Health, University of California at Berkeley. Publications: Women's Health, Politics and Power, Co-editor, 1994; AIDS: The Politics of Survival, 1994; Breast Cancer and Serum, Co-author, 1994; Racism, Sexism and Social Class: Implications for Studies of Health, Disease and Well-Being, 1994. Honours: Jay J Drotman Award, American Public Health Association, 1989. Memberships: American Public Health Association; Society for Epidemiologic Research; National Association of Public Health Policy. Hobbies: Reading; Walking. Address: Division of Research, Kaiver Foundation Research Institute, 3505 Broadway, Oakland, CA 94609, USA.

KRIGER Frank Louis, b. 14 Apr 1951. Medical Educator. m. Education: BSc (hons), 1973, MSc, 1976, MD, 1983, University of Winnipeg, Canada; PhD, York University, Toronto, 1981; Fellow, Nephrology, Johns Hopkins Hospital, Baltimore, 1986-88. Appointments: Clinical Instructor, Albert Einstein Medical Center, Philadelphia, Pennsylvania, USA, 1988-89; Clinical Instructor, Toronto General Hospital, Canada, 1989-92; Assistant Professor, Medicine, North Shore University Hospital, New York, USA, 1992-93; Currently Assistant Professor of Medicine, Co-Director, Dialysis and Transplantation, Medical Director, Home Dialysis Programme, Division of Nephrology, Georgetown University Medical Center, Washington DC. Publications: Theses: Regulation of the Adaptation to Alcohol in the Free-Living Nematode, Panagrellus redivivus, 1976; Neuroendocrine Regulation of Ovulation in an Insect, Rhodnius prolixus (Stal); Co-author, chapters: Fluid Leaks-Prevention and Treatment, 1994; Dialysis and Hemoperfusion in Poisoning, 1994; The Principles and Practice of Nephrology, 1994; Systems and Solutions, 1994; 14 articles. Honours: Dean's Honour List, 1973; Postgraduate Fellow, University of Manitoba, 1975; Postgraduate Scholar, National Science and Engineering Research Council, 1976-77, 1977-78; A E Robertson Bursary, 1981; Genser Bursary, 1982; Alexander Wrightson Hogg Memorial Bursary, 1982. Memberships: New York Academy of Sciences; International Society for Peritoneal Dialysis; American Society for Artificial Internal Organs; American College of Physicians; Johns Hopkins Medical and Surgical Society; American Society of Hypertension; American Association for the Advancement of Science; Smithsonian Institute; Council on the Kidney in Cardiovascular Disease, American Heart Association. Hobbies: Computer programming; Dog training and showing. Address: PHC 6003, Renal Division, Georgetown University Medical Center, 3800 Reservoir Road NW, Washington, DC 20007, USA.

KRISHNAMOORTHY Krish, b. 23 Sept 1949, Sri Lanka. Medical Doctor. m. Shanthy, 18 Jan 1984, 1 son, 2 daughters. Education: MBBS; MRCOG; FACOG. Appointment: Assistant Professor. Publications: Primary Management Melanoma of Cervix, 1985; Placental Masaicism, 1995. Memberships: RCOG; ACOG; SPO; NJPA; NPA; AMA. Hobbies: Fishing; Skiing. Address: 2 Pine Meadow Court, East Brunswick NJ 08816, USA.

KRUGMAN Richard David, b. 28 Nov 1942, New York, USA. Physician. m. Mary Elizabeth Kerber, 9 July 1966, 4 sons. Education: AB, Princeton University, 1963; MD, New York University, 1968. Appointments: Assistant Professor of Pediatrics, 1973-78; Associate Professor of Pediatrics, 1978-88; Professor of Pediatrics, 1988-; Director, C H Kempe National Center for the Prevention & Treatment of Child Abuse. Publications: Editor in Chief, Child Abuse & Neglect, 1987-; Revisal of Pediatrics, 4 editions. Memberships: American Medical Association; International Society for the Prevention of Child Abuse & Neglect. Honours: AOA, 1983; C H Kempe Award for work in child abuse, 1989; Advocacy Award, American Psychological Association. Hobbies: Hiking; Skiing; Music. Address: 4200 E 9th Avenue, Denver, CO 80262, USA.

KRUTOVSKIKH Vladimir Andreevich, b. 17 May 1953, Russia. Experimental Oncologist. m. Korolevskaya Natalia, 14 July 1976, 1 s. Education: Medical Diploma, First Medical Institute, Leningrad, 1976; Candidate of Medical Science, 1980; PhD. Appointments: Postgraduate

Student, 1977-80, Junior Scientist, 1980-87, Senior Scientist, 1988, Cancer Research Centre, Moscow; Researcher, International Agency for Research on Cancer, France, 1988-. Publications: Cntributor of 23 articles in scientific journals and 2 chapters in monographs. Hobbies: Painting; Photography. Address: 150 Cours Albert Thomas, 69372 Lyon, Cedex 08, France.

KRZANOWSKI Joseph John, b. 4 feb 1940, Hartford, Connecticut, USA. Pharmacologist. m. Patricia Teper, 22 June 1963, 2 daughters. Education: BS, Pharmacy, University of Connecticut, 1962; MS, 1965, PhD, 1968, Pharmacology, University of Tennessee, Memphis; MA, Religious Studies, Barry University, 1987; Licensed Pharmacist, Maine, Connecticut; Ordained Deacon, Roman Catholic Church, 1987. Appointments: Postdoctoral Fellow, Department Pharmacology, Washington University, St Louis, 1968-71; Assistant Professor, Department Pharmacology and Therapeutics, 1971-75, Associate Professor, Department Pharmacology and Therapeutics, 1975-83, Professor, 1983-, Vice Chairman, 1981-, Acting Chairman, 1986-88, 1989-91, Interim Associate Dean of Research and Graduate Affiars, 1991-, University of South Florida Coll of Medicine, Tampa; Presenter in field. Publications: Medical Examination Review: Pharmacology, 6th Edition, Co-author, 1987, 7th Edition, 1991, 8th Edition, 1995; Contributor of numerous articles to professional journals and chapters in books. Honours: Outstanding Basic Science Professional, University South Florida College of Medicine, 1984, 1991; Outstanding Faculty Research Award, 1990; Florida Heart Association Grantee, 1974-77; NIH Grantee, 1974-76, 1979-83; Sandoz Incorporated Grantee, 1980-87. Memberships include: American Society for Pharmacology and Experimental Therapeutics; AAAS; American Academy Allergy and Immunology; New York Academy of Sciences; Sigma Xi; Rho Chi. Address: Department Pharmacology and Therapeutics, College of Medicine, University of South Florida, Tampa, FL 33612, USA.

KU David Nelson, b. 15 Mar 1956, St Louis, Missouri, USA. Associate Professor. Education: MS, 1982, PhD, 1983, Georgia Institute of Technology, 1982; MD, Emory University School of Medicine, 1984; Surgical Resident, University of Chicago. Appointments: Fulbright Gastprofessor, Munich, Germany; Fellow, Cardiovascular Surgery, University of Chicago; Assistant Professor of Surgery, currently Associate Professor of Surgery, Emory University School of Medicine, Atlanta, Georgia, USA; Assistant Professor of Mechanical Engineering, currently Associate Professor of Mechanical Engineering, Georgia Institute of Technology, Atlanta. Publications: The mechanical environment of the artery (with C Zhu),, 1990; Fluid wall shear stress measurements in a model of the human abdominal aorta: Oscillatory behavior and relationship to atherosclerosis (with J E Moore, C Xu, S Glagov, C K Zarins), 1994. Honours: Joseph Barrett Award, Harvard University, 1978; President's Award, Southern Association of Vascular Surgery, 1987; National Science Foundation Presidential Young Investigator Award, 1987; Y C Fung Young Investigator Award, Bioengineering Division, American Society of Mechanical Engineers, 1989. Memberships: Georgia Medical Association; American Medical Association; American Society of Mechanical Engineers; Biomedical Engineering Society; American College of Angiology. Hobbies: Piano; Voice; Cycling. Address: Georgia Institute of Technology, School of Mechanical Engineering, Atlanta, GA 30332-0405, USA.

KU (GU) Yun-Hui, b. 9 May 1932, Soochow, China. Professor of Physiology. Education: MD, Tongji Medical University, 1955; Postgraduate study, Department of Physiology, Beijing Medical University, 1955-58; Visiting Researcher, Department of Physiology, Cambridge and Edinburgh Universities, 1965-67. Appointments: Vice-Chairman, Department of Physiology, Beijing Medical University, 1960-80. Publications include: Favored patterns in spontaneous and evoked spike trains, 1991, 1992; RVL area is the intra-brain sympathetic final common path of pressor and depressor areas in brainstem, 1987-93; SI 19, a novel effective depressor acupoint and central mechanisms underlying its effect, 1993. Honours: Model Worker in Beijing, 1960; Scientific awards from Beijing Municipal Government, 1985, Beijing Medical University, 1992, 1993, State Education Commission, 1995. Membership: Chinese Physiological Association. Hobby: Watching TV. Address: Department of Physiology, Beijing Medical University, Beijing 100083, China.

KUANG Guo-Bi, b. 24 Oct 1928, Guangxi, China. Professor of Anatomy. m. Tang Shi-Cong, 8 July 1953, 1 son, 1 daughter. Education: MD. Appointments: Zhong-Shan Medical College; Currently Professor of Anatomy, Sun Yat-Sen University of Medical Sciences. Publications:

Chapters in 9 books; 59 papers. Honours: Best Teacher Awards, Provincial and School, 1983-93; 1st, 2nd, 3rd Prize, Medical Science Research and Natural Science Research, 6 times, 1988-93. Membership: Chinese Society of Anatomical Science. Hobby: Music. Address: Department of Anatomy, Sun Yat-Sen University of Medical Sciences, Guangzhou 510089, China.

KUANG Jian-Quan, b. 1 Oct 1931, Guangzhou, China. Professor of Obstetrics and Gynaecology. m. Li Jin-Fang, 29 Dec 1956, Guangzhou, China, 1 daughter. Education: MD, Sun Yat-Sen University of Medical Sciences, 1955; Appointments include: Currently Professor of Obstetrics and Gynaecology, Sun Yat-Sen Memorial Hospital, Sun Yat-Sen University of Medical Sciences, Guangzhou; Vice-President, Ling-Nan Medical College, Sun Yat-Sen University of Medical Sciences. Publications: Reversal operation after female sterilization by mucilage phenol, 1991; Co-author: A study on cytosol estrogen, Progestin in receptors and secretory endometrium in infertile women, 1989; Obstetrics and Gynecology, textbook, 1990; Pediatric and Adolescent Gynaecology, 1991; Mordern Treatment of Gynecology; Vaginal flora and the relevant factors in young girls, 1992; Experimental research in allogenic transplantation of fetal ovarian cell clusters in rabbits, 1992. Honours: Awards of Scientific and Technological Development, Guangdong Provincial Higher Education Bureau and Guangdong Public Health Department, 1986, 1992. Memberships: Chinese Obstetric and Gynaecologic Association; Guangdong Family Planning Association. Hobbies: Football; Music. Address: Sun Yat-Sen Memorial Hospital, 107 Yan-Jiang Road 1, Guangzhou, China.

KUANG Mingxing, b. 16 Mar 1944, Jiangxi, China. University Teacher. m. 1 Feb 1976, 1 s, 1 d. Education: BS, Beijing University. Appointment: Currently, Professor, Physics Department. Publications: Current Distribution Volume Change Theory of Impedance Plethysmography, 1987; Nonlinear Theory of Cardiac Impedance Plethysmography, 1992; Research on Determination of Left Ventricular Ejection Fraction by Electrical Impedance Method, 1993. Honours: 3 Provincial Scientific Achievement Prizes. Membership: Vice President, National Noninvasive Cardiac Function Examination Association. Address: Physics Department, Jiangxi Medical College, Nanchang, Jiangxi 330006, China.

KUBENA Karen, b. 10 Jan 1945, Madison, WI, USA. Nutritionist. m. Leon F Kubena, 11 Feb 1968, 1 s, 1 d. Education: BS, University of Wisconsin-Madison; MS, Mississippi State University; PhD, Nutrition, Texas A&M University; Registered Dietitian; Licensed Dietitian. Appointments: Lecturer, Assistant Professor, Dietetic Internship Director, Associate Professor and Leader, Human Nutrition Section, Associate Dean, College of Agriculture and Life Sciences, Texas A&M University. Publications: Historical Review of Effects of Marginal Intake of Mg in Chronic Experimental Mg Deficiency, 1990; Role of Magnesium in Immunity, 1993. Honours: Phi Kappa Phi, 1976; Distinguished Teaching Award, Association of Former Students of Texas A&M University, 1992; Outstanding Service Award, American Dietetic Association, 1989, 1990, 1994; Sigma Xi, 1991. Memberships: American Institute of Nutrition; American Dietetic Association; American Society of Clinical Nutrition. Hobbies: Walking; Reading. Address: Human Nutrition Section, Department of Animal Science, Texas A&M University, College Station, TX 77843-2471, USA.

KUEKES Edward Grayson, b. 12 Aug 1924, Berea, Ohio, USA. Clinical Psychologist. m. Roberta Edmonds, 3 June 1950, 1 son, 1 daughter. Education: BS; PhD; Diplomate, International Academy of Behavioral Medicine, Counseling and Psychotherapy. Appointments: Staff Psychologist, San Antonio Mental Health Clinic, San Antonio, Texas; Consultant, San Antonio State Hospital; Currently: Associate Professor of Psychiatry and Behavioural Science, University of Oklahoma; Chief, Psychology Service; Associate Chief, Mental Health Services, Veterans Administration Medical Center, Oklahoma City. Publications: Music in Therapy, 1976; Stroke Lattice, 1984. Honours: Commendation for Contributions to Mental Health Clinic Outsending Service to Veterans, 1959; Superior Performance Award, 1962, 1981, 1982, 1984, 1985, 1987, 1988, 1989, 1990, 1991; Distinguished Service Citation, Oklahoma Psychological Association, 1991. Memberships: American Psychological Association, Divisions 12, 13, 18; Clinical Member, International Transactional Analysis Association; Oklahoma Psychological Association. Hobbies: Sailing; Fishing. Address: 6300 Commodore Lane, Oklahoma City, OK 73162, USA.

KUHSE Helga, b. 26 Mar 1940, Hamburg, Germany. Philosopher. m. Bill Kuhse, 7 Jul 1991, 1 d. Education: BA, Honours, 1978, PhD, 1983, Monash University. Career: Research Fellow, 1982-89; Deputy Director, 1985-91, Senior Research Fellow, 1989-, Director, 1992-, Centre for Human Bioethics, Monash University, Victoria, Australia. Publications: Books: Co-author, Should the Baby Live, 1985, The Sanctity of Life Doctrine in Medicine - A Critique, 1985; Editor, Embryo Experimentation, 1992; Editor, Willing to Listen, Wanting to Die, 1994; Over 100 articles published. Memberships: International Association of Bioethics; Various professional ethics committees. Hobbies: Bush Walking; Gardening; Reading; Skiing. Address: PO Box 218, Beaconsfield, Victoria, Australia.

KUIJPERS-JAGTMAN Anne Marie, b. 11 Feb 1949. Orthodontist. m. Hans Kuijpers, 6 April 1974, 1 s, 1 d. Education: DDS, 1973, PhD, 1978, University of Nijmegen. Appointments: Associate Professor in Orthodontics, 1984-92, Professor of Orthodontics, 1992-, University of Nijmegen; Director, Cleft Palate Centre, University Hospital, Nijmegen, 1980-; Associate University Senior Lecturer, University of Leuven, Belgium, 1987-91. Publications: Contributor of over 75 scientific articles. Memberships include: American Association of Orthodontists; American Cleft palate Association; International Association for Dental Research; Angle Society of Europe; European Orthodontic Society. Address: PO Box 9101, 6500 HB Nijmegen, The Netherlands.

KUKU Stephen Babatunde, b. 9 September 1936, Lagos, Nigeria. Gynaecologist. m. Winifred Geh, 3 sons, 2 daughters. Education: MBBS, London; LRCP; MRCS; DRCOG; FWACS; FICS; FRCOG. Appointments: Consultant, Gynaecology & Obstetrics, Medical Consultants Group. Publications: Inhibition of Lactation with Quinestrol, 1968; Fasting Serum Lipids and Serum Lipoprotein Distribution during Oral Contraceptive Therapy in Nigerians, 1973; Amniotic Fluid Creatinine and Fetal Maturity, 1974; Contribution to the book "Subfertility and Infertility in Africa", 1974; Stein Leventhal Syndrom, 1978. Memberships: Royal College of Obstetricians & Gynaecologists; West African College of Surgeons. Hobbies: Swimming. Address: PO Box 4137, Lagos, Nigeria.

KULIKOWSKI Janus Joseph, b. 28 May 1935, Warsaw, Poland. Neuroscientist. m. Barbara Kulikowska, 30 June 1982. Education: BSc, MSc, Technical University of Warsaw; PhD, Technology; PhD, Physiology; British Council Scholar, Teddington and Cambridge, England, 1964-66; Wellcome Research Fellow, Cambridge, 1970-71. Appointments: Research Officer, 1956, Senior Researcher (Lecturer), 1962, Polish Academy of Sciences; Lecturer, 1971, Reader, 1973, Professor of Visual Neurology, 1989-, University of Manchester, England. Publications: Limiting Conditions of Visual Perception, 1969; Editor: Limits of Vision, 1961; Seeing Contour and Colour, 1989. Memberships: Society of Neuroscience; Association for Research on Vision and Ophthalmology; Physiology Society; European Neuroscience Association; European Brain and Behaviour Society; Brain Research Organisation; International Brain Research Organization. Hobby: Skiing. Address: Visual Sciences Laboratory, JG/126, UMIST, PO Box 88, Manchester M60 1QD, England.

KUMAKURA Hiroo, b. 21 Sept 1955, Kyoto, Japan. Associate Professor. m. Keiko, 5 May 1987, 2 sons. Education: MA, Osaka University, 1982; DMSc, Showa University, 1989. Appointments: Lecturer of Anatomy, Showa University School of Medicine; Associate Professor, Biological Anthropology, Faculty of Human Sciences, Osaka University. Publications: Funcional analysis of the biceps femoris muscles during locomotor behaviour in some primates, 1989; The functional morphology of the epaxial muscles of chimpanzee, 1994. Memberships: International Primatological Society; Japanese Association of Anatomists; Anthropological Society of Nippon; Primate Society of Japan; Human Ergology Society; Japan Neuroscience Society. Address: Onohara higashi 4-3-4-202, Minoo, Osaka 562, Japan.

KUMANA Cyrus R, b. 18 May 1940, Bombay, India. Physician. m. 3 s. Education: BSc, MBBS, University of London; FRCP(C); FRCP. Appointments: Professor of Clinical Pharmacology and Therapeutics, Department of Medicine; University of Hong Kong. Publications: Contributor of professional articles in journals and chapters in books; Antibiotic Guidelines, Co-Editor, 1991. Honours: Editorial Director, JAMA Southeast Asia. Memberships: British Pharmacological Society; Hong Kong Society of Antimicrobial Chemotherapy; Hong Kong Pharmacology Society. Address: Department of Medicine, University of Hong Kong, Queen Mary Hospital, Pokfulam Road, Hong Kong.

KUMAR Vinod, b. 15 Oct 1948, India. Professor of Psychiatry. m. Nita Kumar, 1 Mar 1975, 2 daughters. Education: MBBS; MRCPsych; DPM, London. Appointments: Consultant Psychiatrist, England, 1982; Chief, Geriatric Psychiatry, University of Southern Illinois, Assistant Chairman, Clinical Services, 1985-91. Publications: Several publications on Cholinergic System in Alzheimer Disease and Psychopharmacology. Memberships: American Association of Geriatric Psychiatry; American Psychiatric Association; Royal College of Psychiatrists; International Psychogeriatric Association. Hobbies: Tennis; Jogging. Address: 4300 Allon Road, Main Building, Suite 204, Miami Beach, FL 33140, USA.

KUMMEROW Fred August, b. 4 Oct 1914, Berlin, Germany. Researcher; Teacher. m. Amy L Hilderbrand, 24 June 1942, 1 s, 2 d. Education: BS, 1939, MS, 1941, PhD, 1943, University of Wisconsin, Madison. Appointments: Associate Nutritionist, Clemson College, Clemson, South Carolina, 1943-45; Associate Professor of Chemistry, Kansas State University, Manhattan, Kansas, 1945-50; Professor of Food Chemistry, 1950-; Emeritus, University of Illinois, Urbana, 1985-. Publications: Contributor of over 300 reviewed articles. Honours: Funk Award, Honorary Member, The Purkinje Society; Honorary Member, Czechoslovakian Medical Society; Honorary Member, Physiology in Romania. Memberships: Fellow, Council of Atheriosclerosis; Am Coll Nutrition, AAAS; American Heart Association; American Institute of Nutrition; American Society of Biological Chemistry; Sub Committee, Dietary fats; Society of Experimental Biology and Medicine; American Chemical Society; National Research Delegate to International Union of Pure and Applied Chemistry; Biochemical Soc of Great Britain; Am Soc Microbiology. Hobby: Swimming. Address: Burnsides Research Laboratory, 1208 W Pennsylvania Avenue, Urbana, IL 61801, USA.

KUNDIEV Yuri Illich, b. 2 Oct 1927, Kirovograd, Ukraine. Physician. m. Vasilyeva Svetlana, 14 Feb 1953, 1 s. Education: Kiev State Medical Institute, 1951; Postgraduate Study, Kiev Institute of Labour Hygiene and Occupational Diseases, 1954. Career: Head of Laboratory and Scientific Director, Currently, Director, Kiev Institute of Occupational Health; Academician, National Academy of Sciences and Academy of Medical Sciences of Ukraine; Corresponding Member, Academy of Medical Sciences of Russia. Publications: Absorption through the skin and poisoning prevention, 1975; Co-author, Editor, Labour Hygiene in Agricultural Production, 1982; Co-author, Editor, Occupational Diseases of Agricultural Workers, 1983; Co-author, Epidemiology of Occupational Health, 1986; Co-author, Dust Bronchitis, 1990; Co-author, Co-editor, Chernobyl Disaster, 1995. Honours: Honoured Member, Purkiynye Czechoslovakian Medical Society, 1966; Order of The Red Banner of Labour, 1973; Honoured Scientist of Ukrainian SSR, 1977; Erisman Prize Laureate, 1982; Order of Friendship Among People, 1987. Memberships: World Health Organisation Committee on Occupational Health; Board, International Association on Rural Health; Scientific Committee on Pesticides, International Commission on Occupational Health. Hobbies: Chess; Philately. Address: Institute for Occupational Health, 75 Saksagansky St, 252033, Kiev, Ukraine.

KUNZE Klaus, b. 16 July 1933, Bremen, Germany. Professor of Neurology. m. Anne Kunze, 30 Aug 1963. Education: MD, University of Frankfurt, 1958; Professor of Neurology, 1970. Appointments: Professor of Neurology, Giessen, 1970. Publications: Numerous publications in scientific journals. Memberships: Germany Neurology Society; ENS; EEG. Honours: Schunk-Price, University of Giessen, 1970. Hobbies: Literature. Address: University Kernklin mit Polklin, Hamburg Eppendorf, Martinistrasse 52, D-2000 Hamburg 20, Germany.

KUPERS Terry Allen, b. 14 Oct 1943, Philadelphia, Pennsylvania, USA. Psychiatrist. m. Arlene M Shmaeff, 16 Jan 1982, 3 sons. Education: BA, Psychology, Stanford University, 1964; MD, 1968, MSP, Social Psychiatry, 1974, University of California, Los Angeles; Intern, Kings County, Downstate Medical Center, Brooklyn, 1968-69; Resident, Psychiatry, 1969-72, Fellow, Social and Community Psychiatry, 1972-74, Neuropsychiatric Institute, University of California, Los Angeles; Registrar, Tavistock Institute, London, 1971-72. Appointments: Staff Psychiatrist, M L King Jr Hospital, Los Angeles, Assistant Professor, Charles Drew Postgraduate Medical School, Los Angeles, 1974-77; Staff Psychiatrist, Co-Director, Partial Hospital, Richmond Community Mental Health Center, Richmond, California, 1977-81; Professor, The Wright Institute and private practice of Psychiatry, Oakland, California, 1981-; Staff, Alta Bates Medical Center. Publications include: Public Therapy: The Practice of Psychotherapy in the Public Mental Health Clinic, 1981; Ending Therapy: The Meaning of Termination, 1988; Using Psychodynamic Principles in Public Mental

Health (editor), 1991; Revisioning Men's Lives: Gender, Intimacy and Power, 1993; Articles in journals including Community Mental Health Journal and Free Associations. Honours: Alpha Omega Alpha, 1968; Fellow, American Psychiatric Association, 1984; Fellow, American Orthopsychiatric Association. Memberships: Physicians for Social Responsibility; National Organization for Men Against Sexism. Hobbies: Jazz flute; Wilderness; Sports; Writing. Address: 8 Wildwood Avenue, Oakland, CA 94610, USA.

KURCZYNSKI Elizabeth M, b. 6 Apr 1943, Minnesota, USA. Pediatric Hematology. 1 s, 1 d. Education: BS, University of Wisconsin, USA, 1964; MD, Case Western Reserve University, USA, 1968; Residency in Pediatrics, Cleveland, Ohio; Fellow, Pediatric Hematology-Oncology, University of Michigan, Ann Arbor, MI. Appointments: Assistant Professor of Pediatrics, Albert Einstein Medical School; Assistant Professor, Case Western Reserve; Chief of Pediatrics, Kaiser Foundation Hospital, Parma, OH; Physician in Charge, Kaiser Permanente, Atlanta, GA; Chief of Hematology-Oncology, Scottish Rite Childrens Medical Centre. Publications: Co-author, The Blood and Hematopoietic System in Behrman, Neonatal-Perinatal Medicine, 1983; Co-author, Safety and Efficacy of Monoclonal Antibody Purified Factor IX, in press. Honour: Alpha Omega Alpha. Memberships: American Academy of Pediatrics; American Society of Hematology; American Society of Clinical Oncology; American Society of Pediatric Hematology-Oncology. Hobbies: Biking; Mountain Hiking; Reading; Working Out. Address: 5455 Meridian Mark Road, Atlanta, GA 30342, USA.

KUROKI Yoshikazu, b. 13 Apr 1937, Kagoshima, Japan. Professor. m. Mitsuko Yamagishi, 9 Apr 1967, 1 son, 2 daughters. Education: MD, Kyushu University, 1963. Appointments: Director, Division Medical Genetics, Kanagawa Child Medical Centre. Publications: Clinical Atlas of Human Chromosomes, 1981; Atlas of Congenital Malformation Syndromes, 1990; New Trends in Pediatric Neurology, Co-author, 1993; New Malformation Syndrome (Kabuki Make-up), 1981. Memberships: Japan Society of Human Genetics; Japanese Tetratology Society' European Society of Human Genetics; Japan Pediatric Society. Hobby: Bird Watching. Address: 2-138-4 Mutsukawa, Minami-ku, Yokohama 232, Japan.

KUROL Jüri, b. 23 Sep 1942, Tartu, Estonia. Orthodontist. m. Eva, 1 s. Education: DDS; Odont Dr. Appointments: Head, Orthodontic Department, Institute for Postgraduate Dental Education, JÖnköping; Associate Professor, University of Goteborg. Publications: Contributor of professional articles. Honours: President, Swedish Association of Orthodontists, 1988-95. Hobbies: Music; Fishing; Outdoor Life. Address: Kungsgatan 17, S-561 31 Huskvarna, Sweden.

KURTZKE John Francis, b. 14 Sep 1926, Brooklyn, NY, USA. Neurologist; Epidemiologist. m. Margaret Mary Nevin, 30 Jun 1950, 3 s, 4 d. Education: BS, summa cum laude, St John's University, 1948; MD, Cornell University, 1952; Diplomate in Neurology, American Board of Psychiatry and Neurology, 1958. Career includes: Chief, Neurology Service, VA Hospitals, Coatsville, PA, 1956-63, Washington DC, 1963-; Faculty, Georgetown Medical School, Washington, 1963-; Professor of Neurology, 1968-, Vice Chairman of Department of Neurology, 1976-, Professor of Community and Family Medicine, 1968-, Distinguished Professor of Neurology, Uniformed Services University of Health Sciences, Bethesda, 1992-. Publications include: Author, Co-author: Epidemiology of Multiple Sclerosis, 1968, Epidemiology of Neurologic and Sense Organ Disorders, 1973; Editorial Board, Neuroepidemiology, 1980-, Neurology, 1989-92, Stroke, 1986-, Journal of Clinical Epidemiology, 1988-, Journal of Neurological Science, 1990-, Acta Neurologica Scandinavica, 1990-; Contributor of over 400 articles to professional journals, book chapters. Honours include: Navy Commendation Medal, 1974; Gold Vicennial Medal, Georgetown University, 1982; Armed Forces Res Medal, 3rd award, 1986; Legion of Merit, 1986. Memberships include: Fellow: AAAS, ACP, American Academy of Neurology (various offices held); American College of Epidemiology; NY Academy of Science; American College of Preventive Medicine; Stroke Council, American Heart Association; AAUP; AMA; American Neurological Association; American Epidemiological Society; International Epidemiological Association; Association for Research in Nervous and Mental Disease; Honorary Member, Danish, French, German Neurological Societies; Member: Life, Navy League; Life, Reserve Officers Association; Life, Naval Order of the United States; Life, Naval Institute; Life, The Retired Officers Association; Life, Naval Reserve Association; Life, Fleet Reserve Association, Rear Admiral,

MC, USNR (Ret). Address: 7509 Salem Road, Falls Church, VA 22043-3240, USA.

KUSELMAN Alexey I, b. 7 Feb 1943, Tashkent, Russia. Paediatrician. Education: Paediatrician, Donetsk Medical Institute, 1967; PhD, Leningrad Medical Pavlov Institute, 1974; Postdoctoral, Semipalatonsk Medical Institute, 1984-86; MD, Professor, Scientific Research Institute of Paediatrics, Russian Academy of Medical Sciences, 1989. Appointment: Head, Paediatrics Department, Medical Faculty of Moscow State University, Ulyanovsk. Address: Department of Paediatrics, Medical Faculty of Moscow State University, K Libknecht's Street 1, Ulyanovsk 432601, Russia.

KUSHNER Brian Harris, b. 8 Jul 1951, New York City, USA. Pediatrician. m. Phyllis D Kushner, 22 Feb 1986, 2 children. Education: AB, Biochemistry, Harvard College, Cambridge, MA, 1972; MD, Johns Hopkins University School of Medicine, Baltimore, MD, 1976; Pediatric Intern and Resident, NY, 1976-78; Pediatric Senior Resident, NY, 1978-79; Clinical Fellow, Pediatric Hematology-Oncology, 1979-80; Clinical Research Fellow, Pediatric Hematology-Oncology, 1983-86. Appointments include: Physician, International Rescue Committee, Khao-I-Dang Refugee Camp, Thailand, 1981; Instructor in Pediatrics, Cornell University Medical College, NY, 1987-92; Assistant Attending Pediatrician, New York Hospital, 1988-; Assistant Professor of Pediatrics, Cornell University Medical College, NY, 1992-; Assistant Attending Pediatrician, Memorial Sloan-Kettering Cancer Center, NY, 1992-. Publications include: 25 Peer reviewed primary papers; Many book chapters, reviews and letters to the editor. Honours: Clinical Scholars National Research Service Award, 1988-90; American Cancer Society Career Development Award, 1990-93; American Cancer Society Grant, 1993-95. Memberships: American Academy of Pediatrics; American Association for Cancer Research; American Society of Clinical Oncology; American Society of Hematology; American Society of Pediatric Hematology-Oncology. Hobbies: Reading; Biking; Sport; Stamp Collecting. Address: 1275 York Avenue, Box 299, New York, NY 10021, USA.

KUTTY P T K, b. 23 June 1940, Shoranur, India. psychologist. m. Vimala, 8 Dec 1974, 2 daughters. Education: BA, Delhi University; MA, Annamalai University; Doctoral Fellow, Beahampur Uni. Appointments: Psychologist, Family Counselling Services, Railway Hospital, Shoranur, Kerala. Publications: Management of Alcoholism Among Railway Men - Application of Transactional Analaysis and Behavioural Therapy, 1994. Honours: Railway Hospital Award for Best Psychiatric Research Paper presented in National Industrial Psychiatry Conference, Cuttack, 1993; Railway minister's National Award, India, 1994. Memberships: Life Member: Indian Academy of Applied Psychology' Industrial Psychiatry Association of India; ITAA, USA; ICTA, India. Address: Railway Counselling Centre, Vakkadakalam, By Pass Road, Shoranur, Kerala 679121, India.

KVEDER Rado, b. 26 July 1948, Ljubljana. Physician. m. Dunja Obersnel-Kveder, 26 Aug 1972, 1 son, 1 daughter. Education: MD, MSc, Medical Faculty of Ljubljana. Appointments: Chief, The Nephrological Outpatient Clinic; Head, Department of Nephrology. Address: Univerzitetni Klin, Zaloska 7, Ljubljana 61000, Slovenia.

KWARKO Kwasi Assoku, b. 10 May 1925, Akim Oda, Ghana. Gynaecologist. m. Dora Ama Nyarkoa, 4 Oct 1958, 2 sons, 2 daughters. Education: MB ChB, Glasgow University, Scotland, 1953; Diploma of Tropical Medicine and Hygiene, London, 1955; FRCOG, London, 1962; Fellow, West African College of Surgeons. Appointments: House Officer, Hastings General Hospital, England; House Officer, Merthyr Tydfil Hospital, Wales; Medical Officer, Ghana Government Medical Service; Senior House Officer, Stobhill Hospital, Glasgow Hospital, Scotland; Senior House Officer, Churchill Hospital, Oxford, England; Specialist Gynaecologist, Ghana Government Medical Service; Currently Specialist Gynaecologist in charge of own private clinic. Memberships: British Medical Association; Ghana Medical Association; Private Medical and Dental Practitioners Association, Ghana; Federation of World Gynaecologists and Obstetricians. Hobbies: Reading; Walking. Address: North Ridge Clinic, PO Box 7397, Accra North, Ghana, West Africa.

KWEE James P, b. 24 July 1936, Pare, Indonesia. Clinical Assistant Professor. m. June T Kwee, 24 Nov 1961, 1 s, 2 d. Education: MD, University of Indonesia, Jakarta; Intern, Nassau Hospital, Mineola, USA; Medical Resident, Fellow, Medical Oncology, Nassau Hospital, Mineola. Appointments: Head of Governmental Health Service, West Kalimantan,

Indonesia; Private Practice in Medical Oncology, 1974-; Clinical Assistant Professor, State University of New York at Stoney Brook, USA. Memberships: American Society of Clinical Oncology; American College of Physicians; AMA; Medical Soceity of New York. Hobbies: Tennis; Golf. Address: 520 Franklin Avenue, Garden City, NY 11530, USA.

KWOK Che Ling, b. 24 feb 1946, Hong Kong. Anaesthesiologist. m. Mee Kim Leung, 24 Feb 1975, 1 s. Education: MBBS, Hong Kong; FANZCA; FHKCA. Appointments: Consultant Anaesthetist, 1982-92; Consultant Anaesthetist and Chief of Service, 1983-94. Memberships: Vice President, Society of Anaesthesiologists of Hong Kong. Address: Anaesthetic Department, Princess Margaret Hospital, Hong Kong.

KWON Chul Soo, b. 10 Sept 1948, Seoul, Korea. Psychiatrist. m. Sung Hee, 6 Apr 1974, 1 daughter. Education: MD, College of Medicine, Seoul National University; Residency in Psychiatry, Johns Hopkins Hospital, USA; Fellowship in Psychiatry and Behavioural Sciences, Johns Hopkins University School of Medicine; Diplomate in Psychiatry, American Board of Psychiatry and Neurology. Appointments: Medical Director, Partial Hospitalisation Programme, North Charles Hospital, USA; Medical Director, Homewood Hospital Centre; Currently: Medical Director, Partial Hospitalisation Programme, Department of Psychiatry, Union Memorial Hospital; Clinical Instructor, Psychiatry, Johns Hopkins Hospital. Honours: Chairman, Scientific Committee, Korean Medical Association, District of Columbia, Maryland and Virginia, 1992. Memberships include: American Medical Association; American Psychiatric Association; Maryland Psychiatric Society; Medical and Chirurgical Faculty of State of Maryland; Baltimore City Medical Society; Johns Hopkins Medical and Surgical Association; Southern Medical Association; American Academy of Clinical Psychiatrists; American Association of Geriatric Psychiatry; American Society of Clinical Psychopharmacology; Community Advisory Committee, Partial Hospitalisation Programme, Union Memorial Hospital; Hobbies: Fishing; Listening to music. Address: 2908 Chainita Court, Ellicott City, MD 21042, USA.

KYOMEN Helen Hisae, b. 11 Jul 1959, Long Beach, CA, USA. Physician; Psychiatrist. Education: BA, East Asian Languages and Culture, 1980; BSc, Biological Sciences, 1980; MD, 1993; MSc, Epidemiology, 1993; Appointments: Clinical Fellow, Psychiatry, Harvard Medical School, Boston, MA, 1990-92; Instructor, Psychiatry, Harvard Medical School, Boston, MA, 1992-; Assistant Psychiatrist, McLean Hospital, Belmont, MA, 1992-. Publications include: Aging in Japan, in The Gerontologist, 1989; Co-author, Gender-linked Objections to Hormonal Treatment of Aggression in Men with Dementia, in The Gerontologist, 1991; Co-author, Diagnostic Patterns of Social Phobia: Comparisons in Tokyo and Hawaii, in Journal of Nervous and Mental Disease, 1992; Co-author, Alcohol Abuse in the Elderly, in Principles and Practice of Geriatric Psychiatry, 1994. Honours: Sol Ginsberg Fellowship, Group for Advancement of Psychiatry, 1989-90; John A Hartford Scholar in Geriatric Psychiatry, Harvard Medical School Division on Aging, 1990-91; Biomedical Research Support Grant, Hebrew Rehabilitation Center for Aged, 1992; Pfizer/American Geriatrics Society Postdoctoral Fellowship Award, 1992-94; Harvard Medical School Department of Psychiatry Livingston Fund Award, 1992. Memberships: American Psychiatric Association; American Association for Geriatric Psychiatry; American Geriatrics Society; Gerontological Society of America; American Public Health Association; International Psychogeriatric Association; AMA; ASAM. Hobbies: Playing Guitar; Drawing, pastels, charcoal; Oil Painting; Swimming. Address: 115 Mill Street, Belmont, MA 02178-9106, USA.

L

LA VECCHIA Carlo, b. 27 Feb 1955, Milan, Italy. Epidemiologist. m. Eva Negri, 24 Jul 1987, 1 s, 1 d. Education: MD, University degli Studi di Milan, Italy, 1979; MSc, Clinical Medicine, Oxford University, England, 1983; Diploma in Pharmalogical Research, Institute Mario Negri, Milan, Italy, 1983. Career: Research Fellow, Istituto Mario Negri, Milan, 1979-81, Department of Community Medicine, Oxford, England, 1981-83; Staff Scientist, 1983-86, Currently, Head, Laboratory of Epidemiology, Istituto Mario Negri, Milan; Associate Professor, Epidemiology, University of Lausanne, Switzerland, 1987-92; Currently, Associate Professor, Epidemiology, University of Milan. Publications: Over 700 papers on epidemiology and medicine published in professional journals including: The Lancet, British Medical Journal, Cancer Research, Cancer, American Journal of Epidemiology, American Journal of Obstetrics and Gynaecology, International Journal of Cancer. Honours: Visiting Professor, Royal Society for Medicine, London, England, 1991; Glaxo Prize for Medical Publication, Rome, Italy, 1993. Memberships: Ordine dei Medici, Milan, 1980; Ordine dei Giornalisti, Milan, 1986; Fellowship Committee, UICC, Geneva, Switzerland, 1991-95. Address: Istituto di Ricerche Farmacologiche Mario Negri, Via Eritrea 62, 20157 Milan, Italy.

LABBOK Miriam Harriet, b. 24 Oct 1949, Trenton, NJ, USA. Physician. Education: MMS; MD; MPH; FACPM; MACE; IBCLC. Appointments: Medical Officer, Agency for International Development; Assistant Professor, Johns Hopkins University, Associate Professor, Georgetown University, Adjunct Associate Professor, Johns Hopkins University. Publications include: Breast-Feeding: The Technical Basis, Co-Editor; Breast-Feeding: Protecting a Natural Resource, Co-Author; Tulane Outstanding Alumus, 1995. Honours: NIH Research/Service Award, Johns Hopkins, 1980; Science and Technology in Development Award, 1986; Paul Gyorgy Award, 1976. Memberships: FACPM; MACE; IBCLC. Address: 2115 Wisconsin Ste 602, Washington DC 20007, USA.

LACHIN John M, b. 4 Jul 1942, New Orleans, LA, USA. Biostatistician. m. Teresa Bohan, 18 Jun 1966, 1 s, 2 d. Education: BS, Tulane University, 1965; ScD, University of Pittsburgh, 1972. Career includes: Mental Hygiene Epidemiologist and Director, Program Information and Evaluation, VA State Department of Mental Health and Mental Retardation, Richmond; Adjunct Assistant Professor, Biometry, Medical College of VA, Health Sciences Division, VA Commonwealth Universty, 1972-; Assistant, Associate Research Professor, Professor, Department of Statistics, 1973-; Assistant Director, Co-Director, Director, The Biostatistics Center, George Washington University, 1980-; Statistical Co-ordinating Director for the National Co-operative Gallstone Study 1980-84; Lupus Nephritis Collaborative Study, 1981-88; Diabetes Control and Complications Trail, 1982-96. Publications include: About 90 publications including: Introduction to sample size determination and power analysis for clinical trials, in Controlled Clinical Trials, 1981; Co-Editor, The Randomized Clinical Trial and Therapeutic Decisions, 1982; Co-author, A controlled trial of plasmapheresis therapy in severe lupus nephritis, in New England Journal of Medicine, 1992. Honours: Fellow, American Statistical Association, 1989; Fellow, Royal Statistical Society, 1991; Delta Omega, 1991; Distinguished Graduate Award, University of Pittsburgh, 1992; Elected Member, International Statistical Institute, 1993; Co-recipient, Charles H Best Medal for Distinguished Service in Cause of Diabetes, American Diabetes Association, 1994. Memberships include: American Statistical Association; Biometric Society; International Statistical Institute; American Diabetes Association. Hobbies: Fly Fishing; Jazz. Address: The Biostatistics Center, 6110 Executive Boulevard, Suite 750, Rockville, MD 20852, USA.

LACHMANN Burkhard, b. 5 Oct 1942, Templin, Germany. Physician. m. Dörte Lachmann, 12 Oct 1972, 1 son, 1 daughter. Education: MD, 1970, Habilitation, Dr sc med, 1981, Humboldt University; DrMedSci, Karolinska Institute, Stockholm, 1981. Appointments include: Various visiting positions, Italy, Sweden, Netherlands, Japan, USA, Finland, 1978-85; Guest Professor, 1985-86, Research Director, Anaesthesiology, 1986-, Professor in Experimental Anaesthesiology, 1989-, Erasmus University, Rotterdam, Netherlands. Publications: More than 320, mainly relating to various aspects of experimental and clinical physiology, anaesthesia and intensive care medicine, including surfactant system of the lung, lung function after auto and homo lung transplantation in dogs, experimental RDS after injection of anti-lung serum, neonatal pulmonary mechanics during spontaneous and artificial ventilation, diagnostics and therapy of the RDS in newborns and adults, behaviour of PaO2 in relation to age, weight and sex, high frequency ventilation. Honours: Command Lecture, General Assembly of Societas Europaea, Physiologiae Clinicae Respiratoriae, 1981; Rudolf Virchow Prize, Ministry of Health, German Democratic Republic, 1981; Paper, Improved gas exchange after tracheal instillation of surfactant in animals with adult RDS, selected as 1 of 5 most outstanding among over 9000, World Congress on Critical Care Medicine, 1981. Hobbies: Diving; Sailing. Address: Department of Anaesthesiology, Erasmus University, Postbox 1738, 3000 DR Rotterdam, Netherlands.

LACQUET Albert, b. 24 Oct 1904, Balen-Neet, Belgium. Surgeon. m. Mary-Lucy Nelis, 8 Apr 1931, 3 sons, 2 daughters. Education: MD, Specialist Surgery, University of Louvain, 1928-34; Fellow, Mayo Clinic, USA. Appointments: Assistant; Associate; Chief; Professor of Surgery, 1936-75; Head of Department, 1953-75. Publications: Contributor of numerous professional papers. Honours: First Laureate Competition Travel Awards of the State, 1928; First laureate Inter-university Competition, 1929; Fellow, Royal Society of Medicine, London, 1946; Fellow, American College of Surgeons, 1967; Ennobled with title of Baron, 1977. Memberships: Founding Member, 1938, Permanent Secretary, 1944-94, Royal Academy of Medicine of Belgium; Honorary Secretary, 1995, Elected Member, Academy of Surgery France; Academy of Medicine, Paris. Address: 27 ave Leopold III, 3001 Leuven Heverlee, Belgium.

LACROIX-ARNAUD Marie Blanche, b. 4 Aug 1938, Sevres, France. Psychoanalyst. m. Rolland Lacroix, 12 Sept 1970, 1 son, 1 daughter. Education: Studies, Children Psychoanalysis and Infant Observation. Appointments: MD, Paris, 1965; Psychiatrist, Paris, 1969; Psychoanalyst for Adults & Children. Publications: Je fais ton portait, 1990. Memberships: Groupe Tovlousain de Psychanalyse; Societe Psychanalytique le Paris; International Psychanalytical Association. Hobbies: Flowers; Painting; Walking. Address: 3 Boulevard de la Falaise, 31500 Toulouse, France.

LADISCH Stephan, b. 18 Jul 1947, Garmisch-Partenkirchen, West Germany. Professor of Pediatrics and Biochemistry. m. 2 children. Education: BS, 1969, MD, 1973, University of Pennsylvania, Philadelphia. Appointments include: Visiting Scientist, Institut Pasteur, Paris, France, 1986-87; Assistant Professor 1978-82, Assoc Professor, 1982-86; Professor of Pediatrics, Senior Member, Human Immunobiology Group, Staff Investigator, Jonsson Cancer Center, UCLA School of Medicine, 1986-91; Director, Center for Cancer and Transplantation Biology, Children's Research Institute, Professor of Pediatrics and Biochemistry-Molecular Biology, George Washington School of Medicine, Washington DC, 1991-; Bosworth Chair in Cancer Biology, Children's Research Institute, Washington DC, 1994-. Publications include: Over 80 Research Papers, 1967-; 5 Textbook Chapters; Editorial Review Services to many Medical Publications. Honours include: Phi Beta Kappa; University of Pennsylvania Graduation Award in Cancer Research, 1973; Von L Meyer Travel Fellowship for Study of Malnutrition in Columbia, 1975; Scholar of the Leukemia Society of America, 1982-87; Elaine H Snyder Cancer Research Award, 1994; George Washington University School of Medicine Distinguished Research Award, 1994. Memberships include: Serves on numerous committees; Society for Pediatric Research; American Association of Immunologists; American Federation for Clinical Research; American Society of Hematology; American Association for Cancer Research. Address: Centre for Cancer and Transplantation Biology, Children's Hospital, 111 Michigan Ave NW, Washington DC 20010, USA.

LAGASSE Leo Darrell, b. 13 June 1931. Medicine. m. Ann Atkins, 19 Aug 1961, 1 son, 2 daughters. Education: BA, Loyola University, 1952; MD, University of Virginia, 1959. Appointment: Professor Emeritus, Department of Obstetrics & Gynecology, UCLA School of Medicine. Publications: 110 articles published in medical literature, mostly dealing with Gynecologic Cancer. Honours: Alpha Omega Alpha, 1959; Honoree, Leo D Lagasse Society, 1991. Memberships: American College of Obstetrics & Gynecology; American College of Surgeons; Society of Gynecologic Oncologists; Society of Pelvic Surgeons. Hobbies: Tennis; Reading. Address: 22866 Beckledge Terrace, Malibu, CA 90265, USA.

LAHON Khogeswar, b. 1 Mar 1942, Lengeri, Assam, India. General Practitioner; Obstetrician and Gynaecologist. m. Gitanjali Lahon, 12 Apr 1978, 1 son, 1 daughter. Education: MBBS, Dibrugarh University, Assam; DObstRCOG, 1972, MRCOG, 1976, Royal College of Obstetricians and Gynaecologists, London. Appointments: Registrar, Obstetrics, Gynaecology, All Saint's Hospital, Kent, England, 1976-78; Consultant Obstetrician and Gynaecologist, INAS and Al-Jamahiriya Group of Hospitals, University of Garyounis, Benghazi, Libya, 1978-82; Currently General Practitioner, Private Consultant Obstetrician and Gynaecologist, Hayes, Middlesex, England. Memberships include: Generak Medical Council, UK. Address: 72 Roseville Road, Hayes, Middlesex UB3 4QZ, England.

LAHTI Ilpo Antero, b. 11 Mar 1947, Paattinen, Finland. Chief Physician; Docent in Psychiatry. m. Mervi Remo, 15 June 1983, 1 daughter. Education: MD; MScD; Psychoanalyst, International Psychoanalytic Association; Family Therapy Trainee (SMD). Appointments: Lecturer in Social Psychiatry, Tampere University; Currently Chief Physician in Psychiatry, Turku Student Health Service. Publications: The Adoptive Child in Adolescence, 1991; Co-author: Interaction of Genetic and Psychosocial Factors in Schizophrenia, 1987; The Finnish Adoptive Family Study of Schizophrenia, 1989. Honours: Martti Kaila Award, 1991. Memberships: Finnish Psychoanalytical Society; Finnish Psychiatric Association; Finnish Medical Society. Address: Uudenmaankatu 11 C, 20500 Turku, Finland.

LAI Edward C S, b. 23 Jan 1955, Hong Kong. Surgeon. m. 28 Aug 1983, 1 son, 1 daughter. Education: MBBS (HK); FRCS (Ed); FRACS; FACS; Master of Surgery. Appointments: Senior Lecturer, 1991-93, Chief, Endoscopy Unit, 1991-, Reader, 1993-, Department of Surgery, The University of Hong Kong, Queen Mary Hospital, Pokfulam; Editor-in-Chief, Asian Journal of Surgery, 1991-. Publications: Co-author: Endoscopic biliary drainage for severe acute cholangitis, 1992; Acute pancreatitis - Role of ERCP in 1994, 1994; Preoperative endoscopic drainage for malignant obstructive jaundice, 1994; Hepatic resection for hepatocellular carcinoma: An audit of 343 patients, 1995. Honours: Travelling Fellowship, James IV Association of Surgeons, 1993. Memberships: Advisory Board, Diagnostic and Therapeutic Endoscopy; Advisory Board, Journal of Hepato-Biliary-Pancreatic Surgery; Scientific Committee, International Association of Hepato-Pancreatic-Biliary Association; Treasurer, Hong Kong Society of Gastroenterology; Treasurer, Hong Kong Society of Laparoscopic Surgeons. Hobby: Kendo. Address: Department of Surgery, The University of Hong Kong, Queen Mary Hospital, Pokfulam, Hong Kong.

LAI Eric, b. 20 May 1946, Hong Kong, China. Family Physician. m. Mimi L B Mak, 11 Sept 1972, 1 son, 1 daughter. Education: BSc; BCH; MB; LRCS; LM; LLMRCP. Appointments: Resident in Medicine, Chesterton Hospital, Cambridge, England; Resident, New Addenbrookes Hospital, Cambridge; Resident, Gynecology, Princess Margaret Hospital, Hong Kong; Family Physician in Private Practice, Hong Kong. Publications: Investigations of Medical Care in Hong Kong, 1990; Analysis of Chinese Medicine, 1993. Honours: Chairman of the Board of Education, 1991-92. Memberships: Diplomate, Royal College of Surgeons; Diplomate, Royal College of Physicians in Ireland; Hong Kong College of General Practitioners. Hobbies: Reading; Meditation; Writing Poetry; Walking; Boxing. Address: 140 Healthy Gardens, 560 Kings Road, Hong Kong.

LAJEUNESSE Christine, b. 18 Apr 1962, Montreal, Quebec, Canada. Urologist. m. David J Astles, 24 May 1986, 1 daughter. Education: MD; FRCSC. Appointments: Urologist, Montfort Hospital, Ottawa. Memberships: AUA; CUA; CMA. Hobbies: Chess; Sports; Travel. Address: 406-595 Montreal Road, Ottawa, Ontario, K1K 4L2, Canada.

LAKHOTIA Subhash Chandra, b. 4 Oct 1945, Churu, India. Teaching & Research. m. Sarita Lakhotia, 20 Nov 1971, 1 son, 1 daughter. Education: MSc, Calcutta University; PhD, Calcutta University. Appointments: Lecturer, Zoology, Burdwan University, India; Lecturer, Zoology, Gujarat University, India; Reader, Zoology, Banaras Hindu University, India; Professor, Zoology, Banaras Hindu University. Publications incl: Gelatin as a blocking agent in southern blot and in situ hybridizations, 1993; Drosophila larvae deficient for superoxide dismutase activity are thermosensitive but show normal heat shock response, 1994; The hyperactive X-chromosome is not early replicating in mitotically active somatic cells of Drosophila nasuta males, 1995; RNA metabolism in situ at the 93D heat shock locus in polytene nuclei

of Drosophila melanogaster after various treatments, 1995. Honours: Overseas Scholarship, Royal Commission for the Exhibition of 1851, England, 1972; medal for Young Scientists, Indian National Science Academy, New Delhi, 1975; Career Award, University Grants Commission, New Delhi, 1979; Fulbright Senior Scholar Grant, USA, 1984-85; National Lecturer, University Grants Commission, New Delhi, 1989; SS Bhatnagar Prize, Council of Scientific & Industrial Research, NEw Delhi, 1989; Fellow, Indian National Science Academy, 1993; Fellow, Indian Academy of Sciences, 1994. Memberships: Indian Society of Cell Biology, Life Member; Environmental Mutagen Society of India, Life Member; Genetics Society of America. Address: Cytogenetics Laboratory, Department of Zoology, Banaras Hindu University, Varanasi 221 005, India.

LALA Peeyush K, b. 1 Nov 1934, Chittagong, India. Professor of Anatomy and Oncology. m. (1) Arati Royburman, 7 July 1962, dec, 2 s, (2) Shipra Bhattachareya, 6 Nov 1992. Education: MBBS, 1957, MD, 1962, PhD, Medical Biophysics, 1961, Calcutta University. Appointments: Instructor of Pathology, Calcutta Medical College, 1957-60; Instructor and Lecturer of Pathology and Hematology, NRS Medical College, Calcutta, 1961-62; Instructor and Lecturer of Pathology and Division of Biology and Medical Research, Argonne National Laboratory, Illinois, 1963-64; Assistant Research Biologist and Assistant Professor, Laboratory of Radiobiology, University of California Medical Centre, San Francisco, USA, 1964-66; Research Scientist, Biology and Health Physics Division, Chalk River Nuclear Laboratory, Ontario, Canada, 1967-68; Assistant Professor, 1968-72, Associate Professor, 1972-77, Professor, 1977-83, Department of Anatomy, McGill University, Montreal; Visiting Professor, University of Melbourne and Walter and Elizabeth Hall Institute of Medical Research, 1977-78; Professor and Chairman, Department of Anatomy, 1983-93, Professor, Departments of Anatomy and Oncology, 1990-, University of Western Ontario, London, Ontario, Canada. Publications: Contributor of over 130 original research articles and 15 chapters in books related to Hematology, Immunology, Oncology and Reproductive Medicine. Honours: T Ahmed Medal in Ophthalmology. University of Calcutta, 1957; Fulbright Scholarship, 1962; Discoverer of new mode of Cancer Immunotherapy, 1987; JCB Grant Senior Scientist Award, Canadian Association of Anatomists, 1990. Memberships include: New York Academy of Sciences; American Association for the Advancement of Science; American Association of Cancer Research. Address: 1095 Prince George Road, London, Ontario N6H 4E2, Canada.

LAM Wah-Kit, b. 28 Dec 1947, Hong Kong. Doctor of Medicine. m. Sau-Chi Leung, 27 Mar 1974. Education: MBBS, University of Hong Kong; FHKAM (Med); MRCP (UK), FRCP (Lond); FRCP (Edin); FRACP; FCCP. Appointments: House Officer, 1972-73, Medical Officer, 1973-75; Lecturer, 1975-84, Senior Lecturer, Honorary Consultant Physician, 1984-89, Reader in Medicine, Chief of Respiratory Medicine, 1989-, University of Hong Kong. Publications: Co-author: Analysis of factors associated with bronchial hyperreactivity to methacholine in bronchiectasis, 1991; Incidence of ras oncogene activation in lung carcinomas in Hong Kong, 1992; Non-Respiratory TB, 1994. Honours: Anderson Memorial Medal in Medicine, Hong Kong, 1972; Commonwealth Medical Scholarship for overseas (UK) training in respiratory medicine, 1977-79. Memberships: Hong Kong Medical Association; Hong Kong College of Physicians; Hong Kong Thoracic Society; Royal Colleges of Physicians, London, Edinburgh and Australia; American College of Chest Physicians; British Thoracic Society; Asia-Pacific Society of Respirology. Hobbies: Music; Gardening; Travel. Address: Department of Medicine, University of Hong Kong, Queen Mary Hospital, Pokfulam Road, Hong Kong.

LAM Yin Yuk NG, b. 25 Sept 1954, Hong Kong. Educational Psychologist. m. Shui Yau Stanny Lam, 39 Sept 1980, 1 s, 1 d. Education: MEd, University of Birmingham, 1980; MSc, University of London, Institute of Education, 1983; Advanced Diploma in Educational Studies, University of Cambridge, Institute of Education, 1978. Appointments: Teacher, Hong Kong Association for the Mentally Handicapped, 1979; Supervisor, Wells Green Special Needs Centre, Solihull, UK, 1981; Educational Psychologist, Hong Kong Association for the Mentally Handicapped, 1983; Project Coordinator, Manchester Education Department, UK, 1985; Associate, New Choice Educational Services. Publications: The Effects of Various Seating Arrangements on a Group of ESN(M) Children with Behavioral Problems, 1982; Rows Versus Tables: An Example of the Use of Behavioral Ecology in Two Classes of 11 Year Old Children, 1981; Three Views of Motor Performance in ESN(M) Boys, 1984; Some Applications of the

Henderson Revision of the Test of Motor Impairment, 1987. Honours: Sir Robert Black Trust Fund Scholarship, 1977. Memberships: British Psychological Society, Division of Educational and Child Psychology. Hobbies: Music; Reading; Volunteering; Hiking. Address: 15 Shongum Road, Randolph, NJ 07869, USA.

LAMARCHE Jacques Bernard, b. 18 Feb 1936, Quebec, Canada. Neuropathologist. m. Nicola Guillemette, 10 June, 3 s. Education: BA, 1956, MD, 1961, Universite Laval, Quebec; Diplomate, American Board of Pathology in Anatomical and Neuropathology, USA. Appointments: Assistant Professor of Pathology and Neurology, Boston University, USA; Associate Professor, Professor of Pathology, Chair, Department of Pathology, Universite de Sherbrooke, Quebec. Publications include: Alzheimer's disease and senile dementia as Seen in Mongoloids, Co-author, 1966; Immunologic Mechanisms in Experimental Encephalomyelitis in Nonhuman Primates, Co-author, 1973; The Cardiomyopathy of Friedreich's Ataxia, Co-author, 1980; Necrosis as a Pronostic Criterion in Malignant Astrocytic Supratentorial Gliomas, Co-author, 1983; The Neuropathology of Typical Friedreich's Ataxia in Quebec, Co-author, 1984; Cardiac Iron Deposits in Friedreich's Ataxia, Co-author, 1993. Honours: Scholar, Medical Research Council of Canada, 1971-76. Hobby: Golf. Address: Department of Pathology, Universite de Sherbrooke, Sherbrooke, Quebec J1H 5N4, Canada.

LAMONT Colin Alasdair Robertson, b. 22 Nov 1934, Burnley, England, Medical Practitioner. m. Margaret Woods, 27 Mar 1967, 2 sons. EducationL: BA; MBChB, Edinburgh; MRCOG, 1966; FRCOG, 1979. Appointments: Captain, RMO, Coldstream Guards; Senior Consultant Gynaecologist, Wessex Regional Health Authority; Chairman, Regional Advisory Subcommittee Obstatrics and Gynaecology, 1987-90; Retired, 1992. Publications include: Granulosa Cell Tumours, 1973; Pregnancy Following Renal Transplantation, 1977; Pregnancy and Cyclosporin A, 1983. Honour: Distinction Award, 1986. Memberships: Royal College Obstetricians and Gynaecologists; General Council, University of Edinburgh; The Stevenson Society' CBHS. Hobbies: Equine Breeding; Carriage Driving. Address: The Old Parsonage, Stoughton, Chichester, West Sussex PO18 9JJ, England.

LAMPERI Silvano, b. 31 Oct 1922, Siena, Italy. Nephrologist. m. Maria Lamperi, 31 Jan 1954, 1 son, 1 daughter. Education: Specialist in Endocrinology and recognised Teacher in Clinical Medicine, Genoa University, 1966; Specialist in Nephrology, Turin University, 1974. Appointments: Chief, Medical and Nephrology Department, SPA Hospital, Genoa, 1965-75; Chief, Senior Chief, Nephrology Division, S Martin Hospital, Genoa, 1976-88; Professor, Nephrology School, Genoa University, 1988-89; Currently Consulting Physician. Publications: Eritropoietina, 1990; Co-author: Monocite-Macrophage Mediated Suppression of Erythropoiesis in Renal Anaemia, 1987; Interferon-gamma as In Vitro Enhancing Factor of Peritoneal MO Defective Bactericidial Activity During CAPD, 1988. Honours: Prize for Most Outstanding Scientific Abstract, 4th International Congress, International Society for Peritoneal Dialysis, Venice, 1987. Memberships: Società Italiana di Nefrologia; American Society for Artificial Internal Organs; European Renal Association; International Society of Haematology; The International Society for Peritoneal Dialysis. Hobby: Reading mystery books. Address: Viale Francesco Causa 2-5, Genova CAP 16145, Italy.

LAMPERT Fritz Heinrich, b. 4 May 1933, Frankfurt, Germany. Pediatrician. m. Felicitas Pleitgen, 10 Mar 1961, 2 s, 2 d. Education: MD. Appointments: Chief of Division, Pediatric Hematology, University of Munich, Germany; Currently, Chief, Department of Pediatrics, Haematology and Oncology, University of Giessen, Germany. Publications: Over 300 articles in scientific journals; Over 30 book chapters; 6 Books concerning pediatrics, cancer, blood and chromosomes. Honours: Czerny Prize, 1968; Thiersch Prize, 1968; Certificate of Merit, AMA, 1969. Hobbies: Gardening; Golf; History. Address: Liebigstrasse 48, D-35392 Giessen, Germany.

LAMPERT Lawrence D, b. 10 Feb 1952, Philadelphia, Pennsylvania, USA. Developmental Optometrist. m. Lynn Rosen, 15 Aug 1982, 1 s, 1 d. Education: OD. Pennsylvania College of Optometry; Fellow, College of Optometrists in Vision Devlopment. Appointments: Private Practice and Consultations. Memberships: PBOS; FOA; AOA; FCOUD; OEP; NORA. Hobby: Swimming. Address: 7035 Beracasa Way, Boca Raton, FL 33433, USA.

LAMPKIN Beatrice Campbell, b. 16 Jan 1934, Tuscaloosa, AL, USA. Pediatrician. Education: BS, University of AL, 1956; MD, Medical College of AL, 1960. Career includes: Attending Pediatrician and Hematologist/Oncologist, Children's Hospital, Cincinnati, 1968-; Attending Physician, University of Cincinnati Hospital, 1969-; Professor of Pediatrics, 1975-, Adjunct Professor of Microbiology and Molecular Genetics, 1986-, University of Cincinnati College of Medicine; Professor Emerita, Hematology, Oncology Division, Children's Hospital Medical Center, Cincinnati, 1991-. Publications include: Over 100 professional articles, 29 book chapters, numerous abstracts presented/published, 1974-, and 48 presentations at medical meetings, 1974-. Honours include: Advanced Hematology Fellow, American Cancer Society, 1965-68; Leukemia Scholar, Leukemia Society of America, 1972-77; Outstanding Woman of Year in Medicine, National Board Citation from Medical College of PA, 1976; Jacob G Schmidlapp Professor of Pediatrics, Research Chair, University of Cincinnati School of Medicine, 1983; Pauline Cohen Award, Cancer Family Care, 1986; Founder's Award, Cincinnati Pediatric Society, 1991; Vice President, President Elect, American Society of Pediatric Hematology, Oncology, 1993-95. Memberships include: American Academy of Pediatrics; American Federation for Clinical Research; Phi Beta Kappa; Sigma Xi; Society for Pediatric Research. Address: Division of Hematology and Oncology, Children's Hospital Medical Center, 3333 Burnet Avenue, TCHRF 2367, Cincinnati, OH 45229-3039, USA.

LAMUNYON Guy Clark, b. 17 Mar 1947, Long Beach, California, USA. Nursing. m. Gitte Marwell Johansen, 10Jan 1976, 2 sons. Education: PhD, Religion; Additional Degrees in Business Management & Nursing. Appointments: Associate Faculty, Saddleback College, Mission Viejo, USA. Publications: Multiple articles in professional journals. Honours: Honorary Doctor of Divinity, 1989; Appreciation Award, International Association of Nurses in Substance Abuse, 1988. Memberships: International Association of Nurses in Substance Abuse; National Association of Alcholism & Drug Abuse Counselors. Hobbies: Surfing; Skiing; Reading; Yoga; Meditation. Address: 22332 Torino, Laguna Hills, CA 92653, USA.

LAN Guanghua, b. 9 Sep 1959, Jiangxi, China. Doctor. m. Wu Jing, 20 Oct 1986, 1 d. Education: BM, 1984, MD, 1990, Suzhou Medical College. Appointments: Intern, 1983, Resident and Teaching Assistant, 1985, Attending Doctor and Lecturer, 1992, Attending Doctor of psychiatry and Lecturer, Suzhou Medical College. Publications: A Study of the Coherence of the Intelligence in Twins, 1992; A Study on the Relationship of Type A Behaviour Pattern and Diabetes, 1994. Memberships: Chinese Medical Association. Hobbies: Running; Swimming; Badminton. Address: 96 Shizi Street, Suzhou, Jiangsu 215006, China.

LAN Jingquan, b. 6 Dec 1940, Beijing, China. Neurophysiology. m. Xianglan Ma, 10 Aug 1970, 1 son, 1 daughter. Education: BA, Beijing University, 1966. Appointments: Professor of Neurophysiology & Neuropathology. Publications: Effect of acceleration and acute hypoxia on ultrastructure of Cortex in rats and preventive efficacy of Ginsenosides, 1987; Induction of heat shock protein in cingulate and retrosplanial cortex by anti-ischemic agents, 1993. Memberships: Chinese Physiological Association; Society of Electron Microscopy of China; Society for Neuroscience of Beijing; Chinese Spacescience Association; Society for Space-flight of China. Address: Institute of Space Medico-Engineering, PO Box 5104 (23), Beijing 100094, China.

LAN Mingyang, b. 3 Mar 1937, Jinyun, Zhejiang, China. Parasitology. m. He Dachun, 30 Dec 1963, 1 son. Education: BA, Suzhou Medical College, 1959. Appointments: Head, Department of Parasitology, Suzhou Medical College; Deputy Director, Parasitology Association, Jiangsu Branch of the Chinese Zoological Society; Director, Jiangsu Branch of the Chinese Zoological Society. Publications: Preventing and Cure for Epidemic Hemorrhagic Fever, 1977, 1993; Culturing and Application of Mosquito Cells, 1991; Worm-Bovine Infection Diseases, 1989; Culturing of Medical Parasite in Vitro, 1994; More than 60 articles. Honours: 7 Awards for Science & Technology Achievement of Jiangsu and Public Health Ministry. Membership: Chinese Insectological Association. Hobby: Photography. Address: 402-West-3, 1 Block, Residence of Suzhou Medical College, Suzhou, Jiangsu 215006, China.

LANDALE John Barry, b. 23 Feb 1940. Education: MD, PhD, Sri Lanka; Diploma of Acupuncture, Hong Kong. Appointments: Consultant Acupuncturist, Morningside Acupuncture Clinic, Hebden Bridge,

England. Memberships: International Acupuncture Society, Hong Kong; Medicina Internativa, Sri Lanka; British Acupuncture Association and Register; Society Internationale d'Acupuncture, France. Address: Morningside, Off Savile Road, Hebden Bridge, West Yorkshire HX7 6ND, England.

LANDIS Suzanne Elizabeth, b. 22 Sep 1952, Lancaster, Pennsylvania, USA. Physician. m. William R McKenna, 22 Sep 1979, 1 son, 2 daughters. Education: MD, University of Pennsylvania School of Medicine, 1978; MPH, University of North Carolina School of Public Health, 1986. Appointments: Robert Wood Johnson Clinical Scholar, UNC-CH; Director, Division of Family Medicine. Publications: Results of Randomized Clinical trial of Partner Motification in Cases of HIV Infection in NC, 1992; Focus Groups and Community Mobilization, 1992. Honours: Delta Omega, 1990; Robert C Ney Award, 1981; Tribute to Women in Industry, 1994. Memberships: STFM; AAFP; BCMS; NCMS. Hobbies: Squash; Swimming; Reading; Biking; Sewing; Knitting. Address: 118 Weaver Boulevard, Asheville, NC 28804, USA.

LANG David Michael, b. 21 Nov 1954, Detroit, MI, USA. Medical Doctor. m. Marjory Entus, 28 Oct 1984, 1 s, 1 d. Education: BS, 1976, MD, 1980, University of MI. Career includes: Speaker in field at many meetings, 1984-94; Director, Allergy and Immunology, Co-Director, Hahnemann Allergy and Asthma Center, Hahnemann University, Philadelphia, PA, 1991-; Member of many committees; Assistant Professor of Medicine, Hahnemann University, Philadelphia, 1991-. Publications include: Co-author, Elevated risk for anaphylactoid reaction from radiographic contrast media is associated with both beta blocker exposure and cardiovascular disorders, in Arch Internal Medicine, 1993; Co-author, Gender risk for anaphylactoid reaction from radiographic contrast media, JACI, in press; Co-author, Patterns of asthma mortality in Philadelphia, 1969-1991, in New England Journal of Medicine, in press. Honours include: Fellow, American College of Allergy and Immunology, 1988; Fellow, American College of Physicians, 1989; Fellow, American Academy of Allergy and Immunology, 1991; New Clinical Investigator Award, Henry Ford Hospital, 1989; Pharmacia Allergy Research Foundation Award, International Congress of Allergy and Clinical Immunology, Stockholm, Sweden, 1994. Memberships include: PA Allergy Association; Philadelphia Allergy Society; American Federation for Clinical Research. Address: Hahnemann Univerity Hospital, Broad and Vine Street, MS 107, Philadelphia, PA 19102-1192, USA.

LANG Matti Alarik, b. 1 Apr 1947, Jämsänkoski, Finland. Professor of Toxicology. m. Eija Suomi, 15 Aug 1970, 2 s. Education: PhD. Appointments: Junior Lecturer, University of Kuopio, 1974-76; Research Scientist, Finnish Academy of Science, 1977-78; Visiting Scientist, NIH, USA, 1979-81; Scientific Director, E F Lab Company, Helsinki; Dean, Faculty of Pharmacy, University of Kuopio, 1989-91; Professor of Toxicology, 1984-; Scientist, Staff Member, WHO/SARC, Lyon, France, 1990-; Head, Molecular Toxicology Programme, 1995-. Publications: Contributor of over 100 articles in peer reviewed journals. Memberships: Finnish Society of Toxicology, Chairman, 1986-88; Board. Society of Finnish University Professors. Hobbies: Sport; Music. Address: 150 Cours Albert Thomas, 69342 Lyon, Cedex 08, France.

LANG Zhi Jin, b. 11 July 1932, Peking, China. Doctor. m. Wang Guang Yong, 21 Jan 1961, 2 d. Education: Graduate, Dalian Medical College. Appointments: Resident, 1954, Doctor in Charge and Lecturer, 1962, Associate Professor, 1981, Professor, 1986, Director of Research Institute of Medical Imaging, Dalian Medical University. Publications: Roentgen Diagnosis Diseases of Mediastinum, 1990; Practical Neurology of Children, 1988; CT Diagnosis of Cranial Trauma, 1986; Pathological Studies of CT Findings in Astrocytoma, 1991. Honours: Scientific Progressive Award, Kirin Province, 1987; Scientific Progressive Award, Liaoning Province, 1991. Memberships: Chinese Medical Association; Chinese Association of Medical Imaging Technology; Standing Committee, Chinese Radiological Association. Hobbies: Music; Singing. Address: Department of Radiology, First Affiliated Hospital of Dalian Medical University, Dalian 116011, China.

LANGLEY Ricky Lee, b. 31 Aug 1957, Fountain, North Carolina, USA. Medical Doctor. m. Sandra Ward, 7 June 1980, 2 sons, 1 daughter. Education: BS magna cum laude, North Carolina State University; MD, Wake Forest University; MPH, University of North Carolina, Chapel Hill. Appointments: Assistant Professor, East Carolina University School of Medicine; Assistant Clinical Professor, Duke University. Publications: 27 published manuscripts. Honours: Fellow,

American College of Physicians; Fellow, American College of Preventive Medicine; Fellow, American College of Occupational and Environmental Medicine. Memberships: American Medical Association; American Biological Safety Association. Hobbies: Astronomy; Archaeology. Address: 1506 Miles Chapel Road, Mcbone, NC 28302, USA.

LANSKA Douglas John, b. 6 Aug 1959, Milwaukee, WI, USA. Physician. m. Dr Mary Jo Lanska, 26 June 1982, 2 s. Education: BS, University of Wisconsin, Milwaukee, 1980; MS, 1984, MD, 1984, Medical College of Wisconsin, Milwaukee; Diplomate, National Board of Medical examiners, 1985; Diplomate in Neurology, American Board of Psychiatry and Neurology, 1989. Appointments include: Intern, 1984-85, Neurology Resident, 1985-88, Fellow, Geriatric Neurology and Dementia, 1988-89, Instructor, Department of Neurology, 1988-89; Case Western Reserve University School of Medicine; Assistant Professor, Departments of Neurology, and Preventive Medicine and Environmental Health, University of Kentucky Medical Centre, Lexington, Kentucky, 1989-93; Associate Professor of Neurology, Preventive Medicine and Environmental Health. Publications: Contributor of over 150 professional articles including: Decline in Autopsies for Deaths Attributed to Cerebrovascular Disease; Development of Cerebrovascular Disease Practice Guidelines and Review Criteria: Inter play of Government and Physician Organizations. Honours include: Phi Eta Sigma; Sigma Epsilon Sigma, 1978; Phi Beta Kappa, 1980; Alpha Omega Alpha, 1984; National Research Service Award, National Institutes on Aging, 1989-90; College of Medicine Faculty Research Award, University of Kentucky, 1993. Memberships include: American Academy of Neurology; American Heart Association; American Neurological Association. Hobbies: Hiking; Bicycling; Swimming; Scuba Diving; Sailing; Mathematics. Address: Department of Neurology (MS-129), 800 Rose Street, Lexington, KY 40536-0084, USA.

LANTHONY Philippe Lucien Jacques, b. 8 Dec 1929, Chamalieres, France. Ophthalmologist. m. Duska Radovanovic, 15 Feb 1958. Appointments: Medical Resident, Quinze-Vingts Hospital; Color Vision Laboratory, Quinze-Vingts Hospital, Paris; Chief Ophthalmologist, Troyes Hospital, France. Publications: Co-author, Les Nystagmus, French Society of Ophthalmology, 1973; Co-author, Pathologie du Sens Chromatique, Society of Ophthalmology of Paris, 1975; Dictionnaire du Strabisme, 1983. Memberships: French Society of Ophthalmology; Society of Ophthalmology of Paris; International Research Group on Colour Vision Deficiencies. Hobbies: Study of Art; Novel Writing. Address: 19 Bd 14 Juillet, 10000 Troyes, France.

LAPIERRE Yvon D, Psychiatrist. Education: Graduated in Medicine, University of Ottawa, 1961; Special training in internal medicine and psychiatry; Qualified as Psychiatrist, University of Montreal and at Royal College of Physicians and Surgeons, 1969; Postgraduate Degree in Pharmacology, University of Montreal. Career: After his internship practised general medicine with Canadian Armed Forces for 3 years; In 1970 became Scientific Director at Pierre-Janet Hospital, Hull, Quebec and joined Faculty of Medicine, University of Ottawa; Director of Psycho-Pharmacology, Ottawa General Hospital in 1976; Director of Research, Royal Ottawa Hospital in 1979; Professor and Chairman of Department of Psychiatry, University of Ottawa and Psychiatrist in Chief, Royal Ottawa Hospital, 1986-; Director General, Institute for Mental Health Research. Publications: Author or Co-author of over 200 scientific publications, including over 140 original papers, 20 book chapters and monographs plus a number of educational papers and aids. Honour: Medal of Honour, Canadian College of Neuropsychopharmacology, 1988. Membership: Founding President, Canadian College of Neuropsychopharmacology. Address: 1145 Carling, Ottawa, Ontario, Canada, K1Z 7K4.

LAPIN Boris Arkadievich, b. 10 Aug 1921, Kharkov, Ukraine. m. Professor L A Yakoleva, 20 Dec 1969, 1 son, 1 daughter. Education: Diploma, 2nd Moscow Medical Institute. Appointments: Scientist, Head of Department of Pathology, Deputy Scientific Director, Scientific Director, 1992, IEPT AMSc, Sukhumi; Scientific Director, IMP RAMS, Sochi-Adler. Publications: Monkey Diseases as a Model of Human Diseases, 1959; Comparative Pathology on Primates, Co-author, 1962; Fergleichende Patologie der Affen, 1964; Hemoblastoses in Primates, Co-author, 1979; Role of Viruses in Neoplasms of Hemopeietic System, 1995. Honours: President, International Association Comparative Leukaemia Research and related Diseases; Timakov's Academy of Medical Sciences Prize in Virology, 1984; Korolev's Medal for Space Research, 1981; Gagarin's Medal for Space Research, 1981. Memberships: Chairman, Primate Commission under Presidium of

RAMS, 1965-; Member of several journal editorial boards. Hobbies: Collecting minerals and rosaries. Address: IMP RAMS, Veseloye 1, 354597 Sochi-Adler, Russia.

LAPIS Karoly, b. 14 Apr 1926, Turkeve, Hungary. Pathologist. m. Ibolya Keresztes, 30 Apr 1955, 1 son, 1 daughter. Education: MD; PhD; DSc; Member, Hungarian Academy of Sciences. Appointments: Scientific Research Worker, Institute of Pathology, Debrecen Medical University, 1951-54; Scientific Research Worker, Senior Member, Onco-Pathological Research Institute, Budapest, 1959-63; Professor, Chairman, Department of Pathology, Postgraduate Medical School, 1963-68; · Professor, Director, First Institute of Pathology and Experimental Cancer Research, Semmelweis University of Medicine, Budapest, 1968-93. Publications: The Liver, vol 8 of atlas series Electron Microscopy in Human Medicine, 1979; Regulation and Control of Cell Proliferation (with A Jeney), 1984; Pathologia (in Hungarian), 1989. Honours: Golden Degree, Order of Labour, Hungarian Government, 1978; Honorary Member, Russian Medical Academy; Honorary Member, Serbian Academy of Sciences and Arts. Memberships: Leading body, Hungarian Cancer Society; Pathology Committee, Hungarian Academy of Sciences. Hobbies: Tennis; Gardening. Address: First Institute of Pathology and Experimental Cancer Research, Semmelweis University of Medicine, Üllöi ut 26, H-1085 Budapest, Hungary.

LARAIA Barbara B, b. 3 December 1947, Boston, Massachusetts, USA. Counsellor. Education: BSc, State College at Salem, Massachusetts, USA, 1969; MC, Arizona State University, 1987. Appointments: Instructor, American Culture, John F Kennedy University, Orinda, California; Instructor, College of San Mateo, Intercultural Communication. Publications: A Tribute to the Littlest Mentors, 1990; Looking Back - The Worst and Best of Times, 1992; Audio Tape: The Ethics of Clinical Hypnosis, 1987. Honours: Ethics of Hypnosis Research paper presented at the 1986 Ericksonian Congress, Phoenix, Arizona, USA. Memberships: Mensa; Guide Dogs for the Blind; The Concord Coalition. Hobbies: Walking; Reading non-fiction; Writing; Local Politics. Address: 973 Clark Avenue, San Bruno, CA 94066, USA.

LARAKI Ali, b. 1 Nov 1948, Casablanca. Physician. m. Benchekroun Loubna, 26 Nov 1988, 2 s. Education: High Doctorate, 1978, Paediatrics Certificate, 1980, Strasbourg, France. Appointments: Hospital Paediatrician, Strasbourg, 1975; Taza, Morocco, 1981-; Private Paediatrician, 1984-. Publications: Contributor of articles in professional journals. Memberships: Societe Marocaine de Pediatrie; Amicale des Medecins de Mohammedia. Hobbies: Running; Cycling; Hiking. Address: 21 Av Far, Mohammedia, Morocco 20650, Africa.

LARKIN Catherine Ita, b. 10 Nov 1954, Galway, Ireland. Practitioner of Traditional Chinese Medicine. Education: MB BCh, University College, Galway, 1972-78; FRCR, John Radcliffe Hospital, Oxford, England, 1982-86. Appointments: Junior Medical Doctor, 1978-86. Publications: Edidermolysis Bullosc Acquisitc. Memberships: FRCR' British Acupuncture Society; Professional Registry of Traditional Chinese Medicine; RCHM. Hobbies: Sailing; Reading; Music. Address: 32 Upper Baggot Street, Dublin 4, Ireland.

LARZELERE Robert E, b. 3 Apr 1945, Greensburg, PA, USA. Research Psychologist. m. Rosalie Larzelere, 16 Dec 1972, 1 s, 1 d. Education: MS, Georgia Institute of Technology; PhD, Human Development and Family Studies, PA State University. Career: Associate Professor of Psychology, Rosemead School of Psychology, Biola University; Assistant Professor, Psychology, Western Conservative Baptist Seminary; Assistant Professor and Head of Psychology Department, Bryan College; Currently, Director, Residential Research, Father Flanagan's Boy's Home, Boys Town, NE. Publications include: Co-author, Single-sample tests for many correlations, in Psychological Bulletin, 1977; Co-author, Parental Management: Mediator of the effect of socioeconomic status on early delinquency, in Criminology, 1990; Co-author, The effectiveness of parental discipline for toddler misbehaviour at different levels of child distress, in Family Relations, 1994. Honour: NIMH Traineeship and Postdoctoral Research Fellowships, 1976-77, 1979-80. Memberships: American Psychological Association; Society for Research in Child Development; Association for the Advancement of Behaviour Therapy; National Council on Family Relations; American Professional Society on Abuse of Children. Hobbies: Sport; Camping. Address: Father Flanagan's Boy's Home, Boys Town, NE 68010, USA.

LAST John Murray, b. 22 Sept 1926, Tailem Bend, Australia. m. Janet Margaret Wendelken, 14 Feb 1957, 2 s, 1 d. Education: St Peter's College; University of Adelaide: MB; BS, 1949; MD, 1967; DPH, University of Sydney, 1960. Appointments: Hospital Residencies and Ship's Doctor, 1950-54; General Medical Practice, Australia, 1954-59; Visiting Fellow, Medical Research Council, London, England, 1961-62; Lecturer, University of Sydney, 1962-63; Assistant Professor, University of Vermont, 1964-65; Senior Lecturer, University of Edinburgh, 1965-69; Department Chairman, University of Ottawa, 1970-78; Secretary, School of Medicine, 1980-82; Visiting Professor, Mount Sinai School Medicine, New York, 1978-79; National University of Singapore and Chinese Academy of Medicial Sciences, Beijing, 1982; Emeritus Professor of Epidemiology, University of Ottawa, Canada, 1992-. Publications: Author, Public Health and Human Ecology, 1987; Editor-in-Chief, Maxcy-Rosenau Public Health and Preventive Medicine, 1980, 12th Edition, 1986, 13th Edition, 1991; Editor, A Dictionary of Epidemiology, 1983, 2nd Edition, 1987, 3rd Edition, 1995; Associate Editor, American Journal of Preventive Medicine, 1984-93; Scientific Editor, Canadian Journal of Public Health, 1981-91; Editor, Annals RCPSC, 1990-; Approximately 300 Scientific & Review Articles, Chapters in 40 Books. Honours: include, Recipient Tasmania Prize Royal Australian College General Practitioners, 1967; Distinguished Service Award, American College of Preventive Medicine, 1984; Special Recognition Award, ACPM, 1991; School of Medicine Award for Teaching Excellence, 1988; Scholar in residence, Rockefeller Foundation Villa Serbelloni, 1992; Wade Hampton Frost Lecturer, APHA, 1989; MD (honoris causa, Uppsala), 1993. Memberships: include, American College Epidemiology; American College Preventive Medicine, President 1987-89; Association of Teachers of Preventive Medicine, President, 1983-84; Canadian Public Health Association. Address: 685 Echo Drive, Ottawa, Ontario K1S 1P2, Canada.

LATRENTA Gregory S. Surgeon. Education: MD, New York Medical College, Valhalla, New York, USA; Reconstructive Plastic Surgery Training, New York University Medical Centre; Board Certified, Surgery and Plastic Surgery. Appointments: Reconstructive Surgeon, Americares-Armenian Earthquake Relief Effort, Yerevan, USSR, 1989; Attending Surgeon, Assistant Professor of Surgery, The New York Hospital-Cornell Medical College; Attending Surgeon, The Manhattan Eye, Ear and Throat Hospital. Publications: Aesthetic Plastic Surgery, Editor, 1993; Post-Mastectomy Breast Reconstruction; Contributor of over 50 scientific presentations and articles. Address: New York Hospital-Cornell Medical Centre, 5525 East 68th Street, New York, NY 10021, USA.

LATTO Douglas, b. 13 Dec 1913, Dundee, Scotland. Physician. 1 son, 3 daughters. Education: MBChB; DObst; RCOG; MRCOG; FRCOG. Appointments: Private Practice, Reading, England. Publications: Smoking and Lung Cancer: A Report to all Members of Parliament for the British Safety Council, 1969; Contributor of articles to professional journals. Honours: FRCOG; Queen's Jubilee Medal, 1977. Hobbies: Squash; Travel; Gardening; Philately. Address: Lethnot Lodge, 4 Derby Road, Caversham, Reading, Berkshire RG4 0EY, England.

LAU Chu-Pak, b. 4 Apr 1957, Hong Kong. Cardiologist. Education: MBBS, 1981; MD, 1989; FRCP(Edinburgh), 1992; FRCP, London, 1995; FACC, 1991. Appointments include: Chief of Cardiology Division, Queen Mary Hospital, University of Hong Kong; Publications include: Rate Adaptive Cardiac Pacing: Single and Dual Chamber, 1993 (Monograph); Rate Responsive Pacing, thesis, 1989; The Range of Sensors and Algorithms for Rate Adaptive Pacing, 1992; Sensors and Pacemaker Mediated Tachycardias, 1991; Rate Responsive Pacing: Clinical and Technical Aspects, 1991; Comparative Assessment of Exercise Performance of Six Different Rate Adaptive Right Ventricular Cardiac Pacemaker, 1989; Role of Left Ventricular Function and Doppler Derived Variables in Predicting the Hemodynamic Benefits of Rate Responsive Pacing, Co-author, 1988; Selective Vibration Sensing: A New Concept for Activity Sensing Rate Responsive Pacing, Co-author, 1988; A New Pacing Method for Rapid Regularization and Rate Control in Atrial Fibrillation, Co-author, 1990; A Randomized Double Being Study Comparing the Efficacy and Tolerability of Flecainide Versus Quinidine in the Control of Paroxysmal and Atrial Fibrillation, Co-author, 1992; Editor of Journal, Pacing and Clinical Electrophsiology and European Journal of Pacing and Clinical Electrophysiology; Editor-in-Chief, Journal of Hong Kong College of Cardiology. Honours include: Distinction in Medicine, 1981; Croucher Foundation Scholarship, 1986-88; Sir Patrick Mansion Gold Medal, 1989; KC Wong Foundation Travelling Scholarship, 1990. Address: Department of Medicine, University of Hong

Kong, Queen Mary Hospital, Hong Kong.

LAU David Che Wai, b. 18 Aug 1949, Hong Kong. Physician. m. Dr Marilyn J Mooibroek, 5 July 1986, 1 s. Education: BSc, 1971, MD, 1975, PhD, 1988, University of Toronto, Canada. Appointments: Associate Professor of Medicine and Head, Division of Endocrinology and Metabolism, University of Ottawa. Publications: Contributor of numerous articles including: Regional Differences in the Replication Rate of Cultured Rat Microvascular Endothelium from retroperitoneal and Epididymal Fat Pads, Co-author, 1987; Release of Mitogenic Factors by Cultured Preadipocytes from Massively Obese Subjects, Co-author, 1987; Induction of Preadipocyte Differentiation by Mature Fat cells in the Rat, Co-author, 1989; Influence of Paracrine factors on Preadipocyte Replication and Differentiation, Co-author, 1990; Paradoxically Slow Preadipocyte Replication and Differentiation in Corpulant Rats, Co-author, 1990; Extracellular Matrix Components Secreted by Microvascular Endothelial Cells Stimulate Preadipocyte Differentiation In Vitro, Co-author, 1994; The Regulation of New Fat Cell Formation in Rats: The Role of Dietary Fats, Co-author, 1994. Honour: MRC Scholar, 1985-90. Memberships: American College of Physicians; American Diabetes Association; Endocrine Society; Royal College of Physicians and Surgeons of Canada; North American Association for the Study of Obesity. Hobbies: Jogging; Tennis; Skiing. Address: Division of Endocrinology and Metabolism, Ottawa Civic Hospital, 1053 Carling Avenue, Ottawa, Ontario K1Y 4E9, Canada.

LAU Yun Wah Paul, b. 13 Nov 1960, Hong Kong. Orthodontist. Education: BDS, MDS, Hong Kong; M Orth RCS (Edinburgh); DOrth RCS (Edinburgh); MRCD (Canada). Appointments: Junior Hospital Dental Officer; Part-time Lecturer; Dental Officer; Honorary Clinical Lecturer. Publications: Contributor of articles in professional journals. Memberships: Hong Kong Dental Association; Hong Kong University Dental Alumni Association; Hong Kong Society of Orthodontists; European Orthodontic Society. Address: 26C, Block 18, Chi Fu Fa Yuen, Pokfulam, Hong Kong.

LAUB Dori, b. 6 Aug 1937, Cernauti, Romania. Psychiatrist. 1 s, 1 d. Education: MD, Hebrew University, Hadassah Medical School, Jerusalem, Israel, 1961; MA, Clinical Psychology, Bar Ilan University, Ramat Gan, Israel, 1966. Career includes: Assistant Professor, 1970-77, Associate Professor, 1977-, Department of Psychiatry, Yale University; Part-time Private Practice, 1972-; Senior Attending Physician, CT Mental Health Center, 1993-; Attending Psychiatrist, Homeless Outreach Team, Access Project, 1993-; Co-Visiting Lecturer, Yale Law School, 1994. Publications include: Holocaust Survivors - Adaptation to Trauma, in Patterns of Prejudice, 1979; Failed Empathy - A Central Theme in the Survivor's Holocaust Experience, in Psychoanalytic Psychology, 1989; Truth and Testimony - The Process and The Struggle, in American Imago, 1991; Co-author, Knowing and Not Knowing - Forms of Traumatic Memory, in International Journal of Psychoanalytic Psychology, 1993. Honours: Sigmund Freud Prize for MD Thesis, 1962; Fellow, American Psychiatric Association, 1985. Memberships: American Psychiatric Association; American Association of Directors of Residency Training; International Psychoanalytic Association; Society for Traumatic Stress Studies; AMA. Hobbies include: Boating; Travel; Classical Music. Address: 340 Whitney Avenue, New Haven, CT 06511, USA.

LAUTER Carl, b. 30 Dec 1939, Detroit, MI, USA. Physician. m. Jain Beth Mogill, 21 Dec 1975, 1 s, 2 d. Education: BA, Chemistry, 1962; MD, 1965. Career: Program Director, Internal Medicine, Grace Hospital, 1973-77; Chief of Infectious Diseases, Harper Hospital, 1977-79; Chief of Medical Services, 1982-92, Director, Division of Allergy and Immunology, William Beaumont Hospital, Royal Oak, MI, and, Associate Clinical Professor of Medicine, Wayne State University, Detroit, MI. Publications: 18 Peer reviewed articles, 17 review articles, 7 case reports, 18 published abstracts, several book chapters including: Unexplained Opportunistic Infections and CD4-T Lymphopenia, in New England Journal of Medicine. Honours: Phi Beta Kappa; Alpha Omega Alpha; Teacher of Year Award, Staff Award, Wayne State University Medical School, 1976, 1978; Teacher of Year, Harper Hospital, 1977; Roche Research Award, 1988. Memberships: Fellow, Infectious Diseases Society; Fellow, American College of Physicians; Fellow, American Academy of Allergy and Immunology; Fellow, Clinical Pharmacology. Hobbies: Reading; Films; History. Address: 3601 West 13 Mile Road, Royal Oak, MI 48073, USA.

LAVALLEE Yvon-Jacques, b. 7 May 1945, Quebec, Canada. Psychiatrist. m. Diane Mercure, 14 Aug 1971, 2 sons. Education: MD, Université de Montréal, 1970; Certificat de Spécialiste, Quebec Province, 1974. Appointments: Currently Chairman, Department of Psychiatry, Faculty of Medicine, Université de Sherbrooke. Publications: La thérapie comportementale, in Psychiatrie clinique: Approche bio-psycho-sociale (Lalonde and Grundberg), 1988. Hobbies: Do-it-yourself; Antiques. Address: Université de Sherbrooke, Faculty of Medicine, 3001 12th Avenue N, Sherbrooke, Quebec, Canada J1H 5N4.

LAVIN Thomas Anthony, b. 16 Mar 1949, Garswood, Lancashire. Obstetrician; Gynaecologist. m. Diana Lowe, 23 Jun 1973, 2 s, 1 d. Education: MB, University of Bristol; ChB, University of Bristol; MBA, University of Northumbria; FRCOG; MFFP. Appointments: Lecturer, Obstetrics & Gynaecology, University of Leeds, 1979-82; Consultant/Clinical Director. Address: 6 Rothley Hall, Rothley, Morpeth, Northumberland, NE61 4JX.

LAVIS John Norman, b. 11 June 1965, Montreal, Canada. Physician. Education: BA, MD, Queen's University, Canada, 1989; MSc, London School of Economics, England, 1992. Appointments: Consecutive: General Practitioner; Visiting Research Fellow, London School of Hygiene & Tropical Medicine; Temporary Advisor, World Health Organisation; Research Fellow, Institute for Clinical Evaluative Sciences, Ontario; Research Fellow, Centre for Health Economics & Policy Analysis, McMaster University. Publications: Co-author, The costs of HIV prevention strategies in developing countries, 1993. Memberships: Canadian Medical Association; Canadian Public Health Association; Canadian Society for International Health; College of Physicians & Surgeons of Ontario. Hobbies: Squash. Address: Centre for Health Economics & Policy Analysis, Health Sciences Centre, McMaster University, Hamilton, Ontario, L8N 3Z5, Canada.

LAW David, b. 24 July 1927, Milwaukee, Wisconsin, USA. Physician; Administrator. m. Patricia Thornton, 14 Sept 1949, 5 children. Education: BA, Cornell University; MD, Cornell University Medical College. Appointments: Assistant Professor of Medicine, Associate Professor of Medicine, Chief of Gastroenterology, Vanderbilt University Medical College, 1960-70; Professor of Medicine, University of Mexico School of Medicine, and Chief of Medical Service, Veterans Administration Medical Center, 1970-85; Professor of Medicine, George Washington Medical School, Washington DC, and Associate Deputy Chief Medical Director, Department of Veterans Affairs, 1985-. Publications: Over 100 articles chapters and books, in internal medicine, gastroenterology, nutrition, ethics; International and national presentations. Honours: Alpha Omega Alpha, 1954. Memberships: American College of Physicians, Governor 1986-; Western Association of Physicians; Western Society for Clinical Investigation; American Federation of Clinical Research; American Gastroenterology Association; American Institute of Nutrition; American Society of Clinical Nutrition. Hobbies: Hot air ballooning; Fishing; Gourmet dining. Address: VACO (11), 810 Vermont NW, Washington, DC 20420, USA.

LAWLER Mary K, b. 24 Jul 1942, Washington, DC, USA. Researcher; Educator. m. James J Lawler Jr, 7 Aug 1971, 1 s, 3 d. Education: RN; PhD. Career: Instructor of Nursing, 1982-83; Assistant Professor of Nursing, 1983-84; Graduate Teaching Associate, 1985-87; Visiting Assistant Professor, 1987-89; Graduate Research Assistant, 1989; Assistant Professor, 1989-94; Adjunct Clinical Associate Professor, 1990; Director, 1991-94; Assistant Professor, Department of Family Medicine, University of OK, 1994-. Publications include: Articles published in Maternal Child Nursing, 1972, 1977, 1990, OK Home Economics Association Newsletter, 1989, Family Systems Medicine, 1992. Honours: Phoenix Award, 1987; Outstanding Doctoral Student, 1987; Doctoral Research Fellowship, Omicron Nu, 1987-88; Favorite Teacher, OSU, 1987-88. Memberships: Sigma Theta Tau; Phi Kappa Phi; Kappa Omicron Nu; NAPCRG; STFM; AAPP; AAMFT; NCFR; OCFR; Board of Directors, OK American Diabetes Association. Hobby: Family. Address: Oklahoma University Health Sciences Center, Department of Family Medicine, 900 NE 10th, Oklahoma City, OK 73104, USA.

LAWRENCE H Sherwood, b. 22 Sept 1916, New York City, New York, USA. Physician; Immunologist. m. Dorothea Wetherbee, 13 Nov 1943, 2 sons, 1 daughter. Education: AB, 1938, MD, 1943, New York University; FACP; Diplomate, American Board of Internal Medicine. Appointments: Instructor, 1947-52, Assistant Professor, 1952-55, Associate Professor, 1955-61, Head, Infectious Disease and

Immunology Division, 1959-, Professor, 1961-79, Co-Director, NYU-Bellevue Medical Services, 1964-, Director, Cancer Center, 1974-79, Jeffrey Bergstein Professor of Medicine, 1979-, Director, Center for AIDS Research, 1989-, New York University School of Medicine; Visiting Physician, Tisch Hospital, Bellevue Hospital, 1964-; Consultant, Manhattan Veterans Administration Hospital, 1964-; Harvey Society Lecturer, 1974. Publications: Editor: Medical Clinics of North American, 1957; Cellular and Humoral Aspects of Hypersensitive States, 1959; Mediators of Cellular Immunity, 1969; Immunobiology of Transfer Factor (co-editor), 1983. Honours include: Alpha Omega Alpha Prize, 1943; Von Pirquet Gold Medal, American Forum on Allergy, 1972; Distinguished Achievement Award, American College of Physicians, 1973; Science Medal, New York Academy of Medicine, 1974; Science Achievement Award, American College of Allergists, 1974; Bristol Science Award, Infectious Diseases Society of America, 1974; Lila Gruber Honour Award, American Academy of Dermatology, 1975; Charles V Chapin Medal, 1975; Honorary Fellow: American Academy of Allergy; Royal College of Physicians and Surgeons, Glasgow. Memberships: National Academy of Science; Association of American Physicians; American Association of Immunologists; Infectious Disease Society; Royal College of Physicians and Surgeons, Glasgow. Hobbies: Landscape painting; Mediaeval English history. Address: New York University Medical Center, 550 First Avenue, New York, NY 10016, USA.

LAWRENCE Ruth Edna Anderson, b. 15 Aug 1924, New York City, USA. Paediatrician. m. Dr Robert Marshall Lawrence, 4 July 1950, 5s, 4d. Education: S, Highest Honours, Antioch College, 1945; MD, University of Rochester School of Medicine, 1949. Appointments: Faculty, University of Rochester School of Medicine, 1960-; Director, Finger Lakes Regional Poison Centre, 1958-; Chief of Paediatrics, Highland Hospital, 1960-91; Professor of Paediatrics and Obstetrics/Gynaecology. Publications: Breastfeeding: A Guide for the Medical Profession, 1980, 1985, 1989, 1994; Contributor of numerous professional articles and book chapters. Honours: Alpha Omega Alpha, 1949; Fellow, American Paediatric Society; Fellow, American Academy of Clinical Toxicology; Fellow, American Academy of Paediatrics. Memberships: International Research Society on Human Lactation; American Association Poison Centres; American Women's Medical Society; Academy of Brestfeeding Medicine Board of Trustees. Address: University of Rochester School of Medicine Box 777, 601 Elmwood Avenue, Rochester, NY 14625, USA.

LAWSON Wilfrid Alan, b. 29 Mar 1925, Whitley Bay, England. Dentist. m. Olwen Ann Davies, 2 Oct 1965, 2 daughters. Education: LDS, BDS, University of Birmingham; LDS EDS, Royal College of Surgeons of England; MS, Univesity of Michigan, USA. Appointments: Senior Registrar, Eastman Dental Hospital, London; Lecturer, University of London; Professor of Prosthetic Dentistry, Trinity College, Dublin, Ireland, University College, Dublin and Royal College of Surgeons in Ireland; Professor Emeritus, University College, Dublin; Fellow Emeritus, Trinity College, Dublin. ublications: Contributor of numerous articles on prosthetic dentistry in professional journals. Honours: FEDRCS(Ire), 1965; MA, University of Dublin, 1968; Fellowship of Trinity College, Dublin, 1974. Memberships: Irish Dental Association; British Society for the Study of Prosthetic Dentistry, President, 1972-73; European Prosthodontic Society, Founder Member. Hobbies: Golf; Breeding Horses. Address: Cloncallow, Newcastle, Co Wicklow, Ireland.

LE SOLLEU Gillian Heather, b. 10 May 1960, Colchester, Essex, England. Registered General Nurse. m. Laurent Le Solleu, 8 Sept 1990, 1 s. Education: State registered Nurse Training, St Mary's Hospital, London, 1978-81; Diploma of Osteopathy, European School of Osteopathy, Kent, 1986-90. Appointments: Staff Nurse, St Mary's Hospital, London, 1981-82; Staff Nurse, USAF Lakenheath, Suffolk, 1984-86; Self-employed Osteopath, 1990-. Memberships: United Kingdom COuncil for Nursing, Midwifery and Health Visiting; European Society of Osteopaths; General Council and register of Osteopaths. Hobbies: Horse riding; Gardening; swimming; Badminton; Playing with my children. Address: 13 bd Stalingrad, 24000 Perigueux, France.

LE SOULLEU, Laurent, b. 6 May 1961, Versailles, France. Osteopath. m. Gillian Heather Whybrow, 8 Sept 1990, 1 s. Education: Baccalaureat Construction Mecanique; Diploma in Osteopathy. Appointments: Osteopath in Private Practice. Publications: Thesis: Vestibulocochlear Dysfunction, 1987. Memberships: General Council and Register of Osteopaths; AFDO. Hobby: Car restoration. Address: 20 Cours Montaigne, 24000 Perigueux, France.

LEACH Robert Ellis, b. 25 Nov 1931, Sanford, Maine, USA. Physician; Editor. m. Laurine Seber, 21 Aug 1955, 3 s, 3 d. Education: AB, Princeton University; MD, Columbia University; MS, University of Minnesota. Appointments: Lt Cdm, Ward Medical officer, US Navy, 1962-64; Chairman, Department of Orthopaedics, Lahey Clinic, 1967-70; Chairman, Professor, Boston University Medical School Department of Orthopaedics, 1970-93; Chairman, Department of Orthopaedics, Boston City Hospital, 1974-78; Editor, American Journal of Sports Medicine, 1990-; Professor of Orthopaedics, Boston University Medical School. Publications: Author or Editor of 5 medical books; Contributor of numerous articles. Honours: Certificate of Merit, US Navy, 1964; ABC Travelling Fellow, 1971; Sports Medicine Man of Year, 1988; Honorary Member, German Orthopaedic Trauma Society, 1992 and Hellenic Orthopaedic Association, 1993. Memberships: President, 1993-94, American Orthopaedic Association; President, 1983-84, American Orthopaedic Society Sports Medicine; American Academy of Orthopaedic Surgeons; Boston Orthopaedic Club, President, 1979-81. Hobbies: tennis; Yacht racing. Address: American Journal of Sports Medicine, 230 Calvary Street, Waltham, MA 02154, USA.

LEBEDEV Lev Valerjevich, b. 12 Dec 1923, Pskov, Russia. Surgeon. m. Lebedeva Svetlana, 17 Dec 1968, 3 sons, 1 daughter. Education: Russian Military Medical Academy, 1951. Appointments: Assistant, Docent, Professor, Russian Military Medical Academy; Head Surgoen, Soviet Army in Poland; Chief of Faculty Surgery Clinic, 1st Pavlov Medical Institute, St Petersburg. Publications: Prostheses of Blood Vessels, 1975, 1981, 1994; The Technique of Surgery of Injured and Diseased Blood Vessels, 1978; Surgery of Atherosclerosis and its Complications, 1982; The Surgical Treatment of Obesity and Hyperlipoproteidemia, 1987. Honours: 3 State Orders, 1945, 1957, 1985; State Prize Winner, 1975, 1982. Memberships: Association of Russian Surgeons; Association of Russian Cardiovascular Surgeons; Chairman, Cardiovascular Surgery & Anoiology of Piroor Sugrical Society. Hobbies: Memoirs; History; Skiing. Address: Pr Veteranov, 67-2-28, St Petersburg 198255, Russia.

LEBKOWSKA Urszula Maria, b. 9 Mar 1952, Olsztyn, Poland. Radiologist. m. Wojciech Lebkowski, 30 June 1979, 1 son, 1 daughter. Education: MD; PhD; Board Certified in Ultrasound; Medical Academy, Bialystok, 1978. Appointments: Assistant, Department of Internal Diseases, Hospital for Infectious Diseases; Assistant Lecturer. Publications: The Ultrasound Diagnosis of Lumbar Disc Prolapse, Co-author, 1994. Honour: Scientific Award for Thesis, 1994. Memberships: Polish Society of Ultrasound; European Federation of Societies for Ultrasound in Medicine and Biology. Hobbies: Classical music; Gardening. Address: Bat Chlopskich 10/6, 15-661 Bialystok, Poland.

LEBOWITZ Michael David, b. 21 Dec 1939, Brooklyn, New York, USA. Epidemiologist. m. Joyce M Schmidt, 1960, 1 son, 2 daughters. Education: AB; MA; PhC; PhD. Appointments: Research Associate, University of Washington, department Preventive Medicine and Environmental Health; Assistant and Associate Professor, Professor of Medicine, Pulmonary Section, Department of Medicine, University of Arizona College of Medicine. Honours: University of California Honours Entrance, 1957; California State Scholarship, 1957-60; NIH Research Training Award, 1963-66; Fogarty Senior International Fellow, 1978-79; Honorary Colleague, Polish Society of Hygiene, 1986; Arizona Clean Air Health Award, 1987; Honorary Member, Hungarian Society of Medicine, 1989-. Memberships include: Fellow, American College of Epidemiology; International Academy of Indoor Air Sciences; Italian National Research Council International fellow, 1993; Society for Epidemiologica Research; American Thoracic Society; INternational Epidemiology Society; Fellow, American College of Chest Physicians; American Heart Association; International Society of Exposure Analysis; US-Mexico Border Health Association. Hobby: Outdoor Activities. Address: University of Arizona College of Medicine, Respiratory Sciences Centre, 1501 N Campbell Avenue, Tucson, AZ 85724, USA.

LEDBETTER Elizabeth K, b. 27 May 1940, Columbia, SC, USA. Physician. 5 s, 1 d. Education: MD; MPH; Board Certified in General Preventive Medicine and Public Health, 1993, and Aerospace, 1985. Career: Flight Surgeon, HC3; Flight Surgeon, Mesawa, Japan; Medical Officer, Cubi Pt Clinic; Branch Head, Miami Clinic; Currently, Head, Epidemiology Department, Navy Environmental Preventive Medicine Unit 5; Adjunct Professor, Graduate School of Public Health, San Diego State University, 1994-. Honours: Phi Beta Kappa, 1967; Phi Kappa Phi, 1968. Memberships: Associate Fellow, Aerospace Medical Association;

Fellow, American College of Preventive Medicine; American Society of Tropical Medicine and Hygiene; US Mexico Border Health Association. Hobbies: Travel; Gardening. Address: NEPMU 5, Naval Station, Box 368143, San Diego, CA 92136-5199, USA.

LEDERER Wolfgang, b. 19 Apr 1919, Vienna, Austria. Psychiatrist. m. Alexandra Botwin, 1956, 2 daughters. Appointments: Currently Clinical Professor of Psychiatry, University of California Medical School, San Francisco, USA. Publications: Books: Dragons, Delinquents and Destiny, 1965; The Fear of Women, 1968; The Kiss of the Snow Queen, 1986; Numerous professional and popular papers. Membership: Fellow, American Psychiatric Association. Address: 75 Palm Avenue, San Francisco, CA 94118, USA.

LEDFORD Dennis K, b. 5 Oct 1950, Johnson City, Tennessee, USA. Physician; Academician. m. Jennifer L Shelton, 15 June 1974, 3 sons. Education: BChE summa cum laude, Georgia Institute of Technology, 1973; MD, University of Tennessee Center for Health Sciences, 1976; Intern, Resident, University of Tennessee Affiliated Hospitals, Memphis, 1977-79; Chief Resident in Medicine, City of Memphis Hospitals, 1979-80; Fellow in Clinical Immunology and Rheumatology, New York University, 1980-82; Fellow in Clinical Allergy and Immunology, University of South Florida, Tampa, 1983-85. Appointments include: Assistant Professor of Medicine, 1985-91, Associate Professor of Medicine, 1991-, Director, Training Programme in Clinical and Laboratory Immunology, 1992-, University of South Florida, Tampa. Honours: National Merit Scholarship, 1968; Tau Beta Pi, 1972; Alpha Omega Alpha, 1975; Faculty Medal Winner and Department of Medicine Award as Outstanding Student of Internal Medicine, University of Tennessee Center for Health Sciences, 1976; Fellowship, American Rheumatism Associatin, 1981; Outstanding Speaker Award, Marion County Medical Association, 1987. Memberships: American Medical Association; American College of Physicians; American Society of Internal Medicine; American Rheumatism Association; American Academy of Allergy and Immunology, 3 committees; Florida Allergy and Immunology Society, Secretary 1989-90, Vice-President 1990-91, President 1991-93. Hobbies: Gardening; Hiking; Fishing; Music. Address: University of South Florida, College of Medicine, Division of Allergy and Clinical Immunology, c/o VA Medical Center, 13000 Bruce B Downs Blvd (111D), Tampa, FL 33612, USA.

LEDFORD Janice (Jan) K, b. 19 Feb 1957, Pennsylvania, USA. Medical Writer. m. James L Ledford, 24 Jul 1976, 2 s. Education: AS, General Studies, Biology, 1978, AS, Dental Hygiene, 1980, Columbus College, USA; Certified Ophthalmic Medical Technologist. Appointments: Free Lance Medical Writer; Technical Staff, Eyesight Associates of Middle Georgia. Publications include: Books: Exercises in Refractometry, 1990; In-Office Training Program and Series Review, 1991; Co-author, The Crystal Clear Guide to Sight for Life: A Complete Manual of Eye Care for Those Over 55, 1955. Honour: Achievement in Ophthalmology, 1993. Memberships: Association of Technical Personnel in Ophthalmology; American Medical Writers Association; Editorial Board, The Professional Medical Assistant. Hobbies: Reading; Music. Address: c/o EyeWrite Productions, 112 Victor Street, Warner Robins, GA 31088, USA.

LEE Bee Wah, b. 22 Dec 1954, Singapore. Paediatrician. m. Dr Tan Chai Beng, 29 Jan 1983, 1 s, 2 d. Education: MMed, Paediatrics, Singapore; MBBS; NUS; MD. Appointments: Lecturer, 1981; Senior Lecturer, 1986; Associate Professor, 1990-; Consultant Paediatrician. Publications: IgE Response and Its regulation in Allergic Diseases, 1988; Immunologically-mediated Emergencies, 1989; The Low Affinity fc Receptor for IgE, thesis, 1991. Honour: Singapore President Scholar, 1973. Memberships: American Academy of Allergy and Immunology. Hobbies: Sport; Netball. Address: Department of Paediatrics, National University Hospital, Lower Kent Ridge Road, Singapore 0511.

LEE Chen Hsen, b. 19 September 1946, Chia-yi, Taiwan, China. Surgery Professor. m. Su-Ju, 1 February 1975, 2 sons, 1 daughter. Education: Fellow, American College of Surgeons. Appointments: Professor of Surgery, National Yang-Ming University; Chairman, Emergency Department, Taipei Veterans General Hospital. Honours: President, Chinese Association of Endocrine Surgeons, 1994-; President, Society of Emergency & Critical Care Medicine, Taiwan, 1992-94. Memberships: Societe Internationale de Chirurgie, Collegium Internationale Chirurgie Digestivae; International Association of Endocrine Surgeons. Hobbies: Golf; Music. Address: Chairman,

Emergency Department, Veterans General Hospital, Shih Pai, Taipie, Taiwan, China.

LEE Chung-Hsiang, b. 10 May 1936, Ping-Tong, Taiwan. Prof Paediatrics. m. Hsiu-Hsiu Su, 14 Mar 1964, 1 s, 1 d. Education: MD, 1962, Res, Hosp, 1963-64, Nat Taiwan Univ; DCH, RCP London and RCS England, 1970; DTPH, London Univ, England, 1972-; PhD, Tokyo Women's Med Coll, 1980. Appointments: Res, 1963-64, Vis Staff, Dept of Paediatrics, 1970-73, Nat Taiwan Univ Hosp; Chief, Dept of Paediatrics, 1964-70, Chief, Misurata MCH Ctr, 1968-70, Misurata Hosp, Libya; Instr, Dept of Paediatrics, 1973-76, Assoc Prof, Dept of Paediatrics, 1976-77, Pt-time Prof, Dept of Paediatrics and Dept of Pub Hlth, 1981-94, Coll of Med, Nat Taiwan Univ; Dpty Commnr, 1977-84, Commnr, 1992-93, Hlth Dept, Taipei City Govt, 1977-84; Supt, Taipei Municipal Yang-Wing Hosp, 1984-91; Supt, Taipei Municipal Ho-Ping Hosp, 1991-92. Creative works: Set up MCH Ctr, Misurata Hosp; Promoted child accident prevention, Taiwan; Established Taipei Municipal Yang-Wing Hosp, Childhood Cancer Fndn in Taiwan and Taipei Inst of Pathology; Planned, set up med team to Saudi Arabia; Promoted Taipei City hlth status; Dev, Paediatric Hepatology, Nat Taiwan Univ Hosp; 1st in Taiwan to use steroid test for differential diagnosis of neonatal hepatitis and biliary atresia. Memberships: Chief, Child Hlth Promotion Assn; Hon Chief, Gout Patient Assn; Bd Mbr: Paediatric Assn; Family med Assn; Rehab Med Assn; Taipei Pathology Ctr and Childhood Cancer Fndn. Honours: Ctrl Govt awards: 2nd Publ Award as Fndr, Medical Digest, 1976; Govt Serv Hon Awd, 1992; Outstanding Rsch Award, 1992. Hobbies: Playing tennis and golf; Art collection; Oil painting. Address: 8F 220 Chung-Hsiao East Rd, Sec 4, Taipei, Taiwan.

LEE Gregory Price, b. 3 July 1952, Orange, New Jersey, USA. Doctor of Philosophy (Neuropsychology). m. Susan L Haverstock, 28 Oct 1988, 1 son. Education: BA, University of Northern Colorado, 1975; PhD, Florida Institute of Technology, 1980; Fellow, University of Houston, Baylor College of Medicine, 1984; Fellow, University of Wisconsin Medical School, 1986. Appointments: Associate Professor of Surgery (Neurosurgery) & Psychiatry, Medical College of Georgia. Publications: Neuropsychological evaluation for patients with disturbances of the nervous system; Acute confusional states in toxic and metabolic disorders; Psychological Testing; Co-author: Intracarotid amobarbital assessment; Co-author: Amobarbital effects and lateralized brain function; Co-author: Functional hippocampal assessment with depth electrodes; Co-author: Criteria and validity issues in Wada assessment; Co-author: Issues in clinical memory assessment of the elderly; Over 100 publications in neurological and psychological journals. Memberships: American Academy of Neurology; American Epilepsy Society; American Psychological Association; International Neuropsychological Society; National Academy of Neuropsychology; Sigma Xi; American College of Legal Medicine. Hobbies: Skiing; Scuba Diving; Golf. Address: Section of Neurosurgery, Medical College of Georgia, Augusta, GA 30912-4010, USA.

LEE Harry Antonius, b. 27 June 1954, Jakarta, Indonesia. Physician; Allergist. m. Johanna Francisca, 23 Nov 1977, 1 son, 1 daughter. Education: BS, Fairmont College, 1973-77; MD, St George University School of Medicine, 1978-82. Appointments: Staff Pediatrician, Chief of Allergy Clinic, Tinker Hospital, 1986-89; Chief, Allergy & Immunology Service, Air University Regional Hospital, Maxwell, 1991-93. Publications: Effects of PGE1 or PGE2 on Luteal Function in Pseudopregant Rats, 1979; Analysis of T and B Lymphocyte phenotypes in patients with partial DiGeorge Syndrome, 1991; Soluble FceRII levels in normal children and patients with Immunodeficiency Diseases, 1991. Memberships: American Academy of Pediatrics, 1986; American Academy of Allergy & Immunology, 1991; American College of Allergy & Immunology, 1991; Alabama Society of Allergy & Immunology, 1992; American Association for the Advancement of Science, 1993; Society of Air Force Physicians, 1993; The Medical Association of the State of Alabama, 1994; Joint Council of Allergy & Immunology, 1994. Honours: American Chemical Society Award, 1973; Beta Beta Beta Biological Honor Society, 1975; Schering Travel Grant Award, 1991; The Air Force Commendation Medal, 1994. Hobbies: Computing; Electronics; Philatelic; Water Sports; Tennis; Reading. Address: 6705 Quail Ridge Drive, Montgomery, AL 36117, USA.

LEE Hyung Mo, b. 27 Oct 1926, Tanchon, Korea. Physician; surgeon. m. 2 Jul 1959, 1 s, 1 d. Education: BS, Keijo Imperial University, 1945; MD, Seoul National University Medical School, 1949. Appointments: Instructor of Surgery, Medical College of Virginia,

1963-64; Assistant Professor of Surgery, Medical College of Virginia, 1964-66; Associate Professor of Surgery, Medical College of Virginia, 1966-70; Professor of Surgery, Medical College of Virginia, 1970-; Director, Clinical Transplant Program, Medical College of Virginia, 1973-92; Chairman, Division of Vascular and Transplant Surgery, Medical College of Virginia, 1973-. Publications: include, The Homotransplantation of Kidneys and of Fetal Liver and Spleen after Total Body Irradiation, 1960; The Effect of Antimetabolites of Prolonging of Lymphoid Cells in Vitro, 1963; Some Urological Aspects of 93 Consecutive Renal Homotransplants in Modified Recipients, 1967; Prolongation of Skin Graft Survival with Homologous Antiskin Hyperimmune Serum in Rats, 1972; Use of Plasma Protein Fraction in Preservation of Cadaveric Kidneys, 1976. Honours: Alpha Omega Alpha Medical Honorary Society, 1978; University Award of Excellence, Virginia Commonwealth University, 1990; Second Mainstream America Award for Excellence in Medicine, Asian Pacific Inc. Memberships: include, American College of Surgeons; International Society of Nephrology; Medical Society of Virginia; Society for Clinical Trials; Southeastern Surgical Society; Virginia Surgical Society; Virginia Vascular Society. Hobbies: Reading. Address: Medical College of Virginia, 1200 E Broad Street, Richmond, VA 23298, USA.

LEE Jen-Shih, b. 22 Aug 1940, Canton, China. Educator; Department Chairman. m. Lian-Pin Lee, 11 June 1966, 2 sons, 1 daughter. Education: BS, National Taiwan University, 1961; MSc, 1963, PhD, 1966, California Institute of Technology, USA. Appointments: Research Fellow, Cal tech, 1966; Research Engineer, UC-SD, 1966-69; Assistant Professor, 1969-74, Associate Professor, 1974-83, Professor, 1983-, Chair, Biomedical Engineering, 1988-, University of Virginia; Visiting Associate Professor, Johns Hopkins University, 1979-80. Publications: Microvascular Mechanics, Editor, 1989; Mass Transport in Circulation, 1993; Refereed over 70 publications and book chapters. Honours: Anthony Scholar, California Institute of Technology, 1964-66; Advanced Research Fellowship, San Diego County heart Association, 1966-69; Outstanding Service, Biomedical Engineering Society, 1992. Memberships: President, Biomedical Engineering Society, 1994-95; American Institute of Medical and Biological Institutions, College of Fellows, 1993; Chair, Programmes Committee, Biomedical Engineering Society, 1992; Guest Editor, Annuals of Biomedical Engineering, 1991. Address: University of Virginia, Biomedical Engineering Department, Box 377 Health Sciences Centre, Charlottesville, VA 22908, USA.

LEE Joseph Chuen Kwun, b. 6 Oct 1938, Chungking, China. Physician. m. Pamela Mak, 23 Dec 1967. Education: MB, BS, Hong Kong; PhD, Rochester, USA; American Board of Pathology; FRCP(C); FRCP(A); MRCPath(UK). Appointments: Assistant and Associate Professor of Pathology, University of Rochester, 1972-79; Visiting Professor, NIH, USA, 1980; Research Fellow, AFIP, Washington DC; Professor and Chairman of Pathology, Associate Dean of Medical School, Hong Kong. Memberships: AAAS; American Association of Pathologists; American Society of Clinical Pathology; College of American Pathologists; American Medical Association. Hobbies: Tennis; Reading. Address: Department of Anatomical and Cellular Pathology, The Chinese University of Hong Kong, Shatin, Hong Kong.

LEE Rufus E Jr, b. 10 July 1930, Eufaula, Alabama, USA. Physician. m. Mary Julia Lee, 6 Aug 1954, 2 s, 1 d. Education: MD, 1957, Internship, 1957-58, University of Alabama; Residency, University of Minnesota, 1958-60. Apointments: Southeasst Alabama Medical centre, Dothan, Alabama; Private Practice. Publications include: Practice Patterns of US Board of Certified Allergists; Asthma Practice Parameters, 1991. Honours include: Alpha Epsilon Delta; Delta Phi Alpha' Distinguished Military Graduate, University of Alabama; Pi Tau Chi; American Heart Association Service Recognition Award, 1966; Fellow Distinguished, American College of Allergists, 1985. Memberships include: American Medical Association; Fellow, American Academy of Paediatrics; Fellow, Past President, American College of Allergists; Fellow, American Academy of Allergy; Fellow, Past President, Alabama Society of Allergy and Immunology; Past President, Houston County Medical Society; American Association of Certified Allergists; Secretary, 1983-85, Joint Council of Allergy and Immunology. Address: 1836 West Main, Dothan, AL 36301, USA.

LEE Samuel (Sammy), b. 6 Jan 1958, Hong Kong. Medical Scientist. m. Karen Lee, 7 Dec 1985, 1 son, 1 daughter. Education: BSc, Kings College, University of London, 1979; PhD, University College, University of London, 1984; Diploma, Fertility Counsellor, London Hospital Medical College, 1992. Appointments: Research Fellow, University College,

London, England; Laboratory Director, IVF Unit, Humana Hospital, Wellington; Scientific Director, Northampton Fertility Service; Currently Scientific Director, Colchester Fertility Service. Publications: Numerous scientific publications in various medical journals; Male Infertility, book, 1995. Honours: Medical Research Council Scholar. Memberships: Fellow, Royal Society of Medicine; Fellow, Institute of Biomedical Sciences. Hobbies: Armchair philosopher and raconteur; Cricket. Address: 8 Prince Regent Mews, London NW1 3EW, England.

LEE Shui-shan, b. 10 Apr 1957, Hong Kong. Physician. Education: MBBS; MRCP (UK); FHKAM (Medicine); MD. Appointments: Currently Consultant, AIDS Unit, Department of Health, Hong Kong. Publications: Anti-myeloperoxidase antibody in systemic vasculitis (co-author), 1990; Measurement of whole blood phagocyte chemiluminescence in a microtitreplate format, 1992; HIV infection in Hong Kong, 1992; Profile of opportunistic infections among HIV-1 infected people in Hong Kong (co-author), 1995. Memberships: Hong Kong Advisory Council on AIDS; Hong Kong College of Physicians; Hong Kong Society for Immunology; Royal College of Physicians, Edinburgh; Hong Kong College of Community Medicine. Address: 5/F Yaumatei Jockey Club Clinic, 145 Battery Street, Kowloon, Hong Kong.

LEE Thong Teck, b. 12 Oct 1939, Malaysia. Gynaecologist. m. Gek Sim Yeo, 5 Aug 1967, 2 sons, 2 daughters. Education: MBBS (Singapore), 1963; FRACOG, 1979; FRCOG, 1984. Appointments: Registrar in Obstetrics and Gynaecology, Victoria Hospital, Blackpool, England, 1968-69; Lecturer in Obstetrics and Gynaecology, University of Malaya, Kuala Lumpur, Malaysia, 1969-72; Currently Senior Specialist-in-charge, Obstetrics and Gynaecology, Royal Darwin Hospital, Northern Territory, Australia. Hobbies: Table-tennis; Fishing; Music. Address: 4 Allen Street, Fannie Bay, Darwin, NY 0810, Australia.

LEE Wen-Chung, b. 11 Aug 1962, Taiwan, China. Associate Professor. m. Ru-Lan Hsieh, 29 Mar 1991, 1 daughter. Education: MD; PhD, National Taiwan University. Career: Institute of Epidemiology, College of Public Health, National Taiwan University. Address: No 1, Jen-Ai Road, 1st Sec, Taipei, Taiwan, China.

LEESTMA Jan Edward, b. 30 Nov 1938, Flint, Michigan, USA. Physician; Neuropathologist. m. Louise M Leestma, 4 Apr 1961, 2 d. Education: BA; MD; MM. Appointments: Associate Professor of Pathology and Neucology, Northwestern University School of Medicine, Chicago, 1971-85; Professor of Pathology and Neurology, Prilker School of Medicine, University of Chicago, 1985-87; Dean of Students, Division of Biological Sciences and Prilker School of Medicine, University of Chicago, 1985-87; Associate Medical Director, Chicago Institute Neurosurgery and Neuroresearch. Publications: Contributor of numerous articles and book chapters including: Non-immune Fluorescent Protein Staining of Neoplasms, Co-author, 1963; Paraganglioma of the Urinary Bladder, CO-author, 1971; Velocity Measurements of Particulate Neuroplasmic Flow, 1976; The Pathology of Viral Diseases of the Nervous System, 1985; Natural History of Epilepsy, 1990; Forensic Neuropathology, 1994. Honours: George H Toost Outstanding Teacher of Basic Sciences, Northwestern University, 1978. Memberships: American Association Neuropathologists; International Society Neuropathologists; AAAS; New York Academy of Science; AMA; Illinois Medical Association; Chicago Medical Society. Hobbies: Amateur radio; Watercolours; Skiing; Scuba diving. Address: 428 W Demming Place, Chicago, IL 60614, USA.

LEGGAT Peter Adrian, b. 2 Dec 1961, Brisbane, Australia. Senior Lecturer, Public Health & Tropical Medicine. Education: Bachelor, Medical Science, Distinction; Bachelor of Medicine; Bachelor of Surgery; Postgraduate Diploma, Clinical Nutrition; DSc; Graduate Diploma, Education; Diploma, Tropical Medicine & Hygiene; Certificate in Addiction Studies; Master of Medical Education; Postgraduate Diploma of Industrial Health; Fellow, Australasian College of Tropical Medicine; Fellow, Australian Institute of Company Directors; Member, Australian Institute of Biology. Appointments include: Clinical Tutor, Lecturer, Social & Preventive Medicine, University of Queensland Medical School, 1985-89; Medical Officer, Department of Veterans' Affairs, Repatriation General Hospital, Greenslopes, 1988-89; Medical Officer, Department of Defence (Army), various postings, 1987-91; Attached Defence Officer, Australian Embassy, Bangkok, 1990. Publications include: Microbiological Hazards and Workers, 1986; The Microbiological Hazards posed by Sharps: Complications of Needle Puncture Injuries to Nurses, 1987; Microbiological Hazards and Workers Compensation II, 1987; Insurance against AIDS, 1989; Preventing the Advance of

Legionnaires Disease: An Australian Perspective, 1990; Tour of Duty: Studying Tropical Diseases in Thailand, 1991; Occupational and Environmental Health & Safety: A Regional Perspective, 1992; Australasian Concerns in Environmental Safety & Health Meeting the Challenge, 1992. Memberships: Australasian College of Tropical Medicine; Australian Institute of Company Directors; World Safety Organization; Australian Institute of Biology; Australasian Faculty of Occupational Medicine; American College of Occupational & Environmental Medicine; New York Academy of Science. Honours include: World Safety Person of the Year, 1988; Educational Award, World Safety Organization, 1990; Honorable Mention, American Society of Safety Engineers, 1987. Hobbies: Philatelist; Numismatist; Shell Collector; Artefact Collector; Astronomy; Tennis; Table Tennis; Chess; Travel; Gardening; Medical Writing. Address: Department of Public Health & Tropical Medicine, James Cook University of North Queensland, Townsville, QLD 4811, Australia. 139. 152.

LEGTERS Llewellyn J, b. 23 May 1932, Clymer, NY, USA. Physician. m. 1 s, 1 d. Education: MD; MPH. Career: Medical Officer, US Army, 1957-78, retired as Colonel; Senior Medical Advisor, Environmental Control Inc, 1979; Chairman, Department of Preventive Medicine and Biometrics, Uniformed Services University, 1980-. Publications: Over 40 scientific articles and numerous book chapters in medical publications mainly on infectious disease epidemiology. Honours: Phi Beta Kappa, 1955; Army Commendation Medal, 1960; Legion of Merit w/2 OLC, 1968, 1978, 1978; Meritorious Service Medal, 1971, 1974; Gorgas Medal, 1985. Memberships: New York Academy of Sciences; American Society for Advancement of Science; American Society of Tropical Medicine and Hygiene; American College of Physicians; American Public Health Association. Hobbies: Running; Gardening; Photography; Travel. Address: 9518 Kentstone Drive, Bethesda, MD 20817, USA.

LEI Wei Fu, b. 18 June 1957, Xintai, Shandong, China. Physician. m. LiLi Wang, 10 Oct 1991. Education: MB, Taishan Medical College. Appointments: Resident, 1977-86, Lecturer, 1986-92, Associate professor of Anaesthesia, 1992-, Hospital of Taishan Medical College. Publications: Differentiation and Diagnosis of Pain, 1991; Diagnosis of Therapy of Pain, 1992; Basic Theory of the Treatment of Paries. Honours: Awards of Audiovisual Teaching Material, Chinese Medical Association. Memberships: Chairman, Anaesthesia Association of Taian District; Chairman, Association of Pain Research, Taian District. Address: Hospital of Taishan Medical College, Taian, Shandong 271000, China.

LEIBENSPERGER Stephen, b. 24 Dec 1960, Lancaster, Pennsylvania, USA. Physician. m. Pamela Black, 5 Aug 1990. Education: BA< Duke University, Durham, North Carolina, 1982; MD, Hershey Medical Centre, Penn State University, 1986; Board Certified Family Practice, 1989; Family Practice Residency, St Margaret's Memeorial Hospital, Pittsburgh, 1986-89. Appointments: Medical Director, Community Medical Centre of NW Washington County, Burgettstown, Pennsylvania, 1989-91; Active Medical Staff, Ohio Valley General Hospital, McKees Rocks, Pennsylvania, 1991-; Preceptor, Washington Hospital Family Practice Residency Programme, Washington, Pennsylvania, 1989-. Honours: Alpha Omega Alpha, 1986. Memberships: American Academy of Family Practice; Pennsylvania Academy of Family Practice; American Medical Association. Hobbies: Tennis; Golf; Piano; Scuba diving. Address: Suite 206, 27 Heckel Road, McKees Rocks, PA 15136, USA.

LEIBROCK Lyal G, b. 20 Nov 1940, Alma, Kansas, USA. MD. 1 son, 2 daughters. Education: MD, Neurosurgery. Appointments: Associate Professor of Anesthesiology, 1987-93; Professor of Surgery, Neurosurgery & Professor of Anesthesiology, 1989-93. Publications: The Sealing Action of Subarachnoid Blood, 1971; Arachnoid Clearance of Red Blood Cells, 1974; Simulated Acute Appendicitis Secondary to Ventriculo-Peritoneal Shunt, 1976; A Single Case of Huntington's Disease Simultaneously Occurring with Obstructive Hydrocephalus, 1991; Therapy of Giant Intracranial Aneurysms in the Elderly, 1990; Brachytherapy: A Viable Alternative in the Management of Basal Meningiomas, 1991; IRB review of a Phase II randomized clinical trial involving incompetent patients suffering from severe closed head injury, 1993; Malpositioned endolymphatic subarachnoid shunt causing trigeminal neuralgia: Case report, 1994; An Update on the PEG-SOD study involving incompetent subjects: FDA permits an exception to informed consent requirements, 1994. Honours: Dean's Award, California University, 1965. Memberships: Sigma Xi; American College

of Surgeons. Hobbies: Reading. Address: University of Nebraska Medical Center, 600 South 42nd Street, Omaha, NE 68198, USA.

LEIGH Jonathan Howard, b. 27 Nov 1949, Addiscombe, Surrey, England. Consultant Registered Naturopath and Osteopath; Clinical Director. m. Anne, 15 oct 1972, 1 s, 1 d. Education: DO; ND. Appointments: Consultant, Grayshott Hall Health centre, 1973-75; lecturer, Senior Lecturer in Osteopathic Medicine, British College of Naturopathy and Osteopathy, London, 1977-87; Clinical Supervisor, Senior Clinical Supervisor, BCNO, London, 1977-87; Senior lecturer in Osteopathic Medicine, International College of Osteopathy and Alternative Therapy, Paris, France, 1982-87; Clinical Director, Gillingham Clinic of Complementary Medicine. Memberships: Treasurer, General Council and Register of Naturopaths, 1989-93; Past President, British Naturopathic and Osteopathic Association; President, International Federation of the Practitioners of Natural Therapies. Hobbies: Flying; Dingy sailing. Address: 50 Watling Street, Gillingham, Kent ME7 2YN, England.

LEIKIN Jerrold Blair, b. 28 Aug 1954, Chicago, Illinois, USA. Physician. m. Robin Ellen Goldman, 6 JUne 1982, 1 s, 1 d. Education: BS, University of iowa, 1976; MD< Chicago Medical School, 1980. Appointments: Section Chief, Section of Emergency Medicine, University of Illinois Department of Medicine, 1984-88; Associate Professor of Medicine, Rush Medical College; Medical Director, Rush Poison Control Centre; Associate Director, Rush Emergency Services. Publications include: Acute Lupus Pneumonitis in the post partum state, 1986; Poisoned Patient, 1989; Intravenous Magnesium Sulfate in Pregnant Asthmatics; Skeletaal Muscle relaxant Ingestion, 1990; Oral Labetalol in Hypertensive Urgency, 1991; Noncardiac Chest Pain. A Focus upon Psychogenic Causes; Hypokalemia Following Pediatric Albuterol Overdose: A Case Series, 1994; Headaches in Carbon-Monoxide, Co-author, 1987; Alupent Toxicity, Co-author; Editor: Poisoning and Toxicology Handbook. Honours include: Omnicron Delta Kappa; Phi Eta Sigma; AMA Physician Recognition Award, 1988-93. 1994-97. Memberships: American College of Medical Toxicology; American Medical Association. Address: Rush-Presbyterian-St Luke's Medical Centre, 1653 W Congress Parkway, Chicago, IL 60612, USA.

LEISHMAN Robert Forbes, b. 5 March 1941. Orthodontist. m. Sheila Sayles Crowe, 15 June 1968, 2 sons. Education: BDS, Edinburgh; DD.ORTH, Royal College of Physicians & Surgeons, Glasgow; MScD, University of Wales. Appointments: Orthodontic Practitioner. Publications: An Investigation into the Accuracy of Contour Photography, 1977. Memberships: British Dental Association; New Zealand Dental Association; European Society of Orthodontists; British Association of Orthodontists; New Zealand Association of Orthodontists. Hobbies: Clay Pigeon Shooting; Walking; Photography; Travel; Gardening; Rotary. Address: 876 New North Road, Mt Albert, Auckland 3, New Zealand.

LEITAO Pedro M P S, b. 31 Oct 1962, Lisbon, Portugal. Dentist; Orthodontist. m. Maria Paula Leitao, 30 Aug 1989, 1 son. Education: DMD, Lisbon University; MSc, Speciality in Orthodontics, University of Bergen, Norway, 1990; PhD in progress. Appointments: Currently Assistant Professor in Orthodontics, Lisbon University. Publication: Malocclusion in Lisbon Schoolchildren, 1990. Memberships: Associacao Professional dos Medicos Dentistas; European Orthodontic Society; American Association of Orthodontists; European Society of Lingual Orthodontists. Hobbies: Golf; Swimming. Address: Travessa de Santa Cruz, Lote A, Birre, 2750 Cascais, Portugal.

LENFANT Claude, b. 12 Oct 1928, Paris, France. Scientific Administrator. 2 sons, 3 daughters. Education: BS, University of Rennes, 1948; MD, University of Paris, 1956. Appointments include: Clinical Assistant Professor, 1966-67, Associate Professor, 1968-71, Professor of Medicine and Physiology and Biophysics, 1971-72, University of Washington, Seattle, USA; Director, Division of Lung Diseases, 1972-80, Director, 1982-, National Heart, Lung and Blood Institute, National Institutes of Health, Bethesda, Maryland; Director, Fogarty International Center for Advanced Study in the Health Sciences, National Institutes of Health, 1981-82. Publications: 200 scientific publications; Executive Editor, Lung Biology in Health and Disease monograph series, 82 volumes. Honours: Elected to Institute of Medicine, National Academy of Sciences, 1983; Honorary Member, Royal Society of Medicine, England; Honorary DSc, State University of New York, Buffalo, 1988; Elected to USSR Academy of Medical Sciences, 1988; Honorary Member, French Cardiology Society, 1989; Presidential Distinguished Executive Rank Award, 1991; Fellow, Royal College of Physicians,

London, 1992; Elected to French National Academy of Medicine, 1993; Giovanni Lorenzini Foundation Prize for Advancement of Biomedical Science, 1994; Many more. Memberships: Association of American Physicians; American Society for Clinical Investigation; New York Academy of Sciences; American and French Physiological Societies; American Federation for Clinical Research; Undersea Medical Society; International Federation for Medical Electronics; Society for Experimental Medicine and Biology; American Society of Zoologists; Editorial boards. Address: National Heart, Lung and Blood Institute, Bethesda, MD 20892, USA.

LENG Fangnan, b. 1940, China. Physician. Education: Department of Medical Treatment, Beijing College of Traditional Chinese Medicine, 1957-63. Appointments: Clinic Physician, Physician-in-charge, In-charge of Department of Internal Medicine, 1963-78; Professor, Graduate School, 1978-80, Head, Department of Internal Medicine, Guang An Men Hospital, 1980-87, Chinese Academy of Traditional Chinese Medicine; Vice-President, Correspondence College for Barefoot Doctors, 1986-91; Chief Advisor, Research and Development Centre of Traditional Chinese Medicine, 1987-91; Vice-President, 2nd Attached Hospital, Beijing College of Traditional Chinese Medicine, 1987-. Publications: A Hundred Cases of Saving Patients from Wrong Diagnosis by Famous Doctors of Modern Times; Chief editor or editor: Basic Chinese Patent Medicine, 1989; Treatises on Arthralgia Syndrome; Clinical Treatment of Andriatra by TCM; Treatises on Common Cold Treatment; Clinical Treatment of MBD; Treatises on Nephritis; Food Therapy and Nutrition in TCM; The Standards of Differentiation of Symptoms by TCM; Treatises on Clinical Treatment of Internal Disease; Basic Chinese Patent Medicine, 1989; Holder, several patents for medicine. Honours: National Science and Technology Progress Prize, for patent medicine for rheumatism; Winner, 1st and 2nd Place, National Prize for High Quality Books on Science and Technology. Memberships: Director, Non-Governmental Association for Research and Development of TCM, 1986-91; Evaluation Committee of TCM, National Fund for Natural Science; Secretary-General, Research and Systematisation Committee of TCM Theory, All-China Association of TCM, 1980-91; Deputy Secretary-General, Vice-President, All-China Association of Internal Medicine (TCM). Address: Second Attached Hospital, Beijing College of TCM, Beijing, China.

LENG Nicholas Richard Christopher, b. 13 Nov 1954, England. Clinical Psychologist. m. Jaqueline Macdonald, 23 Oct 1976, 2 sons. Education: BSc, Psychology, 1977; Diploma in Clinical Psychology, 1981; PhD, 1987. Appointments: Principal Clinical Psychologist to Eastbourne Health Authority; Head, Department of Clinical Psychology, Royal Hospital and Home, London; Chartered Clinical Psychologist. Publications: Psychological Care in Old Age, 1990; Neuropsychology of the Amnesic Syndrome (with A J Parkin), 1993; Various papers on the amnesic syndrome. Memberships: Fellow, British Psychological Society; Fellow, Royal Society of Medicine. Hobby: Music. Address: 136 Harley Street, London W1N 1AH, England.

LENG Yan-Jia, b. 6 Nov 1929, Heilongjiang, China. Medical Parasitologist. m. Shu-fan Jing, July 1951, 4 sons. Education: MB, China Medical University, 1950; DTM & H, Liverpool University, England, 1981. Appointments: Assistant, China Medical University; Lecturer, Liaoning University; Associate Professor, Guangdong Medical College; Currently Professor of Medical Parasitology, Faculty of Medicine, Jinan University, Guangzhou. Publications: Human Parasitology, 1955, 1956, 1959; Phlebotomine Sandflies, 1983; Human Parasitology, 1991, 1993; Articles including: Phlebotomine sandflies in limestone caves and a primitive new genus Chinius, 1987; Systematics and distribution of phlebotomine sandflies in China, 1992. Honours: Liaoning Award for Natural Science, 1963; Liaoning Award for Medical Science, 1963; Guangdong Award for Medical Science, 1978; Guangdong Award for Natural Science, 1987; Secretary, Office for China, Royal Society of Tropical Medicine and Hygiene, London. Memberships include: Fellow; Royal Society of Tropical Medicine and Hygiene, London; British Society for Parasitologists; Societas Parasitologica Sinica; Societas Entomologica Sinica; Societas Zoologica Sinica; Chinese Medical Association. Address: 19-202 Yangcheng Yuan, Jinan University, Guangzhou 510632, China.

LENTLE Brian Clifford, b. 23 June 1935, Cardiff, Wales. Physician. m. Jean Margaret Butcher, 3 Jan 1959, 1 son, 1 daughter. Education: MB, BCh, University of Wales; MD; DMRD; FRCPC. Appointments include: Director of Nuclear Medicine, Cross Cancer Institute, Edmonton, Alberta, Canada; Professor of Radiology, University of Alberta; Professor, Head, Division of Nuclear Medicine, University of British

Columbia, Vancouver; Currently Professor, Head, Department of Radiology, University of British Columbia and Vancouver Hospital and Health Sciences Centre; Several Visiting Professorships. Publications: Author or co-author, 10 book chapters including: Ankylosing Spondylitis Radiographic and Scintigraphic Features, 1980; Iatrogenic Alterations in the Biodistribution of Radiotracers Caused by Radiation Therapy, Surgery, and other Invasive Medical Procedures, 1987; Radiology of the Pancreas: Radionuclide Examinations, 1989; Nuclear Medicine, 1991; Liver Tumours, in press; 112 articles; Magnetic Resonance in Cancer (co-editor), 1986. Honours: Exhibit Gold Award, Canadian Association of Radiologists, 1971; Silver Jubilee Medal, Governor General of Canada, 1977; Exhibit Silver Medal, Society of Nuclear Medicine, 1978; Teaching Awards, University of British Columbia, 1988, 1991. Memberships include: Radiological Society of North America; Society of Nuclear Medicine; Council Chair, Canadian Association of Radiologists; Canadian Radiation Protection Association; President, Canadian Heads of Academic Radiology; Canadian Medical Association. Hobbies: Photography; Sailing; Book collecting (1st editions of Joseph Conrad). Address: 6065 Eagleridge Drive, West Vancouver, British Columbia, Canada V7W 1W7.

LEONG John C Y, b. 10 July 1942, Hong Kong. Doctor. m. Annie Leong, 11 Jan 1969, 2 sons. Education: MBBS, 1965; FRCS, 1969; FRCS, 1970; FRACS, 1985. Appointments: Assistant Lecturer, Department of Orthopaedic Surgery, University Hong Kong, 1966-67; Lecturer, Department of Orthopaedic Surgery, University Hong Kong, 1967-75; Honorary Registrar, Department of Orthopaedic Surgery, Nuffield Orthopaedic Center, Oxford, 1969-72; Senior Lecturer, Department of Orthopaedic Surgery, University Hong Kong, 1975-81; Honorary Consultant Orthopaedic Surgeon, Medical & Health Services, Hong Kong Government, 1982-91; Dean, Faculty of Medicine, University Hong Kong, 1985-90; Honorary Consultant of the Hospital Authority, 1991-92. Publications: Tuberculosis of the Spine, 1993; Titanium Mesh Block Replacement of the Intervertebral Disc, 1994; Chapter, Poliomyelitis, 1994. Honour: Non-Official Justice of Peace, appointed by the Governor, 1993-. Membership: President, Western pacific Orthopaedic Association, 1992-95. Hobby: Golf. Address: Department of Orthopaedic Surgery, The University of Hong Kong, Queen Mary Hospital, Hong Kong.

LEPPARD Mandy Yvonne, b. 3 Sept 1965, Elgin, Scotland. Registered Osteopath. m. Roger Charles Anderson, 8 Mar 1991. Education: Diploma in Osteopathy. Memberships: General Council and Register of Osteopaths; Osteopathic Association of Great Britain. Hobby: Horse riding. Address: 31 High Street, Fochabers, Moray, Scotland.

LERMAN Steven Elliot, b. 10 May 1958, Bronx, New York, USA. Physician. m. Wendy Paulette Schwimmer, 21 June 1981, 1 son, 1 daughter. Education: BA, Rutgers University, 1976-80; MD, Washington University School of Medicine, 1980-84; MPH, Robert Wood Johnson Medical School, 1986-88. Appointments: Internal Medicine, Sinai Hospital of Baltimore, 1984-86; Occupational Medicine, Department of Environmental & Community Medicine, University of Medicine & Dentistry of New Jersey Robert Wood Johnson Medical School, 1986-88; Medical Director, EUSA Baytown Refinery, 1988-90; Director of Medicine & Environmental Health, Exxon Chemical Americas, Baytown Area, 1990-. Publications include: Colorectal Polyp Incidence and Prevalence among Polyolefin Unit Workers, 1993; Occupational Health Issues: CME in an Evolving Field, 1993; Colorectal Polyp Incidence Among Polypropylene Manufacturing Workers, 1994; Colorectal Cancer Incidence Among Polypropylene Manufacturing Workers: An Update, 1994; Sleep and Alertness in a 12-hour Rotating Shift Work Environment, 1994; An Evaluation of Scheduled Bright Light and Darkness on Rotating Shiftworkers: Trial & Limitations, 1995. Hobbies: Racketball; History. Address: Exxon Baytown Chemical Plant, PO Box 4004, Baytown, TX 77522 4004, USA.

LERNER Frederick Andrew, b. 27 Dec 1945, Mount Vernon, NY, USA. Information Scientist. m. Sheryl Rubin, 29 Jun 1980, 1 d. Education: AB, 1966, MS, 1969, DLS, 1981, Columbia University. Career: Reference Librarian, Hamilton College; Information Specialist, Research Foundation of City University of New York; Head, Reference Services Unit, Vermont Department of Libraries; Head, Technical Information Services, Spectra Inc; Currently, Information Scientist, National Center for Post-Traumatic Stress Disorder. Publication: Modern Science Fiction and the American Literary Community, 1985. Memberships include: American Society for Information Science;

International Society for Traumatic Stress Studies; Medical Library Association. Hobby: Science Fiction. Address: National Center for PTSD, VA Medical Center 116D, White River Junction, VT 05009, USA.

LEROY Edward Carwile, b. 19 Jan 1933, Elizabeth City, NC, USA. Physician. m. Garnette DeFord Hughes, 11 June 1960, 1 s, 1 d. Education: Fork Union Military Academy, 1951; BS, summa cum laude, Wake Forest University, 1955; MS, University of North Carolina Graduate School, Chapel Hill, 1958; MD, University of North Carolina School of Medicine, Chapel Hill, 1960. Appointments include: Intern, Residency, Presbyterian Hospital, Columbia-Presbyterian Medical Centre, New York City, 1960-62; Associate, 1966-67, Assistant Professor, 1967-72, College of Physicians and Surgeons, Department of Medicine, New York; Professor of Medicine, Director, Division of Rheumatology and Immunology, 1975-, Professor of Immunology and Microbiology, 1976-, College of Medicine, Medical University of South Carolina, Charleston. Publications: Contributor of numerous reviewed reports, reviews, chapters in books and articles in professional journals. Honours include: Phi Beta Kappa; Omicron delta Kappa; Sigma Xi; Alpha Omega Alpha; Distinguished Service Award, University of North Carolina School of Medicine, 1988; President, Waring Medical History Society, Charleston, 1991; President, University of North Carolina Medical Alumni, Chapel Hill, 1991. Memberships include: Vice President, 1971, President, 1973, New York Rheumatism Association; fellow, American College of Physicians; American federation for Clinical Research; American Association of Immunologists; Society for Experimental Biology and Medicine. Address: Rheumatology Division, Medical University of South Carolina, 171 Ashley Avenue, Charleston, SC 29425, USA.

LESAR Colin George, b. 20 Aug 1952, Vanderbijlpark, South Africa. Orthodontist. m. Krystyna Lesar, 29 Nov 1980, 3 daughters. Education: BDS, 1976, Higher Diploma in Dentistry, 1978, MDent, Orthodontics, 1981, University of Witwatersrand. Appointments: Junior Lecturer, Registrar, 1979-81, Senior Specialist, Lecturer, 1982-85, part-time Specialist-Lecturer, 1986-, Department of Orthodontics, University of Witwatersrand; Orthodontist in private practice. Honours: Bronze Medal for Orthodontics, Dental Association of South Africa. Memberships: Dental Association of South Africa; South African Medical and Dental Council; General Dental Council; European Orthodontic Society; South African Society of Orthodontists; Botswana Dental Council. Hobbies: Water-skiing; Squash; Woodworking. Address: 20A Wessel Road, PO Box 1909, Rivonia 2128, South Africa.

LESOURD Bruno Maurice Gabriel, b. 21 Mar 1948, Belleville sur Saône, France. Medical Doctor. m. Brigitte Waternaux, 13 Jul 1974, 1 s, 2 d. Education: AB, Paris, 1966; MD, Pitie-Salpitriere, 1977; PhD, Paris, 1993. Appointments: Assistant in Pathologie Expérimentale; Maitre de Conférence in Pathologie Expérimentale then in Immunologie; Maitre de Conférence, Praticien Hospitalier en Immunologie; Head of Ageing Laboratory Immunology, Paris; Head of Geriatrics Clinical Unit. Publications include: Production de Facteur de Transfert Dialysable de l'immunité Cellulaire par des Cellules Lymphoblastoides en Prolifération Continue, 1975; Influence of Early Maternal Deprivation on Adult Humoral Immune Response in Mice, 1981; Effects of Human Growth Hormone in Men over 60 Years Old, 1990; Decreased Capacity of IL1 Production by Monocytes of Infected Elderly Patients, 1993; Changes of Tall Subjects with Ageing; Influences of Nutritional Status, 1994; Vaccination Antitétanique Chez le Sujet âgé, 1984. Memberships: French Society of Immunology; French Society of Gerontology; French Society of Allergy and Clinical Immunology; French Society of Nutrition; European Society of Nutrition; American Academy of Allergy & Clinical Immunology. Hobbies: History; Politics. Address: Head of Geriatric Clinical Unit of Nutrition, Hospital Charles Foix, 7 Avenue de la Republique, 94200 Ivry sur Seine, France.

LESSER Ruth, b. 2 Aug 1930, Bradford, England. Professor. m. David Lesser, 15 Mar 1952, 3 sons, 2 daughters. Education: BA, University College, London, 1951; BSc, 1971, PhD, 1976, Newcastle University. Appointments: Speech-Language Therapist, Newcastle, 1971; Ridley Fellow, 1972; Lecturer in Education, 1976; currently Professor, Head of Department of Speech, Newcastle University. Publications: Linguistic Investigations of Aphasia, 1978; Co-author: Psycholinguistic Assessments of Language Processing in Aphasia, 1992; Linguistics and Aphasia, 1993. Honours: Honours, College of Speech and Language Therapists, 1991. Memberships: International Association of Logopedics and Phoniatrics, Vice-President 1992; Fellow, College of Speech and Language Therapists; Associate Fellow, British

Psychological Society. Hobby: Her family. Address: Department of Speech, University of Newcastle-upon-Tyne, King George VI Building, Newcastle-upon-Tyne NE1 7RU, England.

LESSER Tristram Hugh John, b. 23 Mar 1956, Bradford, England. Otolaryngoloist. m. Yvonne Lesser, 25 Sep, 1 s, 1 d. Education: AKC, King's College London; MBBS, London; FRCS, Edinburgh; MS, London. Career: Fellow, Skull Base Surgery, Zurich; Fellow, Microvascular and Neurotology, St Louis, USA; Senior Registrar, University Hospital of Wales, Cardiff; Currently, Consultant Otolaryngologist, Walton Hospital, Liverpool. Publications: Editor, Interfaces in Medicine and Mechanics; Numerous publications. Memberships: British Medical Association; BOAC; RSM; Harvian Society; BSBS; YCMONS. Hobby: Golf. Address: Walton Hospital, Rice Lane, Liverpool, L9 1AE, England.

LEUNG Kwok-Sui, b. 23 July 1951, China. Orthopaedic Traumatologist. m. Jennifer P L Ma, 21 Apr 1978, 2 s. Education: MB BS, University of Hong Kong, 1976; MD, The Chinese University of Hong Kong, 1981; FRCS(Edinburgh); Diploma in Biomechanics, University of Strathclyde, Scotland. Appointments: Reader, Department of Orthopaedics and Traumatology, The Chinese University of Hong Kong. Publications: Biodegradable Implants in Fracture Fixation, Chief Editor, 1994; Contributor of 45 papers in professional journals and 7 chapters in various textbooks. Memberships: Fellow, Royal College of Surgeons (Edinburgh), 1980; Founding Fellow, Hong Kong College of Orthopaedic Surgeons, 1992. Hobbies: Tennis; Opera. Address: Department of Orthopaedics and Traumatology, Prince of Wales Hospital, Shatin, New Territories, Hong Kong.

LEUNG Patrick Sai-cheong, b. 7 Aug 1957, Hong Kong. Assistant Professor. m. Barbara F Lam, 10 Aug 1991, 1 son. Education: BSc (Hons) Chinese University of Hong Kong; PhD, University of California, Davis. Appointments: Assistant Professor, University of California School of Medicine, Davis, USA. Publications: Co-author: Biosynthesis of bacterial glycogen: primary structure of Salmonella typhimurium ADPglucose synthetase as deduced from the nucleotide sequence of glgC gene, 1987; The localisation, molecular weight and immunological subclass response to A fumigatus in acute bronchopulmonary aspergillosis, 1988; Site Directed mutagenesis of lysine within the immunodominant autoepitope of PDC-E2, 1990; Molecular structures of autoantigens, 1990; Molecular Characterization of the mitochondrial autoantigens in primary biliary cirrhosis, 1991; Specific Reactivity of recombinant human PDC-E1alpha in primary biliary cirrhosis, 1991; Use of designer recombinant mitochondrial antigens in the diagnosis of primary biliary cirrhosis, 1992; Combinatorial autoantibodies to dihydrolipamide acetyltransferase, the major autoantigen of primary biliary cirrhosis, 1993; Cloning and identification of autoantigens, 1993; Immunoglobulin genes in autoimmunity, 1993; Nucleotide sequence analysis of natural and combinatorial PDC-E2 Antibodies in Patients with Primary Biliary Cirrhosis: Recapitulating Immune Selection with Molecular Biology, 1994. Memberships: American Association for the Advancement of Science; American Society for Microbiology. Hobbies: Bible study; Stamp collecting; Sightseeing. Address: TB192, Division of Rheumatology/Allergy and Clinical Immunology, School of Medicine, University of California, Davis, CA 95616, USA.

LEUNG Ping-Chung, b. 20 Apr 1941, Hong Kong. Surgeon; Professor. m. D P Mak PS, Dec 1974, 1 son, 1 daughter. Education: DSc; MS; FRACS; FRCS; FHKAM; MB BS. Appointments: Consultant Surgeon, Hong Kong Government; Consultant Surgeon, Carutas Medical Centre; United Christian Hospital; Professor of Orthopaedic Surgery; Head, New Asia College, Chinese University. Publications: Current Trend of Bone Grafting, 1989; Modern Trends on Fracture Treatment, 1994; Microsurgery for Orthopaedic Surgeons, 1995; Author of 2 story books, 2 books of essays and over 250 academic works. Honours: OBE, 1994; Victoria Jubilee Prize, Edinburgh College of Surgeons; Fellowship, World Health Organisation. Memberships: Honorary Member, American Orthpaedic Association; Honorary Member, Japanese Orthopaedic Association. Hobby: Sport. Address: Prince of Wales Hospital, Shatin, Hong Kong.

LEVENSON Victor Leonard, b. 22 Feb 1955, Glasgow, Scotland. Psychologist. m. Amanda Levenson, 6 Sept 1987, 2 daughters. Education: BA with honours in Psychology; Diploma in Applied Child Psychology. Appointments: Clinical Psychologist, Child and Family Psychiatry, Paediatrics and Neurology; Senior Clinical Psychologist, Child and Adolescent Psychiatry; Community Psychologist, Learning Disabilities; Senior Community Psychologist, Disabilities; Currently Head of Learning Disability Psychology and Challenging Behaviour Service. Honours: Chartered Psychologist, 1988. Membership: Associate Fellow, British Psychological Society, Division of Clinical Psychology. Hobbies: Skiing; Youth and communal work. Address: 92a Langley Road, Watford, Herts WD1 3PJ, England.

LEVER Alvin, b. 27 Jan 1939, St Louis, MO, USA. Executive Director. m. Norine Schwedt, 27 Jan 1963, 2 s. Education: BS, Architectural Sciences; BArch; MA, Applied Psychology. Career: Project Designer, Sir Basil Spence Architects, 1963-65; Senior Project Designer, Hellmuth, Obata and Kassabaum, 1965-68; Vice President and Project Manager, Hellmuth, Obata and Kassabaum, 1968-72; Vice President, Facility Developer, Michael Reese Medical Center, 1972-74; Vice President, General Manager, Apelco International Ltd, 1974-90; Director of Membership and Finance, 1990-92, Executive Director, 1992-, American College of Chest Physicians. Honour: President, Congregation B'nai Tikvah. Memberships include: American Society of Medical Society Executives; American Society of Association Executives; Chicago Society of Association Executives. Hobbies: Bicycling; Scuba Diving. Address: 3300 Dundee Road, Northbrook, IL 60062, USA.

LEVER Andrew Michael Lindsay, b. 23 June 1953, Sri Lanka. University Lecturer; Honorary Consultant Physician. m. Elizabeth Ann, 22 July 1981, 2 s, 1 d. Education: BSc, 1975, MB Bch, 1978, MD, 1987, University of Wales, MRCP, 1981. Appointments: University Hospital of Wales; Northwick Park Hospital, Newcastle; Royal Free Hospital; Research: Clinical research Centre, Royal Free Hospital; Dana Farber Cancer Institute; Senior Lecturer, St George's Hospital, 1988-91; University of Cambridge, 1991-; University Lecturer, Honorary Consultant Physician. Publications: Contributor of numerous works on professional and scientific subjects. Honours: FRCP, London, 1993; FRCP Edinburgh, 1993; MRCPath, 1993. Memberships: Association of Physicians; Royal College of Physicians, London and Edinburgh; British Society for Study of Infection; Medical Research Society; American Society for Virology. Hobbies: Photography; Wine. Address: Department of Medicine, Level 5, Addenbrooke's Hospital, Hills Road, Cambridge CB2 2QQ, England.

LEVERNES Sverre, b. 25 Mar 1949, Sarpsborg, Norway. Medical Physicist. m. Arnhild Levernes, 7 Mar 1977, 2 sons, 1 daughter. Education: MSc, Institute of Technology, Trondheim, 1974. Appointments include: Currently Researcher, Norwegian Radium Hospital, Oslo. Publications: User Requirements on CT-based Computed Dose Planning Systems in Radiation Therapy, 1983. Memberships: International Organisation of Medical Physicists; European Federation of Organisations for Medical Physics; European Society of Therapeutic Radiology and Oncology. Hobbies: Skiing; Running; Scouting; Classical music. Address: Department of Medical Physics, The Norwegian Radium Hospital, PO Box 20, Montebello, N-0310 Oslo, Norway.

LEVIN Jeffrey Scott, b. 17 Feb 1959, Chicago, IL, USA. Social Epidemiologist. Education: AB, Duke University, 1981; MPH, University of North Carolina, 1983; PhD, University of Texas Medical Branch, 1987; NIH Postdoctoral Fellow, Institute of Gerontology, University of Michigan, 1987-89. Appointments: Associate Professor of Family and Community Medicine, Eastern Virginia Medical School. Publications: Reality and the Mind, Co-Editor, 1995; Religion in Aging and Health: Theoretical Foundations and Methodological Frontiers, Editor, 1994; Contributor of over 70 refereed articles, chapters and reviews. Honours: TREAT Special Recognition Award, 1994; Elias Hochman Award for Research in Environmental Problems, 1987; Rose and Harry Walk Award for Research in Gerontology, 1986. Memberships: American Public Health Association; American Society on Aging; American Sociological Association; Gerontological Society of America; Institute of Noetic Sciences; ISSSEEM; Society for Epidemiologic Research; Society for the Scientific Study of Religion; Society of Teachers of Family Medicine. Hobbies: Country Music Songwriting; Studying Kabbalah; Working Out. Address: 2210 Wolfsnare Road, Virginia Beach, VA 23454, USA.

LEVINE Elena, Physician. Education: BA, University of Pensylvania; MD, New York University School of Medicine. Appointments: Attending Physician & Clincal Instructor, Mt Sinai Medical Center, New York, 1984-85; Attending Physician, Columbia University, 1985-; Board Certified in Family Practice & Preventive Medicine; Certified in Clinical Hypnosis. Publications: The Male Role in Teenage Pregnancy &

Parenting: New Directions for Public Policy, 1990. Memberships: American Public Health Association; American Academy of Family Physicians. Hobbies: Gardening; Travel. Address: Columbia University Health Service, New York, NY 10027, USA.

LEVINE Macy I, b. 19 May 1920, Johnstown, Pennsylvania, USA. Physician. m. Evelyn Finesman, 28 June 1948, 3 s, 1 d. Education: BS, University of Pittsburgh, 1940; MD, University of Pittsburgh School of Medicine, 1943; Internship, University of Pittsburgh Medical Centre; resident, Allergy and Internal Medicine, Veteran's Administration Hospital, Aspinwall, Pennsylvania, 1947-49. Appointments: Fellow in Medicine, Lahey Clinic, Boston, 1950-51; Postdoctorate Research Fellow, USPHS, Peter Bent Brigham Hospital, Boston, 1951-52; private practice of Allergy and Medicine, Pittsburgh, 1952-; Clinical Professor of Medicine, University of Pittsburgh School of Medicine. Publications: Monograph on Insect Allergy, Co-editor, 2nd edition, 1986; Contributor of numerous articles, book chapters, reviews and abstracts. Honours: Distinguished Service Award, American Academy of Allergy and Immunology, 1987; Frederick M Jacob MD Physician Merit Award for Outstanding Service, Allegheny County Medical Society, 1988. Memberships: American Academy of Allergy and Immunology, Fellow, Vice President, 1982-83; American College of Physicians, Fellow; American College of Allergy and Immunology; American Medical Association; Allegheny County Medical Society. Hobbies: Tennis; Cross-Country Skiing. Address: 3347 Forbes Avenue, Pittsburgh, PA 15213, USA.

LEVY David Alfred, b. 27 Aug 1930, Washington DC, USA. Medical Researcher. m. Anne Levy-Badoux, 26 Apr 1985, 2 s, 1 d. Education: BS, Zoology, University of Maryland, Baltimore, 1952; MD, Medicine, University of Maryland, School of Medicine, 1954; Fellow, Immunology, The Johns Hopkins University, School of Medicine, 1966. Appointments include: Directeur Adjoint, Centre d'Immunologie et de Biologie Pierre Fabre, France, 1985-90; Occasional Reviewer for various journals, 1987-; Consultant, Pharmaceutical Research and Development, 1990-; Scientific Advisor, Service d'Allergie, Hôpital Rothschild, Paris, France, 1991-. Publications include: Over 80 presentations at congresses and symposia; Over 80 scientific publications, 1960-, including: Co-author, Psychological Symptoms in Asthma and Chronic Urticaria, 1994. Memberships include: Alpha Omega Alpha, 1954; Emeritus, American Association of Immunologists, 1967; Collegium Internationale Allergologicum, 1976; American Society of Tropical Medicine and Hygiene, 1979; Société Française d'Allergologie, 1986. Address: 11 Quai Saint Michel, 75005 Paris, France.

LEVY Norman B, b. 28 May 1931, New York City, USA. Psychiatrist. m. Dr Carol Lois Spiegel, 26 Dec 1970, 1 s, 3 d. Education: Doctor of Medicine; BA; MD. Appointments: Intern, Maimonides Medical Center, 1956-57; Teaching Fellow, Resident Physician Medicine, University of Pittsburgh, 1957-58; Captain, USAF and Chief of Medicine, 6466 USAF Hospital, Japan, 1958-60; Resident Physician, Pscychiatry, Kings County Hospital, 1960-63; Assistant Professor, Department of Psychiatry, State University of NY, 1963-80; Currently, Director of Liaison Psychiatry Division and Professor of Psychiatry, Medicine and Surgery, NY Medical College. Publications: Living and Dying: Adaptation to Hemodalysis, 1974; Psychonephrology 1, 1976; Psychonephrology 2, 1978; Co-author, Men in Transition: Theory and Practice, 1983; 145 learned articles. Memberships: Fellow of, American College of Psychiatrists; American Psychiatric Association; American College of Physicians; Academy of Psychosomatic Medicine; International College of Psychosomatic Medicine; Council of American Psychosomatic Society. Address: Liaison Psychiatry Division, NY Medical College, Valhalla, NY 10595, USA.

LEW Dukhee Betty, b. 1 June 1952, Seoul, Korea. Physician. Education: BA, 1976, MD, 1980, Temple University, Philadelphia, Pennsylvania, USA; Paediatric Internship and Residency, Shands Medical Center, University of Florida, Gainesville, 1980-83; Allergy and Immunology Training, National Jewish Center for Immunology and Respiratory Medicine, 1983-86; Board Certified, American Board of Pediatrics, 1985; Diplomate, American Board of Allergy and Immunology, 1985. Appointments: Assistant Professor of Paediatrics, 1986-92, Associate Professor of Paediatrics, 1992-, University of Tennessee, Memphis. Publications: Co-author, contributions to: Lung, 1990; Journal of Leukocyte Biology, 1991; Journal of Clinical Investigation, 1991, 1994; American Journal of Respiratory Cellular and Molecular Biology, 1992; Prostaglandins, 1992. Honours: Research Grant, American Lung Association of Tennessee, 1990-91; FIRST

Award, National Institutes of Health, Heart and Lung Institute, 1991-96; Research Grant, American Lung Association, 1991-92. Memberships: American Academy of Allergy and Clinical Immunology; American College of Allergists; Society of Leukocyte Biology; Society of Pediatric Research; Tennessee Thoracic Society. Hobbies: Organ; Photography. Address: Crippled Children's Foundation Research Center, Room 401, 50 N Dunlap Street, Memphis, TN 38103, USA.

LEWIS Barry Victor, b. 8 June 1936. Gynaecologist. Education: MD; FRCS; FRCOG. Appointments: Past President, British Society for Gynaecological Endoscopy; Senior Gynaecological Surgeon, Watford-Mount Vernon Trust, Watford, England. Address: Department of Obstetrics and Gynaecology, Watford General Hospital, Vicarage Road, Watford, Hertfordshire, England.

LEWIS Brian, b. 14 Mar 1955, Donnington, Shropshire, England. Registered Osteopath. Education: DO, British School of Osteopathy, 1975-79; BA, Open University, 1989-91. Appointments: Senior Clinic Tutor, 1987-90, Lecturer in Osteopathic Diagnosis, 1986-90, Clinic Tutor, 1985-87, British School of Osteopathy; Private practice, 1979-. Memberships: General Council and Register of Osteopaths. Hobbies: Music; Chess' Sport; reading. Address: 16 Glamis Close, Hemel Hempstead, Hertfordshire HP2 7QB, England.

LEWIS Philip Christie, b. 19 July 1942. Psychiatrist. m. Rosa Elisa Dragone, 17 Sept 1965, 3 daughters. Education: MD; MA. Appointments: Chief, Community Mental Health Service, Ft Clayton, Panama, 1975-79; Private Practice, Argentina, 1979-88; Chief, Department of Psychiatry, California, 1988-93; Deputy Commander, Clinical Services, California, 1993-94. Honours: Meritorious Service Medal, 1994. Memberships: American Psychiatric Association; Christian Medical & Dental Society. Hobbies: Bicycling; Riding; Hiking. Address: 307 Fitch Avenue, Monterey, CA 93940 6904, USA.

LEYLAND-JONES Brian R, b. 20 June 1949, Shropshire, England. Professor. Education: BSc, 1st Class Honours, 1970, MB BS, St Mary's Hospital Medical School, 1973, University of London; LRCP; MRCS, 1973; Diplomate, American Board of Internal Medicine, 1979; Oncology, 1981. Appointments: Head, Developmental Chemotherapy Section, Investigational Drug Branch, Division of Cancer Treatment, National Cancer Institute, 1983-89; Minda de Gunzburg Professor and Chairman, Department of Oncology, McGill University, Canada, 1990-. Publications: Antineoplastic Drug Sensitivity of Human MCF-7 Breast Cancer Cells Stably Transfected with a Human Alpha Class Glutathione S-Transferase Gene, Co-author, 1991; Two-fluoro-arabinosyl pyrimidines: a study in pre-clinical to clinical translation, 1991; A competitive enzyme-linked immunosorbent assay (ELISA) for the determination of NAT 2 phenotypes, Co-author, 1995; Stereoselective Pharmacokinetics of Ifosphamide and its 2-and 3-N-dechloroethylated Metabolites in Female Cancer Patients, Co-author, Submitted for publication, 1995. Honours: St Mary's Hospital Cheadle Gold Medal in Medicine, 1974; Pharmaceutical Manufacturers Association Foundation Fellowship Award in Clinical Pharmacology, 1978-79. Memberships: British Medical Association; American Society of Pharmacology & Experimental Therapeutics; American College of Physicians; American Society of Clinical Oncology; American Association for Cancer Research; Royal College of Physicians and Surgeons of Canada. Address: McGill University, Department of Oncology, 3655 Drummond, Suite 701, Montreal, Quebec H3G 1Y6, Canada.

LI Arthur Kwok Cheung, b. 23 June 1945, Hong Kong. Professor of Surgery. m. Diana Chester, 24 July 1974, 2 sons. Education: King's College, Cambridge, 1963-66; BA (Cantab), 1966; MB BChir (Cantab), 1969; Middlesex Hospital Medical School, 1966-69; MA (Cantab), 1970; FRCS (Eng), 1973; Full Accreditation, General Surgery, Royal College of Surgeons of England, 1978; ECFMG, 1978; VQE, 1978; Medical Board Licence, Commonwealth of Massachusetts, USA, 1979; MD (Cantab), 1981; FRCS (Edinburgh), 1982; FRACS, 1983; FACS, 1987; FPCS (Hon), 1994; FRCS (Glasgow) (Hon), 1995. Appointments include: Currently Foundation Professor of Surgery, Chairman of Surgical Services, Dean, Faculty of Medicine, Chinese University of Hong Kong and Prince of Wales Hospital, Shatin, New Territories, Hong Kong. Publications include: Reports of trials on surgical aspects of treatment, particularly in areas of upper gastrointestinal surgery and hepatopancreatobiliary surgery. Address: Department of Surgery, Clinical Sciences Building, Prince of Wales Hospital, Shatin, NY, Hong Kong.

LI Baosen, b. 17 May 1937, Tianjin, China. Physician. m. 29 Apr 1961, 3 sons. Education: Medical University. Appointments: Physician, Chief Physician, Director of Gynaecological Department, Director of Obstetrics, Gynaecology Hospital. Publications: Metallic Bead Chain Urethrocystography in the Diagnosis of Urinary Stress Incontinence, 1982; Surgical Treatment of Cervical Incompetence: Report of 23 Cases, 1985; Treatment of Congenital Absence of Vagina with Hemometra, 1985; Spreading Application for TDP, 1987; Clinical Diagnosis and Treatment of First-Aid, 1989; Biofeedback Treatment of Climacteric Syndrome, 1989; Study of Operation Treatment on Heavy Endometriosis, 1992; Type YSZ-1 Remote Control Syringe of Uterus Oviduct, 1994. Honours: 3rd Progress Award of Science and Technology, for Spreading Application for TDP, Tianjin; 2nd Progress Award of Science and Technology, for Study of Operation Treatment on Heavy Endometriosis, Tianjin. Memberships: China Behaviour Medicine Association; Standing Member of Council, Tianjin Overseas Exchange Association of Medicine and Health. Hobby: Fishing. Address: Tianjin Women's Health Care Institution, No 169 Machang Road, Hexi District, Tianjin, China.

LI Bin Zhi, b. 4 Nov 1934, Shandong, China. Professor. m. Miss Wang, 1954, 1 son, 3 daughters. Education: BA, Hebei Traditional Chinese Medicine, 1958. Career: Assistant Researcher, Hebei Traditional Chinese Medicine Research Institute, 1959; Assistant Researcher, Hebei Medicine Department, 1965; Head of Science Research Section, 1978; Professor, Hebei Medical College, currently. Publications: Researchon Radix Aconiti Praeparata, 1983; Effective Recipes of Traditional Medicine, 1985; Questions and Answers about Traditional Chinese Medicine, 1989; Handbook on Diagnosis, 1990. Honours: First Prize of Medical Workers, 1982; Second Prize among Authors of Medical Books, 1984. Memberships: Vice Director, Hebei Chinese Medicine Society; Vice Director, Editors Society of Medical Publications. Hobby: Game of Chess. Address: Medical Periodical of Hebei Medical College, Hebei, China.

LI Bing, b. 28 Jun 1920, Wuhu Anhui, China. Doctor. m. Sun Fang, 12 Dec 1948, 2 s, 1 d. Education: Yanan Medical College. Career: Surgeon in Charge, Central Hospital of Yanan, 1941; Doctor in Charge, Vice-Director, Surgery, 1st Field Hospital of Liberation Army, 1947; Vice-Director, Cancer Institute, Chinese Academy of Medical Sciences, 1956-; Liaison Official of Chinese Party of Cancer Branch of Siho-American Cooperation, 1979-; Vice-Chair and Director General, Chinese Cancer Research Foundation, 1985-. Publications: Editor in Chief, Practical Oncology, 1977; Co-author, Atlas of Cancer Mortality in the People's Republic of China, 1979; Mortality of Chinese Malignant Tumor and Its Distribution Characteristics, 1980; Recent Progress in Research on Esophageal Cancer in China, 1980. Honour: People's Meritorious Cadre Medal, 1st Class, Ministry of Health, 1947. Membership: Chinese Association of Medicine. Address: PO Box 2258, Beijing, China.

LI Chenshan, b. 29 July 1935, Tongshan, China. Docotor of Traditional Chinese Medicine. m. Zhang Xiumin, 8 Dec 1957, 1 son, 2 daughters. Education: BM, Hebei Traditional Chinese Medicine College, 1962. Appointments: The Municipal Red Cross Jian Chang Kang Fu Hospital. Publications: Mini-arterial Pulse Condition, 1987; Broncho-pneumonia Treated by Mini-acupuncture, 1992; Observation on 500 Cases of Tracheitis Treated by In Lian Wan. Hobbies: Swimming; Classic Chinese Liberal Arts; Physics; Music. Address: No A Si Yang Road, Hebei, Tianjin, China.

LI Chun Sang, b. 23 Feb 1951, Hong Kong. Physician. m. Chu Yuk Chun, 19 Nov 1982, 1 son. Education: MB, BS (Hong Kong); MRCP (Hong Kong); FRCP (Glasgow); FRCP (Edinburgh); FHKAM, (Medicine). Appointments include: Currently Consultant Physician, Department of Medicine, Head, Division of Nephrology, Queen Elizabeth Hospital, Kowloon. Publications: Clinical Profile of Chinese Patients with system lupus erythematosus, 1993; Peritoneal equilibration test in Chinese CAPD patients, 1993; Cadaveric Kidney Transplantation in a single center in Hong Kong, 1994. Memberships: International Society for Peritoneal Dialysis; Asian Society of Transplantation. Hobbies: Music; Reading. Address: Medicl Department, Queen Elizabeth Hospital, 30 Gascoigne Road, Kowloon, Hong Kong.

LI Defen, b. 15 July 1931, Guizhou, China. Physician. m. Yang Zhu Xun, 1 Aug 1961, 2 sons. Education: BA, 3rd Military Medical College, 1958. Appointments: Physician, Radiology Department, 2nd Military Medical College, 1959; Attending Doctor, Radiology Department, 1981,

Vice-Director, Ultrasonic Department, 1987, Chief Physician, 1989, Air Force General Hospital, Beijing. Publications: Co-author: Combine Chinese Traditional with Western Medicine in the Study of Tumours, 1988; Practical Medicine Dictionary, 1989; Selections of Rare Cases of Radiology, 1990; The Clinical Ultrasonic Diagnostics, 1991. Honours: Prize of Science and Technology Progress in the Military Forces, 4th degree, 1985, 1991, 1993, 3rd degree, 1991. Memberships include: Councillor, Chinese Medical Imaging Technology Association; Councillor, Military Medical Ultrasonic Special Agency; Chinese Association of Ultrasound in Medicine and Engineering. Hobbies: Travel; Music; Reading. Address: Bld 20, 1-301, Xi Diao Yu Tai No 30, Beijing 100036, China.

LI Dexin, b. 15 Mar 1935, Ying Kou, China. Professor of Medicine. m. Cheng Huiqin, 10 Oct 1966, 2 sons. Education: Graduated, Research Class, Philosophy Department, Liaoning University, 1960; Graduated, Medical Department, Liaoning College of Traditional Chinese Medicine, 1964. Appointments: Assistant, 1964-72, Lecturer, 1973-82, Vice-Professor, 1983-84, Professor, Tutor for doctoral degree, 1985-, Liaoning College of Traditional Chinese Medicine, Shenyang. Publications include: Practical Foundation of the Theory of TCM, 1985; The Basic Theory of TCM, 1985; The Diagnostics of TCM, 1986; Discussion on Qi and Blood, 1990; Andropathy of TCM, 1990; Differentiation of Syndrome of TCM, 1991; Outline of Diagnosis and Treatment of Disease in TCM, 1991; Research on Relationship Between Spleen Deficiency and Bio-membrane, 1992. Honours: Excellent Expert; Excellent Scientist; Excellent Teacher, 1985, Model Researcher, 1987, 1989, 1991, 1993, Liaoning Province and Shenyang City; Special Government Awards for Special Contributor in China, 1991. Memberships: Chairman, Traditional Chinese Medicine Theory Research Committee; Chairman, Professors' Friendship Union of China and Japan Traditional Medicine; Director, Shenyang Promotion Association for Cultural Exchange with Foreign Countries. Hobbies: Literature; Philosophy. Address: Chongshan (East) Road 79, Huanggu District, Shenyang 110032, Liaoning, China.

LI Ding-Guo, b. 7 Sept 1946, Shanghai, China. Doctor. m. Li Li, 14 Apr 1973, 1 son. Education: MSc, Shanghai 2nd Medical University, 1981; MD, PhD, Shanghai 2nd Medical University, 1989. Appointments: Director, Department of Scientific Research & Technology, Xinhua Hospital, Shanghai 2nd Medical University. Publications: Use of calcium-channel blockers in cirrhotic patients with portal hypertension, 1990; Effect of nifedipine on portal venous pressure in patients with cirrhotic portal hypertension, 1990; Significance of serum procollagen-III-peptide in reflecting the therapeutic effects of calcium-channel blockers on hepatic fibrosis, 1991. Honour: Excellent Chinese Doctor, 1989. Memberships: Chinese Medical Association; Society of Gastroenterology; International Gastro-Surgical Club. Hobbies: Table Tennis. Address: 1665 Kong Jiang Road, Shanghai 200092, China.

LI Fang Quan, b. 21 Dec 1937, Nan Kang, Jiangxi. Professor of Urology. m. Mrs Lu Fan, 1 Oct 1966, 1 daughter. Education: Jiangxi Medical College, 1957-62. Career: Resident, 1962-80; Visiting Surgeon, 1980-87; Associate Professor, 1987-94; Professor 1994-; Head of Chinese Medical Team in Kebili Tunisia, 1990-92; Professor of Urology and Head of Department of Surgery, First Hospital Ganzhou, currently. Publications: Management of Bilateral Upper Urinary Tract Calouli with Urinemia, 1983; Treatment of Male Urethra Injury, 1989; Renal Transplant, 1994. Honours: Renal Transplant, acquired the Science and Technical Award of Ganzhou County Government, 1992. Memberships: Society of Urology CMA; Council Member, Society of Urology, CMA Jiangxi Branch; Council Member, Society of Urology. CMA Ganzhou Branch. Hobby: Swimming. Address: Jiangxi Ganzhou First Hospital, Ganzhou, Jiangxi 341000, China.

LI Fengwu, b. 6 Feb 1965, Tianjin, China. University Lecturer. m. Liu Jian, 8 July 1994. Education: BS, Nankai University, Tianjin, 1987; MD, The Capital Medical University, Beijing, 1990. Appointments: Assistant in Parasitology and Medical Entomology, currently Lecturer in Parasitology and Medical Entomology, The Capital Medical University. Publications: Analysis of free amino acids in hemolymph of Aedes albopictus, 1990; Analysis of protein and proteinase in the midgut of Anopheles stephensi and Aedes albopictus, 1991. Honours: 1st Class Science Award, Beijing Bureau of Medicine. Memberships: Chinese Society of Parasitology, Youth Committee Member; Chinese Society of Entomology. Hobbies: Hiking; Badminton; Music; Fine art. Address:

Department of Parasitology, The Capital Medical University, Beijing 100054, China.

LI Fobo, b. 10 Jan 1939, Guangdong, China. Professor of Orthopaedics. m. Pan Xiaobin, 21 Jul 1967, 1 s, 1 d. Appointments: Resident; Lecturer; Associate Professor; Professor of Othopaedics; Head of Orthopaedic Unit. Publications: On the Instruments and Technic for Small Vessel, 1978; The Changes of Somato-Sensory Evoked Potential following Spinal Cord Injury. Memberships: Chinese Medical Association. Hobbies: Tennis; Football. Address: Sun Yan Sen University of Medical Sciences, Guangzhou, China.

LI Guoxian, b. 5 Dec 1938. Physician. m. Yan Yi, 1 Jan 1966, 1 son, 1 daughter. Education: MB, Medical Faculty, Jiangxi Medical College. Appointments: Resident, Assistant, 1963; Visiting Doctor, Lecturer, 1980; Deputy Physician-in-Chief, Associate Professor, 1986, then Professor, Physician-in-Chief, Director, Department of Traditional Chinese Medicine, Jiangxi Medical College. Publications: Editor-in-chief, 5 books, 1986-91, including: Clinical Hemorrheology; Prevention and Treatment of Thrombotic Diseases and Apoplexy; Over 60 theses including: Blood stasis and cancer, extracorporeal thrombosis and blood platelet adherence, 1987, 1988; Hemorheology and blood stasis in 164 cases of nephritis, 1993, 1994; Study of eye-signs in blood stasis; Comparison and study of standards of blood stasis in Japan and China; Comparative study of diagnostic standards of eye-signs in blood stasis and other blood stasis syndrome. Honours: Praise on breakthroughs in National Natural Science Foundation projects, 1992-94; Prizes: Advanced Worker, 1977-78, Best Theses, 1980-84, Excellent Teaching, 1983-85, Jiangxi Medical College; Best Theses: Provincial Public Health Department, 1980-88; Eminent Supervisor, Society of Integrated Chinese and Western Medicine, 1987; 1st Prize, Best Theses, Jiangxi Society of Integrated Chinese and Western Medicine, 1987-90; Advanced Scientific and Technological Worker, Jiangxi Science Commission, 1990; Best Theses, Society of Hemorrheology, China, 1991-93. Memberships: Standing Council, Secretary-General, Jiangxi Branch, Society of Integrated Chinese and Western Medicine; Chinese Medical Association; Member of the International Society of Clinical Haemorheology; New Drugs Assessment and Examination Commission; Jiangxi High Professional Title Judgment Commission for Health Series; 2 editorial boards. Hobbies: Acupuncture; Moxibustion; Growing Chinese medicinal herbs. Address: Department of Traditional Chinese Medicine, The First Affiliated Hospital, Jiangxi Medical College, Nanchang, Jiangxi 330006, China.

LI He, b. 17 Sept 1963, China. Doctor of Chinese Medicine. Education: Diploma, Chinese Medicine. Membership: Register of Traditional Chinese Medicine. Hobby: Music. Address: 75 Gloucester Road, London SW7 4SS, England.

LI Hengyou, b. 1 Feb 1925, Nanchang, Jiangxi, China. Professor of Traditional Chinese Medicine. m. Qi Shu, 6 Nov 1946, 3 sons, 1 daughter. Education: Diplomas, Nanjing Traditional Chinese Medical College, 1959; MD equivalent, Advanced Worker in Tradition Chinese Medicine, 1985. Appointments: Doctor of Chinese Medicine, Chinese Medicine Hospital, Jiangxi, 1954; Doctor of Chinese Medicine, 1955-80, Director of Chinese Medicine, 1984-, Women's Hospital of Jiangxi, Nanchang. Publications: Co-author: The prevention and treatment of early squamous cervical cancer by pharmaco-conization with Chinese traditional drugs, 1983; Treatment of infertility by traditional Chinese medicine, 1988. Honours: National 1st Grade Award for Important Scientific Achievement in Chinese Medicine, 1986; National Development Award, 3rd Grade, 1989; Scientific Achievement Award for Traditional Chinese Medicine, 3rd Grade, Department of Public Health, 1990. Memberships: Committee Member, Chinese Medicine Society of Gynaecology; Major Member of Committee, Chinese Medical Society in Gynaecology, Jiangxi Province; Anti-Tumour Society. Hobbies: Chess; Chinese Taiji. Address: Jiangxi Province Women's Hospital, 72 Ba Yi Ave, Nanchang, Jiangxi 330006, China.

LI Huan-Ying, b. 17 Aug 1921, Beijing, China. Professor; Researcher. Education: MPH, School of Hygiene and Public Health, Johns Hopkins University, Baltimore, USA, 1953; DPH, School of Tropical Hygiene and Medicine, University of London, England, 1957. Appointments: Medical Officer, World Health Organization, 1950-57; Research Associate, Institute of Dermatology, Chinese Academy of Medical Sciences, 1959-78; Currently Senior Research Member, Beijing Tropical Medical Research Institute, 1959-. Publications: Leprosy Control in Shandong Province, China 1955-1983, 1985; Short-term

Multi-drug Therapy in Multi-bacillary Leprosy, 1989; Problems of Leprosy Relapse in Chjina, 1993. Memberships: Indian Leprosy Association; International Leprosy Association; Vice-President, China Leprosy Association. Hobbies: Reading; Listening to classical music. Address: Friendship Hospital, 95 Yong An Road, Beijing 100050, China.

LI Huimin, b. 8 Dec 1928, Xuzhou, China. Teacher. m. Zhai Meide, 25 Jan 1952, 3 s. Education: MD, College of Medicine, Nanking University. Appointments: Assistant Instructor in Anatomy; Lecturer of Anatomy; Professor of Human Anatomy and Neuroanatomy. Publications: Anatomy, Histology and Embryology of the Thyroid Gland, 1979; Skin, 1993; Contributor of numerous professional papers. Honours: 2nd Grade Award of Science and Technology Progress, PLA, 1987. Memberships: Association of Chinese Anatomists; International Association of Study of Pain. Hobby: Music. Address: Department of Anatomy, The Fourth Military Medical University, Xian 710032, China.

LI Jia Zhi, b. 25 Jul 1937, Putian, Fujian, China. doctor of Surgery. m. Yan Chunying, 13 Dec 1969, 1 s, 1 d. Education: MD, Zhejiang Medical University, China, 1960. Appointments: Resident of Second Affiliated Hospital of Zhejiang Medical University, 1960; Doctor-in-Charge, First Affiliated Hospital of Wenzhou Medical College, 1978; Associate Professor of Wenzhou Medical College, 1986; Professor of Wenzhou Medical College, 1991; Professor of Surgery/Chief Physician, Department of Gynaecology, First Affiliated Hospital of Wenzhou Medical College, China. Publications: include, Postoperative Complications of Rectal Malignant Tumour, 1986; Analysis of the Causes of Misdiagnosis and Delayed Treatment in Carcinoma of the Anorectum, 1986; Non-Recurrent Laryngeal Nerve with Report of One Case, 1987; Initial Analysis of the Relationship between Serum T3, T4 and Rectal Cancer, 1987; Analysis of Relationship between Serum T3, T4 and Dukes' Classification in Rectal Carcinoma, 1988; Re-Operation on Postoperative Recurrent Cancer of the Large Intestine, 1990; Management of Primary Carcinoma of the Large Intestine Diagnosed during Pregnancy, 1990. Honours: Two Awards for Excellent Articles, Science Association of Zhejiang Province, China, 1991; Four Awards for Excellent Articles, Science Association of Wenzhou City, Zheijiang, 1989-92; Award for Excellent Articles of Anticancer Association of Zhejiang Province, 1987. Memberships: Chinese Medical Association; Chinese Anticancer Association. Hobbies: Drawing; Sports. Address: Department of Oncology, The First Affiliated Hospital of Wenzhou Medical college, Zhejiang, China.

LI Jiannong, b. 8 Mar 1934, Jiangsu, China. Dentist. m. Feng Yueyi, Feb 1964, 1 son, 1 daughter. Education: MD, Shanghai 2nd Medical University, 1959. Appointments: Currently Professor, Dean, Department of Stomatology, Anhui Medical University, Hefei. Publications: Prescription Handbook of Oral Medicines, 1990; Co-author: The Operation of Peripheral Branch Avulsion for Primary Trigeminal Neuralgia and Its Histo-pathological Study, 1993; Esthetics of Stomatology, 1994; Modern Clinical Genetics, 1994. Memberships: Chinese Medical Association; Vice-Director, Anhui Stomatology Association; Editor, Chinese Journal of Stomatology. Hobbies: Running; Swimming. Address: Department of Stomatology, Anhui Medical University, Hefei 230032, Anhui, China.

LI Jianqing, b. 27 Apr 1937. Professor of Microbiology. m. 1 Oct 1977, 1 s. Education: Graduate, Microbiology, Wuhan University, 1959. Career: Lecturer, Biology, Wuhan University; Currently, Professor and Chairman, Microbiology, Guangzhou Medical College. Publications: Editor and Co-author, A Textbook of Medical Microbiology, 1989, 2nd edition, 1993. Honours: 1st Prize, Science and Technology in Guangzhou, 1978; Excellent Teacher, Guangzhou Medical College, 1984. Membership: Associate Secretary General, Guangdong Association of Microbiology. Hobbies: Chinese Calligraphy; Running; Volleyball. Address: 195 Dongfengxi Road, Guangzhou, China.

LI John Kong-Jiann, b. 28 Aug 1950, Taiwan, China. Professor of Biomedical Engineering. m. Evangeline C-L Sim, 14 July 1973, 2 sons. Education: BSc, Honours, University of Manchester, England; MSE, 1974, PhD, 1978, University of Pennsylvania, USA. Appointments: research Fellow, University of Pennsylvania, 1973-77; Head, Biomedical Engineering in Cardiology, Presbyterian University of Pennsylvania Medical centre, Philadelphia, 1977-79; Assistant Professor of biomedical Engineering, 1979-83, Associate Professor, 1983-89, Professor, 1989-, Rutgers University; Adjunct Professor of Surgery, UMDNJ, Robert Wood Johnson Medical School, New Jersey. Publications: Arterial System Dynamics, 1987; Proceedings of 19th NE Bioengineering Conference,

1993; Feedback Effects in Heart-Arterial System Interaction, 1993; Arterial Compliance, 1994; Transdermal Drug Delivery. 1991. Honours: International Union of Physiological Congress Award, 1982; Elected Fellow, American College of Angiology, 1994; Fellow, American College of Cardiology, 1995. Memberships: American Heart Association; American College of Cardiology; American College of Angiology; Biomedical Engineering Society; Cardiovascular Society; IEEE. Hobbies: Art; Music; Travel; Reading; Tennis. Address: Department of Biomedical Engineering, Rutgers University, Piscataway, NJ 08855, USA.

LI Jun-zhu, b. 10 May 1936, Heilongjiang, China. Ophthalmologist. m. Zhao Gui-shun, 29 July 1960, 1 daughter. Appointments: Professor; Chief Doctor; Director. Publications: Strabismus and Amblyopia; Common Eye Diseases; Vision Protection of Teenagers; Practical Paediatric Ophthalmology. Honours: Both National and Provincial Outstanding Expert and Model Worker. Memberships: National Committee of PBL; Council of Optics; Society of Ophthalmic Genetics, China; Deputy Chief of Ophthalmic Society; Director, Eye Institute, Heilongjiang. Hobbies: Music. Address: The Institute for Prevention and Treatment of Ophthalmic Diseases of Heilongjiang Province, No 151 Eastern Dazhi Street, Nangang, Harvin 150001, China.

LI Juncheng, b. 20 Nov 1938, Jiangxi, China. Teacher. m. Dezho Jiang, 1 Jan 1965, 1 s, 1 d. Education: MD, Hunan Medical College, 1960. Appointments: Assistant, 1961, Lecturer, 1978, Dean, 1984-90, Associate Professor, 1985, Professor, 1991, Chairman, Department of Physiology, 1992-93, Hunan Medical University. Publications: Atrial Natriuretic Factor: Lack of Effect on ATPase Activity of Erythrocyte Membranes, in Proc West Pharmological Society, 1992; Clinical Physiology, book, 1994. Memberships: Chinese Association of Physiological Sciences; Vice Director, Physiological Society. Hobbies: Running; Sport; Fishing. Address: Department of Physiology, Hunan Medical University, Changsha, Hunan 410078, China.

LI Lai-Tian, b. 14 Sept 1937, Jinan, Shandong, China. Professor. m. 1967, 1 son, 1 daughter. Education: Graduated, Department of Biology, Shandong Teachers University. Appointments include: Doctor, Lecturer, 1978; Associate Professor, 1987; Teacher for Master's degree; Established subject of Holographic Medicine, 1989. Publications: 10 books including: Holographic Medicine, 1991; 40 papers especially including comparative physiology on: The Lung Controls the Skin and Hair, 1987. Honours: Gold Medal for Holographic Medical Instrument, 15th World Fair, Zagreb, 1987; Silver Medal, 3rd National Invention Show, 1987; 3rd Science and Technology Prize for HM1 and its Clinical Use, Shandong, 1991. Memberships: Chairman, Chinese Holographic Medical Society; Director, Standing Committee, Chinese Cosmic Holographic Society. Hobbies: Music; Outdoor exercise.

LI Lan-Sun, b. 10 Sept 1932, Changsha, Hunan, China. Cardiology. m. Liu Wei Yong, 19 oct 1956, 1 son, 1 daughter. Education: Graduate, 7th Military Medical University, 1955; Postgraduate of Cardiology, 1965-68; Visiting Scholar, UCLA Medical Center, USA, 1990-91. Appointments: Cardiologist, 1st Teaching Hospital of Fourth Military Medical University, Xian, 1968-83; Associate Professor, Professor, Chief of the Department of Cardiology, 1983-93. Publications: Hand Book of New Diagnosis in Medicine, co-author, 1990; Interventional Cardiology, co-author, 1991; A Modern Clinical Medical Dictionary, co-author, 1993. Memberships: Vice Chairman of Committee, Shaanxi Branch of Chinese Society of Cardiology. Address: Department of Cardiology, Xijing Hospital, 15 West Chang-le Road, Xian 710032, China.

LI Lian-Niang, b. 16 June 1929, Ambarawa, Indonesia. Research. m. Ye Zhe-min, 26 May 1962. Education: BS, Department of Pharmacy, University of Indonesia, 1956; BS, Department of Pharmacy, Beijing Medical University, 1958. Appointments: Research Assistant, 1958-62; Research Associate, 1962-79; Visiting Scholar, Stanford University, 1979-81; Associate Professor, 1982-88; Professor, 1988-. Publications: More than 70 papers in medical natural product chemistry. Honours: National Conference Prize, China, 1978; Prize of Advance Science, CAMS, 1988. Memberships: Chinese Pharmaceutical Society; Chinese Chemical Society. Hobbies: Badminton; Hiking. Address: Institute of Materia Medica, Chinese Academy of Medical Sciences, 1 Xian Nong Tan Street, Beijing 100050, China.

LI Linsun, b. 13 Apr 1936, Shanghai, China. Doctor. m. Liu Xiaohua, 30 Dec 1967, 2 d. Education: BA; Postgraduate Training; Graduated, Nanjing Medical University, 1962. Career: Surgeon, 1962-73;

Radiologist; Professor of Radiology, Nanjing Medical University; Currently, Professor and Chairman, Radiology, Jiangsu Province Hospital, Nanjing. Publications: Infusion of bronchial artery for the treatment of lung cancer, 1986; Clinical Interventional Radiology, 1990; Embolization of suprarenal artery, 1991; Clinical Interventional Therapy, 1994. Memberships: Vice Chairman, Interventional Radiology Society of China; Vice Chairman, Jiangsu Society of Radiology of China. Address: 300 Guangzhou Road, Nanjing 210029, Jiangsu Province Hospital, Nanjing.

LI Meizhi, b. 25 Mar 1932, Beijing, China. Professor. m. 16 Feb 1958, 2 sons. Education: BSc, Beijing Medical University 1955; MSc, Beijing Medical University, 1962. Appointments: Intern, Resident, Associate Professor, 1980; Professor, Obstetrics & Gynaecology, Beijing University of Medical Science, 1985-. Publications: The Clinical Instruction of Obstetrics and Gynaecology, 1988; In Vitro Fertilization and Embryo Transfer (co-author), 1990; Chromosomal Abnormalities and Amenorrhea, 1994. Honours: 2nd Government Prize for IVF/ET, 1989. Memberships: Chinese Medical Association. Address: Obstetrics & Gynaecology Department, Beijing University of Medical Science, Beijing 100083, China.

LI Min Run, b. 15 June 1939, Harbin, China. Researcher. m. Wan Yi Xiang, 31 May 1969, 1 s, 1 d. Education: MD, Harbin Medical University, China, 1962. Appointments: Institute of Blood, Chinese Academy of Medical Science, Tianjin; Institute of Transfusion, Chinese Academy of Medical Science, Chendu; Professor of Biochemistry, Tianjin Institute of Medical and Pharmaceutical Science. Publications: Variation of Activity of cAMP-PDE and r-GT on Breast cancer, 1986; Correlation of r-GT Its Subtypes and Residue of Sialic Acid with Tumor. Honours: Tianjin Scientific and Technical Awards, 1990, 1992. Membership: Chinese Biochemical Society. Hobby: Music. Address: Tianjin Institute of Medical and Pharmaceutical Science, 96 Guizhou Road, Heping District, Tianjin 300070, China.

LI Patrick Chung-Ki, b. 18 Nov 1953, Hong Kong. Medical Doctor. m. Monica Cheung, 27 Sept 1981, 1 son, 1 daughter. Education: MB, BS, University of Hong Kong, 1978; MRCP (UK); FRCP (Edinburgh); FHKAM (Medicine). Appointments: Short-term Consultant, World Health Organization; Currently Consultant, Department of Medicine, Queen Elizabeth Hospital, Hong Kong. Publications: Counselling and AIDS, 1990; Co-author: Current Epidemiological Trends of HIV Infection in Asia, 1992; Penicillium Marneffei: Indicator disease for AIDS in Southeast Asia, 1992; Update on Epidemiology of AIDS in Asia, 1995. Memberships: Hong Kong Neurological Society; Hong Kong AIDS Foundation; International Stroke Society; Hong Kong College of Physicians. Hobby: Music (double bass player). Address: c/o Department of Medicine, Queen Elizabeth Hospital, Gascoigne Road, Kowloon, Hong Kong.

LI Peng, b. 21 Nov 1932, Shanghai, China. Professor of Physiology. m. Liying Zhang, Dec 1992, 1 son, 1 daughter. Education: MD. Appointments: Assistant, 1955-63, Lecturer, 1963-82, Department of Physiology, Shanghai First Medical College; Associate Professor, 1982-86, Professor, 1986-, Chairman, 1988-, Department of Physiology, Shanghai Medical University; Vice-Chairman, National Key Laboratory of Medical Neurosciences, 1992-94. Publications: Mechanism of the modulatory effect of acupuncture on abnormal cardiovascular functions, 1992. Honours: 2nd Class Award for Advanced Sciences and Technology, Ministry of Health, China, 1981; 1st Class Awards, 1986, 2nd Class Awards, 1989, 1990, Educational Committee of China. Memberships: Chinese Physiological Society; International Brain Research Organisation; British Physiological Society; International Physiological Society; American Association for the Advancement of Science. Hobby: Music. Address: Department of Physiology, Shanghai Medical University, Shanghai 200032, China.

LI Ren-li, b. 3 Nov 1930, Beijing, China. University Educator. m. Ying-fen Wang, 26 Oct 1958, 2 sons. Appointments include: Visiting Professor, Department of Chemistry, Pomona College, USA, 1979-81; Currently Professor of Medicinal Chemistry, Beijing Medical University, China. Publications: QSAR studies on dihydrofolate reductase inhibitors, 1982; Journal of Medicinal Chemistry, 31, 366, 1988; QSAR: Quantitative Structure-Activity Relationships in Drug Design, 1989. Memberships: Chinese Pharmaceutical Association; Chinese Chemical Association. Hobbies: Listening to music; Fish. Address: Department of Medicinal Chemistry, Beijing Medical Univesity, 38 Xueyuan Lu, Beijing 100083, China.

LI Sen, b. 7 May 1930, Jiamusi, HeilongJiang Pr, China. Professor of Medicine. Education: Chinese Medical University, 1955. Career: Dean, Department of Internal Medicine, Linyi Medical School; Dean, Department of Internal Medicine, Traditional Chinese Medical Hospital; Dean, Department of Internal Medicine, Red Cross Hospital of Linyi District. Publications: Diagnosis and Treatment of Cardiovascular Disease; Mystery of Longevity of the Aged; More than 80 articles including: Acute Copper Sulfate Poisoning; Pneumonia of Aged; Atypical Myocardial Infarction. Honour: Model Teacher, 1979, 1981; Top-notch Talent of Science & Technology, 1988; Outstanding Member of Red Cross Association, Linyi District, 1991. Memberships: Vice Chairman, Linyi Branch, Chinese Medical Association. Address: QingNian Road 24, Linyi Medical School, Linyi 276002, ShanDong, China.

LI Shaochen, b. 18 Apr 1933, Jinan, Shandong, China. Professor of Epidemiology. m. Cao Ronghua, 10 Feb 1959, 1 daughter. Education: MD; Certification of Public Health, University of Toronto, Canada, 1983. Appointments: Assistant Professor, Harbin Medical University, 1956; Associate Researcher, Physician, Chinese Medical Academy of Sciences, Beijing, 1960; Senior Lecturer, Associate Professor, Professor of Epidemiology and Public Health, Shandong Medical University, Jinan, 1978-. Publications: Applied Clinical Epidemiology (co-author), 1986; First author: Hypertension and lipoprotein cholesterol, 1988; Risk factors for cerebral thrombosis, 1989; Lipoprotein as a screening test for CHD, 1989; Experimental study of wheatgerm for hypecholesterolemia, 1990; Effect inoculated VLDL on AS, 1993. Memberships: Council Member, Chinese Academic Association of Preventive Medicine; Attending Member of Council, Shandong Association of Preventive Medicine; Standing Committee of Clinical Epidemiology (China CLEN). Hobbies: Singing; Painting. Address: Jinan, Shandong, China.

LI Shichuo, b. 10 Apr 1941, Weifang, Shandong Province, China. Professor; Neuroscientist. m. Jing-hua Zhang, 10 Aug 1968, 1 son, 1 daughter. Education: MD, Capital Institute of Medicine, 1965; Visiting Scientist, Diploma, Neuroepidemiology Branch, NINCDS, National Institutes of Health, Bethesda, Maryland, USA, 1988. Appointments: Deputy Director, Attending Neurosurgeon, Jingning County Hospital, Gansu Province, 1977-79; Deputy Director, Chief of Administration, Beijing Neurosurgical Institute, 1985-87; Deputy Director, Beijing Municipal Bureau of Public Health, 1987-92; Currently Director-General, Department of International Cooperation, Ministry of Health, Beijing. Publications include: A Prevalence Survey of Parkinson's Disease and Other Movement Disorders in the P R China, 1985; Epidemiology of Epilepsy in Urban Areas of China, 1985; Cerebrovascular Disease in P R China: Epidemiologic and Clinical Features, 1985. Honours: Awards for Research, Ministry of Public Health and Beijing Municipal Government, for Intervention Trial on Risk Factors for Stroke in 7 Cities of China, 1993; Ministry of Public Health Award for Research Achievements in Neuroepidemiology. Memberships: Neuroepidemiology Research Group, World Federation of Neurology; Vice-Chairman, Chinese Association of Mental Health; Vice-President, Chinese Society of General Medicine; Editorial Committee, Journal of Clinical Neurosciences. Hobbies include: Bridge. Address: Department of International Cooperation, Ministry of Health, 44 Houhai Beiyan, Beijing 100725, China.

LI Shou-xin, b. 1 July 1942, Wanrong County, Shaanxi Province, China. Medical Doctor. m. Tong Li-fang, 8 Mar 1965, 3 sons, 2 daughters. Education: Graduated, Shaanxi Medical College, 1968. Appointments: Ophthalmologist, 1972-85; Associate Professor of Medicine; Currently Physician, Tuberculosis, Director, Yuncheng Municipal Tuberculosis Hospital. Publications: Co-author: 1239 Cases of Lymphoid Tuberculosis with 'Gong-mian-xiao-san' Therapy, 1988; Herbal Drug Series -- Anti-TB Powder, 1993; Observations on Curative Effects on 2139 Cases Treated Mainly with Anti-TB Powder, Journal of Traditional Chinese Medicine, 1994; Clinical Analysis of 511 TB Cases with Anti-TB Powder, 1994. Honours: Shaanxi Provincial 2nd Class Prize of Science and Technology Progress, for Li's TB Therapy, 1990; Gold Medal, National New Well-Known and Best Medicine Fair, 1992, Special Prize, Malaysia International New Technology Products Fair, 1993, for Li's Anti-TB Powder; 1st Class Prize, for article, National Cpmpetition of Learned Articles in Medicine, 1994; Dr Li Shou-xin -- Expert for Tuberculosis, special programme, China Central TV Station, 28 July 1994. Memberships: Shaanx Provincial Society for Science and Technology Information; National Committee of Characteristic Therapies with Traditional Chinese Medicine; Red Cross Society of China; Antituberculosis Association of China. Hobbies: Taking pictures.

Address: Yuncheng Municipal Tuberculosis Hospital, 127 Bei-da Street, Yuncheng, Shaanxi 044000, China.

LI Shu-shen, b. 25 July 1935, Zhejiang, China. Professor of Biology. m. Xu Zhitong, 18 June 1961, 1 son, 2 daughters. Education: BA, Sichuan University, 1959. Appointments: Kunming Institute of Zoology, Academia Sinica, 1959-81; Currently Professor of Biology, Department of Biology, Yunnan University, Kunming. Publications: Systematics Distribution and evolution of Glyptothorax (Sisoridae: Siluriformes), 1986; A karyotypic investigation of five species of lungless salamanders (Family Plethodontidae) from southern Appalachian Mountains, 1987; Cytogenetic study of eight pelobatid toad species belonging to two genera of Scutiger and Oreolalax in China, 1990; Cytogenetic studies on two Leptolalax pelobatoids, 1991; The cytogenetic study of three Megophrys species from Yunnan Province, 1993; The karyotypes and Ag-NORS of three symparicatly paa frogs in Yunnan Province, 1994. Address: Department of Biology, Yunnan University, Kunming, China.

LI Tian-zeng, b. 21 Dec 1941, Dongguan, Guangdong, China. Chief Surgeon; Professsor. m. Lin Hui-lan, 1 son, 1 daughter. Education: BS, Zhong Shan Medical College (now Sun Yat-Sen University of Medical Sciences), 1965; MD. Appointments: Resident Surgeon, Visiting Surgeon and Lecturer, Deputy Chief Surgeon and Associate Professor, currently Chief Surgeon, Professor of Surgery, Supervisor of MM postgraduate students. Publications: 100 Cases of Revival - a collection of experiences in saving patients with grave emergency, 1984; Routine of Diagnosis and Treatment, 1992; A Handbook for Interns, 2nd Edition; A Dictionary of Surgery; Over 40 papers including: The anti-exudation effect of Decoctum with Glochidion Eriocarpus Champ compound in the burned rat, 1978; The fungus infection of severe burns in children, 1981; Experiences in application of Silver Sulphadiazine-Methylene Blue Cream for tangential excision and escharectomy of burn wounds, 1985; Comparative trial between 10% Betadine Ointment and Silver Sulphadiazine in the treatment of burns, 1988; Experience in successful management of a 100% TBSA (third degree 96%) burned patient with severe inhalation injury, 1989; Dermazin in the treatment of burns - a clinical study, 1990; Management of extensive burn patients in shock stage, 1994. Honours include: National Advanced Worker, Ministry of Public Health, 1987; Expert with Special Contribution, Chinese State Council, 1992; Several Science and Technology Advancement Prizes. Memberships: International Society for Burn Injuries; Chairman, Guangdong Society of Burns and Plastic Surgery; Director: Society of Burns Society, Chinese Medical Association; Chinese Medical Association, Guangdong Branch. Hobby: Reading. Address: First University Hospital, Sun Yat-Sen University of Medical Sciences, Zhong Shan Road II, Guangzhou 510080, China.

LI Tong Du, b. 2 Sept 1919, Longkou, Shandong, China. Doctor. m. Ling Pei Fen, 15 Nov 1948, 2 sons, 2 daughters. Education: Dong Nan Medical College Graduate, 1946. Career: Surgical Oncology Professor & Chief, Department of Cancer Research. Chief Author, Cystoscopy, 1979; Co-author, Chemical Prevention and Drug Therapy of Cancer, 1991; Chief Translator, Textbook of Clinical Oncology, 1994; Co-author, Oncology, 1995. Memberships: Chinese Anticancer Association, Head, Department of Social Service & Standing Director; Anhui Provincial Cancer Control Institute, Honorary Director; Anhui Anticancer Association, Chair; Anhui Oncological Association, Honorary Chair. Hobbies: Reading; Music. Address: Anhui Tumor Hospital, Bengbu, Anhui 233004, China.

LI Weixin, b. 6 Apr 1934, Nanking, China. Professor of History. m. Wang Xianglin, 23 May 1959, 1 s, 1 d. Education: Graduated from the First Shanghai Medical College, 1956. Appointments: Assistant, Lecturer, Associate Professor, Chongqing University of Medical Sciences, China; Board Member, Sichuan Board of Sciences and Technique of Family Planning; Counsellor of Chongqing Institute of Family Plannings; Professor of Histology and Director of Laboratory of Electron Microscopy, Chongqing University of Medical Sciences, China. Publications: A Study of Effects of Acupuncture on the Phagocytic Activities of Hepatic Reticuloendothelial System in Rats, 1959; Electron Microscopic Observations of the Effects of Microwave Irradiation on Spermateleosis in the Rabbits, 1983; Effects of Microwave Irradiation on Ultrastructure and Alkaline Phosphatase of the Peritubular Tissue of Ductus Epidymides in Rabbits, 1986; Ultrastructural Studies of the Injurious Action of Cadmium and Protective Action of Zinc on Rat Testis, 1988; Application of Electron Microscopy in the Reproductive Pathology and Contraceptive Studies, 1988; Observation of Ultrastructural and Alkaline Phosphatase Localization of the Peritubular Tissue of

Seminiferous Tubules in Man and Several Rodents, 1989; Ultrastructural Studies of The Effects of Microwave Irradiation on the Seminal Vesicles in Rabbits, 1992. Honours: The Second Award, Sichuan Board of Science and Technique of Family Planning, 1986. Memberships: Chinese Society of Electron Microscopy; Chinese Society of Anatomy; Chinese Medical Association. Hobbies: Singing; Running. Address: Laboratory of Electron Microscopy; Chongqing University of Medical Sciences; Chongqing, Sichuan 630046, China.

LI Wenzhu, b. 15 Oct 1942, Da Pu Commune, Yong Chun County, Fujian, China. Pharmacist. m. Chen Yaohua, Aug 1968, 1 son, 1 daughter. Education: Industry University of Mid-China, Changsha, Hunan; Courses, Medical Training Unit, Chinese People's Liberation Army. Appointments include: Currently Pharmacist, Hospital of Dermatosis Prevention, Zhangzhou, Fujian. Honours: Well-known and honoured locally as Pharmacist Li, for rich knowledge and experience of medicine and magical effect of specially-compounded drugs for dermatosis. Memberships: Association for Leprosy, Fujian Province; Red Cross, Zhangzhou Municipality, Fujian; Medicine Society of Zhangzhou City, Fujian. Address: Room 605, Building 15, Hunei Housing Estate, Zhangzhou Municipality, Fujian, China.

LI Xin, b. 30 Nov 1930, Jinzhou, Liaoning, China. Professor; Doctor. m. Yujie Li, 1951, 2 sons, 1 daughter. Education: BSc, Medical University of China. Appointments: Chief Doctor 1964, Director of Radiotherapy Section 1977, Associate Professor 1978, Professor, Dean 1985, Heilongjiang College of Traditional Chinese Medicine. Publications: X-Ray Bones and Joint Diagnostics; Applied CT Diagnostics; X-Ray and CT Diagnostics; Cardioangiological and X-Ray Diagnostics. Honours: Several 2nd and 3rd Merits in Medicine. Memberships: Dir, China Medicine Image Research Institute; Dir, Northeast Medicine Image Academic Committee; Dir, Heilonghiang Medicine Image Committee. Hobbies: Swimming; Skating; Basketball. Address: Heilongjiang College of Traditional Chinese Medicine, CT Center, Heilongjiang, Harbin, China.

LI Xinsheng, b. 26 June 1929, Heyuan, Guangdong, China. Research Fellow of Philosophy; Professor. m. Nie Zufen, 1 July 1962, 1 son. Education: Studies, Shanghai Amoy University & Zhongshan University, 1948-52; Graduate, South China Teachers College, 1953; Graduate, Chinese People's University, 1962. Appointments: Lecturer, South China Teachers College, 1963-79; Vice Professor, Professor, Chief Tutor, South China Teachers University, 1980-85; Director, Institute of Philosophy Study, Guangdong Academy of Social Science, Commander of Assessment of Academy Titles, 1986-93. Publications: Restoring the Law of the Negation of Negation, 1979; The Universality and Methodological Significance of the Law of the Negation of Negation and the Position and Relation of Negation and Contradiction in Dialectics, 1980; Dialectical Materialism and Historical Materialism, 1983; Dialectical Method and Scientific Exploration, 1988; Dialectical Views on Renewal, Perfection and Development of Socialism, 1991; Perplexity of Freedom A Philosophical Analysis of Sartre's Existentialism, 1991. Honours: Title, Provincial Advanced Te4acher, 1965; 2nd Prize, Research Achievements in Philosophy and Social Science, Guangdong Higher Education Bureau, 1982; Best Provincial Research Achievement in Social Science, 1983; Prize, Outstanding Scientific Research and Merit Certificate, 1984. Memberships Include: Vice President, Guangdong Society of Socialist Dialects. Hobbies: Chinese Ancient Literature; Walking; Mountain Climbing. Address: Institute of Philosophy Study, Guangdong Academy of Social Science, 369 Tian He Bei Road, Guangzhou, China.

LI Xizhen, b. 11 Apr 1932, Harbin, Heilongjiang, China. Professor. Appointments include: Director, Lesser Circulation Research Centre, China Biomedical Engineering Society; Professor of Biomedical Engineering, Northwestern Polytechnical University, China. Publications include: Clinical Impedance Rheography of the Lungs, 1982. Honours include: Major Contribution Award, National Conference on Science, 1976; 2nd award of Science and Technology Progress, PLA, 1976. Address: 304 Building E, Huiyuan INternational House, Asian Olympic Games Village, Beijing, China.

LI Xueru, b. 8 Jan 1938, Sichuan, China. Teaching & Researching. m. Hu Xingyong, 6 Aug 1962, 1 son, 1 daughter. Education: BA, Sichuan University, 1959. Appointments: Assistant of Biology, Ningxia Medical College, 1959; Lecturer of Microbiology, Ningxia Medical College, 1978; Associate Professor of Microbiology, Ningxia Medical College, 1986; Professor of Microbiology, Ningxia Medical College, 1992. Publications:

Study on the Effects of Lycium Barbarum on Immunologic Function, 1984; The Effect of Lycium Barbarum Polysaccharides on C3b and Fc Receptor of Peritoneal Macrophages in Mice, 1990; Study on Anti-bacterial Infective Mechanism of Lycium Barbarum Polysaccharides, 1991. Honours: 4 Prizes for Scientific & Technological Achievements of Ningxia, 1978, 1984, 2 in 1986; Exemplary Teacher of Ningxia, 1994. Memberships: Chinese Microbiology Association Council; Director of Ningxia Microbiology Society; Chinese Medical Association. Hobbies: Walking; Bicycle. Address: Department of Microbiology, Ningxia Medical College, Yinchuan 750004, China.

LI Yi Nong, b. 26 May 1927, Hebei Province, China. Professor of internal Medicine. m. Rui-fang Feng, 14 Aug 1955, 2 d. Appointments: Vice Chairman, Department of internal Medicine, Chairman, Department of Gastroenterology, Professor, Department of Gastroenterology, 3rd Hospital, Beijing Medical University. Publications: The Relation Between Gastric Ca and PCA(+) Atropic Gastritis, Co-author, 1984; The Therapeutic Effect of Amoxycillin on Duodenal Ulcer and Preliminary Study of its Mechanism, Co-author, 1994; Digestive Endoscopy, Editor-in-chief, 1994. Memberships: Chinese Society of Gastroenterology; Chinese Medical Association; Chinese Society of Digestive Endoscopy. Hobby: Photography. Address: Department of Gastroenterology, Third Hospital, Beijing Medical University, 49 Hua Yuan Bei Lu, Beijing 100083, China.

LI Youcai, b. 13 Dec 1935, Gu Lang Lu Island, China. Education: Graduate, 1st Medical Institute, Shanghai, 1958. Appointments: Head Doctor of Orthopaedics. Publications: Results of Treatment of 403 Cases of Congenital Dislocation of Hips in Children, Co-author, 1981; New Surgical Approach in Pediatric Femoral Head Avascular Necrosis, Co-author, 1982. Address: Department of Arthopaedics, The No 1 Hospital of Xiamen, Zhen Hai Road, Xiamen, Fujian, China.

LI Zai-Liu, b. 26 Sept 1934, Andong, Kyungbuk, Korea. University Teacher. m. Jin Sun-Yu, 14 Oct 1960, 1 son, 2 daughters. Education: BA, Yanbian Medical College, 1959; MD, Beijing Medical College, 1965; PhD, Okayama University Medical School, Japan, 1982. Appointments: Assistant, Physiology, 1959, Lecturer in Physiology, 1978, Associate Professor of Physiology, 1983, Professor of Physiology, Chairman, Department of Physiology, 1985-, Yanbian Medical College, Yanji, China. Publications: Co-author: Lecture Manual of Physiology, 1989; Locus coeruleus relays the gastric inhibitory actions of VMH, 1989; The Physiology of Gastrointestinal Tract--basis and clinic, 1990. Honours: Science and Technology Progress Prize, Ministry of Public Health, China, 1984, 1986, 1990. Memberships: Chinese Physiological Society; Jilin Province Physiological Sciences Association. Hobby: Reading newspapers. Address: Department of Physiology, Yanbian Medical College, 121 Juzi Street, Yanji, Jilin 133000, China.

Li Zhanchun, b. 24 Sept 1957, Liaoning, China. Researcher. m. Lijun Zhao, 18 Dec 1982, 1 son. Education: MD, 1991; PhD, 1994; Postdoctoral studies, 1994-. Appointments: Assistant of Histology and Embryology, 1982-87; Lecturer, 1988-90; Associate, 1994-. Publications: Distribution and morphology of IAPP immunoreactive cells in gastroenteropancreatic system of adult rat, 1994; Detection of insulin in RNA by in situ hybridization using digoxienin-labelled dRNA probe, 1994. Honours: Excellent Paper, Third Chinese Young Conference on anatomical Sciences, 1993; Guang Hua Award, Beijing Medical University, 1993. Membership: Chinese Anatomical Society. Hobby: Photography. Address: Department of Pathology 1, University Hospital, S-581 85 Linköping, Sweden.

LI Zhanliang, b. 26 Nov 1933, Guangdong, China. General Surgeon. m. Cui Dejian, 17 Sep 1960, 1 s, 1 d. Education: Physician, Kharkov Medical School, Ukraine, 1960; MD, Military Postgraduate Medical School, 1980; Postdoctoral Fellowship, Loma Linda University Medical Center, 1986-88. Career: Chief, Department of General Surgery, 1984-88, Director, 1988-92, Currently, Professor, Department of General Surgery, 304th Hospital and Trauma Center, PLA, Beijing. Co-author, Huang's Textbook of Surgery, 1988, 1992; Co-author, Management in the Perioperative Period, 1993; Editor, Modern Critical Care Medicine, in press. Honours: Grade 3 Prize, 1990, 1993, Grade 2 Prize, 1995, Armed Forces Science and Technology Advances. Memberships: Vice President, Association of General Surgeons, PLA, 1990-; Chinese Medical Association; Western Returned Student Association. Hobbies: Travel; Music. Address: 304th Hospital and Trauma Center, 51 Fucheng Road, Beijing 100037, China.

LI Zhao-Te, b. 5 Feb 1913, Huhehaote, China. Professor. m. Zha Xiu, 11 Nov 1942, 1 s, 1 d. Education: BS, Yenching University, Beijing, China, 1932; MS, Yenching University, Beijing, China, 1946; PhD, Washington University, St Louis, MO, USA, 1949. Appointments: Associate Professor, Anatomy, Beijing University Medical School, 1949-53; Professor, Histology & Embryology, Beijing Medical University, Beijing, China, 1953-. Publications: Co-Author, The Effect of Lecithin on Tissues, 1962; Histology (A Textbook for Medical Students), 1964; Histology and Embryology, 1987. Honours: 1st Grade Prize awarded by All China Symposium of Science and Technology, 1978; Outstanding Teacher, 1990; Title to Scholars of Extraordinary Contribution to Science and Technology awarded by State Council, 1989. Memberships: Vice President of Chinese Anatomical Association, 1978-87; Honory Presidency, Chinese Anatomical Association, 1987-; President, Beijing Anatomical Association, 1961-90; International Anatomical Nomenclature Committee, 1987; Member of Committee of Science and Technology, Ministry of Health, China, 1978; Advisor of Committee of Academic Degrees, State Council, 1978-83. Hobbies: Chinese Calligraphy. Address: Beijing Medical University, Building 14-3-203, Beijing 100083, China.

LI Zhi, b. 3 Mar 1931, Heibei, China. Physician (Neonatal Medicine). m. Lü Bingxiu, Feb 1952, 2 sons. Education: BM, Bethune's Medical College, Changchun, 1949; Diplomas, Beijing School of Chinese Medicine, 1951, 1976. Appointments: Resident, 1955, Vice-Chief, Beijing Capital University; Associate Professor, 1982, Professor, 1985, Capital Medical University, Beijing; Currently Professor, Vice-Chief, Beijing Children's Hospital, affiliated to Beijing Capital University. Publications: Co-author: Zhu Futang's Practical Pediatrics, 4th edition, 1985; Chin Zhenting's Perinatal Pediatrics, 1987; Papers on neonatal pneumonia and intracranial hemorrhage, Chinese Medical Journal, 1985, 1986, and others. Honours: 3rd Grade Award for Progress in Sciences, Beijing Municipality, 1987, 1991; 2nd Grade Award, Zhu Futang Clinical Research Foundation, 1992. Memberships include: Chinese Medical Association; Chinese Society of Neonatal Medicine; Editorial Board, Chinese Journal of Neonatal Medicine. Hobby: Touring. Address: Beijing Children's Hospital, 56 Nanlishi Road, Beijing 100045, China.

LI Zhi Hui, b. 5 Jul 1936, Shanghai, China. Ophthalmologist. m. 19 Nov 1969, 1 s, 1 d. Education: Graduate, Beijing Medical College, 1959. Career: MD, Tong-Ren Hospital, Beijing, 1959; Currently, Professor of Ophthalmology, Capital University of Medical Sciences, Beijing, China. Publications: Ocular cysticercosis, in Chinese Journal of Ophthalmology, 1980; Co-author, Management of contusion cyclodialysis, in Chinese Journal of Ophthalmology, 1985; Fuchs Syndrome and Glaucoma, in Chinese Journal of Ophthalmology, 1986; Co-author, Treatment of blepharospasm and hemifacial spasm with botulinum A toxin, in Chinese Journal of Ophthalmology, 1993. Membership: Chinese Medical Association. Hobbies: Photography; Music. Address: 2 Chong Nei Street, Tong-Ren Hospital, Beijing 100005, China.

LI Zhi-An, b. 1 Oct 1945, Tianjin City, China. Cardiologist. m. Guifeng Wang, 1 May 1972, 1 son, 1 daughter. Education: MA; PhD. Appointments: Resident, 1970; Physician-in-Charge, 1982; Associate Professor of Cardiology, 1989, Professor of Cardiology, 1990- Deputy Director, Echocardiography Department, UNion Hospital of Tongji Medical University. Publications: Modern COncept of Arrhythmias, 1990; Color Doppler Diagnostics, 1991; Clinical Application of the Three-Dimensional Echocardiography, 1994. Honours: 2nd Class Prize, Science and Technology, Ministry of China Public Health and State Education Commission, 1992; 2nd Class Prize, Science and Technology, China State Education Commission, 1994. Memberships: Chinese Medical Association; International Society of Cardiovascular Ultrasound, USA. Address: Echocardiographic Department, Union Hospital of Tongji Medical University, 575 Jiefang Street, Wuhan 430022, China.

LI Zhi-shang, b. 22 Dec 1916, Honan, China. Professor of Pathology. m. Zhi-Lan Wang, 10 Jan 1941, 3 sons, 1 daughter. Education: MD, Defensive Medical College, 1938; MS, Pathology, University of Kansas Medical School, USA, 1950. Appointments include: Professor of Pathology, Wuhan Medical College; Currently Professor of Pathology, Guangxi Medical University, Nanning. Publications: Co-author: Methods of Autopsy, 1953, 4th edition, 1987; Guide for Autopsy Diagnosis, 1994; Medical Encyclopaedia - Pathology Section (editorial board), 1982. Memberships: International Academy of Pathology; Chinese Medical Association. Hobby: Swimming. Address: Department of Pathology, Guangxi Medical University, Nanning, Guangxi 530021, China.

LIANG Raymond Hin-Suen, b. 4 Apr 1956, Hong Kong. Medical Doctor. m. May Wun, 23 July 1983, 1 daughter. Education: MBBS, 1979, MD, 1990, University of Hong Kong; MRCP (UK), 1983; FRCP (Edinburgh), 1992; FRCPS (Glasgow), 1992; Foundation Fellow, Hong Kong Academy of Medicine, 1993. Appointments include: Lecturer, Guy's Hospital Medical School, London, England, 1984-85; Lecturer, 1985-91, Senior Lecturer, 1991-93, Reader in Medicine (Haematology, Oncology), 1993-, University of Hong Kong and Queen Mary Hospital, Hong Kong; Clinical Associate Dean, Faculty of Medicine, University of Hong Kong, 1992-; Honorary Consultant, Hong Kong Hospital Authority, 1992-. Publications: Over 100 regarding lymphoma, leukaemia, infections in immunocompromised patients, molecular biology, general haematology and oncology, bone marrow transplantation. Honours: Croucher Foundation Scholar, 1983-85; Dr Stephen Chang Visiting Fellowship to Stanford University, USA, 1986; Sir Patrick Manson Gold Medal, University of Hong Kong, 1990; Mary Sun Oncology Fellowship to Bone Marrow Transplantation Unit, Cancer Research Center, University of Washington, USA, 1991. Memberships include: Asian Oceanic Clinical Oncology Association; American Society of Clinical Oncology; New York Academy of Sciences; American Association for the Advancement of Science; International Society for Experimental Hematology; Fellow: Internatioanl Society of Haematology, Asian-Pacific Division; Hong Kong College of Physicians; Founder Member: Hong Kong Cancer Chemotherapy Society; Hong Kong Transplant Club; Hong Kong Society of Antimicrobial Chemotherapy. Hobbies: Tennis; Swimming; Music. Address: Department of Medicine, Queen Mary Hospital, Hong Kong.

LIANG Shao-ai, b. 5 Dec 1929, Yunnan, China. Paediatrician. m. Yang Jin-luan, 30 Aug 1965, 2 sons, 1 daughter. Education: MD, Paediatrics, Medical College, West China Union University, 1954. Appointments: Resident, Paediatrics, 1954-62; Visiting Paediatrician, 1962-83; Assistant Professor of Paediatrics, 1983-87, Professor of Paediatrics, 1988-, Luzhou College; Currently Emeritus Paediatrician. Publications: Clinical analysis of 194 cases of measles, 1963; Clinical observation of 190 cases of favism by combined therapy of traditional Chinese medicine and Western medicine, 1979; Observation of Hb change under therapy of traditional Chinese herbs, 1980; Screening of defect of G-6-PD through umbilical vein in 200 cases of newborn at Luzhou Medical College, 1985; Study of etiology and clinical observation for 74 cases of infantile diarrhoea in autumn and winter (co-author), 1986. Membership: Luzhou Branch, Chinese Medical Association. Hobbies: Reading good books; Running; Watching TV. Address: Ren Min Zhong Road, West 2 AVe 5, Chengdu 610015, China.

LIANG Shao-Ren, b. 20 July 1915, Hei Che County, Yunnan, China. Stomatologist. m. Chen Qiao-pin, 9 Oct 1954, 2 sons. Education: BA, Medicine, West China Union University, 1941; DDS, University of New York State, USA, 1941. Appointments: Tutor, 1941, Lecturer, 1943, West China Union University; Lecturer, Director of Dental Department, 1947, Associate Professor, 1949, Lingnan University, Canton; Head, Stomatological Department, Zhong Shan Medical College, 1953; Professor, Vice-Director, Stomatological Faculty, 1978-86, Honorary Professor, 1990-, Sun Yat Sen University of Medical Sciences, Guangzhou. Publications: The Dental Effects of Water Fluoridation in Canton, 1979; A Preliminary Summary of Water Fluoridation in Canton, 1983 In most regions of China, fluoridation should be applicable, 1984; Prevention of dental caries, 1984; Stomatology section, in Chinese Medicine, 1986; The Effect of Fluorine in Running Water on Infant Teeth (co-author), 1988. Hobby: Playing chess. Address: Zhi Xing Road 119, No 401, Canton, Guangzhou 510080, China.

LIANG Song Ming, b. 27 Nov 1935, Guangzhou, China. Teacher. m. Professor Chen Shu Ying, 12 May 1959, 2 s. Education: Bachelor of Medicine and Pharmacy; PhD, Chinese Traditional Medicine and Acupuncture, North American Branch, Chinese Government. Appointments: Since 1950's worked at Guangzhou College of Traditional Chinese Medicine, currently as Dean of Department of Chinese Materia Medica and Head of Research Institute of Chinese Materia Medica. Publications include: Over 20 research papers including: Application of Chinese Herbal Medicines According to the Zeng-Fu Theory; Application of Chinese Pharmacologic Formulas According to the Zeng-Fu Theory; Treatment of Cancer with Chinese Herbal Medicines; Editor, Co-editor of 12 books; Research paper, Free Radials and Diabetes Mellitus, published in Canada; Editing Committee: A Chinese English Dictionary; China Medical Encyclopedia in Chinese Medicine Pharmacology; Guangdong Chinese Herbal Medicine Encyclopedia, Chinese Herbal Medicine. Honours include: Baccalaureate and Outstanding

Achievements Expert Awarded by Chinese Government; National Excellent Worker Award, Chinese Government; Visiting Professor, Scuala Italiana di Medicina. Membership: President, Council of Chinese Materia Medica Society of China. Hobby: Music. Address: Room 803, Teacher's Building 5, Guangzhou College of Traditional Chinese Medicine, San Yan Li, Guangzhou, China.

LIANG Zhang Ting Zeng, b. 9 Feb 1942, Anxiang, Hunan, China. Medical Doctor. m. Li Juan Liang, 24 May 1970, 1 s. Education: Medical Doctor, Hunan Traditional Chinese Medicine College. Career: Visiting Physician and Lecturer, 1981; Vice Chief Physician, Hunan Children's Hospital, 1987-93; Chief Physician, Zhu Hai Traditional Chinese Medical Hospital, Guangdong, 1993-. Publications: Pediatrics of Traditional Chinese Medicine, in Chinese Medical Encyclopaedia, 1983; Pediatrics of Traditional Chinese Medicine, 1988. Membership: Standing Manager, Pediatrics Committee, Chinese Association of Traditional Chinese Medicine. Hobby: Sports. Address: Pediatrics Department, Zhu Hai Traditional Chinese Medicine Hospital, Guang Dong Province, China.

LIANG Zhi An, b. 20 Sep 1928, Canton, China. Scientist. m. Dian Hua Shao, 11 Aug 1954, 2 d. Education: MD, The 2nd Moscow Medical College, Xiang Ya Medical College, 1958. Appointments: Professor and Head, Laboratory of Audition, Shanghai Institute of Physiology, Academia Sinica. Publications include: Auditory Resolution of Modulation Depth, Proc III Western-Pacific Regional Conference on Acoustics, 1988; Parametric Relation between Impulse Noise and Auditory Damage, in Noise-Induced Hearing Loss, 1991; Auditory Perception and Recognition of Modulator-Speech, Proc 14th ICA, 1992. Membership: Chinese Association of Physiological Sciences. Hobbies: Sport; Music. Address: Laboratory of Audition, Shanghai Institute of Physiology, Chinese Academy of Sciences, 320 Yue-Yang Road, Shanghai 200031, China.

LIAO Caishen, b. 3 Nov 1931, Longnan County, Jiangxi, China. Doctor of Obstetrics & Gynaecology. m. Liu Wuzhen, 4 June 1960, 1 son, 2 daughters. Education: Diploma, Jiangxi Medical College; Diploma, Senior Research Class of Guangzhou College of TCM. Career: Director, Professor, Chief Physician, Section of Cervical Cancer Research. Publications: Author, Female Hygiene, 1972; Co-author, Diagnosis and Treatment Standard of Common Malignant Tumourin China, 1991; Co-author, Epidemic Factors Investigation in Cervical Cancer, Chinese Journal of Oncology, 1986; "Sanpinyitiaoqiang" Conization Therapy for Early Cervical Cancer, Chinese Journal of Traditional Medical, 1983. Honours: Second Award of Invention of China, 1989; Third Award of State Science and Technology, 1989; First Award of State Administration of Traditional Chinese Medicines, 1986. Memberships: Council Member, Chinese Anti-Cancer Association; Vice-Chairman, Chinese Cervical Cancer Research Committee; Chinese Medical Association; Vice-Director, Jiangxi Anti-Cancer Association. Hobbies: Touring; Photography. Address: Women's and Child Health Hospital, Jiangxi Province, Nanchang 330006, China.

LIAO Gong Tie, b. 11 Sep 1917, Chengdu, China. Professor. m. Ho Ling, 13 Aug 1937, 2 sons, 2 daughters. Education: BSc. College of Sciences, University of West China Union, 1941. Appointments: Teaching Assistant, 1941, Lecturer, 1945, Associate Professor, 1948, Director, Pharmaceutical Department, 1952-84, Director, Pharmaceutical Factory, 1948-50, Medical University of West China. Publications: Stability Study of Glucal Injection, CO-author, 1966; Inquire into Preparing and Quality of Chinese Medicine, Co-author, 1982; Study on Sodium Marocmetheridate Albumin Microspheres, Co-author, 1993; Study on Mitoxantrone Polycyanoacrylate Nanoparticles, 1994. Honours: award for Great Achievement in Dosage Form of Chinese Traditional Medicine, Province Government, 1987. Memberships: Committee Member, Pharmaceutics, Chinese Pharmaceutical Society; Chairman, Sichuan Pharmaceutics Committee. Hobby: Cycling. Address: Medical University of West China, 610041 Chengdu, Sichuan, China.

LIAO Mei-Lin, b. 16 Nov 1934, Jiangsu, China. Oncologist. m. Zhao Wei-bin, 4 Apr 1956, 2 sons. Education: MD, Shanghai 2nd Medical University; Fellowship, Ambrose Cardio-Respiratory Unit, McMaster University, Canada. Appointments: Head, Pulmonary Function Group; Chief, Chest Department, Vice Director, Shanghai Research Institute of Chest Tumours. Publications: Practical Oncology, Co-author, 1972; Lung Cancer, 1993; Lung Disease, 1992; Standardized Diagnosis and Treatment of Lung Cancer, 1991; Anathesia and Respiratory. Honours: national Advanced Worker of Merit in Medical Profession, 1987; Winner, Shanghai Science Awards, 1987, 1990; National Model Worker in

Medical Profession, 1992. Memberships: International Association for the Study of Lung Cancwer; Commissioner, Chinese Medical Association and Chinese Cancer Society. Hobbies: Travel; Cinema; Chinese Opera. Address: 241 Hui Hai Road West, Shanghai Chest Hospital, Shanghai 200030, China.

LIAO Qingkui, b. 5 Oct 1935, Pengxi County, Sichuan, China. Medical Doctor; Professor. m. Huang Xianxiang, 1 Oct 1961, 1 son, 2 daughters. Education: BA, West China University of Medical Sciences, 1960; MD, Zhongshan University of Medical Sciences, 1967. Appointments include: Head, Department of Paediatrics, No 1 University Hospital, 1973-87, Vice-Master, No 1 University Hospital, 1987-, Vice-Master, Medical School, 1987-, Head, Haemotology and Oncology Research Laboratory, 1992-, West China University of Medical Sciences, Chengdu. Publications: More than 7 books, 1987-, including: Hematology Atlas, 1987; The Differential Diagnosis in Childhood, 1988; Nutrition and Nutritional Diseases, 1989; The Current Diagnosis and Treatment in Childhood, 1989. Honours include: Science and Technology Progress Award, 1st Degree, Sichuan Province, 1990; Science and Technology Progress Award, 3rd Degree, Ministry of Health, China, 1992. Memberships: Head, Blood Association, Pediatrics Association; Director, China Transfusion Association; National Blood-Quality Assurance Committee. Hobbies: Music; Stamp collection. Address: Department of Paediatrics, No 2 University Hospital, West China University of Medical Sciences, Chengdu, Sichuan 610041, China.

LIAO Yin-Yuan, b. 18 July 1932, Jianglao County, Fujian, China. Doctor. m. Wui Shuxian, 31 Nov 1931, 2 sons, 1 daughter. Publications: Clinical Observations of Emergent Operation for Hernial Hemorrhoid (50 Cases), 1984; Creative Observations of De-Toxius Lotio Fumigated and Washed Treatment of Hemorrhoid Fistula (400 Cases), 1986. Honours: Gold Medal, Diploma, Inheriting and Developing Chinese Medical Heritage. Hobby: Qigong. Address: No 1 Extra Building of 24# Block, Tangshan, Hebei, China.

LICHTENSTEIN Alice H, b. 5 Sept 1949, New York City, USA. Nutrition Biochemist. m. Barry R Geldin, 3 June 1983. Education: BS; MS; DSc. Appointments: Teaching Assistant, The Pennsylvania University State College, 1971-73; Instructor in Nutrition, Queens College, Flushing, 1973-74; Lecturer in Nutrition, Bunker Hill Community College, Charlestown, 1978; Lecturer in Nutrition, Frances Stern Nutrition Center, Boston, 1978-82; Research Associate, Boston University School of Medicine, 1982-83; Adjunct Assistant Professor of Nutrition, Tufts Univerity, 1983-88; Adjunct Assistant Professor, Department of Health Sciences, Sargent College, Boston University, 1983-86; Adjunct Assistant Professor, Department of Biochemistry, Boston University School of Medicine, 1983-88; Assistant Research Professor of Medicine, Boston University School of Medicine, 1983-88; Assistant Professor, School of Nutrition, Tufts University, 1988-94; Scientist II, USDA Human Nutrition Research Center on Aging, Tufts Univerity, 1988-94; Associate Professor, School of Nutrition, Tufts University, 1994-; Scientist I, USDA Human Nutrition Research Center on Aging, Tufts University, 1994-. Publications incl: Trans fatty acids, blood lipids and cardiovascular risk: Where do we stand?, 1993; Hypercholesterolemic effect of dietary cholesterol in diets enriched in polyunsaturated and saturated fat, 1994. Honours incl: Phi Kappa Phi; Omicron Nu. Memberships: American Institute of Nutrition; American Heart Association. Address: HNRCA/Tufts University, Lipid Metabolism, 711 Washington Street, Boston, MA 02111, USA.

LICHTENSTEIN Simon, b. 20 Sept 1961, Wales. Osteopath. 1 s. Education: Diploma Osteopathy, British School of Osteopathy. Appointment: Private Practice. Memberships: General Council and Register of Osteopaths. Hobby: Microlighting. Address 6 Chapel Walk, Burgess Street, Leominster, Herefordshire HR6 8DE, England.

LICHTER Edward A, b. 5 Jun 1928, Chicago, IL, USA. Physician. m. Charlotte Lichter, 2 s. Appointment: Professor and Associate Chief of General Internal Medicine, University of Illinois, Chicago. Honour: Distinguished Service Award, American College of Preventive Medicine, 1990. Memberships: FACP; FACPM; MACE; APHA; ATPM. Address: Department of Medicine M/C 787, 840 South Wood Street, Chicago, IL 60612-7323, USA.

LIEBERMAN Allan Daniel, b. 2 Oct 1934, Brooklyn, New York, USA. Physician. m. Jeanne B Herman, 3 s. Education: BA, New York University, 1956; MD, Chicago Medical School, 1960. Appointments:

Adjunct Assistant Professor, Brown University, 1993; Medical Director, Centre for Environmental Medicine. Publications include: Crytococcus Menngitis in a Child Successfully treated with Amphotericin B with a Review of the Pediatric Literature, Co-author, 1961; Post Vaccinal Eruption - Report of a Case, Co-author, 1962; Health Maintenance Profile for Office and Clinical Use, Co-author, 1974; The Effects of Diet and Provocative Allergy Testing on Eye Movements with Dyslexic Individuals - A Double Blind Study, Co-author, 1989; The Role of the Rubella Virus in the Chronic Fatigue Syndrome, 1990; Has given numerous presentations and lectures. Memberships: AMA; South Caroline Medical Association; American College of Occupational and Environmental Medicine; Fellow, American Academy of Environmental Medicine; President, American Board of Environmental Medicine. Address: Centre for Environmental Medicine, 7510 North Forest Drive, North Charleston, SC 29420, USA.

LIEBERMAN Carole I, b. New York City, New York, USA. Psychiatrist. 1 daughter. Education: BA, State University of New York; MD, Université de Louvain, Belgium; MPH, University of California, Los Angeles; Diplomate, American Board of Psychiatry; National Institute of Mental Health Fellowship; Residencies: New York University/Bellevue Psychiatric Hospital; Maudsley Hospital, London; Hampstead Clinic, London. Appointments: Assistant Clinical Professor of Psychiatry, Neuropsychiatric Institute, University of California, Los Angeles; Psychiatrist specialising in effects of media on society; Script Consultant. Publications: Various scripts; Show Biz Shrink, national weekly print column; Chapters in Encyclopaedia Britannica, Doctors' Book of Home Remedies for Children; Glam Scam; TV/Interactive Toys. Honours: O'Henry Prize for Literature, 1983; Award of Excellence, Film Advisory Council, 1990; Writers Guild Children's Script, 1992; Television Academy EMMY Awards, 1992, 1993. Memberships: Writers Guild of America; AFTRA; Academy of Television Arts and Sciences; Motion Picture Association; Former Chair, National Coalition on TV Violence; American Psychiatric Association. Hobby: Riding. Address: 247 S Beverly Drive, Suite 202Beverly Hills, CA 90212, USA.

LIEBERMAN Phillip Louis, b. 20 Mar 1940, Memphis, USA. Medical Doctor. m. Barbara Jane, 1 Feb 1969, 3 sons. Education: BA, Tulane University; MD, University Tennessee. Appointments: Intern, Medicine, University Tennessee, 1965; Resident, Medicine, University Tennessee, 1966-68; Chief Resident, 1969, Fellow, Northwestern Medical School, 1970-71. Publications: Over 75 professional publications in scientific journals. Honours: Past President, American Academy of Allergy & Immunology. Memberships: AMA; AAAI; ACAI; ACA. Address: 920 Madison Avenue 909N, Memphis, TN 38103 3410, USA.

LIEDTKE A James, b. 10 Jun 1938, McKeesport, PA, USA. Physician. m. Caroline Louise Rodder, 30 Jun 1962, 1 s, 1 d. Education: BS, magna cum laude, Mechanical Engineering, 1960; MD, 1964, University of Pittsburgh. Career: Instructor of Medicine, Harvard Medical School and Peter Bent Brigham Hospital, Boston; Assistant, Associate, Professor of Medicine, Hershey Medical Center, PA State University; Professor of Medicine and Section Head of Cardiology, University of WI, 1983-92; Currently, Professor of Medicine, University of WI Medical School, Madison. Publications: Co-author of 209 peer-reviewed journal articles, review articles, book chapters, book text and published abstracts, 1967-94. Honours: Fellowship, Cardiovascular Medicine, Harvard Medical School and Peter Bent Brigham Hospital, Boston, 1968-70; American Society for Clinical Investigation, 1981; Association of University Cardiologists, 1987; Association of Professors of Cardiology, 1989-93. Memberships: Fellow, Past WI Governor, American College of Cardiology; President, WI Affiliate, American Heart Association. Hobbies: Fossil Collecting; Travel. Address: University of Wisconsin Hospital and Clinics, Cardiology Section H6-3, 600 Highland Avenue, Madison, WI 53792-3248, USA.

LILLEHEI Clarence Walton, b. 23 Oct 1918, Minneapolis, USA. Surgeon. m. Katherine Ruth Lindberg, 31 Dec 1946, 3 s, 1 d. Education: BS, University of Minnesota, 1939; MD, 1942; MS, Physiology, 1951; PhD, Surgery, 1951; Doctor Medicine, University of Oslo, 1976; Honorary Degree, Faculte De Medecinae de Montpellier, France, 1977; Doctor Honoris Causa, University of Paris, France, 1986, University of Rome, 1991; LHD Hon, Oklahoma City University, 1987; DSc, Western VA University, 1993. Appointments include: Diplomate, American Board Surgery, 1951, Diplomate of American Board of Thoracic Surgery, 1954; Private Practice Medicine, 1942-; Lt Colonel MC, Aus, 1942-46; Specializing General Throacic and Cardiovascular Surgery, 1945-; Associate Professor Surgery, 1951-56, Professor Surgery, 1956-67,

Clinical Professor Surgery, 1967-, Director Medical Affairs, St Jude Medical, Inc, St Paul, 1979-; Lewis Atterbury Stimson Professor Surgery Cornell Medical College, New York City, 1967-74; Surgeon-in-Chief, New York Hospital, 1967-70; Board of Directors, Getz Brothers Medical, Tokyo. Honours include: Decorated Bronze Star Medal, 1944; Officer Order of Leopold, Belgium; Theobald-Smith Award AAAS, 1951;Lasker Award, 1955; Ida B Gould Award, 1957; Hektoen Gold Medal, AMA, 1957; Honor Award, Stevens Institute Technology, 1967; Outstanding Achievement Award, Board of Regents, University Minnesota, 1991; Lillehei Endowed Chair, University Minnesota Medical School, 1988; Lillehei Library named in his honour, 1991; Named to Minnesota Inventors Hall of Fame, 1993; Jacob Markowitz Award, Academy of Surgical Research, 1994. Memberships include: Fellow, ACS; American College Chest Physicians; AHA; American Association for Thoracic Surgery; Royal Society Medicine, England; Society Thoracic Surgery; AMA; AAAS; International Cardiovascular Society. Address: 73 Otis Lane, St Paul, MN 55104-5645, USA.

LIM Chin Theam, b. 15 Nov 1951, Penang, Malaysia. m. Tay Kim Yan, 6 Jan 1991, 1 son, 1 daughter. Education: FRCP, England; AM, Malaysia. Appointments: House Officer, University Hospital Kuala Lumpur, Malaysia; Medical Officer, Ministry of Health Hospital; Lecturer, Associate Professor. Publications: A 12 Year Experience of Retinopathy of Prematurity in the Extremely Preterm and Small Infants - 28 Weeks Gestation or 1000g Birthweight, co-author, 1990; Early Congenital Syphilis: Experience with 13 Consecutive Cases Seen at the University Hospital, Kuala Lumpur, 1991; Chapter on Low Birthweight Infants in Paediacric Problems in Tropical Countries, 1991; Effect iof Time of Birth on the Frequency Distribution of Cord Serum Thyroid Related Hormones Level, co-author, 1992; A Rare Cause of Neonatal Intestinal Obstruction in Malaysia, 1994. Honours: Critical Care Medicine Section, B Braun Award, 1995. Memberships: Malaysian Paediatric Association; Malaysian Perinatal Society. Hobbies: Music; Reading; Swimming. Address: 32 Jalan SS15/5G, Subang Jaya 47500, Selangor, Malaysia.

LIM David J, b. 27 Nov 1935, Seoul, Korea. Biomedical Researcher. m. Young Sook Hahn, 2 sons. Education: MD, Yonsei University College of Medicine, 1960; Completed Internship, Certificate, 1961, completed Residency, Otolaryngology, Certificate, 1964, National Medical Centre, Seoul. Appointments: Research Fellow, Department of Otolaryngology, Massachusetts Eye and Ear Infirmary, USA, 1965-66; Assistant Professor, 1966-67, Director, Otological Research Laboratory, 1967-76, Associate Professor, 1976-91, Ohio State University; Professor, Otolaryngology, 1976-91, Professor, Cell Biology, Neurobiology, Anatomy, 1977-91, Professor Emeritus, Otolaryngology, 1991-, Ohio State University College of Medicine; Director, 1992-94, Chief, Laboratory of Cellular Biology, 1992-, Intramural Research Division, National Institute on Deafness and Other Communication Disorders, NIH. Publications: Over 190 scientific papers; 10 textbook chapters; Editor, co-editor, 12 publications. Honours include: Gold Award, Teaching, Ohio State Medical Association, 1970; Gold Award, American Academy of Opthalmology and Otolaryngology, 1972; Fogarty International Fellow, 1982; Javits Award, 1986; Claude Pepper Award, 1989; Shambaugh Prize, 1992; Guyot Prize, University of Groningen, Netherlands, 1994. Memberships include: American Academy of Otolaryngology; American Otological Society; Society for Neuroscience; American Society for Cell Biology; Collegium Oto-rhino-laryngologicum Amicitiae Sacrum; Corresponding Member, Deutsche Gesellschaft für Hals-Nasen-Ohren-Heilkunde, Kopf-und Hals-Chirurgie; Histochemical Society; Society for Mucosal Immunology. Hobbies: Tennis; Skiing. Address: Rm 2A-01, 5 Research Court, Rockville, MD 20850, USA.

LIM Pin, b. 12 Jan 1936, Penang. Vice Chancellor; Professor of Medicine. m. Shirley Loo-Lim, 21 Mar 1964, 2 s, 1 d. Education: MA, Cambridge; MBBChir; FRCP(London); FRCPE; FRACP; FACP; FRACOG(Hon). Appointments: Registrar, Diabetic Department, Kings College Hospital, London, England, 1965; Medical Officer, Ministry of Health, Singapore, 1965-66; Lecturer in Medicine, 1966-70, Senior lecturer in Medicine, 1971-73, Associate professor of Medicine, 1974-77, Professor and Head of Department of Medicine, 1978-81, Deputy Vice Chancellor, 1979-81, University of Singapore; Commonwealth Medical Fellow, Department of Medicine, The Royal Infirmary, Edinburgh, Scotland, 1970. Publications: Contributor of numerous articles in professional journals. Honours: Queen's Scholar, 1957; Honorary Fellow, College of General Practitioners Singapore, 1982; Eisenhower Fellow, 1982; Gold Public Administration Medal, Republic of Singapore, 1984; Officier dans l'Ordre des Palmes Academiques, 1988; Republic of Singapore Meritorious Service Medal, 1990; Honorary fellow, Royal

Australian College of Obstetricians and Gynaecologists, 1992. Memberships: Singapore Medical Association; Academy of Medicine, Singapore; British Medical Association; Singapore Professional Centre. Hobbies: Badminton; Swimming. Address: National University of Singapore, 10 Kent Ridge Crescent, Singapore 0511.

LIM Say Wan, b. 7 June 1939, Malaysia. President; Consultant; Lecturer. m. Jeannie Sek Woo Chung, 7 June 1968, 3 sons. Education: MBBS, University Singapore, 1957-63; FFARCS (Ireland), FFARCS (England), University of Liverpool, 1966-68; FFARACS, 1974. Appointments: Medical Officer, Ministry of Health, Malaysia, 1964-66; Lecturer, University of Malaya, 1966-70; Private Practice, Kuala Lumpur, 1970-; President, Malaysian Society of Anaesthesiologists, 1974-75; President, Malaysian Medical Association, 1982-83; Vice Chairman, Medical Associations of South East Asian Nations, 1982-83; President, Confederation of Medical Associations in Asia & Oceania, 1983-85; Master, Academy of Medicine of Malaysia, 1984-90; Consultant Anaesthesiologist, Pantai Medical Centre, Kuala Lumpur; Honorary Lecturer in Anaesthesiology, National University of Malaysia; President, World Federation of Societies of Anaesthesiologists; President, Alumni Association of Medical Faculties, Universities of Malaya & Singapore; President, Royal Lake Club, Kuala Lumpur. Publications: Papers in Medical Journal of Malaysia & Malaysian Journal of Surgery, 1969-80. Memberships: Council Member, Academy of Medicine, Malaysia; Founding President, Asian & Oceanic Society of Regional Anaesthesia, 1989-91. Honours: Honorary FRACP, 1988; Honorary FACP, 1989; FRCPS,(Glasgow), 1990. Hobbies: Golf; Squash. Address: Pantai Medical Center, 59100 Kuala Lumpur, Malaysia.

LIM Siew Ming Arthur, b. 24 Apr 1934, Hong Kong. Eye Surgeon. m. Chan Poh Geok. Education: BBM, Nat Univ of Singapore; FAMS; FRCS; FRCS(Ed); FRACS; FRACO; FRCOpth; DO. Appointments: Ophthalmic Surgeon, Mt Elizabeth, Mt Alvernia and Gleneagles Hospitals; Currently: Medical Director, Singapore National Eye Centre; Clinical Professor and Head, Department of Ophthalmology, National University of Singapore. Publications include: Practical Ophthalmic Microsurgery, 1980; A Colour Atlas of Posterior Chambers Implants, 1985; A Colour Atlas of Ophthalmology, 1987; Peripheral Iridectomy Surgical-Argon YAG, 1987. Honours: Public Star, Singapore; Honorary Fellow, International College of Surgeons; Steve Charles Gold Medal Oration, 1992; Elected Fellow, Royal College of Medicine and Surgeons. Hobbies: Tennis; Golf; Painting; Sailing. Address: Singapore National Eye Centre Pte Ltd, 11 Third Hospital Avenue, Singapore O316.

LIM Thomas Wee Hwa, b. 29 Mar 1938, Singapore. Obstetrician; Gynaecologist. m. Siew Ying Wong, 24 Jun 1964, 3 d. Education: MBBS, Sydney, Australia; FRCOG(Lon); FAM(Singapore). Career: Registrar, Obstetrics and Gynaecology, Leicester General Hospital, Walsgrave Hospital, Coventry, England; Senior Registrar, Kardang Kerban Hospital, Singapore; Consultant Obstetrician and Gynaecologist, British Australian and New Zealand Forces in Singapore; Currently Consultant in Obstetrics and Gynaecology in private practice. Memberships: Academy of Medicine, Singapore; Singapore Obstetrical and Gynaecological Society; Singapore Medical Association. Hobby: Golf. Address: 277 Orchard Road 07-01-03, Specialist Centre Building, 1026, Singapore.

LIN Chuan-Xiang, b. 4 Apr 1918, China. Professor of Medicine. m. Li Xin-Yuan, 1 June 1948, 1 son, 1 daughter. Education: MD, 1943. Appointments: Instructor, Medicine, Beijing Medical College; Associate Professor, Medicine, Beijing Medical College; Professor of Medicine, Head, Department of Medicine & Chief of Division of Cardiology, First Teaching Hospital of Beijing Medical University. Publications: Fundamentals in Medicine, co-author; Physicial Diagnosis, chief editor; The Electrophysiologic Effect of Atenol and Nitreoipine on Normal and Ischemic Rabbit Myocardium in Situ, co-author, 1989. Memberships: Chinese Medical Association; Standing Committee, Chinese Society of Cardiology. Hobbies: Bridge. Address: Department of Medicine, First Teaching Hospital of Beijing Medical University, 8 Xishiku Street, Beijing 100034, China.

LIN Dao-Ping, b. 9 Jan 1924, Fukien, China. Professor of Thoracic Surgery. m. Professor Xiao Yu-Ying, 2 Feb 1952, 2 sons, 1 daughter. Education: MB, 1949. Appointments: Resident, 1949, Chief Resident, 1952, Lecturer, 1953; Visiting, 1953; Vice Director of Surgery, 1962; Vice Superintendent, 1978; Director of Surgery, 1978; Associate Professor, 1978; Professor, 1983-, President, Guangzhou Medical College, 1983-90. Publications include: Total Excision of Arch of Aorta with

Prosthetic Replacement, 1961; Operation for Double Arches of Aorta, 1963; Lung Function for Prediction of Safety for Pneumonectomy, 1965; Surgery for Advanced Pulmonary Tubercluosis, 1965, 1981; Lung Resection and Mitral Commissurotomy under Acupuncture Anesthesia, 1968; The Successful Operation on Infected Femoral Aneurysm, 1978; Emergency Operation for Lung Cancers, 1985; Sleeve Lobectomy for Lung Cancer, Co-author, 1989; Successful Operation on Infected Femoral Aneurysm, 1978; Co-Chief Editor of several books including: Text Book of Surgery, 1989, 1993; Emergency Management of the Wounded in Earthquake, 1992. Honours include: Model Worker and Teacher of the Province and City, several times, 1951-; Award, First National Science Conference, 1978; Award, provincial Education Bureau, 1981; Award, Association of Science and Technology, several times, 1984-. Memberships: Chairman, Chinese Medical Association, Guangzhou, 1986-91; Chairman, Chinese Association of Science and Technology, Guangzhou, 1991-94. Address: Department of Surgery. Guangzhou Medical College, Guangzhou, China.

LIN Ji, b. 13 Mar 1932, China. Chief Physician. m. Ho Sun Chu, 10 Feb 1960, 2 sons, 1 daughter. Education: Graduated, Medical Department, Fujian Medical School, 1959. Appointments: Clinical practice in Internal Medicine; University Teacher; Scientific Researcher; Currently: Chief Physician, Internal Medicine, Zhangzhou Municipal Hospital, Fujian; Associate Professor, Fujian Medical School, Zhangzhou. Publications: Preliminary Study of 48 Patients in Treatment of Acute Nonlymphocytic Leukemias with Low Dose Homoharringtonine, 1988; Report of 21 Patients with Myelodysplastic Syndrome, 1989; Report on Retinoic Acid in the Treatment of 5 Patients with Acute Promyelocytic Leukemia, 1990; Clinical Study on All Trans-Retinic Acids in the Treatment of 544 Patients with Acute Promyelocytic Leukemia, 1992; A Case of Secondary Therapy-related Leukemia with Multiple Extramedullary Plasmacytoma, 1992; Investigation of 12 Patients with Transformation from Myelodysplastic Syndrome into Acute Leukemia, 1993; Clinicopathologic Analyses of Dry Tap Bone Marrow Aspirations in 47 Patients, 1994; Clinical Analysis of 102 Patients with Complications of Exhaustion of Visceral Function with Acute Leukemia, 1994; Clinical Study on all Trans-Retinoic Acids in the Treatment of 30 Patients with Acute Promyelocytic Leukemia, 1994. Honours: Outstanding Achievements in Haematological Disorder, Leukemia Treatment and Bone Marrow Transplant; Outstanding Teaching Prize, Fujian Medical School, 1991; Outstanding Thesis Prize, 1992; Prize for Scientific Technology Advancement, 1993. Membership: Academician, Chinese Medical Association. Hobbies: Tea drinking; Playing chess; Strolling; Reading. Address: 59 Shengli Road, Zhangzhou, Fujian, China.

LIN Kun, b. 18 Feb 1934, Nanjing, Jiangsu, China. Physician. m. Ying Han, 1 Oct 1958, 2 daughters. Education: MD, China Medical University, 1950-56. Appointments: Physician, Affiliated Hospital of Institute of Hematology, Chinese Academy of Medical Sciences, Tianjin, 1957-69; Attending Doctor, Department of Internal Medicine, 1st Hospital of Panzhihua City, Sichuan, 1970-82; Associate Chief Physician, 1st Hospital of Panzhihua City, Sichuan, 1983-85; Deputy Head, Department of Internal Medicine, Xiqing Hospital, Tianjin, 1986-88; Head, Department of Internal Medicine, Xiqing Hospital, Tianjin, 1988-. Publications incl: Treatment of the bacillary dysentery with retention enema of chloromycetin, 1963; Simplifying the calculating percentage of shunt volume in right cardiac catheterization, 1978; Analysis of 13 right cardiac catheterizations, 1979; Relations between amplitude of Af waves and left atrial dimension in patients with coronary heart disease, 1993. Honours: Title, Advanced Medical Worker, 4 times, 1991-95; Medal of Merit, 8th National 5-Year Plan, Tianjin Municipal General Labour Union. Memberships: Chinese Medical Association; Society of Cardiovascular Disease. Hobby: Playing Weiqi (go). Address: 343 Xiqing Road, Tianjin 300380, China.

LIN Ruey-Shiung, b. 17 Dec 1940, Tainan, Taiwan. Epidemiologist; Educator. m. Feng-Ying Chiu, 15 Aug 1970, 1 son, 2 daughters. Education: MD, 1965, MPH, 1968, National Taiwan University, Taipei; MD, Heidelberg University, Germany, 1970; DPH, Johns Hopkins University, USA, 1977; Diplomate, Board of Preventive Medicine. Appointments: Visiting Associate Professor, College of Medicine, Taiwan University, Taipei, 1970-72; Associate Professor, 1973-75, Visiting Professor, 1986-87, Professor, Director, 1987-93, Institute of Public Health; Assistant Professor, University of Kansas Medical Center, Kansas City, USA, 1977-78; Assistant Professor, University of Maryland School of Medicine, Baltimore, 1978-80; Epidemiologist, Maryland State Health Department, Baltimore, 1980-86; Professor, Dean, College of

Public Health, National Taiwan University, Taipei, 1993-. Publications: A multifactorial model for pancreatic cancer in man: Epidemiologic Evidence; Occupational exposure to electromagnetic fields and the occurrence of brain tumors: an analysis of possible association; Trends in mortality from diabetes mellitus in Taiwan, 1960-88; Maternal role in type 2 diabetes mellitus: Indirect evidence for a mitochondrial inheritance. Honours; National Research Service Award, Public Health Service, DHHS/USA, Baltimore, 1975-77. Memberships: American Public Health Association; Association of Public Health, China, President 1989-91; International Society for Environmental Epidemiology; Bioelectromagnetic Society; Society for Risk Analysis; Society for Epidemiologic Research. Hobbies: Bridge; Mountain climbing; Chess. Address: National Taiwan University, College of Public Health, No 1 Jen Ai Road, 1st Sec, Taipei, Taiwan, China.

LIN Shui-Miao, b. 3 Mar 1941, Shanghai, China. Professor. m. Xia Ai-Zhen, 2 May 1967, 2 daughters. Education: Graduated, Shanghai College of Traditional Chinese Medicine, 1964. Appointments: Associate Professor, Supervisor of Master's degree students, Supervisor of PhD students, Professor of Traditional Chinese Medicine, Traditional Chinese Medicine College, Shanghai; Consultant: Traditional Chinese Medicine and Traditional Chinese Medicine Geriatric Medicine; Vice-President, Shanghai University of Traditional Chinese Medicine; Vice-President, Shanghai Academy of Traditional Chinese Medicine; Head Director, Institute of Geriatric Medicine, Shanghai Academy of Traditional Chinese Medicine; President, Shanghai Academy of Qigong. Publications: Over 20 papers about geriatric medicine with Traditional Chinese Medicine in national Chinese journals and 6 books, 1979-94. Honours: 2nd Class Award of Science and Technology Progress; 2nd Class Award of Shanghai Science and Technology Progress, 1990, 1992; 2nd Class Award of Science and Technology Progress, Government Ministry of Traditional Chinese Medicine, 1991; Special Award, Chinese National Government, 1993-; Honorary President, Japan College of Chinese Medicine. Memberships: Director, 21st Chinese Medical Committee; Deputy Director, Elder Medical Society, Shanghai Traditional Chinese Medical Association; Chief Director, Shanghai Qigong Rehabilitation Association; Vice-Secretary, Traditional Chinese Medical Branch, Shanghai Science and Technology Committee. Hobbies: Chinese calligraphy; Chinese theatre. Address: Shanghai University of Traditional Chinese Medicine, # 530 Ling Ling Road, Shanghai 200032, China.

LIN Yi, b. 20 March 1942, Ganzhou, Jiangxi, China. Surgeon. m. 7 February 1962, 2 daughters. Appointments: Intern, Physician In Charge, Chief Surgeon; Surgeon, Professor, Guangxi Traditional Chinese Medical College; Vice Director, Mastosis Commission of Chinese Traditional Surgeon Institute; Director, National Traditional Chinese Medicine Centre of Prevention and Cure. Publications: Practical Hospital Management, 1990; Practical Chinese Traditional Knowledge, 1992; Practical Traditional Chinese Medicine Mastosology, 1992; Editor, Science and Educational Film, Prevention and Cure Mastosis, 1993. Honours: Title, Outstanding Person of Special Technique, Guilin Municipal Government, 1992; National Excellent Worker in Health, State Council. Memberships: Vice Director, Mastosis Commission of Centre of Chinese Traditional Surgery Institute; Director, National Traditional Chinese Medicine Centre of Prevention and Cure Mastosis; Honorary Presidency, Xiong-Beng Functional Hospital, Japan. Hobbies: Music; Basketball; Swimming; Mountaineering; Lectures; Reading; Travel. Address: Lin Gui Road, Gui Lin Chinese Traditional Hospital, Gui Lin, Guangxi 541002, China.

LIN You-Hua, b. 23 Oct 1927, Fuzhou, China. Professor of Pulmonary Medicine. m. Huan-Mei Lu, 20 Nov 1956, 2 sons. Education: BS, Yanjing University, 1950; Graduated, Peking Union Medical College, 1954. Appointments: Visiting Doctor, 1958, Associate Professor, 1979, Peking Union Medical College Hospital; Professor of Pulmonary Medicine, China-Japan Friendship Hospital, Beijing, 1983-. Publications: Chronic pulmonary sarcoidosis: relationship between lung lavage cell counts, chest radiograph and results of standard lung function tests, 1985; Principles of Pulmonary Function Tests and Their Clinical Application, book in Chinese, 1992. Honours: Award of Science and Technology, Chinese Academy of Medical Science, 1985. Membership: Speciality Society of Chinese Medical Association. Hobbies: Music; Poems. Address: Department of Pulmonary Medicine, China-Japan Friendship Hospital, Beijing 100029, China.

LIN Yu-Chong, b. 24 Apr 1935, Taiwan, China. Professor. m. Dora Liaw, 27 Apr 1960, 2 daughters. Education: PhD, Rutgers University, New Jersey, USA, 1968. Appointments: Research Associate, Rutgers

University; Research Associate, University of California, Santa Barbara; Assistant Professor, Associate Professor, Professor, University of Hawaii, John A Burns School of Medicine, 1969. Publications: More than 100 scientific papers; Hyperbaric Medicine and Physiology, editor, 1988; Man In The Sea, vol 1 and 2, editor, 1990. Honours: Editorial Board, Journal of Applied Physiology; Editorial Board, Chinese Journal of Physiology. Memberships: American Physiological Society; Undersea & Hyperbaric Medical Society. Hobbies: Carpentry; Golfing. Address: Department of Physiology, University of Hawaii, John A Burns School of Medicine, Honolulu, HI 96822, USA.

LIN Zong Guang, b. 26 February 1930, Zhe Jiang, China. Doctor. m. Zhang Xiao Shan, 1 Jan 1958, 2 daughters. Education: Graduate, Zhe Jiang Medical University, 1955; Graduate, Shanghai College of Traditional Chinese Medicine; Integration of Traditional Chinese and Western Medicine, 1961. Appointments: Resident Doctor, 1955-63; Attending Doctor, 1963-82; Associate Professor of Medicine, 1983-87; Professor of Medicine, 1987-. Publications: More than 100 papers on treatment of Cascinoma of the Liver, Hepato-Cirrhosis Ascites, Upper Gastrointestinal Bleeding; 4 books, including: Medical Meals for Cancered. Honours: 2nd Prize, Scientific Research Achievements, Shanghai, 1980; Apartment, Shanghai Municipal Government, Outstanding Contribution, 1989. Memberships: Associate Director, Digestive System Disease Society of Chinese Association of the Integration of Traditional and Western Medicine, 1989-; Standing Director, Shanghai Branch, Chinese Association of the Integration of Traditional and Western Medicine, 1980-; Diretor, Shanghai Association of Traditional Chinese Medicine and Pharmacy, 1978-. Hobbies: Light Music. Address: Rm 504, No 4, Lane 2771, Ping Liang Road, Shanghai 200090, China.

LINDBERG Lene, b. 22 Nov 1957, Engelholm, Sweden. Assistant Professor. 1 d. Education: BSc, 1982, MSc, 1986, PhD, 1994, Uppsala University, Sweden. Appointment: Assistant Professor, Clinical Psychology, Uppsala University. Publications: Co-author, Early feeding problems in a normal population, in International Journal of Eating Disorders, 1991; Co-author, Early food refusal: Infant and family characteristics, in Infant Mental Health Journal, 1994; Co-author, Infant food refusal and parental social support, in Early Development and Parenting, 1994; Co-author, Infantile colic and parental experiences, in Early Development and Parenting, 1994. Memberships: Swedish Psychological Association; Nordic Association of Infant Mental Health; World Association of Infant Mental Health. Hobbies: Travel; Needlework; Computer Games. Address: Margrebelundsv 76, S-161 35 Bromma, Sweden.

LINDON John A, b. 11 Mar 1924, Illinois, USA. Psychoanalyst; Psychiatrist. m. (1) Ruth Blumenson, 1953, dec, (2) Marilyn Becker, 1973, 1 son, 3 daughters. Education: MD, University of Louisville, 1948; PhD, Southern California Psychoanalytic Institute, 1977. Appointments: Assistant Clinical Professor of Psychiatry, University of Southern California; Editor, Psychoanalytic Forum, vol 1-5; Supervising and Training Analyst, Institute of Contemporary Psychoanalysis, Southern California Psychoanalytic Institute. Publications: Castrophilia as a Character Neurosis, 1958; On Freud's Concept of Dream-Action, 1966; Psychoanalysis by Telephone, 1988; Does Technique Require Theory?, 1991; A Reassessment of Little Hans, His Parents and His Castration Complex, 1992; Gratification and Provision in Psychoanalysis: Should We Get Rid of the Rule of Abstinence?, 1994. Honours: Clinical Essay Prize, International Psychoanalytic Association, 1957; Oustanding Faculty Award, Neuropsychiatric Institute, UCLA, 1974; Outstanding Teacher Award, Southern California Psychoanalytic Institute, 1977-78. Memberships: American Psychiatric Association; American Medical Association; Psychiatric Research Foundation; Institute of Contemporary Psychoanalysis; Southern California Psychoanalytic Institute; National Council of Psychoanalytic Self Psychology; International Psychoanalytic Association. Address: 255 S Beverly Glen Boulevard, Los Angeles, CA 90024, USA.

LINDSAY John Spencer Bonar, b. 5 June 1920, Christchurch, New Zealand. Ret Consultant Psychiatrist. Education: John McGlashan College, Dunedin; MBChB, 1943, MD, 1953, Otago University; DPM, London University, 1951; MPhil, Auckland University, 1973; FRCPsych; AFBPsS; CPsychol, 1988. Appointments: Physician in Charge, Psychological Medicine, Auckland Hospital, 1963-75; Tutor, 1964-75. Publications include: Ward 10B, ther Deadly Witch-Hunt, 1992. Honours: Scott Medal; Christie Medal; Senior Scholarship. Address: 1/60 Broadway, Nedlands 6009, Western Australia.

LINDSLEY Donald Benjamin, b. 23 Dec 1907, Brownhelm, Ohio, USA. Professor of Psychology & Physiology. m. Ellen Ford, 16 Aug 1933, 2 sons, 2 daughters. Education: AB, Wittenberg College, 1929; PhD, University of Iowa, 1932; HonoraryDoctorates: Brown University, 1958, Wittenberg University, 1959, Trinity College, Hartford, 1965, Loyola University, Chicago, 1969, Johannes Gutenberg University, Germany, 1977. Appointments: Include: Professor, University of Psychology, Northwestern University, Evanston, 1946-51; Professor, University of California, Los Angeles, 1951-77; Retired, Professor Emeritus, Departments of Psychology & Physiology, University of California. Publications: Numerous publications to professional journals. Memberships: Include: National Academy of Sciences, 1952; American Academy of Arts & Sciences, 1965; American Psychological Association; American Psychological Society; American Physiology Society; American Association for the Advancement of Science; American Academy of Cerebral Palsy; American Academy of Neurology; International Brain Research Organization. Honours: Include: Ralph Gerard Prize, Distinguished Contributions to Neuroscience, Society for Neuroscience, 1988; American Psychological Foundation Gold Medal Award, Lifetime Achievement in Psychological Science, 1989; Awarded Honorary Lifetime Membership, Department of Psychobiology, University of California, Irvine, for Outstanding Contributions to its Founding 25 years ago and in the years since then, 1989; Recipient, herbert Jasper Award, Amer Electroencephalographic Society, 1994. Address: Department of Psychology, University of California, Los Angeles, CA 90024, USA.

LINEHAM Thomas Patrick, b. 18 Apr 1924, London, England. Physician. Education: Md, 1960; DCH, London, 1960; FRCCP, 1972. Appointments: Medical Registrar, St Andrews Hospital London, 1951-52; Medical Registrar, Lambeth Hospital, London, 1952-53; Associate Professor, New York Medical College, 1984. Publications: Various articles. Memberships: British Medical Association. Honours: Knighthood of St Gregory, 1992. Hobbies: Sailing; Skiing; Theatre. Address: 103 Biddulem Mansions, Elerlin Avenue, London W9 1HN, England.

LING Lian-Lian, b. 9 Mar 1947, Wenzhou, China. Obstetrician and Gynaecologist. m. Zhou Rui-zheng, 13 Dec 1977, 1 daughter. Education: Graduated, Zhejiang Medical University, 1969; Master's degree in Medicine and Surgery, Government of Fiji. Appointments: Currently Medical Director, 2nd Affiliated Hospital Wenzhou Medical College; Registrar, Department of Obstetrics and Gynaecology, 3rd Teaching Hospital, Peking Medical University. Publications: Surveillance and treatment of gestational diabetes mellitus of Fiji women, 1994. Membership: Chinese Medical Association, Wenzhou Branch. Address: 2nd Affiliated Hospital, Wenzhou Medical College, Wenzhou 325000, China.

LING Louis J, b. 22 Aug 1954, Minneapolis, USA. Physician. m. Dr Beth Baker, 26 Jan 1980, 1 s, 2 d. Education: BS, Chemistry, 1975, MD, 1980, University of Minnesota. Appointments: Past President, Society for Academic Emergency Medicine; Associate Medial Director. Publications: Emergency Medicine: Concepts and Clinical Practice, Co-editor, 4th edition; Whole Bowel Irrigation for Lithium Overdose, Co-author, 1991. Memberships: American College of Emergency Physicians; Society for Academic Emergency Medicine; American Medical Association. Address: Hennepin County Medical Centre, 701 Park Avenue, Minneapolis, MN 55415, USA.

LINGXU Kong, b. 9 Oct 1939, Beijing, China. Head Department Ageing and Health-Maintaining. m. Zhang Baozhen, 10 Aug 1967, 1 s, 1 d. Education: Studied at Beijing University of Traditional Chinese Medicine, 1958-64. Appointments: Vice Head, 1981-83, Head, 1983-85, Department of Basic Theory, Jilin Provincial Academy of Traditional Chinese Medicine; Currently, Head, Department of Ageing and Health-Maintaining, Institute of Basic Theory. Publications: Summaries on Health-Maintaining Methods of Traditional Chinese Medicine, Chinese Health Education, 1989; Traditional Medicine, in Chinese Encyclopedia, 1992. Membeship: Member of Expert Committee Group in Basic Theory, China Academy of Traditional Chinese Medicine. Hobby: Literature. Address: Dept of Ageing and Health- Maintaining, Institute of Basic Theory, China Academy of Traditional Chinese Medicine, Beijing 100700, China.

LINK Michael P, b. 3 Jan 1949, Cleveland, OH, USA. Professor of Pediatrics. m. Vicki MacKintosh, 30 May 1985, 1 d. Education: AB, summa cum laude, Columbia College, NY, 1970; MD, Stanford

University, CA. Career: Assistant Professor, 1979-85, Associate Professor, 1986-91, Professor, 1991-, Pediatrics, Stanford University School of Medicine; Staff Hematologist and Oncologist, 1979-, Co-Director, Oncology Program, 1990-, Lucile Salter Packard Children's Hospital, Stanford, Palo Alto, CA. Publications: Various. Honours: Phi Beta Kappa, 1969; Alpha Omega Alpha, 1974. Memberships: American Academy of Pediatrics; American Society of Clinical Oncology; American Society of Hematology; American Association of Cancer Research; American Society of Pediatric Hematology and Oncology; Society for Pediatric Research; SIOP. Hobbies: Backpacking; Soaring; Skiing. Address: Hematology/Oncology, Lucile Salter Packard Children's Hospital, 725 Welch Road, Stanford, Palo Alto, CA 94304, USA.

LIPIN Theodore, b. 5 Dec 1920. Physician. Education: MD, Harvard Medical School, 1944; American Board of Psychiatry & Neurology. Appointments: Research, St Gorans Hospital, Stockholm, Sweden. Publications: American Medical Association, Arch Neurology & Psychiatry, 1948, 1955; International Journal Psychoanalysis, 1963; Journal American Psychoanalytic Association, 1969; Journal Clinical Psychoanalysys, 1992. Memberships: Fellow, American Psychiatric Association; Association for Research in Nervous & Mental Disorders; Swedish Medical Association. Address: Messeniusgatan 1, S-112 57 Stockholm, Sweden.

LIPKIN Edward Walter, b. 8 Jan 1949, St Louis, MO, USA. Physician; Scientist. Education: BA, Williams College, 1971; PhD, 1977, MD, 1978, Case Western Reserve University. Appointments: Instructor in Medicine, Boston University School of Medicine, 1980-81; Acting Instructor in Medicine, 1982-84, Assistant Professor of Medicine, 1984-90, Associate Professor of Medicine, University of Washington. Publications: Dynamic Aspects of Oscillatory Glycolysis in Isolated Perifused Fat Cells Synchronized by Insulin and Hydrogen Peroxide, Co-author, 1983; Kinetics of Insulin Binding to Rat White Fat Cells at 15°C, Co-author, 1986. Honours: Phi Beta Kappa, 1970; NIH Clinical Associate Physician, 1984-87; Sigma Xi, 1987; Western Society for Clinical Investigation, 1989. Memberships: American Federation Clinical Research; American Institute Nutritionists; American Society Clinical Nutrition; American Association for the Advancement of Science. Hobbies: Backpacking; Bicycle Touring; Skiing. Address: RG-26, University of Washington, Seattle, WA 98195, USA.

LIPPINCOTT Joseph A, b. 11 Mar 1956, NJ, USA. Psychologist. m. Ruth Bale, 11 Aug 1984. Education: BS, Seton Hall University; MS, Rutgers University; PhD, Lehigh University. Appointments: Psychotherapist, Prince George's County Mental Health Department; Associate, American University Counseling Services; Assistant Professor, Northampton College; Currently, Assistant Professor, Counseling Psychologist, Kutztown University Counseling Services. Publications: Co-author, Group Counseling for Socially Disenfranchised College Students, in Journal of College Student Development, 1994; Co-author, A Comparison of Asian and American Undergraduates: Culture Somatization and Propensity for Seeking Counseling Services, in Journal of American College Health, 1995; 6 State, National and International Presentations. Honours: Recipient Outstanding Research Award, 1990; ERIC/CAPS. Memberships: American Counseling Association; Society for the Exploration of Psychotherapy Integration. Hobbies: Travel; Hunting; Fishing. Address: Counseling Services Admin 215, Kutztown University, PA 19530, USA.

LIPSITT Don R, b. 24 Nov 1927, Boston, MA, USA. Physician. m. Merna Pilot, 9 Aug 1952, 2 sons. Education: BA, New York University, 1949; MA, Boston University, 1950; MD, University of Vermont, 1956. Career: Director, Medical Psychology and Psychiatric Consultation Service, Beth Israel Hospital, Boston, MA; Professor of Psychiatry, Harvard Medical School; Chairman, Department of Psychiatry, Mount Auburn Hospital, Cambridge, MA, USA; Editor-in-Chief, General Hospital Psychiatrist. Publications: Medical and Psychological Characteristics of Crocks, 1970; Co-Editor, Psychosomatic Medicine: Current Trends and Clinical Applications, 1977. Honours: President, American Assoc General Hospital Psychiatrists, 1992-94; President-Elect, Massachusetts Psychiatric Society, 1995; Fellow American Psychiatric Association, 1961; Fellow, International College of Psychosomatic Medicine, 1971; Fellow, American College of Psychiatrists, 1979; Life Fellow, American Psychiatric Association, 1991; President, American Assoc, General Hospital Psychiatrists, 1992, Society of Liaison Psychiatry Achievement Award, 1994, President-Elect, Massachusetts Psychiatric Society, 1995. Memberships: American Psychiatric Association; American

Psychosomatic Society; Executive Secretary, for Academic Psychiatry Association. Hobbies: Music; Sailing. Address: 15 Griggs Road, Brookline, MA 02146, USA.

LIPTON Roger A, b. 6 Dec 1908, Russia. Clinical Associate Professor. m. Pauline Kazar, 6 June 1933, deceased, 2 sons. Education: MD, Syracuse University. Appointments: Diplomate, American Board of Allergy, 1963; Diplomate, American Board Certified Allergist, 1965; Diplomate, American Board of Medicine, 1974; Chief of Allergy, 1959. Publications: Numerous articles in professional journals. Memberships: FAIS; AOA; ASIM; ACP; AACA; AAD. Hobbies: Opera; Ballet. Address: c/o Masonic Home (Weily 224), 2150 Bleecker Street, Utica, NY 13501-1788, USA.

LIPTZIN Benjamin, b. 17 Sept 1945, New York City, USA. Psychiatrist. m. Sharon Leslie Rothstein, 10 June 1968, 1 s, 2 d. Education: BA, Yale University, 1966; MD, University of Rochester School of Medicine, 1971. Appointments include: Assistant Professor of Psychiatry, 1978-89, Associate Professor of Psychiatry, 1990, Lecturer in Psychiatry, 1990-92, Harvard Medical School; Professor and Deputy Chair of Psychiatry, 1990-; Tufts University School of Medicine, Chairman, Department of Psychiatry, Baystate Medical Centre, Springfield, Massachusetts, 1990-. Publications: Contributor of numerous reports, reviews, monographs and letters; Nursing Homes and the Mentally Ill, 1989. Honours include: Phi Beta Kappa, Magna Cum Laude, Honours with Exceptional Distinction, American Psychiatric Association, 1966; Adolf Meyer Award, 1974; PHS Commendation Medal, 1978; Fellow, Gerontological Society of America. Memberships include: Massachusetts Psychiatric Society; Boston Society for Gerontologic Psychiatry. Hobbies: Tennis; Skiing; Music. Address: Baystate Medical Centre, Department of Psychiatry, 140 High Street, Springfield, MA 01199, USA.

LISAK Robert Philip, b. 17 Mar 1941, Brooklyn, New York, USA. Physician. m. Deena Penchansky, 2 Aug 1964, 1 son, 1 daughter. Education: BA, cum laude, Highest Honours, New York University, 1961; MD, Columbia University, 1965. Appointments: Assistant Professor, 1972-76, Associate Professor of Neurology, 1976-80, Professor of Neurology, 1980-87, Vice Chairman of Neurology, 1985-87, University of Pennsylvania; Professor and Chairman of Neurology, Wayne State University School of Medicine. Publications: Myasthenia Gravis, co-author, 1982; Handbook of Myasthenia Gravis and Myasthenic Syndromes, 1994; Contributor of numerous articles, reviews, book chapters and abstracts. Honours: Fulbright-Hays Senior Research Scholar, 1978-79; Lindback Award for Teaching, University of Pennsylvania, 1985; Founders Day Award, New York University, 1961; Phi Beta Kappa. Memberships: American Neurological Association; American Academy of Neurology; AAAS; Society of Neuroscience; American Association Immunologists; International Society Neuroimmunology. Hobbies: Tennis; Photography; Wine; Cooking. Address: Department of Neurology, 6-E University Health Centre, 4201 St Antoine, Detroit, MI 48201, USA.

LISKOW Barry I, b. 6 Jan 1943, Cincinnati, OH, USA. Psychiatrist. m. 1972, 1 s, 1 d. Education: AB, Columbia College, 1964; MD, Columbia College Physicians and Surgeons, 1968. Appointments: Assistant Professor, University of Iowa, 1974-79; Associate Professor, University of Kansas, 1979-86; Professor of Clinical Psychiatry, Ohio State University, 1986-89; Chief of Psychiatry Service, Kansas City VAMC; Professor of Psychiatry, University of Kansas Medical Cntre, 1989-. Publications: Psychotropic Drug handbook, 7h edition, 1995. Memberships: American Psychiatric Association; Royal College of Psychiatrists. Address: 4801 Linwood Boulevard, Kansas City, MO 64128, USA.

LISOWSKI Frederick Peter, b. 31 Aug 1922, Berlin, Germany. Medical Teacher. m. Ei Yoke Lim, 9 Apr 1975. Education: PhD, University of Birmingham, England; LM, Rotunda Hospital, Dublin, Ireland; LRCPI, LRCSI, Royal College of Surgeons, Ireland. Career: Assistant Lecturer, Liverpool University, 1950-54; Lecturer, Senior Lecturer, Birmingham University, 1954-68; Professor, Head of Anatomy, University of Hong Kong, 1969-83, now Professor Emeritus; Currently, Part-time Senior Lecturer, University of Tasmania. Publications include: Numerous books, chapters and articles including: The Variability of Man, in Ethiopian Medical Journal, 1966; Co-author, A New System of Anatomy: A Dissectors Guide and Atlas, 1981; Medical Education in China, in Australia-China Review, 1989; Preventitive Healthcare in China, in Australia-China Review, 1993; China's Rural Healthcare, an example of a county in Sichuan, in Australia-China Review, 1994. Honours: Honorary Professor, Jinan University, Guangzhou, China, 1980-; Honorary Professor, Kumming Medical College, China, 1986-. Memberships: Anatomical Society of Great Britain and Ireland; Fellow, British Association of Clinical Anatomists; International Society for the History of East Asian Science, Technology and Medicine. Hobbies: Reading; Music; Travel. Address: 522 Churchill Avenue, Sandy Bay, Tasmania 7005, Australia.

LISTER Mark Wayne, b. 30 June 1954, Florida, USA. Clinical Laboratory Scientist. m. Elizabeth Steger, 4 Oct 1984, 1 son. Appointments: Laboratory Director, Department of Pathology and Laboratory Medicine, Calhoun General Hospital, Florida; Director of Immunohaematology, Department of Pathology and Laboratory Medicine, Florida Medical Center; Currently Supervisor, Department of Pathology and Laboratory Medicine, Westside Regional Medical Center, Florida. Publications: Presentations on current trends in immunotherapy, clinical aspects of leukemias, resolution of ABO discrepancies, prevalence of human T-lymphotropic retrovirus, 1989; Dipeptidyl pepitase DPPIV/CD6 expression and correlation of short term/long term survivors with HIV infection, 1994; Immune reconstitution and stem cell expansion, 1994; Patents include: Virucidal wipe with hand-protective barrier, 1990; pharmacomechanical applications to HIV infection, pending 1993; Copyright granted on housing and feeding the impoverished, 1990. Honours: Patents and Copyrights involving immune reconstitution, stem cell expansion and immunological therapeutics, 1990-; Presentation at 10th International Conference on AIDS, Yokohama, Japan, 1994. Memberships: National Certification Agency; American Association of Blood Banks; Florida Association of Blood Banks; American Medical Technologists. Hobbies: Woodworking; Cycling; Tennis; Reading. Address: 1729 East Commercial Boulevard, Suite 239, Fort Lauderdale, FL 33334, USA.

LITKIN Mikhail Ivanovich, b. 22 Nov 1919, Solikamsk, Russia. Surgeon. m. Valentina Litkina, 1946, 2 sons. Education: DMS; MD, PhD, Medical Military Academy. Appointments: Chief, Surgical Department, Assistant Professor, Professor, Chief, Department of General Surgery, Chief, Postgraduate Surgical Training, Chief of Hospital Surgery, Professor, General Surgery Department. Publications: Skin Plastic Surgery in Wounds, 1965; Acute Trauma of Main Vessels, 1973; Septic Shock, 1980; Gangrene of the Lungs, 1983; Autotransfusion of the Blood, 1979; Pulmonary Surgery, 1983. Honours: Honourable Researcher of USSR, 1977; Laureat of the Supreme Court Award, 1988; Chief of the Pirogov Surgical Society. Memberships: All-Russia Surgery Association; Pirogov Surgical Society; Honore Cause of Military Surgeons, USA. Hobbies: Fishing; Skiing; Gardens. Address: Apt 136 Av Engels 7, St Petersburg 194156, Russia.

LITTLE Bertis Britt, b. 22 Feb 1957, Whiteville, NC, USA. Medical geneticist. div, 1 s. Education: BA, ASU, 1976; MA, BSU, 1979; PhD, The University of Texas, 1983. Appointments: Instructor, Cape Fear Community College, Wilmington, North Carolina, 1976-78; Lecturer, University of Texas at Austin, 1981-85; Assistant Professor, 1985-92, Associate Professor of Obstetrics and Gynaecology, Southwestern Medical School. Publications: Drugs and Pregnancy, 1992; Contributor of over 100 scientific and medical articles in professional journals. Honours: Academic Scholarship, ASU, 1974-76; Doctoral Fellowship, UT Austin, 1979-83; NIH Junior Investigator Award, 1985. Hobbies: Cycling; Hiking; Camping; Mountain Climbing. Address: Division of Clinical Genetics, Southwestern Medical School, Dallas, TX 75235-9032, USA.

LITVIN Victor Yuryevich, b. 14 Nov 1938, Moscow, Russia. Professor. m. Valentina Pushkareva, 22 July 1989, 1 son. Education: Department of Biology, Moscow State University, 1967; Candidate of Biology, 1970; Doctor of Biology, 1979. Appointments: senior Researcher, 1971-77, Scientific Secretary, 1977-80, Vice-Director, 1980-95, Head, Laboratory of Ecology of Pathogens, Professor, 1991-, Gamaleya Institute of Epidemiology and Microbiology. Publications: Saprophytism and Parasitism of Pathogenic Bacteriae, 1988; Potential Pathogenicity and Incidental Parasitism of Micro-organisms, 1991; Ecological Aspects of Epidemiology, 1993; Contributor of 160 articles. Honours: Corresponding Member, Russian Academy of Medical Sciences, 1994; Corresponding Member, International Academy Science of Eurasia, 1994. Memberships: Russian Society of Epidemiologists, Microbiologists and Parasitologists. Hobbies: Animals; Classical Music. Address: Gamaleya Research Institute of Epidemiology

and Microbiology of RAMS, Gamaleya Street 18, 123098 Moscow, Russia.

LIU Bao-An, b. 15 Sept 1935, Guiyan City, Guizhou Province, China. Physician. m. An Guojun, 29 Mar 1955, 2 sons. Education: BA, Guiyan Medical College, 1963. Appointments: Currently Assistant Chief Doctor of Internal Medicine, Bijie City Hospital, Guizhou. Publication: Misdiagnosis of SLE. Membership: Bijie Medical Association, Head Secretary. Address: Bijie City Hospital, Guizhou, China.

LIU Biansheng, b. 29 Aug 1932, Henan Province, China. Doctor. Education: Tongji Medical University, 1954-59. Appointments: Assistant Military Doctor, 1950-54; Doctor, Head of Endemic Disease Institute, 1959-81; Assistant Professor, Director, Hubei Provincial Institute of Geriatric Medicine, 1981-86; Professor, Master, Liyuan Hospital of Hubei Province, 1986-. Honours: 2nd Award, 1985, 3rd Award, twice, 1985, Science and Technology Success; One of Middle-Youth Age Experts Making Great Contributions, 1990; First Awardee of Excellent Thesis, 1988; Awardee, Whole Country Science and Technology Congress, 1978. Memberships: Standing Council, Society of Geriatric Medicine, Chinese Medicine Association; Standing Council, Chinese Research Association of Trace Element and Health; Director, Hubei Provincial Society of Geriatric Medicine. Address: Hubei Provincial Liyuan Hospital, Wuhan, Hubei 430077, China.

LIU David Tek Yung, b. 26 Apr 1941, Malaysia. Obstetrician and Gynaecologist. m. 26 July 1976, 1 daughter. Education: MB BS, 1966; MRCOG, 1971; MPhil, 1975; Accreditation in Obstetrics and Gynaecology, 1976; FRCOG, 1986; DM, 1991; FRAOG, 1992. Appointments include: Obstetrics and Gynaecology, The Women's Hospital, Sydney, Australia, 1969-70; Canterbury District Memorial Hospital, 1970; Obstetrics and Gynaecology and Research Fellow, University of Sussex and Royal Sussex County Hospital, Brighton, England, 1971-74; Lecturer, Research Registrar, 1974-76, Lecturer, Senior Registrar, 1976, University College Hospital, London; Senior Lecturer, Honorary Consultant, Consultant, Clinical Director, Department of Obstetrics and Gynaecology, University of Nottingham, 1981-. Publications: Labour Ward Manual, Co-author, 1985, 1991; Chorion Villus Sampling, Co-author, 1987; Practical Gynaecology, Co-author, 1989; Ovarian Cysts, 1990; A Practical Guide to Chorion Villus Sampling, 1991; Contributor of professional papers. Memberships: Counsel Member, Birmingham and Midland Obstetrics and Gynaecological Society; Blair Bell Society. Hobbies: Dinghy Sailing; Gardening; Writing Poetry. Address: Department of Obstetrics and Gynaecology, City Hospital, Nottingham NG5 1PB, England.

LIU Duzhou, b. 20 Nov 1917, Liaoning, China. Professor. Appointments: professor, Beijing Traditional Chinese Medicine University, 1978-. Publications: Author of over 20 books in Chinese and Japanese including: Correlation Notes on Treatise on Febrile Disease Due to Invasion of Cold, 1991; Explanation on Chinese Treatise on Febrile Disease Due to Invasion of Cold, 1983; Guide to Empiracal Formulas for Clinic Syndromes, 1993; COntributor of over 100 professional articles. Memberships: Standing Council, China Association of TCM; Director, Zhang Zhongjing's Doctrine; Special Engaged Member, State Council Academy Degree Committee. Address: Beijing Traditional Chinese Medicine University, Beijing 100029, China.

LIU Feng, b. 6 Dec 1963, Shijiazhuang, China. Lecturer of Neurobiology. m. Shiming Xue, 1 Oct 1986, 1 d. Education: MB. 1980, MMed, 1990, Hebei Medical College. Appointments: Assistant Master, Department of Anatomy, Hebei Medical College, 1987. Publications: Ultrastructural Study on the Lobe in Aged Rats, 1993; Measurement of Prostate, Seminal Vesicle and Bulbourethral Gland of Chinese Adult, Co-author, 1987; Electron Microscopic Observrvation of Neurosecretory Fibres of Hypophyseal Neural Lobes in Aged Rats, 1994; Human Anatomy, Co-author. Hobbies: Bridge; Billiards' Chinese Chess. Address: 5 Changan Western Street, Shijiazhuang 050017, China.

LIU Fengzhen, b. 15 Nov 1926, Beijing, China. Professor of Environmental Hygiene. m. Tu Guanpu, Beijing, 2 Aug 1955, 1 daughter. Education: Beijin University, College of Medicine, 1944-50. Career: Director, Department of Environmental Hygiene & Vice Director 1962, School of Public Health 1968, Harbin Medical University; Director, Department of Environmental Health, Tianjin Medical University, 1981-92. Publications: Co-author, Environmental Health, 1966; Author, Cytogenetic Effect of Aluminium, 1990; Neurotoxical Effect of Al in Drinking Water, 1991; Study on Sanitary Standard of Al in Drinking

Water, 1991; Acceptable Daily Intake of Al in Chinese, 1991; Co-author, Wastewater Irrigation and Cancer, 1993. Honours: Prize, 2nd Class, Tianjin Commission of Science & Technology, 1986, 1993; Prize, 3rd Class, Chinese National Commission of Higher Education, 1993; Honour Certificate, 1989. Memberships: Chinese Medical Society; Tianjin Preventive Medicine Society; Tianjin Environmental Science Association; Chinese Environmental Mutagen Society. Address: Department of Environmental Health, School of Public Health, Tianjin Medical University, 22 Qixiang Tai Street, Tianjing 30007, China.

LIU Fu-sheng, b. 27 May 1932, Shandong, China. Professor of Pathology. m. 25 Oct 1958, 1 s, 1 d. Education: MD. Appointments: Visiting Professor, Saint Barnabud Medical Centre, USA; Alexander von Humboldt Scholarship, Stifung, Germany; Visiting Professor, Karolinska Institute, Sweden; Pathologist. Publications: Atlas of Tumor Pathology; Pathology and Prevention of Oesophageal Cancer; Pathology of the Gastro-intestinal Tract; Microinvasive Cancer. Honours: Recipient of Book Award. Memberships: Editorial Committee, Chinese Journal of Pathology; Journal of Pathological Diagnosis' Editorial Committee, National Medical JOurnal of China. Address: Chinese Academy of Medical Sciences and Peking Union Medical College, Cancer Institute, PO Box 2258, Zuanmenwat 100021, China.

LIU Fuxing, b. 21 Apr 1939, Jakarta, Indonesia. Doctor of Traditional Chinese Medicine. m. Zhou Jingfang, 1 July 1968, 1 daughter. Education: Bachelor, Department of Traditional Chinese Medicine, Yunnan College of Traditional Chinese Medicine, 1966. Appointments: Teacher, Traditional Chinese Medicine, 1966-69, Clinical Doctor, 1970-, currently Chief Doctor, Affiliated Hospital of Yunnan College of Traditional Chinese Medicine, Kunming, China. Publications: Diagnosis and Treatment in Surgical Skin and External Diseases; The Knowledge and Treatment of Dermatosis in Chinese Medicine; Co-author: Talking about Medicine along the Changjiang River; Required Readings for Doctors of Traditional Chinese Medicine in Countryside. Honours: Advanced Overseas Chinese: National Award, 1982; Yunnan Provincial Award, 1982, 1987, 1992; Kunming Municipal Award, 1991; Member, 6th and 7th Yunnan Provincial People's Political Consultative Conferences, 1988, 1993. Memberships: Society of Surgery, China's National Association of Traditional Chinese Medicine and Pharmacy; China's Association of Combination of Chinese and Western Medicine, Yang Branch; Yunnan Provincial Association of Dermatology; Standing Committees: Yunnan Provincial Association of Science and Technology; Yunnan Provincial Association of Traditional Chinese Medicine; Yunnan Research Association of National and Folk Medicine; Chief, Specialised Committees: Yunnan Association of Traditional Chinese Medicine; Yunnan Association of Combination of Chinese and Western Medicine. Hobbies: Reading books of medicine and hygiene; Listening to music; Physical exercise; Making friends of all trades and professions. Address: 104 Guanghua Street, Kunming, Yunnan 650021, China.

LIU Geng-Nian, b. 29 Apr 1923, Liaoning, China. Professor of Radiology. m. Xiu Ying Jin, 10 Oct 1946, 4 sons, 1 daughter. Education: MD, Medical School, Beijing University, 1945. Appointments include: Chairman, Department of Radiology, Third Hospital, Beijing Medical University; Chairman, Centre of Magnetic Resonance Institute, Beijing Medical University. Publications: Chief editor: Analysis of Roentgen Signs, 1984; Diagnostic Imaging of Digestive System, 1992; Abdominal Radiology, 1993. Memberships: Committee Member, Chinese Medical Association; Chinese Society of Radiology; Radiological Society of North America. Address: Department of Radiology, Third Hospital, Beijing Medical University, Hua Yuan Bei Lu 49, Beijing 100083, China.

LIU Geng-Tao, b. 5 May 1932, China. Professor of Pharmacology. m. Wu Ruo Shue, 1 May 1960, 1 son, 1 daughter. Education: MD, Medical College. Appointments include: Professor, Chairman, Department of Pharmacology, Institute of Materia Medica, Chinese Academy of Medical Sciences, Beijing. Publications: Author, various publications; Modern Pharmacology (co-editor), 1993. Honours: National Outstanding Expert for Contribution to the State, 1987. Memberships: Chinese Society of Pharmacology; Chinese Society of Free Radicals in Biology and Medicine. Address: Institute of Materia Medica, Chinese Academy of Sciences, 1 Xian Nong Tan Street, Beijing 100050, China.

LIU Gin-Chung, b. 29 Oct 1952. Professor of Radiology. m. Kuei-Li Lee, 15 Mar 1977, 1 daughter. Education: MD, Kaohsiung Medical College, Taiwan. Appointments: Currently: Chairman, Professor, Department of Radiology, Kaohsiung Medical College, Kaohsiung; Dean, School of Technology for Medical Sciences, 1993-. Publications:

Duchenne Muscular Dystrophy: MR grading system with functional correlation in Radiology, 1993. Honours: 1st Prize for Scientific Poster, Annual Meeting of Radiological Society of Republic of China, 1992. Memberships: RSNA; SMRM; Association of Chinese Radiologists; Radiological Society of Republic of China. Hobby: Golf. Address: No 100 Shih-Chuan 1st Road, Kaohsiung Medical College, Kaohsiung, Taiwan, China.

LIU Han Ching, b. 3 July 1933, Guangdong Province, China. Professor of Physiology. m. Hou Chun Liu, 16 Feb 1958, 2 d. Education: Graduate, Jiangxi Medical College, 1954; Postgraduate, Shanghai First Medical College, 1963. Appointments: Chairman, Department of Physiology, Director, Faculty of Basic Medical Sciences, Professor of Physiology, Jiangxi Medical College; Research Fellow, Loyola University Stritch School of Medicine, USA. Publications: Version by Acupuncture and Moxibustion, Co-author, 1984; Anticholinesterase Actions on Sympathetic Ganglia, 1987; High Frequency Ventilation, 1989; Effects of Verapamil on Ganglia, 1990. Honours: Nation Prize for Innovations, China, 1984. Memberships: President, Physiological Society of Jianxi Province; Council Member, Chinese Association for Physiological Sciences. Hobbies: Soccer; Swimming. Address: Department of Physiology, Jiangxi Medical College, Nanchang 330006, China.

LIU Ji-Fu, b. 22 Sept 1952, Hebei Province, China. Cardiothoracic Surgeon; Associate Professor. m. Yu-Hong Li, 26 Jan 1980, 1 daughter. Education: MB, Hebei Medical Institute, 1973; MD, People's Liberation Army Medical Institution, 1985. Appointments: Surgeon, Teacher, People's Hospital of Lang Fang District, Medical School of Lang Fang District, Hebei, 1973; Surgeon-in-charge, Associate Professor, General Hospital of Beijing Military District, Beijing, 1989-. Publications: Bronchoscopy with hematoporphyrin aerosol inhalation for raising the detection rate of lung cancer (1st author), 1986; Clinical application of cryopreserved aortic allografts (co-author), 1993. Honours: Thesis of Excellence, Chinese Medical Association, 1991; Grade 3 Prize in Scientific and Technological Progress of Army, 1991. Memberships: Chinese Medical Association; Society of Cardiothoracic Surgery. Hobbies: Reading; Running; Angling for fish. Address: No 5 Nan Men Cang, Chao Nei Bei Xiao Street, Beijing, China.

LIU Jia-Qi, b. 5 Sept 1929, Guangxi, China. Professor of Surgery. m. Rui-Feng Xu, 28 Nov 1950, 3 sons. Education: Graduated, Guangxi Medical College, 1954; Training, Shanghai Chong Shan Hospital, Shanghai Medical University, 1960-61. Appointments: Resident, Surgery, 1955, Lecturer, Surgery, 1959, Associate Professor of Surgery, 1978, Professor of Surgery, 1985-, Guangxi Medical College Teaching Hospital, Nanning. Publications: 1st co-author: Traumatic Abdominal Aortocaval Fistula caused by Induced Abortion, 1994; An experience of thyroidectomy after paralysis in one side recurrent/superior laryngeal nerve, 1988; The vicissitudes of Choletithiasis over ten years in Guangxi, China, 1994. Honours: 2nd Prize of Science and Technology Progress for a comprehensive study of cholelithiasis, Guangxi; Special Subsidy, Chinese Government, 1993. Memberships: Surgical Committee, Committee of Biliary Surgery Group, Chinese Medical Association; Councillor, Guangxi Branch, Chinese Medical Association; Chairman, Society of Surgery, Guangxi Medical Association; Editorial Committee, Guangxi Medical Journal. Hobbies: Table-tennis; Basketball. Address: 6 Binhu Road, Nanning, Guangxi, China.

LIU Jing Zhang, b. 11 May 1939, Shandong, China. Physiology Teacher. m. Zhou Shu Hua, 16 Jan 1968, 1 s, 1 d. Education: Diploma, Shandong Medical University. Career: Assistant, 1964, Lecturer, 1979, Associate Professor, 1987, Professor, 1992-, Shandong Medical University. Publications: Effects of Dexamethasone on Electroacupuncture Analgesia and Central Nervous System Metabolism, in Acupuncture and Electrotherapeutics Research, 1988; Observation of Neural Influence on the Electromyographic Activity in the Rabbit Oddi's Sphincter Elicited by Electrical Stimulation of the MPO Area of the Hypothalamus, in Acta Academiae Medicinae, Shandong, 1992. Memberships: Chinese Physiological Society; Chinese Association for Study of Pain. Hobbies: Running; Basketball. Address: Department of Physiology, Shandong Medical University, Jinan, Shandong 250012, China.

LIU Jing-Chang, b. 5 Jan 1932, Hebei Province, China. Underwater Physiologist. m. 28 July 1956, 1 son, 1 daughter. Education: MB, First Military Medical University, 1955; MD, PhD, Academy of Military Medical Sciences, USSR, 1961. Appointments: Researcher, Academy of Military Medical Sciences of People's Liberation Army, 1957-61; Researcher,

1964-, currently Professor of Physiology, Naval Medical Research Institute. Publications: Diving Medicine (co-author), 1985; Human Physiology (co-author), 1989; Influence of Hyperbaric Oxygenation on the Microvasculature and Microcirculation, 1991. Honours: 1st Prize, National Technological Advances, 1985. Memberships: Committee Member, China Applied Physiology Society; Advisor, Chinese Society for Hyperbaric Medicine; President, Military Nautical Medical Society. Hobbies: Music; Sport. Address: 880 Xiang Yin Road, Shanghai 200433, China.

LIU Kai, b. 2 June 1938, Tianjin, China. Professor of Physiology.m. Liu Airn, Jan 1964, 1 s, 1 d. Education: Chinese Union Medical College, Beijing, 1962. Appointments: Assistant. Chinese Union Medical College, Beijing, 1962; Lecturer, 1978, Associate Professor, 1987, Professor, 1992, Shandong COllege of Traditional Chinese Medicine. Publications Alcohol and Disease, 1987; The Influence of Electro-acupuncture of Zusantl Point on Single Unit Activity in Cats AHL, 1989; Cardiac Physiology and Clinic, 1990. Honours: Outstanding Accomplishments, Shandong Association of Science and Technology, 1981; Shandong Health department of Government, 1989. Memberships: Chinese Physiological Society; Commissioner, Branch of Traditional Chinese Medicine; Chinese Association of the Integration of Traditional and Western Medicine, Commissioner of Branch of Basic Theory; Chinese Association of Acupuncture and Moxibustion. Hobbies: Table tennis; Sightseeing; Stamp Collecting; Opera. Address: Department of Physiology, Shandong College of Traditional Chinese Medicine, 53 Tingshi Road, Tinan, Shandong 250014, China.

LIU Kan, b. 19 Mar 1928, Hangzhou, Zhejiang, China. Doctor of Traditional Chinese Medicine. m. Zhu Meilin, 10 May 1957, 1 daughter. Education: Graduated, Dalian Medical College, 1954; Graduated, Liaoning College of Traditional Chinese Medicine, 1961. Appointments: Assistant, Internal Medicine, 1954, Lecturer, Traditional Chinese Medicine, 1963, Dalian Medical College; Associate Professor, Traditional Chinese Medicine, Zunyi Medical College, 1978; Full Professor of Traditional Chinese Medicine, Chief, Department of Traditional Chinese Medicine, Dalian Medical University, 1985-. Publications: Treatment of Common Acute Abdomen Based on Differentiation of ZHENG, 1976; Surgery of TCM (co-author), 1987; Basic Theory of TCM (editor-in-chief), 1993. Honours: 1st Class Prize for Excellence in Traditional Chinese Medicine, Ministry of Public Health, China, 1961; Member, Science Committee, Ministry of Public Health, China, 1981-87. Memberships: All-China Association of Traditional Chinese Medicine, Standing Director, Dalian Branch; Chinese Association of the Integration of Traditional and Western Medicine, Director, Dalian Branch; Chinese Association of Rehabilitation Medicine, Standing Director, Dalian Branch. Hobbies: Classical literature; Travel. Address: 4-5-4 Suite, 99 Xi Nan Road, Sha He Kou District, Dalian, Liaoning 116023, China.

LIU Ke-jia, b. 14 May 1930, Beijing, China. Professor of Space Medicine. m. Wu Qin-e, 3 July 1955, 2 sons. Education: MD, Peking Union Medical College, 1957. Appointments include: Vice-Director, Department of Medical Monitoring for Astronauts, Institute of Space Medico-Engineering; Currently Director, Department of Restoration, Health Center, The Chinese Academy of Somatic Science, Beijing. Publications: The systematic response of endocrine axes to diverse environments, 1985; Changes in circadian rhythm of multiple hormones and their relationship with susceptibility to HDT-6°, 1989; Stress and Stress Disorders (with Wu Qin-e), 1991. Honours: National Award of Science, China, 1978. Membership: Academician (Member) of Life Science Section, International Academy of Astronautics. Hobbies: Travel; Swimming; Football, Address: PO Box 5104 (32), Beijing 100094, China.

LIU Ke-Zhou, b. 6 Aug 1937, Guangdong Province, China. Professor of Infectious Diseases. m. 9 Mar 1963, 2 s. Education: Graduate, Zhejiang Medical University, 1960. Appointments: Assistant Professor, 1960-78, Lecturer, Department Infectious Diseases, 1978-86, Associate Professor, Vice Director of Infectious Diseases Institute, 1986-91, Professor, Director of Infectious Disease Institute, 1991-, Zhejiang Medical University. Publications: Infectious Diseases, CO-author, 1979, 1988; Chinese Medical Encyclopaedia Fascicle of Parasitology and Parasitic Diseases, 1984; Infectious Diseases, 1985; Theory of Practice of Medicine, 1985; Handbook of Liver Diseases, 1990; Textbook of Continuing Education of Clinical Medicine, 1990. Honours: Award of Science and Technology Progress in Zhejiang Province, 1984, 1987, 1989, 1990, 1992; Awards from Ministry of Public Health, Zhejiang,

1988, 1989. Memberships: Society of Liver Diseases; Chinese Medical Association; Chinese National Technology Committee of Health Standards. Hobbies: Swimming; Reading. Address: Institute of Infectious Diseases, the First Affiliated Hospital of Zhejiang Medical University, Hangzhou 310003, China.

LIU Linxiang, b. Beijing, China. Professor. m. Guo Ruidin, 1 son, 1 daughter. Education: Graduate, Department of Biology, Beijing University, 1954. Appointments: Teacher, Researcher, Beijing University, 1954-; Beijing Railway Medical College; Professor, Institute of Chinese Materia Medica; Visiting Professor, Toyama Medical and Pharmacueitcal University, Japan. Publications: Contributor of numerous scientific research papers, reviews and translations. Memberships: China Society for Microbiology; China Society for Microecology; Editorial Board, Journal of Microecology. Hobbies: Reading; Classical music; Sport. Address: Institute of Chinese Materia Medica, Academy of Traditional Chinese Medicine, Beijing 100700, China.

LIU Maynong, b. 14 Dec 1934, Taisan, Guangdong, China. Doctor of Gynaecology and Obstetrics. m. Chen Zida, 12 Feb 1964, 1 daughter. Education: Graduate, Guangdong Province Medical College. Appointments: Vice Director, Shenzhen Family Planning Service Centre. Publications: Contributor of professional articles. Honours: Six times Recipient of Award from Guangzhou Science and technology Committee for study combining western and Chinese medical methods. Memberships: Guangdong Province Eugenics Association; Shenzhen Family Planning Association; Chinese Biomedical Engineering Society; Chinese Medical Society. Hobby: Running. Address: Room 104, Building 7, Bi-Bo Garden Shonzhen, Guangdong Province 518003, China.

LIU Mingyuan, b. 3 Feb 1932, Wuhan City, Hubei Province, China. Radiotherapist. m. Jun 1964, 2 s. Education: BS. Appointment: Director, Department of Radiotherapy, Beijing Hospital, 1975-. Publications include: Co-author, IORT for Gastric Carcinoma, 1983; The Treatment Result of 53 Cases of SCLC, 1986; TBI for Allo-BMT, 1987; Practical Dosimetry of Radiation Oncology, 1988; Long Term Result of Medullablastoma, 1989. Memberships: Committee, Chinese Society of Radiation Oncology; Committee, Editorial Board, Chinese Journal of Radiation Oncology. Hobby: Music. Address: Beijing Hospital, 1 Daihua Road, Beijing 100730, China.

LIU Renjie, b. 22 March 1935, Henan, China. Director, Center of Physiological Research, Tianjin Medical University; Vice Director, Department of Physiology. m. Shi-rong Kan, 1 August 1963, 1 son, 1 daughter. Education: Graduated, Department of Medicine, Tianjin Medical University. Appointments: Assistant in Biophysics, Department of Physics, Tianjin Medical College, 1961-64; Assistant of Physiology, Department of Physiology, Tianjin Medical College, 1964-78; Lecturer of Physiology, Department of Physiology, Tianjin Medical College, 1978-86; Associate Professor, 1986-92, Professor, 1992-, Department of Physiology, Tainjin Medical College. Publications: Multiple Choice Questions of Physiology, 1987; Guidebook of Medical Examinations, 1991; Numerous professional articles in scientific medical journals. Honours: Excellent Educator, Tianjin Medical College, 1985, 1986, 1992; Outstanding Achievement Award, Tianjin Municipal Government, 1989. Memberships: Chinese Physiology Society; Chinese Biophysics Society; Council, Society of Physiological Sciences, Tianjin; World Academic Society of Medical Qigong. Hobbies: Growing Flowers; Playing Music. Address: 22 Qixiangtai Road, Department of Physiology, Tianjin Medical University, Tianjin 300070, China.

LIU Tiepu, b. 27 June 1962, Wuhan, China. Epidemiologist. m. Zhen Huang, 16 May 1986, 2 d. Education: MD, 1983, MPH, 1986, Tongji Medical University; DrPH, University of Alabama at Birmingham, USA, 1992. Appointments: Instructor, Assistant Professor, Tongji Medical University, 1986-89; Instructor, Assistant Professor, University of Alabama at Birmingham, 1993-. Publications: Evaluation of Three Nutritional Assessment Methods in a Group of Women, 1992; A Case-Control Study of Nutritional Factors and Cervical Dysplasia, 1993. Memberships: American Public Health Association; Society for Epidemiologic Research; American Association for Cancer Research. Hobby: Fishing. Address: 1791 Napier Drive, Birmingham, AL 35226, USA.

LIU Wei Yong, b. 3 Jan 1929, Nanchang, Jiangxi, China. Cardiovascular Surgeon. m. Li Lan Sun, 19 Oct 1956, 1 son, 1 daughter. Education: Graduate, Seventh Military Medical University, Chong Qing, 1955; Visiting Scholar, Harbor-UCLA Medical Centre, USA.

Appointments: Surgical Resident, 1955-57; Thoracic Surgeon, 1958-63; Cardiac Surgeon and Lecturer, 1964-69; Vice-Chief and Associate Professor, 1970-84; Professor, Chief, Department of Cardiothoracic Surgery, 1985-93; Consultant, Cardiovascular Medical Institute, PLA, 1987; Professor, Nanjing University, College of Medicine, 1994; Professor, Chief-Doctor, 4th Military Medical University. Publications: Cardiovascular Surgery, Co-author, 1985; Practice of Cardiothoracic Surgery, Co-author, 1993; New Clinical Medicine Dictionary, Co-author, 1993; Practical Hypertensionology, Co-author, 1993; Practice of Cardiovascular Surgery, Chief Author, 1994. Memberships: Vice Chairman of Committee, Shaanxi Branch, Chinese Society of Thoracic and Cardiovascular Surgery; Vice Editor-in-Chief, Chinese Journal Thoracic and Cardiovascular Surgery. Address: Department of Cardiovascular Surgery, Xijing Hospital, 15 West Chang-le Road, Xian 710032, China.

LIU Wu-Li, b. 18 Sep 1959, Hunan, China. Doctor. m. Ou Yan Jian Jiung, 16 dec 1987, 1 daughter. Education: BA, 1978-83, MM, 1983-86, Hunan Traditional Chinese Medicine College. Appointments: Professor, Director of Acupuncture Department, First Affiliated Hospital of Hunan Traditional Chinese Medicine College, Chongsha, 1986-. Publications: Treatment of 123 Cases of Migraine with Seven-Star Needles Acupuncture, 1993; Treatment of 116 Cases of Paraplegia with Electropuncture, 1995. Honours: One of Outstanding Young Scientists of all Hunan Province Colleges and Universities, 1994. Memberships: Committeeman of Acupuncture, Chinese National Acupuncture Association; Key Committee Member, Hunan Acupuncture Association. Hobbies: Music; Table Tennis. Address: The First Affiliated Hospital of Hunan Traditional Chinese Medical College, 105 Shaoshan Road, Changsha 410007, China.

LIU Xiao-Ling, b. 3 May 1954, China. Physician (Herbalist). m. 2 Oct 1979, 1 daughter. Education: BSc, Traditional Chinese Medicine; BSc, Class for Traditional Chinese Medical Teachers. Appointments: Physician-in-charge, Clinic in Traditional Chinese Medicine in area of Pulmonary Paediatrics, Asthma, Sun Yat-Sen University of Medical Sciences, Guangzhou, 1976-; Physician, Dr Sun Yat-Sen Memorial Hospital, 1977-91; Physician-in-charge, Sun Yat-Sen University of Medical Sciences. Hobbies: Cooking; Cycling. Address: 3 Inverary Street, Concord, NSW 2137, Australia.

LIU Xue Min, b. 8 Nov 1932, Xian, China. Ophthalmologist. m. Sun Zhihe, 1 Oct 1956, 2 s, 2 d. Education: BA, Shaan Xi Higher Medical College, 1962. Appointments: Eye Doctor, 1962-86; Vice Professor, 1986-93; Professor, 1993-. Publications: Observation of Outerior Chamber Depth in the Elderly, 1986; Clinical Observation of 50 Eye's Artificial Lens, 1990. Honour: Science and Technology Prize. Memberships: Chinese Medical Association. Hobbies: Running; Reading. Address: Shaanxi People's Hospital, Xi'an 710068, China.

LIU Xue-Qin, b. 30 Sept 1941, Yun-Cheng City, Henan, China. Doctor of Chinese Medicine. m. Zhen Xiu-Ying, 15 June 1980, 3 sons, 3 daughters. Education: Henan Medical College, 1957-59. Appointments include: Director, Founder, Shaanxi Traditional Chinese Medicine Institute of Esophagus Cancer, 1982-; Hospital Director. Publications: Treatment of Esophagus Cancer using Liu's Pills Against Cancer, 1993. Honours: Gold Medal for Liu's Pills Against Cancer, China New Medicine and Pharmacy Inventions Exhibition, 1992. Memberships: Shaanxi Anti-Cancer Association; Taiyuan Red Cross. Hobbies: Collector of art curiosities and books. Address: Dong-An Road No 2, Taiyuan, Shaanxi 030013, China.

LIU Yi-De, b. 19 June 1917, Yangzhou, Jiangsu, China. Neuropsychiatrist. m. Jin-Yu Xia, 24 Aug 1964, 3 sons, 1 daughter. Education: MD, Aurora University, Shanghai, 1934; Certificate, Faculte de medecine de Paris, France, 1947. Appointments: Lecturer, Neuropsychiatry, Aurora Medical faculty; Associate Professor of Neuropsychiatry, Tong-ji Medical University; Professor of Neuropsychiatry, Zhejiang Medical College; Professor of Neuropsychiatry, Wannan Medical College. Publications: Clinical Psychiatry, 1953; Diagnosis of Nervous Diseases, 1955; Diagnosis of Height Function Disorders of Nervous system, 1985. Honours: Subsidies of Department of State, 1991-. Memberships: Chinese Neuro-Psychiatry Association; Vice President, Anhui Medical Association. Hobby: Music. Address: Wannan Medical College #85, Wuhu Anhui 241001, China.

LIU Yi-Xun, b. 5 May 1936, Shandong, China. Professor; Departmental Director. m. Zhao Xue-Kun, 1 July 1967, 1 daughter.

Education: Graduate studies, Shanghai Fudan University, 1958-63; Postgraduate studies for PhD, Academia Sinica, 1963-66; Postdoctoral Fellow, University of California, San Diego, 1984-86. Appointments: Research Associate, 1967-73, Assistant Professor, 1977, Professor, Director, Department of Endocrinology, 1990-, Beijing Institute of Zoology; Visiting Scholar, Imperial Cancer Research Fund, London, England, 1974-76; Visiting Professor, Umeå University, Sweden, 1988-90. Publications include: Extrapituitary function of GnRH in uterus, 1980; Theca cells synthesize androgen using granulosa progesterone, 1986; Coordinated tPA and PAI-1 gene expression in ovary causes ovulation, 1987; Increase in tPA activity is correlated with decrease in progesterone production in corpus luteum, 1992; Over 100 articles and reviews in professional journals. Honours include: Natural Science Awards, Academic Sinica, 1982, 1984, 1985, 1992, 1994; Postdoctoral Fellowship, Rockefeller Foundation, 1984-86; Visiting Professor Fellowship Award, Swedish Medical Research Council, 1989-91. Memberships: Society for the Study of Reproduction; Vice-Chairman, Chinese Society for Reproductive Biology; Standing Committee, Chinese Society for Comparative Endocrinology; Standing Committee, Chinese Society of Physiology; Associate Editor-in-Chief, Developmental and Reproductive Biology; Editorial Boards: Acta Physiologica Sinica; Who's Who in Frontiers of Science and Technology in China. Address: State Key Laboratory of Reproductive Biology for Family Planning, Endocrinology Department, Institute of Zoology, Academia Sinica, Beijing 100080, China.

LIU Yu Tan, b. 20 Jan 1937, Muping County, Shandong, China. Acupuncturist. m. Giuo Pei, 1 Jul 1940, 1 s, 1 d. Education: BA, Medicine, Shandong College of TCM, 1965. Appointments: Chairman, Currently, Professor of Acupuncture, Affiliated Hospital of Shandong College of Traditional Chinese Medicine; Standing Committee, Chinese Association of Acupuncturists, Shandong Branch. Publications: Therapeutics of Acupuncture and Moxibustions, 1991; An Improved Acupuncture Method for the Successful Treatment of Renal Colic due to Urolithiasis, in American Journal of Acupuncture, 1993. Honour: 3rd Prize, Scientific Development and Application, Shandong Province. Memberships: Chinese Association of Acupuncture. Hobbies: Mountain Climbing; Hiking. Address: 42 Wen Hua Xi Road, Acupuncture Department, Affiliated Hospital of Shandong College of TCM, Jinan, 250011, China.

LIU Yuabiao, b. 4 June 1965, Hunan, China. Assistant Professor of Pharmacology and Tumour Therapy. m. Chen Ya-jun, 1 June 1989, 1 son. Education: BA, Chongqing University of Medical Sciences, 1986; MS, Beijing Institute of Basic Medical Sciences, 1992. Appointments: Currently Assistant Professor of Pharmacology and Tumour Therapy, North Taiping Road Hospital, Beijing. Publications: The Oncogene C-myc,v-erbB,N-ras Expression in P388/ADR and L1210/cis-platinum Resistant Cell Lines, 1993; The Expression and Amplification of GSTpi Gene in P388/ADR and L1210/cis-platinum Resistant Cell Lines, 1993; The Rapid Methods of DNA,RNA Isolation Studying the Expression of GSTpi and Three Oncogenes in P388/ADR Resistant Line, 1993; The Distribution and Relationship Between GSTpi and C-myc,v-erbB,N-ras Oncogene in Mice and Human Normal Tissues, 1994; The GST Activity and the Gene Expression of GSTpi in Solid Tumour, 1994; The Relationship Between Adriamycin Resistant and GSTpi Tumour, 1994; O2 Consumption in P388/ADR Resistant Lines and P388/ADR Reversed By Verapamil, 1994. Membership: Chinese Medical Association. Hobbies: Poetry; Qigong; Running. Address: 8 Feiren, Zhangshu, Xiangyin County, Hunan, China.

LIU Yunrong, b. 8 March 1939, Beijing, China. Professor of Epidemiology. m. Shi Suoyun, 11 March 1977, 1 son, 1 daughter. Education: MD, Beijing Medical University, 1958-63; John Hopkins University School of Hygiene and Public Health, USA, 1986. Appointments: Assistant Lecturer, Department of Epidemiology, Peking Union Medical College, 1963-82; Associate Professor, Professor, Department of Epidemiology, Department of Social Medicine, NRIFP, Beijing, 1982-. Publications: Co-author: Basics of Applied Immunology, 1976; Co-author: Essentials of Modern Immunology, 1982; Co-author: Biomedical Research Methodology, 1985; Co-author: Statistics and Evaluation of Family Planning, 1992; Co-author: Dynamics and Contraceptive Use in Rural China, 1994; More than 70 papers. Honours: 2nd Prize, National Scientific Achievements, 1986; 3rd Prize, Scientific and Technical Progress, 1987, 1990, 1991, 1992, 1993. Memberships: Expert Committee, State Family Planning Commission of China; Epidemiology Society of the Chinese Medical Association; China Statistics Association; Laws and Regulation Committee of the Chinese

Medical Ethics Association; East-West Center Association, USA. Address: National Research Institute for Family Planning, 12 Da Hui Si, Hai Dain District, Beijing 100081, China.

LIU Zhi-Qing, b. 8 October 1943, Ji-an, Jiangxi, China. Senior Physician. m. Wan Hong, 16 March 1968, 1 son, 1 daughter. Education: Graduated, Department of Medicine, Jiangxi Medical College, 1967. Appointments: Internist, Lou-jia Hospital, Nanchang, 1967-75; Deputy Director of Internal Medicine of Worker's Hospital of the Bureau of Communication, Jiangxi, 1975-92. Publications Include: Co-author: Microcirculatory Changes in Nailfold of Patients with Chronic Obstructive Pulmonary Disease, 1982; Co-author: Microhemorrhages in Hypertension and Massage and Microcirculatory Disturbance, 1987; Co-author: The Clinical Significance of Rheumatoid of Microcirculation on Nailfold, 1993; Co-author: Clinical Application of Microcirculation, 1994. Honours: 3rd Prize, Outstanding Achievement in Science and Technology, Jiangxi, 1984; Prize, Advanced Personality, Nanchang Science Association, 1985; 6 Treatises, Outstanding Academic Treatises, 1985-92. Memberships: Vice President, Jiangxi Society of Microcirculation, 1986-; Director, Chinese Society of Microcirculation, 1994-; Director, China Society of Medicine, Nanchang Branch, 1990-; World Hypentension League and China Hypertension League, 1990-. Hobbies: Swimming; Chinese Character Writing; Travel; Research on Traditional Chinese Drugs. Address: Zhuhai Medical Recovery Centre of Microcirculation, Qianshan Maanshan, Zhuhai, Guangdong, China.

LIU Zhong, b. 23 Mar 1928, Jilin, China. Professor of Human parasitology. m. Xie Jiangli, 14 Apr 1968, 1 s, 1 d. Education: BA, The Third Military University of Medical Sciences, 1952. Appointments: Associate professor, Teacher of Master of Parasitology, 1979; Professor of Human Parasitology, 1985, Norman Bethune University of Medical Sciences. Publications: A Survey of the Aetiological Agent of Rice-Field Dermatitis, 1976; Studies on the Life Cycle of Trichobilharzia Tianens, Co-author, 1977; Studies of the Life History of Prosthogonimus Ovatus and P>Pellucidus, 1983. Honours: 1st award of Scientific Research Achievement of Jilin Province, 1978; 1st Award, Association for Science and technology of Jilin Province, 1987. Memberships: Director of Specoaloty for Parasitology of China; Vice Presidnt, Association for Zoology of Jilin Province; Vice President, Speciality Committee for Parasitology of Jilin Province. Hobbies: Making and flying kites; Table Tennis. Address: Department of Human parasitology of Norman Bethune University of Medical Sciences, Changchun 130021, Jilin, China.

LIU Zhong-Ming, b. 3 Aug 1930, Wuhan, Hubei, China. Professor of Medicine. m. Yun-Jie Zhou, Dec 1932, 1 son, 1 daughter. Education: Wuhan Medical College, 1956; Post Doctorate Fellow, University of South Carolina School of Medicine, USA, 1982-83. Appointment: Professor of Medicine, Henan Medical University, China. Publications: Use of right catheterization on diagnosis of atrial septal defect, 1960; Clinical study on 31 cases of malnutrition edema, 1961; Administration of cortisone and ACTH for cardiovascular diseases, 1964; Problems on quinidine for treatment of chronic atrial fibrillation, 1966; Clinical administration of digitalis, 1974; Treatment of Shock and Heart Failure, 1981; The effects of phentolamine in experimental hemorrhagic shock in the dog, 1984; Acquired cystic disease of kidney and long-term intermediate maintenance hemodialysis, 1987; Superoxide dismutase activity in red blood cell in gentamicine nephrotoxicity: protective effect of ginsensides, co-author, 1990; The effects of thyroxine, camodulin and insulin on CA2-ATPase activity of red blood cell membrane during hemodialysis in patients with uremia, co-author, 1993. Memberships: Chinese Medical Associaiton; Chinese Society of Nephrology; American Medical Association; Chinese Society of Nephrology; American Shock Society; Chinese Medical Center of the North America; International Society of Nephrology. Hobbies: Music; Swimming. Address: 1st Teaching Hospital of Henan Medical University, Zhengzhou, Henan 450052, China.

LIU Zijiang, b. 4 Oct 1925, Shao Xing, Zhejiang, China. Radiologist. m. 31 Dec 1956, 2 sons. Education: MD, Zhejiang University, Medical College, 1953. Appointments: Vice Chairman, 1990-93, Chairman, 1993-, China Interventional Radiology Association; Committee Member, China Radiology Association, 1956-. Publications: Selective Bronchial Artery Infusion of Cisplatin for Inoperable Bronchogenic Carcinoma, 1986; Bronchial Artery Infusion of Anticancer Drugs to Treat 227 Cases of Late Stage Lung Cancer, 1990; Evaluation of Transcatheter Biopsy and Selective Bronchography to Diagnose Lung Cancer, 1982; Comparative Study of Arterial Chemo-embolization of Primary Liver Cancer with Lipidol Plus CDDP-microspheres and Lipidol Emulsion of

Anticancer Drug, Co-author, 1992; The Application of Superselective External Carotid Arteriograph and Preoperative Embolization, Co-author, 1986; The Clinical Application of Selective Celiac and Superior Mesenteric Angiography, 1983; Transfemoral Selective Cerebral Angiography, 1981. Honours: Science and Technology Award, Guizhou People's Government, 1982; Science and Technology Award, Zhejiang People's Government, 1987; Scientific Meeting's Award, Guizhou People's Government, 1978. Memberships: China Radiology Association; China Interventional Radiology Association; Chairman, Zhejiang Provincial Radiology Association. Hobbies: Gardening; Travel; Music; Sports. Address: Department of Radiology, Zhejiang Provincial People's Hospital, Hangzhou, Zhejiang 310014, China.

LIVINGSTON Robert, b. 15 Mar 1939, Portadown, Northern Ireland. Educational Psychologist. m. Catherine Mary Cameron, 21 Oct 1967, 3 daughters. Education: Queen's University, Belfast, 1956-60; BA; MEd; DPhil; DipEd; Chartered Psychologist; AFBPS; Registered Psychologist; AFPSI. Appointments: Lecturer, Senior Course Tutor of MEd courses, University of Ulster, Coleraine, 1969-93. Publications: The Application of Videoconferencing to the Advancement of Independent Group Learning for Professional Development (with L Abbott, J Dallat and A Robinson), 1994. Memberships: British Psychological Society; Psychological Society of Ireland; Association of Educational Psychologists. Hobbies: Mountain walking. Address: 206 Seacon Road, Ballymoney, County Antrim BT53 6PZ, Northern Ireland.

LIVOLSI Virginia A, b. 29 July 1943, New York City, USA. Pathologist. Education: BS cum laude, College of Mount Saint Vincent, New York, 19671-65; MD, Columbia University of Physicians and Surgeons, 1965-69. Appointments: Instructor in Pathology, Columbia University College of P&S, New York, 1974-79, Assistant Professor of Pathology, 1974-79, Associate Professor of Pathology, 1979-83, Yale University; Professor of Pathology and Laboratory Medicine, Department of Pathology, University of Pennsylvania School of Medicine, 1983-; Visiting Faculty, Mount Sinai Hospital and Saint Michael's Hospital, Toronto, Canada, 1993. Publications: Surgical Pathology of the Thyroid Gland, 1990. Memberships: Association of Directors of Anatomic and Surgical Pathology; United States and Canadian Division of the Academy of Pathology; College of American Pathologists; American Society of Clinical Pathologists; American Thyroid Association. Address: University of Pennsylvania Medical Centre, 3400 Spruce Street, Founders Six, Philadelphia, PA 19104-4283, USA.

LIVSHIN N Michael, b. 28 Sept 1943, Russia. Dentist. m. Zhanneta Ostrovskaya, 29 June 1963. Education: DDS-MD, (Physician Stomatologist), First Leningrad Medical Institute, 1966; DMD, University of Medicine & Dentistry, New Jersey, 1978; Fellow, International Congress of Oral Implantologists, 1991. Appointments: Physician Stomatologist, Dentist, 41 United Hospital of Leningrad, 1966-75; Head, Stomatological Department, 1969; Chief Stomatologist, 1970; Dentist, Self Employed, 1978-. Publications: Electrochemical Processes in the Oral Cavity from Different Metals and their Clinical Display, 1970; The Works of the Eighth Stomatological Session of Leningrad. Memberships: Essex County Dental Society; New Jersey Dental Association; American Dental Association; American Academy of General Dentistry; American Academy of Implant Dentistry; Federation Dentaire Internationale; International Congress of Oral Implantologists. Hobbies: Travel; International Politics; Sports. Address: 118 Pompton Avenue, Verona, NJ 07044, USA.

LIYANAGE Piyasena Molligoda, b. 27 Apr 1940, Panadura, Sri Lanka. Medical Officer. m. Padmini Mallika Liyanage, 1 June 1970, 1 son, 1 daughter. Education: MBBS, Ceylon; MRCOG, England; FRCOG, England; FCOG, Sri Lanka. Appointments: Consultant Obstetrician & Gynaecologist, General Hospital, Ratnapura, Badvilla, Nuwora Eliya, Sri Lanka; Locum Consultant Obstetrician & Gynaecologist, Banet General Hospital, England, 1983 & Royal Cornwall Hospital, England, 1991. Publications: Prophylatic Hospitalization of Mothers with Twin Pregnancy - Outcome, 1992. Memberships: Fellow, The Sri Lanka College of Obstetricians & Gynaecologists; Fellow, The Royal College of Obstetricians & Gynaecologists, London. Address: 22/8 Subadra Mawatha, Madiwela, Kotte, Sri Lanka.

LLANOS Roberto T, b. 8 July 1933, Lima, Peru. Medical Doctor; Professor of Psychology and Psychiatry. m. 30 Aug 1967, 1 son, 1 daughter. Education: MD, San Marcos University, Lima; Master in Psychiatry, Max Planck Institute, Munich, Germany, 1968; Doctor in Medicine (Ordination), Cayetano Heredia University, 1990.

Appointments: Currently Professor of Psychology and Psychiatry, University of Sagrados Corazones and Cayetano Heredia University. Publications: Books: El matrimonio Simbiótico, 1991; El encuentro Grupal, 1992; Personalidad y Carácter, 1993. Honours: Honorary Member, German Psychiatric Association, 1984; Honorary Member, Chilean Psychiatric Association, 1985. Memberships: President, Peruvian Society of Bioethics; President, Peruvian Transactional Analysis Association. Hobbies: Opera; Music; Singing; Swimming; Toastmasters Club; Travel. Address: Clínica Ricardo Palma, Ave Javier Prado Este 1038 of 201, San Isidro, Lima 27, Peru.

LLEWELLYN Craig Hartman, b. 5 Sept 1937, Berwick, Pennsylvania, USA. Physician. m. Gail Frederick, 29 Aug 1994, 1 sw, 2 d. Education: BA, 1959, MD, 1963, Yale University; MPH, 1968, MS, 1969, Harvard University; Board Certified, General Preventive Medicine. Appointments: Chief Surgeon, US Army Special Forces, Vietnam, 1965-67; Chief, Communicable Diseases Research, US Army Research Centre; Commander, US Army Medical Research Unit, Trans-Amazon ; Commander, US Army <edical research Institute for Chemical Defense; Professor and Chair, Department of Military and Emergency Medicine, Uniformed Services University of Health Sciences, School of Medicine. Publications: Coontributor of numerous professional articles and book chapters. Honours: Bronze Star with V, 1966; Legion of Merit, 3 times; John Shaw Billuys Award, 1972; Distinguished Service Medal, US Army, 1987. Memberships: Fellow, American College Preventive Medicine; Fellow, American College of Epidemiology; fellow, Royal Society of Medicine; AMA; American Society Tropical Medicine and Hygiene; Association of Military Surgeons of US; WAEDH. Hobbies: Kayaking; Cycling; swimming; Hiking; Sailing. Address: USUHS, 4301 Jones Bridge Road, Bethesda, MD 20814, USA.

LOCKIE Andrew Hart, b. 2 Mar 1947, Glasgow, Scotland. Homeopathic Physician. m. Barbara Lockie, 19 Jun 1976, 3 s, 1 d. Education: MB ChB; MRCGP; MFHom; DipObst; RCOG; FPC. Appointments: SHO, Royal London Homeopathic Hospital; SHO, A & E Northampton General, Royal Surrey County Guildford; SHO, Obstetrics and Gynaecology, Banbury; SHO, Paediatrics, Northampton General; Currently, Homeopathic Physician. Publications: A Study of 4 Types of Diet, in Journal Royal College General Practitioners, 1985; The Family Guide to Homeopathy, 1989; The Women's Guide to Homeopathy, 1992; The Complete Guide to Homeopathy, due 1995. Memberships: MRCGP; MFHom. Hobbies: Guitar; Carpentry; Gym; Walking. Address: 4 Waterden Road, Guildford, Surrey, GU1 2AW, England.

LOCKYER Ruth Barbara, b. 3 Apr 1949, Walsall, Staffordshire, England. Clinical Psychologist. Education: BSc Honours, MSc, Psychology, University of Wales; M App Sci, Clinical psychology, University of Glasgow; Certificate in Egyptology, University of Manchester; CPsychol. Appointments: Clinical Psychologist, Withington Hospital, Manchester; Senior Clinical Psychologist, North Manchester General Hospital, Manchester; Chartered Clinical Psychologist, Preston Guild Community Healthcare Trust. Publications: Haemophilia: Some Implications for Social Work, Co-author, 1977; Self-Perception of Employed and Unemployed Haemophiliacs, Co-author, 1980. Memberships: Associate Fellow, British Psychological Society. Hobbies: Photography; Flying; Reading. Address: 18 Willow Drive, Garstang, Nr Preston, Lancs PR3 1LD, England.

LOEWE-MADSEN Poul, b. 6 Feb 1945, Munkebo, Denmark. Chiropractor. m. Karen Loewe-Madsen, 6 Mar 1971, 2 sons, 1 daughter. Education: Doctor of Chiropractic, Canada. Appointments: Own clinic, primary field. Memberships: Chairman, Student Education, DKF; Chairman, Danish Chiropractic Council; Chairman, Danish Chiropractic Association, Funen; Canadian Chiropractic Association; Alumni CMCC; Alumni AECC. Hobbies: Triathlon; Cooking; Travel. Address: Langegade 89, 5300 Kerteminde, Denmark.

LOEWENTHAL Catherine (Kate) Miriam, b. 29 Oct 1941, Guildford, Surrey, England. Academic Psychologist. m. Naftali Loewenthal, 1 Oct 1964, 5 sons, 6 daughters. Education: BSc, Psychology, 1963, PhD, Psychology, 1967, University College London. Appointments: Assistant Lecturer in Psychology, University of North Wales, 1966-67; Lecturer in Psychology, City University, London, 1968-72; Lecturer, Senior Lecturer in Psychology, Royal Holloway, London University, 1972-; Visiting Lecturer, Department of Theology and Religion, Kings College, London, 1974-93. Publications: Refereed articles including: Psychology and Religion: comments on Giles, Jones, Horton and Lay, 1975; Marriage and religious commitment: the case of hasidic women, 1988;

Depression, Melancholy and Judaism, 1992; Religion, stress and distress, 1993; Family Size and Depressive Symptons in Orthodox Jewish Women, 1993; Gender and Depression in Anglo-Jewry, 1995; Contributions to collections: Effects of understanding from the audience on language behaviour, 1972; Handwriting as a guide to character, 1982; Family planning: Jewish attitudes, 1985; The shape of Jews to come, 1989; Judaism asnd Feminism, 1991; Some correlates of wellbeing and distress in Anglo-Jewish women (with V Goldblatt, V Amos, S Mullarkey), 1993; Publications: Mental Health & Religion, 1994; Introduction to Psychological Tests & Scales, 1995. Honours: Junior Research Fellow, Medical Research Council, 1966-67. Memberships: Associate Fellow, British Psychological Society; Chartered Psychologist. Address: Psychology Department, Royal Holloway and New Bedford College, Egham Hill, Egham, Surrey TW20 0EX, England.

LOGAN George Bryan, b. 1 Aug 1909, Pittsburgh, Pennsylvania. Retired Physician (Paediatrics, Allergy). m. Rhoda Palmer, 24 June 1939, 2 daughters. Education: MD, Harvard, 1934; MS in Paediatrics, University of Minnesota (Mayo Foundation), 1940. Appointments include: Professor of Paediatrics, Mayo Medical School; Retired, 1975.

LOGAN-EDWARDS Robert, b. 24 Oct 1922, England. Obstetrician & Gynaecologist. m. Jean Hazel Stubbs, 23 Feb 1946, 1 son deceased, 2 daughters. Education: MB, BS, Guy's Hospital, 1951; MRCOG, 1953; FRCOG, 1966; FRCS, 1963; MSc Cambridge, 1966. Appointments: Royal Air Force, 1948-51; Registrar, Cambridge, 1952-56; Demonstrator of Anatomy, Cambridge, 1956; Senior Registrar and Elmore Scholar, 1957-60; Senior Lecturer, First Assistant, Professorial Unit, Birmingham, 1960-66; Consultant, United Birmingham Hospitals, 1967-85; Retired. Publications: Numerous articles on obstetrics, gynaecology and reproductive endocrinology; Chapters in books. Memberships: Honorary Fellow, Past President, Birmingham & Midlands Obstetric & Gynaecology Society; Travellers. Hobbies: Art; Music; Travel. Address: Tump House, Abberley, Worcestershire WR6 6BP, England.

LOH Kelvin Hun Yu, b. 18 Dec 1939, Singapore. Consultant Gynaecologist. m. Olivia Loh, 27 Sep 1961, 1 s, 1 d. Education: LRSM(D); LRCP; LRCS(I); LM; DRCOG; AM; FRCOG. Career: SHO, Blackburn and Sheffield's Northern General Hospital; Registrar, Dublin and Northampton General Hospital; Obstetrician and Gynaecologist, General Hospital, Penang; Currently, Consultant Gynaecologist, The Specialists Centre, Penang. Membership: Academy of Medicine, Malaysia. Hobbies: Reading; Golfing; Piano Playing; Travel. Address: 40 Jesselton Crescent, Penang, 10450, Malaysia.

LOMAS Clifford George, b. 17 Nov 1946, England. Osteopath; Naturopath. m. Kathryn Barrow, 11 July 1987, 2 d. Education: BSc, Honours, Geology; Diploma, Osteopathy; Diploma, Naturopathy. Appointments: Geologist; Osteopath; Naturopath. Memberships: Register of Osteopaths; Register of Naturopaths. Hobbies: Natural health topics; Christian activities. Address: 2 Five Ashes Cottages, Kerridge, Nr Macclesfield, Cheshire SK10 5AY, England.

LOMAX James Welton, b. 7 Dec 1944, San Antonio, Texas, USA. Physician; Psychiatrist. m. Nancy Robinson, 9 Mar 1966, 3 daughters. Education: BA magna cum laude, Rice University, 1967; MD with honours, Baylor College of Medicine, 1971. Appointments: Assistant, 1974-79, Associate, 1977-84, Director of Residency Programme, Vice-Chairman for Educational Programmes, 1988-90, Acting Chairman, Department of Psychiatry, 1990-92, currently Associate Chairman and Director of Residency Education, Department of Psychiatry, Baylor College of Education, Houston, Texas; Examiner, Question Writer, American Board of Psychiatry and Neurology. Publications: Psychotherapy Education for Psychiatrists of the '90s, 1990. Honours: Faik Fellow, American Psychiatric Association, 1975-77; Laughlin Fellow, American College of Psychiatrists; Fellow, American Psychiatric Association, 1990; Fellow, American Journal of Psychiatry, 1991. Memberships: Fellow, American Psychiatric Association; Fellow, American College of Psychiatrists; American Psychoanalytic Association; American Association of Directors of Psychiatric Residency Training, President 1994-95. Hobbies: Tennis; Golf; Fishing. Address: Department of Psychiatry, Baylor College of Medicine, One Baylor Plaza, Houston, TX 77030, USA.

LONDON William Thomas, b. 11 Mar 1932, New York City, USA. Physician. m. Linda Greenman, 23 June 1957, 4 daughters. Education: BA; MD. Appointments: Senior Surgeon, USPAS, 1962-66; Research Physician, Fox Chase Cancer Center, 1966-78; Senior Resident

Physician 1978-90, Senior Member 1990-, Assistant Professor, Medicine, University Pennsylvania, 1971-75; Associate Professor, Medicine 1975-78, Adjunct Professor of Medicine, 1978-. Publications: 227 publications in scientific journals. Honours: Medical Excellence Award, American Liver Foundation, Delaware Valley Chapter, 1991; Service Award, American Associationof Ethnic Chinese, 1991. Memberships: American Board of International Medicine; FACP; American Association of Cancer Research; AAAS; AMA. Address: Fox Chase Cancer Center, 7701 Burholme Avenue, Philadelphia, PA 19111, USA.

LONE Asmat Ullah, b. 26 Mar 1944, Nairobi, Kenya. Dental Surgeon. m. Shamim A Lone, 11 Apr 1972, 1 son, 1 daughter. Education: BSc; BDS; MSc, Dentistry; FAACD. Appointments: House Officer; Senior House Officer; Registrar; Currently: Consultant Cosmetic Dental Surgeon, Abu Dhabi; Visiting Adjunct Associate Professor, University of Texas, San Antonio, USA, 1994-95. Memberships: American Equilibration Society; American Academy of Cosmetic Dentistry; Emirates Medical Association. Hobbies: Swimming; Reading. Address: PO Box 26374, Abu Dhabi, United Arab Emirates.

LONG Deirdre, b. 6 July 1969, Pretoria, South Africa. Radiographer. m. Dr M A Long, 1 Aug 1992. Education: BRad Diagnostic; BRad Hon, Oncotherapy. Appointments: Junior Radiographer; Senior Radiographer, Oncotherapy. Honours: Schering A G Berlyn Floating Trophy for Best Final Year Student, 1991; Marie Smit Floating Trophy for Best Final Year Academic Student, 1992; Dean's Medal, 1993; Best Hon Student in Medical Faculty, 1993. Hobbies: Aerobics; Tennis. Address: Pasadena 2, Pres Reitz Avenue, Westdene, Bloemfontein 9301, South Africa.

LONG Donlin, b. 14 Apr 1934, Rolla, MO, USA. Neurosurgeon. m. Harriett Page Kallenbach, 13 Jun, 1 s, 2 d. Education: MD, University MO Medical School, 1959; PhD, Neuroanatomy, University of MN Graduate School, 1964. Career includes: Associate Professor, Neurosurgery, University of MN Hospitals, 1970-73; Neurosurgeon in Chief, Johns Hopkins Hospital, 1973-; Professor and Chairman, Department of Neurosurgery, Johns Hopkins University School of Medicine, 1973-; Principal Staff, Applied Physics Laboratory, Johns Hopkins University, 1976-; Consultant, John F Kennedy Institute, Baltimore, MD, 1977. Publications: Over 265 publications including: Surgery for cervical spine tumors, in The Cervical Spine: An Atlas of Surgical Procedures, 1994; Rehabilitation of the Patient with Persistent Pain, in Neurological Rehabilitation, 2nd edition, 1994; Co-author, Outcome of low back pain therapy, in Perspectives in Neurological Survey, 1994; Editor, Neurosurgery Quarterly; Editorial Board for several professional journals. Honours include: Dean's Honor Five, 7 times; Medical Foundation Award, 1956-67; Jamison Medal, Australian Neurosurgery Society, 1986; Wakeman Award for Research in Neuroscience, 1990; Honoured Guest and Honorary Member, Australasian and Austrian Neurosurgical Societies, 1991. Memberships include: Sigma Xi; American Academy of Neurological Surgeons; American Academy of Pain Medicine; AAAS; American Association of Neuropathologists; American College of Surgeons; AMA; International Society of Pediatric Neurosurgery; Honorary Member, Neurosurgery Society of Peru. Address: Department of Neurosurgery, Johns Hopkins University School of Medicine, 600 North Wolfe Street, Baltimore, MD 21287-7709, USA.

LONTON Anthony Paul, b. 15 January 1940, Swindon, England. Psychologist. Education: BA, Kings College, Cambridge, 1963; MA, Cambridge, 1966; Dip Child Psychology, London, 1967; Chartered Psychologist; Associate Fellow, The British Psychological Society. Appointments: Educational Psychologist, Durham County Council; Senior Lecturer, Bretton Hall College of Education; Consultant Psychologist, Sheffield Children's Hospital; Lecturer, Manchester University. Publications Include: Location of the myelomeningocele, and its relationship to subsequent physical and intellectual abilities in children with myelomeningocele and hydrocephalus, 1977; In infantile hydrocephalus how much brain mantle is needed for normal development?, 1984; The integration of spina bifida children - are their needs being met?, 1986; Conductive education - magic or myth?, 1989; The Special Education Handbook, 1991. Honours: Sir Joseph Barcroft Prizewinner, Kings College, Cambridge, 1965; Visiting Professor of Psychology, Queens University, Belfast, 1981; Leverhulme Fellowship, 1986. Memberships: British Psychological Society; Society for Research into Hydrocephalms and Spina Bifida. Hobbies: History of Ceramics; Languages; Opera; Fell-walking. Address: Wooldale Hall, Wooldale, Huddersfield, West Yorkshire, England.

LOOK-HONG William Andrew, b. 22 Mar 1942, Kingston, Jamaica, WI. Psychiatrist. m. Jeanne Veronica Lyn, 5 Aug 1973, 2 daughters. Education: BSc; MBBS; FRCPC; DABPN. Career: Consultant; Attending Psychiatrist. Honour: Aaron Matalon Prize in Psychiatry, 1973. Memberships: American Psychiatric Association; Canadian Medical Association; Ontario Medical Association; Royal College of Physicians & Surgeons of Canada. Hobbies: Tennis; Golf; Gardening; Swimming. Address: Grey Bruce Regional Health Center, PO Box 1400, Owen Sound, Ontario N4K 6M9, Canada.

LOOMIS William Grant, b. 15 Mar 1931, Waterville, Maine, USA. Physician. m. Jean MacRae, 9 June 1956, 1 son, 4 daughters. Education: AB, Dartmouth College, 1953; MD, Cornell University, 1956; American Board of Psychiatriay and Neurology, Psychiatry, 1969, Child Psychiatry, 1974; Psychiatric Residency, 1963-65, Fellowship, Child Psychiatry, 1965-67, University of Colorado; Rotating Intern, Mary Hetdward Memorial Hospital, New Hampshire. Appointments: Unit manager, Juvenile Court Evaluation and Guidance Unit, Orange County, 1974-90; Staff Psychiatrist, 1990-; Community Mental Health Psychiatrist, County of Orange, California. Publication: Use of Foster Grandparents, 1968. Honour: Phi Beta Kappa, 1952. Address: CA, USA.

LOPATKIN Nikolai Alekseyevich, b. 18 Feb 1924, Moscow, Russia. Urologist. m. Tamara Aleksandrovna Afanassieva, 31 July 1947, 2 daughters. Education: Diploma, 2nd Stalin Medical Institute, Moscow; Professor, DrMedSci; Diploma, Member: USSR and Russian Academies of Medical Science. Appointments: Animal Farm Loader, Saltykov, 1942; Hospital Attendant, Ambulance Service, 1944; Diploma Urologist, 1947; Assistant, Chair of Urology, 2nd Stalin Medical Institute, Moscow, 1964; Professor, 1960, Chief, 1967, Chair of Urology, 2nd Pirogov Medical Institute, Moscow, 1960; Director, Scientific Institute of Urology MH Russia, 1978-; Active Operating Urologic Surgeon; Editor, Urology and Nephrology journal. Publications: Translumbar aortography, 1961; General anaesthesia in urology, 1966; Renal antiography, 1969; Text-book of Urology, 1970, 1977, 1982; Handbook of Urology, 1978; Renal venous stenosis, 1984; Operating urology, 1986; Vesicoureteral reflux, 1990; Great Medical Encyclopaedia (department editor). Honours: State Awards, 1971, 1984, 1990; Hero of Socialist Labour, 1974; Award, Council of Ministers of the USSR, 1981; Order of The Labour Red Banner; Order of Lenin; Order of October Revolution; Korolev Medal; Sofia Municipal Medal, Bulgaria; Other medals: Urologic Society of Bratislava; 1st European Urologic Congress, Padova; Humboldt University. Memberships: Regulartory Body, Russian Scientific Urologic Society; International Urologic Society; European Association of Urology; Honorary Member, Urological and Nephrological Society, Hungary; Purkinier Urologic Association, Czechoslovakia; Editorial Boards: Vestnik mediciny; European Urology. Hobbies: Working in the garden of his country house; Education of his grandchildren; Skiing. Address: Leninsky prospekt 13, apart 23, Moscow, Russia.

LOPES Alberto de Barros, b. 19 Apr 1956, Hong Kong. Doctor. m. Jane, 31 Aug 1985, 3 daughters. Education: MB ChB, Liverpool University, England, 1980; MRCOG, 1986. Appointments: Consultant, Gynaecologic Oncology; Hobby: Sports. Address: Department of Gynaecological Oncology, Queen Elizabeth Hospital, Gateshead, Tyne & Wear, NE9 6SX, England.

LOPEZ G Miryam, b. 13 Jan 1955, Lima, Peru. Biologist. m. Alvaro Marcelo, 11 Mar 1992, 1 daughter. Education: Bachelor of Biological Sciences, 1980, Master in Biochemistry, 1986, University Nacional de San Marcos. Appointments: Instructor, Faculty of Biology, 1980, Assistant Teacher, department of Biochemistry, Faculty of Medicine, 1982; Research Associate, Baylor College of Medicine, USA, 1986; Associate Teacher, Faculty Member, Biochemistry, faculty of Medicine. Publications: Isolation and Characterization of Cysteine Proteinase From Fasciola Adult Worms, Co-author; Molecular and Biochemical Parasitology. Co-author, 1989; Tecnicas Instrumentagas de Uso Mas Frecuente en el Laboratorio Clinico Yde Investigacion, 1992. Memberships: International Union of Biochemistry; Sociedad Quimica del Peru; Sociedad Peruana de Parasitologia. Hobbies: Pastry; Playing the piano. Address: Universite Nacional Mayor de San Marcos, Centro de Bioquimica y Nutricion, Aptdo Postal 1546, Lima 1, Peru.

LOPEZ Victor Francisco, b. 28 July 1929, Moca, Dominican Republic. Physician. m. Luisa Victoria Compres, 29 May 1954, 1 s, 2 d. Education: MD; Board Certified in Anatomic Pathology and Neuropathology, American Board of Pathology. Appointments: Assistant to Associate professor of Pathology, University of Missouri Medical

School, Columbia, Missouri, USA, 1966-71; Associate Pathologist, Genessee Hospital, Rochester, New York, 1971-73; Associate Pathologist, Danbury Hospital, Danbury, Connecticut, 1973-. Publications include: Louis-Bar's Syndrome (ataxia-telangiectasia) Neuropathologic Observations, Co-author, 1967; A Rare Cause of Occlusion of the Internal Carotid Artery, Co-author, 1970; Adenosarcoma of Uterus and Ovary. A Clinicopathologic Study of Two Cases, 1979; Primary Tumor of Spleen with Morphologic Features of Malignant Fibrous Histiocytoma, Co-author. Memberships: American Association of Neuropathologists; American Society of Clinical Pathology; College of American Pathologists; International Academy of Pathology, US Canadian Division. Hobbies: travel; Photography. Address: Danbury Hospital, Department of Pathology and Laboratory Medicine, Danbury, CT 06810, USA.

LOPUKHIN Yuri Mikhailovich, b. 29 Oct 1924, Russia. Professor of Surgical Anatomy. m. 30 June 1955, 1 son, 1 daughter. Education: MD; PhD, Academician. Appointments: Rector, 2nd Moscow Medical School, 1964-84; Professor, Surgical Anatomy Chair; Director, Moscow Physico-Chemical Medicine Research Institute. Publications: Experimental Surgery, 1976; Haemosorption, 1979; Cholesterosis, 1984; More than 300 articles. Honours: Winner, State Science Prizes, 1971, 1978, 1982; MD (Honoris cause), Leipzig University. Memberships: New York Academy of Sciences; Russia Medical Academy of Sciences. Hobby: Tennis. Address: Malaja Pirogovskaja str 1a, 119828 Moscow, Russia.

LORIN Claude, b. 25 June 1949, Saint Cloud, France. Psychologist. 1 son, 1 daughter. Education: Biochemist, 1971; PhD, University of Paris, 1979; Doctor in Psychology, 1980. Appointments: Director of the Laboratory of Applicated Psychology, University of Reims; Professor, University of Reims. Publications: Le Jeune Ferenczi, 1983; L'Inachevé, 1984; Pour Saint Augustin, 1988; Le Fou d'Araucanie, 1990; Fenenczi de la médecine à la psychanalyse, 1993. Memberships: International Association of Psychiatry & Psychoanalysis. Hobbies: Dance; Karate. Address: 11 bis rue Gericault, 750164 Paris, France.

LÖTTER Martha F J, b. 15 Jan 1968, Orange Free State, South Africa. Radiographer. m. Walter Mark Lötter, 28 Sept 1991, 1 daughter. Education: Bacalareus Radiography, Honours. Appointments: Diagnostic Radiographer; Oncotherapy Radiographer; Nuclear Medicine Radiographer, 1986-94. Honours: B(Rad) Honours, Oncotherapy, 1990; B(Rad) Honours cum laude, Nuclear Medicine, 1992. Membership: South African Medical & Dental Board. Address: Hydromed Hospital Bloemfontein, Nuclear Medicine, Orange Free State, South Africa.

LOU Yu Qian, b. 15 Aug 1956, Henan, China. Doctor of Rheumatology & Traditional Chinese Medicine. m. Liu Yamin, 3 July 1984, 1 daughter. Education: Diploma, Henan University of Medicine; Diploma, Succeed Famous & Veteran Expert of China in Herbal Medicine. Appointments: Henan College of Health Staffs Medicine; Henan Province Hospital of Traditional Chinese Medicine. Publications: Self-treatment in Home on Rheumatoid Arthritis, 1989; A Complete Book of China On Rheumatic Diseases, 1993. Memberships: Rheumatic Diseases Committee of Traditional Chinese Medicine, China; Leader, Henan Rheumatic Diseases Committee, Traditional Chinese Medicine, China. Hobbies: Friendship; Sports; Philosophy. Address: Henan College of Traditional Chinese Medicine, Zhengzhou, Henan, China.

LOUJNIKOV Eugeni Alekseevich, b. 27 Sep 1934, Moscow, Russia. Medicine. m. Alina Loujnikova, 28 Jan 1958, 1 s. Education: Doctor of Medical Sciences, Moscow Medical University, 1960. Career: Doctor, Emergency Medicine; Scientist, Moscow Research Institute of Emergency Medicine; Professor of Clinical Toxicology, Russian Academy of Postdiploma Education; Currently, Manager, Moscow Toxicological Centre in Scientific Research Institute of Emergency Medicine. Publications: The principles of reanimatology in acute poisonings, 1977; Acute poisonings, 1989; Clinical Toxicology, 1994. Honour: Russian State Prize Laureate, 1979. Memberships: Russian Scientific Society of Toxicologists; Association of Intensive Care Specialists; Russian Academy of Medical Sciences; Russian Academy of Technological Sciences. Hobbies: Poetry; Skiing. Address: 129010 Moscow, Soukharevskay pl 3, Sklifasovsky Institute, Russia.

LOVE Arthur, b. 31 Aug 1952, Reykjavik, Iceland. Physician; Virologist. m. Margret Hallgrimsdottir, 31 Dec 1984, Divorced 1992, 2 daughters. Education: AA, Reykjavik Junior College, 1972; MD, University of Iceland, 1978; PhD, Karolinska Institute, Stockholm, 1986;

Licenced to Practice Medicine in Iceland, 1982; Certified, Clinical Virology, Iceland, 1986. Appointments: Visiting Scholar, University of California, 1978-81; Resident in Medicine, National University Hospital, Reykjavik, Iceland, 1981-82; Research Fellow, Virology, Neuropathology, Karolinska Institute, Stockholm, 1982-87; Chief Consultant, AIDS & Hepatitis Section, Department of Medical Virology, University of Iceland, 1987-; Associate Professor, University of Iceland, 1988-. Publications: Numerous scientific articles mostly in Virological and Neuropathological Journals. Honours: Numerous research grants, The Karolinska Institute, Swedish & Iceland Science Foundations. Memberships: Icelandic Medical Association; European Group for Rapid Viral Diagnosis; Scandinavian Society for Neuropathology; American Society for Virology; Icelandic Microbiological Society. Hobbies: Hiking; Hunting; Photography. Address: Hraunteigur 16, 105 Reykjavik, Iceland.

LOVE Leon, b. 7 Sept 1923, New York City, USA. Radiologist. m. Rita, 17 June 1956, 2 s, 1 d. Education: MD, Chicago Medical School, 1946; BS; FACR. Appointments: Attending Radiologist, Director of Radiology, Cook County Hospital; Chairman, Department of Radiology, Professor of Radiology, Loyola University Medical Centre. Publications: Contributor of over 75 articles in radiology journals. Honours: AOA Distinguished Alumnus Chicago Medical School; Distinguished Service Award, Chicago Radiological Society; Stritch Medal, Loyola University. memberships: American College of Radiology, Fellow; Radiologic Society of North America; American Roentgen Ray; Association of University Radiology; Society of Uroradiology. Hobby: Tennis. Address: Loyola University Medical Centre, 2160 South 1st Avenue, Room 0067, Bldg 103, Maywood, IL 60153, USA.

LOVE Shirley B, b. 27 Mar 1923. Psychotherapist. m. Dr Sidney I Love, 10 Oct 1958, 2 d. Education: MSW; BCD; ACSW; PhD. Appointments: Therapist, Riverdale Mental Health Clinic; Faculty, LIU Graduate School, Rockland Community College, Mt St Vincent, International School Social Services, Centre for Modern Analytic Studies; Private Practice Psychotherapist; Co-Director, Faculty Supervisor, Riverdale Institute of Psychotherapy. Publications: Contributor of book reviews and articles in journals; Newsletter, Human Services, 1985. Honours: Case Record Award, Children's Aid Society, 1955. Memberships: NAAP; NASW; Association Modern Analysts; Fellow, American Orthopsychiatric Association; Diplomate in Clinical Social Work. Hobbies: Reading; Long walks; Theatre. Address: 2727 Palisade Avenue, Riverdale, NY 10463, USA.

LOVE Susan Margaret, b. 9 Feb 1948, New Jersey, USA. Surgeon. 1 daughter. Education: MD, State University of New York Downstate Medical Centre; FACS; Honorary DSc, Northeastern University; DHS, Simmons College, Boston. Appointments: Clinical Fellow, Instructor in Surgery, Harvard, 1977-87; Director, Breast Clinic, Beth Israel Hospital, Boston, 1980-88; Director, Faulker Breast Centre, Faulkner Hospital, Boston, 1988-92; Director, Revlon/UCLA Breast Centre; Associate Professor of Clinical Surgery University of California Los Angeles. Publications: Dr Susan Love's Breast Book, 1990, 1995; Benign and Malignant Breast Disease, 1995; Inherited Breast and Ovarian Cancer: What Are the Risks? What Are the Choices?, 1993. Honours: 1992 Achievement Award, American Association of Physicians for Human Rights; Women Making History Award, US Senator Barbara Boxer, 1993. Memberships: American Medical Women's Association; American Society of Preventive Oncology; Southwestern Oncology Group; NSABP Oversight Committee. Hobby: Fly Fishing. Address: Revlon/UCLA Breast Centre, 200 Med Plaza, Suite 510 (Box 957028), Los Angeles, CA 90095-7028, USA.

LOWE James E, b. 27 Dec 1946, Brunswick, GA, USA. Cardiac Surgery. m. Lorraine Sassone, 7 Sep 1973, 2 d. Education: BA, Stanford University; MD, UCLA. Appointments: Assistant Professor, 1981-85, Associate Professor, 1986-89, Professor of Cardiovascular Surgery, 1990, Duke University Medical Center, Durham, NC. Publications: Over 200 published manuscripts and book chapters. Honours: AOA, 1973; Outstanding Student in Medicine, UCLA, 1973; Established Investigator, AHA, 1981-86; Cairo University Medal of Honour, 1993. Memberships: ACS; AATS; STS; American Surgical Association; Southern Surgical Association; Society of Clinical Surgeons, AHA. Hobbies: Fishing; Boating; Woodworking; Gardening. Address: Duke Hospital, Box 3954, Durham, NC 27718, USA.

LOWE Sue E, b. 22 July 1954, Scottsburg, Indiana, USA. Optometrist. m. Eric Lundell, 12 Aug 1983, 1 son. Education: BA, Zoology, University of Wyoming, 1976; Doctor of Optometry (OD),

Pacific University College of Optometry, 1980; Fellow, College of Optometrists in Vision Development, 1986; Fellow, American Academy of Optometry, 1987. Appointments: Laboratory Technician, 1972-76; Research Assistant, University of Wyoming, 1975-76; Research Assistant, Teaching Assistant, Pacific University College of Optometry, 1976-78; Bausch & Lomb Diagnostic Soflens Set Technician, 1978-79; Optometrist in private practice, 1980-; Partner, Owner, Snowy Range Vision Center, 1982-; American Optometric Association Spokesperson, National TV's Good Morning America, 1993. Publications: DHEW Region X Optometric Manpower Study, 1980; Patient Care and Management Manual, the Management of Non Strabismic Binocular Vision Problems (co-author), 1986-87. Honours: Alpha Epsilon Delta, 1974; Mortar Board, 1975; Outstanding Greek Woman, 1976; Exemplary Alumni, University of Wyoming College of Arts and Sciences, 1994; Wyoming Optometrist of the Year, Wyoming Optometric Association, 1994. Memberships include: American Optometric Association, committees; Wyoming Optometric Association, President, other offices; Vice-President, Advisory Board Charter Member, Baltimore Academy for Behavioral Optometry; Omega Epsilon Phi; Wyoming Vision Services Inc; Wyoming State Director, Optometric Extension Program Foundation; American Optometric Foundation; American Public Health Association; International Platform Association; American Diabetes Association; Infant Stimulation Education Association; Council for Exceptional Children. Hobbies: Skiing; Fishing; Canoeing.

LOWENGART Ruth A, b. 13 Nov 1954, Cedar Rapids, IA, USA. Physician. Education: BA, University of WI, Madison; MD, MS, Occupational Medicine, University of Southern CA. Career: Manager, Occupational Medicine, ENSR; Manager of Employee Health Program, Contra Costa County, CA; Occupational Physician Consultant, Alta Bates Medical Center, Berkeley, CA; Currently in Private Practice, Orthopedic Medicine and Occupational Health. Publications: Co-author, Childhood Leukemia and Parents Occupational and Home Exposures, JNCI, 1987; Medical and Administrative Guidelines for Use of Respirators, conference proceedings, 1988; Co-author, Methylene Chloride Intoxication in a Furniture Refinisher, JOM, 1990; Guidelines for Hospitals and Emergency Departments: Managing Victims of Hazardous Materials Incidents, 1990. Honour: Phi Beta Kappa. Memberships: Jackson County Medical Association; Oregon Medical Association; American Association of Orthopedic Medicine; American College of Occupational and Environmental Medicine; Western Occupational Medicine Association; American College of Physicians. Hobbies: Dancing; Hiking; Building House. Address: 1648 East McAndrews Road, Medford, OR 97504, USA.

LOWENSTEIN Edward, b. 29 May 1934, Duisburg, Germany. Professor of Anaesthesia. m. 14 May 1989, 5 s, 1 d. Education: MD, University of Michigan, USA; MA, Honorary, Harvard University. Appointments: Intern, University of Oregon; Resident, Massachusetts General Hospital, 1960-63; US Army Surgical Research Unit, 1963-65; Assistant Professor, Associate Professor, Professor of Anaesthesia, MGH and Harvard Medical School, 1965-89; Professor of Anaesthesia, Harvard Medical School; Anaesthetist-in-Chief, Beth Israel Hospital, 1989; Publications: Cardiovascular Response to Large Doses of Intravenous Morphine in Man, 1969; Regional Ischaemic Ventricular Dysfunction in Myocardium Supplied by a Narrowed Coronary Artery with Increasing Halothane Concentration, Co-author, 1981; Catastrophic Pneumonary Vaseconstriction Associated with Protamine Reversal of Heparin, 1983; Editor, Anaesthesiology, 1979-88. Memberships: American Society Anaesthetics; Society Cardiovasular Anaesthetists; American Heart Association. Hobbies: Travel; Cooking; Reading. Address: Department Anaesthesia and Critical Care, Beth Israel Hospital, Boston, MA 02215, USA.

LOWERY Penny Jane, b. 12 June 1954, Leigh-On-Sea, Essex, England. Acupuncture; Gestalt Therapy. Education: Licence in Acupuncture, 1985; 3 Year Training, Gestalt Therapy, 1991. Appointments: Diretor, New Cross Natural Therapy Centre Ltd. Memberships: Traditional Acupuncture Society; British Association for Counselling; Gestalt Association. Hobbies: Ballroom & Latin American Dancing. Address: 51 Mainwood Road, Crofton Park, London SE4 1AB, England.

LOZOFF Betsy, b. 19 Dec 1943, Milwaukee, WI, USA. Pediatrician. 1 d. Education: BA magna cum laude, 1965; MD, 1971; MS, 1981. Appointments: Senior Instructor, Department Medicine, Professor, Department of Paediatrics, 1992-93, Case Western Reserve; Adjunct Assistant Professor, Department Anthropology, 1976-88, Case Western Reserve; Currently, Director and Research Scientist, Centre for Human Growth and Development; Professor of Paediatrics, University of MI, 1993-. Publications: Co-author, Iron Deficiency Anaemia and Iron Therapy: Effects on Infant Development, Test Performance in Paediatrics, 1987; Co-author, Long - Term Development Outcome of Iron Deficiency in Infancy, in New England Journal of Medicine, 1991. Honours: Phi Beta Kappa; Research Career Development Award, National Institute of Health, 1983-88. Address: CHGD, University of Michigan, 300 N Ingalls, Ann Arbor, MI 48109-0406, USA.

LU Chang-lin, b. 26 Nov 1943, Shenyang, China. Medical Professor. m. Gui-zhi Gao, 1 May 1971, 1 son, 1 daughter. Education: MD, 4th Military Medical University, 1968; PhD, 2nd Military Medical University, 1984. Appointments: Lecturer; Professor; Head, Department of Neurobiology; Currently Vice-Chief, Institute of Neuroscience, 2nd Military Medical University. Publications: Effect of Chemical Stimulation in the PAG on Vocalization in the Squirrel Monkey, 1993; Co-author: Dopaminergic Regulation of Quiet Biting Attack Behavior in the Cat, 1991; Behavior Elicited from the Feline Midbrain Periaqueductal Gray is Regulated by and Opioid Receptors, 1991; The Effects of Periaqueductally Injected Transmitter Antagonists on Forebrain-Elicited Vocalization in the Squirrel Monkey. Memberships: International Society for Neuroethology; Chinese Society for Physiology; Chinese Society for Neuroscience. Address: 36-501, 699 Lane, Xiangyin Road, Shanghai 200433, China.

LU Dao Yuan, b. 9 Mar 1939, Shangdong, China. Doctor. m. Tian Changying, 20 Jun 1967, 1 d. Education: BA, Qingdao Medical College. Appointments: Assistant, 1966, Lecturer, 1983, Associate Professor, 1988-. Publications: Co-author, Investigation of patients with Hb disease and G-6PD deficiency, in Shangdong Medicine, 1983; Co-author, The advance and clinical signification about bone marrow necrosis, in Foreign Medicine, 1986; Investigation on 822 pupils with anaemia, in Jou Qingdao Medical College, 1988. Honours: 2nd Class Science Award, Qingdao, 1982; Winner, Achievement in Science Research Award, 1985. Membership: Qingdao Branch of Chinese Medicine Society. Address: No 19, 101 Room, Jiang Su Road, Qingdao, China.

LU Fan, b. 5 Apr 1940, Hefei, AnHui. Professor of Neurology. m. Mr Li Fang Quan, 1 Oct 1966, 1 son, 1 daughter. Education: Jiangxi Medical College, 1958-63. Career: Resident, 1963-80; Visiting Physician, 1980-87; Associate Professor, 1987-93; Professor of Neurology and Head of the Department of Internal Medicine, The First Hospital, Ganzhou, 1993-. Publications: Jiangxi Journal of Medicine, 1972; Epidemiology Survey Disease of Tumor in Ganzhou, 1982; Clinical Analyses on Image of Cerebrovascular Blood Flow, 1982; First Nation Academic Exchanges Meeting on Dopplar, 1993; Chronic Headache and Transcranial Dopplar. Honours: Transcranial Dopplar to Diagnosis of Cerebrovascular Disease, acquired Grade 2 Science and technical award of Ganzhou Zone Government. Memberships: Society of Physician, CMA; Council Member, Society of Neurology, CMA Jiangxi Branch; Council Society, Neurology CMA Ganzhou Branch. Hobby: Painting. Address: Jiangxi Ganzhou First Hospital, Ganzhou, Jiangxi 341000 China.

LU Guishen, b. 23 Sept 1933, Jinan City, Shandong, China. Professor of Medicinal Chemistry. Education: BD, Beijing Medical University; PhD, Peking Union Medical College. Appointments: Research Assistant, Associate, Professor, Institute of Materia Medica, Chinese Academy of Medical Sciences, 1954-83; Professor, Deputy Director, 1983-. Publications: Protective Groups in Organic Chemistry, Co-author, 1984; Improved Synthesis of 4-Alkoxybenzyl Alcohol Resin, Co-author, 1981; Synthesis and Hormonal Activity of (TYR22) Glucagon and (desHis Tyr22) Glucagon, 1987; Synthesis of Small Peptides Containing Hydroxy-Amino-Acid and Its Effects on Profesterone Production, 1994. Honours: Prize of Science and Technology Progress, Ministry of Public Health. Memberships: Committee, Chinese Pharmacy Association; Chinese Association of Chemistry. Hobby: Playing Piano. Address: 1 Xian Nong Tan Street, Beijing 100050, China.

LU Hui Qing, b. 6 Feb 1914, Japan. Professor of Nursing. m. Dr Chen Shih Ti, 4 Feb 1945, 1 s. Education: BS, Science and Nursing, Peking Union Medical College, Beijing, China, 1938. Career: Head Nurse, PUMC Hospital, 1938; Dean of Nursing School of Zhong Shan Hospital, 1946; Director of Nursing of 1st Affiliated Hospital of Chong Qing Medical College, 1956; Currently, Honorary Director of Nursing School and Advisor of Faculty of Nursing, Sun Yat Sen University of Medical Sciences, China. Publications: Translation of nursing magazine from English to Chinese. Honours: Golden Key Award, Yen Jing University, 1938; Academic Excellence Award, PUMC, 1938. Membership: Chinese Nursing Association. Hobbies: Music; Reading; Sport. Address: The Zhongshan Medical University of Guangzhou, 510089 Guangzhou, China.

LU Qi-ming, b. 15 November 1935, Huhot, Inner Mongolia, China. Surgeon. m. 1967, 1 son, 2 daughters. Education: BA, Inner Mongolia Medical College, 1961. Appointments: Assistant Surgeon; Attending Surgeon; Vice Professor; Professor; Chief Surgeon. Publications: Orbital Tumors - Clinical Analysis of 61 Cases, 1982; Clinical Analysis of 22 Cases of Grave Ophthalmic Diseases, 1990. Honours: 4th Award, Science and Technology Advancement, Inner Mongolia, 1981; 3rd Award, Excellent Paper of 30th Anniversary of Inner Mongolia Medical College, 1986. Memberships: Deputy Director, All China Ophthalmology Association, Inner Mongolia Branch. Hobbies: Walking; Table Tennis. Address: Ophthalmic Department, Teaching Hospital, Inner Mongolia Medical College, 010050, China.

LU Rushan, b. 20 Aug 1926, Zhejiang, China. Biochemist; Radiation Biologist. m. Wu Guanyun, 6 Feb 1949, 3 sons. Education: Graduate Diploma, St John's University, Shanghai, 1947; Postgraduate Diploma, First Moscow Medical College, Moscow, 1957. Appointments: Research Associate, Associate Professor, Professor, Director, Institute of Radiation Medicine, Chinese Academy of Medical Science, 1958-78; Vice-President, Branch Academy, Chinese Academy of Medical Science, 1978-81; Assistant Director-General, World Health Organisation, 1982-88; Director, Institute of Medical Information, Chinese Academy of Medical Science, 1988-. Publications: Amino Acid Metabolism, 1957; Radiation Protection and Experimental Therapy, 1980; Acta Pharmacologica Sinicae, 3, 45, 1982; Chinese Journal of Radiation Medicine and Radiation Protection, 4 (2), 20, 1984, and 6, 245, 1986; Chinese Journal of Haematology, 10 (11), 593, 1989. Honours: State Awards, 1978; Ministerial and Provincial Awards, 1982. Memberships: WHO Expert Advisory Panel; Vice-Chair, Chinese Society of Radiation Medicine, 1980-85; Honorary Chair, Chinese Society of Medical Information; Interunion Commission of Comparative Physiology. Address: Institute of Medical Information, Chinese Academy of Medical Science, 3 Yabao Road, Chaoyang District, Beijing 100020, China.

LU Shu-hua, b. 19 October 1935, Shanghai, China. Medical Doctor. m. Kae-yun Sun, 3 October 1971. Education: MD, Shanghai Medical University, 1955; Visiting Scholar, University of California, Los Angeles, USA, 1987-88. Appointments: Head, Department of Obstetrics & Gynaecology, Lu Wan Maternity & Child Health Hospital, China; President, Lu Wan Maternity & Child Health Hospital, Shanghai, China. Publications: Remove Blood Stasis to Promote Regeneration, for the Treatment of Vaginal Bleeding after Artificial and Natural Abortion: An Analysis of 104 Cases, 1975; Qin Gong San, for the Treatment of Chronic Cervicitis, 1982; The Significance of Establishing Special Clinic for Pregnancy Associated with Abnormal Liver Functions, 1982; Activate the blood circulation to eliminate blood stasis, for the Treatment of Membranous Dysmenorrhea, 1983; The Experience of Health Education on Family Planning to Reduce the Contraceptive Failure in Urban China, 1993; Health Education to raise the Continuing Using Rate of IUD in Urban China, 1994. Honours: Scientific Technical Progress Award, Shanghai Municipal Government. Memberships: American Public Health Association; Chinese Medical Association; Chinese Traditional Medical Association; Chinese Association of Integration of Traditional & Western Medicine. Hobbies: Music. Address: 699 Hua Shan Road Apt 32, Shanghai 200040, China.

LU Si Qi, b. 24 Jun 1942, Laoning, China. Professor of Parasitology. m. Di Xim Wang, 8 Nov 1968, 2 s. Education: MD, 2nd Medical College, Beijing, 1967; MPH, Capital University of Medical Sciences, 1983. Appointments: Surgeon, Tongxiang County People Hospital, Gan Su Province, 1968-80; Senior Assistant Research Fellow, Beijing Tropical Medicine Research Institute, Beijing, 1983-89; Currently, Associate Professor, Department of Parasitology, Capital University of Medical Science. Publications: Co-author, Tropical Medicine, 1988; Zoonosis in China, 1988; Establishment of an axenic culture of Giardia lamblia through preliminary passage in suckling gerbils, 1990; Climic Immunology of Parasitic Diseases, 1993. Honour: Award by Government of Beijing Municipality for establishing the first axenic culture strain of Giardia Lamblia in China, 1990. Memberships: Chinese Parasitological Society; The Chinese Protozoological Society. Hobbies: Stamp Collecting; Swimming. Address: 208 3rd Building, Xibahe Zhuonghi,

Zhaoyang District, Beijing 100028, China.

LU Xiang-yun, b. 9 May 1925, Hunan, China. Professor of Obstetrics & Gynecology. m. Lei Xue-xi, 24 Oct 1954, 1 son, 1 daughter. Education: MD, Shanghai Medical College, 1949. Appointments: Resident Physician, Obstetrics & Gynecology Hospital, Shanghai Medical College; Chief Resident Physician, Obstetrics & Gynecology Hospital, Shanghai Medical College; Visiting Doctor, Obstetrics & Gynecology Hospital, Shanghai Medical College; Vice Chairman, Department of Obstetrics & Gynecology, Shanghai Medical College; Vice Director, Institute of Obstetrics & Gynecology, Shanghai Medical College; Chairman, Department of Endocrinology, Institute of Obstetrics & Gynecology, Shanghai Medical University; Chairman, Department of Genetics, Institute of Obstetrics & Gynecology, Shanghai Medical University. Publications: Immunology in "Theory and Practice of Obstetrics & Gynecology", 1983, 1991; Practical Obstetrics & Gynecology, 1987; Gonadotropin Releasing Hormone and its Analogs, 1994; Articles: Safety effects of long acting oral contraceptive Quinestral, 1985; Studies on the clinical use of nonpeptide LHRH-A in diagnosis and therapy, 1987; Studies of domestic LHRH-A for diagnosis and treatment of gynecologic diseases, 1992. Honours: 3rd Award, Promotion of New Products, Shanghai, 1984; 2nd Award, National Family Planning Committee, 1985, 1986; 2nd Award, Scieno-technological Progress, Ministry of Health, 1991; 3rd Award National Scieno-technological Progress, 1992; Honorary Award of Guong Hua, 2nd grade, 1994. Memberships: Expert Advisory Committee, China Family Planning Technical Instruction Center. Hobbies: Drawing. Address: 4 Lane 1674, Apt 201, Xie Tu Road, Shanghai 200032, China.

LU Yu-pu, b. 10 Mar 1917, Suqian, Jiangsu, China. Surgeon. m. Qing Li, 1946, 2 sons, 1 daughter. Education: Graduate, National Central University School of Medicine, China, 1942. Appointments: Lecturer, Department of Surgery, National Central University Medical College; Fellow, University Iowa, USA; Attending Orthopidist, Department of Orthopidist Surgery, Kaiser Foundation Hospital, San Francisco, USA; Chief, Professor, 1st Teaching Hospital, 4th Military Medical University, PLA, China. Publications: Treatment of Congenital Clubfoot by Early Operation, 1988; Successful Replantation in Ten-digit Complete Amputations, 1988; Practical Orthopaedics, 1991. Honours: Model Medical Worker, General Logistics Department of PLA, 1978; Visiting Professor, University Iowa, Louisiana University, Texas Technical University. Memberships: Vice Chairman, Academy for Medical Sciences of PLA; Advisor to the Chinese Orthopaedic Association; Editor Emeritus, Chinese Journal of Orthopaedic Surgery; Editor, International Board of Orthopaedics. Address: Institute of Orthopaedics, Xijing Hospital, Xian 710032, China.

LU Zi-Lan, b. 24 Jan 1914, Shanghai, China. Medical Doctor. Education: BSc; MD, St John's University, Shanghai, 1945. Appointments: Doctor, Obstetrics and Gynaecology, St John's University Affiliated Hospital; Attending Doctor, Chief Doctor, Guangdong Provincial Hospital and Guangdong Maternity and Children's Hospital; Deputy Director, Guangdong Research Institute of Family Planning; Now retired. Publications include: Flower IUD, 1980; Design and Notification of Flower IUD, 1984; Family Planning Principles and Practice, 1988. Honours: 15 honours and awards, National and Provincial Family Planning Committee, Scientific Committee and Ministry of Health, 1950-95; 1st Guangdong Population Award as 1 of 10 contributors of Guangdong Province. Memberships: Chinese Medical Associatin; Chinese Obstetrics and Gynaecology Association, Vice-Director 1955; Chinese Family Planning. Hobbies: Painting; Travel. Address: Guangdong Provincial Research Institute of Family Planning, 12 Shui Jun Nan Street, Guangzhou 510080, China.

LU Zuoxin, b. 30 Jan 1940, Shen Yang, China. Thoracic Surgery. m. 1 Oct 1975, 1 s, 1 d. Education: MD, Chinese Medical University. Career: Thoracic Surgeon, 1974; Thoracic Attending Surgeon, 1978; Thoracic Surgery Associate Professor and Thoracic Surgery Director, 1988-, Thoracic Surgery Professor and Head of Thoracic Surgery. Publications: Treatment of Advanced Bronchogenic Pulmonary Carcinoma by Cryosurgery, 1989; Experimental Study on Frozen Effect on Organs Adjacent to the Lung, 1993; Change of Immunity in Patients with Bronchogenic Cancer after Cryosurgery, 1994. Memberships: CSTCVS Committee, Chinese Medical Association, Sichuan; Chinese Anti-Cancer Association, Sichuan; Committee, Society for Lung Cancer; Chinese Association of Refridgeration. Hobby: Song. Address: Department of Thoracic Surgery, Xinqiao Hospital, Chongqing, Sichuan, 630037, China.

LU-YAO Grace, b. 17 Feb 1963, Taipei, Taiwan. Epidemiology; Outcomes Research. m. Siu-Long Yao, 6 Sept 1990. Education: PhD, Epidemiology; MPH. Appointments: Assistant Professor. Publications incl: Geographic variation in rates of prostat4e cancer and radical prostatectomy in the United States, 1994; Basics and its application in orthopedics, 1994; Transurethral resection of the prostate among Medicare beneficiaries in the United States: Time trends and outcoms, 1994; Internal validation of Medicare claims, 1994; An assessment of radical prostatectomy for prostate cancer: Geographic variations, time trends and the evaluation of medical care outcomes, 1994. Membership: American Public Health Association. Address: 4914 Bramhope Lane, Ellicott City, MD 21043, USA.

LUCE Edward Andrew, b. 3 May 1940, Syracuse, New York, USA. Plastic Surgeon. m. Rebecca, 1 s, 1 d. Education: BS, University of Dayton; Medical School, University of Kentucky; Board Certified in Surgery and Plastic Surgery. Appointments: Assistant Professor of Plastic Surgery, Johns Hopkins; Assistant Professor of Surgery, University of Maryland; Professor and Chief, Division of Plastic Surgery, University of Kentucky. Publications: Contributor of 58 articles in journals, 2 monographs, 11 book chapters, 26 abstracts and 5 movies. Honours: Clinician of the Year, American Association of Plastic Surgeons, 1990. Memberships: AOA; AAPS; ACS; ASPRS' AAST; ASMS; ASA; BRGS; SHNS; PSEF; ABA; PAMAA; PSRC; ACPA; SESPRS; SSA; JHMSA; KSS; KMA; AAAM. Address: Division of Plastic Surgery, KY Clinic Ste K454, Lexington, KY 40536-0284, USA.

LUCHINS Daniel Jonathan, b. 1 July 1948, New York City, New York, USA. Psychiatrist. m. Catherine Meyer, 9 Aug 1988, 1 son, 1 daughter. Education: BSc, 1971, MOCM, 1973, Diploma in Psychiatry, 1978, McGill University, Canada. Appointments: Visiting Scientist, National Institute of Mental Health, 1977-81; Currently Associate Professor of Psychiatry, Chief of Extra-mural Adult Psychiatry, University of Chicago, Illinois. Education: Schizophrenia: Evidence for a subgroup with reversed cerebral asymmetry (co-author), 1979; Mechanism of altered water metabolism in polydipsic, hyponatremic psychiatric patients, 1988; What is appropriate health care for end stage dementia, 1993. Honours: A E Bennett Clinical Science Award, Society of Biological Psychiatry, 1981; President, Illinois Psychiatric Society, 1994. Memberships: American Psychiatric Association; American College of Neuropsychopharmcology; American Association of Geriatric Psychiatry; Society for Biological Psychiatry. Address: Department of Psychiatry, University of Chicago, 5841 S Maryland Avenue, Chicago, IL 60637, USA.

LUCHMANN Dietmar G, b. 4 Dec 1957, Luckau, Germany. Pyschotherapist; Hypnotist. m. Carmen Heerdegen, 28 May 1986. Education: DPsych summa cum laude, Humboldt University, Berlin, 1983; Certified and Approved Consultant in Clinical Hypnosis, Behaviour Therapy, Group Psychotherapy, others; Licensed Psychotherapist, Germany. Appointments: Research Assistant, Institute of Neurobiology and Brain Research, Academy of Sciences of the German Democratic Republic, Magdeburg, 1984-86; Lecturer, Institute of Medical Informatics and Biomathematics, Humboldt University Medical School, Berlin, 1987-89; Department of Psychology, Ruhr University, Bochum, Germany, 1989-91; Senior Psychotherapist, Department of Psychiatry, Eberhard Karls University Medical School, Tübingen, 1992-93; Director, Institute of Modern Psychological Therapy and Unconventional Medicine, Stuttgart, 1993-. Publication: Behavior Therapy Casebook (co-author), 1994. Memberships: American Group Psychotherapy Association; American Psychological Association; American Society of Clinical Hypnosis; German Society of Behaviour Therapy; International Society of Hypnosis; National Academy of Neuropsychology; New York Academy of Sciences. Hobbies: Literature; Yachting. Address: Institut für Moderne Psychologische Therapie und Naturheilkunde, Waldburgstrasse 122, D-70563 Stuttgart, Germany.

LUCIANO Anthony A, b. 22 June 1945, Italy. Physician. m. Mary, 22 Feb 1974, 2 s, 1 d. Education: BA, Chemistry, 1969; MD, 1973; Intern, 1973-74; Resident, 1974-77; Fellowship, Reproductive Endocrinology, 1977-79. Appointments: Assistant of Obstetrics and Gynaecology, University of Iowa, USA, 1979-83; Associate Professor of Obstetrics and Gynaecology, Tufts Univesity, 1983-86; Professor of Obstetrics and Gynaecology, University of Connecticut School of Medicine, 1990-; Director, Centre for Fertility and Reproductive Endocrinology. Publications: Infertility and Reproductive Medicine of North America, Sex Steroids, Associate Editor, 1993; Operative Gynecologic Video Laproscopy-Principles and Techniques, Co-author, 1994. Membership:

sAmerican Board of Obstetrics and Gynecology, 1980, Certification in Division of Reproductive Endocrinology, 1981; Charater Member, Society of Reproductive Surgeons, 1984; Membership, Society for Gynecologic Investigation, 1991; Membership, Endocrine Society. Secretary-Treasurer, 1989, Vice-President elect; American Board of Gynaecologic Laparoscopists, 1993. Hobbies: Tennis; Skiing; Cycling; Music. Address: Centre for Fertility and Reproductive Endocrinology, New Britain General Hospital, 100 Grand Street, New Britain, CT 06050, USA.

LUDLOW Christy L, b. 7 June 1944, Montreal, Canada. Speech Pathologist. m. Gregory Ludlow, 7 Sept 1968. Education: BSc, 1965, MSc, 1967, McGill University; PhD, New York University, USA, 1973. Appointments: Walter A Anderson Fellow, New York University, 1970-73; Project Manager, American Speech Language Hearing Association, 1974; Health Scientisit Administrator, NINCDS-NIH, 1974-83; Chief, Voice and Speech Section, NIDCD, 1985-. PUblications: Treatment of Speech Disorders with Botulinum Toxine, 1990; Genetic Aspects of Speech and Language Disorders, 1983. Honours: Editor's Award, Journal of Speech and Hearing Research, 1987; Honours of the Maryland Speech Language Hearing Association, 1995; Garnett Passe and Rodney Williams Visiting Lecturer, 1994; NIH Directors Award, 1977. Memberships: Society for Neuroscience; American Academy of Otolaryngology, Head and Neck Surgery; Association for Research in Otolaryngology; Acoustical Society of America; Corresponding Fellow, American Laryngological Association; Fellow, Speech-Language Hearing Association; Elected to membership, Academy of Aphasia. Hobby: Gardening. Address: Bldg 10 Room 5D38, National Institutes of Health, 9000 Rockville Pike, Bethesda, MD 20892, USA.

LUEPKER Russell Vincent, b. 10 Jan 1942, Chicago, Illinois, USA. Professor, Director. m. Ellen Thompson, 22 Dec 1966, 2 sons. Education: BA, History, Grinnell College, 1964; MS, Epidemiology, Harvard University, 1976. Appointments: Fellow in Medicine, Cardiology, Harvard University, 1974-76; Professor, Head, Division of Epidemiology. Publications incl: Pulmonary Intra-and Extravascular Fluid Volumes in Exercising Patients, 1969; Pulmonary Intra-and Extravascular Fluid Volumes in Resting Cardiac Patients, 1971; Left Atrial Pressure During Exercise in Hemodynamic Normals, 1971; Putting Medical Practice Guidelines into Practice: The Cholesterol Model, 1994; Apparently Coronary Heart Disease-Free Patients in the Coronary Care Unit: Characteristics, Medical Care and 1-Year Outcome, 1994. Honours: Alfred B Richie Prize for Medical Research, American College of Chest Physicians, 1970; National Research Service Award, NHLBI, 1975-77; Delta Omega; Honorary Public Health Society National Merit Award, 1988;Distinguished Alumni Award, Grinnell College, 1989. Memberships: American Heart Association; Society of Epidemiologic Research; American College of Cardiology; American College of Physicians; American Epidemiological Society. Address: University of Minnesota, School of Public Health, Division of Epidemiology, 1300 South Second Street, Suite 300, Minneapolis, MN 55454-1015, USA.

LUGLIO Joanne, b. 5 Oct 1958, Passaic, New Jersey, USA. Registered Nurse. Education: Associate Degree Nursing, Montclair State College. Appointments: Clara Maas Medical Centre; Emergency Room Technician, Belleville, New Jersey; Hackensack Medical centre; Registered Nurse, Hackensack Burn Unit; St Mary's Hospital; Meadowlands Medical Centre, Secaucus, New Jersey; Account Executive, Manager, Medibar Medical Industries, Philadelphia, Pennsylvania. Honours: Lyndhurst Board of Education for participation in drug awareness programme. Memberships: Education Committee, New Jersey Emergency Nurses Association. Hobbies: Boating; Jet skiing. Address: 720 Stuyvesant Avenue, Apt 2D, Lyndhurst, NJ 07071, USA.

LUI Fred Y H, b. 4 May 1954, China. Physician. Education: BS, Stanford University; MD, Stanford Medical School; FACP. Appointments: Assistant Clinical Professor, UCSF Medical School; Medical Director, Mills Peninsula Renal Services. Honour: National Kidney Foundation Research Fellowship, 1984-85. Memberships: CA Medical Association; International Society of Nephrology; International Society for Peritoneal Dialysis; Vice President and Board of Directors, Transpacific Dialysis Network. Hobbies: Golf; Chess. Address: 1828 El Camino Real 805, Burlingame, CA 94010, USA.

LUK Keith Dip-Kei, b. 6 Nov 1954, Hong Kong. Orthopaedic Surgeon. m. Katherine Mary O'Hoy, 17 Dec 1979, 2 daughters. Education: MBBS (HK), 1977; House Officer, Department of

Orthopaedic Surgery, 1977, House Officer, Department of Medicine, 1978, Medical and Health Officer, Department of Orthopaedic Surgery, 1978-80, General Surgery Training, 1980, University of Hong Kong; Honorary Clinical Assistant, Institute of Orthopaedics, University of London, Royal National Orthopaedic Hospital, Stanmore, 194; Hand Fellow, Princess Margaret Rose Orthopaedic Hospital, Edinburgh, 1984-85. Appointments: Lecturer, 1980-87, Senior Lecturer, 1987-92, Reader, 1992-, Department of Orthopaedic Surgery, University of Hong Kong; Medical Director, 1992-94, Honorary Hospital Chief Executive, 1994-, Duchess of Kent Children's Hospital. Publications: Co-author: The effect on the lumbosacral spine of long spinal fusion for idiopathic scoliosis - a 10-year follow-up, 1987; The comparative results of treatment in idiopathic thoracolumbar and lumbar scoliosis using the Harrington, Dwyer and Zielke instrumentations, 1989; Tuberculosis of the lumbosacral junction, 1990; A critical analysis of motion of the lumbar spine adjacent to an interbody fusion: a clinical radiological study and biomechanical cadaveric study, 1993; Intervertebral disc autografting, 1994; Lumbar spinal mobility following short anterior interbody fusion, 1995; Cord compression due to multiple disc herniations and intra-spinal cyst in Scheuermann's disease, 1995. Memberships: Western Pacific Orthopaedic Association; International Society for the Study of the Lumbar Spine; Royal Colleges of Surgeons, Edinburgh and Glasgow; Royal Australasian College of Surgeons. Address: Department of Orthopaedic Surgery, University of Hong Kong, Queen Mary Hospital, Pokfulam Road, Hong Kong.

LUKA Laszlo, b. 2 Oct 1932, Budapest, Hungary. Psychiatrist; Psychoanalyst. m. Elke Kühne, 5 May 1963, 2 sons. Education: MD, University of Zurich, Switzerland; Diploma in Psychology, University of Geneva. Appointments: Médecin Adjoint, Department of Psychiatry and Psychogeriatrics, University of Geneva, Switzerland; Currently Consultant to Department of Psychiatry, University of Geneva. Publications: Apropos de la prévention de la boulimia nervosa, 1988; La coût de l'alimentation et son influence sur le comportement humain, 1989; Pre-bulimic stages, 1989. Honours: 1st Prize for Prevention in Psychotherapy, Swiss Psychiatric Association, 1987. Memberships: Société Suisse de Psychiatrie et Pédopsychiatrie; Psychoanalyst, International Psychoanalytic Association. Address: 16 plateau de Champel, 1206 Geneva, Switzerland.

LUKYANOVA Elena, b. 13 Jan 1923, Chernigov, Ukraine. Pediatrist. m. 1944, 1 son. Education: MD, Kiev Medical Institute, 1949. Appointments: Scientific Researcher, 1949-63, Chief of Department, 1963, Deputy Director, 1967, Director, 1979-, Institute of Paediatrics, Obstetrics and Gynaecology. Publications: Contributor of 315 works, including 12 monographs; Rickets, 1970; Angiocholecystitis in the Children, 1975; Child's Gastroenterology, 1978; Pharmacotherapy in Pediatrics, 1979, 1993; Vitamins in Pediatrics, 1984; Hereditary Risk Factors of Chronic Digestive Organs Diseases in the Children, 1993; Morphological Changes in Placenta and Health State of Child under the Influence of Low Doses of Radiation, 1993. Honours: Order of the Red Banner of Labour, 1971; Order of October Revolution, 1982; Order of Great Patriotic war, 1st degree, 1985; State Prize Winner of the USSR, 1987; State Prize Winner of Ukraine, 1980. Memberships: European Paediatric Association; European Association of Perinatal Medicine; World Association of Perinatal Medicine; President, Paediatric Soceity of Ukraine; Academician: USSR Academy of Medical Sciences; Russian Academy of Medical Sciences; Ukrainian Academy of Medical Sciences; National Acadey of Ukraine. Hobbies: Classical and folk music. Address: 252002 Kiev, Gorkogo str 8, ap 26, Ukraine.

LUMBIGANON Pisake, b. 28 Aug 1953, Bangkok, Thailand. Physician. m. Pagakrong Teptanavatana, 4 Jan 1979, 1 s, 1 d. Education: MS, Clinical Epidemiology, University of Pennsylvania, USA; Diploma in Clinical Teaching, Johns Hopkins University; MD, Thai Board of Obstetrics and Gynaecology. Appointments: Lecturer, 1979; Assistant Professor, 1982; Associate Professor, 1987. Honours: Technical Consultant, Johns Hopkins Programme for International Education in Reproductive Health, 1991; Steering Committee, Epidemiological Task Force in Reproductive Health, 1992. Memberships: International Epidemiological Association; Supporter for Federation of International Gynaecology and Obstetrics. Hobbies: Jogging; Gardening. Address: 6/3 Klanggmuang Road, Khon Kaen 4000, Thailand.

LUMER Rodney Hugh, b. 19 Sep 1929, Canterbury, Kent, England, Obstetrician and Gynaecologist. m. Susi oppenheimer, 7 feb 1960, 1 son, 1 daughter. Education: MBBS, Sydney University, Australia, 1954; MRCOG, 1959; FRCOG, 1974; FAGO, 1974; FRACOG, 1979.

Appointments: Consultant Obstetrician, Mater Misericordia Mothers Hospital, 19162-78; Visiting Obstetrician and Gynaecologist Royal Brisbane Women's Hospital, 1989-91; Visiting Obstetrician and Gynaecologist, North west Private Hospital, Brisbane, 1984-91; Retired. Membership: Australia Medical Association. Hobbies: Stage Actor; President, Playlab, 1974-78; Editor, Playlab Press, 1978-. Address: 7 Pender Street, The Gap, Queensland 4061, Australia.

LUMSDEN John, b. 27 Apr 1949, Kampala, Uganda. Neurophysiologist. m. Annette Skan, 1 Sep 1978, 1 s, 1 d. Education: BSc, Honours, Biological Sciences, Psychology, Edinburgh University, 1972; PhD, Queen's University of Belfast, Ireland, 1978. Career: Scientist, Neurophysiology Department, Belfast City Hospital; Research Fellow, Queen's University of Belfast; Currently, Head of Neurophysiology Department, Broadmoor Hospital. Publications: Epilepsy and Violence in Mentally Abnormal Offenders in a Maximum Security Hospital, in Journal of Epilepsy, 1994; Activation Sequence of Discrete Brain Areas during Cognitive Processes, in EEG Journal, 1994. Memberships: British Society for Clinical Neurophysiology; British Psychophysiology Society. Hobbies: Swimming; Trout Fishing; Walking. Address: 4 Purcell Road, Crowthorne, Berkshire, RG11 6QN, England.

LUNDBERG Per Olov Magnus, b. 12 Apr 1931, Vänersborg, Sweden. Professor. m. Kerstie Sjöberg, 4 Dec 1960, 2 d. Education: MD, 1957, D Med Sci (PhD) Antomy, 1960, Uppsala. Appointments: Research Assistant, Assistant Professor, Department of Anatomy, 1950-60, Junior Physician,. Assistant Professor, Department of Neurology, 1958-74, Uppsala University; Professor, Head of Department of Neurology, University Hospital, Uppsala. Publications: Corticohypothalmic Connections in the Rabbit, 1960; Textbook of Sexology, 1994; Contributor of numerous professional articles. Honours: Member of Uppsala County Council, 1974-85; Board of Director, Ulleråker Hospital, 1967-78; Medical Adviser, National Board of Health and Welfare, Sweden, 1975-; Advisory Board, Medical Product Agency, Sweden, 1981-. Memberships: Former President, International Academy of Sex Research; Founding Member, Nordic Association for Clinical Sexology; Founding and Honorary Member, Former President, Scandinavian Migraine Society. Address: Tallbacksvägen 19, S-756 45 Uppsala, Sweden.

LUNDIN Tom Karl Vilhelm, b. 12 Dec 1944, Stockholm, Sweden. Psychiatrist. m. Ann-Mari Lundin, 16 Mar 1968, 1 s, 2 d. Education: MD, 1971, PhD, 1982, Uppsala University. Career: Trauma Related Consultations, Sweden, 1988-91; Consultant in Psychiatry, Linköping University, 1991-93; Currently, Consultant and Associate Professor, Department of Psychology and Psychiatry, Karolinska Hospital, Stockholm. Publications include: Co-author, Stress Reactions Among Swedish Health Care Personnel in UNIFIL, South Lebanon 1982-84, in Stress Medicine, 1989; Bereavement in late adolescence - After a major fire disaster, in Bereavement Care, volume 9, 1990; The impact of an earthquake on rescue workers, in Journal of Traumatic Stress, 1993; Co-author, Swedish UN-soldiers in Cyprus, UNFICYP, in Psychotherapy and Psychosomatics, 1992. Memberships: Board, European and International Societies for Traumatic Stress Studies. Address: Department of Clinical Neuroscience, Karolinska Hospital, S-17176 Stockholm, Sweden.

LUO Chuan-Qi, b. 2 Mar 1938, Beijing, China. Ophthalmologist. m. Lo Fu-Sun, 25 Dec 1966, 1 son. Education: MD, Beijing Medical University, 1960; MHS, Johns Hopkins University, USA, 1984. Appointments: Resident, Visiting Doctor, Lecturer, Department of Ophthalmology, Shanghai Medical University, 1960-81; Associate professor, Professor, Department of Ophthalmology, Shanghai Medical University, 1981-94. Publications: Practical Ophthalmology, Co-author, 1984; Ophthalmology, Co-author, 1987; Conjunctival Tuberculosis, 1964; Idiopathic Pre-Retinal Membrane, 1987; Acute Retinal Necrosis, 1991. Honour: 2nd Class prize of Science and Technology, Beijing. Memberships: China Society of Ophthalmology. Address: Eye and ENT Hospital, Shanghai Medical University, 83 Fen-Yang Road, Shanghai 200031, China.

LUO Ding Hui, b. 10 May 1946, Guangzhou, China. Traditional Chinese Medicine Doctor. m. Stanley Takyu Lau, 29 September 1981, 1 son. Education: BA, Guangzhou Traditional Chinese Medical College, 1970. Appointments: Physician, The Hospital of Traditional Chinese Medicine, Guangdong; Paediatrician, The Hospital of Traditional Chinese Medicine, Guangdong; Practitioner of Acupuncture and Moxibustion, The Hospital of Traditional Chinese Medicine, Guangdong;

Consultant Paediatrician. Publications: Co-author, Traditional Chinese Internal Medicines; Co-author, Essential Guidance on Baby and Child Care. Honours: Social Science Research Prize, 1983. Memberships: Chairperson, Association of Traditional Chinese Medicine in England; Honorable Chairperson, Alumni of Guangzhou College of Traditional Chinese Medicine in England. Hobbies: Travel; Drama; Writing. Address: 15 Little Newport Street, London WC2H 7JJ, England.

LUO Guangxiang, b. 12 Feb 1961, Nong-Hui, Hunan, China. Molecular Virologist; Research Investigator. m. Shan-Hong Wang, 5 Mar 1988, 2 daughters. Education: MD, Hunan Medical University, 1983. Appointments: Research Fellow, Beijing Municipal Center for Health and Epidemic Control, 1986-88; Visiting Research Scientist, Fox Chase Cancer Center, Philadelphia, Pennsylvania, USA, 1988-90; Senior Associate, Mount Sinai Medical Center, New York City, 1990-92; Research Investigator, Virology Department, Bristol-Myers Squibb Pharmaceutical Research Institute, Wallingford, Connecticut, 1992-. Publications: First author: Specificities Involved in the Initiation of Retroviral Plus-Strand DNA; A Specific Base Transition Occurs on Replicating Hepatitis Delta Virus RNA; Template Switching by Reverse Transcriptase during DNA Synthesis, 1990; The Polyadenylation Signal of Influenza Virus RNA Involves a Stretch of Uridines Followed by the RNA Duplex of the Panhandle Structure, 1991; Genetic Analysis of Influenza Virus, 1992; Mechanism Attenuation of a Chimeric Influenza A/B Transfectant Virus, 1992. Honours: Scientific and Technological Progress Prize for new discoveries in the study of postnatal transmission and prevention of HBV, Beijing Council for Science and Technology, 1988. Memberships: American Society for Microbiology; American Association for the Advancement of Science. Hobbies: Running; Reading; Basketball; Tennis. Address: Virology Department, Bristol-Myers Squibb Pharmaceutical Research Institute, 5 Research Parkway, Wallingford, CT 06492, USA.

LUO Li-hong, b. 5 Mar 1936, Sichuan, China. Medical Teacher. m. Muo Linghang, 8 Feb 1963, 2 sons, 1 daughter. Education: BSc, Medical Science, Department of Clinical Medicine, Kunming Medical College, 1960; Training courses, Science and Technical Management, China Science and Technical Training Centre. Appointments: Lecturer, Deputy Director, Director, Department of Medical Education, 1st Teaching Hospital, Kunming Medical College, 1978-84; Currently Professor, Vice-President, Kunming Medical College. Publications: A study of the two different administrative systems within the same hospital in China, 1989; More than 10 papers in journals such as: China Hospital Management; Health Science and Management. Memberships: Deputy Director, Yunnan Health Management and Administration Association; Chairman, Coun, Yunnan Nutrition Association; Council Member, China Association of Medical Sciences, Yunnan Branch; Council Member, Yunnan Association of Recovery Medicine; Council Member, Yunnan Red Cross Association. Hobbies: Reading; Football; Music. Address: Kunming Medical College, Kunming 650031, China.

LUO Wei-Wu, b. China. Clinical Psychiatrist. Appointments: Psychiatric Clinical Education and Research, more than 30 years; Currently: Vice-Director, Fuzhou Neuropsychiatric Hospital; Chief Physician, Professor of Psychiatry, Director, Founder, Fuzhou Child Mental Health Institute; Director, Psychiatry Department, Fujian Medical College. Publications: More than 40 research papers including: The Parents' Influence on their Children's Mental Health; Family Rehabilitative Measures for Children; Trauma and Child Mental Health; Antipsychotic drugs in the treatment of Adolescents with Schizophrenia. Honours: Numerous for research. Memberships: China Psychiatry Society; Chairman, Fujian Branch, China Psychiatry Society; Chairman, Fujian Rehabilitation Research Association for Mentally Disabled; Editorial Boards: Chinese Journal of Neurology and Psychiatry; 5 other specialist journals. Address: Fuzhou Child Mental Health Institute, Fuzhou, Fujian, China.

LUO Zhao-zhuang, b. 28 Dec 1936, Tianjin, China. Epidemiologist. Education: MB. Appointments: Attending Physician, 1979-85; Vice Chief Physician, 1985-92; Chief Physician in Epidemiology, 1992-. Publications: Study on Geographic Epidemiology of Epidemic Hemorrhagic Fever (EHF) in China, 1985. Honours: 2nd Award of Scientific Progress of China, 1991. Memberships: Infectious Disease Committee, Military National Public Health. Address: Health and Anti-Epidemic Station of Anhui Province, 125# Wuhu Road, Hefei 230061, China.

LUO Zhen-Lin, b. 14 Oct 1927, Jiangxi, China. Physician; Professor. m. Chen Yong Huo, 4 June 1946, 3 daughters, 1 son. Education: Graduated, Jiangxi Medical College, 1951. Appointments include: Currently Chief Physician and Professor of Medicine. Publications: Major books: Gastrointestinal hemorrhage, 1987; Portal hypertension, 1992; Learned articles: Endotoxemia in liver diseases, 1982; Hepatoencephalopathy, 1985; Co-editor: The etiology of portal hypertension; The Liver and Thyroid, 1986; Noncirrhotic intrahepatic portal hypertension, 1987; The causes and prognosis of liver cirrhosis, 1988; Treatment of hepatic tuberculosis, 1990; Senile liver and its influence on drug therapy, 1990; Treatment of biliary diseases in elderly patients, 1990; Effects of salvia miltiorrhiza bunge complex in the treatment of portal hypertension, 1991; Liver disease complicated with endotoxemia, 1994; Portal hypertension, 1994. Honours: Excelllent Article, International Congress of Liver Diseases, 1986. Memberships: Chinese Medical Association; Editorial Committee, Chinese Journal of Clinical Hepatology; Committeeman, International Research and Exchange Center of Liver Disease. Address: 8-3-8, 4th Area, Xinxiqiao, Nanchang, Jiangxi, China.

LUO Zhengxiang, b. 6 Sep 1927, China. Thoraci-Cardiovascular Surgeon. m. Dorothy Fok, 8 Apr 1950, 3 daughters. Education: MD, Medical College of China Western Union University. Appointments: Associate Professor of Surgery; Professor of Surgery. Publications: Surgery of Cardiothorax, 2nd Edition; Surgical Technic of Cardiothorax, 2nd Edition. Membership: Vice President, Chinese Thoraci Cardiovascular Surgery Association. Address: No 91 Apt 601 Dong Chang Road, Guangzhou 510080, China.

LURAIN John Robert III, b. 27 Oct 1946, Princeton, Illinois, USA. Gynaecologic Oncologist. m. Nell Snavely, 14 June 1969, 2 d. Education: BA, Oberlin College, 1968; MD, University of North Carolina, 1972; Residency, Obstetrics and Gynaecology, University of Pittsburgh Magee-Women's Hospital, 1972-75; Fellowship in Gynaecologic Oncology, Roswell Park Cancer Institute, 1977-79; FACOG. Appointments: Assistant Professor, 1979-83, Associate Professor, 1983-89, Professor, 1989-, Department of Obstetrics Gynaecology, Northwestern University Medical School. Publications: Contributor of over 90 professional articles in scientific journals and books, 1979-. Honours: Magnus P Urnes Resident Teaching Award, 1986-87, 1993-94; American Cancer Society Junior Faculty Clinical Fellowship, 1980-83. Memberships: Society of Gynaecologic Oncologists; American Society of Clinical Oncology; American College of Obstetricians and Gynaecologists; Central Association of Onstetricians and Gynaecologists; American Society of Colposcopy and Cervical Pathology; Chicago Gynaecological Society. Address: Prentice Women's Hospital, 333 E Superior Street, Chicago, IL 60611, USA.

LUSCOMBE Faye A, b. 16 Oct 1939, USA. Epidemiology. m. Robert Lyscombe, 27 Nov 1971. Education: MPH; DrPH. Appointments: Hospital Epidemiologist, St Joseph/Mercy Hospital, Ann Arbor; Public Health Consultant, Michigan Department of Public Health; Research Epidemiologist & Head Epidemiologist, Manager & Health Economist, Healthcare Economics. Honours: Validictorian, Underwood High, 1957; BS cum laude, 1961; Phi Kappa Phi, 1978. Memberships: International Society of Qol Rsearch; International Society for Pharmacoepidemiology; Durg Information Association; American Public Health Association. Hobbies: Sailing; Snorkeling; Music. Address: 2619 Pine Ridge Road, Kalamazoo, MI 49083, USA.

LUSHER Jeanne Marie, b. 9 June 1935, Toledo, Ohio, USA. Physician; Professor. Education: BS summa cum laude, University of Cincinnati College of Arts and Sciences, 1956; MD, University of Cincinnati College of Medicine, 1960. Appointments: Instructor in Paediatrics, Washington University School of Medicine, St Louis, Missouri, 1965-66; Assistant Professor of Paediatrics, 1968-71, Associate Professor of Paediatrics, 1971-74, Professor of Paediatrics, 1974-, currently Marion I Barnhart Haemostasis Research Professor, Wayne State University School of Medicine; Director, Department of Haemtology-Oncology, Children's Hospital of Michigan, Detroit. Publications: Bleeding Disorders of Infancy and Childhood, 1981; Sickle Cell, 1974, 3rd edition, 1980; Hemophilia and Von Willebrand Disease in the 1990's, 1991; The Science and Politics of Women's Health in America, 1995; 160 refereed scientific articles; 35 book chapters; Teaching monographs. Honours: Outstanding Research Award, National Hemophilia Foundation; Named Distinguished Faculty Fellow, Wayne State University, 1987; Lawrence Weiner Award for Outstanding Non-Alumnus Faculty, Wayne State University School of Medicine,

1990; Distinguished Alumnus Award, University of Cincinnati, 1991; Chairman, Medical and Scientific Advisory Council, National Hemophilia Foundation; Member, 4 editorial boards. Memberships: Society for Pediatric Research; American Society of Hematology; Officer, International Society of Thrombosis and Hemostasis; American Society of Pediatric Hematology-Oncology. Hobbies: Wildlife conservation; Travel; Gardening; Humane society activities. Address: 3901 Beaubien Boulevard, Detroit, MI 48201, USA.

LYNCH Alan Russell, b. 29 Dec 1936, London, England. Orthodontist. m. E Margaret Lynch, 29 Dec 1959. Education: BDS, University of London; FDS; RCS (Eng); DOrth; RCS (Eng); Fellow, International College of Dentists; Liveryman, Worshipful Company of Apothecaries. Appointments: House Surgeon, Queen Victoria Hospital, East Grinstead, 1962; Assistentenarzt, Katharinen Hospital, Stuttgart, Germany, 1968; Registrar in Orthodontics, Eastman Dental Hospital, USA, 1972; Currently in private practice. Memberships: British Orthodontic Association; American Association of Orthodontists; European Orthodontic Society. Hobbies: Sailing; Skiing; Music; Cats; Gardening; Forestry.

LYNN Paul, b. 7 Dec 1942, Louisiana, USA. Medical Doctor. m. Bonnie Woodburn, 24 Nov 1989, 1 son, 1 daughter. Education: BS, Louisiana University, 1964; MD, Louisiana University, 1967. Appointments: Owner, Medical Director, San Francisco Preventive Medical Group. Publications: Numerous magazine articles. Memberships: Board Director, American Academy of Advancement in Medicine. Hobbies: Study of Pre Hostoric Cultures. Address: 345 West Portland Avenue, San Francisco, CA 94127, USA.

LYUBIMOV Dmitry Victorovich, b. 6 Feb 1949, Perm, Russia. Physicist. m. 14 Mar 1972, 1 son. Education: Diploma, Perm State University, 1971; PhD, Institute for Problems in Mechanics, Russian Academy of Sciences, Moscow, 1979. Appointments: Assistant Professor, 1974-89, Department Head, 1989-, Theoretical Physics Department, Perm State University, Perm. Publications: Physica D9, 1983; Sov Sci Rev C Math Phys Rev, 8, 1989; Eur J Mech B/Fluids, 10, 1991; Physics D62, 1993. Honours: Grant, Russian Fund of Fundamental Investigation, 1993-94; Grant, International Science Foundation, 1994-95. Address: Theoretical Physics Department, Perm State University, 15 Bukirev Str, Perm 614005, Russia.

M

MA Banyin, b. 26 June 1925, Zhe-jiang, China. Doctor, Professor. m. Dazeng Wang, 7 Oct 1951, 1 son, 1 daughter. Education: Shanghai Medical University, 1949. Appointments: Professor of Pediatrics, Shanghai Medical University (SMU); Consultant, Hematology Branch of Chinese Pediatric Association; Member, Examination & Approval Committee of New Drugs of Shanghai Health Bureau; Vice Editor, Journal of Clinical Pediatrics; Committeeman, Editorial Board, Chinese Journal of Pediatrical & Medical Encyclopedia-Comprehensive Clinical Medicine. Publications: Practical Handbook of Drugs, 1994; Co-author, papers in hematology in 10 books, 1964-91; 11 papers in iron deficiency anemia publised in different journals, 1983-87; 8 papers in acute leukemia publised in different journals, 1982-94. Honours: Science & Technology Award, Shanghai, 1985, 1992; Great Success in 40 Years, National Educational Committee of China, 1990; Excellent Educational Worker of SMU, 1991. Membership: Chinese Pediatric Assocaition. Hobbies: Music; Learning. Address: Children's Hospital of Shanghai Medical University, 183 Feng-lin Road, Shanghai 200032, China.

MA Changjun, b. 18 Dec 1925, Jiangsu, China. Researcher. m. Chen Yuancha, 1 May 1953, 2 daughters. Education: BSc, College of Biology, Zhejiang University, 1949. Appointments: Assistant of Biology, China Medical University; Lecturer in Histology and Embryology, Shanghai First Medical College; Associate Professor of Histology and Embryology, Chongqing Medical College; Currently Professor of Histology, Embryology and Cytogenetics, Sichuan Family Planning Research Institute, Chengdu. Publications: Andrology, book, 1988; Articles: The development of pigment layer of Chinese foetus eye, 1973; Effects of diagnostic ultrasound in SCE frequencies of the amniotic fluid cells, 1987; Simple and effective technique for Chromosome Preparation from chorionic villi samples, 1991. Honours: 3rd Class Science and Technology Awards, Sichuan Province Government, 1978, 1984, 1986, 1990, 1991; Ministry Science and Technology Awards, 2nd Class, 1978, 1994, 3rd Class, 1986, 1990; Winner, State Council Special Subsidy, 1992-. Memberships: Committee Member, China Better Birth Science Association, Associate Chairman of Sichuan Sub-Association; China Family Planning Association. Hobby: Beijing Opera. Address: Sichuan Family Planning Research Institute, No 15, Section 4, People's South Road, Chengdu 610041, China.

MA Chen-Yuan, b. 16 July 1936, Chaoyang, Guangdong, China. Medical Doctor. m. 1 Oct 1965, 1 son, 1 daughter. Education: Graduated, Medical Treatment Department, Xian Medical University, 1961. Appointments include: Vice-Chief, Scientific Research Section, 1984-93, Chief Doctor, 1993-, Guangzhou Medical College; Chairman, Guangzhou Society of General Practice, 1989-92. Publications: Doctor's orders of the first visit in emergency internal medicine, 1987; Doctor's orders of the first visit in general practice, 1993. Honours: Awarded Patent Certificate for Invention, Chinese Patent Office, 1992; Registration Certificate of Key Scientific and Technological Research in Guangdong. Memberships: Chinese Society of General Practice; Chairman, Guangdong Medical Association, Branch of General Practice. Hobbies: Running; Reading. Address: Guangzhou Medical College, Dongfengxi Road, Guangzhou 510182, China.

MA Fujin, b. 6 Nov 1932, Dalian City, Liaoning Province, China. Medical Professor. m. 1 Oct 1960, 2 sons. Education: BS, Chinese Medical University, 1959. Appointments: Doctor, Teacher, Associate Professor, Chinese University of Medicine; Currently Head, Chest Surgery Dpeartment, General Hospital, Shenyang Military District. Publications: The Base and Clinic of Lung Cancer (co-author); Articles in Journal of Chinese Surgery: Surgical Treatment of Benign Esophageal Constriction; Surgical Treatment of Tracheal Tumor; Analysis of Surgical Curative Effect for the Lung Cancer Invading Carina; Surgical Treatment of the Lung Cancer Invading Heart and Main Vessel; Tracheal Reconstruction with Forearm Skin Flap and Titanium Stent; Surgical Treatment of Esophageal Cancer. Honours: Model Teacher; 2nd and 3rd Class Awards of Science and Technology, Liaoning Province; 3rd Class Award of Military Science and Technology. Memberships: Vice-Chairman, Liaoning Branch, Chinese Medical Society of Chest Surgery; Vice-Chairman, Liaoning Branch, Chinese Anti-Cancer Association of Lung Cancer; Chief Editor, editorial boards: Journal of Chinese Practice Surgery; Journal of Liaoning Medicine; Journal of Shenyang Military Medicine. Hobbies: Football; Games. Address: No 85 Wen Hua Road, Shen He District, Shenyang, China.

MA Gui Ying, b. 16 May 1936, Kaifeng, Henan, China. Ultrosonic Diagnosis Doctor. m. Bai Wen-Fu, 3 Sept 1965, 1 daughter. Education: College. Appointment: Head, Ultrasonic Diagnosis, People's Hospital of Henan. Publications: Over 40 articles in various professional journals. Memberships: Vice President, Chinese Ultrasonic Diagnostics Association, Henan Branch; Chairman, CUMEA; Chinese Abdomen Ultrosonic Diagnostic Society; Chinese Ultrasonic Cardiomotitity Diagnostics Society. Address: 7 Wei Wu Road, Zhengzhou, Henan, China.

MA Li, b. 15 Sept 1944, Lintan County, Gansu Province, China. Medical Doctor. m. Wu Guifang, 1 Oct 1974, 1 son, 1 daughter. Education: BA, Lanzhou Medical University, 1967; MD, 2nd People's Liberation Army Medical University, 1982. Appointments: Lecturer in Internal Medicine, 1983, Professor of Gastroenterology, Director, Department of Gastroenterology, 1989-, Tutor for Master's degree Candidates, 1992-, 2nd Affiliated Hospital, Lanzhou Medical College; Chairman, Society for Digestive Endoscopy, Gansu Province, 1993-. Publications: Value of SIgA in gastric cancer screening, 1984; Study on the relation between SIgA content and acidity of gastric juice, 1985; Gastroscopy plus cytology for diagnosis of gastric cancer, 1986; Value of diagnosis of gastric cancer with IgG in gastric juice, 1987; Study on detected SIgA in gastric juice with ELISA and SRID for clinical value, 1987; Value of endoscopy and cytology in 128 cases of esophageal and cardiac cancer, 1992; The value of diagnosis for gastric cancer or non-cancer depending on trace elements in hair in gastric diseases with mathematical model of electric computer, 1993; Gastroscopy and biopsy plus rapid cytology screening diagnosis for 14860 cases of upper gastrointestinal disease, 1993; Application of fibergastroscopy plus Wright-Gimesa rapid dye staining in mass screening of gastric diseases on the spot - report on 7656 cases, 1994. Honours: 8 Awards for Advanced Scientific Results, Provincial and Health Branch Scientific Committee, 1984-94. Memberships: Society of Digestive Endoscopy; Society of Gastroenterology; Society for Medicine, China; Provincial Consultative Conference, Gansu. Hobbies: Table-tennis; Philosophy. Address: Department of Gastroenterology, The Second Affiliated Hospital of Lanzhou Medical University, Lanzhou 730030, Gansu, China.

MA Sanke, b. 19 May 1936, Linxi, Shandong, China. Doctor. m. Yarong Wan, 19 October 1966, 1 son, 1 daughter. Education: Graduated, Dalian Medical College, 1964. Appointments: Director of Internal Medicine, Dandong City People's Hospital, 1964-80; Head of Dandong 1980-. Publications: Liaoning Blood Transfusive Technology Operating Rules, 1992; Clinic Used Blood Transfusive Technology, 1994; Clinic Used Blood Transfusion of Compsition, 1994. Memberships: Director, Transfusive Society and Technical Advisory Society of Liaoning, China. Hobbies: Football. Address: No 27 Chun Wu Road, Dandong Blood Center Station, Dandong 118002, China.

MA Shu-Kun, b. 29 Jan 1931, Tianjin, China. Professor of Cardiology and Cardioangiology. m. Wang Chuan, 20 June 1959, 3 daughters. Education: MD, Peking Union Medical College, 1957. Appointments: Associate Professor; Professor of Cardiology and Cardioangiology, 4th Military Medical University, Xian, 1989-; Member, Editorial Board: Chinese Journal of Pacemaker Technology; Chinese Doctors' Advanced Journal. Publications: Editor-in-chief: Co-author: Rheumatism of heart, 1987; Congenital heart disease, 1987; Pacemaker, 1992; Cardiac irrhythmia, 1993; 53 medical articles in various Chinese medical journals, 1980-. Memberships: Chinese Biomedical Engineering Association; Chinese Cardioelectricity and Electrocardial Vector Association; Chinese Medical Association; Shaanxi Biomedical Engineering Association. Hobbies: Singing; Reading literature; Tennis. Address: Room 14, Building 28, Xi-jing Hospital, Xian 710032, Shaanxi, China.

MA Yongsheng, b. 19 Oct 1961, China. Geologist. m. Zhong Li, 15 July 1987, 1 daughter. Education: BA, Wuhai College of Geology, 1984; Master's degree, China University of Geosciences, 1987; PhD, China Academy of Geology, 1990. Appointments: Head, Research Group of Sedimentology and Reservoirs, Director of Synthetic Research Department, Bureau of Tarim Petroleum Exploration and Development. Education: Carbonate Facies and Deposition Environments of Devonian in Yunnan, 1989; Isochronal study on late Cambrian of North China Platform, 1992; Carbon-isotope..., in Science in China (co-author), 1993. Honours: Engaged as Tutor for Master's degree students, Tongji University, Shanghai, 1993, Petroleum University, Shandong, 1994. Memberships: Association of Chinese Scientists; Association of Chinese Geologists; Association of Chinese Petroleum Geologists. Hobbies:

Running; Tennis; Swimming. Address: Petroleum Geological Research Department, Xueyuanlu 20, PO Box 910, Beijing 100083, China.

MA Zhi Cai, b. 6 Apr 1944, Tangshan, Hebei, China. Doctor; President. m. 6 Dec 1969, 1 d. Education: University. Appointment: Associate Professor, President, Beijing Chengjian Hospital of Traditional Chinese and Western Medicine. Publications: Collate the Classical with the Vernacular Chinese of Ben Cao Gang Mu; Interpretations of the Qian Jin Yi Fang; Analysis of the classical prescriptions, in Guangming Chinese Medicine Magazine, 1989; Analysis on disease case of treated experience by Professor Liu Duzhou, in Chinese Journal of TCM and Pharmacy, 1989; Treated experience by Dan Zhi Xiao Yao Prescription, in TCM Magazine, 1990. Honours: Featured on TV programme, Beijingers, Beijing TV, 1991; 2nd Prize, State Scientific Progress Award, 1992. Memberships: Committee, Zhongjing Theory, Chinese Association of Traditional Chinese Medicine; Ancient Traditional Chinese Medicine Prose Research Council, Chinese Association of Traditional Chinese Medicine; Permanent Member, Beijing Sino-Japanese Folk Literature and Art Exchange Promotion Council. Hobby: Writing. Address: Beijing Chengjian Hospital of Traditional Chinese and Western Medicine, 17 Daliushu Road, Haidian District, Beijing 100081, China.

MA CHUNG Ho Kei, b. 11 Oct 1934, Hong Kong. Obstetrician & Gynaecologist. Education: MBBS; FRCOG. Appointment: Head & Professor of Obstetrics & Gynaecology, University Hong Kong. Publications: Numerous professional publications in scientific journals. Memberships: Several Associations and Societies. Address: Department of Obstetrics & Gynaecology, Queen Mary Hospital, Hong Kong.

MacBETH Robert Alexander, b. 26 Aug 1920, Edmonton, Alberta, Canada. Professor Emeritus Surgery. m. Monique Elizabeth Filliol, 10 Aug 1949, 4 d. Education: BA, 1942, MD, 1944, University of Alberta; MSc, 1947, Diploma in Surgery, 1952, McGill University; Fellow, Royal College of Physicians and Surgeons of Canada, 1952. Appointments: Professor and Chairman, Department of Surgery, University of Alberta, 1960-75; Associate Dean and Professor of Surgery, Dalhousie University, 1975-77; CEO Canadian Cancer Society and National Cancer Institute of Canada, 1977-85; Executive Director, Hannah Institute for the History of Medicine, 1987-91; Currently retired, Professor Emeritus Surgery. Publictions: About 75 publications related to surgery, cancer research, history of medicine and public education about cancer. Honours: Moshier Memorial Medal, University of Alberta, 1944; Nuffield Overseas Travelling Fellowship, 1950-51; Visiting Professor, American School for Classical Studies, Athens, Greece, 1972; Visiting Professor, Pasteur Institute, Paris, France, 1972-73; Corresponding Fellow, Polish Academy of Surgeons, 1972; Outstanding Achievement Award, 1985, Honorary DSc, 1988, University of Alberta; Award of Merit, Union Internationale Contre le Cancer, 1986. Memberships include: Academy of Medicine, Toronto; American Association for History of Medicine; American College of Surgeons; Canadian Society for History of Medicine; International Surgical Group; Royal College of Physicians and Surgeons; International Union Against Cancer; Medical Research Council of Canada. Hobbies include: Voluntary Activities for International Union Against Cancer. Address: 1 Concorde Place, Apt 1506, Don Mills, Ontario, M3C 3K6, Canada.

MacCORQUODALE Donald Willard, b. 12 Nov 1921, San Angelo, TX, USA. Physician. m. Joyce Bloomfield, 24 Mar 1954, 2 d. Education: MD, University of Denver; MSPH, University of North Carolina; Diploma, Statistics, Harvard School of Public Health; BA, Chemistry, University of Denver; Fellow, American College of Preventive Medicine. Appointments: US Navy Medical Corps, 1946-48; Private practice, 1950-64; US Agency for International Development, 1964-82; Civilian, US Army Medical Corps, 1982-86; District Health Director, Virginia Department of Health, 1986-91; Consultant, Public Health, 1991-. Publications include: Analysis of a Famoly Planning Program in Guatemala, 1970; Sex Differentials Among Family Planning Physicians in the Philippines, 1973; The Attitude of Philippine Family Planning Physicians Toward Sterilization, 1974; Education and Fertility in the Dominican Republic, 1978; Primary Health Care in the Dominican republic: A Study of Health Worker Effectiveness, 1982; Some Observations on Military Civic Action and Community Development in Latin America. Honours: Mid-Career Fellowship, Ford Foundation, 1968; Superior Honour Award, USAID, 1969; Special Public Health Award, Virginia Public Health Association, 1991. Memberships: American College of Epidemiology; Society for Epidemiologic Research; International epidemiological Society; American College of Preventive Medicine; American Association for the Advancement of Science.

Hobby: Photography. Address: 4200 Massachusetts Avenue NW, Washington DC, USA.

MacGREGOR J Elizabeth, b. 12 Jan 1920, Glasgow, Scotland. Pathologist. m. Alastair G MacGregor, 13 Oct 1943, 3 sons, 1 daughter. Education: BSc; MBChB; MD; FRCPath; FRCOG. Appointments: Senior Lecturer, Aberdeen University; Honorary Consultant, Grampian Health Board; Retired. Publications: Contributor of numerous professional articles in medical journals. Honour: OBE, 1986. Memberships: College of Pathologists; College of Obstetricians and Gynaecologists; Honorary Vice President, British Society for Clinical Cytology. Hobbies: Sailing; Gardening. Address: "Ardruighe", Clachan, Ilse of Sell, By Oban, Argyll PA34 4QZ, Scotland.

MACHIN Geoffrey Allan, b. 2 May 1940, Carshalton, England. Medicine. m. Ann Hailes, 5 Sep 1964, 2 s. Education: BA; BM; BCh, Oxford University, 1966; FRCPath, UK; FRCP(C); PhD, London University, UK, 1973. Career: Pediatric Pathologist, University of Calgary, Alberta, Canada; Peuiatric Pathologist, Victoria General Hospital, Victoria, BC, Canada; Currently, Professor, Pediatric Pathology, University of Alberta, Canada. Publications: Hydrops fetalis, in American Journal of Med Genet, 1989; Co-author, WT1 Gene Mutations in Denys-Drash Syndrome, in Nature Genetics, 1992; Janiceps Conjoined Twins: Computerized 3-dimensional reconstruction, in March of Dimes, 1993. Memberships: Society for Pediatric Pathology; International Society for Twin Studies. Hobbies: Music; Theatre; Gardening. Address: MacKenzie Health Sciences Centre, University of Alberta, Room 5B4 08 Edmonton, Alberta, Canada, T6G 2R7.

MacKAY Eric Vincent, b. 2 Nov 1924, Melbourne, Australia. Professor Emeritus. m. Gaenor Gregory, 1 s, 1 d. Education: MBBS, DGO, MGO, Melbourne University. Career includes: University of Melbourne, University of California, Los Angeles, Edinburgh University, University of Queensland; Currently, Emeritus Professor, University of Queensland. Publications: Illustrated Textbook of Gynaecology; Obstetrics and The Newborn; The Pregnant Woman and Her Baby; About 150 publications in learned journals. Honour: Member of Order of Australia, 1992. Memberships: FRCOG; FRACOG; FRCS(Ed); F Amer COG(Hon). Hobbies: Reading; Horse Breeding. Address: Lot 2, Upper Camp Mountain Road, Camp Mountain, Queensland 4520, Australia.

MacKAY Gilbert Ferguson, b. 13 Dec 1944, Glasgow, Scotland. Teacher; Psychologist. m. Isobel Spence, 29 Mar 1969, 1 s, 1 d. Education: MA, Dip Ed Psych, PhD, Glasgow University; Chartered Psychologist. Appointments: Teacher, Glasgow, 1967-68; Sole Psychologist, Shetland, 1969-73; Area Psychologist, Chief Psychologist, Whitefield, Lancashire, 1973-75; Senior Psychologist, Banff and Buchan, 1976-78; Research Fellow, Glasgow University, 1978-82; Senior Psychologist, Renfrewshire, 1982-84; Jordanhill College, Faculty of Education, University of Strathclyde, 1984-. Publications: Early Communicative Skills, Co-author, 1989; Supporting Pupils with Physical Disorders, 1993. Honours: Associate Fellow, British Psychological Society. Memberships: British Psychological Society; National Association for Special Educational Needs; Scottish Spina Bifida Association. Hobbies: Running; Cycling; Playing Bagpipes, Violin and Viola. Address: 9 Glebe Lane, Newton Mearns, Renfrewshire G77 6DS, Scotland.

MacKENZIE Donald Bothwell, b. 14 July 1946, Aberdeen, Scotland. Psychologist. m. Eileen Thow, 8 Aug 1969, 3 sons. Education: MA; PGCE; MEd. Appointments: Psychologist, Lindsey County Council Health Department; Psychologist, Lincolnshire County Council Education Department; Currently Director (Studies), Linkage Trust. Honours: AFBPsS, 1977; Chartered Psychologist, 1990; Fellow, Royal Society of Arts, 1993. Memberships: British Psychological Society; Royal Society of Arts. Hobbies: Art; Flyfishing; Filling in forms. Address: 18 Eastfield Road, Louth, Lincs LN11 7AR, England.

MacQUEEN Dawn Jillian, b. 14 Apr 1951, Birmingham, England. Chartered Psychologist. m. John Stewart MacQueen, 4 Sept 1987, 1 daughter. Education: BA, Interdisciplinary Studies, Open University, 1977; BSc (Hons), Upper 2nd Division, Behavioural Science, University of Aston in Birmingham, 1980. Appointments: Personal Assistant to Managing Director, Barnes Group, 1976-80; Hybrid Manager, BL Technology, 1980-82; Senior Research Associate, HUSAT, Loughborough University, 1983-86; Principal Officer, Office of the Chief Scientist, National Health Service, 1986-87; Senior Consultant, Doctus, 1987-88; Managing Consultant, Andersen Consulting, 1988-90;

Freelance Consultant, Sole Practitioner, Corporate Psychologist, 1990-. Publications: Exceptional Children - A Study in Psycho-Linguistic Development, 1979; Implications of Primary Health Data Capture, 1988; Evolving Cultures for New Technologies, 1989. Honours: Distinguished in Economics, Psychology, Philosophy of Science, Economic History, 1977. Memberships include: Associate Fellow, British Psychological Society; Institute of Management Consultants; British Computer Society. Hobbies: Gardening; Genealogy; Countryside pursuits; Local studies. Address: Storrage Grange, Storrage Lane, Alvechurch, Worcs B48 7EP, England.

MACRIS Nicholas Theodore, b. 27 oct 1931, New York City, USA. Physician. m. Efstratia, 21 Aug 1961, 1 s, 2 d. Education: AB; MD. Appointments: Clinical Professor of Medicine, Co-Director, Allergy Immunology Training Programme, Cornell University Medical College; Chief, Allergy Immunology, Lenox Hill Hospital, New York City. Publications include: The Effect of Ficin on the Agglutination of Human red Blood Cells, Co-author, 1955; COntrolled Picrylation of Protein, Co-author, 1966; Effect of Hypothalamic Lesions on Immediate Hypersensitivity, Co-author, 1975; The Evaluation of Immunologic Deficiencies in the Community Hospital, 1978; Arsenic Associated Angioimmunoblastic Lymphadenopathy, Co-author, 1985. Address: Lenox Hill Hospital, 100 East 77th Street, New York, NY 10021, USA.

MADDERN Bruce Robert, b. 1 Nov 1954, New Haven, Connecticut, USA. Paediatric Otolaryngologist. m. Barbara Galli, 18 Aug 1978, 2 s, 1 d. Education: MD; Board Certified Otolaryngologist; Fellowship trained Otolaryngologist; Fellow, American Society of Laser Medicine and Surgery; Fellow, American Academy of Pediatrics. Appointments: Internship, Residency, Tulane University; Instructor, University of Pittsburgh; Cllinical Assistant Professor, Mercer University; Courtesy Assistant Professor, University of Florida; Chief, Pediatric Otolaryngology. Publications include: Laboratory Manual of Cell Structure and Function, Co-author, 1978; Snoring and Obstructive Sleep Apnea Syndrome, 1989; Obstructive Sleep Apnea Syndrome in Sickle Cell Disease, Co-author, 1989; Subglottic Stenosis in Infants and Children, 1990; Hearing Loss in Children, 1993; Voice Disorders in Children, 1994. Memberships include: American Medical Association; Southern medical Association; American Academy of Otolaryngology, Head and Neck Surgery; Duval COunty Medical Society; American Association for the Advancement of Science; Association for Research in Otolaryngology; Society for Ear, Nose, Throat Advances in Children; Northeast Florida Pediatric Society; FLorida Society of Otolaryngology, Head and Neck Surgery. Hobbies: Golf; Fishing; Sailing; Hunting. Address: Nemours Children's Clinic, 807 Nira Street, Jacksonville, FL 32207, USA.

MADORSKY Julie Geiger, b. 1945, Hungary. Psychiatrist. m. Arthur Madorsky, 17 Sept 1978, 3 sons, 2 daughters. Education: MD, Medical College of Pennsylvania, 1969. Appointments: Medical Director, Center for Vrodynamics & Neurology, Casa Colina Hospital for Rehabilitative Medicine, California; Clinical Professor, Physical Medicine & Rehabilitation, University of California, Irvine; Clinical Professor, Rehabilitation Medicine, College of Osteopathic Medicine of the Pacific; Clinical Assistant Professor, Psychiatry & Biobehavioral Studies, University of California, Los Angeles. Publications: Rehabilitation Aspects of Human Sexuality, 1983; Wheelchair Sports Medicine, 1984; The Patient and the Professional: Partners in Sickness and in Health, 1989. Honours: California Physician of the Year, 1987; US Physician of the Year, 1988. Memberships incl: American Academy of Physical Medicine & Rehabilitation; American Medical Association; American Spinal Injury Association; California Medical Association; International Medical Society of Paraplegia.

MADSEN Kirsten Marie, b. 20 Dec 1941, Vinderup, Denmark. Associate Professor of Medicine. Education: MD; PhD. Appointments: Adjunct Lecturer, Institute of Anatomy, University of Aarhus, Denmark; Associate Professor of Medicine, University of Florida, USA. Publications: Effects of Chronic Mercury Exposure and Ageing on the Lysosomal System of the Rat Proximal Tubule, 1982; Structural Functional Relationships along the Distal Nephron, 1986; Structure and Function of the Renal Tubule and Interstitium, 1994. Memberships: American Society of Nephrology; International Society of Nephrology; International Society of Stereology; Microscopy Society of America; American Heart Association. Address: Division of Nephrology, PO Box 100224, University of Florida, Gainesville, FL 32610, USA.

MADURA James Anthony, b. 10 June 1938, Campbell, Ohio, USA. Surgeon; Educator. m. Loretta Jayne Sovak, 8 Aug 1959, 1 s, 2 d. Education: AB, COlgate University; MD, Western Reserve University. Appointments: Assistant Professor of Surgery. 1971-76, Associate professor of Surgery, 1976-81, Professor of Surgery, Indiana University School of Medicine. Publications: Contributor of over 70 scientific articles and book chapters, 1970-94. Memberships: Fellow, American College Surgeons; Central Surgery Association; Midwest Surgical Association; Western Surgical Society; ASPEN; International Biliary Association; SSAT. Hobbies: Photography; Travel; Computers; Cooking. Address: Department of Surgery, 545 Barnhill Drive EM 205, Indianapolis, IN 46202-5125, USA.

MAEDA Kenji, b. 1 Apr 1939, Tsu City, Mie Prefecture, Japan. Professor of Internal Medicine. m. Mayuko Matsunaga, 30 Mar 1975, 2 sons. Education: MD, 1965, PhD, 1978, Nagoya University. Appointments: Associate Professor, 1979-90, Professor of Internal Medicine, Director, 1990-, Nagoya University Branch Hospital. Publications: -Microglobulin modified with advanced glycation endproducts is a major component of hemodialysis-associated amyloidosis, 1993; Effective hemodiafiltration: new methods (editor), 1994. Honours: Japan Kidney Foundation Award, 1993. Memberships: New York Academy of Sciences; American Association for the Advancement of Science; American Society of Nephrology. Address: C-1514 1-2 chome Sunadabashi, Higashi-ku, Nagoya 461, Japan.

MAGNAVITA Jeffrey Joseph, b. 13 Oct 1953, Philadelphia, USA. Psychologist. m. Anne Gardner, 14 Sept 1991, 2 daughters. Education: BA, Temple University; MA, Villanova University; PhD, University Connecticut. Appointments: elmcrest Psychiatric Institute, 1982-84; Glastonbury Psychological Associates, PC. Publications: The treatment of passive-aggressive personality disorder, Part I, 1993; The evolution of short-term dynamic psychotherapy: Treatment of the future?, 1993; The treatment of passive-aggressive personality disorder: Intensive short-term dynamic psychotherapy, Part II, 1993; Psychotherapy update: Research and practice. Psychotherapy: Psychology's forgotten calling, 1993; Psychotherapy update: Research and practice. Psychotherapy: Still the safest and most powerful treatment, 1993; Psychotherapy update: Research and practice: How short is short-term psychotherapy?, 1993; The process of working through and outcome: The treatment of the passive-aggressive personality disorder, Part III, 1994. Memberships: American Psychological Association; Society for Psychotherapy Researchers. Address: Glastonbury Medical Arts Center, 300 Hebron Ave Suite 215, Glastonbury, CT 06033, USA.

MAGOUN George Lester, b. 27 Nov 1952, Albany, GA, USA. Emergency Room Physician. m. Kimberly Crawford, 27 Oct 1990, 4 s, 1 d. Education: BA, Electrical Engineering; MA, Solid State Physics; Associate Civil Engineer; MD. Appointment: Emergency Room Physician. Memberships: AMA; American Academy of Family Practice; Erie County Medical Society. Hobby: Fishing. Address: 680 Wayne Street, Corry, PA 16407, USA.

MAHMOOD Tahir Ahmed, b. 7 Oct 1953, Pakistan. Obstetrician and Gynaecologist. m. Aasia Bashir, 15 Apr 1985, 2 sons. Education: BSc, MBBS, King Edward Medical College, Lahore; MRCOG, 1984; MD (Aberdeen),1990; MRCP (Ireland), 1993; MFFP (RCOG), 1993; FRCP (Ireland), 1994. Appointments: Junior Representative, Scottish Hospital Staffing Review Group, Department of Health and Social Services, UK, 1988; Currently: Consultant Obstetrician and Gynaecologist, Fife Health Board, Scotland; Clinical Senior Lecturer, Obstetrics, Gynaecology, University of Aberdeen. Publications: Author or co-author, papers on pathophysiology of endometriosis, termination of pregnancy, management of labour, medical audit, such as: Maternal height, shoe size and outcome of labour in white primagravidas: a prospective anthropometric study, 1988; A study of the incidence, the trend and the management of patients with ectopic pregnancies in the Scottish Highlands (1976-1987), 1989; The impact of treatment on the natural history of endometriosis, 1990; Menstrual symptomatology in patients with endometriosis, 1991; Peritoneal fluid volume and sex steroids in the preovulatory period in mild endometriosis, 1991; Breech delivery and epidural analgesia, 1992; Role of prostaglandins in the management of prelabour rupture of membranes at term, 1992; The epidemiology of Endometriosis, 1994. Honours: Ethicon Travelling Fund Fellow, Royal College of Obstetricians and Gynaecologists. Memberships: Council, Scottish Executive Council; Royal College of Obstetricians and Gynaecologists; Senatus Academicus, Aberdeen University; British and American Fertility Societies; European Association for Gynaecologists and Obstetricians; European Society for Human Reproduction and Embryology. Hobbies: Walking; Reading history; Squash. Address: 71 Strathallan Drive, Kirkcaldy, Fife, Scotland.

MAHONY Patrick Joseph, b. 11 June 1932, New York City, New York, USA. Professor of Literature; Psychoanalyst. m. Pierrette Senay, 18 July 1954, 2 sons. Education: MA; PhD; Diploma in Psychoanalysis, Canadian Psychoanalytic Society. Appointments: Fulbright Professor, Université d' Aix-en-Provence, France, 1962-63; Professor, Université de Montréal, Canada, 1963-; Medical Scientist, Department of Psychiatry, McGill University, 1979-88. Publications: 5 books, with translations into Portuguese, Japanese, German, Italian, French. Honours: Fulbright Scholar, Sorbonne, 1961-62; Canada Council Fellowship Grants, 1970-71, 1983-84; American Council of Learned Societies, 1973; Miguel Prados Prize, Canadian Psychoanalytic Society, 1985; Holder of Biennial André Ballard Chair, Columbia Psychoanalytic Society, 1989-90; Rockefeller Resident Fellow, Rockefeller Foundation, Bellagio, Italy, 1989; Recipient: Annual International Schmidt Prize in Applied Psychoanalysis; Canadian Killam Award, 1993-94, 1994-95; Mary Sigourney International Award, 1993. Address: 1297 St Viateur, Outremont, Quebec Province, Canada H2V 1Z2.

MAIR Naval, b. 28 Dec 1967, Hampton, Middlesex, England. Osteopath. Education: Diplomate of Osteopathy, British School of Osteopathy, London 1991. Appointments: Principal Osteopath, Battersea Osteopaths; Tutorial Faculty, British School of Osteopathy, London; British College of Naturopathy and Osteopathy, London. Memberships: Register of Osteopaths. Hobbies: Martial Arts; Running; Tennis; Badminton. Address 2b Ashness Road, Battersea, London SW11 6RY, England.

MAJEED Shahul, b. 9 July 1941, Sri Lanka. Medicine. 1 son. Education: MBBS, Ceylon; DRCOG, England; MRCOG, England; FRCOG, England; FACOG, USA; MD, USA. Appointments: Residency MMC, Savannah; Registrar, Obstetrics, St James & Weir Hospital; Private Medical Practice. Memberships: ACOG; AMA; RCOG. Hobby: Boating. Address: 1012 Spring Creek Road, Chattanooga, TN 37412, USA.

MAJTENYI Catherine, b. 3 June 1929, Budapest. Neuropathologist. m. Kornel Lukacs, 7 Apr 1951, 1 son, 1 daughter. Education: Board Certification, Psychiatry, 1957; Neurology, 1963; Certificate of Neuropathology, 1979. Appointments: National Institute of Psychiatry & Neurology, Budapest. Publications: Beitrage Zur Pathologie Der Subakuten Spongiosen Encephalopathie, 1965; Creutzfeldt Jakob Disease, A Neuropathological Study, 1987; Co-author, Cholingergic Fiber Alterations in Alzheimer's Disease, 1992. Memberships: Hungarian Association of Neurologists & Psychiatrists; Hungarian Association of Neuropathologists; International Association of Neuropathology; Belgian Association of Neuropathology. American Association of Neuropathologists. Honours: Santha Award, 1991; Schaffer Award, 1993. Hobbies: Planting Flowers. Address: National Institute of Psychiatry & Neurology, 1281 Budapest, Hungary.

MÄKIPERNAA Anne Marja-Tertiu, b. 30 Nov 1953, Kauhava, Finland. Specialist in Paediatric Haematology and Oncology. Education: Specialist in General Medicine, 1983, in Paediatrics, 1985, in Paediatric Haematological Oncology, 1987. Appointments: Specialist in Paediatric Haematology and Oncology, Tampere University Hospital. Publications: Life After Cure, dissertation, 1990. Memberships: NOPHO; SIOP. Address: Tampere University Hospital, PO Box 2000, 33521 Tampere, Finland.

MAKOWSKI Edgar Leonard, b. 27 Oct 1927, Milwaukee, Wisconsin, USA. Professor Emeritus. m. Patricia M Nock, 1 Nov 1952, 4 sons, 2 daughters. Education: BS; MD. Appointments: Associate Professor, University of Minnesota, 1966; Professor, 1969-88, Chairman, Department of Obstetrics and Gynaecology, 1976-88, Professor Emeritus, 1993-, University of Colorado. Publications: 126 scientific publications. Honours: Special National Institutes of Health Fellow at Yale University, 1963-64; Chairman, Human Embryology and Development, National Institutes of Health Study Section, 1981-82. Memberships: Society for Gynecologic Investigations; Perinatal Research Society; American Gynecology and Obstetrics Society; American College of Obstetricians and Gynecologists. Hobby: Golfing. Address: 1900 E Girard Place, Unit 408, Englewood, CO 80110, USA.

MALHOTRA Rajwant, b. 8 Feb 1948, Narangwal, India. Physician. m. Yash Pal Malhotra, 22 June 1970, 2 daughters. Education: MD, Government Medical College, Rohtak, Punjab University, India, 1970. Appointments: Assistant Professor of Pathology, UMASS Medical School, 1988-93; Associate Professor of Pathology, Medicina & Surgery, UMASS Medical School, Worcester, USA; Professor of Pathology, Medicine & Surgery, UMMC, Worcester, USA; Director Dermatopathology; Associate Director, Surgical Pathology. Publications: The angiogenic properties of psoriatic skin associate with the epidermis not the dermis, 1989; A Malignant gastric leiomyoblastoma presenting as an infected pseudoycst of the pancreas, 1988; A Cronkhite-Canada Syndrome associated with colon carcinoma and adenomatous changes in C-C polyps, 1988; Cyclosporine-ischemia effects in the rat kidney: Biochemical and morphological observation, 1988; Cyclosporine-induced testicular dysfunction: A separation of the nephrotoxic component and an assessment of a 60-day recovery period, 1988; Cyclosporine: Its effects on testicular function and fertility in the prepubertal rat, 1990; Eosinophilia myalgia syndrome: Clinical, histologic, electrophysiologic, pathophysiologic and differential diagnosis considerations, 1990; A new model of nephrolithiasis involving tubular dysfunction/injury, 1991. Honours: Research Fellowship, Yale University School of Medicine, USA. Memberships: American and Canadian Academy of Pathology; Fellow, College of American Pathologists; American Society of Dermatopathology; New England Society of Pathology. Hobbies: Travel. Address: University of Massachusetts Medical School, 55 Lake Avenue, North Worcester, MA 01655, USA.

MALIN Howard Gerald, b. 2 Dec 1941, Providence, Rhode Island, USA. Podiatrist; Journalist; Educator; National and International Lecturer. Education: AB, Biology, University of Rhode Island, 1964; Certificate, Cytotechnology, Our Lady of Fatima Hospital-Institute of Pathology, North Providence, 1965; Certificate, D'Études Françaises, Université de Poitiers, Touraine, France, 1965; SH (Cyt), Université de Tours, France, 1967; MA, Brigham Young University, USA, 1969; BSc, 1969, DPM, 1972, California College of Podiatric Medicine; MSc, Pepperdine University, 1978; Various other certificates. Appointments: Private Practice, Podiatric Medicine and Surgery, Brooklyn, New York, 1974-77; Hospital Staff, Prospect Hospital, New York, 1974-77; Chief Podiatry Service, David Grant USAF Medical Centre, Travis Air Force Base, 1974-77; Instructor, Advanced Cardiac Life Support, 1978-85, Hospital Staff, Podiatrist, 1977-80, David Grant USAF Medical Centre; Editorial Board, Archives of Podiatric Medicine and Foot Surgery, 1978-81, David Grant USAF Medical Centre, 1979-80; Chief, Podiatric Medicine, VA Medical Centre, Martinsburg, 1980-; Hospital Staff, VA Medical Centre, Martinsburg, 1980-; Reserve Staff Podiatrist, Malcolm Grow USAF Medical Centre, Andrews Air Force Base, 1980-. Publications include: An English Translation of Marc-Antoine Muret's Play Entitled Julius Caesar, 1969; The History of the Neuro-Myo-Vascular Glomus and of the Glomus Tumor: A Review of the Literature. Honours: Recipient of numerous honours and awards. Memberships include: American Podiatry Student Association; American Public Health Association; Academy of Podiatric Medicine. Address: 210 Shenandoah Road, Apt 2D, Martinsburg, WV 25401, USA.

MALINDZAK George S, b. 3 Jan 1933. Health Science Administrator. m. Marianne Beamer Malindzak, 27 June 1959, 3 sons, 1 daughter. Education: AB, cum laude, Western Reserve University, Cleveland, 1953-56; MSc, Ohio University, Columbus, 1957-58; PhD, Ohio University, Columbus, 1958-61. Appointments include: Instructor, Associate Professor, Department of Physiology, Bruman Gray School of Medicine, 1962-1973; Professor & Chairman, Department of Physiology, Northeastern Ohio Universities College of Medicine, 1976-85; Professor, Head, Department of Biomedical Engineering, Louisiana Tech University, 1985-88; Health Science Administrator, National Institutes of Health, National Institute of Environmental Health Sciences, Research Triangle Park, North Carolina. Publications include: Coronary Artery Hypercontractility following Myocaridal Wchemia; Echocadiographic Ventricular Function in the Rehabilitating Alcoholic; Personal Monitors for Exposure and Health Effects; Coronary Vasodilatim and Adrenergic Toxicity; Numerical Analysis of Indicator - Concentration Curves. Memberships include: American Physiological Society; Sigma Xi; American Heart Association; American Society for Pharmacology & Experimental Therpeutics, Biomedical Engineering Society. Address: National Institute of Environmental Health Sciences, PO Box 12233, Research Triangle Park, NC 27709, USA.

MALKINSON Frederick David, b. 26 Feb 1924, Hartford, Connecticut, USA. Physician. m. Una, 15 June 1979, 4 s, 1 d. Education:

Harvard College, 1945; DMD, 1947, MD, 1949, Harvard University. Appointments: Instructor, Assistant Professor, Associate Professor, Department of Medicine, Dermatology, University of Chicago, 1954-68; Professor, Department Medicine and Dermatology, University of Illinois, 1968-71; Professor, Chairman, Department of Dermatology, Rush Medical College, 1968-92; Clark W Finnerud MD Professor of Dermatology, Rush-Presbyterian-St Luke's Medical Centre, Chicago, 1981-. Publications include: Studies on the Percutaneous Absorption of C14 Labelled Steroids by Use of the Gas-Flow Cell, 1958; reduction in Rate of hairgrowth in Mice as an Indicator of Exposure to Chronic Low Dosage Ionizing Radiation, Co-author, 1964; Ionizing Radiation Induces Early Sustained Increases in Collagen Biosynthesis: A 48 Week Study in Mouse Skin and Fibroblast Cultures, co-author, 1988; Prostaglandins Protect Against Murine Hair Injury Produced by Ionizing Radiation or Doxorubicin, 1993; Contributor of numerous papers and book chapters. Memberships include: American Academy of Dermatology, Past Vice-President; Society of Investigative Dermatology, Past Vice-President; Chicago Dermatologicl Society, Past President; Fulzberger Institutefor Dermatologic Education, Past President and President again; Dermatology Foundation, Past President; AAAS; American Dermatologic Association. Address: Rush-Presbyterian-St Luke's Medical Centre, 1653 West Congress Parkway, Chicago, IL 60612, USA.

MALLARD John Rowland, b. 14 Jan 1927, England. Medical Physicist. m. Fiona Mackenzie Lawrance, 6 Jun 1958, 1 s, 1 d. Education: University College, Nottingham; BSc, London, 1947; PhD, 1952, DSc, 1972, University of Nottingham; FRSE; F Inst P; FIEE; FRC Path. Appointments: Head, Department of Physics, Hammersmith Hospital, London, 1953-64; Reader in Biophysics, St Thomas Hospital, London, 1964-65; Professor of Medical Physics, University of Aberdeen, 1965-92; Currently, Professor Emeritus, Department of Bio-Medical Physics and Bio-Engineering, University of Aberdeen. Publications: Over 200 papers on medical imaging, including pioneer papers in nuclear medicine and magnetic resonance imaging, 1953-92. Honours: Barclay Prize, 1972, 1991; Silvanus Thompson Medal, 1981; Royal Society Wellcome Gold Medal, 1984; Hevesy Medal, 1984; Royal Society Mullard Medal, 1989; OBE, 1992; Honorary DSc, University of Hull, 1994. Memberships: Honorary Fellow, Institute of Physical Sciences in Medicine; Fellow, Royal Academy of Engineering; Founder President, International Union of Physical and Engineering Sciences in Medicine. Hobbies: Do It Yourself; Jewellery Making; Music; Theatre. Address: 121 Anderson Drive, Aberdeen, AB2 6BG, Scotland.

MALLETTE Lawrence Edward, b. 9 Jan 1942, Wilkinsberg, Pennsylvania, USA. Medical Researcher and Educator. m. 1964, div. 2 s, 1 d. Education: BA, Magna Cum Laude, 1963, PhD, 1968, MD, 1970, Vanderbilt University. Appointments include: Intern, 1970-71, Resident, 1971-72, Internal Medicine, Massachusetts General Hospital, Boston; Clinical Associate, National Institutes of Health, Bethesda, Maryland, 1972-74; Assistant Professor of Medicine, Baylor College of Medicine, Houston, Texas, 1974-84; Staff Endocrinologist, 1974-75, Clinical Investigator, 1975-78, Staff Endocrinologist, 1978-91, Acting Chief of Endocrinology, Houston VA Medical Centre; Associate Professor of Medicine, Baylor College of Medicine, Houston, Texas. Publications: Contributor of 95 research and clinical articles in peer-reviewed journals and 22 textbook chapters on calcium metabolism. Honours: Phi Beta Kappa, 1962; Alpha Omega Alpha, 1970; Fellow, American College of Physicians, 1979; Fellow, American College of Nutrition, 1980. Memberships: New York Academy of Science; American College of Physicians; American College of Nutrition; Endocrine Society; American Federation for Clinical Research; American Association for the Advancement of Science; American Society for Bone and Mineral Research; The Paget's Foundation Scientific Advisory Board. Hobbies: Playing traditional Irish music on flute and pennywhistle and Renaissance and Medieval music on recorder. Address: Medical Service 111E, VA Medical Centre, 2002 Holcombe Boulevard, Houston, TX 77030, USA.

MALLORY Susan Bayliss, b. 12 May 1948. Paediatric Dermatologist. m. George Barron Mallory Jr, 17 may 1975, 2 d. Education: BA, University of Texas at Austin, 1970; MD, University of Texas Medical Branch, Galveston, 1974. Appointments: Assistant Professor of Dermatology and Paediatrics, University of Pittsburgh, 1981-84; Associate Professor of Dermatology and Paediatrics, University of Arkansas, 1984-90; Associate Professor of Medicine and Paediatrics, Washington University School of Medicine, St Louis, Missouri. Publications: Dictionary of Dermatologic Syndromes, 1994;

Topical Lidocaine for Anesthesia, Co-author, 1993. Memberships: American Academy of Dermatology; American Academy of Paediatrics; Society for Paediatric Dermatology. Hobbies: Gardening; Sewing. Address: St Louis Children's Hospital, 1 Children's Place, St Louis, MO 63110, USA.

MALLYA Purandar K, b. 7 Feb 1940, India. Psychiatrist. m. Anurdha Mallya, 15 May 1965, 1 son, 1 daughter. Education: MD; Board Certified in Psychiatry; Diplomate, American College of Utilisation Review and Quality Assurance. Appointments: Programme Director, 1976-78, Associate Medical Director, 1978-82, Rockland Psychiatric Centre, Orangeburg, New York; Currently Senior Psychiatrist. Honours: Physician Recognition Award, American Medical Association, 1971. Hobbies: Raquetball; Aerobics. Address: 32 Choate, Irvine, CA 92720, USA.

MALVERN John, b. 3 Oct 1937, Liverpool, England. Obstetrics and Gynaecology. m. Katharine Malvern, 1 s, 2 d. Education: BSc, first class honours; MB; BS, London; LRCP; FRCS(E); FRCOG. Appointments: Consultant Obstetrician and Gynaecologist, Queen Charlotte and Chezea Hospital; Honorary Senior Lecturer, Charing Cross and Hammersmith Hospital, London. Publications: Contributions to various professional journals inclng: Journal of Gynaecology, Textbook of Obstetrics. Memberships include: Officer of RCOG; Honorary Treasurer of Royal College. Hobbies: Wine Tasting; Travel. Address: 84 Harley Street, London, W1, England.

MANCINI G B John, b. 20 Sept 1952, Toronto, Ontario, Canada. Professor of Medicine. m. Alexandra Skinner, 7 June 1975, 1 son, 2 daughters. Education: MD; FRCP (C); FACC. Appointments: Clinical Assistant Professor, University of California, San Diego, USA; Professor, Chief of Cardiology Section (VA), University of Michigan; Currently Eric W Hamber Professor and Head, Department of Medicine, University of British Columbia, Vancouver, Canada. Publication: Cardiac Applications of Digital Angiography, 1989. Honours: Jerome W Conn Prize in Research, University of Michigan. Hobbies: Guitar; Tennis; Skiing. Address: Koerner Pavillion (S-169), 2211 Wesbrook Mall, Vancouver, British Columbia, Canada V6T 1Z3.

MANDEL H(arold) George, b. 6 June 1924, Berlin, Germany. Pharmacologist. m. Marianne Klein, 25 July 1953, 2 d. Education: BS, 1944, PhD, 1949, Yale University, USA. Appointments include: Laboratory Instructor in Chemistry, Yale University, 1942-44, 1947-49; Research Associate, department of Pharmacology, 1949-50, Assistant Research Professor, 1950-52, Associate Professor of Pharmacology, 1952-58, Professor, 1958-, Chairman, department of Pharmacology, 1960-, George Washington University. Publications: Contributor of numerous publications on professional and scientific subjects. Honours include: Advanced Commonwealth Fund Fellow, Molteno Institue, Cambridge University, England, 1956; John J Abel (Eli Lilly) Award, 1958; Commonwealth Fund Fellow, University of Auckland, New Zealand and University of Medical Sciences, Bangkok, Thailand, 1964; Elanor Roosevelt International Fellow, Chester Beatty Institute, London, 1970-71; Burroughs Wellcome Research Travel Grant, Carshalton, England, 1988; Honorary Research Fellow, Department of Biochemistry and Molecular Biology, University College, London, 1993. Memberships include: AAAS; American Chemical Society; American Society Biochemistry and Molecular Biology; American Society Pharmacology and Experimental Therapeutics, President, 1973-74; American Association Cancer Research; National Caucus of Basic Biomedical Science Chairs, Chairman, 1991-; Sigma Xi; Alpha Omega Alpha. Address: 4956 Sentinel Drive, Bethesda MD 20816-3562, USA.

MANDER John, b. 5 Aug 1924, Sheffield, England. Registered Medical Practitioner. m. Mary Clifford, 24 July 1957, 2 s, 2 d. Education: VRD; MA; MB; BChir; FRCS; FRCOG. Appointments: Registrar, Obstetrics & Gynaecology, St Thomas; Hospital; Senior Registrar, Queen Charlotte's and Chelsea Hospital; Consultant Gynaecologist & Obstetrician, York; Now Retired. Hobbies: Sailing; Lawn Tennis; Walking; Music. Address: 99 Station Road, Upper Poppleton, York YO2 6PZ.

MANN Jillian Rose, b. 29 Apr 1939, Cheltenham, England. Medical Practitioner. Education: Medical Student, St Thomas Hospital, London, 1957-62; Postgraduate Training in London and Birmingham, England; MB; BS, London, 1962; DCH, 1964; MRCP, London, 1966; FRCP, London, 1980. Appointments: Casualty Officer, House Physician, Children's Department; House Physician and Medical Registrar, St

Thomas Hospital, London; House Physician and Registrar, Hospital for Sick Children, Great Ormond Street, London; Registrar and Senior Registrar, Children's Hospital, Birmingham; Consultant Paediatrician, Selly Oak Hospital, Birmingham. Currently, Consultant Paediatric Oncologist, Children's Hospital, Birmingham. Publications include: Over 180 original articles, letters, chapters in books, published abstracts, mainly concerning paediatric oncology and haematology, 1969-94. Memberships: BMA; BPA; British Society of Haematology; CCSG, UK; SIOP; ESPHI; CCSG, US; American Society of Paediatric Haematology and Oncology. Hobbies: Music; Country Pursuits; Mountain Walking; Travel. Address: Children's Hospital, Ladywood Middleway, Birmingham, England.

MANN Richard E, b. 25 Dec 1931, Muncie, Indiana, USA. Psychiatrist. m. Barbara I Irwin, 27 June 1954, 3 sons, 2 daughters. Education: BS; MD; Residency in Psychiatry. Appointments: General Psychiatrist, US Navy (US Medical Corps Recruit Depot), Parris Island, South Carolina; Consultant, US Naval Hospital, Beaufort, South Carolina; Consultant, US Marine Air Station, Beaufort; Consultant, Chatham County Child Guidance Clinic, Savannah, Georgia; Private practice in Psychiatry, Muncie, Indiana; Currently Medical Director, Lindenview Regional Behavioral Center, Fort Wayne, Indiana. Memberships: American Psychiatric Association; American Medical Association; American Academy of Clinical Psychiatrists; American Association of Geriatric Psychiatrists. Hobbies: Fishing; Travel; Learning. Address: Parkview Memorial Hospital, Lindenview Regional Behavioral Center, 1909 Carew Street, Fort Wayne, INa 46805, USA.

MANN Robert W, b. 6 Oct 1924, Brooklyn, New York, USA. Engineer. m. Margaret Florencourt, 4 Sep 1950, 1 son, 1 daughter. Education: SB, 1950, SM, 1951, ScD, 1957, Massachusetts Institute of Technology. Appointments include: Research Engineer, Dynamic Analysis and Control Laboratory, 1951-53, Assistant Professor, 1953-58, Associate Professor, 1958-63, Mechanical Engineering, Professor of Mechanical Engineering, 1963-70, Germeshausen Professor, 1970-72, Professor of Engineering, 1972-74, Whitaker Professor of Biomedical Engineering, 1974-92, Whitaker Professor Emeritus of Biomedical Engineering and Senior Lecturer, 1992-, Massachusetts Institute of Technology. Publications: Author or Co-author of over 330 publications; Holder of 4 patents. Honours include: Tau Beta Pi, 1949; Pi Tau Sigma, 1949; Sigma Xi, 1950; Gold Medal, American Society of Mechanical Engineers, 1977; Bronze Beaver Award, Massachusetts Institute of Technology Alumni Association, 1977; Sigma Xi National lecturer, 1979-81; James R Killian Jr Faculty Achievement Award, MIT, 1983; Fellow, American Academy of Arts and Sciences, 1972; Fellow, IEEE, 1979; Fellow, American Association for the Advancement of Science, 1982; Fellow, American Society of Mechanical Engineers, 1985; Fellow American Institute of Medical & Biological Engineering, 1991. Memberships include: Corporation Member, Mt Auburn Hospital; Corporation Member, Perkins School for the Blind; Trustee, President, National Braille Press Trust; Research Associate in Orthopaedic Surgery, Children's Hospital Medical Centre; Consultant, Engineering Science, Massachusetts General Hospital; Charter Member, Director, Biomedical Engineering Society; National Academy of Sciences; National Academy of Engineering; Institute of Medicine at NAS. Address: Mechanical Engineering Department, Massachusetts Institute of Technology, 77 Massachusetts Avenue, Room 3-137D, Cambridge, MA 02139, USA.

MANNING Everard Alexander Dermot Niall Beresford, b. 20 Feb 1949, Belfast, Northern Ireland. Consultant. m. Ming Choo, 1 Aug 1981, 1 son, 1 daughter. Education: MB, BS, London; Fellow, Royal College of Obstetricians and Gynaecologists. Appointments: Registrar, Obstetrics and Gynaecology, Middlesex Hospital, London, England; Senior Registrar, Obstetrics and Gynaecology, Middlesex and University College Hospitals, London, and Central Middlesex Hospital, London; Currently Consultant Obstetrician and Gynaecologist. Publications: Co-author: Outpatient Excisional Management of Cervical Intraepithelial Neoplasia, 1993; A Comparison between Loop Diathermy Conisation and Cold Knife Conisation of Cervical Dysplasia, 1993. Honours: Honorary Senior Clinical Lecturer, St Mary's Hospital Medical School, University of London, 1987-. Memberships include: Royal Society of Medicine; British Medical Association; British Society for Colposcopy and Cervical Pathology. Hobbies: Photography; Jewellery and Gemmology. Address: Ch'i-Lin, 72 Corringway, Ealing, London W5 3AD, England.

MANNONI Maud, b. 22 Oct 1923, France. Psychoanalyst. m. Octave Mannoni, deceased, 1 son. Education: Diplomate, School of Criminology, Free University of Brussels, 1947; Docteur d'Etat es Letters, Paris, 1982. Appointments: Co-Founder, Ecole-Experimental Day Hospital, Bonneuil-sur-Marne, 1969; Co-Director of Research, Inserm, 1976-79. Publications: L'enfant arrieré et sa mere, 1964; L'enfant sa maladie et les autres, 1967; Le psychiatre son fou et la psychanalyse, 1970; Education Impossible, 1973; Un lieu pour vivre, 1976; La théorie comme fiction, 1979; D'un impossible a l'autre, 1982; Le symptome et le savoir, 1983. Memberships: Founding Member, Centre de Formation de Recherches Psychanalytiques, 1982; Director, Espace Analytique Collection, Denoel, 1983. Address: 35 Avenue Fernand Buisson, F-75016 Paris, France.

MANOHAR Murli, b. 1 Jan 1935, Panchetia, India. Director. m. Bheeke Devi, 21 Jan 1960, 1 son, 1 daughter. Education: ISc, Jaswant College, India, 1955; DVM, College of Veterinary Medicine, University of Rajasthan, India, 1960; MS, University of Minnesota, USA, 1964; MPH, School of Public Health, University of Minnesota, USA, 1965; PhD, University of Minnesota, 1966; MD, Queen's University, Kingston, Canada, 1976. Appointments: Consultant, International Health; Practice of Medicine; Director, Center for Health-care Policies & Planning. Publications: Various articles and papers. Memberships Include: New York Academy of Science; Minnesota Academy of Science; Ohio State Medical Association; Canton Academy of Medicine; Henrici Society of Mocrobiologists; American Academy of Occupational Medicine. Honours: Commemorative Medal of Honor, American Biographical Institute, 1988. Hobbies: Music; Reading; Ball-room Dancing; Travel. Address: 4942 Higbee Avenue NW, Canton, OH 44718, USA.

MANOLESCU Nicolae, b. 21 July 1936, Strunga-Iasi, Romania. Education: PhD, Faculty of Veterinary Medicine, Bucharest, 1969. Appointments: Chief, Morphopatology & Electronmicroscopy Laboratory, Pasteur Institute, Bucharest, 1969-87; Head, Cancer Cell Department, Oncological Institute, Bucharest, 1987-; Professor, Head, Cell Pathology & Veterinary Oncology Department, Faculty of Veterinary Medicine, 1992-; Dean, School of Postgraduate Veterinary Medicine, 1993-. Publications incl: The Medulograme and the Leucoconcentrate in Animals, 1976; Hematological Guide of the Industrial Breeding Animals, 1976; Diagnosis and Epizootiology of Classical Swine Fever, 1976; Leukemical Cells, 1982; Comparative Histology in SEM, 1982; Veterinary Oncology - Compared Study, 1991. Honours: Ion Ionescu de la Brad Prize, Romanian Academy, 1978; Silver International Prize, Nicola Tesla, Belgrade, 1980. Memberships: Romanian Medical Sciences Academy; New York Academy of Sciences. Address: Facultatea de Medicina Veterinara, Splaiul Independentei 105, Sector 5, Bucharest 76201, Romania.

MANOR Filomena Roberta, b. 6 July 1926, Troy, New York, USA. Dietitian. m. Melvin Manor, 3 Sept 1955, div. Education: BS cum laude, Russell Sage College, Troy; Dietetic Internship, Peter Bent Brigham Hospital, Boston, Massachusetts; MS, Ohio State University, 1960; Registered Dietitian. Appointments: Served to Colonel, US Air Force; Dietitian, Consultant, overseas and various commands; Preceptor, Dietetic Residencies and Initiator-Director, US Air Force Dietetic Internship; Associate Chief, Consultant, Nutrition and Dietetics, to US Air Force Surgeon-General. Publications: Military Airlift Command-Cooked Therapeutic Inflight Meals, 1971; Air Force Diet Manual, 1979; Nutrition, education and food service administration articles in Hospitals, Military Medicine, and US Air Force Medical Services Digest. Honours: McLester Award, Association of Military Surgeons, 1962; Distinguished Alumnus Award, Ohio State Univeristy, 1973; Legion of Merit, US Air Force, 1983. Memberships: American Dietetic Association; Association of Military Surgeons of the United States; Aerospace Medical Association; Omicron Nu. Hobby: Worldwide travel. Address: 1830 Avenida del Mundo, Apt 1714, Coronado, CA 92118-3022, USA.

MANSMANN Paris Taylor, b. 19 Feb 1957, Pittsburgh, Pennsylvania, USA. Medical School Faculty. m. Leslie A Windstein, 8 July 1978, 1 son, 2 daughters. Education: BS, Mathematics, St Joseph's University, Philadelphia; MD, Jefferson Medical College, Philadelphia; FACAI; FAAP. Appointments: Resident, Medicine, Paediatrics, 1984-87; Chief Resident, Medicine, Paediatrics, 1987-88, Geisinger Medical Center, Danville, Pennsylvania; Fellow, Allergy, Immunology, Duke University, Durham, North Carolina, 1989-90; Currently Associate Professor, West Virginia University, Morgantown. Publications: Postgraduate Medicine: 82(6),69,1987; Pediatric Asthma, Allergy and Immunology: 4(1),9,1990; 7(4),207,1993; 8(2),1994. Honours:

Outstanding Commitment Award, The Visiting Clinician Programme, 1990; Clinician of the Year, Senior Class of 1993, West Virginia School of Medicine, 1993. Memberships: Fellow: American Academy of Allergy and Immunology; European Academy of Allergology and Clinical Immunology; American College of Physicians; President, West Virginia Allergy Society. Hobbies: Skiing; Farming; Woodworking. Address: Robert C Byrd Health Sciences Center, West Virginia University, Morgantown, WV 26506-9167, USA.

MANSON JoAnn Elisabeth, b. 14 Apr 1953. Ohio, USA. Physician Epidemiologist. m. Christopher Ames, 12 June 1979, 1 s, 1 d. Education: AB, 1975, MPH, 1984, DrPH. 1987, Harvard University; MD, Case Western Reserve University, 1979; Board Certified in Internal Medicine, 1982; Board Certified in Endocrinology, 1987. Appointments: Intern, Resident in Internal Medicine, Harvard Medical School, 1979-82; Fellow in Endocrinology, University Hospital, Boston, 1982-84; Staff Physician and Consulting Endocrinologist, Harvard Community Health Plan, 1986-; Director of Endocrinology, Co-Director of Women's Health, Division of Preventive Medicine, Brigham and Women's Hospital, Harvard Medical School. Publications: Prevention of Myocardial Infarction, Editor-in-chief; Contributor of over 100 scientific articles in professional journals. Honours: Alpha Omega Alpha; Mellon Foundation Fellowship, 1987-89; Tullis Lectureship Award, 1991; Merck SER Fellowship, 1992-95. Memberships: American Medical Association; American College of Physicians; Society for Epidemiologic Research; American Heart Association; American Diabetes Association. Hobbies: Playing with children; Reading; Hiking; Listening to Music. Address: 900 Commonwealth Avenue East, Boston, MA 02215, USA.

MANSTEAD Anthony Stephen Reid, b. 16 May 1950, Liverpool, England. University Professor. Education: BSc, University Bristol, 1968-71; DPhil, University Sussex, 1971-74. Appointments: Lecturer, University of Sussex, 1974-76; Lecturer, Psychology, University Manchester, 1976-88; Senior Lecturer, Psychology, University Manchester, 1988-90; Professor, Psychology, University Manchester, 1990-92; Professor, Social Psychology, University Amsterdam. Publications: The Accountability of Conduct: A Social Psychological Analysis, 1983; Handbook of Social Psychophysiology, 1989; The Blackwell Encyclopedia of Social Psychology, 1995. Memberships: British Psychological Society; European Association of Experimental Social Psychology; Society for Personality & Social Psychology; Society of Experimental Social Psychology. Address: Department of Social Psychology, University Amsterdam, Roetersstraat 15, 1018 Wb Amsterdam, The Netherlands.

MANTHORPE Rolf, b. 19 July 1942, Copenhagen, Denmark. Professor. m. Tove, 4 Dec 1965, 1 son. Education: MD; PhD. Appointments: Associate Professor of Rheumatology and Internal Medicine. Publications: Contributor of articles in international medical journals and books. Honours: Awards, 1st, 2nd, 3rd, 4th, 5th International Congresses on Sjögren's Syndrome; Award, Irish Association for Rheumatology and Rehabilitation. Memberships: Swedish Medical Society; Danish Medical Society. Address: Sjögren's Syndrome Research Centre, Rheumatology Department, Malmö University Hospital, S-205 02 Malmö, Sweden.

MANTIL Joseph, b. 22 Apr 1937, India. Physician. m. Joan Cunningham, 18 June 1966, 2 daughters. Education: BS, Physics; MS, Physics; MS, Biological Sciences; PhD, Physics; MD; Certified: American Board of Internal Medicine; American Board of Nuclear Medicine. Appointments: Research Physicist, Aerospace Research Laboratories, 1964-75; Associate Director, Nuclear Medicine, 1982-86; Director, K-S Magnetic Resonance Laboratory, 1985-; Director, Department of Nuclear Medicine, 1986-; Professor, Department of Medicine, 1990-, Kettering Medical Center, Kettering, Ohio. Publications: Radioactivity in Nuclear Spectroscopy, Vols I and II, 1972; 40 refereed journal articles; 60 presentations; 10 book chapters. Memberships: American Physical Society; Society of Nuclear Medicine; Society of Magnetic Resonance. Hobbies: Running; Travel. Address: Department of Nuclear Medicine (PET), Kettering Medical Center, Kettering, OH 45429, USA.

MAO Bao-Ling, b. 16 Dec 1919, Honan, China. Professor of Medicine. m. Zhou Qiao Yun, 5 Feb 1950, 2 sons, 1 daughter. Education: BM, Army Medical College, 1945. Appointments: Doctor, Medical Department, 1945; Associate Professor, 1962; Professor, Medical Department, 3rd Military Medical University, Xinqiao, Chongqing, 1981-. Publications: Clinical Analysis of Blood Gases, 1985;

Adult Respiratory Distress Syndrome, 1991; Co-author: Fluid, Electrolyte, Acid-base Disturbance, and Coma, 1985; Pulmonary Tuberculosis, 1989; Pleurisy, 1989; Electrolyte, Acid-base Disturbance in Respiratory Diseases, 1991; Adult Respiratory Distress Syndrome, 1992. Honours: Tutor of Doctoral Candidates, 1986; Prominent Contributing Specialist, 1991; Special Subsidy, State Council, 1991. Memberships: Chinese Medical Association; Sichuan Province Medical Association; Medical, Scientific and Technological Committee, People's Liberation Army. Hobby: Football. Address: Respiratory Centre of PLA, Xinqiao Hospital, Third Military Medical University, Xinqiao, Chongqing, Sichuan 630037, China.

MAPSTONE Elizabeth Renee, b. 27 Jan 1937, Kingston, Surrey, England. Chartered Psychologist. m. John Tyerman Williams, 18 Aug 1980, 1 son, 2 daughters. Education: BA, MA(Oxon), DPhil, Oxford University; Advanced Diploma, Institute of Linguists. Appointments: Editor, The Psychologist; Editor, The New Academic; Consultant in Interpersonal Communications. Memberships: Associate Fellow, British Psychological Society; Institute of Linguists. Address: Trethevy. Tintagel, Cornwall PL34 0BE, England.

MARCHER Arlene S, b. 15 May 1953, Miami, FL, USA. Dance and Movement Therapist. m. Gerald R Marcher Jr, 19 Oct 1985. Education: BA, Education and Psychology; Master's MMT, Movement Therapy; Post Graduate Study, Mary S Whitehouse Institute; Currently pursuing PhD in Clinical Psychology, Pacifica Graduate Institute. Career: Movement Therapist at: Cambridgeport Problem Center, New England Rehabilitation Center, Human Resource Institute, Private practice, Market Street Health Association; Currently, Outpatient Dance and Movement Psychotherapist. Publications: From Sorceress to Apprentice, thesis, 1979; Transcendent Art: A symbol of the self, 1994. Memberships: Board, American Dance Therapy Association; Institute of Poetic Sciences; Founder, Ex-officio, Challenge Arts Therapy Center. Hobbies: Dance; Art; Body Oriented Therapies. Address: 22 Chestnut Street, Cambridge, MA 02139, USA.

MARCHESAN Rolando, b. 3 Mar 1923, Grado, Gorizia. Psychologist; Professor; Psychotherapist. Address: Via Le Corsica 57, 20133 Milano, Italy.

MARCO Philip Joseph, b. 20 Sept 1914, Boston, Massachusetts, USA. Medicine. m. Marguerite Barbaso, June 1955, 5 sons, 3 daughters. Education: AB, Boston College; MD, Middlesex University; MD, University of Missouri; Fellow, UCLA. Appointments: Residency, Psychiatry, Duke Hospital; Resident, Instructor, Washington University Medical School, St Louis; Associate Professor, University of Missouri Medical School; Chief Psychiatry, Harry Truman VA Hosptial; Lecturer, University Arizona. Publications: Numerous professional publications in scientific journals. Honours: Past President, Central Missouri Psychiatric Association, 1975-76; Legislative Agent, 1976-78. Memberships: AMA; APA; Massachusetts Medical Society; Missouri Medical Society; US Naval Reserve Voluntary Medical Unit. Hobbies: Golf; Fly Fishing; Movies. Address: 11845 East Speedway, Tucson, AZ 85748 2018, USA.

MARCUS Eric Robert, b. 16 Feb 1944, New York City, New York, USA. Psychiatrist. m. Dr Eslee Samberg, 24 Nov 1985, 1 son, 1 daughter. Education: AB, Columbia University, 1965; MD, University of Wisconsin Medical School, 1969; Diplomate, American Board of Psychiatry and Neurology; Psychoanalysis, Columbia University Psychoanalytic Center, 1987. Appointments: Director, St Mark's Free Clinic, New York City, 1971-75; Co-Director, Director, Neuropsychiatric-Diagnostic Treatment Unit, Columbia-Presbyterian Medical Center, New York City, 1985-84; Director, Medical Student Education in Psychiatry, 1981-, Associate Clinical Professor, then Clinical Professor of Psychiatry and Social Medicine, 1981-, Columbia University College of Physicians and Surgeons; Faculty, Columbia University Center for Psychoanalytic Training and Research, 1987-. Publications: Psychosis and Near Psychosis, 1992; Articles in professional journals; Editor: Intensive Hospital Treatment, 1987; Combined Treatment: Psychotherapy and Medication, 1990. Honours: Weber Award for Psychoanalytic Research, Columbia University Psychoanalytic Center, 1991; Roeske Award for Psychiatric Education, American Psychiatric Association. Memberships: Fellow, American Psychiatric Association; Fellow, New York Academy of Medicine; American Psychoanalytic Association; American College of Psychoanalysts; American Medical Association. Hobbies: Classical music; Reading; Swimming; Photography. Address: College of Physicians and Surgeons of Columbia University, Department of

Psychiatry, 722 W 168th St, New York, NY 10032, USA.

MARDYNSKY Yuriy, b. 16 July 1936, Chita, Russia. Physician. m. Valentina Yelena, 2 Feb 1960, 1 d. Education: Postgraduate Course, 1967; DMS, 1979. Appointments: Junior Researcher; Senior Researcher; Head of Department of Radiation Therapy. Honours: Excellent Worker of Public Health, 1973; Book of Honour, 1975; Diploma of Academy of Medical Science of USSR, 1987. Memberships: Independent Association of Onco-Radiologists. Hobbies: Tourism; Fishing. Address: Medical Radiological Research centre, Koroliov St 4, Obninsk, Kaluga Region, 249020 Russia.

MARGOLIS Doris May Rosenberg, b. 10 May 1936, Washington DC, USA. medical Writer, Editor. m. Judge Lawrence S Margolis, 30 Jan 1960, 1 son, 1 daughter. Education: BA, Psychology, 1958. Appointments: Editor-in-Chief, Journal of Rehabilitation; Contributing Editor, Internal Medicine, Ob-Gyn News & Pediatrics News; Correspondent, Physicians Radio Network; Columnist, Sports Medicine Monthly; Washington Bureau Chief, Pharmacotherapy News Network. Publications incl: To Aid the Disabled, 1963; The Stroke Spectrum-Prevention, Treatment and Rehabilitation, 1963; The Coronary Spectrum-Prevention, Treatment and Rehabilitation, 1966; This Is Goodwill, 1968; Rehabilitation of the Hard-Core Unemployed, 1972. Memberships: American Medical Writers Association; National Press Club; American News Women's Club; National Association of Science Writers. Hobbies: Travel; Music; Dance; Bridge; Ice-Skating; Cross-Country Skiing; Boating. Address: 1101 National Press Building, Washington DC 20045, USA.

MARIN Robert S, b. 24 Apr 1946, New York City, USA. Physician; Psychiatrist. Education: MD; Board Certification, American Board of Psychiatry and Neurology in Psychiatry; Qualification in Geriatric Psychiatry. Appointments include: Assistant Professor, 1979-93, Associate Professor of Psychiatry, 1993-, University of Pittsburgh; Staff Psychiatrist, Western Psychiatric Institute and Clinic, Pittsburgh, 1989-.Publications include: Psychopathology and Hemispheric Dysfunction, Co-author, 1981; A Strengths Oriented Treatment Program, Co-author, 1988; Reliability and Validity of the Apathy Evaluation Scale, Co-author, 1991; Apathy - Who Cares? Ten Reasons Why Every Clinician Should Care About Apathy. Honours: BA cum laude, 1967, Senior Men's Honour Society, 1967, University of Rochester; Alpha Omega Alpha, 1971; Committee on Residents, American Psychiatric Association, 1978; NIA Academic Award, 1984-89; Fellow, American psychiatric Association, 1990. Memberships: American Association of Geriatric Psychiatrists; American psychiatric Association; Gerontological Society of America; International Neuropsychological Society; International Psychogeriatric Association; National Committee for the Prevention of Elder Abuse; American Neuropsychiatric Association. Address: Western Psychiatric Institute and Clinic, 3811 O'Hara Street, Pittsburgh, PA 15213, USA.

MARKEWICH Maurice, b. 6 Aug 1936, Brooklyn, New York, USA. Physician. m. Linda Lawner, 19 June 1960, 2 daughters. Education: AB, Cornell University, 1958; MS, Social Work, Columbia University, 1960; MD, New York Medical College, 1970; Certified Psychoanalyst, Center for Modern Psychoanalytic Studies. Appointments: Social Worker, Jewish Family Service, 1961-64; Psychiatric Consultant, Office of Disability Determination, 1977-; Physician-in-charge, Psychiatric Emergency Service, Associate Attending, Beth Israel Medical Center, New York City, 1977-; Medical Director, Rockland Institute for Psychoanalysis; Assistant Professor, Mount Sinai School of Medicine. Honours: Stephen Jewett Award for Psychiatry, 1970; Max Needleman Award for Teaching, 1993. Memberships: American Psychiatric Association; Medical Society of County of New York. Hobby: Jazz musician. Address: 65 Bacon Hill Road, Pleasantville, NY 10570, USA.

MARKHAM Sanford Max, b. 1 Oct 1934, Pittsburg, Kansas, USA. Physician. m. Ruth H Markham, 1 s, 1 d. Education: BA, University of Kansas, 1956; Doctor of Medicine, University of Kansas, School of Medicine, 1960; Internship, Indiana University, 1960-61; Obstetrices & Gynaecology Residency, The New York Hospital, Cornell Medical Center, 1963-67; Reproductive Endocrinology Fellowship, The Johns Hopkins Hospital, Maryland, 1986-88. Appointments: Assistant Obstetrician and Gynaecologist, New York Hospital, Cornell Medical Center, New York, 1963-67; Visiting Fellow, Columbia Presbyterian Medical Center, New York, 1966; Instructor, The Johns Hopkins University, School of Medicine, Maryland, 1986-88; Assistant Professor, Department of Obstetrics & Gynaecology, Georgetown University

Medical Center, Washington DC, 1990-; Associate Chairman, Department of Obstetrics & Gynaecology, Georgetown University Medical Centre, Washington DC, 1992-. Publications: include, Low Dose Adrenocorticosteroid Maintenance Therapy of Rheumatoid Arthritis, 1961; Full Term Delivery Following Nephrectomy, 1968; Functional Activity of the Corpus Luteum Following Hysterectomy, 1970; Exercise May Reduce Side Effects of Danazol, 1988; A Surgical Isolation System for Gynaecological and Obstetrical Surgery, 1989; Cervical-Utero-Tubal Factors in Infertility, 1991. Memberships: include, American College of Obstetricians & Gynaecologists; American College of Surgeons; American Fertility Society; Washington Gynaecological Society; Aerospace Medical Association; Society for the Study of Fertility. Address: Georgetown YU Medical Center, Obstetrics & Gynaecology, 3800 Reservoir Road NW, Washington, DC 20007-2196, USA.

MARKHAM Thomas N, b. 8 Nov 1934, Middletown, CT, USA. Physician. m. Barbard Halterman, 23 Jun 1980, 3 d. Education: MD, St Louis University; MPH, University of Michigan. Appointments: US Navy; Corporate Medical Director, Brush Wellman Inc, Ohio. Publications: Contributor to: Occupational Medicine, 1994; The Immunology and Management of Interstitial Lung Disease. Memberships: ICOH; WASOG; ACOEM; ATS; FACCP; ACGIH; American Medical Association. Hobbies: Snow Skiing. Address: 17876 St Clair Avenue, Cleveland, OH 44110, USA.

MARKLE William Howard, b. 11 Apr 1947, Pittsburgh, Pennsylvania, USA. Family Physician. m. Mary Pollack Markle, 23 Aug 1969, 1 son, 3 daughters. Education: BA, Washington-Jefferson College, 1969; MD, Pennsylvania State University, M S Hershey Medical Centre, 1973; residency, Family Practice, Medical College of Virginia, Blackstone, 1976; DTM&H, Mahidol University, Bangkok, 1993. Appointments: Family Physician, Mannboro, Virginia, 1976-86; Medical Co-ordinator, Summer Institute of Linguistics, Indonesia, 1987-94; Assistant Professor of Family Medicine, University of Pittsburgh, USA. Publications: Cholesterol Est Content Serum, 1971; Medical Manual for Medics - Thai refugees, 1981; Malaria Incidence Irian Jaya, 1989; Malaria Booklet - Irian Jaya, 1989-92. Honours: Phi Beta Kappa, 1968; Kanjika Devekel Award, Mahidol, 1993. Memberships: AAFP; CMDS; ASTMH; PAAFP; WONCA. Hobbies: Tropical Fish; Gardening. Address: Department Family Medicine and Clinical Epidemiology, University of Pittsburgh School of Medicine, M200 Scaife Hall, Pittsburgh, PA 15261, USA.

MARKOWITZ John C, b. 10 Nov 1954, New York City, USA. Psychiatrist. m. Kathleen F Clougherty, 28 Mar 1980, 1 d. Education: BA. Columbia College, 1976; MA, Columbia University Graduate School of Arts and Sciences, 1978; MD, Columbia College of Physicians and Surgeons, 1982. Appointments: Instructor in Psychiatry, 1986-89, Assistant Professor of Psychiatry, 1989-94, Cornell University Medical College; Lecturer in Psychiatry, Columbia University, 1993-; Associate Professor of Clinical Psychiatry, Cornell University Medical College. Publications: Manual for Interpersonal Therapy with HIV-Seropositive Subjects, Co-author; Manual for Interpersonal Therapy of Dysthymia, co-author; Contributor of over 70 professional articles, reviews and book chapters. Honours: APA-Burroughs Wellcome Fellowship, 1984-86; Payne Whitney Award for Excellence in Teaching, 1986; Junior faculty Member of Year Award, 1992; Teacher of the Year, 1994. Memberships: American Psychiatric Association; Society for Psychotherapy Research. Address: Payne Whitney Clinic, New York Hospital, 445 East 68th Street, New York, NY 10021, USA.

MARKS James E, b. 10 Dec 1939, USA. Physician. m. Janet L Marks, 14 Nov 1983. 1 son, 2 daughters. Education: AB, Knox College, 1961; MD, Washington University School of Medicine, 1965. Appointments: Assistant Professor, University of Chicago; Professor, Radiation Oncology, Washington University; Professor, Chairman, Department of Radiotherapy, Loyola University, Chicago. Publications: Numerous articles. Memberships: American Society of Therapeutic Radiology & Oncology; Radiologic Society of North America. Honours: 2nd Vice President, 1991. Hobbies: Reading; Travel. Address: Loyola University Medical Center, 2160 South First Avenue, Maywood, IL 60153, USA.

MARMER Stephen S, b. 6 Dec 1942, New York, USA. Psychiatry & Psychoanalysis. Education: BA, Philosophy, University of California, Berkeley, 1964; MD, University of Southern California School of Medicine, Los Angeles, 1968; PhD, Psychoanalysis, Southern California Psychoanalytic Institute, Los Angeles, 1978. Appointments: Private Practice of Psychiatry & Psychoanalysis, 1974-; Clinical Faculty, UCLA

School of Medicine, Department of Psychiatry & Biobehavioral Sciences, 1978-; Senior Faculty, Southern California Psychoanalytic Institute, 1979-. Publications: include, Is Psychiatric Consultation in Abortion Obsolete?, 1974; Psychoanalysis of Multiple Personality, 1980; Theories of the Mind and Psychopathology, 1988; The Therapist as a Transitional Object; Theories of the Mind and Psychopathology, 1994; Psychoanalytic Approaches to the Treatment of Dissociative Identity Disorder, 1995; Numerous Papers and Lectures. Honours: include, Outstanding Teacher Award, Southern California Psychoanalytic Institute, 1983; Distinguished Service Award, UCLA School of Medicine, Department of Psychiatry, Neuropsychiatric Institute and Hospitals, 1990; Presidents Award for Distinguished Career Contributions in the Field of Dissociation, International Society for the Study of Dissociation and Multiple Personality Disorder, 1992. Memberships: include, International Psychoanalytic Association; American Psychoanalytic Association; Southern California Psychoanalytic Society; International Society for the Study of Dissociation; International Society for Traumatic Stress Studies. Address: 11611 San Vicente Boulevard, Suite 510, Los Angeles, CA 90049, USA.

MARMOR Michael, b. 13 Feb 1946, Queens, New York, USA. Epidemiologist. m. Gloria, 11 June 1974, 2 sons. Education: BA, Queens College, 1966; MA, State University of New York at Stony Brook, 1968; PhD, State University of New York at Stony Brook, 1972. Appointments: Professor, Environmental Medicine and Medicine. Honour: Phi Beta Kappa, 1965. Memberships: Fellow, American College of Epidemiology; Society for Epidemiologic Research. Address: New York University Medical Center, 341 E 25th Street, New York, NY 10010-2598, USA.

MARMOR Michael Franklin, b. 10 Aug 1941, New York City, USA. Physician. m. Dr Jane Breeden, 20 Dec 1968, 1 s, 1 d. Education: AB, Harvard College, 1962; MD. Harvard Medical School, 1966. Appointments: Assistant Professor of Ophthalmology, University of California School of Medicine, San Francisco, 1973-74; Assistant Professor, 1974, Chairman, department of Ophthalmology, 1987-92, Professor of Ophthalmology, Faculty Member, Programme in Human Biology, Stanford University. Publications: The Retinal Pigment Epithelium, Co-author 1979; Author or Co-author of 3 other books; Contributor of over 25 book chapters and 150 scientific papers. Honours: Honour Award, American Academy of Ophthalmology, 1984; Alcon Research Award, 1989. Memberships: American Academy of Ophthalmology, Fellow; Association for Research in Vision and Ophthalmology; International Society for Eye Research; Retina Society; Macula Society. Hobbies: Music; Clarinet; Tennis; Racewalking; Art; Medical History. Address: Department of Ophthalmology, Stanford University Medical Centre, Stanford, CA 94305-5308, USA.

MARMOT Michael Gideon, b. 29 Jan 1945. Professor of Epidemiology. m. Alexandra Ferster, 1971, 2 s, 1 d. Education: BSc Honours; MBBS Honours; PhD. Appointments: Fellowship in Thoracic Medicine, University of Sydney, Australia, 1970-71; Research Fellow and Lecturer, Department of Biomedical and Environmental Health Sciences, University of California at Berkeley, 1971-76; Lecturer, Senior Lecturer in Epidemiology. London School of Hygiene and Tropical Medicine, 1976-85; Head, Department of Epidemiology, UCL, London; Director, International Centre for Health and Society, UCL, London. Publications: Coronary Heart Disease: Rise and Fall of a Modern Epidemic, 1992; Contributor of over 210 professional papers. Memberships: Chairman, Coronary Prevention Group, Statistics and Epidemiology Advisory Committee; Coordinator, WHO Study on Oral Contraception and CUD. Hobbies: Tennis; Viola. Address: Department of Epidemiology and Public Health, University College London, 1-19 Torrington Place, London WC1E 6BT, England.

MARNEY Samuel Rower Jr, b. 15 Feb 1934, Bristol, Virginia, USA. Physician. m. Elizabeth Ann Bingham, 1 Oct 1966, 1 s, 1 d. Education: BA, Distinction, University of Virginia, 1955; MD, University of Virginia School of Medicine, 1960; Diplomate, American Board of Internal Medicine, 1972; Diplomate, American Board Allergy and Immunology, 1974, 1987; Diplomate, Diagnostic Laboratory Immunology, ABAI, 1988. Appointments: Instructor of Medicine, Vanderbilt University Medical School, 1968; Research fellow, Haematology, NDM, Radcliffe Infirmary, Oxford, England, 1967-68; Clinical Associate. VA Medical Centre, Nashville, Tennessee, 1968-71; VA Clinical Investigator, 1971-74; Chief Allergy, Vanderbilt Medical Centre, 1974; Associate Professor of Medicine, 1976, Director of Allergy and Immunology. Vanderbilt University School of Medicine, Nashville. Publications include: Asthma: Recent Developments in Treatment, 1985; Anaphylaxis and Serum

Sickness, 1992, 1993; Mast Cell Disease, 1992. Honours include: Hal Davidson Award, SEAA, 1981. Memberships: Fellow, American College Physicians, 1975; Fellow, American Academy Allergy and Immunology, 1980; Fellow, American College Allergy and Immunology, 1990; Southeastern Allergy Association. Hobbies: Music; Day Hikes; Bridge. Address: Vanderbilt Allergy Centre, 1500 21st Avenue S, Suite 3500, Nashville, TN 37212, USA.

MAROSY György, b. 21 June 1955, Veszprém, Hungary. Cardiologist. m. Aranka Szi Miklos, 3 Dec 1983, 1 son, 1 daughter. Education: MD, Medical Univerisity of Szeged, 1980; Internist, 1985; Cardiologist, Haemodynamic Laboratory of the Postgraduate Medical University, Budapest. Appointments: Internist, Cardiologist, County Hospital of Veszpreém, 1980-88; Haemodynamic Laboratory of the Postgraduate Medical University, Budapest, 1988-92; Head of CCU, National Koranyi Institute. Publications: Acute dissection of ascending aorta diagnosed by two dimensional echocardiography. Memberships: Working Group on Echocardiography; Working Group on Haemodynamics of the Hungarian Society of Cardiology. Hobbies: Swimming; Riding. Address: Kossuth u 169, Balatonederics, H-8312 Hungary.

MAROTTA Priscilla V, b. 28 Aug 1946, Chelsea, Massachusetts, USA. Psychologist. m. Robert McDonald, Oct 1993, 1 son. Education includes: PhD; Diplomate, American Board of Certified Managed Care Providers. Appointments: President, Broward Psychological Association, 1994. Publications: Quarterly column in Miami Herald. Memberships: Dancing; Theatre; Jazz. Address: 300 NW 70th Avenue 302, Plantation, FL 33317, USA.

MARQUES FERRAZ Olga, b. 8 June 1947, Rio de Janeiro, Brazil. Psychologist. m. Antonio Paulo Ferraz, 19 Feb 1975, 2 daughters. Education: BA, Federal University, 1979; BA, Catholic University, 1980; Postgraduate Diploma, Medical Psychology, 1985. Appointments: Private Psychoanalytic Practice & Special Advisor; Company CEO of CEC; Chairman, Board of Directors, CEC; Board Director, CCN Group. Publications: The Fantasy in an Injured Body, 1985; The Depth of Doubt, 1989. Memberships: Brazilian Psychoanalytical Society; International Psychoanalytical Association, London. Hobbies: Ballet; Tap Dancing; Gymnastics. Address: Othon Bezerra de Melo St, 70 Jandim Botanico, Rio de Janeiro 22460-310, Brazil.

MARSH Laura, b. 16 Dec 1959, Cedar Rapids, Iowa, USA. Psychiatrist. m. Richard Eric Davis, 4 Nov 1992, 1 daughter. Education: BA with highest honours, Psychobiology, 1981; MD cum laude, 1986. Appointments: Currently Assistant Professor, Department of Psychiatry and Behavioral Sciences, Stanford University School of Medicine, Stanford, California. Address: 321 N Clark Avenue, Los Altos, CA 94022-2352, USA.

MARTIN Jay Herbert, b. 30 Oct 1935, Newark, New Jersey, USA. Psychoanalyst. m. Helen Saldini, 9 June 1956, 1 son, 2 daughters. Education: AB with honours, Columbia College, 1956; PhD, Ohio State University, 1960; PhD, Southern California Psychoanalytic Institute, 1983. Appointments: Pennsylvania State University, 1957; Instructor to Associate Professor, Yale University, 1960-68; Leo S Bing Professor of Literature, University of Southern California, 1979-; National Humanities Faculty, 1980-; Faculty, Southern California Psychoanalytic Institute, 1984-88; Professor, Department of Psychiatry, University of California Medical School, Irvine; Coordinator: Committee on Deviations, 1984, 1989, Committee on Psychoanalytic Research, 1988, American Psychoanalytic Association; Editor-in-Chief, Psychoanalytic Education, 1984-89; Speeches, consultations. Publications: Author, editor, books including: Who Am I This Time? Uncovering the Fictive Personality, 1988; Fiction includes: Winter Dreams: An American in Moscow, 1979; Articles include: Psychic Epidemics and American Literary History, 1984; Fictive Personality and the Treatment of Homosexuality, 1990; Book reviews in Los Angeles Times Book Review, New York Times Book Review, International Review of Psycho-Analysis, American Literature, Partisan Review; Psychoanalytic Quarterly. Honours include: Phi Beta Kappa, 1956; Marie E Briehl Essay Prize in Child Psychoanalysis, 1982; Franz Alexander Prize in Psychoanalysis, 1983; Fellowships. Memberships: Southern California Psychoanalytic Institute; Southern California Psychoanalytic Society; American and International Psychoanalytic Associations; International Society for Empirical Aesthetics. Work in progress: Research for biography of John Dewey, philosopher and psychologist. Address: 18651 Via Palatino, Irvine, CA 92715, USA.

MARTIN Lester W, b. 15 Aug 1923, Edwards, MO, USA. Medical Doctor. m. Joan Belanger, 17 Jun 1949, 1 s, 4 d. Education: BS; BSc; MD; FACS. Instructor, Harvard, Simmons College; Assistant Professor, Associate Professor, Professor, University of Cincinnati; Now retired Emeritus Professor of Surgery. Publications: 154 publications. Honours: Numerous. Memberships: American College of Surgeons; American Surgical Association; American Pediatric Surgical Association; British Association of Pediatric Surgeons. Address: Children's Hospital, 3333 Burnet Avenue, Cincinnati, OH 45229, USA.

MARTIN Patricia (Pat) Smith, b. 4 Apr 1949, Alabama, USA. Ophthalmology Assistant. m. Bobby H Martin, 12 Feb 1972, 1 son. Education: Certified Ophthalmology, JCAHPO. Appointments: Telephone Operator; Secretary (Salesman, textile industry); Currently Ophthalmology Assistant. Memberships: Medical Assistants; JCAHPO. Hobbies: Playing the piano; Re-finishing and re-modelling furniture; Reading. Address: 6058 Boeing Drive, Columbus, OH 31909, USA.

MARTIN Robert William III, b. 2 May 1956, Peoria, Illinois, USA. Physician. m. Debra Ann Ring, 22 June 1980, 3 sons, 1 daughter. Education: BS, Southern Illinois University, 1978; MD, Southern Illinois University School of Medicine, 1981; Board Certifications: Family Practice, 1985-92; Dermatology, 1991-2001; Dermatopathology, 1993. Appointments: Senior Clinical Fellow, Department of Dermatology, Johns Hopkins University, 1991-93; Associate Director, Cutaneous Pathology and Immunofluorescence Laboratory, 1993-; Assistant Clinical Professor, Department of Dermatology, Case Western Reserve, 1993-. Publications: Co-author: Conservative excision of penile melanoma, 1988; Teaching third-year medical students how to care for terminally ill patients, 1989; Basex syndrome in a female with pulmonary adenocarcinoma, 1989; Acne fulminans, 1989; Nasal melanoma presenting as nasal obstruction, 1990; Multiple cutaneous granular cell tumors and neurofibromatosis in childhood: A case report and review of the literature, 1990; Pilomatrixoma (calcified epithelioma of Malherbe) with secondary ossification, 1992; Kaposi's Sarcoma, 1993; Benign Leydig cell tumor of the testis associated with human papilloma virus 33 presenting with the sign of Leser-Trelat, 1993; Cutaneous giant cell hyaline angiopathy, 1993; Papillary cystadenoma of the lower lip mimicking hidradenoma papilliferum, 1993; Lichenoid chronic graft versus host disease in an autologous bone marrow transplant recipient, 1994; Papillary squamous cell carcinoma in an immunosuppressed patient, 1994. Memberships: American Academy of Dermatology; American Society of Dermatopathology; American, Ohio State and Southern Medical Associations; The Academy of Medicine, Cleveland. Address: Commerce Park Five, Suite 350, 23200 Chagrin Boulevard, Beachwood, OH 44122-5401, USA.

MARTIN Ronald L, b. 15 June 1945, Cleveland, Ohio, USA. Physician. m. Kathryn J Martin, 2 Aug 1980, 2 s. Education: BA; MD; Certified in Psychiatry and Geriatric Psychiatry, American Board of Psychiatry and Neurology. Appointments: Instructor, 1975-77, Assistant Professor, 1977-80, Psychiatry, Washington University; Associate Professor, 1980-85, Professor, 1985-88, Professor, Department Chair,University of Kansas School of Medicine. Publications: Somatoform Disorders, 1994; DSM-IV in Progress: Diagnostic Issues for Conversion Disorder, 1992; Mortality in a Follow-Up of 500 Psychiatric Outpatients I & II, 1985. Honours: Physician's Recognition Award, American Medical Association, 1984, 1987, 1990, 1993; Appreciation Certificate, American Board of Psychiatry and neurology, 1989. Memberships: Fellow, American Psychiatric Association; Past President, Kansas Psychiatric Society; American College of Psychiatrists; American Psychopathological Association, Fellow. Hobbies: Running; Skiing. Address: Department of Psychiatry, University of Kansas School of Medicine-Wichita, 1010 N Kansas Avenue, Wichita, KS 67214-3199, USA.

MARTIN William W, b. 24 Mar 1951, Albany, Georgia, USA. Clinical Psychologist. m. 7 Nov 1981, 2 sons, 3 daughters. Education: PhD; MA; BS; AA. Appointments incl: Regional Vocational Consultant, Vocational Exploration Services Inc, California, 1984; Psychotherapist & Vocational Consultant, Assessment & Psychotherapy Center, Tustin, California, 1983-89; Private Practice, 1978. Publications: Numerous professional publications in scientific journals. Honours incl: World Lifetime Achievement Award, American Biographical Institute, 1992; Most Admired Man of the Year Nomination, American Biographical Institute, 1992-93. Memberships: American Psychological Association; American Association of Sex Educators, Counselors & Therapists; Timeline Therapy Association. Hobbies: Flying; Scuba Diving; Snow Skiing;

Water Skiing; Horseback Riding. Address: Oceanview Medical Center, 675 Camino de los Mares, Ste 302, San Clemente, CA 92673, USA.

MARTINEZ Ibanez, b. 12 June 1952, Barcelona, Spain. Head, Paediatric Transplant Unit; Paediatric Surgery Department; Children's Hospital of Valle Hebron; Autonomous University of Barcelona. Education: Medical Studies & PhD, Autonomous University, Barcelona, Spain. Appointments: Assistant Fellow, Transplant Division, University of Pittsburgh, USA, 1984; Head, Liver Transplant Unit, Children's Hospital, 1985; Head, Paediatric Transplant Unit, Children's Hospital, Valle Hebron, Barcelona, 1992; Fellow, Barnes Hospital Lung Transplant Unit, St Louis, USA, 1992. Publications: Orthotopic Liver Transplantation in Children, 1987; Liver Transplantation in Metabolic Diseases, 1987; Experimental & Clinical Reduced Sized Orthotopic Liver Transplantation, 1988; Paediatric Liver Transplantation: Life after Portoenterostomy Biliary Atresia, 1992. Memberships: Sociedad Espanola Cirugia Pediatrica; Societat Catalana De Pediatria; Eurpoean Society of Organ Transplantation; Societat Catalana de Transplantament. Honours: Best Research Study Monereo Award, 1985; Marcis Monturiol Award, 1986; Alexander Frias i Roig Award, Paediatric Nutrition, 1990. Hobbies: Jogging; Golf. Address: Manuel Girdna 86, 7-2 D, 08034 Barcelona, Spain.

MARTINEZ SALGADO Homero, b. 4 Nov 1953, Mexico D F, Mexico. Medical Doctor. m. Barbara Loyo, 18 June 1976, 1 son, 1 daughter. Education: MD, Paediatrician; PhD, International Nutrition. Appointments: Currently Senior Investigator. Publications: Co-author, book chapters: La modernizacion de la atencion medica primaria, 1986; Uso de alimentos y bebidas en el manejo de la diarrea aguda en la infancia, 1988; Maternal correlates of infant growth in rural Mexico, 1989; Maternal fatness in Mexican women predicts body composition changes in pregnancy and lactation, 1993; Medidas de control de las infecciones gastrointestinales, 1993; Author or co-author, 22 articles. Memberships: International Union for Nutritional Sciences; American Institute of Nutrition; American Society for Clinical Nutrition; Society for International Nutrition Research; Latinoamerican Society of Nutrition. Hobbies: Hiking; Climbing; Swimming; Biking. Address: Cardenales 76, Las Aguilas, D F Mexico, CP 01710, Mexico.

MARUYAMA Koshi, b. 19 Feb 1932, Sapporo, Hokkaido, Japan. Medical Pathologist. m. Rumy Misawa, 6 May 1961, 2 s, 1 d. Education: MD 1957; PhD, 1962; Japanese Medical License, 1958; Diplomate Japanese Board of Pathology, 1979. Appointments: Staff Pathologist, National Institute for Leprosy Research, Tokyo, 1962-65; Staff pathologist, National Cancer Centre Research Institute, 1965-67; Associate Professor, University of Texas M D Anderson Cancer Centre, Houston, Texas, USA, 1967-75; Head, Department of Pathology, Chiba Cancer Centre, 1975-. Publications: Contributor of over 350 professional articles. Honours: Scholar, Leukaemia Society of America, 1968; Honorary Professor, Liaoning Cancer Hospital & Inst, Shenyang, 1992. Memberships: Fellow, New York Academy of Sciences; World Committee, International Association for Comparative Research on Leukaemia and Related Diseases; Fellow, Japanese Society Pathology; Fellow, Japanese Cancer Association; AAAS; AACR; ASM. Address: Department of Pathology, Chiba Cancer Centre Research Institute, 666-2 Nitona-cho, Chuo-ku, Chiba 260, Japan.

MARWOOD Roger Paul, b. 23 July 1947, Cheltenham, England. Obstetrician & Gynaecologist. m. Suzanne Brown, 21 Feb 1975, 1 son, 2 daughters. Education: FRCOG; MSc; Medical Demography; MB; BS. Appointments: Consultant, Chelsea & Westminster Hospital & King Edward VII Hospital. Publications: Several professional publications in scientific journals. Membership: Vice President, Royal Society of Medicine. Hobbies: Skiing; Opera; Pinball. Address: Chelsea & Westminister Hospital, 369 Fulham Road, London SW10 9NH, England.

MARX Elisabeth Maria, b. 27 Mar 1958, Oberthal, Germany. Psychologist. Education: Diplom, University of Marburg, 1983; DPhil, University of Oxford, England, 1988. Appointments: Lecturer in Psychology, National University of Singapore; Head of International Assessment and Consultancy, NB Selection, London. Publications: Problem-Solving Therapy, 1988; Interpersonal Problem Soving in Depressed Students, Co-author, 1991; Depression and Social Problem Solving, Co-author, 1992. Memberships: British Psychological Society; German Psychological Society. Hobbies: Reading; Swimming; Dancing. Address: 121 Cheyne Walk, London SW10 0ES, England.

MASCARENHAS Lawrence, b. 5 Sep 1955, Reunion, France. Obsterician and Gynaecologist. 1 s, 2 d. Education: MD, Tours, France, 1986; MRCOG, 1991. Career: Senior House Officer: Gynaecology, Churchill Hospital, Oxford, Obstetrics, John Radcliffe Maternity, Oxford; Registrar, Obstetrics and Gynaecology, Northampton General Hospital; Currently, Clinical Research Fellow, Lecturer, Academic Department of Obstetrics and Gynaecology, Birmingham Maternity Hospital, Birmingham Midland Hospital for Women. Publications: Specialist Medical Training and The EC, in Lancet, 1992; Superovulation and timed intercourse: Can it provide a reasonable alternative for those unable to afford assisted conception, in Human Reproduction, 1994; Long acting methods of contraception, in BMJ editorial, 1994; First Clinical Experience with Contraceptive Implants in the UK, in British Journal of Family Planning, 1994; Contraceptive Implants, chapter, Progress in Obstetrics and Gynaecology, in press 1995. Honours: French Government Scholarship to Study Medicine, 1975-82; Northampton General Hospital Registrar Research Prize, 1990; Birmingham and Midland Obstetrical and Gynaecological Society Prize, 1991. Memberships: GMC; BMA; RCOG; Blair Bell Research Society; British Fertility Society; Society for Advancement of Contraception; British Society for Gynaecological Endoscopy. Hobbies: Travel; Watching International Football, Rugby, Tennis, Squash; Cinema; Chess; Current Affairs (International Politics); French Cuisine. Address: Academic Department of Obstetrics and Gynaecology, Birmingham Maternity Hospital, Birmingham B15 2TG, England.

MASHKOVSKY Mikhail, b. 1 Mar 1908, Pinsk, Belorussia. Pharmacologist. m. Education: Physician, Moscow Medical Institute, 1934; MD, 1948; Academician, Russian Academy of Medical Science, 1978. Appointments: Toxicologist, Research Institute, Moscow, 1934-38; Pharmacologist, 1938-41, Senior Scientific Worker, Pharmacology, 1946-48, Head, Pharmacology Department, 1948-, Chemico-Pharmaceutic Research Institute, Moscow; Army Toxicologist, 1941-46. Publications include: Medicinal Drugs, volumes 1 and 2, 15 editions, 1954-94; Structure and Activity of Quinuclidine Derivatives, 1969; Pharmaceutical Properties of Pirlindole, 1981; Further Research of Quinuclidine Derivatives, 1983; Pharmacology of Antidepressants, 1983. Honours: Honoured Scientist, 1968; Hero of Socialist Labour, 1991. Memberships: Honorary President, Russian Pharmacology Society; Chief Expert Consultant, Pharmacopoeia Commission, Ministry of Health, Russian Federation. Address: Chemico-Pharmaceutic Institute, Zubovskaja Str 7, Moscow 119815, Russia.

MASLIKOV Oleg Viktorovitch, b. 26 Apr 1966, Taganrog, Russia. Doctor; Parapsychologist. m. Olga V Bondaletova, 1 Aug 1987, 2 sons. Education: Dr's Cert, High Profl Sch, 1989. Appointments: Researcher in Parapsychology and Non-Traditional Medicine, 1988-; Practitioner, 1989-. Publications: Matter of thought and original possibilities of parapsychology, 1990; Original methods of clearing and treatment for sensation of pain, 1991; Unique methods of auto-treatment, 1992; Clinical statistics and resources of Dr Maslikov's methods, 1992; Lectures on mass-media, 1991-94. Hobbies: Non-traditional medicine; Ancient philosophy. Address: 167/7 Kuznetchnaja Str, Apt 57, Taganrog 347932, Russia.

MASON David Kean (Sir), b. 5 Nov 1928, Paisley, Scotland. Professor of Oral Medicine. m. Judith Armstrong, 3 June 1967, 2 s, 1 d. Education LDS, 1951, BDS, 1952, University of St Andrews; MBChB, MD University of Glasgow; FRCS; FDS' FRCPath. Appointments: Professor of Oral Medicine, 1967-92, Dean of Dental Education, 1980-90, University of Glasgow; President, General Dental Council, 1989-94. Publications: Oral Manifestations of Systemic Disease, 1980, 1990; Salivary Glands in Health and Disease, 1975; Proceedings World Workshop in Oral Medicine, 1988 and 1993. Honours: KB; CBE; Hon DDS, University of Wales; Hon LLD, University of Dundee; Hon FFD RCS I; Hon FDS RCPS G; Honorary Member American Dental Association, 1994; Honorary Fellow British Dental Association, 1993. Memberships: BMA; BDA; International Association of Dental Research; British Society for dental Research; FDI. Hobbies: Golf; Tennis; Gardening. Address: Greystones, Houston Road, Kilmacolm, Renfrewshire PA13 4NY, Scotland.

MASON George Robert, b. 10 June 1932, Rochester, New York, USA. Surgeon. m. Grace Louise Bransfield, 4 Feb 1956, 2 sons, 1 daughter. Education: BA, Oberlin College; MD, University of Chicago; PhD, Physiology, Stanford University; Certified: American Board of Surgery; Board of Thoracic Surgery. Appointments: Faculty, Stanford University, California; Professor and Chairman, Department of Surgery,

Professor of Physiology, University of Maryland; Professor, Chairman, Department of Surgery, University of California, Irvine; Currently Professor, Surgery, Thoracic and Cardiovascular Surgery, Loyola University, Chicago, Illinois. Publications: About 20 book chapters including: The Mesenteric Small Bowel, 1981; Laser Photoradiation Therapy of Recurrent Human Breast Cancer and Cancer of the Head and Neck (co-author), 1983; Tumors of the Duodenum and Small Intestine, 1986; Appendicitis and Appendiceal Abscess (with G R Mason), 1991; Thorascopy: Historical Perspectives, 1994; Over 100 articles in journals; Films: Modified Hill Repair for Hiatus Hernia (Posterior Gastropexy), 1975; Surgery for Chronic Pancreatitis, 1990. Honours: Alpha Omega Alpha, 1957; John and Mary R Markle Scholar in Academic Medicine, 1969-74; Award for Teaching Excellence, University of Maryland, 1977; Distinguished Alumnus, University of Chicago, 1994. Memberships include: American Association for Thoracic Surgery; American College of Chest Physicians; American College of Surgeons; American Gastroenterological Association; American Surgical Association; Sigma Xi, Stanford Chapter; Société Internationale de Chirurgie; Chicago Surgical Society; Baltimore Academy of Surgery; American Physiological Society; Chesapeake Vascular Society. Hobbies: Philately; Photography; History; Gardening. Address: Box 3877, Oak Brook, IL 60522, USA.

MASSERMAN Jules Homan, b. 10 Mar 1905, Russia. Physician. m. Christine McGuire, 20 Feb 1943. Education: MD; Certified in Pharmacology, Neurology and Psychiatry. Career: Assistant Professor of Psychiatry, University of Chicago, 1942-46; Associate Professor, Professor, Psychiatry and Neurology, from 1946 now retired, Co-Chairman Psychiatry and Neurology, from 1952 now retired, Northwestern University; Currently, President, Masserman Foundation for International Accords. Publications: Over 380 articles on neuropsychiatry, history, philosophy, music, and sociology, 1936-; 46 books as author or editor including: Principles of Dynamic Psychiatry, 1946; Practice of Dynamic Psychiatry, 1955; A Psychiatric Odyssey, 1977; Writing and Editing, 1994. Honours: Lasker Award, 1946; Psychiatrist of Year, 1967; Sigmund Freud Award, 1974; Honorary Life President, World Association for Social Psychiatry, 1983. Memberships include: Past President, American Academy of Psychoanalysis; Past President, American Society of Biologic Psychiatry; Past President, APA; Life President, World Association of Social Psychiatry. Hobbies: Violin; Viola; Composing; Golf; Sailing. Address: 2231 East 67th Street, Chicago, IL 60649, USA.

MASSIMO Luisa M E, b. 22 Dec 1928, Genoa, Italy. Paediatrician. Education: Degree in Medicine and Surgery, University of Genoa, 1953; Paediatrics, University of Philadelphia, USA, 1953-54; Specialised in Paediatrics, University of Genoa, Italy, 1955; Studied Paediatric Haematology and Oncology, Centre International de l'Enfance, Paris, France, 1959, Basle, 1962; Habilitation in Clinical Paediatrics, 1965; Habilitation in Child Care, 1965. Appointments include: Various Positions to Assistant Head Physician, Paediatric Clinic, University of Genoa; Professor of Clinical Paediatrics, 1966; Head, Division of Paediatric Haematology and Oncology, G Gaslini Institute, Genoa, 1972-; Co-ordinator for Paediatric Oncology, US-Italy Cancer Agreement and Germany-Italy Agreement; President, National Cancer Research Institute, Institute of Gonova, 1986-94. Publications: Contributor of over 370 papers on Paediatric Haematology, Oncology and Immunology. Honours: G Pauletta Prixe for Oncology. Accademia Nazionale dei Lincei, 1971; Barbara Bohen Pfeifer award for Scientific Excellence, American-Italian Foundation for Cancer Research, 1991. Memberships include: Founder Member, International Society of Paediatric Oncology; European Society of Paediatric Haematology, Past President; Italian Association of Paediatric Haematology and Oncology, Past President; New York Academy of Sciences; American Society of Paediatric Oncology; International College of Paediatrics; College of Italian Clinical Haematologists; Steering Committee, Italian Society of Psycho-Oncology. Hobbies: Abstract Painting. Address: Viale Brigata Bisagno 8, 16129 Genova, Italy.

MASSOF Robert W, b. 2 Jan 1948, Pittsburgh, PA, USA. Professor of Ophthalmology. m. Darcy Rood, 1 Jun 1974, 1 s, 1 d. Education: BA, Hamline University, USA, 1970; PhD, Indiana University, USA, 1975; PhD, Postdoctoral Fellowship, Ophthalmology, Johns Hopkins University, 1976; Director of Lions Vision Research & Rehabilitation Center at Wilmer Eye Institute. Appointments: Professor of Ophthalmology and Neuroscience. Publications: First Order Dynamics of Field Loss in RP, 1990; Rod Sensitivity Relative to Cone Sensitivity in Retinitis Pigmentosa, 1979; Color Vision Theory and Linear Models of Color Vision, 1985; Co-Author of Opinions of Ophthalmologists on the Relation of Disability to Visual Acuity, 1994. Honours: RPB Manpower Award, 1989; Technical Transfer, 1992; Pop Mechanics, 1994; Discover, 1994. Memberships: OSA; ARVO; American Academy Optometry; AER; SID. Hobbies: Skiing; Raquetball; Home Renovations; Archery. Address: Lions Vision Center, 550 North Broadway, 6th Floor, Baltimore, MD 212205, USA.

MATHER Pamela, b. 2 July 1952, Stafford Springs, Connecticut, USA. Nurse; Psychotherapist. 1 son. Education: Diploma, Practical Nursing, New Hampshire Vocational-Technical College, Claremont, 1972; AS, Professional Nursing, Castleton State College, Vermont, 1979; BA, Psychaology, California State University, Long Beach, 1983; MA, Counselling Psychology, Pepperdine University, Irvine, California, 1986; Psychotherapy Internships: Long Beach Community Hospital Adult Day Care, 1985, Family Services of Long Beach, 1985-87, Alternatives Counseling Associates, Long Beach, 1986-87. Appointments: Various nursing positions, 1979-84; Older Adult Specialist, Orange County Mental Health, Santa Ana, California, 1987-; Contract Counsellor, Family Services, Tustin, California, 1990; Marriage, Family, Child Psychotherapist in private practice, 1990-92. Publications: Aging: Arteriosclerotic Changes, Psychological and Social Aspects, 1983; A Humanistic Approach to Aging and Death: An Interview with Carl Rogers, 1993; Interview with Carl Rogers PhD in 1985, forthcoming. Memberships: American Psychological Association; Psi Chi; California Association for Marriage and Family Therapists. Hobbies: Gourmet cooking; Musician (piano, vocal); Gardening. Address: 20232 Santiago Cyn Road, Orange, CA 92669, USA.

MATHOG Robert Henry, b. 13 Apr 1917, New Haven, Connecticut, USA. Otolaryngologist. m. Doona, 14 June 1964, 1 s, 3 d. Education: BA, Dartmouth College; MD, New York University. Appointments: Chief, Hennepin County Medical Centre; Assistant Professor, Associate Professor, University of Minnesota; Professor, Chairman, Department of Otolaryngology, Wayne State University. Publications include: Maxillofacial Trauma, 1984; Contributor of over 200 articles in refereed journals. Honours include: Distinguished Faculty Award, 1993. Memberships: American Medical Association; Society of University Otolaryngologists; American Academy of Facial Plastic Surgery; American Society for Head and Neck Surgery. Address: 5E UHC, 4201 St Antine, Detroit, MI 48211, USA.

MATHUR Krishna Saran, b. 12 July 1912, Shikohabad, India. Cardiologist. m. Radha Rani Mathur, 8 Dec 1936, 1 son, 2 daughters. Education: MD, Lucknow University; DSc, BHU; FRCP(Ed); FACC(USA); FAMS(Ind); FNA(Ind). Appointments: Lecturer in Cardiology, 1946-52, Reader in Medicine, 1952-57, Professor, Head, department of Medicine, 1957-72, S N Medical College, Agra; Eemritus Professor of Medicine. Publications: Contribdutor of 275 papers in national and international journals; Author of chapters in books. Honours: Watumull Memorial Award, 1966; George Coelho Award, 1967; Chaturveoi KJ Memorial Award, 1975; Dr B C Roy National Award, 1979; Dr Jal Rustom Vakil Award, 1982. Memberships: President, Cardiological Society of India; Governing Body, ICMR; Director, India Heart Foundation; President, Indian Medical Association; President, Association of Physicians of India; Indian National Science Academy; National Academy of Medical Sciences. Hobbies: Golf; Photography. Address: 1/130 Professors' Colony, Civil Lines, Agra 282002, India.

MATSU'URA Shuji, b. 16 Feb 1952, Hamamatsu City, Japan. Associate Professor. m. Michiko Kaneko, 5 Dec 1976, 2 sons. Education: BSc, 1974, MSc, Anthropology, 1976, DSc, Anthropology, 1982, University of Tokyo. Appointments: Research Staff, Department of Anthropology, National Science Museum, Tokyo, 1979-87; Associate Professor, Faculty of Home Economics, 1987-92, Associate Professor, Department of Human Biological Studies, School of Human Life and Environmental Science, 1992-, Ochanomizu University, Tokyo. Publications: Co-author: Fraction dependent variation of aspartic acid racemization age of fossil bone, 1980; Primate Evolution, 1986; Anthropology, new 2nd edition, 1989. Memberships: Anthropological Society of Nippon (Japan); American Association of Physical Anthropologists. Hobbies: Driving; Hiking. Address: Department of Human Biological Studies, School of Human Life and Environmental Science, Ochanomizu University, Otsuka 2-1-1, Bunkyo-ku, Tokyo 112, Japan.

MATTHEY Francois Olivier, b. 12 Feb 1954, Morges, Vaud, Switzerland. Orthodontist. m. Breuil Isabelle 8 Dec 1981, 1 s, 2 d (1 deceased 12 Aug 1993). Education: Diplome de Medecin - Dentiste, 1977; Certificate in Orthdontics, 1983. Career: Orthodontist in Private Practice. Honour: Fernex's Prize, 1983. Memberships: Société Suisse d'Odonto-Stomatologie; Société Suisse d'Orthopedie Dentofaciale; Société Française d'Orthopedie Dento-Faciale. Hobby: Cars 1950-1980. Address: 3 Rue de la Treille, 2000 Neuchatel, Switzerland.

MATTHIAS Gamal S H, b. 7 Feb 1955, Cairo, Egypt. Consultant and Senior Lecturer, Obstetrics and Gynaecology. m. Gwyneth Matthias, 21 Apr 1990, 2 s. Education: MB; BCH, Honours; MRCOG; FICS; FRACOG. Appointments: Senior Lecturer and Consultant Obstetrician and Gynaecologist, Roayl Victoria Infirmary, Newcastle-Upon-Tyne; Senior Registrar, Charing Cross and West London Hospital, London; Senior Registrar, Darwin Hospital, Australia; Currently, Consultant and Clinical Senior Lecturer and Director of Obstetrics and Gynaecology, Ipswich, Queensland. Publications: Audit into Stillbirths, in Journal of Obstetrics and Gynaecology, 1992; Perinatal Mortality in Aboriginal and Non-Aboriginal Australians, in Medical Journal of Australia; Fetal Movement, Maternal Serum, AFP and The Mode of Death in Unexplained Stillbirths, in Journal of Obstetrics and Gynaecology. Membership: Society of Gynaecological Endoscopists. Hobbies: Swimming; Table Tennis; Bird Watching. Address: 6/44 Cambridge Street, Epping, New South Wales 2121, Australia.

MATTISON Donald Roger, b. 28 Apr 1944, Minneapolis, MN, USA. Obstetrics and Gynaecology. m. Margaret Libby Mattison, 1967, 1 s, 1 d. Education: BA, cum laude, Chemistry, Mathematics, Augsburg College, MN, 1966; MS, Chemistry, MA Institute of Technology, Cambridge, MA, 1968; MD, College of Physicians and Surgeons, Columbia University, NY, 1973; Diplomate, American Board of Toxicology, 1992. Career includes: Commander, US Public Health Service, Active Duty, 1987-89, Inactive Reserve, 1990-; Various editorial boards; Dean, Graduate School of Public Health, Professor of Environmental and Occupational Health and Obstetrics and Gynaecology, University of Pittsburgh, PA, 1990-; Member of numerous committees. Publications include: Over 150 publications and over 120 abstracts published including: The Impact of Physiologic Pregnancy Adaptations on Maternal and Fetal Pharmacokinetics, in Prenatal Exposure to Toxicants: Developmental Consequences, 1994. Honours: American Chemical Society Medal, 1966; Honor Society, Augsburg College, MN, 1966; Thomas F Cock Award for Excellence in Obstetrics and Gynaecology, Columbia University, 1973; Association of American Publications Award for Best Single Issue, 1983; Delta Omega, 1991. Memberships include: American Public Health Association; Society for Risk Analysis; American Association for Cancer Research; NY Academy of Science; American College of Toxicology; American Fertility Society; Society for Gynaecologic Investigation; Teratology Society. Hobbies: Photography; Computer Sciences; House Restoration; Cross Country Skiing. Address: Graduate School of Public Health, University of Pittsburgh, 111 Parran Hall, Pittsburgh, PA 15261, USA.

MATTOX Kenneth L, b. 25 Oct 1938, Ozark, AR, USA. Medical Doctor. m. Camella June Mattox, 10 Feb 1959, 1 d. Appointment: Professor of Surgery, Baylor College of Medicine. Address: Baylor College of Medicine, Dept of Surgery, 1 Baylor Plaza, Houston, TX 77030, USA.

MATUSZ Petru, b. 8 June 1956, Faget-Timis, Romania. Doctor of Medicine. m. Anca-Alexandra, 28 June 1986, 1 son. Education: Speciality in Plastic & Reconstructive Surgery, 1989. Appointments: Institute of Medicine, Timisoara, 1982. Publications: Co-author: Traumatology in Sportsmen, 1985; Co-author: Vessels and Nerves, 1992; Author: First Aid in Travel Accidents, 1993. Memberships: Anatomische Gesellschaft, 1983; Union Médicale Balkanique, 1987; International Union of Angiology, 1993; European Association of Clinical Anatomy, 1994. Hobbies: Photography. Address: Department of Anatomy, Piata Eftimie Murgu No 2, RO-1900 Timisoara, Romania.

MAURER Harold Maurice, b. 10 Sept 1936 New York City, USA. Professor; Chairman. m. Beverly Bennett, 12 June 1960, 2 d. Education: BA, New York University, 1957; MD, State University of New York, Downstate Medical Centre, Brooklyn, 1961. Appointments: Intern, Paediatrics, Kings County Hospital, Brooklyn, 1961-62; Resident, Paediatrics, Bates Hospital, New York City, 1962-64; Chief, Paediatrics, USPHS Hospital, Norfolk, Virginia, 1964-66; Fellow, Paediatric Haematology and Oncology, Babies Hospital, New York City, 1966-68;

Assistant Professor, 1968-71, Associate Professor, 1971-75, Professor, Chairman, 1976-, Paediatrics, Medical College of Virginia. Publications: Editor of two books; Contributor of over 125 scientific articles. Honours: University Award for Overall excellence, 1986; Dean's Award for Outstanding Contributions to School of Medicine, 1986. Hobbies: Art Nouveau Art Glass; Contemporary Art Glass. Address: Medical College of Virginia, Richmond, VA 23298, USA.

MAUTNER Branco, b. 16 Jan 1938, Zagreb, Croatia. Medical Doctor. m. Renée Yedlin, 16 Aug 1970, 1 son, 1 daughter. Education: MD. Appointments: Staff Cardiologist, Ramos Mejia and Fernandez City Hospitals, Buenos Aires, Argentina; Chief, Coronary Care Unit, Fernandez Hospital; Currently: Vice-director, Professor of Medicine, University Institute of Biomedical Sciences, Buenos Aires; Chief, Emergency Department, Institute of Cardiology and Cardiovascular Surgery. Publications: 105 articles and editorials; 85 abstracts; Co-author, 8 books. Honours: Garfunkel Award, National Academy of Medicine, Argentina. Memberships: Argentine Society of Cardiology, President 1985; Argentine Cardiology Foundation, President 1986-89; Bd Member, Insternational Society and Federation of Cardiologists, 1990-94; International Fellow, Council of Clinical Cardiology; American Heart Association; International Society of Holter Monitoring, Vice-President 1992-93; Member or Honorary Member, other societies. Address: Av Libertador 2200, 1425 Buenos Aires, Argentina.

MAVES Michael Donald, b. 14 Oct 1948, East St Louis, Illinois, USA. Physician. m. Elizabeth Morris, 26 June 1971, 2 s, 1 d. Education: BS, University of Toledo, 1970; MD, Ohio State University College of Medicine, Columbus, 1973; MBA, University of Iowa, College of Business Administration, 1986-88. Appointments include: Assistant Professor, Otolaryngology, Head and Neck Surgery, Indiana University School of Medicine, Indianapolis, 1981-84; Assistant Professor, 1984-87, Associate Professor, 1987-88, Otolaryngology, Head and Neck Surgery, University of Iowa Hospitals and Clnics, Iowa City; Professor, Chairman, Department of Otolaryngology, Head and Neck Surgery, Saint Louis University School of Medicine, St Louis, Missouri, 1988-1994. Publications include: Asymptotic Threshold Shift in Man from 24-Hour Exposure to Noise, Co-author, 1974; Primary Vocal rehabilitation Using Blom-Singer and Panje Voice Prosthesis, 1982; Diagnostic Assessment of the Oral Cavity, Oropharynx and Nasopharynx, 1986; Hodgkin's Disease of the Head and Neck: The University of Iowa Experience, 1987; Editorial Comment on Irradiated Cartilage, 1991; Measures of Harmonic-to-Noise Ratio in Patients with Vocal Pathology. Honours include: 1st Prize, President's Award, Scientific Exhibits, American Academy of Otolaryngology, Head and Neck Surgery, Kansas City, 1991; St Louis University Hospital, Department of Otolaryngology, Outstanding Academic Faculty Member, 1990-91. Memberships include: Research Committee, American Academy of Facial Plastic and Reconstructive Surgery; American College of Surgeons; Association for Research in Otolaryngology. Address: American Academy of Otolaryngology, Head and Neck Surgery, 1 Prince Street, Alexandria, VA 22314, USA.

MAYALL Peter Ronald, b. 16 Apr 1944, Australia. Obstetrician & Gynaecologist. m. Heather, 12 Jan 1970, 1 son, 3 daughters. Education: MBBS, Melbourne University, 1968. Appointments: Geelong Hospital, Australia, 1969; Queen Victoria Hospital, Melbourne, 1970-71; St Albans City Hospital, England, 1978; Barner General Hospital, England, 1974; Honours: United Christian Hospital, Hong Kong, 1975-78; Greelong Hospital, 1978-. Memberships: Australian Medical Association; Royal College of Obstetricians & Gynaecologists; Royal Australian College of Obstetricians & Gynaecologists. Address: 246 Ryvie Street, Geelong, Vic 3220, Australia.

MAYER H Michael, b. 30 Apr 1954, Germany. Chief Consultant Surgeon, Department of Orthopaedic Surgery, Free University of Berlin. m. Isabel Carolin Zöller, 14 Aug 1986, 1 son, 1 daughter. Education: MD, Johannes-Gutenberg University, Germany, 1981; PhD, Free University of Berlin, 1991. Appointments: Resident, Department of Neuropathology, 1982-83; Department of Neurosurgery, 1983-85; Department of Orthopaedic Surgery, 1985-87; Department of Neurosurgery, 1987-89; Senior Lecturer, Consultant, Department of Neurosurgery, 1990-92; Chief Consultant Surgeon, Department of Orthopaedic Surgery, 1992; Assistant Professor, Free University of Berlin. Publications: Percantaneous Lumbar Disectomy, 1987; Numerous articles and contributions to journals. Memberships: German Orthopaedic Society; German Neurosurgery Society; International Society for the Study of the Lumbar Spine. Honours: Award, Young Neurosurgeon, World Federation

of Neurosurgery Society, 1989; Award, Best Presentation, International Intradiscal Therapy Society, 1988. Hobbies: Running; Soccer; Saxophone. Address: Department of Orthopaedic Surgery, Free University of Berlin, Clayallee 229, 14195 Berlin, Germany. 52.

MAYER Kenneth Hugh, b. 27 Dec 1950, New York City, USA. Physician. Education: BA, University of Pennsylvania, 1972; MD, Northwestern University Medical School, 1977; New England Epidemiology Institute, 1991. Appointments include: Intern, Junior, Senior Resident, Internal Medicine, Beth Israel Hospital, Boston, 1977-80; Adjunct Assistant Professor, 1986-89, Adjunct Associate Professor of Epidemiology, 1989, University of Massachusetts, Amherst; Adjunct Assistant Professor of Microbiology, University of Rhode Island, Kingstown, 1988; Consulting Staff, Department of Medicine, Miriam Hospital, Providence, Rhode Island, 1986; Chief, Infectious Disease Division, Memorial Hospital, Pawtucket, Rhode Island. Publications: Contributor of numerous professional articles, book chapters, abstracts and reports. Honours include: Governor's Recognition Award for AIDS Research, Commonwealth of Massachusetts, 1986; Community Recognition Award, AIDS Action Committee, Boston, 1990; Visiting Professor and Medical School Research Week Keynote Speaker, University of Queensland, Royal Brisbane Hospital, Brisbane, Australia, 1991. Memberships include: Fellow, American College of Physicians; American Public Health Association; International Society for Infectious Diseases; Society for Hospital Epidemiology. Address: Infectious Disease Division, The Memorial Hospital of Rhode Island, 111 Brewster Street, Pawtucket, RI 02860, USA.

MAYER Lawrence, b. 14 Nov 1946, Milwaukee, Wisconsin, USA. Epidemiologist. m. Sally Roberts Rohn, 12 Jan 1985. Education: BS, 1967, BA, 1968, MS, 1969, PhD, 1971, Ohio State University; MA Honours, University of Pennsylvania, 1981. Appointments: Associate Professor and Associate Master, Princeton University, 1973-79; Associate Professor and Director, Wharton Analysis Centre, University of Pennsylvania; Visiting Scholar, Stanford University, 1979-83; Professor, Arizona State University and Johns Hopkins, 1989-. Publications: Contributor of numerous professional articles. Honours: Phi Beta Kappa, 1967; Magna cum Laude, 1967; Distinguished Alumni Award, 1974. Memberships: Fellow, Royal Statistical Society; Society for Epidemiologic Research; Society of General Internal Medicine. Address: 3607 N 55th place, Phoenix, AZ 85018, USA.

MAYER Peter Paul, b. 25 May 1943, Nottingham, England. Geriatrician. m. Janet Mary Emery, 12 Aug 1969, div Jan 1993, 4 s. Education: BA, 1st Class Honours, Oxford University, 1965; MA, BM, BCh, 1968; MRCP(UK), 1971; FRCP, 1987. Appointments: Senior registrar, Geriatric Medicine, East Birmingham Hospital, 1974-75; Clinical Lecturer, Geriatric Medicine, 1975-77, Honorary Clinical Senior Lecturer, University of Birmingham; Consultant, 1977-. Publications: Contributor of numerous professional articles in journals. Honours: Goldsmith Entrance Scholarship, 1965; State Scholarship, 1961; Churchill Fellowship, 1988. Memberships: BMA; RCP, London; Midland Medical Society, President, 1992-93; West Midlands Institute of Geriatric Medicine, Director, 1993-. Hobbies: Gardening; Wine; Collecting pictures; Antiques; Swimming. Address: 16 Bryony Road, Selly Oak, Birmingham B29 4BU, England.

MAZUR Artur, b. 17 Mar 1962, Gdansk, Poland. Chiropractor. m. Sophie Nielsen, 23 Sept 1992, 1 son, 1 daughter. Education: BSc; DC. Appointments: Exercise Physiologist, British Olymic Medical Centre & Northwick Park Hospital, England. Memberships: British Chiropractic Association. Hobbies: Reading; Sports. Music. Address: Ham Chiropractic Clinic, 8 Dukes Avenue, Kingston-upon-Thames, KT2 5QY, England.

McBRIDE William Griffith, b. 25 May 1927, Sydney, Australia. Developmental Biologist. m. Patricia Glover, 16 February 1957, 2 sons, 2 daughters. Education:MBBS, 1950; MD, 1962; FRCOG, 1954; FRACOG, 1969; MACT, 1985. Appointments: Medical Superintendent, The Women's Hospital, Sydney, 1955-57; Lecturer in Obsterics & Gynaecology, University of Sydney; Director, Foundation 41, Researching Causes of Birth Defects. Publications: Congenital Malformations Caused by Thahidomide, 1961; Thalidomide May Be A Mutagen, 1994; Autobiography: Killing The Messenger, 1994; Over 85 papers in scientific journals. Honours: CBE, 1969; AO, 1977; Gold Medal, Institut de la Vie Paris, 1971. Memberships: New York Academy of Science; American Association for the Advancement of Science.

Hobbies: Surfing; Golf; Tennis; Cattle Breeding. Address: Foundation 41, 211 Bourke Street, East Sydney 2010, Australia.

McCAFFERY Laurence Andrew, b. 29 Sept 1952, Bournemouth, England. Registered Osteopath; Registered Acupuncturist. m. June Patricia Laxton, 26 may 1982, 2 d. Education: Licentiate with Honours in Acupuncture; Diploma in Osteopathy. Appointments: Assistant to S Korth; Assistant to M Power. Memberships: British Acupuncture Association and Register; Register of Osteopaths. Hobbies: Sailing; Backpacking; Walking; Cycling; Fishing. Address: 114 West Way, Bournemouth, Dorset BH9 3DZ, England.

McCAHAN John F, b. 4 Dec 1936, Philadelphia, Pennsylvania, USA. Physician. m. Kathleen M Baird, 20 June 1959, 2 s, 1 d. Education: AB; MD. Appointments: Associate Dean of Academic Affairs; Associate Professor of Medicine. Memberships: Massachusetts Medical Society; American Academy of Family Physicians; American Geriatric Society. Address: 80 East Concord Street, Boston, MA 02118, USA.

McCARTY Richard Charles, b. 12 Jul 1947, Portsmouth, VA, USA. Professor. m. Sheila Miltier McCarty, 15 Jul 1965, 3 s, 1 d. Education: BS; MS; PhD, Johns Hopkins University, 1976. Career: PRAT Fellow, National Institute of Mental Health, Bethesda, MD, 1976-78; Sr Fellow, National Heart, Lung, and Blood Institute, Bethesda, 1984-85; Visiting Scientist, National Institute of Neurological Diseases and Stroke, Bethesda, 1994-95; Currently, Professor and Chair, Department of Psychology, University of Virginia. Publications: Over 140 articles published including: Co-author, Milk electrolyte content of Dahl hypertensive and normotensive rats, in Physiology and Behavior, 1994; Endangering the aging brain: Glucocorticoids as neuronal assassins, in Contemporary Psychology, 1994; Regulation of plasma catecholamine responses to stress, in Seminars in the Neurosciences, 1994; Editor-in-Chief of Stress, 1995-. Honours include: Fellow, Academy of Behavioral Medicine Research, 1985; NIMH Research Scientist Development Award, 1985-90; Special Editor, Health Psychology, volume 7, 1988; Fellow, American Psychological Society, 1991; Sigma Xi, 1992; Fellow, American Institute of Stress, 1992; Fellow, Society of Behavioral Medicine; Fellow, American Institute on Stress, 1992. Hobbies: Sport; Gardening. Address: Department of Psychology, 102 Gilmer Hall, University of Virginia, Charlottesville, VA 22903, USA.

McCLURE Neil, b. 9 July 1959, County Down, Northern Ireland. Medical Practitioner. m. Jennifer Jane Bunting, 12 Apr 1986, 1 son, 3 daughters. Education: MD; MRCOG; MB BCh BAO, 1983. Appointments incl: House Officer, Royal Victoria Hospital, Belfast 1983-84; Regimental Medical Officer, The Lifeguards Regiment, 1985-86; Regimental Medical Officer, Devonshire & Dorset Regiment, Berlin, 1984-85; Senior Lecturer, Consultant, Queen's University of Belfast & Royal Maternity Hospital, 1994-. Publications incl: Human Follicular Fluid Maturity and Endothelial Cell Mitogenesis, 1993; Human Follicular Fluid Maturity and Endothelial Cell Chemotaxis, 1994; Histochemical Study of Human Ovarian Endothelial Cell Proliferation, 1994; Vascular Permeability Factor and Ovarian Hyperstimulation Syndrome, 1994; Electro cautery endometrial resection compared with Argon laser endometrial ablation, 1992; Luteal Phase support and ovarian hyperstimulation syndrome, 1992. Honours: Matilda Barnett Travelling Scholarship, Queens University of Belfast, 1989, 1990; Boston Fertility Society Tap GnRH Research Award, 1990; Fertility Society of Australia, Organon Young Clinician Award, 1992; Syntex Research Prize, Ulster Obstetrical & Gynaecological Society, 1994. Memberships: Ulster Medcial Society; Ulster Obstetrical & Gynaecological Society; Society for the Study of Fertility; Ulster Architectural Heritage Society; Boston Fertility Society. Hobbies: Organ and Choral Music; Irish Architecture; Horses; Motorcycles. Address: Clifden House, 15 Bangor Road, Holywood, Northern Ireland.

McCORMICK Doreen Susan, b. 24 Apr 1952, Boston, Massachusetts, USA. Clinical Psychologist. m. B McCormick, 28 June 1975, 2 sons. Education: BA, Psychology, Wellesley; MA, Child Psychology, Tufts University; In-service training in Psychology, BPS, 1981; Psychotherapy training, The Tavistock Institute, London, England. Appointments: Currently Senior Clinical Psychologist, Paediatric Oncology and Special Needs of Under 5s. Publications: Research projects: Sleep Problems in Down's Syndrome Children; Behavior Changes Following Chemotherapy for Children with Leukemia. Membership: Associate Member, British Psychological Society. Hobbies: Singing; Squash; Walking. Address: Tanglewood, 36 Greenbank Crescent, Bassett, Southampton, Hants SO16 7FQ,

England.

McCORMICK Marie Clare, b. 7 Jan 1946, Massachusetts, USA. Physician. m. Robert J Blendon, 30 Dec 1977. Education: BA, Emmanuel College, Boston, 1967; MD, Johns Hopkins Medical School, 1971; ScN, Johns Hopkins School of Hygiene and Public Health, 1978. Appointments: Assistant Professor, Johns Hopkins School of Hygiene and Public Health; Assistant Professor of Paediatrics, Associate Professor, University of Pennsylvania; Professor and Chair, Department of Maternal and Child Health, Harvard School of Public Health; Professor of Paediatrics, Harvard Medical School. Publications: Contributor of over 100 articles in professional journals. Honours: Honorary Masters, Harvard University, 1991. Memberships: Fellow, American Academy of Paediatrics; American Paediatric Society; American Public Health Association; Association for Health Services Research. Address: Department of Maternal and Child Health, Harvard School of Public Health, 677 Huntington Avenue, Boston, MA 02115, USA.

McCULLOUGH David Legarde, b. 2 Nov 1938, Chatanooga, TN, USA. Urologic Surgeon. m. Miriam Carroll Lisenby, 1 s, 2 d. Education: BS, Davidson College; MD, Bowman Gray School of Medicine of Wake Forest University. Career: Chairman, University of South AL Medical Center, Mobile, 1975-81; Chairman, Urology Department, Provident Hospital, Mobile, AL, 1978-; Chairman, Urology Department, Knollwood Park Hospital, Mobile, AL, 1982-83; Currently, Professor and Chairman, Bowman Gray School of Medicine, Wake Forest University, Winston-Salem, NC, 1983-. Publications include: Co-author, Correlation of prostate specific antigen (PSA) and prostate specific antigen density (PSAD) with outcome of prostate biopsy, in Urology, 1993; Author, Minimally invasive management of benign prostatic hyperplasia, in Campbell's Urology Update 8, 6th edition, 1993; Co-author, Nephrolithiasis clinical guidelines panel summary report on the management of staghorn calculi, in Journal of Urology, 1994. Honours: Omicron Delta Kappa, 1959; Phi Beta Kappa, 1960; Alpha Omega Alpha, 1964; American Association of Genitourinary Surgeons; Clinical Society of Urinary Surgeons, 1994. Memberships: President, American Board of Urology; Secretary, Southeastern Section of American Urological Association; American College of Surgeons; American Urologic Association; Transamerican Urological Research Association; Southern Society of Urological Surgeons; American Association of Genitourinary Surgeons; Clinical Society of Urinary Surgeons. Hobby: Tennis. Address: Department of Urology, Bowman Gray School of Medicine, Wake Forest University, Winston-Salem, NC 27157, USA.

McCUNE William Stanley, b. 4 June 1909, Petoskey, Michigan, USA. General Surgeon. m. Mary Dykhouse, 22 Mar 1975, 4 daughters. Education: BA with highest honours, Swarthmore College, Swarthmore, Pennsylvania; MD with honours, Harvard University Medical School. Appointments include: Clinical Associate Professor of Surgery, then Clinical Professor of Surgery, George Washington University School of Medicine; Now retired. Publications: Endoscopic Cannalization of Ampulla of Vater, 1967. Honours: Admitted to membership in: Southern Surgical Association, 1949; American Surgical Association, 1953; Southeastern Surgical Congress, 1955. Hobbies: Golf; Novel author. Address: 1134 Charlevoix Avenue, Petoskey, MI 48770, USA.

McDERMOTT John F Jr, b. 12 Dec 1929, Hartford, Connecticut, USA. Professor. m. Sarah Nobel, 27 Dec 1958, 1 s, 1 d. Education: AB, Cornell University; MD, New York Medical College; Residency training in Psychiatry, Child and Adolescent Psychiatry, University of Michigan; FAPA; FAACAP. Appointments: Instructor, Assistant Professor, Associate professor, University of Michigan School of Medicine, 1960-69; Professor and Chair, Department of Psychiatry, University of Hawaii School of Medicine. Publications: Psychiatry for the Pediatrician, Co-author, 1970; Childhood Psychopathology, Co-author, 1972; Mental Health Education in New Medical Schools, Co-editor, 1973; Roles and Functions of Child Psychiatrists, Co-author, 1976; Psychiatric Treatment of the Child, Co-editor, 1977; Adjustment in Intercultural Marriage, Co-editor, 1977; Raising Cain (And Abel Too): The Parents Book of Sibling Rivalry, 1980; New Directions in Childhood Psychopathology Vol 1 Developmental Considerations, Co-editor, 1981; People and Cultures of Hawaii: A Psychocultural Profile, CO-editor, 1980; Culture, Mind and Therapy: Introduction to Cultural sychiatry, CO-author, 1981; New Directions in Childhood Psychopathology Vol II Deviations of Development, Co-editor, 1982; Contributor of over 150 articles in professional journals. Honours include: Distinguished Alumnus Award, New York Medical College, 1976; Visiting Senior Scientist, Department of Experimental psychology, Oxford University, England, 1993; Scholar-in-Residence, Rockerfeller Foundation, Villa Serbelloni, Bellagio, Italy. Memberships include: American College of Psychiatrists; Group for the Advancement of Psychiatry; American Academy of Child and Adolescent Psychiatry; World Psychiatric Association. Address: 1319 Punahou Street No 633, Honolulu, HI 96826, USA.

McDONALD Franklin Delano, b. 11 Nov 1936, Tarraqua, Pennsylvania, USA. Physician. m. Lana Thosteson, 11 Feb 1978, 5 d. Education: BS, St Joseph's University, {hiladelphia; MD, Temple University; Advanced Management, Wharton Business School, University of Pennsylvania. Appointments: Research Fellow, Harvard Medical School, 1966-69; Assistant Professor, 1969-72, Associate professor of Medicine, 1972, University of Michigan; Associate Professor, 1972-76, Professor of Medicine, 1976-, Chief of Nephrology, 1972-91 Wayne State University; Vice President of Medical Services, Hutzel Hospital, Detroit. Publications: Progress in Clinical Kidney Disease and Hypertension, Volumes 1 and 2; Contributor of over 100 refereed papers and over 200 abstracts and presentations. Honours: Distinguished Service Award, National Kidney Foundation, 1979; President's award, National Kidney Foundation, 1987; Rocke Award, Temple University, 1960; AOA, 1961. Memberships: AFCR; American College of Physicians; National Kidney Foundation; Renal Physicians Association; American College of Physician Executives. Hobby: Golf. Address: 4707 St Antoine, Detroit, MI 48201, USA.

McFARLAND Lynne, b. 3 June 1953, San Antonio, Texas, USA. Epidemiologist. m. Marcus Joseph McFarland, 27 July 1975. Education: BS, Biology, 1975, MS, Biology, 1980, Portland State University; PhD, Epidemiology, University of Washington, Seattle, 1988. Appointments: Lecturer, 1988, Research Associate, 1988-91, Research Assistant Professor, 1991-, Department of Medicinal Chemistry, University of Washington, Seattle; Director of Scientific Affairs, Chief Executive Officer, Business Manager, Biocodex Inc, 1988-. Publications: Book chapters: Hospital-Acquired Diarrhea, 1993; Clostridium difficile Associated Disease, 1994; Nosocomial infections, 1994: Over 30 articles mostly on Clostridium difficile infections and their treatment, especially with   Saccharomyces   boulardii;   Antibiotic-Associated Pseudomembranous Colitis (with J Silva and P Lynch), videotape and monograph, 1990. Honours: Air Force Aid Society Scholarship, 1971-75; Graduate School Research Assistantship, University of Washington, Seattle, 1984-87; Poncin Scholarship Fund, Seafirst Bank, Seattle, 1984-87. Memberships: American Society of Microbiology; Society for Epidemiologic Research; Society of Microbial Ecology and Disease; Washington Association of Epidemiology; American Association for the Advancement of Science; Washington State Biotechnology Association; Society for Hospital Epidemiology of America. Hobbies: Photography (medical, environmental, photojournalism); Flute; Piano; Snorkelling; Writing haikus; Skiing; Hiking; Mountain climbing; Literacy plus. Address: 1910 Fairview Avenue East, Suite 208, Seattle, WA 98102, USA.

McFARLANE Alexander Cowell, b. 27 May 1952. Professor of Psychiatry. m. Catherine May McFarlane, 25 June 1977, 2 sons, 1 daughter. Education: MBBS (Hons), 1976, Diploma in Psychotherapy, 1983, MD, 1990, Adelaide University; FRANZCP. Appointments: Senior Lecturer in Psychiatry, 1985-90, Head, Department of Psychiatry, 1989-90, The Flinders University of South Australia; Professor of Communication and Rehabilitation Psychiatry, University of Adelaide, 1990-. Publications: Over 80 including: The severity of Trauma, what is its role in post traumatic stress disorder, 1994; Individual psychotherapy of post traumatic stress disorder. Psychiatric Clinics of North America, 1994. Honours: Frank S Hone Memorial Prize, 1975; H K Fry Memorial Prize for Psychological Medicine, 1975; Organon Junior Research Award, 1986. Memberships: Australian Medical Association; Australian Society for Psychiatric Research; International Society of Traumatic Stress Studies; Australian Society of Traumatic Stress Studies. Hobbies: Tennis; Windsurfing. Address: PO Box 17, Eastwood, South Australia 5062, Australia.

McGANN Duchess Sheila, b. 11 May 1948, Kingston, Jamaica, West Indies. Medical Practitioner. Education: MBBS, Honours in Anatomy, University of West Indies, 1974; ECFMG, 1974; Honorary FACOG, 1980; MRCOG, London, 1982; FMGEMS, NY and Kingston, 1985; FLEX, Seattle, WA, 1980; FRCS, Edinburgh, Scotland, 1990. Appointments: Internship, Pediatric Medicine and Obstetrics and Gynaecology; Elective Microbiology; Completed residency training in obstetrics and gynaecology and general surgery; Staff, Casualty

Department; Currently, Private Practice, General Practitioner. Publications: Research into Maternal Mortality at University Hospital West Indies, for MRCOG Log Book; The Outcome in Women Treated Surgically for Advanced Cerival Cancer; Research into Infections Encountered in the Immunosuppressed. Honours include: Farquharson Scholarship in Natural Sciences. Memberships: Medical Defence Union, UK; Medical Association of Jamaica. Hobbies: Reading; Business Administration Studies.

McGOVERN Dermot Anthony, b. 30 May 1949, Birmingham, UK. Psychiatrist. 3 d. Education: MB, CHB, Birmingham, 1974; MRC Psych. Appointments: Senior Registrar, West Midlands, UK; Staff Psychiatrist, Wollomyong, New South Wales, Australia; Consultant, North East Worcestershire Health Trust. Publications: First Psychiatric Admissions of First and Second Generation AfroCaribbean, 1987; A Follow Up of Second Generation AfroCaribbean and White British with a First Admission Diagnosis of Schizophrenia, 1994. Memberships: Royal College of Psychiatrists. Address: 71 Wentworth Road, Harbonne, Birmingham B17 9SS, UK.

McGOWAN David Alexander, b. 18 Jun 1939, Portadown, Northern Ireland. Oral Surgeon. m. Margaret Macauley, 21 Jun 1968, 1 s, 2 d. Education: BDS, Queen's University, Belfast, 1961; FDSRCS (England), 1964; FFDRCS (Ireland), 1966; MDS, Queen's University, Belfast, 1970; PhD, University of London, 1977; FDSRCPS (Glasgow), 1979. Career: Lecturer in Dental Surgery, Queen's University, Belfast, 1968; Senior Lecturer in Oral Surgery, London Hospital Medical College, 1968-77; Postgraduate Adviser in Dentistry, 1977-89, Currently, Professor of Oral Surgery and Dean of Dental Education, University of Glasgow. Publications: Co-author, Outline of Oral Surgery, Part 1, 1988; An Atlas of Minor Oral Surgery, 1989; co-author, The Maxillary Sinus, 1993. Honour: Dean, Dental Faculty, Royal College of Physicians and Surgeons of Glasgow, 1989-92. Memberships: General Dental Council; EC Advisory Committee on Training of Dental Practitioners; National Dental Advisory Committee (Scotland); Former Councillor, British Association of Oral and Maxillofacial Surgeons. Hobbies: Walking; Sailing; Music. Address: Glasgow Dental Hospital and School, 378 Sauchiehall Street, Glasgow, G2 3JZ, Scotland.

McGREGOR James A, b. 8 Feb 1944. Physician. 1 son, 2 daughters. Education: AB, Dartmouth College, Hanover, New Hampshire, 1966; MDCM, McGill University, Montreal, Canada. Appointments include: Currently Physician, Professor, Obstetrics and Gynaecology, Infectious Desease, University of Colorado Health Sciences Center, Denver. Address: University of Colorado Health Sciences Center, 4200 E 9th Avenue, B-198, Denver, CO 80262, USA.

McINDOE Gerald Angus James, b. 24 Aug 1955, New Zealand. m. Bernadette Bolger, 17 July 1987, 2 sons, 1 daughter. Education: BSc; MB; ChB; PhD; FRCS; MRCOG. Appointments: Senior Registrar, St Mary's Hospital, London & Adenbrooke's Hospital, Cambridge. Address: Institute of Obstetrics & Gynaecology, Hammersmith Hospitals NHS Trust, Du Cane Road, London W12 0HS, England.

McINTIRE Matilda S, b. 15 July 1920. Physician; Paediatrician. m. Dr Waldean C McIntire, 12 July 1947, 1 s. Education: BA, Mount Holyoke College, USA, 1942; MD, Albany Medical College, 1946. Appointments Include: Yellow Fever Programme, Rockefeller Foundation for Medical research, International Health Division, 1942-43; Director, Division of Maternal and Child Health, Omaha/Douglas County Health department, 1966-73; Clinical Professor of Public Health and Preventative Medicine, 1966-, Professor of Paediatrics, 1973-90, Director of Ambulatory Paediatrics, 1973-89, Clinical Professor of Paediatrics, 1990-, Professor of Paediatrics, 1973-90, Professor Emeritus of Paediatrics, 1991, Creighton University School of Medicine; Chief, Ambulatory Paediatric Service, St Joseph Memorial Hospital, 1974-89; Medical Director, Nebraska Poison Control Centre, Children's Memeorial Hospital, 1955-61, 1979-; Clinical professor of Paediatrics, 1984-, Senior Consultant of Paediatrics, 1991, University of Nebraska College of Medicine. Publications: Author of numerous professional articles, reports, abstracts to journals and conferences. Honours sinclude: Honorary DSc, Mount Holyoke, 1989; Distinguished Service Award, Crieghton University, 1989; Certification of Aoppreciation, US Consumer Product Safety Commission, 1972-75. Memberships include: American Association of Poison Cntrol Centers, President, 1978-80; Committee on Accident Prevention, 1974-78, 1977-80; American Association of Medical Colleges, Women's Liaison Officer, Creighton

University School of Medicine, 1977-87. Hobbies: Gardening; Music. Address: 1510 South 80 Street, Omaha, NE 68124, USA.

McINTOSH Shona Anne, b. 21 Mar 1964, Edinburgh, Scotland. Chartered Clinical Psychologist. m. Jonathan N Michaelis, 7 Jul 1988, 1 s, 1 d. Education: MA, Psychology, St Andrews University, 1986; Diploma, Clinical Psychology, Wessex, 1993. Career: Research Psychologist, Department of Rehabilitation Medicine, Southampton University, 1986-89; Currently, Chartered Clinical Psychologist. Publications: Co-author, The prevalence of cognitive impairment in a community survey of multiple sclerosis, in British Journal of Clinical Psychology, 1991; Co-author, The prevalence of multiple sclerosis in Southampton and South West Hampshire Health Authority, in Journal of Neurosurgery and Psychiatry, 1991; Co-author of chapter in, Neurological Rehabilitation, 1993. Memberships: British Neuropsychological Society; British Psychological Society; Associate Member, Group Analytic Society; Associate Member, Society for Research in Rehabilitation; Institute of Group Analysis. Hobbies: Theatre; Vegetarian Cooking; Food; Cello Music. Address: Yalp, 13 Spencer Road, Buxton, Derbyshire, SK17 9DX, England.

McINTYRE John, b. 21 Apr 1942, New York City, USA. Psychiatrist. m. Ann, 20 Aug 1966, 3 s, 1 d. Education: BA, University of Notre Dame, 1963; MD, University of Rochester, 1967. Appointments: President, American Psychiatric Association, 1983-94; Chair, Department of psychiatry, St Mary's Hospital, Rochester, New York; Clinical Professor of Psychiatry, University of Rochester. Publications: Contributor of numerous works in psychiatric and medical journals, 1969-. Honours: Distinguished Service Award, American Academy of Clinical Psychiatrists, 1993; George Ginsberg Award, NYS Psychiatric Association, 1993; Dr Ramon Fernandez Marina Award, Puerto Rico, 1992. Memberships: American Psychiatric Association; Academy of Psychosomatic Medicine; American Academy of Psychiatry and Law; American College of Psychiatry; American Medical Association Hobby: Tennis. Address: 919 Westfall Road, Suite C-210, Rochester, NY 14618, USA.

McKAY Roxane, b. Washington, USA. Congenital Heart Surgeon. Education: BA, magna cum laude, Occidental College, Los Angeles, 1966; MD, University of Chicago, 1970; FRCS; FRCSC; MRCS; LRCP. Appointments: Consultant Paediatric Cardiothoracic Surgeon, The Royal Liverpool Children's Hospital, 1982-92; Professor of Surgery and Paediatrics. Publications: Principles of Cardiac Diagnosis and Treatment - A Surgeon's Guide, Co-author, 1992; Morphology of the Ventriculoaortic Junction in Critical Aortic Stenosis, 1992. Honours: Phi Beta Kappa, 1966; Alpha Omega Alpha, 1970; Annie Wright School Alumnae Award, 1988; Honorary Member, Polish Association Paediatric Surgery, 1992; Merseyside Gold Medal Achievement Award, 1988. Memberships: Royal Society of Medicine; American College of Cardiology; British Cardiac Society; European Association for Cardiothoracic Surgery. Hobbies: Badminton; Classical Music. Address: Department of Surgery, University of Saskatchewan, Saskatoon, Saskatchewan S7N 0W8, Canada.

McKENNA Patricia Kathleen Hilda, b. 10 Mar 1948, London, England. Neuropsychologist. m. William Brian Davies, 27 Sept 1980, 2 d. Education: BSc, PhD, Cardiff, 1994. Appointments: Clinical Psychologist, National Hospital for Neurology, London, 1976-81; Clinical Research Psychologist, Brook Hospital, London, 1984-88; Clinical Psychologist, Brook Hospital, 1988-89; Clinical Psychologist, Rookwood Hospital, Cardiff, 1989-. Publications: Graded Naming Test, 1983; Cognitive Status and Quality of Life Following Subarachnoid Haemorrhage, Co-author, 1989; Recovery after Subarachnoid Haemorrhage, Co-author, 1989; Category-Specificity in Naming Natural and Man-Made Objects: Normative Data from Adults and Children, Co-author, 1994; Category and Modality Deficits of Semantic Memory in Patients with Left Hemisphere Pathology, Co-author, 1994; New Category Naming Test. Address: Rookwood Hospital, Llandaff, Cardiff CF5 2YN, Wales.

McKNIGHT William, b. 15 Feb 1911, Beaver Falls, Pennsylvania, USA. Physician-Psychiatrist. m. Elizabeth Schum, 17 Mar 1938. Education: BS; MD; Fellow, American Psychiatric Association. Appointments: Now retired. Address: 501 S La Posada Circle, Apt 314, Green Valley, AZ 85614, USA.

McLEAN Alexander Cameron, b. 9 July 1914, Dunedin, New Zealand. Retired Dental Surgeon. m. (1) Edith Marion West, 22 Sept

1939 (dec.), 2 sons, 1 daughter, (2) Helen Euphemia McKenzie, 17 Aug 1974. Education: BDS, New Zealand; Postgraduate study, Crown and Bridge, Eastman Dental Hospital, London University. Hobbies: Reading; Golf; Gardening; Painting. Address: 4 Clematis Court, Wanaka, New Zealand.

McLOONE James Brian, b. 21 Mar 1950. Psychiatrist. m. Barbara Bathe, 9 June 1972, 1 son, 1 daughter. Education: BA, University of Arizona, 1972; MD, George Washington University School of Medicine, 1976; Psychiatric Residency, Neuropsychiatric Institute, University of California, Los Angeles, 1976-80; Diplomate, Adult and Geriatric Psychiatry, American Board of Psychiatry and Neurology. Appointments: In-patient Medical Director, Maricopa Medical Center, 1980-81; Director of Residency Training, 1981-, Medical Director, 1986-92, Chairman, 1992-, Good Samaritan Regional Medical Center. Publications: Psychosocial Adaptation Following Myocardial Infarction (with M Stern and L Pascale), 1976. Honours: Alpha Omega Alpha, 1975; Associate Professor of Clinical Psychiatry, University of Arizona, 1995. Memberships: American Psychiatric Association; American Association of Directors of Psychiatric Training; Association for Academic Psychiatry; Association for Hospital Medical Education. Hobbies: Golf; Hiking; Tennis; Gardening. Address: 925 E McDowell Road, Phoenix, AZ 85006, USA.

McMANUS Thomas, b. 24 Oct 1948, Scotland. Doctor of Medicine. Education: MBChB, Glasgow University, 1972; MRCOG, 1977; FRCOG, 1992. Career: Lalor Research Fellow, University of Glasgow; Registrar, Senior Registrar, Genito-Urinary Medicine, St Mary's Hospital, London; Consultant, Genito Urinary Medicine, King's College Hospital, London; Currently, Consultant Physician and Care Group Director, Genito Urinary Medicine, King's College Hospital, London. Publications: Male Homosexual Behaviour, in Counselling HIV Infection and AIDS, 1989; Co-author, Sexually Transmitted Diseases, in Textbook of Medicine, 1994. Memberships: Honorary Secretary, Medical Society for the Study of Veneral Diseases; Royal Society of Medicine; British Medical Association. Hobbies: Opera; Reading; Skiing. Address: Department of Genito Urinary Medicine, King's Healthcare, London, SE5, England.

McMILLAN Euan Murray, b. 17 Dec 1949, Irvine, Scotland. Dermatologist. m. Barbara C Marshall, 1 son, Education: BMed Sci, BSC (Honours) Path, MB ChB, MD, University of Edinburgh. Appointments: Instructor, 1980-81, Assistant Professor, 1981-87, Associate Clinical Professor, 1987-92, USA; Private Practice, Dermatology and Dermatopathology. Publications: Author of 40 scientific publications. Honours: MRCP Diploma, Paediatrics, 1977; American Board of Dermatology, 1982; American Board Dermatopathology, 1983; American Board Dermatologic Immunology, Diagnostic and Laboratory Immunology, 1989. Memberships: Scottish Dermatology Society; Fellow, American Academy of Dermatology; Fellow, American Society of Dermatopathology. Hobby: Cycling. Address: Mercy Doctors Tower, 4200 W Memorial Road, Oklahoma City, OK 73120, USA.

McVIE John Gordon, b. 13 Jan 1945, Glasgow, Scotland. Oncologist; Medical Doctor. m. Evelyn Mary Strang, 16 Sept 1966 (separated), 3 s. Education: BSc Honors, University of Edinburgh, Scotland; MB, University of Edinburgh; ChB, University of Edinburgh; MD, University of Edinburgh; MRCP; FRCP; FRCPS. Appointments: Medical Research Council Fellow, Edinburgh University 1970-71; Lecturer in Therapeutics, Edinburgh University, 1971-76; Senior Lecturer in Clinical Oncology, Glasgow University, 1976-80; Head, Clinical Research Unit, Netherlands Cancer Institute, Amsterdam, 1980-84; Clinical Research Director, Netherlands Cancer Institute, 1984-89; Scientific Director, Cancer Research Campaign, London, 1989-. Publications: Cancer Assessment & Monitoring, 1979; Autologous Bone Marrow Transplantation & Solid Tumours, 1984; Microspheres and Drug Therapy, 1984; Clinical & Experimental Pathology and Biology of Lung Cancer, 1985. Honours: Chairman UICC Fellowships Program, 1990; President, European Organisation for Research & Treatment of Cancer, 1994; European Editor of Journal of National Cancer Institute, 1994. Memberships: Faculty of Medicine, Edinburgh, 1974-76; Council of Scottish Action for Smoking and Health, 1975-80; Royal College of Physicians of Edinburgh, 1976-; Royal College of Physicians & Surgeons, Glasgow, 1978-; Medical Research Council Cancer Therapy Committee, UK, 1984-92; Netherlands Cancer Institute, 1984-89; Permanent Committee on Oncology, Ministry of Health, The Netherlands, 1986-89. Hobbies: Opera; Theatre; Cooking; Italian Wine. Address: c/o Cancer Research Campaign, 10 Cambridge Terrace, London NW1 4JL, UK.

MEAD Beverley Tupper, b. 22 Jan 1923, New Orleans, Louisiana, USA. Physician; Psychiatrist. m. Ruth Cottingham, 8 June 1947. Education: BS, University of South Carolina, 1943; MD, Medical College of State of South Carolina, 1947; MS, Psychiatry, University of Utah, 1958. Appointments: US Army Medical Corp, final rank Captain, 1951-54; Assistant Professor, University of Utah School of Medicine, 1954-61; Associate Professor, University of Kentucky School of Medicine, 1961-65; Professor, 1965-, Department Chairman, 1965-77, Acting Chairman, 1987-89, Associate Dean of Academic Affairs, 1979-88, Creighton University School of Medicine; Professor of Psychiatry, Creighton-Nebraska Department of Psychiatry. Memberships: Fellow, American College of Psychiatry; Fellow, American Psychiatric Association; Former President, Central Neuropsychiatric Association; Former President, Nebraska Psychiatric Society. Hobby: Golf. Address: Creighton-Nebraska Department of Psychiatry, 819 Dorcas Street, Omaha, NE 68108, USA.

MEGGS William Joel, b. 30 May 1942, Newberry, SC, USA. Physician. m. Susan Spring, 11 Jun 1966, 3 s. Education: BS, Physics, Clemson University, 1964; MD, University of Miami; PhD, Physics, Syracuse University. Career includes: Research Physicist, McGill University, Montreal, Canada, 1971-77; Medical Staff Fellow, National Institute of Allergy and Infectious Disease, Bethesda, MD, 1982-85; Director and Chairman, Emergency Department, Lenoir Memorial Hospital, NC, 1990-91; Assistant Professor, Division of Toxicology, Department of Emergency Medicine, East Carolina University School of Medicine, Greenville, NC, 1991-. Publications include: Many articles in refereed journals, a book and book chapters, abstracts and numerous presentations including: Co-author, Biomarkers of Immunotoxicity, book, 1992; Author, Developing clinical research protocols for studying chemical sensitivities, chapter, 1992; Author, Neurogenic inflammation and sensitivity to environmental chemicals, in Environmental Health Perspectives, 1993. Honours: Woodrow Wilson Honorary Fellow, 1964; Clemson University Faculty Medal, 1964; National Science Foundation Postdoctoral Fellow, 1969. Memberships: American College of Emergency Physicians; American Academy of Allergy and Immunology; American College of Physicians; Clinical Immunology Society; International Society of Bioelectricity; AMA; Pitt County Medical Society; NC State Medical Society; Society for Academic Emergency Medicine; Physician's Section, NC Thoracic Society. Address: Department of Emergency Medicine, East Carolina Univerity School of Medicine, Greenville, NC 27858, USA.

MEHTANI Janak, b. 4 Aug 1950, India. Physician. m. Nalini Mehtani,1 son, 2 daughters. Education: MD; Diplomate, American Board of Psychiatry and Neurology. Appointments: Fellow, Department of Psychiatry, Johns Hopkins University Hospital, USA, 1977; Clinical Assistant Professor, UCD Medical Centre, Sacramento, 1978-82; Medical Director, American Fiva Hospital Mental Health Unit, 1981-85; Medical Director, Sutter Hospital, 1983-84; Medical Director, Fairoaks Hospital, 1985-90; Associate Medical Director, CPC Sr Hospital, 1990-; Chief Executive Officer, Fair Oaks Psychiatric Associates. Publications: Contribdutor of articles in professional journals. Honours: Recipient of honours and awards for professional services. Memberships: American Psychiatric Association; American Association of Physician Executives; California Medical Association; American Association of Addiction Medicine. Hobbies: Racquetball; Tennis; Skiing; Biking; Photography. Address: 2277 Fair Oaks #150, Sacramento, CA 95825, USA.

MEI Hua-Jia, b. 10 Mar 1946, Jingjiang City, Jiangsu Province, China. Professor. m. 1 Oct 1968, 1 son, 2 daughter. Appointments: Vice-Doctor in charge of a case; Department of Traditional Chinese Internal Medicine, 1966-79; Department of Anus and Intestines, Municipal Hospital, Jingjiang, 1980-. Publications: Say Something About Spare Time of Examinee, 1991; Co-author: The Practical Prescription and Dosage Dictionary, 1989; Taboo of Medicine Use for Family, 1991; Consulting Service of Pain Disease for Family Treatment, 1994; About 100 sections in provincial magazines. Honours: Young and Middle-Aged Topnotch Professor in Jingjiang, 1989; Science and Technology Worker Contributing Greatly to Medicine, 1990. Memberships: Traditional Chinese Medical Science Institute, China; Secretary-General, Tradition Chinese Medical Science Institute, Jingjiang. Hobbies: Classical poetry; Running. Address: Municipal Hospital, Jingjiang, Jiangsu, China.

MEI Yun Wu, b. 8 Apr 1926, Chekiang Province, China. Teacher. m. 30 Jun 1953, 2 d. Education: Graduate, Shanghai Medical University, 1952. Career includes: Director of Forensic Department, 1982-84, Director of Forensic Biology Department, 1985-, West China University of Medical Sciences, Chengdu. Publications include: Translator and Corrector of 3 books; 80 papers published including: Co-author, Polymorphic analysis of DIS80 locus in a Chinese population by the PCR method, in Chinese Medical Genetics, 1994; Chief Editor, Blood Group Serology and Examination of Physical Evidence, 1990; Contributor to 4 books including, Criminal Sciences of Law Dictionary, Forensic Medicine Section, 1991. Honours: 3rd class prize, Scientific Technical Advance, Quangdong Province Government, 1983; Splendid Book for Teaching Award, Chinese Health Ministry, 1988; 3 Prizes for papers published, 1990, 1991, 1993. Memberships: Chinese Association of Forensic Medicine; Sichuan Province Association of Forensic Medicine; Sichuan Province Appraisal Committee of Forensic Medicine; Chinese Committee Leading Forensic Medicine Program. Hobby: Music. Address: School of Forensic Medicine, West China University of Medical Sciences, 17 South Ren Mind Road, Chengdu 610044, Sichuan, China.

MEI Zhen-Tong, b. 21 Jan 1928, Hangzhou, Zhejiang Province, China. Scientist. m. Professor Xu Ke, 27 July 1956, 2 s. Education: Graduate, Department of Biology, Beijing University, 1949; BS; PhD, Academy of Sciences, USSR, 1955. Appointments: Associate Researcher, 1955, Associate Professor, 1960, Head, department of Physiology, 1960-66, Professor, 1978, Director, 1984-88, Head of Laboratory of Brain and Behaviour, Shanghai Institute of Physiology, Chinese Academy of Sciences. Publications: Contributor of numerous professional articles including: The Role of Monosialoganglioside GMI in LTP-induction in Rat Hippocampal Slices, 1994. Memberships: Chinese Association for Physiological Sciences; Chinese Association for Psychology; IBRO. Hobbies: Gardening; Music. Address: Shanghai Institute of Physiology, Chinese Academy of Sciences, 320 Yue Yang Road, Shanghai 200031, China.

MEIER Helen Margaret Rosemary, b. 6 Jan 1943, Enfield, England. Psychiatrist. m. Peter Meier, 15 July 1967, 1 son, 1 daughter. Education: MB, ChB (Aberdeen); MSc (Toronto); DPM (London); MRCPsych (UK); FRCPC (Canada). Appointments: Coordinator, Geriatric Psychiatry Programme, Toronto Western Hospital, Toronto, Canada; Currently Director, Psychiatry Consultation Programme, St Michael's and Wellesley Hospitals, University of Toronto, Toronto. Publications: Psychogeriatric Admission: Terminable or Interminable?, 1992; Confusion, 1993. Honours: Ontario Volunteer Award, Canadian Centre for the Victims of Torture, 1994. Memberships: Canadian Psychiatric Association; American Psychiatric Association; Canadian Bioethics Society; International Psychogeriatrics Association. Memberships: Reading; Choral singing; Domestic pursuits. Address: 334 Jones Building, The Wellesley Hospital, 160 Wellesley Street East, Toronto, Ontario, Canada M4Y 1J3.

MEISSNER William Walter, b. 13 Feb 1931, Buffalo, New York, USA. Psychiatrist; Psychoanalyst; Clergyman; Professor. Education: BA magna cum laude, 1956, MA, 1957, PhL, 1957, St Louis University; STL, Woodstock College, 1962; MD cum laude, Harvard Medical School, 1967; Postdoctoral Training, 1964-71; Candidate, Boston Psychoanalytic Institute, Boston. Appointments: Faculty member, 1971-, Training and Supervising Analyst, 1980-, Boston Psychoanalytic Institute; Clinical Professor of Psychiatry, Harvard Medical School, 1981-87; University Professor of Psychoanalysis, Boston College, 1987-. Publications: Author of 16 books including: Psychotherapy and the Paranoid Process, 1986; Treatment of Patients in the Borderline Spectrum, 1988; Ignatius of Loyola: The Psychology of a Saint, 1992; Contributor of 168 articles and 41 chapters in books. Honours: Psi Chi; Sigma Chi; Felix and Helene Deutsch Prize, Boston Psychoanalytic Institute, 1969; Oskar Pfister Award, Psychiatric Association, 1989. Memberships: Boston Psychoanalytic Institute; Massachusetts Psychatric Society; American Psychoanalytic Association; American Psychiatric Association; Centre for the Advancement of Psychoanalytic Studies; International Psycho-Analytical Association; Member on 16 Editorial Boards. Address: Carney Hall 420 D, Boston College, Chestnut Hill, MA 02167, USA.

MEKKAWY Emad El, b. 27 Mar 1949, Cairo, Egypt. Gynaecologist and Obstetrician; General Practitioner. Education: MB BCh; MRCOG. Appointments: Currently General Practitioner, Springwell Health Centre, Sunderland, England. Memberships: North of English Society of Obstetricians and Gynaecologists; Vice-Chairman, British Medical Associaton, Sunderland Branch. Address: 50 Killingworth Drive, High Barnes, Sunderland, Tyne and Wear SR4 8QN, England.

MELA David Jason, b. 25 Sep 1958, Washington DC, USA. Research Scientist. m. Ann Patricia Robinson, 26 May 1984, 2 s, 1 d. Education: BS, Animal Sciences, University of VT, 1979; PhD, Human Nutrition, PA State University, 1985; Registered Accredited Nutritionist, Institute of Biology. Career: Postdoctoral Fellow, 1985-87, Assistant Member, 1987-89, Monell Chemical Services Center, Philadelphia, PA; Currently, Head of Food Acceptance Section, Consumer Sciences Department, Institute of Food Research, Reading, England, 1990-. Publications: Author or co-author of over 50 professional and technical articles; Editor, Dietary Fats: Determinants of preference, selection, and consumption, 1992. Honour: Young Scientist Award for research on food choice, British Nutrition Foundation, 1992. Memberships: American Institute of Nutrition; American Society for Clinical Nutrition; Association for Chemoreception Sciences; Institute of Food Technologists; Nutrition Society. Hobby: Mushroom identification and collection. Address: Institute of Food Research, Earley Gate, Whiteknights Road, Reading, Berkshire, RG6 2BZ, England.

MELDRUM Brian Stuart, b. 20 Aug 1935, Ipswich, England. Professor of Experimental Neurology. m. (1) Mary Fryer, 4 Jan 1958, (2) Astrid Chapman, 14 Aug 1981, 2 sons, 1 daughter. Education: BA, Cambridge University, 1956; MA (Cantab); MB BChir, 1959; PhD, University College, London, 1964. Appointments: Research Assistant, Department of Physiology, University College, London, 1961-63; Scientific Staff, Medical Research Council Neuropsychiatric Research Unit, Carshalton, 1963-73; Senior Lecturer, Reader, Professor of Experimental Neurology, Department of Neurology, Institute of Psychiatry, London, 1973-. Publications: Recent Advances in Epilepsy 1-6 (co-editor), 1983-94; Excitatory Amino Acids Antagonists (editor), 1991. Honours: Michael Prize, 1980-81; W G Lennox Lecturer, AES, 1980. Memberships: Society for Neuroscience; British Medical Association; The Physiological Society; British Pharmacological Society; British Neuropathological Society; International Society for Cerebral Blood Flow and Metabolism. Address: Department of Neurology, Institute of Psychiatry, De Crespigny Park, London SE5 8AF, England.

MELDRUM David Roy, b. 28 Feb 1945, Regina, Canada. Physician. m. Claudia Lee Schaefer, 3 May 1970, 2 s, 2 d. Education: BSc, Great Distinction, 1967, MD, 1969, McGill University. Appointments: Clinical Professor, UCLA School of Medicine and Director, Center for Advanced Reproductive Care. Honour: Wood's Gold Medal, McGill University, 1969. Memberships: American Society for Reproductive Medicine; Society for Gynaecologic Investigation; Pacific Coast Fertility Society. Hobbies: Pilot; Scuba Diving; Skiing. Address: 510 North Prospect Avenue, Suite 202, Redondo Beach, CA 90277-3028, USA.

MELLION Morris Bernard, b. 24 Dec 1939, Providence, RI, USA. Physician. m. Irene Mabel Commer, 6 June 1970, 1 s, 1 d. Education: BA, Honours; MD; Diplomate, American Board of Family Practice; Fellow, American Academy of Family Physicians; American Board of Family Practice Certificate of Added Qualigications in Sports Medicine. Appointments include: Medical Director, Sports Medicine Centre, Omaha; Clinical Associate Professor, Departments of Family Practice and Orthopaedic Surgery, University of Nebraska Medical Centre; Team Physician, All Men's and Women's Sports, University of Nebraska at Omaha. Publications: Office Sports Medicine, 2nd Edition, 1995, Editor; Sports Medicine Secrets, 1994; Clinics in Sports Medicine, Guest Editor, 1994; Primary care: Clinics in Office Practice, Guest Editor, 1992; Primary Care: Clinics in Office Practice, Guest Editor, 1991; The Team Physician's Handbook, Co-Editor, 1990; Office Management of Sports Injuries and Athletic Problems, Editor, 1988; COntributor of numerous professional articles. Honours include: NROTC Scholarship, US Navy, Washington DC, 1961-65; Woodrow Wilson National Fellowship, 1965; Phi Beta Kappa; Pi Sigma Alpha; American Medical Association Physician's Recognition Awards, 1973-81, 1985-93. Memberships include: American Academy of Family Physicians; American Medical Association; Nebraska Medical Association. Hobbies: Bicycle touring; Downhill and crosscountry skiing; Nature photography. Address: Sports Medicine Centre, 2255 S 132 Street, Omaha, NE 68144, USA.

MELLSTEDT Håkan, b. 23 Oct 1942, Lund, Sweden. Associate Professor. m. Eva Mellstedt, 21 May 1966. Education: MD, 1969; PhD, 1974. Appointments: Senior Physician, Serafimer Hospital, 1976-80; Head Physician, 1980-86, Deputy Director, 1986-, Department of Oncology (Radiumhemmet), Karolinska Hospital, Stockholm; Associate Professor, Karolinska Institute, Stockholm. Publications: About 350 books and other scientific publications including: Idiotypes in multiple myeloma, 1974; Interferon-alpha therapy in multiple myeloma, 1979;

Cellular idiotypic network response at MAb therapy, 1991; Melphalan, Prednisone, Interferon in multiple myeloma therapy, 1993; MAb 17-1A and GM-CSF for therapy of colorectal carcinoma, 1993. Honours: Alfaferone Prize, Institute of Immunology, Italy, 1989. Memberships include: New York Academy of Sciences; European Society for Medical Oncology; International Society for Interferon Research; Society for Biological Therapy; American Association for Cancer Research. Address: Department of Oncology (Radiumhemmet), Karolinska Hospital, S-171 76 Stockholm, Sweden.

MELMED M Herzl, b. 15 Mar 1937, Port Elizabeth, South Africa. Obstetrician; Gynaecologist. m. Hazel Field, 1 Dec 1965, 1 s, 2 d. Education: BSc, 1958, MBChB, 1963, University of Cape Town; FRCOG; FACOG; Fellow, International Society for the Study of Vulvo-Vaginal Diseases. Career: Chief, Obstetrics and Gynaecology, Rebecca Sieff Medical Centre, Safad, Israel, 1971-74; Currently, Private Practice and Clinical Assistant Professor, University of Colorado Health Sciences Centre. Hobbies: Cycling; Hiking; Skiing. Address: 701 East Hampden Avenue 110, Englewood, CO 80110, USA.

MENDELSOHN Mortimer L(ester), b. 1 Dec 1925, New York, NY, USA. Scientist. m. Laura L Johnston, 5 Dec 1948, 2 s, 1 d. Education: MD, Harvard Medical School, 1948; PhD, Cambridge University, 1958. Career: Assistant, 1957-59, Associate, 1959-64, Professor, 1964-72, Radiology, University of PA; Director, Biomedical and Environmental Research Program, Lawrence Livermore National Laboratory, 1972-92; Currently, Vice Chairman, Radiation Effects Research Foundation. Publications: Co-author of 11 books and 135 research papers. Honours: Alpha Omega Alpha, 1947; Research Career Award, National Cancer Institute, 1962-72; MA, University of PA, 1971; Distinguished Associate Award, Department of Energy, 1990. Memberships: Environmental Mutagen Society; American Association Cancer Research; Radiation Research Society; Commission for Protection Against Environmental Mutagens and Carcinogens. Hobbies: Tennis; Gardening; Hiking. Address: 5-2 Hijiyama Park, Minami-Ku, Hiroshima 732, Japan.

MENDELSON Harold L, b. 25 Oct 1935, New York City, NY, USA. Psychiatrist. m. Mildred Preiss, 28 Jun 1987, 2 s. Education: AB, Williams College, 1956; MD, SUNY, 1960; Board Certified, 1967. Appointments: Director, Glendale Human Services Center, 1980-81; Currently, Director, Department of Psychiatry, Flushing Hospital Medical Center, 1981-. Honour: Fellowship, American Psychiatric Association. Memberships: Queens Psychiatric Society; APA; Queens Medical Society; AMA; American Association for Geriatric Psychiatry; World Federation for Mental Health. Hobbies: Swimming; Titanium Horseshoe Manufacturing and Sales. Address: 146-01 44 Avenue, Suite 311, Flushing, NY 11355, USA.

MENG Pei Lin, b. 30 Nov 1931, Hebei, China. Professor of Internal Medicine. m. Zhou Degin, 1 Aug 1957, 2 sons, 1 daughter. Education: BA, Tianjin Military Medical University, 1953. Appointments: Director, Department of Hematology, Changhai Hospital, Second Military Medical University, China. Publications: Allogeneic Fetal Liver Transplantation in Acute Leukemia, Co-author, 1985; Allogeneic Fetal Liver Transplantation in Acute Leukemia, Co-author, 1986; Autologous Bone Marrow Transplantation in Acute Leukemia, Co-author, 1989; The Experimental Study on Purging Leukemic Cells in Vitro by VP-16 and Hyperthermia, Co-author, 1991; Amplification of VNTR Segment by Polymerase Chain Reaction in Application to Evaluate the Engraftment Following Allogeneic Bone Marrow Transplantation, Co-author, 1992. Membershipss: Chinese Medical Association; Society of Autologous Bone Marrow Transplantation in China; Society of Hematology in Shanghai. Hobby: Chinese Cheese. Address: 174 Chahghai Road, Shanghai 200433, China.

MENG Xian Jun, b. 7 Jul 1931, Beijing, China. Medical Science. m. Mei Yuan, 1 Oct 1956, 2 d. Education: BS, Yenching University, 1951; MD, Peking Union Medical College, 1956. Career: Research Fellow, Academy of Military Medical Science, Institute of Surgical Research, Beijing and Chungking; Associate Professor, 3rd Military Medical College, Chungking; Professor, General Hospital PLA, Beijing; Currently, Director, Surgical Research Laboratory, General Hospital PLA, Beijing. Publications: Multiple organ failure, in Fundamentals of Abdominal Surgery, 1987; Multiple organ failure, in Applied Orthopedics, 1991; Organ association phenomena during sepsis, in Chinese Medical Journal, 1993. Honour: National Award for Advancement in Science and Technology, 1985. Memberships: American Shock Society; Vice President, Society of Experimental Surgery; Chinese Medical

Association. Hobbies: Music; Photography; Cooking. Address: Surgical Research Laboratory, General Hospital PLA, 28 Fuxing Road, Beijing 100853, China.

MENG Xian-Yi, b. 20 Nov 1927, Lin Yi, Shandong, China. Physician; Professor; Tutor. m. Chang Su Ling, 1 Oct 1963, 2 daughters. Appointments: House Physician, Medical Department, Jinan First Municipal Hospital, Jinan, Shandong; House Physician, Attending Physician, currently Chief Physician, Medical Department, Jinan Municipal Zhong Xie Hospital, Jinan; Achievements concerning Cor pulmonale, multiple organ failure, acid and base disorder, blood gas analysis. Publications: Prevention and Treatment of Common Cold, Bronchitis Emphysema and Cor pulmonale, 1977; Cases of Wu Shao Huai, 1978; Saniculture Health Protection, 1987; Pulmonary Emergency, 1992. Honours: Advanced Worker, City of Jinan, 1982; Excellent Professor, Shandong Medical University, 1985. Memberships: Chinese Medical Conference; International Union Against Tuberculosis and Lung Disease. Hobbies: Recreational activities.

MENG Xiang-cheng, b. 26 Sept 1929, Harbin, China. Professor of Ophthalmology. m. Liu Zheng-Rong, 16 Aug 1949, 2 sons, 2 daughters. Education: Graduate, Medical Department, University of Harbin, 1948; Postgraduate study, Ophthalmology, Toyama Medical and Pharmaceutical University, Toyama, Japan. Appointments: Doctor in charge, Lecturer in Ophthalmology, 1961-76, Associate Professor, 1977-84, Professor, 1985-95, Harbin Medical University. Publications: Strabismus and Amblyopia, 1981; Children's Amblyopia and Strabismus, 1988; Pediatric Clinical Ophthalmology, 1992. Honours: 5 Prizes for Science and Research, Heilongjiang Provincial Government, 1979, 1983, 1984, 1986, 1994. Memberships: ISCEV-CB; Advisory Committee, Optometry Research Centre, Ministry of Public Health, China. Hobbies: Appreciating Beijing Opera; Music. Address: The First Affiliated Hospital, Harbin Medical University, Youzheng Road, Nan-gang Qu, Harbin 150001, China.

MERCER Dorothy, b. 12 Dec 1942, Charlevoix, Michigan, USA. Psychologist. 2 sons. Education: BA summa cum laude, Adrian College; MA, University of Michigan; PhD, Counseling Psychology, Michigan State University; Certified Death Educator, American Death Educators and Counselors. Appointments: Special Education Teacher, 1964-68; Psychologist, Jackson Hillsdale Community Mental Health, 1980-84; Psychologist, Stress Management Inc, 1981-85; Psychologist, Michigan State University Counseling Center, 1985-87; Currently: Associate Professor of Psychology, Eastern Kentucky University, Richmond; Consulting Psychologist for National Office of Mothers Against Drunk Driving. Publications: Differences between Older Women Undergraduates when Compared by Marital Status, 1989; Older Co-eds: Predicting Who Will Stay This Time, 1993; Injury: Learning to Live Again, 1994. Memberships: American Psychological Association; American Death Educators and Counselors; International Association for Traumatic Stress Studies. Hobbies: Writing poetry; Playing the piano and organ; Reading. Address: 102 Cammack Building, Eastern Kentucky University, Richmond, KY 40475, USA.

MERCURI Gianni, b. 7 Apr 1967, Nouméa, France. Chiropractic Doctor. Education: BA, Medical Science, Sydney University; BSc, Chemistry, Master of Chiropractice, Macgquerie University. Appointments: Anatomy Tutor, Medical Dissection, University of New South Wales, Australia; Currently, Private Practice as Chiropractor. Publication: Research pilot study of the effects of the chiropractic adjustment on muscle spasms, the rotator muscles, 1992. Honours: Top of Class in Anatomy, Sydney University, Australia. Membership: Association Française de Chiropractic. Hobbies: Deep Water Diving; Big Game Fishing. Address: 11 Rue Jean Mariotti, Haut du Val Plaisance, Nouméa, Nouvelle Calédonie, France.

MERENDA Giuseppe Francesco, b. 28 Sept 1933, Palermo, Italy. Psychiatrist. Education: ITAA Certified Transactional Analyst, Neuro Psychiatry, Psychology. Publications: The Second Chance; The Phobic Child; Contracts, Fictions and Lies; The Mirror Technique. Memberships: SIP; EATA; ITAA; SIMPAT. Address: Via Serradifalco 184, 90145 Palermo, Italy.

MERENDINO Rosario, b. 25 Feb 1931, Messina, Italy. Psychoanalyst. m. Marcella d'Abbiero, 2 June 1978. Education: Doctor in Biblical Theology; Diploma in Organ and Musical Composition. Appointments: Professor of Biblical Language, Abt Herwegen Institut, Maria Laach, Andernach Rh, Germany, 1964-67; Professor of Biblical

Exegesis, Päpstlich Biblical Institute, Rome, Italy, 1969-76. Publications: Sulla coïncidenza, 1980; La protostruttura mente-corpo e la sua patologia, 1981; Struttura prementali e nozione del tempo, 1984; On Epistemiological Functions of Clinical Reports, 1985; Studi di epistemologia psicoanalitica, book, 1990; The Theoretical texts: their functions..., 1992; La recherche historique en psychanalyse, 1993. Memberships: International Psychoanalytical Association; Italian Psychoanalytical Association; Association Internationale pour l'Histoire de la Psychanalyse, Paris; Sigmund Freud Gesellschaft, Vienna. Hobbies: Literature (English, French, German, Italian); Philosphy; History; Philology; Music. Address: via Savoia 51, 00198 Rome, Italy.

MERLE-BERAL Philippe, b. 17 Oct 1942, Albi, France. Stomatologist; Dento-Facial Orthopaedist; Maxillo-Facial Surgeon. m. Marrine Colomb, 2 sons, 2 daughters. Education: Baccalauréat, 1962, Doctor of Medicine diploma, 1969, Toulouse University; Stomatologist, Paris University, 1972; Qualified Orthodontist Specialist, National Board, 1988; Qualified Maxillo-Facial Surgeon, National Board, 1994. Publications: Author or co-author, more than 30 publications in various French or foreign scientific journals, 1972-; More than 30 conference papers, posters and various scientific contributions, 1974-. Honours: Judicial Expert, 1989; Expert for social and private insurances, 1989; Lauréat de l'Académie Nationale de Médecine et des Facultés de Paris et Toulouse. Memberships: Executive Committee, French Society of Dento-Facial Orthopedics; Executive Committee, French Bioprogressive Society; European Orthodontic Society; French Society of Stomatology and Maxillofacial Surgery; International Association of Oral and Maxillo-Facial Surgeons. Hobbies: Golf; Tourism. Address: 2 avenue Gambetta, 81000 Albi, France.

MERRITT Russell James, b. 19 jan 1947, Honolulu, HI, USA. Physician. m. Nancy Walsh, 22 June 1980, 1 d. Education: MD, University of California at Irvine, 1972; BA, Stanford University, 1968; PhD, Massachusetts Institute of Technology, 1977. Appointments: Assistant Professor of Paediatrics, Associate Professor, University of Southern California; Director, Medical and Scientific Affairs, Nestle Nutritional Products USA; Director of Medical and Regulatory Affairs, McNeil Speciality Company; Medical Directoer, Paediatric Nutritionals, Ross Products Division, Abbott Laboratories. Publications: Nutritional Survey pf Hospitalized Patients, 1979; Contributor of articles in professional journals. Honours: President, American Board of Nutrition, 1988-90. Memberships: American Society Clinical Nutrition; American Society of Parenteral and Enteric Nutrition; North American Society for Paediatric GI and Nutrition; American Academy of Paediatrics. Address: 625 Cleveland Avenue, Columbus, OH, USA.

MERRITT Thurman Allen, b. 9 July 1946, Wichita, Kansas, USA. Neonatologist. m. Mary Anne Greninger, 17 Sept 1977, 2 sons. Education: BA (Kansas); MD (Kansas). Appointments: Professor of Paediatrics, University of Rochester, Rochester, New York; Professor of Paediatrics, University of California, San Diego; Currently Professor, Chief, Division of Neonatology, University of California at Davis. Publications: Fetal Growth in Humans (with H C Miller), 1979; Bronchopulmonary Dysplasia (with W H Northway Jr and N Boynton), 1989; 140 peer reviewed articles. Honours: L A Calkins Award for Research, Juselius Foundation, Finland, 1972; Dozer Visiting Scholar, Israel; US Army Commendation Medal, 1990. Memberships: American Academy of Pediatrics; Society for Pediatric Research; American Thoracic Society. Hobby: Children. Address: University of California, Davis Medical Center, 2516 Stockton, Sacramento, CA 95817, USA.

MESBAH Ekram Mohamed M, b. 23 Feb 1955, Cairo, Egypt. Obstetrician & Gynaecologist. m. Elham M Sobhy Said, 21 July 1994. Education: MSc, 1984; MRCOG, 1991; MD, 1992. Appointments: Resident, Obstetrics & Gynaecology; Assistant Specialist, Obstetrics & Gynaecology, Egypt; SHO, Registrar, Obstetrics & Gynaecology, England. Memberships: Royal College of Obstetricians & Gynaecologists; The Egyptian Society for Ultrasound. Hobbies: Reading; Marathon Running. Address: 94 Ahmed Ourahy Street, Flat No 207, El Agouza, Cairo, Egypt.

MESIC Harriet Lee Bey, b. 4 Aug 1937, Norfolk, USA. Executive Director. m. Harry Randolph Mesic, 18 Mar 1956, 1 son, 1 daughter. Education: AD, Computer Programming. Appointments: Executive Director, L E Support Club; Editor, L E Beacon, Lupus Patients. Publications: L E Beacon, vols 1-8, 1954-. Address: 8039 Nova Court, North Charleston, SC 29420-8934, USA. 7.

MESKO Eva, b. 13 Oct 1937, Budapest, Hungary. Physician. Education: Candidate for Medical Sciences. Appointments: Hospital of OZD, 1962; Robert Karoly Hospital, 1964-79; Flor Ferenc County Hospital, 1979-. Publications: The Diagnosis and Therapy of Cerebrovascular Disease, 1986; The Aspect of the Cerebrovascular Diseases in the Internal Medicine, 1987; Diagnosis in Angiology, 1990. Memberships: The Professional Board of Angiology; International Union for Angiology; President, Scientific Board of the Flor Ferenc Hospital. Honours: Markusovszky Prize, 1971. Hobbies: Music; Reading Agatha Christie's Books. Address: Semmelweis Str 1, 2143 Kerepestarcsa, Hungary.

MESSER David John, b. 30 July 1952, Manchester, England. Psychologist. m. L Messer, 15 Sept 1976, 2 sons. Education: BSc (Hons), Psychology; BSc; PhD. Appointments: Senior Lecturer, then Reader in Developmental Psychology; Currently Professor of Developmental Psychology, University of Hertfordshire, Hatfield. Publications: The Development of Communication, 1994. Membership: British Psychological Society. Address: Psychology Division, University of Hertfordshire, Hatfield, Herts AL10 9AB, England.

METHENITIS Nancy Lee, b. 17 Oct 1932, Iowa, USA. Social Worker. m. Louis T Methenitis, 24 Nov 1951, 2 sons, 2 daughters. Education: BA, summa cum laude. Board Certified Diplomate in Clinical Social Work. Appointments: Program Manager, Chief of Service, Out Patient Therapist, Kings View Corporation. Honours: Certificate of Merit, Certificiate of Appreciation, American Cancer Society. Memberships: NASW; Phi Kappa Phi; The Northern California Society of Clinical Hypnosis. Hobbies: Piano; Needlework; Walking; Bicycling. Address: 25520 Via Mariquita, Carmel, CA 93923, USA.

MEUNIER Pierre Jean, b. 5 June 1936, Miribel, France. Professor of Medicine. m. Annie Maries, 27 Dec 1986, 3 sons. Education: MD, Claude Bernard University, Lyons, France, 1967; Professor of Rheumatology, Lyons, 1971. Appointments: Head, INSERM Research Unit, 1979-92; Founder, Groupe De Recherches Et D'Information Sur Les Osteoporoses, 1986. Publications: Osteoporosis, Prevention and Treatment, 1988; Paget's Disease of Bone, 1980; Bone Histomorphometry, Bisphosphonates. Honours: Recipient, International League against Rheumatism Prize, 1989; Recipient, Paget's Disease Foundation Award, 1992. Memberships: Editor in Chief, Osteoporosis International; President, Board of Trustees, European Foundation for Osteoporosis. Hobbies: Tennis; Music. Address: 31 rue du Bois De La Caille, 69004 Lyons, France.

MEURSING Anneke Elina Elvira, b. 15 May 1946, The Netherlands. Anaesthetist. Education: MD; PhD. Appointments: Director, Consultant of Paediatric Anaesthesia. Memberships: Executive Committee, World Federation of Societies of Anaesthesiologists; Secretary, European Federation of Associations of Paed Anaesthesiol; President, Morbi-Dutch. Address: 417 Kleiweg, 3045 PL Rotterdam, The Netherlands.

MEYER Graham Scott, b. 11 Nov 1958. Emergency Specialist. m. Bernadette Fuerth, 10 Sept 1994, 3 sons. Education: BA; BSc; MD; ABEM; FACEP; FRCP (C). Appointments: Chief Resident, Henry Ford Hospital, Detroit, Michigan, USA, 1991-92; Currently Emergency Consultant, 4 hospitals, Ontario, Canada. Publications: Multiple publications with respect to cardiopulmonary resuscitation. Memberships: Ontario Medical Association; Canadian Medical Association; American Medical Association; WAEM; SAEM; Canadian Medical Practitioners Association; Canadian Association of Emergency Physicians; Essex County Medical Society; PGA Charities. Hobbies: Golf; Coins; Horses; Computer games; Dining; Travel. Address: 517 County Rd 46, RR 3, Essex, Ontario, Canada N8M 2X7.

MEYER Greg C, b. 17 Aug 1935, Bismarck, North Dakota, USA. Psychiatrist. Education: Engineering Degree; MSc; MD; Residency in Psychiatry. Appointments: Chairman, Mental Health, Mesa, Arizona; Chairman, Psychiatry, Desert Samaritan Hospital; Chairman, Psychiatry, Mesa Lutheran Hospital; Chief of Staff, Desert Vista Hospital; Psychiatrist, Arizona Central Medical Centre. Memberships: Maricopa Medical Society; Arizona Medical Society; Phoenix Psychiatric Association; American Medical Association. Hobbies: Multi-engine Instrument Pilot; Photography; Sailing. Address: Arizona Central Medical Centre, Florence, AZ, USA.

MEYER John Stirling, b. 24 Feb 1924, London, England. Physician; Neurologist. m. Katharine Sumner, 20 Aug 1987, 5 d. Education: BSc; MD; CM; MSc; Board Certified: American Board of Neurology and Psyuchiatry; American Neurological Associate; American Academy of Neurology. Appointments: Professor, Chairman, Department of Neurology, Wayne State University, USA; Professor, Chairman, Department of Neurology, Baylor College of Medicine; Director, Cerebrovascular Disease Research Centre; President's Commission on Heart Disease, Cancer and Stroke; National Advisory Council, NINDS. Publications: Author of 28 scientific books; Contributor of 780 professional publications. Honours: Honorary Member, Japanese Neurological Society, 1964; Honorary Member, Italian Neurological Soceity, 1974; Harold G Wolff Award, 1977, 1978; Mihaua Award, 1988; Red Oak Award, 1993; Bertha Award, 1992/ Memberships: American Neurological Association; American Academy of Neurology; American Heart Association; World Federation of Neurology, Secretary. Hobbies: Golf; Swimming. Address: Room 225, Building 110, VA Medical Centre 151A, 2002 Holcombe Boulevard, Houston, TX 77030, USA.

MEYERS Christopher D, b. 14 Apr 1941, New Orleans, LA, USA. Physician. m. Mary Rose Jourdan, 27 Dec 1968, 4 d. Education: BA; MD; Certified in Psychiatry and Geriatric Psychiatry, American Board of Psychiatry and Neurology; Ceritified in Adult Psychoanalysis, American Psychoanalytic Association. Appointments: Private Practice of Psychiatry and Psychoanalysis. Memberships: American psychiatric Association; American Psychoanalytic Association. Address: 3525 Prytania Street, Suite 518, New Orleans, LA 70115, USA.

MEYERS Paul Andrew, b. 3 May 1949, Somerville, New Jersey, USA. Physician. m. Maria Luisa Padilla, 24 Nov 1973. Education: BS, Cum Laude, Brown University, Providence Rhode Island, 1970; MD, Mount Sinai School of Medicine, 1973. Appointments: Associate Attending Pediatrician and Vice-Chairman, Department of Pediatrics, Memorial Sloan-Kettering Cancer Center, New York. Address: Department of Pediatrics, Memorial Sloan-Kettering Cancer Center, 1275 York Avenue, New York 10021, USA.

MEYNARDI Pierluigi, b. 20 Jan 1936, Rivarolo, Canavese. Psychologist, Psychsomatist, Sexologist. 2 sons. Education: PhD, Psychology. Appointments: Manager, Psychologist Human Resources; Teacher, Personnel Training Courses; Psychotherapist; Hypnotherapist; Associate Professor, Psychology, Kensington University, Glendale, California. Publications: What's Hidden Behind Our Behaviour, 1992; The Couple, 1993; Self Healing, 1990; Concise View of Psychosomatics. Honours: Knight of Sovereign Military Order of St George. Memberships: Fellow, Clinical Hynotherapists of American Association of Professional Hypnotherapists. Hobbies: Swimming. Address: Via Donatello 32, 20131 Milano, Italy.

MEZA-RUIZ Graciela, b. 6 June 1936, Mexico D F, Mexico. Professor of Neuroscience. Education: BS, Chemistry, 1957; PhD, Biochemistry, 1985, School of Chemistry, National University of Mexico, 1957; MSc, Zoology, University of Illinois, Urbana, 1967. Appointments include: Currently Full-time Professor of Neuroscience, Institute for Cell Phsiology, National University of Mexico. Publications include: Characterization of GABAergic and cholinergic neurotransmission in the chick inner ear, book chapter, 1985; Articles: GABA synthesis in chick vestibullary tissue (with A Carabez and M Ruiz), 1982; Comparative studies on glutamate decarboxylase and choline acetyltransferase activity in the vertebrate vestibule (with I Lopez), 1990; Distribution of GABA-like immunoreactivity in guinea pig vestibular cristae ampullaris (with I Lopez, R A Altschuler, J M Juiz), 1990; Vestibular site of action of hypothyroidism in the pigmented rat (with D Acuna, C Aceves, B Anguiano), 1990; Congenital hypothyroidism: vestibular and auditory damage in the pigmented rat (with D Acuna, Y Penaloza, A Poblano), 1991; GABA is an afferent vestibular neurotransmitter in the guinea pig. Immunocytochemical evidence in the utricular maculae (with J-Y Wu and I Lopez), 1992; Immunocytochemical evidence for an afferent GABAergic neurotransmission in the guinea pig vestibular system (with I Lopez and J-Y Wu), 1992. Honours: President, Mexican Society for Developmental Biology, 1994-. Memberships: Society for Neuroscience; International Society for Developmental Neuroscience; Collegium Otorhinolaryngologicum. Hobbies: Music; Hiking. Address: Department of Neurosciences, Institute for Cell Physiology, National University of Mexico, Apartado Postal 70-253, 04510 Mexico D F, Mexico.

MIAO Hongshi, b. 24 Dec 1932, Guangdong Province, China. Professor of Rehabilitation Medicine. m. 22 Sept 1955, 2 sons.

Education: MD, Qi Lu University, Jinan, Shandong, 1955. Appointments: Staff Physician, Chief Physician, Vice-Director, Beijing Rehabilitation Centre, 1957-85; Vice-Director, 1985-89, Senior Advisor, Professor, 1989-, China Rehabilitation Research Centre, Beijing; Professor of Rehabilitation Medicine, Capital Medical University, Beijing. Publications: China Rehabilitation Medicine, 1990; Rehabilitation Medicine, textbook, 1993; Rehabilitation Medicine - Theory and Practice, in press. Honours: National Science Congress Award, 1976; Ministry of Public Health Awards, 1976; 2 Best Book Awards, China, 1991, 1994. Memberships: Chairman, Society of Physical Medicine and Rehabilitation, 1989-94; Chinese Medical Association. Hobbies: Music; Sports. Address: China Rehabilitation Research Centre, PO Box 2619, Beijing 100077, China.

MIAO Jingliang, b. 2 Nov 1943, Shanghai, China. Researcher. m. Zhang Shurong, 1974, 1 s. Education: BA, Mechanics, University of Spinning and Weaving, 1965; Master, Mechanical Engineering, Mechanical Institute, Chinese Academy of Sciences, 1981. Appointments: Project Manager, Biomechanics, CAS, 1981-88; Software Director, Beijing Computer Technical Institute, 1989-91; Deputy Director, Research Centre, Peking University Branch Campus, Beijing, China, 1992-; Currently Professor. Publications: Articles: Coupling Vibration Analysis of Blood Vessels, 1985; Dynamic Interaction of Elastic Containers with Fluid, 1985; Books: Author, The Technique and Application of Programming Design, 1990; Co-author, Computer Science and Technology Encyclopaedia, 1993. Honours: 1st Inventor Award, Beijing, 1986; ULKA Award, 1988; Found 1st real solution for computer characteristic problem, 1986. Memberships: Vice Chairman, Chinese Microcomputer Medical Application Association; Chinese Vibration Engineering Association in Structural Dynamics; Vice Chairman, Chinese Environmental and Physical Distribution Association. Hobbies: Astrology; Buddhism; Geomancy; Sport. Address: Zhi Xin Block, Building 5, Unit 2, Apt 502, Xue Yuan Rd, Hai Dian District, Beijing 100083, China.

MIAO Tian Rong, b. 24 Jan 1914, Wenzhou, China. Surgeon; Professor. m. Wu Xinghui, 1 Jan 1946, 4 sons. Education: Grad, Zhejiang Provincial Medical College, 1937. Career: Resident Physician, National Jiangsu Medical College, 1937-39; Interpreter & Instructor, Aviation Medicine Training Course with Aviation Commission, 1939-43; Professor of Ophthalmology, Zhejiang Medical College, 1953-58; Professor of Ophthalmology & Chief of Ophthalmologic Optics Institute, Wenzhou Medical College, 1958-. Publications: An Ophthalmic Rule, Chinese Medical Journal, 1946; Logarithmic Visual Acuity Chart, Journal Wenzhou Medical College, 1959; Logarithmic Visual Acuity Chart and 5-Grade Notation, Chinese Journal Ophthalmology, 1983; Logarithmic Visual Acuity Chart and 5-Grade Notation, Acta XXV Concilium Ophthalmologicum, 1986. Honours: Winner, Merit Certificate, National Scientific Conference, 1978; Mr Nan's Medical Scientific Top Prize, 1990; Honorary Certificate, State Educational Commission, 1990; Special Allowance Certificate by State Council, 1991. Memberships: Fellow, Chinese Medical Association; Fellow, China Association Ophthalmology; Editor, Chinese J Ophthalmol; Honorary Committee Member, Wenzhou Scientific Association. Address: Wenzhou Medical College, Zhejiang, China.

MICHAELIDES Doros Nikita, b. 7 Jan 1936, Cyprus. Physician. m. Effie Michaelides, 27 Feb 1965, 2 daughters. Education: MD, cum laude, University of Athens, 1962; DTM&H, University of Liverpool, England, 1967; MS, University of Newcastle-Upon-Tyne, England, 1969. Appointments include: Instructor, Internal Medicine, Creighton University School of Medicine, Omaha, Nebraska, 1977; Assistant Professor of Medicine, Gannon University, Erie, Pennsylvania, 1977-; Assistant Clinical Professor of Medicine, Hahnemann University, Philadelphia, 1978-. Publications include: Clinical aspects of some common causes of chest pain, 1964; Cardiac Failure, 1965; The epidemics of influenza through the centuries, demographic effects, their role in the decline of the Byzantine Empire, 1965; The effects of Levodopa in Chronic Progressive Hereditary Chorea, 1976; Poorly Differentiated Adenocarcinoma of the Prostate presenting as Bilateral Cervical Mass, 1979; Equivalent Potency of Corticosteroid Preparations used in Reversible Airway Obstruction, 1981; Blood gases, Acid-Base and Electrolyte Disturbances, 1980. Honours include: Scholar of the Royal Greek Government, National University of Athens School of Medicine, 1956-62; Citation by the Administrator of Veterans Affairs, 1975, 1978, 1980; Physicians Recognition Award's, American Medical Association, 1979, 1982, 1985, 1991, 1993. Memberships: Committee, Autoimmune Diseases, American College of Allergy & Immunology; Basic & Clinical

Immunology Committee, American College of Allergy & Immunology; Critical Care Council, American College of Chest Physicians; Life Fellow, American College of Physicians FACP; Life Fellow, American College of Chest Physicians FCCP; Fellow, American College of Allergy and Immunology; Fellow, American Association of Certified Allergists; Royal Society of Medicine; Certified American Board, Allergy & Immunology & Conjoint Board of the American Board of Internal Medicine and the American Board of Paediatrics; Certified American Board of Family Practice. Address: 1611 Peach Street, Suite 220, Professional Building, Erie, PA 16501-2172, USA. 2. 6. 15. 52.

MICHAELS Leslie, b. 24 July 1925, London, England. pathologist. m. Edith Waldstein, 21 Sept 1951, 2 d. Education: MBBS, Westminster Medical School, 1949; MD; FRCPath; DPath; FRCP(C). Appointments: Assistant Professor of Pathology. Albert Einstein College of Medicine, Newe York, USA; Professor of Pathology, Institute of Laryngology and Otology, London, England; Professor Emeritus, University of London. Publications: Ear, Nose and Throat Histopathology, 1987; Pathology of Larynx, 1984; Atlas of Ear, Nose and Throat Pathology, 1990. Memberships: British Medical Association; Pathological Society of Great Britain and Ireland. Hobbies: Reading; Walking; Music. Address: Romany Ridge, Hillbrow Road, Bromley, Kent BR1 4SL, England.

MICHALEK Arthur Michael, b. 17 Nov 1953, Lackawanna, NY, USA. Research Scientist. m. Terry O'Dea, 13 May 1977, 1 s, 1 d. Education: BA, Canisius College; MS, PhD, University at Buffalo. Appointment: Currently, Associate Dean, Roswell Park Cancer Institute. Publications: Over 60 articles and 57 presentations; Focusing on Cancer in American Indians; Issues in Cancer Education and Screening; Pediatric and Cancer Epidemiology. Honour: Fellow, American College of Epidemiology. Memberships: American College of Epidemiology; American Association of Cancer Education. Hobbies: Biking; Tennis; Reading. Address: Department of Educational Affairs, Roswell Park Cancer Institute, Carlton and Elm Streets, Buffalo, NY 14263, USA.

MICHALOPOULOS Christos Demetrius, b. 31 Aug 1931, Lyrkeia, Argolis, Greece. Cardiologist. m. Vasiliki P Mitrakos, 21 Feb 1965, 2 d. Appointments: Head, Department of Cardiology, Athens General Military hospital, 1972-74; Head, departments of Medicine and Cardiology, General Military hospital, Tripolis, 1981-82; Head, Department of Cardiology, NIMTS Hospital, 1983-87; Brigadier MC, retired, Hellenic Army; Private Practice; Executive Editor, Hellenic Armed Forces Medical Review, 1968-72; Hellenic Journal of Cardiology, 1991-95; Member of Editorial Board of European Heart Journal, 1992-. Publications: Translator to Greek: Goldberger E, A Primer of Water, Electrolyte and Acid-Base Syndromes, 5th Edition, 1975; J W Hurst, The Heart, 4th Edition, 1978; Cardiology Clinics, WB Saunders Co, 1990. Memberships: Hellenic Cardiological Soceity; European Cardiological Society; New York Academy of Sciences; American College of Angiology. Hobbies: DIY; Chess; Gardening. Address: 9 Neoph Metaxa Street, Athens 104-39, Greece.

MICHELS Karin, b. 7 July 1959, Freiburg, Germany. Epidemiologist. Education: MS, Columbia University School of Public Health, 1991; MPH, Harvard School of Public Health, 1994. Appointments: Editor, Deutscher Arzte Verlag, Cologne, Germany; Editor, Arzte Zeitung, Frankfurt, Germany; Medical Correspondent, Arzte Zeitung, New York; Press Officer, European Society of Cardiology, Nice, France; Medical Correspondent, Suddeutsch Zeitung, Munich, Germany. Publications: Quo vadis Meta-analysis?, 1992; Vitamins and Cancer - A Pracrical Means of Prevention?; The Continuing Unettical Use of Placebo Controls. Honour: Harvard Alumni Fellowship, 1993-94. Memberships: Society of Epidemiologic Research; International Society for Pharmaepidemiologic Research; National Association for Science Writers. Address: 44 Washington St, Ste 1106, Brookline, MA 02146 7106, USA.

MICHLER Markwart Waldemar, b. 30 Apr 1923, Breslau, Silesia. Professor Emeritus. m. Inge Stemmler MD, 20 Dec 1957, 2 sons. Education: Diploma, Surgery, 1958; Diploma, Orthopaedics, 1959. Appointments: Director, Institute for History of Medicine, Fustus Liebig University, Giessen, 1964-73; Founder, Institute for History of Medicine; Arranger, Ludwig Schunk Memorial Lib, Giessen; Emeritus Professor, 1973-. Publications: Books and Autographies; Contributor to numerous journals and reviews; Over 40 articles in Encyclopaedies. Memberships: International Academy of History of Medicine; History of Science Society; Society International ol'Histoire de la Médécine; The New York Academy of Sciences; International Society for the Classical Tradition;

International Gesellsch. für Orthopädie u. Traumatologie. Address: Ernst Putz Str 36, Bad Bruckenau, D-97769, Germany. 139.

MIGONE Paolo, b. 18 Oct 1950, Parma, Italy. Psychiatrist. Education: MD, University of Parma, Italy, 1975. Appointments: Adjunct Professor, Psychiatry Residency, University of Parma, Italy. Publications: Seminari Di Terapia Psycoanacitica, 1995. Memberships: Fellow, American Academy of Psychoanalysis; Rapaport-Klein Study Group. Address: Via Palestro 14, 43100 Parma, Italy.

MILACK Gary Paul, b. 5 July 1949, Floral Park, New York, USA. Podiatric Surgeon. m. Deborah A Stitz, 16 May 1980, 2 sons, 1 daughter. Education: BS; Doctor of Podiatric Medicine. Appointments: Private Practice, Podiatric Medicine, Shoreham, 1978-; Staff, Kings Park Psychiatric Hospital, 1978-; Suffolk Hospital, Riverhead, New York, 1982; Podiatric Medicine Advisor, Matrx Medical Co; Lecturer on Sedation, Emergency Car & Surgical Monitoring of Ambulatory Surgery Cases; Director, shorehans Foot Surgery Complex. Publications: Contibrutor Editor, Current Podiatry Dermatology Section; Editor in Chief, Journal of Current Podiatric Medicine; Derma-Prints Newsletter. Memberships Include: American Podiatric Medical Writers Association; American College of Podiatric Physicians; President, American Board, Podiatric Medical Specialties. Honours: Recipient, Salvation Army Outstanding Service in Clinic Award, 1975; March of Dimes Award for Fitness Walking, 1977. Address: 45 Route 25A Ste 1D, Shoreham, NY 11786-1389, USA.

MILES Timothy Stuart, b. 4 Aug 1946, Adelaide, South Australia, Australia. Lecturer. m. Janet Mary Isaachsen, 20 Dec 1969, 1 son, 1 daughter. Education: BDS; PhD; Postdoctoral Fellow, University of Zurich, Switzerland, 1974-75. Appointments: Lecturer in Physiology, 1975, currently Associate Professor in Physiology, University of Adelaide. Publications: More than 70 in various scientific journals. Memberships: Australian Physiological and Pharmacological Society; Australian Neuroscience Society; Society for Neuroscience, USA. Hobbies: Tennis; Swimming; Cycling; Reading. Address: Department of Physiology, University of Adelaide, SA 5005, Australia.

MILIN Robert Paul, b. 20 Aug 1957, Saskatoon, Saskatchewan, Canada. Psychiatrist. Education: BSc, 1979, MD, 1984, Residency, General Psychiatry, Child and Adolescent Psychiatry, 1985-89, University of Ottawa; FRCPC, 1989; Fellowship, Adolescent and Addiction Psychiatry, University of Ottawa, Canada, University of Minnesota, USA, 1990; Diplomate, 1991, Certificate, added Qualification, Addiction Psychiatry, 1993, American Board of Psychology and Neurology. Appointments: Currently: Assistant Professor of Psychiatry, Faculty of Medicine, University of Ottawa; Director, Adolescent Day Treatment Unit, Royal Ottawa Hospital. Publications: Adolescent Couple Suicide: Literature Review (with A Turgay), 1990; Psychpathology Among Substance Abusing Juvenile Offenders (with J Halikas, J Meller, C Morse), 1991; Drug Preference, Reported Drug Experience and Stimulus Sensitivity (with E Loh and A Wilson), 1992; A Review of Adolescent Substance Abuse and Co-morbidity, Forthcoming. Honours: Physician's Services Incorporated Foundation Award for Resident Medical Research, Faculty of Health Sciences, University of Ottawa, 1989; Annual Resident's Research Award, American Academy of Psychiatrists in Alcoholism and Addictions, 1990. Memberships: American Academy of Child and Adolescent Psychiatry; American Academy of Psychiatrists in Alcoholism and Addictions; American, Canadian and Ontario Psychiatric Associations; American Society of Addiction Medicine; Canadian Academy of Child Psychiatry; Canadian and Ontario Medical Associations. Hobbies: Skiing; Tennis; Swimming; Scuba-diving; Biking; Chess. Address: Royal Ottawa Hospital, 1145 Carling Avenue, Ottawa, Ontario, Canada K1Z 7K4.

MILLER Charles Claude III, b. 23 June 1961, Ft Worth, Texas, USA. Epidemiologist. 1 daughter. Education: BA; MA; PhD. Appointment: Assistant Professor. Publications: Sympathetic denervation blocks blood pressure elevation in episodic hypoxia, 1992; Systemische blutdruckerhoehung als reaktion auf chronische intermittierende hypoxie wird durch carotiskoeperdenervation verhindert, 1992; Joint effects of pulmonary fuction and aerobic power on survival in a cohort of healthy adults, 1993. Memberships: Society for Epidemiologic Research; American Public Health Association. Hobbies: harley-Davidson Motorcycles. Address: Baylor College of Medicine, Pulmonary Disease Section, Smith Tower, Suite 1236, 6550 Fannin Street, Houston, TX 77030, USA.

MILLER Denis R, b. 14 May 1934, Paterson, New Jersey, USA. Physician. m. Dr Linda Patricia Miller, 11 June 1983, 1 s. Education: AB, Cornell University; MD, Cornell University Medical College. Appointments: Director, Paediatric Haematology-Oncology, Assistant Professor of Paediatrics, University of Rochester Medical Centre; Director, Paediatric Haematology-Oncology, New York Hospital-Cornell Medical centre, New York, 1970-75; Associate Professor of Paediatrics, Cornell University Medical College, 1970-75; Professor of Paediatrics, Cornell, 1975-84; Chairman, Department of Paediatrics, Memorial Sloan Kettering Cancer Centre, 1978-84; Head, Division of Paediatric Haematology-Oncology, Children's Memorial Hospital, 1985-88; Professor of Paediatrics, Northwestern University Medical School, Chicago, 1985-88; Associate Medical Director, Cancer Treatment Centres of America, 1990-93; Scientific Director, Cancer Treatment Research Foundation, 1993-; Paediatric Haematology-Oncology Midwestern Regional Medical Centre, Zion, Illinois. Publications: Blood Diseases of Infancy and Children, Editor, 4th, 5th, 6th, 7th Editions, 1978, 1984, 1989, 1995; Contributor of 64 book chapters, 154 peer-reviewed articles and 135 abstracts. Honours: Fulbright Scholar, University of London, St Mary's Hospital Medical School, London, England, 1962-63; Enid A Haupt Chair of Paediatric Oncology, Memorial Sloan Kettering Cancer Centre, 1980-84. Memberships: American Society Clinical Oncology; Society for Paediatric Research; American Paediatric Society; American Society of Haematology; American Society Paediatric Haematology-Oncology; American Association Cancer Research; American Academy of Paediatrics. Address: Cancer Treatment Research Foundation, 3455 Salt Creek Lane, Arlington Heights, IL, 60005, USA.

MILLER Douglas Craig, b. 9 May 1953, New York City, USA. Physician. m. 10 Feb 1979, 3 s. Education: MD, 1978; PhD, Physiology and Biophysics, 1980; Board Certified, Anatomic and Neuropathology, 1985. Appointments: Clinical Assistant Professor of Pathology, UMDNJ, Robert Wood Johnson Medical School; Associate Professor of Neuropathology and Neurosurgery, New York University Medical Centre; Director, Division of Neuropathology, NYUMC. Publications: Atlas of Clinical Neurology, 2nd Edition, 1993; Contributor of over 60 scientific and medical articles and book chapters. Memberships: American Association of Neuropathologists; College of American Pathologists; American Society of Clinical Pathologists; International Society for Neuropathology. Hobbies: Tennis; Baseball; Classical Music; Reading fiction and history. Address: Department of Pathology (Neuropathology), New York University Medical Centre, 550 1st Avenue, New York, NY 10016, USA.

MILLER Harry Charles, b. 22 Sept 1928, Ridgewood, New Jersey, USA. Physician; Urologist. m. Kari Lynn Palmer, 16 June 1969, 2 s, 4 d. Education: BA, Amherst College, 1950; MD, Yale University, 1954. Appointments: Assistant Professor, urology, University of Rochester; Associate Professor of Urology, University of Oklahoma Health Sciences Centre, Oklahoma City; Chair, Department of Urology, George Washington University, Washington DC. Publications: Contributor of over 100 papers and articles, 5 movies and 6 exhibits. Honours: President, American Association of Clinical Pathologists; President, Mid Atlantic Section, American Urological Association; President, Washington Urologic Society; Board of Directors, American Urological Association. Memberships: AUA; AMA; AACU; Society for Paediatric Urology. Hobbies: Golf; Fishing; Tennis; Music; Gardening; Pheasant Hunting; Reading. Address: George Washington University, 2150 Pennsylvania Avenue NW, Washington DC 20037, USA.

MILLER Joseph Morton, b. 9 Nov 1921, Boston, Massachusetts, USA. Medicine. m. Betty Harris, 17 Sep 1976, 3 s, 2 d. Education: AB; MD; MPH; Phi Beta Kappa; Fellow, American College of Physicians. Appointments: Lecturer in Community Medicine, Harvard Medical School; Consultant in Occupational Medicine. Memberships: American Public Health Association. Hobbies: Skiing; Hiking. Address: New Hebron Road, Plymouth, New Hampshire 03264, USA.

MILLER Norman Stanley, b. 1 Aug 1943, Grand Rapids, MI, USA. Physician. m. Nicole Kasten, 30 July 1988, 2 d. Education: AB, Psychology, University of Michigan; MD, Howard University. Appointments: Assistant Professor of Psychiatry, Neurology, Pharmacology, Unviersity of Kansas; Assistant Professor of Clinical Psychiatry, Cornell University Medical College; Associate Professor of Psychiatry, University of Illinois. Publications include: Comprehensive Handbook of Drug and Alcohol Addiction, 1991; The Pharmacology of Alcohol and Drugs of Abuse and Addiction, 1991; Alcohol, 1991;

Principles of Addiction Medicine, 1994. Honours: Alpha Omega Alpha, 1974; American Medical Writers Association Honourable Mention. Memberships: American Psychiatric Association; American Society of Addiction Medicine; American Academy of Clinical Psychiatrists. Address: Department of Psychiatry M/C 913, University of Illinois at Chicago, 912 South Wood Street, Chicago, IL 60612, USA.

MILLER Orlando Jack, b. 11 May 1927, Oklahoma City, Oklahoma, USA. Medical geneticist; Academic. m. Dorothy Anne Smith, 10 July 1954, 1 s, 2 d. Education: BS, 1946, MD, 1950, Yale University; Obstetric/Gynaecology Residency, Yale-New Haven Hospital, 1954-58; genetics, Galton Laboratory, Galton Laboratory, London, England, 1958-60; Certified, Medical Genetics and Clinical Cytogenetics, American Board of Medical Genetics, 1981. Appointments: Assistant, 1961-65, Associate, 1965-69, Full Professor, 1969-85, Obstetrics and Gynaecology and Human Genetics and Development, College of Physicians and Surgeons, Columbia University; Chairman, Department Molecular Biology and Genetics, 1985-93, Director, Centre for Molecular Biology, 1987-90, Professor of Molecular Biology and Genetics and Obstetrics and Gynaecology, 1985-, Wayne State University. Publications: Contributor of over 180 research articles in refereed journals and over 60 reviews and book chapters. Honours: Vice President, 1983; President, 1984-85, American Board of Medical Genetics; Served on numerous editorial boards and study sections; Academy of Scholars, Wayne State University, 1991-(lifetime); President-elect, 1995-96. Memberships: Fellow, American Association for the Advancement of Science; American Society of Human Genetics; American Society for Cell Biology; Genetics Society of America; Genetics Soceity of Australia. Hobbies: Genealogy; Puzzles; Reading. Address: Wayne State University School of Medicine, 3216 Scott Hall, 540 E Canfield, Detroit, MI 48201, USA.

MILLER Raymond Vincent Stephen, b. 31 Jan 1920, Baltimore, Maryland, USA. Mariner. m. Florence J A Miller, 2 sons, 2 daughters. Education: Graduated in Pharmacy and Chemistry, 1940; Atomic, Biological and Chemical courses, 1957. Appointments: Pharmacist, numerous hospitals; Instructor in Pharmacy and Chemistry Schools, US Navy, now retired. Publication: Improving Nutrition Value of Meat using HNI in Commercial Refrigeration, 1993. Memberships: Former Member, Association of Scientific and Technical Mariners; Registered Sanitarian, National Environmental Health Association; Licensed, New Jersey Health Department. Hobby: Studying biometeorology (member, International Society of Biometrology). Address: 1519 Greenwood Avenue, Camden, NJ 08103-2931, USA.

MILLER Robert Harold, b. 2 July 1947, Columbia, Missouri, USA. Physician. m. Martha Guillory, 18 Apr 1981, 1 s, 1 d. Education: BS, Tulane University; MD, Tulane University School of Medicine; American Board of Otolaryngology. Appointments: Associate Professor, Department of Otorhinolaryngology, Baylor College of Medicine, Houston, Texas; Professor, Chairman, Department of Otolaryngology, Head and Neck Surgery, Tulane University School of Medicine. Publications: Airway and Facial Trauma, 1983; Head and Neck Surgery-Otolaryngology, Section Editor, 1993; COntributor of numerous articles, abstracts, videos and book chapters; Numerous presentations given at professional conferences, meetings and symposia. Honours: AOA Medical Society, 1973; Outstanding Senior Medical Student Tulane Medical Alumni Association, 1973; Best Thesis, Tulane Department of Physiology, 1973; Outstansing Man, Houston Chamber of Commerce, 1980. Memberships: American Board of otolaryngology; Triological Society; American Academy of Otolaryngology-Head and Neck Surgery. Hobbies: Tennis; Computers. Address: Tulane University School of Medicine, Department of Otolaryngology-Head and Neck Surgery, SL 59, 1430 Tulane Avenue, New Orleans, LA 70112, USA.

MILLER Thomas Paul, b. 28 July 1961, Detroit, Michigan, USA. Medical Doctor. m. Jill S Christenson, 9 May 1987, 1 son, 1 daughter. Education: BA cum laude, Chemistry, Biology, Spring Arbor College, Spring Arbor, Michigan, 1983; 83; MD, Wayne State University School of Medicine, Detroit, 1987; Intern, Resident, University of Michigan Hospitals, Ann Arbor, 1987-90; Fellowship, Allergy, Immunology, Northwestern University Medical School, Chicago, 1990-92; Diplomate, American Board of Internal Medicine, 1991; Diplomate, American Board of Allergy and Immunology, 1993. Appointments: Clinical Instructor of Medicine: Northwestern University, 1991-92; Clinical Instructor of Medicine, Michigan State University College of Human Medicine, 1992-; Private practice, Immunology in Children and Adults; Academic Faculty, Butterworth Hospital. Publications: Identification, Treatment of Adults at

Increased Risk of Fatal Asthma, 1992; Co-author: Topics in Acute Care; Anaphylaxis: Recognition and Management, 1991; The Diagnosis of Potentially Fatal Asthma in Hospitalized Adults: Patient Characteristics and Increased Severity of Asthma, 1992; Effectiveness of Corticosteroids in Management, and Recurrent SJS, 1992; Asthma in the Adolescent and Adult, 1993; Allergic Rhinitis, 1993; Asthma Classification, 1993; Urticaria and Angioedema, 1993; Circumstances Surrounding Deaths from Asthma in Cook County (Chicago), Illinois, 1993. Memberships: American Academy of Allergy and Immunology; American College of Physicians. Hobbies: Running; Cycling; Reading; Computers. Address: 3625 Clyde Park SW, Grand Rapids, MI 49509, USA.

MILLS Thomas Cooke, b. 24 Nov 1955, San Francisco, California, USA. Psychiatrist. Education: SB, Massachusetts Institute of Technology, 1977; MD, University of Illinois, 1981; MPH, University of California, Berkeley, 1991. Appointments: Resident, University of California, San Francisco; Medical Director, Jail Psychiatric Services of San Francisco; Staff Physician, Veterans Affairs Medical Center, San Francisco; Consultant, Center for AIDS Prevention Studies, University of California, San Francisco; Currently Associate Clinical Professor, University of California, San Francisco. Honours: National Institute of Mental Health fellow in Mental Health Finance and Service Delivery Research, 1990-91. Membership: American Psychiatric Association. Hobbies: Scuba diving; Weight training. Address: PO Box 460520, San Francisco, CA 94114, USA.

MILLSON Richard Case, b. 25 Nov 1951, Kingston, Ontario, Canada. Psychiatrist. m. Karen Schofield, 7 Nov 1992. Education: BA, 1973, MD, 1976, Queen's University; DTM&H, London School of Hygiene and Tropical Medicine, 1978. Appointments: Assistant Professor of Psychiatry, University of Manitoba, 1981-87; Clinical Associate Professor, University of British Columbia. Publications: Self-Induced Water Intoxication and Alcohol Abuse, 1989; Individual Differences in Serum Sodium Levels in Schizophrenic Men with Self-Induced Water Intoxication, 1989; A Survey of Patient Attitudes Toward Self-Induced Water Intoxication, 1992; Self-Induced Water Intoxication with group Psychotherapy, 1993. Memberships: Canadian Psychiatric Association; American psychiatric Association, President, Western Canada District Branch, 1993-94. Hobbies: swimming; Dancing. Address> Riverview Hospital, 500 Longheed Highway, Port Coquitlam, British Columbia V3C 4J2, Canada.

MILNE Eric Nightingale Campbell, b. 8 Feb 1929, Perth, Scotland, England. Professor of Radiology & Medicine, University of California-Irvine Medical Centre. Appointments: Intern, Monmouth Memorial Hospital, New Jersey, 1956-57; Residency, Chest Diseases, Springville, California, 1957-58; Senior House Officer, Royal Infirmary, Edinburgh, Scotland, 1958-60; Radiologist, McKellar General Hospital, Fort William, Ontario, 1961-65; Assistant Professor, University of Western Ontario, 1965-66; Fellow, Cardiovascular Research Institute, University of California, 1966-67; Assistant Professor, Harvard Medical School, Boston, 1967-69; Professor, Founding Director, Radiology Research Institute, University of Toronto, 1969-75; Professor, Chairman, Department of Radiological Sciences, University of California, 1975-78; Professor of Radiology & Medicine, Chief, Chest Radiology, University of California, 1978-. Publications: Models and Techniques in Medical Imaging Research, 1983; Reading the Chest Radiograph: The Physiologic Approach, 1992; 120 articles, 15 book chapters, 5 videotape courses. Memberships: The Fleischner Society; Society of Thoracic Radiology; Association of University Radiologists; Radiological Society of North America. Honours include: Silver Medal, City of Brescia, Italy, 1987; President, Society of Thoracic Radiology, 1988-89; Exchange Scholar, Leningrad University, Russia, 1989; Kaiser-Permanente Distinguished Teaching Award, 1990; Golden Apple Distinguished Teaching Award, 1993. Hobbies: Travel; Photography; Fishing; Sailing; Sking. Address: Department of Radiology, University of California-Irvine Medical Centre, 101 City Drive, Orange, CA 92668, USA.

MILROD David, b. 2 Oct 1924, Toronto, Ontario, Canada. Physician. m. Frances Fleishman, 20 June 1948, 1 daughter. Education: MD. Appointments: Currently Training and Supervising Analyst, New York Psychoanalytic Institute, USA. Publications: Self-Pity, Self-Comforting and the Superego, 1972; The Wished-for Self Image, 1982; A Current View of the Psychoanalytic Theory of Depression, 1988; The Ego Ideal, 1990. Memberships: New York Psychoanalytic Institute; New York Psychoanalytic Society; American Psychoanalytic Association; International Psychoanalytic Association; New York County Medical

Society. Hobbies: Music; Tennis. Address: 7 W 81st Street, New York, NY 10024, USA.

MIN Longrui, b. 23 June 1938, Shanghai, China. Geologist. m. Guanxiang Zhu, 1 Oct 1965, 1 s, 1 d. Education: BSc; MSc. Appointments: Member, Chinese Association of Geology; Member, Quaternary Glacier and Quaternary Geology Committee; Chief, Quaternary Group, Institute of Geology' Chief of Geoenvironment Research Centre. Publications: Atlas of the Palaeogeograpyhy of China, 1985; Discussion about Formation of Luess Plateau in China and Origin of Luess, 1988; Quaternary Map Series of China, 1991. Honours: 2nd Prize, National Natural Science Prize, 1985; 1st Prize, Ministry of Geology and Mineral Resource, 1990. Memberships: Chinese Association of Geology. Hobbies: Reading history books; Watching TV. Address: Institute of geology, Chinese Academy of Gllgcl Sciences, Beijing 100037, China.

MINERBO Marion, b. 18 Sept 1957, Sâo Paulo, Brazil. Psychoanalyst. m. Meier Strengerowski, 18 Dec 1986, 1 son, 2 daughters. Education: MD, 1980, Specialised in Psychiatry, 1982, Faculdade de Medicina da Santa Casa de Sâo Paulo. Appointments: Teacher, Medical Psychology, Faculdade de Ciencias Médicas da Santa Casa de Sâo Paulo. Publications: Interpretaçao: sobre o método da psicánalise, 1989; Contribution to International Journal of Psycho=Analysis, 1993. Honours: Freud Award, XVII Latin-American Psychoanalytical Congress, Sâo Paulo, 1988. Memberships: Full Member: International Psychoanalytical Association; Sâo Paulo Psychoanalytical Society. Hobbies: Biking; Tennis. Address: R Caçapava 49/144, Sâo Paulo, SP, Brazil.

MINNA John Dorrance, b. 19 Dec 1941, San Francisco, CA, USA. Professor of Medicine and Pharmacology. m. Lynn McElhany Minna, 1964, 2 d. Education: BA, Stanford University, 1963; MD, Stanford Medical School, 1967; Board Certified, Internal Medicine, 1973, Medical Oncology, 1977. Career: Chief, NCI VA Medical Oncology Branch, National Cancer Institute, NIH; Chief, NCI Navy Medical Oncology Branch, NIH; Currently, Director, Hamon Research, UT Southwestern Medical Center, Dallas, TX. Publications: Co-author, Neoplasms of the lung, Harrison's Principles of Internal Medicine, 1992; Co-author, Antioncogenes and human lung cancer, 1993; Author, Molecular Biology of Lung Cancer Pathogenesis, 1993. Honours: Rosenthal Prize for Cancer Research, 1984; Woodward Foundation Visiting Professor, Mem Sloan Kettering Cancer Center, 1985; Haddow Lecture, Royal Society of Medicine, London, 1986; Chester Stock Award, Mem Sloan Kettering Cancer Center, 1992. Memberships: American Association for Cancer Research; American College of Physicians; American Society of Clinical Oncology; American Society of Hematology; International Association for the Study of Lung Cancer; The Endocrine Society. Hobby: Tennis. Address: Hamon Research Center, UT Southwestern Medical Center, 5323 Harry Hines Boulevard, Dallas, TX 75235-8590, USA.

MIOTTI Antonio M, b. 30 Sep 1952, Cittadella, Padova, Italy. Surgeon. m. Anna M Tacoli, 18 Jul 1989, 1 s, 1 d. Education: MD, 1977, DMD, 1980, Padova University; MSc, University of London, 1981; Specialist, ENT Surgery, Padova University, 1985; Specialist, Maxillofacial Surgery, Milan University, 1990. Career: Research Assistant, University of Padova, 1977-79, 1982-90; Clinical Assistant, University of London, 1979-81; Consultant Maxillo-Facial Surgeon, Military Hospital, Padova, 1983-93, and Vlss 19, 1983-92; Currently, Head of Department of Oral and Maxillofacial Surgery, Regional Hospital, Udine, Italy. Publications: 185 publications in medical journals. Memberships: Royal Society of Medicine, UK; European Association for Cranio-Maxillo-Facial Surgery; European Skull Base Society. Hobbies: Mountaineering; Sailing; Skiing. Address: Via Modotto 7, Moruzzo, Udine, Italy.

MIR Mohammad Afzal, b. 6 May 1936, Trehgam, Kashmir. Physician. m. Lynda Mir, 7 Mar 1977, 1 son, 2 daughters. Education: MBBS; DCH; FRCP. Appointments: Medical Officer, Agency Hospital Gilgit, Kashmir; Senior House Officer, Alderhey Childrens Hospital; Medical Registrar, North Ormesby Hospital, Middlesborough; Queen Mary's Hospital, Sidcup & Manchester Royal Infirmary; Senior Registrar, Manchester Royal Infirmary. Publications: Publications on Acute Leukaemia, 1972-74; An Aid to the MRCP Short Cases, 1986; An Aid to the MRCP Viva, 1992. Memberships: Medical Research Society; British Diabetic Association; British Hypertension Society; British Cardiac Society. Honours: Young Investigators Research Award, British Cardiac

Society, 1976. Hobbies: Music; Literature; Gardening; Bridge. Address: Iscoed Old Mill Road, Lisvane, Cardiff, CF4 5XP.

MIRAND Edwin Albert, b. 18 Jul 1926, Buffalo, NY, USA. Oncology. Education: BA, 1947, MA, 1949, University of Buffalo, NY; PhD, Syracuse Univerity, NY, 1951. Career: Teaching Fellow, Syracuse University, NY, 1948-51; Instructor, Utica College, NY, 1950; Vice President for Educational Affairs and Dean of Graduate Division, Roswell Park Cancer Institute, Buffalo, NY, 1951-; Professor, Dean, Roswell Park Graduate Division, SUNY, Buffalo, NY, 1968-. Publications: Extrarenal Erythroporietin Activity in Man and Experimental Animals, in Regulation of Hematopoiesis, 1970; Autonomous Erythropoiesis Induced by Virus, in Seminars in Hematology, 1976; Progress in Clinical and Biological Research, 1983; Over 500 publications. Honours: Honorary DSc, Magna University, 1970, D'Youville College, 1973; Margaret Hay Edwards Award for Contributing to Cancer Education, 1992. Memberships: American Association of Cancer Research; American Society of Hematology; President, 1968-69, Association for Gnotobiotics; Secretary-Treasurer, 1968-, Secretary-General, UICC Cancer Congress, 1978-82, Association of American Cancer Institute; American Association for Cancer Education; International Society of Hematology; President, 1983-84, International Association for Gnotobiology; Liaisor to National Cancer Advisory Board, 1972-; Member of New York State Aids Advisory Board, 1982-. Hobby: Classical Music. Address: Roswell Park Cancer Institute, 666 Elm Street, Buffalo, NY 14263, USA.

MIRASSOU Marlene Marie, b. 12 Dec 1948, San Jose, California, USA. Physician; Psychiatrist. Education: BA, San Jose State University, 1971; MD, Medical College of Wisconsin, 1976. Appointments: Assistant Professor, Medical College of Wisconsin, 1980-82; Lecturer, Yale University, 1981-82; Assistant Professor, University of California, Davis, 1982-88; Associate Clinical Professor, Unviersity of California, Davis, 1988-. Publications: Psychiatric Diagnosis Among Female Alcoholics, 1980; A Crisis Intervention Service: Comparison of Younger & Older Adult Clients, 1983. Honours: Fellow, APA, 1992. Memberships: California Medical Society; American Psychiatric Association; Association for Academic Psychiatry; Academy of Psychosomatic Medicine; American Medical Women's Association. Hobbies: Hiking; Cross Country Skiing. Address: University of California Davis, Department of Psychiatry, 2315 Stockton Blvd, Sacramento, CA 95817, USA.

MIREJOVSKY Pavel, b. 10 Sept 1933, Nachod, Czechoslovakia. Pathologist. m. Eliska Bradacova, 12 July 1957, 1 son, 1 daughter. Education: MD, Palacky University, Olomouc; PhD, Charles University Medical School, 1977; DrSc, Charles University, 1988. Appointments: Senior Pathologist, 1960, Head, Laboratory of Electron Microscopy, 1969, Senior Lecturer, 1986-90; Professor of Pathology, Charles University, Medical School, Prague; Currently: Director, Hlava Institute of Pathology, Prague; Editor-in-Chief, Czecho-Slovak Pathology and Forensic Medicine. Publications: Arc Welders' Pneumonia, 1970; Small Cell Carcinoma of Larynx, 1975; Electron Microscopy in Tumour Biopsy, 1978; Bizarre Cells in Pseudotumours, 1987; Ultrastructure of Respiratory Tract Tumours, 1990. Memberships: Czech Society of Pathologists; International Academy of Pathology. Hobbies: Music; Gardening. Address: Hlava Institute of Pathology, Albertov 2039, 128 00 Prague 2, Czech Republic.

MIROW Susan Marilyn, b. 15 Feb 1944, Manhattan, New York, USA. Physician. m. Wayne C Spelius, 21 Mar 1982, 1 s. Education: BA, Temple University, 1964; PhD, Anatomy, 1969; MD, Medical College of Pennsylvania, 1973. Appointments: Clinical Director, Utah State Hospital, 1980-82; Research Director, PMS Center, Western Institute, 1986-87; Assistant Clinical Professor. Publications: Fluoxetine-Induced Cognitive Dysfunction, 1991; Cognitive Dysfunction Associated with Fluoxetine, 1991. Honours: National Science Foundation Fellowships, 1965-1969; Weisman for Excellence in Child Psychiatry, 1973. Memberships: American Psychiatric Association; The New York Academy of Sciences; American Society of Clinical Hypnosis; American Associations for the Advancement of Sciences. Hobbies: Painting; Skiing. Address: 73 G Street, Salt Lake City, Utah 84103-2951, USA.

MIRRAKHIMOV Mirsaid, b. 27 Mar 1927, Frunze, Kyrgyz, Russia. Cardiologist. m. Nelya Usupova, 1955, 1 s, 2 d. Education: Kyrgyz State Medical Institute, 1948; Postgraduate Study, 1950. Career: Lecturer, Therapy, 1950-56, Head of Therapy, 1956-, Pro-rector on Science, 1964-78, Kyrgyz State Medical Institute; Currently, Director, Kyrgyz

Institute of Cardiology; Professor and Academician, Kyrgyz Academy of Sciences and Russian Medical Academy of Sciences. Publications: The cardiovascualr system at high altitude, 1968; The Management of Internal Diseases by High Altitude Climate, 1977; Heart Diseases and Mountains, 1977; Co-author, articles in Journal Clinical Cardiology, 1992. Honours: Badge of Honour, 1961, 1971; Order of October Revolution, 1976; Order of Lenin, 1981; Hero of Socialist Labour, 1987. Memberships: President, Central Asian Association of Cardiologists; Head, Krygyz Society of Internal Medicine; International Society of Human Biology; International Society of Arterial Chemoreceptors. Hobbies: Chess; Classical Music. Address: Toktogul Str 98, Apt 6, Bishkek, 720000, Krygyzstan, CIS.

MISHARI Abdulrahman Al, b. Al Ahsa, Hofuf, Saudi Arabia. Consultant Obstetrician and Gynaecologist. m. Mona Abalkhail, 1 son, 1 daughter. Education: MD; MRCOG. Appointments: Assistant Professor, Medical College, King Saud University, Riyadh; Currently President, Dr Abdul Rahman Al-Mishari General Hospital, Riyadh. Membership: Royal College of Obstetrics and Gynaecology, London. Hobbies: Swimming; Farming; Travel. Address: Dr Abdulrahman Al Mishari General Hospital, PO Box 56929, Riyadh 11564, Saudi Arabia.

MISIASZEK John, b. 12 Oct 1948, London, England. Physician; Psychiatrist. m. Jenifer Davis George, 26 Nov 1983, 1 son, 1 daughter. Education: BS, Distinction, University of Arizona, USA, 1971; MD, University of Arizona College of Medicine, 1975; Flexible Internship, Santa Barbara Cottage and General Hospitals, Santa Barbara, California, 1976-79; Psychaitry Residency, Arizona Health Sciences Centre, Tucson. Appointments: Director of Consultation-Liaison Service in psychiatry; Director, Psychiatry Inpatient Services, Associate Professor of Clinical Psychiatry, Arizona Health Sciences Centre. Publications include: The Effect of Air Pollution and Weather on Lung Function in Exercising Children and Adolescents, Co-author, 1974; Increasing Medical Students' Awareness of Psychological Concomitants of Illness, 1984; An Atypical Case of neuroleptic Malignant Syndrome responsive to Conservative Management, Co-author, 1985; Poor Job Quality and the Decline of Public psychiatry, Co-author, 1985; Air Irons: Past Problems and Future Directions, Co-author, 1986; Psychiatric Morbidity in Heart Recipients, Co-author, 1987; Patients with Combined Physical and Psychiatric Problems, Co-author, 1987; Evaluating the Deaf Patient, Co-author, 1991; Emotional Disorders with Somatic Expressions, 1992. Honours include: Distinguished Psychiatric Educator Award, 1985, 1988, 1995; Fellow, American Psychiatric Association, 1991. Memberships: American and Arizona Psychiatric Associations; Association for Academic Psychiatry' Academy of Psychosomatic Medicine. Hobbies: Softball; Painting; Architecture; Sports. Address: Department of psychiatry, 1501 N Campbell Avenue, Tucson, AZ 85724, USA.

MITCHELL James Edward, b. 19 June 1947, Chicago, USA. Physician; Professor of Psychiatry. m. 6 Dec 1969, 1 son, 1 daughter. Education: BS, Zoology, Indiana University, 1968; MD, Northwestern University, 1972; Psychiatry Fellowship, University of Minnesota, 1976. Appointments: Private Practice, Psychiatry, 1976-79; Faculty, Department of Psychiatry, University of Minnesota, 1979-. Publications: Anorexia Nervosa and Bulimia: Diagnosis and Treatment, 1985; Bulimia Nervosa, 1990; A comparison study of antidepressants and structured intensive group psychotherapy in the treatment of bulimia nervosa, 1990; Cognitive behavioral group psychotherapy of bulimia nervosa: the importance of logistical variables, 1993. Memberships: Academy for Eating Disorders; American Association for Social Psychiatry; American Psychiatric Association; American Psychopathological Association; Hennepin County Medical Society; International Society of Psychoneuroendocrinology; Minnesota Psychiatric Society; North American Association for the Study of Obesity; Sigma Xi; Society for Psychotherapy Research; Society for the Study of Ingestive Behavior. Honours: Distinguished Professor Award, Annual Symposium on Psychiatric Medicine, Florida, 1991; Annual Clinical Scholar Award, University Hospital & University of Minnesota Medical School, 1992. Hobbies: Reading; Canoeing. Address: Department of Psychiatry, University of Minnesota Medical School, 420 Delaware Street SE, Box 393 UMHC, MN 55455, USA.

MITCHELL Jeffrey Thomas, b. 19 Oct 1948. Clinical Associate Professor. Education: PhD; MA; Adv Grad Cert; BA. Appointments: Teacher, Paramedic, Fire Fighter, Regional EMS Coordinator, Psychotherapist, Instructor EHS, Clinical Associate Professor, President of International Critical Incident Stress Foundation. Publications:

Emergency Response to Crisis, 1981; Emergency Services Stress, 1990; Critical Incident Stress, 1993; Debriefing Human Elements Training, 1994. Honour: Instructor of the Year, International Society of Fire Service Instructors, 1984. Memberships: APA; NEMTA; National Registry EMT; NASAR. Hobbies: Photography; Hiking; Sailing; Camping. Address: 5018 Dorsey Hall Road, Suite 104, Ellicott City, MD 21042, USA.

MITCHELL Jo Ellen, b. 6 Oct 1964, Delaware, USA. Ophthalmic Assistant. Education: AA, Delaware Technical and Community College, 1988; Certified Ophthalmic Assistant. Appointments: Certified Ophthalmic Assistant, Eye Care Professionals; Certified Ophthalmic Assistant, Delaware Eye Care Center; Currently Certified Ophthalmic Assistant, Senior Research Interviewer, Wilmer Eye Institute, Johns Hopkins University. Honours: Academic and Achievement Award in Medical Office Assistance, 1988. Membership: Joint Commission on Allied Health Personnel in Ophthalmology. Hobbies: Swimming; Country line dancing. Address: RD 1, Box 38 D, Milton, DE 19968, USA.

MITCHELL Laura, b. 6 Oct 1958, England. Consultant Orthodontist. m. D A Mitchell, 5 Nov 1981. Education: BDS with commendation, Dundee University, 1981; FDS, Royal College of Surgeons Glasgow, 1984; DOrth, Royal College of Surgeons, 1987; MDS, University of Newcastle, 1987; MOrth, 1988. Appointments: Lecturer, Honorary Senior Registrar, Newcastle Dental School, 1987-92; Currently Consultant Orthodontist. Publications: Handbook of Clinical Dentistry (with D A Mitchell), 1991. Memberships: COG; British Dental Association, Cleveland Section Chairman 1995. Address: Orthdontic Department, St Lukes Hospital, Bradford, BD5 0NA, England.

MITCHELL Yasminah, b. 6 June 1956, Cape Town, South Africa. Padiographer. m. A van der Schyff, 4 June 1978, 1 s, 4 d. Appointment: Senior Radiographer. Hobbies: Cooking; Knitting. Address: 109 5th Avenue, Kensington 7405, South Africa.

MITEMA Eric Simon, b. 21 Dec 1951, Kisumu, Kenya. Veterinary Surgeon. 2 sons, 1 daughter. Education: BVM; MS; PhD. Appointments: Lecturer, 1979-86; Senior Lecturer, 1986-90; Professor, 1993-. Publications: More than 40 scientific articles in various journals and conference proceedings. Memberships: Kenya Veterinary Association; American Academy of Clinical Toxicology. Address: University of Nairobi, PO Box 29053, Nairobi, Kenya, Africa.

MITTAL Bharat, b. 2 Feb 1952, India. Radiation Oncologist. m. Raj, 29 Nov 1980, 1 s, 1 d. Education: MBBS; BSc; Board Certified in Radiation Oncology. Appointments: Instructor, Radiation Oncology, Washington University, St Louis, Missouri, USA; Assistant Professor of Radiation Oncology, University of Pittsburgh; Associate Professor of Radiation Oncology, Northwestern University. Publications: Contributor of 40 articles in peer-reviewed journals. Memberships: American College of Radiology; American Society of Therapeutic Oncology. Hobbies: Skiing; Golf; Racquet ball. Address: 250 East Superior Street, Chicago, IL 60611, USA.

MITTAL Veerendra Kumar, b. 15 Sept 1927, Meerut, India. Psychotherapist; Educator. m. Prem Lata Mittal, 14 Apr 1950, 1 s, 1 d. Education: MA, Agra University; MA, Lucknow University; PhD. Appointments: Lecturer in Philosophy, 1952-60, Professor of Psychology, Director, Head of department of Psychology, 1960-88, Meerut University; Director, centre for Psychological research and Psychotherapy; Professor, Indian Institute of Educational Research, Meerut Centre. Publications: Hypnobehavioural Model and Yoga, 1982; A Comparative Study of V-NV and R-C Among College Students with Different Levels of Expediency, 1989; Effect of SSM on Old Students, 1990; Effect of SSM on Reawakening of National Consciousness, 1992. Honours: Travel Grant, UGC and State Government, 1981. Memberships: National Body of Vidya Bharti; International Committee of Scientists, New York-Milan; Governing Body, Indian Institute of Educational research, Lucknow. Hobbies: Visiting new places and old monuments; Social work. Address: 249 Chanakya Puri, Meerut Cantt 250001, India.

MIYATA Hideo, b. 17 Nov 1935, Kyoto, Japan. Physician. m. Nagoya, 25 Apr 1965, 2 daughters. Education: MD, Gifu University School of Medicine, 1961; PhD, Gifu University Graduate School, 1966. Appointments: Associate Professor, Gifu University School of Medicine. Publications: Temporal bone findings in cloverleaf skull syndrome, 1988; Potent activation of phospholipase D by phenylarsine oxide in rat leukemia, 1994. Memberships: Oto-Rhino-Laryncological Society, Japan; Japan Society for Equilibrium Research; Otological Society of Japan; Barany Society. Hobbies: Soft Tennis. Address: Gifu University, 40 Tsukasa-machi, Gifu 500, Japan.

MKRTCHIAN Levon N, b. 8 May 1938, Azerbajian. Physician. m. Lucina, 1965, 1 s. Education: MD; PhD. Appointments: Professor of General and Special Pathology, Yerevan State Medical Institute; Director, Oncology Institute, Yerevan, Armenia; Professor of Medical Sciences. Publications: Introduction to Quantum Medicine, 1994; Geo Onco Pathology of Gastro-Enteric Tract Malignant Neoplasma, 1989; Contributor of 195 scientific articles and monographs. Honours: Designated Honoured Scientist of Armenia, 1990. Memberships: President, Oncology Society of Armenia. Hobbies: Bicycling; Nature Walks and Observations. Address: Oncology Institute, Kanaker 7th Street, Yerevan, Armenia.

MMIRO Francis Anthony, b. 2 Aug 1934. Obstetrics and Gynaecology. m. Sarah Kalibbala, 2 Aug 1968, 4 s, 3 d. Education: MBBS; FRCOG; FICS. Appointment: Professor and Head, Department of Obstetrics and Gynaecology, Makerere Medical School, Kampala, Uganda. Memberships: International College of Surgeons; Fellow, Association of Surgeons of Eastern Africa. Hobby: Golf. Address: Department of Obstetrics and Gynaecology, Makerere Medical School, PO Box 7072, Kampala, Uganda.

MO Qizhong, b. 6 Oct 1938, Guangxi, China. Teacher; Researcher. m. Bin Gong, 28 Dec 1967, 1 son, 1 daughter. Education: BS, Biochemistry, Beijing University, 1964; Molecular Biology, Neuro-Endocrine-Immunology; Advanced studies: Department of Nuclear Medicine, Frankfurt University Hospital and Höechst Company, RCL, Germany, 1988-89; Laboratory for Development of Biochemistry, School of Veterinary Medicine, University of Pennsylvania, 1994. Appointments: Associate Professor, 1988, Professor, 1990-, Biochemistry, Molecular Biology, Nuclear Medicine, Shanghai University of Traditional Chinese Medicine. Publications: Co-author: Experimental NIDDM Rats' Model Rats, 1989; Determination and Significance of a New Carbohydrate Antigen CA50 in the Serum of Patients with Cancer, 1990; The Detection and Value of the New Carbohydrate Antigen CA-50 in Sera of Patients with Different Carcinoma, 1992; Experimental Study on Application of Chinese Herbal Medicine in the Functions of Adrenergic Receptor in Brain Tissues of Analogous Dementia Rats, 1992; The Effect of Kidney-benefiting Chinese Herbal Medicine on the Functions of Neurotransmitter Receptors in Brain and Immunization Organ after Immunizing Rats by SRBC, 1993; The Influence of Acupuncture at Zusanli Point on Cyclic Nucleotide Contents of Plasma, Different Brain Regions and Spleen in Rats, 1994. Honours: 8 2nd and 3rd Class Awards of Science and Technology Progress, Ministry of Public Health and Shanghai Science and Technology Commission, 1980-; Special Contribution Honour, Biomedical Science, State Council, China, 1992. Memberships: Director, Shanghai Nuclear Association; Director, National Biochemistry and Molecular Biology Association; National Senile Biology and Gerontology Association; Editorial Board, Nuclear Techniques; Association of Integrated Traditional Chinese Medicine and Western Medicine. Hobbies: Western music; Basketball; Running. Address: Shanghai University of Traditional Chinese Medicine, 530 Ling Ling Road, 200032 Shanghai, China.

MODEEN Tore Gunnar Werner, b. 25 Sept 1929, Helsingfors, Finland. Professor. m. Herdis Irene Örnhjelm, 14 Jan 1962. Education: Doctorate, University of Helsinki, 1962. Appointments: Bank Lawyer, 1955-57; Court Practice, 1953-57; University Teacher, 1957; Alex Ärt Professor. Publication: The Patient's Rights. Honours: Doctor honoris causa, Aix-Marseille, 1978, Uppsala, 1984. Hobby: Philately. Address: Riddaregatan 9 B, 00170 Helsingfors, Finland.

MODI Vinod Venilal, b. 10 May 1929, Baroda, India. Scientist. m. Bharati Gandhi, 17 Feb 1957, 2 d. Education: PhD, Liverpool University, England, 1955. Appointments: Scientific Officer, Hanna Research Institute, Scotland; Reader, Biochemistry Department, MS University of Baroda, India; Professor and Head, Microbiology Department, MS University of Baroda, India; Chief Coordinator, Biotechnical Program, MS University of Baroda, India; Senior Scientist, Indian National Science Academy. Publications: Numerous Articles on Microbial Detoxification of Hydrocarbons; Biological Nitrogen Fixation; Microbial Production of B-Carotene; Sewage Hygenisation by Gamma Radiation; Fruit Ripening. Honours: Fellow, Indian National Science Academy; Visiting Professor, Nagoya University, Japan; National President, Association of

Microbiologists of India; National Professor, UGC. Memberships: Association of Microbiologists of India; Society of Biological Chemists of India. Hobbies: Classical Music; Social Work. Address: AALAP, 12-A Pratapgunj, Baroda 390002, India.

MOE Peter Johan, b. 21 Oct 1923. Medicine. m. Judith Elisabeth Moe, 20 May 1950, 1 s, 2 d. Education: MD; PhD, Specialist in Pediatrics. Appointments: Professor; Associate Editor; Hospital Consultant. Honours: HM Kings Gold Medal for Science; HM Kings Gold Medal for Clinical Work, St Olav. Memberships include: International Society of Pediatric Oncology; European Society of Pediatric Research; Children Cancer Study Group; ASH; American Society of Hematology. Address: Barneklinikken, RegionSykehuset, 1 Trondheim, 7006 Trondheim, Norway.

MOENS Guido Frans, b. 30 Mar 1949, Aalst, Belgium. MD, Epidemiologist. m. Van Kerckhoven Hilde, 2 sons. Education: MD; DrPH. Appointment: Associate Professor, University Leuven; Scientific Co-ordinator, Occupational Health Service, IDEWE. Publications include: Suicide in Flanders: Epidemiological Aspects, 1993; Increased risk of hepatitis-A among female day nursery workers in Belgium, 1994; Occupation and the prevalence of back pain among employees in health care, 1994; Back pain and its correlates among workers in family care, 1995. Memberships: International Epidemiological Association; International Commission of Occupational Health; Society for Epidemiologic Research. Address: P/2 Idewe Interleuvenlaan 58, B-3001 Leuven, Belgium

MOFID Massoud, b. 4 Jan 1932, Teheran, Iran. Physician. m. Mehri Mofid MD, 1967, 1 s, 1 d. Education: MD; Dr Medicine; FACOG. Appointments: Fellow, UCLA Medical Center, 1971-72; Assistant Professor, Case Western Reserve University, School of Medicine, 1972-77; Associate Professor, Loma Linda University, School of Medicine, 1977-. Publications: 6 Publications in professional journals, 1973-77, including: Co-author: Effects of Intravenous Prostaglandins F20 and Oxytocin on Mother and Fetus in Induced Labor of Near Term High-Risk Pregnancies, in L'union Medicale du Canada, 1976; Effect of Elective Induction of Labor with Prostaglandins F20 and E2 and Oxytocin on Uterine Contraction and Relaxation, in American Journal Obstetrics and Gynaecology, 1977. Memberships: Fellow, American College of Obstetricians and Gynaecologists; Los Angeles Obstetrics and Gynaecology Society. Hobbies: Hiking; Swimming; Reading. Address: 1808 Verdugo Blvd no 408, Glendale, CA 91208, USA.

MOLA Glen Douglas Liddell, b. 9 Jan 1947, Wangaratta, Australia. Obstetrician and Gynaecologist. m. Veronica Mola, 29 May 1994, 1 s. Education: MB; BS, Melbourne; DPH, Sydney; FRCOG; FRACOG. Appointments: Dean, College of Allied Health Sciences; Associate Professor of Obstetrics and Gynaecology, University of Papua New Guinea; Currently, Professor of Reproductive Health. Publications: Manual of Standard Management in Obstetrics and Gynaecology, Papua New Guinea; National Family Planner Guide Lines, Papua New Guinea. Membership: Papua New Guinea Medical Society. Hobbies: Classical Music; Weight Lifting. Address: Box 1421, Boroko, Papua New Guinea.

MOLLER Morten, b. 29 Nov 1942, Odense, Denmark. Medical Doctor; Neuroanatomist. m. Vera K Gudjohnsen, 5 July 1969, 3 sons, 1 daughter. Education: PhD, DrSc, University of Copenhagen; Rotating Intern, Trinity Lutheran Hospital, Kansas City, Missouri, USA, 1969-71. Appointments: Research Assistant, 1971-76, Assistant Professor, 1976-94, Professor in Neuroanatomy, 1994-, Institute of Medical Anatomy, University of Copenhagen. Publication: Neuropeptides and signal transduction in the pineal gland, 1994. Honours: Ulrich and Marie Brinch Award for neuroanatomical studies of rhythm generating centres in the central nervous system, 1990. Memberships: Chairman, Danish Society for Neurosciences; Board Member, European Pineal Society. Address: Institute of Medical Anatomy, Section B, Panum Institute, Blegdamsvej 3, DK-2200 Copenhagen, Denmark.

MONAGHAN Edmond Dupré, b. 4 Sept 1929, Quebec City, Quebec Province, Canada. Professor of Surgery. m. Lise Dufresne, 17 Oct 1959, 3 sons, 1 daughter. Education: BA, MD; MSc; Diploma in Surgery, McGill University; FRCSC; FACS. Appointments include: Professor of Surgery, McGill University; Associate Dean, McGill, 1986-93; Chief, General Surgery Service, Royal Victoria Hospital, Montreal. Honours: Canadian Forces Decoration, 1962; Knight of Malta, 1986. Memberships: Canadian Association of General Surgeons; Canadian Association of Trauma; Canadian Association of Emergency Physicians;

Chairman, Specialty Committee in General Surgery, Royal College. Address: Department of Surgery, Room S10-26, Royal Victoria Hospital, Montreal, Quebec Province, Canada H3A 1A1.

MONCRIEFF Deborah, b. 2 Apr 1949, England. Obstetrician; Gynaecologist. m. Michael Mowbray, 1981, 2 d. Education: MBBS; FRCOG. Appointments: Consultant, Obstetrician & Gynaecologist. Memberships: Royal College of Obstetricians & Gynaecologists. Address: 16 Camelot Close, Wimbledon, London, SW19 7EA, UK.

MONGELLI Joe Max, b. 5 Oct 1956. Obstetrician and Gynaecologist. m. Weizhu Lu, 28 Feb 1993, 1 son. Education: MB, BS; BSc (Medicine); Diploma in Obstetrics and Gynaecology; MRCOG. Appointments: Clinical Research Fellow, Registrar in Obstetrics and Gynaecology, 1992; Currently Lecturer in Obstetrics and Gynaecology. Publications: Screening and assessment of fetal growth (coauthor), chapter; Co-author, articles: Pregnancy after Transcervical Endometrial Resection; Risk assessment adjusted for gestational age in maternal serum screening for Downs syndrome, 1993; Risk assessment and gestation dating for Downs' screening, 1993; Birth weight from pregnancies dated by ultrasonography, 1993. Membership: Royal College of Obstetricians and Gynaecologists. Hobby: Computers. Address: 10 Harrow Gardens, Nottingham, Nottinghamshire NG8 1FH, England.

MONGINI Franco, b. 1 Jun 1939, Turin, Italy. Physician; University Professor. m. Wilhelmine Schmid, 31 Oct 1968, 3 d. Appointment: Professor, Head, Centre for Craniofacial Pathophysiology, University of Turin. Publications: The Stomatognathic System, in 5 languages, 1984; Craniomandibular and TMJ Orthopedics, in 5 languages, 1989; Craniofacial Pain, 1994. Hobbies include: Tennis; Music; Theatre; Literature. Address: Centre for Craniofacial Physiopathology, University of Turin, C South Dogliotti 14, Italy.

MONOD-BROCA Philippe, b. 9 June 1918, France. Surgeon. m. Debre Claude, 1 Apr 1942, 2 sons, 3 daughters. Appointments: Chief of Service, Hopital de Courbevoie, Paris, 1959-65; Hopital de Bicetre, 1965-86. Publications: Chirurgie du vieillaxd, 1968; La Samte a quel prix, 1970; Biographie d'Ed Branly, 1990; Le diverticule de Meckel, 1977. Memberships: Academy of Medicine; Academy of Surgery. Hobbies: Handyman; History. Address: 8 rue Garanciere, 75006 Paris, France.

MONTEAGUDO Emilio, b. 2 May 1959, Valencia, Spain. Medical Doctor. m. Gloria Santolaya, 26 October 1985, 1 son. Education: MD, University of Valencia; Professor of Pediatrics, La Fe School of Nurses, University of Valencia. Appointments: Resident in Pediatrics; Medical Staff, Pediatric Hematology Unit, La Fe Children's Hospital, Valencia. Publications: Co-author: Zinc Nutritional Deficiency in Childhood, 1988; HIV in Hemophiliacs, 1991; Prenatal Diagnosis of Idiopathic Neonatal Hemochromatosis with Magnetic Resonance Imaging, 1994. Honours: Award of the Faculty of Medicine, University of Valencia, 1984. Memberships: American Society of Pediatric Hematology and Oncology; Spanish Society of Pediatrics; Secretary, Spanish Society of Pediatric Hematology. Hobbies: Golf; Music. Address: Guillem De Castro 83, 46008 Valencia, Spain.

MONTES Leopoldo F, b. 22 Nov 1929, Buenos Aires, Argentina. Dermatologist. Education: MD, University of Buenos Aires, 1955; MS, Dermatology, University of Michigan, 1959; DMS, University of Buenos Aires, 1961; Resident in Dermatology, University of Pennysivania Hospital, 1955-56; Resident in Dermatology, University of Michigan, 1956-58; Certified Royal College of Physicians & Surgeons, Dermatology, 1958; Subcertification in Dermatopathology, 1975. Appointments: Instructor in Dermatology, University of Michigan, 1958-60; Instructor to Associate, Department of Dermatology, University of Buenos Aires, 1961-63; Assistant Professor, Dermatology Department, Baylor University, 1963-66; Associate Professor of Dermatology, University of Alabama, 1966-70; Associate Professor of Microbiology, University of Alabama, 1967-70; Professor of Dermatology, University of Alabama, 1970-. Publications: Books, Atlas of Skin Diseases of the Horse, 1983; Scanning Electron Microscopy of Normal & Abnormal Skin, 1985; Numerous Scientific Articles. Honours: Sigma Xi; Third Prize, Annual Essay contest of American Dermatology Association for, The Cytology of the Large Axillary Sweat Glands in Man; Career Development Award, US Public Health Service, Institute of Allergy & Infectious Diseases, 1966-70; Bronze Award, American Academy of Dermatology, 1971. Memberships: Alabama Dermatological Society; American Academy of Microbiology; American Association for

the Advancement of Science; American Society for Cell Research; Association Agrentina de Dermatology; Histochemical Society; International Society of Tropical Dermatology; Societe Argentina de Leprologia. Address: Paraguay 2302, 1121 Buenos Aires, Argentina.

MONTESANO Ruggero, b. 4 Oct 1939, Alba, Italy. Cancerologist. m. C Soden, 2 d. Education: MD; PhD. Appointments: Chief, Unit of Mechanisms of Carcinogenesis and Responsible for the Cancer Research Fellowship Programme. Hobbies: Alpinism; Skiing; Reading. Address: International Agency for Research on Cancer, Unit of Mechanisms of Carcinogenesis, 150 Cours Albert Thomas, 69372 Lyon, Cedex 08, France.

MONTGOMERY Leslie David, b. 4 Sep 1939, Otterbein, Indiana, USA. Biomedical Engineer. m. Patricia Ann Trigg, 3 Aug 1971, 3 sons. Education: BA, Monmouth College, 1961; MS, Iowa State University, 1963; PhD, University of California at Los Angeles, 1972. Appointments: Senior Research Engineer, Centre for Neurodiagnostic Study, 1987-92; SRI International 1980-89; LDM Associates, 1973-; Senior Research Engineer, The Bionetics Corporation. Publications include: Bibliographical Survey f SNAP Fuel Materials: Zirconium-Uranium-Hydride and Related Zirconium and Uranium Systems, Co-author, 1964; Cardiovascular Responses of Men and Women to Lower Body Negative Pressure (LBNP), Co-author, 1977; Limb Blood Flow: Rest and Heavy Exercise in Sitting and Supine Positions in Man, Co-author, 1979; Cardiovascular Dynamics Associated with Tolerance to Lower Body Negative Pressure, Co-author, 1986; Simultaneous Use of Rheoencephalography and Electroencephalography for the Monitoring of Cerebral Function, Co-author, 1992; Body Volume Changes During Simulated Microgravity II: Comparison of Horizontal and Head Down Bedrest, 1993; Effects of Short Term Smoking Cessation Upon Peripheral Circulatory Responses to Reactive Hyperemia and Cold Pressor Stress, Co-author, 1994. Honours include: Sigma Xi, 1971; National Academy of Sciences national Research Council Senior Postdoctoral fellowship at NASA-Ames Research centre, 1992-94. Memberships: American Institute of Aeronautics and Astronautics; Associate Fellow, Aerospace Medical Association; American Society of Aviation Psychologists; Biomedical Engineering Society; Undersea Medical Society. Hobbies: Woodworking; Tropical Fish; Fishing. Address: 1764 Emory Street, San Jose, CA 95126, USA.

MONTO Arnold S, b. 22 Mar 1933. Physician; Epidemiologist. m. Ellyne P Polsky, 15 June 1958, 2 sons, 2 daughters. Education: Cornell University, 1954; MD, Cornell University Medical College, 1958; Intern, Assistant Resident, Vanderbilt University Hospital, 1958-60; US Public Health Service Postdoctoral Fellow, Infectious Diseases, Stanford Medical Center, 1960-62. Appointments: Staff, Virus Diseases Section, Middle American Research Unit, National Institute of Allergy and Infectious Diseases, 1962-65; Research Associate, Assistant Professor, Associate Professor, Professor, Department of Epidemiology, 1965-, Chairman, Department of Population Planning and International Health, 1993-, University of Michigan, Ann Arbor; Visiting Scientist, Clinical Research Centre, Northwick Park Hospital, Harrow, England, 1976; Scholar in Residence, National Academy of Sciences, and Institute of Medicine, 1983-84; Division of Communicable Diseases, WHO, Geneva, Switzerland, 1986-87. Publications include: Epidemiologic designs for the study of acquired immunodeficiency syndrome: Options and obstacles, 1984; Acute respiratory infection in children of developing countries: The challenge of the 90's, 1989; Co-author: Tecumseh Study of Illness. XII, Enteric agents in the community, 1983, XIII. Influenza infection and disease, 1976-81, 1985, XIV. Occurrence of respiratory viruses in the 1976-1981 period, 1986, XVI. Family and community sources of rotavirus infection, 1989; A discrete-time model for the statistical analysis of infectious disease incidence data, 1992; Influenza vaccine effectiveness in preventing hospitalization for pneumonia in the elderly, 1992. Honours: Career Development Award, National Institutes of Health; Pulmonary Diseases Advisory Committtee, NHLBI; National Advisory Allergy and Infectious Diseases Council. Address: SPH 1, 109 Observatory, Ann Arbor, MI 48109, USA.

MOOLGAOKER Arvind Sumant, b. 15 Mar 1934, Bombay, India. Obstetrician and Gynaecologist. m. Jean Moolgaoker, 1 son, 2 daughters. Education: MBBS, 1957; MD, 1960; MRCOG, 1964; FRCOG, 1979. Appointments: Registrar, Obstetrics and Gynaecology, Royal Buckinghamshire and Associated Hospitals, England, 1963-67; Lecturer, Senior Registrar, Obstetrics and Gynaecology, Nuffield Department of Obstetrics and Gynaecology, Oxford, 1967-71; Consultant Obstetrician and Gynaecology, North Hampshire Hospital, 1971-95; Currently in Private Practice. Publications include: A New Design of Obstetric Forceps, 1962; Several articles on management of female urinary incontinence, 1972, 1973, 1974, 1976; Reducing the Hospital Stay following Vaginal Hysterectomy (co-author), 1972. Memberships: Fellow, Royal Society of Medicine, 1964-; International Continence Society. Hobbies: Fly fishing and fly tying; Shooting; Photography. Address: 128 Cliddesden Road, Basingstoke, Hampshire RG21 3HH, England.

MOONEY Ellen, b. 18 Sept 1953, Reykjavík, Iceland. Dermatologist; Dermatopathologist. m. Michael Kissane, 9 June 1974. Education: BS, Biology, University of Utah, USA, 1974; MD, Washington University School of Medicine, St Louis, Missouri, 1978. Appointments: Instructor and Advisor in Establishment of Dermatophyte Laboratory, Department of Microbiology, 1983, Staff Consultant, Department of Pathology, 1983-85, Instructor, Faculty of Medicine, 1983-85, 1987-92, University of Iceland; Instructor, Iceland State School of Nursing, 1983-85; Currently Private Practitioner and Consultant, Reyjavik City Hospital. Publications include: Papers including: The Flushing Patient - A Review, 1985; Dermatophytes in Iceland, 1986; Subacute Cutaneous Lupus Erythematosus in Iceland, 1989; The Immunology of Cutaneous Lupus Erythematosus, 1989; Heavy and Light Chain Isotopes of Epidermolysis. Bullosa Acquisita Antibodies (with W R Gammon), 1990; Alteration of Matrix Molecules at the Basement Membrane Zone in Lupus Erythematosus (with W R Gammon and J C Jennette), 1991; Immunohistologic Detection of the Membrane Attack Complex in Epidermlysis Bullosa Acquisita (with W R Gammon), 1992. Honours: Phi Kappa Phi, 1973; Dean's Letter for High Scholastic Achievement for the Year 1975-76; Physician's Recognition Award, American Medical Association, 1986-89, 1989-92, 1992-95. Memberships: EADV, Board Member, 1991-, Scientific Committee Member, 1991-1994; American Academy of Dermatology; International Society of Derma-Pathology, Executive Committee Member; American Society of Dermatology Practitioners; Association of Icelandic Dermatologists. Address: Laeknastoödin Uppsölum, Kringlunni 8-12, IS-103 Reykjavík, Iceland.

MOORADIAN Arshag D, b. 20 Aug 1953, Syria. Physician. m. Deborah Miles, 21 June 1985, 1 s, 1 d. Education: MD, 1980. Appointments: Assistant Professor of Medicine, UCLA School of Medicine, USA 1985-88; Associate Professor of Medicine, University of Arizona, 1988-91; Professor, Director of Endocrinology, St Louis University. Publications: Contributor of over 170 manuscripts. Honours: Alpha Omega Alpha, 1979; Penrose Award, 1980. Memberships: Endocrine Society; Gelontologic Society. Address: 547 Ballas Trails, St Louis, MO 63122, USA.

MOORE George Eugene, b. 22 Feb 1920, Minneapolis, MN, USA. Physician; Surgeon. m. Lorraine Hammell, 22 Feb 1945, 2 s, 3 d. Education: BA, University of Minnesota, 1942; MA, 1943; BS, 1944; BM, 1946, MD, 1947, PhD in Surgery, 1950; Intern Surgery, University of Minnesota Hospitals, 1946-47; Medical Fellow, General Surgery, 1947. Appointments: Director, Tumor Clinic, 1951-53; Senior Research Fellow, USHPS, 1947-48; Faculty University Minnesota Medical School, 1948-53; Cancer Coordinator, 1951-53; Chief, Surgery, Roswell Park Memorial Institute, Buffalo, 1953-72; Director, Roswell Park Memorial Institute, 1953-67; Director, Public Health Research, New York State Health Department, Albany, 1967-73; Clinical Professor, Surgery, State University of New York, Buffalo, 1962-73; Professor, Research Biology, 1955-69; Director, Surgical Oncology, Denver General Hospital, 1973-; Professor, Surgery, University of Colorado, 1973-. Publications: Author, Diagnosis and Localization of Brain Tumors, 1950; Cancerous Diseases, 1970; Contributed 660 Articles to Professional Journals. Honours: include, Recipient Outstanding Citizen Award, Buffalo Evening News, 1958; Outstanding Scientist Achievement Award, 1959; Distinguished Achievement Award, Modern Medicine Magazine, 1962; Teacher of the Year Award, Department of Surgery, University of Colorado, 1977. Memberships: Society University Surgeons; American Surgical Association; Colorado Oncology Foundation. Address: Denver General Hospital, 645 Bannock Street, Denver, CO 80204, USA.

MOORE James Edward Jr, b. 21 Oct 1964, Toccoa, Georgia, USA. University Professor. m. Margaret Anne Sullivan, 2 Sept 1989, 2 sons, 1 daughter. Education: Bachelor of Mechanical Engineering, Georgia Institute of Technology, 1987; MSc, Mechanical Engineering, Georgia Institute of Technology, 1988; PhD, Georgia Institute of Technology, 1991. Appointments: Sr Research Assistant, Swiss Federal Institute of Technology; Professor of Mechanical Engineering. Publications: Flow Patterns in the Abdominal Aorta, 1988; Hemodynamics in the Abdominal

Aorta, 1994; Fluid Wall Shear Stress Measurements, 1994. Honours: Georgia Tech Presidential Fellow, 1987; ASME Bioengineering Division Student Paper Competition, 1990; Alliance for Engineering in Medicine & Biology Student Paper, 1988. Memberships: American Society of Mechanical Engineers; Biomedical Engineering Society; Swiss Society of Bioengineering; American Heart Association; French Society of Biomechanics. Hobbies: Hiking; Bicycling; Frisbee; Music. Address: Mechanical Engineering Department, Florida International University, Miami, FL 33199, USA.

MOORE Kate H, b. 18 July 1954, Indiana, USA. Gynaecologist. m. Ross Mullane, 25 Sept 1987. Education: MBBS; MRCOG; FRACOG; MD. Appointment: Senior Lecturer, Obstetrics & Gynaecology. Publications: Numerous professional publications in scientific journals. Honours: Robin May Prize for Leadership on the Undergraduate Course, University Sydney, 1979. Memberships: International Conference Society; Continence Foundation of Australia. Address: 1st Floor, Clinical Sciences Building, St George Hospital, Kogarah, Sydney, NSW 2217, Australia.

MORENS David Michael, b. 7 Mar 1948, Detroit, Michigan, USA. Physician. m. Ratna Soetjahja, 22 Dec 1987, 2 s. Education: AB, University of Michigan, 1969; MD, University of Michigan, 1973; Diplomate, National Board of Medical Examiners, 1973; Diplomate, American Board of Pediatrics, 1978; Diplomate, American Board of Preventative Medicine, 1980; Fellow, American College of Epidemiology, 1987. Appointments: Clinical Associate, Children's Psychiatric Center, Michigan, 1975-76; Medical Officer, US Centers for Disease Control, Atlanta, Georgia, 1976-82; Clinical Assistant Professor, Emory University School of Medicine, Atlanta, Georgia, 1978-82; Attending Physician, Grady Memorial Hospital, Atlanta, Georgia, 1978-82; Associate Professor, Department of Tropical Medicine, 1982-87; Professor, Department of Tropical Medicine, 1987-90; Professor, Department of Family Practice, 1987-90; Professor, Department of Public Health Sciences, 1987-; Head, Section of Epidemiology, 1989-; University of Hawaii, Honolulu, Hawaii. Publications: 107 Indexed Publications; 99 Additional Non-Indexed Publications, Presentations or Proceedings in Government Documents or National or International Proceedings. Memberships: American Association for the History of Medicine; American College of Epidemiology; American Society of Tropical Medicine and Hygiene; Hawaii Society for the History of Medicine & Public Health; International Society for Infectious Diseases; Society for Epidemiologic Research. Hobbies: Music; History. Address: Bioneed D103, 1960 Wast-West Road, Honolulu, HI 96822, USA.

MOREY Patricia Sue, b. 17 Nov 1942, Sydney, Australia. Medical Practitioner. Education: MBBS, Sydney, 1967; MPH, Harvard University, USA' FRACP; FRACMA; FAFPHM. Appointments: Director, department of Community Medicine, Royal Prince Alfred Hospital, Sydney, 1976-88; Foundation President, Australasian Faculty of Public Health Medicine, 1990-93; Chief Health Officer, New South Wales Department of Health. Memberships: Australian Medical Association; American Public Health Association; Public Health Association of Australia. Address: 21 Bent Street, Greenwich, New South Wales 2065, Australia.

MORGAN Elaine, b. 22 May 1946, USA. Medical Doctor. 3 s. Education: BA, University of PA, 1967; MD, University of PA Medical School, 1971. Career: Assistant Professor, Currently, Associate Professor of Pediatrics, Northwestern University Medical School. Publications: The Long-term Follow-up Clinic for Survivors of Childhood Cancer at Children's Memorial Medical Center, in The Journal, 1992-93; Late Manifestations of Curative Therapy for Hodgkin's Disease, in Contemporary Oncology, 1994. Memberships: ASCO; ASH; AAP; ASPHO. Address: Hematology, Oncology, Children's Memorial Hospital, 2300 Children's Plaza, Chicago, IL 60614, USA.

MORGAN Howard E, b. 8 Oct 1927, Bloomington, IL, USA. Physiologist. m. Donna M Morgan, 1 Jul 1986. Education: MD, Johns Hopkins University, 1949. Career includes: US Army, 1955-57; Instructor, 1957-59, Assistant Professor, 1959-62, Associate Professor, 1962-65, Professor of Physiology, 1965-67, Evan Pugh Professor, Chairman, 1967-87, Physiology, PA State University, Hershey; Senior Vice President, Director, Research, Geisinger Clinic, Danville, PA, 1987-. Publications: 170 Peer-reviewed publications on cardiovascular physiology and biochemistry, 1959-94; Editor, Physiology Review, 1973-79, American Journal of Physiology: Cell Physiology, 1981-84. Honours: National Heart, Lung and Blood Advisory Council, 1979-83;

Carl Wiggers Award, 1984, President, 1985, Daggs Award, 1992, American Physiology Society; Award of Merit, 1979, President, 1987, Distinguished Achievement Award, 1988, Gold Heart Award, 1994, American Heart Association; Howard Hughes Scholar, 1982. Memberships: American Society of Biology, Chemistry and Molecular Biology; Biochemistry Society; Biophysiology Society; President, International Society of Heart Research; Institute of Medicine NAS. Hobbies: Golf; Reading. Address: Weis Center for Research, Geisinger Clinic, 100 North Academy Avenue, Danville, PA 17822-2601, USA.

MORGAN Samuel Kirkpatrick, b. 9 Sep 1930, Selma, AL, USA. Pediatrician. m. Patricia Gainey, 21 Dec 1953, 2 s, 2 d. Education: Pre Medical, Vanderbilt University, 1951; MD, Tulane University, 1955. Career: Assistant Professor, 1967-71, Associate Professor, 1971-76, Professor of Pediatrics, 1976-90, Profesor Emeritus, Pediatrics, Pathology and Laboratory Medicine, 1990-, Medical University of Southern Carolina, Charleston. Publications: Numerous including: Carcinoma and other uncommon tumors, in Neoplastic Diseases of Childhood, 1995. Honour: Fellow, International Society of Hematology. Memberships: American Academy of Pediatricians; American Society of Pediatric Hematology and Oncology; American Society of Hematology; American Society of Clinical Oncology. Hobby: Golf. Address: 275 North Hobcaw Drive, Mount Pleasant, SC 29464-2557, USA.

MORGENSTERN Leon, b. 14 Jul 1919, Pittsburgh, PA, USA. General Surgeon. m. Laurie Mattlin, 1 s. Education: BA, magna cum laude, Brooklyn College; MD, NY University College of Medicine. Career: Clinical Professor of Surgery, UCLA, 1960-70; Director of Surgery, Cedars of Lebanon Medical Center, 1960-70; Director of Surgery, 1970-88, Currently, Director of Surgery Emeritus, Cedars Sinai Medical Center. Publications: Over 225 publications including: Diogenes in the biliary tract, in Archives of Surgery, 1994; Non-parasitic splenic cysts, 1994; The art of sitting, in Western Journal of Medicine, 1994; Achilles' Heel and Laparoscopic Surgery, editorial, Surgical Endoscopy, 1994. Honours: Maimonides Award, American Technion Society, 1985; Golden Apple Award for Excellence in Teaching and Outstanding Contributions to Medical Education, Cedars Sinai Medical Center, 1986; Ralph Colp Prize, Mount Sinai School of Medicine, NY, 1986-87; Pioneer of Medicine Award, Cedars Sinai Medical Center, 1990. Memberships include: Alpha Omega Alpha; American College of Surgeons; Los Angeles Surgical Society; Society for Surgery of Alimentary Tract; American Gastroenterological Association; AMA; Societe Internationale de Chirurgie; American Surgical Association; Honorary Member, Society of American Gastrointestinal Endoscopic Surgeons. Hobbies: Writing; Medical History; Classical Music; Painting; Sculpture. Address: Cedars Sinai Medical Center, 444 South San Vincente Boulevard 602, Los Angeles, CA 90048, USA.

MORHENN Vera Beatrix, b. 22 Dec 1941, Heidelberg, Germany. Dermatologist. 2 s. Education: MD. Appointments: Co-Director, Psoriasis Research Institute, Palo Alto, California, USA. Publications: Activiated Human Langerhans Cells Express RNA for IL-id and IL-IB Cytokine 4, 1992. Memberships: SID; American Academy Dermatology. Address: 600 Town and Country Village, Palo Alto, CA 94301, USA.

MORI Kazu, b. 26 November 1936, Japan. Professor Emeritus. Education: Training course of Teachers of Acupuncture Medicine, Tokyo University of Education, 1961; Special Research Student, Faculty of Medicine, University of Tokyo, 1961-71; PhD, Tokyo University, 1971. Appointments: Assistant Professor, Tokyo University of Education, 1976; Assistant Professor, University of Tsukuba, 1978; Professor, Meiji College of Oriental Medicine, 1983; Professor, Postgraduate School, Meiji College of Oriental Medicine, 1991-; Guest Professor, Shanghai University of Traditional Medicine & Pharmacology, 1992-; Professor Emeritus, Liaoning College of Traditional Chinese Medicine, 1993-; Professor Emeritus, Beijing College of Acupuncture & Orthopedics, 1993-. Publications: Approaching acupuncture research through image technology and nuclear medicine methods, 1983; A scientific study of Qi using image technology and multivariate statistical analysis, 1991; Stress reduction effect of acupuncture as an Oriental approach, 1992. Memberships: Councilor, Japanese Association of Physical Medicine, Balneology and Climatology; Advisor, The Japan Society for Dentistry Oriental Medicine; President, Japan-China Society for Systematizing Traditional Chinese Medicine Theories; Advisor, Japan Holistic Medical Society; Honorary Advisor, College of Chinese Traditional Medicine and Pharmacy of Beijing Union University; Advisor, Chinese Scalp Acupuncture Association; Advisor, Chinese Acupuncture Institute of

USA. Address: #708 40-1 Takehana-donomae-cho, Yamashina-ku, Kyoto, Japan.

MORIARTY Sean, b. 11 Jul 1966, Cork, Ireland. Dental Surgeon. m. Louise Casey, 19 Sep 1992. Education: BDS; NUI. Appointment: General Dental Practitioner. Membership: Irish Dental Association. Hobbies: Football; Hurling; Music. Address: Library Road, Listowel, Co Kerry, Ireland.

MORIMOTO Iwataro, b. 5 June 1928, Matsumoto, Japan. Teacher. m. Keiko Nakada, 18 Oct 1956, 3 daughters. Education: MD, 1955, PhD, 1962, Shinshu University. Appointments: Associate Professor of Anatomy, Niigata University, 1963-72; Professor of Anatomy, St Marianna University, 1972-93; Professor of Anatomy and Physiology, The Japanese Red Cross College of Nursing, Tokyo. Publications: Influence of Squatting Posture on Talus and Calcaneus in Japanese, 1960; A Decapitated Human Skull from Medieval Kanakura, 1992; A Bolivian Mummy Eviscerated, Dating to 100 BC, 1993; Speciality and Variability of Embalming Methods Seen in Human Mummies from Qurna, Egypt, 1993. Honours: Professor Emeritus, St Marianna University, 1993; Honorary Member, Japanese Association of Anatomists, 1993. Memberships: Anthropological Society, of Nippon, 1956-. Hobbies: Walking; Travel. Address: Department of Fundamental Nursing, The Japanese Red Cross College of Nursing, 4-1-3 Hiro-o, Shibuya-ku, Tokyo 150, Japan.

MORIN Richard Lewis, b. 18 Mar 1949, Miami, FL, USA. Medical Physicist. m. Carol Nellen, 14 Aug 1971, 1 s. Education: MS, Radiation Biophysics, University of FL; PhD, Medical Physics, University of OK. Career: Director of Physics, Radiology, University of MN, 1981-87; Director of Physics, Radiology, 1987-90, Currently, Professor and Consultant, 1990-, Mayo Clinic, Jacksonville. Publications: Monte Carlo Simulation in Radiological Sciences, 1988; 50 Papers, 10 chapters and 1 book. Honours: Fellow, American College of Radiology; Diplomate, American Board of Radiology; Chairman, American Association of Physicists in Medicine, 1994; Chairman, American Board of Radiology Diagnostic Physics Examination Committee. Memberships: AAAS; RSNA; AAPM; ACR; Sigma Xi; IEEE. Hobbies: Golf; Biking; Tennis. Address: Department of Radiology, Mayo Clinic Jacksonville, 4500 San Pablo Road, Jacksonville, FL 32224, USA.

MORING Jan, b. 2 June 1954, Doncaster, England. Consultant Clinical Psychologist. m. Eric Moring, 22 July 1989, 1 son, 1 daughter. Education: BSc (Hons), University of Leeds, 1976; PhD, Psychology, University of Birmingham, 1980; MSc, Clinical Psychology, University of Manchester, 1982. Appointments: Senior Clinical Psychologist, Principal Clinical Psychologist in Drug Dependence, 1986-89, Top Grade Clinical Psychology in Drug and Alcohol Dependence, 1989-92, Head, Psychological Services for Addictive Behaviours, 1992-, Oldham Health Authority. Publication: Cue Exposure as an Assessment Technique in the Management of a Heroin Addict, 1989. Honours: Churchill Fellowship, 1986. Memberships: Associate Fellow, British Psychological Society; British Association for Behavioural and Cognitive Psychotherapy. Hobbies: Miniature crafts; Walking in the countryside. Address: 1 Redclyffe Road, West Didsbury, Manchestger M20 3JR, England.

MOROZ Vladimir, b. 1 Nov 1958, Moscow, Russia. Surgeon. m. Olga Mishuk, 3 Nov 1979, 1 s, 1 d. Education: MD; DSc; PhD; Kharkiv Medical Institute, 1981; Academy Institute of Radiology, Obninsk, Russia, 1985; Oncology Institute, Kiev, Ukraine, 1987; Institute of Oncology, Vilnus, Lituvania, 1989. Career: Surgeon, Angiology, Kharkov Institute of Surgery, Ukraine, 1981; Scientist, Institute of Medical Radiology, 1985; Head of Late Radiation Injuries Group, 1992; Chief of Local Radiation Injuries Department, Institute of MR, 1993-. Publications: Co-author, Roentgenoradionuclide diagnostics of late radiation injuries of soft tissue, 1988; Surgical treatment of late radiation injury, 1993. Membership: World Federation of Ukranian Medical Societies. Hobbies: Mountain Skiing; Chess. Address: 58 Pobedy Avenue, R 64, 310202 Kharkiv, Ukraine.

MORRIS Anthony Michael, b. 3 Oct 1950, Leeds, England. Psychology. m. Felicity Morris, 13 Jul 1985, 1 s, 1 d. Education: BSc. Honours, University of Aston, Birmingham; PhD, University of Leeds; AFBPsS. Appointments: Department of Education, University of Manchester, Department of Social and Psychological Studies; Chelsea College, University of London; Department of Psychology, Warwick University; Human Movement Studies, West Sussex Institute of Higher

Education; Currently, Senior Lecturer in Sport Psychology, Department of Physical Education and Recreation, Victoria University of Technology, Melbourne, Australia. Publications: Senior author, Overview of Mental Training, 1991; Senior author, Sport Psychology: Theory Applications and Issues, 1994; Sport Psychology in Australia, in Australian Psychologist, in press. Honours: Social Science Research Council Scholarship, 1974-77; Social Science Research Council Research Award, 1980-82. Memberships: BPS; APS; BASES; NASPSPA; AAASP; BSECH; ISSP; Board of Sport Psychologists, Chair, 1991-94. Hobbies: Table Tennis; Tennis; Cricket; Films; Archaeology. Address: Centre for Rehabilitation, Exercise and Sport Science, 300 Flinders St, Victoria University of Technology, PO Box 14428, Melbourne Mail Centre, Melbourne, Vic 3000, Australia.

MORRIS David Perry, b. 4 June 1922, Wellsburgh, West Virginia, USA. Physician. m. Elizabeth A Jones, 10 Mar 1952, 2 sons, 3 daughters. Education: BS; MD; PhD. Appointments: Head of Launch Site Medical Operations, NASA, Cape Kennedy; Medical Director, Naval Aerospace Medical Research Laboratory; Currently Medical Director, Amethyst, Charlotte, North Carolina. Honours: Member, International Academy of Astrontic; ACPM. Membership: American Medical Association. Hobby: Gardening. Address: 6558 Folger Drive, Charlotte, NC 28270, USA.

MORRIS Peter Delaney, b. 22 Dec 1954, Fort Worth, Texas, USA. Public Health Physician. m. Ellen Ruben, 1 son. Education: BA, Biology, University of North Texas, 1977; MD, Southwestern Medical School, 1981; MPH, University of Washington School of Public Health, 1984; Board Certified, Family Practice and General Preventive Medicine/Public Health. Appointments: Family Practice Resident, University of Texas at San Antonio, 1984-86; Epidemic Intelligence Service Officer, Centers for Disease Control, 1987-89; Currently Medical Epidemiologist, North Carolina State Health Department. Publications: Articles in: Journal of the National Cancer Institute, 1986; American Journal of Preventive Medicine, 1988; American Journal of Epidemiology, 1989, 1992; Southern Medical Journal, 1990; American Journal of Industrial Medicine, 1991; American Journal of Public Health, 1991; New England Journal of Medicine, 1994; Environmental Research, 1995. Memberships: American Public Health Association; Society for Epidemiologic Research; American College of Preventive Medicine; American College of Epidemiology. Hobbies: Travel; Hiking; Photography. Address: North Carolina Department of Environment, Health and Natural Resources, Division of Epidemiology, PO Box 27687, Raleigh, NC 27611-7687, USA.

MORRIS Robert DuBois, b. 8 Dec 1956, New Haven, CT, USA. Epidemiologist. m. Astrid Mueller, 20 Dec 1994. Education: BA, Yale University, 1978; PhD, University of Wisconsin, 1986; MS, Medical College of Wisconsin, 1988; MD, Medical College of Wisconsin, 1991. Appointments: Lecturer, University of Wisconsin; Visiting Scientist, Harvard University, School of Public Health; Assistant Professor. Publications: include, Localization of Disease Clusters using Regional Measures of Spatial Autocorrelation; Drinking Waters and Cancer; Cancer and the Environment; Meta-Analysis in Cancer Epidemiology; Increased Mortality from Brain Tumors: A Combined Outcome of Diagnostic Technology and Change of Attitude Toward the Elderly; A Clinical Trails Data Base as a Research Tool in Health Care; Association of Waist Hip Ratio and Family History with the Prevalance of NIDDM among 25,272 Adult White Females; Obesity and Heredity in the Etiology of Non-Insulin Dependent Diabetes Mellitus in 32,662 Adult White Females; Geostatistics and the Optimal Design of Water Quality Sampling Networks. Honours: Phi Kappa Phi, Academic Honor Society, 1986. Memberships: American Medical Association; Society for Epidemiological Research; International Society for Environmental Epidemiology. Hobbies: Scuba Diving; Mountain Climbing. Address: Department of Family and Community Medicine, Medical College of Wisconsin, 8701 Watertown Plank Road, Milwaukee, WI 53226, USA.

MORRISON David Campbell, b. 1 Sept 1941, Stoneham, USA. Professor. m. Pamela Wentworth, 9 May 1981, 1 son, 1 daughter. Education: PhD, Molecular Biology & Biophysics, Yale University, New Haven, 1969. Appointments: Postdoctoral, Bethesda, 1969-71; Postdoctoral, Scripps Clinic, La Jolla, 1971-74; Assistant, 1975-78, Associate, 1978-80, Professor & Director of Graduate Studies, Emory University School of Medicine, 1980-85; Professor & Chairman, 1985-91, Professor, 1991-. Dept of Microbiology Molecular Genetics & Immunology, Univ of Kansas Medical Center, Kansas City, Kansas. Publications: Numerous professional scientific publications in journals.

Honours: Merit Award, 1990; Higuchi Research Award, 1994. Memberships: International Endoctorine Society; American Society of Microbiology; American Academy of Microbiology. Address: Department of Microbiology, University of Kansas Medical Center, 3901 Rainbow Blvd, KS 66160, USA.

MORROW Linda Ann, b. 14 May 1954, New Castle, Pennsylvania, USA. Physician; Scientist; Educator. m. Dr Robert J Schott, 5 May 1985, 1 s, 1 d. Education: BA, Westminster College, New Wilmington, Pennsylvania, 1976; MD, Medical College of Paynnsylvania, Philadelphia, 1980. Appointments include: Instructor of Medicine, Harvard Medical School, 1990-; Attending Physician, department of Medicine, Veterans Administration Medical Centre, Ann Arbor, Michigan, 1989-90; PHysician Scientist, Geriatric Research, Education and Clinical Centre, Brockton/West Roxbury Department of Veterans Affairs Medical Centre, 1990-; Staff Physician, Division of Gerontology, Department of Medicine, Beth Israel Hospital, 1990-; Investigator, Aging with a Long-Term Disability Research Project, Brokton/West Roxbury, 1990. Publications: Contributor of numerous articles in professiona journals, abstracts and chapters in books. Honours: Alpha Omega Alpha; Associate Editor, Journal of Gerontology, Medical Sciences, 1992-; Advisory Board, Harvard Health Letter,, 1993-. Memberships: American Geriatrics Association; Gerontological Society of America; American Paraplegia Society; American Diabetes Association. Hobbies: Skiing; Gardening. Address: GRECC (182), 1400 VFW Parkway, West Roxbury, MA 02132, USA.

MORTON John, b. 1 Aug 1933, Lancashire, England. Psychologist. 1 d. Education: BA, Psychology, Cambridge University, 1957; PhD, Reading University, 1961. Appointments: Scientist, MRC Applied Psychology Unit, Cambridge, 1960-82; Lecturer in Psychology, Yale, 1967-68; Scientist, Unite de Researches Neuropsycholiques, Paris, France, 1974-75; Consultant, Max Planck Gesellschaft, Nijmegen, 1977-80; Unit Director, MRC Cognitive Development Unit, 1982-. Publications: Editor, Biological and Social Factors in Psycholinguistics, 1971; Co-author, Headed Records: A Model for Memory and Its Failures, 1985; Co-author, Biology and Cognitive Development, 1991. Honours: Fellow, British Psychological Society, 1974; BPS President's Award, 1988. Memberships: Fellow, British Psychological Society; Academia Europaea. Hobbies: Theatre; Food. Address: MRC Cognitive Development Unit, 4 Taviton Street, London, WC1H 0BT, England.

MOSES Rafael, b. 31 May 1924, Berlin, Germany. Psychiatrist; Psychoanalyst. m. Rena Moses-Hrushovski, 24 Apr 1982, 3 sons, 3 daughters. Education: MD, University of Zurich, Switzerland, 1951. Career: Professor & Chairman, Department Behavioral Sciences Faculty of Life Sciences, BenGurion University, Beer Sheba, Israel, 1974-76; Director, Esrat Nashim Hospital, Jerusalem, 1976-78; Medical Director, Summit Institute, Jerusalem, 1977-89; Sigmund Freud Professor of Psychoanalysis & Director, S Freud Center for Psychoanalysis Hebrew University, Jerusalem, 1987-88; Training & Supervising Psychoanalyst, Israel Psychoanalytic Institute, currently. Publications: Co Editor, Psychological Bases of War, 1973; 130 articles on psychotherapy, psychoanalysis, psychosomatic medicine teaching & political psychology; Persistent Shadows of the Holocaust; Editor, International Universities Press Corr, 1992; Honour: Resident Erikson Scholar, Austen Riggs Center, Stockbridge, MA, USA, 1988-89. Memberships: Israel Psychiatric Assocation; Israel Psychotherapy Association; Israel Psychoanalytic Society; Internationa; Psychoanalytic Association. Hobbies: Collects old maps; Swimming; Travel. Address: 9 Molcho Street, Jerusalem 42185, Israel.

MOSES-HRUSHOVSKI Rena, b. 27 May 1930, Neisse, Germany. Psychoanalyst. m. Rafael Moses, 24 Apr 1982, 3 sons, 3 daughters. Education: BA, Hebrew University of Jerusalem, 1953; MA Columbia Univ, NY, 1960; PhD The Wright Institute, Berkely, CA, 1972. Career: Director, Educational-Psychological Clinic, Jerusalem Municipality, 1960-62; Founding Staff Member, Counseling Division of School of Education, Hebrew University, Jerusalem, 1962-73; Clinical Psychologist, Child Guidance Clinic, Jerusalem, 1962-72; Supervising & Training Psychoanalyst, Israel Institute of Psycho Analysis, currently. Publication: Deployment - A Narcissistic Character Defense, 1994. Memberships: Israel Clinical Psychology Section of Psychological Association; Israel Psychoanalytic Society; International Psychoanalytic Association. Hobby: Swimming. Address: 9 Molcho Street, Jerusalem 92185, Israel.

MOSIN Alexei Fedorovich, b. 1 Oct 1931, Volgograd Region, Russia. Scientist. m. Kseniya Petrova, 25 Oct 1958, 2 daughters. Education: Diploma, 1st Medical Institute, St Petersburg, 1957; PhD 1st stage diploma, Institute of Experimental Medicine, RAMH, 1963; PhD 2nd stage diploma, Medical Radiological Research Centre, RAMN, 1977. Appointments: Physician, Kareliya, 1957-59; Research Assistant, Institute of Experimental Medicine, St Petersburg, 1959-62; Chief of Research Group, Medical Radiological Research Center, RAMN, Obninsk, 1962-72, 1985-; Chief of Research Group, Institute of Arctic Biology, RAN, Magadan, 1972-85. Publications: ATP-synthesis and cellular recovering after UV- or gamma damages, 1969; Phage reaction to UV-irradiation: Recovery of phage DNA during its penetration through cell membrane, 1975; On the energy fuel in small wild rodents during their starvation, 1983; Energy balance and death of tumor cells under oxidative stress, 1990. Hobby: Fishing. Address: Medical Radiological Research Center, Korolev str, Obninsk 249020, Russia.

MOSSOP Diana Frances, b. 22 May 1947. Practitioner of Complementary Medicine. m. Lt Col RNC Mossop, 17 May 1971, 2 sons. Education Include: Various Courses in Iridology, Polarity Therapy, Nutrition and Herbalism, 1987-90; MD, Open International University for Complementary Medicine, 1990; PhD, 1992. Appointments: Officer, Womens Royal Army Corps; Owner, Diana's Health & Beauty Clinic Ltd; Dean, Institute of Phytobiophysics. Publications: Numerous professional publications. Honours: Knighthood, Order of Malta, St John of Jerusalem. Memberships: British Association of Beauty Therapy and Cosmetology. Hobbies: Travelling; Research; Reading; Music; Sailing. Address: Le Prevot, St Clement's Inner Road, St Clement, Jersey, Channel Islands.

MOSTOFSKY David I, b. 19 Sep 1931, Boston, MA, USA. Behavioural Neuroscience. m. Rita Rottenberg, 20 Jul 1975, 1 s, 1 d. Education: BA, Yeshiva College, 1953; PhD, Boston University, 1960. Appointment: Professor, Boston University. Publications: Neurobehavioral Treatment of Epilepsy, 1993; Pain and Aging, in press. Honours: Switzer Memorial Award, 1978; NIH Fogarty Fellow, 1980; Fulbright Award, 1991. Memberships: Behavioral Neuroscience Society; American Psychology Assn; Society of Behavioral Science. Address: Boston University, 64 Cummington Street, Boston, MA 02215, USA.

MOTULSKY Arno Gunther, b. 5 Jul 1923, Fischhausen, Germany. Geneticist; Physician; Educator. m. Gretel C Stern, 22 Mar 1945, 1 s, 2 d. Education: Student, Central YMCA College, Chicago, 1941-43; Yale University, 1943-44; BS, University of Illinois, 1945; MD, University of Illinois, 1947; DSc, 1982; MD, 1991; Diplomate, American Board International Medicine; American Board Medical Genetics. Appointments: Intern Fellow, Resident Michael Reese Hospital, Chicago, 1947-51; Staff Member/Charge Clinical Investigation, Department Hematology, Army Medical Service Graduate School, Walter Reed Army Medical Center, Washington, 1952-53; Research Associate, Internal Medicine, George Washington University, School of Medicine, 1952-53; Instructor to Associate Professor, Department of Medicine, University of Washington School of Medicine, Seattle, 1953-61; Professor of Medicine/Professor of Genetics, 1961-; Head, Division Medical Genetics/Director, Genetics Clinic, University Hospital, Seattle, 1959-89; Childrens Medical Center, Seattle, 1966-72; Director, Center for Inherited Diseases, Seattle, 1972-90; Attending Physician, University Hospital, Seattle. Publications: Editor, American Journal Human Genetics, 1969-75; Human Genetics, 1969-. Honours: include, Commonwealth Fund Fellow in Human Genetics, University College, London, 1957-58; John & Mary Markel Scholar in Medical Science, 1957-62; Fellow, Center for Advanced Study in Behavioral Sciences, Stanford University, 1976-77. Memberships: include, International Society of Hematology; American Federation of Clinical Research; Genetics Society of America; American Association of Physicians. Address: Department of Medicine & Genetics, University of Washington, Seattle, WA 98195, USA.

MOURSY Mohamed Nayer Abul Moneim, b. 16 Apr 1943, El-Mansora, Egypt. Medical Doctor. m. Edith Moursy, 10 Aug 1969, 2 sons. Education: MB, ChB; Diploma in Obstetrics, Royal College of Physicians, Dublin; MRCOG, London. Appointments: House Surgeon, Resident, Cairo; Senior House Officer, Registrar, Locum Consultant, England; Acting Specialist, Zambia, Liberia and Nigeria; Consultant, Medical Director, Medical Centre, Qatar; Currently Consultant Obstetrican and Gynaecologist, Medical Director, Medical Centre, Alexandria, Egypt. Publications: Alpha-Foto Protein and Neural Tube Defects, 1978; Textbook on obstetrics and gynaecology today (co-author), in progress. Memberships: Royal College of Physicians, Ireland; Royal College of Obstetricians and Gynaecologists, London; Medical Syndicates of Egypt, Zambia, Liberia, Nigeria and Qatar. Hobbies: Swimming; Gardening. Address: 4 Rue Mohamed Moussa, Azarita, Alexandria, Egypt.

MOUTAERY Khalaf Reden, b. 1 July 1948, Dhamir in Al Sham, Saudi Arabia. Neurosurgeon. 1 son, 3 daughters. Education: MBChB; Dr.med; Facharzt; FRCS (Edinburgh). Appointments: Consultant in Neurosurgery, 1985, Head, Division of Neurosurgery, 1986-, Director of Clinical Neuroscience, 1987, also Chairman of Medical Staff, Riyadh Armed Forces Hospital, Riyadh. Publications: RSA Presentation. Memberships: German Society of Neurosurgeons; Fellowship of Royal College of Surgeons, Edinburgh; Pan Arab Society of Neurosurgeons. Hobbies: Table-tennis; Swimming. Address: Riyadh Armed Forces Hospital, PO Box 7897, Riyadh 11159, Saudi Arabia.

MOYO Geoffrey N, b. 2 Nov 1960, Chililabombwe, Zambia. Lecturer. m. Maggie Chilengwe, 29 Oct 1989, 1 son, 1 daughter. Education: Diploma, Physiotherapy, Evelyn Hone College, 1984. Appointments: Secretary General, Zambia Society of Physiotherapy, 1990-92; WCPT Africa Regional Representative, 1992-95; Vice Secretary of Zambia Society of Physiotherapy. Memberships: Zambia Society of Physiotherapy; Medical Council of Zambia. Honours: Best Student Certificate, 1985. Hobbies: Volley Ball; Badminton; Current Affairs; Watching Videos; Computer Games. Address: c/o Physiotherapy Department, Evelyn Hone College, PO Box 30029, Lusaka, Zambia.

MSAPENDA George Chrysostom, b. 7 Oct 1957, Kabwe, Zambia. Ultrasonographer. m. Maria Kapula, 2 Jan 1981, 6 sons. Education: Diploma, Diagnostic Radiography, University Teaching Hospital, Zambia, 1979; Certificates, Medical Ultrasound: Aarhus, Denmark, 1983; Middlesex Hospital, London, England, 1985; Tokyo, Japan, 1987; Certificates, Clinical Instructing, Radiography and Radiation Protection, Ipswich, England. Appointments: Principal Radiographer/Ultrasonographer, part-time Lecturer, University Teaching Hospital, Lusaka, Zambia, 1984-87; Senior Radiographer/Ultrasonographer, Princess Marina Hospital, Botswana, 1988-92; Senior Radiographer/Sonographer, Debswana Diamond Company, Jwaneng, 1992-. Publications: Medical Ultrasound Problems in Developing Countries, 1987; Ultrasound Evaluation of Liver Disease in Botswana - Hepato Cellular Carcinoma, 1994. Honours: Certificate of Recognition for paper Ultrasound Problems in Developing Countries, International Society of Radiographers and Radiological Technologists, Singapore, 1994. Memberships: Secretary, Radiological Society of Botswana; Associate Member, International Society of Radiographers and Radiological Technologists; Corresponding Member, South African Association of Medical Physicists in Medicine and Biology. Hobbies: Golf; Gymnastics; Round Table; Church. Address: Debswana Diamond Company, Jwaneng Hospital, Private Bag 08, Jwaneng, Botswana.

MUELLER Rudhard Klaus, b. 20 Aug 1936, Glauchau, Saxony, Germany. Chemist; Forensic Toxicologist. m. Ursula Hanni Rossberg, 5 May 1961, 3 d. Education: Dip Chem, 1960, Dr rer nat, Dr rer nat habil, 1977, Leipzig. Appointments: Institute of Forensic Medicine, Leipzig University, 1960-; Head, PGS Toxicology, Leipzig University; Director, Insitute Doping Analysis, Kreischa, Dresden. Publications: Toxicological Analysis, 1976, English edition, 1992; Author of several books and contributor of over 170 scientific papers. Honours: Leibniz Award' Virchow Award; Member, Academy of Sciences of Thuringia; Richard Kockel Medal, 1982. Memberships include: TIAFT; International Academy of Legal Medicine; German Society of Legal Medicine; Society of German Chemists. Hobbies: Chamber music; Organ playing. Address: Johannisallee 28, D-04103 Leipzig, Germany.

MUKHERJEE Sushanta K, b. 29 Jan 1942, India. Medical Doctor. m. Savita Mukherjee, 15 Dec 1967, 1 son. Education: MB; BS; DGO; D Obst RCOG; MRCOG; ECFMG; FACOG; DOG; FRCOG. Appointments incl: Clinical Assistant Professor, Department of Obstetrics & Gynecology, College of Medicine, Downstate Medical Center, University New York, Brooklyn, 1978-; Private Practice, Brooklyn, New York, 1983-. Publications incl: Respiratory Distress Syndrome, 1966; Correspondence on Ruptured Ectopic Pregnancy 31 days after Laparoscopic Sterilization, 1974; The Tesicular Feminization Syndrome: A Report of Two Cases, 1977; Recurrence of Tubal Stump Pregnancy Following Female Sexual Tubal Sterilization, 1977; Intravenous Leiomyomatosis Diagnosis and Management, 1979. Memberships: Fellow, American College of Obstetricians & Gynecologists; Royal

College of Obstetricians & Gynecologists, England; Fellow, Brooklyn Gynecological Society; International Correspondence Society of Obstetricians & Gynecologists. Hobbies: Tennis; Photography; Travel. Address: 15 Waldo Place, Staten Island, NY 10314, USA.

MUKHERJEE Trishit Kumar, b. 1 Jan 1934, Konnagar, India. Physician. m. Anna Purna, 6 Aug 1962, 3 sons. Education: MD; PhD; FRCS; FRCOG; FACOG. Appointments: Clinical Associate Professor, New York Medical College, USA. Honours: Best Doctors in New York City, 1991. Address: PO Box 150, Orangeburg, NY 10962-0150, USA.

MULAZZI Luigi, b. Feb 1953, Paicenza, North Italy. Forensic Doctor. Education: Doctor in Medicine; Specialisation in Forensic Medicine and Criminology; University Diploma in Document Examination. Appointments: Private Expert in Forensic Psyciatry, Impairment Evaluation, Disability Pensions and Malpractice. Address: C.so Vitt. Emanuele 212, 29100 Piacenza, Italy.

MULDER David S, b. 28 July 1938, Eston, Saskatchewan, Canada. Surgeon. m. Norma D Johnston, 19 Aug 1961, 2 sons, 1 daughter. Education: MD; MSc; FRCS; FACS. Appointments: Currently: Surgeon-in-Chief, Montreal General Hospital; Professor, Chairman, Department of Surgery, McGill University, Montreal. Publications: More than 150 scientific publications; Textbook on Surgical Research. Memberships: American Surgical Association; Royal College of Surgeons; Many other surgical societies. Hobby: Professional hockey health care. Address: Room D-6-136, Montreal General Hospital, Montreal, Quebec, Canada H3G 1A4.

MÜLLER Christian, b. 11 Aug 1921, Berne, Switzerland. Medical Doctor. m. M Schaetti, 18 Oct 1947, 1 son, 2 daughters. Education: MD. Appointments include: Professor, Head, Department of Psychiatry, University of Lausanne; Now retired. Publications: Lexikon der Psychiature, 1983; Die Gedanken werden handgreifliche, 1993; Vom Tollhaus zum Psychozentrum, 1993. Honours: Dr h c, University of Heidelberg; Member, Academia Leopoldina. Memberships: Swiss Society of Psychiatry; Swiss Society of Psychoanalysis. Hobby: Gardening. Address: Herrengasse 23, 3011 Berne, Switzerland.

MULLER Donna Sue, b. 5 Jan 1954, Houston, Texas, USA. Physician; Naval Officer. m. Dr Daniel James Beless, 7 Jun 1980, 2 s. Education: BS, Biology/BA, Chemistry, Emory University, 1976; MD, Emory University School of Medicine, 1980; MPH, Emory University, 1986. Appointments: Senior Medical Officer/Senior Flight Surgeon, NAS, New Orleans; Flight Surgeon, VP67, NAS, Memphis. Publications: 2nd Author, Aortoiliac Occulusion Secondary to Atherosclerotic Placgue Ruptere, The Result of Blunt Trauma, 1990. Honours: Comnavairres for Fligh Surgeon on the Year, 1983, 1984; Navy Achievement Medal; Navy Commendation Medal, 1994. Memberships: Aerospace Medical Association; Society of US Naval Flight Surgeons; Association of Naval Aviators; Tailhook Association; Naval Reserve Association. Hobbies: Skiing; Antiques; English History. Address: NAS Branch Clinic, NAS Atlanta, Marietta, GA 30060-5099, USA.

MULLER Nestor L, b. 5 June 1948, Brazil. Radiologist. m. Ruth Muller, 19 Oct 1975, 1 son, 1 daughter. Education: MD; PhD; Fellow, Royal College of Physicians & Surgeons of Canada; American Board of Pediatrics & American Board of Radiology. Appointments: Fellow, Thoracic Imaging, University of California, San Francisco; Assistant Professor, Department of Radiology, UBC; Associate Professor, Department of Radiology, UBC; Professor of Radiology, Department of Radiology, UBC. Publications: Imaging of Diffuse Lung Disease, 1991; Diseases of the Lung: A Team Approach, 1991; High Resolution CT of the Lung, 1991; Author or Co-author of more than 20 book chapters and more than 180 manuscripts. Honours: Award of Honour, Radiological Society of North America, 1991; Cum Laude Award, Society of Computed Body Tomography & Magnetic Resonance, 1993. Memberships: Fleischner Society; Society of Thoracic Radiology; Radiological Society of North America; American Roentgen Ray Society; American College of Chest Physicians; Canadian Association of Radiologists. Hobbies: Tennis; Gardening; Skiing. Address: Department of Radiology, Heather Pavilion Room 63, Floor A, Vancouver Hospital & Health Sciences Center, 855 West 12th Avenue, Vancouver, V5Z 1M9, Canada.

MULLOL Joaquim, b. 24 Apr 1957, Catalonia, Spain. Otolaryngologist. m. Concepcio Marin, 25 June 1991, 1 d. Education: MD; PhD. Appointments: Resident; Fellow in Training; Senior

Investigator. Publications: Numerous articles in scientific journals. Memberships: SCAIC; SEAIC; EAACI; AAAI; SOCAP; SEPAR; ERS. Honours: Young Investigator Award, 1990; Award for Excellence in Research, 1990. Hobbies: Soccer; Music; Coin & Stamp Collecting. Address: Servei De Pneumologia, Hospital Clinic Villarroel 170, Barcelona 08036, Catalonia, Spain.

MULROW Patrick J, b. 16 Dec 1926, New York City, New York, USA. Physician; Researcher. m. Jacquelyn Pinover, 8 Aug 1953, 1 son, 3 daughters. Education: AB, Colgate University, 1947; MD, Cornell University, 1951; Intern, New York Hospital, 1951; Resident, 1952-54; Research Fellow, Stanford University, 1955-57. Appointments: Instructor, Physiology, Cornell University, 1954-55; Instructor, Medicine, 1957-60, Assistant Professor, 1960-66, Associate Professor, 1966-69, Professor, 1969-75, Yale University; Currently Professor, Chairman, Department of Medicine, Medical College of Ohio, Toledo. Publications: Over 200 in various journals. Honours: MSc (honorary), Yale University, 1969; Humboldt Senior Scientist Award, West Germany, 1987; 1 of US's foremost endocrinologists, Town and Country, 1989; Research Merit Award, American Heart Association, 1993. Memberships: American College of Physicians; American Society of Clinical Investigation; American Association of Physiology; American Physiology Society; Endocrine Society; AFCR; ACCA; American Health Association; APM; APDIM; ISH; IASH; Alpha Omega Alpha; Chairman, Council for High Blood Pressure Research, American Health Association. Hobbies: Golf; Tennis; Skiing. Address: PO Box 10008, Toledo, OH 43699-0008, USA.

MUMCUOGLU Kosta Y, b. 3 Feb 1946, Istanbul, Turkey. Parasitologist. m. Madeleine Bliah, 6 Jul 1978, 1 s. Education: PhD. Career: Visiting Scientist, Department of Medical Entomology, Hebrew University, Jerusalem; Research Biologist, Department of Dermatology, University of Basel, Switzerland, 1975-80; Visiting Scientist, Pest Control Department, Teheran University, 1978; Research Biologist, Department of Parasitology, University of Zurich, Switzerland, 1980-83; Senior Investigator, Department of Parasitology, Hebrew University, Jerusalem, Israel, 1983-. Publications: Dermatological Entomology, in German, 1982; Co-author, Allergy and Asthma, in German, 1988. Honour: Wilhel-Lutz Award, Swiss Society of Dermatology and Venerology, 1983. Memberships: Entomological Society of America; Entomological Society of Israel; Entomological Society of Switzerland; Israel Society for Parasitology; Israel Society for Skin Research; Swiss Parasitological Society. Hobbies: Squash; Folk Dance; Sailing; Swimming; Travel. Address: Department of Parasitology, Hebrew University, Hadassah Medical School, POB 12272, 91120, Jerusalem, Israel.

MUNEER Razia Sultana, b. 11 Nov 1938, Nizamabad (A P), India. Assistant Professor of Paediatrics. m. Mohamed Muneer, 22 Dec 1958, 2 sons, 2 daughters. Education: BSc, Osmania University, Hyderabad, 1958; MS, Florida State University, USA, 1964; PhD, Washington University, 1969. Appointments: Graduate Research Assistant, Florida State University, Tallahassee, USA, 1961-64; Graduate Teaching Assistant, Washington University, St Louis, Missouri, 1965-69; Research Associate, Department of Biochemistry and Molecular Biology, 1974-78, Assistant Professor, Department of Paediatrics, 1978-, University of Oklahoma Health Sciences Center, Oklahoma City; Section Chief, Scientific Director, Cytogenetics, Children's Hospital of Oklahoma, Oklahoma City, 1978-. Publications: Effects of LSD on Human Chromosomes, 1978; Co-author: Human breast tumor cell membrane function by CMGT, 1979; Complex translocation of chromosomes, 1981, 1988, 1993; Microchromosome in Amniotic Cells, 1984; Renal Cell Carcinoma, 1988; Tetrasomyd, 1990. Honours: Watumal Foundation, PhD dissertation, 1969; Medical Genetics Fellowship, National Institutes of Health. Memberships: American Association for Advancement of Science; American Society of Human Genetics; Great Plains Genetics Service Network; American College of Medical Genetics; Association of Cytogeneticists. Hobbies: Cooking; Gardening; Reading; Sewing. Address: Department of Paediatrics, University of Oklahoma Health Sciences Center, Children's Hospital of Oklahoma, Oklahoma City, OK 73190, USA.

MUNGER Bryce Leon, b. 20 May 1933, Everett, Washington, USA. Anatomist. m. Donna Bingham, 3 sons, 1 daughter. Education: MD, Magna Cum Laude. Appointments: Intern, Assistant in Pathology, 1958-59; Investigator in Experimental Pathology, 1959-61; Assistant Professor of Anatomy, 1961-65; Associate Professor of Anatomy, 1965-66; Chairman of Anatomy, 1966-87; Professor of Neuroscience and Anatomy, 1966-91; Professor, Head, Department of Anatomy, University of Tasmania, Australia. Publications: The Biology of Merkel

Cells, 1991; Neurocutaneous Interactions in Development: Implications for Medical Dermatoglyphics, 1991; Intravascular Plastic Catheters. How They Potentiate Tumor Necrosis factor Release and Exacerbate Complications Associated with Sepsis, Co-author, 1991; Trigeminal System, Somatic Sensory Receptors, 1991; The Differentiation of the Skin and its Appendages, I, Normal Development of Papillary Ridges, 1992, II, Altered Development of Papillary Ridges Following Neuralectomy, 1992, Co-author; An Experimental Painful Peripheral Neuropathy Due to Nerve Constriction. L. Axonal Pathology in the Sciatic Nerve, Co-author, 1992; Normal Development of the Skin and Subcutis of the Albino Rat, Co-author, 1993; The General Somatic Afferent Teriunals in Oral Mucosae, 1993. Honours include: Phi Beta Kappa, 1954; Alpha Omega Alpha, 1957; Roche Award, 1956; Sigma Xi, 1962; Purkinje Medal, 1987. Memberships: American Association of Anatomists; American Association for the Advancement of Science; American Society for Cell Biology; Society for Neuroscience. Address: Anatomy Department, University of Tasmania, GPO Box 252C, Hobart, Tasmania 7001, Australia.

MURALEEDHARAN, D, b. 24 Apr 1947, Kerala, India. Educator; Researcher. m. Usha Muraleedharan, 11 Dec 1974, 1 son. Education: MSc; PhD; Post-doctoral Fellowship, Council of Scientific and Industrial Research; Professional training in Analytical Techniques. Appointments: Lecturer, 1980; Reader, 1988; Currently Professor in Insect Physiology; Sucessfully guided several PhD and MPhil students. Publications: Chapters: Insect Neurochemistry and Neurophysiology, 1986; Agricultural Zoology Review, 1992; Article, Chronobiology International. Honours: UGC National Associate; Nuffic Fellowship. Memberships: International Society of Invertebrate Reproduction; Life Member: Indian Society of Chronobiology; AAE, Trivandrum. Hobbies: Travel; Music; Shuttle badminton. Address: Damusha, Thekkummoodu, Trivandrum, India 6955037.

MURATKHODJAEV Nariman, b. 17 June 1928, Tashkent, Russia. Professor of Oncology. m. Karimova Sevar, 24 May 1952, 2 sons, 1 daughter. Education: Diploma of Physician. Appointments: Military Doctor, 1951-55; Research Worker of Leningrad Military Medical Academy, 1955-63; Chief of Radiological Sector, Institute of Oncology of Uzbekistan, 1963-68; Deputy Director, Institute of Oncology, 1968-73. Publications: 210 articles; 5 monographs. Hobbies: History of Ancient East. Address: Institute of Oncology and Radiology, Farobi Street, 700095 Tashkent, Uzbekistan.

MURAVSKAYA Galina Vladimirovna, b. 7 Jun 1939, Tver, Russia. Therapeutic Radiologist. Divorced, 1985, 2 s. Education: Physician's Diploma, Tver State Medical Institute, 1962; Candidate Science, Medicine, 1971, MD, 1986, Moscow Roentgen, Radiological Research Institute, 1986. Career: Therapeutic Radiologist, Senior Research Associate, Head of High Energy Department, Professor of Radiology, Currently, Head of Radiodiagnosis and Radiotherapy Department, Research Institute of Oncology and Medical Radiology, Minsk. Publications: Co-author, Directory on Surgical Oncology, section of Radiotherapy, 1979; Co-author, Oropharynx, in Principles of Cobalt-60 Therapy, including the introduction to the Compendium, 1984; Co-author, The Role of Radiotherapy in Combined Treatment of Breast Cancer, in Cancer Research and Clinical Oncology, 15th International Cancer Congress, 1990; Co-author, Non-Traditional Regimens of Fractionation of Dose for Radiotherapy of Unoperated Epidermoid Lung Cancer, in International Congress of Radiation Oncology, 1993. Honour: Badge for Excellent Results in Health Services; Corresponding Member, Byelorussian Engineering Academy. Memberships: Chair, Byelorussian Society of Radiologists; Vice-President, Byelorussian Association of Radiodiagnosticians and Radiotherapeutists; Board, Byelorussian Society of Oncologists; Associated Member, Radiobiology Scientific Board at Russian Academy of Sciences; ESTRO; Invited Member, New York Academy of Sciences. Hobbies: Chess; Swimming. Address: 29 Pushkin Street Apt 152, Minsk, 220015, Belarus, Russia.

MURPHY Karl William, b. 10 Dec 1957, Ireland. Consultant. Education: MB BCh; BAO; DCH; MRCOG; MRCP; MD. Appointments include: Currently: Consultant Obstetrician and Gynaecologist; Subspecialist in Fetal Medicine. Publications: Various on birth asphyxia and fetal monitoring. Honours: Gold Medal, MRCOG. Memberships include: Blair Bell Research Society; Royal Society of Medicine, London. Hobbies: Art; Food and wine. Address: St Mary's Hospital, Praed Street, London W2 1NY, England.

MURRAY John Joseph, b. 28 Dec 1941, Bradford, West Yorkshire, England. Dentist. m. Valerie, 28 Mar 1967, 2 sons. Education: BDS, Honours, 1966, MDS, 1968, PhD, 1970, Leeds; FDSRCS(Eng), 1973; MCCD, RCSEng, 1989. Appointments: Research Fellow, Children's and P{reventive Dentistry, University of Leeds, 1966-70; Senior Lecturer in Children's Dentistry, 1970-75, Reader in Children's Dentistry, 1975-77, Institute of Dental Surgery and Eastman Dental Hospital, London; Professor, Head of Department, Child Dental Health. 1977-92, Dental Postgraduate Dean, 1982, Dean of Dentistry, 1992-, University of Newcastle upon Tyne. Publications: Fluorides in Caries Prevention, 1976; Fluorides in Caries Prevention, CO-author, 2nd Edition, 1982 3rd edition, 1991; The Prevention of Dental Disease, Editor, 1983, 1989, 1995; Contributor of articles in professional journals. Honours include: Distinction in Clinical Dental Surgery; Maccabaean Essay Prize, 1972; Tomes Medal, British Dental Association, 1993. Memberships: Chairman, Standing dental Advisory Committee, 1992-96; Committee on Continuing Education and Training, Department of Health, 1988-; General Dental Council, 1992-; Dentifrice Accreditation Panel, BDA, 1990-. Hobbies: Golf; Photography; Bridge. Address: The Dental School, University of Newcastle upon Tyne, Framlington Place, Newcastle upon Tyne NE2 4BW, England.

MURRELL Helen Calvert, b. 21 May 1928, Adelaide, South Australia. Retired Obstetrician and Gynaecologist. Education: BSc; MBBS, Adelaide University, South Australia; Diploma Obstetrics Reg, 1962; MRCOG, London, 1963; Diploma Tropical Public Health, University of London, 1975; Fellowship RCOG, 1985; MFFP, 1993; FFCH, 1992. Appointments: Associate Professor Obstetrics and Gynaecology, Christian Medical College, Ludhiana Punjab, India, 1963-71; Lecturer, 1963-67; Consultant Obstetrician and Gynaecologist, Christian Hospital, Shiraz, Iran, 1972-73; Clinical Assistant, Diagnostic Ultrasound Department of Obstetrics and Gynaecology, Withington Hospital, Didsbury, Manchester, 1973-74; Principal, General Practice, Brooke Lane Medical Mission, Bromley, Kent, 1974-78; Senior Medical Officer, Department of Health, London, 1978-88; Now retired. Memberships: BMA; Royal Society of Public Health; Windsor and District Medical Society; Christian Medical Fellowship. Hobbies: Bird Watching; Swimming; Walking. Address: 8 Lawkland, Farnham Royal, Slough, Bucks SL2 3AN, England.

MUSANTE Gerard John, b. 3 Apr 1943, New York City, USA. Psychologist. m. Rita Glasser, 9 June 1965, 3 s. Education: BS, New York University; PhD, University of Tennessee, Knoxville; Licensed, North Carolina and New York; Diplomate, American Board of Professional Psychology in Clinical Psychology, National register of Health care Providers in Psychology. Appointments: Psychologist, Oak Ridge Community Mental Health Centre, 1969-70; Assistant Professor, Duke University Medical Centre, 1971-77; Director and Chief Executive Officer, Structure House, 1977-. Publications: Book Chapters: Affective and Cognitive Behavior Change: Essential Components to Comprehensive Obesity Treatment, 1980; Behavioral and Dietary Treatment of Obesity: A Follow Up, 1979; Application of Multidimensional Scaling of Rating Up Foods for Obese and Normal Psychology and Behavior, 1978. Memberships: American Psychological Association; Association for Advancement of Behavior Therapy; North Carolina Psychological Association. Hobbies: Golf; Skiing. Address: Structure House, 3017 Pickett Road, Durham, NC 27705, USA.

MUSE Mark Dana, b. 1 Mar 1952, California, USA. Psychologist. Education: BS; MA; EdD; PsyD. Appointments: Director, Pain Clinic, Sacred Heart Hospital, Cumberland, USA, 1981-83; Director, Centre Mensana, Girona, Spain, 1987-94; Professor, Universitat Ramon Llull, Barcelona, Spain, 1994. Publications: Stress & Relaxation, 1983; Exercise for the Chronic Pain Patient, 1984; Manual for Sex Therapy, 1993; Numerous articles in professional scientific journals. Memberships: American Psychological Association; College of Psychologists, Catalonia, Spain. Address: Centre Mensana, Migdia 16 2 2, 17002 Girona, Spain.

MUSMAND Jonathan, b. 5 July 1962, New York City, USA. Physician. Education: BA, Johns Hopkins University, 1984; ScM, Johns Hopkins University School of Hygiene and Public Health, 1987; MD, New York University Medical School, 1988. Appointments: Intern, 1988-89, Residency, 1989-91, INternal Medicine, University of California, San Diego; Research fellowship, 1991, Clinical fellowship, 1992-93, Clinical Immunology and Allergy, Tulane University; Assistant Professor, Tulane University, New Orleans. Publications include: Crustacea Allergy, Co-author, 1993; Surimi: A hidden, Potentially

Serious, Cause of Fish Allergy, Co-author, 1993; Fish Sensitivity and the Oral Allergy Syndrome, Co-author; Analysis of High Molecular Weight Cockroach Allergen Isolation by Preparative SDS-PAGE, Co-author, 1993; The Acute Effect of Environmental Tobacco Smoke on Bronchial Reactivity to Ragweed, Co-author; Immunopathogenesis of Fish Allergy: Identification of Fish-Allergic Adults by Skin Test and RAST, Co-author. Honours include: Travel Grant, 1992, 1993, Special 50th Anniversary Award, American College of Allergy and Immunology; Travel Scholarship, University of Texas Medical Branch, Galveston, 1993; DuPont Young Investigators Award, American College of Chest Physicians, 1993. Memberships: American Academy of Allergy and Immunology; American College of Allergy and Immunology; American College of Chest Physicians; American College of Physicians; American Thoracic Society. Hobbies@ Skiing; Biking. Address: Tulane University, Section of Allergy and Immunology, SL-75, 1430 Tulane Avenue, New Orleans, LA 70112, USA.

MUSSON Frances Ann, b. 20 Mar 1930, Birmingham, England. Obstetrician & Gynaecologist. Education: MRCS; LRCP; MRCOG. Appointments: General Duties Medical Officer, North Nigeria; Clinical Senior Lecturer, Obstetrics & Gynaecology, University of Ahmadu Bello, Nigeria. Publications: Preoperative Hydrocortisone & Fetal Survival Following Early Elective Caesarian Section for Severe Pre-eclamptoxaemia, 1968; Pregnancy After Haematocolpos, 1972; Early Symptomatology to Select Cases for Ultrasound Screening for Ovarian Reoplasm, 1983. Memberships: FRS Medicino. Address: Strand House, Topsham, Exeter, Devon, England.

MWAMBINGU Faulos Thomas, b. 25 December 1950, Tukuyu, Tanzania. Gynaecologist. m. 4 September 1976, 1 son, 2 daughters. Education: MB ChB, Makerere, 1976; DCH, Glasgow, 1980; MRCOG, England, 1983; MFFP, England, 1993. Appointments:Assistant Professor, Obstetrics and Gynaecologist, King Saudi University, Medical College; Registrar, Chester and Wrexham Hospitals; Principal Research Practitioner in Family Medicine. Publications: Water Intoxication in Obstetrics, 1985; Association of Unexplained Raised Maternal Alpha Feto Protein with Adverse Fetal Outcome, 1988; Pregnancy Outcome in Grand Multiparity, 1988. Honours: Makerere University Outstanding Student, 1974. Hobbies: Squash; Travel. Address: 44st James Avenue, Upton, Chester, England.

MYBURGH Johannes Albertus, b. 31 May 1928, Lindley, South Africa. Emeritus Professor of Surgery. m. Marie-Louise Mullen, 13 Feb 1993, 1 son, 2 daughters from previous marriage. Education: MB; ChB; FRCS; FACS; FRCS(Ed); FACP; FRACS; MD; FRSSAF. Appointments: Surgeon, Johannesburg Hospital; Professor of Surgery, 1966; Professor, Head of Department of Surgery, University of Witwaterstrand & Johannesburg Hospital, 1977-94. Publications: Over 200 papers in scientific journals; Chapters in 3 books. Honours: Honorary Fellowships; Past President, College of Medicine, South Africa; Association of Surgeons of South Africa, Surgical Research Society of South Africa, South Africa Transplantation Society. Memberships: International Transplantation Society; International Hepato-pancreato-biliary Association; International Society of Surgery. Hobbies: Reading; Music; Golf. Hobbies: Reading; Music; Golf. Address: 23 Edward Avenue, Sandringham, Johannesburg 2192, South Africa.

MYERS Allen Richard, b. 14 Jan 1935, Baltimore, MD, USA. Physician. m. Ellen Patz, 26 Nov 1960, 3 s. Education: BA, University of PA, 1956; MD, University of MD, 1960; American Board of Internal Medicine, 1967; Rheumatology Subspeciality Board, 1972. Appointments include: Director of Clinical Training Program, 1969-72, Chief, 1972-78, Rheumatology Section, University of PA; Director, Internal Medicine Resident Training Program, 1978-86, Deputy Chairman, 1978-84, Acting Chairman, 1984-86, of Department of Medicine, Associate Vice President, 1988, Dean, 1991-, Temple University School of Medicine. Publications: 76 Professional Articles and Chapters, 1966-, including: Co-author, Insulin-like growth factor-1 is partially responsible for fibroblast proliferation induced by bronchoalveolar lavage fluid from patients with systemic sclerosis, in Clinical Science, 1994; Co-editor, Systemic Sclerosis (Scleroderma), 1985; Co-editor, Medicine, 1993; 29 Abstracts, 1967-90; Book reviews and teaching programs. Honours: Margaret Whitaker Prize, University of MD, 1960; La Asociocion Colom de Rheum, 1973; Lindback Award, Distinguished Teacher, 1981; Physician of Year, Temple University Hospital, 1986; Memberships: Philadelphia Rheumatology Society; Philadelphia College of Physicians; American Federation for Clinical Research; American College of Rheumatology; American College of

Physicians; NY Academy of Sciences; British Society of Rheumatology. Hobbies: Classical Music; Walking. Address: Temple University School of Medicine, 3420 North Broad St, Philadelphia, PA 19140, USA.

MYERS Stan M, b. 26 June 1951, Martinsburg, West Virginia, USA. Health Educator. Education: BS, Mathematics, Shepherd College; MS, Counselling, Shippensburg University; Certificate in Healthcare Administration, West Virginia University; Certified Health Education Specialist, Certified Nuclear Medicine Technologist. Appointments: Nuclear Medicine Technologist and Supervisor, Division of Nuclear Medicine, City Hospital Inc, Martinsburg, West Virginia, 1973-84; Currently Health Education Instructor. Honours: MacMurran Scholar, Shepherd College, 1972; Golden Poet Award, American Poetry Association, 1991. Memberships: American Registry of Radiologic Technologists; American Association of Christian Counselors; Association for the Advancement of Health Education. Hobbies: Skiing; Hunting; Fishing. Address: Route 1, Box 241-B, Martinsburg, WV 25401, USA.

MYERSON Ross Steven, b. 26 Nov 1950, Englewood, NJ, USA. Physician. m. Karin Dale Larson, 14 Feb 1981, 2 d. Education: BA, Washington University St Louis, MO, 1973; MD, George Washington University, 1979; MPH, Boston University School of Public Health, 1985. Appointments: Senior Managing Physician, IBM Corporation; Associate Corporate Medical Director, Digital Equipment Corporation; Medical Director, Occupational Medical Clinics of America; Currently, Senior Clinical Associate, WA Occupational Health Associates. Honours: Phi Beta Kappa, 1973; Alpha Omega Alpha, 1979; Fellowship in Occupational and Environmental Medicine, Boston University Medical Center, MA. Membership: Fellow, American College of Occupational and Environmental Medicine. Hobbies: Skiing; Scuba Diving. Address: 1120 19th Street NW Ste 410, Washington DC 20036, USA.

N

NACHIN Claude, b. 6 Nov 1930, France. Psychiatrist-Psychoanalyst. m. Anne-Marie Guenot, 6 Mar 1954, 1 son, 3 daughters. Education: Diploma of Neuropsychiatry. Appointments: Private practice. Publications: Le deuil d'amour, 1989; Les fantômes de l'âme, 1993. Memberships: Paris Psychoanalytical Society; International Psychoanalytic Association; Medicopsychological Society; Psychiatric Evolution. Hobbies: Reading; Writing. Address: 33 rue Debray, 80000 Amiens, France.

NADER Kathleen Olympia. Psychotherapist. Education: BA, Psychology, Duke University, USA, 1970; MSW, 1974, DSW, Clinical Social Work, 1989, Tulane University. Appointments: Social Worker, Department of Social Services, Santa Ana, California, 1975-78; Lecturer, University of California, Irvine, 1977-78; Family Therapist, Youth Services Programme, Fountain Valley, California, 1976-82; Psychotherapist, private practice, Laguna Beach area, California, 1978-; Lecturer, California State University, Fullerton, 1980-81; Psychotherapist, Child Psychiatry, Tulane School of Medicine, New Orleans, Louisiana, 1983; Director of Evaluations, Trauma, Violence and Sudden Bereavement Programme, University of California, Los Angeles, 1984-93; Lecturer, Cypress College, Cypress, California, 1986; Consultant in Trauma and Traumatic Grief. Publications include: Childhood post-traumatic stress reaction: A response to violence, 1990; Countertransference in treating trauma and victimization in childhood, 1994; Co-author: Grief reactions in school age children following a sniper attack at school, 1987, 1988; Children who witness the sexual assaults of their mothers, 1988, 1989; Post-traumatic stress reactions in preschool children with catastrophic illness: Assessment needs, 1991; Post-traumatic stress disorder in adolescents, 1992; The children of Kuwait following the Gulf Crisis, 1993. Memberships: National Registry of Social Workers; International Society for Traumatic Stress Studies; Trauma, Grief and Mourning Interest Group; Consortium for Children in War and Community Violence. Address: PO Box 2251, Laguna Hills, CA 92654, USA.

NAFTOLIN Frederick, b. 7 Apr 1936, Bronx, New York, USA. Physician. m. Marcie Myerson, 1 Nov 1987, 2 sons. Education: BA with honours, University of California, Berkeley, 1958; MD with honours, University of California, San Francisco, 1961; PhD, University of Oxford, 1970. Appointments: Assistant Chief, Gynaecology, Endocrine Fellow, US Public Health Service, Seattle, Washington, 1966-68; National Institutes of Health Fellow, Oxford University, England, 1968-70; Assistant Professor, University of California, San Diego School of Medicine, 1970-73; Associate Professor, Harvard Medical School, 1973-75; Professor, Chairman, Obstetrics-Gynaecology Department, McGill Faculty of Medicine, Montreal, Canada, 1975-78; Professor, Chairman, Obstetrics-Gynaecology Department, 1978-, Professor, Department of Biology, 1983-, Yale Medical School, New Haven, Connecticut; Director, Yale University Center for Research in Reproductive Biology, 1986-; Visiting Professor, University of Geneva, Switzerland, 1982-83. Publications: Subcellular Mechanisms in Reproductive Neuroendocrinology, 1976; Abnormal Fetal Growth, 1978; Clinical Neuroendocrinology, 1979; Dilatation of the Uterine Cervix, 1980; Basic Reproductive Medicine, Vol I, Basis of Normal Reproduction, Vol II, Male Reproduction, 1981, Metabolism of Steroids by Neuroendocrine Tissues, Follicle Stimulation and Ovulation Induction, 1986; Articles in medical journals. Honours: Fogarty International Fellow, 1982; Guggenheim Fellow, 1983; Berlex International Scholar, 1991. Memberships: American Gynecology and Obstetrics Society; Society for Gynecologic Investigation; Endocrine Society; International Society of Neuroendocrinology; Canadian Fertility Society; International Society of Psychoneuroendocrinology; Society for Neuroscience; New Haven Obstetrics-Gynecology Society. Address: Yale Medical School, Department of Obstetrics-Gynaecology, 333 Cedar Street, New Haven, CT 06520-8063, USA.

NAGASAKA Masahito, b. 22 Jan 1924, Fukuoka, Japan. Physician. m. Setsuko Yokohama, 19 Apr 1955, 1 s. Education: MD, 1947, DMS, 1959, University of Tokyo; Certified Med Diplomate. Appointments: Research Fellow, 1949-62, Assistant, 1951-53, 1962-70, Lecturer, 1970-83, University of Tokyo; Assistant Director, 1984-89, Advisor, 1989-, Tachikawa Sogo Hospital, Tokyo. Publications: Contributor of numerous research papers and reviews and textbook chapters. Memberships: Japan Society Internal Medicine, Local Councillor, 1986-;

Local Honorary Member, Japanese Circulation Society; Special Member, Japanese College Angiology;Special Member, Japan Society Applied Physiology; Japan Society Nephrology, Councillor, 1962-. Hobbies: Collecting books; Music. Address: 5-15-13 Higashinakano, Nakanoku, Tokyo 164, Japan.

NAGATOMI Akira, b. 10 Dec 1928, Kitakyushu, Japan. Entomologist; Professor Emeritus. m. Miyo Maruyama, 28 May 1953, 2 daughters. Education: BA, 1951, PhD, 1961, Kyushu University. Appointments include: Professor of Entomology, currently Professor Emeritus, Kagoshima University. Publications include: Aquatic snipe flies, 1958-62; Genera of Rhagionidae, 1982; Structure of mouthparts of orthorrhaphous Brachycera (senior author), 1985. Memberships: Entomological Society of Japan; Japan Society of Sanitary Zoology. Hobby: Garden seeing. Address: 4-30-7 Murasakibaru, Kagoshima 890, Japan.

NAGEL Joachim Hans, b. 22 Feb 1948, Haustadt, Saarland, Germany. Professor. m. Dr Monika Nagel. 1985. Education: Diploma, Applied Physics and Electrical Engineering, 1973; DSc, Biomedical Engineering, 1979. Appointments: Professor, BME Director, Behavioural Medicine Research Centre, University of Miami, USA. Publications include: Biotelemetry, 1988; Medical Imaging - Beam/Ray Imaging, 1988; Biopotential Amplifiers, 1995; New Diagnostic and Technical Aspects of Fetal Phonocardiography, 1986; Invariant Image Description for the Improvement of Medical Diagnostics, 1994; Assessment and Diagnostic Applications of Heart Rate Variability, 1993; Proceedings of the Annual International Conference of the IEEE Engineering in Medicine and Biology Society, Volume 15, Editor, 1991; Evaluation of a Neural-Network Classifier for PET Scans of Normal and Alzheimer's Disease Subjects, Co-author, 1992; Differential Patterns of Dynamic Cardiovascular Regulation as a Function of Task, Co-author, 1993; Neural-Network Classification of Normal and Alzheimer's Disease Subjects Using High-resolution and Lo-Resolution PET cameras, Co-author, 1994. Honours include: fellowships, Commission of the EC-Medical and Public Health Research, 1976-86; Consultant to NIH, American Cancer Society and Scientists Institute for Public Information. Memberships: IEEE; SPIE; BIOmedical Engineering Society; New York Academy of Sciences; Sigma Xi. Hobbies: Reading; Fishing. Address: Department of Biomedical Engineering, University of Miami, PO Box 248294, Coral Gables, FL 33124, USA.

NAGLER Willibald, b. 23 Oct 1929, Austria. Physician. m. Marion Plitt, 15 Apr 1969, 2 sons. Education: Matura Degree, Gymnasium Linz, Ooe, 1949; MD, Medical School of the University of Vienna, 1958. Appointments include: Provisional Assistant Physician to Outpatients, New York Hospital, 1963-65; Assistant Physician, New York Hospital, 1965-66; Physician to Outpatients, New York Hospital, 1966-67; Acting Director, Department of Physical Medicine & Rehabilitation, New York Hospital, 1967-69; Head, Department of Physical Medicine & Rehabilitation, New York Hospital, 1969-71; Physiatrist in Chief, Department of Physical Medicine & Rehabilitation, New York Hospital, 1971-; Professor, Rehabilitation Medicine in Surgery, Cornell University Medical College, 1978-. Publications include: Unruptured primary ovarian pregnancy, 1961; Fluorine 18, a new radioisotope for bone localization, 1962; Radioisotope photoscanning of the liver, 1963; Vertebral artery obstruction by hyperextension of the neck: Report of three cases, 1973; Peripheral nerve damage resulting from local hemorrhage and ischemia, 1973; Mechanical obstruction of vertebral arteries during hyperextension of the neck, 1973. Spinal accessory nerve palsy: An unusual complication of coronary artery bypass, 1991; The neuromotor behavior of full term and preterm children by 3 years of age: Quality of movement and variability, 1991; Complications associated with intermittent pneumatic compression, 1992. Memberships include: American Medical Association; New York Medical Society; New York Society of Physical Medicine & Rehabilitation; British Association of Sport & Medicine; American Congress of Rehabilitation Medicine; Academy of Pain Research; American Heart Association. Honours: Medical Student Essay Award, Austrian Ministry of Culture & Education, 1956; Gold Medal Award, 6th International Congress of Physical Medicine, Barcelona, Spain, 1972; Endowment of Chair, Jerome & Anne Fisher Physiatrist in Chief, 1983; Conrad Jobst Award, Outstanding Contributions in Vascular Research, American Congress of Rehabilitation Medicine, 1990. Address: 525 E 68th St, New York, NY 10021, USA.

NAGY Zoltan George, b. 22 June 1942, Budapest, Hungary. Neurologist. m. Mary Manninger, 8 Jan 1972, 1 son, 1 daughter.

Education: DSC; PhD; MD. Appointments: Assistant Professor, Department of Pathology; Associate Professor, Department of Psychiatry, Semmelweis Medical School; Visiting Scientist, Department of Pathology, McGill University; Professor of Neurology, Director, National Stroke Centre. Publications: 82 papers; 1 book; 5 chapters. Honours: Excellent Medical Doctor Award, 1989. Memberships: IBRO. Hobbies: Painting; Fine Arts; Gardening; History. Address: Bogar 17, Budapest, Hungary.

NAHUM Gerard Georges, b. 23 Sept 1956, Paris, France. Obstetrician & Gynaecologist. m. Margaret M Nahum, 7 May 1989, 1 son, 1 daughter. Education: BS, Chemistry & Engineering, Yale University, 1978; MD, Stanford University, 1984. Appointments: Clinical Instructor, Santa Clara Valley Medical Center. Publications: Correlation Between First and Early Third Trimester Glucose Screening Test Results, 1990; Racial Differences in Oral Glucose Screening Test Results: Establishing Race-Specific Criteria for Abnormality in Pregnancy, 1993; Fetal Weight Gain at Term: Linear with Minimal Dependence on Maternal Obesity, 1995. Honours: California State Fellowship in Medicine, 1980-83; Yale University, Dual Degrees in Chemistry & Engineering, cum laude with Departmental Distinction, 1978. Memberships: American College of Obstetricians & Gynaecologists; American Fertility Society; American Association of Gynaecologic Laparoscopists; American Chemical Society; Flying Physicians Association. Hobbies: Tennis; Jogging; Chess; Writing; Piloting Light Aircraft. Address: 2440 Samaritan Drive, Suite 2, San Jose, CA 95124, USA.

NAKOWA Anastassia, b. 13 July 1942, Sofia, Bulgaria. Ophthalmology. Education: MD, Medical Academy, Sofia, 1968. Appointments: Scientist, Postgraduate Medical Institute, Sofia, 1967; Thesis, Postgraduate Medical Institute, Sofia, 1971; Doctorat-Habil. Thesis, Medical Academy, Sofia, 1989; Head, Department of Ocular Functional Diagnostics. Publications: The Second Eye in Retinal Detachment, 1971; Photopic Functions in Retinitis Pigmentosa Cross-Correlations, 1989; Modern Problems in Ophtalmology, 1981; Clinical Ophtalmology, co-author, textbook, 1994. Honours: Diploma for Young Scientist, Moscow University, Russia, 1974. Memberships: International Society of Clinical Electrophisiology of Vision; International Research Group of Colour Vision Deficiencies; President of the Bulgarian Section of the Association for Eye Research, 1995-. Hobbies: Classical Music; Literature. Address: San Stephano 9, Sofia 1504, Bulgaria.

NAMAZOVA Adilia, b. 9 Sep 1926, Agdam, Azerbaijan. Professor; Pediatrician. m. Suleymanov Fazil, 20 May 1968, 1 s. Education: Azerbaijan Medical University, Baku, 1949; Postgraduate, Central Advanced Training Institute for Doctors, Moscow, 1954-57; Scientific Research, Institute of Pediatrics, Moscow. Career: Manager of Children's Hospital, Agdam, 1949-54; Assistant Lecturer, 1958-60; Currently, Head of Department of Pediatrics, Azerbaijan Medical University; Professor, Academician, Azerbaijan Academy of Sciences; Academician of Medical Sciences Academy of Russian Federation. Publications: Over 200 books and articles including: Surgery of septal defects of the heart, 1966; Congenital Heart Disease, 1967; Diseases of Children, 1969; Uvinel Arterial Hypotension of Children, 1979; Endocrine disease of children, 1978; Pediatrician's Reference Book. Honours: Honoured Scientist of Azerbaijan; State Prize Winner; Merited Worker of Health Care System of Russia. Memberships: President, Pediatric Association of Azerbaijan; Pediatric Society of Turkey; Vice President, Union of National Pediatric Society of Turkey. Hobbies: Music; Needlework. Address: 370000, Prosp Bul-Bul 21 kv 33, Azerbaijan.

NANDI Panna Lal, b. 6 Jan 1940, India. m. Anita, 15 Aug 1974, 2 daughters. Education: University of Calcutta, Calcutta Medical College Hospitals, 1956-61; ISc (Calcutta), 1956; MBBS (Calcutta), 1962; FRCS (Edinburgh), 1968; FRCS (England), 1969; FCCP (USA), 1973; FACS (USA), 1979. Career: Senior Lecturer in Surgery, The University of Hong Kong, Queen Mary Hospital, Hong Kong; Consultant Cardiothoracic Surgeon, 1980-. Publications include: Books: The Gastrointestinal Tract, Foreign Bodies in Oesophagus, 1981; Lung Tuberculosis in Surgery in Tropical Diseases, in press; Articles: Bronchogenic Carcinoma in Hong Kong: Review of 390 Cases, 1978; Surgery of Isolated Patent Ductus Arteriosus - review of 188 Cases, 1978; Sarcoidosis in Hong Kong Chinese, 1983; The Patient with Pneumothorax: Causes and Managements, 1988; Foreign Body in the Bronchus, 1989; Percutaneous Fine Needle Aspiration Cytology for Solid Pulmonary Lesions, 1993. Memberships include: American College of Chest Physicians, Fellow; American College of Surgeons, Fellow; British Medical Association; British Thoracic Society; Hong Kong Surgical Society, Fellow; Society of Thoracic and Cardiovascular Surgeons of Great Britain and Ireland. Address: Department of Surgery, University of Hong Kong, Queen Mary Hospital, Pokfulam, Hong Kong.

NAQSHBANDI Jahan Ara, b. 8 August 1935, India. Obstetrician and Gynaecologist. m. 5 September 1969, 1 daughter. Education: MBBS, India; MRCOG, London. Appointments: Professor, Obstetrics and Gynaecology, Gort Medical College, 1967-. Publications: Numerous articles in professional medical journals. Memberships: Royal College of Obstetricians and Gynacologists, London. Hobbies: Classical Music, Indian and Western. Address: White House, Raja Bagh, Srinagar, Kashmir, India.

NARULA Surinder Kaur, b. 21 Oct 1951, New Delhi, India. Doctor. m. H S Narula, 21 Feb 1975, 1 son, 1 daughter. Education: MBBS; DRCOG; D-Obs; MRCOG. Appointment: General Practitioner. Memberships: Royal College of Obstetrics & Gynaecology, London; Local Medical Committee. Hobbies: Swimming; Entertaining. Address: 18 Shepherd Drive, Langstone, Newport, Gwent, Wales, England.

NASSAR Munir, b. 21 June 1934, Beirut, Lebanon. Physician. m Leila George, 17 June 1959, 1 son, 1 daughter. Education: BSc; MD. Appointments: Assistant in Medicine, Baylor College of Medicine, USA; Visiting Scholar, Columbia University; Associate in Medicine, American University of Beirut; Visiting Adjunct Docent, Uppsala University Academic Hospitals, Sweden; Staff Physician, Internal Medicine and Cardiology, Medical Service, Veterans Affairs Medical Department: Medical Education. Publications: Tricuspid Regurgitation, 1964; Master's Test and Mitral Stenosis, 1964; The I C U, 1968; Lung Function Norms in Lebanese Children, 1970; M Myeloma, 1983; Editorial, JRSM, 1991; JRSM, 1994: Appraisal of US Health Care. Honours: Fellow, American Heart Association, 1965-66; Fellow, American College of Physicians. 1987. Memberships: Royal Society of Medicine; American Society of Internal Medicine; Cardiological Society, NY State. Hobbies: Classical Music; Bridge; Tennis; Walking; Travel; History of Medicine. Address: 176 Holley Brook Road, Brockport, NY 14420, USA.

NATH Aruna, b. 5 Nov 1942, Lahore, India. Obstetrician and Gynaecologist. m. Narindar Nath, 15 May 1066, 2 sons, 1 daughter. Education: MBBS, Lady Hardinge Medical College, Delhi, 1965; DObstRCOG, 1968, MRCOG, 1970, FRCOG, 1987. MFPM, 1988, FFPM, 1990, MFFP, 1993, London. Appointments: House Surgeon, King's College Hospital, London, England, 1968-69; Registrar, Westminster Medical School Group of Hospitals, 1970-72; Instructing Medical Officer, Family Planning and Joint Committee on Contraception, London, 1970-; Lecturer, Honorary Senior Registrar, St Bartholomew's Medical School, 1973; Senior Registrar, Medical Officer in-charge, Council for Investigation of Fertility Control, 1974-70; Medical Officer, Redhill General Hospital, Surrey, Principal in general practice, Beckenham, Kent, Consultant to Wembley Hospital, Middlesex, 1980-82; Medical Officer, 1982-90, Senior Medical Officer, 1990-, Senior Assessment Consultant, Medicines Control Agency, 1990-, Department of Health; Senior OP Obstetrician and Gynaecologist, St George's Medical School and Hospital, London, 1992-. Publications: The Problem of Cervical Smears, 1974; The Effect of Prolonged Oral Contraceptive Steroid Use on Enzyme ACtivity and Vitamin Status, 1981; Abridged Medical Applictions-Recent General and Medical Experiences, 1990. Honours include: Hindi Rattan, 1991. Memberships include: Fellow, Royal Society of Medicine; Faculty of Pharmaceutical Medicine, Royal College of Physicians; Blair Bell Research Society; International Society of Psychosomatic Obstetrics and Gynaecology; IPMS; Medical Women's Federation; International Medical Association; NAFPD; Overseas Development Administration; School Governors, Applegarth School. Hobbies: Music; Reading; Comparative study of religions. Address: Abbotswood, Bridle Way, Shirley Heath, Croydon, Surrey CR0 5AH, England.

NATH Indira, b. 14 Jan 1938. Scientist. 1 d. Education: MBBS; MD(Path); FRC (Path); National Academy of Sciences, India; Indian National Sciences Academy; National Academy of Sciences, Allahabad; Indian Academy of Sciences, India. Career: House Surgeon, 1963, Tutor, 1966-70, Lecturer, Biochemistry, 1972-80, Assistant Professor, Pathology, 1980-86, Associate Professor of Pathology, 1986-87, Professor and Head, Biotechnology, 1987-, All India Institute of Medical Sciences, New Delhi, India. Oration Award, ICMR-JALMA Trust Fund, 1981; SS Bhatnagar Award, 1983; Kshanika Oration, 1984; Dr Nitya

Anand Endowment, 1987; ShOm Prakash Bhasin Foundation Award, 1990. Memberships: Elected, Guha Research Conference; Life, Indian Association of Leprologists; Founder Life Member, Indian Immunology Society; Elected Fellow, College of Allergy and Applied Immunology; Indian Association of Pathologists and Microbiologists; Life, Association of DNA Fingerprinting. Address: Department of Biotechnology, All India Institute of Medical Sciences, New Delhi 110-029, India.

NATHAN David Gordon, b. 25 May 1929, Boston, MA, USA. Pediatrician. m. Jean L Friedman, 1 Sep 1951, 1 s, 2 d. Education: AB; MD. Appointments: Research Associate in Medicine, Assistant Professor of Pediatrics, Associate Professor of Pediatrics, Professor of Pediatrics, Harvard Medical School; Currently, Physician-in-Chief, Children's Hospital Boston and Robert A Stranahan Professor of Pediatrics at Harvard Medical School. Publications: Hematology of Infancy and Childhood, 4 editions; Blood, Genes and Courage, in press. Honours: Phi Beta Kappa; National Medal of Science, 1990; Fellow, American Association of Advancement of Science, 1991. Memberships: President, 1984, American Society of Hematology; American Society of Clinical Invest; Association of American Physicians; American Pediatric Society. Hobbies: Tennis; Sailing; Grandchildren. Address: Children's Hospital Medical Ctr, 300 Longwood Ave, Boston, MA 02115, USA.

NATHANSON Neal S, b. 1 Sept 1927, Boston, Massachusetts, USA. Virologist. m. Dr P S Leboy, 10 July 1984, 2 s. 1 d. Education: MD, Harvard Medical School, 1953. Appointments: Chair, Microbiology, Microbiology, 1979-94, Vice Dean for Research, University of Pennsylvania Medical Centre; Professor, Epidemiology, Johns Hopkins University, 1968-79. Publications: Editor-in-Chief, Viral Pathogenesis, 1995; Contributor of 170 primary articles. Address: 1600 Hagys Ford Rd, Narbeath PA 19072-1049, USA.

NATTA Clayton Lyle, b. 17 Nov 1932, Trinidad, West Indies. Physician. m. Stephanie Natta, 4 July 1962, 2 daughters. Education: BA, McMaster University; MD, University of Toronto; FRCP (C), 1972; FRC Path, London, 1990. Appointments include: Chief, Haematology Laboratories, Attending Haematologist, Harlem Hospital Center, NYC, USA, 1970-; Assistant Attending Physician, 1970-85, Co-Director, Comprehensive Sickle Cell Center, 1977-, Associate Attending, Department of Pathology, 1980-89, Associate Attending Physician, Department of Medicine, 1985-, Attending, Department of Pathology, 1989-, Harlem Hospital; Instructor, 1970-72, Assistant Professor, Medicine, Pathology, 1973-81, Associate Professor, Clinical Medicine, 1981-, Columbia University, NYC; Assistant Physician, Medicine Service, 1973-85, Associate Attending Physician, Department of Medicine, 1985-, Presbyterian Hospital. Publications: Failure of the Alpha Thalassemia Gene to Decrease the Severity of Sickle Cell Anemia, 1978; Painful Crises Due to Sickle Cell Anemia: Effect of Vitamin B6 supplementation, 1986; Co-author: Alteration in IgG Subclass Distribution in AIDS, 1989; IgG Subclass Levels in Adult Asthma; Many others, mainly regarding sickle cells. Honours include: Fellow, International Society of Hematology, 1980. Memberships include: American Society of Hematology; American Society of Internal Medicine; New York Academy of Sciences; International Society for Experimental Hematology; American Institute of Nutrition; American Association for Advancement of Science. Hobbies: Table-tennis; Weightlifting. Address: Department of Medicine, Columbia University College of Physicians, 630 West 168th Street, New York, NY 10032, USA.

NAVAR Luis Gabriel, b. 24 Mar 1941, El Paso, Texas, USA. Physiology Educator. m. Randa Ann Bumgarner, 15 Oct 1965, 2 s, 2 d. Education: BS, Texas A&M University; PhD, Univrsity of Mississippi. Appointments include: Instructor, 1966-67, Assistant Professor, 1967-71, Associate Professor, 1971-74, University of Mississippi Medical Centre, Jackson, Mississippi ; Associate Professor, 1974-76, Professor, 1976-79, Associate Professor, Department of Medicine, Senior Scientist, Nephrology Research and Training Centre, 1979-83, Professor, Department of Medicine, 1983-88, Adjunct Professor, 1988-90, University of Alabama at Birmingham, Alabama; Chairman and Professor, Department of Physiology, Tulane University School of Medicine, New Orleans, Louisiana, 1988-. Publications: Microcirculation of the Kidneys, Co-author, 1983; Regulation of Body Fluid Balance, 1984; Renal Hemodynamics, Co-author, 1992. Honours include: Phi Eta Sigma, 1959; Phi Kappa Phi, 1962; Sigma Xi, 1966; Research Career development Award, National Heart, Lung and Blood Institute, 1974-79; Merit Award, 1988-. Memberships include: American Association for the Advancement of Science; American Heart Association, Council on Kidney in Cardiovascular Disease, Council on High Blood Pressure; American Physiological Society; American Society of Nephrology; International Society of Hypertension; Microcirculatory Soceity; National Kidney Foundation. Hobby: Racquetball. Address: Tulane University School of Medicine, Department of Physiology SL39, 1430 Tulane Avenue, New Orleans, LA 70112, USA.

NAVARRE Gerald Leo, b. 10 Apr 1931, Ecorse, Michigan, USA. Obstetrics & Gynecology. m. Rita Osweiler, 11 June 1960, 4 sons, 1 daughter. Education: MD. Appointments: Head, Colposcopy Laser & Leep Kaiser Hospital Anaheim, California; Staff Physician, Chief Colposcopy & Leep. Publications: Colposcopy in Prepaid Group Practice, 1976; Trends in Colposcopy; Screening colposcopy; Office Biopsy as Treatment. Honours: Clinical Professor, 1990. Memberships: ASCCP. Hobbies: Golf, Scuba. Address: 3rd Floor, 5 Centerpointe Drive, La Palma, CA 90623-1084, USA.

NEAL-SMITH Denys John, b. 7 Aug 1915, Richmond, Surrey, England. Medical Practitioner. m. Margaret Anne Westcott, 24 Sep 1983. Education: MD, BS, London; LRCP; MRCS; DOMS, England; FRCOG; FRCO, CHM. Appointments: Ophthalmic Specialist, RAF; Senior Registrar, Chelsea Hospital for Women; Currently, Consultant Obstetrician and Gynaecologist, St Mary's Hospital and University College Hospital, London. Memberships: BMA; Past Chairman, West Sussex Division, BMA. Hobby: Musically qualified and has been professionally employed as a church organist. Address: 10 Kings Walk, Shoreham-By-Sea, West Sussex, BN43 5LG, England.

NEALE Anne Victoria, b. 14 Feb 1953, Garden City, Michigan, USA. Research Psychologist. 1 son, 1 daughter. Education: MA; PhD, Social Psychology, Wayne State University, 1981; MPH, University of Texas, 1983; Specialist Certificate in Aging. Appointments: Currently Assistant Professor, Director, Division of Research Support, Department of Family Medicine, Wayne State University. Publications: Widows in a Florida retirement community, 1987; Work stress in emergency medical technicians, 1991; Behavioural contracting as a tool to help patients achieve better health, 1991; Racial and marital status influences on 10 year survival from breast cancer, 1994; Co-author, about 20 others including: Behavioral contracting in an urban health promotion project, 1987; Incongruence between self-reported symptoms and objective evidence of respiratory disease among construction workers, 1990; Validation of the Hwalek-Sengstock Elder Abuse Screening Test, 1991; Activity levels, fitness status, exercise knowledge, and exercise beliefs among healthy older African American and white women, 1994. Honours: Examination for Professional Practice in Psychology, 1983. Memberships: American Public Health Association; Gerontological Society of America; American Psychological Association; Association for Women in Science; Society for Epidemiological Research. Hobby: Gardening. Address: Department of Family Medicine, 4201 St Antoine, VHC 4-J, Detroit, MI 48201, USA.

NECHAI Anatoly, b. 5 Jul 1927, Poltava, Ukraine. Surgeon. m. Lidia Nechai, 29 Jan 1949, 2 s, 1 d. Education: MD, Military Medical Academy, Leningrad, Russia. Career: Military Surgeon, 1949-53; Adjunct Professor, 1953-56, Lecturer, Associate Professor of Abdominal Surgery, Professor and Head of Department of Abdominal Surgery, 1977-88, Currently, Professor of Abdominal Surgery, Military Medical Academy, St Petersburg. Publications: Postcholecystectomy syndrome and repeated operations on bile duct, in Medicina, 1982; Duodenal ulcers treatment by vagotomy, 1986; Cancer of Stomach, 1987; Non-operative removal of biliary stones with outside drainage, in Medicina, 1987; Editor, Icenko-Cushing Syndrome, 1988; Postcholecystectomy Syndrome, in St Petersburg Medical News, 1994. Honours: Laureate, State Prize of Russia; Honoured Board Member, Pirogov Surgery Society. Memberships: Association of Surgeons - N Pirogov; Pirogov Surgical Society; Editorial Board, Vestnik Kbirurgii. Hobbies: Old Russian Romance Songs; Fishing. Address: Military Medical Academy, Pyrogov St 3, St Petersburg 194175, Russia.

NEELY John Gail Henry, b. 10 Dec 1939, Oklahoma City, USA. Medical Doctor. m. Susan Neely, 2 sons, 4 daughters. Education: BS, University of Central Oklahoma; MD, University of Oklahoma School of Medicine; Internship, University of Oregon; Resident, Baylor College of Medicine. Appointments: Associate, Baylor College of Medicine; Professor, Department of Otorhinolaryngology & Communicative Sciences, 1980-81; Professor, Chairman, University of Oklahoma Health Sciences Center, 1981-91. Publications: Include: Impedance Audiometry: Interpretation of Tympanograms, 1975; Treatment of the

Uncomplicated Aural Cholesteatoma (Keratoma), 1977; Complications of Suppurative Otitis Media, Part I: Aural Complications, 1978; Complications of Suppurative Otitis Media, Part II: Intracranial Complications, 1979; Evaluation of the Patient with Hearing Difficulty, 1980; Seminars in Hearing: The Neuro-Audiologic Examination, 1983; Vestibular System Testing-Special Issue, 1986; Head and Neck Surgery-Otolaryngology, 1993; Seminars in Hearing, 1995. Memberships: Include: American Auditory Society; American College of Surgeons; American Medical Association; American Otological Society; North American Skull Base Society; Society of University Otolaryngologists; New York Academy of Sciences. Honours: Best Doctor in America, 1991, 1994; Broncho Award, University of Central Oklahoma, 1990; Two Patents, US Patent Office, 1991, 1993. Hobbies: Computers; Hunting; Fishing; Family; Religion. Address: WA University School of Medicine, Department of Otolaryngology Head & Neck Surgery, 517 South Euclid, Box 8115, St Louis, MO 63110, USA.

NEGOVSKY Vladimir A, b. 19 Mar 1909, Kozelets, Ukraine. Academician; professor; Scientific Adviser. Education: MD, 2nd Moscow State Medical Institute, 1928-33; Candidate of medical Sciences, 1942; DMS, 1943. Appointments: Founder, Director, Research Laboratory of General Reanimatology, USSR Academy of Medical Sciences, 1936-85; Director, 1985-88, Scientific Adviser, 1988-, Institute for General Reanimatology, USSR Academy of Medical Sciences. Publications: Cntributor of over 300 original works including 10 monographs translated into many languages and published worldwide. Honours include: Doctor Honoris Causa, Medical Academy of Poznan, Poland, 1973; Gold Medal, Messina University, Italy, 1985; Gold Medal, Italian Radio and Television, 1988; certificate of Recognition, University of Pittsburgh, USA, 1981; Gold Medal, Soviet Peace Fund, 1987. Memberships include: Honorary member, German Society of Clinical Medicine, 1966; Honorary Member, USSR Society of Anesthesiology and Reanimatology, 1966; Honorary Member, Society of Anesthesiologists, Poland, 1973; Honorary member, USSR Society of Pathophysiology, 1982; Honorary Member, Society of Emergency Medicine, Germany, 1988. Address: Institute for General Reanimatology, Academy of Medical Sciences of Russia, 25 Petrovka Street, Building 2, Moscow 103031, Russia.

NEILSON James Purdie, b. 28 Nov 1951, Falkirk, Scotland. Obstetrician and Gynaecologist. 1 d. Education: BSc; MB; ChB; MD; MRCOG. Appointments: Research Fellow, University of Glasgow; Senior Registrar, Harare Central Hospital, Zimbabwe; "New Blood" Lecturer, University of Glasgow; Senior Lecturer, University of Edinburgh; Currently, Professor of Obstetrics and Gynaecology, University of Liverpool. Publications: Many articles published; Books Co-authored, Edited: Obstetrics and Gynaecology, 4th edition, 1991; Obstetric Ultasound 1, 1993; Obstetric Ultasound 2, 1994; Guide to Effective Care in Pregnancy and Childbirth, 2nd edition, 1995; Scientific Essentials of Reproductive Medicine, 1995. Memberships: Royal College of Obstetricians and Gynaecologists; British Association for Perinatal Medicine. Hobbies: Golf; Squash; Travel; Mountaineering. Address: Dept of Obstetrics and Gynaecology, University of Liverpool, PO Box 147, Liverpool, L69 3BX, England.

NEL Johan Theron, b. 17 July 1947, Port Elizabeth, South Africa. Gynaecologist and Obstetrician. m. Marthie Jansen, 15 Nov 1975, 1 son, 2 daughters. Education: MB ChB with 6 distinctions, MMed, Obstetrics and Gynaecology, University of Stellenbosch; FCOG (SA), 1985; MRCOG (London); FRCS (Edinburgh). Appointments: Senior Specialist, Department of Obstetrics and Gynaecology, Head, Gynaecological Urology Unit, Microsurgeon, Infertility Unit, University of Stellenbosch, 1982-87; Associate Professor, Professor, Head, Urogynaecology and Reproductive Surgery, Department of Obstetrics and Gynaecology, University of Orange Free State, 1987-; Leader, team for 1st ever ovarian autotransplantation to the axilla, 1990. Publications: Author or co-author, 72 scientific publications including: Core Obstetrics and Gynaecology with Examination Guidelines for MB ChB, 1995. Honours: Winner: Prize, Best Undergraduate Student in Obstetrics and Gynaecology, University of Stellenbosch, 1971; Daubenton Medal, Most Outstanding Candidate, Examinations for Fellowship, College of Obstetricians and Gynaecologists of South Africa, 1985. Memberships: Representative for Africa, International Board, International Urogynaecology Association; Founder Member, Committee Member, South African Society of Endoscopic Surgery and Microsurgery; Committee Member, Faculty of Obstetrics and Gynaecology, College of Medicine, South Africa; Founder Member, South African Microsurgery Society; Elected to New York Academy of Sciences; Fallopius

International Society. Hobbies: Scuba diving; Mountaineering; Long distance running; Waterskiing. Address: Department of Obstetrics and Gynaecology, Internal Box G71, University of the Orange Free State, PO Box 339, Bloemfontein 9300, South Africa.

NELSON Harold Stanley, b. 17 Jan 1930, New Britain, Connecticut, USA. Physician. m. Sarah Millage, 23 July 1953, 3 s. Education: BA; MS; MD. Appointments: residency, Internal Medicine, Letterman Army Medical Centre; Fellowship, Allergy/Immunology, University of Michigan Medical centre; Chief of Medicine, Ft Rucker, US Army Hospital; Chief of Medicine, 5th general Hospital, Bad Cannstedt, Germany; Chief, Allergy/Immunology Service, Fitzsimmons Army Medical Centre; Senior Staff Physician, Department of Medicine, National Jewish Centre for Immunology and Respiratory Medicine; professor of Medicine, University of Colorado Health Sciences Centre. Publications: Contibutor of over 140 publications. Honours: James J Waring Award, American Lung Association of Colorado, 1989; American College of Allergy and Immunology, Bela Schick Lecturer, 1985, fellow, Distinguished Award, 1986, Jaros Lecturer, 1989, McGovern Lecturer, 1990./ Memberships: Fellow, American Academy of Allergy and Immunology; Fellow, American College of Allergy and Immunology; Editorial Board, Annals of Allergy, Journal on Allergy and Clinical Immunology and American Thoracic Society. Hobbies: Tennis; Scuba diving. Address: National Jewish Centre for Immunology and Respiratory Medicine, 1400 Jackson Street, Denver, CO 80206, USA.

NELSON Ralph A, b. 19 June 1927, Minneapolis, Minnesota, USA. Physician. m. Rose Marie Pokele, 7 Aug 1954, 3 s, 2 d. Education: PhD, Physiology, MD, BA cum laude, University of Minnesota. Appointments: Associate Professor of Physiology and Nutrition, Mayo Medical School, 1973-78; Associate Professor of Medicine, University of South Dakota School of Medicine, 1978-79; Executive Head, Department of Medicine, University of Illinois College of Medicine. Publications: Author or Co-author of over 200 publications. Honours: Fulbright Lecturer Award to Morocco, 1988. Memberships: American Physiological Society; American Society for Clinical Nutrition; Central Society for Clinical Research. Hobbies: Hiking; Biking. Addresws: Carle Foundation Hospital, 611 WE Park, Urbana, IL 61801, USA.

NEMCSICS Antal, b. 9 Jun 1927, Pápa, Hungary. University Professor. m. Magda Takács, 14 Aug 1951, 3 s. Education: MSc; PhD; DSc. Appointment: Technical University of Budapest, 1951-, Current position: Professor. Publications: The Role of the Coloured Environment in Diagnostic and Therapy, 1976; Experimental Determination of a Perceptively Equidistant Scale in the Colour Space, 1980; Coloroid Colour System, 1980; Coloroid Colour Atlas, 1988; Colour Harmonies, 1991; Colour Dynamics, 1993. Honours: International VIT, 1949; International Giorgione, 1963; International Design, 1984; Prize of the Hungarian Academy of Sciences, 1994. Memberships: Association Internationale de la Couleur; International Academy of Coloursciences; Association of Colour Consultants. Hobbies: Painting; Fine Arts. Address: Ungvár u 42, H-1185, Budapest, Hungary.

NEMETH Magdolina, b. 19 Mar 1924, Miskolc, Hungary. Physician. m. Laszlo Nemeth, 23 Dec 1950. Education: MD; LRCP; LRCS; LRFPS; LMCC; FRCPS, Canada; Diplomate of American Board of Psychiatry & Neurology; Post-Doctoral Fellowship in Psychiatry and the Law, University of Southern California, USA. Appointments: Psychiatric Residency, Ipsi County, Michigan, 1964-69; Senior Resident, Clark Institute, Toronto, Ontario, 1970-71; Director of Adolescent Sciences, Elmida Psychiatric Center, Elmida, New York, 1972-79; Staff Psychiatrist. Publications: Psychosis In a Concentration Camp Survivor, 1971; Whose Life Is It Anyway? Memberships: Forensic Mental Health Association of California. Hobbies: Piano; Back Packing; Bird-Watching; Creative Writing. Address: 2560 Alturas, Atascadero, CA 93422-1175, USA.

NEMIRO Eugeni, b. 16 Dec 1926, Kraslava, Latvia. Radiologist. m. Rasma Tseplite, 18 Aug 1958, 1 son. Education: MD, Medical Institute of Riga, 1951. Appointments: Assistant, Department of Roentgenology, 1956-67, Assistant Professor, Head, Department of Roentgenology, 1967-91, Professor, Department of Roentgenology, 1991-, Medical Academy of Latvia. Publications: Roentgenology and Radiology, 1973; Medical Roentgenology, 1983; Regional System of Individual Dosimetry Based on TLD, Co-author, 1987; Roentgendiagnostic of Mediastinal Tumors, 1988. Memberships: Latvian Association of Roentgenology and Radiology; European Radiology Association. Address: Dselsavas Street 33-11, LV 1084 Riga, Latvia.

NEUBERGER John Stephen, b. 29 Jun 1938, New York City, NY, USA. Teacher. m. Geri C Budesheim, 13 Jul 1980, 1 s. Education: BME, Cornell University; MBA, Columbia University; MPH, PhD, Johns Hopkins University. Appointments: Assistant Professor, 1978-84, Currently, Associate Professor of Preventive Medicine, University of Kansas. Publications: Senior Author, Health Problems in Galena, Kansas: A Heavy Metal Mining Superfund Site, in Science Tot Environment, 1990; Senior Author: Residential radon exposure and lung cancer: An overview of ongoing studies, in Health Physics, 1992; Senior Author, Residential radon exposure and lung cancer: Evidence of an urban factor in Iowa, in Health Physics, 1994. Honour: Sigma Xi, 1984. Memberships: American Association for the Advancement of Science; American Association for Cancer Research, Health Physics Society; American Public Health Association. Hobbies: Tennis; Swimming; Jogging; World War II History. Address: University of Kansas School of Medicine, Department of Preventive Medicine, Rainbow Boulevard at 39th, Kansas City, KS 66103, USA.

NEUSPIEL Daniel Robert, b. 15 May 1952, Haifa, Israel. Paediatrician; Epidemiologist; Addictionologist. m. Cathy Cánepa, 12 Apr 1987, 1 son, 1 daughter. Education: BA, Rutgers University, 1975; MD, New Jersey Medical School, 1979; Resident in Paediatrics, Children's Hospital, Pittsburgh, 1979-82; Fellow in Epidemiology, Graduate School of Public Health, 1982-84, MPH, 1984, University of Pittsburgh. Appointments: Assistant Professor, 1984-90, Associate Professor, Paediatrics, Epidemiology and Social Medicine, 1990-, Albert Einstein College of Medicine, Bronx, New York, USA. Publications: Sudden and unexpected natural death in childhood and adolescence, 1985; Parental smoking and post-infancy wheezing, 1989; Maternal cocaine use and infant behavior, 1991. Honours: Phi Beta Kappa, Rutgers University, 1976; University Scholar, University of Pittsburgh, 1985. Memberships: American Academy of Pediatrics; American Public Health Association; Ambulatory Pediatric Association; American Society of Addiction Medicine. Hobbies: Family activities; Music; Computers. Address: University Avenue Family Practice, 105 West 188 Street, Bronx, NY, 10468, USA.

NEUTRA Raymond Richard, b. 12 Mar 1939, Los Angeles, CA, USA. Physician; Epidemiologist. m. Penelope Der Yuen, 17 Jun 1977, 3 s. Education: MDCM, McGill University; MPH, Dr PH, Harvard University. Career includes: Assistant Professor, University of Valle Cali Colombia, 1970-73; Assistant Professor, Harvard Medical School and School of Public Health, 1974-77; Associate Professor, UCLA School of Public Health, 1977-80; Lecturer, Epidemiology, Chief, Exposure Assessment Section, Chief, Environment Health Investigations Branch, California Department of Health Services, Emeryville, CA, 1980-; Numerous lectures and presentations. Publications: Numerous publications including: Risk Factors for Eclampsia, in Acta Medica del Valle, 1973; Author, Counterpoint from A Cluster Buster; American Journal of Epidemiology, 1990; Co-author, Clinical Decision Analysis W B Saunders, 1980. Honours: President, International Society of Enviromental Epidemiology. Memberships: Emeritus, American Epidemiological Society; Society of Epidemiological Research; International Society for Environmental Epidemiology; International Society for Exposure Analysis. Hobbies: Singing; Swimming. Address: 956 Evelyn Avenue, Albany, CA 94706, USA.

NEVES-PINTO Roberto Machado, b. 9 June 1935, Maceio, Alagoas, Brazil. Physician. m. Dirlene Neves-Pinto, 14 Mar 1962, 2 d. Education: MD, 1958. Appointments:Otolaryngologist, Varig Brazilian Airlines, 1961-92; Otolaryngologist, Brazilian Air Force Medical Corps, 1960-84; President, Brazilian Rhinologic Society, 1978-86; First President, Latin American Rhinologic Society, 1982-84; Orienting Professor, Postgraduate Course of ORL, Escola Paulista de Medicina, Sao Paulo; Head, ORL Department, St Vincente de paulo Hospital, Rio de Janeiro; Scientific Editor, Section of ORL, A Folha Medica, Rio de Janeiro; Adjudant Editor, Rhinology, Utrecht. Publications: Functional Rhinoplasty, 1980; Incision in the Gingival Margin for Approaching the Maxillary Sinus, 1981; Nasal Lobule Surgery: A Simple Manoeuvre for Precise Resection of Part(s) of the Lower Lateral Cartilage Through Intercartilaginous Approach, 1990; A Double-Blind Study on the Effect of Loratadine Versus Placebo on the Performance of Pilots, 1992. Honours: President of Honour, Brazilian Rhinological Society, 1988; The Golden Head-Mirror Award, American Rhinological Society, 1988. Memberships: Representative for Latin-America, International Rhinologic Society; International Committee for Standardization of Rhinometry. Hobbies: Vocal erudite music; History; Geography. Address: Voluntários de Patria 445, Suite 1304, 22270-000 Rio de Janeiro, RJ, Brazil.

NEVINS Thomas, b. Rockford, IL, USA. Pediatrician. m. Joyce Nevins, 1 s, 6 d. Education: BS, Rockhurst College, 1965; MD, Washington University, 1969. Appointments: Pediatric Resident, 1969-72; LCDR US Navy MC, 1972-74; Fellow, 1974-; Assistant Professor; Associate Professor; Currently, Professor of Pediatrics. Honours: Certified in Pediatrics; Certified in Pediatric Nephrology. Memberships: International Society of Nephrology; American Society of Nephrology; American Society of Investigative Pathology; International Society of Pediatric Nephrology; American Society of Pediatric Nephrology; American Society of Transplant Physicians. Address: University of Minnesota Hospital and Clinic, Box 491, Minneapolis, MN 55455, USA.

NEWBOWER Ronald S, b. 19 Oct 1943, Gloversville, New York, USA. Medical Centre Administrator. m. Donna Denekamp, 27 Aug 1967, 2 sons. Education: BS, Physics, Massachusetts Institute of Technology, 1965; MA, Applied Physics, 1967, PhD, Applied Physics, 1971, Harvard University; Postdoctoral fellow, NSF Harvard University and Massachusetts General Hospital, 1971-72. Appointments: Director, Biomedical Engineering, 1984-87, Deputy Director, Research Affairs, 1989-90, Vice President and Associate General Director for Research and Technology Affairs, 1990-94, Vice President for Research and Technology, 1994, Senior Vice President, 1994-, Massachusetts General Hospital. Publications: IEEE Transactions on Biomedical Engineering, Associate Editor, 1982-85; Journal of Clinical Anesthetics, Editorial Board, 1988; The Automated Anesthesia Record, Co-author, 1987; Integrated Approaches to Monitoring, 1983; Essential Non-Invasive Monitoring in Anesthesia, 1980. Honours: National Alumni Fund Scholar, 1961-65; Watson Honorary Fellow, Harvard University, 1976-80; NSF Graduate Fellow, 1965-70; NSF Postdoctoral Fellow, 1971-72; NIH Special Research Fellow, 1973-74; Arnold O Beckman Award, 1978. Memberships: American Physical Society; Association for Advancement of medical Instruction; The Engineering in Medicine and Biology Society; Institute of Electronics and Electrical Engineers; Instructors Society of America, Senior member; Biomedical Engineering Society, Senior Member; Licenced Engineers Society; Society of Research Administrators. Address: Massachusetts General Hospital, 40 Blossom Street, Boston, MA 02114-2605, USA.

NEWBURG David Stephen, b. 2 Apr 1948, Boston, Massachusetts, USA. Biochemist. m. Kathryn J Woolley, 3 Jun 1973, 1 s, 2 d. Education: BS, Chemistry, University of Massachusetts, Amherst, Massachusetts; PhD, Biochemistry, Boston University, Boston, Massachusetts. Appointments: Assistant Professor, University of Kentucky; Associate Professor, University of Kentucky; Instructor, Harvard Medical School; Associate Professor, Massachusetts General Hospital; Senior Biochemist, Shriver Center for Mental Retardation. Publications: Characterization of a Human Milk Factor the Inhibits binding of HIV gp120 to its CD4 Receptor, 1991; Human Milk Mucin Inhibits Rotavirus Replication and Prevents Experimental Gastroenteritis, 1991; Human Milk Contains the Shigatoxin and Shiga-like Toxin Receptor Glycolipid, Gb3, 1992; Susceptibility to Hemolytic-Uremic Syndrome Relates to Erythrocyte Glycosphingolipid Patterns, 1993. Memberships: American Chemical Society; American Institute of Nutrition; Society for Research in Human Milk and Lactation; American Association for the Advancement of Science. Hobbies: Running; Camping. Address: 15 Harrington Street, Newtonville, MA 02160, USA.

NEWMAN TURNER Roger, b. 29 Apr 1940, Radlett, Herts, England. Naturopath, Osteopath, Acupuncturist. m. Birgid, 1966, 1 son, 1 daughter. Education: BAc; ND; DO. Appointments: Editor, British Journal of Acupuncture, 1981-92; Chairman, Governors British College of Acupuncture, 1982-85; Trustee, Research Council for Complementary Medicine, 1983-, Chairman 1993-96. Publications: Diets to Help Hay Fever and Asthma, 1970; Diets to Help Control Cholesterol, 1978; Principles and Practice of Moxibustion, 1981; New Self Help For Angina, 1987; Naturopathic Medicine, 1984; Banish Back Pain, 1989. Memberships: General Council & Register of Naturopaths; General Council & Register of Osteopaths; Fellow, British Acupuncture Association. Hobbies: Acting; Singing; Theatre; Opera; Walking; Gardening. Address: 1 Harley Street, London W1N 1DA, England.

NEWNHAM John Phillipps, b. 10 Mar 1952, Perth, Western Australia. Obstetrician. m. Sue-Anne Patricia Jenkins, 14 Mar 1980, 1 son, 2 daughters. Education: MBBS; MRCOG; FRACOG; MD; DDU; CMFM. Appointments: Resident Medical Officer, Royal Perth Hospital, 1976-78; Registrar, King Edward Memorial Hospital, Perth, 1978-80; Registrar, Edendale Hospital, South Africa, 1980; Registrar, St

Bartholomew's Hospital, England, 1981-82; Fellow, University of California, Los Angeles, USA, 1982-84; Staff Specialist, King Edward Memorial Hospital, Australia, 1984-. Publications: More than 70 original articles in scientific journals, 1982-. Honours: Gold Medal, Royal College of Obstetricians & Gynaecologists, London, England, 1980. Memberships: Royal College of Obstetricians & Gynaecologists. Hobbies: Tennis; Swimming; Agriculture. Address: King Edward Memorial Hospital for Women, Subiaco, Perth, Western Australia 6008.

NEZIROGLU Fugen, b. 6 Jan 1953, Istanbul, Turkey. behavioural Psychologist. m. 21 Oct 1978. Education: BA, Psychology, 1974, Doctoral Programme, School Community Psychology, 1977, Clinical Psychology Certificate, Doctoral Programme, 1982, Hofstra University; The Institute for Advanced Study in Rational Psychotherapy, 1976-77. Appointments include: Counsellor, Nassau County Children's Shelter, USA, 1970-72; Counsellor, Nassau County Jail, New York, 1976-77; Intake Examiner, Intake Counsellor, 1972-76, 1972-79, Assistant research Psychologist, 1972-79, Chief, department of Experimental Psychology, 1979, North Nassau Mental Health Centre, Manhasset, New York; Research Associate, Hofstra University, New York, 1985-86; Clinical Director, Research Associate, Administrator, SUpervisor of Clinical Psychology Interns, Institute for Bio-Behavioural Therapy and Research, Great Neck, New York, 1979-. Publications: Contributor of numerous articles in professional journals. Honours: Magna Cum Laude; Phi Beta Kappa; Psi Chi. Memberships include: American psychological Association; Association for Advancement of Behaviour Therapy; Anxiety Disorders Association of America; New York State Psychological Association; Nassau County psychological Association. Address: 935 Northern Boulevard Suite 102, Great Neck, NY 11021, USA.

NG Alan Beh Puan, b. 8 Feb 1934, Kuala Lumpur, Malaysia. Pathologist. m. Enid Charters, 2 Nov 1958, 2 sons, 2 daughters. Education: MB, BS, University of Melbourne; Certified, Board of Anatomic Pathology, USA; Anatomic Pathology Speciality, Australia. Appointments: Pathology Registrar, St Vincent's Hospital, Melbourne, Victoria, Australia, 1961-62; Lecturer, Pathology, 1963-67, Acting Head, 1965-66, University of Malaya, Kuala Lumpur, Malaysia; Visiting Fellow, 1963-64, Assistant Professor, Associate Professor, Professor, 1967-75, Case Western Reserve University, Cleveland, Ohio, USA; Professor, Director of Surgical Pathology and Cytology, Schools of Cytotechnology and Histotechnology, Professor, Obstetrics, Gynaecology, Jackson Memorial Hospital, University of Miami, Florida, 1975-80; Head, Department of Pathology, Professor, Pathology, Royal Prince Albert Hospital, University of Sydney, New South Wales, Australia, 1981-; Visiting Professor, Pathology, University of Zurich, Switzerland, 1987-88. Publications: Co-author, books: Cells of Uterine Adenocarcinoma; Gynecologic Cytology and Cancer Screening in Gynecologic Practice; 60 book chapters and 120 articles in journals on cancer and cytology. Honours: President, 1976-77, G N Papanicolaou Award, 1980, American Society of Cytology; President, Australian Society of Cytology, 1984-85. Memberships: Fellow: American Society of Clinical Pathologists; International Academy of Cytology; American Society of Dermatology; Royal College of Pathologists of Australia. Hobbies: Tennis; Theatre; Travel. Address: Royal Prince Albert Hospital, Department of Anatomic Pathology, Missenden Rd, Camperdown 2050, New South Wales, Australia.

NG Ho Keung, b. 5 Jun 1958, Hong Kong. Pathology. m. Yuen Fun Ng, 21 Jul 1984, 1 s. Education: Chinese University of Hong Kong; MBChB, Edinburgh; MRCPath; FRCPA; FCAP; FFPathRCPI; MIAC; FHKAM, Pathology. Appointments: Lecturer, Senior Lecturer, Currently, Reader, Department of Pathology, Prince of Wales Hospital, Hong Kong. Publications: Professional publications concerning, brain tumours and neuropathology in: Histopathology, Cancer, Surgical, Neurology Journals and British Journal of Neurosurgery. Memberships: American Association of Neuropathology; Australian and New Zealand Society of Neuropathology; International Society of Neuropathology. Address: Dept of Pathology, Prince of Wales Hospital, Chinese University of Hong Kong, Shatin, Hong Kong.

NG Kwee-Boon, b. 6 Sept 1959, Kuala Lumpur, Malaysia. Doctor. Education: MB; BS; MRCOG. Appointments: Registrar, Obstetics & Gynecology, Inverness, Scotland, 1987-88; Registrar, Obstetics & Gynecology, Western General Hospital, Edinburgh, 1988-91; Lecturer, Obstetics & Gynecology, University Hospital, Kuala Lumpur, 1991-94. Publications: Several professional publications in scientific journals. Memberships: Malaysian Medical Association; British Menopause

Society; Obstetric Surgery of Malaysia. Hobbies: Outdoor Activities; Golf; Tennis; Travelling; Small Dinner Parties. Address: 13 Road 14/48, 46100 Petaling Jaya, Malaysia.

NG Man Lun, b. 14 Oct 1946, Hong Kong. Psychiatrist; Sexologist. m. Sui May, 19 Sept 1972, 1 son, 1 daughter. Education: MB, BS (Hong Kong); MD (Hong Kong); DPM (Eng); FRANZCP; FRCPsych (UK); FHKAM (Psychiatry); Dip Am Board (Sexology); FAACS. Appointments: Medical Officer, 1972; Lecturer, 1973, Senior Lecturer, 1981, Reader, 1992-, Department of Psychiatry, University of Hong Kong. Publications include: Psychoanalysis for the Chinese - applicable or not applicable, 1985; Homosexuality in Chinese culture (with M P Lau), 1989; Sexual attitudes in the Chinese (with M P Lau), 1990; The community meeting - a review, 1993; Books: Sexual Medicine, a Modern Perspective (with W Y Ng), in Chinese, 1991; Sexual Behavior in Modern China - A report of the nationwide Sex-Civilization Survey on 20,000 subjects in China (contributor, edited with D L Liu and L P Chou), in Chinese, 1992; Chinese Dictionary of Sexology (edited with D L Liu), 1993; Sexuality in Asia (edited with L S Lam), in English, 1993. Honours: Sexologist of Asia, Asian Federation for Sexology, 1994. Memberships include: Hong Kong College of Psychiatrists. Hobbies: Music; Computers. Address: Department of Psychiatry, University of Hong Kong, Pokfulam, Hong Kong.

NG Oi Lin Irene, b. 13 July 1957, Hong Kong. Pathologist. m. Matthew Ng, 24 Mar 1984, 2 sons. Education: MD, MB BS, 1980, University of Hong Kong; MRCPath(UK); FHKAM(Pathology). Appointments: Clinical Pathologist, 1981-86, Lecturer, 1986-92, Senior Clinical Pathologist, 1992-, Department of Pathology, University of Hong Kong. Publications include: Encapsulation in Hepatocellular Carcinoma - A Pathologic Study of 189 Cases, Co-author, 1992; Use of CEA Tissue Staining in Colorectal Cancer Patients - Correlation with Plasma CEA, Histology and Staging, Co-author, 1993; P53 Gene Mutation Spectrum in Hepatocellular Carcinomas in Hong Kong Chinese, Co-author, 1994; Flow Cytometrics Analysis of DNA Ploidy in Hepatocellular Carcinoma, Co-author, 1994; Prognostic Significance of Proliferating Cell Nuclear Antigen (PCNA) Expression in Hepatocellular Carcinoma, Co-author, 1994; Better Survival in Female Patients with Hepatocellular Carcinoma - Possible Causes from a Pathological Approach, Co-author, 1995; Hospital Mortality Hepatectomy for Hepatocellular Carcinoma Associated with Cirrhosis, Co-author, 1995. Memberships: Hong Kong Academy of Medicine; International Academy of Pathology; American Association for the Study of Liver Diseases; American Society of Clinical Pathologists. Address: Department of Pathology, The University of Hong Kong, Queen Mary hospital, Hong Kong.

NG Soon-Chye, b. 17 Feb 1950, Singapore. Gynaecologist. m. Kiat-Piah Tan, 5 April 1979, 1 son. Education: MBBS, University of Singapore, 1974; MMed, Obstetrics, Gynaecology, 1980, MD, 1989, National University of Singapore; MRCOG (London), 1981; FRCOG (London), 1994. Appointments: Lecturer, 1980-83, Senior Lecturer, 1984-89, Associate Professor, 1990-93, Professor, 1993-, National University of Singapore. Publications include: Co-author: Pregnancy after transfer of multiple sperm under the zona, 1988; Improved quality of human embryos when co-cultured with human ampullary cells, 1989; Micro-manipulation: its relevance to human IVF, 1990; Co-cultures: their relevance to assisted reproduction, 1990; Microinjection of human oocytes: a technique for severe oligoasthenoteratozoospermia, 1991; Centrioles in the beginning of human development, 1991; In vitro decondensation of mammalian sperm and subsequent formation of pronuclei-like structures for micromanipulation, 1992; Visual atlas of early human development for assisted reproductive technology, 1993; Microinjection of human sperm directly into human oocytes, 1993; Isolation and culture of inner cell mass cells from human blastocysts; Intracytoplasmic sperm injection of mouse oocytes with 5mM Ca++ at different intervals. Honours: National Science and Technology (part of team), Singapore Government, 1988; 8th Henry Benjamin Henry Sheares' Memorial Lecture, Singapore, 1989; William Blair Memorial Lecture, Royal College of Obstetricians and Gynaecologists, 1990. Memberships: Academy of Medicine, Singapore; Society for the Study of Reproduction; New York Academy of Sciences; American Fertility Society; Smithsonian Institute, USA; American Association for the Advancement of Science. Hobbies: Bird watching; Wildlife conservation. Address: Department of Obstetrics and Gynaecology, National University Hospital, Lower Kent Ridge Road, Singapore 0511.

NGAN Hextan Yuen Sheung, b. 12 Aug 1955, Hong Kong. Gynaecological Oncologist. Education: MBBS (HK); MRCOG (UK);

1983. Appointments: Medical and Health Officer, 1979-84; Lecturer, 1985-89, Senior Lecturer, 1990-, Queen Mary Hospital, Hong Kong. Publications: Co-author, about 20 including: Psychosocial aspects of gestational trophoblastic disease in Chinese residents of Hong Kong, 1986; Diagnosis of endometrial carcinoma by histopathological examination of the endometrial aspirate by the Curity-Isaacs sampler, 1987; Multicentric neoplasia of the lower female genital tract - a case report of neoplastic change at an unusual site, 1988; Further study on sexual function following treatment of carcinoma of cervix in Chinese patients, 1988; Role of CA 125 and abdominal pelvic computerized axial tomogram in the monitoring of chemotherapy treatment of ovarian cancer, 1990; Cervical human papilloma virus infection of women attending the social hygiene clinic in Hong Kong, 1993; The prognostic value of TPA and SCC in squamous cell carcinoma of cervix, 1994; HPV by PCR/SB and p53 by immunohistochemical staining in squamous cell carcinoma of cervix, 1994. Honours: Mary Sun Oncology Fellowship, 1991; Croucher Foundation Fellowship, 1992. Memberships: Asian Oceanic Clinical Oncology Association; Hong Kong College of Obstetricians and Gynaecologists; Hong Kong Medical Association; Hong Kong Surgical Laser Association; International Gynaecologic Cancer Society; Hong Kong Cancer Chemotherapy Society. Hobbies: Swimming; Tennis. Address: Department of Obstetrics and Gynaecology, Queen Mary Hospital, Pokfulam Road, Hong Kong.

NGO Giang Lien, b. 11 Nov 1961, Hanoi, Vietnam. Lecturer. Education: BSc Biology w high distinction, USSR; MSc Biology, Vietnam; PhD Study, 1992-95. Career: Project Coordinator; Lecturer. Publications: 2 books: Practical Course on Cell and Molecular Biology, 1993; Co-author, Cell Biology, 1984. Honours: Research Training Award, NUFFIC 1986, WHO 1991, NUFFIC 1992, Women in Science Club 1994; Research Award, WHO, 1993-94; Full support, Colorado State University & British Council for Training Course, USA 1993, UK 1994. Membership: Executive Member, Women in Science Club, Vietnam (VINAWIS). Hobbies: Love of Music; Painting. Address: Phong 6, Nha D6 Trung Tu, Hanoi, Vietnam.

NGUYEN Philip Hiep, b. 8 May 1931, Hanoi, Vietnam. m. 9 Oct 1970, 1 s, 1 d. Education: Diploma of Tropical Public Health, London; Diploma of Malariology; Diploma of Epidemiology; Diploma of Acupuncture. Appointments: Head, Department of Infectious Diseases, Children's Hospital, Saigon, Vietnam; Professor of Tropical Diseases, Hue Medical School, Vietnam; Professor of tropical Diseases and Child Health, Minh Duc Medical School, Saigon; Private Practice, general Medicine and Acupuncture, Winter Park, Florida, USA. Publications: Communicable Diseases in the Tropics, 1972; Child Health in the Tropics, 1973; Preventive Medicine and COmmunity Health, 1974; Dictionary of Acupuncture and Moxibustion, 1987. Honour: Colombo Plan Scholarship, 1965. Memberships: Fellow, Royal Society of Tropical Medicine and Hygiene, London; Vietnamese Medical Association of Florida, USA. Hobbies: Photography; Reading; Writing. Address: 2020 W Fairbanks, Winter Park, FL 32789, USA.

NGUYEN Xuan Dung, b. 7 May 1940, Quynhdoi, Nghean, Vietnam. Professor Teacher; Researcher. m. Ta Thi Khoi, 25 Dec 1970, 1 son, 1 daughter. Education: Doctor of Chemistry. Appointments: Head, Department of Technical Chemistry, University of Hanoi, 1975-90; Managing Director, Centre for Education and Development of Chromatography of Vietnam. Publications: Author of 2 books and contributor of over 150 papers. Memberships: Executive Member, International Association for Study of Medicinal Forest Plants; Editorial Board of the Journal of Chemistry, Vietnam. Hobby: Basketball. Address: Centre for Education and Development of Chromatography of Vietnam, 3 Giai Phong Str, Quan Haiba, 10000 Hanoi, Vietnam.

NGUYEN-LEGROS Jeanine Marie Antoinette, b. 16 Jan 1936, Paris, France. Researcher. m. A Nguyen, 31 Oct 1957, 1 son. Education: Docteur es Sciences. Appointments: Attaché de Recherche, 1963; Chargé de Recherche, 1969; Maitre de Recherche, 1978; Directeur de Recherche, 1984. Publications: More than 100 papers in international research journals in Neurosciences & Ophthalmology. Memberships: New York Academy of Sciences; International Society Eye Res. Honours: IPSEN Research Prize in Ophthalmology, 1989. Hobbies: Divinities; Sacred Art; Painting. Address: 4 Villa Marces, 94-160 Saint Mandé, France.

NI Gua-chen, b. 24 August 1940, Beijing, China. Doctor. Appointments: Doctor, Beijing Childrens Hospital, 1965; Visiting Doctor, 1987; Associate Professor, Beijing Second Medical College, 1987;

Chief, Childrens Department, Beijing Childrens Hospital; Professor, Beijing Childrens Hospital, 1994-. Publications Include: Clinical analysis of juvenile thyrotoxicosis in 66 cases, 1985; Preliminary observation of betacell function in diabetic children, 1983; Children's sella turaca region tumor, 1991; Management of IDDM in children, 1992; Obesity and hypertension in children, 1992; Retinopathy in children with IDDM, 1994. Memberships: Society of Pediatrics, Chinese Medical Association; Society of Medicine, China and Germany. Hobbies: Music. Address: Beijing Childrens Hospital, Nan Lishi Road, Beijing 100045, China.

NI Guo Tan, b. 16 Feb 1925, Qidon, Jiangsu, China. Profesor Of Diving Medicine and Physiology. m. Ji Ying, 4 Feb 1954, 1 son, 2 daughters. Education: BS, Fudan University, 1949. Appointment: Professor of Diving Medicine and Physiology, Department of Diving Medicine, Faculty of Naval Medicine, Second Military Medical University. Publications: Normal Human Physiology, Chief Editor, 1961; Naval Diving Medicine, Chief Editor, 1965, 1973, 1981, 1988; Practical Diving Medicine, Chief Editor, 1980; Nautical and Diving Medicine (A Fascicle of The Chinese Medical Encyclopaedia), Vice CHief Editor, 1984; Physiological Principles and Medical Problems of Diving Practice, 1987. Memberships: Chinese Medical Association; Chinese Physiological Society; International Society of Hyperbaric Medicine. Hobbies: Chinese Classical Poetry; Piping of Vertical Bamboo flute. Address: 972 Xiang Yin Road, Shanghai 200433, China.

NI Zhi-Quan, b. 15 Aug 1947, Qidong, Jiangshu, China. Doctor. m. 1 Jan 1974, 2 d. Education: Masters Degree, Suzhou Medical College. Appointments: Vice President, Department of Internal Medicine of Tumour. Publications: Clinical feature of Extrohepatic Metastases in Primary Cancer: A Report of 63 Cases; A Study on the Efficiency of Hepatitis B Vacinne in Sole Anti-HBclgCt Positive Persons; Advances in Liver Cancer and Hepatitis Research, 1991. Hobbies: Listening to Music. Address: Qidong Liver Cancer Institute, Jiangshu, China.

NICHOLAS Christopher Eustace, b. 22 May 1929, Colombo, Sri Lanka. Medical Practitioner. m. Venita Koch, 29 Dec 1971. Education: MBBS (Ceylon), 1955; Fellow, Gemmological Association of Great Britain, 1982; PhD, 1983, MD, 1984, Medicina Alternativa, Open International University. Appointments: Medical Officer, Government hospitals, Sri Lanka (formerly Ceylon), 1955-65; Private Medical Practitioner, 1965-70; Director, full-time Medical Officer, Medical Centre Ltd private hospital, Colombo, 1971-89; Daily professional practice, mostly psychic healing and planetary propitiation for all human problems, also occultism, astro-palmistry, numerology and Feng-Shui, 1990-. Membership: British Acupuncture Association. Hobbies: Yogic exercises; Study of German, French and Japanese for conversational purposes. Address: 24/1 Sudarshana Mawatha, Rajagiriya, Sri Lanka.

NICKEL Ruth, b. 20 Dec 1950, Tübingen, Geermany. Psychologist. Education: Diploma in Psychology; Studies in Islamic Sciences; Clinical Psychologist/Psychotherapist BDP. Appointments: Teacher for German Language, Istanbul, Turkey, 1980-85; Clinical Psychologist, University of Freiburg, Germany, 1986-88; Clinical Psychologist, Essen, Germany, 1988-90; Clinical Psychologist, Centre for Migration, Diak, Werk, Hagen, Germany, 1990-. Publications: include, Eine empirische Untersuchung über Zusammenhänge zwischen Persönlichkeit. Stil und Falsifikationsgrad von kognitiven Systemen. Zur Oberprüfung von Ertels D Stilmerkmalen, 1978; Räubertheater, 1984; Einführung und Obung von Relativsätzen mit Präpositionen, 1985; Fehldiagnosen und kulturelle Interpretationsmuster, 1990. Memberships: German Association of Transactional Analysis. Hobbies: Bicycle Riding; Horseback Riding; Swimming; Hiking. Address: Schillstr 5, 58097 Hagen, Germany.

NICULESCU Virgiliu, b. 8 Jan 1939, Arad, Romania. Doctor of Medicine. m. Viorica, 24 Dec 1963, 1 son. Education: MD; Speciality in Legal Medicine & Pathologic Anatomy, 1974. Appointments: Institute of Medicine, Timisoara, 1973. Publications: Co-author: Practical Anatomy, 1972; Neuroanatomy, 1975; The Surgical Diseases of the Pancreas, 1984; The Surgery of the Abdominal Wall, 1987; Lessons of Clinical Nephrology, 1992; Guide for Abdominal Echography, 1993; The Branchial Nerves, 1993; The Interdisciplinarity of the Internal Medicine, 1993; Author: The Masticatory Apparatus, 1991; Anatomical Sections at the Level of Head and Neck, Limbs, Trunk, 1992; Vessels and Nerves, 1992; Transversal Anatomical Sections, 1993 Honours: President, Society of Romanian Anatomists. Memberships: Societe Anatomique de Paris, 1975-; The International Federation of Associations of Anatomists, 1994-; Anatomische Gesellschaft, 1983; Society on

Romanian Anatomists, 1992. Hobbies: Music. Address: Department of Anatomy, Piata Eftimie Murgu No 2, RO-1900 Timisoara, Romania.

NIE Huimin,b. 28 Feb 1935, Beijing, China. Doctor and Professor. m. Zhang Ji, 12 August 1962, 1 son, 2 daughters. Education: Bachelor Degree, Traditional Chinese Medicine, Beijing College of Traditional Chinese Medicine. Appointments: Chief, Heilongjiang Province Traditional Chinese Medicine College Clinic, 1973; Chief, Teaching & Researching Section of Theory on Febrile Diseases, 1984. Publications: Elucidate the meaning of the theory of Febrile Diseases, 1987; The theory of Febrile Diseases, 1993; Collate & Annotate the addenda for the theory of Febrile Diseases, 1994. Honours: 1st Prize, Traditiobnal Chinese Medicine, 1992. Memberships: Vice President, Secretary, Professional Committee, Zhang Zhongjing's Doctrine of China Association for Traditional Chinese Medicine. Hobbies: Swimming; Table Tennis; Listening to Music. Address: Department of Traditional Chinese Medicine, Beijing Traditional Chinese Medicine University, Beijing 100029, China.

NIEBYL Jennifer Robinson, b. 5 Dec 1942, Montreal, Canada. Professor; Department Head. Education includes: BSc, McGill University, Canada, 1963; MD, Yale University School of Medicine, 1967; Diplomate, Medical Examiners, 1968; FACOG, 1977. Career includes: Assistant Professor, 1974-79, Associate Professor, 1980-88, Department of Obstetrics and Gynaecology, Associate Professor, Pediatrics, 1985-88, Johns Hopkins University School of Medicine; Director, Division of Maternal and Fetal Medicine, Department of Gynaecology and Obstetrics, Johns Hopkins Hospital, Baltimore, 1982-88; Professor and Head, Department of Obstetrics and Gynaecology, University of Iowa Hospitals and Clinics, Iowa City, 1988-. Publications include: Co-Editor-In-Chief, American Journal of Perinatology; Associate Editor and Editorial Board Member of several professional journals; Numerous refereed articles, books, book chapters, review articles, book reviews, audio-visual productions and abstracts including: Drug Use in Pregnancy, 2nd edition, 1988; Co-author, Eastman's Expectant Motherhood, 1989; Co-author, Obstetrics: Normal and Problem Pregnancies, 2nd edition, 1991. Honours include: Examiner, American Board of Obstetrics and Gynaecology, 1984-. Memberships: Council, 1992-95, Society for Gynaecologic Investigation; Board of Directors, 1984-87, Society of Perinatal Obstetricians; Central Association of Obstetricians and Gynaecologists; American Gynaecologic and Obstetrical Society; Association of Professors of Gynaecology and Obstetrics. Address: Department of Obstetrics and Gynaecology, University of Iowa Hospitals and Clinics, Iowa City, IA 52242, USA.

NIEDERHUBER John Edward, b. 21 Jun 1938, Steubenville, OH, USA. Surgeon. m. Tracey Niederhuber, 1 s, 1 d. Education: BS, Bethany College, 1960; MD, Ohio State University, 1964. Career includes: Professor of Surgery, Professor of Oncology and Professor of Molecular Biology and Genetics, The Johns Hopkins University School of Medicine; Currently, Emile Holman Professor and Chairman, Department of Surgery, Professor of Microbiology and Immunology, Stanford University School of Medicine; Editorial Board for 10 professional journals. Publications include: Over 200 presentations and abstracts; Atlas of General Surgery, book in progress; Fundamentals of Surgery, book in progress; Over 100 articles in professional journals including: Colon and Rectum Cancer: Patterns of Spread and Implications for Workup, in Cancer, volume 71, 1993; Current Therapy in Oncology, 1993; Clinical Oncology, 1995; Many invited reviews and chapters in books. Honours include: US Public Health Service Research Career Development Award, National Institute of Allergy and Infectious Diseases, 1974-79. Memberships include: American Association for Cancer Research; American Association of Immunologists; Fellow, American College of Surgeons; American Society of Clinical Oncology; American Society of Transplant Surgeons; American Surgical Association; Central Surgical Society; Coller Surgical Society; Society of University Surgeons; The Transplantation Society; Zollinger/OSU Surgical Society. Address: Stanford University Medical Center, Medical School Office Building, Room X300, Stanford, CA 94305-5408, USA.

NIENABER Christoph Anton Theodor, b. 13 Sept 1955, Hamm, Westphalia, Germany. Physician; Cardiologist; Internist. Education: MD; Fellow, American College of Cardiology; Fellow, European Society of Cardiology. Appointments: Instructor in Internal Medicine and Cardiology, University Hospital Eppendorf, Hamburg; Assistant Professor, Department of Radiological Sciences, School of Medicine, University of California, Los Angeles, USA; Currently Associate

Professor of Internal Medicine and Cardiology, University Hospital Eppendorf, Hamburg. Publications: Imaging and Intervention (edited with U Sechtem); Diagnosis of aortic dissection by non-invasive imaging procedure, 1993; Flow and Metabolism in Hypertrophic Cardiography, 1993. Memberships: International Society of Angiology; German Cardiovascular Society. Hobbies: Foreign languages; Sailing; Indian-American history, Address: Department of Cardiology, University Hospital Eppendorf, 20247 Hamburg, Germany.

NIKOLIC George, b. 7 Feb 1945, Belgrade, Yugoslavia. Physician. m. Annette Courtney Smith, 7 Feb 1978, 1 s, 1 d. Education: MB,BS, Honours; FRACP; ABIM Intern Med, 1980; ABIM Cardiovascular Dis, 1981; ABIM Critical Care Med, 1991. Career includes: Research, Clinical Fellow, Cardiology, St Vincent's Medical Center of Richmond, NY, 1979-80; Instructor in Physical Diagnosis, 1980, Assistant Professor of Medicine, 1981-82, University of Massachusetts Medical School; Advanced Cardiology Fellow, St Vincent Hospital, Worcester, MA, 1980-81; Director, Intensive Care Unit, 1982-91, Senior Specialist, Intensive Care Unit, 1991-, Consultant Physician in Cardiology, 1984-, Woden Valley Hospital, Canberra, ACT, Australia. Publications include: Over 60 articles in peer reviewed journals including: Co-author, Sudden death recorded during Holter monitoring, Circulation, 1982; Co-author, LBBB with RAD, in Journal of Electrocardiology, 1985; Empty Wenckebach pauses, in Heart and Lung, 1992; Myocardial infarction and cerebral hemorrhage, in Heart and Lung, 1993; Other articles in various journals. Honour: Graduation Honours, University of Sydney, 1970. Memberships: RACP; ACC; ACCP; GCCM; AMA; Australia and New Zealand Cardiac Society; ANZICS. Address: Woden Valley Hospital, PO Box 11, Woden, ACT 2606, Australia.

NININGER James Edward, b. 31 Oct 1948, Fort Worth, TX, USA. Psychiatrist. m. Margaret Van der Meden, 13 May 1989, 1 s, 1 d. Education: BA cum laude, Biology, Kenyon College, Gambier, OH, 1970; MD, University of Cincinnati College of Medicine, 1974. Appointments: Residency in Psychiatry, Mt Sinai Hospital, NY, 1974-77; Clinical Affiliate in Psychiatry, 1977-79, Assistant Attending Psychiatrist, 1979-89; Associate Attending Psychiatrist, 1989-, NY Hospital; Clinical Instructor and Instructor in Psychiatry, 1977-79; Assistant Professor, 1979-83, Clinical Assistant Professor, 1983-89, Clinical Associate Professor, 1989-, of Psychiatry, Cornell University Medical College; Private Practice. Publications: 15 Professional articles, 1978-93, including: Inhibition of Ejaculation at Orgasm, in NY State Journal Medicine, 1979; Co-author, Medical Student Attitudes towards Electroconclusive Therapy, in Journal Psychiatric Education, 1984; American Psychiatric Association Practice Guidelines for Eating Disorders, in American Journal Psychiatry, 1993; 2 Book Chapters. Honours: Outstanding Teaching of Medical Students, Richard L Scharf, MD, Memorial Award, Mt Sinai Hospital. 1979; Fellow, American Psychiatric Association, 1989; Significant Achievement Certificate, American Psychiatric Association, 1991. Memberships: Various offices, APA, NY District; Treasurer, 1994, Vice President, 1994-, NY State Psychiatric Association; Board of Trustees, Kenyon College, Gambier, OH, 1990-; President, Kenyon Alumni Council, 1989-90. Hobbies: Tennis; Fishing; Arctic Travel. Address: 17 East 76th Street, New York, NY 10021, USA.

NISTRI Andrea, b. 15 Jan 1947, Florence, Italy. University Professor. Education: MD, University of Florence, 1971. Appointments: Senior Lecturer, Pharmacology, St Bartholomews Hospital Medical College, London, England, 1985-87; Reader, Pharmacology, St Bartholomews Hospital Medical College & Queen Mary & Westfield College, London, England; Professor, Cellular & Molecule Pharmacology. Publications: Co-author, Pharmacological Characterization of Different Types of GABA & Glutamate Receptors in Vertebrates and Invertebrates, 1979; GABA Receptor Mechanisms in the Central Nervous System. Memberships: International Society of Neurochemistry; British Pharmacological Society; Society for Neuroscience. Honours: CIBA Foundation Royal Society of Medicine Fellow, 1974-75; MRC Fellow, McGill University, Montreal, 1977-78. Hobbies: Classic Cars; Hiking; History of Painting. Address: International School for Advanced Studies, Via Beirut 4, 34013 Trieste, Italy. 52.

NIU Yuanqi, b. 27 Jan 1941, Tianjin, China. Doctor. m. Dr Yuan Yijun, 4 Feb 1976, 1 s. Education: BA, Tianjin College of Traditional Chinese Medicine, 1962. Appointments: Physician-in-Charge, 1979; Vice-Professor, 1983; Director Doctor, 1988; Professor, 1990; Honored by National Expert of Febrile Disease, 1991; Professor, Expert of Febrile Disease/Director Doctor. Publications: Treatment of Peptic Ulcer with

Decoction of Ophiopogonis, 1964; The Proper Dosage of Pinelliae, 1986; How To Learn to Use Decoction of Ephedrae, 1983; Research of Anti-Pain Ointment, 1988; Research on Treatment of Endotoxinic-Shock of Rabbit with Sheng-jin Injection, 1992. Hobbies: Chinese Classical Literature; Chess. Address: The 1st Hospital att to Tianjin College of Traditional Chinese Medicine, Tianjin 300193, China.

NIU Zheng Xian, b. 20 May 1936, Zheng Zhou, China. Professor of Medicine. m. 22 Jan 1963, 3 d. Education: BA, Henan Medical University, 1961; Diploma, Undergraduate, 1961. Appointments: Resident Physician, 1961-78; Attending Physician 1978-86; Associate Professor, 1987-91; Professor of Medicine, 1991-; Director, Internal Medicine Department. Publications: Co-Author, Chinese Large Intestine and Anus Diseases, 1985; A Statistical Analysis of 734 Cases of Digestive Diseases in the Elderly, 1989. Honours: Diploma by Ministry of Health of People's Republic of China, 1993. Memberships: Chinese Medical Association. Hobbies: Tennis; Running. Address: The First Affiliated Hospital of Henan Medical University, 1 Jian She Road, Zheng Zhou 450052, China.

NIVEN Peter Ashley Robertson, b. 3 Mar 1938, London, England. Consultant Obstetrician & Gynaecologist, United Bristol Healthcare Trust. m. Peta Callaway, 20 June 1964, 3 sons. Education: BA, 1959, MA, 1963, MB BChir, 1962, FRCS, 1966, MRCOG, 1969, FRCOG, 1982, from Dulwich College, Gonville & Caius College, Cambridge, St Bartholomews Hospital. Appointments: Senior Registrar, St Bartholomew's Hospital; Consultant Obstetrician & Gynaecologist, Newcastle General & Hexham Hospitals. Honours: Purdue Frederick Award, American College of Obstetricians & Gynaecologists, 1975; Eden Travelling Fellow, Royal College of Obstetricians & Gynaecologists, 1972; Open Exhibition, Gonville & Caius College, Cambridge, 1955. Memberships: Fellow, Royal Society of Medicine; Gynaecological Visiting Society, Great Britain & Ireland. Hobbies: Skiing; Golf; Rugby Football; Cricket; Long Distance Walking. Address: 2 Clifton Park, Bristol BS8 3BS, England.

NIZAMI Riaz Munir, b. 27 Nov 1930, Raipur, India. Physician; Allergist. m. Rabia E May, 15 May 1960, 2 s, 2 d. Education: MD; FRCPC; FACAI; FAAAI; DTM & H, England; DOHS, McMasters; Honorary Consultant, Hospital for Sick Children, Toronto, Canada. Appointments: Senior Registrar, Burnley, England, 1960-64; Fellow, N I H, Bethesda, Maryland, USA, 1966-67; Fellow, Allergy & Immunology, University of Toronto, Canada, 1968-70; Assistant Professsor, University of Toronto, Canada. Publications: include, Occupational Asthma: Causes and Diagnostic Procedures, 1981; Co-Author, Allergies in Children, Handbook for Parents; Treatment of Seasonal Conjunctivitis: Comparison of 2% & 4% Sodium Cromoglycate Ophthalmic Solutions, 1984; Hyper-Carotenemia - A Case Report & Review of the Literature, 1985; A Double-Blind, randomized study of Pelletized Cromolyn Versus Cromolyn Blend in the Treatment of Asthma, 1985. Honours: Special Honorary Member, American Medical Association. Memberships: Ontario Medical Association; Canada Medical Association; American Medical Association. Hobbies: Travel; Research; Reading. Address: 559 College Street, Suite #302, Toronto, Ontario M6G 1A9, Canada.

NIZNY Melvyn M, b. 15 Nov 1937, Dayton, Ohio, USA. Psychiatry. Education: BSc, 1956-60; MD, 1960-64. Appointments: Major, US Army as Psychiatrist, including Vietnam Tour, 1969-70; Private Practice; Volunteer Instructor in Psychiatry, University Cincinnati Department of Psychiatry. Honours: Fellow, American Psychiatric Association. Memberships: Cincinnati, Ohio & American Psychiatric Associations; Academy of Organizational & Occupational Psychiatrists; International Society for Traumatic Stress Studies. Address: 3001 Highland Avenue, Cincinnati, OH 45219, USA.

NOCHLIN-SOTO David, b. 12 Apr 1947, Mexico City, Mexico. Physician. m. M Eugenia, 27 Apr 1973, 2 s. Education: BS, Instituto Vasco de Quiroga, Mexico, 1964; MD, Faculty of Medicine, National Autonomous University of Mexico, 1971. Career includes: Assistant Professor of Pathology, University of Washington School of Medicine, Seattle, 199; Attending Neuropathologist, Department of Pathology, University of Washington School of Medicine, Seattle, 1988-; Consultant Neuropathologist, Department of Pathology, Children's Hospital and Medical Center and Veterans Affairs Medical Center, Seattle, WA, 1992-. Publications: 12 Articles in professioal journals including: Co-author, Comparison of the severity of neuropathologic changes in familial and sporadic Alzheimer's disease, Alzheimer Disease Association Disord, 1993; Co-author, A simple method of rapid freezing

adequately preserves brain tissue for immunocytochemistry and light and electron microscopic examination, Acta Neuropathology, 1993. Honour: Certificate in Neuropathology, American Board of Pathology, 1980. Memberships include: American Academy of Neurology, 1976-; International Academy of Pathology, 1980-; New York Academy of Sciences, 1984-; AAAS, 1985-; Society for Neuroscience, 1985-; American Registry of Pathology, 1992-. Hobby: Running. Address: Neuropathology Laboratory, RJ-05, Department of Pathology, University of Washington School of Medicine, Seattle, WA 98195-0001, USA.

NOLLERT Georg Daniel Andreas, b. 24 Oct 1964, Duisburg, Germany. Cardiac Surgeon. Education: Dr Med, University of Luebeck, Germany. Career: Resident, Department of Cardiac Surgery, University of Munich, Germany. Publications: Use of the IMA after Failed PTCA Thorac Cardiovasc Surg, 1995; CABG after Failed PTCA Thorac Cardiovasc Surg, 1995; Neuropsychological Dysfunction After Cardiac Surgery; Determinants of Cerebral Oxygenation during Cardiac Surgery. Memberships: German Society of Thoracic, Cardiac and Vascular Surgery. Hobbies: Computers; Modern Art; Fitness. Address: Klinikum Grosshadern, Marchionistr 15, 81366 Munich, Germany.

NOMANI M Zafar A, b. 14 Jun 1935, India. Dietetics and Nutrition. m. Sajida Nomani, 31 Jan 1962, 1 s, 1 d. Education: PhD; Registered Dietician. Appointments: Associate Professor, 1979-83, Associate Professor, Currently, Professor, West Virginia University. Publications: Professional articles in: American Journal Clinical Nutrition, 1988, 1989; Journal of American Dietetic Association, 1990; International Journal of Science and Technology, 1993. Honours: Fellow, International College of Nutrition; King Hassan II Award, Morocco, for Research Contributions in Health and Ramadan Area. Memberships: American Institute of Nutrition; American Society for Clinical Nutrition; International College of Nutrition; American Dietetic Association. Hobby: Gardening. Address: 704 Allen Hall, West Virginia University, Morgantown, WV 26506-6124, USA.

NOONAN Charles (Chuck) A, b. 9 Aug 1949, Valparaiso, Indiana, USA. Physician. m. Jill E Short, 12 Feb 1967, 1 son, 2 daughters. Education: BS, Purdue University, 1971; MD, Indiana University Medical School, 1971-75; Internship, Residency, Psychiatry, University of California, Davis, Sacramento Medical Centre. Appointments include: Acting Clinical Director, La Porte County Comprehensive Mental Health Centre, 1979; Co-Chairman, 1979-80, Chairman, 1979-80, Department of psychiatry, La Porte Hospital; Consultant, Sierra Clinic, San Francisco, 1983-84; Consultant, Health Analysis, Evaluation of Disability Claims, 1983-84; Medical Director, Mt Diablo Hospital Eating Disorders Programme, 1984-86; Consultant, US District Court, 1982-; Consultant, Contra Costa County Superior Court, 1982-; Qualified Medical Evaluator, California Industrial Council, 1993-. Publications include: Holiday depression, 1979; Depression, Anyone Can Be Affected, 1980; Adolescence and Today's Society, 1981; The Resident as Child; Reduction of Depressive and Paranoid Groups by Dexotroamphetamine TX, 1979. Honours: Physician's Continuing Education Certificate, American Psychiatric Association, 1978, 1981; Physician's Recognition Award, American Medical Association, 1978, 1981; Board Certification, 1981. Memberships: American Psychiatric Association; Southern Medical Association; Northern California Psychiatric Society; Alameda-Contra Costa Medical Association; California Medical Association. Hobbies: Astronomy; Photography. Address: 2001 Salvio Street, Suite 22, Concord, CA 94520, USA.

NOONAN Jacqueline Anne, b. 28 Oct 1928, Burlington, VT, USA. Physician. Education: BA, Albertus Magnus College, New Haven, CT, 1950; MD, University of Vermont Medical School, Burlington, 1954. Career includes: Professor of Pediatrics, Cardiology, 1969-, Chairman, Department of Pediatrics, 1974-92, University of Kentucky College of Medicine; Editorial Board, Clinical Pediatrics, 1990-; University of Kentucky Press Committee, 1993-96; University Senate, 1993-96; Faculty Council, 1993-96. Publications include: Numerous international presentations; 56 Peer reviewed publications, 26 invited publications and book chapters and 58 abstracts. Honours include: Alpha Omega Alpha, 1965; KMA Faculty Scientific Award, 1971; Helen B Fraser Award, 1971; UK Distinguished Professor Alumni Award, 1975; Honorary Doctor of Science Degree, University of Vermont, 1980; ODK Leadership, 1983; AAP Section on Cardiology Founders Award, 1994. Memberships include: American Academy of Pediatrics; Various positions, American College of Cardiology; American Federation for Clinical Research; American Heart Association; AMA; American Medical Women's Association; American Pediatric Society; Association of American

Medical Colleges; Various positions, National Board of Medical Examiners; Society for Pediatric Research; Williams Syndrome Association. Address: 2980 Four Pines, Lexington, KY 40502, USA.

NORIEGA Gloria Isabel, b. 29 July 1949, Mexico City, Mexico. Psychologist. div., 1 son, 1 daughter. Education: Specialisation, Transactional Analyst with Clinical Work, 1983; Licensed Psychologist, 1990; Master in Clinical Psychology, 1993. Appointments: Primary School Teacher, 1968; Currently: Psychotherapist; Co-Founder, Director, Instituto Privado de Análisis Transaccional de México SC. Publications: A TA techniquye used with juvenile female delinquents, 1990; Diagnosis and Treatment of Ego States Boundary Problems, 1994; Various articles in The Transactional Analysis Journal. Honours: Graduated with honours, 1990; Gustavo Baz Prada Social Service Award, Universidad Nacional Autonoma de México, 1991. Memberships: Clinical Teaching Member, Instructor, Supervisor, Editorial Board Member, International Transactional Analysis Association. Hobbies: Reading; Swimming; Snorkelling. Address: Agrarismo 21, Col Escandon, Mexico DF, CP 11800, Mexico.

NORMAN Philip Sidney, b. 4 Aug 1924, Pittsburg, Kansas, USA. Physician. m. Marion Birmingham, 15 Apr 1955, 1 son, 2 daughters. Education: AB, Pittsburgh State University; MD, cum laude, Washington University. Appointments: Instructor, Medicine, 1956, Assistant Professor of Medicine, 1959, Associate professor of Medicine, 1964, Professor of Medicine, Johns Hopkins University. Publications: Contributor of 270 articles in medical journals. Honours: President, American Academy of Allergy and Immunology, 1975. Memberships: American Federation for Clinical Research; American Soceity for Clinical Investigation; American Association of Physicians; American Thoracic Society; American Academy Allergy and Immunology; American Clinical and Climatological Association; American Association Immunologists. Address: Johns Hopkins Asthma and Allergy Centre, 5501 Hopkins Bayview Circle, Baltimore, MD 21212, USA.

NORMAN Robert John, b. 19 June 1949, England. Medical Specialist. m. Susan Gay, 24 June 1972, 2 sons, 1 daughter. Education: MBChB, hons; MD; FRCAP; FRCOG; MRCPath; CREI. Appointments: Associate Profesor, University of Natal; Associate Professor, University Adelaide. Publications: 150 Publications in referred journals. Memberships: British Endocrine Society; Australia Society of Reproductive Biology; Endocrine Society of Australia; Fertility Society Australia. Hobbies: Sport; Current Affairs. Address: Department of Obstetrics & Gynawcology, The Queen Elizabeth Hospital, Woodville, SA 5011, Australia.

NORRIS H(erbert) Thomas, b. 24 Nov 1934, Johnson City, TN, USA. Doctor of Medicine. m. Patricia Henry, 19 Jun 1956, 1 s, 2 d. Education: BS, Honours, Washington State University, Pullman, WA, 1956; MD, University of Southern California, Los Angeles, 1959. Career includes: Associate Professor of Pathology, 1971-76, Professor of Pathology, 1976-83, University of Washington; Director of Hospital Pathology, University Hospital, Seattle, WA, 1974-83; Professor and Chairman, Pathology and Laboratory Medicine, East Carolina University School of Medicine, Greenville, NC, 1983-; Chief of Pathology, Pitt County Memorial Hospital, Greenville, NC, 1983-. Publications: Editor: Contemporary Issues in Surgical Pathology, volume 2, 1983, volume 17, 1991; Associate Editor, Current Surgery, 1990-; Author of 61 articles, abstracts and editorials in professional journals; 11 Contributions to textbooks and encyclopaedias; 6 Book reviews. Honours: Alpha Omega Alpha, 1959; Certificate Oustanding Achievement, US Army Science Conference, West Point, NY, 1964. Memberships include: Pitt County Medical Society; North Carolina Society of Pathologists; Sigma Xi; New York Academy of Sciences; American Gastroenterological Association; AMA; AAAS; Fellow, American Pathology Foundation; Founding Member, Gastrointestinal Pathology Club; Fellow, College of American Pathologists; Fellow, American Society of Clinical Pathologists; Fellow, American College of Physicians; International Academy of Pathology. Hobbies: Water Sports; Photography. Address: 403 Wesley Road, Greenville, NC 27858, USA.

NORWICH Kenneth Howard, b. 8 May 1939, Toronto, Canada. Professor; Physician. m. Barbara Gross, 18 June 1963, 3 daughters. Education: MD; BSc; MSc; PhD. Appointments: Scholar, Medical Research Council of Canada, 1970-75; Physician, University of Toronto Health Service, Assistant Professor, Faculty of Biomedicine, Associate Professor, 1975-80; Professor, 1980-. Publications: Molecular Dynamics in Biosystems, 1977; Information Sensation and Perception, 1993; 60

journal articles. Memberships: Canadian Medical Association; Canadian Medical & Biological Engineering Society; Biomedical Engineering Society. Hobbies: Reading; Theoretical Studies in Biology and Medicine. Address: Institute of Biomedical Engineering, University of Toronto, 4 Taddle Creek Road, Toronto, Ontario M5S 1A4, Canada.

NOSHPITZ Joseph Dove, b. 31 Aug 1922, New York, NY, USA. Child and Adolescent Psychiatrist. m. Charlotte Sorkine, 20 Sep 1956, 1 s. Education: BA; MD; Graduate, Psychoanalysis and Child Analysis, DC Institute for Psychoanalysis. Appointments: Professor of Psychiatry, George Washington University; Currently: Private Practitioner; Clinical Professor of Psychiatry. Publications: Editor in Chief, Basic Handbook of Child Psychiatry, 5 volumes, 1979, 1980, 1985. Memberships: American Academy of Child and Adolescent Psychiatry; American Psychiatric Association; American Orthopsychiatric Association; Group for the Advancement of Psychiatry. Hobbies: Reading; Fossil Collecting. Address: 3141 34th Street NW, Washington, DC 20008-3308, USA.

NOUJEIM Ziad Fouad, b. 2 Nov 1958, Beirut, Lebanon. Clinical Assistant Professor, Lecturer, Department of Oral Surgery, St Joseph University, Beirut, Lebanon. Education: Oral Biology Advanced Certificate, Paris VII University, France, 1982; Oral Surgery Advanced Certificate, Paris VI University, France, 1983. Appointments: Former Clinical Assistant Professor, Lecturer, Department of Oral & Maxillofacial Surgery, Lebanese University, Faculty of Medical Sciences, Beirut, 1985-85; Former Clinical Fellow, Oral & Maxillofacial Surgery, Massachusetts General Hospital, Harvard School of Dental Medicine, Boston, 1991. Memberships: Lebanese Dental Association; American College of Oral & Maxillofacial Surgeons; International Association of Oral & Maxillofacial Surgeons. Honours: Research Fellow, Oral Pain Project, St Joseph University, Beirut, Lebanon; Auvergne-Clermont I University, Clermont-Ferrand, France. Address: Oral Surgery & Implantology Clinic, PO Box 166496, Ashrafieh, Beirut, Lebanon.

NOURI Soraya, b. 9 April 1940, Tehran, Iran. Physician; Professor of Pediatrics; Professor of Internal Medicine; Professor of Radiology. m. Michael Wolverson, 1 son, 2 daughters. Education: MB, BS, 1965; MRCP, 1971; MBA, 1994. Appointments include: Senior Registrar, Honorary Lecturer, Hospital for Sick Children, Great Ormand Street, London, England, 1971-75; Assistant Professor, Pediatrics Department, Baylor College of Medicine, Houston, Texas, 1975-77 and St Louis, 1978-81 Assistant Professor, Division of Cardiology, Department of Internal Medicine, Baylor College of Medicine, 1975-77, and St Louis University, 1977-83; Associate Professor of Pediatric & Radiology, St Louis University 1981-89, School of Medicine, Missouri, 1986-90; Professor of Internal Medicine, St Louis University School of Medicine, 1991; Director of Pediatric Cardiology, St Louis University, 1978-92. Publications include: Sever Pulmonary Stenosis in Infancy & Childhood, 1969; The mechanism responsible for echogenicity of blood, 1983; Infantile cardiac fibromatosis: correlation of antemortem and necropsy findings, 1984; Management of infants with univentricular heart, 1984; Dysrhythmias after the modified fontan procedure, 1989; Clinical profile of dilated cardiomyopathy in children, 1990; The cardiovascular benefits and complications of habitual strenuous exercise in children, 1990; Reliability of echocardiography in the diagnosis of anomalous origin of the left coronary artery from the pulmonary trunk, 1991; Pediatric cardiac rehabilitation, 1992. Memberships include: British Medical Association; British Cardiac Society; Harris County Medical Society; American College of Cardiology; American Heart Association; Council for Cardiovascular Diseases for the Young; American Association of University Professors; American Federation for Clinical Research. Honours: Annual Award, Outstanding Academic Achievement, 1960; Representative Student, RFH London University to European Students Conference, Denmark, 1963; Traveling Scholarship, Royal Free Hospital Medical School, London, England, 1964; Certificate of Merit, London University, 1965; YWCA Special Leadership Award, 1993. Hobbies: Walking; Music; Reading; Swimming. Address: 1465 South Grand Blvd, St Louis, MO 63104, USA.

NOVEMBER Abigail, b. 4 Dec 1944. Nutritionist. m. Richard Dusansky, 1 son, 1 daughter. Education: BS, New York University; MS, University of Wisconsin; PhD, New York University. Appointments: Assistant Professor, SUNY, Stony Brook, 1979-82; Visiting Assistant Professor, West Australian Institute of Technology, 1982; Consultant, Woodhaven Nursing Home, 1975-84; Director, Research, Bureau of Nutrition Services, Texas, 1993-; Assistant Professor, Incainate Word College, 1990-92; Nutrition Education Training Co-Director, Texas Human Services, 1989-90. Publications: Burns, 1981; Several professional publications in scientific journals. Honours: Omicron Nu, 1965. Memberships: Society of Nutrition Educators; Texas Public Health Association. Hobbies: Stand-up Comedy. Address: Box 27203, Austin, TX 78731, USA.

NOVOA-MONTERO Darío A, b. 13 July 1937, Venezuela. Medical Doctor. m. Sildren Vergara, 27 August 1981, 1 son, 3 daughters. Education: MD, Barcelona, Spain, 1961; DrM, Universidad de Los Andes, Venezuela, 1967; MHS, 1977, PhD, 1983, The Johns Hopkins University, Baltimore, USA. Appointments: Director, Clínica San Carlos, San Carlos de Zulia, Venezuela, 1961-68; Professor, School of Medicine, Universidad de Los Andes, Mérida, (ULA) Venezuela, 1969-94; Chairman, Lab-MICE, ULA, 1989-94; Visiting Professor, The Johns Hopkins School of Public Health, 1992-93. Publications: Congenital Cardiovascular Abnormalities, 1974; Chagas' Disease and Chronic Myocardiopathy, 1983; Co-author: Protozoan Infection in Man-Color Atlas, 1988; Comparability and Reliability of ELISA, 1993. Honours: 1st Prize, Venezuelan Medical Federation, Scientific Activities, 1967; Scientific Medical Activities, 1969; Literary Activities, 1970. Memberships: Venezuelan Association for Advancement of Science; APH USA; ACPM USA; International Epidemiological Association; New York Academy of Sciences; World Federation for Education and Research. Hobbies: Farming; Travel. Address: Apartado de Correos No 6, Merida 5101A, Venezuela.

NURCOMBE Barry, b. 11 Jan 1933, Brisbane, Australia. Child Psychiatry. m. Alison Carson, 7 Dec 1956, 2 s, 1 d. Education: MD; BS; DPM; FRANZCP; FRACP; FAACAP; FACP; FAPA; MRC Psych; Board Certified in General and Child Psychiatry. Appointments: Associate Professor Psychiatry, University of New South Wales, 1967-76; Professor of Psychiatry, University of Vermont, 1976-84; Professor of Psychiatry, Brown University, 1984-89; Currently, Director of Child and Adolescent Psychiatry, Vanderbilt University School of Medicine. Publications: Children of the Dispossessed, 1976; The Clinical Process in Psychiatry, 1986; Child Mental Health and The Law, 1994. Honour: Gold Medal, University of Queensland, 1956. Memberships: American Psychiatric Association; American Academy of Child and Adolescent Psychiatry; Royal Australian and New Zealand College of Psychiatry; American College of Psychiatry. Hobbies: Japanese; Music; Tennis. Address: The Psychiatric Hospital at Vanderbilt, 1601 23rd Ave S, Nashville, TN 3271, USA.

NURMAMEDOV Narzy, b. 27 May 1932, Chardjoy Region, Turkmenistan. Ophthalmologist. m. Zoya Mamedovna, 13 Mar 1956, 1 son, 1 daughter. Education: MD. Appointments: Ophthalmologist, Kizyl-Ayakskaya Region Hospital; Scientific Worker, Deputy Scientific Director, Turkmen Scientific Ophthalmologic Institute; Rector, Turkmen State Medical Institute; Currently: Head, Ophthalmologic Faculty, Turkmen State Medical Institute; President, Academy of Medical Sciences of Turkmenistan. Publications: Surgical Treatment of Eye Cicatrical Xerosis, 1974; Children's Paratrachome, 1984; Children's Eye Tumors, 1985; Ophthalmoherpes in Turkmenistan Arid Zone, 1994. Honours: Order of the Red Banner of Labour, 1981; State Prizewinner in Science and Technology of Turkmenistan, 1981; Gayrat Medal. Memberships: Chairman, Turkmen Scientific Ophthalmologic Society; Academy of Medical Sciences of Turkmenistan; Academy of Sciences of Turkmenistan. Hobbies: Drawing; Photography. Address: Lermontov st 27, 744012 Ashgabat, Turkmenistan.

NUTTALL James B, b. 8 July 1914, Schley, Virginia, USA. Physician of Aerospace Medicine. m. Virginia B Richardson, 8 Mar 1941, 1 son, 1 daughter. Education: BS, MD, University of Maryland; MPH, Johns Hopkins University; Fellow, American College of Physicians; Fellow, Aerospace Medicine; Fellow, International Academy Aviation & Space Medicine. Appointments: Director, Department of Aviation Medicine, USAF School of Aviation Medicine; Deputy Director of Professional Services, Officer Surgeon General, USAF; Commander, USAF School of Aviation Medicine; Medical Director, McDonnel Douglas Aerospace Co; Associate Medical Director, Transamerica Occidental Life. Publications: Numerous professional publications in scientific journals. Honours: University Gold Prize Award, School of Medicine, University of Maryland, 1939; USAF Certificate of Achievement in Aviation Medicine, 1958; Distinguished Flying Cross, 1944; Legion of Merit, 1960; Distinguished Service Medal, 1969. Memberships: American Medical Association; Aerospace Medical Association; American College of Physicians; American College of Occupational & Environmental Medicine. Hobby: Running. Address: 7046 Vista De Mar Lane, Playa Del Rey, CA 90293, USA.

NUTTALL Richard Norris, b. 7 Feb 1940, Ontario, Canada. Physician. m. Jane Pickering, 9 July 1977, 2 sons. Education: BSA, Toronto, 1961; MPA, Harvard, 1964; MB, BS, London, 1974; Certified, American Board of Preventive Medicine. Appointments: Regional Director, Alberta, Medical Services Branch, Health Canada; Medical Health Officer, Government of Northwest Territories; Medical Health Officer, Regina Health District. Honours: Fellow, American College of Preventive Medicine, 1985; Fellow, American College of Healthcare Executives, 1990; Fellow, Canadian College of Health Service Executives, 1994. Memberships: Saskatchewan Medical Association; Canadian Medical Association. Hobbies: Hiking; Jogging. Address: 1910 McIntyre Street, Regina, Saskatchewan S4P 2R3, Canada.

NWOSU Ezechi Callistus, b. 19 Jun 1953, Nigeria. Obstetrician and Gynaecologist. m. Beverley Nwosu, 21 Jun 1981, 2 s, 1 d. Education: BM; ChB; MRCOG, 1989; Master Obstetrics and Gynaecology, Liverpool, 1992. Appointments include: Registrar, 1985-90; Postmembership Research Registrar, 1990-92; Senior Registrar, Obstetrics and Gynaecology 1993-. Publications: Co-author, Tubal Pregnancy in Microsurgery, in British Medical Journal, 1991; Carcinoid Tumor and Infertility, in Journal of Obstetrics and Gynaecology, 1992; Longit Assessment of Amniotic Fluid Index, in British Journal Obstetrics and Gynaecology, 1993; Two Cases of Cardiomyopathy, in British Journal Obstetrics and Gynaecology, 1993; Assessment of Amniotic Fluid Volume Using Maximum Pool Depth, in Contemporary Reviews in Obstetrics and Gynaecology, 1994. Memberships: North of England Obstetrics and Gynaecology Society; British Medical Ultrasound Society; BMA; Medical Defence Union; Blair Beli Research Society. Hobbies: Football; Table Tennis; Lawn Tennis. Address: Countess of Chester, Department of Obstetrics and Gynaecology, Liverpool Road, Chester, CH2 1BQ, England.

NYE Emil Bowden, b. 10 Feb 1940, Skelmorlie, Ayrshire, Scotland. Gynaecologist and Obstetrician. m. Judith Ann Cannell, 25 Feb 1965, 1 son, 2 daughters. Education: MB BS; MRCS; LRCP; FRCOG; FRNZCOG. Appointments: Lecturer, Senior Registrar, Obstetrics, Royal Free Hospital, London, England, 1972-76; Senior Lecturer, Department of Obstetrics and Gynaecology, University of Auckland, New Zealand, 1976-80; Currently Obstetrician and Gynaecologist in private practice and Honorary to Greenlane and National Women's Hospitals. Publications: Ovarian Carcinoma - improvement in survival with chemotherapy, 1972; Gynaecological symptoms following rectal excision, 1973; Others including papers on placental size, 1980. Hobbies: Instrumental and vocal music; Sailing; Windsurfing; Woodwork; Restoration crafts; Clocks. Address: 81 Bell Road, Remuera, Auckland 5, New Zealand.

NYGAARD Randi, b. 17 Aug 1945, Trondheim, Norway. Consultant in Paediatric Oncology. m. Per Fridtjov Bonsaksen, 17 Aug 1985. Education: Cand Med, Medical School, University of Oslo, 1970; Specialist in Paediatrics, 1977; PhD, Scientific Research, University of Trondheim, 1991. Career includes: Paediatric Resident, Wisconsin, USA as Fulbright Fellow, 1971-72; Senior Lecturer in Paediatrics, 1979-84, Child Oncologist and Research Fellow, 1984-91, Consultant in Paediatric Oncology, 1991-, University of Trondheim. Publications: 15 Scientific articles in child oncology and medical ethics, 1985-92; Long-term Survival in Childhood Leukemia: Relapses and Late Effects after Completed Therapy, thesis, 1991. Memberships: Norwegian Medical Association; Norwegian Paediatric Society; Nordic Society for Paediatric Haematology and Oncology; International Society for Paediatric Oncology. Hobbies: Music; Skiing; Hiking. Address: Department of Paediatrics, University Hospital of Trondheim, N-7006 Trondheim, Norway.

O

O'BRIEN James Gerard, b. 25 Feb 1943, Thurles, Co Tipperary, Ireland. Medicine, Family Practice. m. Margaret Kelly, 7 Jan 1968, 2 s, 1 d. Education: MB; B Ch; BAO; Geriatric Fellow, Center for Study of Aging and Human Development, Duke University, Durham, NC. Career: Director of Graduate Education, Department of Family Practice, CHM, Michigan State University, 1977-84; Director, Clinical Geriatrics, College of Human Medicine, 1984-87, Interim Chair, Department of Family Practice, 1991-92, Currently, Professor and Senior Associate Chairperson, Department of Family Practice, College of Human Medicine, Michigan State University, East Lansing. Publications: Co-author, Abuse of the Elderly: An Annotated Bibliography, 1985; Co-author, Elder Abuse: An Educational Program for Physicians, 1991; Ethical and Legal Issues in Care of the Elderly, 1991. Honours: V K Volk Award, Michigan Gerontological Society, for Outstanding Contribution to the Health Care of The Elderly in Michigan, 1987; Educator of the Year, Michigan Academy of Family Physicians, Michigan Family Practice, 1993. Memberships: AMA; American Academy of Family Physicians; American Geriatrics Society; Michigan State Medical Society; Michigan Academy of Family Physicians; Gerontological Society; Society of Teachers of Family Medicine. Hobby: Soccer. Address: B106 Clinical Center, College of Human Medicine, Michigan State University, East Lansing, MI 48824, USA.

O'BRYAN Thomas Dorin, b. 1 Jan 1952, Detroit, Michigan, USA. Chiropractor. m. Wendy Selin, 7 Mar 1977, 1 son, 1 daughter. Education: Bachelor's degrees in General Studies and Human Biology; Doctorate, Chiropractic. Appointments: Secretary, President, Chicago Chiropractic Society; Director, Illinois Chiropractic Scoeity; Lecturer, National Chiropractic College; Currently, Director, Omnis Chiropractic Group. Honours: Chiropractor of the Year, Chicago Chiropractor Society, 1989. Memberships: International Academy of Preventive Medicine; American Chiropractic Association; International College of Applied Kinesiology. Hobbies: Den Leader, Cub Scouts; Coach, Minors Baseball; Triathlete. Address: 1500 Waukegan, Suite 200, Glenview, IL 60025, USA.

O'CONNELL Edward J, b. 30 May 1934, Rochester, Minnesota, USA. Physician; Paediatrician. m. Maureen D Gallagher, 9 June 1958, 1 son, 4 daughters. Education: BS, St Thomas University, 1956; MD, St Louis University Medical School, 1960. Appointments: Professor of Paediatrics, Allergy-Immunology; Consultant, Mayo Medical School, Mayo Clinic. Honours: Teacher of the Year, Paediatrics, 1971, 1978, 1989; Hall of Fame Teachers, 19184; Master in Allergy, 1992; Best Doctors in America, 1994; Distinguished Fellow, ACAI, 1992. Memberships: AMA; ACAI; AAP; AAAI; IAPS. Hobbies: Golf; Fishing; Woodworking. Address: Department of Paediatrics, Mayo Clinic, Rochester, MN 55905, USA.

O'CONNELL John B, b. 27 July 1949, Chicago, Illinois, USA. Physician. m. Mary Owens O'Connell, 1 Dec 1980, 1 son, 4 daughters. Education: MD. Appointments: Medical Director, Utah Cardiac Transplant Program; Assistant Chief of the Medical Service, Hines Veterans Administration Hospital; Medical Director, Cardiac Transplantation Program, Loyola University Medical Center; Professor of Medicine, University of Mississippi School of Medicine; Chairman, Department of Medicine, University of Mississippi School of Medicine. Publications: Over 160 publications; 8 in press. Memberships: Association of Professors of Medicine; Mississippi Affilate; American Heart Association; Internal Society of Heart & Lung Transplantation; American Society for Transplant Physicians; Fellow, American College of Physicians. Honours: Alpha Omega Alpha, Honor Medical Society; Robert Kark MD Research Award, Chicago Society of Internal Medicine; Outstanding Young Citizen Award, Chicago Junior Associates of Commerce & Industry; Shinshu University Medal, Matsumoto City. Hobbies: Golf; Travel. Address: Department of Medicine, University of Mississippi Medical Center School of Medicine, Jackson, MS 39216, USA.

O'CONNELL Laurence Joseph, b. 12 May 1945, Chicago, USA. President; Chief Executive Officer. m. Angela Schneider, 1 son. Education: BA, Philosophy, Loyola-Chgo; BA, Theology, University Catholique de Louvain, Belgium; MA, Religious Studies, Louvain; PhD, Religious Studies, Louvain; STD, Theology, Louvain. Appointments: Assistant Professor of Theology, St Louis University; Associate Professor of Theology, St Louis University; Chair, Department of Theological Studies, St Louis University; Vice President, Theology, Mission & Ethics, The Catholic Health Association of the US; President, Chief Executive Officer, The Park Ridge Center for the Study of Health, Faith & Ethics, Chicago; Adjunct Assistant Professor, Department of Medicine, Stritch School of Medicine, Loyola University. Publications: Ethics Committees: A Practical Approach, 1986; The Gospel Alive: The Care of Persons with AIDS and Related Diseases, 1988. Memberships: Director, Division of Philosophy & Theology, The Albert Schweitzer Institute for the Humanities; Fellow, The Institute of Medicine, Chicago; Board Member, The Acadia Institute; Board Member, International Association of Law, Ethics & Science; Board Member, SSM Health Care System; Board Member, American Health Decisions; Scientific Committee, San Raffaele School of Medical Humanities, Milan; Public International Panel Member, American Council on Pharmaceutical Education. Honours: Outstanding Young Man of the Year Award, 1978, 1981; St Louis University Speakers Award, 1979. Hobbies: Travel; Boating. Address: 507 W Barry, Chicago, IL 60657, USA. 8. 15.

O'CONNELL Walter Edward, b. 2 Aug 1925, Reading, Massachusetts, USA. Clinical Research Psychologist. m. Gloria O'Connell, 5 Aug 1960. Education: BA, University of Massachusetts, 1950; MA, University of Texas, 1952; PhD, 1958; Diplomate, American Board of Professional Psychology; Licensed Psychologist. Appointments: Research & Clinical Psychologist, Veterans Administration Medical Centre, 1955-86; Clinical Associate Professor, Baylor College of Medicine, Houston, 1967-93, University of Houston, 1967-86; Director, Professor, University of St Thomas, Houston, 1966-86, Baylor University, Waco, 1959-66, Union Institute, Cincinnati, 1984-; Private Practice in Psychotherapy, Houston, 1973-86; Consultant to Hospitals, Universities, Schools and Business, 1965-86. Publications: Action Therapy and Adlerian Theory, 1975, 1980; Contributing Chapters to books and 350 articles to Voices, The Art and Science of Psychotherapy, Individual Psychology, Adlerian Journal of Research, Theory & Practice; Columnist: Bastrop Advertiser, 1991-. Honours: Roth Foundation Award, 1977; Annual National Veterans Administration Professional Service Award, 1983; Fellow, APA International Academy of Electric Psychotherapists; Outstanding Performance Awards, 1977, 1992. Memberships: North American Society Adlerian Psychology; American Academy of Psychotherapists; Fellow, Academy of Clinical Psychology. Hobbies: Dancing; Animals. Address: 106 Kelly Road, Bastrop, TX 78602, USA.

O'DORISIO Thomas Michael, b. 29 May 1943, Denver, Colorado, USA. Physician. m. M Sue Wedemeyer, 8 June 1968, 2 sons, 1 daughter. Education: BS cum laude, Biology, Regis College, Denver, 1965; MS, Thesis in Anatomy, 1967, MD, 1971, Internship, 1971-72, Creighton University; Residency, 1972-74, Fellow, Endocrinology, 1974-77, Ohio State University. Appointments: Assistant Professor, 1977-79, Associate Professor, 1979-84, Professor, Medicine, 1984-, Physiology, 1985-, Pathology, Human Nutrition, 1993-, Director, Division of Endocrinology and Metabolism, 1989-, Ohio State University, Columbus; Associate Programme Director, Ohio State University Clinical Research Center, 1984-; Associate to Vice-President for Industrial Relations. Publications: About 30 book contributions; Nearly 200 refereed articles in physiology, pathology, gastroenterology, endocrinology, nutrition; Reviews. Honours include: Academic Scholarship, Creighton University School of Medicine, 1967-71; Ohio State University: Golden Apple Teaching Award, 1974; Research Merit Award, Department of Medicine, 1980; Professor of the Year Award, Class of 1983; Donald V Unverferth Research Award, Department of Internal Medicine and Division of Cardiology, 1992. Memberships: Sigma Xi; American Federation of Clinical Research; Central Society of Clinical Research; The Endocrine Society; American College of Physicians; Alpha Omega Alpha; American Association for the Advancement of Science; Honorary Member, Phi Zeta, Delta Chapter; American Gastroenterology Association; American Society of Clinical Endocrinologists. Address: Division of Endocrinology and Metabolism, The Ohio State University Medical Center, Room N1123, Doan Hall, 410 W 10th Avenue, Columbus, OH 43210-1228, USA.

O'FARRELL Timothy James, b. 22 Apr 1946, Lancaster, Ohio, USA. Clinical Psychologist. m. Jayne Sara Talmage, 19 May 1973, 1 son. Education: BA, University of Notre Dame, 1968; PhD, Psychology, Boston University, 1975. Appointments: Instructor, Harvard Univeristy Medical School, Boston, 1977-82; Assistant Professor, 1982-86, Associate Professor, 1986-; Staff Psychologist, VA Medical Center, Brockton, 1975-78; Director, Alcoholism Clinic, 1978-83; Director,

Counseling for Alcoholics' Marriaages Project, 1978-; Chief, Alcohol & Family Studies Lab, 1981-; Associate Chief Psychology Service, 1988-. Publications: Alcohol and Sexuality; Treating Alochol Problems Manual and Family Intervention. Memberships: Smithers Foundation; Guggenheim Foundation; Fellow, Behavior Therapy & Research Society; NIAAA, Psychosocial Research Rev Group; Editorial Board, Journal, Family Psychology; Editorial Board, Family Dynamics Addition Quarterly; American Psychology Association; Association for the Advancement Behavior Therapy; Eastern Psychology Association. Address: 260 High Street, Duxbury, MA 02332-3406, USA. 6. 52.

O'HARE KNIGHT Margaret Howden, b. 16 Mar 1934. Secretary General. m. David Knight, 2 sons. Education: University of London, 1953-56; University of Grenoble, 1961-65; Imperial College London, 1966-68; City University, London, 1969-70. Appointments: Engineer, I.T.T; Academic Researcher, Semiconductors; British Civil Service; Secretary General, World Confederation for Physical Therapy. Memberships: International Association Forum. Hobbies: Swimming; Camping; Theatre. Address: 2 Viga Road, London N21 1HJ, England.

O'LEARY Eleanor Anne, b. 15 Apr 1947, Cork, Ireland. Statutory Lecturer. Education: MA; PhD; MDip in Education; Diploma in Gestalt Therapy. Appointments: Guidance Counsellor, 1973-81; University Lecturer. Publications: Psychology of Counselling, 1986; Gestalt Therapy: Theory, Research and Practice, 1992. Honour: Governor, University College Cork, 1991-. Memberships: British Psychological Society; Psychological Society of Ireland; European Association of Counselling; Irish Association of Humanistic & Integrative Psychotherapy. Hobbies: Swimming; Singing; Dancing; Reading; Gymn. Address: Department of Applied Psychology, University College, Cork, Ireland.

O'LOUGHLIN John Augustine, b. 30 Apr 1938, Adelaide, Australia. Medical. m. Tanya Sue Frahn, 1981, 3 sons, 1 daughter. Education: MBBS; MS; FRCOG; FRACOG; FRANZCOG. Appointments: Past President, Royal Australian College of Obstetricians & Gynaecologists, 1986-89; Honorary Treasurer, International Federation of Gynecology & Obstetrics; Consultant Obstetrician & Gynaecologist, Adelaide, Australia. Address: 53 Walter Street, North Adelaide, SA 5006, USA.

O'REILLY-KNAPP Mary Elizabeth, b. 4 Dec 1940, Philadelphia, PA, USA. Psychotherapist. m. Barton W Knapp, 29 Aug 1981. Education: Doctor in Nursing Science; Registered Nurse; Certified Clinical Specialist; Member of Sigma Theta Tau International Honor Society of Nursing. Appointments: Instructor in Medical-Surgical Nursing, 1962-72; Assistant Professor, University of Pennslyvania School of Nursing, 1974-78; Private Practice, 1979-; Co-Director, Pheonix Centers, 1981-; Publications: The Myth of the Cave, 1989; The Dissociative Process: Theoretical Considerations and Therapeutic Implications, 1991; Baccalaureate Nursing Students' Reports of Social Support, 1994; Guest Editor of Transactional Analysis Journal on Shame, 1994. Memberships: American Group of Psychotherapy Association; American Nurses Association; Sigma Theta Tau; International Society for the Study of Multiple Personality. Hobbies: Builds Miniature Houses and Furniture; Gardening. Address: 905 Newtown Road, Devon, PA 19333, USA.

O'SULLIVAN Mary Josephine, b. 22 Mar 1938, USA. Physician. Education: BS; MD. Appointments: Assistant Professor, New York Medical College; Senior Lecturer; Assistant Professor, Associate Dean, New York Medical College; Director, New York Medical College; Professor Obs & Gyn & Hematology Director, Obstetric Service. Honour: US PHS Award, 1993. Address: Department OB GYN, University of Miami, PO Box 016960, Miami, FL 33101, USA.

O'SULLIVAN Victor Robin, b. 16 May 1948, Cork, Ireland. Anatomist. m. Marian Kelleher, 25 June 1976, 2 sons, 1 daughter. Education: BDS, 1971, MB BCh, BAO, 1976, MSc, 1980, PhD, 1988, National University of Ireland. Appointments: General Dental Practitioner, Cork; Registrar in Dental Surgery, Cork Dental Hospital; Currently Lecturer in Anatomy, University College, Cork. Publications include: The Dental Remains from Newgrange, 1982; Co-author: A Review of Current Local Anaesthetic Techniques in Dentistry for Children, 1986; Age Changes in Axon Number Along Rat Cervical Ventral Spinal Nerve Roots, 1989; Segment Length and Root Orientation in Normal and Sacrally Attached Spinal Cords: A Morphometric Study, 1993. Honours: FICD, 1987. Memberships: Anatomical Society of Great Britain and Ireland; Royal Academy of Medicine in Ireland; International Association for Dental Research. Hobbies: Papier mâché modelling;

Pteridology; Genealogy; Port wine. Address: Oakhurst, Donovan's Road, Cork, Ireland.

OAKLEY Stanley Preston, b. 11 May 1956, Charlotte, North Carolina, USA. Psychiatrist. m. Vickie E Wilson, 27 May 1978. Education: BS, Chemistry, University North Carolina, Chapel Hill, 1978; MD, East Carolina University School of Medicine; Certified, American Board of Psychiatry and Neurology in Psychiatry, 1990; Geriatric Psychiatry qualifications, 1991. Appointments: Senior registrar, Forensic and Geriatric Psychiatry, Hillcrest Hospital, Adelaide, South Australia, 1986-87; Associate Professor of Psychiatric Medicine, Director, residency Training. Publications: Psychiatric Aspects of Organ Transplantation, 1991. Memberships: American Psychiatric Association; American Association of Directors of Psychiatric Residency Training; American Association for Geriatric Psychiatry. Hobbies: Travel; Science Fiction; Maritime History. Address: Grenville, NC 27858-4354, USA.

OBAS Remy, b. 1 Oct 1940, Haiti. Medical Director. m. 4 June 1966, 1 son. Education: BSc, 1959; MD, 1965. Appointments: Medical Director, Reynots Aluminium Mines, Haiti; Depty Chief of Surgery, USPHS Hospital, New York; Cheif of Surgery, USPHS Hospital, Staten Island, New York; Attending Surgeon, Bayley Seton Hospital, Interfaith Medical Center, St Marys Hospital; Medical Director, Department of Sanatation, New York. Publications: Papillary Carcinoma in Hyroslossal Cyst, 1976. Memberships: American College of Surgeons; American Medical Association; Biomedical Foundation. Honours: Vice President, Public Affairs, Biomedical Society; 1st Vice President, Association of Physicians Abroad. Hobbies: Swimming; Racquet Ball. Address: 86-92 Dunton Street, Helliswood, NY 11423, USA.

OBEREM Maria-Luise Annegret, b. 8 Aug 1954, Mönchengladbach, Germany. Dance Therapist. Education: MA, Free University Berlin, 1980; MA, California State University, Hayward, 1987; Certificate in Authentic Movement, Centre for the Study of Authentic Movement, Eastchester, New York, 1991. Appointments: Dance Therapist, San Francisco's Mayor's Council for the Disabled, California, USA; Dance Therapist, Coordinator, Creative Arts Therapy Programme, Booth Memorial Hospital, Flushing, New York; Dance Therapy Educator and Supervisor, Vienna, Austria, and Berlin, Germany; Currently Clinical Dance Therapist and Educator. Publications: Mary Wigman: The Origins of Expressive Dance, 1991; Possibilities of using Dance Therapy to master our past: Dance Therapy with Jewish Senior Citizens, 1994. Honours: Co-organiser, 1st International Clinical Conference on Dance Therapy, NKS, Berlin, Germany, 1994. Memberships: Member of The Academy of Dance Therapists Registered; American Dance Therapy Association, Columbia, Maryland; Gesellschaft für Tanzforschung, Bremen. Hobbies: Swimming; Dancing; Reading. Address: Roemer, Riemannstr 4, 10961 Berlin, Germany.

OBRAMS Gunta Iris, b. 2 Sept 1953, Germany. Physician. m. Malcolm Patterson, 21 Dec 1975, 1 son. Education: BS, 1977; MD, 1977; MPH, 1982; PhD, 1988. Appointments: Medical Officer, 1986-89; Deputy Branch Chief, 1989-90; Branch Chief, 1990-. Publications: Epidemiology and Biology of Multiple Mycloma, 1991. Honours: Delta Omega, 1982; Phi Beta Kappa, 1988; PHS Achievement Medal, 1989; PHS Commendation Medal, 1990. Memberships: Fellow, American College of Preventive Medicine; Society for Epidemiologic Research; American Public Health Association. Hobbies: Golf; Tennis; Swimming. Address: National Cancer Institute, 6130 Executive Blvd 535, Bethesda, MD 20892, USA.

ODELL William D, b. 11 June 1929. Professor, Chairman, Department of Internal Medicine, University of Utah. m. Margaret F Reilly, 19 Aug 1950, 4 sons, 1 daughter. Education: MD, University of Chicago, 1956; PhD, Phsiology, George Washington University, 1965; MACP, American College of Physicians, 1988. Appointments: Internship, King County Hospital, Seattle, 1956-57; Endocrinology & Metabolism Fellow, Washington, 1958-59; Chief Resident in Medicine, University Hospital, University of Washington, 1959-60; Senior Investigator, Attending Physician, National Cancer Institute, Bethesda, 1960-65; Associate Professorial Lecturer, George Washington University, 1965-66; Head, Endocrinology Service, National Institute of Child Health & Human Development, Bethesda, 1966; Associate Professor, University of California, 1966-68; Professor, UCLA School of Medicine, 1968-75; Chairman, Harbor-UCLA Medical Center, 1972-80; Professor, University of California, 1976-80; Visiting Professor, University of Auckland, New Zealand, 1979-80; Professor, University of Utah College of Medicine, 1980-. Publications: Over 300 scientific publications; 7 books. Honours: University of Chicago, Distinguished Alumni; Science & Technology Governor's Award, Utah, 1987; Endocrine Society Distinguished Leadership Award, 1991; Western Society for Clinical Investigation, Mayo Soley Award, 1993. Memberships: American Society Clinical Investigation; Association of American Physicians; Endocrine Society; Western Association of Physicians; American Society of Andrology; Society of Pediatric Research; Western Society of Clinical Investigation; American Physicians Society. Hobbies: Golf; Backpacking; Fly Fishing; Running; Cross Country Skiing. Address: Department of Medicine, 50 North Medical Drive, Salt Lake City, UT 84132, USA.

ODENDAAL H, b. 17 July 1942, Vrede, South Africa. Professor of Obstetrics & Gynaecology. m. Elizabeth Schobort, 4 Dec 1976, 1 son, 1 daughter. Education: MB, ChB, University Pretoria; MMed, cum laude, University Stellenbosch. Appointments: Senior Lecturer, University Stellenbosch; Professor, Chairman, Department of Obstetrics & Gynaecology, University of the Orange Free State. Publications: Ginekologie, 1986; Decision Making in Obstetrics, 1990; Clinical Gynaecology, 1993; More than 100 articles in scientific journals. Honours: Albert Strating Medal of South African Academy of Science & Art for Community Medicine; FOGSI Rallis Oration, 1993. Memberships: South African Society of Obstetricians & Gynaecologists; Royal College of Obstetrics & Gynaecology; South African College of Medicine; International Society for the Study of Hypertension in Pregnancy. Hobbies: Hiking; Bird Watching; Classical Music. Address: Department of Obstetrics & Gynaecology, PO Box 19063, 7505 Tugerberg, South Africa.

ODUNUGA James Olumuyiwa, b. 27 Nov 1960, Lagos, Nigeria. Artist; Tchr. m. Folake Odunuga, 2 Nov 1991, 2 s. Education: NCE: Nigeria Cert in Educ, Fine & Applied Art, Fed Coll of Educ, Abeokuta. Appointments: Art Instr; Yth Dev, Fed Min Educ. Creative Works: paintings, num, incl: Abstract Drummer with 4 Drums, 1994; Gwoje Player, 1988; Drummer Traditional, 1987; Lake Scene, 1994. Honours: Life Mbr Cert, Fine Arts Student Assn. Hobbies: Paintings; Music. Address: Fed Gov Coll, PMB 1054, Idoani, Ondo State, Nigeria.

OEHLING Albert K, b. 19 Aug 1928, Granada, Spain. Professor; Doctor. m. Blanca Duran, 3 sons, 3 daughters. Education: MB, University of Granada, 1955; MD, University of Granada, 1956; Specialist in Internal Medicine, Allergie Forschungs-Institut, Bad Lippspringe, Germany, 1960; Specialist in Allergology & Clinical Immunology, University of Navarra, 1970; Specialist in Immunology, University of Navarra, 1970; Dr (Honoris Causa), University of Montevideo, Uruguay, 1991; Clinical Professor, Internal Medicine, South Florida University, 1982. Appointments: Resident, Assistant Professor, Clinica de Patologia Medica, University of Granada, 1955-56; Resident, Krankenhaus Sued, Medizinische Klinik Luebeck, Germany, 1957; Resident, Allergologie Forschungsinstitut und Asthmaklinik, Bad Lippspringe, Germany, 1958-59; Consultant, Allergologie Forschungsinstitut, Bad Lippspringe, Germany, 1959-61; Professor, University of Navarra, Spain, 1961-93. Memberships include: European Academy of Allergology & Clinical Immunology; Deutsche Gesellschaft für Allergie und Immunitatsforschung; Spanish Society of Allergology & Clinical Immunology; Gesellschaft für Immunology. Address: Dept Allergology, University Clinic Aptd 192, Pamplona 31080, Spain.

OEHME Frederick Wolfgang, b. 14 Oct 1933, Leipzig, Germany. Veterinarian; Toxicologist. m. Pamela Sheryl Ford, 2 Oct 1981, 1 s, 4 d. Education: BS, Biological Science, 1957, DVM, Veterinary Medicine, 1958, Cornell University, Ithaca, NY; MS, Toxicology and Medicine, Kansas State University, Manhattan, KS, 1962; Dr Med Vet, Pathology, Justus Liebig University, Giessen, Germany, 1964; Radioisotope training, Oak Ridge Institute of Nuclear Studies, TN, 1967; PhD, Toxicology, University of Missouri, Columbia, 1969. Career includes: NIH, Special Postdoctoral Fellow in Toxicology, University of Missouri, 1966-69; Director of Comparative Toxicology Laboratories, 1969-, Professor of Toxicology, Medicine and Physiology, 1973-, Kansas State University. Publications: 650 Scientific papers published as books or in professional journals including: Toxicity of Heavy Metals in the Environment, Part 1 and 2, 1978, 1979; Textbook of Large Animal Surgery, 2nd edition, 1988; Co-author, The Effects of Various Dietary Zinc Concentrations in the Biological Interactions of Zinc, Copper and Iron in Rats, in Biological Trace Elements Res, 1991; 560 Papers presented to national and international professional and scientific groups. Honours include: Fellow, American College of Veterinary Toxicologists, 1962; Fellow, American Academy of Clinical Toxicology,

1976; Kansas Veterinary Medical Association President's Oustanding Committee Member Award, 1992; John Doull Award, Central States Society of Toxicology, 1994; International Guest Professor, University Medallion of Azabu University, Japan, 1994. Hobbies: Travel; Reading; Walking Tours. Address: Comparative Toxicology Laboratories, Kansas State University, Manhattan, KS 66506-5606, USA.

OFFOBOCHE Matthias Oko, b. 30 Dec 1936, Ugaga, Yala, Nigeria. Medicine. m. Juliana Odo, 4 Oct 1969, 3 s, 3 d. Education: MB; BCh; BAO, National University of Ireland, 1966; MRCOG, 1973; FMCOG, 1981; FWACS, 1982; FRCOG, 1987; FICS, 1991. Appointments: Medical Superintendent, Joint Hospital, Ikom, 1969-71; Consultant Obstetrician and Gynaecologist, Moniaya Hospital, 1973-78; Currently, Proprietor and Medical Director, Offoboche Specialist Hospital, Okuku, Nigeria. Honours: Chieftaincy title of NTUL Ochima Biji of Ikom; Distinguished Medical Practitioner of Nigeria, 1993; Fellow Institute of Sales Management of Nigeria, 1994. Memberships: Irish, British and Nigerian Medical Associations; Society of Gynaecologists of Nigeria; International Federation of Gynaecologists. Hobbies: National Politics; Gaming. Address: Ugalashi, 61 Mission Road, Igoli, Box 80, Ogoja, Nigeria.

OGDEN Thomas Henry, b. 4 Dec 1946, New York City, New York, USA. Psychiatrist; Psychoanalyst. m. Sandra Prissy, 29 Aug 1970, 2 s. Education: BA, Amherst College, Phi Beta Kappa; MD, Yale University. Appointments: Director, Center for the Advanced Study of the Psychoses, San Francisco. Publications: Books, Projective Identification and Psychotherapeutic Technique; The Matrix of the Mind; The Primitive Edge of Experience; Subjects of Analysis. Memberships: International Psychoanalytical Association; American Psychoanalytic Association; American Psychiatric Association. Hobbies: Squash. Address: 306 Laurel Street, San Francisco, CA 94118, USA.

OGLE Clive William, b. 21 Aug 1933, Penang, Malaya. Medical Practitioner. m. Eileen Ogle, 11 June 1960, 1 son, 2 daughters. Education: MB, BS (Malaya), with distinction in Obstetrics and Gynaecology; PhD (West Australia); CBiol; FIBiol. Appointments: Houseman, Orthopaedics and General Medicine, 1958-59; Medical Officer, Singapore General Hospital, 1959-60; Assistant Lecturer in Pharmacology, 1960-63, Lecturer in Pharmacology, 1963-69, University of Singapore; Riker Research Fellow, University of Western Australia, 1964-67; Senior Lecturer in Pharmacology, 1969-76, Reader in Pharmacology, 1976-82, Professor of Pharmacology, Head of Department, 1982-94, Deputy Director, School of Postgraduate Medical Education and Training, 1994-, University of Hong Kong; Commonwealth Fellow and Registrar, Department of Clinical Pharmacology, St Bartholomew's Hospital, University of London, England, 1973-74. Publications: Over 340 research papers, chapters in books, abstracts and technical papers. Memberships: British Pharmacological Society; British Medical Association; New York Academy of Sciences; Fellow, Institute of Biology, UK. Hobbies: Chess; Driving. Address: School of Postgraduate Medical Education and Training, Faculty of Medicine, The University of Hong Kong, 1/F Patrick Manson Building South Wing, 7 Sassoon Road, Hong Kong.

OGUEH Onome, b. 19 Jan 1964, Nigeria. Obstetrician and Gynaecologist. m. Mabel Erebor, 4 June 1993, 1 daughter. Education: MB, BS; MRCOG; MFFP. Appointments: Currently Registrar, Obstetrics and Gynaecology. Honours: Best Graduating Student in Medicine. Hobbies: Music; Squash; Travel. Address: 33 Palamon Court, Cooper's Road, London SE1 5EE, England.

OGUNSANWO Olugbenga Adeleke, b. 12 Aug 1956, Ibadan, Nigeria. Obstetrician and Gynaecologist. m. Olufunmiso Oyediran, 10 Dec 1983. Education: MB, BS, University of Ibadan, 1979; MRCOG, 1985; Diploma in Addictive Behaviour, 1994. Appointments: Registrar in Obstetrics/Gynaecology, Musgrove Park Hospital, Taunton, England, 1984-86; Registrat in Obstetrics/Gynaecology, Cuckfield Hospital, Cuckfield, 1989-91; Locum Consultant, Obstetrics, Gynaecology, Princess Royal Hospital, Haywards Heath, 1991-92; Currently Senior Medical Officer, Director of Health Care, HM Prison, Swaleside. Memberships: Medical Protection Society. Hobby: Preaching the Gospel. Address: 9 Goosander Way, Thamesmead West, London SE28 0ER, England.

OH Teik Ewe, b. 15 May 1945, Georgetown, Australia, Physician. m. Lala Ann Irene Tabecki, 8 May 1976, 1 son, 1 daughter. Education: MB (Queensland); MD (Queensland); FRCP (Edinburgh); FRCP (London);

FRACP; FRCA; FANZCA; FFICANZCA; FHKAM. Appointments: Resident Medical Officer, Brisbane Hospital, Queensland; Resident Medical Officer, Royal Canberra Hospital, Australian Capital Territory; Senior House Officer, Whittington Hospital, London, England; Registrar, Royal Free Hospital, London; Registrar, Sir Charles Gairdner Hospital, Perth, Western Australia; Director, Intensive Care Unit, Woden Valley Hospital, Canberra, Australian Capital Territory; Head, Department of Intensive Care, Sir Charles Gairdner Hospital, Perth; Currently Chairman, Department of Anaesthesia and Intensive Care, Chinese University, Prince of Wales Hospital, Shatin, Hong Kong. Publications: Butterworth's Intensive Care Manual (editor), 4th edition, 1995; 60 book chapters; 135 papers in idexed journals. Memberships: Australian Medical Association; British Medical Association; Hong Kong Medical Association; Australian and New Zealand Intensive Care Society; Hong Kong Society of Critical Care Medicine; Western Pacific Association of Critical Care; Australian Society of Anaesthetists; Royal Colleges of Physicians of London, Edinburgh, Australasia; Royal College of Anaesthetists; Australian and New Zealand College of Anaesthetists. Hobbies: Sailing; Saxophone. Address: Department of Anaesthesia and Intensive Care, Chinese University of Hong Kong, Prince of Wales Hospital, Shatin, Hong Kong.

OH William, b. 22 May 1931, Philippines. m. Mary Q-Ang, 4 June 1960, 1 son, 1 daughter. Education: MA, honorary, Brown University School of Medicine; DSc, Honorary, Rhode Island College. Appointments: Professor of Pediatrics & OB/GYN, University of California School of Medicine, Los Angeles; Sylvia Kay Hassenfeld Professor, Chairman, Department of Pediatrics, Brown University School of Medicine. Publications: Numerous professional scientific articles in journals. Honours include: Rhode Island Governor's Award for Scientific Achievement, 1985; Virginia Aggar Award, American Academy of Pediatrics, 1995. Memberships include: American Academy of Pediatrics; American Institute of Nutrition; American Society of Photobiology; The American Thoracic Society; European Society for Pediatric Research. Address: 593 Eddy Street, Providence, RI 02903, USA.

OHNO Shigeaki, b. 21 Aug 1944, Hakodate, Japan. Ophthalmology. m. Chizuko Onoe, 5 Sept 1971, 2 s, 1 d. Education: MD, Doctor of Medical Science. Appointments: Associate Professor, Department of Orthalmology, Hokkaido University, School of Medicine, Sapporo, Japan; Professor & Chairman, Department of Orthalmology, Yokohama City University, School of Medicine, Yokohama, Japan. Publications: Ocular Immunology Today, 1990. Address: Department of Opthalmology, Yokohama City University, School of Medicine, 3-9 Fukuura, Kanazawa-ku, Yokohama, 236 Japan.

OHRY Abraham, b. 24 Sept 1948, Natanya, Israel. Physician; Associate Professor of Rehabilitation Medicine. m. Karin Ohry-Kossoy MA, 3 April 1973, 2 daughters. Education: MD, 1973, Diploma, Rehabilitation Medicine, School of Continuing Medical Education, 1978, Tel Aviv University. Appointments include: Consultant, Physiotherapy School, 1982-80, currently Director, Department of Neuro-Rehabilitation, Sheba Medical Centre, Tel Hashomer; Senior Lecturer, 1982-88, Chairman, School of Occupational Therapy, 1984-88, Associate Professor, Rehabilitation Medicine, 1989-, Sackler School of Medicine, Tel Aviv University; Senior Consultant Physician, Israeli Ministry of Defence and Israeli Medical Corps, 1982-; Other consultancies. Publications: Co-author: Spinal cord injuries in the 19th century-background research and treatment, 1989; The Feldsher: Medical, Sociological and Historical Aspects of Practitioners of Medicine with below University Level Education, 1992; Introduction to Rehabilitation Medicine (co-editor), 1990; Co-author, articles including: The prevalence of hypertension, ischemic heart disease and diabetes in traumatic spinal cord injured patients and amputees, 1989; Hyperprosexia in the traumatic brain injured patients: a forgotten term to an old problem, 1990; Upper limb functions regained in quadriplegia: a hybrid computerized neuromuscular stimulation system; Arm crank ergometry in spinal cord injured patients, 1990; Assessment of PTSD: Validation of the revised PTSD inventory, 1993. Honours: Maimonides Fellow, Australoasian Jewish Medical Federation, 1990; Research grants. Memberships include: Chairman, Israeli Association of Rehabilitation Medicine; Israel Medical Association; Israeli Society of Sports Medicine; American Society of Neuro-rehabilitation; International Medical Society of Paraplegia, American Spinal Injury Association, American Academy of Physical Medicine and Rehabilitation. Hobbies: Music; History; Art of medicine; Literature; Medicine. Address: Rehabilitation Centre, Sheba Medical Centre, Tel Hashomer 52621,

Israel.

OJUKWU Clifford Ikechukwu, b. 6 May 1959, Onitsha, Nigeria. Obstetrician; Gynaecologist. m. Chinwe Ezeiru, 8 June 1991, 2 sons. Education: MBBS, University of Ibadan, 1984; MRCOG, London, 1992. Appointments: Obstetrician and Gynaecologist, Alexandra Hospital, Redditch, England. Publications: Thromboembolism in Pregnancy and Heparin Hypersensitivity, 1995. Memebrships: Medical Defence Union; British Medical Association. Hobbies: Squash; Badminton; Computing. Address: Gynaecology Department, Alexandra Hospital, Redditch, Worcestershire, England.

OKTAY Ahmet, b. 28 Sep 1953, Ankara, Turkey. Medical Doctor. m. Dr Sule Oktay, 29 Jun 1979, 1 s. Education: MD, 1976; Cardiologist. Appointments: Research Assistant, Departments of Internal Medicine and Cardiology, Hacettepe University School of Medicine, Ankara, Turkey; Currently, Head, Cardiology Department, Marmara University School of Medicine, Istanbul, Turkey. Publications: 2 Books on Internal Medicine, translations from English to Turkish; Over 40 Articles and Case Reports, in English and Turkish. Membership: Turkish Society of Cardiology. Hobbies: Classical Music; Playing Tennis. Address: Marmara University Hospital, Department of Cardiology, Altunizade, Istanbul, Turkey.

OKUSUN Onoagbe Henry, b. 17 Feb 1956, Nigeria. Obstetrican and Gynaecologist. m. 31 Mar 1984, 3 sons. Education: MB, BS; MRCOG, Royal College of Obstetricians and Gynaecologists; MFFP; MMedSc, Assisted Reproduction, 1995; Training, National Postgraduate College of Nigeria. Appointments: Registrar, Obstetrics and Gynaecology, Whipps Cross Hospital, England; Registrar, Obstetrics and Gynaecology, St Bartholomew's Hospital, London. Honours: National Merit Scholarship, 1978. Hobbies: Chess; Swimming; Lawn tennis. Address: 2 Arrowhead Court, James Lane, Leytonstone, London E11 1NY, England.

OLDHAM Keith Thomas, b. 24 Aug 1950, St Louis, MO, USA. Pediatric Surgeon. m. Karen S Guice MD, 9 May 1981, 2 s. Education: MD, Medical College of VA, 1976. Appointments: Assistant Professor of Surgery, University of TX, Medical Branch, 1983-85; Associate Professor of Surgery, University of MI, 1985-91; Currently, Professor and Chief, Division of Pediatric Surgery, Duke University Medical Center. Publications: Surgery: Scientific Principles and Practice, 1992; 75 Peer reviewed articles. Honours: AOA, 1975; ACS Fellow, Australia and New Zealand, 1992. Memberships: American Surgical Association; Society of University Surgeons; Association for Academic Surgery; American Pediatric Surgery Association. Hobbies: Running; White Water Canoeing. Address: Box 3815, Duke University Medical Center, Durham, NC 27710, USA.

OLESKOWICZ Jeanette, b. 10 Oct 1956, New York City, New York, USA. Medicine; Military Psychiatrist. Education: BA; MS; MD; DC; Psychiatry Internship and Residency, DD Eisenhower Army Medical Center, Georgia; Diplomate of American Board of Medical Examiners; Combat Casualty Care Training. Appointments: US Immigration Officer; Banking Administration; Adult Education Teacher; Instructor for Military Paraprofessional Personnel in area of Mental Health; Stress Management; Staff Psychiatrist, US Army, Vicenza, Italy. Publications: Psychotherapy No Bovvice for the Aged, 1994. Honours: National Service Defense Medal, for serving the Military during Operation Desert Storm, 1993; Us Army Indoctrination, 1990. Memberships: American Medical Association; American Psychiatric Association. Hobbies: Roller Skating; Travel; Church Activities; Prayer Group. Address: c/o John Oleskowicz, 2254 Massachusetts Avenue, Naperville, Illinois 60565, USA.

OLIVER Guy Fergus, b. 24 Jul 1957, Auckland, New Zealand. Dermatologist. m. Carol Ann Oliver, 6 Sep 1986, 2 s, 1 d. Education: BHB; MB Ch B; FRACP. Appointments: Registrar, Department Dermatology, Auckland Hospital; Fellow, Department Dermatology, Mayo Clinic, Rochester, MN, 1988; Senior Registrar, St John's Hospital for Diseases of Skin, London, 1988-89; Currently: Private Dermatologist; Visiting Specialist, Auckland Hospital; Consultant in Dermatopathology, Medlab Limited. Publications: 19 Professional Publications, 1989-, including: Cutaneous follicular lymphoma, in Current Problems in Dermatology, 1989; Current management of urticaria, in New Ethicals, in progress; Co-author, Inflamatory elastolysis in a patient with dermatomyositis, in progress. Memberships: New Zealand Society of Dermatologists; New Zealand Society of Pathologists; Non-Resident

Associate, American Society of Dermato- pathology; Executive Member, Australian Society of Dermatopathology. Hobbies: Soccer; Squash; Jogging; Chess; Music. Address: 15 Gilgit Road, Epsom, Auckland, 1003, New Zealand.

OLIVIERI Nancy Fern, b. 1 June 1954, Hamilton, Canada. Physician. Education: BSc; MD; Fellow, Royal College of Physicians & Surgeons of Canada. Appointments: Research Fellow, Harvard University, 1984-86; Assistant Professor, Pediatrics University of Toronto, Canada, 1986-92; Career Scientist, Ministry of Health, 1986-. Publications: Over 80 articles on Hemoglobinopathies, Iron Chillation Therapy. Honours: Recipient of Research Grants and Fellowships, Medical Research Council of Canada, Canadian Heart & Stroke. Memberships: American Society of Hematology; American Society of Pediatric Hematology & Oncology; Society for Pediatric Research. Hobbies: Tennis; Travel; Music. Address: The Hospital for Sick Children, 555 University Avenue, Toronto, M5G 1X8, Canada.

OLKEN Melissa Hendrix, b. 22 Jan 1956, Chicago, IL, USA. Physician. m. Norman M Olken, 28 Jun 1987, 2 s. Education: BS Education, University of MI, 1978; MS, Exercise Physiology, 1980, PhD, Nutritional Sciences, 1988, MD, 1988, University of IL. Appointments: Internal Medicine Residency, House Staff, University of MI Medical Center, 1988-91; Physician, Scientist, Ann Arbor VA Medical Center, 1991-94; Lecturer, University of MI School of Medicine, 1991-94; Currently: Core Faculty, Department of Internal Medicine, St Joseph Mercy Hospital, Ann Arbor; Adjunct Assistant Profesor, Human Nutrition, School of Public Health, University of MI. Publications: 3 Peer Reviewed Articles, 1988-, including: Co-author, Hydration of the Fat-Free Body in Children During Maturation, in Human Biology, 1984; 3 Chapters in Books; 5 Abstracts, 1981-93. Honour: NIH Pre-Doctoral Clinical Nutrition Fellowship, 1986-88. Memberships: AMA; American College of Physicians; American Institute of Nutrition; American Society for Clinical Nutrition; American Diatetic Association. Address: Medicine Faculty Associates, 5333 McAuley Dr, Ste 5008-5010, Ipsiland, MI 48197, USA.

OLSEN Ingar, b. 11 Sep 1942, Drammen, Norway. Dentist. m. Britt Spinnangr, 4 Aug 1967, 1 son, 1 daughter. Education: Dr Odont. Appointments: Dental Instructor; Associate Professor; Professor. Publications: Contributor of over 100 articles on microbiology, oral surgery, oral medicine, pharmacology and toxicology. Honour: Doctor Odontologiae, University of Oslo, 1976. Memberships: IADR; ASM. Hobby: Mountain Hiking. Address: Department of Oral Biology, Dental Faculty, University of Oslo, POB 1052 Blindern, 0316 Oslo, Norway.

OLSEN Jan Nymark, b. 25 Aug 1967, Glostrup, Denmark. Chiropractor. Education: BSc, Chiropractic; Doctor of Chiropractic. Appointments: Currently Associate Chiropractor, Worthing Chiropractic Clinic, Worthing, Suxxex, England. Memberships: British Chiropractic Association; Sacro-Occipital Technique Organisation of Europe. Hobby: Golf. Address: Worthing Chiropractic Clinic, 25 Shakespeare Road, Worthing, West Sussex BN11 4AS, England.

OLSZEWER Efrain, b. 3 Dec 1954, Bolivia. Clinical Director. m. Melany Olszewer, 5 Oct 1980, 1 son, 2 daughters. Education: MD, Universidad Mayor De San Simon; Revalidated, Universidad Federal De Juiz De Fora. Appointments: Internship, Hospital Viedma, Bolivia, Incor, Fmusp, Cardiology, Brazil; Visitor Program, Jewish Home for Ageing, USA. Publications: 7 Health Books; 1 Medical Book; Numerous Articles. Memberships: President, Medical Brazilian Oxidology Society; Scientific Director, Sobramo Brazilian Society of Orthomolecular Medicine; The Rheumatoid Foundation. Honours: Lecturer, 6 times, American College for the Advancement of Medicine. Hobbies: Soccer; Reading; Basket Ball; Tennis. Address: Rua Campevas 211, Perdizes, 05016-010 Sao Paulo, Brazil.

OMELUTA Victor Pavlovich, b. 1 November 1941, Kurakhovo, Ukraine. Doctor of Plant Protection. m. Kurakhovo, 30 October 1965, 2 daughters. Education: Diploma, Kharkov Agriculture Institute, 1967; Diploma, Ukrainian Academy of Agriculture, Kyiv, 1972. Appointments: Agronomist, 1961-69; Postgraduate, Institute of Plant Protection, 1969-72; Scientist, Institute of Plant Protection, 1972-75; Head of Labour, 1975-. Publications: The photoperiod reaction of the larvae of Grapholitha molesta, 1974; On Photoperiodic reactivation of diapausing pronymphae of Pyrausta sticticalis, 1981; Co-author: Physiological state and reproductive ability of Codlin Moth after chemical treatments of orchards, 1978; Co-author: Influence of photoperiod on fecundity of beet webworm, 1983; Recomendation in control of orchards in USSR, 1981;

Registration of pest and diseases agricultural crops, 1986; Determinant main pests of field crops, 1987; Reference book of protection field crops, 1985, 1993; The pests of agricultural crops and forest ranges, 1987, 1988, 1989. Memberships: Ukrainian Entomological Society. Hobbies: Flowers and Citrus. Address: Generala Naumova Street, 37-b, Flat 77, Kyiv 252164, Ukraine.

OMENN Gilbert Stanley, b. 30 Aug 1941, Chester, PA, USA. Professor and Dean. m. Martha Darling, 1 Jan 1984, 2 s, 1 d. Education: AB, Princeton University, 1961; MD, Harvard Medical School, 1965; PhD, University of WA, 1972. Appointments include: Science and Public Policy Fellow, Brookings Institute, Washington DC, 1981-82; Professor of Environmental Health, University of WA, 1981-; Dean, School of Public Health and Community Medicine, University of WA, 1982-. Publications: Author and co-author of 117 peer reviewed published papers concerning experimental and clinical research; 171 Review and policy papers; Editor and co-editor of 14 books and 38 book reviews; Over 100 abstracts. Honours include: US Public Health Service, Special Fellow, 1969-71; Fellow, National Genetics Foundation, 1971-72; Research Award, National Institute of General Medical Sciences, 1972-76; White House Fellow, Atomic Energy Commission, MD, 1973-74; Howard Hughes Medical Institute Investigator, 1976-77; Fellow, American College of Physicians, 1978. Memberships include: Institute of Medicine; National Academy of Sciences; Western Association of Physicians; Royal Society of Medicine, London; Board, National Research Council; Board, Biomembrane Institute; Board, Fred Hutchinson Cancer Research Center; American Association for the Advancement of Science; Many Advisory boards and Committees. Hobbies: Political Involvement; Music including piano and supporting local syphonies; Tennis. Address: University of Washington, Dean's Office, School of Public Health & Community Medicine, Box 357230, Seattle, WA 98195-7230, USA.

OMER George A Jr, b. 23 Dec 1922. Medicine. m. Wendie V Omer, 2 s. Education: BA, Chemistry, Fort Hays Kansas State University, 1944; MD, University of Kansas, 1950; MS, Orthopaedic Surgery, Baylor University, 1955; FACS, 1960. Appointments: Assistant Clinical Professor, University of Colorado, 1961-63; Clinical Associate Professor, University of Texas, 1966-70; Professor, University of New Mexico, 1970-. Publications: 123 Peer Reviewed Papers; 54 Chapters; 70 Abstracts; 2 Books. Honours: Alumni Achievement Award, Fort Hays Kansas State University, 1973; Recognition Award for Devotion to Education, American Society for Surgery of the Hand, 1989. Memberships: American Orthopaedic Association; American College of Surgeons; American Society of Surgery of the Hand; Western Orthopaedic Association. Hobbies: Single Airplane Pilot. Address: 316 Big Horn Ridge Road, CE, Saudia Heights, Alberquerque, New Mexico 87122, USA.

OMURA Emily Fowler, b. 19 Oct 1938, Oklahoma City, Oklahoma, USA. Medicine. m. Dr George A Omura, 27 Dec 1962, 1 s, 3 d. Education: BA, Barnard College, New York, 1960; MD, Cornell University Medical College, New York, 1964; Board-Certified in Dermatology, 1970; Board-Certified in Dermatopathology, 1974. Appointments: Clinical Instructor in Dermatology, Cornell University Medical College, 1969-70; Instructor, University of Alabama, Birmingham, Alabama, 1970-71; Assistant Professor, University of Alabama, Birmingham, Alabama, 1971-75; Associate Professor, University of Alabama, Birmingham, Alabama, 1975-83; Professor of Dermatology & Director of Dermatopathology, University of Alabama Medical Center, Birmingham, Alabama, 1983-. Publications: Co-Author, Histologic Variation in the Glucagonoma Syndrome, 1986; Editor, Dermatological Disorders, 1988; Benign and Malignant Adnexal Tumors, 1990. Honours: National Merit Scholar, 1956; Phi Beta Kappa, 1960. Memberships: Fellow, American Academy of Dermatology; Fellow, American Society of Dermatopathology; Alabama Dermatology Society; American Medical Association. Hobbies: Dance Aficionado; Sewing; Reading; Art History. Address: Department of Dermatology, University of Alabama at Birmingham, Medical Center, Birmingham, AL 35294, USA.

ONABOWALE Babatunde Oladipo, b. 5 Dec 1942, Lagos, Nigeria. Medicine; Orthopaedic Surgery. m. Charis Onabowale, 25 Aug 1973, 3 sons, 2 daughters. Education: MA; MB; Bch; BAO; TCD; FMCS; FWACS; FICS. Appointments: Chief Consultant Orthopaedic Surgeon, Head of Research Education Training, National Orthopaedic Hospital, WHO Collaborating Centre, Lagos; Honorary Consultant to University Postgraduate Nsukka, Enugu; Medical Director & Chief Consultant

Orthopaedic Surgeon. Publications: Supracondylar Fracture of The Humerus in Children and Industrial Crush Injuries of The Hand; Several other publications. Honour: Distinction in Physics, TCD Metric. Memberships: Overseas Fellow (BOA, Menter Siwt, Sirot, WOC, Vice President of WAOA, W. Hobbies: Music; Sports; Golf; Photography. Address: National Orthopaedic Hospital, Enugu, Nigeria.

ONAT Teoman, b. 8 Nov 1931, Istanbul. Pediatric. m. Ruth Fontana, 25 Apr 1959, 1 son, 1 daughter. Education: BSc; MD; PhD. Appointments: Resident, Zurich Kinderspital; Pediatrician in Chief for New Born Department, Admiral Bristol Hospital, Istanbul; Assistant Professor, Associate Professor, Professor of Pediatrics, Cerrahpasa Medical Faculty, University Istanbul. Publications: Books on Paediatric Cardiology, Development and Maturation of Girls During Adolescence; Over 150 papers in the field of Pediatric Cardiology, Adolescence, Sexual Development, Skeletal Development. Honours: International Schleussner Prize for Radiology, Montreal, Canada, 1962; Eczacibasi Scientific Award, 1976; Myrtle Watt Award, 1990; Haktan Scientific Award in Pediatrics, 1995. Memberships: President, Turkish Paediatric Association; President, Association of European Paediatric Cardiologists; Board of Turkish Cardiology Society. Hobbies: Jazz; Sports. Address: Cerrahpasa Tip Fak, Cocuk Klinigi, Cerrahpasa, Istanbul.

OPHIR Yael, b. 17 Aug 1932, Jerusalem, Israel. Dance-Movement Therapist. m. Gideon Ophir, 30 Apr 1959, 2 sons. Education: Feldenkraize Practitioners Programme, 1980-83; Dance-Therapy Programme, Antioch and Haifa Universities, 1981; Registered Dance-Movement Therapist; Authorised Practitioner, Feldenkraize Method. Appointments: Therapist, Psychiatric Day-Care Unit for Children, Sheba Hospital; Teacher, Superviser, Levinsky College, Tel Aviv. Publications: Articles: I belong to Myself, 1983, published in Germany, 1986, 1988; To move, to touch, to create meaning, 1987, published in Germany, 1990; Interaction, Group Therapy with Autistic Children, 1992. Memberships: Israeli Association of Creative and Expressive Therapy; American Dance Therapy Association; Israel Association of Growth and Development. Address: 7 Hardof Street, Ramat Efal 52960, Israel.

OPPENHEIMER Agnes, b. 19 Apr 1948, Neuilly Sur Seine 92, France. Psychoanalyst. div. 1 s, 1 d. Education: Master in Philosophy and Psycology; Licensed Psychologist; Doctorate in Psychology. Appointments: Psychologist Centre, Alfred Binet, Paris, 1974-84; Lecturer, University of Paris V, 1980-89; Associate Professor of Clinical Psychology, Paris V, 1989-. Publications: Le Choix du Sexe, 1980; The Wish for Sex Change: A Challenge to Psychoanalysis, 1991. Memberships: The Paris Psychoanalyst Society; International Psychoanalysts Association. Address: 134 Rue de Grenelle, 75007 Paris, France.

ORCHBERG Frank M, b. 7 Feb 1940, New York City, USA. Psychiatrist. m. Lynn J Wescott, 1 July 1962, 1 son, 2 daughters. Education: AB, Harvard, 1961; MD, Johns Hopkins, 1965; Resident Psychiatry, Stanford, 1969. Appointments: Associate Director, National Institute for Mental Health; Director, Michigan Department of Mental Health; Clinical Professor, Psychiatry; Adjunct Professor, Criminal Justice, Michigan University. Publications: Violence & The Struggle for Existence, co-editor, 1970; Victims of Terrorism, co-editor, 1982; Post Traumatic Therapy, editor, 1989. Honour: Best Expert Witnesses in America, Forensic Psychiatry, 1992. Memberships: International Society for Traumatic Stress Studies; American Board of Psychiatry & Neurology; Red Cross Disaster Volunteer; Primatology Field Research Volunteer. Address: 4211 Okemos Road #6, Okemos, MI 48864, USA.

OREN Joseph, b. 24 Mar 1932, Albany, NY, USA. Physician. m. Sonja Porter, 23 Nov 1979, 2 s, 2 d. Education: BA, Cornell University, 1953; MD, Cornel Medical School, 1956. Appointments: Practice of Allergy, Honolulu, 1963-70; Associate Medical Director, Syntex, 1971-79; Senior Director, Schering Fisons Agriculture, Vice President, Schering, Nelson Research & Development, Praxis Biologics; President, Clinicom Consultancy. Honours: Phi Beta Kappa, 1952; Alpha Omega Alpha, 1956; Allergy Foundation Fellowship, 1970; Board Certification Pediatrics, 1962; Allergy, 1972. Memberships: American Medical Association; American Academy of Allergy; American Thoracic Society; Royal Society of Medicine. Hobbies: Gardening; Wines; Skiing; Baseball; Cooking; Travel. Address: P O Box 2339, Napa, CA 94558, USA.

OREOPOULOS Dimitrios G, b. 24 May 1936, Alexandropolis, Greece. Physician; Nephrologist. m. Nancy Hooker, 19 Sep 1971, 3 s, 1 d. Education: MD; PhD; FRCPC; FACP; Corresponding Member Academy of Athens, Greece. Appointments: Intern, 1961, Resident, 1961-64, Chief Resident, 1965-66, Research Fellow, Hippokratean Hospital, Athens; Resident Fellow, Dialysis Unit, Queen's University of Belfast, Ireland, 1966-69; Research Fellow, Toronto Western Hospital, 1969-70; Currently, Director, Peritoneal Dialysis Unit, The Toronto Hospital, Western Division. Publications: Nephrology and Urology in the Aged Patient; Principles of Peritoneal Dialysis; Editor-in-Chief: Peritoneal Dialysis International; Humane Medicine; Geriatric Nephrology and Urology Journal. Honours: Charles Mickle Fellow, 1981; Gardiner Award, Metro Toronto Citizen of the Year, 1989; Distinguished Physician of The Year, Hellenic Medical Society, NY, 1993; National Torchbearer Award, American Kidney Fund, 1994. Memberships include: International Society of Nephrology; American Society of Nephrology; Canadian Society of Nephrology; Hellenic Society of Nephrology; President Elect, International Society of PD; Order of St Andrew the Apostle. Hobby: Volunteer Work. Address: c/o The Toronto Hospital, Western Division, 399 Bathurst Street, Suite 6 EW - 539, Toronto, Ontario, Canada, M5T 2S8.

ORFORD Robert Raymond, b. 18 Apr 1948, Winnipeg, Manituba, Canada. Physician. m. Dale Laura Stuart, 2 Jun 1972, 2 s, 1 d. Education: BSc, McGill University, Montreal, Canada, 1964-67; MD, CM, McGill University, Montreal, Canada, 1967-71; MS, Medicine, University of Minnesota, Mayo Graduate School of Medicine, Rochester, 1972-75; MPH, University of Washington, 1976; Certified by American Board of Internal Medicine; Certified by American Board of Preventivie Medicine; Certified by Royal College of Physicians and Surgeons of Canada. Appointments: Plant Physician, Dow Chemical Company, 1976-77; Occupational Medicine Consultant and Manager, Government of Alberta, Canada, 1977-84; Deputy Minister/Community Manager, Government of Alberta, Canada, 1985-88; Senior Associate Consultant, Mayo Clinic, Rochester, Minnesota, 1988-91; Consultant, Mayo Clinic, Rochester, Minnesota, 1991-. Publications: include, Pre-Employment and Periodic Physical Examiniation of Airline Pilots at the Mayo Clinic, 1939-1974, 1976; Hemorrhagic Pneumonitis Due to Inhalation of Resins Containing Trimellitic Anhydride, 1978; Epidemiologic and Immunologic Studies in Processors of the King Crab, 1985; Injury and Prevention, 1988. Honours: National Health Fellowship, Canada, 1975-76. Memberships: include, The Royal College of Physicians and Surgeons of Canada; American College of Preventative Medicine; Canadian Public Health Association; Alberta Medical Association; International Commission on Occupational Health; Aerospace Medical Association; Mayo History of Medicine Society; North Central Occupational Medical Association. Address: BA5A, Mayo Clinic, Rochester, Minnesota 66905, USA.

ORNE Martin Theodore, b. 16 Oct 1927, Austria. Psychiatrist. m. Emily Carota, 3 Feb 1962, 1 s, 1 d. Education: AB, 1948; AM, 1951; MD, 1955; PhD, 1958. Career includes: Director, Studies in Hypnosis Project, 1958-64, Senior Research Psychiatrist, 1960-64, Massachusetts Mental Health Center; Currently, Director, Unit for Experimental Psychiatry, Institute of Pennsylvania Hospital. Publications: Co-author, On the differential diagnosis of multiple personality in the forensic context, in International Journal of Clinical and Experimental Hypnosis, 1984; Co-author, Hypnosis, in Comprehensive Textbook of Psychiatry, 1989. Honours: Honoris Causa Doctor of Science, John F Kennedy University, 1980; Distinguished Scientific Award, Applications of Psychology, APA, 1986; Seymour Pollack Award, American Academy of Psychiatry and Law, 1991; Honoris Causa Doctoral Degree, Hofstra University, 1993. Memberships: Life Fellow, American Psychiatric Association; Fellow, Editor, 1961-92, President, 1971-73, Society for Clinical and Experimental Hypnosis. Hobbies: Art Collecting; Travel; Investments. Address: Institute of Pennsylvania Hospital, 111 North 49th Street, Philadelphia, PA 19139, USA.

ORR James Cameron, b. 10 Aug 1930, Paisley, Scotland. Teacher. m. Dr Robin D Moore, 1 s, 1 d. Education: BSc, Honours, Chemistry, Imperial College, London; ARCS; PhD, Chemistry, Glasgow University, Scotland. Appointments: Assistant Lecturer, Glasgow University; Research Chemist, Syntex Inc, Mexico City; Associate Professor of Biological Chemistry, Harvard Medical School; Currently, Professor of Biochemistry, Memorial University, Newfoundland, Canada. Publications: Biochemical Applications of Mass Spectometry: Hormones; Over 50 research papers. Hobbies: Sailing; Tennis; Scottish Country Dancing; Glassblowing. Address: 360 Hamilton Ave, St John's, Newfoundland, Canada, A1E 1K2.

ORRINGER Mark Burton, b. 19 Apr 1943, Pittsburgh, PA, USA. Thoracic Surgeon. m. Susan Michaels, 20 Jun 1964, 1 s, 1 d. Education: BA, 1963, MD, 1967, University of Pittsburgh, USA; Residency in General and Thoracic Surgery, The Johns Hopkins Hospital, 1967-73. Appointments: Assistant Professor of Surgery, 1973-76, Associate Professor of Surgery, 1976-80, Professor of Surgery, 1980-, Head of Section of Thoracic Surgery, 1985-, University of Michigan. Publications: Over 140 publications in peer reviewed surgical literature, 1970-, including: Over 70 book chapters in surgical textbooks, 1977-. Honours: Phi Beta Kappa, 1963; Alpha Omega Alpha, 1966. Memberships: American College of Surgeons; Society of University Surgeons; American Surgical Association; American Board of Thoracic Surgery. Address: Section of Thoracic Surgery, University of Michigan Medical Center, Taubman Health Care Center, 1500 East Medical Center Drive, 2110 Box 0344, Ann Arbor, MI 48109, USA.

ORTH David Nelson, b. 5 Mar 1933. Professor of Medicine. m. Linda Diana D'Errico, 9 Jun 1979, 1 s, 2 d. Education: ScB, Chemistry, Brown University, 1954; MD, Vanderbily University, 1962; John & Mary R Markle Scholar; Howard Hughes Medical Institute Investigator; Resident Scholar, Rockefeller Foundation, Bellagio Study Center, Italy; Secretary/Treasurer, The US Endocrine Society. Appointments: Instructor in Medicine, Johns Hopkins School of Medicine; Instructor in Medicine; Assistant Professor of Medicine; Associate Professor of Medicine; Profe anssor of Medicine; Professor of Molecular Physiology and Biophysics; Director, Division of Endocrinology, Vanderbilt University Medical Centre. Publications: 202 Articles, Chapters, Reviews including, The Adrenal Cortex in Williams Textbook of Endocrinology, 8th Edition, 1992. Honours: Fellow, American College of Physicians, 1971; Alpha Omega Alpha, Vanderbilt University, 1961; Sigma Xi, Vanderbilt University, 1967; Markle Scholar, 1968-73; Investigator, Howard Hughes Medical Institute, 1969-75. Memberships: American Association for Advancement of Science; American College of Physicians; American Federation of Clinical Research; American Society of Clinical Investigation; Association American Physicians; Endocrine Society; Endocrine Society of Republic of China; International Society of Endocrinology; Nashville Academy of Medicine; Southern Society for Clinical Investigation: New York Academy of Science. Hobbies: Bronze Sculpture; Trout Fishing. Address: Division of Endocrinology, Vanderbilt University Medical Center, Nashville, TN 37232, USA.

ORTIZ CABANILLAS Pedro, b. 31 July 1933, Cajamarca, Peru. Medical Surgeon. Education: MD, San Marcos University, Lima, 1974. Appointments: Assistant Neurologist, The Neurological Service, Hospital Central del Empleado, Lima, 1962; Fellow, Department of Neurology, University of Newcastle upon Tyne, England, 1969-70; Head, Department of Neurology, The National Hospital E Rebagliati, Lima, 1978-91; President, Peruvian Society of Psychiatry, Neurology & Neurosurgery, 1982-83; Dean, The Medical College of Peru, 1987-89; Member, National Commission for the Formulary & Registration of Drugs, Ministry of Health, 1991-92; Professor of Medicine, Neurology & Neuropsychology, San Marcos Uniersity, Lima; Professor of Psychophisiology, Faculty of Psychology, University of Lima. Publications: Subarachnoid Hemorrhage: A Follow up of 225 Patients, 1974; Cysticercosis of the Nervous System: A short-term follow up after its Treatment with Praziquantel, 1984; The National Guide of Farmacotherapeutics, 1993; The System of the Personality, 1994; Personality Disordeers due to Cerebral Lesions: A Reinterpretation, 1994. Honours: Gold Medal, Diploma al Merito Extraordinario, The Medical College of Peru, 1990; Diploma, The Medical Association of the Peruvian Institute of Social Security, 1994. Memberships: Peruvian Society of Neurology; Peruvian Society of Neurosurgery. Address: Rodolfo Beltran 155, Urb Sta Catalina, La Victoria, Lima 13, Peru.

OSBORN John Frederick, b. 5 Apr 1943, Portsmouth, England. University Teacher. m. Angela Spinelli, 17 Apr 1993, 1 d. Education: BSc, University of Durham, England; PhD, University of London, England; FRSS. Appointments: Senior Lecturer in Medical Demography, London School of Hygiene and Tropical Medicine, University of London; Currently, Professor of Epidemiological Methodology and Hygiene, University of Rome, La Sapienza. Publications: Statistical Exercises in Medical Research, 1979; Statistics in Dentistry, 1989. Membership: Fellow, Royal Statistical Society. Hobby: Sailing. Address: Via Tolmino 43-2, 00198 Rome, Italy.

OSBORNE Michael P, Surgeon. Education: University of London, England; Surgical Training, Royal College of Surgeons of England,

Charing Cross Hospital, St James' Hospital, Brompton Hospital. Appointments include: Honorary Lecturer, Royal Marsden Hospital and Institute of Cancer Research, London; Director, Strang-Cornell Breast Centre, New York City, USA; Chief, Breast Service, Attending Surgeon, Department of Surgery, The New York Hospital-Cornell Medical Centre; President, Strang Cancer Prevention Centre; Professor of Surgery, Cornell University Medical College; Visiting Associate Physician, The Rockefeller University Hospital; Head, research group, Cornell University Medical College; Head, Breast Cancer Research Laboratory, Member, Breast Service, Memorial Sloan-Kettering Cancer Centre, 1991. Publications: Contributor of over 100 articles on breast disease. Honours: Recipient of numerous prizes for professional services. Address: Strang-Cornell Breast Centre, 428 East 72nd Street, New York, NY 10021, USA.

OSEROFF Allen, b. 20 Jan 1953, Washington DC, USA. Cardiologist. m. Amy Oseroff, 20 Jan 1983, 2 s. Education: BS, University of Michigan, Ann Arbor, MI; MD, George Washington University, Washington DC. Career: Internist, US Army, 1983-85; Cardiologist, US Army, 1987; Currently, Cardiologist. Memberships: Fellow, American College of Physicians; Fellow, American College of Cardiologists. Hobbies: Sailing; Bicycles. Address: 620 South Memorial Drive, Greenville, NC 27834, USA.

OSHIYOYE Adekunle Emmanuel, b. 5 Jan 1951, Lagos, Nigeria. Obstetrician-Gynaecologist; Physician; Educator. m. Oluwatoyin Osinowo Oshiyoye, 28 Dec 1991. Education: Howard University, USA, 1972-73; BS, State University of New York, 1974; Postgraduate, Columbia University, 1974-78; MD, American University, 1979; Intern: South Chicago Community Hospital, 1980-81, Obstetrics-Gynaecology, Cook County Hospital; Resident, 1982-84, Chief Resident, 1984-86, Obstetrics-Gynaecology, Cook County Hospital-Chicago Medical School. Appointments: Associate Professor, Department of Obstetrics and Gynaecology, Chicago College of Osteo Medicine, 1986-; Attending Physician; Hyde Park Hospital, 1986, Mercy Hospital, 1987-, Roseland, Provident, Columbus, Jackson Park and Grant Hospitals, 1988-; Physician, Chicago Department of Health, 1988-. Publications: Medical editor, African Connections; Articles on hypertension, diabetes mellitus, ante myocardial infarction, obesity; Columnist, Newsbreed magazine, 1990. Honours include: Shell Scholar, 1965-69; Scholar, 1972-74, Postgraduate Medical School, 1975-79, Federal Government of Nigeria; Howard University Scholar, 1973-74; Cerebral Palsy Research Award, 1977; Recognition Awards: American Medical Association, 1986; Alpha Phi Alpha, 1991. Memberships include: Fellow, American College of International Physicians; American College of Obstetricians and Gynecologists; American College of Legal Medicine; American Society of Law and Medicine; American, National, Illinois, Chicago and Cook Country Medical Associations; Cook County Physicians Association. Hobbies: Ping-pong; Swimming; Fishing; Travel. Address: 920 S Washington Street, Lansing, MI 48910, USA.

OSOJNIK Jani, b. 18 Nov 1952, Ljubljana, Slovenia. Acupuncturist. m. Melita Avsenak, 29 Nov 1987, 3 sons, 1 daughter. Education: MSc, Traditional Chinese Medicine University of Ljubljana, 1987; BSc, Psychology, University of Ljubljana, 1980; Undergraduate Studies, Chinese Language, Beijing College of Languages, 1980-82; Postgraduate Studies, Guangzhou College of Traditional Chinese Medicine, 1982-85; Postgraduate Studies, Beijing College of Traditional Chinese Medicine, 1985-86. Publications: Co-author: Chinese Traditional Medicine and Acupuncture part 1, 1993. Memberships: Associate Member, Slovenian Acupuncture Association; President, Slovenian Association of Taijiquan. Hobbies: Astronomy; Playing Flute; Painting; Travel. Address: Gerbiceva 3, 61000 Ljubljana, Slovenia.

OSTERGAARD Keld, b. 19 Feb 1965, Denmark. Chiropractic & Medicine. Education: DC, Anglo-European College of Chiropractic; BS, University of Odense, Denmark; MD, University of Copenhagen. Appointments: Chiropractor; Research Fellow, National University Hospital, Copenhagen. Honours: Best Academic Student, Anglo-European College of Chiropractic, 1990; Gold Medal, University of Copenhagen for Research on Molecular Biology & Osteoarthritis, 1993. Membership: Danish Chiropractic Association. Hobby: Mountain Biking. Address: Rodovre Centrum 16, DK-2610 Rodovre, Denmark.

OSTRZENSKI Adam, b. 29 Aug 1940, Poland. Professor of Obstetrics and Gynaecology. m. Maria Molenda, 17 Feb 1987, 1 son, 1 daughter. Education: MD; PhD; Dr hab med. Appointments include: Director, Institute of Video Endoscopy and Laser, Wash DC, USA;

Currently Director, Operative Gynaecology-Endoscopy-Laser Surgery, Department of Obstetrics and Gynaecology, Howard University College of Medicine, Wash DC. Publications: Laparoscopic Panhysterectomy with Posterior Culdeplasty and Vaginal Vault Suspension, book, 1993; Co-author, 6 books; Pioneering papers on new endoscopic operation including: Laparoscopic Radical Hysterectomy with Extended Pelvic Lymphadenectomy; Over 100 publications and abstracts. Honours: Honorary Member, Polish Gynaecological Society; Medal Award, Pelviscopy International Society; Medal Award, Gynecological Urology International Society; Medical Staff Award, Howard University Hospital. Memberships: American Association of Gynecological Laparoscopists; International Society of Prenatal and Perinatal Psychology and Medicine. Hobbies: Reading; Running. Address: 2041 Georgia Avenue, Washington, DC 20060, USA.

OURIEFF Arthur J, b. 20 Jan 1924. Psychoanalyst. m. Vernie Gusack, 17 Aug 1947, 1 son, 2 daughters. Education: MD, Harvard Medical School; Psychoanalysis, Los Angeles Psychoanalytic Institute. Appointments: Currently Training and Supervising Analyst, Los Angeles Psychoanalytic Institute. Memberships: American Psychoanalytic Association; American Association of Child Psychoanalysts; Los Angeles Psychoanalytic Society and Institute, President 1965-67, Dean 1967-73. Hobbies: Skiing; Hiking; Mountain climbing; Trekking; Travel. Address: 320 N Clifford Avenue, Los Angeles, CA 90049, USA.

OUVRIER Robert Arthur, b. 17 May 1940, Perth, Western Australia. Paediatric Neurologist. m. Margo Johnson, 1967, 1 son, 2 daughters. Education: MB, BS, BSc, MD, Sydney University; Fellow, Royal Australasian College of Physicians. Appointments: Honorary Assistant Physician, Royal Children's Hospital, Melbourne, 1969; Fellow in Neurology, University of Kentucky, Lexington, USA, 1969-70; Fellow in Neurology, Johns Hopkins Hospital, Baltimore, USA; Head, Department of Neurology, The Children's Hospital, New South Wales, Australia. Publications: Peripheral Neuropath in Childhood, 1990; Numerous book chapters and scientific articles in Child Neurology. Memberships: Fellow, Royal Australasian College of Physicians; Australian Association of Neurologists; Australian College of Paediatrics. Hobbies: Music; Tennis; Surfing. Address: Department of Neurology, The Children's Hospital, Bridge Road, Camperdown 2050, Australia.

OVERVAD Jesper, b. 1 May 1957, Denmark. Chiropractor. m. Annjette Handberg, 30 Jul 1988, 1 s, 1 d. Memberships: Danish Chiropractor Association; European Chiropractor Association. Hobbies: Hunting; Fishing. Address: Vorregaards Alle 99, 8200 Aarhus N, Denmark.

OWNBY Dennis Randall, b. 14 Jul 1948, Athens, OH, USA. Doctor. m. Helen Engelbrecht, 1 s, 1 d. Education: BS, Ohio University; MD, Medical College of Ohio. Career: Intern Resident, Fellow, Research Fellow, Duke University School of Medicine; Senior Staff Physician, Currently, Director of Allergy Research Laboratory, Henry Ford Hospital. Publications: Many book chapters, reviews, editorials and publications in referred journals including: Co-author, Why mix ROC with RAST?, guest editorial, Ann Allery, 1992; Co-author, Testing for Latex Allergy, in Journal of Clinical Immunoassay, 1993. Honours: Alpha Omega Alpha, 1972; Young Investigator Award, NIH, 1989. Memberships: Past President, Michigan Allergy Society; American Board of Allergy, Asthma and Immunology; American Academy of Allergy and Immunology; American Academy of Pediatrics. Hobby: Scuba Diving. Address: 858 Bedford Road, Grosse Pointe Park, MI 48230, USA.

OWOLABI Makanjuola Akindele, b. 8 Aug 1953, Ife-Ife, Nigeria. Aviation Medicine. m. Edna Aiyekeyi, 24 Dec 1978, 1 son, 3 daughters. Education: MBBS; D Av Med; MRAeS; FRSM; FIAMN(Hon); College of Medicine, University of Ibadan, 1971-76; British Postgraduate Medical Federation, University of London and RAF Institute of Aviation Medicine, Farnborough, England, 1978-80. Appointments: Flight Surgeon, Specialist in Aviation Medicine, Nigerian Air Force, Kaduna, 1980-92; Senior Aviation Medical Examiner, FAA, USA, 1982-; Consultant/Authorised Medical Assessor, Federal Civil Aviation Authority, Lagos, Nigeria, 1990-; Medical Director, Aeromedical Consultant. Publications include: Aeromedical Evacuation: Clinical and Operational Aspects, 1983; Sickle Cell Trait and Flying, 1984; The Sickle Cell Trait in Relation to Military and Civil Aviation, 1984; Medication and Flying, 1988; Medical and Psychological Certification of Aircrew, 1990; Drugs and Alcohol Problems in Civil Aviation, 1991; Do's and Dont's by the Crew and Passengers on Board a Commercial Aircraft, 1994. Honours: Certificate of Merit, 1986. Memberships:

Aerospace Medical Association; Royal Aeronautical Society of London; Royal Society of Medicine of London; Nigerian Association of Aviation Medical Examiners; Guild of Medical Directors of Nigeria; New York Academy of Sciences. Address: Medical Director, Mends Hospital, 5B Old Dawaki Road, PO Box 3001, Kaduna, Nigeria.

OZORES Julio, b. 1 Nov 1958, Havana, Cuba. Physician. Education: BS, University of Miami, 1979; MD, University of Miami School of Medicine, 1984. Appointment: Physician. Address: 2041 Bancroft Way, Suite 307, Berkeley, CA 94704, USA.

OZUMBA Benjamin Chukwuma, b. 21 Mar 1954, Onitsha, Nigeria. Professor of Obstetrics and Gynaecology. m. Chinelo Udokwu, 29 Jan 1994, 1 son. Education: MB,BS, Lagos, 1979; FMCIG, Nigeria, 1987; FICS, USA, 1991; FWACS, West Africa, 1994; MRCOG, England, 1993. Appointments: Medical Officer, General Hospital, Minna Niger State, Nigeria, 1980-81; Resident, University of Nigeria Teaching Hospital, Enugu, 1981-88; Senior Lecturer, Consultant Obstetrician and Gynaecologist, 1988-93; professor of Obstetrics and Gynaecology. Publications: Contributor of numerous professional publications. Honours: American Association for Advancement of Science, 1993; New York Academy of Sciences, 1994. Memberships: Nigerian Medical Association; Enugu Medical Society; Society of Gynaecologists of Nigeria; Royal College of Obstetricians and Gynaecologists. Hobbies: Table Tennis; Lawn Tennis. Address: 115 Agbani Road, Uwani, Enugu, Enugu State, Nigeria.

P

PAASCH Ronald N, b. 22 Apr 1961, New York City, USA. Physical Medicine and Rehabilitation. Education: BA, Neurobiology; MD; Board Certified, Physical Medicine and Rehabilitation; ACLS Certified, UCI Medical Center, 1989; Special Training in Peripheral Nerve Blocks and Facet Injections, 1990-91. Career: Internship, UCI Medical Center, 1987-88; Residency in PM and R, UCI Medical Center, 1988-91; Family Practice, FHP Fountain Valley, CA, 1988-90; Currently, Doctor, Physical Medicine and Rehabilitation, EMG. Honours: Alpha Lambda Delta, Cornell University; Most Valuable Player Award, Championship Hockey Team, Cornell University; Committee of Cardiology Awards, Rutgers Medical School, 1986. Memberships: California Society of PM and R; American Academy of PM and R; American Congress of Rehabilitation; AMA; American Running and Fitness Association; National Conditioning and Fitness Association. Hobbies: Sports - Hockey, Soccer, Golf, Skiing, Triathlon Training, Biking; Travel; Photography; Antique Car Body Rebuilding and Restoration; Home Design and Remodeling; Business Management and Financial Consultant. Address: Sports and Rehabilitation Medicine, PC, 201 Park Avenue, West Springfield, MA 01089, USA.

PAFFENBARGER Ralph Seal Jr, b. 21 Oct 1922, Columbus, Ohio, USA. Professor of Epidemiology. m. (1) Mary Dale Higdon, 19 Sept 1943, 6 children, 1 deceased, (2) Jo Ann Schroeder, 20 July 1991. Education: AB, Ohio State University, 1944; MD, Northwestern University, 1947; MPH, Johns Hopkins University, 1952; DrPH, Johns Hopkins University, 1954. Appointments: Lecturer on Biostatistics, Clinical Associate Professor, Preventive Medicne, Lecturer on Epidemiology, Visiting Professor of Epidemiology, Harvard School of Public Health, 1961-88; Adjunct Professor of Epidemiology, Harvard School of Public Health, 1988-; Professor of Epidemiology, Stanford University School of Medicine, 1977-93; Emeritus Professor, 1993-; Resident Epidemiologist, University of California, 1993-. Publications: Physical Activity, all-cause mortality, 1986; The Association of changes in physical-activity level and other lifestyle characteristics with mortality among men, 1993; 208 publications in all. Honours: Johns Hopkins Society of Scholars, 1980; Sports Medal Honour Award, 1994. Memberships: American Epidemiological Society; American Public Health Association; American Heart Association; American Medical Association; American College of Sports Medicine. Hobbies: Long Distance and Trail Running. Address: 892 The Arlington, Berkeley, CA 94707, USA.

PAGE Ian John, b. 6 Apr 1955, Kingston, Surrey, England. Medical Practitioner. m. Suzanne, 17 Oct 1992, 1 son, 2 daughters. Education: LRCP, MRCS, 1978; MB, BS, 1979; MRCOG, 1985. Appointments: Consultant Obstetrician & Gynaecologist, Royal Army Medical Corps; Consultant Obstetrician & Gynaecologist, Royal Lancaster Infirmary. Publications: Preparation & Revision for the DRCOG, 1990. Memberships: Blair-Bell Research Society; British Society for Colposcopy & Cervical Pathology; National Association of Clinical Tutors. Hobbies: Music; Golf; Gardening. Address: Departement of Gynaecology, Royal Lancaster Infirmary, Ashton Road, Lancaster LA1 4RP, England.

PAHKALA Riitta Helena, b. 21 Dec 1963, Sonkajärvi, Finland. Dentist. m. Dr Ari Pahkala, 16 Aug 1986. Education: DDS, 1987, PhD, 1993, University of Kuopio. Appointment: Assistant Professor, Department of Orthodontics, Faculty of Dentistry, University of Kuopio, Finland. Publication: Thesis, Orofacial dysfunctions and development of occlusion: A longitudinal study of articulatory speech disorders, craniomandibular disorders and orofacial motor skills in children from 7 to 10 years of age, University of Kuopio, 1993. Honours: WJB Houston Research Award, 1993; Finnish Dental Society's Award, 1990, 1992. Memberships: International Association for Dental Research; European Orthodontic Society; Finnish Dental Society. Hobbies: Cycling; Skiing; Tennis. Address: Käpykuja 4, 70150 Kuopio, Finland.

PAHOR, Ahmes Labib, b. 15 sep 1942, Cairo, Egypt. Consultant Ear, Nose and Throat Surgeon. Education: MB, BCh, 1964, DLO, 1966, Cairo University; DMSc (Path), Ain Shams University, Cairo, 1968; FRCS(Edin), 1974; Certificate Higher Surgical Training, ENT RCS Edinburgh, 1977; MRCS, LRCP, London, 1978; ECGMG, Philadelphia, USA, 1974; Gold Medal, Public Speaking, London Academy Music and Dramatic Art, 1976; Certificate, English Speaking Board, 1984; MA,

Institute of Higher Coptic Studies, Cairo, 1986. Appointments include: Senior Registrar, Birmingham Hospitals, 1974-76; St Cross Hospital, Rugby. George Eliott Hospital, Nuneaton, Staffordshire, 1976-77; City general Hospital, North Staffordshire Royal Infirmary, Stoke-on-Trent, 1977-78; Consultant Ear Nose and Throat Surgeon, Dudley Road Hospital, West Buirmingham Health Authority and Sandwell District general Hospital, Sandwell District Health Authority, 1978-; Honorary senior Clinical Lecturer, Birmingham University Medical School. Publications include: Homologus and Heterologus Materials in Tympanoplasty, (Co-author, 1973; Papers in proceedings include: Otology in Ancient Egypt, 1984; History of Removal of Nasal Polyps. Co-author, 1991; History of Nasal Snare, 1993;; Contributor of articles in professional journals. Honours include: Scholarship to National Research Centre, Cairo; Recipient of several; grants. Memberships include: British Medical Association; Royal Society of Medicine; British Association of Otolaryngologists; British Association for Cancer Research; Midland Institute of Otology; Founder Member, Imhotep Scientific Society, Cairo. Address: City Hospital-NHS Trust, Dudley Road, Birmingham B18 7QH, England.

PAHWA Jagdish Chander, b. 1 Mar 1940, Rahimyarkhan, India. Acupuncturist; Physiotherapist; Chinese Herbal Medicine Practitioner. m. Krishna Kumari, 12 June 1966, 2 daughters. Education: Diploma in Physiotherapy; Diploma in Occupational Therapy; Bachelor of Acupuncture; Licentiate in Chinese Herbal Medicine; Doctor of Alternate Medicine; Fellow, Indian Institute of Homoeopathy. Appointments: In charge, Physiotherapy, Occupational Therapy, Rehabilitation Centre, Saket, India; Superintendent Physiotherapist, St Andrews Hospital, London, England, to 1981; Currently: Visiting Consultant, Lecturer in Acupuncture, British College of Acupuncture; Director, private health clinic, London. Publications: Approximately 200 articles on homoeopathy in Hanemannian Gleanings, Calcutta, and several other homoeo journals. Honours: Fellowship in Homoeopathy, Indian Institute of Homoeopathy, 1964; Doctorate in Alternative Medicine, Open University, Colombo, Sri Lanka, 1985-86. Memberships: British Acupuncture Association; Society of Orthopaedic Medicine. Hobbies: Reading; Music. Address: Charlbury House, 41 Rectory Lane, Loughton, Essex IG10 1NZ, England.

PAINE Jeannette Abigail, b. 10 Feb 1916, Denver, Colorado, USA. Nutritionist. m. Frederic C Paine Jr, 16 Oct 1943, 1 son, 1 daughter. Education: BS, Colorado University, 1938; Internship, Dietetics, University Colorado School of Medicine & Hospitals, 12 months; MPH, University California, Berkeley, 1958. Appointments: Asbury Protestant Hospital, Salina, Kansas, 1940; Dietitian, St Luke's, Tokyo, 1940-41; Dietitian, Colorado Hospital, Pueblo, 1943-45; Dietitian, Suburban Hospital, South Gate, California, 1950; Teacher, High School in Colorado, 1951-57; Dietitian, San Joaquin General Hospital, French Camp, California, 1958-78; Private Consulting Nutritionist, 1978-86; Retired. Memberships: American Dietetic Association; American Public Health Association; American Association of University Women; Society of Nutrition Education; California Nutrition Council; Home Economics Association. Hobbies: Antiques; Stamp Collecting; Organ; Swimming. Address: PO Box 511, 225 NW 3rd Cedaredge, CO 81413, USA.

PAKES Eddy Hymie, b. 16 Mar 1937, Edmonton, Alberta, Canada. Physician; Psychiatrist; Psychoanalyst. m. Dr Judith Pakes, 28 Jun 1967, 1 s, 2 d. Education: MD; FRCP(C); FAPA; DPsych, Psychoanalysis. Career: Director, In-Patient Unit for Children and Families, Hospital for Sick Children; Consultant, Hematology, Oncology and Psychotherapy; Supervisor, Clark Institute of Psychiatry, Family Therapy; Currently, Director, Bereavement Clinics, Hospital for Sick Children and Families, Mount Sinai, Toronto. Publications include: Many articles and book chapters including: Is Suicide Catchy? Are There Risks in Treating the Suicidal?, Proceedings on Conference on Suicide, Kings College, London, Ontario, 1986; Treating The Grieving Patient, in Ontario Medicine, 1993; Bereavement coping with the loss of a loved one, in Mount Sinai Health Report, 1993; TV appearances, 1985, 1988; In Our Sorrow - Hope, video tape, 1983. Honour: Fellow, American Psychiatric Association, 1975. Memberships: Canadian Psychiatric Association; American Psychiatric Association; Canadian Medical Association. Hobbies: Skiing; Sailing; Tennis; Jogging; Golf. Address: Mount Sinai Hospital, 600 University Avenue, Toronto, Canada, M5G 1X5.

PAL Sekhar Kanti, b. 6 Jan 1942, Calcutta, India. Obstetrician & Gynecologist. m. Gayatri Pal, 8 Aug 1969, 1 son, 1 daughter. Education: ISc, Calcutta University, 1960; MBBS, Calcutta University, 1966; DGO,

Calcutta University, 1968; MRCOG, London, England, 1978. Appointments: Lecturer, Medical Faculty of Garyounis University, Benghazi, Libya, 1979; Consultant Gynecologist, Gujrati Relief Society Hospital, Calcutta. Memberships: Indian Medical Association; Bengal Obstetric & Gynecology Society. Hobbies: Obstetrics & Gynecology. Address: GA 40 Narayantala West, PO Deshbandhunagar, Calcutta 59, Pin 700059, India.

PALMA-CARLOS Antero G, b. 21 Mar 1933, Lisbon, Portugal. Professor of Medicine. m. M Laura Almeida, 22 Dec 1956. Education: MD, Lisbon University, 1959; PhD, Lisbon University, 1969; Resident, Lisbon University Hospital, 1958-65; Karolinska Hospital, Stockholm, 1958; Lausanne University Policlinics, 1961-62. Appointments: Associate Professor, Internal Medicine, Lisbon School of Medicine, 1969-79; Head, 1st Medical Clinic, Lisbon School of Medicine, Immunology Institute, Lisbon School of Medicine; Coordinator for Portuguese Histocompatibility Centers. Publications: Immunodeficiencies, 1992; Drugs, 1992; Treatment of Asthma in Europe Bronchial Asthma, 1994. Memberships: Portuguese Society of Allergology; European Academy of Allergology; British Society of Allergy; AAAI; ACAI; GAILL. Honours: Knight French Order of Merit, 1980; Honorary Member, Czech Medical Academy, 1989; Gold Medal, Nagoya University, 1990; Distinguished Fellow, ACAI, 1993. Hobbies: Classical Music; Fine Arts; Walking. Address: CAIC, Sampaio e Pina 16-40, 1000 Lisboa, Portugal.

PALMEIRO Joao Francisco, b. 25 Mar 1937, Beja, Portugal. Neurologist. m. Cecilia Mota, 23 June 1963, 1 son, 2 daughters. Education: MD, Neurology. Appointments: Resident, Max-Planck Institute for Brain Research, Germany, 1964-65; Assistant of Neurology, Coimbra University, 1966; Director of the Neurological Department, Central Hospital, 1974. Publications: Several in Neurological Topics, mainly in Cerebro-Vascular Diseases and Haedechs. Memberships: Sociedade Das Ciencias Médicas De Lisbon; Sociedade Portuguesa De Neurologia; Ordem Dos Médicos. Hobbies: Gardening; Tennis. Address: R Jose Maria De Abreu 15, 3000 Coimbra, Portugal.

PALMER Monica, b. 7 May 1944, Hatton, England. Orthodontist. m. Raymond Palmer, 9 July 1968. Education: BDS (Hons); FDS; RCS (Edinburgh); DDO; RCPS (Glasgow). Appointments: Lecturer in Child Dental Health; Registrar in Dental Surgery; Senior Registrar in Orthodontics; Consultant Orthodontist; Private Orthodontic practice. Publications: Addent, 1969; Evaginated Odontomes in Caucasians, 1973; Severe Hypodontia of the Permanent Dentition with Bilateral Dilated Odontomes in the upper incisor region, 1976; The Universal Appliance: a segmental approach, 1977; Indirect Direct-Bonding, 1977; Bonded Space Maintainers, 1979; A Fixed Appliance Manual for Community in-service Orthodontic Trainees; Multibracket Bonding, 1979; Memberships: Scientitfic Committee Member, Journal Coordinator, Angle Society of Europe; American Association of Orthodontists; European Orthodontic Society; British Association of Orthodontics; Editorial Board, Praktische Kieferorthopädie journal. Hobbies: Painting; Music; Literature. Address: Berkaer Str 30, 14193 Berlin 33, Germany.

PALO Nicholas Edwin, b. 18 Nov 1945, Waukegan, IL, USA. m. Lauren M Reynolds, 18 Aug 1990 (deceased). Education: BA, University of Wisconsin, Eau Claire, 1971; MS, University of Missouri, 1975. Career: Instructor and Coordinator, University of Missouri Extension, Columbia, 1974-85; Executive Officer, American Board of Professional Psychology, Columbia, 1984-. Memberships: President, Columbia Community Band, 1987; Chairman, Arts Resources Council, Columbia, 1988; American Society Association of Executives, Psychology Executives, Roundtable; Mensa; Windjammers Unlimited; Club, American Association Concert Bands; Honorary, Phi Delta Kappa; Honorary, Phi Mu Alpha. Hobby: Music. Address: American Board of Professional Psychology, 2100 East Broadway Suite 313, Columbia, MO 65201-6082, USA.

PALOFF Adrian Milenov, b. 29 Jan 1941, Bulgaria. Medical Doctor. m. Dimka Hinova, 9 July 1976, 1 daughter. Education: MD; PhD. Appointments: Assistant; Assistant Professor; Associate Professor. Publications: Numerous articles to professional journals and magazines. Memberships: Bulgarian Society of Anatomists; Anatomische Gesellschaft; Bulgarian Society for Neuroscience; International Brain Res Organization. Hobbies: Running; Swimming. Address: Department of Anatomy, Histology & Embryology, Medical Academy Base 1, 1431 Sofia, Bulgaria.

PALOMINO Robert Miguel, b. 31 Aug 1940, Peru. Medical Doctor. m. Marta Nuñez, 11 July 1970, 5 sons. Education: MD, Specialist in Internal Medicine, San Marcos University, Lima; Physician, San Agustin University, Arequipa. Appointments: Assistant in Internal Medicine, currently Chief of Internal Medicine, Peruvian Naval Hospital; Auxiliary Professor in Internal Medicine, Associate Professor in Internal Medicine,, currently Chief of Internal Medicine, San Marcos University, Lima. Publications include: Atopia, 1994; Nuevos conceptos con la biología y la inmuno patogenisis de la infeción por HIV, 1995. Honours: Observership in Internal Medicine at Oakland Naval Hospital, California, Jan 1984. Memberships: American College of Physicians, USA; Phoenix Alliance Inc, St Paul, Minnesota; WHO Expert Advisory Panel on the Health of Seafarers; Peruvian Internal Medicine Society, Lima. Hobby: Activities in International Lions clubs. Address: Jacaranda 912, Lima 33, Peru.

PALOYAN Edward, b. 19 Mar 1932, Paris, France. Surgeon. m. Geraldine P Richveis, 7 Jul 1957, 1 s, 3 d. Education: MD. Career includes: Associate Professor of Surgery, University of Chicago, 1968-73; Professor of Surgery, Chief of Endocrine Surgery, Loyola University of Chicago, 1973-94; Currently, Associate Chief of Staff. R and D, Veteran's Administration Hospital, Hines, IL. Publications include: Numerous books, book chapters, publications, abstracts and editorials including: Coexistence of Hypothyroidism and Hyperparathyroidism, in Essays in Surgery, 1989; Co-author, Parathyroidectomy for Primary Hyperparathyroidism, in Mastery of Surgery, 1992; Co-author, An Alternative Approach, in Surgery of the Thyroid and Parathyroid Glands, 3rd edition, 1990, in press. Honours include: Sigma Xi, 1957; Fellow, American Diabetes Association, 1962-63; McClintock Award, 1971; Special Invitation by French College of Surgeons, Bicentennial Celebrations at 91st Congress, 1989. Memberships include: American Surgical Association; American College of Surgeons; Endocrine Society; American Thyroid Association; International Association of Endocrine Surgeons; Society for Experimental Biology and Medicine; American Federation for Clinical Research; Founding Member, Board of Directors, 1991-94, American Association of Clinical Endocrinologists. Address: Endocrine Loyola University of Chicago, 2160 South First Avenue, Maywood, IL 60153, USA.

PAN Bo-Rong, b. 15 Aug 1932, Yixing, Jiangsu, China. Consultant; Professor. m. Wang Xiu-Zhen, 28 Dec 1960, 2 s. Education: BM, China Medical University, Shenyang, 1956; MD, Fourth Military Medical University, 1965. Appointments: Registrar, 1956-, Medical Assistant, 1971-, Consultant and Professor, 1983-, Xijing Hospital, Fourth Military Medical University; Research Fellow, Royal Postgraduate Medical School, London, 1982; Editor-in-Chief, Editorial Department, Journal of Fourth Military Medical University, 1987-. Publications: 218 Learned articles, including, Pan B-R, in Clinical Exp Immunology, 1984; Chief Editor of 22 Books and Co-author of 18 Books including, Current Therapy for Peptic Ulcer, 1990. Honours: Honorary Consultant and Professor of Jilin 222th Army Hospital, Lazhou Air Force Hospital, Minsen Pharmaceutical Factory, and other organizations. Memberships include: President: China Gastrology Committee; Chinese Association of Medical Writing; China Society of Study on Clinical Misdiagnosis and Mistreatment. Hobby: Gardening. Address: Building 621, No 12, Fourth Military Medical University, 17 Changlexilu, Xi'an 710033, China.

PAN Ci-Kang, b. 3 July 1926, Chengdu, China. Urologist. m. Feng-Zhai Tao, 12 Dec 1953, 1 daughter. Education: The Medical College of The National Central University. Appointments: Resident Surgeon, 1949-54; Visiting Surgeon, 1954-75; Assistant Head of Surgical Department, 1975-83; Director, Sichuan Provincial People's Hospital, 1983-88. Publications: The Principles and Clinical Application of Extracorporeal Shock Wave Lithotripsy, 1991; The Clinical Significance of Prostatic Acid Phosphatase and Prostate-specific Antigen in Prostate Cancer, 1994. Memberships: 10 Societies and Associations. Hobbies: Music; Flowers and Plants. Address: Qing Yang Gong, Chengdu, Sichuan, China.

PAN Xiaoping, b. 23 Mar 1964, Meishan, Sichuan, China. Teacher. m. Qingxiu Liao, 1 May 1987, 1 son. Appointments: Assistant Professor of Health Statistics; Deputy Director, Department of Health Statistics. Publications: Prediction of the Prognosis on the Outcome of Gyaves Disease after Cessatium of Antithyroid Drug Therapy, 1990; Evaluation of a Logistic Regression Model in Predicting the Progress of Graves Disease Treated by Anthyroid Drugs, 1991. Honours: Advanced Teacher, 1989, 1990. Memberships: Editor, Chinese Journal of Health Statistics; Commissioner, The Health Statistics Society for China

Preventive Medical Association. Hobbies: Table Tennis; Chinese Chess; Computers. Address: Department of Health Statistics, West China University of Medical Sciences, Chendu, Sichuan 610041, China.

PAN Zhuo-Ru, b. 2 Feb 1940, China. Obstetrician. m. 8 Feb 1968, 2 d. Education: Shanghai Second Medical University. Appointments: Resident Doctor, 1964; Visiting Docotr, 1982; Associate Professor, 1988; Professor, 1994. Publications: Intraamniotic instillation of Dexamethasong to enhance fetal lung maturity - Analysis of 315 cases of high risk pregnancies with long follow-up, 1992; Analysis on indications of 393 cases prenatal chromosomal karyotyping diagnosis, 1993. Honours: Visiting Scholar, Lying-in Hospital, American University of Chicago, 1986-88. Memberships: OBS/GYN Society; Chinese Medical Association. Hobbies: Music. Address: Department of Obstetrics, Xin Hua Hospital, Shanghai 2nd Medical University, 1665 Kon Jiang Road, Shanghai 200092, USA.

PANCER Stephen Mark, b. 26 Jun 1949. Professor of Psychology. m. Karen Golets, 15 Sep 1974, 2 s. Education: BSc, University of Toronto, 1972; MA, 1974, PhD, 1977, University of Waterloo. Career: Assistant Professor, Department of Psychology, University of Saskatchewan; Director, Research and Evaluation, The Dellcrest Children's Centre; Currently, Professor of Psychology, Wilfrid Laurier University, Canada. Publications: Co-author, A developmental stage approach to program planning and evaluation, in Evaluation Review; Co-author, Community-based approaches to health promotion and guidelines for community mobilization, in International Quarterly of Community Health Education. Honour: Fellow, Canadian Psychological Association, 1993. Memberships: Canadian Psychological Association; American Psychological Association; Society for the Psychological Study of Social Issues. Hobbies: Guitar; Violin; Golf. Address: Department of Psychology, Wilfrid Laurier University, Waterloo, Ontario, Canada, N2L 3C5.

PANDYA Rooshikumar, b. 27 Mar 1940, Ahmedabad, India. Trainer; Consultant. m. Annapurna Devi, 9 Dec 1982. Education: BA (Hons), 1960, BA (Hons), 1961, Gujarat University; MA, Humboldt State University, 1965; Permanent Professional Teaching Certificate for College Teaching, Department of Education, State of Iowa, 1968; MA, Montreal, PhD studies, Concordia University, Canada, 1972; Certified Sex Educator, American Association of Sex Educators, Counsellors and Therapists, 1976; Postgraduate studies, Psychology of Education, 1976-79, University of Sherebrooke, Canada. Appointments: Teaching Assistant, Humboldt State University, California, USA, 1964-66; Faculty Member, North Iowa Area Community College, 1968; Humanities Faculty, John Abbott College, Montreal, Canada, 1971-82; Currently Consultant and Trainer, India; Guest Lecturer, numerous bodies. Publications: Articles: Hypnosis in the Current of Time, 1977; Stress Management for the Professional Negotiator, 1982; Therapeutic Aspects of New Religious Movement (with Fredrick Bird), 1993; Books: Assert and Succeed, 1994; Hypnose Thérapeutique et Pratique (with Dr Verma), in press. Honours: Rotary Fellowship, 1964-65; Fulbright Fellowship, 1966-68; USA Research Fellowship, 1975; Shastri-Canadian Fellowship, 1979; Honorary Fellow, College of Human Sciences, Canada, 1982. Memberships: American Association of Sex Educators, Counsellors and Therapists; International Transactional Analysis Association. Hobbies: Indian classical music; Reading; Helping people to succeed; Making audio-visual material on health and related subjects (has produced over 40 audio cassettes and 3 video cassettes). Address: 6-A Akashganga, 89 Warden Road, Bombay 400 026, India.

PANDYA Sugna Vasudeo, b. 5 Aug 1936, Ahmedabad, India. Medical. Education: MBBS, Gujrat University, 1959; MRCOG, 1965; FRCOG, 1978. Appointments: Honorary Professor, Obstetrics & Gynaecology, SMT. NHL. Municipal Medical College & Sheth KM School of Postgraduate Medicine & Research, Ahmedabad, India, 1979-94. Publications: Endodermal Sinus Tumor - A Case Report; Caesarean Hysterectomy. Honours: Fellow, International Council of Sex Education & Parenthood, USA, 1984. Memberships: Ahmedabad Medical Association; Ahmedabad Obstetric & Gynecological Society. Hobbies: Reading; Music; Scrabble. Address: Gayatree, Bansidhar Society, Sarkhej Road, Ahmedabad 380007, India.

PANETH Nigel Sefton, b. 19 Sep 1946, London, England. Physician. m. Ellen M Pollak, 16 Dec 1973, 2 d. Education: AB, Columbia, 1968; BMS, Dartmouth, 1970; MD, Harvard, 1972; MPH, Columbia, 1978. Career: Assistant Clinical Professor of Pediatrics, Albert Einstein College of Medicine, NY, 1977-78; Assistant Professor, Associate

Professor of Pediatrics and Public Health, Columbia University, 1978-89; Visiting Lecturer in Neurology, Harvard Medical School, 1988-89; Associate Professor, Professor of Pediatrics and Epidemiology and Director of Program in Epidemiology, Michigan State University, East Lansing, MI, 1989-. Publications: Co-author, Brain Damage in the Preterm Infant, 1994; 66 articles in professional journals; Many chapters in books, committee publications, book reviews, abstracts and presentations. Honours: Rose Segal Award, Harvard Medical School, 1972; Kathleen Lyle Murray Award, American Academy of Cerebral Palsy and Developmental Medicine, 1986. Memberships: American Academy of Pediatrics; Society for Pediatric Research; Society for Epidemiologic Research; Executive Committee, Society for Pediatric Epidemiologic Research; International Epidemiologic Association; American Epidemiologic Society; National Board, Committee for Health in Southern Africa. Address: A 206 East Fee Hall, Michigan State University, East Lansing, MI 48824, USA.

PANG Jonathan Chi Kin, b. 6 July 1940, Hong Kong. Obstetrician and Gynaecologist. m. Elizabeth Sheila Watson, 3 May 1970, 4 daughters. Education: BA, 1961, MA, 1964, Trinity College, Cambridge; St Thomas's Hospital Medical School, London; MB BChir (Cantab), 1964; Diploma, Obstetrics, Royal College of Obstetricians and Gynaecologists; FRCOG; FHKCOG; FHKAM (Obstetrics and Gynaecology). Appointments: Registrar, Obstetrics and Gynaecology, Mile End Hospital, London, England; Lecturer in Obstetrics and Gynaecology, University of Hong Kong; Consultant Obstetrician and Gynaecologist, Nethersole Hospital, Hong Kong; Currently Consultant Obstetrician and Gynaecologist, Dr Vio and Partners, Hong Kong. Publications: The induction of therapeutic abortion using intravenous prostaglandin E2 in Chinese patients, 1973; Cryosurgery in the treatment of cervical erosions, 1974; Co-author: The use of the foetal electrocardiogram in the detection of foetal distress, 1974; Induction of labor by acupuncture electro-stimulation, 1976; Oral prostaglandin E2 and F2oC in the induction of labour, 1977; Cytology and Colposcopy in the diagnosis of cervical neoplasia, 1977; Hyperosmolar urea for elective midtrimester abortion, 1978. Memberships include: British Medical Association; Hong Kong Medical Association. Hobbies: Golf; Wine; Swimming. Address: Dr Vio and Partners, 604 Gloucester Tower, 11 Pedder Street, Central, Hong Kong.

PANG Peter A, b. 20 Feb 1940, Kedah, Malaysia. Modern & Traditional Acupuncture Practitioner; Community Pharmacy Practitioner. m. Helen S P Lee, 7 May 1965, 1 son, 1 daughter. Education: BSc, Pharmaceuticals; BAc, Advance Acupuncture, British College of Acupuncture; Advance Auricular Medicine, International Society of Bio-physical Medicine. Appointments: Pharmacy Manager, Boots The Chemist, Merseyside Branches; Consultant Acupuncturist, Merseyside Drug Dependent Initiative, 1987. Memberships: Academy of Western Acupuncture; British Acupuncture Association; Association of Auricular Therapy; Royal Pharmaceutical Society, England; National Pharmceutical Association. Hobbies: Badminton; Table Tennis. Address: 223 Stanley Road, Bootle, Merseyside L20 3DY, England.

PANG Ru-yan, b. 6 Apr 1945, Beijing, China. Associate Professor of Paediatrics. m. Shou-yong Yan, 14 Feb 1970, 1 son. Education: MD, Beijing Medical University, 1969; Specialist training in Paediatrics, Peking Union Medical College, 1982; MPH, Emory University, USA, 1990. Appointments: Assistant Professor of Paediatrics, Shaanxi Medical School, 1970-79; Associate Professor of Paediatrics, Peking Union Medical College, University, Beijing, 1978-90; National Programme Officer, UNICEF, Beijing, 1990-94; Currently Deputy Director-General, MCH Department, Ministry of Public Health. Publications: Strategy View of Perinatal Care in Different Birth Weight Groups, 1985; The Diagnosis and Treatment of Respiration Failure, 1986; The Diagnosis and Treatment of Neonatal Pneumothorax, 1987; Etiology and Clinical Study of Neonatal Diarrhoea, 1990; Epidemiology Study on Hypothermia in Newborns, 1993; The Impact of BFHI Activities in the Program of Support and Promotion of Breast Feeding, 1993. Memberships: Chairman, Chinese Child Health Association; Vice-Chairman, Chinese Family Education Association. Hobby: Cooking. Address: 44 Houhai Beiyan, Beijing 100725, China.

PANG Shiu Fun, b. 22 Feb 1945, Hong Kong. Teacher; Scientist. m. Celia Sook-Fun Ho, 18 Jun 1971, 2 s. Education: BSc, Chinese University of Hong Kong; MA, CA State University, USA; PhD, Pittsburg University, USA. Appointments: Graduate Assistant Biology, CA State University, 1970-71; Teaching Assistant and Fellow, Biology, University of Pittsburgh, 1971-74; Research Associate, Psychology, University of

IA, 1974-75; Research Associate, Clarke Institute of Psychiatry, 1975-76; Lecturer, Senior Lecturer, Reader, Head, Physiology, University of Hong Kong, 1976-; Associate Executive Editor, Editor, Chinese Journal Physiological Sciences, 1986-91; Editor, Journal of Pineal Research, 1987-91; Editor-in-Chief, Managing Editor, Biological Signals, 1990-95; Honorary Professor, Physiology, 2nd and 3rd Military Medical Universities, 1994-96; Visiting Professor, Institute of Physiology, China, 1994-97. Publications: Advances in Pineal Research Volume 3, 1989; Special Neuroendocrine Systems, 1991; Putative Melatonin Receptors in Peripheral Tissues, 1993; 2[125] Iodomelatonin Binding Sites in Endocrine and Immune Systems, 1994. Memberships: AAAS; American Society of Zoology; European Pineal Society, 1981-; European Society Neuroscience; IBRO, 1985-; Chinese Association of Physiological Sciences, 1988-; Hong Kong Society of Neurosciences Biochemistry, 1978-. Hobbies: Reading; Music; Soccer; Basketball; Badminton. Address: Department of Physiology, University of Hong Kong, 5 Sassoon Road, Hong Kong.

PANIAGUA Cecilio, b. 1944, Madrid. Psychoanalyst. Education: Medical Doctor; DSc. Appointments: Training and Supervising Analyst, Madrid Psychoanalyst Association. Memberships: American Psychoanalytic Association; Madrid. Address: c. Corazon de Maria 2, 28002 Madrid, Spain.

PANIZZON Renato G, b. 12 Dec 1944, Basel, Switzerland. MD. m. Nicole Guisan, 30 Sept 1972, 1 son, 2 daughters. Education: MD, University of Basel, 1971; Dermatologist, University Hospital, Berne, 1978; Visiting Professor, Rush University, Chicago, USA. Appointments: Associate Professor of Dermatology, University of Zurich. Publications: Modern Dermatologic Radiation Therapy, 1991. Memberships: Swiss Dermatologic Society; German Dermatologic Society; American Academy of Dermatology; Society of Investigative Dermatology. Honours: President, Board of Examination, Swiss Dermatology Society; President, Nelanoma Group, Swiss Society of Clinical Cancer Research. Hobbies: Skiing. Address: Deptartment of Dermatology, University Hospital, Gloriastrasse 31, CH-8091 Zurich, Switzerland.

PANJE William R, b. 22 Dec 1942, Amarillo, Texas, USA. Head and Neck Surgeon. m. Helen Panje, 2 daughters. Education: BS, Iowa Wesleyan College, 1965; MS, Department of Zoology, 1967, MS, Otolaryngology, 1977, University of Iowa; MD, University of Iowa College of Medicine, 1971; Board Certified, American Academy of Otolaryngology, 1977. Appointments: Assistant Professor, 1977-80, Director, Head and Neck Surgical Oncology Division, 1977-84, Associate Professor, 1980-83, Professor, Director, 1983-84, Department of Otolaryngology-Head and Neck Surgery, University of Iowa, Iowa City; Professor of Surgery, Chairman, Otolaryngology, University of Chicago Pritzker School of Medicine, Illinois, 1984-92; Professor, Director, Head and Neck Reconstruction and Skull Base Surgery, Rush Medical College, Chicago and Rush-Presbyterian-St Luke's Medical Center, 1992-. Publications include: Iowa Head and Neck Cancer Course Book, 1979; Co-author: Microsurgical Reconstruction of Head and Neck, 1989; Musculocutaneous Flap Reconstruction of the Head and Neck, 1989; Endoscopic Sinus Surgery, 1992; Co-editor, 2 books; Numerous papers and chapters. Honours include: Developmental Biology Award, Oogenesis Research, 1968; Co-participant, paper for Benjamin Schuster Award, 1977; President's Award, Best Free Paper, Vancouver; Teacher of Year Award, 1982, 1983; 2nd Place, Scientific Exhibit, American Academy of Otolaryngology, 1989; 1st Place, Scientific Exhibit, North American Skull Base Society, 1991; Sir William Wilde Medal, Irish Otolaryngological Society, Dublin, 1992. Memberships include: American Medical Association; Fellow: American Society of Head and Neck Surgery; American College of Surgeons; American Academy of Facial Plastic and Reconstructive Surgery; American Academy of Otolaryngology-Head and Neck Surgery; American Academy of Ophthalmology and Otolaryngology. Hobbies: Golf; Fishing; Reading; Medical history. Address: 1725 W Harrison, Suite 340, Chicago, IL 60612, USA.

PANTSYREV Yuri Michaylovich, b. 9 May 1929. Surgeon. m. F Polykarpova, 20 Sept 1951, 1 son, 1 daughter. Education: PhD, 1959; DMS, 1970. Appointments: Fellowship, 1954; Assistant Professor, 1964-; Professor, Chairman, Department of Surgery, 1971-, Russian National Medical University. Publications: Vagotomy Complicated Duodenal Ulcer, 1979; Operative Endoscopy in Gastrointestinal Tract, 1984; Clinical Surgery, Chief Editor, 1988. Honour: National Premium for Outstanding Achievements in Medicine. Memberships: International Surgical Society; Russian Academy of Medical Sciences. Hobby: Skiing.

Address: Russian National Medical University, Department of Surgery, 42 Lobachevsky Street, Moscow, Russia.

PAPADOPOULOS Andrew, b. 18 Jan 1956, London, England. Clinical Psychologist. 1 s, 1 d. Education: BSc, Honours; MSc; C Psychol. Appointments: Clinical Coordinator, Coventry Psychology Services; Head of Speciality, Older Adults, Coventry; Currently, Consultant, Head of Physical Health for Older Adults. Publications: Counselling Carers, 1990; Care Management in Practice, 1992; Working with Elder Abuse, due 1995. Memberships: British Psychological Society; West Midlands Institute of Gerontology; Honorary Tutor, Birmingham University. Hobbies: Gardening; Cooking; DIY. Address: 15 Cotton Lane, Moseley, Birmingham, B13 9SA, England.

PAPARELLA Michael Mauro, b. 13 Feb 1933, Detroit, Michigan, USA. Physician; Surgeon. m. Treva Crane, 1 Oct 1992, 2 s, 1 d. Education: BS; MD. Appointments include: Clinical Professor, Chairman Emeritus, Department of Otolaryngology, University of Minnesota Medical School, Minneapolis, 1984-; Director, Otopathology Laboratory, Department of Otolaryngology, University of Minnesota, 1984-; President and Staff, Minnesota Ear, Head and Neck Clinic, Minneapolis, 1984-; member of Staff and Hospital Committees, Fairview Riverside Medical Centre, Minneapolis, 1984-; Secretary and Founder, Member of Board of Directors, International Hearing Foundation, 1984-; Director, Midwestern Centre, National Temporal Bone Bank Programme, 1979-. Publications include: Editor and Co-Editor of numerous books; Contributor of numerous articles in professional journals. Honours: Recipient of numerous honours and awards including: Kobrak Research Award, 1960; Award of Merit, American Academy of Ophthalmology and Otolaryngology, 1975; Award for Outstanding Service in Education and Research, International Hearing Foundation, 1985; Distinguished Harper Alumnus Award, Outstanding Dedication and Contributions to Research and Medicine, 1990; Honored for 30 Years of Dedication to Research and Medicine, University of Minnesota and International Hearing Foundation, 1993; Achievement Award for Scientific and Clinic Efforts in Otolryngology, University of Rome, Department of Otolaryngology, 1993. Hobby: Tennis. Address: 701 25th Avenue S #200, Minneapolis, MN 55454, USA.

PAPP Mátyás I, b. 24 July 1927, Vajdácska, Hungary. Neurologist. m. Julia Nemes, 14 Aug 1967, 2 daughters. Education: MD, Medical University Budapest & 1st Institute of Medicine, Leningrad, 1955; Specialist in Neurology, 1960, Specialist in Psychiatry, 1974. Appointments: Assistant Professor, 1975; Associate Professor of Neurology, Semmelweis Medical University, 1985-. Publications: Glial cytoplasmic inclusions: in 'J Neurol Sci' 1989, 1992; in 'Brain', 1994. Memberships: International Society of Neuropathology; Hungarian Society of Neurology & Psychiatry. Hobbies: Running; Music. Address: 1035 Budapest, Miklos u 7-507, Hungary.

PAPPER Emanuel Martin, b. 12 Jul 1915, New York City, USA. Physician. m. Patricia M Meyer, 30 Nov 1975, 2 s, 2 d. Education: AB, Columbia University, NY, 1935; MD, NY University, 1938; Hon MD, Sweden, 1964; Hon MD, Italy, 1969; Hon MD, Austria, 1977; Hon DSc, Columbia University NY, 1988; PhD, English Literature, University of Miami, FL, 1990. Appointments include: Professor of Anesthesiology, University of Miami, 1969-; Vice President, Medical Affairs, Dean, University of Miami School of Medicine, 1969-81; Professor of Pharmacology, University of Miami, 1974-81; Dean Emeritus, Professor of Pharmacology Emeritus, 1981-. Publications: 256 Scientific papers published in various medical and scientific journals; Author of 4 books; Author of 15 book chapters; Editor of 3 books; Foreward of 3 books; Many Editorials. Honours include: Honorary Professor, University of Santiago de Chile, South America, 1980; Honorary Member, Panamanian Society of Anesthesiologists, 1981; Honorary Fellow, Royal College of Anaesthetists of England, 1982; Endowed Chair, E M Papper Chair in Anesthesiology, Columbia University, 1984; Ralph M Waters Award, Midwest Anesthesia Conference, 1989; Honorary Fellowship, Royal Society of Medicine, England, 1990. Memberships: Fellow Senior Member, American Surgical Association, 1981; Honorary Member, Anesthesia History Association, 1990; Residency Review Committee, 1960, Chairman Committee, 1963-64, AMA, 1946-; Diplomate, American Board of Anesthesiology, 1956-65, Vice President, 1963-64, President, 1964-65, American Board of Anesthesiology. Hobbies: Tennis; Collecting Rare Books. Address: 1 Grove Isle Drive, Apt 1501, Miami, FL 33133, USA.

PARER Julian Thomas, b. 2 Sept 1934, Melbourne, Australia. University Professor. m. Robin M W Parer. Education: BA, University Melbourne, 1959; MRur Sc, University of New England, 1962; PhD, Oregon University, 1965; MD, University Washington, Seattle, 1971. Appointments include: Co-Director, North Coast Perinatal Access System, University California, San Francisco, 1984-89; Visiting Scientist, Laboratorio de Fisiologia y Fisiopatologia del Desarrollo, Chile, 1985, 1986, 1987, 1988, 1989, 1991, 1993; Associate Vice Chairman, Department of Obstetrics, Gynecology & Reproductive Sciences, University California, San Francisco, 1987-. Publications include: Cerebral blood flow and metabolism in ovine fetuses during asphyxia resulting in seizures, 1994; Glyceryl trinitrate stops active labour in sheep, 1994; Cardiovascular response to hypoxemia in near-term chronically catheterized fetal llamas, 1993; Blood pressure responses to changes in head position in pregnant and nonpregnant llamas, 1993. Honours: Phi Kappa Phi, 1963; Phi Sigma, 1964; Seattle Gynecology Society Annual Student Award, 1970; John J Bonica Annual Student Award, 1971. Memberships include: Society for the Study of Fetal Physiology; Society for Gynecologic Investigation; American College of Obstetricians & Gynecologists; Australian Perinatal Society. Address: University of California, Obstetrics & Gynecology Department, San Francisco, CA 94143, USA.

PARK Joon Bu, b. 20 June 1944, Pusan, Korea. Professor. m. Bea Young, 11 Sep 1963, 2 sons, 1 daughter. Education: BS, Boston University, USA, 1967; MS, Massachusetts Institute of Technology, 1969; PhD, University of Utah, 1972. Appointments: University of Washington, 1972-73; University of Illinois, Champaign-Urbana, 1973-76; Clemson University, 1976-81; Tulane University, 1981-83; University of Iowa, 1983-. Publications: Biomaterials: An Introduction, 1979; Biomaterials Science and Engineering, 1984; Biomaterials: An Introduction, Co-author, 2nd edition, 1992; Contributor of 80 refereed papers, 88 abstracts and 5 patents. Honours: Cum Laude, Boston University, 1967; McQueen Quattlebaum Award, Clemson University, 1980; Best Teacher, BME, University of Iowa, 1989. Memberships: Society for Biomaterials; Biomedical Engineering Society. Hobbies: Reading; Golf. Address: 1212EB Department of Biomedical Engineering, University of Iowa, Iowa City, IA 52242, USA.

PARK MinSun, b. 11 Apr 1958, Seoul, Korea. Medical Doctor; Researcher in Nephrology. 1 son, 1 daughter. Education: MD, Ehwa Women's University, 1983; MSc, Han Yang University, 1986. Appointments: Currently Instructor in Medicine, Soon Chun Hyang University Hospital, Seoul; Researcher, Hyonam Kidney Laboratory, Soon Chun Hyang University. Publications: Co-author: CAPD in Korea 1981-89, 1992; Peritoneal membrane function after 5 years of CAPD, 1992; Outcome of dialysis in the elderly, 1992; Effects of erythropoietin-induced hemopoiesis on peritoneal transfer and on in vitro T cell responses in CAPD, 1992; Subcutaneously implanted catheters reduce the incidence of peritonitis during CAPD by eliminating infection by preluminal route, 1992; Supplemented dialysis. Amino acid based solutions in peritoneal dialysis, 1993; Peritoneal transport during dialysis with amino acid based solutions, 1993; The effect of alternative osmotic agents on peritoneal transport, 1993; Effect of anemia with EPO on peritoneal dialysis, 1994; Dialysate to plasma solute concentration (D/P) versus peritoneal transport parameters in CAPD, 1994; Bi-directional solutes transport in peritoneal dialysis, 1994. Memberships: Korean Society of Nephrology; International Society of Peritoneal Dialysis; International Society of Blood Purification. Address: Shindonga Apt 15-401, Subingo-dong, Yongsan-koo, Seoul, Korea 140.

PARKE Ross, b. 17 Dec 1938, Canada. Professor. Education: PhD, University of Waterloo. Appointments: Assistant Professor, Professor, University Wisconsin, 1964-71; Senior Scientist, Fels Research Institute & Fels Clinical Professor of Research Pediatrics, University Cincinnati Medical School, 1971-75; Professor, University Illinois, 1975-90. Publications: Father, 1981; Child Psychology, 1993; Family-peer Relationships, co-editor, 1992; Children in Time & Place, co-editor, 1993; More than 100 articles and chapters. Memberships: American Psychology Association; American Psychological Society; Society for Research in Child Development. Address: Department of Psychology, University California, Riverside, CA 92521, USA.

PARKER James William, b. 1 Nov 1948, Osaka, Japan. US Army Physician. m. Mary Carolyn Clayton, 21 Nov 1975, 1 son, 1 daughter. Education: BA, University of Texas, 1971; MD, University Hospital of Texas Medical School, 1975; Internship, University of South Florida, 1975-76. Appointments: Chief, Department of Pediatrics, Winn Army

Hospital, 1981-84; Chief, Department of Pediatrics, 130th Station Hospital, Heidelberg, Germany, 1984-88. Publications: Injury Sites in Child Abuse Cases: A Preliminary Report, 1980; Two Child Abuse/Child Neglect Examinations for the Dentist, 1981; Child Abuse/Child Neglect Documentation Kit, 1982. Memberships: Fellow, American Academy of Pediatrics; Fellow, American College of Allergy & Immunology; Fellow, American Academy of Allergy & Immunology; Allergy & Immunology Society of Georgia; Association of Military Allergists. Address: 402 Yeager Avenue, Ft Benning, Georgia, USA.

PARKER Robert George, b. 29 Jan 1925, Detroit, MI, USA. Medicine. m. Diana Davis, 30 Jun 1977, 2 s. Education: BS, 1946, MD, 1948, University of Wisconsin; Board Certified, Radiology, 1955. Career: Director, Division of Radiation Oncology, University of Washington, 1958-87; Currently, Professor and Chairman, Department of Radiation Oncology, UCLA School of Medicine. Publications: Over 200 scientific publications. Honours: Fellowship, American College of Radiology, 1973; Citation, University of WI Medical Alumni Association, 1990. Memberships: President, American Board of Radiology, 1988-90; President, American Society of Therapeutic Radiology and Oncology, 1975-76; President, American Radium Society, 1990-91; President, Radiological Society of North America, 1991-92; American Medical Association; RSNA. Hobbies: Jazz Piano; Rose Gardening; Swimming. Address: Department of Radiation Oncology, 200 Medical Plaza, University of California, Los Angeles, CA 90024, USA.

PARKIN James L, b. 2 June 1939, Salt Lake City, Utah, USA. Surgeon. m. Bonnie Rae Dansie, 4 Aug 1963, 4 s. Education: BS, 1963, MD, 1966, University of Utah; MS, Physiology and Biophysics, University of Washington, 1970. Appointments: Instructor, Department of Otolaryngology, University of Washington; Assistant Professor, Associate Professor, Professor of department of Surgery, Professor and Chairman, Division of Otolaryngology-Head and Neck Surgery, University of Utah; Hetzel Professor and Chairman, Department of Surgery, University of Utah School of Medicine. Publications: Multichannel Cochlear Implant, 1993; Multichannel Cochlear Implantation with Percutaneous Pedestal, 1994; Laser Use in Otolaryngology-Head and Neck Surgery, 1987. Honours: Alpha Omega Alpha; Phi Kappa Phi; American Academy of Otolaryngology Honour Award; Coates Memorial Lecturer, 1986. Memberships: American College of Surgeons; American Society for Head and Neck Surgery; American Laryngological, Rhinological and Otological Society; American Otological Society. Hobbies: Family life; Skiing; Athletics; Reading; Church and community service. Address: Department of Surgery, University of Utah, 50 North Medical Drive, Salt Lake City, UT 84132, USA.

PARKS Thomas Norville, b. 27 May 1950, Berkeley, California, USA. Neurobiologist. m. Dr Patricia Legant, 6 July 1980, 1 d. Education: BS, Biology, University of California, Irvine, 1972; PhD, Psychobiology, Yale University, 1978. Appointments: Lecturer in Psychology, Yale University, 1977; Postdoctoral Fellow, Developmental Neurology, University of Virginia, 1977-78; Assistant Professor of Anatomy, 1978-83, Associate Professor, 1983-87, Professor, 1987-92, George and Lorna Winder Professor of Neuroscience, Chairman, Department of Neurobiology and Anatomy, University of Utah School of Medicine. Memberships: Sigma Xi; Soceity for neuroscience; Centurions of the Deafness Research Foundation. Hobbies: friut-growing; Winemaking. Address: Department of Neurobiology and Anatomy, University of Utah School of Medicine, Salt Lake City, UT 84132, USA.

PARMET Allen J, b. 25 Nov 1950. Medicine. 2 s. Education: MD; MPH; D AV MED. Appointments: MD, Eastern Test Range, Space Operations, 1982-84; Medical Director, Western Test Range, Space Shuttle Operations, 1984-87; Professor, Aerospace Medicine, USAF School of Aerospace Medicine, 1987-92; Currently, Medical Director: TranWorld Airlines; St Luke's Occupational Medicine. Publications: Study Guide for Preventive Medicine, 1989, revised editions, 1990-95; Over 100 articles; Assistant Editor, AVIAT Space and Environmental Medicine. Honours: Unger Award, 1986; Resident's Teaching Award, 1989; MSM 2, 1992. Memberships: AMA; Fellow, Aerospace Medical Association; Fellow, American College PREV Medicine. Address: 2025 SWIFT, NKC, MO 64116, USA.

PARPIANI Priya, b. 24 Sept 1936, Karachi, Pakistan. Obstetric & Gynecology Docotr. m. 3 Feb 1973. Education: MD; FCPS; DGO; DFP; FACOG. Appointments: Obstetrics & Gynecology Physician, California, USA. Memberships: Fellow, American College of Obstetrics &

Gynecology. Hobbies: Travell; Golf. Address: 18831 Winnwood, Santa Ana, CA 92705, USA.

PARRES Ramon, b. 21 May 1920, Chiapas, Mexico. Psychiatrist. m. Amparo Romero, 24 Oct 1946, 2 d. Education: BSc, cum laude, University of Mexico, 1938; MD, Honorary Mention, University of Mexico, 1945; Psychiatrist, Psychologist, Columbia University, 1948-52. Career: Director, Psychoanalytic Institute, 1957-60; Director, Psychoanalytic Clinic, 1960-70; Assistant Professor of Psychiatry, 1954-68; Currently, Professor, Faculty, Training Analyst, Psychoanalytic Institute, Faculty of Medicine. Publications: History of Psychiatry - Mexico, in World Studies in Psychiatry, 1979; 50 articles published. Honour: Medal of Merit, Mexican Society of Neurologic Psychiatry, 1970. Memberships include: President, Mexican Society of Neurologic Psychiatry, 1968-69; President, Mexican Psychoanalytic Association, 1957-60; Life Fellow, American Psychiatric Association; American Academy of Psychoanalysis; International Psychoanalytic Association. Hobbies: Swimming; Sailing; Golf; Photography; Woodwork. Address: Prado Norte 655-40 Piso Col, Lomas de Chapultepec Deleg, Miguel Hidalgo, 11000 Mexico DF, Mexico.

PARSON Erwin Randolph, b. 5 June 1943, Honduras, Central America. Psychoanalyst; Clinical Psychologist. m. 15 Dec 1972, 1 son, 1 daughter. Education: BS; MA, PhD, Clinical Psychology, 1977; Postdoctoral Certificate, Psychoanalysis, Psychotherapy, Derner Institute for Advanced Psychological Studies, USA, 1984. Appointments: Regional Manager, Region I (Northeastern USA), Veteran Centers, 1981-84; National Programme Specialist, Veterans Administration Central Office, 1984-85; Director of Research, VA Medical Center, Northport, New York, 1985-88; Consultant in Post-Traumatic Stress Disorder, Albany, New York, 1985-91; Visiting Professor, War and Its Social Consequences, University of Massachusetts, 1988-89; Veterans Administration Medical Center, Perry Point, Maryland, 1991-. Publications include: Vietnam Veterans: The Road to Recovery (with Joel O Brende), 1985; Ethnicity and Traumatic Stress: The Intersecting Point in Psychotherapy, 1985; Post-Traumatic Stress Disorder, 1992; Culture and Stress, 1992; Post-Traumatic Group Psychotherapy: A Handbook on Treating Victims of Violence, Rape, Technological Disasters and War, forthcoming; About 45 articles and Book Chapters mainly regarding stress disorders of war veterans and Inner City Children Affected by Violence; Editor-in-chief, Journal of Contemporary Psychotherapy, 1986-. Honours: Dr Martin Luther King Jr Award, New York Society of Clinical Psychologists, 1982; Key to City of Des Moines, Iowa, 1985; Honorary Citizen, State of Iowa, 1985; US Congressional Award for Community Development, 1990; New York State Department of Labor Service Award, 1990. Memberships: American Psychological Association, Division of Psychoanalysis; International Society for Traumatic Stress Studies; Many others. Hobbies: Woodworking; Creative writing; Music; Travel. Address: 1093 Fourth Street, PO Box 62, Perry Point, MD 21902-0062.

PARTIDA Pedro, b. 1 Sept 1959, Saginaw, Michigan, USA. Certified Ophthalmic Assistant; Optician. Appointments: Medical Assistant; Ophthalmic Photographer; Radial Keratotomy Coordinator; Currently: Certified Ophthalmic Assistant; Registered Dispensing Spectacle Optician. Memberships: Joint Commission of Allied Health Personnel; State of Texas Opticians Registry; Ophthalmic Photographers Society. Hobby: Member, Conté De Loyo Flamenco Dance Theatre. Address: 8225 Southwestern Boulevard 1029, Dallas, TX 75206, USA.

PASHIKOV Ata, b. 24 June 1935, Turkmenistan. Cardiology. m. Maya Pashikova, 25 June 1960, 5 sons, 2 daughters. Education: Turkmen State Medical Institute, 1963; Postgraduate, Moscow Medical Institute, 1968; Doctorate Course, 1976. Appointments: Doctor Radiologist, 1963-65; Assistant Professor, Medical Institute, Turkmenistan, 1977; Doctor of Radiology, 1979; Professor of Radiology, 1980. Publications: Clinic and Menodynamics of Congenital Heart Defects with Increased Pulmonary Blood Flow, 1991; Complex Diagnostics and Surgical Treatment of Cholecystites, 1990. Memberships: Corresponding Member, Academy of Medicine of Turkmenistan; Chairman, Association of Medicine of Turkmenistan. Hobbies: Weight Lifting; Swimming. Address: Erevanskij pr 27, 744008 Ashgabat, Turkmenistan.

PASNAU Robert Ottus, b. 8 July 1934, Mason City, Iowa, USA. Professor of Psychiatry. m. Janet Worden, 13 Aug 1955, 3 s. Education: BS, MD, 1959, University of Illinois; MS, UCLA. Appointments: Director, Residency Education, Department Psychiatry, Director, Consultation

Liaison Service, Department Psychiatry. Director, Clinical Service, Neuropsychiatric Institute, Assistant Dean, School of Medicine, Professor, Department of Psychiatry, UCLA Director, Mental Health Services for Physicians in Training. Publications: Consultation Liaison Psychiatry, 1975; Diagnosis and Treatment of Anxiety Disorders, 1995; Author of 6 other books; Contributor of over 100 professional articles. Honours: Gold Medal, Scientific Writing, Academy of psdychosomatic Medicine, 1964; Bowis Award, American College of Psychiatrists, 1986; Distinguished Service Award, UCLA, 1993. Memberships: President, Southern California Psychiatric Society, 1975; President, American College of Psychiatrists, 1984; President, American Psychiatric Association, 1986. Hobbies: Skiing; Philately; Piano playing; Music; Reading; Hiking; Doll houses. Address: UCLA Neuropsychiatric Institute, 760 Westwood Plaza, Los Angeles, CA 90024, USA.

PATEL Ambrish Janardanbhai, b. 11 Dec 1940, Baroda, India. Neurobiologist. m. Gwyneth Mary Evans-Patel, 29 Feb 1980. Education: BSc, Honours, Gujarat University, 1961; MSc, Baroda University, 1963; PhD, Baroda University, 1967; DSc, London University, England, 1984; FRCPath, 1991. Appointments: Lecturer, Baroda University, 1966-67; Scientist, MRC Neuropsychiatry Unit, Carshalton, England, 1967-75; Senior Scientist, Honorary Lecturer, MRC Developmental Neurobiology Unit, Institute of Neurology, London; Senior Scientist, National Institute for Medical Research, London, 1988-93; Senior Scientist, Medical Research Council, Honorary Reader, Charing Cross and Westminster Medical School, London. Publications: Contributor of over 150 research papers in international scientific journals and 40 reviews or chapters in books. Honours: Dr C S Patel Gold Medal, Baroda University, 1972; Silver Jubilee Medal, HM Queen Elizabeth II, 1977; Government of India Merit Scholar, 1963-66. Memberships: International Brain Research Organisation; International Soceity for Neurochemistry; Biochemical Society; British Pharmacological Society; British Neuropathological Society. Hobbies: Walking; Reading; Writing; Finance; Gardening. Address: MRC Neurodegenerative Disorders Group, Charing Cross and Westminster Medical School, Fulham Palace Road, London W6 8RF, England.

PATEL Amrish K, b. 13 Mar 1959. Physician. m. Vaishali, 3 Aug 1986. Education: MB,BS; MD; MRCP(UK). Appointments: Allergist and Immunologist in private practice. Memberships: American College of Physicians; American College of Allergy and Immunology; American Academy of Allergy and Immunology. Address: 3535 W 13 Mile Road #240, Royal Oak, MI 48073, USA.

PATEL Jyotsna Navalrai, b. 12 May 1936, Ahmedabad, India. Physician. Education: MBBS, Gujarat University, 1960; MD, Gujarat University, 1964; MRCOG, 1969. Appointments incl: Private Practice, Bombay, India, 1974-75; Resident Registrar, Various Hospitals, England, 1975-76; Private Practice, Ashland, Kentucky, 1978; Resident House Officer, St Raphael Hospital, New Havenm, 1978-79; Fellow, Obstetrics & Gynaecology, Franklin Hospital, Long Island, 1979-80; Group Practice, Obstetrics & Gynaecology, La Guardia Medical Group, New York, 1981-83; Consulting Obstetrician & Gynaecologist, Ahmedabad, India, 1983-86; Obstetrician & Gynaecologist, SEWA, Rural, Jhagadia, Bharuch District, 1986-87; Honorary Technical & Medical Consultant, Family Planning ICE Project, Gujarat State Crime Prevention Trust, 1992-. Honours: Fellow, American College of Obstetricians & Gynaecologists, 1983; Fellow, Royal College of Obstetricians & Gynaecologists, England, 1992. Memberships: Indian Medical Association; Fedeeration of Obstetrics & Gynaecology Society of India. Hobbies: Music; Reading; Yoga. Address: 3 Hindu Colony, opp Stadium Navarang-Pura, Ahmedabad 380009, India.

PATEL Mukesh P, b. 16 Feb 1957, Nasik, India. Medical. m. Falguni Patel, 15 Jul 1983, 2 s. Education: MBBS; MD; Certified in Adolescent Psychiatry, and Additionology. Appointments include: National Merit Scholarship, Ministry of Education, Government of India, 1974-79; Commissioned Officer, Medical Corps, US Army Reserve, 1983; Lectures, Seminars and Publications, Roanoke Valley Professional and Community Education, 1986-92; Medical Director, Mount Regis Center, 1987-; Program Medical Director, Respond and Day Treatment Program, LGPC, Salem, VA, (for Profit Psychiatric Hospital), HCA Columbia GRP. Publication: Article, Cocaine and Crack, Its Impact in the Roanoke Valley, in Roanoke Memorial Hospital On-Call Newsletter. Memberships: Roanoke Valley Academy of Medicine; Committee, State Level, American Psychiatric Association; Southern Medical Association; American Society of Addiction Medicine; American Academy of Psychiatrists in Alcohol and Addictions; National Alliance for the

Mentally Ill. Hobbies: Tennis; Tabletennis; Soccer; Yoga. Address: 16, Walnut Ave. SW, Roanoke, VA 24018, USA.

PATEL Thakor G, b. 5 Jan 1945, Nairobi, Kenya. Physician. m. Usha Patel, 10 May 1970, 2 d. Education: MD; Board Certified in Internal Medicine and Nephrology. Appointments: Clinical Associate Professor of Internal Medicine, Eastern VA Medical School, Norfolk, VA; Currently, Director, Surface Medicine, US Navy. Publications: Several articles on renal diseases. Honours: Admiral Joel T Boone Award of AMSUS, 1989; Laureate Award of the American College of Physicians. Memberships: American Society of Nephrology; International Society of Nephrology; International Society of Peritoneal Dialysis; National Kidney Foundation; Indian Society of Nephrology; Fellow, American College of Physicians; ACPE; AMSUS. Hobbies: Jogging; Trains; Cars. Address: 10980 Rice Field Place, Fairfax Station, VA 22039, USA.

PATEL Yogini Nandubhai, b. 24 Sep 1952, Lamu, Kenya. Doctor. Education: MBBS; MRCOG. Appointments: Registrar in Obstetrics and Gynaecology: Great Yarmouth District Hospital, England, 2 years; Park Hospital, Deryhulm, Manchester, England, 4 years; Currently, Consultant Obstetrician and Gynaecologist. Honour: Gold Medal, Physics. Memberships: Indian Medical Association; Royal College of Obstetricians and Gynaecologists; Federation of Obstetricians and Gynaecologists Societies of India. Hobbies: Cooking; Sewing; Reading; Interior Decorating. Address: Kantalaxmi Hospital, Desai Vago, Rabari Wado, Nadiad PC 387001, Gujarat, India.

PATIL Mothiram K, b. 3 Sept 1940, Keelanje, India. Professor of Biomedical Engineering. m. Pushpa, 7 May 1969, 1 son, 1 daughter. Education: BSc, 1961; ME, 1967; DSc, 1971. Appointments: Assistant Professor, Department of Applied Mechanics, IIT, Madras, 1972-84; Associate Professor, IIT Madras, 1984-85; Professor of Biomedical Engineering, IIT Madras, 1985-; Professor, Chairman, Department of Applied Mechanics, IIT Madras, 1991-94. Publications: Over 115 professional publications in journals. Honours: Alexander von Humboldt Fellow, Germany, 1980-81; Visiting Scientist Award, Eindhoven University of Technology, 1989-90. Memberships: Biomedical Engineering Society, USA; Life Member, Biomedical Engineering Society of India; Life Member, Indian Foot Society; Life Member, Indian Society of Biomechanics. Hobbies: Reading Philosphy Books. Address: Biomedical Engineering Division, Department of Applied Mechanics, Indian Institute of Technology, Madras 600036, India.

PATSOURIS Efstratios, b. 19 Aug 1951, Athens, Greece. Medical Doctor. m. Anna Maria Maruantonaui, 9 July 1992, 1 son, 1 daughter. Education: MD, University of Athens Medical School, 1976; PhD, University of Athens Medical School, 1980; Fellow, Pathology, University of Athens Medical School, 1989. Appointments: Lecturer, Department of Pathology, University of Athens Medical School, 1981; Assistant Professor of Pathology, University of Athens Medical School, 1990. Publications: Histological and Immunohistological findings in Lennet's Lymphosis, 1988; Relationship between Ui-67 Positive Cells Growth and Histological Type of Human Intracoxinal Tumor, 1988; Angioiumnoblestic Lymphodenopathy Type of T-Cell Lymphonia with a high content of Epithelioid Cells, 1989; Cytohistologic and Immunohistochemical findings in Hodgkins Disease, mixed Cellularity Type with a high content of Epithelioid Cells, 1989; Immunocytomia with a high content of Epithelioid Cells, Histologic and Immunohistochemical findings, 1990; Cellular Composition and Distribution of Gliomesenchyual Nodules in the CNS of AIDS Patients, 1990; Lennert's Lymphonea: Clinical Features derived from analysis of 108 cases, 1993. Memberships: European Society of Pathology; International Society of Pathology; Greek Society of Pathology; European Lymphonea Group; German Society of Neuropathology; International Society of Neuroethology; International Brain Research Organization. Honours: Deutscher Akademischer Austauschdiensy, 1984; Heineuan Foundation Scholarship, 1984; Herman and Lilly Schilling Stiftung für Medizinische Fozschung, 1985; Deutscher Akademischer Austauschdiensy, 1994. Hobbies: Travel; Studying History. Address: Tritonos 100, Paleo Faliro 17562, Athens, Greece.

PATTERSON Charles Wilmot, b. 5 Aug 1940, Minnesota, USA. Psychiatrist. m. Stephanie Hamlin, 28 Dec 1968, 2 s. Education: BS, South Dakota State University, 1962; MD, University of Minnesota, 1967; Board Certification, American Board of Psychiatry and Neurology, 1974. Appointments: Chief, Mental Health, USAF Hospital, Malmstrom AFB, Montana; Ward Chief, Adult INpatient Service, LAC+USC Medical Centre, Los Angeles; Acting Chairman, USC Department of Psychiatry,

1991; Director of Graduate Education, Department of Psychiatry, University of Southern California School of Medicine. Publications: Psychiatrists and Physical Examinations: A Survey, 1978; Some Characteristics of Inpatient Psychiatric Training, Co-author, 1985. Honours: Fellow, American Psychiatric Association, 1992; Phi Kappa Phi, 1962. Memberships: American Psychiatric Association; Southern California Psychiatric Society; West Coast College of Biological Psychiatry. Hobbies: Golf; Model building. Address: USC Department of Psychiatry, 1934 Hospital Place, Los Angeles, CA 90033, USA.

PATTERSON Paula C, b. 18 Mar 1946, Norfolk, Virginia, USA. Creative Arts Therapist. m. Richard Frazier Patterson, 1 Jan 1990, 2 sons, 1 daughter. Education: BA, Scripps College, 1968; MA, Dance/Movement Therapy, Columbia College, 1987; Registered Dance/Movement Therapist. Appointments include: Dance/Movement Therapist, Drama Therapist: Forest Hospital, Des Plaines, Illinois, 1971-76; Old Orchard Hospital, Skokie, Illinois, 1981-85; Hanbleceya Hospital, 1990-91, Charter Hospital, 1991-95, Kaiser Permamente Hospital, San Diego, California, 1993-95; Founder & Director, San Diego Playback Theatre, San Diego, California. Publications: Humanistic Dance/Movement Therapy, article, 1990; Dancing Colors - The Use of Scarves in Dance Therapy, Education, Performance and Ritual (co-produced with Emily Day), video, 1992. Memberships: American Dance Therapy Association; American Drama Therapy Association; American Society of Group Psychotherapy and Psychodrama; International Association of Humanistic Psychology; International Playback Theatre Network. Address;: 1725 Woodmere Drive, Jacksonville, FL 32210, USA.

PATTERSON Stuart Drew, b. 3 June 1958, South Africa. Hand Surgeon. m. Haydee B M Yell, 6 July 1991, 2 sons. Education: MBChB, University of Cape Town; FRCSC, McMaster University. Appointments: Assistant Professor, Orthopaedic Surgery. Publications: Multiple publications in various journals and magazines. Memberships: Canadian Orthopaedic Association; American Academy of Orthopaedic Surgeons. Hobbies: Scuba Diving; Skiing. Address: Hand & Upper Limb Centre, St Joseph's Health Centre, 268 Grosvenor Street, London, Ontario N6A 4L6, Canada.

PATTON David, b. 2 Apr 1954, Larne, North Ireland. Psychologist. 3 s. Education: BA, Honours, University of Western Ontario, Canada; MA and PhD, Psychology, University of Manitoba, Winnipeg, Canada. Appointments: Research Associate School of Child and Youth Care, University of Victoria, BC; Research Associate, Family Studies Department, University of Manitoba, Winnipeg. Publications: Sex and Marital Therapy, 1985, 1986; Personality and Individual Differences, 1993; International Journal of Addictions, 1994; Journal of Studies on Alcohol, 1994. Honours: Doctoral Fellowship, SSHRC, 1990; Manitoba Health Research Council, 1992-93; National Health Research and Development Grant, 1994-95. Memberships: American Psychological Association; Canadian Psychological Association; International Society for the Study of Individual Differences. Hobbies: Soccer; Swimming; Coaching and Referee. Address: Manitoba Centre for Health Policy and Evaluation, Department of Community Health Sciences, University of Manitoba, 750 Bannatyne Ave, Winnipeg, Manitoba, Canada, R3E 0W3.

PATY Donald Winston, b. 25 Sept 1936, Peking, China. Neurologist. m. Jo Anne Haymore, 28 Dec 1958, 3 s, 1 d. Education: BA, Emory University, 1958; MD, 1962; Intern, Duke University, 1962-63; Resident in Medicine and Neurology, Emory University, 1965-70; Fellow in Immunology, MRC Demyelinating Diseases Unit, University of Newcastle-Upon-Tyne, England, 1970-72. Appointments: Assistant Professor, then Professor of Neurology, University of Western Ontaria Medical School, 1972-80; Professor of Neurology/Head of Division, Univ of BC Medical School, Vancouver, 1980-; Secretary General, XV World Congress of Neurology, Vancouver BC, 1993. Publications: Interferon beta - Ib is Effective in Relapsing-Remitting Multiple Sclerosis II; Results of a Multicentre, Randomized Double-Blind, Pacebo Controlled Trial, 1993. Honours: Certificate of Honour for Outstanding Contribution, Vancouver Hospital, 1993; Honorary Member, ABN, 1993; National Certificate of Merit, Multiple Sclerosis Society of Canada, 1993; Abstract Neurological Psychiatry, Doctor of the Year, France, 1993. Memberships: American Academy of Neurology; Canadian Neurological Society; American Neurological Association; British Association of Neurologists; World Federation of Neurology; Multiple Sclerosis Research Group; Alpha Omega Alpha. Hobbies: Music; Hiking; Scubadiving. Address: 2657 West 24th Avenue, Vancouver, BC B65 1L7, Canada.

PAUL-CAVALLIER François, b. 4 Aug 1945, Bayonne, France. Psychotherapist. m. Brigitte du Parc, 25 May 1968, 1 s, 1 d. Appointments: Founder of Édition de la Tortue; Publishing Director, Luter Editions. Publications: Visualisation 1989; Le Empreuiter de Corps, 1984; Mauris Vincent au risque de l'amaus, 1989; Accompaquer la Vie, 1990; Jauous, 1993; Co-Author, Grandir Ensemble, 1993. Memberships: Titulaire Fromation; SNP Psychotherapy. Hobies: Gardening; Writting Novels. Address: 56 Rue Madama, 75006 Paris, France.

PAUSAWASDI Somsri, b. 30 Apr 1940, Petchaburi Provinces, Thailand. Chairman, Department of Anesthesiology. m. Professor Arun Pausawasdi, 10 Aug 1966, 3 s, 2 d. Education: MD, 1963; Doctor Medicine, DTM, Hamburg University, 1966-69; Diploma, Thai Board of Anesthesiology, 1971. Appointments include: Assistant Professor, 1975-78, Associate Professor, 1979-87, Professor, 1987-, Professor and Chairman, Department of Anesthesiology, 1988-. Ramathibodi Hospital, Mahidol University, Bangkok; President, Examiners Committee of Thai Board of Anesthesiology, 1989-; Special Lecturer, Faculty of Medicine, Chiengmai Hospital, 1986-; Special Lecturer, Rungsit University, Bangkok, 1991-. Publications include: 37 articles in professional journals, 1977-92; Many Chapters and contributions to textbooks, 1983-90. Honours: Knight Grand Cross, First Class, The Most Noble Order of the Crown of Thailand, 1986; Mahidol University Prize for Best Textbook of Year for, Neuroanesthesia, from the King, 1988; Knight Grand Cross, First Class, The Most Exalted Order of the White Elephant, 1990; Knight Grand Cordon of the Most Noble Order of The Crown of Thailand, 1990. Memberships include: Editorial Board: Thai Journal of Anesthesiologists, 1984-; Journal Medical Association Thailand, 1987-; Medical Council Bulletin, 1990-; Immediate Past President, The Royal College of Anesthesiologists of Thailand, 1991-93; Secretary General, Internal Association for the Study of Pain, 1990-92. Address: Department of Anesthesiology, Ramathibodi Hospital, 270 Rama VI Road, Bangkok 10400, Thailand.

PAVSIC Ivo, b. 25 Dec 1932, Maribor, Slovenia. Professor of Orthodontics. m. Apolonia Mejac, 20 Feb 1954, 1 son, 2 daughters. Education: Doctor of Stomatology, 1965, Specialist of Jaw Orthopaedics, 1969, DSc, 1979, Faculty of Medicine, Ljubljana. Appointments: Assistant, 1968-80, Docent, 1980-86, Professor, 1986-, Head, Orthodontic Department, 1990-, Faculty of Medicine, Ljubljana. Publications: 7 scientific and clinical publications in international journals, 19 in national journals, pre-1994; Dilemmas Arising in Orthodontic Corrections of Post-Traumatic Disorders of the Anterior Teeth, 1994; Retrospective Evaluation of Orthodontics Care in Slovenia, 1994; Orthodontic Care of Patients with Cleft Lip and Palate, 1994. Memberships: Slovenian Medical Society, Orthodontic Association; European Orthodontic Society. Hobby: Magic. Address: Stantetova 10, SLO-61000 Ljubljana, Slovenia.

PAWSON Michael Edward, b. 10 Jun 1937, Edgbaston, England. Gynaecologist. m. Carolyn Pawson, 12 Aug 1961, 1 s, 2 d. Education: MBBS; FRCOG. Career includes: Examiner to Central Midwives and Conjoint Board; Currently, Examiner to University of London and Royal College of Obstetrics and Gynaecology and Consultant Gynaecologist. Publications: Numerous on infertility. Memberships: British Fertility Society; Worshipful Society of Apothecaries; Chairman, British Society of Psychosomatic Obstetrics, Gynaecology and Andrology; UK representative, International Executive Committee of the International Society of Psychosomatic Obstetrics and Gynaecology. Hobbies: Modern First Editions; Vegetable Horticulture; Beekeeping; Escapism. Address: Braywood House, Drift Road, Windsor Forest, Berkshire, SL4 4RR, England.

PAYEUR Richard, b. 28 Jan 1960, Quebec, Canada. Psychiatrist. Education: MD, University of Montreal, 1984; Psychiatry, McGill University, 1990; Anxiety Disorder Fellowship, Medical University, South Carolina, USA, 1990-92; FRCPC, Royal College, 1991; Pharmacology, University of Nantes, France, 1993. Appointments: Clinical Teacher, McGill University & University of Ottawa. Publications: Co-author, Cholecystokinin and Panic Disorder, 1992; CSF DBI Concentrations in Panic Disorder, 1992; The Role of CCR in Schizophenia, 1993. Memberships: American Psychiatric Association; Canadian Psychiatric Association; Canadian College of Neuropharmacology. Address: 20 rue Pharand, Hull, Quebec J9A 1K7, Canada.

PEACOCK Warwick John, b. 27 Oct 1940, Johannesburg. Neurosurgeon. m. Ann Taylor, 5 Mar 1971, 1 son, 4 daughters. Education: BSc, University of Stellenbosch, 1962; MB ChB, University of Cape Town, 1966. Appointments: Family Practice, 1968-70; Lecturer in Anatomy, University of Durban, 1970-72; Associate Professor, University of Cape Town, 1979-85; Chief, Spinal Defects Clinic, Cape Town, 1979-85; Associate Professor, UCLA School of Medicine, 1986-90; Attending Pediatric Neurosurgeon, Harbor UCLA Medical Center, 1986-; Attending Pediatric Neurosurgeon, Shriner's Hospital, Los Angeles, 1986-; Professor, Department of Surgery, UCLA School of Medicine, 1990-. Publications Include: A Review of 450 Stab Wounds to the Spinal Cord, 1977; The Neurosurgical Management of Spasticity, 1981; Tuberculous Osteitis of the Skull, 1982; Results of Epilepsy Surgery, 1992; Behavioral and anatomical features of a rabbit model for infantile hydrocephalus, 1992; Developmental outcomes in children receiving surgery for medically intractable spasms, 1993; Surgical Treatment of epilepsy in children, 1992; Selective posterior rhizotomy, 1992; Pediatric Moyamoya, 1993. Honours: Taljaard Prize, 1962; Outstanding Physician of the Year Award, UCLA Medical Center, 1990; Folke Bernadotte Lecture Award, 1992. Memberships: American Society of Pediatric Neurosurgeons; California Neurosurgical Association for Pediatrics; California Association of Neurological Surgery; Southern California Neurosurgical Surgery; International Society for Paediatric Neurosurgery. Hobbies: Jogging; Skiing. Address: Division of Neurosurgery, UCLA School of Medicine, Los Angeles 90024, USA.

PEARLMAN David Samuel, b. 20 Jan 1934, Syracuse, New York, USA. Physician. m. Doris Greenberg, 1966, 1 son, 1 daughter. Education: MD, University of New York, 1958. Appointments: Instructor, University of Colorado Medical School, 1962-63; Assistant Professor, University of Colorado Medical School, 1964-68; Associate Professor, University of Colorado Medical School, 1969-72; Clinical Associate Professor, University of Colorado Medical School, 1972-78; Clinical Professor, University of Colorado Medical School, 1978-. Publications include: Antibody Formation in Infancy, 1961; Complement Components of Paired Mother-Cord Sera, 1961; Effects of Exercise and Anemia on Coronary Arteries of Small Animals as Revealed by the Corrosion-Cast Technique, 1961; Asthma Therapy: A Total Approach, 1972; Management of Atopic Dermatitis: An Allergist's Point of View, 1974; Rationale for Therapy of Allergic Disorders, 1975; The Relationship Between Allergy and Croup, 1989; Systemic Anaphylaxis During Rectal Manometry with a Latex Balloon, 1989; Asthma (Reactive Airways Disorder), 1990. Honours: Best Doctors in the US, 1980, 1982; Town & Country's The Best Medical Specialists in the US, 1984, 1989; The Best Doctors in America, 1992, 1994. Memberships: Executive Committee, Section on Allergy & Immunology, American Academy of Pediatrics; Chairperson, Section on Allergy & Immunology, 1992-94. Hobbies: Running; Skiing; Travel. Address: 1450 S Havana Street, Aurora, CO 80012, USA.

PEARSE Warren Harland, b. 28 Sept 1927, Michigan, USA. Physician. m. Jacqueline A Langan, 15 June 1950, 4 daughters. Education: BS, Michigan University, 1948; MB, MD, Northestern University, 1951. Appointments: Instructor to Professor & Chairman, University Nebraska, 1959-71; Dean, Medical College of Virginia, 1971-75; Executive Director, American College of Obstetricians & Gynecologists, 1975-93. Publications: 115 articles in scientific literature; Editor, Journal, Women's Health Issues. Honours: Fellow, Royal College of Obstetricians & Gynecologists, London. Memberships: ACOG; AMA; American Gynecological & Obstetrical Society; Society for Gynecologic Investigation. Hobbies: Curling; Philately; Model Rail Roading; American Highway History. Address: 350 South River Landing, Edgewater, MD 21037, USA.

PEARSON Althea Mary, b. 30 May 1955, London, England. Chartered Counselling Psychologist. m. Brian Pearson, 27 Apr 1974, 2 s. Education: BA, 1978, PhD, 1985, University of London; Diploma in Counselling, Brighton Polytechnic, 1984. Appointments: Counselling Psychologist in Private Practice; Bishops' Advisor on Counselling, Diocese of Canterbury. Publications: Many Professional Publications, 1977-91, including: The Handwriting of Children with Spina Bifida, Z Kinder Chirurgie, 1988; Stress, in Church of England Newspaper, Jul 1988; Bi-Monthly Discussions on Emotional and Psychological Issues, Woman Alive, 1991; Book, Growing Through Loss and Grief, 1994. Honour: Associate Fellow, British Psychological Society. Memberships: British Psychological Society; Accredited Counsellor, 1986-, British Association for Counselling, 1985-; Network of Christians in Psychology, 1990-; Christians in Caring Professions, 1986-; West Kent Association for Pastoral Care and Counselling, 1991-. Hobbies: Committed Christian; Theatre. Address: 20 Pilgrims Way, Canterbury, Kent, CT1 1XU, England.

PEAT John Humphrey, b. 3 Oct 1927, Palmerston North, New Zealand. Orthodontics. m. Lana Rainey, 28 Sept 1953, 4 sons. Education: BDS (NZ), 1950; DDS (North Western), 1952; DOrth RCS (Eng), 1959; DDS (Otago), 1966; FRACDS, 1968; FCID, 1986. Career: Consultant Orthodontist, Plastic Surgical Unit, Middlemore Hospital, Auckland, NZ, 1963-92; Retired Orthodontist. Publications: Cephalometric Study of Tongue Position, 1968; Orthodontics for Cleft Palate Child, 1970; Early Orthodontic Treatment for Complete Clefts, 1974; Pre-Surgical Oral Orthopaedics, 1982. Memberships: NZ DA, NZ AO; AAO; ASO. Hobbies: Tennis; Golf; Swimming; Reading. Address: 130 Point View Drive, RD1 Papatoetoe, Auckland, New Zealand.

PEATTIE Robert Addison, b. 8 Aug 1956, Greenwich, CT, USA. Professor. Education: BS, Trinity College, 1979; PhD, Johns Hopkins University, 1988. Career: Postdoctoral Fellow, Johns Hopkins University, 1988-89; Currently, Assistant Professor, Biomedical Engineering, Tulane University. Publications: Contributor to: Journal of Physics, International Journal of Heat and Mass Transfer, Investigative Radiology, Journal of Ultrasound in Medicine, Annals of Biomedical Engineering, Experiments in Fluids. Honours: Mary A Terry Fellowship, 1979; Alpha Eta Mu Beta, 1990; Sigma Xi, 1990; National Science Foundation Research Initiation Award, 1990; Teacher of Year, Department of Biomedical Engineering, Tulane University, 1993; Tau Beta Pi, 1995. Memberships: Chairman of Finance, 1993-, Biomedical Engineering Society; American Physical Society; American Academy of Mechanics. Hobbies: Swimming; Biking; Running; Carpentry; Gardening. Address: Department of Biomedical Engineering, Tulane University, New Orleans, LA 70118, USA.

PECK William Arno, b. 28 Sept 1933, New Britain, Connecticut, USA. m. (1) 2 s, 1 d, (2) Patricia Hearn, 10 July 1982, 3 d. Education: AB, harvard University, 1955; MD, University of Rochester, 1960. Appointments: Intern, resident, Internal Medicine, Barnes Hospital, St Louis, 1960-62; Fellow, Metabolism, Washington University School of Medicine, St Louis, 1963; Professor of Medicine and Biochemistry, University of Rochester 1973-76; Head, Division of Endocrinology and Metabolism, 1969-76; John E and Adaline Simon Professor of Medicine, Co-Chairman, Department of Medicine, Washington University School of Medicine, St Louis, 1976-89; Physician-in-Chief, Jewish Hospital, St Louis, 1976-89; Professor of Medicine, Executive Vice Chancellor of Medical Affairs, Dean, School of Medicine, President, University Medical centre, Washington University, St Louis, 1989-. Publications: Bone and Mineral Research Annuals, editor, 1982-88; Contributor of articles in medical journals. Honours: Mosby Book Award, Alpha Omega Alpha, 1960; Doran J Stephens Award, University of Rochester School of Medicine, 1960; Lederle Medical faculty Award, 1967; NIH Career Programme award, 1971; Commissioner's Special Citation, FDA, 1988. Memberships include: Fellow, ACP; Fellow, AAAS; American Society Biological Chemists; American Physiology Society; American Society Clinical INvestigation; American Federation Clinical Research; American Diabetes Association; American Society Bone and Mineral Research, President, 1983-84; Association American Physicians; Endocrine Society; Orthopaedic Research Society; National Institute Arthritis; Sigma Xi; Alpha Omega Alpha, Board Directors, 1992-. Address: 2 Apple Tree Lane, St Louis, MO 63124-1601, USA.

PECKHAM Michael John, b. 2 Aug 1935, Pontypool, Wales. University Professor; Civil Servant. m. Professor Catherine Stevenson King, 7 Oct 1958, 3 sons. Education: BA; MA; FRCP; FRCR; FRCPath. Career: Junior Hospital Posts, Military Service, 1959-65; Clinical Research Scholar, Institute Gustave Roussy, Paris, 1965-67; Lecturer/Senior Lecturer Institute of Cancer Research, 1967-73; Professor of Radiotherapy, Institute of Cancer Research, Royal Marsden Hospital, 1974-86; Dean Institute of Cancer Research, 1984-86; Director, British Postgraduate Medical Federation, 1986-90; Director of Research and Development, Dept of Health, 1991. Publications: Over 270 research papers; Editor-in-Chief, European Journal of Cancer, 1990-95; Co-editor (with H Pinedo & U Veronesi), Oxford Textbook of Oncology, 1995. Honours include: Université de Franche-Compté, Besançon, Doctor Honoris Causa, 1991; Katholieke Universiteit Leuven, Doctor Honoris Causa, 1993; Fellow, Royal Society of Arts, 1993; Foreign Associate Member, National Academy of Sciences, Institute of Medicine, Washington DC, 1994. Hobby: Painting. Address: Department of Health, Richmond House, 79 Whitehall, London SW1A 2NS, England.

PEDERSON Sanford L, b. USA. Psychologist. Education: BA, Psychology, University of California, Riverside, 1974; MA, General and Experimental Psychology, California State University, San Bernardino, 1978; PhD, Clinical Psychology, University of Maine, Orono, 1984.

Appointments include: Staff Psychologist, VA Medical Center, Togus, Maine, 1983-85; Neuropsychologist, VA Medical Center, North Chicago, Illinois, 1985-91; Clinical Assistant Professor, Psychology, University of Health Sciences/The Chicago Medical School, North Chicago, 1986-91; Psychologist in private practice, Arlington Heights, Illinois, 1987-91; Chief, Psychology Service, Department of Veterans Affairs Medical Center, Livermore, California, 1991-94. Publications include: Co-author: Personality styles and psychopathy, 1982; A proposal for a computerized APIC National Intern Matching Program, 1988; Effects of Post-traumatic stress disorder on neuropsychological test performance, 1989; Refining psychological testing for PTSD, 1990; Co-author, papers: APIC's study of computerized internship matching: Issues and information, 1989; The Results of the APIC Pilot Study of the Computerized Internship Matching Program, 1990; Others. Honours: National Institute of Mental Health Fellowship, 1978-81; Certificate of Recognition, National Organization of VA Psychologists, 1989. Memberships: Trustee, Training and Education Committee Chair, Research Committee Member, National Organization of VA Psychologists; Division 18 Executive Committee and Fellowship Chair, American Psychological Association; Psi Chi; Board of Directors, Secretary-Treasurer, Newsletter Editor, Association of Psychology Postdoctoral and Internship Centers; International Neuropsychological Society. Address: 4685 Duarte Avenue, Oakley, CA 94561, USA.

PEEBLES-KLEIGER Mary Josephine, b. La Jolla, California, USA. Clinical Psychologist. m. James H Kleiger, 18 Mar 1989, 1 son, 1 daughter. Education: BA, Wellesley College, 1972; PhD, Psychology, Case Western Reserve University, 1977. Appointments: Staff Psychologist, The Menninger Clinic, 1980-89, 1992-; Staff Psychologist & Consulting Staff Psychologist, Chestnut Lodge Hospital, Rockville, 1989-92; Private Practice, Wheaton, Maryland, 1989-92. Publications incl: Using Countertransference in the Hypnosis of Trauma Victims: Hazards That Can Facilitate Healing, 1989; Toward a Conceptual Understanding of the DR Response in the Comprehensive Rorschach System, 1993; Re-integration Stress for Desert Storm Families: Wartime Deployments and Family Trauma, 1994. Honours incl: National Merit Scholar, 1968; Phi Beta Kappa; Publications Award, Topeka Institute for Psychoanalysis, 1987. Memberships: American Psychological Association; International Neuropsychological Society; The Society for Clinical & Experimental Hypnosis; International Society for Traumatic Stress Studies. Hobbies: Piano; Reading; Cycling. Address: Menninger, PO Box 829, Topeka, KS 66601, USA.

PEELE Roger, b. 24 Dec 1930, Elizabeth City, NC, USA. Psychiatry. m. Gail Peele, 15 Oct 1992, 1 s, 2 d. Education: MD. Appointments: Assistant Director of NIMH for Treatment; Assistant Superintendent and Acting Superintendent, St Elizabeth's Hospital; Currently, Chair, Department of Psychiatry and Medical Director, CMHS, DC. Publications: Clinical Manual of Supportive Psychotherapy, 1993; Force into Treatment: The Role of Coercion in Clinical Practice, 1993. Honour: Administrative Psychiatrist of Year, 1989. Memberships: American Psychiatric Association; AMA; Group for the Advancement of Psychiatry; President, American Association for Social Psychiatry; Past President, American Association of Psychiatric Administrators. Hobby: Jogging. Address: St Elizabeth's Campus, Washington, DC 20032, USA.

PEERLINGS Robertus Henricus Josephus, b. 8 Jul 1963, Nederweert, The Netherlands. Orthodontist. m. M Tieleman, 14 Oct 1993. Education: Dr, Dentistry, Orthodontics. Career: Dentist; Currently, Orthodontist in Private Practice. Publications include: Transverse Resistance of Composite Resin Restorations on Denture, 1989; The Occlusal Contact Status of Extensive Amalgam Restorations, 1988; Development of an Illustrated Scale to Measure Facial Esthetics, 1991; Orthodontics and dento-facial esthetics, thesis, 1992; Co-author, Improvement of facial appearance after orthodontic treatment, in European Journal of Orthodontics, 1993; Co-author, A photographic scale to measure facial esthetics, in European Journal of Orthodontics, 1995. Memberships: European Orthodontic Society; American Association of Orthodontists; Nederlandse Vereniging van Orthodontische Studie; Nederlandse Vereniging van Specialisten in de dento-maxillaire Orthopedie. Hobbies: Tennis; Cooking. Address: Papegaaienburg 48, 4386 DA Vlissingen, The Netherlands.

PEEVY Keith Jackson, b. 28 Dec, Baton Rouge, LA, USA. Neonatal Medicine. m. Micki Denny Baswell, 3 sons, 1 daughter. Education: BS, Louisiana University, 1971; MD, Louisiana University School of Medicine, 1974; Residency, Pediatrics, University of South Alabama, 1977; Fellowship, Neonatal Medicine, Duke University, 1979.

Appointment: Professor of Pediatrics & Neonatal Medicine, University of South Alabama. Publications: Myocardial Dysfunction in Group B Streptomocal Shock, 1985; Mechanisms of Ventilator Induced Lung Injury, 1993; Association Between Maternal-Fetal HLA-DR Relationships and Fetal Growth, 1993. Honours: AOA, 1974; OKO, 1971. Memberships: Society for Pediatric Research; American Academy of Pediatrics. Hobbies: Family; Golf; Aerobic Exercise. Address: University of South Alabama, Department of Pediatrics, Mobile, AL 36619, USA.

PEH Wilfred C G, b. 21 Apr 1958, Singapore. Diagnostic Radiologist. m. Angeline Yue, 28 July 1988. 2 sons, 1 daughter. Education: MB, BS, National University of Singapore, 1982; DMRD, 1989, FRCR, 1990, Royal College of Radiologists, UK; FHKAM (Hong Kong), 1993; FAMS (Singapore), 1993. Appointments: Registrar in Diagnostic Radiology, Royal Infirmary, Glasgow, Scotland; Senior Registrar in Diagnostic Radiology, West Midlands Regional Health Authority, England; Currently Senior Lecturer in Diagnostic Radiology, University of Hong Kong. Publications: Co-author: Tarlov Cysts - Another Cause of Sacral Insufficiency Fractures, 1992; The Role of Computerized Tomography in Shoulder Arthrography, 1994; Imaging of the Wrist. A Customized Approach, 1994. Memberships include: British Institute of Radiology; American Roentgen Ray Society; Radiological Society of North America. Hobbies: Golf; Riding. Address: Department of Diagnostic Radiology, The University of Hong Kong, Queen Mary Hospital, Pokfulam, Hong Kong.

PEI Xue Yi, b. 14 Feb 1926, Beijing, China. Director; Doctor of Chinese Herbs Medicine. m. Zhao Xiu Qing, 9 Sept 1950, 2 sons. Education: Degree, Beijing Chinese Medicine College, 1947. Publications: Treatment for 150 Cases of Lepatitis by Chinese Traditional Herbs Medicine; Dialectical Theory for Acute Adrenitis by Chinese Traditional Herbs Medicine; Treatment for Prevalent B Encephalitis by Herbs Medicine; Treatment for Bronchietasis by Herbs Medicine; Treatment for Dance Illness by Herbs Medicine; My Opinion for Longevity. Hobbies: Fishing; Beijing Opera. Address: Beijing Childrens Hospital, 56 Nalishi Road, Xichang District, Beijing 100045, China.

PEI Zhu Guo, b. 17 Oct 1936, Heishan, Liaoning Province, China. Doctor. m. Xing Fuqin, 5 May 1956, 2 s, 1 d. Education: MD, China Medical University. Appointments: Resident, 1960, Lecturer, 1970, CMU; Director of Nuclear Medicine Department, 2nd Hospital of CMU, 1978; Assistant Professor of Nuclear Medicine, 1982; Visiting Scholar, Harvard Medical School, MGH, USA, 1985; Professor of Nuclear Medicine, CMU, 1989. Publications: Clinical Technic Application in Medical Imaging, 1988; The Asynchronism of Left Ventricular Diastolic Filling in Patients with AMI, 1990; The Development and Application of the Computer Program for Left Ventricular Function, 1993; Nuclear Imaging in Clinical Cardiology, 1995; Chief Editor, Imaging of Nuclear Medicine, 1993; 83 articles, 9 books. Honours: 3rd Achievement Prize, National Ministry of Public Health, 1990; 3rd Prize of Provincial Government Achievement, 1988, 1994; The Government Allowance for Speical Contribution, 1993. Memberships: Member, World Federation of Nuclear Medicine and Biology; Standing Member, Chinese Society of Nuclear Medicine; President, Liaoning Provincial Academy of Nuclear Medicine. Hobbies: Walking; Literature; Art. Address: 2nd Affiliated Hospital, China Medical University, No 36 San Hao Street, Shen Yang 110003, China.

PEIFFER Jurgen, b. 1 Dec 1922, Berlin, Germany. Neuropathologist. m. Dr Hanna Greuel, 28 Apr 1951, 1 s, 3 d. Education: MD, University of Munich, 1950; Habilitation in Neurology and Psychiatry, Würzburg, 1961. Appointments: Psychiatric University Clinic, Munich, 1951-52; Max-Planck-Institute Psychiatry, Institute of Neuropathology, 1952-56; University Clinic of Nervous Disease, University of Würzburg, 1956-61; University Clinic of Neurology, Glessen, 1962-64; Full Professor of Neuropathology, Director, Institute of Brain Research, University of Tübingen, 1964-88. Publications: Morphological Aspects of Epilepsies, 1963; Brain Aging, 1981; Neuronal Lesions by Epilepsies, 1993; Neuropathology, 1995; Contributor of chapters in books. Honours: Rector and Prorector, University Tübingen, 1968-71; Member, German Scientific Council, 1972-77; Senator, Max-Planck-Society, 1974-87; Member, Heidelberg Academia of Sciences, 1973-. Memberships: German Association Neuropathology; German Association Neurology; German Association Pathology; European Association Neuropathology; Liga Against Epilepsy. Hobbies: History of Medicine; Archaeology. Address: Institute of Brain Research, University Tübingen, Calwerstrasse 3, 72076 Tübingen, Germany.

PEIPHO Robert W, b. 31 July 1942, Chicago, IL, USA. Dean and Professor. m. Mary Lee Peipho, 10 Dec 1981, 3 sons, 3 daughters. Education: BS Pharmacy, University of Illinois College of Pharmacy; PhD Pharmacology, Loyola University School of Medicine. Career: Assistant/Assoc Professor, University of Nebraska College of Pharmacy; Professor/Assoc Dean, University of Colorado School of Pharmacy; Dean and Professor, University of Missouri-Kansas City School of Pharmacy. Publications: Antihypertensive Therapy in the Elderly Patient, 1991; Heterogeneity of Calcium Channel Blockers, 1991; Antihypertensive Therapy in the Geriatric Patient, 1993. Honours: Honorary President, Missouri Pharmacy Association, 1993-94; Board Certification, American Board of Clinical Pharmacology, 1991; Outstanding Teaching Award, University of Nebraska, 1974; Lederle Pharmacy Faculty Award, 1974. Memberships: American Board of Clinical Pharmacology, Counselor; American College of Clinical Pharmacology, Secretary; American College of Apothecaries, Fellow; American Pharmaceutical Assocation; American Society of Hospital Pharmacists. Hobby: Cycling. Address: University of Missouri, Kansas City School of Pharmacy, 5005 Rockhill Road, Kansas City, MO 64110, USA.

PEKKANEN Juha Raimo, b. 1 Apr 1957, Helsinki, Finland. Physician. m. Dr Riitta Erkinjuntti, 19 Apr 1985, 1 son, 1 daughter. Education: MD, University of Helsinki, 1987. Career: Researcher, Department of Epidemiology and Health Promotion, National Public Health Institute, 1984-87, 1988-91; Visiting Scholar, University of North Carolina, NC, USA, 1987-88; Head, Department of Environmental Epidemiology, National Public Health Institute, currently. Publications: Articles on cardiovascular and environmental epidemiology. Memberships: Finnish Medical Association; Society of Social Medicine in Finland. Hobby: Badminton. Address: National Public Health Institute, PO Box 95, 70701 Kuopio, Finland.

PELETMINSKIY Sergey, b. 14 Feb 1931, Tyotkino Kursk Region, Ukraine. Physicist. m. Prohorova Valentina, 26 Nov 1960, 2 s. Education: Doctor of Science in Physics and Mathematics, 1966; Senior Scientific Worker, 1961; Professor, 1969; Master of Science, Kharkov State University, 1953; Doctor of Philosophy in Physics and Mathematics, 1959. Appointments: Head, Department of Theoretical Physics, National Science Center, Kharkov Institute of Physics and Technology. Publications: Books, Spin Wavers, 1968; Methods of Statistical Physics, 1981; Fields and Fundamental Interactions, 1986; The Thoery of Fundamental Interactions, 1993. Honours: Diploma of Discovery of Phenomenon of Magneto-Acoustic Resonance, Committee on Inventions and Discoveries of Council of Ministers of the USSR; State Prize of the Ukrainian SSR in Science and Technology, 1986; The K D Sinelnikov Prize of the Prezidium of Academy of Sciences of the Ukrainian SSR, 1978; The MM Krylov Prize of Prezidium of Academy of Science of the Ukrainian SSr, 1986. Memberships: National Academy of Sciences of Ukraine; Ukrainian Physical Society. Address: Evpatorijskij Proezd 3, Apt 13, Kharkov 310108, Ukraine.

PELTOLA Heikki Olavi, b. 26 Dec 1943, Angola. Professor of Infectious Diseases. m. Sinikka Peltola, 15 Aug 1970, 2 daughters. Education: MD; Specialist, Paediatrics, General Surgery and Traumatology, Infectious Diseases; Diploma in Tropical Medicine and Hygiene, London. Appointments: Consultant, Infectious Diseases, Helsinki, Finland; Head of Infectious Diseases, University of Helsinki. Publications: Over 200, mostly in peer-reviewed journals; 4 books; 7 CD and LP records. Honours: Award for Medical Science, University of Nizza. Memberships: Board Member, International Society for Infectious Diseases; Past President, local and European scientific societies. Hobby: Music: singer and conductor, Kamariherrat-The Chamberlains vocal ensemble. Address: Children's Hospital, University of Helsinki, 11 Stenbäck Street, FIN-00290 Helsinki, Finland.

PEÑA Carlos E, b. 26 May 1931, Bogata, Colombia. Physician. m. Carol Ammann, Oct 1967, 1 s, 1 d. Education: MD, National University School of Medicine, Bogata. Appointments: Senior Staff Pathologist, Mercy Hospital Pittsburgh, USA, 1973-85; Assistant Professor of Pathology and Neurology, Georgetown University School of Medicine, 1969-73; Clinical Associate Professor of Pathology, University of Pittsburgh. Publications: Aspergillosis, chapter, 1971; Contributor of over 60 professional articles. Honours: British Council Scholar, 1960; French Government Scholar, 1958-59. Memberships: Societe Anatomique de Paris; College of American Pathologists; American Association of Neuropathologists; Latin-American Pathology Society' Colombian

Pathology Society. Hobby: Painting. Address: 3600 Ridgewood Drive, Pittsburgh, PA 15235, USA.

PENG Bin, b. 28 Aug 1953, Yichun City, China. Medical Doctor. m. Huang Hua, 15 Mar 1990, 1 son. Education: BM, 1983; MS, 1986; PhD candidate, University of Newcastle-upon-Tyne, 1992-. Appointment: Lecturer, Sun Yat-Sen University of Medical Sciences, 1988-92. Publications: Nomogram for Drug Dosage Adjustment in Patients with Renal Failure, 1989; Co-author: A Computer Program for Calculating Pharmacokinetic Constants Following IV Administration of Drug, 1987; Pharmacokinetic Studies of Cis-diaminedichloroplatinum in Patients with Neoplastic Disease, 1987; Determination of Cis-diaminedichloroplatinum in plasma by Atomic Absorption Spectrometry and Pharmacokinetics in Rabbits, 1987; Dosage Schedules of Digitalis, 1989; Phase I Clinical Pharmacokinetics of Carboplatin, 1990; Preclinical Pharmacokinetics of b-carboxyethylgermaniumsesquioxide (Ge-132), 1991; A Comparative Study of the Clinical Pharmacokinetics and Molecular Pharmacology of Carboplatin and Cisplatin in Children with Cancer, 1994; The Comparative Pharmacokinetics and Pharmacodynamics of Cisplatin and Carboplatin in Paediatric Patients: A Review, 1994. Honours: ORS Award, UK, 1991-94. Memberships: Chinese Medical Association; Chinese Pharmacological Society. Hobby: Table-tennis. Address: Cancer Research Unit, The University of Newcastle-upon-Tyne, Newcastle-upon-Tyne NE2 4HH, England.

PENG Han Chu, b. 8 July 1930, Hunan, China. Professor of Clinical Medicine. m. 21 October 1961, 2 sons. Education: Hunan (Xiang-Yale) Medical University, 1956. Appointments: Professor of Otorhinolaryngology, Shanxi Medical College, China, 1987; Professor of Laser Medicine, 1992. Publications: Coriolis Accelerational Endurance Test, 1986; Observation on Ultrastructional Study of Inner Ear in Ototoxic Cases, 1993; Nd: Yag Laser Treated the Nasal Polyps, 1994; Co-author: An Electron Microscopic Study of Thyroxine Against Ototoxicity of Kanamycin, 1993. Memberships: Chinese Medical Society; Chinese Otorhinolaryngology Association; Society of Chinese Laser Medicine and Surgery. Hobbies: Singing; Dancing. Address: 13 Jie-fang South Road, Taiyuan, Shanxi 030001, China.

PENG Jie Qing, b. 4 May 1928, Jiaoling, Guangdong, China. Professor of Pathology. m. Xiu Gan Wu, 28 Dec 1955, 2 d. Education: Diploma, Zhongshan Medical College, Guangdong, 1954; Advanced studies at Pathological Institute of Munich University, Germany, 1986-87. Career: Assistant, 1954-62, Lecturer, 1963-79, Associate Professor, 1980-85, Wuhan Medical College, China; Professor, Pathology, Tongji Medical University, 1986-; Chief of Pathological Department, Tongji Hospital; Member, Assessing Degree Committee, Tongji University. Publications: Books: Co-author, Surgical Pathology I, 1978, II, 1983, Textbook of Pathology, 1989, Pathology, 1991; Other publications include: The Establishment of Experimental Model of Glomerulonephritis, 1984, Pathological Change, Diagnosis and Differential Diagnosis of Renal Cyclosporine An Intoxicant Injury, 1992. Honours: Excellent Academic Thesis Awards, Province Academic Association, 1981, 1986; Advanced Educationlist Awards of Province and University, 1983, 1989; Advanced Scientific Worker of Province, 1983. Memberships: International Academy of Pathology; Chinese Medical Association. Hobbies: Music; Sport. Address: Department of Pathology, Tongji Medical University, Wuhan 430030, China.

PENG Lin, b. 25 November 1943, Cheng Zhou City, Henan, China. Chief Physician of Neurosurgery. m. Mianyang Wang, 16 July 1968, 1 son, 1 daughters. Education: MD, Henan Medical University, 1962-68; MD Training, Shanghai Medical University, 1978-80; Visiting Scholar, UTMB Galveston, USA, 1989. Appointments: Associate Professor of Neurosurgery, Qinghai Medical College, 1984; Professor of Neurosurgery, Henan Medical University, 1992; Chief Physician of Neurosurgery, Henan Medical University, 1993. Publications: Tregeminus Schnannoma of 17 Cases: A Review of Recent Experience, 1988; The Diagnosis and Treatment of the Brain Stem Hematoma, 1990; Co-author: The Guide of Emergency Medicine, 1991. Honours: Contributed Neurosurgery Expert, The Association of Science of China, 1984. Memberships: The Medical Society of China; The Neurosurgery Society of China; The Society of Henan Medical Branch at Zheng Zhou; Editor, Journal of Nervous Diseases. Address: 2nd Teaching Hospital, Henan Medical University, Jingba Road 2, Zheng Zhou, Henan, China.

PENG Shi-sheng, b. 23 Dec 1932, Beijing, China. Orthodontist. Professor. m. Gu Zhi-cheng, 1 daughter. Education: Diploma, Dental School, Beijing Medical College, Beijing University. Appointments:

Resident, Department of Orthodontics and Prosthetic Dentistry, 1955-62; Visiting Dentist, 1962-71, St Mary Hospital, Shanghai Second Medical College; Member, 1971-82, Associate Professor, 1982-90, Professor, Chief Doctor, 1990-, Department of Orthodontics, Shanghai Second Medical College. Publications: Chapter on Orthodontics, Stomatology Section, Encyclopedia Medicinae Sciencae, 1985; Steiner Norms for Shanghai Adults, 1991. Honours: Science Fund, sponsored by US National Academy of Sciences, Visiting Scholar Exchange Programme to Harvard School of Dental Medicine and Children's Hospital, 1987-88. Memberships: Shanghai Association for Science and Technology; China Medical Association; China Red Cross Society. Hobbies: Stamp collecting; Taking photographs. Address: No 10 Lane 23 Changde Road, Shanghai 200040, China.

PENG Shiqi, b. 8 Oct 1947, Jiangxi, China. Medical Chemist. m. 8 Mar 1974, 1 son. Education: BA, 1969, PhD, 1984, Beijing Medical University; Humboldt Fellow, Hannover University, Germany, 1987-89. Appointments: Chairperson, Department of Medicinal Chemistry, Beijing Medical University. Publications: Medicinal Chemistry of Peptides, 1994; Spectroscopy in Stereochemistry, 1994; Contributor of 80 papers. Hobbies: Reading; Writing. Address: College of Pharmaceutical Sciences, Beijing Medical University, Beijing 100083, China.

PENG Shu You, b. 7 Nov 1932, Gangdong, China. Professor of Surgery; Chairman, Department of Surgery, Zhejiang Medical University; Director, Surgical Institute, Zhejiang Medical University. m. Xie Long Hua, 30 Sept 1967, 1 son. Education: MBBS; MD. Appointments: Surgical Resident, Zhejiang Medical University, 1955-62; Attendant Surgeon, Zhejiang Medical University, 1963-77; Lecturer of Surgery, Zhejiang Medical University, 1978-80; Associate Professor of Surgery, Zhejiang Medical University, 1981-85; Visiting Professor, Sheffield, London, England, Belfast, Ireland, 1981-85; Professor of Surgery, Zhejiang Medical University, 1986-. Publications: More than 80 articles published: Sequential external & internal drainage of pancreatic pseudocyst, 1984; Closed mansulpialization and delayed open in the treatment of severe pancreatitis, 1991; A new technique for hepatectomy with Peng's multifunctional operative dissector, 1993. Memberships: International Microsurgical Society; British Society of Acupuncture; Comm, Chinese Society of Organ Transplantation; Comm, Chinese Association of Experimental Surgery. Honours: National Award, Outstanding Contribution in Higher Education, China, 1991. Hobbies: Sport; Music. Address: Department of Surgery, No 2 Affilliated Hospital, Zhejiang Medical University, Hangzhou 310009, China.

PENG Xianguang, b. 15 Apr 1928, Anyue County, Sichuan, China. Proctologist. m. Zhou Shanxian, 26 Dec 1948, 2 sons, 1 daughter. Appointments: Vice Chairman, Academic Committee, Guiyang College of Traditional Chinese Medicine; Director, Institute of Miscellanous Diseases of South-West China, Guizhou Province. Publications: Deputy Editor-in-Chief of TCM Proctology, 1994. Hobbies: 7 Award's by the Ministry of Public Health of China or by the Provincial Government of Guizhou. Memberships: Society of Proctology of China; Society of Proctology of South-West and North-West China. Hobbies: Cao Bo; Peng Weihong. Address: Guiyang College of Traditional Chinese Medicine, 1 Shidong Road, Guiyang, Guizhou, China.

PENG Xing, b. 8 Sept 1932, Chong Qing, China. Doctor and Professor. m. Lan-ying Sun, 10 May 1964, 2 s, 1 d. Education: Bachelor of Medicne, Chinese Medical University, China, 1956. Appointments: Doctor, People;s Hospital of Gansu Province, 1956-86; Doctor and Professor, Department of Medicine, People's Hospital of Gansu Province, 1986-95; Publications: Jaundice of the Heart Failure, 1959; Pleural Vascular-Murmur with Pulmonary Abscess, 1959; The Diagnostic Value of Adrenal CT Scanning for Addison Disease, 1992; The Diagnostic Value of Thyroid Vascular Murmurs for Grave's Disease, 1993; rT3 Hyperthyroidism, 1993. Memberships: Chinese Medical Association; Chinese Rheumatismal Association; Medical Association of Gansu Province. Hobbies: Reading; Writing; Swimming. Address: 96 Dong Gang West Road, Lanzhou 730000, Gansu Province, China.

PENG Ying-Xiu, b. 25 June 1933, Chengdu, Sichuan, China. Professor of Physiology. m. Huang Kai-sheng, 16 Aug 1957, 1 son, 2 daughters. Education: BS, Southwest Normal University; MS, Physiology, Beijing Normal University. Appointments: Assistant, 1959-78, Lecturer, 1978-85, Professor of Physiology, 1985-, Sun Yat-sen University of Medical Sciences, Guangzhou. Publications: The effects of gonadal hormones on Met-enkephalin in brain, 1989; The effects of gonadal hormones and gonads on contents of MEK and LEK in hypothalamus-pituitary gland, 1990, 1992, 1993. Membership: Chinese Physiological Society. Hobby: Reading; Music; Dancing. Address: 501/53 Cai Yuan Xi St, Zhong Shan Road II, Guangzhou 510080, China.

PENG Zhouhui, b. 1 May 1952, Shanxi province, China. Professor; Director. m. Jiang Zhaorong, 9 Apr 1979, 1 daughter. Education: PhD; MD. Appointments: Assistant Professor, 1983-87, Associate Professor, Director, 1989-92; Department of Biochemistry, First Military Medical University; Professor, Director, 1992-, Institute of Molecular Biology, First Military Medical University; Vice Secretary-General, Professor, The South China Center for Biological Science and Biotechnology, 1994-; Guest Researcher, Chiba University, Japan, 1987-88; Guest Researcher, University of California, Los Angeles, USA, 1995-. Publications: Molecular Biology of the Gene, 1992; Gene Therapy - Principal and Applications, 1994; Contributor of articles in professional journals. Honours: Outstanding Scientist in Biochemistry and Molecular Biology, Guangdong Province. Memberships: Vice President, Society of Biochemistry and Molecular Biology, Guangdong Province. Hobbies: Mountaineering; Music. Address: Institute of Molecular Biology, First Military Medical University, Guangzhou 510515, China.

PEPPAS Nicholas A, b. 25 Aug 1948, Athens, Greece. Professor. m. Lisa Brannon-Peppas. Education: ScD, Chemical Engineering, MIT; Diploma, Chemical Engineering, National Technical University of Athens, Greece. Appointments: Assistant Professor, School of Chemical Engineering, Purdue University, 1976-78; Associate Professor, School of Chemical Engineering, Purdue University, 1978-82; Professor, School of Chemical Engineering, 1982-; Showalter Distinguished Professor, School of Chemical Engineering, 1993-. Publications: Numerous professional publications to scientific journals. Honours include: AA Potter Award, Best Engineering Professor, Purdue University, 1994; Silver Medal of the University of Parma, 1994; Bioengineering Award, American Inst of Chemical Engineers, 1994. Memberships include: American Institute of Medical & Biological Engineers; American Institute of Chemical Engineers; American Physical Society; American Chemical Society; American Association for the Advancement of Sciences. Address: School of Chemical Engineers, Purdue University, West Lafayette, IN 47907-1283, USA.

PEPPERCORN (Anne) Gillian, b. 27 Aug 1938, London, England. Chartered Psychologist. m. (John) Julian Peppercorn, 4 Sept 1976, 1 daughter. Education: BSc Honours, Psychology, University College London, 1959; Associate Fellow, British Psychological Society; Postgraduate courses on Organisation Behaviour and Process Intervention, Columbia Business School, New York City and Massachusetts Institute of Technology. Appointments: Research Officer, Ashridge Management College; Manager, Personnel Research, IBM Americas/Far East Corporation, USA; Personnel Research and Development Manager, IBM UK; Senior Research Fellow, Ashridge Management College; Currently Consultant, Tutor. Publications: International Cultural Mobility, 1970; Profile of British Industry, 1987; Managing Tomorrow's Employee, 1990. Honours: IBM Outstanding Contribution Award for Excellence in Personnel Research Programme Development, 1974. Hobbies: Travel; Theatre; Antiques; Gardening; Bridge; Tennis. Address: Stratone Cottage, Strettington, Chichester, West Sussex PO18 0LA, England.

PEPPERELL Roger James, b. 7 Jan 1942, Melbourne, Australia. Obstetrician & Gynaecologist. m. Betty, 9 Sept 1977, 1 son, 2 daughters. Education: MD, 1976; FRACP; FRCOG; FRACOG. Appointments: Research Fellow, Prince Henry's Hospital, 1972-73; Commonwealth Registrar, Queen Mothers Hospital, Glasgow, 1974; First Assistant, University Melbourne, 1975-77. Publications: The Infertile Couple. Honours: BDH Research Fellow in Endocrinology, 1972-73; Arthur Nyulasy Prize, University Melbourne, 1973. Memberships: RCOG; RACP; RACOG; American Fertility Society. Hobbies: Golf; Music. Address: 28 Alfred Street, Kew, Victoria 3101, Australia.

PERAICA Margarita, b. 28 Dec 1924, Split, Croatia. School Medical Doctor. m. Ivo Peraica, 23 Aug 1952, 1 son, 2 daughters. Education: School of Medicine, University of Zagreb, 1952; Specialist, School & University of Medicine, 1956; Primarius, 1980. Appointments: MD, School of Medicine, University of Zagreb, 1952-56; Specialisation, School of Medicine, 1956-58; School Physician, 1958; Chief Medical Officer, School Health Service Centre, Zagreb; Lecturer in School, Health & Medicine, Postgraduate Education, Andrija Stampar School of Public Health. Publications: The nourishment and locomotory system

abnormality in school children and adolescents in Zagreb and Samobor District, 1969; Acute infectious diseases in school children and youth, 1972; Current status and possibility of development of School Medicine in Croatia, 1978; Effect of atmospheric pollution in the child's respiratory system in urban environment, 1978; Bibliography of Croatian School Medicine Association Members, 1924-1988, 1991. Memberships: Croatian Medical Association; Croatian Society for School & University Medicine; Croatian Catholic Medical Society, Zagreb. Hobbies: Folk Handicrafts Collecting. Address: Baruna Filipovica 26/IX, 41000 Zagreb, Croatia.

PEREKLAD Elena Leonidovna, b. 2 Apr 1951, Kirhizia, Russia. Physician; General Practitioner. m. Vladimir Pereklad, 21 Feb 1976, 1 son, 1 daughter. Education: 2nd Medical Institute, Moscow, 1975. Appointments: District Physician, Municipal Polyclinic, Medical Sanitary Department N8. Honours: Best Physician of the Polyclinic, 1985, 1987, 1989. Hobbies: Reading; Skiing; Walking in the Forest; Nontraditional Medicine. Address: 19-8 Korolev Street, 249021 Obninsk, Kaluga Region, Russia.

PERELMAN Mikhail Israel, b. 20 Dec 1924, Minsk, Byelorussia. Physician. 2 sons. Education: DMS, Medical Institute, Jaroslavl, 1945. Appointments: Junior Research Assistant, 1945; Leading Surgeon, City Hospital, 1951; Chief, Department of Thoracic Surgery, National Centre of Surgery, 1963; Chief, Chair of Pulmonology and Thoracic Surgery, Medical Academy, Moscow 1981; Academician, Russian Academy of Medical Science. Publications: Resection and Plastic of Bronchi, 1968, 1969; Surgery of the Trachea, 1972, 1976; Tracheobronchial Surgery, 1978; Author of 10 books in Russian and contributor of 8 book chapters in English and 200 articles. Honours: USSR State Prize, 1974; Bakulev Prize, 1977; Pirogov Prize, 1978; USSR Council of Ministry Prize, 1985; Spasokukotskiy Prize, 1989; USSR Government Prize, 1991. Memberships: Societe INternationale de Chirurgie; European Association for Cardio-Thoracic Surgery; International College of Surgeons. Hobby: Photography. Address: Centre Pulmonology, 4 Dostoevsky str, Moscow, Russia.

PEREZ-LOPEZ Manuel, b. 17 Dec 1941, Madrid, Spain. Psychiatrist; Psychoanalyst. Memberships: Colegio de Medicos de Madrid; Asociacion Psicoanalitica de Madrid; International Psychoanalytical Association; Instituto de Estudios Psicosomaticos y Psicoterapia Medica. Address: General Moscardo 7 4o B, 28020, Madrid, Spain.

PERLSTEIN Abraham Phillip, b. 15 Apr 1926, New York, NY, USA. Psychiatry. m. Shirley Anne Rubenstein, 10 Jul 1949, 1 s, 2 d. Education: BS, Chemistry; MD; Certified in Psychiatry, 1960; Additional qualification in Geriatric Psychiatry, 1992. Career: Medical Director, SUNY, Alcohol Clinic, 1958-68; Medical Director, Peninsula Counseling Center, 1973-78; Associate Director, Psychiatry, Franklin General Hospital, 1980-88; Currently, Psychiatrist in Private Practice, Clinical Assistant Professor, Psychiatry, SUNY, Brooklyn. Publications: The Use of Drugs in the Treatment of Alcoholism in the Young, Alcoholism Clinics of North American, 1963; Suicide in Adolescence. in NY St Journal Medicine, 1966; Co-author, Sleep Disturbances and Hallucinations in the Acute Alcoholic Psychoses, JN and MD, 1966; Hospitalized Suicidal Adolescents, Two Generations, in Journal of Academy of Child Psychiatry, 1975. Honours: Fellow, Life Fellow, American Psychiatric Association. Memberships: American Psychiatric Association. Hobbies: Music; Art; Literature; Sport. Address: 1800 Dutch Broadway, Elmont, NY 11003, USA.

PERRY Joy S, b. 26 July 1941, South Bend, IN, USA. Medical Editor. m. 1) Tomas M Russell, 15 June 1963, div 1983, 2) Matthew C Perry, 3 Aug 1985, 2 daughters, 1 stepdaughter, 1 Stepson. Education: BS, University of Wisconsin-Madison, 1963. Career: Research Assistant, University of Wisconsin Medical School, 1963-67; Yearbook Medical Publishers, 1967-81; Chicago Heart Association, 1972-73, 1979-85; Freelance Medical Editor, 1967-. Publications: Edited numerous medical/nursing texts and journal articles for many different publishers. Memberships: American Medical Writers Association; Council of Biology Editors; National Association of Female Executives; American Heart Association; American Association Advancement of Science; NY Academy Sciences. Hobbies: Music - Singing, Piano; Sailing; Hiking; Traveling. Address: 974 Upland Drive, Elmira, NY 14905, USA.

PERSAD Prakashbhan Sharma, b. 15 Oct 1961, Trinidad. Obstetrician & Gynaecologist. m. Shastri Maharaj, 9 Mar 1986, 1 son, 1 daughter. Education: DGO, 1990; MRCOG, 1992; MRCP, 1993;

MFFP, 1994. Appointment: Honorary Clinical Lecturer, Birmingham University, 1993; Research Fellow, Department of Fetal Medicine, University of Birmingham. Publications: Adolescent Triplet Pregnancy, 1992; Congenital Heart Block in Pregnancy, 1992; Outcome Following Vaginal Hysterectomy, 1990. Honour: Additional National Scholarship, Trinidad & Tobago, 1981. Memberships: British Society of Cytologists and Colposcopists; European Society of Ultrasound in Medicine; British Menopause Society; British Medical Ultrasound Society; Caribbean Institute of Perinatology. Hobbies: Cricket; Reading; Running. Address: Lot 2, Warner Street, St Augustine, Trinidad.

PESONEN Erkki Juhani, b. 29 Mar 1943, Helsinki, Finland. Paediatric Cardiologist. m. Irma Vesalainen, 31 May 1969, 1 s, 1 d. Education: MD, University of Helsinki, 1970; DMS, 1974. Appointments: Paediatrician, 1979; Paediatric Cardiologist, 1980; Docent in Paediatric Cardiology, 1984; Chief of Paediatric Cardiology, Children's Hospital, University of Helsinki. Publications include: Thickening in the Coronary Arteries in Infancy as an Indication of Genetic Factors in Coronary Heart Disease, 1975; Geographic Origin of the Family as a Determinant of Serum Levels of Lipids in Finnish Children, Co-author, 1986; Correlation of Patent Ductus Arteriosus Shunting with Plasma Atrial Natruiuretic Factor Concentration in Preterm Infants with Respiratory Distress Syndrome, Co-author, 1990; Intimal Thickening of the Coronary Arteries in Infants in Relation to Family History of Coronary Artery Disease in Infants as Determining Mortality for Coronary Heart Disease, 1993; Value of Absent or Retrograde End Diastolic Flow in Fetal Aorta and Umbilical Artery as a Predictor of Perinatal Outcome in Severe Pregnancy Initiated Hypertension, 1993. Honours: Thomas Peltonen Award for Research in Paediatric Cardiology, 1994. Membership: Association of European Paediatric Cardiologists. Hobbies: Marathon Running; Skiing. Address: The Children's Hospital, University of Helsinki, Finland.

PESTKA Sidney, b. 29 May 1936, Drobin, Poland. Department Chairman. m. Joan Sparacin, 19 June 1960, 2 s, 1 d. Education: BA, summa cum laude, Princeton University, 1957; MD, University of Pennsylvania, 1961; DSc, honoris causa, Rider College, 1987. Appointments include: Intern, Pediatrics and Medicine, Baltimore City Hospital, 1961-62; Researcher in Biochemistry Genetics Laboratory, NIH, 1962-66; Researcher, National Cancer Institute, 1966-69; Section Chief, Associate Member, Department Biochemistry Roche Institute Molecular Biology, 1969-74; section Chief, Full Member, Department Biochemistry, 1975-79, Full member, Head of Laboratory of Molecular Genetics, 1980-86, Professor, Chairman, Department of Molecular Genetics and Microbiology, RWJMS, University Medicine and Dentistry of New Jersey, 1986-. Publications: Molecular Mechanisms and Protein Biosynthesis, 1977; Interferons Methods in Enzymology, 1981-86; Contributor of over 400 scientific papers. Memberships: N Caldwell Board of Health, 1973; Past Councillor, Secretary, International Society for Interferon Research; President, 1994, 1995, International Society for Interferon and Cytokine Research. Address: department Molecular Genetics and Microbiology, University Medicine and Dentistry of New Jersey, Robert Wood Johnson Medical School, 675 Hoes Lane, Piscataway, NJ 08854-5635, USA.

PETER Jonathan Clemence, b. 25 Jan 1942, Cape, South Africa. Paediatric Neurosurgeon. m. Elizabeth M Ross, 9 Oct 1969, 1 s, 1 d. Education: MB, ChB, University of Cape Town; FRCS Edinburgh. Appointments: Head of Paediatric Neurosurgery, Red Cross War Memorial Children's Hospital; Mauerberger Professor of Neurosurgery, University of Cape Town; Head, Department of Neurosurgery, Groote Schuur Hospital and Red Cross War Memorial Children's Hospital. Publications include: Selective Posterior Rhizotomy: A Long-term Follow-up Study, Co-author, 1989; Subacute Traumatic Extradural Haematomas of the Posterior Fossa: A Clinicopathological Entity of the 5-10 Year Old Child, Co-author, 1990; The Incidence of Spinal Deformity in Children after Multiple Level Laminectomy for Selective Posterior Rhizotomy, Co-author, 1990; Midline Dermal Sinuses and Cysts and Their Relationship to the Central Nervous System, Co-author, 1991; Occult Dysraphism: A Retrospective Analysis of 88 Operative Cases, 1992; Acute Spinal Epidural Abscess, Co-author, 1992; Hydatid Infestation of the Brain. Difficulties in Diagnosis and Treatment, Co-author, 1994 Memberships: Secretary, Society of South African Neurosurgeons; South African Association of Paediatric Surgeons; World Federation of Neurosurgeons; International Society of Paediatric Neurosurgeons. Hobbies: Jogging; Birdwatching; Music. Address: Department of Neurosurgery, Medical School, University of Cape Town, South Africa.

PETERS Alan, b. 6 dec 1929, Nottingham, England. Anatomist. m. Verona M Shipman, 30 Sept 1955, 3 d. Education: BSc, 1951, PhD, 1954, Bristol University. Appointments: Lecturer, Anatomy, Edinburgh University, Scotland, 1958-66; Visiting Lecturer, Harvard University, USA, 1963-64; Chairman, Waterhouse Professor of Anatomy and Neurobiology, Boston University, 1966-. Publications: The Fine Structure of the Nervous System, Co-author, 3rd edition, 1991; Myelination, Co-author, 1970; Cerebral Cortex, series of books, Co-editor; Contributor of over 140 scientific articles. Honours: Senator Javits Neuroscience Investigator award, 1986; Cortical Discover Award, Cajal Club, 1990. Memberships: American Anatomical Association, President, 1992-93; Association Anatomy Chairman, President, 1976-77; American Society Cell Biology; Society for Neuroscience. Hobby: Model shipbuilding. Address: Department of Anatomy and Neurobiology, Boston University School of Medicine, 80 East Concord Street, Boston, MA 02118, USA.

PETIN Vladislav G, b. 29 Dec 1939, Stepnyak, Kazakhstan. Biophysicist. m. Valentina Matrenina, 22 June 1963, 1 son. Education: Moscow University, 1962; Candidate of Biological Sciences, 1969; Doctor of Biological Sciences, 1984. Appointments: Engineer, 1962; Senior Research Scientist, 1970; Leader Research Scientist, 1972; Head, Biophysical Laboratory, 1978; Head, Biophysical Laboraty, Medical Radiological Research Centre. Publications: Pecularities of Mechanisms of Action of Densely Ionizing Particles, Co-author, 1985; Genetic Control of Cell Radiosensitivity Modification, 1987; Quantitative Description of Cell Radiosensitivity Modification, Co-author, 1989; Radio Biological Aspects of Combined Action of Damaged Factors, Co-author, 1993. Memberships: Medical Radiology Society; All Russian Society of Genetics and Selection. Hobbies: Running; Chess. Address: 22-A Kurchator Street, Suite 35, Obninsk 249020, Russia.

PETRAKIS Nicholas Louis, b. 6 Feb 1922, Bancroft, IA, USA. Medicine. m. Patricia E Kelly, 24 Jun 1947, 1 s, 2 d. Education: BA, Augustana College, 1943; BS, Medicine, University of South Dakota School of Medical Science, 1944; MD, Washington School of Medicine, St Louis, 1946. Career: Lt JG, US Navy, 1947-49; Senior Assistant Surgeon, National Cancer Institute, 1950-54; Assistant Clinical Professor, Cancer Research Institute, 1954-56, Assistant Professor of Preventive Medicine, 1956-62, Associate Professor, Preventive Medicine, 1962-68, Professor of Preventive Medicine, 1968-, Professor and Chairman, Department of Epidemiology, and International Health, 1978-88, Professor and Chairman Emeritus, Preventive Medicine, 1990-, University of California, San Francisco. Publications: Over 250 publications on clinical oncology, genetics and breast cancer epidemiology, 1950-. Honours: Eleanor Roosevelt International Cancer Fellowship, 1962-63; Lewis C Robbins Award, Society of Prospective Medicine, 1985; Distinguished Achievement Award, American Society of Preventive Oncology, 1992. Memberships: American Society of Preventive Oncology; American Association for Cancer Research; Western Association of Physicians; American Society for Clinical Investigation. Hobbies: Travel; Reading; Computers. Address: Department of Epidemiology and Biostatistics, University of California, School of Medicine, San Francisco, CA 94143, USA.

PETRALIA Ronald Sebastian, b. 7 Nov 1954, Lawrence, USA. Scientific Researcher. Education: BS, Entomology, University of Massachusetts, 1972-75; PhD, Entomology, Biology, Texas A & M University, 1979. Appointments: Graduate Research Assistant, Texas A & M University, 1975-79; Research Associate, Texas A & M University, 1979-80; Assistant Professor of Biology, St Ambrose College, 1980-85; Postdoctoral Research Fellow, Department of Anatomy, George Washington University School of Medicine, 1985-90; Senior Staff Fellow, National Institute on Deafness & Other Communication Disorders, National Institutes of Health, 1991-. Publications: Numerous articles in scientific journals and books; Presentations at national and foreign conferences. Memberships: Society for Neuroscience; Association for Research in Otolaryngology; Microscopy Society of America; Sigma Xi; Chesapeake Society for Microscopy. Hobby: Natural History. Address: 78 Boston Street, Methuen, MA 01844, USA.

PETRIDES Simon Peter, b. 10 Mar 1961, England. Orthopaedic, Osteopathic and Sports Physician. m. Kathleen, 28 Mar 1992. Education: MBBS; DO; MRO; Dip Sports Med. Appointments: Director, Milton Keynes Orthopaedic and Sports Clinic; Councillor, British Institute of Musculoskeletal Medicine; Treasurer; Education Committee, British Association Sports Medicine. Memberships: BIMM; BASM; BMA; SOM/

Hobbies: Rugby; Travel. Address: Blackberry Orthopaedic Clinic, Blackberry Court, Walnut Tree, Milton Keynes, Buckinghamshire. England.

PETROV Rem Victorovich, b. 22 Mar 1930, Serafimovich, Russia. Physician; Immunologist. m. Kook Tatiana, 12 Apr 1951, 1 s, 1 d. Education: Physician, Voronez Medical University, 1953. Appointments: Staff, Institute of Biophysics, Moscow, 1953-58; Senior Member Science Staff, 1958-62, Laboratory Chief, 1962-83, Department Chief, 1970-83, Director, 1983-88, Institute of Immunology; Vice President of Russian Academy of Sciences, 1988-. Publications: Immunology of Acute Radiation Injury, 1962; Immunology and Immunogenetics, 1976; Immunology, 1982; Me or Not Me, 1987; Synthetic Antigens and Vaccines, 1988; Cell Membranes and Immunity, 1991. Honours: Decorated Order of October Revolution, Russia; Gold Star of Hero of Socialist Labor, Russia; Academician, Russian Academy of Medical Sciences, 1978; Academician, Russian Academy of Science, Russia, 1984. Memberships: Vice Chairman, UNESCO Committee; Council of International Union of Immunology Societies; Doctor Honoris Causa Bar-Ilan University (Israel) and Madrid Politechnical University. Hobbies: Hunting; Fishing; Woodworking. Address: Russian Academy of Sciences, 14 Leninsky Prosp, Moscow, Russia.

PETROVA Galina Alexeyevna, b. 12 Mar 1943, Kalouga, Russia. Research Worker. m. Yu V Volkov, 28 Nov 1970. Education: Diploma, Moscow Institute of Fine Chemical Technology, 1969; DBiol. Appointments: Assistant, Biological Department, Moscow State University, 1969-70; Research Worker, Medical Radiological Research Centre of RAMS, Obninsk, 1970-. Publications: Pharmacokinetc of Tritium Labelled Melatonin, Co-author, 1989; Autoradiological and Immunohistochemical Analysis of 3H-Melatonin Distribution in the Endocrine and Non-Endocrine Organs, Co-author, 1990. Memberships: Mendeleyev Chemical Society; Russian Society of Immunologists. Hobbies: History; Religions; Biographies of Scientists; Pets. Address: 124 Ap 51, Av Marx, 249020 Obninsk, Kalouga Region, Russia.

PETROVSKY Boris Vasilyevich, b. 27 Jun 1908, Stavropol, Russia. Professor; Academician, Academy of Science of Russia and Academy of Medical Sciences of Russia. m. Timofejeva Ekaterina, 15 Dec 1934, 1 d. Education: Medical Faculty of M V Lomonossov's Moscow State University, 1926, 1930; Candidate, MSc, 1937; Medical Doctor, 1947; Senior Resident Fellow, Moscow, 1940-41; Professor Academician, 1953, 1966. Career: Junior Medical Staff, Technical Secretary, Medsantrud, Kislovodsk City, 1924-26; Military Service, Soviet Army, 1941-44; Senior Assistant, Military Medical Academy, Leningrad, 1944-45; Professor, Chair of General Surgery, 2nd Moscow Medical Academy, 1948-49; Currently, Honorary Director, Research Centre of Surgery, RAMS. Publications: 300 publications including 28 books; Chief Editor of 30 volumes of The Large Medical Encyclopaedia. Honours: State Prize Winner, 1960; Lenin's Prize Winner, 1975; Bernard's Prize Winner, International Health Organization; 28 Orders; State title of Hero; Golden Star of the Hero of Labour. Memberships: Minister of Health Service of Russia, 1965-80; President, Council of Elders of Russian Academy of Medical Sciences. Hobbies: Photography; Fishing; Hiking. Address: Ulitza Burdenko, 14 N 26 Moscow, Russia.

PETTERSON Claire Dianne, b. 26 March 1954, Melbourne, Australia. Obsterician, Gynaecologist. Education: MBBS; MRCOG; FRACOG. Appointments: Lecturer, Obstetrics and Gynaecology, Melbourne University; Assistant Obstetrician; Consultant in Charge, Family Birth Centre. Memberships: Royal College of Obstetrics & Gynaecology; Royal Australian College of Obstetrics & Gynaecology. Hobbies: Music; Opera; Art. Address: 109, 320 Victoria Parade, East Melbourne, Victoria, Australia.

PEVET Paul, b. 27 May 1945, Moutiers sous Chantmerle, France. Medical Director. m. Dr Mireille Masson-Pevet, 11 Sep 1971, 1 d. Education: 3rd Cycle Doctorate, Université de Poitiers, France, 1972; PhD, University of Amsterdam, Netherlands, 1976. Career: Scientist, The Netherlands Institute for Brain Research, Amsterdam, 1973-83; Scientist, CNRS, University Louis Pasteur, Strasbourg, France, 1984-. Currently, Director of Research, CNRS; Director of the Laboratory, Neurobiologie des fonctions rythmiques et saisonnières, Université L Pasteur, Strasbourg, France. Publications: 10 Books and 127 articles on biological rhythms. Memberships include: European Pineal Society; European Neurosciences Association; American Neurosciences Association. Address: Neurobiologie des Fonctions Rythmiques et Saisonnières, Université L Pasteur, 12 rue de l'Université, 67000 Strasbourg, France.

PEYSER Herbert Stanley, b. 4 Nov 1924, NY, USA. Psychiatry. m. 28 Dec 1978, 1 s, 2 d. Education: MD, Columbia College of Physicians and Surgeons, 1948. Appointments: Assistant Clinical Professor of Psychiatry, Mt Sinai Medical School, NY; Associate Attending Physician, Mt Sinai Medical Center; Consultant Psychiatrist, St Luke's-Roosevelt Hospital Center. Publications: Alcoholism: A Practical Treatment Guide, 2nd edition, 1988; Chapter on Alcohol, Alcoholism and Stress, in Handbook of Stress, 2nd edition, 1990. Memberships: Life Fellow, American Psychiatric Association; Medical Society, State of NY; Fellow, New York Academy of Medicine; American Society of Addiction Medicine; American Academy of Psychiatrists in Alcoholism and Addiction. Address: 110 East 87th Street, New York, NY 10128, USA.

PFEFFER Robert I, b. 4 Aug 1939, Buffalo, New York, USA. Professor. Education: AB cum laude, Princeton Univerity, 1960; MD, Harvard Medical School, 1964; MSPH, UCLA School of Public Health, 1984-85. Appointments: Laboratory Assistant, Princeton University, 1959-60; Student Summer Fellow, Harvard Medical School, 1962; Assistant Professor-in-Residence of Neurology, University California, Irvine, 1972-79; Director, Neurology & Multiple Sclerosis Clinics, University California, Irvine Medical Center, 1972-; Associate Professor-in-Residence, University California, Irvine, 1979-; Consultant, University California, Irvine, 1986-. Publications incl: Measurement of functional activities in free-living older adults, 1982; Use of the mental function index in older adults: Reliability, validity and measurement of change over time, 1984; Prevalence of Alzheimer's disease in a retirement community, 1987; Olfactory tests as possible probes for detecting and monitoring Alzheimer's disease, 1988. Memberships: American Academy of Neurology, Fellow; Society for Epidemiologic Research; Orange County Neurological Society; American Association for Advancement of Science. Hobbies: Music; Model Railroads. Address: UCT Study Group, 24411 Health Center Drive, Suite 660, Laguna Hills, CA 92653, USA.

PFEIFFER Ronald Frederick, b. 11 Aug 1947, Racine, Wisconsin, USA. Physician. m. Breanda Haarberg, 6 Jun 1969, 1 s, 1 d. Education: BS, University of Nebraska, Lincoln, 1969; MD, University of Nebraska Medical Center, 1973; Neurology Residency, Waller Reed Army Medical Center, 1977. Appointments: US Army, 1973-80; University of Nebraska Medical Center, 1980-94; Professor of Neurology and Pharmacology, University of Nebraska Medical Center. Publications: 89 Manuscripts and Book Chapters; 82 Abstracts. Memberships: American Neurological Association; American Academy of Neurology; Movement Disorders Society. Address: Section of Neurology, University of Nebraska Medical Center, 600 South 42nd Avenue, Omaha, NC 68198-2045, USA.

PFEIFFER Steven Ira, b. 10 Nov 1950, NY, USA. Psychologist. m. Jan Pfeiffer, 26 Aug 1979, 1 d. Education: BA, Psychology, State University of New York, 1972; MA, Psychology, Fairleigh Dickinson University, Teaneck, NJ, 1974; PhD, Psychology, University of North Carolina, Chapel Hill, 1977; Clinical Internship, The Astor Home and Child Guidance Clinic, Rhinebeck, NY, 1976-77. Career includes: Clinical Psychologist (Reserves), US Navy Medical Service Corps, 1986-; Executive Director, The Devereux Foundation, Institute of Clinical Training and Research, 1987-1995; Clinical and Consulting Psychologist, 1988-; Professor, Adjunct Faculty, Psychological Studies, Temple University, 1989-; Adjunct Research Associate, Philadelphia Child Guidance Centre, 1990-; Adjunct Professor, Educational Services and Research, Ohio State University, 1990-; Adjunct Professor of Psychology and Psychiatry, University of Pennsylvania Medical School, 1991-; Adjunct Associate Professor, Graduate School of Education, University of Pennsylvania, 1991-. Publications include: Numerous articles in referred journals, monographs and book chapters, books, book reviews, conference presentations; Various editorial boards and reviewer for several professional publications. Honours include: Diplomate, American Board of Professional Psychology; Fellow, American Psychological Association; Fellow, American Orthopsychiatric Association; Fellow, American Association of Children's Residential Centres. Memberships include: American Association of Mental Retardation; APA; Council for Exceptional Children. Hobbies: Tennis; Jogging; Sailing. Address: 1301 Lancaster Avenue, Berwyn, PA, 19312, USA

PHANTHUMCHINDA Kammant, b. 28 Feb 1952, Bangkok, Thailand. University Professor. Education: BSc, Honours; MD, Honours; MSc,

Clinical Epidemiology, McMaster University; FRCP(T); Thai Board of Neurology. Appointments: Assistant Professor, Associate Professor of Medicine; Professor of Medicine, Head, Division of Neurology. Publications: The Effect of Gangliosides in Non-Insulin-Dependent Diabetes Mellitus with Peripheral Neuropathy: A Preliminary Study, Co-author, 1990; Prevalence and Clinical Features of Migraine Headache, Co-author, 1989. Honour: Award for Best Teacher, Chulalongkorn University, 1993. Memberships: Neurological Society of Thailand. Hobby: Classical Music. Address: Division of Neurology, Faculty of Medicine, Chulalongkorn University, Bangkok, Thailand.

PHILIPP Elliot Elias, b. 20 Jul 1915, London, England. Gynaecologist. m. Lucie Hackenbroch, 22 Mar 1939, dec, 1 s, 1 d. Education: MA, MB BCh, Cambridge; FRCS(Eng); FRCOG. Career: Senior Registrar, Royal Free Hospital; Consultant, Old Church Hospital, Romford, Royal Northern Hospital, Whittington Hospital, London. Publications: Co-Editor, Obstetrics and Gynaecology for Students, 1970; Scientific Foundations of Obstetrics and Gynaecology, 1970, 1976, 1980, 1990; Co-author, The History of Obstetrics and Gynaecology, 1994. Honour: Chevalier de la Legion d'Honneur. Memberships: Royal Society of Medicine; Past Pres: Medical Society of London; Hunterian Society. Hobbies: Travel; Walking; Theatre; Opera. Address: 166 Rivermead Court, Ranelagh Gardens, London, SW6 3SF, England.

PHILLIPS Carol, b. 17 Dec 1932, Bridgeport, CT, USA. Medicine. m. Charles A Phillips, 30 Aug 1954, 1 s, 3 d. Education: BS, Douglass College; MD, Yale University. Appointments: Associate Dean for Admissions, University of Vermont, 1977-83; Chariman, Department of Pediatrics, University of Vermont, 1983-93; Professor of Pediatrics/Associate Dean for Academic Affairs, University of Vermont. Publications: Associate Editor, Redbook - American Academy of Pediatrics, 1988, 1991; Contributor, Nelsons Textbook of Pediatrics, 1976 to latest edition. Memberships: American Academy of Pediatrics; American Pediatric Society; Infectious Diseases Society; Pediatric Infectious Diseases Society. Hobbies: Reading; Swimming. Addess: Department of Pediatrics, University of Vermont, Burlington, VT 05406, USA.

PHILLIPS John Patrick Norman, b. 15 Apr 1931, Horsham, Sussex, England. University Lecturer; Clinical Psychologist. m. Moira Forsyth Reid, 17 Oct 1959, 2 s. Education: MA(Oxon); Diploma, Psychology, London; PhD, London; BA, MSc, Open. Career: Senior Clinical Psychologist, Springfield Hospital; Lecturer, Senior Lecturer, University of Hull; Currently, Reader, Psychology Department, University of Hull, Principal Clinical Psychologist, East Yorksire Community Health Trust. Memberships: Fellow, British Psychological Society; Chartered Psychologist Member, British Association of Behavioural and Cognitive Psychotherapy. Hobbies: Reading; Music; Languages; Horse Riding; Ice Dancing; Skiing; Lakeland Fell Walking; Sailboarding. Address: Psychology Department, The University of Hull, Cottingham Road, Hull, HU6 7RX, England.

PHILLIPS Michael Ian, b. 30 July 1938, London, England. Professor. m. Sara Galli, 14 June 1985. Education: BSc, Exeter University, 1962; PhD, Birmingham University, 1967; DSc, Birmingham University, 1986. Appointments: Visiting Assistant Professor, University of Michigan, 1967-69; Fellow, California Institute of Technology, 1969-70; Assistant Professor, University of Iowa, 1970; Associate Professor, University of Iowa, 1973; Professor, University of Iowa, 1978-80; Professor, Chairman, University of Florida, 1980-; Program Director, Neurobiology National Science Foundation, 1990. Publications: Brain Unit Activity During Behavior, 1973; The Renin Angiotensin System in the Brain, 1980; Insulin and Insulin-like Peptides, 1988; Cellular and Molecular Biology of the Renin Angiotensin System, 1993; Neuroimmunology: Methods in Neuroscience, 1994. Memberships: American Physiological Society; American Heart Association, (Fellow); International Society of Hypertension; American Society of Hypertension. Honours: NIMH Career Development Award, 1973; Teacher of the Year, University of Iowa, 1975; Teacher of the Year, University of Iowa, 1976; Humboldt Foundation Scholar, Heidelberg University, 1976-77; Artur Lucian Award for Cardiovascular Research, McGill University, 1989; President, Association Chairman Departments of Physiology, 1989; Chairman, ExperimentCardiovascular Study Section NIH, 1992-94. Hobbies: History; Art; Dog Walking. Address: Department of Physiology, Box 100274, College of Medicine, University of Florida, Gainesville, FL 32610-0274, USA.

PHILLIPS William Thomas, b. 29 Jun 1952, Ulysses, Kansas, USA. Physician. m. Lauren, 20 Oct 1981, 2 s, 1 d. Education: BA, Eastern New Mexico University; MD, University of Texas at Galveston. Appointments: Resident Family Practice, Lubbock, Texas, 1980-83; Resident, Nuclear Medicine, University of Texas, San Antonio, 1985-87; Associate Professor, University of Texas, San Antonio. Publications: Rapid Gatric Emptying of an Oral Glucose Solution in Type 2 Diabetic Patients, 1992; A Simple Method for Producing a Technetium-99m-Labelled Liposome which is Stable, 1992. Memberships: Society of Nuclear Medicine; American Medical Association; American Diabetes Association. Address: Department of Radiology, University of Texas, Health Sciences Center, 7703 Floyd Curl Drive, San Antonio, Texas 78209, USA.

PHILPOTT John Frederick, b. 31 Mar 1961, Chatham, NB, Canada. Physician. Education: BSc, 1982; MD, 1987; Paediatrician, 1991; FRCP(C); FAAP. Career: Physician, Mount Sinai Hospital, Toronto, Canada, 1991-93; Physician, Hospital for Sick Children, Toronto, Canada, 1993-. Hobby: Sports. Address: 3210 99 Harbour Square, Toronto, Ontario, Canada, M5J 2H2.

PHIPATANAKUL Chintana, b. 2 July 1941, Bangkok, Thailand. Physician. m. Supote Phipatanakul, 16 June 1968, 1 son, 1 daughter. Education: MD. Appointments: Currently Assistant Clinical Professor of Medicine. Publications include: Letters to the Editor: Metaproterenol Metered Dose Inhalers over the Counter Medication?, 1988. Memberships: St Louis Metropolitan Medical Society; Fellow, American College of Physicians; American Academy of Allergy and Immunology. Hobbies: Arts; Music. Address: 1125 Graham Road, Suite 2091, Florissant, MO 63031, USA.

PI Chihong, b. 26 Dec 1940, Nankang, Jiangxi, China. Physician. m. He Zhizhi, Jan 1968, 2 sons. Education: MB. Appointments: Resident, Attending Doctor, Lecturer, Associate Professor, Senior Doctor of Chinese Medicine, Professor, Vice-President, Jiangxi Institute of Traditional Chinese Medicine. Publications: Chinese Herbal Medicine, Co-author, 1992; Traditional Chinese Medicine Emergency, Co-author, 1994; Author of 7 other books and 19 essays in medicine. Honours: Special Allowance. Jiangxi Provincial Government, 1992; Special Allowance, State Council, 1994. Memberships: National Chinese Medical Society; Special Committee of Spleen and Stomach; Jiangxi Qigong Research Society. Hobbies: Sports; Music. Address: Yangming Road 20, Nanchang 330006, China.

PICARD Pierre, b. 8 July 1931. Doctor of Chiropractic. m. Nathalie Picard, 5 June 1982, 1 son, 1 daughter. Education: Doctor of Chiropractic, Palmer School of Chiropractic, Davenport, Iowa, USA, 1955; Intern, B J Palmer Chiropractic Clinic, Clearview Sanatarium for Nervous and Mental Disorders, Davenport. Appointments: Independent Practitioner. Memberships: Swiss Chiropractic Association; European Chiropractic Association. Hobbies: Golf; Sailing; Fitness. Address: Rue de Flore 32, 2502 Bienne, Switzerland.

PICCIRILLO A V, b. 12 Nov 1928, New Haven, CT, USA. Physician. m. Jeanne Pieroway, 29 May 1953, 2 s, 2 d. Education: BA, MD, Yale University. Career: Associate Clinical Professor, Pediatrics, Yale School of Medicine; Currently in Private Practice. Memberships: Fellow, American College of Allergy and Immunology; Fellow, American Academy of Allergy and Immunology; State Allergy Society; Medical Society. Hobbies: Gardening; Home Maintainance; Classical Music. Address: 1550 Elm Street, Wallingford, CT 06492, USA.

PICHLER John Frank, b. 6 Apr 1964, Cuckfield, England. Osteopath. Education: Diploma in Osteopathy, ESO; Clinical Competence, International College of Applied Kinesiology; Master Hypnotherapist and Neurolinguistic Programmer, Harrisonian Associates; Qualified Chiropodist, SMAE Institute. Career: Currently: Registered Osteopath, Applied and Clincial Kinesiologist, Hypnotherapist and Neurolinguistic Programmer, Chiropodist. Memberships: General Council and Register of Osteopaths; Osteopathic Association of Great Britain; International College of Applied Kinesiology; Harrisonian Associates; British Chiropody Association. Hobbies: Playing Guitar; DIY; Photography; Cinema; Theatre; Concerts; Post Graduate Courses. Address: The Horsted Green Health Centre, Horsted Pond Cottage, Little Horsted, Uckfield, East Sussex, TN22 5TR, England.

PICK Susan, b. 31 July 1952, Mexico DF. Psychologist. 2 sons, 1 daughter. Education: PhD. Appointments: Professor, National University of Mexico. Publications: Cano Investigation in Clinical Society, 1981; Planendo tu uda, 1990; Yo Adolscente, 1991; Yo, Mipannithia by Mis Medio Anliate, 1994. Honours: PhD Honour, 1978; National University Prize for Social Science Research, 1991. Memberships: American Psychological Association; Mexico Society for Social Psychology; American Public Health Association. Hobbies: Swimming; Hiking. Address: Apdo Postal 41-595, Mexico DF 11001, Mexico.

PICKERING Thomas George, b. 5 May 1940, Buckingshire, England. Physician. m. Janet Pickering, 16 Oct 1965, 2 sons. Education: BA, 1962, MB, BChir, 1966, MA, 1968, Cambridge University; DPhil, Oxford University, 1970. Appointments: House Physician, Middlesex Hospital, Lndon, 1966-68; Medical Research Council Fellow, 1968-71, Registrar, 1971-72, Lecturer, 1974-76, Radcliffe Infirmary, Oxford; Assistant Professor, Rockefeller University, New York City, USA, 1972-74; Currently Professor of Medicine, Hypertension Center, New York Hospital, Cornell Medical Center, New York City. Publications: How Common is White Coat Hypertension?, 1988; Ambulatory Monitoring and Blood Pressure Variability, 1991; Relation between Job Strain, Alcohol Intake and Ambulatory Blood Pressure, 1992; Ambulatory Monitoring and the Definition of Hypertension, 1992. Honours: Young Investigator Award, British Cardiac Society, 1975; President, Academy of Behavioral Medicine Research, 1994. Memberships: Fellow, Royal College of Physicians; Secretary, American Society of Hypertension; Society of Behavioral Medicine. Hobbies: Gardening; Running. Address: Hypertension Center, New York Hospital-Cornell Medical Center, New York, NY 10021, USA.

PICKLE Linda Williams, b. 19 July 1948, Hampton, Virginia, USA. Biostatistician. m. James B Pearson Jr, 14 Oct 1984, 1 daughter. Education: BA, Quantitative Studies, Johns Hopkins University, 1974; PhD, Biostatistics, Johns Hopkins University, 1977. Appointments: Computer Programmer, 1966-72; Staff Fellow, 1977-80; Senior Staff Fellow, 1980-84; Statistician, 1984-88; Director of Biostatistics, VT Combardi Cancer Research Center, Georgetown University, 1988-91. Publications: Over 100 publications in medical/Statistical Literature; Atlas of US Cancer Mortality Among Whites: 1950-1980, 1987; Atlas of US Cancer Mortality Among Nonwhites: 1950-1980, 1989. Honours: Phi Beta Kappa, 1973; Department of Health & Human Services Awards, 1986, 1988. Memberships: Biometric Society; American Statistical Association; Society for Epidemiologic Research; Society for Industrial & Applied Mathematics; Sigma Delta Epsilon; Graduate Women in Science. Hobbies: Fitness Walking; Mystery Reading. Address: National Center for Health Statistics, Hyattsville, MD 20782, USA.

PIDDOCK Marianne, b. 11 Feb 1936, East Molesey, Surrey, England. Diagnostic Radiographer. m. David John Piddock, 5 July 1958, 2 sons. Education: Diploma, Society of Radiographers. Appointments: Radiographer: Kent and Canterbury Hospital; Ashford Hospital; St Mary's Hospital, Luton; Crawley Hospital; Germiston Hospital, South Africa; Dr V Heerden and Partners, Germiston and Alberton; Vanderbiltpark Hospital; Currently Senior Radiographer (part-time), Dr Bloch and Partners, Sandton Clinic. Memberships: Society of Radiographers; Society of Radiographers of South Africa; South African Medical and Dental Council. Hobbies: Swimming; Gardening; Travel. Address: PO Box 209, Wilgeheuwel 1736, South Africa.

PIECZYNSKI Natasha, b. 26 Oct 1964, Mansfield, Ohio, USA. Marriage and Family Therapist. m. Richard Michael Pieczynski, 26 Sept 1987, 1 son. Education: BA, Sociology, Religion, Westminster College, New Wilmington, Pennsylvania, 1985; MDiv, 1990, MA, 1993, Louisville Presbyterian Theological Seminary, Louisville, Kentucky; Family Court Appointed Mediator. Appointments: Interim Minister; Psychotherapist; Minister of Christian Education; Consultant, Stress in the Family Life Cycle and Issues of Sexuality in Professionalism and Pastoral Care; Currently Marriage and Family Therapist, Family Mediator, Chemical Dependency Counsellor in Training. Honours: John Hanley Speech Award, 1985. Memberships: Clinical Member, American Association for Marriage and Family Therapy; Regular Member, American Society of Group Psychotherapist and Psychodrama; Regular Member, International Transactional Analysis Association. Hobbies: Walking; Reading; Travel; Racquetball. Address: 420 Ethridge Avenue, #205, Louisville, KY 40223, USA.

PIETRA Giuseppe G, b. 30 Dec 1930, Piacenza, Italy. Pathologist. m. Kathy Pietra, 23 Nov 1957, 2 sons. Education: MD; MA, honoris. Appointments: Resident in Pathology, Massachusetts General Hospital, 1960-62; University of Zurich, 1962-64; Assistant Professor, Oncology,

Chicago Medical School, 1964; Assistant Professor, Pathology, University Illinois, 1968; Assistant Professor, Pathology, 1969-70; Associate Professor, 1971-77; Professor of Pathology, University of Pennsylvania School of Medicine, 1977-. Publications: Author and Co-author of more than 150 papers and chapters, including: Pseudomesotheliomatous carcinoma of the lung, an immunohistochemical and ultrastructural study of the thress cases, 1991; Primary pulmonary hypertension in association with human immunodeficiency virus infection: A possible viral etiology for some forms of hypertensive arteriopathy, 1992; Extranodal lymphoid disorders, 1993; The histopathology of primary pulmonary vasculature and heart, 1993. Memberships: International Academy of Pathology; American Thoracic Society; Microscopic Society of America; Society of Investigative Pathology; Fellow, College of Physicians; College of American Pathologists. Honours: MA, University of Pennsylvania School of Medicine. Hobbies: Art; Music; Travel. Address: University of Pennsylvania Medical Center, Division of Anatomic Pathology, 6 Founders, 3400 Spruce Street, Philadelphia, PA 19104-4283, USA.

PIETTE Etienne Marie Ghislain, b. 4 Dec 1950, Kinshasa, Zaire. Maxillofacial Surgeon. m. Andrée Grandjean, 22 Dec 1973, 3 sons, 1 daughter. Education: MD, University of Liège, Belgium; BDS, University of Louvain; Specialist in Oral and Maxillofacial Surgery, University of Louvain; ECFMG Certificate, USA, 1973; PhD, University of Hong Kong, 1993. Appointments: Assistenz-Ärzt, University of Kiel, Germany, 1982-83; Spécialiste, University of Louvain, Belgium, 1983-88; Chief (part-time), Department of Oral and Maxillofacial Surgery, Ougrée Hospital, University of Liège, 1983-88; Senior Lecturer, 1988-92, Reader, 1992-93, University of Hong Kong; Consultant in Maxillofacial Surgery, Belgium 1994-. Publications: More than 85 publications in learned journals; Piette E and Reychler H: Traité de Pathologies Buccale et Maxillofaciale (editor), 1991; Editor, 2 small monographs. Memberships: Belgian Society of Oral and Maxillofacial Surgery; French Society of Oral and Maxillofacial Surgery; German Society of Oral and Maxillofacial Surgery; International Association of Oral and Maxillofacial Surgeons; European Association for Craniomaxillofacial Surgery. Hobbies: Reading; Tennis; Swimming. Address: Allée de la Meuse 6, B-5530 Godinne, Belgium.

PIHL Robert O, b. 2 Feb 1939, Wisconsin, USA. Professor. m. Sandra Woticky, 10 Oct 1973, 2 sons. Education: BA, Lawrence University, 1961; MA, Arizona University, 1965; PhD, Arizona University, 1966. Appointments: Assistant Professor, Department of Psychology, McGill University, 1966-71; Director, Department of Psychology, Lakeshore General Hospital, 1967-94; Co-Director, Alcohol Studies Group, Douglas Hospital, Montreal. Publications: Introduction to Abnormal Psychology: A compendium of readings, 1993; Cognitive deficits and autonomic reactivity in boys at high-risk for alcoholism, 1994; Predicting early onset of male antisocial behaviour from preschool behaviour: A test of two personality theories, 1994. Honours: Fellow, The American Psychological Association, 1994; Lehmann Award, Canadian College of Neuropsychopharmacology, 1994. Memberships: Fellow, The Canadian Psychological Association; Fellow, The American Psychological Association. Address: McGill University, Department of Psychology, 1205 Docteur Penfield Avenue, Montreal, Quebec H3A 1B1, Canada.

PIKE Steven. Medical Director. Education: BSc, magna cum laude, Chemistry, 1973, BSc, magna cum laude, Mathematics, 1973, College of Santa Fe; MD, University of New Mexico, 1979; MSc, Toxicology, University of Arizona, 1990; Internship, Tucson Medical Center, Kino Community Hospital, 1979-80. Career includes: President, EnviroMD Inc, 1986-; Emergency Physician, St Joseph's Hospital, Tucson, 1987-; President, TEMalytics Inc, 1989-; Director, Arizona Chapter, American College of Emergency Physicians, 1990-96; Consultancy to the Lesotho Highlands Development Authority, Africa, 1992; Director, Western Occupational Medical Association, 1992-94; Tucson Medical Center, Employee Health Physician and Occupational and Environmental Health Consultant, 1993-94; Health Partners, Medical Director, Occupational and Environmental Health, 1994-; Editor, Western Occupational and Environmental Medical Association Newsletter, 1994. Publications: Many publications, EnviroMD reports, presentations and many continuing education presentations. Honours: President's Award for Outstanding Student in Physical Sciences and Mathematics, College of Santa Fe; National Science Foundation Recognition; Undergraduate Research Participant. Memberships: Fellow, American College of Emergency Physicians; Fellow and Master, American College of Occupational and Environmental Medicine; American Academy of

Clinical Toxicologists; American College of Preventive Medicine; Permanent Commission and International Association on Occupational Health; American Academy of Consulting Toxicologists. Address: EnviroMD Inc, 4400 East Broadway, Suite 300, Tucson, AZ 85711, USA.

PILET Charles, b. 22 Feb 1932, Coëx, France. Veterinary Medicine. m. Lyon, 5 Apr 1958, 1 s. Education: Professor of Microbiology and Immunology, Alfort-Paris Veterinary School; Doctor of Veterinary Medicine, Pasteur Institute, Paris. Appointments: Assistant in Alfort-Paris Veterinary School; Lecturer, Alfort-Paris Veterinary School; Professor, Alfort-Paris Veterinary School; Dean, Alfort-Paris Veterinary School, 1976-84; Professor and Director of Animal and Comparative Immunology Institute. Publications: Co-Author of 2 Books of Microbiology; Author/Co-Author of over 170 Scientific Papers in Microbiology, Immunology or Infectious Diseases field. Memberships: French Medicine Academy, 1982-; French Sciences Academy, 1980-; President, World Association of Veterinary Microbiologists & Immunologists of Infectious Diseases; Vice-President, World Veterinary Association. Hobbies: Golf. Address: ENVA/7 A General de Gaulle, 94704 Maisons-Alfort, France.

PILIPENKO Nikolay Ivanovitch, b. 9 May 1937, Kharkiv, Ukraine. Radiologist. m. (1) 11 Apr 1963, (2) Irene Shestitko, 22 Jun 1983, 1 s, 1 d. Education: Physician, Kharkiv Medical Institute, 1960; Postgraduate, Radiologist, Candidate of Medical Sciences, Department of Radiology, Kharkiv Medical Institute, 1966; Doctor of Medical Sciences, 1986. Career: Assistant, 1966, Assistant Professor, 1969, Head of Department of Radiology and Oncology, 1982-, Kharkiv State Medical University; Currently, Director of Kharkiv Institute of Medical Radiology. Publications include: Co-author, Theoretical basis for calculation of physiological values of some organism systems functions at radionuclide diagnosis, 1993; Co-author, Cesium-137 incorporation levels in the residents of the regions of Ukraine which were not considerably contaminated after Chornobyl accident, 1994; Co-author, On history of medical radiology in Ukraine, 1993-94; Editor in Chief, Ukranian Journal of Radiology. Memberships: Vice President, Ukranian Association of Radiologists; Vice President, Kharkiv Regional Charity Anti-Cancer Foundation. Hobbies: Gardening; Skiing; Tennis. Address: Kharkiv, Sumska St 116, Apt 7, 310023, Ukraine.

PILKINGTON Raymond, b. 30 Apr 1932, Blackpool, Lancashire, England. Doctor. m. Phyllis Mary Worseley, 5 Sep 1959, 2 s, 1 d. Education: MB Bs, St Bartholomews Hospital, London, 1958; MRCOG, 1964; MD, 1966; FRCOG, 1978. Career includes: House Surgeon, St Bartholomews Hospital, 1959; Research Registrar, University of Newcastle upon Tyne, 1962; Senior Registrar, University of Liverpool, 1964; Consultant Obstetrican and Gynaecologist, now retired. Publications: Malignant Melanoma of Vagina, in British Journal of Obstetrics and Gynaecology, 1961; Biliary Peritonitis in Pregnancy, in British Medical Journal, 1963; Rhesus Isoimmunization, Some Aspects, thesis, 1966. Memberships: Royal College of Obstetricians and Gynaecologists; Medical Defense Union. Hobbies: Golf; Watercolour Painting; Books; Philately. Address: 67 Cartmell Road, St Annes on Sea, Lancashire, FY8 1DF, England.

PINAEV George, b. 29 Jan 1929, Leningrad, Russia. Biochemist. m. Alexandra Are, 15 July 1988, 2 sons. Education: Leningrad State University, 1955; PhD, Leningrad Paediatric Medical Institute, 1965; DS, Institute of Cytology, RAS, 1981. Appointments: Laboratory Assistant, Junior Scientist, 1965, Senior Scientist, 1970, Head of Department, 1975, Head, Cell Culture Department, Institute Cytology, RAS. Publications: Biochemistry of Muscles, Co-author, 1977; Synthesis of Specific Contractile Proteins as Biochemical Markers of Myogenic Cell Differentiation in Problems of Myogenesis, 1981; Cell Cultures Banks in General Problems of Biology, 1984. Memberships: World Federation Culture Collection; European Culture Collection Organisation; Society for In Vitro Biology; European Tissue Culture Society; Russian Academy of Science, Councils in Cell Biology in Biophysics and in Biotechnology; Russian Cell Culture Association. Hobbies: Ballet dancing; Ballet Master; Skiing. Address: Butlerova Str 24, ap 32, 194220 St Petersburg, Russia.

PINARD Gilbert Daniel, b. 19 Jul 1940, Montreal, Canada. Psychiatrist. m. Andrée Pouliot, 17 Aug 1963, 2 s. Education: BA, 1961, MD, 1965, Diploma in Psychiatry, 1970, University of Montreal, Canada. Career: Assistant Professor, Associate Professor, 1975-76, University of Montreal; Associate Professor, 1976-78, Chairman, Department of Psychiatry, 1976-82, Professor, 1978, Associate Dean of Medicine,

1983-85, University of Sherbrooke, Canada; Visiting Professor, Psychiatry, University of Texas, Dallas, South Western Medical School, USA, 1982-83; Currently, Chair, Department of Psychiatry, McGill University. Publications: 1st Author, The Language of Psychotics and Neurotics, in Aphasia, 1983; Author, Brief Psychotherapy of the Elderly, in Klinische Psychiatrie, 1986; Co-author, Idiopathic Constipation by Colonic Dysfunction: Relationship with Personality and Anxiety, in Digestive Diseases and Sciences, 1989; Author, Quality of Life in Insomnia, in Journal of American Medical Association, 1993. Memberships: Fellow, Royal College of Physicians and Surgeons; Fellow, American Psychiatric Association; Canadian Psychiatric Association; Association des Médecins de Langue Française du Canada; Canadian College of Neuropsychopharmacology; Quebec Psychiatric Association. Address: 3430 Peel Street, Apt 11-C, Montreal, Quebec, Canada, H3A 3K8.

PINHEIRO A Daniel Alves, b. 28 Nov 1962, Port, Portugal. Medical Student. m. Janice Blakeman, 28 Dec 1985, 1 d. Education: BA, Mid-America Nazarene College, USA, 1986; MA, 1988, PhD, 1994, MD, 1996, University of Missouri-Columbia. Appointments: Graduate Teaching Assistant: Histology, 1991-92; Physiology, 1990-91; Biology, 1989-90. Publications: Encoding Repetition rate and Duration in the Inferior Colliculus of the Big Brown Bat, Eptesicus Fuscus, Co-author, 1991; Naxolone Eliminates Passive Avoidance Retention Deficits Produced by Pretest Exposure to Novelty in Rats, 1991; Directional Sensitivity of Bat Inferior Collicular Neurons Determined under Normal and Moaurally Plugged Conditions, 1991. Honours: Rhoads Scholar, 1993-94; Research Fellow in Biological Sciences, 1990, 1991; Outstanding Biology Graduate Teaching Assistant, 1990-91. Memberships: American Medical Association; Association for Research in Otolaryngology; Society for Neuroscience. Hobbies: Skiing; Running; Sailing. Address: Columbia, MO 65202-1228, USA.

PINILLOS ASHTON Luis, b. 1 Feb 1945, Lima, Peru. Medical Doctor. m. Teresa, 14 May 1971, 1 son, 2 daughters. Education: DMRT. Appointments: Radiotherapist, Cancer Institute; Director, Peruvian Cancer Institute; Minister of Health, Peruvian Representative to the UN Scientific Committee on The Effects of Atomic Radiation; UNSCEAR Head, Academic Department of Radiology, Per Universidad Cayetano Heredia. Publications: Problematica Del Sector Salud, 1988; Un Ano De Gestion, 1988-89; La Salud En El Peru, 1988; El Medico Y El Tabaquismo En El Peru, 1993. Honours: Daniel A Carrion, Great Cross, 1988; Hipolito Unanue, Great Cross, 1988; Concytec, Honour Diploma, 1990; Paho, Medal for Anti Tobacco Activities. Memberships: UNSCEAR; Cancer Society; Radiology Society. Hobbies: Water Skiing. Address: Paseo De La Republica 3650, San Isidro, Lima 27, Peru.

PINKERTON John Henry McKnight, b. 5 June 1920, Belfast, Ireland. Physician. m. Florence McKinstry, 30 Sept 1947, 4 sons. Education: MB, BCh; BAO, Queens University, Belfast. Appointments: SHR Lecturer Consultant, UCWI; Professor, Obstetrics & Gynaecology, University of London; Surgeon, Queen Charlottes & Chelsea Hospitals; Professor, Obstetrics & Gynaecology, Queens University, Belfast; Surgeon, Royal Maternity & Royal Victoria Hospitals, Belfast. Publications: Numerous contributions in books and journals to medical literature. Honours: CBE, 1983; Hon DSc, 1986. Memberships: RCOG, Vice President 1977-80; RCPI, Censor 1985-87; Institute of Obstetrics & Gynaecology, RCPI, Chairman 1984-87. Address: 41C Sans Souci Park, Belfast, BT9 5BZ, Ireland.

PINTO DE SA Carlos Jose, b. 31 July 1940, Palmeira, Brazil. Physician. m. Ligia Pereira De Sa, 25 Dec 1966, 1 son, 1 daughter. Education: MD, Federal University of Rio Grande De Sul, 1969. Appointments: President, Rio De Sul Syndicate of Physicians; President, Vice President, National Association of Physicians; Vice President, Brazilian Medical Association; President, Brazilian Society of Vascular Surgery & Angiology; President, Brazilian Society of Orthomolecular Medicine. Publications: Translation & Adaptation of Chelation, A New Weapon for Medicine, 1986; Flaps, Chapter on Free Radical and Plastic Surgery, 1990. Memberships: American College for Advancement in Medicine; International Society of Oxicology; American Association of Orthomolecular Medicine. Hobbies: Reading; Jogging; Sail Boats; Water Sking; Music. Address: Rua Marcilio Dias, 1056-90130000 Porto Alegre RS, Brazil.

PIOT Peter, b. 17 Feb 1949, Leuven, Belgium. Public Health Official. m. Greet Kimzeke, 1975, 1 son, 1 daughter. Education: MD, University of Ghent, 1974; PhD, Microbiology, University of Antwerp, 1981.

Appointments include: Associate Professor, 1982-86, Head, Division of Microbiology, 1982-86, 1987-92, Professor, 1987-92, Chairman, Department of Infection and Immunity, 1989-92, Institute of Tropical Medicine, Antwerp; Associate Professor, Department of Medical Microbiology, University of Nairobi, Kenya, 1986-87; Associate Professor, Epidemiology, Free University of Brussels, Belgium, 1989-92; Associate Director, 1992-93, Director, Division of Research and Intervention Development, 1993-94; Executive Director, Joint United Nations Programme on AIDS, Geneva, 1995. Publications: Co-editor: Chlamydial Infection, 1982; AIDS and HIV Infection in the Tropics, 1988; The Handbook on AIDS Prevention in Africa, 1990; AIDS in Africa, 1991; Basic Laboratory Procedures in Clinical Bacteriology, 1991; Hepatitis B, and STD in Heterosexuals, 1991; Reproductive Tract Infections in Women, 1992; AIDS in Africa: A Handbook for Physicians, 1993. Honours: AMICON Prize for Medical Research, Antwerp, 1990-91; Officier, Ordre du Lion, Sénégal, 1991; H Breurs Award, Free University of Brussels, 1992; A Jauniaux Award for Social Action, Brussels, 1992; Van Thiel Lecturer, University of Leiden, Netherlands, 1992; Honorary Member, Dutch Society for the Study of Sexually Transmitted Diseases, 1992; Fogarthy Scholar, National Institutes of Health, USA, 1993; F R Rice STD Memorial Lecture, Indiana University, USA, 1993; Glaxo Award for Infectious Disease, 1994; Doctor honoris causa, Free Univeristy, Brussels, 1995. Memberships: Royal Academy of Medicine, Belgium; Royal Academy for Overseas Sciences, Brussels; International Society for STD Research, Secretary 1981-86; International AIDS Society, President 1992-94. Hobbies: Cooking; Reading; Opera. Address: Joint United Nations Programme on AIDS, World Health Organization, 20 Avenue Appis, CH-1211 Geneva 27, Switzerland.

PIPER Claire, b. 29 Apr 1969, Middlesex, England. Registered Osteopath. Education: Diploma in Osteopathy; MRO. Memberships: General Council and Register of Osteopaths; Osteopathic Association of Great Britain; Society of Osteopaths. Hobbies: Swimming; Keep Fit; Reading; Cross-Stitch; Needlework. Address: 6 Springfield Road, St Leonards-on-Sea, East Sussex TN38 0TU, England.

PIRANI Bahadurali B K, b. 8 May 1939, Uganda. Physician. m. Carolyn T Brown, 1 July 1967, 1 son, 1 daughter. Education: MD, Aberdeen; MBChB, St Andrews; FRCOG; FACOG; FRCSC. Appointments: Head, Department of Obstetrics and Gynecology, Grace General Hospital, Winnipeg, Manitoba, 1989-93; Vice President of Medical Staff, Grace General Hospital, Winnipeg, Manitoba, 1991-93; President of Medical Staff, Grace General Hospital, Winnipeg, Manitoba, 1993. Publications Include: Serum heat stable alkaline phosphatase in normal pregnancy and its relationship to urinary oestriol and pregnanediol excretion, placental weight and baby weight, 1972; The cause of the fall in serum folate in normal pregnancy, 1976; Smoking during pregnancy. Review article, 1978; Abruptio placentae and smoking in pregnancy, 1979. Memberships: Manitoba Medical Association; Canadian Medical Association; Royal College of Obstetricians and Gynaecologists; American College of Obstetricians and Gynaecologists. Hobbies: Cricket; Tennis; Jazz. Address: 3151 Vialoux Drive, Winnipeg, Manitoba R3R 0A1, Canada.

PISANI-CROCKFORD Audrey, b. 3 Jan 1938, Sliema, Malta. Naturopath. m. Alfred, 20 Apr 1961, 2 s, 1 d. Education: Diploma in Music Performance Violin, 1956; Diploma in Acupuncture, 1986; Diploma in Homeopathy, 1984; Diploma in Osteopathy, 1985; Diploma in Naturopathy, 1985; Fellow, Commonwealth Institute of natural Medicine and Acupuncture; D Hom Med, London; MAcF. Appointments: Hotelier, Co-Founder, Corinthia Group of Companies; Naturopath; Physician of Alternative Medicine. Publications: COntributor of several papers read at distributed in international conventions on alternative medicine, 1985-. Honours: FCINM&Ac, Sri Lanka, 1986. Memberships: Register of Osteopaths, United Kingdom;'Register of Homeopaths, United Kingdom; Register of Naturopaths, United Kingdom; Institute of Management, Malta. Hobbies: Violinist; Scuptor; Painter. Address: Krypton Chemists, Tal-Ibragg, Malta.

PISTOLESI Massimo, b. 1 Aug 1948, Pisa, Italy. Chest Physician. m. Vanna Ciampalini, 23 Feb 1974, deceased, 1 daughter. Education: MD, Catholic University, Rome, 1973; Diploma, Respiratory Diseases, University of Pisa, 1975; Diploma, Nuclear Medicine, University of Pisa, 1977. Appointments: Career Investigator, National Research Council, Italy; Visiting Associate Professor, University of California, USA; Associate Professor, Respiratory Pathophysiology, University of Rome; Currently Associate Professor of Respiratory Pathophysiology, University of Pisa. Publications: Assessment of Extravascular Lung

Water, 1978; Injury Versus Hydrostatic Lung Edema, 1982; The Vascular Pedicle of the Heart and the Vena Azygos, 1984; The Chest Roentgenogram in Pulmonary Edema, 1985; Pleural Liquid and Solute Exchange, 1989; Reading the Chest Radiograph, 1993. Memberships: European Respiratory Society; Italian Association of Nuclear Medicine; Italian Association of Respiratory Medicine; Fleischner Society for Chest Diagnosis. Address: Pulmonary Unit, CNR Institute of Clinical Physiology, Via Savi 8, 56127 Pisa, Italy.

PITKIN Roy Macbeth, b. 24 May 1934, Anthon, Iowa, USA. Physician; Educator. m. Marcia Jenkins, 17 Aug 1957, 2 sons, 2 daughters. Education: BA, University Iowa, 1956; MD, University Iowa, 1959. Appointments: Assistant Professor, Obstetrics & Gynecology, University Illinois, 1965-68; Associate Professor, Professor, Chairman, Department of Obstetrics & Gynecology, University Iowa, 1968-87; Professor, Chair, Department of Obstetrics & Gynecology, UCLA School of medicine, California. Publications: Several publications in medical journals; Editor, Obstetrics and Gynecology, 1985-; Editor, Clinical Obstetrics and Gynecology, 1975-. Honours: Fellow ad eundem Royal College of Obstetricians & Gynaecologists; Member, Institute of Medicine; Honorary Fellow, German Society of Gynecology & Obstetrics. Memberships: FRCOG; FACOG; American Gynecological & Obstetrical Society; Society for Gynecologic Investigation. Address: UCLA Department of Obstetrics & Gynecology, 10833 Le Conte Avenue, 27-117 CHS, Los Angeles, CA 90024-1740, USA.

PITT Ian Thomas, b. 1 Sept 1960, Coventry, England. Osteopath. Education: Diploma in Osteopathy. Appointment: Private Practice. Memberships: General Council and Register of Osteopaths; Osteopathic Association of Great Britain. Hobbies: Golf; Football; Acupuncture. Address: 127 Milton Road, Weston-Super-Mare, Avon BS23 2UY, England.

PITTS Kenneth E, b. 3 Feb 1924, Missouri, USA. Psychiatrist. m. jacqueline Brookes, 25 June 1949, 3 s. Education: MD; FAPA. Appointments: Director, Detroit Psychiatric Institute; Medical Director, Orchard Hills Psychiatric Centre. Memberships: American psychiatric Association; Michigan state Medical Society; American Medical Association. Address: 42450 West Twelve Mile Road, Suite 305, Novi, MI 48377-3011, USA.

PLASCHKES Jack, b. 13 Apr 1932, Czechoslovakia. Surgeon. Education: MD, Berne, Switzerland, 1957; Accreditation Paediatrics, 1964, Accreditation General Surgery, 1969, Israel Ministry of Health; Accreditation Paediatric Surgery, Swiss Medical Association, 1977; Accreditation Paediatric Surgery, Royal College of Surgeons, England, 1979; FRCS, England, 1978. Appointments: Registrar, Senior Registrar, 1971-72, Resident Assistant Surgeon, 1974-75, Paediatric Surgery, Hospital for Sick Children, Great Ormond Street, London, England; Senior Surgeon, Paediatric Surgery, 1972-74, 1980-, University Children's Hospital, Berne, Switzerland; Associate Surgeon, Paediatric Surgery, Emma Children's Hospital, Amsterdam, Netherlands, 1977-78; Locum Consultant Surgeon, University Hospital. Queen's Medical Centre, Nottingham, England, 1979-80. Publications: Cancer in Childhood, chapter, 1989; Surgical Oncology in Children, chapter, 1992; Adult Tumours in Children, Is There a Difference, 1991. Memberships: International Society of Pediatric Surgical Oncology, President; Swiss Pediatric Oncology Group; Swiss Association of Paediatric Surgeons; Paediatric Oncology Group, USA; International Society of Paediatric Oncology; British Association Paediatric Surgeons; British Association Surgical Oncology. Address: University Children's Hospital, Department of Paediatric Surgery, Inselspital, 3010 Berne, Switzerland.

PLATA MUJICA Carlos, b. 15 Aug 1922, Socorro, Colombia. Medical Psychoanalyst; Training Analyst. m. 10 Dec 1951, 1 s. Education: Medicine, Psychiatric Hospital, Buenos Airies, 1950; Asst Psychoanalyst, 1956, Argent, 1958, Soc Colomb de Psico, 1959. Career: Director, Institute of Psychoanalysts; President, College of Psychoanalysts, 1962-65; Secretary Copal, 1968-70, President Copal, 1970-72, Vice President Copal, 1973-75, International Psycho Assn; President, Consej Direc, University College of Colombia, 1982-91. Publications: El dinitil succinico en Psiquiatria El Psiquismo Fetal (en colaboracion CAP VI) Ed Paidos Buenos Aires, 1960; Metapsicologia y tecnica psicoanalitica Tercer Mundo Bogota, 1989; Algunos aspectos psicoanaliticos de Sancho y Don Quijote Rev Soc Col Psicoan, 1983. Memberships: Society of Colombian Psychoanalysts; International Psychoanalytical Association; Society College of Psychiatry; Federation of Medicine of Colombia. Hobbies: Historic Buildings and Surroundings. Address: Avda 15 No 127-A-33 apto 1408, Bogota, Colombia.

PLOTH David William, b. 22 Jun 1941, IA, USA. Physician. m. Janis M Ploth, 1961, 3 d. Education: MD, University of IA, College of Medicine, 1967; Diplomate, American Board of Internal Medicine, 1972, Nephrology Subspeciality, 1978. Appointments include: Professor of Medicine, University of AL at Birmingham; Professor and Director, Division of Nephrology, Medical University of SC; Medical Director, Dialysis Clinics Inc Program, Charleston, SC, 1989-. Publications include: 64 Professional publications, 1967-, including: Renovascular hypertension, in Principles and Practice of Nephrology, 1994; Mechanisms of acute renal failure in one-kidney, one-clip hypertensive rats in response to Na+ nitroprusside, mechanically reduced blood pressure, or Ca++ channel Blocking agents, 1994; Co-author, Glomerular hemodynamics in normal and 1-kidney, 1-clip hypertensive rats, 1994; 85 Abstracts, 1973-. Honours include: American Chemical Society Award, Inorganic Chemistry, 1960; National Kidney Foundation Renal Research Fellowship, University of IA, College of Medicine, 1973-74; Fellow, American College of Physicians, 1977; Many Awards and Grants; NIH RO-1 Award, 1987; VA Merit Review Award, 5 years. Memberships include: National Kidney Foundation; American College of Physicians; AMA; American Society of Nephrology; American Physiological Society, Committee on Committees, 1993-; International Society of Nephrology; Southern Society for Clinical Investigation, Nominating Committee, 1993-; Central Society for Clinical Research; Charleston County Medical Society. Address: Director, Div of Nephrology, Medical Univ of SC, 171 Ashley Avenue, Charleston, SC 29425-2220, USA.

PLOUFFE Leo Jr, b. 26 Nov 1957, Montreal, Canada. Reproductive Endocrinologist. m. Evelyn W White, 22 Sep 1990. Education: MD, CM, McGill University, Montreal, 1980; Residency, McGill University Dept of Ob/Gyn, 1981-85; Fellowship, Medical College of Georgia, Dept of Ob/Gyn, Reproductive Endocrinology, Augusta, Georgia, USA, 1985-87. Appointments: Assistant Professor, 1987-92, Associate Professor of Obstetrics and Gynaecology, 1992-, Chief, Reproductive Endocrinology Infertility and Genetics section, 1994-, Medical College of Georgia. Publications: Screening for Sexual Problems Through a Simple Questionnaire, 1985; Biological Modeling on a Microcomputer Using Standard Spreadsheet and Equation Solver Programs: The Hypothalamic-Pituitary-Ovarian Axis as an Example, 1992; Repeated Fetal Losses with Antiphospholipid Antibodies: A Collaborative Randomized Trial Comparing Prednisone to Low-Dose Heparin Treatment, 1992; Comprehensive Management of the Menopause, 1993. Honours: McGill Faculty of Medicine, W W Chapman Gold Medal in Ob-Gyn, 1980; McGill Alumnae Society Scarlet Key Award, 1981; Outstanding Young Clinical Faculty Award. School of Medicine, Medical College of Georgia, 1992. Memberships: American Society for the Advancement of Science; American College of Ob/Gyn, Fellow; American Society of Reproductive Medicine; American Fertility Society. Hobbies: Bicycling; Poetry. Address: Medical College of Georgia, Department of OB/GYN, 1120 15th Street, Augusta, GA 30912-3360, USA.

POCHA Nusly Piloo Jehangir, b. 7 Oct 1944, Bombay, India. General Practitioner; Aviation Medicine Specialist. m. Sherna Dubash, 9 Apr 1973, 1 son, 1 daughter. Education: MB, BS; FRSH (Eng); FCIP; AFAsMA (USA); MCSAM (Can); Course in Aviation Medicine for AME Flight Surgeons. Appointments: Senior Medical Officer, Bombay Dyeing and Manufacturing Co Ltd, 1973; Medical Officer: Singapore Airlines, 1973, Air Canada, 1984, Air France, 1990, ModiLuft, 1993, Alitalia, 1994, Lufthansa German Airlines, 1994, El Al Israel Airlines, 1994, Swissair, 1994; Medical Officer: Consulate General of Israel, 1980, Consulate-General of the United States of America, 1985-91, Consulate of Australia, 1988, Consulate of Canada, 1991, Consulate-General for Germany, 1991; Senior Aviation Medical Officer for Federal Aviation Administration, 1991; Only Indian designated Medical Examiner for Department of Transportation of Canada and Ministry of Australia. Publications: Papers: Experiences in the Textile Industry, 1981; India - Experiences, 1990. Memberships: Associate Fellow, Aerospace Medical Association; Airlines Medical Directors Association; Canadian Society of Aerospace Medicine; Fellow, College of Independent Practitioners of India. Hobbies: Philately; Reading. Address: Carmel, 30 Nepean Sea Road, Bombay 400 006, India.

PODDAR Nises Chandra, b. 31 Dec 1946, Bangladesh. Obstetrician and Gynaecologist. m. Kalyani Ray, 12 May 1980, 1 daughter.

Education: MBBS; DGO (Calcutta); DObstRCOG (London); DObstRCP (Ireland); DipFPA (London); FRCOG (London); FHKCOG; FHKAM (Hong Kong). Appointments: Registrar and Locum Consultant, England; Senior Medical Officer, Hong Kong; Currently Consultant Obstetrician and Gynaecologist, Kwong Wah Hospital, Kowloon, Hong Kong. Honours: Certificate of Merit Award, Calcutta National Medical College, India, 1965. Memberships: Obstetrics and Gynecological Society of Hong Kong; Hong Kong Surgical Laser Association; Hong Kong Gynecological Endoscopy Society. Hobbies: Reading; Debating; Current affairs. Address: Department of Obstetrics and Gynaecology, Kwong Wah Hospital, 25 Waterloo Road, Kowloon, Hong Kong.

PODRUG Dinko, b. 1 Feb 1952, Zagreb, Croatia. Psychiatrist. m. Nena Ilic, 1975, 1 d. Education: Doctor Medical Science, SUNY, 1988. Appointments: Currently, Attending Physician, University Hospital and Assistant Professor, SUNY, Brooklyn. Publication: Co-author, Transference in Brief Psychotherapy, Analytic Press, 1985. Memberships: APA; SPR; ISSTS. Address: 52 East End Avenue, New York, NY 10028, USA.

POGATSA Gabor, b. 25 Feb 1932, Budapest, Hungary. Professor of Cardiology. m. Gizella Pogatsa, 31 July 1957, 1 son, 2 daughters. Education: MD, Semmelweis University Medical School, Budapest, 1956; PhD, Semmelweis University Medical School, Budapest, 1967; DSc, Hungarian Academy of Sciences, Budapest, 1980. Appointments: Resident, 3rd Medical Department, 1956-59; Professors' Assistant, 2nd Medical Department, 1959-64; Assistant Professor, 2nd Medical Department, 1964-67; Senior Member, 1967-80; Head of Research Department, 1980-92; Vice Director, National Institute of Cardiology, Budapest, 1993. Publications: Effect of diabetes therapy on the myocardium in experimental diabetes', 1979; Possible cardiac benefits of hypoglycaemic sulphonylures', 1987; Effect of prostaglandins on the diabetic heart and coronary circulation, 1991. Memberships: European Association for the Study of Diabetes; International Society of Heart Research; Federation European of Associations Medical Catholic; International Union of Physiological Sciences; Hungarian Diabetes Association; Hungarian Society of Cardiology; St Luke's Society of Hungarian Catholic Physicians; Hungarian Society of Physiology. Honours: Hetényi Award, 1986. Address: Maros utca 28, H-1122 Budapest, Hungary.

POIRIER-BRODE Karen Yvonne, b. 2 Dec 1949, Canada. Physician. m. Cal Barwick, 26 Aug 1989, 2 sons, 5 stepsons. Education: BSc, 1971, MD, CM, 1973, McGill University; Residency, 1974-77, Fellowship, 1977-79, University of California Davis, Medical Centre, Sacramento, USA. Appointments include: Contract Physician, Planned Parenthood Association of Butte, Solano, Contra Costa and Napa Counties, 1983-85, 1988-90; Contract Physician, Planned Parenthood of Sacramento Valley, 1982-90; Assistant Clinical Professor, Department of Obstetrics and Gynaecology, University of California, Davis, 1983-89, 1989-; Private Practice, Obstetrics and Gynaecology, Valley Centre for Women's Health, sacramento, 1983-90; Kaiser Permanente Obstetrics and Gynaecology Medical Offices, Stockton, California, 1990-. Publications include: Sickle Cell Disease, 1988; Adolescent Pregnancy and Prenatal Care, 1987; Hematological Complications in Pregnancy, 1983; Vascular Complications in Pregnancy, 1983; Leiomyoma of the Female Urethra, 1979. Memberships: AMA; AMWA; SAM; CMA; AAGL. Hobbies: Skiing; Fabric Arts; Travel; Reading. Address: Kaiser Permanente Medical Centre, 7373 West Lane, Stockton, CA 95210, USA.

POKROVSKY Anatoly V, b. 21 Nov 1930, Minsk. Vascular Surgeon. m. Ekaterina Pokrovskaya, 1 daughter. Education: MD. Appointments: A N Bakulev Institute of Cardiovascular Surgery, 1959-83; Chief, Vascular Department, Chief, Chamber of Vascular Surgery, Advanced Training Institute for Doctors, 1986-, Professor of Surgery, A V Vishnevsky Institute of Surgery. Publications: Contributor of 12 monographs including: Clinical Angiology, 1979; Diseases of Aorta and Its Branches, 1979; Contrisbutor of book chapters. Honours: Laureate of the USSR State Prize, 1975. Memberships: President, Russia Society of Angiologists; Editor-in-Chief, Russian-English Journal on Vascular Surgery; International Cardiovascular Surgery; Honorary member, Society for Vascular Surgery, USA; European Society Cardiovascular Surgery; European Society Vascular Surgery. Hobby: Tourism. Address: 27 B Serukhovskaya Street, 113811 Moscow, Russia.

POKROVSKY Valentin Ivanovich, b. 1 Apr 1929, Ivanovo, USSR. Professor. m. 1 son. Education: DMS, I M Setchenov 1st Moscow

Medical Institute, 1952. Appointments: Head, Chair of Infectious Diseases and Epidemiology, Semasko Moscow Medical Stomatology Institute, 1965-; Deputy Director, Central Scientific Research Institute of Epidemiology, 1968-; President, Russian Academy of Medical Sciences, 1987-. Publications include: Meningococcus Infections, 1976; Manual in Infectious Diseases, 1977; Cholera, 1978; Dysentery, 1979; Rotaviral Infections, 1982. Honours: Timakov Prize, 1979; Ivanovsky Prize, 1986; Chairman of the Board, Mechnikov Russian Microbiology, Epidemiology and Parasitology Scientific Society; Board Member, International Federation of Infectionists. Membership: World Health Organisation Expert Committee. Address: Presidium of the Russian Academy of Medical Sciences, Solianka 14, 109801 Moscow, Russia.

POLANI Paul Emanuel, b. 1 Jan 1914, trieste, Italy. Professor Emeritus. m. Nina Ester Sullam, 24 Aug 1944. Education: MD; FRCP; FRCOG; Honorary FRCPath; FRP(Ir); DCH; FRS; CM(IT). Appointments: Senior MO and SO, Evelina Hospital for Sick Children; National Birthday Trust Research Fellow; Assistant Director, Paediatrics, Guy's Hospial Medical School; Director, National Spastics Society Research Unit; Prince Philip Research Professor; Director, SE Thames Genetics Centre; Professor Emeritus, London University; Honorary Geneticist, Division Medical Molecular Genetics, Paediatric Research Unit, Guy's and St Thomas' Hospitals Medical Schools. Publications: Impact Genetics on Medicine, 1990; Contributor of numerous articles in professional journals. Honours: CM(IT), 1980; International Cerebral Palsy Gold Medal, 1979; Bailey Gold Medal, Royal College of Physicians, London, 1985. Hobbies: Reading; Horse-riding. Address: Little Meadow, West Clandon, Surrey, GU4 5TL, England.

POLKE David Richard, b. 22 Apr 1957, Bridgeport, Connecticut, USA. Physician. m. Linda Richter, 12 Oct 1989, 2 sons, 2 daughters. Education: BS, 1979, MD, 1986, University of Connecticut; MS, University of Bridgeport, 1982; Diplomate, National Board of Medical Examiners, 1987; Speciality, American Board of Obstetrics and Gynecology, 1992. Appointments: Supervisor, Research and Development, Uniroyal Chemical, 1980-81; Currently in private practice, Naugatuck Valley Obstetrics and Gynecology Associates PC, Waterbury, Connecticut; Staff, St Mary's Hospital, 1990-; Visiting Courtesy Staff, Bridgeport Hospital, 1990-; Courtesy Staff, Waterbury Hospital, 1994-. Honours: Phi Kappa Phi, 1978; Phi Beta Kappa, 1979; Recognition Award, American Medical Association. Memberships: Fellow, American College of Obstetrics and Gynecology; American Medical Association; American Institute of Ultrasound and Medicine; New Haven Medical Society; New York Academy of Sciences; Connecticut State Medical Society; Connecticut Society of Obstetrics and Gynecologists; American Association of Gynecologic Laparoscopists; Society of Laparoendoscopic Surgeons. Hobbies: Fishing; Hunting. Address: 133 Scovill Street, Suite 303, Waterbury, CT 06706, USA.

POLLACK Shimon, b. 20 June 1946, Israel. Professor. m. Miriam, 26 May 1971, 2 sons, 1 daughter. Education: MD. Appointments: Chief Physician, department of Medicine, Director, Immunology, Allergy and AIDS Institute, Rambam Medical Centre, Haifa. Publications: The Macrophage, Co-author, 1992; Recurrent severe Infections Caused by a Novel Leukocyte Adhesion Deficiency, Co-author, 1992. Memberships: American Association of Immunology; International Society of Allergy and Clinical Immunology. Hobby: Reading. Address: 5 Ranas Street, Kiriat Motzkin 26317, Israel.

POLLACK William, b. 7 Nov 1950, New York City, USA. Psychologist. m. Dr Marsha Padwy, 7 Nov 1982, 1 daughter. Education: PhD; MA. Appointment: Director, Continuing Education, McLean Hospital. Memberships: Fellow, Massachusetts Psychology Association; American Psychology Association. Address: 115 Mill Street, Belmont, MA 02178, USA.

POLLOCK George Howard, b. 19 Jun 1923, Chicago, Illinois, USA. Psychoanalyst. m. Beverly Yufit, 3 Jul 1946, 3 s, 2 d. Education: MD; PhD, Physiology. Appointments: President/Director, Institute for Psychoanalysis, Chicago; Ruth and Evelyn Dunbar Distinguished Professor of Psychiatry and Behavioral Sciences, Northwestern University Medical School. Publications: Co-Editor, The Course of Life; Co-Editor, Psychoanalytic Explorations of Music; Author, The Morning-Liberation Process; Numerous Scientific Articles. Memberships: Past President, American Psychiatric Association; American Psychoanalytic Association; Illinois Psychiatric Society; Chicago

Psychoanalytic Society. Address: 30 North Michigan Avenue, Chicago, Illinois 60602, USA.

POLS Jan, b. 25 Mar 1936, Alblasserdam. Psychiatrist. m. R P Mast, 15 Oct 1976, 3 sons, 1 daughter. Appointments: Psychiatrist in Private Practice; Director of Psychiatrist Training Department. Publications: Mythe en Macht. Over de Kritische Psychiatrie, 1984; Mental Illness and Rationality: A Critique, 1989. Memberships: KNMG; NV Psychatrie; NV Psychothreapie; VRT. Address: Cederlaan 4, 9401 Assen, The Netherlands.

POMERANCE Herbert Hart, b. 28 Mar 1918, New York, USA. Professor, Pediatrics, University of South Florida. m. Ruth E Segal, 25 Dec 1940, 2 sons. Education: MD, Columbia University, 1941; Diplomate, American Board of Pediatrics, 1951; Fellow, American Academy of Pediatrics, 1951. Appointments: Professor, Chairman, Department of Pediatrics, West Virginia University, Charleston, 1973-84; Emeritus Professor, Pediatrics, West Virginia University, 1984; Professor, Department of Paediatrics, University of South Florida, Tampa, 1984-; Interim Chairman, 1990-1991. Publications: Growth Standards in Children, 1979; Topics in Pediatrics, A Festschrift for Lewis A Barness, 1990. Memberships: American Academy of Paediatrics; Florida Pediatric Society. Address: Department of Paediatrics, University of South Florida College of Medicine, Box MDC015, Tampa, FL 33612, USA.

POON Chi-Sang, b. 12 Nov 1952, Hong Kong. Research Scientist. m. Sau-Chun Ng, 12 Aug 1978, 1 son. Education: BSc, University of Hong Kong, 1975; MPhil, The Chinese University of Hong Kong, 1977; PhD, University of California, Los Angeles, 1981. Appointments: Assistant, Associate Professor of Electrical Engineering, North Dakota State University; Adjunct Assistant, Associate Professor of Medicine, University of North Dakota; Principal Research Scientist, Massachusetts Institute of Technology. Publications: Over 60 research articles, 1978-. Honours: Harold Lamport Award, Biomedical Engineering Society, 1983; Human Frontier Science Program Fellowship, 1994. Memberships: American Physiological Society; Biomedical Engineering Society; Neural Networks Society; Society for Neuroscience; American Association for the Advancement of Science. Hobbies: Music; Singing. Address: Massachusetts Institute of Technology, 77 Massachusetts Avenue, Cambridge, MA 02139, USA.

POON Kwong Chiu, b. 2 Nov 1927, Hong Kong. Medical Practitioner. m. Chee Hing Kwan, 1 Jan 1957, 2 daughters. Education: MB BS, University of Hong Kong; FACCP; FAGS; FRCG; FHKGP' FHKAM(Family Medicine). Appointments: Clinical Assistant Medical Unit, University of Hong Kong; Medical Officer, Ruttonjee Hospital; Medical Officer, Wing on Life Assurance Company; Private Practice. Memberships: Hong Kong Medical Association; American College of Chest Physicians; American Geriatrics Soceity; Royal College of General Practitioners; Hong Kong College of General Practitioners; Hong Kong Academy of Medicine. Address: B2, Park Villa, 2 Park Road, Hong Kong.

POON Wai-Sang, b. 20 Dec 1953, Canton, China. AcademicNeurosurgeon. m. Gillian Kew, 15 Sept 1984, 2 sons, 1 daughter. Education: MB, ChB, Glasgow University, Scotland; FRCS, 1983. Appointments: Currently Senior Lecturer, Chief in Neurosurgery, Chinese University of Hong Kong. Publications: Hyponatraemia in neurosurgical patients, 1989; Traumatic extradural haematoma of delayed onset, 1992; Laser-induced fluorescence in brain tumours, 1992. Membership: International Brain Research Organisation. Hobby: Chinese instrumental music. Address: Department of Surgery, Prince of Wales Hospital, Shatin, Hong Kong.

POPA Valentin Tudor, b. 17 Feb 1932, Romania. Physician. m. Opritsa Popa, 28 Jan 1968, 1 daughter. Education: MD, with honors. Appointments: Assistant Professor of Medicine, University of Illinois, 1973-74; Assistant Professor of Medicine, University of Chicago, 1973-74; Associate Professor of Medicine, Director, Palm Medical Centre, 1977-82; Associate Professor of Medicine, University of California, 1982-87. Publications: 116 articles; Contributions to 5 books. Memberships: California Medical Society; American Medical Association. Honours: NIH Grant, 1984; Merit Review Grant, 1984. Hobbies: Classical Music. Address: 7501 Timberlake 205, Sacramento, CA 95823, USA.

POPESCU Valerian, b. 26 Oct 1912, Negresti, Romania. Professor of Maxillo-Facial Surgery. m. 5 Dec 1943, 2 d. Education: MD, 1939; DDS; PhD; Specialist Stomatology, 1943; Specialist, Maxillo-Facial Surgery, 1947; Doctor Docent, 1960; Faculty of Medicine and Surgery, University of Bucharest, Institute of Stomatology and Maxillo-Facial Surgery. Appointments: Intern, Hospital Surgery, 1935-41; Resident, Maxillo-Facial Surgery, 1942-47; Professor, Maxillo-Facial Surgery, 1947-49; Professor, Head of Chair of Maxillo-Facial Surgery, Institute of Medicine, Bucharest, 1949-85; Professor of Maxillo-Facial Surgery, Ecological University, 1990; Dean, Faculty of Stomatology, 1962-76; Director, Hospital Clinic Maxillo-Facial Surgery, 1948-85; Professor of Maxillo-Facial Surgery, Ecol University. Publications: Author of 19 books including: Maxillo-Facial Surgery, 1956, 1966, 1977; Oral Surgery techniques, 1961-66; Anesthesia in Stomatology, 1971; Emergencies in Stomatology, 1969; Maxillo-Facial Traumatology, 1967; Stomatological Radiology, 1977; Radiodiagnostic in Oral Surgery, 1985; Early Diagnostic in Oral Cancer, 1984; Salivary Gland Pathology, Co-author, 1987; Contributor of over 400 scientific works in journals and congress; 12 original methods and techniques of surgery. Honours include: Gold Medal Academy, Art Science et Lettres, 1979; Prix Magitot, Academie de Medicine de France, 1968; Medaille de la Ville de Paris, 1968; Medal Sanitary Merit, 1943, 1973. Memberships include: President, 1948-73, Society of Stomatology; President, 1969-71, Union of Societies Medical Sciences; President, Association Stomatologique Internationale, 1975-79. Address: Strada Inocentei No 1, Bucharest SII, Romania.

POPLACK David Gerson, b. 3 May 1943, Taunton, MA, USA. Physician. m. June Takenaga, 1 son, 2 daughters. Education: BA, Tufts University; MD, Boston University School of Medicine. Career: Sr Investigator, Pediatric Branch, National Cancer Institute, National Institutes of Health, Bethesda, MD; Deputy Chief, Pediatric Branch, National Cancer Institute, National Institutes of Health; Director, Texas Children's Cancer Center. Publications: Co-author, Principles and Practice of Pediatric Oncology, 1988; Second Edition, 1993. Memberships: American Society of Clinical Investigation; Society for Pediatric Research; Fellow, American Academy of Pediatrics; American Society of Clinical Oncology; American Association of Cancer Research; American Society of Pediatric Hem/Onc; International Society of Pediatric Oncology; American Soc of Hematology. Hobbies: Gardening; Tennis; Fishing. Address: Texas Children's Cancer Center, 6621 Fannin St, MC 3-3320, Houston, TX 77030, USA.

POPOVICIU Liviu, b. 8 Feb 1927, Bran, Romania. Physician; Neurologist. m. Adriana Popoviciu, 7 July 1957, 1 daughter. Education: MD, PhD, Faculty of Medicine; Postdoctoral Research, France. Appointments: University Assistant, 1954; Lecturer, 1958; Assistant Professor, 1966; University Professor, Head of Neurological Clinic, 1970; Research Director, 1984. Publications: 40 books, include: Normal and Pathologic Sleep, 1972; Pathology of the Wake-sleep States, 1984; Pathology of Autonomic Nervous System, 1990; Articles: Electroclinical correlations in temporal lobe epilepsy, 1991; Polysomnographic and computerized electroencephalographic studies in myoclonic petit mal epilepsies, 1993; Clinical EEG electromyographic and polysomnographic studies in restless legs syndrome caused by magnesium deficiency, 1993. Honours: G Marinesco Prize, 1972; Medaille de bronze, National Academy of France, 1984. Memberships: Society Francaise d'EEG; EMG et Neurophysiologie; International College of Angiology; International Society of Magnesium Research. Hobbies: Skiing. Address: Academy of Medical Sciences, G Marinescu Street 40, 4300 Targu Mures, Romania.

PORADZISZ Adam, b. 10 Dec 1944, Karkow, Poland. Physician. m. Janina Poradzisz, Aug 1972, 1 son, 1 daughter. Education: MD, Medical Faculty, Jagiellonian University, Poland, 1962. Appointments: Anesthetist, Researcher in Social Medicine & Cardiology. Publications: Over 300 professional articles; Podveczuik Pievwszej Powoucy, 1994. Memberships: International Association for Medical Assistance to Travellers. Hobbies: Wood Working; Target Shooting; Travel. Address: Box 130, Empress, Alberta T0J 1E0, Canada.

PORT Friedrich K, b. 17 Mar 1938, Heidelberg, Germany. Nephrologist. m. Evelyn Port, 2 sons, 1 daughter. Education: MD; MS; FACP. Appointments: Associate Consultant, Mayo Clinic; Professor of Internal Medicine; Professor of Epidemiology. Publications: Morbidity and Mortality in Dialysis Patients, 1994; Comparison of Survival Probabilities for Dialysis Versus Transplant. Honours: Deputy Director, US Renal Data System-CC; Best Physicians in America Award. Memberships: American Society of Nephrology; International Society of

Nephrology. Hobbies: Antique Maps; Outdoors. Address: University of Michigan, 315 West Huron, Suite 240, Ann Arbor, MI 48103, USA.

PORTER Arthur Thomas, b. 11 June 1956, Sierra, Leone, USA. Medical Doctor; Oncologist. m. Pamela Porter, 28 Aug 1982, 4 daughters. Education: BA, Anatomy, Cambridge; MD, Cambridge; MA, Cambridge. Appointments: Senior Radiation Oncologist, Universityof Alberta, Canada; Chief Radiation Oncologist, University of Western Ontario & London Regional Cancer Centre; President, Radiation Oncology Research & Development Centre; Professor, Chairman, Depart of Radiation Oncology, Wayne State University. Publications: Musde Invastive Bladder, 1990; Prostate Brach Therapy, 1993. Memberships: President, American Cancer Society (Michigan). Honours: Annual Award, Detroit Medical Society, 1993. Hobbies: Automobiles; Boats. Address: Department of Radiation Oncology, Wayne State University, 4201 81 Antoine, Detroit, MI 48201, USA.

PORTER Stephen R, b. 13 Sept 1957, Scotland. Doctor; Dentist. Education: BSc; BDS; PhD; MD; MB; ChB; FDSRCS; FDSRCSE. Appointments: Dental Surgeon, Bristol, 1982-83; MRC Research Training Fellow, 1983-86; Oral Surgery Registrar, 1986-87; Honorary Lecturer in Oral Medicine, 1987-92; Lecturer in Oral Medicine, 1992-93; Consultant Senior Lecturer in Oral Medicine. Publications: Several professional publications. Memberships: Royal College of Surgeons of Edinburgh. Hobbies: Tennis; Skiing. Address: Department of Oral Medicine, Eastman Dental Institute for Oral Health Care Sciences, 256 Gray's Inn Road, London WC1X 8LD, England.

PORTNEY Robert, b. 25 Sept 1952, New York City, New York, USA. Physician; Violinist. m. Stacey Channing, 8 Apr 1984, 2 daughters. Education: BA with honours, Harvard College; MD, Yale University School of Medicine. Appointments: Psychiatrist-in-Charge, Dementia Unit, McLean Hospital; Neuropsychiatrist, Behavioural Cognitive Unit, Massachusetts General Hospital, Boston. Address: 835 ACC, Neurology Clinics, Massachusetts General Hospital, Boston, MA 02114, USA.

POULSEN Lars Kaergaard, b. 29 Jan 1958, Copenhagen, Denmark. Laboratory Head. m. Lisbeth E Hansen, 1 s, 1 d. Education: MSc, Chemistry, Technical University of Denmark, 1984; PhD, University of Copenhagen, 1988. Appointments: Head of Laboratory; Research Co-ordinator. Publications: Diagnostic Tests for Allergy, Co-author, 1993. Memberships: European Academy of Allergy and Clinical Immunology; American Academy of Allergy and Immunology; Danish Society for Allergy; Danish Society for Immunology. Address: National University Hospital TTA 7542, Laboratory of Medical Allergology, Tagensvej 20, Copenhagen DK-2200, Denmark.

POUNDSTONE John Walker, b. 1 May 1940, Lexington, Kentucky, USA. Physician. m. Mary Lucas Powell, 30 Mar 1991, 2 daughters. Education: MD; MPH; FACPM. Appointments: Head, TB & VD Control, Burea of Medicine & Surgery, US Navy, Washington DC; Chief, Epidemiology & Biometrics Division, US Navy Medical Research Unit, Great Lakes, Illinois; Chief, Occupational & Preventive Medicine, Navy Regional Medical Center, Great Lakes; Officer-in-Charge, US Navy Preventive Medicine Unit, Naples, Italy. Honours: Scholar, Public Health Leadership Institute, 1991; Fellow, US Public Health Service Primary Care Policy Fellowship, 1995. Memberships: American Association of Public Health Physicians; American Medical Association; AAAS; Fellow, American College of Preventive Medicine. Hobbies: Photography; Gardening; Hiking; Railroad History. Address: Lexington/Fayette Co Health Department, 650 Newtown Pike, lexington, KY 40508 1113, USA.

POWELL Don W, b. 29 Aug 1938, Gadsden, AL, USA. Academic Physician. Married, 1 s, 2 d. Education: BS, Honours, Auburn University, 1960; MD, Highest Honours, Medical College of AL, 1963; Diplomate, American Board Internal Medicine, American Board Gastroenterology. Appointments include: Special NIH Fellow, Physiology, 1969-71; Assistant Professor Medicine, University of NC, Chapel Hill, 1971-74; Associate Professor, 1974-78, Professor, 1978-91, Chief of Division Digestive Diseases, 1977-91, University of NC; Director, Center for Gastrointestinal Biology and Diseases, University of NC, 1985-91; Associate Chairman for Clinical Affairs, Department of Medicine, 1989-91; Professor and Chairman of Department of Internal Medicine, Professor Physiology and Biophysics, University of TX Medical Branch, 1991-. Publications include: Over 100 articles to professional journals; Associate Editor and Editorial Board Member to several professional journals and textbooks. Honours: Research Career Development Award, NIH, 1973-78; Merit Award, 1987; Fellow, ACP; Physician of the Year,

Crohn's and Colitis Federation of Ammerica, Gulf Coast Chp, 1994. Memberships: Merit Review Board, VA, 1977-80; General Medicine A-2 Study Section, NIH, 1985-89; Advisory Council, NIDDK, 1994-; American Physiology Society; American Gastroenterological Association, Vice President, 1991-92, President Elect, 1992-93, President, 1993-94; Gastroenterology Research Group, President, 1988-89; Southern Society Clinical Investigation; American Society Clinical Investigation; Association American Physicians; Association Professors Medicine. Hobby: Singing. Address: University of Texas Medical Branch, 301 University Blvd, 4.108 John Sealy Annex, Galveston, TX 77555-0567, USA.

POWER Michael John, b. 10 Aug 1954. Senior Lecturer. m. Lorna Champion, 31 Aug 1985, 2 s. Education: BSc, University College London, 1976; PhD, University of Sussex, 1981; MSc, University of Birmingham, 1982. Appointment: Senior Lecturer in Clinical Psychology, Royal Holloway, University of London. Co-author, Adult Psychological Problems: An Introduction; Founding Editor of Journal, Clinical Psychology and Psychotherapy. Honour: Associate Fellow, British Psychological Society, 1987. Membership: New York Academy of Sciences, 1991. Address: 19 Chestnut Road, Kingston-upon-Thames, Surrey, England.

POZZATO Gabriele, b. 26 Mar 1951, MonFalcone, Italy. Medical Doctor. m. Dr Maria Lorenzon, 29 Jun 1978, 3 d. Education: MD, University of Trieste. Appointment: Assistant Professor of Medicine. Publications: Low-Grade malignant lymphoma, mixed cryoglobulinemia and MCV infection, in Blood, 1989; Different Genotypes of MCV are associated with different severity of chronic liver disease, in Journal Medical Virology, 1989; Co-author, High blood alcohol levels in women in northern England, 1990. Memberships: NY Academy of Science; European Association for The Study of the Liver; Associazione Italiana Studio Figato; Societa Italiana Ematologia. Hobby: Running. Address: Instituto di Patalogia Medica, c/o Ospedale di Cattinara, Strada di Fiume 447, 34100 Trieste, Italy.

PRACY Martin Power, b. 26 Mar 1947, Hertfordshire, England. Medical Physics, Management. m. Susan, 6 May 1972, 1 son, 1 daughter. Education: ARCS, 1968; MSc, 1974; MPhil, 1984; Fellow, Institute of Physical Sciences in Medicine, England. Appointments: Basic Grade Physicist, Cookridge Hospital, Leeds, England, 1968-72; Physicist, Waikato Hospital, hamilton, New Zealand, 1972-73, 1974-81; Senior Scientist, Waikato Hospital, 1981-85; Manager, Scientific Services, Health, Waikato, New Zealand. Publications: External beam radiotherapy in a hyperbaric oxygen tank, 1972, 1974; Neutron howitzer design, 1976; External beam radiotherapy planning: The Edinburgh algorithm, 1980; A retrieval facilty for computed radiotherapy plans, 1980; Automated photon field measurements for computer assisted radiotherapy treatment planning, 1987. Memberships: Institute of Physical Sciences in Medicine; Institute of Physics, England; Australasian College of Physical Scientists & Engineers in Medicine. Hobby: Photography. Address: 27 McCracken Avenue, Hamilton, New Zealand.

PRAGAY Desider Alexander, b. 12 Aug 1921, Transylvania. Scientist; Professor. m. Eva Bakay, 20 July 1956. Education: MS, University of Budapest, Hungary, 1950; PhD, University of Budapest, 1956; Certificate of Registration, 1968. Appointments Include: Assistant Professor, Medical University of Budapest, 1950-56; Assistant Professor, State University of Utrecht, Holand, 1957-60; Associate, Buffalo University, USA, 1960-63; Advanced Postdoctral Fellow, Massachusetts General Hospital, Harvard University, 1964-66. Publications: Numerous professional articles. Honours: Diploma of Recognition, 1979;Fisher Award, 1981; Somogii Award, 1982. Memberships: Life Fellow, American Institute of Chemists; New York Academy of Sciences; American Chemical Society; American Public Health Association; Sigma Xi. Hobbies: Historical Research; Photography; Travel. Address: c/o Dr Rosler, Wilhelm Nieswaldt Allee 133, 45326 Essen, Germany. 6. 52. 188.

PRAKASAN Kollara Chathunny, b. 18 Aug 1946, Edathiruthy. Doctor. m. Shyama Prakasan, 6 Feb 1972, 4 daughters. Education: MS. Appointments: Assistant Surgeon, Keral Health Service; ENT Consultant, Elite Mission Hospital. Publications: Radio Talks on All India Radio, several times. Memberships: Association of Otolaryngologists, India; Life Member, Indian Medical Association; Life Member, Indian Society of Otology. Hobbies: Cycling; Swimming. Address: Elite Mission

Hospital, Koorkkenchery, Thrissur 680007, PO Box 1414, Kerala State, India.

PRAKASH Pranav, b. 4 June 1952, Delhi, India. Andrologist; Gynecologist. m. Madhavi Ratnam, 11 Apr 1976, 2 daughters. Education: MBBS; MD; MRCOG (London). Career: Lecturer, Obs & Gynae, Allms, ND, India, 1981-83; Assistant Professor, Obs & Gynae, Allms, ND, India, 1983-86; Consultant Obs & Gynae, Ministry of Health, Saudi Arabia, 1986-87; Lecturer, Bristol Hospital, England, 1987; Registrar Obs & Gynae, Sheffield Health Authority, England, 1987-90; Associate Andrologist & Director, Andrology Laboratory, currently. Publications: Serum Gonadotrophins Histopatholol gy in Primary Amenorrhoea, 1979; Experimental Hybrids of Rana Tigrina & Rana Cyanophlyctis, 1978; Antisperm Antibodies in Archives of Andrology, 1995. Memberships: Royal College of Obstetricians & Gynaecologists, London; American Fertility Society; American Society of Andrology. Hobbies: Swimming; Walking. Address: Vincent Ob-Gyn Service, Massachusetts General Hospital, Boston, MA 02114USA.

PRASAD Rama Narayana Vara, b. 7 May 1948, Singapore. Professor of Obstetrics and Gynaecology. m. Vijayalakshmi Prasad, 9 Feb 1973, 1 son. Education: MBBS (Singapore); MMed, Obstetrics and Gynaecology; MD; DSc; FRCOG; FACS; FICS; DClinPharm (London); FAMS. Appointments: Captain, Singapore Armed Forces; Associate Professor, National University of Singapore; Senior Consultant, Kandang Kerbau Hospital; Senior Consultant, National University Hospital. Publications: Over 150 refereed articles including: Vaginal administration of 16-16-dimethyl PGE2 p-benzaldehyde semicarbazone ester for preoperative cervical dilatation, 1977; Postponement of preterm birth with Salbutamol, 1979; New approaches to female fertility regulation, 1983; Termination of early human pregnancy with RU486 (mifepristone) and the prostaglandin analogue sulprostone, 1989; Management of abnormal pregnancy, 1990; The epidemiology of venous disease in Oral Contraceptive users, 1994; Author, Co-author, book chapters, including: Singapore experience with termination of pregnancy, 1979; Oral contraceptives, 1983; Medical menstrual regulation with prostaglandin analogues, 1986; Antiprogestogens, 1991; World Population trends and ethics, 1994. Honours: Jane Prize in Paediatrics for work on Tracheal Anatomy in children, 1971; Surgical Society Prize, 1972; DSc (Hon), 1988. Memberships: Singapore Medical Association; Academy of Medicine; Obstetrical and Gynaecological Society of Singapore; Singapore Institute for Standards in Industry and Research. Hobbies: Reading; Motor racing; Vintage sports cars; Gardening. Address: 88 Duchess Road, Singapore 1026.

PREHEIM Laurel C, b. 14 July 1947, USA. Professor of Medicine. m. Twila Friesen, 1 Sept 1968, 1 s, 2 d. Education: BA, Bethel College, 1969; MD, Northwestern University, 1973. Appointments: Professor of Medical Microbiology and of Medicine, Creighton University School of Medicine and University of Nebraska College of Medicine; Chief, Creighton University of Nebraska Section of Infectious Diseases. Publications: Pneumoccal Pneumonia in a Rat Model of Cirrhosis, Co-author, 1992; A Model of Pneumoccal Pneumonia in Chronically Intoxicated Rats, Co-author, 1993. Honours: Alpha Omega Alpha, 1987; Fellowship, American College of Physicians, 1984; Fellowship, Infectious Diseases Society of America, 1989. Memberships: American Society for Microbiology; Society for Hospital Epidemiology of America; American Federation for Clinical Research; American Medical Association. Hobbies: Tennis; Music; Golf; Gardening. Address: VA Medical centre, 4101 Woolworth Avenue, Omaha, NE 68105, USA.

PRESLAND John Leslie, b. 2 Nov 1935, London, England. Educational Psychologist. m. Patricia Mabel Presland, 27 Aug 1960, 1 s, 1 d. Education: MA, Cantab, 1958; Cert Ed, External, Dip Ed Psych, University of Birmingham, 1963-64; FBPsS; C Psychol. Appointments: Educational Psychologist, Birmingham and Warwickshire; Deputy Chief Educational Psychologist, Birmingham; Principal Educational Psychologist and Senior Advisor for Special Education, Wiltshire County Council. Publications include: Numerous articles concerning, teaching literacy and numeracy, helping overcome behaviour problems, teaching children with severe learning difficulties and continuing professional development; 84 Publications, 1969-, including: Applied Psychology and Reading Problems: An Approach to Teaching Children with Learning Difficulties, 1975; Paths to Mobility in "Special Care": A Guide to Teaching Gross Motor Skills to Very Handicapped Children, British Institute of Mental Handicap, 1982; Overcoming Problem Behaviour, 1989; Co-author, Preparing teachers for a support role in dealing with adjustment problems in secondary schools, in Intervention with Children,

1990. Memberships: British Psychological Society; Association of Educational Psychologists; National Council for Special Education. Hobbies: Natural History, mainly Botannical; Italian Language and History; Reading. Address: 175C Ashley Lane, Winsley, Bradford-on-Avon, Wiltshire, BA15 2HR, England.

PREZZIA Charles Paul, b. 3 June 1956, East Liverpool, Ohio, USA. Physician. m. Karen Long, 9 Nov 1982, 3 sons, 3 daughters. Education: MPH; MD; BA, Physics. Appointments: Staff Physician, MECC, 1985-87; Private Practice, 1987-89; President, Occupational Care Consultants of Toledo, 1990-. Memberships: Fellow, ACOEM; Fellow, AAFP; Fellow, RSM; Fellow, ACPM. Hobbies: Chess; Wine; Computers: Theology; Classical Music. Address: Work Injury Network, St Charles Hospital, 2600 Navarre Avenue, Oregon, OH 43616, USA.

PRICE Sandra M, b. 16 July 1965, Erith, Kent, England. Osteopath. Education: DO; MRO. Appointments: Opened Croydon practice, 1988; Harley Street, Devonshire and Lister Hospitals, 1989; Harley Street and Croydon, 1989-. Memberships: Register of Osteopaths. Hobbies: Tennis; Drawing and design; Skiing. Address: 144 Harley Street, London W1, England.

PRIER Ronald Eugene, b. 30 Apr 1950, Tacoma, WA, USA. Psychiatrist; Epidemiologist. m. Deborah Fyffe, 22 Sep 1988, 1 d. Education: MD; MPH, Johns Hopkins University. Appointments include: Active Duty, USMA, US Military Academy, West Point, NY, 26 years service; Chief Department of Epidemiology, Walter Reed Institute of Research; Epidemiology Consultant, US Army Europe; Chief, Department of Psychiatry, Fort Jackson, SC; Currently, Associate Professor, University of SC School of Medicine. Publications include: Co-author of 11 Professional Publications, 1984-91, including: Changes in Hepatitis Morbidity in the United States Army Europe, in Military Medicine, 1984; Intradermal and Intramuscular Rabies Immunization: Failure to Achieve Anticipated Antibody Responses, in The Lancet, 1984; A Comparison of Rates of Child Abuse in US Army Families Stationed in Europe and in the United States, in Military Medicine, 1987; Inpatient Psychiatric Morbidity of HIV-Infected Soldiers, in Hospital and Community Psychiatry, 1991. Honours include: Phi Kappa Phi; Alpha Omega Alpha; Distinguished Graduate, USMA, West Point; National Defence Service Medal, with Service Star; Overseas Service Ribbon, 1985; Army Achievement Medal, 1985; Meritorious Service Medal, 1982, 1985; Order of Military Medical Merit, 1990; Legion of Merit, 1994. Memberships: Fellow, American College of Preventive Medicine, 1980; SC Medical Association; American Psychiatric Association; SC Psychiatric Association; Columbia Medical Society. Hobbies: Microcomputer Hardware and Software. Address: 3555 Harden Street, Ste 104A, Dept of Neuropsychiatry, Univ of SC School of Medicine, Columbia, SC 29203, USA.

PRIKHODKO Alexandr, b. 18 Mar 1945, Krasnodar, Russia. Professor. m. Ivanova Elena, July 1969, 1 son, 1 daughter. Education: Candidate of Science, 1976; Doctor of Science, 1983; The Rank of Professor, 1990. Appointments: Roentgenologist, Radiologist, Medical Institutions, Russia; Clinical Intern, SRI of Diagnosis Department; Vice Director for Science Work. Publications incl: The Nuclear Medical Tumour Diagnosis with Tumourtropic Radiopharmaca, 1981; The Use of 111 In-Citrine for Bone Marrow Scintigraphy, 1988; Computer-Aided Tomography and Positive Scitigraphy in The Diagnosis of Tumors of The Head and Neck, 1993. Memberships: Editorial Board, Ukrainian Radiological Journal; Russian Association of Radiologists. Hobbies: Horticulture. Address: Krasnodar ul Gudimy 32, kv 60, Russia.

PRILLELTENSKY Isaac, b. 18 Sep 1959, Cordoba, Argentina. Associate Professor of Psychology. m. Ora Rapaport, 14 Dec 1982, 1 s. Education: BA, Bar Ilan University, Israel, 1979; MA, Tel Aviv University, 1982; PhD, University of Manitoba, Canada, 1989. Career includes: School Psychologist, Child Guidance Clinic, Winnipeg, 1985-91; Assistant Professor, 1991-94, Associate Professor of Psychology, 1995-, Wilfrid Laurier University. Publications: The Morals and Politics of Psychology: Psychological Discourse and the Status Quo, book, 1994; Co-editor, Special Issue of Canadian Journal of Community Mental Health on Prevention: Focus on Children and Youth, volume 13, no 2. Memberships: American Psychological Association; Canadian Psychological Association. Hobby: Reading. Address: Department of Psychology, Wilfrid Laurier University, Waterloo, Ontario, Canada N2L 3C5.

PRINZ Richard Allen, b. 13 May 1946, Chicago, Illinois, USA. Medical Doctor. m. Lorraine Adams, 1 son, 3 daughters. Education: BA, Chemistry, Northwestern University, 1968; MD, Loyola University Stritch School of Medicine, 1972. Appointments: Honorary Lecturer, Royal Postgraduate Medical School, Hammersmith Hospital, London, England; Professor of Surgery, Loyola University Stritch School of Medicine, Maywood, Illonis, USA. Helen Shedd Keith Professor & Chairman, Department of General Surgery. Publications: Laparoscopic and Thoracosopic Surgery, 1994; Numerous professional articles and book chapters. Honours: Evans Scholar, 1964-68; Plotkin Award, 1970-72; Australia & New Zealand Chapter of American College of Surgeons Travelling Fellowship, 1990. Memberships: American College of Surgeons; American Association of Endocrine Surgeons; American Surgical Association; International Association of Pancreatology. Hobbies: Travel; Antique Car Restoration. Address: Rush-Presbyterian, St Luke's Medical Center, 1653 West Congress Parkway, Chicago, IL 60612, USA.

PRIOR David Charles, b. 18 January 1935, Chester, England. Gynaecologist. m. Jane Ann Venner, 27 October 1962, 2 sons. Education: MRCS, England; LRCP, London; LMSSA; FRCOG. Appointments: Honorary Senior Registrar, Department of Investigative Medicine, University of Cambridge, England; Consultant Obstetrician and Gynaecologist, Chief of Surgery, Clinical Assistant Professor, Memorial University of Newfoundland, Canada. Publications: Co-author: The Effect of Maternal Hypercapnea on Oxygenation of Foetal Blood and Uterine Blood Flow in the Pig, 1970, 1975. Memberships: Royal College of Obstetricians & Gynaecologists; Newfoundland Medical Association. Hobbies: Collector of Musical Instruments; Canadian Art Collector. Address: Site 4, Box 24, Appleton, Newfoundland, A0G 2K0, Canada.

PRISCO Luigi M, b. 5 Nov 1954, Milano. Career: Anthropotherapist; Psycographotherapist. Hobbies: Classical Music; Piano Playing. Address: via Podgora 15, Milano, Italy.

PRITCHARD Jon, b. 7 Mar 1942, Cheshire, England. Physician. div. 1 s, 1 d. Education: BA, MB BChir, Cambridge University; MRCP(UK), 1970; FRCP, 1981. Appointments include: Paediatric House Physician, St Thomas' Hospital, London, 1967-68; Paediatric Senior House Officer, University of Rhodesia Medical School, Harare Hospital, Salisbury, Rhodesia, 1968; Senior House Officer, Medicine and Paediatrics, Burton-on-Trent General Hospital, England, 1969-70; research fellow, Department of Haematology, Liverpool University and Liverpool Royal Infirmary, 1971-74; Honorary Senior registrar in Paediatric Haematology/Oncology, Alder Hey Hospital, Liverpool, 1973-74; Research Fellow, Haematology, Children's Hospital Medical Centre, Fellow in Medicine, Harvard University, Boston, Massachusetts, USA, 1974-75; Lecturer, Institute of Child Health and Honorary Senior registrar in Haematology, 1976-78, Senior Lecturer, Leukaemia Research Fund, 1978-83, Senior Lecturer, Imperial Cancer Research Fund, Honorary COnsultant in Paediatric Oncology, 1983-, Hospital for Sick Children, Great Ormond Street, London; Honorary Consultant, Paediatric Oncology, St Bartholmew's Hospital, London, 1980-; Honorary COnsultant, Paediatric Oncology, SE Thames Regional Health Authorities, 1985-. Publications: Contributor of numerous articles in professional journals. Honours include: Honorary Fellow, American Academy of Paediatrics, 1991. Memberships include: British Paediatric Association; British Association of Paediatric Surgeons; Association of Cancer Physicians; International Society of Paediatric Oncologists. Address: Department of Haematology and Oncology, Hospital for Sick Children, Great ormond Street, London WC1N 3JH, England.

PRITCHARD-JONES Kathryn, b. 20 Feb 1958, Coventry, England. Physician. m. Bruno Girardeau, 1 s, 1 d. Education: MA, BMBCh, Oxford University, 1977-83; PhD, Medical Research Council and Council for National Academic Awards, 1992. Appointments: Paediatric Senior House Officer, Newcastle-upon-Tyne, 1985-87; Registrar, Paediatric Haematology/Oncology, Adelaide Children's Hospital, South Australia, 1987; MRC Recombinant DNA Training Fellow, MRC Human Genetics Unit, Edinburgh, Scotland, 1987-91; Paediatric Registrar, Royal Hospital for Sick Children, Edinburgh, 1991-92; Honorary Senior Registrar, Department of Paediatric Oncology, Royal Marsden Hospital, Sutton, Surrey, England, 1992-94; Currently: Senior Lecturer in Paediatric Oncology, Institute of Cancer Research/Royal Marsden Hospital, Sutton, Surrey, England, 1994-. Publications: The Candidate Wilms' Tumour Gene is Involved in Genitourinary Development, 1990; Cell Types Expressing the Wilms' Tumour Gene in Wilms' Tumours, 1991. Honours: Odile Schweisguth Prize, International Society of Paediatric Oncology,

1991; Donald Patterson Prize, British Paediatric Association, 1991. Membership: Royal College of Physicians; UK Children's Cancer Study Group; International Society of Paediatric Oncology (SIOP). Address: Department of Paediatric Oncology, Royal Marsden Hospital, Sutton, Surrey SM2 5PT, England.

PROCTER Desmond Stephen Collacott, b. 15 Aug 1924, Kimberly, South Africa. Senior Surgical Consultant. m. Blanche Mary Dobson, 10 Jan 1948, 4 sons, 2 daughters. Education: MB, ChB, University of Cape Town; FRCS, England; FACS, USA; DCH, Royal College of Surgeons and Physicians, London. Appointments include: Registrar; Medical Superintendent, Mission Hospital; Specialist Surgeon in private practice; Senior Surgical Specialist. Publications: Full Term Extrauterine Pregnancy, 1952; Angiosarcoma of the Breast, 1958; Treatment of Fractures of the Femur, 1962; Coma in Burns, 1966; Treatment of Burns, 1966; Oesophageal Reconstruction, 1967; Oesophageal Intubation in Carcinoma of the Oesophagus, 1968; Clandestine Cancer, 1968; Carcinoma of the Oesophagus, 1968; Treatment of Burns, 1971; Burns in Children, 1971; Butterworth Diagnostic Clinic for Carcinoma of the Oesophagus, 1970; Children's Tumour Clinic, 1971; Oesophageal Intubation for Carcinoma of the Oesophagus: A New Oesophageal Dilator, 1994. Memberships: British Paediatric Surgical Society; South African Paediatric Surgical Society; Royal Society of Medicine; International Burns Society; Société Internationale de Chirurgie; South African Gastroenterology Society. Hobbies: Squash; Hockey; Water-skiing; Photography; Gardening; Wildlife. Address: 9 Joycelyn Rd, Bluewater Bay, Port Elizabeth 6210, South Africa.

PROSCHIN Anatoly Dmitrievisch, b. 20 Nov 1948, Bryansk, Russia. Physician. m. Linda Tselichtchewskaia, 22 Apr, 2 sons. Education: State Medical Institute, Imolensk, 1973. Appointments: Head, Department of Cardiology, Hospital, Bryansk, 1982; Mean Specialist in Therapeutics; Deputy Chief, Public Health, Bryansk region. Publications: Thyroid Pathology in Children and Adolescents in the Most Radio-Contaminated Areas of Bryansk Region (Russia) Sfter the Chernobyl Accident,Co-author, 1994. Memberships: International Consortium for Research on the Health Effects of Radiation. Hobbies: Tourism; Music. Address: Lenin Av 35, Bryansk 241000, Russia.

PROTSYK Vladimir, b. 10 Aug 1940, Poltava, Ukraine. Physician; Professor. m. 31 July 1971, 1 son. Education: MD, High Medical School, Odessa, 1963; Dr sci (med). Appointments: Physician, Kirovograd Hospital, 1963-65; Physician, Kiev Oncology Institute, 1965-71; Physician, 1971-, currently Head, Department of Head and Neck Tumours, Institute for Oncology and Radiology, Kiev. Publications: Combined therapy of malignant tumour, 1979; Combined therapy of malignant tumour maxila, 1985; Local UHF-Hyperthermia and Intra-arterial Hyperglycaemia in the Complex Treatment of Patients with Advanced Oral, Oropharyngeal and Maxillary Sinus Carcinomas, 1991; Enhancement of radiotherapy efficacy by trimodality (chemo/hyperglycaemia/hyperthermia) treatment, abstract, 1993; Trimodality (Radiation/Chemo/Hyperthermia) Treatment Supplemented with i.a Regional Glucose Infusion in Head and Neck Tumours, 1994. Memberships: Scientific Boards: Oncology; Otolaryngology; Cranial-Facial Surgery. Hobbies: Music; Aesthetical surgery. Address: Lomonosov St 33, 252022 Kiev, Ukraine.

PSIMENOU Erasmia, b. Athens, Greece. Nephrologist. m. 15 May 1983, 2 daughters. Education: Medical School, Athens University. Career: Athens Naval Hospital; Laiko General Hospital, Athens; Research Fellow, Department of Nephrology, Royal Free Hospital, London, England. Memberships: Athens Medical Association; Hellenic Society of Nephrology; General Medical Council (British). Address: Anatolis Str 88A, Papagos 15669, Athens, Greece.

PTOK Martin U, b. 10 June 1955, Marburg, Germany. Otorhinolaryngologist. m. Dr Angelika Noodt, 21 Sept 1985, 2 s. Education: MD, Medical School, University of Goettingen, 1981. Appointments: Vice Chairman, Department of Communication Disorders, University of Tuebingen; Chairman/Professor, Department of Communication Disorders, Medical School, Hannover. Honour: Annelie Frohn Prize, 1993. Memberships: Association for Researching Otorhinolaryngology, USA; Voice Foundation, USA; Society of Neuroscience, USA; Deutsche Gesellschaft für HNO-Heilkunde; Deutsche Gesellschaft für Phoniatrie und Pädaudiologie. Hobbies: Modern Art; Jogging. Address: Department of Communication Disorders, MHH, Konstanty Gutschow Strasse 8, 30625 Hannover, Germany.

PU Shouyue, b. 11 Sep 1926, Beijing, China. Medical Doctor. m. Deshing Wan, 12 Feb 1953, 2 s, 1 d. Education: MD, Shanghai Medical College, 1950; MGH, Boston, USA, 1980, 1981. Appointments: Co-Director Medical Department, Zhong Shan Hospital, Shanghai Medical University, 1978; Co-Director, Cardiology, 1979, Professor of Internal Medicine, 1980-, Shanghai Medical University. Co-author, Practice of Internal Medicine, 1972, 1980, 1984, 1988, 1992; Co-author, Chinese Medical Encyclopaedia, Volume of Cardiology, 1981; Co-author, Practice of Cardiology, 1992. Honours: Fellow in Cardiology, Brigham and Women's Hospital, USA; National Science and Technology Progress Award, 1989; Science and Technology Progress Award of Shanghai, 1992. Memberships: Shanghai Medical Association; Chinese Medical Association; Shanghai Association of Cardiology; Chinese Association of Cardiology. Hobbies: Gardening; Reading; Travel. Address: Zhong Shan Hospital, Shanghai Institute of Cardiovascular Diseases, 180 Feng Lin Road, Shanghai 200032, China.

PUGET Janine, b. 19 Dec 1926, Marseille, France. Psychoanalyst. m. Enrique Aisiks, 25 July 1970, 1 son. Education: MD, Buenos Aires University, Argentina; Appointments: Currently: Private practice, Buenos Aires; Chair, Psychoanalysis of Couple Marital Department, Argentine Association of Group Psychology and Psychotherapy. Publications: Co-author: The Group and its Configurations, 1982; Psychoanalysis of the Marital Couple, 1988; Social Violence and Psychoanalysis, 1989; Author, more than 100 papers and psychoanalytical subjects in Argentinian, Brazilian, UK, Colombian, French, Italian, US and other international journals. Honours: Honorary membership: French Society of Group Psychotherapy; Columbian Society of Link Psychoanalysis; Uruguayan Society of Link Configuration. Memberships: Board Member, International Association of Group Psychotherapy; International Psychoanalytic Association; Latin American Federation of Psychoanalysis; Chair, XIIth International Congress of Group Psychotherapy;Full Member, Training Analyst, Argentine Association of Group Psychology and Psychotherapy, 1957; Associate Member, 1959, Full Member, 1967, Training Analyst, 1974, Argentine Psychoanalytical Association. Hobbies: Skiing; Swimming; Music. Address: Paraguay 2475 7o, 1121 Buenos Aires, Argentina.

PUNATAR Ila, b. 9 July 1950, Ahmedabad, Gujarat, India. Medical. m. Dr Bharat Punatar, Orthopaedic Surgeon, Jamnagar, India, 4 Dec 1973, 3 sons. Education: MBBS; DGO; MD (Obst & Gynae); DRCOG; FRCOG. Career: Assistant Professor of Obstetrics & Gynaecology, MP Shah Medical College & Irwin Group of Hospitals, Jamnagar, India, 1985-94; Associate Professor of Obstetrics & Gynaecology, MP Shah Medical College & Irwin Group of Hospitals, Jamnagar, India. Honours: Nominated as West Zone (India) Representative, Royal College of Obstetricians & Gynaecologists, London, England; Undergraduate & Postgraduate Teacher & Examiner for MBBS, DGO & MD Exams. Memberships: President, Jamnagar Obstetric & Gynaecological Society; Federation of Obstetric & Gynaecological Societies of India; Royal College of Obstetricians & Gynaecologists, London. Hobby: Cooking. Address: Nalin Niwas, Victoria Bridge Road, Jamnagar 361 001, India.

PURGER John Clayton, b. 6 Nov 1925, Columbus, Ohio, USA. Obstetrician & Gynaecologist. m. Mary Irene Purger. Education: BS; MS; MD. Appointments: US Marine Corps, 1942-47. Memberships: American College of Obstetrics & Gynaecology; American Fertility Society; Florida Obstetrics & Gynaecology Society; Miami Obstetrics & Gynaecology Society; Fort Lauderdale Obstetrics & Gynaecology Society. Hobbies: Pilot. Address: 3080 NE 42nd St, Ft Lauderdale, FL 33308, USA.

PUSCEDDU Fulvia, b. 28 Dec 1935, Taranto, Italy. Psychologist; Psychotherapist. m. Walter Molinas, 31 Jan 1960, 2 sons. Education: Degree, Tutogenous Training; Degree, Psychosomati Medicine; Degree, Hypnosis; Degree, Clinical Sexuology. Appointments: Support Teacher, Handicap Bearing Children, Junior High School; Psychotherapist. Publications: Several publications on clinical cases of omosexual pedofilia and a case of incestuous rape. Memberships: Ordine Degli Psicologi Italiani; Ordine Degli Psicoterapeuti Italiani. Hobbies: Travel; Swimming. Address: via Garibaldi 51, 26025 Pandino, Italy.

PUSZET Joseph, b. 6 Dec 1937, Warsaw, Poland. Obstetrician & Gynaecologist. m. Sarah E W Andrews, 2 May 1992, 1 son. Education: MB, BS, Kings College Hospital, London, 1962; FRCOG, 1990. Appointments: Consultant, Obstetrics & Gynaecology, Royal Army Medical Corps, 1978-86; Consultant, Obstetrics & Gynaecology, King Khalid National Guard Hospital, Jeddah, Saudi Arabia, 1987-94; Senior Consultant, Obstetrics, Gynaecology, Sultan Qaboos. Memberships:

Royal College of Obstetricians & Gynaecologists, London. Hobbies: Military History; Bridge. Address: Willowtree Bungalow, 19 Bicester Road, Long Crendon, Bucks HP18 9BP, England.

PYERITZ Reed Edwin, b. 2 Nov 1947, Pittsburgh, Pennsylvania, USA. Physician; Researcher. m. Jane E Tumpson, 1972, 2 s. Education: MD; PhD. Appointments: Professor of Human Genetics, Paediatrics and Medicine, Medical College of Pennsylvania and Hahnemann University; Chairman, Department of Human Genetics, ASRI; Director, Institute for Medical Genetics, AHERF. Publications: Principles and Practice of Medical Genetics, Co-editor; Editorial Board, New England Journal of Medicine; Contributor of over 300 articles in professional journals. Honours: Taylor Award, 1968; Piersol Research Scholar, American College of Physicians, 1979; Antoine Marfan Award, National Marfan Foundation, 1986; Alumni Wall of Fame, University of Delaware, 1994; Memberships: American Heart Association; American Soceity of Human Genetics; American College of Medical Genetics; American College of Physicians. Hobby: Athletics. Address: Department of Human Genetics, Allegheny-Singer Research Institute, 320 East North Avenue, Pittsburgh, A 15212, USA.

PYLE Hoyte R, b. 25 Apr 1937, Ft Smith, AR, USA. Physician. m. Dianna Wingfield, 16 June 1963, 1 son, 1 daughter. Education: BA; MD; Residency in Internal Medicine; Fellowship in Nephrology. Appointments: Associate Clinical Professor of Medicine, University of Arkansas for Medical Sciences; Private Practice of Internal Medicine. Memberships; FACP; ASN. Hobbies: Camping; Hunting; Photography. Address: 5918 Lee Avenue, Little Rock, AR 72205, USA.

Q

QI Ji, b. 29 Aug 1945, Tianjin, China. Radiologist. 1 son. Education: Masters Degree; MD. Appointments: Assistant, 1985, Associate Professor, 1985-90, Vice Director, 1990-92, Professor, Director of Radiology, 1992-, Tianjin First Central Hospital. Publications: Principle of DSA, 1990; DSA Paramatric Imaging: I Videodensity, Iodine Concentration Translation; II Blood Perfusion Study of Brain, Kidneys and Lungs, 1989. Memberships: Radiological Society of North America; Commission, Chinese Radiological Society. Hobby: Music. Address: 24 Fukang Road, Tianjin, China.

QI Liyi, b. 1 Mar 1933, Shanghai, China. Physician. m. Hui Kang Han, 8 Feb 1964, 2 d. Education: Chinese Medical University, 1951-59; MD, Course for Traditional Chinese Medicine, 1959-62. Appointments: Head, Nervous Disease Research Group, 1978-89; Director, Acupuncture Department, Guang-am-Men Hospital, Academy of Traditional Chinese Medicine, 1985-89; Member, Scientific Commission in Hospital, 1986-89; Associate Professor, Neurology and Traditional Chinese Medicine, Academy of Traditional Chinese Medicine, Beijing, 1984; Visiting Worker, MRC Cyclotron Unit, Hammersmith Hospital, 1989-93; Honorary Acupuncturist, Hammersmith Hospital, London, 1989-93. Publications: Author of numerous works. Honours: Certificate of Merit, Chinese Ministry of Public Health, 1963. Memberships: Society of Neurology and Psychiatry, China Medical Association; Chinese Association of the Integration of Traditional and Western Medicine; China Association of Acupuncture and Moxibustion; Honorary Member, Australian Medical Acupuncture Society; British Acupuncture Association and Register. Address: MRC Cyclotron Unit, Hammersmith Hospital, Dulane Road, London W12 0HS, England.

QI Ri-Mai, b. 27 Nov 1927, Fuxin, Liaoning, China. Mongolian. Medical Professor. m. Liu Ruen Hua, 15 Mar 1954, 2 daughters. Education: MB, China Medical University, Shenyang, 1951. Appointments: Doctor, Shenyang Infectious Disease Hospital, 1951-58; Teacher, Doctor, currently Professor of Infectious Diseases, Inner Mongolia Medical College, Hohhot, 1950-. Publications: Typhoid Fever and Salmonellosis, 1976; Chinese-Mongolian Dictionary of Classification (Medicine), 1990; In Mongolian: Infectious Diseases, 1975; Undulant Fever, 1980; Viral Hepatitis, 1985; Encephalitis and Meningitis, 1986. Honours: Advanced Teacher Award, Universities of Inner Mongolia Autonomous Region, 1983; Model Worker Award, Inner Mongolia Autonomous Region, 1986. Memberships: China Infectious Diseases and Parasitosis Society; Vice-Chairman, Inner Mongolia Internal Medicine Society. Hobby: Literature. Address: Xin Hua Street 5, Inner Mongolia Medical College, Hohhot 010051, China.

QI Wen-Hang, b. 18 November 1937, Jiangsu, China. Doctor and Professor of Medicine. m. You Ya-xi, 18 November 1962, 2 sons. Education: Diploma, Shanghai Second Medical University. Appointments: Associate Professor of Medicine, 1985; Professor of Medicine, 1989-. Publications: 81 articles published during 1983-94; Timing of PVE initiating VT, 1984; Polymorphons VT, 1993; Verapanil Treatment of TpVT, 1988. Honours: Honorary Certificate of Recognition of Outstanding Contribution, Indiana University, USA, 1982. Memberships: European Society of Cardiology; New York Academy of Sciences; Committee Member, Chinese International Medical Association. Hobbies: History; Reading; Travel. Address: Rui-Jin Hospital, 197 Rui-Jin No 2 Road, Shanghai 200025, China.

QIAN Keda, b. 20 Feb 1934, Shanghai, China. Professor of Medicine. m. Xu Wang Sun, 1 May 1960, 3 sons. Education: MD, Zhejiang Medical University, Hangchow, 1957. Appointments: Resident Doctor, 1957, Visiting Doctor, 1978, Associate Professor, 1983, Professor of Medicine, 1988-, Zhejiang Medical University, 2nd Affiliated Hospital, Hangzhou. Publications: Gastric carcinoma in the youth, 1981; The relationship between gastric lesion and duodenal ulcer, 1985; Endoscopic diagnosis of depth invasion in early gastric cancer, 1991; The alteration and significance of tissue fibrinolytic activity in gastric malignant and benign ulcer, 1993; The Clinical Manual of Nutriology for diagnosis and treatment (co-author), 1993. Honours: Educational Honours of Wang Ji Wu Professors, Zhejiang Medical University, 1993; 2nd Science and Technology Award, Public Health Department, Zhejiang. Memberships: Chinese Medical Association; Chinese Anti-Cancer Association; Zhejiang Medical Association; International Gastro-Surgical Club,

Belgium. Hobbies: Photography; Music. Address: 2nd Affiliated Hospital, 68 Jie Fang Road, Hangzhou 310009, China.

QIAN Li Juan, b. 29 Jul 1932, Shanghai, China. Medical Doctor. m. Cheng Zhen Ya, 15 May 1958, 1 s, 1 d. Education: Graduate of 2nd Shanghai Medical University, 1955. Appointments: MD, Tianjin Medical University Hospital No 1, 1955-75; Appointment Director Doctor, 1985; Professor of Obstetrics & Gynaecology, Tianjin Medical University Hospital No 2, 1990. Publications: Clinical Study of Three Types of Intrauterine Devices, 1986; A Randomized Comparative Study of the Performance of Seven Different Size of the Mahua Ring Inserted Following Measurement of the Uterine Cavity and One Size of the Mahua Ring, 1990; A Multicenter Comparitive Clinical Study of 4 Types of Domestic Intrauterine Devices, 1992; Basic Technology of Gynaecology and Obstetrics, 1994. Honours: Achievement and Contribution to the Science and Research of Family Planning Nationwide, Ministry of Public Health of China, 1989; Advancer of Family Planning Science and Research, State Committee of Family Planning, China, 1991; Science and Technique Progress Prize of Ministry Committee of Family Planning, China, 1991; Predominent Contributor to Family Planning Technique, 1993. Memberships: Academic Committee Member, State Family Planning in Special Subject, 1984-91; Advisory Committee on Science and Technique of Family Planning; Tianjin Family Planning Association; Editorial Committee, Foreign Medicine Journal in Family Planning. Hobbies: Peking Opera. Address: Tianjin Medical University Hospital No 2, Ping Jiang Road, Jian Shan, He Xi District, Tianjin, China.

QIAN Liming, b. 8 Jan 1956, Guangdong, China. Teacher. m. Ling Xiaoshan, 27 Dec 1991, 1 son. Education: BS, Guangzhou Teachers College, 1983. Appointments: Electrician, 1974-83; Professor, Director, Bio-Sciences Laboratory, Guangzhou Teachers College. Publications: Studies on the Genotoxicities of Organic Extracts from Source water with Ames test and SOS Chromotest,1994; A Study on Nuclear Anormalities of Oral Mucosal Cells in the Mentally Handicapped, 1989. Honours: One of Ten Outstanding Teachers of GTC, 1991; Future Star Honour for Teachers, 1994. Memberships: International Association of Environmental Mutagen Society; EMS; Microbiology Society Guangzhou. Hobbies: Music; Philately; Running; Basketball. Address: Rm 305 Bldg No 17, Huanghua Xin Cun, Guangzhou 510600, China.

QIAN Wen Yan, b. 30 June 1936, Changchun, China. Physician. m. 17 March 1962, 1 daughter. Education: MD, Beijing Traditional Chinese Medical College, 1956-62. Appointments: Resident, 1962-65, Attending Doctor, 1965-75, Beijing City Hospital of Traditional Chinese Medicine; Associate Professor, 1975-84, Professor, 1984-, Sino-Japanese Hospital. Publications: A Practical Textbook of Dermatology in Traditional Chinese Medicine, 1978; Differential Diagnosis of the Symtoms in Traditional Medicine, 1984; A Clinical Research in the Treatment of SLE with Traditional Chinese Medicine, 1990. Memberships: Beijing Association of Traditional Chinese Medicine; Chinese Association of Traditional Chinese Medicine Dermatology. Hobbies: Music; Tennis. Address: Ying Hua Block, Chao Yang District, Beijing, China.

QIAN Xuexian, b. 11 Jan 1934, Shanghai, China. Doctor. m. Qingyun Zhou, 1 Jul 1964, 2 s, 2 d. Education: Graduated from Fourth Military Medical University, Xi'an, China, 1956; Doctorial Director. Appointments: Resident Physician, 1956-62; Assistant Professor, 1962-74; Physician in Charge, 1974-78; Lecturer, 1978-83; Associate Professor, 1983-88; Professor and Director, Department of Cardiology, Zhujiang Hospital, 1st Military Medical University, China, 1988-. Publications: Current Coronary Heart Disease Care Medicine, 1993; 70 articles, 1956-94. Honour: Outstanding Achievements in Medical Health, State Council, 1992. Memberships: Vice President, PLA Cardiovascular Medical Group; Research Committee, Chinese Interventional Cardiology; Editorial Committee, Chinese Journal of Internal Medicine; Editorial Standing Committee, Chinese Journal of Interventional Cardiology; Editorial Committee, Chinese Journal of Cardiac Function. Hobbies: Swimming; Music. Address: Department of Cardiology, Zhujiang Hospital, Industry Road 253, 1st Military Medical University, Guangzhou City, Guangdong Province, 510280, China.

QIAO Zhi-Heng, b. 5 May 1932, Luo-yan, Henan Province, China. Medical Doctor. 3 d. Education: MD, Dep of Medicine, Huaxi Medical College, Si Chan Province. Career: Director of Physical Medicine; Professor, Department of Physiotherapy. Publications: Simple and Easy Physiotherapy, 1982; Question and Answer Physiotherapy, 1987; China

Rehabilitation Medicine, 1990; Rehabilitation, 1992; A New Edition Physiotherapy, 1994. Honours: Award of Congress of National Science; Award of Excellent Research Paper of Beijing Branch, Chinese Medicine Association. Memberships: Standing Member, Society of Physical Medicine Rehabilitation, Chinese Medicine Association; Chief, Society of Physical Medicine, Beijing Branch. Hobby: Traditional Chinese Medicine. Address: China Rehabilitation Research Centre, Box 2619, Beijing, China.

QIN Chao, b. 26 Oct 1955, Xian, China. University Teacher. m. 1 July 1983, 1 daughter. Education: MD, 1978, MS, 1986, PhD, 1992, Xian Medical University. Appointments: Assistant, 1978-86, Instructor, 1987-93, Associate Professor, Vice-Chairman, Department of Physiology, 1994-, Xian Medical University. Publications: Over 50 papers; 10 books including: Qigong-Feedback Therapy, 1990; How to Cope with Pain, 1993; Co-author: The World of the Electroencephal Wave, 1991; Co-author: Review of Physiology, 1992; Neurophysiology, 1992; The Science of Pain, 1993; Physiology; Over 120 popular medicine articles. Honours: Over 20 including: National Excellent Young Scientist, Chinese Association of Science and Technology, 1988; Excellent Academic Paper, Chinese Association of Physiological Science, 1988; Excellent Paper in Natural Science, Shaanxi Association of Science and Technology, 1991; Silver Medal for DQF-I Multichannel Qigong-Feedback Instrument, 6th National Invention Exhibition, China, 1991; Chinese Inventor, Chinese Association of Inventors, 1992. Memberships include: Chinese Association of Physiological Science; International Brain Research Organization; International Association for the Study of Pain; Chinese Traditional Medicine Society; Standing Member, Chinese Association of Psychosomatic Medicine; Vice-President: Shaanxi Academic Committee of Qigong Scientific Society; Shaanxi Association of Young Scientific Workers; Standing Councillor: Chinese Association for the Study of Pain; Shaanxi Association of Scientific Workers. Hobbies: Music; Photography; Postage stamps. Address: Department of Physiology, Xian Medical University, Xian, Shaanxi 710061, China.

QIN Dayi, b. 28 Dec 1949, Jiangxi, China. Professor of Physiology. m. Zhang Xiaoxin, 15 Aug 1978, 1 daughter. Education: BA, Jiangxi College of Traditional Chinese Medicine, 1976; MS, Shanghai College of Traditional Chinese Medicine, 1982; PhD, Kyushu University, Japan, 1990. Appointments: Teaching Assistant, Jiangxi College of Traditional Chinese Medicine, 1976; Research Associate, Jiangxi Institute of Medical Science, 1982; Assistant Professor, Physiology, 1987, now Professor, Jiangxi Medical College; Guest Professor, University of Science and Technology of China; Visiting Professor, State University of New York, USA. Publications: ATP-dependent decay and recovery of K channels in guinea pig cardiac myocytes (co-author), 1990; 1st author: A new oil-gate concentration jump technique applied to inside-out patch-clamp recording, 1988; Kinetics of ATP-sensitive K channel revealed with oil-gate concentration jump methods, 1989; Limitations due to unstirred layers in measuring channel response of excised patch using rapid solution exchange methods, 1991; Model gating kinetics of cardiac Na channel induced by anthopleurin-A, 1993. Honours: 3rd Prize for Scientific Research Contributing to Chinese Traditional Medicine and Combined Chinese-Western Medicine, Shanghai Municipality, 1981; 2nd Prize for Advancement of Science and Technology, State Education Commission, China, 1992; 4th Prize, National Natural Science Prizes, 1993. Memberships: American Association for the Advancement of Science; Physiological Association of China; Biophysical Association of China. Hobbies: Reading; Photography. Address: Cardiology Divisiosn (111A), Brooklyn VA Medical Center, 800 Poly Place, Brooklyn, NY 11209, USA.

QIN Junfa, b. 24 Aug 1936, Jiangyin, Jiangsu Province, China. Scientific Researches. m. Peng Yuqing, 5 Sept 1963, 2 s. Education: Fudan University, 1958. Appointments: Chief of Researching Group; Deputy Director of Dept. Publications: 125 scientific papers about trace elements, 1978-94; 114 in Chinese, 11 in English; 1 book in Chinese, 1994. Honours: 5 awards of Advance Scientific & Technological Achievement: Shanghai 1977; Academia Sinica, 1979; Shanghai 1981, 1984. Memberships: Vice Chairman, Trace Element Science Society of China, 1988-; Vice President, Shanghai Trace Element Society, 1992-; China Creative Studies Institute, 1994-. Hobbies: Studies of Trace Elements in Traditional Chinese Medicine and Materia Medica. Address: Shanghai Institute of Nuclear Research, Academia Sinica, Shanghai 201800, China.

QIU Lianbin, b. 28 Jul 1931, Xiamen, China. Ophthalmologist. m. Chenghuei Wang, 10 Aug 1959, 2 s. Education: Dalian Medical College, China, 1956. Career: Director, Ophthalmology Department, Affiliated Hospital of Xiamen Medical College, 1962; Director, Ophthalmology Department, Zeimei Hospital, Xiamen, China, 1970; Currently, Director, Ophthalmology Department, Xiamen First Hospital, China, 1982-. Publications: Co-author, U-Flap Conjunctival Transplantation for Pterygium Excision, 1984; Double-Flap Conjunctival Transplantation for Thick Pterygium, 1985. Honours: Xiamen City Science and Technological Prize, 1978; Xiamen City Technology Progressive Achievement Prize, 1979-84. Memberships: Chinese Medical Association; Chinese Science and Technological Association; Chinese Association of the Integration of Traditional Chinese and Western Medicine. Hobby: Philately. Address: Xiamen The First Hospital, Xiamen, Fujian 361003, China.

QIU Weiliu, b. 13 Oct 1932, Chengdu, Sichuan, China. Surgeon; Teacher. m. Wang Xiaoyi, 15 Feb 1955, 3 daughters. Education: DDS, Faculty of Stomatology, West China University of Medical Sciences, 1955; FICD. Appointments: Professor, Chairman, Oral and Maxillofacial Surgery, Shanghai 2nd Medical University; Director, Affiliated No 9 People's Hospital, Shanghai 2nd Medical University; Dean, School of Stomatology, Shanghai 2nd Medical University; Surgeon-in-Chief, Oral and Maxillofacial Surgery. Publications include: Editor-in-chief, 5 books including: Hand Book of Oral and Maxillofacial Surgery, 1980; Oral and Maxillofacial Surgery, 1987; The Advances in Stomatology, 1992; Author or co-author, journal contributions including: Cryotherapy in oral and maxillofacial surgery, 1976; Evaluation of free flaps transferred by microvascular anastomosis in oral and maxillofacial surgery, 1984; A preliminary experience of chemotherapy using Cisplatinum (CDDP) for oral and maxillofacial carcinoma, 1989; Cleft lip and palate, 1991; Clinical experiences and research work of oral and maxillofacial tumors in China--prospective and perspective, 1993. Honours: National Excellent Teacher, Chinese Committee of Higher Education, 1990; National Expert of Great Contributions, State Council, 1991; 13 Prizes for Science and Technology, 1980-94. Memberships: Fellow, International Association of Oral and Maxillofacial Surgeons; American Society of JMJ Surgeons; President, Chinese Society of Oral and Maxillofacial Surgery; Vice-President: Chinese Society of Stomatology; Chinese Society of Head and Neck (Tumour) Society; Chinese Society of Reparative and Reconstructive Surgery. Hobbies: Watching sports or games; Reading and writing Chinese poems. Address: Affiliated 9th People's Hospital, School of Stomatology, Shanghai 2nd Medical University, 639 Zhi-Zao-Ju Rd, Shanghai 200011, China.

QU Heng-Tian, b. 22 Mar 1934, Zaozhuang, Shandong, China. Professor of Surgery. m. Jia Peilan, 15 Sept 1962, 1 son, 1 daughter. Education: BA, 7th Military Medical University, Chngqing, 1960. Appointments: Resident Physician, 1961; Visiting Physician, 1969; Vice-Chief Physician, 1982; Currently Professor of Surgery, Hospital No 113, People's Liberation Army, Ningbo. Publications include: 20 treatises; 2 inventions. Honours include: Famous Doctor of People's Liberation Army, 1988. Memberships: Chinese Medical Association; Chinese Adenocarcinoma Association; Chinese Anti-Cancer Association; 6th Medical Committee, Nanjing Unit, People's Liberation Army. Hobby: Running. Address: 171 Dahe Road, Ningbo, Zhejiang 315040, China.

QU Mian-Yu, b. 18 Mar 1925, Shandong, China. Orthopaedic Doctor. m. Han Zhong-min, 14 Aug 1952, 3 daughters. Education: Medical College, Peking University. Appointments:President, 1983-91, Department Head, Sports Medicine, 1955-, Director, Institute of Sports Medicine, Beijing Medical University. Publications: Practical Sports Medicine, 1982; China's Sports Medicine, 1988. Honours: Honorary Member, FIMS, Gold Medal, 1994; Founding President, Asian Federation of Sports Medicine, Gold Medal. Memberships: Chinese Association of Sports Medicine; Former Vice President, International Federation of Sports Medicine, 1986-94. Address: Institute of Sports Medicine, Beijing Medical University, Beijing 100083, China.

QU Yu-rong, b. 30 Aug 1940, Ji Lin, China. Professor of Medicine. m. Professor Gao Zi-jin, 15 Mar 1967, 1 son, 1 daughter. Education: MB, Norman Bethune University of China, 1965. Appointments: Doctor, Professor, Department of Obstetrics and Gynaecology, Nanfang Hospital. Publications: Studies on Microsurgical ASnastomosis of Fallopian Tubes, 1988; Studies on Blocking Hepatitis B for the Transmission During the Perinatal Period, 1990. Honour: Guangdong Lingnan Famous Doctors in Medicine, 1990. Memberships: Chinese

Medical Committee; Director, Guangdong Association of Improving Birth Quality and Child Upbringing. Hobbies: Running; Climbing. Address: Hui Qiao Building, Nanfang Hospital, Tong He, Guangzhou 510515, China.

QUEN Jacques M, b. 23 Oct 1928, New York City, USA. Psychiatrist. Education: BSc, Bethany College, 1944; MSc, Brown University, 1950; MD, Yale University, 1954; Graduate, William A White Psychoanalytic Institute, 1973. Appointments: Clinical Professor of Psychiatry, New York Hospital, Cornell Medical Centre. Publications: American Psychoanalysis: Origins and Development, Co-editor, 1978; Split Minds/Split Brains, Editor, 1986; Kraepelin's Psychiatry: A Textbook for Students and Physicians, Editor, 1990. Memberships: American Psychiatric Association; American Academy Psychoanalysis; American Academy Psychiatry and the Law; American Association for the History of Medicine. Hobby: Fly Fishing. Address: 141 East 55th Street, Suite 10-C, New York, NY 10022, USA.

QUI Xiaozhi, b. 23 October 1935, Shanghai, China. Professor of Ophthalmology. m. Zhou Haizhen, 1 May 1961, 2 sons. Appointments: Resident of Ophthalmology, EENT Hospital, 1959; Attending Ophthalmologist, EENT Hospital, 1978; Associate Professor, 1986, Professor of Ophthalmology, 1989, EENT Hospital. Publications: Large grafts for penetrating keratoplasty, 1986; The experimental research and clinical observation on the corneal cryopreservation, 1988. Honours: Outstanding Citizenship Award, Los Angeles, 1994. Memberships: International Federation of Eye Banks. Hobbies: Music; Translating. Address: Eye & ENT Hospital, Shanghai Medical University, 83 Fen Yang Road, Shanghai 200031, China.

QUICK Jonathan D, b. 5 June 1951, Albany, New York, USA. Medical Officer, World Health Organization. m. Tina Lee Burdick, 1 May 1982, 3 daughters. Education: AB, magna cum laude, Harvard University, 1974; MPH, University of Rochester, 1979; MD, with distinction in research, University of Rochester School of Medicine, 1979. Appointments: Clinical Director, Chief of Staff, USPHS Hospital of Talihina; Director, Drug Management Program, Management Sciences for Health; Health Development Advisor, Management Sciences for Health, Peshawar, Pakistan; Health Planner, Health Care Financing Project, Kenya. Publications: Senior Editor: Managing Drug Supply, 1995; Co-Author: Stress and Challenge at the Top, 1990; CO-Author: Clinical Guidelines, 1994; Author/Co-Author, over 30 articles and seven books on Health Management, Stress, Public Health. Honours: Achievement Medal, US Public Health Service, 1984; Citation for Outstanding Performance, US Public Health Service, 1984; Family Medicine Staff Award, 1982. Memberships: Fellow, Royal Society of Medicine; Fellow, American College of Preventative Medicine; American Board of Family Medicine; Rotary International; National Council for International Health. Hobbies: Jogging; Drumming; Tennis. Address: Action Programme on Essential Drugs, World Health Organization, CH-1211 Geneva 27, Switzerland.

QUINN Phillip D R, b. 1946, Bromley, Kent, England. President, Federation of Hypnotherapists; Director, Association for Applied Hypnosis; Consultant, UK Training College of Hypnotherapy & Counselling. Publications: The Role of Hypnotherapy Interventions in Medically Unexplained Infertility. Memberships: British Psychosocial Oncology Group, Kings College Hospital; British Infertility Counselling Association. Address: The Hale Clinic, 7 Park Crescent, London W1N 3HE, England.

QUINTYN Luc, b. 26 Feb 1950, Genth, Belgium. Psychologist. Education: PhD, Clinical Psychology; Family Sex SC; BACC Phil. Career: Chief, Department of Clinical Psychology, Queen Astrid Military Hospital, 1980-89; Currently, Director, National Centre for Crisis Psychology. Publications: 112 Articles on psycho-traumatology and victimology in 7 languages. Honours: Honorary member, Russian Society of Traumatic Stress; Professor, Mil Academy and Moscow State University. Memberships: International Society of Post Traumatic Stress Studies; Flemish Society of Clinical Psychology. Hobby: Restoration of Furniture. Address: CCP-QAMH, Bruynstraat, B-1120, Brussels, Belgium.

QUIROZ Q Guillermo, b. 18 June 1941, Lima, Peru. Medical Doctor. m. Nancy Portella, 9 June 1977, 2 sons, 1 daughter. Education: MD. Career: Assistant Cardiologist, Chief Coronary Care Unit, Chief ofCardiology Department, National Police Hospital, Lima, Peru. Publications: Editor, several medical journals: Symposium, 1975-76; Diagnostico, 1977-95; Acta Medica, 1990-92; Journal of The Police

Hospital, 1985-95; Contemporary Medicine, 1992-95. Memberships: Vice President, Peruvian Cardiology Society; Fellow, American College of Cardiology. Hobbies: Reading - Fronton Paddle - Windsurf. Address: Madreselvas 327, Lima 33, Peru.

R

RABIN David L, b. 14 July 1932, New York City, New York, USA. Professor; Physician. m Laurel H Kagan, 2 Sept 1963, 2 daughters. Education: AB, University of Arizona, 1954; MD, Washington University, St Louis, Missouri, 1958; MPH, Harvard University, 1964. Appointments: Assistant in Medicine, University of Chicago School of Medicine; Research Associate in Preventive Medicine, Cornell University School of Medicine; Junior Associate in Medicine, Harvard Medical School; Assistant Professor of Public Health Practice, Harvard University School of Public Health; Assistant Professor, Johns Hopkins University School of Hygiene and Public Health; Currently Professor, Associate Chair, Department of Family Medicine, Director, Division of Community Health Care Studies, Georgetown University School of Medicine, Washington, District of Columbia. Publications: Fact Book on Long Term Care, 1987; 100 articles on health care organisation, primary care, prevention, long term care. Honours: Milbank Foundation Faculty Fellowship, 1968-73; Health Policy Fellowship, Robert Wood Johnson, 1981-82; Chair, Governing Board, American Journal of Preventive Medicine. Memberships: President, Association of Teachers of Preventive Medicine; President, Metropolitan Washington Public Health Association; Gerontological Health Section Chair, Executive Board, Programme Development Board, American Public Health Association; National Co-ordinating Committee for Preventive Health Services; American College of Preventive Medicine; American Geriatric Society; Association for the Advancement of Science; Association of Teachers of Preventive Medicine. Hobbies: Music; Hiking; Tennis. Address: Division of Community Health Care Studies, Department of Family Medicine, Georgetown University School of Medicine, 3750 Reservoir Road NW, Washington, DC 20007, USA.

RABINOWITZ Jack Grant, b. 9 Jul 1927, Monticello, New York, USA. Physician. m. Rica Guadalia, 19 Jun 1972, 3 s, 2 d. Education: BA; MD; FACR. Appointments: Professor & Chairman, University of Tennessee; Professor, State University of New York; Professor & Chairman, Department of Radiology, Mount Sinai Medical Center, New York. Publications: Pediatric Radiology Textbook; Emergency Radiation Textbook. Memberships: ACR; AUR; RSNA. Hobbies: Music; Piano; Skiing. Address: Mount Sinai Medical Center, New York 10029-6574, USA.

RABKIN Charles, b. 1 Apr 1957, Washington, DC, USA. Physician. m. Mari L Plagge, 1 June 1987, 1 son, 2 daughters. Education: BSc, MD, Brown Univ; MSc, London School of Hygiene & Tropical Medicine. Career: HIV/Cancer Coordinator, Viral Epidemiology Branch, NCI. Publications: 35 journal articles. Address: Viral Epid Branch, 6130 Executive Boulevard EPN/434, Rockville, MD 20852 4910, USA.

RADOS Aldo, b. 6 August 1933, Pazin (Istra), Croatia. Medical Doctor. m. Ljiljana Kopic, 30 Sept 1972, 1 son, 1 daughter. Education: MD, University of Medicine, Zagreb, 1961; Specialisation in Neurology and Psychiatry; Magister scientiae, Clinical Pathophysiology, University of Rijeka; Degree in Transactional Analysis, University of Zagreb; Postgraduate Diploma, Alcoholism and Drug Addictions, Zagreb; Degree in Psychosomatic Medicine, Degree in Medical and Psychological Hypnosis degree, University of Milan, Italy. Appointments: General Practitioner, former Yugoslavia, to 1965; US Military Doctor, Germany, to 1971; Neurologist, Psychiatrist, 1971-, currently Chief of Staff, Psychiatric Department, General Hospital, Pula, Croatia. Publications: Various papers in neurology and psychiatry and pathophysiology in Proceedings of the International Neuropsychiatric Symposium of South-Eastern Europe; Others in foreign editions. Honours: Silver Cross of Honour for Merit to the Republic of Austria, President of Austria, 1981. Memberships: International TAA; Croatian Medical Association; International Society for Medical and Psychological Hypnosis; General Secretary, International Neuropsychiatric Symposium of the South-East, Pula. Hobbies: Skiing; Swimming; Collecting paintings. Address: Gortanova Uvala 12, 52000 Pula, Croatia.

RAGHUVARAN Sumithra, b. 9 Oct 1941, Blantyre, Malawi, South Africa. Gynaecologist and Obstetrician. m. G Raghuvaran, 12 May 1967, 1 son. Education: BSc, Chemistry; MBBS, DRCOG (Lond), 1971; MRCOG (Lond), 1975; FRCOG (Lond), 1990. Appointments: Senior House Officer, Obstetrics and Gynaecology, 1970-71, Registrar, 1973-77, Nottingham University, England; Senior House Officer, Birmingham Solihull University, 1972-73; Registrar, Clatterbridge Hospital, Liverpool, 1977; Currently Consultant Gynaecologist and Surgeon, Dr M Gopalapillai's Jawahar Hospital, Nagercoil, India. Publications: Articles; Conference papers. Honours include: Paul Harris Fellow, Rotary, 1992; Fellowship, International College of Surgeons, 1993; Invited to organise Asia Oceania Federation of Obstetricians and Gynaecologists workshop, 1992; Organiser, continuing Medical Education Progress, Nagercoil. Memberships: Obstetric and Gynaecological Society, FOGSI; Nagercoil Obstetric and Gynaecological Society, Secretary 1985-88, President 1988-93; All India International Medical Association Central Working Committee; Indian Academy of Reproduction; Life Member, Central Working Committee Member, International Medical Association; Representative, South Zone Fellows, All Indian Coordination Committee, Royal College of Obstetricians and Gynaecologists; Life Member: Indian Association of Infertility and Sterility; Indian Association of Gynaecological Endoscopists; Indian Academy of Juvenile and Adolescent Gynaecology and Obstetrics. Hobbies: Music; Social service; Playing tennis and badminton (formerly State team player for basketball, badminton, tennis, hockey). Address: Dr M Gopalapillai's Jawahar Hospital, Ramavarmapuram, Nagercoil 629 001, South India, India.

RAJA Rasib, b. 2 Feb 1943, Pakistan. Physician. m. 1969, 2 sons. Education: MD; Fellow, American College of Physicians; Fellow, Philadelphia College of Physicians. Career: Professor of Medicine, Temple Univeristy, Philadelphia; Chief, Kraftsow Div Nephrology. Publications: Multiple Nephrology publications. Memberships: American Society of Nephrology; American College of Physicians; International Society of Nephrology; American Society of International Organizations; National Kid Foundation. Hobbies: Tennis; Jogging. Address: 5501 Old York Road (AEMC), Philadelphia, PA 19141, USA.

RAJAB Khalil Ebrahim, b. 14 June 1941, Manama. Doctor. m. Elizabeth MacPherson, 8 Apr 1968, 3 sons. Education: MChB, Baghdad University, 1965; MRCOG (London), 1972; FRCOG (London), 1989; MFFP (London), 1994. Career: Assistant Associate Professor, Arabian Gulf University, Faculty of Medicine; Chairman, Department of Obstetrics & Gynaecology, Salmaniya Medical Centre. Hobbies: Community Work - Philathletic. Address: POB 26752, Bahrain.

RAJAKUMARAN Nadarajah, b. 12 Feb 1946, Sri Lanka. Doctor. m. 9 Feb 1977, 1 daughter. Education: MBBS; MRCOG; MFFP. Appointments: SHO, Registrar; Staff Grade Obstetrician & Gynaecologist. Memberships: Royal College of Obstetricians & Gynaecologists; Faculty of Family Planning. Hobbies: Badminton; Tennis; Fitness. Address: St Cross Hospital, Rugby, Warwickshire CV22 5PX, England.

RAKEL Robert Edwin, b. 13 Jul 1932, Cincinnati, OH, USA. Physician. m. Peggy Rakel, 20 Aug, 1 s, 3 d. Education: BS, Zoology, University of Cincinnati, 1954; MD, University of Cincinnati, College of Medicine, 1958. Career includes: Private Practice, Newport Beach, CA, 1962-69; Chairman, Family Practice Program, University of CA, Irvine, College of Medicine, 1969-71; Professor and Head, Family Practice, University of Iowa College of Medicine, 1971-85; Richard M Kleberg Senior Professor and Chairman, Department of Family Medicine, Associate Dean for Academic and Clinical Affairs, Baylor College of Medicine, Houston, TX, 1985-. Publications: Books include: Principles of Family Medicine, 1977; Textbook of Family Practice, 3rd edition, 1984, 4th edition, 1990; 5th edition, 1995; Essentials of Family Practice, 1992; Editor, Saunders Manual of Medical Practice, 1996; Numerous articles in professional journals, chapters, forewards, editorials; Editorial Board Member for several journals including: Your Patient and Cancer, 1984-, Advances in Therapy, 1986-, Internal Medicine Bulletin, 1993-. Honours: Mead-Johnson Scholarship Award, 1971; Thomas W Johnson Award, American Academy of Family Physicians, 1973; F Marian Bishop Leadership Award, STFM Foundation, 1992. Memberships include: President, 1993-94, American Osler Society; Cosmos Club, Washington DC; American Medical Association; Texas Medical Association; Association of American Medical Colleges; American Academy of Family Physicians; World Organization of National Colleges, Academies and Academic Associations of Family Practice. Hobbies: Boating; Writing. Address: 5510 Greenbriar, Houston, TX 77005, USA.

RAMAKRISHNAN S, b. 25 Oct 1927, Dhalapathi Samudram, Tamil-Nadu, India. Teacher; Researcher. m. Smt A Meenakshi, 8 Apr 1955, 3 daughters. Education: PhD, Biochemistry, 1962; Master's Degree, 1954; FAMS, 1989. Appointments: Lecturer, Madurai Medical College, 1955-63; Lecturer, Medical College, Pondicherry, Government of India, 1963-67; Reader, Biochemistry, 1967-75, Professor of Biochemistry, Head, 1975-85, Jawaharlal Institute of Postgraduate Medical Education and Research, Pondicherry, Government of India; Professor of Biochemistry, Head, Rajah Muthia Medical College, Annamalai University, 1985-91; Professor of Biochemistry, Head, Sankara Nethralaya Vision Research Foundation, Madras, 1991-. Publications: Author of 7 textbooks; Contributor of 175 research papers in national and international journals. Honours: FAMS for Excellence in Research and Academics; Hari Om Ashram Alembic Research Award, Medical Council of India; Professor Shadaksharaswami Endowment Lecture Award, Society of Biological Chemists, India; Silver Jubilee Oration Award, Medical College, Trivandrum; Oration Award, Jawaharlal Institute of Postgraduate Medical Education and Research; Oration Award, Association of Clinical Biochemists of India Rajasthan Chapter, Jaipur. Memberships: Society of Biological Chemists India; Indian Society of Atherosclerosis Research; Advisor, International Students' Association, Annamalai University; Advisor, Clinical Laboratory Services, Lion's Club Hospital, Madras. Hobby: Social Service in the Temple. Address: Sankara Nethralaya Vision Research Foundation, 18 College Road, Madras 600 006, India.

RAMALINGAM Raghupathy, b. 19 Sept 1932, Colombo, Sri Lanka. Obstetrician and Gynaecologist. m,. Thilakeswari Sabharatnam, 5 June 1965, 1 son, 2 daughters. Education: MBBS (Ceylon); FRCSE; FRCOG; FRACOG; FCOG (Sri Lanka). Appointments: Consultant Obstetrician and Gynaecologist, General Hospital, Kandy; Lecturer, Obstetrics and Gynaecology, Chinese University, Shatin, Hong Kong; Specialist in Obstetrics and Gynaecology, Broken Hill Base Hospital, Broken Hill, New South Wales, Australia; Currently Visiting Medical Officer, Obstetrics and Gynaecology, North-West Regional Hospital, Mersey Division, Latrobe, Tasmania. Publications: Repair of Partial Vaginal Atresia, 1966; Primary Ovarian Pregnancy, 1967; Placenta Percreta, 1967. Address: 53 Nixon Street, Devonport, Tasmania 7310, Australia.

RAMASAMY Ranjan, b. 1 June 1949, Colombo, Sri Lanka. Biochemist. m. Manthri, 11 Sept 1975, 1 daughter. Education: BA, University of Cambridge, England, 1971; MA (Honorary), University of Cambridge; PhD, University of Cambridge, 1974. Career: Senior Lecturer, University of Nairobi, Kenya; Professor and Head, Department of Biochemistry, University of Jaffna, Jaffna, Sri Lanka; Head, Division of Life Sciences, Institute of Fundamental Studies, Sri Lanka. Honours: Wellcome Trust Scholar, 1971-74; Senior Scholar, Christs College, University of Cambridge, 1970. Memberships: British Society for Immunology; Biochemical Society, England; American Society for Tropical Medicine & Hygiene; Sri Lanka Association for the Advancement of Science. Hobbies: Tennis; Swimming; Chess. Address: 137/3 Kirula Road, Colombo 05, Sri Lanka.

RAMIREZ Carlos A, b. 4 Feb 1953, Puerto Rico, USA. Professor of Chemical Engineering. m. Ana L Brana, 1 son, 1 daughter. Education: BS, Chemical Engineering, University of Puerto Rico, 1974; ScD, Chemical Engineering, Massachusetts Institute of Technology, 1979. Appointments: Chemical Process Development Engineer, Fine Chemicals Division, The Upjohn Company, Kalamazoo, Michigan, 1979-82; Associate Professor, Chemical Engineering, UPR, 1982-92; Professor, Chemical Engineering, UPR, 1992-. Publications: Numerous professional scientific articles in journals. Honours include: Travel Fellowship Awards, ASAIO Annual Meeting, 1992 and 1995. Memberships: American Association for the Advancement of Science; American Chemical Society; American Institute of Chemical Engineers; American Society for Artificial Internal Organs; Biomedical Engineering Society; The Controlled Release Society; The Microcirculatory Society; The New York Academy of Sciences; Sigma Xi. Hobbies: Various Sports; Classical Music; Reading; Chess; Photography. Address: Department of Chemical Engineering; University of Puerto Rico, Mayagüez, Puerto Rico 00681-5000, USA.

RAMJHUN Ahmad Faoud, b. 18 Sep 1952, Mahebourg, Mauritius. Child and Educational Psychologist. m. June Ramjhun, 2 s. Education: BSc, Honours, Leicester University; PGCE, Southampton University; MSc, London; DSE, CNAA. Appointments: Child and Educational Psychologist; Principal Officer in Children's Special Needs, Hampshire County Council; Currently, Principal Officer and Psychologist, Hampshire County Council. Publications: Appraisal in Education, 1994; Principles of Good Practice: A Guide to Stautory Assessment Procedures for Children with Special Educational Needs, in progress. Honours: Associate Fellow, British Psychological Society, 1985; Chartered Psychologist, 1990. Memberships: British Psychological

Society. Hobbies: Soccer; Snooker. Address: 46 Hammonds Way, Totton, Southampton, Hampshire SO40 3HF, England.

RAMPERSAUD Olga Mavis, b. Trinidad, West Indies. Obstetrician & Gynaecologist; Community Medicine Specialist. Education: St Joseph Convent POS, Trinidad; McGill University, Montreal, Canada; University Liverpool, England; MRCS, LRCP, London, England, 1950; LM Rotunda, DGO Dublin, 1954; MRCOG 1959, FRCOG 1988, London, England; LMCC, Toronto, Canada, 1969; DPH, University Toronto, Canada, 1969. Appointments: hexham General Hospital, Northumberland, England; Jessop Hospital for Women, Sheffield, England, 1954; University West Indies, Jamaica, 1960; Sangre Grande Hospital, Trinidad, 1960; Consultant Specialist Obstetrician & Gynaecologist, Government Service, Trinidad & Tobago, 1962; Director of Medical Services, Department of Public Health, Toronto, 1973; Associate Medical Officer, Health & Preventive Clinical Services Manager, City of Toronto, Canada, 1982; Lecturer, Faculty of Medicine, Unviersity Toronto, Canada, 1981. Memberships: CPHA; OPHA; CARIPHA; Public Health Associations; AICP. Address: 18 Lower Village Gate, Suite 411, Toronto M5P 3M1, Canada.

RAMSEY Julie, b. 20 Oct 1956, San Francisco, California, USA. Social Worker. m. Derek Ramsey, 1 son. Education includes: MSW, University of Hawaii, Manoa. Appointments: Tripler Army Medical Center for Discharge Planning; Pearl Harbor Family Advocacy for Prevention of Domestic Violence; Currently Family Advocacy Outreach Manager for Prevention of Domestic Violence. Honours: Outstanding Performance Award for Professional Services, 1991, 1992, 1993. Memberships: National Association of Social Workers; ACSW. Hobbies: Camping; Dancing; Bowling; Fishing; Puzzles; Roller blading. Address: 7032 Fair Oaks Blvd 20, Carmichael, CA 95608, USA.

RAMSEY-GOLDMAN Rosalind, b. 22 Mar 1954, NY, USA. Physician. m. Glenn Ramsey, MD, 29 Jun 1975, 1 s, 1 d. Education: BA, summa cum laude, MD, 1978, MPH, 1988; PhD, 1992. Career: Instructor, Assistant Professor of Medicine, University of Pittsburgh, 1986-91; Currently, Assistant Professor of Medicine, Northwestern University, 1991-. Publications: Many reports, abstracts, books and monographs including: Co-author, Previouspregnancy outcome in an important determinant of subsequent pregnancy outcome in women with systemic lupus erythematosus, in American Journal of Reprod Immunology, 1992; Co-author, Red cell serology in systemic lupus erythematosus, ASCP Check sample, Transfusion Medicine, in press. Honours: Undergraduate Book Prize for Research, 1974; Phi Beta Kappa, 1974; Judy S Finkelstein Award, 1986; Outstanding Student, University of Pittsburgh, 1991. Memberships: American College of Rheumatology; Society for Epidemiologic Research; Central Society for Clinical Research. Travel; Music. Address: Arthritis Ward, 3-315, 303 East Chicago Avenue, Chicago, IL 60611, USA.

RAN Maosheng, b. 12 Mar 1964, Sichuan, China. Psychiatrist. m. 1987, 1 son. Education: BSc, 1985, MSc, 1991, West China University of Medical Sciences. Appointments: Assistant, Resident, of Psychiatry, 1985-91, Chief Resident, 1991-92, Senior Lecturer, Attending Doctor, West China University of Medical Sciences. Publications: A Study of Schizophrenic Patient's Treatment Compliance in a Rural Community, 1995; A Controlled Evaluation of Psycho-educational Family Intervention in Rural Chinese Community, 1994. Honours: Three Articles Awarded Excellent Article Award, Association of Chinese Mental Rehabilitation. Memberships: Committee Member, Association of Chinese Transcultural Psychiatry; Member, Association of Chinese Neurology and Psychiatry. Hobbies: Swimming; Music. Address: Institute of Mental Health, First School of Clinical Medicine, West China University of Medical Sciences, Xiaoxue Lu No 7, Chengdu, Sichuan 610041, China.

RAN Wei, b. 12 Dec 1954, Zhengzhou, China. Oral Surgeon. m. Dr Guo Bing, 28 Mar 1991, 1 daughter. Education: BS, Stomatology, 1977; MS, Oral and Maxillofacial Surgery, 1986. Appointments: research Assistant, Department Oral and Maxillofacial Surgery, 1983-86; Lecturer, Department of Oral and Maxillofacial Surgery; Surgical Dean, Department of Oral and Maxillofacial Surgery, 1990-. Publications include: The Miscrovasculature of Human Oral Mucosa Using Vascular Corrosion Casts and Indian Ink Injection I Tongue Papillae, Co-author, 1992; Studies of the Factor of Genetics in Congenital Cleft Lip Methods of Twin, CO-author, 1989; A Clinical Study of COngenital Palatopharyngeal Atresuia, Co-author, 1990; Three Dimensional Survey of Trend of Whole Interior Alveolar Nerve Canal and its Relation to Adjacent Structure and Their Values in Operation, Co-author, 1988;

Observation on Microvascular Corrosion Casts of the Periosteum of Infant mandibular Ramus by SEM, Co-author, 1987;' A Clinical Survey of 306 Cases of Elective Radical Neck Dissection Surgery in Maxillofacial Tumor, Co-author, 1981. membership: Chinese Medical Association. Hobbies: Swimming; Fishing. Address: Department of Oral and Maxillofacial Surgery, First Affiliated Hospital, Sun Yat-Sen University of Medical Sciences, Guangzhou, China.

RAN Zhingqi, b. 26 dec 1938, Guiyang, China. Leprologist. m. Song Guang Xian, 15 Mar 1963, 2 sons. Education: Medical School of Guiyang. Appointments: Leprologist, Leprosy Hospital of Salaxi, Guizhou; Teacher, 2nd Medical and Health School of Bie-Jie Prefecture. Guizhou. Publication: Leprologia, Co-author, 1986. Honours: Advanced Worker of the Precautions Against Leprosy of Province Guizhou, 1982; Advanced Worker in Medicine or Province Guizhou, 1984. Memberships: Society of Dermatology, Guizhou Province; Society of Leprosy Guizhou Province. Hobbies: Study; Reading. Address: Second Medical and Health School of Bie-Jie Prefecture, Guizhou, China.

RANA T Geetha, b. 11 August 1956, Kerala, India. Obstetrician and Gynaecologist. m. Dr Suraj S J B Rana, 28 April 1979, 1 son, 1 daughter. Education: MBBS; DGO; MRCOG. Appointments: Consultant Obstetrician and Gynaecologist. Publications: Case Report, Prolapse of an Ovarian Tumor during Labour, 1987; Some Fetal and Pregnancy Parameters in Nepal, 1988; A Multicentre Study of Perinatal Mortality in Nepal, 1990; Perinatal Mortality, Prospects for Improvement in Developing Contries, 1992; A Prospective Randomized Controlled Trial of Perineal Repair after Childbirth Comparing Interrupted Chromic Catgut to Subcuticular Prolene for Skin Closure, 1993; A Random Allocation Comparison of Silicone and Santoprene Soft Vacuum Extractor Cups for Assisted Delivery, 1993. Honours: Best Out-Going Student, Karnatak Medical College, Hubli, 1978; 1st, Stanley Medical College, 1984. Memberships: Nepal Medical Association; Nepal Society of Obstetricians and Gynaecologists; Royal College of Obstetricians and Gynaecologists, London. Hobbies: Reading. Address: Patan Hospital, GPO Box 252, Kathmandu, Nepal.

RANADIVE Kamal, b. 8th Nov 1917, Pune, Maharashira, India. Cancer Research. m. Jayasing Ranaine, 13 May 1938, 1 s. Education: MSc; PhD; FNA Padmabhushan; FMAS. Career: First lady Professor of Biology, Fergusson College, Poona, 1939-41; Doctoral Work, Tata Memorial Hospital Laboratory, 1943; Currently, Emeritus Scientist, ICMR. Publications: Over 200 research publications on cancer and leprosy. Honours: Rockefeller Foundation Fellowship, 1949-51; Basantidevi Amirchand Award, Indian Council of Medical Research, 1958; Medical Council Award for Cancer Research, 1964; G J Watumull Award for Leprosy Work, 1964; Sandoz Award, 1976; Padmabhushan Award, Government of India, 1982; Distinguished Woman Award, Banaras Hindu University, 1983; Tata Memorial Hospital Golden Jubilee Award for Outstanding Work in Cancer Control, 1991. Memberships: Several committees of Indian Council of Medical Research and Council of Scientific and Industrial Research; Editorial Board of 3 Indian journals and International Journal of Cancer; International Committees of Cancer Research and Tissue Culture; Board of Studies, Chancellor's Nominee of Academic Council of Universities of Bombay and Poona; Founder Member, Chairperson, Board of Trustees, Indian Women Scientists Association; Founder Fellow, Maharashtra Academy of Sciences; Fellow, Indian National Science Academy. Hobbies: Reading; Medico-Social Work, Tribals and Rural. Address: 1127, Nishigandh, Poopnagar, Bandra East, Bombay 400051, India.

RANATUNGA Gunasiri Ananda, b. 30 Apr 1951, Kalutara, Sri Lanka. Obstetrician & Gynecologist. m. 4 Aug 1981, 2 sons, 1 daughter. Education: MBBS, Ceylon; MS, Sri Lanka; MRCOG, England. Appointments: Resident Obstetrician, General Hospital of Kurunegala, Sri Lanka; Consultant Obstetrician & Gynecologist, Bane Hospital, Kegalle, Sri Lanka. Honours: Wiserama Award, Sri Lanka Medical Association for Best Free Paper, 1994. Memberships: Royal College of Obstetricians & Gynecologists, England; Sri Lanka College of Obstetricians & Gynecologists. Hobbies: Swimming; Reading; Sight Seeing; Nature. Address: No 40/13 Lake Gardens, Off Lake Drive, Rajagiriya, Srijayawardanapura, Sri Lanka.

RANDERIA Jamshed Pestonji, b. 21 May 1938, Ahmedabad. Visiting Professor of Medicine, CMP Homoeopathic Medical College, Bombay University; Professor, London College of Osteopathic Medicine; Consultant, British Osteopathic Association Clinic. m. Hella Randeria, 12 Oct 1971, 1 son, 1 daughter. Education: Diploma, Faculty of Homoeopathy, Royal London Homoeopathic Hospital, 1966; Doctor of Medicine, Homoeopathic; Member, London College of Osteopathic Medicine, elected to the Fellowship, 1967. Appointments: House Physician, Government Homoeopathic Hospital, Bombay, 1963; Clinic Assistant, Royal London Homoeopathic Hospital, 1966; Clinical Lecturer, London College of Osteopathic Medicine. Publications: The Osteopathic Lesion, 1969; The Role of Psoas Muscle in low back pathology, 1974; Homoeopathy in the Light of Modern Science, 1987; Homoeopathy Planatory Notes and a General Guide, 1990; Homoeopathic Bowel Nosodes, 1993. Memberships: British Association of Manipulative Medicine; British Osteopathic Association; Fellow, Royal Society of Health; International Homoeopathic Medical League; International Homoeopathic Medical Organization. Hobbies: Classical Music; Tennis; Weight Training. Address: 138 Harley Street, London W1N 1AH, England.

RANGA Viorel, b. 15 July 1926, Pojejena, Romania. Physician. m. Brunhilde Ciesla, 1963, 1 daughter. Education: BA, General Dragalina Collage, Oravita, Romania; MD, Faculty of General Medicine, Bucharest. Appointments: Assistant, 1953; Lecturer, 1962; Docent, 1970; Professor of Anatomy, 1974-; Scientific Leader of Anatomy, 1981-; Chairman, Head, Department of Anatomy, Faculty of Medicine, 1977-90; Prodean, 1972-77; Dean, 1991-. Publications: Human Anatomy, 1961; Human Anatomy and Physiology, 1970; Human Anatomy, 1990; Atlas of Human Anatomy: Systema Nervosum Centrale, 1993. Memberships: USSM, Romania; Anatomische Gesellschaft, Germany; Association des Anatomistes, France; International Federation of Anatomists; Society of Neuropathology; Union Medicale Balcanique. Address: Str Anastasie Simu Nr 6, Sector 1, Bucharest, Romania.

RANKIN Diane, b. 13 May 1939, Houston, TX, USA. Psychiatry. m. William V Miller, MD, 15 Oct 1975, 1 s. Education: BA, 1962, MD, 1968, University of CO; Adult Psychoanalysis; Candidate, Child and Adolescent Psychoanalyst. Appointment: Private Solo Practice, Psychiatry and Psychoanalysis. Honour: Fellow, Child Psychiatry, 1974. Memberships: American Psychoanalytic Association; American Academy of Child and Adolecent Psychiatry; International Psychoanalytical Association. Hobbies: Tennis; Skiing; Biking. Address: 141 N Meramec Suite 110A, St Louis, MO 63105, USA.

RANNEY Robert John, b. 16 Apr 1943, Fort Dodge, IA, USA. Management Consultant to Rural Health Clinics. Education: BS, Human Relations, Missouri Valley College; MPA, University of Missouri, Kansas City. Career: Executive Director, Central Ozarks Medical Center; CEO, Midwest Rural Health Association; Senior Consultant, National Rural Health Association; Manager, Practice Support Initiative, American Academy of Family Physicians; Owner and Consultant, Ranney Associates; Rural Health Care Specialist, Health Care Consulting Inc. Publications: Community Caring: A Model for Health Care Delivery Through Community Interaction, 1986; Rural Health Crisis: The Effects of The Rural Economy on Primary Health Care, 1986; Policy and Procedures Manual for Rural Health Clinics, 1992. Honours: Outstanding Young Man of the Year, 1978; National Honor Society for Public Affairs and Administration, 1988. Memberships: Chair, 1982-83, Vice Chair, 1985-86, Missouri Coalition for Primary Care; Chair, 1981, Vice Chair, 1984-85, Midwest Rural Health Association; Medical Group Management Association, 1979-84; Society of Medical and Dental Consultants. Hobbies: Reading; Music; Fishing; Hunting. Address: 120 Cedar Valley Road, Fairfield Bay, AR 72153, USA.

RANSOM James Harley, b. 9 Mar 1936, Des Moines, Iowa, USA. Physician. m. Marcia Mohler, 21 May 1972, 1 s, 3 d. Education: BA, Magna Cum Laude, University of Iowa, 1958; MD, University of Iowa, 1962. Appointments: Physician, Topeka Allergy & Asthma Clinic. Publications: Co-Author, Allergic Reactions to Plant Cloning Enzymes, 1981; Dust Mite Assays in Clinical Practice, 1990. Honours: President of Medical Staff, Stormont-Vail Regional Medical Center, 1974-75. Memberships: Fellow, American College of Allergy & Immunology; American Academy of Allergy Immunology. Hobbies: Fly Fishing; Shooting. Address: 1123 SW Gage, Topeka, Kansas 66604, USA.

RAO D C, b. 6 Apr 1946, India. Academic. m. Sarada, 31 July 1974, 1 son, 1 daughter. Education: BStat 1967, MStat 1968, PhD 1971, Indian Statistical Institute, Calcutta, India. Career: Postdoctoral Fellow, University of Sheffield, England, 1971-72; Assistant Geneticist, 1972-78; Associate Geneticist, 1978-80; University of Hawaii, Honolulu; Associate Professor & Director, 1980-82; Professor & Director, Washington University, currently. Publications include: The Relation Between

Tongue Pigmentation and Mental Ability, 1970; On Haldane's Exact Text Test for Random Mating, 1974; Complex Segregation Analysis of Tongue Pigmentation: A Search for Residual Family Resemblance, 1978; A Genetic Study of Hypoalphalipoproteinemia, 1984; Blood Pressure in a Rural West Bengal Fishing Community: An Epidemiologic Profile, 1988; Assessing Genetic and Cultural Heritability, 1994. Memberships: President Elect, International Genetic Epidemiology Society, 1994-96; Member, several societies. Hobbies: Photography; Gardening. Address: Washington University, Division of Biostatistics, Box 8067, 660 S Euclid Avenue, St Louis, MO 63110, USA.

RAO Gullapalli Nageswara, b. 21 Sept 1945, Chodavaram, AP, India. Physician. m. Pratibha, 24 May 1973, 1 son, 1 daughter. Education: MD (Ophthalmology). Career: Fellow in Ophthalmology, Tufts New England Medical Center, Boston, USA; Associate Clinical Professor & Director, Cornea Research Lab, University of Rochester, Rochester, USA; Director, LV Prasad Eye Institute. Publications: Contact Lenses: Endothelim Cell Morphology and Cornea Deturgescence; Cell Size - Shape Relationships in Corneal Endothelium. Honours: Honour Award, American Academy of Ophthalmology, 1983; Silver Medal, International Council of Contact Lenses, 1994. Memberships: Fellow, American Academy of Ophthalmology; Association for Research in Vision & Ophthalmology. Hobby: Reading Biographies. Address: L V Prasad Eye Institute, Road No 2, Banjara Hills, Hyderabad 500034, India.

RAO Gyaneshwar, b. 11 Jan 1950, Lautoka, Fiji. Physician. m. Ragini Rao, 11 Nov 1978, 2 sons. Education: MB. BS, University of Bombay, India, 1976; Medical Registrar, Colonial War Memorial Hospital, Suva, 1978-82; Medical Registrar, Christchurch and Princess Margaret Hospitals, Christchurch, New Zealand, 1983-89; FRACP, 1990. Appointments: Consultant Physician, Colonial War Memorial Hospital, Suva, 1989-. Publications: Multiple Melanoma (with P Ram), 1982. Honours: Indian Government Scholarship for undergraduate medical studies, 1968-76; New Zealand Bilateral Aid Scholarship for postgraduate medical studies, 1983-89. Memberships: Fellow, Royal Australasian College of Physicians; Asia Pacific Committee; Fiji Medical Association. Hobbies: Reading; Gardening. Address: c/- Colonial War Memorial Hospital, Suva, Fiji.

RAO Kalluri Subba, b. 18 Aug 1939, Pedapadu, India. Teaching; Research. m. Kameswari Devi, 7 Feb 1965, 1 son, 1 daughter. Education: MSc; PhD; FARS. Appointments incl: Professor, School of Life Sciences, University of Hyderabad, 1979-; Visiting Fulbright Professor, University of Washington School of Medicine, Seattle, USA, 1982-83; Dean, School of Life Sciences, University of Hyderabad, 1986-89; Biotechnology Overseas Visiting Fellowship, University of Washington School of Medicine, 1991; Biotechnology Visiting Scientist, Department of Biochemistry, I.I.Sc, Bangalore, 1993. Publications: Several professional articles in scientific journals. Honours incl: Sigma Xi; Senior Fulbright Fellows, 1982, 1983; GJS Rao Memorial Lecture Award, Biochemical Society, 1994. Hobbies: Reading; TV; Cricket. Address: Department of Biochemistry, School of Life Science, University of Hyderabad, Hyderabad 500134, India.

RAO Satyanarayana M, b. 21 Jan 1948, Mysore, India. Scientist. m. Padma S Rao, 7 May 1981, 2 sons. Education: MSc, Biochemistry; PhD, Biochemistry; FASC; FNASc; FNA. Appointments: Assistant Professor, Baylor College of Medicine, Houston, Texas, USA, 1975-76; Assistant Professor, 1982-87, Associate Professor, 1987-91, Professor, 1991-, Indian Institute of Science, Bangalore. Publications: Contributor of 80 papers; Co-author of paper discovering the gene responsible for colorectal cancer. Honours: S S Bhatnagar Award. CSIR, 1988; Eleanor Roosevelt Cancer Fellowship, 1993. Membership: Society of Biological Chemists India. Hobby: Music. Address: Department of Biochemistry, Indian Institute of Science, Bangalore 560012, India.

RAO Sreedhar, b. 2 Jan 1943, India. Medicine. m. Dr Sarojini Rao, 1 June 1967, 1 son, 1 daughter. Education: MD. Career: Assistant Professor, 1975-81; Associate Professor, 1981-93; Professor, Department of Pediatrics, Director, Ped Hematology/Oncology, 1994. Publications: Bone Scintigraphy in Patients with Sickle Cell Disease and Osteomyelitis, 1989. Memberships: American Academy of Pediatrics; American Society of Pediatric Hematology/Oncology; American Society of Hematology; American Society of Clinical Oncology. Hobbies: Tennis; Music; Travel. Address: SUNY Health Science Center at Brooklyn, 450 Clarkson Avenue, Brooklyn, NY 11203, USA.

RAPAPORT Judith, b. 27 Feb 1928, Myjava, Czechoslovakia. Psychoanalyst; Psychiatrist. m. Dr Chanan Rapaport, 1 May 1957, 1 s, 1 d. Education: Baccalaureate, Bratislava High School, 1946; MD, Hadassah Medical School, Hebrew University, Jerusalem, 1954; Specialist, Diploma in Psychiatry, Israeli Ministry of Health, 1964; Graduate, Israeli Psychoanalytic Society, 1970. Appointments include: Talbieh, University Mental Hospital, Jerusalem, 1954-56, 1965-71; Psychiatric Consultant, Well Baby Clinics of Jerusalem, 1956-58; Children's Hospital, Creedmoor, NY, 1958-62; Psychiatric, Psychoanalytic Fellowship, JBG, New York City, 1962-64; Professor of Psychiatry, Columbia University Medical School, NY, 1972-73; Department Head, Eitanim Psychiatric Hospital, Jerusalem, 1975-76; Senior Psychiatrist, Talbieh Hospital, Jerusalem, 1977-93. Publications include: 15 Professional Publications, 1954-, including: Stuttering and Tic among Children, The Academy of Medicine, Jerusalem, 1970; Adolescence and Suicide, Medical Monographs, 1971; Sexual Deviations, The Academy of Medicine, 1972; Co-author, The Late Effects of Nazi Persecution among Elderly Holocaust Survivors, Acta Psychiatrist Scand, 1990; Co-author, Retraumatization of Holocaust Survivors During the Gulf War and Scud Missile Attacks on Israel, accepted for publication, British Journal of Medical Psychology. Memberships: Israeli Medical Association; Israeli Psychiatric Society; Israeli Society for Child Psychiatry; Israeli Psychoanalytic Society; New York Council for Child Psychiatry, 1961-65. Address: 21 Shmuel Hanagid St, Jerusalem 945 92, Israel.

RAPHLING David L, b. 8 June 1937, Washington, District of Columbia, USA. Physician. m. Lois Schwartzman, 19 July 1959, 1 son, 1 daughter. Education: BA, George Washington University, 1958; MD, George Washington University School of Medicine, 1962; Internship, Barnes Hospital, St Louis, Missouri, 1963; Residency in Psychiatry, Massachusetts General Hospital, Boston, 1969; Psychoanalytic training, Washington Psychoanalytic Institute, 1976; Certified: Psychiatry, American Board of Psychiatry and Neurology; Psychoanalysis, American Psychoanalytic Association. Appointments: Instructor, Harvard Medical School; Associate Clinical Professor of Psychiatry, Georgetown University Medical School; Currently Professor of Psychiatry, US University of Health Sciences Medical School; Currently Training and Supervising Analyst, Washington Psychoanalytic Institute, District of Columbia. Publications: Incest: A Genealogic Study, 1969; Technical Issues of the Opening Phase, in Adult Analysis and Childhood Sexual Abuse, 1990; Some Vicissitudes of Aggression in the Interpretive Process, 1992; A Patient Who Was Not Sexually Abused, 1994. Honours: Alpha Omega Alpha, 1962; Smith Reed Russell Honor Society, 1962; Fellow, American Psychiatric Association, 1981; Research Prize, Washington Psychoanalytic Society, 1984, 1994; Center for Advanced Psychoanalytic Studies, 1990. Memberships: American Psychoanalytic Association; International Psychoanalytic Association; Princeton Centre for Advanced Psychoanalytic Studies. Hobbies: Art; Literature; Travel; Tennis. Address: 5225 Connecticut Ave NW, Washington, DC 20015, USA.

RAPINI Ronald Peter, b. 15 Feb 1954, Akron, Ohio, USA. Dermatologist. m. Mary Jo Beigel, 16 Jun 1979, 2 d. Education: MD, Medicine, Ohio State University, Columbus, Ohio, 1978. Appointments: Internship, University of Wisconsin & Marshfield Clinic, 1978-79; Dermatology Residency, University of Iowa, 1979-82; Dermatopathology Fellowship, University of Colorado, 1982-83; Assistant & Associate Professor, University of Texas, Houston, 1983-93; Professor & Chairman, Department Dermatology, Texas Technical University, Lubbock, Texas, 1993-. Publications: Over 150 Publications including, Atlas of Dermatopathology, 1988; Special Dermatopathology Techniques, 1991. Honours: Dean's Teaching Excellence Award, 1986, 1987, 1988, 1989, 1990, 1991. Memberships: American Society of Dermatopathology; American Academy of Dermatology; Society of Investigative Dermatology; American Society Dermatology Surgery; American Medical Association; Southern Medical Association; International Society of Dermatopathology. Hobbies: Tennis; Entomology. Address: Department of Dermatology, Texas Tech University, 3601 Fourth Street, Lubbock, TX 77430, USA.

RAPP Dorrie Louise, b. 14 Sep 1949, Chicago, IL, USA. Neuropsychologist. Education: Doctorate in Experimental Psychology, Cambridge University, England; Chartered Psychologist, UK; Diplomate, American Board of Professional Neuropsychology. Appointments: Psychologist, Spastics Society, UK, 1976-79; Assistant Director, Psycholgical Services, 1981-83, Neuropsychologist, Drucker Brain Injury Center, 1984-85, Moss Rehabilitation Hospital, Philadelphia, PA;

Currently, Private Practice, Neuropsychology. Publications: Numerous including: Brain Injury Case Book: Methods for Reintegration to Home, School and Community, 1986. Honours: Richmond Cerebral Palsy Center, AACPDM, 1980; Executive Board and Examiner for Diplomate in Neuropsychology. Memberships: APA; ABPN; NAN; INS. Hobbies: Skiing; Scuba Diving; Underwater Photography. Address: 53 Neal Road, White River Jct, Vermont, USA.

RAREY Kyle Eugene, b. 13 May 1948, Elwood, IN, USA. Professor; Researcher. m. Donna Susan Pugh, 12 Nov 1976, 3 s, 1 d. Education: BA, Zoology; PhD, Anatomy. Career: Science Teacher; Associate Instructor; Teaching Associate; Instructor; NIH Postdoctoral Fellow; Assistant Research Scientist; Assistant Professor; Associate Professor; Currently, Professor, University of Florida College of Medicine, Gainesville. Publication: Rarey's Video Manual of Human Dissection, 1994. Honours: Graduate Research Fellowship, 1976; National Research Service Award, 1979-81; Basic Science Teacher of the Year, 1987-88; Outstanding Teacher of the Year, 1989-90, 1993-94. Memberships: American Association of Anatomists; American Association of Clinical Anatomists; American Association for Research in Otolaryngology; American Academy of Otolaryngology, Head and Neck Surgery. Hobbies: Guitar; Marathon Running. Address: University of Florida College of Medicine, Box 100235 JHMHC, Gainesville, FL 32610, USA.

RATANAKORN Disya, b. 15 Oct 1960, Bangkok, Thailand. Neurologist. Education: BSc, Faculty of Science, 1982, MD (Hons), Faculty of Medicine, 1984, Mahidol University; Diploma, Clinical Neurology, University of London, 1987; Diplomate, Thai Board of Neurology, 1990. Appointments: Neurological Consultant, Prasat Neurological Hospital and Institute, Ministry of Public Health, Thailand, 1986-93; Lecturer in Clinical Neurology, Faculty of Dentistry, Mahidol University, Bangkok, 1991-; Guest Lecturer in Neurology, Neurology Unit, Department of Medicine, Faculty of Medicine, Ramathibodi Hospital, Mahidol University, 1991-93, Instructor, 1994-, Faculty of Medicine, Ramathibodi Hospital, Mahidol University. Publications: Co-author: Acute intermittent porphyria crisis with good functional recovery, 1988; Oral loading and maintenance doses of phenytoin in Thai patients - a pharmacokinetic study, 1990; Delayed cerebral swelling complicating intracerebral hematoma, 1991; Myasthenia Gravis and Thyrotoxicosis: A review of 51 Thai patients, 1991; A genetic fragment of Dyssynergin Cerebellaris Myoclonica (Ramsay-Hunt Syndrome) in a Thai family: a preliminary study, 1992; Abnormal topographic brain mapping in patients with normal conventional electroencephalography: a preliminary study, 1993; Long term follow up of patients with Myasthenia Gravis and Thyrotoxicosis, 1993; Neuroeysticercosis, 1995. Memberships: Neurosonology Research Group, World Federation of Neurology; American Society of Neuroimaging; International Brain Research Organization; American Institute of Ultrasound in Medicine. Hobbies: Reading; Travel. Address: 356/7, Sri-Ayudhaya Road, Phyathai, Bangkok 10400, Thailand.

RAVALICO Giuseppe, b. 14 Aug 1941, Trieste, Italy. Associate Professor. m. Ida Frattarold, 19 Mar 1968, 2 daughters. Education: MD, University of Rome, 1966; Special Ophthelmology University, Rome, 1970. Appointments: Assistant, University Eye Clinic of Rome, 1967; Associate Professor. Publications: Numerous publications in professional journals. Memberships: ISCEV; ESCRS. Hobbies: Golf. Address: Clinica Oculistica, Universita, 34129 Trieste, Italy.

RAWLINGS Charles Adrian, b. 11 Nov 1936, Paducah, Kentucky, USA. Biomedical Engineering. Education: BSEE; MS, Engineering; PhD, Physiology & Engineering. Appointments: Engineer, Sperry Rand Corporation, 1959-61; Field Engineering Training Representative, Rockwell International, 1961-65; Senior Logistics Field Engineer, Rockwell International, Apollo Program, 1965-66; Instructor to Professor, Southern Illinois University, Carbondale, 1965-; Founder, Director, Seminar in Biomedical Instrumentation, 1972-. Publications: Electrocardiography, 1993; Occupational Biohazards Affecting Clinical Engineers and Biomedical Equipment Technicians; A Computer Model to Study Norepinephrine-Induced Oscillation of Contraction in Tail Arteries of Spontaneously Hypertensive Stroke-Prone Rats. Honours: Member, Technical Staff, Rockwell Corporation, 1967, 1968, 1969. Memberships: American Society for Hospital Engineering; Association for the Advancement of Medical Instrumentation; Instrument Society of America. Hobbies: Electronics; Woodworking; Gardening. Address: Department of Electrical Engineering, Biomedical Engineering Laboratory, Southern Illinois University, Carbondale, IL 62901, USA.

RAZZOLI DELLA MADDALENA VON ALLESTEIN Guy, b. 25 Mar 1925, Genoa, Italy. Research Fellow; Technical Co-ordinator; Professional Physician. m. Paola C Gonella, 28 Mar 1973, 4 sons, 2 daughters. Education: Specialist, Science of Nutrition, Paris, France, 1958, Modena, Italy, 1968; Specialist, Psychosomatics & Clinical Psychology, Milan, 1973; MD, University of Pavia, Italy. Appointments: Medical Assistant, Medical Service, Vatican City; Vice Director, Clinic La Tour de Baousset of Mentone, France; Technical Manager, Biological Research Centre, Nice, France; Technical Manager, Institute for the Scientific Nutrition Spreading of Nice; Committee Member, Dietetique et Nutrition, Paris; Human Nutrition Research Lab, Hopital Bichart, Paris; Technical Adviser, Microalgae Research Lab of Bologna, Italy; Director, Centre de Medicine Psychosomatique, Cannes, France; Technical Advisor, Juridic International Association, Vienna, Austria; Technical Advisor, Radio TV Suisse for programmes on Nutrition; Research Fellow, Center on Bioclimatology, Biotechnologies & Natural Medicine, University of Milan, Italy; Technical Co-ordinator, Lab on Eating Disorders, University of Milan, Italy; Professional Physician, (nutritionist & psychologist) Milan, Italy. Publications: A New Proteic Source: Chlorella, 1966; A Physician in a Kitchen - A Dietetic Guide, 1976; An Alimentary Guide to Aesthetics, 1975; Food Biochemistry, 1965; The Italian Gourmet Diet, 1983; Een Neuw Sportman Voeding, 1979; and many others. Memberships include: Italian & French Medical Associations; Association for Fighting against Obesity, Rome. Honours: Borromini Prize for Dietetics, 1970; Academia Teatina per le Scienze, 1971; UNAMSI Prize, 1972; Seville City Prize, 1972; Academia Gentium Pro Pace, 1976; Accademia Tiberina, 1978; Lacan Prize, 1983; International Prize "Tema Medicina", 1994. Hobbies: Music; Archaeology; Foreign Languages. Address: Chateau Amiral, 42 Boulevard d'Italie, MC 98000 Monte Carlo.

READER George, b. 8 Feb 1919, Brooklyn, New York, USA. Physician. m. Helen C Brown, 23 May 1942, 4 sons. Education: BA, 1940, MD, 1943, Cornell University; Fellow in Medicine, New York Hospital-Cornell University, 1946-47; Assistant Resident, Cornell University Medical College, 1947-49; Certified in Internal Medicine, 1951. Appointments: Assistant Professor of Medicine, 1951, Associate Professor, 1953, Professor, 1957, Professor of Public Health, Department Chair, 1972-92, Livingston Farrand Professor of Public Health Emeritus, 1992-, Cornell University Medical College. Publications: The Student Physician (with Merton and Kendall); Comprehensive Medical Care (with Goss); Welfare Medical Care (with Goodrich and Olendsky); Editor, Milbank Memorial Fund Quarterly, Health and Society, 1973-76. Honours: Stockard Prize in Anatomy, 1941; Alpha Omega Alpha, 1942; Sigma Xi, 1947; DSc honoris causa, Drew University, 1988. Memberships: Senior Member, Institute of Medicine, 1985; American College of Physicians; American College of Preventive Medicine; New York Academy of Medicine, Vice-President 1980; American Sociological Association; American Public Health Association. Hobbies: Gardening; Fishing; Hiking. Address: 155 Stuyvesant Avenue, Rye, NY 10580, USA.

READING Anthony John, b. 10 Sep 1933, Sydney, Australia. Physician. m. Elisabeth Hoffman, 27 Jul 1975, 2 d. Education: MB; BS, University of Sydney, 1956; MPH, 1961, DSc, 1964, Johns Hopkins University. Career: Assistant Professor, 1968, Associate Professor, Johns Hopkins University; Currently, Professor and Chair, Department of Psychiatry, University of South Florida, Tampa. Publications: Psychiatry in Medicine, 136-144, in Principles and Practice of Medicine, 1972; Illness and Disease, in Medical Clinics of North America, 1977; Proprietary Chains in Academic Centers, in NEJM, 1985. Honour: Certificate of Merit, 1992. Memberships: AAAS; AMA; APA; American Psychosomatic Society. Hobby: Tennis. Address: University of South Florida, 3515 East Fletcher Avenue, Tampa, FL 33613, USA.

REALI Grazia, b. 2 Oct 1948, Riccione, Italy. Professor of Psychology of Writing; Specialist of Relaxation Techniques. m. Enzo Bernardini, 19 July 1970, 1 son, 1 daughter. Education: Degree, Literary Subjects, Urbino University, Italy, 1970. Appointments: Teacher, Literary Subjects, High School, 1971-89; Professor, Psychology of Writing, International University of New Medicine, Milan, 1988-. Publications: Mental Anorexy: A Clinical Case, 1991; Two Clinical Cases about Alcohol Addiction, 1992; A Fascinating Clinical Case about Possession, 1993. Memberships: Psychological Expert Witness, to the Court of Justice, Rimini, Italy, 1992; International Society for Medical & Psychological Hypnosis, New York, Milan; Theatine Academy of Sciences. Hobbies: Swimming; Skiing; Aerobics. Address: Via Mondaino 2, 47036 Riccione, Forli, Italy.

REBHUN Joseph, b. 10 July 1921, Poland. Physician. m. 8 Oct 1945, 2 sons, 1 daughter. Education: MD, Innsbruck, Austria; MS, Medicine, Northwestern University, Chicago, Illinois, USA. Appointments: Fellow, Instructor, Northwestern University Medical School, 1954; Assistant Clinical professor of Medicine, Loma Linda University, 1957-; Clinical Professor of Medicine, USC; Chief Allergy,, Chicago Eye Ear Nose and Throat Hospital, 1953-55; Chief Allergy, Letterman Army Hospital, 1955-57; Consultant: pacific State Hospital, Spadra, Pomona Valley Community Hospital, Pomona and Casa Colina Hospital, Pomona. Puboications: SOS The Cry of Democracy for Help; God and Man in Two Worlds; The Embers of Michael; Contributor of 44 articles in professional journals. Memberships: Fellow, American Academy of Allergy, Research Council, 1960-65; American College of Allergists; American Association for Clinical Immunology and Allergy; West Coast Allergy Society; California Allergy Association; Los Angeles Society of Allergy; Los Angeles Medical Association; California Medical Association. Address: 1481 Lafayette Road, Claremont, CA 91711, USA.

REDMAN Christopher Willard George, b. 30 Nov 1941, Pretoria, South Africa. Physician. m. Corinna Susan Page, 8 Aug 1964, 4 sons, 1 daughter. Education: MA, MB, BChir, Cambridge University; FRCP; FRCOG. Appointments: Lecturer, Regius Department of Medicine, Oxford University; Lecturer, Clinical Reader, Nuffield Department of Obstetrics and Gynaecology, Oxford University; Clinical Professor, Oxford University Medical School. Publications: Contributor of numerous papers on hypertension and other complications of pregnancy. Memberships: Fellow, Lady Margaret Hall, Oxford; Fellow, Royal College of Physicians; Fellow, Royal College of Surgeons. Hobby: Hill Walking. Address: Nuffield Department of Obstetrics and Gynaecology, John Radcliffe Hospital, Oxford OX3 4DU, England.

REDMAN Theodore Francis, b. 3 Mar 1916. Consultant Ostetrician and Gynaecologist. m. Jenanne Mary Houston Everett, 4 Jun 1955, 2 s, 1 d. Education: TD; MBChB; FRCSE; FRCOG. Career: Senior Lecturer in Obstetrics and Gynaecology, University of Bristol; Senior Clinical Lecturer in Obstetrics and Gynaecology, University of Leeds; Consultant Obstetrician and Gynaecologist, St James' University Hospital, Leeds, now retired. Publications: Lecture notes on midwifery. Honours: Territorial Decoration and Bar. Memberships: Royal College Obstetricians and Gynaecologists; Fothergill Club; North of England Obstetrical and Gynaecological Society. Hobbies: Opera; Travel. Address: 5 Mayo Close, Leeds LS8 2PX, England.

REES Margaret, b. 26 Jan 1951, London, England. Honorary Senior Clinical Lecturer in Obstetrics and Gynaecology. m. Russell Egdell, 16 Aug 1980, 1 son, 1 daughter. Education: MA; DPhil; MRCOG. Appointments: Parke Davis Fellow, 1984-93; MRC Training Fellow, 1979-83. Publications: On Menstruation, Endmetrial Function and the Menopause. Memberships: Endocrine Society; Society for the Study of Fertility; British Menopause Society. Address: Nuffield Department of Obstetrics & Gynaecology, John Radcliffe Hospital, Oxford OX3 9DU, England.

REES William James, b. 13 Jul 1922, Kansas City, MO, USA. Medicine. m. Marybeth Smith, 31 Jan 1950, 5 d. Education: BA; MD; MPH; Graduate US Army War College Courses, US Naval War College, US Marine Corps Institute. Career: Assistant Clinical Professor of Dermatology, University of San Francisco Medical Center; Director of International Clinical Medical Affairs, G D Searle and Co; Currently, President and Managing Director of RXHYS International Associates. Publication: Handbook of Regulations in European Countries for Clinical Investigational Studies of New Drugs and Food Additives, 3 volumes, 1971. Honour: Meritorious Service Medal, US Army, 1987. Memberships: Life Member, American Academy of Dermatology; AMA; American Academy of Medical Directors; American Academy of Clinical Toxicology; American Public Health Association; American Medical Society of Vienna. Hobbies: Photography; Philately; Railroadiana. Address: 550 Seamont Lane, Edmonds, WA 98020, USA.

REGAN David M, b. 5 May 1935, Scarborough, England. University Professor. m. Dr Marian P Regan, 14 Aug 1959, 2 sons. Education: DSc, PhD, MSc, BSc, Imperial College, London University, England. Career: Lecturer, Physics, London University, 1961-65; Reader, Department of Neuroscience & Communication, Keele University, England, 1964-75; Professor, Departments Ophthalmology & Medicine, Dalhousie University, Canada, 1975-85; Industrial Research Professor, York University Professor of Ophthalmology, University of Toronto, Canada, currently. Publications: Human Brain Electrophysiology, 1989; Binocular

Vision, 1991; Spatial Vision, 1991; 237 publications. Honours: DSc, 1974; Fellow, Royal Society of Canada, 1989; Prentice Medal, 1991; Killam Fellow, 1991; Killam Research Professor, 1978. Memberships: Association for Research in Vision & Ophthalmology; American Academy of Optometry; Optical Society of America. Hobbies: Cricket; Walking; Modern History. Address: 785 Cummer Avenue, North York, Ontario, Canada M2H 1E8.

REIBALDI Alfredo, b. 5 Apr 1942, Cerignola, Italy. Ophthalmologist. m. Finaguerra M Grazia, 11 Nov 1971, 1 s, 1 d. Education: Degree in Medicine, University of Rome, Italy, 1968; Specialist in Ophthalmology, University of Bari, Italy, 1972. Appointments: Assistant, University of Bari, Italy, 1976-82; Associated Professor, University of Bari, Italy, 1982-86; Ordinary Professor, Catania University, 1986-; Head of Institute of Ophthalmology, Catania University, 1986-. Publications: 480 Papers in different languages; One Book on Pharmacology of Glaucoma, 1990. Honours: Favaloro Prize, 1971; Motolese Prize, for Scientific Qualities, 1990. Memberships: SIEO; SCM; Ocular Pharmacology Study Association. Hobbies: Tennis; Skiing; Soccer. Address: Via Androna N 5, 95100 Catania, Italy.

REICHGOTT Michael J, b. 26 July 1940, Newark, New Jersey, USA. Professor of Medicine. m. Lynn Haar, 22 Dec 1962, 3 sons. Education: AB, Chemistry, Gettysburg College, 1961; MD, Albert Einstein College of Medicine, 1965; PhD, University of California, San Francisco, 1973; Intern, Resident, Internal Medicine, 1965-66, Fellow, Clinical Pharmacology, 1969-72, University of California, San Francisco. Appointments include: Associate Chief of Staff, Ambulatory Care, 1980-82, Chief, Section of General Internal Medicine, 1980-84, Philadelphia Veterans Administration Medical Center; Associate Professor, Medicine, Pharmacology, University of Pennsylvania School of Medicine, 1981-84; Adjunct Associate Professor, Pharmacy, Philadelphia College of Pharmacy and Sciences, 1982-84; Medical Director, Bronx Municipal Hospital Center, 1984-89; Associate Professor of Medicine, 1984-1994, Professor, 1994-, Assistant Dean, 1984-89, Associate Dean, 1989-, Albert Einstein College of Medicine. Publications include: Original papers and book chapters relating to hypertension; Several papers on administrative matters such as: Training for interprofessional collaboration in a VA mental hygiene clinic; CaseLog: Semantic Network Interface to a Student Computer-based Patients Record System, 1993. Honours include: Alpha Omega Alpha, 1965; Fellow, American College of Physicians, 1975; Fellow, Philadelphia College of Physicians, 1980; New York Academy of Medicine, 1991. Memberships: American Federation for Clinical Research; American Heart Association, Southeastern Pennsylvania; Society for Research and Education in Primary Care Medicine; American Association of Medical Directors; American Association of Medical Colleges; American Medical Association; Several committees. Address: 210 Belfer, 1300 Morris Park Avenue, Bronx, NY 10461, USA.

REID Lynne McArthur, b. 11 Nov 1923, Melbourne, Australia. Pathologist. Education: MB, BS, Melbourne, 1946; MRACP, 1950; MRCP, 1951; MRCPATH, 1964; FRACP, 1964; FRCPATH, 1966; FRCP, 1969; MD, Melbourne, 1969; MA, (Hon) Harvard College, 1975. Appointments Include: Junior, Senior Staff, Royal Melbourne Hospital, 1946-49; Junior, Senior Research Fellow, National Health & Medical Research Council, Royal Melbourne Hospital & Walter & Eliza Hall, 1949-51; Research Assistant, Institute of Diseases of the Chest, London University, 1951-55; Lecturer, Senior Lecturer, London University, 1964-67; Professor, Experimental Pathology, Cardio-thoracic Institute London University, 1967-76; Dean Cardio-thoracic Institute, London University, 1973-1976; Simon Burt Wolbach Professor of Pathology, Harvard Medical School, Boston, 1975-; Pathologist-in-Chief, Children's Hospital, Boston, 1976-1989; Pathologist-in-Chief, Emeritus, Children's Hospital, Boston, 1990-. Publications: Numerous scientific articles and chapters. Memberships Include: Royal College of Physicians; Royal Australian College of Physicians; Royal College of Pathologists; Thoracic Society; American Thoracic Society; Canadian Thoracic Society; Fleischner Society; Pathological Society of Great Britain & Ireland; American Pathological Society; United States & Canadian Academy of Pathology; American College of Chest Physicians; Perinatal Research Society; New England Pediatric Pathology Club. Honours Include: President Fleischner Society, 1977, President, Perinatal Research Society, 1987; Keynote Speaker, NIH Workshop, 1991; Honor Lecture, American College of Chest Physicians, Florida, 1993. Hobbies: Travel; Reading. Address: Harvard Medical School, Department of Pathology, Children's Hospital, 300 Longwood Avenue, Boston, MA 02115, USA.

REIFLER Burton Victor, b. 18 Jul 1944, Chicago, IL, USA. Psychiatrist. m. Frances Reifler, 18 Oct 1970, 1 s, 1 d. Education: BA; MD; MPH. Career: Instructor through to Associate Professor, Department of Psychiatry, University of Washington, Seattle, 1978-87; Professor and Chairman, Department of Psychiatry, Bowman Gray School of Medicine, Wake Forest University, 1987-. Contributions to: Co-author of: A clinic for the impaired elderly and their families, in American Journal of Psychiatry, 1980; Excess disability in demented elderly outpatients: the rule of halves, in Journal of American Geriatric Society, 1988; A National demonstration program on dementia day centers and respite services: an interim report, in Behavior, Health and Aging, 1992. Honours: Robert Wood Johnson Clinical Scholar, University of Washington, 1976-78; National Institute on Aging Visiting Research to Tokyo Metropolitan Institute of Gerontology, 1986; Leadership Award Winston-Salem, 1990-91. Memberships: American Psychiatric Association; Gerontology Society of America; International Psychogeriatric Association; American Geriatrics Society; AMA. Hobbies: Swimming; Golf. Address: Bowman Gray School of Medicine, Department of Psychiatry, Medical Center Boulevard, Winston-Salem, NC 27157-1087, USA.

REINHARDT-RUTLAND Anthony Hope, b. 13 Oct 1950, Reading, Berkshire, England. Lecturer. m. Frances Hanvey, 19 Jul 1980. Education: BSc, Edinburgh University, 1973; MSc, Bristol University, 1977; DPhil, Ulster University, 1987; AFBPsS; CPs. Appointments: Lecturer at Ulster Polytechnic; Currently, Lecturer in Psychology, University of Ulster. Publications: Over 100 articles published including: Perception, 1991; Approaches to Poor-Visability Road Accidents: Motivation and Perception, in Safety in Transportation, Delft University; Journal of General Psychology, 1992. Honours: Research Grants from various organizations including: Science and Engineering Council, UK, European Union. Memberships: British Psychological Society; Psychological Society of Ireland. Hobbies: Cycling; Railways; Orchestral Music. Address: Psychology Dept, University of Ulster, Shore Road, Newtownabbey, Northern Ireland, BT37 0QB.

REINISCH John, b. 7 Apr 1944, Holyoke, MA, USA. Surgeon. m. Nancy Dodge, 30 Jun 1990, 3 d. Education: AB; BS; MD, Harvard Medical School, 1970; FACS. Career: Assistant Professor, University of Missouri, 1978-82; Head of Division of Plastic Surgery at Children's Hospital, Los Angeles, 1983-; Chairman, Division of Plastic Surgery, University of Southern California, 1984-94. Memberships: American Society of Reconstruction Surgeons; American Association of Plastic Surgeons; American College of Surgeons. Hobbies: Skiing; Running; Photography. Address: 654 South Rimpau Boulevard, Los Angeles, CA 90005, USA.

REISS-SCHIMMEL Ilana, b. 16 Jan 1935, Haifa, Israel. Psychoanalyst. m. Dr F Schimmel, 19 Dec 1960, 1 son, 1 daughter. Education: DESS; DEAD; DPsy, University of Paris. Appointments: Psychoanalyst. Publications: La Psychanalyse et L'Argent; Ed Odile Jocub, Paris, 1983; Contributor of articles in professional journals. Memberships: Societe Psychoanalytique de Paris. Address: 134 rue d'Assas, Paris 75006, France.

REKERS George Alan, b. 11 Jul 1948, Waterloo, IA, USA. Clinical Psychology. m. Sharon Lee Chapin, 26 Aug 1972, 5 s. Education: BA, magna cum laude, Psychology, Westmont College, 1969; MA, 1971, CPhil, 1972, PhD, 1972, Psychology, University of California, Los Angeles; MDiv, Columbia International University. Career includes: Visiting Scholar and Research Fellow, Harvard University; Assistant Research Psychologist and Adjunct Assistant Professor, University of California, Los Angeles; Associate Professor and Chief Psychologist, Division of Child Psychiatry, University of Florida College of Medicine; Professor and Department Head, Kansas State University; Currently, Professor of Neuropsychiatry and Behavioral Science, University of South Carolina School of Medicine. Publications include: Over 100 scholarly and public service publications, 1971-92; Cross-Sex Problems in Primary Pediatric Care, 1991; Development of Problems in Puberty, in Handbook of Clinical Child Psychology, 1992; Handbook of Child and Adolescent Sexual Problems, 1994. Honours: Diplomate in Clinical Psychology, American Board of Professional Psychology, 1979; Diplomate and Fellow in Medical Psychotherapy, American Board of Medical Psychotherapists, 1987; Fellow, Academy of Clinical Psychology, 1993. Memberships: American Psychological Society. Hobbies: Racquetball; Piano. Address: Department of Neuropsychiatry and Behavioral Science, University of South Carolina School of Medicine, 3555 Harden Street Extension, Columbia, SC 29203, USA.

RELACION José, b. 21 May 1929, Libon, Albay, Philippines. Obstetrician and Gynaecologist. m. Eugenia Querol, 13 Sept 1953, 2 sons, 1 daughter. Education: AA, 1950, BS, 1955, MD, 1959, University of the Philippines. Appointments: Resident, Instructor to Professor of Obstetrics and Gynaecology; Administrator, Maternity Center, Manila; Budget Director; Chief of Professional Services; Vice-President for Administration; Currently: President, Hospital Director, Medical Center Manila; President, MASEAN Obstetrics-Gynaecology; Trustee, Yaman Lahi Foundation Inc, House of Knowledge; Executive Secretary, Metro-Manila Health Science Commission; Consultant in Obstetrics and Gynaecology. Publications: Enzymes of Normal and Malignant Trophoblast, 1975; Delineation of Function, 1984; Obstetric Care in the Philippines, 1985; Adolescent Pregnancy in the Philippines, 1985; Ethical Issues in OB-Gyn, 1994. Honours: University of the Philippines Medical Alumni, 1984; Distinguished Service Award, University Physicians Services, 1987. Memberships: President-Elect, Asia Oceanic Federation of Obstetrics and Gynaecology; Fellow, Philippine Obstetrics and Gynaecology Society; Philippine College of Surgeons; American College of Surgeons; International College of Surgeons; American Fertility Society; Philippine Society of Endocrinology and Metabolism. Hobbies: Biking; Swimming. Address: 47 Gen Malvar, Bgy San Antonio, Pasig, Metro Manila, Philippines.

REMIS Robert S, b. 17 Nov 1948, Winnipeg, Canada. 1 son. Education: MD; MPH; FRCPC. Appointments: Epidemic Intelligence Service Officer, Centers for Disease Control, Atlanta, 1981-83. Publications incl: Report on the health and health services of Quebec Indians, 1975; Improvisation of medical equipment in developing countries, 1983; Outbreaks of hemorrhagic colitis associated with a rare Escherichia Coli Sterotype, 1983; Laboratory investigation of hemorrhagic colitis outbreaks associated with a rare Escherichia Sterotype, 1983; The epidemiology of heterosexually acquired HIV infection and AIDS in Western industrialized countries, 1994. Honour: University Scholarship, 1966, 1967. Memberships: Canadian Public Health Association; American Public Health Association. Hobbies: Travel; Photography; Model Gliders. Address: 4145 Marcil Avenue, Montreal, Quebec H4A 2Z7, Canada.

REMUZZI Giuseppe, b. 3 Apr 1949, Italy. Medical Doctor. m. Nadia Ghisalberti, 3 Apr 1993, 2 sons, 1 daughter. Education: MD, 1974; Specialisation in Lab & Clin Hematology; Specialisation in Clin Nephrology, 1980. Appointments: Research Fellow, Cell Biology Laboratory, Institute of Animal Phys, Cambridge, England; Research Fellow, Clinical Science Laboratory, Guy's Hospital, London, England; Consultant Nephrologist, Mario Negri Institute of Pharm, Res, Milan, Italy; Head, Laboratory of Kidney Diseases, Negri Bergamo Laboratories, Italy. Publications: 400 papers in nephrology journals; 4 books: Hemostasis, Prostaglandins and Renal Disease, 1980; Glomerular Injury: 300 years after Morgangi, 1983; Drugs and Kidney; Haemostasis and the Kidney, 1989. Memberships: International Society of Nephrology; American Society of Nephrology; Italian Society of Nephrology; International Advisory Board of the International Nephrology Research & Training Center, Hungary; International Registry for HUS, Milan; Society of Italian-American Society of Nephrology. Address: Negri Bergamo Laboratories, Via Gavazzeni 11, 24125 Bergamo, Italy.

REN Ming Zhong, b. 4 December 1940, Shanghai, China. Doctor. Education: Graduated, Medical Faculty of Tianjin Medical University, 1963. Appointments: Resident Doctor; Attending Doctor; Lecturer; Assistant Professor; Professor. Publications: On Schwannoma of the head and neck region, 1988; Anatomic research relative to retrosigmoid-internal auditory canal approach operation, 1992; Retrosigmoid-internal auditory canal approach operation, 1993. Honours: Award, Advance of Science and Technology, Tianjin, 1993; Government Special Subsidy for Outstanding Achievements, 1993. Hobbies: Travel; Social Dancing. Address: 132 Ma Chang Road, 3rd Hospital of Tianjin Medical University, Tianjin, China.

REN Pei-xian, b. 25 Feb 1933, Shanghai, China. Ophthalmologist. m. 26 Dec 1954, 2 sons. Education: MD, Shanghai Medical University, 1955. Appointments: Assistant, 1955, Lecturer, 1986, Associate Professor, 1988, Professor of Ophthalmology, 1991-, Shanxi Medical College, Taiyuan. Publications: Subretinal neovescular membrane in senile macular degeneration, 1990; Experimental autoimmune uveitis - A clinical and pathological study, 1992; Cellular immunoreaction to S-antigen in patients of uveitis and neuritis, 1993; Experimental retinal photic injury, 1994. Honours: Lifelong Government Special Scientific Allowance, 1993-; Editor, Chinese Journal of Ophthamology; Editor,

Chinese Journal of Ocular Fundus Diseases. Memberships: Chinese Medical Association; Committee Member, Shanxi Ophthalmology Branch, Chinese Medical Association. Hobbies: Classical music; Reading novels; Travel. Address: 1st Teaching Hospital, Shanxi Medical College, Taiyuan 030001, Shanxi, China.

REN Shou-zhong, b. 7 Nov 1918, Liaoyang, Liaoning, China. Professor of Acupuncture. m. Lee Qi Fang, 10 Aug 1946, 2 sons. Education: BM, National Kweiyang Medical University, 1944. Appointments include: Chief Physician, Department of Acupuncture, Beijing Children's Hospital, 1955-89; Professor of Medicine, Capital Institute of Medicine, China, 1986-; Professor of Acupuncture, Australian Medical Acupuncture Training Centre, Cairns, Queensland, 1990-. Publications: Pediatric Acupuncture, 1985; Medical Acupuncture - Acupuncture, Laser Acupuncture, 1995. Honours: Famous Specialist of Acupuncture; Prize for Scientific Achievement, Beijing Bureau of Health. Memberships: Standing Governor, All-China Acupuncture Society; Standing Governor, Beijing Acupuncture Society. Hobbies: Playing table-tennis. Address: 12th Floor, National Mutual Tower, 15 Lake Street, PO Box 6711, Cairns, Queensland, Australia.

REN Xue Dao, b. 12 Feb 1943, Le Ning County, Henan Province, China. Medicine. m. Qiu Yu Li, 26 Dec 1968, 1 s, 1 d. Education: Graduated Xian Health School, 1965. Career includes: Director, Department of Coloproctology, Visiting Physician, 1984-90, President, Vice Chief Physician, 1990-, Affiliated Hospital of Shaanxi Academy of Traditional Chinese Medicine; Adviser of Coloproctology Center, Takano Hospital, Japan. Publications: Co-author, Chinese Coloproctology, 1989; Editor in Chief, Chinese Complete Works of Anal Fistula, 1993; Research articles published in China and presented at national and international scientific conferences. Honours: Grade A Prize of Scientific and Technical Achievement, Chinese Public Health Ministry, 1980; Grade B Prize, Chinese Public Health Ministry, 1982; Grade B Prize, National Scientific and Technical Advanced Prize, Chinese Scientific and Technical Committee, 1985; Golden Prize, International Fair of Invention and Creation, Yugoslavia, 1986. Memberships: Councillor, Chinese Society of Coloproctology; Vice Director, Secretary, Chinese South West Sectional Association of Coloproctology; President, Shaanxi Society of Coloproctology; Editorial Board of Chinese Journal of Coloproctology. Hobby: Chinese Chess. Address: Shaanxi Academy of Traditional Chinese Medicine, 20 Xi Hua Men, Xi'An, Shaanxi Province, 710003, China.

REN Zhi Dong, b. 12 December 1928, Shandong, China. Doctor. m. Li Gui Xiang, 23 November 1947, 2 sons, 1 daughter. Appointments: Assistant Doctor, 1953; Chief Doctor of Chinese Medicine, 1978; Associate Senior Physician of Chinese Medicine, 1988. Publications: Chinese Medicine Experimental Conference of Tong Gu, 1980; The Treatment of using retention of Senible Hypertriopty of Prostate. Memberships: Tianjin Chinese Medicine Institute. Address: Hong Zhou Pao Section Hospital, Tang Gu District, Tianjin, China.

RERAT Alain André, b. 16 July 1926, Nancy, France. Researcher. m. Kirsten Halsteen, 20 Apr 1957, 2 daughters. Education: Diploma, Ecole Nationale Vétérinaire d'Alfort, 1949; DVM, Paris, 1951; Lic és sciences, Paris, 1955; DSc, Paris, 1960. Appointments: Head, Station de Recherches sur l'Elevage des Porcs, INRA, 1962-72; Head, Centre National de Recherches Zootechniques, INRA, 1970-72; Head, Department of Nutrition, INRA, 1972-84; Head, Laboratoire de Physiologie de la Nutrition, INRA, 1972-89; Head, Centre de Recherches sur la Nutrition, Centre National de Recherche Scientifique, 1972-82; Director of Research Emérite á l'INRA, 1993-; Vice President, IUNS, 1989-; Member, Superior Council of Public Hygiene in France, 1992-. Publications: Digestive Physiology in the Pig, Co-editor, 1982; Le Porc et son Elevage, Co-editor, 1986; Biotechnology of Control of Growth and Product Quality in Swine, Co-editor, 1989; Intestinal Flora, Immunity, Nutrition and Health, Co-editor, 1993; Production Alimentaire Mondiale et Environnement, Author, 1994. Honours include: Member, Royal Academy of Veterinary Sciences, Madrid, 1979; Member, Académie Veterinaire de France, 1980; Member, Académie d'Agriculture de France, 1983; Member, Académie Nationale de Médecine, 1987; Chevalier de la Légion d'Honneur, 1980; Officier du Mérite Agricole, 1980I Officier de Mérite National, 1988; Prix Fondation Française pour la Nutrition, France, 1988; FAO Distinction, 1992; Distinguished Services Award, European Association Animal Production, 1994. Memberships include: American Society for Animal Science; French Society of Physiologists. Address: CRJ-INRA, Domaine de Vilvert, 78352 Jouy-en-Josas, Cedex, France.

RESCALDINI Giuseppe, b. 10 Oct 1957, Magenta, Milan, Italy. Psychologist. m. Nadia Scioscia, 29 Oct 1983, 1 daughter. Education: Degree in Psychology, University of Padova; Specialist in Psychosomatic Medicine and Psychotherapy. Appointments: Psychologist, Drug Addiction Department, 1981-93, Psychologist, Obstetrical and Gynaecological Department, 1983-87, Magenta Hospital, Magenta; Currently: Freelance Professional; Chief, Psychological Service, Centro Studi Coppia; Lecturer in Psychomatic Medicine, International University of New Medicine, Milan. Publications: Analisi psicosociale dell'isterectomia, 1984; Dubbi e paure della contraccezione in rapporte con la richiesta de IUG, 1985; Peter Pan, Edipo e gli Altri, 1994. Hobby: Scuba diving. Address: V Ticino 28/A, 20010 S Stefano T (MI), Italy.

RESKE-NIELSEN Edith, b. 24 Apr 1918, Tranekaer, Denmark. Neuropathologist. m. Erik Reske-Nielsen, 22 Oct 1943, 2 sons, 1 daughter. Education: MD, University of Copenhagen, 1947; MD, Aarhus University, 1961. Appointments: Resident, Radiology, Copenhagen, Aarhus, 1948-53; Resident, Aarhus, 1953-56, 1959-63; Scientific Assistant, Institute of Pathology, Aarhus University, 1956-59; Head, Department of Neuropathology, Aarhus University Hospital, 1962-88; Assistant Professor, 1967-88. Publications: Neurological and neuromuscular changes in mice with transplanted reticulosarcom, 1961; Articles on Normal Muscle, Muscular and Neuromuscular Diseases, Malignant Hyperthermia, Inherited Brain Diseases, Astrocytes in Normal Fetuses. Honours: Prize, Faculty of Medicine, Aarhus University, 1963; Tagea Brandt Travel Prize, 1976. Memberships: Scand Society of Neuropathology; World Commission on Muscular Diseases; British Neuropathology Society; International Society of Neuropathology. Hobbies: Gardening; Travel. Address: Joenhoejvej 4, DK-8230 Aabyhoej, Denmark.

RETCHIN Sheldon Michael, b. 2 Apr 1950, Charlotte, North Carolina, USA. Physician. m. Tracy Fields, 16 June 1989, 1 daughter. Education: BA, University of North Carolina, 1972; MD, University of North Carolina School of Medicine, 1976; MSPH, University of North Carolina School of Public Health, 1982. Appointments include: Instructor, 1979-80, Chairman, Division of Geriatric Medicine, 1986-93, Assistant Professor of Medicine, Department of Internal Medicine, 1986-, Research Associate, Williamson Institute for Health Studies, 1987-, Associate Professor, Department of Gerontology, 1987-93, Associate Professor, Health Administration, 1992-93; Professor, Gerontology, Health Administration, Internal Medicine, 1993-, Virginia Commonwealth University/Medical College of Virginia, Richmond; Director of Ambulatory Care, 1982-86, Clinical Assistant Professor, School of Public Health, 1982-86, Assistant Professor of Medicine, School of Medicine, 1982-86, Research Associate, Health Services Research Center, 1984-86, University of North Carolina, Chapel Hill; President, MCV Associated Physicians, Richmond, 1993-. Publications include: Co-author: The impact of echocardiographic results on treatment decisions for patients suspected of mitral valve prolapse, 1987; The management of geriatric hypertension in health maintenance organizations, 1991; Medical Considerations in the Older Driver (editor), 1993. Honours: Elected Fellow, American College of Physicians, 1991. Memberships include: Medical Society of Virginia; Richmond Academy of Medicine; American College of Physicians Health Care Executives; Gerontological Society of America. Address: MCV Associated Physicians, PO Box 980270, Richmond, VA 23298-0270, USA.

RETNAKARAN Arthur, b. 28 Aug 1934, Trichy, India. Entomologist. m. Sarsi Retnakaran, 25 Apr 1961, 1 son, 1 daughter. Education: MSc, Zoology; MS, Entomology; PhD, Insect Physiology; Postdoctoral Fellow, 1967-68. Appointments: Lecturer in Zoology, 1955-58; Professor of Zoology, 1958-62; Research Scientist, 1968-. Publications: Benzoylureas, 1986; Physiology of the Insect Epidermis, 1992. Honours: Fulbright Fellow, 1962; Visiting Professor, University of Louis Pasteur, Strasbourg, France, 1974; Visiting Scientist, Council of Scientific and Industrial Research, Canberra, Australia, 1982. Memberships: American Entomological Society; Canadian Entomological Society. Hobbies: Cross-country skiing; Travel. Address: Forest Pest Management Institute, 1219 Queen Street E, Sault Ste Marie, Ontario, Canada P6A 4X2.

REVELEY Ted, b. 10 Apr 1944, Camden, AR, USA. Psychiatrist. m. Suzanne Marie Smith, 28 Feb 1984, 1 s, 2 d. Education: BS, Hendrix College, 1966; MD, Tulane University, 1970. Career: Medical Director, Outpatient Psychiatry Clinic, Tulane Medical Center, 1988-94; Currently: Associate Clinical Professor of Psychiatry, LSU School of Medicine and

Tulane University School of Medicine; Training and Supervising Analyst, New Orleans Psychoanalytic Institute. Honours: Bick Psychiatry Award, 1970; Outstanding Teaching Award, Tulane Department of Psychiatry, 1989. Memberships: Affiliate, Center for Advanced Psychoanalytic Studies, Princeton; Affiliate, Psychoanalytic Studies, Aspen; American Psychiatric Association; American Psychoanalytic Association. Address: 3525 Prytania Street, Suite 514, New Orleans, LA 70115, USA.

REVES Joseph Gerald, b. 14 Aug 1943, Charleston, South Carolina, USA. Physician. m. Virginia Cathcart, 1 Sept 1968, 3 daughters. Education: NA; MS; MD. Appointments: Currently Professor of Anaesthesiology, Chairman, Director, Duke Heart Center, Durham, North Carolina. Publications: Common Problems in Cardiac Anesthesia, 1986; Intravenous Anesthesia and Analgesia, 1987; Cardiac Anesthesia - Principles and Practice, 1994. Honours: Alpha Omega Alpha; Sigma Xi; President, Society of Cardiac Anesthesiologists; Board of Directors, International Anesthesiology Research Society. Memberships: American Medical Association; Society of Cardiovascular Anesthesiology; American Society of Anesthesiology. Hobbies: Tennis; Sailing. Address: Box 3094, Duke University Medical Center, Durham, NC 27710, USA.

REVILLA AVALOS José, b. 24 Sept 1932, Lima, Peru. Physician. m. Gloria Cárdenas Gereda, 13 Mar 1965, 4 sons, 2 daughters. Education: MD; Internist, 1988. Appointments: Medical Doctor, 1963; Auxiliary Professor, 1976; Associate Professor, Faculty of Medicine, Universidad Nacional Mayor de San Marcos, Lima,1981-. Publications: Rheumatoid Arthritis in Inca-Peru, 1968; Ergometry in Service of Cardiology of Universidad Nacional Mayor de San Marcos, 1989; Medicinal and Nutritive Plants of Selva, in press. Honours: Correlative Member, Chilean Society of Rheumatology, 1968. Memberships: Peruvian Society of Rheumatology; Chilean Society of Rheumatology. Hobbies: Reading; Going to the beaches and to Selva. Address: Universidad Nacional Mayor de San Marcos, Faculty of Medicine, Apartado 529, Lima 1, Peru.

REYCHLER Herve Paul Marie, b. 28 Nov 1949, Bruges, Belgium. University Professor. m. Claeys Yvette, 17 Aug 1974, 2 sons. Education: MD, 1974; BDS, 1975; DMD, 1978; Oral & Maxillofacial Surgeon, 1979. Appointments: Professor, Faculté Medecine UCL; Head, Department of Stomatology & Maxillofacial Surgery. Publications: Traité De Pathologies Burrale Et Maxillofaciale, 1991. Memberships include: European Association of Maxillofacial Surgery. Hobbies: Tennis; Windsurfing. Address: Maxillofacial Surgery Unit, University Clinic St Luc, 15 Avenue Hippocrate, B-1200 Brussels.

REYNOLDS Herbert Young, b. 20 Aug 1939, Richmond, Virginia, USA. Medicine. m. Anne B Leavell, 11 July 1964, 2 sons, 1 daughter. Education: BA, MD, University Virginia, 1961, 1965; MA, Yale University, 1979. Appointments incl: Assistant Physician, Fellow in Medicine, The New York Hospital, Cornell Medical Center, 1966-67; Professor, Internal Medicine, Head, Pulmonary Section, Department of Internal Medicine, yale University School of Medicine, 1979-88; J Lloyd Huck Professor of Medicine, Chairman, Department of Medicine, Pennsylvania University, Milton S Hershey Medical Center, 1988-. Publications incl: Chronic Bronchitis and Acute Infectious Exacerbations. in Principles and Practice of Infectious Diseases, 1994; Diffuse Interstitial and Alveolar Inflammatory Diseases in Chest Medicine: Essentials of Pulmonary and Critical Care Medicine, 1994; Pulmonary Host Defense. Alcoholism: Clinical and Experimental Research, 1994. Honours incl: Sigma Xi, 1965; John Edward Nobel Fellowship, 1961-65; Fellow, Saybrook College, Yale University, 1984-88; Outstanding Medical Specialists in the US, 1989. Memberships: All Saints Episcopal Church, Hershey; Hershey Country Club; Pennsylvania Farmington Country Club. Hobbies: Tennis; Music; Violin. Address: 226E Caracas Avenue, Hershey, PA 17033, USA.

RHAME Frank Scorgia, b. 11 Sept 1942, Pittsburgh, USA. Physician. m. Betsey Clark Ingraham, 30 May 1966, 2 daughters. Education: MD, Columbia University, 1968. Appointments: Staff Physician, Veterans Administration Hospital, 1975-79; Assistant Professor, University Minnesota, 1980-92; Associate Professor, Division of Infectious Diseases, Department of Medicine, School of Medicine & Division of Epidemiology, School of Public Health. Publications: AIDS: Testing and Privacy, 1989; A Look Back Investigation of Patients of an HIV-Infected Physician, 1991. Honours: Alexander D Langmuir Prize, 1972; Best Manuscript of the Year, Epidemic Intelligence Service. Memberships: Fellow, Infectious Diseases Society of America; Fellow, American College of Epidemiology; Society of Health Care Epidemiology of America; Physicians for AIDS Care; Association for Practitioners in

Infection Control; International AIDS Society; American Society for Microbiology. Hobby: Running. Address: Box 421 UMHC, Minneapolis, MN 55455, USA.

RHOADS George Grant, b. 2 Nov 1940, Philadelphia, USA. Medical Epidemiologist. m. Frances, 6 May 1965, 2 sons. Education: BA, Haverford College, 1961; MD, Harvard University, 1965; MPH, University Hawaii,1970. Appointments: Associate Professor, Professor, Public Health, University Hawaii, 1974-82; Chief, Epidemiology Branch, National Institute of Child Health, NIH, 1982-89; Professor, Director, New Jersey Graduate Program in Public Health. Publications: More than 120 journal articles on Epidemiology of Non-infectious Diseases. Honours: Director's Award, National Institutes of Health, 1987. Memberships: Society for Epidemiologic Research; American Epidemiological Association; American Public Health Association; International Epidemiological Association. Address: UMDNJ-Robert Wood Johnson Medical School, Environmental & Occupational Health Sciences Institute, 681 Frelinghuysen Road, Piscataway, NJ 08855-1179, USA.

RHOADS Jonathan Evans, b. 9 May 1907, Philadelphia, Pennsylvania, USA. Professor of Surgery. m. (1) Teresa Folin, 4 July 1936, 5 sons, 1 daughter, (2) Katharine Goddard, 13 Oct 1990. Education: BS, Haverford College, 1928; MD, Johns Hopkins School of Medicine, 1932; DScMed, University of Pennsylvania, 1940; Intern, Resident, University of Pennsylvania Hospital, 1932-39. Appointments: Assistant Instructor to Professor of Surgery, 1934-49, J Wm White Professor of Surgical Research, 1949-51, Provost, 1956-59, John Rhea Barton Professor of Surgery, Chairman, Department of Surgery, 1959-72, Provost Emeritus, 1977, University of Pennsylvania; Director, Department of Surgery, Pennsylvania Hospital, 1972-74. Publications: Surgery: Principles and Practice, 4th Edition (with J G Allen, H N Harkins, C A Moyer), 1970; Physiologic Factors Regulating the Level of the Plasma Prothrombin, 1940; Co-author: The Use of Diuretics as an Adjunct in Parenteral Hyperalimentation for Surgical Patients with Prolonged Disability of Gastrointestinal Tract, 1965; Can Intravenous Feeding as the Sole Means of Nutrition Support Growth of the Child and Restore Weight in an Adult? - An Affirmative Answer, 1969. Honours: Honorary degrees: LLD, DSc (5), DMedSci (3), MA, DLitt; Foreign Fellowships; Distinguished Service Medals; College of Physicians of Philadelphia; American Trauma Society; American Surgical Association; Philadelphia Award; Benjamin Franklin Medal, American Philosophical Society; Prix de la Société Internationale de Chirurgie. Memberships: Phi Beta Kappa; Ampha Omega Alpha; Sigma Xi; Philadelphia Academy of Surgery; College of Physicians of Philadelphia; American College of Surgeons; American Surgical Association; American Philosophical Society; Institute of Medicine. Address: 3400 Spruce Street, Philadelphia, PA 19104, USA.

RHODES Philip, b. 2 May 1922, Sheffield, England. Dean. m. Elizabeth Worley, 26 Oct 1946, 3 s, 2 d. Education: Clare College, Cambridge; St Thomas' Hospital Medical School; MA; MB B Chir (Cantab); FRCS(Eng); FRCOG; FRACMA; FFOM(RCP); FRSA. Career: Obstetric Physician; Professor of Gynaecology; Dean, all three departments, St Thomas' Hospital; Dean, Faculty Medicine, University of Adelaide; PG Dean, Newcastle upon Tyne; PG Dean, University of Southampton, now retired. Publications: Fluid Balance in Obstetrics, 1960; An Introduction to Obstetrics and Gynaecology, 1967; Woman: A Biological Study, 1969; Reproductive Physiology for Medical Students, 1969; The Value of Medicine, 1976; Doctor John Leake's Hospital, 1977; Letters to a Young Doctor, 1983; An Outline History of Medicine, 1985; A Short History of Clinical Midwifery, 1995. Honour: Brontë Society Prize, 1974. Membership: British Medical Association. Hobbies: Photography; Writing; Reading. Address: 1 Wakerley Court, Wakerley, Oakham, Leicestershire, LE15 8PA, England.

RHODES Robert Shaw, b. 3 Mar 1936. Medicine. m. Gwendolun Malone, 1 Feb, 1 son, 4 daughters. Education: MD; MPH. Appointment: Regional Director of Health Services. Hobbies: Golf; Tennis. Address: 2615 Walden Avenue, Cheektowaga, NY, USA.

RHYS William Joseph St Ervyl-Glyndwr, b. 6 July 1924, Newport, Gwent, Wales. Retired Consultant Physician. m. Dr Ann Rees, 29 April 1961, 6 daughters, 1 son. Education: BSc 1945, DPH 1966, University of Wales; MB, BS, Guy's Hospital, London University, 1948; MA, St John's College, Cambridge University, 1950; MRCOG, 1961; MFCM, RCP, UK, 1974. Appointments: Squadron Leader, RAF Institute of Aviation Medicine, University Demonstrator, Cambridge, 1949-54; Hs Surgeon, Registrar, Senior Registrar, Consultant, Obstetrics &

Gynaecology. including Royal Postgraduate Medical School, London, Welsh National School of Medicine, Cardiff, Welsh Hospital Board, 1954-63; Assistant MOH, Glamorgan, 1964-66; MOH, Cardiganshire, 1966-74; Consultant Physician, Community Medicine, Dyfed, 1974-82; Honorary Medical Adviser,Welsh National Water Authority, 1966-82; Honorary Chairman of Medical Services, Royal National Eisteddfod of Wales, 1976, 1984, 1992. Publications: Papers on High Altitude Flying, Medical History, Obstetrical and Public Health Topics. Honours: Lord of the Barony of Llawhaden, Lord of the Manor of Llanfynydd (Celtic, Pre-Norman); High Sheriff County of Dyfed, 1979; Honorary Member, White Robe, Gorsedd of Bards of Wales, 1986; Commander, Most Venerable Order of St John of Jerusalem, 1987; Freeman, City of London, 1987; Liveryman, Worshipful Society of Apothecaries, 1990. Memberships: Cambridge University Representative, Council of University Colleges Wales, 1979-86; Chairman, Trustees, St John's College, Dyfed; Commissioner, St John's Ambulance, Ceredigion; President, Scout Association, Ceredigion; Chairman, Hospitallers Club, Dyfed; Chairman, Governors Ceredigion Schools; Trustee, The Two Red Dragons Education Trust, Wales and Japan; Executive Committee, Association of Friends of National Liberty of Wales; RAF Club; Shrievalty Association; International Society for the History of Medicine. Hobbies: Swimming; Celtic History; Poetry; Musing in Churchyards. Address: Plas Bronmeurig, Ystrad Meurig, Dyfed, Wales.

RIBER Charlotte, b. Denmark. Chiropractor. m. Lars Erik Nielsen, 1 son, 1 daughter. Education: Doctor of Chiropractic. Appointment: Chiropractor, Private Practice. Publications: Take Care of Your Child's Back; Skan bit Barns Ryg. Memberships: Junior Chamber, Svendborg. Hobbies: Sailing; Swimming. Address: Centrumpladseen 21 1, Svendborg 5700, Denmark.

RIBON Arie, b. 14 Sept 1930, Bucharest, Romania. Medical Doctor. m. Marsha Goldstein, 10 Sept 1967. Education: MD, Bucharest, Romania, 1954. Appointments: Associate, Flower & Fifth Avenue Hospital, New York Medical College, 1967-79; Assistant, Associate Professor, Clinical Pediatrics, New York Medical College, 1967-81; Chief, Allergy & Immunology Section, Director, Allergy & Immunology Training Program, New York Medical College, 1969-81; Chief, Pediatric Allergy Clinic, Metropolitan Hospital Center, 1969-81; Chief, Pediatric Allergy Clinic, Lincoln Hospital Center, 1979-81. Publications: Bronchial Asthma in Children and its Occurrence in Relation to Weather and Air Pollution, 1972; Chapter, Pediatric Allergy, Survey of Clinical Pediatrics, 1974; Immunodeficiency with Congenital Rubella, 1974; Immunodeficiency with Ataxia-Telangiectasia, 1975; Air Pollution: Its Effects on Health and Respiratory Disease - A Review, 1977; Standardization of Allergenic Extracts, 1978; Drug Induced Asthma, 1980; Is There Any Relationship Between Food Additives and Hyperkinesis?, 1982. Honours: American Medical Association Physician's Recognition Award; American Academy of Human Services Outstanding Professional in Human Services. Memberships include: Fellow, American Academy of Allergy, 1967-85; Fellow, American College of Allergists; Fellow, American Association for Clinical Immunology & Allergy; Executive Committee, New York Allergy Society, 1975-77. Hobbies: Art History; Classical Music; Swimming; Travel. Address: 305E 86th St, Apt 9N-West, NY 10028, USA.

RICHARD Norman B, b. 16 Mar 1926, NJ, USA. Medicine. m. Rachel D Richard, 12 Jul 1981, 2 s, 3 d. Education: MD. Career: President, Buffalo Allergy Society; President, Buffalo Pediatric Society; Currently, Assistant Clinical Professor, State University of New York, School of Medicine; Private Practice. Contributions to: Journal of Allergy, 1956. Memberships: Fellow, American Acadmey of Allergy; Fellow, American College of Allergy; Fellow, American Association of Certified Allergists. Hobbies: Tennis; Travel; Theatre. Address: 1077 Delaware Road, Buffalo, NY 14223-1099, USA.

RICHARD William Wilson Jr, b. 22 Oct 1941, St Louis, MO, USA. Psychiatrist. m. Maribeth Conley, 14 Sept 1969, 1 d. Education: BS, University of California, Berkeley; MD, University of California Medical School; Intern, Los Angeles General Hospital; Psychiatric Residency, University of California at Los Angeles, Neuro Psychiatric Institute; Board Certified in Psychiatry. Appointments: Director, Area Division of Behavioral Health, Alaska Area Native Health Service, Anchorage, Alaska. Publications: Numerous articles on Rural Mental Health, Fetal Alcohol Syndrome, Alaska-Russian Far East Mental Health Exchange Projects. Honours: Fellow, American Psychiatric Association. Memberships: Group for Advancement of Psychiatry; American College of Psychiatry; American Psychitric Association. Hobbies: Aerobics;

Weight Lifting. Address: A-DBH Alaska Area Native Health Service, 250 Gambell Street, Anchorage 99501, AK, USA.

RICHARDSON David Ian, b. 16 Jan 1962, Hastings, England. Osteopath. Education: BSc, Honours; Diploma in Osteopathy. Appointment: Registered Osteopath. Memberships: General Council and Register of Members of Osteopaths. Hobbies: Wind Surfing; Surfing; Hockey. Address: 4 Station Road, Keynsham, Bristol, BS18 2BN, England.

RICHARDSON Robert Edward, b. 4 Apr 1959, Lincoln, England. Doctor. m. D L Shier, 13 Sept 1987, 1 son, 1 daughter. Education: BSc, Hons, Pharmacology, Leeds; MBBS, London; MRCOG. Appointments: Research Registrar, Royal Free Hospital, London; Senior Registrar, Obstetrics & Gynaecology, Chelsea & Westminster. Publications: Is Laparoscopic Hysterectomy A Waste of Time?, 1995. Hobby: Fly Fishing. Address: 10 St Pauls Road, Islington, London, N1 2QN, England.

RICHTER Derek, b. 14 Jan 1907, Bath, England. Psychiatric Research; Writer. m. (1) Beryl A Griffiths, 27 Dec 1937, (2) Winifred M Hoskin, 18 Nov 1953, 1 s, 2 d. Education: MA; BSc (Oxon), 1930; PhD (Munich), 1932; MRCS; MRCP(London), 1965. Career: Biochemical Laboratory, Cambridge, 1933-37; Maudsley Hospital, London, 1938; Mill Hill Emergency Hospital, 1939; Addenbrookes Hospital, Cambridge, 1945; Whitchurch Hospital, Cardiff, 1946; Director, MRC, Neuropsychiatric Research Unit, Carshalton and Epsom, Surrey, 1959-72; Currently, Writer. Publications: Perspectives in Neuropsychiatry, 1950; Schizophrenia Somatic Aspects, 1957; Metabolism of the Nervous System, 1957; Comparative Neurochemistry, 1964; Aspects of Learning and Memory, 1966; The Challenge of Violence, 1972; Addiction and Brain Damage, 1981; Women Scientists, 1982; Research in Mental Illness, 1984; Life in Research, 1989; English Usage Guide, 1992. Honours: Honorary Consultant, West Park Hospital, 1960; Honorary FRCP, 1980; Honorary FRC Psych, 1993. Memberships: Former Trustee of Mental Health Foundation; Former Secretary General of IBRO. Hobbies: Gardening; Writing. Address: Deans Cottage, Walton on the Hill, Surrey, KT20 7TT, England.

RIEDESEL William M, b. 4 May 1946, Denver, CO, USA. Psychiatrist. Education: MD, Cornell University; Certified in Psychiatry and Addiction Psychiatry, American Board of Psychiatry. Appointment: Associate Clinical Professor Psychiatry, Washington University, St Louis; Certified in Psychiatry, Addiction and Forensic Psychiatry. Memberships: American Psychiatric Association; American Academy of Psychiatry and The Law. Hobbies: Travel; Music; Art Collecting. Address: 7165 Kingsbury Boulevard, St Louis, MO 63130-4307, USA.

RIEGNER Elizabeth Jane, b. 3 Sept 1944, West Reading, USA. Therapist; Nurse. 3 sons. Education: RN, Methodist Hospital, Philadelphia, 1966; BSEd, Millersville University, 1968; MS, West Chester University, 1977; PhD, 1993. Appointments: Instructor, Reading Hospital School of Nursing; Nurse Specialist, Wilmington Medical Center; Pediatric RN, Jameston, New York; Therapist; Hospice Nurse; Psychiatric Nurse, Florida; Nurse Consultant. Publications: Several professional articles to scientific journals. Memberships incl: American Mental Health Association; Association of Play Therapy. Address: 3954 S Nova Road, Ste 5, Port Orange, FL 32125, USA.

RIES Richard K, b. 6 Dec 1947, Seattle, WA, USA. Psychiatrist. m. Sarah Ries, 1 child. Education: MD. Appointments: Director, Harborview Chemical Dependency Project, 1988-; Director, Inpatient Psychiatry, Harborview Medical Center, 1988-92; Medical Director, Outpatient Psychiatry and Dual Disorders Program, Harborview Medical Center, 1992-. Memberships: American Psychiatric Association; Society of Biological Psychiatry; American Society of Addiction Medicine; American Academy of Psychiatrists in Alcoholism and Addictions. Address: Harborview Medical Center ZA-31, 326 Ninth Avenue, Seattle, WA 98104, USA.

RIGA Dan, b. 19 Sept 1947, Bucharest, Romania. Scientist; Neurologist. Education: BSc magna cum laude, 1971, PhD, Brain Research (Neuropathology), 1976, Principal Neurologist, MD, Neurology, 1982, Senior Neurologist, 1990, Carol Davila Medical University, Bucharest; Scientific Researcher, 1974; Senior Researcher, 3rd degree, 1980; Senior Researcher, 2nd degree, 1993. Appointments: Victor Babes Institute of Morphopathology, Bucharest, 1971-73; Research Centre, 1974-86, Head, Brain Research Laboratory, 1978-85,

Institute of Neurology and Psychiatry, Bucharest and Gh Marinescu Hospital of Psychiatry and Neurology, Bucharest, 1986-95. Publications: Over 100 scientific papers including: Lipofuscin Decrease by Centrophenoxine Co-author, 1974; Lipofuscin Subcellular Genesis, 1977; Lipofuscin Research Methodology, 1978; Mécanismes de la vitalité cérébrale, 1984; Aging Deceleration and Brain Lipofuscinolysis by Antagonic-Stress. I. Light Morphometry. II. Electron Microscopy, 1994; Antagonic-Stress: New Treatment in Gerontopsychiatry, 1994; About 30 patents including: Anti-stress and anti-aging drug Antagonic-Stress, Romanian Patent, 1992, Patent Cooperation Treaty and European Patent registrations, 1994. Memberships: International Society of Neuropathology; Union Médicale Balkanique; International Brain Research Organization; International Association of Biomedical Gerontology; New York Academy of Sciences; World Stress Society. Hobbies: Science fiction; Yoga. Address: 7 Belgrade Street, RO-71248 Bucharest 63, Rumania.

RIGA Sorin, b. 19 Sept 1947, Bucharest, Romania. Scientist; Psychiatrist. Education: BSc magna cum laude, 1971, PhD, Brain Research (Neurochemistry), 1976, Principal Psychiatrist, MD, Psychiatry, 1982, Senior Psychiatrist, 1990, Carol Davila Medical University, Bucharest; Scientific Researcher, 1974; Senior Researcher, 3rd degree, 1980; Senior Researcher, 2nd Degree, 1993. Appointments: Institute of Biochemistry, Bucharest, 1971-73; Research Centre, 1974-86, Associate Head, Brain Research Labatory, 1978-85; Institute of Nuerology and Psychiatry, Bucharest and Gh Marinescu Hospital of Psychiatry and Neurology, Bucharest, 1986-95. Publications: Over 100 scientific papers including: Lipofuscin Decrease by Centrophenoxine, 1974; Lipofuscin Subcellular Genesis, 1977; Lipofuscin Research Methodology, 1978; Mécanismes de la vitalité cérébrale, Co-author, 1984; Aging Deceleration and Brain Lipofuscinolysis by Antagonic-Stress, I. Light Morphometry, II. Electron Microscopy, 1994; Antagonic Stress: New Treatment in Gerontopsychiatry, 1994; About 30 patents including: Anti-stress and Anti-aging Drug Antagonic-Stress, Romanian Patent, 1992, Patent Cooperation Treaty and European Patent Registrations, 1994. Memberships: International Society of Neuropathology; Union Médicale Balkanique; International Brain Research Organisation; International Association of Biomedical Gerontology; World Psychiatric Association; New York Academy of Sciences; World Stress Society. Hobbies: New Age Philosophy, Yoga. Address: 7 Belgrade Street, RO-71248 Bucharest 63, Romania.

RIGGS Lorrin Andrews, b. 11 Jun 1912, Harput, Turkey. Psychologist. m. (1) Doris Robinson, 28 Aug 1937, dec 1943, 2s, (2) Caroline Cressman, 1994. Education: AB, Dartmouth, 1933; MA, 1934, PhD, 1936, Clark University. Career: NRC Fellow Biological Sciences, University of Pennsylvania, 1936-37; Instructor, University of Vt, 1937-38, 1939-41; Instructor, 1938-39, Research Associate, Assistant Professor, Associate Professor, Professor of Psychology, 1951-77, Brown University; Professor of Psychology, L Herbert Ballou Foundation, 1960-68; Edgar J Marston University, Professor, 1968-77, University Professor Emeritus, 1977-. Publications: Co-author, Vision and Visual Perception, 1965; Numerous articles and book chapters. Honours include: Howard Crobsy Warren Medal, Society of Experimental Psychologists, 1957; Friedenwald Award, 1966, President 1977, Association of Research in Ophthalmology; Tillyer Medal, 1969, Ives Medal 1982, Optical Society of America; Guggenheim Fellow, 1971-72; Distinguished Scientific Contribution Award, American Psychological Association, 1974; Kenneth Craik Award, Cambridge University, 1979; William James Fellow, American Psychological Society, 1989. Memberships include: National Academy of Sciences; Fellow, American Academy of Arts and Sciences; American Physiological Society; Psychonomics Society, Board of Governors, 1967-72; International Brain Research Organisation; National Advisory Eye Council, 1975-79. Address: 80 Lyme Road, Kendal at Hanover, Hanover, NH 03755-1225, USA.

RIKKERS Layton Frederick, b. 31 Jan 1944, Fond du Lac, Wisconsin, USA. Physician; Surgeon. m. Diane Lynn Foster, 20 Aug 1966, 1 son, 1 daughter. Education: BS with honours, University of Wisconsin, 1966; MD, Stanford University School of Medicine, 1970. Appointments: Consultant, Omaha Veterans Administration Medical Center, Omaha, Nebraska, 1984-; Professor, Chairman, Department of Surgery, 1984-, M M Musselman Professor of Surgery, 1990-, Interim Dean, 1991-93, University of Nebraska Medical College, Omaha; Chief of Surgery, University of Nebraska Medical Center. Publications: Surgical Clinics of North America - Management of Variceal Hemorrhage, 1990; Digestive Tract Surgery: A Text and Atlas (with R H

Bell and M Mulholland). Honours: Phi Eta Sigma, 1963; Phi Kappa Phi, 1965; Phi Beta Kappa, 1966; Candidate, Alumni Scholar, 1970; Alpha Omega Alpha, 1970; Distinguished Professor for Teaching Excellence, 1981, 1982. Memberships include: Past President, Collecion Internationale Chirurgiae Digestivae; Councillor, Société Internationale de Chirurgie; American Medical Association; American College of Surgeons; Halsted Society. Address: University of Nebraska Medical Center, 600 S 42nd St, Omaha, NE 68198-3280, USA.

RIKLI Arthur E, b. 2 Dec 1917, Aurora, Illinois, USA. Physician. m. Frances L Mayer, 17 Sep 1944, 2 sons, 2 daughters. Education: MD; MPH; Certified as Medical Specialist, American Board of Preventive Medicine and Public Health. Appointments: Regular Corps, USPHS, US Representative to Health Agencies in Geneva, Switzerland, 1945-68; Visiting Professor, NIPPON Medical School, Tokyo, Japan, 1974-75; Visiting Lecturer, Wuhan, China, 1993; Visiting Scholar, National Library of Medicine. Publications: Diagnostic Computers, Co-author, 1969. Honours: Recognized as Friend, Pioneer and Founder of the national organization for State Kidney programmes, 1988. Memberships: American College of Preventive Medicine; International Society of Cardiology. Hobbies: Philately; Photography; Computers. Address: 4003 Faurot Drive, Columbia, MO 65203-0311, USA.

RIOS TEJADA Francisco, b. 5 June 1954, Malaga, Spain. Medical Doctor. m. Paloma Alvarez Pato, 20 Nov 1992. Education: PhD, Medicine, University of Madrid; Board Certified in Respiratory Medicine; Diploma in Aerospace Medicine; Fellowship in Hyperbaric Medicine. Appointments: Medical Director, Baromed Hyperbaric Medicine Unit, Madrid; Chief, Aeromedical Branch, Institute of Aerospace Medicine, Madrid. Publications: Hypoxia and exercise in simulated C-212 flight profile, 1987; Incapacitation time in the Pilot. A new method for measuring intellectual performance during hypoxia, 1989; Limitaciones Humanas en Medicina Aeronautica, 1994. Honours: Aeronautical Merit Award, 1992. Memberships: Associate Fellow, Aerospace Medical Association; Undersea and Hyperbaric Medical Society; Iberoamerican Aerospace Medical Society; Executive Secretary, Spanish Aerospace Medical Association; Panel Member, AGARD. Hobbies: Mountain bike; Photography. Address: Alcala 411 3F, 28027 Madrid, Spain.

RITCHIE Elspeth Cameron, b. 22 Mar 1958. Psychiatrist. Education: BA cum laude, Biology, Harvard, 1980; MD, George Washington University Medical School, Washington DC, 1986; Psychiatric Resident, 1987-90, Fellow, Forensic Psychiatry, 1993-, Walter Reed Army Medical Center. Appointments: Division Psychiatrist, 2nd Infantry, Camp Casey, Korea, 1990-91; Unit Director, Ward 54, Department of Psychiatry, 1991-92, Assistant Chief, Inpatient Psychiatry Service, 1992, Unit Director, Ward 55, 1993, Walter Reed Army Medical Center, Washington DC, USA; Executive Director, 528th Combat Street Control Univ, Mogadishu, Somalia, 1993; Clinical Assistant Professor, Psychiatry, Bethesda, Maryland, USA, 1994-. Publications: Treatment of gas mask phobia; Co-author: Bullet in the brain: A case of an organic psychosis, 1986; Acute generalized myoclonus following buspirone administration, 1988; Depression and support systems in HIV+ patients, 1992; Cognitive therapy in US psychiatry residency programs, 1992; Being a successful Division Psychiatrist: Preparation for and making the Assignment a successful one, 1993; Depersonalization Disorder and Associated Depression Treated with Electroconvulsive Therapy, 1994; A Case of Ketamine Dependence. Honours include: Lewis A Mologne Award, Excellence as Scholar, Soldier, Physician, Teacher, 1990; Albert Glass Award, Outstanding Psychiatric Resident. Memberships: American Medical Association; Washington Psychiatric Society; American Psychiatric Association; Association of Convulsive Therapy; American Academy of Psychiatry and the Law; Society of American Military Psychiatrists, Vice President; Association of Military Surgeons of the US; American Academy of Forensic Sciences. Hobbies: Gardening; Windsurfing; Reading crime novels; Birding. Address: 10014 Portland Place, Silver Spring, MD 20901, USA.

RITCHIE James Whiteford Knox, b. 22 Apr 1944, Belfast, Northern Ireland. Obstetrician and Gynaecologist. 1 son, 1 daughter. Education: MD; FRCOG; FRCS (Canada). Appointments: Currently Chairman, Department of Obstetrics and Gynaecology, University of Toronto, Canada; Obstetrician and Gynaecologist-in-Chief, Mount Sinai Hospital. Publications: Chapters in Dewhurst's Textbook of Obstetrics and Gynaecology for Postgraduates: Diabetes and other endocrine diseases in pregnancy, 1986, updated, 1991; Malformations of the occiput and malpresentations, 1986, updated, 1991; Obstetric operations and procedures, 1986, updated, 1991; Fetal Surveillance, 1986, updated,

1991; The fetus, placenta and amniotic fluid, 1991; Other book chapters; Author or co-author, numerous contributions to journals include: Fetal breathing movements and lung maturation in the congenitally abnormal human fetus, 1984; Effect of placental resistance, arterial diameter, and blood pressure on the uterine arterial velocity waveform: a computer modeling approach, 1989; Site-dependent effects of increases in placental vascular resistance on the umbilical arterial velocity waveform in fetal sheep, 1990; Localization of two angiogenic growth factors (PDECGF and VEGF) in human placentae throughout gestation, 1994. Memberships include: Fellow, American College of Obstetricians and Gynaecologists; Canadian Gynaecological Society; Society of Perinatal Obstetricians; Society for Gynecologic Investigation; Association of Professors of Obstetrics and Gynaecology of Canada; College of Physicians and Surgeons of Ontario; Blair Bell Research Society. Hobbies: Sailing; Gardening. Address: 92 College Street, Toronto, Ontario, Canada M5G 1L4.

RIVKIND Nickolay Borisovich, b. 8 Aug 1951, Bryansk, Russia. Laboratory Medicine. m. Tatyana Aleschenkova, 11 Nov 1972, 1 son, 1 daughter. Education: MD, Moscow State Medical Institute, 1975. Appointments: Research Worker, Institute of Clinical and Experimental Medicine, Siberian Department, USSR Academy of Medical Sciences, Novosibirsk, 1975; Chief, Clinico-Biochemical Laboratory, Central Hospital No 1, Bryansk, 1981; Head, Dosimetry Department, Bryansk Diagnostic Centre. Memberships: Russian Association of Medical Laboratory Diagnostics; International Consortium for Research on the Health Effects of Radiation. Hobbies: Tourism; Fishing. Address: 2 Bejitzzkaya Str, Bryansk 241007, Russia.

RO Long Sun, b. 19 Nov 1959, Taipei, Taiwan. Neurology; Neuropathology. m. Chih Ying Yang, 7 Apr 1989, 1 s, 1 d. Education: MB, Chung Shan Medical and Dental College, Taiwan; PhD, Institute of Neurology, The National Hospital, Queen Square, London, England, 1990-93; Specialist in Neurology, Accredited by Department of Health, Taiwan, 1990; ECFMG Certificate, USA, 1992. Career: Resident, Department of Medicine, Cathy General Hospital, Taipei, 1987; Resident, Department of Neurology, National Taiwan University Hospital, Taipei, 1987-90; Currently, Consultant and Associate Professor of Neurology, Chang Gung College of Medicine, Taipei. Publications: Behavioural and morphological studies on experimental chronic compression of peripheral nerve in rats, in University of London, 1993; Co-author, The role of the sophenous nerve in experimental sciatic nerve mononeuropathy produced by loose ligatures, in Pain, 1993; Co-author, A morphological study of experimental mononeuropathy in the rat, in Journal of Neurological Science, 1994. Honours: Ministry of Education Grant, Taiwan, 1989; Overseas Research Student Awards, CVCP, UK, 1992. Memberships: Medical Society of Fiormosa; Neurological Society, China; American Academy of Neurology. Hobbies: Running; Tennis; Swimming; Table Tennis. Address: Department of Neurology, Chang Gung Memorial Hospital, 199 Tung Hwa North Road, Taipei, Taiwan.

ROACH Frederick O'Neale, b. 12 June 1945, Bridgetown, Barbados. Clinical Psychologist. m. Marvalene Marguerita, 6 Sep 1970, 2 sons, 1 daughter. Education: Cert Ed, Merit, 1972, BA, Honours, 1986, BSc, Honours, 1986, London University, England; PhD, Southbank University, 1989; MSc, Surrey University, 1979. Appointments: Consultant Psychologist and Specialist in Forensic P{sychology and Alcohol and Substance Misuse, Mid-Surrey Health Authority, Surrey Heartlands, west Park Hospital, Epsom, Surrey. Publications: Self-labelling and Personality factors in Alcoholism, CO-author, 1980; The Behavioural Management of Neurosis by the Psychiatric Nurse Therapist, Co-author, 1986; Primary Health Care - Strategies for Change, Co-author, 1988; Community Mental Health Services for Black and Ethnic Minorities, 1982. Memberships: Associate Fellow, British Psychological Society; British Society for Experimental and Clinical Hypnosis; Barbados Paramedical Association; Chartered Clinical Psychologist. Hobbies: Golf; Chess; Photography. Address: 8 Southlands Road, Bromley, kent BR2 9QP, England.

ROB Charles Granville, b. 4 May 1913, Weybridge, England. Surgeon. m. Mary Doroty Elaine, 2 sons, 2 daughters. Education: MD; MA; FRCS. Appointments: Surgeon, St Thomas's Hospital; Resdence in Surgery, University of Hadi; Professor of Surgery, St Marys Hospital; Professor, Chairman, Department of Surgery, University of Richester; Professor of Surgery, East Catholic School of Medicine. Publications: Several professional publications from 1952-95. Memberships: AMA. Hobbies:Skiing. Address: 4935 Crescent Street, Bethesda, MD, USA.

ROBBINS Edwin, b. 11 Jan 1925, USA. Psychiatrist. m. Lillian Cukici, 8 May 1956, 1 son, 1 daughter. Education: MD. Appointments include: Currently Clinical Professor, Department of Psychiatry, New York University Medical Center and Albert Einstein College of Medicine. Publications: Psychiatric Emergencies (with R Glick, A Meyerson and J Talbott), 1976. Memberships: Academy of Psychoanalysis; American Psychiatric Association; Society of Medical Psychoanalysts; New York Academy of Medicine. Hobbies: Ballroom dancing; Skiing; Gardening; Tennis; Reading. Address: 49 East 96th Street, New York, NY 12188, USA.

ROBBINS Richard George, b. 11 July 1947, Brooklyn, New York, USA. Medical Entomologist. m. Fu-meei Yeh, 17 June 1978, 1 daughter. Education: BS, State University of New York, College of Environmental Science and Forestry, 1970; MS, Oregon State University, 1975; PhD, George Washington University, 1990. Appointments: Museum Specialist, Department of Entomology, Smithsonian Institution, 1977-83; Museum Specialist, National Institute of Allergy and Infectious Diseases, National Institutes of Health, 1983-90; Currently: Civilian Entomologist, Defense Pest Management Information Center, Armed Forces Pest Management Board, Walter Reed Army Medical Center, Washington, District of Columbia. Publications: About 40 scientific papers and reports; Systematics and ecology of the subgenus Ixodiopsis (Acari: Ixodidae: Ixodes), book, 1992. Honours: Phi Kappa Phi, 1970; Phi Sigma, 1970; Sigma Xi, 1994; Adjunct Assistant Professor, Department of Preventive Medicine and Biometrics, Uniformed Services University of the Health Sciences, Bethesda, Maryland, 1989-. Memberships: Acarological Society of America; American Entomological Society; American Society of Parasitologists; Entomological Society of Washington; New York Entomological Society; Society for Vector Ecology. Hobbies: Architecture; History; Music. Address: Armed Forces Pest Management Board, Walter Reed Army Medical Center, Washington, DC 20307-5001, USA.

ROBBOY Merle, b. 9 Feb 1941, Cleveland, Ohio, USA. Physician. m. Christine Stevens, 8 Feb 1991, 1 son, 1 daughter. Education: AB, Western Reserve University; MD, Ohio State University. Appointments: Active Staff, Chairman, Hoag Memorial Hospital, Department Ob-Gyn, 1981-83; Clinical Associate Professor, Department Ob-Gyn, University of California, Irvine, 1973-. Publications: The Hypercarotenemia in Anorexia Nervosa, 1974; The Management of Cervical Incompetence, 1973; Idiiopathic Peripartum Cardiomyopathy, 1988. Honours: Roessler Research Scholarship, Ohio State University, 1964. Memberships: President, 1983-84, Vice President, 1982-83, Secretary, 1981-82, Treasurer, 1980-81, Orange County Ob-Gyn Society. Hobbies: Judge, American Dahlia Society; Lecturer, American Orchid Society. Address: 1401 Avocado Avenue Suite 801, Newport Beach, CA 92660, USA.

ROBERTS Elizabeth H, b. New York, USA. Podiatry. m. Nathan Wasserheit, 25 Nov 1951, 1 daughter. Education: DPM; Fellow, American Society of Podiatry Dermatology; Professor Emeritus, New York College of Podiatric Medicine; Fellow, American Society of Podiatry Medicine; Fellow, American Association of Practice Administration. Appointments: Chair, Department of Special Anatomy; Creator, Director, Department of Practice Administration; Freelance Writer. Publications: Manual of Practice Administration, 1951; On Your Feet, 1975; Numerous articles, radio, television appearances. Memberships: Founder, President, American Podiatric Medical Writers Association; American Association for Women Podiatrics. Honours: Vice Chair, Board of Trustees, New York College of Podiatric Medicine; Distingushed Practitioner, National Academies of Practice. Hobbies: Writing; Travel. Address: 210 West 90th Street, New York, NY 10024, USA.

ROBERTS Judith Mary, b. 17 Dec 1936, Broken Hill, New South Wales, Australia. Voluntary Community Worker. m. Bruce Mallan Roberts, 21 Apr 1961, 1 s, 1 d. Education: Registered Nurse, South Australia, 1957; State Registered Nurse, UK, 1958. Career: Vice President, Australian Council of Social Service, 1985-88; Presiding Member, Senior Secondary Assessment Board of South Australia, 1988-94; Currently: President of Relationships, Australia, South Australia; Chair, The South Australian Council on Reproductive Technology; Chair, The Helpmann Academy; Deputy Chair, The Royal Adelaide Hospital, South Australia. Publications: Ministerial Review of Cancer in Women in South Australia, 1986; Review of Management and Administration of Women's Shelters in South Australia, 1987; Guidelines for Genetic Registers - NHMRC, 1990; Review of Disability Services in South Australia, 1993; Women's Health Strategy and Implementation

Plan, NHMRC, 1993. Honours: Gold Medal, South Australia Nurses Board Final Examination, 1957; Order of Australia, 1984; Commander of the Order of St Lazarus of Jerusalem, 1985; South Australia Great Award, 1986. Memberships: Inaugural National Womens Advisory Council, 1978-81; National Health and Medical Research Council, 1986-94. Hobbies: Contract Bridge; Opera; Music; Theatre. Address: 10 Commercial Road, Hyde Park, South Australia 5061, Australia.

ROBERTS Kenneth Boyett, b. 7 Nov 1944, Martin, Tennessee, USA. Dean, School of Pharmacy. m. Kittye Louise Rice, 20 October 1968, 2 daughters. Education: BSc, Pharmacy; MBA; PhD. Appointments: Assistant Director of Pharmacy, US Naval Hospital, Great Lakes, Illinois, 1967-68; Director of Pharmacy, US Naval Hospital, Taipei, Taiwan, 1969-71; Pharmacist, various practice locations, 1971-75; Executive Director, Missouri Foundation for Pharmaceutical Care, 1977-79; Director of Administrative Affairs, American College of Apothecaries, Memphis, 1979-84; Executive Director, American College of Apothecaries, Memphis, 1984-86; Director of Research, American College of Apothecaries, Memphis, 1986-87; Dean, School of Pharmacy, University of Mississippi, 1989-; Professor, Department of Pharmacy Administration, School of Pharmacy, University of Mississippi, 1989-; Adjunct Professor of Pharmacy Administration, College of Pharmacy, University of Tennessee, 1989-. Publications: Managing Pharmacy Support Personnel, 2nd edition, 1988; Guidelines for Establishing Pharmacy Service for Hospice, 1987; Co-author: Marketing a Community Pharmacy Practice, 1983; Guidelines for Pharmacy Management by Self Study, 1984. Honours: Phi Kappa Phi, 1992; Rho Chi Honour Society, 1974; Phi Lambda Sigma, 1980; Charles R Walgreens Memorial Fellow, 1974; Sigma Xi Scientific Research Society, 1981. Memberships: American Association of Colleges of Pharmacy; American College of Apothecaries; American Society of Hospital Pharmacists; American Pharmaceutical Association; Mississippi Pharmacists Association; National Council of University Research Administration; American Association of Pharmaceutical Scientists. Hobbies: Genealogy; Stamp and Coin Collecting; Reading. Address: University of Mississippi, School of Pharmacy University, MS 38677, USA.

ROBERTS Lyndel Rene, b. 20 June 1957, Salina, USA. Medical Technologist. 1 daughter. Education: Associate of Applied Science, Southwestern Oklahoma University, 1977; Bachelor of General Studies, Texas Technical University, 1991. Appointments: Medical Technologist, 1977-83; Fire Department Dispatcher, Secretary, Emergency Medical Technician, 1983-88; Medical Technologist, 1988-. Publications: Non-Traditional HIV/AIDS Therapy, 1991. Memberships: American Medical Technologists. Hobbies: Sports; Music; Reading; Movies. Address: 2102 W Yoop 289, Apt #29, Lubbock, TX 79407, USA.

ROBERTSON George Irvine, b. 20 May 1919, Stirling. Physician. Education: MBE; MD; FRCP Ed. Career: Physician, Nairobi Hospital. Publications: Transactions of the Royal Society of Tropical Medicine & Hygiene, Vol 51, 450-504, 1957. Address: PO Box 20005, Nairobi, Kenya.

ROBERTSON Susan Elizabeth, b. 10 Dec 1950, Highland Park, Illinois, USA. Physician; Epidemiologist. Education: BA, Northwestern University, 1972; MD, Medical College of Pennsylvania, 1978; MPH, Harvard University, 1984; MS, Harvard University, 1985. Appointments: Internship, Naval Hospital, San Diego, 1978-79; Medical Officer, US Navy, Atsugi, Japan, Maine, Rhode Island, 1979-83; Fellowship, Harvard University, 1983-85; Epidemic Intelligence Service Officer, Centers for Disease Control, Atlanta, 1985-88; Medical Officer, Global Programme for Vaccines & Immunization, World Health Organization, Geneva, Switzerland, 1988-. Publications include: Research and Development within the Expanded Programme on Immunization: The First Five Years, 1993; Studies of Missed Opportunities for Immunization in Developing and Industrialized Countries, 1993; Poliomyelitis: The Immunological Basis For Immunization, 1993. Honours: Mortar Board National Honour Society, 1972; Commendation Medal, US Navy, 1981; Arkansas Traveler Award, 1986. Memberships: American Public Health Association; International Epidemiology Association; European Association of Science Editors. Address: Global Programme for Vaccines & Immunization, World Health Organization, 1211 Geneva 27, Switzerland.

ROBINOWITZ Carolyn Bauer, b. 15 Jul 1938, Brooklyn, NY, USA. Psychiatrist. m. Max Robinowitz, 1962, 2 s. Education: AB, Wellesley College, 1959; MD, Washington University, St Louis, 1964. Career:

Director of Child Psychiatry Training and Pediatric Psychiatry, University of Miami, 1970-72; Director of Education, George Washington University, Department of Psychiatry, 1972-74; Private Practice, Psychiatry and Director of EDPE Project, 1974-76; Director of Education, American Psychiatric Association, 1976-86; Senior Deputy Medicine, Director, APA, 1986-. Honours: NIMH Career Development Award, 1966-90; AAP First Educator of the Year Award, 1988; Distinguished Service Award, APA, 1991; Bowis Award, ACP, 1994. Memberships: Fellow, American Psychiatric Association, 1968-; Fellow, American College of Psychiatrists, 1972; Board of Regents, 1993-; Board of Directors, 1982-84, President Elect, 1987-89, President, 1989-91, Group for Advancement of Psychiatry, 1973-; Board of Directors, 1979-86, Secretary, 1984, Vice President, 1985, President, 1986, American Board of Psychiatry and Neurology. Address: 1400 K Street NW, Washington, DC 20005, USA.

ROBINSON Daniel N, b. 9 Mar 1937, NY, USA. Professor. m. Francine S Malasko, 18 Sep 1967, 2 d. Education: BA, Colgate University; MA, Hofstra University; PhD, City University of NY. Appointments: Columbia University Electronics Research Laboratories, 1960-68; Visiting Lecturer, Princeton University, 1965-68; Professor: Amherst College, 1968-71; Georgetown University, 1971-; Visiting Professor, University of Oxford, 1991-. An Intellectual History of Psychology, 1976; Co-author, The Wonder of Being Human: Our Mind and Our Brain, 1982; Co-author, Foundations of Psychobiology, 1987; Aristotle's Psychology, 1989. Honour: President's Medal, Colgate University, 1986. Memberships: Fellow, American Psychological Association; Fellow, British Psychological Society. Address: Dept of Psychology, Georgetown University, Washington, DC 20057, USA.

ROBINSON David Errol, b. 6 Mar 1939, Brisbane, Australia. Research Engineer. m. Helen Gordon, 6 Jan 1962, 1 son, 2 daughters. Education: BE, ME, DSc, University of New South Wales. Appointments: Research Scientist, National Acoustic Laboratories; Project Leader, Ultrasonics Laboratory, Division of Radiophysics, CSIRO. Publications: Contributor of 90 articles in professional journals. Memberships: Fellow, Institution of Engineers Australia; Fellow, Institution of Radio and Electronics Engineers Australia; Honorary Fellow, Royal Australasian College of Radiologists. Hobbies: Outdoor Activities; Hobby Farm. Address: 73 The Outlook, Bilcola Plateau, New South Wales 2107, Australia.

ROBINSON Eliezer, b. 17 June 1931, Vienna, Austria. Clinical Oncologist. m. Tova Leszcz, 10 Oct 1957, 2 sons, 1 daughter. Education: MD; Oncology Specialist. Career: Director, Department of Oncology, Rambam Medical Center, Haifa, Israel, 1968-; Professor, Faculty of Medicine, Israel Institute of Technology, Haifa, Israel, 1978-; Chairman, Northern Israel Oncology Center, 1975-. Publications: Over 200 original publications in journals; 170 abstracts; 21 publications in books. Memberships: Israel Medical Association; Israel Radiological Society; Israel Society for Nuclear Medicine; Israel Society for Clinical Oncology & Radiation Oncology; American Society of Clinical Oncology; American Society of Therapeutic Radiology; British Institute of Radiology. Address: Northern Israel Oncology Center, Rambam Medical Center, POB 9602, 31096 Haifa, Israel.

ROBINSON Robert G, b. 22 May 1945, Pittsburgh, PA, USA. Physician. m. Gretchen P Smith, 5 Jan 1974, 2 s. Education: MD. Career: Assistant Professor, Associate Professor, 1977-90, Professor, 1990-91, Johns Hopkins University; Professor and Head, Psychiatry, University of Iowa College of Medicine, 1991-. Publications: 197 Articles, 34 book chapters and 2 books: Depression and Coexisting Disease, 1989, Depression in Neurological Disease, 1993. Honours: Mullen Engineering Scholarship, 1967; Sandra Lee Shaw Award for Research in Neurology and Pharmacology, 1969; Mellon Fellowship, 1977; Research Scientist Award, 1989. Memberships: Society for Neuroscience; American Psychiatric Association; Royal College of Psychiatrists; AAAS; American Association for Geriatric Psychiatry; Psychiatric Research Society; American College of Neuropsychopharmacology. Hobbies: Running; Tennis. Address: Department of Psychiatry, University of Iowa College of Medicine, 200 Hawkins Drive, 2887 JPP, Iowa City, IA 52242, USA.

ROBITAILLE Yves, b. 11 Mar 1941, Montreal, Canada. Neuropathologist. m. Juleana C Sonka, 1 d. Education: BA, cum laude, 1962; MD, cum laude, 1966; CSPQ; FCAP; Certified Pathologist, Anatomic Pathology, Neuropathology. Career includes: Associate Professor, Neuropathology, Departments of Neurology, Neurosurgery and Pathology, Adjunct Professor, McGill University, Montreal. Publications include: Over 100 articles, 1974-92 including: Co-author, Retrospective assessment of relative risks of coronary arteriosclerosis and myocardial infarct in autopsy confirmed dementias of the AD and non AD types, in Alzheimer's Disease: Advances in Clinical and Basic Research, 1993; 69 Abstracts published. Honours: Fellow, College of American Pathologists. Memberships: Canadian Association of Neuropathologists; American Association of Neuropathologists; Société Française de Neuropathologie. Hobbies: Jogging; Swimming; Reading; Travel. Address: Ste-Justine Hospital, Department of Pathology, 3175 Côte Ste-Catherine Road, Montreal, Quebec, Canada, H3T 1C5.

ROCCO Michael Vito, b. 12 July 1959. Physician. m. Mary Ruth Gore, 21 Aug 1993. Education: BS, Seton Hall University, 1981; MD, Vanderbilt University, 1985; MS, Wake Forest University, 1994. Appointments: Assistant Professor of Medicine and Nephrology, Bowman Gray School of Medicine. Publications: Determination of Peritoneal Transport Characteristics Using 24 Hour Dialysate Collections, 1994; The Effect of Increasing hematocrit on Peritoneal Transport Kinetics, Co-author, 1994; Prevalence of Missed Treatments and Early Signoffs on Hemodialysis Patients, 1st author, 1993; The Efficacy Number as a Predictor of Morbidity and Mortality in Peritoneal Dialysis Patients, 1993; Assessment of Dialysis Dose by Measured Clearance vs Extrapolated Data, Co-author, 1993. Memberships: American Society of Nephrology; National Kidney Foundation; American College of Physicians; International Society of Nephrology; International Society of Peritoneal Dialysis. Address: Bowman Gray School of Medicine, Medical Centre Boulevard, Winston-Salem, NC 27157-1053, USA.

ROCK John Aubrey, b. 21 Oct 1946, Corpus Christie, Texas, USA. Physician. m. Dr Barbara McAlpine Rock, 8 Oct 1976, 2 sons, 1 daughter. Education: BS, Zoology, 1968; MD, 1972; Ob/Gyn Residency, 1976; fellowship, Reproductive Endocrinology, 1978. Appointments: Chairman, Department of Gyn/Ob, Union Memorial Hospital, Baltimore, Maryland, 1991-92; Director, Division of Reproductive Endocrinology, Johns Hopkins Medical Institutions, Baltimore, 1978-91; Professor, Chairman, Department of Gynaecology and Obstetrics, Emory University School of Medicine, Atlanta, Georgia. Publications: TeLinde's Operative Gynecology, 7th Edition, 1991, 8th edition; Reproductive Endocrinology, Surgery and Technology, 1995; Advances in Obstetrics and Gynecology, Mosby Year Book, 1994. Honour: President, Society for Reproductive Medicine, 1997. Memberships: AMA; American College of Ob/Gyn; Society for Reproductive Medicine; Society of Gynecologic Surgeons; Society of Gynecologic Investigation. Address: Department Gyn/Ob, PO Box 21246, Emory University, Atlanta, GA 30322, USA.

ROCKER Israel. Education: MD, London; FRCOG. Appointments: Consultant Obstetrician & Gynaecologist, 1964-; Hon Tutor, Welsh College of Medicine, 1964-91. Publications: Frtoscopy Elsevier, 1981; Pelvic Pain in Women Springer Verlag, 1990; Articles on Infertility, Prenatal Diagnosis, Ovarian Cancer. Honours: Examiner & Welsh Regional Advisor, RCOG. Memberships: Fetoscopy Group, British Gynaecology Cancer Society. Hobbies: Golf; Reading. Address: Lawnside, 2 Stow Park Circle, Newport, Gwent NP9 4HE, Wales.

ROCKETT Ian R H, b. 3 Oct 1943, Perth, Western Australia, Australia. Epidemiologist. m. Sandra L Putnam, 26 Feb 1983, 1 son. Education: BA, University of Western Australia, 1965; MA, University of Western Ontario, 1973; PhD, Brown University, 1978; MPH, Harvard University, 1986. Appointments: Senior Research Fellow, Department of Community Medicine, Melbourne, Victoria, Australia; Professor of Epidemiology, University of Tennese, Knoxville. Publications: First author: Adolescent Risk Takers: A Trauma Center Study, 1991 & Covert Suicide Among Elderly Japanese Females, 1993; Population and Health, 1994; Honours: Ontario Graduate Fellowship, 1972-73; Canada Council Fellowship, 1973-74; Population Council Fellowship, 1974-76. Memberships: Society for Epidemiological Research; International Epidemiological Association; International Union for the Scientific Study of Population. Hobbies: Tennis; Golf. Address: 2617 Delrose Drive, Knoxville, TN 37914, USA.

RODDIE Thomas Wilson, b. 19 Aug 1921, Belfast, Northern Ireland. Obstetrician and Gynaecologist. m. Alix P M Hurst, 21 Apr 1949, 2 d. Education: MB, B Ch, BOA, Royal College of Obstetricians and Gynaecologists; FRCOG. Career: House Surgeon and House Physician, Royal Victoria and Royal Maternity Hospitals, Belfast; Obstetrical Officer, Princess Mary Maternity Hospital, Newcastle upon Tyne;

Resident Medical Officer, Jessop Hospital for Women, Sheffield; Senior Registrar and Tutor, Royal Maternity Hospital, Belfast; Consultant Obstetrician and Gynaecologist, Kandang Kerban Hospitals, Singapore; Senior Lecturer and Associate Professor, University of Malaya, Singapore; Consultant Obstetrician and Gynaecologist, Eastern Health and Social Services Board, Belfast; Surgeon Lieutenant Commander, Ulster Division RWVR. Publications: Various publications on Obstetrics and Gynaecology. Memberships include: British Medical Association; Royal College of Obstetrics and Gynaecology; Ulster Medical Society; North of England Obstetrics and Gynaecology Society. Hobby: Foreign Travel. Address: Lodge Farm, Kirkby Fleetham, Northallerton, North Yorkshire, DL7 0SN, England.

RODGERS Catherine, b. 28 Mar 1962, Dublin, Ireland. University Lecturer. Education: BA (Hons), Psychology, Trinity College, Dublin University, 1984; PhD, Strathclyde University, 1988. Appointments: Research Officer, University of Strathclyde, Scotland, 1988; Research Officer, King's College, University of London, England, 1990; Currently University Lecturer, Department of Psychology, Monash University, Gippsland Campus, Victoria, Australia, 1991-. Publications include: Co-author: Maternal Support for the Down's Syndrome Stereotype: The Effect of Direct Experience of the Condition, 1987; Peer Interaction and the Development of Physical Causality: An Investigation through Children's Understanding of Floating and Sinking, 1988; The Stress of Parents Caring for Children with Handicaps, 1991; Interim Report on the Evaluation of the Nutrition Section of the LaTrobe Valley Better Health Project, 1993; Breast Cancer Prevention and Detection Behaviors Across the Lifespan: A Pilot Study, 1993; The Relationship Between Preventive Health Behaviours and Screening for Breast Cancer: An Issue for Perceived Control, 1994. Membership: British Psychological Society. Hobbies: Aerobics; Skiing. Address: 81 Henry Street, Traralgon, Victoria 3844, Australia.

RODRIGUEZ Gilberto E, b. 14 Apr 1941, San Juan, Puerto Rico. Medicine. m. Maryanne Anglade, 18 Aug 1965, 3 s. Education: BS, University of Notre Dame; MD, Temple University School of Medicine. Appointment: Professor of Pediatrics. Memberships: AAAI; ACAI; AAAS; NYAS; ASM; AMLI. Address: PO Box 225, MCV Station, Richmond, VA 23298, USA.

RODRIGUEZ Jorge, b. 21 Feb 1947, Lima, Peru. Physician. m. Blanca Lozano, 26 Jan 1980, 1 son, 1 daughter. Education: MD, Specialist in Gynaecology and Obstetrics. Appointments: Resident, Gyn-Obstetrics, Hospital E Rabagliati, 1978-80; Obstetrics Department, 1981-84; Gyn Department, 1985-95; Temporary Chief of Gynaecology Service, Chief, Gynaecology Unit; professor of Gynaecology and Obstetrics, Faculty of Medicine, Universidad San Marcos, 1990-. Publications: Contributor of articles in professional journals. Honours: Scholarship, Hospital E Rebagliati to St george's Hospital, London, England, 1994. Memberships: Colegio Medico del Peru; Sociedad Peruana de Obstetricia y Ginecologia; Og Gestosis Associacion Peruaa de Perinatalogia. Hobbies: Reading; Music; Travel; Photography. Address: Calle 30 (Buenos Aires), Monzana P-1 Loto 39 Urbanizacions Santa Patricia (Primera Etapa). La Molina, Lima 12, Peru.

ROE Benson Bertheau, b. 7 July 1918, Los Angeles, California, USA. Surgeon (retired). m. Jane F St John, 20 Jan 1945, 1 son, 1 daughter. Education: AB, University of California, Berkeley, 1939; MD cum laude, 1943, Research Fellow, Department of Physiology, 1948-49, Harvard Medical School; Surgical Residency, Massachusetts General Hospital, 1943-50; University of Edinburgh, Scotland, 1950-51. Appointments: Chief, Cardiothoracic Surgery, 1958-76, Co-Chief, Cardiothoracic Surgery, 1976-86, Professor of Surgery, Emeritus, 1989, University of California, San Francisco; Senior Scientist, Cardiovascular Research Institute, University of California, San Francisco, 1958-86; Director, 1971-83, Chairman, 1981-83, American Board of Thoracic Surgery; President, Miranda Lux; Director: International Biothics Institute; Avery Fuller Foundation; Point Reyes Bird Observatory; Medical Consultant, Proclosure Inc; Consultant, Blue Shield of Northern California; Several Visiting Professorships, 5 countries. Publications: 175, including 2 textbooks, 21 textbook chapters. Honours: National Research Fellowship, 1948-49; Moseley Travelling Fellow, 1950-51; American Heart Assn, Silver Medal. Memberships include: President, Society of Thoracic Surgeons, 1973; President, Thoracic Surgery Directors Association, 1979-81; President, California Academy of Medicine; Vice President, Society for Vascular Surgery; President, San Francisco Heart Association; Editorial Board, PHAROS; American College of Surgeons, Chairman, Advisory Committee for Thoracic

Surgery, 3 years, Chairman, Thoracic Surgery Programme Committee, 2 years, Cardiovascular Committee, 6 years; Director, Control Laser Corporation; Director, Planned Parenthood, Alameda-San Francisco. Address: M 593 University of California, San Francisco CA 94143-0118, USA.

ROEDER Lois Marie, b. 13 Feb 1932, Baltimore, Maryland, USA. Research Biochemist. Education includes: ScD, Biochemistry, Graduate School, Johns Hopkins University School of Hygiene and Public Health, 1971. Appointments: Research Chemist, National Institutes of Health, 1954-67; Assistant Professor, Biochemistry, Maternal and Child Health, The Johns Hopkins University School of Hygiene and Public Health; Currently Associate Professor, Paediatrics, University of Maryland School of Medicine, Baltimore. Publications: Sudden Infant Death Syndrome, 1982; Metabolic Regulation in Brain Cells, 1986; Articles in: Biochemistry Journal, 1983, 1984; Journal of Neurochemistry, 1984, 1985; Brain Research, 1987; American Journal of Physiology, 1988. Memberships: American Society for Neurochemistry; American Institute of Nutrition. Hobbies: Gardening; Travel. Address: 116 Forest Avenue, Baltimore, MD 21228, USA.

ROEMER Milton Irwin, b. 1916, Paterson, New Jersey, USA. Physician. m. Ruth Rosenbaum, 1939, 1 son, 1 daughter. Education: BA; MA; MD; MPH. Appointments: New Jersey Department of health, 1941-42; Public Health Service, 1943-51; World Health Organization, 1951-53; Saskatlhewan Department of Health, 1953-56; Cornell University, 1957-62; University of California, Los Angeles, 1962-. Publications: Doctors in Hospitals, 1971; Comparative National Policies on Health Care, 1977; Ambulatory health Services in America, 1981; National Health Systems of the World, 1991, 1993. Honours: Phi Beta Kappa, 1935; Phi Kappa Phi, 1941; Alpha Omega Alpha, 1945; Delta Omega, 1967; Sigma Xi, 1972. Memberships: American Public Health Association; International Epidemiological Association; Physicians Forum; national Academy of Social Insurance; Association of Teachers of Preventive medicine. Hobbies: Photography; Travel. Address: 365 South Westgate Avenue, Los Angeles, CA 90049, USA.

ROGERS Eugene J, b. 13 Jun 1921, Vienna, Austria. Physician; Educator. m. Joyce M Lighter, 9 Feb 1952, 2 s. Education: BSc, 1943; Bachelor of Medicine, 1946; Medical Degree, 1947. Career: Fellow, Public Health Service, 1947; Ship's Surgeon, 1948; Private Practice, 1949-73; Professor and Chairman, Department of Rehabilitation Medicine, Finch University of Health Sciences, Chicago Medical School, 1973-. Publications: Numerous in referenced journals on pain, strokes, fibrositis and back pains; Textbook on Rehabilitation in Cancer. Honours: Presidential Plaques, Greater NY Chapter, Chicago Medical School Alumni Association, 1971-73; Distinguished Alumni Award, Chicago Medical School; Honorary Staff for Contributions to Science and Medicine, St Mary of Nazareth Hospital Center, 1986; Presidential Plaque, IL Society Phys Medical and Rehabilitation, 1983-84; Service Award, Faculty of Chicago Medical School as Speaker of Assembly, 1987. Memberships include: Treasurer, Alumni Association, Chicago Medical School; University Senator, University of Health Sciences, Chicago Medical School; Delegate, Chicago Medical Society; Fellowships: American College of Physicians, Academy of Phys, Medical and Rehabilitation, American Medical Society, Illinois Medical Society. Address: Finch University of Health Sciences, The Chicago Medical School, 3333 Green Bay Road, North Chicago, IL 60064, USA.

ROGERS Gary, b. 31 Aug 1950, Loudon, Tennessee, USA. Psychologist. m Beverly Law, 18 Aug 1990, 1 son, 1 daughter. Education: BA, Interdisciplinary Studies, Univ of Alabama, 1984; MS, Psychology, 1986, PhD, Psychology, 1989, California Coast University; National Defense University, 1990. Appointments include: Served US Marines, Vietnam, 1968-70; Readjustment Counselling Service, US Department of Veteran Affairs, 1984-93; Founder, Executive Director, Center for Traumatic Stress, Atlanta, Georgia, 1993-94; Currently Chairman, Chief Executive Officer, Genesis Behavioral Health Care Services. Publications include: People in Crisis, 1984; Grief Resolution Therapy, 1987; The Grieving Process: Social, Psychological and Religious Aspects, 1989; Post-Traumatic Stress Disorder: A New Challenger for the Helping Professional, 1991; Does What We Cannot Hear Really Influence Us?, 1993; Behavioral Medicine and Christian Counseling, 1993; Traumatic Stress! What is it? Who is at risk? How do we cope?, 1993. Memberships include: American Psychological Association, General Psychology, Humanistic Psychology, American Psychology-Law Society divisions; Georgia Psychological Association; International Society of Traumatic Stress Studies; Piedmont Mental

Health Association; American Health Care Association-College of Chaplains. Hobby: Golf. Address: 110 South Main Street, Suite 101, Woodstock, GA 30188, USA.

ROGERS Michael Scott, b. 21 Apr 1953, England. Obstetrician and Gynaecologist. m. Kay Rogers, 3 Jan 1976, 2 s, 1 d. Education: MBChB, Birmingham, 1975; MRCOG, 1980; FRCS, 1983; FRCOG, 1993. Career: Lecturer, Currently, Senior Lecturer, Obstetrics and Gynaecology, Chinese University of Hong Kong. Publications include: Co-editor, Analysis of Complex Data in Obstetrics, in Balliere's Clinical Obstetrics and Gynaecology, 1994; Many articles in peer reviewed journals including: Co-author, Prediction of caesarian section from ultrasound and clinical assessment of fetal size, in ANZ Journal of Obstetrics and Gynaecology, 1994; Co-author, A reapraisal of second trimester mean arterial pressure in the prediction of pre-eclampsia, in Journal of Obstetrics and Gynaecology, 1994; Co-author, Lararoscopic hysterectomy: do we need to remove the cervix?, in ANZ Journal of Obstetrics and Gynaecology, 1994. Memberships: Royal College of Obstetrics and Gynaecology; Royal College of Physicians and Surgeons of Glasgow. Address: Department of Obstetrics and Gynaecology; Prince of Wales Hospital, Shatin, New Territories, Hong Kong.

ROGERS Robert Jeffrey, b. 30 Apr 1956, New York City, New York, USA. Physician. Education: MD; Diplomate, American Board of Anesthesiology; Diplomate, American Board of Internal Medicine. Appointments: Assistant Clinical Professor, University of California, Los Angeles Medical Center; Attending Physician, Cedars-Sinai Medical Center; Founding Partner, Gerskal Anesthesia Specialists Partnership. Publications: Multiple articles. Honours: Beta Sigma Award, Sigma Alpha Mu. Memberships: American Medical Association; ASA; American College of Physicians; Los Angeles (California) Medical Association; California Medical Association; FUHS; The Chicago Medical School Alumni Association. Hobbies: Skiing; Sailing. Address: Cedars-Sinai Medical Center, Department of Anaesthesis, 8700 Beverly Blvd, Rm 8211, Los Angeles, CA 90210, USA.

ROGERS Roy Steele III, b. 3 Mar 1940, Hillsboro, OH, USA. Professor of Dermatology; Dean, Mayo School of Health Related Services. m. Susan Hudson, 22 Aug 1964, 1 s, 1 d. Education: AB, cum laude, Denison University, 1962; MD, cum laude, Ohio State University, 1966; MS, University of Minnesota, 1974. Career: Associate Dean for Student Affairs, 1982-84, Associate Dean for Academic Affairs, 1984-88, Mayo Medical School; Board of Directors, American Academy of Dermatology, 1986-90; President, American Dermatological Society for Allergy and Immunology, 1982-83; Professor of Dermatology, 1983; President, Minnesota Dermatological Society, 1985; Dean, Mayo School of Health Related Sciences, 1991-. Publications: Recurrent Aphthous Stomatitis, in Journal of Investigative Dermatology, 1977; Dapsone and Sulfapyridine Therapy of Pemphigoid Diseases, in Australian Journal of Dermatology, 1986; Co-author, Melkersson-Rosenthal Syndrome, in Journal of American Academy of Dermatology, 1989. Honours: AOA, 1965; Alumni Citation, Ohio State University College of Medicine, 1991; Mayo Medical School Faculty Service Award, 1993; Alumni Achievement Award, Denison University, 1993. Memberships: American Academy of Dermatology; American Dermatological Association; Society for Investigative Dermatology; American Dermatologic Society for Allergy and Immunology; Association of Schools of Allied Health Professions. Hobbies: Walking; Reading; Travel; Family. Address: Department of Dermatology, Mayo Clinic, Rochester, MN 55905, USA.

ROGOZEA Radu, b. 21 June 1931, Cluj, Romania. Professor; Doctor; Scientific Researcher. m. Dr Doina Rogozea, 24 October 1960. Education: MD, highest honours, University of Cluj, Romania, 1956; PhD, highest honours, Neurophysiology, Institute of Neurology & Psychiatry, Bucharest, 1971. Appointments: Chief Senior Researcher, 1980-89, Head, Neurological & EEG Departments, 1989-, Scientific Director, Institute of Neurology & Psychiatry, Bucharest. Publications Include: Handbook of Neurology, 1979; Negative learning: habituation, 1982; Numerous professional papers in scientific journals. Honours: Gh Marinescu, Award of The Romanian Academy, 1978. Memberships Include: Honorary Member, British Brain Research Association; Honorary Member, European Brain & Behaviour Society; Fellow, American Electro Encephalegraphic Society; American Academy of Neurology; International Brain Research Organization; The New York Academy of Science; Australian Neuroscience Society. Hobbies: Classical Music; Literature; Dogs; Car Driving. Address: Institute of Neurology and Psychiatry, 10 Berceni Road, PO Box 6180, RO-75622, Bucharest, Romania.

ROGOZHIN Vladimir Alexeevich, b. 10 Apr 1951, Leningrad, USSR.Radiologist. m. Gorelik Zoya, 24 Aug 1973, 1 son. Education: MD, Odessa Medical University, Ukraine, 1974; Radiologist, Kiev Medical University, 1975. Appointments: Radiologist, Filator's Eye Research Institute, Odessa, 1974-80; Chief, CT Department, Ukrainian Government Hospital, Kiev, 1980-89; Chief Doctor, Ukrainian Government Hospital, Kiev, 1989-94; Chief, Radiological Centre, Ukrainian Government Hospital, Kiev, 1994-. Publications include Introduction to CT, Co-author, 1983; CT in Diagnosis of Extraorganic Pelvic Neoplasms, 1987. Memberships: Ukrainian Radiological Association; Kiev Radiological Association. Hobby: Gardening. Address: Raisy Okipnoy Street b1, Flat 27, Kiev 252167, Ukraine.

ROLA-PLESZCZYNSKI Marek, b. 9 Aug 1947, Fermo, Italy. MD. 1 s, 1 d. Education: BA, Séminaire de Sherbrooke, 1966; MD, Université de Sherbrooke, 1970. Appointments: Associate Dean for Research and Graduate Studies, Faculty of Medicine, 1988-92; Professor of Pediatrics and Immunology, Faculty of Medicine, University of Sherbrooke; Head, Allergy and Immunology Division, Director, Clinical Research Center, University Hospital. Publications include: Co-author, Transcriptional modulation of PAF receptor gene expression by cyclic AMP, in Journal of Biology Chemistry, 1993; Co-author, Interferon-gamma regulates platelet-activating factor receptor gene expression in human monocytes, in Journal of Immunology, 1994. Honours: Young Investigator Award, CRCQ, 1986; Excellence Award for Pediatric Research, 1990. Memberships: Canadian Society for Immunology; Society Leukocyte Biology; American Association of Immunologists; Club de Recherche Clinique du Québec. Hobbies: Skiing; Canoeing; Hiking. Address: 3001 N 12th Ave, Sherbrooke, Quebec, J1H 5N4, Canada.

ROLAND Jay Alan, b. 20 Jun 1930, Brooklyn, NY, USA. Psychoanalyst. m. Joan Gardner, 30 Sep 1962, 1 s, 1 d. Education: BA, Sociology, Antioch College; PhD, Clinical Psychology, Adelphi University; Certificate in Psychoanalysis, National Psychologists Association for Psychoanalysis (NPAP). Appointment: Faculty and Member, Board of Trustees, NPAP. Publications: Psychoanalysis, Creativity and Literature: A French-American Dialogue, over 30 pages, 1978; In Search of Self in India and Japan: Toward a Cross-Cultural Psychology, 1988. Contributions to: Co-editor and contributor, Career and Motherhood: Struggles for a New Identity, 1978. Memberships: American Psychological Association; American Academy of Psychoanalysis; National Psychological Association for Psychoanalysis; Association for Asian Studies; American Society of Contemporary Artists. Hobbies: Skiing; Theatre. Address: 274 West 11th Street, New York, NY 10014, USA.

ROLLMAN-BRANCH Hilda S, b. Essen, Germany. Psychoanalyst; Psychiatrist. Education: BS, Chemistry, Columbia University, USA, 1943; MD, University of Southern California, Los Angeles, 1947. Appointments include: Private practice, Psychiatry, Psychoanalysis, Los Angeles, 1952-; Staff Psychiatrist, then Attending Psychiatrist, Los Angeles Psychiatric Services, 1952-64; Attending Psychiatrist, Reiss-Davis Clinic for Child Guidance, 1956-64; Clinical Instructor, 1957-60, Assistant Clinical Professor, 1960-66, Associate Clinical Professor, Psychiatry, 1966-74, Clinical Professor, Psychiatry, 1974-, University of California, Los Angeles; Director, Extension Division, Los Angeles Institute for Psychoanalysis, 1963-66; Lecturer, 1966-70, Associate Clinical Professor, Law in Psychiatry, 1970-74, Clinical Professor, Law in Psychiatry, 1974-82, University of Southern California Law School; Assistant Instructor, 1962-63, Instructor, 1963-67, Senior Faculty Member, 1967-, Training Analyst, 1968-, Supervising Analyst, 1969-, Chairman, Admissions Committee, 1970-72, Assistant Director, 1970-72, Director, 1975-76, Chairman, Candidates Evaluation Committee, 1980-84. Publications include: Plasma Levels of Radioactive Iodine (I131) in Human Tracer Studies (with D W Petit), 1949; Freud and Schnitzler (Doppelganger) (with H I Kupper), 1959; Psychoanalytic Reflections on Verdi's Don Carlo, 1963; El Ideal Hermafrodita y La Voz, 1967, as The Hermaphroditic Ideal and the Voice, 1972; Review of technik zur Dialektic der Psychoanalytischen Praxis, 1984; Review of ubersicht der ubertragungsneurosen, 1989. Memberships: Los Angeles County, California State and American Medical Associations; Southern California Psychiatric Society; Fellow, American Psychiatric Association; Los Angeles Psychoanalytic Society and Institute; American and International Psychoanalytic Associations; Corresponding Member, Mexican and Israel Psychoanalytic Associations. Address: 1505 Sorrento Drive, Pacific Palisades, CA 90272, USA.

ROMANO Paul Edward, b. 30 Oct 1934, New York City, USA. Pediatric Ophthalmologist; Educator; Editor and Publisher of Professional Journal. m. Judith Ann Robinson, 18 Oct 1969. Education: AB, Cornell University, 1955; MD, 1959; MS, Distinction, Ophthalmology, Georgetown University, 1967; Diplomate in Ophthalmology; Intern in Surgery, Albany Medical Center, NY, 1959-60. Career includes: Fellow in Ophthalmology, Armed Forces Institute of Pathology, WA, 1967, Wilmer Ophthalmology Institute, Johns Hopkins Hospital, Baltimore, 1967-69; Director of Ophthalmology, Children's Memorial Hospital, Chicago, 1970-80; Assistant Professor, 1969-73, Associate Professor, 1973-80, Professor of Ophthalmology, 1980-89, University of Florida College of Medicine, Gainesville; Consultant, VA Medical Center, Gainesville, 1980-89, Naval Regional Medical Center, Jacksonville, FL, 1981-89; Founding Editor and publisher, Binocular Vision and Eye Muscle Surgery Quarterly, 1985-. Contributions to: Over 300 articles to scientific journals. Honours: Fellow, Heed Foundation, 1968, NIH, 1968-69; Fellow, American Academy of Ophthalmology. Memberships: American Academy of Pediatrics; Charter Member, International Association of Ocular Surgeons; International Strabismus Association; Charter Member, American Association for Pediatric Ophthalmology; Association for Research in Vision and Ophthalmology; AAUP; Florida Medical Association; Florida Society of Ophthalmology; Alachua County Medical Society; Society of Heed Fellows; Wilmer Residents Association. Address: 2500 NW 23rd Terrace, Gainesville, FL 32605-2811, USA.

ROOS Stefanus David, b. 9 Dec 1948, Christiana, South Africa. Nurse. m. Elizabeth Susanna Roos, 26 Apr 1989, 1 s, 1 d. Education: BA, Cur, M Cur, D Cur (PhD); Registered as Community Health Nurse, Nurse Tutor, Nurse Administrator, General Nurse, Psychiatric Nurse, Supplementary Diagnostic Radiographer. Career: Student Nurse, Anglo American Mines; Charge Nurse, Mine Hospital; Senior Matron, Department of Health; Medical Station Superintendant, Mines; Nursing Service Manager, Department of Health; Lecturer, Senior Lecturer, Rand Afrikaans University. Publications: Geneskunde, 1993; Curationis, 1994; Higher Education, 1994. Memberships: SA Nursing Council, South Africa Nursing Association; CHASA; SAMDC. Hobby: Racing Pigeons. Address: Azalealaan 156, Wilropark, Roodepoort 1725, South Africa.

ROOT Caroline, b. 16 June 1956, Cambridge, England. Acupuncturist; Chinese Herbalist. m. Alan Hext, 18 Aug 1984. Education: BA, Oxford; MA, Notre Dame, USA; Lic AC; BAc; Dip SCHM. Appointments: Director, Cambridge Traditional Acupunture Centre; Partner, Monkey Press. Memberships: Traditional Acupuncture Society; Register of Chinese Herbal Medicine. Hobbies: Literature; Movies. Address: Cambridge Traditional Acupuncture Centre, 5 Tredgold Lane, Napier Street, Cambridge CB1 1HN, England.

ROOT Harlan D, b. 16 Jan 1926, USA. Physician; Teacher. m. Catherine B Friedrich, 26 June 1953, 2 sons, 2 daughters. Education: MD; PhD. Appointments: Assistant Professor of Surgery, 1961-65; Associate Professor of Surgery, 1966-67; Professor of Surgery, 1967-. Publications: Numerous professional publications in scientific journals. Memberships: Secretary, President, TX Chapter of American College of Surgeons, 1981-86; Governor, American College of Surgeons, 1988-94; American Cancer Society Fellow, 1955-57; President, American Association for Surgery of Trauma, 1988-89. Hobbies: Hunting; Tennis; Automotives. Address: 216 Village Circle, San Antonio, TX 78732, USA.

ROSADO Jorge L, b. 28 Jan 1959, Mexico City, Mexico. Scientist. m. Norma Rico, 7 Dec 1985, 3 d. Education: MSc, MIT; PhD, University of CT. Appointments: Visiting Scientist, INCAP, 1986; Professor, National University of Mexico, 1988-. Publications: About 30 scientific articles in major journals, 1983-94; 4 Chapters in books concerning nutrition. Honours include: National Prize in Food Research, 1987; National Prize in Human Nutrition, 1992. Memberships: American Institute of Nutrition; Latin American Society of Nutrition; Society International Nutrition Research; Institute of Food Technology. Hobby: Exercise. Address: National Institute of Nutrition, Vasco de Quinogo no 15, Halpan, Mexico DF 14000, Mexico.

ROSE Cynthia, b. 26 Apr 1936, Boston, MA, USA. Psychiatry. m. Cameron E Berry, MD, 6 Jun 1964, divorced, 2 s. Education: AB, Tufts University, Medford, MA, 1959; MD, Boston University Medical School, 1963. Career: Executive Director, 1970, Medical Director, 1970-83, Pikes Peak Medical Health Center; Currently, Private Practice Psychiatry; Associate Clinical Professor of Psychiatry, University of Colorado, Health Sciences Center. Honours: Fellow, American

Psychiatric Association; President, Colorado Psychiatric Society, 1980-81; Spokesperson of the Year, Colorado Psychiatric Society, 1991. Memberships: American Psychiatric Association; American Medical Association; Royal Society of Medicine; International Women's Forum. Hobbies: Single Engine Pilot - Instrument Rated; Skiing; Tennis; Hiking. Address: 730 No Cascade Avenue, Colorado Springs, CO 80903, USA.

ROSE Frank Clifford, b. 29 Aug 1926, London, England. Neurologist. m. Angela Rose, 16 Sep 1963, 3 s. Education: MB; FRCP; MBBS; DCH. Career: Consultant Neurologist, Royal Eye Medical Ophthalmology Unit, 1963; Consultant Neurologist, Charing Cross Hospital, London, Currently, Director, London Neurological Centre. Publications: 60 Books on neurology including: Advances in Headache Research, No 4, 1994; Advances in ALS Research, 1994. Honours: Harold Wolff Award, American Association for Study of Headache, 1981, 1984; Distinguished Clinical Award, American Association for Study of Headache, 1986. Membership: Secretary, Treasurer General, World Federation of Neurology. Hobbies: Travel; History; Wine. Address: London Neurological Centre, 110 Harley Street, London, W1N 1AF, England.

ROSEN Jay Scott, b. 3 Apr 1965, New York, USA. Optometrist. Education: BS; OD; FAAO. Appointments: Chief, Cornea & Contact Lens Service, Assistant Clinical Professor. Publications: Accommodation to Naturalistic Stimuli, 1990; Making Corneal Toricity, Does it Work, 1991; Accommodation during Distance Ophmetric Test Procedures, 1991; Amber Discoloration of Contact Lenses, 1992; Parameter Consistency of Disposable Lenses, 1993. Honours: Bausch & Lomb Contact Lens Award; Alcon Research Award. Memberships: American Academy of Optometry; American Optometric Association. Hobbies: Music; Reading. Address: 949 Siems Ct, N Bellmore, NY 11710, USA.

ROSEN Leonard J, b. 9 Aug 1946, Detroit, MI, USA. Psychiatrist. m. Sharon Rosen, 22 Jun 1969, 2 s, 2 d. Education: MD; Diplomate, American Board of Psychiatry. Appointment: Medical Director, Mental Health Services, Macomb Hospital Center. Honour: Alpha Omega Alpha. Memberships: American Medical Association; American Psychiatric Society. Address: 11800 East 12 Mile Road, Warren, MI 48093, USA.

ROSEN Maria Rosaleen Barron, b. 1 Dec 1941, Scotland. Psychiatrist. m. Frederick Rosen, 25 May 1968, 2 sons. Education: MB ChB, Glasgow University, 1965; DPM, 1971; MRC Psych, 1974. Appointments: Tavistock Clinic, London, 1981-90; Currently Psychiatrist and Psychoanalyst in private practice, London. Publications: Group Therapy in a Marital Group, 1975; A Project in Reinforcing the Effectiveness of the Primary Care Team in the Area of Mental Health, 1991; The Demosthenes Complex Revisited, 1991; Enuresis, 1992; Electra Complex in Development of Femininity, 1994. Memberships: British Medical Association; Royal College of Psychiatrists; British Association of Psychotherapists; British Psychanalytical Society. Hobbies: Reading; Walking; Music. Address: 40 Priory Gardens, Highgate, London N6 5QS, England.

ROSEN Michael, b. 17 Oct 1927, Dundee, Scotland. Anaesthetist. m. Sally Barbara, 17 Oct 1955, 2 sons, 1 daughter. Education: MB ChB; FRCA; FRCOG; FRCS(Eng). Appointments: Cnsultant Anaesthetist, 1962-93; University Hospital of Wales; President, Association of Anaesthetists, 1986-88; President, College of Anaesthetists, 1988-91. Honours: CBE, 1989; Honorary FFARCSI, 1984; Gold Medallist, Association of Anaesthetists of Great Britain and Ireland, 1993. Memberships: Honorary Member, University Anaesthetists Assocviation, USA, 1989. Hobbies: Work; Music; Family. Address: 45 Hollybush Road, Cardiff CF2 6SZ, Wales.

ROSENBAUM Arthur L, b. 30 Jan 1933, Lorain, OH, USA. Medicine. m. Marcia Selzman, 19 Aug 1956, 2 s, 1 d. Education: BA, University of Michigan; MD, Western Reserve University, CWRU; Graduate, Cleveland Psychoanalytic Institute. Career includes: Chairman, Educational Committee, Cleveland Psychoanalytic Institute, 1989-; Chairman, Committee of Certification, Board of Professional Standards, American Psychoanalytic Association, 1990-; Currently, Private Practice and Assistant Clinical Professor, Department of Psychiatry, School of Medicine, Central Western Reserve University. Publication: Assessment of Parental Function, in Psychoanalytic Quarterly, 1994. Memberships: American Psychoanalytic Association; International Psychoanalytic Association; Association for Child Psychoanalysis; OH State Medical Association; Academy of Medicine, Cleveland; Cleveland Psychoanalytic Society; Cleveland Psychoanalytic Institute. Address: 2680 Fairmount Boulevard, Cleveland Heights, OH 44106-3647, USA.

ROSENFIELD Allan Garber, b. 28 Apr 1933, USA. Medical Doctor. m. Clare Stein Rosenfield, 31 July 1966, 1 son, 1 daughter. Education: BA, Harvard College; MD, Columbia University College of Physicians & Surgeons. Appointments: Population Council Representative, Thailand, 1967-93; Population Council, Director, MCH/FP Programs, 1973-75; Director, Center for Population & Family Health, Columbia University, 1975-88; Acting Chairman, Department of Obstetrics & Gynecology; DeLamar Professor of Public Health; Professor of Obstetrics & Gynecology; Dean, Columbia University School of Public Health. Publications: Over 100 articles on population, MCH family planning, obstetrics & gynecology, international health. Memberships: American Public Health Association; American College of Obstetrics & Gynecologists. Hobbies: Tennis; Skiing; Music. Address: Columbia School of Public Health, 600 West 168th St, NY 10032, USA.

ROSENMAN Kenneth D, b. 2 Feb 1951, NY, USA. Professor of Medicine. Education: AB, Cornell University, 1972; MD, NY Medical College, 1975. Career: Assistant Professor of Epidemiology, University of MA; Director of Occupational and Environmental Health, NJ Department of Health; Currently, Professor of Medicine, MI State University College of Human Medicine, East Lansing, MI. Publications: Cardiovascular Disease and Workplace Exposures, in Archives of Environmental Health, 1984; Co-author, Does Silicosis Still Occur?, in JAMA, 1989; Asthma and Work: How Do You Diagnose the Association?, 1991. Memberships: Collegium Ramazzini; American College of Epidemiology; American College of Preventive Medicine. Address: Michigan State University, 117 West Fee, East Lansing, MI 48824-1316, USA.

ROSENMAN Stephen, b. 4 Sept 1945, Brooklyn, New York, USA. Physician. m. Aelette de Grect, 26 Dec 1970, 1 s, 1 d. Education: MD; BA, Biology; Fellow, American College of Obstetrics & Gynaecology; Diplomate of American Board of Obstetrics & Gynaecology. Appointments: Practising Physician. Hobbies: Computer. Address: 1735 Post Road, Fairfield, CT 00430, USA.

ROSENOW Edward C III, b. 2 Feb 1934, Columbus, OH, USA. Medicine. m. Constance Grahame, 31 Aug 1957, 1 s, 1 d. Education: MD; MS, Medicine. Appointment: Arthur M and Gladys D Gray Professor of Medicine, Mayo Medical School. Publications: Over 100 articles including 43 book chapters; Co-author, Diffuse Diseases of The Lung: A Team Approach, book, 1991. Honours: President, Mayo Clinic Staff, 1986; President, American College of Chest Physicians, 1989-90; Ohio State University College of Medicine, Alumni Achievement Award, 1989; Henry S Plummer Award, Department of Internal Medicine, Mayo Clinic, 1994;Distinguished Mayo Clinician award 1994; Ralph O Claypoole Sr Memorial award, American College of Physicians 1995. Numerous Teacher of The Year in Internal Medicine Awards, Mayo Clinic. Memberships: American College of Chest Physicians; Fellow, Governor, 1987-91, American College of Physicians; American Medical Association. Hobbies: Exercise; Reading. Address: Mayo Clinic, 200 First Street SW, Rochester, MN 55905, USA.

ROSENSTREICH David L, b. 16 Nov 1942, New York City, NY, USA. Physician. m. Victoria Abokrek, 2 s, 1 d. Education: BS; MD; FACAI; FAAAI. Career: Senior Investigator, NIH, Bethesda, MD; Visiting Associate Professor, Rockefeller University, NY; Currently, Professor of Medicine and Microbiology, Immunology, Albert Einstein College of Medicine. Honours: Alpha Omega Alpha, NY University School of Medicine, 1966; Founder Award, New York University School of Medicine, 1967; US PHS Commendation Medal, 1975; Danziger Professorship of Microbiology and Immunology, 1983. Memberships: American Association of Physicians; American Society for Clinical Investigation; American Academy of Allergy and Immunology; American College of Allergy and Immunology; American Association of Immunologists. Hobby: Oenology. Address: 1300 Morris Park Avenue, Bronx, NY 10461, USA.

ROSS Colin Andrew, b. 14 July 1950, Sarnia, Ontario, Canada. Psychiatrist. m. Nancy Eleanor Keys, 8 Feb 1986, 3 s, 2 d. Education: MD, 1981; Canadian speciality in psychiatry, 1985. Appointment: Currently, Director, Dissociative Disorders Unit, Charter Behavioral Health System of Dallas. Publications: Pseudoscience in Biological Psychiatry, 1995; Adenocarcinoma and Other Poems, 1989; Multiple Personality Disorder, Diagnosis, Clinical Features and Treatment, 1989; The Osiris Complex, Case Studies in Multiple Personality Disorder, 1994. Honours: Laughlin Fellow, American College of Psychiatrists, 1985; President, International Society for Study of Dissociation, 1994.

Memberships: International Society for Study of Dissociation; APA; American College of Psychiatrists. Hobbies; Running; Writing. Address: 1701 Gateway, 4349 Richardson, TX 75080, USA.

ROSS Elliott D, b. 3 Jan 1945, Queens, New York, USA. Physician. m. Stephanie Silverman, 7 Jan 1970, 1 son, 1 daughter. Education: BA, College of Liberal Arts, 1968, MD, School of Medicine, 1968, Boston University; Board Certified, Neurology, American Board of Psychiatry and Neurology. 1978. Appointments: Clinical Fellow, Harvard Medical School, Boston, Massachusetts, 1972-75; Assistant Professor, Neurology, 1975-81, Psychiatry, 1979-81, Associate Professor, Neurology, Psychiatry, 1981-88, University of Texas Southwestern Medical Center, Dallas; Professor, Chair, Neurology, Department of Neuroscience, University of North Dakota School of Medicine, Fargo, 1988-; Director, Senior Research Scientist, Clinical Research Programme, Neuropsychiatric Research Institute, Fargo, 1988-. Publications include: Sensory Specific and Fractional Disorders of Recent Memory in Man, I and II, 1980; The Aprosodias: Functional-Anatomical Organization of the Affective Components of Language in the Right Hemisphere, 1981; Nonverbal aspects of language, 1993; Co-author: Dominant Language Functions of the Right Hemisphere?: Prosody and Emotional Gesturing, 1979; Diagnostic Issues and Neuroanatomical Correlates of Depression in Brain Damaged Patients: Implications for a Neurology of Depression, 1981; Differential Hemispheric Lateralization of Primary and Social Emotions: Implications for Developing a Comprehensive Neurology for Emotions, Repression and the Subconscious, 1994; Lateralization of Affective Prosody in Brain a. nd the Callosal Integration of Hemisphere Language, forthcoming. Honours include: 1st Award, NASA, 1st Award, US Navy, National and International Science Fair, Kansas City, 1961; Westinghouse Science Honours Group, 1962. Memberships: American Academy of Neurology; American Neurological Association; Behavioral Neurology Society; International Neuropsychology Society. Hobbies: Skiing; Golf; Riding. Address: Department of Neuroscience, UND Education Bldg, 1919 N Elm St, Fargo, ND 58102, USA.

ROSS Helen Elizabeth, b. 2 Dec 1935, London, England. University Lecturer. Education: MA, University of Oxford, 1959; PhD, University of Cambridge, 1966. Career: Lecturer in Psychology, University of Hull, 1965-68; Lecturer, 1969-72, Senior Lecturer, 1972-83, Reader, 1983-94, Honorary Senior Research Fellow, 1994-, University of Stirling. Publications: Behaviour and Perception in Strange Environments, 1974; Co-author, E H Weber: The Sense of Touch, 1978; Co-author, The natural moon illusion: a multi-factor angular account, in Perception, 1994. Honours: ESA and Royal Society of London Fellowships at DLR, Cologne, 1980-81; Leverhulme Fellowship, University of Stirling, 1983-84. Memberships: Fellow, 1986, Chartered Psychologist, 1988, British Psychological Society; Fellow, 1990, Fellowships Secretary, 1994, Royal Society of Edinburgh. Hobbies: Skiing; Hill Walking; Curling; Traditional Music, Concertina and Small Pipes. Address: Department of Psychology, University of Stirling, Stirling, FK9 4LA, Scotland.

ROSS Henry George Tiley, b. 23 Apr 1917, Johannesburg, South Africa. Obstetrics and Gynaecology. m. Moyra Florence Mackenzie, 12 Dec 1949, 3 s, 1 d. Education: MBChB; MRCOG; FRCS(C); FRCOG; FACOG. Career: Obstetrician and Gynaecologist now retired. Address: 976 Lands End Road, Sidney, BC V8L 5L3, Canada.

ROSS William Ross, b. 13 Sept 1913, Hamilton, Ontario, Canada. Psychiatrist; Psychoanalist. 1 s. Address: Dept of Psychiatry Coll of Med, ML 559 231 Bethesda Ave, Cincinnati, OH 45267, USA.

ROTH Karl Sebastian, b. 3 Mar 1941, New York City, New York, USA. Paediatrician. m. Carole N Roth, 27 July 1984, 4 sons. Education: AB, Biology, University of Rochester, 1963; MA, Physiology, City University of New York, 1965; MD, Wake Forest University, 1969. Appointments: Assistant Professor of Paediatrics, University of Pennsylvania School of Medicine, 1975-81; Currently Professor of Paediatrics, Biochemistry and Molecular Biology, Virginia Commonwealth University-Medical College of Virginia, Richmond. Publications: Prenatal Administration of Biotin in Biotin Responsive Multiple Carboxylase Deficiency, 1982; Metabolic Disease: A Guide to Early Recognition (co-author), 1983. Honours: Daland Fellowship, American Philosophical Society, 1972-75; National Institutes of Health Research Career Development Award, 1976-81. Memberships: American Pediatric Society; Society for Pediatric Research; Society for Inborn Errors of Metabolism. Hobbies: Violin and string quartets;

Authoring novels. Address: Box 239, MCV Station, Richmond, VA 23298, USA.

ROTH Loren H, b. 9 May 1939, Cleveland, OH, USA. Psychiatrist. m. Ellen Roth, PhD, Aug 1973, 1 s, 2 d. Education: BA, Philosophy, Cornell University, Ithaca, NY, 1961; MD cum laude, Medicine, Harvard Medical School, Boston, 1966; MPH, Behavioral Sciences, Harvard School of Public Health, Boston; 1972. Appointments include: Chief, Clinical Services, 1989-, Western Psychiatric Institute and Clinic, University of Pittsburgh; Chief of Psychiatry, 1990-, Presbyterian University Hospital, Pittsburgh; Vice Chairman, Department of Psychiatry, University of Pittsburgh, 1988-; Medical Staff, Chief of Psychiatry, Montefiore University Hospital, Pittsburgh, 1990-; Vice President for Managed Care, University of Pittsburgh Medical Center, 1993-. Publications include: Over 60 refereed articles, 1961-, including: Psychological predictors of vulnerability to distress in the year following heart transplantation, Psychological Medicine, in press; Numerous books, book chapters, monographs, reviews, articles and abstracts; Numerous presentations, workshops, symposium and book forewards. Honours include: Phi Beta Kappa; Outstanding Teacher Award, WPIC Psychiatric Residents, 1983; Commission on mentally disabled, American Bar Association, 1987; Isaac Ray Award, American Psychiatric Association, 1988; Exemplary Psychiatrist Award, National Alliance for Mentally Ill, 1992. Memberships include: Fellow, American Psychiatric Association, 1971; American Society of Criminology, 1975; AMA, 1983; Fellow, Royal Society of Medicine, London, 1992. Address: 200 Lothrop, Pittsburgh, PA 15213-2582, USA.

ROTH Robert Howard, b. 15 Jan 1933, Newark, USA. Psychologist. m. Estelle Goldstein, 16 June 1957, 1 son, 1 daughter. Education: BS, Juilliard School; MA, Columbia University; EdD, Columbia University. Appointments: Professor of Psychology; Instructor of Psychology; Assistant Professor of Psychology; Associate Professor of Psychology; Staff Clinical Psychologist; Consultant Clinical Psychologist. Publications: Psychopathologies and Treatments, 1991; Ego Self Person Context, 1992; Tempest in the Mind: Behavioural and Experimental Pathologies, 1994. Honours: Life Fellow, American Orthopsychiatric Association, 1992. Memberships: American Psychological Association; American Orthopsychiatric Association; New York Academy of Sciences; American Association for the Advancement of Science. Life Fellow, American Orthopsychiatric Association, 1992. Hobbies: Classical Music. Address: 111 Gallinson Drive, Murray Hill, NJ 07974-2723, USA. 188.

ROTHBAUM Barbara Olasov, b. 7 Jul 1960, Charleston, SC, USA. Psychologist. m. John E Rothbaum, 19 Jun 1988, 2 s. Education: BA, Highest Honours, Psychology, University of NC, 1982; MA, 1984, PhD, 1986, University of GA; Certified in Behavioral Psychology, ABPP. Career: Assistant Professor, Medical College of Pennsylvania; Currently, Assistant Professor, Psychiatry, Emory University School of Medicine. Publications: Female assault victims: A treatment manual for PTSP, in press; Numerous journal articles. Honours: Award for Research on Women, American Psychological Association, 1991; Award for Research on Women, Georgia Psychological Association. Memberships: APA; GPA; AABT; Society for Traumatic Stress. Hobbies: Family; Reading. Address: Department of Psychiatry, The Emory Clinic, 1365 Clifton Road NE, Atlanta, GA 30322, USA.

ROTHMAN Kenneth Jay, b. 2 Nov 1945, Brooklyn, NY, USA. Epidemiologist. m. Nancy A Dreyer, 30 Aug 1980, 3 d. Education: AB, Colgate University, 1966; DMD, 1969, MPH, 1970, DrPh, 1972, Harvard University. Career: Assistant and Associate Professor of Epidemiology, Harvard School of Public Health; Professor of Community Medicine, University of MA Medical School; Currently: Editor, Epidemiology, Professor of Public Health, Boston University. Publications: Modern Epidemiology, 1986; Casual Inference, 1988; Conflict of Interest - The New McCarthyism in Science, in JAMA, 1993; The Continuing Unethical Use of Placebo Controls, in New England Journal of Medicine, 1994. Honour: Adolph G Kammer Award, American Occupational Medicine Association, 1983. Memberships: Society for Epidemiologic Research; International Society for Environmental Epidemiology; Council of Biology Editors; Biometric Society. Hobbies: Running; Sailing; Hiking; Orienteering; Bicycling. Address: Epidemiology, One Newton Executive Park, Newton Lower Falls, MA 02162, USA.

ROTHSCHILD Henry, b. 5 Jun 1932, Horstein, Germany. Physician. m. Tanea Miller, 2 d. Education: BA, Cornell University, Ithaca, NY; MD, University of Chicago, IL; PhD, Johns Hopkins University, Baltimore, MD. Career includes: Instructor in Medicine, Massachusetts General

Hospital; Associate Research Professor of Medicine and Anatomy, Research Professor of Medicine and Anatomy, Head of Section of Genetics and Geriatrics, Adjunct Professor of Department of Psychology, LSU Medical Center. Publications include: Over 65 articles in professional journals from 1963, and over 40 abstracts from 1958; Co-author, Doctors for The President, book, 1981; Editor or Co-Editor of 4 books. Honours: MBRS Visiting Professor, Universidad de Puerto Rico, Colegio Univeristario de Cayey, 1989; MBRS Visiting Professor, University of Houston, 1991. Memberships: American Society on Aging; New Orleans Academy of Internal Medicine; American Association for the Advancement of Science; The Gerontological Society of America; American Society of Human Genetics. Hobbies: Racquetball; Reading; Art. Address: LSU Medical Center, 1542 Tulane Avenue, New Orleans, LA 70117, USA.

ROTONDO Gaetano Mario, b. 30 January 1926, Taranto, Italy. Aerospace and Forensic Medicine Physician. m. Vittoria Beltrami, 23 June 1957. Education: MD, University Bari,Italy, 1949; PhD, University of Rome, Italy, 1969. Appointments: Chief, Italian Military School of Medicine, Rome, 1974-75; Deputy Chief, 1975-78, Chief, 1979-82, Italian Air Force Medical Service; Surgeon, General Italian Air Force, 1980-86. Publications: Editor, 4 Books: Military Forensic Medicine, 1983, 1989; Forensic Aeronautical Medicine, 1988; Aviation Medicine, 1990; Co-editor, Review "Minerva Aerospaziale", 1980-95; More than 300 scientific publications in aerospace and forensic medicine. Honours: Grand Officer Cross Order of Merit, Italy; Golden Medal of Merit for Public Health, Italy; Italian Red Cross Meritorious Service Golden Medal; Golden Medal for Senior Military Service, Italy; Honorary Flight License and Wings, Germany; Theodore C Lyster International Award, Aerospace Medical Association, Washington. Memberships: Vice President, Italian Society of Aerospace Medicine; Fellow, Royal Aeronautical Society and British Interplanetary Society; Fellow, USA Aerospace Medical Association; American Astronautic Society; Academician, International Academies of Aerospace Medicine and Astronautics; Roman Academy of Medical & Biological Sciences; Lancisiana Academy of Rome. Hobbies: Private Pilot. Address: 348 Via Conca d'Oro 348, Ò 0141, Rome, Italy.

RÖTTINGER Erwin M, b. 11 Mar 1940, Augsburg, Germany. Professor of Radiotherapy. Education: MD; Doctor of Medicine; Professor. Career includes: Resident, Harvard Joint Center for Radiation Therapy, Boston and Clinical Fellow in Radiation Therapy, 1970-72; Instructor in Radiation Therapy, Harvard Medical School and Clinical and Research Fellow in Radiation Therapy, Massachusetts General Hospital, Boston, 1972-73; Currently, Director, Department of Radiotherapy, University of Ulm. Memberships: American Society of Therapeutic Radiology and Oncology; European Society of Therapeutic Radiology and Oncology; Societé International Oncologique Pediatrique; Deutsche Röndgengesellschaft. Address: Department of Radiotherapy, University of Ulm, 7900 Ulm, Germany.

ROUTSONIS Kornilios, b. 28 July 1925, Thessaloniki, Greece. Professor of Neurology. m. Alexandra Koklitou, 28 Apr 1958, 4 sons. Education: MD, University of Thessaloniki, 1952; Training, Innsbruck, Austria Psychiatry University Clinic, 1953; Training, Neuropathology Department, Medical School, Hamburg, Germany, 1959-61; MA, Theology, University of Thessaloniki, 1970; Professor of Neurology & Psychiatry, University of Thessaloniki, 1978. Appointments: Medical Assistant, 1953; Assistant, University of Neurology Clinic, Thessaloniki, 1957; Private Doctor, Neurology & Psychiatry, 1963; Associate Professor, Neurology & Psychiatry, University of Thessaloniki, 1970; Professor, University of Thessalouiki. Publications: Temporal Lobe Epilepsy, 1956; Postvaccinale Encephalopathic, 1960; Enzymhistochemistry at the Punct Wound of the Brain, 1962; Entamarkumgsenzephalitis, 1962; Hallucinations Hemianopsiques Chez des Vieillards, 1972. Memberships: Hellenic Neurology Society; Southern Europe Society for Neurology & Psychiatry. Honours: President, Societyof Neurology & Psychiatry, Northern Greece; President, Society for Neuropathology of Greece. Hobbies: Painting. Address: Kambouridou St 47, Panorama, Thessaloniki, Greece.

ROWLEY Peter Templeton, b. 29 Apr 1929, Greenville, Pennsylvania, USA. Doctor of Medicine; Professor. m. 19 Mar 1967, 2 sons. Education: MD. Appointments: Assistant Professor of Medicine, Stanford University California; Currently Professor of Medicine, Paediatrics, Genetics, Microbiology/Immunology, Oncology, University of Rochester School of Medicine, Rochester, New York. Publications: 122 apart from abstracts, 1956-94. Memberships: American Society of

Human Genetics; American Society of Hematology; American College of Medical Genetics; American College of Medical Genetics. Address: University of Rochester School of Medicine, Divison of Genetics, Box 641, 601 Elmwood Avenue, Rochester, NY 14642, USA.

ROXBURGH David Russell, b. 31 Oct 1945, Sydney, Australia. Obstetrics and Gynaecology. m. Anne Sullivan, 18 Dec 1968, 2 s, 2 d. Education: MBBS, Sydney University; FRCOG; FRACOG. Appointment: Visiting Medical Officer, Nepean Hospital. Memberships: Australian Menopause Society; Australian Perinatal Society. Hobbies: Cross Country Skiing; Sailing. Address: 150 Lethbridge Street, St Penrith, NSW 2750, Australia.

ROZEN Lynn Marie, b. 4 July 1966, Westerly, Rhode Island, USA. Dance/Movement Therapist. Education: MA, Dance/Movement Therapy & Counseling Psychology, Antioch New England Graduate School, Keene, New Hampshire, USA; BA, Psychology, University of Washington, Seattle, WA, USA; Registered Dance Therapist. Career: Activities Therapist, Wild Acre Inns, Belmont, MA, USA; Children's Dance Teacher, Newton Arts Center, Newton, MA; Dance/Movement Therapist, Boston Institute for Arts Therapy, Boston, MA; Children's Program Coordinator, Nurturance Program, Child Abuse Prevention Service of Tuscaloosa. Publications: Chaos Theory: A Model for Dance/Movement Therapy, American Dance Therapy Association 28th Annual Conference Proceedings, 1993. Memberships: American Dance Therapy Associaton; Chaos in Praxis Network. Hobbies: Reading; Swimming; Hiking; Dance. Address: 1629 1st Avenue, Tuscaloosa, AL 35401, USA.

RUAN Changgeng, b. 8 Aug 1939, Shanghai, China. Professor of Medicine. m. Huiyu Gu, 1 May 1969, 2 daughters. Education: BA; Diploma, Peking University, 1964; MD; PhD; Diplôme d'Etude et de Recherche en Biologie Humaine (Hématologie), 1980, Doctorat d'Etat en Biologie Humaine, 1981, Université de Paris VII. Appointments: Resident, Suzhou Medical College Hospital, 1965-73; Assistant Professor, 1973-79, Associate Professor, 1982-86, Professor of Medicine, 1986-, Suzhou Medical College; Fellowship, Institut des Maladies du Sang, Hôpital St Louis, Paris, France, 1979-81. Publications: Study with monoclonal antibodies on normal and diseased platelets (co-author), 1982; The Platelets - Basics and Clinicals (author, editor), 1987; Studies on platelet membrane glycoproteins using monoclonal antibodies, 1989; Von Willebrand Disease, 1991; Thrombosis and Haemostasis - Current Concept and Clinical Practice (author, editor), 1994. Honours: National Distinguished Specialist, 1986; Chevalier de l'Ordre National du Mérite, France, 1994. Memberships: Chinese Medical Association; Chinese Society of Haematology; Chinese Society of Biochemistry; Société Française d'Hématologie; American Society of Haematology; American Heart Association; International Society of Thrombosis and Haemostasis; International Society of Haematology; International Society for Fibrinolysis and Thrombolysis. Hobbies: Running; Collecting stamps, pictures, other objects. Address: Jiangsu Institute of Haematology, Suzhou Medical College, 48 Renmin Road, Suzhou 215007, China.

RUAN Shi-Yi, b. 21 Feb 1920, Tianjin, China. Medical Doctor (Internal Medicine of Combined Chinese and Western Medicine). m. 16 Aug 1945, 4 daughters. Education: MD, 1945. Appointments: Visiting Doctor, 1952, Vice Chief Doctor, Vice Professor, 1956, Chief Doctor, Professor, 1965, Vice-President, 1969, 1st Teaching Hospital of Traditional Chinese Medicine of Tianjin. Publications: Internal Medicine of Traditional Chinese Medicine, 1973; Articles: Prevention and treatment of coronary heart disease by 651 pill, 1981; Experimental research of atherosclerosis prevention and treatment by "jangzhiruanmai tablet", 1990. Honours: Advanced Worker of Scientific Research, Tianjin, 1989, 1992; 2nd Degree Award of Scientific Research, Tianjin, 1989, 1992, 1993. Memberships: Association of Combined Chinese and Western Medicine of China; Tianjing Branch Association, Traditional Chinese Medicine Association of China. Hobbies: Fishing; Peking Opera. Address: The 1st Teaching Hospital of the Traditional Chinese Medicine College of Tianjin, 314 Anshanxi Road, Nankai District, Tianjin, China.

RUBEN Robert Joel, b. 2 Aug 1933, New York City, New York, USA. Otolaryngologist. m. Yvonne Korshak, 1 son, 3 daughters. Education: AB magna cum laude, Princeton University, 1955; MD, Johns Hopkins School of Medicine, 1959; FACS; FAAP. Appointments include: Professor, Chair, Otolaryngology Department, 1971-, Professor, Paediatrics Department, 1983-, Albert Einstein College of Medicine,

Yeshiva University, New York City; Director, Institute for Communication Disorders, 1986-; Attending, Chair, Otolaryngology Department: Albert Einstein College of Medicine Hospital, 1971-, Montefiore Medical Division and Center, 1971-, Bronx Municipal Hospital Center, 1971-, North Central Bronx Hospital, 1976-; Consultant: Misericordia Hospital Medical Center, 1971-, St Barnabas Hospital, 1973-. Publications: Co-editor: Electrocochleography, symposium proceedings, 1974; The Biology of Change in Otolaryngology, 1986; Otology: Medicine and Surgery, 2 vols, 1988; The Genetics of Hearing Impairment, 1991; Numerous articles and book chapters; General Otorhoinolaryngology (with S Thaler and A Eviatar), slides, 1970; Extracorporeal Development of the Ear, film, 1977; Terminal Mitosis, film 1980; Recognition and Management of the Hearing-Impaired Infant, 1983; Voice Problems in Children, TV tape, 1985; Hearing Impairment in Children (moderator), audio-tape, 1993. Honours: Sigma Xi, Princeton, 1955; 1 Gold and 2 Silver Medals for Extracorporeal Development of the Ear; Gold Medal, Schreiber Award, Deafness Research Foundation and National Association of the Deaf, 1980; Many others. Memberships include: American Otological Society; ARO; American Board of Otolaryngology; American Academy of Otolaryngology-Head and Neck Surgery; American Neurotological Society; Many committees and boards. Hobby: Book collecting. Address: Montefiore Medical Center, Department of Otolaryngology, 111 East 210th Street, Gold Zone Ste 100, Bronx, NY 10467, USA.

RUBEN Samuel M, b. 4 Mar 1950, PA, USA. Public Health Officer. Divorced, 1 d. Education: BS, Biology, Chemistry, 1974; MD, 1979; MPH, Johns Hopkins University, 1981; FAAFP. Career: Occupational Medical Physician, Preventive Medicine Officer, US Army; Currently, District Health Officer, Island of Hawaii; Medical Director, Big Island Substance Abuse Council, HI; Part Time Emergency Room Physician, Ka'u Community Hospital, HI. Publications include: The AIDS Epidemic: The Cultural Response to a Natural Phenomenon, 1988; Ecological Ethics and The Workplace, 1989; Co-author, High Altitude Reactive Hypertension in National Guard Personnel at Annual Training, in Military Medicine. Honours: Expert in the Field Medical Badge, 1982; FAAFP, 1991. Memberships: AMA; AAFP; IAMAT. Hobbies: Microcomputers; Bicycling; Kayaking. Address: PO Box 6088, Hilo, HI 96720, USA.

RUBENSTEIN A Daniel, b. 19 Nov 1907, Lynn, MA, USA. Physician. m. Delilah Riemov, MD, 26 Dec 1936, 2 d, 1 d. Education: AB, Harvard College, 1928; MD, Boston University School of Medicine, 1933; MPH, Harvard School of Public Health, 1940. Career includes: Instructor, Clinical Professor of Epidemiology, Harvard School of Public Health, 1945-60; Visiting Professor of Epidemiology, MA Institute of Technology, Department of Food Science, 1960-69; Currently, Consultant in Hospital Administration and Preventive Medicine. Publications: Many publications in Epidemiology and Hospital Administration, 1945-65. Honour: A Daniel Rubenstein Lectureship in Geriatrics, Boston College School of Nursing, 1965-. Memberships: AMA; MA Medical Society; American Hospital Association; Fellow, American Public Health Association. Address: 164 Ward Street, Newton, MA 02159, USA.

RUBENSTEIN Edward, b. 5 Dec 1924. Medicine. m. Nancy Mill, 20 Jul 1954, 3 s. Education: MD. Appointment: Associate Dean, Postgraduate Medical Education and Professor of Medicine. Publications: As author or author/editor, Textbooks on intensive medical care, internal medicine, synchrotron radiation research, synchrotron radiation in the life sciences and molecular medicine. Honours: Alpha Omega Alpha, 1947; Kaiser Award, 1989; Albion Walter Hewlett Award, 1993. Memberships: Institute of Medicine of the National Academy of Sciences, USA; Master, American College of Physicians; Fellow, American Association for the Advancement of Science. Address: Stanford University School of Medicine, Stanford, CA 94305, USA.

RUBENSTEIN Laurence Z, b. 15 Oct 1948, Los Angeles, CA, USA. Physician. m. Lisa Van Horne Rubenstein, 14 Apr 1969, 2 s, 1 d. Education: BA, University of CA, 1970; MD, Albert Einstein College of Medicine, NY, 1974; MPH, UCLA School of Public Health, Los Angeles, 1979; FACP; AGSF. Appointments: Professor of Medicine, UCLA; Director, Geriatric Center, Sepulreda, VA Medical Center. Publications include: Over 180 research articles, books and chapters including: Co-author, Quality of care for elderly people: The state of the evidence, Institute of Medicine Report, 1989; Co-editor, Falls Balance and Gait Disorders in the Elderly, 1992; Co-author, Medicare: Challenges and future directions in a changing health care environment, in Gerontologist, 1994. Honours: Board Certified, Internal Medicine, 1980, Preventive Medicine, 1981, Geriatric Medicine, 1988; FACP, 1983; AGSF, 1990.

Memberships: American College of Physicians; American Geriatric Society; American Public Health Association; Gerontological Society of America. Hobbies: Music; Hiking. Address: GRECC (11E), VA Medical Center, Sepulveda, CA 91343, USA.

RUBIANES-CILLAZO Yvette, b. Denver, Colorado, USA. Cytologist. Education: BA cum laude, Inter-American University, 1979; MD, World University School of Medicine, 1984; CT(ASCP), Memorial Sloan-Kettering Cancer Centre, 1987. Appointments: Cytologist, 1987-. Honours: 1st Student Honour Citation Award, New York City; Gold Medal of Music; Dean's National List, 1978-79; Inter-American Representative, National Institute of Health Biomedical Support Programme, Atlanta, Georgia; Participant at Concert given at the United Nations for the Diplomatic Families with New York City Wide Band; Vice-President of Medical School Class; Memberships: American Management Association; Washington Association of Cytology; American Society of Cytology; Greater New York Association of Cytology; National Association for Female Executives. Hobbies: Art; Music including singing in church choir; Some sports. Address: PO Box 341416, Bethesda, MD 20827, USA. or 2590 39th St. SW, Naples, Florida, 33964.

RUBIN John Stephen, b. 7 July 1953, Massachusetts, USA. Medical Doctor. m. Kristine M Carroll-Porczyaski, 26 Mar 1977. Education: BA, English Literature, Dartmouth College, 1974; MD, New York Medical College, 1977. Appointments: Lecturer, London, England, 1983-84; Assistant Professor, Department of Surgery, University of Maryland School of Medicine, 1984-86; Assistant Professor, Albert Einstein College of Medicine, 1986-92; Director, North Central Bronx Hospital; Director, Voice Center, Montefine Medical Center. Publications: Diagnosis and Treatment of Voice, 1994. Memberships: AMA; AAOHNS; ACS; SUO; RSM, Voice Foundation; AAFPRS. Honours: Phi Beta Kappa, 1974; New York Magazine, 1000 Best MS's in New York, 1992. Hobbies: Sculpture; Poetry. Address: 48 Sagamore Road, Bronxville, NY 10708, USA.

RUBIN Judith Aron, b. 12 Sep 1936, New York City, USA. Psychotherapist. m. Herbert Rubin, 28 Nov 1957, 1 s, 2 d. Education: BA, Art, Wellesley College, 1957; MEd, Elementary Education, Harvard Graduate School of Education, 1959; PhD, Counselling, University of Pittsburgh, 1976; Postgraduate study: Pittsburgh Psychoanalytic Institute; Graduate: Psychoanalysis of Adults, 1982, of Children and Adolescents, 1983. Career: Art Therapist, Pittsburgh Child Guidance Center, 1969-81; Co-Director, Creative and Expressive Arts Therapy Department, Western Psychiatric Institute and Clinic, 1981-85; Currently, Clinical Assistant Professor, Department of Psychiatry, University of Pittsburgh; Faculty, Pittsburgh Psychoanalytic Institute. Publications: Child Art Therapy: Understanding and Helping Children Grow Through Art, 1978, revised edition, 1984; The Art of Art Therapy, 1984; Approaches to Art Therapy: Theory of Technique, 1987. Honours: Phi Beta Kappa, 1956; Pi Lambda Theta Award, 1959; Honorary Life Member, American Art Therapy Association, 1981. Memberships: President, 1977-79, American Art Therapy Association; Chairman, 1973-75, Pittsburgh Association for the Arts in Education and Therapy; American Psychological Association; American Psychoanalytic Association. Hobbies: Writing; Filmmaking; Painting; Grandchildren. Address: 128 North Craig Street, Pittsburgh, PA 15213, USA.

RUBIN Saul Howard, b. 15 Oct 1912, New York City, New York, USA. Biochemist (retired). m. Anne Bisom, 2 Aug 1932, 1 son, 1 daughter. Education: BS; MS; PhD. Appointments: Fellow in Biochemistry, New York University Medical School; Instructor in Medicine, New York University Medical College; Director of Nutrition Research, Hoffmann LaRoche. Publications: 75 on nutritional and medical problems. Honours: Sigma Xi Award, 1939; Scientific Advisory Board, Quartermaster Food Institute, US Army, 1948; Scientific Research Society, 1949; President, Association of Research Directors. Memberships: American Institute of Clinical Nutrition; American Institute of Biochemistry; American Pharmaceutical Association; Society for Experimental Biology and Medicine. Hobby: Photography. Address: 12401 Rock Garden Lane, Miami, FL 33156, USA.

RUDDY Shaun, b. 27 Feb 1935. Rheumatologist. m. Millicent Kavanagh, 21 Jun 1961, 2 d. Education: MD, cum laude, Yale University, 1961; FACP; FACR. Career includes: Professor of Internal Medicine, Microbiology and Immunology, Chairman, Division of Rheumatology, Allergy and Immunology, Medical College of VA, VA Commonwealth University, Richmond, VA, 1974-93; Elam C Toone

Professor of Internal Medicine, Microbiology amd Immunology, 1987-; Acting Chairman, Department of Internal Medicine, 1993-. Publications: 96 articles and 46 reviews including: Co-author, Covalent linkage of C3 to properdin (P) in the formation of activated P, in Journal of Immunology, in press; Co-author, Changes in immunologic cell surface markers during cocaine withdrawal, submitted. Honours include: Alpha Omega Alpha, 1960; Howard Hughes Medical Foundation Investigatorship, 1968-72; Eminent Scholar, Commonwealth of Virginia, 1974; Fogarty Senior International Fellowship, NIH, 1980-81; National Volunteer Service Award, Arthritis Foundation, 1981; Dean's Award, VA Commonwealth University, 1982; Outstanding Faculty Award, State Council on Higher Education in VA, 1990. Memberships include: Fellow, American College of Physicians; Fellow, American College of Rheumatology; Fellow, American Academy of Allergy and Immunology; British Society for Immunology; American Society for Clinical Investigation; AMA; AAAS. Hobby: Sailing. Address: Department of Internal Medicine, PO Box 980663, Medical College of VA, VA Commonwealth University, Richmond, VA 23298-0663, USA.

RUEDA Joaquin, b. 12 Aug 1957, Leon, Spain. Physician. m. Mercedes Rueda, 22 Oct 1983, 1 son, 2 daughters. Education: MD, University of Valladolid, Spain, 1980; PhD, University of Valladolid, Spain, 1982; Post-Professor Resident, Department of Otolaryngology, Ohio University, 1986-87. Appointments: Assistant Professor of Anatomy, University of Valladolid, 1982; Associate Professor of Histology, University of Alicante, 1983; Professor, Institute of Neurosciences, University of Alicante, 1988; Full Professor of Histology, University of Alicante, 1993. Publications: Neuronal loss in the Spiral Ganglion, 1987; Possible transient adhesion molecules expressed during Cochlea Development, 1988; Structural Development of the Cochlea, 1992; Dev tectal cells, 1993. Memberships: European Neuroscience Association; Association for Research in Otolaryngology; International Brain Research Organization. Address: University of Alicante, Department of Histology, Faculty of Medicine, Alicante 03080, Spain.

RUNDEN Ingrid, b. 23 Mar 1952, Bloomington, Indiana, USA. Doctor of Medicine. Education: AB, Sarah Lawrence College; MD, University of Medicine and Dentistry of New Jersey, 1979; Internship, State University of New York at Stony Brook, 1979-80; Residency, St Vincent's Hospital and Medical Center of Greater New York, New York City, 1980-83; Fellowship, Bronx Veterans Administration Medical Center, 1983-84; Diplomate, Psychiatry, and added qualifications in Geriatric Psychiatry, American Board of Psychiatry and Neurology. Appointments: Currently locum tenens Psychiatrist. Publications: Schizotypal and Borderline Personality Disorder (with Larry J Siever, Howard N Klar, and others), poster, 1984. Honours: Karl Jasper Research Award, St Vincent's Hospital, 1983. Memberships: American Psychiatric Association; American Association for Geriatric Psychiatry; American Medical Association; American Medical Women's Association. Address: 1229 Broadway, Suite 382, Bangor, ME 04401, USA.

RUSHTON John Philippe, b. 3 Dec 1943, Bournemouth, England. Professor of Psychology. m. (1) Doylene Rushton, 22 Dec 1962, div. 1973, (2) Serpil Rushton, 2 Jan 1992. Education: BSc, Psychology, 1970, PhD, Psychology, 1973, University of London. Appointments: Assistant Professor of Psychology, York University, Canada, 1974-76; Assistant Professor of Psychology, University of Toronto, Canada, 1976-77; Currently Professor of Psychology, University of Western Ontario. Publications: Altruism, Socialization, and Society, 1980; Race, Evolution, and Behavior, 1995. Honours: DSc, University of London, 1992. Memberships: American Association for Advancement of Science; American, British and Canadian Psychological Societies. Hobby: Walking. Address: Department of Psychology, University of Western Ontario, London, Ontario, Canada N6A 5C2.

RUSHWAN Hamid M E, b. 18 Jan 1940, Sudan. Professor of Obstetrics and Gynaecology. m. Laila Oreibi, 18 Apr 1968, 1 son, 4 daughters. Education: MB, BS, 1965, MD, 1977, University of Khartoum, Sudan; MRCOG (London), 1971; FRCOG (London), 1983. Appointments: Lecturer, 1973-77, Associate Professor, 1977-82, Full Professor, 1982-90, Department of Obstetrics and Gynaecology, University of Khartoum; WHO Regional Adviser on Maternal and Child Health, 1989-. Publications: Epidemiological and Clinical Aspects of Incomplete Abortions in Khartoum, 1976; Traditional Practices Affecting Health of Women and Children (co-editor), 1980; Epidemiological Study of Female Circumcision in the Sudan, 1983; Over 50 articles on topics related to reproductive health and clinical obstetrics and gynaecology,

including: The Hidden Costs of Abortion, 1978; Etiologic Factors in Pelvic Inflammatory Disease in Sudanese Women, 1980; The Impact of Traditional Practices on Family Health Services, 1981; Female Circumcision. Present position and future outlook. Honours: Distinction in Public Health, 1964, Prize and Distinction in Obstetrics and Gynaecology, 1965, University of Khartoum; Honorary Fellowship, International Council for Management of Population Programmes, Kuala Lumpur, Malaysia, 1989. Memberships: Scientific Council, International Association for Maternal and Neonatal Health; Honorary Fellow, International Council for Management of Population Programmes; Fellow, American Fertility Society; Founding Committee, Pan-African Federation for Maternal and Neonatal Health, Cairo. Hobbies: Reading; Travel. Address: PO Box 830824, Amman 11183, Jordan.

RUSSELL Anthony Science, b. 6 Mar 1939, Newcastle, England. Physician. m. J Alison Russell, 18 Dec 1972, 2 s. Education: MA; MB; BChir; FRCP; FRCP(C); FACP. Appointment: Professor of Medicine, University of Alberta, Edmonton. Memberships: Canadian Rheumatism Association; American College of Rheumatology; British Society of Rheumatology. Hobbies: Skiing; Squash. Address: 562 Heritage Medical Centre, University of Alberta, Edmonton, Alberta, Canada, T6G 2S2.

RUSSELL Glenda Marie, b. 21 Jul 1949, Leonardtown, MD, USA. Clinical Psychologist. 1 d. Education: BA, summa cum laude, 1979, MA, 1983, PhD, 1984, University of CO, Boulder. Career: Instructor, University of CO, Boulder; Instructor, Boulder Valley School District, Boulder County; Currently, Psychologist in Private Practice and Researcher. Publications: Co-author, Structure and Ideology of Shelters for Battered Women, in American Journal of Community Psychology, 1988; Hospice Programs and the Hospice Movement: An Analysis Based on General Systems Theory, in Hospice, 1989; Co-author, Homophobia within the supervisory relationship: An invisible intruder, in Psychologist Psychoanalyst, 1994. Honours: Phi Beta Kappa, 1978; J Van EK Award, 1979; Summa cum laude, 1984; Research Grant-in-Aid, Society for Psychological Study of Social Issues, 1993; Boulder County Women's Hall of Fame, 1994. Memberships: American Psychological Association; American Orthopsychiatric Association; International Society for the Study of Traumatic Stress. Hobbies: Singing; Dolphins; Music. Address: 2315 Broadway, Boulder, CO 80304, USA.

RUSSELL John Gordon, b. 21 Aug 1928, Killgreel, Co Antrim, Northern Ireland. Oral Medicine; Stomatologist. m. Mary Ferguson, 12 Aug 1964 (sep Aug 1994), 6 s, 3 d. Education: BDS; MB; BCh; BAO, National University of Ireland, 1951, 1957; LAH, Ireland, 1956; FDSRCS Eng, 1959; FFDRCSI, without examination, 1965. Appointments: House Surgeon, Sheffield Dental Hospital; Dental Registrar, Central Middlesex Hospital, London; House Physician, St Finbars Hospitals, Cork; House Surgeon, Birmingham and Midland Ear and Throat Hospital; Dental Registrar, University College Hospital, London; Clinical Tutor, Cork Dental Hospital; Currently, Emeritus Professor of Dental Surgery, University College, Cork; Retired. Publications: Many publications concerning: dental examinations, medical and legal aspects of dentistry, implications of HIV infection for dental education and treatment. Memberships: Vice President, Association Stomatologique International; Irish Medical Organization. Hobbies: Folk Dancing; Archaeology; Sailing. Address: 3 Ferryview Cottages, World's End, Kinsale, Co Cork, Ireland.

RUSSELL Steven Laurence, b. 4 June 1950, Derby, England. Homoeopath. m. Jacqueline Russell, 20 Dec 1971, 1 son, 1 daughter. Education: Diploma in Homoeopathy, Medical Herbalism, Auricular Acupuncture; MD (Medicina Alternativa). Appointments: Royal Naval Shipwright Artificer; Royal Naval Helicopter Pilot; Teacher, Lecturer in Further Education; Homoeopath, part-time, then full-time; Currently: Director, Natural Therapy Centre, Guisborough; Consultant Holistic Practitioner; Dean, International College of Holistic Medicine; Visiting Professor, Open International University for Complementary Medicines. Publications: Holistic Approach to Arthritis, 1984; Nutshell Series of Homoeopathy, Herbalism, Auriculotherapy, Holistic First Aid, Nutrition, Aromatherapy, 1984-94. Honours: Runner-up, Practice of the Year, 1989; Runner-up, Practitioner of the Year, 1989; Certificate of Excellence, 1994. Memberships: Fellow, Homoeopathic Foundation; Medicina Alternativa; Holistic International Society; Association of Schools and Colleges of Holistic Medicine. Hobbies: Science; Conservation; Wildlife. Address: International College of Holistic Medicines, 7 Westgate Road, Guisborough, Cleveland TS14 6EA, England.

RUSSELL-CURRY Patricia Ann, b. 28 June 1956, Merced, California, USA. Psychotherapy. m. John William Russell, 15 January 1977, 2 sons, 1 daughter. Education: BA; MA; Licensed Marriage, Family and Child Counselor; Registered Dance-Movement Therapist; Trained in MediationCommunity College; Life Credentials in Psychology and Counseling; Teacher Examination Certificates in Classical Ballet, Cecchetti Method. Appointments: Coordinator, Merced County Sexual Abuse Treatment, 1983; Inpatient Psychiatric Social Worker Therapist, Dance Therapist and Creative Arts Coordinator, Marin County, 1986; Program Manager, Community Outreach Services and Program Manager for Children and Youth Services Merced County Mental Health, 1990; Mental Health Consultant to Merced County Head Start Program; College Adjunct Instuctor in Eary Childhood Education and Psychology; Classical Ballet Instructor, 1977-; Private Practice, 1994. Publications: Unpublished Thesis: There's An Armadillo in My Chest: The Significance of Psychotic Metaphor, 1983; Published: ADTA Conference Presentation Monograph, 1991; California State Department of Mental Health Programs of Excellence, 1993. Honours: Lori Hogan Award for Statewide Mental Health Prevention Programs of Excellence. Memberships: California Association of Marriage and Family Therapists; American Dance Therapy Association and Northern California Chapter; Sacred Dance Council; Cecchetti; Council of America. Hobbies: Dance; Geneology; Collecting Antiques; Unusual Dolls; Cross-Country Skiing. Address: 2750 N 'G' Street, Suite D, Merced, CA 95340, USA.

RUTHERFOORD Gerald Stuart, b. 16 Nov 1941, Cape Town, South Africa. Doctor. Education: MB Ch B, 1969, MMed Path, 1975, University of Cape Town; MRCPath, Royal College of Pathologists, London, 1984. Career: Senior Specialist, Department of Anatomical Pathology, Groote Schliur Hospital and University of Cape Town; Senior Consultant, Department of Neuropathology, Frenchay Hospital, Bristol, England; Currently, Head of Neuropathology Unit, Tygerberg Hospital and University of Stellenbosch, Cape Town, South Africa. Publication: Co-author, Atlas of Correlative Neuropathology and Imaging, 1994. Memberships: Royal College Pathologists; British Neuropathological Society; International Academy of Pathology; International Society of Neuropathology. Hobbies: Squash; Photography; Travel. Address: Neuropathology Unit, 6th Floor Clinical Building, Medical Faculty, University Stellenbosch, PO Box 19063, Tygerberg 7505, South Africa.

RUTHERFORD Robert B, b. 29 July 1931. Surgeon. m. Kay Folk, 20 Aug 1955, 2 sons, 3 daughters. Education: BA Biology; MD. Career: Assistant, Associate Professor of Surgery, Johns Hopkins University; Associate Professor, then Professor, University of Coloardo; Chief, Vascular Surgery; Professor of Surgery, University of Colorado Health Sciences Center. Publications: 300 articles; 5 books, 2 reached 4 editions: Vascular Surgery, 1978, 1984, 1989, 1994; Management of Trauma, 1967-82; Atlas of Vascular Surgery, 1992. Honours: PBK with AB, 1952; ADA with MD, 1956. Memberships: Fellow, ACS; American Surgical Association; Society of University Surgeons; Society for Vascular Surgery; Western Vascular Society, President; Western Surgical Associaton; International Society for Cardiovascular Surgery, President; Director, American Board of Surgery, 1990-96. Hobbies: Skiing; Biking; Windsurfing; Tennis. Address: C-312 Vascular Surgery, University of Colorado Health Sciences Center, Denver 80262, Colorado, USA.

RUTISHAUSER Wilhelm Jakob, b. 2 Sept 1931, Amriswil, Switzerland. Director, Cardiology Center. m. Lilly Leuener, 5 Apr 1975. Education: Medical Studies, Basle, Paris, Vienna; Swiss Federal Diploma, MD, Basle, 1957; Assistant, University Hospital of Zurich, 1958-63; Research Fellow, Mayo Clinic, Rochester, USA, 1963-65. Appointments: Chief Resident, Lecturer, University of Zurich, 1965-70; Chief of Cardiology, Associate Professor, University of Zurich, 1970-76; Professor of Cardiology, University of Geneva, 1976-. Publications: Kreislaufdiagnostik mit der Farbstoffverdünnungsmethode, Kreislaufanalyse mittels Röntgendensitometrie; Vasodilators in heart failure for cardiovascular pharmacotherapy. Memberships: Swiss Society of Cardiology; Swiss Society of Internal Medicine; Swiss Foundation of Cardiology; German Society for Heart & Circulation Research; Swiss & German Society for Biomedicine Techniques; European Society of Cardiology; International Society of Cardiovascular Pharmacotherpay (President 1987-89); International Society and Federation of Cardiology (President 1991-92). Honours: Prize, Swiss Society of Cardiology, 1967; Prize, Swiss Society of Radiology, 1968; Prize, Goetz of the University of Zurich, 1975; Prize, Morawitz of German Society of Heart & Circulation Research, 1991. Hobbies: Skiing;

Golf; Sailing. Address: Centre de Cardiologie, Hopital Cantonal Universitaire, CH-1211 Geneve 14, Switzerland.

RUTLAND Andrew, b. 30 May 1943, Lake Alfred, Florida, USA. Physician. m. (1) Sidney Woods, 19 Jan 1970, div, 2 sons, 2 daughters, (2) Diana, 10 Sep 1988. Education: BS, 1965, MD, 1969, Howard University; JD, University of West Los Angeles Law School, 1988; Diplomate, National Board Medical Examiners, 1970; Diplomate, American Board Obsstetricians Gynaecologists, 1977. Appointments: Resident, Chief Resident, Ob-Gyn, University Southern California, Los Angeles County general Hospital, 1973-76; Fellow, Gynaecologic Oncology, 1976-77; Served to Lieutenant Colonel, US Air Force, 1969-81; Chief, Professional Services, Vice Commander, Medical Clinic, USAF Spangdahlem, Germany, 1970-73; Family Practice Resident Instructor, University California, Los Angeles, 1977-81; Physician, Corporate Secretary, Prairie Avenue Medical Group, Inglewood, 1985-91; Medical Staff, Chief, department OB/Gyn, Centinela Hospital, 1989-. Publications: Contributor of articles in professional journals. Honours: Book Review Editor, Law Review, University West Los Angeles Law School, 1987-88. Memberships: Aerospace Medicine Soceity; National Health Lawyers Association; Medical Group Management Association. Hobbies: Skiing; Fishing; Hunting; Painting. Address: 1736 Medical Centre Drive #B, Anaheim, CA 92801, USA.

RUTTER Michael Llewellyn (Sir), b. 15 Aug 1933, Brumanna, Lebanon. Child Psychiatrist. m. Marjorie Heys, 1958, 1 s, 2 d. Education includes: MD Honours, 1963; FRCPsych, 1971; FRCP, 1972; FRS, 1987. Appointments include: Nuffield Medical Travelling Fellow, Albert Einstein College of Medicine, NY, 1961-62; Senior Lecturer, Reader, 1966-73, Professor, Child Psychiatry, 1973-, Institute of Psychiatry; Honorary Director, MRC Child Psychiatric Unit, 1984-; Honorary Consultant Psychiatrist, Joint Bethlem and Maudsley Hospitals; Director, MRC Research Centre in Social, Genetic and Developmental Psychiatry, Institute of Psychiatry, 1994. Publications include: Numerous publications, 1966-, including: Co-editor, Education, Health and Behaviour, 1970; Editor, Infantile Autism, 1971; Author, Helping Troubled Children, 1975; Author, Changing Youth in a Changing Society, 1979; Co-author, Lead Versus Health, 1983; Co-editor, Stress, Coping and Development, 1983; Co-author, Developing Minds: Challenge and continuity across lifespan; Co-editor, Child and Adolescent Psychiatry Modern Approaches, 4th edition, 1994; Co-editor, Development Through Life: A Handbook for Clinicians, 1994; Co-editor, Stress, Risk and Resilience in Children and Adolescents: Processes, Mechanisms and Interventions, 1994; Honours include: Honorary FBPsS, 1978; Honorary CBDSSc, University of Leiden, 1985; CBE, 1985; Honorary Doctor of Science, University of Birmingham, 1990; Honorary Doctor of Medicine, University of Edinburgh, 1990; Honorary Doctor, Leuven, 1990; Honorary Doctor of Science, University of Chicago, 1991; Honorary Doctor of Science, University of Minnesota, 1993; Honorary Doctor of Science, University of Ghent, 1994; Numerous other awards in UK and USA. Kt, 1992. Memberships include: Founding Member, Academy Europaea, 1988; Foreign Associate Member, Institute of Medicine of the National Academy of Sciences, USA, 1988; Foreign Honorary Member, American Academy of Arts and Sciences, 1989; Foreign Associate Member, US National Academy of Education, 1990; Honorary Member, British Paediatric Association, 1994. Hobbies: Fell Walking; Tennis; Wine Tasting; Theatre. Address: Institute of Psychiatry, De Crespigny Park, Denmark Hill, London, SE5 8AF, England.

RYAN Julie M, b. 3 Sep 1951, Des Moines, IA, USA. Optometry. m. Patrick O Ryan, 27 Jun 1976. Education: AA, Southwestern Community College; BS, Visual Science, IL College of Optometry; OO, IL College of Optometry, 1975; MS, Education, CA State University, Fullerton; Diplomate, Binocular Vision and Perception, 1981. Career: Chief, Pediatric Optometry Services, Southern CA College of Optometry; Currently, Private Practice, Irvine, CA and Associate Professor, Southern CA College of Optometry, Fullerton, CA. Publications include: A Needs Analysis for Teachers of the Visually Handicapped, in American Journal of Optometry and Physiological Optics, 1986; Teacher's Guide to Vision Problems, in The Reading Teacher, 1984; Co-author, Personal Characteristics of Optometry Students at the Southern California College of Optometry, in Journal of Optometry Education, 1987. Honours include: Fellow, American Academy of Optometry, 1979; Fellow, College of Optometrists in Vision Development, 1992. Memberships: CA Optometry Association; American Optometry Association; Optometric Extension Program Foundation; Soroptimists International of Irvine. Hobbies: Aerobic

Exercise; Sewing; Reading. Address: 4950 Barranca Pakway, Suite 310, Irvine, CA 92714, USA.

RYAN Stephen J, b. 20 Mar 1940, Honolulu, Hawaii, USA. Physician. m. Anne Christine Mulladay, 1 d. Education: MD, Johns Hopkins University School of Medicine, Baltimore, MD, 1965. Career includes: Fellow, Armed Forces Institute of Pathology, NIH Ophthalmic Pathology Branch, Washington, DC, 1970-71; Professor and Chairman, Department of Ophthalmology, LAC & USC Medical Center, Los Angeles, CA, 1974-95; President, Doheny Eye Institute, Los Angeles, CA, 1987-; Dean, School of Medicine, University of Southern California, Los Angeles, CA, 1991-. Publications: Over 200 published papers in peer-reviewed ophthalmic medical journals; Co-author of 6 medical books including: Retina, volumes I-III, 1989, Medical and Surgical Retina, 1994. Honours: Louis B Mayer Scholar Award, Research to Prevent Blindness, 1973; Award of Merit, American Academy of Ophthalmology, 1975; The Rear Admiral William Campbell Chambliss Award, United States Navy, 1982; Society of Scholars, Johns Hopkins University, 1984; Senior Honour Award, American Academy of Ophthalmology, 1988. Memberships: American Academy of Ophthalmology; The Macula Society; The Retina Society; American Association of Ophthalmology; Pan-American Association of Ophthalmology; Club Jules Gonin; American Ophthalmological Society; Academic Ophthalmologica Internationalis. Address: Doheny Eye Institute, 1450 San Pablo Street, Los Angeles, CA 90033-4681, USA.

RYBICKI Benjamin Anthony, b. 14 Oct 1961, Detroit, MI, USA. Epidemiology; Genetics. m. Erin O'Shea, 25 Jun 1988, 1 s, 3 d. Education: Masters of Health Science, Johns Hopkins, 1988; Currently pursuing DPhil, University of MI. Career: Research Associate, Kennedy Institute for Handicapped Children, Balto, MD, 1987-88; Clinical Research Manager, Bassett Hospital, Cooperstown, NY, 1988-91; Currently, Epidemiologist, Henry Ford Hospital. Publications: Co-author, Major genetic mechanisms in pulmonary function, 1990; Co-author, Demographic differences in referral rates to neurologists of patients with suspected PD, 1994. Honour: Alpha Omega Delta, 1988. Memberships: Society of Epidemiologic Research; American Society of Human Genetics. Hobbies: Bowling; Golf; Boxing. Address: Henry Ford Hospital, 2799 West Grand Boulevard, Detroit, MI 48202, USA.

S

SAARMA Jüri, b. 24 Oct 1921, Viljandi, Estonia. Physician. m. Valve Luberg, 6 May 1943, 2 s, 1 d. Education: Physician, 1945; Doctor of Medical Science, University of Tartu, 1964. Career: Lecturer, 1945, Assistant Professor, 1954, Professor, 1964, Head of Department, 1975, Consulting Professor, 1983, Professor Emeritus, 1994, Department of Psychiatry, University of Tartu; Dean, Medical Faculty, University of Tartu, 1963-66. Publications include: Forensic Psychiatry, 1970; Psychopathology, 1977; Clinical Psychiatry, 1980; Narcology, 1989. Honours: Deserved Physician of Estonia, 1973; Member of Russian Academy of Medical Sciences, 1974. Memberships include: Estonian Society of Psychiatrists; International Society of Social Psychiatry; International Brain Research Organization. Hobbies: Gardening; Swimming. Address: Taara Boulevard 1A-5, Tartu, EE2400, Estonia.

SAATCI BIBERCI Pinar, b. 23 May 1966, Ankara, Turkey. Orthodontist. m. Osman Saatci, 16 Jun 1989. Education: Hacettepe University, Faculty of Dentistry, Department of Orthodontics; DDS; MS. Appointment: Research Assistant. Publication: Occlusal contact changes after the active phase of treatment, in American Journal of Orthodontics, 1992. Membership: European Orthodontic Society. Hobbies: Reading; Fine Arts; Aerobics; Cooking. Address: Iran Cad 49-9, 06700 Gaziosmanpasa, Ankara, Turkey.

SABATÉ Joan, b. 10 Sep 1954, Barcelona, Spain. Teacher; Researcher. m. Carmen Llorca, 3 s. Education: MD; Dr PH; MPH, Health Education; MPH, Epidemiology. Career: Assistant Research Professor, 1990-92, Associate Professor, 1992-, Department of Public Health and Preventive Medicine, School of Medicine, Loma Linda University, CA; Associate Professor, Department of Epidemiology and Biostatistics, Loma Linda University, CA, 1992-; Associate Professor, Department of Nutrition, School of Public Health, Loma Linda University, CA, 1992-. Publications: Many publicationsin professional journals including: Co-author, Attained Height of Lacto-ovo Vegetarian Children and Adolescents, in European Journal of Clinical Nutrition, 1991; Co-author, A Possible protective effect of nut consumption on risk of coronary heart disease: The Adventist Health Study, in Archives of Internal Medicine, 1992; Co-author, Effects of walnuts on serum lipid level and blood pressure in normal men, in New England Journal of Medicine, 1993. Honours: Fulbright Scholar, Loma Linda University, 1984-86; Dean's Award, Loma Linda University, 1988; Overseas Training Grant, National Institute of Health, Spain, 1988; Delta Omega, 1988; Advanced Research Fellow, American Heart Association, 1988-90. Memberships include: American Institute of Nutrition; Catalonian Academy of Medical Sciences; International Epidemiological Association; Society for Pediatric Epidemiologic Research; Council of Epidemiology and Prevention, International Society of Cardiology. Hobbies: Hiking; Camping; Travel. Address: Loma Linda University, School of Public Health, Nutrition Department, Nichol Hall 1102, Loma Linda, CA 92350, USA.

SABISTON David Coston Jr, b. 4 Oct 1924, Onslow County, NC, USA. Surgeon. m. Agnes Foy Barden, 1955, 3 d. Education: BS, University of NC, Chapel Hill, 1944; MD, Johns Hopkins University School of Medicine, 1947. Career: Assistant Professor, 1955, Associate Professor, 1959, Professor, 1964, Johns Hopkins University School of Medicine; Fulbright Research Scholar, University of Oxford, 1960-61; James B Duke Professor of Surgery and Chairman, 1964-, Chief of Staff, 1994-, Duke University Medical Center. Publications include: Textbook of Surgery, 15 editions; Surgery of the Chest, 6 editions; Essentials of Surgery, 2 editions; Pulmonary Embolism, 1980; Atlas of General Surgery, 1994; Atlas of Cardiothoracic Surgery, 1995. Honours: Golden Apple Award, 1966, 1977, 1993; TD Kinney Outstanding Teacher of Year, 1976, 1981-83; ME DeBakey Award, 1984; Honorary Degree, University of Madrid, 1994; Gimbernat Prize, Societat Catalana de Cirurgia, 1994. Memberships: American College of Surgeons; American Surgical Association; American Association for Thoracic Surgery; Society of University Surgeons; Society of Clinical Surgery; Institute of Medicine; NIH. Address: Department of Surgery, Duke University Medical Center, PO Box 3621, Durham, NC 27710, USA.

SABOE Gerald Wayne, b. 30 June 1953, Waterloo, Iowa, USA. Physician. m. Julie Ann Miller, 13 Aug 1977, 1 son, 1 daughter. Education: BA; MPH; DO. Appointments: Chief Aeromedical Services, 1979-83; Commander, 49th Tactical Hospital & Chief, Aerospace Medical Services, 1985-87; Chief, Aeromedical Advisor, Aeronautical Equipment/Human Systems Program Officer, Wright-Patterson AFB OH, 1987-91; Chief, Professional Services, Armstrong Laboratory Aeromedical Consultation Service, Brooks AFB TX, 1992-95. Publications: The effects of hypoxia induced by hypobaric pressure on soft contact lens wear, co-author, 1986; Aeromedical risk associated with asymptomatic cholelithiasis in USAF pilots and navigators, co-author, 1995. Honours: USAF Air Training Command Flight Surgeon of the Year, 1982; Fellow, American College Preventive Medicine, 1986; Fellow, American Osteopathic College of Occupational & Preventive Medicine, 1989. Memberships: Aerospace Medical Association; American Osteopathic Association; American College Physician Executives; American Osteopathic College of Occupational & Preventive Medicine. Hobbies: Amateur Radio; Flying; Hunting; Fishing. Address: Armstrong Laboratory, Aerospace Medicine Directorate, Clinical Sciences Division, 2507 Kennedy Circle, Brooks AFB, TX 78235-5117, USA.

SACHAN Dilep Singh, b. 18 Dec 1938, Makhauli, India. Educator. m. Cheryl Hill, 2 Nov 1968, 2 sons, 1 daughter. Education: BVSc; MVSc; MS; PhD. Appointments: Instructor, Obstetrics and Gynaecology; Research Assistant, Nutrition; Research Associate, Pharmacology; Assistant Professor, Pharmacology; Research Chemist, Lipid Pharmacology; Associate Professor, Nutrition, Paediatrics, Environmental Practice; Currently Professor of Nutritional Biochemistry, Director of Nutrition Institute, University of Tennessee, Knoxville. Publications: Research papers in the area of nutrition, microbiology, pharmacology, drug metabolism, drug-nutrient interactions, nutrient-interactions, alcoholism, cancer, low birth weight infants, mould toxins, others. Honours: University Gold Medal, 1961; University Honours, 1963. Memberships: American Institute of Nutrition; American Society for Clinical Nutrition; American College of Nutrition; International College of Nutrition; Sigma Xi; Gamma Sigma Delta; Phi Zeta. Hobbies: Travel; Real estate. Address: Department of Nutrition, University of Tennessee, 1215 Cumberland Avenue, Knoxville, TN 37996-1900. USA.

SACKEIM Harold A, b. 13 July 1951, Hackensack, New Jersey, USA. Professor of Psychiatry. m. Donna M Zucchi, 9 Oct 1977, 1 son. Education: BA, Columbia University; Magdalen College, Oxford; BA (Oxon); MA (Oxon); PhD, University of Pennsylvania. Appointments: Assistant Professor, Department of Psychology, Columbia University, New York; Associate Professor, Department of Psychology, New York University; Currently Chief, Department of Biological Psychiatry, Columbia University. Publications: 200 including contributions to Science, New England Journal of Medicine, Archives of General Psychiatry, Archives of Neurology. Honours: Established Investigtor Award, NARSAD, 1989; Merit Award, National Institute of Mental Health, 1990; Honorary Fellow, American Psychiatric Association, 1993; Joel Elkes International Award, American College of Neuropsychopharmacology, 1994. Memberships: American College of Neuropsychopharmacology; American Psychological Society; International Neuropsychological Society. Hobby: Skiing. Address: Department of Biological Psychiatry, New York State Psychiatric Institute, 722 West 168th Street, New York, NY 10032, USA.

SACKETT Richard Stuart, b. 4 Apr 1955, Rhode Island, USA. Psychologist. m. Sheila Karr, 2 Aug 1980, 1 s, 1 d. Education: PhD, Psychology; Certified in Cognitive Therapy. Career: Coordinator, 1985-87, Adjunct Assistant Professor, 1986-87, Baruch College, City University of NY; Clinical Director, 1987-89, Supervising Psychologist, 1989-92, Cognitive Therapy Center of NY; Currently: Director of Integrative Psychotherapy Services and Psychologist in Private Practice. Publication: Integration of Existential and Cognitive Therapies, article in preparation. Honour: Phi Kappa Phi, 1983. Memberships: American Psychological Association; Association for the Advancement of Behavior Therapy; Manhattan Psychological Association; NY State Psychological Association. Hobbies: Basketball; Blues; Reading; Ocean Activities; Family. Address: 2 Tudor City Place, New York, NY 10017, USA.

SACKS Seymour, b. 1 July 1918. Physician. m. (1) Mary Marx, 12 May 1944, 3 sons; (2) Beatrice K Brown, 30 July 1995. Education: AB; MED. Appointments: Chief of Obstetrics, Glover Memorial Hospital; Retired. Memberships: Boston Obstetrical Society; American College of Obstetrics and Gynaecology. Hobbies: Tennis; Music. Address: 3570 S Ocean Boulevard, Palm Beach, FL, USA.

SADAVOY Joel, b. 5 Feb 1945, Ottawa, Canada. Psychiatrist. m. Sharian Smolack, 20 Nov 1977, 2 s, 2 d. Education: MD, 1968; Diploma, Psychiatry, 1972; FRCP(C), 1973. Career: Staff Psychiatrist, Mount Sinai Hospital, 1973-79; Assistant Professor, 1977-86, Associate Professor, 1986-, Psychiatry, University of Toronto; Head of Psychiatry, Baycrest Centre for Geriatrics Care, 1980-91; Head of Division of Geriatric Psychiatry, University of Toronto, 1991-94; Psychiatrist in Chief, Joint Department Psychiatry, Mount Sinai Hospital, Princess Margaret Hospital and Ontario Cancer Institute, 1993-. Publications: Assistant Editor, American Journal of Geriatric Psychiatry; Editorial Board, Journal of Geriatric Psychiatry; Senior Editor, Compr. Rev. Geriatric Psychiatry; Editor, Treating The Elderly with Psychotherapy, 1987; Co-Editor, Psychiatric Consequences of Brain Disease in the Elderly, 1989; Numerous articles, Book chapters and other publications. Memberships: Director, Canadian Psychiatric Association; Founding President, Canadian Academy Geriatric Psychiatry; Founding Chair, Council of Academies, Canadian Psychiatric Association; Corresponding Member Council on Aging; American Psychiatric Association; American Association of Geriatric Psychiatry. Hobbies: Travel; Camping; Reading. Address: Mount Sinai Hospital, 600 University Avenue, Suite 925, Toronto, Ontario, Canada, M5G 1X5.

SADEGH Ali M, b. 1 Sep 1950, Tehran, Iran. Researcher; Professor. m. Guita, 10 July 1980, 2 sons, 3 daughters. Education: BS, Arya-Mehr University of Technology, Tehran, 1972; MS, Mechanical Engineering, 1975, PhD, Mechanics, 1978, Dostdoctoral, 1979, University of Michigan, USA. Appointments include: Assistant Professor, Arya-Mehr University of Technology, 1979-81; Visiting Assistant Professor, Michigan State University, USA, 1981-82; Assistant Professor, 1982-87, Associate professor, 1987-91, Professor, 1991-, Chairman, Department Mechanical Engineering, 1992-, City University of New York; Coonsultant, Delopment Iranian Heavy Industries, Tehran, 1979-81; Technical Consultant, AC Rochester General Motors Company, 19186-92; Consultant to Industry, 1988-; Expert Witness, 1990-. Publications: Contributor of 80 articles in professional and scientific journals; Owns 2 US Patents in field; Contributor of numerous technical reports and presentations at national and international conferences. Honours: Best Paper Awardm 1942, Melville Medal, 1993, ASME Recipient of 22 Research Awards from National Scientific Foundation, AT&T Foundation, PSC-CUNY and others. Memberships: American Academy Mechanics; Society of Manufacturing Engineers, Chairman, Chapter 320; Sigma Xi. Hobbies: Tennis; Swimming. Address: City University of New Yorkm 140th Street and Convent Avenue, New York, NY 10031, USA.

SADOFF Robert L, b. 8 Feb 1936, Minnesota, USA. Physician. m. Joan A Handleman, 21 June 1959, 1 son, 3 daughters. Education: BA, University of Munnesota, 1956; BS, 1957; MD, 1959; MS, UCLA, 1963. Appointments: Clinical Director, 1968; Clinical Professor of Psychiatry. Publications: Forensic Psychiatry: A Practical Guide for Lawyers and Psychiatrists, 1975; Psychiatic Melpractice, 1992. Memberships: American Psychiatric Association; American College of Psychiatrists. Honours: Manfred Guttmacher Award, 1993. Hobbies: Book Collecting. Address: Suite 326, Jenkintown, PA 19046 3706, USA.

SADWIN Arnold, Assistant Clinical Professor of Psychiatry and Neurology, retired. Education: BA, Boston University, 1948; Special Postgraduate Student, Brown University, 1948-49; Northwestern Dental School, 1951-52; MD, Chicago Medical School, 1956. Career includes: US Navy, 3/C Personnel Interviewer, Honorably Discharged, 1945-46; Lecturer in Clinical Neurology and Psychiatry,Retired Acting Chairman of Psychiatry and Chief of Neuropsychiatry, Graduate Hospital, University of PA, 1960-93; Assistant Clinical Professor of Psychiatry, 1972-87, of Neurology, 1972-84, Admitted to 25 Year Faculty Club, 1986, University of Pennsylvania School of Medicine, now retired; Senior Staff Psychiatrist, Institute of Pennsylvania Hospital, 1979-; Honorary Lifetime Consultant in Psychiatry and Neurology, Pocono Medical Center, PA, 1983-; Senior Staff Psychiatrist, Belmont Center for Comprehensive Treatment, PA, 1985-; Clinical Assistant Professor, Volunteer Faculty Appointment, Department of Family Practice, University of Medicine and Dentistry of NJ School of Medicine, 1993; Inventor of the word Dysconscious (To be Published in 27th Edition Stedmans Medical Dictionary). Publications: Numerous original papers published including research papers on the Post Concussion Syndrome and the Psychiatrist on the Cardiac Surgery Team. Honours include: Secretary of Navy Commendation Medal; World War II Medal; Associate of Chicago Medical School, 1971; Humanitarian of the Year Award, MSA, 1975; Physicians Recognition Award, AMA, 1975-; Four Chaplains

Legion of Honour Membership, Chapel of the Four Chaplains, 1977; Fellow, Philadelphia College of Physicians, 1981; Fellow, Behavioral Neurology International, 1990. Memberships include: AMA; Life Member, APA; Fellow, American Academy of Psychosomatic Medicine, 1977; Vice President, 1980-83, American Institute of Bio-Medical Climatology; National Head Injury Foundation. Address: 1205 Heartwood Drive, Cherry Hill, NJ 08003, USA.

SAGGINO Aristide, b. 3 Sep 1956, Naples, Italy. Psychologist. m. Michelina Loré, 22 Feb 1986, 1 s. Education: Degree in Applied Psychology, 1979, PhD, Clinical Psychology, 1992, University La Sapienza, Rome, Italy. Appointments: Junior Clinical Psychologist, Senior Clinical Psychologist, National Health Service, Italy. Publications: The Rorschach in the John E Exner's Comprehensive System, book, 1989; The Myers-Briggs Type Indicator: Normative Data and Contribution to The Italian Standardization of the Form F, book, 1993; Co-author, Item Factor Analysis of the Italian Version of The Myers-Briggs Type Indicator, submitted 1994. Memberships: Italian Committee for the Study of Autogenic Training; British Psychological Society; Society for the Exploration of Psychotherapy Integration; Society for Personality Assessment; Italian Association of Behavioural Analysis and Modification; Foreign Affiliate, American Psychological Association. Hobbies: Art; Philosophy. Address: Via Nazario Sauro, 12-80026 Casoria, NA, Italy.

SAHAY Glenys Madeline, b. 30 Jul 1928, UK. Lecturer in Health Studies, retired. m. Shraddhanand Sahay, 2 Jun 1951, 1 s, 1 d. Education: Bachelor of Acupuncture, Honours; City and Guilds Further Education Teachers Certificate. Career: Physiotherapist, St James Hospital, Leeds; Superintendent Physiotherapist, Leeds Education Committee; Private Practice, Calcutta, India; Lecturer in Health Studies, North East Surrey College of Techology, now retired; Faculty of British College of Acupuncture. Honours: MCSP; Member and Register, British Acupuncture Association. Memberships: FRSH; FRIPHH; MIHE; Founder and Life Member, Health Service Careers Tutors Association. Hobbies: Reading; Theatre; Gardening; Great Dane Dogs. Address: Moombaville, Box Hill Road, Tadworth, Surrey, KT20 7JQ, England.

SAHN Steven Alan, b. 25 Jan 1943, Brooklyn, New York, USA. Physician. m. Eleanor Elizabeth Jones, 4 Nov 1974, 2 sons, 3 daughters. Education: BA, Duke University, 1964; MD, University of Louisville, 1968; Intern, Resident, Internal Medicine, University of Iowa Hospitals, 1968-71; Fellow, Pulmonary Disease, University of Colorado Health Sciences Center, 1971-73. Appointments: Instructor, 1973-74, Assistant Professor of Medicine, 1974-78, Associate Professor of Medicine, 1978-83, University of Colorado Health Sciences Center, Denver; Professor of Medicine, Director, Division of Pulmonary and Critical Care Medicine, Medical University of South Carolina, Charleston, 1983-. Publications include: With J E Heffner: Pulmonary pearls, 1988; Critical care pearls, 1989; Pulmonary pearls II, 1994; Editor or co-editor, several other books and monographs; Over 150 original papers and over 75 book and monograph chapters, mainly in field of pulmonary and critical care medicine; Over 100 abstracts. Honours: Research Scholarship, University of Louisville, 1966, 1967; Young Investigator Pulmonary Research Award, NHLBI, 1975-77; Nominee, Golden Apple Award, Medical University of South Carolina, 1992. Memberships: Fellow, American College of Chest Physicians; Fellow, American College of Physicians; Fellow, American College of Critical Care Medicine; American Federation for Clinical Research, Southern Section; American Thoracic Society; Charleston County Medical Society; South Carolina Thoracic Society. Address: Division of Pulmonary and Critical Care Medicine, Medical University of South Carolina, 171 Ashley Ave, Charleston, SC 29425, USA.

SAID Emilio, b. 10 Mar 1936, Mexico. Medical Doctor. 2 sons, 2 daughters. Education: MD. Appointments: Medical Doctor, Surgeon, 1963; Specialization in Transactional Analysis, 1983; Psychotherapist; President, Instituto Privado de Analisis Transaccional, Mexico. Publications: Psycho Transactional Diagnosis Instrument, 1981; Various articles in professional journals. Honours: Red Cross International, Recognition for Social Service. Memberships: Co-founder, President, Privado de Analisis Transaccional de Mexico; Clinical Teaching Member Instructor & Supervisor, The International Transactional Analysis Association. Hobbies: Reading; Baseball. Address: Agrarismo 21, Col Escandon, 11800 Mexico City, Mexico.

SAIDA Toshiaki, b, 5 July 1943, Gunma, Japan. Dermatologist. m. Keiko Okuyama, 2 sons. Education: MD, 1971, PhD, 1983, University of

Tokyo; Visiting Fellow, Harvard Medical School, USA, 1984; Certified, Board of Dermatology, Japan. Appointments: Head, Dermatology Clinic, Saitama Cancer Center, 1975; Associate Professor, University of Tokyo Branch Hospital, 1983; Professor, Chairman, Department of Dermatology, Shinshu University School of Medicine, Matsumoto, 1989-. Publications: Malignant melanoma in situ on the sole of the foot, 1989; Clinical and Histopathologic characteristics of early lesions of subungual malignant melanoma, 1989; The concept of de novo origin of cutaneous malignant melanoma, 1994. Honours: Makoto Seiji Memorial Award, 1991. Memberships: Japanese Dermatological Association; American Academy of Dermatology; International Society of Dermatopathology. Hobbies: Reading essays; Playing golf; Cultural history. Address: Department of Dermatology, Shinshu University School of Medicine, 3-1-1 Asahi, Matsumoto 390, Japan.

SAING Htut, b. 11 Apr 1935, Bassein, Burma. Paediatric Surgeon. m. Tin Tin Oo, 7 Nov 1965, 2 sons, 1 daughter. Education: MBBS (Rangoon); FRCS (Edin); FAAP; FACS. Career: House Officer 1960-61, Assistant Surgeon 1961-65, Rangoon General Hospital, Rangoon, Burma; Assistant Surgeon 1965-73, Consultant Paediatric Surgeon 1973-78, Consultant Paediatric Surgeon & Head of Department of Surgery 1978-79, Rangoon Children's Hospital, Rangoon, Burma; Senior Lecturer & Chief 1979-84, Reader in Surgery & Chief 1984-90, Division of Paediatric Surgery, University of Hong Kong, Queen Mary Hospital, Hong Kong; Professor of Pediatric Surgery, Chief of Division of Paediatric Surgery, The University of Hong Kong, Queen Mary Hospital, Hong Kong, 1990-. Publications: Surgical Management of Choledochal Cysts: A Review of 60 Cases, 1985; The Use of the Disposable Intraluminal Stapler in the Definitive Management of Hirschsprung's Disease, 1986; Problems in the Surgery of Conjoined Twins, 1987; Advanced Necrotizing Enterocolitis: An Indication for Emergency Separation of Omphalopagus Conjoined Twins, 1987; A Method of Repair of Thoracic Cage Defects after Separation of Thoraco-omphalopagus Twins, 1987; Biliary Atresia - The Hong Kong Experience, 1987; Childhood Recurrent Pyogenic Cholangitis, 1988; Pediatric Pyeloplasty: 50 Patients with 59 Hydronephrotic Kidneys, 1989; A Prospective Randomized Trial Comparing Cefoperazone Versus Ampicillin-Gentamicin-Metronidazole in the Empirical Treatment of Postoperative Cholangitis in Biliary Atresia, 1991. Honours include: Depelchin Gold Medal, Award for Character, Studies and Gams before St Joseph's College, Darjeeling, India, 1952; Gold Medal, Sportsman of the Year Award, Burma, 1958. Memberships include: President, Asian Association of Paediatric Surgeons; Pacific Association of Pediatric Surgeons; British Association of Paediatric Surgeons; Societe Internationale de Chirurgie; International Hepatobiliary Pancreatic Association; Editorial Board, Hong Kong Journal of Paediatrics. Hobbies: Rowing; Tennis. Address: Department of Surgery, The University of Hong Kong, Queen Mary Hospital, Pokfulam Road, Hong Kong.

SAITOU Naruya, b. 14 Jan 1957, Sabae-shi, Fukui-ken, Japan, Scientist. m. Ayako Saitou, 1983, 2 daughters. Education: PhD, University of Texas at Houston, Graduate School of Biomedical Sciences, USA, 1986; DSc, University of Tokyo Graduate School of Sciences, Japan, 1994. Appointments: Assistant Professor, Faculty of Science, University of Tokyo, 1989-91; Associate Professor, National Institute of Genetics, Japan, 1991-. Publications: Contributor of over 40 articles and co-author of several books. Honours: Research Grant, Toyota Foundation, 1991; Fulbright Scholarship, 1982-84. Memberships: Numerous professional societies and organisations. Address: National Institute of Genetics, 1111 Yata, Mishima-shi, Shizuoka-ken 411, Japan.

SAKIN Laurence Albert, b. 24 Feb 1960, Tucson, Arizona, USA.Appointments: Manager, Hollywood Records & Tapes; Owner, Awareness Music Productions; Partner, PDQ Records & Tapes; Owner, Kept in the Dark Record Productions; Chairperson, United Federation of CFS Organizations. Honours: Member of Delegation Meeting with First Lady Barbara Bush at White House, 1992. Hobbies: Music Composition; Bowling; General Philanthropy. Address: Box 12345, Tucson, AZ 85732, USA.

SAKSENA Manu, b. 26 Oct 1958, Lucknow, India. Doctor. m. Poonam Saksena, 24 Feb 1987, 1 son, 1 daughter. Education: MBBS, DVD, Delhi University. Career: Junior Resident, Safdarjang Hospital, New Delhi; Medical Officer, BHEL; Senior Medical Officer, BHEL; Currently, Assistant Chief Medical Officer, BHEL. Publications: Co-author, Central Hyperthermic Effect of Arsenic in Rabbits, Indian Journal of Medical Research, 1991. Honours: Regularly attend and also present papers, annual National Level Dermatology Conferences;

Presented Poster, World Congress of Dermatology, New York, USA, 1992; Awarded Research Project, Indian Council of Medical Research, New Delhi. Memberships: Indian Medical Association; Indian Association of Dermatologists, Venereologists and Leprologists; Delhi Medical Association. Hobbies: Swimming; Golf; Chess; Table Tennis. Address: BHEL Clinic, 5 Parliament Street, New Delhi 110001, India.

SAKUA Hajime, b. 13 Jan 1930, Tokyo, Japan. Professor. m. Tomoko Hasegawa, 21 Apr 1963, 3 daughters. Education: BSc, D Med Sci, Anthropological Institute, School of Science, University of Tokyo. Appointments: Research Assistant of Anatomy, Chiba University; Assistant Professor, Tokyo Medico-Dental College; Senior Curator of Anthropology, National Science Museum, Tokyo; Professor of Anthropology, Sapporo Gakuin University. Publications: Historical Changes in the Frequency of Dental Caries among the Japanese People, 1964; Dentition of the Amud Man, 1970. Memberships: Anthropological Society of Nippon; Japanese Society of Legal Medicine; International Association of Human Biologists; Associate, Current Anthropology. Hobby: Go. Address: 7-28-5 Shakujii-machi, Nerima, Tokyo, Japan.

SALAMAH Mohammed Muraweh, b. 9 Mar 1947, Turmusaiya, Jordan. Medical Doctor. m. 27 Oct 1973, 3 sons, 1 daughter. Education: MD, 1971; Fellowship in Pediatric Hematology/Oncology, 1978-80; University of Illinois, Chicago, USA. Career: Instructor, University of Illinois; Instructor, Rush Presbyterian Saint Luke Medical School; Consultant Pediatric Hematologist/Oncologist. Publications: Saudi Arabian Sickle Cell Anemia, Amolccular Approach, 1989. Honours: Honor Degree, University of Alexandria, Egypt, 1971; Resident of the Year, Christ Hospital, 1978. Memberships: Fellow, American Academy of Pediatrics; American Society of Hematology; ASH. Hobbies: Soccer; Reading. Address: c/o Saudi Aramco, PO Box 9870, Dhahran 31311, Saudi Arabia.

SALAMEH Yaser, b. 28 July 1952, Gaza. Gynaecologist. m. K Yasin, 20 June 1979, 3 sons, 1 daughter. Education: MBBS; MSc Obs & Gynae; MCROG. Career: Senior Resident, University Hospital Jordan Medical School; Consultant, Obstetrics & Gynaecology, Amman; Registrar, Obstetrics & Gynaecology, England; Senior Registrar, Obstetrics & Gynaecology, College of Medicine, Kingland University, KSA. Memberships: MRCOG, Member, Royal Colege of Obstetricians & Gynaecologists, England; Member, Jordan Society of Obstetricians & Gynaecologists. Hobbies: Travelling; Painting. Address: Jabal Hussein, PO Box 921517, Amman, Jordan.

SALIBA Isabelle Ann, b. 16 Nov 1960, Malta. Gynaecologist. m. Dr Christopher Saliba, 18 Dec 1988. 1 s, 1 d. Education: MD; MRCOG. Appointments: Senior Registrar. Publications: Pharmacological Agents in Urinary Retention; Gynaecological Surgery. Honours: 1st Prize for Best Presentation, First Joint Obstetrics & Gynaecological Meeting, Malta, 1991. Memberships: MD, Malta; Royal College of Obstetrics & Gynaecology, England. Hobbies: Sailing; Piano Playing. Address: 45 St Aristarkis Street, Rabat, RBT07, Malta.

SALIMI ESHKEVARI Hadi, b. 18 Jul 1938, Rasht, Iran. Child Psychiatrist. m. Zahra Moghaddami, 6 Aug 1975, 1 s, 1 d. Education: MD, Tehran University School of Medicine, 1967; DPM, UK, 1973; MRCPsych (UK), 1974. Career includes: Private Practice, Child and Adolescent Psychiatry and Mental Retardation, Iran, 1975-87; Sole Consultant, Child Psychiatric Unit, Department of Psychiatry, Assistant Professor, Tehran University School of Medicine, Iran, 1977-80; Staff Psychiatrist, Adelaide Children's Hospital, Department of Psychiatry, Professorial Unit, Australia, 1987-91; Currently, Senior Consultant Psychiatrist, Women's and Children's Hospital, Adelaide, Australia. Publications include: Books, papers, translations, and articles in various journals, in Tehran and Australia including: Development in the first three years of life: A cultural perspective, 1988; Stress, in The News, Adelaide, 1990; Aggressiveness in Children, in The News, Adelaide, 1991. Memberships include: American Academy of Child and Adolescent Psychiatry; National Society for Autistic Children and Adults, USA; American Society for Human Genes; American Association on Mental Deficiency; World Psychiatric Association, Section of Psychiatric Rehabilitation; NY Academy of Sciences; World Association for Infant Psychiatry and Allied Disciplines. Hobby: Reading. Address: 22 Mayflower Crescent, Hallett Cove, SA 5158, Australia.

SALINAS Pedro José. b. 23 June 1939, Caracas, Venezuela. Agronomist. div. 1 son, 3 daughters. Education: Agronomist Engineer,

Central University of Venezuela, 1962; Diploma, Imperial College of Science, Technology and Medicine, University of London, England, 1966; MSc, 1966, PhD, 1972, University of London. Appointments: Shell Foundation, venezuela, 1962-68; University of the Andes, Merida, Venezuela, 1968-. Publications: Practical Inimitation to Scientific Research; Comparative Clnical Study after One Year in Children Born Alive in the Area of Merida, 1992; Relationship Between Nutritional Status and SocioEconomic Characteristics in Pre-School Children, Merida, venezuela, 1992; Heterosexual Behaviour in a Group of University Students, 1992; Cholera: An Updated Review, Part 1, 1992, Part II, 1993, Part III, 1993. Honours: Order Henri Pittier, First Class, 1983, 2nd Class, 1981; Merida County Award for Environmental Conservation, 1983; Award the Golden Book, 1986, 1987; Honorary Professor, Technological University Institute of Ejido, 1994; Honorary Member of several institutions, societies, scientific meetings and conferences. Membership: Society of Family Medicine. Hobbies: Numismatics; Philately; Poetry; Camping; Music; Travel. Address: PO Box 241, Merida, Venezuela.

SALIVE Marcel Edward, b. 8 Jun 1960, Bethesda, MD, USA. Physician. m. Carolyn Susan Pollard, 6 Jun 1987. Education: BS, Chemistry, 1981, MD, 1985, University of MI; MPH, Johns Hopkins University, 1987; Certified in General Preventive Medicine and Public Health. Career: Medical Officer, MD Division of Corrections, 1988; Associate, Johns Hopkins University, 1988-89; Medical and Research Officer, US Public Health Service, 1988-; Currently: Senior Research Investigator, National Institute on Aging, National Institutes of Health. Publications: Suicide mortality in the Maryland state prison system, 1979-88, in JAMA, 1989; Left-handedness and Mortality, in American Journal of Public Health, 1993; Co-author, Serum albumin and physical disability as predictors of mortality in older persons, in JAMA, 1994. Honours: Jay S Drotman Award, American Public Health Association, 1990; Unit Commendation, 1990, Achievement Medal, 1993, US Public Health Service. Memberships: Fellow, American College of Preventive Medicine; AMA; American Public Health Association. Hobbies: Travel; Bicycling. Address: 7201 Wisconsin Avenue, Gateway Building, Suite 3C309, Bethesda, MD 20892-9205, USA.

SALLUZZO Richard F, b. 27 Dec 1950, Gloversville, New York, USA. Medical Doctor. 3 daughters. Education: BA summa cum laude, University of Massachusetts, 1973; MD, Tufts University School of Medicine, 1978; Board Certified: Internal Medicine; Emergency Medicine; Certifications: Instructor, Advanced Cardiac Life Support, American Heart Association; Advanced Trauma Life Support, American College of Surgeons. Appointments: Attending Physician, Emergency Department: Danbury Hospital, Danbury, Connecticut; Charlotte Hungerford Hospital, Torrington, Connecticut; Albany Medical Center, Albany, New York; Currently: Associate Professor of Emergency Medicine, Chairman, Department of Emergency Medicine, Albany Medical College. Publications: Over 25 articles in Journal of Emergency Medicine, Annals of Emergency Medicine, Res Staff Phys, Emergency Reports, Academic Emergency Medicine, other journals; Book chapters include: Rhabdomyolysis, 1992; Development of Clinical Indicators in Emergency Medicine, 1992; Evaluating the Effectiveness of CQI Programs in Emergency Medicine (with J Bartfield); Insect and Spider Bites; Enhancing Patient Through Put; Case Studies in CQI. Memberships: Society of Academic Emergency Physicians; Fellow, American College of Physicians; Fellow, American College of Emergency Physicians; Board of Directors, Secretary-Treasurer, American College of Emergency Physicians, New York State; American College of Emergency Physicians, New York; Fellow, American College of Physicians Executives; Society of Critical Care; American Medical Association; Various committees and editorial boards. Address: Albany Medical College, Department of Emergency Medicine A-139, 47 New Scotland Avenue, Albany, NY 12208, USA.

SALMUN Luis Marcelo, b. 8 Nov 1961, Buenos Aires, Argentina. Physician. m. Nancy Ann Salmun, 3 Aug 1986, 2 sons. Education: MD, University of Buenos Aires, 1984. Appointments: Instructor in Paediatrics, Harvard Medical School, Massachusetts, USA; Assistant in Medicine, Children's Hospital, Boston. Publications: Basophil releasability in atopic asthmatic patients, 1988; Cotinine-measured environmental tobacco smoke intake and childhood asthma morbidity, 1993. Memberships: American Academy of Allergy and Clinical Immunology; Massachusetts Medical Society; American College of Allergy and Immunology; Asociacion Argentina de Alergia e Inmunologia. Address: Division of Immunology, Children's Hospital, Fegan 6, Boston, MA 02115, USA.

SALNER Andrew Lister, b. 16 May 1951, Philadelphia, Pennsylvania, USA. Physician. m. Patricia Madfis, 14 June 1975, 1 son, 2 daughters. Education: ScB, 1973, MD, 1976, Brown University. Appointments: Instructor in Radiation Oncology, Joint Center for Radiation Therapy, Harvard Medical School, 1981-82; Currently: Director of Radiation Oncology and the Cancer Programme, Hartford Hospital, Hartford, Connecticut; Director of Radiation Oncology, Clinical Assistant Professor of Radiology, University of Connecticut Health Center, Farmington. Publications: Multiple articles on breast cancer, brain tumours. Honours: Sigma Xi. Memberships: ASTRO; ASCO. Address: 80 Seymour Street, CT 06102-5037, USA.

SALTISSI David, b. 8 Feb 1948, Leeds, Yorkshire, England. Physician. Education: MBBS; MRCP (UK); MD (London). Appointments: Director of Renal Medicine, Senior Staff Specialist, Royal Brisbane Hospital, Herston, Queensland, Australia. Publications: Papers on a variety of nephrological topics. Memberships: Royal College of Physicians, London; London University Convocation; Australia and New Zealand Society of Nephrology; Many others. Hobbies: Golf; Tennis; Theatre. Address: Department of Renal Medicine, Royal Brisbane Hospital, Herston, Queensland 4029, Australia.

SALVAGGIO John Edmond, b. 19 May 1933, New Orleans, Louisiana, USA. Physician. m. Anne Poillon, 18 Apr 1957, 3 sons, 1 daughter. Education: BS, Chemistry; MD, Medicine; Intern, Resident, Charity Hospital; Fellow, Massachusetts General Hospital. Appointments: Assistant Professor, Associate Professor, Louisiana State University Medical School; Professor, University of Colorado Medical School; Henderson Professor, Chairman, Department of Medicine, Tulane Medical School; Currently Henderson Professor, Vice-Chancellor, Tulane University Medical Center. Publications: Over 375 original articles, books and book chapters; 178 published abstracts and/or brief presentations. Honours: Alpha Omega Alpha; William Peck National Scientific Award; Henry Salter Distinguished Clinician Award; Louisiana State University Hall of Distinction Award; Medallion, University of Padova; National Institutes of Health Career Investigation Award; H Davidson Teaching Excellence Award. Memberships: American Society for Clinical Investigation; Association of American Physicians; American Association of Immunologists; American Academy of Allergy and Immunology, President; American Board of Internal Medicine, Board of Governors. Hobbies: Sailing; Golf; Medical history; Oil painting. Address: 5726 St Charles Avenue, New Orleans, LA 70115, USA.

SALZBERGER Ruth Caro, b. Frankfurt-am-Main, Germany. Psychologist; Social Anthropologist. Education includes: MA (Hons), Psychology & Social Anthropology (Edinburgh); DPhil, Social Anthropology (Oxon); Chartered Psychologist. Appointments: Tutor, Oxford University Delegacy for Extra-Mural Studies; Lecturer, Goldsmiths' College, University of London; Health Research Officer, Cambridgeshire and Isle of Ely; Supervisor, University of Cambridge; Lecturer, Extra-Mural Department, University of Manchester; Currently: Psychoanalytic and Existential Counsellor; Counselling Supervisor. Publications: Cancer: Attitudes and Social Action in two Cambridgeshire Villages, 1971; Attitudes to Pain, Illness and Death, 1971; Death: Beliefs, Activities and Reactions of the Bereaved, 1975; Cancer: Assumptions and Reality concerning Delay, Ignorance and Fear, 1976. Honours: Calouste Gulbenkian Research Fellow, Lucy Cavendish College, University of Cambridge, 1970-72, 1974-75; Simon Research Fellow, University of Manchester, 1972-74. Memberships: Associate Fellow, British Psychological Society; Association of Social Anthropologists; European Association of Social Anthropologists; The Higher Education Network for Research and Information in Psychoanalysis; Associate Member, NW Institute of Dynamic Psychotherapy. Hobbies: Composing songs; Writing poetry; Painting. Address: 6 Highover House, The Beeches, West Didsbury, Manchester M20 8PG, England.

SAMAJA Michele, b. 13 Apr 1951, Milano, Italy. Researcher. m. Ilaria Vannini Parenti, 3 Oct 1981, 1 d. Education: Summa cum laude, University of Milano, 1975. Career: Visiting Fellow, NIH Bethesda, MD, USA, 1976-77; National Research Council, Italy, 1977-81; Assistant Professor, University of Milano School of Medicine, 1981-, University of Brescia, 1995-; Publications: 100 Full papers in professional journals, over 85 congresses and 1 patent, 1975-95. Honours: Milano Medicina Award, 1986, 1992; XIII Congress of Clinical Chemistry, 1987. Memberships: American Physiological Society; International Society for Heart Research; International Society for Mountain Medicine; International Society Oxygen Transport to Tissue; Scientific Expeditions to High Altitude 1976, 1981, 1986, 1991, 1994 (Himalayas and Andes). Hobbies: Mountain Climbing; Skiing. Address: 1 Cso Sempione, I-20145 Milano, Italy.

SAMARAJALINGAM S Shanmuganandan, b. 13 May 1951, Trichy, Tamilnadu, India. Teaching; Research. m. 7 May 1981, 1 s. Education: BA, 1st Rank; Higher Diploma in French, Madurai University; MPhil, MA, 2nd Rank, Merit Scholarship, PhD, Madras University. Career: Lecturer, 1977-87; Reader, 1987-93; Professor of Medical Geography, Madurai Kamaraj University, 1994-. Publications: Presented and published research papers at international conferences on social science medicine in India and abroad including 40 national conferences in India and over 19 international conferences abroad. Honours: ICSSR Regular Doctoral Institutional Fellowship; Queen Mary's College Jawaharlal Nehru Memorial Fund Award; Editorial Committee, International Journal on Health and Place. Memberships: Life Member, International Union for Health Education; Life Member, International Association of Geographers; Corresponding Member, IGU Commission on Health, Environment and Development. Hobbies: Attending Conferences; Social Services. Address: Ishwarya Plot 72, Pasupathy Nagar, Madurai 625014, Tamilnadu, India.

SAMARANAYAKE Lakshman Perera, b. 16 Dec 1947, Colombo, Sri Lanka. University Reader. m. Yuthica Hemamala, 22 Jun 1981, 1 s, 1 d. Education: BDS, Sri Lanka; DDS, Glasgow, Scotland; MRCPath, UK; MI Biology, C Biology, UK; FHKCPath, Hong Kong; FCDSHK, Hong Kong. Appointments: Consultant Senior Lecturer in Oral Microbiology, University of Glasgow, 1984-89; Associate Professor in Oral Biology, University of Alberta, Edmonton, Canada, 1989-90; Reader and Head, Oral Biology Unit, Prince Philip Dental Hospital, University of Hong Kong. Publications: Co-author, Clinical Oral Microbiology, 1989; Co-editor, Oral Candidosis, 1990; Co-author, Infection Control for the Dental Team, 1991; Clinical Virology in Oral Medicine and Dentistry. Memberships: Royal College of Pathologists; Hong Kong Academy of Medicine. Hobbies: Reading; Music; Tennis; Walking. Address: K14 Scenic Villas, Victoria Road, Hong Kong.

SAMET Jonathan Michael, b. 26 Mar 1946, Newport News, Virginia, USA. Epidemiologist; Physician. m. Shirley Murphy, 21 Jan 1990, 1 son. Education: AB, Harvard College, 1966; MD, University of Rochester School of Medicine and Dentistry, 1970; MS, Harvard School of Public Health, 1977. Appointments include: Chief, Pulmonary and Critical Care Division, Department of Medicine, University of New Mexico School of Medicine, Albuquerque, 1986-94; Professor, Chairman, Department of Epidemiology, School of Hygiene and Public Health, The Johns Hopkins University, Baltimore, Maryland, 1994-. Publications: The Epidemiology of Lung Cancer, book, 1994; Co-author, books: Indoor Air Pollution: A Health Perspective, 1991; Smoking Cessation, 1991; Racial and Ethnic Patterns of Mortality in New Mexico, 1993. Honours: Surgeon General's Medallion, 1990; American Epidemiological Society, 1992. Memberships: Society for Epidemiologic Research; American Thoracic Society; New Mexico Thoracic Society; International Epidemiological Association. Address: The Johns Hopkins University, School of Hygiene and Public Health, Department of Epidemiology, 615 N Wolfe Street, Suite 6039, Baltimore, MD 21205, USA.

SAMMAD Mohamed A, b. 30 Nov 1953, Misurata, Libya. Cardiovascular Surgeon. m. Moufeda A Fituri, 3 daughters. Education: MD; Austria Board of Surgery; Fellow of Cardiovascular Surgery. Appointments: House Officer in Surgery; Senior House Officer in Surgery; Resident in Cardiovascular Surgery; Senior Resident in Cardiovascular Surgery. Publications: Hypertension & Related Illness Risk Factors and Prevention; Atherosclerosis Curr Concept Pathphysiology Risk Factors & Prevention. Memberships: International Society for Heart & Lung Transplantation; New York Academy of Sciences; American Association for the Advancement of Science. Honours: Man of the Year, 1993; International Man of the Year, 1993-94; Certificate of Meritorious Achievement. Hobbies: Music; Violin; Soccer. Address: 19 Silbergasse 11/15, 1190 Vienna, Austria.

SAMMAN Nabil, b. 3 Sept 1953, Beirut, Lebanon. Surgeon. m. A M O'Regan, 2 Sept 1982, 3 sons. Education: MRCS (England); LRCP (London); BDS (Sydney); FDSRCS (England). Appointments: Senior House Surgeon, Middlesbrough Hospital, England; Registrar, Royal Infirmary, Leicester; Lecturer, currently Senior Lecturer, Oral and Maxillofacial Surgery Department, University of Hong Kong. Publications: Disseminated intravascular coagulation and facial injury, 1984; Co-author: Feasibility of osteotomies in fibrous dysplasia of the

jaws, 1991; Analysis of 300 dentofacial deformities in Hong Kong, 1992; The buccal fat pad in oral reconstruction, 1993; Immediate reconstruction following maxillectomy: a new method, 1993; A comparison of alveolar bone grafting with and without simultaneous maxillary osteotomies in cleft palate patients, 1994. Honours: Commonwealth University Scholarship, 1972. Membership: Life Fellow, International Association of Oral and Maxillofacial Surgeons. Hobbies: Tennis; Travel; Languages. Address: Department of Oral and Maxillofacial Surgery, University of Hong Kong, Hong Kong.

SAMMAN Samir, b. 20 May 1960, Lebanon. Lecturer. m. Marija, 4 July 1987, 3 daughters. Education: BSc; PhD. Appointments: Postdoctoral Fellow, Canadian Heart Foundation, 1987-89; Clinical Research Fellow, Royal Prince Alfred Hospital, 1989. Publications: 1 monograph, 49 publications in refereed international journals. Memberships: Nutrition Society of Australia; Australian Atheroslerosis Society. Address: Human Nutrition Unit, University of Sydney, Sydney, Australia.

SAN ANDRES Rafael, b. 28 Apr 1951, Bizkaia, Spain. Psychiatrist. m. Irune Gonzalez, 27 Feb 1974, 1 son, 1 daughter. Education: Licentiate in Medicine and Surgery, University of Bilbao, 1979; Specialised in Psychiatry, Universidad del Pais Vasco, 1982. Appointments: Professor of Behavioural Sciences, Nursery School, Universidad del Pais Vasco, 1979-87; Currently Psychiatrist in private practice. Publication: The Specifically Human Basic Need and Personality Disorders, 1992. Memberships: Academia de Ciencias Medicas, Bilbao; Society for the Exploration of Psychotherapy Integration. Hobbies: Languages; Travel. Address: Juan Bautista Zabala 10 3, Algorta, 48990 Bizcaia, Spain.

SAN ROMAN Federico, b. 4 Apr 1942, Mexico City, Mexico. Psychiatrist. m. Rosario Sarmiento, 27 Feb 1975, 1 daughter. Education: MD, Faculty of Medicine, 1967, Psychiatry Speciality, 1970, National Autonomous University of Mexico; Specialisation in Psychoanalysis, Mexican Institute of Psychoanalysis, Mexican Psychoanalytical Association, 1973-77. Appointments: Former Professor, Psychiatry, Psychotherapy: Hospital Central Militar; Comision Extension Academica de Asociacion Psicoanalitica Mexicana; Instituto Mexicano de Psicoterapia Adolescencia; Currently in private practice. Publications: Dreaming, a psychotic rehearsal with minimum energy cost, 1982. Honours: Chairman, Scientific Committee, 1980-82, Chairman, Academic Extension, 1984-86, Treasurer, 1984-86, Mexican Psychoanalytical Association. Memberships: International Psychoanalytical Association; Mexican Psychoanalytical Association; Latin American Federation of Psychoanalytical Societies; Sociedad Mexicana de Neurologia y Psiquiatria. Hobbies: Tennis; Journalism. Address: Insurgentes Sur 1188-804, México DF, Mexico.

SANCHEZ Albert, b. 10 Feb 1936, Solomonsville, Arizona, USA. Educator. m. Aneva Louise Allred, 11 Feb 1962, 1 son, 3 daughters. Education: BA, Chemistry, La Sierra University, 1959; MS, Biochemistry, Loma Linda University, 1962; DPH, Nutrition, University of California at Los Angeles, 1968. Appointments include: Assistant Professor, Nutrition, 1968-73, Associate Professor, Nutrition, 1973-74, 1980-82, Professor, Nutrition, 1982-91, Professor, Nutrition, International Health, 1986-, Loma Linda University School of Public Health, Loma Linda, California; Professor, Biochemistry, Nutrition, 1974-80, Assistant Dean, 1978-80, Adjunct Professor, 1985-, Universidad de Montemorelos School of Medicine, Montemorelos, Mexico; Programme Coordinator, Pacific Health Education Center, Bakersfield, California, 1991-. Publications include: Co-author, about 50 on nutrition including: Plasma amino acids in humans fed plant proteins, 1983; Vegetarianism and health, 1985; Zinc, vitamin B-6 and other nutrients in pregnant women attending prenatal clinics in Mexico, 1987; Dietary protein modulation of serum cholesterol: the amino acid connection, 1989; Atherogenic effect of oxidized products of cholesterol, 1989; Dietary protein control of serum cholesterol by insulin and glucagon, 1990; Profile of blood elements in leprosy patients, 1991. Honours: USPHS Trainee, 1965-68; Delta Omega, UCLA, 1968-. Memberships: American Institute of Nutrition; American Society for Clinical Nutrition; Society for International Nutrition Research; Sociedad Latinoamericana de Nutrición; American Dietetic Association; National Coalition of Hispanic Health and Human Services Organization. Hobbies: Gardening; Mountain biking; Walking. Address: Public Health Education Center, 5300 California Avenue, Bakersfield, CA 93309, USA.

SANDBLOM J Philip, b. 29 Oct 1903, Chicago, IL, USA. Professor Emeritus; University President. m. Grace Schaefer, 2 s, 2 d. Education: MD, Karolinska Institute, 1930; MS, North West, 1932; PhD, Karolinska Institute, 1944. Career includes: Assistant Head, Serafimerlasarettet, 1940-45; Surgeon in Chief of Surgery, Kronprinsessan Lovisa Children's Hospital, Stockholm, 1945-50; Professor of Surgery, Lund University, Surgeon in Chief of Surgery, Lund Hospital, 1950-70; Deputy Vice Chancellor, 1956-57, Vice Chancellor, 1957-68, Lund University; Currently, Professor Emeritus of Surgery. Publications: Tensile Strength of Healing Wounds, 1944; Haemobilia, Charles Thomas, 1972; Creativity and Disease, Marion Boyars, 8th edition, 1995. Honours include: Reuterskiold Prize, Stockholm, 1945; Opening Speech, President of Congress of the International Surgical Society, 1967; Speech as Rector Magnificus at celebration of 300th year of University of Lund, 1968; R Moore Memorial Lecture, Dallas, 1978; Honorary Member of many Societies and Associations; Honorary Fellow: ACS, RCS, RCSE, RCSI; Doctor honoris causa at 5 Universities. Hobbies: Art and Literature; Sailing; Skiing. Address: 2 Chemin des Bluets, 1009 Pully, Switzerland.

SANDBORG Shirlee J, b. 4 Aug 1934, IL, USA. Laboratorian; Manager of Clinical Laboratory. m. C Richard, 1952, deceased 1991, 2 s, 2 d. Education: Knox College, University of Kansas, Galesburg; Postgraduate in Medical Technology. Career: Supervisor, Clinical Laboratory, Galesburg State Research Hospital; Laboratorian, St Mary's Hospital and Cottage Hospital Laboratories, Galesburg; Supervisor, Medical Arts Clinic Laboratory; Supervisor and Manager, Galesburg Clinic Laboratory. Memberships: Clinical Laboratory Managers Association; American Association of Clinical Chemistry; American Medical Technologists; National Agency of Laboratory Medical Personnel; International Society of Clinical Laboratory Technology; American Association of Bioanalysts. Hobbies: Reading; Computers; Sewing. Address: The Galesburg Clinic Laboratory, 3315 North Seminary Street, Galesburg, IL 61401, USA.

SANDERS Wyman, b. 10 Apr 1931, Boston, MA, USA. Physician. Divorced, 2 s. Education: BA; MD. Career includes: Associate Clinical Professor, Psychiatry, University of CA, Los Angeles, 1978-; Associate Clinical Professor, Psychiatry, USC School of Medicine, Los Angeles, 1980-82; Medical Director, The Bresler Center Medical Group Inc, Los Angeles, 1981-87; Associate Member, UCLA Jonsson Comprehensive Cancer Center, Los Angeles, 1983-; President and Founder, Optimal Health Management Inc, Los Angeles, 1987-. Publications include: Integrating Wellness into the Workplace, in California Broker, 1989; Smoking Cessation: Selecting an Approach and Appropriate Support for Success, in Optimal Health Management Inc, 1989; Health Care Cost Containment, in Open Forum, 1990. Honours: Commendation Award for Caring for Children of the Military Command, 1964; Physician's Recognition Award, American Medical Association, 1969. Memberships: Fellow, American Orthopsychiatric Association; APA; Game Inventors of America; MA Medical Society; National Wellness Association; Society for Public Health Education; Southern CA Psychiatric Society; Southern CA Society for Child Psychiatry. Hobbies: Music; Theatre; Dance; Exercise. Address: 12122 Greenock Lane, Los Angeles, CA 90049, USA.

SANDERSON John Elsby, b. 1 May 1949, Iraq. Physician. m. Dr Julia Billingham, 19 May 1981, 1 s, 1 d. Education: BA, Cambridge University, 1970; MB B Ch, St Bartholomew Hospital Medical College, London, 1973; MA, 1974; MD, Cantab, 1981; MRCP, 1975; FRCP, 1991. Appointments: House Physician, St Bartholomews Hospital, London, 1973-74; SHO, Brompton Hospital, London, 1974; SHO, Hammersmith Hospital, London, 1977; Research Fellow, Hammersmith Hospital, London, 1974-78; Lecturer in Cardiovascular Medicine, University of Oxford, 1978-81; Lecturer, St Mary's Hospital, London, (Wellcome/St Mary's/Univ of Nairobi Project), 1981-83; Consultant Physician and Cardiologist, Taunton and Somerset Hospital, 1983-92; University Tutor, University of Bristol, 1985-92; Senior Lecturer in Medicine and Consultant Cardiologist, Chinese University, Hong Kong, 1992. Publications: Many publications on Cardiomyopathy, Heart Failure, Treatment of Angina, Pacemakers. Honours: FRCP, 1991; Fellow, American College of Angiology, 1994. Memberships: British Cardiac Society; European Society of Cardiology; British Hypertension Society; North American Society of Pacing and Electrophysiology; American College of Angiology; Hong Kong College of Cardiology. Hobbies: Sailing; Music; Tennis; Travel. Address: Dept of Medicine, Chinese University of Hong Kong, 9Fl Clinical Science Bldg, Prince of Wales Hospital, Sha Tin, Hong Kong.

SANDLER Bernard Maurice, b. 7 Mar 1923, South Africa. Obstetrician and Gynaecologist. m. Carla Schoenlank, 16 Oct 1949, 2 s, 1 d. Education: MB; BCH, 1946; MRCOG, 1954; FRCOG, 1971. Career: Consultant Obstetrician and Gynaecologist: Rhodesian Government Hospitals, Rhodesia Railways, Rhodesian Forces (later Zimbabwe); Currently Retired. Memberships: Zimbabwean Medical Association; President, Matabeleland Branch, 1977-83. Hobbies: Golf; Bridge. Address: 2 The Red House, Brick Kiln Lane, Limpsfield, Surrey, RH8 0QG, England.

SANDOR George Kalman Bela, b. 6 Apr 1954, Toronto, Canada. Surgeon. m. Cecilia Sandor, 2 daughters. Education: DDS, University of Toronto, 1978; Oral Maxillofacial Surgery, University of Washington, 1982; MD, University of Toronto, 1986; Plastic Surgery, University of Toronto, 1991. Appointments: Staff Oral & Maxillofacial Surgeon, The Hospital for Sick Children, Toronto, 1991; Staff Plastic Sureon, Humber Memorial Hospital, 1993. Publications: Numerous significant publications in professional journals. memberships: Omicron Kappa Upsilon, 1978; Alpha Omega Alpha, 1984. Honours: Sopman Humanitarian Award, 1987; Teaching Excellence in Medical Education, 1989, 1991; A-O International Scholarship; Semmelweis Medallion. Hobbies: Travel. Address: The Hospital for Sick Children, 555 University Avenue, Toronto, Ontario, M5G 1X8, Canada.

SANTOS-HERNANDEZ Erick F, b. 24 May 1942, Rio Piedras, Puerto Rico. Psychiatrist. m. Dr Gladys N Visgal de Santos, 27 May 1967, 3 sons. Education: BS, 1964; MD, 1968; Psychiatrist, 1972; ABPN Psychiatry, 1979; ABPN Addiction Psychiatry, 1993; FAPA, 1992. Appointments: Chief, Mental Health Clinic, Homestead AFB, 1972-74; Director, San Ruan State Psychiatric Hospital, 1974-76; Director, Student's Health Service, UPR, 1977-78; Chief Co-ordinator, San Juan VAMC, 1978-94. Honours: Secretary, Peurto Rican Psychiatric Society, 1991-94; Deputy Representative to APA from Puerto Rican Society, 1994-96. Memberships: Puerto Rican Medical Association; APA; AAPAA; American College of Physicians Executives. Hobbies: Tourism; Reading; Walking. Address: Harvard 270, University Gardens, Rio Piedras, PR 00927, USA.

SAPIR Paul Edward, b. 21 Jun 1928, Chicago, IL, USA. Psychiatrist; Psychoanalyst. m. Sylvia L Kutik, 8 Nov 1964, 2 s. Education: AB, 1950, AM, 1952, MD, 1959, Harvard; Graduate, New York Psychoanalytic Institute, 1973. Career: Assistant Professor of Psychiatry, Albert Einstein College of Medicine, 1967-74; Clinical Assistant Professor of Psychiatry, Brown University, 1974-. Honour: Fellow, American Psychiatric Association, 1991. Memberships: American Psychoanalytic Association; American Psychiatric Association; New York and Boston Psychoanalytic Societies; Past President, RI Psychiatric Society. Address: 112 Prospect Street, Providence, RI 02906-1445, USA.

SARFEH I James, b. 2 Nov 1940, Tehran, Iran. General Surgeon. m. Sharon Lynette (Haney), 23 Apr 1983, 1 son, 2 daughters. Education: MD, Albany Medical College, Albany, ND, USA. Career: Professor of Surgery, University California Irvine; Attending Surgeon, University California Irvine Medical Center; Staff Surgeon, Long Beach, VACC, CA & Consultant Surgeon, St Joseph Hospital, Orange, CA. Publications include: Hepatic Dysfunction Following Trauma: Experimental Studies, 1977; The Gastric Mucosa in Portal Hypertension: Effects of Topical Bile Acid, 1984; Gastric Bleeding in Portal Hypertension Inflammatory or Congestive?, 1986; Partial Shunting for Portal Hypertension: Surgical Technique, 1988; The Surgical Management of Variceal Hemorrhage, 1994. Honours: Outstanding Faculty Member Award, University of California, Irvine, 1982; Golden Apple Award, University of California, Irvine, 1994. Memberships include: American Association for the Study of Liver Disease; American Surgical Asociation; American Surgical Liver Group; International Society of Surgery; Pacific Coast Surgical Association; Society of University Surgeons; Western Surgical Association. Hobbies: Skiing; Piano. Address: University of California, Irvine Medical Center, 101 City Drive, Orange, CA 92613-4091, USA.

SARIRIAN Kris Koroush, b. 10 Oct 1961, Isfahan, Iran. Physician. Education: BA, Biology, University of South Florida, USA, 1983; MD, St George's University School of Medicine, Grenada, West Indies, 1988. Appointments: Clinical Fellow, The New York Hospital, Cornell Medical College, 1991-93; Currently in private practice. Publications: Enhancements of murine in vitro antibody formation by hyperthermia, 1982; Allergy to latex surgical gloves: an unfamiliar cause of intraoperative anaphylaxis, 1992; Correlation between the ability of elderly individuals to respond to influenza vaccination and the capacity of their peripheral blood lymphocytes to express receptors for IgD, 1992; Increased serum HLA class I molecule levels in elderly who responded to influenza vaccination, 1993; Serum HLA class I levels in elderly humans: Utilization in following the response to influenza vaccine; Several abstracts. Honours: Recipient, R G Thompson Fellowship, American Cancer Society, Florida Division (University of South Florida School of Medicine), 1981; Phi Sigma. Memberships: American Medical Association; American College of Physicians; American Academy of Allergy and Immunology; New York Allergy Society; European Academy of Allergology and Clinical Immunology. Address: 2919 Swann Avenue, Suite 403, Tampa, FL 33609, USA.

SARIS Nils Erik Leo, b. 2 Nov 1928, Helsinki, Finland. Biochemist. m. (1) Eva Maria Wollitz, (2) Margita Solveig Lund, 2 s, 1 d. Education: DSc, University of Helsinki, 1964. Career: Clinical Biochemist, Aurora Hospital, Helsinki; Principal Clinical Biochemist, Meilahti Hospital, Helsinki; Currently, Chairman of Institute of Biomedicine, University of Helsinki. Recommendations and Related Documents, International Federation of Clinical Chemistry, volume 1, 1978-83; W de G Berlin and New York, 146 pages, 1984. Honours: Doctor Honoris Causa, Medicine and Surgery, University of Helsinki, 1990; Commander of the Order of the Finnish Lion, 1990. Memberships: American Association of Clinical Chemistry; Finnish Society of Sciences and Letters; Finnish Medical Society; Societas Biochemica, Biophysica et Microbiologicae Fennicae. Hobbies: Entomology; Fishing. Address: Ostra Allén 16A1, Fin-00140 Helsinki, Finland.

SARKAR Jaladhi Kumar, b. 1 Aug 1916, Burdwan, West Bengal, India. Professor, Medical Service. m. Gita Sarkar, 18 May 1944, 2 daughters. Education: MBBS, Calcutta University; Dip. Bact. London University; PhD, Calcutta University; Honours Certificates in Physiology and Midwifery, Calcutta Medical College. Appointments: Specialist, Pathology, Indian Army; Professor, Virology, Calcutta School of Tropical Medicine; Director, School of Tropical Medicine; Emeritus Medical Scientist, Indian Council of Medical Research. Publications: Reviwer, Smallpox and its Eradication, WHO 1988; Author: Physician of Sri Rama Krishna - Dr Mahendraeal Sarkar, 1990; Articles: Haemorrhagic Fever in Calcutta, 1967; Concurrent Smallpox and Chickenpox, 1976. Honours: Coates Medal, Calcutta University, 1965; Col. Calvert Memorial Oration Award, Indian Medical Association, 1979; Y.S.N. Rao Oration Award, India, 1980, Council of Medical Research. Barclay Medal from Asiatic Society, 1992. Memberships: WHO Expert Advisory Panel on Virus Diseases; Fellow, Ind National Science Academy; Fellow, National Academy of Medical Sciences; Fellow, Ind Virological Society. Hobbies: Sciencie Fiction writing. Address: 87 Golf Club Road, Calcutta 700033, India.

SARKISOV Donat S, b. 5 Sept 1924, Moscow, Russia. Pathologist. m. Sarkisova Lydia, 1958, 1 daughter. Education: Navy Medical Academy, St Petersburg, Russia. Career: Hospital Prosecutor, Senior Lecturer, Navy Medical Academy, Leningrad, 1949-58; Head of Department of Pathology, A V Vishnevsky Institute of Surgery, Moscow, 1958-; Academician Secretary, Department of Medico-Biological Sciences, Russian Academy of Medical Sciences, 1984-85; Chief Scientific Secretary, Presidium of USSR Academy of Medical Sciences, 1985-. Publications: Regeneration: Clinical Significance, 1968; Essays on the Structural Bases of Homeostasis, 1977; Electronic & Microscopic Radioautography of the Cell, 1981; Essays on the History of General Pathology, 1994; Author, over 300 scientific works, including 20 monographs. Honours: Several government awards of Russian Federation. Membership: President, Association of Pathologists of the Community of Indepedent States. Membership: International Academy of Pathology, 1993. Hobbies: History of Science; Philosophy. Address: Russian Academy of Medical Sciences, 14, Solianka St, Moscow 109801, Russian Federation.

SASCO Annie Jeanne, b. 4 Dec 1951, Talence, France. Medical Epidemiologist. m. Elio Riboli, 7 Mar 1983, 1 son, 1 daughter. Education: BS, 1969, Educational Commission for Foreign Medical Graduates Certification, 1977, MD, 1978, Occupational and Social Medicine, Aeronautical and Spatial Medicine, 1978, Bordeaux University; Specialised studies, Preventive Medicine, Toulouse University, 1977; MPH, 1979, MS, Biostatistics, Epidemiology, 1980, DPH, Epidemiology, 1986, Harvard University School of Public Health. Appointments: Public Health Research, Bordeaux University, 1976-78; Public Health and Epidemiology Research, Harvard University, USA, 1978-83; Medical Cancer Epidemiologist, Institut National de la Santé et de la Recherche Médicale, seconded to International Agency for Research on Cancer,

Lyon, 1983-. Publications: 1st author, articles, books, including: Measles infection and Parkinson's disease, 1985; Case-control studies for the evaluation of screening, 1986; Risques pour la santé dans les laboratoires de recherche biologique et médicale. Le point sur les connaissances épidémiologiques actuelles, 1989; Smoking and Parkinson's disease, 1990; Comparative study of anti-smoking legislation in the Member States of the EEC, 1992; Smoking habits in French adolescents. 1993. Honours: Fellowship, Ministère des Affaires Etrangères, 1978-80; Victor Emmanuel Chapman Memorial Fellowship, Harvard, 1980-83; Prix de la Charente de la Ligue nationale contre le Cancer, 1994. Memberships: American Association for the Advancement of Science; American Public Health Association; International Epidemiological Association; Society for Epidemiologic Research; New York Academy of Sciences; Association des Epidémiologistes de Langue française. Hobby: Reading. Address: 26 rue du Professeur Florence, 69003 Lyon, France.

SATIN David G, b. 16 July 1933, Brooklyn, New York, USA. Psychiatrist. m. Bernice A Perlmutter, 1 June 1958, 2 daughters. Education: AB with honours, Princeton University, 1954; MD, Harvard Medical School, 1958; Medical-Paediatric Internship, North Carolina Memorial Hospital, 1958-59; Psychiatric Residency, Massachusetts General and McLean Hospital, 1959-62. Appointments: Assistant Professor, Associate Professor, Psychiatry, Boston University School of Medicine; Assistant Attending Psychiatrist, Associate Attending Psychiatrist, Boston University Medical Center and Boston City Hospitals; Currently Assistant Clinical Professor, Psychiatry, Harvard Medical School; Assistant Psychiatrist, McLean Hospital; Medical Director, EXCEL Geriatric Program, Bournewood Hospital. Publications: The Clinical Care of the Aged Person: An Interdisciplinary Perspective (contributing author and editor), 1994; Insights and Innovations in Community Mental Health (edited with E B Lindemann and J Farrell), 1994. Honours: National Institute of Mental Health Fellow in Community Mental Health, 1961-62, 1964-66, in Research Training for Psychiatrists, 1966-68. Memberships: Fellow, American Psychiatric Association; Fellow, Massachusetts Psychiatric Society; American Geriatric Association; American Association for Geriatric Psychiatry; Gerontologic Society of America. Address: 21 Whittlesey Road, Newton Centre, MA 02159-2621, USA.

SATKUNARAJAH Somasundram, b. 19 Dec 1928, Manipay, Sri Lanka. Obstetrician and Gynaecologist. m. J Soundraranee, 27 Aug 1958, 3 sons. Education: MBBS, Ceylon; FRCOG (UK); FRACOG (Australia). Appointments: Registrar, Obstetrics and Gynaecology, Rush Green Hospital, Romford, England; Obstetrician and Gynaecologist, Cooperative Hospital, Moolai, Sri Lanka; Currently Visiting Obstetrician and Gynaecologist, Camden and Campbelltown District Hospitals, New South Wales, Australia. Memberships include: National Association of Specialist Obstetricians and Gynaecologists, (NASOG), Australia; Australian Medical Association, Rotary Club. Address: 5 Southdown Road, Camden, New South Wales 2570, Australia.

SATOH Chiyoko, b. 1 Jan 1937, Hiroshima, Japan. Molecular Geneticist. 1 son, 1 daughter. Education: BA, 1960, PhD, 1968, Tokyo University. Appointments: Research Associate, Tanabe Pharmaceutical Co; Research Associate, Pennsylvania State University School of Medicine, USA; Research Associate, Atomic Bomb Casualty Commission; Laboratory Chief, Radiation Effects Research Foundation; Senior Research Associate, University of Michigan School of Medicine, USA; Currently Chief, Department of Genetics, Radiation Effects Research Foundation. Publications: Biochemical genetic studies on the children of the atom bomb survivors, 1992; Variations among Japanese of the factor IX gene (F9) detected by PCR-denaturing gradient gel electrophoresis, 1993. Memberships: Japan Society of Human Genetics; Genetics Society of Japan; Japan Radiation Research Society; Molecular Biology Society of Japan. Hobbies: Tennis; Scuba diving. Address: 4-23-602 Fujimi-cho, Naka-ku, Hiroshima 730, Japan.

SATOYOSHI Eijiro, b. 11 Feb 1924, Tokyo, Japan. Clinical Neurologist. m. Mitsuko Satoyoshi, Oct 1960, 1 son. Education: MD, Keio University School of Medicine, 1946. Appointments: Professor of Internal Medicine and Neurology, 1968; Director, National Centre Mental and Muscular Diseases, 1978; Director, National Institute Neuroscience, 1986; President, President Emeritus, National Centre Neurology and Psychiatry, 1989. Publications: Myopathy in Thyrotoxicosis, 1963; A Syndrome of Progressive Muscle Spasms, Alopecia and Diarrhoea, 1978; Text Book of Neurology, Co-editor, 1980. Honours: President, Japanese Soceity of Neurology, 1978; President, 8th International

Congress Neuro-muscular Diseases, 1994; Vice President, World Federation of Neurology, 1993. Memberships: Japanese Society Child Neurology; Japanese Society Internal Medicine; American Neurological Association; Royal Society of Medicine; New York Academy of Sciences; French Neurological Society. Hobby: Sports. Address: 4-20-33 Shiromeguro, Meguroku, Tokyo 153, Japan.

SAUBERLICH Howerde Edwin, b. 23 Jan 1919, Ellington, Wisconsin, USA. Biochemist; Nutritionist. m. 15 Sept 1945, 1 son, 1 daughter. Education: BA summa cum laude, Physical Chemistry, Lawrence University, 1944; MS, Biochemistry, 1946, PhD, Biochemistry, 1948, University of Wisconsin. Appointments include: Chief, Nutrition Technology Division, Letterman Army Institute of Research, Presidio of San Francisco, California, 1974-80; Acting Director, Western Human Nutrition Research Center, USDA-ARS, Presidio of San Francisco, 1980-82; Affiliate/adjunct Professor, University of California, Berkeley, 1974-82; Professor, Nutrition Sciences Department, University of Alabama, Birmingham, 1983-; Adjunct Professor, School of Medicine, University of Miami, Florida, 1990-. Publications: Over 300 including: Specific nutrient abnormalities in asymptomatic HIV-1 infection (co-author), 1992; Antagonists of folate - Their biochemical and clinical importance, 1994; Antithiamins - Their biochemical and nutritional importance, 1994; Effects of the consumption of an umbelliferous vegetable beverage on constituents in human sera (co-author), 1994; Vitamin C and cancer, book chapter, 1994. Honours: Mead-Johnson Award for Vitamin B-complex research, American Institute of Nutrition, 1952; McLester Award, research in human nutrition, 1965; Award, Canadian Society for Clinical Chemistry, 1983; Many more. Memberships include: American Society for Biochemistry and Molecular Biology; American Society of Clinical Nutrition; American Association for Cancer Research; American Chemical Society; American Society for Microbiology; Society for Experimental Biology and Medicine; American Society of Animal Sciences; European Academy of Nutritional Sciences; New York Academy of Sciences. Hobbies: Gardening; Travel; Hiking; Botany; Antiques; Photography; Music. Address: 1512 Kestwick Drive, Hoover, AL 35226, USA.

SAUCIER Jean François, b. 14 Feb 1930, Quebec, Canada. Professor of Psychiatry. m. Janet Futvoye, 18 Oct 1969, 1 d. Education: BA, 1949, MD, 1958, Laval University, Canada; PhD, Columbia University, USA, 1974. Career: Lecturer, Department of Psychiatry, McGill University, Montreal, 1965-67; Associate Professor, Department of Sociology and Anthropology, Carleton University, Ottawa, 1972-75; Professor, Department of Psychiatry, University of Montreal, 1982-. Publications: Correlates of the long postpartum taboo: a cross cultural study, 1972; Co-author, Perceived vulnerability in children and adolescents, 1982; Co-author, Adolescents, self-reported mental health and parents marital status, 1983. Honours: Graduate Faculties Fellowship, Columbia University, USA, 1970; Academic Excellence Award, University of Montreal, 1993. Memberships: Canadian Psychiatric Association; Canadian Medical Association; American Anthropological Association. Hobbies: Outdoor Exercise; Skiing. Address: 3100 Ellendale Avenue, Montreal, Quebec, Canada, H3S 1W3.

SAUNDERS John Rudolf, b. 15 Jan 1926, Aberdeen, Scotland. Medicine. m. Patricia Ann Cosyns, 2 Feb 1952, 3 d. Education: MB; BS; MRCS; LRCP; FRCOG. Career includes: Senior Obstetric and Gynaecological Registrar, University College Hospital, Ibadan, Nigeria, 1956-58; Currently retired from practice of Obstetrics and Gynaecology. Publications: The Oxytorin Sensitivity Test, British Congress of O and G, Cardiff, in Journal of O and G, 1959; Vacuum Extractor, Proc Royal Society of Medicine, 1960; Vacuum Extraction, in The Medical World, 1962. Honour: Liston Gold Medal in Senior Clinical Surgery, 1949. Memberships: Fellow, Royal Society of Medicine; British Medical Association. Hobbies: Music; Drama; Archaeology; Wine; Commercial Fishing; History of Medicine. Address: 25 Biddenham Turn, Bedford, MK40 4AZ, England.

SAVAGE Charles, b. 25 Sep 1918, Berlin, CT, USA. Physician. m. Ethel Truss, 9 May 1940, 1 s, 1 d. Education: BA; SM; MD; Graduate WA-Baltimore Psychoanalytic Institute, 1957. Appointments: Assistant Director, MD Psychiatry Research Center, Baltimore, 1965-72; Professor of Psychiatry, University of MD, 1965-82; Chief of Psychiatry and Drug Dependency Treatment, VA Medical Center, Baltimore, 1972-82; Psychiatrist, Department of Health, US Virgin Islands, 1986-92; Consultant Geriatric Psychiatry, Eastern Shore Hospital Center, Cambridge, MD, 1992-94; Currently, Volunteer Physician and Translator, Iglésia Santa Ana, Chichicastenango, Guatemala; Assistant

Emeritus Professor, Johns Hopkins University. Publications: Co-editor, Research in Psychotherapy, 1968; Co-editor, Drug Abuse Controversy, 1972; Sex and Heroin, in American Journal of Psychiatry, 1980. Honours: Fellow, Centre for Advanced Study, Behavioural Science, Stanford, CA, 1957-58; David C Wilson Honorary Lecturer, University of VA, 1967. Memberships: International Psychoanalytic Association; American Psychiatric Association; American EEG Society; American Psychoanalytic Association. Hobbies: Sailing; Scuba Diving; Cycling. Address: Box 945, Coral Bay, St John, VI 00831, USA.

SAVAGE Wendy Diane, b. 12 Apr 1935, Thornton Heath, Surrey, England. University Lecturer; Obstetrician and Gynaecologist. div., 2 sons, 2 daughters. Education: Girton College, Cambridge; The London Hospital Medical College; BA; MBBCh (Cantab), 1960; MRCS LRCP (London), 1960; MRCOG, 1971; FRCOG, 1985; FPA, Contraception and Vasectomy. Appointments: Specialist, Obstetrics, Gynaecology, Venereology, Family Planning, Cook Hospital, Gisborne, New Zealand, 1973; Press Officer, Doctors for a Woman's Choice on Abortion, 1977-; Senior Lecturer, Obstetrics and Gynaecology, 1977-, Honorary Consultant, 1977-85, 1986-, London (now Royal London) Hospital Medical College; Honorary Visiting Professor, Middlesex University, 1991; Clinical Tutor, Royal London Hospital Trust, 1994-. Publications: Author or co-author, several books including: Coping with Caesarian Section and Other Difficult Births, 1983; Savage Enquiry, 1986; Caesarean Birth in Britain, 1993; Book chapters; Papers on abortion, bacteriuria in pregnancy, cytology, Depo-Provera, perinatal death, antenatal care, gonnorrhoea. Honours: Elected Member, General Medical Council, 1989, 1994. Memberships: Fellow, Royal Society of Medicine; Founder Member, Women in Medicine; Founder Member, Women in Gynaecology and Obstetrics; Trustee, Pregnancy Advisory Service; Executive Committee, Birth Control Campaign; Medical Society, Institute for Psychosexual Medicine. Address: Room EWS49, 2nd Floor, Talbot Wellington Corridor, Royal London Hospital, Whitechapel, London E1 1BB, England.

SAVONA-VENTURA Charles, b. 18 Feb 1955, Cospicua, Malta. Obstetrician and Gynaecologist. m. Marylene Simler, 24 Aug 1980, 1 son, 1 daughter. Education: MD, University of Malta, 1979; AccCertObsGyn, Catholic University of Leuven, Belgium, 1985; MRCOG, Royal College of Obsetricians and Gynaecologists, London, 1986. Appointments: Lecturer, University of Malta, 1981-87; Currently Specialist Obstetrician and Gynaecologist, St Luke's Teaching Hospital, Gwardamangia, Malta. Publications: Analysis of perinatal deaths occurring in Malta (with E S Grech), 1986; Risk factors in elderly obstetric patients (with E S Grech), 1987; A prospective multicentre study to determine the influence of pregnancy upon the 75-g oral glucose tolerance test (OGTT) (co-author), 1989; Outlines of Maltese Medical History, 1995; Mammals and Reptiles in the Mediterranean Sea, in preparation; Author or co-author, articles in journals including Animalia, Medical History, International Journal of Obstetrics and Gynaecology, International Journal of Risk and Safety Medicine. Honours: Craig Memorial Research Scholarship, University of Malta, 1988; Medical Research Project Grant, British Medical Association, (Malta Branch)-BUPA Foundation, 1991. Memberships: European Association of Obstetricians and Gynaecologists; Malta College of Obstetricians and Gynaecologists; New York Academy of Sciences. Hobbies: Medical history and folklore; Natural history and environmental studies; Computing; Hiking. Address: NorthWynds, 40 Antonio Zammit Street, Ix-Xwieki, L/O Gharghur, Malta NXR 08.

SAXENA Nirmala, b. 19 Dec 1938, India. Medical Gynaecologist. m. D V Saxena deceased, 1 daughter. Education: MS, Patna; MRCOG, London; F Jhapiego, USA; FRCOG, London; FIMCH, India. Registrar, Darbhanga Medical College, India; SHO, Basildon Hospital, Essex; Registrar, South London Hospital; Assistant Professor, Patna Medical College; Associate Professor, Professor, Nalauda Medical College, Patna. Publications: Articles published in national journals. Memberships: Life Member, FOGST & IMA; Federation of Ultrasound. Hobbies: Travel; Social Work. Address: Justice Raj Kishore Path - New Area, Kadamkuan, Patna 800003, India.

SAXENA Prem Narain, b. 15 Sept 1925, Bareilly District, Uttar Pradesh, India. Teacher in Medicine. m. Rajeshwari Saxena, 5 May 1944, 1 son, 2 daughters. Education: MB BS, Medicine; MD, Pharmacology; PhD; DSc. Appointments: House Physician, Demonstrator, Lecturer, Reader, Professor, K G Medical College, Lucknow, 1947-64; Professor, Chairman, Pharmacology, 1964-87; Professor Emeritus, Pharmacology Department, 1987-, Aligarh Medical

University, Aligarh; Emeritus Medical Scientist, ICMR, 1987-90. Publications: 85 published research papers, 60 presented at conferences; Practical Pharmacy, 1965, revised editions, 1978, 1983; J N Medical College Pharmacopoeia, 1978; Manual of Experimental Pharmacology, 1979, revised edition, 1984. Honours: Rockefeller Foundation Fellow, USA, 1960-61; Commonwealth Medical Fellow, 1969-70; Wellcome Trust Medical Fellow, UK, 1970-71, 1974; Dr B N Ghosh Memorial Lecturer and Gold Medallist, Calcutta University, 1981; B N Ghosh Memorial Oration Award, 1986. Memberships: Indian Pharmacological Society; Indian Medical Association; International Brain Research Organization; Fellow, Indian Academy of Neurosciences; Fellow, International Medical Sciences Academy; Fellow, National Academy of Medical Sciences, India; Fellow, Indian National Sciences Academy. Hobbies: Philately; Literature. Address: HIG-3Q, ADA Colony, Ram Ghat Road, Aligarh, UP 202 002, India.

SAYERS Janet Virginia, b. 26 Oct 1945, London, England. Professor of Psychology. m. Sean Philip Sayers, 19 Sep 1970, 2 s. Education: MA, Cambridge; Diploma in Clinical Psychology, London; PhD, Kent. Career: Clinical Psychologist, Tavistock Clinic, 1968; Clinical Psychologist, St Augustine's Hospital, Canterbury, 1970; Educational Psychologist, Canterbury Child Guidance Clinic, 1971; Currently, Professor of Psychoanalytic Psychology, Keynes College, University of Kent, Canterbury. Publications: Biological Politics, book, 1982; Sexual Contradictions, book, 1986; Mothering Psychoanalysis, book, 1991; The Man Who Never Was, book, 1995. Honour: Walford Exhibition, New Hall, Cambridge, 1966-68. Memberships: British Psychological Society; Association of University Teachers. Hobbies: Knitting; Theatre; Opera. Address: Keynes College, University of Kent, Canterbury, Kent CT2 7NP, England.

SAYK Johannes, b. 28 Sep 1923, Hirschen, Germany. Clinic Director. m. Sömmerda Sayk, 14 Jan 1947, 2 d. Education: MD, Friedrich Schiller University, Jena, 1945-50. Career: Docent and Head of Department of Neurology, University Jena, 1958-60; Director of Clinic of Neurology, University Rostock, 1960-89, Emeritation, 1989-. Publications: Cell Sediment Chamber Sayk's Method, 1954; Cytology of Cerebrospinal Fluid, Fischer Jena, 1960; The cerebrospinal fluid in brain tumours, chapter 12 in Handbook of Neurology, volume 16, 1974. Honours: Rudolf Virchow Prize, 1965; Honorary Member, Academia de Brasil, 1988; Karl Bonhoeffer Medaille, 1988; Doctor Honoris Causa. Memberships: Founding Member, Research group, World Federation of Neurology; German Academy of Nature Researcher "Leopoldina", 1968; Academia Medyczney Poznan, Poland, 1989; Fellow, Royal Society, London, 1990; Honour Needle of University Rostock. Address: Lewarkweg 4, 18146 Rostock, Germany.

SBARDOLINI Alessandra, b. 27 August 1963, Milan, Italy. Psychologist. Education: Psychologist; Doctor. Appointments: Clinical Psychologist & Hypnologist. Memberships: Centro Internazionale Di Ipnosi Medica e Psicologica. Address: Via Dei Grimani, 4-20144 Milano, Italy.

SCANNELL John Gordon, b. 13 May 1914, Cambridge, MA, USA. Surgeon. m. Helen L Jones, 8 June 1940, 1 son, 6 daughters. Education: AB (Harvard); MD cum laude (Harvard). Career: Resident Surgeon, Visiting Surgeon, Massachusetts General Hospital; Editor, Harvard Medical Alumni Bulletin; Clinical Professor of Surgery, Harvard Medical School/Senior Surgeon, Massachusetts General Hospital. Publications: Wanderjahr, Education of a Surgeon, 1992; Numerous papers. Honour: Henry Christian Prize, Harvard Medical School, 1940. Memberships: American Surgical Association; American Association for Thoracic Surgery; New England Surgical (President); Boston Surgical (President); Society of University Surgeons. Address: Massachusetts General Hospital, Clinic 375, Boston, MA 02114, USA.

SCARLATO Guglielmo, b. 20 June 1931, Naples, Italy. Medical Doctor. m. Bernasconi Mariangela, 19 Nov 1964, 2 sons, 1 daughter. Education: Degree in Medicine. Appointments: Assistant Professor of Neurology; Chairman, Department of Neurology, University of Milan; Professor of Neurology. Publications: More than 400 scientific papers and several books in different fields of neurology. Memberships: Medical Faculty, University Milan. Honours: Honorary Member, French Swiss Society of Neurology; Honorary Corresponding Member, American Academy of Neurology. Hobbies: Fishing. Address: Department of Neurology, University Milan Medical School, Via F Sforza 35, Milan 20122, Italy.

SCASSELLATI SFORZOLINI Guido, b. 22 May 1927, Perugia, Italy. Ophthalmologist. m. Vincenza Riccardi, 20 Oct 1958, 2 sons, 1 daughter. Education includes: Qualified as University Lecturer of Ophthalmology. Appointments: Assistant, then Associate Professor, Bologna University (Ophthalmology Clinic); Professional Ophthalmologist, 1980-. Publications: Various in clinical and pathological fields, semiotic topics in ophthalmology, surgical topics. Memberships: Italian Ophthalmology Society; Professional Ophthalmological Association; French Society for Ophthalmology; European Strabismological Association; Tosco-Umbro-Emiliana Society of Ophthalmology; Barraquer Institute, Spain. Hobby: Fine arts. Address: Via dei Poeti, 6 Bologna, Italy.

SCHACHTER Joseph, b. 26 Aug 1925, New York City, New York, USA. Psychoanalyst. m. Judith A Spector, 6 Dec 1949, 1 son, 2 daughters. Education: MD; PhD. Appointments include: Associate Professor of Psychiatry, University of Pittsburgh, Pennsylvania; Currently in private practice. Publications: Concepts of termination and post-termination patient-analyst contact, 1992; Abstinence and neutrality: development and diverse views, 1994. Memberships: American Psychoanalytic Association; American Psychiatric Association. Hobbies: Antiques; Travel; Tennis. Address: 401 Shady Avenue, Pittsburgh, PA 15206, USA.

SCHAINBERG Helio, b. 4 Apr 1957, Sao Paulo, Brazil. Physician. m. Claudia G Schainberg, 2 Mar 1986, 1 daughter. Education: MD. Appointments: Fellow, Allergy & Immunology, New England Medical Center, Boston, USA, 1986-88; Chief, Allergy & Inflammation Division, Instituto do Cancer, Sao Paulo, 1988-. Publications: Inflammation, 1986; Clinical Trials, 1986; Clinical Immunology, 1987; Immunology, 1988. Memberships: American Academyof Allergy & Immunology; American College of Allergy & Immunology; Braxilian Society of Allergy & Immunopathology. Honours: Travel Grant Award; Special Honor Award; Young Investigator Award, American Academy of Allergy & Immunology; Israel Bonomo Award. Hobbies: Photography. Address: Rua Diogo Jacome 341, 04512-001 Sao Paulo SP, Brazil.

SCHALIN Lars-Johan Fredrik, b. 21 Mar 1931, Helsinki, Finland. Psychoanalyst. m. 5 Sept 1953, Yvonne Beaurain, 1 son, 3 daughters. Education: PhilMag, University of Helsinki, 1954; Associate Member, Swiss Psychoanalytical Society, 1960; Full Member, 1966, Training Analyst, 1967, Finnish Psychoanalytical Society. Appointments: Currently Training Analyst. Publications: Books in Finnish: Articles: in Scandinavian Psychoanalytic Review Aspects on the Personality of the "ILLA FACIET" Daughter, 1979; On the Problem of Envy. Social, clinical and theoretical considerations, 1979; Phallic integration and male identity development, 1983; On the Normal and Pathological Middle-age Crisis - Eric Maria Remarque, a Lost Survivor, 1985; Narsismin kohtaloita, 1986; On Phallicism, 1989; Perheen ihmissuhteista, 1991; Hobbies: Sailing; Music; Literature. Address: Grundvägen 13, 00330 Helsinki, Finland.

SCHALLER Jane Green, b. Cleveland, Ohio, USA, 26 June 1934. Paediatrician. 2 sons, 1 daughter. Education: AB, Hiram (Ohio) College, 1956; MD cum laude, Harvard University, 1960; Resident, Paediatrics, 1960-63, Fellow, Immunology, Arthritis, 1963-65, Children's Hospital, University of Washington, Seattle; Diplomate: American Board of Pediatrics, American Board of Medical Examiners. Appointments: Faculty, 1965-83, Professor, Paediatrics, 1975-83, University of Washington Medical School; Head, Division of Rheumatic Diseases, Children's Hospital, Seattle, 1968-83; Visiting Physician, Medical Research Council, Taplow, England, 1971-72; Professor, Chairman, Department of Paediatrics, Tufts University School of Medicine/New England Medical Center, Boston, Massachusetts, 1983-; Paediatrician-in-chief, Boston Floating Hospital, 1983-. Publications: Articles in field. Memberships include: Institute of Medicine, NAS; American Association for the Advancement of Science, Science and Human Rights Programme; Society for Pediatric Research; American Pediatric Society; American Academy of Pediatrics, Chairman, Subcommittee on Children and Human Rights 1989-; Member, Committee on International Child Health 1990; American College of Rheumatology; New England Pediatric Society, Prsident 1991-93; Association of Medical School Pediatric Chairmen, Executive Committee 1986-89; Committee for Health in Southern Africa, Executive Committee 1986-; Physicians for Human Rights, Executive Committee 1986-, President 1986-89; Aesculapian Club, President 1988-89; Harvard University Medical School Alumni Council, Vice-President 1977-80,

President 1982-83; Editorial boards, professional journals. Address: 287 Kent Street, Brookline, MA 02146, USA.

SCHARFF Jill Savege, b. 28 Mar 1944, Arbroath, Scotland. Psychoanalyst. m. David E Scharff, 12 Oct 1994, 1 s, 2 d. Education: MB Ch B, University of Aberdeen Medical School, Scotland, 1967; MD, Flex 1975; Scottish Conjoint Diploma in Psychological Medicine; MRCPsych; Certified, American Boards of: Psychiatry and Neurology, Child Psychiatry; Certification: Psychoanalysis and Child Analysis, American Psychoanalytic Association. Appointments: Senior House Officer, Ross Clinic, Aberdeen, Scotland; Registrar, Dingleton Hospital, Melrose, Scotland; Registrar, Senior Registrar, Royal Edinburgh Hospital, Scotland; Senior Registrar, Tavistock Clinic, London; Special Research Fellow, George Washington University and The National Medical Center of Childrens Hospital, WA; Currently, Co-Director, International Institute of Object Relations. Publications: Co-author, Object Relations Family Therapy, 1987; Editor, Foundations of Object Relations Family Therapy, 1989; Author, Projective and Introjective Identification and the Case of The Therapist's Self, 1992; Co-author, Object Relations Couple Therapy, 1992; Co-author, Scharff Notes: A Primer of Object Relations Therapy, 1993; Editor, The Autonomous Self: The Work of John D Sutherland, 1994; Co-author, Object Relations Therapy of Physical and Sexual Trauma, 1994. Memberships: American Psychoanalytic Association; WA Psychoanalytic Association. Hobby: Theatre. Address: 6612 Kennedy Drive, Chevy Chase, MD 20815, USA.

SCHATZBERG Alan Frederic, b. 17 Oct 1944, New York, USA. Psychiatry. m. 27 Aug 1974, 2 daughters. Education: BS, New York University, 1965; MD, New York University School of Medicine, 1968. Appointments: Instructor of Psychiatry, Harvard Medical School, 1974-77; Assistant Professor of Psychiatry, Harvard Medical School, 1977-82; Associate Professor of Psychiatry, Harvard Medical School, 1982-88; Professor of Psychiatry, Harvard Medical School, 1988-91; Kenneth T Norris Jr, Professor and Chairman of Psychiatry, Stanford University School of Medicine, 1991-. Publications: Manual of Clinical Psychopharmacology, 1991; Co-editor, Textbook of Psychopharmacology, 1994. Memberships: American Psychiatric Association; American College of Neuropsychopharmacology. Honours: Meritorious Service Medal, US Air Force, 1974; Fellow, American Psychiatric Association, 1978; Fellow, American College of Neuropsychopharmacology. Hobbies: Fine Arts; Theater; Ballet; Sports. Address: Department of Psychiatry & Behavioral Sciences, Room 300, 101 Quarry Road, Stanford, CA 94305-5548, USA.

SCHEER Peter J Z, b. 7 May 1951, Tel-Aviv, Israel. Paediatrician. Divorced, 2 s, 2 d. Education: BA, Philosophy, University of Vienna, 1974; MD, University of Vienna; Certified Doctor for Psychosocial, Psychosomatic and Psychotherapeutic Medicine and Teaching Analyst, Austrian Medical Society. Career: 1st Assistant, Institute for Medical Psychology, Medical Faculty at University of Vienna, 1981-85; Lecturer, University of Vienna, Klagenfurt, Zurich; Currently, Head of Psychotherapeutic and Psychosomatic Division, Univerity of Kinderklinik, Graz, Austria. Publications include: Co-author, Präventive Pädiatrie, 1991; Co-author, Kinderpsychosomatik, 1984, revised edition, 1994. Honour: Award for Cultural Philosophy, City of Vienna, 1980. Memberships: Task Force Zero to Three, National Clinical Infant Programs, Washington DC, USA; MRSM; CM AACAP; World Association for Infant Mental Health. Hobbies: Music; Walking; Cycling. Address: University of Kinderklinik, A-8036 Graz, Austria.

SCHEIBEL Arnold Bernard, b. 18 Jan 1923, New York City, New York, USA. Psychiatrist; Neuroscientist. m. Marian Diamond, 9 Oct 1982. Education: BA, Columbia University; MD, Columbia University Postgraduate School; MS, Neuroscience, University of Illinois, Chicago. Appointments: Assistant Professor, Associate Professor, Anatomy, Psychiatry, University of Tennessee Medical School, 1952-55; Currently Director, Brain Research Institute, Professor of Anatomy and Psychiatry, University of California at Los Angeles Medical Center. Publications: 200 articles on brain structure; Books with Adam Wechsler: Biological Substrates of Alzheimer's Disease, 1986; Neurobiology of Higher Cognitive Function, 1990. Honours: Lennox Lecturer, 1978; American Academy of Arts and Sciences, 1983; Norwegian Academy of Sciences, 1984; University of California at Los Angeles Faculty Lecturer, 1985. Memberships: American Association for Advancement of Science, Society for Neuroscience; American Psychiatric Association; American Neurological Association. Hobbies: Painting; Sculpture; Short story writing. Address: Brain Research Institute, UCLA Medical Center, Los Angeles, CA 90024, USA.

SCHEIBNER Horst, b. 3 May 1929, Freiburg i Br., Neurophysiologist. Education: Diplomingenieur, Doktoringenieur; Habilitation in Biophysics. Career: Assistent, Lichttechnisches Institut of the Technical University of Karlsruhe; Scientific Co-worker, Max-Planck Institut Bad Nauheim; Universitaetsprofessor, University Düsseldorf. Publications: Articles in: Journal Optical Society of America; Vision Research; Die Farbe; Proceedings of the International Research Group on Colour Vision Deficiencies; Memberships: Optical Society of America; International Research Group of Colour Vision Deficiencies; Deutsche Physiologische Gesellschaft. Address: Oberbilker Allee 78, D 40227 Düsseldorf, Germany.

SCHEINMAN Jonathan I, b. 20 Nov 1940, Chicago, IL, USA. Pediatric Nephrologist. 2 children. Career: Faculty, Pediatrics, University of MN Hospital, 1975-83; Chief, Pediatric Nephrology, Duke University Medical Center, 1983-92; Faculty, Pediatrics, Medical College of VA. Publications: Over 40 articles on glomerulae cell culture, immunohistopathology, basement membrane collagens, and oxalosis. Honour: NIH Career Development Award, 1978-83. Membership: Pediatric Nephrology. Address: Medical College of VA, Box 980498, Richmond, VA 23298, USA.

SCHELLENBERG Jean Claude, b. 8 Feb 1945, Basel, Switzerland. Physician. m. Christine Basham, 14 Dec 1985, 3 sons. Education: Diploma of Medicine (Switz); Specialist in Obs & Gynae (Switz); Registration in Medicine, Massachusetts, USA and New Zealand; Diplomate Am B Anesthesiology; FRNZCOG; MRCOG; Specialistin Obs & Gynae (NZ). Career: District Hospital, Lachel, Switzerland; Department of Obs & Gynae, University Hospital, Lauranne; Massachusetts General Hospital, Boston, USA; Department of Anaesthesia, University Hospital, Basel, Switzerland; Department of Obs & Gynae, National Women's Hospital, Auckland, NZ; Senior Lecturer in Obstetrics & Gynaecology. Publications: Dr Med Thesis, 1977; PhD Thesis, 1988; Journal Applied Physiology, 1988, 1992; Journal Clinical Investigation, 1995. Honours: Prize, Swiss Society of Gynaecology, 1988; Lectureship of the RNZCOG, 1988. Memberships: Swiss Society of Gynaecology; RCOG; RNZCOG; ASA; ASP; NY Academy of Science; American Association Adv Science. Hobbies: Windsurfing; Skiing; Music. Address: Department of Obstetrics & Gynaecology, National Women's Hospital, Claude Road, Auckland, New Zealand.

SCHENKENBERG Thomas, b. 3 Nov 1943, St Louis, MO, USA. Psychology. m. Christine Currey, 16 Dec 1981. Education: AB; MA; PhD. Career: Currently: Associate Professor, Department of Neurology, Resident Professor, Department of Psychology, Adjunct Professor, Department of Psychology, Adjunct Associate Professor, Department of Psychiatry, University of Utah; Adjunct Clinical Professor, Department of Psychology, Brigham Young University; Adjunct Professor, Department of Psychology, Utah State University; Chief of Psychology, VA Medical Center. Publications: 25 papers and book chapters, EEG and Clinical Neurophysiology, Neurology, Diseases of the Nervous System, Journal of Clinical Psychology. Honours: Diplomate in Clinical Psychology, 1982; Clinical Neuropsychology, 1985, American Board of Professional Psychology. Membership: American Psychological Association. Hobbies: Skiing; Fly Fishing. Address: 116B VA Medical Center, Salt Lake City, Utah 84148, USA.

SCHER Jordan Mayer, b. 20 Nov 1924, Baltimore, MD, USA. Physician; Psychiatrist. m. Linda Anderson, 25 Jun 1975, 4 d. Education: BS, Wesleyan University, Middletown, CT, 1945; MD, University of MD School of Medicine, Baltimore, MD, 1949; PhD, Psychoneuropharmacology, Hamilton University, 1952; Diplomate, Psychiatry and Neurology, 1957, Medical Hypnosis, 1972. Career includes: Director, Chicago Psychiatric Institute; Director, Methodone Maintenance Institute, Chicago; Founder and Editor, The Journal of Existential Psychiatry; Director, Psychiatry Unit, Cook County Jail, Chicago; Advisor to Mayor's Office, St Louis; Currently, Director, Drug Abuse Center, New Life, Jerusalem, Israel. Publications: Over 100 papers and 4 books including: Co-author, Chronic Schizophrenia, 1959; Theories of The Mind, 1963; Drug Abuse in Industry: Growing Corporate Dilemma, 1973; Co-author, Drugs and The Law, volume 1, Perspectives in Drug Abuse, 1989. Honours: Wesleyan University Prize in Biology; Binwanger Prize, International Existential Society; Carl Jasper Medal, International Ontoanalytic Association; Gold Medal Commemorative Award, Britain. Memberships: American College of Forensic Psychiatry; American Academy of Psychiatry and The Law; American Academy of Psychiatry in Alcohol and Drug Abuse; Royal Society of Medicine, UK.

Hobby: Work. Address: 13 Naomi Street, Abu Tor, Jerusalem 93552, Israel.

SCHERB Elena Diana, b. 14 July 1956, Buenos Aires, Argentina. Psychologist. m. Eduardo Nicenboim, 28 Mar 1979, 1 son. Education: PHO; Residency in Clinical Psychology, Borda Psychiatric Hospital. Appointments: Group Therapy Psychologist, private psychiatric clinic; Founding Member, Clinical Psychologist, private practice, Aigle, Centros de Estudios Humanos, 1979-; Professor in training psychotherapists; Supervisor. Publications: As research work collaborator, 1993, 1994, in 2do Encuentro Latinoamericano de SPR, Santiago, Chile. Honours: Vice-President, Society for Psychological Research, South American Chapter, 1994-96. Memberships: SEPI; IACP; Aigle; Society for Psychological Research. Address: Vieery Loreto 2544 4o A, 1426 Buenos Aires, Cap Fed, Argentina.

SCHERER Ronald Callaway, b. 11 Sep 1945, Akron, OH, USA. Voice Science. m. Mary Ellen Angel, 14 Aug 1971, 1 s, 1 d. Education: BS, Mathematics; MA, Speech Pathology and Audiology; PhD, Speech Science. Appointments: Assistant Clinical Professor, University of CO Medical School; Adjunct Associate Professor, University of IA and University of OK; Affiliate Clinical Professor, University of Northern CO; Associate Professor Adjoint, University of CO, Boulder; Senior Scientist, Wilbur James Gould Voice Research Center, Denver, CO. Publications: Co-Editor, Vocal Fold Physiology: Biomechanics, Acoustics and Phonatory Control, 1985; 67 Publications. Honours: Fellow, International Society of Phonetic Sciences; Sigma Xi. Memberships include: Association Research Otolaryngology; Acoustical Society of America; American Speech Hearing Language Association; International Arts Medicine Association. Hobbies: Music; Sport. Address: Wilbur James Gould Voice Research Center, 1245 Champa Street, Denver, CO 80204, USA.

SCHETKY Diane, b. 8 Feb 1940, NY, USA. Physician. m. Edward T Keenan, 17 Jun 1992, 2 s from previous marriage. Education: BA, Sarah Lawrence College, 1961; MD, Case Western Reserve University, 1966; Internship in Pediatrics, Residency in Adult Psychiatry, Fellowship in Child Psychiatry, University Hospitals Cleveland, OH. Career: Assistant Clinical Professor of Psychiatry, University of Oregon Health Sciences Center; Associate Clinical Professor of Psychiatry, Yale University Child Study Center; Currently, Associate Clinical Professor of Psychiatry, University of Vermont College of Medicine, and in Private Practice, Child and Adult Forensic Psychiatry. Books: Co-editor, Child Psychiatry and The Law; Co-editor, Emergency Issues in Child Psychiatry and The Law, 1985; Co-author, Child Sexual Abuse: A Handbook for Health Care and Legal Professionals, 1992; Articles and chapters in books published. Honours: Diplomate, American Board of Psychiatry and Neurology, Adult Psychiatry, 1974, Child Psychiatry, 1976; Fellow, American Psychiatric Association and American Academy of Child and Adolescent Psychiatry. Memberships: American Psychiatric Association; American Academy of Child and Adolescent Psychiatry; American Academy of Psychiatry and Law; Maine Medical Association. Hobbies: Sailing; Cross Country Skiing; Singing; Music. Address: Fox Ridge Office Park, 247 Commercial Street Box 515-6, Rockport, ME 04856, USA.

SCHEWITZ Lionel Joseph, b. 27 Feb 1928, Pretoria, South Africa. Obstetrics & Gynaecology. m. Sheila Yedeikin, 7 July 1951, 1 son, 2 daughters. Education: MBBcH; FRCOG; Diploma in Obstetrics & Gynaecology; FACS; FACOG. Appointments: Assistant, Baragwanath Hospital, Johannesburg, 1957-59; Senior Lecturer, Charing Cross Hospital, London, 1959-60; Research Fellow, Hektoen Pathological Institute, Chicago, 1960-61; Director, Researcher, Assistant, Associate, Presbyterian St Lukes Hospital, Chicago, 1961-69; Clinical Assistant, Professor, University of Illinois Medical College, 1963-69; Attending Obstetrian & Gynaecologist, Lake Forest Hospital, Illinois; Assistant Professor, RUSH Presbyterian St Lukes University. Honours: Outstanding New Citizen, 1965. Hobbies: Tennis; Model Building; Music. Address: 900 North Westmoreland Road, Suite 228, Lake Forest, IL 60045, USA.

SCHEXNAYDER Donald Alfred, b. 4 Dec 1940, New Orleans, USA. Medical Doctor. Education: BS, Chemistry, LA State Univeristy, 1963; PhD, Organic Chemistry, Northwestern University, 1967; MD, Tulane University Medical School, 1976; Training, General Psychiatry, Tulane University Medical School, 1979; Child Psychiatry, Hartford Consortium, 1979-80; Tulane University Medical School, 1980-81. Appointments: Clinical Assistant Professor, Child Psychiatry, Tulane University Medical School, 1981-; Private Practice, Child Adolescent & Adult Psychiatry,

1981-; Clinical Director, Colisum Medical Center, Adolescent Substance Abuse Tract, 1988-89. Publications: Adolescent Suicide, 1992. Memberships: American Psychiatric Association; LA Psychiatric Medical Association; New Orleans Psychiatric Association; American Academy of Child Psychiatry; LA State Medical Society; Orleans Parish Medical Society. Hobbies: Classical Piano; World Travel; Jogging; Weightlifting; Scuba-diving. Address: 1421 Napoleon Avenue, New Orleans, LA 70115, USA.

SCHLEIFER Steven J, b. 10 Mar 1950, NY, USA. Psychiatry. m. Sarah L Rosenberg, 3 s, 1 d. Education: BA, Columbia College, NY, 1971; MD, Mt Sinai School of Medicine, 1975; Resident, Intern, in Psychiatry, 1975-76, USC-LA County Hospital, Los Angeles; Resident in Psychiatry, Mt Sinai School of Medicine, 1976-79. Appointments: Instructor in Psychiatry, 1978-81, Assistant Professor in Psychiatry, 1982-87, Mt Sinai School of Medicine; Associate Professor, 1987-92, Professor of Psychiatry, 1992-, UMDN, NJ Medical School; Director of Consultation Liaison Psychiatry, 1987-91; Acting Chairman, Psychiatry, 1991-92, Chairman, Department of Psychiatry, 1992-, UMDNJ, NJ Medical School. Publications: About 40 original articles, 25 book chapters, 100 abstracts, in the fields of psychoneuroimmunology and psychosomatic medicine. Memberships include: Fellow, American Psychiatric Association; Society of Biological Psychiatry; American Psychosomatic Society; ISPNE; AAAS; American Society of Psychiatric Oncology/AIDS; American Academy of Psychiatrists in Alcoholism and Addictions. Address: Dept of Psychiatry, UMDNJ New Jersey Medical School, 185 South Orange Avenue, Newark, NJ 07103, USA.

SCHLESSINGER Nathan, b. 31 Oct 1924, Ciechanow, Poland. Psychoanalyst. m. Alice Wiley, 7 Sep 1947, 4 s, 1 d. Education: MD, University of Cincinnati, 1949; Certificate, Institute of Psychoanalysis, Chicago, 1962. Appointments: Clinical Professor Psychiatry, University of IL; Senior Attending Physician, Michael Reese Hospital; Currently: Private Practice; Clinical Emeritus Professor of Psychiatry, University of IL; Training and Supervising Analyst, Institute for Psychoanalysis, Chicago. Publications: Co-author, A Developmental View of the Psychoanalytic Process: Follow up Studies and Their Consequences, IUP, 1983; On Analyzability In Psychoanalysis: The Vital Issues Vol II, 1984; A Developmental View of Converting Psychotherapy to Psychoanalysis, in Psychoanalytic Inquiry, 1990. Memberships: Alpha Omega Alpha; AMA; American Psychoanalytic Association; Center for Advanced Studies in Psychoanalysis; American Psychiatric Association; IL Psychiatric Society; Chicago Psychoanalytic Society. Address: 35E Wacker Drive, Chicago, IL 60601, USA.

SCHLOERB Paul R, b. 22 Oct 1919, Buffalo, New York, USA. Surgeon. m. Louise Grimmer, 25 Feb 1950, 2 sons, 3 daughters. Education: AB, Harvard University, 1941; MD, University of Rochester, 1944; Diplomate, American Board of Surgery, 1953. Appointments: Assistant to Professor of Surgery, University of Kansas Medical Centre, 1952-79; Professor of Surgery, University of Rochester, Strong Memorial Hospital, 1979-88; Professor of Surgery, University of Kansas Medical Centre, 1988-. Publications: Contributor of over 100 research and clinical studies papers. Honours: Research Career Development Award, NIH, 1962-67. Memberships: American College of Surgeons; American Medical Association; American Surgical Association; Central Surgical Association; Society University Surgeons; American Association for Surgery of Trauma; APS. Hobby: Swimming. Address: Department of Surgery, University of Kansas Medical Centre, Kansas City, KS 66160, USA.

SCHMID Lynette Sue, b. 28 May 1958, Tecumseh, Nebraska. Child & Adolescent Psychiatrist. m. Vijendra Sundar, 13 June 1987, 2 sons. Education: BS, University of Nebraska, 1979; MD, University of Nebraska, 1984; General Psychiatry Residency, University of Missouri, 1984-87; Child & Adolescent Psychiatry Fellowship, University of Missouri, 1988-89. Appointments: Psychiatrist, Fulton State Hospital, 1990-91; Clinical Assistant Professor of Psychiatry, University of Missouri, 1990-; Psychiatrist, Mid Missouri Mental Health Center, 1991-. Memberships: University of Nebraska Alumni Association; American Psychiatric Association; American Academy of Child & Adolescent Psychiatry; Central Missouri Psychiatric Association. Honours: Phi Beta Kappa, 1979; Alpha Omega Alpha, 1984. Hobbies: Walking; Reading; Studying Scriptures. Address: Mid Missouri Mental Health Center, 3 Hospital Drive, Columbia, MO 65201, USA.

SCHMID Wilhelmine, b. 9 Aug 1940, Vienna, Austria. Orthodontist. m. Franco Mongini, 30 Oct 1968, 3 daughters. Education: MD, Specialist in Stomatology, University of Turin, Italy. Appointments: Currently Lecturer, Postgraduate School in Orthopaedics, University of Turin. Publications: Co-author: Treatment of mandibular asymmetries during growth, 1987; Craniomandibular and TMJ orthopedics, 1989; Computer based assessment of structural and displacement asymmetries of mandible, 1991; Improvement of masticatory function after orthopedic treatment, 1994. Memberships: American Association of Orthodontics; European Association of Orthodontics. Hobbies: Music; Theatre; Sport. Address: Corso Massimo D'Azeglio 76, I-10126 Turin, Italy.

SCHMID-SCHOENBEIN Geert W, b. 1 Jan 1948, Albstadt, Germany. Bioengineer. m. Renate E, 3 July 1976, 3 sons. Education: MS; PhD, Bioengineering. Appointments: Assistant Professor, 1979-84, Associate Professor, 1984-89, Professor, 1989-, Department of Bioengineering. Publications: Physiology and Pathophysiology of Leukoujke Adhesion, 1995; Frontiers in Biomechanics, 1986. Honours: Lafon Award, 1994; Melville Medal, 1990. Memberships: American Society of Mechanical Engineering; Biomedical Society; European & American Society for Microcirculation. Hobbies: Hiking. Address: Department of Bioengineering, University of California, San Diego, La Jolla, CA 92093-0412, USA.

SCHMIDT Dietmar, b. 18 Mar 1952, Altena, Germany. Assistant Medical Doctor; Assistant Professor of Pathology. m. Dietlind Schmidt, 7 Jul 1978, 1 s, 2 d. Education: MD, 1979; Assistant Professor of Pathology, 1986. Career: Resident and Instructor, 1979-86; Assistant Professor of Pathology, 1986-; Assistant Medical Director, 1991-, University of Kiel. Publication: Nephroblastome (Wilms-Tumoreu) and Nephroblastom Sonder-varianten, Gustav Fischer Verlag, 1989. Memberships: German Society of Pathology; International Academy of Pathology; Society of Pediatric Oncology and Hematology; International Society of Pediatric Oncology; Histiocyte Society. Hobbies: Photography; Sport; Hiking. Address: Institute of Pathology, University of Kiel, Michaelstrasse 11, DW-2300 Kiel 1, Germany.

SCHMIDT Robert Milton, b. 7 May 1944, Milwaukee, Wisconsin, USA. Scientist; Educator. 2 sons. Education: AB, Northwestern University, 1966; MD, Columbia University, 1970; MPH, Harvard University, 1975; PhD, Law, Medicine and Public Policy, Emory University, 1982; Diplomate, American Board Preventive Medicine. Appointments include: Director, Haematology, National Centre for Disease Control, Atlanta, 1971-78; Special Assistant to Director, 1978-79, Inactive Reserves, 1979-, National Centre for Disease Control; Clinical Assistant Professor of Paediatrics, Tufts University Medical School, 1974-86; Clinical Assistant Professor of Medicine, Emory University Medical School, 1971-81; Clinical Associate Professor of Humanities in Medicine, Morehouse Medical School, 1977-79; Attending Physician, Department of Medicine, California Pacific Medical Centre, San Francisco, 1983-; Director, Centre Preventive Medicine and Health Research, 1983-; Director, Health Watch, 1983-; Professor of Haematology and Gerontology, Director, Centre Preventive Medicine and Health Research, Chair, Health Professions Programme, San Francisco State University, 1983-. Publications: Author of 17 books and manuals including: Hematology Laboratory Series, 4 volumes, 1979-86; CRC Handbook Series in Clinical Laboratory Science, 1976-; Contemporary Gerontology, Associate Editor, 1993-; Alternative Therapies in Health and Medicine, 1995-; Contributor of over 260 articles in professional journals. Honours: Recipient of numerous awards for professional services. Memberships include: AMA; American Public Health Association; American Society of Haematology; Sigma Xi Address: 25 Hinckley Walk, San Francisco, CA 94111-2303, USA.

SCHNEIDER Achim, b. 17 Sep 1950, Augsburg, Germany. Gynaecologist. Education: MD; MPH. Appointment: Currently, Chairman, Department of Gynaecology. Publications: Articles on epidemiology, morphology, natural history of genital human papillomavirus infections. Honour: Fellowship, Gynaecology and Oncology, University of Arizona, 1991-92. Memberships: German Society of Obstetrics and Gynaecology; Honorary Member, Canadian Society of Colposcopists. Hobbies: Tennis; Skiing. Address: Dept of Gynaecology, Friedrich-Schiller University, Bachstr 18, Jena 07740, Germany.

SCHNEIDER Fiona Mary, b. 16 May 1959, Rawdon, England. Obstetrician and Gynaecologist. m. Jens Schneider, 30 May 1987, 2 sons. Education: MB BS, St Bartholomew's Medical College, London, 1982; Trainee, Obstetrics and Gynaecology, Hammersmith Hospital, London, John Radcliffe Hospital, Oxford, St James University Hospital, Leeds; MRCOG, 1988. Appointments: St Bartholomew's Hospital London; Currently Obstetrician and Gynaecologist, American Clinic, Frankfurt, Germany. Publications: Papers on antibiotic prophylaxis during hysterectomy, 1984. Memberships include: European Association of Obstetricians and Gynaecologists. Address: Burgstrasse 5, 30826 Schloß, Ricklingen, Germany.

SCHNEIDER Lon. Psychiatrist. Appointments: Associate Professor of Psychiatry and Neurology. Memberships: American Association of General Practitioners; American Psychiatry Association; AGS. Address: USC School of Medicine, 2250 Alcazar Street, Room 135E, Los Angeles, CA 90033, USA.

SCHNEIDER Pierre-Bernard, b. 29 Sep 1916, S-Imier, Switzerland. Professor of Psychiatry and Medical Psychology. m. Isabel Huguenin, 21 Jun 1941, 3 d. Education: MD, University of Lausanne; MD; Psychoanalyst, IAP; Specialist FMH, Psychiatry and Psychotherapy. Appointments: Director, Psychiatric University Outpatients Clinic, Lausanne, 1948-82; Professor of Psychiatry and Medical Psychology and Forensic Psychiatry, University of Lausanne, 1957-82; Currently, Honorary Professor. Publications: La tentative de suicide, 1954; Psychologie médicale, 1969; Pratique de la Psychothérapie de Groupe, 1965, 2nd edition 1968, 3rd edition 1972; Propédentique d'une psychotherapie, 1976; La dépression, 1980; Regards discrets et indiscrets sur le médecin. Honours: Honorary President: Societe de Psychologie Médicale; International Federation of Medical Psychotherapy; International Federation of the Organizations of Medical Psychology and others. Hobbies: Sailing; Literature. Address: 19 Ave General Guisan, CH 1009, Pully, Switzerland.

SCHNITT Jerome M, b. 2 Feb 1947, Huntington, WV, USA. Physician. Education: AB, Yale University, 1969; MD, WV University, 1973; MD, 1978; Certified in Psychiatry, American Board of Psychiatry and Neurology with Added Qualifications in Addiction Psychiatry, 1993. Appointments: Assistant Chief, Alcoholism PGM, VA Medical Center, West Haven, CT, 1976-87; Private Practice, 1987-; Associate Clinical Professor of Psychiatry, Yale University, School of Medicine. Publications: Issues in Developing Alcoholism Screening Models, in Substance Abuse, 1986; Double Diagnosis Treatment, in Jnl Substance Abuse Treatment, 1985; Co-author, Psychological Issues in Dance, 1988; Co-author, Eating Disorders in Dancers, 1987. Memberships: Fellow, American Psychiatric Association; Secretary, CT Psychiatric Society; Past President, New Haven Cty Psychiatric Society; Director, Section on Treatment, New England Director, American Academy Psychiatrists in Alcoholism and Addictions. Address: 2A, 123 York Street, New Haven, CT 06511, USA.

SCHOBER Edward Albert, b. 20 Mar 1969, Park Ridge, Illinois, USA. Biomedical Engineer. Education: BS, Biology, 1990; PhD, Biomedical Engineering, 1992. Appointments: Research Assistant, Department of Biomedical Engineering, University of California, Chapel Hill; Scientist, Smith & Nephew General Research Centre, York, England. Publications: Effect of thickness on the mechanical characteristics of the chorioamniotic membrane, 1994; Resistance of fetal membranes to the concentrated application of force and reconciliation of puncture and burst testing, 1994; Ionic control of the rupture of fetal membranes, 1995. Honours: Delta Phi Alpha, 1988. Memberships: Biomedical Engineering Society; American Society of Biomechanics. Hobbies: Russian; Guitar; Snow Skiing; Photography. Address: 65 Millfield Road, York, Y02 2NH, England.

SCHOENHERR Joachim Horst, b. 23 Feb 1926, Oelsa, Germany. University Professor. m. 14 July 1951, 1 daughter. Education includes: Dr phil; Studies in Forest Zoology, Entomology. Appointments include: Currently Professor of Forest Zoology and Entomology. Publications: 85 in various journals. Honours: Doctor honoris causa. Address: Am Schlosspark 6, D-79252 Stegen, Germany.

SCHOENWETTER William Frederick, b. 10 Mar 1935, Milwaukee, Wisconsin, USA. Physician. m. Barbara Lee Barney, 25 June 1960, 2 sons, 1 daughter. Education: MD. Appointments: Currently Director, Asthma and Allergy Research Center, Park Nicollet Medical Center, Minneapolis, Minnesota. Memberships: Fellow, American College of Physicians; Fellow, American Academy of Allergy and Immunology; Fellow, American College of Allergy and Immunology. Address: Park Nicollet Medical Center, 5000 w 39th Street, Minneapolis, MN 55416, USA.

SCHOLL Susie Marie Elisabeth, b. 8 June 1950, Ettelbruck. Physician. m. Jos Even, 1 son, 1 daughter. Education: MD; MRCOG(UK); HDR. Appointments: Senior House Officer, Cambridge, England, 1982-84; Registrar, Obstetrics and Gynaecology, Romford, Essex and The London Hospital, London, 1984-86; Assistant, Institut Curie, Paris, France, 1986-. Publications: Molecular Carcinogenesis, 1993; Contributor of articles in professional journals. Honour: The Lancet Award, 1994. Memberships: European Society of Mastology. Hobbies: Skiing; Gastronomy; Botany. Address: Institut Curie, 26 rue d'Ulm, 75231 Paris, Cedex 05, France.

SCHÖNBERGER Winfried Josef, b. 2 Apr 1940, Wiesbaden, Germany. Pediatrician. m. Gisela Schönig, MD, 8 Apr 1971. Education: MD; PhD; Pvt Docent. Career: Assistant Professor, 1972-75, Private Docent, 1975-77, Professor of Pediatrics, 1977-, University of Mainz. Publications: Anatomie und Physiologie, Gustav Fischer Verlag, Stuttgart, 8th edition, 1991; Kinderheilkunde, Gustav Fischer Verlag, 1992; Over 105 papers in national and international journals. Honours: Annual Award, German Society of Dentistry, 1977; Boehringer Prize, Ingelheim, 1980. Memberships: German Society of Pediatrics, South German Society of Pediatrics; German Society of Endocrinology. Address: Pfahler Strasse 43, D-55 193 Wiesbaden, Sonnenberg, Germany.

SCHRAUB Simon, b. 1 Jan 1940, Bordeaux, France. Physician. m. Aurore Abclewicz, 20 Aug 1969, 2 sons, 1 daughter. Appointments: Professor of Oncology; Head, Radiotherapy and Oncology Department. Publication: La magie et la raison, 1987. Honour: Chevalier de la Legion d'Honneur, 1994. Memberships: Administration Staff, Anticancer French League; Administrative Staff, University Hospital of Besancon. Hobbies: Photography; Mountaineering. Address: CHR, 1 bld Fleming, 25030 Besancon, France.

SCHRIER Robert William, b. 19 Feb 1936, Indianapolis, Indiana, USA. Physician. 3 sons, 2 daughters. Education: BA, DePauw University, 1957; MD, Indiana University School of Medicine, 1962. Appointments: Assistant Professor of Medicine and Cardiovascular Research Institute, 1969-72, Associate Member, Cardiovascular Research Institute, 1970-72, Associate Director, Renal Division, 1971-72, Associate Professor of Medicine and Cardiovascular Research Institute, 1972, University of California Medical Centre, San Francisco, California; Professor of Medicine, Head, Division of Renal Diseases and Hypertension, 1972-92, Professor, Chairman, Department of Medicine, 1976-, University of Colorado School of Medicine, Denver, Colorado. Publications include: The Clinical Use of Drugs in Renal Failure, Co-editor, 1976; Renal and Electrolyte Disorders, Editor, 1980; Current Medical Therapy, Editor, 1984; Vasopressin, Editor, 1985; Geriatric Medicine: The Care of the Elderly, 1990; Manual of Nephrology, 1990, 4th edition, 1994; Advances in Internal Medicine, Volume 39, Co-editor, 1994, Volume 40, 1995. Honours: Numerous including: John Phillips Memorial Award, American College of Physicians, 1992; Mayo Soley Award for Biomedical Research, Western Society for Clinical Investigation, 1989; David M Hume Memorial Award, National Kidney Foundation, 1987; Louis Pasteur Medal for Research in Acute Renal Failure, University of Strasbourg, France, 1987. Memberships include: National Kidney Foundation; American Society of Nephrology; International Society of Nephrology; American College of Physicians; American Heart Association. Address: University of Colorado School of Medicine, 4200 East Ninth Avenue, B-178 Denver, CO 80262, USA.

SCHROCK Theodore Ross, b. 21 Oct 1939, Berne, Indiana, USA. Professor of Surgery. m. Barbara Schrock, 21 Oct 1939, 2 sons. Education: BS with highest honours, 1961, MD, 1964, University of California, San Francisco. Appointments: Assistant Professor of Surgery, 1971-76, Associate Professor of Surgery, 1976-84, Professor of Surgery, Interim Chairman, Department of Surgery, 1984-, University of California, San Francisco. Publications: The Endosurgery Evolution: No Place for Sacred Cows, 1992; Colonoscopy versus barium enema in the diagnosis of colorectal cancers and polyps, 1993; Colonoscopy for colorectal cancer: Too much, too little, just right, 1993; Principles of colectomy for malignant disease: Can laparoscopy meet the challenge; Co-author: Ileoanal pouches; comparison of CT, scintigraphy, and contrast enemas for diagnosing postsurgical complications, 1990; The Efficacy and Limitations of Percutaneous Endoscopic Gastrostomy, 1991; Editor: Handbook of Surgery, 1978, 1982, 1985, 1989, 1994; Perspectives, Colon and Rectal Surgery Outlook, 1988-. Honours: Phi Beta Kappa; Alpha Omega Alpha; Gold-Headed Cane Award; Crohn's and Colitis Award; Gerald Marks Lecturer, Society of American Gastrointestinal Endoscopic Surgeons; American Society for Gastrointestinal Endoscopy Lecturer. Memberships: American College of Surgeons; American Society of Colon and Rectal Surgeons; Society of American Gastrointestinal Endoscopic Surgeons; Pacific Coast Surgical Association; American Society for Gastrointestinal Endoscopy. Hobby: Deep sea diving. Address: Department of Surgery, University of California at San Francisco, 513 Parnassus Avenue S-320, San Francisco, CA 94143-0104, USA.

SCHRÖDER J Michael, b. 12 Nov 1937, Hamburg, Germany. Professor of Neuropathology. m. Monika Schröder, 2 s. Education: MD, 1962; Habilitation, 1971; Leiter des Referenzzentrums für Neuromuskuläre Krankheiten bei der Dt Gesellschaft für Neuropathologie und Neuroanatomie eV. Career: Max Planck Institut für Hirnforschung, Koln, Frankfurt, 1963-74; Harvard Medical School, Boston, MA, 1965-66; Abteilung für Neuropathologie der Universität Mainz, 1974-80; Currently, Director of The Institute of Neuropathology, Aachen. Publications: 160 Articles in scientific journals, 1964-93; Pathologie der Muskulatur, 1982. Honour: Duchenne-ERB Prize der Deutschen Gesellschaft Bekämpfung der Muskelkrankheiten. Memberships: Executive Committee of the Research Group on Neuromuscular Disorders of the World Federation of Neurology; International Society of Neuropathology; 5 other German Societies; Royal Society of Medicine, London. Hobbies: Tennis; Sailing, Skiing. Address: Klinikum der RWTH Aachen, Direktor des Institutes für Neuropathologie (Hochschulmedizin, Neuropathologie), Pauwelsstrasse, D-52074 Aachen, Germany.

SCHUCKIT Marc Alan, b. 5 Mar 1944, Milwaukee, USA. Psychiatrist. m. Judith Schrinsky, 7 Feb 1967, 1 s, 1 d. Education: BS, University of Wisconsin, 1964; MD, Washington University, St Louis, 1968; Board Certified, Psychiatry, 1974. Appointment: Professor of Psychiatry, University of California, San Diego Medical School and San Diego Veterans Hospital. Publications include: 8 Books; 320 publications. Honours: Distinguished Scientist, Research Society on Alcoholism, 1993; Isaacson Award, 1994. Memberships: American College of Neuropsychopharmacology, Fellow; Fellow, American Psychiatric Association; Board, International Society of Biomedical Research on Alcohol. Hobbies: Music; Literature; Hiking; Racquetball. University of California, School of Medicine and San Diego Veterans Hospital, 3350 La Jolla Village Drive, San Diego, CA 92131, USA.

SCHUHL Juan Francisco, b. 15 Dec 1938, Montevideo, Uruguay. Medical Doctor. m. Ilene Alves da Silva, 8 Apr 1965, 1 son, 4 daughters. Education: MD, postgraduate study in Pneumology, Faculty of Medicine, Montevideo; Allergology, Institut d'Immunobiologie, Paris, France. Appointments: Chief, Allergy and Clinical Immunology Department, Military Hospital, Montevideo, 1970-90; Assistant Professor of Allergy and Clinical Immunology, Faculty of Medicine, Montevideo, 1977-. Honours: Prize for Best Free Paper at International Meeting on Allergy, Asthma and Immunology, Buenos Aires, 1986. Memberships: Allergy Societies of Uruguay, Argentina, Brazil, Chile and Paraguay; American Academy of Allergy; American College of Allergy. Hobbies: Music; Collecting and repairing watches. Address: Casilla de Correos 12245, 11300 Montevideo, Uruguay.

SCHUKER Eleanor, b. 3 Jan 1941, New York City, USA. Psychiatrist. m. Dr Alan Melowsky, 26 Dec 1974, 1 daughter. Education: BA, Swarthmore College, 1961; MD, Columbia University, 1965. Career: Attending Psychiatrist, Columbia University Health Service, 1969-90; Co-Director, Psychiatric Emergency Services, St Luke's Hospital, New York City, 1970-72; Founding Director, Rape Intervention Program, St Luke's Hospital, 1977-80; Collab Psychoanalyst, Columbia University Psychoanalytic Center, 1975-85; Training & Supervising Analyst, Columbia University Psychoanalytic Center; Associate Clinical Professor of Psychiatry, Columbia University, currently. Publications: Contributor of several chapters; Editor (with Nadine Levinson), Female Psychology = An Annotated Psychoanalytic Bibliography; Contributor, several articles to professional journals. Memberships: Fellow, American Psychiatric Association; American Psychoanalytic Association; President Elect, 1993-95, Association for Psychoanalytic Medicine (Columbia University). Address: 150 West End Avenue #26A, New York, NY 10023, USA.

SCHULMAN Harold, b. 26 Oct 1930, Newark, New Jersey, USA. Physician. m. Rosemarie Vincenti, 27 Jan 1980, 1 son, 2 daughters. Education: BS, University of Florida, Gainesville, 1951; MD, Emory University School of Medicine, Atlanta, 1955. Appointments include:

Assistant Professor, Department of Obstetrics and Gynaecology, Temple University School of Medicine, Philadelphia, 1961-65; Assistant Professor, 1965-67, Associate Professor, 1968-71, Professor, 1971-83, Acting Chairman, 1972-73, Chairman, 1973-81, Department of Obstetrics and Gynaecology, Albert Einstein College of Medicine, Bronx, New York; Associate Director, 1067=70, Deputy Director, 1970-72, Department of Obstetrics and GYnaecology, Bronx Municipal Hospital Centre, Bronx, New York; Professor, Department of Obstetrics and Gynaecology, State University of New York at Stony Brook, 1984-93; Chairman, Department of Obstetrics and Gynaecology, WInthrop-University Hospital, Mineola, New York, 1984-93; Private Practice, Vero Beach, Florida. Publications include: A Comparison of the Accuracy of Punch and Cone Biopsies, 1959; Practical Applications of the Graphic Portrayal of Labor, 1964; Induced Abortion in a Municipal Hospital, 1970; Maternal and Fetal Acid-Base Balance in Labor, 1974; Effect of Ritodrine Infusion on Pregnancy Rabbit Vena Cava Blood, 1977 Doppler Ultrasound in Pregnancy, 1990. Honours include: E G Winkler Memeorial Lecture, Buffalo Gynaecologic and Obstetric Society; 1st Annual Onstetric and Gynaecology Recognition Lecture, Bronz lebanon Hospital, 1987. Memberships include: Phi Beta Kappa; Alpha Omega Alpha; Fellow, American College of Obstetricians and Gynaecologists. Address: 4605 N A1A, Vero Beach, FL 32963, USA.

SCHULTZ Jean, b. 12 Jan 1929, New Jersey, USA. Psychiatrist. m. Ron Judd, 23 May 1959, 1 son, 2 daughters. Education: MD, Medical College of Pennsylvania; MPH and Residency in Psychiatry, Columbia Presbyterian Medical Center; Board Certified in Psychiatry, Certificate of added qualifications in Geriatric Psychiatry, American Board of Psychiatry and Neurology. Appointments: Currently Director, Adult Ambulatory Services and Geriatric Psychiatry, Department of Psychiatry, North Shore University Hospital, Manhasset, New York. Honours: Fellow, American Psychiatric Association. Address: North Shore University Hospital, 400 Community Drive, Manhasset, NY 11030, USA.

SCHULTZ Richard Michael, b. 28 Oct 1942, Philadelphia, PA, USA. Biochemist; Research. m. Rima Lunin, 3 Jul 1965, 2 s. Education: BA, State University of New York, Binghamton; PhD, Brandeis University. Career: Assistant Professor, 1971-76, Associate Professor, 1976-84, Professor, 1984-, currently Professor and Chair, Department of Molecular and Cellular Biochemistry, Loyola University of Chicago, Stritch School of Medicine. Publications: Chapters on proteins, in Textbook of Biochemistry (T. Devlin, Editor); Research articles including: Co-author, Fibroblasts Transformed by Different ras Oncogenes Show Dissimilar Patterns of Protease Gene Expression and Regulation, in Cancer Research, 1992. Honours: NIH Predoctoral Fellowship, 1967-69; NIH, Postdoctoral Fellowship, 1969-71; NIH Research Awards, 1972-. Memberships: American Society for Biochemistry and Molecular Biology; American Chemical Society; Protein Society; American Association for the Advancement of Science; New York Academy of Sciences. Address: Department of Molecular and Cellular Biochemistry, Loyola University Stritch School of Medicine, 2160 South 1st Avenue, Maywood, IL 60153, USA.

SCHULZ Jan Ivan, b. 3 Feb 1946, Bratislava, Slovakia. Medical Doctor. m. Mary Grossman, 5 Apr 1975, 1 son, 1 daughter. Education: MD, University of Western Ontario, London, Canada, 1970; FRCPC; FACP. Appointments: Currently Associate Professor of Medicine, St Mary's Hospital, Montreal, Canada. Publications: Delayed Tumor Growth Caused by a Combined Treatment with B16 and Pseudomonas Agruginosa etc, 1978; Exercise-Induced Asthma, 1986. Memberships: American Academy of Allergy and Clinical Immunology; Canadian Society of Allergy and Clinical Immunology. Hobbies: Running; Skiing; Scuba diving. Address: 3830 Lacombe Avenue, Montreal, Quebec, Canada H3T 1M5.

SCHUMACHER Raymond John, b. 21 July 1952, LeMars, Iowa, USA. Physician. m. Nancy, c16 June 1994. Education: MD; MPH. Appointments: Internal Medicine Residency, Maricopa County Hospital, Phoenix; Indian Health Service, San Carlos; Good Samaritan Hospital Emergency; Tcson Medical Associates; Western Occupational; Private Practice. Memberships: ACOEM; ACPM; APHA. Address: Tucson Medical Associates, 116 North Tucson Blvd, Tucson, AZ 85716, USA.

SCHUYLER Dean, b. 15 Sep 1942, NY, USA. Psychiatry. m. Terry Herman, 25 Jun 1967, 2 d. Education: AB, Highest Honours in Psychology, NY University, 1963; MD, NY University School of Medicine, 1967; FAPA. Career: Psychiatrist in Private Practice, 1971-;

Faculty, Georgetown University Department of Psychiatry, NIMH, 1971-74; Consultant, Sheppard Pratt Hospital, 1983-86. Publications: The Depressive Spectrum, 1974; A Practical Guide to Cognitive Therapy, 1991; 16 papers on aspects of depression and cognitive therapy. Honours: Psi Chi Prize, 1963; Psi Chi, 1963; Diplomate in Psychiatry, ABPN, 1974; Fellow, American Psychiatric Association, 1978. Memberships: American Psychiatric Association; Society for Psychotherapy Research. Hobby: Hockey Journalist, Washington Capitals Hockey Club. Address: 6280 Montrose Road, Rockville, MD 20852, USA.

SCHWAB John Joseph, b. 10 Feb 1923, Cumberland, Maryland, USA. Professor; Psychiatrist. m. Ruby E Baxter, 4 Aug 1945, 1 daughter. Education: BS; MS; MD; Diplomate, Psychiatry; Diplomate, Internal Medicine; AOA. Appointments: Internist, Psychosomatist, Gallipolis, Ohio, 1954-59; Resident to Professor of Psychiatry and Medicine, University of Florida, 1960-73; Professor, Chairman, Department of Psychiatry, 1973-91, Professor Emeritus, 1993-, University of Louisville, Louisville, Kentucky. Publications: Handbook of Psychiatric Consultation, 1968; Mental Health and Social Order, 1978; The Sociocultural Roots of Mental Illness, 1979; Evaluating Family Mental Health, 1993; 250 scientific articles. Honours: Fellow in Psychomatics, Duke University, 1951-52; Teacher Fellowship, National Institute of Mental Health, 1962-64. Memberships: American Psychiatric Association, Chairman, Council of Research and Development, 1974-75; American Medical Association; GAP; Academy of Psychosomatic Medicine, President 1971; American Association for Social Psychiatry, President 1970; Board of Regents, American College of Psychiatrists. Address: Department of Psychiatry, School of Medicine, University of Louisville, Louisville, KY 40292, USA.

SCHWARTZ Allan J, b. 8 Dec 1939, Brooklyn, New York, USA. Psychologist. m. Sharon B Hoffman, 30 Oct 1987, 2 sons. Education: BA, Chemistry; MA, Educational Psychology; MS, Natural Sciences; PhD, Clinical Psychology; Diplomate, American Board of Sexology; Registrant, National Council of Health Care Providers in Psychology; Certificate of Completion, Sexual Dysfunction Treatment, Center for Marital and Sexual Studies. Appointments: Staff Writer, Science, Technology, Crowell-Collier Publishing Co, New York City; Faculty, Science Department Chairman, Riverdale Country School, New York City; Research Associate, The Diebold Group, New York City; Currently Associate Professor, Psychiatry, Psychology, Director, Counselling and Mental Health Services, University of Rochester, Rochester, New York. Publications include: The epidemiology of suicide among students at colleges and universities in the United States, 1990; Suicide and Stress Among College Students, 1992; Co-author: Returning Students, 1989; Suicide among students at colleges and universities in the United States, 1990; Suicide among college students: assessment, treatment, and intervention, 1990; Research in college health 4: analyzing and communicating results, 1993. Honours: Teacher Recognition Award, American Association of Physics Teachers, 1965; Poster Excellence Award, American College Health Association, 1990 & 94. Memberships: American Association of Sex Educators, Counselors and Therapists; Fellow, American College Health Association; International Transactional Analysis Association; American Psychological Association. Hobbies: Cycling; Photography; Skiing; Travel; Tennis. Address: University of Rochester, 107 Lattimore Hall, Rochester, NY 14627-0356, USA.

SCHWARTZ Elias, b. 30 Aug 1935, New York, NY, USA. Physician. m. Esta Rosenberg, 12 June 1960, 2 sons. Education: AB, Columbia College, summa cum laude, 1956; MD, Columbia College of Physicians & Surgeons, 1960. Career: Associate Professor of Pediatrics, Jefferson Medical College, Phila, PA, 1968-72; Professor of Pediatrics, University of PA School of Medicine, Phila, 1972-. Publications include: The Silent Carrier of Beta Thalassemia, 1969; Regulation of Hemoglobin Synthesis in Beta Thalassemia, 1974; Management of Strokes in Patients with Sickle Cell Disease, 1975; Hematology of the Newborn, 1983; Structure of the Platelet Membrane Glycoprotein IIb: Homology to the Alpha Subunits of the Vitronectin and Fibronectin Membrane Receptors, 1987; Thalassemia Syndromes, in Hematology: Basic Principles and Practice, in press. Honours: MA, University of PA, 1972; Many visiting professorships in US and abroad. Memberships include: American Academy of Pediatrics; American Medical Informatics Association; American Society of Hematology; Association of American Physicians; Eastern Society for Pediatric Research; Philadelphia Health Care Congress; Society for Pediatric Research. Hobbies: Tennis; Early music (viola da gamba, recorder); Piano; Jazz. Address: The Children's

Hospital of Philadelphia, Room 2143, 324 S 34th Street, Philadelphia, PA 19104, USA.

SCHWARTZ Richard Stanton, b. 30 Mar 1948, New York City, New York, USA. Psychiatrist. m. Jacqueline Olds, 25 Aug 1978, 1 son, 1 daughter. Education: AB magna cum laude, Harvard College, 1970; MD, Harvard Medical School, 1974. Appointments: Currently Director, Adult Outpatient Clinic, McLean Hospital; Assistant Clinical Professor of Psychiatry, Harvard Medical School. Publications: Multiple articles in professional journals. Memberships: American Psychiatric Association; American Psychoanalytic Association. Address: 115 Mill Street, Belmont, MA 02178, USA.

SCHWARTZ Stanley, b. 20 July 1941, Newark, New Jersey, USA. Professor of Medicine. m. Diane, 20 June 1965. Education: AB, 1963, MS, 1965, Rutgers University; PhD, University of California, San Diego, 1968; MD, Albert Einstein College of Medicine, 1972. Appointments: Associate Professor of Paediatrics and Communicable Diseases, 1978-83, Associate Professor of Microbiology and Immunology, 1978-83, Associate Professor of Epidemiology, 1981-84, Professor of Immunology, 1983-92, School of Public Health, University of Michigan; Director, Divsiion of Allergy/Clinical Immunology, Professor of Medicine, State University of New York at Buffalo. Publications include: Immunology Section, Birth Defects Encyclopedia, Editor, 1990; New Directions in the Clinical Use of Intravenous Immune Globulin, Volume III, Editor, 1990; Future Directions of Immunoglobulin Therapy, Associate Guest Editor, 1990; Clinical Use of Immune Serum Globulin as Replacement Therapy in Patients with Primary Immunodeficiency Syndromes, 1992; Two Siblings With Recurrent Infections, Co-author, 1993; Paradoxical Immunoregulatory Activities of Interferon on Natural Killer Cells, Co-author. Honours: UN World Travel Fellow; NSF Undergraduate Fellow; Henry Rutgers Scholar; Graduate Research Fellowship, Rutgers University. Memberships: American Academy Allergy and Immunology; American Association of Immunologists; American Federation for Clinical Research; American Pediatric Society; American Society for Clinical Investigation; Society for Pediatric Research; Midwest Society for Pediatric Research. Address: State University of New York at Buffalo, Buffalo General Hospital Division of Allergy/Clinical Immunology, 100 High Street, Buffalo, NY 14203, USA.

SCHWARZ Eitan Daniel, b. 12 Mar 1943, Israel. Physician. m. Carolyn M Singer, 21 Jun 1969, 2 d. Education: AB, Cornell University, 1965; MD, Johns Hopkins University, 1969. Appointments include: Office Clinical Practice, 1973-; Senior Attending Physician, Evanston/Glenbrook and Highland Park Hospitals, 1979-; Examiner, American Board of Psychiatry and Neurology, 1979-; Consultant, Alternative School, Evanston High School, IL, 1981-; Head, Division of Child and Adolescent Psychiatry, Department of Psychiatry, Head, Division of Pediatric Psychiatry, Department of Pediatrics, Evanston Hospital, IL, 1988-; Assistant Professor of Psychiatry and Behavioral Sciences, Northwestern University Medical School, Chicago, IL, 1990-. Publications: Numerous peer reviewed publications and invited presentations including: Co-author, Malignant Memories: Effect of a Shooting in the Workplace School Personnel's Attitudes, in Journal of Interpersonal Violence, 1993; Co-author, Adolescent partial hospitalization: Developmental Considerations, in Adolescent Psychiatry, in press. Honours: Grants: IL Department of Mental Health and Developmental Disabilities, 1988-90, Bureau of Maternal and Child Health, 1989-93, Kramer Foundation, 1992-93. Memberships include: Fellow, American Academy of Child and Adolescent Psychiatry, 1989; AMA; Fellow, APA, 1989; Professional Advisory Board, Evanston Mental Health Association; Meetings Planning Committee, International Society for Adolescent Psychiatry; Society for Traumatic Stress Studies. Hobbies: Cello; Photography; Computers; Exercise. Address: 2650 Ridge Avenue, Suite 5306, Evanston, IL 60201-1718, USA.

SCHWARZ I Gene, b. 20 Nov 1930, New York City, NY, USA. Physician. m. Joan Weyand, 13 Jun 1954, 2 s, 1 d. Education: BS, 1951, MA, 1953, Wagner College, Staten Island, NY; MD, Medical College of GA, Augusta, 1960; Postgraduate Training includes: Institute for Psychoanalysis, Chicago, IL, 1965-71; Diplomate, American Board of Psychiatry and Neurology, 1968; Certified in Psychoanalysis, American Psychoanalytic Association, 1973. Appointments include: CO General Hospital, University of CO Health Sciences Center, CO, 1970-; Psychoanalytic Training and Education, Denver Institute of Psychoanalysis, 1970-; Faculty, Denver Institute for Psychoanalysis, University of CO School of Medicine, 1973-; Associate Director, 1986-89, Director, 1989-92, Denver Institute for Psychoanalysis,

University of CO School of Medicine; Clinical Professor, Department of Psychiatry, University of CO School of Medicine, 1992-. Publications: Many publications and papers presented, 1970-91, including: A Developmental Perspective to Psychiatric Residency Training, in The Cincinnati Journal of Medicine, 1975; The Attorney-Client Relationship, in The Colorado Lawyer, 1991. Honours: Service Award, Supreme Court Grievance Committee, CO, 1978; Commendation, Chief Justice Pringle, Supreme Court of State of CO, 1978; Fellowship, American Psychiatric Association, 1985. Memberships include: Fellow, CO Psychiatric Association; Secretary, 1973-75, Chairman Membership Committee, 1982-85, Vice President, 1985-87, Denver Psychoanalytic Society; International Psychoanalytic Association; Fellow, Board of Professional Standards, 1984-, American Psychoanalytic Association. Address: Ste 2, 4900 Cherry Creek So Drive, Denver, CO 80222, USA.

SCHWEISS John Francis, b. 25 Jun 1925, St Louis, MO, USA. Physician. m. Mary Virginia Shriner, 24 Jun 1950, 3 s, 2 d. Education: MD. Appointment: Professor and Chairman, Department of Anesthesiology, St Louis University School of Medicine. Memberships include: AMA; ASA; St Louis Medical Society; Missouri State Medical Society; St Louis Society of Anesthesiologists; IARS; SPA; SNA; Society of Regional Anesthesiologists. Address: St Louis University School of Medicine, 3635 Vista Avenue, St Louis, MO 63110, USA.

SCHWEITZER Laurence R, b. 15 May 1937, Brooklyn, NY, USA. Psychiatry. Education: AB; MD. Appointments: Deputy Chief of Psychiatry, Methodist Hospital, Houston, TX; Chief of Psychiatry, St Francis Hospital, Hartford, CT; Director, Substance Abuse Treatment Program, UTMB, Galveston; Currently, Chief of Psychiatry, Newington VA Medical Center, CT. Publications: 11 refered publications. Memberships: American College of Psychiatrists; Society of Biological Psychiatry. Address: VA Medical Center, 555 Willard Avenue, Newington, CT 06111, USA.

SCILLIGO Pio, b. 8 Jan 1928, Formazza, Itlay. Psychologist. Education: PhD, Stanford, USA. Appointments: Founder and Editor of journal, Incontri; President of IRPIR; Director of IFREP-93, an institute for training psychotherapists; Currently, University Profesor and Psychotherapist. Publications: Ricerca in Psicologia in 6 volumes. Memberships: Ordine degli Psicology; American Psychological Association. Address: Piazza Ateneo Salesiano 1, 00139 Rome, Italy.

SCOTCHMER Sheila Paterson, b. 27 Oct 1920, Glasgow, Scotland. Gynaecologist (retired). m. Arthur J Scotchmer, 30 Apr 1960. Education: MB ChB; FRCOG. Appointments: Registrar, Ayrshire Central Hospital; Consultant, Aga Khan Hospital, Nairobi, Kenya; Private practice, Nairobi. Membership: Fellow, Royal College of Obstetricians and Gynaecologists. Hobbies: Gardening; Music; Embroidery. Address: Pear Tree Cottage, Longborough, Moreton-in-Marsh, Gloucestershire GL56 0QQ, England.

SCOTT Henry G, b. 5 July 1944, New Jersey, USA. Psychoanalyst. m. Yumi Ninomiya, 10 June 1972, 2 sons. Education: Bachelor Degree, University of Rochester, 1966; Doctor of Psychoanalysis, Heed University, 1981. Appointments: Broomall Clinic, Pennsylvania. Publications: Psychoanalysis and Stage Fright, 1985. Memberships: National Association for the Advancement of Psychoanalysis; American Boards for Accreditation & Certification. Hobbies: Running. Address: 1200 Sandringham Road, Bala Cynwyd, PA 19004, USA.

SCOTT James Raymond, b. 24 June 1937, Mediapolis, Iowa, USA. Physician. m. Mary Jo Putney, 14 June 1958, 1 son, 3 daughters. Education: BS; MD; Resident in Obstetrics and Gynaecology, University of Iowa; Fellowships in Reproductive Endocrinology and Immunology, Universities of Iowa and Texas. Appointments: Assistant Professor, Obstetrics, Gynaecology, University of Texas at Dallas, 1973-74; Assistant Professor, Obstetrics, Gynaecology, 1974-75, Associate Professor, Obstetrics, Gynaecology, 1975-77, University of Iowa; Currently Professor, Chairman, Department of Obstetrics and Gynaecology, University of Utah Medical Center, Salt Lake City. Publications: 102 papers in peer reviewed journals, 59 books and chapters; Immunology in Obstetrics and Gynecology (editor), 1984; Co-editor: Danforth's Obstetrics and Gynecology, 5th-7th editions; Clinical Obstetrics and Gynecology (editor). Honours: Alpha Omege Alpha; Outstanding Teaching Awards, 1982, 1983, 1984, 1985, 1993; Many invited lectures; Best Medical Specialist in Obstetrics and Gynaecology in US, Town and Country magazine, 1984, 1985; 1 of 107 Best Doctors for Women, 1988. Memberships: American College of

Obstetricians and Gynecologists; American Medical Association; Examiner, American Board of Obstetrics and Gynecology; SGI; University Chairs of Obstetrics and Gynecology, President 1992-93; APGO; American Gynecology and Obstetrics Society, Secretary 1988-92; American Society of Reproductive Immunology, President 1985-86. Hobbies: Golf; Skiing; Family; Travel. Address: Department of Obstetrics and Gynaecology, University of Utah Medical Center, Salt Lake City, UT 84132, USA.

SCOTT Jonathan Woodforde, b. 20 Jan 1945, Petersfield, Hampshire, England. Medicine. m. Sarah T Taylor, 10 Jul 1971, 1 s, 2 d. Education: MRCS, LRCP, MBBS, Westminster Medical School, 1968; FRCS(Eng); FRCOG. Career: House Surgeon, Resident Obstetric Assistant and Obstetric Registrar, Westminster Hospital; RMO Hospital San José, San Bernado Colombia; RMO, Queen Charlotte's Maternity Hospital; Senior Registrar, O and G, Bath and Bristol; Currently, Senior Consultant Obstetrician and Gynaecologist, Poole Hospital. Publications: Management of Cervical Pregnancy, British Medical Journal, 1978; Scotts Primary Paternal Bonding Manouvre, Journal of Maternal and Child Health, 1981; A New Uterine Manipulator for Use at Laparoscopy, in American Journal of O and G, 1983. Memberships: British Medical Association; Fellow, RSM; Honorary Secretary, Nuffield Visiting Society. Hobbies: Carpentry; Wood Turning; Kite Making and Flying; Fell Walking; Paragliding. Address: Merton Grange, Wheelers Lane, Bear Wood, Bournemouth, BH1 9QJ, Dorset, England.

SCOTT William Clifford Munro, b. 11 Mar 1903. Consulting Psychiatrist. Education incl: Parkdale Collegiate, Toronto; BSc, University of Toronto; MD, Toronto; DPM, London; LMSSA, James H Richardson Fellow, 1922-24. Appointment: Postgraduate Teacher, Psychiatry & Psycho-analysis, 1945-. Publications: Numerous professional publications in scientific journals. Memberships incl: Royal Society of Medicine; American Psychiatric Association. Address: 488 Mount Pleasant, Westmount, Quebec H3Y 3H3, Canada.

SCRIMGEOUR John Beocher, b. 22 Jan 1939, Elgin, Scotland. Obstetrician and Gynaecologist. m. Joyce Morrin, 22 Sept 1963, 1 son, 1 daughter. Education: MB, ChB, Edinburgh University Medical School; FRCOG; FRCP; FRCS. Appointments: General Practitioner, 1963-65; Senior House Officer, Stirling, 1965; Registrar, Eastern General Hospital, Edinburgh, 1966-69; Senior Registrar, Royal Infirmary, Edinburgh, 1969-72; Currently Obstetrician and Gynaecologist, and Medical Director, Western General Edinburgh Hospitals Trust. Publications: Towards the Prevention of Fetal Malformation, 1978; Articles on early diagnosis of fetal abnormalities. Membership: Gynaecological Visiting Society of Great Britain and Ireland. Hobbies: Golf; Gardening; Tennis. Address: Western General Hospital, Crewe Road, Edinburgh EH4 2XU, Scotland.

SCRIMSHAW Nevin Stewart, b. 20 Jan 1918, Milwaukee, WI, USA. University Director. m. Mary Ware Goodrich, 26 Aug 1941, 4 s, 1 d. Education: BA, OH Wesleyan University, 1938; MA, Biology, 1939, PhD, Physiology, 1941, Harvard University; MD, University of Rochester, 1945; MPH, Honours, Harvard University, 1959. Career includes: Visiting Lecturer, Columbia University, NY, 1961-66, Harvard University, 1968-86; Visiting Professor, Tufts University, 1987-; Director, Food and Nutrition Program, 1975-, Director, Developmental Studies Division, 1985-86, United Nations University, Boston, MA. Publications: Over 600 articles on human and clinical nutrition, nutrition and infection, agricultural and food chemistry, food science, food and nutrition policy and public health; Co-author: Amino Acid Fortification of Protein Foods, 1971; Nutrition, National Development and Planning, 1973; Chronic Energy Deficiency, 1987; Activity, Energy Expenditure and Energy Requirements of Infants and Children, 1989; Protein-Energy Interactions, 1992. Honours include: Osborne-Mendel Award, 1960; International Award, Institute of Food Technologists, 1969; Medal of Honour, Fundacion F Cuenca Villoro, Spain, 1978; Bristol-Myers Prize, 1988; Alan Shawn Feinstein Award, 1991; World Food Prize, 1991. Memberships include: Fellow, AAAS; Fellow, American College of Nutrition; Fellow, American Epidemiological Society; Fellow, American Institute of Nutrition; Corresponding Member, National Academy of Medicine, Argentina; International Union of Nutritional Sciences; Fellow, Royal Society of Health, UK. Hobbies: Skiing; Gardening. Address: Food and Nutrition Program Human Social Development, United Nations University, 134 Charles Street, PO Box 500, Boston, MA 02114-0500, USA.

SCULLY Anne Marie, b. 24 Dec 1952, Melbourne, Australia. Nurse. div, 1 son, 1 daughter. Education: BASc, Nursing; Certificate, General Nursing and Midwifery. Appointments: Project Officer, National Breast and Cervical Programmes, Victoria, 1993-94; Nurse Adviser, Health Department, Victoria, 1989-93; Federal Nurse Adviser, Australian Nursing Federation. Memberships: Royal Australian College of Nursing; Public HealthAssociation. Hobbies: Perusing and Carousing. Address: Australian Nursing Federation, 373-375 St Georges Road, North Fitzroy, Victoria 3068, Australia.

SCULLY Crispian, b. 24 May 1945, Hove, Sussex, England. Professor. m. Zoe Boucoumani, 5 Jan 1977, 1 daughter. Education: BDS; BSc; MBBS; PhD; MD; LDSRCS; MRCS; LRCP; FDSRPS; MRCPath; FFDRCSI; FDSRCS; FRCPath. Appointments: Lecturer, University of Glasgow, 1979-81; Senior Lecturer, University of Glasgow, 1981-82; Professor of Oral Medicine, University of Bristol, 1982-93; Director, Centre for Study of Oral Disease, University of Bristol, 1989-93. Publications: Clinical Virology in Oral Medicine and Dentistry, co-author, 1992; Colour Guide of Medicine and Surgery for Dentistry, co-author, 1993; A Colour Atlas of Oral Diseases in Children and Adolescents, co-author, 1994; Colour Atlas for Oral Pathology, co-author, 1995. Honours: Colgate Prize for Dental Research, 1979. Memberships: British Dental Association; British Society for Oral Medicine; British Society for Dental Research; International Association of Oral Pathology; European Academy of Oral Medicine; General Dental Council; British Society of Dentistry for the Handicapped. Hobbies: Swimming; Music; Organ Playing; Skiing; Hill Walking; Travel. Address: Eastman Dental Institute for Oral Health Care Sciences, 256 Gray's Inn Road, London WC1X 8LD, England.

SEALY Vernol St Clair. Laboratory Scientist. m. Josephine S D Nanton, 12 May 1965, 1 son, 1 daughter. Education: LLB. La Salle Extension University, Chicago, USA, 1967; BS, 1968, Medical Technology, 1969, MS, Microbiology, 1971, Howard University; MPH, Epidemiology and Public Health Laboratory Practice, University of Michigan, 1974; PhD summa cum laude, Religion, Trinity Theological Seminary, Newburgh, Indiana, 1988. Appointments: High School Teacher and Physiotherapist, Trinidad, West Indies, pre-1963; Nursing: Eugene Leland Hospital, Riverdale, Maryland, 1965-67; Freedmen's Hospital, Washington, District of Columbia, 1970-73; Medical Technologist, District of Columbia General Hospital, Washington, 1970-73; Clinical Laboratory Haematologist, St Joseph Mercy Hospital, Ann Arbor, Michigan, 1973-93; Chaplain Resident, Children's Hospital of Michigan, Detroit, 1993-94. Publications: Kinetics of Simian Hemorrhagic Fever Virus Neutralization Test, MS thesis; Suffering: A Biblical Perspective, PhD thesis. Honours include: Invited to submit questions for proficiency examination for Clinical Laboratory Technologists, Professional Examination Service, New York, 1974; Cultural Doctorate in Sacred Philosophy, World University, 1984. Memberships: American Society of Clinical Pathologists; Fellow, Royal Society of Health; American Public Health Association; National Registry of Microbiology; Royal Institute of Public Health and Hygiene, England; American Association for the Advancement of Science; New York Academy of Sciences; Academy of Political Science. Hobbies: Reading; Walking. Address: 3667 Helen Ave, Ypsilanti, MI 48197-3760. USA.

SEALY Will Camp, b. 6 Nov 1912, Roberta, GA, USA. Doctor of Medicine. m. Jacqueline Womble, 20 Apr 1965, 3 sons, 3 daughters. Education: BS; MD. Career: Professor of Surgery, Duke University, 1946-82; Chief, Division of Thoracic Surgery, Duke Hospital, 1950-77; Professor of Surgery, Mercer University, 1984-. Publications include: Paradoxical Hypertension, 1957; Surgical Treatment, 1969. Honours: Bronze Star, Army of USA, 1945; Fish Award, Texas Heart Institute, 1979; Scientific Award, North American Soc Pacing, 1987. Memberships: American Surg Association; American Association for Thoracic Surgeons; Society of Thoracic Surgeons; Society of University Surgeons; South Surgical Association; American College of Surgeons. Hobby: Medical History. Address: 3186 Vista Circle.

SEGAL Hanna, b. 20 Aug 1918, Lodz, Poland. Psychoanalyst. m. Paul Segal, 16 Nov 1946, 3 sons. Education: MB ChB; FRCPsych. Appointments: President, British Psychoanalytical Society; Vice-President, International Psychoanalytical Association; Visiting Professor, Freud Memorial Chair, University College, London, England. Publications include: Introduction to the Work of Melanie Klein, 1964; Melanie Klein, 1979; The Work of Hanna Segal, 1981; Dream, Phantasy and Art, 1991. Honours: Mary Sigouuly Award for Services to Psychoanaylsis, American Psychoanalytic Association, 1992.

Memberships: British Psychoanalytical Society; Royal College of Psychiatry. Hobbies: Reading; Writing; Watersports. Address: 44 Queen's Avenue, London N10 3NU, England.

SEGGEV Joram Simon, b. 7 Apr 1944, Tel-Aviv, Israel. Physician. m. Varda Alexandri, 3 Oct 1968, 2 s, 1 d. Education: MD, Hebrew University, Jerusalem, Israel, 1970. Appointment: Head, Allergy and Immunology Division, University of Nevada, School of Medicine Las Vegas. Publications include: Many articles in professional journals including: Co-author, Anaphylaxis due to surgical glove powder, in Ann Allergy, 1990; Co-author, Modulation of pulmonary perivasculitis in MRL/MpJ-1pr/1pr mice by cyclophosphamide and sex hormones, in Clinical Immunology Immunopathology, 1991. Honours: Fellow, American College of Physicians; Fellow, American Academy of Allergy and Immunology; Fellow, American College of Allergy and Immunology. Memberships: American Association of Immunologists; Clinical Immunology Society; American Thoracic Society; New York Academy of Sciences; Western Society of Allergy and Immunology. Hobbies: Music; Swimming. Address: 2040 West Charleston Boulevard, No 503, Las Vegas, NV 89102, USA.

SEIBERT-LARKE Grace, b. 14 Aug 1946, Wheeling, WV, USA. Psychology; Social Work. m. Dr Jerry Larke, 8 Jun 1968, 1 s, 2 d. Education: BA, WV University, 1968; Masters Social Work, KS University, 1970; Doctorate in Clinical Psychology, Antioch Univerity, 1993; Certified Social Worker. Career: Assistant Professor, Syracuse University; Brockton/West Roxbury Veteran's Administration Medical Center, 1990-92; Currently, Assistant Director, Bridgewater State College Counseling Center. Publications: Death Education of Children, article, 1986; Social-Psychological dimensions of low-income and middle-income, dissertation, 1993. Honours: Psi Chi, 1968; NIMH Award, 1969, 1970; Harvard Clinical Appointment, 1990-92. Memberships: American Psychological Association; MA Psychological Association; National Association of Social Workers. Hobbies include: Canoeing; Sailing. Address: 2016 Ocean Street, Marshfield, MA 02050, USA.

SEICOL Noel H, b. 5 Nov 1923, Hartford, CT, USA. Physician. m. Betty Jean Friedman, 26 Dec 1945, 2 s, 1 d. Education: MD, 1950. Career: Physician in Private Practice. Honour: Fellow, American College of Chest Physicians. Memberships: American College of Allergists and Immunologists; American Academy of Allergy and Immunology. Hobbies: Travel; Gardening; Bridge; Photography; Philately; Numismetics. Address: 33 Cedar Street, Rye, NY 10580, USA.

SEIDEN Anne Maxwell, b. 22 May 1936, Durham, NC, USA. Psychiatrist. m. Lewis S Seiden PhD, 27 Dec 1962, 2 s, 1 d. Education: BA, 1959, MD, 1964, University of Chicago; FAPA. Appointments: Assistant Chief, Outpatient Psychiatry, Michael Reese Hospital; Coordinator of Research Education in Psychiatry, 1972-74; Director of Research Institute for Juvenile Research, 1973-78; Currently, Chairperson, Department of Psychiatry, Cook County Hospital. Publications: Parenting: Child Care/Parent Care, 1987; Psychiatric issues for women through out the life cycle, in Psychiatric Clinics of North America, 1989; Measures of Pregnant, Drug Abusing Women for Treatment Research, in National Institute on Drug Abuse, NIDA Research Monograph Series, 1992. Honour: Feminist Physician Service Award, National Women's Health Network, 1977. Memberships: American Psychiatric Association; American Orthopsychiatric Association; American Association of Psychiatrists in Alcohol and Addictions. Hobbies: Shoemaking; Sewing; Crafts; Gardening; Sailing. Address: Dept of Psychiatry, Cook County Hospital, 1825 W Harrison Street, Chicago, IL 60612, USA.

SEIDERMAN Arthur S, b. 28 Nov 1936, Philadelphia, USA. Doctor of Optometry. m. Susan Levin, 19 Aug 1965, 2 sons, 1 daughter. Education: AB, Central High School, Philadelphia, 1954; AB, West Virginia Wesleyan College, 1959; BS, Pennsylvania College of Optometry, 1962; Doctor of Optometry, Pennsylvania College of Optometry, 1963; MA, Fairleigh Dickinson University, 1973; Postgraduate Study, University of Vienna Medical School, 1966; Postgraduate Study, Indiana University, 1968; Certification, Gesell Institute of Child Development, Yale University, 1971; Certification, Pennsylvania College of Optometry, 1976. Appointments: Adjunct Faculty, Pennsylvania State University; Professional Advisory Board, Journal of Learning Disabilities; Vision Consultant, US Olympic Team & Philadelphia Flyers. Publications: 20/20 Is Not Enough, 1990; The Athletic Eye, 1983; Over 30 Chapters; Published Manuscripts and Research. Honours: Recognition Award, 1978; Special Award, 1980, 1989; Outstanding Alumnus of Year, West Virginia Wesleyan College, 1990. Memberships: Board Director, College of Optometrists in Vision Development; American Optometrists Association; American Academy of Optometry; American Psychology Association; Council for Exceptional Children. Address: 2401 Pennsylvania Avenue 6B24, Philadelphia, PA 19130, USA. 15.

SEIM Anders Johan Blystad, b. 24 Apr 1954, Namsskogan, Norway. Medical Doctor. Education: MD, University of Saarland, 1982; Specialty Psychotherapy, 1992. Appointments: Medical Doctor, Fachklinik Munchwies, 1982-85; Medical Director, Schaumberger Hof, Centre for Drug Addiction, 1986-88; Medical Doctor, Tagesklinik Acteburger Strasse, Cologne, 1989-91; Director, Private Management Consulting, 1991-. Publications: Susto-Eine Angstkrankheit in Den Anden, 1993; Ausnahmen Vom Fahrerlaubnisenteug Bei Alkoholauffalligen Kraftfahrern, 1993. Memberships: The Norwegian Medical Soceity; AMEE Association for Medical Education in Europe. Hobbies: Skiing; Jogging; Badminton. Address: Grossherzog Friedrich Str 72, D-66121Saarbruecken, Germany.

SEKERAK Robert John, b. 10 Feb 1942, Ohio, USA. Medical Librarian. m. Judith Mlac, 8 Aug 1964, 1 son, 2 daughters. Education: BS, John Carroll University, 1964; MSLS, Case Western Reserve University, 1972. Appointments: Currently Associate Professor, Information Specialist, University of Vermont. Publications: Hospital Library Development Services, 1975; Cooperative Serials Acquisition and Retention, 1986; Harbeson v Parke-Davis and the United States of America: an Overview, 1986; Librarians Contract to Provide Bibliographic Support for the Creation of a Medical Text (co-author), in press. Honours: National Library of Medicine Management Intern, 1980-81; Distinguished Member, Academy of Health Information Professionals, 1990. Memberships: Medical Library Association; North Atlantic Health Sciences Libraries; Health Sciences Libraries of New Hampshire and Vermont. Hobbies: Running; Fishing; Gardening. Address: Dana Medical Library, University of Vermont, Burlington, VT 05405, USA.

SELIDOVKIN Georgii Dmitrievich, b. 30 June 1946, Kursk, Russia. Haematologist. div. 2 daughters. Education: Candidate of medicine, 1975, MD, 1994, Institute of Biophysics. Appointments: Moscow Medical Institute, 1970; Institute of Biophysics, 1970-. Publications: The Radiological Accident in oiania, CO-author, 1988; Bone Marrow Transplantation after Chernobyl Nuclear Accident, Co-author, 1989; Hematopoietic Recovery After 1 Gy Acute Total Body Radiation, Co-author, 1994. Honours: Badge of Honour, 1987; Member of Scientific Council, Institute of Biophysics, 1990. Memberships: Moscow Therapeutic Society; Moscow Haematological Society. Hobbies: Skiing; Horticulture. Address: 123098 Bochvar st, 15, 94 fl Moscow, Russia.

SELJESTAD Ingegerd, b. 1 Apr 1925, Sorreisa, Troms, Norway. Psychologist. Education: Teaching Certificate, University of Oslo; MA, University of Minnesota, USA; University of Bergen, Norway. APpointments: Teacher, Sorreisa Osto Nes Hedmark School; Psychologist, Leader, Narvik Ofotin Noroland; Psychologist, trondheim Sor-Trondelag; teacher, Dronning Mauds Minne, Trondheim; Consultative Psychologist, Lira School; Environmental Worker, Dormitories and Psychologist, Centre for Visually Handicapped, Gimse; Private Practice, Trondheim and Finnsneg. Honours: National Society of Colonial Dames of America, State of Minnesota, 1953; University of Minnesota, 1953; University of World Affairs, 1954. Memberships: Rorsehach Comprehensive System Association of Norway; World Association for Infant Mental Health. Hobbies: Handicrafts; Skiing; Walking; Family Farming. Address: Postboks 67, N-9301 Finnsnes, Norway.

SELKOE Dennis J, b. 25 Sep 1943, NY, USA. Physician; Scientist. m. Polly Ann Strasser, 24 Jun 1967, 1 s, 1 d. Education: AB, Columbia University, 1965; MD, University of Virginia School of Medicine, 1969; MA, Honours, Harvard University, 1990. Career: Resident in Neurology, Peter Bent Brigham, Children's Hospital, Boston, 1972-75; Fellow in Neuroscience, Harvard Medical School, 1975-78; Assistant Professor, Neurology, 1978-82, Associate Professor, Neurology and Neuroscience, 1982-90, now Professor of Neurology and Neuroscience, Harvard Medical School. Publications include: Over 100 original reports, 1969-, including: Co-author, Polarized secretion of ß-amyloid precursor protein and amyloid ß-peptide in MDCK cells, PNAS, 1994; 47 Reviews and over 200 abstracts. Honours: Medical Research Award, Metropolitan Life

Foundation, 1986; Leadership and Excellence in Alzheimer's Disease Award, National Institute of Health, 1988; Potamkin Prize, American Academy of Neurology, 1989. Memberships: Society for Neuroscience; American Academy for Advancement of Science; American Academy of Neurology; American Neurological Association; World Federation of Neurology. Address: Center for Neurologic Diseases, Harvard Medical School, Brigham and Women's Hospital, 221 Longwood Avenue, Boston, MA 02115, USA.

SELLEVOLD Olav F Münter, b. 31 Jul 1947, Oslo, Norway, Anaesthesiologist. m. Anne Brit M Sellevold, 2 s, 1 d. Education: MD; PhD. Appointments: Specialist Anaesthesiology, 1982; Editorial Board, 7 Cardiothoracic Vascular Anesthesia, 1993-; Referee, European and American Journals; Head Section of Cardiothoracic Anaesthesia and Intensive Care, University Hospital, Trondheim, 1993-. Publications: Thesis, Glucocorticoids and myocardial protection, 1988, University of Trondheim; Scientific articles published in professional journals on concentrated subjects linked to anaesthesia myocardial protection and postoperative care; Over 40 internationally published papers. Memberships: Board, 1987-92, Chairman of Board, 1992-93, Committee Chairman on Quality Assurance, 1992-, Norwegian Society of Anaesthesiology; Specialist Committee, 1979-83, 1993-, Norwegian Medical Association; Board, Scandinavian Society of Anaesthesiology; European Committee, 1993-, Union European Medicin Specialist; Representative Council, 1986-92, Directory Board, Deputy Chairman, Scientific Committee, 1992-, European Association of Cardiothoracic Anaesthesiologists (EACTA); Scientific and Organizing Committee, Scandinavian Congress of Anaesthesiology; Scientific Program Committee, 1994-, Society of Cardiovascular Anaethesia. Hobbies: Literature; Classical Music; Classical Languages and Culture; Winter Sports. Address: Department of Anaesthesia, University Hospital, N 7006 Trondheim, Norway.

SELTZER Ronni Lee, b. 24 Apr 1952, New York City, New York, USA. Physician. m. Gary Broder, 20 Jan 1980. Education: BA, Syracuse University; MD, Chicago Medical School; Diplomate, American Board of Psychiatry and Neurology. Appointments: Currently Psychiatrist, Chief, Division of Psychiatry, Holy Name Hospital. Publications: Dealing with Psychiatric Problems After Eye Surgery, 1983; Spotting Probable Contact Lens Failures, 1983; Coping with the Patient's Pre-Op Fears, 1983; Coping with Career Stress, 1984; Happy Retirement, 1984; Lithium Carbonate and Gastric Ulcers; Monoamine-Oxidase-Inhibitor-Induced Rapid Cycling Bipolar Affective Disorder in an Adolescent. Memberships: American Psychiatric Association; New Jersey Psychiatric Association; President, North Jersey Psychiatric Society; American Medical Association; BCMS. Hobbies: Skiing; Golf; Sportfishing; Tennis. Address: 200 Engle Street, Englewood, NJ 07631, USA.

SEMAN Elvis Ivan, b. 26 July 1960, Broken Hill, NSW, Australia. Obstetrician & Gynaecologist. m. Marija Pedisic, 24 July 1993. Education: MBBS; MRCOG; FRACOG; EUCOGF. Career: Intern, 1983; RMO, 1984; Obs & Gynae Registrar, 1985, 1986; Surg Reg, 1987; Senior Registrar, Obs & Gynae, 1988; Reg, Obs & Gynae, UK, 1989; Chief Resident, Obs & Gynae, 1990; Consultant Gynaecologist, Flinders Medical Centre, 1991-. Publications: Australian Medical Journal: 1991 Methotroxate Treatment of Ectopic Pregnancy, 1991; Antenatal Diagnosis - Protest Counselling, 1994; Australian Journal Obs & Gynae: Endocervicosis of Urinary Bladder, 1994. Memberships: AMA; Guild of St Luke; Australian Gynaecologic Endoscopy Society; World Association of Doctors Who Respect Human Life. Hobby: Music. Address: 18 Bickford Terrace, Somerton Park, 5044, Australia.

SEMKE Valentin, b. 8 Sep 1936, Krasnodar, USSR. Psychiatrist. m. Galina, 22 Feb 1984, 1 son, 1 daughter. Education: MD; PhD; Clinical Studies, Filtai Medicval Institute; Postgraduate Studies, Altai Medical Institute; Moscow Medical Institute. Appointments: Assistant, senior lecturer, Head, psychiatry Chair, Altai Medical Institute; Vice-Director, Director, Mental Health Institute. Publications: Hysterical Disorders, 1988; Psychopathology of Teenagers, 1994; Borderline Disorders and Mental Health, 1990. Memberships: European Council, World Federation of Mental Health; International College of Psychosomatic Medicine; Russian-German Unity. Hobbies: Chess; Touring. Address: Uchebnaya Sts 42, Apt 11, Tomsk 634014, Russia.

SEMLITZ Linda, b. 15 Feb 1953, NY, USA. Psychiatry. m. 30 Mar 1985, 1 s, 1 d. Education: MD; Certifications by American Boards of: Psychiatry and Neurology, 1983, Psychiatry - Neurology Child

Psychiatry, 1984, Psychiatry and Addiction Medicine. Appointments: Medical Director, Child and Adolescent Inpatient Services, Providence Medical Center; Psychiatric Consultant, Parry Center School Based Day Treatment, Alder School, Portland; Currently: Chairman, Department Psychiatry, Providence Medical Center; Assistant Clinical Professor, OR Health Sciences University. Publications: 10 Professional publications, 1982-, including: Psychiatric Findings that Obscure Diagnosis of Tourettes Syndrome in Children, in Hong Kong Practitioner; Treatment Planning, in Adolescent Substance Abuse, in press; 11 Presentations, in USA and Hong Kong, 1981-1987. Memberships: American Psychiatric Association, 1981-; American Academy of Child Psychiatry, 1981-; Hong Kong Psychiatric Association, 1986-; American Association of Psychiatrists in Addictions Medicine; OR Psychiatric Association, 1989-; OR Medical Association, 1989-; OR Council of Child and Adolescent Psychiatry, 1990-; Association of Substance Abuse Medicine, 1994-. Hobbies: Travel; Art; Cooking. Address: 2386 NW Hoyt, Portland, OR 97210, USA.

SEMMLOW John, b. 12 Mar 1942. Professor. Education: PhD; BSEE; Fellow, IEEE. Appointments: Senior Engineer, Motorola Inc; Assistant Professor, Biomedical Engineering, University of Illinois; Professor, Surgery, Bioengineer, UMDNJ Robert Wood Johnson Medical School and Rutgers University. Publications: Referred journals include: Coronary Artery Disease; Ischemic Intestinal Disease; Motor Control Systems. Honours: Fellow, IEEE, 1994; NSF-CNRS Exchange Fellow, France, 1995. Memberships: IEEE; BMES; Sigma Xi. Hobbies: Skiing; Tennis; Flying; Gardening; Sailing; Travel. Address: 81 Louis Street, New Brunswick, NJ 08901, USA.

SEN Amiya Bhushan, b. 31 May 1926, Calcutta, India. Medical Parasitologist. m. Dr Kanika, 29 Apr 1961, 1 s. Education: MSc, Zoology, Entomology; MBBS with residentship in clinical medicine; DPhil, Medicine, Parasite Chemotherapy; FNA; FAMS; FISP; FISCD. Career: Deputy Director and Head, Parasitology Division, Central Drug Research Institute, CSIR, Lucknow, India, to 1986; Director, Rajendra Memorial Research Institute of Medical Sciences, JCMR, Patna, 1986-90; Emeritus Scientist, CSIR, 1991-; Currently, Honorary Advisor, Central Drug Research Institute, CSIR, Lucknow, India. Publications: Co-editor, Malaria, Filariasis and Leishmaniasis, 1983; Perspectives in Parasitology, volume 1, 1986, volume 2, 1991; Over 175 original research papers in national and international journals. Honours: Fellow: Indian National Science Academy, 1981, National Academy of Medical Sciences, India, 1985, Indian Society for Parasitology, 1986, Indian Society for Com Diseases, 1984; Oration Awards: Dr B N Singh Memorial, 1988, Sir U N Brahamachari Memorial, 1991. Memberships: Life Member, U P Academy for Advancement of Sciences; Life Member, Indian Association for Laboratory Animals. Hobbies: Reading; Birdwatching; Gardening; Cooking. Address: 148 Rabindra Palli, Off Faizabad Road, Lucknow, PIN 226016, India.

SENERICHES Juliana Sustento, b. 6 Feb 1943, Philippines. Psychiatrist. m. Candido Seneriches, 20 June 1970, 2 daughters. Education: BS, Zoology; MD; Diplomate, American Board of Psychiatry and Neurology; Diplomate, Philippine Board of Psychiatry. Appointments: Teaching Fellow, Harvard Medical School, USA, 1967-79; Chief Resident, Outpatient Psychiatry, Boston City Hospital, 1968-69; Associate Professor, Chief, Psychiatry Department, Iloilo Doctors School of Medicine, 1977-84; Private Practice. Publications: Depression and Other Mental Health Issues: The Filipino American Experience, Co-author, 1994; Practical Psychiatry in the Philippine Setting, 1983; Handbook of Psychiatry, 1980. Memberships: Past President, East Bay Psychiatric Association; Counciller, Northern California Psychiatric Association. Hobbies: Swimming; Writing. Address: 287 Old Bernal Avenue, Pleasanton, CA 94566-7015, USA.

SENSEMAN Laurence A, 21 May 1911, New Jersey, USA. Psychiatrist. m. Ervel Anderton 3 May 1934, 1 son, 2 daughters. Education: BS, Columbia Union College, 1932; MD, Loma Linda University, 1937. Appointments include: Chief, Neuropsychiatry, Memorial Hospital, Pawtucket, Rhode Island, 1946-66; Consultant, Neuropsychiatry, Sturdy Memorial Hospital, 1950-61; Notre Dame Hospital, Woonsocket Hospital, Miriam Hospital, 1946-69; Senior Psychiatrist, Butler Hospital, 1965-69; Medical Director, Fuller Memorial Sanitarium, South Attlebore, Massachusetts, 1937-69; Medical Diretor, Glendale Adventist Hospital, 1971-79. Publications include: Attempted Suicides in Adolescents, 1968; Alcohol A Health Hazard, 1971; Alcohol and the Nervous System, 1971; Transcultural Psychiatry, 1977. Honours include: Alumnus of the Year, Loma Linda University, 1966; President,

First & Third International Congress for the Prevention of Alcoholism Kabul, Afganistan. Memberships include: American College of Physicians; American Medical Association, Fellow; Life Fellow, American Psychiatric Association; Life Member, Indian Psychiatric Association. Hobbies: Painting. Address: 1365 Pine Avenue, Carsbad, CA 92008 1941, USA.

SERAFINI Paulo C, b. 28 Nov 1950, Brazil. Medical Doctor. m. Elizabeth, 21 Feb 1976, 2 s. Education: MD; Fellow, American College of Obstetrics & Gynaecology. Appointments: Co-Director, Huntingdon Reproductive Center. Memberships: American College of Obstetrics & Gynaecology; American Fertility Society. Hobbies: Basketball; Jogging. Address: 39 Congress Street, Suite 202, Pasadena, CA 91105-3021, USA.

SEREBRYAKOVA Galina Vasiljevna, b. 1 Jan 1942, Nazhnij Novgorod Region, Russia. Paediatrician. m. Valierij Serg Serebryakov, 15 July 1967, 1 son. Education: State Nizhnij Novgorod Medical Institute, 1967; Advance of Professional Qualification, State Research Institute for Paediatrics, Moscow, 1976-78. Appointments: Polyclinic Paediatric Doctor, 1967-76; Clinic Doctor, 1976-78; School Paediatric Doctor, 1978-79; Head, School Department, Child Polyclinic, 1979-83; Head, School Polyclinic, 1983-89; Head, Polyclinic Paediatric Department, 1989-. Honours: Recipient of several awards from central Medical Sanitary department and 3rd Main Management, Moscow. Hobbies: Knitting; COuntryside. Address: 249020 Obninsk, Kaluga Region, Mark's Str 106-8, Russia.

SERGEEV Michael G, b. 11 Sep 1957, Nikolaev, Ukraine. Biologist. m. Galina I Sergeeva, 14 Feb 1981, 2 d. Education: MSc, Biology, Novosibirsk State University, Russia; PhD, Entomology, 1984; DSc, Entomology, 1992; Professor of Biology, 1994. Career: Junior Science Researcher, 1982-86, Science Researcher, 1986-91, Biological Institute, Novosibirsk, Russia; Associate Professor, 1990-93, Currently, Professor of General Biology, Novosibirsk State University; Currently, Senior Scientific Researcher, Institute for Systematic and Ecology of Animals, Novosibirsk. Publications: Patterns of Orthoptera Distribution in North Asia, 1986; Articles: Distribution Patterns of Orthoptera in North and Central Asia, in Journal of Orth Research, 1992; The General Distribution of Orthoptera in the Main Zoogeographical Regions of North and Central Asia, in Acta, 1993. Memberships: Orthopterists' Society; Species Survival Commission; Russian Entomological Society. Hobby: Hiking. Address: 14-21 Zhemchuzhraja Street, Novosibirsk 630090, Russia.

SERLIN Ilene Ava, b. 18 Sep 1948. psychologist. Education: PhD; ADTR. Appointments: Director, Arts Medicine, programme, California Pacific Medical Centre, USA; Director, Driago Centre for psychotherapy and the Counselling Arts; Assistant Professor, University of California at Los Angeles; Professor of Psychology, Saybrook Institute. Publications: The Anne Sexton Complex, 1994; Root Images of Healing in Dance Therapy, 1994. Honours: Phi Beta Kappa, 1970; Dean's List, 1966-70; Flow Fund Grant, 1994. Memberships: Executive Board, Division of Humanistic Psychology, American Psychological Association; Board, Tamalpa Institute. Hobbies: Dance; Reading. Address: Saybrook Institute, 450 Pacific Street, San Francisco, CA 94133, USA.

SEROV Roman, b. 5 Oct 1945, Moscow, Russia. Anatomical Pathologist. m. Olga Schaposchnicova, 15 Aug 1970, 1 son. Appointments: Assistant, Docent, Department of Patholgoical Anatomy, 2nd Moscow Medical Institute; Chief, Department of Pathological Anatomy. Publications: Diseases of Veins, 1982; Comparison of the Injurious Effects of Catecholamines and Ischemia on the Myocardium, 1987; Alterations of the Myocardium and Adrenergic Nerves of Heart During Ischemia and Reperfusion, 1991, Hobby: Lawn tennis. Address: Krasnii Majak Str 11-1-56, 113570 Moscow, Russia.

SEVCIK Pavel, b. 14 Aug 1953, Cesky, Tesin, Czechoslovakia. Head, Intensive Care Unit, University Hospital Brno. m. Alena Slavikovà, 7 July 1978, 2 daughters. Education: MUDr, Purkyne University, Brno, 1978; Postgraduate Diplomas, Anaesthesiology & Resusitation, 1st Grade, 1982; Anaesthesiology & Resusitation, 2nd Grade, 1986. Appointments: House Officer, Anaesthesiology, University Hospital, Brno, 1978-83; Registrar, Intensive Care, University Hospital, Brno, 1983-88; Head, Department of Anaesthesiology, Municipal Hospital, Brno, 1989-91. Publications: In Czech, Dissertation: Multiple Organ Failure and Septic Shock in Intensive Care, 1988; Monograph: Sepsis in Intensive Care, 1993; Co-author: The Control of Pain, 1994.

Memberships: Editorial Board, Czech Journal, Anaesthesiology and Critical Care, since 1991; Scientific Board, Czech Chamber of Medicine since 1993; Czech Society for Study & Control of Pain. Honours: Secretary, Czech Society of Anaesthesiology & Resuscitation, since 1990. Hobbies: Running; Skiing; Hiking. Address: Coupkovych 32, 63500 Brno-Komin, Czech Republic.

SEWARD James Pickett, b. 14 Oct 1949, New York, USA. Physician. m. Laura Morgan. Education: MD; MPP; FACOEM; FACPM. Appointment: Director, Occupational Health, University California, Berkeley. Honours: John Harvard Scholar; Fulbright Scholar. Memberships: American College of Occupational Environmental Medicine; American College of Preventive Medicine; American Public Health Assocaition. Address: University California, Berkeley Occupational Health Training Center, Berkeley, CA 94720, USA.

SEYAL Arif M, b. 1 Jan 1949, Multan, Pakistan. Physician. 1 son, 1 daughter. Education: MBBS, University of Punjab, Nishtar Medical College, Multan, Pakistan, 1971; Certificate, American Board of Internal Medicine, 1982; Certificate, American Board of Allergy & Immunology, 1987. Appointments: Chief, Department of Allergy & Clinical Immunology, Kaiser-Permanente, Rancho Cordova, California; Assistant Clinical Professor, Department of Internal Medicine, University of California, Davis. Publications: Coauthor: Future Trends in Understanding and Treatment of Asthma; Co-author: Response of Asthmatics and Normal Volunteers to Sulfiting Agents in Wine, 1984. Honours: Chief Resident Award, Altoona Hospital, Pennsylvania, 1980. Memberships: American Academy of Allergy & Immunology; Fellow, American College of Chest Physicians; American College of Physicians. Hobbies: Travel; Cycling; Photography. Address: 1348 Kingsford Drive, Carmichael, CA 95608, USA.

SFERRAZZA Joseph, b. 15 Nov 1930, New York City, USA. Private Medical Practice, Internal Medicine. m. Marilyn Licitra, 6 Jun 1959, 1 s, 4 d. Education: BA; MD. Career: Associate Attending in Medicine, St Francis Hospital, Roslyn, NY; Currently in Private Practise, Internal Medicine. Publications: Natural History of Anuerysm of Ventricle, New York State Journal of Medicine, volume 62, No 2, 1962. Memberships: New York State Medical Society; American Society of Internal Medicine. Hobbies: Classical Music; Golf; Travel. Address: 259-10 Hillside Avenue, Floral Park, NY 11001, USA.

SHADER Richard Irwin, b. 27 May 1935, Mount Vernon, NY, USA. Physician. m. Aline Brown, 21 Sep 1958, 1 s, 2 d. Education: BA, Harvard College, Cambridge, MA, 1956; MD, New York University School of Medicine, NY, 1960; Candidate and Graduate, Boston Psychoanalytic Society and Institute, Boston, MA, 1964-70. Career includes: Professor, 1979-, Chairman, Department of Psychiatry, 1979-91, Professor, 1989- (with tenure from 1992), Chairman, 1991-93, Department Pharmacology and Experimental Therapeutics, Tufts University School of Medicine; Editor in Chief, Journal of Clinical Psychopharmacology, 1980-. Publications include: Many books and monographs including: Co-author, Drug Interactions in Psychiatry, 1989, Second Edition, 1995; Co-editor, Clinical Manual of Chemical Dependence, 1991; Editor, Manual of Psychiatric Therapeutics, 2nd edition, 1994. Honours include: Seymour Vestermark Award, American Psychiatric Association, 1988, and co-winner, 1990; Fellow, Center for Advanced Study in Behavioral Sciences and Visiting Scholar, Stanford University, CA, 1990-91; Good Housekeeping Magazine's List of Best Mental Health Experts, 1994. Memberships include: Medical and Scientific Advisory Board, Alzheimer's Disease and Related Disorders Association, 1988-94; President, American College of Neuropsychopharmacology, 1990; AMA; American Society for Clinical Pharmacology and Therapeutics; American Society of Clinical Psychopharmacology Inc. Address: Department of Pharmacology and Experimental Therapeutics, Tufts University School of Medicine, 136 Harrison Avenue, Room 208, Boston, MA 02111, USA.

SHAFFER Natalie, b. Montreal, Canada. Doctor; Lawyer. Education: MD, CM, McGill University, Canada; FRCPC; DABD; CSPQ; BCL; LLB; FCLM. Appointments: Currently, Dermatologist and Dermatologic Surgeon; Attorney. Publications: Pagetic Spinal Stenosis with Extradural Pagetoid Ossification, in Spine, 1988; Nodular Vasculitis (Erythema Induratum) Treatment with Auranotin, in Jourani of the American Academy of Dermatology, 1991; Perifolliculitis Capitis Abscedens et Suffodiens: Complete and Lasting Resolution with Combination Therapy, in The Archives of Dermatology, 1992. Honours: Zimmer Prize, 1986; Eugene Rogala Award, 1986. Memberships: Canadian and Quebec

Medical and Dermatology Associations; Quebec Bar Association; Lord Reading Law Society. Hobbies: Most Winter and Summer Sports; Travel; Music. Address: Decelles Medical Centre, 5757 Decelles Avenue, Suite 555, Montreal, Quebec, Canada, H3S 2C3.

SHAGYLYJOV Kakabai, b. 10 Jan 1929, Murgab, Turkmenistan. Forensic Doctor. m,. Nasarova Ogulbibi, 2 Feb 1947, 1 son, 3 daughters. Education: Diploma, Turkmen Medical Institute; Postgraduate Study, MD, Leningrad. Appointments: Chief, Department of Forensic Medicine, Turkmen Medical Institute, 1958-; Chairman, Medical Scientific Board, Health Ministry of Turkmenistan. Publications: Pathology Anatomy Diagnostic of Ischemic Heart Disease, 1978; Contributor of over 120 professional articles including: The Analysis of Criminal Affairs Against Doctors for the Professional Violations, 1994. Honours: The Order, SDign of Honour, 1980; Recipient of 5 medals; Honoured Man of Science and Technology of Turkmenistan, 1991. Memberships: Chairman, Turkmen Society of Forensic Medicine; Board, Russian Society of Forensic Medicine. Hobby: Gardening. Address: Stepnaya Street 28, Ashgabat 744006, Turkmenistan.

SHAH Shahnaz, b. 15 Feb 1949, Pakistan. Obstetrician & Gynacologists. divorced, 2 sons. Education: MBBS; DGO; MRCOG. Career: Senior Registrar in Obstetrics & Gynaecology; Registrar in Obstetrics & Gynaecology; Consultant Obstetrician & Gynaecologist. Honours: Edwin Lillie Medal, 1980; Dedication Beyond Duty, 1980; Ethicon Travel Fund Award, 1992. Memberships: BMA; British Colposcopy & Cervical Cytology Society; Emirates Medical Association. Hobbies: Travelling; Music; Computers. Address: Corniche Hospital, PO Box 3788, Abu Dhabi, United Arab Emirates.

SHAMOIAN Charles A, b. 10 May 1931, Worcester, MA, USA. Psychiatrist. m. Paule Faye Shamoian, 10 Aug 1961, 1 s, 1 d. Education: AB; MA; PhD; MD. Career: Assistant Professor, Associate Professor, Professor of Clinical Psychiatry, Cornell University Medical College. Publications: Biology and Treatment of Dementia in the Elderly, APPI, 1984; Treatment of Affective Disorders in the Elderly, APPI, 1985; Psychopharmacological Treatment Complications in the Elderly, APPI, 1992. Honour: J Weinburg Award in Geriatric Psychiatry, APA, 1994. Memberships: Past President, American Association of Geriatric Psychiatry; Fellow, American College of Psychiatrists; American Physiological Society; Society of Biological Psychiatry. Hobbies: Gardening; Walking. Address: New York Hospital, Cornell Medical Center, Westchester Division, 21 Bloomingdale Road, White Plains, NY 10605, USA.

SHAN Lai Jia, b. Aug 1934, Wenchang County, Hainan province, China. Head of Department. Appointments: Head, Department of Ophthalmology, Director, Department of Teaching Hospital, Hainan Medical College; Associate Director, Society of Combination of Traditional Chinese aand Western Medicine; Standing Committee Member, China Ophthalmology Society; Editor, Contemporary Ophthalmology Theses Selection; Research, Director, China Optical Science Institute, Hainan Centre; Adviser, Hua Tai Pharmaceutical Factory; Research Fellow, Lu's Ophthalmology Research Institute. Publications: Contributor of 48 theses published national and internationally. Honours: 2nd Prize, Hainan Science Soceity; Golden prize, International Exhibition of Chinese Medicines, USA. Address: Ophthalmology Department, Hainan Medical College, No 33 Longhua Road, Haikou, Hainan province, China.

SHAN Tuo-Sheng, b. 24 Mar 1928, Hunan, China. Biochemist. m. He Suyun, 6 Sept 1953, 2 daughters. Education: BM, Guiyang Medical College, 1952. Appointments: Currently Professor of Biochemistry, Guiyang Medical College. Publications: The carotene content of certain Chinese herbs for "Hwenmong" (night blindness), 1958; The method determination of urinary 17-Hydroxycorticosterone, 1963; Biochemical studies of experimental fluorosis in rat, 1985; The changes of serum concentration of Neurotransmitter Monoamines and its metabolites in the essential hypertension, 1991. Memberships: Board Member, Chinese Biochemistry Society; Chairman, Guizhou Biochemistry Society. Address: 4 Beijing Road, Guiyang, Guizhou, China.

SHAN Zhao Wei, b. 19 Oct 1940, Nantong, Jiangsu, China. Professor. m. Mei Yun Tao, 8 Feb 1968, 1 son, 1 daughter. Education: Bachelor of Medicine, Nangjing University of Traditional Chinese Medicine. Appointments: Resident Physician, 1965; Attending Physician, Lecturer, 1980; Deputy Director, Associate Professor, 1983; Tutor of PhD Graduates, 1993. Publications: Co-author, Internal Medicine of

TCM, 1988; Co-author, Spleen and Stomach Theory and Clinical Practice, 1990; Co-author, Qing You Tang in the treatment of helicobacter pylori infected Gastritis and Peptic Ulcers, 1991; Co-author, Treatment and Syndrome of Acute Gastric Disease, 1991; Co-author, Gastroenterology of TCM, 1993. Honours: 2nd Prize, Scientific Advances, State Traditional Chinese Medical & Pharmaceutical Administration, 1994. Memberships: China Association of Traditional Chinese Medicine & Pharmacy; Jiangsu Research Institute of Spleen & Stomach Disease. Hobbies: Calligraphy; Literature. Address: 155 Hanzhong Road, Nanjing, Jiangsu, China.

SHANG De Jun, b. 10 Mar 1932, He Nan, China. Vascular Surgeon. m. Qin Chuan Qiu, 1 Jul 1957, 1 s, 2 d. Education: Shandong Chinese Traditional Medicine College. Appointment: Professor, Director of Surgery, Teaching and Research Section, Chinese Traditional Medical College. Publications: Surgeon of Chinese Traditional Medicine, 1986; Treatment of angiopathy with combination of Chinese traditional and Western medicine, 1990. Honour: 1st Class Award for Research on Buerger Disease, Chinese National Science and Technology, 1978. Memberships: Chairman, Chinese Angiopathy Medical Association for Combining Chinese Traditional and Western Medicine. Hobbies: Literature; Writing. Address: Shandong Chinese Traditional Medicine College, Jiana, Shang Dong, China.

SHANG Fang, b. 20 Nov 1930, Peking, China. Professor of Physiology. m. Yue Wen Hao, 8 Apr 1956, 1 daughter. Education: BD, Chinese Medical University, 1950-55; Higher Electro-Physiology studies, Shanghai Medical University, 1966-67. Appointments: Physiological Assistant, Lecturer, Associate Professor, 1956-87, Professor of Physiology, 1988-95, Shandong Medical University. Publications: Physiological, 1958; Physiological Experiment, 1958; Contributor of 15 professional papers, 1957-90. Honours: Recipient of 4 Awards for Scientific Study. Membership: Chinese Physiological Association. Hobbies: Travel; Reading; Music. Address: Department of Physiology, Shandong Medical University, Jinan, 250012 Shandong, China.

SHANG Kezhong, b. 22 August 1923, Jiongsu, China. Doctor; Professor. m. Wenlam Li, 30 September 1952, 3 sons. Education: BA, MD, Medical College of National Defense, Shanghai, 1948; Certified of Radiation Oncology, Shanghai 1st Medical College, 1964. Appointments: Assistant Professor of Pathology, Medical College of National Defense, 1948; Radiologist, Associate Professor, Professor, Chairman, Department of Radiology, 6th Hospital, Shanghai, 1955-. Publications: GI double-contrast radiography interpretation on dynamic mechanics, 1985; Experiment and application of DC diagnosis, 1993; Videofluorography during Qi-Gong, 1990. Honours: Shanghai Government Award on Science and Medicine, 1986, 1993; National Health Administration Award, 1993. Memberships: Standing Member, Chinese Medical Association; Chinese College of Radiology; Chinese Journal of Radiology. Hobbies: Fishing; Table Tennis. Address: Department of Radiology, Shanghai 6th People's Hospital, Shanghai 200433, China.

SHANG Tao, b. 2 Oct 1956, Xianmen, Fujian, China. Visiting Doctor of Dermatology. m. Li Ping Chen, 20 Nov 1992, 1 s. Education: No 1 Graduate, Xiamen Medical College. Appointment: Visiting Doctor of Dermatology, Department of Dermatology, First Hospital Xiamen, Fujian, China. Publications: Co-author: Analysis of 120 cases of cosmetic dermatitis, 1988; A clinical study on condyloma acuminate treated with CO2 laser, 1990; Analysis of 241 cases of condyloma acuminate, 1991. Membership: Xiamen Branch of Chinese Medical Association. Hobbies: Literature; Philosophy, especially Ancient Chinese philosophy. Address: Department of Dermatology, Xiamen First Hospital, Xiamen, Fujian 361003, China.

SHAO Dian Hua, b. 16 Mar 1928, Hangchow, China. Scientist. m. Zhi An Liang, 11 Aug 1954, 2 d. Education: MD, Xiang Ya Medical College, 1952. Career: Resident Neurosurgeon and Assistant, Hu Nan Medical College, 1952-64; Research Assistant, 1964-78, Research Associate, 1978-86, Associate Professor, 1986-, Shanghai Institute of Physiology, Academia Sinica, China. Publications include: Noise-induced neuronal facilitation in the brain cortices, in Applied Acoustics, 1988; Slow cortical responses and auditory difference limens in Macaca monkeys, in Chinese Journal of Physiological Sciences, 1988; Noise-induced neuronal activation in the monkey cortex, in Chinese Journal of Physiological Sciences, 1990; Changes in Auditory Differential Sensitivity After Impulse Noise Exposure, 14th International Congress on Acoustics, 1992. Memberships: Chinese Association of Physiological

Sciences; Association for Research in Otolaryngology, USA. Hobbies: Travel; Gardening. Address: Laboratory of Audition, Shanghai Institute of Physiology, Chinese Academy of Sciences, 320 Yue Yang Road, Shanghai 200031, China.

SHAO Jingming, b. 14 March 1911, Xihua, Henan, China. Professor of Acupuncture. m. Xu Junqing, 8 June 1931, 1 son, 4 daughters. Education: Graduate, Old-style School, Equal to a University. Appointments: Researcher, Traditional Chinese Medicine, 1927; Doctor, Traditional Chinese Medicine, 1933; Doctor in Charge, 1952; Member, Acupuncture Institute of China; Chief Member, Acupuncture Institute of Henan. Publications: Selective Points of Acupuncture; Acupuncture Treatment and Prevention on Asthma; Excellent Prescriptions of Acupuncture Compendium of Chinese Acupuncture, etc. Honours: 1st Prize, Henan Province; 2nd Prize, Education Department of Henan. Memberships: Consultant, Clinical Research of Acupuncture Institute, China; Honorary President, Henan Acupuncture Institute; Director, Science and Technology Association, Zhengzhou. Hobbies: Calligraphy. Address: Henan College of Traditional Chinese Medicine, Jinshui Dadao Dungduan, Zhenzhou, Henan 450003, China.

SHAO Mingjian, b. 10 Sept 1936, Linhai, Cheking, China. University Teacher; Ophthalmology Clinician. m. Xu Zaie, Mar 1963, 1 son, 1 daughter. Education: Graduated, Medical Department, Cheking Medical University, 1960. Appointments: Assistant and Oculist, 1960; Lecturer in Ophthalmology and Attending Oculist, 1981; Higher Lecturer in Ophthalmology and Associate Chief Oculist, 1987; Associate Professor in Ophthalmology, Dean of Teaching and Research Group in Ophthalmology and Otolaryngology, Cheking Medical University, Ningbo, 1993-; Member, Editorial Committee, Ningbo Medical Journal, 1994. Publications: Analysis of 59 Cases of Serious Rupture of Cornea and Sclera, 1986; Summing-up of 60 Cases of the Treatment of Glaucoma by Schie's Operation, 1988; Clinical Analysis of 50 Cases of Trabeculectomy, 1990; Significance of the Diagnosis of Retina Pigment Epithelia Disease on Electrophysiological Test of Vision, 1992; Co-author, textbooks: Otolaryngology, 1983; Otolaryngology and its Nursing, 1983; Otolaryngology Book Two (chief editor), 1992. Honours: 3rd Prize for Outstanding Paper, Ningbo Medical Association, 1986; Advanced Worker, Cheking Ningbo Health School, 1993. Memberships: Committeeman, Ophthalmic Institute; Cheking Branch, Chinese Medical Association; Chief Committeeman, Ophthalmic Institute; Cheking Ningbo Branch, Chinese Medical Association. Address: Cheking Ningbo Health School, Ningbo 315010, China.

SHAO Qiyun, b. 12 Nov 1939, Zhejiang Province, China. Teacher. m. Jin Feng Dai, 23 Mar 1967, 1 s, 1 d. Appointment: Associate Professor, Department of Physics, Fudan University, Shanghai. Publications: Theoretical calculations of axial blocking dips (1) Monte Carlo simulation, in Chinese Physics, USA, 1989; Monte Carlo calculation of surface peak intensity, in Nuclear Technology, China, 1990; Quantitative study of ablation of bone tissues by Er: YAG laser light, in Chinese Laser, 1991. Memberships: Chinese Nuclear Association; Chinese Computational Physics Association. Hobbies: Painting; Watching Football. Address: Department of Physics No 2, Fudan University, Shanghai 200433, China.

SHAO Xiaohong, b. 15 Jun 1922. Physician. m. Dr Guo Yingxian, 5 Apr 1952, 1 s, 1 d. Education: MD, Cheeloo University Medical College, 1950. Appointment: Professor, Department of Emergency Medicine, PUMC Hospital, Beijing, China. Publications: Editor, Emergency Clinic, 1985; The role of health sectors in disaster preparedness - Floods in South Eastern China, 1991; Editor, Emergency Medicine, 1992; Prehospital Disaster Medicine, 1993. Honour: Honorary President, Chinese Association of Emergency Medicine, 1994. Membership: Board of Directors, World Association for Disaster and Emergency Medicine. Hobby: Drawing. Address: Department of Emergency Medicine, PUMC Hospital, 1 Shuaifuyuan, Wangfujing, Beijing 100730, China.

SHAPIRO Marc Jerome, b. 29 Apr 1953, Detroit, MI, USA. Physician. m. Joanne Shapiro, 2 s. Education: BS, 1974, MS, 1975, MD, 1979, University of Michigan, Ann Arbor. Career includes: Internship and Residency, Surgery, Henry Ford Hospital, Detroit, MI, 1979-84; Associate Professor of Surgery; Director, Trauma Surgery and Surgical Intensive Care Unit, Assistant Director, Emergency Department, St Louis University Medical Center, MO, 1986-; Courtesy Staff, John Cochran Veterans Administration Hospital and St Mary's Health Center, St Louis, MO, 1986-; Assistant Professor of Surgery, St Louis University School of Medicine, 1986-90, and currently at St Louis University Health

Sciences Center; Many committees and directorships. Publications: Many articles published including: Co-author, Computed tomography in the diagnosis of blunt thoracic injuries, American Journal of Surgery, 1994; Co-author, The perils of bungee jumping, Journal of Trauma, 1994; Many book contributions, abstracts, and international presentations. Memberships include: Association for Academic Surgery; Society of Critical Care Medicine; Midwest Surgical Association; St Louis Surgical Society; National Association of EMS Physicians; Missouri Medical Society; St Louis Medical Society; Shock Society; Fellow, Guidelines Committee, American College of Critical Care Medicine, 1989-; Fellow, American College of Surgeons, 1989-; American Association for Surgery of Trauma, 1989-; Societe Internationale de Chirurgie, 1991-. Address: Department of Surgery, 3635 Vista Avenue at Grand Boulevard, PO Box 15250, St Louis, MO 63110-0250, USA.

SHAPIRO Robyn S, b. 19 July 1952, Minneapolis, Minnesota, USA. Attorney. m. Charles Barr, 27 June 1976, 2 sons, 1 daughter. Education: BA summa cum laude with highest distinction, University of Michigan; JD, Harvard Law School. Appointments: Attorney, Foley & Lardner, Milwaukee, 1977-79; Adjunct Assistant Professor of Law, Marquette University Law School, Milwaukee, 1979-83; Associate Director, 1982-85, Director, Associate Professor, 1985-, Center for the Study of Bioethics, Medical College of Wisconsin, Milwaukee; Attorney, Quarles & Brady, Milwaukee, 1987-92; Partner, Michael, Best & Friedrich, health law special practice group, 1992-. Publications: Unanswered Questions Surrounding the PSDA, 1992; Legal Basis for the Control of Analgesic Drugs, 1994; Willingness to Perform Euthanasia: A Survey of Physician Attitudes, 1994. Honours: Phi Beta Kappa, 1973; Included in Best Lawyers in America, 4th edition, 1993; Golden Compass Award, 1994. Memberships: American Bar Association, Coordinating Committee on Bioethics; American Society of Law and Medicine; International Association of Bioethics; National Health Lawyers Association. Address: Medical College of Wisconsin, Bioethics Center, 8701 Watertown Plank Road, Milwaukee, WI 53226, USA.

SHAPIRO Sumner L, b. 15 May 1926, Boston, MA, USA. Psychoanalyst. m. Jacqueline Dovcette, 19 Mar 1956, 1 s, 2 d. Education: AB, AM, Harvard University; MD, Boston University. Appointment: Psychoanalyst. Publications: Moment of Insight, 1976; Beyond Insight, 1979; Beyond Case Histories, 1984; Well-Kept Secrets, 1994; Moment of Insight, audiocassette; Lost and Found, audiocassette. Hobbies: Writing, Reading Classics; DIY. Address: 16780 Oak View Drive, Encino, CA 92436, USA.

SHARMA Om Prakash, b. 4 July 1936, Gwalior, India. Physician. m. Maggie Sharma, 1 son, 3 daughters. Education: BSc; MD; DTM&H; FACP; FCCP. Appointments: Research Registrar, Royal Northants, London, England, 1966-69; Assistant Professor of Medicine, USC School of Medicine, 1969; Associate Professor of Medicine; Professor of Medicine. Publications: Sarcoidosis: A Clinical Approach, 1975; Sarcoidosis: Clinical Management, 1984; Hypersensitivity Pneumonitis: A Clinical Approach, 1989. Memberships: Royal Society of Medicine, England; British Thoracic Society; American Thoracic Society; American College of Chest Physicians. Honours: Andrew Balfour Scholar, London School of Tropical Medicine, 1961; Prophit Research Scholar, Roy College of Physicians, 1966-69; Honorary Member, Japanese Sarcoidosis Association. Hobbies: History of Medicine; Shakuhachi. Address: 1200 N State St, Los Angeles, CA 90033, USA.

SHARMA Santosh, b. 24 Feb 1934, Kenya. Medicine. Education: MBBS, BJ Medical School, Pune, India; FRCOG; FACOG. Career: Lecturer and Senior Lecturer, Obstetrics and Gynaecology, Makerere University School of Medicine, Kampala, Uganda, 1967-72; Assistant Professor, Obstetrics and Gynaecology, Howard University, Washington DC, USA, 1972-74; Associate Professor, 1974-78, Professor, 1978-, John A Burns School of Medicine, University of HI at Manoa, USA. Publications include: Prostaglandins for Termination of Pregnancy, in Journal of Obstetrics and Gynaecology British Commonwealth, 1971; Cancer of The Cervix, Abortion, Breast, chapters in Textbook of Gynaecology, 1982; Maternal Physiology in Pregnancy, chapters in Concise Textbook in Obstetrics, 1987. Honour: Lifetime Achievement Award, Federation of International Gynaecology and Obstetrics, 1994. Memberships: American College of Obstetrics and Gynaecology; Royal College of Obstetrics and Gynaecology; Federation of International Gynaecology and Obstetrics; International Menopause Society; American Society of Colposcopy and Cervical Pathology. Hobbies: Travel; Photography; Walking. Address: John A Burns School of

Medicine, University of Hawaii, 1319 Punahou Street 801, Honolulu, HI 96826, USA.

SHARMA Subhash Shelly, b. 16 Sep 1948, Nairobi, Kenya. Doctor, GP. m. Anjali Sharma, 4 Aug 1984, 1 s, 2 d. Education: BSc, Honours, Engineering, England; MPhil, Leicester, England; MB Ch B, Leicester, England; DCH; DROCG; MRCGP; CCFP. Appointments: Lecturer, Computer Science, England, 1974-77; General Practitioner, England, 1987-91; Family Physician, Canada, 1991-. Publication: Co-author, Contraception in Asian Women, 1987. Honour: Justice of the Peace, England, 1991. Memberships: Royal College of General Practitioners; Canadian Family Physicians; Manitoba Medical Association. Hobbies: Reading; Computer Education in Schools; Voluntary Work, Medical Officer for British Diabetic Association, for Children's Holiday Camps. Address: Box 344, Eriksdale, Manitoba, Canada, R0C 0W0.

SHARMAN William Angus, b. 24 Feb 1936, Edinburgh, Scotland. Medical Practitioner. m. Ramona Helen Robertson, 16 Sept 1958, 1 s, 2 d. Education: MB, Edinburgh, 1960; ChB, Edinburgh, 1960; MRCOG, 1973; FRCOG, 1992. Appointments: Senior Partner in General Practice; Hospital Practitioner in Obstetrics & Gynaecology. Memberships: British Medical Association; Royal College of Obstetricians & Gynaecologists. Hobbies: Photography; Scuba Diving; Bird Watching; Sailing. Address: 19 Colley Rise, Lyddington, Oakham, Rutland, Leics, LE15 9LL, UK.

SHARPE Robert, b. 5 Jul 1946, Coventry, England. Chartered Psychologist. m. Kerstin Sharpe, 19 Sep 1983, 2 s, 2 d. Education: BSc, Honours; PhD, Psychology, Nottingham University, England; C Psychol; Post-Doctoral Studies at Middlesex Hospital, London. Appointment: Consultant Behavioural Psychologist. Publications: Thrive on Stress, 1977; Assert Yourself, 1989; Self Help for Your Anxiety, 1991. Membership: British Psychological Society. Hobbies: Equestrian Sports; Classical Music. Address: 30 Weymouth Street, London, W1N 3FA, England.

SHARPS John Geoffrey, b. 29 July 1936, Weaverham, Cheshire, England. Psychologist. m. Heather Acheson, 19 Aug 1966, 1 son, 1 daughter. Education: MA, Edinburgh University, 1958; DipEd, 1962, MEd, 1963, Queen's University, Belfast; MLitt, Oxford University, 1964; BTh, Hull University, 1992; Chartered Psychologist. Publications: Mrs Gaskell's Observation and Invention: A Study of Her Non-Biographic Works, 1970. Memberships: Associate Fellow, British Psychological Society; Fellow, Royal Economic Society; Fellow, Royal Geographical Society; Fellow, Royal Society of Arts. Address: Sarda Lapis, 25 Cornelian Drive, Scarborough, North Yorkshire YO11 3AL, England.

SHAW Peter John, b. 17 Jul 1956, Manchester, England. Staff Oncologist. Education: MB BS, London, 1980; MA, Cambridge, England, 1981; MRCP, 1983; FRACP, 1989. Career: Leukaemia Research Fund Fellow, Edinburgh, Scotland, 1989-90; Staff Oncologist, The Children's Hospital, Camperdown, Sydney. Publications: On paediatric oncology and bone marrow transplantation. Memberships: International Society of Paediatric Oncology; Co-responding Member, United Kingdom Children's Cancer Study Group; Australian and New Zealand Children's Cancer Study Group; Medical Oncology Group. Address: The Children's Hospital, Camperdown, Sydney, Australia.

SHAW Robert Wayne, b. 25 Jun 1946, Shrewsbury, England. Obstetrician and Gynaecologist. m. Mae McGovern, 6 Mar 1980, 1 s, 1 d. Education: MBChB, Honours; MD, Honours; FRCS(Ed); FRCOG; MFFP. Career: Senior Lecturer, Department of Obstetrics and Gynaecology, Edinburgh University; Professor and Head, Academic Department of Obstetrics and Gynaecology, Royal Free Hospital School of Medicine, London; Currently, Professor and Head of Department of Obstetrics and Gynaecology, University of Wales College of Medicine. Publications: LHRH and Its Analogues, 1989; Co-author, Gynaecology, 1992. Honour: Honorary Member, Finnish Society of Gynaecologists and Obstetricians, 1991. Memberships: American Fertility Society; Gynaecological Visiting Society; Blair Bell Research Society; British Fertility Society. Hobbies: Sailing; Hill Walking. Address: Department of Obstetrics and Gynaecology, University of Wales College of Medicine, Heath Park, Cardiff, CF4 4XN, Wales.

SHEA William D, b. 1 Mar 1939. Assistant Professor in Orthopedics; Clinical Instructor. m. Laura Shea, 2 s, 2 d. Education: BS, St Francis Xavier University, Nova Scotia, 1960; MD, University of Ottawa, Faculty of Medicine, Ottawa, 1964. Career includes: Private Practice from 1973 including: Sports Medicine Boston Inc, Medical Directory, 1988-;

Surgeon, New England Baptist Hospital, Boston, 1973-; Courtesy Staff, Mount Auburn Hospital, Cambridge, MA, 1973-, Kennedy Memorial Hospital, Brighton, MA, 1975-, New England Rehabilitation Hospital, Woburn, MA, 1976-; Clinical Instructor, Orthopedic Surgery, Tufts University, 1971-; Assistant Professor in Orthopedic Surgery, University of MA Medical School, 1983-; Clinical Instructor in Orthopedic Surgery, Harvard University, 1973-83. Publications: Many papers presented, 1968-82; Indications and Contraindications in Surface Replacement Arthroplasty of The Hip, in Orthopedic Clinics of North America, volume 13, No 4, 1982. Honours: Joseph Collins Foundation Scholarship, NY, 1962, 1963, 1964; Massachusetts Medical and Dental and Nursing Scholarship, 1962, 1963, 1964; US Navy Senior Medical Student Scholarship, 1964; Orthopedic and Research Education Foundation Traveling Fellowship, 1972; Operation Desert Storm, Walter Reed Army Medical Center, Army Commendation Medal, 1991. Memberships include: American Academy of Orthopedic Surgeons; AMA; American College of Sports Medicine; American College of Surgeons; Canadian Orthopedic Association; International Arthroscopy Association; Diplomate, American Board of Orthopedic Surgery; Royal Society of Medicine. Address: 1 International Place, Suite 420, Boston, MA 02110, USA.

SHEEN Alan Edward, b. 1 May 1950, New Orleans, USA. Physician. m. Joan Carolyn Kessler, 10 Jan 1981, 2 daughters. Education: New Orleans Academy, 1964-68; Tulane University, 1968-71; MD, Louisiana University, 1971-74. Appointments: LSU Medical Center, New Orleans, 1973-74; King's College Hospital Medical School, London, England, 1974; Ochsner Clinic, Ochsner Foundation Hospital, New Orleans, 1975; LSU Medical Center, New Orleans, 1978; Children's Hospital National Medical Center, Washington, 1978-79; Private Practitioner. Publications: Serum Theophylline Concentrations in Asthmatic Children, 1978; Comparison of Serum Theophylline Concentrations Measured by High Pressure Liquid Chromatography and Quantitative Enzyme, 1979; Simultaneous use of Rapidly Absorbed and Sustained Release Theophylline Preparations in Children, 1979; Comparison of Theolair SR and Theodur Tablets, 1979; Evaluation of Calibration of Spirometers, 1980; Status Asthmaticus and Bleeding Duodenal Ulcer Disease, 1980. Memberships includes: Alph Epsilon Delta; American Medical Association; American Academy of Allergy & Immunology; American College of Allergy; American College of Chest Physicians; American Thoracic Society; American Lung Society. Honours: Gold Medal Scholastic Award, 1964-68; Physics Award, 1968; Special Service Award, Tulane University Pre-Medical Society, 1972. Hobbies: Sailing; Fishing; Tennis; Golf. Address: 3701 Houma Blvd, Ste 101, Metairie, Louisiana, USA.

SHEIKH Kazim, b. 21 Sep 1936, Hyderabad, Pakistan. Physician. m. Parveen Fahim, 1 Jan 1969, 2 s. Education: MBBS; DIH; MFOM. Career includes: Chronic Disease Epidemiologist, Office of Epidemiology and Health Promotion, WV Department of Health, Charleston, 1987-89; Director, Division of Industrial Hygiene, WV Department of Health, Charleston, 1988-89; Currently, Medical Ofrficer, US Health Care Financing Administration. Publications include: Occupational injury, chronic low back pain and return to work, in Public Health, 1987; Co-author, Mortality of workers at acetylene production plants, in British Journal of Industrial Medicine, 1988. Memberships: Faculty of Occupational Medicine, Royal College of Physicians of London; Society of Occupational Medicine; Society for Social Medicine; Society for Epidemiologic Research; American College of Occupational Medicine; American College of Preventive Medicine; American College of Epidemiology. Address: 315 West 99th Street, Kansas City, MO 64114, USA.

SHEN Eh, b. 9 Nov 1928, Zhejiang, China. Scientific Researcher. m. Liang-Qing Qiu, 16 Mar 1960, 1 son, 1 daughter. Education: BS, Zhejiang University, 1951; Postgraduate studies, Neurobiology, Biochemistry, Institute of Physiology and Biochemistry, Academia Sinica, 1951-55. Appointments: Research Instructor, Institute of Physiology and Biochemistry, 1956; Associate Professor, 1960, Professor, 1983, Institute of Physiology; Professor of Neurobiology, Shanghai Brain Research Institute, 1984-. Publications: Over 80 papers including: Vagal expiratory afferent discharges during spontaneous breathing, 1985; Respiratory neurons in the medulla of the rabbit: distribution, discharge patterns and spinal projections, 1991; Spontaneous and transmitter-induced rhythmic activity in neonatal rat sympathetic proganglionic neurons in vitro, 1994. Honours: 1st Grade Prize, Academia Sinica, 1980. Memberships: International Brain Research Organization; Society for Neuroscience, USA; Chinese

Association for Physiological Sciences. Hobby: Chinese calligraphy. Address: Shanghai Brain Research Institute, Yueyang Road, Shanghai 200031, China.

SHEN Hefei, b. 24 Dec 1932, Jiangsu Pr, China. Clinical Medicine. m. 5 Dec 1955, 1 son. Education: Bachelor of Medicine. Career: Doctor in Charge of Inter Medicine; Vice Chief Doctor of Geriatrics; Vice Professor of Cardiology in the Elderly, Chief Doctor and Professor 1988-. Publication: Emergent Medicine in China, 1983. Honours: Third and Second Awards of Scientific Progress, Jan & Dec 1988. Memberships: Chinese Association of Geriatrics; Chief Member, Hebei Branch of CAG; Director of Emergency, Hebei Province. Hobby: Music. Address: Institute of Geriatric Medicine, People's Hospital of Hebei Province, 64 Beima Road, Shijiazhuang, 050071, China.

SHEN Huai Xin, b. 27 July, Shanghai, China. Orthopedic Surgeon. m. Chen Cui Xia, 3 Dec 1949, 2 daughters. Education: MD, Medical College, West China Union University, Chengdu, 1945. Appointments: Vice Chairman, Chairman, Department of Surgery; Professor of Orthopedic Surgery. Publications: Textbook of Surgery, 1984; China Medical Encyclopedia, Orthopedic Section, 1984; China Modern Medicine, 1985; Handbook for Emergencies, 1985; Operative Spine Surgery, 1993. Honours: 3rd Prize, Sichuan Science & Technology Committee, 1980; 3rd Prize, Sichuan Provincial Health Department, 1981. Memberships: China Orthopedic Society; Chairman, Sichuan Orthopedic Society & Chengdu Orthopedic Society; Honorary Advisor, Chinese Journal of Reparative and Reconstructive Surgery. Address: 16-6 Xiao Xue Road, Chengdu, Sichuan 610041, China.

SHEN Huanxin, b. Jul 1919, Shanghai, China. Orthopedic Surgeon. m. Chen Cuixia, 3 Dec 1949, 2 d. Education: MD; Professor of Surgery. Appointments: Head of Department of Surgery, 1980; Professor of Orthopedic Surgery, 1980-. Publications: China Medical Encyclopaedia, Orthopedic Volume, 1982; Handbook of Emergency, 1983; China Modern Medicine, 1984; Textbook of Surgery, 1984; Co-author, Operative Orthopedics of the Spine, 1993. Honours: 3rd Prize, Science and Technology Committee of Sichuan Province, 1980; 3rd Prize, Department of Public Health of Sichuan Province, 1984. Memberships: Chinese Orthopedic Association; Chairman, Honorary Chairman, Sichuan Orthopedic Association; Advisor, Journal of Reparative and Reconstruction Surgery; Editorial Board, Journal of Biomedical Engineering. Address: 16, 6 Xiao Xue Road, Chengdu, Sichuan 610041, China.

SHEN Jenta, b. 20 Mar 1945, Taiwan. Medical Doctor. m. 2 sons, 1 daughter. Education: MD; PhD. Appointments: Assistant Professor, Director of Gynecologic Oncology, Attending Gynecologic Oncologist, Acting Director of Gynecologic Oncology, Attending Gynecologic Oncologist; Teaching-Columbia/Presbyterian Medical Center, New York, 1984-87. Memberships: American College of Obstetricians & Gynecologists; American College of Surgeons; Society of Genecologic Oncologists. Hobbies: Classical Music; Museums; Travel. Address: 3905 Sacramento Street, Suite 302, San Francisco, CA 94118, USA.

SHEN Kang, b. 18 Sep 1941, Jiaxin, Zhejiang Province, China. Teacher. m. Qiu Xiaochun, 21 July 1970, 1 son, 1 daughter. Education: BA, Biology, Hangzhou University. Appointments: Middle School Teacher; Technician; Secretary; Lecturer, Associate Professor, Wenzhou Medical College; Associate Professor, Hangzhou Medical College. Publications: Effects of TDP and Infrared Rays on the Abdominal Subcutaneous Macrophages in Mice, 1992; A Regression Analysis of the Relationship Between the Age, Length and Weight of Fetuses, 1993; Mice Under the Irradiation of Infrared Rays and TDP, 1994; The Influence of Centipede (Traditional Chinese Medicine) on the Embryo Development of Mice, 1994; A Guide to the Study of Histology and Embryology, Co-Editor, 1993. Honours: Guanghua Award in the Study of Fundamental Medicine, 1991. Memberships: Chinese Academy of Medical Sciences; Histology and Embryology, Chinese Society of Natural Sciences. Hobbies: Weightlifting; Music; Travel. Address: Department of Histology and Embryology, Hangzhou Medical College, Wenyi Road, Hangzhou 310012, China.

SHEN Liande, b. 26 May 1930, Chung King, Sichuan, China. Teacher. m. 8 Feb 1958, 2 s. Education: BSc, West China University granted by College of Science, Chendu, Sichuan, China. Appointments: Assistant Instructor, 1953-77, Lecturer, 1977-81, Associate Professor, 1981-87, Professor, 1987-, Head of Department, Department of Pharmacognosy, West China University of Medical Sciences, Chengdu,

Sichuan, China. Publications: Codonopsis Wall, in Flora Reipublicae Popularis Sinicae, 1983; Pharmacognosy, 1987; Identification of Chinese Materia Medica, 1991; Pharmaceutical Botany, 3rd edition, 1993. Honour: Award of Progress of Science and Technology, for Codonopsis Wall, 1983. Membership: Chairman, Branch of Chinese Materia Medicae, Chengdu Pharmacy Society, Chengdu, China. Hobbies: Painting; Singing; Dancing. Address: Dept of Pharmacognosy, Faculty of Pharmacy, West China University of Medical Sciences, Chengdu, Sichuan, 610044, China.

SHEN Ming, b. Shenyang, China. Education: Graduate, Manchuria Medical College. Appointments: Leadership, Associate Professor of Abdominal Surgery, China Medical University, Shenyang; Chief, Gastroenterology Department, Beijing Railway Medical College; Chief of Cancer Institute, Beijing Railway General Hospital, 1980. Publications: Advanced gastric cancer of "Lymphoid Stromal Type", 1983; Modified radical mastectomy, 1988; Epidemiologic study of Chinese large bowel carcinomas, 1994; Clinico-epidemiological survey of colorectal cancer in southern area of China, 1994; Long term survival effect of modified radical mastectomy, 1988; Acupuncture for acute appendicitis, 1988; Cancer of the Stomach and Intestine, 1983; Early Diagnosis and Teatment of Breast Cancer, 1990. Memberships: Beijing Surgery and Oncology Society; China Anticancer Society. Address: Department of Oncology, Beijing Railway General Hospital, Beijing 100038, China.

SHEN Wei-Zai, b. 7 Feb 1956, Shanghai, China. Doctor of Medicine; Anatomist. m. Zhang Ning, 11 Mar 1982, 1 daughter. Education: MD; MSc, Medical Sciences. Appointments: Currently Associate Professor of the Department of Anatomy, Faculty of Medicine, Jinan University. Publications: 4 chapters in 3 books; 11 original papers in scientific journals. Honours: Third Prize, Adv in Medicine and Health Science and Technology, Guandong, 1993; Man of the Year, ABI, 1994; The 20th Century Award for Achievement, IBC. Memberships: Chinese Society of Anatomy; Guangdong Anatomical Society; The Hong Kong Society of Neurosciences. Hobbies: Music; Swimming. Address: Department of Anatomy, Faculty of Medicine; Jinan University, Guangzhou 510632, China.

SHEN Yanmin, b. 3 Dec 1933, Zhejiang Province, China. Dentist. m. Mo Deyu, 1 Oct 1962, 2 daughters. Education: Diplomas, Second Medical College, Shanghai, 1957. Appointments: Chief, Department of Stomatology; Vice-dean, Faculty of Stomatology; Vice-chief of National Expert Committee to Prevent Dental Caries with Fluorides; Professor of Oral Medicine and Preventive Dentistry. Publications: Water Fluoridation in Guangzhou and Guancheng, Guangdong, China, 1988; Change Dental Caries Prevalence in Preschool Children after Water Fluoridation Discontinuance, Co-author, 1989; An Investigation on Prevalence of Dental Fluorosis in Fangcun, Guangzhou and Hong Kong Fluoridated to 0.7mg/L, Co-author, 1993. Memberships: Group of Technical Direction on National Epidemiologic Survey of Oral Health, China; Standing Committee, Society of Stomatology, Guangdong, Branch, Chinese Medical Association. Address: Department of Stomatology, First Affiliated Hospital, Sun Yat-sen University of Medical Sciences, Guangzhou 510080, China.

SHEN Yiping, b. 30 Apr 1926, Wuxi, Jiangsu, China. Professor of Medical Parasitology. m. Wang Heyu, 1 Jan 1953, 3 daughters. Education: BSc, Jiangsu Medical College, 1952; Senior Visiting Scholar, London School of Health and Tropical Medicine, London University, 1983. Appointments: Assistant in Medical Parasitology, 1953-56, Lecturer in Medical Parasitology, 1957-77, Jiangsu Medical College; Associate Professor of Medical Parasitology, 1978-85, Professor of Medical Parasitology, 1986-, Nanjing Medical University. Publications: Parasite and Clinic, 1991; Co-author: Control, chapter 12 in Schistosomiasis, 1963; Discovery of an endemic area of paragonimiasis in Jiangsu, 1979. Honours: Special Allowance granted by State Council of China, 1992-. Memberships: Society of Zoology, China; Jiangsu Parasitic and Endemic Disease Association. Hobbies: Music; Sports. Address: 19 E-Mei-Lin, Hanzhong Road, Nanjing 210029, China.

SHENG Can Ruo, b. 12 Nov 1935, Nan Tong, Jiangsu, China. Chinese Physician; Acupuncturist. m. Zhu Guiying, 1 Oct 1956, 2 sons. Education: Graduate, NanTong Medical School, 1954; Graduate, Nanjing College of Traditional Chinese Medicine, 1958; BA, Acupuncture, Nanjing College of Traditional Chinese Medicine. Appointments: Acupuncture Department, Jiangsu Hospital of Traditional Chinese Medicine 1954-; Chinese Medical Team, Tanzania, 1968-71; Lectures given worldwide. Publications: Practical Handbook of

Acupuncre in Clinic, 1988; Practical handbook of Relieving Pains with Acupuncture, 1989; Clinical Acupuncture and Moxibustion, 1990; Chinese Acupuncture and Moxibustion. Honours: national Science and Technology Award, 1978; Science and Technology Award, National Health Department, 1985; Science and Technology Award, Jiangsu provincial Health Department, 1985. Memberships: Councillor, Chinese Acupuncture and Moxibustion Society; Head, Acupuncture Department, Irish Acupuncture and Moxibustion. Hobby: Fishing. Address: Acupuncture Department, Jiang su Provincial Hospital of Traditionl Chinese Medicine, 155 Hanzhong Road, 210029 Nanjing, China.

SHENG Jinde, b. 29 Jun 1926, Changsha, Hunan, China. Professor of Parasitology. m. 12 Mar 1953, 1 s, 1 d. Education: Graduated from Tong-Ji Medical University, Shanghai, 1952; 2 Years advanced studies of Medical Parasitology. Appointments: Department of Parasitology: 4th Military Medical University, Xian, 1953-65; 1st Military Medical University, Guangzhou, 1965-. Publications: 8 Professional articles in professional journals including: Cryopreservation of Trypanosome, in Bulletin of Biology, 1992; Cryopreservation of Protozoa, in Chinese Journal of Zonoses, 1993; Cryopreservation of Muscle Stage Larvae of Tricinells, in Chinese Journal of Parasitology and Parasitic Diseases, 1993. Honour: Military Science and Technology Advanced 3rd Award, 1991. Hobbies: Touring; Reading. Address: Dept of Parasitology, First Military Medical University, Guangzhou, Guangdong Province, 510515, China.

SHENG Zhi-Yong, b. 1 July 1920, Shanghai, China. Surgeon. m. Yun-xue Zhang, 9 Oct 1943, 1 son, 2 daughters. Education: MD; Shanghai Medical College, 1942; Research fellow, Surgical Research Labaoratory, Department of Surgery, University of Texas Medical Branch, Galveston, Texas, USA, 1947-48. Appointments: Resident, 1942-45, Chief Resident, 1945-46, Visiting Surgeon, 1946-47, Department of Surgery, Red Cross First Hospital, Shanghai; Visiting Surgeon, Yangtzepoo Hospital, Shanghai, 1949-50; Visiting Surgeon, Chongsan Hospital, Shanghai, 1950-52; Associate researcher, Department of Experimental Surgery, Academy of Military Medical Sciences, 1952-61; Chief, Department of Surgery, Surgical Emergency Hospital, Shanghai, 1956-57; Chief, Faculty Topographical Anatomy and Operative Surgery, 2nd Military Medical College, Shanghai, 1956-57; Deputy Chief, Department Experimental Surgery, Academy of Military Medical Sciences, 1959-61; Chief, Department Trauma and Burns, General Hospital of PLA, Beijing, 1961-82; Professor of Surgery, 1978-, Director, Trauma Centre, 1982-, Vice Superintendent, 1982-88, Postgraduate Medical College and 304th Hospital, Beijing. Publications: Contributor of numerous articles in professional journals; Advances in Burns, Editor, 1992; Modern Treatment of Severe Burns, Editor, 1992. Honours include: Merit of Honour, 1987, Merit of Honour, 1987, 2nd Class Merit, 1987, 3rd Class Merit, 1989, General Department of Logistics, PLA. Memberships include: Honorary Chairman, Chinese Burns Society; Board of Trustees, Chinese Medical Association; Chinese Surgical Society. Hobby: Classical Music. Address: 304th Hospital, 51 Fu-Cheng Road, Beijing 100037, China.

SHENG Zhuoren, b. 3 Oct 1928, Shanghai, China. Professor of Anaesthesiology. m. 1 Mar 1952, 3 daughters. Education: MD, China Medical University, 1953. Appointments: Associated Professor, 1978-82, Professor, Chairman of Anaesthesiology, China Medical University; International Visiting Professor, Cleveland Clinic Foundation, USA, 1984. Publications: Editor-in-Chief, Clinical Anesthesiology in Practice, 1987, 1995; Hemodilution Affects the Pressor Response to Norepinephrine, Co-author, 1987. Memberships: Vice President. Chinese Society of Anaesthesiology; Chairman, Liaoning Section, CSA; Chinese Medical Association. Hobbies: Swimming; Cycling; Cooking. Address: Affiliated First Hospital, China Medical University, 155 Nanjing N Street, Shenyang, Lioaning 110001, China.

SHEPHARD Robert Adrian, b. 12 Nov 1955, Ipswich, England. Academic. m. Shan Thomas, 23 Aug 1980. Education: BSc, Pharmacology, University of Leeds, 1976; PhD, Psychology, University of Birmingham, 1980; AFBPsS; C Psychol. Appointment: Senior Lecturer in Psychology, University of Ulster, Ireland. Publications: Many articles in professional journals including: Psychopharmacology; Neuropharmacology; Pharmacology, Biochemistry and Behaviour; Life Sciences; European Journal of Pharmacology; Behavior Genetics; Physiology and Behavior. Membership: Associate Fellow, British Psychological Society. Hobbies: Chess; Weight Training. Address: Dept of Psychology, University of Ulster at Jordanstown, Newtown Abbey, Northern Ireland, BT37 0QB.

SHEPHERD John Henry, b. 11 July 1948, Enfield, Middlesex, England. Registered Medical Practitioner. m. Alison Sheila, 27 May 1972, 1 son, 2 daughters. Education: MB BS; FRCS; MRCOG; FACOG. Appointments: Consultant Surgeon, Chelsea Hospital for Women; Gynaecological Oncology Fellow, University of South Florida, Tampa, Florida, USA; Consultant Gynaecological Surgeon and Oncologist, St Bartholomew's Hospital and The Royal Marsden Hospital, London, England. Publications: Clinical Gynaecological Oncology Blackwell Scientific, Co-Editor, 1990; Contributor of numerous articles and book chapters on gynaecological cancer and surgery. Honours: Gold Medal, MRCOG Examination, 1978; Fulbright-Hays Scholarship, 1979. Memberships: Society of Pelvic Surgeons; Society of Gynaecologic Oncologists; British Gynaecological Cancer Society. Hobbies: Skiing; Sailing; Beethoven; Opera. Address: 149 Harley Street, London W1N 2DH, England.

SHEPHERD Robert Keith, b. 13 Sep 1953, Victoria, Australia. Scientist. m. Ursula Schuster, 25 Jan 1975, 1 s, 1 d. Education: BSc, Deakin University; DipEd, Hawthorn State College; PhD, University of Melbourne; Diploma of Applied Science. Career: Research Fellow, currently, Senior Research Fellow, Department of Otolaryngology, University of Melbourne. Publications: Senior Author, Electrical Stimulation of the Auditory Nerve: Effect of electrode placement on neural excitation, in Hearing Research, 1993; Senior Author, Deaf Animal Models, in Hearing Research, 1994. Memberships: Australian Neuroscience Society; Association of Research in Otolaryngology; New York Academy of Sciences; Victorian Tinnitus Association. Hobbies: Camping; Reading; Bush Walking; Squash; Cycling. Address: 50 Monash Avenue, Ascot Vale, Victoria 3032, Australia.

SHEPS Cecil George, b. 24 July 1913, Winnipeg, Manitoba, Canada. Doctor of Medicine. m. Ann Mann, Aug 1973, 2 sons. Education: MD, University of Manitoba, 1936; MPH, Yale University, 1947. Appointments: Professor of Social Medicine, University of North Carolina, Chapel Hill, 1947-53; General Director, Beth Israel Hospital & Clinic, 1953-60; Professor of Preventive Medicine, Harvard Medical School, 1960-65; Professor of Medicine & Hospital Administration & Director of Program in this field, Graduate School of Public Health, University of Pittsburgh. Publications: The Sick Citadel: The American Academic Medical Center and the Public Interest, 1983. Honours: Miles Award for Scientific Achievement, Canadian Public Health Association, 1970; Louis Gorin Award, National Rural Health Association, 1985; Duncan Clark Award, Association of Teachers of Preventive Medicine, 1988; Sedgwick Memorial Medal, American Public Health Association, 1990. Memberships: American Public Health Association; Institute of Medicine, National Academy of Sciences. Address: Sheps Center for Health Services Research, University of North Carolina at Chapel Hill, 725 Airport Road, CB# 7590, Chapel Hill, NC 27599-7590, USA.

SHERMAN Charles Daniel, b. 10 May 1920, Avon Park, FL, USA. Surgeon. m. Jean Reibling, 13 Aug 1943, 2 s, 1 d. Education: BS, University of FL, 1942; MD, Johns Hopkins University, 1945; Fellowship in Surgery, Memorial Sloan Kettering, 1950-51. Career includes: President, Monroe City Cancer Association, 1961-65; Secretary-Treasurer, Health Council of Monroe City, 1970-73; NYS Cancer Program Association President, 1970; Clinical Professor of Surgery, University of Rochester School of Medicine and Dentistry, 1970-; Councillor, 1970-80, Assistant Treasurer, 1980-84, NY State Medical Society; President, NY State Medical Society, 1988-89; Chair, Professional Education, UICC, 1986-94; Currently, Head, Surgical Oncology, Highland Hospital, Rochester. Publications include: Numerous papers, books and chapters, lectures, demonstrations and exhibits including: Clinical Oncology: A Manual for Students and Doctors, 2nd edition, 1978; Co-editor and contributor, Concepts in Cancer Medicine, 1983; Editor, Revised Directory of Oncologists, 1983. Honours: Phi Beta Kappa; Phi Kappa Phi; Alpha Omega Alpha; Phi Eta Sigma; Fulbright Grant, University of Mendoza, Argentina, 1963; Edward Speno Award in Health Education, NY State Public Health Association, 1973; Edward Mott Moore Award, Monroe County Medical Society, 1978; Honorary Professor Extraordinario, University of Salvador, Buenos Aires, 1982. Memberships include: American Board of Surgery; American College of Surgeons; American Radium Society; Royal Society of Surgeons; NY Academy of Science; President, 1976, American Association for Cancer Education; American Society for Preventive Oncology. Hobbies: Music; Squash. Address: Highland Hospital, 1000 South Avenue at Bellevue, Rochester, NY 14620, USA.

SHERMAN Donald J, b. 18 Mar 1934, Philadelphia, Pennsylvania, USA. Physician. m. Elaine Schwartz, 21 Dec 1958, 1 son, 2 daughters. Education: BA, Temple University, 1955; MD, Hahnemann University, 1959; Certified in Occupation Medicine, American Board of Preventive Medicine. Appointments: Plant Physician, Ford Motor Company Automotive Assembly Plant, Edison, New Jersey; Physician-in-Charge, Central Medical Services, Ford Motor Company, Dearborn, Michigan; Director, Occupational Medicine, Henry Ford Hospital, Detroit; Associate Medical Director, BP America, Cleveland, Ohio; Corporate Medical Director, The Goodyear Tire & Rubber Company. Publications: Carpal Tunnel Syndrome: Biomechanical Aspects of the Occupational Etiology and Implications Regarding Surgical Management, Co-author, 1978. Honours: Distinguished Service Awards: Michigan Occupational Medical Association; Middlesex County, New Jersey, Medical Society. Memberships: Fellow, American College of Occupational and Environmental Medicine; Fellow, American College of Preventive Medicine; American Medical Association; Ohio State Medical Association; Cleveland Academy of Medicine; Tri-State Occupational Medical Association. Address: 1144 E Market Street, Akron, OH 44316, USA.

SHETH Ketan Kumudchandra, b. 20 Apr 1962, Rome, Italy. Physician. m. Tanuja R Sheth, 14 June 1987, 2 daughters. Education: AB, Chemistry, Duke University, Durham, North Carolina, USA, 1983; MD, 1987, Fellow, Allergy, Immunology, 1990-92, University of Wisconsin Medical School, Madison; Internship, Residency, Paediatrics, Children's Hospital Medical Center, Cincinnati, Ohio, 1987-90; Certifications: American Board of Pediatrics, 1990; American Board of Allergy and Immunology, 1993. Appointments: Director, Paediatric Allergy, Arnett Clinic, Lafayette, Indiana, USA, 1992-. Publications include: Co-author: Pathogenesis of Asthma, 1991; Dissociation of Pulmonary Late Allergic Responses and Airway Hyperresponsiveness by Treatment with Dexamethasone, 1991; Asthma in the Adolescent and Adult, 1992; Cellular Mechanisms of Nocturnal Asthma: The Role of the Eosinophil, Neutrophil and Mast Cell, 1993; Respiratory Tract Infections and Asthma, 1994; Reversal of Persistent Post-Bronchiolitis Airway Abnormalities with Dexamethasone in Rats, 1994. Memberships: Fellow, American Academy of Pediatrics; American Academy of Allergy and Immunology; Associate Member, American Thoracic Society; American College of Allergy and Immunology; State Medical Society of Indiana; Tippecanoe County Medical Society; Advisory Boards: National Faculty, New Developments in Bronchodilator Therapy; American Lung Association, Indiana West Central Region; Editorial Board, Current Allergy Practice. Address: Arnett Clinic, 1500 Salem Street, Lafayette, IN 47904, USA.

SHETH Rekha, b. 25 Jan 1946, Bombay, India. Dermatologist. m. Ashit Sheth, 22 Jan 1971, 2 sons. Education: MD; DVD. Appointment: Practising Dermatologist. Publications: Hair & Nutrition, 1979; Indigenous Cosmetics of India, 1979; Dandruff Assessment & Management, 1984; Cosmetics in Dermatology. Memberships: Indian Association of Dermatology & Venereology; International Society of Dermatology; American Academy of Dermatology. Hobbies: Swimming. Address: 105 Maker Bhavan 3, New Marine Lines, Bombay 400 020, India.

SHEVIN Frederick F, b. 15 Nov 1921. MD; Psychoanalyst. m. Helen Dante, 22 Dec 1945, 2 s, 1 d. Education: BS; MD; Certified, American Psychoanalytic Association. Career: Private Practice. Publication: Countertransference, in Journal of American Psychoanalytic Association, 1963. Honour: Ira Miller Essay Award, Michigan Psychoanalytic Society, 1963. Memberships include: American Psychoanalytic Association; International Psychoanalytic Association. Hobbies: Theatre; Films. Address: 31151 Sunset, Franklin, MI 18025, USA.

SHI Airong, b. 9 Feb 1925, Shandong, China. Professor. m. Zhou Jiayin, 17 Feb 1952, 1 son, 1 daughter. Education: BS, Fu-Ren Catholic University, Beijing, 1949; Yale Medical College, Changsha, China, 1951. Appointments: Vice Director, Laboratory of Neuroendocrinological Histochemistry, 1982; Professor, Histology and Embryology, 1985; Supervisor of Graduate Students, Beijing Medical University, 1981. Publications: Books Co-author: The Effects of Lecithin on Tissues, 1963; Gastroenterology, 1993; 40 Papers: Morphological Studies of the Hypophysis-adrenal Cortex Axis and Gastroenteropancreatic (GEP) Endocrine Cells During Experimental Gastric Ulcer, 1982-94; Immunocytochemical Localization of Islet Amyloid Polypepticle in GEP System, 1993-94; Insulin mRNA Expression, 1994. Honours: 1st and 3rd

Awards of Gansu, Scientific Achievement, 1981; 2nd and 3rd Awards of Hebei, Scientific Progress, 1990, China. Memberships: Chinese Anatomical Society; Associate Editor, Acta Anatomica Sinica; Committee, Histology & Embryology; Editorial Board, Chinese Journal of Histochemistry Cytochemistry. Hobbies: Painting. Address: Department of Histology & Embryology, Beijing Medical University, Xueyuan Lu, Beijing 100083, China.

SHI De, b. 31 Aug 1935, Shanghai, China. Surgeon. m. Professor Wu Qing-ling, 31 Dec 1966, 2 sons. Education: MD, Shanghai Medical University, 1959. Appointments: Lecturer, 1980-86, Associate Professor, 1987-90, Professor, 1991-, Surgeon of General and Vascular Surgery, First Hospital, Chongqing University of Medical Sciences. Publications: Alimentary Canal Disease, Co-author, 19877; Principle of Outpatient Management, CO-author, 1991; Contributor of over 30 articles. Honours: 3rd Class Prize, 1989, 1st Class, 1992, 2nd Class, 1994, China. Memberships: Vice Chairman, Society of Surgery of Sichuan Branch, Chinese Medical Association; Chairman, Society of Surgery of Chongqing Branch, CMA. Hobbies: Music; Cinema. Address: First Hospital of Chongqing University of Medical Sciences, Chongqing 630042, China.

SHI Hongyu, b. 28 June 1968, Yichun, Heilongjiang, China. Surgeon. m. Zhao Xin, 5 July 1993. Education: MB. Appointments: Surgeon. Publications: Damage of Thoracic and Abdomen in Diagnosis and Treatment, 1994. Memberships: Chinese Medical Association. Hobbies: Reading; Running; Singing. Address: department Thoracic Surgery, The Affiliated Hospital Jiamusi Medical College, Jiamusi, Heilongjiang 154002, China.

SHI Junnan, b. 16 Sept 1919, Yixing City, Jiangsu Province, China. Dentist. m. Xinzhang Ma, 13 Nov 1937, 3 sons, 2 daughters. Education: BA, National Central University, China, 1948. Appointments: Professor of Dental Operative Dentistry and Endodontics. Publications: Dental Pulpology, 1955; Dental Thereopitics, 1986. Honours: Visiting Professor, School of Dentistry, Meikai University, Japan; Chinese Science Progress Award, 3rd level, 1988. Memberships: Head of Division of Operative Dentistry and Endodontics, Chinese Stomatogical Association. Hobby: Playing the Erhu (a Chinese traditional instrument). Address: College of Stomatology, Fourth Military Med University, Xian 710032, Shaanxi, China.

SHI Renfang, b. 29 Nov 1955, Dandong, Liaoning, China. Anaesthesiologist. m. 8 Jan 1983, 1 daughter. Education: MD. Appointments: House Officer, 1982-88; Registrar, 1988-94; Junior Consultant, 1994-95. Publications: Effects of H1 and H2 Receptor Blockers on Revension of Cardiovascular Adverse Reactions of Protamine, 1994. Membership: Chinese Medical Association. Hobby: Swimming. Address: Department of Anaesthesia, Liaoning Province Tumour Hospital Shenyang 110042, China.

SHI Shu-Jun, b. 7 Aug 1932, Shenyang, China. Professor of Prosthodontics; Dentist. m. Zhou Hong, 1964, 2 daughters. Education: DDS, Beijing Medical University, 1957. Appointments: Resident Doctor, 1957; Doctor in charge, 1972; Head, Dental Department, 1st Attached Hospital, 1978, Chairman, Faculty of Stomatology, 1984-; Director Doctor, 1987-, Professor, 1991-, Tianjin Medical University; Dean, Dental Hospital, Tianjin Medical University. Publications: Emergency in Dentistry, 1974; Conservative treatment in patients with poor crown and roots, 1981; Synthesis and Investigation of New Type Casting Glass Ceramic, 1991; Stress Distribution of Tilt Abutment Teeth in the Periodontum, 1992. Honours: 2nd Class Science Award, Chinese Ministry of Public Health, 1982; 1st Class Science and Invention Award, 1982; 3rd Class Science Awards, Tianjin Municipality, 1985, 1993. Memberships: Vice-President, Tianjin Chapter of Stomatology, Chinese Medical Association; Fellow, International College of Dentistry; Council Member, Tianjin Biomedical and Engineering Association. Hobbies: Swimming; Skating. Address: Department of Stomatology, Tianjin Medical University, Tianjin 300070, China.

SHI ShuiSheng, b. 16 Sept 1937, Hebei, China. Senior Medical Doctor of Surgery. m ShiYuan Zheng, 12 Feb 1967, Tianjin, China. 1 son, 1 daughter. Education: MD, Tianjin University of Medical Sciences, 1963. Appointments: Chief Surgeon, Zhuhai Poeple's Hospital; Chairman, Chinese Society of Surgery, Zhuhai Branch; Vice-Chairman, The Research Institute of Acute Abdominal Diseases, Guangdong Branch; Vice-Chairman, The Research Institute of Hepatic Cancer, Guangdong; Editor, Clinics in Hepato-Biliary Pancreatic and Splenic

Surgery; Editor, Chinese Journal of Surgery of Integration of Traditional and Western Medicine. Publications: The Advancement of the Integration of Traditional and Western Medicine on Acute Abdominal Diseases, 1983; Coroli's Disease Complicated by Choledochal Stenosis, 1987; Surgical Treatment of Cholecystolithiasis and Cholecystitis, 1994; Co-author: The Diagnosis of Acute Abdominal Diseases, 1981; Treatment of Common Acute Abdominal Diseases with Traditional and Western Medicine, 1982; A Handbook of Diagnosis and Surgical Treatment of Common Diseases, 1984; Practices of Abdominal Surgery, 1990. Honours: 1st Place for book Treatment of Common Acute Abdominal Diseases with Traditional and Western Medicine, National Excellent Technology and Science Publications Annual Competition, 1982. Memberships: Chinese Medical Association; Chinese Association of Integration of Traditional and Western Medicine; Society of Surgery. Address: 21-301 QianJin Street, Xiangzhou, Zhuhai, China.

SHI Yangshan, b. 17 Mar 1931, Shanghai, China. Professor. m. Jinlin Li, 1974, 2 sons, 4 daughters. Appointments: Vice Director, Shanghai Huangpu Area Centre Hospital; Director, Shanghai Huangpu Traditional Chinese Medicine Hospital. Memberships: Vice Chairman, Shanghai Huangpu Area, Chinese People's Political Consultative Conference. Hobbies: Music; Peking Opera; Reading. Address: Shanghai Huangpu traditional Chinese Medicine Hospital, 130 Bei Jing Road (W), Shanghai 200003, China.

SHI Yongming, b. 27 May 1929, Rushan, Shandong, China. Professor of Rehabilitation Medicine. m. Zu Qi, 8 February 1954, 1 son, 3 daughters. Education: MD, Shandong Medical University, 1952. Physiatrist, Beijing Soviet Union Hospital, class for Advanced Studies, 1955. Appointments: Professor, Rehabilitation Medicine, Affiliated Hospital of Shandong Medical University. Publications: Mineral bath and ultraviolet treated Psoriasis, 1958; Mineral mud and ultraviolet treated Dermatoneuritis, 1959; Treatment of Hyperosteogeny by vineger iontophoresis, 1961; Effect of mineral mud on patients with circulation function, 1981; Electrodiagnosis and impulse current therapy for nerve injuries, 1980; Effect of pain by square wave, 1988; Effect of He-Ne laser and Exponential curve current on nerve injuries, 1988. Memberships: Committee Member, Society of Physical Medicine and Rehabilitation, Chinese Medical Association; Council, Shandong Medical Association; Chairman, Society of Physical Medicine and Rehabilitation, Shandong; Council, Association of Rehabilitation Medicine, China Deformity Union; Council, Society of Shandong Rehabilitation Medicine; Chairman, Society of Physiotherapy and Exercise of Shandong. Address: No 107 Wenhua West Road, Jinan 250012, China.

SHI Yu-Wu, b. 12 Sep 1925, Jiangsu Province, China. Professor of Anesthesiology. m. Ren-Xin Chen, 26 Jan 1954, 1 d. Education includes: BS, Biology, Yenching University, Peking, 1950; MD, Peking Union Medical College, 1954. Appointments: Teaching Assistant and Resident, Surgery Department, 1954-56, Teaching Assistant and Resident, Anesthesiology Department, 1956-63, Lecturer and Visiting Physician, Anesthesiology Department, 1963-80, Deputy Director, Anesthesiology Department, 1979-87, Associate Professor, Anesthesiology Department, 1980-84, Xijing Hospital, 4th Military Hospital Medical University, Xian; Associate Professor, 1984-87, Professor and Chief Anesthetist, 1987-, Director of Department, 1987-90, all Anesthesiology Department, Nanfang Hospital, 1st Military Medical University, Guangzhou; Currently, Advisory Board of Anesthesiology, 1990-. Publications include: Co-author, Modern Anesthesiology, 1987, 2nd edition, submitted 1994; 34 Professional articles published. Memberships: Executive Committee, 1979-84; Executive Committee of the Chinese Anesthesiology Society, 1979-84; Vice Chairman, Chapter of Shanxi Province of the Chinese Anesthesiology Society, 1979-84, Executive Committee, Anesthesiology Society of PLA, 1962-; Editorial Board: Journal of Chinese Anesthesiology, 1979-84; Foreign Medicine-Section of Anesthesiology and Resusitation, 1979-91, Executive Editor, 1991-; Journal of Clinical Anesthesiology, 1986-. Hobby: Music. Address: Department of Anesthesiology, Nanfang Hospital, Guangzhou 510515, China.

SHI Yuhua, b. 9 Jan 1926. Professor of Traditional Chinese Medicine. m. Mao Zeng Rong, 19 Aug 1952, 1 s, 1 d. Education: Graduate, Zhong Zheng University, 1949. Appointments: Worked at Department of Histology and Embryology for more than 44 years, studying, Nourishing Kidney Herbs; Currently, Professor of Shanghai University of Traditional Chinese Medicine. Publications: Co-author of over 30 original academic papers. Honours: 14 Awards including: Shanghai Municipality, 2nd Prize, for Science and Technology Progress, 1987; Ministry Level, 2nd Prize, for Science and Technology Progress,

State Education Commission, 1988, 1989; Shanghai Municipality Level Prize for Distinguished Women, 1988; Shanghai Excellent Worker of Education, 1989; Ministry Level, 2nd Prize, for Science and Technology Progress, National Administration of Traditional Chinese Medicine, 1992; Shanghai Municipality, 3rd Prize, for Science and Technology Progress, 1990; Outstanding Worker of Science and Technology of Nationwide Institutions of Higher Learning, State Education Commission and State Science and Technology Commission.

SHI Yunfeng, b. 17 Nov 1923, Hebei, China. Professor. m. Su Jingfang, Jan 1946, 2 sons, 2 daughters. Education: MD, Medical University of Bethune, China; MD, Department of Aviation Physiology, Kupov Medical College, Leningrad, Russia. Appointments: Director, 2nd Rear Hospital; Vice Director, Space-Medico-Engineering Institute, Beijing; President, Honour President, Somatic Science Academy of China. Publications: Astonishment 99 Parapsychology, 1993; Brilliant Prospect of Somatic Science and its Application in Research, 1995. Honours: National Scientific & Technological Progress Award, 1986. Memberships: Space Medico-Engineering Committee, Chinese Society of Astronautics; Somatic Science Association of China; Somatic Science Academy of China; Research Association of Haidian Somatic Science, Beijing. Address: PO Box 5104 (31), Beijing 100094, China.

SHIAU Edwin, b. 13 Dec 1934, Bangkok, Thailand. Pathologist. m. Peta Shiau, 13 Sept 1978, 2 sons, 2 daughters. Education: BSc (Hons), MD, CM, McGill University, Canada; FRCPC. Appointments: Currently Pathologist, Royal Columbian Hospital, New Westminster, British Columbia, Canada. Memberships: British Columbia Medical Association; BCALP; PNSP; ASCP; NAME; Canadian Association of Neuropathologists; International Society of Neuropathology. Hobbies: Badminton; Tennis; Photography; Philately; Rhododendrons. Address: 3362 Darwin Avenue, Coquitlam, British Columbia, Canada V3B 7M9.

SHIELDS Robert (Sir), b. 8 Nov 1930, Paisley, Scotland. Surgery. m. Grace Marianne Swinburn, 19 Jan 1957, 1 son, 2 daughters. Education: MD, University of Glasgow, Scotland; FRCSE; FRCS. Career: House Officer, Western Infirmary, Glasgow; Fellow, Mayo Foundation, New York, USA; Lecturer in Surgery, University of Glasgow; Senior Lecturer/Reader in Surgery, Welsh National School of Medicine, Cardiff; Professor of Surgery, University of Liverpool; President, Royal College of Surgeons of England. Publications: Surgical Management, 1984; Gastrointestinal Emergencies 2, 1982; Gastrointestinal Emergencies, 1992; Clinical Gastroenterology: Portal Hypertension, 1992. Honours: Knight Bachelor, 1990; Deputy Lord Lieutenant of Merseyside, 1991. Memberships: President and Member of Council, The Royal College of Surgeons of Edinburgh; Surgical Research Society. Hobbies: Walking; Reading. Address: 81 Meols Drive, West Kirby, Wirral L48 5DF, England.

SHIGEOKA Ann O'Neill, b. 18 Jan 1947, Philadelphia, PA, USA. Medicine. m. John W Shigeoka, MD, 4 Jul 1971, 2 d. Education: BS, PA State University; MD, Jefferson College of Medicine; Board Certified in Pediatrics and Pediatric Hematology and Oncology. Appointment: Associate Professor of Pediatrics, University of Utah School of Medicine, Salt Lake City. Publications: Co-author, Protective efficacy of hybridoma type-specific IgM against experimental group B strep, in Journal of Infectious Diseases, 1984; Regional localization of a novel X-linked immunodeficiency to Wiskott-Aldrich locks, 1993. Memberships: Society for Pediatric Research; American Federation for Clinical Research; American Society for Pediatric Hematology-Oncology; American Academy of Pediatrics. Hobbies: Swimming; Skiing; Horseback Riding; Hiking. Address: Department of Pediatrics, University of Utah Hospital, 50 North Medical Drive, Salt Lake City, UT 84132, USA.

SHIMADAS Toru, b. 31 May 1959, Tokyo, Japan. Entomologist. Education includes: PhD, University of Tokyo, 1987. Appointments: Research Entomologist, Department of Medical Entomology, National Institute of Health, Japan; Currently Assistant Professor, Department of Agrobiology, University of Tokyo. Publications: Polymorphism and linkage analysis of the prothoracicotropic hormone gene in the silkmoth Bombyx mori (with T Hasegawa, K Matsumoto, N Agui, M Kobayashi), 1994. Honours: Award for Promotion of Sericultural Science, 1993. Memberships: Japanese Society of Sanitary Zoology; Japan Molecular Biology Society. Address: Department of Agrobiology, University of Tokyo, Yayoi, Bunkyo-ku, Tokyo 113, Japan.

SHIMBERG Elaine Fantle, b. 26 Feb 1937, Yankton, SD, USA. Writer. m. Mandell Shimberg, 10 Jan 1961, 3 s, 2 d. Education: BS; MS,

Health and Human Services. Career: Writer; TV appearances and numerous national and local radio talk shows; Many writing workshops and speeches given. Publications include: Books: Teenage Drinking and Driving: A Deadly Duo, 1984, Relief from IBS: Irritable Bowel Syndrome, 1988, paperback, 1991, German edition, 1991, Strokes: What Families Should Know, 1990, Depression: What Families Should Know, 1992, Tourette Syndrome: Understanding and Coping with TS, due 1995; Coping with Tourette Syndrome: A Parent's Viewpoint, booklet, 1979, 2nd edition, 1981, 3rd edition, 1983, revised edition, 1993; How to Avoid Injury in Youth Sports, booklet, 1985; Many articles in various journals. Honours: Co-winner, FL Hospital Association's Public Relations and Media Awards for seminar and booklet, 1985; National Honour Citation for booklet, Living in a Strange World, American Cancer Society; Best Lay Medical Books for Public Libraries for, Relief from IBS, Library Journal, 1988-89; Finalist, June Roth Memorial Award for Medical Journalism, for Gifts of Time, 1994. Memberships: American Society of Journalists and Authors; American Medical Writers' Association; National Association of Science Writers; St Joseph's Health Services Ethics Committee, 1993-98 and Hospital Board, 1993-98; Council on Ethical and Judicial Affairs, FL Medical Association, 1993-98. Address: 100 South Ashley Drive, Suite 820, Tampa, FL 33602, USA.

SHIMIZU Yukiko, b. 3 Mar 1951, Hiroshima, Japan. Statistical Epidemiologist. Education: BA, 1973, Doctor of Medical Science, 1982, Hiroshima University. Appointment: Assistant Chief, Department of Epidemiology, Radiation Effects Research Foundation, Hiroshima. Publications: Studies of the mortality of A-Bomb survivors. 9. Mortality, 1950-1985: Part 2. Cancer mortality based on the recently-revised doses (DS86) in Radiation Research, 1990; Cancer risk among atomic bomb survivors. The RERF Life Span Study in J. American Medical Association, 1990. Memberships: Japan Radiation Research Society; Japan Statistical Society; Japanese Society of Public Health; Japanese Society of Hygiene; Japan Epidemiological Association. Hobby: Tea ceremony. Address: Radiation Effects Research Foundation, 5-2 Hijiyama Park, Minami-ku, Hiroshima 732, Japan.

SHIN Tae Ho, b. 18 Sep 1927, Hamkyungbookdo, Korea. Acupuncturist. m. Bong Sook Lee, 27 May 1945, 3 s, 2 d. Education: Graduate, Hambook Chunjin Industrial High School; Acupuncturist. Appointments: Acupuncturist; Chairman, Korean Acupuncture Association. Publications: 6 Publications including: Diagnosis and Healing. Honours: Elected to Chairman: Seoul Acupuncture Association, 1976, Korean Acupuncture Association, 1992. Membership: WFAS. Address: 276-10 Suckchon-Dong, Songpo-Ku, Seoul.

SHIRES George Thomas, b. 22 Nov 1925, Waco, TX, USA. Surgeon; Physician; Educator. m. Robbie Jo Martin, MD, 1948, 1 s, 2 d. Education: MD, University of TX, Dallas, 1948. Career includes: Surgeon in Chief, New York Hospital, NY, 1975-91; Lewis Atterbury Stimson Professor and Chairman, Department of Surgery, 1975-91, Stephen and Suzanne Weiss Dean and Provost for Medical Affairs, 1987-91, Adjunct Professor of Surgery, 1991-, Cornell University Medical College; Professor of Surgery and Chairman, Texas Tech University Health Sciences Center, Lubbock, TX, 1991-. Publications include: Editorial Board, American Journal of Surgery, 1968-; Associate Editor, Advances in Surgery, volumes IX and X, 1974-; Editorial Board, Archives of Surgery, 1977-; Over 300 manuscripts and abstracts, 100 chapters in books and over 50 books including: Co-author, Advances in Surgery, volume 26, 1993; Co-editor, Surgical Intensive Care, 1993; Co-author, Principles of Surgery, 6th edition, 1993. Honours include: Many Honorary Memberships and Fellowships; Dr Roswell Park Medal for Eminent Service to Profession and Humanity, Buffalo Surgical Society, 1975; Distinguished Achievement Award, American Trauma Society, 1981; Sheen Award for The Outstanding Doctor of Medical Science in US, 1985; Harvey Stuart Allen Distinguished Service Award, American Burn Association, 1988; Robert Danis Prize, International Surgical Society, Hong Kong, 1993. Memberships include: Numerous offices, American Board of Surgeons; American Burn Association; AMA; ASA; Founder, Digestive Disease Foundation; NY Academy of Medicine; NY Academy of Sciences. Address: Surgery, Texas Tech University, Health Sciences Center, 3601, 41st Street, Lubbock, TX 79430, USA.

SHIZGAL Harry Morris, b. 23 Jun 1938, Montreal, Canada. Surgeon. m. Wendy Fine, 7 Dec 1990, 1 s, 2 d. Education: BSc, 1st Class Honours, Physics and Physiology, 1959, PhD, 1963, McGill University. Career includes: Assistant Professor, 1971-77, Associate Professor, 1977-80, Professor of Surgery, 1980-, Associate Member, Nutrition and Food Science Centre, 1984-, McGill University; Senior Surgeon, 1984-,

Acting Director, Research Institute, 1984, Director, Research Institute, 1985-, Attending Physician, Palliative Care Service, 1990-, Royal Victoria Hospital. Publications include: Associate Editor, Nutrition and Cancer, 1977-; Reviewer for 9 professional journals; Numerous book chapters, papers, abstracts and letters, lectures and presentations, including: Co-author, Peripheral amino acids, in Total Parenteral Nutrition, 2nd edition, 1991; Author, Parenteral and Enteral Feeding, in Annual Review of Medicine, 1991; Author, Body composition in acute disease, in Shock, in press. Honours include: Centennial Fellow, Medical Research Council of Canada, 1970-71; James IV Traveller Fellowship, 1984. Memberships include: AAAS; American College of Surgery; American Society for Clinical Nutrition; American Surgical Association; Canadian Association for Advancement of Computers in Health; Canadian Critical Care Society; Osler Reporting Society; Fellow, Royal College of Physicians and Surgeons of Canada. Address: Royal Victoria Hospital, 687 Pine Avenue West, Montreal, Quebec, Canada, H3A 1A1.

SHOKER Ahmed Said, b. 9 Feb 1952, Cairo, Egypt. Physician. 1 s, 2 d. Education: MD; FRCPC. Career: Physician; Currently, Head, Division of Nephrology and Director, Transplant Program; Assistant Professor. Publications: The Sensitized Patient: A single centre study, Clinical Transplants UCLA Tissue Typing Laboratory, chapter 19, 1988. Address: Division of Nephrology, Department of Medicine, Royal University Hospital, Saskatoon, SK S7N 0X0, Canada.

SHOPE Robert E, b. 21 Feb 1929, Princeton, NJ, USA. Physician. m. Virginia Barbour, 27 Dec 1958, 2 s, 2 d. Education: BA, Cornell University, 1951; MD, Cornell Medical College, 1954. Career: Intern, 1954-55, Resident, 1957-58, Internal Medicine, Grace-New Haven Hospital; Captain, Medical Corps, US Army, Kuala Lumpur, Malaya, 1955-57; Staff, Rockefeller Foundation, Belem, Brazil, 1958-65; Assistant, Associate Professor, 1965-75, Professor, 1975-, Yale University School of Medicine; Director, Yale Arbovirus Research Unit, 1972-. Publications: Over 150 including: Emerging Infections, 1992. Honour: Walter Reed Medal, American Society of Tropical Medicine and Hygiene, 1993. Memberships: American Society of Tropical Medicine and Hygiene; American Society for Virology; American Epidemiological Society; American Academy of Microbiology; Infectious Diseases Society of America. Hobby: Travel. Address: Yale Arbovirus Research Unit, Box 208034, NewHaven, CT 06520-8034, USA.

SHORT Elizabeth Meehan, b. 2 June 1942, Boston, Massachusetts, USA. Physician. m. 21 Dec 1975, 3 daughters. Education includes: MD cum laude, Yale University School of Medicine, 1968; Postdoctoral Fellowships, 1968-75. Appointments include: Assistant Professor, 1975-83, Assistant Dean, Student Affairs, 1978-90, Associate Dean, Student Affairs, Medical Education, 1980-83, Stanford University School of Medicine; Staff Physician, Palo Alto Veterans Medical Center, Stanford, 1975-80; Visiting Professor, Human Biology, Stanford University, 1983-86; Director, Division of Biomedical Research and Faculty Development, Deputy Director, Department of Academic Affairs, 1983-87, Deputy Director, Biomedical Research, 1987-88, Association of American Medical Colleges, Washington DC; Deputy Associate Chief Medical Director, Academic Affairs, 1988-92, Associate Chief Medical Director, Academic Affairs, 1992-. Department of Veterans Affairs, Washington DC. Publications: Articles and book chapters including: Evidence for X-Linked Inheritance of Ornithine Transcarbamylase Deficiency, 1973; Genetic Hyperammonemias, 1977; The Role of Abstracts and Meeting Presentations in the Communication of Scientific Information, 1982; Fetal Research and Fetal Tissue Research, 1988; Hyperuricemia and Gout, 1992; Medical Education and the Department of Veterans Affairs. Honours include: Phi Beta Kappa, 1962; Alpha Omega Alpha, 1967. Memberships: American Federation for Clinical Research, National Council and Executive Committee 1976-84; American Council for Human Genetics, Public Policy Committee Chair 1986-; American Association of Women in Science; American Association for the Advancement of Science; American Society of Bone and Mineral Metabolism; Western Society for Clinical Investigation; California Academy of Medicine. Address: Department of Veterans Affairs, 810 Vermont Avenue (14), Washington, DC 20420, USA.

SHORTER Nicholas Andrew, b. 14 Oct 1953, London, England. Paediatric Surgery. m. Sally Jo Trued, 28 Aug 1982, 2 s, 1 d. Education: AB, Harvard College, Cambridge, MA, 1975; AM, Harvard University, Cambridge, MA, 1975; MD, Johns Hopkins University, Baltimore, MD, 1979. Career: Intern and Resident, surgery, Johns Hopkins Hospital, 1979-85; Research Fellow, Children's Hospital Medical Centre, Boston, MA, 1982-83; Resident in Paediatric Surgery, Children's Hospital of

Philadelphia, 1985-87; Attending Surgeon, Duke University Medical Centre, Durham, NC and Assistant Professor of Paediatric Surgery and Paediatrics, Duke University, 1987-91; Currently: Associate Professor of Surgery and Paediatrics, Dartmouth Medical School, and Director of Paediatric Surgical Services, Dartmouth-Hitchcock Medical Centre, Lebanon, NH. Publications include: Many publications, book chapters and abstracts, including: Co-author, Suction drain injury in a public wading pool North Carolina, 1991; Co-author, Autoregulation of Neuroblastoma growth by vasoactive intestinal peptide, in Journal of Paediatric Surgery, 1992. Honours: Cum Laude Society, 1970; Phi Beta Kappa, 1979; Alpha Omega Alpha, 1979. Memberships: Fellow, American College of Surgeons; Speciality Fellow, American Academy of Pediatrics; American Pediatric Surgical Association; Fellow, Southeastern Surgical Congress; International Society of Paediatric Oncology; Founding Member, International Society of Paediatric Surgical Oncology; American Association for Cancer Research; Association for Academic Surgery. Hobby: Collecting US Political Memorabilia. Address: Department of Surgery, Dartmouth-Hitchcock Medical Center, Lebanon, NH 03756, USA.

SHORTRIDGE Kennedy Francis, b. 6 Apr 1941, Mt Isa, Queensland, Australia. Microbiologist. m. Dilys Roberts, 10 Sep 1966, 1 son, 2 daughters. Education: BSc, University of Queensland, 1962; PhD, University College Hospital Medical School, University of London, 1971; CBiol; FIBiol, Institute of Biology, London, 1985; Certificate, Art Conservation and Restoration, University of Hong Kong, 1991. Appointments: Bacteriologist, Royal Brisbane Hospital, Queensland, 1963-64; Lecturer, Department of Bacteriology, University College Medical School, London, England, 1965-71; Senior Lecturer, 1972-76, Reader, 1976-81, Professor, 1981-, Department of Microbiology, University of Hong Kong. Publications: Avian influenza A viruses of Southern China and Hong Kong: Ecological aspects and implications for man, 1982; Pandemic influenza: a zoonosis?, 1992; Co-author: Persistence of Hong Kong influenza virus variants in pigs, 1977; An Influenza Epicentre?, 1982; The nucleoprotein as a possible major factor in determining host specificity of influenza H3N2 viruses, 1985; Rapid diagnosis of equine influenza by Directigen FLU-A enzyme immunoassay, 1994. Honours: Member, 1984-, Chairman, 1989-, Commonwealth Scholarship and Fellowship Plan Selection Committee; Member, UK/Hong Kong Scholarship Selection Committee, 1992-; Expert Consultant, Centers for Disease Control and Prevention, Atlanta, Georgia, USA, 1993; Adviser or Consultant, Ecology of Influenza Viruses, World Health Organization, on occasion. Memberships: Society for General Microbiology; Institute of Biology. Hobbies: Conservation of objects; Rotary International; Hockey. Address: Department of Microbiology, University of Hong Kong, Pathology Building, Queen Mary Hospital Compound, Hong Kong.

SHU Hui-Hua, b. 25 Nov 1938, Wuhan, China. Paediatrician. m. Mar 1972, 1 son, 1 daughter. Education: Bachelors degree, Tongji Medical University. Appointments: Resident, 1963-79, Attending Doctor, 1979-87, Vice Chief Doctor, 1987-93, Chief Doctor, 1993-, Vice Director, 1990-, Guangzhou Children's Hospital. Publications: Clinical Study of Abdominal Epilepsy, 1987; Clinical and Pathological Study of Nine Cases Aspergillosis of Central Nerve System, 1987; Study of Clinical Treatment and Misdiagnosis of 30 Cases Progressive Tics, 1994; Etiologic Analysis of 770 Cases in Child Neurological Rehabilitation Clinic, 1992; Intracranial Hemorrhage due to delayed Vitamin K Deficiency: Analysis of Head CT Scan and Head Type B Untrasound, 1989; Association of Trace Element Cu, Zn, Ca and Grand Mal, 1993; Combined Treatment with Chinese Traditional and Western Medicines in 266 Cases of Viral Encephalitis in Childhood; The Association of Multiple System Organ Failure with Childhood Central Nerve System Diseases: A Study of 409 Autopsy Cases. Membership: Vice President, Guangzhou Society of Paediatrics. Hobbies: Music; Singing. Address: Guangzhou Children's Hospital, 318 Renmin Road, Guangzhou, China.

SHU Si-Yun, b. 1 Aug 1937, Wuhang, China. Neurobiologist. Education: Medical Education, Fourth Military Medical University, 1954-60; MD, West Medical University of China, 1967. Appointments: Teaching Associate, 1960-63, Lecturer, 1967-82, Associate Professor, 1983-86, Fourth Military Medical University; Visiting Professor, USA, 1986-88; Professor of Neurobiology, Institute of Neurosciences, Xian, China, 1988-90; Professor of Neurobiology, Chairman of Department, Co-Director, Centre of Neuromedicine, Pearl River Hospital, Guangzhou, 1990-; Editor: Journal of Medical College of People's Liberation Army (English issue) and Journal of the First Medical University of People's Liberation Army, 1990-. Publications: About 150 papers relating to

research on the connection between the spinal cord and brain stem, degeneration and regeneration of the nervous system, the basal ganglia and the hypothalamus. Honours: 2nd Prize for Science and Technology, 1980, 1981, 1991, 3rd Prize, 1981, 1991, People's Liberation Army; National Distinguished Scientist, Chinese Government, 1992-; Guest Chairman, Department of Biochemistry, Guangzhou Pharmaceutical Industrial Research Institute, 1993-. Memberships: Chinese Society of Anatomy; Chinese Society of Cell Biology; Chinese Society of Immunology; Chinese Society of Electronmicroscopy; International Brain Research Organization; American Society for Neuroscience; Council Member, Chinese Paralysis Association, Xian Branch; Council Member, Chinese Neurobiochemistry Society. Address: Department of Neurobiology, Centre of Neuromedicine, Pearl River Hospital, Huangzhou 510282, China.

SHU Yu, b. 22 Nov 1930, Beijing, China. Chief Physician. m. Huang Nian Tang, 1 Oct 1958, 2 s. Education: Biology, Wuhan University, 1949-50; Bachelor of Medicine, Tongji Medical University, 1950-55; Visiting Scholar, Cleveland Clinic, OH, USA, 1982-83. Appointments: Resident Physician, 1955-60, Attending Physician, Lecturer, 1961-80, Vice Chief Physician, Associate Professor, 1981-86, Chief Physician, Professor of Cardiology, Chairman of Department of Cardiology, 1987-, Tongji Hospital. Publications: Choice of lasers for laser angioplasty, 1989; Photosensitizing effects of tetracycline, chlorophyll and hematoporaphyrin clerivativeson laserablation of atherosclerotic plaques, 1991; Clinical Cardiopathology, in press. Memberships: Deputy President, Cardiology Association, Hubei Branch; Chinese Medical Association; Chinese Society of Biomedical Engineering Council on Cardiac Pacing Technology. Hobbies: Music; Gardening. Address: Dept of Cardiology, Tongji Hospital, Tongji Medical University, 515 Jie Fang Da Dao, Wuhan, China.

SHULAN David Jay, b. 16 Jun 1951, Akron, OH, USA. Physician. m. Dr Mollie Shulan, 14 Mar 1982, 2 s. Education: BA, MS, Northwestern University; MD, Medical College of OH; Board Certified: American Board of Internal Medicine; American Board of Allergy and Immunology. Appointments: Research Assistant, Northwestern University Medical School, IL, 1974-77; Intern in Medicine, 1980-81, Resident, Internal Medicine, 1981-83, Evanston Hospital, IL; Fellow, Allergy-Immunology, University of IA, 1983-85; Teacher of Residents and Medical Students; Assistant Clinical Professor, Assistant Attending, Albany Medical College, NY; Assistant Attending, St Peter's Hospital, Albany, NY; Currently, Attending Physician Certified Allergy Consultants; Attending Physician, Albany Allergy and Asthma Services. Publications: 13 Professional papers and abstracts published including: Co-author: Double-Blind, placebo-controlled study of terfenadine and hydroxyzine in patients with chronic idiopathic urticaria, in Annals of Allergy, 1989; Comparison of Azelastine and Clemastine to Placebo in the Management of Perennial Allergic Rhinitis, American Academy of Allergy and Clinical Immunology Meeting, 1990. Honour: Fellow: American College of Physicians; American Academy of Allergy and Immunology; American College of Allergy and Immunology. Memberships: American Thoracic Society; New England Allergy Society. Hobbies: Golf; Computers; Gardening. Address: c/o Certified Allergy Consultants, 62 Hacket Blvd, Albany, NY 12209, USA.

SHUMACKER Harris B Jr, b. 20 May 1908, Laurel, Mississippi, USA. Surgeon (retired). m. Myrtle Landau, 1 Dec 1933, 2 sons. Education: BS, University of Tennessee, 1927; MA, Vanderbilt University, 1928; MD, Johns Hopkins University, 1932. Appointments: Assistant in Surgery, 1932-35, Instructor in Surgery, 1938-41, Assistant Professor, 1941-46, Johns Hopkins University; Assistant in Surgery, 1936-37, Instructor, 1937-38, Associate Professor, 1946-48, Yale University; Professor of Surgery, 1948-70, Chairman, 1948-68, Distinguished Professor, 1970-, Indiana University; Professor of Surgery, 1979-86, Distinguished Professor, 1986-, Uniformed Services University. Publications: 650 including: Evolution of Cardiac Surgery, 1992; 5 other books and chapters in 50 books. Honours: Roswell Park Award, 1968; Distinguished Service Award, American College of Surgeons, 1968; Medal of Honour, University of Evansville, 1970; Honorary DSc, Indiana University, 1985; Distinguished Service Medal, Uniformed Services University, Department of Defense, 1988; Réné Leriche Prize, Société Internationale de Chirurgie, 1994. Memberships: American Surgical Association, Vice-President 1960-61, Secretary 1964-68; Society of University Surgeons, President 1951-52; Society of Vascular Surgery, President 1958-59; Society of Clinical Surgeons, President 1960-62; Pan-Pacific Surgical Association, President 1975-78; International Surgical Group, President 1975-78; Honorary Member: Royal College of Surgeons, England; Italian Surgical Society; Polish Surgical Association; Society of Thoracic Surgeons; International Surgical Group. Address: 1000 Lowry Street, Delray Beach, FL 33483, USA.

SHUN Zhu Yue, b. 26 Dec 1917, Yong Chun County, Fujian Province, China. Chief Physician. m. Zheng Min Zhong, 22 Oct 1939, 4 s, 1 d. Education: Fuijian Medical College, 1947. Appointments: Administrator of Yong Chun Hospital; Head of Health Quarantine Institute; Chairman of Quanzhou Medical Science Research Institute; Deputy Administrator of Quanzhou People's Hospital; Currently, Chief Physician of Public Hygiene, People's Hospital of Quanzhou. Publications: Shun Zhu Yue Medical Essays, Quanzhou Hygiene Bureau, 1988. Honours: Advanced Personnel of Fujian Province Hygiene Bureau; Advanced Science and Technology Personnel, Fujian Science Workers Association. Memberships: Committee, Fujian Association of the Integration of Traditional and Western Medicine, and Chairman of Quanzhou Branch. Hobbies: Sport; Chinese Chess. Address: The People's Hospital of Quanzhou, Quanzhou, Fuijian, China.

SHUPERT Charlotte Lee, b. 23 Oct 1953, Lancaster, USA. Neuroscientist. m. Erik Dana Westman, 5 May 1982, 2 sons. Education: BA, Michigan University, 1975; MA, University of Illinois, 1976; MS, Pennsylvania University, 1980; PhD, Pennsylvania University, 1985. Appointments: Senior Research Fellow, University of Washington; Researcher, Teaching Assistant, Pennsylvania University; Assistant Scientist, R S Dow Neurological Sciences Institute. Publications: Co-author: Effect of unilateral loss of vestibular function on VOR and posture, 1989; Hip sway associated with vestibulopathy: Voluntary hip sway, 1992; Reactive and predictive scaling of postural responses in patients with diabetic peripheral neuropathy, 1993; Vestibular ataxia following shuttle flights: Effects of microgravity on otolith-mediated sensorimotor control of posture, 1993; Hip sway associated with vesibulopathy, 1993; Responses to head and support surface displacements: Vestibular and somatosensory contributions to postural stability in normals, 1993; Responses to head and support surface displacements: Patients with adult and child onset vestibular loss, 1993. Memberships: Society for Neuroscience; Barany Society; Association for Research in Vision & Ophthalmology; Association for Research in Otolarying. Honours: Tower Guard Honour Society; Phi Beta Kappa; University Fellow, University of Illinois, 1975-76. Hobbies: Skiing; Gardening; Cooking. Address: 1120 NW 20th Avenue, Portland, OR-97209, USA.

SHUTE Wallace Beresford, b. 4 June 1911, London, Ontario, Canada. Gynaecologist & Obstetrician. m. Eileen Elizabeth Radcliff, 7 Oct 1937,1 son, 1 daughter. Education: BA (Hon Science); MD; FRCS(C); FRCOG; FACOG; FACS; FSOGC; DABOG. Career: Major Specialist, Obs & Gynae, RCAMC, 1945-46; Active Staff in Obstetrics & Gynaecology, Ottawa Civic Hospital, Riverside Hospital of Ottawa; Courtesy Staff, Obstetrics, Grace Hospital, Ottawa, 1946-retirement; Innovations: Invention of Three-Way Uterine Cell Collector, 1962; Rapid, Improved Method of Vaginal Sterilisation with Instrumentation, 1973; New Method of Suprapubic Catheter Insertion Preventing Post-Op Bladder Infection after Vaginal Surg, 1970; Publications include: Congenital Absence of the Vagina, 1958; A New Painless Episiotomy Repair, 1960; Vaginal Repair and Abdominal Suspension of the Vagina with Resultant Cure of Stress Incontinence, 1973; Paraesthesias of the Hand: A Conservative, Non-Surgical Approach, unpublished; Shute Parallel Obstetrical Forceps; Migraine Headache: Its Long Term Cure, 1990; 4 published plays in verse & prose: Christus; Deus; Terra Nova; The Nativity. Honours: 1st Phyllis Graveley Humanitarian Award, 1987; Achievement of Arms, College of Heralds, London, 1981; Matriculated by Lord Lyon of Scotland, 1981; Matriculated by Canadian Heraldic Authority, 1990; Fellowship, The Royal College of Obstetricians & Gynaecologists, 1994. Memberships: Canadian Medical Association; Ontario Medical Association; Society of Obstetrics & Gynaecology of Canada; Royal College of Physicians & Surgeons, Canada; Royal College of Obstetricians & Gynaecologists, England; Canadian Authors' Association; American College of Obstetricians & Gynaecologists; American College of Surgeons; American College of Abdominal Surgeons. Address: 300 Island Park Drive, Ottawa Ont, K1Y 0A7, Canada.

SICARD André, b. 1 Dec 1904, Paris, France. 1 son, 2 daughters. Publications: Chiurgie du Rachis et autres publications orthofediques. Honours: Commandeur de la Légion d'Hommeur et de l'Ordre; National du Merit. Memberships: Professeur Honoraire. Address: 18 Avenue de Villars, 75007 Paris, France.

SIDORCHENKOV Vyacheslav Olegovich, b. 30 Jan 1938, Smolensk, Russia. Radiologist. m. Shalatova Alla, 22 July 1962, 1 daughter. EducationL: DMS; Smolensk State Medical Institute, 1956-62; Postgraduate Student, Research Institute of Medical Radiology, 1971-73. Appointments: Junior Researcher, Radiotherapy, 1973-81, Senior Researcher, 1981-90, Leading Researcher, 1990-, Research Institute of Medical Radiology of AMS. Publications: Intracavity Brachytherapy for Rectal Cancer, 1991; Tumor Brachytherapy with Californium-252 Endocurietherapy/Hyperthermic Oncology, Co-author, 1992. Memberships: Problem Committee on Radiation Therapy, RAMS; Society of Roentgenologists and Radiologists of Russia. Hobby: Playing with Grandchildren. Address: Medical Radiological Research centre of RAMS, ul Koroliova 4, 249020 Obninsk, Kaluga Region, Russia.

SIDORENKO Yuri Sergeevich, b. 8 Nov 1939, Kherson, Ukraine. Oncologist. Widower, 1 daughter. Education: MD, Uzhgorod University, Ukraine, 1968; Qualified as Professor of Oncology. Appointments: Chief Physican, Rostov Cancer Research Institute, Russia, 1976-79; Chief Physician, City Hospital No 20, Rostov, 1979-82; Currently: Chief Oncologist, Rostov-on-Don Region; Director, Rostov-on-Don Cancer Research Institute; Head, Chair of Oncology, Rostov Medical Institute. Publications: Some Aspects of Diagnostics, Treatment and Dispensary System of Oncogynecologic Patients, 1987; New Operative Technique in Oncogynecology, 1990; Neuro-endocrine aspects of Vulvar Cancer, 1994. Honours: Honorary Inventor of Russian Federation, 1990; National Prize Winner, 1991. Memberships: Society of Oncologists; Ecological Academy of Russia. Hobbies: Art; Reading and writing books. Address: 63, 14 Line, 344037 Rostov-on-Don, Russia.

SIEGAL Gene Philip, b. 16 Nov 1948, Bronx, NY, USA. Physician. m. Sandra H Meyerowitz, 2 Aug 1972, 2 d. Education: BA, Adelphi University, 1970; MD, University of Louisville, 1974; PhD, University of Minnesota, 1979; Certified in Hospital Management, University of NC, 1988. Career includes: Fellow in Surgical, Pathology, University of Minnesota, 1981-82; Assistant Professor of Pathology, 1982-88, Associate Professor of Pathology, 1988-90, University of NC; Member, Lineberger Comprehensive Cancer Centre, 1983-90; Currently: Professor of Pathology, Cell Biology and Surgery, University of Alabama, Birmingham; Senior Scientist, UAB Comprehensive Cancer Centre. Publications: Over 150 manuscripts, monographs, book chapters and abstracts including: Co-editor, Monoclonal Antibodies in Diagnostic Immunohistochemistry, 1988. Honours: Alpha Epsilon Delta, 1968; Beta Beta Beta, 1968; Omicron Delta Kappa, 1974; Sigma Xi, 1976; Clinical Fellow, American Cancer Society, 1981; Junior Faculty Fellow, American Cancer Society, 1983; Jefferson Pilot Fellow in Academic Medicine, 1986; Fellow, Royal Society of Medicine, 1992; Phi Beta Delta, 1993; International Skeletal Society, 1994. Memberships: US-Canadian Academy of Pathology; Metastasis Research Society; AAAS; AACR; ASIP; AMA; CAP; Stout Society of Surgical Pathologists; Association of Directors Surgical Pathology; Editorial Board, Arch Pathology Laboratory Medicine. Address: Department of Pathology, University of Alabama, UAB Station, Birmingham, AL 35294, USA.

SIEGEL Daniel, b. 17 July 1957, USA. Psychiatrist. Education: BS, USC; MD, Harvard Medical School; Diplomate, American Board Psychiatry and Neurology, General Psychiatry, Child and Adolescent Psychiatry. Appointments: Acting Director, University of California Los Angeles Child and Adolscent Psychiatry. Publications: Handbook of Psychiatry, Co-editor, 1991; Memory, Trauma aand Psychotherapy: A Cognitive Sciences View on Psychotherapy Practice and Research, 1995. Honours: APA Burroughs Wellcome Fellow, 1984-86; American College of Psychiatry Laughlin Fellow, 1988. Membership: American Psychiatric Association. Address: UCLA-NPI, 760 Westwood Plaza, Los Angeles, CA 90024-1759, USA.

SIEGEL Michael Alan, b. 6 Feb 1953, Baltimore, USA. Dentist. m. Sharon Crane, 22 July 1979, 1 daughter. Education: BS, Zoology, 1975; DDS, 1979; MS, Oral Pathology, 1986; Fellow, Academy of General Dentistry, 1986; Diplomate, American Board of Oral Medicine, 1988; Fellow, American Academy of Oral Medicine, 1990. Appointments: Dental Officer, US Army, Walter Reed Army Medical Center, Washington, 1979-82; Associate Professor of Oral Medicine. Publications: Intraoral Biopsy Technique for Direct Immunofluorescent Studies, 1991; Oral Presentation and Management of Vesiculobullous Disease, 1993; Direct Immunofluorescence of Detached Gingival Epithelium for the Diagnosis of Cicatricial Pemphigoid, 1993. Memberships: American Dental Association; Maryland State Dental Association; American Academy of Oral Medicine; American

Association of Dental Schools. Honours: Fellow, Academy of Dentistry International, 1988; Meritorius Award, Distinguished Service, American Academy of Oral Medicine, 1991; Outstanding Faculty Award, American College of Dentists, Maryland, 1993. Hobbies: Sports; Music; Family. Address: Department of Oral Medicine & Diagnostic Sciences, Dental School, University of Maryland, 666 W Baltimore Street, MD 21201, USA.

SIEGEL Norman Joseph, b. 8 Mar 1943, Houston, TX, USA. Professor of Pediatrics and Medicine. m. Rise Joan Ross, 24 Dec 1967, 1 s, 1 d. Education: BA, Mathematics; MA, Physiology; MD, Medicine. Career: Fellow, Nephrology, 1970-72, Assistant Professor, 1972-76, Associate Professor, 1976-82, Professor of Pediatrics and Medicine and Vice Chairman, Department of Pediatrics, 1982-, Yale University School of Medicine. Publications: 89 Original papers including: Co-author, ddAVP does not stimulate acute changes in levels of medullary trimethylamines in man, in Journal of American Society Nephrology, 1993; Co-author, Immature renal tubules are resistant to prolonged anoxia, in Pediatric Research, 1994; Case Reports and Editorials; Numerous reviews, chapters and books including: Co-author, Acute Renal Failure: B Clinical, in Pediatric Nephrology, 3rd edition, 1993. Honours: Examiner, American Board of Pediatrics, Sub Board of Pediatrics, 1983; Special Recognition Award, Society for Pediatric Research, 1985; Medical Editor, 1990-; Secretary Treasurer, American Pediatric Society, 1993; Chairman, Pediatric Test Committee, National Board of Medical Examiners, 1993-95. Memberships: Society for Pediatric Research; American Pediatric Society; American Society for Clinical Investigation; American Board of Pediatrics, Sub Board of Pediatric Nephrology; American Society of Pediatric Nephrology; National Kidney Foundation. Address: Yale University School of Medicine, Department of Pediatrics, 333 Cedar Street, PO Box 208064, New Haven, CT 06520-8064, USA.

SIEGEL Stuart Elliott, b. 16 Jul 1943, Plainfield, NJ, USA. Paediatric Hematologist and Oncologist. m. Linda Wertkin, 1 s. Education: BA, summa cum laude, Boston University, 1967; MD, magna cum laude, Boston University, 1967. Appointments: Currently: Associate Director for Paediatric Oncology, Kenneth Norris Junior Comprehensive Cancer Center, 1989-; Associate Chair, Department of Paediatrics, Children's Hospital, Los Angeles; Vice Chair, Department of Paediatrics, USC School of Medicine; Head, Division of Hematology and Oncology, Children's Hospital, Los Angeles. Publications: 140 peer reviewed articles in professional journals including: Co-author, Long-term follow-up of patients treated with COMP or LSA2L2 therapy for childhood non-Hodgkin's lymphoma, in Journal of Clinical Oncology, 1993; Co-author, Establishment and characterization of a human mixed-lineage, T-lymphoid/myeloid cell line (USP-91), in Blood, 1993; Co-author, A Phase II Study of carboplatin in children with recurrent or progressive solid tumours: a report from the Children's Cancer Group, in Cancer, 1994. Honours include: Medical Staff of Children's Hospital of Los Angeles, Distinguished Service Award, 1984; Concern II Foundation Honoree, 1991; Israel Cancer Research Fund Honoree, 1994. Memberships: American Paediatric Society; American Association for Cancer Research; American Society for Clinical Oncology; American Association for Cancer Education; Society for Paediatric Research; Societe Internationale d'Oncologie Pediatrique. Hobby: Hockey. Address: 4650 Sunset Boulevard m/s 54, Los Angeles, CA 90027, USA.

SIEGLER Richard Louis, b. 5 May 1939, Vallejo, CA, USA. Pediatric Nephrologist. m. Karen Koenig, 25 Jun 1963, 2 s, 1 d. Education: BA, CA State University, Sacramento, 1961; MD, Creighton University College of Medicine, 1965. Appointments: Medical Advisor to Republic of Vietnam, MILPHAP, MACV, 1967-68; Assistant Professor, 1972-78, Associate Professor, 1978-90, Currently, Professor of Pediatrics, Chief, Division of Pediatric Nephrology and Hypertension, University of Utah School of Medicine. Publications: Prostacyclin in the Hemolytic Uremic Syndrome, Journal of Nephrology, 1993; A 20-Year Population-Based Study of Post-Diarrheal Hemolytic Uremic Syndrome in Utah, Pediatrics, 1994; The Spectrum of Extra-Renal Involvement in Post-Diarrheal Hemolytic Uremic Syndrome, Journal of Pediatrics, 1994. Honours: Bronze Star, Department of Army, Meritorious Achievement in Public Health, South Vietnam, 1967; Excellence in Teaching Award, Department of Pediatrics, 1977-78. Memberships: American Academy of Pediatrics; Society for Pediatric Research; Western Society for Pediatric Research; American Society of Nephrology; American Society of Pediatric Nephrology; International Society of Nephrology; International Pediatric Nephrology Association. Hobbies: Playing violin in an amateur symphony orchestra; Skiing; Jogging. Address: Division

of Nephrology, Department of Pediatrics, University of Utah School of Medicine, 50 North Medical Drive, Salt Lake City, UT 84132, USA.

SIERRASESUMAGA Luis, b. 20 Sept 1955, Bilbao, Spain. Consultant, Pediatrics Department, University of Navarra, Spain. m. Isabel Martin Montaner, 19 Dec 1987, 1 son, 1 daughter. Education: MD, University of Navarra, 1978; Fellowship, Bone Marrow Transplantation, New York University, USA, 1982; PhD, University of Navarra, 1988. Appointments: Assistant, Pediatric Department, University Clinic of Navarra, 1982-88; Consultant, Pediatric Department, University Clinic of Navarra, 1988-93, Chairman of Department, 1993-. Publications: Pediatric Oncology, 1992; Few articles in journals of Pediatric Oncology. Memberships: International Society of Pediatric Oncology; Spanish Pediatric Association. Hobbies: Mountaineering; Swimming; Reading. Address: Department of Pediatrics, University Clinic of Navarra, Pamplona 31008, Navarra, Spain.

SIERVOGEL Roger M, b. 17 Dec 1944, Phoenix, AZ, USA. Fels Professor of Community Health. m. Renée Harber, 30 Jun 1990, 1 s, 1 d. Education: BS, 1967, MS, 1968, AZ State University; PhD, University of OR, 1971; Board Certified, PhD Medical Geneticist, 1992. Career includes: NIH Postdoctoral Fellow, Department of Biostatistics, School of Public Health, University of NC, Chapel Hill; Fels Professor and Head, Division of Human Biology, Department of Community Health, Wright State University, School of Medicine. Publications: Over 175 publications including: Heredity and hypertension, in NHLBI Workshop on Juvenile Hypertension, 1984; Co-author, Fat distribution and blood pressures, in Fat Distribution During Growth and Later Health Outcomes, 1988; Genetic and familial factors in human obesity, in Childhood Obesity: A Behavioral Perspective, 1988; Co-author, Patterns of change in weight stature2 from 2 to 18 years: long term serial data from children in the Fels Longitudinal Growth Study, in International Journal of Obesity, 1991. Honour: Outstanding Faculty Member Award, Academy of Medicine, Wright State University School of Medicine, 1993. Memberships: American Society of Clinical Nutrition; American Society of Human Genetics; American College of Medical Genetics; Epidemiology Council of the American Heart Association; American College of Sports Medicine. Hobbies: Skiing; Scuba Diving; Sailing; Theatre. Address: Division of Human Biology, Department of Community Health, WSU School of Medicine, 1005 Xenia Avenue, Yellow Springs, OH 45387-1695, USA.

SIGNORELLI Carlo, b. 23 July 1962, Milan, Italy. University Researcher. Education: MD, 1986, DPH, 1990, Law degree, 1993, University of Milan; MSc, Epidemiology, 1989, PhD, 1994, University of London. Appointments include: University Researcher, Deputy Head, Centre for Diagnosis and Prevention of Toxoplasmosis and Perinatal Infections, Institute of Hygiene, Faculty of Medicine, La Sapienza University, Rome, 1992-; Teacher of Enviromental Hygiene, Politechnik of Milan, 1994-; Coordinator, Ministry of Health sponsored project, on Sexual Behaviour of Young Italians and HIV Infection; Coordinator, project on Epidemiology of Caesarean Section; Director, View and Review Hospital scientific journal. Publications: Textbook of Epidemiological Methods for University Students, 1989, 4th edition, 1995; Legal problems related to the method of delivery, 1993; Co-author, 4 textbooks and about 150 scientific papers in Italian and international scientific journals; Articles on hygiene, public health and sanitary legislation, in popular press. Honours: Luigi Moneta Foundation Scholarship, 1986; Anna Villa Rusconi Scholarship, 1987; Rotary International Scholarship, 1988-89; Scholarship for doctoral students, Ministry of University, Italy, 1986-89; Scholarship for AIDS Prevention, Ministry of Health, Italy, 1990-92. Memberships: Italian and British Medical Council Registration; Italian Journalist Council; Italian Council of Solicitors; International Epidemiological Association; Society for Epidemiological Research; Hospital Infection Society; Italian Society of Hygiene, Preventive Medicine and Public Health, Committee of University Teachers; Italian Association of Epidemiology. Hobbies: Skiing; Golf; Bridge. Address: Piazza Otto Novembre 6, 20129 Milan, Italy.

SIGNORELLI Innocenzo, b. 10 March 1928, Milan, Italy. Gynacologist. m. 1 son. Education: Postgraduate Course, Gynacology Surgery, University of Florence, Italy, 1970; University Roma, 1972; Degree in Med and Surgery, University of Milan; Specialist in Clinical Obst and Gyn, University of Milan; University of Winnipeg, 1985. Appointments: Houseman, Osp Magg, Milan, Italy, becoming Assistant, then Hospital Assistant; Assisant Director of The Autonomous Isolation Section; Director of 3 Div Obst OSP Maggiore; Head, 2 Obstetrics and

Gynaecology Division. Publications: 60 medical papers and 3 monographs. Memberships: National Society of Obstetrics and Gynaecology; AOGOI; FIGO. Hobbies: Travel; Literature Studies; Golf. Address: Via Calzecchi 6, 20133 Milan, Italy.

SILA Misiada Vunisau, b. 14 Feb 1930, Rewa, Fiji Islands. Doctor. m. Makereta Nakalevu, 27 Dec 1960, 2 sons, 3 daughters. Education: Diploma of Surgery & Medicine, Fiji School of Medicine, 1957; Diploma of Anaesthetics, Phillippines, 1977; Fellow, Phillippine Board of Anaesthesia, 1979. Appointments: Junior Surgical Registrar, 1959-60; Trainee Anaesthetic Registrar, 1961-67; Anaesthetic Registrar, Lautoka Hospital, Fiji 1968-70; Anaesthetic Registrar, Labasa, Fiji, 1971-74; Anaesthetic Registrar, CWM Hospital, 1975-94; Chief Medical Officer, 1985. Publications: Exciting Moments of Anaesthetic Practice, 1991; Reminiscence of My Medical Career, 1992. Memberships: Pacific Society of Anaesthetists; Fiji Medical Association. Hobbies: Mixed Farming; Swimming; Travel; Reading Books. Address: c/o CWM Hospital, Box 115, Suva, Fiji.

SILBERBERG Donald H, b. 2 Mar 1934, Washington DC, USA. Neurologist. m. Marilyn A Damsky, 31 May, 2 s. Education: MD, University of Michigan, 1958; MA Honorary, University of Pennsylvania, 1971. Appointments: Chairman, Department of Neurology, 1982-94; Professor of Neurology and Associate Dean of International Medical Programmes, University of Pennsylvania. Publications: Contributor of numerous works. Hobby: Photography. Address: Department of Neurology, University of Pennsylvania Medical Centre, Philadelphia, PA 19104-4283, USA.

SILBERFELD Michel, b. 15 Feb 1946, Paris, France. Psychiatrist. m. Susan Fremes, 1 son. Education: BSc cum laude, 1966, MDCM, 1970, McGill University, Canada; Medical Intern, Queen Elizabeth Hospital, 1970; MSc, Biostatistics, 1963, Postgraduate Programme in Psychiatry, 1973-76, University of Toronto; Certificate, Royal College of Physicians and Surgeons, 1976; FRCP (C); Graduate, Institute for Psychoanalysis, 1983. Appointments: Assistant Professor, Department of Psychiatry, University of Toronto; Senior Research Scientist, Staff Psychiatrist, Addiction Research Foundation, Associate, Biological Research Division, Ontario Cancer Institute, Head, Division of Psychological Medicine, Department of Medical Oncology, Associate Staff, Princess Margaret Hospital, Director, Psychiatric Emergency Service, Senior Staff, Psychiatry, Wellesley Hospital, 1978-85; Coordinator, Community Psychiatric Service, 1985-88, currently Coordinator, Competency Clinic, Baycrest Centre for Geriatric Care, North York. Publications: Evaluating decisions in Mental Capacity Assessment, 1994; Co-author: Prescreening competency assessments, 1993; A randomized trial of a decision aid for mental capacity assessments, 1993; Capacity to complete an advance directive, 1993; Living with incompetency: a guide to those encountering it, 1994. Honours: Founding Member, Centre for Bioethics, University of Toronto. Memberships: Canadian Psychiatric Association; Ontario Psychiatric Association; Canadian Society of Bioethics; Canadian Psychoanalytic Society; International Psychoanalytic Society. Address: Baycrest Centre for Geriatric Care, 3560 Bathurst Street, North York, Ontario, Canada M6A 2E1.

SILBERGELD Ellen, b. 29 July 1945, USA. Scientist. m. A M Silbergeld, 19 Apr 1969, 1 son, 1 daughter. Education: AB, Vassar College; PhD, Johns Hopkins University; Honorary LLD. Appointments: Scientist, NIH; Senior Toxicologist, Environmental Defense Fund; Professor of Epidemiology and Toxicology. Publications: Over 200 works. Honours: Phi Beta Kappa, 1967; AB summa cum laude, 1967; Fulbright Fellow, 1967; Kennedy Fellow, 1974-75; MacArthur Fellow, 1993-; Fellow, Collegium Ramazzini, 1993-. Memberships: Society Occupational Environmental Health; American Public Health Association; American Society Pharmacology Experimental Therapy; Society Neuroscience; Society of Toxicology. Hobbies: Fly Fishing; Gardening; Harpsichord Playing. Address: University of Maryland Medical School, 660 W Redwood Street, Baltimore, MD 21201, USA.

SILLANPÄÄ Matti Lauri, b. 4 Aug 1936, Noormarkku, Finland. Physician. m. Pirjo Huida, 30 Oct 1964, 1 s. Education: MD, 1962, PhD, 1973, University of Turku. Career includes: Senior Consultant, Department of Paediatrics, Turku, 1969-76; Acting Professor, Public Health, 1977-88; Associate Professor, Department of Public Health, University of Turku, 1976-90; Currently, Professor and Head of Department of Child Neurology, University and Hospital of Turku. Publications include: Many articles in professional publications from 1973: Social adjustment and functioning of chronically ill and impaired

children and adolescents, 1987; Co-editor, Paediatric Epilepsy, in Wrightson Biomedical, 1990; Children with epilepsy, as adults, 1990; Co-editor, Pseudo-epileptic Seizures, in Wrightson Biomedical, 1993. Honours: Ribbon of Merit, Students Union, 1960; Medal of Merit, Finnish Red Cross, 1970; Honorary Member, Academia Medicorum Litteratorum, Italy, 1980; Silver Medal of Merit, National Epilepsy Association, 1984; Paul Harris Fellow, Rotary Foundation of Rotary International, 1985; Silver Medal of Merit, Order of the St Constantine the Great, Athens, 1986; Golden Medal of Merit, National Epilepsy Association of Finland, 1993; Ambassador Award, International Bureau for Epilepsy and International League Against Epilepsy, 1993. Hobbies: Music; Clubs; Forestry. Address: Honkatie 32 B 1, FIN-20540 Turku, Finland.

SILVER Ann-Louise Schesinger, b. 3 Mar 1942, Syracuse, NY, USA. Psychiatrist; Psychoanalyst. m. Stuart Beal Silver MD, 2 Apr 1962, 2 s, 1 d. Education: MD, Johns Hopkins University, School of Medicine; Graduate, Adult Psychoanalysis, WA Psychoanalytic Institute; Family Therapy Training Program, WA School of Psychiatry. Appointments: Staff Psychiatrist: Springfield Hospital, Sykeville, 1974; Clifton T Perkins Hospital, 1974-76; Private Practice, 1974-; Chestnut Lodge Hospital, Rockville, 1976-; Clinical Associate Professor, US University of Health Sciences, Bethesda, 1980-; Civilian Consultant, Walter Reed Army Medical Center, WA, 1987-. Publications: Editor, Psychoanalysis and Psychosis, 1989; Psychoanalysis and Severe Emotional Illness, 1990; Illness in the Analyst, 1990; Articles in professional journals. Honours: Fellow, American Psychiatric Association; Board Certified in Psychiatry, 1976; Trustee, American Academy of Psychoanalysis, 1993. Memberships: American Psychiatric Association; American Academy Psychoanalysis; American Psychoanalytic Association; American Medical Women's Association; Association of Women Psychiatrists; MD Psychiatric Society; WA Psychoanalytic Society; International Psychoanalytical Association. Hobby: Gardening. Address: Chestnut Lodge Hospital, 500 W Montgomery Ave, Rockville, MD 20850, USA.

SIMAIKA Samir Mahfouz, b. 27 Feb 1936, Cairo, Egypt. Obstetrician and Gynaecologist. m. Yolande Cassab, 2 July 1967, 1 son, 1 daughter. Education: MB, BCh; DGO, DS; FRCOG; FICS. Appointments: House Officer, then Resident in Obstetrics and Gynaecology, Kasr El Ainy University Hospital, Cairo; Registrar, Obstetrics and Gynaecology, Hammersmith Postgraduate Hospital, London, England; Consultant, Obstetrics and Gynaecology, Head, Department of Obstetrics and Gynaecology, Coptic Hospital, Cairo, Egypt. Publications: Leucorrhea in Egyptian Females, 1965; Rare Functioning Ovarian Tumours, 1966; A History of Egyptian Obstetrics, 1976. Honours: Madden Gold Medal in Clinical Surgery, 1959. Memberships: Fellow, Royal College of Obstetricians and Gynaecologists, London; Fellow, International College of Surgeons. Hobbies: Reading; Stamp collecting; Travel. Address: 80 Gomhoriya Street, Cairo, Egypt.

SIMANOVSKAYA Yevgeniya Yudovna, b. 15 June 1916, Perm, Russia. Stomatologist. m. Pupko Ph A, 1942 (dec 1986), 2 d. Education: Honoured Diploma in Stomatology, Perm State Stomatological Institute, 1939; DMed, 1970. Appointments: The Soviet Service, 1941-46; Assistant Chair, 1946-63, Assistant Professor, 1963-70, Surgical Stomatology; Head of Chair of Childrens Stomatology, Perm State Medical Institute, 1970-87. Publications: Face & Jaw Tumours, 1964; Face & Jaw Benign Tumours, 1969; co-author, Children Orthopedic Stomatology, 1989; 282 works published, 16 invention authorized certif. Honours: The Order of the World War; Ten Medals; Title and Badge, Otlichnik zdravoochranenia, 1967. Memberships: Chairman, Perm Regional Scientific Stomatological Society, 1969-95; Honorary Member, Russian Stomatological Scientific Society, 1982-. Hobbies: Classical Music; Playing the Piano. Address: Geroev Hasana Street 10-1, Perm 614010, Russia.

SIMBIRTSEV Semyon A, b. 15 Sep 1929, Chapaev, Ural Region, Russia. Pathophysiology. m. Lidia Simbirtseva, 21 Jan 1954, 1 s. Education: MD, Leningrad Medical Institute, 1955. Career: Scientific Worker, Emergency Medicine; Chief, Department of Experimental Pathology; Rector, Medical Academy Postgraduate Studies; Chief, Department of Operative Surgery and Experimental Pulmonology. Publications: Acute Renal Insufficiency by Injury, in textbook, Military Surgery, 1973; Crash Syndrome and Acute Renal Insufficiency, lecture, 1978; Co-author, Isolated Lung, 1983; Microembolism of Lung, 1986. Honours: Honoured Science Worker, RF, 1985; Gold and Silver Medals in Exhibition Achievement of Science, Russia, 1987-89. Memberships include: Corresponding Member, Academy of Medical Sciences of

Russia; Academy of Science and Art of Peter; American Academy of Health Care Addictions. Hobby: Gardening. Address: 195009, St Petersburg, Finskiy per 7, No 26, Russia.

SIMMONS Henry Clifton, b. 21 Dec 1949, Nashville, USA. Dentist. m. Joan Peyton Jacobs, 16 June 1975, 1 son, 2 daughters. Education: BS, Tennessee Technological University, 1971; DDS, University of Tennessee, 1977. Appointments: President, Old Hickary Dental Study Club; President, Middle Tennessee Academy of Implant Dentistry; Program Chairman, Nashville Dental Society; Editor, Tennessee Academy of General Dentistry; President, Tennessee CRANIO; General Dentist, Assistant Clinical Professor, Vanderbilt University. Publications: Newsletter of Tennessee Academy of General Dentistry, Spring & Fall, 1993. Memberships: American Dental Association; American Academy of Head, Neck, Facial Pain & TMJ Orthopedics; Academy of General Dentistry; Tenessee CRANIO; American Academy of Implant Dentistry; Middle Tennessee Academy of Implant Dentistry; American Dental Society of Anesthesiology; American Society of Osseointegration. Honours: Dean's Honorary Odoutological Society, 1976; Psi Omega Fraternity Scholastic Award; Omicron Kappa Upsilon, Dental Fraternity, 1977. Hobbies: Gardening; Boating; Travel. Address: 1916 Hayes Street, Nashville, TN 37203, USA.

SIMON Bennett, b. 6 Nov 1933, Brooklyn, NY, USA. Psychiatrist. m. Dr Roberta J Apfel, 5 Jan 1978, 2 s, 3 d. Education: AB, summa cum laude, Harvard College, 1955; MD, Columbia University, 1959. Career: Fellow in Psychiatry through to Assistant Professor, Albert Einstein College of Medicine, 1960-71; Lecturer through to Clinical Professor, Psychiatry, Harvard Medical School, 1971-. Publications: Mind and Madness in Ancient Greece: The Ancient Roots of Modern Psychiatry, 1978; Tragic Drama and The Family, 1988. Honours: Guggenheim Fellowship, 1976; Fulbright Lecturer, Hebrew University of Jerusalem; Sigmund Freud Professor of Psychoanalysis, 1989-90. Memberships: American Psychiatric Association; American Psychoanalytic Association; American Philological Association; Society for Psychotherapy Research. Hobbies include: Walking; Talking; Reading. Address: Department of Psychiatry, Cambridge Hospital, Cambridge, MA 02139, USA.

SIMON Helen Hemalatha, b. 28 Sept 1938, Andhra Pradesh, India. Doctor of Medicine. Education: DGO; MD (Gynae); FRCOG (London); FICOG (India). Career includes: Associate Professor, Obstetrics & Gynaecology, Miraj Medical College and Waneless Hospital, Miraj, Maharashtra, India, 1971-72; Head of Department & Consultant, Obstetrics & Gynaecology, Kugler Hospital, Guntur, Andhra Pradesh, India, 1976-77; Associate Professor, Obstetrics & Gynaecology & Project Director 1979-, 80, Professor and Head, Department of Obstetrics & Gynaecology & Project Director 1982-88, All India Postpartum Programme, Christian Medical College, Ludhiana, Punjab, India; Director, currently. Publications include: Intra Amniotic Injection of Hypertonic Solution as a Method for Termination of Pregnancy; Abortion Hazards, Renal Failure, Journal of Obstetrics & Gynaecology, 1975; Epidemiological Factors in Ovarian Malignancy in Punjab, 1986; Medical Education in India, Health and Population Perspective and Issues, 1989. Honours: Best Teacher Award, CMC, Ludhiana by Students Union, 1988; Award for services for home club, Lions Club, Phillaur (Dist), Punjab, 1983; Second Prize, Science Essay Competition, Govt Girls' College for Women, Guntur, 1957; Award for Best Outgoing Student of Stall Girls' High School, Guntur, 1954. Memberships include: Indian Medical Association of India; International Union for Health Education; International Society for Community Education; Delhi Association of Obstetrics & Gynaecology; Indian College of Obstetrics & Gynaecology; Indian Society of Perinatology & Reproductive Biology. Address: National Institute of Health and Family Welfare, New Mehrauli Road, Munirka, New Delhi 110 067, India.

SIMON James, b. 18 Dec 1951, Chicago, Illinois, USA. Physician. m. Debra D, 22 Dec 1974, 3 daughters. Education: MD, Rush Medical College; BA, Washington University. Appointments: Instructor, Assistant Professor, Division of Reproductive Endocrinology & Infertility, Department of Obstetrics & Gynecology, Harbor-UCLA Medical Center, Torrance, 1984-85; Assistant Professor, Section of Pregnancy Research, The Jones Institute for Reproductive Medicine, Norfolk, Virginia, 1985-87; Associate Professor, Chief, Division of Reproductive Endocrinology & Infertility, Georgetown University School of Medicine, 1987-. Publications incl: Leuprolide Acetate and Bone Mineral Density Measured by Quantitative Digitized Radiography, 1993; Progesterone Antgonist RU 486 Accommodates, But does not induce labour and

delivery in primates, 1993; Familial Adenomyosis: A Case Report, 1994; Adenomyosis: Evidence for Genetic Cause, 1994. Honours: Junior Fellow Prize Paper, ACOG District IV Annual Meeting, 1980; Squibb Prize Paper, Pacific Coast Fertility Society, 1983; Associate Member Prize Paper, American Fertility Society, 1984; Upjohn Prize Paper, ACOG Annual Meeting, 1986; Selected to Top Washington Physicians, Washington Magazine, 1993; Elected to Best Doctors in America, 1993; Resident Clinical Teaching Award, Department of Obstetrics & Gynecology, 1993. Memberships incl: American Association for the Advancement of Science; American College of Nutrition; American Medical Association; International Menopause Society; The Endometriosis Alliance of Washington DC; Washington Gynecological Society. Hobby: Baseball. Address: 3800 Reservoir Road NW, 3 PHC, Washington DC 20007-2197, USA.

SIMON Jonathan Edward, b. 19 Oct 1949, Watford, England. Medical Practitioner. m. Josephine Susan, 2 Jan 1976, 2 s, 1 d. Education: BSc, Bristol; BM BCh, Oxford; MRCGP; FRNZCGP; DA; DCH' DMJ; DRCOG. Appointments include: Principal in General Practice, Oxford, 1979-82; Assistant in General Practice, Ratanui Medical centre, Henderson, Auckland, New Zealand, 1982; Principal in General Practice, Otumoetai Health Centre, Tauranga, 1982-. Publications include: Family Medicine and Primary Care in America, 1981; The DMJ Casebook, 1982; Observations on Family Medicine in America, 1983; A Community Oriented Medical in New Zealand?, 1989; The Practice Nurse in a New Zealand General Practice, 1989; Contributor of various articles in professional journals, book reviews and radio interviews. Honours include: Recipient of various grants; W G Johnson Memorial Trust Special Award, 1982; Pilot Funding, Midland Regional Health Authority, 1993-94; RNZCGP Gold Medal, 1995. Memberships: British Academy of Forensic Sciences; Associate, Faculty of Homoeopathy, London; New Zealand Medical Association; Founder Member, National IPA Network. Hobbies: Reading; Writing; Music; Theatre. Address: PO 8010, Tauranga, New Zealand.

SIMON Michael R, b. 12 Oct 1943, New York City, New York, USA. Academic Physician. m. Carol Herman, 1 son, 1 daughter. Education: BA, Harpur College, State University of New York, Binghamton, 1965; MD, New York University School of Medicine, 1969; MA, Stanford University, 1973; Fellow, American College of Physicians; Fellow, Royal College of Physicians and Surgeons of Canada. Appointments: Currently: Associate Professor of Internal Medicine and Paediatrics, Training Programme Director, Allergy and Immunology Fellowship, Wayne State University School of Medicine. Publications: Epidemiology of Sarcoidosis (co-author with S G Desai), 1985; Method for the derivation of clinical and laboratory indices in relation to disease activity and outcome in sarcoidosis (author), 1986; Serum antibodies from patients and household contacts of patients with Crohn's disease react with murine lymphomas induced by Crohn's tissue filtrates (co-author), 1986. Memberships: Fellow, American Academy of Allergy and Immunology; American Federation for Clinical Research; Society of Experimental Biology and Medicine. Address: 111F VA Medical Center, Allen Park, MI 48101, USA.

SIMONOVA Larisa I, b. 3 May 1937. Pathophysiologist. m. Dr N S Pushkar, 1960, 1 s. Education: Dnepropetrovsky Medical Institute, 1960; Candidate of Medical Sciences, 1969; MD, 1986. Career: Junior Scientific Assistant, 1960, Senior Scientific Assistant, 1969, Chief of Laboratory of Radiation Pathophysiology, Currently, Chief of Radiation Medicine Department, Institute of MR. Publications: Over 170 publications including: Co-author, Pathogenesis and Treatment of Combined Radiation Injuries, 1989. Memberships: Pathophysiological Society; Presidium of Radiobiological Society. Hobbies: Country Estate Management; Ballet. Address: 52 Lenin's Prospekt, Apt 34, Kharkiv 310, Ukraine.

SIMONS F Estelle R, b. 26 Apr 1945, Vancouver, Canada. Doctor of Medicine. m. Keith John Simons, 21 Dec 1968, 1 son, 1 daughter. Education: BSc, 1965; MD, 1969; Fellow, Royal College of Physicians; Fellow, American Academy of Pediatrics; Fellow, American Academy of Allergy and Immunlolgy. Appointments: Deputy Chairman, Department of Pediatrics & Child Health, University of Manitoba; Chairman, Medical Advisory Committee, Children's Hospital Research Foundation; Director of Research & Clinical Invesitgation, Children's Hospital; Professor, Head of the Section of Allergy & Clinical Immunology. Memberships: Chairman, Royal College of Physicians & Surgeons of Canada Speciality Committee in Allergy & Clinical Immunology. Honours: Numerous awards for research, including: The Medical Research

Council Queen Elizabeth II Scientist Award, 1975-81; the Rh Award, University of Manitoba, 1988; the Dr Bruce Chown Professorship, University of Manitoba, 1989; The Canadian Society of Allergy and Clinical Immunology Research Award, 1991. Hobbies: Music; Arts. Address: 840 Sherbrook Street, Winnipeg, Manitoba R3A 1S1, Canada.

SIMPSON Roderick Howard Wallace, b. 10 Jan 1951, London, England. Physician. m. Alethea Avrille Milborrow, 10 Nov 1979, 3 s, 1 d. Education: BSc, University of St Andrews, 1971; MB ChB, University of Dundee, 1974; MMed, University of Stellenbosch, 1981; MRC Pathology 1983. Appointments: Registrar in Pathology, Guy's Hospital; Senior Registrar in Anatomical Pathology, University of Stellenbosch, South Africa; Consultant, senior Lecturer, University of Witwatersrand, South Africa; Consultant, Senior Lecturer in Histopathology, University of Exeter, England. Publications include: Classification of Tumours of the Salivary Glands, 1994. Memberships: International Academy of Pathology; European Society of Pathology; Pathological Society of Great Britain; Association of Clinical Pathologists. Hobbies: Cricket; Travel; The Past; Dining well with good company. Address: Area Department of Pathology, Church Lane, Heavitree. Exter, Devon, England.

SINCLAIR Graeme Craig, b. 30 Oct 1947, Balclutha, New Zealand. Periodontist. m. Diane Lesley Ridge, 8 Jan 1987, 1 s, 2 d. Education: BDS, University of Otago Dental School, 1970; MSc, Periodontics, London, 1975. Career: Registrar in Periodontics, Eastman Dental Hospital, London; Clinical Demonstrator, Royal Dental Hospital, London; Visiting Honorary Periodontist for Auckland Hospital Board; Currently in Private Practice, Periodontics and Dental Implants. Honours: Fellow, International Congress of Oral Implantologists, 1990; Diplomate, American Society of Osseointegration, 1992. Memberships: President, New Zealand Society of Periodontology; Auckland Dental Association; New Zealand Dental Association; ICOI. Hobbies: Swimming; Fishing; Golf; Tennis; Running. Address: 188 Gillies Avenue, Epsom, Auckland, New Zealand.

SINEL Michael S, b. 1 Mar 1960, New York, USA. Assistant Clinical Professor; Director, Physical Medicine & Rehabilitation. Education: BA, Phychology, Stony Brook University; MD, SUNY, Brooklyn; Internship, General Medicine, Staten Island Hospital; Residency, Physical Medicine & Rehabilitation, New York Hospital, Cornell Medical Center, Memorial Sloan Kettering Cancer Center. Appointments: Director of Out Patient Services; Attending Physician, Physical Medicine & Rehabilitation. Publications: Two Unusual Bad Disturbances, 1990; Thalamic Infraction Secondary to Chiropractic Cervical Manipulation. Memberships: American Back Society; American Academy of Physical Medicine & Rehabilitation; American Academy of Pain Management; American Pain Society; International Association for the Study of Pain; American Medical Association; California Medical Association; Young Physicians Association, Los Angeles. Honours: Blue Ribbon Presentation Award, Academy of Physical Medicine & Rehabilitation, 1988. Hobbies: Sailing; Travel; Sking; Poetry; Charity Work. Address: 9911 W Pilo Blvd 200, Los Angeles, CA 90035, USA.

SINGH Bawa Prehlad, b. 22 Feb 1923, Lucknow, India. Medicine. m. Renate Maria Trawniczek, 20 Jan 1962, 1 s. Education: BSc; MBBS; FACS; FACOG; FICS. Appointments: Instructor, Assistant Clinical Professor, Associate Clinical Professor, Obstetrics and Gynaecology, UCLA Medical School, Los Angeles. Publications include: Protein-bound Iodine and Radioactive Iodine Uptake Studies in the Normal Menstrual Cycle, in American Journal of Obstetrics and Gynaecology, 1956; Leiomyosarcoma of the Uterus, in American Journal of Obstetrics and Gynaecology, 1958; Intra-aortic Nitrogen Mustard Therapy in Advanced Pelvic Malignancies, in Surgery, 1959. Honour: Outstanding Teacher Award, Harbor-UCLA Medical Center, Torrance, CA, 1971; Fellow, Oncologic Surgery, City of Hope Medical Center, CA; Diplomate, American Board of Obstetrics and Gynaecology. Memberships: Life Fellow, Los Angeles Obstetric and Gynaecological Society; Life Fellow, American College of Surgeons; Life Fellow, American College of Obstetrics and Gynaecology; Life Fellow, International College of Surgeons. Hobbies: Photography; Tennis; Travel. Address: 1300 West 155th Street, Gardena, CA 90247-4048, USA.

SINGH Keshaw, b. 20 Jul 1947, Ghazipur, India. Teacher. m. Baleena Singh, 26 Jul 1969, 1 s, 3 d. Education: BSc, MSc, PhD, Banaras Hindu University. Appointments: Head of Physics Department, Dean, Faculty of Science, University of Science and Technology, Kumasi, Ghana. Publications: Over 24 research articles; Instability phenomenon in thin insulating films on silicon, review article in Journal

of Microelectronics and Reliability, 1976. Honour: Fellow, Ghana Institute of Physics. Membership: ISES. Hobbies: Swimming; Playing Guitar. Address: Faculty of Science, University of Science and Technology, Kumasi, Ghana, West Africa.

SINGH Meharban, b. 14 Oct 1937, Amritsar, India. Doctor. m. Mrs Kaushal, 2 Oct 1965, 1 s, 1 d. Education: MBBS, 1960; MD, Pediatrics, 1964. Appointments: Assistant & Associate Professor of Pediatrics, AIIMS, New Delhi, 1966-86; Direcot, Institute of Child Health, kabul, Afghanistan, 1979-83; Professor of Pediatrics, AIIMS, New Delhi, 1987-; Visiting Professor of Pediatrics and Examiner to several Universities in India and Afghanistan, Iran, Libya, Kuwait and Sri Lanka. Publications: More that 230 Research Papers and Review Articles and 15 Chapters published in Medical Textbooks in India and Abroad; Author of 5 Monographs and 6 Textbooks pertaining to Health Problems of Newborn Babies and Children. Honours: British Commonwealth Fellow, 1970-71; Fellow, National Academy of Medical Sciences, 1988; Honory Fellow, American Academy of Pediatrics, 1991; Dr L H Lobo Oration Award, 1992; Glaxo Oration Award, 1994. Memberships: President, Indian Academy of Pediatrics, 1993; President, National Neonatology Forum of India, 1989-90; Secretary, National Neonatology Forum of India, 1988-89. Hobbies: Medical Writing; Reading Spiritual Literature. Address: Department of Pediatrics, All India Institute of Medical Sciences, Ansari Negar, New Delhi, 110029, India.

SINGH Ravi P, b. 30 May 1948, Sitapur, UP, India. Psychiatrist. 1 s, 2 d. Education: BS, Jodhpur University, India, 1967; MD, S N Medical College, Jodhpur, University of Rajasthan, Jaipur, India, 1972; MPH, Johns Hopkins University, 1978. Appointments include: Consultant Coordinator, Behavior Associate, Alcohol and Drug Rehabilitation Program, Baltimore, MD, 1986; Resident, 1987-90, Chief Resident, 1990, Department of Psychiatry, Meharry Medical College, Nashville, TN; Clinical Director, Substance Abuse and Adult Psychology, 1991-92; Instructor and Clinical Director of Consultation, Liaison and Emergency Psychiatric Services, Meharry Medical College, Nashville, TN, 1992-. Publications: Several publications and presentations, 1978-92, including: Epidemiology of Colon Cancer, in Review of Literatures, 1978; Genetics of Alcoholism (presentation), First LC Elam Mental Health Symposium, 1990. Honours include: Best Essay Writer, Rotary International of Rajasthan, 1968; Citation for Community Services, Mayor of Baltimore, 1983; Mini Fellowship, American Psychiatric Association, 1988. Memberships include: American Society of Addiction Medicine; American Association of Psychiatrists in Alcoholism and Addictions; American Psychosomatic Society; American Geriatric Society; American Public Health Association; AMA; American Psychiatry Association; Southern Medical Association; National Medical Association; American Society of Clinical Psychopharmacy. Hobbies: Writing short stories, one-act plays and poems in Hindi; Contemporary Religions; Travel; Hiking; Photography. Address: 745 South Church St, Ste 309, Murfreesboro, TN 37130, USA.

SINGH Sant P, b. 2 Oct 1936, India. Physician. m. Satinder, 21 Apr 1968, 1 d. Education: MBBS; Masters in Experimental Medicine; FACP; Fellow, American College of Clinical Endocrinologists. Appointments: Assistant Professor of Medicine, State University of New York, USA, 1970-73; Associate Professor of Clinical Medicine, Northwestern University, Chicago, 1973-76; Professor of Medicine and Physiology, Chicago Medical School, 1976-. Publications: Contributor of over 60 articles in scientific journals. Honours: Performance Award, US Veterans Administration, 1976; Lawrence Medoff Award, Chicago Medical School, 1990. Memberships: American College of Physicians; American Endocrine Society; American Diabetes Association; International Diabetes Federation; American Society of Alcohol Research. Hobbies: Tennis; Golf. Address: Department of Endocrinology, Chicago Medical School, 3333 Greenbay Road, North Chicago, IL 60064, USA.

SINGH Sukeshi, b. 23 Mar 1943, Bihar, India. Gynaecologist. m. Hari N Sharma, 13 June 1962, 1 son, 1 daughter. Education: MBBS (honours in Surgery); MS, Obstetrics and Gynaecology; FRCOG (London). Appointments: Assistant Professor, Associate Professor, Obstetrics and Gynaecology, S K Medical College, Bihar; Consultant Gynaecologist. Memberships: Indian Medical Association; Royal College of Obstetricians and Gynaecologists; FOGSI; Saudi Obstetric Society. Hobbies: Music; Reading. Address: Shubhprad, B-48-49, Kankarbag, P C Colony, Patna 800020, India.

SINGHAL Madhu, b. 8 Jan 1947, India. Obstetrician and Gynaecologist. m. Dr Grish Mohan Singhal, 9 Nov 1970, 1 s, 1 d.

Education: BSc; MBBS; MRCOG, 1974; FRCOG(Eng), 1990. Career: Registrar, Obstetrics and Gynaecology, Huddersfield Royal Infirmary, 1974-76, Bolton General Hospital, 1976-78; Consultant Obstetrician and Gynaecologist, Singhal Nursing Home, Muzaffarnagar, 1978-. Publications: Paper on Development of Medical Facilities in Muzaffarnagar, Royal Society of Medicine, Surgical Section, England, 1986, and on Development of Obstetric and Gynaecological Facilities in Muzaffarnagar in meeting of Royal College of Obstetrics and Gynaecology, Chandigarh. Honour: Outstanding President, Innerwheel Club, Muzaffarnagar. Memberships: FOGSI; Gynaecology Endoscopy Society of India; Fellow, Royal College of Obstetricians and Gynaecologists, England. Hobbies include: Photography; Rotary Activities; Interior Decoration. Address: Singhal Nursing Home, Meerut Road, Opp Company Bagh, Muzaffarnagar 251002, India.

SIOW Yong-Chai, b. 22 June 1935, China. Physician. m. Wong Yee-Koong, 7 June 1964, 2 sons, 1 daughter. Education: MB, China; FACA, UK. Appointments include: Physician to HRH Prince Bernhard of the Netherlands; Currently Doctor in Acupuncture, London, England. Membership: British Acupuncture Association. Address: 10 Harley Street, London W1N 1AA, England.

SIOW Yung-Ching,b. 2 April 1946, Singapore, China. Practitioner; Acupuncturist. m. Yong Chai-Fong, May 1974, 2 daughters. Education: BSc, Biology; Diploma in Clinical Medicine. Appointments: Practitioner in Chinese Medicine; Acupuncturist. Memberships: British Acupuncture Association; Singapore Chinese Physicians Association. Hobbies: Music, Vocal, Conductor of Choir. Address: 6001 Beach Road # 02-19, Golden Mile Tower, Singapore 0719, China.

SIPEK Jiri, b. 7 Mar 1950, Ceska Trebova, Czech Republic. Clinical Psychologist. m. Eva Sipkova, 2 Apr 1981, 2 daughters. Education: MA, 1973, PhDr, 1974, Charles University, Prague; CSc, Academy of Sciences. Appointments: Assistant Researcher, Psychology Institute, Academy of Sciences, Prague, 1973-79; Clinical Psychologist, Faculty Hospital, Prague, 1979-82; Clinical Psychologist and Psychotherapist, Psychiatric Centre, Prague, 1982-. Publications include: Integration in Psychotherapy, 1993; Time in Psychotherapy, 1994; A Case of Multimodal Therapy, 1991. Memberships: Association of Clinical Psychologists; Society for CBT; Society for the Exploration of Psychotherapy Integration. Hobbies: Yoga; Jogging. Address: Veronske Nam 382, 10900 Prague, Czech Republic.

SIREGAR Erwin, b. 21 May 1946, Padangsidempuan, Indonesia. Medical Doctor. m. Riseptina, 7 Dec 1978, 3 daughters. Education: MD, University of Indonesia; Certified Anesthesiologist, University of Indonesia. Appointments: Consultant Anesthesiologist, Medical Faculty, University of Indonesia; Consultant Anesthesiologist, Medical Faculty, Gajah Mada University, Indonesia; Head, Department of Anesthesiology, National Cardiac Center, Jakarta. Publications: Cardiac Anesthesia, 1993. Honours: Scientific Advisor, Clinical Research, Janssen Research Council, 1987. Memberships: Indonesian Society of Anesthesiologists; Society of Cardiovascular Anesthesiologists; Council on Cardio-thoracic & Vascular Surgery; World Association of Cardiac, Thoracic & Vascular Anesthesiology. Hobbies: Tennis; Swimming; Chess. Address: Department of Anesthesiology, National Cardiac Center, J1 S Parman Kav 87, Jakarta 11420, Indonesia.

SIRIS Ethel Martha Silverman, b. 21 Aug 1945, Clifton, New Jersey, USA. Physician. m. Dr Samuel Siris, 2 June 1971, 1 s, 1 d. Education: AB, Harvard University, 1967; MD, Columbia University, 1971. Appointments include: Intern, Assistant Resident, Department of Medicine, Presbyterian Hospital, 1971-74; Assistant Professor, 1977-84, Associate Professor of Clinical Medicine, 1984-91, Professor of Clinical Medicine, 1991-, Columbia University; Attending Physician, Presbyterian Hospital, New York, 1991-; Director, Programmes in Osteoporosis, Centre for Women's Health, Columbia Presbyterian Medical Centre, 1993-. Publications include: Effects of Childhood Leukemia and Chemotherapy on Puberty and Reproductive Function in Girls, Co-author, 1976; Paget's Disease, Co-author, 1980; Current Concepts Regarding the Nature and Management of Paget's Disease of Bone, Co-author, 1982; COmmentary: Information, not Unnecessary Alarm, Co-author, 1985; Cases in Paget's Disease of Bone, Co-author, 1991; Paget's Disease of Bone, Co-author. Honours: Phi Beta Kappa; Alpha Omega Alpha; Upjohn Award, Colubia University College of Physicians and Surgeons, 1971; Mary Putnam Jacobi Award for Clinical Research, 1979; The Paget's Disease Foundation Research Award, 1986, 1987. Memberships: Endocrine Society; American Society for Bone and

Mineral Research. Hobbies: Reading; Travel. Address: Columbia Presbyterian Hospital, 630 W 168th Street, New York, NY 10032, USA.

SIRIS Samuel Gidding, b. Philadelphia, PA, USA. Psychiatry. m. Ethel M Silverman MD, 2 Jun 1971, 1 s, 1 d. Education: BA, 1966, MS, Biology, 1967, Lehigh University; MD, Columbia University, 1970; Certificate in Psychoanalysis, Columbia University, 1982. Appointments: Assistant Professor, Clinical Psychiatry, Columbia University, 1977-79; Assistant Professor, 1979-84, Associate Professor, 1984-88, Psychiatry, Mount Sinai School of Medicine; Currently, Director, Adult Day Programs, Hillside Hospital, Long Island Jewish Medical Center; Professor of Psychiatry, Albert Einstien College of Medicine, 1989-. Publications: Over 100 articles and book chapters including: Adjunctive medications in the maintainance treatment of schizophrenia and their conceptional implications, in British Journal of Psychiatry, 1993; Maintainance imipramine for secondary depression in schizophrenia: A controlled trial, Arch General Psychiatry, 1994. Honours: Research Grants: National Institute of Mental Health; National Institute of Drug Abuse. Memberships: American College of Neuropsychopharmacology; Group for the Advancement of Psychiatry. Address: Hillside Hospital, 75-59 263rd Street, Glen Oaks, NY 11004, USA.

SIROIS Pierre, b. 12 Dec 1945, Quebec City, Quebec, Canada. Professor. 1 daughter. Education: BA; BSc; MSc; PhD. Appointments: Research Fellow, Royal College of Surgeons of England, London, 1975-77; Visiting Scientist, Imperial College of Science and Technology, London, 1976-77; Research Fellow, The Hospital for Sick Children, Toronto, Ontario, Canada, 1977-78; Visiting Scientist, Centre d'Etude Nucléaire, Saclay, France, 1984; Currently Full Professor, Chairman, Department of Pharmacology, Faculty of Medicine, University of Sherbrooke, Sherbrooke, Quebec. Publications: More than 500 papers and abstracts. Honours: Medical Research Council Scientist Award, 1987-92. Memberships: British Pharmacological Society; ACFAS; Club de recherches cliniques du Québec; Société canadienne d'immunologie; Société canadienne d'investigation clinique; International Society of Immunopharmacology; The Pharmacological Society of Canada. Hobby: Flying. Address: Department of Pharmacology, Faculty of Medicine, University of Sherbrooke, 3001 12e AVenue Nord, Sherbrooke, Quebec, Canada J1H 5N4.

SIVASURIYA Mailvahanan, b. 20 Apr 1933, Kajang, Malaysia. Professor of Obstetrics & Gynaecology; Consultant. m. Shanthini Vallipuram, 30 Mar 1963, 1 son, 1 daughter. Education: MBBS (Cey); FRCS (Eng); FRCS (Edin); FRCS (Glasg); FCS (SL); FACS; FRCOG (Gt Brit); FCOG (SL). Career: Associate Professor & Consultant Obstetrician & Gynaecologist, General Hospital Kandy, Sri Lanka; Senior Professor & Head, Department of Obstetrics & Gynaecology, University of Jaffna, Sri Lanka/Consultant Obstetrician & Gynaecologist, General Hospital Jaffna (Teaching), Jaffna, Sri Lanka, currently. Publications: Author, Ectopic Pregnancy, Obstetrics & Gynaecology for Postgraduates, vol 2, 1994. Honours: Commonwealth Senior Medical Fellow, 1994; Visiting Professor, Royal Postgraduate Medical School, Hammersmith Hospital, London, 1994. Memberships: Sri Lanka Medical Association; Jaffna Medical Association. Address: Department of Obstetrics & Gynaecology, University of Jaffna, PO Box 57, Jaffna, Sri Lanka.

SIVATHASAN Sivalingam, b. 27 May 1951, Sri Lanka. General Practitioner. m. 1978, 1 son, 1 daughter. Education: MBBS; LRCP (Lon); MRCS (Eng); DRCOG; MRCOG. Career: Obstetrics & Gynaecology Registrar, 7 years; General Practitioner with Special Interest in Obstetrics & Gynaecology, currently. Memberships: Royal College of Obstetricians & Gynaecologists, England; Medical Protection Society. Hobby: Gardening. Address: 2a Oakfield Gardens, Beckenham, Kent BR3 3AZ, England.

SKINNER Gordon Robert Bruce, b. 21 Feb 1942. Doctor. m. Janet, 4 Jan 1968, 2 sons, 1 daughter. Education: MD (first class hons); DSC; FRCPath; FRCOG. Career: Lecturer, University of Birmingham, England, 1976; Senior Lecturer, University of Birmingham, currently. Publications: Many articles on prevention of microbiol and neoplastic disease. Memberships: British Medical Association; Birmingham Inventors Club. Address: Harborough Banks, Old Warwick Road, Lapworth, West Midlands B94 6LD, England.

SKINNER James E, b. 15 Apr 1940, Okmulgee, Oklahoma, USA. Neuroscientist. m. Mary Jeanne Skinner, 2 sons, 2 daughters. Education: AB with distinction, Pomona College, 1962; PhD, University of California, 1967. Appointments: Assistant Professor of Physiology, Associate Professor of Physiology, Associate Professor of Neurology, Professor of Neurology, Adjunct Professor of Neurology, Baylor College of Medicine; Currently Director of Research, Totts Gap Medical Research Laboratory. Publications: Neuroscience: A Laboratory Manual, 1971; Co-author: Brain Dynamics Progress and Perspectives, 1990; An International Perspective on Self Regulation and Health, 1991; Arrhythmia: A Clinical Approach, 1994. Honours: USPHS Predoctoral Fellow, 1964-66; Creative Talent Award, American Institute of Research, 1968; President, Pavlovian Society, 1994. Memberships: Society for Neuroscience; American EEG Society, 1982; Pavlovian Society of North America. Hobbies: Skiing; Squash; Tennis. Address: RR 1 Box 1120-G, Bangor, PA 18013, USA.

SKOLNIKOFF Alan Zachary, b. 25 Sep 1932, NY, USA. Psychoanalyst. m. Suzanne Chevalier, 22 Sep 1965 (div 1991), 2 s. Education: MD, State University of NY, Downstate Medical Center, 1959; Psychiatric Residency, Langley Porter Psychiatric Institute, 1963-66; Psychoanalytic Training, San Francisco Psychoanalytic Institute, 1965-73. Appointments: MD; Psychiatrist; Community Psychiatrist; Currently, Training and Supervising Psychoanalyst at San Francisco Psychoanalytic Institute; Associate Clinical Professor, University of CA, San Francisco. Publications: Analysis of the Transference: Implications for Theory and Research, 1984; Configurational Analysis: A Method to Measure Change in Psychotherapy, 1984; Consensual Analysis: A Case Study with Verbal Report and Process Notes, 1985; The Emotional Position of the Analyst in Psychoanalysis and Psychotherapy, 1990; The Evolution of the Concept of Interpretation, 1992; The Analyst's Experience in the Psychoanalytic Situation: A Continuum Between Objective and Subjective Reality, 1993. Memberships: American Psychoanalytic Association; International Psychoanalytic Association; American Psychoanalytic Psychiatric Association. Hobby: Backpacking. Address: 205 Edgewood Avenue, San Francisco, CA 94117, USA.

SKONER David Peter, b. 10 Mar 1954, Johnstown, PA, USA. Doctor. m. Janet Skoner, 1 s, 4 d. Education: BS, Juniata College, Huntingdon, PA, 1976; MD, Temple University, Philadelphia, PA, 1980. Career includes: Assistant Professor of Pediatrics, 1985-91, Associate Professor of Pediatrics, 1991-, University of Pittsburgh School of Medicine, PA; Associate Director, Allergy and Immunology Training Program, 1993-, Chief, Laboratory Research, Division of Allergy, Immunology and Rheumatology, 1994-, Children's Hospital of Pittsburgh, PA; Numerous seminars and invited lectures. Publications include: Editorial Board, American Journal of Rhinology; Numerous refereed articles, reviews, books, chapters, published abstracts including: Co-author, Pediatric Allergy and Immunology, in Atlas of Pediatric Physical Diagnosis, 2nd edition, 1992; Guest Editor, Breathing Free, patient education newsletter, 1994; Co-author, Diseases of the Ear, in Allergy, Clinical Immunology and Asthma, Management in Infants, Children and Adults, 3rd edition, 1994, in press. Honours include: Various travel grants; Ross Award for Excellence in Ambulatory Pediatrics, Children's Hospital, Cincinnati, OH, 1983; Young Investigator Award, American Academy of Allergy and Immunology, 1985; Geigy Fellowship for Excellence in Allergy and Immunology Research, 1985. Memberships include: Fellow, American Academy of Pediatrics; Society for Pediatric Research; PA Thoracic Society; Pittsburgh Allergy Society. Address: Children's Hospital, 3705 Fifth Avenue, Pittsburgh, PA 15213, USA.

SLADEN Robert Neil, b. 7 Sept 1946, Cape Town, South Africa. Anesthesiologist-Intensivist. m. Maureen Elizabeth Greenblo, 17 Jan 1976, 2 daughters. Education: MBChB, University of Cape Town, 1970; MRCP (UK), 1974; Diplomate, American Board of Anesthesiology, 1979; FRCP (C), 1981; Special Qualifications in Critical Care, American Board of Anesthesiology, 1987. Appointments: Assistant Professor of Anaesthesia, 1978-84, Associate Professor of Anaesthesiology, 1984-86, Stanford University Medical Center, California, USA; Chief, Anaesthesiology Service, Veterans Affairs Medical Center, Durham, North Carolina, 1986-92; Associate Professor of Anaesthesiology and Surgery, 1986-, Co-Director, Surgical Intensive Care, 1991-, Vice-Chairman, Department of Anaesthesiology, 1992-, Duke University Medical Center, Durham, North Carolina. Publications include: Report on Midazolam infusion in the surgical ICU, 1989; Intensive Care: Editorial overview, 1993; Accurate estimation of glomerular filtration in the intensive care unit: another Holy Grail?, editorial, 1993; Co-author: Use of Midazolam infusion for sedation following cardiac surgery, 1987; Labetalol for the control of elevated blood pressure following coronary artery bypass grafting, 1990; Anesthesia and Sedation by Continuous

Infusion: Proceedings of a Symposium (edited with J G Reves), 1992. Honours: University Gold Medal in Medicine, University of Cape Town, 1970. Memberships: American Society of Anesthesiologists; Society of Critical Care Medicine; Society of Cardiovascular Anesthesia. Hobbies: Cycling; Jogging; Hiking; Skiing. Address: Department of Anaesthesiology, Box 3094, Duke University Medical Center, Durham, NC 27710, USA.

SLAKTER Edmund Lee, b. 9 Sep 1932, New York City, USA. Psychiatrist; Psychoanalyst. m. Ruth Goldfarb, 4 Sep 1955, 2 sons, 2 daughters. Education: MD, State University of New York, 1957. Appointments: Associate Professor of Psychiatry, Mt Sinai School of Medicine; Associate, Attending, Mt Sinai Hospital. Puiblications: Countertranference, 1988; Problems in Supervising Aftercare Therapy, 1967. Memberships: International Psychoanalytic Association; American Psychoanalytic Association; New York Psychoanalytic Society; New York State Medical Society; Medical Society of County of New York. Hobbies: Tennis; Music; Theatre. Address: 311 E 72nd Street, Apt 15F, New York, NY 10021, USA.

SLAVNOV Valentin Nickolayevich, b. 18 Jan 1924, Kiev, Ukraine. Professor of Nuclear Medicine. m. Inna Miagkaya, 20 Dec 1967, 1 son. Education: Medical Institute, Kiev, 1955; PhD, 1959, MD, 1967, Institute of Radiology and Roentgenology, Leningrad; DMA. Appointments: Postgraduate Student, 1955-58; Senior Scientist, 1958-60, Assistant, Assistant Professor, 1960-68, Head, Department of Radiology, 1968-90, Professor, Head of Group, 1990-95, Institute of Endocrinology AMS, Ukraine. Publications Radioisotope and Radioimmunological Investigations Function of Endocrine Glands, 1978; Radioummunological Analysis in Oncology, 1984; Radioimmunological Analysis in Clinical Endocrinology, 1988. Honours: Order Patriotic War; Recipient of 11 Medals; Honorary Member, Association of Radiology Ukraine; Sign Excellent Public Health. Memberships: Association of Radiology and Endocrinology; Special Council, Ukrainian Institute of Oncologyn and Radiology. Hobbies: Swimming; Travel. Address: Department of Radiology, Institute of Endocrinology and Metabolism, Vyshgorodskaya 69, Kiev 254114, Ukraine.

SLEGE William Hurt, b. 26 Jan 1945, Greensboro, Alabama, USA. Academic Psychiatrist. m. Elizabeth Travis Rose, 21 Dec 1968, 3 d. Education: AB, Washington Lee University, 1967; MD, Baylor College of Medicine, 1971; Residency in Psychiatry, Yale University School of Medicine, Department of Psychiatry, 1972-75; Graduate, Western New England Institute for Psychoanalysis, 1986. Appointments: Staff Psychiatrist, USAF School of Airspace Medicine, 1975-77, 1977-79; Assistant Clinical Director, Yale Psychiatric Institute, 1979-86; Director, Graduate Education, Yale University School of Medicine, Department of Psychiatry, 1986-89; Director, Outpatient Division of Connecticut Mental Health Centre; Professor of Psychiatry, Yale University School of Medicine; Clinical Director, Connecticut Mental Health Centre; Associate Chair for Education, Department of Psychiatry. Publications: Core Readings in Psychiatry, Co-editor, 1984; Contribdutor of 40 peer-reviewed scientific articles. Honours: Air Force Commendation Medal, 1977; Phi Beta Kappa, 1989; Excellence in Residency Education, 1989; Roerig Visiting Professor, Eastern Tennessee State University, 1991. Memberships include: Aerospace Medical Association; American Association of Directors of Psychiatric Residency Training; American College of Psychiatry; American Medical Association; American psychiatric Association; American Psychoanalytic Association; Association of Academic Psychiatry; Association of American Medical Colleges' Group for the Advancement of Psychiatry. Hobbies: Running; Biking; History; Swimming; Dancing. Address: 701 Prospect Street, New Haven, CT 06511, USA.

SLOBODA Zili, b. 17 Dec 1940, Philadelphia, PA, USA. Epidemiologist. m. Walter Sloboda, 31 Jul 1991, 2 s, 1 d. Education: BA; MD; ScD. Career includes: Research Epidemiologist, Clinical Medicine Branch, 1987-89, Chief, Prevention Research Branch, 1989-91, Acting Director, Division of Epidemiology and Prevention Research, 1991-92, Associate Director, Planning and Services Coordination, Division of Clinical Research, 1992-93, Director, Division of Epidemiology and Prevention Research, 1993-, National Institute on Drug Abuse; Member of many committees. Publications: Many publications and scientific presentations including: Making research useful to the policymaker: drug abuse as an example, in Prevention in Human Services, forthcoming; Co-author, Gender differences in drug use patterns, in progress; Co-author, HIV risk factors among injecting drug users in five US cities, in AIDS, forthcoming. Honours: Administrator's Award for Meritorious

Achievement, Alcohol, Drug Abuse and Mental Health Administration, PHS, 1989; Delta Omega, 1993; Director's Award, National Institutes of Health, 1993. Memberships: Founder, Society for Prevention Research; American Public Health Association; Society for Epidemiologic Research; American College of Epidemiology. Hobby: Word Puzzles. Address: 15700 Buttonbush Court, Rockville, MD 20853, USA.

SLONECKER Charles Edward, b. 30 Nov 1938, Gig Harbor, Washington, USA. University Professor. m. Jan Hunter, 1961, 3 sons. Education: DDS, University of Washington, Seattle, 1965; PhD, Biological Structure, University of Washington Graduate School, 1967. Appointments: Scientific Assistant, University of Bern, Switzerland, 1967-68; Assistant Professor, 1968-73, Associate Professor, 1973-78, Professor of Anatomy, 1978-, Head, Department of Anatomy, 1981-92, Director of Ceremonies and University Relations, 1989-, University of British Columbia, Vancouver, Canada. Publications: Grant's Method of Anatomy (co-author), 11th edition, 1989. Honours: Master Teacher Merit Award, 1977; Centennial Gold Medal, American Association of Anatomists, 1987; President, American Association of Anatomists, 1994-95. Memberships: American Association of Anatomists; Canadian Association of Anatomists; Sigma Xi. Hobbies: Reading; Gardening; Travel. Address: University Relations, The University of British Columbia, 6251 Cecil Green Park Road, Vancouver, British Columbia, Canada V6T 1W5.

SLOTS Jorgen, b. 16 Apr 1944, Denmark. Dentistry. m. Maritza Slots, 2 Aug 1980, 2 sons, 1 daughter. Education: DDS; DMD; MS; PhD; MBA; FACD. Appointments include: Teacher, Royal Dental College, 1969-71; Doctoral Candidate, Royal Dental College, 1971-74; Private Practice, Copenhagen, Denmark, 1969-76; Assistant Professor, Department of Periodontology & Bacteriology, Royal Dental College, 1974-76; Professor, Department of Periodontology, University of Southern California, 1990-; Associate Dean for Research, University of Southern California, 1990-; Chairperson of Periodontology, University of Southern California, 1991-; Head, Oral Micro Testing Laboratory, University of Southern California, 1991-. Publications: More than 200 articles and book-chapters in periodontology, microbiology, immunology, molecular genetics. Honours: Award, Danish Society to the Study of Periodontology, 1985; Honorary Master's Degree, University of Pennsylvania, 1986; Basic Research in Periodontal Disease Award, International Association for Dental Research, 1990; Correspondence Member, Finnish Dental Society, 1990; Gies Periodontology Award, 1990. Memberships include: International Association of Dental Research; American Association of Dental Research; American Association of Microbiology; Academy of Osseointegration. Hobbies: Hiking; Golfing. Address: University of Southern California School of Dentistry, MC-0641, Los Angeles, CA 90089-0641, USA.

SLOVENTANTOR Vladimir Jurjivich, b. 12 Nov 1938, Parfonovo, Altai, USSR. Anaesthetist. m. O J Davidova, 22 Dec 1959, 1 son, 1 daughter. Education: Graduate, Kalinin Medical Institute, 1963; DMS. Appointments: Surgeon regional hospital, 1963-65; Anaesthesiologist, regional hospital, 1965-70; Anaesthesiologist, 1970-78, Senior Research Worker, 1978-90, Chief Research Worker, 1990-, Medical Radiological Research Centre of RAMS, Obninsk. Publications: The Metabolic and Medical rehabilitation during the Combined Therapy of Oncologic Patients (Radionuclide Evaluation), dissertation, 1993; recipient of 3 Certificates for inventions, 1988-92. Hobbies: Reading Poetry; Skiing; Swimmng. Address: Russian Federation, 249020 Obninsk, Kaluga Region, Kurchatova Street, 15, Apartment 124, Russia.

SLOWIK Felicia, b. 2 Apr 1932, Pecs, Hungary. Pathologist. m. Janos Sandor, 23 Dec 1965. Education: Board Certificated General Pathologist, 1960; Board Certificated Neuropathologist, 1980; MD. Appointments: Department of Pathology, University School, Debrecen, 1956-61; Department of Radiology, National Institute of Nervous & Mental Diseases, Budapest, 1962; National Institute of Neurosurgery, Department of Pathology, 1962. Publications: Co-author: Data on the biology of medulloblastoma, 1982; Co-author: Primary non-Hodgkin lymphomas of the CNS, 1986; Co-author: Pathologie und immunomorphologie primärer Lymphoma des ZNS, 1988; Co-author: Membraneous changes in primary malignant CNS lymphomas, 1989. Memberships: Hungarian Society of Pathology & Neuropathology; International Society of Neuropathology. Hobbies: Travel; Music. Address: National Institute of Neurosurgery, 1145 Budapest, Amerikai ut 57, Hungary.

SLUNSKY Rudolf, b. 24 November 1926, Dobré Pole, Czechoslovakia. Professor; Med-Rat; Cand Sci Med; Obstetrician and Gynaecologist. m. Silvia, 12 June 1954. Education: Specialist, Obstetrics & Gynaecology, 1st Degree, 1955; 2nd Degree, 1960. Appointments: Physician, Hospital of Ostrava, 1951; Specialist, Department of Ostetrics & Gynaecology, Ostrava, 1961; Vice Chief, 1964; Chief, 1968, Hospital Havirov; Emigration Assistant, 1st Clinic of Obstetrics & Gynaecology, University Wien, Austria, 1968; Chief, Hospital Klosterneuburg, 1976-91. Publications: 4 books and monographs, 9 brochures, 536 scientific articles, reports, lectures. Honours: Prize, Czechoslovak Society of Obstetricians & Gynaecologists, 1958; Swiss Society of Gynaecologists, 1974; Senior Officer of Health, Vienna, 1990; Professor, Vienna, 1995. Memberships: Czech Society of Obstetricians & Gynaecologists; Austrian Society of Obstetricians & Gynaecologists. Hobbies: Nature; Gardening; Music; Summer-house; Travel. Address: Vorgartenstrasse 27/7/4, A 1200 Wien, Austria.

SLUTSKY Arthur Samuel, b. 31 Dec 1948, Toronto, Ontario, Canada. Physician. m. Myra Schwartz, 31 Oct 1971, 2 sons. Education: BASc cum laude; MASc; MD. Appointments: Instructor, 1980-81, Assistant Professor, 1981-84, Harvard University, USA; Associate Professor, 1984-88, Professor of Medicine, 1988-, University of Toronto; Professor of Surgery and Biomedical Engineering, 1988-; Division Director, Respiratory Medicine. Publications: Contributions to books and proceedings include: Measurement of ventilatory responses to hypercapnia and hypoxia (with A S Rebuck), 1981; Control of breathing in diseases of the respiratory tract and lungs (with A S Rebuck), 1986; Non-conventional techniques of ventilatory support (with J Villar and B Winston); Mechanical Ventilation, 1992; Stress proteins and acute lung injury (with J Villar), 1994; Over 125 in peer-reviewed journals, mainly relating to respiration and ventilation. Honours: Ontario Government Scholar, 1966; Ashrae Bursary, 1966; National Research Council Scholar, 2nd Grand Prize for Medical Students, Mead Johnson, 1971; Excellence in Research Award, SAMA-UTMB; Medical Research Council: Fellowship, Canada, 1978, 1979, 1980, Scientist Award, 1985, 1986, 1987, 1988, 1989, 1990; Elected to American Society for Clinical Investigation, 1987; William Goldie Prize for Research, University of Toronto, 1992. Memberships: American Association for the Advancement of Science; American College of Chest Physicians; American College of Physicians; American Physiological Society; American Thoracic Society; Association of Professional Engineers of Ontario; Canadian Society for Clinical Investigation; Ontario Medical Association; Operations Research Society of America; Society of Critical Care Medicine. Address: Mount Sinai Hospital, 600 University Avenue, Ste 656A, Toronto, Ontario, Canada M5G 1X5.

SLY Ridge Michael, b. 3 Nov 1933, Seattle, Washington, USA. Physician. m. Ann Turner Jennings, 12 June 1957, 2 daughters. Education: AB, Kenyon College, Gambier, Ohio, 1956; MD, Washington University, St Louis, 1960; Editor, Annals of Allergy, 1990. Appointments: Assistant Professor, Associate Professor, Professor of Pediatrics, Louisiana University School of Medicine, 1967-78; Chairman of Allergy & Immunology, Childrens' National Medical Center; Professor of Pediatrics, George Washington University School of Medicine & Health Sciences. Publications: Pediatric Allergy, 1977; Textbook of Pediatric Allergy, 1985; 14 chapters in various textbooks; 127 articles in medical journals. Memberships: American College of Allergy & Immunology; American Academy of Allergy & Immunology; American Academy of Pediatrics; American Thoracic Society; Council of Biology Editors; American Medical Writers Association. Honours: AB magna cum laude, 1956; Phi Beta Kappa, 1956; Louisiana Plaque of the American League Association of Louisiana, 1978; M Murray Peshkin Memorial Award of Association for the Care of Asthma, 1983; Distinguished Fellow Award, American College of Allergy & Immunology, 1993. Hobbies: Piano; Organ. Address: 111 Michigan Avenue NW, Washington, DC 20010-2970, USA.

SMETANA Karel, b. 28 Oct 1930, Prague, Czech Republic. Physician, Scientist. m. Vlasta Smetanova, 24 Oct 1953, 1 son. Education: MUDr, 1955; CSc, 1962; DSc, 1967. Appointments: Lecturer, Department of Histology, Charles University, Prague, 1955-62; Scientific Officer, Laboratory of Ultrastruct Research, Academy of Science, Prague, 1962-84; Director, Institute of Hematology & Blood Transfusion, Prague, 1984-90; Head, Laboratory of Ultrastruct Cytology, 1990-. Publications: 253 scientific publications in scientific journals on Nuclear Components in Normal and Malignant Cells. Honours: State Prize, 1986; Prize of the Minister of Health, 1973. Memberships: Czech

Histochemical Society; Czech hematological Society. Hobbies: Cytology. Address: Puchovska 2, Prague 4, Czech Republic 14100.

SMITH David Michael, b. 11 Dec 1940, Birmingham, England. Medical Osteopath. Education: MB ChB, University of St Andrews, Scotland; MRCGP, South Birmingham Vocational Trainee Scheme; MFHom, Liverpool, 1983; MLCOM, London, 1983. AppointmentsL General Practitioner Principal, Castlefields Health Centre, Runcorn, Cheshire, 1974-83; Medical Osteopath, Sutton Coldfield, 1984-. Memberships: RCGP; Faculty of Homoeopathy; Register of Osteopaths; British Association Manipulative Medicine. Address:222 Lichfield Road, Four Oaks, Sutton Coldfield, B74 2UB, England.

SMITH Edward Durham, b. 27 May 1922, Sunderland, England. Surgeon. m. Dorothy Lois Bennetts, 29 Dec 1948, 4 s. Education: MBBS, 1948, MD, 1967, MS, 1972, Melbourne; FRACS, 1956; FACS, 1963. Career: Intern, Resident, Registrar, Alfred and Royal Children's Hospitals, Melbourne, 1949-56; Assistant Surgeon, Alfred Hospital, 1956-60; Assistant Neurosurgeon, Alfred and Royal Children's Hospital, 1956-60; Consultant Paediatric Surgeon, Alfred Hospital, 1956-65, Royal Children's Hospital, 1965-87; President, 1987-89, Executive Director, 1989-92, Royal Australasian College of Surgeons; Currently, Honorary Senior Surgeon, Royal Children's Hospital, Melbourne and Honorary Secretary, International Federation of Surgical Colleges. Publications: Spina Bifida, book, 1963; Co-author, Rectal Malformations in Children, book, 1971, revised edition, 1985; Co-editor, Congenital Anomalies of Urinary Genital and Cloacal Tracts, in press; Chapters in 8 books and many papers in surgical journals on Paediatric Urology. Honours: Gold Medal, Royal Children's Hospital, 1987; Honorary FRCSI, 1987; Honorary, FRCS, 1988; Honorary FRSC Ed, 1988; Honorary Member, British Association of Paediatric Surgeons, 1988; Honorary, FRSC (Glasg), 1990; Honorary FCS(SA), 1990; AO, 1991; Honorary Fellow, American Paediatric Surgeons Association. Memberships: President, 1984-85, Pacific Association of Paediatric Surgeons; President, 1987-88, Australian Association of Paediatric Surgeons; Vice President, 1984, World Federation of Paediatric Surgeons; RACS; ACS; AMA; Urology Society of Australia; BAPS; APSA. Hobbies: Music; Tennis; Gardening; Travel. Address: 12 Hardy Terrace, Ivanhoe, Victoria 3079, Australia.

SMITH Edwin Ide, b. 13 May 1924, Norfolk, Virginia, USA. Paediatric Surgeon; Educator. m. Matilda Janet Snelling, 31 Mar 1951, 1 son, 2 daughters. Education: Student, Harvard College, 1942-44; Student, Georgetown University School of Medicine, 1944-46; MD, Johns Hopkins University, 1948. Appointments: Private practice in Paediatric Surgery, Norfolk, Virginia, 1956-63; Associate Professor of Surgery, University of Missouri College of Medicine, Kansas City, 1963-68; Associate Professor of Surgery, 1968-71, Professor of Surgery, 1971-89, University of Oklahoma College of Medicine, Oklahoma City; Professor of Surgery, University of Texas Southwestern Medical Center, Dallas, 1989-94; Emeritus Professor of Surgery, 1994-. Publications: 89 articles in professional journals; 10 chapters in books. Memberships: American Academy of Pediatrics; Charter Member, American Burn Association; American College of Surgeons; Founding Member, American Pediatric Surgical Association; American Surgical Association; Society of Surgical Oncology; Southern Surgical Association; Lilliputian Surgical Society. Hobbies: Tennis; Music; Travel. Address: University of Texas, Southewestern Medical Center at Dallas/Southwestern Medical School, 5323 Harry Hines Blvd, Dallas, TX 75235, USA.

SMITH Elizabeth M, b. 15 Dec 1940, McCook, Nebraska, USA. Social Psychologist; Social Worker. m. Richard M Stout, 18 June 1983. Education: BA, 1960, MSW, 1962, University of Nebraska, Lincoln; PhD, Washington University, St Louis, Nebraska, 1978. Appointments: Chief Social Worker, Psychiatry Clinic, Barnes Hospital, St Louis, Missouri, 1963-67; Instructor, Department of Psychiatry, 1967-75, Assistant Professor, 1975-92, Associate Professor, 1992-, Washington University School of Medicine, St Louis. Publications: 55 including: Acute Post-disaster psychiatric disorders, 1990; Alcohol, drugs and psychiatric comorbidity among homeless women, 1993; Psychosocial Consequences of Sterilization, in Comprehensive Psychiatry, 1994. Honours: American Academy of Clinical Psychiatrists Award for Best Published Paper, 1992; Fellow, American Psychopathological Association. Memberships: American Psychological Association; International Society for Traumatic Stress Studies; Research Society on Alcoholism; American Public Health Association; National Association of Social Workers. Hobbies: Photography; Antiques; Travel. Address:

Department of Psychiatry, Washington University School of Medicine, 4940 Children's Place, St Louis, MO 63110, USA.

SMITH Gary A, b. 19 Nov 1952, California, USA. Physician. m. Morna Smith. Education: MD; DrPh; MS; MPH. Appointments: Director of Emergency Medicine & International Health, Department of Pediatrics, Ohio State University College of Medicine. Honours: One of the Ten Outstanding Young Americans, US Jaycees, 1988; One of the Ten Outstanding Young Persons of the World, Jaycees International, 1988. Memberships: Fellow, American Academy of Pediatrics; Fellow, American College of Preventive Medicine. Hobby: Scuba Diving. Address: Children's Hospital, Section of Emergency Medicine, 700 Children's Drive, Columbus, OH 43205, USA.

SMITH Gordon Stephen, b. 10 Oct 1951, Dunedin, New Zealand. Physician; Epidemiologist. m. Katy Lisa Benjamin, 18 Jun 1982, 1 s, 1 d. Education: MBChB, Otago University Medical School, Dunedin, 1975; MPH, Harvard School of Public Health, Boston, 1981. Career includes: Director, Tari Research Unit, Papua New Guinea, 1978-80; Teaching Assistant, Harvard School Public Health, 1981-82; Epidemic Intelligence Service Office, Centers for Disease Control, 1982-85; Assistant Professor, 1985-92, Associate Professor, 1992-, Johns Hopkins School of Public Health. Publications: 4 Books and book chapters and about 57 articles in professional journals including: Unintentional Injuries in Developing Countries: The epidemiology of a neglected problem, 1991; Methodologic issues in using hospital discharge data to determine incidence of hospitalized injuries, in American Journal of Epidemiology, 1991. Hobbies: Biking; Skiing; Hiking. Address: Johns Hopkins Injury Center, 624 North Broadway, Baltimore, MD 21205, USA.

SMITH James Cecil, b. 17 Jan 1934, Maryland, USA. Nutritionist. m. Kay L Plummer, 19 Aug 1961, 1 son, 2 daughters. Education: BS; MS; PhD; Postdoctorate, UCLA. Career: Health Service Office, National Institutes of Health, 1959-61; Biological Chemist, University of California, LA, 1964-66; Research Chemist, California Medical Center, Washington DC, 1966-70; Research Leader, VA Medical Center, 1970-77; Research Leader, US Department Agriculture, 1977-93; Research Chemist, US Department Agriculture, 1993-. Publications: Author or Co-author, 300 scientific articles & abstracts in journals & books including: Science, Lancet & Methods of Enzymology. Honours: Klaus Schwarz Award for Excellence in Trace Element Research, 1982. Memberships: American Institute of Nutrition; American Society for Clinical Nutrition; Commissioned Officers Association; US Public Health Service. Hobbies: Auto Mechanics; Woodsman; Travel. Address: Building 307, Room 122, US Department of Agriculture, Beltsville, MD 20705, USA.

SMITH James Richard, b. 15 Jan 1960, Falkirk, Scotland. Gynaecologist. m. Valerie Smith, 20 Mar 1993. Education: MB ChB; MRCOG, London, 1988; MD, Glasgow, 1992. Appointments: Currently Senior Lecturer and Consultant, Charing Cross and Westminster Medical School, Chelsea and Westminster Hospital, London. Publications: Co-author: Is HIV associated with cervical neoplasia?, 1993; Infection in Gynaecology, book, 1994. Memberships: Royal Society of Medicine; BGLS; MSSUD; BSCCP. Hobbies: Reading; Skiing; Rough shooting. Address: Department of Obstetrics and Gynaecology, Charing Cross and Westminster Medical School, Chelsea and Westminster Hospital, London SW10, England.

SMITH Joanne Victoria Elizabeth, b. 30 Mar 1960, Stone, Staffordshire, England. Chartered Clinical Psychologist. m. William David Norton, 13 June 1992, 1 son. Education: BSc (Hons), Psychology, 1981; MSc, Clinical Psychology, 1984; PhD, Psychology, 1991. Appointments: Research Associate, Senior Clinical Psychologist, West Birmingham Health Authority; Principal Clinical Psychologist, Rehabilitation, then Change Facilitator for Mental Services, Bromsgrove and Redditch Health Authority; Currently Head, Adult Clinical Psychology Service, NE Worcestershire Community Healthcare Trust. Publications: Co-author, over 20 including: Syntactic Comprehension in Downs Syndrome Children, 1984; Understanding Schizophrenia, 1985; Schizophrenia and the Family, 1987; Specific and non-specific effects of Educational Intervention with families living with a Schizophrenic Relative, 1987; Predicting and Controlling Relapse in Schizophrenia: early signs monitoring system, 1990; Informing People with Schizophrenia about their illness: the effect of Residual Symptoms, 1992; Family Interventions: service practice, 1992. Memberships: British Psychological Society; Division of Clinical Psychology, British Psychological Society; British Association for Cognitive Behavioural Psychotherapy. Hobbies: Squash; Sailing; Tennis. Address: c/o

Psychology Department, Smallwood House, Church Green West, Redditch, Worcestershire B97 4BD, England.

SMITH Josephine Ann, b. 19 Nov 1937, Leicester, England. Traditional Chinese Acupuncturist. m. Arthur J Smith, 13 May 1974, 2 sons. Education: Bachelor of Acupuncture; Licensed Acupuncturist. Appointments: Currently Acupuncture Practitioner. Membership: Traditional Acupuncture Society. Address: 123 Station Road, Glenfield, Leicester LE3 8GS, England.

SMITH Karl Ulrich, b. 1 May 1907, Zanesville, OH, USA. Professor. m. Margaret Foltz, 2 Aug 1937, 3 s, 2 d. Education: MA, Brown University, 1933; PhD, Brown University, 1935. Career: Instructor, Brown University, 1935-36; Instructor, 1936-38, Assistant Professor, 1938-43, University of Rochester; Research Director, NORC, 1943-45; Director, Bur Ind Psychology, University of WI, 1945-47; Visiting Professor, University of Trondheim, 1974; Professor of Psychology, University of WI, 1947-77, now retired. Publications: Behaviour of Man, 1958; Perception and Motion, 1962; Feedback and Behaviour, 1962; Behaviour, Organisation and Work, 1962; Cybernetic Prin Learning, 1966; Co-author, Psychology: Ints to Behavioural Science, 1973. Honours: National Science Research Awards, 1959-77; Distinguished Professor, Ford Foundation, 1960-61, 1971-72; Distinguished Professor, 1972, 1974, 1980; Human Factors Society Award, 1986; Paul Fritts Award, 1986; Meritorious Award, International Congress Cybernetics. Memberships include: Honorary Member, Human Factors Society; Phi Beta Kappa; Society of Experimental Psychologists; American Physiological Society. Hobbies: Horticulture. Address: 1001 Tower Boulevard, Lake Wales, FL 33853, USA.

SMITH Richard John Howard, b. 23 Feb 1953. Medical Doctor. m. Lynne Dorris Lanning, 22 Aug 1981, 2 s, 2 d. Education: BA, magna cum laude; MD, Pediatric Otolaryngology; FACS; FAAP. Assistant Professor, 1983-88, Associate Professor, 1988-90, Department of Otolaryngology, Baylor College of Medicine; Professor, Department of Otolaryngology, HNS, University of Iowa College of Medicine, 1990-. Publications: 95 Publications including: Co-author, Localization of two genes for Usher syndrome type 1 to chromosome II, in Genomics, 1992; Co-author, Localization of the gene for branchiootorenal syndrome to chromosome 8q, in Genomics, 1992; Co-author, Polymerase chain reaction amplification of DNA from archival celloidin-embedded human temporal bone sections, in Laryngoscope, 1993. Honours: Phi Beta Kappa, 1974; Phi Lambda Upsilon, 1974; Queeny Foundation Academic Scholarship, 1974; A B Cohn Academic Scholarship, 1975; Harriet Cunningham Citation for Meritorious Scientific Writing, 1982; Certificate of Appreciation, TX Department of Health, 1985; Barry J Anson Outstanding Teacher Award, 1991; Shirley Baron Award for Outstanding Research, 1992. Memberships include: AMA; American Academy of Otolaryngology, Head and Neck Surgery; International Society for History of Otolaryngology; Charter Member, American Society for Pediatric Otolaryngology; Fellow, American College of Surgeons; Fellow, American Academy of Pediatrics; American Society of Human Genetics; Research Association in Otolaryngology. Hobbies: Music; Sports. Address: 11 Cherry Lane, Iowa City, IA 52240, USA.

SMITH Robert Boulware III, b. 15 June 1933, Atlanta, Georgia, USA. Vascular Surgeon. m. Florence Limehouse, 22 Aug 1953, 2 sons, 1 daughter. Education: MD. Appointments: Instructor in Surgery, Columbia University College of Physicians and Surgeons, 1965; Associate in Surgery, 1966-67, Assistant Professor of Surgery, 1967-69, Associate Professor of Surgery, 1969-77, Professor of Surgery, School of Medicine 1977-, Head, General Vascular Surgery, 1984-, Acting Chairman, Department of Surgery, School of Medicine, 1990-91, Emory University; Chief, Surgical Service, VA Medical Centre, Atlanta, 1969-88; Associate Chief of Surgery, 1989-, Associate Medical Director, 1992-, Emory University Hospital. Publications: Contributor of numerous articles in professional journals. Honours: Phi Beta Kappa; Alpha Omega Alpha' Distinguished Service Award, Association of VA Surgeons, 1988. Memberships include: Medical Association of Atlanta; Medical Association of Georgia; American Medical Association; Southern Medical Association; Southeastern Surgical Congress; Atlanta Clinical Society; Association for Academic Surgery; Georgia Surgical Society; Society for Surgery of the Alimentary Tract; International Society for Cardiovascular Surgeons; American Surgical Association; American Heart Association, Council on Cardiothoracic and Vascular Surgery. Address: Emory University, Department of Surgery, 1364 Clifton Road NE, Atlanta, GA 30322, USA.

SMITH Thomas Elijah, b. 11 Apr 1933, North Augusta, SC, USA. Biochemist. m. W Arrena McKoy, 19 May 1953, 1 s, 1 d. Education: BS, Benedict College, 1953; MS, George Washington University, 1959; PhD, George Washington University, 1962. Appointments: Senior Scientist, Research Group Leader, Melpar Incorporated, 1963-65; Senior Scientist and Biochemist, Biomedical Division, Lawrence Livermore Laboratory, 1965-74; Associate Professor of Biochemistry and Assistant Dean of Graduate School of Biomedical Sciences, University of TX Health Sciences Center, Dallas, 1974-80; Professor and Chairman, Department of Biochemistry and Molecular Biology, Howard University College of Medicine, 1980-. Publications include: Molecular Cell Biology (book chapter), in Textbook of Biochemistry with Clinical Correlations, 1992; 7 Articles in professional journals, 1977-87, including: Co-author, The Use of Immunoblotting to Study Mutant Enzymes,' in BioTechniques, 1987. Honour: Percy L Julian Research Award, Sigma Xi, 1991. Memberships: American Chemical Society; Society of Sigma Xi; American Association for Advancement of Science. Hobbies: Photography; Reading; Cabinet Making. Address: Department of Biochemistry and Molecular Biology, Howard University College of Medicine, 520 W Street NW, Washington DC 20059-0001, USA.

SMITHSON William Anthony, b. 3 Oct 1942, Charlotte, NC, USA. Pediatric Hematology/Oncology. m. Judith Tyson, 3 Aug 1963, 2 sons, 1 daughter. Education: BA History; MD. Career: Associate Professor Pediatrics, Mayo Medical School, 1976-. Memberships: ASCO; ASH; AAP; ASPHO. Address: Department of Pediatrics, Mayo Clinic, Rochester, MN 55905, USA.

SNELLING Nicholas John, b. 22 Mar 1965, Purley, Surrey, England. Registered Osteopath. Education: BSc, Honours, Biology and Psychology; Diploma in Osteopathy. Membership: Register of Osteopaths. Hobbies: Gym; Swimming; Tennis. Address: 106 High Street, Rottingdean, Brighton, Sussex, England.

SNOW Diana Doyle, b. 31 July 1939, Mobile, Alabama, USA. Counsellor & Psychotherapist, Private Practice, 1973-. m. Nelson M Snow III, 8 Apr 1961, 2 sons. Education: BS, 1961, MA, 1970, PhD, 1981, University of Alabama. Appointments: Senior Unit Psychologist, Bryce State Psychiatric Hospital; Psychologist, University of Alabama, Birmingham Medical Centre; Counsellor, Frank Kay Clinic, Birmingham; Mental Health Planning Consultant, Baldwin County Mental Health Project, Spring Hill College, Psychology Department. Publications: Expression of Anger as a Variable in Cancer Patients: Implications for Psychological Treatment, 1981; A Time For Change, 1973; Early Decisions and the Cancer Patient, 1979. Memberships: American Psychological Association; American Association for Marriage & Family Therapy; International Transactional Analysis Association; Society for Behavioral Medicine; American Board for Medical Psychotherapy; National Board for Certified Counsellors. Hobbies: Hiking; Sailing; Golf; Cross Country Skiing; Guitar Playing; Art & Sculpting. Address: 113 West Volanta Avenue, Fairhope, AL 36532, USA.

SOBKOWICZ Hanna Maria, b. 1 Jan 1931, Warsaw, Poland. Scientist. m. Jerzy E Rose, 12 Mar 1972. Education: MD, 1954, PhD, 1962, Medical Academy, Warsaw, Poland; Board Certified in Neurology, 1959. Career: Resident, Senior Assistant in Neurology, Neurological Clinic of Medical Academy of Warsaw, Poland, 1955-63; Research Fellow, Mount Sinai Hospital, Columbia University, NY, 1963-66; Assistant Professor, 1966-72, Associate Professor, 1972-79, Professor, 1979-, Tissue Culture Laboratory, Department of Neurology, University of WI, Madison. Publications: Articles in medical journals on development and regeneration of the nervous system and hearing organ. Honours: NIH Grantee, 1968-; Editorial Board, International Journal of Developmental Neuroscience, 1984-; Member of NASA Grant Review Session. Hobbies: Books; Dogs; Flowers. Address: 4169 Cherokee Drive, Madison, WI 53711, USA.

SODERBERG-WARNER Margaret Louise, b. 2 May 1948, Escanaba, Michigan, USA. Allergist and Immunologist. div., 1 son, 1 daughter. Education: BS, Zoology, University of Michigan, 1970; MD, University of Michigan Medical School, 1974; Fellowship, Paediatric Allergy-Immunology: LAC-USC Medical Center, Los Angeles, 1976-77, UCLA Medical Center, 1977-79. Appointments include: Private practice, Allergy and Clinical Immunology (Adults, Children), 1979-; Assistant Clinical Professor, Paediatrics: University of California, Irvine, 1984-; UCLA Medical Center, 1985-. Publications: Co-author: Emergency Room Treatment of Status Asthmaticus in Children, 1977; Pharmacokinetics of Oral Theophylline in Asthmatic Children: Evaluation of New Preparation "Theolair", 1978; Cell-Mediated Immune Defects and Infection in Malnourished Hospitalized US Children, 1980; Lectin-Dependent T-Lymphocyte and Natural Killer Cytotoxic Deficiencies in Human Newborns, 1982; Reversal of Enterocolitis-associated Combined Immuno-deficiency by Plasma Therapy, 1982; Scanning and Transmission Electron Microscopic Aspects of the Nasal Acilia Syndrome, 1982; Neutrophil and T-Lymphocyte Characteristics of Two Patients with the Hyper-IgE Syndrome, 1984; Lack of Suppression by Concanavalin A-Activated Neonatal Mononuclear Cells, 1985. Honours include: Scholarships; Alpha Lambda Delta; Foundation for Children's Health Care Humanitarian Award, 1986. Memberships include: American Academy of Allergy and Immunology; Fellow, American Academy of Pediatrics; Joint Council of Allergy and Immunology; Western Society of Allergy and Immunology; Fellow, American College of Allergists; American and California Medical Associations; California Society of Allergy and Immunology, Executive Council 1988-90. Address: 4132 Katella Avenue, Suite 201, Los Alamitos, CA 90720, USA.

SOEPRONO Fred Fermin, b. 1 Aug 1947, China. Physician. m. Lorraine Medford, 9 Sep 1973, 5 children. Education: MD; MPH. Appointment: Associate Professor of Medicine, Loma Linda University. Publications: Contributions to Professional Journal. Honour: Alpha Omega Alpha. Memberships: AFIP; AAD; ASDS; ASD; CMA; AMA. Hobby: Skiing. Address: Loma Linda Skin Center, 1115 Mountain View Avenue, Suite 101, Loma Linda, CA 92354, USA.

SOIDLA Tonu, b. 28 May 1939, Rakvere, Estonia. Biologist. m. Olga Nevzglyadova, 16 Sep 1987, 1 son. Education: Diploma with Honour, Tartu University, 1963; PhD, 1969, DSc, 1990, Leningrad University. Appointments: Research Scientist, Leningrad University, 1966-83; Head of laboratory, Hydroloysis Research Institute, 1983-86; Senior Scientist, Institute Agricultural Microbiology, Leningrad, 1986-88; Leading Scientist, Leningrad Nuclear Physics Institute, 1988-91; Leading Scientist, Institute Cytology, St Petersburg, 1991-. Publications: Super-Suppressor Induced Interallelic Complementation, Co-author, 1966; Negative Complementation in ADE2 Locus in Saccharomyces, Co-author, 1976; Mechanisms of Translation Termination, Co-author, 1981; A Possible Enzymatic Role of Imported trNAlys in Splicing of Yeast Mitochrondrial Transcripts, 1986; Open Mouth, Open Mind, 1995. Honours: Stipend, Russian Academy of Sciences for Outstanding Scientist, 1994. Memberships: Vavilov's Genetical Society, Russia; European Society for the Study of Science and Theology. Hobby: Music. Address: Institute of Cytology, Tikhoretsky Ave 4, St Petersburg 194064, Russia.

SOKOL Ronald Jay, b. 18 July 1950, Chicago, Illinois, USA. Physician (Paediatric Gastroenterology and Nutrition). m. Lori Lubman, 20 Aug 1990, 2 sons. Education: BS, University of Illinois, Urbana, 1972; MD, University of Chicago School of Medicine, 1976; Paediatric Residency, University of Colorado Medical Center, Denver, 1976-80; Fellow, Paediatric Gastroenterology and Nutrition, Children's Hospital, Cincinnati, Ohio, 1980-83. Appointments: Currently Associate Professor of Paediatrics, University of Colorado School of Medicine, Denver. Publications: 60 articles; 31 chapters, symposia, reviews; 27 other publications. Honours: Edward J James Scholar, 1968-72; Phi Beta Kappa, 1971; Bronze Tablet, 1972; Alpha Omega Alpha, 1976; Mead Johnson Award for Nutrition Research, 1990. Memberships: Society for Pediatric Research; American Gastroenterology Association; American Association for Study of Liver Disease; American Institute of Nutrition; North American Society for Pediatric Gastroenterology and Nutrition. Hobbies: Hiking; Climbing; Camping; Windsurfing; Gardening; Basketball. Address: Box B290, The Children's Hospital, 1056 E 19th Ave, Denver, CO 80218-1088, USA.

SOKOLOV Boris A, b. 30 Dec 1930, Moscow, Russia. Geologist. m. J N Sokolova, Mar 1957, 1 s, 1 d. Education: Doctor of Geology. Career: Professor, 1980, Head of Fossil Fuel Geology and Geochemistry Chair, 1992, Dean of Geology Department, 1992, Moscow State University; Academician of Russian Academy of Natural Sciences and Academy of High Education. Publications: 15 Books in Russian including: Oil and Gas Basins of the Earth, 1965; Features of Geology of Pakistan, 1971; Evolution and Oil and Gas Potential of Sedimentary Basins, 1980; Oil and Gas Formation in Eastern Pre-Caucasus, 1990. Honours: Honoured Diploma, Moscow Society of Nature Investigators, 1976, 1983; Honoured Scientist of Russia, 1991. Memberships: Moscow Society of Nature Investigators; Scientific Council on Fossil Fuel Geology and Geochemistry, Moscow. Hobbies: Travel; Dogs. Address: Moscow State University, Department of Geology, Vorobjovy Gory, 119899 Moscow, Russia.

SOKOLOV Eugeni Ivanovich, b. 21 Nov 1929, Moscow, Russia. Professor of Internal Diseases. m. Alexandra Klimenko, Aug 1949, 1 son. Education: Diploma, Second Moscow Medical Institute; Candidate of Medical Sciences, DMS, State Higher Certifying Commission. Appointments: Assistant Lecturer, 1960-68, Senior Researcher, Assistant Professor, 1968-71, Professor, Head, Internal Diseases Department, 1971-, Rector, Moscow Medical Stomatology Institute. Publications: Emotions and Arterosclerosis, 1983; Emotions, Hormones and Arterosclerosis, 1993. Honour: Order of Friendship, 1976. Memberships: Therapeutics Society; Cardiologists Soceity. Hobby: Swimming. Address: 114a Mir Prospect, Moscow 129141, Russia.

SOKOLOV Viktor, b. 26 Sept 1937, Odessa, Ukraine. Radiologist. m. L D Moros, 19 Apr 1958, 1 son. Education: BA, 1960, MD, 1974, Odessa University. Appointments: Professor, Head Chair, Medical Institute, Odessa, 1966-76; Head Chair, Department of Medical Sciences, Kremlin, Moscow, 1976-80; Head, Department of Gastroenterology, Moscow Scientific Institute, 1980-83, 1983-87; Head, Chair, X-Ray department, Odessa, 1987-95. Publications: Radiocirculography in Clinical Practice, 1974; Tumors of Eyes, Its Appendages and Orbits, 1978; Rentgenological of Diseases of the Digestive Organs, 1980; Pulmonological Atlas, 1985. Honours: Honorary Member of Sciences and Technology of Ukraine. Memberships: Vice President, Republic Association of Radiologists; Computer Medicine Association. Hobby: Running. Address: Street Torgova, House 8, Flat 42, Odessa, 270100 Ukraine.

SOLANKE Toriola Feisetan, b. 9 Mar 1930, Ijebu-ode, Ogun State. Medical Professor. m. Olufolake Solanke, 6 Oct 1956, 1 son, 2 daughters. Education: MB, ChB, St Andrews; CHM, Dundee, FRCS, England; FNMC, Nigeria. Appointments: Professor of Surgery, University of Ibadan, 1970-90; Provost, Ladoke Akintola University of Technology, 1990-93; Chairman, Co-ordinator, National Headquarters of Cancer Registries in Nigeria. Publications: Co-author: Cancer in Nigeria, 1982; Co-author: Breast Lumps in Western Nigeria, 1986; Manual on Superficial Tumours, 1992. Memberships: Nigeria Medical Association; British Medical Association. Hobbies: Hunting. Address: National Headquarters of Cancer Registries in Nigeria, University College Hospital, PMB 5116, Ibadan, Nigeria.

SOLNIT Albert J, b. 26 Aug 1919, CA, USA. Physician. m. Martha Benedict, 22 Oct 1949, 3 s, 1 d. Education: University of CA, San Francisco and Berkeley; MD. Appointments: Former Director of Yale Child Study Center, 1966-83; Coordinator of Muriel Gardiner Program in Psychoanalysis and The Humanities at Yale, 1987-; Commissioner, CT Department of Mental Health; Sterling Professor Emeritus, Pediatrics and Psychiatry, Yale University Child Study Center, New Haven, CT. Publications: Beyond Best Interests of the Child, 1973; Before the Best Interests of The Child, 1979; In the Best Interests of The Child, 1986; When Home is No Haven, 1992; Many Meanings of Play, 1993. Honours: Honorary President, International Association for Child and Adolescent Psychiatry, 1990; Distinguished Service Award, American Psychiatric Association, 1992. Memberships: Institute of Medicine; American Academy of Child and Adolescent Psychiatry; International Psychoanalytical Association; Association for Child Psychiatry. Hobbies: Travel; Reading; Grandchildren. Address: PO Box 207900, New Haven, CT 06520-7900, USA.

SOLOMAN Laurence Richard, b. 26 Aug 1948, Beaconsfield, England. Physician. m. Judith Ann Bingham, 23 Jan 1982, 2 d. Education: MA; MD; FRCP; MB; BCLir. Appointments: Consultant Physician, General & Renal Medicine, Royal Preston Hospital, Preston, UK. Publications: Numerous on Renal Disease. Memberships: Renal Association; European Dialysis and Transplant Association; International Society of Nephrology. Address: Renal Unit, Royal Preston Hospital, Sharoe Green Lane, Preston, UK.

SOLOMON Brenda Rae Clorfene, b. 7 Dec 1939, Chicago, IL, USA. Psychiatrist; Psychoanalyst. m. David Solomon MD, 26 Jun 1961, 2 s. Education: MD. Appointments: Currently, Faculty, Chicago Institute for Psychoanalysis; Clinical Assistant Professor, University of IL College of Medicine, Department of Psychiatry. Honour: Fellow, American Psychiatric Association, 1977. Memberships: American Psychiatric, Psychoanalytic Adolescent Associations; International Psychoanalytic

Association. Hobbies: Bicycling; Rollerblading; Piano. Address: 150 Park Avenue, Glencoe, IL 60022, USA.

SOLOMON George Freeman, b. 25 Nov, Freeport, New York, USA. Physician. m. Susan Keran, 22 July 1974, 2 sons. Education: AB, Stanford University, 1952; MD, Stanford University School of Medicine, 1955. Appointments: Assistant & Associate Professor of Psychiatry, Stanford, 1962-73; Professor of Psychiatry, University California, San Francisco 1976-84; University of California, Los Angeles, 1984-95; Professor Emeritus, 1995-. Publications: 68 papers, 54 book chapters, 11 commentaries, 2 books, From Psyche to Soma and Back, 1995. Honours: Dedication of Textbook, Psychoneuroimmunology, 1991; Fellow, Royal College of Psychiatrists, England; Fellow, American Psychiatric Association; Fellow, International College of Psychosomatic Medicine; Fellow, Academy of Behavioral Medicine Research; Fellow, Society of Behavioral Medicine; Fellow, American College of Forensic Psychiatry. Address: 19054 Pacific Coast Highway, Malibu, CA 90265, USA.

SOLOMON Steven L, b. 13 Jan 1951, New York City, USA. Physician. Education: BA, Rutgers University, 1971; MD, Tufts University, 1975. Appointments: Epidemic Intelligence Service, Center for Disease Control(CDC); Acting Chief, Epidemiology Branch, Hospital Infections PGM, CDC; Assistant Director for Prevention, Training & Laboratory Program Office, CDC. Honours: Public Health Service Meritorious Service Medal; Oustanding Service Medal; Alexander D Langmuir Prize. Memberships: Fellow, American College of Physicians; Infectious Diseases Society of America; Society for Healthcare Epidemiology of America. Address: 1600 Clifton Road NE, Mailstop A-07, Atlanta, GA 30333, USA.

SOLOMON Zahava, b. 31 May 1950, Israel. Psychiatric Epidemiology. m. 25 July 1972, 1 son, 1 daughter. Education: PhD. Appointments: Head of Research Branch, Department of Mental Health; Dean, School of Social Work. Publications: Combat Stress Disorder - The Enduring Toll of War, 1993; Coping with the Gulf War; Over 140 scientific articles. Memberships: ISTSS. Hobbies: Music; Sailing. Address: 5 Haprachin Street, Heizeliya, Israel.

SOLORZANO del RIO Hector E, b. 11 May 1955, Guadalajara, Mexico. Surgeon; Doctor of Science. m. Cecilia G Flores Becerra, 27 Dec 1992, 2 sons, 2 daughters. Education: MD; DSc; Doctor of Naturopathy. Appointments: Professor of Microbiology, University of Guadalajara, 1974; Professor of Cybernetics, University of Guadalajara; Professor of Pharmacology, University of Guadalajara; Adjunct Professor, University of Durango; Adjunct Professor of Acupucnture, UNAM. Publications: Enzimoterapia, 1991; Masaje Tuina, 1994; Probiotica, 1994; Over 100 articles to professional journals and magazines. Honours: Honorary Member, Sociedad Mexicana de Medicos Acupunt, 1976; Honorary Member, Medizinische Forshung Gesellschaft Enzimatisch, 1990; Honorary Member, Policlinic University of Guadalajara, 1976; Two Golden Needle Awards, ORICI, Canada, 1980. Memberships: Sociedad de Investigacion de Acupuntura y Medicina Oriental; Association Medica de Jalisco; Sociedad Mexicana de Medicos; World Federation of Acupuncture. Hobbies: Jogging; Aerobics; Camping; Swimming. Address: Los Alpes 1022, Col Independencia, Jal 44340, Guadalajara, Mexico.

SOLURSH Lionel Paul, b. 14 Jan 1936, Toronto, Canada. Psychiatrist. m. (1) Marcia Persin, divorced, 1 s, 2 d, (2) Diane Sue Mullenax, 2 d. Education: MD, University of Toronto, 1959; Diploma in Psychiatry, University of Toronto, Canada, 1962; CRCPC, Royal College of Physicians, 1964; FRCPC, 1965; Diplomate, American Board of Sexology; Board Certified, Sex Educator and Clinical Supervisor. Career includes: Associate Professor, 1974-86, University of Toronto; Director, PTSD Out-Patient Psychiatry, VA Medical Center, Augusta, 1986-; Professor of Psychiatry and Health Behaviour, Medical College of GA, Augusta, 1986-; Consultant Psychiatrist, Augusta Correctional Medical Institute, GA, 1990-; Medical Director, Special In-Patient Unit, Post Traumatic Stress Disorder, 1991-, Assistant Chief, Psychiatry, 1991-, VA Medical Center, Augusta; Consultant, GA Regional Hospital, Augusta. Publications: Human Sexuality, audiotape, 1967, 1971; Art, Symbolism and Mental Health, videotape, 1991; Contributor of book reviews, over 148 papers to professional journals and book chapters. Honours: RS McLaughlin Travelling Fellow, 1966; Outstanding Young Canadian, 1974; Minister of Health Gold Medalist, University of Toronto, 1962; Fellow, American Orthopsychiatric Association. Memberships: Associate Fellow, American Academy of Clinical Sexologists; American Psychiatric

Association; American Academy of Psychiatrists in Alcoholism and Addictions; AMA; CPA; International Society for Traumatic Stress Studies; American Association of Sex Educators, Counselors and Therapists. Hobbies: Photography; Scuba Diving; Travel; Performing Arts; Cyberspace Touring. Address: VA Medical Center 116AU, 2460 Wrightsborg Road, Augusta, GA 30904, USA.

SOMMER Alfred, b. 2 Oct 1942, New York, USA. Ophthalmologist. m. Jill Abramson, 3 Sept 1963, 1 son, 1 daughter. Education: MD, Harvard Medical School, 1967; MHS, Johns Hopkins, 1972. Appointments: Dean, Johns Hopkins School of Public Health; Professor of Ophthalmology; President, International Federation of Eye Banks;. Publications: Epidemiology & Statistics for Ophthalmology, 1980; Vitamin A Deficiency, 1994; Control of Vitamin A Deficiency, 1994; Over 270 professional articles. Honours: Phi Beta Kappa, 1963; Dana Award, 1988; E V McCollum Award, 1988; Joseph Smadel Medal, 1991; Gold Medal, Saudi Ophthalmological Society, 1992; National Academy of Science, Institute of Medicine, 1992 Memberships: American Academy of Ophthalmology; American Ophthalmological Society; APHA. Hobbies: Travel; Reading. Address: Suite 1041, Johns Hopkins School of Hygiene & Public Health, 615 N Wolfe Street, Baltimore, MD 21205, USA. 2.

SOMMER Joachim R, b. 11 Apr 1924. Pathologist. m. Doris M Fischer, 14 July 1951, 1 son, 1 daughter. Education: MD, University of Munich, Germany. Appointments: Duke University Medical Center, 1958-. Publications: The Ultrastructure of Cardial Muscle, 1979; Comparative Auatomy: In Praise of a Powerful Approach to Elucidate, 1995. Memberships: American Society of Cell Biology; American Society of Investigative Pathology; Microscopy Society of America; AAAS. Hobbies: Carpentry. Address: Department of Pathology, Duke University Medical Center, Box 3548, Durham, NC 27710, USA.

SONDEL Paul M, b. 14 Aug 1950, Milwaukee, USA. Physician; Researcher. m. Sherie Ann Katz, 1 Jan 1973, 1 son, 3 daughters. Education: BS, Honours, 1968-71, PhD, 1971-72, 1974-75, University of Wisconsin, Madison; MD, Magna cum laude, Harvard Medical School, Boston, Massachusetts, 1972-74, 1975-77. Appointments include: Intern, Department of Paediatrics, University of Minnesota Hospital, Minneapolis, 1977-78; Resident, Department of Paediatrics, University of Wisconsin Hospital and Clinics, Madison, Wisconsin, 1978-80; Visiting Scientist, Department of Cell Biology, Weizmann Institute of Science, Rehovot, Israel, 1987; Assistant Professor, Department of P{aediatrics, Human Onc9ology and Genetics, 1980-84, Associate Professor, 1984-86, Professor, Departments of Paediatrics, Human Oncology and Genetics, 1987-, Head, Division of Paediatric Haematology and Oncology, department of Paediatrics, 1990-, Program Leader, Clinical Cancer Centre Programme in Biological Therapy and Immunology, 1990-, Programme Leader, Comprehensive Cancer Centre Program in Paediatric Oncology, 1990-, University of Wisconsin. Publications: Contributor of over 200 professional articles in medical journals. Honours include: Phi Eta Sigma, 1969; Phi Beta Kappa, 1971; Alpha Omega Alpha, 1977; University of Wisconsin Romnes Faculty Research Award, 1986-90; State of Wisconsin Combined Health Appeal Advancement Award, 1993; Dean's Award for Excellence in Health Communication, University of Wisconsin Medical School and Public Affairs Department of the Centre for Health Sciences, 1994. Memberships include: Transplantation Society. Address: Departmenmt Paediatrics, University of Wisconsin Centre for Health Sciences, 600 Highland Avenue, Madison, WI 53792, USA.

SONG Dandan, b. 29 July 1951, Harbin, Heilongjiang, China. Director; Editor. 1 daughter. Education: Department of Medicine, Jiamusi Medical College. Appointments include: Director, Lesser Circulation Cardiac Function Section, Harbin Children's Hospital; Director, Physical Diagnosis section, Harbin Institute of Paediatrics; Editor, Chinese Journal of Medical Electric Impedance. Publications: Over 10 treatise including: The Study of Lesser Circulation Cardiac Function in China; The Study of Lesser Circulation Cardiac Function and Its Progress, 1991. Honours include: 4th Harbin Science and Progress Award, 1991; 1st Heilongjiang New Technology in Medicine Award, 1993; 2nd Award, Harbin Science and Technology Progress, 1993. Address: 55 Youyi Road, Daoli District, Harbin 150010, Heilongjiang, China.

SONG Gang, b. 18 Feb 1959, Jilin City, China. Physician. m. Feb 1985, 1 daughter. Education: MB, Third Army Medical University, Chongqing City. Appointment: Doctor in Digestive Medicine. Publications: Effect of Endoscopic Electrochemical Treatment on Esophageal and Crdiac Carcinoma, 1995. Membership: China Medical

Association. Address: Army Hospital 222, 47# Yue Shan Road, Jilin City, Jilin 132011, China.

SONG Guo-Xiang, b. 25 Oct 1928, Tianjin, China. Ophthalmologist. m. 20 Apr 1956, 2 sons. Education: Graduate, Beijing Medical University, 1955. Appointments: Intern, Affiliated Hospital, Beijing Medical University, 1955; Resident, Visiting Ophthalmologist, Associate Professor, Affiliated Hospital, Tianjin Medical College, 1955-86. Publications: Eye Changes in Internal Disease, 1977; Orbital Lesions: The Enlightenment from 1012 Operations, 1989; Ultrasound in Medicine, 1994. Honours: Scientific Advance Award, 1993. Memberships: Standing Committee, Chinese Society of Ophthamology; Chairman, Chinese Society of Ophthalmic Ultrasound. Address: Department of Ophthalmology, 2nd Hospital of Tianjin Medical University, Tianjin, China.

SONG Ming, b. 8 Dec 1928, Liaoning, China. Professor of Paediatric Cardiology. m. Fang Chen Shi, 8 Feb 1950, 1 son, 1 daughter. Education: National Medical College of Sheng Yang, 1946-48; BD, China Medical University, 1951. Appointments: Doctor, 1951-52, resident Doctor, 1952-56, Chief Doctor, 1956-78, Vice Professor, 1978-85, Professor of Paediatric Cardiology and Director of MD, 1955-, First Teaching Hospital of Harbin Medical University. Publications: Pediatrics, 1979; Practical Healthology of Children, 1988; Pediatric Cardiology, 1995; Analysis of 1165 Cases of Viral Myocarditis, 1984; Clinical Observation of Rheumatism of Children, 1957. Honours: 2nd Class Award of Scientific Achievement, Ministry of Public Health, 1982; 1st Class Award of Developing New Technology, Office of Public Health of Heilongjiang Province, 1984. Memberships: Committeeman of Appraisal, State Natural Science Fund; Deputy Secretary-General, HLJ Province Branch, Department of Paediatrics, China Medicine Commission; Vice Chairman, Harbin City Branch Department of Paediatrics, China Medical Commission. Hobby: Swimming. Address: The First Hospital of Harbin Medical University, 110 4-201 You Zheng Street, Nan Gang Ha-Er-Bin 150001, China.

SONG Nai Yun, b. 10 Mar 1942, Chongin, China. Doctor. m. Huo Chen Yu, 23 Nov 1944, 1 s, 1 d. Education: BA, West University, China. Appointment: Professor. Publications: Campycobacter pyloridis in chronic gastritis, analysis of 324 cases, 1990; Clinical Analysis of 88 patients with ACI with MSOF, 1993. Membership: Chinese Medical Association, Chongqin Branch. Hobbies: Running; Photography. Address: Chong Qin The 9th People's Hospital, Chongqin 630700, China.

SONG Shi-Lian, b. 8 May 1933, Liaoning, China. Professor of Biochemistry. m. Wang Mei-zhen, 26 Jan 1955, 2 daughters. Education: BS, Beijing University. Appointments: Technician, 501 Factory, 1954-57; Assistant Professor, Director of Business Department, Director of Research Section, Zoological Institutem, Chinese Academy of Sciences, 1963-82; Professor of Biochemistry and Food Nutrition, Director of Research Section, Director of MD Programme, Dalian Light Industry Institute, 1982-; Director, Liaoning Biochemical Academy. Publications: Study on the friction of secreting glue by Saccifer lasca (Kerr), 1964; Research on effect of stiff silkworm and musk, 1971-72; Systematic research on effect of snake venom, 6 papers; Study on new process of ferment of citric acid, 1992; Study on soybean, 8 papers, 1984-94. Honours: 1st Prize for Scientific Research, Chinese Academy of Sciences, 1977; 1st Prize for Science and Technology Development, Yunnan Province, 1980; Excellent Teacher, Light Industry Ministry of China, 1989; 1st Prize for Science and Technology, Hunan Province, 1991. Memberships: Biochemical Academy of China; Director, Liaoning Biochemical Academy. Hobbies: Travel; Music. Address: Dalian Institute of Light Industry, Dalian, Liaoning 116001, China.

SONG Xiu-Jun, b. 20 October 1949, Hubei, China. Doctor, Professor. m. Zhi-chen Cao, 21 July 1977, 1 daughter. Education: MD, Tangshan Medical College, China, 1976. Appointments: Resident, Assistant, Department of Ophthalmology, 3rd Affiliated Hospital, Hebei Medical University, 1976-85; Chief Resident, Lecturer, Department of Ophthalmology, 3rd Affiliated Hospital, Hebei Medical University, 1985-86; Assistant Professor, Hebei Medical University, Attending Doctor, 3rd Affiliated Hospital, Hebei Medical University, 1986-90; Visiting Scholar, Fellowship from WHO, University of Houston, College of Optometry, USA, 1990-93; Associate Professor, Hebei Medical University, Ophthalmic Surgeon-in-Vice-Chief, 3rd Affiliated Hospital, Hebei Medical University, 1993-. Publications: Ocular symptom in patient with botulism, 1983; Observation in medicinal curative effect in

experimental hyphema using method of isotope mark (co-author), 1984; Ocular fundus fluorescein angiography, 1986; Survey of blindness and ocular diseases in rural of Zhengding County of Hebei Province, 1986; Epithelial ingrowing glaucoma (co-author), 1988; Dislocation of lens, 1989; Analysis of flow cytometry of the retinoblastoma and its clinical significance, 1990; Epidemiologic investigation of blind and low vision in Hebei Province, 1992. Honours Include: Award, Provincial Achievement in Scientific Research, 1986, 1989 1993, 1994; Title, Advanced Worker in Prevention & Treatment of Blindness in Hebei, 1988; Fellowship, World Health Organization in Ophthalmology, 1989; Title, Advanced Individual in Low Vision Rehabilitation, 1994. Memberships: Chinese Medical Association. Hobbies: Table Tennis; Beijing Opera. Address: Hebei Medical University, Shijiazhuang, Hebei 050051, China.

SONG Zhen-Ying, b. 24 Jan 1920, Yanshi, Henan, China. Ophthalmologist. m. 10 Oct 1948, 2 sons, 2 daughters. Education: National Military Medical College, Shanghai, 1941-47. Appointments: Ophthalmic Assistant Resident Doctor, Shanghai General Hospital, 1947-52; Ophthalmic Instructor, 5th Military Medical College, Nanjing, 1953-56; Ophthalmic Chief Physician, General Hospital of Jinan Command, Jinan, 1957-94. Publications: Co-author: Ophthalmic Therapeutics, 1983; Ophthalmic Traumatology, 1988; Practical Ocular Fundus Diseases; Current Ophthalmology; Chief editor: Ocular Syndromes, 1st Edition, 1964, 2nd Edition, 1975, 3rd Edition, 1994; Handbook of Ophthalmic Emergency; Diagnostic Handbook of Ocular Symptoms, 1988; Ophthalmic Diagnosis, 1985. Honours: Permanent National Special Subsidy for Outstanding Medical Achievement, 1992-; Science Awards for: Conjunctival flap operation for pterygium, 1958; The levator muscle advancement for ptosis, 1964; The classification of retinal arteriosclerosis, 1982; Removal of foreign bodies from the transparent lens, 1986; The classification of conjunctival microcirculation, 1988; Angiogenesis and development of corneal neovascularization, 1988; Morphometric study of endothelial wound-healing following penetrating keratoplasty, 1993. Memberships: Chinese Medical Association; Adviser, Jinan Ophthalmic Association; Adviser, Ophthalmic Institution, People's Liberation Army. Hobbies: Cultivating flowers; Strolling: Appreciating cartoons and humorous pictures. Address: Ophthalmic Department, General Hospital of Jinan Command, People's Liberation Army, No 25 Shifan Road, Jinan 250031, China.

SONG Zheng Lian, b. 26 Dec 1926, Sichuan, China. Doctor. m. Zhu Xiue Xian, 6 Mar 1953, 1 son, 1 daughter. Education: BM, Hubei College of Medicine, 1951; Master, China Academy of Traditional Chinese Medicine, 1958. Career: Surgeon, Hubei Huang Shi Hospital, 1951; Physician, China Academy of Traditional Chinese Medicine, 1953; Vice Director, 1962; Director, 1974; Professor, 1981; Professor, Institute of Acupuncture and Moxibustion, Academy of Traditional Chinese Medicine; President & Professor, Chinese Medical Centre in Dubai UAE. Publications: Co-author, Treatment of Common Diseases Manual, 1970; Clinical Application of Acupuncture and Moxibustion, 1975; An Outline of Chinese Acupuncture, 1975, 1977; Practical Traditional Chinese Medicine, 1989, 1992; 46 learned articles. Honours: The Ministry of Public Health, People's Republic of China Medaled Certificate of Honour, 1958; Certificate of Honour, 1988; Medal of Brilliant Development of Acupuncture and Moxibustion for Thirty Years, 1991. Memberships: All-China Society of Acupuncture and Moxibustion; Australia Society of Acupuncture and Moxibustion; Expert Committee, Institution of Acupuncture and Moxibustion of China. Hobbies: Swimming; Running. Address: Chinese Research Institute of Traditional Chinese Medicine, Beijing, China.

SONG Zhong-Lin, b. 1 Nov 1936, Jiangxi, China. Surgeon. m. 20 Jan 1962, 3 sons. Education: Jiangxi 1st Medical Institute, 1953. Appointments: Assistant Surgeon, Hangchan 1st Hospital, 1953; Surgeon, Jingdezheng 1st People's Hospital, 1961; Surgeon, Affliated Hospital of Shanghai Railway Medical College, 1964; Assistant Chief Surgeon, 1978, Vice-Director, 1979, Surgeon-in-Chief, 1987, Director, 1988, currently President, Surgeon-in-Chief, Jingdezheng 3rd People's Hospital, Jiangxi. Publications: Intestinal Obstruction Caused by Splenectopia, 1959; Traumatic Pseudo-Mesentery Cyst and Mesenteric Hiatal Hernia, 1962; Some Technical Improvement in Pancreatic Cyst Intragastric Drainage, 1981; Co-author: Congenital Caecal Ureter, 1983; Cholangiothoracic Fistulae. 1989; Diagnosis and Treatment of Surgical Emergency, 1992. Honours: Director Member of Development of Spiritual Culture, Jingdezhen City Government, 1985; Honorary Professor, Jiangxi Medical College, 1990; Special Technical Excellent Personage, Jingdezheng City Government, 1993. Memberships: Integrated Traditional and Western Medical Research Association;

Jiangxi Provincial Society of Surgery; Lung Cancer Association of Jiangxi; Acute Abdominal Association of Jiangxi; Micro-Circulation Research Association of Jiangxi. Hobbies: Poetry; Novels; Chinese history. Address: Affiliated Hospital of Shanghai Railway Medical College, Shanghai, China.

SONMEZ Bingur, b. 3 May 1952, Turkey. Doctor of Medicine. m. Nilgun Sonmez, 3 Dec 1978, 1 son, 1 daughter. Education: MD, Istanbul University; Qualification as Professor. Appointments: Assistant, 1978, Senior Registrar, 1985-87, currently Chief of Department, Istanbul University; Honorary Registrar, Research Fellow, 1984-85, Registrar, Senior Registrar, 1987-90, St Thomas Hospital. Publications: Co-author: Les ruptures bronciques post-traumatiques, complètes et muettes de l'enfant, 1983; Implantation of expanded politetrafluoroethylene grafts on peripheral arterial occlusions, 1985; Particle-Induced Coronary Vasoconstriction in the Rat Heart: Pharmacological Investigation of Underlying Mechanisms, 1986; Ruptured abdominal aortic aneurism with fistula into the right iliac vein, 1987; A usual vascular complication following partial nephrectomy, 1988; Late Vascular Complication of Lumbar Disc Surgery Case Reports, 1988; Traction injury in the internal mammary artery, 1990; Postoperative cardiac surgical care: an alternative approach, 1993; About 30 publications in Turkish. Memberships: Society of Thoracic and Cardiovascular Surgeons of Great Britain and Ireland; European Society of Cardiovascular Surgery; International Society for Heart Research; Cardiac Muscle Research Group; The International College of Angiology; Turkish Cardiology Society; Turkish Respiratory Research Society; Turkish Oncology Society. Hobbies: Skiing; Gardening. Address: Florence Nightingale Hastanesi, Caglayan, Istanbul, Turkey.

SOOD V P, b. 13 Apr 1936, Amb, India. Surgeon. m. 14 Feb 1966, 2 d. Education: MBBS, Punjab University, 1961; MS, Otorhinolaryngology, All India Institute of Medical Sciences, New Delhi, 1965; FICS, 1980. Appointments include: Teaching Fellow, Department of Otolaryngology, All India Institute of Medical Science, New Delhi, 1963-65; Registrar, 1965-68, Lecturer, 1968-69, Assistant Professor, 1969-70, ENT Department, Maulana Azad Medical College and associated Irwin and GB Pant Hospitals, New Delhi; Assistant Professor, Head of ENT Department, Medical College, Shimla, 1970-71; Assistant Professor, Department of Otorhinolaryngology, All India Institute of Medical Sciences, New Delhi, 1971-81; Senior ENT Consultant, Moolchand Hospital, New Delhi, 1981-; Senior ENT Consultant, Batra Hospital, New Delhi, 1986-; Senior ENT Consultant, Central Railway Hospital, New Delhi, 1986-. Publications: Contributor of over 55 clinical and research papers; Presentations at numerous professional conferences. Honours include: Shri Gauravashali Award, International Milan Club, Delhi, 1992; Awarded Rajdhani Ratna by Ex-President of India, 1992. Memberships include: International Rhinology Society; Fellow, International College of Surgeons; Founder Secretary, All India Rhinology Society, 1986-; President, 1992-93, Association of Otolaryngologists of India. Address: 48 New Rajdhani Enclave, Vikas Marg, Delhi 110092, India.

SOOKNANAN Narine Datt, b. 31 October 1940, Crabwood Creek, Guyana. Doctor of Medicine. m. Eliska, 22 July 1977, 3 sons, 1 daughter. Education: MD, Charles University, Prague; LRCP, London; MRCS, England; FRCOG, London. Appointments: Senior Consultant Obstetrician & Gynaecologist. Memberships: Royal College of Obstetricians & Gynaecologists; British Medical Association; The British Medical Ultrasound Society. Hobbies: Fishing; Farming. Address: 5-11 Coburg Street, New Amsterdam, Berbice, Guyana.

SOOTHILL Peter William, b. 30 Oct 1957, Droitwich, England. Professor of Fetal Medicine. m. Caroline Jane MacKenzie, 3 daughters. Education: MBBS; BSc; MRCOG; MD; University of London, England. Career: Guys Hospital, King College Hospital, 1982-85; Research Fellow, King's College Hospital, 1985-87; Oxford, 1987-88; Bristol, 1988-89; Lecturer in Obstetrics & Gynaecology, 1989-92; Senior Lecturer/Consultant, University College Hospital, London, England, 1992-94; Professor of Maternal and Fetal Medicine, University of Bristol, currently. Publications: Over 100 publications on aspects of fetal medicine. Membership: Royal Society of Obstetrics & Gynaecology. Hobbies: Music; Family. Address: St Michael's Hospital, University of Bristol, Southwell Stret, Bristol, England.

SORENSEN Ricardo U, b. 13 May 1939, Valdivia, Chile. Physician. m. Sally O Bruch, 1 Aug 1970, 3 daughters. Education: Medical degree, University of Chile, Santiago, 1964. Appointments: Assistant Professor, Associate Professor, Department of Paediatrics, Calvo Mackenna

Hospital, University of Chile; Assistant Professor of Paediatrics, Associate Professor of Paediatrics, Associate Professor of Pathology, Case Western Reserve University, Cleveland, Ohio, USA; Currently Professor of Paediatrics and Immunology, Head, Division of Allergy and Immunology, Department of Paediatrics, Louisiana State University Medical Center, New Orleans. Publications: About 3 dozen original articles in Chilean medical journals, mostly in paediatrics; Over 50 in American medical journals including: Lymphocyte responses to bacterial antigens in human neonates (with H Rubin and S H Polmar), 1981; Efficacy and safety of high dose IVIG therapy for antibody deficiency syndromes (with S H Polmar), 1984; Studies of the mechanism of T cell inhibition by the Pseudomonas aeruginosa phenazine pigment pyocyanine (co-author), 1987; Antibody levels and response to pneumococcal vaccine in steroid dependent asthmatics (with N Lahood, S S Emerson, P Kumar), 1993; Disseminated bacillus Calmette-Guerin (BCG) infections in patients with primary immunodeficiencies - Pathologic findings (with C Abramowsky and B Gonzalez), 1993; Book chapters. Memberships: American College of Allergy and Immunology; Louisiana Allergy Society; Clinical Immunology Society; Association of Medical Laboratory Immunologists; American Association of Immunologists; Society for Pediatric Research; Northern Ohio Pediatric Society. Address: Department of Pediatrics, LSU Medical Center, 1542 Tulane Avenue, New Orleans, LA 70112-2822, USA.

SOSA Baldemar (Bill), b. 15 Jan 1934, TX, USA. Teacher. m. Angela N Sosa, 13 Feb 1952, 2 s, 2 d. Appointment: Chief Instructor and Director of Southwestern Aikido Institute. Publications: Co-author, Essence of Aikido, 1987; Internal Arts, Health and Fitness Magazine, 1987, 1988, 1989; Author, PACT Police Aikido Controlling Tactics, 1993. Honour: 6th Degree Black Belt in Aikido, one of highest ranking non-oriental in the world. Memberships: Masonic Organization; The Mayan Organization. Hobbies: Reading; Travel. Address: 1703 Melbourne Ave, Dallas, TX 75224, USA.

SOTELO-AVILAA Cirilio, b. 9 July 1938. Physician. m. Andrea J Fish, 26 Aug 1967, 5 d. Education: MD, National Autonomous University of Mexico; Dilomate, Anatomic Pathology, Clinical Pathology, Paediatric Pathology, American Board of Pathology. Appointments: Assistant Professor of Pathology, University of Tennessee; Assistant Professor of Pthology, Northwestern University; Associate Professor of Pathology and Professor of Pathology and Paediatrics, St Louis University; Director of Pathology and Laboratory Medicine. Publications: Congenital Tumours, 1991; Nephroblastoma and other Paediatric Renal Cancers, 1990. Memberships: Fellow, College of American Pathologists; Fellow, American Society of Clinical Pathologists; Society for Paediatric Pathology. Hobbies: Racquetball; Classical music. Address: Department of Pathology, Cardinal Glennon Children's Hospital, 1465 South Grand Boulevard, St Louis, MO 63104-1003, USA.

SOVIE Margaret Doe, b. 7 Jul 1934, Ogdensburg, NY, USA. Registered Nurse. m. Alfred L Sovie, 8 May 1954, 1 s. Education: BSN, summa cum laude, 1964, MS, Education, 1968, PhD, Adult Education, 1972, Syracuse University, NY. Appointments include: Instructor of Nursing, School of Nursing, St Lawrence State Hospital, NY, 1954-62; Education Director and Coordinator, Nursing Service, SUNY Upstate Medical Center, 1965-71; Associate Dean for Nursing Practice, Associate Professor of Nursing, 1976-85, Professor of Nursing, 1985-88, School of Nursing, University of Rochester; Since 1988: Associate Deputy Executive Director and Chief Nursing Officer, Hospital of University of PA; Jane Delano Professor, Nursing Administration, Associate Dean for Nursing Practice, University of PA School of Nursing. Publications include: Numerous professional publications, 1967-, including: Clinical Nursing Practices and Patient Outcomes: Evaluation, Evolution and Revolution, in The Best of Nursing Economics, 1990; Numerous papers presented, 1962-. Honours: Special Nurse Research Fellowship, NIH, 1971-72; Sigma Theta Tau; Pi Lambda Theta; Fellow, American Academy of Nursing, 1978; Honorary DSc, SUNY Health Science Center, Syracuse, 1989. Memberships include: American Nurses Association; American Academy of Nursing; American Organization of Nurse Executives; Institute of Medicine; Zonta International; Many committees and task forces. Hobbies: Golf; Music. Address: Hosp of Univ of Pennsylvania, 21 Penn Tower, 3400 Spruce Street, Philadelphia, PA 19104, USA.

SPASOV Alexander Alexeyevich, b. Baku, Azerbaijan. Doctor of Medical Sciences. m. Galina, 1 daughter. Education: MD, Volgograd Medical Academy; Postgraduate, Department of Pharmacology, Volgograd Medical Academy. Appointments: Head, Department of

Pharmacology, Medical Academy and Department of Drugs Pre-clinical Toxicity Testing, Scientific Research Institute of Pharmacology. Publications: Author of 135 printed works and 45 patents. Memberships: Russian Society of Biochemists; Russian Society of Pharmacologists. Hobbies: Theatre; Reading; Basketball; Swimming; Travel; Canoes. Address: Medical Academy, Pl Pavshikh Bortsov 1, Volgograd 400066, Russia.

SPECIANI Paolo M, b. 12 Dec 1952, Milan, Italy. Physician. m. Barbara Zanini, 2 sons. Education: MD, Milan University, 1978. Career: Co-Founder, Integrated Medicine School, Milan, 1981; Experience in Homeopathy, Bioenergetics, Psychosomatic Cancer; Currently freelance professional. Publications: Co-Director, Rivista Psicosomatica, 1980-84. Address: 48 Legnano St, 20121 Milan, Italy.

SPECKHARD Anne Catherine, b. 29 Nov 1957, Wausau, Wisconsin, USA. Psychologist. m. Daniel Speckhard, 23 Aug 1980, 1 son, 2 daughters. Education: MS; PhD. Appointments: Public Health Service Fellow, Department of Health & Human Services, Office of Population Affairs & Adolescent Pregnancy. Publications: Post Abortion Syndrome: An Emerging Public Concern, 1992; Post Abortion Trauma: Incidence & Diagnostic Considerations, 1993; Informed Consent & Abortion: Issues in Medicine & Consulting, 1993; Treatment of Dissociative Disorders: A Developmental Contextual Model, 1994; Complicated Mourning: Dynamics of Impacted Post Abortion Grief, 1994; Traumatic Death in Pregnancy: Diagnosis & Treatment, 1995. Memberships: International Society of Traumatic Stress; International Association of Trauma Counselors; American Association of Marriage & Family Therapists. Hobbies: Nature; Swimming; Travel. Address: 4009 David Lane, Alexandria, VA 22311, USA.

SPECTOR Novera Herbert, b. 23 Aug 1919, Ohio, USA. Physiologist. 1 son, 3 daughters. Education: BS; PhD. Appointments include: Consultant in Patent Development and Inventions; National Institutes of Health Pre-doctoral Fellow, University of Pennsylvania; Visiting Professor of Physiology, Claude Bernard University, Lyon, France; Chief, Neurophysiology, Walter Reed Institute of Research, USA; Director, Neurobiology, National Science Foundation; Professor or Adjunct Professor, Physiology, Biophysics, Anatomy, Neuroscience, Microbiology, other disciplines, USA, France, Italy; Currently Vice-President for Research, Director, Scientific Research, American Institute for Neuroimmunomodulation Research, Phoenix, Arizona. Publications: Editor or co-editor, 8 books on neurosciences, immunology, neuroimmunomodulation; Principal author, approximately 150 research papers and reviews in scientific journals in 10 countries. Honours include: Honorary Member: Rumanian Academy of Medical Sciences; Association des Physiologistes; Academy of Behavioral Medicine; 1st Metalnikov Gold Medal; Best Teacher Awards. Memberships include: International Society for Neuroimmunomodulation, First President; American Physiological Society; Society for Neuroscience; Sigma Xi; American Association for the Advancement of Science; Federation of American Scientists; Academy of Behavioral Medicine. Hobbies: Epistemology; Education of children; Fencing, including in 6 US Olympic Squads and Championships in USA and France. Address: American Institute for Neuroimmunomodulation Research, 45 East Osborn Road, Phoenix, AZ 85012, USA.

SPECTOR Sheldon L, b. 13 Feb 1939, Detroit, MI, USA. m. Judith Spector, 1 s, 2 d. Education: MD, Wayne State University, Detroit, MI, 1960-64; Internship, Medicine, Mount Sinai Hospital, NY, 1964-65; Residency: Internal Medicine, 1965-66, Research Investigator, 1966-68, Internal Medicine, 1968-69; Fellowship, Allergy and Clinical Immunology, National Jewish Hospital, Denver, 1969-71. Appointments include: Commissioned Officer, US Public Health Service, Bethesda, MD, 1966-68; Assistant Professor, 1971-77, Associate Professor, 1977-81, Medicine, University of CO, Denver; Associate Clinical Professor, 1981-82, Clinical Professor, 1982-, Medicine, UCLA School of Medicine, Los Angeles; Peer Reviewer, Board of Medical Quality Assurance, CA, 1983; Editorial Board, Journal of Asthma, 1993-. Publications include: Over 200 professional papers published, 1963-, including: Allergic and nonallergic rhinitis: Update on pathophysiology and clinical management, in Journal Clinical Pharmacology, 1993; Update on exercise-induced asthma, in Ann Allergy, 1993; 24 Non-peer reviewed papers, 1975-93; Numerous editorials, consultative letters, essay, monographs, chapters and books, and 89 published abstracts. Honours include: Lady Davis Post-Doctoral Fellow in Allergy, Hebrew University, Israel, 1977-78; Research Award, William Beaumont Society,

Wayne State University School of Medicine; Distinguished Physician's Award, American College of Allergy; President, Los Angeles Society of Allergy and Immunology, 1993; Distinguished Service Award, American Academy of Allergy and Immunology, 1994. Memberships include: Various offices and Fellow, American Academy of Allergy and Immunology; American College of Physicians; AMA; American Thoracic Society. Address: 11620 Wilshire Blvd, ste 200, Los Angeles, CA 90025, USA.

SPEIRS Andrew Lennox, b. 22 Feb 1946, Australia. Gynaecology. m. Susan Rodd, 19 Dec 1970, 2 sons. Education: MB, BS, Melbourne, 1969; MRCOG, 1975; FRACOG, 1979; FRCOG, 1988. Appointments: Director, Reproductive Biology Unit, The Royal Women's Hsopital, Melbourne. Publications: Pregnancy Following Implantation of an Embryo by IVF, 1980; 40 further publications on infertility. Memberships: Australian Medical Association; Royal Australian College of Obstetrics & Gynaecology; Royal College of Obstetrics & Gynaecology; Fertility Society of Australia; ISFAHSIM. Hobbies: Golf; Skiing; Sailboarding; Bridge. Address: Ste 3, 320 Victoria Road, East Melbourne, Vic 3002, Australia.

SPELLMAN Mitchell W. Appointments: Dean, Medical Services, Professor of Surgery, Harvard Medical School; Executive Vice President, Harvard Medical Center; Dean Emeritus for International Projects, Boston; Director of International Exchange Programs, Harvard Medical International, Brookline, MA. Publications: Numerous publications in professional journals. Honours: Alpha Omega Alpha; Honorary degrees, Georgetown Univ, 1974, Univ of Florida, 1977, Dillard Univ, 1983; PhD Thesis, Univ of Minnesota, 1955; Who's Who in America, 1984-1985. Memberships include: Society of University Surgeons; American College of Surgeons; American College of Cardiology; American Surgical Association; Institute of Medicine of National Academy of Sciences. Hobby: Gardening. Address: Harvard Medical International, 138 Harvard Street, Brookline, MA 02146-6418, USA.

SPENCER Richard P, b. 7 June 1929, New York City, USA. Physician; Scientist. m. Gwendolyn E Williams, 7 Apr 1954, 3 d. Education: AB, Dartmouth College, 1951; MD, University of Southern California, 1954; MA, 1958, PhD, Biochemistry, 1961, Harvard University. Appointments: Assistant and Associate Professor of Biophysics, University of Buffalo School of Medicine, 1961-63; Associate Professor, Professor of Nuclear Medicine, Yale University School of Medicine, 1963-74; Professor, Chairman, Department of Nuclear Medicine, University of Connecticut Health Centre. Publications: Author of 10 books; Contributor of over 850 scientific publications. Honours: Honorary MA, Yale University, 1968; Editorial Boards, Nuclear Medicine and Biology and CRC Critical Reviews of Imaging. Memberships: Chairman, Committee on Ethics, Society of Nuclear Medicine; Biophysical Society; American Physiological Society; American Association Advancement of Science. Hobby: History. Address: Department of Nuclear Medicine, University of Connecticut Health Centre, Farmington, CT 06030, USA.

SPENCER-GREGSON Richard Nicholas, b. 8 Dec 1931, Whitburn, County Durham. Doctor of Medicine. m. Maureen Spencer-Gregson, 3 daughters. Education: MSc; MB; BS; DObst; RCOG; FRCOG. Appointments: HS.RVI. Newcastle on Tyne; Senior Registrar, Leeds General & St James; Consultant, NHS. Publications: Shutes Parallel Forceps, 1966; Bradykinin & Polypertides in Vitro Human Hypertension, 1969. Memberships: Royal College of Obstetricians & Gynaecologists. Hobbies: MCC Cricket. Address: Pinfold House, 11 Main Road, Long Bennington, Newark, Notts NG23 5EH, England.

SPERLING George. Cognitive Scientist; Educator. Education: BS, UNiversity of Michigan, 1955; MA, Columbia University, 1956; PhD, Psychology, Harvard University, 1959. Appointments include: Research Assistant, Biophysics, Brookhaven National Laboratories, Upton, New York, USA, 1955; Technical Research Staff, Acoustical and Behavioural Research Centre, AT&T Bell Laboratories, Murray Hill, New Jersey, 1958-86; Professor of Psychology and Neurological Science, New York University, 1970-92; Distinguished Professor of Cognitive Sciences, University of California at Irvine, 1992-. Honours include: Meritorious Civilian Service Medal, USAF, 1993; Guggenheim Fellow, 1969-70; Phi Beta Kappa; Sigma Xi. Memberships include: Fellow, AAAS; American Academy Arts and Sciences; American Psychological Association; Optical Society of America; NAS; Association for Research in Vision and Ophthalmology; Board Directors, 1982-85, Eastern Psychological

Association; Steering Committee, 1974-78, Society for Computers in Psychology; Society of Experimental Psychologists; Chairman, 1983-84, Executive Board, 1979-85, Society for Mathematical Psychology. Address: Department of Cognitive Science, SST, University of California, Irvine, CA 92717, USA.

SPIEKSMA Frits Th M, b. 18 May 1936, Rijswijk, Netherlands. Aerobiologist. m. Marise Boezeman, 25 May 1963, 2 sons, 1 daughter. Education: MSc, 1961, PhD, 1967, University of Leiden. Appointments: Currently Associate Professor of Allergological Aerobiology, Head, Laboratory of Aerobiology, University Hospital, Leiden. Publications: Author or co-author, over 120 publications including: The house-dust mite and the allergens it produces, 1967; Daily hay-fever forecast, 1980; Evidence of grass-pollen allergenic activity in the smaller micronic aerosol fraction, 1990; Allergenic Pollen and Pollinosis in Europe, book, 1991; Pictorial key for the identification of domestic mites, 1992. Honours: Honorary Member, South African Allergy Society, 1992; Honorary Member, Italian Association for Aerobiology, 1993. Memberships: President, International Association for Aerobiology; European Academy for Allergy and Clinical Immunology. Hobbies: Nature photography; Geography. Address: Laan van Alkemade 1, NL-2341 LJ Oegstgeest, Netherlands.

SPIELBERGER Charles Donald, b. 28 Mar 1927, Atlanta, USA. Research Professor, University of South Florida. m. Carol G Lee, 2 June 1971, 2 sons, 1 daughter. Education: BA, 1951, MA, 1953, PhD, 1954, all at The University of Iowa; Doctor of Humane Letters, Pacific Graduate School of Psychology, 1990; Honoraris Doctoris Causa, Hungarian University of Physical Education, Budapest, Hungary, 1991. Appointments: Assistant, Associate Professor, Department of Psychiatry, Duke University, 1955-63; Professor, Psychology, Vanderbilt University, 1963-66; Professor, Psychology, Director of Clinical Training, Florida University, 1967-71; Professor, Psychology, Director, Research Professor, University of South Florida, 1972-. Publications: Anxiety: Current trends in theory and research, 1972; Understanding Stress and Anxiety, 1979; Stress and Anxiety, 1991; Stress and Emotion, 1991; Personality Assessment in America, 1992; Motivation: Theory and Research, 1994; Professional Manual: Job Stress Survey, 1994. Memberships: American Psychological Association; APA Division of Community Psychology; Southerneastern Psychological Association; Interamerican Society of Psychology; International Association of Applied Psychology; International Council of Psychologists; International Society for Test Anxiety Research; Society for Personality Assessment; Council of Scientific Society Presidents. Honours include: Distinguished Scholar Award, University of South Florida, 1973; Sigma Xi Award, Outstanding Faculty Researcher, University of South Florida, 1985; Centennial Award, Distinguished Sustained Contributions to Education in Psychology, American Psychological Association, 1992. Hobbies: History; World Travel. Address: Department of Psychology, University of South Florida, Tampa, FL 33620-8200, USA.

SPITZER John J, b. 9 Mar 1927, Baja, Hungary. Research Scientist. m. Judy A Gottfried, 30 June 1951, 1 s, 1 d. Education: MD Magna Cum Laude, University of Munich, Germany, 1950. Appointments include: Demonstrator, Department of Physiology, School of Medicine, University of Budapest, 1947-49; Assistant Professor, Department of Physiology, Florida State University, 1952-54; Assistant Professor, 1957-58, Associate Professor, 1958-61, Consultant, Division of Cardiology, Department of Medicine, 1958-64, Professor, 1961-73, Department of Physiology and Biophysics, Hahnemann Medical College; Visiting Scientist, Laboratory of Physiology, University of Oxford, England, 1963-64; Professor and Head, Department of Physiology, 1973-91, Boyd Professor and Head, 1991-, Louisiana State University; Medical Centre. Publications: Contributor of over 225 articles in scientific journals, 1952-. Honours include: Research Fellowship, Hungarian National Research Council, Biological Institute, 1948; Honours Achievement Award, Angiology Research Foundation, 1964-65; Burroughs Wellcome Visiting Professor, 1983; Boyd Professorship, Louisiana State University, 1991-. Memberships include: Shock Society, President, 1988-89; Charter Member, International Endotoxin Society; Society for Leukocyte Biology; Research Society on Alcoholism; American Physiological Soceity, Committee on Committees, 1981-83; New York Academy of Sciences. Hobby: tennis. Address: Department of Physiology, LSU Medical Centre, 1901 Perdido Street, New Orleans, LA 70112, USA.

SPITZER Peter G, b. 3 Dec 1955, Albany, New York, USA. Physician. m. Wendy C Pollock, 1978, 2 s, 1 d. Education: BA, Brown University, 1977; MD, Louisiana State University Medical School, New Orleans, 1981. Appointments include: Clinical Fellow in Medicine, 1981-85, Research Fellow in Medicine, 1985-86, Clinical Instructor in Medicine, 1987-89, Harvard Medical School; Associate Staff, 1986-89, Senior Staff, 1989, Department of Internal Medicine, Section of Infectious Disease, Lahey Clinic Medical Centre, Burlington, Massachusetts; Assistant Attending Physician, 1989-92, Associate Attending Physician, 1992-95, Attending Physician, 1995-, Department of Internal Medicine, Service of Infectious Disease, Bryn Mawr hospital, Bryn Mawr, Pennsylvania. Honours: Sigma Xi, 1977; Aesculapian Society, Louisiana State University Medical School, 1978-81; Dr james L Tullis Award, New England Deaconess Hospital, 1983; Distinguished Teaching Award, Medical House Staff, Bryn Mawr Hospital, 1991. Memberships: Associate, 1983-86, Member, 1986-90, Fellow, 1990-. American College of Physicians; American Medical Association; Fellow, Massachusetts Medical Society. Hobbies: Sports with the children. Address: 933 Haverford Road, Bryn Mawr, PA 19010, USA.

SPIVAK Leonid Ivanovich, b. 23 Oct 1925, Lubny, Ukraine. Psychiatrist. m. Nonna Yastrebova, 13 Mar 1952, 1 son. Education: MD, Psychiatry, 1950; DSc, Psychiatry, 1961. Appointments: State Military Academy of Russia: Associate Professor, Professor, 1950-85; Head of Chair of Psychiatry, Asuman Brain Institute, Russian Academy of Sciences, 1986-. Publications: Knee Reflex in Normal and Pathological State, 1957; Psychotomimetics, 1971; Side Effects of Psychopharmacological Therapy, 1988; Psychogenic States in Extreme Conditions, 1991; Drug Research in The Soviet Scientific Tradition, 1991. Honours: USSR State Prize, Research in Psychopharmacology, 1980. Memberships: Honorary Member, Russian Psychiatric Association; Scientific & Medical Network, England. Hobbies: Collecting Old Russian Coins and Clocks. Address: PO Box 19, St Petersburg 191 186, Russia.

SPOTNITZ Henry Michael, b. 7 July 1940, New York City, USA. Surgen. m. Sharon Meryl Hertz, 2 Jan 1977, 1 s, 1 d. Education: BA, Harvard College, 1962; MD, Columbia University, 1966. Appointments: Assistant Professor, Associate Professor, Professor, George H Humphreys II, Professor of Surgery, College of Physicians and Surgeons, Columbia University; Assistant Attending Surgeon; Associate Attending Surgeon; Attending Surgeon' President, New York Society for Thoracic Surgery; Member, NIH Surgical Study Section. Publications: Contributor of over 105 professional papers. Honours: NIH RO-1 Research Grants, 1978, 1982, 1988, 1992; Established Investigator, American Heart Association, 1977-82. Memberships: American Surgical Association; American Association for Thoracic Surgery' Society of Thoracic Surgeons; Society of University Surgeons. Hobbies: Computers; Football; Model railways; Jogging. Address; 630 West 168th Street, New York, NY 10032, USA.

SPOTO Angelo Peter, b. 25 Mar 1933, Tampa, FL, USA. Physician; Allergist and Immunologist. m. Carolyn Jeanette Barbee Spoto, 30 Aug 1958, 1 s, 2 d. Education: AA, University of FL, 1953; BS, Medicine, Duke University, 1956; MD, 1957; Diplomate: American Board of Internal Medicine; Board of Allergy; American Board of Allergy and Immunology. Appointments include: Past Clinical Associate Professor of Medicine, University of South FL College of Medicine; Executive Committee, Watson Clinic, 1984-93; Currently, Partner, Watson Clinic. Publications include: 5 Papers published, 1960-90, including: Executive Focus: Wellness I Learned From My Father, in Group Practice Journal, 1990; 15 Presented papers. Honours include: Fellow, American College of Physicians, 1974; Fellow, American Academy of Allergy and Immunology, 1969; Fellow, American College of Allergy and Immunology, 1974; Alpha Epsilon Delta; Sigma Chi. Memberships include: Board of Directors, Watson Clinic Foundation, 1984-; Polk County Medical Association, 1966-; FL Medical Association, 1966-; FL Allergy Society, 1967-; FL Society of Internal Medicine, 1968-; Southern Medical Association, 1957-; American Medical Association, 1959-; Past President, American Group Practice Association, 1966-; American Society of Internal Medicine, 1968-; American Association of Certified Allergists, 1971-. Hobbies: Tampa Bay Buccaneer's; Swimming; Tennis. Address: The Watson Clinic, 1600 Lakeland Hills Blvd, Lakeland, FL 33804-5000, USA.

SPREHE Daniel Joseph, b. 21 Feb 1932, Oklahoma, USA. Psychiatrist. 1 son, 1 daughter. Education: BS, University of Oklahoma, 1950-53; MD, University of Oklahoma, 1953-57; Internship, Charity Hospital of Louisiana, 1957-58; Resident, Tulane University, 1961-64; Postgraduate, Tulane University, 1963-66. Appointments include: Clinical Assistant, University of South Florida, 1971-75; Assistant

Professor, University of South Florida, 1975-77; Clinical Associate Professor, University of South Florida, 1977-93; Chief, Section on Forensic Psychiatry, University of South Florida, 1978-. Publications include: Observations with Indoklon, 1963; A Quantitative Comparison of Electroconvulsive Therapy with Hexafluorodiethyl Ether, 1963; A Controlled Evaluation of Butaperazine in Chronic Schizophrenic Patients, 1964; Workers Conpensation: What Happens After the Ratings?, 1981; Use of Psychiatrists in Insanity Defense, 1981; Stalking the Expert, 1984; Does the Greenback Poultice Improve Stress Related Trauma?, 1988; Geriatric Psychiatry and the Law, 1993. Memberships: AMA; APA; AAPL; American Academy of Forensic Sciences. Honours: Phi Beta Kappa; Alpha Omega Alpha; Appreciation Award, Criminal Defense Lawyers of Hillsborough County; Recognition Plaque, The Florida Bar Convention, 1981; Outstanding Service Award, Department of Psychiatry, USF, 1982; Recognition Award, Mental Health Association of Hillsborough County; Outstanding Clinical Faculty Award, USF Department of Psychiatry, 1989. Hobbies: Snow Skiing. Address: 800 West Martin Luther King Avenue #4, Tampa, FL 33603 3302, USA.

SQUIRE Edward Noonan, b. 27 Nov 1948, Lancaster, PA, USA. Medicine. m. Quida Carden, 3 Apr 1973, 1 s, 2 d. Education: BS; MPH; MD. Career: Chief, Allergy and Immunology, Florence A Blanchfield Army Community Hospital, Fort Campbell, KY; Currently, Assistant Chief, Allergy and Immunology Service, Walter Reed Army Medical Centre, Washington DC; Assistant Professor of Pediatrics and Medicine, Uniformed University of Health Sciences. Publications include: Numerous publications and abstracts including: Co-author, Corticosteroids and theophylline clearance, in North England Reg Allergy Proce, 1987; Co-author, Chronic sulfasalazine therapy in the treatment of delayed pressure urticaria, in press. Honours include: Alpha Zeta Foundation Scholarship, 1968; White Fellowship Award, 1970; Legion of Valor Bronze Cross, PSU Army ROTC Program, 1969; Evan Pugh Gold Medal, PA State University, 1969; Phi Kappa Phi; Omicron Delta Kappa, 1972; Roche Medical Publishing Company Book Award, University of KY College of Medicine, 1973; Army Commendation Medal, 1979; Meritorious Service Medal, 1991. Memberships include: Fellow, American Academy of Pediatrics; Fellow, American College of Allergists; Fellow, American College of Allergy and Immunology; Chairman, 1988-90, Association of Military Allergists. Hobbies include: Reading; Travel. Address: 2535 Remington Street, Falls Church, VA 22046, USA.

SRIVASTAVA Rajendra Nath, b. 10 Jul 1937, Barabanki, India. Physician. m. Manju Srivastava, 22 Jul 1961, 1 d. Education: MBBS; DCH; MRCP(Ed); Diplomate, American Board of Pediatrics. Career: Director, Institute of Child Health, Kabul, Afghanistan, 1974-79; Visiting Professor of Pediatrics, University of Texas Medical Branch, Galveston, USA, 1990-91; Currently, Professor of Pediatrics, All India Institute of Medical Sciences, New Delhi, India. Publications: Pediatrics, 1989; Co-author, Pediatric and Neonatal Emergencies, 1990; Co-author, Pediatric Nephrology, 1994. Honours: B L Khullar Award of Indian Society of Nephrology, 1989; Kamala Menon Award of Indian Council of Medical Research, 1993. Memberships: President, Indian Society of Nephrology, 1990; President, Indian Academy of Pediatrics, 1996; International Society of Nephrology; International Pediatric Nephrology Association; Asian Pediatric Nephrology Association. Hobbies: Reading Books; Classical Music. Address: Department of Pediatrics, All India Institute of Medical Sciences, New Delhi 110029, India.

ST CLAIRE Lindsay, b. 17 Oct 1951, England. Psychologist. m. J G Telfer, 30 Apr 1989, 2 sons. Education: BA; BSc; PhD; Chartered Psychologist. Appointments: Department of Child Health, Department of Epidemiology, currently Lecturer, Research Fellow, Department of Psychology, Bristol University. Publications include: Articles in: General Practice, 1991-1995; Medical Teacher, 1992; Journal of Community and Applied Psychology, 1993. Membership: British Psychological Society. Hobby: Singing. Address: Department of Psychology, Bristol University, 8 Woodland Road, Clifton, Bristol BS8 1TN, England.

ST PIERRE Jean-Paul, b. 26 July 1944, Riviere-Bleue, Quebec. Medical. m. Diane Robert, 7 Aug 1965, 2 daughters. Education: BA; MD. Career: Medical Director, Sandoz Canada; Vice President, Medical Affairs, Hoechst-Rousee, Canada Inc. Publications include: La Dermite Atopique, 1972; Le Traitement des Maladies Allergiques, 1981; The Pharmacological Control of Asthma; La Rhinite Allergique, 1985; L'Urticaire au froid: Une Maladie frequente et mal connue, 1985; Double-blind Multicentre Study of Ketitofen (Zaditen) in Chronic Idiopathic Urticaria, 1991. Honours: 1st Prize, Obstetrics, Faculty of

Medicine, University of Montreal; Conseil de Recherches Medicales du Quebec, 1972-73. Memberships include: American Society of Microbiology; Canadian Medical Association; The Asthma Society of Canada; Insead Alumni Association; Canadian Cardiovascular Society; Canadian Paediatric Society. Hobby: Fishing. Address: Hoechst-Roussel Canada Inc, 4045 Cote Vertu, Montreal, Que H4R 2E8, Canada.

STABRUN Anne Elisabeth, b. 24 Jan 1949, Oslo, Norway. Orthodontist. m. Erik J Stabrun, 15 Aug 1970, 1 s, 1 d. Education: DDS, Oslo, 1972; Dr odont, Oslo, 1991. Appointments: Research Fellow; Currently, Private Practice, Orthodontics. Publications: About 6 articles published in orthodontic and rheumatologic scientific literature. Memberships: Norwegian Dental Association; European Orthodontic Society; Norwegian Orthodontic Society. Hobby: Childcare. Address: Fagertun Vn 125, 1342 Jar, Norway.

STAFFORD-BELL Martyn Anthony, b. 13 Oct 1942, Enfield, Middlesex, England. Gynaecologist. m. Julie, 10 Mar 1989, 3 sons, 1 daughter. Education: MB; BS; LRCP; MRCS; FRCOG; FRACOG. Appointments: Registrar, Obstetrics & Gynaecology, The Royal London Hospital, 1969-71; Senior Registrar, Obstetrics & Gynaecology, Guy's Hospital, London, 1971-74; Private Practice. Memberships: AMA; AAS; FSA; ESHRE; ESH; AFS; AGES. Hobbies: Golf; Skiing. Address: Suite 8, The Australian Surgeons Building, 13 Napier Close, Deakin, Canberra, ACT 2600, Australia.

STALAND John Gustaf Bertil, b. 24 May 1913, Råggärd, Sweden. Retired Physician. m. Britt Frick, 8 June 1946, 2 sons. Education: MM, Authorized Physician; Specialist, Obstetrics Gynecology & General Surgery. Appointments: Assistant Physician, Surgeon, Various Hospitals in Sweden, 1942-53; Gynecologist, Uppsala, Sweden, 1953-79; Retired, 1979. Publications: Articles to various professional journals. Memberships: Swedish Association of Gynacologists & Obstritricians; American Association for the Advancement of Science. Address: Hästeskovägen 22, S 311 37 Falkenberg, Sweden.

STALLONES Lorann, b. 5 June 1952, San Francisco, California, USA. Epidemiologist. m. John R Nuckols, 5 July 1985, 1 son, 2 daughters. Education: PhD; MPH. Appointments: Public Health Analyst, NIH/NHLBI; Research Fellow, Mary Imogene Bassett Hospital, Cooperstown, New York; Assistant to Associate Professor, University Kentucky, College of Medicine; Associate Professor, Colorado University. Publications: Education equipment modification and injury control among farm workers in Kentucky, 1989; Fatal injuries among Kentucky farm children, 1989. Surveillance of fatal and nonfatal injuries in Kentucky, 1990. Memberships: American College of Epidemiology; American Public Health Association; National Rural Health Association; Society for Epidemiologic Research. Hobbies: Reading; Skiing; Doll Making. Address: Department of Environmental Health, Colorado University, Ft Collins, CO 80523, USA.

STAMPFER Meir Jonathan, b. 3 May 1950, Lincoln, Nebraska, USA. Physician; Epidemiologist. m. Claire Blum Stampfer, 1 son, 2 daughters. Education: AB, Columbia University, 1973; MD, New York University School of Medicine, 1977; MPH 1980, DrPH 1985, Harvard School of Public Health. Appointments: Resident, Mt Sinai Hospital, 1978-79; Instructor in Medicine 1982-85, Assistant Professor in Medicine 1985-, Harvard Medical School; Associate Professor 1988-93, Professor of Epidemiology & Nutrition 1993-, Harvard School of Public Health. Publications: Three major areas of interest are dietary etiologies of chronic disease, health effects of exogenous hormones and the effect of aspirin on platelets & heart disease; Over 200 original articles, 36 reviews and 4 collaborative publications to date. Honours: Jones Prize for Logic & Philosophy of Science, Columbia University, 1973; NIH National Research Service Award, 1979-82; Distinguished Alumnus Speaker, Maimonides Hospital, 1989. Memberships: Society for Epidemiologic Research; International Society & Federation of Cardiology; Fellow, American Heart Association; Fellow, American College of Nutrition; Elected Member, American Epidemiologic Society. Hobbies: Skiing; Hiking. Address: Channing Laboratory, 180 Longwood Avenue, Boston, MA 02115, USA.

STANDEN Clive Struan, b. 31 Aug 1952, London, England. Osteopath. m. Anne Margaret Shee, 5 Jan 1974, 2 s, 1 d. Education: City and Guilds Further Education Teachers' Certificate; DO. Appointments: Honorary secretary, Osteopathic Association of Great Britain, 1981-86; Vice Principal, 1986-90, Principal, British School of Osteopathy, London. Memberships: General Council and Register of

Osteopaths; Osteopathic Association of Great Britain. Hobbies: Gardening; Walking; Reading; Squash. Address: 3 The Drive, Kettering, Northamptonshire NN15 7EX, England.

STANNERS Clifford Paul, b. 19 Oct 1937, Sutton, Surrey, England. Director; Professor. m. Dorothy Bird, 8 Aug 1959, 3 sons. Education: BSc, McMaster University, Hamilton, Ontario, Canada, 1958; MA, 1960, PhD, 1963, University of Toronto. Appointments: Assistant Professor, Associate Professor, Professor, Medical Biophysics, University of Toronto, 1964-82; Research Scientist, Ontario Cancer Institute, 1964-82; Professor, Biochemistry, 1982-, Director, Professor, Research Division, Oncology, 1989-, McGill University, Montreal; Director, McGill Cancer Centre, 1988-. Publications: 77 including: DNA synthesis in individual L-strain mouse cells, 1960; The effect of cycloheximide on polyrib Hoosomes from hamster cells, 1966; Control of macromolecular synthesis in proliferating and resting Syrian hamster cells in monolayer culture, I Ribosome function, 1971; Two types of ribosomes in mouse-hamster hybrid cells, 1971; A mammalian cell mutant with a temperature sensitive leucyl-tRNA synthetase, 1973; Analysis of a vesicular stomatitis virus mutant with attenuated cytopathogenicity: Mutation in viral function, P, for inhibition of protein synthesis, 1977; Stuttering: High level mistranslation in animal and bacterial cells, 1978; Effect of extreme amino acid starvation on the protein synthetic machinery of CHO cells, 1978; Transformed cells have lost control of ribosome number through their growth cycle, 1979; Molecular cloning of a functional gene responsible for the expression of a cell surface antigen correlated with human chronic lymphocytic leukemia, 1981; The use of the E coli gene for asparagine synthetase as a selective marker in a shuttle vector capable of dominant transfection and amplification in animal cells, 1987; Isolation and characterization of full length functional cDNA clones for human carcinoembryonic antigen (CEA), 1987; Carcinoembryonic antigen (CEA), a human tumour marker, functions as an intercellular adhesion molecule, 1989; A genetic element that increases the frequency of gene amplification, 1991; Homophilic adhesion between Ig superfamily carcinoembryonic antigen molecules involves double reciprocal bonds, 1993; Human carcinoembryonic antigen, an intercellular adhesion molecule, blocks fusion and differentiation of rat myoblasts, 1993. Honours: Union Carbide Scholarship, McMaster University, 1954-58; Reeve Prize for Research, 1960. Memberships: Canadian Society of Cell and Molecular Biology; American Association for the Advancement of Science; American Association for Cancer Research. Hobbies: Wine making; Photography; Running. Address: McGill Cancer Centre, 3655 Drummond Street, Room 701, Montreal, Quebec, Canada H3G 1Y6.

STARINSKY Valery Vladimirovich, b. 3 July 1940, Smolensk, Russia. Doctor. m. Helen, 21 Sept 1962, 1 son. Education: Postgraduate Course; Degree of the Candidate of Medical Sciences. Appointments: head Physician, Distric Hospital; Junior Research Associate, Scientific Secretary, Chief of the Department; Deputy Director. Publications: Planning and Evaluation of Russian Cancer Control Program, 1992; Early Diagnostics of Cancer, 1994. Membership: All-Russian Oncological Society. Hobbies: Outdoor Activities. Address: Moscow Certsen Cancer Research Institute, 125284 Moscow, 2nd Botkinsky pr 3, Russia.

STARK Richard Boies, b. 31 Mar 1915, Conrad, Iowa, USA. Plastic Surgeon. m. Judy Thornton, 31 Oct 1967. Education: BA, Stanford University; MD, Cornell University Medical College; FACS, American Board of Plastic Surgeons, 1952, recertified, 1977. Appointments: Associate Professor, 1958, Professor of Clinical Surgery, currently Emeritus Professor, College of Physicians and Surgeons, Columbia University. Publications: History of Plastic Surgery at New York Hospital, 1952; Plastic Surgery, 1963; Cleft Palate, 1968; Aeathetic Plastic Surgery, 1980; Reconstruction of Total Face, 1985; Plastic Surgery of Head and Neck, 1987. Honours: Bronze Star, US Army, 1945; Medal of Honour, 1st Class, Republic of Vietnam, twice; Order of San Carlos, Colombia, South America; Dieffenbach Medal, Berlin; Gold Medal, National Institute of Social Sciences. Memberships: American College of Surgeons; American Surgical Association; American Association of Plastic Surgery; Halsted Society. Hobby: Exhibiting artists with 19 solo exhibitions. Address: 35 E 75th Street, New York, NY 10021, USA.

STARKE Rodman David, b. 2 March 1933, USA. Physician. m. Esther Benedict, 8 August 1957, 2 sons, 1 daughter. Education: AB, cum laude BK; MD, AOA. Appointments: Chief of Cardiology, RK Davies Medical Centre, San Francisco; Clinical Professor of Medicine, Emeritus, University of California, San Francisco. Memberships: Fellow,

American College of Cardiology. Current Senior Vice President, Scientific Affairs, American Heart Association; Executive Board, International Society and Federation of Cardiology. Address: 7272 Greenville Avenue, Dallas, TX 75231, USA.

STARLING James R, b. 2 Sept 1943, Madison, WI, USA. Physician. Education: BA, Carroll College, Wisconsin; ESA, 1965; MD, University of Rochester, New York, 1969. Appointments: Professor of Surgery, University of Wisconsin, Madison. Memberships: Society of University Surgeons; American Surgical Society. Address: Department of Surgery H4/750, University of Wisconsin Clinical Science Center, Madison, WI 53792, USA.

STATHOPOULOS Vassilios, b. 10 June 1961, Athens, Greece. Orthodontist. m. 26 Sept 1987, 2 sons, 1 daughter. Education: Dental Diploma, Athens University; Certificate in Orthodontics, Master in Dentistry, University of the Pacific, USA. Appointments: Currently private practice in Orthodontics, Athens. Publications: Evaluation of Rare Earth Intensifyuing Screens in Cephalometric Radiography (co-author), 1990. Memberships: American Association of Orthodontics; European Orthodontic Society; Greek Orthodontic Association. Hobbies: Swimming; Running; Gymnastics. Address: 10 Botasi Str, Athens 10682, Greece.

STAVE Gregg Martin, b. 10 May 1957, New York, USA. Physician. m. Christine Marie Hunt, 12 Sep 1987, 1 daughter. Education: SB, Massachusetts Institute of Technology, 1979; JD, Duke University School of Law, 1983; MD, Duke University School of Medicine, 1984; MPH, Epidemiology, University of North Carolina, Chapel Hill, 1990. Appointments: Research Assistant, 1976-77, 1978-79, Massachusetts Institute of Technology; Summer Intern-Regulatory Affairs, Merck, Sharpe and Dohme, West Point, Pennsylvania, 1983; Emergency Room Physician, McGuire VA Medical Centre, Richmond, Virginia, 1986-88; Consultant, Occupational Health and Safety Programme, Burroughs-Wellcome Company, 1988-90; Occupational Physician, 1990-91, Associate Director, Occupational Health Services, 1990-, Glaxo Inc; Consulting Associate, Department Community and Family Medicine, Division of Occupational and Environmental Medicine, Duke University Medical Centre, 1990-. Publications include: Physical and Biological Hazards of the Workplace, Co-Editor, 1994; Effect of a Total Worksite Smoking Ban on Employee Smoking and Attitudes, Co-author 1991; Adult Respiratory Distress Syndrome From Sulfuric Acid Fume Inhalation, Co-author, 1991; The Effect of Age and Gender on the Activity of Human Hepatic CYP3A, Co-author, 1992. Honours: Fellow, American College of Occupational and Environmental Medicine, 1993; Fellow, American College of Preventive Medicine, 1992; Fellow, American College of Physicians, 1991; 2nd Place, Abstract/Presentation Competition, American College of Physicians, Virginia Chapter, 1988. Memberships include: American Medical Association; American Public Health Association; North Carolina Medical Society. Address: 6407 Stoneridge Place, Chapel Hill, NC 27514, USA.

STAVROU Dimitrios K, b. 19 Dec 1935, Arta, Epirus, Greece. Professor of Neuropathology. m. Dr med Rosemarie Stavrou, 5 Jan 1970, 1 son. Education includes: University of Vienna; Aristoteles University of Thessaloniki; University of Munich; MD; Dr phil; Dr med habil. Appointments: Assistant, Institute of Pathology, University of Vienna, Austria, 1964-66; Assistant, Department of General Pathology and Neuropathology, University of Munich, 1966-71; Lecturer in Pathology, 1971; Professor of Pathology, 1977; Professor of Functional Pathology, University of Munich, 1980; Professor, Head, Department of Clinical and Experimental Neuro-Oncology, University of Munich, Germany, 1984; 1989- , Director, Department of Neuropathology, University of Hamburg, Hamburg, Germany. Publications include: Contributions to: Journal of Neurochemistry, 1973; Journal of Neurological Science, 1973; Cancer Research, 1977; European Journal of Cancer, 1977; Neurosurgical Review, 1990; Other journals. Honours: Research Award, C Bohnewand Foundation for Cancer Research, University of Munich, 1976. Memberships: International Society of Neuropathology; German Society of Pathology; German Society of Neuropathology; European Association for Cancer Research; Federation of European Biochemical Societies; International Union of Biochemistry. Address: Berner Stieg 51, 22145 Hamburg, Germany.

STEBNICKY Milan, b. 27 Nov 1958, Presov, Czechoslovakia. Surgeon. m. 24 Sept 1983, 2 sons. Education: Degree, Bratislava, 1988; Degree, Clinical Oncology, Bratislava, 1992. Appointments: Department of Surgery, Hospital with Policlinic, Krompachy, 1984-87; 2nd Clinic of

Surgery, L Pasteur Faculty Hospital, Kosice, 1987-. Memberships: International Society of Paediatric Oncology-SIOP; International Society of Pediatric Surgical Oncology-IPSO. Hobbies: Karate; Sport; Travel. Address: Huskova 25, 04011 Kosice, Slovak Republic.

STEELE Margaret Mary, b. 25 Aug 1960, Toronto, Canada. Child Psychiatrist. Education: BS; MD; Fellow, Royal College of Physicians & Surgeons; Diploma, University of Western Ontario. Appointments: Child Psychiatrist; Clinical Lecturer, University of Western Ontario. Memberships: Ontario Medical Association; Canadian Academy of Child & Adolescent Psychiatry; American Association of Child & Adolescent Psychiatry; Canadian Psychiatric Association; World Federation for Mental Health. Hobbies: Travel; Reading; Swimming. Address: Childrens Hospital of Western Ontario, 800 Commissoners Road E, London, Ontario, N6C 2V5, Canada.

STEELE Stuart James, b. 13 Jan 1930. Medicine. m. Jill Westgate Smith, 23 Oct 1965, 2 sons. Education: MA; MB; BChir; FRCS; FRCOG; MFFP. Appointments: Former Director, Department of Obstetrics & Gynaecology, Middlesex Hospital Medical School, London; Associate Director, Department of Obstetrics & Gynaecology, University College, London. Publications: Gynaecology, Obstetrics And The Neonate. Honour: WHO Fellow, 1969. Memberships: BMA; British Fertility Society; British Medical Laser Association; British Society for Colposcopy & Cervical Pathology; Blair Bell Society; Royal Society of Medicine. Hobbies: Gardening; Opera; Ballet. Address: 35 Tring Avenue, Ealing Common, London, W5 3QD, England.

STEGINK Lewis D, b. 8 Feb 1937, Holland, Michigan, USA. Biochemist. m. Carol N Kallio, 30 June 1962, 2 sons. Education: BA, Chemistry; PhD. Appointments: Biochemist, Assistant Professor of Paediatrics, 1965-67, Assistant Professor of Paediatrics and Biochemistry, 1967-71, Associate Professor of Paediatrics and Biochemistry, 1971-76, Professor of Paediatrics and Biochemistry, 1976-, University of Iowa, Iowa City. Publications: 178 published papers including: Intravenous lipid emulsions in the treatment of essential fatty acid deficiency: studies in young pigs (with D W Andersen and L J Filer Jr), 1984; Aspartame: Physiology and Biochemistry (edited with L J Filer Jr), 1984; Effects of diets high in sucrose or aspartame on the behavior and cognitive performance of children (with M I Wolraich, S D Lindgren, P J Stumbo, M I Appelbaum, M C Kiritsy), 1994. Honours: Mead Johnson Award, American Institute of Nutrition, 1976. Memberships: American Chemical Society; American Association for the Advancement of Science; American Institute of Nutrition; American Society of Clinical Nutrition; American Society for Biochemistry and Molecular Biology; Society for Parental Alimentation; Society for Pediatric Research; Perinatal Research Society; American Pediatric Society; American Pediatric Society for Parenteral and Enteral Nutrition. Address: Department of Pediatrics, The University of Iowa, S385 Hospital School, Iowa City, IA 52242-1011, USA.

STEINBERG Hannah. Honoary Research Professor. Education: Certificate Commerce, University of Reading; BA, 1st class honours, Psychology, 1948, Troughton Scholarship, Post-Graduate Studentship, PhD, Psychopharmacology, 1954, University College, London. Appointments include: Professor of Physchopharmacology, 1st in Europe, Department of Pharmacology, UCL, 1970-78; Research Professor, Psychopharmacology and Head of Group, Department of Psychology, UCL, 1978-92; Emeritus Professor, University of London, 1989-; Honorary Research Fellow, Department of Psychology, UCL, 1992. Publications include: Joint Editor, about 170 publications on psychopharmacology and physical exercise and mental health, including: Motivation, Winning and Sport, in The Psychologist, 1994; Exercise and Mood, in The Psychologist, 1994; Co-author, Aerobic Exercise and Type A Behaviour, in Journal Sports Sciences, in press; Articles and reviews in newspapers and magazines including: The Times; Daily Telegraph; Several radio programmes and advice given on television programmes; About 60 invited lectures and seminars given at universities, research institutes, learned societies, various organizations in UK and abroad. Honours include: Fellow, British Psychological Society; Distinguished Affiliate, American Psychological Association, 1978; Chartered Psychologist, 1990-; Accredited Sports Psychologist, British Association of Sport Sciences, 1992. Memberships include: British Pharmacological Society; Experimental Psychology Society; Founder Member: European Behavioural Pharmacology Society, 1986-; European College of Neuropsychopharmacology, 1986-. Address: Health Res Centre, Sch of Psychology, Middx Univ Queensway, Enfield, Middx EN3 4SF, England.

STEINBERG Martin H, b. 2 July 1936, New York City, USA. Physician. m. Susan McDaniel, 24 Nov 1973, 1 d. Education: AB, Cornell University, 1958; MD, Tufts University, 1962. Appointments: Intern, Bellevue Hospital, New York, 1962-63; Captain, US Army Medical Corps, 1963-66; Resident in Medicine, Fellow in Haematology, New England Medical Centre, Boston, 1966-70; Assistant and Associate Professor, University of Mississippi, 1970-77; Visiting Professor of Medicine, Tufts University, 1987; Professor of Medicine, University of Mississippi; Chief Research, Jackson VAMC. Publications: Sickle Cell Disease: Basic Principles and Clinical Practice, 1994; Contributor of over 160 original scientific articles, book chapters and review articles, 1970-94. Honours: AOA, 1961; Fellow, AAAS, 1989; President, Southern Society Clinical Investigation, 1993-94. Memberships: Association of American Physicians; American Society Clinical Investigation; Southern Society Clinical Investigation; American Society Haematology; Central Soceity Clinical Research. Hobbies: Music; History. Address: VA Medical Centre, 1500 E Woodrow Wilson Drive, Jackson, MS 39216, USA.

STEINBERG Paul, b. 11 Apr 1937, New York City, USA. Physician. m. Vivian Claire Gallo, 26 June 1960, 2 s. Education: BS, 1959, MD, 1963. Appointments: Staff Member, 1971-72, Consultant in Medicine, 1971-72, The Good Samaritan Hospital, Baltimore, Maryland; Consultant in Medicine, Allergy, Wayne County General Hospital Detroit, 1972-76; Consultant in Medicine, Allergy, US Veterans Administration Hospital, Ann Arbor, 1972-76; Allergist, Park Nicollet Medical Centre, Minneapolis, 1976-85; Attending in Medicine, Allergy and Immunology, 1976-, Director, Division of Allergy and Immunology, 1985-, Hennepin County Medical Centre, Minneapolis; Staff, Methodist Hospital, Minneapolis, 1985-. Publications include: The Cause of Gigantism and Cannibalism in Blepharisma Undulans, 1959; Allergy, Chapter, 1981; Diagnostic Tests Used in the Evaluation of Allergic Conditions, 1989; Common Sense Approach to Avoiding Anaphylaxis, 1989; Anaphylaxis Following Oral Ingestion of Psyllium in Breakfast Cereal, Co-author; Co-author: Reflex Sympathetic Dystrophy: An Adverse Reaction to Immunotherapy, 1995; Noncardiogenic Pulmonary Edema Induced by Non-Ionic Low Osmolality Radiographic Contrast Media, 1995; Double Blind Placebo Controlled Study of the Efficacy of Oral Terfenadine, forthcoming. Honours: Phi Beta Kappa, 1959; Sigma Xi, 1959. Memberships: Fellow, American Academy of Allergy and Immunology; Fellow, American COllege of Allergy and Immunology. Hobby: Antiquarian Medical Books. Address: Hennepin County Medical Centre, 701 Park Avenue, Minneapolis, MN 55415, USA.

STEINER Hans, b. 27 June 1946, Vienna, Austria. Physician. m. Judith Harrison, 6 May 1967, 2 sons, 1 daughter. Appointments incl: Consulting Psychiatrist, Downriver Child Guidance Clinic, Seaway Unit, Detroit, 1976-78; Consulting Psychiatrist, Psychological Clinic, University of Michigan, 1977-78; Consulting Psychiatrist, Peninsula Children's Center, Palo Alto, California, 1979-91; Assistant Director, Psychosomatic Inpatient Service, Children's Hospital at Stanford, California, 1978-79; Chief, Pediatric Psychiatry, Lucile Salter Packard Children's Hospital at Stanford, 1988-; Acting Chief, Division of Child Psychiatry & Child Development, Stanford University School of Medicine, 1995. Publications incl: Psychic Survival After the Burn, 1978; Defense Styles and Family Environment, 1995; Menstrual Outcome in Anorexia Nervosa in Adolescents, 1995; Personality Traits Predict Recidivism in Adolescent Delinquents, 1995; Differences in Caloric Utilization in Eating Disordered Adolescents, 1995; Memberships incl: Austrian Medical Association; Local & National American Psychiatric Associations; Regional Organization of Child & Adolescent Psychiatrists; American Association of Directors of Psychiatric Residency Training; Academy of Psychosomatic Medicine; American Academy of Child & Adolescent Psychiatry; American Medical Association. Hobbies: Skiing; Tennis. Address: 401 Quarry Road, Stanford, CA 94305-5540, USA.

STEINMETZ Philip Rolf, b. 10 Jun 1927, De Bilt, The Netherlands. Physician; Scientist. m. Micheline Osmont, 14 Apr 1955, 2 s. Education: Bacc, Rynlands Lyceum, Leiden University, 1939; MD, Arts, 1954, PhD, 1975, Leiden University; Boards Internal Medicine, 1963, Nephrology, 1976. Career: Instructor, 1961-65, Assistant, Associate and Professor of Medicine, 1965-73, New York University Medical School; Professor of Medicine, University of Iowa, 1973-81; Professor of Medicine, University of Connecticut School of Medicine, 1981-. Publications: 75 Papers published including: Cellular mechanisms of urinary acidification in Physiology Review, 1974; Cellular organization of urinary acidification, in American Journal of Physiology, 1986. Honours: Josiah Macy Scholar Award, 1979; Homer Smith Award in Renal Physiology, 1985.

Memberships: American Society of Nephrology; American Physiological Society American Society for Clinical Investigation; Association of American Physicians. Hobbies: Tennis; Literature; Travel. Address: University of Connecticut School of Medicine, Department of Medicine, Farmington, CT 06030-1405, USA.

STEPANOV Konstantin, b. 24 Mar 1930, Leningrad, USSR. Physicist. m. Timochina Elena, 29 Aug 1965, 1 s, 1 d. Education: Doctor of Science in Physics and Mathematics, 1965; Senior Scientific Worker, 1961; Professor, 1969; MSc, Kharkov State University, 1952; Doctor of Philosophy in Physics and Mathematics, 1958. Appointments: Head, Department of Plasma Theory, Institute of Plasma Physics, National Science Center, Kharkov Institute of Physics & Technology. Publications: Collective Oscillations in a Plasma, 1967; Plasma Electrodynamis, 1975; Radio-Frequency Heating in the Ion-Cyclotron Frequency Range, 1992. Honours: Order of Labour Red Banner, 1970; List of Honour of Ukrainean SSR Supreme Soviet Prezidium, 1978. Memberships: National Academy of Sciences of Ukraine; Bureau of Physics Astonomy Division of Academy; Academy of Applied Radio Electronics Belorussia; National Council of Science and Technologies of Ukraine. Address: P Morozova Str 2, Apt 9, 310108 Kharkov, Ukraine.

STERIOFF Sylvester, b. 19 Jan 1938, St Louis, MO, USA. Surgeon. m. Yvonne Carey, 14 Sep 1991, 2 s, 1 d. Education: AB, Harvard College; MD, Washington University, St Louis, MO; American Board of Surgery, 1969. Career: Associate Professor of Surgery, Johns Hopkins School of Medicine, Baltimore, MD; Currently, Professor of Surgery and Director of Transplantation, MAYO Clinic. Publications: Over 100 articles and book chapters. Memberships: American College of Surgeons; American Society of Transplant Surgeons; Society for Surgery of the Alimentary Tract; Transplantation Society; International Cardio-Vascular Society. Address: Department of Surgery, MAYO Clinic, Rochester, MN 55905, USA.

STERLING Theodore David, b. 3 July 1923, Vienna, Austria. Epidemiologist. m. Nora Mostalik, 20 June 1948, 2 sons. Education: BA, MA, University Chicago; PhD, Tulane Unversity. Appointments: Professor, Computer Science; Professor, Applied Mathematics. Publications: 8 books and over 300 scientific articles. Address: School of Computer Science, Simon Fraser University, BC, V5A 1S6, Canada.

STEUBER Marlene, b. 24 June 1940, Potsdam, Germany. Psychotherapist; Supervisor. 1 son. Education: Diploma in Psychology, University of Cologne; Psychoanalyst, DPV/IPV; Clinical Psychologist/Psychotherapist, BDP; Psychoanalytic-Systemic Psychotherapy, APF. Appointments: Assistant, Institute of Psychology, University of Cologne; Educational Adviser, Family Therapist, Heinrich-Meng Institute, Brühl; Psychotherapist, Cologne Psychiatric Hospital; Currently private practice as Psychoanalyst, Family Therapist, Teacher in Psychoanalytic-Systemic Psychotherapy. Memberships include: German Society of Psychotherapy (DGPT). Hobbies: Friends; Music; Sports. Address: Alteburgerstrasse 288, 50968 Cologne, Germany.

STEVENS Barbara Christine, b. 4 Sept 1939, Guildford, Surrey, England. Clinical Psychologist. m. John Ridsdale, 21 Nov 1974 (dec). Education: BA Hons, Sociology, London School of Economics, 1961; BA Hons, Psychology, University College, London, 1962; PhD, Institute of Psychiatry, London, 1967; Clinical Psychology Diploma, British Psychological Society, 1982. Appointments: Scientific Staff, Medical Research Council Social Psychiatry Unit, 1962-72; Research Staff, Institute of Psychiatry, 1972-77; Senior Psychologist, H M Prison Service, 1977-83; Regional Forensic Psychologist, Runwell Hospital, Essex, 1983-. Publications: Marriage and Fertility of Women Suffering from Schizophrenia or Affective Disorders, 1969; Over 30 articles including: Impact of Community-Orientated Psychiatry on Marriage and Fertility of Psychotic Women, 1969; Frequency of Separation and Divorce among Women Suffering from Schizophrenia and Affective Disorders, 1970; Illegitimate Fertility of Psychotic Women, 1970; Psychoses Associated with Childbirth, 1971; Dependence of Schizophrenic Patients on Elderly Relatives, 1972; Evaluation of Rehabilitation for Psychotic Patients in the Community, 1973; The Role of Fluphenazine Decanoate in Lessening the Burden of Chronic Schizophrenics in the Community, 1973; The Social Value of Fluphenazine Decanoate, 1976; Deaths Due to Drug Addiction in Greater London 1970-4, 1978; Clinical Psychological and Social Problems of Patients with Multiple Sclerosis, 1978; Alternatives to Custody: The Essex Community Orientated Forensic Psychology

Service 1983-93, 1994. Honours: Mapother Research Fellow, Medical Research Council, 1963-66. Membership: Associate Fellow, British Psychological Society. Address: Psychology Department, Runwell Hospital, Essex SS11 7QE, England.

STEVENS Richard Frederic, b. 21 Apr 1949, Leeds, England. Consultant Paediatric Haematologist. Education: BSc, Honours, Mb ChB, University of Birmingham Medical School; FRCP; MRCPath. Career: Senior Registrar in Haematology, North West Regional Health Authority; Currently, Consultant Paediatric Haematologist, Royal Manchester Children's Hospital. Publications: Handbook of Haematological Investigations in Children, 1989; Chapters and articles on all aspects of Paediatric Haemotology and bone marrow transplantation. Memberships: Medical Research Council, Childhood Leukaemia Working Party; United Kingdom Children's Cancer Study Group. Hobbies: Gardening; DIY; Music. Address: Royal Manchester Children's Hospital, Pendlebury, Manchester, M27 1HA, England.

STEVENS Rudolph Alonzo, b. 30 July 1953, Old Harbour Bay, Jamaica. Consulting Obstetrician & Gynaecologist, Gynae Associates. m. Rachel Cartie, 18 December 1993. Education: MB.BS honours in medicine and therapeutics, University of the West Indies, Mona, Jamaica, 1981; DM, University of the West Indies, 1986; MBA, Barry University, Miami Shores, Florida, USA. Appointments: Medical Officer, Ministry of Health; Co-ordinator/Lecturer, BSc Health Services Administration, College of Arts, Science & Technology; Editor-in-Chief, The Health Executive journal. Publications: In medicine and health care management. Conducts seminars in the management of medical practice. Memberships: Fellow, American College of Obstetricians & Gynaecologists; Royal College of Obstetricians & Gynaecologists; American Society of Colposcopy & Cervical Pathology; Jamaica Association of Health Services Executive (JAHSE) Medical Association of Jamaica. Hobbies: Badminton; Reading; Poetry; Listening to Music. Address: 19 Ravinia Mews, Kingston 6, Jamaica.

STEVENSON Jim Eric, b. 14 Jan 1947, London, England. Psychologist. m. Pamela May Connor, 24 Nov 1973, 1 son, 2 daughters. Education: BA, University of Oxford, 1968; MSc, University of Sussex, 1969; PhD, University of Surrey, 1990. Appointments: Reserch Fellow, Institute of Child Health, University of London, 1971-81; Lecturer, then Senior Lecturer, University of Surrey, 1981-92; Reader, Institute of Child Health; Professor of Psychology and Health, Department of Psychology, University of Southampton, 1995-. Publications: Co-author: Preschool to school: a behavioural study, 1982; ADMD and spelling disability: testing for a shared genetic aetiology, 1993. Membership: Fellow, British Psychological Society. Hobbies: Tennis; Music. Address: Department of Psychology, University of Southampton, Highfield, Southampton, Hants, SO17 1BJ, England.

STEWART Ian James, b. 7 Mar 1943, Sydney, Australia. Obstetrics & Gynaecology. m. Merilyn, 17 Oct 1981, 2 sons, 1 daughter. Education: MBBS, University Sydney, 1967; BA, University of New England, New South Wales, 1993; FRACOG, 1979; FRCOG, 1982. Appointments: Resident MO, Royal Prince Alfred Hospital,Sydney, 1967-68; Registrar, Obstetrics & Gynaecology, King George Hospital, Sydney, 1969-71; Obstetric & Gynaecology Registrar, Bradford, West Yorkshire, England, 1972-73; MO, Wagga Base & Calvary Hospitals, 1974-94. Memberships: AMA, 1974-94; RACOG, 1979-94. Hobbies: History; Bush Walking; Birds; Pop Music; Old Books. Address: PO Box 976, Wagga Wagga, NSW 2650, Australia.

STEWART Jonathan Taylor, b. 15 Mar 1956, Bethpage, New York, USA. Geropsychiatrist. m. Linda Sue Irvin, 27 Oct 1984, 2 sons. Education: Honours BA, Rollins College, Winter Park, Florida, 1976; MD, University of South Florida, Tampa, 1979; Psychiatric Residency, University of Florida, Gainesville, 1983; Board Certified, Psychiatry, 1985, Geriatric Psychiatry, 1991, American Board of Psychiatry and Neurology. Appointments: Associate Professor, Psychiatry, University of Florida, 1983-94; Currently: Chief, Geropsychiatry Section, Veterans Administration Medical Center, Bay Pines, Florida; Professor in Psychiatry, University of South Florida, Tampa. Publications: Approximately 40 articles and chapters in geropsychiatry, neuropsychiatry, dementia, psychopharmacology, 1985-. Honours: Samuel Harris Award, 1986, 1993, Teacher of the Year Award, 1988, 1990, Department of Psychiatry, University of Florida. Memberships: Fellow, American Psychiatric Association; Florida Psychiatric Society, CME Committee Chair; American Geriatrics Society; American Association of Geriatric Psychiatry. Hobbies: Flying; Cooking; Scuba diving; Travel. Address: Psychiatry Service (116A), VA Medical Center, Bay Pines, FL 33504, USA.

STEWART Kenneth Sloan, b. 15 Oct 1938, Clydebank, Scotland. Obstetrician and Gynaecologist. m. Sally McKenzie, 19 Sept 1963, 3 sons, 2 daughters. Education: MB ChB (Edinburgh), 1962; FRCS, 1967; MRCOG, 1969; MD (Edinburgh), 1977; FRCOG, 1983; DFM, 1988. Appointments: Registrar, Aberdeen Royal Infirmary, 1967-69; Senior Registrar, Clinical Tutor, Queen Elizabeth Hospital, Birmingham, England, 1969-72; Consultant in Obstetrics/Gynaecology, Harari Hospital, Rhodesia and Senior Research Fellow, University of Rhodesia, 1972-74; Currently Consultant Obstetrician/Gynaecologist, Stirling, Scotland; Examiner: Royal College of Surgeons, Edinburgh, Royal College of Obstetricians and Gynaecologists, and for PLAB. Publications: Cephalo pelvic disproportion in the African Premigravid: Intensive Care of the High Risk Fetus in Africa, 1977; Bacterial Infections in Pregnancy, 1981; The Second Stage of Labour, 1984; Medical Hazards of Aqualung Diving, 1989. Memberships: President, Glasgow Obstetrical/Gynaecological Society; Fothergill society. Hobbies: Mountaineering; Sub-aqua diving; Sailing; Swimming. Address: 19 Clarendon Place, Stirling, Scotland.

STEWART Sarah Barton, b. 2 Jun 1961, Boston, MA, USA. Psychologist. Education: BA, Harvard-Radcliffe College, 1984; Doctor of Psychology, MA School of Professional Psychology, 1991. Career: Psychology Fellow, Harvard Community Health Plan, 1991-92; Clinical Instructor, Psychology, Harvard Medical School, 1994-; Clinical Associate, Psychology in Psychiatry Service, MA General Hospital, 1994-; Currently, Clinical Psychologist in Private Practice. Publication: Phenomenological Study of the Experience of Dissociation, 1991. Memberships: American Psychological Association; MA Psychology Association; International Society for Traumatic Stress Studies; International Society for Study of Dissociation; National Organization of Women; Society for Exploration of Psychotherapy Integration; Executive Committee, 1990, Treasurer, 1992-94, New England Society for the Study of Dissociation. Hobbies: Jogging; Hiking; Wildlife; Cooking; Swimming. Address: 263 Concord Avenue 2nd Floor, Cambridge, MA 02138-1336, USA.

STIERLIN Helm, b. 12 Mar 1926, Mannheim, Germany. Psychiatrist. m. Dr Satuila Zanolli, 11 Jun 1965, 2 d. Education: MD; PhD. Appointments: Acting Chief, Family Studies Section, Adult Psychiatry Branch, National Institute of Mental Health, Bethesda, MD; Faculty Member, WA School of Psychiatry; Currently, Professor Emeritus of Psychiatry and Psychotherapy, University of Heidelberg. Publications: Editor and co-founder of magazine, Familiendynamik, Stuttgart; Books: Conflict and Reconciliation, 1969; Separating Parents and Adolescents, 1974; Psychoanalysis and Family Therapy, 1977; The Language of Family Therapy: A Systemic Vocabulary and Sourcebook, 1985. Honour: Distinguished Professional Contribution to Family Therapy Award, American Association of Marital and Family Therapysts, 1985. Memberships: Corresponding member, American Psychiatric Association; American Family Therapy Academy; International Psychoanalytic Association; Deutsche Arbeitsgemeinschaft für Familientherapie. Hobbies: Theatre; Skiing; Swimming; Hiking. Address: Kapellenweg 19, D 69121Heidelberg, Germany.

STINE Susan Marie, b. 25 Sep 1949, Miami, FL, USA. Psychiatrist. Education: BA cum laude, Biology and German Literature, Tulane University, New Orleans, LA, 1971; PhD, Neuroscience, Center for Brain Research, University of Rochester, NY, 1979; MD, University of Miami School of Medicine, PhD to MD Program, 1983. Appointments include: Internship, St Raphael's Hospital, New Haven, CT, 1983-84; Residency, Yale Psychiatry Program, 1984-87; Assistant Professor, Yale Department of Psychiatry, 1987-; Director of Outpatient Substance Abuse Clinic, West Haven VA Medical Center, 1989-. Publications include: Numerous original articles, 1980-94, including, Co-author, Reduction of Opiate Withdrawal-Like Symptoms by Cocaine Abuse During Methadone and Buprenorphine Maintainance, In American Journal of Drug and Alcohol Abuse, 1994; Many Chapters, Books, Letters and Book Reviews; 15 Presentations, 1979-. Honours: Tulane University Scholarships; Beta Beta Beta; NIH and NIMH Training Grant Awards, University of Rochester; Sigma Xi. Memberships: CEGO, 1985, 1986, 1987, 1988; Peer Review Board, The American Journal on Addictions and Harvard Review of Psychiatry; American Academy of Psychiatrists in Alcoholism and the Addictions committee on Military Veterans. Address: Yale Department of Psychiatry, VA Medical Center, West Haven, CT 06516, USA.

STOLLAR B(ernard) David, b. 11 Aug 1936, Saskatoon, Sask, Canada. Medical Scientist. m. Carol Ann Singer, 7 Oct 1956, 2 s, 1 d. Education: BA, 1958, MD, 1959, University of Saskatchewan; Internship, University of Saskatoon Hospital, 1959-60. Career: Postdoctoral Fellow, Brandeis University Biochemistry, 1960-62; Department Chief, Biology Science Division, US Air Force Office of Scientific Research, 1962-64; Assistant Professor of Pharmacology, 1964-68, Associate Professor, 1968, Professor of Biochemistry, 1974, Tufts University; Professor and Chairman of Department of Biochemistry, Tufts University Schools of Medicine, Dental Medicine, Veterinary Medicine and Sackler School of Graduate Biomedical Sciences. Publications: 182 Original scientific articles in various journals and 29 review articles and chapters. Honours: Copland Prize, University of Saskatchewan, 1958; Gold Medallist, University of Saskatchewan, 1959; Commendation Medal, US Air Force, 1964; Senior Fellow, Weizmann Institute, 1971-72; Third Alumni Lecturer, University of Saskatchewan, 1989. Memberships include: American Society of Biological Medical Molecular Biology; American Association of Immunologists; American College of Rheumatology; American Association of Advancement of Science. Hobbies: Photography; Music Appreciation; Swimming. Address: Department of Biochemistry, Tufts University School of Medicine, 136 Harrison Avenue, Boston, MA 02159, USA.

STOLLEY Paul David, b. 17 June 1937, Pawling, New York, USA. Physician. m. Jo Ann Goldenberg, 13 June 1959, 1 son, 2 daughters. Education: AB, summa cum laude, Lafayette College, 1957; MPH, Johns Hopkins University, 1968. Appointments: Assistant Associate Professor of Epidemiology, Johns Hopkins University School of Public Health, 1968-76; Herbert Rorer Professor of Medicine, University of Pennsylvania School of Medicine, 1976-91; Professor, Chairman, Department of Epidemiology and Preventive Medicine, University of Maryland School of Medicine, Baltimore. Publications: Case Control Studies, 1982; Epidemiology: Investigating Disease Patterns, 1995; Foundations of Epidemiology, 1994. Honours: Phi Beta Kappa, 1956; National Academy of Sciences, 1981; Johns Hopkins Society of Scholars, 1983. Memberships: Institute of Medicine; Society for Epidemiologic Research; American Epidemiological Society. Hobbies: Music; Jogging; Literature. Address: 660 West Redwood Street, Baltimore, MD 21201, USA.

STONE Alan Abraham, b. 15 Aug 1929, Boston, MA, USA. Psychiatrist. Divorced, 2 s, 1 d (deceased). Education: BA, Harvard, 1950; MD, Yale, 1955. Career: President of American Psychiatric Association, 1979-80; Currently, Touroff-Glueck Professor of Law and Psychiatry, Harvard Law School, Cambridge, MA. Publications: Longitudinal Studies of Child Personality, 1959; The Abnormal Personality Through Literature, 1966; Mental Health and Law: A System in Transition, 1976; Law, Psychiatry and Morality, 1987. Honours include: Isaac Ray Award, 1982; Guggenheim; Tanner Lecturer. Address: Harvard Law School, Cambridge, MA 02138, USA.

STONE Leroy Allen, b. 13 Sep 1931, San Francisco, CA, USA. Forensic Clinical Psychologist. m. Patricia Joan Snider, 28 Dec 1957, 1 d. Education: AB, 1953, MA, 1954, San Jose State University; PhD, University of North Dakota, 1962; Diplomate in Forensic Psychology. Career: Professor of Psychology, University of North Dakota, 1965-75; Senior Clinical Psychologist, National Security Agency, 1975-88; Chief Research Psychologist, National Security Agency, 1988-; Forensic Clinical Psychologist. Publications: 2 Books, 1969; Over 200 articles in refereed journals. Honours: NIMH Research Fellow, 1966-68; Fellow, American Academy of Forensic Psychology, 1987. Memberships: American Psychology Association; Psychonomic Society; Sigma Xi; American Psychology - Law Society; Military Testing Association. Hobbies: Antique Glass and Print Collecting; Computers. Address: P O Box 395, Harpers Ferry, WV 25425-0395, USA.

STONES Christopher Robin, b. 13 Jan 1952, Bulawayo, Zimbabwe. Psychologist. m. Annette Marie Stones, 5 Aug 1978, 1 s. Education: MSc, Psychology; SAMDC, 1984; AFBPsS, 1988; PhD, Psychology, Rhodes University; C Psychol, 1989. Appointments: Lecturer in Psychology, Rhodes University, South Africa, 1975-86; Research Fellow, Durham University, 1987-88; Principal Clinical Psychologist, National Health Service, UK; Currently, Professor and Head of Department of Psychology, Rhodes University. Publications include: Prejudice and Conflict in South Africa: The Ghost and Spirit of Apartheid?, 1988. Honours include: St Aidan's College Fellowship, Durham University, 1987-88. Memberships include: British Psychological Society; Chairman, South Africa Society for Clinical

Psychology. Hobbies: Golf; Scuba Diving; Road Running. Address: Dept of Psychology, Rhodes University, Grahamstown 6140, South Africa.

STOREY Kenneth B, b. 23 Oct 1949, Taber, Alberta, Canada. Biochemist. m. Janet M Collicut, 6 June 1975, 2 daughters. Education: BSc Hons, Biochemistry, University of Calgary, 1971; PhD, Zoology, University of British Columbia, 1974. Appointments: Assistant Professor, Zoology, Duke University, USA, 1974-79; Currently Professor of Biochemistry, Carleton University, Ottawa, Canada. Publications: 303 research publications in refereed journals. Honours: E W R Steacie Memorial Fellowship, 1984-86; Ayerst Award, Canadian Biochemical Society, 1989; Elected Fellow, Royal Society of Canada, 1990; Killam Senior Research Fellowship, 1993-95. Memberships: Society for Cryobiology; Canadian Biochemical Society; American Society of Biochemistry and Molecular Biology; Canadian Society of Zoologists. Address: Institute of Biochemistry, Carleton University, Ottawa, Ontario, Canada K1S 5B6.

STRADER Kyle W, b. 24 June 1955, Clarksburg, USA. Clinical Assistant Professor. m. Deborah Cain, 11 Nov 1978. Education: BA, West Virginia University, 1973-77; MD, West Virginia Medical School, 1977-81; Residency, Milton S Hershey Medical Center, 1981-84; Fellowship, Bowman Gray School of Medicine, 1984-86. Appointments: Clinical Assistant Professor, University of North Carolina, Chapel Hill. Publications: Disseminated Gonococcal Infection caused by Chromosomally-Mediated Penicilin-Resistant Organisms, 1986. Memberships: American College of Physicians; American Medical Association; American College of Allergist; American College of Rheumatology. Honours: Phi Beta Kappa, 1973; Lange Book Award, Academic Achievement, 1978; Mosby Book Award, Academic Achievement, 1979; Resident of the Year, Milton S Hershey Medical Center. Hobbies: Billiards; Stamp Collecting. Address: 3831 Merton Drive, Raleigh, NC 27609, USA.

STRAEDE William Thomas Charles, b. 14 Aug 1916, Melbourne, Australia. Medical Practitioner, retired. m. Kay Miller, 1 Dec 1942, 2 s. Education: MBBS, Melbourne, 1950. Career: Resident, Clinical Assistant, Alfred Hospital; Lecturer and Examiner, Northern District College of Nursing; Honorary Allergist and Dermatologist, Bendings Base Hospital; Now retired. Honour: Knight of The Most Venerable Order of St John of Jerusalem, 1989. Hobbies: Gardening; Walking. Address: 17 Flinders Street, Queenscliffe, Victoria 3225, Australia.

STRAHAN Thomas Martin, b. 8 Oct 1956, Rockhampton, Queensland, Australia. Internist. m. Jeanne Eloise Booth, 22 Dec 1977, 3 s. Education: MB; BS; DrPH; FRACP; FAFPHM; FACPM. Appointments: Director of Medicine. Address: Department of Medicine, Bundaberg Base Hospital, Bundaberg, Queensland 4670, Australia.

STRASBERG Steven Martin, b. 10 Oct 1939. Surgeon. m. Yona, 13 June 1963, 1 son, 3 daughters. Education: MD; FRCSC; FACS. Career: Professor of Surgery, University of Toronto, Canada; Professor, Head Hepatobiliary-Pancreatic & Gastrointestinal Surgery, Washington University School of Medicine. Publications: 125 original publications. Honour: Lester Prize, 1980. Memberships: American Surgical Association; American Association for Study of Liver Diseases; American College of Surgeons. Address: Barnes Hospital, Suite 6107 Queeny Tower, One Barnes Hospital Plaza, St Louis, MO 63110, USA.

STRASZAK-SURI Marina Anna, b. 3 Aug 1959, Ottawa, Canada. Assistant Professor. m. Permjit Suri, 29 June 1992, 1 son, 2 daughters. Education: BSc, McGill University, Canada, 1981; MD, University of Ottawa, 1986; FRCSC, Obstetrics & Gynecology, University of Ottawa, 1991. Publications: Family Studies of Epileptiform EEG Abnormalities and Photosensitivity in Focal Epilepsy, 1982; The Medical Management of Uterine Hyperstimulation, 1992; The Use of Transvaginal Ultrasound in the Management of Early Pregnancy Loss, 1993. Memberships: Society of Obstetricians & Gynecologists of Canada; American College of Obstetricians & Gynecologists; Canadian Society for International Health; American Association of Gynecolobic Laparoscopists; Ontario Medical Association; Canadian Medical Association. Honours: Winnifred Cullis Grant, 1984; International Health Exchange Program, 1984, 1989. Hobbies: Travel; Swimming; Reading. Address: 1919 Riverside Drive, Suite 302, Ottawa, Ontario K1H 1A2, Canada.

STRAUCH Berish, b. 19 Sept 1933, New York City, New York, USA. Plastic Surgeon. m. Rena Feuerstein, 12 Jun 1955, 1 son, 1 daughter. Education: BS, 1955, MD, College of Physicians and Surgeons, 1959,

Columbia University; Internship, Bellevue Hospital, New York City, 1959-60; Residencies: Montefiore Medical Center, Bronx, 1960-64; Plastic and Reconstructive Surgery, Roosevelt Hospital, New York City, 1961, Stanford University, 1966-68. Appointments include: Assistant Professor, Associate Professor, 1970-81, Professor of Plastic Surgery, 1981-, Chairman, Plastic and Reconstructive Surgery, 1989-, Albert Einstein College of Medicine, Bronx, New York; Assistant Attending, Adjunct Attending, Associate Attending, 1968-76, Plastic Surgeon-in-Chief, 1978-79, Attending Surgeon, 1978-, Chairman, Plastic and Reconstructive Surgery, 1989-, Montefiore Medical Center; Other attending positions. Publications: Co-editor: Textbook on Microsurgery, 1976; Grabb's Encyclopedia of Flaps, 3 vols, 1990; Atlas of Microvascular Surgery: Anatomy and Operative Approaches (co-author), 1992; Microsurgical Thumb Reconstruction: Toe-to-Thumb Transplant, film, 1977; Numerous articles and book chapters. Honours: Fellowship in Plastic and Reconstructive Surgery, 1966-68; Emanuel Kaplan Award, Outstanding Anatomic Study, American Society for Surgery of the Hand, 1987; Founder's Lecturer, American Society for Reconstructive Microsurgery, 1988; Association of American Publishers Award, Outstanding Publication in Clinical Medicine, 1990. Memberships: President, Montefiore Physician Practice Association; American Association for the Advancement of Science; President, American Society for the Peripheral Nerve; American Society of Plastic and Reconstructive Surgeons; Many more. Address: 3331 Bainbridge Ave, Bronx, NY 10467, USA.

STRICKLAND Maurice Henry Van, b. 24 Mar 1951, Atlanta, Georgia, USA. Physician. m. Cathy Eileen O'Shea, 16 June 1979, 3 daughters. Education: MD, Baylor College of Medicine, 1974; Residency, Baylor College of Medicine, 1974-77; Fellowship, National Jewish Hospital, 1977-79; Diplomate, American Board of Pediatrics, 1979; Diplomate, American Board of Allergy & Immunology, 1979. Appointments: The Wichita Clinic, 1979-82; Private Practice, Wichita, 1982-83; Wyoming Chest & Allergy Clinic, 1983-84; The Olive Garvey Center for the Improvement of Human Functioning, Wichita, 1984-85; The Allergy Clinic of Garland, 1985-86; American Allergy Consultants, 1986-87; The Olive Garvey Center for Improvement of Human Functioning, 1987-90. Memberships: American Medical Association; Sedgwick County Medical Society; Kansas Medical Society; American Academy of Allergy & Immunology; Fellow, American College of Allergy & Immunology; Fellow, American Academy of Pediatrics; Fellow, Southern Medical Association; International Academy of Nutrition & Preventive Medicine. Hobbies: Aviation; Photography; Running Marathons; Hiking; Mountaineering. Address: 710 N Woodchuck, Wichita, KS 67212, USA.

STRIKER Gary E, b. 7 Mar 1934. Physician. m. Dr Liliane Striker. Education: BS, University of Washington, USA; MD, UNiversity of Washington Medical School. Appointments: US Army Medical Corp; Assistant Professor, Department of Pathology, Associate Professor, Department of Pathology, Dean, Curriculum School of Medicine, Professor, Department of Pathology, University of Washington; Maitre de Conference, Agrege, Section de Pathologie Experimental, University Pierre et Marie Curie, Paris, France; Director, Division of Kidney, Urological Haemtologic Disorders, NIH. Publications: Contributor of 192 articles in professional journals. Honours: Malphigi Gold Medal, 1994;; Honorary Member, Italian Society of Nephrology, 1994; Ambord Award for Scientific Achievement, 1991; Department of HHS senior Executive Service Awards, 1986, 1987, 1988, 1990; Distinguished Visiting Professor, Cambridge University, England, 1991; American Association Physicians, 1990. Memberships: American Association Cell Biology; American Association Physicians; American Federation Clinical Research; American Association Pathology; American Society nephrology; National Kidney Foundation; International Society Nephrology; Endocrine Society; King County medical Society; Washington State Medical Society; American Society Cell Biology; American Heart Association. Address: NIH NIDDK, Building 10 Room 3N110, Bethesda, MD 20892, USA.

STROUD Robert Malone, b. 12 Mar 1931, St Louis, Missouri, USA. Physician; Professor. m. Gloria June Flowers, 19 June 1955, 1 son, 1 daughter. Education: BA cum laude, Mathematics, Harvard College, 1952; MD, Harvard Medical School, 1956. Appointments include: Professor of Medicine, Professor of Microbiology, University of Alabama; Currently Clinical Professsr of Medicine. Publications: 75 articles in refereed medical journals relating to biochemistry of complement, to food allergy and to arthritis. Memberships: American Society of Clinical Investigation; American College of Rheumatology; American Academy of Allergy; American College of Allergy. Hobbies: Swimming; Travel. Address: 32 Iroquois Trail, Ormond Beach, FL 32174, USA.

STRYDOM Wynand Johannes, b. 11 Mar 1946, Bloemfontein, South Africa. Professor of Medical Physics. m. Jeanette Kleingeld, 12 Dec 1970, 2 sons, 1 daughter. Education: BSc, distinction; BSc (Hons), distinction; MSc, distinction; PhD in Biophysics. Appointments: Lecturer; Senior Professional Officer, Senior Lecturer; Chief Medical Physicist, Professor; Currently Director, Professor of Physics. Publications include: Energy sensitivity of LiF thermoluminescent dosimeters for different electron energies, 1982; A study of pelvimetry dose-CT against conventional X-rays, 1985; Evaluation of different formulae for the study of platelet survival, 1987; Comparative study of six analytical expressions to calculate the percentage depth dose for 6 MV photos, 1991; Central axis depth dose curve for electron beams, 1991; Co-author: The Relevance of Ethnic Differences in Haemodynamic Responses to the Head-up Tilt Manoeuvre to Clinical Pharmacological Investigations, 1985; Comparative pharmacokinetics of intravenous propranalol in Black and White volunteers, 1985; The importance of cholescintigraphy and interior vena cava flow studies in the deferential diagnosis of Hepatocellular carcinoma, 1989; A two detector system to measure SeHCAT retention in the human body to determine malabsorption of the terminal ileum, 1990; Use of indium-111-labelled platelets in black stroke patients, 1990; The assessment of mucociliary clearance using monodisperse 99m-Tc-tagged red blood cells, 1991; Normalization of GFR measurements, 1991. Memberships: Professional Board of Medical Scientists; South African Association of Physicists in Medicine and Biology; South African Institute of Physics; South African Medical Physics Society; South African Radiation Protection Society; South African Society of Nuclear Medicine; South African Society of Magnetic Resonance. Hobbies: Tennis; Squash. Address: 54 Kameeldoring Avenue, Wonderboom 0182, South Africa.

STUART Robert Kenneth, b. 6 Jul 1948, Baton Rouge, LA, USA. MD. m. Charlene Gates, 2 Nov 1991, 1 s, 1 d. Education: BS, magna cum laude, Psychology, Georgetown University, WA, 1970; MD, Johns Hopkins University School of Medicine, Baltimore, MD, 1974. Appointments: Assistant Professor of Medicine, 1985-85, Associate Professor of Medicine, 1984-85, Johns Hopkins University School of Medicine, Baltimore, MD; Currently, Professor of Medicine, Director of Hematology and Oncology Division, Medical University of SC. Publications include: Author, Co-author of 8 publications, 1980-, including: Autologous Bone Marrow Transplantation in Patients with Acute Nonlymphocytic Leukemia, Using ex Vivo Marrow Treatment with 4-Hydroperoxycyclophosphamide, in New England Journal of Medicine, 1986; Autologous Bone Marrow Transplantation for Leukemia, Seminars in Oncology, 1993; Disposition of Folic Acid and its Metabolites: A Comparison with Leukovorin, Clinical Pharmacy and Therapeutics. Honours: Henry Strong Denison Scholar, 1973-74; Mosby Scholarship Award, 1974; Junior Faculty Clinical Fellow, American Cancer Society, 1979-80; Special Fellow, Leukemia Society of America Inc, 1980-82. Memberships: Phi Beta Kappa, 1969; Alpha Omega Alpha, 1974; International Society for Experimental Hematology, 1980; American Society of Hematology, 1981; American Society of Clinical Oncology, 1982; American Association for Cancer Research, 1986; Charleston County Medical Society, 1992. Hobby: Bicycling. Address: Medical University of SC, Hematology/Oncology Division, 171 Ashley Avenue, Charleston, SC 29425, USA.

STUHLMILLER Cynthia, b. 27 Oct 1956, Buffalo, NY, USA. Nursing Professor. Education: MSc, Nursing; DSc, Nursing. Career: Clinical Nurse Specialist, National Center for Post Traumatic Stress Disorder, 1981-91; Clinical Professor, University of San Francisco, 1991-93; Currently, Visiting Professor, University of Tromso, Department of Nursing Science. Publications: Book Chapters: Action-Based Therapy for Post Traumatic Stress Disorder, in Handbook of Post Traumatic Therapy, 1994, Narrative Methods in Disaster Studies: Rescuers of Cyprus, in Interpretive Phenomenology; Articles: Rescuers of Cyprus: Work Meanings and Practices that Guided Appraisal and Coping, in Western Journal of Nursing Research, 1994. Honours: Volunteer of Year Award, American Red Cross, Palo Alto, CA, 1986; Distinguished Dissertation, UCSF School of Nursing, 1992; Fulbright Senior Scholar, 1993-94. Memberships: International Society of Traumatic Stress Studies; Nurses Organization of the Veterans Administration. Hobbies: Camping; Rollerskating; Skiing; Hiking; Biking.

STVRTECKY Roberto Orlando, b. 11 Feb 1940, Buenos Aires, Argentina. Oral Surgeon. m. Zulma Borgetti, 29 Apr 1990, 2 sons, 1 daughter. Education: Doctor in Dentistry; Professor of Surgery. Appointments: Chief, Oral and Maxillofacial Surgery Department, Air Force Hospital; Chief, Maxillofacial Department, Falklands Islands Interforce Hospital, during Falklands War; Currently Chief, Dental Department, Main Air Force Hospital, Buenos Aires. Publications: Epithelial Adhesion of Subperiosteal Implants, 1989; Subperiosteal Implants, 1993. Memberships: Life Fellow, International Association of Oral and Maxillofacial Surgeons; American Academy of Implant Dentistry. Hobbies: Golf; Skiing. Address: Vicente Lopez 1931 - 1o B, 1128 Buenos Aires, Argentina.

SU Hanlian (Jiuru), b. 1938, Xianzhou County, Guangxi, China. Doctor of Traditional Chinese Medicine. Education: University. Appointments include: Researcher, Ancient Zhuang Minority's Medicine and Guangxi Ethnic Minority's Medicine, 1960s-; Currently: Chief, Researcher, Guangxi Medical and Cultural Research Centre, Shanghai Oriental Research Institute; Professor, World Confucius University, USA; President, Professor, Chinese Affiliated College, Asia Correspondent College, Hong Kong; Invited Lecturer, Taiwan and USA. Publications include: Ethnic Minority Medical Knowledge; Concise Course of Zhuang's Medicine; Introduction to Zhuang's Medicine; Over 50 theses in medical journals, China and abroad. Honours: Gold Cup, 1st World Meeting of Traditional Medicine, 1994; Certificate of Appreciation, American Institute of Chinese Medicine Inc, 1994; 3rd Award for Thesis and Works, 1st International Academic Meeting of Traditional Chinese Medicine; 1st National Prize for Excellent Medical Thesis. Memberships: Standing Committee, Asia Confucius Academy Association, Japan; Standing Council, International Letters and Artists Sodality; Special Committee of Traditional Medicine, Chinese Culture Research Association; Editing Committee, Chinese Contemporary Senior Science and Technology Talents Dictionary Series.

SU Hongxi, b. 30 Jan 1915, Jiangsu, China. Cardiac Surgeon. m. H Jane McDonald, 15 Sept 1956, 2 sons, 2 daughters. Education: MB, National Central University Medical College; Residency, Surgery, Northwestern University School of Medicine, Wesley Memorial Hospital, Chicago, USA; Fellowship in Cardiovascular Surgery, Illinois Research Hospital, University of Illinois, Chicago. Appointments: Professor, Department of Thoracic Surgery, 4th Army Medical University, successfully performed first case of heart surgery under extracorporeal circulation in China, 1958; Professor of Surgery and Department Head of Cardiac Surgery, General Hospital of People's Liberation Army. Publications: Contemporary Treatment of Multiple Trauma, 1993; Contemporary Intensive Care for Critical Patients, Chief Editor, 1995; Contributor of over 180 articles in professional journals. Honours: Award, Chinese Ministry of Health for Technical Innovation, 1958; 1st Class Award for Achievement in Scientific Research, Chinese People's Liberation Army, 1964; 2nd Grade Award for Progress in Science and Technology, PLA, 1985; 3rd Grade Awards for Progress in Science and Technology, PLA, 1986, 1986; Certificate of Honour, 20 Years Contributions to National Defence, education and Construction, PLA, 1986; Certificate of Honour for Important Contributions to Military Science and Technology, PLA, 1987. Memberships: Chinese Medical Association; Chinese Society for Thoracic and Cardiovascular Surgery; Chinese Society for Cardiovascular Diseases; Fellow, American College of Chest Physicians; International Society of Surgery. Hobby: Writing Poetry. Address: Building 8, 28 Fuxing Road, Beijing 100853, China.

SU Jing-Yi, b. 7 Aug 1928, Zhejiang, China. Professor of Pathophysiology. m. Jiabin Wang, 1 Oct 1955, 2 s, 1 d. Education: Premedicine, School of Science, 1946-48, School of Medicine, 1948-53, Peking University; MD, Beijing Medical College, 1953. Appointments include: Professor of Pathophysiology, 1973-, Chairman, Department of Pathophysiology, 1973-93, Professor, Cardiovascular Research Laboratory, 1993-, Beijing Medical University. Publications: Textbook of Pathophysiology (co-editor), 1984, (editor), 1991; Pathophysiological Basis of Cardiovascular Diseases (editor), monograph, 1994; More than 80 articles in Chinese and foreign journals. Honours: Awards of Progress in Science and Technology, Chinese Ministry of Health, 1988, 1990, 1991. Memberships: Chinese Pathophysiological Society, Past President; Chinese Physiological Society; Committee Member, International Society of Pathophysiology; Shock Society, USA. Address: Department of Cardiovascular Pathophysiology, Beijing Medical University, Beijing 100083, China.

SU Liaoyuan, b. 20 Feb 1930, Xiamen, China. Professor of Medicine. m. Wenying Xiao, 6 Sept 1958, 1 daughter. Education: Graduate Diploma, Shanghai Medical College; Postgraduate Diploma, Regular

Training System of Medicine, Shandong Medical College. Appointments: Assistant, Department of Pathology, Guiyang Medical College; Currently Professor, Tutor of PhD Candidates, Department of Radiomedicine, Suzhou Medical College. Publications: Introduction to Radiation Biology, 1994; Encyclopaedia of Science and Technology Integration, 1994; 121 articles, 1972-94. Honours: 10 Science and Technology Prizes, Jiangsu Province and Nuclear Industry Ministry, 1979-93; Prize of Medical Education, China International Medical Exchange Foundation, 1993; National Medal, Excellent Teacher, China Education Committee; Outstanding Researcher of Jiangsu Province, Jiangsu Education Committee. Memberships: Director, China Radiation Research and Radiation Processing Association; Editorial Board, Textbook in Radiomedicine. Hobbies: Music lover; Accordion player; Chinese chess; Basketball. Address: Department of Radiomedicine, Suzhou Medical College, Suzhou 215007, China.

SU Qing-Fen, b. 20 Feb 1932, Shanghai, China. Professor of Physiology. m. Jing-Ru Zhang, 4 Apr 1952, 2 sons, 1 daughter. Education: MD, Shanghai 1st Medical College, 1955. Appointments: Assistant in Physiology, 1955; Lecturer in Physiology, 1963; Associate Professor of Physiology, 1982; Currently: Professor of Physiology, Shanghai Medical University, 1989-; Director, Central Laboratory of Physiology. Publications: Human Physiology (co-author), 1989; Effect of Deep Peroneal Nerve Stimulation on the Carotid Chemoreceptor Afferent Discharges in Rabbits, 1989. Memberships: Chinese Association for Physiological Sciences; International Society of Arterial Chemoreception. Address: Department of Physiology, Shanghai Medical University, 138 Yi Xue Yuan Road, Shanghai 200032, China.

SU Qingping, b. 1 Aug 1934, Shaowu, Fujian, China. Professor. m. Husong Gao, Jul 1957, 2 s. Education: Graduated from Fujian Medical College, 1958. Publications: Observation on cryptosporidium of ultrastructure and oocyst shedding, in Chinese Journal of Zoonoses, 1992; Studies of blastocystis hominis by culture, in Chinese Journal of Zoonoses, 1993. Membership: Protozoological Society of China. Hobbies: Sport; Physical Training. Address: Dept of Parasitology, Fujian Medical College, 88 Jiaotong Road, Fuzhou, Fujian 350004, China.

SU Shu Yong, b. 10 Jan 1919, Hang Zhou, China. Chinese Medical Doctor. m. (1) Jul 1945, (2) Oct 1970, 2 s, 1 d. Education: BA, Shanghai Chinese Medical College, 1938; MD, 1942. Career: Chief, Chinese Medical Department, Jiang Fang Hospital, 1964; Director, Chinese Medical Department, Huang Pu Central Hospital, Shanghai, 1987; Currently, Daily Care Specialist Consultant, Chinese Medical Department of Huang Pu Central Hospital, Shanghai. Publications include: Study on Traditional Chinese Medicine for ascites of hepatocirrhosis, 1977; Clinical observation of 55 cases of Yin-Deficiency tongue, 1983. Honours: Outstanding Doctor Group, 1983; Grand Prize for Best Paper presented at Seminar of World's Traditional Medicine, 1994. Memberships: Chinese Medical Society; Research Society of Combined Use of Chinese and Western Medicine; Chinese Science and Technology Association; Most Wellknown Chinese Medical Doctors of Academic Society. Hobbies: Music; Running. Address: Room 302, No 19, 120 Lane, Ningbo Road, Shanghai 200002, China.

SU Xue-zeng, b. 22 Feb 1925, Tianjin, China. Professor of Diagnostic Radiology. m. 1 Oct 1956, 2 sons. Education: MD Diploma, Peking Union Medical College, 1953. Appointments include: Associate Professor, 1978; Professor of Diagnostic Radiology, Supervisor, MR Unit, Cancer Hospital, Academy of Medical Sciences, Beijing. Publications: Clinical Body CT Diagnosis (vice-editor), 1986; Computed Tomography of Hepatoma, Chapter 33 of Primary Liver Cancer (in English), 1989. Honours: Special Contributor Award, State Council of China, 1983. Memberships: Faculty of American College of Radiology, 1991; Chinese Medical Association. Hobby: Chinese chess. Address: MR Unit, Cancer Institute (Hospital), Chinese Academy of Medical Sciences, PO Box 2258, Beijing 100021, China.

SU Zaifu, b. 2 May 1927, Hunan, China. Professor. m. Zeng Xianjing, 4 Aug 1961, 1 son, 1 daughter. Education: BS, Wuhan University, 1955. Appointments: Assistant of Physics, Lecturer, Associate Professor; Currently Professor, Director, Department of Informatics, Tongji Medical University, Wuhan, Hubei. Publications: The First-Order Artificial Intelligence Diagnosis System of Chinese Traditional Medicine, 1983; Fuzzy Mathematics and Medicine, 1986; Brain Mapping of Running Fractal, 1994. Honours: 2nd Award for Development of Science and Technology, Hubei, 1990; 2nd Award for Excellent Paper, China Medical Informatics Association, 1991. Memberships: China Medical Informatics

Association; China Traditional Medicine Engineering; Vice-Chairman, Hubei Medical Informatics Association. Hobbies: Penmanship; Beijing Opera. Address: Department of Physics, Tongji Medical University, 13 Hangkong Road, Wuhan, Hubei, China.

SUAREZ CUNZA Silvia, b. 17 July 1959, Huaral, Lima, Peru. Chemist; Pharmacist. m. Jose Ernesto Gonzalez, 23 June 1989, 1 son, 1 daughter. Education: Bachelor, 1985, Maestria en Bioquimica, 1988, University Nacional Mayor de San Marcos. Appointments: Auxiliary Professor of Biochemistry, Medical Faculty, University Nacional Mayor de San Marcos. Publications: Antioxidants Effects of Vit E, 1993; Food Nitrates Effects on Rat hepatic Metabolism, 1994. Memberships: Colegio Quimico Farmaceutico; Chemical Society of Peru; Peruvian Society of Biochemistry. Hobbies: Camping; Painting; Football; Basketball. Address: Centre of Investigation of Biochemistry and Nutrition, Av Grau Cda 7, Lima 1, Peru.

SUEDFELD Peter, b. 30 Aug 1935, Budapest, Hungary. Psychologist. m. Dr Phyllis J Johnson, 19 Oct 1961, 2 s, 1 d, previous marriage. Education: BA, Queens College; MA, PhD, Princeton University. Career: Visiting Assistant Professor, University of IL, 1964-65; Assistant Professor to Professor and Department Chair, University College, Rutgers University, 1965-72; Professor of Psychology, 1972-, Head, Department of Psychology, 1972-84, Dean, Faculty of Graduate Studies, 1984-90, University of British Columbia. Publications: Restricted Environmental Stimulation: Research and Clinical Applications, 1980; Psychology and Torture, 1990; Co-author, Psychology and Social Policy, 1991; About 150 scientific articles and book chapters in anthologies. Honours: Fellow, Royal Society of Canada; Fellow, American and Canadian Psychological Associations; Academy of Behavioral Medicine Research; Fellow, Society of Behavioral Medicine; Fellow, American Psychological Society; Killam Senior Fellow, 1987; Canada Council Leave Fellow, 1978. Memberships include: Chairman, Canadian Antarctic Research Program; Associate Editor, Environment and Behavior; Book Review Editor, Political Psychology; Member 3 Editorial Boards. Hobbies: Travel; Scuba Diving; Fishing; Skiing; Military History. Address: Department of Psychology, University of British Columbia, 2136 West Mall, Vancouver, BC, Canada, V6T 1Z4.

SUEN James Yee, b. 10 Sep 1940, Dermott, AR, USA. Otolaryngology - Head and Neck Surgery. m. Karen Hannahs, 3 Nov 1983, 3 s, 1 d. Education: BA, University of Texas; BS, MD, University of Arkansas, General Surgery; Otolaryngology Residency, University of Arkansas, Head and Neck Fellowship, MD Anderson Cancer Centre. Career: Faculty Associate, MD Anderson Cancer Center, 1974; Professor and Chairman, Department of Otolaryngology - Head and Neck Surgery, University of Arkansas, 1975-. Publications: Cancer of The Head and Neck, 1981, 2nd edition, 1989; Emergencies in Otolaryngology, 1986; 22 Book chapters and 38 scientific journal articles. Honours: Distinguished Faculty Award, 1991; Arkansas Citizen of the Year Award, 1991; President, American Society of Head and Neck Surgeons, 1993-94. Memberships: American Society of Head and Neck Surgeons; American Academy of Otolaryngology - Head and Neck Surgery; Society of University Otolaryngologists; Alpha Omega Alpha. Hobbies: Sculpturing; Karate. Address: Department of Otolaryngology - Head and Neck Surgery, University of Arkansas for Medical Sciences, 4301 West Markham, S-543, Little Rock, AR 72205, USA.

SUGARMAN Alan, b. 17 July 1947, Detroit, Michigan, USA. Psychologist. m. Julie Diane Cooper, 1 July 1993, 2 sons. Education: BA with distinction and honours in Psychology, Wayne State University, 1969; Psychology Intern, Department of Psychiatry, McMaster University, 1973-74; PhD, University of Tennessee, 1974; Postdoctoral Fellow, Clinical Psychology, The Menninger Foundation, 1974-76; San Diego Psychoanalytic Society and Institute, 1981-87; Certified in Psychoanalysis, Board of Professional Standards, American Psychoanalytic Association. Appointments: Assistant Professor of Psychiatry, Yale University, 1976-81; Associate Professor, California School of Professional Psychology, 1981-84; Currently: Private Practitioner; Senior Faculty, San Diego Psychoanalytic Institute; Associate Clinical Professor of Psychiatry, University of California, San Diego. Publications: Borderline Phenomena and the Rorschach Test, 1980; The Technique and Practice of Psychoanalysis, Vol 2, 1992; On Loving, Hating, and Living Well, 1992; Victims of Abuse, 1994. Honours: Psi Chi, 1969; Phi Beta Kappa, 1970; Fellow, Society for Personality Assessment, 1987; Professional Writing Award, Menninger Foundation Alumni, 1993. Memberships: American Psychological Association;

American Psychoanalytic Association; International Psychoanalytical Association; Association for Child Analysis; Society for Personality Assessment. Hobbies: Bodybuilding; Baseball. Address: 4180 La Jolla Village Drive, Suite 550B, La Jolla, CA 92037, USA.

SUGITA Chizuko, b. 28 Aug 1936, Osaka, Japan. Professor. Education: Graduated, doctor's course, Kyoto University. Appointments: Assistant Professor (Lecturer), of Kyoto University; Associate Professor, currently Director of Psychology and full Professor, Bukkyo University; Arbitrator, Kyoto District Court. Publications: Educational and Psychological Evaluation and Measurement, 1976; Editor: Factors to Contribute to Assist and Disturb Human Development, 1982; Educating and Learning, 1989; Contemporary Psychology, 1994. Honours: Awards for Contribution to Long-Term Arbitration, Kyoto District Court. Memberships: Trustee, Centre of Disaster Prevention, The Association of Kyoto City Fire Authorities; Member of Steering Committee, The Kyoto Seminar on Psychology under the Auspices of Kyoto University; Japanese Psychological Association; International Association of Applied Psychology; Japanese Association of Social Psychology; Japanese Association of Group Dynamics; International Council of Psychologists. Address: 26-4 Shibamoto-cho, Shimogamo, Sakyo-ku, Kyoto 606, Japan.

SUKHOMLINA Angelina N, b. 27 Aug 1926, Ukraine. Physician of Radiology. Education: Medical University, Leningrad, Russia, 1958; Postgraduate, Institute of Radiology Hygiene, Leningrad, Russia, 1967. Appointments: Chief, Radiology Laboratory, Regional Sanitary-Epidemiology Institute, 1958-88; Regional Clincial Hospital Doctor of Radiology, 1988-. Publications: 36 professional articles in scientific journals; Hygiena and Sanitariya, 1963; Radiology Hygina, 1967; Medical Radiology, 1976; Hygiena and Sanitariya, 1977; The Works of Republic Conference on Medical Geography, 1977. Address: X-Ray Department, Regional Clinical Hospital, 330110 Zaporozhy, Orekhovskoye sh 10, Ukraine.

SULLIVAN Lorne Donald, b. 3 July 1936, Expanse, Saskatchewan, Canada. Urologist. m. Alma Elaine Sullivan, 9 April 1939, 2 s, 1 d. Education: ARCT; AA; MD; FRCSC. Appointments: President, British Columbian Urological, 1974; President, NW Urological, 1982; President, Canadian Urological, 1983; President, Western section, American Urological, 1992; Head, Division of Urology, University of British Columbia, 1991. Publications include: Co-Author: Management of Priapism, 1972; Primary Malignant Tumors Associated with Renal Cell Carcinoma, 1979; Re-alignment of Damaged Membranous Urethra, 1979; Penile Prosthesis for Organic Impotence, 1981; Evaluation of a Specific Radioimmunoasssay for Prostatic Acid Phosphatase, 1982; Vesico-psoas Hitch: A Versatile Procedure, 1982; Intraoperative Balloon Catheter Control of Renal Arteriovenous Fistula, 1984; Renal Matrix Calculus. Sonographic Appearance, 1990; Major Vessell Excision in Retroperitoneal Lymph Node Dissection, 1992; The management of Clinical T3, Carcinoma of the Prostate C1 C2, 1994. Honours include: Touring Fellowship, Canadian Cancer Society, 1970-71; Merit Award, UBC Department of Surgery, 1982, 1986; Merit Award, VGH Medical Staff, 1989; Best Clinical Teacher, Urology Residents, 1993; Recipient of numerous prize presentations and exhibits. Memberships: BCMA; CUA; CMA; AMA; Western section, AWA; BC Urological; Northwest Urological; BC Surgical. Hobbies: Cycling; Windsurfing. Address: John Balfour Urology Clinic, D9 Heather Pavillion, Vancouver Hospital, Vancouver, BC, V5Z 3J5, Canada.

SULLIVAN Peter John, b. 10 July 1947, Waratah, New South Wales, Australia. Obstetrician; Gynaecologist. m. Wendy, 27 Mar, 2 daughters. Education: MB,BS, Sydney University; FRCOG(London); FRACOG(Australia). Appointments: JRMO, Royal South Sydney Hospital, 1971; SRMO, St Vincents Hospital, Sydney, 1972; Womens Hospital, Crown St, Sydney, 1973; SHO Leicester General Hospital, 1974; Registrar, Southampton General Hospital, 1975; Senior Registrar, King Edward Hospital, Perth, 1977; Senior Registrar, Queen Victoria Hospital, Adelaide, 1978; Private Practice, Obstetrics and Gynaecology. Publications: Second Ectopic Pregnancy After Laparoscopic Sterilisation, 1978; Handbook of Office Gynaecology. Memberships: ASCCP; Australian Menopause Society; Australian Perinatal Society; Australian Gynaecological Endoscopy Society; Australian Association for Adolescent Health. Hobby: Travel. Address: 139 Mary Street, Toowoomba, Queensland 4350, Australia.

SULTAN Abdul Hameed, b. 29 Aug 1954, South Africa. Obstetrician & Gynaecologist. m. Razia, 18 Dec 1976, 1 son, 1 daughter. Education:

MB; ChB; MRCOG. Appointments: Registrar, North Middlesex Hospital, 1988-90; Research Fellow, St Bartholomews & St Mark's Hospitals, 1990-93; Senior Registrar, Whipp's Cross Hospital, London, 1993-94. Publications: Anal Sphincter Disruption During Vaginal Delivery, 1993; Third Degree Anal Sphincter Tears, 1994. Honours: The Victor Bonney Shield, 1993; The Gladys Dodds Prize, 1993. Memberships: British Medical Association; Royal College of Obstetricians & Gynaecologists. Hobbies: Cycling; Fishing. Address: 39 Avonwick Road, Hounslow, Middlesex TW3 4DX, England.

SULTANOV Fuat Fayzrachmanovich, b. 30 Mar 1928, Tashauz, Turkmenistan. Pathophysiologist. m. Lale Mird Salichovna, 29 May 1951, 1 son, 1 daughter. Education: MD. Appointments: Academician Secretary of the Biology Department, Head Academic Secretary, Vice President, Academy of Sciences, Turkmenistan. Publications: Hormonal Mechanisms of Temperature Adaptation; High Temperature and Hemodynamics. Honours: Honorary Diploma of the Presidium Supreme Soviet of Turkmenistan, 1972; Badge of Honour, 1978; Friendship of People, 1986. Memberships: Chairman, Turkmen Scientific Physiologic Society; International Pathophysiologic Society. Hobbies: Gardening; Floriculture. Address: Razin Passage 62-10, Ashgabat, 744025 Turkmenistan.

SUMAYA Ciro V, b. 8 Jan 1941, Texas, USA. Health Administrator. Education: BA, University of Texas, Austin, 1962; MD; MPH. Appointments: Assistant Professor, Department of Paediatrics, Division of Infectious Diseases, School of Medicine, University of California at Los Angeles, 1973-76; Assistant Professor, Paediatrics, Pathology, 1976-77, Associate Professor, Paediatrics, Pathology, 1978-83, Associate Dean of Continuing Medical Education, 1987-90, Associate Dean for Affiliated Programmes and Continuing Medical Education, 1990-94, University of Texas Health Science Center, San Antonio; Director, 1996-77, Consultant, 1978-83, Diagnostic Virology Laboratory, Bexar County Hospital; Served on President Clinton's Health Task Force, 1993; Administrator, Health Resources and Services Administration, PHS/DHHS, 1994-. Publications: 74 original articles and invited articles or editorials and 28 book chapters, including contributions regarding infectious mononucleosis infections in children, seroepidemiology, immunology and Epstein-Barr virus. Honours: Avalon Foundation Scholarship, 1962-66; Phi Beta Kappa, 1963; Alpha Omega Alpha, 1966; Scholar in Health Policy and Academic Administration, Association of Academic Health Centers, 1991-94. Memberships: American Academy of Pediatrics; Texas Medical Association; Editorial Board, Texas Medicine; Consultant, PAHO. Hobbies: Classical piano; Writing historical fiction; Family. Address: Parklawn Bldg, Rm 14-05, 5600 Fishers Lane, Rockville, MD 20857, USA.

SUMERFIELD James Ian, b. 15 Oct 1956, London, England. Osteopath; Lecturer. m. Penelope Susan Green, 18 Jul 1987, 1 s. Education: BA, Honours, Law and English, University of Sussex, 1978; Diploma of Osteopathy, European School of Osteopathy, 1987. Career: Senior Partner of own business in private practice; Part-time Lecturer at the European School of Osteopathy. Publications: Editor: Tibetan Medicine and Other Holistic Healthcare Systems, and, Osteopathic Textbook. Memberships: Member of General Council and Register of Osteopaths; The Sutherland Society. Hobbies: Travel; Walking; Music; Gardening. Address: 31 Harley Street, London, W1N 1DA, England.

SUMMERS Frank Leslie, b. 19 May 1945, Chicago, Illinois, USA. Clinical Psychologist. m. Renee Summers, 15 Aug 1981, 1 s, 2 d. Education: BA, University of California, Berkeley; MA, Columbia Teachers College; PhD, University of Chicago; Psychoanalytic Training, Chicago Institute for Psychoanalysis, 1983-91. Appointments: Assistant Professor, Northwestern University Medical School, 1976-80; Associate Professor, 1980-88; Associate Professor, Voluntary Faculty; Faculty, Chicago Institute for Psychoanalysis; Faculty, Chicago Center for Psychanalsis; Private Practice of Psychoanalysis and Psychotherapy. Publications include: Object Relations Theories and Psychotherapy: A Comprehensive Text, 1994; A Manual for the Measurement of Symbiosis in Human Relationships, 1978; The Effects of Aftercare After One Year, 1981; The Post-Acute Functioning of the Schizophrenic, 1981; Psychoanalytic Therapy of the Borderline Patient: Treating the Separation-Fusion Contradiction, 1988; Implications of Object Relations Theories for the Psychoanalytic Process, 1993. Honours: PhD Honours Graduate. Memberships: American Psychoanalytic Society; Pratitioners Section Division of Psychoanalysis; American Psychological Association; Chicago Association for Psychoanalytic Psychology.

Hobbies: Running; Soccer coach. Address: 333 E Ontario, Suite 4509B, Chicago, IL 60611, USA.

SUN Cheng-Lu, b. 10 October 1936, Tang Shan, Hebei, China. Doctor. m. Zhouke Jing, 20 June 1957, 2 sons, 1 daughter. Education: Tang Shan Medical College. Appointments: Attending Physician, 1972-80, Vice-Doctor Director, Professor, 1980-87; Currently Doctor Director, Professor, Tang Shan Medical College; Treatment of retinosis by transplanting musculi oculi onto choroid. Publications: Surgery of lacrimal drainage, 1982; Co-author: Advances in ophthalmology, 1980; Treasuring the eye, 1994; 95 learned articles including: A statistical study on configuration of the eye among healthy male youths, 1979; Circling operation with fascia lata strips and into air for retinal detachment, 1984; A clinical analysis of hereditary types and complications of primary retinitis pigmentosa (co-author), 1993. Honours: Encouragement of Science and Technology, Tianjin, 1980, 1990; Scientific Achievement, Chinese Committee of Science and Technology; Special Allowance for Expert, State Council of China. Hobbies: Running; Playing basketball. Address: Baodi Hospital, Tianjin, China.

SUN Fan, b. 13 Nov 1957, Changchun, Jilin, China. Management in Science & Technology. m. 4 Aug 1985, 1 daughter. Education: Bachelor, Northeast Normal University, Changchun, China. Career: Assistant, 1982; Lecturer, 1986; Manager, 1992. Publications: China Animals in Medicine Geographical Distribution, 1987; Jilin Provincal Preliminary Research for the Organization of Soil and Animal and the Biological Distribution, 1991; Changchung Land Resources, 1990; Jilin Province Natural Geography, 1992. Honours: Second Award for Progress in Science & Technology, China National Education Committee, 1992; First Award for Excellent Paper in Science & Technology, Jilin Province, 1988. Memberships: China Institute on Animal and Geography; China Geography Institute; China Biology Institute. Address: Guangdong, 519000, China.

SUN Jiurong, b. 3 Aug 1944, China. Physiologist. 1 son. Appointments: Assistant, 1970, Lecturer, Department of Biology, 1978, Professor, College of Life Sciences, 1991-, Peking University. Publications: Neuroplasticity of Vestibular Neurons in Cat, 1995; Effect of B-B12 on Activity of Hypothalamic Neurons in Rat, 1993; Effect of Low Temperature on Contraction of Cutaneous Muscle of Hedgehog, 1989. Memberships: Chinese Physiological Society; Japanese Society of Sleep Research. Hobbies: Table Tennis; Swimming. Address: Department of Physiology and Biophysics, College of Life Sciences, Peking University, Beijing 100871, China.

SUN Ming, b. 15 Jan 1931, Changsha, Hunan, China. Cardiologist. Education: BA, Hunan Medical College, 1950-55. Appointments: Resident, Internal Medicine Department, 1955-57, Chief Resident, 1957-58, Attending Physician of Medicine, Lecturer, 1958-80, Associate Professor of Medicine, 1980-85, Professor of Medicine, 1985-, First Affiliated Hospital. Publications: Modern Treatment, Co-author, 1984; Modern Diagnostic and Therapeutic Technique, Co-author, 1987; Multiple Choice Questions of Clinical Medicine, 1983; Multiple Choice Questions and Answers of Clinical Medicine, 1986; Textbook of Bare-Foot Doctors, Co-editor, 1982; Hypertension, 1989; Coronary Heart Disease, 1989; Practical Hypertensionology, Co-author, 1993; Contributor of 110 medical scientific papers. Honours include: 1st Prize, Provincial Using Doppler Echocardiogram to Measure Left and Right Ventricular Heart Function, 1988; 4th prize, Cold Pressor Test on Apical Cardiogram in Diagnosis of Coronary Heart Disease, 1986; 3rd prize, National, Multiple Choice Question on Internal Medicine, 1988. Memberships include: Chairman, Chinese Cardiovascular Disease Association, Hunan Branch, 1987-; Executive Committee, Chinese Medical Association, Hunan Branch, 1987-; Committee, National Chinese Cardiovascular Disease Association, 1987-; Committee, National Chinese Nephrology Association, 1983-; Chairman, Judge Group of malpractice in Internal Medicine, Hunan Province, 1988-. Address: Department of Internal Medicine, First Affiliated Hospital, Hunan Medical University, Changsha, Hunan, China.

SUN Nianhu, b. 5 Dec 1929, Jiangsu, China. Medical Doctor. m. Xu De-Gui, 1 Oct 1952, 2 sons, 1 daughter. Education: MD, Peking Union Medical College, 1954; Fellow, Medical Genetics, University of California, San Francisco, 1981-82. Appointments include: Associate Professor, Obstetrics and Gynaecology, 1983-, Full Professor, Obstetrics and Gynaecology, 1985-, Peking Union Medical College Hospital; Vice-Director, National Center of Medical Genetics, Beijing,

1986-; Visiting Professor: Department of Medical Genetics, Mount Sinai Medical School, USA, 1982-83, 1989-90, 1993-94; Visiting Professor, Medical Genetics, Erasmus University, Netherlands, 1987. Publications: High Risk Pregnancy, 1982; Prenatal Diagnosis of Inherited Diseases, 1983; Chapter on Prenatal Diagnosis, in Textbook of Medical Genetics. Honours: Award for Science and Technology, 1st Grade, Ministry of Health, China, 1981; National Award for Science and Technology, 2nd Grade, 1985; Award for Science, 2nd Grade, Ministry of Family Planning, 1986; Award for Science, 2nd Grade, Ministry of Health, 1990, 1994. Memberships: Standing Board Member, Association of Medical Genetics of China; Evaluation Group for Awards, Ministry of Health, China, 1985-94. Address: Department of Obstetrics and Gynaecology, Peking Union Medical College Hospital, Beijing 100730, China.

SUN Rui-Long, b. 22 Feb 1928, Shanghai, China. Doctor. m. Dai Xi-Zhen, 7 May 1955, 2 sons. Education: MD. Career: Resident 1954-58; Attending Physician, 1958-78; Associate Professor, 1979-84; Professor, 1985-94. Publications: A Concise Electrocardiography, 1975; Cardiac Catheterization, Technique and Diagnosis, 1979; Atlas of Clinical Vectorcardiogram, 1988; Electrophysiologic Study on PSVT. Memberships: Chinese Medical Association; Chinese Bio-Medical Eng Association; NASPE; ISPE. Address: Fu Wai Hospital, Beijing 100037, China.

SUN Shiquan, b. 28 Jan 1927, Liaoning, China. Pathology; Radiation Protection. m. You Zhanyun, 20 Jan 1954, 1 s, 1 d. Education: Graduate from China Medical University, Shenyang, China, 1949. Appointments: Director of Department of Radiation Medicine, China Institute for Radiation Protection; Currently, Professor, China Institute for Radiation Protection. Publications: Radon and Arsenic in the Etiology of Yunnan Tin Miner Lung Cancer, 1991; Radiation Epidemiology of Nuclear Industry in China, 1994. Honour: Prize Cup from National Committee on Science and Technology, for the study of miner lung cancer. Memberships: Deputy Director of Chinese Society of Radiation Medicine and Protection; Vice President of Asia-Pacific Association of Surgical Tissue Banking; Vice Chairman of Shanxi Provincial Medical Association. Address: Xuefu Street 270, Taiyuan PO 120, China Institute for Radiation Protection, Shanxi Province, China.

SUN Wei Zheng, b. 2 July 1942, Harbin, China. Physician. m. Shen Hua fang, 18 Jan 1968, 1 son, 1 daughter. Education: BA, Heilongjiang College of Traditional Chinese Medicine, 1966. Appointments: Assistant, 1966-80, Lecturer, 1980-85, Deputy Professor, 1985-91, Professor, 1991-93, Tutor of Doctors, 1993-95, heilongjiang College of Traditional Chinese Medicine. Publications include: Collections of Multi-Choosing Question of TCM, 1986; Internal Medicine of TCM, 1987; Diagnosis and Treatment of TCM on Diseases of Spleen System, 1987; Internal Medicine of Acupuncture and Moxibustion, 1987; Internal Medicine of TCM, 1988; Diagnosis and Treatment of TCM on Diseases of Lung System, 1989; A Guide to Clinical Practice of TCM, 1991; Internal Medicine of TCM, 1991; Collection of Theses Written by Famous Scholars from Various TCM Colleges All Over the Country, 1993. Honours: Excellent Prize for Results of Scientific Research, heilongjiang Provincial Government, 1979; Excellent Prize for Results of Scientific Research, Office of Culture and Education, heilongjiang Province, 1980; Excellent Prize for Results of Scientific Research, Health Bureau, heilongjiang Province, 1980; 2nd Prize for Results of Scientific Research, Health Ministry of China, 1981; 2nd {rize for Scientific Research of TCM, Heilongjiang Provincial Government, 1991; Special Allowance of State Council of China, 1991; Elected Famous Doctor of TCM in Heilongjiang Province, 1994. Memberships include: International Traditional Chinese Medicine Committee of USA; Vice Director, Promoting Committee, TCM Research of Heilongjiang Province. Hobbies: Running; Philately. Address: 14 Heping Road, Harbin, China.

SUN Weirong, b. 28 Oct 1936, Jimo City, Qingdao, China. Medical Doctor. m. Shumei Wang, 26 Dec 1965, 1 son, 2 daughters. Education: Bachelor's degree, Qingdao Medical Collge, 1963. Appointments: Assistant Lecturer, Lecturer, Vice-Professor; Currently Professor, Director, Laboratory of Ocular Pathology, Department of Ophthalmology, Qingdao Medical College. Publications: Books: Ocular Pathology, 1984; Practicala Ocular Hereditism, 1992; Immunology of the Cornea, 1993; Articles including: Histopathological Observation of Phacalytic Glaucoma, 1986. Honours: Prize for Science and Technology, 2nd Class, Shandong Province, 1981, 1987, 1989; Scientific and Technical Prize, Education Department, Shandong Province, 1984, 1987. Memberships include: Ocular Pathology, Branch, China Medical Association; Editorial Board, China Journal of Ophthalmology; China

Recovery Association, Shandong Branch; China Biogeography Project Association. Hobbies: Plants; Swimming. Address: No 14 First Guanxiang Road, Qingdao, Shandong, China.

SUN Wenzhuo, b. 17 May 1944, Zhuanghe County, Liauning Province, China. Teacher; Professor of Anatomy. m. Shuxia Zhang, 1 Oct 1970, 1 s, 1 d. Education: BM, Jiamusi Medical College, 1969. Appointments: Lecturer of Anatomy, Mudanjiang Medical College, 1983; Head of Teaching and Research Section of Anatomy, 1989; Dean of Preclinical Medicine Department. Publications: The Measurement of Chinese Lumbar Vertebrae, 1989; The Observation of Gall Bladder Septum, 1990; Co-author, Anatomy of Human Body, 1992; Anatomical Observation and Clinical Significance of the Thickness of Sternum, 1994. Honours: Scientific and Technological Prize, Mudangjing City, 1989; Excellent Teacher Achievement Prize, Heilongjiang Province, 1991. Memberships: Vice Chairman Board, Society of Anatomical Sciences of Heilongjiang Province; Director, Chinese Society of Anatomical Sciences. Hobbies: Reading; Playing Basketball; Running. Address: Teaching and Research Section of Anatomy, Mudanjiang Medical College, 157011 Heilongjiang Province, China.

SUN Yan-Ching (Yan-Qing), b. 22 July 1923, Yantain, Shandong, China. Cardiovascular Surgeon. m. 1 Oct 1950, 2 sons, 1 daughter. Education: MD, Beijing University, 1949. Appointments include: Director, Beijing Heart, Lung and Blood Vessel Research Centre, Anzhen Hospital, Beijing; Professor, Advisor, Beijing Municipal Government; Currently: Professor of Surgery, Capital University of Medical Science; Editor-in-Chief, Chinese Journal of Thoracic Cardiovascular Surgery; Consultant Professor, Beijing Medical University. Publications: Editor-in-Chief, 12 books including: Thoracic Cardiovascular Surgery; 112 articles including: Surgical Treatment of Aortic Dissection (first author). Honours: 2 China Science and Technology Awards; 2 Beijing Science and Technology Awards; Health Ministry Award. Memberships: President, Chinese Society for Thoracic-Cardiovascular Surgery; President, Chinese Society of Beijing Bio-Medical Engineering. Hobby: Classical music. Address: Beijing Heart, Lung and Blood Vessel Research Centre, Anzhen Hospital, Capital University of Medical Science, Andingmenwai, Beijing 100029, China.

SUN Yonghua, b. 6 Dec 1935, Hebei, China. Medical Doctor. m. Ni Guichen, 27 Feb 1967, 1 son, 1 daughter. Education: MD. Appointments: Doctor, 1960, Visiting Doctor, 1972, Chief Doctor, 1986-, Beijing Jishuitan Hospital; Department Chief Physician, Associate Professor, Beijing Medical College, 1982; Professor, Beijing Medical University, 1990-. Publications include: Extraordinary Severe Burn Cases Treated with Integrated Chinese Traditional and Western Medicine, 1977; Early Vascular Grafting to Prevent Upper Extremity Necrosis after Electrical Burns, 1981; Early Excision and Immediate Repair with Skin Flap in Treatment of Electric Burn of the Wrist, 1982; Greater Omentum - Cutaneous Axial Flap, 1982; The Treatment and Research in Burns, 1983; Tangential Excision of Eschar for Deep Burns of the Hand, 1984; The Tangential Excision of Extensive or Deep Burns, 1984; Early Treatment of Burned Scalp and Skull, 1984; Successful Reconstruction of Both Buttocks with Musculocutaneous Flap in Extensive Deep Burns, 1985; Candida Infection in Severe Burns, 1985; Use of Autogenous Omentum for Grafting Electrical Injury Affecting the Scalp and Skull, 1985; Autogenous Omentum for Grafting Scalp and Skull, 1986; Advance in Burns, 1992. Honours: Alexander von Humboldt Scholar, Germany, 1984; National Scientific and Technical Specialist, 1990. Memberships: International Society for Burn Injury; Council Member, Chinese Medical Association; Deputy Chief of Chinese Society of Burn Injury, 1994. Address: Beijing Jishuitan Hospital, 31 Xin-Jie-Kou DongJie, Beijing 100035, China.

SUN Yuhua, b. 29 Oct 1955, Beijing, China. Registered Nurse; Associate Professor. m. Yinhe Qin, 16 July 1979, 1 son. Education: Nursing School, 1975-78, BS, Superior Nursing Department, 1984, The Third Military Medical College, Chongqing. Appointments: Registered Nurse, Head Nurse, 1978-92, Associate Professor, 1993-, Department of Orthopaedics, Xinqiao Hospital, Chongqing. Publications: Postoperative nursing for prosthetic replacement of elbow, 1988; Postoperative nursing for congenital dislocation of the hip in juvenile, 1989; Postoperative nursing for excision and reconstruction of the humeral malignant tumour, 1991. Memberships: Council Member, Rehabilitation Nursing Research Association of China; Deputy Secretary-General, Poliomyelitis Nursing Research Association of China. Hobbies: Music; Swimming. Address: Department of Orthopaedics, Xinqiao Hospital, Chingqing 630037, China.

SUN Yuqing, b. 10 Oct 1930, Yantai, Shandong, China. Professor. m. Zhuyan Wang, 1 son, 1 daughter. Education: Qilu University, Shandong; BS, China University of Pharmacy, Nanking, 1954. Appointments: Faculty, 1954, Teacher Researcher, Professor, PhD Supervisor, Department of Analytical Chemistry, Shenyang Pharmaceutical University; Visiting Scholar, School of Pharmacy, University of California, USA, 1986. Publications: Author of numerous books. Honours: Named National Expert, Committee of Science of State Council of China. Memberships include: Committee, Chinese Pharmacopoeia; Committee, Pharmaceutical Society of China; Permanent Director, Chromatographic Society of China. Address: Shenyang Pharmaceutical University, 103 Wenhua Road, Shenyang 110015, China.

SUN Zhongxing, b. 5 April 1937, Shenyang, China. Professor of Clinical Epidemiology. m. 30 August 1965, 2 sons. Education: Harbin Medical University, 1957-62. Appointments: Toxicologist; Physician in Charge; Lecturer of Environmental Medicine; Vice Professor of Oological Epidemiology; Professor of Clinical Epidemiology. Publications: Co-author: Evaluation of Environmental Quality in Shenyang City, 1980; Co-author: Modern Medicine, 1985; Co-author: Stomach Cancer, 1987; Chief Editor: Clinical Epidemiology, 1989, Clinical Epidemiology, 1995; Articles: Correlation of morbidity rate of pulmonary tuberculosis with natural infection rate of tuberculosis, 1983; The effect of air pollution on T-lyocyte of peripheral blood in children, 1984; Multifactory analysis influenced long-term survival in postoperation of gastric cancer, 1987; Relationship of chronic superficial, atrophic gastritis and gastric cancer, 1990; Geophysical, cultural and behavioral differences between high and low risk areas of gastric cancer in Liaonin Province, 1992. Memberships: Standing Committee, Chinese Society of Clinical Epidemiology and Chinese Society of General Practice. Hobbies: Basketball; Ping-pong Ball. Address: China Medical University, First Clinical College, Shenyang 110001, China.

SUNEJA Sudarshan K, b. 22 May 1942, Amritsar, India. Psychiatry. m. Veena Suneja, 28 Nov 1971, 2 d. Education: MD; PhD. Appointments: Consulting Psychiatrist; Chairman of several committees. Honour: Exemplary Psychiatrist Award, 1994. Membership: St Louis Metropolitan Medical Society. Hobbies: Travel; Gardening; Reading. Address: 12847 Hickory Woods Drive, St Louis, MO 63131, USA.

SUNG Lanping Amy, b. 25 Feb 1949, Dow-Len, Taiwan, China. Associate Professor of Bioengineering. m. Kuo-Li Paul Sung, 17 Aug 1974, 1 son, 1 daughter. Education: BS, National Taiwan University, 1971; MA, College of William and Mary, USA, 1974; MPH, 1980, PhD, 1982, Columbia University. Appointments: Staff Scientist, 1983, Associate Research Scientist, 1983-88, Columbia University; Associate Research Bioengineer and Lecturer, 1988-94, Associate Professor, 1994-, University of California San Diego. Publications: Contributor of articles in professional journals. Honours: National Taiwan University Award, 1968. Memberships: American Society of Hematology; American Society for Cell Biology. Hobbies: Reading; Biking. Address: Department Bioengineering, University of California San Diego, La Jolla, CA 92093, USA.

SUNG Shih, b. 1 March 1930, Beijing, China. Medical Doctor. m. Hsi-yi Yang, 24 October 1957. Education: BS MD, St John's University School of Medicine, Shanghai Second Medical College, 1954. Appointments: Professor, Senior Consultant of Obstetrics/Gynecology and Fertility Regulation, Tianjin First Central Hospital, Tianjin Medical University, Publications: Two-year Comparative Clinical Experience with 3 IUDs', 1984; Investigation of Genetic Influence of the Contraceptive Film on the Hunan Fetus and A Study on the Long Term Use of the Vaginal Contraceptive Film, 1985; Pathologic Changes of Endosalpinx in Relation to Tubal Pregnancy in IUD Users, 1986; Conception, Birth and Baby Care, 1995. Honours: Certificates of, for: Outstanding Contribution in Medical Health Service, State Council, 1992; Outstanding Achievement on National Research of Fertility Regulation, Ministry of Health, 1989; Outstanding Achievement on National Scientific Research, National Commission on Fertility Regulation, 1986; Advanced Worker of Family Planning & Medal of Honour, Tianjin Municipal Government, 1985; Outstanding Achievement on Technical Work of Fertility Regulations, Tianjin Health Bureau jointly with Tianjin Commission of Fertility Regulation, 1993; Outstanding Achievement of Research, Tianjin Commission of Fertility Regulation, 1991; Advanced Worker, Tianjin Health Bureau, 1983, 1984; Outstanding Teaching for the Year, Tianjin Second Medical College, 1993. Memberships: Editor, Foreign Medical Literature of Obstetrics & Gynaecology; Chinese Medical

Association; Chinese Association of Eugenics; Tianjin Board of Assessment for Scientific Achievement on Medical Research of Obstetrics & Gynaecology. Hobbies: Horticulture; Aerobics. Address: Tianjin First Central Hospital, 24 Fu Kang Road, Tianjin 300192, China.

SUO Jing Xian, b. 3 May 1922, Changchun, Jilin Province, China. Neurosurgery. m. Di Xiu Wen, 10 Jun 1943, 1 s, 2 d. Education: Ha Er Bin Medical Officer College, 1943. Appointments: Lecturer of Abdominal and Thoracic Surgery, Changchun Medical College of Chinese People's Liberation Army; Currently, Professor of Neurosurgery, Norman Bethune University of Medical Sciences. Publications: Practical Neurosurgery, 1976; Clinical Manifestation and Pathology of Moyamoya Disease in Northeast China, 1988; Giant Arterior Communicating Aneurysm, Chinese Society of Neurosurgery, 1985; Over 40 articles in national journal. Memberships: Chinese Neurosurgery Association; Chinese Society of Nervous and Mental Diseases; Chinese Society of Neurology and Psychiatry; Chinese Society of Apoplexy and Nervous Diseases; Jilin Society of Surgery. Address: 21 second Mingde Road, Chao Yang District, Changchun, Jilin Province, China.

SUPERKO H Robert, b. 1 Jan 1949, Bethesda, Maryland, USA. Research Physician. Education: BA, Biology, University of California, San Diego, 1971; MD, State University of New York, Stony Brook, 1975; Fellow, American College of Sports Medicine; Fellow, American College of Cardiology. Appointments include: Medical Director, Lipid Research Clinic, Lipoprotein Laboratory, 1983-91, Clinical Assistant Professor, 1985-91, Stanford University School of Medicine; Director, Center for Progressive Atherosclerosis Management, Alta Bates Medical Center, Berkeley, 1990-92; Co-Medical Director, American Heart Association, Lipid Disorders Training Center, Lawrence Berkeley Laboratory, 1990-, Medical Director, Research Scientist, Cholesterol Research Center, Lawrence Berkeley Laboratory, Donner Laboratory, 1991-, University of California, Berkeley; Director, Lipid Institute, Sequoia Hospital, Redwood City, 1992-. Publications include: The scientific basis for designing an exercise prescription for optimal health (with W L Haskell), 1984; Decreasing blood cholesterol levels with a dietary additive: an additional approach to diet and drugs, 1985; Drug therapy and the prevention of atherosclerosis in humans, 1988; Beneficial angiographic and clinical response to multifactor modification in the Stanford Coronary Risk Intervention Project (SCRIP) (co-author), 1994; Book chapters. Honours include: Fellow, American Heart Association Council on Arteriosclerosis, 1988. Memberships include: New York Academy of Sciences; American Heart Association, Chapter President 1985-87; American Society of Clinical Nutrition; Fellow, American Association of Cardiovascular and Pulmonary Rehabilitation, Public Education Committee 1987-, Board of Directors 1987-. Address: Lipid Institute, Sequoia Hospital, 170 Alameda de las Pulgas, Redwood City, CA 94062-2799, USA.

SUREAU Claude, b. 27 Sept 1927, Paris, France. MD. m. Janine Murset, 6 Oct 1956, 1 s, 2 d. Education: PhD, University of Paris, 1953; MD, University of Paris, 1955; French Academy of Medicine, 1978. Appointments: Professor/Chairman, Obstetrics & Gynaecology Department, St Vincent de Paul Hospital, 1974-76; Professor/Chairman, University Clinic, Baudelocque, Paris, 1976-89; Head, Obstetrics & Gynaecology Unit, American Hospital, Paris, 1990-93; Director, U.262, National Institute of Health & Medical Research, 1983-90; Medical Director, American Hospital, Paris, 1994-95. Publications: Le Danger De Naitre, 1978; Clinical Perinatology, 1980; Uterine Contraction, 1987; Immunologie De La Reproduction, 1990; Aux Debuts De La Vie, 1990; Ethical Aspects of Human Reproduction, 1995. Honours: Officier Legion D'Honneur, 1989. Memberships: President, International Federation of Obstetrics & Gynaecology, 1982-85; President, Federation of French Speaking Gynaecological Obstetricians, 1986-88; President, European Association Gyn, 1988-91. Address: 9 Boulevard De Chateau, 92200 Neuilly, France.

SURENDRAN Indira, b. 12 Oct 1936, Malawi. Obstetrician and Gynaecologist. m. G Surendran, 26 Jan 1961, 1 son, 1 daughter. Education: MD; DGO; FICOG. Appointments: General Practitioner, Nagercoil, India; Senior House Officer in Obstetrics, then Department Head, hospital, Leicester, England; Currently Head, Department of Obstetrics and Gynaecology and IVF Centre, Dr Gopala Pillai's Hospital, Nagercoil. Publications: A few original articles presented at various professional conferences. Honours: Outstanding Citizen Award, 1993; Chief Minister's Medal for Best Area Home Guard Commander, 1993; Many district level awards. Memberships: Past President, Obstetrics and Gynaecology Society; Past President, Indian Medical Association; Vice-President, Indian Society of Ultrasound. Hobbies: Gardening;

Farming; Tree planting; Classical music. Address: Dr Gopala Pillai's Hospital, Nagercoil 629001, Tamil Nadu, India.

SURIA Amin Mohammad, b. 24 Aug 1942, Dhoraji, India. Professor and Chairman of Pharmacology. m. Khairunnisa Suria, 19 Jan 1974, 1 s, 3 d. Education: BSc, Honours, Chemistry, Karachi University, Pakistan, 1963; MSc in Organic Chemistry; Classical Physiology with Modern Instrumentation, Baylor University School of Medicine, Houston, TX, 1968; PhD, Pharmacology, Vanderbilt University, USA, 1970. Career includes: Assistant Professor, 1975-77, Associate Professor of Pharmacology, 1977-80, George Washington University Medical School, Washington DC; Associate Professor of Pharmacology, King Saud University, Riyadh, Saudi Arabia, 1980; Currently, Professor and Chairman, Department of Pharmacology, The Aga Khan University, Karachi; Invited speaker at many international seminars and symposia. Publications include: Numerous articles in many professional journals from 1971, including: Co-author, The effect of aspirin on 5-HT amplification of platelet aggregation produced by arachidonic acid and PAF, American Society of Pharmacology and Experimental Therapeutices, 1993. Honours include: Honorary Professor of Pharmacology, HEJ Postgraduate Institute of Advanced Chemistry, University of Karachi; Fellow, Pakistan Academy of Medical Sciences; Professor of Clinical Pharmacology, College of Physicians and Surgeons, Karachi, 1994-. Memberships include: New York Academy of Sciences; President, Medical Research Society of Pakistan; Councillor, Pakistan Pharmacological Society; President, Dhoraji Youth Services; Trustee, Dhoraji Foundation. Hobbies: Music; Sufism; Reading; Philosophy. Address: Aga Khan University, Medical College, Department of Pharmacology, Stadium Road, PO Box 3500, Karachi 74800, Pakistan.

SUSKIND Robert Morris, b. 29 Jul 1937, Elmira, NY, USA. Physician. m. Leslie Lewinter, 6 Feb 1963, 2 s, 2 d. Education: BA, University of Pennsylvania, 1959; MD, University of Pennsylvania School of Medicine, 1963; Postdoctoral Degree in Tropical Medicine, University of Dakar, Senegal, 1966. Career includes: Visiting Professor of Pediatrics to Thailand, China, Israel, Samoa and Scotland; Editorial Board, Journal of American College of Nutrition, 1982-; Honorary Board of Advisors, Georgia Institute of Human Nutrition, Augusta, 1982-; Professor and Chairman, Department of Pediatrics, Louisiana State University Medical Center, New Orleans, LA, 1984-. Publications include: Over 110 articles; Editor or Co-editor of 6 textbooks; 138 Invited presentations; 136 Abstracts and papers presented at scientific meetings. Honours include: Travelling Fellowship for the Study of Medical Facilities in the Tropics, 1966-67. Memberships include: American Academy of Pediatrics, 1970-; American Institute of Nutrition, 1975-; American Society for Clinical Nutrition, 1977-; Society for Pediatric Research, 1979; American Pediatric Society, 1992-. Address: LSU School of Medicine, Department of Pediatrics, 1542 Tulane Avenue, New Orleans, LA 70112, USA.

SUSSKIND Herbert, b. 23 Mar 1929. Biomedical Engineer. m. E Suzanne Lieberman, 18 June 1961, 2 sons, 1 daughter. Education: BChE cum laude, CUNY, 1950; MChE, New York University, 1961. Appointments: Chemical Engineer, Section Supervisor, Brookhaven National Lab, Upton, 1950-77; Biomedical Engineer, Brookhaven National Lab, 1977-94; Associate Professor of Medicine, SUNY, Stony Brook, 1979-; Assistant to Chairman, Medical Department, Brookhaven National Lab, 1989-94; Research Collaborator, Brookhaven National Lab, 1994-. Publications: 8 chapters in books, 66 articles in journals, 91 abstracts, 3 patents. Memberships: Biomedical Engineering Society; Society of Nuclear Medicine; American Institute of Chemical Engineers; American Nuclear Society; American Thoracic Society. Hobbies: Geneology; Stamp Collecting. Address: Brookhaven national Lab, PO Box 5000, Upton, NY 11973-5000, USA.

SUTER Paolo Mirco, b. 12 July 1956, Zurich, Switzerland. Physician. Education: MD, University of Zurich, 1982; MS, Tufts University School of Nutrition, Boston, USA, 1986. Appointments: Assistant, Medical Policlinic, University Hospital, Zurich. Publications: Vitamin Requirements in the Elderly, 1987; Reversal of Protein-bound Vitamin B12 Malabsorption with Antibiotics in Atrophic Gastritis, 1991; The Effect of Ethanol on Fat Storage in Healthy Subjects, 1992; The Effect of Ethanol on Energy Expenditure, 1994. Honours: Prix Gabriel Baud, 1992. Memberships: ASCN; American Institute of Nutrition; New York Academy of Sciences; Swiss Hypertension Society; Swiss Society for Nutrition Research. Address: University Hospital, Medical Policlinic, Raemistrasse 100, CH-8091 Zurich, Switzerland.

SUTHERLAND Arthur Maclennan, b. 30 Sep 1909, Glasgow, Scotland. Gynaecologist. m. Barbara Stewart Ness, 18 Mar 1988. Education: MBChB (Glasgow), 1932; MRCOG, 1936; Robert Jardine Research Scholar, 1936; FRFPSG, 1937; MRC Research Scholar, 1938; MD (Glasgow), 1944; FRCOG, 1954; FRCPG, 1987. Career: House Officer, Western Infirmary, Glasgow, 1932, 1934, Victoria Infirmary, Glasgow, 1933, Royal Infirmary, Glasgow, 1934, Samaritan Hospital, Glasgow, 1935, Maternity Hospital, Glasgow, 1935, Staff, 1938-49, Staff Samaritan Hospital, Glasgow, 1935-49 (4 years part-time pathologist), Glasgow Corporation Hospitals, 1939-44, Lanarkshire Hospitals, 1946-48, Southern General Hospital, Glasgow, 1949-77 (consultant in charge); Lecturer, Glasgow University; Examiner to CMB, Glasgow University, 1936; Gynaecologist, Endocrine Clinic, Royal Samaritan Hospital for Women, 1956-58; Researcher on Gynaecological Tuberculosis, Scottish Home and Health Department, 1974-77; Numerous lectures and memorial lectures in UK and abroad; Member of various professional committees. Publications: Over 70 original articles as author or co-author in many countries, mainly on aspects of tuberculosis of female genital tract. Honours: Hall Fellow, Glasgow University, 1938; Corresponding Member, Portuguese Society of Obstetrics and Gynaecology, 1957. Memberships include: BMA; Royal Society of Medicine, Board of Management; Glasgow Medical Journal Board of Management, Southern General Hospital. Hobbies: Swimming; Black Belt First Dan, Aikido; Travel; Gastronomy; Reading. Address: 48 St Germains, Bearsden, Glasgow, G61 2RS, Scotland.

SUTMOLLER Frits, b. 8 Nov 1952, Winterswijk, Netherlands. Physician. m. Cloris M A C Sutmoller, 6 Jan 1977, 1 son, 1 daughter. Education: MD, Rijksuniversiteit Leiden, Netherlands, 1979. Career: Coordinator STD/AIDS Prevention Program, Private Practice as Family Physician. Membership: American Academy of Family Physicians. Hobby: Swimming. Address: R Visconde de Piraja, 414/802, Ipanema, 22471-002 Rio de Janeiro, RJ, Brazil.

SUTTON Paul, b. 23 Aug 1945, Brooklyn, New York, USA. Paediatric Allergist. m. Marian Miraglilo, 27 Oct 1973, 1 s. Education: BS; MS; MD; Fellow, American Academy of Paediatrics; Fellow, American Academy Allergy Immunology; Fellow, American College Allergy Immunology. Appointments: Associate, Department of Paediatrics, Geisinger Medical Centre, Danville. Memberships: American Academy of Paediatrics; Pennslvania Allergy Association; American Academy Allergy Immunology; American College Allergy Immunology. Address: Geisinger Medical Centre, No Academy Avenue, Danville, PA 17822, USA.

SUZUKI Makoto, b. 9 Dec 1933, Yokohama, Japan. Professor. m. 1964, 2 daughters. Education: Graduate, School of Medicine, Keio University, 1958; MD, 1965. Appointments: Associate Professor of Medicine, Department of Community Medical Service, University of Ryukyus, 1976; Professor of Medicine, Department of Community Medical Service, University of Ryukyus, 1983; Director, Research Center of Comprehensive Medicine, University of Ryukyus, 1987. Publications: Centenarian's Science, 1983; Clinical Investigation for Cardiovascular System. Memberships: Japanese Gerontological Association; Japanese Hospital Administration Society. Honours: Mitsukoshi Medical Award, 1981. Address: Research Center of Comprehensive Medicine, University of the Ryukyus, 207 Uehara Nishihara-cho, Nakagami-gun, Okinawa 903-01, Japan.

SVENSON Ernest Olander, b. 16 Oct 1923, Duluth, MN, USA. Psychoanalyst; Psychiatrist. m. Shirley Svenson, 2 s. Education: MD; Psychoanalytic Training. Appointments: Chairman, Department Psychiatry, Tovro Infirmary; President, New Orleans Area Psychiatric Association; President, New Orleans Psychoanalytic Society; President, New Orleans Psychoanalytic Institute; Clinical Professor Psychiatry, LSU and Tulane Medical Schools; Currently, Private Practice, Staff, VA Hospital, Post Traumatic Stress Center and Clinical Professor Psychiatry, Tulane and LSU. Honours: Distinguished Alumni Award, Augustan College, 1990; Alpha Omega Alpha. Memberships: Fellow, American Psychiatric Association; Diplomat, American Board of Psychiatry; Life Member, American Psychoanalytic Association; International Psychoanalytic Association. Hobbies: Tennis; Art; Camping. Address: 1301 Antonine Street, New Orleans, LA 70115, USA.

SVINDLAND Aud Dorthea, b. 21 July 1947, Oslo, Norway. Leading Pathologist. 1 son, 1 daughter. Education: MD, University of Oslo, 1975; PhD, Localization of Atherosclerotic Lesions in Human Arterial Bifulcations, 1984. Appointments: Research Fellow, Norwegian Research Council for Science & Humanities, 1981-84; Resident

Pathologist, 1984-90; Leading Pathologist, Oslo University Hospital, 1990-. Publications: Papers of, Localization of Atherosclerotic Lesions in Human Arteries, 1981-85; Atherosclerotic Carotid Diseases and Pathogenesis of Carotid Thrombosis, 1989; Model for Skeletal Muscle Ischemia in Rat Hindlimb, 1991; Effect of Different Factors on Muscle Ischemia, 1991-94. Hobbies: Sking; Sailing. Address: President Harbitz Gate 23A, 0259 Oslo, Norway.

SWARTZ Donald Percy, b. 12 Sep 1921, Kitchener, Canada. Physician. m. (1) Norma Mae Woolner, deceased, (2) Isabelle L Dale, 21 Apr 1984, 1 s, 1 d. Education: BA; MD, cum laude; MSc, cum laude; FRCS(C); Diplomate, ABOG. Career: Professor and Director, Obstetrics and Gynaecology, Harlem Hospital, New York City; Professor, Obstetrics and Gynaecology, Columbia University, New York City; Professor and Chairman, Currently Professor and Head, Division of General Gynecology, Department of Obstetrics and Gynaecology, Albany Medical College, Albany, New York. Publications: Abnormal Uterine Bleeding, in Telinde's Operative Gynaecology, 7th edition, 1991; Editor, Hormonal Replacement Therapy, 1992. Honours: Alpha Omega Alpha, 1949; Hippocratic Honor Medical Society, 1951; John and Mary Markle Scholar in Medical Science, 1958-63; Fellow, ACOG; Fellow, American Board of Obstetrics and Gynaecology; Fellow, AGS; Senior Resident Award for Excellence in Teaching of Operative Gynaecology, 1983, 1987; Life Member, Society of Gynaecological Surgeons, 1990. Memberships: ACOG; ABOG; ISFAHSIG; NA Menopause Society; International Menopause Society; Society of Gynaecological Surgeons; American Association of Laparoscopists; NE Obstetric and Gynaecological Society. Hobbies: Skiing; Golf; Theatre. Address: Department of Obstetrics and Gynaecology A-74, Albany Medical Center, Albany, NY 12208, USA.

SWASH Michael, b. 29 Jan 1939. Consultant Neurocologist. m. Caroline Mary Payne, 3 sons. Education: MD; FRCP; FRCPath; MBBS, London University. Appointments: Consultant Neurologist, Royal London Hospital; Senior Lecturer in Neuropathology, The Medical College of the Royal London Hospital; Honorary Consultant Neurologist, Honorary Consultant to the Sir Alan Parks Anorectal Physiology Laboratory, St Mark's Hospital, London; Consultant Neurologist, The London Independent Hospital; Consultant Neurologist, The London Bridge Hospital; Honorary Consultant Neurologist, St Luke's Hospital for the Clergy, London; Chief Medical Officer, Swiss Reinsurance (UK) Ltd, London. Publications: 12 books on Neurology, Neuromuscular Disease, Neuropathology & Coloproctology; More than 350 papers on medical science. Memberships Include: Royal College of Physicians; Royal College of Pathologists; American Neurological Association; American Academy of Neurology; Australian Association of Neurologists; British Association of Clinical Neurophysiologists; British Neuropsychiatry Society. Address: Neurology Department, The Royal London Hospital, Whitechapel E1 1BB, London, England.

SWE Kyu Kyu, b. 29 Mar 1929, Rangoon, Burma. Professor of Obstetrics and Gynaecology (retired). m. Pe thein, 26 Mar 1961, 2 sons. Education: MB, BS, Rangoon, 1953; MRCOG, London, 1961; FRCOG. Appointments include: Professor, Head, Department of Obstetrics and Gynaecology, Institute of Medicine, Mandalay, Burma, 1983-86; Professor, Head, Department of Obstetrics and Gynaecology IM 2, 1986-88, Professor, Head, Department of Obstetrics and Gynaecology IM 1, 1988-89, Yangon, Myanmar. Publications: Rupture of Gravid Uterus at Mandalay General Hospital, 1971; Laparoscopy in Gynaecology, 1972; Maternal Mortality at MGH, 1983; Gestational Trophoblastic Diseases at MGH, 1985; A study of Menopause at North Okkalapa, 1991. Memberships: President, Myanmar Medical Association; Vice-President, Myanmar Maternal and Child Welfare Association; Chairman, Myanmar Reference Committee, Royal College of Obstetricians and Gynaecologists, London; International Federation of Gynaecology and Obstetrics; AOFOG. Hobbies: Tennis; Gardening. Address: 314 U Wisara Road, University PO, Yangon, Myanmar.

SWEET William Herbert, b. 13 Feb 1910, Kerriston, Washington, USA. Emeritus Professor of Surgery. m. Elizabeth Jane Dutton, 29 july 1978, 1 son, 2 daughters. Education: SB. University of Washington, 1930; BSc, 1934, DSc, 1957, Magdalen College, Oxford University, England; MD, Harvard University Medical School, USA, 1936; Diplomate, American Board of Neurological Surgery, 1946; American Board of Psychiatry and Neurology, 1946. Appointments include: Acting Chief, Neurosurgical Service, Birmingham United Hospital, England, 1942-45; Regional Cnsultant in neurosurgery, British Emergency Medical Service, 1942-45; Assistant in neurosurgery, 1945-47, Assistant

Neurosurgeon, 1947-48, Associate Visiting Neurosurgeon, 1948-57, Visiting Neurosurgeon, 1957-61, Chief, Neurosurgical Service, 1961-77, Consusltant Visiting Neurosurgeon, 1977-80, Massachusetts General Hospital, USA; Assistant in Surgery, 1945-46, Instructor in Surgery, 1946-47, Associate in Surgery, 1947-48, Assistant Professor of Surgery, 1948-54, Associate Clinical Professor of Surgery, 1954-58, Associate Professor of Surgery, 1958-65, Professor of Surgery, 1965-76, Harvard Medical School. Publications include: Pain: Its Mechanisms and Neurosurgical Control, Co-author, 1955; Neurosurgical Treatment of Persistent Pain: Physiological and Pathological Mechanisms of Human Pain, Co-author, 1989; Operative Neurosurgical Techniques: Indications, Methods, and Results, 2 volumes, 1982, 2nd edition, 2 volumes, 1988, 3rd edition, 2 volumes, 1995. Honours include: Phi Beta Kappa; Sigma Xi; Alpha Omega Alpha. Memberships include: American Academy of Neurological Surgery. Address: Massachusetts General Hospital, 309 Goddard Avenue, Brookline, MA 02146-7425, USA.

SWENSON Orvar, b. 7 Feb 1909, Sweden. Professor of Surgery (retired). m. Melva Swenson, 6 Nov 1941, 3 daughters. Education: MD, Harvard Medical School, 1937; AB, William Jewelle College; DSc, William Jewelle College. Appointments include: Professor of Paediatric Surgery, Tufts University Medical School, USA; Professor of Surgery, Northwestern University Medical School; Professor of Surgery, University of Miami, Florida. Publications: Textbook of Pediatric Surgery, 1958, 8th Edition, 1990; Many papers describing his discovery and cure of Hirschsprung's Disease. Honours: Mead Johnson Award, 1952, Ladd Award, 1969, American Academy of Pediatrics; Denis Brown Medal, London, 1967; Dr honoris causa. Memberships: American Surgical Association; Society of University Surgeons; American Pediatric Surgery Association, President 1973. Hobby: Furniture making. Address: PO Box 41, Rockport, ME 04856, USA.

SWERDLOW Martin Abraham, b. 7 July 1923, Chicago, Illinois, USA. Physician. m. Marion Levin, 19 May 1945, 2 s. Education: BS; MD. Appointments: Pathologist, Hospitals in Kansas City and Chicago; Professor of Pathology and Associate Dean, University of Illinois College of Medicine; Professor and Chairman, University of Missouri Kansas City; Chair of Pathology, Michael Rees Hospital and Professor and Associate Dean, University of Chicago; Geever Professor, Head, University of Illinois College of Medicine; Emeritus Professor. Publications: Iga deposition in Liver, 1982; Iga Subclasses in Liver, 1983; Atlas of Urinary Sediments, 1989; Skin, chapter, 1959. Honours: Alumnus of Year, University of Illinois College of Medicine, Teaching and Research, 1973; Frances B Geever Professorship in Pathology, 1991; Golden Apples for Teaching, 1960, 1965, 1968, 1971, 1972. Memberships: US Canadian Academy of Pathology; College of American Pathologists; American Society of Clinical Pathology; American Society Dermpathology; American Association Study of Liver Disease. Hobbies: Music; Photography; Making Learning Programmes. Address: 5757 S Dorchester Avenue, Chicago, IL 60637, USA.

SWIDERSKI Gerwazy, b. 26 May 1920, Kobylrim Wlkp, Poland. Professor of Spinal Surgery. m. Krystyna Soldernhof, 4 June 1954, 1 son, 1 daughter. Education: MD. University of Poznan. Appointments: Docent, University Orthopaedic Department, Poznan; lecturer, University Institute for Anatomy; Director, University Orthopaedic Institute, Wroclaw; President, World Federation of Spondylologists; Rector, International Academy of Spine Surgery; Dean of Faculty Nations Co-operation. Publications: Author of several professional works; Editor of professional journals. Honours: Order of Poland, Resurrection 2nd Class, 1975, 1977; Cross for Bravery, 1939. Memberships: Corresponding Member, German Association for Spine Study; Club for Spine Surgeons USA; German Association for Orthopaedics. Hobbies: Gardening; Sportt; Philosophy. Address: Asmyka-str 30, PL 51143 Wroclaw, Poland.

SWYGERT Leslie Ann, b. 20 March 1957, USA. Independent Medical Epidemiology Consultant. Education: MD; MPH; Board Certified by The American Board of Preventitive Medicine. Appointments: General Medicine Practioner, 1985-88; EIS Officer, US Centers for Disease Control, 1988-90; Chronic Disease Epidemiologist, Hawaii Department of Health, 1990-91. Publications: Eosinophilia-Myalgia Syndrome: Results of National Surveillance Jama, 1990; Eosinophilia-Myalgia Syndrome: Mortality Data From The US National Surveillance System, 1993. Honours: Phi Beta Kappa, 1978; Alpha Epsilon Upsilon, 1978; Phi Sigma, 1978; ADA, 1983; Janet M Glasgow Memorial Achievement Citation, 1984; Four Commissioned Corps Citations, 1989-91. Memberships: ACOEM; ACPM; APHA; ARHP;

ATPM; GEENET (WHO); ISDE; RSM; SER. Hobbies: Scuba Diving; Underwater Photography; Naturalist. Address: 4104 24th Street, #540, San Francisco, CA 94114-3615, USA.

SYED Saadat, b. 10 May 1933, Nairobi, Kenya. Family Physician. m. Shaista Syed, 6 Sept 1970, 1 son, 1 daughter. Education: MD; MRCOG (Eng). Appointments: Registrar, Obstetrics and Gynaecology, Herefordshire Hospitals, England; Currently Active Staff, York Finch General Hospital and Secretary of Medical Staff Association. Honours: Gold Medal in Internal Medicine, Richmond Hospital, Dublin, Republic of Ireland, 1960. Memberships: Ontario Medical Association; Royal Society of Medicine, Ontario; Royal College of Obstetricians and Gynaecologists, England. Hobbies: Arts; Reading; Squash; Cricket. Address: 4640 Jane Street, Suite 201, Downsview, Ontario, Canada M3N 2K5.

SYMBAS Panagiotis N, b. 15 Aug 1925, Greece. Surgeon. m. Hytho Bagatis, 3 sons. Education: MD, University of Salonika Medical School, 1954; Internship and Residencies, Vanderbilt University, Nashville, Tennessee, USA, 1956-61. Appointments include: Associate Professor of Surgery, 1968-73, Director, Daniel C Elkin Surgical Research, 1970-, Professor of Surgery, 1973-, Emory University School of Medicine, Atlanta, Georgia; Director, Thoracic and Cardiovascular Surgery, Grady Memorial Hospital, Atlanta, Georgia, 1964-. Memberships include: Fellow, American Surgical Association; Fellow, American College of Surgeons; Fellow, American College of Cardiology; Fellow, American College of Chest Physicians; American Association for Thoracic Surgery; Society of Thoracic Surgeons; Association of Academic Surgery; International Society of Cardiovascular Surgery, North American Chapter; Southern Medical Assocaition; Medical Society of Georgia; The Georgia Surgical Society. Hobbies: Attending and supporting my three sons athletic participation. Address: Emory University School of Medicine, Thoracic Cardiovascular Surgery, 69 Butler Street NE, Atlanta, GA 30303, USA.

SYMINGTON Neville, b. 3 July 1937. Psychoanalyst. m. Joan Cornwell, 21 Dec 1974, 2 sons. Education: BSc; DCP; Read Philosophy, Theology, St Edmund's College, 1958-64; Psychology, Brunel University, 1968-72. Appointments: Psychotherapist, Grendon Prison, 1971-75; Director, Personal Consultation Centre Psychotherapy Unit, London, 1975-78; Senior Staff Member, Adult Department, 1978-85, Head, Psychology Discipline, Adult and Adolescent Departments, 1979-82, Tavistock Clinic, London; Private practice as Psychoanalyst, Sydney, New South Wales, Australia, 1985-93; Chairman, Sydney Institute for Psycho-Analysis, 1987-93. Publications: Books: The Analytic Experience, 1986; Narcissism: A New Theory, 1993; Emotion and Spirit: Questioning the Claims of Psycho-Analysis and Religion, 1994; The Making of a Psychotherapist, forthcoming; The Clinical Theory of Wilfred Bion (with Joan Symington), forthcoming; Book chapters; Articles in journals. Memberships: British Psycho-Analytical Society, Scientific, Curriculum and Application of Psycho-Analysis committees 1980-85; Australian Psycho-Analytical Society; Australian Psychological Society. Address: 88b Warragal Road, Turramurra, NSW 2074, Australia.

SZANIAWSKI Wojciech Kazimierz, b. 7 Apr 1942, Lodz, Poland. Physician. m. Ewa Romanowska, 3 Aug 1968. Education: MD, Medical School of Lodz, Poland; Doctor of Medical Sciences. Appointments: Ajunct, Section of Pathology, Research Centre, Medical School of Lodz, Poland; Clinical Assistant Professor of Dermatology, Albert Einstein College of Medicine, Bronx, NY; Currently, Partner, Dermatopathology Associates of NY, New Rochelle, NY; Clinical Associate Professor, Professor of Dermatology, NY Medical College, Valhalla. Publications: Epithelioid Angiomatosis, in Journal Amercian Academy Dermatology, 1990; Co-author, Giant Cell Lichenoid Dermatitis, in Journal Cutan Pathology, 1994. Honour: Faculty Prize, NY Medical College, 1991. Memberships: Fellow, American Academy of Dermatology; American Society of Dermatology; International Society of Dermatopathology. Hobby: Scuba Diving. Address: 91 Weyman Avenue, New Rochelle, NY 10805, USA.

SZASZ Thomas Stephen, b. 15 Apr 1920, Budapest, Hungary. Psychiatrist. 2 daughters. Education: AB with honours, Physics, 1941, MD, 1944, University of Cincinnati; Diplomate, National Board of Medical Examiners, Residencies: Medicine, 1945-46, Psychiatry, 1946-49; Diploma, Chicago Institute for Psychoanalysis, 1950; Diplomate, Psychiatry, American Board of Psychiatry and Neurology, 1951. Appointments: Professor of Psychiatry, 1956-90, Professor Emeritus, 1990-, State University of New York Health Science Center, Syracuse;

Adjunct Scholar, The Cato Institute, Washington DC. Publications: 22 books including: Pain and Pleasure: A Study of Bodily Feelings, 1957, 2nd edition, 1975, new preface, 1988; Psychiatric Justice, 1965, new afterword, 1988; Sex by Prescription, 1980, UK edition as Sex: Facts, Frauds, and Follies, 1981, new preface, 1990; The Therapeutic State: Psychiatry in the Mirror of Current Events, 1984; Our Right to Drugs: The Case for a Free Market, 1992; Cruel Compassion: Psychiatric Control of Society's Unwanted, 1994; About 600 articles, book chapters, reviews, newspaper columns. Honours: Alpha Omega Alpha, 1944; Holmes-Munsterberg Award, International Academy of Forensic Psychology, 1969; Root Tilden Lecturer, New York University School of Law, 1971; DSc honoris causa: Allegheny College, 1975, Universidad Francisco Marroquin, Guatemala, 1979; Distinguished Lecturer, The Cato Institute, 1993; Many more. Memberships: Life Fellow, American Psychiatric Association; Life Member, American and International Psychoanalytic Associations; Fellow, International Academy of Forensic Psychology; Honorary Life Member, American Humanist Association. Address: 750 East Adams Street, Syracuse, NY 13210, USA.

SZEIFERT György Tamas, b. 4 Dec 1953, Debrecen, Hungary. Neurosurgeon. m. Illona Guth, 28 Dec 1992, 1 son, 1 daughter. Education: Diploma; Board Certificated Pathologist; Neurosurgeon; Paediatric Neurologist. Appointments: General Pathologist, Department of Pathology, University Medical School of Debrecen, 1978-86; Neurosurgeon, National Institute of Neurosurgery, Budapest, Hungary, 1986-. Publications: Atlas of Fetal Diagnosis, 1992; Pathological Characteristics of surgically removed craniopharyngiomas: Analysis of 131 Cases, 1993. Hobbies: Organ Playing. Address: National Institute of Neurosurgery, Amerikai Str 57, H-1145 Budapest, Hungary.

SZIKLAI Istvan, b. 28 Feb 1954, Kalocsa, Hungary. ENT Surgeon. m. Marianna Hejja, 1984, 3 daughters. Education: MD, Szentgyörgyi Albert University; PhD. Appointments: Hugh Knowles Visiting Professor, Northwestern University, Evanston, Illinois; Senior Assistant, ENT Surgery, Semmelweis Medical University, Budapest. Publications: Co-author: Time related alteration of endolymph composition in an experimental model of endolymphatic hydrops, 1992; ACh controls the gain of the voltage to movement converter in isolated OHCs, 1993. Memberships: Collegium Oto-Rhino-Laryngologicum Amicitiae Sacrum; Association for Research in Otolaryngology. Hobbies: Classical Music. Address: Eotvos u 32, 1067 Budapest, Hungary.

SZPYTMA Roman Jozef, b. 26 June 1956, Rzeszow, Poland. Ophthalmologist. m. Teresa Chudzik, 12 Aug 1980, 1 son. Education: BA, The Copernicus Academy of Medicine, Poland, 1981; MD, The Copernicus Academy of Medicine, Poland, 1991. Appointments: Doctor, Cracow Oculistic Hospital, 1981-84; Department of Pathophysiology of Vision & the Neuro-ophthalmology Clinic, Cracow Academy of Medicine, 1985-93. Publications: Co-author, Botulinum A Toxin Injections into Extraocular Muscles for Correction of Strabismus, 1986; Botulinum Toxin A Injections into Extraocular Muscles in Paralytic Strabismus, 1991; Cockayne's Syndrome. Memberships: European Strabismological Association; Polish Oculistic Association; Polish Strabismological Association; Polish Acupuncture Association. Honours: Diploma of Distinction, Lisbon, 1988. Hobbies: Photography; Climbing. Address: ul Targowa 1/6, 30-529 Krakow, Poland.

SZYDLO Kon David, b. 7 Mar 1954, Mexico City, Mexico. Psychiatrist; Psychoanalyst. m. Janet Shein, 9 Dec 1978, 1 son, 2 daughters. Education: BSc, ITAM, Mexico, 1976; MD, Autonomous Metropolitan University, 1981; Psychiatry, University of London, 1984; Psychoanalysis, Institute of Psychoanalysis, London. Appointments: Psychiatry, Maudsley Hospital, London, England; Psychoanalyst, Researcher, Brent Consultation Centre, London; Clinical Director, MIND, Hammersmith, London; Various teaching positions, England and Mexico; Currently: Psychiatrist, American British Hospital, Mexico; Honorary Consultant in Psychiatry, National Nutrition Institute, Mexico. Publications: Psychiatric Services in Mexico, 1984; Group Psychotherapy (co-author), 1986; New Understanding in the Dynamics of Psychosomatic Disorders; Relevances of Baby Observation Research for Psychosomatic Disorders. Honours: National Award El Ateneo, Mexico City, 1981. Memberships: British Psychoanalytic Association; Mexican Psychiatry Association; Mexican Society for Neurology and Psychiatry; Mexican Psychoanalytic Association. Hobbies: Scuba diving; Tennis. Address: Vicente Guemes 135, Lomas Virreyes, Mexico DF 11000, Mexico.

T

TAGLIAVINI Fabrizio, b. 4 Sept 1950, Traversetolo, Parma, Italy. Neurologist. m. Lucilla Schianchi, 23 Dec 1978, 1 daughter. Education: MD, University of Parma, Italy, 1975; Certified Specialist in Neurology, University of Parma, 1979; Certifield Specialist in Neuropathology, University of Milano, 1985. Appointments: Postdoctoral Fellow, Neurology, University of Parma, 1975-80; Assistant Professor, Neurology, University of Bern, Switzerland, 1981-84; Associate Neurologist, Associate Scientist, Istituto Neurologico Besta. Publications: Neuronal counts in basal nucleus of Meynert in Alzheimer disease and in simple senile dementia, 1983; The basal nucleus of Meynert, 1987; Preamyloid deposits in the cerebral cortex of patients with Alzheimer's disease and nondemented individuals, 1988; Amyloid protein of Gerstmann-Sträussler-Scheinker disease, 1991; Gerstmann-Sträussler-Scheinker disease, 1991; Prion protein preamyloid and amyloid deposits in Gerstmann-Sträussler-Scheinker disease, 1992; Down syndrome as a key to the time sequence of brain changes in Alzheimer disease, 1992; Neurotoxicity of a prion protein fragment, 1993. Memberships: Italian Society of Neurology; Italian Association of Neuropathology; Swiss Society of Neuropathology; International Society of Neuropathology. Honours: Executive Committee, Italian Association of Neuropathology, 1990-93; Honorable Mention, Moore Award, American Association of Neuropathologists, 1991. Hobbies: Music. Address: Via G Pascoli 18, 20129 Milano, Italy.

TAI Teik Huat, b. 7 Mar 1945, Malaysia. Obstetrician & Gynaecologist. m. Tipawan Dechaboonako, 1971, 2 sons, 1 daughter. Education: MRCOG, 1978; FRCS Ed, 1979; FRACOG, 1980. Memberships: Australian Medical Association; Royal College Obstetricians & Gynaecologists (London); Royal College of Surgeons Edinburgh; Royal Australian College of Obstetricians & Gynaecologists. Hobby: Travelling. Address: 5/64 Arnisdale Road, Duncraig, WA 6023, Australia.

TAKAHASHI Ryo, b. 28 Feb 1911, Yokohama, Japan. Medical Doctor; Emeritus Professor. m. 30 Oct 1935, 1 son, 2 daughters. Education: MD, Jikeikai University School of Medicine. Appointments include: Chief Professor, now Emeritus Professor, Emeritus President of Nasal Surgeries course, Jikeikai University School of Medicine; Emeritus President, ORL Tokyo magazine. Publications: A collection of ENT studies, in English, 1971; Takahashi-collection in Archaeology, 7 vols; The formation of nasal septum (the concept of evolutional paradox), in English. Honours: Award, 18th Congress, Japan Society of Logopedics and Phoniatrics; Award, 74th Congress, Otorhinolaryngology Society of Japan, 1973; Award, ISIAN, Tokyo, 1976. Hobby: Archaeological collection (displayed in Fujisawa City, Kanagawa Prefecture). Address: Kugenuma-Kaigan 2-11-34, Fujisawa-shi, Kanagawa-ken, Japan.

TAKAHASHI Susumu Y, b. 13 Apr 1938, Kamakura City, Japan. Biochemist; Molecular Biologist. m. 1964, 1 daughter. Education: Master's degree, DSc, Tokyo Metropolitan University. Appointments: Associate Professor, Research Associate, Department of Biology, Nagoya University, Nagoya; Currently Professor, Department of Biology, Yamaguchi University, Yamaguchi. Publications: Cysteine proteinases from Bombyx silkmoth, 1990, 1992, 1993; Recent Advances in Insect Physiology, 1991; Recent Advances in Insect Biochemistry and Molecular Biology, in press. Memberships: Japanese Society of Biochemistry; Japanese Society of Zoology. Hobbies: Playing tennis; Music, especially Latin music. Address: Department of Biology, Faculty of Liberal Arts, Yamaguchi University, Yamaguchi 753, Japan.

TAKAISHI Noboru, b. 2 Jan 1928, Kobe, Japan. Psychiatrist. m. Hideko Tatsumi, 1958, 2 sons, 1 daughter. Education: MD, Nippon Medical School, 1954; Diplomate, Japanese National Board of Medical Examiners, 1955; DrMedSc, 1959; Senior Visiting Fellow, Psychiatry, University of Oregon Medical School, USA, 1964-65; Research Fellow, Psychiatry, Albert Einstein College of Medicine, USA, 1983. Appointments: Assistant Professor, Psychiatry, 1966-69, Lecturer, Psychiatry, 1969-, Osaka University Medical School; Chief of Psychiatry, Osaka University Branch Hospital, 1966-69; Private practice, 1969-. Publications: 22 papers mainly on behavior therapy and hypnotherapy including: Psychosomatic Studies on Chronic Urticaria, 1963; Translations: Oskar Vogt's Work and Autogenic Training (W Luthe), 1970; Use of Hypnosis in the Control of Organic Pain and Functional

Symptom Control (H B Crasilneck), 1972; Strategies of Psychotherapy (J Haley), 1973, 1986; Ordeal Therapy (J Haley), 1988; Therapeutic Patterns of Ericksonian Influence Communication (J Zeig), 1990. Memberships: Japanese Psychiatry Association, Board Member 1979-81; Approved Consultant, Japanese Society of Psychosomatic Medicine; Japanese Society of Hypnosis, Board Member, International Communication Committee Chair, Past Editor-in-Chief, Past Research Committee Chair; Approved Consultant, Fellow, American Society of Clinical Hypnosis; Board Member, Japanese Society of Behaviour Therapy; Board Member, Japanese Union of Associations for Psychomedical Therapy; Scientific Associate, American Academy of Psychoanalysis; Fellow, Association for Advancement of Behavior Therapy; Society for Exploration of Psychotherapy Integration; Swedish Society of Clinical and Experimental Hypnosis. Address: 1-2-2-200 Umeda, Kita-ku, Osaka 530, Japan.

TAKANO Takehito, b. 3 Apr 1949. Professor. Education: MD, 1975; PhD, Tokyo Medical and Dental University, 1979. Appointments: Lecturer, Department of Hygiene, 1979, Associate Professor, Department of Hygiene, 1981, Professor, Public Health and Environmental Science, 1987-, Tokyo Medical and Dental University; Visiting Associate Professor, Duke University Medical Center, USA, 1983-84. Publications: Baseline Data for Healthy City Tokyo, 1990; Editor: Formulation and Development of a Research Base for Healthy Cities, 1992; Urban Health, 1993. Memberships: Japanese Society of Public Health; Japanese Society for Hygiene; Society of Environmental Science, Japan; American Public Health Association. Address: Department of Public Health and Environmental Science, Tokyo Medical and Dental University, Yushima 1-5-45, Bunkyo-ku, Tokyo 113, Japan.

TALBERT Frances Suzanne, b. 1 Dec 1949, Oxford, Mississippi, USA. Psychologist; Educator. Education: PhD; BA; Master in Human Development & Hearing. Appointments: Reporter, The Columbus Commercial Dispatch, 1971-72; Copy Editor, The Evansville Press, 1972-75; Assistant City Editor, Night City Editor, Wire Editor, Copy Editor, The Charlotte News, 1975-82; Psychology Intern, University Georgia, 1988-89; Director, Medical College of Georgia Learning Support Center, 1989-90; Counseling Psychologist, Counseling & Testing Center, Augusta College, 1989-90; Research Psychologist, Medical Research, Augusta VA Medical Center, 1990-91. Publications: MMPI profiles in PTSD as a function of comorbidity; A comparison of MMPI and MMPI-2 in PTSD assessment; Evaluation of Publication Productivity in Academic Family Medicine Departments; Relationship of NEO-PI to Personality Styles and Severity of Trauma in Chronic PTSD Patients. Memberships: American Psychological Association; American Association of Applied & Preventive Psychology; Society of Teachers of Family Medicine; Southeastern Psychological Association; Georgia Psychological Association; Family Medicine Educators in Georgia; International Society for Traumatic Stress Studies; Augusta Area Psychological Association. Hobbies: Tennis; Reading; Gardening. Address: PO Box 2712, Augusta, GA 30914, USA.

TALLENT Marc Andrew, b. 3 Dec 1954, Newport News, VA, USA. Clinical Psychologist. Education: PhD, Adelphi University, 1983. Career: Independent practice, Supervising Psychologist and Consultant. Publication: Oedipal and Preoedipal Factors Related to Fear of Success, 1982. Honour: Phi Beta Kappa, 1978. Memberships: American Psychological Association; New York State Psychological Association; National Association for the Advancement of Psychoanalysis. Hobby: Travel. Address: 51 Fifth Street, Professional Suite B, New York, NY 10003, USA.

TALLEY Joseph Eugene, b. 27 May 1949, Springfield, Massachusetts, USA. Psychologist. m. Vibeke Absalon, 3 Jan 1981,2 s, 1 d. Education: BA, University of Richmond, 1971; MA, Radford College, 1973; PhD, University of Virginia, 1977; Diplomate, American Board of Professional Psychology, 1986. Appointments: Psychologist, Co-ordinator of Research Programme Evaluation and Testing Counselling and Psychological Services, Clinical Faculty, Department of Psychiatry, Duke University; Certified Practitioner and Consultant, Clinical Hypnosis. Publications: The Predictors of Succesful Very Brief Psychotherapy, 1992; Performance Prediction of Public safety and Law Enforcement Personnel, 1990; Counselling and Psychotherapy with College Students, 1985; Counseling and Psychotherapy Services for University Students, 1985; Study Skills, 1981; Multicultural Needs Assessments at the College and University. Honours: Psi Chi, 1971; Omicron Delta Kappa, 1971. Memberships: American Psychological Association; North Carolina Psychological Association; American Board of Professional Psychology; American Soceity for Clinical Hypnosis. Hobbies: Music; Theological Studies. Address: Counselling and Psychological Services, PO Box 90955, Suite 214 Page Building, Duke University, Durham, NC 27708, USA.

TALLEY Nicholas Joseph, b. 9 Jan 1956, Perth, Australia. Professor of Medicine. m. Penelope Ann Steele, 9 Feb 1985, 2 sons. Education: MBBS, 1979; FRACP, 1985; PhD, 1987; FACG, 1988; FACP, 1989; FAFRHM, 1991; MD, 1993; MRACMA, 1994. Appointments: Intern Resident, Registrar, Prince of Wales Hospital, Sydney, 1979-83; N Hard MRC Research Fellow, Royal North Shore Hospital, Sydney, 1983-86; Professional Registrar, Royal North Shore Hospital; Research Fellow, Consultant, Mayo Clinic, Rochester, 1980-93. Publications: Over 300 publications, books, original articles, reviews and abstracts; Textbooks: Examination Medicine, 1985; Clinical Examination, 1988; Internal Medicine, 1990. Honours: Graduated Honours, Medical School; NH+MRC Postgraduate Research Scholar. Memberships: Royal Australasian College of Physicians, Fellow; American College of Physicians, Fellow; American College of Gastroenterology, Fellow. Hobbies: Chess; Running; Tennis; Squash; Martial Arts; Writing. Address: Clinical Sciences Building, Nepeon Hospital, Box 63, Penrith, NSW, Australia.

TALLIS Frank, b. 1 Sept 1958, London, England. Clinical Psychologist. BSc (Hons); MSc; PhD. Appointments: Lecturer in Clinical Psychology, Institute of Psychiatry, London; Lecturer in Psychology, King's College, London; Clinical Psychologist, Chelsea and Westminster Hospital, London; Currently Consultant Clinical Psychologist. Publications: How To Stop Worrying, 1990; Understanding Obsessions and Compulsions, 1992; Coping with Schizophrenia (with S Jones), 1994; Worrying: Perspectives on Theory, Assessment, and Treatment (with G C L Davey), 1994. Membership: British Psychological Society. Hobby: Creative writing. Address: Charter Nightingale Hospital, London, England.

TALOB Edmund Ramon Corpuz, b. 2 Nov 1961, Philippines. Counsellor; Educator; Therapist. m. Lourdes S Ramos, 9 June 1990, 1 daughter. Education: BS, Psychology major, University of the Philippines, Diliman, Quezon City; MA in Education, Guidance and Counselling major, Ateneo University Graduate School of Education. Appointments: Clinical Counsellor, Euphrasian Residence, Quezon City and St Mary's Theologate, Ozamiz City; Consulting Psychologist, L S Cunanan Psychiatric Clinic (Multi-test Diagnostic Centre), Davao City; Consulting Psychologist, Davao Mental Hospital, Davao City; Assistant Professor, Honours Programme, St Scholastica's College, Manila. Publication: Using Transactional Analysis to Enhance Adjustment of Filipino College Students, 1994. Honours: Scholarship Grant for Advanced Training in Transactional Analysis, International Transactional Analysis Association, 1987-91; Best Faculty Moderator, St Scholastica's College, 1992-93. Membership: Regular Member in Clinical Training, International Transactional Analysis Association Inc. Hobbies: Swimming; Ballroom dancing; Photography. Address: 3 Pearl Street, Millionaire's Village, 1117 Novaliches, Quezon City, Metro Manila, Philippines.

TAM Alfred Yat-Cheung, b. 28 Aug 1953, Hong Kong. Paediatrician. Education: MB, BS, Hong Kong University; MRCP (UK); FRCP (Edin); FCCP; FHKAM (Paediatrics). Appointments: Medical and Health Officer, Paediatrics, 1979-84, Paediatrician-in-charge, Paediatric and Neonatal Intensive Care Units, 1984-92, Queen Mary Hospital, Hong Kong; Honorary Registrar, Respiratory Univ, Hospital for Sick Children, London, England, 1982-83; Lecturer, Department of Paediatrics, HKU, 1984-89; Consultant Paediatrician, Department of Paediatrics, Queen Mary and Grantham Hospitals, 1989-92; Currently Honorary Clinical Lecturer in Paediatrics, University of Hong Kong; Consultant Paediatrician, Canossa and Matilda Hospitals, Hong Kong. Publications: Author or co-author, about 30 articles including: Is pertussis still with us?, 1985; Systemic Staphylococcal infection in the neonatal nursery, 1985; Haemorrhagic shock encephalopathy, 1989; Brain death in the PICU, 1989; Asthma in the PICU, 1989; Studies on the respiratory health of primary school children in urban communities of Hong Kong, 1991; Development of paediatric intensive care in Hong Kong, 1992; Allergic profile of Chinese Children in Hong Kong: a skin prick test and Elisa Comparative study, 1992. Honours: Commonwealth Scholarship, 1982-83; Ho Hung Chiu Medical Education Foundation Fellowship, 1991. Memberships: Hong Kong Branch, British Medical Association; Council Member: Hong Kong College of Paediatricians; Hong Kong Thoracic Society; Hong Kong Paediatric Society; Chartered Member, Hong Kong

Association of Sports Medicine and Sports Science; European Society of Intensive Care Medicine; Society of Critical Care Medicine, USA; Hong Kong Medical Association; Fellow: American College of Chest Physicians; Centre of Asian Studies University of Hong Kong. Address: Room 1213, Melbourne Plaza, 33 Queen's Road Central, Hong Kong.

TAMMET Hannes, b. 5 Aug 1937, Tallinn, Estonia. Environmental Physicist. m. Eve-Reet Tammet, 30 Aug 1958, 2 sons. Education: Diploma, Tartu University, 1959; PhD, Tartu University, 1964; DSc, Main Geophysical Observatory, St Petersburg, 1979. Appointments: Assistant, Tartu University; Lecturer, Tallinn Pedagogical Institute; Professor, Environmental Physics, Tartu University. Publications: The Aspiration Method for the Determination of Atmospheric Ion Spectra, 1970. Memberships: Honorary Member, American Institute of Biomedical Climatology, 1980-; International Commission on Atmospheric Electricity, 1980-. Hobbies: Wandering in the Wilderness. Address: 56-6 Ravila Street, Tartu EE2400, Estonia.

TAN Hai-dong, b. 16 Sept 1939, Tianjin City, China. Professor of Surgery; Chief Surgeon. m. Shu Feng-yong, 11 Apr 1969, 1 son, 1 daughter. Education: Bachelor's degree, 4th Military Medical University, People's Liberation Army, 1966. Appointments: Resident Surgeon, 1966, Attending Surgeon, 1978; Chief Surgeon, Norman Bethune International Peace Hospital, 1993-; Professor, Department of Surgery, Hebei Medical College, 1993-. Publications: Premonition of injury of recurrent nerve in thyroidectomy, 1982; Clinical observations on selective distal splenorenal shunt, 1983; Percutaneous transhepatic catheting and drainage of liver abscess, 1985; Diagnostic analysis of 71 cases of hepatic abscess, 1985; Condyloma acuminatum, 1992. Honours: Scholarship Awards of Scientific Progress, People's Liberation Army, for distal spelenorenal shunt, 1987, clinical analysis of 54 cases of hepatic lobectomy, 1987, percutaneous transhepatic catheting and drainage of liver abscess, 1992, 122 cases of hepatic lobectomy, 1993. Memberships: Medical Society of Hebei Province; Surgical Society of Beijing Military Region; Medical Association of China. Hobby: Swimming. Address: Department of Surgery, Norman Bethune International Peace Hospital, Shi Jia Zhuang, Hebei 050082, China.

TAN Ramon K, b. 27 Oct 1936, Manila, Philippines. Psychiatrist. m. Josephine Tan, Oct 1965, 2 s. Education: MD; Fellow, American Psychiatric Association. Appointments: Chief Psychiatrist: Erie County Medical Center, Buffalo, NY; Sheehan Memorial Hospital of Buffalo, NY; Currently: Clinical Associate Professor of Psychiatry, State University of NY, Buffalo; Chief of Psychiatry, Sisters of Charity Hospital of Buffalo and St Mary's Hospital of Lewiston, NY. Memberships: American Psychiatric Association; American Medical Association. Hobbies: Golf; Tennis; Bowling. Address: 10158 Niagara Falls Blvd, Niagara Falls, NY 14304, USA.

TAN Seang Lin, b. 4 Sept 1952, Malaysia. Obstetrician and Gynaecologist. m. Grace Tai Han U, 28 Mar 1981, 2 sons. Education: MBBS; MMed (Obstetrics and Gynaecology); MRCOG, London, 1993. Appointments: Formerly Senior Lecturer, Consultant, Department of Obstetrics and Gynaecology, King's College School of Medicine and Dentistry, Denmark Hill, London, England; Currently: Professor, Chairman, Department of Obstetrics and Gynaecology, McGill University, Montreal, Quebec, Canada; Obstetrician and Gynaecologist in Chief, Royal Victoria Hospital, Montreal. Publications: Co-author, books: Infertility - Your Questions Answered; Recent Advances in the Management of Infertility; Frontiers in Reproduction and Endocrinology and Infertility; Pregnancy and Childbirth; Co-author, papers: Cumulative conception and live birth rates after invitro fertilisation, 1992; A prospective randomised study of the optimum timing of human chorionic gonadatrophin administration after pituitary desensitisation in in vitro fertilisation, 1992; Obstetric outcome of in vitro fertilisation pregnancies compared with normally conceived pregnancies, 1992. Honours: Howard Eddey Gold Medal, Royal Australasian College of Surgeons, 1980; Benjamin Henry Sheares Gold Medallist, 1986; MRCOG Gold Medal, Royal College of Obstetricians and Gynaecologists, London, 1993. Memberships: British Fertility Society; American Fertility Society; Fellow, Royal Society of Medicine, UK; Society of Endocrinology, UK. Hobbies: Tennis; Golf; Fine cuisine. Address: Department of Obstetrics and Gynaecology, McGill University, Women's Pavilion, 687 Pine Avenue West, Montreal, Quebec, Canada H3A 1A1.

TAN Shih-Chieh, b. 4 Apr 1909, Hua-Shi, Xiang-Tan, Hunan Province, China. Teacher; Researcher. m. 12 Aug 1938, 4 sons, 1 daughter. Education: MD, Hsiang-Ya Medical College, 1936; Advanced

Study in Pharmacology, PUMC, Peiping, 1936-37; Central Pharmaceutical Institute, Kunming, 1938-40. Appointments: Professor of Pharmacology; Head, Pharmacological Department. Publications include: Isolated Crystals from Yun-nan White Powder, Its Physical Properties and Biological Effects Very Like Those of Scopolomine, 1939; Toxicological Investigation on Yo-Tan-Tzu, An Amebicidal, 1944. Honours: Golden Plate for Graduation Thesis. Memberships: Chinese Pharmacological Society; Chinese Physiological Society; IUPS; Editorial Board, Acta Pharmacologica Sinica. Address: No 23,, 699 Xiang Yin Road, Shanghai 200433, China.

TAN Xuezhong, b. 18 Apr 1948, Harbin, Heilongjiang, China. Doctor. m. 28 Dec 1975, 1 son. Education: BM, Heilongjiang Traditional Chinese Medical College, 1982. Appointments: Doctor, 1982-87, Doctor-in-Charge, 1987-94, Associate Chief Physician (Associate Professor), 1994-, First Hospital of Harbin. Publications: Clinical Treatment of Ulcerative Stomatitis and Knowledge from Practice, 1987; Treatment of Periarthritis of Shoulder by Attacking Points, 1987; Clinical Application of Decoction of Five Drugs Containing Radix Astragali Sea Hedysari and Ramulus Cinnamomi, 1987. Honours: Most famous Doctor of Harbin City, 1987. Membershis: Secretary, Harbin Branch, Traditiona Chinese Medical Association. Hobbies: Chess; Swimming. Address: 4 Ground Floor, Second Unit, 74 Dongfeng Street, Daoli District, Harbin City, Heilongjiang Province, China.

TAN Yunliang, b. 8 Sept 1963, Wuhan, China. Vice Chief, Clinical Department, Hubei Provincial Institute of Geriatric Medicine. m. Li Yianling, 23 July 1987, 1 daughter. Education: MD, Internal Medicine, Shanghai University of Traditional Chinese Medicine. Publications: Guide of Prevention and Treatment of Common Diseases for Older Persons, book, 1990; Aging Mechanism, 1992; Study on Changes of Liver LDL Receptors in Aged Rats, article, 1994. Honours: Invention Prize, Hubei Provincial Youth Scientifical & Technological Foundation, 1989-91. Memberships: Chinese Medicine Society. Hobbies: Reading. Address: Liyuan Hospital, East Lake, Wuhan 430077, China.

TAN Zan, b. 8 Apr 1940, Hunan, China. Doctor. m. Xue Ling Liu, 1971, 1 d. Education: BS, Hunan Medical University; Professor. Appointments: Professor; Instructor; MD; Currently, Professor of China Qigong Science Research Association. Membership: Special Member of China Qigong Science Research Association; World Calligraphy. Hobbies: Chinese Painting; Calligraphy; Painting. Address: Dept of Physiology, Hunan Medical University, Zhangsha 410000, China.

TAN Zeng Lu, b. 26 Jan 1926, Beijing, China. Doctor; Educator. m. 24 Feb 1953, 2 s. Education: MD; PhD; Postgraduate Student, Department of Anatomy, Leningrad 1st Medical College, Russia. Career: Teaching Assistant, Anatomy and Neuroanatomy, 1951-54; Instructor and Associate Professor, Anatomy and Neuroanatomy, Chairman of Department of Anatomy, 1957-78; Associate Professor, Professor of Cell Biology and Neurobiology, Chairman, Department of Cell Biology, 1978-94; Currently, Doctor and Professor, Preclinical Medical Academy, Beijing Medical University. Publications: Over 30 articles mainly on blood supply of the central nervous system and the mechanism of recovery from isochemical damage of the cerebral cortical neurons, 1957-92; Chief Editor and Publisher, Human Anatomy, 1961-65, Medical Cell Biology, 1992. Honours include: Advanced Worker of Medical Education, Beijing City Government, 1960. Memberships: Board of Directors, Chinese Society of Anatomical Sciences; Vice Editor, Acta Anatomica Sinica. Hobbies: Classical Music; Chinese Chess; Walking. Address: Department of Cell Biology, Beijing Medical University, Xie-Yuan Road, 100083 Beijing, China.

TANAAKA Issei, b. 25 Nov 1950, Fukuoka, Japan. Associate Professor. m. Fujiko Yamauchi, 9 Sep 1984, 2 sons. Education: MD, 1975, PhD, 1983, Kyoto University. Appointments: Research Associate in Bochemistry, Vanderbilt University School of Medicine, USA; Assistant and Associate Professor, Hamamatsu University School of Medicine; Associate Professor of Medicine and Clinical Science, Kyoto University Graduate School of Medicine, Japan. Publications: Contributor of articles in professional journals. Memberships: Japanese Society of Internal Medicine; Japanese Society of Nephrology' Japanese Society of Endocrinology. HobbiesL: Golf; Travel. Address: 31018 Momoyama-cho Taichoro, Fushmi-Ku Kyoto 606, Japan.

TANG De-An, b. 18 Mar 1935, Hunan, China. Professor. m. Wan Hui-Jun, 22 Aug 1960, 1 son. Education: Graduate, Beijing University, 1965. Appointments: Assistant Research Fellow, Bio-philosophy, The

Chinese Academy of Sciences, 1965; Lecturer, Professor, Experimental Acupuncturology, The Tianjin College of Traditional Chinese Medicine, 1980, 1986. Publications: Experimental Acupuncturology, book, 1990; Effects of opposite needling on rheoencephalograms of cerebral infaction, 1990. Honours: 2nd Prize, Science & Technology Advance, Ministry, 1986; Highest Prize of Teaching, State of China, 1989. Memberships: Vice President, Experimental Acupuncturology Society of Chinese Association of Acupuncture & Moxibustion. Hobbies: Qigong; Taijiquan. Address: Tianjin College of Traditional Chinese Medicine, Tianjin, China.

TANG Fai, b. 13 Nov 1947, Hong Kong. University Teacher; Researcher. m. Regina Lai Ching Yu, 2 Aug 1990. Education: BSc, MSc, University of Hong Kong; PhD, University of Hull, England. Appointments: Assistant Lecturer, 1977-79, Lecturer, 1979-91, Senior Lecturer, 1991-, Department of Physiology, Faculty of Medicine, University of Hong Kong. Publications: Some age-related changes in pituitary-adrenal function in the male laboratory rat, 1978; Increase of proenkephalin mRNA and enkephalin content of rat striatum following daily injection of haloperidol for 2 to 3 weeks, 1983; Endocrine control of hypothalamic and pituitary met-enkephalin and beta-endorphin contents, 1991; Age-related changes in the contents of neuropeptides in the rat brain and pituitary, 1993. Honours: Commonwealth Scholar to UK, 1972-75; Ames Research Associate, National Aeronautics and Space Administration (NASA), Moffett Field, California, USA, 1993-. Memberships: Society for Endocrinology, UK; Endocrine Society, USA; Society for Neurosciences, USA; New York Academy of Sciences; International Brain Research Organization; Chinese Association for Physiological Sciences. Hobbies: Poetry; Ballroom dancing; Chinese Opera music; Soccer; Tennis. Address: Department of Physiology, Faculty of Medicine, University of Hong Kong, 7 Sassoon Road, Pokfulam, Hong Kong.

TANG Pei-Hsien, b. 26 Dec 1930, Shanghai, China. Professor of Medical Basic Research. m. Esther Y S Fu, 22 Dec 1956, 3 sons. Education: BS, Biology, Yenching University, 1952; MD, Peking Union Medical College, 1957. Appointments: Visiting Professor, Biochemistry Department, Munich University, 1980-82; Guest Professor, Ulm University, 1982-83; Director, Senior Scientist, Institute of Basic Medical Sciences, 1983-90; Director, Sinochem Institute of Biotechnology; Vice President, Chinese Academy of Medical Sciences, 1987-90. Publications: More than 110 original papers during 1978-93 on hematopoietic regulation, heterogeneity of hemopoietic stem cells, effects of pleiotropic and redundant hemopoietic growth factors and their gene transduction; 2 books on hematopoiesis and hemopoietic growth factors. Honours: Awards of Hematology, Oncology Research Program from the National Science & Technology Progress Prize. Memberships: President, Chinese Society for Experimental Hematology, 1986-; Scientific Advisor, US Cancer Research Council; Editorial Member, International Journal of Cell Cloning and Journal of Stem Cells. Address: Sinochem Institute of Biotechnology, PO Box 130(3), Beijing 100850, China.

TANG Sibiao, b. 7 May 1939, Wenzhou, Zhejiang, China. Chinese Traditional Medicine Doctor. m. Jan 1970, 1 son, 1 daughter. Education: Graduate, Chinese Traditional Medical College, Shanghai, China. Appointments: Director, Chinese Traditional Medicine, Huimin Hospital, Beijing, China; Team Leader, Chinese Abroad Treatment Team to North Africa. Publications: Clinical Differentiating Diagnosis in Chinese Traditional Medicine, 1986; Guide to Medicine and Nursing in Chinese Traditional Medicine, 1987. Honour: Advanced Medical Scientist of Beijing Health Bureau. Memberships: Chinese Traditional Medicine Association, China. Hobbies: Music; Chinese Chess; Sports. Address: Building 14, Unit 3 No #14, Chaoyangan Erligou, Xicheng District, Beijing 100084, China.

TANG Xilin, b. 8 Apr 1925, Shenyang, China. Professor.m. Wenyan Zhang, 1945, 1 s, 2 d. Appointments: Lecturer, China Medical University, 1954; Professor, Harbin Medical University, 1982; Currently, Professor, Hygiene of Children and Adolescents. Publications: Hygiene of Children and Adolescents, 1980, 2nd edition, 1986; Growth and Development of Children and Adolescents, 1991. Memberships: Vice Chairman, Chinese Association for Hygiene of Children and Adolescents; Chairman, Heilongjiang Association for Hygiene of Children and Adolescents. Address: No 199, Dazhijie, Harbin, China.

TANG Yong, b. Sichuan, China. Teacher. m. 31 Oct 1985, 1 son. Appointments: Currently Visiting Scholar. Publications: 1st author:

Application of stereological method to measure the capillary density in human nasal mucosa, 1992; A quantitative study of the number of Purkinje cells in the human cerebellum, 1992; The architecture and ultrastructure of the microvessels in human nasal mucosa, 1992; Scanning electron microscopy of the microvessel wall in human nasal mucosa, 1993; A quantitative study of the volume and surface area of the grown-up cortex, 1993; Estimation of lateral ventricular volume with stereological method, 1994; A quantitative study of parapharyngeal space and adjacent structure on CT, 1994. Memberships: Chinese Society of Anatomical Sciences; Chinese Society of Stereological Sciences. Address: Department of Anatomy, North Sichuan Medical College, Nanchong 637007, China.

TANNEN Richard L, b. 31 Aug 1937, New York City, USA. Physician. m. Vivien Baraban, 17 Nov 1990, 1 s, 4 d. Education: Undergraduate, Vanderbilt University, 1957; MD, University of Tennessee, 1960. Appointments: Co-Director, Nephrology Unit, University of Vermont, 1969-78; Professor and Director, Nephrology Division, University of Michigan, 1978-88; Professor, Department of Medicine, University of Southern California, Los Angeles. Publications: Fluids and Electrolytes, Co-author, 1986, 2nd edition, 1990; Contributor of over 130 articles. Honours: Established Investigator, American Heart Association; Merit Award, National Institutes of Health; President's Award, National Kidney Foundation; Pasteur medal, University of Strasbourg; Distinguished Alumnus, University of Tennessee. Memberships: Past President, American Society of Nephrology; Past Regional Vice President, National Kidney Foundation; American Society for Clinical Investigation; Association of American Physicians; Fellow, American College of Physicians. Hobby: Tennis. Address: 2020 Zonal Avenue, IRD 220, Los Angeles, CA 90033, USA.

TANPHAICHITR Kongsak, b. 22 Feb 1946. Physician. m. Sirirat Tareesung, 17 Jun 1973, 1 s, 1 d. Education: MD, cum laude; Diplomate: Internal Medicine, Rheumatology, Allergy and Immunology; Certificate in Rheumatology, Royal College of Physicians of Canada. Career: Instructor in Medicine, 1976-77, Currently, Assistant Professor in Medicine, Washington University, St Louis, MO. Publications: Amyloid Fibrils in Joint Fluid, 1976; Studies of Tolerance in NZB/NZW Mice, 1977; Vasculitis and Multiple Sclerosis, 1980; Buddhism - Answers to Common Questions, 1990; Buddhism Answers Life, 1995. Memberships: Fellow, American College of Physicians; Fellow, American Academy of Allergy and Immunology; Fellow, American College of Rheumatology; Fellow, Royal College of Physicians of Canada; President, Thai Association of Greater St Louis. Hobbies: Insight Meditation; Karate. Address: Allergy, Rheumatology and Immunology Specialists, 11115 New Halls Ferry Road, Suite 102, St Louis, MO 63033, USA.

TANUMIHARDJO Sherry Ann, b. 29 Jan 1961, Mauston, WI, USA. Research Scientist. m. Idarto Tanumihardjo, 11 Aug 1984, 3 s. Education: BS, magna cum laude, University of Wisconsin, Eau Claire, 1983; MS, PhD, Iowa State University, Ames. Career: Research Associate I, 1987-90, Research Associate II, 1990-91, Assistant Scientist II, 1991-93, Assistant Scientist III, 1993-, Iowa State University. Publications: Many articles in professional journals. Honour: Salutatorium High School, 1979. Memberships: American Institute of Nutrition; American Society of Clinical Nutrition. Hobby: Refinishing Furniture. Address: Iowa State University, 3258 Molecular Biology Building, Ames, IA 50011, USA.

TAO Chunxiang, b. 19 February 1943, Jiangsu, China. Physician of Chinese Medicine. m. Feng Lanzi, 6 November 1964, 1 son, 2 daughters. Education: College Diplomas. Appointments: Physician, 1962-; Vice Director Physician of Chinese Medicine. Publications: The Usage of Fuzzy Mathematics in Chinese Medicine, 1990; Experiences of Curing Parkinson Dialectically, 1994; New Interpretation of Treatise on Febrile Disease, 1994; Numerous articles published in scientific journals. Memberships: Chinese Association of Traditional Chinese Medicine; Chinese Association of the Integration of Traditional and Western Medicine. Hobbies: Taijiquan; Table Tennis. Address: Xuyi Hospital of Traditional Chinese Medicine, West Wuden Road, Xuyi, Jiangsu 211700, China.

TAO Shou-Chi, b. 31 March 1918, Shanghai, China. Cardiologist. m. September 1945, 3 sons, 2 daughters. Education: Postgraduate Fellow, Cardiology, Massachusetts General Hospital, 1947-48; MB. Appointments: Resident Physician, Teaching Hospital of Shanghai Medical College, 1941-45; Physician, Cardiologist, Chung Shan Hospital, Shanghai, 1948-74; Professor of Medicine, Shanghai First Medical College, 1958-74; Director, Fu Wai Hospital, Beijing, 1980-83. Publications: Practical Cardiology, 1962, 1978, 1993; More than 80 original articles in cardiology and cardiovascular epidemiology. Memberships: Council Member, Chinese Medical Association; President, Chinese Society of Cardiology, 1983-88; WHO Expert Advisory Panel on Cardiovascular Disease; Council Member, Section of Epidemiology and Prevention ISFC, 1986-92. Address: Fu Wai Hospital, Beijing 100037, China.

TAO Yixun, b. 2 July 1926, Jiangsu, China. Professor of Medical Laboratory Sciences. m. Qian Qinghua, 29 Mar 1948, 3 sons, 1 daughter. Education: MD, Aurora University, Shanghai, 1951. Appointments: Assistant Research Fellow, Chinese Academy of Medicine, 1956; Research Fellow, Shanghai Centre for Clinical Laboratory, 1965; Professor of Medical Laboratory Sciences, Shanghai Second Medical University. Publications: Clinical Biochemical Laboratory Technology, Chief Editor, 1982. Immunology and Immunological Laboratory Technology, Chief Editor, 1989; Honours: Distinguished Fellow, Queensland Institute of Medical Research, Australia 1989; Member, WHO Expert Advisory Panel on Health Laboratory Services, 1992-; Memberships: Chinese Medical Association; Asian and Pacific Federation of Clinical Biochemistry; Société Française de Biologie Clinique. Hobby: Music. Address: Shanghai Second Medical University, 280 South Chongqing Road, Shanghai 200025, China.

TAPP John Cecil, b. 1 Dec 1940, Horse Cave, Kentucky, USA. Physician. 2 sons. Education: MD; Diplomate, American Board of Family Practice; Diplomate, National Board of Medical Examiners; Fellow, American Academy of Family Physicians; Master Practitioner, Neurolinguistic Programming. Appointments: University of Louisville Medical School; Voluntary Faculty, Vanderbilt University; Clinical Instructor, Voluntary Faculty, Travacca-Nazarene College; Associate Clinical Professor, Voluntary Faculty Maj US Public Health Service; Active Staff, Greenview Hospital, Bowling Green Medical Center, Bowling Green, Kentucky; Training Consultant, Division of Regional Medical Programming; Currently: Practising Family Physician; Trader, Futures Markets. Honours: Member: Alpha Omega Alpha Medical Honorary Society; Honorable Order of Kentucky Colonels. Memberships: Kentucky Medical Association; American Association of Family Physicians; Kentucky Chapter, American Association of Family Physicians; American College for the Advancement in Medicine; Warren County Medical Society. Hobbies: Martial arts; Raquetball. Address: 414 Old Morgantown Road, Bowling Green, KY 42101, USA.

TARDIFF Kenneth J, b. 20 Oct 1944, New Orleans, LA, USA. Psychiatry. m. Kathleen Deane Tardiff, 2 Feb 1974, 1 d. Education: MD, Tulane Medical School, 1969; MPH, Harvard School of Public Health, 1973. Career: Medical Director, Payne Whitney Clinic, New York Hospital; Professor of Psychiatry and Public Health, Cornell Medical College. Publications: Psychiatric Uses of Seclusion and Restraint, 1984; Assessment and Management of Violent Patients, 1989; Homicide in New York City, in JAMA, 1994. Honours: Alpha Omega Alpha; Guttmacher Award for Forensic Psychiatry, APA, 1985. Memberships: Fellow, American Psychiatric Association; American Academy of Psychiatry and Law; Association for Academic Psychiatry. Hobbies: Sailing; Figure Skating; Skiing. Address: Department of Psychiatry, Cornell Medical College, 525 East 68th Street, Box 147, New York, NY 10021-4873, USA.

TARIOT Pierre N, b. 9 Oct 1952, USA. Medicine. m. Laura Jakimovich, 18 Oct 1991, 2 d. Education: AB, Amherst College, 1974; MD, University of Rochester, 1978; Board Certified, Internal Medicine, 1981, Psychiatry, 1985. Career: Resident, in Medicine, 1978-81, in Psychiatry, 1981-83, University of Wisconsin; Medical Staff Fellow, 1983-85, Senior Staff Fellow, 1985-86, NIMH; Assistant Professor of Psychiatry, 1986-90, Currently, Associate Professor of Psychiatry, Medicine, and Neurology, and Director of Psychiatry, Monroe Community Hospital, University of Rochester. Publications include: Numerous articles, books, monographs, chapters and review articles including: Co-author, Treatment of Alzheimer's Disease: Glimmers of Hope?, in Chemistry and Industry, 1993; Co-author, Emerging Drugs for Dementia, in Medical Clinics of North America, in press. Honours: Phi Beta Kappa, 1974; New Investigator Award for Neuroscience, American Geriatrics Society, 1988; NIMH Mental Health Academic Award, 1988-93; Fellow, Gerontological Society of America, 1992. Memberships: AAAS; AAGP; American Geriatric Society; GSA;

International Psychogeriatric Association; APA. Address: Monroe Community Hospital, University of Rochester School of Medicine, Psychiatry Unit, 435 East Henrietta Road, Rochester, NY 14620, USA.

TARRO Giulio, b. 9 July 1938, Messina, Italy. Medical Doctor. Education: MD, University of Naples, 1962; PhD, University of Rome, 1971. Appointments: Assistant in Medical Pathology, 1964-66, Professor of Oncological Virology, 1972-85, Division Chief of Virology, 1985-, University of Naples; Assistant Professor of Research, Paediatrics, University of Cincinnati, Cincinnati, Ohio, USA, 1968-69; Research Chief, National Research Council, Italy, 1972; Currently President, De Beaumont Ronelli Foundation for Cancer Research. Publications: Virology Trends, 1978; Oncological Virology, 1979; Virus Origin, 1979; AIDS, What To Do, 1987; Pathology of AIDS, 1991; With Cancer One Can Live, 1992; AIDS: What We Can Do, What We Must Know, 1994. Honours: Gold Medal of Culture, Rome, 1975; Knights of Humanity Award, Malta, 1976; Prime Minister's Award, Rome, 1985; Decorated Commander, National Order of Merit, 1991; Gold Cesare Award, Padua, 1992; Honorary degrees in Immunology and Medicine, Albany and New York. Memberships: Academic Senate, Constantinian University; Dean of Natural and Physical Sciences Faculty, Noble Academy of St Theodora. Hobbies: Soccer; Swimming; Art history. Address: Via Posillipo 286, 80123 Naples, Italy.

TASHNER Michael, b. 8 Nov 1966, WI, USA. Optometry. m. Julie A Engelke, 14 Aug 1993. Education: Doctor of Optometry, IL College of Optometry, 1993. Optometrist in Private Practice, Platteville, WI. Honour: WI Vision Awareness Award, 1993. Memberships: American Optometric Association; WI Optometric Association; Southwest WI Optometric Society. Hobby: Golf. Address: 350 West Pine Street, Platteville, WI 53818, USA.

TATHAM Alan, b. 26 Dec 1949, England. Clinical Psychologist. m. Lorraine Tatham, 21 Aug 1971, 2 d. Education: BSc, Honours, Psychology, Bristol University, 1971; D Clinical Psychology, British Psychological Society, 1974. Appointments: Clinical Psychologist, Oldham Health Authority, 1974-81; Currently, Head of Salford Clinical Psychology Services. Memberships: Associate Fellow, British Psychological Society; BPS Division of Clinical Psychology; British Association of Cognitive Behavioural Psychology. Address: Department of Clinical Psychology, Mental Health Services of Salford, Bury New Road, Prestwich, Manchester, M25 3BL, England.

TATSUMURA Toshiki, (Alias Lauw Tiong Kee), b. 21 Aug 1943, Palembang, Indonesia. Thoracic Surgeon. m. Sawako Higashi, 10 Jan 1970, 2 daughters. Education: MD 1971, PhD 1976, Kanazawa University School of Medicine, Japan. Career: Assistant Professor, Department of Thoracic Surgery School of Medicine, Toyama Medical and Pharmaceutical University, 1979-88; Visiting Research Scientist, Department of Pharmacology, Yale University, USA, 1984-85; Associated Professor, Department of Emergency, Thoracic Surgeon, 1988-. Publications: Changes in Glycosphingolipids Accompanying the Differentiation of Human Squamous SQCC/Y1 Cells, 1988; A New Technique for One-Stage Radical Eradication of Long-Standing Chronic Thoracic Empyema, 1990; Further Study of Nebulisation Chemotherapy, A New Chemotherapeutic Method in the Treatment of Lung Carcinomas: Fundamental and Clinical, 1993; Practical Emergency Medicine (Textbook), Editor, 1993; A New Surgical Approach to Apical Segment Lung Diseases, Including Carcinomas and Inflammatory Diseases, 1994; Experimental Tracheal Reconstruction with Interposing Autogenous Main Bronchus in Dogs, 1995; Preoperative and Intraoperative Ultrasonographic Examination as An Aid in Lung Cancer Surgery, 1995. Memberships include: Corresponding Member, American Association for Cancer Research; Active Member, American Society of Clinical Oncology; Japan Lung Cancer Society; Japanese Cancer Association; Councilor, Japanese Society for Chest Surgery; Active Member, Japan Surgical Society; Fellow, American Association of Chest Physicians; Active member, American Association for Bronchology; Councillor, Japanese Association for Clinical Surgery. Hobbies: Golf; Skiing; Fishing; Reading; Music. Address: Department of Emergency, School of Medicine, Toyama Medical and Pharmaceutical University, 2630 Sugitani, Toyama 930-01, Japan.

TATTERSALL Martin Henry Norman, b. 7 June 1941. Physician. m. Dr Susan F Pearsall, 18 Sep 1971, 3 sons. Education: BA, MB BChir, MA, MD, University of Cambridge, England; MSc, University of London; FRCP, London; FRACP. Appointments: House Physician, University College Hospital; Medical registrar, Royal Postgraduate Medical School; Research Fellow, Harvard Medical School, USA; Consultant Physician, Charing Cross Hospital; Professor of Cancer Medicine, University of Sydney, Australia. Publications: Basic Principles of Cancer Chemotherapy, Co-author, 1981; Gynecological Oncology, Co-author, 1992. Honours: Liston Gold Medal, Magrath Clinical Scholar, University College Hospital, 1964, 1965. Hobbies: Fishing; Music; Tennis. Address: 2 View Street, Woolwich, New South Wales 2110, Australia.

TAVERNE Aart Alexander Richard, b. 19 Feb 1945, The Hague, Netherlands. Orthodontist. 1 daughter. Education: BDSc, University of Queensland; Specialist DMO; DDM; Dr Dentistry. Appointments: Currently Senior Lecturer in Orthodontics, University of Queensland Dental School, Brisbane. Publications: The Role of Collagen in Eruption, 1989; Articles in Archives of Oral Biology and Australian Journal of Orthodontics, 1978-93. Memberships: Australian Dental Association; Australian Society of Orthodontics; American Association of Orthodontics; EBS; EOS. Hobby: Horse Riding. Address: University of Queensland Dental School, Turbot Street, Brisbane, Queensland 4000, Australia.

TAVILL Frederick, b. 20 Feb 1925, Manchester, England. Physician. m. Joyce Libman Tavill, 19 Mar 1983, 3 s, 2 d. Education: DPH(Lond); MRCS(Eng); LRCP(Lond); Diplomate, American Board of Preventive Medicine. Career: Medical Director, American Joint Distribution Committee, Iran and Morocco, 1954-67; Associate Professor, 1968-93, Associate Dean, 1973-85; Program and Medical Director, Milwaukee International Center, Medical College of Wisconsin, USA, 1986-93; Director, Metro Health Clement Center, Metro Health System, Cleveland, OH, 1993-. Publications: Traitement de Masse des Teignes par lu Grisedfulvive, in Maroc Medical, 1964; Co-author, Use of Fish Protein Concentrate in the Diets of Weanling Infants, in American Journal of Clinical Nutrition, 1969; Contributor, A Course Book in Health Care Delivery, 1976; Co-author, Living Will in Wisconsin, in Wisconsin Medical Journal, 1986. Membership: Faculty of Public Health Medicine. Address: 21500 Shelburne Road, Shaker Heights, OH 44122, USA.

TAWANSI Abdullah Yassin El, b. 25 Sep 1947, Cairo, Egypt. Professor of Solid State Physics. m. Regaa Abdel-Hamid Kasim, 29 Dec 1977, 1 son, 1 daughter. Education: BSc, Distinction, Applied Physics, Cairo University, 1970; PhD, Physics, Moscow University, Russia, 1977. Appointments: Demonstrator, Lecturer, Assistant Professor, Professor, Physics department, Faculty of Science, Mansoura University. Publications: Micromagnetism, 1990; Experimental Electronics, 1984; Contributor of over 55 research papers in international journals and periodicals. Honours: Award of State in Physics, 1988; Award of Intellectual Members of Egyptian Scientific Association, 1989. Memberships: Executive Member, Regional Association of Materials Scientists Islamabad, 1986; International Member, American Association for the Advancement of Science, 1995. Hobbies: Swimming; Music; Walking. Address: Department of Physics, Faculty of Science, Mansoura University, 35516, Egypt.

TAY John Sin Hock, b. 8 Oct 1942, Tangkak, Johor, Malaysia. Professor of Paediatrics. m. Ivy Gom Kim Kee, 10 Aug 1968, 1 son, 1 daughter. Education: MBBS, 1st Class Honours, University of Sydney, Australia; MMed, Paediatrics, Singapore; MD, Singapore; PhD, National University of Singapore; BD (Hons), University of London; FRACP; FRCPE; FACC; FAMS; FACMG. Appointments: Lecturer, Senior Lecturer, Associate Professor, Professor of Paediatrics, Head, Department of Paediatrics, National University of Singapore. Publications: Over 200 inclng: The Genetics of Palmar Creases. A study in the inheritance of liability estimated from the incidence among relatives, 1979; Dermatoglyphics in children with febrile convulsions, 1979; Co-author: New prognostic criteria for cyanotic congenital heart disease, 1982; Parental age and birth order effects in Chinese children with congenital heart disease, 1982; Mathematical function for maternal age in Down's syndrme, 1984; The estimation of inbreeding from isonymy: relationship to the average inbreeding coefficient, 1984; Dermatoglyphics in children with mitral valve prolapse, 1985; An index for measuring changes in the shape of the left ventricle in two-dimensional echocardiography, 1985; Genetic Heterogeneity among the Negroid and Arab Tribes of Sudan, 1988; Dystrophin function: calcium related rather than mechanical, 1990. Honours: University Medal and Arthur Edward Mills Graduation Prize for Distinction over Whole Medical Course, University of Sydney; Young Investigators Award, Academy of Medicine, Singapore, 1977; 9th Haridas Memorial Lecture, 1982. Hobbies: Music; Chess. Address: 24 West Coast Place, Singapore 0512.

TAYEAU Francis Emile, b. 24 Nov 1913, Boulogne sur mer, France. Professor. Education: MD; DSc; PharmD; Agrege des Facultes de Medecine. Appointments: Assistant, 1943, Maitre de conferences, 1950, Professor, 1950; Docent, 1961-69, Faculty of Medicine, Bordeaux; Retired. Publications: Contributor of 372 articles in professional journals. Honours: Recipient of numerous honours and awards for professional services. Hobby: Music. Address: Residence Borghese A, 25 rue Duvergier, 33200 Bordeaux, France.

TAYLOR Andrew Barrie Wilson, b. 23 Nov 1939, Ambala, India. Obstetrician and Gynaecologist. m. Sheila Anderson, 6 Jul 1963, 2 s, 1 d. Education: MBChB; FRCOG; FRCS(Ed). Career: Registrar, Western General Hospital, Edinburgh; Senior Registrar and Clinical Tutor, Royal Postgraduate Medical School, Hammersmith Hospital and Northampton General Hospital; Currently, Consultant Obstetrician and Gynaecologist, Kings Lynn and Wisbech NHS Hospitals Trust. Publications: Papers on fetal monitoring and epidural anaesthesia in British Journal of Obstetrics and Gynaecology, 1975, British Medical Journal, 1977, Anaesthesia, 1979. Memberships: British Medical Association; East Anglian Obstetric and Gynaecology Society; Nuffield Visiting Society. Hobbies: Private Pilots License IMC; Sailing; Skiing. Address: Easter Cornhill, South Creake, Fakenham, NR21 9LX, England.

TAYLOR Antony James William, b. 14 Aug 1926, London, England. Psychologist. Education: Certificate in Science and Administration; MA, New Zealand University; PhD, Victoria University; DHC, Reims; FNZPsS; FBPsS. Appointments: Probation Officer; Prison Psychologist; Professor of Clinical Psychology; Chief Selection Adviser Volunteer Service Abroad; Consultant Antarctic Division DSIR; Police; Fire; Conservation; Currently, Emeritus Professor, Trauma Consultant. Publications: 217 Deviant Behaviour, New Zealand Studies, 1979; Antarctic Psychology, 1987; Disaster Stress, 1989; Psychological Aspects of Disaster, in press. Honours: Carnegie Fellow, 1966; British Council, 1968; DAAD, 1975; Fulbright, 1985; British Council Study Award, 1989; Docteur Honoris Causa, Reims, 1990. Memberships: British Psychological Society; New Zealand Psychological Society; New Zealand Royal Society; Australia and New Zealand Society for Study of Traumatic Stress. Hobbies: Odd Jobs. Address: Psychology Department, Victoria University, Box 600 Wellington, New Zealand.

TAYLOR David Samuel Irving, b. 6 June 1942. Paediatric Ophthalmologist. m. Anna Rhys-Jones, 5 July 1979, 2 sons. Education: MB, ChB, University of Liverpool; University of California, 1976-77; DO; FRCS; FRCP; FRCOphth. Appointments: Consultant Ophthalmologist, National Hospital for New Diseases, 1976-89; Consultant Ophthalmologist, Hospital for Sick Children, London. Publications: Paediatric Ophthalmology: Current Aspects, 1983; Pediatric Ophthalmology, 1990; About 120 articles in reviewed journals. Memberships: Royal College of Physicians; Royal College of Surgeons; Royal College of Ophthalmologists; British Medical Association. Honours: Teacher Collins Prize, 1982; Richardson Cross Medal, 1991. Hobbies: Tennis; Forestry; Skiing; Carpentry. Address: 1 Harmont House, 20 Harley Street, London W1N 1AL, England.

TAYLOR Hugh Ringland, b. 10 Nov 1947, Melbourne, Australia. Professor of Ophthalmology. m. Elizabeth M Dax, 2 Dec 1968, 2 s, 2 d. Education: MBBS, Melbourne; BMedSc, Melbourne; DO, Melbourne; MD, Melbourne; FRACS; FRACO; FACS; FAAO. Appointments: Intern and Resident, Austin Hospital, Melbourne, 1972-73; Ophthalmic Registrar, Royal Victorian Eye and Ear Hospital, 1974-76; Fellow, Wilmer Institute, Baltimore, USA, 1977-79; Assistant Professor, 1979-83, Associate Professor, 1983-90, Professor, 1990, Johns Hopkins University, USA; Currently, Ringland Anderson Professor and Head of Department of Ophthalmology. Publications: Over 300 scientific articles published since 1970 including: Effect of UV radiation on cataract formation, in NEJM, 1988; Epidemiology and diagnosis of acute conjunctivitis at an inner city hospital, in Ophthalmology, 1989; Impact of mass treatment of onchocerciasis with ivermectin on the transmission of infection, in Science, 1990. Honours: Fight for Sight, 1981; RPB Award, Genive, 1989; International Organization against Trachoma, 1990; Alcon, 1993. Memberships: AMA; ARVO; RACS; RACO; AAO; ASTMA; RSTM. Hobbies: Sailing; Golf; Oenophilia. Address: Department of Ophthalmology, 32 Gisborne Street, East Melbourne, Victoria 3002, Australia.

TAYLOR Patrick J, b. 23 Aug 1941, Blackpool, Lancashire, England. Physician. m. Kathleen Withers, 1 Apr 1967, 1 s, 1 d. Education: MD; FRCS(C); FRCOG. Career: Assistant Professor of Obstetrics and

Gynaecology, 1971, Associate Professor, 1976, Professor, 1981-87, University of Calgary; Director, Department of Medicine, 1987, Director, 1988, Professor of Obstetrics and Gynaecology, Bourne Hall Clinic, Cambridge; Chief of Section of Reproductive Endocrinology, University of Man, 1989-91; Currently, Professor of Obstetrics and Gynaecology, University of BC; Chairman, Department of Obstetrics and Gynaecology, St Paul's Hospital, Vancouver, 1991-. Publications: Co-author, Laparoscopy and Hysteroscopy in Gynaecologic Practice, 1986; Unexplained Infertility, 1992; Practical Hysteroscopy, 1993; Practical Laparoscopy, 1993; Translator, Hysteroscopy Atlas and Text, by J Hamou, 1990; Over 170 articles in scientific journals. Memberships: Editor in Chief, Journal Society, 1990-; Member various editorial boards; Vice President, 1985-87, FSOGC; FACOG; Charter Member, Society of Reproductive Surgeons; President, 1980-81, Canadian Fertility Society. Hobbies: Sailing; Fly Fishing. Address: St Paul's Hospital, 1081 Burrard Street, Vancouver, BC V6Z 1Y6, Canada.

TEFUARANI Nakapi, b. 4 Apr 1956, Mortlock, Papua New Guinea. Senior Lecturer. m. 12 Apr 1979, 1 s, 3 d. Education: MBBS; DCH; MMED. Appointments: Residency, 1980-82; Junior Registrar, 1983-84; Senior Registrar, 1985-86; Lecturer, Child Health, 1987-90; Currently, Senior Lecturer, Child Health. Memberships: International Paediatric Association; International Society of Tropical Paediatrics; Australasian College of Tropical Medicine. Hobbies include: Running; Gym Work. Address: PO Box 5623, Boroko, Papua New Guinea.

TEICH Malvin Carl, b. 4 May 1939, New York City, NY, USA. College Professor. Education: SB, Physics, MA Institute of Technology, Cambridge, MA, 1961; MS, Electrical Engineering, Stanford University, CA, 1962; PhD, Quantum Electronics, Cornell University, Ithaca, NY, 1966. Appointments: MIT Lincoln Laboratory, Lexington, MA; Faculty, 1967, Chairman, 1978-80, Department of Electrical Engineering, Columbia University, NY; Faculty, Department of Applied Physics and Columbia Radiation Laboratory. Publications: About 200 technical publications; Co-author, Fundamentals of Photonics, 1991; Editorial Advisory Panel, Optics Letters, 1977-79; Editorial Board, Journal of Visual Communication and Image Representation, 1989-92; Deputy Editor of Quantum Optics, 1988-92; Board of Editors, Jemná Mechanika a Optika, 1994-. Honours: IEEE Browder J Thompson Memorial Prize Award, 1969; Guggenheim Fellowship, 1973; Citation Classic Award, Institute for Scientific Information, 1981; Memorial Gold Medal, Palacký University, Czechoslovakia, 1992; Fellow: American Physical Society; Optical Society of America; Institute of Electrical and Electronics Engineers; American Association for the Advancement of Science; Acoustical Society of America. Memberships: Sigma Xi; Tau Beta Pi; Association for Research in Otolaryngology; NY Academy of Sciences; Scientific Board, Czech Academy of Sciences' Institute of Physics. Address: Columbia University, New York, NY 10027, USA.

TEMPLE Christine Margaret, b. 9 Jul 1958, Glasgow, Scotland. Neuropsychologist. m. Leslie McCune, 9 Jul 1994. Education: BSc, 1st class honours, Psychology, University of St Andrews, 1980; MA, Cognitive Psychology, University of CA, Los Angeles, 1981; DPhil, Neuropsychology, University of Oxford, 1984; CPsychol; As FBPS; FRSM. Appointments: Weir Research Fellowship, University College, Oxford, 1984-86; Research Officer, MRC Neuropsychology Unit, Radcliffe Infirmary, Oxford, 1984-85; Lecturer, Senior Lecturer, Reader, Neuropsychology, University of London, 1985-91; Head of Department, Psychology, University of Essex, 1991-94; Currently, Director of Developmental Neuropsychology Unit, University of Essex. Publications: The Brain: An Introduction to the Psychology of Brain and Behaviour, 1993; Over 50 published academic research papers and chapters. Honours: Taylor Thomson Bursary, University of St Andrews, 1976-80; EAP Scholarship, University of CA, 1980-81; Wolfson Research Award, 1989-92. Memberships: Fellow, Royal Society of Medicine; Associate Fellow of British Psychological Society; Chartered Psychologist; Experimental Psychology Society. Address: Developmental Neuropsychology Unit, Department of Psychology, University of Essex, Wivenhoe Park, Colchester, CO4 3SQ, England.

TEMPLE Linda, b. 23 Apr 1948, London, England. Chartered Clinical Psychologist. Divorced, 1 s, 1 d. Education: Trilingual Secretarial Diploma, 1967; BA, First Class Honours, Open University, 1984; MSc, Clinical Psychology, 1988. Career: Marriage Guidance Counsellor, National Marriage Guidance Council, 1983-85; Clinical Psychologist, Hillingdon Hospital, 1988-93; Clinical Affiliate, Personal Performance Consultants (UK) Ltd and ICAS Ltd, 1990-; Partner, clinical psychology consultancy, Harris Thomson Associates, 1992-; Clinical Psychologist,

Northwick Park Hospital, Harrow, 1993-; Consultant Psychologist, Bowden House Clinic, Harrow, 1993-; School Counsellor, St Helen's School, Northwood, 1994-. Membership: British Psychological Society. Hobbies: Theatre; Cinema; Sport. Address: Bowden House Clinic, London Road, Harrow on the Hill, Middlesex, HA1 3JL, England.

TEMPLETON Allan, b. 28 Jun 1946. Gynaecologist. m. Gillian Penney, 17 Dec, 3 s, 1 d. Education: MBChB, 1969; MRCOG, 1974; MD, Honours, 1982; FRCOG, 1986. Career: Junior Hospital Posts and Shert Research Fellow, Aberdeen Royal Hospitals, 1969-75; Lecturer and Senior Lecturer, Edinburgh, 1976-85; Currently, Regius Professor of Obstetrics and Gynaecology, Aberdeen Maternity Hospital, Scotland. Publications: Books: The Early Days of Pregnancy, 1988; Reproductive Medicine and The Law, 1990; Infertility, 1992. Memberships: British Fertility Society; European Society for Human Reproduction and Embrology. Hobby: Mountaineering. Address: Knapperna House, Uony, Aberdeenshire AB41 0SA, Scotland.

TEMPLETON Bryce, b. 28 Jun 1932, Floral Park, NY, USA. Medicine. m. Dorothy B Templeton, 1 s, 1 d. Education: MD, 1957; MEd, 1969. Appointment: Professor, Medical College of Pennsylvania, Hahnemann University School of Medicine, Department of Psychiatry Sciences. Publication: Co-author, Evidence of role of psychosocial factors in diabetes mellitus: A review, in American Journal Psychiatry, 1990. Honours: Alpha Omega Alpha; Associate of Academic Psychiatry Education Award; RJF Weiner Award, Philadelphia County Medical Society, 1993. Memberships: American Psychiatric Association; AMA; Association Academic Psychiatry; Director, Residency Training in Psychiatry; AAAS; AAMC. Address: Department of Psychiatry, Hahnemann University, MS 403, Broad and Vine, Philadelphia, PA 19102-1192, USA.

TEMPLETON John Young III, b. 1 July 1917, Portsmouth, Virginia, USA. Physician. m. Dorothy E Fraley, 30 Apr 1943, 1 son, 3 daughters. Education: BS; MD. Appointments include: Professor of Surgery, University of Pennsylvania, 1964; Samuel D Gross Professor of Surgery, 1967, Emeritus Professor of Surgery, 1987-, Thomas Jefferson University. Publications: Experimental Reconstruction of Cardiac Valves by Venous and Pericardial Grafts, 1949. Honours: Honorary DSc, Davidson College, 1987; Honorary Doctor of Laws, Thiomas Jefferson University, 1987. Memberships: American Association of Thoracic Surgery; American Surgical Association; American College of Surgeons; Société Internationale de Chirurgie; Society of Vascular Surgery; International Cardiovascular Society. Hobbies: Wood and canvas canoes; Hunting; Fishing. Address: 311 Airdale Road, Rosemont, PA 19010, USA.

TEPPER Lloyd Barton, b. 21 Dec 1931, Los Angeles, CA, USA. Physician. m. Lamonte Leverage, 22 Jun 1957, 2 s. Education: AB, Dartmouth College; MD, MIH, ScD in Hygiene, Harvard University. Appointments: Professor, Environmental Health, University of Cincinnati, 1965-72; Associate Commissioner for Science, US Food and Drug Administration, 1972-76; Corporate Medical Director, Air Products and Chemicals Inc. Memberships: American College of Occupational and Environmental Medicine; American Board of Preventive Medicine. Address: Air Products and Chemicals Inc, 7201 Hamilton Boulevard, Allentown, PA 18195-1501, USA.

TERBLANCHE John, b. 10 Sept 1935, Cape Town, South Africa. Professor of Surgery. m. Anne C L Ansley, 9 Jan 1960, 3 s, 1 d. Education: MBChB, 1958, ChM, 1964, University of Cape Town; FCS, 1964; FRCS(Eng), 1965; FRCPS(Glas); FACS(Hon); Honorary FRCS, England; FRCSC(Hon); FRCS(Ed)(Hon); FACP(Hon). Appointments: Lecturer in Surgery, University of Bristol, England, 1965-67; Senior Lecturer, 1967-72, Professor of Surgery, 1973, University of Cape Town; Professor and Chairman, Department of Surgery, University of Cape Town and Groote Schuur Hospital, Cape Town, 1981-. Publications: Hepatobiliary Malignancy, Editor, 1994; Author of 3 books and 80 invited chapters in textbooks; Contributor of over 219 articles in refereed journals. Honours: Fellow, University of Cape Town, 1980-; Hans Snykers Memorial Award, 1985; Silver Medal, Medical Association of South Africa, 1991; Sims Visiting Professor, Surgical Colleges, United Kingdom, Ireland and Canada, 1991; Honorary Fellowship, American Surgical Association, 1994. Memberships: President Elect, International Association for the Study of the Liver; President, Association of Surgeons of South Africa; Past President, COllege of Medicine of South Africa; Surgical Research Society of South Africa; South African Transplantation Society. Hobbies: Outdoors; Photography. Address:

Department of Surgery, University of Cape Town, J Floor, Old Main Building, Groote Schuur Hospital, Observatory 7925, South Africa.

TERVO Timo Martti Tapio, b. 9 Mar 1950, Helsinki, Finland. Chief Physician. m. Kaarina Tervo, 10 Aug 1977, 2 sons. Education: MB, 1972; MD, 1975; PhD, 1977; Docent, 1978. Appointments: Assistant, University of Helsinki, 1972-79; Physician, Helsinki Naval Station, 1979-80; Resident, University of Helsinki, 1980; Chief Physician, 1989-. Publications: 270 scientific publications and congress abstracts. Memberships: Association of Research in Vision & Ophthalmology. Hobbies: Sailing; Skiing. Address: Jatasalmentie 9, 00830 Helsinki, Finland.

THADEPALLI Haragopal, b. Nov 1936, India. Physician. m. Carmen, 1 s, 5 d. Education: MD. Appointments: Associate Dean, Academic Programs, 1983-88, Chairman, Department of Medicine, 1986-89, Drew University School of Medicine; Professor of Medicine and Pathology, Chief of Division of Geriatrics and Gerontology, drew University of Medicine and Science s and Professor of Medicine, UCLA School of Medicine. Publications: Anatomical Basis of Infectious Disease, 1992; Antimicrobial Therapy in Intestinal Surgery, 1990; Diagnosis of Infectious Disease, 1980; Contributor of 220 works. Honours: Heritage Award, 1994; Outstanding Professor, 1992, 1993, 1994; Distinguished Physician, 1990. Memberships:: Fellow, Academy of Microbiology; Fellow, American College of Chest Physicians; Fellow, Infectious Disease Society of America. Hobby: Movies. Address: 1621 E 120th Street, Los Angeles, CA 90059, USA.

THAM Elizabeth, b. 7 Nov 1946, Singapore. Educational Psychologist. Education: BA, Honours, Singapore; LLAM, Speech and Drama, London; RT Certified, USA; MEd, Birmingham, England. Appointments: Member of Canossian Daughters of Charity, religious Order; Lecturer, Catholic Junior College; Educational Psychologist, Ministry of Education, Singapore; Director, Canossaville Children's Home, Singapore. Publications: Re-definitions of Pastoral Care from the Perspective of Sixth-Form Students, 1992. Memberships: British Psychological Society; British Association for Counselling; Singapore Psychological Society; British Alumni Association. Hobby: Swimming. Address: Canossaville Children's Home, 1 Sallim Road, Singapore 1438.

THAVARAJAH Maniccam, b. 13 May 1950, Jaffna, Sri Lanka. Dentist; Assistant Professor. m. Shantharanjani Thavarajah. 2 daughters. Education: BDS, University of Ceylon; MMedSc, PhD, Sheffield University, England. Appointments: Dental Surgeon, 1974-75, Lecturer in Human Anatomy, 1975-84, Sri Lanka; Research Scientist, Monash University, Victoria, Australia, 1982-84; Research Associate, Sheffield University, Sheffield, England. 1987-93; Assistant Professor in Human Anatomy, Sultan Qaboos University College of Medicine, Al-Khod, Muscat, Oman, 1993-. Publications: Several scientific articles in international journals. Honours: Oral Health Fellowship, 1980; Monash Research Scholar, 1982-84; Yorkshire Cancer Research Council Scholar, 1984-87; Medical Research Council Award, 1987-92. Hobbies: Photography; Current affairs. Address: College of Medicine, Sultan Qaboos University, PO Box 35, Post Code 123, Al-Khod, Muscat, Sultanate of Oman.

THEISS Phyllis Brooks, b. 3 Aug 1926, Ashtabula, Ohio, USA. Retired Counsellor. m. Chester B Theiss Jr, 19 June 1949, 1 son, 3 daughters. Education: Registered Nurse; Bachelor of Professional Arts. Appointments: Psychiatric Nurse, Louisville Veterans Administration Hospital, Kentucky, 1948, 1949; Private practice in Counselling, Louisville, 1971-89; Now retired. Memberships: Kentucky Board of Nursing; Clinical Member in International Transactional Analysis Association. Hobbies: Swimming; Scuba diving; Gardening; Birding; Reading. Address: 1808 Valley Vista Drive, Borden, IN 47106, USA.

THENABADU Pujitha Nihal, b. 29 Jul 1941, Badulla, Sri Lanka. Cardiologist. m. Shiranie R Thenabadu, 23 Jan 1967, 2 d. Education: MBBS, 1965; MD, 1969; MRCP, 1971; FACC, 1983; FRCP, 1988; FCCP, 1990. Appointments: Resident Physician, 1969-71, Cardiologist, 1972-83, General Hospital, Colombo; Consultant Cardiologist, Institute of Cardiology, General Hospital, Colombo. Publications: 12 Articles in international scientific journals; 17 Articles in national medical journals; 45 Presentations at international and national scientific congresses. Honours: Commonwealth Scholar, 1970; Invited to give the Sri Lanka Medical Association Oration. Memberships: Fellow, American College of Cardiology; Fellow, Royal College of Physicians, London, England;

Fellow, Ceylon College of Physicians; Councillor, Asian Pacific Society of Cardiac Pacing and Electrophysiology. Hobbies: Golf; Tennis. Address: 4 Charles Drive, Colombo, Sri Lanka.

THENUWARA Clarence Dayasiri, b. 12 Sept 1938, Ceylon. General Practitioner. m. Chinta Gunawardene, 19 Jul 1947, 3 sons. Education: MBBS; MB AcA; DMICAc. Appointments: District Medical Hospital, Ceylon; Currently General Practitioner, London, England. Memberships: British Medical Acupuncture Society; British Medical and Dental Hypnosis Society. Hobbies: Painting; Swimming; Manipulatioh healing; Reflexocoly. Address: 118 Restons Crescent, Eltham, London SE9 2JJ, England.

THIBAULT DE BOESINGHE Léopold A G (Baron de), b. 4 Sept 1943, Gent, Belgium, Physician. m. Isabel, 26 Mar 1981, 1 son, 1 daughter. Education: MD, Occupational Health; Special courses in Radiotherapy, Nuclear Medicine, Forensic Medicine, Radiation Protection. Appointments: Medical Director, Department of Occupational Health, University of Gent; Chief, ASZ Clinic Aalst, Department of Nuclear Medicine. Publications: Several scientific articles published abroad and in Belgium. Honours: Honorary Member, American Academy of Thermology; Officer, Order of Leopold II; Commander, Order of Saint Sepulchri; Knight, Order of the Constantinian of St Georges. Memberships: Past President, Association Européenne de Thermologie; Provincial Chamber, Board of Physicians of Oost-Vlaanderen; International College of Thermology; President, Provincial Medical Commission of OVP; Belgian Association of Radiation Protection; Ste Litt Club Gand; Société des Redoutes; University Foundation; Association of Foreign Scientists. Hobby: Photography. Address: St Martensstraat 10 B, 9000 Gent Belgium.

THIERY Michel, b. 14 Nov 1924, Gent, Belgium. MD; Gynaecologist. m. Huguette Descheemaeker, 28 Aug 1957, 1 d. Education: PhD; FRCOG. Career includes: Postgraduate Fellow, College of Physicians and Surgeons, Columbia University, NY, 1952-53; Postgraduate, Oncology, Radiology, Stockholm, 1955; Assistant Professor, 1954-63, Professor and Department Head, Obstetrics, 1963-89, Currently, Emeritus Professor, University of Gent. Publications: Books on experimental carcinoma of the cervix uteri, contraception, abortion, and induction of labour; Many articles in professional journals. Memberships: President, 1962-63, Belgian Royal Society of Obstetrics and Gynaecology; President, European Society of Perinatal Medicine, 1983; Belgian Royal Academy of Medicine, Brussels. Hobbies: History of Medicine; Hiking; Botany; Bird Watching. Address: 6 Aan de Bocht, B-9000 Gent, Belgium.

THIRION Jean Paul Joseph Marie, b. 30 Jul 1939, Metz, Moselle, France. Professor. m. Nancy Ouei, 12 Oct 1967, 2 s. Education: DSc, Institut Pasteur, Paris, France; PhD, University of WI, Madison. Appointments: CNRS, Institut Pasteur; Fellow, Academy of Science, Israel, Weizman Institut; Fellow, Oxford University, England; Professor, University of Sherbrooke. Publications: 66 Articles published, 1966-94. Honours: Fulbright Scholar; Scholar of Medical Research Council of Canada and Quebec. Membership: Genetics Society. Address: Department Microbiology, Faculty of Medicine, University of Sherbrooke, Sherbrooke, Canada, J1H 5N4.

THOMAS Eric Jackson, b. 24 Mar 1953, Hartlepool, England. Medical Practitioner. m. Narell Rennard, 23 Oct 1976, 1 s, 1 d. Education: MBBS, 1976, MD, 1987, University of Newcastle upon Tyne; MRCOG, 1983. Career: Research Fellow, 1984-85, Lecturer, 1985-87, Obstetrics and Gynaecology, University of Sheffield; Senior Lecturer, Obstetrics and Gynaecology, University of Newcastle upon Tyne, 1987-90; Currently, Professor of Obstetrics and Gynaecology and Head of the School of Medicine, University of Southampton. Publications: Co-author, The Impact of Gestrinone on The Natural History of Endometriosis, in British Medical Journal, 1987; Co-editor, Modern Approaches to Endometriosis, 1991; The Effect of Smoking on Reproductive Hormones, in Human Reproduction, 1993. Honour: William Blair Bell Memorial Lecturer, Royal College of Obstetricians and Gynaecologists, 1987. Memberships: British Association for Advancement of Science; BMA; American Fertility Society; Society for Study of Reproduction; Society for Study of Fertility. Address: Department of Obstetrics and Gynaecology, Princess Anne Hospital, Coxford Road, Southampton, SO16 4XY, England.

THOMAS Francis T, b. 24 June 1939, Hibbing, Minnesota, USA. Physician; Surgeon. m. Judith M Thomas, 21 June 1968, 3 sons.

Education: BA, BS, MA, MD, University of Minnesota; Board Certified in General Surgery, Cardiac Surgery, Transplant Surgery. Appointments: Resident, Chief Resident, Surgery, New York University, Bellevue Medical Centre; Fellow, Cardiac Surgery, Case Western Reservce Medical centre; Associate Professor, Medical College of Virginia; Professor of Surgery, University Medical Centre, University of North Carolina. Publications: Author of 1 book, 11 book chapters and 320 peer-reviewed articles, 1964-94. Memberships: American College of Surgeons; American Surgical Association; Society of University Surgeons; Societe Internationale de Chirigury. Address: 400 Wesley Drive, Greenville, NC 27834, USA.

THOMAS José Honoré Armand, b. 17 Nov 1946. Doctor. m. Lommee Christine Thomas, 23 Mar 1979, 2 s. Education: Internal Medicine; Medical Oncology. Appointments: Joint Chief of Staff; Protocol Review Committee, EORTC. Memberships: Founding Member, Belgian Society of Medical Oncology; Secretary EORTC Cooperative Lymphoma Group; ESMO. Address: Hof 10 Bekelaan 4, B-3020 Herent, Belgium.

THOMAS Joseph Paul, b. 11 Oct 1947, Biloxi, Mississippi, USA. Physician; Psychiatrist. m. Sandra Elam, 26 Jan 1974, 1 s, 2 d. Education: BA; MA; MD. Appointments include: Chairman, Department of Psychiatry, Providence Hospital, 1986; Sleep Disorders Committee, 1991, Psychiatric Services Committee, 1984-92, The Mobile Infirmary; Mental Illness Awareness Week Publicity Committee, The Mental Health Association, 1991-92; Chairman, Ethics Committee, Alabama Psychiatric Society, 1988-91; Private Practice. Publications: Contributor of numerous professional articles and television programmes. Honours: Fellow, American Psychiatric Association; President, Alabama Psychiatric Society, 1993-94. Memberships: AMA; APA. Address: PO Box 8309, Mobile, AL 36689-8309, USA.

THOMPSON E(dward) Brad(bridge), b. 20 Dec 1933, Burlington, Iowa, USA. Professor (Human Genetics, Internal Medicine). m. Lynn Parsons, 1 son, 1 daughter. Education: BA, Rice University, Houston, Texas; MD, Harvard Medical School, Boston, Massachusetts; Residency, Presbyterian Hospital, Columbia University, New York City, 1961-62. Appointments: National Institutes of Health, Bethesda, Maryland, 1962-84; I H Kempner Professor of Human Genetics, Chairman, Department of Human Biological Chemistry and Genetics, Professor of Internal Medicine, University of Texas Medical Branch, Galveston, 1984-; Founding Editor, Molecular Endocrinology, 1986-93. Publications: Over 200 articles in journals, books in his field; Editor, 6 books in field. Honours: Phi Beta Kappa; Alpha Omega Alpha; Fulbright Scholar, 1992; American Cancer Society Research Scholar, 1992. Memberships: American College of Medical Genetics; American Association for Cancer Research; American Society for Biochemistry and Molecular Biology; American Society for Cell Biology; American Society of Human Genetics; American Society for Microbiology; Endocrine Society; Tissue Culture Association; Southwest Environmental Mutants Society. Hobbies: Sailing; Tennis; Gardening. Address: Department of Human Biological Chemistry and Genetics, The University of Texas Medical Branch, 603 Basic Science Bldg 0645, Galveston, TX 77555-0645, USA.

THOMPSON James Lloyd, b. 26 June 1927, New Haven, USA. Counselor. m. Barbara Longfellow, 17 Nov 1955, 3 sons. Education: AB, University of Missouri; MS. Appointments: Director of Intelligence, Na Trang, Vietnam & Whiteman AFB, 1965-69; Vocational Rehabilitation Counselor, 1969-77; Executive Director, Covenant House Inc. Publications: History of Foster-Parenting in Lafayette County, 1978. Honours: Psi Chi National Honour Society, 1950; Honorary Life Member, USC Alumni Association, 1964; Bronze Star Medal, USAF, 1968. Memberships: NAR; AAMD; MCDD. Hobbies: Music; Boating; Renovating. Address: 740 E Eastwood, Marshall MO, USA.

THOMPSON William Moreau, b. 20 Oct 1943, Philadelphia, PA, USA. Medicine. m. Judy Ann Seal, 27 Jul 1968, 2 s. Education: BA, Colgate; MD, University of PA; Radiology Residency, Duke University Medical Center, Durham, NC. Appointments: Assistant Professor, 1975-77, Associate Professor, 1977-82, Professor, 1982-86, Duke University; Diagnostic Radiologist, Professor and Chairman, University of MN, 1986-. Publications: Over 200 articles and book chapters. Honours: James Picker Scholar, 1975-79; Fellow, American College of Radiologists, 1982; Vilholmina and Eugene Gedguadas Chair in Radiology, 1988-. Memberships: President, Association of University Radiologists, 1990; President, Society GI Radiologists, 1994-95; RSNA; AUR; Society of Gastrointestinal Radiologists; ACR; American

Radiology Society. Hobby: Sport. Address: Box 292 UMHC, Department of Radiology, 420 Delaware Street, Minneapolis, MN 55455, USA.

THORBURN Dennis Newstead, b. 14 June 1940, Morrinsville, New Zealand. Specialist Dental Practitioner. m. Susan Eggleton, 9 Dec 1968, 1 son, 3 daughters. Education: BDS, University of Otago, NZ, 1968; FDSRCS, Edinburgh, 1972. Career: Lecturer, Guys Hospital, University of London, 1972-74; Senior Lecturer, School of Dentistry, University of Otago, Dunedin, New Zealand; Visiting Specialist in Oral Medicine, Canterbury Area Health Board, New Zealand; Senior Clinical Lecturer, Christchurch Clinical Medical School, New Zealand. Publications: 11 papers in refereed journals including: Mandibular Dysfunction in Children with Otalgia, 1985; Exposure Factors and Film-Screen Combinations in Temporomandibular Joint Radiography, 1991; Familial Ogee Roots, Tooth Mobility, Oligodontia and Microdontia, 1992; Topical Steroids and Lesions of the Oral Mucosa, 1994; The Anterior Displaced Disc: Aetiology and Diagnosis, 1994. Honour: University of Otago School of Dentistry Travelling Scholar, 1970; NZ Dental Association Inaugural Travelling Fellow, 1988. Memberships: NZDA; British Association Oral & Maxillofacial Surgeons; NZ Health Boards Dental Surgeons Association; NZ Pain Society. Hobbies: Hill-Walking; Music; Gardening. Address: 50 Cannon Hill Crescent, St Andrews Hill, Christchurch 8008, New Zealand.

THORNE Elizabeth, b. 14 Apr 1919, Evanston, Illinois, USA. Clinical Psychologist. Education: PhD Clinical Psychology, New York University, 1967; JD, Law, University of Michigan, Ann Arbor, Michigan, 1943; AB, Vassar College, Poughkeepsie, New York, 1940. Appointments: Lawyer, Dewey Ballantine, New York, 1943; Lawyer, Private Practice, New York, 1952-; Psychologist, Private Practice, New York, 1969-. Publications: Psychoanalysis Today : A Case Book. Memberships: American Psychological Association; New York State Psychological Association; National Psychological Association for Psychoanalysis Inc. Address: 265 East 66 Street, New York, NY 10021, USA.

THORNGATE George, b. 18 June 1921, Madison, WI, USA. Physician. m. Helen McFarland, 25 June 1944, 5 daughters. Education: BA, Milton College; MD, University at Buffalo. Appointments: Medical Staff, Monterey County Hospital; President, Medical Staff, Monterey Hospital; Chairman, Obstetrics & Gynecology Staff, Chomp; Retired. Memberships: Monterey County Medical Society; California Medical Association; American Medical Association; American College of Obstetrics & Gynecology; San Francisco Gynecological Society. Hobbies: Skiing; Hiking; Travel; College Courses in Western Civilization History. Address: 4134 El Bosque Drive, Pebble Beach, CA 93953-3013, USA.

THORNTON Steven, b. 4 Nov 1959, Lincoln, England. Obstetrician. m. Georgina Thornton, 9 May 1993, 1 son. Education: BM, 1983, DM, 1989, Southampton University; MRCOG, 1989. Appointments: Clinical Scientist. Publications: British Medical Journal, 297, 167-9, 1988; American Journal of Physiology, 259, F21-24, 1990; Experimental Physiology, 72, 293-305, 1992. Honour: Blair Bell Memorial Lecture, 1994. Memberships: The Physiological Society; Society for Endocrinology; East Anglian Obsterical and Gynaecological Society. Hobbies: Squash; Motor sport. Address: Department of Obstetrics, Rosie Maternity Hospital, Robinson Way, Cambridge CB2 2SW, England.

THREEFOOT Sam A, b. 10 Apr 1921, Meridian, Mississippi, USA. Physician. m. Virginia Rush, 6 Feb 1954, 4 daughters. Education: BS, College of Arts and Sciences, Tulane University, 1943; MD, 1945, Fellowship, 1947-49, Tulane University School of Medicine. Appointments include: Consultant, Charity Hospital, New Orleans, 1969-70, 1976-; Professor, 1963-70, 1975-91, Assistant Dean, Veterans Affairs, 1979-91, Professor Emeritus, 1991-; Professor, Assistant Dean, Medical College of Georgia, Augusta, 1970-76; Chief of Staff, VA Medical Center, Forest Hills Division, Augusta, 1970-76; Associate Chief of Staff for Research, 1976-79, Chief of Staff, 1979-91, Consultant, 1991-, VA Medical Center, New Orleans; Professor of Medicine, 1979-91, Coordinator, Veterans Affairs, 1979-91, Louisiana State University School of Medicine, New Orleans. Publications: Articles, papers, chapters, including: Hypotension, 1949; A Shielded Coil for Continuous Scintillation Monitoring of Circulating Radioactivity, 1966; Physiology and Pathophysiology of Lymphaticovenous Communications, 1969; Disordered Lymph Flow-An Overview, 1977; Co-author: Theoretic Consideration of Biologic Decay Rates of Isotopes, 1949; Clinical Problems in Fluid and Electrolyte Balance in the Aged, 1957; Collateral

Circulation, Renal Function and Histology after Experimental Obstruction of Renal Veins, 1970. Honours include: Honour Scholarship, Tulane University College of Arts and Sciences, 1938-41; Beta Mu, 1940; Phi Beta Kappa, 1943; Award of Merit, American Heart Association, 1976. Memberships include: Sigma Xi; Fellow, American College of Physicians; Fellow, American College of Cardiology; National Association of VA Chiefs of Staff, Executive Committee 1984-, President 1988; American, Louisiana and Georgia Heart Associations, committees, offices; New York Academy of Sciences. Address: 347 Millaudon St, New Orleans, LA 70118, USA.

THUN Michael John, b. 29 Sep 1944, Reading, Pennsylvania, USA. Epidemiologist. m. Patricia Lynn Moody, 22 Dec 1974, 2 sons, 1 daughter. Education: BA, cum laude, Harvard College, 1970; MD, University of Pennsylvania, 1975; MS, Epidemiology, Harvard University, 1983; Diplomate, American Board of Occupational Medicine, American Board Preventive Medicine. Appointments: Medical Intern, University of Florida, Gainesville, 1975-76; Medical Resident, 1976-77; Medical Officer, New Jersey State Health Department, Trenton, 1978-80; EPidemic Intelligence Service Officer, US Centres for Disease Control, National Institute for Occupational Safety and Health, Cincinnati, 1980-82; Supervisor, 1983-89; Clinical Associate Professor, Emory University School Public Health, 1990-; Director, Analytic Epidemiology, American Cancer Society. Publications: Teaching Epidemiology in Occupational Health, Associate Edityor, 1987; Author of chapters in books; Editorial Board Member, Epidemiology; Reviewer in several professional journals; Contributor of articles to professional journals. Honours: Charles C Sheppard Science Award, 1993; Alice Hamilton Science Award, 1993; Captain, USPHS, 1980-89. Memberships: APHA; AAAS; Society for Epidemiologic Research; Physicians for Social Responsibility. Hobbies: Hiking; Camping; Travel; Birdwatching. Address: American Cancer Society, 1599 Clifton Road NE, Atlanta, GA 30329, USA.

TIAN Chang Ying, b. 14 Sep 1937, Shang Dong, China. Doctor. m. Lu Dao Yuang, 20 Jun 1967, 1 d. Education: Graduate, Medical College. Career: Nurse, 1961; Doctor, 1972; Physician in Charge, 1987; Associate Professor, 1992. Publications: Clinical survey of 80 infants with poor appetite by Tui Na treatment, in Shan Dong Chinese Medicine, 1983; Qi Lu Tui Na Medicine, 1987; Treatment on infants with convulsions by Tui Na, in Journal of Chiropody, 1991. Honours: Woman Heroine Cup, 1990; World Life Cup, Chinese Traditional Medicine, 1993. Membership: Society of Chinese Traditional Medicine. Hobby: Tui Na. Address: No 19 Room 101, Jiang Su Road, Qing Dao, China.

TIAN Fenlan, b. 2 June 1936, Hebei Province, China. Doctor. m. Zhao Jingzhou, 8 Aug 1965, 2 daughters. Education: BM, Tianjin College of Traditional Chinese Medicine. Appointments: Director, Internal Department, 1977, Vice-President, 1981, President, 1983, No 2 Hospital Attached to Tianjin College of Traditional Chinese Medicine; Consultant, Association of Chinese Traditional Medicine in Canada. Publications: Clinical Observation on 210 Coronary Heart Disease by the Method of Activating the Blood and Eliminating Stagnant, 1985; Longlife For You, Co-author, 1986; The Research on Mechanism and Reason of Acute Myocardial Infarct by Traditional Chinese Medicine, 1987; Research of the Relation Between the Hour and Acute Myocardial Infarct, 1987; Review of the Clinical Research on Acute Myocardial Infarct by Traditional Chinese Medicine, 1990; Modern Internal Medicine of Traditional Chinese Medicine, Co-author, 1991; The Curing of Heart Failure by Qiangxinling-some Medicine Helping Heart Working, 1994. Honours: 2nd Grade Medal for Great Achievement in Science and Technology, Public Ministry, 1988; 2nd Medal of Achievement in Science and Technology, Tianjin Science Committee; Specialist Enjoying Privileged Allowance by State Council. Memberships: Internal Medicine of China Association of Traditional Chinese Medicine; Tianjin Association of Traditional Chinese Medicine; China Professional Committee in Candiopathy. Hobby: Qi Gong. Address: 1 Shanlin Li, Beian Street, Hebei District, Tianjin 300010, China.

TIBBLES Paul Nicholas, b. 10 Feb 1958, Isle of Wight, England. Clinical Psychologist. Education: BA (Hons), Psychology; MSc, Human Communication; MSc, Clinical Psychology; Plymouth Polytechnic, 1979; Guy's Hospital Medical School, 1980; Surrey University, 1988. Appointments: Mental Health Officer, London Borough of Merton; Currently Principal Clinical Psychologist, Adult Mental Health. Publications: The Very Small Group (co-author), 1986; Changes in Depression and Personal Construing, 1992; Silence of Symbiosis, 1992. Honours: Chartered Psychologist, 1990; Elected Associate Fellow,

British Psychological Society, 1992. Hobbies: Sculpture; Painting; Drama and mime; Riding. Address: Department of Psychology, The Gordon Hospital, Bloomburg Street, Westminster, London SW1, England.

TICHENOR Wellington S, b. 29 Oct 1950, New York City, USA. Physician. Education: MD, New York Medical College; BSE cum laude, Princeton University, 1972. Appointments: Associate Medical Director, American International Group, 1978-80; Private Practice, 1981-. Publications: Sulfite Sensitivity, Co-author, 1985; Fiberoptic Laryngoscopy in an Allergy Practice, Co-author, 1986. Honours: Leonard P Wershub MD Award for Academic Excellency, Cor et Manus, 1975; Sigma Xi. Memberships: American College of Physicians; American Academy of Allergy and Immunology; American College of Allergy and Immunology; New York State and County Medical Society; New York State Allergy Society; AMA. Hobbies: Skiing; Tennis. Address: 642 Park Avenue, New York, NY 10021, USA.

TILSON Donald H Jr, b. 23 Mar 1930, Tarrytown, New York, USA. Doctor of Medicine. m. Kirtley Jane Gunn, 26 July 1952, 2 s, 2 d. Education: MD, Washington University, School of Medicine, 1955; AB, Harvard College, 1951; MHA, Baylor, 1968. Appointments: Lt to Col, United States Army Medical Corps, 1956-77; NW Permanente PC (Kaiser), Portland, Oregon, USA, 1977-; Physician in Charge, Fracture Clinic, Kaiser West Interstate Medical Offices, Portland, Oregon. Honours: Phi Beta Kappa, 1950; Alpha Omega Alpha, 1955; Army Decorations: Army Commendation Medal (Oak Leaf Cluster); Bronze Star Legion of Merit; Distinguished Service Medal; Vietnam Campaign Medal. Memberships: American Academy of Orthopaedic Surgeons; American Academy of Occupational & Environmental Medicine. Hobbies: Walking; Swimming; Reading; Music. Address: Kaiser West Interstate Medical Offices, 3325 No. Interstate Ave, Portland, OR 97227-1099, USA.

TILSON Hugh Hanna, b. 6 Jan 1940, Pennsylvania, USA. Physician. m. Judith Scullion, 10 June 1961, 2 sons, 2 daughters. Education: BA, Reed College, 1963; MD, Washington University School of Medicine, St Louis, Missouri, 1964; Medical Field Service School, Fort Sam Houston, Texas, 1965; MPH, 1969, DPh, 1972, Harvard School of Public Health, Boston; Government Executives Institute Certificate, University of North Carolina School of Business Administration, 1980; Physician Retraining Programme Certificate, Medical College of Pennsylvania, Philadelphia, 1981; London Business School, Senior Management Forum, 1993. Appointments include: Preventive Medicine Officer, US Army, Germany, 1965-68; Health Officer, Multnomah County, Oregon, 1971-78; Health Officer, State of Noerth Carolina; International Vice President, Burroughs Wellcome Company. Publications: Author or Editor of over 120 articles, abstracts, book chapters and monographs. Honours include: Phi Beta Kappa; Alpha Omega Alpha; Mosby Book Prize, Washington University; Army Commendation Medal, 24th Infantry Division, 1966; Army Commendation Medal, 1st Oak Leaf Cluster, 1968; Special Award for Outstanding Contribution, Northwest Oregon Health Systems Agency, 1978; Distinguished Service Award, American College of Preventive Medicine, 1991; Lifetime Member, American Association of Pharmaceutical Physicians, 1994-. Memberships include: American Board of Preventive Medicine, Vice Chairman; American College of Preventive Medicine, President, 1995-97; Drug Information Association; Oregon Public Health Association. Hobbies: Music; Travel. Address: Burroughs Wellcome Company, 3030 Cornwallis Road, Research Triangle Park, NC 27709, USA.

TIMMS Michael William Hector, b. 21 Mar 1947, Dorchester, England. Psychologist. m. Joyce Taylor, 29 Aug 1975, 1 son, 1 daughter. Education: BA; MSc; PhD; CPsychol; AFBPsS; AFpsSI. Appointments: Psychologist to Dublin Health Authority and Eastern Health Board; Coordinator of Counselling, Irish Multiple Sclerosis Society; Senior Psychologist to Eastern Health Board; Currently Senior Psychologist to Irish National Rehabilitation Board. Publications: Genesis of a Drug Abuse Epidemic - A Case of Social Imitation (with Carney), 1977; Survey of the Needs for a Clinical Psychologist for Wicklow General Practitioners, 1979; Treatment of Chronic Blushing by Paradoxical Intention, 1980; The Treatment of Urinary Frequency by Paradoxical Intention, 1985; Psychology and Cancer: A Review, 1989; Psychologists Working with General Practitioners, 1990. Honours: English Speaking Union Scholar to USA, 1965-66; Japanese Department of Foreign Affairs European Community Scholar to Tokyo, 1981. Memberships: British Psychological Society; Psychological

Society of Ireland. Hobby: Canoeing. Address: 201 Ardmore Park, Bray, Co Wicklow, Republic of Ireland.

TING Bau-luo, b. 3 Aug 1923, Zhengzhou, Honan, China. Teacher; Doctor. m. Li Shu-Ren, 6 June 1949, 1 son, 2 daughters. Education: Graduate, West China Medical University Dental College, 1954. Appointments: Head, Department of Dental Medicine, Secondary Medical School, 1954-62; Director, Dental Department, Affiliated Hospital of Luzhou Medical College, 1963-93; Dean, Yan-King Correspondence Medical College, Luzhou. Publications: Dental Medicine, 1960; Preventive Dentistry, 1987; Prevented and Treated Dental Caries for Children in Luzhou, 1988; Prevented and Treated Endemic Fluorosis in Gu-Len County, 1988; Honours: Excellent Teacher, 1985; Excellent Educationalist, 1989; Excellent Member, Chinese People's Political Consultative Conference, Luzhou, 1992. Membership: Director, Chinese Medical Association, Luzhou. Hobby: Music. Address: The Affiliated Hospital of Luzhou Medical College, Luzhou 646000, Sichuan, China.

TINKLE James S, b. 1947, Oregon, USA. Endodontist. m. Sandra McCoy. Education: BS, Portland State University, 1974; DMD, University of Oregon, 1979; FACD; FICD. Appointment: Associate Professor of Endodontology. Memberships: Fellow, American College of Dentists; Fellow, International College of Dentists; Fellow, Pierre Fanchard Academy; American Association of Endodontists; American Association of Dental Schools. Address: Oregon Health Sciences University School of Dentistry, 611 SW Campus Drive, Portland, OR 97201, USA.

TINKLENBERG Jared R, b. 25 Nov 1939, Madison, South Dakota, USA. Psychiatrist. m. Mae Van Der Weerd, 8 Aug 1964, 2 d. Education: BA, Medical Degree, 1965; University of Iowa. Appointments: Instructor, Associate Professor, Stanford University; Professor, Stanford Medical Centre. Publications: Marijuana Hazards, 1965; Drug and Criminal Assaults by Adolescents, 1981. Honours: Medical AOA, Honours Scholar, University of Iowa Medical School, 1965. Memberships: Fellow, American Psychiatric Association; Fellow, American College of Neuropsychopharmacology. Hobbies: Jogging; Hiking. Address: Palo Alto Veterans Affairs Medical centre, 3801 Miranda Avenue, Palo Alto, CA 94305, USA.

TIOLLAIS Pierre, b. 8 Dec 1934, Rennes, France. Professor. m. Iréne Manheimer, 18 July 1987, 1 son. Education: MD. Appointments: Professor, University Paris VII, 1972; Chef de laboratoire, 1979, Professor, 1988, Institute Pasteur, Paris. Publications: Contributor of articles in professional journals. Honours: Prix SOVAC, 1988; Prix Athena, 1990; Prix de la fondation pour la Recherche Médicale, 1990. Memberships: French Academy of Sciences. Hobbies: Fishing; Magic. Address: Institut Pasteur, 28 rue du Docteur Roux, 75724 Paris Cedex 15, France.

TIPANS Igors, b. 7 Feb 1953, Riga, Latvia. Associate Professor of Mechanics. 1 son, 1 daughter. Education: Graduate, St Petersburg Polytechnic Institute, Russia, 1976; Postgraduate, Riga Technical University, Latvia, 1985; Postdoctoral Research, Duke University, 1988-89. Appointments: Researcher, Riga Polytechnic Institute; Assistant Professor, Riga Technical University. Publications: The Quantitative Investigation of the Binding Process of Calcium Blocking Drugs, 1991. Memberships: Senior Member, Biomedical Engineering Society; National Mechanics Committee; Latvian Scientists Union. Hobbies: Model Trains; Swimming; Boat Tours. Address: Department of Theoretical Mechanics, Riga Technical University, Kalku St 1A, Riga, LV-1658, Latvia.

TIPIRNENI Padma, b. 7 Dec 1945, India. Medicine. m. Haranath Tipirneni, 10 Feb 1967, 1 s, 1 d. Education: MD; FAAA; FACA; FAAP; Diplomate, American Board of Pediatrics and Allergy, Immunology. Appointment: Consultant Allergist and Immunologist. Membership: American Medical Association. Address: 903 Burroak Court, Oakbrook, IL 60521, USA.

TIRIBELLI Claudio, b. 6 Oct 1946, Venice, Italy. Professor of Medicine. m. Rita Russo, 27 May 1972, 1 son. Education: MD, University of Padova, 1971; PhD, Gastroenterology, University of Trieste, 1975. Appointments: Research Professor, 1972-74, Research Associate, 1974-80, Research Professor of Medicine, 1980-82, 1983-90, Full Professor of Medicine, 1990-, University of Trieste; Visiting Scientist, University of Groningen, Netherlands, 1982; Visiting Professor, Polytechnic University, New York, 1989-. Publications: Several papers in peer-reviewed international journals; Co-author, reviews on bilirubin metabolism. Honours: Secretary, European Association for the Study of the Liver, 1983-85; Secretary, Educational Council, European Association for the Study of the Liver, 1992-. Memberships: European Association for the Study of the Liver; International Association for the Study of the Liver; American Society for the Study of Liver Disease; Sigma Xi; New York Academy of Sciences. Hobbies: Various sports; Flying. Address: Centro Studi Fegato, University of Trieste, 34100 Trieste, Italy.

TITTMAR Heinz-Günther, b. 18 June 1945, Ehrhorn/Soltau, Federal Republic of Germany. Academic. m. Joan Elizabeth Gray, 16 Dec 1967, div 1995, 2 sons. Education: BA, 1969, PhD, 1973, Queen's University, Belfast; Chartered Psychologist. Appointments: Demonstrator, 1968-73, Teaching Assistant, 1973, Queen's University, Belfast, Northern Ireland; Temporary Lecturer, Ulster College, Jordanstown, 1974-75; Lecturer II, 1975-82, Senior Lecturer, 1982-84, Ulster Poly, Newtownabbey; Lecturer, 1984-85, Reader, 1985-, University of Ulster. Publications: Editor and author: Advanced Concepts in Alcoholism, 1984; Spiegelbilder, 1988; Chapters to books and articles on fetal alcohol syndrome, alcoholism, biorhythms, sex and reproduction, time, sport, social skills training. Honours: Honorary Mention, Gravity Research Foundation, 1972; Postdoctoral Research Fellow, Medical Council for Alcoholism, London, 1975-78; Recipient, Territorial Decoration, 1982, 1988; DSc, 1989, MD (MA), 1990, Open International University, Colombo. Memberships: Associate Fellow, British Psychological Society; Psychonomic Society; British Institute of Sport Coaches; Knight Templar. Hobby: Full-bore target shooting; Coaching (sport). Address: Department of Psychology, University of Ulster, Newtownabbey BT37 0QB, Northern Ireland.

TITUS George, b. 23 Sept 1951, Johor Baru, Malaysia. Medical Doctor. m. Susy Mathews, 22 Sept 1990. Education: MBBS. Appointments: Medical Officer, General Hospital, Johor Baru; Currently General Practitioner, own clinic. Memberships: Malaysian Medical Council; Malaysian Medical Association. Hobbies: Reading; Cycling; Fishing; Gardening. Address: Kelinik Sawit, S-82 Jalan Selamat, Kelapa Sawit, 81030 Kulai, Johor, West Malaysia, Malaysia.

TIU Nanneth, b. Dumaguete City, Philippines. Physician. Education: MD; Fellow in Allergy-Immunology. Appointments include: Currently, Consultant. Publications: Co-author: Incidence of Dust Mite Allergy in Blacks, 1986; A Case Report of Schwachmann's Syndrome, 1988. Honours: Model Student of the Year, Cebu Eastern College, 1971; Cum laude, Pre-Med, 1974; Scholar, 1st Year Medicine, 1974; Gold Medallist in History of Medicine, 1978. Memberships: Secretary, Manila Medical Society; Vice President, Association of Asia Brewery Medical Scholars; American Academy of Allergy and Immunology; American College of Allergy; Philippine Medical Association; Philippine Society of Allergy and Immunology. Hobbies: Swimming; Singing. Address: Chinese General Hospital and Medical Center, 286 Blumentritt Street, Sta Cruz, Manila, Philippines.

TIZON Jorge L, b. 20 Apr 1946, La Coruña, Spain. Psychiatrist; Psychoanalyst. m. Maria J Marcos, 31 July 1971, 1 son, 1 daughter. Education: MD, University of Salamanca; PsD, Universidad Pontificia de Salamanca; PhD; Universidad de Barcelona. Appointments: Associate Professor, University of Barcelona; Titular Professor, University School of Social Work, University of Barcelona; Director, Mental Health Unity La Verbeda-La Pau-La Mina, Barcelona. Publications: Introducción Epistemología de la Psicopatología, 1978; Apuntes para una Psicología basada en la Relación, 1988, 1992, 1993; Componentes psicologicos de la práctica mèdica, 1988; Atenció Primaria en Salud Mental, 1992. Honours: Luis Martin Santos National Prize in Neuropsychiatry, 1993. Memberships: Asociación Española de Neuropsiquiatría; Sociedad Española de Psicología; Sociedad Española de Psicoanálisis. Hobbies: Mountaineering; Cycling. Address: Lauría 130, 1o 3a, 08037 Barcelona, Spain.

TKACHENKO Grigory Ivanonich, b. 13 Mar 1939, Trylisy, Ukraine. Physician. m. Albina Trush, 23 Feb 1972, 1 son. Education: Candidate of Science, Medicine; Diploma of Physician, Kharkov Medical Institute, 1956-62. Appointments: Researcher, 1965-91, Head, Department of Radiodiagnosis, 1991-95, Kharkiv Research Institute of Medical Radiology. Publications: Diagnosis and Treatment of Thyroid Diseases in Children, 1993; Radionuclide Diagnosis for Thyroid Diseases Diagnosis, 1992. Membership: Ukrainian Society of Radiologists.

Hobbies: Gardening; Fishing. Address: Institute of Medical Radiology, Pushkinska 82, Kharkiv 310024, Ukraine.

TOBIN Colm, b. 17 Apr 1943, Co Clare, Ireland. Psychologist. m. Emer, Aug 1992. Education: BA; HDE; Dip Psych; AFPsS; CPsychol; AFBPhS. Appointments: Teacher; Company Director; Careers Officer, University College Dublin. Publications: Contributor of several articles in journals. Memberships: BPS; PSI. Hobby: Golf. Address: 99 Rowanbyrn, Blackrock, Co Dublin, Ireland.

TOBOLOWSKY David Martone, b. 22 Jul 1953, Dallas, TX, USA. Psychiatrist. m. Patrice Robbins, 28 Dec 1980, 1 s, 2 d. Education: BS, Southern Methodist University, 1974; MD, University of TX, Southwestern Medical School, 1978; Resident, Psychiatry, University of Miami, Jackson Memorial Hospital, 1978-82. Appointments: Private Practice in Psychiatry; Clinical Associate Professor, Department of Psychiatry, University of Miami School of Medicine. Honour: Fellow, American Psychiatric Association, 1993. Memberships: American, Florida and Dade County Medical Associations; American Psychiatric Association; South FL Psychiatric Society, Secretary, 1992-94. Hobby: Chess. Address: 7400 N Kendall Drive No 310, Miami, FL 33156-7706, USA.

TOCK Edward Peng Chong, b. 10 May 1934, Singapore. Pathologist; University Professor. m. Lim Wen Mei, 5 Aug 1961, 2 daughters. Education: MB BS, MD, Singapore; PhD, London; FRCPath, London, FRCPA; FCAP; FAMS; FCPS. Appointments: Medical Officer, Ministry of Health, Singapore; Assistant Lecturer, Lecturer, Senior Lecturer, Associate Professor in Pathology, National University of Singapore; Currently: Professor, Head, Department of Pathology, Dean, Faculty of Medicine, National University of Singapore; Chief of Pathology, Chairman of Medical Board, National University Hospital, Singapore. Publications: More than 100 scientific papers in regional and international refereed journals including British Medical Journal, British Journal of Urology, Journal of Anatomy, American Journal of Obstetrics and Gynecology, American Journal of the Diseases of Children, Thorax, American Review of Respiratory Diseases, Pathology, Quarterly Journal of Medicine, American Journal of the Medical Sciences, Journal of Pathology, American Journal of Clinical Pathology, Acta Oncologica. Honours: Public Administration Medal, President of the Republic of Singapore, 1980; Officier, Ordre des Palmes Académiques, President of the Republic of France, 1984; Honorary Fellow, College of General Practitioners, Singapore. Memberships: Singapore Medical Association; Singapore Society of Pathology; Academy of Medicine, Singapore. Hobbies: Swimming; Jogging; Bush trekking; Tennis; Music. Address: Department of Pathology, National University of Singapore, National University Hospital, Singapore 0511.

TODD Christopher James, b. 1 Dec 1956, Bournemouth, England. Health Psychologist. Education: BA, Honours, Psychology, 1978, MA, 1981, PhD, 1988, University of Durham, England; CPsychol; AFBPsS. Career: Research Officer, Centre for Applied Health Studies, University of Ulster, Northern Ireland, 1987-90; Research Associate, 1990-92, Currently, Senior Research Associate and Director, Health Services Research Group, University of Cambridge, England; Fellow, Wolfson College Cambridge, 1995-. Memberships: British Psychological Society. Hobbies: Greenhouse Gardening; Wine Tasting; Squash. Address: Health Services Research Group, Institute of Public Health, University of Cambridge, Robinson Way, Cambridge, CB2 2SR, England.

TODUA Fridon Ippolit, b. 9 Jan 1944, Zugdidi. Radiologist. m. Shenelaia Tina, 12 Nov 1974, 1 d. Education: Tbilisi State Medical Institute, 1962-68; MD, 1984; PhD, 1989; Academician, 1994. Career: Junior Research Assistant, Senior Research Assistant, Thoracic Department, Moscow Institute of Surgery; Senior Research Assistant, Chief of CT Department, Contrast and Intravenous Rontg Investigating Laboratory; Currently, Radiologist. Publications: Co-author, Diagnostic problems of local diseases of the liver, 1992; Computed tomography of the abdomen, 1992; US diagnostic of surgical diseases of the liver and biliar ducts, 1993. Honour: State Award of Russia, 1988. Memberships: European Radiology Association; North American Radiology Association; International Gastro-Surgical Club; Georgian Radiology Association. Hobbies: Tennis; Travel. Address: Chavchavadze av 19-19, Tbilisi 380079, Republic of Georgia.

TOMAR Russell Herman, b. 19 Oct 1937, Philadelphia, PA, USA. Physician. m. Karen Kent, 29 Aug 1965, 1 s, 1 d. Education: AB, Journalism, MD, Medicine, George Washington University.

Appointments include: Senior Assistant Surgeon, NIH Division of Biologics Standards, 1981-; Interim Director of Clinical Pathology, SUNY Health Science Center, 1986-87; Professor of Medicine, Professor of Pathology and Laboratory Medicine, Director of Clinical Laboratories, University of WI Center for Health Sciences, 1988-. Publications include: Co-author, Manual of Laboratory Immunology, 2nd edition, 1990; Author, Serological factors in the pathogenesis of HIV infection, in AIDS and Other Manifestations of HIV Infection, 2nd edition, 1992; Author, Breaking the asymptomatic phase of HIV 1 infection, in Journal of Clinical Laboratory Anal, 1994. Memberships: American Society of Clinical Pathology; Clinical Immunology Society; College of American Pathologists; American Association for Advancement of Science; American Association of Immunology. Hobbies: Tennis; Dramatic and Music Theatre; Classical Music. Address: University of WI Hospital and Clinics, 600 Highland Avenue, Madison, WI 53792-2472, USA.

TOMLINSON Brian, b. 24 Jan 1950, Beverley, England. Physician. m. Ruth Newbon, 9 Jul 1983. Education: BSc, Middlesex Hospital Medical School, London, 1970; MBBS, London, 1973; MRCP(UK), 1976; MD, London, 1993; FRCP(London), 1994; FRCP(Edin), 1994; FHKAM(Medicine), 1994. Career: Lecturer in Medicine, University College Hospital, London, 1980-83; Lecturer in Clinical Pharmacology, University College and Middlesex School of Medicine, 1983-90; Currently, Senior Lecturer in Clinical Pharmacology, Chinese University of Hong Kong. Publications: Co-author, Clinical Pharmacology of Urapidil, in Journal Hypertens, 1988; Co-author, Clinical Pharmacology of Drugs Acting on the Sympathetic Nervous System, in Current Opinion in Cardiology, 1989; Co-author, Clinical Pharmacology of Carvedilol, in Clinical Investigating, 1992; Co-author, Chinese Herbal Medicines Revisited - A Hong Kong Perspective, Lancet, 1993. Memberships: Fellow, Royal College of Physicians, London; Royal College of Physicians, Edinburgh; Hong Kong Academy of Medicine; International Hypertension Society; British Pharmacological Society; British Hyperlipidaemia Association. Hobbies: Travel; Sailing. Address: Department of Clinical Pharmacology, Prince of Wales Hospital, Shatin, Hong Kong.

TONG (TUNG) Tan-jun (Tan-chun), b. 15 Aug 1934, Zhejiang, China. Biochemist. m. Zong-yu Zhang, 17 July 1963, 2 daughters. Education: MD, Beijing Medical University, 1959; Visiting Scholar, The Johns Hopkins University, USA, 1979-80; Postdoctoral Fellow, National Institutes of Health, USA, 1980-81. Appointments: Faculty Member, 1964-78, Associate Professor, Vice-Chairman, Department of Biochemistry, 1985, Professor, Director, 1988-, Beijing Medical University; Visiting Associate Professor, Department of Biological Chemistry, University of California at Davis, USA, 1986-87. Publications: Cancer-suppressive activity of biological fluids, 1979; Purification and characterization of a tumor-associated high molecular weight serum DNA binding protein, 1991; Nuclear mechanisms of peptide growth factor action, 1994; Medical Gerontology, in press. Honours: International Research Fellowship, Ministry of Education, 1978-80; NIH Fellowship, USA, 1980-81; Outstanding Contribution for Medical and Health Development Award, State Council of China, 1992. Memberships: Chinese Biochemical Society; Chinese Physiological Science Society; Chinese Gerontological Society; Chinese Cancer Research Foundation. Hobby: Reading. Address: Department of Biochemistry and Molecular Biology, Beijing Medical University, 38 Xue-yuan Road, Beijing 100083, China.

TOON Kay, b. 7 Feb 1952. Clinical Psychologist. Education: BS, Honours; MPhil; MS; Chartered Clinical Psychologist; AFBPsS. Appointments Systems Engineer, ICL; Lecturer in Psychology, University of Leeds, England; Consultant Clinical Psychologist. Publications: Breaking Free - Help for Survivors of Sexual Abuse, Co-author, 1993. Memberships: Associate Fellow, British Psychological Society. Hobbies: Adventure holidays; Walking; Dancing. Address: Department of Clinical Psychology, H Gwynne Jones Centre, Stanley Royd Hospital, Wakefield, North Yorkshire, England.

TORRENS Paul Roger, b. 14 Dec 1934, San Francisco, California, USA. Physician. 3 sons, 1 daughter. Education: MD, Georgetown University, 1958; MPH, Harvard University, 1962. Appointments: Chief, Community Health Studies Unit, St Luke's Hospital, New York City, 1962-69; Director, Maryknoll Hospital, Kowloon, Hong Kong, 1969-72; Professor, University of California at Los Angeles School of Public Health, USA, 1972-. Publications: Introduction to Health Services, Co-author, 4 Editions. Address: 410 19th Street, Santa Monica, CA 90402, USA.

TOSKAS Phillip P, b. 4 Jan 1940, Baltimore, Maryland, USA. Physician. m. Patricia A Sponsel, 3 June 1961, 1 son, 2 daughters. Education: BA, Johns Hopkins University; MD, University of Maryland. Appointments: Internist, Walter Reed Army Institute of Research, 1970-73; Assistant Professor of Medicine, 1973-75, Associate Professor of Medicine, 1975-78, Professor, Director, Division of Gastroenterology, 1978-, also Associate Chairman, Department of Medicine, University of Florida, Gainesville. Publications: Gastrointestinal Diseases, 1993; Harrison's Textbook of Medicine, 1994; Oxford Textbook of Medicine, 1994; Bockus Gastroenterology, 1994; Cecil's Textbook of Medicine, 1995. Honours: ASCI, Career Investigator, Veterans Administration, 1973-78; Distinguished Achievement Award, Canadian Gastroenterology Association, 1982. Memberships: American College of Physicians; ASCI; American Gastroenterology Association; American Physicians Association; International Association of Physicians. Hobbies: Travel; Boating. Address: Division of Gastroenterology, University of Florida, Box 100214, Gainesville, FL 32610, USA.

TOWNES Brenda Dessau, b. 11 Jan 1936, Norwalk, CT, USA. Clinical Psychologist. 2 s, 2 d. Education: BA, Antioch College, 1957; MA, Mills College, 1958; PhD, University of WA, 1970. Appointments include: Assistant Professor, 1976-81, Associate Professor, 1976-81, Professor, 1981-, Department of Psychiatry and Behavioral Sciences, University of WA; Adjunct Professor, Department of Psychology and Department of Anesthesiology, University of WA, 1981-; Head, Neuropsychology Laboratories, Department of Psychiatry and Behavioral Sciences, University of WA, 1986-. Publications: 76 Articles in professional journals, 1966-, including: Co-author, Neurobehavioral outcomes in cardiac operations: A prospective controlled study, in Journal of Thoracic and Cardiovascular Surgery, 1989; Co-author, The cost to the central nervous system of climbing to extremely high altitude, in New England Journal of Medicine, 1989. Honours: Honorary Visiting Fellow, Murdoch University, Perth, Australia, 1977-78; Harold and Margaret Feldman Research Award, 1980; Visiting Scholar, Hunan Medical University, Changsha, China, 1985; Visiting Scholar, Center for Rehabilitation of Brain Damage, University of Copenhagen, 1987; Diplomate, Clinical Psychology, 1980; Diplomate, Clinical Neuropsychology, 1987. Memberships: Fellow, American Psychological Association; International Neuropsychological Society; National Academy of Neuropsychology. Hobbies: Hiking; Kayaking; Tennis; Music. Address: University of Washington, ZA-41, Department of Psychiatry and Behavioral Sciences, Seattle, WA 98195, USA.

TOWNS Melanie Jane, b. 28 Apr 1953, Cheshire, England. Educational Psychologist. m. Charles Towns, 17 Sept 1971, 1 son, 2 daughters. Education: BA Hons Psychology 1975, MSc Educational Psychology 1981, University of Newcastle Upon Tyne, England. Career: Teacher, Dudley MBC, 1976-78; Teacher, Newcastle, 1978-79; Educational Psychologist, currently. Publications: Publications in: ACCP Newsletter, 1985; OECP Newsletter, 1994. Memberships: Associate Fellow, British Psychological Society; Division of Ed & Child Psychologists; Association of Child Psychologists & Psychiatrists; British Society for Experimental & Clinical Hypnosis. Hobbies: Sailing; Gardening. Address: 136 Woodstock Road, Oxford OX2 7NG, England.

TRASLER Gordon Blair, b. 7 Mar 1929, Bournemouth, England. Psychologist. m. Kathleen Fegan, 19 Sept 1953. Education: MA, Exeter; PhD. London; FBPsS; Chartered Forensic Psychologist. Appointments: Psychologist. HM Prisons, Wandsworth and Winchester, 1955-57; Lecturer, University of Southampton, 1957-64; Professor of Psychology, 1964-94; Emeritus Professor of Psychology, University of Southampton; Leverhulme Emeritus Fellow, 1995-. Publications: In Place of Parents, 1960; The Explanation of Criminality, 1962; The Shaping of Social Behaviour, 1967; The Formative Years, Co-author, 1968; Behaviour Modification with Offenders, Co-author, 1980. Honours: Justice of the Peace; Sellin-Glueck Award for Distinguished Contributions to Criminology, American Society of Criminology, 1990. Memberships: American Society of Criminology; British Psychological Society; Institute for the Study and Treatment of Delinquency; Liberty. Hobbies: Reading; Photography; Writing. Address: Fox Croft, Old Kennels Lane, Oliver's Battery, Winchester SO22 4JT, England.

TRAUB-WERNER Daniel, b. 16 Apr 1946, Prague, Czech Republic. Psychoanalyst. m. Beatrice Traub-Werner, 3 sons. Education: MD, University of Buenos Aires, 1969; Fellow, Royal College of Physicians and Surgeons (Canada), 1975; Supervising and Training Psychoanalyst, Toronto Institute of Psychoanalysts. Appointments: Currently Assistant Professor of Psychiatry, University of Toronto, Canada. Publications: A note on counter-transference and anti-Semitism, 1979; Towards a theory of prejudice, 1984; The place and value of bestophilia in perversions, 1986; Affect deficit: A vicissitude of the phenomenon and experience of affect, 1990; The occurrence of mirroring in psychotherapy supervision (with K Manassis), 1994. Honours: Miguel Prados Prize, Canadian Psychoanalytic Society, 1986. Memberships: International Psychoanalytic Association; Canadian Psychiatric Association; Canadian Medical Association. Address: 43 Oriole Gardens, Toronto, Ontario, Canada M4V 1V9.

TRAVIS Susan, b. 12 Oct 1940, New York, USA. Physician. m. Dr Melvin Grossman, dec, 1 son, 1 daughter. Education: AB, Syracuse University; MD, New York University Medical School. Appointments: Teaching ASsistant, New York University; Teaching Assistant, Children's Hospital of Philadelphia; Instructor in Paediatrics, Associate in Paediatric Haematology, New York University; Assistant, Associate Professor of Paediatrics, Cardeza Foundation, Thomas Jefferson University, Philadelphia; Associate Professor of Paediatrics, Robert Wood Johnson Medical School, UMDNJ, Camden, New Jersey. Publications: Contributor of 27 articles and 28 abstracts including: Spontaneous Hemorrhage Associated with Accidental Brodifacoum Poisoning in a Child, 1933. Honours: phi Beta Kappa; Alpha Epsilon Delta; Phi Sigma Phi; Best Teacher Award, Paediatric Residents, Thomas Jefferson University Medical School, 1985; Best Teacher Runner-Up Award, Paediatric Residents, Cooper Hospital University Medical Centre, Camden, New Jersey, 1987. Memberships: American Society of Paediatric Haematology and Oncology; American Association of Haematology; American Academy of Paediatrics. Address: Division of Paediatric Haematology/Oncology, Cooper Hospital University Medical Centre, Three Cooper Plaza, Camden, NJ 08103, USA.

TRAVLOS Andrew, b. 29 Apr 1961, Johannesburg, South Africa. Medical Doctor. m. Lee Ann Travlos, 8 Feb 1986, 2 d. Education: MBBCh; FRCP(C); Witwatersrand Medical School, South Africa, 1984; Physical Medicine and Rehabilitation Speciality, 1993; Electrophysiology Fellowship, 1994. Appointments: Clinical Instructor, University of British Columbia; Residency Program Director, Division of Physical Medicine and Rehabilitation, University of British Columbia, 1994-. Publications: 6 Professional articles, 1991-, including: Co-author, Steroid Psychosis: A cause of confusion on the acute spinal cord injury service, in Archives of Physical Medicine and Rehabilitation, 1993; Co-author, Cerebrospinal fluid cell count following spinal cord injury, in Archives of Physical Medicine and Rehabilitation, 1994. Honours: Resident Research Award, Canadian Association of Physical Medicine and Rehabilitation, 1991; Resident Research Awards, University of British Columbia, Division of Physical Medicine and Rehabilitation, 1991, 1993. Memberships: Canadian Congress of Neurologic Sciences; American Congress of Physical Medicine and Rehabilitation; British Columbia Medical Association. Address: Division of Physical Medicine and Rehabilitation, 4255 Laurel Street, Vancouver, BC, Canada, V52 2G9.

TRENERRY Selwyn Peter, b. 26 Apr 1927, Sydney, Australia. Allergist. m. Naomi Stevenson, 1 May 1953, 4 d. Education: MB; BS; FACA. Appointments: RMO, Royal South Sydney Hospital; Government MO, New South Wales; Currently, Consultant Physician. Memberships: Australian Society of Immunology and Allergy; American Academy of Allergy and Immunology; AMA. Hobbies: Golf; Tennis; Cattlebreeding. Address: A M P Boulevard, Hobart Place, Canberra, Australia.

TRENOUTH Michael John, b. 2 June 1946, Grange-Over-Sands. Education: University of Manchester; BSc Hons; BDS; MDS; PHD; FDSRCPS; DDORCPS; DOrth RCS. Career: House Officer 1971-72, Lecturer in Oral Surgery 1972-75, Lecturer in Dental Anatomy and Orthodontics 1975-85, Manchester Dental Hospital; Consultant Orthodontist, Royal Preston Hospital, Currently. Publications: Publications on Bruxism and TMJ Dysfunction; Foetal Craniofacial Growth; Twin Block Functional Orthodontic Appliances; Normative Cephalometric Data; Tooth Lead in Relation to Environmental Pollution. Memberships: British Dental Association; British Orthodontic Society; European Orthodontic Society; American Association of Orthodontists. Hobbies: Skiing; Ice Skating; Sailing; Fell Walking. Address: Department of Orthodontics, Royal Preston Hospital, Sharoe Green Lane, Preston PR2 4HT, England.

TREPKA Christopher J S, b. 13 Dec 1955, Warsaw. Consultant Clinical Psychologist. m. Penelope Cook, 21 Sept 1981, 1 s. Education: BA, Hull University, 1977; MPhil, Edinburgh University, 1981. Appointments: Senior Clinical Psychologist, Bangour Village Hospital,

West Lothian, Scotland; Specialist in Cognitive Therapy; Community Mental Health Centre Co-ordinator. Publications: Hopelessness and Depression, 1983; Perfectionism and the Threat to Self-Esteem in Clinical Anxiety. 1984; Group Treatment of Anxiety, 1986; Activities From an Outpatients Psychology Clinic, 1986; A Clinical Psychology Service to the Elderly, 1987; The Evaluation of Psychological Treatment in Primary Care, 1987; Predicting Return to Work After Myocardial Infection, 1988; Co-ordinating Supply And Demand in a Clinical Team, 1989; Community Mental Health Teams on the Role Security of Clinical Psychologists, 1990; A Survey of Clinical PsychologyRegional Advisory Groups, 1991; Contributor of professional articles. Memberships: Associate Fellow, British Psychological Society. Hobbies: Chess; Computing; Weight training; Camping. Address: Ashgrove CMHRC, 48 Ashgrove, Bradford, West Yorkshire BD9 4AH, England.

TRESTRAIL John Harris, b. 4 May 1944, Battle Creek, MI, USA. Toxicologist. m. Mary Lee Wenzel, 15 Oct 1971, 1 s, 1 d. Education: BS, Honours, Pharmacy, 1967; Diplomate, American Board of Applied Toxicology. Appointments: Volunteer, US Peace Corps, 1968-70; Hospital Pharmacist, 1971-76; Co-director, Blodgett Regional Poison Center, 1976-. Publications: 20 Published papers; 235 Published book reviews. Honours: Phi Eta Sigma, 1962; Rho Chi, 1966; Dean's Award, 1967; NAMA Prexy's Award, 1993. Memberships: American Association of Poison Control Centers; American Academy of Clinical Toxicology; International Society on Toxicology; American Academy of Forensic Sciences; Toxicological History Society. Hobbies: Singing Barbershop Harmony; Book Collecting; Travel. Address: 1840 Wealthy Street SE, Grand Rapids, MI 49506, USA.

TREW Geoffrey Howard, b. 19 Jan 1961, Gower. Gynaecologist. m. Alison, 16 Jul 1994. Education: MBBS; Master, Royal College of Obstetrics & Gynaecology. Appointments: Senior Registrar in Reproductive Medicine. Memberships: Blair Bell Society; Treasurer, Victor Bonney Society; Fellow, Royal Society of Medicine. Hobbies: Riding. Address: 19 Queensland Avenue, Wimbledon, London, SW19 3AD, UK.

TRINKLE David Ball, b. 28 Mar 1961, Roanoke, VA, USA. Geriatric Psychiatry. m. 30 May 1992, 1 s. Education: MD; Board certified in Psychiatry and Geriatric Psychiatry, American Board of Psychiatry and Neurology. Career: Psychiatry Residency Program, University of Virginia Medical School, Medical College of Virginia; Fellowship in Geriatric Psychiatry, Northwestern Memorial Hospital; Currently, Assistant Clinical Professor of Psychiatric Medicine, University of Virginia, Roanoke; Geriatric Psychiatrist, Roanoke Memorial Hospital. Memberships: AMA; APA; American Association of Geriatric Psychiatry; International Psychogeriatric Association. Address: 213 McClanahan Street SW, Suite 310, Roanoke, VA 24014, USA.

TRINKOFF Alison Miller, Nurse. m. Paul Trinkoff, July 1979, 2 sons. Education: BSN, University of Rochester, USA; MPH, University of North Carolina, 1978; ScD, Johns Hopkins University, 1987. Appointments: Research Associate, University of North Carolina, Chapel Hill; Research Analyst, Maryland Department of Health and Mental Hygiene, Baltimore; Associate Professor, School of Nursing, University of Maryland, Baltimore; Associate Professor, Department of Psychiatric and Community Nursing. Publications: Poisoning Hospitalizations and Deaths from Solids and Liquids Among Children and Teenagers, Co-author, 1986; Predictors of the Iniation of Psychotherapeutic Medicine Use, Co-author, 1990; The Prevalence and Self-Reported Consequences of Cocaine Use: An Exploratory and Descriptive Analysis, Co-author, 1990; The Prevalence of Substance Abuse Among Registered Nurses, Co-author, 1991; Infant Walker-Related Injuries: Preventive Strategies, Co-author, 1993; Relationship of Speciality and Access to Substance Use Among Registered Nurses: An Exploratory Analysis, Co-author, 1994. Honours: Principal Investigator, Substance Abuse Among Registered Nurses, National Institute on drug Abuse; Individual National Research Service Award; National centre for Nursing Research, 1985-87; Travel Award, College on Problems of Drug Dependence, 1991; Delta Omega, 1988; Sigma Theta Tau, 1980. Memberships: American Nurses Association; American Public Health Association; National Nurses Society on Addictions; Association for Medical Education and Research in Substance Abuse. Hobbies: Music; Cooking. Address: 622 W Lombard Street, Rm 720, Baltimore, MD 21201, USA.

TRIVEDI Rajendrakumar, b. 2 Oct 1951, Rajkot, India. Physician. Education: MBBS; FCCP; FAAAI; FACAI; FAAP. Appointments:

Paediatric and Internal Meeicine residency; Fellowship in Allergy and Immunology; Physician. Memberships: American College of Chest Physicians; American Academy of Allergy and Immunology; American College of Allergy and Immunology; American Academy of Pediatrics. Hobbies: Travel; Sightseeing. Address: University Medical Centre, INternal Medicine, 2390 West Congress Street, Lafayette, LA 70506, USA.

TROJANOWSKI John Q, b. 17 Dec 1946, Connecticut, USA. Scientist. m. Virginia Lee. Education: BA, King's College, 1970; PhD, Tufts University School of Arts and Sciences, 1976; MD, Tufts University School of Medicine, 1976. Appointments include: Assistant Professor, 1981-86, Associate Professor, 1986-90, Director, Medical Pathology, 1989-, Professor, Department of Pathology and Laboratory Medicine, 1990-, Professor of Pathology and Laboratory Medicine in Psychiatry, 1991-96, Director, National Institute on Aging Alzheimer's Disease Centre Core, 1991-96, University of Pennsylvania School of Medicine, Philadelphia; Adjunct Professor, Wistar Institute, Philadelphia, 1992-. Publications: Contributor of numerous articles in professional journals, pamphlets, teaching aids and invited lectures. Honours include: Magna Cum Laude, King's College, 1970; Wm Dameshek Research Award, Tufts University School of Medicine, 1976; Metropolitan Foundation Award for Alzheimer's Disease Research, 1991; Established Investigator Award, National Alliance for Research on Schizophrenia and Depression, 1994. Memberships: Society for Neuroscience; American Society for Cell Biology; American Association of Pathologists; International Academy of Pathologists; European Neuroscience Association; American Association of Neuropathologists. Address: University of Pennsylvania Medical Centre, Department of Pathology and Laboratory Medicine, 3400 Spruce Street, Philadelphia, PA 19104-4283, USA.

TROMPETER Richard Simon, b. 27 Jan 1946. Consultant Paediatrician. m. Barbara Maislish, 26 Mar 1978, 2 s, 2 d. Education: MB; BS; MRCP; FRCP. Appointments: Consultant Paediatrician, The Royal Free Hospital, London, 1983-87; Currently, Consultant Paediatric Nephrologist, Hospital for Sick Children, London. Publication: Editor, The Haenolytic Uremic Syndromes and TTP, 1993. Memberships: International, European and British Paediatric Nephrology Associations. Hobby: Theatre. Address: Hospitals For Sick Children, Great Ormond Street, London, WC1N 3JH, England.

TROSMAN Harry, b. 9 Dec 1024, Toronto, Ontario, Canada. Psychiatrist. m. Marjorie Susan, 22 June 1952, 2 s, 1 d. Education: Certification, Chicago Institute for Psychoanalysis, 1962; MD. Appointments: Professor of Psychiatry, University of Chicago. Publications: Freud and the Imaginative World, 1985. Honours: Franz Alexander Prize, Chicago Institute for Psychoanalysis, 1965. Memberships: American psychoanalytic Association; American College of Psychoanalysts; International Psychoanalytic Association; Chicago Psychoanalytic Society; American Psychiatric Association. Address: Department of Psychiatry (MC 3077), The University of Chicago, 5841 S Maryland Avenue, Chicago, IL 60637, USA.

TRUSLER George Aubrey, b. 17 Nov 1926, Toronto, Canada. Cardiac Surgeon. m. Constance Sparrow, 4 sons, 1 daughter. Education: MD, 1949; BSc, 1953; FRCS(C), 1956; FACS, 1962; MS, 1962. Appointments: Former Head, Division of Cardiovascular Surgery, Staff Surgeon, Cardiovascular Surgery, Hospital for Sick Children, Toronto. Publications: Contributor iof 56 book chapters and 198 professional articles. Honours: Aide de Camp, Lt Governor of Ontario; Honorary Lt Colonel, 25th Medical Co; Lister Prize in Surgery, 1962; Centennial Medal, 1967; Jubilee Medal, 1978; Canada 125 Medal, 1992. Memberships: AATS; STS; ACS; ASA; CACS; CCS; CMA; CPSO; Jones Surgical Society; OMA; RCPSC. Hobbies: Skiing; Gardening; Woodcarving; Fishing; Hunting; Photography. Address: 138 Douglas Drive, Toronto, Ontario M4W 2B7, Canada.

TSAI Hao-Jan, b. 22 Dec 1938, Jiangxi, China. Professor. m. 8 Mar 1965, 2 sons. Education: BSc, Peking University, 1963; PhD, Kassel University, Germany, 1983. Appointments: Research Assistant, 1963, Associate Researcher, 1973, Associate Professor, 1986, Professor, 1989. Publications: Basis pf Molecular Physiology in Vision, 1978; Visual Physiology and Bionics, 1979; Contributor of 34 professional papers. Honours: Research Fellowship, Alexander von Humboldt Foundation, 1981-83; Fellowship, JSPS, 1987-88; Fellowship, ANU, Australia, 1992. Memberships: Biophysical Society of China; Chinese Medical Society; International Society for Neuroethology. Hobby:

Photography. Address: Department of Paediatric ophthalmology, First School of Clinical Medicine, Beijing Medical University, 8 Xishiku Street, Beijing 100034, China.

TSANG Reginald C, b. 20 Sep 1940, Hong Kong. MD; Professor. 1 s, 1 d. Education: MBBS, Medicine, Hong Kong University Medical School, 1964; Pediatrics, 1966-69, Neonatology, 1967-69, Michael Reese Hospital, Chicago; Neonatology, Children's Hospital, Cincinnati, 1969-71. Career includes: Attending Pediatrician, Children's Hospital, Cincinnati, 1971-, Cincinnati General Hospital, University Hospital, 1971-, Jewish Hospital, Cincinnati, 1971-, Good Samaritan Hospital, 1986-, Bethesda Hospital, 1988-, Christ Hospital, 1989-; Professor of Pediatrics, Obstetrics and Gynaecology, University of Cincinnati, 1979-; Director, Division of Neonatology, 1983-; Chief, NIH Perinatal Emphasis Research Center, 1985-; David G and Priscilla R Gamble Professor of Neonatology, 1986-; Director, NIH Program Project Grant Diabetes in Pregnancy, 1987-; Director, Neonatology Training Program, 1987-; Executive Director, Perinatal Research Institute, 1990-. Publications: Books include: Nutrition and Child Health: Perspectives for the 1980s, 1981; Nutrition in Infancy, 1988; Beginning an Academic Medical Career, 1993; Growth Factors in Perinatal Development, 1993; Numerous articles in professional journals. Honours include: Sigma Xi, 1976; Nutrition Award, American Academy of Pediatrics, 1989; George Rieveschl Award for Distinguished Scientific Research, University of Cincinnati, 1991. Memberships include: American Federation for Clinical Research, 1974-; Endocrine Society, 1975-; Various offices, Fellow, American College of Nutrition; American Pediatric Society, 1976-; Perinatal Research Society, 1978-; National Perinatal Association, 1983-. Address: College of Medicine, Department of Pediatrics, University of Cincinnati, PO Box 670541, Cincinnati, OH 45267-0541, USA.

TSANKOV Georgi, b. 15 July 1930, Rabisha, Bulgaria. Forest Entomologist. m. Rositsa Ivanova, 7 Mar 1954, 1 s, 2 d. Education: DSc, 1966. Appointments: Professor, University Santiago de Cuba, 1970-73; President, Commission Forest Biological Control, East Palearctic Section, 1984-, Chief of Laboratory, 1987-89, Chief of Department, 1989-93, IOBC Moscow. Publications: Biological Control with Disease and Insect Pests in Forestry, 1984; Microbial Preparations fort he Regulatio of the Number of Defoliators in Bulgarian Forests, 1985; Author of textbooks. Memberships: Forest Research Institute; President, Bulgarian Entomological Union. Hobby: Collecting insects. Address: Kliment Ochridski 132, 1756 Sofia, Bulgaria.

TSAO Edmund, b. 19 June 1930, Hong Kong. Professor of Surgery. m. Ana Leung, 1 daughter. Education: MD, Ling-Nan University School of Medicine, 1948-54. Appointments: Resident, Chief Resident, Attending Surgeon, 1954-60, Attending Surgeon, 1960-70, Lecturer of Surgery, 1970-78; Associate Professor, Vice Chairman, Department of General Surgery, 1978-85, Professor, Director, Department of HPB Surgery, 1994, Professor, Supervisor Director, Department of HPB Surgery, 1994-, First Affiliated Hospital of Sun Yat-Sen University. Publications: The Principle and Practise of Biliary Surgery, Co-author, 1991; Surgical Treatment of Hepatocellular Carcinoma, 1990; Extrahepatic Bile Duct Cancer, 1992; Diagnosis and Treatment of Biliary Tract Tumours, 1994. Honour: Best Teacher Award, 1984. Memberships: Senior Member, Chinese Medical Association; Chinese Society of Hepatic Surgery; Chinese Society of Biliary Surgery; Standing Committee, Guandong Society of General Surgery; Chairman, Guangdong Society of Hepatobiliary Surgery. Hobbies: Classical Music; Volleyball; Table-tennis. Address: 12 Hung Yu Dao 2/F, Yue Xiu Bei Road, Guangzhou 510055, China.

TSENG Quen, b. 18 August 1935, Shanghai, China. Professor; Researcher. m. Ling Sue-Jin, 1956, 2 sons. Education: Graduate, Department of Physiology, Fudan University, Shanghai, 1964. Appointments: Engineer, Institute of Shanghai Medical Instruments; Director, Institute of Biological Signes, Researcher of Tumor Signes, China Developing Academy of Science and Technology; Director, Institute of Biological Signes. Publications: Nature Journal, vol 5 no 7, 1982; Nature Journal, vol 12 no 7, 1989; Later in Life Sciences p. 227, 1990. Honours: Award, National 4th Grade, Technological Achievement, 1990. Hobbies: Swimming; Basketball. Address: China Developing Academy of Science and Technology Science Center, 7th Floor, Shang Bu Road (middle), Zhen Zhen 518031, China.

TSENG Robert Ying Mei, b. 3 Nov 1950, Hong Kong. Paediatrician. m. Nancy Loo. 29 Feb 1979, 2 sons, 2 daughters. Education: BSc, St

Andrews University, Scotland, 1973; MB ChB, University of Manchester, England; Diploma, Child Health, London, 1979; MRCP, England, 1982; FCCP, 1990; Fellow, Hong Kong College of Paediatricians, 1992; FRCP, Edinburgh, 1994. Appointments: Several hospital posts, England; General Practice, Gosbury Hill Health Centre, Chessington, Surrey, 1983-84; Lecturer, Paediatrics, Chinese University of Hong Kong, Prince of Wales Hospital, 1984-92; Private Practice, Kowloon, Hong Kong, 1992-; Consultant Physician, Evangel Hospital, Kowloon, 1992-; Honorary Lecturer, Paediatrics, Chinese University of Hong Kong, 1992. Publications include: Self-directed learning in history taking in childhood asthma, 1988; Prevention of Childhood Asthma - Facts, Fantasies and Prospects, 1990; Co-author: Post-streptococcal glomerulonephritis in Hong Kong, 1987; Umbilical cord serum IgE concentration of Chinese babies in Hong Kong, 1987; Rising hospitalisation of childhood asthma in Hong Kong 1976-1985, 1987; Setting up of a clinical audit of Paediatric morbidity in Hong Kong, 1987; Maternal hepatitis B infection affects fetal IgE synthesis, 1988; Seasonal asthma in Hong Kong and its management implications, 1989; Breast feeding babies of HbsAg positive mothers, 1988; Low level atmospheric sulfur dioxide pollution and childhood asthma, 1990; Particulate air pollution and asthma hospitalisation, 1992. Honour: Syntex Award for Research Paper, University of Surrey, 1984. Memberships include: Corresponding Member, American Academy of Allergy and Clinical Immunology. Hobbies: Tennis; Music; Food. Address: Room 1005 B, Argyle Centre Phase 1, 688 Nathan Rd, Kowloon, Hong Kong.

TSOUKAS Christos Michael, b. 2 Apr 1948, Kastoria, Greece. Associate Professor. m. Nadine Nicolopoulos, 2 Dec 1979, 4 sons. Education: BSc, McGill University, 1968; MSc, University of Hawaii, 1970; MD, University of Athens, 1977; FRCP (C), 1982; FACP, 1989. Appointments: Currently: Associate Professor, Faculty of Medicine, McGill University, Montreal, Canada; Associate Director, McGill University AIDS Centre; Director, Immune Deficiency Treatment Centre, Montreal General Hospital. Publications: Co-author, 50 articles including: Liposomal Encapsulation of Azidothymidine Results in Decreased Hematopoietic Toxicity and Enhanced Activity Against Murine Acquired Immunodeficiency Syndrome, 1992; Effect of Ultraviolet Irradiation on Selected Host Cell Proteins Including Ro/SS-A and Epstein-Barr Virus in Cultured Lymphoblastoid Cell Lines, 1992; Clinical Correlates in In Vitro HIV-1 Resistance to Zudovudine; Results of the Multicentre Canadian AZT Trial, 1993; Effects of Lovastatin on Natural Killer Cell Function and Other Immunological Parameters in Man, 1993; Markers Predicting Progression of Human Immunodeficiency Virus Related Disease, 1994; Book chapters; Reports. Honours: Achievement Award, Canadian Hemophilia Society, 1989; Commemorative Medal, Governor General of Canada, 125th Anniversary of Confederation of Canada, 1992. Memberships include: World Federation of Hemophilia; Canadian Hemophilia Society; Canadian and Quebec Medical Association; New York Academy of Sciences; Canadian Society for Clinical Investigation; American Academy of Allergy and Immunology; Montreal Medico-Chirurgical Society; Clinical Immunology Society; Canadian Society for Immunology; International AIDS Society; American Association for the Advancement of Science; Canadian Society for HIV Research. Address: Immune Deficiency Treatment Centre, Montreal General Hospital, B7-117, 1650 Cedar Avenue, Montreal, Quebec, Canada H3G 1A4.

TSUI Siu Lun, b. 15 Jan 1956, Hong Kong, China. Anaesthesiology & Pain Management. m. Ivy S K Yu, 2 daughters. Education: MB, BS, Faculty of Medicine, University of Hong Kong, 1080; Fellow, Royal Australasian College of Surgeons, 1986; Fellow, Australian & New Zealand College of Anaesthetists, 1992; Fellow, Hong Kong College of Anaesthesiologists, 1991; Foundation Fellow, Hong Kong Academy of Medicine (Anaesthesiology), 1993. Appointments: Consultant Anaesthetist, Queen Mary Hospital, Hong Kong, 1991-; Head, Pain Management Team, Assistant Equipment Manager, Honorary Clinical Lecturer,Department of Anaesthesiology, Queen Mary Hospital; Member, Hong Kong Regional Project Subcommittee, Training Committee of the Faculty of Anaesthetists, Royal Australasian College of Surgeons. Publications: Anaesthetic Management of a two month old infant for laser resection of laryngeal granuloma, 1991; A comparaison of two lung high frequency positive pressure ventilation (HFPPV) and one lung ventilation (OLV) plus 5 cm water non-ventilated lung CPAP, in patient undergoing anaesthesia for oesophagectomy, 1991; High frequency jet ventilation in the anesthetic management of a patient with tracheo-esophageal fistula complicating carcinoma of esophagus, 1991; Postoperative analgesia for oesophagectomy: A comparison of three analgesic regimens, 1991; Anaesthesia for oesophageal cancer surgery,

1993. Memberships: Hong Kong College of Anaesthesiology; Society of Anaesthetists. Hobbies: Personal Computers; Reading; Tourism. Address: Queen Mary Hospital, Pokfulam Road, Hong Kong, China.

TU Ying, b. 24 Sep 1925, Jiangxi, China. Professor of Epidemiology. m. Xiao Lu-yan, 10 June 1953, 1 son, 2 daughters. Education: Medical Student, Sixth Military Medical College, 1951. Appointments: Member, Distinction Specialist Committee, Ministry of Public Health, 1986-; Professor of Epidemiology, Third Military Medical College. Publications: Practical Handbook of Control of Infectious Diseases, CO-author, 1987; Disinfection in Chinese Encyclopedia of Medicine, Co-author, 1988; Pest Control in Hygiene, Co-author, 1992. Honours: Advanced Worker, Third Military Medical College, 1961; Advanced Worker of Science and Technology, Third Military Medical College, 1992. Memberships: Council, Chinese Disinfection Association; Council, Preventive Medicine Association, Sichuan. Address: Department of Epidemiology, Third Military Medical College, Gao Tanyan Road, Chengqing 630038, China.

TU Yun ren, b. 15 Mar 1934, Yuhang, Zhejiang, China. Epidemiologist. m. Bing Hu, 9 Jan 1959, 1 son. Education: MD, Public Health College of West China University of Medical Science, 1957. Virology Department, China Military Medical Academy, 1959. Appointments: Epidemiologist, Department Chief, Deputy Centre Director, Director, Sichuan Provincial Health Anti-Epidemic Centre. Publications: Management of Health and Epidemic Prevention, 1990; Manual for Polio Surveillance, 1992. Honours: 1st Prize of Science and Technology Advance, Sichuan Province, 1992. Memberships: Standing Committee, Chinese Epidemiology Association; Deputy Director, Sichuan Preventive Medicine Association; IEA. Hobby: Music. Address: 40 Huai Shu Street, Chengdu, Sichuan 610031, China.

TUCKER Landrum Sylvanius, b. 7 Dec 1939, Nashville, Tennessee, USA. Psychiatrist; Psychoanalyst. m. Eleanor Muenzer, 19 Aug 1970, 1 son, 2 daughters. Education: AB, Philosophy, University of Tennessee, 1961; MD, Stanford University, 1966; Residency, Adult and Child Psychiatry. University of North Carolina; Graduate, University of North Carolina and Duke Psychoanalytic Institute; Child and Adolescent Psychoanalysis, Washington DC Psychoanalytic Institute. Appointments: Chief Resident, Child Psychiatry, University of North Carolina, 1973; Assistant Professor, 1974-78, currently Clinical Associate Professor, Child Division, Department of Psychiatry, University of North Carolina, Chapel Hill. Publications: Partial G/D Translocation in 2 members of a family (with Kongoo Goh), 1964; A Case of Foliéa Deux: The Influenced One (with Thomas Cornwall), 1975. Honours: Omicron Delta Kappa, Alpha Epsilon Delta, University of Tennessee, 1960; Fellow, American Psychiatric Association, 1984; Fellow, American Academy of Child and Adult Psychiatry, 1991. Memberships include: American Psychoanalytic Association; Board Member, Lucy Daniels Foundation; Board Member, Lucy Daniels Preschool. Hobbies: Music; Painting and drawing; Tennis; Swimming. Address: 2005 N Lakeshore Drive, Chapel Hill, NC 27514, USA.

TUER William F P, b. 10 Feb 1944, Ottawa, Canada. Physician. m. Diane Bednarek, 6 Jun 1970, 2 d. Education: BSc, St Michael's College, University of Toronto, Canada; 1967; MD, Faculty of Medicine, University of Toronto, Canada, 1970. Appointments: Chief Pediatrician, McDonald Army Hospital, Fort Eustis, VA; Chief, Department of Medicine, Silas B Hays Hospital, Fort Ord, CA; Commander, 8th Evac Hospital, Saudi Arabia; Director, Gorgos Hospital, Ancon, Panama; Diplomat, American Board of Pediatrics; Diplomat, American Board of Allergy and Immunology. Memberships: Fellow, American Academy of Pediatrics; American Academy of Allergy and Immunology; British Allergy Society; European Academy of Allergology and Immunology; Canadian Pediatric Society. Hobbies: Running; Diving. Address: Box 1834, PSC 03, APO, AA 34003, USA.

TUGWELL Peter, b. 30 Mar 1944, Egypt. Medicine. m. Jane Katherine Tugwell, 26 Jun 1971, 1 s, 1 d. Education: MD; MSc; FRCP(UK); FRCPC; FACP. Appointments: Chairman, Department of Clinical Epidemiology and Biostatistics, 1979-89, McMaster University; Currently, Professor and Chair, Department of Medicine, University of Ottawa. Address: University of Ottawa Faculty of Medicine, 451 Smyth Road, Ottawa, Ontario, Canada, K1H 8M5.

TUNBRIDGE William Michael Gregg, b. 13 Jun 1940, Leeds, England. Medicine. m. Dr Felicity K E Tunbridge, 1965, 2 d. Education: MA; MD; FRCP. Appointments: Consultant Physician, Newcastle

General Hospital; Senior Lecturer in Medicine, University of Newcastle upon Tyne; Director of Postgraduate Medical Education and Training, Oxford University, 1994-. Publications: Diabetes and Endocrinology in Clinical Practice, 1991; Thyroid Disease - The Facts, 1991; Rationing Health Care in Medicine, 1993. Memberships: Royal College of Physicians; Royal Society of Medicine; Society for Endocrinology; British Diabetic Association. Hobby: Yoga. Address: Medical School Officer, John Radcliffe Hospital, Headington, Oxford, OX3 9DU, England.

TUPIN Joe P, b. 17 Feb 1934, Comanche, Texas, USA. Psychiatry. m. Betty Thompson, 19 June 1955, 2 sons, 1 daughter. Education: BS; MD, University of Texas, Galveston. Appointments: Assistant Professor, University of Texas, 1964-66; Associate Professor, University of Texas, 1966-69; Associate Professor, Professor, University of California, Davis, 1971-92; Chair Psychiatry, University of California, Davis, 1977-83; Medical Director, University of California, Daivs, 1983-92. Publications: Over 70; Transient Psychosis; Handbook of Clinical Psychopharmacology. Memberships: American Psychiatric Association, Fellow; American College of Psychiatrists, Fellow. Hobbies: Fly Fishing; Art. Address: 1108 Kent Drive, Davis, CA 95616, USA.

TUPPY Hans, b. 22 Jul 1924, Vienna, Austria. Scientist. m. Erika Fuchs, 3 Dec 1992, 3 d. Education: PhD, University of Vienna, 1948. Appointments: Dean, Medical Faculty, University of Vienna, 1970-72; President, Austrian Science Foundation, 1974-82; Rector, University of Vienna, 1983-85; President, Austrian Academy of Sciences, 1985-87; Austrian Federal Minister of Science and Research, 1987-89; Currently, Professor of Biochemistry, University of Vienna, Austria. Memberships: Deutsche Akademie der Naturforscher Leopoldina; Osterreichische Akademie der Wissenschaften; Pontificia Academia Scientiarum; Academia Europaea. Address: Hockegasse 17, A-1180 Vienna, Austria.

TURGAY Atilla, b. 16 Jun 1946, Ankara, Turkey. Psychiatrist. m. Cigdem Turgay, 1 s, 1 d. Education: Medicine and Psychiatry, University of Ottawa and Hacettepe University. Appointments: Director, Division of Child and Adolescent Psychiatry, University of Ottawa, Canada; Director, Medical Student Education in Psychiatry, Wayne State University, Detroit, MI, USA; Currently, Professor of Pediatric Psychiatry, MI State University. Publications: 2 Books; Over 200 papers, chapters and abstracts concerning: suicide, brain mapping, psychopharmacology, conversion hysteria. Honour: Distinguished Service Award, State Of MI, 1991. Memberships: Over 30 national and international organizations in Turkey, Canada and USA. Hobby: Playing classical guitar. Address: 3219 Bloomfield Shores, West Bloomfield, MI 48323, USA.

TURK Dennis Charles, b. 15 Mar 1946, NY, USA. Psychologist. m. Lorraine Meichenbaum, 7 Sep 1969, 1 s, 1 d. Education: BA, University of FL; MA, PhD, University of Waterloo, Canada. Career: Assistant Professor, Associate Professor, Yale University; Professor, University of Pittsburgh School of Medicine; Currently, Professor of Psychiatry, Anesthesiology and Behavioural Science and Director of Pain Evaluation and Treatment Institute, University of Pittsburgh School of Medicine. Publications: Pain and Behavioral Medicine, 1983; Health, Illness and Families, 1985; Psychological Assessment in Terminal Care, 1986; Pain Management, 1986; Facilitating Treatment Adherence, 1987; Reasoning, Inference and Judgement in Clinical Psychology, 1988; Handbook of Pain Assessment, 1992. Honours: Yale University Junior Faculty Fellowship, 1981-82; American Association of Diabetes Educators Award, 1981; Boehringer Ingelheim Foundation for Basic Research Lecturer, 1987. Memberships: Fellow, American Psychology Association; Fellow, Society of Behavioral Medicine; Fellow, Academy of Behavioral Medicine Research; Founding Member, International Association for Study of Pain; Founding Member, American Pain Society. Address: Pain Evaluation and Treatment Institute, University of Pittsburgh School of Medicine, 3601 Baum Boulevard, Pittsburgh, PA 15213, USA.

TÜRKOGLU Cüneyt, b. 5 January 1950, Izmir, Turkey. Medical Doctor. m. Melis Acaroglu, 9 June 1983, 2 daughters. Education: PhD, Cardiology, Ege University. Appointments: Director, Cardiology Department; Chief of Invasive Cardiology. Publications: Heart Catheterization and Angiography, 1990. Memberships: Turkish Society of Cardiology. Hobbies: Running; Football. Address: Ali Getinkaya Bulvari No 31, D.6 Alsancak, Izmir, Turkey.

TURNBULL Gordon James, b. 22 Dec 1948, Edinburgh, Scotland. Consultant in Psychiatry. m. Alison Grey, 22 Oct 1977, 3 s. Education: BSc, Medical Sciences; MBChB, Edinburgh, 1973. Career: RAF Medical

Branch, Head of Psychiatry, RAF Wroughton, Wiltshire; Consulting Psychiatrist to Civil Aviation Authority, UK; Currently, Clinical Director, Traumatic Stress Unit, Ticehurst House Hospital. Publications: Various articles and chapters on aviation psychiatry, pilot selection, psychological debriefing of prisoners of war and hostages. Honours: Winston Churchill Memorial Fellowship, 1976; Whittingham Memorial Prize for Aviation Medicine, 1990; People of the Year Award, 1993. Memberships: Royal College of Physicians; Royal College of Psychiatrists. Hobbies: Golf; Garening; Reading; Family. Address: Ticehurst House Hospital, Ticehurst, Whd Hurst, East Sussex, TN5 7HN, England.

TURNER Stuart William, b. 1 Sep 1952, Sheffield, England. Psychiatry. m. Morag Brocklehurst, 16 Mar 1991, 1 s, 1 d. Education: Gonville and Caius College Cambridge and Middlesex Hospital Medical School; MA(Cantab); MD; B Chir; MRCP(UK); FRCPsych. Career: Lecturer in Psychological Medicine, King's College School of Medicine and Dentistry and Institute of Psychiatry; Senior Lecturer in Psychiatry, University College , London Medical School; Currently, Medical Director, Camden and Islington Community Health Services, NHS Trust. Publications: Numerous articles on traumatic stress reactions including torture, homelessness and schizophrenia. Memberships: Vice-President, European Society for Traumatic Stress Studies; Editorial Boards of Journal of Traumatic Stress, and, Torture. Address: Camden and Islington Community Health Services NHS Trust, 112 Hampstead Road, London, NW1 2LT, England.

TURO Joann Katherine, b. 13 Feb 1938, Westerly, Rhode Island, USA. Psychoanalyst. Education: BS, University of Rhode Island, 1959; MA, Ohio University, 1964; Postgraduate, New York University, 1966-71; Freudian Institute, New York City, 1977-85; Mental Health Institute, New York City, 1977-80. Appointments: Research Assistant, Harvard University Medical School, Boston, 1959-60; Industrial Psychology Assistant, NY Telephone Company, New York City, 1964-66; Staff Psychologist, Testing and Advisement Centre, New York University, 1966-70; Staff Psychologist, MDC Psychology Services, New York City, 1971-72; Clinical Director, Greenwich House Substance Abuse Clinic, New York City, 1973-76; Consultant Psychotherapist, Mental Health Consultation Centre, New York City, 1977-82; Private Practice Psychoanalysis and Psychotherapy, New York City, 1981-; Mental Health COnsultant, Brooklyn Centre for Psychotherapy, 1976-78. Memberships: International Psychoanalytic Association; Society for Personality Assessment; New York Freudian Society, Co-chairman, Graduate Committee, 1985-86, Continuing Education Committeee, 1986-94; New York Council Psychoanalytic Psychotherapists; Metropolitan Association for College Mental Health Practitioners, Public Relations Committee, 1983-99; Psychoanalytic Consultation Service, 1994-. Address: 15 West 12th Street #12D, New York, NY 10011-8556, USA.

TURSKI Lechoslaw, b. 10 Aug 1955, Opole-Lubelskie, Poland. Neuropharmacologist. m. Hrissanthi Ikonomidou, 12 Oct 1985, 1 s, 1 d. Education: MD, Medical School, Lublin, Poland, 1980; PhD, University of Göttingen, Germany, 1988. Appointments: Research Assistant, Institute of Clinical Pathology, Lublin Medical School, 1978-85; Research Assistant, Department of Biochemical Pharmacology, Max-Planck Institute Exceptional Medicine, Göttingen, 1981-84, 1985-86; Research Assistant, Department of Neurology, Institute of Psychiatry, University of London, 1984; Head, Amino Acid Research, Schering AG, Berlin, 1987-; Professor of Neuropharmacology, University of Göttingen, 1993-. Publications: Editor, Frontiers in Excitatory Amino Acid Research, 1988; Editor, Excitatory Amino Acids and Second Messenger Systems, 1991. Honours: Polish Academy of Science Award, 1983; Polish Ministry of Health, 1984; Michael Award in Epilepsy Research, Jerusalem, 1986. Memberships: Society for Neuroscience; International Basal Ganglia Society; Polish Pharmacological Society. Address: Schering AG, Müllerstr 178, 13342 Berlin, Germany.

TWARDOWSKI Zbylut Józef, b. 2 Jun 1934, Stanislawice, Poland. Professor of Medicine. m. Halina Nowosielska, 26 Sep 1958, 2 s. Education: PhD; MD, Medical Academy, Kraków, Poland, 1959. Appointments: Chairman, Department of Medicine, Hospital for Miners, Bytom, Poland; Chairman, Department of Nephrology, Medical Academy, Lublin, Poland; Professor of Medicine, University of Missouri. Publications: Peritoneal Dialysis - New Concepts and Applications, 1990; Over 230 original publications and book chapters. Honours: Torchbearer of the American Kidney Foundation, 1993; Best Doctors in America, 1994. Memberships: Founder Member, Polish Society of

Nephrology; Founder Member, International Society for Peritoneal Dialysis; Honorary Member, Colombian Society of Nephrology. Hobbies: Sport; Travel. Address: University of Missouri, MA 436 Health Sciences Center, Columbia, MO 65212, USA.

TYERS G Frank O, b. 6 Nov 1935, Giroux, MON, Canada. CVT Surgeon. m. Phyllis Randall, 14 May 1960, 2 s. Education: MD; FRCSC; FACS; FACC. Appointments: Professor and Head, Division of Thoracic Surgery, University of Texas, Medical Branch; Professor and Head, Division of Cardiovascular and Thoracic Surgery, University of BC, Vancouver, Canada. Publications: About 200 contributions. Memberships: AATS; ABS; ABTS; ACC; ACS; AHA; ASA; AATS; BCCS; BCCPS; BCMA; CCS; CMA; CSCVTS; ISCVS; NASPE; RCPSC; STS; TSDA. Address: Floor C, Room 314, 700 West 10th Avenue, Vancouver BC, V5Z 4E5, Canada.

TZAFETTAS John Menelaos, b. 12 July 1943, Greece. Associate Professor in Obstetrics and Gynaecology. m. Sandra Whiting, 21 Sept 1980, 1 son, 2 daughters. Education: MD; DrMed (Greece), 1979; MRCOG (London), 1979; FRCOG (London), 1992. Appointments: Registrar, Lecturer in Gynaecology, St Thomas Hospital, London, England, 1977-78; Assistant Professor, 1985, Associate Professor, Obstetrics, Gynaecology, 1987-, Thessaloniki, Greece. Publications: The purpose of prelaparoscopy, transvaginal retrieval and evaluation of oocytes in a modified GIFT procedure, 1979; l/s ratio, biochemical and clinical changes after vitrodine IV infusion, 1983. Transvaginal intra-amniotic injection of Methotrexate in early ectopic pregnancy. Advantages over the laparoscopic approach, 1994; Transvaginal intra-fallopian insemination, GIFT/ZIFT, 1994. Memberships include: American Fertility Society; Hellenic Gynaecological Society; New York Academy of Sciences Hobby: Painting. Address: 30 Karolou Diehl Str, Thessaloniki, Greece.

TZORTZATOU-STATHOPOULOU Fotini, b. 6 April 1939, Kefalonia, Greece. Physician; Professor of Pediatric Hematology/Oncology. m. Jim Stathopoulos, 2 February 1980, 1 son, 1 daughter. Education: BA, MD, University of Athens, 1965, 1969; Specialist in Pediatrics, 1969; PhD, University of Cambridge, 1975. Appointments: Resident in Pediatrics, 1967; Senior Resident, 1969-72; Postdoctorate Researcher, 1972-75; Lecturer, University of Athens, 1976-81; Professor, 1981-93; Professor of Pediatric Hematology/Oncology, 1993-. Publications: Various professional publications in scientific medical journals. Honours: Choremis Award for the Highest Pediatric Researcher in Greece. Memberships: ASPHO; ESPHI; ISH; SIOP. Hobbies: Swimming. Address: Oncology Unit, First Department of Pediatrics, University of Athens, Aghia, Sophia Childrens Hospital, Goudi, Athens 11527, Greece.

U

UDEGBE Idayat Bolarinwa, b. 15 May 1961, Ibadan, Nigeria. Lecturer in Psychology. m. Joseph E Udegbe, 3 Aug 1985, 1 s, 1 d. Education: BEd, Science; MSc, Psychology; PhD, Psychology. Career: Graduate Research Assistant, 1984-87, Assistant Lecturer, 1987-91, Lecturer, 1991-, University of Ibadan, Nigeria. Publications: About 15 articles mainly on women's adjustment and health from adolescence to old age. Memberships: Social Sciences and Reproductive Health Network; Society for Psychological Study of Social Issues. Address: Department of Psychology, University of Ibadan, Ibadan, Nigeria.

UDELMAN Harold, b. 21 Mar 1933, Hamilton, OH, USA. Psychiatrist. m. Linda Chaisson, 25 Apr 1993, 1 s, 2 d. Education: BS, University of Cincinnati, 1954; MD, University of Cincinnati, College of Medicine, 1958. Appointments: Assistant Clinical Professor, University of California, Irvine; President, American Institute for Neuroimmunomodulation Research, Inc. Publications: Hope As A Factor in Remission of Illness, 1985; Concurrent Use of Buspirone in Anxious Patients During Withdrawal from Alphrazolam Therapy, 1990; A Preliminary Report on Anti-Depressant Therapy and Its Effects on Hope and Immunity, 1986. Honours: Fellowship APA, 1972; Fellowship, Academy of Psychosomatic Medicine, 1981. Memberships: American Psychiatric Association; American Medical Association; Academy of Psychosomatic Medicine. Hobbies: Tennis; Music. Address: 45 E Osborn Road, Phoenix, AZ 85012, USA.

UJHAZY Viliam, b. 18 Apr 1926, Likier, Czechoslovakia. Physician. m. Dr Dagmar Kralikova, 15 Oct 1955, 1 son, 1 daughter. Education: MD, 1951; PhD, 1966; DSc, 1978. Appointments: Resident, General Hospital, Banska Bystrica, 1951-55; Scientist, Senior Scientist, 1955-, Director, 1983-91, Cancer Research Institute, Slovak Academy of Sciences, Bratislava. Publications: Contributor of over 110 scientific articles in professional journals. Honours: National Prize of Slovakia for Science, 1983; Golden Medal, Slovak Academy of Sciences, 1986; Consultant, Chief Editor, Neoplasma. Memberships: Council, International Union Against Cancer; UICC. Hobbies: Music; Swimming. Address: Medena 4, 81102 Bratislava, Slovakia.

ULDALL-HANSEN Mogens Christian, b. 15 Dec 1913, Copenhagen, Denmark. Chiropractor. m. Tove Larsen, 14 Jan 1939, 2 s, 2 d. Education: Doctor of Chiropracty, 1938. Career includes: President, Danish Chiropractic Association; Chiropractor; Currently, Unitarian Pastor, 1986-. Publications: The Upright Posture of Man; Several learned articles. Honour: Honorary Member of Danish Chiropractic Association, 1991. Memberships include: Honorary Member, Archeological Society, 1982. Hobbies: Music; Astronomy. Address: Mejsevej 3, Holbaek 4300, Denmark.

UMEDA Masaru, b. 5 December 1957, Sakai, Japan. Doctor. m. Miho Yamanaka, 28 October 1989, 1 son, 1 daughter. Education: MD, PhD, Osaka City University Medical School, 1987. Appointments: Head, Department of Hemodialysis, Tadaoka Municipal Hospital; Director, Kidney Center, Nogami Hospital. Publications: Ca kinetics in Hemodialysis Patients, 1994; RBC AL in Renal Failure, 1990; Polymyxin Sepharose, 1983; Carbocyanine Stain, 1987. Honours: Osaka City Mayor's Award, Osaka Medical Association, 1988. Memberships: Council, Japanese Society of Artifical Organs; American Society of Artificial Internal Organs. Hobbies: Fishing; Japanese Chess. Address: Kidney Center, Nogami Hospital, 1-2-5 Tarui, Sennnann-Shi, Osaka 590-05, Japan.

UNGER Gerald, b. 15 May 1949, New York City, New York, USA. Physician; Attorney. m. Alicen-J McGowan, PhD; 2 sons, 1 daughter. Education: JD, Bernedean University, 1979; MD, Escuela Libre and Instituto Politecnico Nacional, 1986; Advanced training in Arbitration, American Arbitration Association, 1992; Certificate Programme in Health Care Negotiation and Conflict Resolution, Boston University School of Public Health, 1993; Harvard Law School, Credentialed in Negotiation, 1994; Board Certified in Medical Jurisprudence, by the American Board of Forensic Examiners; Board Certified, American Board of Medical Legal Analysis in Medicine and Surgery. Appointments include: Medical Director, Vietnam Veterans Post-Traumatic Stress Disorder Programme, 1988-90; Senior Partner, Consultant in Clinical Legal Medicine, Paladin Professional Group PA, Fort Lauderdale, Florida, 1988-; Surgeon and Consultant in Medical Fraud, Bronx-Lebanon Hospital, 1990-92;

Reviewer, Hospital and Community Psychiatry, American Psychiatric Association publication, 1993. Publications: On Call: The Law and Ethics of Patient Dumping, 1992. Introduction to Ethical Decision Making in Surgery, 1994. Honours: Honorary Doctorate in Physical Medicine, Clinica Moderna and Metropolitan University, 1987. Memberships include: International College of Surgeons, Ethics Committee; Fellow, American College of Legal Medicine; Federal Bar Association; International Bar Association; American Bar Associations Centre for Professional Resposibility; American College of Physician Executives; Incoming Chairman, Forum on Medicine and Law, Admitted to Practice before the Maritime Administration and its Subsidy Boards, US Department of Transportation; Broward County Mediation Association; Editorial Review Board, Journal of Neurological and Orthopaedic Medicine; American Society of Critical Care Medicine, Surgical Critical Care Committee; New York State Captain, American Trial Lawyers Exchange. Address: 2800 E Commercial Blvd, Suite 212, Ft Lauderdale, FL 33308, USa.

URSANO Robert J, b. 26 May 1947. m. Education: BS, Magna Cum Laude, Chemistry, University of Notre Dame, 1969; MD, Yale University, 1973; Resident in Psychiatry, Wilford Hall USAF Medical Center, 1973-75; Postdoctoral Fellow, Psychiatry, Yale University and Yale Psychiatric Institute, 1975-77; USAF Primary Course in Aerospace Medicine, Brooks Air Force Base, Texas, 1977; Washington Psychoanalytic Institute, 1980-86. Appointments: Staff Psychiatrist, USAF School of Aerospace Medicine, Brooks Air Force Base, Texas, 1977-79; Clinical Assistant Professor, University of Texas, 1977-79; Consultant & Supervisor, Psychotherapy, Wilford Hall USAF Medical Center, 1977-79; Consultant, National Naval Medical Center, Bethesda and Walter Reed US Army Medical Center, Washington, 1979-; Uniformed Services University of the Health Sciences, Department of Psychiatry, Bethesda, Maryland: Assistant Professor/Director, Third Year Clerkships, 1979-81; Associate Professor/Director, Third Year Clerkships, 1981-83; Professor & Associate Chairman, 1987-90; Professor & Acting Chairman, 1990-92; Professor & Chairman, 1992-. Publications: Numerous Original Articles, Books, Book Chapters, Monographs, Reviews, Letters, Abstracts and Presentations. Honours: include, Alpha Epsilon Delta; Phi Beta Kappa; Falk Fellow, American Psychiatric Association; Special Assistant to USAF Surgeon General. Memberships: include, International Psychoanalytic Association; American Psychosomatic Society; Washington Psychiatric Society; Aviation Space and Environmental Medicine. Address: Department of Psychiatry, Uniformed Services University of the Health Sciences, 4301 Jones Bridge Road, Bethesda, Maryland 20814, USA.

USHIO Yukitaka, b. 1 Nov 1937, Hiroshima, Japan. Professor of Neurosurgery. m. Kazuko Tomomatsu, 13 Jan 1969, 2 d. Education: MD, Osaka University Medical School. Appointments: Assistant Professor of Neurosurgery, Osaka University Medical School; Currently, Professor and Chairman, Department of Neurosurgery, Kumamoto University Medical School. Publications: Chemotherapy of metastatic brain tumors from lung carcinoma, in Neurosurgery, 1991; Chemotherapy of malignant gliomas, in Critical Reviews of Neurosurgery, 1992; Treatment of supratentorial low-grade astrocytoma, in Critical Reviews of Neurosurgery, 1993. Memberships: American Congress of Neurosurgery; Japanese Society of Neurosurgery; Japanese Congress of Neurosurgery; Japanese Society of Cancer Research. Hobbies: Skiing; Tennis. Address: 1-1-1 Honjyo, Kumamoto 860, Japan.

UTIAN Wulf Hessel, b. 28 Sep 1939, Johannesburg, South Africa. Obstetrics and Gynaecology. m. Moira Mervis, 4 Oct 1964, 1 s, 1 d. Education: MBBCH; PhD; FRCOG; FACOG; FICS. Career: Full Time Consultant, 1968-69, Part Time Consultant, 1970-76, University of Cape Town; Associate Professor, Obstetrics and Gynaecology, 1976-89, Currently, Arthur H Bill Professor and Chairman, Reproductive Biology, 1989-, Case Western Reserve University School of Medicine, Cleveland; Director, Obstetrics and Gynaecology, Mount Sinai Medical Center, 1980-89. Publications: 8 Books and over 120 scientific articles including: The Menopause Manual, 1978; Menopause in Modern Perspective, 1980; Your Middle Years, 1980; Managing Your Menopause, 1990. Memberships: International Menopause Society; North American Menopause Society; ACOG; RCOG; AFS. Hobbies: Hiking; Sailing. Address: 9725 Lake Shore Boulevard, Bratenahl, OH 44108, USA.

UTIDJIAN Haig Michael Dikran, b. 11 Aug 1931, London, England. Physician. m. Lesley Helen Jukes, 24 Jan 1954, 3 sons, 2 daughters. Education: MB BS,(London), UCH, 1954; DIH, 1962; Boards in

Occupatrioonal Medicine, USA, 1975; MFOM. Appointments: Pipeline Medical Officer, Iraq Petroleum Company; Assistant Industrial Medical Officer, Slough Industrial Health Service; Industrial Medical Officer, Caroni Limited (Tate and Lyle), Trinidad; Assistant Professor of Edipdemiology, University of Pittsburgh, USA; Vice President, Health Sciences, Equitable Environmental Health Incorporated, USA; Associate Corporate Medical Director, Union Carbide; Corporate Medical Director, American Cyanamid Company, 1981-95; International Consultant in Occupational Medicine, Toxicology and Epidemiology. Publications: Ferruginous Bodies in Human Lungs - Prevalence at Random Autopsies, Co-author, 1968; Sputum Cytology and Occupational Pulmonary Disease, Co-author, 1973. Memberships: Britiah Medical Association; Society of Occupational Medicine; Faculty of Occupational Medicine, RCp, London; Fellow, American College of Occupational and Environmental Medicine; American College of Epidemiology. Hobbies: Classical Numismatics; Travel in Mediterranean and Near and Middle East. Address: 3 The Spinney, Sudbury Hill Close, Wembley, Middlesex HA0 2QS, England.

UTSUNOMIYA Toshinori, b. 14 Feb 1951, Kyoto, Japan. Cardiologist. m. Yasuko Utsunomiya, 29 Apr 1977, 2 sons, 3 daughters. Education: Diploma in Medicine; MD. Appointments: Assistant, 3rd Department of Internal Medicine, Nagasaki University; Visiting Researcher, University of California, Irvine, USA; Currently Lecturer in Internal Medicine, Saga Medical School, Saga, Japan. Publications: Effect of machine parameters on variance display in Doppler color flow mapping, 1990; Doppler color flow proximal isovelocity surface area method for estimating volume flow rate, 1991. Memberships: Fellow, Japanese Society of Internal Medicine; Fellow, Japanese Circulation Society; The Japan Society of Ultrasonics in Medicine; American Society of Echocardiography. Hobbies: Jogging; Music. Address: 1-17-30 Nabeshima, Saga 849, Japan.

UYANWAH Philomena Obiageliuwa, b. 28 March 1940, Enugu, Nigeria. Obstetrician and Gynaecologist. Education: MB CHB, Aberdeen, Scotland 1964; MD, Manchester University, England, 1978; MRCOG, England, 1973. Appointments: Senior Consultant, Senior Lecturer, University of Lagos, Nigeria; Advisor, Cancer of Cervix, WHO Africa. Publications Include: Fibrinolytic Enzyme System in Pregnancy in Nigeria, 1984; Influence of Maternal Factors in the Post Natal Smear, 1985; A Preliminary Study of an Open Clinical Comparative Evaluation of Tioconazole "Trysod", 1986; Control of Cancer of the Cervix Uteri, 1986. Honours: Ministerial Merit Award, 1994; Senior Fellowship Award, 1987; International University Fellowship Award, 1985; Pfizer Fellowship Award, 1978. Memberships: Royal College of Obstetricians & Gynaecologists, England; Nigerian College of Obstetricians & Gynaecologists Society. Hobbies: Crossword Puzzles; Reading; Table Tennis; Television. Address: 24 Princess Road, Primrose Hill, Regents Park, London NW1 8JL, England.

UYS Johanna Beatrix, b. 1 May 1948, Heidelberg, Transvaal, South Africa. Radiographer. m. Dietloff J Uys, 2 May 1970, 3 sons, 1 daughter. Education: Dipl Radiography, University of Pretoria, 1968. Appointment: Housewife. Memberships: South African Medical and Dental Council; South African Woman Agricultural Union. Hobbies: Sewing; Gardening; Pottery; Silk Painting. Address: 14 Nagtegal Avenue, Birch Acres x 2, Kempton Park 1619, South Africa.

UZEL Ilter, b. 29 Oct 1944, Bor, Turkey. Professor of Orthodontics. m. A Aysel, 5 July 1967, 2 sons. Education: DDS, Istanbul University, 1965; Specialist, Orthodontics, 1976; PhD, History of Medicine, Medical Ethics, 1979; Private Dozent, 1981; Professor of Orthodontics, 1985. Appointments: Dental Surgeon, Trabzon Military Hospital, 1965-72; Assistant, Orthodontics, 1972-76; Orthodontist, Professor of Orthodontics, Gülhane Medical Academy, 1976-90; Private Practice in Orthodontics, 1990-94; Professor of Orthodontics and Medical Ethics, çukurava University, Adana, 1994-. Publications: Co-author, books: Orthodontics and Cephalometrics, 1984; Cerrâhiyyetü'l - Hâniyye (The Imperial's Surgery), 1992; Handbook of Orthodontics, 1993; Introduction of History of Dentistry in Turkey, 1993. Memberships: European Orthodontic Society; Société Internationale de l'Histoire de la Médecine. Hobbies: Painting Islamic miniatures; Collecting antique medical instruments. Address: Resit Galip C 130-3, 06700 GÓP Ankara, Turkey.

V

VAGUE Jean Marie, b. 25 Nov 1911, Draguignan. Professor of Endocrinology. m. Denise Jouve, 3 Sept 1936, 3 sons, 1 daughter. Education: Resident, Marseille, 1932; MD, Marseille, 1935; Lic Sc, 1935. Appointments: Physician, Hospital, 1943; Associate Professor, 1946; Professor, Endocrinology Unit, Marseille, 1957; Academy of Science, New York, 1980; Academy of Medicine, France, 1980; Academy of Medicine, Spain, 1980; Emeritus Professor, 1981; Academy of Science & Letters, Marseille, 1986; Academy of Medicine, Italy, 1989; Academy of Medicine, Belgium, 1993. Publications: First demonstration of diabetogenic and atherogenic effect of android obesity with topographic distribution of fat in upper and deep parts of the body, evolution of android obesity from 1st stage of efficacious hyperinsulinism to less efficacious hyperinsulinism and hypoinsulinism, 1947-56; Books: Acute Hepatonephritis, 1935; Creatine, 1939; Cardiac Liver, 1939; Meagernesses, 1945; Human Sexual Differentation, 1953; Notions of Endocrinology, 1965; Diabetic's Adviser, 1971; Obesities, 1991; Dawn over Iaboc's Ford, History of Men, 1993. Memberships: President, National Syndicate of French Professors of Medicine, 1967-81; American Diabetic Association; Europe Diabetic Association; Endocrinology Society of America, France, Spain, and Italy; Royal Society of London. Honours: French Academy Medical Prize's, 1938-39; French Academy of Science Prize's, 1938-53; War Cross, 1940; Officer Légion d'honneur & Academy Oalms, 1973; International Willendorf Award, 1990; French Maurice Dérot Prize, 1991; French Academy Prize, 1994; French Academy of Moral and Politic Sciences Prize, 1994. Address: 6 Prado Parc, 411 Avenue du Prado, F-13008 Marseille, France.

VAISMAN Nachum, b. 3 Sep 1948, Jerusalem, Israel. Paediatrician. m. Tamar Vaisman, 13 May 1971, 1 s, 2 d. Education: BSc, Chemistry, Clinical Nutrition, Gastroenterology; MD, Tel Aviv University Medical School, 1979; Paediatrics, Clinical Nutrition, 1984-87, Sick Children Hospital, Toronto, Canada. Appointment: Paediatrician, Head of Nutritional Clinic, Kaplan Hospital, Rehovot, Israel. Publications: REE Expenditure in patients with CF, in Journal of Paediatrics, 1987; Changees in body composition during refeeding patients with AN, in Journal of Paediatrics, 1988; Changes in REE and substrate utilization during refeeding patients with AN, in European Journal of Clinical Nutrition, 1991; Protein turnover and REE in patients with undernutrition and chronic lung disease, in American Journal of Clinical Nutrition, 1992; Change in body composition of children with subnormal secretion of growth hormone during first year of treatment, in Metabolism, 1992. Memberships: Israeli Medical Association; Israeli Association for GI and Nutrition; American Association for Clinical Nutrition. Hobbies: Gardening; Books; Music. Address: Kaplan Hospital, Pediatrics Department B, Rehovot, Israel.

VALEK Albert, b. 16 April 1925, Prestice, Czechoslovakia. Professor of Medicine; Physician. m. Dina Melicharova, 22 April 1977, 3 sons. Education: MD; PhD; DSc. Appointments: Head, Department of Internal Medicine, Charles University Medical School, Prague; Head, Department of Nephrology and Dialysis. Publications: Books: Acute Renal Failure, 1967; Chronic Renal Failure, 1973; Regular Dialysis Treatment, 1977; Clinical Nephrology, 1984; 268 other professional publications. Honour: International Medal of the National Kidney Foundation, USA; Honorary Member, Society of Nephrology, Bulgaria, Czechoslovakia, Germany, Hungary, Poland, Russia, Slovak Society of Medicine, EDTNA. Memberships: EDTA; ISAO; ESAO; Czechoslovakia Society of Nephrology. Hobbies: Tennis. Address: Karenova 14, 150 00 Prague 5-Kosire, Czechoslovakia.

VAN ASSCHE Frans Andre, b. 17 Dec 1937, Liezele, Belgium. Obstetrician and Gynaecologist. m. Liddy Tierens, 2 sons, 2 daughters. Education: Classic Humanities, Sint-Jan College, Antwerp, 1949-56; MD, KU Leuven, 1963; PhD, 1970; FRCOG, 1990. Appointments: Associate Professor, 1970, Professor of Obstetrics and Gynaecology, 1974, Board Member, Faculty of Medicine, 1982, Professor, Chairman, Department of Obstetrics and Gynaecology, 1983, Head, Education Committee, Faculty of Medicine, 1990, K U Leuven; Secretary-General, ECOG, 1992; Secretary-General, EBGO, 1994; President-Elect, ISSHP, 1994. Publications: Contributor of numerous professional articles, proceedings, papers and reports on medical and scientific subjects. Memberships include: Executive Member, Flemish Obstetrical and Gynaecological Society' Past President, Royal Belgian Society of Obstetrics and Gynaecology; Executive Member, International Society of Hypertension in Pregnancy; Past President, European Diabetic Pregnancy Study Group; Honorary Member, Ulster Obstetric and Gynaecological Society, United Kingdom; Honorary Member, Gynaecological Club, United Kingdom. Address: Herestraat 49, 3000 Leuven, Belgium.

VAN BOEMEL Gretchen, b. 29 December 1955, Glendale, California, USA. Director, Ocular Electrophysiology. Education: BA, California State University, Long Beach, 1980; MA, University of California, Irvine, 1992; PhD Candidate, University of California, Irvine, 1993. Appointments: Director, Ocular Electrophysiology Department, Doheny Eye Institute, Los Angeles, California. Publications: The Diagnosis of Retinal Disease: A Practical Guide, 1989; Psychological Effects of Abuse on Older Cambodian Female Refugees, 1989; Outreach and Education: Reduction of Black Market Enrollment, 1991; Treatment for Psychosomatic Blindness Among Cambodian Refugee Women, 1992; Education and Outreach Extending SSI Benefits to the Blind, Newly Blind Aged and Visually Disabled, 1994. Honours: Distinguished Publication Award, Association of Women in Psychology, 1990; Science Directorate Award, American Psychological Association, 1990; Distinguished Faculty Award, Joint Commission on Allied Health Personnell in Ophthalmology, 1990. Memberships: American Psychological Association; Association for Research in Vision and Ophthalmology; California Association of Ophthalmology. Hobbies: Fly Fishing; Reading; Camping; Gardening. Address: Doheny Eye Institute, 1450 San Pablo Street, Suite 5200, Los Angeles, CA 90033, USA.

VAN DEN BOUT Jan, b. 30 Oct 1994, Tiel, Netherlands. Psychologist. m. Kienhorst Van Den Bout, 2 s. Education: Doctor of Psychology. Appointments: Assistant Professor, University of Nijmegen, Netherlands; Professor, University of Utrecht, Netherlands. Publications: 3 contributions concerning inpatients with spinal cord injuries to Journal of Clinical Psychology, 1988. Honour: Associate Fellow, Institute for Rational - Emotive Therapy. Address: Department of Clinical Psychology, University of Utrecht, Heidelberglaan 1, Utrecht 3584 CS, Netherlands.

VAN DEN BRANDT Piet A, b. 21 Oct 1957, Vlijmen, Netherlands. Epidemiologist; Nutritionist. 1 s. Education: MSc, Nutrition, Agricultural University, Wagemingen, NL, 1983; SM, Epidemiology, Harvard School of Public Health, Boston, MA, 1984; PhD, University of Limburg, Maastricht, NL, 1993. Career: Research Fellow, Dutch Cancer Society, 1983-85; Assistant Professor, Epidemiology, University of Limburg, Maastricht, 1986-; Consultant Epidemiologist, Comprehensive Cancer Centre, Limburg, Maastricht, 1987-. Publications: Numerous articles and abstracts including: Co-author, A prospective cohort study on dietary fat and the risk of postmenopausal breast cancer, in Cancer Research, 1993; Co-author, Epidemiology of selenium status and cancer, chapter in Free Radicals in Biology and Medicine, 1994; Co-author, Toenail selenium levels and the risk of breast cancer, in American Journal of Epidemiology, 1994. Honour: Edmond Hustinx Science Prize, University of Limburg, Maastricht, 1994. Memberships: Society for Epidemiologic Research; Netherlands Epidemiological Society; International Epidemiological Association; American Association for Cancer Research. Hobbies: Running; Volleyball. Address: University of Limburg, Department of Epidemiology, PO Box 616, NL-6200 MD, Maastricht, Netherlands.

VAN DER KOLK Bessel A, b. 7 Aug 1943, Netherlands. Psychiatrist. m. Elisabeth de Boer, 13 Jun 1971, 1 s, 1 d. Education: MD. Career: Director, Psychpharmacology Training, Cambridge Hospital, MA, 1982-87; Director, Trauma Clinic, MA Health Center, Boston, 1982-90; Director, Trauma Clinic, MA General Hospital, 1990-94; Currently, Director, HRI Training Center, Associate Professor of Psychiatry, Harvard Medical School. Publications: PTSD: biological and psychological sequence, 1985; Psychological Trauma, 1987; Pierre Janet and the breakdown of adaptation in psychological trauma, 1989; Co-author, The Black Hole of Trauma, 1995. Honours: Fernandez Marina Award, Puerto Rico Psychiatric Association, 1989; David Schaffer Award for Research on Traumatic Stress, 1992; Eli Lilly Lecturer, Royal College of Psychiatrists, 1994. Memberships: International Society for Traumatic Stress Studies; American Psychiatric Association; American Group Psychotherapy Association. Hobbies: Cello; Hiking; Tennis; History; Art. Address: 16 Braddock Park, Boston, MA 02116, USA.

VAN DER LINDEN Frans P G M, b. 7 Apr 1932, Helmond, Netherlands. Orthodontist. m. Pim J Van Der Linden-Hage, 3 Feb 1960, 1 s, 4 d. Education: DDS, University of Groningen, 1957; PhD, University of Groningen, 1959. Appointment: Professor of Orthodontics, University of Nijmegen, 1962-. Publications include: 140 articles in international scientific journals including: Consequences of functional aspects and growth changes for retention and relapse, in Retention and Long Term Stability, 1993; Books and book chapters include: Orthodontie in de praktijk, 1992. Honours include: Honorary Member Belgian Dental Association, 1972; De Dentz Award, Dutch Society of Dentistry, 1979; Award of Associated Orthodontic Journals of Europe, 1991; Royal Netherlands Academy of Arts and Sciences, 1992; Professor Lammers Prize for Excellence in Teaching Achievements, 1993; Fellow, Royal College of Physicians and Surgeons of Glasgow, 1995. Memberships include: Netherlands Dental Association; Netherlands Association of Orthodontists; European Orthodontic Society; Deutsch Gesellschaft für Kieferothopädie; Angle Society of Europe; International Society of Cranio-Facial Biology; International Association for Dental Research. Hobbies include: Sailing; Golf. Address: Philips van Layenlaan 25, 6500 HB Nijmegen, Netherlands.

VAN DER WESTHUIJZEN Albert, b. 22 Jan 1955, Cape Town, South Africa. Oral and Maxillofacial Surgeon. Education: BCHD, University of Stellenbosch, South Africa, 1979; MCHD, University of Stellenbosch, South Africa, 1990, FFD (SA) MFOS; FDSRCS (Eng). Appointments: Dentist, Addington Hospital, Durban, 1979-80; Dentist, Private Practice, Wimbledon, London, 1980-85; Registrar in O & FMS, University of Stellenbosch, South Africa, 1985-90; Visiting Registrar, Department of Oral & Maxillofacial Surgery, Guy's Hospital, London, 1991-92; Senior Specialist/Senior Lecturer, Department of Oral & Maxillofacial Surgery, University of Stellenbosch, South Africa; Consultant, Department of Oral and Maxillofacial Surgery, University of Stellenbosch, South Africa. Publications: A Rapidly Fatal Palatal Ulcer: Rhinocerebral Mucormycons, 1989; A Randomized Double Blind Comparison of Tiaprofenic Acid and Diclophenic Sodium following Third Molar Surgery, 1994. Memberships: South African Society of Maxillofacial & Oral Surgeons; British Association of Oral & Maxillofacial Surgeons; International Association of Oral & Maxillofacial Surgeons; Dental Association of South Africa. Address: Department of Oral & Maxillofacial Surgery, Dental Faculty, University of Stellenbosch, Private Bag XI, Tygerberg 7505, South Africa.

VAN DYCK Christopher H, b. 25 Aug 1955, Wichita, Kansas, USA. Research Psychiatrist. m. Dr Amy F T Arnsten, 25 Apr 1987, 1 s, 1 d. Education: BA, Yale University, 1978; MD, Northwestern University, 1984. Appointments: Assistant Professor of Psychiatry, Geopsychiatry, Yale University School of Medicine. Memberships: Society of Nuclear Medicine; Society of Neuroscience; American Association of Geriatric Psychiatry; American Psychiatric Association. Hobbies: Chess; Astronomy; Gardening. Address: CB 2041, Yale University School of Medicine, 333 Cedar Street, Hew Haven, CT 06510, USA.

VAN GELDER Nico M, b. 24 Dec, Indonesia. Neurobiologist. m. Louise M Singer, 30 May 1959, 2 s, 1 d. Education: BSc; PhD, Montreal Neurological Institute, McGill University. Career: Life Insurance Medical Research Fellow, Cambridge, England, 1959; Research Associate, Harvard Medical School, 1960-62; Assistant Professor, Tufts University, 1962-67; Visiting Professor, IVIC, Venezuela; Advisor, Pan American Health Organization; Associate Professor, 1967-73, Affiliate Professor of Nutrition, Currently, Professor of Physiology, University of Montreal, Canada. Publications: Contributions to: Journal of Neurochemistry, 1958, Progress Brain Research, 1966, Brain Research, 1972, Canadian Journal of Physiology and Pharmacology, 1978, EEG Supplement, 1982, Journal of Neuroscience Res, 1988, Advanced Experimental Medical Biology, 1992, Basic Mechanisms Hyperexci, 1983, Malnutrition Infant Brain, 1990. Memberships: American Society of Neurochemistry; International Society of Neurochemistry; European Society of Neurochemistry; Spinal Cord Research Foundation (PVA); Goteborg Epil Center; NY Academy of Sciences; IBRO; Society of Neuroscience, Venezuela. Hobbies: Sailing; Ecology. Address: University of Montreal, Faculty of Medicine, Department of Physiology, CP 6128 succursale A, Montreal, Quebec, Canada, H3C 3J7.

VAN GILDER John Corley, b. 14 Aug 1935, Huntington, West VA, USA. Physician. m. Kerstin Olesson, 3 Jun 1965, 2 s, 2 d. Education: MD, 1961, AB, Arts and Sciences, 1957, Bachelor of Medicine, 1957. Appointment: Professor and Chairman, Department of Neurosurgery, University of Iowa. Hobbies: Sport; Fishing; Motorcycle Touring. Address: Department of Neurosurgery, University of Iowa, Iowa City, Iowa 52242, USA.

VAN THIEL David, b. 5 sept 1941, Cutbank, Montana, USA. Physician. m. Judith Gausler, 2 s, 3 d. Education: MD, UCLA, 1967; AOA. Appointments: Professor of Medicine, Surgery, Psychiatry; Chief of Gastroenterology, University of Pittsburgh School of Medicine; Medical Director, Transplantation. Publications: Contributor of over 700 works. Honours: President, AASLD; President, RSA. Memberships: AGA; AASLD; RSA; Endocrine Society; Transplant Society. Hobbies: Collecting stamps, masks and maps. Address: 3300 Northwest Expressway, Oklahoma Transplant Institute, Baptist Medical Centre, Oklahoma City, OK 73112, USA.

VAN WANING Adeline, b. 12 Aug 1946, Rotterdam, Netherlands. Psychiatrist. Education: MD, University of Leiden, 1972; Psychiatrist, 1976; PhD, Doctorate in Medical Science, 1994. Appointments: Staff Member, Child Psychiatry, Adolescent Psychiatry, University of Amsterdam; Currently Staff Member, Psychoanalytical Institute, Amsterdam. Publications: To be the best or not to be, that's the question, 1991; The works of pioneering psychoanalyst Sabina Spielrein, 1992; Geen woorden maar daden - over ageren, 1994. Memberships: Dutch Society of Psychiatry; Dutch Psychoanalytical Association; International Psychoanalytical Association. Hobbies: Drawing; Writing; Cycling; Swimming. Address: Den Texstraat 51 II, 1017 XZ Amsterdam, Netherlands.

VAN WOUWE Jacobus Pieter (Ko), b. 27 Jan 1950, Rotterdam, Netherlands. Consultant in Paediatrics. m. Eva Elbaum, 2 May 1989, 1 son. Education: BSc thesis, Community Hospital, Roanoke Valley, Virginia, USA, 1972; MD, Erasmus University, Rotterdam, 1979; Resident in Paediatrics, 1979-89; PhD, 1991, Leiden University. Appointments: Counsellor, Frost Valley, New York, USA, 1967-71; Case Worker, Municipal Health Service, Rotterdam, Netherlands, 1973-76; Researcher, Delft University of Technology, 1983-89; Currently Consultant in Paediatrics. Publications: Published on Medical Genetics, 1985, on Trace Elements Cu and Zn, 1986-95; Review on Acrodermatitis Enteropathica, 1989. Honours: Grantee, Prevention Fund. Memberships: American Society for Clinical Nutrition; European Society for Clinical Investigation; Fellow, Royal Society of Medicine, UK. Hobbies: Piano playing; Windsurfing; Philately. Address: Rijnsburgerweg 102, 2333 AE Leiden, Netherlands.

VANCE Dennis E, b. 14 July 1942, Idaho, USA. Professor of Biochemistry. m. Jean Eaton, 10 June 1967, 1 son, 1 daughter. Education: BS, Dickinson College; PhD, University of Pittsburgh. Appointments: Assistant Professor, 1973; Associate Professor, 1978; Professor, 1982, Head, 1982-86, Department of Biochemistry, University of British Columbia, Canada; Currently Professor of Biochemistry, Director of Lipid and Lipoprotein Research Group, University of Alberta, Edmonton. Publications: Biochemistry of Lipids and Membranes (edited with Jean Vance), 1985; Phospholipid Metabolism (editor), 1989; Biochemistry of Lipids, Lipoproteins and Membranes (edited with Jean Vance), 1991; Principles of Biochemistry (G Zubay and W Parsons), 1994. Honours: Postdoctoral Fellowship, National Institutes of Health, 1968; Established Investigator, American Heart Association, 1973-78; Boeringher-Mannheim Canada Prize, Canadian Biochemistry Society, 1989; Heinrich Wifland Prize from Germany, 1989. Memberships: Canadian Society of Biochemistry and Molecular Biology; American Society of Biochemistry and Molecular Biology. Hobbies: Golf; Skiing; Fishing; Camping; Hiking. Address: Lipid and Lipoprotein Research Group, University of Alberta, Edmonton, Alberta, Canada T6G 2S2.

VANDENBOS Gary Roger, b. 16 Dec 1943, Grand Rapids, MI, USA. Psychology. m. Jane Annunziata, 16 Dec 1983, 1 s. Education: PhD, Clinical Psychology, University of Detroit; Diplomate, Forensic Psychology. Appointments: Director, Howell Area Community Mental Health, 1973-77; Director, National Policy Studies, APA, 1977-82; Professor of Clinical Psychology, University of Bergen, Norway, 1982-84; Executive Director, Communications, APA, 1984-. Publications: Psychology and National Health Insurance, 1979; Psychotherapy of Schizophrenia: The Treatment of Choice, 1981; Psychological Aspects of Serious Illness, 1990; Psychopharmacology: Basic Mechanisms and Applied Interventions, 1992. Honour: Fellow in Psychotherapy. Memberships: Society for Psychotherapy Research; American Psychological Association. Address: American Psychological Association, 750 First Street NE, Washington, DC 20002-4242, USA.

VARMA Thankam Rama, b. 2 Oct 1937, India. Medical Doctor. m. Dr Rama Varma, 1 s, 1 d. Education: PhD; FRCS; MRCOG; FRCOG. Career includes: Registrar to Professor of Obstetrics and Gynaecology, Women and Children's Hospital, Madras, India, 1964-65; Senior Registrar, Research Fellow, Professor Curzen, Westminster Medical School, Queen Mary's Hospital, Roehampton, 1970-73; Currently, Senior Lecturer and Consultant in Obstetrics and Gynaecology, St George's Hospital and Medical School, London; Medical Examiner. Publications include: Numerous articles, books, and chapters including: Books: Manual of Gynaecology, 1986, Postgraduate Gynaecology, 1991, Tuberculosis of the Genital Tract in Clinical Gynaecology and Obstetrics, 1993. Honours include: First Woman Surgeon Appointed at St George's Hospital; Mrs Rukmani Memorial Gold Medal for Ophthalmology, Bradfield Prize for Anatomy and Surgery, Madras Medical College; Balfour Memorial Medal, Dr T M Nair Memorial Medal, The Rajah of Pangal Gold Medal, Madras University. Memberships include: Royal College of Surgeons, Edinburgh; Royal College of Obstetricians and Gynaecologists, London; British Fertility Society; British Menopause Society; Medical Advisory Committee. Hobbies: Travel; Music; Classical Dance; Writing. Address: 3 Woodcote Drive, Purley, Surrey. CR8 3PD, England.

VARTANIAN Genrikh Aramaisovich, b. 6 Dec 1930, Krasnodar, Russia. Neurobiologist. m. Emma A Vartanian, 17 Feb 1962, 1 s, 2 d. Education: PhD, 1954, MD, 1958, Leningrad Medical Institute. Career: Professor of Physiology, Legon University, Gana and Makerere University, Kampala, Uganda; Head, Laboratory of Memory; Head, Pavlovian Physiology Department, Institute of Experimental Medicine, St Petersburg, Russia. Publications: 7 Books in Russian including: Organization and Modulation of Memory Processes, 1981, Emotions and Behaviour, 1989, Chemical Symmetry and Asymmetry of the Brain, 1991, Neurobiological Bases of the Higher Nervous Activity, 1991, Emotional Analizator of the Brain, 1994; 279 Articles in Russian and English. Memberships: Corresponding member, Russian Academy for Medical Sciences; IBRO; Russian Physiological Society; Expert, World Health Organization. Hobby: Painting. Address: Barmaleeva Str 18, Apt 11, St Petersburg 197136, Russia.

VASCO Antonio José Branco, b. 22 Jan 1955, Abrantes, Portugal. Psychologist. Education: MA, Catholic University of America, Washington DC, 1985; PhD, University of Lisbon, Portugal, 1993; Doctorate in Counselling and Psychotherapy, University of Lisbon, 1993. Career: Lecturer, 1980-83, Senior Lecturer, 1985-93, Assistant Professor, 1993-, Counselling and Psychotherapy, University of Lisbon, Portugal; Teaching Assistant, Catholic University of America, Washington DC, 1983-84. Publications include: Co-author, Psychotherapist know thyself!: Dissonance between metatheoretical and personal values in psychotherapists of different theoretical orientations, in Psychotherapy Research, 1993; Author, Correlates of constructivism among Portuguese therapists, in Journal of Constructivist Psychology, 1994; Co-author, The development of psychotherapist's theoretical orientation and clinical practice, in British Journal of Guidance and Counselling, 1994. Honour: Fulbright Grantee, Catholic University of America, 1983-84. Memberships: Portuguese Association of Psychotherapy; Portuguese Association of Cognitive-Behaviour Therapy; American Psychological Association; American Psychological Society; International Association of Cognitive Therapy; Society for the Exploration of Psychotherapy Integration; Society for Psychotherapy Research. Hobbies: Reading; Films; Travel. Address: Rua Goncalo Nunes 49-B, 1400 Lisboa, Portugal.

VASILYEV Valentine A, b. 27 Aug 1933, Olaneshti, Moldova. Cardiosurgeon. m. Larisa Vasilyeva, 29 Sept 1965, 3 daughters. Education: MD with honours, Kishinev State University, 1958; Training, 1960-63; Associate Professor qualification. Appointments: General Surgeon, 1958-60; Assistant Professor, 1963-70; Associate Professor, Department of Surgery, Kishinev State Medical University, 1970-. Publications include: Constrictive Pericarditis in Childhood, 1963; The Immediate and the Late Results after Subtotal Pericardectomy, 1964; Surgical treatment of foreign bodies from weapons in the lungs, 1964; Chronic Constrictive Pericarditis, 1969. Honours: Excellent Doctor, 1966. Memberships: Moldavian National Society of Surgery; Moldavian National Society of Cardiology. Hobby: Gardening. Address: Apartment 41, House 22, Miron Costin str, 277068 Kishinev, Moldova.

VASSILYEV Grigory Alekseevich, b. 14 Sept 1944, Olaneshty, Moldova. Anaesthesiologist. m. Liudmila Vassilyeva, 3 Nov 1977, 2 sons. Education: PhD, 1978. Appointments: Anaesthesiologist, 1967-73;

Assistant Professor, 1973; Associate Professor, Kive Advanced Training Institute for Physicians Anaesthesiology & Intensive Care Department, 1982. Publications: Co-author: Reference Book for Doctors of the First Aid, 1972; Co-author: Ukranian Soviet Encyclopaedia, 1979; Co-author: Infection-Allergic Polyradiculoneuritis in Children, 1982; Co-author: Anaesthesiology and Intensive Care Reference Book, 1982; Co-author: Acute Neuroinfections in Children, 1986; Co-author: Anaesthesiology and Intensive Care, 1992; 81 other publications. Memberships: Ukrainian Society of Anaesthesiologists; Chief Pediatric Anaesthesiologist & Intensive Care of Ukraine, 1973-85. Honours: Graduated with Honours, Medical Institute. Hobbies: Stamp Collecting; Tennis. Address: Flat 21, House 92, Acad Zabolotniy Str, Kiev 252187, Ukraine.

VAUGHAN Christopher Leonard, b. 21 Apr 1953, Blyvoorvitzicht, South Africa. Biomedical Engineer. m. Joan Blair, 23 July 1977, 1 son, 1 daughter. Education: BSc, hons, Rhodes University, South Africa, 1975; PhD, University of Iowa, USA, 1980; Postdoctoral Fellow, Oxford University, England, 1983. Appointments: Senior Lecturer, University of Cape Town, 1980-86; Chief Biomedical Engineer, Groote Schuur Hospital, Cape Town, 1980-86; Associate Professor of Bioengineering, Clemson University, 1986-89; Professor of Orthopaedics & Biomedical Engineering, University of Virginia, 1989-95. Publications: Cerebral Palsy and Rhizotomy: A Three Year Follow-up with Gait Analysis, 1991; Gait Analysis Laboratory, 1992. Honours: President's Award, CSIR, 1984; Barclays Bank Industrial Inventiveness Award, 1985. Memberships: International Society of Biomechanics; American Society of Biomechanics; IEEE. Hobbies: Golf; Squash; Fly Fishing. Address: University of Cape Town, Biomedical Engineering, Observatory, Cape 7925, South Africa.

VAUGHAN John Thomas Jr, b. 1 June 1957, Columbus, Georgia, USA. Biomedical Engineering. m. Jacqueline E, 21 Oct 1989, 1 son, 1 daughter. Education: BS, Biology; BE, Electrical Engineering; PhD, Biomedical Engineering. Appointments: Design Engineer, NASA, 1979-82; Electronic Design Engineer, Texas Instruments, 1982-84; Research Engineer, University of Texas Southwestern Medical School, 1984-89; Chief Biomedical Engineer, 1989-93, Assistant Professor of Medicine and Biomedical Engineering, 1994-95, University of Alabama at Birmingham; Radiofrequency Scientist, Philips Medical Systems, 1989-92; Assistant Professor, Harvard Medical School; Adjunct Assistant Professor, Massachusetts Institute of Technology; Director of Engineering, Massachusetts General Hospital, Nuclear Magnetic Resonance Centre. Publications: RF Front End for a 4.1 Tesla Clinical NMR Spectometer, 1995; High Frequency Volume Coils for Clinical Nuclear Magnetic Resonance Imaging and Spectroscopy, 1994. Honours: Pi Mu Epsilon, 1980; Tau Beta Pi, 1981; Eta Kappa Nu, 1981; Dean's Award, Outstanding Engineering Student, 1994; Outstanding Engineering Student, Biomedical Engineering Deparrtment, 1994. Memberships: Society of Magnetic Resonance; Institute for Electrical and Electronics Engineers; Biomedical Engineering Society. Hobbies: Flying; Backpacking; Biking. Outdoors. Address: Massachusetts General Hospital, Nuclear Magnetic Resonance Centre, Building 149 13th Street, Mailcode 1492301, Charlestown, MA 02129-2060, USA.

VEGH Arthur B, b. 2 Sep 1955, Szombatheley, Hungary. Clinical Instructor. m. 1982, 2 s, 1 d. Education: BS, Cellular and Molecular Biology, 1977, MD, 1983, University of WA, Seattle; Resident, Internal Medicine, University of SD, Yankton, 1983-86; Fellow, Allergy and Immunology, University of IA Hospitals, IA, 1986-89. Appointments: Course Instructor, University of SD School of Medicine, 1985-86; Assistant Clinical Instructor of Medicine, University of WA, Seattle, 1991-. Publications: 6 Professional papers; 6 Abstracts; Numerous presentations to both professional and non-professional assemblies. Memberships: AMA; WA Medical Association; American College of Physicians; Fellow, American Academy of Allergy and Immunology; Fellow, American College of Allergists; American Thoracic Society; Joint Council of Allergy and Immunology; WA Thoracic Society; Northwest Allergy Society; Pierce County Medical Society. Address: Allergy Associates of Tacoma B-6010, Allenmore Medical Center, Tacoma, WA 98405, USA.

VEITH Richard Charles, b. 23 May 1947, Seattle, Washington, USA. Physician. m. Marcella Pascualy, 2 sons, 1 daughter. Education: BA, Western Washington University, 1969; MD, 1973, Internship, Internal Medicine, 1973-74, Psychiatry Residency, 1974-77, University of Washington School of Medicine, 1973; Board Certified: National Board of Medical Examiners, 1974; American Board of Psychiatry and

Neurology, 1979; Added Qualification in Geriatric Psychiatry, American Board of Psychiatry and Neurology, 1991. Appointments include: Assistant Professor, 1980-83, Associate Professor, 1983-89, Professor, 1989-, Head, Division of Gerontology and Geriatric Psychiatry, 1991-, Department of Psychiatry and Behavioural Sciences, University of Washington School of Medicine, Seattle; Director, Geriatric Research, Education and Clinical Center, Veterans Administration Medical Center, Seattle. Publications: Co-author: Cardiovascular effects of tricyclic and antidepressants in depressed patients with chronic heart disease, 1982; Age differences in plasma norephinephrine kinetics in humans, 1986; Sympathetic nervous system activity in major depression: basal and desipramine-induced alterations in plasma norepinephrine kinetics, 1994. Honours: Scholarship, Overlake Service League, 1965-66; President's Scholar, 1966-69. Memberships: Society of Biological Psychiatry; Fellow, American Psychiatric Association; American Geriatrics Society; Gerontological Society; American Association of Geriatric Psychiatry; Psychiatric Research Society; Society for Neuroscience; Several editorial boards. Address: GRECC (182B), VA Medical Center, 1660 South Columbian Way, Seattle, WA 98108, USA.

VELASCO CAMPOS Francisco, b. 2 May 1939, Mexico D F, Mexico. Neurosurgeon. m. Manuela Canales, 21 May 1966, 3 daughters. Education: MD; Resident, Internal Medicine, Nutrition Disease Institute; Resident, Neurosurgery, The Johns Hopkins Hospital, USA; Certified, Mexican Board of Neurological Surgery; Senior Investigator, National Research Council; Senior Investigator, National Institutes of Health and National Medical Centre; Postdoctoral Professor, University of Mexico. Appointments: Chief, Neurophysiology Unit, National Medical Centre; Currently Chief Neurosurgeon, General Hospital of Mexico, D F Mexico. Publications: Further Definitions of the Subthalamic Target for the Arrest of Tremor, 1972; Electrical Stimulation of the Thalamus for Control of Epilepsy; Textbook on Stereotactic and Functional Neurosurgery, 1994; 138 international publications; 38 book chapters. Honours: National Award, Pharmaceutical Industry, 1972, 1987; National Award, Mexican Academy of Surgery, 1974; Award, National Council of Health, 1987; Iberoamerican Award, International League Against Epilepsy, 1987. Memberships: American Association of Neurological Surgeons; Congress of Neurosurgery; French Society of Neurological Surgeons; Society for Neuroscience; Research Society of Neurological Surgeons; International Brain Research Organization. Hobbies: Pianist; Water sports. Address: Creston 116, Jardines del Pedregal, Mexico D F 01900, Mexico.

VELLEMAN Richard David Benjamin, b. 1 Aug 1952, London, England. Clinical Psychologist. m. Gill, 16 Dec 1991, 2 d. Education: BSc, University of Sussex; MSc, PhD, University of Exeter; FRSS; FBPS; CPsychol. Appointments include: Research Fellow in Clinical Psychology, 1980-84; Consultant Advisor, Northern Ireland Council on Alcohol, 1984-87; Senior Lecturer in Psychology, University of Bath; Manager, Addiction Services, Consultant Clinical psychologist, Director of Research and Development, Bath Mental Health Care NHS Trust. Publications: Training Volunteers to Counsel Problem Drinkers and Their Families, Co-author, 1985; Counselling for Alcohol Problems, 1992; Adults Who Were the Children of Problem Drinkers, Co-author, 1995; Contributor of numerous professional papers, book chapters and conference proceedings. Memberships: British Psychological Society; Royal Statistical Society. Hobbies: Squash; Music; Dining; Travel. Address: School of Social Sciences, University of Bath, Claverton Down, Bath, Avon BA2 7AY, England.

VENTRIGLIA Salvatore, b. 24 Nov 1956, S Maria Capus Vetere Ce, Italy. Physician; Doctor. m. Rita Della Valle, 1984. Education: Honours in Medicine, Naples General Hospital, 1982. Career: Specialist in Neurology, Naples General Hospital, 1987; Positions held at Chiangiano, Italy, 1993-. Publications: L'A T meobirniana nel Triatiamento della psicori maniaco de prenila im Abstrach 19th EATA Conference, 1993; Il matrimonio bianco: l'approccio A T con l'ausilio di Tecniche fisiche, 1994. Memberships: Ordini du medici de Caserta, Italio; Consylio Diretivo della SIAT; EATA S Ginopre di Inolini Transepionsle. Hobbies: Piano; Photography; Ping Pong. Address: Via G Paolo 1 Coop, Giglio 2, Guistizia, 81055 s Maria Capus Vetere Ce, Italy.

VERCO Christopher Johnson, b. 5 Sep 1948, Australia. Obstetrician and Gynaecologist. m. Judith Sloan, 14 Feb 1981, 2 d. Education: MBBS; MD; FRCOG; FRACOG. Career: RMO, Royal Adelaide Hospital, Adelaide Children's Hospital, Queen Victoria Hospital, Adelaide; Registrar, Royal Aedlaide Hospital, The London Hospital; Senior Registrar, Hammersmith Hospital, Fliners Medical Centre;

Currently, Head, Obstetric and Gynaecological Services. Publications: Fallopian Tube Microvasculature, MD Thesis; Articles on Fallopian Tube Anatomy and Micro Anatomy, Tubal Vasculature, Basic Studies on Fallopian Tube, 1986, 1994. Honour: Reserve Force Decoration. Memberships: AMA; BMA; RCOG; RACOG; American Fertility Society; Fertility Society of Australia. Hobbies: Golf; Swimming. Address: 120 Mills Terrace, North Adelaide, SA 5006, Australia.

VERKAUF Barry Stephen, b. 28 Dec 1940, Tampa, Florida, USA. Physician. m. Arline Laviage, 22 Aug 1964, 2 daughters. Education: MD. Appointments: Associate Professor of Obstetrics and Gynaecology. Publication: Congenital Anomalies of the Female Reproductive Tract, 1993. Honours: Certificate of Special Competence in Reproductive Endocrinology, American Board Obstetricians and Gynaecologists, 1980. Memberships: American Society of Reproductive Medicine; Society of Reproductive Endocrinologists; Society of Reproductive Surgeons; Howard Kelly Society; SART. Hobby: Golf. Address: 2919 Swann Avenue, Suite 305, Tampa, FL, USA.

VERMA Pramod K, b. 7 Mar 1959, New Delhi, India. Doctor. m. Puja Verma, 14 Nov 1989, 1 s. Education: MD; FRCSC; Specialist, Obstetrics and Gynaecology. Appointment: Staff, Grey Nuns Hospital, Edmonton, Alta Canada. Memberships: AMA; CMA; SOGC. Address: 2911-66 St, Cedar Professional Park, Edmonton, Alta Canada.

VERNY Thomas Raphael, b. 26 Jan 1936, Bratislava, Slovakia. Psychiatrist. m. Sandra Collier, 11 Aug 1983, 2 s. Education: MD, University of Toronto, 1961; DPsych, University of Toronto, 1964; FRCPC, Fellowship of the Royal College of Physicians and Surgeons of Canada, 1972. Appointments: Teaching Fellow, Harvard University, 1965; Clinical Instructor, Department of Psychiatry, University of Toronto, 1966; Director of Psychiatric In-Patient Service, Toronto East General Hospital, 1968-70; Programme Director, Centre for Continuing Education, York University, 1969-74; Currently in Private Practice. Publications include: Analysis of Attrition Rates in a Psychiatric Clinic, 1970; The Psychiatrist as Radical Humanist, 1971; Adults Relive the Moment of Birth, 1975; A Baby Sound in Mind and Body, 1977; The Secret Life of the Unborn Child, 1981; Prenatal Psychology: Implications for the Practice of Medicine, 1984; The Psycho-Technology of Pregnancy and Labor, 1985; Parenting Your Unborn Child, 1988; The Biopolitics of Womb Life, 1989. Honours: Eli Lilly International Fellowship, 1985. Memberships: Canadian Medical Association; Ontario Medical Association; Canadian Psychiatric Association; Ontario Psychiatric Association; American Psychiatric Association; Pre and Peri-Natal Psychology Association of North America; International Society for the Study of Prenatal Psychology and Medicine; The Writer's Union of Canada; Canadian Authors Association. Hobbies: Chess; Skiing; Squash; Yoga; Writing (poetry/short fiction). Address: 36 Madison Avenue, Toronto, Ontario M5R 2S1, Canada.

VERSTRAETE Marc, b. 1 Apr 1925, Brugge, Belgium. Professor of Medicine. m. Bernadette Moyersoen, 12 July 1955, 1 son, 4 daughters. Education: MD, 1951; PhD, 1955. Appointments: Currently Professor of Medicine, Center for Molecular Biology, University of Leuven. Publications: Hemostasis, in Dutch, French, Spanish, Italian, Portuguese, Russian; Thrombosis, in Dutch, French, Spanish, Italian; Thrombosis in Cardiovascular Disorders, 1992, 2nd edition, 1995. Honours: Doctor honoris causa: University of Cordoba, Argentina, 1983, University of Bologna, Italy, 1988, University of Bordeaux, France, 1989; Visiting Professor, Harvard Medical School, Boston, USA; Knighted Baron, 1995. Memberships: Royal Academy of Belgium, Past President; International Society of Thrombosis and Hemostasis. Hobbies: Tennis; Skiing. Address: 29 Minderbroedersstraat, 3000 Leuven, Belgium.

VESTFRID Mario Alberto, b. 28 Mar 1944, Rivera, Buenos Aires Province, Argentina. Pathology Specialist. m. Clara Silvia Suckewer, 8 July 1971, 1 son, 2 daughters. Education: BA, 1969, MD, 1972, La Plata University. Appointments include: Currently: Chairman, Department of Pathology, Dr Ricardo Gutierrez General Acute Hospital, La Plata; Professor of Human Biology and Neurobiology, La Plata National University. Publications: Philosophy Biology, 1988; Articles: Paneth's cells in human appendix. A statistical study, 1977; Ectopic adrenal cortex in neonatal liver, 1980; Papillary carcinoma of the thyroid gland with lipomatous stroma: Report of a peculiar histological type of thyroid tumour, 1986; The ovaric lobule: A histoembryological unit, 1986. Honours: Award for Anatomy of Human Development, Rioplatense Association of Anatomy, 1991. Membership: Argentinian Society of

Pathology. Hobbies: Reading, especially selected political topics; Chess; Paddle-tennis. Address: Calle 26, No 119, 1900 La Plata, Argentina.

VETOSHCHUK Vasiliy, b. 23 Sept 1920, Zabie, Ilcia, Ukraine. Professor of Roentgenology. m. Nina Panchenko, 25 Oct 1952, 1 son, 1 daughter. Education: BA, Institute of Medicine, Stanislav, Ukraine, 1947; MD, Institute of Roentgenology & Radiology, Moscow, 1968. Appointments: Roentgenologist, Municipal Hospital, Stanislav, Ukraine, 1947-56; Holder, Professor of Chair, Roentgenology & Radiology, Ivano-Frankovsk Institute of Medicine, Ukraine, 1956-92. Publications: Eponymic symtoms and syndromes in Roentgenology, 1976; Optic modelling of the tomographic effect, 1966; Concerning the technological indistinctness of tomographic image and the permissible values in tomographic units, 1968; Author and Co-Author of 14 Inventions. Memberships: Ukrainian Association of Radiology. Hobbies: Photography; Design of Medical Tomographs. Address: 284000 Ivano-Frankovsk, Pershotravneva 3 kv 20, Ukraine.

VIACAVA Claudio, b. 21 Apr 1948, Milan, Italy. Medical Doctor. m. Elisabeth Restelli, 23 Sept 1974, 1 son, 1 daughter. Education: MD, Biology, Psychology. Appointments: Researcher in Biology, Ecology, Geobiology, Geopathology, Ecology of the Body and of the Mind, Psychosomatic Disease, Energo-Medicine, Oriental Medicine, Hypnosis; Currently: Professor in Psychobiology; Medical Doctor. Publications: Books: Biology and Genetics, 1991; Bioenergetica, 1991; Omeopatia e Terapie Naturali, 1992; Visibile e Invisible (Geobiology-Geopathology), 1992; Psychosomatic Disease, 1993. Honours: Senatore onorevole accademico, Accademia Medicea, Florence, 1990; Distinguished Professor, Centro Universitario Ticinese, Lugano, Switzerland, 1991. Memberships: ALBO Profl of Biology; ALBO Profl of Psychology. Hobbies: Volleyball; Football; Historic cars. Address: via Beato Angelico 23/5, 20133 Milan, Italy.

VIANO David C, b. 7 May 1946, San Mateo, California, USA. Auto Company Research Scientist. m. Sharon Lynn Henderson, 7 Dec 1975. Education: BS, Electrical Engineering, Cum Laude, University of Santa Clara, California, 1968; MS, Applied Mechanics, California Institute of Technology, 1969; PhD, Applied Mechanics, California Institute of Technology, 1972; Postdoctorate in Biomechanics, University and ETH Zurich, Switzerland, 1973-74. Appointments: Senior Research Engineer, 1972-76; Staff Research Engineer, 1976-78; Assistant Department Head, 1978-87; Principal Research Scientist, Biomedical Science Department, General Motors Research and Development Centre, Michigan, and Safety Research Program Leader, 1988-92; Adjunct Assistant Professor, 1981-86; Ajunct Associate Professor, 1986-89; Adjunct Professor, 1989-, General Motors Research Laboratories. Publications: Editor 18 Symposia Publications in Automotive Safety Engineering; Associate Editor, Accident Analysis and Prevention, 1988; Editorial Consultant, Journal of Trauma, 1988; Contributed Journal Articles on Technologies to Improve Occupant Protection, The Biomechancis of Trauma and Disability, Transportation Safety and Public Health Approaches to Injury Control. Memberships: AAAM; AAAS; ASB; ASME; ISO; MVMA; NAS; National Science Foundation Bioengineering Committee; SAE; Del Harder Rehabilitation Foundation; National Head Injury Foundation; Board of Review for Property Tax Assessment, City of Bloomfield Hills, Michigan. Address: General Motors Research and Development Center, Warren, Michigan 48090-9055, USA.

VICKERS Michael Douglas Allen, b. 11 May 1929, London, England. Doctor. m. Ann Hazel, 16 July, 1 son, 1 daughter. Education: MBBS, London; DA; FRCA; FANZCA. Appointments: President, Associate of Anaesthetists, 1952-54; President, European Academy, 1988-91; Vice Provost, Professor of Anaesthetics and Intensive Care Medicine, University of Wales College of Medicine; SGC General World Federation of Societies of Anaesthesiologists, 1992-96. Publications: Drugs in Anaesthetic Practice, 3rd-7th editions; Medicine for ANaesthetists, 1-3rd editions; Principles of Measurement, 1st-3rd editions; Ethical Issues in Anaesthesia, 1994; OSCEs in Anaesthesia, 1995. Honours: John Snow Lecturer, 1984; Honorary Fellow, Faculty of Anaesthetists, RCS Australasia. Memberships: BMA; RSM; RCA. Hobbies: Music; Writing. Address: 2 Windsor Close, Radyr, Cardiff CF4 8BZ, Wales.

VICTOROFF Jeff, b. 9 May 1952, Cleveland Heights, Ohio, USA. Neurologist. Education: MA; MD. Appointments: Instructor in Neurology, University of California at Los Angeles School of Medicine; Assistant Professor of Neurology, University of Southern California School of Medicine. Memberships: American Academy of Neurology; American Psychiatric Association; American Society for Neurorehabilitation; Behavioral Neurology Society. Address: Department of Neurology, Rancho Los Amigos Medical Centre, 7601 E Imperial Highway, Downey, CA 90242, USA.

VICTOROV Vladimir, b. 25 Jan 1933, Bobruisk Region, Russia. Biomedical Technology. m. Olga Victoroya, 30 Dec 1969, 1 s. Education: Moscow Aviation Institute, 1957; Radio Engineer Candidate, Technical Services, 1964; DEng, 1969; Professor, 1972; DSc. Appointments: Engineer, Science Fellow, Head of Laboratory, Institute of Control of Problems, Automatics and Telemechanics, 1957-77; General Director, Research Institute of Medical Engineering. Publications: Invariablility Principles in Measuring Engineering, 1976; Control in Biosystems, 1984; Trends in Medical Engineering, 1991. Honour: The State Award of Russia, 1977. Memberships: Chairman, Scientific Board on Medical Engineering with Presidium of RAMS; Jury Member for State Awards of Russia; Chief Editor of Meditsinskaya Tekhnika Journal; Academician, Russian Academy of Medical Engineering; Associate Member, Academy of Medical Sciences. Hobbies: Car Driving; Hunting. Address: 1, Timiryazevskaya Street, Moscow 125422, Russia.

VIDOVICH Marea, b. 27 Feb 1939, Perth, Australia. Nurse. Education: BA; Registered Nurse. Appointments: President, Western Australian Branch of Australian Nursing Federation; Nurse Adviser, ANF; Currently, Assistant Secretary, Australian Nursing Federation. Memberships: ANF; Royal College of Nursing, Australia. Hobbies: Politics; Current Affairs; Music; Tropical Fish. Address: 373 St George's Road, North Fitzroy, Victoria, Australia.

VIEDERMAN Milton, b. 17 Feb 1930, New York City, New York, USA. Physician. m. Brigitte R G Gervaise, 26 Mar 1956, 1 son, 1 daughter. Education: AB, Columbia College, 1951; MD, Harvard, 1955; Certificate in Psychoanalytic Medicine, Columbia Psychoanalytic Center, 1964. Appointments: Assistant Clinical Professor, Columbia P & S, 1971-75; Currently: Professor of Clinical Psychiatry, Cornell University Medical School; Associate Director, Training Analyst, Columbia Psychoanalytic Center. Publications: René Magritte: Coping with Loss, 1987; Nature of Passionate Love 1-14, in Passionate Attachments, 1987; Impact of Personality of Analyst on Psychoanalytic Cure, 1991; Picasso and Matisse, 1993; Uses of PAST, 1994; Edvard Munch, 1994. Honours: Distinguished Lecturer, Oxford, 1982; Visiting Professor: Duke University, 1984, Michael Reese University, 1985, University of California, Los Angeles, 1987; Richard Sterba Lecture, 1985; Anchin Lecture, 1987; Sidel Lecture, 1988; Liebert Lecture, 1990. Memberships: American Psychoanalytic Association; Association for the Advancement of Science; American Psychosomatic Society; New York Academy of Medicine; American College of Psychoanalysis; New York Psychiatric Society. Hobbies: Art; Applied psychoanalysis. Address: 525 East 68th Street, New York, NY 10021, USA.

VIEGAS Osborn Anacleto Casimir, b. 4 Mar 1946, Kenya. Obstetrician and Gynaecologist. m. Claire M Mascarenhas, 4 Jan 1975, 1 son, 2 daughters. Education: MBChB, Honours in General Surgery, University of East Africa, 1971; Diploma in Anaesthesia, Royal College of Physicians and Surgeons, Dublin, 1974; MRCOG (London), 1976; MD, University of Birmingham, 1982; AM, Academy of Medicine, Singapore, 1983; FRCOG (London), 1989. Appointments: Registrar, Good Hope Maternity Hospital, Birmingham, England, 1975-78; Senior Registrar, Research Fellow, Sorrento Maternity Hospital, Birmingham, 1978-82; Lecturer, Obstetrics, Gynaecology, 1982-83, Senior Lecturer, Obstetrics, Gynaecology, 1984-89, Associate Professor, Senior Consultant Obstetrician and Gynaecologist, 1990-, National University Hospital, Singapore. Publications: Two Aspects of Fetal Welfare: (i) Diagnostic: The assessment of non-stress antepartum cardiotocography. (ii) The promotion of intrauterine growth by nutritional supplementation, doctoral thesis, 1982; Numerous articles, papers, contributions to books in the field. Honours: Mary Crosse Research Fellowship to present doctoral thesis, Birmingham University, 1978-81. Memberships include: Catholic Medical Guild, Singapore. Hobby: Tropical fish. Address: 15 B Jalan Tempua, Singapore 1129.

ViiNIKKA Lasse Untamo, b. 10 May 1948, Virrat, Finland. Senior Physician. m. Tuula Oikarinen, 7 Dec 1974, 2 daughters. Education: Licentiate of Medicine, 1974; Doctor of Medical Science, 1978; Specialist in Clinical Chemistry, 1979; Docent in Clinical Chemistry, 1981. Appointments: Research Associate, Department of Clinical

Chemistry, University of Oulu; House Officer, Assistant Senior Physician, Oulu University Central Hospital; Visiting Scientist, Department of Chemical Pathology, St Bartholomew's Hospital, London, England; Head of Laboratory Services, Children's Hospital, Helsinki University Central Hospital. Publications: About 200 full length scientific articles on different aspects of endocrinology. Honours: President, Finnish Sauna Society, 1991-; President International Sauna Association, 1994-. Memberships: Finnish Medical Association; Finnish College of Physicians; Finnish Society of Clinical Chemistry; American Association for Clinical Chemistry; The Association of Clinical Biochemists; The New York Academy of Science. Hobbies: Books; Finnish Sauna. Address: Helsinki University Central Hospital, Laboratory/Children's Hospital, FIN-00290, Helsinki, Finland.

VIKMAN Yan Eduard, b. 31 Oct 1958, Kharkov, Ukraine. Doctor; Radiologist. m. Raisa Chernets, 24 Jul 1982, 1 s, 1 d. Education: MD, Zaporozhye Medical Institute, Ukraine, 1981; MSO, Kharkov Institute of Medical Radiology, Ukraine, 1989. Appointments: Scientific Researcher, Kharkov Institute of Medical Radiology, Ukraine, 1981-88; Deputy Head, Krasnodar Diagnostic Centre, Russia, 1989-91; Chief, Radionuclide and Ultrasound Diagnostics Group, Kharkov; Currently, Radiologist, Institute of Medical Radiology, Ukraine. Publications: Co-author, Present State of Nuclear Cardiology With Radiopharmaceuticals, 1993; Co-author, An Organization of Medical Radionuclide Production in Ukraine, 1994. Membership: Association of Radiologists of Ukraine. Hobbies: Bicycling; Chess. Address: 154A Klochkovskaya Street, Flat 065, Kharkov, 310145, Ukraine.

VILLAVECES James W, b. 4 Nov 1933, San Louis Obispo, CA, USA. Physician. Education: AA, Ventura College, 1953; BA, UCLA, 1955; MD, University of CA, San Francisco School of Medicine, 1960; Certified, American Board of Allergy and Immunology, 1974, 1994. Appointments: Co-director, Allergy Clinic, Ventura County Hospital, 1969-88; President, Lung Association, Ventura County; Film and Filmstrip Consultant, 1973; Air Pollution Control Advisory Committee, Ventura Co, 1973-74; President, Tri-co Gold Coast Allergy Society, 1990; Consultant to, Fisons, 3M, Pharmacia, Boeringer, Ingelheim, Enviracare Corp, Norwich Erton Corp; Co-founder, Ventura Co Sports Hall of Fame; Annual Tri-county Allergy Wild Walk; Assistant on set of slides for NIH Asthma Education Program, 1991; Publications: 14 Articles in professional journals, 1968-88, including: Co-author, Testing a new Sphygmomanometer: Observer Reliability, in Urban Health Journal, 1980; Co-author, Experience with an Elemental Diet, in Ann Allergy, 1985; Co-author, Fibrositis - Diagnostic Dilemmas in Allergy Observer, 1988; Created a series of film and filmstrips concerning drunk driving and on allergies. Honours: Physician Recognition Awards, AMA, 1968-; Commendation for Community Service, Ventura Board of Supervisors, 1972; Member of MENSA Society, 1981, Who's Who in America, in the West, in California & in Ventura County. Memberships include: Board, American Lung Association of Ventura County, 1968-; CA Medical Association; Ventura County Medical Association; CA Allergy Society; Fellow, American Academy of Allergy and Immunology; Fellow, American College of Allergy and Immunology. Hobbies: Computers; Photography; Fresh and Salt Water Fishing. Address: 4080 Loma Vista Road No M, Ventura, CA 93003, USA.

VINCENT Charles Anthony, b. 12 July 1952, London, England. Psychologist. Education: BA, Oxford, 1975; MPhil, 1978, PhD, 1987, London. Appointments: Clinical Psychologist, 1978-84; Research psychologist, 1985-88, Senior Lecturer in Psychology, University College London. Publications: Clinical Risk Management, Editor, 1995; Medical Accidents, Co-editor, 1993. Membership: British Psycological Society. Address: Department of Psychology, Phillips House, University College London, Gower Street, London WC1E 6BT, England.

VINIKER David Alan, b. 1 Jun 1948, Luton, Bedfordshire, England. Obstetrician; Gynaecologist. m. Simone Viniker, 31 Aug 1975, 1 s, 1 d. Education: Whipps Cross Hospital, London; University College, London; University College Hospital, London; MB; BS; MD; MRCOG; RCOG, London, 1984. Appointments: Senior Registrar, Leicester Royal Infirmary; Senior Registrar, Research, University College Hospital, London; Registrar, The London Hospital; Senior Officer, Royal Post Graduate Medical School; Currently, Clinical Director, Obstetrics and Gynaecology. Publications: The Fetal EEG (Detection of Oxygen Deprivation), in Journal of Hospital Medicine, 1979; Monitoring the Neonate With the Cerebral Function Monitor in Fetal and Neonatal Physiological Movements, 1986. Honour: Blair Bell Memorial Lecturer, Royal College of Obstetricians and Gynaecologists, 1984. Memberships

include: British Fertility Society; American Fertility Society; European Fertility Society. Hobbies: Computers; Music; Photography. Address: Bourne House, 6 Spareleaze Hill, Loughton, Essex, IG10 1BT, England.

VIOQUE Jesus, b. 21 Sept 1956, Seville, Spain. Associate Professor of Public Health. m. Manoli Garcia, 1990, 2 daughters. Education: MD, University of Alicante, 1987; MPH, Harvard University School of Public Health, 1988. Appointments: General Practitioner, 1983; Assistant Professor of Public Health, University of Alicante, 1989-91. Publications: Trends in mortality from lung cancer in Spain (co-author), 1987; A meta-analysis of alcoholic beverage consumption in relation to risk of colorectal cancer, 1990; A Changing Mortality Patterns for major cancers in Spain, 1991; Esophageal Cancer Mortality: Relationshop with alcohol intake and cigarette smoking in Spain, 1991. Honours: Special Distinction, School of Medicine, University of Alicante, Spain, 1984. Memberships: Sociedad Espaniola de Epidemiologia; International Epidemiological Association; Society for Epidemiologic Research, USA. Hobbies: Sports; Cooking; Reading; Movies. Address: Depto Salud Publica, University of Alicante, Apd 374, Alicante 03080, Spain.

VISHA Carla A, b. 28 Mar 1944, The Netherlands. Psychiatrist. div. 1 son. Education: AB, Highest Honours, San Diego State University, USA. 1977; AA, Southwestern College, 1974; MD, University of California, Davis, 1981; Board Certified in Psychiatry, American Board Psychiatry and Neurology. Appointments: Founder, Director, The Organic Healing Centre, Davis, California; Consulting Psychiatrist, Solano County Mental Health, Adolescent Treatment Programme and University of California at Davis Student Health Services; Private Practice in General and Child Psychiatry. Publications: Mothers': Societies Unrecognised Dictators, 1993; Loss of the Extended Family as a Function of a Deeply Rooted Prenatal or Newborn-Developed Fear of Intimacy, 1991. Honours: Phi Beta Kappa, 1977; Phi Kappa Phi, 1977. Memberships: American Psychiatric Association; Central California Psychiatric Society; Yolo County Mental Health Association. Hobbies: Acting; Singing; Swimming; Bicycling. Address: 2655 Portage Bay Avenue #7, Davis, CA 95616, USA.

VISHNEVSKAYA Ekaterina Efimovna, b. 25 Dec 1930, Gomel, Belarus. Surgeon; Oncologist. m. 1 June 1960. Education: MD. Appointments: Junior Research Worker, 1963; Senior Research Worker, 1971; Head, Oncogynecologic Department, 1973. Honours: Prize Winner, USSR Council of Ministers, 1990; Honorary Diploma of the Supreme Soviet of RB, 1994. Memberships: European Society of Oncogynecologists, 1984; Expert Council in Oncoradiology, Academy of Medical Science, 1988. Hobbies: Growing Flowers; Mushroom Picking; Berrying. Address: Yakub Kolas-str 52/53, 220113 Minsk, Belarus.

VISOTSKY Harold M, b. 25 May 1924. Medicine. m. Gladys R Maurich, 18 Dec 1955, 1 s, 1 d. Education: BS; MD. Appointments: Director, Psychiatric Training, University of IL; Director, Department of Mental Health, State of IL; Chairman, Department of Psychiatry and Behavioral Sciences, Northwestern Medical School; President, Habscor Corporation; President, Center for Transcultural Studies; Currently, Director, Research and Educational Development, Northwestern Medical School, Department of Psychiatry. Publications: Legal Rights of Mentally Handicapped, 1975; Psychiatric Services in USA, 1985; Future Directions in Psychiatry, 1989. Honours: Strecker Award, Institute of PA Hospital, 1969; Alumnus of Year, University of IL, 1976; E B Bowis Award, American College of Psychiatrists, 1981; Simon Bolivar Award, 1982; American Psychiatric Association Admininstration Psychology Award, 1986; Gold Medal, American College of Psychiatrists, 1988; President's Award, 1990. Memberships: American Psychiatric Association; World Psychiatric Association; World Association for Social Psychiatry; American Orthopsychiatry Association. Hobbies: Tennis; Walking; Travel. Address: 303 East Ohio Street, Northwestern University Medical School, Department of Psychiatry, Chicago, IL 60611, USA.

VITTONE Bernard John, b. 5 Oct 1951, Latrobe, USA. Psychiatrist. 1 son. Education: BS, Psychology, cum laude, Georgetown University, Washington, 1969-73; MD, Georgetown University Medical School, 1973-77. Appointments include: Intern, Flexible Medicine, St Vincent's Hospital & Medical Center, New York, 1977-78; Resident, Ophthalmology, The Wills Eye Hospital, Philadelphia, 1978-79; Resident, Psychiatry, St Vincent's Hospital & Medical Center, 1979-81; Chief Resident, Psychiatry, St Vincent's Hospital & Medical Center, 1981-82; Medical Staff Fellow, Unit on Anxiety & Affective Disorders, National Institute of Mental Health, Bethesda, 1982-84; Psychiatric

Consultant, Roundhouse Square Psychiatric Center, Alexandria, 1983-85; Director, National Center for the Treatment of Phobias, Anxiety & Depression, Washington, 1985-; Director, Advisory Board, America Against Drugs, Washington, 1990-; Member, Headquarters Committee Under Council on Internal Organization of American Psychiatric Association, 1992-. Publications include: Differential Diagnosis and Treatment of Panic Disorder: A Medical Perspective, 1985; Blunted Growth Hormone Response to Clonidine in Panic Disorder Patients, 1986; Glucose Tolerance Testing in Panic Disorder, 1986; Major Depression in Patients with Social Phobia, 1990; Cognitive Behavioral and Pharmacological Treatments for Social Phobia: A Controlled Study, 1991; Panic Disorder Syndrome, 1993. Memberships include: American Medical Association; American Psychiatric Association; Alpha Omega Alpha; Washington Psychiatric Society. Honours include: Award, Outstanding Achievement in MicroBiology, Georgetown University, 1977; Certificate, Continuing Medical Education, American Psychiatric Association, 1988; Physician's Recognition Award, American Medical Association, 1991. Hobbies: Tennis; Table Tennis; Snorkeling. Address: 1755 S Street NW, Washington, DC 20009 6117, USA.

VLAHOV Vitan, b. 6 July 1937, Sofia, Bulgaria. Physician. m. Natalia Vlahova, 16 June 1966, 3 sons. Education: MD, Medical Academy, 1961; Research Fellow, Humboldt Foundation, Germany. Appointments: General Practitioner, 1962; Assistant Professor, 1967; Associate Professor, 1976; Professor of Pharmacology, 1984; Visiting Lecturer in Russia, China, Nepal, Germany, 1988-89; Head, Department of Clinical Pharmacology, Medical Faculty, Sofia. Publications: Pharmacology of Cerebral Circulation, 1983, 1991; Co-author, Dose Response Relationship of Drugs, 1989; Textbook of Clinical Pharmacology, 1993. Memberships: Union of the Scientific Medical Societies of Bulgaria (General Secretary; Bulgarian Drug Commission; Bulgarian Pharmacological Society; German Society of Clinical Pharmacology. Hobbies: Skiing; Tennis; Tourism. Address: 1000 Sofia, 4 Levski Street, Bulgaria.

VLASOV Pavel V, b. Aug 1929, Krasnoyarsk, Russia. Radiologist. Education: Graduate, Krasnoyarsk Medical Institute, 1952; Radiological Diagnostics Postgraduate Course, Central Institute for Postgraduate Education, Moscow, 1958. Appointments: Physician, Norilsk, Taymir; Institute of Medical Radiology, Obninsk; Moscow Stomatological Medical Institute, 1973-77; Professor, Moscow Institute of Roentgenology and Radiology, now Institute of Diagnostics and Surgery, 1977-; Chief Radiologist, Ministry of Health, 1986-. Publications: Author of over 300 research papers, books and monographs including: Clinical-Radiological Semiotics odf Gastric cancer; Relief of the Gastric Mucous Membrane in the Radiological Imaging; Complex Diagnostics of the Breast Cancer; Radiodiagnostics of the Pleural Tumours; Technical Means of the Radiodiagnostics; The Conversation on X-Ray; The Refuge of the Charity. Honours: Honorary MD, 1972. Membership: President, 1986-m, Russian Radiological Association. Address: Department of Diagnostical Radiology, Moscow Institute of Diagnostics and Surgery, Moscow, Russia.

VOGE-BLACK Victoria Mae, b. 27 June 1943, Minneapolis, Minnesota, USA. Physician. m. Gerald R Black, 10 Jan 1976, 2 sons, 2 daughters. Education: BA; MD; MPH, Occupational Medicine; MPH, Aerospace Medicine. Appointments include: Head, Acceleration Physiology Branch, NADC, 1974-76; Head, Aeromedical Division, Naval Safety Centre, 1978-81; Chief, Occupational Medicine and Preventive Medicine Department and Aviation Medicine, Corpus Christi Naval Hospital, 1984-88; Chief, Aviation Medicine Department, Code 6025, NADC, 1988-91; Researcher, Aircrew Standards, Armstrong Laboratory, 1991-. Publications: Contributor of numerous articles on aviation safety, clinical aviation medicine and acceleration physiology. Honours: Fellow: Aerospace Medical Association, 1982; International Academy of Aviation and Space Medicine, 1983; American Occupational and Environmental Medicine Association, 1988; American College of Preventive Medicine; Aerospace Human Factors Association, 1994; Wiley Post award for Operational Aerospace Physiology, 1980. Memberships: AMA; ACOEM; ASMA; ACPM; SUSNFS; ANA; International Academy of Aviation and Space Medicine; SMA; TOMA. Hobbies: Flying; Travel; Scuba Diving. Address: RR3 Box 73, Gonzales, TX 78629, USA.

VOGEL Victor Gerald, b. 14 Mar 1952, Bethlehem, PA, USA. Academic Medicine. m. Sarylyn Schaffner, 25 Jun 1977, 1 s, 1 d. Education: BA, Natural Sciences, Johns Hopkins University, 1974; MD, Temple University, 1978; Master of Health Science, Johns Hopkins University, 1986; Fellow, American College of Physicians; Fellow,

American College of Preventative Medicine. Appointments: Resident in Internal Medicine, Baltimore City Hospitals, 1978-81; US Public Health Service, 1981-83; Fellow in Medical Oncology, Johns Hopkins University, 1983-86; Andrew W Mellow Fellow in Clinical Epidemiology, 1984-86; Associate Professor of Medicine and Epidemiology; Deputy Chairman, Department of Clinical Cancer Prevention, University of Texas, MD Anderson Cancer Center. Publications: Numerous Articles published in Refereed Journals; Numerous Abstracts, Books and Chapters; Videotape on Breast Health, 1989. Honours: Fellow, American College of Preventive Medicine, 1987; Fellow, American College of Physicians, 1993; Susan G Komen Foundation Fellow, 1989. Memberships: American College of Physicians; American Society of Clinical Oncology; American Society of Preventive Oncology; American Association for Cancer Research. Address: Univerity of Texas, MD Anderson Cancer Center, 1515 Holcombe Boulevard, Box 236, Houston, Texas 77030-4009, USA.

VOGT Guido, b. 22 July 1945, Glucksburg, Germany. Physician. m. Ursula Rasch, 31 Dec 1969, 1 son, 1 daughter. Education: MD. Appointment: Occupational Medicine, Radiation Protection. Memberships: International Radiation Protection Association; International Research Group on Colour Vision Deficiencies. Hobbies: Sailing; Skiing; Art; Painting. Address: Heinz-Hilpert-Straße 8, 37085 Göttingen, Germany.

VOIGT Lynda Fay, b. 6 Feb 1945, Longview, WA, USA. Epidemiologist. m. Michael R Turner, 8 Sep 1990, 2 d. Education: BS; MSN; PhD. Career: Statistical Research Associate, Staff Scientist, Currently, Senior Staff Scientist, Fred Hutchinson Cancer Research Center. Publications include: Co-author, Smoking, obesity and alcohol consumption and the risk of rheumatoid arthritis, in Epidemiology, 1994; Co-author, Recency, duration and progestin content of oral contraceptives in relation to the incidence of endometrical cancer, in Cancer Causes and Control, 1994; Co-author, Risk of breast cancer associated with induced abortion, in JNCI, 1994, in press. Honours: Faculty Commendation, University of WA, 1967; Outstanding Student Award, Emory University, 1969. Memberships: Society for Epidemiologic Research; American Association of Public Opinion Research. Hobbies: Dancing; Astronomy; Bird Watching; Hiking. Address: Fred Hutchinson Cancer Research Center, 1124 Columbia, MP381, Seattle, WA 98104, USA.

VOIGT Monique Maria Johanna Petronella de, b. 30 June 1967, Hertogenbosch, The Netherlands. Resident. Education: MA, University of Utrecht, 1993. Memberships: International Federation of Medical Students Associations; President, Netherlands Medical Students International Committee; Royal Dutch Medical Association. Hobbies: Travel; Karate; Aerobics; Drawing. Address: Mgr v d Wetering straat 120 bis, 3581 EM Utrecht, The Netherlands.

VOIGTS Matthew Frederick, b. 13 Feb 1965, Romford, Essex, England. Osteopath. m. Petrina Montrose, 9 Sep 1989. Education: Diploma in Osteopathy. Appointment: Osteopath. Memberships: General Council and Register of Osteopaths; Osteopathic Association of Great Britain. Hobbies: Golf; Tennis; Squash. Address: 14 Elm Grove, Thorpe Bay, Essex, SS1 3EZ, England.

VOLZ Michael Alan, b. 15 Oct 1957, Milwaukee, Wisconsinm, USA. Allergologist and Immunologist. m. Laura Volz, 18 Apr 1994, 1 son. Education: BS, Zoology; MD; Resident, Internal Medicine, Jackson Memorial Hospital, University of Miami, 1985-88; Fellow, Allergy and Immunology, National Jewish Hospital, University of Colorado, Denver, 1988-92. Career: Practising Physician. Publications: Drug Allergy: Postgraduate Medicine, 1990; Ureaplasma Urealyticum chronic osteomyelitis in a patient with hypogamino globulinemia, 1991; Interferons, 1992; Drugs, 1992. Honours: Jerome A and Simona Chazen Fellow in Immunology, 1990-91. Memberships: American Medical Association; New York Academy of Sciences; Association for the Advancement of Science; American Academy of Allergy and Immunology. Hobbies: Golfing; Reading; Travel; Theatre. Address: 7474 E Arkansas Avenue 2406, Denver, CO 80231, USA.

VON AULOCK Maryna, b. 11 Mar 1957, Allanridge, South Africa. Lecturer in Radiotherapy. m. Hubertus Hans Christoph Von Aulock, 11 Oct 1980, 1 s, 1 d. Education: National Diploma in Diagnostic Radiography; National Diploma in Therapeutic Radiography; Advanced Diploma in Teaching Radiography, University of Cape Town. Appointments: Radiographer, Radiotherapy; Senior Radiographer,

Radiotherapy; Lecturer in Radiotherapy, Peninsula Technikon. Memberships: South African Society of Radiographers; SAMDC. Hobbies: Art; Gardening; Interior decorating. Address: Radiotherapy Department, X Block, Tygerberk Hospital, 7500, South Africa.

VON EUW Arnold Josef, b. 18 Mar 1949, Schwyt. Dentist. Education: Orthedonics. Appointments: Assistant, Volkstahuklinik Basel; Assistant, Kliuik für Kieferorthopadie der Universtat Bern. Memberships: EOS; SGK; SSO; SGDTIFR. Hobbies: Violin; Running. Address: Bahnhofstrasse 21, CH-6430 Schwyz, Swizerland.

VON GIERKE Henning Edgar, b. 22 May 1917, Karlsruhe, Germany. Professor of Bioengineering. m. Hanlo Weil, 22 Oct 1950, 2 daughters. Education: Diploma Ingenieur, Technical University Karlsruhe, Germany, 1943; Doctor of Engineering, Technical University Karlsruhe, Germany, 1944. Appointments: Research Assistant, Institute for Theoretical Electrical Engineering & Communications Technique, Technical University Karlsruhe, 1943-47; Lecturer, Technical University Karlsruhe, 1946-47; Project Engineer, Section Chief, Branch Chief, Aerospace Medical Research Laboratory, US Air Force, Ohio, 1947-56; Director, Biodynamics & Bioengineering Division, Armstrong Aerospace Medical Research Laboratory, 1956-88; Clinical Associate Professor, Department of Preventive Medicine, Ohio University, 1963-; Clinical Professor, Department of Community Medicine, Wright State University School of Medicine, Ohio, 1980-; Technical Advisor, Consultant, Armstrong Aerospace Medical Research Laboratory, 1988-. Publications: Author or co-author of over 170 scientific-technical publications and 5 patents. Memberships incl: National Academy of Engineering; International Academy of Aviation and Space Medicine; Acoustical Society of America; Aerospace Medical Association; Biomedical Engineering Society; Institute of Noise Control Engineering; Numerous International and National Awards. Address: 1325 Meadow Lane, Yellow Spring, OH 45387, USA.

VON KUSTER Larry Carl, b. 2 Feb 1949, Walla Walla, Washington, USA. Pathologist. m. Paula Revolinski, 24 Aug 1969, 2 sons. Education: BA, Walla Walla College, 1971; MD, Loma Linda University, 1977; Pathology Residency, Hershey Medical Center, Hershey, Pennsylvania, 1977-81; Diplomate, American Board of Pathology (AP/CP), 1982; Dermatopathology Fellowship, University of Cincinnati, 1981-82; Certification in Dermatopathology, 1983. Appointments: Assistant Professor of Clinical Pathology, University of Cincinnati, Cincinnati, Ohio, 1983-89; Currently Chairman, Department of Pathology, Memorial Hospital, Fremont, Ohio, and Director of Laboratory, Bellevue Hospital, Bellevue, Ohio. Publications include: Traumatic Aneurysms of the Ulnar Artery (with A B Abt), 1980; Malignant Mixed Tumor of the Gallbladder: Report of Two Cases and a Review of the Literature (with C Cohen), 1982; Concanavalin A and Lens culinaris Binding Patterns in Normal and Neoplastic Sebaceous Epithelium (with D E Ward and B H Liwnicz), 1986; Complement and Antibody Deposition in Brazilian Pemphigus Foliaceus Correlation of Disease Activity with Circulating Antibodies (with I T de Messias, J Santamaria, A Kajdacsy-Balla), 1988; Cutaneous Manifestation of Strongyloidiasis (with R M Genta), 1988. Memberships: American Academy of Pathology; Canadian Academy of Pathology; American Society of Dermatopathology; College of American Pathologists; American Association of Blood Banks. Hobbies: Cycling; Reading. Address: 811 Northwest Street, Bellevue, OH 44811, USA.

VON SEGESSER Ludwig Karl, b. 15 Mar 1952, Lucerne, Switzerland. Cardiovascular Surgeon. m. Marie Dinh, 27 Jun 1979, 1 s, 1 d. Education: MD, University Basel, 1979; PD, 1989; Certified, Surgical Board, Switzerland, 1985. Appointments include: Fellow, Cardiovascular Surgery, TX Heart Institute, Houston, USA, 1986; Staff Surgeon, Clinic for Cardiovascular Surgery, University Hospital, Zurich, 1987-; Academic Appointee, Zurich University, 1989-; European Board of Cardiovascular Perfusion, Chairman, 1993-. Publications: Arterial Grafting for Myocardial Revascularization, 1990; Assistant Editor, Perfusion, 1992-; Assistant Editor, European Journal of Cardio-Thoracic Surgery, 1994-; Over 300 articles to professional journals. Honours: Goetz-Preis Award, University of Zurich, 1991; Swiss Cardiology Foundation Award, 1991; Fellow, ACS. Memberships: Swiss Society Thoracic and Cardiovascular Surgery, Secretary, 1989-; Swiss Society of Surgery; Swiss Society of Cardiology; German Society Thoracic and Cardiovascular Surgery; European Association Cardio-Thoracic Surgery; European Society Artificial Organs; Society Critical Care Medicine; International Society Heart and Lung Transplantation; International Society Surgery; Society Thoracic Surgeons; Association for Advancement of Medical Instruction;

American Society Artificial Internal Organs. Address: Weinbergstrasse 45, Zurich CH-8006, Switzerland.

VON ZIELINSKI Theodor Von Beringe, b. 6 Feb 1953, Virginia, USA. Obstetrician; Gynaecologist. m. Betty Kerns, 7 April 1979, 1 son, 2 daughters. Education: AB, Honours, Princeton University; MD, University of Virginia; Board Certified, American Board of Obstetrics and Gynaecology. Appointments: Formerly Chairman, Department of Ob-Gyn, Currently Vice Chief of Staff, Member of Board of Directors, Staff Obstetrician and Gynaecologist, Indian River Memorial Hospital. Memberships: Gynaecologic Laser Society; American Association of Gynaecologic Laparoscopists; Indian River County Medical Society; Florida Medical Association; Fellow, American College of Obstetricians and Gynaecologists. Address: 777 37th Street, Suite C-104, Vero Beach, FL 32960, USA.

VOORBERG Robert, b. 3 Dec 1945, Naaldwyk, The Nethelands. Managing Doctor in Travel Medicine. m. T J P Govens, 14 May 1989, 3 sons, 1 daughter. Education: MD; Specialisation in Occupational Health. Appointments: Technical Engineer, Medical School, University of Amsterdam; Head of Medical Services, Schipol Amsterdam Airport. Hobby: Sailing. Address: Medical Services, Schipol Amsterdam Airport, PO 7501, 1118 ZG Schipol, The Netherlands.

VOORHORST Reindert, b. 15 Jun 1915, Wijhe, Netherlands. Allergologist. m. Frieda Smeenk, 13 Nov 1940, 3 s. Education: MD. Appointments: General Medicine; Assistant, Department Internal Medicine, University Hospital Groningen; Staff, Department Internal Medicine, Mil Hospital Utrecht; Staff, Laboratory Microbiology, University Utrecht; Head Department of Allergology, University Hospital Leiden; Now Retired. Publications: Basic Facts of Allergy, 1962; Het atopie Syndroom, 1966; First author, House-Dust and the House-Dust Mite, 1969; Over Asthma, Bronchitis en Allergie, 1975; Many publications in Annals of Allergy. Honours: Corresponding Member, German Allergy Society, 1971; Honorary Fellow, American College of Allergists, 1979; Storm van Leeuwen Medal, Dutch Society of Allergology, 1984; Karl Hansen Medal, German Society of Allergy and Immunology, 1984. Membership: Dutch Society of Allergology. Hobby: Philosophy. Address: Tivolistraat 62-29, 5017 HR Tilburg, Netherlands.

VORA Shailesh C, b. 1 Aug 1958, Bombay, India. Physician. m. Chetna S Vora, 16 Feb 1982, 2 daughters. Education: MD with speciality in Neurology, Psychiatry, Sleepdisorders & Clinical Neurophysiology. Owner: Neurology Clinic of South Arkansas. Career: Private Practice with Affiliation, MCSA; Staff Psychiatrist, SARHC; Medical Director, Sleep Disorder Lab, MCSA; Clinical Professor (Assistant), UAMS-AHEC Eldorado. Honours: Best Intern, Bombay, India, 1982; National Scholar, India, 1974. Memberships: AMA; American Psychiatric Association; American Academy of Neurology; Sleep Disorder Society. Hobbies: Play Tennis; Swimming; Sightseeing. Address: 2402 Pathway, Eldorado, Arkansas 71730, USA.

VORTEL Vladimir, b. 19 Jan 1916, Nachod, Czech Republic. Pathologist. m. Eliska Starova, 16 Sept 1944, 3 sons. Education: MUDr, 1946; Professor, Charles University, 1961; DrSc, 1963; Vice Dean, Faculty of Medicine, Hradec Kralove. Appointments: Assistant, Associate, Full Professor, Department of Pathology, Faculty Hospital Hradec Kralove, 1946-75; Head, Department of Pathology, Research Institute for Pharmacy & Biochemistry, 1975-. Publications: Proteus Encephalitis bei neugeborenen Kindern, 1960; Co-author Pathology of BCG Vaccine, 1962; Pulmonary adiaspiromycosis in man, 1971; Co-author, Cytomegalovirus-Virology, Pediatrics, Pathology, 1979. Memberships: Czech Medical Society; Czech Society of Pathologists. Honours: J E Purkyne Medal, 1963; Charles University Medal, 1965; Professor Emeritus, 1992; Honorary Member, Society of Pathologists, 1993. Hobbies: Gardening. Address: Na Jezirkach 303, 500 11 Hradec Kralove, Czech Republic.

VOTYAKOV Veniamin Iosifovich, b. 1 Aug 1921, Buguruslan, Russia. Virologist. m. Evdokiya Pozydevskaya, 10 July 1962, 1 son, 1 daughter. Education: MD, 2nd Medical Institute, Mscoow, 1939-43; Postgraduate Student, Institute of Bacpreparations Control, 1947-50. Appointments: Military Physician, 1943-46; Director, Byelorussian Research Institute for Epidemiology and Microbiology, 1950-86; Head, Department of Virus Activity Inhibitors, Research Institute of Epidemiology. Publications: Western Tick-borne Encephalitis, 1978; Amyotropic Leukospongiosis, 1990; Viruses as Risk factors of Atherosclerosis, series of articles, 1989-95; Diploma on Discover N322,

1988. Honours: 5 Governmental Orders, 1943-80; Diploma of the Supreme Soviet of the Republic of Belarus; Diplomas from scientific societies, 1975-85. Memberships: Russian Academy of Medical Sciences; Academy of Life Sciences; Editorial Boards of scientific journals; Byelorrusian Academy of Sciences. Hobbies: Walking; Painting. Address: K Zetkin Street 4, Minsk 220050, Belarus.

VOÛTE P A, b. 21 Jun 1936, Amsterdam, Netherlands. Professor. m. M M de Gaay Fortman, 27 Apr 1963, 1 s, 2 d. Education: MD; PhD. Appointments: Professor in Paediatric Oncology, University of Amsterdam; Head, Department of Paediatric Oncology, Academic Medical Center, Emma Kinderziekenhuis, Amsterdam. Publication: Editor, Cancer in Children, Clinical Management, 1993. Memberships: International Society of Paediatric Oncology; American Society of Clinical Oncology; American Association of Cancer Research. Address: Academic Medical Center, Emma Kinderziekenhuis, Dept Paediatric Oncology, Meibergdreef 9, 1105AZ, Amsterdam, Netherlands.

VOWELS Marcus Rex, b. 15 June 1941, Australia. 2 sons, 1 daughter. Education: MB BS, 1966; FRACP, 1971; MD, 1993. Appointments: Director, Haematology, Oncology, Bone Marrow Transplantation. Honour: Order of Australia, 1993. Memberships: ASH; ISEH; HSA; TSANZ; ACP; COSA; ANZCCSC. Hobby: Sailing. Address: Prince of Wales Children's Hospital, Randwick, New South Wales 2031, Australia.

VROEGOP Peter, b. 28 Nov 1934, The Hague, Netherlands. Clinical Psychologist and Psychotherapist. m. 14 July 1970, div., 2 sons. Education: Studies in Clinical and Industrial Psychology, Behavioural Medicine; Drs Clinical Psychology, State University of Utrecht; Registered Clinical Psychologist, Dutch Association of Psychologists; Registered Psychotherapist, Dutch Government; Client-centered Therapist; Gestalt Therapist. Appointments: Head, Department of Special Psychological Investigations, Royal Dutch Navy, Medical Department; Currently: Supervisor, Teaching Therapist, Instructor in Psychotherapy; Head, Department of Psychology, Bosch Medicentrum. Publications: On diving fear, 1968; Qualities of character and psychological stress, 1974; Prolonging of life by chemotherapy: worthwhile?, 1989; Cancer and chemotherapy, a behavioural medicine approach, 1990. Memberships: Dutch Institute of Psychologists; British Psychological Society; Association for Client-Centered Therapy; Association for Behavioural Therapy; Association for Gestalt Therapy; Association for Psychosocial Oncology; Behavioural Medicine Federation; Association for Psychotherapy. Hobbies: Skiing; Skating; Mountain walking; Piano; Cabaret. Address: Eerste morgen 18, 5233 NB 's Hertogenbosch, Netherlands.

VUJCICH John Michael, b. 24 Aug 1943, Kalgoorlie, Western Australia. Obstetrician; Gynaecologist. m. Beth Oldfield, 26 Jul 1969, 2 s, 2 d. Education: MBBS, Western Australia, 1969; MRCOG, 1975; FRACOG, 1980; FRCOG, 1988. Career: Private Practice, Obstetrician and Gynaecologist. Memberships: AMA; AGES; ASUM; FRACOG. Address: 108 Outram 8th, West Perth, Australia.

VYAS Mahesh, b. 17 Jun 1953, Rajkot, India. MD. m. Jayshree Vyas, 6 Dec 1976, 3 s, 1 d. Education: MD, Paediatrics and Allergy and Immunology. Career: Allergist in Private Practice. Address: 1424 South Euclid, Fullerton, CA 92632-3152, USA.

W

WACHS Harry, b. 24 May 1924, Pittsburgh, PA, USA. Developmental Optometrist. m. Ruth W Weissman, 20 May 1959, 1 s, 2 d. Education: Doctor of Optometry. Appointments include: Founder and Director, Pennsylvania Vision Institute, Pittsburgh, PA, 1952-92; Team Optometrist, Vision and Conceptual Development, WA Redskins Football Team, 1985-; Director and Coordinator, Vision and Conceptual Development Centre, Washington DC, 1991-; Professor School of Education, Reading Centre, George Washington University, Washington DC, 1982-91; Recipient, College of Vision Development, AM Skeffington Award, Excellence in Optometric Writing, 1994; Consultant to WA Capitals Hockey Team 1992- and Numerous School Systems. Publications: Co-author, Thinking Goes to School, Piaget's Theory in Practice, 1974, 8th printing, in seven languages, 1974; Co-author, Wachs Analysis of Cognitive Structures, Western Psychological Services, 1977; Piaget's Theory and Special Education, in Advances in Special Education, 1980. Memberships: American Optometric Association; Fellow, Diplomate, Contact Lenses, American Academy of Optometry; Fellow, College of Vision Development; Washington DC Optometric Association; Board of Directors, Multi-Disciplinary Academy of Clinical Education, 1989-; Board of Directors, Hands on Science, 1988-. Hobbies: Horses; Farming; Wildfowl; Exercise. Address: 2460 Huntingfields Drive, Huntingtown, MD 20639, USA.

WADA Ibrahim, b. 19 Aug 1957, Ayangba, Nigeria. Physician. m. Rabi Halidu, 20 Aug 1988, 2 daughters. Education: MBBS, 1980; MRCOG, 1988. Appointments: Consultant, Gynaecologist, Bourn Hall Clinic, Bourn, Cambridge, England; Consultant, Special Grade 1, Obstetrics and Gynaecology. Publications: E;ective Cryopreservation of All Embryos in Obts, 1993; Los Dose Aspirin Therapy in Assisted Conception, 1994. Memberships: Society of Obstetricians and Gynaecologists of Nigeria. Hobbies: tennis; Golf. Address: Department of Obstetrics and Gynaecology, Gwagwalada Specialist Hospital, PMB 228, Abuja, Nigeria.

WADDELL William Joseph, b. 16 Mar 1929, Commerce, GA, USA. Toxicology; Medicine. m. Carolyn Marlowe, 19 Oct 1974, 2 s, 1 d. Education: MD; AB, Chemistry, University of North Carolina. Appointments: Assistant Professor, Pharmacology, University of NC, 1958-62; Associate Professor, 1962-69; Professor, 1969-72, Professor of Pharmacology, 1972-76, University of KY; Professor and Chairman, University of Louisville, 1977-. Publications: Over 100 peer reviewed articles in Toxicology and Pharmacology. Honour: Centennial Alumnus Distinguished Visiting Professor, School of Medicine, University of NC, 1979. Memberships include: Society of Toxicology; American Society for Pharmacology and Experimental Therapeutics; International Society for the Study of Xenobiotics; American Physiological Society; Fellow Academy of Toxicological Sciences. Hobbies: Music; Reading; Travel. Address: Department of Pharmacology and Toxicology, School of Medicine, University of Louisville, Louisville, KY 40292, USA.

WADE Gillian Sarah, b. 24 June 1954, St Annes-on-Sea, England. Chartered Psychologist. Education: BA (joint honours), Psychology, Sociology, 1975, PhD, Psychology, 1981, University of Leeds. Appointments: Research Associate, Department of Psychiatry, University of Manchester, 1980-82; Research Fellow, University of Kent, 1982-83; Research Associate, Health Care Research Unit, Newcastle-on-Tyne, 1987; Divisional Director, Health Care Division, The Produce Studies Group, 1990-94; Senior Manager, Head of Regional Project Unit, District Audit Service, Cardiff, 1994-. Publications: Combination therapies: what is their impact on prescribing budgets?, 1994; Co-author: Specialist Care for the Elderly, 1984; Explaining inter-group differentiation in an industrial organisation, 1986; Partners in recall: Collaborative order in the recall of a police interrogation, 1986; Meetings make evidence? An experimental study of collaborative and individual recall of a simulated police interrogation, 1986; Superordinate goals and interpersonal behaviour: the effects of role ambiguity and relative status on interorganisational attitudes and task performance, 1987; What makes people with diabetes measure their own blood glucose?, 1994. Honours: Honorary Research Fellow, Kent University, 1984; Awarded entry as Chartered Psychologist, 1988. Memberships: Associate Member, Market Research Society; British Psychological Society; Institute of Health Services Management; District Audit Society. Hobbies: Sailing; Cooking. Address: District Audit, 2nd Floor, 2-4 Park Grove, Cardiff, South Glamorgan CF1 3PA, Wales.

WADLOW Geoffrey Philip, b. 17 July 1945, England. Acupuncturist. m. Dr Virginia Laurence, 20 Oct 1990, 1 daughter. EducationL: BA, Honours, University of Kent, Canterbury; BAc, International College of Oriental Medicine, East Grinstead; CAc, Nanjing College of Traditional Chinese Medicine, Nanjing, China. Appointments: Director, Senior Lecturer, Clinical Supervisor, London School of Acupuncture, England. Publications: Alternatives in Healing Co-author, 1988; Well's Supportive Therapies in Health Care, Co-author, 1994. Membership: Register of Traditional Chinese Medicine. Hobbies: Reading; Hillwalking; Swimming; Taiji; Qigong. Address: 8 Pound Hill, Cambridge CB3 0AE, England.

WAGNER Franklin C, b. 13 Dec 1938, Chicago, IL, USA. Neurosurgeon. m. Sarah L Latta, 4 Sep 1965, 1 s, 2 d. Education: AB, Princeton University, 1961; MD, Bowman Gray School of Medicine, 1966. Appointments: Associate Professor of Surgery, Neurosurgery, Yale University School of Medicine, 1972-82; Currently, Professor and Chairman of Department of Neurological Surgery, University of CA, Davis. Honours: Alpha Omega Alpha; Wakeman Award for Research in the Neurosciences. Memberships: Society of Neurological Surgeons; American Association of Neurological Surgeons; American Medical Association; American College of Surgeons; Cervical Spine Research Society. Hobbies: Running; Music; Reading. Address: 2516 Stockton Boulevard, Sacramento, CA 95817, USA.

WAGNER Hans Peter, b. 13 Nov 1930, Frauenfeld, Switzerland. Head, Division of Paediatric Hematology & Oncology. m. Anne Lucie Perrinjaquet, 22 Dec 1956, 2 sons, 4 daughters. Education: Matura, Städtisches Gymnasium, Bern, 1950; MD, University of Bern Medical School, 1956; Paediatric Board Certificate, 1964; Professor of Paediatrics, 1971; Paediatric Hematology Board Certificate, 1974; Paediatric Hematology & Oncology Board Certificate, 1987. Appointments: Intern, Department of Paediatrics, University of Bern, 1957-58; Rotating Internship, Stamford Hospital, Connecticut, USA, 1958-59; Research Fellow, University of Madison, USA, 1959-61; Resident, Department of Paediatrics, University Hospitals, Bern, 1961-63; Consultant, Department of Paediatrics, University Hospitals, Bern, 1964-67; Research Collaborator, Brookhaven National Laboratory, Upton, NY, USA, 1964-75; Consultant, University Hospitals Lausanne, Switzerland, 1966-81; Consultant, Children's Hospital, Geneva, 1967-75; Head, Division of Cell Kinetics, Institute for Clinical & Experimental Cancer Research, University of Bern, 1967-88; Head ,Divisionof Paediatric Hematology/Oncology, University Hospitals of Bern, 1968-. Publications: Over 250 publications: Original articles, case histories, reviews, chapters of books.Honours: San Salvatore Prize, 1982. Memberships: Founding Member, International Society for Paediatric Oncology; Founding Member, Swiss Society for Oncology; Founding Member, Cell Kinetics Society; Swiss Society of Paediatrics; Founding Member European Society for Paediatric Hematology & Immunology; International Society for Experimental Hematology; Swiss Society for Hematology. Hobbies: Architecture; Building Decoration; Reading; Jazz; Sking; Travel. Address: Schneiderstrasse 45, 3084 Wabern, Switzerland.

WALKER Elizabeth Helen May, b. 1 May 1928, London. England. Obstetrician and Gynaecologist. Education: MA; MB BChir (Cantab); FRCOG; DCH. Appointments: Medical Officer, St Luke's Hospital, Chabua, Assam, India; Registrar, Obstetrics and Gynaecology, Newcastle General Hospital, England; Consultant in Obstetrics and Gynaecology, Lincoln Group of Hospitals; Now retired. Publications: The management of pregnancy in Vol Willebrand's Disease, 1968; Successful pregnancy in a patient with Thalassaemia major, 1969. Membership: Emeritus Member, Women's Visiting Gynaecological Club. Hobbies: Painting; Ecumenical concerns; Churches Ministry of Healing. Address: 10 Curle Avenue, Lincoln LN2 4AN, England.

WALKER Leslie Gresson, b. 17 May 1949, Glasgow, Scotland. Clinical Psychologist. m. Mary Birnie Durno, 6 Sept 1974, 2 s. Education: MA. Honours, 1971, PhD, 1975, University of Aberdeen; Dip Clin Psychol, British Psychological Society, 1976; AFBPsS; CPsychol. Appointments: Clinical Psychologist, Grampian Health Board, 1974; Lecturer, department of Mental Health, 1976, Senior Lecturer, 1989, Director, Behavioural Oncology Unit, departments of Mental Health and Surgery, 1993-, Aberdeen University Medical School. Publications: Models of Psychotherapy: A Primer, Co-author, 1982; Police Stress at Work, Co-author, 1993. Memberships: British Society of Experimental and Clinical Hypnosis, Council Member; Associate Fellow, British Psychological Society; British Psychosocial Oncology Group, Chairman Elect. Hobbies: Family; Photography. Address: Behavioural Oncology

Unit, Departments of Mental Health and Surgery, Aberdeen University Medical School, Foresthill, Aberdeen AB9 2ZD, Scotland.

WALKER Mark Lamont, b. 5 Jan 1952, Brooklyn, NY, USA. Surgeon. m. Alicia Walker, Nov 1975, 1 s, 4 d. Education: BS; MD; FACS; FICS. Appointments: Trauma Fellow, 1982-83; Instructor, Howard University, Department of Surgery, 1983-85; Assistant Professor of Surgery, MSM, 1985-87; Clinical Assistant Professor of Surgery, 1987-89; Associate Professor, 1990-present; Chairman and Program Director, Morehouse School of Medicine, 1990-94. Hobbies: Piano; Basketball; Novels; Films. Address: 22 Piedmont Avenue, Atlanta, GA 30335, USA.

WALLACE Helen Margaret, b. 18 Feb 1913, USA. Physician. Education: AB, Wellesley, 1993; MD, Columbia University College of Physicians & Surgeons, 1937; MPH, Harvard School of Public Health, 1943. Appointments: Junior Health Officer; Assistant Health Officer; Chief, Maternity and Newborn Division; Director, Bureau for Handicapped Children, New York City Department of Health, 1943-55; Professor & Chairman, Department of Preventative Medicine, New York Medical College, 1955-56; Professor, Maternal and Child Health, University of Minnesota, School of Public Health, 1956-59; Chief, Professional Training & Chief, Child Health Research, US Children's Bureau. 1959-62; Professor & Chairman, Maternal & Child Health Program, University of California, School of Public Health, 1962-80; Professor & Head, Division of Maternal and Child Health, Graduate School of Public Health, San Diego State University, 1980-85; Director, Study of Infant Mortality, San Diego County, 1988-; Director, Study of Prenatal Care in Hispanic Women in San Diego County, 1991-; Professor, Maternal and Child Health, Graduate School of Public Health, San Diego State University, 1985-. Publications: Author of 12 Books and 325 Articles in various journals. Honours: Martha May Eliot Award, 1978; Lewis Award - American Academy of Pediatrics, 1980; Wellesley College Alumnae Achievement Awards, 1982; University of Minnesota Award in Maternal and Child Health, 1985; Alumi Award for Teaching and Scholarship, San Diego State University, 1983; Fulbright Award, Czechoslovakia, 1992. Memberships: New York Philanthropic League; Muscular Dystrophy Association of New York City; American Academy of Pediatrics, 1989. Address: 850 State Street, San Diego, CA 92101, USA.

WALLACE Leon, b. 7 July 1925, Syracuse, New York, USA. Medical Doctor. m. Div, 2 sons, 1 daughter. Education: AB magna cum laude, Physics, 1944; MD (Case) Western Reserve University School of Medicine, 1949; Resident: Psychiatry, Compton Sanitarium, California, 1950-52, Psychosomatic Medicine, Los Angeles County General Hospital, 1952-53; Certified: Psychiatry, American Board of Neurology and Psychiatry, 1955, Psychoanalysis, American Psychoanalytic Association, 1977. Appointments: Private practice, 1955-; Assistant Clinical Professor, UCLA School of Medicine, 1968-. Publications: The Mechanism of Shame, 1963; Psychotherapy of a Male Homosexual, 1969; The Psychoanalytic Situation and the Transference Neurosis, 1974; Observations on the Psychoanalytic Treatment of a Patient with Multiple Sclerosis, 1975; Psychoanalytic Observations on Marijuana Use, 1978; The Transference Neurosis and the Therapeutic Process, 1979; Silence, Sleep and the Psychoanalytic Situation, 1980; Assimilation and the Jewish Group Identity: A Dialogue (with Ernest Lewy), 1983; Pleasure and Frustration: A Resynthesis of Clinical and Theoretical Psychoanalysis, 1984; Normality, Psychosomatic Disorders and Schizophrenia, 1993. Honours: Phi Beta Kappa; Sigma Pi Sigma; Pi Mu Epsilon. Memberships: American Medical Association; California Medical Association; American Psychiatric Association; Life Member, Southern California Psychiatric Society, Ethics Committee 1977-78, 1987-88; Founding Member, South Bay Psychiatric Society; Corresponding Member, Israel Psychoanalytic Society; American Society of Psychoanalytic Physicians; American and International Psychoanalytic Associations; Medical Education Committee, Torrance Memorial Hospital, 1975-78; Honorary Member, Torrance Memorial Hospital Medical Staff; Certified in Psychoanalysis, American Psychoanalytic Association. Address: 25202 Crenshaw Blvd, Suite 207, Torrance, CA 90505-6151, USA.

WALLACH Stanley, b. 10 Dec 1928, Brooklyn, New York, USA. Physician. m. Pearl Small, 26 Aug 1973, 2 sons, 6 daughters. Education: AB, Cornell University, 1948; MA, Columbia University, 1949, MD, SUNY Downstate Medical Center, Brooklyn, 1953; Resident, Internal Medicine, 1954-56; Fellow, Endocrinology, Metabolism, Massachusetts General Hospital, Boston, 1956-57; Diplomate: American Board of

Internal Medicine; American Board of Endocrinology and Metabolism. Appointments include: Chief, Medical Services, VA Medical Center, Bay Pines, Florida, 1983-90; Professor, 1983-92, Associate Chair, 1988-92, Department of Internal Medicine, University of South Florida College of Medicine; Consultant, VA Medical Center, Tampa, Florida, 1991-92; Attending Physician, Moffatt Cancer Center, 1991-92, Tampa General Hospital, 1991-92; Director, Medical Education, Catholic Medical Center, Jamaica, New York, 1992-; Director, Endocrinology, Metabolic Bone Disease Center, Hospital for Joint Diseases, New York City, 1993-; Executive Director, American College of Nutrition, 1993-. Publications: Numerous articles in professional journals. Honours: Co-recipient, Hektoen Silver Award, American Medical Association, 1959; John J Johnson Award, Paget's Disease Foundation, 1989. Memberships include: Fellow, American College of Physicians; Fellow, American College of Clinical Pharmacology; Fellow, American College of Nutrition, Board of Directors 1982-, President 1987-89, Secretary-Treasurer, 1991-; Sigma Xi; Association of American Physicians; American Association of Clinical Endocrinology; American Society for Magnesium Research; American Society for Bone and Mineral Research; Paget's Disease Foundation; International Conference on Calcium Regulating Hormones. Hobbies: Riding; Physical fitness; Scuba diving. Address: Hospital for Joint Diseases/Orthopedic Institute, 301 East 17th Street, New York, NY 10003, USA.

WALLER John Louis, b. 1 Dec 1944, Loma Linda, California, USA. Anaesthesiologist. m. Jo Lynn Marie Haas, 4 Aug 1968, 1 s, 2 d. Education: BA, Southern College, 1967; MD, Loma Linda University, 1971; FACA; FACCP; Intern, Hartford Hospital; Resident in Anaesthesiology, Harvard University; Fellow in Cardiac Anaesthesiology, Harvard University Medical School, Massachusetts General Hospital; Diplomate, American Board of Anaesthesiology, 1975. Appointments: Major M C, USAF, 1975-77; Assistant Professor of Anaesthesiology, 1977-80, Associate Professor of Anaesthesiology, 1980-86; Professor, Chairman, Department of Anaesthesiology, 1986-, Emory University School of Medicine; Medical Director, Emory University Hospital, 1993-. Publications: Contributor of articles in professional journals and chapters in books. Honours: Certificate of Appreciation, Office of Secretary of Defence, 1983; Board of Directors, Clifton Casualty Co, 1985; Trustee, International Anaesthesia Research Society, 1985; Consultant, Arrow International Incorporated, 1988; Member, Advisory Committee on Anaesthesia and Life Support Drugs Food and Drug Administration, 1986-92; Best Doctors in America, 1992. Memberships include: American Medical Association; American Society of Anaesthesiologists; Society of Academic Anaesthesia Chairs; Association of Cardiac Anaesthesiologists; European Association of Cardiothoracic Anaesthesiologists; Society of Cardiovascular Anaesthesiologists. Hobbies: Tennis; Sailing; Swimming. Address: Emory University Hospital, Department of Anaesthesiology, 1346 Clifton Road NE, Atlanta, GA 30322 1104, USA.

WALLER Julian Arnold, b. 17 Apr 1932, New York City, USA. Professor Emeritus of Medicine. m. Elsa M Neipris, 17 Nov 1956, 1 son, 1 daughter. Education: AB, Columbia University, 1953; MD, Boston University, 1957; MPH, Harvard University, 1960. Appointments: US Public Health Service, 1958-64; California Department of Public Health, 1964-68; Professor of Community Medicine, University of Vermont, 1968-73; Chairman, Department of Edipdemiology and Environmental Health, 1973-79; Professor of Medicine, 1979-94; Professor Emeritus, 1994-. Publications: Report to Congress on Alcohol and Highway Safety, 1968; Medical Impairment to Driving, 1973; Safe Practices in the Arts and Crafts. A Studio Guide, 1985; Injury Control, 1985; Injury in America - A Continuing Public Health Problem, Co-author, 1985. Honours: National Safety Council Metropolitan Life Award of Merit for Accident Research, 1972; Alpha Omega Alpha, 1988; American Public Health Association ICEHS Career Achievement Award, 1989; Association for the Advancement of Automotive Medicine Award of Merit, 1994. Memberships: American Public Health Association; Association for the Advancement of Automotive Medicine; Human Factors and Ergonomics Society; American College of Preventive Medicine; American College of Epidemiology. Hobbies: Ceramics; Assemblage; Writing Poetry. Address: 125 Holmes Road, S Burlington, VT 05403, USA.

WALLER Kathleen Grace, b. 18 Feb 1964, St Albans, England. Physician. Education: BA; BM BCh; MRCOG. Appointments: Research Fellow to Professor Shaw, University Hospital of Wales, Cardiff, 1991-93; Registrar in Obstetrics and Gynaecology, Hammersmith Hospital, London. Publications: Gonadotrophin-Releasing Hormone Analoges for the Treatment of Endometriosis: Long-Term Follow-Up,

1993; Endometriosis, Pelvic Pain and Psychological Functioning, 1995. Membership: Royal College Obstetricians and Gynaecologists, 1993. Address: 32 Waverley Road, St Albans, Hertfordshire AL3 5PE, England.

WALLER Richard Maxwell, b. 27 June 1954, Nairobi, Kenya. Podiatric Surgeon; Specialist in Biomechanics and Podo Paediatrics. m. Susan Pinchen, 16 Sept 1978, 1 son. 1 daughter. Education: Distinction, Physics, 1973, DPodMed, 1975, Chelsea School of Chiropody; SRCh; MChS; FPodA, 1989. Appointments: Contractual Chiropodist, North Hampshire Health Authority, England, 1975-78; Private Practice, Podiatry, Boston, Lincolnshire, 1979-; Specialist, Podiatric Surgery, Pilgrim Hospital, Boston, 1994-; Lecturer, 2-day Podopaediatrics course, London Business School, 1985; Lecture series include: Brighton Health Authority, St James Hospital Postgraduate Group, Leeds, 4 days; Harringay Health Authority, Grimsby Health Authority (Biomechanics and Surgical lectures); Podopaediatrics lecture, London Postgraduate Group, Austria, 1990; Lectures, Royal Society of Medicine, Society of Chiropodists Conferences, World Podiatric Conference, 1993; Consultancy, Mr B Francis, Enfield and Harley Street, London, 1987-91. Publications: Contributor to professional publications; Parents Magazine, 1994. Honours: Member, 1978, Fellow, 1989, Podiatry Association; Awarded Tankard, Boston Fenland Round Table, 1991; Many sporting and school honours and awards include: Croydon Discus Champion, 1968-71; Junior Gold, Senior Silver Medals, Discus, age 16. Memberships include: Chairman, Lincolnshire Branch, Society of Chiropodists; Founder Member, Pilgrim Technologies; Chairman, Ecology Study Group, Boston; 1st Chairman, Ecology Party, South Lincolnshire. Hobbies: Hillwalking; Windsurfing; Gardening; Reading detective novels; Travel, especially in Africa; Tropical fish; Cycling; Swimming; Music; Family.

WALSH B Timothy, b. 17 Oct 1946, USA. Psychiatrist. m. Mary Beth Walsh, MD, 2 s, 1 d. Education: AB cum laude, Chemistry, Princeton University, 1967; MD cum laude, Harvard Medical School, 1972. Appointments: Instructor in Psychiatry, 1978-79, Visiting Assistant Professor, Psychiatry, 1979-82, Albert Einstein College of Medicine; Coordinator, Medical Student Teaching in Psychiatry, Montefiore Hospital, 1978-79; Assistant Professor, 1979-85, Associate Professor, 1985-90, Professor, 1990-, Clinical Psychiatry, College of Physicians and Surgeons, Columbia University. Publications: Co-author: Long-term outcome of antidepressant treatment for bulimia nervosa, in American Journal of Psychiatry, 1991; Binge Eating Disorder: Reliability and validity of a new diagnostic category, in Journal Consultant and Clinical Psychology, in press. Honours: American Institute of Chemists Undergraduate Award, 1967; Sigma Xi; Phi Beta Kappa; Alpha Omega Alpha. Memberships: American Psychiatric Association; American Psychosomatic Society; Fellow, American Psychopathological Association; American Society of Clinical Psychopharmacology Inc; Academy for Eating Disorders. Address: 722 West 168th Street, Unit 98, New York, NY 10032, USA.

WALSH Fiona Mary, b. 23 Dec 1953, Romford, Essex, England. Osteopath; Instructor. Education: Diploma in Osteopathy, British School of Osteopathy, 1977. Appointments include: Assistant Osteopath, 1977-82; Private Group Practice, London, 1978-; Regional Osteopathic Careers Officer for SE London, 1980-; Osteopathic Lecturer, 1983-, Principal Tutor, 1988-, British School of Osteopathy, London. Honours: Osteopathic Technique I Prize, Applied Anatomy and Physiology I Prize, Pathology Prize, Clinical Practice Prize, British School of Osteopathy. Memberships: General Council and Register of Osteopaths, 1977-; Osteopathic Association of Great Britain, 1977-82; Member of several professional committees. Hobbies: Opera; Ballet; Theatre; Golf; Skiing. Address: 20 Sundial Avenue, South Norwood, London, SE25 4BX, England.

WALSH John Patrick (Sir), b. 5 July 1911, Melbourne, Australia. Dentist. m. Enid Morris, 10 Dec 1934, 1 son, 3 daughters. Education: MB BS, DDSc, Melbourne; FDSRCS, England and Edinburgh; MDS; FRS(NZ); Honorary DSc. Appointments: Dean, University of Otago Dental School, New Zealand; Emeritus Professor; Retired. Publications: A Manual of Stomatology, 1957; Living with Uncertainty, 1968; Psychiatry and Dentistry, 1976. Honour: KBE, 1960. Memberships: NZDA; BMA. Address: Unit 29 Hillsborough Heights Village, 1381 Dominion Road, Auckland, New Zealand.

WALSH Patricia Noonan, b. New York City, USA. Psychologist. m. Brendan M Walsh, 2 s, 1 d. Education: BA, Newton College; MEd, Tufts University; MSc, PhD, Trinity College, Dublin, Ireland; Dip Clin Psych, British Psychological Society. Appointments: Senior Psychologist, Research Associate, Director of Research, St Michael's House, Dublin; Part-time Lecturer, UCD, Dublin. Publications include: The Partners Project: II Using a Repertory Grid to Evaluate Change, Co-author, 1988; Job Coaches: A User's Guide, Co-author, 1992; Assessing the Support Needs of Ageing Carers, Co-author, 1994; Determinants of the Costs of Providing Services to Persons with Intellectual Disability, Co-author; Creating Work Opportunities for Europeans with Mental Handicap, Editor, 1991. Memberships: British Psychological Society; Psychological Society of Ireland; American Association on Mental Retardation, Academy. Hobbies: Travel; Theatre; Reading. Address: 20 Palmerston Gardens, Rathmines, Dublin 6, Ireland.

WALTERS Judith R, b. 20 Jun 1944, Concord, NH, USA. Neuropharmacologist. 3 s. Education: BA, Biochemistry, Mount Holyoke College, 1966; PhD, Pharmacology, Yale University, 1972. Appointments: Assistant Professor, Department of Psychiatry, Yale University School of Medicine; Currently, Chief, Neurophysiological Pharmacology Section, ETB, NINDS. Publications: Contributor of over 90 articles on neuropharmacology and neurophysiology to professional journals. Memberships: Editorial Board of Synapse; Board of Scientific Counselors; NIAAA; Society of Neuroscience; American Society of Pharmacology and Experimental Therapeutics. Address: National Institutes of Health, Bldg 10, Room 5C214, 9000 Rockville Pike, Bethesda, MD 20892, USA.

WALTERS Penelope Jane, b. 1 July 1959, Westminster, England. Management Consultant; Dentist. m. Ian Walters, 5 Jan 1993, 2 sons. Education: BDS, University of London, 1981; MBA, University of Auckland, 1991. Appointments: Dental Practitioner, England and New Zealand, 1982-93; Director, Insight Medix Ltd, 1989-; Director, Waitemata Health Limited, 1992-94; Chairman, Pragmatix Limited, 1993-; Management Consultant. Memberships: Institute of Directors, New Zealand; New Zealand Dental Association; Strategic Management Society, New Zealand. Hobbies: Contract bridge; Photography; Reading; Sports. Address: 42 Marine Parade, Herne Bay, Auckland 1002, New Zealand.

WALTON Henry John, b. 15 Feb 1924, Botswana. Professor of Psychiatry; Professor of Medical Education; Federation President. m. Sula Wolff. Education: MD; PhD; FRCP; FRCPsych. Appointments include: Professor of Psychiatry, to 1986, then Professor of International Medical Education, University of Edinburgh, Scotland; President, World Federation for Medical Education; Editor, Medical Education. Appointments: Editor: Small Group Psychotherapy, 1974; Dictionary of Psychiatry, 1985; Report of World Conference on Medical Education, 1988; Proceedings of World Summit on Medical Education, 1994. Honours: Academician, Academy of Medicine, Buenos Aires, 1988, Poland, 1993, Belgium, 1994; Medal, World Health Organization, 1998; Medicus Magnus Medal, Poland, 1994; Honorary MD, Universities of Uppsala, Lisbon and Tucuman. Membership: Life President, Association for Medical Education in Europe. Hobbies: Literature; Visual arts, particularly Western, Chinese and Japanese. Address: 38 Blacket Place, Edinburgh EH9 1RL, Scotland.

WALTON OF DETCHANT John Nicholas (Lord), b. 16 Sep 1922, Rowlands Gill, Co Durham, England. President, World Federation of Neurology; Member of UK House of Lords. m. Mary Elizabeth Harrison, 31 Aug 1946, 1 s, 2 d. Education: MBBS, 1st Class Honours, King's College University, Durham, 1945; MRCP, 1950; MD, University of Durham, 1952; DSc, University of Newcastle upon Tyne, 1972; Certified Physician, Neurologist. Appointments include: Director, Muscular Dystrophy Research Laboratories, Newcastle General Hospital, 1965-83; Professor of Neurology, 1968-83, Dean of Medicine, 1971-81, University of Newcastle upon Tyne; Warden, Green College, Oxford, 1983-89; Patron, International Spinal Research Trust, 1981-; President, World Federation of Neurology, 1989-; President, Little Foundation, 1991-; Member, House of Lords Select Committee on Science and Technology, 1991-; Numerous visiting professorships and named lectures in UK and abroad. Publications include: Many books and chapters to medical and neurological textbooks and over 200 papers published in journals including: Introduction to Clincial Neuroscience, 2nd edition, 1987; Co-editor, Skeletal Muscle Pathology, 2nd edition, 1992; Co-editor, Oxford Medical Companion, 1994. Honours include: Numerous Honorary Degrees; Knight Bachelor, 1979; Life Peerage, 1989; Gaetano Conte Award, 1993; Harben Medal, 1993; Fellow, Honoris Causa, Institute of Education, University of London, 1994.

Memberships include: Numerous Honorary Memberships; Chairman, Muscular Dystrophy Group of Great Britain and Northern Ireland, 1971-95; Neuropathological Society. Hobbies: Cricket; Golf; Music; Reading; Walking. Address: 13 Norham Gardens, Oxford, OX2 6PS, England.

WAN Xiaogang, b. 8 Aug 1963, Jiangan County, Sichuan Province, China. Associate Professor of Traditional Chinese Medicine. m. Liao Jianling, 12 Mar 1986, 1 son. Education: MB, 1982; MMed, 1990. Appointments: Physician; Assistant of Medicine; Currently Associate Professor, Hubei College of Traditional Chinese Medicine, Wuhan. Publications: Analysis and Comments on Diagnostic Theories in the Analysis and Comments on the Treatise on Febrile Diseases, 1990; Research on Pathologic Model and Plasma ANP about Cold-stasis with Blood-deficiency Syndrome, 1993; Practical Cardioangiology of TCM, 1993. Honours: Progress Awards in Science and Technology, Hubei Province, 1992. Hobbies: Chinese ancient literature; Physical culture. Address: Hubei College of Traditional Chinese Medicine, Wuhan 430061, China.

WAN Xuancai S T, b. 16 Nov 1930, Kunming, China. Chairman; Professor, Anatomy & Neurobiology. m. Q Hong, 14 Feb 1955, 1 son, 1 daughter. Education: MD, Medical College, Peking University, 1953; Postdoctor, Peking Union Medical College, 1953-56. Appointments: Lecturer, Department of Anatomy, Peking Union Medical College, 1956-69; Clinical Doctor, Wuwei, Gansu, 1970-74; Lecturer, Associate Professor, Lanchow Medical College, 1974-79; Visiting Associate Professor, School of Medicine, University of Pennsylvania, USA, 1980-82; Associate Professor, Department of Cell Biology, 1982-85; Professor, Chairman, Department of Anatomy & Neurobiology, 1986-; Visiting Professor, University Fribourg, Suisse, Oxford University, England, 1991-. Publications: Development of ligand-HRP method and the discovery of Golgi-phobic dendrites, 1986; The theoretical model of the brain, 1987. Memberships: IBRO; Vice President, Neuroscience Society of China; Vice President, Anatomy Society of Beijing; Board Member, Chinese Society of Cell Biology; Foreign Member, AAA. Honours: Honorary Professor, Capital Medical University, Beijing; Honorary Chief Editor, Chinese Journal of Neuroscience; First Degree Scientific Award, National Health Ministry, 1984; Second Degree Scientific Award, National Committee for the Promotion of Science & Technology, 1985. Hobbies: Philosophy of Science; Poetry. Address: Chinese Academy of Medical Sciences, Peking Union Medical College, 9 East Dan 3rd Tiao, Beijing 100005, China.

WAN Zi-an, b. 1950, Huining County, Gansu Province, China. Doctor. m. Feng Ya-Fang, 1979, 2 d. Education: Traditional Chinese Medicine; Paediatrics. Appointment: Physician-in-Charge, Jingyuan Worker's Hospital of Coal Administration, Gansu, China, 1977-. Publications: Clinical Observation on the Treatment of Coal Silicosis Caused by Insufficiency of Q and Stasis; Clinical Observation on Shengi Bufei Decoction on 40 Cases of Coal Silicosis; Co-author, The Essence of Modern Prescriptions, in progress; About 10 articles published. Honours: Award for Excellent Learned Articles on Traditional Medicine, 1992; Award, 1st Competition of International Traditional Medical Science. Membership: Chinese Learned Society of Acupuncture and Moxibustion. Hobby: Calligraphy. Address: Jingyuan Worker's Hospital of the Mine Administration, Gansu Province, 730913, China.

WANG Bao-mei, b. 8 Sept 1926, Tsingtao, China. Pathologist. m. Shou-yan Guo, 15 Jan 1956, 1 d. Education: BS, Catholic University, Peking, 1948; MD, Peking Union Medical College, Peking, 1952. Appointments: Professor, Department of Pathology, Shanghai Second Medical University, Shanghai; Chief, Laboratory of Immunopathology, Shanghai Institute of Immunology. Publications: Pathologic Study of 21 Autopsy Cases of Extensive Burn, 1962; Acute Hemorrhagic Enteritis. A Pathologic Study of 21 Autopsy Cases, 1964; SEM & TEM Study on Activated Macrophages, 1988; Flow Cytometric Analysis of the Effect of Activitated Macrophages on Alveolar Cell Carcinoma of Lung in Vitro, 1989; Thin Basement Membrane Nephropathy and Asymptomatic Hematuria in Children, 1992; Diseases of Hematopoietic and Lymphoid System, Deept Mycotic Infections, Diseases of Urinary System, 1979, 1990; Effect of Corynebacterum Parvum Activated Macrophages on Tumor Cells, Co-author, 1982; Classification and Incidence of Alveolar Bronchiolar Neoplasms in BALB/C Female Mice, Co-author, 1982. Honours: Shanghai Science and Technology Award, 1982; Shanghai Distinguished Woman Scientist. 1985. Memberships: Chinese Medical Association; Chinese Society of Pathology; International Academy of Pathology, Chinese Division; Asia Pacific Association of Societies of

Pathologists; Chinese Society of Immunology. Hobby: Music. Address: Department of Pathology, Shanghai Second Medical University, 280 South Chongqing Road, Shanghai 200025, China.

WANG Bi, b. 7 Nov 1929, Wu Xi, China. Professor of Thoracic Surgery. m. Jian-yun Song, 24 Aug 1959, 3 sons. Education: BA, Shanghai Second Medical University, 1956; MD, 1961. Appointments: Professor of Thoracic Surgery, Shanghai Railway University, College of Medicine; Director, Department of Thoracic Surgery, Gan Quan Hospital affiliated to Shanghai Railway University, China. Publications: Diagnosis and Treatment of Leiomyoma of the Esophagus, in Chinese Journal of Surgery, 1980; The Complications of Esophagus Disease After Operation, 1984; 3 books and 60 articles in Specialty of Thoracic Tumor Surgery (Carcinoma of Cardia-Esophagus, Lung and Tumor of Mediastinum), 1984-94. Memberships: Chinese Medical Association; UICC (International); Director, Chinese Railway Cancer Foundation. Hobbies: Swimming; Travelling. Address: 123 Zhi Jiang Xi Road, Suite 6/101, Shanghai 200070, China.

WANG Bing-sheng, b. 4 Feb 1941, Jiangsu, China. Professor of Surgery. m. Ni Hong, 10 May 1969, 2 daughters. Education: Diplomate, Shanghai First Medical College, 1965. Appointments: Visiting Surgeon, 1980; Associate Professor, 1989, Professor, 1993-, Department of Surgery, Zhongshan Hospital, Shanghai Medical University. Publications: Some Aspects of Smooth Muscle Tumours of the Digestive Tract, 1987; Choice of operation in congenital dilatation of the bile ducts, 1988; Extracorporeal Shock Wave Lithotripsy: Experience in Treating 245 Patients with Gallbladder Stones, 1990; Combined non-operative intervention for retained bile duct stones, 1994. Address: Department of Surgery, Zhongshan Hospital, Shanghai Medical University, Shanghai 200032, China.

WANG Cephas Hsun-Keng, b. 4 Feb 1915, Long-Kou, Shandong, China. Surgeon. m. Judy Wang, 1 Aug 1945, 1 son, 1 daughter. Education: BM; MD. Appointments: Resident Surgeon, Cheeloo and West China University Hospital; Surgeon, Cheeloo University (affiliated) Hospital; Surgeon, Affiliated Hospital of Shandong University School of Medicine; Chief Surgeon, Vice-Superintendent, currently Emeritus Superintendent, Tsingtao Municipal Hospital; Currently Professor of Surgery, Tsingtao University School of Medicine. Publications: Biliary Ascariasis - Report of 141 cases, 1956; Relationship between Biliary Ascariasis and Choledocholithiasis, 1957; Cholelithiasis, 1980; Oriental Choledocholithiasis, 1982; Treatment of Choledocholithiasis by Combined Western and Chinese Traditional Medicine, 1982. Membership: Chairman, Tsingtao Surgical Association. Hobbies: 27 Su-Chow Road, Tsingtao 266003, China.

WANG Chuan, b. 3 Dec 1931, Shanghai, China. Professor of Otorhinolaryngology and Clinical Ecology. m. Ma Shu Kun, 20 June 1959, 3 daughters. Education: MD, Peking Union Medical College, 1957. Appointments include: Associate Professor, 1985; Professor of Otorhinolaryngology and Clinical Ecology, 4th Military Medical University, 1989-; Member, Editorial Board, Chinese Journal of Medicine and Philosophy, 1991; Editor, Journal of Conservative Dentistry, China, 1992. Publications: More than 30 medical articles in various Chinese medical journals, 1958-94; Co-author: Noise disease, 1987; Clinical, 1993. Memberships: Chinese Ecology Association; Chinese Medical Association. Hobbies: Bridge; Photography; Chinese chess; Tennis. Address: Room 14, Building 28, Xi-jing Hospital, Xian 710032, Shaanxi, China.

WANG Chun-Xiang, b. 13 Jan 1925, Zhejiang, China. Professor. m. Mr Liu Li-Chang, 31 Dec 1953, 1 son, 1 daughter. Education: BA, Zhejiang University, 1951; Graduate Student of Microbiology, Beijing Medical University, 1953. Career: Assistant of Pathophysiology, Xian Medical University, 1953; Lecturer, Zhejiang Medical University, 1978; Associate Professor, ibid, 1986; Professor of Microbiology and Immunology, ibid, 1991. Publications include: Agglutination of Red Blood Cells and Tumor Cells by CONA in J. Zhejiang Medical University, 1980; The Effect of CONA on Proliferation of Sarcoma Cell S180, ibid, 1983; The Intensifying Effect of Cyclophosamide on CONA in Inhibiting Proliferation of Sarcoma Cell S180 in Mice, ibid, 1983; A Preliminary Report on the Agglutination and Haemolysis of Red Blood Cell by Anti-CONA Antibody, ibid, 1984; The Effect of Senility on Expression of HLA Class-II Antigens on the Surface of Monocyte in Chinese J. Geriatrios, 1992. Honours: Class three commendation for achievement in natural science and liberal arts, Zheijing Institutions of Higher Learning, 1987. Memberships: Chinese Medical Association; China

Society of Microbiology; Sino-German Medical Association. Hobby: Table Tennis. Address: Zhejiang Medical University, Yan-an Street, Hangzhou 310006, China.

WANG Daozhuang, b. 17 May 1943, Chengdu City, Sichuan Province, China. Doctor. m. Liang Runxi, 1 May 1972, 1 d. Education: Bachelor of Medicine, Chongqing University of Medical Sciences, 1965; Advanced Studies, Surgical Department of Third University Hospital, Beijing University of Medical Sciences, 1973; Advanced Studies, Department of Cardiac Surgery, Institute of Cardiovascular Diseases, Chinese Academy of Medical Sciences, 1985. Appointments: Resident Doctor, Surgical Department, People's Hospital of Sichuan Province, China, 1965; Attending Doctor, Department of Thoracocardiac Surgery, People's Hospital of Sichuan Province, China, 1987; Professor, Department of Thoracocardiac Surgery, People's Hospital of Sichuan Province, China, 1988-. Publications: The Danger of Indiscriminate Use of Adrenal Cortical Hormone, 1976; Congenital Mesenteric Hiatus Hernia, 1981; Turning-out Suture Versus Enucleation Method in Treatment of Ganglion, 1981; Cardiac Myxoma, 1985; Diagnosis and Treatment of the Ventricular Membranous Septus Aneurysm, 1992; The Diagnosis and Therapeutic Experience of Ruptured Congenital Aortic Sinus Aneurysm, 1993; Injuries of Heart and Great Vessels in Open Heart Surgery, 1994; Surgical Treatment of Primary Mediastinal Tumor, 1994; Therapy of Thoracic Open Wound, 1994. Memberships: Society of Thoracocardiac Surgery; Chinese Medical Association. Hobbies: Photography; Music. Address: Department of Thoracocardiac Surgery, People's Hospital of Sichuan Province, Chengdu 610072, China.

WANG Dazeng, b. 26 June 1924, Shanghai, China. Physician; Professor. m. Professor Banyin Ma, 7 oct 1951, 1 son, 1 daughter. Education: Shanghai Medical University, 1943-49; Postgraduate, Shangai University of Traditional Chinese Medicine and Pharmacology. Appointments include: Professor, Chief PHysician, Gynaecology Department, Long-hua Hospital; Academic Committee, Shanghai University of Traditional Chinese Medicine and Pharmacology; Committeeman, Editorial Board, Chinese Journal of Integrated Traditional and Western Medicine. Publications: Conttributor of numerous research papers and articles in professional journals. Honours: Recipient of several awards and grants for professional services. Membership: Committee, Chinese Association of the Integration of Traditional and Western Medicine. Hobbies: Music; Drawing. Address: Longhua Hospital, Shanghai University of Traditional Chinese Medicine and Pharmacology, 725 Wan Pin Nan Road, Shanghai 200032, China.

WANG De, b. 23 Nov 1945, Yu-ci, Shanxi Province, China. Surgeon. m. 4 May 1975, 1 daughter. Education: BA, Shanxi Medical College, 1970. Appointments: Vice Chairman, 1987-88, Chairman, 1988-, department of Thoracic Surgery, people's Hospital of Shanxi. Publications: Experience of Using GF-1 Anastomotic device in the Prophylaxis of Anastomotic Stenosis, 1991; Self-designed Prodecure by using GF-1 device prevented anastomotic stenosis; The Surgery of Esophageal Cancer invading trachea. Memberships: Chinese Medical Association; Chinese Anti-Cancer Association. Hobbies: Music; Physical Culture. Address: Department of Thoracic Surgery, People's Hospital of Shanxi Province, Taiyuan 030012, China.

WANG De-quan, b. 4 Oct 1953, Qu-Fu, Shandong, China. Medical Doctor. m. Li Yun-qiu, 1 Oct 1978, 1 son. Education includes: Postgraduate studies; Master's degree. Appointments: Doctor: Department of Medicine, 1975-86, Department of Endocrinology, 1987-, Affiliated Hospital of Shandong Medical University, Jinan; Royal Melbourne Hospital, Victoria, Australia, 1986-87; Currently Professor. Publications: The treatment of type I diabetes mellitus with insulin pump, 1989; The determination of six antibodies and its clinical significance in Graves' disease, 1990; Pedigrees of 110 patients with Graves' disease and the determination of antithyroid antibodies in their first-degree relatives, 1994; Clinical and Laboratory diagnosis of endocrine disorders (editor), 1991. Honours: 2nd Prize for Theoretical Research, Education Council of Shandong Province, 1991; 1st Prize for Scientific Research, Science Council of Shandong Province, 1994. Memberships: Councillor, Chinese Gerontology Association; Vice-President, Shandong Diabetes Mellitus Association. Hobby: Climbing. Address: Department of Endocrinology, Affiliated Hospital of Shandong Medical University, 107 Wenhua Xilu, Jinan, Shandong 250012, China.

WANG De-Yuan, b. 7 Feb 1924, Tianjin, China. Surgical Oncologist. m. Z S Wang, 17 Aug 1958, 1 son, 1 daughter. Education: MB, Beijing

Medical University. Appointments: Intern, Affiliated Hospital, Beijing Medical University, 1948-49; Assistant Resident Surgeon, Surgical Department, 1949-52, Chief Resident, Surgical Department, 1952-53, Visiting Surgeon, 1953-56, Tianjin First Central Hospital; Visiting Surgeon, Associate Attending Surgeon, Attending Surgical Oncologist, Chest Department, Tianjin Cancer Hospital and Institute, 1956-85; Currently: Senior Attending Surgeon, Chest Department, Tianjin Cancer Hospital; Research Fellow, Cancer Institute. Publications: Numerous including: A Comparison of Results of Type I and II Radical Operations for Carcinoma of the Gastric Cardia (co-author), 1986; Tumors of the Chest, 1994. Memberships: Chinese Medical Association; Chinese Association of Oncology; Chinese Anticancer Association. Address: Tianjin Cancer Hospital, Hexi District, Tianjin 300060, China.

WANG Guilan, b. 1 Dec 1937, Yantai, Shandong, China. Professor of Internal Medicine. m. Futang Guo, 18 Oct 1962, 2 s. Education: Bachelor of Medical Science. Appointments: Doctor, 1961-77, Attending Doctor, 1977-85, Associate Professor, 1985-92, Professor, Vice Chairman, Department of Internal Medicine, Affiliated Hospital of Shandong Medical University. Publications: Mauriac Syndrome: Diabetic Pseudodwarf, 1985; Allotransplantation of Parathyroid Treated Hypoparthyroidism, 1987; Diagnosis and Treatment of Hyperadrenocorticism, 1991; Heart Disease Due to Abnormal Parathyroid Functions, 1993. Honours: 3rd Award, Shandong Committee of Science, 1986; 2nd Award, Shandong Medical University, 1986; 1st Award, Shandong Bureau of Public Health, 1994. Memberships: Shandong Division of Endocrine, Chinese Association of Medicine. Hobbies: Reading; Dancing; Watching television. Address: Department of Internal Medicine, The Affiliated Hospital of Shandong Medical University, Jinan, Shandong 250012, China.

WANG Guoxiong, b. 27June 1940, Zhejiang, China. Professor of Environmental Health. m. Zhong Benying, 27 January 1973, 1 son, 1 daughter. Education: MD, Nanjing Railway Medical College, China, 1963. Appointments: Professor of Environmental Health. Publications: Author: Multivariate analysis of casual factors including cooking oil fume and others in matched case-control study of lung cancer, 1992; Co-author: Analysis of PAH in cooking oil fume, 1994. Memberships: Chinese Society of Medicine; Chinese Society of Preventive Medicine; Chinese Society of Environmental Science. Address: Nanjing Railway Medical College, 87 Ding Jia Qiao Road, Nanjing 210009, China.

WANG Haiyan, b. 8 July 1937, Shandong, China. Medical Doctor. m. Jian Li, 26 Jan 1968, 1 son, 1 daughter. Education: MD; Postgraduate training, Department of Medicine, Beijing Medical University. Appointments: Currently Professor of International Medicine, Chief, Institute of Nephrology, Beijing Medical University. Publications: 209 original articles, 1980-; Glomerular diseases, in Internal Medicine, 1979, 1984, 1990; Nephrology (editor), 1994; Co-editor: New Advances in Nephrology; Internal Medicine of Today. Honours: Distinguished National Expert, 1990; Unique Scientific Technologist of National Universities, 1991. Memberships: Outstanding Committee, Chinese Society of Medicine; Outstanding Committee, General Secretary, Chinese Society of Internal Medicine; President, Chinese Society of Nephrology. Hobbies: Classical music; Travel. Address: Building 12-8, No 156 North-Xishi Street, Beijing 100034, China.

WANG Helen H, b. 4 Jun 1950, Taipei, China. Pathologist. Education: MD; MPH; PhD. Appointment: Assistant Professor in Pathology, Harvard Medical School, Boston, MA. Address: Beth Israel Hospital, 330 Brookline Avenue, Boston, MA 02215, USA.

WANG Heng, b. 3 Feb 1936, Jiangsu, China. Physician. m. Qin Qi, 10 Feb 1963, 2 d. Education: MD. Appointments: Associate Professor, 1985-88, Professor of Endocrinology, 1988-, PUMC Hospital. Publications: HLA-DQA and DQB Alleles Contribute to Susceptability to Insulin Diabetes Mellitus, 1993; Expression of HLA Class II Genes of IDDM Patients on the Surface of the Ltk-cells, 1994. Honours: Scientific Advanced Award, Ministry of Public Health, 1994. Memberships: Life Member, International Diabetes Federation. Hobby: Reading. Address: Peking Union Medical College Hospital, Beijing 100730, China.

WANG Hong Tu, b. 12 Apr 1937, Hebei Province, China. Internal Medicine. m. 1 May 1964, 2 s. Education: MD, Beijing College of Traditional Chinese Medicine. Career: Teaching Assistant, Lecturer, Assistant Professor, Professor, Currently, Director of Internal Medicine, Beijing University of Traditional Chinese Medicine. Publications: Composite Treatment of the Yellow Emperor's Classic of Internal

Medicine, I, 1993, II, III, IV, V; The Advanced Internal Medicine, 1993. Honours: Certificate for Achievement in Teaching Research, 1993; Certificate for Achievement in Teacher of China, 1993. Memberships: Director, Section of Internal Medicine, Chinese Medicine and Pharmacology Association. Hobby: Qi Gong Exercise. Address: Department of Internal Medicine, Beijing University of Traditional Chinese Medicine, Beijing 100029, China.

WANG Hongbo, b. 25 Dec 1962, Shen Yang, China. Anaesthesiology. m. 10 Feb 1988, 1 d. Education: Bachelor Degree, Dalian University College of Medicine, 1986. Career: Junior Doctor; Home Officer; Junior Registrar; Currently, Senior Registrar, Department of Anaesthesiology, Liaoning Province Tumour Hospital. Publication: Effect of Metoprolol on Reducing Stress Response Induced by Endotracheal Intubation in Old Patients with Essential Hypertension, 1995. Membership: Chinese Medical Association. Hobby: Music. Address: Department of Anaesthesiology, Liaoning Province Tumour Hospital, 110042, China.

WANG Huei-Shyong, b. 18 Apr 1955, Tainan, Taiwan. Child Neurologist. m. Meng-Fai Kuo, 22 Dec 1987, 1 daughter. Education: MD, Taipei Medical College, 1979. Appointments: Resident, 1979-83, Attending, 1983-93, Department of Paediatrics, Chang Gung Memorial Hospital; Attending, Department of Paediatrics, Director, 1st Paediatric Department, 1993-, Chang Gung Children's Hospital; Associate Professor of Paediatrics and Neurology, Chang Gung Medical College. Publications: Salmonella meningitis, 1982; Brainstem abscess, 1992; Infantile panthalamic infarct with sonographic "Bright Thalamus", 1993; Herpes simplex encephalitis, 1994; Sonographic lenticulostriate vasculopathy in infants, 1995; Supraorbital approach for transcranial Doppler sonography, 1995. Memberships: Chinese Taipei Pediatric Association; Neurological Society ROC (Taiwan); Epilepsy Society ROC; American Institute of Ultrasound in Medicine. Hobbies: Audio and video; Travel. Address: 199 Tung-Hwa North Road, Taipei, Taiwan, China.

WANG Jia-Yu, b. China. Professor. 1 son, 1 daughter. Education: BA, Beijing Medical University, 1960; Visiting Scholar, University of Pittsburgh, USA, 1985. Appointments: Teaching Assistant, 1960, Lecturer, School of Pharmacy, 1978, Associate Professor, Analytical Computational Centre, 1985, Professor, Analytical Computation Centre, 1990-, currently Standing Director, Analytical Computational Centre and Spectral Analysis Laboratory, Beijing Medical University; National Grade Adjuster, Chinese Measurement Accreditation. Publications include: 1st author: Fluorometric Determination of Free Salicylic Acid in Preparations of Acetylsalicylic Acid, 1983; The Study of Analytical Method for Preparation of Chinese Herbal Medicines, 1984; Quaternary Alkaloids of Thalictrum Cultratum, 1986; NMR Study on the Chemical Structure of a New Flavonoloside, 1994; Co-author: The Study of Chromatography and Spectrometry for Chinese Medicines, 1984; New Bisbenzylisoquinoline Alkaloids from Pycnarrhena Manillensis, 1987; New Bisbenzylisoquinoline Alkaloids from Daphnadra Diclisii, 1989; Structure Investigation of a New Alkaloid from Zanthoxylumm Schinifolium Sieb et Zucc, 1992. Honours: Visiting Professor, Tianjin Medical University, 1988. Memberships: Chinese Pharmaceutical Association; Beijing Chemical Association; Chinese Analytical Measurement Association; Beijing New Drugs Committee for Examination and Approval. Hobbies: Swimming; Chinese chess; Table-tennis; Music. Address: PO Box 219, Beijing Medical University, 38 Xueyuan Road, Beijing 100083, China.

WANG Jialing, b. 2 Dec 1930, Wuhan, China. Professor. m. 20 Oct 1956, 2 s. Education: Graduate, Postgraduate, Hwazhong Agricultural College, 1956. Appointments: Assistant, 1956-59, Lecturer, 1959-68, Engineer, 1969-78, Lecturer, Associate Professor, Professor, 1978-94, Tong Ji Medical University. Publications: Environmental Microbiology, 1988; Study on the Mutagenecity of Non-Volatile Trace Organics in Drinking Water, 1987. Honours: Award. EPA of China, 1987; Award, Ministry of Health, China, 1988. Memberships: Council Committee, Chairman of Commisssion of Environmental Microbiology, Chinese Society of Microbiology. Address: Department of Environmental Microbiology, Tongji Medical University, Wuhan, Hubei, China.

WANG Jian Zhang, b. 5 Nov 1928, Jiangsu, China. Doctor. m. Professor He Cui Hua, 17 Nov 1953, 2 s. Education: Medical College, Nanking University. Career: Surgeon, Deputy Chief of Department of Surgical Oncology, Chief of Office of Medical Administration, Scientific Res, Department of Cancer Prevention, Cancer Hospital, CAMS,

1953-80; Vice Director of Cancer Institute and Hospital, 1980-92; Chief, WHO Collaborating Centre for Cancer Research, 1986-93; Currently, Professor of Cancer Prevention, Cancer Hospital, CAMS. Publications: The Early Warnings of Cancer and Its Prevention and Treatment, 1992; Etiology and Prevention of Commonly Seen Cancers, 1994. Honours: Honorary Awards for Miner's Lung Cancer Control in Yunnan Tin Mine, 1991; Governmental Special Allowance for Medicine and Health Contributions, 1992. Memberships: Council, Chinese Cancer Research Foundation; Council, Chinese Anti Cancer Society; Council, Chinese Association on Smoking and Health. Hobby: Painting. Address: Cancer Institute and Hospital, Chinese Academy of Medical Sciences; Panjiayuan, Chaoyang District, 100021 Beijing, China.

WANG Jing Hua, b. 25 dec 1942, Jinan, China. Oculist. m. Zhang Ping, 1 Oct 1968, 2 sons. Education: MD, Qingdao Medical College, 1981 Appointments: Resident, Fangi Commune Hospital and Workers Hospital of Ziyang Locomotive Works, 1967-68; Assistant Professor, Instructor, Ophthalmology Department, QMCH, 1992-. Publications: Development of Glaucoma Research, 1993; Studies on Embryonal Development of Lamins Cribosa of Human Eyes, 1994; COntributor of over 50 articles,. Honours: Prize, Provincial Authority, 1993; Prize, Municipal Authority, 1989, 1990; Prize, College, 1990. Membership: China Ophthalmology Society. Hobbies: Volleyball; Music. Address: Ophthalmology Department of QMCH, 16 Jiangsu Road, Qingdao, China.

WANG Jue-Sheng, b. 12 May 1931, Beijing, China. Professor. m. Zeqi Luo, 20 Oct 1956, 1 son, 1 daughter. Education: MD, Sichuan Medical College, 1955; MSc, McMaster University, Canada, 1982. Appointments include: Currently Professor of Internal Medicine, Professor of Clinical Epidemiology, West China University of Medical Sciences, Chengdu, Sichuan; Member of the Committee, Hematological Society, CMA Sichuan Branch. Publications: Investigation of Prevalence of Chronic Leukopenia, 1985; Guide for Clinical Medical Research, 1986; Peripheral Hemogram Changes in Plastics Workers, 1988; Clinical Epidemiology, 1990; Cross-Over Trial in the Prevention of Blood Transfusion Febrile Reactions, 1992. Honours: Provincial 4th Award, 1986; Provincial 1st Award, 1992; National 1st Award, 1993. Memberships: Chinese Medical Association; International Epidemiological Association. Hobbies: Photography; Music. Address: Department of Clinical Epidemiology, West China University of Medical Science, Chengdu, Sichuan 610041, China.

WANG Ke-Cheng, b. 6 Oct 1939, Hebei, China. Doctor; Professor. m. Shu-ling Li, 17 Feb 1965, 2 d. Education: MD, Hebei Medical College, China, 1963. Appointments: Resident and Assistant, Department of Surgery, 3rd Hospital of Hebei Medical College, 1963-67; Chief Resident and Lecturer, Department of Surgery, 3rd Hospital of Hebei Medical College, 1967-68; Assistant Professor, Hebei Medical College, 1978-87; Associate Professor, Hebei Medical College, 1987-91; Professor, Hebei Medical College, 1991-93; Director of Hospital; Professor of Surgery; Surgeon-in-Chief, 3rd Hospital of Hebei Medical College, 1993-. Publications: Diagnosis and Treatment for Primary Hepatic Cancer, 1983; Recent Development of Anastomosiswares on Rectal Precarcinectomy, 1988; Experience of Treatment in 40 Cases with Severe Thorcoabdominal Injuries, 1993; The Diagnosis Value of Rheophlebogram on Thromboangiitis Obliterans and Deep Thrombophlebitis, 1992. Honours: Recipient of Provincial Achievement Award in Scientific Research, 1989, 1993; Awarded title of Provincial Outstanding Teacher, 1991; Owner of Special Allowance from the State Council, 1992. Memberships: Chinese Medical Association. Hobbies: Smoking. Address: 16 Weiming Street, Shijiazhuang, Hebei 050051, China.

WANG Kewei, b. 20 dec 1923, Shen Yang, China. Professor of Radiation Medicine. m Zheng Mengzhen, 25 Nov 1947, 2 sons, 2 daughters. Education: MB, Jike Kai University, Tokyo, Japan. Appointments: Lecturer, Vice Professor, Vice Dean, Dean of Radiation Medicine, Professor of Radiation Medicine, 4th Military Medical University. Publications: Irradiation Induced Biochemical Reaction in Small Intestines of Mice, 1988; The Inhibitory Effect of Earthworm Extract on the Transplanted Tumor in Mice, 1991. Memberships: Chinese Association of Radiological Medicine and Protection; Chinese Association of Radiation Research; Chinese Medical Association. Hobby: Music. Address: Department Radiation Medicine, 4th Military Medical University, Xi'an, Shaanxi 710032, China.

WANG Lisheng, b. 10 Apr 1934, Shenyang, China. Professor. m. Jin Zuomei, 26 Aug 1958, 1 son, 1 daughter. Education: BA, Chengdu University of Science and Technology, 1955; PhD, Leningrad Chemical Engineering College, 1962. Career: Research Director; Director of Phosphoric Chemical Engineering Research Center. Publications: Chemistry of Resources, 1994; Technology of Phosphates and Phosphoric Fertlizer, 1993; Technology of Inorganic Chemical Industry, 1988; Kinetics of Calcium Carbonate Crystallization in Ammonium Sulphate Solution, 1989; Study on Mechanism of Production of Feed Grade Dicalcium Phosphate by Wet-Process Phosphoric Acid; Phosphoric and Comp Fertilizer, 1992; Study on Deflourination in Wet-Process Acid, 1994; A Study on the Kinetics for Reusing Waste Phosphogypsum, 1994. Honours: Awarded with five prizes for achievements in research, Ministry of Chemical Engineer 1988, National Committee of Science & Technology 1994, Sichuan Committee of Science & Technology 1978, 1990, 1994. Memberships: Councilor, Applied Chemistry, The Chemical Society of China; Councilor, Design Center, The Sulfuric Acid and Phosphoric Fertilizer. Hobby: Swimming. Address: Department of Applied Chemistry, Chengdu University of Science & Technology, Chengdu 610065, China.

WANG Mei-Ying BS RNS, b. 18 Aug 1918, Beijing, China. Nurse. Education: Postgraduate Student, Collombia University, New York, USA, 1947; Midwifery School Diploma, New York City, Maternity Center Association, 1948. Career: Head Nurse, Public Health, 1940-42; Head Nurse, Xie Ji Hospital, Tianjin, 1946; Nursing Instructor, PUMC, Beijing, 1951; Head of Nursing Department, Jian Zhu Gong Ren Hospital, Beijing, 1954-66; Teacher by appointed. Publications: Hurting the Field Works Foot by the Nail is Danger, 1955; Syringe and Needle, 1957; Basic Nursing: Psychophysiologic Approach, 1976. Honour: First Prize, Children's Care School, 1957; Second Prize for Coworks in Second Nursing School, 1957. Hobbies: Make Medal; Plant Flowers; Singing. Address: 102, Unit I, 5th Building, Xi Ba He Dong Li, Chao Yong Qu, Beijing 100028, China.

WANG Meng-Ya, b. 19 Mar 1959, Anhui, China. Teacher. m. Rong Zhu, 19 Sept 1987, 1 son. Education: MD, 1982, MS, 1985, Wannan Medical College; PhD, Shanghai Brain Research Institute, Academia Sinica, 1993. Appointments: Teaching Assistant, 1985, Lecturer, 1987, Wannan Medical College, China; Research Associate, Loyola University, Chicago, Illinois, USA, 1988; Associate Professor, 1993, currently Professor of Physiology, Wannan Medical College, Wuhu, China. Publications: 1st author: Mathematical Models for Hyperbolic Type of Timed Dose-Response Relationship of Drugs, 1987; Phaclofen-insensitive presynaptic inhibitory action of l-baclofen in neonatal rat motoneurones in vitro, 1990; 5-Hydroxytryptamine responses in neonate rat motoneurones in vitro, 1990. Memberships: Chinese Association for Physiological Sciences; Chinese Pharmacological Society; Society for Neuroscience, USA; New York Academy of Sciences. Hobbies: Badminton; Running. Address: Cell Electrophysiology Laboratory, Wannan Medical College, Wuhu 241001, China.

WANG Naiqian, b. 4 Nov 1931, Chang Shu, China. Professor of Stomatology. m. Zhijie Gu, 1 Oct 1961, 1 daughter. Education: beijing University College of Medicine. Appointments: Professor of Stomatology, Chief, Department Oral and Maxillofacial Surgery, Chief Doctor, Harbin Medical University; Guest Professor, Academy of Medical sciences, Xapbkob University yxpanb; Guest Professor, Academy of Medical sciences, Mapnynonb University. Publications include: Oral and Maxillofacial Surgery, 1978; The Recent Advance of Cryosurgery, 1985; Low-Temperature Medicine, 1990; Dictionary of Nature Scientific System, 1991. Honours: Outstanding Scientific Award, 1978; Advanced Scientific and Technical Worker, Heilongjiang Province, 1985; National Outstanding Person, 1985. Memberships: International Society of Cryosurgery; Ordinary Commissioner, Chinese Society of Stomatology; Chief of Group for Freezing Therapy of Oral Diseases, Chinese Society of Freezing Engineering; Chief, Chinese Surgery Society for Head and Neck Tumor; Chief, Heilongjiang Provincial Society of Stomatology; Chief, Heilonjiang Provincial Surgery Society for Head and Neck Tumor. Hobbies: Basketball; Swimming. Address: First Affiliated Hospital, Harbin Medical University, Harbin, Heilongjiang Province, China.

WANG Pei-Yen, b. 1 Feb 1926, Honan, China. Surgeon. m. Chu, Shu-Mei, 10 Nov 1954, 2 s, 1 d. Appointments: Chief of Thoracic Surgery, Veterans General Hospital, Taipei; Chief of Experimental Surgery, Veterans General Hospital, Taipei; Professor of Surgery,

National Defense Medical Center; Chairman of Surgical Department, Taichung Veterans General Hospital; Surgical Consultant, Surgical Department, Taichung Veterans General Hospital. Publications: Surgical Treatment of Carcinoma of the Esophagus & Cardia Among The Chinese, 1983; A Spiral-Grooved Endoesophageal Tube for Management of Malignant Esophageal Obstruction, 1985; A Check-Valve Device for Prevention of Regurgitation after Endoesophageal Intubation, 1986. Memberships: Council Member of the International Society for Disease of the Esophagus; Council Member of Asian Thoracic and Cardiovascular Surgical Association. Hobbies: Golf; Go-Go Cheese. Address: Taichung Veterans General Hospital, 160 Taichung Kang Road, Section 3, Taichung 405, Taiwan, China.

WANG Pei-Yi, b. 9 September 1948, Zhucheng, Shandong, China. Doctor. m. Zhang Gui-Hua, 17 July 1950, 1 daughter. Education: Graduate, Medical College. Appointments: Responsible Doctor, 1987; Associate Professor, 1992. Publications: Observations on Experimental Infection of Periodic Brugia Malayi in Man, 1991; Treatment of Filarial Elephantiasis by the Injection of 25% Extracts from Mulberry Leaves, 1989; A ten-year Observation on Experimental Infection of Periodic Brugia Malayi in Man, 1994. Honours: 2nd Award, Shandong, 1984. Memberships: Medical Parasitological Association. Address: Shandong Institute of Parasitic Diseases, 13 Tabai Zhong Lu, Jining, Shandong 272133, China.

WANG Peishan, b. 17 Jun 1945, Tianjin, China. Professor of Epidemiology. m. Shujin Li, 1 May 1971, 1 s, 1 d. Education: Medicine, Tianjin Medical College, 1970; Master, Epidemiology, Tianjin Medical University, 1981. Career: Physician, Tianjin Xiaozhan Clinic, 1970-78; Teacher of Epidemiology, Tianjin Medical College, 1981-; Currently, Professor of Epidemiology, Tianjin Medical University. Publications: Epidemiology of Infectious Diseases, in General Epidemiology, 1990; Subarachnoid hemorrhage and family history, in Arch Neurology, 1994. Memberships: Committee, Chinese Society of Clinical Epidemiology; Chinese Society of Epidemiology. Hobbies: Music; Billiards. Address: Department of Epidemiology, Tianjin Medical University, Tianjin 300070, China.

WANG Pen-Jung, b. 7 Apr 1951, Tainan, Taiwan, China. Physician. m. Liow-Shoiw Lee, 24 Jan 1978, 2 sons, 1 daughter. Education: MD, China Medical College, Taiwan, 1977; PhD, Tokyo Women's Medical College, Japan, 1986. Appointments: Resident, Research Fellow, Tokyo Women's Medical College, 1980-86; Research Fellow, National Epilepsy Centre, Japan, 1991; Associate Professor, Attending Staff, Department of Paediatrics, National Taiwan University Hospital, China. Publications: Partial Inhibitory seizures, 1984; A Study of Genetic Leukodystrophy in Chinese Children, 1992; Segawa Syndrome in Taiwan, 1994; Neurophysiologic Studies and MRI in Pelizanes-Merzbacher Disease, 1995. Hobbies: Reading; Sports. Address: 6th Floor, No 27, Yi-Ting Street, Taipei, Taiwan, China.

WANG Qi-Lu, b. 25 Jan 1933, Shandong, China. Professor. m. Liu Fu-sheng, 25 Sept 1958, 1 son, 1 daughter. Education: MD PhD. Appointments: Vice Chairman, Department of Medical Oncology. Publications: Editor of several Chinese journals of medicine; Articles: Pathology of Gastrointestinal Tract; Malignant Lymphoma; Lung Cancer; Pathology and Prevention of Esophageal cancer. Memberships: Int Study of Lung Cancer. Address: Zuanumenwai 100021, PO Box 2258, Peking, China.

WANG Qingqi, b. 15 December 1944, Shanghai, China. Educator; Doctor. m. YaJuan Cheng, 1 December 1968, 1 son. Education: MA of Medicine, China Academy of Traditional Chinese Medicine, 1981. Appointments: Shanghai Jiading Hospital; China Traditional Chinese Medicine Academic School; Shanghai University of Traditional Chinese Medicine. Publications: Traditional Chinese Medicine Basic Theory, 1987; Traditional Chinese Medicine Theory Collection, 1993; Traditional Chinese Medicine Pathology of Syposium, 1994; Practical Huang-di's Internal Classic Dictionary, 1994; 10 books; More than 100 articles. Honours: Shanghai City Excellent Teacher, 1989; 1st Award, National Traditional Chinese Medicine Department, 1991. Memberships: Traditional Chinese Medicine Academic Association; Vice President, Huang-di's Internal Classic Division. Hobbies: Writing; Reading; Carving. Address: Shanghai University of Traditional Chinese Medicine, Lingling Road 530#, Shanghai 200032, China.

WANG Rong-Guang, b. 11 Jan 1952, Tianjin, China. Professor of Otolaryngology. m. Li Yu-Qing, 25 Feb 1975, 1 son, 1 daughter.

Education: MD, Military Postgraduate Medical School, 1981; Research Fellow, University of Toronto, Canada. Appointments: Associate Professor, 1987, Professor of Otolaryngology, Hebei Medical College. Publications: Clinical Otology, 1990; Clinical Rhinology, 1995. Hobbies: Photography; Chinese Literature. Address: Institute of Otolaryngology, PLA General Hospital, 28 Fuxing Road, Beijing 10085, China.

WANG Ru-Kuan, b. 15 May 1941, Haian, Jiangsu, China. Biomedical Information Science. m. Song Xiao-ming, 24 Jan 1976, 1 daughter. Education: Graduated, Peking University, 1965. Appointment: Vice Director, CIMI, CAMS, PUME; Chief, Information Administration Office, Ministry of Health, China. Publications incl: Progress in Liver Cancer Research in China, 1977; Advances in Cancer Research in China, 1987; Reviews and Prospects of Chinese Cause of Medical Science and Technology, 1987; Anti-Cancer Work in Progress in China, 1987; Generally Studying Designing and Planning of the Chinese Biomedical Literature Retrieval and Analysis System, 1988; Prospects for Medical Science and Technology in 21 Century and our Strategy, 1995. Honours incl: Special State Councils Allowance; Prize of National Outstanding Information Research Achievements. Memberships: New York Academy of Science; Chinese Medical Association; Chinese Society of Genetics of Oncology; Standing Vice Chairman, Chinese Society of Medical Information Science; Standing Council, ChineseSociety of Science & Technology Information. Hobbies: Swimming; Fishing; Collecting Stamps & Coins from Various Countries. Address: Institute of Medical Information, 3 Yabo Road, Beijing 100020, China.

WANG Rui-zhong, b. 26 May 1941, Shanhaiguan, Hebei, China. Medical Doctor. m. Yao Zhen-juan, 1 Oct 1965, 2 daughters. Education: Graduated, Chengde Medical Institute, Hebei Province. Appointments: Doctor in Tumour Department, Surgeon, Physician, Shijiazhuang City First Hospital; Currently Chief Physician, Professor, Medical Laser Research Institute, Shijiazhuang City First Hospital. Publications: Medical Laser, 1987; The Study of Acute Digestive Disease (co-author), 1989; International articles: Clinical Experience in Endoscopic YAG Laser Therapy for Large Intestine Polyps, 1987; Clinical Experience in Applying Endoscopic YAG Laser to Treat Alimentary Canal Polyps, 1988; Clinical Experience in Applying Endoscopic Nd:YAG Laser to Treat Cancers in Esophagus and in Orifice of Stomach, 1990; Clinical Experience in Applying Endoscopic Laser to Treat 451 Esophagostenotic Cases, 1991; A Clinical Summary on 769 Cases Treated by Using YAG Laser, 1991, 1992; 29 national articles in Chinese Digestion Magazine, Endoscopy Magazine, Chinese Medical Laser Magazine, others. Honours: Special Classification as Doctor, Hebei Province. Membership: Committee Member, Alimentary Canal Endoscopy Institute of China. Hobbies: Fishing; Flower planting. Address: Medical Laser Research Institute, Shijiazhuang City First Hospital, Shijiazhuang, China.

WANG Shih-Chen, b. 7 Mar 1916, Chiba, Japan. Professor of Nuclear Medicine. m. Chien Chou, 10 Jan 1980, 1 son, 1 daughter. Education: BS, Tsinghua University, 1938; MS, University Iowa, USA, 1948; PhD, University Iowa, USA, 1950. Appointments: Instructor, Guiyang Medical College, 1940; Assistant Professor, Guizhou University, 1942; Res Associate, University Iowa, 1950; Associate Professor, Peking Union Medical College, 1951; Professor, PUMC, 1956; Honorary Director, Institute of Radiation Medicine, 1985. Publications: Editor of 12 books incl, Nuclear Medicine & Biology, 1990, Chinese Medical Encyclopaedia on Nuclear Medicine, 1986 and a series of monographs on Nuclear Techniques and their Biomedical Applications, 1980-92; Author of over 200 journal articles. Honours: Phi Lambda Upsilon, 1948; Sigma Xi, 1948; Life Member, Chinese Academy of Sciences, 1980; Outstanding Achievement in Nuclear Medicine Award, 1986. Memberships: Chinese Chemical Society; Chinese Nuclear Society; Chinese Medical Association; Chinese Society of Nuclear Medicine; Chinese Society of Physiological Sciences; Chinese Society of Biochemistry; Chinese Society of Nuclear Electronics. Hobbies: Table Tennis; Bike Riding; Stamp Collecting. Address: Peking Union Medical College Hospital, Beijing 100730, China.

WANG Shijun, b. 18 Aug 1922, Beijing, China. Professor. m. Chen Jianhong, 5 Oct 1947, 3 sons. Education: Medical College of Peking University, Beijing, China. Appointments: Vice Director, Department of Internal Medicine, Third Teaching Hospital of Beijing Medical College, 1958-83; Director, Department of Occupational Medicine, Third Teaching Hospital of Beijing Medical College, 1977-84. Publications: Chelating therapy with Na-DMS in occupational lead and mercury intoxications, 1965; Chelating therapy in occupational metal intoxications in China,

1988; Lead poisoning, 1979; Metal intoxications, 1988; Clinical occupational medicine, 1994. Memberships: Chinese Medical Association; Consultant, Society of Occupational Medicine; Chinese Preventive Medical Association; Vice Editor, Chinese Journal of Industrial Hygiene & Occupational Diseases. Address: Department of Occupational Disease, Third Teaching Hospital, Beijing Medical University, Beijing 100083, China.

WANG Shou Chan, b. 12 June 1946, Jiangsu, China. Professor of Medicine. m. Ling Ling, 1973, 2 daughters. Education: MB, 1970, MMed, 1982, Nanjing College of Traditional Chinese Medicine. Appointments: Vice President of Paediatrics of Traditional Chinese Medicine, Nanjing College of TCM, 1987; Vice Director of Paediatrics of Traditional Chinese Medicine, Jiangsu Hospital of TCM, 1987; Director, Professor of Paediatrics of TCM, Nanjing College of Traditional Chinese Medicine. Publications: Contemporary Pediatrics of TCM, CHief Editor, 1994; Practical Clinical Handbook of Pediatrics, Chief Editor, 1993; Practical Prescriptions of Pediatrics, CHief Editor, 1993; Health Preservation and Rehabilitation of TCM, Associated Editor, 1989. Honours: Jiangsu's Progress Prize on Science and Technique, 1991; Huadong's Highly Rated Books on Science and Technique for Medical Prescriptions of Pediatrics, 1994. Memberships: China Traditional Chinese Medicine and Pharmacy Association. Hobbies: Running; Tourism. Address: 61# Nanjing College of Traditional Chinese Medicine, Nanjing, Jiangsu 210029, China.

WANG Shouyi, b. 2 Feb 1938, Heilongiang Province, China. Teacher; Researcher. m. Yingbo Su, 8 Feb 1960, 2 sons, 1 daughter. Education: Graduate, Qiqihar Medical College, 1963; Training, Department of Medical Jurisprudence, West China Medical University. Appointments: Teaching Assistant, 1964; Lecturer, 1978; Associate Professor, 1987; Associate Professor; Tutor, Graduate Students for Master Degree; Director, Department of Medical Jurisprudence. Publications: Quantification of the Standards for Injury Identification, Editor-in-Chief, 1985; Psychology in Hospital Management, Editor-in-Chief, 1994; An Introduction to Medical Philosophy - On the Subject, Object and Entirety of Medicine, Co-author, 1993. Honours: Twice Recipient, Title of Exemplary Teacher from the University. Memberships: Board of Directors, Guangzhou Association of Medical Jurisprudence; Military Pathology Committee, Pathology Society of the Army; Editorial Board, Human Nature and Society. Hobbies: Qigong; Long distance running. Address: Department of Medical Jurisprudence, The First Military Medical University, Tonghe, Guangzhou 510515, China.

WANG Shu-hui, b. 31 Dec 1938, Hebei Province, China. Ear, Nose and Throat Specialist. m. Wang Xian-xi, 1 Oct 1965, 1 son, 1 daughter. Education: MB, Medical College, Tianjin. Appointments: Resident Physician, Ear, Nose and Throat, 1963-74; Attending Physician, Ear, Nose and Throat, 1975-85; Associate Chief Physician, 1986-92; Associate Professor, 1992; Chief Physician, Director, Ear, Nose and Throat, Tianjin Hospital, 1993-. Publications: Glomus Jugular Tumor (Tympanic Type), 1989; Multiple First Branchial Cleft, 1989; Operating Analysis of 553 cases (592 ears) of Chronic Suppurative Otitis Media, 1993. Membership: Society of Otorhinolaryngology, Chinese Medical Association. Hobby: Drawing. Address: ENT, Tianjin Huanhu Hospital, Tianjin, China.

WANG Soo Ray, b. 2 Aug 1940, Taiwan. Physician. m. Sharon Wang, 20 Dec 1969, 2 s, 1 d. Education: MD; PhD. Career: Section Chief, Section of Allergy and Immunology, Chang Gung Memorial Hospital, Taipei, Taiwan; Currently: Professor of Medicine, National Yang-Ming University, School of Medicine; Section Chief, Allergy, Immunology and Rheumatology, Veterans General Hospital, Taipei. Publications: Over 90 refereed papers including: Co-author, Serum arginase level in patients with gastric cancer, in Journal of Clinical Gastroenterology, 1994; Co-author, The serum levels of soluble CD23 in rheumatoid arthritis and its correlation with C-reactive protein, in Journal of Rheumatology ROC, 1994. Memberships: Fellow, American Academy of Allergy and Immunology; Clinical Immunology Society; Fellow, American Association of Certified Allergists. Hobby: Mountain Climbing. Address: Section of Allergy, Immunology and Rheumatology, Veterans General Hospital, Taipei 112, Taiwan.

WANG Sunjing, b. 1 April 1913, Zhong-Xian, Sichuan, China. Professor of Stomatological Education. m. Tang Zhifang, 10 December 1947, 1 son, 2 daughters. Education: Graduate, College of Dentistry, West China Union University, 1942; DDS, Diploma, State University of

New York, USA. Appointments: Assistant, 1942, Instructor 1944, Associate Professor, Head, Department of Periodontology, College of Dentistry, West China Union University; Head, Oral Medicine, Department of Stomatology, Sichuan Medical College, 1954; Professor of Oral Medicine, Sichuan Medical College and West China University Medical Sciences, 1978; Director of Research Institute of Stomatology, Sichuan Medical College and West China University of Medical Sciences, 1979. Publications: Pericoronal infection and eruption time of third molar, 1948; Study and analysis of Periodenitis in the Chinese People, 1949; Textbook of Oral Medicine, 1960. Memberships: Stomatological Branch of Chinese Medical Association. Address: College of Stomatology, West China University of Medical Sciences, Renmin Nanlu Section 3 No 19, Chengdu 610041, Sichuan, China.

WANG Teh-Hong, b. 2 Oct 1926, Taipei, Taiwan. Gastroenterologist. m. Li-Tsu Yang, 2 Dec 1956, 3 daughters. Education: MD, Taiwan University, 1954; PhD, Tokyo University, 1968; Speciality, Internal Medicine, Subspeciality, Gastroenterology, Digestive Endoscopy. Appointments include: Chief Editor, The Taiwan Journal of Gastroenterology, 1984-88; President, The Gastroenterological Society of Taiwan, 1991-94; Currently President, The Digestive Endoscopy Society of Taiwan. Publications: What kind of digestive endoscopy unit should we have at teaching hospitals, 1994; Clinicopathologic study of 208 patients with early gastric cancer in Taiwan (co-author), 1994. Honours: Republic of China Premier's Award for Science and Technology, 1982, for Service, 1991. Memberships include: OMGE; OMED; APAGE; APADE; Formosan Medical Association. Hobbies: Fishing; Taiwan chess; Table-tennis. Address: F11-7, No 25, Sec 3, Chung-Shan N Road, Taipei, Taiwan, China.

WANG Tian-you, b. 23 Apr 1942, Honan, China. Professor, Director of Thoracic Cardiovascular Surgery. Education: Graduate, Beijing University College of Medicine, 1963. Appointments: Surgeon, Department of Surgery, 1963-74; Attending Surgeon, Lecturer of Surgery, 1974-84; Vice Director, Associate Professor of Surgery, 1984-89; Director, Professor, Department of TC Surgery, 1989-, all at Beijing Friendship Hospital. Publications: Mammary Disease, 1981; Surgical Treatment of Aneurysm of Ascending Aorta with Aortic Insufficiency; Dynamic Cardiomyoplasty. 1st Science Technologic Prize of Beijing Government, 1989; The First Successful Case in China. Honours: 2nd Science Technologic Prize, 1990. Memberships: General Secretary, Standing Committee, Chinese Society for Thoracic Cardiovascular Surgery; Vice Chairman, Beijing Society of Thorac Cardiovascular Surgery. Hobbies: Music; Singing; Chinese Writing. Address: Department of Thoracic Cardiovascular Surgery, Beijing Friendship Hospital, Capital University of Medical Science, 95 Yong-An Road, Beijing 100050, China.

WANG Wei, b. 18 July 1937, Jian Su, China. Medical Doctor. m. Dr Zheng Sun-yi, 9 Feb 1964, 2 daughters. Education: Shanghai Second Medical University, 1956-61, Postgraduate, 1965-68. Appointments: Director, Department of Plastic and Reconstructive Surgery, Shanghai Second Medical University Ninth People's Hospital. Publications include: The Extended Second Toe-to-Hand Transfer, 1978; Temporo-Fascia Flap with Skin Graft Transfer for the Treatment of Postburn Claw Hand deformity, 1978; Mamaplasty with Tree Flaps Method for the Huge or Ptosis Breasts, 1987; The Thumb Reconstruction, 1990; Congenital Hand Deformities, 1992; Modern Microsurgery, 1994; The Application of Microsurgery in the Plasti and Reconstructive Surgery, 1995; Facial Reanimation with a Single-Stage Free Transfer of Split and Segmental Latissmus Dorsi Flap, 1994. Honours include: Recipient of several Certificates of Merit from central Health Ministry of China; Money award, Certificate of Merit, Shanghai Scientific Committee, 1992; National Inventor Money award and Certificate of Merit, National Scientific Committee of China, 1994. Memberships include: President, Shanghai Branch, Chinese Association of Plastic and Reconstructive Surgery; Vice President, Chinese Association of Plastic and Reconstructive Surgery; Vice President, Chinese Association of Reparative and Reconstructive Surgery; Chinese Medical Association of Rehabitation. Address: Shanghai Ninth People's Hospital, Shanghai Second Medical University, Shanghai 200011, China.

WANG Wei Qi, b. 30 May 1939, Shanghai, China. Professor. m. 1968, 1 s, 1 d. Education: Fudan University, China, 1961. Appointments: Professor, Supervisor of PhD Program, Fudan University, Shanghai. Publications: 84 Papers published including: Optimum Position and Quans: Compensation, in Journal of Cardio Ultrasonography, 1986; Fractal of Simulated and Real Doppler Signal, in Ultrasound in Medicine

and Biology, 1994; Adaptive - Autoregressive Spectrum of Doppler Ultrasound, in Ultrasound in Medicine and Biology, 1994. Honours: National Invention Award, 1985; Shanghai Science and Technology Award, 1987, 1991, 1993; Pioneer Award of History and Medical Ultrasound, WFUMB and AIUM, 1988. Memberships: Foreign Member, AIUM; Council, Acoustical Society of China; Council, Chinese Society of BME. Address: Department of Electric Engineering, Fudan University, 220 Handan Road, 200433 Shanghai, China.

WANG Weicheng, b. 9 Oct 1949, Hubei, China. Medical Chemist. m. Tian Deying, 1 May 1979, 1 son. Education: BA, Wuhan University, 1977; Diploma, Tianjin University, 1982. Appointments: Assistant, 1978-86, Lecturer, 1986-92, Professor of Chemistry, 1992-, Tongji Medical University, Wuhan. Publications: A Method for Determining the Trace Cobalt in the Human Body by Differential Pulsed Adsorptive Voltammetry, 1991. Membership: Chinese Chemical Society. Hobby: Chinese chess. Address: Department of Chemistry, Tongji Medical University, Wuhan, Hubei 430030, China.

WANG Wen-Wei, b. 7 July 1938, Shanghai, China. Ophthalmologist. m. Dai-Wei Xu, 21 Oct 1963, 1 d. Education: Beijing Medical University. Appointments: Internship and Residency, 1962-78; Visiting Doctor, 1978-87; Associate Professor, 1987-, Head of Trauma Department of Ophthalmology, 1990-, Beijing Tong Ren Hospital. Publications: Senile Retinoschisis, 1981; Application of the Soft Contact Lens Soaked in EDTA in Cases of Chemical Burn, 1988; Analysis of 72 Cases of Closed Pars Plana Vitrectomy, 1990. Honour: 3rd Award, Bureau of Beijing Health,1990. Memberships: Society of Ophthalmology; Chinese Medical Association. Hobby: Playing Piano. Address: Liu Jia Nan Li, 16-1-30I Feng Tai District, Beijing 100075, China.

WANG Xiang Pu, b. 14 Dec 1930, Shandong, China. Teacher. m. Yingshi Han, 24 Jul 1954, 1 s, 2 d. Education: MD, Graduated from Shandong Medical University, 1953. Career: Lecturer of Hygiene; Associate Professor of Occupational Health; Director of Department of Occupational Health; Director of Faculty of Hygiene; Professor of Toxicology, Head of Department of Health Toxicology; Currently, Professor of Occupational Health and Toxicology and Director of Institute for Preventive Medicine, Hunan Medical University, China. Publications: Method in Health Toxicology, 1979; Textbook of Hygiene, 1979, 1984, 1989, 1994; Dictionary on Hygiene, 1984; Lecture on Health Toxicology, 1994; 68 Original articles in industrial toxicology. Honours: Public Health Ministry Award; 5 Awards for Scientific Research, Hunan Province. Memberships: Chinese Association of Preventive Medicine; Chinese Society of Health Toxicology; Hunan Preventive Medicine Society. Hobbies: Running; Swimming. Address: Hunan Medical University, 22 Beizan Road, Changsha, Hunan 410078, China.

WANG Xin-de, b. 24 Nov 1924, Zhejiang Province, China. Professor of Neurology. m. Tang Ci-mei, 4 July 1931, 1 daughter. Education: MD, Shanghai Medical College, 1950; Candidate of Medicine degree, Institute of Neurology, Academy of Medical Sciences, USSR, 1956. Appointments: Assistant Professor of Neurology, 1956, Associate Professor, 1959, Shanghai 1st Medical College; Associate Professor, 1961, Professor of Neurology, 1978-, Beijing Hospital; Professor of Neurology, Beijing Medical University, 1992-. Publications: Cerebrovascular Disease, 1962, 2nd edition, 1984; Geriatric Medicine, 1981; Geriatric Neurology, 1990. Honours: Medical Sciences and Technology Awards, 2nd Prize, 1993, 3rd Prize, 1994, Ministry of Public Health, China. Memberships: 21st Council, Chinese Medical Association; Chairman, Chinese Society of Neurology, Chinese Medical Association; Chairman, Chinese Society of Geriatrics; Research Committee of Extrapyramidal Disease, World Federation of Neurology. Address: Department of Neurology, Beijing Hospital, Dongdan, 100730 Beijing, China.

WANG Xin-Fang, b. 28 Sept 1934, Luoyang, Henan, China. Physician. m. Yu-E Guo, 28 Dec 1958, 1 son, 2 daughters. Education: BA, 1958, MD, 1980, Tongji Medical University. Appointments include: Head, Ultrasound Department, 1980, Professor of Medicine, 1986, Tongji Medical University; Deputy Director, Cardiovascular Disease Institute, Tongji Medical University. Publications: Textbook of Echocardiography, 1985; Biplane transesophageal echocardiography, 1992; Three-dimensional transesophageal echocardiography, 1994. Honours: History of Medical Ultrasound Pioneer Award, Washington DC, 1988; Best Abstract Award, ISCU, Nice, France, 1994. Memberships: Vice-President, Society of Ultrasound, Chinese Medical Association; Board of Directors, International Cardiac Doppler Society. Hobby:

Chinese classical literature. Address: Union Hospital, 575 Jiefang Road, Wuhan, 430022, China.

WANG Xin-Xiang, b. 23 Mar 1923, Szechuan, China. Teacher. m. Fu Jia-hua, 16 July 1946, 1 son, 2 daughters. Education: graduate, Nanking Traditional Chinese Medicine College. Appointments: District Vice Health Bureau, 1955-78; Chief, Department of Traditional Chinese Medicine, Adviser, Institute Pharmaceutical Medicine, Luzhou Medical College. Publications: Textbook of Traditional Chinese Medicine College, 1987; Treatment of 50 Patients with Liquor Bupleuri, 1986. Honours: 2nd Prize, Szechuan Province, 1993; Excellent Teacher, LuZhou Medical College, 1985, 1988. Memberships: Szechuan Branch, Chinese Traditional Medicine and Pharmacy Association. Hobby: Playing Chess. Address: LuZhou Medical College, LuZhou, China.

WANG Xingzhen, b. 6 Jan 1929, Shandong, China. Professor. m. Robert C Yu, 1953, 3 daughters. Education: MD, West China University, Chengdu, Sichuan, 1952. Appointments: Assistant Professor of Parasitology, Associate Professor of Parasitology, currently Professor of Parasitology, West China University of Medical Sciences, Chengdu. Publications: Production and screening of monoclonal antibodies against Plasmodium vivax, 1985; Recognition and detection of antigenic molecular weight by McAb against erythrocytic stages of P. vivax, 1988; Monoclonal antibodies against erythrocytic stages of P. vivax: Inhibitory effect on gametocyte infectivity and development within mosquitoes, 1988; The preparation and identification of anti-idiotypic antibody against P. vivax at erythrocytic stages, 1992; Field evaluation of QBC technique and fluorochrome stain applied to the rapid diagnosis of vivax malaria, 1993; Contributor to Human Parasitology, 2nd Edition, 1994. Honours: Certificates of Merit for Important Science and Technology, Sichuan Province, 1979, 1988; Research Grant, Science Fund, Chinese Academy of Sciences, 1984; Special Research Grant, Sichuan Public Health Bureau, 1985; Research Grant, National Natural Science Fund, 1986; Research Grant, National Education Ministry Fund, 1988; WHO/TDR Grant, 1991. Memberships: Chinese Society of Zoology; Board of Directors, Chinese Society of Zoology, Sichuan Division; Chinese Society of Parasitology; Vice Committee Director, Sichuan Society of Parasitology; Deputy Editor in Chief, Sichuan Journal of Zoology; Editor, Journal of Practical Parasitic Diseases. Hobby: Classical music. Address: Department of Parasitology, West China University of Medical Sciences, Chengdu, Sichuan 610041, China.

WANG Xiu Ying, b. 28 May 1908, Ding Hsian County, He Bei Province, China. Nursing Education. Education: Registered Nurse, 1931; PUMC School of Nursing, 1931-35; MS, Columbia University, NY, USA, 1935-36; Nursing Professor, Professor of Science, Beijing, China, 1981. Appointments include: Public Health Nursing Assistant and Instructor of Health Education, 1931-35; Associate Professor, PUMC; Associate Chairman of CNA, 1950-87; Established and was first Dean of the Third Nursing School, 1954; Advisor, Nursing Health Bureau, Beijing, 1954-61; Advisor, Capital University of Medical Sciences, Beijing, 1961-. Publications include: Books: Public Health Nursing Progressive History; Common Knowledge of Health; Primary School Health Text Books; The Development of Chinese Nursing History; Co-Author, New Scientific Knowledge for Nurses, 1983; Contributor of many professional articles, 1945-; Given numerous lectures, interviews, official visits; Co-producer of various educational films including: How to Bear a Healthy Baby; Disinfection and Isolation. Honours include: Excellent Health Worker, Chinese Nursing Association; 1st Chinese Nurse awarded the 29th Florence Nightingale Model and Certificate, International Red Cross Association, 1983; 1st Chinese Nurse to receive Honorary Fellow of the Royal College of Nursing, London, 1985. Memberships include: Honorary Life Member, Chinese Association Council; European American and Chinese Classmates Association, China. Hobbies: Playing Piano; Writing; Plants and Flowers; Birds. Address: 102 Unit 1, 5th Building, Xi Ba He Dong Li, Chao Yong Qu, Beijing 100028, China.

WANG Xuehao, b. 1 Mar 1942, Jiangsu, China. Surgeon. m. Fengxia Fu, 1 May 1967, 1 s, 1 d. Education: MD, Nanjing Medical University, 1982. Appointments: Assistant Professor and Attending Doctor, 1976, Vice Professor and Chief Doctor, 1987, Professor and Chief Doctor, 1970; Chairman and Professor of Surgery, First Affiliated Hospital of Nanjing Medical University. Publications: Targeted Therapy for Primary Hepatoma with a Report of 44 Cases, 1990; Seceral Improvemenets in Liver Surgery, 1989; Current Spleen Surgery, 1990. Honour: Distinguished Expert of China, 1990. Memberships: Vice Chairman, Anti-Cancer Association of China, Jiangsu Branch. Hobby: Table tennis. Address: 300 Guangzhou Road, Nanjing 210029, China.

WANG Yifang, b. 11 May 1958, Hunan Province, China. Editor; Doctor. m. Liyun Ni, 1984, 1 daughter. Education: MB, Department of Medicine, 1983, MSc, Medicine, Department of Internal Medicine, 1986, Hunan College of Traditional Chinese Medicine. Appointments: Research Assistant, 1986-87; -; Senior Editor, Director of Medicine Department, Hunan Science and Technology Press, Changsha, 1987-; Associate Professor, Shanghai Traditional Chinese Medicine University, 1994-; Visiting Professor, Hunan College of Traditional Chinese Medicine, 1994- Publications: Co-author: Introduction of TCM, 1986; Medicine in Jin-Chu Area, 1991; Illustration of Acupuncture, Moxibustion and Qigong in China, 1991; Follow Me To Learn TCM, 1994; Tension and Balance of Humanistic Tradition and Scientific Construction of Chinese Medicine in 20th Century, forthcoming; Various articles on Traditional Chinese Medicine, including its history and Medical Humanistic; 6 publications on publishing. Honours: 2nd Award for Science, Art and Literature, 1987; Second Class Award as Scientific Editor. Address: Hunan Science and Technology Press, Exhibition Hall Road No 3, Changsha 410005, Hunan, China.

WANG Yixun, b. 4 Aug 1940. Gynaecologic Oncology. m. Wu Guang Zheng, 1 Oct 1966, 1 s, 1 d. Education: MD; Post Doctoral Research at Yale University, 1986-87, 1991-93. Career: Resident, Ying Ko Hospital, 1962-78; Attending Doctor, 1978-87; Vice Chief Doctor, 1987-93, Chief and Chairman, 1993-, Liaoning Tumour Hospital, Gynaecologic Oncology Department. Publications: Chemoresistance of Chpriocarcinoma with 9 Cases Report, 1986; Urinary Gonadotropin Fragments (UGF) in Cancers of The Female Reproductive System, 2 initial serial study, in Gynaecologic Oncology, 1988. Honours: Member, Liaoning Anti-Cancer Council, 1989-; Editorial Board, Foreign Medicine Journal and Clinical Obstetric and Gynaecologic Journal, 1989-; Board of Directors, Liaoning Branch of Chinese Obstetrics and Gynaecology and Tumour Society; Model Doctor of Liaoning Province. Memberships include: Shen Yang Tumour Society. Hobby: Reading. Address: Liaoning Tumour Hospital, Shen Yang, 110042 Liaoning, China.

WANG Zhao-ming, b. 20 Mar 1931, Tianjin, China. Medical Doctor. m. Men Yu-mei, 1 May 1956, 2 sons, 1 daughter. Education: Graduated, 1952; Postgraduate studies, Chinese Medicine, Tianjin Academy of Research in Integration of Traditional Chinese Medicine and Western Medicine, 1964-67. Appointments: Physician, Tianjin No 1 Hospital, 1952-64; Class Leader, specific training in integration of Traditional and Western Medicine, 1964-67; Director, Nankai Hospital, Tianjin, 1967-69; President, Daxinganling Special Hospital, Heilongjiang, 1969-79; President, Jinhua Rheumatism Hospital and Tianjin Institute of Traditional Chinese Medicine, 1979-. Publications: Treatment of Haemorrhoids by the Integration of Traditional and Western Medicine, 1962; Treatment of Rheumatism by the Integration of Traditional and Western Medicine, 1989; About 100 papers in research on rheumatism and haemorrhoids in Chinese medical journals. Honours: Prize for Scientific Advancement, Tianjin Science and Technology Committee, 1982, 1984, 1992; Gold Prize, All-China Health Product, 1992; Gold Prize, US Chinese Medical Association 1993. Memberships: Director, All-China Committee of Rheumatism; Vice-Director, All-China Committee of Refractory Disease; Leader, All-China Committee for Prevention and Treatment of Rheumatism; Director, All-China Society of Rheumatism; Vice-President, US Chinese Medical Association. Hobbies: Painting; Calligraphy; Associating with friends. Address: 3 Baokangli, Apt 3-405, Yuquan Road, West Anshan Avenue, Tianjin 300073, China.

WANG Zhao-pu, b. 11 Nov 1924, Gansu Province, China. Orthopaedic Surgeon. m. Yu Meng-Lu, 1 Apr 1959, 1 son, 1 daughter. Education: Graduated, MMed, Medical College, Lanzhou, 1951; Postgraduate study, First Medical College, Moscow, 1952-56. Appointments: Doctor-in-charge, Traumatology Department, Ji Shui Tan Hospital, 1957-78; Assistant Professor, Professor, Institute of Ortho-Trauma, China Academy of Traditional Chinese Medicine, 1978-; Currently Director, Bone Disease Department, Institute of Ortho-Trauma. Publications: Clinical Research on Rheumatoid Arthritis, special issue, 1981; Clinical Essential Point Precussion Therapy, 1989; Acupressure Therapy, 1991; Orthopedics in China issue (compiler). Honours: 5 Advanced Worker Awards, 1959-64; Civilised Medical Worker, Institute of Ortho-Traume, 1984. Membership: Specialist Commission, China Academy of Traditional Chinese Medicine.

WANG Zhen-Xi, b. 20 Dec 1933, Jiangsu, China. Researcher in Molecular Biology. m. Qian Yizhen, 10 Aug 1965, 2 daughters. Education: MD, Department of Medicine, Zhejiang Medical University,

1958. Appointments: Teaching Assistant and Medical Practitioner, 1958-76; Lecturer in Biochemistry, 1978-85, Associate Professor of Biochemistry, 1986-92, Zhejiang Medical University, Hangzhou; Visiting Scholar, State University of New York at Buffalo, 1980-82; Visiting Scientist, Harvard University, Cambridge, Massachusetts, USA, 1989-90; Visiting Research Scientist, Yale University, New Haven, Connecticut, 1990-94. Publications: 1st author: Androgen regulation of seminal vesicle protein II mRNA, 1986; Synthesis of thymosin alpha-1 gene, 1987; Isolation of androgen-regulated secretory protein from rat seminal vesicle by FPLC, 1989; Antifertility effect of sperm coating protein in rat seminal vesicle by isoimmunization, 1990; Mutational Analysis of the CR2 site of EIA and its effect on binding to the retinoblastoma gene product: Use of the "Double Tagging" assay, 1995; Vectors for the "Double Tagging" assay for protein-Protein interactions, 1995; Co-author: Study of fluorescent localization of seminal vesicle II protein on rat sperm surface, 1990; A contingent replication assay for the detection of protein-protein interactions in animal cells; Screening for in vitro protein-protein interactions (2nd author), 1993; Two schistosome cDNA encoding ATP-binding cassette (ABC) family proteins, (2nd author) 1994. Membership: Chinese Biochemical Association. Hobbies: Walking; Running; Table-tennis. Address: 258 Har Er Lane, Apt 403, Hangzhou 310006, China.

WANG Zheng-min, b. 19 Nov 1935, Shanghai, China. Professor of Otolaryngology. m. Feng Junshi, 15 Oct 1960, 2 daughters. Education: Graduated, Shanghai Medical University; MD, Zurich, Switzerland; Resident, 1955-60. Apppointments: Assistant Professor, Associate Professor, 1960-85, Professor, 1986-, Eye and Ear Hospital, Shanghai Medical University; Chairman, Department of Ear, Nose and Throat, Eye and Ear Hospital; Visiting Professor: Hongkong University, 1986; Wright University, Ohio, USA, 1991. Publications: The Textbook of Otolaryngology, 1988; Microsurgery of the Ear, 1989; Surgery of the Skull Base, 1994; Selection and Fitting of Hearing Aid, 1994. Honours: 1st Award of Science and Technology, Shanghai; 1 of 10 Talents in Shanghai Scientific and Technical Circles, 1993. Memberships: Executive Committee, International Association of Audiology; Commission of Medicine, WFD. Address: 83 Fen Yang Road, Shanghai, China.

WANG Zhi Jin, b. 24 Dec 1937, Shanghai, China. Professor. m. 21 Oct 1960, 1 s, 1 d. Education: MD; MSc. Career: Zhongshan Medical College, 1961-84; University of Calgary, Canada, 1984-87; Professor and Head, Department of Epidemiology, Sun Yat Sen University of Medical Sciences, Guangzhou, 1987-. Publications: Birth Patterns: Are the Chinese in Guangzhou City Different, in International Journal of Gynaecology and Obstetrics, 1988; Cancer Mortality of Chinese in Canada, in International Journal of Epidemiology, 1989; Medical Epidemiology, 1992. Honours: International Development Research Centre, Canada, 1984-87; New South Wales University, 1991. Memberships: International Epidemiological Association; Chinese Medical Association; Chinese Clinical Epidemiological Association. Hobbies: Swimming; Reading; Writing. Address: Department of Epidemiology, Sun Yat Sen University of Medical Sciences, Guangzhou 510089, China.

WANG Zi-Dong, b. 22 Nov 1937, Qin-Huang-Dao, China. Physician. m. 31 Dec 1959, 1 s, 1 d. Education: MD, Hopei Medical College. Appointments: Associate Professor, Deputy Director, 1980, Professor and Chairman, Department of Physiology, 1985-, Medical College of Jinan University. Honours: Guangdong Province Advanced Teacher Award, 1993; Medical Advance Prize, 1993. Memberships: Chinese Physiological Society; Chinese Biomedical Engineering Society. Hobbies: Running; Swimming; Travel. Address: Department of Physiology, Medical College of Jinan University, Shipai Street, Guangzhou, Guangdong Province, China.

WARD Joel, b. 18 May 1948, Los Angeles, CA, USA. Pediatric Medicine. 1 s, 2 d. Education: BS, 1969, MD, 1973, University of CA. Career includes: Consultant: Arctic Investigations Laboratory, Centers for Disease Control, Anchorage, Alaska, 1977-, Alaska Area Native Health Service, Indian Health Service, 1977-; Chairman, Infection Control Committee, 1980-, Director, Medical Epidemiology Unit, 1980-, Director, UCLA Center for Vaccine Research, 1988-, Chief, Division of Pediatric Infectious Diseases, 1990-, Harbor-UCLA Medical Center, Torrance, CA; Professor of Pediatrics, University of CA, Los Angeles, CA, 1989-. Publications: Many editorial activities, 1980-, including: American Journal of Diseases of Children, American Journal of Epidemiology, Annals of Internal Medicine, Editorial Board, Infection and

Immunity, Journal of American Medical Association, Journal of Pediatrics. Memberships include: American Epidemiologic Society; Fellow, American Pediatric Society; Fellow, American Academy of Pediatrics; Fellow, Infectious Disease Society of America; Society for Pediatric Research. Address: UCLA Medical Center, Research and Education Institute, Building E 6 170738, Torrance, CA 90502, USA.

WARD Malcolm Russell, b. 7 Nov 1946, Worthing, England. Dentist. m. Marie-Louise, 28 Mar 1972, 3 daughters. Education: BDS, Otago University, 1971; Diploma, Clinical Dentistry, Otago University, 1990. Appointments: Executive, Auckland Branch Nzda, 1989-95; Assistant Secretary, 1991-92, Secretary, 1993, Nzda Practice Management Committee, 1994; Executive, Prosthodontic Society, 1985-. Memberships: Auckland Dental Association; New Zealand Dental Association; New Zealand Prosthopontic Society; New Zealand Society of Endodontics. Hobbies: Sailing; Skiing; Vintage Sports Cars; Steam Machinery. Address: Floor 10, Southern Cross Building, Victoria Street, Auckland, New Zealand.

WARD Michael Alvin, b. 1 Jul 1951, Providence, KY, USA. Director, Contact Lens Service. m. Alice Ward, 1 Aug 1981, 2 s. Education: GA State University, 1969-71; University of Puget Sound, 1972; BSc, Microbiology, 1978; Postgraduate Study in Biochemistry, GA State Univ, 1978-79. Appointments include: Ocular Microbiologist, Contact Lens Specialist, 1980-84, Director, Contact Lens Service, 1984-, The Emory Clinic, Section of Opthalmology, Atlanta, GA; Instructor in Opthalmology, Emory University School of Medicine, 1987-. Publications include: Many contributions to medical journals, 1985-1994; Numerous meetings and lectures, 1979-; Reviewer for 3 medical journals. Honours include: Honoured Fellow, Contact Lens Society of America; Delivered the Theodore E Obrig Memorial Lecture, Las Vegas, 1990. Memberships include: President, Contact Lens Society of America, 1991-93; American Association for the Advancement of Science; International Academy of Sports Vision; American Society for Microbiology; Henderson Mill Civic Association; Steering Committee, The Paideia School. Hobbies: Hiking; Camping; Travel; Woodworking. Address: Department of Opthalmology, Emory University School of Medicine, 1327 Clifton Road NE, Atlanta, GA 30322, USA.

WARD Susan Jennie, b. 19 Jul 1957, Chester, England. Doctor. m. Andrew Theuring, 30 Aug 1993, 1 s, 1 d. Education: Nottingham University; Bachelor Medical Science; BM; BS; FRCS; MRCOG. Appointment: Senior Registrar in Obstetrics and Gynaecology. Publications: The Role of Cartilage Canals in the Formation of Secondary Centres of Ossification, 1979; The Characteristics of the Carbon Dioxide-Haemoglobin Dissociation Curve in Pregnancy, Clinical Science, 1993. Membership: Careers Advisor, Medical Women's Federation. Address: 160 Edwards Lane, Sherwood, Nottingham, NG5 3HZ, England.

WARDEN Karen Elizabeth, b. 12 Aug 1959, Minneapolis, Minnesota, USA. Engineer. Education: BSME, West Virginia University; MEBE, University of Virginia; PhD in progress, Case Western Reserve University. Appointments: Research Associate, Department of Orthopaedic Surgery, Johns Hopkins Medical Institutions; Manager, Engineering Research, AcroMed Corporation; Currently Engineering Consultant. Publications: Co-author: The Effect of Implant Rigidity on Vertebral Bone Density; Predicting Femoral Neck Strength from Bone Mineral Data; Device-Related Osteoporosis with Spinal Instrumentation. Honours: Recipient, Volvo Award on Low Back Pain Research, 1989. Memberships: American Society of Mechanical Engineers; Orthopedic Research Society; ASTM; BMES; ASB; ISB; Johns Hopkins Medical and Surgical Association. Address: 2249 Elm Street, Suite 415, Cleveland, OH 44113-2307, USA.

WARNER Mark, b. 5 Jul 1956, Leicester, England. Naturopath; Osteopath. m. Brigid Thesen, 7 Jun 1985, 1 s, 1 d. Education: Diploma in Naturopathy, Diploma, Honours, in Osteopathy, British College of Naturopathy and Osteopathy, London; MRN; MRO. Appointments: Medical Laboratory Scientific Officer: Leicester Royal Infirmary; Leicester General Hospital; Volunteer Scientific Officer, Savar Gonoshasthaya Kendra, Bangladesh; Currently in Private Practice, Naturopathy and Osteopathy. Memberships: General Council and Register of Osteopaths; General Council and Register of Naturopaths. Hobbies: Walking; Cooking. Address: 26 West Street, Cromer, Norfolk, NR27 9DS, England.

WARREN George Lewis, b. 7 Feb 1940, Jacksonville, Florida, USA. Psychiatrist. m. Carol K Miller, 13 May 1994, 1 s, 1 d. Education: BS, 1961; MD, 1965; Board Certified, 1974; FAPA, 1985; Added Qualification of Geriatric Psychiatry, 1991; Certified, American Board of Addiction Medicine, 1990. Appointments: Committee Chair, Florida Psychiatric Society, 1984-; Secretary, 1985, Vice President, 1986, Counsellor, 1983, 1984, 1989, President-elect, 1991, President, 1992; Vice President, Southern Psychiatric 1991; President-elect, Florida Psychiatry, 1992; President, Florida Psychiatry, 1993; APA Assembly Rep, 1995; Newsletter Editor, Florida Psychiatric Soceity. Publications: Mental Health and Abuse Treatment, 1993; Healthcare Reform and Mental Health Practice, 1993. Honours: Medical Diretor, Medfield Hospital, 1986-94. Memberships: American Psychiatric Association; American Medical Association; American Group Psychotherapy Association; Southern Psychiatric Association. Hobbies: Bicycling; Boating; Scuba diving. Address: 516 Lakeview Road, Clearwater, FL 34616, USA.

WARRIER Rajasekharan P, b. 22 Apr 1946, Kerala, India. Pediatrics, Hematology, Oncology. m. Jaya Warrier, 18 Mar 1974, 1 son, 1 daughter. Education: MBBS; MD; DCH; Diplomate of American Branch of PENS; Diplomate of American Bord of Pediatrics, Hematology, Oncology. Publications: More than 75 papers and abstracts on childhood blood disorders. Honours: Best Clinical Professor, Louisiana State University, 1990, 1991, 1992. Memberships: ASH; AAP; AAPI; ASCO; Indian Academy of Pediatrics. Hobbies: Tennis. Address: Louisiana School of Medicine, 1542 Tulane Avenue, New Orleans, LA 70112, USA.

WARTENBERG Daniel Everett, b. 15 Mar 1952, NY, USA. Professor. m. Caron Chess, 10 Sep 1993. Education: AB, cum laude, Cornell University; MS, University of WA, Seattle; MPhil, Columbia University; PhD, SUNY, Stony Brook. Career: Fellow, Interdisciplinary Programs in Health, Harvard School of Public Health; Currently, Associate Professor. Publications: Co-author, Defining Exposure in Case-Control Studies: A New Approach, in American Journal Epidemiology, 1991; Co-author, Cluster Methods: What Works, When and Why?, in Statistics in Medicine, 1993; Co-author, Risky Business: The Inexact Art of Hazard Assessment, in The Sciences, 1994. Memberships: International Society for Environmental Epidemiology; American Public Health Association; Society for Epidemiological Research; Society for Risk Analysis. Hobbies: Scuba Diving; Photography. Address: EOHSI, PO Box 1179, Piscataway. NJ 08855, USA.

WARWICK Hilda Maude, b. 26 Oct 1919, Alberta, Canada. Biochemist. m. James Cochrane Warwick, 19 Dec 1962. Education: BA, University of Alberta; B Education, University of Alberta; MA, Biochemistry, University of Toronto; Honours BA, magna cum laude, Art History, Honours in Biochemistry and Physiology, University of Toronto; BA, Visual Arts, University of Ottawa. Appointments: Teacher, Dramheller Schools, Alberta; Teacher, High School Maths and Science, Wainwright Schools; Professor of Maths, St Hilda;s College, Calgary, Alberta; Assistant Chemist, NRC, Ottawa, Canada; Medical Chemist, Ayerst Research Laboratories, Montreal; Medical Writer and Editor; President, H M Warwick Biomedical Communications. Publications: include, Isolation of B, Dihydroequilin and a Dihydroequilenin from Urine Pregnant Mares, 1956; Absorption and Excretion Studies of Certain Alkyl Sugar Derivation, 1951; Synthese de quelques derives du benzothazoline, 1968. Honours: Intramural Sports Crest, Athletic A, University of Alberta. Memberships: Organizing Committee, International Physiological Congress, Montreal; Board of Governor's, Montreal General Hospital; Research Partner, Mount Sinai Hospital, Toronto; New York Academy of Science; AAAS; American Medial Writers Association; Council of Biology; Editors Faculty Club, University of Toronto. Hobbies: Sports; Music; Art. Address: 507-1171 Ambleside Drive, Ottawa, Ontario, Canada, K2B 8E1.

WASZ-HÖCKERT Ole, b. 28 Aug 1918, Helsinki, Finland. Pediatrician. m. Nina Gorbatow, 19 Sept 1940 (dec. 1988), 3 daughters. Education: MD, 1946; PhD, 1950; Docent, 1954; Board specialised in Paediatrics and Infectious Diseases. Appointments: Professor, Head of Children's Hospital, Department of Paediatrics, University of Oulu, Oulu, 1964-72; Professor, Head, Chair of Paediatrics, 1972-85, now Emeritus Professor, University of Helsinki, 1972-85; Member, Helsinki City Council, 1980-; Member of Finnish Parliament, 1983-91; Member, Committees of Education, Health, Defence and International Parliamentarians Union. Publications: 300 original scientific articles (mostly in English), monographs, chapters in textbooks, in fields of paediatrics, infectious disease, tuberculosis and social paediatrics. Honours: Wartime medals, 1940-44; Commander, Order of the Finnish Lion, 1978; Honorary memberships, Finnish, Swedish and Nordic Paediatric Associations, Finska Läkaresällskapet, Folkhälsan; Several corresponding memberships including Leopoldiner. Memberships: President, 4 international congresses: Finnish IPPNW, 1981-94, Arctic Medicine, CRW Research, and Folkhälsan, 1980-92. Hobbies: Archipelago; Skiing (formerly); Politics, 1980-; His Spanish home, 1990-. Address: Dragonvägen 7, 00330 Helsingfors, Finland.

WATANABE Hisako, b. 2 Mar 1948, Tokyo, Japan. Child Psychiatrist. m. Ryo Watanabe, 29 Apr 1973, 1 son, 1 daughter. Education: MD, 1973, PhD, 1994, Keio University. Appointments: Paediatrician, Director of Department of Psychiatry, Yokoham City Hospital; Director, Infant, Child and Adolescent Mental Health Unit, Department of Paediatrics, School of Medicine, Keio University. Publications: Establishing Emotional Mutuality in Infancy with Japanese Families, 1987; Difficulties in Amae: Clinical Perspective, 1992. Honours: Sanshiki Award, 1993; Tokyo Medical Association Award, 1994. Memberships: Executive-at-large, World Association of Infant Mental Health; Advisory Board, Perinatal and Prenatal Psychology of North America; Japan Medical Association; Japan Paediatric Association. Hobbies: Piano; Tennis. Address: 2740-56 Takatacho, Kohokuku, Yokohama 223, Japan.

WATERHOUSE Ian Kellie, b. 30 May 1921, Sydney, Australia. Psychologist. m. Marie Jeanette Young, 12 Aug 1958, 2 s. Education: BA, Sydney; MA, PhD, Yale; Hon DSc, Macquarie. Appointments: Senior Lecturer, Reader, University of Melbourne, 1963-65; Professor of Psychology, Macquarie University, 1966-86; Chairman, New South Wales Institute of Psychiatry, 1978-86; Retired. Publications: Australian Journal of Psychology, Editor, 1961-65. Memberships: Fellow, British Psychological Society; Fellow, Australian Psychological Society; Australian Psychoanalytic Society; Sigma Xi. Hobbies: Gardening; Walking; Camping; Fishing. Address: 107 Hunter Avenue, St Ives, New South Wales 2075, Australia.

WATKINS Joan Marie, b. 9 Mar 1943, Anderson, IN, USA. Physician. Education: Doctor of Osteopathic Medicine; Master of Health Professions Education; Master of Public Health. Appointments: Director, Minor Emergency Center, Mercy Hospital and Medical Center, Chicago, IL, 1984-88; Resident in Occupational Medicine, University of Illinois, 1988-90; Corporate Medical Director, University Community Hospital, Occupational Health Services. Honours: Fellow of American College of Preventative Medicine. Memberships: Secretary/Treasurer, Florida Association of Occupational and Environmental Physicians; American College of Occupational and Environmental Medicine. Hobbies: Sailing; Needlework; Reading. Address: 4306 Harbor House Drive, Tampa, FL 33615 5408, USA.

WATSON Mary Ellen, b. 29 Oct 1931, San Jose, CA, USA. Ophthalmic Medical Technologist. m. Joseph Garrett Watson, 11 May 1950, 2 sons, 1 daughter. Education: Certified Ophthalmic Medical Technologist, with special certification in Surgery, 1984. Career: Ophthalmic Technician, Kent W Christoferson, MD Eugene, 1965-80; Administrator, Surgical Assistant, Technologist, I Howard Fine, MD Eugene, 1980-. Publications: Journal of Ophthalmic Nursing & Technology, 1989; Today's Dr Nurse, 1989; Journal of Ophthalmic Nursing & Technology, 1991; Today's Dr Nurse, 1991. Honours: Course Director, Joint Commission Allied Health Personnel in Ophthalmology, 1976-; Faculty Award, 1989. Memberships: Joint Commission Allied Health Personnel in Ophthalmology; Allied Technical Personnel in Ophthalmology; American Society of Ophthalmic Administrators; International Women's Pilots Association. Hobbies: Flying; Travel. Address: 2560 Chaucet Ct, Eugene, OR, USA.

WATTS Jenny, b. 13 Nov 1946, Tonbridge, Kent, England. Psychologist. Education: Certificate in Education, Biology, Psychology, 1968, BSc (Special), Psychology, 1972, MSc, Psychology of Education, 1973, London University; PhD, Psychology, Open University, 1986. Appointments: Teacher, schools, Lecturer, London Colleges of Further Education; Lecturer in Social and Cognitive Psychology, Birkbeck College, University of London (Extra-Mural Studies), and Open University; Senior Tutor, London Fire Brigade; Principal Research Officer, Head of Assessment and Evaluation Unit, Croydon; Currently Consultant Research Psychologist and Honourary Research Fellow in the Division of Psychiatry and Psychology, Guy's, Hospital, London;

Examiner for Diploma in Psychology, London University. Publications: Cognitive Complexity: A Summary of doctoral research; A new approach to Cognitive Complexity; Cognitive Complexity Revisited: A Monograph of Some New Ideas; How I got my PhD; The Watts-Moore Report: A survey of UK establishments awarding PhDs. Honours: Associate Fellow, 1988, Chartered Psychologist, 1989, British Psychological Society. Memberships include: Senator, Convocation, London University; Education Faculty Representative, Graduates Society, London University. Hobbies: Golf; Opera; Ballet; Theatre; Art exhibitions; Travel; Places of interest. Address: 67 Sevenoaks Road, Crofton Park, London SE4 1RF, England.

WAXMAN Stephen George, b. 17 Aug 1945, Newark, New Jersey, USA. Neurologist. m. Merle Applebaum, 25 June 1968, 2 sons. Education: BA, Harvard College, 1967; PhD, Albert Einstein College of Medicine, 1970; MD, Albert Einstein College of Medicine, 1972; MA, Yale University, 1986. Appointments: Clinical Fellow in Neurology, Harvard Medical School; Visiting Assistant Professor of Neuroscience, MIT; Associate Professor, Associate Chairman, Department of Neurology, Stanford University School of Medicine, 1978-86; Professor, Chairman, Department of Neurology, Yale University School of Medicine, 1986-. Publications: Spinal Cord Compression, 1990; Molecular & Cellular Approaches to the Treatment of Neurological Disease, 1993; Over 250 published articles. memberships: American Society for Cell Biology; American Academy of Neurology; Society for Neuroscience; American Neurological Association; World Federation of Neurology; Society for Neurotrauma. Honours: Tuve Award, NIH, 1972; Research Career Development Award, NINDS, 1975; Established Investigator, National MS Society, 1987; Distinguished Alumus Award, Albert Einstein College of Medicine, 1991; Fellow Royal Society of Medicine, 1991; President, Association for Research in Nervous & Mental Diseases, 1991-92. Hobbies: Running; Gardening. Address: Department of Neurology, PO Box 208018, New Haven, CT 06520-8018, USA. 2.

WAYNE Victor Samuel, b. 7 Jan 1953, Melbourne, Australia. Consultant Cardiologist. m. Karen Elsinger, 21 Dec 1976, 2 daughters. Education: MBBS; FRACP; FACC; FCCP; FESC; FICA; DDU. Appointments: Senior Cardiology Fellow, St Vincent Hospital & Instructor in Medicine, University of Massachusetts Medical School, 1982-83; Visiting Physician & Cardiologist, Monash University of Medicine, 1983-84. Publications: Author and Co-author of numerous articles in professional journals. Honours: Honours Degree in Medicine, Monash University, 1976; National Heart Foundation of Australia Overseas Travel Grant, 1982. Memberships: Fellow, Royal Australian College of Physicians; American College of Chest Physicians; European Society of Cardiology; American College of Cardiology; International Academy of Chest Physicians & Surgeons; Cardiac Society of Australia & New Zealand. Hobbies: Travel; Reading; Theatre; Property Investments. Address: 44 Grange Road, Toorak, Vic 3142, Australia.

WAYNIK Cyril, b. 3 May 1928, Cape Town, South Africa. Psychiatrist. m. Loraine Katz, 21 Dec 1950, 1 s, 1 d. Education: MD; MBChB, University of Cape Town Medical School, 1950; American Board of Psychiatry and Neurology, 1969; FAPA, 1973. Appointments: Private Practice; Past President, Connecticut Psychiatric Society. Memberships: American Psychiatric Society; Connecticut Medical Society. Hobbies: Golf; Whitewater Rafting; Gardening. Address: The Inwood, 3200 Park Avenue, Bridgeport, CT, USA.

WEATHERHOGG Deborah Jacqueline, b. 24 Jun 1961, Ilford, Essex, England. Osteopath. Education: Diploma in Osteopathy, British School of Osteopathy, 1983. Appointment: Osteopath. Membership: General Council and Register of Osteopaths. Hobbies: Christianity; Horse Riding; Handcarft; Jigsaw Puzzles. Address: Cwch Gwenyn, 13 Fairfield Road, Bude, Cornwall, EX23 8DH, England.

WEAVER C Phillip, b. 24 July 1940, Detroit, MI, USA. MD. m. Carol, 11 Nov 1994, 2 sons, 3 daughters. Education: AB, Stanford University, 1962; MD, University of South California School of Medicine, 1962. Appointments: Fellowship, 1971-72; Chief, Obstetrics & Gynaecology, Irwin Army Hospital, Ft Riley, Kansas, 1974; Medical Director, Ft Sanders Center for Women's Health, 1994. Publications: Urinary Estrial in Diabetic Pregnancies, 1968. Memberships: American College of Obstetrics & Gynaecology; American Association of Gynaecological Laparoscopists. Hobbies: Photography; Boating. Address: Ft Sanders Center for Women's Health, PO Box 1037, Lenoir City, TN 37771, USA.

WEBB Maurice James, b. 27 Sep 1941, Brisbane, Australia. Gynaecologic Surgeon. m. Val Skerman, 29 Apr 1966, 1 s, 2 d. Education: MBBS, University of Queensland; FRCOG(London); FRACOG; CGO; FACOG; FACS. Career: State Coordinator of Gynaecologic Oncology, Queensland, Australia, 1981-88; Currently, Consultant Gynaecologic Surgeon, Mayo Clinic; Professor of Obstetrics and Gynaecology, Mayo Medical School. Publications: Editor, Surgical Gynaecologic Oncology, 1993; Author, Manual of Pelvic Surgery, 1994. Honours: Teacher of Year, Mayo Clinic, 1979, 1989, 1993; Excellence in Teaching Award, Association of Professors of Obstetrics and Gynaecology, 1993. Memberships: Society of Pelvic Surgeons; Society of Gynaecologic Oncologists. Hobbies: Travel; Photography; Gardening. Address: Department of Obstetrics and Gynaecology, Mayo Clinic, Rochester, MN 55905, USA.

WEBBER Sandra Nell, b. 13 Feb 1951, South Africa. Radiographer. Education: National Diploma in Diagnostic Radiotherapy, 1971. Appointments: Diagnostic Radiographer. Red Cross Childrens Hospital, Cape Town; Diacnostic Radiographer. Addington Hospital, Durban; Senior Diagnostic Radiographer. Memberships: South African Medical and Dental Council. Hobbies: Travel; Reading; Theatre. Address: 8 Antigua. Chartwell Drive, Umhlanga Rocks 4320, South Africa.

WEBSTER John Goodwin, b. 27 May 1932, Plainfield, New Jersey, USA. Biomedical Engineering Educator; Researcher. m. Nancy Egan, 27 Dec 1954, 2 sons, 2 daughters. Education: BEE, Cornell University, 1953; MSEE, University of Rochester, 1965; PhD, 1967. Appointments: Registered Professional Engineer, Wisconsin; Engineer, North American Aviation, Downey, California, 1954-55; Engineer, Boeing Airplane Company, Seattle, 1955-59; Radiation Incorporated, Melbourne, Florida, 1959-61; Staff Engineer, Mitre Corporation, Bedford, Massachusetts, 1961-62; IBM Corporation, Kingston, New York, 1962-63; Assistant Professor of Electrical Engineering, 1967-70, Associate Professor of Electrical Engineering, 1970-73, Professor of Electrical and Computer Engineering, 1973-, University of Wisconsin-Madison; Consultant, General Electric Company, 3M Company, Johnson and Johnson. Publications include: Co-Author: Medicine and Clinical Engineering, 1977; Sensors and Signal Conditioning, 1991; Medical Instrumentation: Application and Design, Editor, 1978, 2nd Edition, 1992; Clinical Engineering: Principles and Practices, 1979; Design of Microcomputer-Based Medical Instrumentation, 1981; Therapeutic Medical Devices: Application and Design, 1982; Electronic Devices for Rehabilitation, 1985; Interfacing Sensors to the IBM-PC, 1988; Encyclopedia of Medical Devices and Instrumentation, 1988; Design of Cardiac Pacemakers, 1995. Honours include: Theo C Pilkington Outstanding Educator Award, 1994. Memberships include: Fellow, IEEE; American Institute Medical and Biological Engineering; Biomedical Engineering Society. Address: University of Wisconsin, Department Electrical and Computer Engineering, 1415 Engineering Drive, Madison, WI 53706-1691, USA.

WEEKS David Joseph, b. 25 May 1944, Elizabeth, New Jersey, USA. Clinical Psychologist. 1 son, 1 daughter. Education: BA (Hons), Strathclyde University, Glasgow, Scotland, 1975; MPhil, 1977, PhD, 1981, University of Edinburgh. Appointments include: Senior Clinical Psychologist, Royal Victoria Hospital; currently Principal Clinical Psychologist, Royal Edinburgh Hospital, Edinburgh, Scotland. Publications: Ageism and Loneliness, 1982; Transcutaneous Nerve Stimulation, 1984; Eccentrics, 1995. Honours: First Inaugural Lecturer, Carr-Gomm Society, London, 1990. Membership: British Psychological Society. Hobbies: Hi-fi; Walking; Music; Painting; Photography; Cooking. Address: 75 b Leamington Terrace, Edinburgh EH10 4JT, Scotland.

WEEKS Paul Martin, b. 11 June 1932, Clinton, North Carolina, USA. Surgeon. m. Doris Hill, 28 Apr 1956, 4 sons, 2 daughters. Education: AB, Duke University, 1954; MD, University of North Carolina, Chapel Hill, 1958; Certifications: American Board of Surgery, 1964; American Board of Plastic Surgery, 1967; Surgery of the Hand, American Board of Surgery, 1989. Appointments include: Assistant Professor, 1965-68, Associate Professor, 1968-70, University of Kentucky Medical Center; Professor of Surgery, Head, Division of Plastic and Reconstructive Surgery, Washington University School of Medicine, 1971-; Plastic Surgeon-in-Chief, Barnes Hospital and Children's Hospital, St Louis, Missouri, 1971-. Publications: Management of Acute Hand injuries: A Biological Approach (with R C Wray), 1973, 2nd edition, 1978; Acute Bone and Joint Injuries of the Hand and Wrist: A Clinical Guide to Management, 1981; About 30 chapters; Over 150 articles. Honours: Distinguished Service Award, University of North Carolina, 1992.

Memberships: American College of Surgeons, Governor; American Society of Plastic and Reconstructive Surgeons; American Society for Surgery of the Hand; American Association of Plastic Surgeons, Past Vice-President, Past President; American Board of Plastic Surgery, 1981-87; American Board of Surgery, 1983-87; Plastic Surgery Research Council; Society of University Surgeons; Association of Academic Chairmen in Plastic Surgery; Nathan Womack Surgical Society, Vice-President; St Louis Medical Society; Canadian Society of Plastic and Reconstructive Surgeons; American and Southern Surgical Associations; American Society for Peripheral Nerve; Missouri State Medical Association; Wound Healing Society. Hobbies: Skiing; Sailing; Fishing; Woodworking. Address: One Barnes Hospital Plaza, Suite 17424, St Louis, MO 63110, USA.

WEERASEKARA Muthu Banda, b. 24 Apr 1937, Sri Lanka. Medical Physicist. m. Jan 1971, 1 son, 1 daughter. Education: BSc; Diploma, Radiological Physics. Appointments: Chief Physicist, Cancer Institute, Maharagama. Publications: Physics of Radiology, Contributor. Membership: IOMP. Hobby: Swimming. Address: Medical Physics Department, Cancer Institute, Maharagama, Sri Lanka.

WEERASEKERA Deepal Senaka, b. 16 Mar 1960, Horana, Sri Lanka. Obstetrician & Gynaecologist. m. Saumya Kamaleen Goonethileke, 24 June 1988, 1 son, 1 daughter. Education: MBBS, Colombo; MS, Sri Lanka; MRCOG; FRCS. Appointments: Registrar in Obstetrics & Gynaecology, Solihull Maternity Hospital, West Midlands; Consultant Obstetrician & Gynaecologist, General Hospital, Badulla, Sri Lanka. Publications: A retrospective evaluation of early carcinoma of the cervix treated surgically in a Provincial General Hospital, 1994. Honours: Distinction in Physiology, Faculty of Medicine, Colombo, 1980. Memberships: Sri Lankan College of Obstetricians & Gynaecologists; Royal College of Obstetricians & Gynaecologists; Fellow, Royal College of Surgeons. Hobbies: Tennis; Swimming. Address: No 33/1, 2nd Lane, Galpotta Road, Nawala, Rajaginya, Sri Lanka.

WEGMAN David Howe, b. 13 Mar 1940, Baltimore, MD, USA. Professor. m. Peggy, 7 Jun 1969, 1 s, 1 d. Education: BA, History, Swarthmore College, 1963; MD, Medicine, Harvard Medical School, 1966; MS, Occupational Health, Harvard School of Public Health, 1972. Appointments: Medical Intern, Cleveland Metropolitan Hospital, Ohio, 1966-67; Medical Epidemiologist, National Communicable Disease Center, New York City Health Department, 1967-69; Director, Urban Planning Aid, Inc, Industrial Health and Safety Project, Cambridge, Massachusetts, 1969-71; Occupational Hygiene Physician, Division of Occupational Hygiene, Department of Labor and Industries, Massachusetts, 1972-78; Assistant Professor, Occupational Health, Harvard School of Public Health, Massachusetts, 1972-77; Associate Professor, Occupational Health, Harvard School of Public Health, Massachusetts, 1977-83; Professor and Director, Division of Environmental and Occupational Health Sciences, University of California, Los Angeles School of Health, California, 1983-87; Professor and Department Chair, Department of Work Environment, College of Engineering, University of Massachusetts Lowell, Massachusetts, 1987-. Publications: include, Pilot Application of a Teaching Technique in Social Medicine, 1969; EpidemicKeratoconjunctivitis, 1970; Interactive Electronic Computing of the Mortality Odds Ratio, 1983; Work and Pregnancy, 1984. Honours: Aldred L Frechette Award, 1979; Delta Omega, 1987; Harriet L Hardy Award, 1994. Memberships: include, American Conference of Governmental Industrial Hygienists; American Public Health Association. Hobbies: Hiking; Swimming. Address: Department of Work Environment, University of Massachusetts, Lowell, MA 01854, USA.

WEI Jia, b. 24 July 1933, Jiangxi, China. Professor of Acupuncture. m. Jiang Cu Ying, 1949, 3 sons, 2 daughters. Education: Nanjing College of Traditional Chinese Medicine, 1958. Appointments include: Senior Doctor of Acupuncture, 1986; Professor of Acupuncture, 1987; Currently Dean of Studies, Jiangxi College of Traditional Chinese Medicine, Nanchang. Publications: Different Schools of Acupuncture and Moxibustion (editor-in-chief), college textbook, 1987; Acupuncture and Moxibustion without Harm and Pain (adviser), 1992; 96 learned articles in over 10 periodicals, 1955-. Honours: Named Scholar Who Makes an Outstanding Contribution, Chinese State Council; Special Allowance, Chinese State Council, 1990. Memberships: Committee Member, Chinese International Examination Centre for Acupuncture and Moxibustion; Acupuncture Representative to Medical Science Commission, Ministry of Public Health, China. Hobbies: Calligraphy;

Walking. Address: Jiangxi College of Traditional Chinese Medicine, 20 Yang Ming Road, Nanchang, Jiangxi 330006, China.

WEI Jinhe, b. 30 Sep 1940, Henan, China. Professor of Space Medicine. m. Zhizhen Shi, 28 Dec 1969, 2 daughters. Education: Graduate, Department of Biology, Postgraduate in Biology, Peking University. Appointments: Deputy Director, Gravitational Physiology, 1983, Director, 1987-93, Director, Space Life Sciences Projects, Institute of Space Medico-Engineering. Publications: Cardiogenic Motion in Dogs, 1985; Open-Loop Gain of Baroreceptor Reflex, 1985; Brain response Change by Simulated Weightlessness, 1992; Level Characteristics in Effect of Weightlessness on Physiological Systems, 1994. Honour: National Awards in Space Medicine Research, 1994. Memberships: Life Sciences Committee, IAF IAA; Standing Council, Chinese Society of Space Sciences; Council, Chinese Society of Astronautics; Chinese Society of Physiology. Hobby: Music. Address: Institute of Space Medico-Engineering, PO Box 5104, Beijing 100094, China.

WEI Neng-Run, b. 18 Nov 1919, Nanjing, China. Professor of Otorhinolaryngology. m. Zhao Shu-yan, 4 Aug 1921, 1 son, 1 daughter. Education: BM, Tong-ji University, Shanghai, 1944; MD, Tong-ji University, Wuhan. Appointments: Chief, Professor, ENT, Tong-ji Medical University, Wuhan, 1956-; Research Professor, HNO-Klinik, University of Tübingen, Germany, 1984-. Publications include: A small fenestra established in the footplate of stapes for otosclerosis: 1) The development of stapes operation in China, Chinese Journal of Otolaryngology, 1959; 2) Personal experience of stapes operation for otosclerosis in the three years (1957-59), Chinese J of Otolaryngol, 1960; 3) Histopathological findings in the inner ear of cats following stapes operation, Acta Academiae Medicinae, Wuhan, 1981; 4) Die Zweietagenfensterung, Arch Otohinolaryngol, 1983; Allografts applied in tympanoplasty: 1) Clinical application of allografts stored in Wuhan Medical College Type I Ear Bank, Chinese Med Journal, 1983; Immunology of inner ear diseases tested with patientw' own inner ear tissue: 1) Immunhistochemie am Ganglion Scarpae und an der Crista ampullaris von Ménière-Patienten, Laryngo-Rhino-Otol, 1992; 2) Die immunpathologische Bedeutung von humoralen Antikörpern bei der Otosklerose, HNO-Information, 1995; Bücher: 1) Co-author: Deutsch-chinesisches Wörterbuch der Medizin, 1985; 2) Co-author: Reference book of ENT, 1977; 3) Chief Editor: Textbook of Otorhinolaryngology for Chinese Students, 1959, 1963, 1979, 1985; Former Editor, Chinese Journal ENT. Honours: 1st Scientific Prize for Allografts stored in Wuhan Medical College Type I Ear Bank for Tympanoplasty, Chinese Public Health Ministry, 1980; Man of the Year, ABI, USA, 1994. Memberships: Standing Committee, Chinese Association of Otorhinolaryngology, 1956-87; Chinese Association of Otorhinolaryngology, China, 1947-; International Association of Logopedics and Phoniatrics, Basel, 1980-; Korrespondierendes Mitglied der Deutschen Gesellschaft für Hals-Nasen-Ohren-Heikunde, Kopf-und Hals-Chirurgie, Bonn, 1982-; Neurootological and Equilibriometric Society, Germany, 1980-; American Association for the Advancement of Science, USA, 1994. Hobbies: Acupuncture practice and research; Chi-Gong; Chinese calligraphy and painting. Address: Universitäts-HNO-Klinik, Silcherstrasse 5, 72076 Tübingen, Germany.

WEIL Ellen Kathleen, b. 8 Feb 1954, Binghamton, New York, USA. Pharmacist; Editor. Education: BA, Music, State University of New York, Binghamton, 1978; BS, Pharmacy, 1982, Lasdon Research Fellow, 1987, MS, Drug Information and Communications, 1988, Long Island University. Appointments: Pharmacist, Long Island College Hospital, Brooklyn, New York; Assistant Professor of Clinical Pharmacy, Long Island University, Brooklyn; Currently Editor, Prescribing Reference Inc. Honours: Music Activities Award, 1979-81. Memberships: American Medical Writers Association; American Pharmaceutical Association; Drug Information Association; Lambda Kappa Sigma. Hobbies: Music; Basketball; Travel; Skiing. Address: 146 Saint Johns Place, Brooklyn, NY 11217, USA.

WEINBERGER Miles, b. 28 Jun 1938, McKeesport, PA, USA. Physician. m. Dr Leslie Kramer, 22 Aug 1992, 2 s, 2 d. Education: AB, 1960, MD, 1965, University of Pittsburgh; Board certified: Pediatrics, 1970; Allergy and Immunology, 1972; Pediatric Pulmonology, 1986. Appointments include: Associate Professor of Pediatrics, 1975-80, Director, Pediatric Allergy and Pulmonary Division, 1975-, University of IA College of Medicine; Director, Cystic Fibrosis Center, University of IA Hospitals and Clinics, 1976-; Professor of Pediatrics, University of IA College of Medicine, 1980-. Publications include: Managing Asthma (book), 1990; 125 Articles published in professional journals; 25 Book

Chapters. Honours: Fellow, American Academy of Pediatrics, 1970; Clemens von Pirquet Award, American College of Allergy, 1974; Fellow, American College of Allergy, 1983; Walter Bierring Award, American Lung Association of IA, 1986. Membership: SPR; AAP; AAAI; ACAI; ATS. Address: Department of Pediatrics, JCP, University of Iowa Hospitals, Iowa City, IA 52242, USA.

WEINER Richard, b. 25 Nov 1945, Brooklyn, NY, USA. Psychiatrist. m. 7 Jul 1968, 1 s, 1 d. Education: MD; MSE; PhD. Appointment: Currently, Chief, Psychiatry Services, Durham VAMC, Associate Professor of Psychiatry, Duke University Medical School. Publications: The Practice of ECT, 1990. Honour: NIMH Merit Award, 1988. Memberships: Fellow, American Psychiatric Association; American EEG Society. Address: PO Box 3309, DUMC, Durham, NC 27710, USA.

WEINSHILBOUM Richard Merle, b. 31 Mar 1940, Eldorado, KS, USA. Physician; Pharmacologist. m. Lily Shuling Feng, 4 Jun 1965, 1 s, 1 d. Education: BA, Highest Distinction, Honours in Zoology, University of KS, 1962; MD, University of KS Medical School, 1967. Appointments: Professor of Pharmacology and Internal Medicine; Director for Education, Mayo Foundation. Publications: 178 Scientific articles published; 143 Scientific abstracts published. Honours: Phi Beta Kappa; Alpha Omega Alpha; Faculty Development Award, Pharmaceutical Manufacturers Association, 1973-75; Established Investigatorship, American Heart Association, 1976-81; Burroughs Wellcome Scholar, Clinical Pharmacology, 1981-86; Mayo Distinguished Investigator, 1989; American Society for Clinical Pharmacology and Therapeutics Rawls Palmer Award, 1979. Memberships: American Society for Clinical Pharmacology and Therapeutics; American Society for Pharmacology and Experimental Therapeutics; American Federation for Clinical Research; American Society for Clinical Investigation; Association of American Physicians. Hobbies: Tennis; Art; Music. Address: Department of Pharmacology; Mayo Medical School, Mayo Foundation, Mayo Clinic, Rochester, MN 55905, USA.

WEISS Carol Juliet, b. 5 Mar 1957, New York City, USA. Physician. m. Martin A Koshakow, 19 Aug 1990, 1 s. Education: BA, Wesleyan University; MD, Johns Hopkins University School of Medicine. Psychiatry Residency, 1987, Chemical Dependancy Fellowship, 1979, Cornell University Medical Centre. Appointments: Clinical Assistant Professor of Psychiatry and Public Health. Publications include: Alcohol-Drug Abuse in Workplace, 1989; Hallucinogens, 1990; AIDS, 1991. Honours: Phi Beta Kappa; Magna Cum Laude, 1977. Memberships: American Psychiatric Society; American Society Addiction Medicine; American Society Clinical Psycopharmacology. Address: 55 East 72nd Street #W, New York, NY 10021, USA.

WEISS Margaret Danielle, b. 25 Apr 1955. Child Psychiatrist. 2 d. Education: MD; PhD; FRCP(C). Appointment: Child Psychiatrist. Address: British Columbia Children's Hospital, Division of Child Psychiatry, 4480 Oak Street, Vancouver BC, V6H 3V4, Canada.

WEISS Scott T, b. 16 Apr 1946, NY, USA. Physician. m. Deb Weiss, 2 Jun 1968, 2 s. Education: BA, Honours, Haverford College; MD, Case Western Reserve Medical School, 1972; MS, Epidemiology, Harvard School of Public Health, 1977. Career includes: Chief Resident, Medicine, Beth Israel Hospital, 1977-78; Instructor in Medicine, 1977-80; Assistant Professor in Medicine, 1980-85; Associate Professor, AMS, 1985-; Associate Physician, Brigham and Women's Hospital; Currently, Associate Professor of Medicine, Harvard Medical School. Publications: 170 articles on epidemiology of asthma, chronic obstruction lung disease, hypertension, coronary disease. Honours: Alpha Omega Alpha, 1972; Albert S Award for Excellence in Art and Practice of Medicine, 1972; Future Leader in Pulmonary Medicine, ACCP, 1983; American Epidemiology Society, 1989. Memberships: American Thoracic Society; American College of Chest Physicians; European Respiratory Society; Society for Epidemiological Research; American College of Epidemiology; American College of Physicians. Hobbies: Cooking; Reading; Ice Hockey. Address: Rm 305 Chenning Laboratory, Brigham and Women's Hospital 180 Longwood Avenue, Boston, MA 02115, USA.

WEISS Stanley H, b. 28 Jan 1954. Medicine. m. Robin Joanna Kase Weiss, 12 Jan 1981, 1 s, 1 d. Education: BA, summa cum laude, Molecular Biophysics and Biochemistry, Yale College, 1974; MD, Infectious Diseases, Harvard Medical School, 1978. Appointments include: Chief of AIDS and Retroviral Epidemiology, Department of Preventive Medicine, NJMS, UMDNJ, 1987-; Assistant Professor, Medicine, NJ Medical School, 1988-; Executive Scientific Committee, NJ

Community Research Initiative, 1988-; Director of Division of Infectious Diseases Epidemiology, 1989-; Associate Attending in Medicine, UMDNJ, University Hospital, 1989-; AIDS Faculty, Academy of Medicine of NJ, 1989-; National Faculty, Infectious Disease Challenges in AIDS, 1992-; Associate Professor, Department of Preventive Medicine and Community Health, UMDNJ, NJMS, 1993-. Publications include: Over 75 publications and over 80 published abstracts. Honours include: NY State Governor's Committee Award for Academic Achievement, 1971-74; Joseph Collins Scholar, Harvard Medical School, 1975-78; Humanities Fellow, University of Medicine and Dentistry of NJ, 1988; Fellow, Infectious Diseases Society of America, 1989-; Fellow, American College of Physicians, 1992-. Memberships include: Advisory Board, International Retrovirology Association, HTLV and Related Viruses, 1994-97. Hobbies: Bridge; Travel. Address: 30 Bergen Street, Room ADMC 1614, Division of Infectious Diseases Epidemiology, Newark, NJ 07107, USA.

WELCH Laura Stewart, b. 27 Nov 1951, New York, USA. Physician. m. Harry Feifelbaum, 10 Dec 1987, 1 son, 1 daughter. Education: MD, University of New York, Stony Brooke, 1978. Appointments: Director, Division of Occupational & Environmental Medicine, The George Washington University School of Medicine, 1988-; Associate Professor of Medicine & Health Care Sciences, The George Washington University School of Medicine, 1989-. Publications incl: Development of Multiple Chemical Sensitivity after an Outbreak of Sick-Building Syndrome, 1992; Occupational exposure to dust and lung disease among sheet metal workers, 1993; Improving education and resources for health care providers: Occupational and environmental reproductive hazards, 1993; Musculoskeletal symptoms among electricians, 1994; Surveillance of construction worker injuries through an urban emergency department, 1994; Asbestos-Related Disease among Sheet Metal Workers, 1994. Memberships: American College of Occupational & Environmental Medicine; American Public Health Association; Society for Occupational & Environmental Health; Association of Occupational & Environmental Clinics. Address: 23W 11 St NW, Washington, DC 20037, USA.

WELLER Elizabeth B, b. 7 Aug 1949. Psychiatrist. m. Ronald A Weller, 18 Feb 1978, 1 s, 1 d. Education: BS, MD, American University of Beirut; Board certified in, Psychiatry, Child Psychiatry. Appointments: Intern, Pediatrics, American University of Beirut, 1974-75; Residency and Resident in Psychiatry and Child Psychiatry, WA University School of Medicine, Fellow in Child Psychiatry, University of KS Medical Center, 1975-78; Currently: Professor of Psychiatry, Pediatrics and Neuroscience; Associate Chair, Department of Psychiatry; Director of Training, Child and Adolescent Psychiatry, OH State University, Columbus, OH. Publications: Steady-State Plasma Imipramine Levels in Prepuberal Depressed Children, 1982; Psychiatric Disorders in Children and Adolescents, 1990; DST and Depressive Symptoms in Bereaved Children: A Preliminary Report, 1990; Depression in Recently Bereaved Prepubertal Children, 1991. Honours: American Academy of Clinical Psychiatry Research Award, 1982, 1984, 1988; Professor of Year, 1990; Distinguished Award, Program Chair, American Academy of Clinical Psychiatry, 1992. Memberships: American Academy of Child and Adolescent Psychiatry; American Psychiatric Association; AMA; Society of Biological Psychiatry; OH Psychiatric Association. Hobbies: Cooking; Antique Collecting; Volunteer work with non-English speakers. Address: Division of Child Psychiatry, Ohio State University, 473 West 12th Avenue, Columbus, OH 43210-1252, USA.

WELLS Adrian, b. 2 Feb 1962, Yorkshire, England. Clinical Psychologist. Education: BSc, Honours, 1984, PhD, 1987, Aston University; MSc, Leeds University, 1989; Cognitive Therapy Diploma, University of Pennsylvania, 1990. Appointments: Postdoctoral Research fellow, University of Pennsylvania, Centre for Cognitive Therapy; Chartered Clinical Psychologist, University of Oxford, Department of Psychiatry. Publications: Relationships Between Anxiety, Self-Counsciousness and Cognitive Failure, Co-author, 1988; Panic Disorder in Association with Relaxation Induced ANxiety: An Attentional Training Approach to Treatment, 1990; A Multi-Dimensional Measure of Worry, 1994; Attention and the Control of Worry, 1994; Negative Outcome in Cognitive-Behaviour Therapy: A Case Study, 1992; Imagery and Core Beliefs in Health Anxiety: Content and Origins, Co-author, 1993; Attention and Emotion: A Clinical Perspective, Co-author, 1994. Honours: Associate Fellow, British Psychological Society; Chartered Clinical Psychologist. Memberships: British Psychological Society; British Association of Behavioural and Cognitive Psychotherapy. Hobby: Watercolour painting. Address: University of Manchester, Department of Psychiatry, Oxford Road, Manchester, M13 9PT, England.

WELLS Lionelle D, b. 22 Nov 1921, Winnsboro, North Carolina, USA. Psychiatrist. m. (1) Mildred Wohltmann, 28 June 1945 (dec. 1986), 2 sons, 2 daughters, (2) Eileen Bromfield, 23 Sept 1989. Education: BS, University of South Carolina, 1943; MD, Medical University of South Carolina, 1945; Postgraduate, Boston Psychoanalytic Society and Institute, 1960; Certified: Psychiatry, American Board of Psychiatry and Neurology, 1952; Psychoanalysis, Professional Standards Board of American Psychoanalytic Association, 1963; Medical Management, American College of Physician Executives, 1990. Appointments: Private practice, Psychiatry and Psychoanalysis, 1959-; Hospital and academic positions include: Courtesy Staff, Waltham Weston Hospital and Medical Center, 1977-; Lecturer, Psychiatry, Boston University School of Medicine, 1977-; Assistant Clinical Professor, Psychiatry, Harvard Medical School, 1978-93; Consulting Staff, Newton-Wellesley Hospital, 1980-; Lecturer, Psychiatry, Tufts University Medical School, 1981-; Psychiatrist, Massachusetts General Hospital, Boston, 1982-; Psychiatrist, South Bay Mental Health Center, 1993-. Honours: Phi Beta Kappa, 1942; Robert Wilson Award, 1943; Medical University of South Carolina, 1944; 1st Honours Graduate, Medical University of South Carolina, 1944. Memberships: Fellow, American College of Physician Executives; Fellow, American Psychiatric Association; Massachusetts Psychiatric Society; American Medical Association; Massachusetts Medical Society; Boston Psychoanalytic Society and Institute Inc; American Psychoanalytic Association; Boston Society for Gerontologic Psychiatry Inc; American Geriatric Society; American Association for the Advancement of Science. Address: 73 Rolling Lane, Weston, MA 02193, USA.

WEN Ha Xian. Appointments: Professor and Vice Director of Surgical Oncology; Chairman, Department of Head and Neck Surgery; Vice Director, Cancer Institute and Hospital, CAMS. Publications: Practical Oncology, 3 volumes, author and Co-editor, 1978; China Encyclopaedia of Oncology, author and co-editor, 1980; Etiology and Prevention of Esophageal Cancer, 1981. Honours: A-Grade Scientific Achievement Awards, Ministry of Public Health, China, 1986. Memberships: China Medical Association; Corresponding Fellow, American Society for Head and Neck Surgery. Hobbies: Fishing; Reading. Address: Residential Quarter of Cancer Institute, PO Box 2258, Panjiayao, Beijing 100021, China.

WEN Hanzhang, b. 25 March 1932, Kunming, China. Teacher; Professor. m. 1956, 1 son, 2 daughters. Education: Diploma, Yunnan University, 1957. Appointments: Assistant, 1957; Instructor, 1978; Associate Professor, 1985; Director of Hygienic Chemistry, Guanxi Medical University, 1982; Retired, 1992. Publications: Co-author, 3 books including: Analytical Chemistry, 1990. Honours: Selected through Public Appraisal as Activist of Guanxi Chemistry-Chemical Industry, 1983; Numerous Professional Articles. Memberships: Chinese Chemical Society. Hobbies: Reading; Preparing New Tools and Instruments. Address: Guanxi Medical University, Nanning, Guanxi 530021, China.

WEN Jin-Kun, b. 9 May 1954, hebei, China. Teacher. m. Yang Yan, 29 july 1979, 1 daughter. Education: MD; PhD. Appointments: Assistant, Lecturer, Associate Professor, Dean Basic Medical department, Hebei Medical College. Publications: Molecular Analysis of Human Acatalasemia, Identification of a Splicing Mutation, 1990. Memberships: Chinese Biochemical and Molecular Biology Society. Hobby: Fishing. Address: Department of Biochemistry, Hebei Medical University, Shijiazhuang 050017, China.

WEN Qixiang, b. 11 Mar 1943, Chongqing, China. Cardologist; Perfusionist. m. Dr Tong Shiying, 27 Nov 1968, 1 son, 1 daughter. Education: Graduate, Third Military Medical University, 1967. Appointments: Residence, Department of Cardiology, 44 Hospital, 1967-78; Visiting Doctor, Intensive Care Unit, Department of Cardiac Surgery, 1978-89; Chief of Anaesthesia, Perfusion and ICU, Tianjin Chest Hospital. Publications: Postoperative Monitoring and Management of Rheumatic Heart Disease after Valve Replacement, 1983; Control Study of Postoperative Hemodynamic Monitoring in Congenital and Rheumatic Heart Disease, 1989; Monitoring and Managing of CAGB During CPB, 1992; Management of Water and Electrolytes During CPB in 66 Infants, 1994. Memberships: Chinese Extracorporal Circulation and Cardiovascular Surgery, Chinese Medical Association. Hobbies: Painting; Table-tennis. Address: No 97 Xian Road, Hopen District, Tianjin 300051, China.

WENG Tiandian, b. 5 June 1950, Gutian, Fujian, China. Teacher. m. Yun Huang, 11 nov 1981, 2 d. Education: Graduate, Fujian Medical University, 1977. Appointments: Lecturer, Ningde Medical School. Publications: Distribution of Finger Hair of She Nationality, 1994. Memberships: Chinese Society of Anatomical Sciences; Chinese Society of Medicine. Hobbies: Table-tennis; Swimming; Photography. Address: Ningde Medical school, Fuan, Fujian 355000, China.

WENZEL Richard P, b. 8 Jan 1940, Philadelphia, PA, USA. Physician. m. Jo Gail Hunt, 13 Jul 1968, 1 s, 1 d. Education: MD, Internal Medicine; MSc, Epidemiology, Infectious Diseases. Career: Professor of Internal Medicine, University of VA, 1971; Currently, Professor of Internal Medicine, University of Iowa College of Medicine, Iowa. Publications: 4 Books and over 350 articles. Honours: Sir Henry Wellcome Prize and Medal; Major Louis Livingston Seaman Prize, 1973; Fogarty NIH Award, 1985; Abbott Achievement Award, 1994. Memberships: Association of American Physicians; American Society of Clinical Investigators; Infectious Diseases Society of America. Address: Department of Internal Medicine, University of Iowa College of Medicine, Iowa City, IA 52242, USA.

WERBART Andrzej B, b. 19 Sept 1946, Katowice, Poland. Psychologist; Psychoanalyst. 3 s. Education: Philosophy, Universities of Warsaw and Uppsala, Sweden; Psychology, University of Stockholm; Licensed Psychologist. Appointments: Research Porgramme Leader; Private Practice. Publications: Psychotherapy Research Between Process and Effect: The Need of New Methodological Approaches, 1989; How to Use Therapeutic Environments in the Treatment of Schizophrenia? Common Ground and Areas of Disagreement, 1992; Psychotherapy of Schizophrenia: Facilitating and Obstructive Factors, Co-editor, 1992; Exploration and Support in Psychotherapeutic Environments for Psychotic Patients, 1992; The "Living Dead" - Survivors of Torture and Psychosis, Co-author, 1993. Memberships: Associate Member, Swedish Psychoanalytical Association; Associate member, International Psychoanalytical Association; Society for Psychotherapy Research. Address: Psychosocial Research Unit, Ektorpsvagen 2, 131 47 Nacka, Sweden.

WERBLOWSKY Joshua H, b. 25 May 1942, Brooklyn, NY, USA. Psychiatry. m. 17 Mar 1968, 1 s, 2 d. Education: BA, Yeshiva University; MD, Albert Einstein College of Medicine; FAPA. Career: Lecturer, Psychiatry, University of PA; Clinical Associate Professor, Psychiatry, Medical College of PA/Hahnemann University. Publication: Co-author, A Controlled Clinical Trial of Alprazolan for Treatment of Anxiety, in American Journal of Psychiatry, 1983. Memberships: Fellow, American Psychiatric Association; Fellow, American Academy of Forensic Sciences. Address: Presidential Apartments, Suite D-111, Philadelphia, PA 19131, USA.

WERMAN David Sanford, b. 1 Jan 1922, New York City, New York, USA. Physician. m. Marjolijn de Jager, 25 Oct 1958, 1 son, 1 daughter. Education: MA; MD; Certificat d'Etudes Médicales. Appointments include: Associate Professor, Department of Psychiatry, University of North Carolina, 1967-76; Currently Professor Emeritus of Psychiatry. Publications: The Practice of Supportive Psychotherapy, book; Chance, Ambiguity and Psychological Mindedness; Hardy's The Well Beloved, and the Nature of Infatuation; 40 others. Honours: Outstanding Teacher, Department of Psychiatry, University of North Carolina, 1975; Honoured Professor, Department of Psychiatry, Duke University, 1978, 1990. Memberships: American Psychoanalytic Association; American Psychiatric Association; American College of Psychoanalysts. Hobbies: Reading; Music; Gardening. Address: Department of Psychiatry, Box 3812, Duke University Medical Center, Durham, NC 27710, USA.

WERNER Eric James, b. 24 Dec 1953, Hartford, Connecticut, USA. Physician. m. Alice L Werner, MD, 2 s, 1 d. Education: MD with Postdoctoral Pediatric Hematology/Oncology; Board Certification Speciality : Pediatrics; Board Certification Subspeciality : Pediatrics/Hematology/Oncology. Appointments: Associate Professor, Pediatrics, Eastern Virginia Medical School; Medical Director, Hemophilia Comprehensive Program of Tidewater, Virginia; Elected Chief, Department of Pediatrics, Medical Staff at Children's Hospital of The King's Daughters. Honours: Phi Beta Kappa Society; Teacher of the Year, Wright State University; USAF Commendation Medal; Resident Teaching Award, CHKD; Young Faculty Award, Southern Section American Federation for Clinical Research; Mid-Atlantic Region, American Red Cross Award. Memberships: Fellow, American Academy of Pediatrics; American Federation for Clinical Research; American Society of Pediatric Hematology/Oncology; American Society for Hematology; Hemophilia Research Society; Southern Society for

Pediatric Research; Virginia Pediatric Society; World Hemophilia Foundation; Tidewater Pediatric Society. Address: 601 Children's Lane, Norfolk, Virginia 23507, USA.

WERTH Russ G, b. 8 Dec 1952, Jamestown, ND, USA. Educator. m. Betty Aslakson, 2 Aug 1975, 1 son, 1 daughter. Education: BA, Jamestown College. Appointment: Health Eductor. Honours: North Dakota Health Educator of the Year, 1993; US Central Distric Health Educator of the Year, 1993-94. Memberships: NEA; NDEA; AAHPERD. Hobbies: Walking; Biking; Wrestling; Hunting; Politics. Address: 310 2nd Avenue South West, Bowman, North Dakota 58623, USA.

WEST Clive Eric, b. 27 July 1939, Griffith, New South Wales, Australia. Nutritionist. m. Helen J Chambers, 22 Aug 1964, 1 son, 1 daughter. Education: BSc (Sydney), 1960; PhD (New England), 1966; DSc (New England), 1991; FRACI. Appointments: Lecturer, University of New England, 1965; Scientist, Unilever Research, UK, 1965-68; Fellow, Senior Fellow, Australian National University, Canberra, 1968-76; Senior Lecturer, Reader, Ahmadu Bello University, Nigeria, 1976-79; Currently: Associate Professor, Department of Human Nutrition, Wageningen Agricultural University, Netherlands; Visiting Professor in International Nutrition, Emory University School of Public Health, Atlanta, Georgia, USA. Publications: 175 papers in refereed scientific journals. Memberships: Nutrition Society, UK; American Institute of Nutrition.

WESTERMEYER Joseph John, b. 8 Apr 1937, Chicago, IL, USA. Physician; Psychiatrist. m. Rachel Mary Moga, 4 Aug 1962, 1 s, 1 d. Education includes: BS, Biology, Chemistry, 1959, MD, Medicine, 1961, MA, Anthropology, 1969, MPH, Public Health, 1970, PhD, Psychiatry, Anthropology, 1970, University of Minnesota; Board Certified, 1974, Addiction Psychiatry, 1993, American Board of Psychiatry; Board Certified, American Board of Family Practice, 1974. Appointments include: Psychiatry Staff, University of Minnesota Hospital and Clinic, 1970-89; Professor and Chair, Department of Psychiatry and Behavioral Sciences, University of Oklahoma Health Sciences Center, 1989-92; Professor, Department of Psychiatry, University of Minnesota, 1992-; Chief of Psychiatry, Minneapolis VA Hospital, 1992-. Publications include: Over 150 manuscripts in various professional journals; Over 50 chapters in books and monographs; Numerous book reviews, communications, editorials and other articles; Many books including: The Psychiatric Care of Migrants: A Clinical Guide, 1989; The Big Smoke: Opium and Its Uses in Asia, in progress. Honours include: Fellow: American Anthropolgical Association, 1976; American Association of Family Practice, 1976; American Psychiatric Association; American College Psychiatrists; Numerous grants, 1971-. Memberships include: Aerospace Medical Association; AMA; American Psychiatric Association; Kittil Bruun Society; Society of Biological Psychiatry; Society for Traumatic Stress Studies; World Psychiatric Association; Special Consultant, WHO Advisory Panel. Hobbies: Swimming; Hiking; Running; Skiing; Flying Aeroplane; Sailing. Address: 1935 Summit Avenue, St Paul, MN 55105, USA.

WESTLAKE Robert A, b. 7 Sept 1035, Ohio, USA. Physician. m. Christiane, 2 s. Education: BA, Allegheny College, 1957; MD, University of Pennsylvania, 1961. Appointments: Clinical Associate, NIMH Bethesda, Maryland; Assistant Professor of Psychiatry, University of Pennsylvania School of Medicine; Medical Director, Medical Administrator, Butler Hospital. Publications: Age and Personality Diagnosis with major Depression, 1990; Differential Diagnosis of Primary and Secondary Delusions, 1992. Memberships: Fellow, American Psychiatric Association; Fellow, American College of Psychiatrists. Address: Butler Hospital, 345 Blackstone Boulevard, Providence, RI 02906, USA.

WESTON (Henry) Jeffray, b. 9 Sep 1926, New Plymouth, New Zealand. Medicine. m. Dr Ann Coates, 7 Oct 1961, 1 s, 3 d. Education: FRCP; FRACP; DCH; EDMB; GLB; MB; 6LB (NZ); ADMS Defence HQ, 1967-72. Appointments: Registrar, Wellington Hospital, 1953-54; HP, Hammersmith Hospital, 1955, Brompton Hospital, 1955; Resident Assistant Physician, Great Ormond Street Hospital for Sick Children; Paediatrician, Wellington; Foundation Professor of Paediatrics, Wellington School of Medicine, 1975-91; Currently, Emeritus Professor and Locum Paediatrician. Memberships: New Zealand Medical Association; Honorary Fellow, Australian College of Paediatrics; Paediatric Society of New Zealand. Hobbies: Golf; Geology. Address: 6 Hauraki Street, Karori Wellingtons, New Zealand.

WESTWOOD Christine Muriel, b. 2 Aug 1954, England. Training & Consultancy Communication. Education: ACCA, East London University, 1978-79; Findhorn Foundation, 1982; Durham University, 1992-93; South Bank University, 1993-95. Appointment: Private Practice, 10 Years Counselling and Natural Therapies. Publications: Aromatherapy: A Guide for Home Unse, 1991; Aromatherapy: A Guide to Stress Management, 1993; Aromatherapy: Healthy Legs & Feet, 1995. Memberships: Fellow, Association of Certified Accountants;; London & Counties Society of Physiologists; British Association of Counselling; International Federation of Aromatherapists. Address: 25 Kite House, The Falcons, Grant Road, London SW11 2NJ, England.

WETMORE Ralph Frederick, b. 23 Nov 1950, Allentown, USA. Pediatric Otolaryngologist. m. Mary Cantalupo, 22 May 1976, 1 son, 1 daughter. Education: BA, Franklin & Marshall College, 1972; MD, University of Pennsylvania School of Medicine, 1976. Appointments: Assistant Professor, Otolaryngology, University of Pennsylvania School of Medicine; Associate Professor, Otolaryngology, University of Pennsylvania School of Medicine. Publications: Pediatric Effects otracheostomy: Experience during the past decade, 1982; f acid on the larynx of the maturing rabbit and their possible significance to the sudden infant death syndrome, 1993. Memberships: American College of Surgeons; American Medical Association; American Academy of Otolaryngology: Head & Neck Surgery; American Academy of Pediatrics; American Society of Pediatric Otolaryngology. Honours: Phi Beta Kappa, 1972; Alpha Omega Alpha, 1976; The Best Doctors in America, 1992-93; Edmund Prince Fowler Award, 1993. Address: Department of Otolaryngology, 34th Street and Civic Center Blvd, Philadelphia, PA 19104, USA. 6.

WETTSTEIN Robert M, b. 4 Jun 1950, New York, USA. Psychiatrist. m. Stacey Wettstein, 1 s, 1 d. Education: MD; Board Certified, Forensic Psychiatry. Appointment: Co-Director Law and Psychiatry Program, University of Pittsburgh School of Medicine. Publication: Co-author, Legal Issues in Mental Health Care, 1993. Memberships: American Academy of Psychiatry and The Law; American Psychiatric Association. Address: Western Psychiatric Institute and Clinic, 3811 O'Hara Street 1174, Pittsburgh, PA 15213, USA.

WHEATER Andrew William, b. 1 December 1956, Rochdale, Lancashire, England. Gynaecologist. m. Margaret Drinkwater, 25 October 1994, 1 son, 1 daughter. Education: BSc, St Andrews, 1978; MBBS, Newcastle, 1981; MRCOG, 1989; MSc Manchester, 1995. Appointments: Consultant, BPAS, Austy Manor, Solihull, England. Publications: Co-author: Obstetric Outcomes in West Cumbria - Is There A Risk From Sellafield?, 1989; Co-author: A Simple Test For Bleeding From Vasa Praevia Lancet, 1987. Memberships: British Medical Association; Royal College of Obstetricians and Gynaecologists. Hobbies: Skiing; Golf; Cooking. Address: Aldwych, 15 Milner Avenue, Bury, Lancashire BL9 6NG, England.

WHETSELL William Otto Jr, b. 25 Sept 1940, South Carolina, USA. Physician. m. Anne E Rodgers, 14 Oct 1967, 1 son, 1 daughter. Education: BS, Wofford College, 1962; MS, Medical University of South Carolina, 1964; MD, Medical College of South Carolina, 1966. Appointments: Assistant Professor, Neurology & Pathology, Mt Sinai, New York; Adjunct Assistant Professor, Rockefeller University; Associate Professor, Neurology & Pathology, Mt Sinai; Professor, Pathology, University of Tennessee; Professor, Pathology & Psychiatry, Vanderbilt University. Publications: Co-author: Quinolinic Acid produces axon-sparing lesions, 1983; Co-author: Prolonged Exposure to Quinolinic acid in vitro, 1989; Co-author: Extrastriatal Dopamine Receptors in Human Brain, 1993; Biology of Disease: Neuroexcitation, Excitotoxicity, Human Neurological Disease, 1993. Memberships: American Association of Neuropathologists; American Medical Association; Society for Neuroscience; College of American Pathologists. Honours: Fellow, College of American Pathologists, 1985; Phi Beta Kappa Alumni Citation, 1989; Distinguished Alumnus Award, MUSC, 1991. Hobbies: Gardening; Studying Operatic Music; Skiing. Address: Division of Neuropathology, Department of Pathology, Vanderbilt University School of Medicine, Nashville, TN 37215-2561, USA.

WHITAKER Linton Andin, b. 16 Nov 1936, Navasota, TX, USA. Plastic Surgeon. m. Renata Grasmanis, 20 Dec 1963, 1 son, 1 daughter. Education: BA; MD. Assistant Professor, Associate Professor, University of Pennsylvania School of Medicine; Professor of Plastic Surgery. Publications: 160 papers and 5 books including: Clinics in Plastic

Surgery, 1987; Aesthetic Surgery of the Facial Skeleton, 1991. Memberships: AAPS; ASA; ASPRS; ACS; ISCFS. Honours: James IV Surgical Traveler, 1979; Award, 1984; Honorary Member, Mt Kenya Safari Club, 1984; Honorary Fellow, American Society of Ophthalmic Plastic & Reconstructive Surgery, 1990; Honours of the League of Children's Hospital of Philadelphia for contributions to Children & Craniofacial Surgery. Hobbies: Mountaineering; Snow Skiing; Wines. Address: Hospital of the University of Pennsylvania, 10 Penn Tower, 3400 Spruce Street, PA 19104, USA.

WHITE Anthony Gilbert Browning (Tony), b. 5 Mar 1957, Perth, Australia. Psychologist. m. gaile Golding, 27 Feb 1987, 2 s. Education: BA, Honours; CTM, International Transaction Analysis Association. Appointments: Psychologist in Private Practice; Director, T A Training Institute. Publications: New Ways in Transactional Analysis, 1984; Transference Based Therapy: Theory and Practice, 1985; How Kids Grow Up and Leave Home, 1986; Creative Feeling: How to Understand and Deal with Your Child's Feelings, 1986; The Treatment of Character, 1987; Adolescence, Anger and What To Do: A Happy Teenager is not a Healthy Teenager, 1990; Employee Support Programme, 1991; Staying Alive: A Handbook on the No-Suicide Contract, 1991; Psychotherapy: And the Art of Being Human, 1993; Contributor of numerous articles in journals and magazines. Honours: Inaugural Goulding Award for Excellence in Transactional Analysis, 1988. Memberships: Australian Psychological Society; International Transactional Analysis Association. Address: 16 Claverton Street, North Perth, 6006 Western Australia, Australia.

WHITE Christopher Michael, b. 22 Aug 1947, Adelaide, South Australia, Australia. Psychoanalyst. m. Wendy Una Royans, 3 Apr 1971, 2 sons, 2 daughters. Education: MB, BS, University of Adelaide, 1971; Resident Medical Officer, Royal Adelaide Hospital, 1971; Psychiatric Registrar, Glenside and Royal Adelaide Hospitals and Child Guidance Clinic, 1972-75; MANZCP, 1975; Senior Registrar, Royal Adelaide Hospital, 1976; FRANZCP, 1980. Appointments include: Captain, 1973, Major, 1978, Lieutenant-Colonel, 1984-, currently Consultant Psychiatrist, 4th Military District, Royal Australian Army Medical Corps; Private Practice in Psychotherapy and Psychoanalysis, 1978; Supervisor, Lecturer, 1979-94, External Examiner, 1983-, Royal Australian and New Zealand College of Psychiatrists; Visiting Specialist, Senior Visiting Specialist, currently Senior Visiting Consultant, Royal Adelaide Hospital; Part-time Lecturer, South Australian Institute of Technology; Lecturer, Tabor College, 1992-; Currently Clinical Lecturer in Psychiatry, Adelaide University. Publications: Training Programs in Psychiatry, 1973; A Fragment from the Analysis of a Man with a Perversion, 1986; Discussion Paper on Psychoanalytic Training, 1988; Discussion Paper on Assessment of Control Cases, 1989; Oedipus is Complex - So is the Myth; Freud, Religion and Psychoanalysis. Honours: Prizes for Ophthalmology, Psychiatry, Gynaecology, Clinical Medicine, University of Adelaide, 1970. Memberships include: Australian Psychoanalytic Society; Founding Member, President, Psychotherapy Association of South Australia; Medical Defence Association of South Australia; Australian Medical Association; International Psychoanalytical Association. Address: 31 Cheltenham Street, Highgate, South Australia 5063, Australia.

WHITE Craig Allen, b. 23 Feb 1971, Irvine, Scotland. Clinical Psychologist. m. Gwen H McPhail, 9 July 1994. Education: BSc, Honours 1st class, University of Glasgow, 1988-92. Appointment: Clinical Psychologist. Honours: Dr Alaistair Weir Prize in Psychology, 1991, Henry J Watt Prize in Experimental Psychology, 1992, University of Glasgow. Memberships: Division Clinical psychology, British Psychological Society; British Association of Behavioural and Cognitive Psychotherapy. Hobbies: Swimming; Reading; Cooking; The Media. Address: Department Clinical psychology, School of Psychiatry and Behavioural Sciences, University Hospital of South Manchester, West Didsbury, Manchester M20 8LR, England.

WHITE Elissa Josefa Queyquep, b. 26 Aug 1933, Chicago, Illinois, USA. Dance and Movement Therapist. m. Robert Wickey White, 11 Oct 1968, 1 son. Education: BA, Human Development; Registered, Academy of Dance Therapists; Certified Movement Analyst; Certified Practitioner, Jin Shin Do Body-Mind Acupressure. Appointments: Dance Therapist and Coordinator, Dance Therapy Unit, Bronx Psychiatric Center, New York, 1967-77; Lecturer, Hunter College, City University of New York, 1971-; Coordinator, Dance Therapy Programme, Sound Shore County Mental Health Center, Harlem Valley Psychiatric Center, 1977-88; Senior Rehabilitation Counsellor, Dance Therapist, Creedmoor

Psychiatric Center, 1988-92. Publications: Introduction to Dance Therapy (with C Schmais), 1986; Movement Analysis: A Must for Dance Therapists, (with C Schmais) 1989. Honours: Annual Lecturer, Marian Chace Memorial Fund, 1993; Former Co-Editor, American Journal of Dance Therapy; Former Secretary and Treasurer, American Dance Therapy Association. Memberships: American Dance Therapy Association; Lims/Bartenieff Institute for Movement Studies; American Oriental Bodywork Therapy Association; Jin Shin Do Foundation. Hobbies: Music; Gardening; Dance. Address: 87-89 Columbia Street 16 J, New York, NY 10002, USA.

WHITE Robert Silliman, b. 28 Apr 1947, New Haven, Connecticut, USA. Psychiatrist. m. Charlotte Birchbill, June 1984. Education: BA, Haverford College, 1969; MD, University of Virginia School of Medicine, 1973. Appointments: Clinical Director, Altobello Psychitric Hospital for Adolescents; Director, Psychiatric Clinic, Hospital of St Raphaels; Assistant Clinical Professor of Psychiatry, Yale University. Publications: Transformations of Transferences, 1992. Memberships: American Psychiatric Association; American Psychoanalytic Association; Connecticut Medical Society.

WHITE Susanne, b. 13 Apr 1949, New Orleans, Louisiana, USA. Paediatrician; Associate Professor. m. James Carnell White, 10 Apr 1971, div. Mar 1992, 1 son, 2 daughters. Education: BS, Bennett College; MD, MPH, University of North Carolina at Chapel Hill; Board Certified. Appointments: Instructor, Assistant Professor, University of North Carolina/Wake Area Health Education Center; Director, Paediatric Emergency Room, then Division Chief of Ambulatory Services, currently Division Chief of Community Paediatrics and Adolescent Medicine, Louisiana State University, New Orleans. Publications: Am J Dis Child, 136:994, 1982; Pediatrics, 72:16-21, 1983; Ped Infect Dis J, 3(2):97-99, 1984, 5(2):266-229, 1986, 11(ii):945-950, 1992; Child Abuse and Neglect, 9:342-352, 1985, 13(2):217-224, 1989, 16(2):265-272, 1992, 16(2):847-853, 1992. Honours: Delta Omega. Memberships: American Association of Pediatricians; American Pediatric Association; American Medical Association. Hobbies: Singing; Bowling; Sewing. Address: 8140 Morrison Road, New Orleans, LA 70126, USA.

WHITEHEAD Paul Leon, b. 23 May 1936, Salt Lake City, Utah, USA. Physician. m. Marilyn Davis, 5 Sept 1964, 1 son, 3 daughters. Education: BS, University of Utah, 1957; MD, University of Utah School of Medicine, 1960; Residency in Psychiatry, 1963-65; Fellowship, Child and Adolescent Psychiatry, University of Cincinnati Medical Center, 1965-67; Diplomate, General Psychiatry, American Board of Psychiatry and Neurology; Additional Qualification in Child and Adolescent Psychiatry. Appointments: Director, Children's Psychiatric Center, and Chairman, Department of Child Psychiatry, Primary Children's Medical Center, 1967-81; Director, Division of Child and Adolescent Psychiatry, 1977-78, Clinical Professor of Psychiatry, 1978-, University of Utah School of Medicine; Medical Director, CPC Olympus View Hospital, 1986-88; Private practice in Child, Adolescent and Adult Psychiatry, Salt Lake City. Publications: Cooperation for Mental Health, 1972; Changes in Religious Doctrines and Practices, 1979; Co-author: Effect of Lithium Carbonate, Placebo and Thioridazine on Hyperactive Children, 1970; Religion as Ego Support, 1989; History of Child Psychiatry in Utah, 1989. Honours: Phi Beta Kappa, 1957; Admitted to membership, 1958, President, 1959-60, Alpha Omega Alpha; Norman S Anderson MD Award, 1989. Memberships: American Medical Association; Utah State Medical Association; Fellow, American Psychiatric Association; Fellow, American Academy of Child and Adolescent Psychiatry; Utah Psychiatric Association, President 1977-78. Hobbies: Organist; Gardening; Hiking. Address: 1580 East 3900 South, Salt Lake City, UT 84124, USA.

WHITELAW Robert George, b. 29 Apr 1913, Motherwell, Scotland. Consultant Gynaecologist. m. Cicely Mary Ballard, 14 Jun 1944, 1 s. Education: MA, Honours, English Language and Literature, MBChB, University of Glasgow; MRCOG, 1948; MD, Commend, 1956; FRCOG, 1963. Career: Consultant Obstetrician and Gynaecologist, West Fife Group of Hospitals, 1956-78; Clinical Teaching Staff, University of Edinburgh, 1976-78; Now retired. Publications: Ovarian Activity Following Hysterectomy, 1958; A New Operation for Reconstruction of Fallopian Tubes, 1971; Ten Year Survey of 485 Sterilisations, 1979; Pathology and The Conserved Ovary, 1985. Honours: Deputy Lieutenant, County of Fife, 1969-; Honorary Sheriff, County of Fife. Memberships: President, Fife Branch of British Medical Association, 1966; Council, Edinburgh Obstetrical and Gynaecological Society.

Hobbies: Photography; Golf; Travel. Address: 64 Garvock Hill, Dunfermline, Fife, KY12 7UU, Scotland.

WHITLOCK James Alan, b. 17 July 1958, Kingsport, TN, USA. Pediatric Educator. m. Deborah A Wrenn, 26 Apr 1986, 1 son. Education: BS, Southwestern at Memphis, 1980; MD, Vanderbilt University, 1984; Resident, Vanderbilt, 1984-87. Appointments: Assistant Professor of Pediatrics. Publications: Inherited hypercoagulable states in children, 1989; Epipodophyllotoxin-related secondary leukemia: Identification of a new subset of secondary leukemias, 1991; Acute lymphocytic leukemia with variant t(5;14) preleukemia: Expanding the spectrum of the 5q-abnormality?, 1992; Childhood acute lymphocytic leukemia with a preleukemic phase: Report of an associated translocation and review of the literature, 1993; t(5;14) (q33-34;q11): A new recurring cytogenetic abnormality in childhood acute leukemia, 1994. Honours: Phi Beta Kappa, 1980. Memberships: American Society of Hematology; American Society of Pediatric Hematology/Oncology; American Association for Cancer Research; Children's Cancer Group; Histiocyte Society. Address: T-3320 Medical Center North, Nashville, TN 37232, USA.

WHITMER Gilbert G, b. Pittsburgh, Pennsylvania, USA. Orthopaedic Surgeon. m. Julie, 3 s. Education: BSc, Johns Hopkins University; MD, Johns Hopkins School of Medicine; Orthopaedic Training, University of South Carolina, Columbia. Appointments: Private Orthopaedic Practice, Rocky Mount, North Carolina, 1993-. Publications: Contributor of articles to international medical journals. Honours: Phi Beta Kappa; Award for Excellence in Research, Johns Hopkins School of Medicine; National defence Service Medal. Hobbies: Reading; Writing; Weightlifting; Jogging; Skiing; Racquet Sports. Address: 813 Joshua Clay Drive, Rocky Mount, NC 27803, USA.

WHITTAKER Paul, b. 1 Oct 1943, Spokane, Washington, USA. Food and Drug Administrator. Education: BA, Whitworth College, 1965; MA, Western Michigan University, 1967; PhD, Utah State University, 1983. Appointments: University of Kansas Medical Center, 1984-86; Supervisory Research Chemist, Food and Drug Administration, 1986-. Publications: Co-author: Iron fortification of infant cereals: a proposal for the use of ferrous fumarate or ferrous succinate, 1989; Comparison of in vitro, animal and clinical determinations of iron bioavailability: International Nutritional Anemia Consultative Group Task force report on iron bioavailability, 1989; Duodenal iron proteins in idiopathic hemochromatosis, 1989; Study of iron bioavailability in a cereal for young children produced from native Nigerian grain amaranth, 1990; Effect of EDTA on the bioavailability of fortification iron used in Egyptian balady bread, 1990; Calcium supplementation: effect on iron absorption, 1991; Prolonged acetaminophen ingestion by mice fed a methionine-limited diet does not affect iron-induced liver lipid peroxidation or S-adenosylmethionine, 1992; Effect of chronic iron overload on iron status, lipid peroxidation, cell proliferation, and DNA damage, 1992; Toxicological profile, current use and regulatory issues of EDTA compounds for assessing potential use of sodium iron EDTA for food fortification, 1993; Acute asthma drug enhancement of myocardial lesions in rats, 1994. Honours: Phi Kappa Phi, 1983. Memberships: American Society of Clinical Nutrition; American Institute of Nutrition; American Association for Cancer Research; Society of the Sigma Xi. Hobbies: Running; Biking; Camping. Address: Food and Drug Administration, 8301 Muirkirk Road, Laurel, MD 20708, USA.

WHITTAKER Robert Charles Miller, b. 25 Apr 1947, Portmadoc, North Wales. Physician. m. Annette Marie Lumbleau, 27 Jan 1990, 1 son. Education: MB BChm Wales, 1972; DCH, London; MRCOG(London), 1985. Appointments: Registrar, Obstetrics, Northwick Park Hospital, Harrow, Middlesex; Senior Medical Officer, Nigerian Christian Hospital, Nigeria. Hobbies: Golf; Watercolour painting. Address: Nigerian Christian Hospital, Box 823, Aba, Abia State, Nigeria.

WIBELL Lars Bertil, b. 3 Feb 1937, Sweden. Physician. Education: MD, 1970; Dissertation, 1974. Appointments: Assistant Professor, Lecturer in Internal Medicine, Uppsala University. Publications Include: Autologous transfusions in uraemic patients, 1970; The use of a calcium infusion test in the diagnosis of hyperparathyroidism, 1972; Gamma-camera scintigraphy after kidney transplant, 1973; Side effets of benoxaprofen, 1982; Chronic pulsatile low dose GnRH therapy for induction of testosterone production and spermatogenesis in a man with secondary hypogonadotropic hypogonadism, 1982; The effect of Fish Oil on Triglycerides, Cholesterol, Fibrinogen and Malondialdehyde in Humans Supplemented with Vitamin E, 1991; Mortality of all incident cases of diabetes mellitus in Sweden, 1992; Prevalences of risk factors and angiopathy in diabetic patients in Uppsala, 1992. Memberships: Swedish Society of Medicine; European Association for the Study of Diabetes; Swedish Medical Society for Endocrinology & Nephrology. Hobbies: Literature; Chess. Address: Statarvagen 24, 75245 Uppsala, Sweden.

WICK Paul H, b. 2 Aug 1936, Victoria, Texas, USA. Psychiatrist. m. D'Anna Poole, 19 June 1960, 2 sons, 1 daughter. Education: BA, University of Texas, Austin; MD, Residency in Psychiatry, University of Texas Medical Branch, Galveston; Board Certified in Psychiatry, 1970, added qualifications in Geriatric Psychiatry, 1992, American Board of Psychiatry and Neurology. Appointments: Captain, US Air Force Medical Branch, 1962-64; Currently: Psychiatrist in private practice; Medical Director, University Park Hospital, Tyler, Texas. Honours: Fellow, American Psychiatric Association, 1976. Memberships: American Psychiatric Association, Fellow, Assembly Representative; Texas Society of Psychiatric Physicians, Past President; American Association of Psychiatry and Law; Association for Geriatric Psychiatry; Central Neuropsychiatric Association. Hobby: Travel. Address: Tyler Psychiatry Clinic, 3300 S Broadway, Tyler, TX 75701, USA.

WICKHAM Newton Ernest, b. 14 May 1917, Stratford, New Zealand. Periodontist. m. Keitha Maud Adelaide Kenrick, 27 Mar 1948, 2d. Education: BDS, University of Otago Dental School, 1939; DDS University of Toronto Dental School, 1946. Appointments include: New Zealand Dental Corps, Military Service, World War II, 1939-45; Post War Territorial Army, 14 Years; Private Practice, Auckland, 1947-49; Periodontics and Preventive Dentistry, Auckland, 1949-76; Lecturer in many countries including: New Zealand, USA, United Kingdom, Japan, Thailand, Singapore, and Australia. Contributor of numerous articles in national and international professional journals including: Care of Gums; Be a Non-Smoker. Honours: Honoured by HM Queen Elizabeth II, CBE 1993. Memberships include: NZDA; Dental Health Council of NZDA; NZ Society of Periodontology; NZ Society of Anaesthesia in Dentistry; NZ Society of Endodontics; NZ Society of Prosthdontics. Address: 1 Wootton Road, Remuera, Auckland, New Zealand.

WIDDOWSON Elsie May, b. 21 Oct 1906. Medical Researcher. Education includes: DSc, London. Appointments include: Assistant Director, Department of Experimental Medicine, Cambridge; Head, Medical Research Council's Infant Nutrition Research Division, Cambridge; Now retired. Publications: Composition of Foods, 1940, 5th edition (as McCance and Widdowson's Composition of Foods), 1991; More than 300 papers in scientific journals on aspects of preseral metabolism, infant physiology, undernutrition, growth and development, body composition. Honours: James Spence Medal, British Paediatric Association, 1981; 2nd British Myers Award for Distinguished Achievement in Nutrition Research, 1982; 1st European Nutrition Award, 1983; Prize for Nutrition, Rank Prize Funds, 1984; 1st Nutricia Award, 1988; Companion of Honour; Commander, Order of the British Empire; Fellow, Royal Society; DSc (Hon), Manchester, Salford. Memberships: Nutrition Society, President 1977-80; Neonatal Society, President 1978-81; British Nutrition Foundation, President 1986-; Honorary Fellow, Royal College of Physicians, 1994. Hobbies: Gardening; Apple growing. Address: Orchard House, 9 Boot Lane, Barrington, Cambridge CB2 5RA, England.

WIGGINS Roger Charles, b. 26 May 1945, Tetbury, Gloucestershire, England. Physician. m. Jocelyn Kent Wiggins, 2 sons. Education: BA, 1968, BChir, 1971, MB, 1972, MA, 1972, Cambridge University. Appointments include: Registrar, 1974-75, Research Registrar, 1975-76, The Middlesex Hospital Medical School, London; Postdoctoral Fellow, 1976-78, Research Associate, 1978-79, Assistant Member 1, 1979-81, Department of Immunopathology, Scripps Clinic and Research Foundation, La Jolla, California, USA; Assistant Professor, 1981-84, Associate Professor, 1984-90, Chief, 1988-, Professor, 1990-, Division of Nephrology, Department of Internal Medicine, University of Michigan at Ann Arbor. Publications: Contributor of numerous peer reviewed articles, book chapters and monographs; Invited Lecturer at numerous conferences and symposia worldwide. Honours include: First Broderip Scholarship, 1971; Berkeley Fellowship, Gonville and Caius College, Cambridge and Middlesex Hospital Medical School, 1976; Established Investigator, American Heart Association, 1984; Internal Medicine Residents Award for Excellence in Teaching, 1992; Recipient of numerous grants. Memberships include: American Society of Nephrology; Central Society of the American Federation for Clinical Research; American Federation for Clinical Research; American Society of Clinical Investigation; Association of American Physicians; Fellow, Royal College of Physicians, United Kingdom. Address: Department Medicine, Division Nephrology, University of Michigan, Ann Arbor, MI 48109, USA.

WIJESUNDERE Ajita Pinkumara Desilva, b. 21 Aug 1948, Colombo, Sri Lanka. Obstetrician; Gynaecologist. m. Dr Anula Wijesundere, 6 May 1976, 1 s, 2 d. Education: MBBS, Sri Lanka, 1975; MS, Obstetrics and Gynaecology, Sri Lanka, 1983; Diploma, International Maternal Health Care, Uppsala University, Sweden, 1992; FRCOG, United Kingdom, 1994. Appointments: Consultant Obstetrician and Gynaecologist: Base Hospital, Polonnaruna, Sri Lanka, 1985-89; Base Hospital, Kulmapitiya, Sri Lanka, 1990; Base Hospital, Wathupitiwela, Sri Lanka, 1991-92; Currently, Base Hospital, Gampaha, Sri Lanka. Publications: Contributor to Books: Medical Complications of Pregnancy, 1992; The Challenge Beyond the Year 2000, 1992; Malaria in Pregnancy, 1992; Malaria and It's Prevention, 1994. Honour: Outstanding Young Gynaecologist, FIGO, 1991. Memberships: Fellow, The Royal College of Obstetricians and Gynaecologists; Council Member, Sri Lanka College of Obstetricians and Gynaecologists; Life Member, Sri Lanka Medical Association. Hobbies: Swimming; Jogging. Address: 147 Model Farm Road, Colombo 8, Sri Lanka.

WIKLUND Knut Lars Carl, b. 10 Oct 1943, Uppsala, Sweden. Anaesthetist. m. Ulla Birgitta Wiklund, 19 Apr 1969, 1 son, 1 daughter. Education: MD; PhD; FRCA. Appointments: Anaesthesiologist, Assistant Professor, 1976-77; Associate Professor, Head, Neuroanaesthesia, 1977-86; Professor and Chairman, Department of Anaesthesiology, Uppsala University Hospital, 1987- Publications: 80 major original scientific articles in professional journals. Honours: The Laerdal Honorary Prize in Acute Medicine, Oslo University, 1991. Memberships: Swedish Society for Anaesthesia & Intensive Care; American Society of Anaesthesiologists; Critical Care Society; European Academy of Anaesthesiology. Hobbies: Sailing; Skiing. Address: Sveavagen 2, S 75236 Uppsala, Sweden.

WIKSTROM Sakari, b. 26 Apr 1943, Helsinki, Finland. Medical Doctor. 1 son, 1 daughter. Education: MD, University of Helsinki, 1970; PhD, University of Helsinki, 1981. Appointments: Consultant in Paediatric Surgery & Urology, Children's Hospital, University of Helsinki. Publications: Co-author: Renal Transplantation in children with congenital mephrotic syndrome of the finnish type, 1990; Co-author: Localized amuloidosis of the urinary bladder, 1991; Co-author: Percutaneaus needle biopsy preceding preoperative chemotherapy in the management of renal tumors in children, 1991; Co-author: Late urologic sequelae after surgery for congenital sacrococlygeal teratoma, 1992. Memberships: Nordic Association of Urology; Nordic Association of Paediatric Surgery; Nordic Association of Paediatric Haematology & Oncology; European Association of Paediatric Urology. Hobbies: Sailing; Wandering in the Wilderness. Address: Children's Hospital, University of Helsinki, Stenbackinkatu 11, 00290 Helsinki, Finalnd.

WILBUSH Joel, b. 27 Sep 1918, Heathera, Canada. Academic; Retired. m. Margaret Cox, 23 Jul 1945, 1 d. Education: MBChB, Sheffield, 1943, DObstRCOG, 1948; MRCOG(London); 1950; Diploma, Ethnology, Honours, Oxford, 1972; DPhil, Oxford, 1980; FRCOG, 1984. Career includes: War Service, Captain, RAMC, 1943-47; Registrar, Lincoln, 1950-51; Obstetrician and Gynaecologist in Private Practice, 1951-60; Obstetrician and Gynaecologist in Nigeria, Israel, Arctic Canada, Zambia among others, 1961-71; General and Specialist Practice, Alberta, 1971-79; Part Time Relief Medical Practice, Academic, 1979-91; Currently, Adjunct Professor of Anthropology, University of Alberta, Edmonton. Publications include: Series of papers on history of the menopausal syndrome, 1980-93; Papers on social aspects of the climacteric, 1981, 1982, 1985; Major papers on menonliagia and menopause maturitas, and research trends in these studies, diagnostic process, bioethics, environment and anthropology. Honour: Gold Medal in Psychiatry, Sheffield, 1943. Memberships: Fellow, Royal Society of Medicine, London; Founding Member, International Menopause Society; Life Member, College of Family Physicians of Canada. Hobbies: Travel; Biology; Bird Watching. Address: 11027 87th Avenue 203, Edmonton, Alberta, Canada, T6G 2P9.

WILDER Walter Llewellyn, b. 23 May 1926, Ann Arbor, MI, USA. Medicine. m. Rosemary Ruzicka, 24 May 1952, 3 s, 1 d. Education: MD. Career includes: Currently in private practice. Honour: President's Award, MMA, 1988. Memberships: AMA; MMA; AAP; ACAI; AAEM;

AAPS. Hobbies: Lake Cabin; Fishing; Travel; Reading; Sport. Address: 6525 Drew Avenue South, Edina, MN 55435, USA.

WILDING John Martin, b. 1 Sept 1936, Newbury, Berkshire, England. University Lecturer. 3 sons. Education: St John's College, Oxford, 1958-64; MA (Oxon); University College, London, 1964-70; PhD (London). Appointments: Assistant Lecturer in Psychology, 1964-66, Lecturer in Phychology, 1966-84, Reader in Psychology, 1985, Bedford College, University of London; Currently Reader in Psychology, Royal Holloway and Bedford New College, University of London. Publications: Perception: from sense to object, 1983; Superior memory ability, in Memory: neurochemical and abnormal perspectives, 1992; Papers in British Journal of Psychology, British Journal of Developmental Psychology, Applied Cognitive Psychology, others. Memberships: British Psychological Society; Experimental Psychology Society; European Society for Cognitive Psychology; Society for Applied Research in Memory and Cognition. Hobbies: Gardening; Cricket. Address: Department of Psychology, Royal Holloway and Bedford New College, University of London, Egham Hall Egham, Surrey TW20 0EX, England.

WILHELMSEN Lars Wilhelm, b. 31 Dec 1932, Kristianstad, Sweden. Professor. m. Kerstin W, 17 May 1986, 2 daughters. Education: MD. Appointments: Registrar, Consultant, Head, Department of Medicine, Sahlgrenska Hospital, Goteborg, -1978; Physician-in-Chief, Department of Medicine, Östra Hospital, Gothenburg. Publications: Lung Mechanics in Mitral Valvular Disease, 1968; Recurrent Pulmonary Embolism, 1963; Epidemology of Coronary Heart Disease, 1994-95. Honour: Lars Werkös Award, 1994. Memberships: International Society of Cardiology; International Society of Hypertension. Hobbies: Music; Tennis. Address: Department of Medicine, Östra University Hospital, S-41685 Gothenbörg, Sweden.

WILKINS Alan Keith, b. 20 Nov 1956, Usk, Wales. Psychologist. m. Frances Gurdler, 1 Aug 1981, 1 son. Education: BEd, Honours, London University; MEd, MSc, University of Wales; CPsychol. Appointment: Area Educational Psychologist. Brecon, Powys. Memberships: Association of Educational Psychologists; British Psychological Society. Hobbies: Sailing; Walking; Reading; Painting. Address: Kohinur, Harpers Road, Garndiffaith, Pontypool, Gwent NP4 8QO, Wales.

WILKINSON Michael Ian, b. 20 Sept 1953, Darlington, England. Clinical Psychologist. m. Vivien Grace, 7 July 1979, 1 son, 1 daughter. Education: BA (Nottingham); MPhil (Edinburgh); PhD (Leeds); Chartered Psychologist; Associate Fellow, British Psychological Society. Appointments: Clinical Psychologist, Child Speciality, Darlington, 1980-; Currently Academic Tutor, Newcastle University and Consultant Psychologist. Publications include: Family assessment: a basic manual for practitioners, book, 1993; Cognitive style in depressed and recovered depressed patients (with Blackburn), 1981; Family assessment: a review, 1987; The reliability and validity of a system for family assessment (with Stratton), 1991. Honours: Darlington Research Prize, 1987; Sir William Lee Research Prize, 1989. Memberships: DCP (British Psychological Society); AFT; ACPP. Hobbies: Creative writing; Cycling; Soccer; Food. Address: Ridley Building, Claremont Place, Newcastle-upon-Tyne NE1 7RU.

WILKINSON Sherri Ann, b. 4 Oct 1955, San Antonio, Texas, USA. Wellness Teacher. m. Ricky D Wilkinson, 11 Jan 1980, 2 sons,. Education: AA, 1974, BS, 1976, Freed-Hardeman College; MS, Memphis State University, 1978. Appointments: Teacher, Chester County Junior High, 1976; Teacher, Health, Physical Education, St Agnes Academy, 1979; Scrub Nurse, Memphis Eye and Ear Hospital, Memphis, Tennessee, 1981; Scrub Nurse, Magnolia Hospital, 1982; Biology Teacher, Perquimans High School, 1985; Teacher, Health, Physical Education, Corsicana High School, 1987; Teacher, Health, Physical Education, Collins Middle School, 1990; Wellness Teacher, Bowie Elementary School, 1994. Honours: Honour Graduate, 1974, 1976; Outstanding Graduate, Department of Health, Physical Education and Recreation, 1976; Recipient, Excell Grant, 1994. Memberships: Association of Texas Professional Educators; Texas Association of Health, Physical Education and Dance; American Alliance for Health, Physical Education, Recreation and Dance. Hobbies: Running; Guitar; Riding. Address: 3000 FM 2452, Corsicana, TX 75110, USA.

WILLIAMS Christopher, b. 7 Nov 1943, Wolverhampton, England. Clinical Psychologist. m. Philippa Warin, 28 July 1984, 2 sons, 2 daughters. Education: BSc (Hons), University of Manchester, 1967; MSc, 1969, PhD, 1975, University of Birmingham; FBPsS; Chartered

Psychologist. Appointments: Currently Director of Psychology Services, National Health Service Community Trust, Exeter. Publications: Autism (co-author), 1971; Language development, 1973; Behaviour Modification, 1974; Hearing loss, 1976; Community Living, 1979; Deafness and mental handicap, 1982; Social Training Record, 1985; Head Injury, 1990; Sexuality and disability, 1993; Post-traumatic strees, 1994. Memberships: British Psychological Society; British Neuropsychological Society; British Association of Behavioural Psychotherapy. Hobbies: Sailing; Bridge; Skiing; Music. Address: The Old Vicarage, Holman Way, Topsham, Exeter, Devon, England.

WILLIAMS George Wynns, b. 31 Oct 1946, Nashville, TN, USA. Biostatistics. m. Wanda L Mead, 1 s, 2 d. Education: BS, Bucknell University, 1968; MA, George Washington University, 1970; PhD, University of NC, 1972. Career: Assistant Professor, Associate Professor, Professor, University of MI, 1972-81; Chairman, Department of Biostatistics and Epidemiology, Cleveland Clinic, 1980-91; Currently, Executive Director, Biostatistics and Research Information Management, Merck Research Laboratories. Publications: In peer-reviewed medical and statistical literature. Honours: Pi Mu Epsilon, 1967; Phi Beta Kappa, 1968; Sigma Xi, 1978. Memberships: American Statistics Association; Biometric Society; Society for Epidemiologic Research; American Association for Advancement of Science; American Heart Association; Council on Epidemiology. Address: Merck Research Laboratories, West Point, PA 19486, USA.

WILLIAMS (John) Mark Gruffydd, b. 23 July 1952, Hawarden, Wales. Clinical psychologist. m. Phyllis Patricia Simpson, 6 Oct 1973, 1 s, 2 d. Education: MA, 1970-73, MSc, 1973-76, DPhil, 1976-79, St Peter's College, Oxford; CPsychol; FBPsS. Appointments: Lecturer in Applied Psychology, University of Newcastle upon Tyne, 1979; Research Scientist, Medical Research Council, Applied Psychology Unit, Cambridge, 1982; Professor of Clinical Psychology, University of Wales, Bangor. Publications: Author of several books including: Psychological Treatment of Depression, 1984, 2nd edition, 1992; Cognitive Psychology and Emotional Disorders, 1988; Cognitive Therapy in Clinical Practice, 1988; Contributor of numerous learned articles in professional journals. Honours: BPS Mary Davidson Award, 1986; Mental Health Foundation Award, 1994. Memberships: British Psychologicol Society; Society for Psychotherapy Research; International Association of Suicide Prevention. Hobbies: Music; Family; Psychology of Religion. Address: Department of Psychology, University of Wales, Bangor, Gwynedd LL57 2DG, Wales.

WILLIAMS Paul V, b. 10 Aug 1949, USA. Physician. Education: BS, Biology, Seattle University, 1971; MD, 1975, Fellow in Allergy and Immunology, Department of Paediatrics, 1988-91, University of Washington School of Medicine, Seattle; Resident, 1975-77, Chief Resident, 1977-78, Paediatrics, Strong Memorial Hospital, Rochester, New York; Bd Cert: Paediatrics, 1981; Allergy, Immunology, 1991. Appointments: Instructor, University of Rochester School of Medicine, 1977-78; Paediatrician, Skagit Valley Medical Center, Mt Vernon, Washington, 1978-91; Clinical Assistant Professor, Department of Paediatrics, 1983-88, Clinical Associate Professor, Department of Paediatrics, 1988-, Clinical Professor, 1994-, Clinical Associate Professor, Department of Environmental Health, 1993-, Education Coordinator, Chief, Resident Education, 1993-, University of Washington School of Medicine, Seattle; Allergist, Northwest Asthma and Allergy Center PS, Seattle and Mount Vernon, 1991-. Publications: Book chapters, co-author: Bronchial Hyperreactivity in Childhood, 1990; Asthma in Children, 1996; Inhalation bronchoprovocation in children; Non-allergic environmental factors; Pulmonology-Allergy Drugs; Articles; Abstracts. Memberships: President, Vice-President, Secretary, Skagit-Island Counties Medical Society; Puget Sound Pediatric Society; Puget Sound Allergy Society; North Pacific Pediatric Society; Washington State Medical Association; Washington State Society of Allergy; Washington State Society of Pediatrics, Committee Chairman; American Medical Association; American College of Allergy and Immunology; American Academy of Pediatrics; American Academy of Allergy and Immunology. Address: Northwest Asthma and Allergy Center, 120 North 17th, Mount Vernon, WA 98273, USA.

WILLIAMS Stephen, b. 31 Aug 1944, Bristol, England. Specialist Orthodontist. m. Kirsten Williams, 22 Nov 1969, div., 1 daughter. Education: BDS; DDS; Diploma in Orthodontics (DEN). Appointments: Associate Professor, University of Århus, Denmark; Currently Private Practitioner, Horsens; Guest Lecturer, Vienna. Publications: Over 25 publications on orthodontics, diagnosis and evaluation of patients,

therapy - adult orthodontics and biomechanics. Membership: Former Vice-President, Danish Society of Orthodontic Specialists. Hobby: Music; Opera; Travel; European history. Address: Borgergade 3, 8700 Horsens, Denmark.

WILLIAMS Stephen Meredith, b. 2 Feb 1950, London, England. Psychologist. m. Brigitte Strater, 4 July 1980, 1 s, 1 d. Education: BA, Honours, Trinity College, Cambridge, 1972; DPhil, Sussex; MA. Appointments: Research Consultant, Open University, 1978-79; Lecturer in Psychology, University of Ulster at Coleraine, 1979-90; Lecturer in Psychology, North Essex Institute for Health Studies, 1990-94; Chartered Psychologist. Publications: Psychology on the Coach, 1988; Environment and Mental Health, 1994; Contributor of over 40 articles in professional journals. Honours: Entrance Scholar, Senior Scholar, Trinity College, Cambridge. Memberships: AFBPS; European Society for the Study of Cognitive Systems; Society of Authors. Hobbies: Chess; Numerical Computing; Social Democratic Politics. Address: 66 Mile End Road, Colchester, Essex CO4 5BY, England.

WILLIAMS Timothy Ivor, b. 15 June 1955, Oxford, England. Clinical Psychologist. m. Dr V N Healy, 11 June 1986, 1 s, 2 d. Education: MA, Cambridge; MSc, DPhil, Oxford; Associate Fellow, British Psychological Society; Chartered Clinical Psychologist. Appointments: Research Psychologist, EEG Department, Park Hospital, Oxford, 1978-79; Clinical Psychologist, Smith Hospital, Henley, 1979-84; Honorary Research Tutor, Oxford Regional Health Authority, 1985-90; Honorary Research fellow, Department of Psychology, University of Reading, 1988-; Consultant Psychologist, WBPCS NHS Trust. Publications include: Mental Disorder and The Law, Co-editor, 1983; A Social Skills Group for Autistic Children, 1989; Language Acquisition in Autistic Children, 1990; Vocabulary Development in an Autistic Boy, 1993; A Comparison of the Social Behaviour of Autistic and Down's Syndrome Children with Their Siblings, Co-author, 1995; Intrusive Thoughts in a Non-Clinical Adolescent Population, Co-author, 1995. Honours: honorary Research Fellow, University of Reading,, 1987; ESF Scholarship, 1990. Membership: British Psychological Society. Hobbies: Model Engineering; Ornithology; Music; Swimming. Address: CHASAC Team, Wokingham Hospital, Barkham Road, Wokingham, RG41 4RE, England.

WILLIAMS William Joseph, b. 8 Dec 1926, Bridgton, New Jersey, USA. Physician; Educator. m. Karen A Hughes, 18 Feb 1989, 1 son, 3 daughters. Education: Bucknell University, 1943-45; MD, 1949, Intern, 1949-50, Resident, 1954-55, University of Pennsylvania; American Cancer Society Research Fellow, Biochemistry, 1950-52. Appointments: Senior Instructor, Microbiology, Case Western Reserve University, 1952; Associate Assistant Professor, Medicine, 1955-58, Associate Professor, Professor, Medicine, Chief, Haematology, 1961-69, University of Pennsylvania; Assistant Professor, Medicine, Washington University, St Louis, 1959-60; Research Fellow, Oxford University, England, 1960-61; Research Career Development, National Heart and Lung Institute, National Institutes of Health, 1963-68; Professor, Medicine, 1969-, Chairman, Medicine, 1969-92, Interim Dean, College of Medicine, 1991-92, State University of New York Health Science Center, Syracuse. Publications: Hematology (editor-in-chief), 2nd, 3rd, 4th editions, 1972, 1983, 1989; Many articles in medical literature. Honours: Deland Fellow for Research, American Philosophical Society, 1955-57; Markle Scholar, 1957-62; Research Career Development Award, National Institutes of Health, 1963-68. Memberships: National Arthritis, Metabolism and Digestive Disorders Advisory Council 1975-79; Thrombosis Advisory Committee, National Heart and Lung Institute, 1969-73; RRC-ACGME, Vice-Chair 1983-89; Board of Appeals 1989-; Association of American Physicians; American Society of Clinical Investigation; American Society of Biochemistry and Molecular Biology; American Society of Hematology; Interurban Clinical Club. Address: Department of Medicine, SUNY Health Science Center at Syracuse, 750 E Adams Street, Syracuse, NY 13210. USA.

WILSON Clare Eleanor, b. 3 Aug 1947, Leeds, England. Clinical Psychologist. m. Neil Murray Drew, 6 Dec 1987, 2 d. Education: BSc, 1st Class Honours, The City University, London, 1970; MSc, University of Birmingham, 1972. Appointments: Lecturer in Psychology, Middlesex Hospital Medical School, 1972; psychologist, Government of Seychelles, 1973-76; Senior Clinical Psychologist, St Brendan's Hospital, Bermuda, 1976-77; Senior Clinical Psychologist, Isle of Wight, England, 1978-80; Head of Counselling Centre, James Cook University of North Queensland, Australia, 1980-89; Head of College, St Catherines College, University of Western Australia, 1989-94; Therapy Team Manager, Cambridge Hospital, Western Australia. Memberships:

Associate Fellow, British Psychological Society; Australian Psychological Society; Member, College of Clinical Psychologists; Member, College of Counselling Psychologists. Hobbies: Music; Theatre; Travel; Outdoors. Address: 36 Robinson Street, Nedlands, WA 6009, Australia.

WILSON Frederick Allen, b. 22 Aug 1937, Winchester, Massachusetts, USA. Physician. m. Lynne Cantley, 24 Feb 1962, 1 son, 1 daughter. Education: BA, Colgate University, 1959; MD, Albany Medical College, Union University, 1963, Intern, Resident, Hartford Hospital, Connecticut, 1963-66; Gastroenterology Fellow: Albany Medical College, New York, 1966-67, University of Texas Southwestern Medical School, Dallas, 1969-72. Appointments: Major, US Army Medical Corps, 1967-69; Assistant Professor, Associate Professor of Medicine, Vanderbilt University School of Medicine, Nashville, Tennessee, 1982-90; Professor of Medicine, Pennsylvania State University School of Medicine, Hershey, 1990; Currently Professor of Medicine, Medical University of South Caroline, Charleston. Publications: Co-author: Unstirred water layers in intestine: rate determinant of bile acid absorption from micellar solutions, 1971; Sodium-coupled taurocholate transport in proximal convolution of rat kidney, 1981; Identification of cytosolic and microsomal bile acid binding proteins in rat ileal enterocytes, 1990; Molecular cloning of 14kDa bile acid binding protein. Honours: Clinical Investigator, Veterans Administration, 1972-75; Investigator, Howard Hughes Medical Institute, 1975-78; Senior International Fellowship, NIH Fogarty International Center, 1979-80. Memberships: American Federation for Clinical Research; Central Society for Clinical Research; American Gastroenterological Association; American Association for the Study of Liver Disease; American Society for Clinical Investigation; South Carolina Medical Association. Hobbies: Fishing; Gardening. Address: 916 Clinical Science Building, The Medical University of South Carolina, 171 Ashley Avenue, Charleston, SC 29425, USA.

WILSON Glenn Daniel, b. 29 Dec 1942, Christchurch, New Zealand. Psychologist. m. Judith Ann Holden, 24 Feb 1967, 2 daughters. Education: MA (Hons); PhD; Chartered Psychologist; FRPsS. Appointments: Visiting Professor, California State University, Los Angeles, USA; Visiting Professor, Stanford University, California; Adjunct Professor, University of Nevada, Reno; Currently Reader in Personality, Institute of Psychiatry, University of London, England. Publications: Love and Instinct, 1981; The Great Sex Divide, 1989; Psychology for Performing Artists, 1994. Memberships: British Psychological Society; International Society for Study of Individual Differences. Hobbies: Tennis; Golf; Opera singing. Address: 24 Dorchester Drive, London SE24 0DQ, England.

WILSON Michael, b. 26 Jan 1953, Brooklyn, New York, USA. Podiatric Medicine. m. 13 July 1978, 3 daughters. Education: BS, Delaware University; MS, Tuskegee Institute; DPM, New York College of Podiatric Medicine; Fellow, American Society of Podiatric Dermatology. Appointments: Assistant Professor, South Carolina University; Staff Podiatrist, Regional Medical Center, Orangeburg; Baker Hospital, Charleston. Publications: Pompholyx (Dyshidrosis), 1985; Two Foot One Hand Disease, 1988; Charcot Foot Osteoarthropathy in Diabetes Mellitus, 1991. Honours: South Carolina Podiatrist of the Year, 1992; Beta Kappa Chi National Honour Scoeity; Citation, South Carolina State House of Representatives, 1994. Memberships: Association of Military Surgeons of the US; American Association of Podiatric Physicians & Surgeons; American Diabetes Association; American Podiatric Medical Association; Alpha Phi Alpha. Hobbies: Long Distance Running; Political Action. Address: 2180 Pineridge Drive NE, Orangeburg, SC 29115, USA.

WILSON Michael David, b. 5 Aug 1959, Wimbledon, England. Psychologist. m. Fiona Gunn, 26 Feb 1994. Education: BSc, Sussex University, 1980; PhD, Cambridge University, 1984; AFBPsS; CPsychol. Appointments: Research Student, MRC Applied Psychology, Cambridge, 1980-83; Research Scientist, MRC APU, Cambridge, 1983-86; Research Associate, Rutherford Appleton Laboratory. 1986-91; Principal Research Fellow, SERC, 1991-92; Senior Scientific Officer, Central Laboratory of the Research Councils. Wealth, Healthcare and the State, 1984; The MRC Psychological Database: Machine Readable Dictionary, Volume 2, Behaviour Research Methods, 1987; Contributor of over 50 works. Memberships: British Psychological Society; Association of Computational Machinery. Hobbies: Cinema; Bridge. Address: Computing and Information Systems Department, Rutherford Appleton Laboratory, Chilton, Didcot, Oxfordshire OX11 0QX, England.

WILSON Ronald Gene, b. 23 Jan 1941, Hemet, California, USA. Physician. Education: BA, University of Colorado, 1962; MD, George Washington University, 1966; DTMH, Mahidol University, Bangkok, Thailand, 1971; MPH, University of Hawaii, 1972; Diplomate, American Board of Preventive Medicine; Appointments: Staff Physician, USPHS US Peace Corps, Thailand, 1967-69; Staff Physician, US State Department, 1969-71; Associate Director, MEDEX/Micronesia Programme, Hawaii and Micronesia, 1972-74; Project Manager, Lampang Health Development Project Ministry Public Health, Thailand, 1974-81; Health Programme Officer, 1981-85, Director, Health Programmes, 1985-, Aga Khan Foundation, Geneva, Switzerland. Publications: Lampang Health Development Project Series, 7 volumes, Editor, 1981; Planning and Managing Primary Health Care Programs, 1984; Primary Health Care Technologies, 1986; Management Information Systems and Microcomputers in Primary Health Care, 1988; Primary Health Care Management Advancement Program Series, 22 volumes, 1993 Contributor of chapters in books. Honours: Most Honourable Order of the Crown of Thailand, His Majesty Bhumibol Adulyadej, 1978. Memberships: American College Preventive Medicine; American Society Tropical Medicine and Hygiene. Hobbies: Skiing; Scuba Diving; Birdwatching. Address: The Aga Khan Foundation, PO Box 6179, 7 rue Versonnex, 1211 Geneva 6, Switzerland.

WINER Colin John, b. 23 Feb 1938, Clacton-on-Sea, England. President of British Naturopathic and Osteopathic Association. m. Jill Patricia Osborn, 27 Aug 1964, 2 s, 1 d. Education: ND, DO, British College of Naturopathy and Osteopathy, 1964; DC, Lincoln Chiropractic College, IN, USA, 1965; MRO; MRN. Appointments: Private Practice, London and Rome, 1965-; Lecturer in Orthopaedics, Radiology and Diagnosis, BCNO, 1965-75; Council, BNOA, 1969-; Head of Radiology, Turingham Clinic, Newport Pagnell, 1969-76; Lecturer, European School of Osteopathy, 1970-75; President, BNUA, 1974-75, 1987-88, 1991-; Council, GCRN, 1988-; Currently. President, British Naturopathic and Osteopathic Association. Memberships: British Naturopathic and Osteopathic Association, 1964-; General Council and Register of Osteopaths, 1989-; General Council and Register of Naturopaths, 1991-; American Chiropractic Association; Osteopathic Association of Great Britain, 1991-. Hobbies: Photography; Classic Car Restoration. Address: 31 Weymouth Street, London, W1N 3FT, England.

WINER Conrad Edward Robert, b. 11 Jan 1931, Essex, England. Clinical Director; Lecturer. m. Marguerita Anne Dutton, 13 Apr 1957, 3 s. Education: LLB, London; MB; BS, London; MRCS, England; LRCP, London; DObst RCOG; MF Hom; MLCOM; DPRM, Sydney; FACRM; FAFRM(RACP). Appointments include: Captain, RAMC, 1960-63; VMO, Clinic of London College of Osteopathy, 1964-67; Visiting Senior Specialist, Department Rehabilitation Medicine, Royal Prince Alfred Hospital, 1967-79; Post-Graduate Course Supervisor, Spinal Manipulation, University of Sydney, 1974-; Clinical Director, Department of Rehabilitation Medicine, Royal Prince Alfred Hospital, 1980-; Lecturer, Rehabilitation Medicine, Sydney University, 1981-. Publications: Chapter in, Aspects of Manipulative Therapy, 1980, 1985; Manual Medicine, 1984; Papers in national medical journals in Britain, Australia, New Zealand, France, and in conference proceedings in England, Australia, New Zealand, France, Germany, Denmark, Switzerland, Spain and Russia. Honours: Past President and Honoary Life Member, Australian Association of Musculo-Skeletal Medicine; Honorary Life Member, Childbirth Education Association. Memberships: Past President, Australian College of Rehabilitation Medicine; Royal Australian College of Physicians; Australian Rheum Association; Australian Medical Association; British Osteopathic Association. Address: Royal Prince Alfred Hospital Medical Centre, Sydney 2042, Australia.

WINGARD Deborah, b. 20 Aug 1952, San Diego, CA, USA. Epidemiologist. m. Pierre P Vaughn, 4 Sep 1976, 2 s. Education: BA, Zoology, 1974, MS, Epidemiology, 1976, PhD, Epidemiology, 1980, University of CA, Berkeley. Career: Epidemiologist, Human Population Laboratory, 1977-78; Assistant Professor, 1980-86, Associate Professor, 1986-, Epidemiology, University of California, San Diego. Publications: Over 100 articles and book chapters on women's health and diabetes. Honours: Shannon Award with Dr Barbara Cohn, 1991-93; Mentor Award, American Medical Women's Association, Upjohn, 1994. Memberships: Society for Epidemiologic Research; American Public Health Association; American Diabetes Association; American Heart Association; Association of Women in Science. Hobbies: Photography; Dancing. Address: University of California, Department of Family and Preventive Medicine, Division of Epidemiology, 0607, 9500 Gilman Drive, La Jolla, CA 92093-0607, USA.

WINIKUR Bernard, b. 31 Jan 1922, New York City, New York, USA. Aerospace Engineer; Instructor in Nutrition. m. (1) Sylvia Golden, 18 April 1942, 2 sons, (2) Benice Lindo, 1 July 1985, 1 daughter. Education: BS; MS, Financial Planning; PhD, Human Behaviour, Nutrition: California Teaching Credential. Appointments: Formerly Aerospace Engineer, Hughes Aircraft; Instructor, Nutrition, Beverly Hills Adult and South Bay Adult School, California. Publications: An Integrated Approach of Financial Planning, 1986; The Arthritis Treatment Dilemma, 1988; Nutrition for Health, 1993. Membership: Past Chairman, Hughes Aircraft Salaried Retirees Action Committee. Hobbies: Skiing; Cycling; Tennis; Hiking; Helicopter piloting. Address: 1232 Corona Stret, Hermosa Beach, CA 90254, USA.

WINKELMAN James, b. 29 Oct 1935, Brooklyn, New York, USA. Medical Doctor. m. Rina LaVie, 1 son, 3 daughters. Education: AB; MD, Johns Hopkins University. Appointments: Assistant Professor of Pathology, New York University School of Medicine, New York, 1965-67; Associate Clinical Professor of Pathology, University of California at Los Angeles School of Medicine, Los Angeles, California, 1969-80; Professor of Pathology, SUNY-HSC, New York, 1980-86; Chairman, Division of Clinical Pathology, 1980-86; Acting Chairman, Department of Pathology, 1985-86; Professor of Pathology, Harvard Medical School, Boston, Massachusetts, 1986-; Director of Laboratories, SUNY-HSC, New York, 1980-86; Vice President/Director of Clinical Laboratories, Brigham & Women's Hospital, Boston, Massachusetts, 1986-; Assistant Director, 1960-70, Director, 1970-77, Vice-President, 1970-72, President, 1972-77, Bio-Science Laboratories, USA; Executive Vice-President, Director of Scientific Affairs, National Health Laboratories, La Jolla, California, 1977-80. Honours: Alpha Omega Alpha, 1959; Career Scientist, Health Research Council, New York City, 1965-67; MA (Hon), Harvard University, 1981; Pioneer of PDT, International Photodynamic Association, New York, 1990. Memberships: American Association of Pathologists; College of American Pathologists; American Society of Clinical Pathologists; American Association of Clinic Chemists; Academy of Clinical Laboratory Physicians and Scientists; American Medical Association; Council of Academic Societies. Address: Brigham and Women's Hospital, 75 Francis Street, Boston, MA 02115, USA.

WINN Katherine, b. 29 July 1964, Riverside, California, USA. Ophthalmic Technician. Education: Physical/Life Sciences, Riverside Community College & Chaffey College. Appointments: Ophthalmic Technician for Daniel J Sigband; Manager, Optician, Price Savers; Optician, Contact Lens Technician, Sun City Vision Clinic. Honours: Health Fair Expo, 1994. Memberships: JCAHPO; ABO; AAO; NAO. Hobbies: Drawing; Water Colour Painting; Jewelery Making; Billiards; Poetry; Botany. Address: 6000 Garden Grove Blvd # 273, Westminster, CA 92683, USA.

WINSTEAD Daniel Keith, b. 30 Dec 1944, Cincinnati, OH, USA. Psychiatrist. m. Jennifer Winstead, 1 s, 1 d. Education: BA, University of Cincinnati, OH, 1966; MD, Vanderbilt University School of Medicine, Nashville, TN, 1970; Residency, Psychiatry, 1970-72, Child Psychiatry Fellowship, 1972-73, University of Cincinnati, Cincinnati General Hospital; Certified, Psychiatry, 1975, Geriatric Psychiatry, 1992. Appointments include: Consultant, Department of Energy, Strategic Petroleum Reserve, 1983-; Professor of Psychiatry, with Tenure, Tulane University School of Medicine, 1984-; Staff Psychiatrist, New Orleans Veterans Administration Medical Center, 1987-; Senior Visiting Physician, Psychiatry, Charity Hospital of New Orleans, 1990-; Consultant Psychiatrist, Feliciana Forensic Facility, Jackson, LA, 1993-; Robert G Heath Professor and Chairman, Department of Psychiatry and Neurology, Tulane University School of Medicine. Publications include: Over 70 articles in professional journals, 1973-, including: Co-author, The Risk of HIV Infection in Homeless and Chronically Mentally Ill, in Southern Medical Journal, 1993; 2 Audio tapes; Numerous presentations; 2 Editorial Boards; Reviewer for 4 professional journals. Honours include: Army Commendation Medal, 1976; Fellow, American Psychiatric Association, 1984; Distinguished Professor Award, 1990; Fellow, Academy of Psychosomatic Medicine, 1990; Psychiatrist of Year, LA Psychiatric Association, 1993. Memberships include: Society of Biological Psychiatry; Association for Academic Psychiatry; AMA; American Society for Clinical Pharmacology and Therapeutics; American Academy of Psychiatry and the Law; American College of Psychiatrists, Fellow; New Orleans Neurological Society. Address: Dept of Psychiatry, Tulane University Medical Center, 1430 Tulane Ave, New Orleans, LA 70112-2699, USA.

WINSTON Robert Maurice Lipson, b. 15 July 1940, London, England. Physician. m. Lira Feigenbaum, 3 Mar 1973, 2 sons, 1 daughter. Education: MB; MRCS; FRCOG; FRSA. Appointments: Senior Resident Accoucheur, The London Hospital; Wellcome Senior Research Fellow, Hammersmith Hospital, 1973-76; Research Fellow, Leuven University, Belgium, 1977; Professor of Gynaecology, University of Texas, San Antonio, 1980-81; Professor of Fertility Studies, Royal Postgraduate Medical School, London University. Publications: Over 200 articles on Tubal Disease and IVF; Articles in Nature and Science on Preimplantation Genetic Disease; Various books on Infertility. Honour: Blair-Bell Lecturer Recognition, 1978. Memberships: Royal Society of Medicine; British Fertility Society; American Fertility Society; Society for Study of Reproduction. Hobbies: Skiing; Music; Arts; Theatre; Pond Building. Address: Hammersmith Hospital, Du Cane Road, London W12, England.

WINTERKORN Jacqueline Schuker, b. 2 January 1947, Queens, New York, USA. Associate Professor, Cornell University Medical Colege NY. m. Thomas H Meikle Jr, 2 daughters. Education: AB, Wellesley College, Massachusetts, 1963-65; Barnard College of Columbia University, 1965-67; PhD, Cornell University Graduate School of Medical Sciences, 1967-73; MD, Cornell University Medical College, 1981-83. Appointments: Cornell University: Instructor, Department of Anatomy 1975-76, Assistant Professor 1976-81, Lecturer 1981-86, Assistant Professor 1989-93, Associate Professor of Ophthalmology 1993-, Associate Professor of Neurology and Neuroscience 1994-. Publications Include: Similar deficits in visual learning by cats with lesions of the frontal cortex or the superior colliculus, 1975; Visual discrimination between spatially separated stimuli by cats with lesions of the superior colliculus-pretectum, 1974; The effect of monocular paralysis on the lateral geniculate nucleus of the cat, 1981; Ergotamine headache mistaken for temporal arteritis, 1990; Optic chiasmal neuritis, 1991; Treatment of vasospastic amaurosis fugax with calcium channel blockers, 1993; Recovery from ocular ischemic syndrome after treatment with Verapamil, 1994; Pioneered usage of video tapes for teaching Neuro-Opthalmology. Honours: National Merit Scholar, Andrew Mellon Teacher-Scientist, Cornell University Medical College, 1976-78; William Warner Hoppin Award, Residents Night, New York Academy of Medicine, 1985; Heed Fellowship in Ophthalmology, 1987-88; Recognition Award, North Shore University Hospital, 1991. Memberships Include: American Academy of Ophthalmology; New York State Medical Society; Sigma Xi; Women in Ophthalmology; Editorial Boards: J. Neuro-Ophth; Rev Ophth; Survey Ophth. Address: 900 Northern Boulevard, Great Neck, NY 11021, USA.

WISEMAN Gloria Diana, b. New York, USA. Physician. Education: BS, City University of New York, 1977; MD, Columbia University College of Physicians & Surgeons, 1981. Appointments: Teaching Assistant, New York University Medical Centre, 1983-84; Staff Associate, Columbia University, 1984-86; Instructor, New Jersey Medical School, 1986-87; Assistant Professor, Clinical Paediatrics, New Jersey Medical School, 1987-88; Research Fellow, Albert Einstein College of Medicine, 1988-91; Assistant Professor of Paediatrics, Mount Sinai School of Medicine, 1991-; Director of Neonatology, Englewood Hospital, 1991-. Publications: Levels of Insulin and Somatomedin-C in Small for Gestational Age Infants, 1986; Effect of Chronic Maternal Hypovolemia on the Foetus, 1986; Lung of the Premature Infant 1994; Proliferative and IL2 Secretory Responses Directed Against Various HIV-1 Peptides in Children of HIV-1 Infected Mothers; Cellular and Antibody Responses directed against the HIV-1 Principal Neutralising Domain in HIV-1 Infected Children, 1991. Honours: College Dean's List, 1974-77; Urology Prize, Medical School; Fellowship, American Medical Association Physician's Recognition Award; Certificate of Recognition by UMDNJ-New Jersey Medical School for Service in the education of New Jersey Students and Professional Practitioners of Emergency Cardiac Care; Who's Who in the East. Memberships: American Medical Association; Fellow, American Academy of Pediatrics; New York Perinatal Society; American Academy of Allergy & Immunology; Clinical Immunology Society; Joint Council of Allergy & Immunology. Address: 570 Fort Washington Avenue, New York, NY 10033, USA.

WIST Abund Ottokar, b. 23 May 1926, Vienna, Austria. Radiation Physicist; Retired. m. Suzanne Smiley Wist, 30 Nov 1963, 2 sons. Education: BS, MS, PhD, 1951, University of Vienna; Certified Biomedical Engineer, 1990; Certified Computer Manufacturing Engineer. Appointments: Research and development Engineer, Phillips, Siemens, 1957-59; Director of Research. Brinkmann Instruments, 1959-64; Senior Scientist, Fisher Scientific, 1963-69; Research Associate, University of

Pittsburgh, USA, 1970-73; Assistant Professor of Radiology, Medical College of Virginia/VCU, 1973-93; Retired; Adjunct Professor of Radiology, MCU/VCU; Radiation Health Specialist, State of Virginia. Publications: Electronic Design of Microprocessor-Based Instruments and Control Systems, Co-author, 1986; Contributor of over 70 articles in professional scientific journals; Ten patents in Germany and USA. Honours: Biomedical Engineering Delegate to China, 1987, 1993, Russia, 1993; NASA-ASEE Summer Faculty Fellowship, 1975. Memberships: IEEE, Senior member; New York Academy of Sciences; Sigma Xi; American Association of Physicists in Medicine; Associate Member, American College of Radiology/ Hobbies: Swimming; Skiing. Address: 9304 Farmington Drive, Richmond, VA 23229-5336, USA.

WITHAM Gary Elmer, b. 17 June 1938, Rockland, Maine, USA. Dentist. m. Louise Frost, 18 Jan 1986, 1 son, 1 daughter. Education: DMD, Tufts Dental School; American Academy of Implant Dentistry; Mastership, Academy of General Dentistry. Appointments: Private Dental Practice. Honours: Fellowship, Society of Generalists in Dentistry; Diplomate, American Society of Osseointegration; Fellow, Academy of Dentistry International; Founder, American Society of Preventative Dentistry. Memberships include: American Society for Geriatric Dentistry; American Academy of Orthodontics for the General Practitioner; Maine Dental Association; American Dental Association; American Academy of Peridontology; American Academy of Cosmetic Dentistry; American Equilibration Society; Northeastern Prosthodontic Society. Hobbies: Croquet; Fishing. Address: One Pearl St, Camden, ME 048043, USA.

WOLCHUK Luba Nadia, b. 6 Oct 1954, Toronto, Ontario, Canada. Author; Editor. m. Anthony A Shardt, 14 July 1981, 2 sons, 1 daughter. Education: MD, 1979, MHSc, 1986, University of Toronto, 1979; Certificant, College of Family Physicians of Canada, 1981. Appointments: Chief Resident, Family Practice, Women's College Hospital, Toronto, 1981; Family Physician, 1981-84; Currently Editor-in-Chief, Biograf Canada Inc. Publications: Essays on history of medicine, 1992-; Numerous review articles on primary care and various subspeciality topics including: A Painless Approach to Migraine. Honours: W J Taylor Scholarship, 1975; Invited Speaker, American Medical Writers Association Annual Conference, 1991, 1993. Memberships: American Medical Writers Association; College of Family Physicians of Canada; Paleopathology Association. Hobbies: Gardening; Painting. Address: PO Box 805, Lewiston, NY 14092, USA.

WOLFF James Alexander, b. 19 Jun 1914, New York, NY, USA. Retired MD. m. Janet Loeb, 24 Jun 1946, 3 s, 1 d. Education: BA; MD. Appointment: Professor of Pediatrics, College of Physicians and Surgeons, Columbia University, NY, USA. Publications: Over 100 peer reviewed articles in medical journals. Honour: Named professorship, James A Wolff, College of Physicians and Surgeons, Columbia University, 1991. Memberships: American Pediatric Society; Society for Pediatric Research; American Society of Pediatric Hematology and Oncology; American Society of Clinical Oncology; International Society of Pediatric Oncology. Hobby: Tennis. Address: 518 Isle of Capri, Fort Lauderdale, FL 33301, USA.

WOLKE Dieter, b. 19 Mar 1957, Aschendorf, Germany. Psychologist. m. Patricia Rios, 13 Dec 1986. 1 s, 1 d. Education: Dipl Psych, Christian Albrecht University, 1982; PhD, University of London, England, 1989; AFBPsS, 1987; CPsychol, 1987. Appointments: Research Assistant, University of London Institute of Education, 1982; Research Officer, Clinical Psychologist, King's College Hospital, London, 1984; Research Fellow and Lecturer, Institute of Child Health, University of London, 1986; Director of Psychology, University of Munich Children's Hospital, Germany. Publications include: Comparison of Mothers' with Trained Observers' reports of Neonatal Behavioral Style, Co-author, 1984; Supporting the Development of Lo-Birthweight Infants, 1991; Feeding and Sleeping Across the Lifespan; Excessive Infant Crying: A Controlled Study of Mothers Helping Mothers; The Cognitive Outcome of Very Preterm Infants May Be Poorer than Often reported: An Empirical Investigation of How Methodological Issues Make a Big Difference, Co-author. Memberships: Association for Child Psychology and Psychiatry, British Psychological Society; Deutsche Gesellschaft fuer Psychologie; Society for Research in Child Development; Society for reproductive and Infant Psychology; Deutsche-Osterreichische Gesellschaft fuer Perinatologie. Hobbies: Swimming; Skiing; Cinema. Address: University of Munich Children's Hospital, Lindwurmstrasse 4, 80337 Munich, Germany.

WOLMAN Moshe, b. 19 Oct 1914, Warsaw, Poland. Pathologist. m. Brigitte Koebbel, 25 Jan 1939, 2 sons, 2 daughters. Education: MD, Rome, 1938; Associate Professor of Pathology, Jerusalem, 1956; Professor of Pathology, Tel-Aviv, 1964. Appointments: Pathologist, British Army, 1945-46; Resident to Chief Physician in Pathology, Hadassah Hospital, Jerusalem, 1946-59; Head of Pathology, Tel Hashomer Hospital, 1959-79; Head, Professor of Pathology & of Histology, Tel-Aviv University Medical School, 1964-85; Professor Emeritus, Tel-Aviv University, 1985-. Publications: Described and delineated the disease known as Wolman's disease in 1956, with Abramov and Schorr; Histochemistry of Lipids in Pathology, 1946; Pigments in Pathology, 1969; Demagoguery and Rhetoric, 1990; Co-author: Lipid Pigments, 1993. Memberships: Israel Pathology Society; Israel Society of Histochemistry & Cytochemistry; World Academy of Neurology; American Society of Neuropathology. Honours: 1st Recipient of the Pearse Prize of Royal Microscopical Society, England, 1988; Pioneer Award, International Federation Histochemical Societies, 1988; President, Israel Society of Histochemistry, 1984-90. Hobbies: Family; Sightseeing; Swimming. Address: Tel-Aviv University Sackler Faculty of Medicine, Department of Pathology, 69978 Tel-Aviv, Israel.

WOLRAICH Mark Lee, b. 30 Jun 1945, Bronx, New York, USA. Developmental Pediatrician. m. Debra J Kowaloff, 23 Jun 1968, 2 s, 1 d. Education: BA, SUNY Harpur College, Binghamton, New York, 1966; MD, SUNY Upstate Medical Center, Syracuse, New York, 1970. Appointments: Assistant Professor of Pediatrics, University of Iowa, 1976-81; Associate Professor, University of Iowa, 1981-86; Professor of Pediatrics, University of Iowa, 1986-90; Professor of Pediatrics/Chief of Division of Child Development, Vanderbilt University, Tennessee, 1990-. Publications: Papers include, Stimulant Drug Therapy in Hyperactive Children: Research and Clinical Implications, 1977; Pediatric Practitioners' Knowledge of Developmental Disabilities, 1980; Counseling Parents of Children with Cerebral Palsy, 1986; The Treatment of Attention Deficit Hyperactivity Disorder with Methylphenidate, 1991; Books include, What You Should Know About Your Child with Spina Bifida, 1979; Advances in Developmental and Behavioral Pediatrics, Volumes 3-8, 1982-89; The Practical Assessment and Management of Children with Disorders of Development and Learning, 1987; Numerous Chapters and Reviews. Honours: Distinguished & Dedicated Service Award, Spina Bifida Association of Iowa, 1979; Lou Holloway Award for Research in Health Sciences Education, University of Iowa. Memberships: include, American Board of Pediatrics; American Academy of Pediatrics; Society for Behavioral Pediatrics; American Academy of Cerebral Palsy and Developmental Medicine; Society of Developmental Pediatrics; Society for Pediatric Research; Society of Pediatric Psychology Association. Hobbies: Skiing; Canoeing; Wood Work. Address: Vanderbilt Child Development Center, 2100 Pierce Avenue, Nashville, TN 37232-3573, USA.

WONG Alan Yau Kuen, b. 6 Feb 1937, Hong Kong. Professor. m. 31 July 1967, 2 sons, 1 daughter. Education: BSc, 1962, MSc, 1963, PhD, Biophysics, 1967, Dalhousie University, Canada. Appointments: Canadian Heart Research Fellow, 1968-71; Assistant Professor, Medical Research Council (Canada) Scholar, 1971-76; Senior Canadian Heart Research Fellow, Visiting Scientist, University of Washington, Seattle, USA, 1976-77; Associate Professor, 1977-84, Professor, 1984-, Department Physiology and Biophysics, Dalhousie University. Publications: Stress Distribution within Left Ventricular Wall Approximated as a Thick-Walled Ellipsoidal Shell, 1968; Mechanics of Cardiac Muscle Based on Huxley Model, 1971, 1972; Model of Excitation-Contraction Coupling in Mammalian Cardiac Muscle, 1981; Dynamics of Coronary Venous System in Dog, 1984; Hemodynamics of Coronary Artery Stenosis, 1984; Model of $Ca2+$ induced $Ca2+$ Release Mechanism in Cardiac Cell, 1992; Model of Cytosolic $Ca2+$ Regulation and Autacoids Production in Vascular Endothelial Cell, 1992; Model of $Ca2+$ Regulation in Smooth Muscle Cell, 1993. Honour: Fellow, Council in Circulation, American Heart Association. Memberships: Biophysical Society; Society Mathematical Biology; New York Academy of Science; Cardiovascular System Dynamic Society; Biomedical Engineering Society. Hobbies: Tennis; Ballroom Dancing; Oil Painting . Address: Department Physiology and Biophysics, Faculty of Medicine, Dalhousie University, Halifax, Nova Scotia B3H 4H7, Canada.

WONG Felix, b. 28 April 1951, Hong Kong. Professor in Obstetrics & Gynaecology. m. 29 October 1984, 2 sons. Education: MMed, Singapore; MD, Hong Kong; FRCS, Edinburgh; FRCS, Glasgow; FRCOG, England; FRACOG, Australia; FHKCOG, Hong Kong; FHKMA,

Hong Kong. Appointments: Medical Officer, 1976-83; Lecturer, 1983-87; Senior Lecturer, 1987-92. Publications: 100 articles in various international journals, from 1984-94. Honours: Croucher Foundation Fellowship; Honorary Professorship in Sun Yat-Sen University, Yangzhou Medical College, Peking Union Medical College. Memberships: Fellow, Royal Society of Medicine, Professional Colleges, Hong Kong & Australian Medical Associations. Hobbies: Swimming; Tennis; Stamp Collecting; Reading; Computers. Address: Department of Obstetrics & Gynaecology, Liverpool Hospital, Liverpool, NSW 2170, Australia.

WONG Nathan, b. 18 Apr 1961, Downey, CA, USA. Medicine; Epidemiology. Education: PhD; MPH. Appointments: Associate Professor and Director, Preventive Cardiology Program, University of California, Irvine. Publications: About 75 peer reviewed articles, abstracts and scientific symposia including publications in Annals of Internal Medicine, Circulation and American Journal of Cardiology. Honour: Fellow, Council on Epidemiology, American Heart Association. Memberships: American Heart Association; American College of Cardiology. Hobbies: Skiing; Photography; Running. Address: Preventive Cardiology Program, C240 Medical Sciences 1, University of California, Irvine, CA 92717, USA.

WONG Otto, b. 14 Nov 1947, China. Epidemiologist. m. Betty Yeung, 14 Feb 1970, 1 s, 1 d. Education: DSc, Epidemiology and Biostatistics; MS, Biostatistics; MS, Physics; BS; FACE. Career: Assistant Professor of Epidemiology, Georgetown University School of Medicine, 1975-79; Director of Epidemiology, Tabershaw Occupational Medicine Association, 1980; Chief Epidemiologist, Environmental Health Association, 1980-90; Chief Epidemiologist, Applied Health Sciences, San Mateo, CA, 1991-. Publications: Considerations of specificity in researching the relationship between asbestos and cancer, in American Journal of Industrial Medicine, 1993; An epidemiologic study of workers exposed to ethylene oxide, in British Journal of Industrial Medicine, 1993; Health Effects of Gasoline, in Environmental Health Perspectives, 1993; An updated cohort mortality study of workers exposed to styrene, in Occupational and Environmental Medicine, 1994. Honour: Fellow, American College of Epidemiology. Memberships: Fellow, Human Biology Council; Society for Epidemiologic Research; International Commission on Occupational Health; NY Academy of Science. Address: Applied Health Sciences, 181 Second Avenue, Suite 628, PO Box 2078, San Mateo, CA 94401, USA.

WONG Po-Yee, b. 7 July 1944, Haifeng, Guangdong, China. Acupuncture Specialist. m. Kam-On Chan, 18 Mar 1973, 1 son, 1 daughter. Education: Chinese Medicine Certificate in Acupuncture, Chengdu College of Chinese Medicine, China. Appointments: Assistant to Dr Y K Wong, Hong Kong; Specialist in curing or curtailing: Psoriasis, Colitis, Asthma, Raynaud's Disease, Back Pains, Migraine, Hay-fever, PMT, etc. Memberships: Chinese Medical Association, United Kingdom; Chung San Acupuncture Society, London. Hobbies: Country Walks; Research in Chinese Ancient Medicine; Flower Arranging; Address: 2 Harlington Road East, Feltham, Middlesex TW14 0AB, England.

WONG Shou Pang, b. 9 Sep 1946, China. Doctor. Education: MBBS, Distinction in Biochemistry; MRCP(UK); FRCP(Edin). Appointments: Medical Officer, 1971-72, Medical and Health Officer, 1972-79, Senior Medical Officer, 1979-86, Consultant Physician and Cardiologist, 1986-, Honorary Lecturer, Department of Medicine, University of Hong Kong and Chinese University of Hong Kong; Chief of Service, Department of Medicine, Queen Elizabeth Hospital, Hong Kong. Publications include: Parenteral Salbutamol in the Treatment of Cardiogenic Shock, Co-author, 1975; Inotropic Agents in the Treatment of Congestive Heart Failure, 1979; Lipid Profile in Acute Myocardial Infarction Patients, Co-author, 1990; Left ventricular Thrombux after Acute Myocardial Infarction, Co-author, 1990; Experience of Implantation dof Dual Chamber Pacemaker, CO-author, 1990; Sensing Performance of Unipolar and Bipolar Leads in Dual Chamber Pacing, Co-author, 1990; Use of Terazosin in Treatment of Hypertension, Co-author, 1990; Prospective in Treatment of Dilated Cardiomyopathy, 1991. Memberships: American College of Chest Physicians; COuncil Member, Hong Kong Medical Association; Council; Member, Hong Kong College of Cardiology; Fellow, Hong Kong Academy of Medicine; Council Member, Hong Kong College of Physicians. Address: Queen Elizabeth Hospital, Department of Medicine, 30 Gascoigne Road, Kowloon, Hong Kong.

WONG Tak Ming, b. 8 June 1943, China. University Reader. m. Joanne Jo Lan Wong, 22 Jan 1978, 1 son, 1 daughter. Education: BSc (General), Chinese University of Hong Kong; BSc (Special Honours), MSc, PhD, University of Hong Kong. Appointments: Lecturer, Senior Lecturer, Currently Reader, Department of Physiology, University of Hong Kong; Visiting Professor, Zhejiang Medical University, Xuzhou Medical College, and Nanjing Medical University, China. Publications: Co-author, articles: Journal of Experimental Zoology, 1977; International Journal of Peptide and Protein Research, 1981; British Journal of Pharmacology, 1986; Journal of Molecular and Cellular Cardiology, 1990; Brain Research, 1991; Journal of Pharmacology and Experimental Therapeutics, 1994. Memberships: International Brain Research Organization; International Narcotic Research Conference; Hong Kong Society of Neuroscience. Hobby: Tennis. Address: C8, 350 Victoria Road, Hong Kong.

WONG Yong-Chuan, b. 7 June 1942, Malaysia. Eductor; Scientist. m. Chook-Yee, 28 Dec 1971, 2 s. Education: BSc, Nanyang University, Singapore, 1966; MSc, 1968, PhD, 1971, University of Western Ontario, Canada. Appointments: Lecturer in Anatomy, 1971-77, senior Lecturer, 1977-84, Reader in Anatomy, 1984-93; Head of Dept of Anatomy, 1991-; Associate Dean, Faculty of Medicine, University of Hong Kong; Honorary Research Associate, University of Birmingham, England, 1974; Visiting Lecturer, Flinders University, Australia, 1981; Visiting Professor, University of Chicago, USA, 1977-78; Visiting Professor, UCSF, 1988-89; Visiting Professor, Sun Yat-Sen University of Medical Sciences, 1992. Honours:CMB Fellowship; Wellcome Foundation Fellowship; Lee Foundation Fellowship. Memberships: American Association of Anatomists; Canadian Association of Anatomists; New York Academy of Science; Anatomical Society of Great Britain and Ireland; Institute of Biology; Hong Kong Institute of Science; American Association for the Advancement of Science; Hong Kong Society of Endocrinology Metabolism and Reproduction. Hobbies: Swimming; Badminton. Address: Department of Anatomy, Faculty of Medicine, The University of Hong Kong, 5 Sassoon Road, Hong Kong.

WOO Jean, b. 14 Apr 1949, Hong Kong. Professor of Medicine. m. C M Wong, 16 Aug 1975, 2 daughters. Education: BA (Cantab); MA (Cantab); MB BChir (Cantab); MD (Cantab); FRCP (Edinburgh); FRCP (London). Appointments: Senior House Officer, Hammersmith Hospital, London, England; Senior House Officer, Brompton Hospital, London; Lecturer, Senior Lecturer, Reader, currently Chairman and Professor, Department of Medicine, The Chinese University of Hong Kong, Shatin, New Territory. Publications: Nutritional indices in healthy active Chinese elderly, 1988; Biochemical predictors for osteoporotic fractures in elderly Chinese - a longitudinal study, 1990; Hypertension, lipoprotein (a), and apolipoprotein A-I are independent risk factors for stroke in a Chinese population, 1991. Memberships: Fellow, Hong Kong Academy of Medicine; Fellow, Hong Kong College of Physicians; British Geriatrics Society; American Geriatrics Society. Hobbies: Swimming, Tennis, Cycling. Address: Department of Medicine, Prince of Wales Hospital, Shatin, NT, Hong Kong.

WOOD Edwin Charles, b. 27 May 1925, Washington DC, USA. Psychiatrist; Psychoanalyst. m. Constance D Wood, 17 Dec 1977, 1 s, 1 d. Education: MD. George Washington University School of Medicine, 1950; Graduate, The Western New England Institute of Psychoanalysis, 1962; Life Fellow, American Psychiatric Association; Life Member, American Psychoanalytic Association. Appointments: Associate Director, Psychiatric Education, The Institute of Living, Hartford, Connecticut; President, Supervising and Training Psychoanalyst, The Houston-Galveston Psychoanalytic Institute; Clinical Professor of Psychiatry, Baylor College of Medicine. Publications: Some Observations on the Psychoanalytic Institute Site Visit Experience, 1988; Tearfulness: A Psychoanalytic Interpretation, 1984; Evolutions of an Orientation Concerning the Nature of Male Homosexualities, 1994. Honours: John Ordronaux Award for Scholarship, 1950. Memberships: American Medical Association; American Psychiatric Association; American Psychoanalytic Association. Hobbies: Tennis; Horticulture. Address: 5300 San Jacinto, Ste 150, Houston, TX 77004-6886, USA.

WOOD Tracey Gillian, b. 4 Sep 1966, Surrey, England. Osteopath. m. S M Green, 3 June 1989, 1 d. Education: Diploma in Osteopathy. Appointment: Registered Osteopath. Membership: General Council and Register of Osteopaths. Address: The Albion Clinic, 4 Albion Place, Bennetthorpe, Doncaster, DN1 2EG, England.

WOOD William C, b. 3 May 1940, Illinois, USA. Professor; Surgeon. m. Judith Lindsell, 15 Aug 1964, 1 son, 2 daughters. Education: BS, Wheaton College; MD, Harvard. Appointments: Joseph Bilolon Whitehead Professor and Chairman, Department of Surgery, Emory University School of Medicine; Clinical Director Winship Cancer Centre of Emory University. Publications: Numerous articles in journals and magazines. Honours: Nathanson Scholar, American Cancer Society, 1978-82. Hobbies: Tennis.Memberships: American Surgical Association; New England Surgical Society; Surgical Society of Oncology; Fellow, American College of Surgeons. Address: Emory University School of Medicine, 1364 Clifton Road, Atlanta, GA 30322, USA.

WOODRUFF Bradley A, b. 24 May 1953, Jamestown, New York, USA. Epidemiologist. Education: BA, University College at Fredonia, New York and University of New York, Buffalo, 1976; MD, Upstate Medical Center, Syracuse, New York, 1980; MPH, The Johns Hopkins University School of Hygiene and Public Health, Baltimore, 1986. Appointments: Technical Advisor, Operations Research, Columbia University, 1987; Epidemic Intelligence Service Officer, US Public Health Service, 1987-89; Resident in Preventive Medicine, US Public Health Service, 1988-90; Medical Epidemiologist, US Public Health Service, 1990-. Publications Include: Disease surveillance and control after a flood in Khartoum, Sudan, 1988; A new look at typhoid vaccination: Information for the practicing physician, 1991; Early diagnosis and survival of ruptured abdominal aortic aneurysms, 1991; Hospital outbreak of hepatitis E, 1992; A description of non-fatal spinal cord injury using a hospital-based registry, 1994; Nosocomial transmission of hepatitis A in a pediatric hospital traced to an anti-HAV negative patient with immunodeficiency. Honours Include: Unit Commendations (5), US Public Health Service, 1989 (2), 1992, 1993 (2); Group Special Recognition Award, US Public Health Service, 1992; Achievement Medal, US Public Health Service, 1993. Memberships: American Public Health Association; Physicians for a National Health Plan; American College of Preventive Medicine; Physicians for Social Responsibility. Address: PHS/Region IX, 50 United Nations Plaza, Room 349-A, San Francisco, CA 94102, USA.

WOODRUFF Michael Francis Addison (Sir), b. 3 Apr 1911. Surgeon (retired). m. Hazel Gwenyth Ashby, 12 Jun 1946, 2 s, 1 d. Education: MD; MS; DSc, Melbourne; FRCS; FRCSE; FRACS; FACS (Hon); FRCPE (Hon); FRSE; FRS. Career includes: Tutor in Surgery, Sheffield, 1946-48; Lecturer in Surgery, Aberdeen, 1948-52; Professor of Surgery, Otago, New Zealand, 1953-57; Professor of Surgery, Edinburgh, 1957-76, now retired. Publications: Co-author, Deficiency Diseases in Japanese Prison Camps, 1951; Transplantation of Tissues and Organs, 1960; On Science and Surgery, 1976; The Interaction of Cancer and Host, 1980; Co-author, Surgery for Dental Students, 4th edition, 1984; Cellular Variation and Adaptation in Cancer, 1990; Articles on surgical topics and transplantation and tumour immunology. Honours include: Associé Etranger de Chirurgie, 1964; FRS, 1968; Corresponding Member, Deutsche Gesellschaft Chirurgie, 1968; Lister Medal, 1969. Memberships include: Royal College of Surgeons; FRACS; FACS. Hobbies: Walking; Sailing; Reading. Address: University of Edinburgh, 506 Lanark Road, Juniper Green, Edinburgh, EH14 5DH, Scotland.

WOOLDRIDGE Thomas Dean, b. 25 Feb 1946, Grenada, MI, USA. Physician, Nephrology. m. Luanne Lyle, 25 Oct 1975, 1 son. Education: BS, BA, Millsaps College, 1968; MD, University of Mississippi, 1972. Appointments: Practice of Nephrology, Director, Artificial Kidney Unit, North Mississippi Medical Center, 1977-. Publications: LeVeen Shunt (LS): Long Therm Therapy for Idiopathic Ascites of Chronic Renal Failure, 1976; Peritoneal Dialysis: A Review, 1977; Rhabdomyolysis As A Complication of Parathyroidectomy and Calcium Supplementation, 1978; Graft Infection and Bacteremia, 1983; Immunoregulatory Studies in Patients with IgA Nephropathy, 1988. Honours: President, Mississippi Nephrologic Society, 1994. Memberships: American Society of Nephrology; International Society of Nephrology; American Society of Hypertension; American Medical Association. Hobbies: Running; Tennis; History. Address: 4 Medical Park Circle, Tupelo, MI 38801, USA.

WOOSLEY Raymond L, b. 2 Oct 1942, Kentucky, USA. Medical Educator. m. Julianne. Education: BS, Western Kentucky University, 1964; PhD, Louisville, 1967; MD, University of Miami, 1973; Intyern, Resident, Vanderbilt University Hospital, Nashville, 1973-76. Appointments: Senior Pharmacologist, Director of Rese4arch, Meyer Laboratories, Ft Lauderdale, 1968-71; Instructor, Department of Medicine and Pharmacology, Vanderbilt University, 1976-77; Assistant Professor, 1977-79, Associate Professor, 1979-84, Associate Director of Clinical Research centre, 1981-88, Professor, 1984-88, Professor of Pharmacology and Medicine, Chairman of Department of Pharmacology, 1988-, Georgetown University School of Medicine, Washington DC; Chief of Division of Clinical Pharmacology, 1988-94. Publications: Clinical Application of Zinc Metabolism, 1975; Cardiovascular Pharmacology and Therapeutics, 1994; Contributor of chapters in books and articles in professional journals. Honours: NIH Postdoctoral Fellow, 1964-67; Postdoctoral fellow, University of Louisville, 1967-68, Vanderbilt University,1976-77; American College Clinical Pharmacology, Fellow, 1974; Ogden Scholar, Western Kentucky University, 1960-64l Cancer Devlopment Award in Clinical Pharmacology. Pharmaceutical Manufacturers Association Foundation, 1977-80. Memberships include: Fellow, American College Clinical Pharmacology; American College of Physicians; American Heart Association, COuncil, Clinical Cardiology, 1985-. Address: Georgetown University School of Medicine, Department of Pharmacology, 3900 Reservoir Road NW, Washington DC 20007-2100, USA.

WORRALL Joseph Allen Jr, b. 12 Aug 1924, Brooklyn, New York, USA. Physician. m. Mary Worrall, 3 sons, 3 daughters. Education: MD; RDMS. Appointments: Practice of Gynecology & Obstetrics & Gynecology Sonography. Memberships: ACOG; FACS; Diplomate of American Board of Obstetrics & Gynecology; AIUM; SDMS; International Society of Ultrasound in Obstetrics & Gynecology. Hobbies: Computers; Ham Raido. Address: 120 Eureka Avenue, Fairbanks, AK 99701-3618, USA.

WORTHINGTON-WHITE Diana Alice, b. 7 Jan 1956, Cleveland, Ohio, USA. Research Scientist. Education: BS, Biology, 1977, MEd, Health Education, 1978, University of Cincinnati. Appointments: Instructor in Health, University of Cincinnati, Ohio, Research Technician, University Hospitals of Cleveland, Ohio, 1979-81; Associate Research Scientist, University of Florida, Gainesville, 1981-. Publications: Editor with S Gross and A P Gee: Bone Marrow Purging and Processing, 1990; Advances in Bone Marrow Purging and Processing, 1992; Advances in Bone Marrow Purging and Processing, 1994; Co-author, book contributions: Transplantation for neuroblastoma using immunomagnetically purged autologous bone marrow, 1987; Serine proteases promote human CFU-GM in methylcellulose culture systems, 1988; Transporting bone marrow for in vitro purging for autologous reinfusion, 1990; A dozen refereed articles in journals including American Journal of Hematology, International Journal of Cancer, Blood, Experimental Hematology. Honours: Award Winner, University of Florida Paediatric Science Day, 1984; Organising Secretary, Bone Marrow Purging and Processing Conferences, 1989, 1991, 1993; Founding Member, 1992, Secretary, 1992-, International Society of Hematotherapy and Graft Engineering; Editorial Assistant, Cancer Research, Therapy and Control, 1993-. Memberships include: American Association for the Advancement of Science; American Medical Writers Association. Hobbies: Classical flautist; Volleyball; Physical Fitness; Vocal ensembles. Address: Department of Paediatrics, PO Box 100296, University of Florida, Gainesville, FL 32610, USA.

WRAITH James Edmond, b. 30 Oct 1953, South Shields, England. Paediatrician. m. Elizabeth Susan Ellison, 21 Aug 1976, 2 sons, 1 daughter. Education: MB ChB, 1977; MRCP, 1980; FRCP, 1993. Appointments: Clincial Research Fellow, Murdoch Institute, Children's Hospital, Melbourne, Australia; Consultant Paediatrician, Royal Manchester Children's Hospital. Publications: Many articles on inherited metabolic disease. Memberships: FRCP. Hobbies: Squash; Gardening. Address: Willink Gntcs Unit, Royal Manchester Childrens Hospital, Pandlebury, Manchester M27 1HA, England.

WREN Barry George, b. 8 Apr 1932. Gynaecologist. m. Loloma Cochrane, 2 Jan 1957, 3 s. Education: MD; MBBS; MHPEd; FRACOG; FRCOG. Career: Registrar, Hammersmith Hospital, London; Director, Maternity Services, Western Nigeria; Associate Professor of Obstetrics and Gynaecology, University of New South Wales; Currently, Director, Centre for Management of Menopause. Publications: Handbook of Obstetrics and Gynaecology, 1980, 1985, 1989; Your Choice, 1994; Many papers on menopause, hormone replacement treatment therapy, and HRT following genital tract cancer. Honours: Fotheringham Fellowship, 1958; Novo-Nordisk Distinction Award, 1994. Memberships: Australian Medical Association; Australian Menopause Society; Amarant Foundation; International Menopause Society; International Gynaecology Society. Hobbies: Golf; Gardening. Address: 506-180 Ocean Street, Edgecliff, NSW 2027, Australia.

WRETLIND Karl Arvid Johannes, b. 19 Jan 1928. Professor Emeritus. m. Astrid, 1 s, 1 d. Education: MD, Karolinska Institute, Stockholm, 1949. Appointments: Head of Vitrum Institute of Human Nutrition, Kabi-Vitrum AB, 1975-; Lecturer, Department of Chemistry and Pharmacology, 1941-62, Professor of Nutrition, 1970-75, Karolinska Institute; Professor of Nutrition, Swedish Institute of Health, 1962-70. Publications: Contributor of over 275 professional papers. Honours: Honorary Member, European Society of Parenteral and Enteral Nutrition; American Society of Clinical Nutrition; Swedish Royal Order of Polar Star, 1965; Commander of the Swedish Royal Order of Vasa, 1972; Annual Golden Prize Medal, Swedish Royal Academy of Engineering Sciences, Stockholm, 1979; 4th W H Sebrell Jr International Lecturer on Nutrition, Columbia University, USA, 1979; Honorary DSc, Rutgers University, USA, 1980; 6th Annual Bristol-Myers Award for Distinguished Achievement in Nutrition Research, 1986. Address: Floragatan 2, S-11431 Stockholm, Sweden.

WRIGHT Harry Hercules, b. 4 Jan 1948, Charleston, SC, USA. Child and Adolescent Psychiatrist. 1 d. Education: MD, 1976, MBA, 1976, University of PA; Certified in Psychiatry, 1982 and Child Psychiatry, 1984. Appointment: Professor, Neuropsychiatry, University of SC. Publications: Huntington's Disease, in Arch Neurology, 1981; Elective Mutism, in JAACAP, 1985; Pediatric C/L, in Journal Dev Bch Pediatrics, 1987; Serotonin in Autism, in Journal of Autism and Development Disorders, 1989. Honours: Sigma Xi, 1972; Falk Fellow, American Psychiatric Association; Laughlin Fellow, American College of Psychiatry; Omicron Delta Kappa. Memberships: American Psychiatric Association; American Academy of Child and Adolescent Psychiatry; American Public Health Association; World Association for Infant Mental Health. Address: PO Box 12474, Columbia, SC 29211, USA.

WRIGHT Liam Hugh, b. 9 Dec 1926, Opuwake, New Zealand. Gynaecologist. m. M Barbara Brosnan, 19 Jan 1952, 3 sons, 1 daughter. Education: BSc; MB; ChB; FRCOG; FRCS; FRCSEd. Appointments: RMO, Palmerston North; Registrar, Senior Registrar, National Women's Hospital, Auckland; Lecturer, Nuffield, Department of Obstetrics & Gynaecology, Oxford; Visiting Obstetrician & Gynaecologist, National Women's Hospital. Memberships: Royal New Zealand College of Obstetrics & Gynaecology. Hobbies: Gardening; Travel; Bridge. Address: 100 Arney Road, Auckland 5, New Zealand.

WRIGHT Stephen James, b. 15 Feb 1957, Manchester, England. Clinical Health Psychologist. Education: BA (Hons), Psychology, Goldsmiths College, London; PhD, St George's Hospital Medical School, London; MSc, Clinical Psychology, University of Leeds. Appointments: Research Fellow in Social Psychology; Lecturer in Health Psychology; Currently Clinical Psychologist and Honorary Lecturer in Health Psychology. Publication: Measures in Health Psychology: A User's Portfolio (with M Johnston and J Weinman). Membership: Associate Fellow, British Psychology Society. Hobbies: Cycling; Cinema; Folk music. Address: Department of Medical Psychology, CSSD, Leicester General Hospital NHS Trust, Leicester LE5 4PW, England.

WU Aiqin, b. 20 Aug 1956, Huzhou, China. Psychiatrist. m. Li Lin, 11 Feb 1983, 1 son. Education: MD; MSc, Suzhou Medical College, 1989. Appointments: Internist (Attending Doctor), 1981; Currently Associate Professor, Head, Department of Psychiatry, 1st Affiliated Hospital, Suzhou Medical College. Publications: Study on Psychosocial Factors and CHD, 1990; Psychosomatic Research, 1992; The Relationship between Arrhythmia and Psychological Stress, 1992. Honours: 1st Prize of Advancement of Science and Technology, for research project, Chinese Suzhou Academy of Sciences. Memberships: American Psychosomatic Society; Chinese Medical Association; Secretary-General, Council Member, Suzhou Mental Health Association. Hobbies: Penmanship; Singing. Address: Department of Psychiatry, First Affiliated Hospital, Suzhou Medical College, Suzhou 215006, China.

WU Airu, b. 10 Feb 1931, Beijing, China. Professor of Gynaecological Oncology. m. Liu Ke-jun, 10 Nov 1956, 1 son, 1 daughter. Education: BA, Beijing Medical University, 1955; MD, First Moscow Medical College, Russia, 1958; Visiting Scholar, Ludwig Institute for Cancer Research, Sydney University, Australia, 1983. Appointments: Head, Professor of Gynaecological Oncology Department, 1984-93; Vice Director, Cancer Insitute Hospital, Chinese Academy of Medical Sciences, 1984-85. Publications: Epidemiology of Cancer of the Cervix; Combined Treatment with Radiotherapy and Surgery for Invasive Carcinoma of Cervix; Pharmacology and selection

of Anticancer Drugs, Co-author, 1994; Cancer of the Uterus and Cervix, 1991; Etiology and Prevention of Cancer of the Cervix, Endometrium and Ovary, 1994; Early Diagnosis of Cancer of the Cervix, 1994; Flow Cytometric Analysis of DNA Content in Cancer of the Cervix, 1988; The Application of Monoclonal Antibody OC125 in Gynecologic Cancer, 1988; A Study of Relationship between HPV Infection and Cervical Cancer in High Incidence Area in Xiang Yuan County, 1992. Honours: Award of Science and Technology Commission, 1978; Award of Science and Technology Achievement, CAMS, 1993. Memberships: Chinese Cancer Control Consultative Committee; Vice Chairman, Research Committee, Cancer of the Cervix, Chinese Anticancer Society; AOCOA. Hobbies: Travel; Music. Address: Cancer Institute (Hospital), Chinese Academy of Medical Sciences, Zuoanmenwai, Panjiayao, Beijing 100021, China.

WU Ben-Jie, b. 14 July 1932, Jiangsu, China. Teacher. m. Professor Wang Xiu-bi. 14 July 1957, 2 s. Education: MB, Dalian Medical College, 1954. Appointments: Dean, Professor of Biophysics, Department of Biophysics, Beijing Medical University. Publications: Contributor of professional articles including: The Principle of Acupuncture Analgesia, Co-author, 1987; A Study of Magnetic Signal During Qigong State with Superconducting Biomagnetometer, Co-author, 1993. Memberships: Biophysical Society of China; Physiological Society of Beijing; Chinese Society of Somatic Science. Hobbies: Literature; Music. Address: Department of Biophysics, Beijing Medical University, Beijing 100083, China.

WU Dunxu, b. 27 Feb 1939, Chendu, Sichuan, China. Professor; Physician. m. Peilun Zhu, 30 Dec 1969, 2 daughters. Education: Graduation Certificate, Master's Degree, Shanghai College of Traditional Chinese Medicine. Appointments: Paediatrician, Shanghai Shuquang Hospital, 1962-71; Head, Department of Chinese Medicine, Jiaotong Hospital, Yunnan Province, 1971-78; Instructor, Associate Professor, Professor, Doctoral Heacher, Head of Teaching and Research, Dean, Department of Basic Medicine, Shanghai College of Traditional Chinese Medicine, 1982-. Publications: Paediatrics Volume, A Complete Book of China's TCM Secret Prescriptions, Chief Editor, 1984; Diet Therapy of Common Diseases of Children, Chief Editor, 1981; A Study of TCM Pathology and Pathogenesis, Chief Editor, 1987; Food Nutrition and Medical Diet, Deputy Editor, 1981. Honours: 2nd Prize, TCMP Administrative Bureau, 1991; 3rd Prize, TCMP Administrative Bureau, 1991; 2nd Prize, Shanghai Health Bureau, 1980, 1984. Memberships: Routine Director, Research Committee, Shanghai Traditional Chinese Medicine Nutrition and Medical Diet; TCM Basic Theory Committee, Society of Traditional Chinese Medicine, Chinese Medical Association. Hobby: Chinese Martial Art. Address: Shanghai University of Traditional Chinese Medicine and Pharmacology, 530 Ling Ling Road, Shanghai 200032, China.

WU George Yung-hsing, b. 10 Nov 1948, NY, USA. Physician; Scientist. Education: MD; PhD. Appointments: Assistant Professor of Medicine, Associate Professor of Medicine, Currently Professor of Medicine and Chief of Gastroenterology-Hepatology. Publications: Co-editor, Liver Diseases: Diagnosis and Therapy Using Specific Receptors, 1991; 60 Professional articles, 1974-, including: Co-author, Fate of DNA targeted to the liver by asialogly coprotein receptor-mediated endocytosis in vivo: prolonged persistence in cytoplasmic vesicles after partial hepatectomy, in Journal Biology Chemistry, 1993. Honours include: Phi Beta Kappa and Magna Cum Laude, 1970; Gail I Zuckerman Foundation Fellowship, 1979; American Liver Foundation Postdoctoral Fellowship, 1980-81; NIH Research Career Development Award, 1986-91; Stuart F Wilson Young Faculty Research Award, 1987; Chinese American Medical Society Scientific Award, 1992; Herman Lopata Chair in Hepatitis Research, 1992. Memberships: National Board of Medical Examiners; American Board of Internal Medicine; American Association for Study of Liver Diseases; American Gastroenterological Association; American Society of Clinical Investigations; Association of American Physicians. Hobbies: Piano; Camping; Sport. Address: University of CT School of Medicine, 263 Farmington Avenue, Room AM-044, Farmington, CT 06030-1845, USA.

WU Guande, b. 29 Feb 1931, Zhejiang Province, China. Teacher. m. Zhang Qingxian, 1 May 1960, 1 son, 1 daughter. Education: Graduated, Medical University of West China, 1954. Appointments include: Vice-Director, Basic Medical Department, Luzhou Medical University, 1978-86; Various higher professional posts, Basic Medical Assessment Group, Sichuan Province, 1986-93; Currently Director, Department of Pathology, Luzhou Medical University. Publications: Study of 1541 cases of AGC in China, 3441 cases of benign and malignant ulcers, poster, 1990; Articles in Chinese Journal of Cancer Research, 1992, 1993. Honours: Honoured as Excellent Teacher and Advanced Worker, 1986, 1990, 1993; Scientific Prize, Sichuan Province, 1989, 1993; Honourable Certificate in APCC. Memberships: Director, Anti-Cancer Cooperation Association; Chinese Medical Association, Sichuan Branch. Hobbies: Playing tennis and table-tennis. Address: Department of Pathology, Luzhou Medical University, Sichuan 646000, China.

WU Han Wen, b. 10 Mar 1925, Hong Kong. Doctor; Teacher; Researcher. m. Hai Qui Wu, 7 Dec 1984, 3 d. Appointments: Professor of Medicine and Medical genetics, Head of Research Institute of Endocrinology and Metabolism, Hunan Medical University; Visiting Professor of medicine, University School of Medicine, USA, 1981-82; Dean, Hunan Medical University 2nd Affiliated Hospital, 1984-86. Publications: COntributor of 257 medical articles in professional journals, 1950-94. Honours: Scientific and Technological Advance Prize4 of National Grade, 1978, 1992; Ministerial Grade, 1992; Provincial Grade, 1980, 1986, 1987, 1992, 1992; Title of Person with Special Contribution in Science in China, 1992. Memberships: Standing Council, Chinese Medical Association; Committee Member, Internal Medicine, CMA; Committee Member, Endocrinology, CMA; Head, Metabolic Bone Disease Group, China. Hobby: Vocal music. Address: The Second Affiliated Hospital, Clinical College, Hunan Medical University, 156 Renmin Road, Changsha, Hunan, China.

WU Huai-Shen, b. 21 July 1944, Shanghai, China. Professor of Thoracic Surgery. m. Yi-Liang Huang, Wuwei, China, 10 July 1969, 2 sons. Education: MD, Nanjing Railway Medical College, China, 1971. Career: Visiting Physician, Roswell Park Memorial Institute, USA, 1985; Research Associate, University of Chicago, USA, 1986; Visiting Scholar, Tokyo Medical College, Japan, 1987; Visiting Scholar, University of Hong Kong, Hong Kong, 1988; Visiting Professor of Surgery, University of Palermo, Italy, 1989; Fellow, Austin Hospital, Australia, 1992; Professor; Vice Chief Surgeon; Tutorship of Postgraduate, Shanghai Chest Hospital, China. Publications: Co-author: Bronchiectasis & Mediastinitis in Operative Surgery of Cardio-Thoracic Disease, 1993; Results of Surgical Treatment of Lung Cancer in China, in 93 China Annual of Clinic Oncology, 1994; Advance on Prevention and Treatment of Lung Cancer, in 94 China Annual of Clinic Oncology, 1995; Super-Long-Term Survival over 15 Years of 128 Postoperative Patients with Lung Cancer, in Lung Cancer (Greece), 1994; Author: A Study on Pulmonary Scar Cancer, in National Med J China, 1984; Perioperative Blood Transfusions and Cancer Recurrence, in J Clin Oncology (USA), 1988; Cardiac Arrhythmia after Lung Cancer Surgery, in Chinese J Oncol, 1994. Honours: Honorary Scholar, Peter MacCallum Cancer Institute, Australia, 1991; Honorary Member, Hellenic Society Against Lung Cancer, Greece, 1994. Memberships: Standing Director, Chinese Cancer Research Foundation; Commissioner, Shanghai Society of Surgery; Fellow, UICC; Fellow, American College of Chest Physicians; International Society for Disease of Esophagus. Hobby: Social Dancing. Address: Department of Thoracic Surgery, Shanghai Chest Hospital, 241 West Huai-Hai Road, Shanghai 200030, China.

WU Jianguang, b. July 1938, Fuding, China. Director, Doctor. Education: MS, Collegiate Graduation. Appointments: Academy Member, Chinese Cancer Research Foundation; Member, Chinese Anticancer Association; Member, Editorial Committee, Chinese Anticancer Newspaper; Special Director, Editor, Chinese Medical Symposium; Standing Committee, Oncology, Academy of Fujian; Member, Oncology Academy of Integreted Traditional & Western Medicine, Fujian; Vice-Pres, Fujian Anticancer Association; Chief, Ningde District Anticancer Association. Publications: Clinical Study of Integration of TCM and Chemotherapy for Cancer of Stomach and Colon in the Middle and Late Stages, 1990; Hepatic Artery Ligation and Infusion of Anticancer Chemotherapy Agents through Hepatic Artery Combined with Intratumoral Injection of Absolute Alcohol in the Treatment of Unresectable Liver Cancer, An Experience in 24 cases, 1993. Honours: Award by State Council of PRC, Great Contribution to Chinese Medical & Health Undertaking, 1992. Address: Ningde District Second Hospital, 5 Jiaocheng Bang Road, Ningde City 352100, Fujian, China.

WU Jin Zhi, b. 10 July 1938, Shanghai, China. Doctor. m. 12 June 1966, 2 daughters. Education: MD. Appointments: Physician, Shanghai First Steel Plant; Zhongshan Hospital, Shanghai; International Peace Maternity & Child Health Hospital. Publications: Serum FSH.LH Estrodial and Progesterone Levels During Menstrual Cycle in Healthy Women,

1983; Preliminary Report on Human Chorionic Gonadotropin in the Treatment of Habitual Abortion; Livial in the Treatment of Menopaused Syndrome, 1992. Memberships: Chinese Medical Association. Hobbies: Music; Sports. Address: Room 408 No 900 Cao-Qi Road North, Shanghai 200030, China.

WU Jinmin, b. 28 Aug 1939, Shanghai, China. Surgical Oncologist. m. Song Xiaoyan, 7 Jan 1967, 2 sons. Education: MD, Zhejiang Medical University, 1962; Visiting Fellow, Harvard Medical School, USA, 1983-85; Visiting Fellow, Loma Linda University, USA, 1988. Appointments: Attending Surgeon, 1978-86, currently President, 2nd Affiliated Hospital, Zhejiang Medical University, Hangzhou, 1978-86; Associate Professor, Zhejiang Medical University, 1986-90; Currently Dean, 2nd Clinical College. Publications: Cancer metastasis, 1990; Screening of Colorectal Cancer - the Protocol and its Evaluation, 1991. Honours: Winner, Government Special Allowance, 1990; 1st Grade Provincial Science and Technology Achievement Award, 1992; 3rd Grade State Science and Technology Achievement Award, 1993. Memberships: Chinese Medical Association; Chinese Anti-Cancer Association; Society of Colorectal Disease, USA. Hobbies: Tennis; Swimming. Address: 2nd Affiliated Hospital, Zhejiang Medical University, 68 Jiefang Road, Hangzhou 310009, China.

WU Ke-fu, b. 12 Jan 1938, Shanghai, China. Scientist. m. Yu-hua Song, 1 Jan 1963, 1 son, 2 daughters. Education: BA, Peking University, 1959; MD, Peking Union Medical College, 1964. Appointments: Chinese Academy of Medical Sciences: Research Assistant, Institute of Medical Biology, Kunming, 1964-71; Assistant, Institute of Blood Transfusion, Chengdu, 1971-72, Research Assistant, 1973-79, Lecturer, 1980-81, Institute of Hematology, Sichuan; Visiting Scientist, University of Hong Kong, 1981; Visiting Fellow: Queensland Institute of Medical Research, Brisbane, Australia, 1982-84; Peter McCulum Cancer Institute, Melbourne, 1984; Lecturer, 1985-86, Associate Professor, 1986-90, Professor, Chairman, Department for Cell Biology, 1990-, Institute of Hematology, Tianjin; Visiting Professor, University of Nebraska Medical Center, Omaha, USA, 1991. Publications include: Cell Growth Factors, 1988; Co-author: Inhibition of growth of certain human tumor cell lines by a factor derived from human fibroblast-like cell line, 1985; Expression of Transforming Growth Factor-beta, Tumor Necrosis Factor-alpha and Leukemia Inhibitory Factor mRNAs in rodent and human hematopoietic cells, 1991; Enhancement of J6-1 human leukemic cell proliferation by cell-cell contact: Role of an M-CSF-like membrane-associated growth factor, 1994. Honours: 1st Class Prize, 1980, 2nd Prize, 1992, Chinese Public Health Ministry; Cytology Specialist, Tianjin Science and Technology Commission, 1992. Memberships: Chinese Society of Cell Biology; Fellow, International Union Against Cancer; Standing Director, Chinese Society of Experimental Hematology; Leukocyte Biology Society; International Society for Experimental Hematology. Hobby: Music. Address: Institute of Hematology, Chinese Academy of Medical Sciences, 288 Nanjing Road, Tianjin 300020, China.

WU Ke-Rang, b. 13 August 1935, Yi-Wu City, Zhejiang, China. Professor. m. Nan-Hua Xu, 1 May 1967, 2 daughters. Education: The Pharmacy College of Beijing Medical University, 1953-58; The 7th Study Class of Traditional Chinese Medicine of Shanxi, 1975-76. Appointments: Pharmacist, Taiyuan Central Hospital, Shanxi, 1958-78; Zhejiang College of Traditional Chinese Medicine, 1979-; Director, Chinese Traditional Medical Research Centre. Publications: 40 Journal Articles, 9 Textbooks and other works, 5 Popular Articles. Honours: The Excellence Award and Honour of Zhejiang College of Traditional Chinese Medicine for Distinguished Educational Reforms, 1989; The 3rd Chinese Outstanding Textbook Award, 1993. Memberships: Committee, Zhejiang Association of Pharmacology; Editorial Board, Chinese Materia Medica, State Bureau of Traditional Chinese Medicine; Director, Zhejiang College of Traditional Chinese Medicine of 9-3 Party. Hobbies: Travel; Sport. Address: Zhejiang College of Traditional Chinese Medicine, Hangzhou 310009, China.

WU Lezheng, b. 6 June 1935, Shaoxing, Zhejiang, China. Medical Doctor. m. 8 Jan 1970, 2 sons. Education: MD, Medicine, 1957, Completed postgraduate studies in Ophthalmology, 1962, Sun Yat-Sen University of Medical Sciences. Appointments: Ophthalmologist, 1957-72, Associate Professor, Professor, Chairman, Department of Ophthalmology, Director, Eye Research Institute, 1982-, Sun-Yat Sen University of Medical Sciences; Attending Ophthalmologist, Guangdong Province, and Peking (Beijing) Medical College, 1972-79; Research Scientist, Fellow, Stanford and Johns Hopkins Universities, National Institutes of Health, USA, 1979-82; Director, National Ophthalmological

Laboratories, Ministry of Public Health, China, 1991-. Publications: Artificial Vision, 1980; Ocular Differential Diagnosis, Chinese version, 1981; Electroretinogram, 1989; 170 articles. Honours include: Honorary Guest, 91st Japan National Ophthalmological Congress, 1987; Guest Professor, University Eye Hospital, Munich, 1991; Distinguished Specialist, Ministry of Public Health, 1992; Awards: Menpower, Research to Prevent Blindness, USA, 1980; Distinguished Service, World Eye Foundation, 1982; Advance in Science and Technology, National Education Commission and Ministry of Public Health, 1987, 1989, 1991, 1993; Distinguished Service, Asia-Pacific Academy of Ophthalmology, 1991. Memberships: Secretary, International Society for Clinical Electrophysiology of Vision; Board, Afro-Asian Council of Ophthalmology; Committeeman, Ophthalmological Society, China Medical Association; Consultant, Helen Keller International; President, International Society on Tropic and Subtropic Ophthalmology. Hobbies: Stamp collecting; Photography. Address: 54 Xianlie Nan Road, Guangzhou 510060, China.

WU Min, b. 10 Mar 1958, Zhejiang, China. Teacher. m. 21 Dec 1987, 1 d. Education: BA, Xinjiang University, 1982. Appointments: Associate Professor of Genetics,Department of Biology, Xinjiang Normal University. Publications: A Preliminary Study of the Karyotype of Bufo Viridis, 1987; A Study of the Karyotype of Three Species of Phrynocephalus from Xinjiang, 1989; A Preliminary Report on the Kind of rare Wildlife-Ranodon Sibiricus, 1990; The Study of the RELPs of TK-C Gene of Weiwuer and Hui Nationalities, 1994. Memberships: Chinese Genetics Soceity; Council Member, Xinjiang Zoology Society. Hobby: Running. Address: Department of Biology, Xinjiang Normal University, Urumqi 830053, China.

WU Peng Nian, b. 1 May 1921, Jiang Du County, Jiang Su Province, China. Preventive Medicine. m. Lai Qi Ling, 1 Oct 1951, 1 s, 1 d. Education: MD, Hsiang Ya Medical College; Advanced study at Shanghai Medical University, 1955-57. Career: Assistant, 1949-54, Lecturer, 1954-55, Tropical Medicine, Lecturer, 1955-79, Associate Professor, 1979-85, Professor of Epidemiology, 1985-, Hunan Medical University, Changsha, China. Publications include: Co-author, Diphtheria Malaria Filaraisis, in Textbook of Epidemiology, 1984; Typhoid Fever Enteritis, in Advance of Epidemiology, 1986; Risk Factors of Nasopharyngeal Carcinoma, Bulletin Hunan Medical College, 1987. Honours: 2nd Class Award, Scientific and Technical Advances, Hunan Province, 1987; Long Service and Achievement Award, State Education Commission of China, 1990. Memberships: Hunan Preventive Medical Association; Hunan Epidemiological Association; National Epidemiology Association. Address: Department of Epidemiology, Hunan Medical University, Changsha 410078, China.

WU Ruimei b. 15 Oct 1935, Anhui, China. Teacher. m. Shi-yuan Cheng, 1 May 1967, 2 d. Education: Graduation Certificate, Anhui Medical College, 1961. Appointments: Assistant of Histology and Embryology, 1961-78. Lecturer of Histology and Embryology, 1979-84, Associate Professor, 1985-92, Professor of Histology and Embryology, 1993-, Anhui Medical University. Publications: Practical Histology and Embryology, Co-author, 1987, 1989; Pharmacological Experimental Methods, Co-author, 1991; Quantitative Study of Neurons Within the Mucosa of Human Small Intestine, Co-author, 1991; Intramucosal Nerve Cells in Human Small Intestine, Co-author, 1993; Histochemical and Immunohistochemical Observations on Neurons within the Mucosa of Human Small Intestine, Co-author, 1993; Concomitance of Ganglion Plexus and Blood Vessel in the Submucosa of Gastrointestinal Tract of the Guinea-Pig, Co-author, 1993. Membership: Chinese Society of Anatomy. Hobbies: Running; Table-tennis. Address: Department of Histology and Embryology, Anhui Medical University, Hefei 230032, China.

WU Shaoting, b. 26 Jan 1945, Hubei, China. Professor, Doctor. m. 11 January 1976, 1 son. Education: Graduate, Tongji Medical University, 1970. Appointments: Department Parasitology, Tongji Medical University, 1994-. Publications: Toxoplasma Gondii-infection of Pregnant Women in Wuhan and Heidelberg: A Comparative Study, 1991; Study of Sarcolystis Fusiformis from Water Buffalo in China, 1992; Hepatology, 1994. Memberships: Chinese Medical Association; Zoological Society of China; Chinese Protozoological Society; Chinese-German Medical Association. Address: Department of Parasitology, Tongji Medical University, Wuhan, Hubei 430030, China.

WU Tiefeng, b. 18 Sept 1927, Nanjing, Fujian, China. Teacher; Professor of Dermatology. m. Guoying Jin, 8 July 1952, 1 son, 1

daughter. Education: MB, Third Military Medical University, 1951. Appointments: Assistant in Dermatology, 1951, Lecturer in Dermatology, 1956, Associate Professor of Dermatology, 1981, Professor of Dermatology, 1987-, Jiangxi Medical College, Nanchang. Publications: Symptom Diagnosis of Skin Diseases, book, 1985; Dermatosis linearis alba, 1986; Leukoderma and Melanoderma, book, 1993; Treatment of keloids with triamcinolone and 5-fluorouracil injected intralesionally, 1994. Honours: 1st Award of Technical Innovation, Jiangxi Health Department, 1993. Memberships: Committee Member, Dermatological Association, Chinese Medical Association; Head of Committee, Jiangxi Dermatological Association. Hobbies: Swimming; Music. Address: Department of Dermatology, Second Affiliated Hospital, Jiangxi Medical College, Nanchang, Jiangxi 330006, China.

WU Wei-Fong, b. 12 Aug 1951, Chang-Hwa, Taiwan. Physician. m. Helen Chen, 7 Jan 1982, 2 sons. Education: MD, China Medical College, Taichung, Taiwan, 1976. Appointments: Resident, Chief Resident, Department of Paediatrics, Fellow, Paediatric Allergy and Immunology, Taipei Municipal Jen-Ai Hospital; Visiting Fellow, University of California, San Francisco, USA; Currently Director, Paediatric Allergy and Immunology, Taipei Municipal Jen-Ai Hospital. Publications: Co-author: Evaluation of Pulmonary Function in Children with Bronchial Asthma by Berodnal MDI, 1991; Paediatric Respiratory Allergy and Asthma: An Update (in Chinese), 1992. Honours: Outstanding Physician, China Culture Association, 1983. Memberships: American Academy of Allergy and Immunology; American College of Allergy and Immunology; International Association of Allergy and Clinical Immunology. Hobbies: Squash; Swimming; Golf. Address: 10 Sec 4, Jen-Ai Road, Taipei 10650, Taiwan.

WU Xi Ru, b. 19 Nov 1933, Shanghai, China. Peadiatrician; Paediatric Neurologist. m. 12 Feb 1961, div. 2 s. Education: Bachelor, Beijing Medical University, 1950-55. Appointments: Resident, Attending Associate Professor, 1955-85, Director, Professor, 1985-, First Teaching Hospital, Beijing Medical University; Honorary fellow, Minnesota Medical School, USA, 1979-82; Adjunct Scientist, NIH, USA, 1990. Publications: Molecular Neurobiology Basis of Nervous System Disorders, Chief Editor, 1994; Contributor of articles in numerous professional journals. Honours: Chinese Ministry of Health Award for Science and Technology, 1990; Chinese Nationwide Award for Science and Technology, 1992. Memberships:IBRO; AOACN; Deputy Director, Chinese Paediatric Society; Council Member, ICNA, Beijing Epilepsy Association of China. Hobbies: Music; Piano. Address: Paediatrics, First Teaching Hospital, Beijing Medical University, Beijing 100034, China.

WU Xinyan, b. 20 July 1933, Shanghai, China. Radiologist. m. 31 September 1962, 2 sons. Education: MD; PhD. Appointments: Resident, Assistant Professor, Department of Radiology, Qingdao Medical College Affiliated Hospital; Professor, Qingdao Medical College; Clinical Professor, Qingdao Municipal Hospital. Publications: Co-author: Radiology of Bone and Joint, 1982; Co-author: Imaging Diagnosis of Liver Bilebladder, Pancreas and Spleen, 1980; Co-author: Imaging Diagnosis of Obstetrics and Gynaecology, 1989; Author: The Clinico-Radiological Diagnosis of Lymphoma of Stomach, 1977; Author: Radiologic Diagnosis of Rickets in Infancy Using Molybdenum Target, 1987; Author: The Clinico-Radiologic Diagnosis of Thoracic Sarcoidosis, 1990; Author: CT Study of Asbestosis in Chinese Journal of Industrial Hygiene and Occupational Disease, 1992; Author: CT Features of Wilson's Disease and Clinical Significances, 1994. Honours: National Prize, 1992; Excellent Scientific Worker of Shandong, 1988; Outstanding Scientific Talent of Qingdao, 1988, 1992. Memberships: Chairman, Qingdao Branch Society of Radiology; Chinese Medical Association. Hobbies: Football; Basketball; Classical Music. Address: 1 Jiaozhou Road, Qingdao Municipal Hospital, Qingdao, Shandong 266011, China.

WU Xirui, b. 16 Aug 1923, Tianjing, China. Medical Doctor. m. Ma Tingyuan, 14 Nov 1953, 2 daughters. Education: MD, Tongji University, 1949; PhD, All-Soviet Academy of Medicine, 1961. Appointments: Tongji Medical University, 1949-80, 1984-94, currently Professor and Director, Centre of Reproductive Medicine; World Health Organization, 1981-83. Publications: Uterotonic effect of Lenurus Sibiricus, 1954; Female oral contraceptives, 1964; Trichosanthin for contragestion, 1965; Gossypol for male antifertility, 1972; Chlormadinone for female contraception, 1978; Mifepristone for female contragestion, 1986, 1989. Honours: National Advanced Scientist in Fertility Regulation Research, 1989, 1991; 24 awards in fields of fertility regulation and reproductive medicine. Membership: President, Society of Fertility Regulation, Chinese Medical Association, 1985-94. Hobbies: Music; Sport. Address:

Centre of Reproductive Medicine, Tongji Medical University, Wuhan 430030, China.

WU Xiu-Gan, b. 10 Mar 1928, Zhongshan, Guangdong, China. Professor of Pathology. m. Jie-Qing Peng, 28 Dec 1955, 2 daughters. Education: Graduate Diploma, Zhongshan Medical College, Guangzhou, 1954. Appointments: Assistant, Tongji Medical College, Wuhan, 1954-62; Lecturer, 1963-79, Associate Professor, 1980-89, Wuhan Medical College; Professor of Pathology, Tongji Medical University, Wuhan, 1990-; Member, Academic Committee, International Research and Exchabnge Centre of Liver Diseases. Publications: The influence of vitamin B2 on the development of experimental hepatoma, 1985; The pathologic change, diagnosis and differential diagnosis of lobular virus hepatitis, 1986; The role of Ito cells in liver cirrhosis of rats induced by DEN, 1988; The influence of ginseng on the development of DEN hepatoma of rats, 1990; The study of curative effects of ginseng on DEN hepatoma of rats, 1991; Books: Pathology of Liver Diseases, 1987; Basic Pathology of Liver Diseases, 1992. Honours: Excellent Academic Thesis Awards, Provincial Academic Association, 1981, 1985, 1986; Advanced Academic Work Award, Tongji Medical University, 1991. Memberships: Chinese Medical Association; International Research and Exchange. Hobbies: Music; Sports. Address: Department of Pathology, Tongji Medical University, Wuhan 430030, China.

WU Xu, b. 8 Jan 1940, Nantong, Jiangsu, China. Acupuncturist.m. Feng Xingyuan, 1 son. Education: Undergraduate. Appointments: Vice Dean; Doctor; Tutor of MD. Publication: Clinical Acupuncture. Honour: Famous Traditional Chinese Medicine Doctor of Jiangsu, 1994. Membership: Vice President, Jiangsu Acupuncture Association. Hobby: Music. Address: Nanjing College of Traditional Chinese Medicine, Nanjing, Jiangsu, China.

WU Xuezhou, b. 27 Nov 1938, Nankang, Jiangxi, China. Medical Education. m. Zeng Linglian, 8 Feb 1967, 4 daughters. Education: MB, Jiangxi Medical College, China, 1962. Career: Physician, 1963; Instructor, Jiangxi College of Traditional Chinese Medicine (JCTCM); Head and Professor, Department of Microbiology, JCTCM; Associate Professor, 1987; Professor, 1993. Publications: Microbiology and Parasitology, 1980; Medical Microbiology, 1991; Methodology of Studying Pharmacology of Chinese Medicines, 1993; Microbiology and Parasitology, 1993. Honours: 3rd Prize, Scientific-Technology Achievement, JCTCM, 1993; 1st Prize, Scientific-Technology Invention, Jiangxi Department of Public Health, 1994; 3rd Prize, Scientific-Technology Invention, Jiangxi, 1994. Memberships: Standing Counil & Vice Secretary General, Jiangxi Microbiology Association (JMA); Director, Jiangxi Med Microbiology Council, JMA; Vice Director and Member of Standing Council, Microbiology & Immunology Association, Jiangxi Branch, CMA. Hobby: Stamp Collection. Address: Jiangxi College of Traditional Chinese Medicine, No 20 Yangming Road, Nanchang, Jiangxi 330006, China.

WU Yijing. Director. Appointments: Direcotr, Yijing Institute for the Treatment of Cancer, Lin Fen, China. Publications: Numerous Papers including, Selection from Natural Organic Embryo Cell Modification Treatment; Research of 242 Cases of Cancer with Reference Between Tianhua Anticancer Pill Treatment and Chemot Therapy Treatment; Books include, Natural Organic Embryo Cell Modification Treatment; A New View on Cancer Treatment. Honours: Rewarded 4 Gold Medals, National and International; Second Prize of National Science Development; Gold Medal of the World Traditional Science Papers of Excellence Competition in America, 1994; Grant to set up Wuerpeng Medicine Research Center, New York; Grant to set up Shanxi Asian - Pacific Cancer Research Center by Chinese Government. Address: Linfen Prefectural Holistic Medicine, Cancer Curing Research Institute of Shanxi Province, 74 Pingyang Nanjie, Linfen City, Shanxi Province, China.

WU Ying-Kai, b. 8 May 1910, Liao-ning, China. Thoracic Surgeon. m. Li Shih-yan, 1 Jan 1950, 2 sons, 1 daughter. Education: MB ChB; FACS(Hon). Appointments: Professor, Chair, Department of Surgery, Peking Union Medical College; Director of Cardiovascular Institute, Chinese Academy of Medical Sciences; Honorary Director, Beijing Heart Lung and Blood Vessel Medical Centre. Publications: Chest Diseases, 1959; Cancer of Esophagus, 1964; Chest Surgery, 1974; International Practice of Cardiothoracic Surgery, 1985. Memberships: Permanent Member, Chinese Medical Association; Chairman, Society of Surgery; Chairman, Cardiovascular Society of China; Honorary Fellow, American Surgical Association; Honorary Member, USSR Surgical Association;

Honorary Fellow, American Association of Thoracic Surgery. Address: Beijing Heart Lung and Blood Vessel Medical Centre, 100029 Beijing, China.

WU Zhi-li, b. 20 Aug 1915, Anhui Province, China. Medical Doctor; Professor (retired). m. Zhang Yang-fen, 28 Dec 1941, 3 sons. Education: Bachelor of Medicine, National Medical College, Shanghai. Appointments: Director of Medical Service (MS), 3rd Division, New 4th Army, 1943-47; Vice Director of Medical Services, North-Eastern Military District, 1948-50; Surgeon General to Chinese People's Volunteer Army (CPVA), Korea, 1950-54; Principal, 1954-59, 2nd Military Medical University, PLA, 1954-59; Vice-President, Chinese Medical Association, 1952; Surgeon General, Air Force, PLA, 1962-65; Vice-Director, Academy of Military Medical Sciences (AMMS), 1978-85. Publications: Chief Editor, Report of Medical Service, CPVA, 4 Volumes; Chief Editor, Practical Medical Dictionary, editions 1-2; Wounded Patient Flow, Medical Corps Intern. Vol 2, #6, 1987; Associate Editor, Military Medicine, Encyclopedia Medica Sinica. Honours: 3 pcs of 2nd class medal from PLA; 5 pcs of 2nd class medal from N.Korea; Honourable Professor of Military Medicine, AMMS. Hobbies: Tennis; Billiards; Bridge. Address: 27 Taiping Road, Beijing 100850, China, T 8211994.

WU Zhong-yao, b. 1 Sep 1938, Goungdon, China. Ophthalmologist. m. 8 Sep 1967, 1 son, 1 daughter. Education: Postgraduate. Appointments: Resident of Ophthalmology, 1961-68; Attending Ophthalmologist, 1969-78; Postgraduate of Ophthalmology, 1978-81; Lecturer and Attending Ophthalmologist, 1978-85; Associate Professor, 1985-87, Professor, 1991-, Zhongshan Ophthalmic Centre. Publications: The Research of Biometric Measurement in Primary Closed-Angle Glaucoma, 1983; The Diagnosis of Retinoblastoma with Ultrasound (A- and B- Scan), 1985; The Diagnosis of Choroidal Tumors with Ultrasound - Report of 43 Cases, 1988; The Diagnosis of Intracranial AV Malformation with orbital Involvement by B-scan, Colour Doppler and CT-Scan, 1989; CT Scan in 52 Cases of Retinoblastoma, 1993; Color Doppler in the Diagnosis and Follow-up of Carotid Cavernous Sinus Fistulas, 1994. Memberships: Chinese Medical Association; Guangdong Ophthalmological Society; Biological Medicine and Engineering; Ultrasonic Society. Address: Zhongshan Ophthalmic Centre, Sun Yat-Sen University of Medical Sciences, Guangzhou 510060, China.

WU Zhongbi, b. 19 Mar 1919. Medical Professor. m. Yidi Yang, 25 Feb 1952, 2 d. Education: Graduate, National Tongji University, 1945. Appointments: Assistant of Pathology, Tongji University, 1945-50; Lecturer, 1950-56, Associate Professor, 1956-77, Professor, 1978-, Tongji Medical University, Wuhan. Publications: Textbook on Pathology; System Research on the Old Cadavers from Western Han Dynasty, 1981; Basis of Ultrastructural Pathology, 1990; Primary Liver Cancer, 1989. Honours: 1st rate National Prize, 1978; Large Cross for Distinguished Service, Germany, 1985; Honorary Medal, Heidelberg University, 1986; Honorary Prize, National education Committee, 1989, 1993; Dr Honoris Causa. Memberships: Chinese Association of Pathology; International Academy of Pathology; German Association of Pathology; German Academy Natural Sciences. Address: Tongji Medical University, 13 Hangkong Road, Wuhan 430030, China.

WU Zhunian, b. 10 Mar, Beijing, China. Chinese Medical Doctor. m. Liu Chun Hua, 24 Oct 1942, 3 d. Education: Pharmacist, Chinese Medical College, 1942. Career: Doctor, Private Clinic, 1946-59; Beijing TB Hospital, 1959-84; Beijing Anzhen Hospital, 1984-89, now retired. Publications: Treatment of Tuberculosis Pulmonary by Traditional Chinese Medicine, in Journal of Traditional Chinese Medicine, 1980; Handbook of Traditional Prescriptions, in China Selected Works of Traditional Prescriptions, 1984; Treatment of Cough, in China Selected Works of Famous Prescriptions, 1993. Honour: Senior Doctor, Over 30 Years Service, Beijing Bureau of Health. Memberships: Beijing Cancer Association; Beijing Chinese Medical Association. Address: 5-102 Building No 1, Anzhen Hospital, Beijing 100029, China.

WU Ziliang, b. 25 Oct 1932, Bo-Yang, Jiangxi Province, China. Paediatrician. m. Liang Shengqiong, 30 Sept 1989, 1 son, 3 daughters. Education: MD, 1958, Intern, Resident, 1958-61, Postdoctoral research, Paediatric Infectious Disease, 1961-64, Zhongshan Medical College; Fellow, Paediatric Haematology and Oncology, Zhejiang Medical College, 1974-75. Appointments: Assistant Professor, Paediatrics, General Hospital, 1964-71, Associate Professor, Paediatrics, General Hospital, 1971-81, Zhongshan Medical College, Guangzhou; Vice-Chairman, Department of Paediatrics, 1981-82, Chairman, Professor, Paediatrics, 1986-, 1st Affiliated Hospital, Guangzhou

Medical College; Visiting Associate Professor, Paediatrics, Haematology-Oncology Division, School of Medicine, University of California, Los Angeles, USA, 1982-85. Publications: Co-author: Lectures in Clinical Pediatrics, 1977; Hematological Diseases of the Newborn, 1980; Jaundice in the Newborn, 1982; Case Discussion on Pediatric Hematology, 1987; Textbook of Pediatrics, 1990; Author, book contributions: Glucose-6-Phosphate Dehydrogenase Deficiency in Erythrocytes, Pyruvate Kinase Deficiency in Erythrocytes, 1990; Primary Immunodeficient Diseases, 1993; 97 papers, 1960-. Honours include: Silbert Scholar, University of California, Los Angeles, 1982-83; 6 Research Awards, Guangdong Province and City, 1986-89; Outstanding Teacher, Guangzhou City, 1989; Expert of Great Contribution, Guangdong Province, 1991; Outstanding Expert and Scholar, Teacher with Great Contribution, Guangzhou City, 1992. Memberships include: Vice-President, Guangzhou City Branch, Chinese Medical Association; Pediatric Association, Chinese Medical Association, Guangzhou City Branch Chairman, Vice-Chairman 1986-88; Leading Group, Hematological Association, Chinese Medical Association. Hobbies: Reading, especially historical subjects. Address: Department of Pediatrics, 1st Teaching Hospital, Guangzhou Medical College, 151 Yan Jiang Road, Guangzhou 510120, China.

WYKES Til, b. 14 Mar 1953, Cheshire, England. Psychologist. Education: BSc, Honours; MPhil; DPhil. Appointments: Scientific Officer, MRC; Visiting Research Fellow, Department of Health, New South Wales, Australia; Lecturer, Department of Psychology, Institute of Psychiatry; Senior Lecturer and Honorary Consultant Clinical Psychologist. Publications: Violence and Health Care Professionals, 1994; Contributor of 35 learned articles. Memberships: Fellow, British Psychological Society, Clinical Pathology Section; Chartered Clinical Psychologist. Address: Department of Psychology, Institute of Psychiatry, De Crespogny Park, London SE5 8AF, England.

WYNN Susan Rudd, b. 25 Dec 1955, Louisville, KY, USA. Physician. 2 s. Education: BSc, MD, TX A and M University, College Station, TX; Residency Training in General Pediatrics, Pediatric Allergy and Allergy Research, Mayo Clinic, Rochester, MN. Appointments: Instructor, Mayo Medical School, 1986-87; Associate Consultant in Pediatrics, Mayo Clinic, 1987; Currently, Allergist, Fort Worth Allergy and Asthma Associates, Fort Worth, TX. Publications: Over 20 articles in professional journals, 1984-93, including: Anticholinergics, Corticosteroids, Troleandomycin, and Immunosuppressives, In Annals Allergy, 1991; Co-author: Anaphylaxis at School: Etiologic Factors, Prevalence, and Treatment, in Pediatrics, 1993; The Effect of Heating-Ventilation-Air Conditioning (HVAC) System Sanitation on Airborne Fungal Populations in Residential Environments, in Annals Allergy, 1993. Honours: Distinguished Student, TX A and M University, 1975; Outstanding Pediatrics Student, TX A and M University College of Medicine, 1981; Various Awards and Travel Grants; Geigy Fellowship Award, American College of Allergists, 1987. Memberships: Alpha Omega Alpha; American Medical Association; American Academy of Pediatrics; American Academy of Allergy and Immunology; American College of Allergy and Immunology. Hobbies: Choral Music; Piano; Photography; Gardening. Address: Fort Worth Allergy and Asthma Associates, 5929 Lovell Avenue, Fort Worth, TX 76107, USA.

X

XI Jiu-Yi, b. 22 January 1923. Doctor of Traditional Chinese Medicine. m. Zhao Ling Zhao, 2 February 1987, 2 sons, 2 daughters. Appointments: Chairman, Doctoral Tutor, Director, Shanghai Traditional Chinese & Western Medicine Integrated Institute for Peripheral Vascular Disease; Chairman, Department of National Traditional Chinese Medicine Medical Center for Peripheral Vascular Disease. Publications Include: Treatment of DVT (deep vein thrombosis) with principle of clearing up Ying (nutrient) and removing blood stasis, 1982; Experience of treatment of peripheral vascular disease based on the concept of "stasis due to evils", 1987; Clinical experience of foot tendon degeneration caused by diabetes mellitus, 1989; Treatment of peripheral vascular disease with Traditional Chinese Medicine, 1992. Honours: Award, Excellence in Developing Traditional Chinese Medicine, Ministry of Public Health, 1959; Award, Distinguished Person in Integrating Traditional Chinese Medicine-Western Medicine Work, Ministry of Public Health, 1982; Award, National Advanced Worker, State Council of China, 1989; Award, Special Subsidy Certificate, Government of China for Great Contribution to the Cause of Health, 1991. Memberships: Vice Chairman, National Specialized Committee of the Peripheral Vascular Disease of Integrating Traditional Chinese Medicine-Western Medicine; Senior Technical Rank Approval Committee, Shanghai Public Health Bureau; Shanghai Advisory Committee of Traditional Chinese Medicine Work. Hobbies: Qigong (breathing exercise). Address: Room 202, No 2, Lane 103, Kun Shan Road, Shanghai 200080, China.

XI Zhong Yi, b. 1 Oct 1932, Xiao Yi County, Shanxi Province, China. Professor. m. 26 feb 1961, 1 son, 2 daughters. Education: BA, Medical Academy of Hebei, 1960. Appointments: Surgical Doctor, Director Doctor, Shanxi Province Tumour Hospital; Director, Shanxi Anus Rectum Hospital; Director, Institute of Combined Traditional Chinese and Western Medicine in Shanxi Province. Publications: An Improved Technique for Urinary Diversion After Total Cystectomy, 1985; Method of Artificial Anus at the Perineum after Miles' Operation, 1986; Blood Supply in Anal region, 1986; Intussusception-Like Artificial Preineal Anus After Miles' Radical Surgery, 1988; Transposition of the Abdominal Colostomy to Perineum to Form the Intussuscepted Artificial Anus, 1989; Anoplasty by Colic-Invagination with the External Sphincter retained in Treatment of Mid-Rectal Cancer, 1991; Contemporary Anus Rectum Surgery, 1993; The Advanced Therapeutics of Surgical Disease, 1993. Honours: Shanxi Special-Class Working Hero, 1985; National Exemplary Science-Technology Worker and May 1 Medal, 1986; 2nd Prize, Provincial Achievement in Science and Technology, 1986; Expert of Prominent Contribution of National Level. Memberships: Delegate, Chinese Institute of Combined Traditional Chinese and Western Medicine. Hobby: Football. Address: Shanxi Tumour Hospital, Taiyuan, Shanxi, China.

XIA Dezhao, b. 15 Jan 1918, Siping, Jilin Province, China. Ophthalmologist. m. Ke Wang, Mar 1946, 3 sons, 4 daughters. Education: MD. Appointments: Associate Professor, Professor in Ophthalmology, 1945-, Department Chairman, 1948-83, currently Director, postgraduate students for Doctor's degree, Department of Ophthalmology, 1st Hospital, China Medical University, Shenyang; Editor-in-chief, The Journal of Practical Ophthalmology, 1983-. Publications: Ophthalmology, 3rd Edition (chief editor), 1989; Surgical Anatomy - Eye section (editor-in-chief), 1992. Honours: Deputy to National People's Congress, 1983-92. Memberships: Ophthalmological Society, Chinese Medical Association, Past Standing Committee Member. Hobbies: Hunting; Swimming; Skating. Address: Department of Ophthalmology, The 1st Hospital, China Medical University, 155 North Nanjing Street, Shenyang 110001, China.

XIA Kangtai, b. 9 May 1950, Anhua County, Hunan Province, China. Anaesthetist. m. Zhu Xili, 10 Jan 1978, 1 son, 1 daughter. Education: BM, 1973, MMed, 1993, First Military Medical College of PLA. Appointments: Teaching Assistant, 1973-88, Resident Doctor, General resident Doctor, 1985-88, Lecturer, Doctor-in-Charge, 1989-93, Associate Chief Doctor, 1994-, Nan Fang Hospital. Publications: Cytological Examination of CSF for 29 Cases of Peripheral Nerve Diseases, Co-author, 1994; TV-AV Type Anesthetic Breathing Machine, 1987; Anesthesia for 2815 Cases of Epidural Space Nerve Block, 1981. Honours: Prize for Rescuing Dying Patients, Nan Fang Hospital, 1982; Honour of Model General resident Doctor, nan Fang Hospital, 1985; Model Medical Team Worker, 1986; Excellent Teacher of Clinica

Medicine, Nan Fang Hospital, 1992. Memberships: Guangdong Association of Anesthesiology; Chinese Anesthesiology Society. Hobbies: Chess; Swimming. Address: Anaesthetic Department, Nan Fang Hospital, Tong He, Guangzhou 510515, China.

XIANG Meng Ze, b. 26 April 1929, Sichuan, China. Professor of Psychiatry. m. Guan Ming Sun, 7 November 1952, 2 sons, 1 daughter. Education:BM, MD, West China Union University, Chengdu, Sichuan, China, 1952. Appointments: Psychiatrist, The Mental Hospital of Sichuan Medical College, 1952-57; Lecturer in Psychiatry, Sichuan Medical College, 1958-80; Associate Professor of Psychiatry, Sichuan Medical College, 1980-85; Professor of Psychiatry, West China University of Medical Sciences, Chengdu, China, 1985-. Publications: Co-author: Child Psychiatry of Modern China, 1994; Community Rehabilitation of Mental Disease, 1993; A Comprehensive Book of Psychological Health, 1993; A Textbook of Psychiatry, 1964, 1973. Honours: 2nd Prize Award, Ministry of Health, China, 1985; 2nd Prize Award, Sichuan Science and Technology Committee, 1985, 1993. Memberships: Committee Member, Chinese Academy of Medicine, Section of Social Psychiatry; Advisor, Chinese Association of Mental Health Rehabilitation; WHO Section of Trans-Cultural Psychiatry. Hobbies: Bridge. Address: 15, 3rd Section of Renmin Nan Lu, Chengdu, Sichuan 61004, China.

XIAO Changsi, b. 2 Feb 1930, Hunan, China. Professor of Anaesthesiology. 2 sons. Education: BA, Medical University of China; MD, Shanghai Medical University. Apointments: President, Department of Anaesthesia, Children's Hospital of Shanghai Medical University; President, Department of Anaesthesia, Zhongshan Hospital, Shanghai Medical University; Vice Director, Pain Research Centre, Shanghai Medical niversity. Publications: Bupivacaine in Glycerine for Analgesia, 1993; Mechanical Ventilation During Mitral Valve Surgery, 1985; The Eliminative Effect of Drugs on Oxygen Radical Generated in Pulmonary Artery, 1992; Anesthesia for Heart Surgery of Valve Replacement, 1982. memberships: Vice President, Shanghai Medical Society; Committee Member, Anesthesia Society of China. Hobbies: Taiji; Quan. Address: Zhong Shan Hospital, Shanghai Medical University, 136 Yi Xue Yuan Road, Shanghai 200032, China.

XIAO Guan Hui, b. 3 Nov 1930, Guangzhou, China. Doctor. m. Gui Zhi Ning, 1 Oct 1960, 2 d. Education: Medical Degree, South China University of Medical Sciences, Guangzhou, China; Medical Diplomate. Appointments: Doctor, Department Head of Radiology, Sun Yat Sen University of Medical Sciences, 1955-. Publications: Radiographic changes in bone and joint in 244 cases of Pine Caterpillars disease, in Chinese Journal of Radiology, 1979; Ewing Sarcoma, in Chinese Journal of Radiology, 1986; Chondromy Fibroma of bone, in Chinese Journal of Orthopedics; Co-author, Pathological and Radiological study of Parenteal Sarcoma, in National Medical Journal of China, 1989. Membership: Chinese Medical Association. Address: 11-2 Ma Pang Gang Street, Guangzhou, Guangdong, China.

XIAO Taosheng, b. 9 Sep 1946, Chengdu, China. Oil Painter. m. Yuan Dalin, 1 Jan 1978, 1 son. Appointments: ASssociate Professor; Director; Deputy President, Sichuan Academy of Sculpture and Arts. Publications: A Selection of Sketchesd bu Xiao Taosheng, 1994; A Selection of Oil-Paintings by Xiao Taosheng, 1995; Contributor to magazines and television worldwide. Honours: 1st prize, Chinese Oil Painting Exhibition, 1984; 1st Prize, Chinese National Sports-Arts Exhibition, 1990; 1st prize, China National Painting Exhibitions, 1984; Chinese Self-Educated Experts prize, 1994. Membership: Chinese Artists Association. Hobbies: Football; Music. Address: 73 Xi Mian Qiao Xia Jie, Chengdu 610041, China.

XIAO Xuehe, b. 28 Apr 1936, Tianjin, China. Doctor. m. 12 Mar 1963, 2 daughters. Education: Graduate, 4th Military Medical College, 1962. Appointments: Attending Doctor, Vice Chief, ENT Department, No 161 Central Hospital, 1969; Vice-Archiater, Chief, 1989; Archiater, Professor, Chief, 1990-. Publications: 5 medical books including: Review the Development of Ear Operation, Editor-in-Chief, 1985; Failure and Experience of Head and Neck Operation, Editor-in-Chief, 1994; Contridbutor of 40 medical theses including: Preparing and Clinical Use of Suction-Cutter of Polyp of Vocal Cord, 1991; Modified IV Tympanoplasty, 1994; Longterm Observing of Hemoe-auditory Ossicles Postoperatively, 1994. Honours: Advanced Model in Science and Technology of PLA, 1982; 3rd Class Merit, 1985, 1991; Special Government Allowance of the State Council. Memberships: Professor, Research Institute of Biological Material, Wuhan Industrial University, 1992; Professor, First Military Medical College, 1991; Committee

Member, ORL Academy of PLA; Language and Hearing Academy of Hubei, Chinese Medical Academy; Committee Member, Secretary, ORL Academy of Chinese Medical Academy; editor, Clinical ORL Journal and Practical Medical Journal. Hobbies: Beijing Opera. Address: ENT Department, Hospital of PLA 161, Wuhan 430010, China.

XIAO Yin-Qi, b. 3 July 1938, Feshan, Guangdong Province, China. Medical Doctor. m. 1 Oct 1966, 2 daughters. Education: MB, 4th Military College, Xian, 1962. Appointments: Resident, 1962-77; Doctor in charge, 1977-83; Dean, Department of Hepatobiliary Surgery, 309th Hospital of People's Liberation Army, Beijing, 1983-94. Publications: More than 60 articles in Chinese Medical Surgery, 1980-. Honours: 6 Scientific Awards, 1989-93; Special Awards of Chinese Government, monthly 1992-. Membership: Chinese Medical Institute. Hobbies: Sports. Address: Department of Hepatobiliary Surgery, 309th Hospital, Beijing, China.

XIE Guorong, b. 2 Feb 1935, Taohuayuan, Hunan, China. Doctor of Traditional Chinese Medicine. m. Chen Fuzhi, Jan 1964, 3 daughters. Education: Graduate, Hunan Continuation School of Traditional Chinese Medicine. Appointments: Doctor; Attending Doctor; Lecturer; Associate Professor; Director Doctor, Director, Teaching and Research Section; Tutor, Master Candidates; Currently Director Doctor, Director, Acupuncture Teaching and Research Department, Hunan College of Traditional Chinese Medicine, Changsha; Developer, burnproof medicinal sticks for flaming moxibustion. Publications: Concise Acupuncture, Popular Acupuncture and A Chart of the Commonly-Used Acupoints of the Fourteen Channels, 1958-59; Observation of Channel Phenomena by Finger-Pressure and Needling Therapy, 1973; On the Pecularities of Stream Points and Careful Selection of Acupoints, and An Analysis of the Mechanical View of Classical Acupuncture Manipulation, 1986, 1990, 1993, 1994. Honours: Honour Certificates: 30 Years' Service in Education, Hunan Provincial People's Government, 1986; 30 Years' Service of Traditional Chinese Medicine, Hunan Public Health Department, 1989; Medical Team in Aid of Sierra Leone, Ministry of Public Health, China, 1993; Prizes for Research into the Anatomy of Acupoints: Hunan Educational Commission, 1987; China Medicine Society, 1990; Hunan Public Health Department, 1991. Memberships: Director, China Acupuncture Society; Director, Clinical Society, China Acupuncture Society; Chairman, Hunan Acupuncture Society; Standing Director, All-China Traditional Chinese Medicine Society, Hunan Branch; Adviser, Hunan Massotherapy; Chinese Culture Society. Hobby: Reading literature of traditional Chinese medicine and stories about Chinese physicians of all ages. Address: Hunan College of Traditional Chinese Medicine, 107 Shaoshan Road, Changsha, Hunan 410007, China.

XIE Hai-bao, b. 9 June 1935, Shanghai, China. Geriatrician. m. 1 May 1958, 2 daughters. Education: BM; Shanghai Second Medical University. Appointments: Resident Doctor, Attending Doctor, Vice-Chief of Physicians, Chief of Physicians; Director of Research Students, Zhejiang Medical University; Currently Vice-President, Zhejiang Geriatrics Institute, Hangzhou. Publications: Co-author: Determination of Serum Cortisol in 200 Elderly, 1984; Observation of Cardiopulmonary Function, Immunity and Hemorrheologic Changes in Joggers During Rest, 1984; Serum TSH, TT4, TT3, T3uR, FT4I, FT3I and T3/T4 Ratio in the Elderly, 1985; Effects of Bee Pollen on Blood Glucose and Serum Lipid Level in Diabetic Patients, 1991; Examination of Basal Cerebral Arteries with Transcranial Doppler Ultrasound in Healthy Aged, 1991. Memberships: Director, Chinese Association of Geriatrics Research; Vice-Chairman, Zhejiang Geriatrics Association. Hobby: Music. Address: Zhejiang Hospital, 12 Lingyin Road, Hangzhou 310013, China.

XIE Minhao, b. 9 Aug 1960, Beijing, China. Associate Professor of Sports Physiotherapy. m. 22 Nov 1988, 1 daughter. Education: MB, Beijing Medical University; MEd. Physiology, National Research Institute of Sports Science. Appointments: Research Assistant, Biochemical Department, The Second Institute of Clinical Medicine, Chinese National Academy of Traditional Medicine; Lecturer, Sports Nutrition Centre, Associate Professor of Sports Physiology and Biochemistry, National Research Institute of Sports Medicine. Publications: Contributor of articles in professional journals. Memberships: Chinese Association of Sports Medicine. Hobbies: Sport; Making Friends; Reading. Address: National Research Institute of Sports Medicine, 1st Anding Road, Beijing 100029, China.

XIE Nian Ming, b. 19 Jun 1929, Jiang Su Province, China. Scientific Research. m. 1956, 2 s. Education: BA, Biology, Nanjing University.

Career: Director of Culture Medium Laboratory, 1966-77; Professor of Biology, Director of Pathology, National Insititute for Control of Pharmaceutical and Biological Pdts, 1977-. Publication: Atlas of the Electron Micrography of Medical Bacteria, Chinese and English editions, 1994. Memberships: Chinese Association of Electron Microscope; Chinese Association of Microbiology. Address: National Institute for The Control of Pharmaceutical and Biological Pdts, Beijing 100050, China.

XIE Ruping, b. 3 Oct 1943, Beijing, China. Clinical Doctor. Professor. m. Yuan Guan, 1 Jan 1967, 2 daughters. Education: Graduated, Tianjin Medical University, 1965; Visiting Scholar, Department of Neurology, Yale University School of Medicne, USA, 1993-94. Appointments: Resident, 1965-70, Chief Resident, 1971-74, Instructor, Attending Doctor, 1975-84, Associate Professor, 1985-91, Professor, Neurology and Electroencephalogram Laboratory, 1992-, Department of Neurology, Beijing Medical University. Publications: Co-author: Creutzfeldt-Jakob Disease, 1987; The Important Appearance of Multiple Sclerosis as Neuromyelitis optica, 1989; Statistical Analysis of Brain Electrical Activity Mapping with Cerebral Hemorrhage Patients, 1990; Clinical Analysis of Primary Pontine Hemorrhage, 1990; Cerebral Amyloid Angiopathy, 1992. Honours: Excellent Clinical Teacher, Beijing Medical University, 1987, 1992. Memberships: Neurological Branch, Chinese Medical Association; Chinese Electroencephalogram Society, Chinese Medical Association. Hobby: Walking. Address: Department of Neurology, The Third School of Clinical Medicine, Beijing Medical University, 49 North Garden Road, Beijing 100083, China.

XING Yi-Shan, b. 6 Oct 1936, Hainan Province, China. Professor of Gastroenterology. m. 1 July 1967, 1 son, 1 daughter. Education: Bachelor, Wuhan Medical College (Toongji Medical College), 1960. Appointments: Resident Physician, Attending Physician, Wuhan Military Medical School, 1960-66; Currently Professor in Gastroenterology, 1st Military Medical University, Zhujiang Hospital, Guangzhou. Publications: Health Care in Gastroenterology for Middle and Old Ages, 1994; Articles: Study on preventive effect of trace elements combined with herbal medicine on liver disease deteriorative progression (co-author), 1993; Treatment of irritable bowel syndrome by dual regulation of gastrointestinal dynamics, 1993. Honours: Nice Doctor Award, 1978; Excellent Teacher Award, 1993; Prize for Pharmacy Research, People's Liberation Army, 1993. Memberships: Chinese Association of Digestion; Chinese Association of Medicine; Chinese Association of the Integration of Traditional and Western Medicine. Hobby: Tradition Chinese culture. Address: Department of Gastroenterology, Pearl River Hospital, 253 Industrial Road, Guangzhou, China.

XING Yu-lan, b. 8 Nov 1937, Henan, China. Physician; Research Professor. m. Fu Xin, 29 July 1961, 2 sons. Education: Graduated, Department of Public Health, Beijing Medical University (now Public Health College, Medical Sciences University of Beijing), 1961. Appointments: Doctor, Microbiology; Visiting Physician, 1978; Associate Chief Physician, 1982-; Chief Physician, 1991; Vice-Director. Publications: Laboratory Manual for Rapid Diagnosis of Viral Infections, 1984; Serological screening of HIV antibody in China, 1988; Rules of Operation Microbiological Examinations, 1990; Studies on Prevention and Therapy of Viral Hepatitis, 1993. Honours: Awards for Achievements in Scientific Research: 2nd Class, 1985, 3rd Class, 1987, 1989, 1st Class, 1990; Honorary Title, Advanced Individual of Widespread Achievement, Beijing City Government, 1992. Memberships: International AIDS Society; Chinese Medical Association, Virology Branch; China Microbiology Society; Council, Beijing Prevention and Therapy Association of STD and AIDS. Hobbies: Music; Watching television. Address: Beijing Municipal Centre for Hygiene and Epidemic Control, 16 Hepingli Zhongjie, Beijing 100013, China.

XIONG Rongchao, b. 12 Oct 1909. Tangshan, Hopei, China. Obstetrician and Gynaecologist. m. 15 Oct 1938, 1 son, 1 daughter. Education: BS, Beiping Yenching University, 1933; MD, Beiping Union Medical College and State University of New York, 1937; Training in Gynaecological Pathology, Harvard Medical School, 1946. Appointments: House Staff, Obstetrics and Gynaecology, Peiping Union Medical College Hospital; Head, Obstetrics and Gynaecology Department, Shanghai National Defence Medical College; Head, Obstetrics and Gynaecology Department, Dalian Medical University; Retired, 1984. Publications: Clinical Gynecology (co-author), 1993; Ovarian Carcinoma, 1955; Cisplatinum Therapy of Late Ovarian Carcinoma, 1984. Honours: Honorary Certificate, Dalian Medical College, 1987; Honorary Certificate, Chinese Government, 1993. Memberships: China Medical Association, Dalian and Liaoning branches; Obstetrical and Gynaecological Association of Dalian; Obstetrical and Gynaecological Association of Liaoning. Hobbies: Stamp collection; Bridge; Dancing. Address: Dalian Medical University, Dalian, Liaoning, China.

XU Baozhen, b. 1 Sept 1945, Anhui Province, China. Doctor; Paediatrician. m. Chen Xiaoqian, 9 Dec 1971, 1 son, 1 daughter. Education: BM, Beijing Medical University, 1970; Training, Uppsala University, Sweden, 1989. Appointments: Editor, medical books at publishing house, 1970; Paediatrician, 1974; Visiting Physician, Paediatrics and Child Health, 1987, Chief Physician, Paediatrics and Child Health, 1992-, Anhui Provincial Children's Hospital, Hefei. Publications: Child Health, 1990; Facilitating Rural Maternal and Child Health, 1990; Guide to Improving Birth and Development, book, 1993. Honours: Superior Article for Risk Factors of Child Cardiovascular Disease, Gaojinlang Fund, 1987; China National Education Prize as Editor and Director for TV series on Improving Birth and Development, 1993. Memberships: Anhui Provincial Paediatric Society; Anhui Provincial Maternal and Child Health Association. Hobbies: Fashion design; Cycling. Address: Anhui Provincial Children's Hospital, 39 Wang Jiang East Rd, Hefei 230051, China.

XU Benyuan, b. 28 Aug 1940, Yugan, Jiangxi, China. Paediatric Surgeon. m. Liu Weishih, 21 Jun 1939, 2 daughters. Education: Jiangxi Medical College. Appointments include: Associate Professor, 1986-91; Professor, 1991-; Tutor to Postgraduates; Director, Surgery Department Chief, Jiangxi Children's Hospital, Nanchang. Publications: Repair of Acquired Preanal Fistula in Childhood, 1981; Acquired Preanal Fistula in Childhood, 1986. Honours: Gold Medal, Fistullography, Brussels Eureka, Salon Mondial de l'invention de la recherche et de l'innovation industrielle, 40th Anniversary, 1991. Memberships: Chinese Medical Association; Chinese Paediatric Surgery Society; Editorial Board, Pediatric Surgery. Address: Children's Hospital, Nanchang, Jiangxi 330006, China.

XU Bing-ze, (HSU Ping-tze), b. 10 Feb 1927, Hubei Province, China. Urologist. m. Li-li Yang, 1 Nov 1953, 3 sons. Education: Graduated, National Medical College, Shanghai, 1951; MD, Peking Union Medical College, 1952; Intern, 1950-52, Resident, 1952-56, Department of General Surgery, Peking Union Medical College Hospital. Appointments: Visiting Surgeon, Urological Section, Department of General Surgery, Peking Union Medical College Hospital, Beijing, 1956-79; Visiting Surgeon, Department of General Oncology, 1979-85, Deputy Chief, Chief, Associate Professor, Professor, Department of Urological Surgery, 1985-94, Cancer Institute Hospital, Chinese Academy of Medical Sciences, Beijing. Publications: Diabetes in the cases of Pheochromocytoma, Review of the Literature and report of 2 cases, 1961; Surgical Treatment of Urogenital Tuberculosis, 1965; Virilism caused by Big Adrenal Cortical Tumour, Report of 3 cases, 1981; LASER in the Treatment of Urogenital Cancer, 1989; The value of clinical use of PDT with HpD-laser in the Treatment of Bladder Cancer, 1988; A Clinical Analysis of 131 cases of Bladder Cancer Treated by PDT with HpD-Laser and Nd:YAG laser, 1993. Honours: 1st Prize of Scientific and Technical Achievement for research work on Photodynamic Therapy (PDT) with Haematoporphyrin Derivative (HpD) in the Treatment of Bladder Cancer, Ministry of Public Health, China, 1985; Special State Subsidy, Chinese Government, 1993-. Memberships: Chinese Medical Association; Chinese Optical Society; Regular Member, The Society for Experimental Biology and Medicine, New York. Hobbies: Likes most things. Address: No 17 Panjiayuan Nanli, Chaoyang District, PO Box 2258, Beijing 100021, China.

XU Changxi, b. 24 Oct 1933, Zhejiang Province, China. Professor of Biomaterials. m. Hu Lida, 1 July 1957, 2 sons. Education: BA, Shanghai Medical University, 1955. Appointments: Scientific and Technological Adviser, Sichuan Province Government; Professor of Biomaterials, Medicinal Chemistry; Director, Department of Biomedical Engineering, Chongqing University of Medical Sciences. Publications: Studies of Adsorbents for Hemoperfusion in Artificial Liver Support I CAAC-1, 1981; Prep of CAAC-III, Co-author, 1991; Biosynthesis High Concentration Fructose Diphosphate, 1995. Memberships: Council, Chinese Society for Biomedical Engineering; Editorial Board, Journal of Functional Materials. Hobby: Reading newspapers. Address: Department of Biomedical Engineering, Chongqing University of Medical Sciences, Chongqing 630046, China.

XU Chengbin, b. 5 Jan 1932, Zhejiang, China. Professor of Medicine. m. Yang Jiyun, 7 Sep 1957, 2 sons. Education: MD. Appointments:

Chairman, Professor, Department of Internal Medicine, 1985-88; Senior Visiting Professor, University of Mississippi Medical Centre, USA, 1988-89; Research Associate, Visiting Professor, Wayne State University, 1989-90; Vice President, Cardiovascular Research Institute; Chairman, Cardiology Department, People's Hospital, Beijing Medical University. Publications: Phonocardiograph, 1982; How to Analyse Cardiac Arrhythmias, Co-author, 1981; Cardiac Electrophysiology and Pharmacology, 1995; Clinical Guide to the Diagnosis and Treatment of Cardiovascular Diseases Update, 8 books, 1995; Contributor of over 200 medical papers. Honours: Outstanding Research in α HANP and Chinese Herb Mai-ji, Chinese Ministry of Public Health, 1985; Excellent Contribution to Medical Science, State Council of China, 1992. Memberships: Chinese Medical Association; Cardiac Function Society of China; Microcomputer Medical Applications Association of China; North American Society of Pacing and Electrophysiology; Soceity of Chinese Bioscientists in America. Hobbies: Walking; Exercise. Address: People's Hospital, Beijing Medical University, 42 North Li Shi Road, Beijing 100044, China.

XU De Li, b. 2 Sep 1957, Dandong, Liaoning, China. Professor of Pediatrics. m. Gao Wei Wei, 18 Sep 1983, 1 d. Education: MB, Chinese Medical University, 1982; Graduate, Da Lian Foreign Language College, 1992. Career: Chief Surgeon, Dandong First Hospital, 1982-86; Director, Department of Pediatrics, 1994, Currently, Professor of Pediatrics, Dandong Women and Children's Hospital, Liaoning. Publications: PTC in Children, in International Symposium on Pediatric Surgery, 1993; Co-author, Handbook of Clinical Diagnosis and Treatment, 1993; Eosinophilic Granuloma in Children, in Chinese Journal of Pediatric Surgery, 1993. Honours: Excellent Worker in Science, Dandong, 1993; Second Class Medical Youth Award for New Operational Method, 1994. Membership: Commission, Dandong Medical Association. Hobbies: Running; Skating; Swimming. Address: Dandong Women and Children's Hospital, Liaoning 118002, China.

XU De-Zheng, b. 8 Mar 1936, Shanghai, China. Professor of Surgery. m. Han Kai-Nan, 1 May 1962, 1 Son, 1 daughter. Education: MB, Shandong Medical College, 1960. Appointments include: Professor of Surgery, 1st Affiliated Hospital, Xingjiang Medical College; Director, Department of Surgery, Hangzhou 2nd Hospital, 1994-. Publications include: The Clincal Application of Percutaneous Transhepatic Cholangiography, 1981; The Clinical Application of Percutaneous Transhepatic Internal Cholangio-drainage, 1990; The Special Type of Obstructive Jaundice, 1990; Biliary Surgical Principle and Practice, book, 1990. Honours: Excellent Scientist, Xiangjiang Autonomous Region; 3rd Award for Science and Technology Progress, Xiangjiang Autonomous Region, 1985, 1986, 1988, 1992; Special Lifetime Subsidy, Chinese Government, 1992-. Memberships: Chinese Biliary Surgery Association; Chinese Hepatic Surgery Association; Chinese Medical Association. Hobbies: Basketball; Running. Address: No 1 Wenzhou Road, Hangzhou 310015, China.

XU Guang-Lu, b. 19 July 1933, Nanjing, China. Professor of Pharmacology. m. Rui Yang, 15 Jan 1960, 2 sons. Education: Diploma, Shanghai Medical University, 1954; Visiting Scholar, Department of Biochemistry and Chemistry, Guy's Hospital Medical School, London, 1980-82. Appointments: Assistant, Lecturer, Department of Pharmacology, Xi'an Medical College, 1954-60; Currently Professor, Head, Research Laboratory of Keshan Disease and Trace Element and Endemic Disease Research Laboratory, Xi'an Medical University. Publications include: Investigations on the distributional relationship between Keshan Disease and selenium-deficiency in animals in Shaanxi Province, 1981; GSH-Px, GST, SOD and CAT activities in tissues of ducklings deprived of vitamin E and selenium, 1983; Keshan disease and selenium deficiency, 1985; The prevention of Keshan disease with sodium selenite and the relation of selenium deficiency to the disease, 1987; Platelet aggregability and thromboxane of children from a low selenium Keshan disease area, 1992; Effects of sodium selenite and selenium-yeast on blood selenium levels of residents in a Keshan disease area, 1994. Honours: Certificate of Merit, National Conference on Science, China, 1978; Klaus Schwarz Commemorative Medal, International Association of Bioinorganic Scientists, 1984; Award for Progress in Science and Technology, Shaanxi Provincial Government, 1993. Memberships: Chinese Society of Endemiology; Chinese Medical Association; Chinese Medical Trace Element Association; Chinese Biochemical Society; Geographical Society of China; Chinese Pharmacological Society; Editorial Board, J Trace Elem Electrolytes Health Dis. Hobbies: Photography; Ball games. Address: Research

Laboratory of Keshan Disease, Xi'an Medical University, Xi'an, Shaanxi 710061, China.

XU Guang-wei, b. 25 Oct 1934, Shanghai, China. Surgical Oncologist. m. Lin-lin Song, 14 July 1958, 1 son. Education: MD. Appointments: Deputy Director, Department of Surgery, Head, Department Surgical Oncology, Professor of Surgical Oncology, Beijing Institute for Cancer Research. Publications: Author of 5 books and contributor of over 80 articles in professional journals, 1959-94. Honours: Recipient of 9 Awards. Memberships: Member of nine professional bodies. Hobby: Bridge. Address: Beijing Institute for Cancer Research, Da-Hong-Luo-Chang Street, Western District, Beijing 100034, China.

XU Ji-Sheng, b. 27 July 1917, Baoding, China. Professor of Ophthalmology. m. Zhao Ai Mei, 29 Apr 1951, 1 son, 2 daughters. Education: BA, Beijing Medical University, China. Appointments include: Director, Eye Department, Vice-President, Jinan Central Hospital. Publications: Co-author, books: Intraocular Lens, Monograph I, 1980; Intraocular Lens, Monograph II, 1992; Ophthalmology Diagnostics, 1993; Co-author, articles: Research of Axis Depth of Chinese Anterior Chamber, 1956; Initial Summing-up Report of Intraocular Lens Implantation, 1981; Manufacture of Artificial Vitreous and Evaluation of Rabbit's Eye Possibility, 1993. Honours: Nationwide Model Staff Member, 1960. Memberships: China Intraocular Lens Association; Shandong Province Ophthalmology Association; Jinan City Ophthalmology Association. Hobby: Beijing Opera. Address: 105 Jiefant Road, Jinan, Shandong 250014, China.

XU Jie, b. 7 Mar 1936, Shenyang, China. Ophthalmology. m. Ma Shengyun, 20 Oct 1967, 1 s, 1 d. Education: MD, China University of Medical Science, Shenyang, China, 1959. Career: Professor of Ophthalmology, 2nd Clinical Medicine College, Norman Bethune University of Medical Sciences, Changchun, China; Currently, President, First Clinical Medicine College, Norman Bethune University, Changchun. Publications: Recession of anterior chamber angle glaucoma, 1990; HLA DRZ and primary glaucoma, 1992; Co-author, Detecting herpes simple virus DNA of the tear by PCR, 1992. Honours: 1st Prize for Scientific Achievement, Norman Bethune University, 1989; 3rd Prize for Scientific Achievement, China Public Health Bureau, 1989. Memberships: Chairman, China Ophthalmological Association, Jilin and Changchun Branches; Chinese Medical Association, Jilin Branch. Hobbies: Chess; Music. Address: First Clinical Medicine College, Norman Bethune University of Medical Science, 1 Xin Min Street, Changchun, 130021, China.

XU Jin-tang, b. 15 Feb 1931, Hebei Province, China. Professor of Ophthalmology. m. Mei-hua Shi, 27 Aug 1958, 1 son, 1 daughter. Education: MD, Dalian Medical College, 1955; PhD, Moscow Second Medical College, USSR, 1959; Visiting Scholar, Certificate, University of Louisville, USA, 1988. Appointments include: Associate Professor, Harbin Medical University, 1980; Professor of Ophthalmology, College of Medicine, 1985-; Adviser of postgraduates for doctoral degree, 1990-, Jinan University. Publications: Co-author: Pseudo-tumors in orbit, 1964; Clinical application in lamellar keratoplasty with homografts and heterografts preserved in dehydrated honey medium, 1985; Experimental heterokeratplasty with human corneal grafts in monkey eyes, 1992; Prevention and treatment of ophthalmologic emergencies (editor-in-chief), 1973; Keratoplasty (co-editor), 1980; Corneal Disorders - basic theory and clinical practice (editor-in-chief), 1994. Honours: Top Grade Science and Technology Progress Prize, Education Committee of China, 1991. Memberships: Chinese Ophthalmology Association, Chairman, Corneal Disorders Branch; Chinese Medical Association; Deputy Director, Guangdong Ophthalmology Society; Editorial Boards: Ophthalmological Research; Clinical Ophthalmology; Ophthalmology; Eye Science. Hobbies: Running; Badminton; Table-tennis. Address: Department of Ophthalmology, Medical College, Jinan University, Guangzhou 510632, China.

XU Lili, b. 3 Apr 1934, Hunan, China. Medical Doctor. m. Lin Yi-Zhen, 15 Feb 1964, 2 daughters. Education: Graduated, Hunan Medical College, 1957; Visiting Scholar, Yale University School of Medicine, 1985-86. Appointments include: Consultant, Chinese Eugenics Association; Professor of Obstetrics and Gynaecology, Chairman, Department of Obstetrics and Gynaecology, Hunan Medical University, Changsha; Consultant, China Sexology Association; Visiting Professor, University of Tennessee Medical College, 1991-92. Publications: Treatment for cervical cancer with Chinese Traditional Medicine, 1973; Regional intra-arterial chemotherapy for cervical cancer from abdominal aorta via inferior epigastric artery, 1979; Atlas of Colposcope, 1983; Traditional Chinese Gerontology, 1986; Successful Pregnancy and Birth after transfer of donated embryo fertilized in vitro, 1988; 2nd Prize in Progress of Science and Technology, China, 1989; 1st Prize, 1988, 3rd Prize, 1989, in Progress of Science and Technology, Hunan Province; Title of Advanced Individual in Family Planning Research, China, 1989. Memberships: Chinese Medical Association; Chinese Eugenics Association; Chinese Sexology Association; Vice-Chairman, Chinese Association of the Integration of Traditional and Western Medicine, Hunan, China. Hobbies: Reading; Walking; Music. Address: Department of Obstetrics and Gynaecology, 2nd Affiliated Hospital, Hunan Medical University, 156 Renming Rd, Changsha, Hunan 410011, China.

XU Qunyuan, b. 2 Oct 1941, Yunnan, China. m. Li Guixian, 6 Jan 1968, 1 son, 1 daughter. Education: PhD, Medicinsk Vetenskap, Karolinska Institute, Sweden. Appointments: Director, Department of Anatomy; Assistant President of CUMS; Senior Assistant Director, Beijing Institute of Neurosciences. Publications: 8 books incl, Neuroanatomy, 1987; 63 papers incl, Course of Spinocerebellar Axons, 1994. Honours: Model Worker in Beijing, 1984; Excellent Scientist of National Education Commission, 1990; Prize of Science & Technology, Ministry of Public Health, 1994. Memberships: Chinese Society of Anat Sci; International Brain Research Organization; International Society of Development Neuroscience; Europ Neuroscience Association. Hobbies: Painting; Swimming. Address: Capital University of Medical Sciences, You An Men, Beijing 100054, China.

XU Shao-ting, b. 10 Nov 1921, Shandong Province, China. Orthopaedic Surgeon. m. Fei Shi-ying, 20 May 1948, 2 sons, 2 daughters. Education: MD (equivalent to rank of Lieutenant-General), National Defence Medical College. Appointments: Head, Orthopaedic Department, 1956, Chief, Traumatology and Orthopaedics Centre, People's Liberation Army, 1980-92, Honorary Chief, Orthopaedics Centre, People's Liberation Army, 1992-, Beijing Army General Hospital. Publications: Peripheral nerve injury (co-author), 1981; Orthopaedics, 1992; SCI, 1993; Translations from Surgery in World War II, 1989: Spinal cord injury; Peripheral nerve injury. Honours: Distinctions for Research, 1962, 1978, 1981, 1983, 1984, 1988, 1990, 1991; Distinction for Education of Young Doctors. Memberships: International Medical Society of Paraplegia; Committee Member, Chinese Spinal Surgery Association. Hobbies: Swimming; Tai-ji exercise. Address: 2 Bei Xao Street, Dong-si, Beijing 100700, China.

XU Xue-Mei, b. 16 Nov 1929, Jianying, Jiansu, China. Professor. m. Yang Ming-li, 10 Sept 1952. Education: Graduate, Jiansu Medical College, 1952. Appointments: Assistant, Shandong University and Qingdao Medical College, 1953-58; Assistant, Lecturer, Associate Professor, Professor, 1958-92, Guide Teacher of Postgraduate Master, 1986-91, Weifang Medical College. Publications: Discovery of Keshan Disease in Shandong, 1962; Detection of Epidemic Hemorrhagic Fever Antigen on Necrosy Tissues by Inm Gold-Silver Meth, 1990; Pathological Analysis on Heavy Deep Inters Keratitis, 1989. Honours: Science Technical Prize of Weifang City, 1962; Science Prize, Health Bureau of Shandong, 1982; Excellent Paper, 1st Grade Prize, Weifang Medical College. Memberships: Pathology Council of Shandong Ch Medical Association. Hobbies: Reading the Bible; Qigong. Address: Pathology Department, Weifang Medical College, Weifang, Shandong 261042, China.

XU Yan Ying, b. 22 July 1963, Hebei, China. Dentist. m. Dr Songlin Wang, 18 Jan 1988, 1 daughter. Education: DDS, PhD, Beijing Medical University. Appointment: Doctor-in-Chief. Publications: Studies on Diagnosis of Oral Candosis, 1993. Membership: Chinese Medical Association. Hobbies: Sport; Arts. Address: Department of Oral Medicine, School of Stomatology, Beijing Medical University, Beijing 100081, China.

XU Zhi-Biao, b. 21 October 1930, Zhejiang, China. Physician; Professor. m. 2 February 1959, 2 sons. Education: MD, Beijing Medical University, 1954. Appointments: Vice Director of the Institute, 1987-92. Publications: Co-author: Theoretics & Practice in Internal Medicine, 1984; Co-editor: Tropical Medicine, 1986; Editor: Section of Parasitology & Parasitic Diseases in Volume of Medicine, Chinese Encyclopaedia, 1993. Honours: 2nd Class Award, Ministry of Public Health for Achievement in Science and Technology, 1982; Special Subsidy, State Council of China, 1992-. Memberships: Vice Chairman, 4th Session Council, Society of Infectious & Parasitic Diseases; Vice Chairman, 1st Session, Council, Society of Tropical Medicine & Parasitology, Chinese

Medical Association. Hobbies: Chinese Chess. Address: Beijing Tropical Medicine Research Institute, 94# Yong An Road, Beijing 100050, China.

XU Zhi-Jie, b. 21 Aug 1936, Shao Xing, Zhejiang Province, China. Parasitologist; Professor. m. Wang Chun-Rong, 14 Apr 1965, 1 son, 1 daughter. Education: BA, Harbin Medical University, 1959. Appointments: Parasitologist, 1959-63, 1973-; Physician, 1963-73; Currently Professor of Medical Parasitology, Harbin Medical University. Publications: Seroepidemiological survey of human cysticercosis in the NeHe county of Heilongjiang Province, 1988; Preliminary observation on the detection time of circulating antigens in pigs artificially infected with cysticercus cellulosae, 1993; Comparative study on antigens of cysticercus cellulosae by ELIB and ELISA, 1993; Alteration in lipid peroxide content in cerebral cysticercosis, 1994; Cysticercosis, 1994. Honours: 2nd Grade Prize for Science and Technology Accomplishment, Provincial Medical Department, 1988; 2nd Grade Prize of National Excellent Television Programme of Special Theme, 1988; Outstanding Researcher, Harbin Technical Market, 1989; 1st Grade Prize for Science and Technology Progress, Provincial Education Committee, 1992; 2nd Grade Prize for Science and Technology Progress, Heilongjiang Province, 1992. Memberships: Secretary, Medical Parasitology Committee, Chinese Zoological Society, Heilongjiang Branch; Director, Committee of Chinese Medical Prevention Society, Heilongjiang Branch, Medical Parasitology Society; Standing Committee, Society of Tropical Medicine and Parasitic Diseases, Chinese Medical Association. Hobbies: Travel; Bridge. Address: Department of Parasitology, Harbin Medical University, Harbin 150086, China.

XUE Miao, b. 24 Jun 1929, Shanghai, China. Professor of Biomaterial and Prosthetic Dentistry. m. Zong Lan Shen, 15 Jun 1949, 2 d. Education: DDS, Shanghai Second Medical University, 1953. Appointments: Assistant Department of Prosthetic Dentistry Science, 1953-60, Lecturer, Assistant Professor, Dental Material Research Laboratory, 1960-82, Vice Head, Associate Professor, 1982-87, Vice Head, Associate Professor, Biomaterial Research Laboratory, 1982-87, Head, Professor of Department of Dental Material Science, 1987-91, Head, Professor of Dental Material and Biomaterial Research Laboratories, 1988-91, Professor, 1988-, Director, Professor of Shanghai Biomaterial Research and Test Center, 1989-, Shanghai Second Medical University. Publications: Co-author, Science of Applied Dental Material, 1963; Editor, China Yearbook of Dentistry, 1984, 1986, 1988, 1990, 1992, 1994; Material Science of Prosthetic Dentistry, 1987; Chief Editor, Chinese Journal of Dental Materials and Devices, 1992-. Honours: Certificate of Merit Medal, Chinese Ministry of Public Health, 1960, 1988; Merit Certificate, Shanghai Scientific and Technological Commission, 1984, 1990, 1992; State Education Commission of China, 1988, 1992; National Government Special Subsidy, 1992; Shanghai Advanced Worker, 1995. Memberships: ASTM; Board of Directors, Chinese Dental Material Society; Board of Directors, Chinese Maxillofacial and Dental Implant Society; Chief, Shanghai Biomaterial Committee; Committee, Shanghai Association for Stomatology; Standing Committee, Shanghai Medical Engineering for Stomatology; Chinese Shape Memory Alloy Committee; Standing Committee, Chinese Biomaterial Society. Address: Shanghai Second Medical University, Shanghai Biomaterial Research and Test Center, 716 Xie Tu Road, Shanghai 200023, China.

Y

YADDANAPUDI Ravindranath, b. 12 Feb 1942, Narsipathnam (AP), India. Physician. m. Kanta Bhambhani, 8 May 1976. Education: MBBS. Career: Assistant Professor, Wayne State Univ (WSU), 1975-78; Associate Professor, (WSU), 1978-88; Professor (WSU), 1988-; Co-Director, Division of Pediatric Hematology/Oncology. Publications: 155 includes original articles, book chapters, published abstracts. Memberships: American Society of Hematology; American Societyof Clinical Oncology; International Society Pediatric Oncology. Address: Children's Hospital of Michigan, 3901 Beaubien Boulevard, Detroit, MI 48201, USA.

YAHR Melvin D, b. 18 Nov 1917, New York, USA. Neurologist. Widower. 4 d. Education: AB, Washington Square College, New York City, 1939; MD, New York University, College of Medicine, New York, 1943. Appointments: College of Physicians & Surgeons, Columbia University: Professor of Neurology, 1962-70; Associate Dean, 1967-73; H Houston Merritt Professor of Neurology, 1970-73; Mount Sinai School of Medicine, City University of New York: Professor and Chairman, Department of Neurology; Henry P and Georgette Goldschmidt Professor of Neurology, 1973-92; Aidekman Family Professor of Neurological Research, 1992-. Publications: 299 Publications in total, including, Treatment of Thrombophlebitis, 1945; Painful Sensory Syndrome during Nerve Regeneration, 1950; Digital Vasomotor Responses following Nerve Root Stimulation, 1955; Current Status of the Drug Therapy of Epileptic Seizures, 1956; Long-Term Follow-Up of Patients with Petit Mal, 1967; Treatment of Parkinsonism, 1972; Corticothalamic Projections and Sensorimotor Activities, 1972. Honours: include, Annual Award, United Epilepsy Association, 1960; Award of Merit, United Parkinson's Foundation, 1965; Lucy Moses Award - Neurology, Columbia University, 1972; Soloman A Berson Award - Clinical Science, NYU College of Medicine, 1985. Memberships: include, Alpha Omega Alpha; American Academy of Neurology; American Medical Association; American Epilepsy Society; Harvey Society; New York Academy of Medicine; New York Academy of Science; Pan American Medical Association. Hobbies: Golf. Address: Mount Sinai Medical Center, Department of Neurology, Box 1139, One Gustave lane, Levy Place, New York, NY 10029, USA.

YAKIMETS Walter William, b. 4 Aug 1935, Redwater, Alberta, Canada. Professor of Surgery. m. Katherine Yorke, 6 June 1959, 3 sons, 1 daughter. Education: MD; FRCS (C); Diploma, American Board of Surgery. Appointments: Assistant Professor, Associate Professor, Full Professor, Department of Surgery, Director of Continuing Medical Education, Chairman to Admissions Committee to Faculty of Medicine, Director to Division of General Surgery, University of Alberta. Publications: 4 chapters in Pharmacologic Aspects of Nursing, 1986; Aortoesophageal Fistula Secondary to Benign Barrett Ulcer-A Rare Cause of Massive GI Hemorrhage, 1993. Honours: Visiting Professor to Sweden, 1981, Korea, 1986, Cameroon, 1987, China, 1991; External Examiner to Saudi Arabia, 1991. Memberships: Fellow, Royal College of Physicians and Surgeons of Canada; American College of Surgeons; American Society of Colon and Rectal Surgeons; Canadian Association of Gastroenterological Surgery; Canadian Medical Association; Alberta Medical Association. Hobbies: Travel; Wine. Address: 2D4.44 Mackenzie Centre, 8440 112 Street, Edmonton, Alberta, Canada T6G 2B7.

YAMAMOTO Joe, b. 18 Apr 1924, Los Angeles, California, USA. Psychiatrist. m. Maria Fujitomi, 9 May 1947, 2 s. Education: BS, 1946, MB, 1948, MD, 1949, University of Minnesota. Appointments: Assistant Professor of Psychiatry, University of Oklahoma Medical centre, 1955-58; Assistant Professor, USC School of Medicine, 1958-60; Associate Professor, 1961-68, Professor, 1969-77, Director, Adult Ambulatory care Services, UCLA, 1977-88; Professor of Psychiatry, Neuropsychiatric Institute, 1977-. Publications: Effective Psychotherapy for Low-Income and Minority Patients, Co-editor, 1982; The Psychosocial development of Minority Group Children, Co-editor, 1983. Honours: Asian/Asian American Award, American Psychoatric Association, 1993. Memberships: Life Fellow, American Psychiatric Association; President, American Orthopsychiatric Association; Group for Advancement of Psychiatrists. Address: UCLA Neuropsychiatric Institute, 760 Westwood Plaza, Los Angeles, CA 90024-1759, USA.

YAN Caijie, b. 5 May 1932. Surgeon. m. Zhu Shunqing, 1 Apr 1957, 1 son, 2 daughters. Education: MD; Studied Oncology and Surgery, Brigham and Women's Hospital and Sidney Farbor Cancer Institute, Harvard Medical School, 1981-83. Appointments: Visiting Surgeon, 1959, Professor of Surgery, Director, Department of Surgery, 1985, Southwest Hospital, Chongqing, China; Professor of Surgery, Director, Department of General Surgery, 1988, currently Chief Surgeon, Xinqiao Hospital, Chongqing. Publications: Surgical management of gastric adenocarcinoma, 1985; Pylorus and antroseromuscular flap-preserving gastrectomy - A new type of reconstruction after subtotal gastrectomy for treatment of peptic ulcer, 1991. Honours: 2nd Grade Award for Progress of Science and Technology, People's Liberation Army, China, 1991. Memberships: Chinese Medical Association; Gastroenterologic Surgery Group, Chinese Medical Association; Committee of General Surgery, People's Liberation Army. Hobbies: Music; Singing; Dancing. Address: Department of Surgery, Xinqiao (Newbridge) Hospital, Chongqing, Sichuan 630037, China.

YAN Heping, b. 9 Sept 1946, Chengdu, Sichuan, China. Associate Professor of Parasitology. Education: MD, 1969, Master's degree, 1982, West China University of Medical Sciences. Appointments: Lecturer, Department of Parasitology, 1986-88, Director, Department of Parasitology, 1986-, Associate Professor of Parasitology, 1988-, West China University of Medical Sciences, Chengdu, Sichuan; Research Associate, Department of Biology, Vanderbilt University, USA. Publications: Effect of eosinophils on the growth and development of Paragonimus skrjabini in rats, 1986; Recognition and detection of antigenic weight by McAb against Paragonimus, 1987; McAb-Immunobloting assay for detecting circulating antigen of Paragonimus skrjabini (co-author), 1988; Monoclonal antibodies and Zoonosis (co-author), book, 1989; Preparation of McAb against Trichinella spiralis and localization of antigen, 1990. Honours: Certificate of Honour for Outstanding Paper, Science and Technology Committee, Sichuan, 1986; Certificate of Honour for research on Monoclonal Antibodies against Paragonimus, Sichuan People's Government, 1987. Memberships: Chinese Zoological Society; Chinese Society of Parasitology; American Society of Parasitologists. Hobby: Swimming. Address: Department of Parasitology, West China University of Medical Sciences, Chengdu, Sichuan 610041, China.

YAN Yi, b. 1 Jan 1939, Fengcheng, Jiangxi, China. Physician. m. Li Guoxian, 1 Jan 1966, 1 son, 1 daughter. Education: MB, Medical Faculty, Jiangxi Medical College. Appointments: Resident, Assistant, 1965; Visiting Doctor, Lecturer, 1980; Currently Associate Professor, Deputy Physician-in-Chief, First Affiliated Hospital, Jiangxi Medical College. Publications: Co-author, 4 books including: Clinical Haemorrheology - Questions and Answers; On Promoting Blood Circulation and Removing Blood Stasis; More than 30 theses including: Treatment of 35 cases with acute early granulocytic leukemia with Integrated Chinese and Western Medicine, 1991. Honours: Prize for Advanced Worker, 1986, Prize for Advanced Teaching Work, 1988, Jiangxi Medical College. Memberships: Chinese Medical Association; Society of Integrated Chinese and Western Medicine of China; Member of the International Society of Clinical Haemorrheology. Hobbies: Chinese traditional medicine; Knitting. Address: Department of Blood, The First Affiliated Hospital, Jiangxi Medical College, Nanchang, Jiangxi 330006, China.

YANG An Li, b. 12 Dec 1938, Shanghai, China. Medicine. m. 1 Aug 1960, 2 daughters. Education: Bachelor of Medical Science, Nanjing Medical College; Postgraduate Training in Orthopedic Surgery. Appointments: General Surgery, 1963-70; Vice Director, Vice Chief Doctor, 1970-90; Director, Chief Doctor, 1990-94; Vice President, 1994-. Honours: 3rd Award of National Creation, 1990; Honour of National Special Intellectual, 1990; The Award of National Patent, 1991, 1992, 1992. Memberships: Association of Poliomyelitis; Association of China Creation; Society of China Ache. Hobbies: Travel; Reading. Address: Bo Yang Road 130, Shanghai 200090, China.

YANG Bing-Xiu, b. 8 Mar 1936, Hunan, China. Gynaecologist and Obstetrician. m. Chen Ning-Sheng, 6 Aug 1961, 2 sons. Education: MB, Guangzhou Traditional Chinese Medicine College. Appointments: Doctor, 1977-, Doctor-in-charge, 1978-, Deputy Professor, 1986, Professor, 1992-, currently Director, Department of Gynaecology and Obstetrics, First Affiliated Hospital, Hunan Traditional Chinese Medicine College, Changsha; Beijing Traditional Chinese Medicine, 1962-77. Publications: A Report of Treatment on Pregnant Women with Pain in the Back and Legs, 1986; Clinical Study on 80 Cases of Sterility with

Syndrome Differentiation and Treatment, 1987; Clinical Report of 123 Cases of Sterility Cured with Chinese Herbs; Clinical Study on 149 Cases of Tube Blocking with Personally Made ShuTong Decoction, 1991; Clinical Study of 215 Cases of Sterility with TCM Treatment, 1991; Research on 78 Cases of Male Sterility with Syndrome Differentiation and Treatment, 1992; Clinical Effect of SheTaoShuTong on Tube Blocking; Clinical Analyses of Syndrome Differentiation and Treatment for 89 Cases of Benlou, 1993. Honours: Outstanding Paper Prize, 1st World Traditional Medicine Competition, 1991. Memberships: Chinese Medical Association; State Association of Traditional Chinese Medicine of China. Hobby: Listening to Chinese classical music. Address: The First Affiliated Hospital of Hunan College of Traditional Chinese Medicine, 105 ShaoShan Road, Changsha, China.

YANG Donghua, b. 21 Jan 1954, China. Professor of Gastroenterology. m. 28 Dec 1980, 1 daughter. Education: PhD; MD. Appointments: Resident Physician. Guizhou Perovincial Hospital, 1982; Attending Physician, Lecturer, Southwest Hospital, 1985; Associate Professor, 1991, Professor, 1993-, Zhu Jiang Hospital. Publications: Changes of Blood Selenium Level and Ghitathion Peroxide Activity and Their Clinical Significance in Primary Liver Cancer and Benign Liver Disease, 1988. Memberships: Chinese Medical Society; Chinese Anti-Cancer Society; Councillor, Guangdong Digestive Diseases Society. Hobbies: Pingpong; Tennis; Driving; Travel. Address: Department of Gastroenterology, Zhu Jiang Hospital, Guangzhou 510282, China.

YANG Guodong, b. 2 Aug 1937, Jiangshu, China. Professor of Medicine. m. Wenying Shou, 6 June 1961, 1 son, 1 daughter. ERducation: BA, Zhejiang Medical University, 1956; Shanghai No 1 College of Medicine, 1961. Appointments: Zhejiang Medical University, 1960; Ningbo Medical College, 1962; Ningbo Institute of Medical Science, 1976; Ningbo Institute of Micro-circulation and Henbane, Director, Ningbo Drug Withdrawal Research Centre, 1986-. Publications: Clinical Applications of Henbanes in Microcirculation Disturbance, 1987; New Therapy for Drug Withdrawal, 1993; Critical Care Medicine, Co-author, 1993. Honours: National Specialist of Great Attribation, 1986; National 5.1 Labour Model, 1986; Science and technology Award of Zhejiang Province, 1992. Memberships: Dir4ector, China College of Microcirculation CAIM; Associate Editor-in-Chief, Integrated Traditional Chinese and western medicine in Practice of Critical Care Medicine. Hobbies: Running; Reading. Address: 42 Xibeijie Street, Ningbo 315010, China.

YANG Hsing Yun, b. 1 Mar 1931, Henan, China. Physician; Acupuncturist. m. 15 Oct 1961, 2 sons. Education: MD; HMD, British Institute of Homeopathy; Doctor of Acupuncture; Doctorate, Present Day Chinese Medicine, Hong Kong; Residency, 1970-74. Appointments: Chief Flight Surgeon, Hsin-Chu Air Force Hospital, Taiwan, 1975; Commander, 3rd Medical Squadron, retired as Lieutenant-Colonel, 1976; Senior Aviation Medical Doctor, 1976-80; American Aviation Medical Examiner, USA, 1977; Currently: Acupuncture Doctor, Acting Director, Centre for Traditional Medicine, Veterans General Hospital, Taipei; Clinical Associate Professor, National Yang Ming University. Publications: Naturopathy for essential hypertension, 1978; General introduction of aviation medicine, 1979; General introduction to ear acupuncture; Primary report for quitting smoking by acupuncture, 1981. Honours: Kai-Me Medal; Chung-Chen Medal (military). Memberships: Chinese Medical Association, Taiwan; British Acupuncture Association; Homeopathic Association of Delhi, India; National Center for Homeopathy, USA; Director, Association of Naturopathy, Taiwan; Family Physicians Association, Taiwan; Pain Control Medical Association, Taiwan; Medical Laser Association, Taiwan; Chinese Acupuncture Research Association, Hong Kong; Vocational Medical Association, Taiwan; Gerontology Medical Association, Taiwan; International Federation of Homeopathic Physicians, India; Several others. Hobbies: Watching television; Yoga exercise; Jogging. Address: 316 6F 2nd Section, Shih-Pai Road, Taipei, Taiwan, China.

YANG Hsiu-Ying Tsai, b. 17 Aug 1931, Taiwan, China. Scientist. m. 7 Aug 1959, 1 son. Education: BS, National Taiwan University, 1954; MS, Louisiana State University, USA, 1958; PhD, 1962, Postdoctoral Fellow, 1962, University of Oklahoma. Appointments: Research Associate, 1964-66, Instructor, 1966-68, Assistant Professor, 1968-70, University of Oklahoma, USA; Currently Pharmacologist, National Institute of Mental Health, Washington, DC. Publications: Co-author: New enzymatic route for the inactivation of angiotensin, 1968; Characterization of a dipeptide hydrolase (Kinase II; Angiotensin I

converting enzyme), 1971; The monoamine oxidases of brain: Selective inhibition with drugs and the consequences for the metabolism of the biogenic amines, 1974; An enkephalin-generating enzyme in bovine adrenal medulla, 1982; Isolation, sequencing, synthesis and pharmacologic characterization of two new brain neuropeptides that modulate the action morphine, 1985; Origin of neurohypophyseal neuropeptide FF (FLFQPQRFamide), 1993; Neuropeptide FF receptors: Structure-activity relationship and effect of morphine, 1993. Memberships: American Society for Pharmacology and Experimental Therapeutics; Neuroscience; American Peptide Society. Address: 6108 Beech Tree Drive, Alexandria, VA 22310, USA.

YANG Jin, b. 22 Jun 1925, Taiyuan, Shanxi Province, China. Teacher. m. Zhang Jinxin, 2 s, 2 d. Education: MD, School of Medicine, Peking University. Appointments: Assistant, 1950-56, Lecturer, 1956-60, Department of Histology and Embryology, Beijing Medical College; Lecturer, 1960-79, Associate Professor, 1979-86, Professor, 1986-, Department of Histology and Embryology, Capital University of Medical Science. Publications: Co-author, Histology, 1981, 2nd edition, 1993; Co-author, Neuroanatomy, 1988; Vice Editor, Chinese Encyclopaedia: Histology and Embryology Volume, 1988; Co-author, Textbook of Histology and Embryology, 1978, 1982, 1988, 1994. Honour: Excellent Scientist with Outstanding Achievements, State Council of China. Memberships: Standing Council, Chinese Society for Anatomical Sciences; Editor-in-Chief, Acta Anatomica Sinica; International Anatomical Nomenclature Committee. Hobby: Music. Address: Ste 443, Unit 21, Building 8, Dormitory of Beijing Medical University, Haidian District, Beijing 100083, China.

YANG Jun, b. 10 Feb 1919, Hobei, China. Professor of Ophthalmology. m. Jiang Run Jin, 12 Sept 1950, 1 s, 3 d. Education: MD, College of Medicine, Peking University, 1947. Appointments: Assistant and Resident, Ophthalmology Department, 1947, Instructor, Visiting Physician, Ophthalmology department, 1953, Associate Professor, Director, Ophthalmology department, 1962, Professor and Director, 1980, Ophthalmology department, First Affiliated Hospital and Beijing Medical University; Professor and Director, Ophthalmology Department, Guang An Men Hospital, CATCM, 1981; Professor of Ophthalmology, People's Hospital, BMU and China-Japan Hospital, Beijing; Professor Emeritus, Guang An Men hospital, 1991-. Address: Guang An Men Hospital, Beijing 100053, China.

YANG Jun-shan, b. 1 May 1942. Harbin, China. Scientist. m. 28 Dec 1968, 1 son, 1 daughter. Education: BA, Shengyang Pharmaceutical University, 1965. Appointments: Assistant Professor, Associate Professor, Institute of Materia Medica, CHinese Academy of Medical Sciences, 1965-92; Professor, Vice Director, Institute of Medicinal Plant Development. Publications: Handbook of Analytical Chemistry V The Spectrum of Nuclear Magnetic Resonance, 1989. Memberships: Chinese Chemical Society; Academic Committee, Chinese Pharmaceutical Society; Standing Committee, Chinese Botanical Society. Hobbies: Chinese Chess; Photography. Address: No 100 Xi Bei Wang, Hai Dian District, Beijing 100094, China.

YANG Liande, b. 29 Jan 1924, Hangzhou, Zhejiang, China. Professor. m. Zhang Jun, 13 Nov 1956, 1 son, 1 daughter. Education: Graduate, Beijing College of Traditional Chinese Medicine, 1956; Dr Med. Appointments: Doctor, 1949, Attending Doctor, 1954, Associate Chief Doctor, 1980, Chief Doctor, Director of Teaching and Research section of Channel and Acupuncture, Professor, 1989, Tutor, Master Degree Students, 1992, Gansu College of Traditional Chinese Medicine. Publications: A Clinical Observation and Study on Chronic Bronchitis and Bronchial Asthma by the Therapy Applying Semen Sinapis Albae Paste on Certain Acupost; Acupuncturist Huang Fu Mi in Jin Dynasty, 1982; Essentials of Dialectical Method of Traditional Chinese Medicine, 1983; Cases Report of Famous Acupuncturist in Contemporary China, 1991; State of Traditional Chinese Medicine in China and Abroad, 1991; A Guide to Acupuncture Clinic, 1991. Honours: Scientific and Technical progressive Medal, Higher education Committee of Gansu Province, 1992-93. Membership: Vice Chairman, Gansu Acupuncture and Moxibustion Association. Address: Gansu College of Traditional Chinese Medicine, 35 Din Xi Dong Lou Road, Lanzhou, gansu province 730000, China.

YANG Meilin, b. 10 June 1932, Harbin, China. Professor. m. Zeyong He, 10 Aug 1954, 2 s, 1 d. Education: MD, Shanxi Medical College, 1956. Appointments: Assistant, Lecturer, Associate Professor, Professor of Histology and Embryology, Shanxi Medical College. Publications:

Blood, Co-author, 1993; Mast Cells in Esophageal Cancer: A Histochemical and Electron Microscopic Study, 1994. Memberships: Chinese Society of Anatomy; Vice President, Society of Anatomy of Shanxi Province. Hobbies: Music; Taijiquan. Address: Shanxi Medical College, 86 Xin Jian Nan Road, Taiyuan 03001, China.

YANG Ming-li, b. 8 Sept 1924, Nanjing, China. Professor. m. Xu Xue-Mei, 10 Sept 1952. Education: BM, Jiansu Medical College, 1949. Appointments: Assistant Surgeon, Central Hospital, Nanjing, 1949-50; Assistant, Lecturer, Shandong University, 1951-54; Instructor, Qingdao Medical College, 1954-58; Instructor, 1958-77, Associate Professor, 1978, Professor, 1981-, Weifang Medical College. Publications: Discovery of Kershan Disease in Shandong, 1962; Epidemic Hemorrhagic Fever 18 Necropsy Cases Analysis, 1982; Study on Trace Elements in Renal Tissue, 1992; Contributor of professional papers. Honours: Science Technical Prizes, Weifang City, 1962; Science Prize of Health Bureau of Shandong, 1982; Excellent Teacher in 3 Classes, College, Municipal and Province. Memberships: Vice Chairman, Pathology Council of Shandong, Chinese Medical Association. Hobbies: Chinese Calligraphy; Qugong. Address: Pathology Department, Weifang Medical College, Weifang, Shandong 261043, China.

YANG Si-Qi, b. 10 Mar 1931, Hunan, China. Professor; Physician. m. Bing-wen Yu, 1 July 1957, 3 daughters. Education: MA, China Medical University, 1955. Appointments: Assistant, Resident, 1956, Attending Physician, 1963, Lecturer, 1980-82, Hunan Medical University; Lecturer, 1982, Associate Professor, 1983, Professor, Chief Physician, Tutor, postgraduate students, 1991-, Medical College, Jinan University. Publications: Practical Infectious Diseases (co-author), 1989, 1994; Over 40 scientific papers on infectious diseases, mainly viral hepatitis, 1974-, including: The first case of Angiostrongyliasis cantonensis on the Mainland of China, 1988. Memberships: Chinese Medical Association; Infectious Diseases Branch, Epidemiology Branch, Chinese Medical Association; Editorial Board, Chinese Journal of Clinical Hepatology; Committee Member, International Research and Exchange Center of Liver Diseases. Address: Department of Infectious Diseases, Affiliated Hospital of Medical College, Jinan University, Guangzhou 510630, China.

YANG Victor Chi-Min, b. 2 July 1949, Shanghai, China. University Educator. m. Iris Y Yang, 25 Aug 1979, 1 son, 1 daughter. Education: BS, Chemistry, Tamkang University, Taipei, Taiwan; MS, Biochemistry, East Texas State University, Commerce, Texas, USA; PhD, Physical Biochemistry, Brown University, Providence, Rhode Island. Appointments: Postdoctoral Research Associate, Department of Applied Biological Sciences, Massachusetts Institute of Technology, Cambridge, USA, 1982-85; Assistant Professor, 1986-91, Associate Professor of Pharmaceutics, 1991-, College of Pharmacy, The University of Michigan, Ann Arbor. Publications: 65, mostly in peer-reviewed scientific journals such as Analytical Chemistry, Journal of Biochemistry, Analytical Biochemistry; 10 patents. Honours: Most Outstanding Manuscript Award, American Association of Medical Instrumentation, 1989; Arthur Doolittle Award, American Chemical Society, 1990; Fellows, American Association of Pharmaceutical Scientists, 1995. Memberships include: American Society for Artificial Internal Organs; American Association of Pharmaceutical Scientists; American Chemical Society. Address: College of Pharmacy, The University of Michigan, 428 Church Street, Ann Arbor, MI 48109-1065, USA.

YANG Wen-Xiu, b. 20 Apr 1938, Henan, China. University Teacher. m. 23 Apr 1966, 1 son, 1 daughter. Education: BA, Nankai University, 1961. Appointments: Assistant, 1961-77, Instructor, 1978-84, Associate Professor, 1985-92, Professor of Biophysics and Medical Physics, 1992-, Nankai University. Publications: Co-author: A model of sodium channel in nerve axons, 1982; Gating current and gating kinetics of sodium channel in nerve membranes, 1985; Effects of sennosides on cellular electric activities, 1993. Memberships: Council Member, Chinese Biophysical Society; New Techniques Committee of Chinese Medicine. Address: Department of Biophysics, Nankai University, Tianjin 300071, China.

YANG Wenguang, b. 12 March 1930, Rong Xian, Guangxi, China. Professor. m. Li Jiafang, 29 December 1960, 2 daughters. Education: Graduated, Guangxi Medical College, 1956. Appointments: Physician, Teaching Assistant, 1956-76; Lecturer, 1977; Associate Professor, 1985; Professor, 1990-. Publications: The relation betweeen gastroducdenal disease and the "Iliac painful point", 1980; A stereotaxic Atlas of the Brain of Tupaia Belangeri and Macague Monkey living in Guangxi, 1990;

Breeding of a New Variety GMm-Ns of Guangxi Monkey for Brain Research, 1993. Honours: Advanced Element on the Work of Chinese Medicine, 1960; 3rd Prize, Guangxi Science and Technology Progress, 1985; 1st Prize, Guangxi Medicine Technology Progress, 1993; 2nd Prize, Guangxi Science and Technology Progress, 1993; 3rd Prize, Medicine Technology Progress, Ministry of Health, China, 1994. Memberships: China Zoology Society; China Anatomy Society. Hobbies: Traditional Chinese Painting; Penmanship; Chinese Poems; World Classical Music. Address: Guangxi Medical University, Nanning, Guangxi 530021, China.

YANG Xi-Qiang, b. 3 June 1938, Chongqing, Sichuan Prov, China. Pediatrician. m. Zhou Kang-Ru, 9 Sept 1961, 1 son. Education: MD, Chongqing University of Medical Sciences, 1966. Career: Head, Division of Immunology, Children's Hospital, Chongqing University of Medical Sciences (CUMS), 1981-89; Vice Chairman, Department of Pediatrics, CUMS, 1983-89; Vice Director, Institute of Pediatrics, 1992-; Director, Children's Hospital, Chairman, Department of Pediatrics, Chongqing University of Medical Sciences. Publications: IqG Subclass Deficiency in Children with Recurrent Respiratory infections, 1991; IqG Subclasses in Serum and Circulating Immune Complexes of Children with Kawasaki Syndromes, 1990; Immunologic Abnormalities in Acute Stage Kawasaki Disease, 1993. Honours: 2nd Prize of Scientific & Technical Progress, Sichuan Province, 1990, 1994; 2nd Prize of Scientific Progress, National Health Bureau, 1990. Memberships include: Chairman, Association of Pediatrics in Chongqing; Vice Chairman, Association of Pediatrics in Sichuan. Address: Children's Hospital, Chongqing University of Medical Sciences, Chongqing 630014, China.

YANG Zhen-hua, b. 4 Aug 1935, Shanghai, China. Clinical Chemist. m. Shen Yan, 23 Apr 1957, 1 son, 1 daughter. Education: Graduated, Medicine major, Chinese Medical University, 1956; MD. Appointments: Junior Researcher, Academy of Chinese Military Medicine, 1956; Laboratory Scientist, Nantong Medical College Teaching Hospital, 1958; Deputy Chief, Institute of Navigation Medicine, 1979; Director, Department of Laboratory Medicine, Beijing Hospital. 1983-. Publications: Clinical Enzymology, book chapter, 1989. Memberships: Vice-Chairman, Chinese Society of Medical Laboratory Sciences. Hobbies: Sightseeing; Reading. Address: Department of Laboratory Medicine, Beijing Hospital, No 1 Dahua Road, Beijing 100730, China.

YANG Zhijun (Chih-chun), b. 22 Nov 1930, Shanghai, China. Professor of Surgery. m. Ding Huai-yi, 18 Feb 1958, 1 son. Education: MD, Shanghai Second Medical College, 1954. Appointments: Resident Doctor, Visiting Doctor, Vice-Chief of Burn Unit, Chief of Burn Unit, Professor of Surgery, Rui Jin Hospital, Shanghai Second Medical University. Publications: Resurfacing acute extensive deep burn (co-author), 1985; Co-editor: Treatment of Burns, 1982, 2nd Edition, 1985; The Treatment and Research in Burns, 1983. Honours: Special Reward, Minister of Health, China, 1964; Outstanding Expert Certificate, Minister of Human Resources, China, 1984. Memberships: International Burn Association; Chinese Burn Association. Hobby: Playing the violin. Address: Burn Unit, Rui Jin Hospital, Shanghai 200025, China.

YANOWITZ Edward Stanley, b. 4 Jul 1950, New York, NY, USA. Physician. m. Jean W Temeck, MD, 25 Oct 1986. Education: BA, Yale University, 1972; MD, Autonomous University of Guadalujara, Mexico, 1978. Career: Pediatric Intern, Roosevelt Hospital, NY, 1979-80; Pediatric Residency, St Luke's-Roosevelt Hospital Center, NY, 1980-82; Clinical Fellow, Division of Allergy and Immunology, Department of Pediatrics, NY Hospital, Cornell Medical Center, 1982-84; Instructor in Pediatrics, Cornell University Medical Center, NY, 1984-87; Currently, Assistant Professor of Medicine; George Washington University. Publication: Co-author, Asthma Therapy in Handbook of Pulmonary Drug Therapy, 1994. Memberships: Fellow, American Academy of Pediatrics; Fellow, American Academy of Allergy and Immunology; AMA; Joint Council of Allergy and Immunology. Hobbies: Baseball; Tennis; Hiking; Music. Address: George Washington University Medical Center, Ambulatory Care Center, Room 4-241, 2150 Pennsylvania Avenue NW, Washington, DC 20037, USA.

YAO He-Xiang, b. 29 Dec 1936, Henan Province, China. Director of General Surgery. m. Sun Zhi Xian, 8 Feb 1963, 2 sons, 1 daughter. Education: Graduated, Second Military Medical University, Shanghai. Appointments: The Military Hospital 180, Quanzhou; Currently Director of General Surgery, Fuzhou Military General Hospital, Fuzhou, Fujian. Publications include: Human Orthotopic Liver Transplantation: A Report of 1 Case, 1982; Experience in Selective Celiac and Superior

Mesenteric Arteriography, 1983; Human Orthotopic Liver Transplantation: A Report of 3 Cases, 1984; The Surgical Anatomy of the Second and Third Order Biliary Ducts and Application, 1989. Membership: Chinese Medical Association. Hobby: Travel. Address: Fuzhou Military General Hosptal, Fuzhou, Fujian 350001, China.

YAO Ji Lu, b. 29 Sep 1939, Macau. Medical Doctor. m. Dr Li Lei, 3 Mar 1963, 1 s, 1 d. Education: Diplomate, Medicine. Appointments: From Doctor to Professor, Director of Department of Infectious Diseases, Sun Yat-Sen University of Medical Sciences, Guangzhou, 1961-. Publication: Co-author, Textbook of Infectious Diseases, 3rd edition, 1994. Honour: Outstanding Middle Age Scientist, State Government China, 1988. Memberships: Fellow, Society of Infectious Diseases and Parasitic Diseases; Chinese Medical Association; Fellow, Royal Society of Tropical Medicine and Hygiene, UK. Hobby: Swimming. Address: The Third Hospital Sun Yat Sen, University Medical Sciences, Guangzhou, China.

YAO Jiasheng, b. 15 June 1924, Wuxi, Jiangsu, China. Professor of Obstetrics and Gynaecology. 1 son, 3 daughters. Education: Bachelor, Military Medical College, Central-Southern China, 1950. Appointments: Resident, Visiting, Chief Physician; Assistant, Lecturer, Professor; Currently Director, Obstetrics Department, Maternal and Child Health Hospital, Jiangxi Province. Publications: Hand-Book of Technicology and Management of Perinatal Health Care in Rural Areas, 1989; Discussion on Indications and Rate of Caesarean Section in Breech Presentation, 1986; Pregnancy Induced Hypertension Score and Immunoglobulin Levels, 1988; Systemic Control in Rural Areas, 1991. Honours: 2nd Prize for Achievement in Medical Scientific Research, Ministry of Public Health, China. Memberships: Chinese Obstetrics and Gynaecology Association; Chinese Perinatalogy Association; Director, Jiangxi Provincial Perinatalogy Association; Vice-Director, Jiangxi Obstetrics and Gynaecology Association. Address: Maternal and Child Health Hospital, Nanchang, Jiangxi 330006, USA.

YAO Ke, b. 17 September 1950, Hangzhou, China. Ophthalmology. m. 31 July 1979, 1 son. Education: MD; PhD. Appointments: Resident, 1983-85; Attending Surgeon, 1985-90; Associate Professor, 1991-92; Professor, 1992-. Publications: Endothelium-dependent regulation of the vascular tone of ophthalmic artery, 1991; Influence of cataract on automated perimetry, 1993; Influence of pupil size on Opacity Lens Meter (701) Measurements, 1993; Relationship between cataract density and visual field damage, 1993; Small incision extracapsulaz cataract extraction with a manual nucleus division technique and intraoculaz lensimplantation, 1994. Honours: National Science and Technology Advance Prize, 2nd Class, 1990; Alfred-Vogt Prize, Switzerland, 1990; The Scientist of Outstanding Contribution Award, Chinese Government, 1992. Memberships: Committee Member, Society of Ophthalmology; Chinese Medical Association. Hobbies: Photography. Address: Department of Ophthalmology, 2nd Teaching Hospital, Zhejiang Medical University, Hangzhou 310009, China.

YAO Yu-chun, b. 9 Feb 1941, Jinzhou, Liaoning, China. Physician; Professor (Occupational Disease). m. 25 Mar 1968, 2 daughters. Education: No 2 Shanghai Military Medical College, 1961-66; Medical English major, grade Excellent, Jinzhou Science and Technology Training Institute, 1981-83; Clinical Department, Occupation Toxicity Training for Qualified Doctors in the 3 Northeast Provinces, 1984; Liaoning Occupational Diseases Diagnosis Criteria, 1988. Appointments: Surgeon, 1968; Visiting Physician, 1983; Professor, 1991-; Currently Professor, Occupational Disease, Internal Medicine; Leader, Pneumoconiosis Diagnosis Group; Committee for Assessment of Labour Ability in Patients of Jinzhou with Occupational Diseases. Publications include: Standard-sized Administration of Occupational Health Check, 1992; On the Administrative System of Occupational Health Surveillance, 1993; Occupational Health Surveillance, book, 1994; Co-author: Monitoring Specification of Industrial Labour Hygiene in Liaoning Province, book, 1988; Preliminary Investigation of Contest of Cholylglycine Acid in Serum (SGCA) of Workers Operating with TNT, 1990; The Influence of Malathion on the Worker's Immunity, 1991; Labour Hygiene Monitoring and Occupational Health Surveillance, book, 1991; Electro Hydraulic Lithotripsy of Bile Duct and Stomach Stones, 1993; Immune Toxicity of Organophosphorus Pesticides (summary), 1993. Honours: Prize, Certificate, Advanced Worker in Industrial Hygiene, Public Health Department, Liaoning Province. Memberships: Chinese Medical Association; Chinese Preventive Medical Association; Special Department of Natural Science, Jinzhou Science Association;

Health Supervisor, People's Government of Jinzhou. Address: Jinzhou Science and Technology Training Institute, Jinzhou, Liaoning, China.

YAO Zhen Xiang, b. 5 Nov 1933, Zhejiang, China. Surgeon. m. Tang Wei Ling, 1 Oct 1957, 1 s, 2 d. Education: MD, Hunan Medical College, China, 1956. Appointment: Professor of Surgery, Chongqing University of Medical Sciences, China. Publications: 3 Studies in Medical Journals, 1986, 1989, 1991. Memberships: Council of Chongqing Branch of Chinese Anti-Cancer Association; Vice Director, Committee of Surgery, Chongqing Branch of Chinese Medical Association. Hobbies: Swimming; Chinese Violin. Address: Department of Surgery, First Affiliated Hospital of Chongqing University of Medical Sciences, Chongqing 630042, China.

YAREMCHUK Michael John, b. 8 Feb 1950, Detroit, MI, USA. Assistant Professor of Plastic Surgery. m. Marilyn Kraft, 26 Dec 1977, 1 s. Education: BA, Yale College; MD, Columbia College of Physicians and Surgeons. Appointments: Assistant Professor of Plastic and Orthopaedic Surgery, Johns Hopkins University, Baltimore, MD; Assistant Director of Plastic Surgery, MD Institute for Emergency Medical Services Systems; Assistant Professor of Plastic Surgery, University of MD; Currently: Associate Visiting Surgeon, MA General Hospital; Assistant Professor of Plastic Surgery, Harvard Medical School. Publications: Lower Extremity Salvage and Reconstruction: Orthopedic and Plastic Surgical Management, 1989; Rigid Fixation of the Craniomaxillofacial Skeleton, 1992. Honour: Kappa Delta Award for Outstanding Orthopedic Research, 1991. Memberships: American Society of Plastic and Reconstructive Surgeons; American College of Surgeons; Plastic Surgery Research Council; American Society of Craniofacial Surgery. Hobby: Rowing. Address: MA General Hospital - WACC 453, Boston, MA 02114, USA.

YE Chun-Xiu, b. 6 Feb 1924, Shanghai, China. Physician. m M H Wang, 6 Apr 1952, 2 daughters. Education: BSc, 1946, MD, 1950, St John's University and Medical School. Appointments: Surgeon-in-Chief, Ren-Ji Hospital, Shanghai; Consultant, Guangdong Provincial Research Institute on Cardiovascular Diseases, Guangdong; Professor of Surgery, Cardiothoracic and Director, Surgical Reseach on Cardiovascular Surgery, Ren-Ji Hospital, Shanghaio Second Medical University. Publications: Assissted Circulation and Cardiac Replacement, Editor, 1990; Hemodynamic and Metabolic Effects of Aortic Counterpulsation on Canine Heart under Anesthesia, 1984; In-Vitro and Invivo Evaluation of the Antithrombogenic Properties of the Spiral Vortex for Temporary Left Heart Bypass, 1991. Honours: National 1st Grade award, 1964; Mational Health Bureau Award, 1984; Polystan Travelling Award, 1984. Memberships: Fellowship Committee, International Society of Artificial Organs; Consultant, Chinese Society for Extracorporeal Circulation; Advisory Editorial Board, Perfusion, London, England. Hobby: Classical Music. Address: No 11 Lane 930. Yen-an Zhong Lu, Shanghai 200040, China.

YE Daxun, b. 25 Sept 1931, Beijing, China. Doctor. m. Wang Wenhua, 1 Oct 1959, 3 d. Education: MD, department of medicine, Beijing Medical University, 1950-56. Appointments: Director of Paediatric Depaertment; Professor. Publications: Practical Endocrinology, CO-author, 1994; Practical Paediatrics, Co-author, 1995. Memberships: Tianjin Branch, Paediatric Soceity of Chinese Medical Association, Vice Chairman Hobbies: Music; Fishing. Address: Department of Paediatrics, General Hospital of Tianjin Medical University, Tianjin 300052, China.

YE Rengao, b. 27 Sep 1932, Guangzhou, China. Nephrologist. m. Li Yaji, Sep 1959. Education: MD, Zhongshan Medical University. Appointments: Resident, Attending Physician, Associate Professor, Professor, Sun Yat-sen University of Medical Sciences. Publications: Author of 8 books and Co-author of 9 books about nephrology; Contributor of over 450 articles and reviews in medical journals. Honours: Recipient of Awards and Honours of Medicine and Scientific Technology from National Ministries and Guangdong Province. Memberships: Chairman, Chinese Kidney Association of Integrated Traditional and Western Medicine; Director Member, Chinese Society of Nephrology; International Dialysis Association. Hobbies: Reading; Writing. Address: Renal Department, Sun Yat-sen University of Medical Sciences, Guangzhou 510080, China.

YE Shunzhang, b. 26 Feb 1937, Zhejiang, China. Doctor, Professor. m. Wang Heying, 1 Aug 1962, 2 daughters. Education: MD, Chinese Academy of Medical Sciences. Appointments: Deputy Director, STD Department of Institute of Dermatology, 1986-92; Deputy Director,

Institute of Dermatology, 1992-93; Director, Institute of Dermatology, 1993-. Publications: Handbook, Laboratory Diagnosis on Sexually Transmitted Diseases, 1991; Article, Survey on antibiotic sensitivity of neisseria gonohoal strain isolated in china, 1987-1992, 1994. Hobbies: Music. Address: Institute of Dermatology, 100 Jiangwangmiao Road, Nanjing 210042, China.

YE Songbei, b. 25 Oct 1934, Chengdu, China. Pharmacologist. m. Dr Tian Mingyi, 10 Aug 1962, 1 d. Education: MD, Zhejiang Medical University, 1956. Appointment: Professor of Pharmacology, West China University of Medical Sciences. Publications: Co-author, A Textbook of Clinical Pharmacology, 1987; A Guide for Clinical Use of Drugs, 1989; Co-author, Methods in Experimental Pharmacology, 1991; Co-author, Hormone Receptors and Their Clinical Uses, 1993. Memberships: Chinese Pharmacological Society; Chinese Pharmaceutical Society; Society of Sichuan Physiological Sciences. Hobby: Playing Chess. Address: Dept of Pharmacology, West China University of Medical Sciences, Chengdu, Sichuan, China.

YE Tiehu, b. 18 Aug 1946, Fujian, China. Anesthesiologist. 2 daughters. Education: Master Degree, Peking Union Medical University. Appointments: Surgeon, 1970-83; Anesthesiologist, 1983-. Publications: Changes of Pulmonary Function During HFJV, 1984; 20 articles in professional journals. Memberships: Chinese Association of Anesthesiology. Hobbies: Fishing; Cooking; Sport. Address: Department of Anesthesiology, Peking Union Medical College Hospital, Beijing 100730, China.

YE Weihsin, b. 8 Apr 1929, Wuhan, Hubei, China. Professor of Nuclear Medicine. m. 8 Apr 1955, 2 sons. Education: Clinical Medicine Faculty, Tongji Medical College, 1955. Appointments: Assistant, Resident of Surgery, 1955, Lecturer, Attending Surgeon, 1960, Associate Professor of Nuclear Medicine and Radiation Medicine, 1978, Professor of Nuclear Medicine, 1985-, Director, Department of Nuclear Medicine, Tongji Medical University. Publications: Chief Editor: Nuclear Medicine, 1986; Experimental Nuclear Medicine, 1990; Experimental Nuclear Medicine Techniques, 1991; Guide to Diagnosis and Therapy of Nuclear Medicine, 1991; Nuclear Medicine, Co-author, 3rd edition, 1987; Clinical Nuclear Medicine, CO-author, 1993; Clinical Cardiology, 1994; Symposium on the Clinical Research of Acute Radiation Sickness, 1990. Honours: National Science and Progress Prize, 1978; Science and Progress, Ministry of Health 1986, 1992, 1993; National Family Planning Committee Prize, 1987. Memberships: World Federation of Nuclear Medicine and Biology; Standing Committee, Society of Nuclear Medicine, CMA; Council, Chinese Association of Medical Imaging Technology. Hobby: Football. Address: Department of Nuclear Medicine, Tongji Medical University, Hongkong Road 13, Wuhan, Hubei 430030, China.

YE Yaoguang, b. 1938, Wenzhou, Zhejiang, China. Education: Graduate, Medical Department, Suzhou Medical College, 1962. Appointments: Visiting Scholar, Jiangsu Institute of Hematology, 1976; Professor, Internal Medicine, Berthume Medical University, Chief Physician, Head, Department of Internal Medicine & Hematology Research Unit, Liaoyuan Center Hospital. Publications: Clinic Crisis; Nature Therapy for Common Diseases; A Handbook of Modern Practical Hematology Diseases; Author of over 80 academic papers. Honours: Title, Excellent Expert at Provincial Level; Provinical Berthume-like Medical Worker and National Advanced Individual of Democratic Parties for the Service of Four Modernizations; Elite Medal of Jilin Province; Certificate of Govermental Special Allowance. Memberships: Standing Committee, Hematology Society; Director, Jilin Provincial Branch of Chinese-Western Medicine Unition Association; Chairman, Liaoyuan Branch, Standing Director, Liaoyuan Anticancer Association and Geriatric Medicine Association. Address: Central Hospital, Liaoyuan, Jilin, China.

YEE Bill, b. 14 Apr 1952, China. Physician. m. Karen Yasuda, 2 d. Education: MD. Appointments: Director of In Vitro Fertilization; Associate Professor of Obstetrics and Gynaecology. Publications: Transvaginal Sonography in Infertility, 1995. Memberships: American College of Obstetricians and Gynaecologists; Pacific Coast Obstetrical and Gynaecological Society. Address: 701 East 28th Street, Suite 202, Long Beach, CA 90806, USA.

YEH Tsu Fuh, b. 13 Oct 1942, LuKang, Taiwan. Medicine. m. Ya Fei Yang, Feb 1986, 1 d. Education: Doctor of Medical Science. Career: Professor of Pediatrics, College of Medicine, University of IL, Chicago,

USA, 1986-90; Acting Director, Division of Neonatology, Cook Councty Hospital, Chicago, IL, USA; Currently, Vice Superintendent, Chairman, Professor of Pediatrics, National Cheng Kung University Hospital, Taiwan. Publications: Editor, Drug Therapy in Newborn Infants, 1985; Editor, Neonatal Therapeutics, 1991. Memberships: Society of Pediatric Research, USA; Affiliated Member, European Society of Pediatric Research. Hobby: Fishing. Address: 138 Sheng Li Road, Tainan, Taiwan.

YELISEENKO Vladimir Ivanovich, b. 6 Aug 1942, Trkutsk, Russia. Pathologist. m. Nataly Makarova, 1 Oct 1966, 1 d. Education: Diploma, Medical Institute, Rjazan, 1965; Candidate of Medical Sciences, 1969; Assistant Professor, 1975; Doctor of Medical Science, 1983; Professor of Pathology, 1992. Appointments: Aspirant of the Chair of Pathological Anatomy, 1965-68; Assistant of the Chair of Pathological Anatomy, 1968-73; Assistant Professor, 1973-78; Chief, Department of Morphology, National Centre for Laser Medicine, Russia, 1978-93; Chief, Scientific Department, Laser Medical Center, Interlas, 1993-. Publications: Co-Author: Morphology of Reparative Processes after Laser Photocoagulation of an Acute Gastro-Intestinal Hemorrhages, 1981; Morphology of Purulent Wounds in the Treatment by Means of CO_2 Laser, 1984; Morphological Basis of Laser Revascularisation of Myocard, 1984; Lasers in Surgery, 1989; Laser Wound Morphology, 1992. Memberships: Moscow Society of Pathologists; Russian Laser Association; International Society for Optical Engineering. Hobbies: Swimming; Skiing. Address: Krylatskiye Holmy Ste, 21 Ap 419, Moscow 121360, Russia.

YEN Samuel S C, b. 22 Feb 1927. Professor. Education: MD; DSc. Appointments: Professor, Chairman, Department of Reproductive Medicine, UCSD, 1972-83. Publications incl: Inappropriate secretion of follicle-stimulating hormone and luteinizing hormone in polycystic ovarian disease, 1970; The effect of ovariectomy on gonadotropin release, 1971; Expression of the insulin-like growth factor (IGF)-1 and IGF-11 and the IGF-1, IGF-11 and insulin receptor genes and localization of the gene products in the human ovary, 1993; Effects of Replacement Dose of Dehydroepiandosterone (DHEA) in Men and Women of Advancing Age, 1994. Honours incl: Chancellor's Award for Excellence in Research, 1981; Distinguished Scientist Award, Society for Gynecological Investigation, 1992; Distinguished Achievement Award, The American Fertility Society, 1992. Memberships: International Society of Neuroendocrinology; Society for Gynecological Investigation; The Endocrine Society; Association of American Physicians "The Old Turks"; American College of Obstetricians & Gynecologists; Association of American Gynecologists & Obstetricians; Royal College of Obstetricians & Gynecologists, London. Hobby: Tennis. Address: Department of Reproductive Medicine, UCSD School of Medicine, La Jolla, CA 92093, USA.

YEO Richard, b. 4 Jun 1964, Dover, England. Surgeon. m. Carmel Llewellyn, 19 Aug 1993, 2 s, 1 d. Education: MBBS; D Obst RCOG; MRCOG; FRCOG; AKC. Career: Registrar, Tunbridge Wells, Kent; Registrar and Senior Registrar in Obstetrics and Gynaecology, Charing Cross Hospital, London; Currently, Consultant in Obstetrics and Gynaecology, Westwood Hospital, Beverley, North Humberside. Memberships: Royal College of Obstetricians and Gynaecologists; London Obstetric and Gynaecologic Society. Hobbies: Antiques; Clocks. Address: Westwood Hospital, Beverley, North Humberside, England.

YEUNG Chap Yung, b. 29 Dec 1936, Hong Kong, China. Professor of Paediatrics, University of Hong Kong. m. Helen Chiu, 1963, 2 daughters. Education: MBBS, Hong Kong, DCH, London; MRCP, Edinburgh, 1967; MRCP, Glasgow, 1967; CRCP, 1972; FRCP, 1973; FRCP, Edinburgh; FRCP, Glasgow; FRCP, London. Appointments: Consultant, Queen Elizabeth Hospital, Hong Kong, 1970-72; Assistant Professor of Paediatrics, McMaster University, 1972-76; Associate Director, McMaster University, 1974-76; Consultant, Toronto, 1977-80; Professor of Paediatrics, Hong Kong, 1980-. Publications: 145 articles and 3 chapters; Immunoglobulin Levels in Newborn, 1967; Phenobarb Therapy for Neonatal Jaundice, 1969; Automatic End Oxpiratory Sampler for Small Infants, 1991. Memberships: British Paediatric Association; International Perinatology Collogium; Hong Kong College of Paediatricians; Hong Kong Maternal & Neonatal Health Association. Honours: Commonwealth Medical Scholar to England, 1966-68; Commonwealth Visiting Fellow to Australia, 1970; Honorary Member, Americam Pediatric Society, 1992-. Hobbies: Cross Country; Reading. Address: Department of Paediatrics, University of Hong Kong, Queen Mary Hospital, Pokfulam Road, Hong Kong, China.

YEW Tai-Wai David, b. 8 July 1947, Hong Kong. University Academic. m. Lily K Kuin, 1970, 1 son, 1 daughter. Education: BSc; PhD; DSc (Medicine); Postdoctoral Fellow, Wayne State University, USA. Appointments: Lecturer in Biology, Chinese University of Hong Kong; Lecturer in Anatomy, Hong Kong University; Senior Lecturer in Anatomy, currently Reader of Anatomy, Chinese University of Hong Kong. Publications: 110 full papers; 3 books. Honours: Visiting Scientist, Hubrecht Laboratory, Netherlands, 1980; Visiting Associate Professor, University of Pennsylvania, USA, 1988; Visiting Professor, Sun Yat Sen Medical University and Jinan University, China. Memberships: International Society of Developmental Biologists; American Association of Anatomists; Anatomical Society of Great Britain and Ireland; New York Academy of Sciences. Hobbies: Antique studies; Tennis. Address: Department of Anatomy, Chinese University of Hong Kong, Shatin, New Territories, Hong Kong.

YI Yong Lu, b. 24 Jan 1937, Tianjin, China. Professor; Diet Physician. m. 4 May 1968, 2 sons. Education: Graduate, Department of Medicine, Hebei Medical College, 1961. Appointments: Deputy Director, Emergency Department, First Hospital, Tianjin College of Traditional Chinese Medicine, Tianjin. Address: 4th gate 501, Geng Yu Li, Lin-xi Road, He-ping District, Tianjin, China.

YIN Bingsheng, b. 28 Jan 1938, Shouguan, China. Pathophysiology. m. 14 Oct 1966, 2 daughters. Education: Graduate, 1961, Postgraduate, 1966, Fourth Military Medical University, China. Appointments: Assistantship, Fourth Military Medical University, 1966; Lecturer 1979, Associate Professor 1987, Professor 1989, First Military Medical University. Publications: On the hypothesis of the electrocardial quasi-spheriod field, 1983; The normal limits of HCECG, 1991; An enourmous concept of the cardiac electrophysiology, 1993. Memberships: International Society for Heart Research; Chinese Electronics Institute; Chinese Medical Informatics Association; Electrocardiological Informatics Congress. Hobbies: Music; Sport. Address: The Centre for Electrocardic Research, First Military Medical University, Tonghe, Guangzhou 510515, China.

YIN Frank Chi-Pong, b. 21 June 1943, Kunming, China. Professor of Medicine. m. Grace Lu-Chi Chen, 19 Apr 1975, 2 sons. Education: BS, 1965, MS, 1967, Massachusetts Institute of Technology, USA; PhD, 1970, MD, 1973, University of California at San Diego. Appointments: Assistant Professor, 1978, Associate Professor, 1983, professor of Medicine and Biomedical Engineering, Johns Hopkins Medical Institute. Publications: Ventricular Vascular Coupling, 1987; Contributor of over 100 articles and book chapters. Honours: Founding Fellow, AIMBE, 1993; American Society Clinical INvestigation, 1987; Fellow, American physiological Society, 1986; established Investigator, American Heart Association, 1983. Memberships: AIMBE; AHA; APS; ASCI; BMES. Hobbies: Photography; Skiing; Tennis. Address: Johns Hopkins University School of Medicine, Carnegie Room 530, 600 N Wolfe Street, Baltimore, MD 21287, USA.

YIN Hui-Zhen, b. 1 Feb 1935, Nanjing, China. Professor of Physiology. m. Ming-Hai Mu, 8 Jan 1961, 1 son, 1 daughter. Education: BA, Department of Biology, East China Normal University, 1956. Appointments: Lecturing to Physiology students, 1956-73, research, Brain Function Research Laboratory, 1973-86, Professor of Physiology, 1986-94, East China Normal University, Shanghai. Publications include: Responses of Pain-sensitive Neurons of the Thalamic Rf to Stimulation of Anterior Cingulate Gyrus in Rabbits, Acupuncture Research 13(4), 1988; Acta Physiologica Sinica 36 (3), 1984; Shanghai Journal of Traditional Chinese Medicine, Sept 1990; April 1993. Honours include: 3rd Prize, for Influence of cingulate gyrus on analgesic effect of acupuncture, Shanghai Sanitary Board, 1989. Memberships: Chinese Physiological Association; Shanghai Physiological Association; Shanghai Neuroscience Association. Hobbies: Listening to music; Reading. Address: Rm 402, No 221 Lane 3671, Zhong Shan Bei Rd, Shanghai 200062, China.

YIN Kejing, b. Sep 1941, Sanyuan, Shaanxi, China. Professor. m. Wang Aning, May 1964, 1 son, 2 daughters. Education: MB, Shanxi College of Traditional Chinese Medicine, 1963. Publications: Introduction to Acupuncture, 1994; China Magnetic Needles, 1994; Acu-diagnostics for Emergency, 1989; Traditional Chinese Health Caring Therapies, 1992. Honours: Model Teacher Award, Shaanxi Provincial Government, 1985; Book Experimental Acupuncture awarded 1st Prize, Shaanxi provincial Educational Committee, 1991; 3rd Prize, Shaanxi provincial Science and technology Committee, 1994. Memberships: Meridian

Committee, China Acupuncture and Moxibustion Association; Shaanxi Acupuncture and Moxibustion Association. Address: Shaanxi COllege of Traditional Chinese Medicine, Shaanxi Province, China.

YIN Shu Zhen, b. 26 Mar 1929, Tianjin, China. Professor of Cardiovascular-Thoracic Surgery. m. He Shu Lan, 1 Jan 1950, 1 s, 2 d. Education: BA, Hopei Medical College, 1952. Appointments: Chief Resident Doctor, First TB Centre of Tianjin, 1956; Visiting Doctor, 1959, Associate Professor, 1978, Tianjin Chest hospital; Professor, Affiliated Hospital of Tianjin 2nd Medical College, 1985; Surgeon-in-Chief. Publications: Surgical Anatomy of Chest, 1987; Myxoma of RA, 1982; Surgical Treatment of Fallot's Tetralogy, 1983; Surgical Anatomy of Fallot's Tetralogy, 1983; Tricuspid Atresia. 1986; Double-Outlet Ventricles, 1986; Univentricular Heart, 1988; Persistent Truncus Arteriosus, 1986; Clinical Anesthesiology, CO-author, 1992. Memberships: Chinese Medical Association. Address: 13 Jiu-Jiang Road, Hexi District, Tianjin, China.

YIN Xing, b. 14 Feb 1933, Shanghai, China. Consultant. m. Chen Ding-Hua, 4 Nov 1962. Education: MD, Shanghai Second Medical University, 1956. Appointments: Technician, Department of Bacteria Vaccines, 1956, Head, Department of Bacterial Vaccines, 1980, Head, Department of Bacterial Diagnositc Reagents, 1986, Head, Department of Bacterial and Immune Diagnostic Reagents, 1989, Professor, 1987-, Consultant, 1991-, Shanghai Institute of Biological Products; Council Member, Shanghai Association for Anti-Tuberculosis, 1986-; Editorial Board, Journal of Microbiological Volume of Medical Abroad, 1989-. Publications: Control and Preparation of Purified Endotoxin, 1981; Leptospirosis of Serodiagnosis, 1986; Immune-Therapy of Vesica Tumor of Human by Oral Administration with Killed BCG Vaccines, 1989; Comparative Intradermal Reactions of Human Purified Tuberculin; Manual of Practical Pharmacology, Co-author, 1991; Manual of Medical Laboratory Diagnostic, Co-author, 1992. Memberships: National Medical Society; Chinese Microbiology Society; Shanghai Microbiology Society; Shanghai Immunology Society. Hobbies: Television; Sightseeing. Address: 1262 Yan An Road (Western), Shanghai 200052, China.

YING Da-ming, b. 13 Jan 1931, Shanghai, China. Paediatrician. m. Wang Xian-yuan, 22 Apr 1956, 3 daughters. Education: Graduated, Shanghai Second Medical College, 1954; WHO Fellow, St Louis Hospital, University of Paris VII, France, 1980. Appointments include: Professor of Paediatrics, Shanghai Second Medical University; Director, Department of Paediatric Haematology, Xin Hua Hospital; Director, Laboratory of Immunology, Shanghai Institute for Paediatric Research. Publications: Childhood solid tumor, 1994; Co-author: Bone marrow transplantation in a case with Severe Aplastic Anemia, 1981; Treatment of 139 cases with Childhood Acute Lymphoblastic Leukemia, 1990; Effect of IL-2 on NK cell activity in children with malignant solid tumors, 1991. Memberships: Chairman, Committee of Paediatric Oncology, China Anti-Cancer Association; Committee Member, Chinese Paediatric Medical Association; Shanghai Society of Immunology. Hobbies: Travel. Address: 1665 Kong Jiang Road, Shanghai 200092, China.

YING Jiang, b. 1934, Fuxhou, China. Professor. m. Chen Yuanyi deceased, 1962, 1 daughter. Education: Graduated, Shanghai Medical University, 1956. Appointment: Professor, China Pharmaceutical University. Publications: Numerous professional publications in scientific journals. Honour: 3rd Prize, Health Ministry of China. Address: Majia Street, No 40, 1-2-202, Nanjing, Jioangsu 210009, China.

YING Mingde, b. 26 Feb 1929, Wuzi, Jiangsu, China. Physician; Teacher. m. Jianming Bei, 27 Mar 1958, 1 son. Education: BM; MD. Appointments: Assistant, Lecturer, Associate Professor; Resident Physician, Visiting Physician, Vice-Chief Physician; Currently Professor and Chief Physician, First Affiliated Hospital, Nanjing Medical University. Publications: Books: Emergency Otolaryngology; Fundamentals of Otolaryngology; Dizziness; Articles: Immunological Basis of indications for tonsillectomy and adenoidectomy; Pediatric tonsillectomy; Specific desensitization for allergic rhinitis. Honours: 3rd Municipal Science and Technology Award, for development of new oesophageal bougies; 4th Provincial Science and Technology Award, for investigation in genetic deafness in a big family; Central People's Government Allowance. Memberships: Chairman, Society of O-HNS, Chinese Medical Association, Jiangsu and Nanjing Branches; Chairman, Committee of Otolaryngology, Chinese Association of the Integration of Traditional and Western Medicine, Jiangsu Branch; Allergy Committee, Chinese Society of Microbiology and Immunology; ARS; AAO-HNS. Hobbies: Music; Poetry; Literature; Art. Address: The First Affiliated Hospital of Nanjing

Medical University (The Jiangsu Provincial Hospital), 300 Guangzhou Road, Nanjing 210029, China.

YING Yue-Ying, b. 18 Dec 1926, Zhejiang, China. Pathologist. m. Bao-Rong Zhu, 25 Oct 1952, 1 son, 1 daughter. Education: MD, Hsiang Ya Medical College (now Hunan Medical University), Changsha, 1947; Postdoctoral Fellow in Neuropathology, 1988-92, Certificate, 1992, Loma Linda University, California, USA. Appointments: Assistant Professor of Pathology, 1951-55, Lecturer in Pathology, 1955-62, Associate Professor of Pathology, 1963-80, Professor of Pathology, 1980-, Shanghai Medical University; Visiting Professor of Neuropathology, Loma Linda University, California, USA, 1990-92, Postdoctoral Neuropathology Research Fellow, Childrens Hospital, Los Angeles, California, USA, 1992-. Publications: Pathology of Liver Cancer, 1983; Pathology of Subclinical Liver Cell Cancer, 1985; Text Book of Pathology (chief editor, co-author), 1988; Pathology (co-author), 1989; Pathology and Immunopathology of Viral Hepatitis, 1992. Honours: 1st Class National Science and Technology Award, China, 1985; Awards, Ministry of Health, China, 1982, 1986; Award, Ministry of Education, China, 1990. Memberships: Committee of Medical Science, Ministry of Health, China; Vice-President, Chinese Society of Pathology; Standing Committee, Chinese Medical Association. Hobbies: Music; Reading; Swimming. Address: 1929 N Vermont Avenue 3, Los Angeles, CA 90027, USA.

YOGANANDAN Narayan, b. India. Professor. Education: BSC; BSCE; MSCE; PhD. Appointments: Visiting Professor; Assistant Professor; Associate Professor; Currently Professor, Department of Neurosurgery, Medical College of Wisconsin, Milwaukee. Publications: Over 200 articles in national and international medical and engineering journals, books, handbooks, conferences, symposia and others. Honours: Valedictorian, 1973-79; Gold Medals, 1974-80. Memberships: AANS; American Society of Mechanical Engineers; SAE; CSRS; American Association for the Advancement of Science; BMES; ASTMI; EMBS; ASB. Address: Department of Neurosurgery, Medical College of Wisconsin, 9200 W Wisconsin Avenue, Milwaukee, WI 53226, USA.

YOO Tai June, b. 3 July 1935, Seoul, Korea. Professor. m. Marie Ann Yoo, 3 daughters. Education: MD, Seoul National School of Medicine, 1959; PhD, Biophysics, University of California, Berkley, 1963. Appointments include: Professor, Medicine, Associate Professor, Microbiology, Immunology, 1980-87, Director, Clinical Immunology, 1980-81, Chief, Immunology and Allergy Division, Department of Medicine, 1982-, Professor, Neuroscience programme, 1985-, Professor, Medicine, Microbiology, Imunology, 1987-, University of Tennessee, Memphis, USA; Chief, Allergy-Clinical Immunology Section and Allergy Research Programme, VA Medical Center, Memphis, 1980-; Attending and Consultant Staff, University of Tennessee Medical Center, Memphis, City of Memphis and Baptist Memorial Hospitals, 1980-; Consultant, St Joseph's and Eastwood Hospitals, Memphis, 1983-. Publications: Author or co-author, over 125 papers and book chapters including: Florescence Probe for Antibody Active Sit, 1976; Immunologically-Induced Temporal Bone Lesion: An Animal Model, 1985; Autoimmune Diseases of the Cochlea, 1986; Animal Model of Autoimmune Ear Disease; The study of collagens and transgenic mice models for ear disease, 1991. Honours: Postdoctoral Research Fellowship, Korea Atomic Energy Office; National Institutes of Health Postdoctoral Fellowship; Clinical Investigatorship, Veterans Administration, 1972-75. Memberships: Biophysical Society; American Association for the Advancement of Science; American Academy of Allergy; New York Academy of Sciences; American Association for Cancer Research; American Association for Immunologists; American Society for Experimental Pathology; Reticuloendothelial Society; Central Society; Association of Research in Otolaryngology; American Federation for Clinical Research. Hobby: Golf. Address: 956 Court Avenue, Room H300, Memphis, TN 38163, USA.

YOON Ji-Won, b. 28 Mar 1939, Kan-jin, Chonnam, Korea. Professor; Diabetes Researcher; Director. m. Chungja Rhim, 17 Aug 1968, 2 sons. Education: MS, University of Connecticut, 1971; PhD, University of Connecticut, 1973. Appointments: Senior Investigator, NIH, 1978-84; Professor, Chief, Division of Virology, University of Calgary,1984-; Professor, Associate Director, Diabetes Research Centre, 1985-90. Publications: Author of over 150 papers in journals. Memberships: American Society of Microbiology; New York Academy of Science; American Diabetes Association; International Diabetes Federation. Honours: NHI Director Award, 1984; Heritage Medical Scientist Award, Alberta Heritage Foundation for Medical Research, 1984; Lectureship

Award, 3rd Asian Symposium of Childhood Diabetes, 1989; Lectureship Award, 8th Annual Meeting of Childhood Diabetes, Osaka, 1990. Hobbies: Hiking in the Mountains. Address: Julia McFarlane Diabetes Research Centre, University of Calgary, Faculty of Medicine, 3330 Hospital Drive, NW Calgary, Alberta T2N 4N1, Canada. 52.

YOSHIMURA Takesumi, b. 23 Feb 1943, Tokyo, Japan. Professor. m. 19 May 1968, 2 sons. Education: MD, Kyushu University, Faculty of Medicine, 1967; Dr Medical Sciences, Kyushu University Graduate School in Medical Sciences, 1971; MPH, Harvard School of Public Health, USA, 1975. Appointments: Research Associate, Department of Public Health, Faculty of Medicine, Kyushu University, 1971-79; Associate Professor, Department of Human Ecology, School of Medicine, 1979-84, Professor, Director, 1992-95, Department of Clinical Epidemiology, Institute of Industrial Ecological Sciences, 1984-, University of Occupational and Environmental Health. Publications: New Epidemiology, 1991; Industrialization and Emerging Environmental Health Issues: Risk Assessment and Risk Management, 1991; Papers: Epidemiologic Study on Yusho, 1972; Prevalence and Incidence of Onchocerciasis as Baseline Data for Evaluation of Vector Control in SVP Guatemala, 1982. Honours: Cancer Fellowship, US National Cancer Institute, 1973-74; International Cancer Fellowship, International Agency for Research on Cancer, Lyon, 1974-75. Memberships: Japanese Society of Public Health; Japan Society of Tropical Medicine; International Epidemiological Association; Society for Epidemiological Research International Commission on Occupational Health. Hobbies: Travel; Culture. Address: Department of Clinical Epidemiology, Institute of Industrial Ecological Sciences, University of Occupational and Environmental Health of Japan, 1-1 Iseigaoka, Yahatanishiku, Kitakyushu 807, Japan.

YOSHIZAKI Shiro, b. 17 Feb 1944, Tokushima, Japan. Medicinal Chemist. m. Ayako Ohno, 31 May 1970, 2 sons. Education: Bachelor of Engineering, Tokushima University, 1966; Master of Engineering, Tokushima University, 1968; Doctor of Pharmacy, Osaka University, 1981. Appointments: Researcher, Otsuka Pharmaceutical Co, Ltd, Tokushima, 1968-81; Senior Researcher, Otsuka Pharmaceutical Co, Ltd, 1982-89; Senior Researcher, NKK Corporation, Kawasaki, Japan, 1989-. Publications: Preparation of Procaterol, 1976; Preparation of Carteolol, 1974. Memberships: Fellow, American Chemical Society; New York Academy of Sciences; Charles Darwin Associates; Pharmaceutical Society of Japan; Kinki Chemical Society; Japan Consulting Engineers Assocaition. Honours: Kagaku-Gijyutsu Prize, Kinki Chemical Society, 1983. Hobbies: Fishing; Go; Walking. Address: Research & Development Division, NKK Corporation, 1-1 Minamiwatarida-Cho, Kawasaki-Ku, Kawasaki 210, Japan.

YOU Dayu, b. 25 Aug 1929, Suzhou, China. Physician. m. Baowang Zheng, 1 May 1959, 1 d. Education: BS, Suzhou University, 1947-50; MD, Peking Union Medical College, 1950-55. Appointments: Resident, Visiting Physician, PUMC Hospital, 1955-65; Lecturer, Associate Professor, Norman Bethune University of Medical Sciences, 1965-80; Associate Professor, Professor, Nanjing Railway Medical College, 1980-. Publications: Fatty Liver in Clinical Hepatology, Co-author, 1983; Treatment of Portal Hypertension in Therapy of Liver Disease, Co-author, 1992. Memberships: Academic Committee, International Research and Exchange Centre of Liver Disease; Director, Medical Branch, Chinese Railway Association. Address: Nanjing Railway Medical College, Nanjing, Jiangsu, China.

YOU Rui-lin, b. 10 Aug 1935, Yangzhou, Jiangsu, China. Professor of Botany. m. Wang Mo-shan, 30 Apr 1963, 1 son, 1 daughter. Education: Graduated, Department of Plant Molecular and Developmental Biology, College of Life Sciences, Peking University, 1957. Appointments: Assistant, 1957-79; Instructor, 1979-85; Associate Professor, 1985-92; Professor, Peking University, 1992-. Publications Include: Ultrastructural observations of mature megagametophyte and the nucellar cells in wheat (Triticum aestivum), 1985; The influence of space conditions on the seeds and their offsprings of cucumber, 1992; Transcriptional regulation of a seed-specific carrot gene, 1992; Impact of temperature of callus growth and somatic embryogenesis in carrot haploid cell line HA and its temperature-sensitive mutant lines, 1993; Primary study of callus induction and plantlet regeneration in Arabidopsis thaliana, 1994. Memberships: Chinese Societies of Botany, Cell Biology & Electron Microscopists; International Association of Sexual Plant Reproduction Research. Address: Bldg No 306, Apt No 105, Yan Bei Yuan, Peking University, Beijing 100091, China.

YOUNG Charles Gibson, b. 18 Oct 1926, Winston-Salem, NC, USA. Physician. m. Marie Kyum, 18 Feb 1949, 3 s, 1 d. Education: BS, Wake Forest College, 1946; MD, Duke University, School of Medicine, 1953. Appointments: Private Practice, Greensboro, NC, 1955-64; Assistant Medical Director, E I DuBut Chambers Works, 1964-69; Assistant Medical Director, Exxon Research & Engineering Co, 1969-73; Medical Director, Fieldcrest, 1973-77; Solo Private Practice, Internal Medicine, Reidsville, NC, 1973-. Honours: Certified by The American Board of Preventative Medicine in Occupational Medicine. Memberships: AMA; North Carolina Medical Society; American College of Preventative Medicine; Rockingham County Medical Society; Omicron Delta Kappa. Hobbies: Golf; Instrumental Music; Aviation. Address: 671 Highland Park Drive, Eden, NC 27288, USA.

YOUNG Gordon Neville, b. 10 Jul 1913, Sydney, Australia. Medicine. m. Edna Spencer, 27 Dec 1939, 3 s. Education: MBBS, Honours, Sydney; FRACS; FRCOG; FRACOG. Career includes: Honorary Obstetrician, Royal Prince Alfred Hospital, Sydney, 1945-73; Honorary Consultant Obstetrician and Gynaecologist, Ryde and Parramatta Hospitals; Consulting Gynaecologist, Australian Army HQ, Honorary Surgeon, 6th Governor General, 1965-68; Representative Honorary Colonel RAAMC, 1974-77; Chief Commissioner, 1979-84, Knight of Grace, St John Ambulance Brigade, Australia; Retired Medical Practitioner in Obstetrics and Gynaecology. Honours: ED, Three Bars, 1952; KStJ, 1981. Memberships: British Medical Association; Australian Medical Association; Fellow, 1966, Royal Society of Medicine. Hobbies: Travel; Oil Painting. Address: 30-28 Curagul Road, North Turramurra, NSW 2074, Australia.

YOUNG Grace, b. 22 Apr 1941, MI, USA. Psychiatrist. m. G L Whitecotten, MD, 21 May 1967, 2 s. Education: MD, University of MI; Postdoctoral Training, Cleveland Clinic, Cleveland, OH; George Washington University, Washington DC. Appointments: CMHC, Beaufort, SC; CMHC and Private Practice, Savannah, GA; Private Practice, Guam; Currently, Private Practice, Los Alamos, NM. Memberships: National Council on Psychiatry and The Law, Representative to Assembly from NM, National Committee on Confidentiality, American Psychiatric Association; Psychiatric Medical Association, NM; NM Medical Society; Los Alamos County Medical Society; President, Board of Directors, Family Council. Hobbies: Reading; Family Activities; Community Service. Address: Los Alamos Medical Center, Los Alamos, NM 87544, USA.

YOUNG Jacqueline, b. 15 Jan 1955, London, England. Health Consultant; Writer. Education: BA, Psychology, Newcastle University, 1977; MA, Clinical Psychology, Liverpool University, 1981; Diploma in Acupuncture, International Institute of Oriental Medicine, Tokyo, Japan, 1985; Certificate of Advanced Acupuncture, Academy of Traditional Chinese Medicine, Beijing, China, 1984; Currently pursuing a PhD at Exeter University. Appointments: Clinical Psychologist, Mersey Regional Health Authority, 1979-81; Researcher, Motoyama Institute for Life Physics, Tokyo, 1981-85; Co-Founder and Practitioner, Whole Woman Clinic, London, 1985-88; Faculty Coordinator and Lecturer, International College of Oriental Medicine, 1988-90; Consultant, New Momentum Health Care Centre, Hilversum, Netherlands and Guest Lecturer, International University of Lugano, Switzerland, 1988-90; Visiting Lecturer, Centre for Complementary Health Studies, University of Exeter and Private Practice, London, 1990-. Publications: Vital Energy, 1991; Self Massage, 1992; Acupressure for Health, 1993; other titles in press; Numerous articles to professional journals. Memberships: British Acupuncture Association and Register; Council for Acupuncture Research Committee. Hobbies: Martial Arts; Walking; Singing. Address: PO Box 2211, Barnet, Hertfordshire, EN5 4QW, England.

YOUNG Rosie, b. 23 Oct 1930, Hong Kong. Physician. Education: MD, University of Hong Kong; FRCP, London, Edinburgh, Glasgow; FRACP. Career: Assistant Professor, 1957, Professor, 1974-, Medicine, University of Hong Kong; Sino British Research Fellow, 1958-59; Smith and Nephew Research Fellow, 1963-64; China Medical Board Fellow, 1968, 1970. Publications: Over 100 articles in international medical journals mainly on diabetes, CHO metabolism and endocrinology. Honours: JP, Hong Kong, 1971; Officer of the Most Excellent Order of the British Empire, 1987; Honorary Fellow, Newham College, University of Cambridge, 1988. Memberships: American Diabetes Association; Association of Physicians of Great Britain and Ireland; American Endocrine Society; Founding Member, Past President, Society for the Study of Endocrinology, Metabolism and Reproduction, Hong Kong;

Australian Endocrine Society. Address: Department of Medicine, Queen Mary Hospital, Pokfulam Road, Hong Kong.

YTREHUS Kirsti, b. 2 June 1953, Drammen, Norway. Medical Physiology. m. Svein J Karoliussen, 3 children. Education: MD, University of Oslo, Norway, 1980; PhD, University of Tromso, Norway, 1988. Appointments: Internship, Narvile Hospital, Norway, 1981; Research Fellow, University of Tromso, 1982; Visiting Associate Professor, University of South Alabama, 1992; Professor, University of Tromso, Norway. Publications incl: Estimates of free radical production in rat and swine hearts: Method and application of measuring malondialdehyde levels in fresh and frozen myocardium, 1984; Influence of oxygen radicals generated by xanthine oxidase in the isolated perfused rat heart, 1986; A comparison of six laboratory models of experimental infarction in rat and rabbit hearts: The effect of species, anesthesia, perfusate, risk sixe and method of infarct size evaluation; Endothelin-1 causes accumulation of inflammatory cells in the pulmonary circulation in rats. Memberships: Norwegian Medical Association; Norwegian Society of Cardiology; American Heart Association; Nordic Council for Artic Medical Research. Address: Department of Medical Physiology, Institute of Medical Biology, University of Tromso, N-9037 Tromso, Norway.

YU Anke, b. 13 Oct, Mindung, Shandong, China. Teacher. m. 1 July 1962, 3 s. Appointments: Teacher, Lecturer, Associate Professor of Parasitology. Publications: Study on Parasitological Biology, 1986. Honours: Award for Excellent Medical paper. Memberships: Chinese Biological Association, Parasitology Branch; CHinese Medical Association; Hygienic Biology Association. Hobbies: Swimming; Running. Address: Yinchuan Scientific and Technological Information Research Institute, Yinchuan, China 750001.

YU Bao Ming, b. 23 Dec 1934, Shanghai, China. Surgeon. m. Yin Zai Mei, 2 Nov 1958, 2 sons. Career: Assistant Professor of Surgery, Shanghai 2nd Medical University, 1985-89; Vice Chairman, Department of Surgery, Rui Jin Hospital, 1985-89; Professor of Surgery, Shanghai 2nd Medical University, Chief Surgeon & Vice Chairman, Department of Surgery, Rui Jin Hospital, 1990-. Publications: Co-author, Abdominal Surgery, 1992; Co-author, Modern Oncological Surgery, 1994; Co-author, Clinical Theory and Practice, 1994; Co-author, Atlas of Gastrointestinal Operations, 1994. Memberships: Chinese Medical Association; Shanghai Branch of Chinese Medical Association; Society of Surgery; Society of Oncology; Shanghai Anti-Cancer Society. Hobbies: Swimming; Dancing. Address: Department of Surgery, Rui Jin Hospital, 197 Rui Jin Er Road, Shanghai 200025, China.

YU Bing-wen, b. 6 Oct 1931, Hongkong. Professor; Physician. m. Si Qi Yang, 1 July 1957, 3 daughters. Education: MA, Sun Yat-Sen University of Medical Science, 1956. Appointments: Assistant, Resident, 1957, Attending Physician, 1964, Lecturer, 1980-82, Hunan Medical University; Lecturer, 1982, Associate Professor, 1986, Chief Physician, Professor, Tutor, postgraduate students, 1993-, Jinan University. Publications include: Practical Infectious Diseases (co-author), 1989, 1994; About 20 scientific papers on hepatitis research, 1984-; The first human case of Angiostrongyliasis cantonensis on the Mainland of China (co-author), 1988. Memberships: Chinese Medical Association; Committee Member, International Research and Exchange Center of Liver Diseases. Hobbies: Traditional Chinese Medicine; Sewing. Address: Department of Infectious Diseases, Affiliated Hospital of Medical College, Jinan University, Guangzhou 510630, China.

YU Byung Ho, b. 15 Oct 1958, Seoul, Korea. Physician. m. Joo Yu Byung, 23 Apr 1988, 1 s, 1 d. Education: BA, Knox College, 1982; MD, Loyola University Medical School, Chicago. Appointment: Clinical Instructor, Allergy and Immunology, Rush Pres St Luke Medical Center. Memberships: American Academy Allergy and Immunology; American College Allergy and Immunology; American Medical Association. Address: 1725 West Harrison Street 207, Chicago, IL 60612, USA.

YU Chuan Ling, b. 27 Sept 1922, Hupeh, China. Professor of Immunology. m. Zhi-Xi King, 15 July 1950, 3 d. Education: BA, National Shanghai Medical College; MD, Shanghai Medical University. Appointments: Assistant, Instructor, Shanghai First Medical College; Vice Head, Microbiological Department, Chungking Medical College; Associate professor of Microbiology and Immunology, Professor of Immunology, Shanghai Medical University. Publications: Textbook of Virology, 1953; Liquid Culture Medic for Typhoid Vaccine, 1954; Laboratory Diagnosis for Japanese B Encephalitis Virus Infection, 1956;

Advances in Cellular Immunology, 1980; Medical Basic immunology, 1990. Memberships: Chinese Microbiological Association; Chinese Immunological Association; Shanghai Immunological Association. Hobby: Beijing Opera. Address: 20/273 Ping-Jiang Road, Shanghai 200032, China.

YU Chun-zhi, b. 25 Aug 1925, Shandong, China. Doctor; Professor. m. Hua Yu, 9 Oct 1954. Education: MD, Shenyang Medical College, 1948. Appointments: Resident, Department of Surgery, Third Municipal Hospital, Beijing, 1948; Instructor, Department of Anatomy, Fourth Military Medical University, Xian, 1949; Instructor, Department of Histology & Embryology, Fourth Military University, Xian, 1950; Resident, Department of Ophthalmology, Xijing Hospital, Fourth Military Medical University, Xian, 1953; Visiting Doctor, Department of Ophthalmology, Xijing Hospital, Fourth Military Medical University, Xian, 1962; Associate Professor, Department of Ophthalmology, Xijing Hospital, Fourth Military Medical University, Xian, 1979; Professor, Department of Ophthalmology, Xijing Hospital, Fourth Military Medical University, Xian, 1983. Publications incl: Observations on the effect of "Tong-mai-ling" on corneal scar, 1982; The morphologic distinction between lamellar cornea preserved by anhydrous calcium chloride and normal fresh cornea, 1986; An experimental study on the treatment of corneal scar with "Hua-yun-ning", 1988; Discussion on the time for surgery of glaucoma with narrow angle on the histological ground, 1994. Memberships: Chinese Medicical Association; Vice Chairman, Xian Ophthalmologic Association; Committee, Chinese Ophthalmic Pathologic Association. Hobbies: Athletics. Address: 15 Chang Le West Road, Department of Ophthalmology, Xijing Hospital, Fourth Medical University, Xian, China.

YU Da Nian, b. 17 Oct 1926, Shanghai, China. Orthopaedic Surgeon. m. Van Min-Xian, 25 Aug 1953, 2 s, 1 d. Education: BSc, University of Shanghai, 1946; MD, West China Medical University, 1954. Appointments: Visiting Professor, Institute of Royal National Orthopaedics, London, England, 1987; Deputy Director, Institute of Traumatology and Orthopaedics, Professor of Orthopaedics and Consultant, Beijing Ji Shui Tan Hospital. Publications: Recent Advances of Surgical Treatment of Rheumotoid Arthritis, 1986, 1987; History of Orthpaedics Surgery in China From Ancient to 1949, 1993. Memberships: Member of 105 professional institutions. Address: No 19 Hu Jia Yuan 501, Dong Zhi Men Wei Xiao Jia, Beijing, China.

YU Fang Ting, b. 25 Aug 1946, Hunan Province, China. Chinese Medicine. m. Sun Li Jun, 12 Dec 1972, 2 s. Education: Master of Medicine, Hunan College of Traditional Chinese Medicine, 1970. Career: Physician, 1970, Lecturer, 1987, Currently, Associate Professor, Department of Chinese Medicine, Nanfang Hospital of the First Military Medical University; Medical Adviser, China Guang Xi Wu Zhou Xi Jiang Instrument Factory. Publications: Clinical effect study on Sanjiu Weitai of 112 cases of chronic gastritis, 1986; Observation of tongue picture and tongue and nail-bed microcirculation before and after blood dialysis in 125 uremic patients with deficiency of kidney-yang, 1991; The characteristics of treatment on differentiation of symptoms of coughing in the synopsis of presciptions of the Golden Chamber, 1993. Honours: Excellent Achievement Award, Meeting of Science and Technology of PLA, 1987; Special Grade Award for the making of the presciption, Sanjiu Weital, 1st Military Medical University of PLA, 1992. Memberships: Guangdong Branch, Promoting Blood Circulation to Remove Blood Stasis of Chinese Association of Integration of Traditional Chinese and Western Medicine; Guangdong Branch, Society of Association of Traditional Chinese Medicine and Pharmacy. Hobbies: Chinese Literature; Music. Address: Department of Medical, Nanfang Hospital, Tonghe, Guangzhou 510515, China.

YU Fu Li, b. 2 May 1934, Peking, China. Cancer Researcher. m. Jie Feng, 20 Apr 1980, 1 s, 1 d. Education: BS, Agriculture and Chemistry, Chung Shing University, Taiwan, 1966; MS, Biochemistry, University of Alabama, 1962; PhD, Biochemistry, University of CA, San Francisco, 1965. Appointments: Research Associate, Institute of Cancer Research, Columbia University, NY, 1966-73; Assistant Professor, Department of Biochemistry, Jefferson Medical College, PA, 1973-79; Associate Professor, 1980-85, Professor, 1985-, Head, University of IL College of Medicine, Rockford, IL. Publications include: 100 Articles published including: Nature, Journal of Biological Chemistry, 1977, 1981; Carcinogenesis, 1983, 1990, 1993. Honours include: Research Awards: American Cancer Society; National Institutes of Health. Memberships include: American Society of Biological Chemists; American Association for Cancer Research; American Chemical Society. Address: Department

of Biomedical Sciences, University of IL College of Medicine, 1601 Parkview Avenue, Rockford, IL 61107, USA.

YU Guo-Zhong, b. 1 March 1934, Shandong, China. Surgeon. m. Zhang Ai-Xin, 6 September 1960, 1 son. Education: MD, Zhong Shan Medical College, 1957; Certificate of Fellow in Hand Surgery, University of Louisville Hospitals, USA, 1990. Appointments: Surgical Resident, Acting Attending Surgeon, Attending Surgeon, 1957-78; Lecturer of Plastic and Micro Surgery, 1978-85; Associate Professor of Plastic & Micro Surgery, 1985-91; Professor of Plastic & Micro Surgery, 1991-. Publications: Operative Treatment of Lymphedema of Limbs, 1983; The Scapular Free Flap, 1985; The Lateral Abdominal Free Flap, 1985; Lymphatic Vessel Transplantation for Treatment of Lymphedema of the Lower Extremity, 1992. Honours: Division of Plastic & Reconstructive Surgery, Medical College of Virginia, conferred Certificate for Visiting Professor, 1982; American Plastic Surgery Educational Foundation Awarded Certificate of Merit for Visiting Professor, 1987. Memberships: Chinese Medical Association; Standing Committee Member, Plastic Surgery Society of Chinese Medical Association; Vice Chairman, Burns & Plastic Surgery Society, Guangdong Branch, Chinese Medical Association. Hobbies: Watching TV; Reading; Riding a Bicycle. Address: Division of Plastic & Micro Surgery, Affiliated First Hospital, Sun Yat-Sen University of Medical Sciences, Guangzhou, China.

YU Guomao, b. 2 Apr 1946, Wen Zhou, China. Teacher. m. Jinhua Zhen 7 Feb 1972, 1 s, 1 d. Education: Zhejian Medical University, 1968. Appointments: Doctor; Teacher; Currently, Director of Department of Histology and Embryology; Council, Xhejian Society of Anatomical Sciences. Publications: Co-author: The measurement and the morphological observation of the induced abortion fetal thymus in 105 cases, 1988; Studies of relationship between the hand length, the foot length and the body length in different fetal ages, 1991; Effects of whitmania pigra decoction on embryos of mice, 1991; Effects of TDP and infrared rays on the abdominal subcutaneous macrophages in mice, 1992; Regression analysis of relationship between fetal age length of external shape and body weight in human fetus, 1993; Observation on the hand skin-prints of patient arteriosus ducts, 1993; Observation on the SCE and mitotic index of chorionic villi in drug abortion caused by mifepristone, 1994; Influence of infrared ray and specific electromagnetic wave radiation on the peripheral blood picture of mice, 1994; The effect of scolopendra decoction on embryos of mice, 1994; Author: Anhidrotic etoctodermal dysplasia, 1988; A comparison of weight and volume between the fetal adrenal gland and kidney report of 192 cases, 1989. Honour: National Excellent Worker in Pepular Science, 1990. Membership: Chinese Society of Anatomical Sciences. Hobbies: Skiing; Volleyball; Literature; Photography; Touring. Address: Department of Histology and Embryology, Wen Zhou Medical College, Wen Zhou 325003, China.

YU He-Chun, b. 1 July 1938, Tangshan, Hebei, China. Professor of Surgery. m. 4 May 1963, 2 sons, 1 daughter. Education: Graduated, Tianjin Medical College, 1963. Appointments: Teacher, Hebei Cangzhou Medical School, 1963-73; Surgeon, Wushir Hospital, 1973-80; Editorial Director, Chinese Journal of Physical Medicine, 1985-92; Associate Editor-in-Chief, Editorial Director, Chinese Journal of Ultrasonography, 1992-; Professor of Surgery, Hebei Medical College, 1980-. Publications: General Publishing Conditions of Ultrasonic Journal, 1988; Diagnosis of Acute Abdomen by B-mode Ultrasound, 1990; 1959-1989 Years Titles of Diagnosis by Ultrasound, 1990; Common Handbook of Making a Diagnosis and Giving Treatment in Acute Disease, 1993. Honours: Medical Information Prize, Hebei Province, 1992; Special Prize, Society of Ultrasound in Medicine, Chinese Medical Association, 1992. Memberships: Trustee, Chinese Medical Association; Senior Editor, Society of Ultrasound in Medicine, Chinese Medical Association. Hobbies: Tourism; Recreational activities. Address: Hebei Medical College, Chanan Road, Shijiazhuang, Hebei 050017, China.

YU Hui-Qin, b. 1 Dec 1928, Shanghai, China. Pharmacologist. m. Lu Ke Ping, 1 July 1951, 2 sons. 1 daughter. Education: Graduated, Dong Wu University, Suzhou, 1951. Appointments: Pharmacist; Vice-Chief Pharmacist; Currently Chief Pharmacist, Professor, Pharmacy Department, 88th Hospital, People's Liberation Army, Tai An, Shandong. Publications: The Handbook of Operating Technique of Hospital Pharmacy, 1982; The Operating Technique of the Hospital Pharmacy, 1992. Honours: Advanced Woman and Female Pacesetter of China, Son of the East programme, CCTV, 1993. Memberships: Medical Science and Technology Committee, People's Liberation Army; Vice-Chief, Pharmacy Committee, People's Liberation Army; Hobbies: Piano playing; Reading books. Address: 88th Hospital, People's Liberation Army, Tai An, Shandong 271000, China.

YU Jen, b. 23 Jan 1943, Taipei, Taiwan. Medical Doctor. m. Janet Chen, 16 Jun 1973, 2 s. Education: MD, National Taiwan University; PhD, Physiology, University of PA. Appointments: Assistant Professor, Department of Physical Medicine and Rehabilitation, University of PA School of Medicine, 1975-76; Assistant Professor, 1976-79, Associate Professor, 1979-81, Department of Physical Medicine and Rehabilitation, University of TX Health Science Center, San Antonio; Professor, 1981-, Chair, 1982-, Department of Physical Medicine and Rehabilitation, University of CA, Irvine College of Medicine. Publications: 96 Research papers and 6 books or book chapters concerning neuroscience and physical medicine and rehabilitation. Memberships: American Academy of Physical Medicine and Rehabilitation; Society for Neuroscience; American Association of Anatomists; American Congress of Rehabilitation Medicine; Association of Academic Physiatrists; International Rehabilitation Medicine Association. Address: Dept of Physical Medicine and Rehabilitation, UCI Medical Center, 101 The City Drive, Orange, CA 92668, USA.

YU Jian-Min, b. 20 May 1938, Guangfeng, Jiangxi, China. Physician and Professor. m. Zhao Chun-yi, 1 May 1960, 1 son, 1 daughter. Education: Bachelor of Medicine, Jiangxi Medical College; Academic Research, Shanghai Medical University; Tokai University and Tokushukai Medical Centre, Japan. Appointments: Physician, 1960-, currently Chief Physician and Professor, People's Hospital of Jiangxi Province, Nanchang. Publications: Applying Chinese Medicinal Herbs in the Treatment of Malignant Histiocytosis, in Practice of Internal Medicine, 1981; A Comprehensive Book for the Health Care of the Old, 1988; A New Practical Handbook for Doctors; Some 100 academic papers including: Changes of Plasma Colloid Osmotic Pressure (COP) in Cor Pulmonale with Respiratory Failure, 1987. Honours: Prize of Achievement in Scientific and Technological Research, for A Clinical and Experimental Study for Applying Gautheria yunnanens is (Fr) Rehd in the Treatment of Virus Infection, Jiangxi Provincial Science and Technology Commission, 1982; Heated Ultrasonic Aerosol Spray appraised by the Administrative Medicine Bureau, Jiangxi Province, 1985; Prize of Achievement in Scientific and Technological Research, for A Computer Analysis of Pulmonary Function, Science and Technology Commission, Jingdezhen Municipality, 1992. Memberships: International Asian Pacific Society of Respirology; China Medical Association; China Association of Anti-Cancer. Hobbies: Running; Reading. Address: People's Hospital of Jiangxi Province, 104 Ai Guo Road, Nanchang, Jiangxi 330006, China.

YU Man, b. 6 Nov 1970, Jiangxi, China. Basic Medical Research Doctor. Education: MD, Tongji Medical University, China, 1993. Appointments: Assistant Professor, Chinese Academy of Medical Sciences, 1993-. Publications: Primary Tracheal Carcinoma Report of the Clinicopathological Findings, 1991; A New Practical Handbook for Doctors, 1994. Honours: Award, Excellent Thesis Prize, Tongji Medical University, 1990. Memberships: Chinese Pathophysiological Society. Hobbies: Dancing; Music; Tennis. Address: Department of Pathophysiology, Institute of Basic Medical Sciences, Chinese Academy of Medical Sciences, Peking Union Medical College, 5 Dong Dan San Tiao, Beijing 100005, China.

YU Mao-Lan, b. 21 Feb 1935, Shanghai, China. Chief Physician. m. Hao-Bai Zhou, 1 Feb 1960, 1 s, 1 d. Education: Nanjing Medical College, 1958. Appointments: Department of Gastroenterology, Department of Endoscopy, People's Hospital of Jiangsu Province. Publications: Analysis of the Complications From Endoscopic Polypectomy with High-Frequency Current, 1990; Ultrastructure Change of Gastric Mucosa due to Bile Reflux, Co-author, 1985; Equal Inspection of Cancerous Focus of Familical Large Intestine Carcinoma under Endoscope, Co-author, 1990. Memberships: Jiangsu Endoscopy and Gastroenterology Society. Hobby: Music. Address: 300 Guangzhou Road, Nanjing, Jiangsu 210029, China.

YU Ming-Whei, b. 6 Nov 1960, Taiwan, China. Associate Professor. Education: PhD, National Taiwan University College of Medicine. Career: Lecturer, Associate Professor, Department of Public Health, College of Public Health, National Taiwan University. Publications: Association Between Heptitis C Virus Antibodies and Hepatocellular Carcinoma in Taiwan, in Cancer Research, 1991; Elevated Serum Testosterone Levels and Risk of Hepatocellular Carcinoma, in Cancer Research, 1993. Hobbies: Reading; Music. Address: College of Public

Health, National Taiwan University, Rm 1545, No 1 Jen-Ai Road, Sec 1, Taipei 10018, Taiwan, China.

YU Pei Lan, b. 2 Feb 1921, Beijing, China. Pediatrician. m. Professor Mei Hong Cao, 1 Dec 1950, 1 s, 1 d. Education: BA, Medicine, 1946; Special Training in Beijing Traditional Medical College organised by Ministry of Public Health of China for high grade traditional and western medical doctors, 1958-61. Career: Committee, Chinese Pediatric Association of Hunan, 1979-82; Chairman, Chinese Association of Traditional and Western Medicine, Hunan, 1985-90; Standing Committee, Chinese Association of Traditional and Western Medicine, 1985-90; Currently, Professor of Pediatrics, Hunan Medical University and Adviser of Postgraduate PhD, 1987-. Publications: Co-author, Brain edema model induced with typhoid endotoxin in rabbit, in Inaba Y et al: Brain Edema, 1985; Co-author, Bacterial infection complicated brain edema in children in Cervés-Navarro Journal, Stroke and Microcirculation, 1987. Honours: Prominent Scientific Worker for 40 Years, State Educational Commission of China, 1990; Advance Prize of National Scientific Technology, 2nd grade award, 1991. Memberships: Traditional and Western Medicine, 1984-; Chinese Association of Traditional and Western Medicine, 1984-; Neurological Association of Asia-Pacific. Hobbies: Singing; Learning. Address: The First Affiliated Hospital, Hunan Medical College, Changsha, China.

YU Shang-Ming, b. 1 Apr 1947, Taipei, Taiwan, China. Doctor; Teacher. m. Lin Kwan-Hwa, 5 Feb 1976, 2 sons, 1 daughter. Education: BS, National Taiwan University, 1971; MS, National Taiwan University, 1977; PhD, University of Kentucky, USA, 1982. Appointments: Research Associate, Kansas State University; Research Associate, UCLA School of Medicine; Associate Professor, Chang-Gung Medical College; Visiting Associate Professor, Yale University School of Medicine. Publications: Co-author: Soluble prolactin may be directly released from cellular compartments other than secretory granules, 1982; Author: Prolactin immunoreactivity in the rat pituitary glands: Comparison of immunofluorescence, immunoperoxidase and immunogold techniques, 1993. Honours: Scholarship, Dr Sun Yat-sen, Ministry of Education, 1968; Research Award, National Science Council of China, 1992. Memberships: American Society for Cell Biology; Society for Neuroscience; Microscopy Society of America; Association for Research in Otolaryngology. Hobbies: Chinese Martial Arts; Aikido. Address: National Yang-Ming University, Institute of Anatomy, 155 Section 2, Lee-Nung Street, Shih-Pai, Taiwan 11221, China.

YU Yang, b. 25 Jan 1925, Anhui, China. Professor of Internal Medicine; Respirologist. m. Wang Yin, 4 May 1949, Nanjing, China, 1 son, 2 daughters. Education: MD, National Jiangsu Medical College, 1949. Appointments: Emeritus Professor of Internal Medicine, Nanjing Medical University; Respirologist, Jiangsu Provincial Hospital. Publications: Contributor of over 300 professional papers including: A Clinical Analysis of 42 Cases of ARDS, 1983; Ten-Year Study on the Treatment of Chronic Cor Pulmonale in Remission Period with Therapeutic Exercise, 1984; Clinical Analysis of 64 Cases of Pulmonary Fungal Infections, 1984; Treatment of 148 Patients of Obstructive Lung Diseases with d-asarone, 1986; A Clinical Analysis of 54 Cases of Pulmonary Infiltration with eosinophilia, 1987; The Effect of Tranilast on the Down-Regulation of Beta-Adrenoceptors, 1993. Honours: 14 prizes of Scientific and Technological Advance by State, Ministry and Province, 1978-92. Memberships: International Union Against Tubercluosis and Lung Disease; Asian Pacific Society of Respirology; Chinese Respirology Association, Standing Council; Jiangsu Province Antituberculosis Association, Honorary President. Hobbies: Chess; Table Tennis. Address: 19 Emeiling Street, Nanjing, Jiangsu 210029, China.

YU Yong-qiang, b. 20 August 1938, Wendong, Shandong, China. Professor of Toxicology. m. Zhang Xiu-lan, August 1967, 2 daughters. Education: BS, Shandong University, 1965. Appointments: Staff, Department of Radiobiology, Kuming Animal Research Institute, China Academy of Science, 1965-76; Department of Immunology, Shandong Medical Scientific Research College, 1976-84; Chief, Department of Industrial Health, The Research Institute of Occupational Safety and Health, Ministry of Chemical Industries, 1984-. Publications: Risk assessment of genetoxic chemicals with chromosome analysis of mouse zygotes, 1990; The effects of potassium dichromate on the chromasomes of human spcrmatozoa in vitro, 1994; The frequency of micronuclei of exfoliated mucosa cells of the workers exposed to Chromium, 1991; Editor: Male reproductive toxicology, 1994; 60 papers published. Honours: Certificate of Merit, Scientist with Outstanding

Contribution to the Nation, State Ministry of Chemical Industry, Shandong & Qingdao, 1978-94; Outstanding Scientist, Ministry of Chemical Industries, 1990; Certificate of Commendation, Chinese Government, 1992. Memberships: IAEMS; Committee Member, Mutagenicity Committee; Vice Chairman, Genetics of Reproductive Cell Zygote Sub-division; Committee Member, China Toxicological Society, Reproductive Toxicological Division. Address: The Research Institute of Occupational Safety and Health, 218 Yanan Road 3rd, Qingdao, Shandong 266071, China.

YU Yongmin, b. 19 Jun 1928, Jinan, Shandong, China. Doctor. m. 15 Feb 1959, 1 s, 1 d. Education: Graduated from Peking University Medical College, 1954. Career: Assistant of Medical Department, Sian Medical College, 1955; Chief Director, Department of Traditional Chinese Medicine, 1961; Professor, Department of Traditional Chinese Medicine, Sian Medical College, 1983; Currently, Director, Department of Integration of Traditional and Western Medicine, Shanghai Oriental Hospital, China. Publications: Clinical Application and Study on The Method of Activating the Blood Circulation and Removing the Blood Stasis, 1981. Membership: Chinese Association for The Integration of Traditional and Western Medicine. Hobby: Music. Address: Room 16-5, 235 Chong Qing Bai Road, Shanghai, China.

YU Yuk-Ling, b. 29 Sept 1947, Hong Kong. Medical Practitioner. m. Vivienne, 26 July 1975, 1 s. Education: MD(HK); FRCP, Edinburgh and London. Appointments: Registrar, Senior Registrar, National Hospital for Neurology and Neurosurgery, Queen Square, London, England, 1978-83; Lecturer, Senior Lecturer, Reader, Department of Medicine, Queen Mary Hospital, Hong Kong, 1984-. Hobbies: Reading; Swimming; Walking. Address: Department of Medicine, University of Hong Kong, Pokfulam Road, Hong Kong.

YU Zhenrong, b. 25 Nov 1961, Hebei, China. Teacher; Researcher. m. 11 June 1988, 1 d. Education: BS, MS, Doctorate, 1990, Beijing Agricultural University; Diplomas of Soil Geography, WAU, Netherlands. Appointments: Associate Professor. Publications: Comprehensive Control of Salt-Affected Land, Co-author, 1990; Approach to Land Use Planning and Designing, 1992; Modelling the Sufficiency of Soil Water to Crop Growth; Impacts of Landscape Pattern on Plant Diversity, CO-author, 1993. Honours: National Awards for Outstanding Research on Comprehensive Control of Soil-Affected Land. Memberships: Association of International Landscape Ecology; Chinese Ecological Association; Association of Chinese Soil Science. Hobbies: Mountaineering; Running. Address: Department of Agrocological Environment, Beijing Agricultural University, Beijing 100094, China.

YU Zhi-Qiang, b. 4 Dec 1931, Kilin Province, China. Head Doctor. m. Du Su-Nian, 24 June 1955, 2 s, 1 d. Education: BA, Dalian Medical Institute, 1958. Appointments: Clinical Head Doctor, Professor of Gynaecology and Obstetrics, Hospital for Gynaecology and Obstetrics in Changchun, Kilin. Publications: The Clinical Analyses of 1.858 Cases for Treating Cervical Erosion with CO2 Laser, 1989. Memberships: China Medical Laser Specialist Cultivation Centre; China Combination of Western Medicine with Traditional Chinese Medicine Research Institute; Changchun Sex Disease Specialist Association. Hobbies: Literature; Sport. Address: The Hospital for Gynaecology and Obstetrics in Changchun, Kilin Province, China.

YUAN Jiaji, b. 26 Jul 1913, Guiyang, Guizhou, China. Traditional Chinese Medicine. m. Yao Jingying, 18 May 1937, 3 s, 2 d. Education: Graduated from Beijing North China College of TCM, 1931-35; National Noted Veteran Doctor of TCM; Pedagogic Expert. Appointments: Vice-Director, Guiyang Municipal Health Bureau, 1954-64; Vice-President/President/ Emeritus President of Guiyang College of TCM, 1984-91; Professor. Publications: The Folk Medicinal Herbs in Guizhou, 1985; Experience of Treating Apoplexy, 1973; A Study on Jueyin Disease Described in TCM Classic Treatise on Fevers, 1983; The Pick of Medical Circle - Experience of the Noted Veteran TCM Doctors in Guizhou Province, 1985; Experience of Treating Coronary Heart Disease, 1988; A Collection of Academic Experience of All China Noted Veteran TCM Doctors and Pharmacologists, 1994. Honours: 2nd Prize for Clinical Study on treating Coronary Heart Disease with Tongluoshuya Bolus, Medicinal & Hygienic Achievements of Guizhou Province, China, 1990; Vice-Chairman of 4th, 5th & 6th People's Political Consultative Conference; Delegate & Model Worker to Multi-Session National Provincial & Municipal Model Worker's Conference, 1978. Memberships: All China TCM Council; Chairman, All China TCM Council, Guizhou Branch; Emeritus Chairman of All China Red Cross,

Guizhou Branch. Hobbies: Chinese Calligraphy; Chese; Weiqi. Address: Guiyang College of TCM, Guiyang, Guizhou 550002, China.

YUAN Jiurong, b. 5 Nov 1935, Caoxian County, China. Educator. m. 7 Feb 1959, 1 son, 2 daughters. Education: BSc, Shandong University. Appointments: Head, Department of Traditional Chinese Materia, 1985-93, Head, Laboratory of National Drugs of Medicine, Shandong College of Traditional Chinese Medicine. Publications: Chinese Patent Medicines, 1990; Recent Development and Future Prospects sof the Research on Contraception and Antifertility by Using Chinese Materia Medica. Honours: National Science Meeting Award, 1978; National Science Progress Award on TCM, 1990. Memberships: Director, Chinese Pharmaceutical Association; Standing Director, Shandong Branch, Chinese Pharmaceutical Association. Hobby: Chinese Drawing. Address: No 53 Jingshi Road, Jinan 250000, China.

YUAN Shi Zhen, b. 26 Feb 1935, Guangdong, China. Attending Physician. m. He Ying Zhi, 30 Mar 1968, 2 daughters. Education: MD, Sun Yat-sen University of Medical Sciences, 1959. Appointments: Physician, Sun Yat-sen Memorial Hospital, 1959-; Visiting Scholar, University of Chicago & California, USA, 1981-83; Chief, Clinical Pharmaceutical Research Laboratory, 1993; Vice Chairman, Guangdong GI Medical Association, 1994. Publications: Gastroenterology, 1983; Cancer Research, 1985; Inflammatory Bowel Disease, 1993. Honours: Scientific & Technical Progression Awards of Educational Committee of China, 1989; Outstanding Contribution Prize of China, 1992. Memberships: Chinese Medical Association. Hobbies: Reading; Music. Address: Department of Gastroenterology, Sun Yat-sen Memorial Hospital, 107 Yan Jiang Road 1, Guangzhou 510120, China.

YUAN Xinchu, b. 15 July 1953, Yueyang, Hunan, China. Teacher. m. 1981, 1 daughter. Appointments: Department of Histology and Embryology, Wuhan Medical School Metallurgical Industry, China. Publications: The Anionic Sites at the Surface of Granulocytes in Acute Myelkiogenous Leukemia, 1993; Morphometry Study on the Development of Reticular Fiber in Fetal Liver, 1994. Memberships: Anatomy Committee of China. Address: Department of Histology & Embryology, Wuhan Medical School, Metallurgical Industry, Wuhan 430080, China.

YUAN Yusun, b. 10 December 1931, Shanghai, China. Professor. m. Xui Aizhen, 4 May 1958, 1 son, 1 daughter. Education: Fudan University. Appointments: Lecturer, 1960; Associate Professor, 1981; Professor, 1985; Vice Chairman, Biological Department, 1982; Chairman, Biochemistry Department, 1985; Pharmaceutical Developing And Research Institute of Nanjing University, 1989. Publications: Two books and 30 articles. Honours: Outstanding Teacher in Nanjing University. Memberships: China Biochemical Association; Chairman, China Biochemical Pharmaceutical Association, Jiangsu Branch; Vice Chairman, Jiangsu Province Biological Engineering Society. Hobbies: Music. Address: The Biochemical Pharmaceutical Factory of Zhuhai, Yuanlin Road, Jida Area, Zhuhai, Guangdong, China.

YUE Song-ling, b. 24 Apr 1920, Chengdu, Sichuan, China. Professor, Dentistry, Cariology. m. Tan Mei-yu, 1 July 1949, 1 son, 3 daughters. Education: DDS, New York State University, 1946; Bachelor of Medicine, West China Union University. Appointments: Assistant, 1946-48; Instructor of Oral Histopathology & Conservative Dentistry, 1948-63; Associate Professor, Oral Therapeutics, 1963-83; Professor of Cariology, 1983-. Publications: Cariology, 1982; Textbook of Oral Therapeutics, 1987; Modern Cariology, 1994. Honours: Prizes of Science and Technology, 1979, 1986, 2nd Degree Award, Sichuan; Prize of Science Advancement, 1992, Ministrial. Distinguished Tutor of Postgraduates of Sichuan, 1992. Memberships: Conservative Dentistry Group, Dental Association of China. Hobbies: Picture Drawing; Music; Reading. Address: College of Stomatology, Medical University of West China, Chengdu 610041, China.

YUE Wen Hao, b. 21 Nov 1930, Anhwei Feng Tair, China. Professor of Psychology. m. Shang Fang, 8 Apr 1956, 1 d. Education: BD, Chinese Medical University, 1955; Psychological Studies, Hurnan Medical University and Syhchuan Medical University, 1983-84. Career: Physiological Assistant, Lecturer, Associate Professor, 1956-83; Professor of Department of Basic Medical Science, 1984-91; Professor of Psychology, 1984; Currently, Professor of Medical Psychology, Shandong Medical University. Publications: Physiology, 1977; Theory of Neural EMG, 1983; Applied Brain Science, 1988; Medical Psychology, 1994; Modern Behavioural Medicine, 1994; Editor of 30 books; 169 Papers published, 1957-. Honours: Recipient of 18 Results in Scientific Study, Health Department of Shandong, 1981-93; Progressive Scientist Award of Shandong, 1986. Memberships: Director, Psychological Health Association; Director, Medical Psychology of China; Director, Psychosomatic Association of Chinese Medical Association. Hobbies include: Reading; Travel. Address: Department of Medical Psychology, Shandong Medical University, Jinan, Shandong 250012, China.

YUE Yun, b. 12 Mar 1952, Shanghai, China. Professor. m. Zhao Weili, 23 Sept 1978, 1 son. Education: Graduate, Fourth Military Medical University, 1974; MD, Peking Union Medical University, 1983. Appointments: Anaesthesiologist, 2nd Affiliated Hospital of the FMMU, 1974-79; Postgraduate, Pekin Union Medical University, 1979-83; Associate Professor, Tangdu Hospital of FMMU, 1987-90; Professor, Chairman, Department of Anaesthesiology, Fourth Military Medical University. Publications: Interaction Between Calcium Channel Blocker and High Dose Epinehrine During CPR, 1994; The Kinetics of Carbon Dioxide During CPR, 1992; Effect of Verapamil Administered Before CPR on Cardiac Resuscitation Myocardial or Cerebral Blood Flow and Hemodynamics, 1990. Memberships: Vice Chairman, Society of Anaesthesiology of Shaanxi Branch, Chinese Medical Association, 1992-; Editorial Board, Journal of Medical Colleges of PLA, 1992-; Chinese Journal of Anesthesiology, 1994-. Address: 18-404 Xinsi Road, Xian, Shaanxi 710038, China.

YUNG Man Bun Paul, b. 15 Mar 1951, Hong Kong. Clinical Psychologist. m. 16 Jul 1994. Education: MA, CA State University, Los Angeles, USA; Honorary BA. Appointments: Lecturer, School of Social Work, Hong Kong Polytechnic; Clinical Psychologist, Psychological and Counseling Services, Hong Kong Christian Service, Hong Kong; Currently, Lecturer in Clinical Psychology, Department of Health Sciences, The Hong Kong Polytechnic University. Publications: Co-author, Stress: A Practical Guide to Coping, Hong Kong, 1992; Treatment for Trichotillomania, in Journal of American Academy of Child and Adolescent Psychiatry, 1993; Co-author, Maintainance Effects of Long-Term Relaxation Training in a Case of Hypertension, in International Journal of Stress Management, 1994. Memberships: Chartered Clinical Psychologist, UK; Registered Psychologist, Australia; Associate Fellow, British Psychological Society, UK; Board of Directors, International Stress Management Association. Hobbies: Running; Swimming. Address: The Department of Health Sciences, Hong Kong Polytechnic University, Hung Hom, Kowloon, Hong Kong.

YUSEV Eugene Ivanovich, b. 23 May 1939, Moscow, Russia. Neurologist. m. Mazina Yugel, 4 Oct 1961, 1 daughter. Education: MD, Russian State Medical University, 1962. Appointments: Chief Physician, District Hospital, 1962-64; Lecturer, Assistant Professor, Department of Neurology, 1964-75, Head, Neurology and Neurosurgery, Russian State Medical Univeristy; Professor, Academician, Russian Academy of Medical Sciences. Publications include: Cerebrovascular Disorder, 1984; Intensive Care in Neurology, 1982; Comatose States; Hereditary Diseases of Metabolism and Phacomatoses, 1981. Honours: Honourable Worker of Science of Russian Federation, 1994; Order of the Red Banner of Labour, 1990; Badge of Honour. Memberships: President, All-Russian Society of Neurologists; Chief Editor, Journal of Neurology and Neurosurgery. Hobby: Travel.

Z

ZACARIAS Fernando, b. 9 September 1944, Mexico City, Mexico. Physician. m. Annette Norrelund, 12 October 1968, 2 daughters. Education: BSc, French-English College, Mexico, 1961; MD, National Autonomous University of Mexico, 1969; MPH, Harvard University, 1980; Diplomate, American Board of Preventive Medicine, 1985; DrPH, Harvard University, 1986. Appointments: Visiting Scientist, Centers for Disease Control, Atlanta, Georgia, USA; Regional Advisor on STD, PAHO/WHO; Senior Regional Advisor on AIDS/STD-PAHO/WHO, Washington DC, USA. Publications: AIDS: Profile of an Epidemic, 1989; More than 35 scientific articles on AIDS/HIV and STD. Honours: National Council for Science and Technology, 1979; Technical Advisory Boards, World Health Organization; NIAID (Fogarty) USAID-FHI. Memberships: American Public Health Association; US-Mexico Border Health Association. Hobbies: Music; Motion Pictures; Linguistics; Travel. Address: 12309 Donaldson Ct, Fairfax, VA 22033 2850, USA.

ZACHERT Virginia, b. 1 Mar 1920, Jacksonville, Alabama, USA. Industrial Psychologist. Education: AB; MA, Emory University; PhD, Purdue University. Appointments: Research Professor Emerita, Department Obstetrics and Gynaecology. Publications: Essentials of Gynecology Oncology, 1967; Applications of Gynaecology Oncology, 1967; Delegate, White House Conference on Aging, 1981, 1995. Memberships: Fellow, AAAS; American Psychological Association; AAUP; Sigma Xi. Hobbies: Fishing; Gardening. Address: 1126 Highland Avenue, Augusta, GA 30904, USA.

ZAGORSKI Maria T, b. 18 Dec 1953, Trenton, New Jersey, USA. Physician; Gynaecologist. m. Floyd Katske, 10 July 1983, 1 son, 1 daughter. Education: BS, Biochemistry, Cornell University, 1975; MD, George Washington University, 1979; Chief Resident, 1982-83, completed Residency, 1983, Obstetrics and Gynaecology, University of California, Los Angeles, 1983. Appointment: Assistant Clinical Professor of Obstetrics and Gynaecology, University of California, Los Angeles, 1983-. Honours: Board Certification in Obstetrics and Gynaecology, 1985. Memberships: American Medical Association; California Medical Association; American College of Obstetricians and Gynecologists; American Fertility Society; Pacific Coast Fertility Society. Hobbies: Greek mythology; Gardening. Address: 23928 Lyons Avenue, Suite 202, Newhall, CA 91321, USA.

ZAKHARCHENKO Gheorgii Semionovich, b. 23 Sept 1943, Ukraine. Physicist; Radiologist. m. Starikova Stetlana, 17 Apr 1978 (div), 1 daughter. Education: Military Naval College, Baku, 1966. Appointments: Military Student, 1963; Officer, Submariner, 1966; Physicist, Radiologist, Moldova Oncological Institute, 1970. Publications: New Methods of External Beam Therapy; Technology of Programmated External Beam Therapy and complex for Her Using; Programmated Changing of densitive structure of material medium and External Beam Therapy. Memberships: President, Moldova Association of Medical Physicists, 1992. Hobbies: Reading; TV. Address: 277039 Kishinyov, Str Alba Julia 2, Ap 54. Moldova.

ZANE Manuel David, b. 4 Jan 1913, Chattanooga, TN, USA. Medicine Doctor. m. Judith Sophia Richmond, 18 Jun 1944, 2 d. Education: BS; MD; Diplomate, American Boards of Internal Medicine, 1948 and Psychiatry and Neurology, 1951. Career includes: Associate Attending Psychiatrist, Division of Rehabilitation Medicine, Montefiore Hospital, Bronx, NY, 1961-81; Assistant Clinical Professor of Psychiatry, Albert Einstein College of Medicine, 1966-81; Currently, Attending Psychiatrist, Founder and Director Emeritus, Phobia Clinic, White Plains Hospital Center. Publications: Co-author, Your Phobia, 1984; Articles: Co-author, Agoraphobia: Contextual Analysis and Treatment, in Agoraphobia, 1982; Co-author, The Management of Patients in a Phobia Clinic, in American Journal of Psychotherapy, 1985. Membership: American Psychiatric Association. Address: 130 Havilands Lane, White Plains, NY 10605, USA.

ZANG Xu, b. 18 May 1923, Hobei, China. Neuropathology. m. Su Hua Jin, 27 Jul 1952, 1 s, 1 d. Education: MD, PUMC Hospital. Career: Assistant, Lecturer, Associate Professor, Professor, PUMC Hospital, now retired. Publications: Practical Neuropathology, 1980; Autopsy study of 200 cases of stroke, in Chinese Medical Journal, 1980; Pathological analysis of 150 cases of pituitary adenoma with light, electronic and inmunocytochemical methods, in Chinese Medical

Journal, 1987. Honour: Grade 1 Prize, National Scientific Progress, 1992. Membership: Chinese Medical Association. Hobby: Television. Address: Department of Pathology, PUMC Hospital, Beijing 100730, China.

ZARAND Pal, b. 15 May 1939, Kispest, Hungary. m. Biborka Csentes, 1 son, 1 daughter. Education: MD, Budapest, 1963; MSc, Budapest, 1969; PhD, Budapest, 1979; DSc, Budapest, 1986. Appointment: Head, Medical Physics Laboratory. Publications: Several professional publications in scientific journals. Memberships: Hungarian Medical Physics Society; International Organization of Medical Physics. Hobbies: Classical Music. Address: Badacsony U 8, H-1029 Budapest, Hungary.

ZARR Michael Lester, b. 2 Nov 1949, Brooklyn, NY, USA. Consultant-Liaison Psychiatrist. m. Sandra C Sarner, 10 Aug 1975, 1 d. Education: BS cum laude, Brooklyn College, 1971; CSM, University of Liege, 1975; MD, Albany Medical College, 1979; FAPA; Fellow, Chief Resident, Intern, Albany Medical Center Hospital, 1979-84. Appointments: Psychiatrist: Samaritan Hospital, Troy, NY; Albany VAMC, NY; Capital District Psychiatric Center, 1982-85; Psychiatric Consultant and Clinical Director, CMHC Fulton-McDonough Counties, 1985-86; Director, Consultation-Liaison Psychiatry, Hurley Medical Center, 1987-. Publications: Therapeutic Usefulness of Amitriptyline in Spastic Colon Syndrome, 1981-82; Psychobiology of The Borderline Disorders - A Heuristic Approach, 1985; Computer-Mediated Psychotherapy: Toward Patient Selection Guidelines, 1984. Honours include: Fellow, American College of Medical Quality; Fellow, American Board of Medical Psychotherapists; Semi Finalist, Clinical Psychiatric Paper Contest, Hillside Journal of Clinical Psychiatry, 1982. Memberships: AMA; American Psychiatric Association; American Association Community Mental Health Center Psychiatrists; Association Advancement Psychotherapy; American Society Clinical Hypnosis; President MI Psychiatric Society, 1995-97; President Genesee Chapter, 1989-; Chair, Peer Review Committee. Hobby: Computers. Address: Hurley Medical Center, 1 Hurley Plaza, Flint, MI 48502, USA.

ZAUBER Ann Graham, b. 23 May 1947, Birmingham, Alabama. Biostatistician. m. Peter Zauber, 5 June 1971, 1 son, 1 daughter. Education: BA, Statistics, Hollins College, 1969; PhD, Biostatistics, Johns Hopkins University, 1976. Appointments: Research Associate, Health Services Research & Development Center, Johns Hopkins University; Associate Attending, Department of Epidemiology & Biostatistics. Publications: Randimized Comparison of Surveillance Intervals After Colonoscogic Removal of Newly Diagnosed Adinomatus , 1993; Prevention of Colorectal Cancer by Colonoscopic Polypectomy, 1993. Memberships: Biometric Society; American Statistical Association; Society of Epdemiology Research; American Society of Preventive Oncology; International Genetic Epidemiology Society; International Society for Pharmacoepidemiology, Hobby: Tennis. Address: Box 44, Department of Epidemiology & Biostatistics, Memorial Sloan Kettering Cancer Center, 1275 York Avenue, NY 10021, USA.

ZAYID Ismail, b. 14 Mar 1933, Beit Nuba, Palestine. Physician. m. Greta Herbert, 20 Aug 1960, 1 son, 4 daughters. Education: MB, BS (London); MRCS (England); LRCP (London); DCP; DPath; DTM&H; FRCPC; FRCPath. Appointments: Director, Department of Pathology, Main Hospital, Amman, Jordan, 1966-69; Honorary Consultant, Department of Morbid Anatomy, Hammersmith Hospital and Royal Postgraduate Medical School, London, England, 1970-71; Currently Professor of Pathology, Dalhousie University and Director, Anatomical Pathology, Victoria General Hospital, Halifax, Nova Scotia, Canada. Publications: Numerous including: Synthetic Progestogen-Oestrogen Therapy and Uterine Changes, 1967; Familial Multicentric Fibromatosis, 1969; Familial Histocytic Dermatoarthritis, 1973; Familial Histocytic Dermatoarthritis (Zayid-Farraj Syndrome), 1990. Honours: Graduated with distinction, National College, Ramallah, Jordan, 1949; Jordan State Scholarship, 1951; Jordan Medical Journal, 1972. Memberships: International Academy of Pathology; International Society of Gynecologic Pathologists; Director, Canadian Reference Center for Cancer Pathology. Hobbies: Reading; Bridge, Address: 531 Young Avenue, Halifax, Nova Scotia, Canada B3H 2V4.

ZBAR Lloyd I S, b. 2 Jun 1939, NJ, USA. Head and Neck Surgery; Private Practice. m. Margo Wally, 28 Mar 1965, 2 s, 2 d. Education: BA, 1961, MD, 1964, Queens University, Kingston, Ontario. Appointments: Private Practice; Head and Neck Surgery; Clinical Associate; Professor Otolaryngology, New York University School of Medicine. Contributions to: New England Journal of Medicine, 1989. Memberships: American Academy of Otolaryngology - Head and Neck Society; Royal Society of Medicine. Hobbies: Cross Country Skiing; Medical Antiques. Address: 200 Highland Avenue, Glen Ridge, NJ 07028, USA.

ZEHM-WILTSCHKE Elisabeth Waltraud, b. 22 Oct 1929, Radeburg, Dresden, Germany. Orthodontist. m. (1) Siegfried Zehn, Oct 1955 (dec), 1 son, (2) Horst Wiltschke, Feb 1981 (dec). Education: Dental degree; Degree in Orthodontics. Appointments: Teaching courses in Prosthetics, Dental School of Jena; Currently own office, Training Centre for Orthodontics. Memberships: Deutsche Kieferorthopädische Gesellschaft; European Orthodontics Society; FDJ. Hobbies: Sport; Music; Information trips. Address: Wockel u Co KG, Kurfürstendamm 92, Berlin 31, Germany.

ZEIDMAN Heywood William, b. 30 Jan 1941, Brooklyn, New York, USA. Psychiatrist. m. Ronni Beres, 27 Nov 1982, 1 son, 2 daughters. Education: MS, Pharmacology; MD; Certified, American Board of Psychiatry and Neurology, American Board of Adolescent Psychiatry and American Society Addiction Medicine. Appointments: Private Practice; Medical Director, VillaView Hospital. Honours: Certificate of Appreciation, San Diego County, 1977; Appreciation for Teaching, University of California, San Diego, School of Medicine; Fellow, American Society Adolescent Psychiatry. Memberships: American Medical Association; American psychiatric Association; American Society Addiction Medicine. Hobbies: Skiing; Golf; Tennis. Address: 6719 Alrarado Road, San Diego, CA 92120, USA.

ZEIGER Robert, b. 31 Jul 1942, Brooklyn, NY, USA. Physician. m. Karen Jacobson, 25 Jun 1967, 2 d. Education: BA, Honours, Tulane University, 1963; MD cum laude, Downstate Medical Center, NY, 1969; PhD, 1969. Appointments include: Instructor in Pediatrics, Harvard Medical School, Boston, MA, 1975-76; Chief, Department of Allergy, Southern CA Permanente Medical Group, SD, 1977-; Clinical Associate Professor, Department of Pediatrics, UCSD, 1984-90; Clinical Professor, Department of Pediatrics, UCSD; Currently, Chief of Allergy, Kaiser Permanente Medical Center. Publications: 100 Original articles in referred journals, 1971-95 including: Co-author: Facilitated referral to asthma specialist reduces relapses in asthma emergency room visits, in Journal Allergy Clinical Immunology, 1991; Genetic and environmental factors affecting the development of atopy through age 4 in children of atopic parents: A prospective randomized study of food allergen avoidance, in Pediatric Allergy Immunology, 1992; Development of nasal basophilic cells and nasal eosinophils from age 4 months through 4 years in children of atopic parents, in Journal Allergy Clinical Immunology, 1993. Honours include: Phi Beta Kappa, 1962; AOA, 1968; Pfizer Honor Scholar, 1967-69; Charles A Janeway Scholar of Pediatric Medicine, 1975; Hood Foundation Grantee, 1975-77; Mead Johnson Clinical Pediatric Scholar, USCD, 1991. Memberships include: FAAP; FAAAI; SPR; ATS; JCAI; LAAS; SDAS. Hobbies: Tennis; Golf; Swimming. Address: 7060 Clairemont Mesa Blvd, San Diego, CA 92111, USA.

ZEMZARI Abdelkrim, b. 3 Apr 1949, Kébili, Tunisia. Physician. m. 5 Jul 1980, 2 s. Education: MD, Constantine University, 1977; CESAM, Villejuif University, 1979; FRCP, Arab Medical Board, Damascus, 1991; MPH, Tulane University, 1993. Appointments: Medical Chief, Testour District, 1978; Coordinator of Comprehensive Medicine Project of Mejez-El-Bab, 1980; Endemic Diseases Control Chief, Basic Health Care Department, 1982; Currently, Deputy Director for Programming, School Health Department, Ministry of Public Health, Tunis; Senior Physician, Specialist in Preventive Medicine; Consultant in Basic Health Care (Chad 1989, Burkina Faso, 1994). Publications: Co-author, The Teacher's Guide in Health Education for Basic Schoolchildren, 1990; Translation of the Manual of Taking Children's Weight and Height, French to Arabic, 1991. Honours: National Public Health Union Board, 1979; Medal of the Republic, 1980; Blood Donor Medal, 1990. Memberships: American School Health Association; French School Health Association; American Public Health Association; Association of Teacher of Preventive Medicine; ADELF. Hobbies: Swimming; Travel. Address: 54 Cite Faiza El Manar 2, Tunis 2092, Tunisia.

ZENG Renduan, b. 17 June 1935, Surabaya, Indonesia. Professor of Medical Physics. m. He Shiwen, 1 July 1962, 2 daughters. Education: BSc, Physics Department, Central China Normal University, Huazhong, 1959. Appointments: Teaching, Research, Medical Physics, Physics Method of Medical Imaging, 1959-, currently Department Head, Department of Physics, Tongji Medical University, Wuhan. Publications

include: Editor-in-Chief: Modern Medical Imaging, 1985; A Textbook of Experiments in Medical College Physics, 1990; Human Body Imageology, 1994; Chinese Journal of Medical Physics; Co-author: Physics for Medicine and Biology, 1987; Medical Physics, 1989; Electronics for Medicine, 1991; B Mode Ultrasonic Diagnostics, 1992. Honours include: 2nd Prize for Excellent Essay, The MRI of the Heart Propagated by ECG, Hubei Province Science and Technology Association, 1990; Honorary Title of Expert Having Significant Contribution, Government of China, 1992. Memberships: International Organization for Medical Physics; Council Member, Chinese Society of Medical Physics; Council Member, Chinese Society of Medical Imaging Technology. Hobby: Photography; Painting. Address: Department of Physics, Tongji Medical University, No 13 Hangkong Road, Wuhan, Hubei 430030, China.

ZERIN Edward, b. 5 May 1920. New York City, USA. Rabbi; Psychotherapist. m. Marjory Bernice Fisher, 27 Oct 1946, 2 sons, 1 daughter. Education: BA, University of Delaware, 1941; MS, 1950, Phd. 1953, University of Southern California; Honorary DD, 1971. Appointments: Rabbi, 1946-74; Co-Director, Westlake Centre for Marital and Family Counselling, 1974-; Faculty: Drake University, 1955-66, Grinnell College, 1964-66, Boston University, 1970-72, University of California, Los Angeles, 1975-76. Publications: Living Judaism, Volume I, 1958, II, 1959, III, 1962; Teacher's Guide to Justice and Juaism, 1958; Our Jewish neighbors, 1959; The Birth of the Torah, 1963; What Catholics (and other Christians) Should Know About Jews, 1980; The "Q" Model for the Effective Management of Personal Stress, Co-author, 1985; Contriburos of articles in professional journals; Jewish Consultant for 45 To Live As Christ Catholic textbooks, 1960-85. Honours: Phi Kappa Phi, 1941. Memberships include: American Association Marriage and Family Therapists; International Transactional Analysis Association; Central Conference of American Rabbis; National Chair, Chesky Institute for Judaism and Psychotheray. Hobbies: Philately; Travel; Swimiming. Address: 3823 Bowsprit Circle, Westlake Village, CA 91361, USA.

ZERIN Marjory, b. 17 Feb 1925, Richmond, Virginia, USA. m. Edward Zerin, 27 Oct 1946, 2 sons, 1 daughter. Education: BA, University of Michigan, 1946; MA, Drake University, 1967; PhD, Clinical Psychology, Fielding Institute, 1982. Appointments: Executive Director, Municipal Community Relations Commission, Newton, Massachusetts, 1969-72; Consultant to Readers Digest, Educational Book Division, 1969; Faculty, UCLA School of Densistry, Department Public Health, 1975-77; Lecturer, Mo9orpark College, California Lutheran University, Pepperdine University, The Police Academy, 1973-74. Memberships: American Association of Marriage and Family Therapists; California Association of Marriage and Family Therapists; Southern California Association of Marriage and Family Therapists; Society for Scientific Study of Sex; American Association of Sex Educators and Therapists; International Transactional Analyst Association; Charter Member, Conejo Women in Business; Ventura Professional Women's Network. Address: Westlake Centre for Marital and Family Counselling, 3823 Bowsprit Circle, Westlake Village, CA 91361, USA.

ZETIN Mark, b. 19 June 1948. Psychiatrist. div, 1 son, 1 daughter. Education: MS, Applied Physics; MD, Universityu of California, Irvine, USA, 1976; Diplomate, American Board of Psychiatry and Neurology. Appointments: Clinical Professor of Psychiatry, University of California at Irvine; Private Practice of Adult Psychopharmacology. Membership: American psychiatric Association. Hobby: Computer Diagnostics. Address: 12443 Lewis Street #101, Garden Grove, CA 92640, USA.

ZETTERMAN Rowen K, b. 30 July 1944, York, Nebraska, USA. Professor of Internal Medicine. m. Emily Joan Clark, 4 June 1966, 3 sons. Education: BA, Nebraska Wesleyan University, Lincoln, 1966; MD, University of Nebraska Medical School, Omaha, 1969. Appointments: Chief, GI Service, 1976-82, Associate Chief of Staff/Research, 1980-87, Omaha VAMC; Chief, GI Service, University of Nebraska, 1984-91; Currently Professor of Internal Medicine, University of Nebraska Medical Center, Omaha. Publications: 68 original manuscripts; 17 book chapters; 1 book. Honours: Editor, American Journal of Gastroenterology, 1991-97; Governor, Nebraska Chapter, American College of Physicians, 1992-96. Memberships: American College of Physicians; AASLD; IASL; American Gastroenterological Association; American College of Gastroenterology; AFCR. Hobbies: Fishing; Stained glass. Address: University of Nebraska Medical Center, 600 S 42nd Street, Omaha, NE 68198. USA.

ZHA Xi-Liang, b. 2 Feb 1949, Shanghai, China. University Teacher. m. Zhang Weihua, 9 Feb 1983, 1 daughter. Education: MD; MS, PhD in Biochemistry. Appointments: Teacher; Currently Full Professor, Shanghai Medical University. Publications: Structural Analyses of Oligosaccharides by Lectin Affinity Chromatography, 1990; Retinoic Acid Affects Oligosaccharide Structure of Cultured Keratinocytes, 1991. Honours: Science Star in Medical Field, Nationwide; Fellowship Award, Faculty of Medicine, University of Manitoba, Canada. Memberships: Chinese Biochemical Society; Society of Chinese Bioscientists in America; Canada Biochemical Society. Hobbies: Travel; Sports. Address: Department of Biochemistry, Shanghai Medical University, Shanghai 200032, China.

ZHA PING Wu Ping, b. 28 Jan 1963, Anqing, China. Doctor. Education: College of Traditional Chinese Medicine, Anhui. Appointment: Resident Physician. Publications: An Analysis of Traditional Chinese Medicine Treatment in Chronic Golomerulonephritis According to Histopathologic Type; Observation of therapy of The Kidney's anemia patients treated with method of Bu Shen Sheng Xue; Observation of therapy in 45 CGN patients treated with method of Hurishing Qi invigorating blood circulation, cleaning heat and drying dampens; Examples of Chen Yi-ping's cure of suspicious and difficult affectins. Memberships: China Academy of Traditional Chinese Medicine; Academy of Traditional Chinese Medicine Nephrology. Hobbies: Literature; Drama; Music; Reading; Philosophy. Address: 110034 Shen Yang City, Liaoning, China.

ZHAI De-pei, b. 10 Nov 1929, Hebei, China. Physician. m. Chun-yun Zhao, 14 Jan 1957, 2 sons. Education: Hebei Medical College, 1955; Physical Therapy Course, Beijing, 1957; Veterans' Administration Lakeside Medical Centre, Northwest University, Chicago, 1981-83; MD. Appointments: Resident, Assistant Lecturer, 1955-60; Visiting Lecturer, 1961-80; Deputy Chief Doctor, Lecturer, 1981-86; Assistant Professor, 1986-90; Director of Internal Medicine, 1989-92; Professor, Director of Nephrology Department, 1991-. Publications: Diagnostics, 1979; Medicine, 1981; Basic Training for Internal Medicine, 1991; Clinical Endocrinology, 1993; The Significance of Determining HDL2-Ch/MOL3-Ch in Renal Disease with Hyperlipid, 1988; Serum Epo Levels in CRI, 1985. Honours: Chu H I Medical Prize, Tianjin Medical College, 1984; Achievement Prize in CAPD Research, Tianjin Health Bureau, 1981; Chu H I Medical Scholarship for Aluminium & Old Research, 1994. Memberships: Associate Member of EDTA-ERA; Standing Committee, China National Society of Nephrology; Editor, Chinese Journal of Nephrology; Chairman, Tianjin Society of Nephrology. Hobbies: Fishing; Table Tennis. Address: Department of Medicine, Tianjin Medical University, General Hospital, 154 An-shan Road, Tianjin 300052, China.

ZHAI Jing Zhi, b. 11 Oct 1934, China. Professor. m. 4 Nov 1958, 1 son, 1 daughter. Education: Bachelor Degree. Appointment: Head, Department of Pediatrics, Head, PICU of The 2nd Clinical College. Publications incl: Treatment of respiratory failure with ventilator (44 cases), 1985; Clinical use of transcutaneous monitor of oxygen pressure, 1988; Analysis of foreign body in traches and bronchus (120 cases), 1990; Clinical analysis of acute poisining of 140 children, 1994; Talks on emergency work in pediatric clinic (225 cases), 1995. Membership: Chinese Medical Society. Hobbies: Music; Dance; Sports. Address: Dept of Pediatrics, The 2nd Clinical College, China Medical University, 110003 China.

ZHAN Chuoran, b. 15 Feb 1928, Taiyuan, China. Doctor. m. Yiepen Zhoo, 4 May 1952, 2 sons. Education: Sanxi Medical College. Appointments: 1st Hospital, 2nd Hospital, Tianjin Medical College; Doctor, Head of Otorhinolarngology, Huan Hu Hospital, Tianjin. Publications: The Error in ENT Surgery, Co-author, 1988; The Modern Otorhinolarngology, Co-author, 1994. Membership: Head, Rhino-Telescopic Surgery, Chinese Medical Association. Address: Huanhu Hospital, Tianjin 300060, China.

ZHANG An, b. 20 Feb 1916, Tianjin, China. Physician; Haematologist. m. Qi Fan, 16 July 1944, 2 sons, 2 daughters. Education: BS, Yenching University, Beijing, 1939; MD, Peking Union Medical College, 1943. Appointments: Physician, Beijing Zhong-He Hospital, 1943-48; Chief Resident, 1948, Instructor, 1949, Associate Professor, 1953, Chief, Haematology Unit, 1957-83, Vice-Chairman, Department of Medicine, 1959-83, Professor of Medicine, 1978-88, Emeritus Professor of Medicine, 1988-, Peking Union Medical College, Hospital Beijing. Publications: Co-author: Pharmacology, 1952; Fundamentals in

Diagnosis, 1964; Practical Oncology, 1979; Chinese Medical Encyclopedia, 1985; Clinical Hematology, 1985; Medicine - Theory and Practice, 1988; More than 60 medical papers. Honours: From: Chinese Medical Association, 1985; Chinese Medical Association, Beijing Branch, 1988; Peking Union Medical College and Chinese Academy of Medical Sciences, 1990; Ministry of Education, 1990; Special Government Subsidy, Chinese State Council, 1992. Memberships: Formerly: Vice-Chairman, Chinese Society of Hematology and Chairman, Beijing Branch; Standing Committee, Chinese Anti-Cancer Association; Council Member, Chinese Medical Association, Beijing Branch; Chinese Society of Internal Medicine. Hobbies: Sports; Bridge; Reading detective novels. Address: 59 Wai Jiao Bu Jie, House 34, Beijing 100005, China.

ZHANG An-Yu, b. 29 July 1931, Guangzhou, China. Professor. m. Lu-xian Zou, 30 Dec 1958, 2 sons, 1 daughter. Education: MBBS; MD. Appointments: Assistant, 1956-59; Lecturer, 1960-79; Associate Professor, 1980-87; Professor, 1988-. Publications: Tianjin Four Disease Program and Its Health Education, 1988; The Study on Risk Factors Associated with Breast Cancer among Women in Tianjin, China & Adelaide, Australia, 1989; Epidemiological Studies on Diet and Risk of Breast Cancer, 1991; Evaluation of Health Education Program, 1993. Honours: National Award for Key Science & Technology in Sixth-Five Years in 1988; Awarded a Distinguished Scientist and Given Government Allowance, 1993. Memberships: Committee, Tianjin Cancer Society; Breast Cancer Committee, China Anti-Cancer Association; Standing Member, Council, China Health Education Talent Development Society. Hobbies: Reading Literature Works; Music; Calligraphy. Address: Department of Epidemiology, School of Public Health, Tianjin Medical University, Tianjin 300070, China.

ZHANG Bai-he, b. 20 Aug 1946, Jin City, China. Surgeon. m. Xue Xiao Hua, 8 Jan 1979. 1 son. Education: MD, 7th Medical Military College, Chongqin, 1970; PhD, 2nd Military Medical University, Shanghai, 1989. Appointments: Resident, Chief Resident, 94th Hospital, People's Liberation Army, Nanchang, 1970-86; Attending Surgeon, Associate Professor, Professor, Institute of Hepatobiliary Surgery, Shanghai Hospital, 2nd Military Medical University, Shanghai, 1986-. Publications: Answer and Analysis for 5000 Items of Physiology, 1982; Abdominal Surgery, 1992; Atlas of Operations, 1994; 18 articles on hepatic cancer research. Honours: 2nd Prize of National Science and Technology Progress, 1990; Eminent Doctor of the Nation, 1991. Membership: Chinese Medical Council. Hobbies: Reading; Chinese calligraphy; Gardening. Address: Institute of Hepatobiliary Surgery, Changhai Hospital, 174 Changhai Road, Shanghai 200433, China.

ZHANG Bao-ren, b. 19 Mar 1933, He Nan Province, China. Surgeon. m. Cai Kai-hua, 19 Mar 1960, 1 son, 2 daughters. Education: Graduate, Haerbing Medical University, 1950-56. Appointments: Resident, General Surgery, 1956-59, Resident, Department Thoracic and Cardiovascular Surgery, 1959-62, Visiting Surgeon and Lecturer, 1962-77, Director, professor, 1978-87, Changhai Hospital and Second Military Medical University, Shanghai; Chief, Professor, Institute of Thoracic and Cardiovascular Surgery, Chairman, teaching and Research section of Surgery, Changhai Hospital, Second Military Medical University, 1987-. Honours: 1st National Scientific Reward, 1978; 1st Military Scientific Reward, 1981; 2nd National Scientific Reward, 1985, 1994; 2nd Military Scientific Reward, 1988. Hobbies: Chinese Opera; Basketball; Football. Address: Department of Thoracic and Cardiovascular Surgery, Changchai Hospital, Second Military Medical University, Shanghai 200433, China.

ZHANG Cheng-yuan, b. 18 Mar 1950, Lintao, Gansu, China. Doctor of Clinical Medicine. m. Yang Ai-guo, Feb 1977, 1 son. Education: Graduated, Military Medical College, Lanzhuo Military Command. Appointments: Medical Officer, People's Liberation Army, 1975; Doctor, currently Director, Surgical Department, Transport Co Hospital, General Company of Oil and Gas, Wurumuqi. Publications: Surgical treatment on transformation of carcinoma from stomach to liver, 1989; Clinical observation of an anti-cancer prescription in treatment of liver cancer, 1990; Differential diagnosis on clinical aches (co-author), 1992. Honours: 3rd Grade Award, Health Department of Xijiang Autonomous Region; 3rd Grade Award, Wurumuqi Health Department. Membership: Hepatocellular Carcinoma Research Society. Hobbies: Running; Biking. Address: 374 Altai Road, Wurumuqi 830014, China.

ZHANG Chuanhan, b. 2 May 1955, Wuhan, Hebei, China. Anaesthesiologist. m. Zeng Cuiqiong, 2 Feb 1983, 1 d. Education: BA,

Tongji Medical University, 1982; MD, Ruprecht-Karls-University, Heidleberg, Germany, 1990. Appointments: Professor of Anaesthesiology, Tongji Hospital of University. Publications: Effect of Relaxant Pipercurium, 1988; Wie Sinnvoll ist die ZVD Messung Uber Infusionsfilter, Co-author, 1990; Relationship between PetCO2 and PaCO2 dueing One-lung Ventilation, 1993. Memberships: Chinese and Germany Medical Association; Chinese Society of Anaesthesiology; Chinese Medicine Association. Hobbies: Music; Reading; Running; Travel. Address: Department of Anaesthesiology, Tongji Hospital of Tongji Medical University, 515 Jie-Fang-Da-Dao, Wuhan, China.

ZHANG Daning, b. 11 September 1944, Tianjin, China. Doctor. m. Zhang Lina, 6 February 1972, 1 son. Education: College Graduate; PhD. Appointments: Doctor; Lecturer; Vice Director of Tianjin Traditional Chinese Medical Hospital; Professor of Nephrology. Publications: A Collection of Medical Essays by Zhang Daning, 1986; Practical Traditional Chinese Medicine Nephrology, 1990; Scientific Traditional Chinese Medicine Foundations, 1991; A Dictionary of Traditional Chinese Medicine Nephrology, 1993. Honours: Visiting Professor; Honourable PhD, Chinese Academy of Sciences, Taiwan, 1990; China's National Achievement Prize for Traditional Chinese Medicine, 1992. Memberships: Chairman of International Society on Traditional Chinese Medicine Nephrology; Vice Chairman, China Conference for the Study and Promotion of Traditional Chinese Medicine. Hobbies: Calligraphy; Chinese Painting. Address: 1206 17th Building, Feng Hu Li, Nankai, Tianjin, China.

ZHANG Dong-Ming, b. 8 Sept 1929, Kaifeng, Henan, China. Professor of Anatomy. m. Rong Lin, 12 Apr 1957, 1 son, 1 daughter. Education: BA, Medicine, 2nd Army Medical College, Shanghai. Appointments: Assistant, 1953, Lecturer, 1964, Associate Professor, 1985, Professor, 1989-, Department of Anatomy, 2nd Army Medical College, Shanghai; Deputy Editor-in-Chief, Chinese Journal of Coloproctology. Publications include: Books: Science of Colo-Anal Diseases in China, 1985; Anatomical physiology of coloproctology, 1989; Papers: Blood supply in anal region, 1986; Anatomy of anal nerve, 1987; Morphological studies on the nerve to the Levator Ani, 1987; Morphological studies on the puborectalis, 1987; Morphology and innervation of anal sphincter muscle complex, 1991. Honours: 2nd Class Prize for Achievement, All-Army Science and Technology, 1988. Memberships: Chinese Association of Anatomy; Committee member, Association of Chinese Coloproctology; Vice-Director, Association of People's Liberation Army Coloproctology. Hobbies; Drawing; Swimming. Address: Department of Anatomy, 2nd Army Medical College, Shanghai, China.

ZHANG Fengshan, b. 26 June 1938, Dunhua County, Jilin Province, China. Medical Doctor; Professor; University Vice-President. m. 26 Dec 1966, 2 sons. Education: MB, Western Medicine, Department of Medical Science, Harbin Medical University; Traditional Chinese Medicine courses, Ministry of Public Health, 1960-63. Appointments include: Currently Vice-President, Harbin Medical University; Member, Reward Assessing Committee for Science and Technology Progress, Director, Clinical Pharmacology Base of Harbin Medical University, Ministry of Public Health. Publications: Over 60 articles; Chief editor: Connective Tissue Diseases, 1982; Autoimmunity and Rheumatic Diseases, 1993; Doctrine of Epidemic Febrile Disease (chief translator into Japanese); Co-author: Diagnosis and Treatment of Rheumatic Diseases by the Combination of Traditional Chinese and Western Medicines; Dictionary of Chinese Natural Sciences, 1990. Honours: 2nd Grade Science and Technology Achievements Prize for diagnosis and treatment of SLE, Heilongjiang Cultural and Educational Office and Heilongjiang Province Public Health Department, 1982; 1st Grade Science and Technology Achievements Prize for finding new methods of curing RA, Heilongjiang Public Health Department, 1990. Memberships: Chinese Academy of Medical Sciences, Heilongjiang Branch Vice-President; Traditional Chinese and Western Medicines Combination Institute of China, Council Member, Deputy Director of Heilongjiang Specialised Rheumatism Committee; Standing Committee, Chinese Institute of Rheumatology; Traditional Chinese Medicine Association of China, Director 1976-86, Deputy Director of Standing Committee; Heolongjiang Science and Technology Association, Vice-Chairman. Hobbies: Skating; Swimming; Gymnastics. Address: President's Office, Harbin Medical University, Harbin 150086, China.

ZHANG Guangshu, b. 10 Apr 1924, Anhui Province, China. Physician. m. Huijun Leu, 26 Sept 1957, 3 daughters. Education: BA, Medical College of Nanjing University, 1952. Appointments:

Vice-Director, 88th Hospital of PLA; Director, Infectious Diseases Department and Centre, Head, Professor, Institute of Liver Diseases, Jinan Military region, Publications: Prevention and Treatment of Water and Electrolyte Disorder, 1980; Laboratory Researches and Clinical Applications of Placenta Transfer Factor, 1992; Investigation and Treatment of Anthropozoonosis, Co-author, 1986; Advances in the Researches of Transfer Factor, Co-author, 1990. Hobby: Gardening. Address: The 88th Hospital, Taian City, Shandong 271000, China.

ZHANG Guo Zhen, b. 26 Apr 1926, Shanghai, China. Internal Medicine, Hematology. 1 son, 1 daughter. Education: MD, School of Medicine, St John's University, Shanghai, 1951; Research Fellowship, Hematology, Postgraduate School, Zhe Jiang University, 1957-60. Appointments: Visiting Doctor, 1964-80, Lecturer, 1968-80, Associate Professor, 1980-83, Professor of Medicine, 1983-, Shanghai Medical University; Department Head of Hematology, Director of Clinical Hematological Laboratory, Zhong Shan Hospital, 1982-91. Publications: Medicine in Clinical Practice, 1993; Chinese Medical Encyclopedia, 1994. Honours: National Award on Research, 1983, 1990, 1992. Memberships: Chinese Medical Society, Hematological Section, Shanghai. Hobbies: Western Classical Music; Chinese Folk Music. Address: Qing Zhen Road 1615-6-101, Shanghai 200032, China.

ZHANG Hua Nan, b. 15 June 1926, Shandong, China. General Surgeon. m. Li Ai Ling, 1 Dec 1954, 1 daughter. Education: Graduate, Cheeloo University School of Medicine, 1952. Appointments: Lecturer, Shandong Medical College, 1978; Associate Professor, Shandong Medical College, 1984; Professor, Shandong Medical University, 1986-. Publications: Reginal Heitis, 1955; Treatment of Hernia in Children, 1982; Management of Portul Hypertension, 1984; Management of Severe Hepatic Trauma, 1990. Honours: Honorable Title of Outstanding Scientific Worker of Jinan Municipality, 1983, 1986, 1989. Memberships: Chinese Medical Association; Jinan Medical Association. Hobbies: Literature; Classical Music. Address: Jinan Central Hospital, Jinan, Shandong 250013, China.

ZHANG Huai-bin, b. 15 Feb 1920, Hubei, China. Professor; Thoracic Surgeon. m. Chu Ling, 1 July 1947, 1 daughter. Education: Medical School, Cheeloo University, Shandong, 1940-47; MD, approved by University of Toronto, Canada, 1947. Appointments: Resident, Surgery, 1947-50, Chief Resident, Orthopaedics, General Surgery, 1950-51, University Hospital, West China Union University, Chengdu; Consultant Surgeon, General Surgery, Lecturer, 1951-55, Consultant Surgeon, General Thoracic Surgery, Associate Professor, Professor, Surgery, 1956-, Sichuan Medical College (former West China Union University, now West China University of Medical Sciences); Editor, Sichuan Medicine. Publications: Treatment of Large Area Gangrene of Afferent Loop of Jejunal Wall after Subtotal Gastrectomy, 1965; Follow-up Results of Surgical Resection of Different Types of Esophageal Carcinoma, 1981; Late Results of Combined Bleomycin and Resection Therapy of Carcinoma of the Esophagus, 1984; Carcinoma of the Esophagus, 1986; Co-author: Early Esophageal Squamous Carcinoma - A Clinico-pathologic Analysis of 20 Cases, 1979; Pre- and Postoperative Sequential Study on the Immunosuppressive Activity of Serum and Cell-free Skin Bleb Fluid of Patients with Lung Cancer and Esophageal Cancer, 1989; The Diagnostic Significance of Gastrin Measurement of Bronchoalveolar Lavage Fluid for Lung Cancer, 1992; Pre- and Postoperative Sequential Study on the Serum Gastrin Level in Patients with Lung Cancer, 1992; Pre- and Postoperative Sequential Study on the Serum Carcinoembryonic Antigen in Patients with Lung Cancer, 1993; Surgical Treatment of Patients with Lung Cancer Involving Left Atrium, 1994. Honours: Monthly Lifelong Bonus, Central Government, China, 1992-. Membership: Chinese Medical Association, Chairman, Sichuan Thoraco-cardiovascular Branch, 1986-93. Hobbies: Classical Music; Photography. Address: 15th Building, Guang Ming Lu, West China University of Medical Sciences, Chengdu, Sichuan 610041, China.

ZHANG Hui Lan, b. 8 Mar 1918, Shandong, China. Nursing. m. 7 July 1937, 1 son. Education: Diploma, School of Nursing, Peking Union Medical College, 1941. Appointments: Supervisor, Instructor, Peking Union Medical College Hospital & School of Nursing, 1951; Director, Nursing Department, Cancer Institute/Hospital (Chinese Academy of Medical Science), 1957-83; Advisor and Professor, 1983-. Publications: Vol Nursing, Chinese Medical Encyclopedia, 1984; The Nursing Care of Cancer Patients, 1991; The Role of Traditional Chinese Medicine in Supportive Care of Cancer Patients, 1991; Editorial Board of Encyclopedia of China, the modern medicine section; Nursing, 1993;

Editorial Board of Chinese Journal of Nursing, 1954-. Honours: Delegate to the 3rd National People's Congress, 1964; Member of the CPPCC, 1978-93; Awarded by the State Council a special allowance for the contribution in the promotion of medicine and health in China, 1992-. Memberships: Chairman, Oncology Nursing Committee, Chinese Nursing Association; Board Director, International Society of Nurses in Cancer Care. Address: Building No 1, Residential Area, Cancer Hospital, Chinese Academy of Medical Sciences, Panjiayuan, Beijing 100021, China.

ZHANG Hui-Rong, b. 2 Nov 1931, Si Chuan, China. Doctor, Professor. m. Li Qian-Sheng, 12 June 1964, 1 son. Education: Postgraduate Student. Appointments: Vice Chairman 1961-82, Chairman, Professor 1983-93, Ophthalomolgy, Third Hospital, Beijing Medical University. Publications: Practical Ophthalmology, 1984; New Concept in Ophthalmology, 1991; Ocular microcirculation and its relative diseases, 1993; Current Ophthalmologic Manual, 1993; Lasers in Ophthalmology, 1994; 84 papers. Honours: The Science & Technical Prize of Beijing Science & Technical Committee, 1979; The Science & Technical Prize of Ministry Health, 1991; Book Chapter in Spirit of Enterprize, The 1990 Rolex Award. Memberships: Executive Member, Standing Committee, Society of Ophthalmology, CMA; Vice Chairman, Beijing Society of Ophthalmology; Editor, Seven Sorts of Chinese Journals of Ophthalmology. Hobbies: Music; Shadow Boxing. Address: Department of Ophthalmology, Third Hospital, Beijing Medical University, Beijing 100083, China.

ZHANG Ji, b. 21 May 1930, Jinzhou, Liaoning, China. Professor of Acupuncture and Moxibustion. m. Nie Hui Min, 12 Aug 1962, 1 son, 2 daughters. Education: Graduate, China Medical University, 1950; Graduate, Beijing Traditional Chinese Medical College, 1962. Appointments: Dean, Department of Acupuncture and Moxibustion, Beijing University of Traditional Chinese Medicine, 1984-92; Professor, Advisor, PhD Program, Beijing University of Traditional Chinese Medicine. Publications: A Differentiation of Syndromes in the Canon of International Medicine, 1988; Acupuncture & Moxibustion, 1990; Acupoints, 1992; Papers: Dongyuan's Acupuncture Methods, 1990. Honours: Award of Honour of Expert who has made great Contribution to the Nation, Special Government Allowance, 1993-. Memberships: Director, China Association of Acupuncture * Moxibustion; Director, China Academy of Acupuncture & Moxibustion. Hobbies: Swimming; Chinese Taiji Boxing. Address: Department of Acupuncture & Manipulation, Beijing Traditional Chinese Medical University, Beijing 100029, China.

ZHANG Ji-Zhi, b. 1 Oct 1925, WeiFang, Shandong, China. Professor of Psychiatry. m. Shu-xue Ji, 20 Nov 1954, 1 son, 1 daughter. Education: Graduate, Shandong University School of Medicine; Advanced Studies for Clinical Psychiatry, Beijing Medical University. Appointments: Resident, Clinical Reader, Consultant Psychiatrist, Vice Superintendent, beijing An Ding Hospital; Associate Professor, Professor of Psychiatry, Capital University of Medical Science. Publications: Psychiatry, 2nd, 3rd editions, 1988, 1993; Mental Health, Chief Editor, 1994; Psychotropic Drugs in Clinical Practice, Chief Editor, 1994; COntributor of numerous papers and lectures. Honours: Award for Science and Technology, Beijing, 1986, 1990. Memberships: Standing Member of Council, Chinese Association for Mental Health; Vice Chairman of Psychiatry, Beijing Medical Society. Hobbies: Planting Flowers; Collecting Coins. Address: Beijing An Ding Hospital, De Sheng Men, Beijing 100088, China.

ZHANG Jiajun, b. 28 Jan 1939, Shanghai, China. Doctor of Traditional Chinese Medicine. m. 15 July 1969, 2 daughters. Education: BM, Shanghai Traditional Chinese Medicine and Pharmacology University, 1965; Institute of Traditional Chinese Medicine, Shanghai Municipality, 1981-82; Seminar on Academic Thoughts of Nationwide Senior Traditional Chinese Medicine Physicians, 1991-93. Appointments: Resident Physician, Department of Traditional Chinese Medicine, 1965; Visiting Doctor, 1978; Deputy Chief Doctor, 1989; Chief Physician, Director, Department of Traditional Chinese Medicine, 1993-, Shanghai 2nd Municipal People's Hospital. Publications include: Textual Research on the Authenticity of the Japanese Kangping Edition of 'Treatise on Febrile Diseases', 1982; Famous Senior TCM Dr Wang Zheng-gong's Way to pursue his studies, 1991; Satisfactory Result of Asthma Treated with Diaphoresis, Emesis and Purgation by Senior TCM Dr Wang Zhenggong; Experience in Treating Diseases of the Respiratory System by Senior TCM Dr Wang Zhenggong (co-author), 1993; Collection of Famous Textual Research on the Editions of

'Treatise on Febrile Diseases' (Shang Han Lun), 1994; The 18 Programmed Prescriptions in the Treatment of Asthma. Honours: 2 Excellent Theses, 1st Conference on World Traditional Medicines, 1994; Top-Grade Honours for Excellence, 2 theses, 1994; Excellent Thesis, National Seminar on Clinical International Medicine of Traditional Chinese Medicine. Memberships: Fellow: Chinese Society of Acupuncture and Moxibustion; Chinese Society of Combined TC and Western Medicine; Chinese Society of TCM and TC Medicinal Herbs; Director, Medico-Pharmacological and Health Society, Nanshi District, Shanghai; Board of Specialists, Shanghai 2nd Municipal People's Hospital; China Catholic Intellectual Fellowship Party; Intellectual Fellowship Party, Nanshi District. Hobbies: Tours; Swimming. Address: 2nd Municipal People's Hospital, No 1 Duo Jia Road, Shanghai 200011, China.

ZHANG Jin-Shan, b. 28 Jan 1947, Beijing, China. Professor. m. Zhai Fei, 4 May 1976, 1 son, 1 daughter. Education: BA, Qin Hai Medical College; PhD, MD, Nagasaki University, Japan. Appointments: Director, Professor of Diagnostic Radiology, Great Wall Hospital. Publications: Interventional Radiology, Co-author, 1st edition, 1994; Bronchial Arteriography and Transcatheter Embolization Management of Hemoptysis, Co-author, 1994; TIPSS, 1994. Honours: 3 times Recipient of Bronze Medal, Chinese Government. Memberships: Committee Member, Chinese Medical Association; Chinese Association of Radiology; Standing Editor, Chinese Journal of Radiology; COntributing Editor, Clinical Imaging. Hobbies: Swimming; Hunting. Address: Department of Diagnostic Radiology, Great Wall Hospital 301, 28 Fuxing Road, Wu-Ke-Song, Beijing 100853, China.

ZHANG Jing Xia, b. 23 Apr 1933, Nanjing, Jiangsu Province, China. Professor. m. Professor Lin Zhenshen, 20 Aug 1961, 2 d. Education: BS, Nanjing University, 1953; Advance Study, Department of Biology, Beijing University, 1956-57; Advance Study, Institute of Biophysics, China Acadamia Sinica, 1958-59; Visiting Scholar, Michigan University, 1959. Appointments: Assistant Professor, Lecturer, Beijing Medical University, 1953-65; Associate Professor, Xi'an Medical University, 1965-85; Professor, Department of Biophysics, Beijing Medical University, 1986-. Publications: Co-author, Application of Radioisotope in Medicine, Biophysics, 1962; Vice-editor, Activation Analysis and Proton Induced X-Ray Emission Analysis, Experimental Nuclear Medicine, 1988; Tracer Technique in Trace Elements Research, Trace Element and Health, 1990. Honours: 1st Class Award of Progress of Science and Technology, Ministry of Public Health, China, 1979, 1982, 1983; 2nd Class Award of Achievement of Science and Technology, Shanxi Province, 1981, 1986. Memberships: The Biophysics Society in China; Chinese Medical Association; Chinese Nuclear Society. Hobbies: Reading Novels; Travel. Address: Beijing Medical University, Department of Biophysics, Xue Yuan Road, 100083, Beijing, China.

ZHANG Jing Yuann, b. 4 Feb 1925, Peking, China. Professor of Parasitology. m. Sheng Zhi jie, 4 Aug 1951, 1 son, 2 daughters. Education: Graduate, medical College of Nanking University, 1953. Appointments: Professor of Parasitology, Parasitology Head Ningxia Medical College. Publications: Literature Index of Hydatidosis, 1987; Immunology and Immunodiagnosis of Hydatidosis, 1991; Contributor of numerous articles in professional journals. Honours: Honorary Credential, Medicine and Health Conference of Ningxia Hui Autonomous region, 1978; 3rd Awards, department of Public Health, Ningxia Hui Autonomous Region, 1984; 4th Awards, Scientific and Technological Commisssion of Ningxia Hui Autonomous Region, 1984; 2nd Award, Public Health department of Ningxia Hui, Autonomous Region, 1991; 4th Awards, Scientific and Technological Commission, Ningxia Hui, Autonomous Region, 1992. Memberships: Institute of Parasitology; Commissioner, Parasitic Disease Expert Advisory Committee, Public Health Ministry, 1987-; Invited Editor, Endemic Diseases Bulletin, 1985-; Advisor, National Hydatid Disease Centre of China, 1989-; Commissioner, Infective and Parasitic Disease Society, 1982-; Commissioner, Ningxia New Drug Judgement Committee, 1985-; Commissioner, Editorial Board, Ningxia Medical College Journal, 1987-. Hobbies: Walking; Chess; Qigong. Address: department of Parasitology, Ningxia Medical College, Yinchuan, 750004 Ningxia, China.

ZHANG Jing Zhen, b. 23 October 1935, Xi Feng, Liao Ning, China. Chief Physician. Education: Graduate, Liao Ning College of Traditional Chinese Medicine. Appointments: Chief Physician; Director of the Tumour Department; Director, Traditional Chinese Medicine Association of China, Guangxi. Publications: Variation Profile of the Blood Pressure and the Pulse Rhythm Along the Day, 1992; Physiocracy for the

Gerontal Male's Sexual Disorders, 1991; 18 academic thesis published, two of which exchanged in International Medical Conferences. Address: Guiling Nanxishan Hospital, Guiling, Guangxi 541002, China.

ZHANG Jing-Ru, b. 21 May 1929, Shanghai, China. Professor of Physiology. m. Dr Qing-Fen Su, 4 Apr 1952, 2 sons, 1 daughter. Education: MD, Shanghai First Medical College, 1947-53. Appointments: Associate professor, 1978, Professor, 1982, President, 1984, Shanghai Medical University; Vice Chairman, Chinese Association for Physiological Sciences, 1985; Chairman, Academic Committee, State Key Laboratory of Medical Neurobiology. Publications: textbook of Physiology, Editor-in-Chief, 1983, 1989; Human Physiology, Editor-in-Chief, 1978, 1989; Contributor of over 50 research papers on neural regulation of respiration. Honours: Honorary Citizenship of Baltimore, USA, 1986; Thomas Hart Benton Mural Medallion, Indiana University, 1986. Memberships: Honorary Member, Standing Committee, Chinese Association for Physiological Sciences; International Organisation of Brain Research. Address: Department of Physiology, Shanghai Medical University, Shanghai 200032, China.

ZHANG Ju-zhi, b. 31 Dec 1925, Sichuan, China. Professor of Periodontology. m. Xiu-Kun Zhou, 31 Dec 1956, 1 son, 1 daughter. Education: Graduated, College of Stomatology, 1952; DDS, Hua-Xi Medical University. Appointments: Lecturer, 1956, Associate Professor, 1980, Chairman, Oral Medicine, 1983, Dean, Dental College, 1984, Professor of Periodontology, 1985-, Hua-Xi Medical University, Chengdu. Publications: The mechanism of therapeutic effect by tooth-firming pills, 1991; Oral Medicine, 3rd edition, 1996. Honours: Scientific and Technological Awards, Sichuan Government, 1984. Memberships: Chairman, Chengdu Dental Branch, Chinese Medical Association; International College of Dentistry; Chinese Association of Periodontology. Hobby: Playing bridge. Address: Hua-xi Medical University, 19 3rd Section, Ren Men Nan Road, Chengdu 610041, China.

ZHANG Jun, b. 29 Dec 1940, Jiangsu Province, China. Medical Doctor. m. Gan Fangmei, Mar 1962, 1 son, 1 daughter. Education: BA, Chinese Medicine, Shanghai Chinese Medicine Research Institute. Appointments include: President, Shanghai Jingsan Sanyan Hospital, 1985-93; Dean, Tingling Hospital of Jinshan County, 1993-. Publications: Regulation Law of Cassia Twig Soup, 1993; Theory of Curing Chronic Liver Disease, 1994. Honours: 2nd Prize for Excellent Thesis, Liaoning Province. Membership: Committee Member, Jingshan Chinese Medicine Association. Hobby: Chinese medicine research. Address: Tingling Hospital of Jingshan County, Shanghai 201505, China.

ZHANG Li-He, b. 8 Sept 1937, Yangchow, Jiansu, China. Professor. m. Zhang Pei-in, 23 Dec 1938, 1 s, 1 d. Education: BS, 1958, Diploma, 1967, Beijing Medical University. Appointments: Lecturer, 1967-81. Associate Professor, 1983-86, Professor, 1986-, Dean, School of Pharmaceutical Sciences, Beijing Medical University; Research Associate, Department of Chemistry, University of Virginia, USA, 1981-83; Visiting Professor, Tsukuba Research Centre, Eisai Co, Japan and University of Missouri, USA. Publications: Contributor of 88 papers in professional journals. Honours: National Scientific Research Excellence Award, 1964; Science and Technology, Beijing, 1980; Otani Prize, Japan, 1988; Colorcon Award, FIP, 1993; Honorary Doctorate, Hoshi University, Japan. Memberships: Chinese Chemical Society; Chinese Pharmaceutical Association. Hobbies: Sport; Music. Address: School of Pharmaceutical Sciences, Beijing Medical University, Beijing 100083, China.

ZHANG Liang. Address: Zhuhai Hospital of Traditional Chinese Med, Guang Dong, China.

ZHANG Maohong, b. 5 Feb 1929, Xuqian, Jiangsu, China. Professor of Haematology. m. Zhang Yu Xing, 26 Jan 1957, 1 son, 2 daughters. Education: MD, Shandong Medical University, 1953; Postdoctoral Fellow, Hematology Institute, Chinese National Academy of Medical Science, Tianjin, 1959-60. Appointments: Assistant, Lecturer, Associate Professor of Internal Medicine, Department of Internal Medicine, 1954-85, Head Chief, Hematology Institute, 1980-, Professor of Internal Medicine, Chairman, Department of Internal Medicine, 1985-88, Shandong Medical University, Jinan. Publications: Veteran Health Care, 1987, 2nd edition, 1993; Co-author: Internal Medicine, 1980; Clinical Hematology, 1985; Chinese Modern Medicine, 1985; Chief editor: Ask and Answer on Nursing, 1982; Practical Hematology, 1990. Honours: Member of Pathology, National Nature Science Foundation of China,

1991-; Member, Clinical Medical Appraisal Group, Academic Degree Committee, State Council of China, 1993-. Memberships: Standing Committee, Chinese Association of Hematology; Head Chief Member, Shandong Provincial Association of Hematology; Editorial Committees: National Medical Journal of China; Chinese Journal of Hematology. Address: Department of Internal Medicine, Affiliated Hospital, Shandong Medical University, Jinan, Shandong, China.

ZHANG Mengliang, b. 28 Apr 1963, Liaoning, China. Lecturer in Anatomy. m. Yi Liu, 2 Aug 1988, 1 daughter. Education: MB, Jinzhou Medical College, 1986; MMed, Dalian Medical College, 1991. Appointments: Doctor, Tiefa Municipal Hospital; Currently Lecturer in Anatomy, Dalian Medical University. Publications: The synaptic relationship between the medial lemniscal terminals and thalamocortical projecting neurons in the VPL thalamic nucleus of the cat, 1992; The ultrastructure of the thalamocortical projecting neurons in the VPL thalamic nucleus of the cat, 1993; The synaptic organization of medial lemniscal terminals in the VPL thalamic nucleus of the cat, 1994. Honours: 2nd Grade Award for Excellent Paper, 1992; 2nd Grade Award for Teaching Achievement, 1993. Memberships: Society of Chinese Medicine; Society of Chinese Anatomy. Hobbies: Swimming; Running. Address: 465 Zhongshan Road, Sha He Kou District, Dalian 116023, China

ZHANG Ming-heng, b. 7 June 1936, Shanghai, China. Ophthalmologist. m. Yuan-gie Ding, 12 Mar 1959, 1 son, 2 daughters. Education: MB, Shanghai Second Medical University, 1959. Appointments: Shanghai Sixth People's Hospital, 1959-62; Chief Doctor, Professor of Ophthalmology, Rui Jin Hospital, 1962-; Consultant, Si Jin Hospital, Nam Hae Guang Ming Hospital, North Shanghai Hospital. Publications: Ar Laser Photocoagulation in Ophthalmology, CO-author, 1978; Ar Laser Photocoagulation of Von Hippel Disease, Co-author, 1978; Q-Switched Nd: YAG Laser Posterior Capsulotomy, Co-author, 1988; The Pharmacological and Clinical Studies of Bß-Acetoxynortropane in Ophthalmology, Co-author, 1991; Toxoplasmic Retinochoroditis, 1992. Honours: Shanghai Higher Educational Bureau Significant Achievement Prize, 1979; Combined Traditional Chinese and Western Medicine Prize, 1st prize, 1981; Shanghai Scientific Progress Prize, 2nd Prize, 1990. Memberships: Shanghai Laser Society; CHinese Optical Society; Chinese Medical Association. Hobbies: Music; Travel. Address: 343 Hua SDhan Road, Shanghai 200040, China.

ZHANG Mingzheng, b. 20 Sept 1931, Harbin, China. Surgeon. m. Wang Yan, 1 May 1956, 1 son, 1 daughter. Education: China Medical University, 1950-55; Research Scientist, training, Karolinska Hospital, Stockholm, Sweden, 1979-1981. Appointments: Surgeon, 1956-, Full Professor, Chairman, Department of Urology, 1985-, 1st Clinical College, China Medical University, Shenyang, Liaoning. Publications: Transurethral prostatectomy, 1984; Experience in transurethral resection of BPH, 1986; Transurethral resection of superficial bladder tumors, 1987. Honours: 2nd Class Scientific Research Prize, Ministry of Health, China, 1984; Silver Medal, Karolinska Institute, 1985. Memberships: Standing Committee, Urologic Society, Chinese Medical Association; Chairman, Urologic Society of Liaoning Province. Hobby: Music. Address: 1-3-2 No 68 8 Jing Street, Heping District, Shenyang 110003, Liaoning, China.

ZHANG Ru-Fu, b. 31 Aug 1924, Shandong, China. Medical Doctor; Professor. m. Ji Gao, 19 Apr 1952, 1 son, 1 daughter. Education: MD, Cheeloo University; Postgraduate Diploma, Pathology, Peking Union Medical College; DrAc (Acupuncture). Appointments: Assistant, Department of Pathology, 1953-57, Assistant, Lecturer, Department of Pathophysiology, 1957-76, 4th Military Medical University; Vice-Director, Associate Professor, Department of Cell Biology, 1976-78, Director, Professor, Department of Cancer Etiology, 1978-93, Beijing Institute for Cancer Research, Beijing Medical University; Currently Doctor of Acupuncture and Therapeutic Massage, Canada. Publications: Contributions to books include: Cerebral edema, 1978; N-nitroso compounds and the etiology of stomach cancer, 1987; Host factors and the etiology of gastric cancer, 1987; Experimental atrophic gastritis and experimental stomach cancer, 1987; Role of nitrosamides in the high risk for gastric cancer in China, 1991; Journal articles; Induction of Gastric Adenocarcinoma in Wistar Rats Following Neonatal Exposure to MNNG and Neoplastic Transformation Assay of DNA of the Induced Cancer, 1994; Honours: 2nd Prize, Science and Technology Achievement, Beijing, 1981; 2nd Prize, Science and Technology Progress, Beijing, 1986, Putian, Fujian, 1988; 3rd Prize, Science and Technology Progress, Beijing, 1994; Specialist, Outstanding

Contribution to Science, Technology and Management, Bejing, 1988; 3rd Prize of Progress on Science and Technology, Beijing, China, 1994. Memberships: China Anti-Cancer Association, Vice-Chairman, Cancer Etiology and Prevention Committee; China Medical Association, Board of Directors of Gastric Cancer Research Committee; Vice-Director, Society for Carcinogenesis, Teratogenesis and Mutagenesis, Beijing; Chinese Medicine and Acupuncture Association of Canada; Board of Directors: Chinese Society for Environmental Mutagens, Beijing Branch; China Association for Laboratory Animal Science; American Society for Experimental Biology and Medicine, Beijing Branch; Board, Beijing Society for Oncology; 2 editorial boards. Hobbies: Tennis; Skating; Cycling. Address: 96 Westpointe Crescent, Nepean, Ontario, Canada K2G 5Y8.

ZHANG Ru-Ping, b. 14 Aug 1934, Jiangsu, China. Dr of Stomatology. m. Zhong Zhi-Ming, 7 Nov 1963, 1 daughter. Education: Grad, Faculty of Stomatology, Shanghai Second Medical University, 1956. Career: Head, Department of Oral Medicine, GPSH, 1984-89; Associate Chief Physician, Guangdong Provincial Stomatological Hospital (GPSH), currently. Publications: Author, A Survey of Oral Leukoplakia in 5400 Persons, Chinese J Stomatology, 1981; Author, The Role of Spirochetes in Periodontal Disease, J Clinical Stomatology, 1988. Membership: Chinese Medical Association. Hobby: Playing Piano. Address: 366 Jiangnan Boulevard, Guangzhou 510260, China.

ZHANG Shao-Jing, b. 25 Mar 1917, Zhongshan City, Guangdong, China. Cardiologist. m. Cheng Wang, 1 Jan 1945, 1 son, 1 daughter. Education: MB, Medical College, Sun Yat-Sen University, 1942. Appointments: Vice-Director, 1956-59, Director, 1960-87, Vice-Professor, 1978-87, Professor, 1987-, Department of Internal Medicine, Guangzhou Medical College; Currently Adviser, 1st Affiliated Hospital, Guangzhou Medical College. Publications: The Statistics of 2522 aged in-patients, 1981; Heart failure of the aged complicated by multiple organ failure: an analysis of 54 cases, 1988; The effect of inderol, prazosine and nifedipine on blood lipids, 1987. Honours: Attended National Clinical and Hygienic Conference for Progressive Experience Exchange, Beijing, 1958; Active Working Member, Guangzhou Science and Technology Association and Chinese Medical Association, Guangzhou Branch, 1982; Special Subsidy, State Council of China, 1992-. Membership: Chairman, Cardiovascular Division, Chinese Medical Association, Guangzhou Branch. Hobbies: Music; Photography. Address: 75 Friendship Road 2/F, Overseas New Village, Guangzhou 510060, China.

ZHANG Tian-xi, b. 21 Jan 1925, Hangzhou, Zhejiang, China. Professor. m. Yan Yue-xian, 1 Oct 1953, 2 sons, 2 daughters. Education: Graduated, Shanghai Aurora University School of Medicine, 1950. Appointments: Resident, Attending Doctor, Associate Professor, Professor, Chairman, Neurosurgeon, Department of Neurosurgery, former Ste Marie Hospital, RUI-JIN Hospital, 1950-. Publications: Basic Neurosurgery and Clinical Practice, 1991; Long Term Result of VM26-CCNU Chemotherapy in Brain Glioma, 1995. Honours: 2nd Award, Shanghai Medical Science Progress, 1994 and 1995. Memberships: Standing Member, Chinese Association of Neurosurgery; Chinese Association of Neurology; Division of Clinical Neurochemistry. Address: Department of Neurosurgery, RUI-JIN Hospital, SSMU, 197 Rui-Jin Er Road, Shanghai 200025, China.

ZHANG Tian-Ze, b. 2 Apr 1920, Liaoning, China. Oncologist. m. Pei-Lan Zhu, 1954, 3 s. Education: MBChB. Appointments: Chief, Abdominal Tumour Service, Tianjin Cancer Hospital, 1982-88; Director, Tianjin Cancer Institute, 1985-92; Honorary Director, Tianjin Cancer Institute. Publications: Cancerology, Chief Editor; Gastric Cancer Volume 10, Guest Editor, 1994. Memberships: Executive Committee, APFOCC; President, China Anti-Cancer Association; Vice Chairman, China Cancer Society; Asia-Australian Oncology Association, (AOCOA). Hobbies: Auctions; Bridge. Address: 108 Macang Street, He-Ping District, Tianjin 300050, China.

ZHANG Tianmin, b. 25 July 1925, Jiangsu, China. Professor of Internal Medicine. m. Yunzhong Su, 1949, 1 daughter. Education: MB, National Kiangsu Medical College, 1949. Appointments: Resident, 1949, Visiting Physician, 1953, Vice Chief Physician, 1981, Chief Physician, 1987, Nanking Central Hospital; Professor of Internal Medicine, Wuhan Medical School of Metallurgical Industry, 1992. Publications: Tuberculosis, 1983; Disease of the Pleura, 1993; Co-author: Mycobacterial Morphological Study by Electron Microscopy and Thin Section, 1984; Effect of Rifandin on Ultrastructure of Tubercle Bacilli,

1985. Honours: 2nd Class Prize for Achievement in Science and Technology, People's Government, Hubei Province, 1982; 2nd Class Prize for Achievement in Science and Technology, Health Bureau, Hubei Province, 1984; Special Allowance, State Council, China, 1992. Memberships: International Union Against Tuberculosis and Lung Disease; Chinese Medical Association; Hubei Medical Association; Chinese Antituberculosis Association; Hubei Antituberculosis Association. Hobbies: Classical music; Playing bridge. Address: 25 Metallurgic Boulevard, Wuhan 430080, Hubei, China.

ZHANG Wan Hua, b. 14 Sep 1921, Jiangxi, China. Surgeon. 1 son, 1 daughter. Education: National Chung Zheng Medical College, 1941-47. Appointments: Associate Professor, 1962, Professor of Surgery, 1980, Vice Chairman, 1962, Chairman, Surgical Department, 1978, Beijing Medical University. Publications: Surgical Fundamentals, Chief Editor, 1987; Clinical Guide of Surgery, 1988; Gastroenterology, Editorial Board, 1986; English-Chinese Word-ocean Dictionary, 1987. Honours: Awards in Science and Technology, Beijing Municipal Government, 1981, 1985; Honourable Document for Success in Works of Science, 1990. Memberships: Chinese Medical Association; Chinese Surgical Association; FOunder Member, World Associartion of Hepato-Pancreato-Biliary Surgery. Hobbies: Tennis; Swimming. Address: Surgical Department, The Third Clinical Faculty, Beijing Medical University, 100083 Beijing, China.

ZHANG Xibin, b. 30 July 1930, Henan, China. Teacher, Clinical & Researching of Orthopaedics Department. m. Zhang Lirong, 8 June 1955, 1 son, 1 daughter. Education: Master Degree. Appointments: Vice Chairman, Out-patient Department, Chengdu Hospital of Physical Training, 1962; Chairman, Athletic Hurt Teaching & Research Station, Department of Athletic Medicine, 1978; Vice President, Chengdu Hospital of Physical Training, 1981; Chairman, Department of Athletic Medicine. Publications: Chinese Traditional Medical Treatment of Kneecap Injury; Science of Sports Injury; On the Types and Mechanism of Humeral Neck Fracture; Disorder of Lower Joint of Femer; Chinese Orthopaedics. Memberships: Director of a Standing of the Fourth Session of Chinese Medicine of Sichuan; Vice Chairman, First To the Fourth Session of Orthopaedics Department; Profession Committee of Chengdu & Sichuan. Hobbies: Dance. Address: Department of Athletic Medicine, Chengdu Institute of Physical Training, West Yihuan Road, Chengdu, Sichuan 610041, China.

ZHANG Xiran, b. 22 Nov 1941, Shandong, China. Cytogeneticist. m. 23 Ma4r 1968, 1 s, 1 d. Education: Shandong University, 1965. Appointments: Assistant Professor, Kunming Institute of Zoology, Academia Sinica, 1979; Associate Professor of Cytogenetics. Publications: Establishment of Lung Cell Strain K12-81A of the Tufted Deer, co-author, 1984; Comparative Investigation on the Chromosomes of Panthera Tigri's Amureusis and P t Amoyensis, Co-authpr, 1993. Memberships: Chinese Society for Cell Biology; Chinese Society for Genetics. Hobbies: Beijing Opera; Shadowboxing. Address: Department of Biology, Nanjing Normal University, China.

ZHANG Xiuzhi, b. 11 Feb 1931, City Qing Dan, China. Professor. m. Prof Sun Mengju, Jul 1963, 2 s. Education: Harbin Institute of Technology, 1950-56; PhD, USSR, 1960. Appointments: Teacher of Welding, Division of Harbin Institute of Technology, 1956; Associate Professor, 1980; Professor, 1985-. Publications: 4 Monographs; Numerous research papers published in the field of new welding technology, metal weldability and welding expert systems. Honours: Awarded the level degree by Ministries of China, Provinces and Harbin City, 1980-85. Memberships: Vice-Chairman of IXB Committee of CMES WI; Member of WI of CS for Modern Technical Equipment. Hobbies: Chinese Chiguang; Music. Address: Welding Department of Harbin Institute of Technology, Harbin 150001, China.

ZHANG Xun, b. 30 Apr 1933, Beijing, China. Doctor. m. Yei Jin-shang, 4 Sept 1957, 2 sons, 1 daughter. Education: MD, Peking Union Medical College, 1957. Appointments: Deputy Director, Department of Nephrology, Jinling Hospital, Nanjing, 1973-87; Visiting Physician, Department of Nephrology, Jinling Hospital, Nanjing, 1966-73; Professor, Medical Director, Department of Nephrology, Nanfang Hospital. Publications: Hypertension in Renal Parenchymal Diseases: Renovasuclar Hypertension, 1987. Honours: National Science & Technology Award, 1985. Memberships: International Society of Nephrology; Chinese Medical Association; Chinese Society of Nephrology. Hobbies: Music; Peking Opera. Address: Department of Nephrology, Nanfang Hospital, Guangzhou 510515, China.

ZHANG Yin-Chang, b. 26 Apr 1923, Shenyang, China. Pathologist. m. Wang Qian-Lan, 5 May 1942, 1 son, 1 daughter. Education: BA, China Medical University, 1949; MD. Appointments: Assistant, Pathology, 1949-60, Assistant Professor, Cancer Research Department, 1961, Associate Professor, 1978, currently Professor of Pathology, China Medical University, Shenyang; Visiting Professor, Department of Pathology, Temple University School of Medicine, Philadelphia, Pennsylvania, USA, 1981-82; Deputy Director, Cancer Institute, China Medical University, Shenyang, 1985-. Publications: Epithelial dysplasia of the stomach and its relationship with gastric cancer, 1984; Histopathologic types of gastric dysplasia, 1988; Editor: Gastric Cancer, 1988; Precancerous Conditions and Lesions of the Stomach, 1993. Honours: Awards for Excellent Research, Ministry of Health, China, and Liaoning Province Government. Memberships: Chinese Medical Association; Permanent Council, Chinese Cancer Research Foundation; Council, Chinese Anticancer Association; Honorary Chairman, Liaoning Province Cancer Association. Hobbies: Oil painting; Chinese traditional painting; Art photography. Address: 155 Nanjingbei Street, Heping, Shenyang 110001, China.

ZHANG Yingqing, b. 28 Mar 1947, Inner Mongolia, China. Professor of ECIWO Biology and Medicine. m. Zhaoqin Wang, 7 Jan 1970, 1 son, 1 daughter. Education: Neimenggu Telecourse University, 1982. Appointments: Researcher, Biological and Medical Information, Institute of Science and Technology, Wulanchabu, Inner Mongolia, 1974-84; Lecturer, Biology, Department of Philosophy, 1984-85, Associate Professor of Biology, 1985-87, Professor of ECIWO Biology and Medicine, Director, ECOWO Biology Institute, 1990-, Shandong University, Jinan. Publications: Books: The Materialistic Principles of Acupuncture Anesthesia and Critique of Pavlovian Physiology and Modern Anatomy, 1974; Three Laws of Organism Structure, 1982; Bio-holographic Biology Research (editor), 1985; Bio-holographic Diagnosis and Therapy, 1987; ECIWO Biology and Medicine: A New Theory for Conquering Cancer and a Completely New Acupuncture Therapy, 1987; ECIWO Biology, 1987; A New View of the Organism: The ECIWO Theory and Its Solution of Some Challenging Problems in the Frontiers of Biology and Medicine, 1991; ECIWO and Its Application to Medicine: New Discoveries of the Unity of the Different Structural Units of an Organism and the Physiological or Pathological Correlation in a Human Body, 1991; ECIWO Theory in Medicine (editor), 1992. Honours: Laureate, Prix de la Mairie de Paris, Highest Prize of 80th International Inventions Fair, Paris, 1989; Laureate, National Outstanding Expert, China, 1990; Laureate, Outstanding Expert, Shandong Province, 1993. Membership: Lifelong President, International Society of ECIWO Biology. Hobby: Reading. Address: ECIWO Biology Institute, Shandong University, Jinan, Shandong 250100, China.

ZHANG Yishen, b. 2 Nov 1920, Pingjiang, Hunan, China. Biochemistry Educator and Researcher. m. Ruli Zheng, 1 Dec 1945, 3 sons, 1 daughter. Education: Bachelor's degree, Wuhan University, 1944. Appointments: Teacher, Chongqing University and elsewhere, 1944-49; Lecturer, Northeast Normal University, Changchun, 1949-58, 1961-78; Lecturer, Jilin University, Changchun, 1958-60; Associate Professor, 1978-83, Professor, 1983-, Northeast Normal University, Changchun. Publications: A Brief Course in Biochemistry, 1982; Over 50 research articles on Polysaccharides to journals. Memberships: Chinese Biochemistry Society; Society of Chinese Bioscientists in America. Hobby: Volleyball. Address: Department of Biology, Northeast Normal University, Changchun 130024, China.

ZHANG Yisheng, b. 15 Mar 1930, Jiangxi, China. Research Professor in Clinical Neurophysiology. m. Niu Linzhi, 15 Oct 1957, 3 daughters. Education: BA, 3rd Militaryu Medical College, 1955. Appointments: Research Trainee, Naval Medical Institute, People's Liberation Army, Shanghai, 1955-62; Lecturer in Physiology, Naval Medical College, Nanjing, 1962-82; Research Professor of Clinical Neurophysiology, Changhai Hospital, 2nd Military Medical College, Shanghai, 1982-. Publications: A study on spatial vectogram of BAEPs in normal subjects, 1987; A spatial-temporal system for EPs, 1990; Role of Nu.vestibularis Med. in vestibulo-sympathetic response, 1991; Central pathway of VSR, 1993; Brain-stem and motor control (co-author), 1993. Honours: 2nd Class Award of Science and Promotion, People's Liberation Army, 1992. Memberships: Chinese Society of Physiology; Chinese Society of EMG and Clinical Neurophysiology. Hobby: Classical music. Address: Rm 401, No 14 Lane 170, Changhai Road, Shanghai 200433, China.

ZHANG Yong Fang, b. 15 May 1929, China. Professor; Doctor. m. Professor Jingya Jiyaang, 20 May 1958, 1 s, 1 d. Education: Chinese Medical University of China. Appointments: Doctor of Department of Psychiatry, The Shanghai Medical University, 1955-59; Doctor, Professor of Department of Psychiatry, First Teaching Hospital, Chong Qing University of Medical Science. Publications: Differentiation of Medicine; Psychiatry; Contributions to Medical Journals. Memberships: Chief, Association of Psychiatry, Chong Qing Branch, CMA; Vice-Chairman, Association of Psychiatry, Sichuan Branch, CMA. Address: West China University of Medical Science, Chengdu, Sichuan, China.

ZHANG Yongfu, b. 19 Mar 1932, Chongqing, China. Oral Surgeon. m. 1 Jan 1958, 2 sons, 1 daughter. Education: West China University of Medical Science, 1949-55. Career: Professor of Oral and Maxillofacial Surgery, 1987; Dean of Faculty of Stomatology, Director of Oral Hospital, Professor, Director of Institution of Stomatology of Jiangxi Medical College. Publications: Books: Practical Oral and Maxillo-facial Surgery, 1989; Health Cure for Child, 1988; Articles: Cleft Lip Repair, 1963; Anatomic Research and Clinical Application of Facial Nerve, 1988; Nasolabial Flap for Tongue Reconstruction, 1992. Honours: 3rd Class Awards of Science and Technology, 1989; Special Subsidy for Outstanding Contribution, 1992. Memberships: Specialty Society Membership of Chinese Medical Association; Fellow, International Association of Oral and Maxillo-facial Surgeons. Hobbies: Reading; Playing Chess. Address: 161 Bayi Road, Jiangxi Medical College, Nanchang City, China.

ZHANG Yongmu, b. 25 July 1940, Jiangxi, China. Doctor. m. Zhong Xenzhen, 10 March 1968, 2 sons. Education: BA, Jiangxi Medical College, 1964. Appointments: Lecturer, Jiangxi Medical College, 1980-88; Vice Professor, Jiangxi Medical College, 1988-93; Professor, Jiangxi Medical College, 1993-. Publications: Appendical mucus cystis, 1982; The clinc application of the improvement of 3 style shunt with the Y-style, 1984; The learning from the operation of portacatal shunt, 1986; The experimental study about the effect of man-made vascular bridge-style of mesenteric vena caval anastomsis on hemodynamics of syndrome, 1988; Co-author: High frequency ventilate, 1987; Diagnosis and therapy of portal hypertension, 1993. Hobbies: Running; Swimming. Address: 1st Affiliated Hospital, Jiangxi Medical College, Nanchang, Jiangxi, China.

ZHANG You Jun, b. 13 Feb 1940, Hebei, China. Doctor. m. Wang Mu Zhi, Dec 1970, 1 son, 1 daughter. Education: Bachelor of Medicine, TJ TCM College, 1966. Career: Professor, Tianjin College of TCM; Director of Department, Psychosmatic Medicine, 1st Hospital att to Tianjin College. Publications: How to Keep Healthy by TCM, 1988; Selection of Sexial Knowledge, 1989; Andriatry Case Reports, TCM, 1990; Treasure of Gerocomy, 1991; Treasure of Andriatry, 1992; Sexology of TCM, 1992. Honours: Best Lecturer Award, TCM, 1987, 1992; Award for Most Advanced Scientific Research, TCM, 1991. Memberships: Chinese Association of Sexology; Institute of Chinese Medicine. Hobbies: Reading; Writing; Art; Literature. Address: The 1st Hosp att to Tianjin College of Traditional Medicine, Tianjin, China.

ZHANG You-duan, b. 14 Aug 1919, Changsha, Hunan, China. Biochemist. m. Rui-Ming Chen, 3 Apr 1948, 1 daughter. Education: BSc; MSc; PhD. Appointments: Instructor, Tsinghua University, 1943-47; Experimental Officer, Low Temperature Research Station, Department of Scientific and Industrial Research, Cambridge, England, 1954-58; Senior Scientist, Vitamin C Research Group, 1958-66, Senior Scientist, Division of Radiation Biochemistry, 1966-78, Chief, Division of Steroid Biochemistry, 1978-89, Emeritus Professor, Research Section on Gene Regulation, and Member of Council of Specialists, 1989-, Shanghai Institute of Biochemistry, Academia Sinica. Publications: Synthesis of L-ascorbic acid, 1954; Studies on the oxidation of succinate by rat liver mitochondria, 1964; Expression of androgen receptor on a prostatic steroid binding protein, 1988; Determination and characterization of androgen receptor, 1990. Memberships: Chinese Society of Biochemistry; Chinese Society of Physiological Sciences; Chinese Society of Radiation Research. Address: Shanghai Institute of Biochemistry, Academia Sinica, 320 Yua-Yang Road, Shanghai 200031, China.

ZHANG Yue-Qing, b. 30 Sept 1937, Zhu County, Hebei, China. Research Worker. m. 26 Aug 1962, 1 s, 1 d. Education: BS, Nankai University, Tianjin, China, 1962. Appointments: Assistant, 1962-67; Senior Assistant, 1967-78; Instructor, 1978-87; Associate Professor,

1987-92; Professor of Tropical Medicine, 1992-. Publications: include, Investigation on Giardia Lamblia and Giardiasis, 1984; Diagnosing Trichinella Spiralis Infection in Man by Detecting CAg with McAb & Polyclonal Ab, 1992. Honours: 18 Awards including Ministry, Municipal and Bureau Level Awards in 1977-94. Memberships: Chinese Microbiology & Immunology Association; Chinese Association of Zoology. Hobbies: Singing. Address: Beijing Friendship Hospital, Beijing Tropical Medicine Research Institute, 94# Yong An Road, Beijing 100050, China.

ZHANG Yun, b. 18 May 1928, Beijing, China. Professor of Radiology. m. 27 dec 1957, 2 sons. Education: MD, Shanghai Medical University Appointments: Resident to Professor, Supervisor, Department of Radiology, Chang Hai Hospital. Publications: The Evaluation of Pulmonary Hypertension in Rheumatic Valvular Disease, Co-author, 1988; Valvular Heart Diseases and prosthetic Valve Replacement, Co-author, 1986; Current Clinical Cardiology, CO-author, 1991; English Chinese Clinical Radiological Vocabulary, Vice CHief Editor, 1983. Memberships: Committee, Society of Radiology, CMA; Committee, Shanghai Biomedical Engineering. Address: Chang Hai Hospital, Second Military Medical College, Shanghai 2000433, China.

ZHANG Zhen-Xiang, b. 25 Nov 1920, Hobei, China. Professor of Surgery (retired). m. Qing-Guo Zhou, 15 May 1947, 1 son, 1 daughter. Education: BS, Yenching University, Beijing, 1942; MD, Medical College, West China Union University, Chengdu. Appointments include: Medical Director, Kienshi Hospital, Yunnan; Vice-Chairman, Associate Professor, Department of Surgery, Shandong Medical College; Chairman, Professor, Department of Surgery, Shandong Medical University. Publications: Emergency Surgery (chief editor), 1980; Cardiovascular Surgery in China, 1984; Superior Vena Cava Syndrome, 1984; Surgery of Lymphatic System (chief editor), 1985; Saphenojugular Shunt for Treatment of Superior Vena Cava Syndrome, 1985; Articles: Vesical Calculi in Shandong, 1954; Principles and Techniques of Surgical Treatment of Varicocele, 1954; Timing and Technique of Surgical Treatment of Undescended Testis, 1956; Surgical Treatment of Scrotal Elephantiasis, 1956; Bilateral Giant Renal Calculi Treated by Surgical Removal and Pyeloplasty, 1957; Carcinoma of Bladder Treated by Total Cystectomy, Rectal Bladder and Perineal Colostomy, 1957; Surgical Treatment of Fusiform Aneurysm of the Ascending Aorta, 1976; Complication of Mitral Valve Replacement, 1976; Diagnosis and Surgical Removal of Left Ventricular Myxoma, 1980. Honours: Provincial 2nd Prize Award for Accomplishment in Medical Science Writings, 1980, 1982. Memberships: Committee Member, Chinese Cardiothoracic Surgical Association; Chairman, Cardiothoracic Surgical Association of Shandong. Hobby: Painting. Address: 44 Neilson Avenue, Scarborough, Ontario, Canada M1M 2S2.

ZHANG Zheng-Gang, b. 30 Oct 1956, Beijing, China. Physician. m. Ming Li, 10 Feb 1983, 1 son. Education: MB, Beijing 2nd Medical College, 1982; MM, Union Medical University of China, Beijing, 1985; PhD, State University of New York, Buffalo, 1992. Appointments: Intern Physician, Beijing Friendship Hospital, 1981-82; Resident Physician, Cancer Institute, Chinese Academy of Medical Sciences, Beijing, 1983-85; Research Assistant, Roswell Park Cancer Institute, Buffalo, New York, USA, 1985-91; Postdoctoral Research Fellow, Biochemical and Molecular Pharmacology, Department of Experimental Therapeutics, Roswell Park Cancer Institute, USA, 1991-92; Resident Physician, Millard Fillmore Hospitals, State University of New York, Buffalo, 1992-. Publications include: Co-author: Role of dose, schedule and route of administration of 5-formyltetrahydrofolate: preclinical and clinical investigations, 1988; Effects of diastereoisomers of 5-formyltetrahydrofolate on cellular growth, sensitivity to 5-fluoro-2'-deoxyuridine, and methylenetetrahydrofolate polyglutamate levels in HCT-8 cells, 1991;   Mechanisms of resisitance to fluoropyrimidines, 1992; Quantitation of dihydrofolate reductase and thymidylate synthase mRNAs in vivo and in vitro by polymerase chain reaction, 1992; Pharmacologic rationale for fluoropyrimidine-leucovorin combination: biochemical mechanisms, 1992; Isolation and characterization of a human ileocecal carcinoma cell line (HCT-8) subclone resistant to fluorodeoxyuridine, 1993; 5-fluoro-2'-deoxyuridine: Role of schedule in its therapeutic efficacy, 1993. Honours: Dave Fellowship, Department of Pharmacology, Roswell Park Graduate Division, State University of New York, Buffalo, 1986; Winner, Medical Biostatistics Workshop Competition, Roswell Park Cancer Institute, 1991. Memberships: Associate Member: American Association for Cancer Research; American College of Physicians. Hobby: Bridge. Address: 174 Thistle Lea, Amherst, NY 14221, USA.

ZHANG Zhengguo, b. 31 July 1949, Beijing, China. Biomedical Engineer. m. Qingping Liu, 5 Jan 1976, 1 daughter. Education: MMedicine; Beijing TV University, 1979-82; Peking Union Medical College, 1982-85; Postdoctoral, University of California, San Francisco, School of Medicine, 1989-90. Appointments: Assistant, 1985, Research Associate, 1987, Professor, 1993-, Peking Union Medical College. Publications: Single Channel Inductive Cochlear Implant, 1986; Inventor of several medical prostheses. Honours: Ministry of Public health Award, 1986; Ministry of Civil Affairs Award, 1987; World Health Organization Award, 1989; Beijing Public Health Bureau Award. 1990. Memberships: IEEE; IAA; ASHA; Chinese Society of Biomedical Engineering; Beijing Psychological Health Association; Chinese Society of Acoustics. Hobbies: Reading Kung-fu novels. Address: 5 Dong Dan San Tiao, Beijing 100005, China.

ZHANG Zhengru, b. 1924, Nanchang, Jiangxi Province, China. Physician. Appointments: Professor of Traditional Chinese Medicine. Publications: Theory of Yin-Refreshing; Theory of Emergy regulating; Zhang's Decatheory of TCM; Contributor of over 60 professional papers. Membership: Director, China Association of Traditional Chinese Medicine. Address: 49 LiHuangPi Road, Wuhan 430014, China.

ZHANG Zhixian, b. 12 Nov 1934, Hunan, China. Professor of Radiation Oncology. m. Yulan Li, 1 May 1966, 2 sons, 1 daughter. Education: Diplomas, Hunan (Xiangya) Medical College, 1959; Professor's Certificate, CAMS and Peking Union Medical College, 1993; Expert's Certificate, Chinese Science and Technology Association, 1994. Appointments: Intern, 1959-60, Resident, 1961-63, Chief Resident, 1964-77, Visiting Radiotherapist, 1978-85, Associate Professor, 1986-92, Professor, 1993-, Cancer Institute Hospital CAMS and PUMC. Publications: Radiation Oncology, Co-author, 1983; Modern Oncology, 1993; Radiation Oncology, 1993; Radiation Treatment of Carcinoma of the Oropharynx, 1983; Value of Preoperative Radiotherapy for Adenocinoma of the Gastric, 1991; Value of Preoperative Radiotherapy for Esophageal Carcinoma, 1992. Honours: Expert's Special Subsidies and Certificate, Government of China, 1993-. Memberships: Society of Radiation Oncology, CMA; Society of Oncology, CMA; Chinese Medical Association; Chinese Science and Technology Association. Hobbies: Reading; Walking; Light Music. Address: No 17 Panjiayang, Chaoyang District, Beijing 100021, China.

ZHANG Zhongbing, b. 18 Mar 1945, Danyang, Jiangshu province, China. Professor of Gastroenterology. m. Yuan Shufen, 10 dec 1973, 1 son. Education: MB, MMed, MD. Appointments: Associate Professor, 1986, Professor, 1992, Xijing Hospital; Director, Changzheng Hospital, Shanghai, 1994-. Publications: Immunocytochemical and Histochemical Studies on T and Antibody-Producing Cells within and Around Carcinoma, 1985; Applied Value of ANHE Stain in Paraffin Embed Gastrointestinal Tissue, 1986; Antral G Cells and D Cells in Gastric and Duodenal Ulcer, 1987; Preliminary Studies on Relationship Between the Distribution of Antral G Cells and Gastrin Contents in Gastric Juice, Gastric Tissue and Serum, 1987; SC IgA and IgA-Producing Cells in Gastric Mucosa of Chronic Gastritis and Gastric Carcinoma and Their Clinical Significance, 1988; Study on Gastrin in Duodenal Ulcer, 1990; Preliminary Study on VIP and SP in Ulcerative Cells, Chronic Colitis and Irritable Bowel Syndrome, 1992. Honours: 2nd Award, Chinese PLA Advanced Science and Technology Award. 1987, 1992, 1993; 3rd Award, Chinese PLA Advanced Science and technology, 1984, 1985, 1986, 1991; 1st Award, 4th Chinese Medical Association Conference on Middle and Young Age Excellent Medical Themes. memberships: Chinese Society of Gut Hormone; Standing Committee, Shaanxi Society of Gastroenterology; Vice Chairman, Xian Internal Medicine Society. Hobbies: Running; Pingpong. Address: Department of Gastroenterology, Changzheng Hospital, 415 Fengyang Road, Shanghai, China.

ZHANG Zidong, b. 21 Sept 1934, Hubei, China. Teacher of Physiology. m. Dec 1961, 1 s, 1 d. Education: Graduate, Wuhan Medical College; Postgraduate Training, Chinese Academy of Medical Sciences. Appointments: Assistant of Physiology, 1958, Lecturer, 1978, Associate Professor, 1985, Professor of Physiology, 1990-, Department of Physiology, Tongji Medical University. Publications: Author of textbooks and reference books in Chinese; Contributor of professional articles. Memberships: International Association for the Study of Pain; Chinese Association for the Study of Pain; Chinese Association for Physiological Science; Member of Council, Hubei Association for Neuroscience. Address: Department of Physiology, Tongji Medical University, Hang Kong Lu 13, Wuhan 430030, China.

ZHANG Zi-ying, b. 4 Jan 1943, Henan Province, China. Professor of Ophthalmology. m. Hue-qin He, 27 Dec 1968, 1 son, 1 daughter. Education: MB, Henan Medical University, 1967; Graduate Student, Beijing Medical University, 1986. Appointments: Professor of Ophthalmology. Publications: The Treatment of Traumatic Iridic Cyst and Its Complication, 1988; Sympathetic Ophthalmia, 1988, Diagnosis and Surgery of Melanoma of Choroid, 1993; relations Between the Conversion of Vogt-Koyanagi Syndrome and the Using Dosage of Corticosteroid, 1990; Central Exudative Chorioretinitis, 1994; Modern Diagnosis and Treatment of Ophthalmology, Co-author, 1992; New Treatment of Ophthalmopathy, Co-author, 1994. Membership: Chinese Medical Association. Hobbies: Literature; Badminton.

ZHANG Zong-Yu (Chung-Yu), b. 17 Jan 1935, Nanking, China. Biochemist. m. Tan-Jun Tong, 17 July 1963, 2 daughters. Education: MD, Beijing Medical University, 1959; Visiting Fellow, National Institutes of Health, Bethesda, USA, 1981. Appointments: Faculty Member, 1959, Associate Professor, 1985, Professor, Laboratory Chief, 1990-, Department of Biochemistry, Beijing Medical University; Visiting Professor, Thomas Jefferson University, Philadelphia, Pennsylvania, USA, 1991-92. Publications: S-adenosyl homocysteine hydrolase from hamster liver, 1983; Inactivation of S-adenosyl-homocysteine hydrolase by nucleosides, 1985; Cell aging of human diploid fibroblasts is associated with changes in responsiveness to EGF and changes in HER-2 expression, 1994. Honours: Outstanding Contribution for Medical and Health Development, State Council of China, 1993. Memberships: Chinese Biochemical Society; Chinese Gerontology Society; Chinese Medical Gerontology Society. Address: Department of Biochemistry and Molecular Biology, Beijing Medical University, 38 Xue-yuan Road, Beijing 100083, China.

ZHANG Zuosheng, b. 30 Dec 1937, Ningde, Fujian, China. Bioelectronic Engineer. m. 8 July 1968, 2 sons. Education: BS, Fudan University, 1961. Appointments: Director, Biocybernetics Committee, Biophysics Society of China; Director, Biocybernetics and Medical Engineering Committee, Automation Society of China; Director, BME Society of China; Director, Professor, Biomedical Engineering Institute, USTC. Publications: Neural Network and Its Application, 1993; The Advance of Biomedical Engineering, 1993; Estimation of Single Trial Evoked Potentionals Using Parametric Modeling, 1990; Investigation of Evoked EEG Response Driven by Sine Modulated Light, 1991. Honours: Prize of Science and technology Progress, National Education Committee of China, 1994. Memberships: Head, Academic Committee, Biomedical Engineering in Anhui. Hobbies: Classical Music; Bridge; Stamp Collecting; Photography. Address: Department of Electronic Engineering, University of Science and Technology of China, Hefei, Anhui 230026, China.

ZHAO Da-Zheng, b. 24 July 1936, Shanghai, China. Orthopaedist. m. Cheng Shi Ming, 1 Oct 1962, 1 son, 1 daughter. Education: MD, Zhejiang Medical University, 1959. Appointments: Currently Director, Orthopaedics Department, Zhejiang Hospital, Hangzhou; Director, Orthopaedics Divsion, Zhejiang Research Institute of Gerontology. Publications: Clinical advance of the calcaneal fracture, 1989; Manual reduction for intra-articular fracture of the calcaneus, 1991; Co-author: Continuous direct current in treatment of nonunion and delayed union, 1986; Treatment for osteoporosis accompanied by diabetes after menopause with Salmon calcitonin in a small dosage, 1992. Honours: Title of Advanced Worker for Public Health, Chinese Ministry of Public Health, 1987; Special Allowance, State Council of China, 1993-. Memberships: Council Member, All-China Association for the Extension and Application of New Techniques in Orthopaedics; Council Member, Orthopaedics Department, Zhejiang Branch, Chinese Medical Association; Council Member, Bone Tumour Division, Zhejiang Branch, CAA; Council Member, Orthopaedics Department, Zhejiang Branch, Chinese Association for the Combination of Traditional Chinese and Western Medicine. Hobbies: Basketball; Swimming. Address: Department of Orthopaedics, Zhejiang Hospital, Hangzhou, Zhejiang 310013, China.

ZHAO Dianchang, b. 2 May 1933, Jinan Shandong Province, China. Doctor. m. Li Jingyi, 10 Aug 1954, 1 s, 1 d. Appointments: Secretary, Association of Burns and Plastic Surgery of Shandong Province; Surgeon-in-Charge, 1978-84, Associate Professor, 1984-91, Professor of Surgery, 1992-, Affiliated Hospital of Shandong Medical University. Publications: Emergency Surgery, Co-author, 1980; Neonatal Surgery, Co-author, 1981; Clinical Burns, Co-author, 1984; Surgical Nurse; Disorders of Micro-Circulation and Surgical Illness, 1980. Honours:

Governmental Allowance for Specialist, 1993-. Memberships: Association of Burns and Plastic Surgery of Shandong Province; Association of Large Intestine Cancer of China. Hobbies: Mountain Climbing; Swimming. Address: The Affiliated Hospital of Shandong Medical University, China.

ZHAO Hui-yang, b. 20 July 1931, Beijing, China. Professor of Medicine. m. Qiang-sun Zhang, 15 Jan 1958, 1 son, 1 daughter. Education: MD. Appointments include: Currently Director, Institute of Nuclear Medicine, Shanghai. Memberships: American Association of Physicists in Medicine; Chinese Society of Nuclear Medicine. Hobbies: Music; Sports. Address: Department of Nuclear Medicine, Zhongshan Hospital, Shanghai Medical University, Shanghai 200032, China.

ZHAO Junyong, b. 2 June 1940, Fuping, Shaanxi, China. Professor. m. Professor Meiju Cao, 28 Dec 1940, 1 son, 1 daughter. Education: Diploma, Faculty of Medicine, Xian Medical University, 1958-63. Appointments: Assistant, Department of Biochemistry, 1963-78, Lecturer, Department of Biochemistry, 1978-87, Associate Professor, 1987-93, Professor, 1993-, Department of Biochemistry, Xian Medical University. Publications include: Comparative Studies on Catalytic Properties of Rat Pyruvic Kinase Isoenzyme, 1980; Effects of Selenium on RNA Synthesis and Content in Rat Pancreas, 1990; Detection of Mycobacterium Tubercluosis DNA in Pleural Effusion by PCR, 1994. Honours: Exemplary Teacher, Xian Medical University, 1986; Prize of Science and Technology Progress in Shaanxi province, 1993. Memberships: Society of Chinese Biochemistry and Molecular Biology; Society of Chinese Biophysics. Hobbies: Reading; Chinese Classical Literature; Walking; Tourism. Address: Department of Biochemistry, Xian Medical University, 205 Scarlet-Bird Avenue, South Suburb, Xian, Shaanxi, China.

ZHAO Shilin, b. Shaanxi Province, China. Professor. m. Wang Wei, dec, 2 sons, 2 daughters. Education: Studied Medicine, Medical College of Northwest University. Appointments include: Doctor, Dermatology Department, Shaanxi Zhen An County Hospital; Director, Medical History Department Professor, Shaanxi Academy of Traditional Chinese Medicine; Edit Committee, CChinese Medical History of Public Health Ministry. Publications include: Shaanxi Collected Works on Medical History, volume 1; Famous Doctor Dun Simiao; Developing History on Chinese Dermatology; Who's Who of Doctors in Shaanxi, Gansu and ninxia Region; Achievement n Syphilis Made by Chen Sicheng in Min Dynasty; Contributor of over 60 scientific papers in magazines. Memberships: Director, Medical History Committee, Shaanxi Academy of Science and Technique History; Adviser, Chinese Medical History Association, Shaanxi Branch; Honorary Director, Sun Simiao Research Association. Hobbies: Reading; Music; Opera; Travel. Address: Shaanxi Academy of Traditional Chinese Medicine, Shaanxi, China.

ZHAO Shufen, b. 5 Apr 1945, Liaoyuan, China. Associate Professor of Physiology. m. Li Rui Wu, 1 Dec 1970, 1 son. Education: MD, China Medical University, 1970; Postdoctoral Fellow, Department of Pharmacology, Temple University, Philadelphia, Pennsylvania, USA, 1994-95. Appointments: Instructor, 1979, Assistant Professor, 1983, Associate Professor of Physiology, 1992-, China Medical University, Shenyang. Publications: Co-author: Effect of electroacupuncture on the activity of thermosensitive neurons of the preoptic anterior hypothalamus in the cat treated with pyrogen, 1983; Effects of electroacupuncture at acupoint Quchi and electric stimulation to type A Fibrils of saphenous nerve on the spontaneous firing of the preoptic anterior hypothalamic neurons in the cat, 1985; The neurotoxic effect of monosodium glutamate on ventromedical neurons of hypothalamus in the infant rat, 1992; Effect of arcuatus nucleus lesion on body temperature regulation in the rat (1st author), 1992. Membership: Physiological Society of China. Hobby: Basketball. Address: Department of Physiology, China Medical University, Shenyang 110001, China.

ZHAO Songquan, b. 12 July 1915, Beijing, China. Medical Professor. m. Wu Yuzhen, 8 Oct 1935, 4 sons, 3 daughters. Education: Bachelor Degree, Medicine, 1935. Appointments: Beijing Hospital for Gynecology & Obstetrics, 1935-94. Publications: Female Sterility Caused by Functional Insufficincy of Ovary, 1958; Treating Haemolysis of ABO, 1985: reating Pelvis Infection & Impassibility of Oviduct, 1992. Honours: Gold Cup Prize, 1994. Membership: Institute of Chinese Herb Medicine. Hobbies; Chess; Chinese Martial Arts. Address: 43 Yaer Hutong, Xuan Wu District, Beijing 100050, China.

ZHAO Tiping, b. 21 July 1933, Shanghai, China. Medical Oncologist. m. Tienji Feng, 8 Dec 1967, 1 son, 1 daughter. Education: Shanghai Medical University, 1956; Fellow, Istituto Nazionale Tumori, Milan, Italy, 1980; Fellow, Hospital Paul-Brousse, Paris, France, 1981. Appointments: Chief, Research Laboratory of Clinical Pharmacology for Antitumour Agents, Cancer Hospital, Shanghai Medical University. Publications: Contributor of numerous works. Memberships: Committee of Drug Evaluation, Commission of CHinese Pharmacopeia, Ministry of Public Health, China; Board, Asian-Oceanian Clinical Oncology Association; Managing Director, Shanghai Antitumour Association; Academic Committee, Chinese Cancer Research Foundation; Board, Chinese Society of Oncological Pharmacology and Chemotherapy. Hobby: Detective Stories. Address: 399 Ling-Ling Road, 200032 Shanghai, China.

ZHAO Xue Zhong, b. Jul 1939, Beijing, China. Master of Chi Kung. Education: Studied Chi Kung. Career: Chi Kung Doctor: Beijing Employees Infirmary of the Water Conservancy, 1984-85, Hua-Y Clinic, Beijing, 1985-88, Beijing and Western Medical Expert Centre, Master of Chi Kung, 1988-89, Consultant and Instructor at the Master Zhao Institute, California, USA, 1989-. Honours: 1st Chi Kung doctor licensed by the Beijing Bureau of Health; Honoured by the Mayor of Beijing City; Honoured Member, Beijing Chi Kung Association; Honoured Consultant, American Chinese Chi Kung Research Association; Special Consultant of the President of World Chi Kung Medicine Association. Hobbies: Reading; Travel; Singing; Dancing. Address: Master Zhao Institute, 43176 Christy Street, Fremont, CA 94538, USA.

ZHAO Xuejian, b. 5 Mar 1939, Tonghua, Jilin, China. Professor of Pathophysiology. m. 24 May 1967, 1 son, 1 daughter. Education:BA, Norman Bethune University of Medical Sciences, 1964. Appointments: Physician, Teaching Hospital, 1964; Lecturer, Department of Pathophysiology, 1978, Vice Professor, Department of Pathophysiology, 1985, Professor, Director of Postgraduate for MD, 1992, Norman Bethune University of Medical Sciences. Publications: Study of Causes of Infetility of Vasovasestomized Rabbits: Analysis of Antisperm Antibodies, Co-author, 1992; The Influence of Vasectomy and Vasovasostomy on testicular ATPase, cAMP, ABP and Androgen Receptor in Rabbits, Co-author, 1994. Honours: State Family Planning Commission Science and technology Development Award, 2nd Award, 1988; State Education Commission Science and Technology Development Award, 3rd Award, 1994. Memberships: Chinese Pathophysiological Society; Chinese Productive Immunological Society. Hobbies: Tennis; Running; Music. Address: Department of Pathophysiology, Norman Bethune University of Medical Sciences, Xinming Street, Changchun 130021, China.

ZHAO Yu-hua, b. 14 Mar 1934, Beijing, China. Medical Doctor. m. Yang Rei He, 25 Aug 1960, 2 sons. Education: MD, First Military Medical University, 1957. Appointments: Surgeon, 1958; Ultrasound Doctor, 1960; Physician, 1972; Currently Director, Department of Ultrasound, Professor, Changhai Hospital, Second Military Medical University, Shanghai, 1979-95. Publications: Co-author, chapters on ultrasound diagnosis in Liver Surgery, 1982, Handbook for Physicians, 1985, Basis of General Surgery, 1985, Valvular Disease and Prosthetic Replacement, 1986, Ultrasound Diagnosis of Abdominal Diseases, 1990, Clinical Ultrasonic Diagnostics, 1991, Color Doppler Diagnostics, 1991; 50 learned articles, 1980-94. Honours: Special Lifelong Prize, Government of China, 1993. Memberships: Committee Member, Society of Ultrasound, Chinese Medical Association; Council Member, Society of Chinese Ultrasound in Medicine and Engineering; Committee Member, Shanghai Ultrasound Branch, Chinese Medical Association; WFUMB; AFSUMB. Hobbies: Singing; Chinese music. Address: Changhai Hospital, 174 Changhai Road, Shanghai 200433, China.

ZHEN Xiang, b. 3 Apr 1954, Wuhan, China. Professor. m. Lu Guiming, 1982, 1 son. Education: Graduate, Wuhan Retraining College for Physicians. Appointment: Associate Professor of Internal Traditional Chinese Medicine. Publications: Practising Syndromes with TCM; Contributor of 48 papers. Membership: Wuhan Board, China Association of Traditional Chinese Medicine. Hobbies: Basketball; Table tennis;l Micro-computers. Address: 49 LittiangPi Road, Wuhan 430014, China.

ZHEN Yao, b. 12 Feb 1930, Hebei, China. Professor of Medicine. m. Lin Sulan, 30 July 1954, 2 sons, 1 daughter. Education: BMed, 1952, MMed, 1954, Dalian Medical College. Appointments: Assistant, 1954; Lecturer, 1958; Associate Professor, 1980; Professor of Medicine and Biomedical Ultrasonics, Chief Physician, Department of Infectious

Diseases and Department of Ultrasonics, 2nd Affiliated Hospital, Harbin Medical University, 1985-; Director, Editor-in-Chief, Journal Prov Cure VH, 1989. Publications: 10 books including: Clinical Hepatology, 1985; Ultrasonics, 1993; English-Japanese-Chinese Lexicon of Ultrasonics, 1993; 70 papers. Honours: Award, National Health Scientific Conference, 1978; 1st Prize for National Excellent Thesis, 1992; 1st Prize, Heilongjiang Scientific and Technological Association, 1993. Memberships: IASL; Academic Committee, IRECLD; Committee Member, CEACB. Hobbies: Reading; Visits. Address: The 2nd Affiliated Hospital of Harbin Medical University, Harbin 150086, China.

ZHENG Bao Qian, b. 7 Feb 1927, Beijing, China. Surgeon. m. Zhang Gini Yein, May 1964, 1 s. Education: MD, Medical College Beijing University, 1953. Career: General Practitioner, 1953-57; Staff, Surgical Department, Tianjin Red Cross Hospital, 1957-58; Currently, Chief Surgeon, Department of Surgery, Tianjin Second Medical College. Hobbies: Playing Violin; Etiology and Treatment of Cancer. Address: Surgical Department, Tianjin Second Medical College, Tianjin, China.

ZHENG Chuan Jing, b. 8 Sep 1928, Kumming, Yunan Province, China. Paediatrician; Educator. m. Guan Xian Lin, 28 July 1959, 2 sons, 2 daughters. Education: MB, Shan Yale Medical College, Changsha, 1952; MD, Beijing Medical College, 1959; Advanced Study in Haematology, Tokyo Medical College, Japan, 1983. Appointments: Assistant, Lanchow Medical College, 1953-56; Postgraduate, Beijing Medical College, 1956-59; Instructor, Associate Profesor, Professor, 1960-89, Ningxia Medical College; Consultant Professor, Hainan Medical College, 1990-93; Professor of Paediatrics, Ningxia Medical College. Publications: ß-Thalassemia in Northwest China, 1978; Relationship of Iron Metabolism Between Mother and Newborn, 1985; Iron deficiency in Pregnant Women, 1985; Chemotherapy of ALL in Children, 1986; ITP in Child, 1988. Honours: Award on Iron Deficiency in Children, Ningxia Government, 1988; Advanced Medical Worker Prize, Health Ministry, 1987. Memberships: Committee, Chinese Paediatric Soceity; editorial Board, Chinese Journal of Paediatrics, 1978-94; Editorial Board, Journal of Clinical Paediatrics, Journal Practical Paediatrics. Hobbies: Music; Running; Tourism. Address: Department of Paediatrics, Affiliated Hospital of Ningxia Medical College, Yinchuan, Ningxia 750004, China.

ZHENG Fang, b. 23 Feb 1926, Liaoning, China. Professor of Anaesthesiology. m. 2 Oct 1952, 3 sons. Education: BA, Chang Chun University, 1948. Appointments: Preceptor of Master, 1981; Preceptor of Doctor, 1990; Preceptor of Postdoctoral Research centre, 1994; Editor, Journal of Chinese Anesthesiology, 1985-95; Chairman, Anaesthesiology, 2nd Hospital of Harbin Medical University. Publications: Anesthesia Physics, 1991; Modern Anesthesiology, Co-author, 1987; Therapeutics of Pain, Co-author, 1993; Application of Gaschromatography in Anesthesiology, 1979. Honours: Award of Science and Technology Advance, Ministry of Health of China, 1990; Award of Science and Technology Advance, Heilongjiang Provincial Government, 1989. Memberships: International Trauma Anaesthesia and Critical Care Society; Vice-Chairman, Anesthesia Society of Heilongjiang Province, 1972-95. Hobby: Classical Literature of China. Address: Department of Anaesthesiology of 2nd Affiliated Hospital of Harbin Medical University, Harbin, Heilongjiang, China.

ZHENG Jian Wei, b. 30 Apr 1963, Xiamen, Fujian, China. Physician. m. Zheng Ying Yang, 23 Apr 1993. Education: Masters Degree in Medicine; Advanced Training in Gastroenterology, Utah Medical Association, USA; ACLS training, American Heart Association. Appointment: Attending Doctor. Publications: Dexamethosome therapy in rats of acute hepatic failure induced by D-galactosamine, in Acta Academine Medicine Nantong, 1990; Study on brain edema in rats with D-galactosamine induced fulminant hepatic failure, in Chinese Journal of Clinical Hepatology, 1991. Membership: Xiamen Branch, Chinese Medical Association. Address: Department of Digestive Diseases, Xiamen First Hospital, Xiamen, Fujian 361003, China.

ZHENG Jing Chen, b. 3 Sept 1947, Wenzhou, China. Physician. m. Wu Difan, 6 Apr 1973, 2 sons. Education: MBBS, 2nd Military Medical University, Shanghai, 1969; Diploma, Endocrinology, Shanghai Medical University, 1985. Appointments: Medical Official, 413th Hospital of PLA, 1970; Physician, 1st Affiliate Hospital, Wenzhou Medical College, 1978; Lecturer, Consultant, Ibid, 1987; SMO, Colonial War Memorial Hospital, Suva, Fiji, 1988-92. Publications: Speical manifestations in hypothyroidism, 1983; The relationship between oral glucose and insulin secretion in type II diabetes mellitus, 1989; Analysis on diabetic acute myocardial infarction in 72 cases, 1993. Memberships: International Medicine Society, Wenzhou Branch of China Medical Association; Fiji Medical Association. Hobbies: Swimming; Table Tennis. Address: 95 Jiefan South Road, Wenzhou, Zhejiang, China.

ZHENG Jinhua, b. 20 Sep 1947, Wen Zhou, China. Nurse. m. Guo mao Yu, 7 Feb 1972, 1 s, 1 d. Education: Wen Zhou Health Polytechnic School, 1966. Appointments: Nurse; Chief of Nurses in Surgery. Publications: Co-Author: Studies of the relationship between the hand length, the foot length and the body length in different fetal age, 1991; Effects of whitmania pigra decoction on embryos of mice, 1991; Measurement of the induced fetal placenta and umbilical cord of different fetal age in 218 cases, 1992; Influence of infrared ray and specific electromagnetic wave radiation on the peripheral blood picture of mice, 1994; The effect of scolopendra decoction on embryos of mice, 1994; Author: Observation on the hand skin-prints of patient arteriosus ducts, 1993; Study on congenital malformations in pediatric surgery, 1994; Care of patient malformation of the anus and rectum, 1994. Honour: One of 10 Best Nurses of Wen Zhou City, 1994. Membership: Chinese Nursing Association. Hobbies: Horticulture; Literature. Address: Wen Zhou Medical College, 2nd Affiliated Hospital, Wen Zhou 325003, China.

ZHENG Pinru, b. 15 July 1933, Shanghai, China. Professor of Cardiology and Geriatrics. m. Song Guo-pei, 26 Jan 1961, 2 sons. Appointments: Assistant Professor of Cardiology, 1956-73, Lecturer in Cardiology, 1973-80, Vice-Professor of Cardiology and Geriatrics, 1980-85, Professor of Cardiology and Geriatrics, 1985-, Norman Bethune University of Medical Science, Changchun; Director, Geriatric Department, First Teaching Hospital, Norman Bethune University of Medical Science; Director, Geriatric Research Institute, Jilin Province. Publications: Co-author: The characters of natural killing cells in healthy elderly, 1991; To evaluate the diabetes in the elderly by means of pulsed Doppler Echocardiography, 1992; Research of the relationship of natural killing cells and Type II white cells in healthy elderly, 1992. Honours: 3rd Degree Award of Scientific Progress, Jilin Province, 1992. Memberships: Chief Editor, Editorial Board, Chinese Journal of Gerontology; Editorial Standing Committee, Chinese Journal of Geriatrics. Address: No 1 Xinmin Street, Changchun 130021, Jilin, China.

ZHENG Qian, b. 17 May 1924, Changtu, Liaoning, China. Physiologist. m. Jingquan Wu, 8 Aug 1955, 3 sons. Education: Bachelor of Mathematics, Jilin Normal University; Bachelor of Public Hygiene, China Medical University. Appointments: Assistant, Lecturer, then Associate Professor; Currently Full Professor in Physiology, China Medical University, Shanghai. Publications: Study on unit discharges of posterior nucleus (PO) in thalamus evoked by stimulating splanchnic afferent fibre in cat, 1983; Electrical membrane properties of neurones of mesencephalic nucleus of Vth nerve in rats, 1989. Honours: 2nd Prize for Scientific and Technical Progress, National Committee of Education, 1988; 3rd Prize for Scientific and Technical Progress, National Ministry of Health, 1989. Memberships: China Physiology Association; Biomedical Engineering Association. Hobby: Game of go. Address: Department of Physiology, China Medical University, Shanghai 110001, China.

ZHENG Richard Qi Hao, b. 5 Feb 1963, Shanghai, China. Medical Scientist; Acupuncturist. Education: Medical Graduate, Shanghai Medical University; PhD, University of London; Studied Western and Traditional Chinese Medicine, Shanghai Medical University; Immunology, University of London. Appointments: Research Assistant, Acupuncturist, 1987; Postdoctoral Scientist, Acupuncturist, 1990; Senior Research Scientist, Acupuncturist, 1993-. Publications: Various on immunology, 1990-, including T-cell activation, antigen presentation, cytokines, adhesion molecules, auto-immunity, in situ hybridisation. Honours: Top Student, Shanghai Medical University, 1985; Overseas Student Award, University of London, 1987. Memberships: Fellow, Royal Microscopical Society; British Society of Immunology; Biochemical Society; Register of Traditional Chinese Medicine. Hobbies: Tennis; Opera; Ballet. Address: 3 Laurel House, Little Ealing Lane, London W5 4EG, England.

ZHENG Shoujin, b. 3 Jan 1930, Shanghai, China. Medical Doctor. m. Shen Biru, 23 Sept 1956, 2 sons, 1 daughter. Education: Diploma, China Medical University, 1955. Appointments: Surgeon, Tongchuan Mining Hospital, 1955-73; Consulting Surgeon, Hanjiang Worker's Hospital, 1973-79; Associate Professor, Nanjing Railway Medical College, 1979-88; Professor, 1988-. Publications: Clinical Syndromology, 1989; Selection of Orthopaedic Cases, 1987; Orthopaedic Geriatrics, TJSTPH,

1989. Honours: Science & Technology Progress Award, 1987; Outstanding Textbook Writer Award, 1993. Memberships: Standing Director, Chinese Medical Association Medical Information Society; Director, Chinese Railway Association Medical Society. Hobbies: Classical Music; Opera; Novels; News Reports. Address: Room 104, No 129, Qingshicun, Nanjing 210037, Nanjing, China.

ZHENG Shu-sen, b. 27 January 1950, China. Associate Professor. m. 2 children. Education: Medical School, Zhejiang Medical University, 1970-73; Postgraduate, Zhejiang Medical University, 1983-86; Medical Sciences Doctor Degree, West China University, 1986-89. Appointments: Resident, Department of Surgery, First Affiliated Hospital, Zhejiang Medical University, 1973-86; Lecturer, Department of Surgery, First Affiliated Hospital, Zhejiang Medical University, 1986-92; Associate Professor, Department of Surgery, First Affiliated Hospital, Zhejiang Medical University, 1992-. Publications Include: Scanning transmission electron microscope observaion on mucosas of alkaline reflux gastritis of dog, 1989; Experimental studies of pathogenesis of alkaline reflux gastritis, 1989; Primary ileal lymphosarcoma: Analysis of 2 cases, 1990; Analysis of 78 cases with gallbladder polyp, 1991; Combined kidney and pancraticodudenal transplantation in one Diabetics patient with End-stage kidney disease, 1994; Orthotopic liver transplantation, 1995. Honours: Excellent Thesis Prize, 3rd Chinese National Congress on Treatment of Acute Abdominal Diseases by Integrated Traditional and Western Medicine, 1988; 2nd Prixe, Chinese Medical Association; 1st Class Prize, Sichuan Province National Science and Technic, 1992; 3rd Class Prize, Science and Technic Improvement of Zhejiang University and Colleges. Address: Hepatobiliary Pancreatic Surgery, Zhejiang Medical University, First Affiliated Hospital, Hangzhou, Zhejiang, China.

ZHENG Si Jin, b. 5 Jan 1915, Jiangsu, China. Professor of Anatomy. m. Dr Lin Mei Shang, Sep 1945, 2 sons. Education: BS, 1937, MS, 1940, Soochow University; PhD, Harvard University, USA, 1951. Appointments: Assistant of Biology, Soochow University, 1936; Lecturer of Human Anatomy, Shanghai Medical College, 1941; Associate professor of Human Anatomy, 1952, Professor of Human Anatomy, 1958. Shanghai Medical University; Visiting Professor of Anatomy, School of Medicine, University of Massachusetts, USA, 1980; Professor Emeritus. Publications: Survey of Anatomical Data and Variations of Chinese, volume 1, 1980, volume 2, 1990; Nomina Anatomica Sinica, 1982; Human Anatomy, 1983; Systemic Anatomy, 1990. Memberships: President, Shanghai Association of Anatomical Sciences, 1978; International Anatomical Nomenclature Committee, 1983; Honorary President, Chinese Association of Anatomical Sciences, 1990. Hobby: Travel. Address: Department of Anatomy, Shanghai Medical University, Shanghai 200032, China.

ZHENG Wanchuen, b. 21 July 1941, Haikou, Hainan, China. Physician. m. Jiqiong Ge, 24 May 1970, 1 daughter. Education: MB. Zhongshan Medical University, 1959-64; Postgraduate, Nishimoto Research Room, No 2 Internal Medicine Department, Hiroshima University, Japan, 1982-84; Visiting Scholar, Chest Research Institute, Kotoy University, Japan, 1993-94. Appointments: Resident Doctor, 1964, Attending Doctor, 1978, Vice Clinical Professor, 1989, Clinical Professor, 1992, 1st Vice Director of Hospital, Hainan Provincial People's Hospital. Publications: Lung Tissue Volume Changes Before and After the Treatment of Radiation Pneumonitis, 1988; Contributor of 46 articles in professional journals. Honours: Award, Hainan Science Development, 1989, 1992; First Award of Excellent Essays, 1993; National Special Award for Outstanding Specialists, 1992. Memberships: Chinese Respiratory Association; Chinese Hospital Administrative Association; Director Member, Hainan Respiratory Association. Hobbies: Music; Reading. Address: Hainan Provincial People's Hospital, Haikou, Hainan 570311, China.

ZHI Qu, b. 1928, Beijing, China. |BNiophysicist. Education: Graduate, China Medical University, 1950; Beijing University; Studied Theoretical Biophysics, China Medical University, 1982-. Appointments: Tutor, Master and Doctorate Degrees on Biophysics; Founder, Academic leader, Department of Biophysics, China Medical University, Shenyang. Honours: Prize for Advance of Science and Technology, National Education Commission. Memberships: Chairman, Liaoning Biophysics Society; Standing member, China Biophysics Society; Vice Chairman, China Microcomputer Medical Application Society; Vice Chairman, China Life Science Society. Hobbies: Qigong. Address: Department of Biophysics, China Medical University, Shenyang 110001, China.

ZHONG Baoren, b. 10 July 1925, Shanghai, China. Medical Doctor; Emeritus Professor. m. 14 Apr 1951, 2 sons. Education: MD, Faculty of Medicine, Shanghai Université de l'Aurore. Appointments include; Chief, Renal Diseases Research Group, Combined Traditional and Western Medicines, Shanghai Guang Hospital, affiliated to Shanghai College of Traditional Chinese Medicine; Currently Emeritus Professor. Publications include: Clinical study of 290 cases of chronic glomerulonephritis with TCM treatment, 1965; Clinical study of 358 cases of primary glomerulopathy with traditional and Western combined medical treatment, 1978; Treatment of Primary Glomerulopathy with TCM, 1981; Chinese-French Medical Dictionary, 1992. Membership: Chinese Scientific Association. Hobbies: Chinese Beijing Opera; Ping-pong. Address: Room 403, No 98 Ri Hui Lane, No 6 Ling Ling Road, Shanghai, China.

ZHONG Ru Chuan, b. 22 Nov 1925, Zhuangdong, China. Professor. m. Z X Yan, Feb 1959, 1 son, 1 daughter. Education: BS, Tongi University, 1951. Appointments: Professor of Histology, Embryology & Electron Microscopy; Assistant 1951-55, Lecturer, 1956-80, Associate Professor, 1981-85, Professor, 1986-. Publications: Microscopic Research in Loose Cells of Nasophaynx Cancer Prevention and Treatment of Guangdong Cancer, 1978; Histology of Human Small Blood and Lymphatie Vessels, 1991. Honours: Prize, Research Work, Guangzhou & Guangdong Government, 1979, 1983, 1984, 1986. Memberships: Chinese Anatomy Association; Chinese Zoology Association; Vice Principal Editor, Guangdong Anatomy Bulletin. Hobbies: Bridge; Music. Address: Bldg 25, Room 503, Guangzhou Medical College, Dongtong Xi Road, Guangzhou 510182, China.

ZHONG Zhi-ming, b. 28 June 1930, Guangdong, China. Stomatologist. m. Zhang Ru-ping, 7 Nov 1963, 1 daughter. Education: Graduated, Faculty of Stomatology, Fourth Military Medical University, 1955. Appointments include: Vice-Director, Department of Oral Medicine, Faculty of Stomatology, 1985, Associate Professor, Head, Department of Oral Medicine, Centre of Stomatology, 1987-, Sun Yat-Sen University of Medical Sciences. Publications: Premenstrual oral ulceration, 1985; Systemic side effects during topical oral application with triamcinolone acetonide, 1994. Memberships: International Association for Dental Research; Chinese Medical Association. Hobbies: Enjoying movies; Soccer; Boxing. Address: 366 Jiangnan Boulevard, Guangzhou 510260, China.

ZHOU Ai-Qing, b. 2 Mar 1937, Jiangsu, China. Professor of Paediatrics and Cardiology. m. Fei Yue Ying, 3 Dec 1967, 2 daughters. Education: MD, Shanghai Second Medical University, 1961; MD, Université Claude Bernard, Lyon, France; Professor, 1988. Appointments: Instructor, 1978; Associate Professor, 1982; Professor, Chief Physician of Paediatrics and Division of Cardiology, Vice-Director, Shanghai Institute for Paediatric Research. Publications: Contributor to The Reduction of Pediatric Cardiology; 50 articles including: China-made inplantable pacemakers in children, 1976; Balloon atrial septostomy for TGA in infancy, 1981; Torsade de pointes, 1982; Selective angiocardiography, 1983; Using Prostaglandin E in the treatment of CHD in newborn, 1984; Cardiac catheterization in newborn, 1990; China-made balloon dilation catheter and its applications, 1990; Balloon angioplasty for congenital aortic coarctation, 1990; Balloon valvuloplasty for AS, 1990; PBPV using overised balloon, 1991; Double umbrella closure of PDA, 1994; Pediatric Cardiology, 1994; Cardiac catheterization, 1994. Honours: 7 prizes, Ministry of Health and Shanghai Municipality. Memberships: Chinese Medical Association; Council Member, Chinese Society of Paediatric Cardiology. Hobbies: Music; Literature. Address: 1665 Kong Jiang Road, Shanghai 200092, China.

ZHOU Dingbiao, b. 30 Oct 1944, Jiangsu, China. Neurosurgeon. m. Xiuying Guo, 1 May 1972, 1 son. Education: MD; Master, Military Postgraduate Medical College; Visiting Scholar, University of Minnesota Medical School, USA. Appointments: Associate Professor, 1987, Professor, 1989, Professor, Chairman, 1993-, Neurosurgery Department, General Hospital of PLA, Beijing. Publications: Diagnosis and Treatment of Congenital Atlanto-Axial Dislocation, 1992; Microsurgery of Cavernous Sinus Tumors, 1992; Neurosurgical Operation, Co-author, 1994; Neurosurgery, Co-author, 1994; Surgery of Skull Base Tumors, 1995; Honours: Awards, Military Science and Technical Advances, 1986, 1987, 1990, 1992, 1994. Memberships: Leading Member, Study group of CVD, China; Committee Member, Neurosurgeons Association, China; Vice Chairman, Neurosurgeons Association, Beijing. Hobbies: Basketball; Painting. Address:

Neurosurgical Department, General Hospital of PLA, 28 Fuxing Road, Beijing 100853, China.

ZHOU Fang Jian, b. 15 May 1962, Hunan, China. Vice Professor of urology. m. Xiong Yong-Hong, 8 Mar 1990, 1 son. Education: MB, 1984, MMed, 1987, MD, 1992, Hunan Medical University. Appointments: Resident of urology, 1984-88; Research Fellow of Urology, 1989; Chief Resident of Urology, 1990; Visiting Urologist, 1991-94; Vice Professor of Urology, XiangYa Hospital. Publications: The Effect of Bladder Filling on urodynamics of the Upper Tract, Co-author, 1994; The Constant Pressure Perfusion of the renal Pelvis in Diagnosing Upper Tract Obstruction, Co-author, 1994. Membership: Chinese Urological Societyl. Hobby: Swimming. Address: Department of Urology, XiangYa Hospital, Hunan Medical University, Changsha 410008, Hunan, China.

ZHOU Gang, b. 28 Nov 1958, MuDan Jiang, Heilongjiang, China. Surgeon. m. Yu Ying, 31 July 1986, 1 daughter. Education: MMed. Appointments: Surgeon; Surgeon-in-Charge. Publications: Computerized Tomographic Scanning and Pathological Studies of the Extent of Infiltration of Esophageal Carcinoma, Co-author, 1993. Membership: Chinese Medical Association. Hobbies: Swimming; Running; Readinh. Address: Department of Thoracic Surgery, The Affiliated Hospital, Jiamusi Medical College, Jiamusi, Heilongjiang 154002, China.

ZHOU Hancha, b. 16 May 1932, Wuhan, Hubei, China. Surgeon. m. Disheng Liu, 16 July 1960, 1 son, 2 daughters. Education: BA, Xiang-ya Medical College, 1958; MD, Heart and Vascular Institute, Medical Sciences Academy of China, Beijing, 1964. Appointments: Attending Surgeon, 1964, Senior Attending Surgeon, 1972, Chief of Surgery, 1976, Professor of Surgery, Hunan Medical University. Publications: Successful Replantation of a Traumatic Cmplete severed Upper Arm, 1971; Transplantation of Pedicled Omentum in the Management of Chronic Empyema, 1980; Clinical Heart Transplantation, editor, 1993. Memberships: Chinese Medical Association; Hunan Thoracic and Cardiovascular Surgery Association. Hobbies: Music; Running; Swimming. Address: Cardiothoracic Division, Xiangya Hospital, Hunan Medical University, Beizhan Road, Changsha 410008, China.

ZHOU (CHOU) Jia-Yin (Chia-Yin), b. 25 Aug 1927, Beijing, China. Professor of Physiology. m. Shi Ai-Rong, 17 Feb 1953, 1 son, 1 daughter. Education: Graduated in Biology, Catholic University, China; Studied Medicine, Yale Medical College, China. Appointments: Assistant to Professor, Beijing Medical University, 1951-92; Visiting Professor, China Academy of Traditional Chinese Medicine, Beijing, 1980-84; Visiting Professor, Karolinska Institute, Stockholm, Sweden, 1985-86; Medical Adviser, Director of Acupuncture, Chinese Swedish Acupuncture Center, Malmö, 1986-92; Currently working in own acupuncture clinic, Malmö. Publications: 42 original scientific papers, 1955-90; Laboratory Manual of Physiology (chief author), 1963; Fundamentals of Electrophysiology, 1980; Laboratory Manual of Electrophysiology (chief author), 1987; System Physiology (co-author). Honours: Honorary Diploma of Acupuncture, MD, PhD, Norway, 1988. Membership: Chinese Physiological Society, China, Secretary-General, Standing Councillor, Main Editor of News Communications. Hobbies: Volleyball; Swimming; Enjoys music and nature. Address: Kiviksgatan 4 A, 214 40 Malmö, Sweden.

ZHOU Jing-xiu, b. 10 Jan 1925, Zhe Zhang, China. Professor of Neurobiology. m. Gu Jing-Hwa, 25 May 1955, 2 sons. Education: BE, Nanjing Aeronautical University, 1982; BT, Fu-Dan University, 1984. Appointments: Professor of Neurobiology, College of Basical Medical School, Shanghai University. Publications: Afferent Connections of the Entopeduncular Nucleus in the Rat, 1982; Afferent Connections of the Periaqueductal Grey in the Rat, Co-director, 1982; Distribution of Substance P CCK-8, 5-HT and Neurotensin Immunoreactive Neurons and their Co-existence in the Ventral Medulla of Rat, Co-director, 1988; Neurons in Paragigantocellularis Lateralis of Rats, Co-director, 1993; Colocalization of Serotonim and Fos-like Protein in the Rat CNS After Electroacupuncture and Pain Stimulation, Co-director, 1993; Mechanism of Acupuncture Analgesia of Quanliao Point-Role of NTS and RVM, Co-director, 1994; COntributor of 58 papers. Memberships: Summit County Anatomical Soceity; Chinese Acupuncture and Moxibus Association; Chinese Association for the Study of Pain. Address: Room 20-202, 170 Lane, Ping Jiang Road, Shanghai 200032, China.

ZHOU Juechu (Betsey), b. 17 Jan 1934, Zhejiang, China. Radiation Oncologist. m. Xie Shouchi, 1 Dec 1957, 1 son. Education: MB,

Shanghai 2nd Medical College. Appointments: Head, Radiotherapy Group, 1970-84, Deputy Director, Radiotherapy department, 1985-89, Director, Radiotherapy Department, 1989-, Professional Staff, Scientific and Technical Committee, 1987-, PUMC. Publications: Treatment and Prognosis of Giant-cell Tumor of the Bone: Analysis of 44 Patients, 1987; Radiotherapy of Pituitary of Cushing's Disease, 1989; Oncology of Radiotherapy, 1992. Memberships: Society of Radiation Oncology, CMA; Committee, SRO; Editorial Committee, Chinese Journal of Oncology. Hobby: Classical Music. Address: Department Radiotherapy, Peking Union Medical College Hospital, Chinese Academy of Medical Science, Wangfujing, Beijing 100730, China.

ZHOU Mei-rong, b. 3 Nov 1924, Shanghai, China. Professor of Obstetrics and Gynaecology. m. Zhao-chang Wu, Apr 1953, 1 son. Education: BA, Shanghai Medical University, 1950; MD. Appointments: Committee member, Shanghai Medical Association, 1958; Standing Committee, Shanghai Biomedical Engineering Association, 1985; Vice Chairman, Shanghai Preventive MCH Association, 1986; Honorary President, Shanghai Luwan MCH Hospital. Publications: Clinical Evaluation Fetal EKG, 1959; Advanced Pulmonary TB in Parturient Women, 1966; Fetal Movement Monitoring for High Risk Pregnancy, 1981; HE to reduce Contraceptive Failure, 1994. Honours: Shanghai Important Science and Technical Contribution Reward, 1982; Shanghai Women's Science and Technical Reward, 1987. Address: Shanghai Luwan MCH Hospital, 393 Yan An Zhong Road, Shanghai 200020, China.

ZHOU Meng-Sheng, b. 9 July 1932, Zhejiang Province, China. Biochemist. m. Chen Yin Hui, 25 Aug 1957, 2 sons, 1 daughter. Education: Studied at Dalian Medical College, 1951-56. Appointments: Assistant, Department of Biochemistry, Dalian Medical College, 1956-59; Assistant, 1959-78, Lecturer, 1978-83, Associate Professor, 1983-85, Professor, Department Director, 1985-, Department of Biochemistry, Liaoning College of Traditional Chinese Medicine. Publications: From History of Chinese Medicine to Know Recognition of Ancients regarding Food Nutrition, 1960; Study of Catharsis Treatment on Poisoning Nephritis in Rabbit, 1978; Textbook of Biochemistry Experiments, 1988; Biochemistry, 1988; Study of Replication of Mimicked Qi Deficiency in Animal Models, 1989. Honours: Advanced Worker, 1985, Exemplary Teacher, 1990, Model Teacher, 1992, Liaoning College of Traditional Chinese Medicine; Exemplary Teacher, City of Shenyang, 1993. Memberships: Standing Council, Chinese Biochemistry Society, Liaoning Branch; Consultant, Liaoning Society of Geriatric Nutrition and Health. Hobby: Ping-pong. Address: 79 Chongshan East Road, Huang-qu District, Shenyang, China.

ZHOU Qinghua, b. 16 October 1955, Zigong, China. Doctor; Professor of Thoracic Surgery. m. Guanglin Zeng, 13 August 1983, 1 son. Education: MD 1978, MSc 1984, West China University of Medical Sciences. Appointments: Intern, 1977-78; Assistant Resident, 1978-79; Resident, 1979-84; Chief Resident, 1984-85; Lecturer and Attending Surgeon, 1986-91; Associate Professor, 1991-94; Professor, 1995-. Publications Include: Pre and postoperative sequential study on the function of cell-mediated immunity of patients with lung cancer and esophageal cancer, 1986; Pre and postoperative serial study on the immunosuppressive activity of serum in patients with lung cancer, 1988; Co-author: Treatment of disseminated lung cancer with cryosurgery, 1989; Pre and postoperative sequential study on the immunosuppressive activity of serum and cell-free skin bleb fluid of patients with lung cancer and esophageal cancer, 1989; A study on the expression of oncogenes in patients with primary lung cancer, 1991; A study on the relationship between mutation of Ki-ras oncogenes and long-term survival rate in patients with lung cancer, 1994. Honours: Doctor of the Year of China Award, The Sackler Foundation, USA, 1991. Memberships: IASLC; Chinese Medical Association; Chinese Association of Thoracic and Cardiovascular Surgery; Lung Cancer; Anti-cancer. Hobbies: Swimming; Basketball. Address: Department of Thoracocardiac Surgery, 1st University Hospital, West China University of Medical Sciences, 37 Guo Xue Xiang, Chengdu, Sichuan 610041, China.

ZHOU Ren-Hou, b. 22 Mar 1922, Hebei Province, China. Medical Doctor. m. May 1950, 2 sons, 2 daughters. Education: BM, Medical College of Peking University, 1948; MD. Appointments: Resident, Chief Resident, 1948-51; Visiting Physician, 1951; Lecturer, 1954; Head, Orthopaedic Department, 1958-85; Associate Professor, 1960; Professor, 1982-; Consulting Orthopaedist, First Hospital, Beijing Medical University. Publications: About 50 learned articles, 1953-88;

Translated Russian textbooks of surgery, 1955. Honours: Numerous selections as Advanced Physician, 1955-86; 3 Excellent Article Awards, 1960, 1962, 1985. Memberships: Beijing Orthopaedic Association, Chairman 1978-87; National Orthopaedic Association, Standing Committee 1980-92. Hobbies: Drawing pictures; Engraving stamps. Address: First Hospital of Beijing Medical University, No 8 Xishiku Street, Beijing 100034, China.

ZHOU Renfeng, b. 28 Mar 1930, Ran Ge, Bai Guan, Hebei, China. Professor of Health Care Sport and Qi Gong. m. Meng Qing Fen, 28 Aug 1956, 2 sons. Education: Graduated, Beijing Medical College, 1955. Appointments: Chief Doctor, Shanxi Provincial Hospital, 1955-65; Vice-Professor of Martial Arts, Researcher, Xian Sport Institute, 1965-81; Chief, Professor of Health Care Sport and Qi-Gong Research, Tianjin Chinese Medical Institute, 1981-90. Publications: Common Sense of Medical Sports, 1976; Taijiquan Practice, 1977; Taijiquan Common Sense, 1978; Health Care Sport, 1978; Wu Shu, 1980; Regime for Old and Middle-Aged Persons, 1986; Taiji 13 Forms, 1986; Summary of Qi Gong, Regime and Recovery, 1987; Tortoise and Snake Gong, 1988; Regime with Qi Gong and Dao Yin, 1988; Qi Gong Taijiquan, 1989; Medical Qi Gong, 1989; Yijin Xi Sui Gong, 1989; Video tapes: Ba Duan Jin, 1986; Taijiquan, 1986; Tu Nai Dao Yin Gong, 1987; Video tapes with book: Hua Tuo Five Animals Forms, 1986; Yijin Xi Sui Jin, 1988. Honours: Research Fellow, Qi Gong Research, Beijing Chinese Medical Institute; Honorary Chairman, Qi Gong Research of Australia. Memberships: Board Vice-Chairman, Tianjin Human Body Science Institute; Board Vice-Chairman, Tianjin Tibet Qi Gong Institute. Hobbies: Qi Gong; Wu Shu. Address: 105-3-3 Bao Kang Li, Yu Quan Road, Xi-Hu, Nankai, Tianjin 300073, China.

ZHOU Shuxia, b. 23 June 1923, Zhejiang, China. Surgeon. m. Dr Kao Yuan, 1 Jan 1954, 2 daughters. Education: DDS, Dental College of National Central University, Nanking. Appointments: Resident, Assistant, 1947; Physician-in-Charge, Lecturer, 1953; Vice Chief Physician, Associate Professor, 1963; Chief Physician, Professor, 1981; Professor, Chief Physician of Oral and Maxillofacial Surgery, 4th Military Medical University, Xian; Director of PhD. Publications: Therapeutics of Trauma of Oral and Maxillofacial Region, Chief Editor, 1988; Operative for Oral and Maxillofacial Surgery, Chief Editor, 1994. Honours: 2nd Prize, Medical Science Achievement in the Army, 1986, 1990, 1991, 1992. Memberships: Chinese Medical Association; Society of Traumatology; Society of Stomatology; Society of Oncological Surgery of Head and Neck. Hobby: Basketball. Address: Department of Oral and Maxillofacial Surgery, Stomatological College, 4th Military Medical University, 1 KangFu Road, Xian, Shanxi 710032, China.

ZHOU Xiao Si, b. 25 Apr 1933, Sichuan, China. Professor and Doctor of Surgery. m. Shi Mei Zhou, 31 Mar 1957, 1 s, 2 d. Education: College (BMC), Beijing Medical University, 1955. Appointments: Resident, 1st Affiliated Hospital of BMC, 1955-58; Resident, Visiting Surgeon, 3rd Hospital of BMC, 1958-80; Associate Professor of BMC, 1980-85; Professor of Surgery, Chief of Division of General Surgery, 3rd Hospital of Beijing Medical University, 1985-. Publications: Pigment Gallstone Study, in Chinese Medical Journal, 1982; Bilirubin-calcium compound precipitation and the effect of bile salts on it, in Chinese Medical Journal, 1985; Gallstone Disease and Biliary Infection, in Gastroenterology Beijing, 1993. Honours: Third Award of Science, Scientific and Technological Committee of Beijing City, 1980; Second Award for Progress in Science and Technology, The Ministry of Public Health, China, 1988. Memberships: Society of Surgery, Chinese Medical Association; International Hepato-Pancreato-Biliary Association. Hobby: Computers. Address: Department of Surgery, Third Hospital of Beijing Medical University, 49 North Garden Road, Beijing 100083, China.

ZHOU Xiaophong, b. 16 Mar 1958, Hangzhou, China. Cardiologist. m. Hongli Xia, 12 May 1986, 1 s. Education: MD, 1982, Masters degree. 1985, Zhejiang Medical University. Appointments: Assistant Professor, 1986-87, 1990, 1991-92, Zhejiang Medical University; Research Associate, 1987-90, 1990-91, 1992-94, Duke University Medical centre, USA; Senior Research Associate, UAB Medical Centre, 1994-. Publications: Contributor of numerous professional articles; Method and Apparatus for the Prevention of Arrhythmia by Nerve Stimulation, patent. Honours: 2nd Prize, Zhejiang Biological Science, 1988; Principal Investigator, Chinese NSF Grant, Zhejian NSF Grant, American Heart Grant. Memberships: American Heart Association; Chinese Society of Physiology. Hobbies: Reading; Basketball. Address: PO Box 201, Cardiology/Medicine, University of Alabama at Birmingham, Birmingham, AL 35294-0019, USA.

ZHOU Xigeng, b. 21 Apr 1920, Shanghai, China. Surgeon; Colorectal General. m. Zheng Huai Mei, 3 Nov 1951, 3 sons, 1 daughter. Education: BSc, St John's University, Shanghai, 1942; MD, St John's University Medical School, Shanghai, 1945. Appointments: Resident, General Surgery, Mt Sinai Hospital, New York, USA, 1949-50; Assistant Surgeon, 1951; Deputy Chairman, Department of Surgery & Chief of Colorectal Surgery, 1957, RuiJin Hospital, Shanghai No 2 Medical University; Associate Professor, 1963, Professor of Surgery, 1980, Shanghai No 2 Medical University. Publications: Chapters on Surgical Treatment & Adjuvant Therapies of Colorectal Cancer, 1994; Progress in the Surgical Treatment and Late Results in 1597 Cases of Rectal Cancer, 1992; Surgical Treatment & Late Results in 1226 Cases of Colorectal Cancer, 1983; Re-appraised of Posterior Pelvic Exenteration for Low-Rectal Cancer in Females, 1991. Honours: Certificate of Honour on Meritorious Work in Research, National Council of Education, China, 1990; Awards of Meritorious Work in High Education, State Department, China, 1992; Progress Award, Shanghai Council of Science & Technology, 1994; Progress Award, Ministry of Health, China, 1994. Memberships: Consultant, Committee of Colonectal Cancer; Hinese & Shanghai Anticancer Associations; Consultant, Committee Coloanal Diseases; Chinese Society of Traditional-Western Medicine; International Society of University Colon & Rectal Surgeons. Hobbies: Classical Music; TV. Address: RuiJin Hospital, Shanghai No 2 Medical Unviersity, 34 W Fuxing Road, Suite 7C, Shanghai 200031, China.

ZHOU Xiu-Kun, b. 30 Jan 1929, Sichuan, China. Professor of Orthodontics. m. Ji-Zhi Zhang, 31 Dec 1956, 1 son, 1 daughter. Education: DDS, College of Stomatology, 1952. Appointments: Lecturer, 1956; Associate Professor, 1979; Professor of Orthodontics, 1985-, Superior Advisor of PhD graduates, 1987-, Hua-Xi Medical University, Chengdu. Publications: Orthodontics, textbook, 1988, 2nd edition, 1992; Study of resistance center of dental facial structure, 1989; The removable orthodontic appliance in clinical practice, 1991; Holographic determination of forward, backward traction of maxila, 1991. Honours: Scientific and Technological Awards, Sichuan Government, 1990. Memberships: Chinese Medical Association, Dental Branch; Orthodontic Association. Hobbies: Dancing; Reading novels. Address: Hua-Xi Medical University, 19 3rd Section, Ren Min Nan Road, Chengdu 610041, China.

ZHOU Ya-de, b. 5 June 1932, Liaoning, China. Paediatrician. m. Deng Lei-li, 3 Nov 1964, 1 son. Education: BS, Chinese Medical University, Sheng Yang, 1954; MD, 2nd Medical University, Moscow, 1960. Appointments: Resident, Visiting Doctor (Lecturer), Associate Professor of Paediatrics, 1960-83; Vice-President, 1983-89, Professor of Paediatrics, 1987-94, President, 1989-94, Chongqing University of Medical Sciences; Director, Paediatrics Research Institute, Chongqing University of Medical Sciences. Publications: Bacterial liver abscess in children, 1980; Congenital leukemia: A comprehensive report of 28 cases, 1982; IgG subclass platelet-associated antibody in children with idiopathic thrombocytopenic purpura, 1992; The small megakaryocytes and degenerate megakaryocytes in children with ITP, 1992; Co-author: Diseases of children, 1984; Hand-book of applied clinical paediatrics, 1987; Nutrition and nutritional diseases in childhood, 1990. Memberships: Board Member, China Medical Association; Vice-President, Sichuan Branch, China Medical Association; Board Member, China Higher Medical Education Society; Vice-Chairman, Chongqing Science and Technology Association. Hobbies: Music; Fine arts. Address: Chongqing University of Medical Sciences, Chongqing, Sichuan 630041, China.

ZHOU Yi-Ping, b. 1 August 1932, Liyang, Jiangsu, China. Director of Research Institute of Meridian Channels; Director of Acupuncture & Moxibustion Hospital of Anhui College. m. Shu-qing Zhao, 8 August 1956, 2 sons, 1 daughter. Education: Shanghai Medical University, 1953; Anhui Medical University, 1955. Appointments: Dean, Department of Physiology, Benxi Medical School, 1953; Hefei Junior Medical School, 1958; Anhui College of Traditional Chinese Medicine, 1959; Head, Research Institute of Merdian Channels, Anhui College of Traditional Chinese Medicine, 1971. Publications: The Influence of Acupuncture on Hemodynai Change in Experimental Acute Myocardial Infraction of Dogs, 1981; Effect of Acupuncture on Angina Pectoris and so on, 1993. Honours: Four National Prizes, One Provincial Prize, 1978; One Provincial Prize, 1987; One Provincial Prize, 1989; One Provincial Prize, 1992. Memberships: Science Committee, Chinese Public Health Ministry; Acupuncture & Moxibustion Lecturers' Group of China; Anhui Society of Biomedical Engineering. Hobbies: Qigong; Music. Address:

Research Institute of Meridian Channels of Anhui College of Traditional Chinese Medicine, Meishan Road, Hefei, Anhui, China.

ZHOU Zhi-Long, b. October 1926, Shanghai, China. Education: Graduate MD, St John's University Medical School, 1950. Appointments: Head, Chairman, Obstetrics & Gynaecology Department, Xinhua Hospital, Shanghai Second Medical University. Publications: Editor of 5 books on Perinatal Medicine and 60 papers in Chinese, English and Spanish, in Chinese, American and Spanish journals. Memberships: Chinese Society f Obstetrics & Gynaecology; Shanghai Obstetric & Gynaecology Society; Shanghai Bio-Medical Engineering Society. Address: Xinhua Hospital, Shanghai Second Medical University, Shanghai, China.

ZHOW Wen-Quan, b. 23 Sep 1940, Jielin, China. Professor of Geriatrics. m. 1970, 1 daughter. Education: MD, Jielin College of Traditional Chinese Medicine, 1963. Appointments: Physician, 1963-78, Physician-in-Charge, 1978-83, Associate Professor of Geriatrics, 1983-90, Professoro f Geriatrics, 1990-; Director, National Centre of Geriatrics of Traditional Chinese Medicine. Publications: The Practical TCM Geriatrics, Editor-in-Chief, 1994; The Cream of the Chinese Geriatric Books, 1988; Contributor of over 100 academic papers. Honours: Recipient of 3 National Awards; Recipient of 5 Awards, China Academy of Traditional Chinese Medicine. Memberships: Vice Chairman, Geriatric Society; Chinese Association of Traditional Chinese Medicine-Western Medicine; Chairman, Chinese Association of Medical Dietetics. Address: Department of Geriatrics, Xiyuan Hospital, China Academy of Traditional Chinese Medicine, Xiyuan, Beijing 100091, China.

ZHU Cheng Mo, b. 27 Mar 1930, Jiangsu, China. Prof, Medicine, Education. m. Wen Ying Hu, 9 Nov 1959, 1 daughter. Education: BS, St John's University, 1949; MD, St John's Medical School & Shanghai 2nd Medical College, 1954; Postdoctoral, Shanghai 1st Medical College, 1957. Appointments: Residency of Internal Medicine, 1955-60; Physician of Nuclear Medicine, 1960-80; Associate Professor of Nuclear Medicine, 1980-85; Professor of Nuclear Medicine, Rui Jin Hospital, Shanghai 2nd Medical University, 1985-. Publications: CEA RIA, 1984; Myocardial Image, 1992; Books: Radiommunoassay, 1986; Clinical Nuclear Medicine, 1994. Honours: Municipal Award, 1985; Ministry Award, 1986; Nation Award, 1992. Memberships: Chinese Society of Nuclear Science; World Union of Nuclear Medicine. Hobbies: Photography; Music. Address: Rui Jin Hospital, 197 Rui Jin 2nd Road, Shanghai 200025, China.

ZHU Chun-Wei, b. 18 Jan 1932, Shanghai, China. Professor of Pathology. m. Shi-Min Zhang, 28 Jan 1959, 1 son, 1 daughter. Education: BA, Yanching University; MD, Peking Union Medical College; Postgraduate Course, Shaanxi Chinese Traditional Medical College. Appointments: Vice Professor, Department of Pathology, Fourth Military Medical University, 1957-59, 1962-84; Head of Research Group on Chronic Bronchitis, PLA, 1971-77. Publications: Pathology of Thyroid Gland in Surgery of Thyroid Gland, 1983. Honours: 2nd Grade Prize, PLA Scientific & Technical Progress, 1989, 1993. Memberships: Chinese Medical Association. Address: 26 Fangtai Road 5-3-3, Beijing, China.

ZHU Hong Yang, b. 9 Jul 1960, Nanjing, China. Assistant Researcher. m. Shun Geng Zhang, 30 Jul 1986, 1 s. Education: Third Military Medical University, Chongqing. Appointments: Associate Researcher, Department of Microbiology, Third Military Medical University, Chongqing, 1977-85; Assistant Researcher, Jiangsu Provincial Sanitary and Anti-Epidemic Station, Nanjing, 1985-89; Assistant Researcher, Cell and Molecular Biology Laboratory, Department of Biology, Nanjing Normal University, 1989-. Publications: 12 Articles published in professional journals, 1985-94, including: The Hemogram and Blood Chemical Values of Panthera Tigris Amoyenses and P T Amoyenses, in Acta Theriologica Sinica, 1993; Comparative Investigation on the Chromosomes of Panthera Tigris Amureusis and P T Amoyenses, in Acta Zoologica Sinica, 1993; The Karyotype G-bands and Ag-Noks of Rattus Edwardsi in Guangdong, in Heredias, 1994. Memberships: Society of Microbiology in Chongqing; Society of Psychology in Jiangsu Province. Hobbies: Reading; Travel; Stamp Collecting. Address: Department of Biology, Nanjing Normal University, Nanjing 210024, China.

ZHU Hongda, b. 27 May 1940, Suzhou, China. Professor of Radiation Hygiene. m. Dong Qinglian, 20 Sep 1968, 2 sons. Education:

MB, Nanjing Medical College, 1962; Diploma, IAEA/RCA Training Course on Development of Infrastructures for Ensuring Radiation Protection, Sydney, Australia, 1988. Appointments: Professor of Radiation Hygiene, Institute of Radiation Medicine, Chinese Academy of Medical Sciences; Academic Committee, Institute of Radiation Medicine; Specialized Committee on Radiation Hygiene, Chinese Association of Preventive Medicine. Publications: Radioactivity in Chinese Foods and Resultant Internal Doses, Chief Editor, 1989; Chinese Diet Composition, Resultant Intake Estimation of Nutrients, Elements and Radionuclides by Ingestion, 1993; Determinations of 90Sr, 137Cs, 226RA, 228Ra, 210Pb and 210Po Contents in Chinese Diet and Estimation of Internal Doses due to these Radionuclides, 1993; Basic Principles for Establishment of Chinese National Health Standard - Limited Concentrations of Radioactive Materials in Foods, 1990; Bases for Establishment of Standard Methods - Radiological Examination of Food Hygiene, 1990. Honours: Title of Expert on Radiation Hygiene, Tianjin Scientific and Technical Committee, 1991; 2nd Prizes Scientific and Technical Achievement, Ministry of Public health, 1987, 1993. Memberships: Chinese Nuclear Society; Tianjin Branch, Chinese Association of Preventive Medicine. Address: PO Box 71, Tianjin 300192, China.

ZHU Huiming, b. 4 Nov 1951, Wuhan, China. Gastroenterologist. m. Deng Chuanzheng, 1 Oct 1979, 1 son. Education: BA, Hubei Medical University; MD, PhD, Tongji Medical University; Fellowship, Milan University, Italy. Appointments: Associate Professor of Gastroenterology, Hubei Medical University, 1980; Professor of Gastroenterology, Tongji Medical University, 1986; Currently Professor Gastroenterology, Shen Zhen People's Hospital. Publications: Co-author: Clinical Hepatology, 1980; Helicobacter Pylori and Gastroduodenal Pathology, 1993; Therapeutic Endoscopy, 1993; Esophageal Diseases, 1993. Memberships: Chinese Medical Association; Guangdong Medical Association; Chinese Association of Gastroenterology; Hubei Medical Association. Hobbies: Running; Stamp collecting; Swimming. Address: Department of Gastroenterolgy, Shenzhen People's Hospital, No 3 Dong Men Bei Lu, Shen Zhen 518001, China.

ZHU Jia-Jai, b. 21 Feb 1931, Hong Kong. Surgeon. m. deng Gui-fen, 27 Mar 1952, 2 sons. Education: Graduate, Medical School, Zhong-shan University, 1952; Beijing University, UCSF, USA. Appointments: Professor of Microsurgery, 1983, Vice President, Sun Yat-sen University of Medical Sciences. Publications: Surgery of Peripheral Nerve Surgery, 1991; Advances in Peripheral Nerve Surgery, 1991; Advances in Microsurgery, 1990. Honours: Recipient of 18 Awards from Chinese Central Government and Central Educational Committee, 1978-84. Memberships: Chinese Medical Association; Chinese Rehabilitative Medicine Association. Hobby: Stamp collecting. Address: Department of Microsurgery, 1st Affiliated Hospital, Sun Yat-sen University of Medical Sciences, Guangzhou 510080, China.

ZHU Jiazhen, b. 15 July 1928, Shanghai, China. University Teacher. m. Jianjian Ping, 1 Oct 1954, 1 daughter. Education: MD, Shanghai Medical College, 1952. Appointments include: Professor of Forensic Medicine, 1983-, Vice-President, 1984-90, Head, Faculty of Forensic Medicine, 1984-92, Head, Department of Forensic Pathology, 1984-92, Co-Editor in Chief, Academic Journal, 1985-, Supervisor, Doctorate Students, 1986-, Sun Yat-Sen University of Medical Sciences, Guangzhou; Vice-President, Chinese National Committee for the Guidance of Education in the Speciality of Forensic Medicine, 1985-; Co-Editor in Chief, Chinese Journal of Forensic Medicine, 1985-; Member, Speciality Appraisal Group, Academic Degree Committee, Chinese State Council, 1985-; Editor in Chief, Textbook of Forensic Pathology for the Student of Speciality of Forensic Medicine, 1985-; Member, Editorial Board, Forensic Science International, 1993-. Publications: Textbook of Forensic Pathology (editor in chief), 1989; Lexicon of Forensic Medicine (co-editor in chief), 1994; 25 articles in Chinese Journal of Forensic Medicine; 7 articles in Forensic Science International. Honours: 1st Class Award for Textbook of Forensic Pathology, Chinese National Committee of Education; 3rd Class Award for Research on Eye Changes in Abused Children, Guangdong Provincial Committee of Sciences, 1993. Membership: Chinese Society of Forensic Medicine, Vice-President 1985-. Hobbies: Reading; Swimming; Photography; Chinese seal carving. Address: 24-601 Zhu Si Cun, S Zhi Xin Road, Guangzhou 510080, China.

ZHU Maosheng, b. 12 Dec 1948, Heyuan, Guangdong, China. Health Toxicology. m. Tu Yuying, 6 May 1978, 1 son. Education: Zhongshan

Medical College, China, 1973. Career: Associate Chief, Toxicology Department, 1986-92. Publications: Co-author: The Research of Lethal Mutation of Sodium Flouride Using Sex-Linked Recessive Lethal, 1989; Potential Genotoxicity of Chemicals Using Protophage Inducement Test, 1989. Honour: Second Class Award of Science & Technology Results, Municipal Health Bureau of Guangzhou, China, 1990. Memberships: Standing Committee, Guangdong Association of Health Toxicology; Chinese Association of Preventive Medicine; International Association of Environmental Mutagen Society (IAEMS). Hobbies: Football; Chinese Chess. Address: No 23 3rd Zhongshan Road, Guangzhou 510080, China.

ZHU Mei-Guang, b. 15 Jan 1932, Shanghai, China. Obstetrician and Gynaecologist. m. You Ziang Bian, 7 Feb 1961, 2 sons. Graduated, Shanghai First Medical University, 1955; Fellow, Obstetrics and Gynaecology Department, Brigham and Women's Hospitals, Boston, USA, 1 year. Appointments: Resident, Chief Resident, Attending, Tianjin General Hospital, Tianjin Medical College; Attending Chief Doctor, Laboratory Deputy Director and Director, Tianjin Central Hospital for Obstetrics and Gynaecology. Publications: Colpomicroscopy in the diagnosis of cervical carcinoma, 1959; New approach in contraceptive agents and devices, 1981; Gynecologic endocrine therapy, 1992. Honours: Specialist of Obstetrics and Gynaecology, 1993. Memberships: Chinese Medical Association of Obstetrics and Gynaecology; Chinese Traditional Medicine and Western Medicine Association; Chinese Immunology Association; Chinese Nuclear Medicine, Tianjin Branch; Editorial Boards: Journal of Reproductive Medicine; Journal of Practical Obstetrics and Gynaecology; Foreign Medicine of Obstetrics and Gynaecology. Hobby: Listening to music. Address: Tianjin Central Hospital for Obstetrics and Gynaecology, 210 Ying Kou Dao, Heping Qu, Tianjin 300052, China.

ZHU Shou-peng, b. 20 June 1931, Hangzhou, China. Professor of Radiotoxicology. m. Zhang L S, 15 Feb 1956, 1 son, 1 daughter. Education: BA, Zhejiang Medical University; MD, Soviet Academy of Medical Sciences. Appointments: Director, Laboratory of Radiation Injury; Director, Department of Radiotoxicology. Publications: Experimental Radiotoxicology, 1983; Radiogenotoxicology, 1988; Isotopic Tracers in Medicine, 1989; Autoradiography, 1990; Radiotoxicology, 1992; Radiotoxicology of 147 Pn', 1994. Honours: Grade 2 Major Progressive Award of Science by national Science Committee, 1986; Grade 2 of Major Progressive Award of Science by Ministry of Public Health, 1992. Memberships: Chief of the Chinese Radiation Medical Association. Hobbies: Swimming. Address: 48 Renmin Road, Faculty of Radiological Medicine, Suzhou Medical College, Suzhou, Jiangsu 215007, China.

ZHU Wen Yu, b. 20 Oct 1934, Shanghai, China. Professor of Physiology. m. Wu Guangzhang, 7 Feb 1961, 2 s. Education: MD, Shanghai Medical University, 1959. Appointments: Lecturer and Associate Professor of Physiology, Now Professor of Physiology, Beijing Medical University. Publications: Co-author: Gut Hormones, 1985; Textbook of Physiology, 1991; Gastrointestinal Physiology, 1991; Gastroenterology, 1993. Honours: Fellow, University of Liverpool, England, 1979-81; Visiting Associate Professor, University of Michigan, USA, 1989-90. Membership: Chinese Society of Physiological Sciences. Hobbies: Reading; Music. Address: Department of Physiology, Beijing Medical University, Beijing 100083, China.

ZHU Wu-nan, b. 23 Feb 1920, Changsha, Hunan, China. Professor of Medicine. m. Di Xi-yin Zhang, 1 Oct 1954, 1 son, 1 daughter. Education: MB, Graduate, Hsiang Ya Medical College, 1946. Appointments: Resident Physician, Central Hospital, Nanjing, 1946-48; Chief Resident, Visiting Physiciabn, Lecturer of Medicine, College Hospital of Hunan Medical College, 1949-54; Visiting Physician, Lecturer of Medicine, Associate Professor, Vice Head, Medical Department, Professor and Director, Medical department, Concurrent Chief of Gastroenterologic Division, Zhong Shan Hospital, Shanghai Medical University, 1954-84; Emeritus Professor of Medicine, Committee of Specialist, 1984-, Honorary Professor, Zhong Shan Hospital, 1994-, Shanghai Medical University. Publications: Practical Medicine, Section editor, 5th-9th editions, 1958-90; Textbook of Internal Medicine, 1st to 3rd editions, Section editor, 1979-90; Contributor of over 90 scientific papers. Memberships: Chinese Medical Association; Committee Member, Standing Committee, Nationwde Society of Digestive Diseases; Vice Chairman, Shanghai Society of Digestive Diseases; Asian-Pacific Association for the Study of Liver. Address: Zhong Shan Hospital, Shanghai Medical University, Shanghai 200032, China.

ZHU Xianli, b. 25 Mar 1933, Ningbo, Zhejiang Province, China. Professor of Neurological Surgery. m. Qing-Xiang Luo, 8 Mar 1966, 2 daughters. Education: Graduated, Tongji Medical University, 1956; Microneurosurgery training under Professor Yasargil, University Hospital, Zurich, Switzerland, 1979-81. Appointments: Resident, Assistant, Surgery, 1956, Attending Surgeon, 1961, Lecturer, Surgery, 1965, Vice-Chief Surgeon, Associate Professor, Neurological Surgery, 1980, Tutor, Postgraduates for Master's degree, 1983, Chief Surgeon, Professor, Neurological Surgery, 1986, currently Professor and Director of Neurosurgical Department, Tutor of Postgraduates for Doctorate, Union Hospital, Tongji Medical University, Wuhan; Guest Academician, Academy of Sciences, Zurich University, Switzerland, 1980. Publications: Microsurgical Technique for Intracranial Aneurysms, 1986; Microsurgical Technique for Total Resection of Cranionpharyngioma, 1992; Clinical Research on Bipolar Coagulation Techniques in Neurosurgical Hemostasis, 1992; Microsurgical Treatment of Tumours in Pineal Region, 1993; An Introduction to Microneurosurgery, video tape in 8 cassettes, 1990. Honours: Science and Technology Awards, Hubei Province Government, 1987, 1991, 1993. Memberships: Vice-President, Wuhan Neurosurgical Society; Standing Committee, Hubei Neurosurgical Society; Secretary, Standing Committee Member, Hubei Surgical Society; Board of Directors, Hubei Division, Chinese Medical Association. Hobbies: Table-tennis; Running; Harmonica. Address: Neurosurgical Department, Union Hospital, Liberation Avenue 1277, 430022 Wuhan, China.

ZHU Yong Zhi, b. 16 Sep 1947, Rong Chen County, Hebei Province, China. Doctor. m. 30 Jan 1975, 1 s. Education: Master of Medicine, 1981; Professor of Traditional Chinese Medicine. Appointments: Rural Doctor, 1968; Graduate, Doctor, Assistant, Heillongjiang College of Traditional Chinese Medicine, 1975; Lecturer, Doctor in Charge, 1983; Director of Channels Callaterals Section, Heilongjiang College, 1986-91; Associate Professor, Vice Chief Doctor, 1991. Publications include: Acupuncture Dictionary, 1987; Brief Acupuncture Dictionary, 1988; Applied Acupuncture, 1989; Collection of Mr Zhang Qi Clinical Experiences, 1993; 18 Academic Theses published in provincial and country medical journals. Honour: Excellent Scientific Achievement Award, Heilongjiang Province Government, 1985; Excellent Achievement Award, 2nd World Traditional Medicine Symposium, 1995. Membership: Chinese Acupuncture Society. Hobby: Chinese Chess. Address: 1st Teaching Hospital of Provincial College of Traditional Chinese Medicine, Harbin Heilongjiang Province, 150040, China.

ZHU Yuangen, b. 8 Feb 1936, Jiangsu, China. Research Fellow (Professor) of Physiology and Acupuncture. m. Zhu Bojun, 30 May 1967, 1 son, 1 daughter. Education: MD, Shanghai Medical University, 1959. Appointments: Currently Director, Department of Acupuncture Physiology, Institute of Acupuncture, China Academy of Traditional Chinese Medicine, Beijing. Publications: Co-author: The investigation on the relationship between the changes of sensation thresholds underlying propagated sensation along meridians and peripheral sensory nerves, 1979; The response of auricular resistance during stimulation of rabbit's heart and the study of its mechanism, 1981; The effect of electroacupuncture on viscera-auriculopoint response, 1986; Effects of humoral factors in viscera-auriculopoint response, 1990; Viscera-auriculopoint response in Yang-Deficiency Syndrome, 1992. Honours: Prize for Study on Propagated Sensation along Meridians, National Science Convention, 1978; Prize for Study on Effects of the Sympathetic Nerve and Adrenal Gland in Viscera-Auriculopoint Response, State Administration of Traditional Chinese Medicine, 1993. Memberships: China Association of Physiology; Beijing Association of Physiology; China Association of Acupuncture and Moxibustion; China Association of Health Care Science and Technology. Hobby: Chinese chess. Address: Department of Physiology, Institute of Acupuncture, National Academy of Traditional Chinese Medicine, No 18 Beixincang, Dongzhimennei, Beijing, China.

ZHU Zhi Zhong, b. 12 Dec 1942, Hei Long Jiang Province, China. Medicine. m. Zheng Yanxia, 1 July 1970, 1 son, 1 daughter. Education: BS Medicine, Qi Qi Ha Er Medical College. Career: Resident Doctor and Assistant Professor, 1962-81; Doctor in Charge, Lecturer, Chairman of Department of Surgery, 1981-91; Professor and Chairman, Department of Surgery, 1991-. Publication: The Color Atlas for the Disease of Anus and Colon, 1991. Honour: Researching Awards, Hei Long Jiang Province Government, 1987. Memberships: National Anus and Colon Surgery Association; Vice Director-General, National Higher Medical Education Association. Hobby: Photography. Address: The Affiliated Hospital of Hei Long Jiang Chinese Trad Medical College, Hei Long Jiang, China.

ZHU Zongling, b. 9 Oct 1947, Qingdao, China. Teacher. m. Suyun Li, 8 Mar 1982, 1 daughter. Education: MD. Appointments: Resident, Lecturer, Associate Professor; Currently Professor, Head, Department of Pathology, Qingdao Medical College. Publications: Protective Effects of Solcoseryl on Experimental Postischemic Renal Injury, 1991. Address: Department of Pathology, Qingdao Medical College, 16 Song Shan Road, Qingdao 266021, China.

ZHUANG Xiangchang, b. 11 Sept 1928, Ningbo, Zhejiang Province, China. Professor. m. 29 Mar 1956, 2 sons, 1 daughter. Education: MD, Medical College, National Central University. Appointments: Director, Research Department, 1971, Vice-Director, 1983-, Institute of Space Medico-Engineering; Vice-Director, Academic Committee, Chinese Academy of Somatic Science. Publications: Co-author: A History of Chinese Physiology, 1993; Studies on atrophic change of soleus muscle and its countermeasures in suspended rats, 1994. Honours: State Award for Scientific and Technological Progress, 1985; State Prize for Outstanding Contributions in Research Work, 1991. Memberships: Trustee, International Society for Gravitational Physiology; Director, Chinese Society of Somatic Science. Hobbies: Table tennis. Address: Suite 302, Building 6, No 1 West Yuan Ming Yuan Road, Beijing 100094, China.

ZIEGLER Moritz Matthew, b. 25 Oct 1942, Ann Arbor, Michigan, USA. Pediatric Surgeon. m. Barbara S Ziegler, 8 Jan 1970, 2 sons. Education: BS, Capital University; MD, University of Michigan; MA, hons, University of Pennsylvania. Appointments: Professor of Surgery, University of Pennsylvania; Associate Surgeon, Childrens Hospital of Philadelphia; Professor of Surgery & Pediatrics, University of Cincinnati College of Medicine, Surgeon-in-Chief, Children's Hospital Medical Center. Publications: 134 articles, 32 book chapters. Memberships: American College of Surgeons; American Pediatric Surgical Association; Surgical Section of American Academy of Pediatrics; Society of University Surgeons; American Surgical Association. Hobbies: Outdoor Activities; Music. Address: Department of Surgery, Children's Hospital Medical Center, 3333 Burnet Avenue, Cincinnati, OH 45229, USA.

ZIGMOND Michael Jonathan, b. 1 Sep 1941, Waterbury, CT, USA. University Professor. m. Naomi Zigmond, 4 Apr 1966, 1 s, 1 d. Education: BS, Chemical Engineering, Carnegie Institute of Technology, Pittsburgh, PA, 1963; PhD, Biopsychology, University of Chicago, II, 1968; Postdoctoral training in Neuropharmacology, Massachusetts Institute of Technology, Cambridge, MA, 1967-70. Career includes: Associate Director for Basic Research, Clinical Research Center for Affective Disorders, 1977-90, Professor of Psychiatry, 1983-, Professor of Neuroscience, 1986-, University of Pittsburgh; Instructor, Minority Fellowship Program, Marine Biological Laboratory, Woods Hole, MA, 1991-. Publications: About 100 referred research articles and 45 review articles including: Compensations after lesions of central dopaminergic neurons: some clinical and basic implications, TINS, 13, 1990, 290-296; Editorial Board for 5 professional journals. Honours: Research Science Awardee, NIH, 1985-; Merit Awardee, NIH, 1993-. Memberships include: Executive Committee, Center for Neuroscience, University of Pittsburgh, 1983-; Scientific Advisory Board, Dystonia Medical Research Foundation, 1991-; Scientific Advisory Board, Tourette Syndrome Association, 1992-; Board of Directors, Winter Conference on Brain Research, 1992-96; Advisory Board, Society of Neuroscientists of Africa, 1993-. Address: 570 Crawford Hall, Department of Neuroscience, University of Pittsburgh, Pittsburgh, PA 15260, USA.

ZILBACH Joan J, b. 12 Mar 1927, Brooklyn, NY, USA. Psychoanalyst. m. Marc Fried, 1 May 1953, 1 s, 3 d. Education: BS; PhB; MD, Boston University School of Medicine, 1951; Certificate in Psychoanalysis, 1964. Career: Staff Psychiatrist, Judge Baker Guidance Center, 1955-76; Professor, Fielding Institute, 1976-. Publications: Young Children in Family Therapy, 1986; Children in Family Therapy: Treatment and Training, 1988; Many articles on family development and women's issues. Memberships: American Psychiatric Association; American Psychoanalytic Association; American Group Therapy Association; American Academy of Family Therapy; Boston Psychoanalytic Society; International Psychoanalytic Association. Hobbies: Outdoor Activities. Address: 36 Amory Street, Brookline, MA 02146-3909, USA.

ZIMET Carl N, b. 3 Jun 1925, Vienna, Austria. Psychology. m. Sara Goodman, 4 Jun 1950, 2 s. Education: BA, Cornell University; PhD, Syracuse University; Postdoctoral Fellow, Stanford University. Career: Assistant Professor of Psychology and Psychiatry, Yale University School of Medicine, 1956-63; Currently, Professor and Head, Division of Psychology, University of Colorado School of Medicine. Publications: Co-author, An Ego-Psychological Approach to Character Assessment, 1964; Co-author, The Interpretation of Psychological Tests, 1968; The Mental Health Care Revolution, in American Psychologist, 1989; Psychology's Role in a National Health Program, in Journal of Clinical Psychology, 1994. Honours: Diplomate in Clinical Psychology, 1959; Distinguished Service Award, Colorado Psychological Association; Distinguished Contributions to Professional Psychology Award, Division of Clinical Psychology, APA, 1981 and 1987; Distinguished Psychology Award, Division of Psychotherapy, APA, 1981; Alfred M Wellner Memorial Award, The National Register of Health Service Providers in Psychology, 1993. Memberships: Chair, Board of Directors, Association of Psychology Postdoctoral and Internship Centres; Task Force on Human Development, NIH, 1992-; APA; President, Association of Medical School Professors of Psychology, 1992-94; President of Academy of Clinical Psychology, 1993-. Hobbies: Skiing; Biking. Address: University of Colorado Health Sciences Centre, 4200 East 9th Avenue C256-47, Denver, CO 80262, USA.

ZIMMERMAN Richard Kent, b. 29 Aug 1960, Toledo, Ohio, USA. Medical Doctor. m. Elizabeth Wellhousen Zimmerman, 25 June 1989, 2 sons. Education: MD; MPH; ABFP; ABPM. Appointments: Clinical Instructor, Department of Family Medicine, OSU School of Medicine, 1986-89; Assistant Professor, Department of Family Medicine & Clinical Epidemiology, University of Pittsburgh School of Medicine, 1991-. Publications: Childhood Immunizations: A Practical Approach for Clinicans, 1992; Adult Immunization: A Practical Approach for Clinicians, Part I & II, 1995. Honours: OSU Department Award in Preventive Medicine, 1989; Outstanding Young Man of America, 1991; 3rd Place, National Immunization Scientific Poster Award, 1992. Memberships: Christian Medical Society; Fellow, American Academy of Family Physicians; Society of Teachers of Family Medicine; Fellow, American Academy of Preventive Medicine. Hobbies: Current Events; Jogging; Church. Address: Department of Family Medicine & Clinical Epidemiology, University of Pittsburgh, M-200 Scaife Hall, Pittsburgh, PA 15261, USA.

ZIMMERMAN Thom J, b. 5 Oct 1942, Lincoln, IL, USA. Ophthalmologist. 1 d. Education: BS, Zoology, University of IL, Champaign Urbana, 1964; MD, University of IL School of Medicine, Chicago, 1968; PhD, Pharmacology, University of FL College of Medicine, 1976. Career includes: Surgeon, US Public Health Service, Jacksonville, FL, 1969-71; Chairman, Department of Ophthalmology, Ochsner Clinic, New Orleans, 1979-86; Professor of Ophthalmology and Pharmacology and Experimental Therapeutics, Louisiana State University Medical Center, School of Medicine, 1979-86; Guest Lecturer at many international seminars, 1982-; Professor of Pharmacology and Toxicology, University of Louisville School of Medicine, 1986-; Professor and Chairman, Department of Ophthalmology and Visual Science, University of Louisville, 1986-. Publications include: 7 Books including, Co-author, Ophthalmic Drug Facts, 1989; 6 Videos; Over 300 articles in professional Journals, 1964-, including, Safety of Beta Blockers in Clinical Practice, in Journal of Ophthalmology, volume 10 No 3, 1993; Board of Editors for various journals. Honours include: Alpha Omega Alpha, 1968; Physician's Recognition Award, AMA, 7 times; Fellow, American College of Clinical Pharmacology, 1974; Several Memorial Lectures; Lederle Award, 1987; Heed Award, 1987; President's Award for Outstanding Scholarship, Research and Creative Activity, University of Louisville, 1990. Memberships include: AMA, 1968-; Association for Research in Vision and Ophthalmology, 1972-; International Glaucoma Congress, 1978-; International Society of Ocular Toxicology, 1988-. Address: Ophthalmology and Visual Sciences Department, University of Louisville Health Science Center, Louisville, KY 40292, USA.

ZIMMERMANN Werner, b. 18 Jul 1941, Rio de Janeiro, Brazil. Psychoanalyst; Psychiatrist. m. Anne Pearson, 2 Feb 1967, 1 s, 1 d. Education: Psychiatric Specialization, Bern University, Switzerland, 1981; Psychotherapy in Guided Affective Imagery, 1981; Psychoanalyst, IPA, 1991. Appointments: Fellow, Institute Microbiology, UFRJ, 1966-71; Fellow, Laboratoire de Cytogenetique, Universite Louvain, Belgium, 1969-71; Professor Adjunto, Institute Microbiologia, Rio de Janeiro, 1972; Medical Adviser, Boehringer Mannheim, Rio, and Ciba Geygi, Switzerland, 1972-75; Psychiatrist, University of Bern, Switzerland,

1975-81; Psychiatrist, Pestalozzi, Rio de Janeiro, 1982-83; Private Practice, Consultation, 1982-; Currently, Physician, Vila Serena, Drug Addiction Treatment; Psychoanalyst, Family Therapy, Institute MOSAICO, Rio de Janeiro. Memberships: Swiss Psychiatric Association; Brazilian Association of Psychiatry; Brazilian Association for Alcohol and Drug Studies; International Society for Guided Affective Imagary; International Psychoanalytical Association. Hobbies: Tennis; Reading. Address: Instituto MOSAICO, Rua Ramon Franco 79, 22290-290 Rio de Janeiro, Brazil.

ZIYAL Nüzhet, b. 16 Mar 1922, Kemaliye, Turkey. President of Turkish Acupuncture Association; Medical Chief, Gamlica Senatorium. m. Rezzan Ziyal, 16 June 1991, 1 daughter. Education: Graduate, Istanbul University, Department of Medicine; Specialist Doctor of Chest Diseases. Appointments: Assistant Doctor, State Hospital, 1947; Medical Chief of Sureyyapasa Senatorium, 1952; Founder, Medical Chief, Gamlica Senatorium, 1960; Founder, President, Turkish Acupuncture Association, 1985. Publications: Acupuncture, 1978; Scientific Acupuncture, 1990; Alternative Medicine Magazine, 5 volumes. Memberships: Japanese Ryodoraku Association; German Acupuncture Association; British Acupuncture Association; SIA. Honours: Stockholm International Congress of Acupuncture: Doctor of Philosophy and Honore Causa. Hobbies: Golf; Photography. Address: Bagdat Cad No 459, Suadiye, Istanbul 81070, Turkey.

ZLOTKIN Stanley Howard, b. 5 Feb 1948, Toronto, Ontario, Canada. Medical Doctor; Faculty Member. m. Judith Wolfson, 7 June 1970, 3 sons. Education: BSc; MD; FRCO (C); PhD. Appointments: Attending Paediatrician, Clinique de Jeunesse de Montréal, 1975-77; Staff Physician, University of Toronto Health Service, 1977-80; Lecturer, School of Continuing Studies, 1978-79, Assistant Professor of Nutrition and Paediatrics, 1980-87, Associate Professor of Nutrition and Paediatrics, 1987-93, currently Professor, Departments of Paediatrics and Nutrition, Coordinator, Continuing Medication, Department of Paediatrics, University of Toronto; Chair, Research Ethics Board, Hospital for Sick Children, Toronto. Publications: Numerous refereed articles, book chapters and papers including: Protein and energy requirements for parenterally fed premature infants, 1981; Meeting zinc, copper and manganese requirements in the parenterally fed preterm and fullterm infant, 1985; Protein Energy-Interactions in Humans, 1986; Nutrient interactions with TPN: The effect of histidine and cysteine intake on urinary zinc excretion, 1989; Iron deficiency in Canadian Children? Implications and prevention, 1992; How nutrients influence growth, 1993. Honours: Honours List Award, Innis College, University of Toronto, 1971; Colin R Woolf Continuing Education Award, University of Toronto, 1992; Borden Award in Nutrition, Canadian Society of Nutritional Sciences, CFBC, 1992. Memberships: Nutrition Committee, Canadian Pediatric Society; Scientific Advisory Council, National Institute of Nutrition; Joint Canadian Pediatric Society/HPB Working Group on Fat in the Diet of Growing Children. Address: Hospital for Sick Children, 555 University Avenue, Toronto, Ontario, Canada.

ZOLLINGER Robert Milton Jr, b. 4 Feb 1934, Boston, Massachusetts, USA. Physician. m. Ruth L R Harold, 6 June 1959, 3 sons. Education: BA, Harvard College, 1955; MD, Harvard University, 1959; Surgical Intern, Resident, Chief Resident, 1959-67, Postdoctoral Fellow, National Institutes of Health, 1962-65, Peter Bent Brigham Hospital. Appointments: Instructor, Harvard Medical School, 1968; Assistant Professor, Associate Professor, Professor, Vice-Chairman, Department of Surgery, Case Western Research University School of Medicine. 1969-. Publications: Atlas of Surgical Operations (co-author), 7th edition, 1993; 90 scientific articles. Memberships: American College of Surgeons; American Surgical Association; Central Surgical Association; Society of International Surgeons; American Medical Association; Ohio State Medical Society. Hobbies: Gardening; Electronics. Address: Department of Surgery, University Hospitals of Cleveland, 11100 Euclid Avenue, Cleveland, OH 44106, USA.

ZOLOV David Mitchell, b. 5 Aug 1937, Portland, Maine, USA. Physician. m. Eleanor Kessler, 10 Apr 1969, 4 s. Education: MD; Diplmoate, American Board Internal Medicine; Diplomate, American Board Allergy and Immunology; FACP; FACA; FAAA. Appointments: President, New York Allergy Society, 1980-81; President, Connecticut Allergy Society, 1984-86; President, New England Allergy Society, 1992-93; President, Medical Staff, Dandbury Hospital, 1990-92; Chief, Allergy, Danbury Hospital. Publications include: The Effect of Posture on Respiratory Function in Patients with Obstructive Emphysema, CO-author, 1966; Prediction of Penicillin Allergy by Immunological

Tests, Co-author, 1967; Penicillin Hyersensitivity and the Doctrine of Original Antigenic Sin, Co-author, 1968; Prediction of Penicillin by Immunological Tests, Co-author, 1969; Penicillin-related Exanthems in Infectious Mononucleosis Identical to Those Associated with Ampicillin, Co-author, 1972. Memberships: FACP; FACA; FAAAI. Hobbies: Hunting; Fishing; Automobiles; Travel. Address: 62 Sugar Lane, Newtown, CT 06470-1768, USA.

ZONANA Howard V, b. 16 Mar 1938, USA. Psychiatrist. m. Linda Howard, 14 May 1966, 1 s, 2 d. Education: BA, magna cum laude, Syracuse University, NY, 1958; MD, Johns Hopkins School of Medicine, Baltimore, MD, 1962; Candidate, Western New England Institute of Psychoanalysis, 1968-71. Career includes: Director, PGY V Law and Psychiatry Fellowship Training Program, 1979-, Director, Law and Psychiatry Division, 1986-, Acting Clinical Director, 1994-, Secretary and Treasurer, Medical and Professional Staff, 1994-, Connecticut Mental Health Center; Chair, Bioethics Committee, Yale New Haven Hospital, 1985-; Consultant and Chair Coordinator, State Department of Mental Health, 1991-; Professor of Psychiatry, Yale University School of Medicine. Publications include: Over 20 original articles, 1958-93, including, Co-author, Prosecuting Assaultive Psychiatric Patients in Journal of Forensic Sciences, 1992; Over 20 book chapters and other publications. Honours include: Fellow, American Psychiatric Association, 1976; Outstanding Faculty, Psychiatric Residents Association Teaching Award, Yale University School of Medicine, 1990; Outstanding Service Award, American Acadmey of Psychiatry and The Law, 1991; Honorary Master of Arts, Yale Corporation, 1993. Memberships include: APA; Many positions held, American Academy of Psychiatry and the Law; Group for The Advancement of Psychiatry; Various positions, American Board of Forensic Psychiatry; American Board of Psychiatry and Neurology. Address: Yale University School of Medicine, Connecticut Mental Health Center, 34 Park Street, New Haven, CT 06519, USA.

ZONG Xiuying, b. 25 July 1926, Beijing, China. Medical Doctor; Professor. m. 20 Aug 1944, 5 sons, 1 daughter. Education: BA, Chinese Literature, Christian Furen University, Beijing. Appointments: Doctor of Traditional Chinese Medicine, 1976-87; Associate Professor, Traditional Chinese Medicine, 1976-87; Professor, Traditional Chinese Medicine, 1987; Director, Department of Traditional Chinese Medicine, Beijing Friendship Hospital; Director, Department of Teaching and Research of Traditional Chinese Medicine, Faculty No 2 of Medicine, Capital Medical University; Special Consultant, Hospital of Traditional Chinese Medicine, Xishan Badachu, Beijing. Publications include: Curing a Case of Thrombocytopenic Purpura Subsequent to Pulmonary Abscess, 1965; Experience Curing Fever Caused by Affection of Exopathogen, 1979; A Report of Treatment of Metrorrhagia with Decoction of Colla Corri Asini and Flos Carthami, 1980; Experience in Treatment of Angular Gyrus Syndrome, 1982; Treatment for Diseases in Accordance with Seasonal Conditions, 1985, in English, 1987; Application of Removing the Phlegm in Gynecology, 1987; Emotion and Health Care, 1990; Three Cases of Thrombocytosis, 1991. Honours: Model Worker, Beijing, 1985; Highest Techno-Scientific Prize, Gold Prize, International Convention Fair, Paris, 1989. Memberships include: Society of Internal Medicine, Chinese Society of Beijing Traditional Chinese Medicine; Director, Consulting Division, Beijing Overseas Chinese for Traditional Chinese Medicine; Standing Director: Exploitation Association of Folk Traditional Chinese Medicine; Chinese Society of Beijing Traditional Chinese Medicine. Hobbies: Chinese history; Literature; Peking Opera; Chinese calligraphy with writing brushes; Flower growing; Fish raising; Tourism. Address: Department of Traditional Chinese Medicine, Beijing Friendship Hospital, 95 Yong'anlu Road, Xuanwu District Beijing 100050, China.

ZOU Hong-en, b. 25 Dec 1936, Zhen-Ping County, Henan, China. Professor. m. 6 Jan 1956, 1 son, 2 daughters. Education: Graduate, Bachelor, University of Medical Sciences. Appointments: Assistant, Resident Surgeon, Lecturer, Visiting Doctor, Associate Professor, Vice Director Doctor, Professor of Orthopaedics, 4th Military Medical University, Xian. Publications: Applied Biomechanics of the Hip Joint, 1993; Applied Anatomy of the Orthopaedic Surgery, 1993; Studies on Interface Mechanism of Porous Titanium, 1991; The Study on the Mechanism of Crack Pattern of Interface between Bone and Porous Coated TC4 Implants with BMP, 1993. Honours: Improving Prize of Science and Technology, China; Subsidy, National Fund of Natural Sciences, China. Memberships: Chinese Medical Society; Technological Committee for Standardization of Surgical Implants and Orthopaedic Instruments in China. Hobbies: Music; Travel. Address: Department of Orthopaedic Surgery, Tang-du Teaching Hospital, The Fourth Military Medical University, Xi'an, Shaanxi 710038, China.

ZOU Sheng Quan, b. 8 Jul 1943, Wuhan, China. Surgeon. m. Hong Chang, 12 Apr 1969, 1 s, 1 d. Education: MD; PhD. Appointment: Department of Surgery, Tong Ji Hospital, Tong Ji Medical University. Publications include: Experimental studies on the effect of duodenal contents on canine gastric mucosa, in Chinese Journal of Surgery, 1984; Calculi formation and biliary hydromechanics, in Chinese Journal of Surgery, 1990. Memberships: Secretary, Society of Surgery, Hubei Branch, Chinese Medical Association; IHPBS; World Association of HPB Surgery. Hobby: Music. Address: Department of Surgery, Tong Ji Hospital, Tong Ji Medical University, 515 Jie Fang Da Dao, Wuhan 430030, China.

ZOU Zhongshou, b. 27 Apr 1935, Wanxian, Sichuan Province, China. Professor of Surgery. m. Wei Lizhu, 1 Oct 1960, 1 son, 2 daughters. Education: Bachelor's Diploma, 4th Military Medical College. Appointments: Physician-in-charge, 1978-85, Vice-Director, Department of Abdominal Surgery, 1989, Director, Department of Abdominal Surgery, 1989-, General Hospital, Nanjing Military Command; Professor, 2nd Military Medical College, 1989-; Professor, School of Medicine, Nanjing University, 1990-. Publications: First author: Clinical application of gastro-intestinal staplers, 1988; Parietal cell ultrastructure and acid secretory function before and after vagotomy, 1990; Intraoperative coronary venography in observing changes of portal blood flow after portal azygos disconnection, 1990; The density and immunoelectronmicroscopic picture of G cells before and after vagotomy, 1991; Long-term therapeutic effects of selective vagotomy based on types of gastric secretion in treating duodenal ulcer, 1991; PCV and SV+A in treatment of duodenal ulcer - A follow-up of 10 years, 1991. Honours: Winner, 7 Technological Progress Awards, People's Liberation Army, 1980-. Memberships: Vice-President, Gastroenterology Surgery Department, National Surgery Association of China; Academic Secretary, General Surgery Committee, People's Liberation Army; Medical Science Committee, Nanjing Unit, People's Liberation Army; Editorial Board, Journal of Practical Surgery of China. Hobbies: Chinese Taiji Kongfu; Fishing; Music. Address: 520 East Zhangshan Road, 210002 Nanjing, China.

ZRENNER Eberhart, b. 18 Oct 1945, Munich, Germany. Ophthalmologist. m. Claudia Bulle, 7 Apr 1979, 2 sons, 1 daughter. Education: MD summa cum laude, Technical University of Munich; Habilitation (Dr med habil), University of Giessen. Appointments: Research Fellow, Max Planck Institute for Physiology and Clinical Research; Fogarty Fellow, National Institutes of Health, Laboratory of Vision Research; Clinical Fellow, University Eye Hospital, Munich; Head, Max Planck Research Group; Chairman, Department of Pathophysiology of Vision and Neuro-ophthalmology; Dean, Medical Faculty, Tübingen University; Currently: Full Professor of Ophthalmology, Chairman, Department of Ophthamology, Tübingen University; Executive Director, University Eye Hospital, Tübingen. Publications: Over 140, including: Colour mechanisms in primates, Studies of brain function 9, 1983; The physiological basis of the pattern electroretinogram, 1989; Colour perception, 1990; Tests of retinal function in drug toxicity, 1992. Honours: Fogarty Fellowship Award, 1977; Franceschetti-Liebrecht Award, German Ophthalmological Society, 1981; Honorary Professor in Physiology. Memberships: President, International Society of Clinical Electrophysiology of Vision; Board of Directors, International Society of Ophthalmological Toxicology; ARVO; German Ophthalmological Society; Section Editor: Vision Research; Neuro-ophthalmology. Hobbies: Music; Electronics; Swimming. Address: University Eye Hospital, Schleichstrasse 12-16, 72076 Tübingen, Germany.

ZSIGMOND Andrew, b. 17 Nov 1935, Nyaradszentlaszlo, Hungary. Occupational Health Physician. m. Carol Ann Zsigmond, 6 Oct 1979, 2 sons, 1 daughter. Education: LRCP; MRCS; CGAM; MFOM. Appointments: House Officer, Royal Southern Hospital and Walton Hospital, Liverpool, England; Senior House, Clatterbridge Hospital, Bebington; Currently Occupational Health Physician. Publications: Sudden Onset of Irritant Dermatitis in a Car Component Factory, 1985. Memberships: Pres, Liverpool Medical Institution, 1995-96; Conservative Medical Society; Society of Occupational Medicine. Hobbies: Opera; Classical music; Skiing; Golf. Address: 43 Rodney Street, Liverpool L1 9EW, England.

ZUNICH Kathryn Margaret, b. 12 Feb 1953, NY, USA. Physician. Education: BA, Fordham University, NY; MD, SUNY Upstate Medical Center, Syracuse, NY. Career: Medical Officer, Laboratory of Immunoregulations NIAID NIH, 1988-89; Chief Transplantation Section, DAIT NIAID NIH, 1989-90; Chief, Asthma Section, DAIT NIAID NIH,

1990-91; Associate Medical Director, Institute of Clinical Medicine, Syntex Research, 1992-94; Currently, Director of Clinical Research, Viral and Immunologic Diseases, Univax Biologics Inc, Rockville, MD. Publications: 10 Articles in professional journals including: Co-author, Methionine-enkephalin as immunomodulator therapy in human immunodefeciency virus infections: Clinical and immunological effects, in Journal of Clinical Immunology, 1988. Memberships: American academy of Allergy and Immunology; American College of Allergy and Immunology; American College of Physicians. Address: Univax Biologics Inc, 12280 Wilkins Avenue, Rockville, MD 20852, USA.

ZUO-FENG Zhang, b. 9 June 1953, Nantong, Jiangsu, China. Epidemiologist. m. Qing-Yi Lu, 6 Dec 1985. Education: MD, Shanghai Medical University, China, 1983; PhD, University New York, Buffalo, 1991. Appointments: Research Fellow, International Agency for Research on Cancer, Lyon, 1987-88; Research Instructor, University New York, Buffalo, 1988-91; Assistant Professor, Cornell University Medical College, 1991-. Publications: Over 35 professional publications in scientific journals. Honours: 2nd Class Scientific & Technology Award, Ministry of Health, China; Rong-Lin's Prize, Shanghai Medical University, 1983. Memberships: Society of Epidemiology Research; American Association of Cancer Research; American Society of Preventive Oncology; American college of Epidemiology. Hobbies: Swimming; Fishing. Address: 401 East 89th Street, Apt 10H, NY 10128, USA.

ZWART Benton P, b. 7 Oct 1952, Stamford, Connecticut, USA. Physician. m. Kathryn, 20 Aug 1983, 3 daughters. Education: MD, University of Connecticut, 1982; Aerospace Medicine Primary, 1982; MSEE, Lehigh University, 1976; BSEE, 1974; MPH, Harvard School of Public Health, Boston, 1989-90. Appointments include: Medical Inspector, Air Force Inspection Agency, Kirtland AFB, New Mexico, 1994-; teaching Assistant, 1974-75, Research Assistant, 1976, Department of Electrical Engineering, Lehigh University; Faculty of School of Aerospace Medicine, Brooks AFB, Texas, 1992-94. Publications: The Story of Pokey 55, 1987; You're the Flight Surgeon, 1991; Tracking and Analyzing Illness and Morbidity Among Active Duty Air Force Aviators, 1993; A New Method for Tracking and Analyzing Illness and Morbidity Among Active Duty Air Force Aviators, 1994. Honours include: USAF MSM, First Oak Leaf Cluster, 1989, Second Oak Leaf Cluster, 1994; Tau Beta Pi; Eta Kappa Nu. Address: 23622 Hartwick Lane, San Antonio, TX 78259 1604, USA.

ZWEIMAN Burton, b. 7 June 1931, New York City, New York, USA. Physician. m. Claire Zweiman, 30 Dec 1962, 2 daughters. Education: MD. Appointments: Assistant Professor, 1967; Associate Professor, 1969; Professor of Medicine and Neurology, Chief of Allergy and Immunology, University of Pennsylvania School of Medicine, Philadelphia, 1975-. Publications: The skin as a site of allergic reactions, 1992; Cell-Mediated Immunity in Allergy Principles and Practice (with A I Levinson), 1992; The late-phase reaction: role of IgE, its receptor and cytokines, 1993. Honours: Phi Beta Kappa, 1952; Alpha Omega Alpha, 1956; Merck Award, 1967; Lindback Teaching Award, 1967. Memberships: Fellow, American College of Physicians; Fellow, President, American Academy of Allergy and Immunology; American Association of Immunologists; American Federation for Clinical Research; Clinical Immunology Society. Hobbies: Tennis; Swimming; Music. Address: 512 Johnson Pavilion, 3610 Hamilton Walk, Philadelphia, PA 19146-4257, USA.

ZYBINA Eugenia Victorovna, b. 5 Jul 1927, Engels, Russia. Biologist. m. Gennadius P Zybin, 1 Jun 1951, 1 d. Education: Doctor of Biological Sciences, Leningrad State University, 1952; Candidate Thesis, 1958; Doctoral Thesis, 1981. Career: Junior Researcher, Institute of Experimental Medicine, Leningrad, 1952; Junior Researcher, 1955, Senior Researcher, 1973, Leading Researcher, 1993-, Institute of Cytology, Leningrad. Publications: Co-author, Polyploidization and endomitosis in giant cells of rabbit trophoblast, in Cell Tissue Research, 1975; The Trophoblast Cytology, 1986. Honour: Labour Veteran, 1985. Membership: Russian Association of Anatomists, Histologists and Embryologists. Hobbies: Paintings; Travel. Address: Institute of Cytology, RAS, Tikhoretsky Ave 4, St Petersburg 194064, Russia.